PAPERBACK

# Encyclopedia

HarperCollins *Publishers*
Westerhill Road, Bishopbriggs, Glasgow G64 2QT

www.**fire**and**water**.com

First published 1995
Updated edition 1998
Third edition 2000

© Helicon Publishing Ltd 2000
www.helicon.co.uk

Maps and diagrams © Helicon Publishing Ltd 2000

ISBN 0 00 472520-4

British Library Cataloguing in Publication Data

A catalogue record for this book is available from the British Library

Typesetting by TechType, Abingdon, Oxon
Printed and bound in Great Britain by Omnia Books Ltd, Glasgow G64

# CONTENTS

# CONTRIBUTORS

Owen Adikibi PhD, CIM, IBIM
Lesley Adkins MPhil, FSA, MIFA
Roy Adkins MPhil, FSA, MIFA
Alain Anderton MA (Oxon)
Christine Avery MA (Bryn Mawr College, Pennsylvania), PhD
Tim Ayers MA (Courtauld Institute, London), PhD
John Ayto MA
Paul Bahn PhD, FSA
Anne P Baker BA (Oxon)
Stephen Ball
Tallis Barker AB (Harvard University), DPhil (Oxon), ARCM
Gordon Bloomer MA (Oxon), BScEcon (London), MEd (Manchester), FRGS
Dr Roy Bradshaw
Elizabeth Breuilly
Michael Broers MA, DPhil
Joanna E Bullard PhD.
Liu Hong Cannon
Carolyn Carter BLS (Hons), ALA
Ev Charlton
Ian Chilvers BA
Professor Hugh Clout
Ian Crofton
Nigel Davis BSc
Ian D Derbyshire MA (Cantab), PhD, FCA
Denis Derbyshire PhD, FInstM
Col Michael Dewar MA
Mawil Izzi Dien PhD
Dougal Dixon MSc
Nigel Dudley BSc
Dr Rebecca Elmhirst
Georgina Endfield PhD
Richard English MA, PhD
Dr June Evans FRGS
Eric Farge
Anna V Farkas MA
Christine Finn PhD
Peter W Fleming PhD
Eamonn Gaffney PhD
Lawrence Garner BA
Tim Hall PhD
Oliver C G Harris DPhil (Oxon)
Bill Hartston MA
Jackie Herald
Julie Hickey

Michael Hitchcock DPhil
Chris Holdsworth BSc, MA, PhD
Stuart Holroyd
Sara Hulse
John Ingerson MA
Evelyn Jenkyns BSc, MSc (Texas)
H G Jerrard PhD
Richard Johnson
Tony Jones
Rob Jones
Anthony Kamm
Eileen Kamm
Charles W Kidd
Helen King
Peter Lafferty MSc
G R Peter Lawrence, BSc, MSc, ARICS
Graham K H Ley MPhil
Carol Lister PhD, FSS
Graham Littler MSc, FSS
Alan Marriott
Richard Martin PhD
S P Martland PhD
Patrick Maume BA, MA, PhD
Tom McArthur PhD
Helen McCurdy BA
Lindsey McEwen PhD
John McKendrick BA (Hons), PhD, FRGS, FRSGS
Julie Scott Meisami
Richard Milbank
David Milsted
Tim Morris
Ann Mummery
David M Munro PhD, FSA (Scot)
Hilary Murphy
Chris Murray
David J Nash PhD
Rewi M Newnham PhD
Sarah O'Hara PhD
Joanne O'Brien MA
Maureen O'Connor BA
Jonathan D Oldfield
Robert Paisley PhD
Martin G Palmer MA (Cantab)
Douglas Palmer
Cliff Pavelin
Alice Peebles BA, BPhil
Roy Porter MA, PhD (Cantab), FBA
Paulette Pratt

Andrew Puddephatt
Tim Pulleine
Ben Ramos
Glyn Redworth MPhil (Oxon)
Chris Rhys
Christine Riding
Ian Ridpath FRAS
Carolyn Roberts
Adrian Room MA, DipEd, FRGS
Simon Ross BA (Hons)
Jonathan E Rowe
Julian Rowe PhD
Theodore Rowland-Entwistle
Paul Rowntree BA (Hons)
Stephen A Royle PhD
Jack Schofield MA
Emma Shackleton MA
Denis J B Shaw PhD
Matthew Shepherd PhD
Mary R Shields PhD, CertEd
Peter Shoebridge PhD
Anne Shukman
Jane Sillery
Andrew Skilton DPhil
Laura Smethurst PhD
Conor G Smyth PhD
Penny Sparke
Deborah Sporton PhD
Joe Staines BA
Callum Storrie BSc (Arch)
Chris Stringer
Richard Tames
Catherine Thompson MA (Oxon)
Richard Thomson
Jason Tomes DPhil (Oxon)
Matthew Tonts PhD
Graham Topping MA
Norman C Vance DPhil (Oxon)
Ingrid von Essen
Martin Walters
Patricia Warner
Mary Warren
Judith Webb PhD
Dr Stephen Webster MPhil, PGCE
Marcus Weeks
John C Wells PhD
Diana Whaley
Caroline Whitehand
Elizabeth L Whitelegg BSc
John Wright

# EDITORS

*Editorial Director*
Hilary McGlynn

*Managing Editor*
Roger Tritton

*Editor*
Catherine Thompson

*Technical Project Editor*
Claire Lishman

*Database Managing Editor*
Louise Richmond

*Production Director*
Tony Ballsdon

# PREFACE

*The Collins Paperback Encyclopedia* is an illustrated single-volume companion to world events, history, arts, science, medicine, and information technology for home, school, and library use. The aim throughout has been to provide up-to-date, readable entries, using clear and non-technical language.

## Arrangement of entries

Entries are ordered alphabetically, as if there were no spaces between words. Thus, entries for words beginning 'national' follow the order:

national insurance
nationalism
nationalization
National Security Agency

However, we have avoided a purely mechanical alphabetization in cases where a different order corresponds more with human logic. For example, sovereigns with the same name are grouped according to country before number, so that King George II of England is placed before King George III of England, and not next to King George II of Greece. Words beginning 'Mc' and 'Mac' are all treated as if they begin 'Mac'; 'St' is treated as if spelt out in full.

## Foreign names

Names of foreign sovereigns and places are usually shown in their English form, except where the foreign name is more familiar, for example Juan Carlos and not John Charles, but Florence and not Firenze.

## Titles

Entries for people with titles are under the name by which they are best known, for example the entry for Anthony Eden is under E for Eden and not under A for Lord Avon.

## Cross references

These are indicated by a ◊ symbol. Cross referencing is selective; a cross reference is shown when another entry contains material directly relevant to the subject matter of an entry, and to where the reader may not otherwise think of looking.

## Units

SI (metric) units are used throughout for scientific entries. Measurements of distances, temperatures, sizes and so on include an imperial conversion after the metric measurement.

## Science, technology, and medicine

Many scientific, technical, and medical terms also have common names that are more widely used. Both technical and common names are often listed, the main entry being given under the term the general reader is most likely to be familiar with. For example, the entry for rubella is a cross reference to the main entry under German measles.

## Chinese names

Pinyin, the preferred system for transcribing Chinese names, is generally used: thus, there is an entry at Mao Zedong and not Mao Tse-tung. The former (Wade-Giles) forms, for example Chiang Kai-shek are given as cross references where appropriate.

## Comments and suggestions

We welcome comments from readers on suggested improvements or alterations to the Encyclopedia.
*Please send them to*
*Reference Department,*
*HarperCollins Publishers,*
*Westerhill Road,*
*Bishopbriggs,*
*Glasgow G64 2QT.*

**A** in physics, symbol for ◊ampere, a unit of electrical current.

**Aachen** French *Aix-la-Chapelle,* cathedral city and spa in the *Land* (state) of North Rhine-Westphalia, Germany, 64 km/40 mi southwest of Cologne, near the Dutch and Belgian borders; population (1995) 247,400. It has thriving electronic, glass, food, woollen textile, and rubber industries, and is one of Germany's principal railway junctions. It also lies at the centre of a coalmining district, although coal and lignite production is in decline. Aachen was the Roman *Aquisgranum* and was the site of baths in the 1st century AD. Charlemagne, Holy Roman Emperor from 800, founded the cathedral in 796.

**Aalto, Alvar (Hugo Alvar Henrik)** (1898–1976) Finnish architect and designer. He was a pioneer of the ◊Modern Movement in his native Finland. Initially working within the confines of the ◊International Style, he later developed a unique architectural style, characterized by asymmetry, curved walls, and contrast of natural materials. He invented a new form of laminated bent-plywood furniture 1932 and won many design awards for household and industrial items.

**aardvark** (Afrikaans 'earth pig') nocturnal mammal *Orycteropus afer,* the only species in the order Tubulidentata, found in central and southern Africa. A timid, defenceless animal about the size of a pig, it has a long head, a piglike snout, large ears, sparse body hair, a thick tail, and short legs.

**abacus** ancient calculating device made up of a frame of parallel wires on which beads are strung. The method of calculating with a handful of stones on a 'flat surface' (Latin *abacus*) was familiar to the Greeks and Romans, and used by earlier peoples, possibly even in ancient Babylon; it survives in the more sophisticated bead-frame form of the Russian *schoty* and the Japanese *soroban.* The abacus has been superseded by the electronic calculator.

**Abadan** Iranian oil port in Khuzestan province, situated on an island on the east side of the Shatt-al-Arab waterway at the head of the Gulf, 675 km/420 mi southwest of Tehran; population (1997 est) 308,000. Abadan is the chief refinery and shipping centre for Iran's oil industry, nationalized in 1951. This measure was the beginning of the worldwide movement by oil-producing countries to assume control of profits from their own resources. Oil installations were badly damaged during the Iran–Iraq war from 1980–88.

**abalone** edible marine snail of the worldwide genus *Haliotis,* family Haliotidae. Abalones have flattened, oval, spiralled shells, which have holes around the outer edge and a bluish mother-of-pearl lining. This lining is used in ornamental work.

**Abbasid dynasty** family of rulers of the Islamic empire, whose ◊caliphs reigned in Baghdad 750–1258. They were descended from Abbas, the prophet Muhammad's uncle, and some of them, such as Harun al-Rashid and Mamun (reigned 813–33), were outstanding patrons of cultural development. Later their power dwindled, and in 1258 Baghdad was burned by the Tatars.

**abbey** in the Christian church, a building or group of buildings housing a community of monks or of nuns, all dedicated to a life of celibacy and religious seclusion, governed by an abbot or abbess respectively. The word is also applied to a building that was once the church of an abbey; for example, Westminster Abbey, London.

**Abbott and Costello** stage names of William Abbott (1895–1974) and Louis Cristillo (1906–1959) US comedy duo. Having formed a successful vaudevillian stage act during the 1930s, Abbott and Costello went on to make a number of films together that showcased their routines between 1940 and 1956.

**abdication crisis** in British history, the constitutional upheaval of the period 16 November 1936 to 10 December 1936, brought about by the British king ◊Edward VIII's decision to marry Wallis ◊Simpson, a US divorcee. The marriage of the 'Supreme Governor' of the Church of England to a divorced person was considered unsuitable and the king abdicated on 10 December and left for voluntary exile in France. He was created Duke of Windsor and married Mrs Simpson on 3 June 1937.

**abdomen** in vertebrates, the part of the body below the ◊thorax, containing the digestive organs; in insects and other arthropods, it is the hind part of the body. In mammals, the abdomen is separated from the thorax by the ◊diaphragm, a sheet of muscular tissue; in arthropods, commonly by a narrow constriction. In mammals, the female reproductive organs are in the abdomen. In insects and spiders, it is characterized by the absence of limbs.

**Abdullah, Sheikh Muhammad** (1905–1982) Indian politician, known as the 'Lion of Kashmir'. He headed the struggle for constitutional government against the Maharajah of Kashmir, and in 1948, following a coup, became prime minister. He agreed to the accession of the state to India, but was dismissed and imprisoned from 1953 (with brief intervals of freedom) until 1966, when he called for Kashmiri self-determination. He became chief minister of

Jammu and Kashmir in 1975, accepting the sovereignty of India.

**Abdullah ibn Hussein** (1882–1951) King of Jordan 1946–51. In 1921, after the collapse of the Ottoman empire, he became emir of the British mandate of Transjordan, covering present-day Jordan, and became king when the mandate ended in May 1946. In May 1948 King Abdullah attacked the newly established state of Israel, capturing large areas. He retained the area called the West Bank (Arab Palestine) after a ceasefire in 1949 and renamed the country the Hashemite Kingdom of Jordan. He was assassinated in July 1951 by a Palestinian Arab fanatic.

**Abdullah ibn Hussein** (1962– ) King of Jordan from 1999. Abdullah was crowned king of Jordan after his father, ◊Hussein ibn Talal, who had ruled the Hashemite Kingdom since 1952, died. Abdullah, who was an army major general, and untested in the affairs of state, became the fourth leader of this small but strategically vital state. He promised to maintain Hussein's legacy, continuing the course of moderation and commitment to Middle East peace.

**Abelard, Peter** English form of Pierre Abélard (1079–1142) French scholastic philosopher who worked on logic and theology. His romantic liaison with his pupil ◊Héloïse caused a medieval scandal. Details of his life are contained in the autobiographical *Historia Calamitatum Mearum/The History of My Misfortunes.*

**Aberdeen, George Hamilton Gordon**, 4th Earl of Aberdeen (1784–1860) British Tory politician, prime minister from 1852 until 1855, when he resigned because of criticism provoked by the miseries and mismanagement of the ◊Crimean War.

**Aberdeen City** city and unitary authority in northeast Scotland. The unitary authority was created in 1996 from the district of the same name that was part of Grampian region from 1975; before that it was part of Aberdeenshire. The city of Aberdeen, as well as being the administrative headquarters of the Aberdeen City unitary authority, is the administrative headquarters of Aberdeenshire unitary authority
*area* 185 sq km/71 sq mi
*physical* low-lying coastal area on the banks of the rivers Dee and Don; it has 3 km/2 mi of sandy beaches
*features* St Andrew's Episcopal Cathedral (consecrated in 1816), King's College (from 1500) and Marischal College (founded in 1593, and housed in one of the world's largest granite buildings constructed in 1836), which together form Aberdeen University, Brig O'Balgownie (1314–18), Municipal Buildings (1867), St Machar Cathedral (from 1370). Aberdeen's granite buildings have given it the name of 'Silver City', although the last granite quarry, in Rubislaw, closed in 1971
*agriculture* white and salmon fishing
*industries* North Sea oil (it is the main centre in Scotland and Europe for offshore oil exploration and there are shore-based maintenance and service depots for the North Sea oil rigs; an

airport and heliport at Dyce, 9.6 km/6 mi northwest of the city, link the mainland to the rigs), oil and gas service industries, paper manufacturing, textiles, engineering, food processing, chemicals, fish processing
*population* (1996) 219,100
*famous people* poet John Barbour, archdeacon of Aberdeen; Scottish historian Hector Boece (*c.* 1465–1536), principal of King's College; theologian George Campbell; the poet Lord ◊Byron received his early education at the grammar school here.

**aberration of starlight** apparent displacement of a star from its true position, due to the combined effects of the speed of light and the speed of the Earth in orbit around the Sun (about 30 km per second/18.5 mi per second).

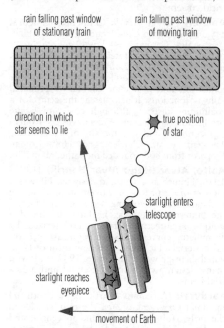

**aberration of starlight** *The aberration of starlight is an optical illusion caused by the motion of the Earth. Rain falling appears vertical when seen from the window of a stationary train; when seen from the window of a moving train, the rain appears to follow a sloping path. In the same way, light from a star 'falling' down a telescope seems to follow a sloping path because the Earth is moving. This causes an apparent displacement, or aberration, in the position of the star.*

**aberration, optical** any of a number of defects that impair the image in an optical instrument. Aberration occurs because of minute variations in lenses and mirrors, and because different parts of the light ◊spectrum are reflected or refracted by varying amounts.

**Abidjan** port and former capital (until 1983) of the Republic of Côte d'Ivoire; population (1988) 1,929,100. Products include coffee, palm oil, cocoa, and timber (mahogany). There are tourist markets trading in handicrafts and traditional medicines. Yamoussoukro became the new capital in 1983, but was not internationally recognized as such until 1992. Around 10% of adults carry the AIDS virus (1996).

**Abkhazia** also *Abkhaziya,* autonomous republic in northwestern Georgia
*cities* Sokhumi (capital), Ochamchire, Gagra
*area* 8,600 sq km/3,320 sq mi
*physical* located between the main range of the ◊Caucasus Mountains and the ◊Black Sea, with a subtropical climate on the latter's shores; densely wooded foothills of the Caucasus
*industries* mining of tin and coal, lumbering and sawmilling; fruit, tobacco, and tea are cultivated; tourism and health resorts
*population* (1991) 525,000
*history* Abkhazia was part of the ancient province of Colchis, and later belonged to Pontus, Rome, and Byzantium; it became independent in 756 and was merged in the all-Georgian state in 985. It became a separate principality in the 16th century, fell under Turkish rule in 1578, under the Russians in 1810, and was absorbed into Russia in 1864. There were uprisings against Russian rule and many Abkhazians emigrated to Turkey. An autonomous Soviet Socialist republic was formed in 1921. In 1938–53 Abkhazians were subjected to a policy of assimilation by the Georgian authorities.

From the late 1980s onwards, the region was the scene of secessionist activity on the part of the minority Muslim Abkhazi community, culminating in the republic's declaration of independence in 1992, and the invasion by Georgian troops, who took control in August 1992. However, secessionists subsequently gained control of the northern half of the republic, taking the region's capital, Sokhumi, in October 1993, as well as much of the republic's remaining territory. A UN Observer Mission in Georgia (UN OMIG) was stationed in the country in 1993. A ceasefire was agreed in 1994. Many ethnic Georgians fled Abkhazia during the four-year war, which claimed around 3,000 lives. In May 1998 the ceasefire broke down temporarily and renewed fighting led to 20,000 Georgians fleeing the country.

**Åbo** Swedish name for ◊Turku, a port in southwest Finland.

**abolitionism** a movement culminating in the late 18th and early 19th centuries that aimed first to end the slave trade, and then to abolish the institution of ◊slavery and emancipate slaves.

**aborigine** (Latin *ab origine* 'from the beginning') any indigenous inhabitant of a region or country. The word often refers to the original peoples of areas colonized by Europeans, and especially to ◊Australian Aborigines.

**abortion** (Latin *aborire* 'to miscarry') ending of a pregnancy before the fetus is developed sufficiently to survive outside the uterus. Loss of a fetus at a later gestational age is termed premature stillbirth. Abortion may be accidental (◊miscarriage) or deliberate (termination of pregnancy).

**Abraham** (lived *c.* 2300 BC) in the Old Testament, the founder of the Jewish nation. In his early life he was called Abram. God promised him heirs and land for his people in Canaan (Israel), renamed him Abraham ('father of many nations'), and tested his faith by a command (later retracted) to sacrifice his son Isaac.

**Abraham, Plains of** plateau near Québec, Canada, where the British commander James ◊Wolfe defeated the French under ◊Montcalm, 13 September 1759, during the French and Indian (or Seven Years) War (1754–63). The outcome of the battle established British supremacy in Canada.

**abrasive** (Latin 'to scratch away') substance used for cutting and polishing or for removing small amounts of the surface of hard materials. There are two types: natural and artificial abrasives, and their hardness is measured using the ◊Mohs scale. Natural abrasives include quartz, sandstone, pumice, diamond, emery, and corundum; artificial abrasives include rouge, whiting, and carborundum.

**Abruzzi** mountainous region of southern central Italy, comprising the provinces of L'Aquila, Chieti, Pescara, and Teramo; area 10,800 sq km/4,169 sq mi; population (1992) 1,255,500. L'Aquila, the capital, and Pescara are the principal towns. Gran Sasso d'Italia, 2,914 m/9,564 ft, is the highest point of the ◊Apennines.

**abscissa** in ◊coordinate geometry, the $x$-coordinate of a point – that is, the horizontal distance of that point from the vertical or $y$-axis. For example, a point with the coordinates (4, 3) has an abscissa of 4. The $y$-coordinate of a point is known as the ordinate.

**absolute value** or *modulus,* in mathematics, the value, or magnitude, of a number irrespective of its sign. The absolute value of a number $n$ is written $|n|$ (or sometimes as mod $n$), and is defined as the positive square root of $n^2$. For example, the numbers $-5$ and $5$ have the same absolute value:

$$|5| = |-5| = 5$$

**absolute zero** lowest temperature theoretically possible according to kinetic theory, zero kelvin (0 K), equivalent to $-273.15°C/-459.67°F$, at which molecules are in their lowest energy state. Although the third law of ◊thermodynamics indicates the impossibility of reaching absolute zero in practice, a temperature of $2.8 \times 10^{-10}$ K (0.28 billionths of a degree above absolute zero) has been produced in 1993 at the Low Temperature Laboratory in Helsinki, Finland, using a technique called nuclear demagnetization. Near absolute zero, the physical properties of some materials change substantially; for example, some metals lose their electrical resistance and become superconducting.

**absolutism** or *absolute monarchy,* system of government in which the ruler or rulers have unlimited power and are subject to no constitutional safeguards or checks. The principle of an absolute monarch, given a right to rule by God (the ◊divine right of kings), was extensively used in Europe during the 17th and 18th centuries; it was based on an earlier theory of papal absolutism.

**absorption** the taking up of one substance by another, such as a liquid by a solid (ink by blotting paper) or a gas by a liquid (ammonia by water). In physics, absorption is the phenomenon by which a substance retains radiation of particular wavelengths; for example, a piece of blue glass absorbs all visible light except the wavelengths in the blue part of the spectrum; it also refers to the partial loss of energy resulting from light and other electromagnetic waves passing through a medium. In nuclear physics, absorption is the capture by elements, such as boron, of neutrons produced by fission in a reactor.

**abstract art** nonrepresentational art. Ornamental art without figurative representation occurs in most cultures. The modern abstract movement in sculpture and painting emerged in Europe and North America between 1910 and 1920. Two approaches produce different abstract styles: images that have been 'abstracted' from nature to the point where they no longer reflect a conventional reality, and nonobjective, or 'pure', art forms, without any reference to reality.

**Abstract Expressionism** movement in US painting that was the dominant force in the country's art in the late 1940s and 1950s. It was characterized by the sensuous use of paint, often on very large canvases, to convey powerful emotions. Some of the artists involved painted pure abstract pictures, but others often retained figurative traces in their work. Most of the leading Abstract Expressionists were based in New York during the heyday of the movement (they are sometimes referred to as the New York School), and their critical and financial success (after initial opposition) helped New York to replace Paris as the world's leading centre of contemporary art, a position it has held ever since.

**Absurd, Theatre of the** avant-garde drama originating with a group of dramatists in the 1950s, including Samuel Beckett, Eugène Ionesco, Jean Genet, and Harold Pinter. Their work expressed the belief that in a godless universe human existence has no meaning or purpose and therefore all communication breaks down. Logical construction and argument gives way to irrational and illogical speech and to its ultimate conclusion, silence, as in Beckett's play *Breath* 1970.

**Abu Bakr** also known as *Abu-Bekr* (573–634) Muslim ◊caliph (civic and religious leader of Islam) from 632 to 34. Born Abd-al-Ka'aba, he adopted the name Abu Bakr ('Father of the virgin') about 618 when the prophet ◊Muhammad married his daughter Ayesha. He was a close adviser to Muhammad in 622–32 and succeeded the prophet as political leader at his death. As the first Muslim caliph he imposed Muslim authority over all the Arab tribes, added Mesopotamia to the Muslim world, and instigated expansion of Iran into Iraq and Syria.

**Abu Dhabi** sheikhdom in southwest Asia, on the Gulf, capital of the United Arab Emirates; area 67,350 sq km/26,000 sq mi; population (1995) 928,400. Formerly under British protection, it has been ruled since 1971 by Sheikh Sultan Zayed bin al-Nahayan, who is also president of the Supreme Council of Rulers of the United Arab Emirates.

**Abuja** capital of Nigeria (formally designated as such 1982, although not officially recognized until 1992); population of Federal Capital District (1991) 378,700; population of city alone (1992 est) 305,900. Shaped like a crescent, the city was designed by Japanese architect Kenzo Tange; it began construction in 1976 as a replacement for Lagos, and is still largely under construction. The main functions of the city are administrative, with only light industry.

**abyssal plain** broad expanse of sea floor lying 3–6 km/2–4 mi below sea level. Abyssal plains are found in all the major oceans and they extend from bordering continental rises to mid-oceanic ridges.

**abyssal zone** dark ocean region 2,000–6,000 m/6,500–19,500 ft deep; temperature 4°C/39°F. Three-quarters of the area of the deep-ocean floor lies in the abyssal zone, which is too far from the surface for photosynthesis to take place. Some fish and crustaceans living there are blind or have their own light sources. The region above is the bathyal zone; the region below, the hadal zone.

**abzyme** in biotechnology, an artificially created antibody that can be used like an enzyme to accelerate reactions.

**a/c** abbreviation for *account.*

**AC** in physics, abbreviation for ◊alternating current.

**acacia** any of a large group of shrubs and trees that includes the thorn trees of the African savanna and the gum arabic tree (*Acacia senegal*) of North Africa, and several North American species of the southwestern USA and Mexico. The hardy tree commonly known as acacia is the false acacia (*Robinia pseudacacia*, of the subfamily Papilionoideae). True acacias are found in warm regions of the world, particularly Australia. (Genus *Acacia,* family Leguminosae.)

**Academy Award** annual honour awarded since 1927 by the American Academy of Motion Picture Arts and Sciences in a number of categories that reflect the diversity and collaborative nature of filmmaking. The Academy Award is one of the highest accolades in the film industry, and a virtual guarantor of increased financial returns. The trophy itself is a gold-plated statuette which since 1931 has been popularly nicknamed an 'Oscar'. The most prestigious awards are for Best Picture, Best Director, Best Actor, and Best Actress.

**acanthus** herbaceous plant with handsome lobed leaves. Twenty species are found in the Mediterrranean region and Old World tropics, including bear's-breech (*Acanthus mollis*) whose leaves were used as a motif in classical architecture, especially on Corinthian columns. (Genus *Acanthus*, family Acanthaceae.)

**Acapulco** or *Acapulco de Juarez,* port and holiday resort in southern Mexico; population (1990) 593,200. There is deep-sea fishing and tropical products are exported.

Acapulco was founded 1550 and was Mexico's major Pacific coast port until about 1815.

**acceleration** rate of change of the velocity of a moving body. It is usually measured in metres per second per second (m s$^{-2}$) or feet per second per second (ft s$^{-2}$). Because velocity is a vector quantity (possessing both magnitude and direction) a body travelling at constant speed may be said to be accelerating if its direction of motion changes. According to Newton's second law of motion, a body will accelerate only if it is acted upon by an unbalanced, or resultant, ◊force.

Acceleration due to gravity is the acceleration of a body falling freely under the influence of the Earth's gravitational field; it varies slightly at different latitudes and altitudes. The value adopted internationally for gravitational acceleration is 9.806 m s$^{-2}$/32.174 ft s$^{-2}$.

**accelerator** in physics, a device to bring charged particles (such as protons and electrons) up to high speeds and energies, at which they can be of use in industry, medicine, and pure physics. At low energies, accelerated particles can be used to produce the image on a television screen and generate X-rays (by means of a ◊cathode-ray tube), destroy tumour cells, or kill bacteria. When high-energy particles collide with other particles, the fragments formed reveal the nature of the fundamental forces.

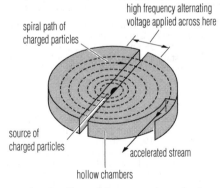

spiral path of charged particles

high frequency alternating voltage applied across here

source of charged particles

accelerated stream

hollow chambers

*accelerator The cyclotron, an early accelerator, consisted of two D-shaped hollow chambers enclosed in a vacuum. An alternating voltage was applied across the gap between the hollows. Charged particles spiralled outward from the centre, picking up energy and accelerating each time they passed through the gap.*

**acclimation** or *acclimatization,* the physiological changes induced in an organism by exposure to new environmental conditions. When humans move to higher altitudes, the number of red blood cells rises to increase the oxygen-carrying capacity of the blood in order to compensate for the lower levels of oxygen in the air.

**accommodation** in biology, the ability of the ◊eye to focus on near or far objects by changing the shape of the lens.

**accomplice** in law, a person who acts with another in the commission or attempted commission of a crime, either as a principal or as an accessory.

**accordion** musical instrument of the free-reed organ type, comprising left and right wind chests connected by flexible, pleated bellows. The accordionist's right hand plays the melody on a piano-style keyboard of 26–34 keys, while the left hand has a system of push buttons for selecting single notes or chord harmonies.

**accounting** the principles and practice of systematically recording, presenting, and interpreting financial accounts; financial record keeping and management of businesses and other organizations, from balance sheets to policy decisions, for tax or operating purposes. Forms of inflation accounting, such as CCA (current cost accounting) and CPP (current purchasing power), are aimed at providing valid financial comparisons over a period in which money values change.

**Accra** capital and port of Ghana; population (1988 est) 949,100. It is an important political, commercial, and administrative centre. The port trades in cacao, gold, diamonds, and timber. Industries include light engineering, brewing, and tobacco and food processing. Osu (Christiansborg) Castle is the presidential residence. The National Museum of Ghana is here, and the University of Ghana is at nearby Legon.

**accumulator** in electricity, a storage ◊battery – that is, a group of rechargeable secondary cells. A familiar example is the lead–acid car battery.

**acetone** common name for ◊propanone.

**acetylene** common name for ◊ethyne.

**Achaea** or *Achaia,* in ancient Greece, an area of the northern Peloponnese. The *Achaeans* were the predominant society during the Mycenaean period and are said by Homer to have taken part in the siege of Troy. The larger Roman province of Achaea was created after the defeat of the Achaean League 146 BC; it included all mainland Greece south of a line drawn from the Ambracian to the Maliac Gulf.

**Achebe, Chinua (Albert Chinua-lumogo)** (1930– ) Nigerian novelist. His themes include the social and political impact of European colonialism on African people and the problems of newly independent African nations. Among his works are the seminal *Things Fall Apart* 1958, one of the first African novels to achieve a global reputation, and *Anthills of the Savannah* 1987.

**Achernar** or *Alpha Eridani,* brightest star in the constellation Eridanus, and the ninth-brightest star in the sky. It is a hot, luminous, blue star with a true luminosity 250 times that of the Sun. It is 125 light years away from the Sun.

**Achilles** Greek hero of Homer's *Iliad*. He was the son of Peleus, King of the Myrmidons in Thessaly, and of the sea nymph Thetis, who rendered him invulnerable, except for the heel by which she held him, by dipping him in the River Styx. Achilles killed ◊Hector at the climax of the *Iliad* and, according to subsequent Greek legends was himself killed by ◊Paris, who shot a poisoned arrow into Achilles' heel.

**Achilles tendon** tendon at the back of the ankle attaching the calf muscles to the heel bone. It is one of the largest tendons in the human body, and can resist great tensional strain, but is sometimes ruptured by contraction of the muscles in sudden extension of the foot.

Ancient surgeons regarded wounds in this tendon as fatal, probably because of the Greek legend of ◊Achilles, which relates how the mother of the hero Achilles dipped him when an infant into the River Styx, so that he became invulnerable except for the heel by which she held him.

**acid** in chemistry, compound that releases hydrogen ions ($H^+$ or protons) in the presence of an ionizing solvent (usually water). Acids react with ◊bases to form salts, and they act as solvents. Strong acids are corrosive; dilute acids have a sour or sharp taste, although in some organic acids this may be partially masked by other flavour characteristics. The strength of an acid is measured by its hydrogen-ion concentration, indicated by the ◊pH value. All acids have a pH below 7.0.

**acid rain** acidic precipitation thought to be caused principally by the release into the atmosphere of sulphur dioxide ($SO_2$) and oxides of nitrogen, which dissolve in pure rainwater making it acidic. Sulphur dioxide is formed by the burning of fossil fuels, such as coal, that contain high quantities of sulphur; nitrogen oxides are contributed from various industrial activities and from car exhaust fumes.

**aclinic line** the magnetic equator, an imaginary line near the Equator, where a compass needle balances horizontally, the attraction of the north and south magnetic poles being equal.

**acne** skin eruption, mainly occurring among adolescents and young adults, caused by inflammation of the sebaceous glands which secrete an oily substance (sebum), the natural lubricant of the skin. Sometimes the openings of the glands become blocked, causing the formation of pus-filled swellings. Teenage acne is seen mainly on the face, back, and chest.

**acorn** fruit of the ◊oak tree, a nut growing in a shallow cup.

**acoustic** term describing a musical instrument played without electrical amplification or assistance, for example an acoustic guitar or acoustic piano. It is also a term used by musicians to characterize room response, an important factor in performance. A so-called 'bright' acoustic provides a lively reverberation while a 'dry' or 'muddy' acoustic is lacking in response; see ◊acoustics.

**acoustics** in general, the experimental and theoretical science of sound and its transmission; in particular, that branch of the science that has to do with the phenomena of sound in a particular space such as a room or theatre. In architecture, the sound-reflecting character of an internal space.

**acquired character** feature of the body that develops during the lifetime of an individual, usually as a result of repeated use or disuse, such as the enlarged muscles of a weightlifter.

**acquired immune deficiency syndrome** full name for the disease ◊AIDS.

**acquittal** in law, the setting free of someone charged with a crime after a trial.

**acre** traditional English land measure equal to 4,840 square yards (4,047 sq m/0.405 ha). Originally meaning a field, it was the size that a yoke of oxen could plough in a day.

**acronym** word formed from the initial letters and/or syllables of other words, intended as a pronounceable abbreviation; for example, NATO (*N*orth *A*tlantic *T*reaty *O*rganization), radar (*ra*dio *d*etecting *a*nd *r*anging), RAM (*r*andom-*a*ccess *m*emory) and FORTRAN (*for*mula *tran*slation).

**acropolis** (Greek 'high city') citadel of an ancient Greek town. The Acropolis of Athens contains the ruins of the Parthenon and surrounding complexes, built there during the days of the Athenian empire. The term is also used for analogous structures.

**acrostic** (Greek 'at the extremity of a line or row') a number of lines of writing, usually verse, whose initial letters (read downwards) form a word, phrase, or sentence. A *single acrostic* is formed by the initial letters of lines only; a *double acrostic* is formed by the first and last letters.

**Acrux** or *Alpha Crucis,* brightest star in the constellation of Crux, marking one of the four points of the ◊Southern Cross, and the 12th-brightest star in the night sky. It is a binary star comprising two blue-white stars, and is 510 light years away. Together with nearby Gacrux, it points towards the south celestial pole.

**acrylic fibre** synthetic fibre often used as a substitute for wool. It was first developed in the mid-1940s but was not produced in large quantities until the 1950s. Strong and warm, acrylic fibre is often used for sweaters and tracksuits and as linings for boots and gloves, as well as in furnishing fabrics and carpets. It is manufactured as a filament, then cut into short staple lengths similar to wool hairs, and spun into yarn. *Modacrylic* is a modified acrylic yarn.

**acrylic paint** any of a range of synthetic substitutes for ◊oil paint, mostly soluble in water.

Acrylic paints are used in a variety of painting techniques, from wash to impasto. They dry quicker than oil paint and are waterproof and remain slightly flexible, but lack the translucency of natural substances.

**actinide** any of a series of 15 radioactive metallic chemical elements with atomic numbers 89 (actinium) to 103 (lawrencium). Elements 89 to 95 occur in nature; the rest of the series are synthesized elements only. Actinides are grouped together because of their chemical similarities (for example, they are all bivalent), the properties differing only slightly with atomic number. The series is set out in a band in the ◊periodic table of the elements, as are the ◊lanthanides.

**actinium** (Greek *aktis* 'ray') white, radioactive, metallic element, the first of the actinide series, symbol Ac, atomic number 89, relative atomic mass 227; it is a weak emitter of high-energy alpha particles.

Actinium occurs with uranium and radium in ◊pitchblende and other ores, and can be synthesized by bombarding radium with neutrons. The longest-lived isotope, Ac-227, has a half-life of 21.8 years (all the other isotopes have very short half-lives). Chemically, it is exclusively trivalent, resembling in its reactions the lanthanides and the other actinides. Actinium was discovered 1899 by the French chemist André Debierne (1874–1949).

**action** in law, one of the proceedings whereby a person or agency seeks to enforce rights or redress a wrong in a civil court.

**action painting** or *gesture painting,* in abstract art, a form of ◊Abstract Expressionism that emphasized the importance of the physical act of painting. Jackson ◊Pollock, the leading exponent, threw, dripped, and dribbled paint on to canvasses fastened to the floor. He was known to attack his canvas with knives and trowels and bicycle over it. Another principal exponent was Willem de Kooning.

**Actium, Battle of** naval battle in which Octavian defeated the combined fleets of ◊Mark Antony and ◊Cleopatra on 2 September 31 BC to become the undisputed ruler of the Roman world (as the emperor ◊Augustus). The site of the battle is at Akri, a promontory in western Greece.

**act of Congress** in the USA, a bill or resolution passed by both houses of Congress, the Senate and the House of Representatives, which becomes law with the signature of the president. If vetoed by the president, it may still become law if it returns to Congress again and is passed by a majority of two-thirds in each house.

**act of Parliament** in Britain, a change in the law originating in Parliament and called a statute. Before an act receives the royal assent and becomes law it is a *bill.* The US equivalent is an ◊act of Congress.

**acupuncture** in alternative medicine, a system of inserting long, thin metal needles into the body at predetermined points to relieve pain, as an anaesthetic in surgery, and to assist healing. The needles are rotated manually or electrically. The method, developed in ancient China and increasingly popular in the West, is thought to work by stimulating the brain's own painkillers, the ◊endorphins.

**acute angle** an angle between 0° and 90°; that is, an amount of turn that is less than a quarter of a circle.

**AD** in the Christian chronological system, abbreviation for anno Domini.

**Adam** family of Scottish architects and designers. *William Adam* (1689–1748) was the leading Scottish architect of his day, and his son *Robert Adam* (1728–1792) is considered one of the greatest British architects of the late 18th century, responsible for transforming the prevailing Palladian fashion in architecture to a Neo-Classical style.

**Adam** (Hebrew *adham* 'man') in the Old Testament (Genesis 2, 3), the first human. Formed by God from dust and given the breath of life, Adam was placed in the Garden of Eden, where ◊Eve was created from his rib and given to him as a companion. Because she tempted him, he tasted the forbidden fruit of the Tree of Knowledge of Good and Evil, for which trespass they were expelled from the Garden.

**Adams, Gerry (Gerard)** (1948– ) Northern Ireland politician, president of ◊Sinn Fein (the political wing of the Irish Republican Army, IRA) from 1978. He was elected member of Parliament for Belfast West in 1983 but declined to take up his Westminster seat, as he refused to take an oath of allegiance to the Queen; he lost his seat in 1992 but regained it in 1997, still refusing to sit in the Westminster Parliament. Despite doubts about his ability to influence the IRA, he has been a key figure in Irish peace negotiations. He was the main architect of the IRA ceasefire in 1994 and in 1997 he entered into multiparty talks with the British government which, on Good Friday, 10 April 1998, resulted in an agreement accepted by all parties and subsequently endorsed in referenda held simultaneously in Northern Ireland and in the Irish Republic. However, Sinn Fein lost support to the moderate republican Social Democratic Labour Party (SDLP) in the June 1998 elections to the new Northern Ireland Assembly.

**Adams, John** (1735–1826) 2nd president of the USA 1797–1801, and vice-president 1789–97. He was a member of the Continental Congress 1774–78 and signed the Declaration of Independence. In 1779 he went to France and negotiated the treaty of 1783 that ended the American Revolution. In 1785 he became the first US ambassador in London.

**Adams, John Quincy** (1767–1848) 6th president of the USA 1825–29, eldest son of President John Adams. He negotiated the Treaty of Ghent to end the ◊War of 1812 (fought with Britain) on generous terms for the USA. In 1817 he became President James Monroe's secretary of state, formulating the ◊Monroe Doctrine 1823. As president, Adams was an advocate of strong federal government.

**Adamson, Robert** (1821–1848) Scottish photographer. He collaborated with fellow Scottish photographer David Octavius Hill. See ◊Hill and Adamson.

**Adana** capital of Adana (Seyhan) province, southern Turkey; population (1990) 916,150. It is a major cotton-growing centre and Turkey's fourth-largest city.

**adaptation** (Latin *adaptare* 'to fit to') in biology, any change in the structure or function of an organism that allows it to survive and reproduce more effectively in its environment. In ◊evolution, adaptation is thought to occur as a result of random variation in the genetic make-up of organisms coupled with ◊natural selection. Species become extinct when they are no longer adapted to their environment – for instance, if the climate suddenly becomes colder.

**adaptive radiation** in evolution, the formation of several species, with ◊adaptations to different ways of life, from a single ancestral type. Adaptive radiation is likely to occur whenever members of a species migrate to a new habitat with unoccupied ecological niches. It is thought that the lack of competition in such niches allows sections of the migrant population to develop new adaptations, and eventually to become new species.

The colonization of newly formed volcanic islands has led to the development of many unique species. The 13 species of Darwin's finch on the Galápagos Islands, for example, are probably descended from a single species from the South American mainland. The parent stock evolved into different species that now occupy a range of diverse niches.

**Ad Dakhla** port and southern region in Western Sahara; population (1982) 17,800. The town was first established as a Spanish trading port in 1476, when it was known as *Villa Cisneros*.

**adder** (Anglo-Saxon *naedre* 'serpent') European venomous snake, the common ◊viper *Vipera berus*. Growing on average to about 60 cm/24 in in length, it has a thick body, triangular head, a characteristic V-shaped mark on its head and, often, zigzag markings along the back. It feeds on small mammals and lizards. The puff adder *Bitis arietans* is a large, yellowish, thick-bodied viper up to 1.6 m/5 ft long, living in Africa and Arabia.

**addiction** state of dependence caused by habitual use of drugs, alcohol, or other substances. It is characterized by uncontrolled craving, tolerance, and symptoms of withdrawal when access is denied. Habitual use produces changes in body chemistry and treatment must be geared to a gradual reduction in dosage.

**Addis Ababa** or *Adis Abeba* (Amharic 'new flower'), capital of Ethiopia; population (1992) 2,213,000. The city is at an altitude of 2,500 m/8,200 ft. It was founded in 1887 by Menelik II, chief of Shoa, who ascended the throne of Ethiopia in 1889. His former residence, Menelik Palace, is now occupied by the government. Industries include light engineering, food processing, brewing, livestock processing, chemicals, cement, textiles, footwear, clothing, and handicrafts.

**Addison, Joseph** (1672–1719) English poet and dramatist, and one of the most celebrated of English essayists. In 1704 he commemorated Marlborough's victory at Blenheim in a poem commissioned by the government, 'The Campaign'. He subsequently held political appointments and was MP for Malmesbury from 1708 until his death. From 1709 to 1711 he contributed to the *Tatler* magazine, begun by Richard ◊Steele, with whom he was cofounder in 1711–12 of the *Spectator*.

**addition reaction** chemical reaction in which the atoms of an element or compound react with a double bond or triple bond in an organic compound by opening up one of the bonds and becoming attached to it, for example

$$CH_2 = CH_2 + HCl \rightarrow CH_3CH_2Cl$$

An example is the addition of hydrogen atoms to ◊unsaturated compounds in vegetable oils to produce margarine. Addition reactions are used to make useful polymers from ◊alkenes.

**additive** in food, any natural or artificial chemical added to prolong the shelf life of processed foods (salt or nitrates), alter the colour, texture, or flavour of food, or improve its food value (vitamins or minerals). Many chemical additives are used and they are subject to regulation, since individuals may be affected by constant exposure even to traces of certain additives and may suffer side effects ranging from headaches and hyperactivity to cancer. However, it can be difficult to know how to test the safety of such substances; many natural foods contain toxic substances which could not pass the tests applied today to new products.

Food companies in many countries are now required by law to list additives used in their products. Within the European Union, approved additives are given an official E number.

**Adelaide** capital and chief port of ◊South Australia; population (1996) 978,100. Adelaide is situated on the River Torrens, 11 km/7 mi from the Gulf of St Vincent. Industries include oil refining, shipbuilding, electronics, and the manufacture of electrical goods and cars. Grain, wool, fruit, and wine are exported from Port Adelaide, 11 km/7 mi northwest of the city. Adelaide was founded in 1836 and named after the queen of William IV. The city's fine buildings include Parliament House, Government House, the Anglican cathedral of St Peter, and the Roman Catholic Cathedral of St Francis Xavier (built 1856–1926).

**Aden** Arabic *'Adan,* main port and commercial centre of Yemen, on a rocky peninsula at the southwest corner of Arabia, commanding the entrance to the Red Sea; population (1995) 562,000. The city's economy is based on oil refining, fishing, and shipping. A British territory from 1839, Aden became part of independent South Yemen in 1967; it was the capital of South Yemen until 1990.

**Adenauer, Konrad** (1876–1967) German Christian Democrat politician, chancellor of West Germany 1949–63. With the French president Charles de Gaulle he achieved the post-war reconciliation of France and Germany and strongly supported all measures designed to strengthen the Western bloc in Europe.

**adenoids** masses of lymphoid tissue, similar to ◊tonsils, located in the upper part of the throat, behind the nose. They are part of a child's natural defences against the entry of germs but usually shrink and disappear by the age of ten.

**adhesive** substance that sticks two surfaces together. Natural adhesives (glues) include gelatin in its crude industrial form (made from bones, hide fragments, and fish offal) and vegetable gums. Synthetic adhesives include thermoplastic and thermosetting resins, which are often stronger than the substances they join; mixtures of epoxy resin and hardener that set by chemical reaction; and elastomeric (stretching) adhesives for flexible joints. Superglues are fast-setting adhesives used in very small quantities.

**adiabatic** in physics, a process that occurs without loss or gain of heat, especially the expansion or contraction of a gas in which a change takes place in the pressure or volume, although no heat is allowed to enter or leave.

**Adi Granth** or *Guru Granth Sahib*, the holy book of Sikhism; see ◊*Guru Granth Sahib*.

**adipose tissue** type of ◊connective tissue of vertebrates that serves as an energy reserve, and also pads some organs. It is commonly called fat tissue, and consists of large spherical cells filled with fat. In mammals, major layers are in the inner layer of skin and around the kidneys and heart.

**admiral** any of several species of butterfly in the same family (Nymphalidae) as the tortoise-shells. The red admiral *Vanessa atalanta*, wingspan 6 cm/2.5 in, is found worldwide in the northern hemisphere. It either hibernates, or migrates south each year from northern areas to subtropical zones.

**Admiralty Islands** group of small islands in the southwest Pacific, part of Papua New Guinea; area 2,071 sq km/800 sq mi; population (1980) 25,000. The islands form part of the ◊Bismarck Archipelago and constitute with the North Western Islands the Manus district of Papua New Guinea. The largest island (about 80 km/50 mi long) is Manus of which Lorengau is the chief town. Exports are copra and pearls. The islands became a German protectorate in 1884 and an Australian mandate in 1920.

**adobe** in architecture, a building method employing sun-dried earth bricks; also the individual bricks. The use of earth bricks and the construction of walls by enclosing earth within moulds (*pisé de terre*) are the two principal methods of raw-earth building. The techniques are commonly found in Spain, Latin America, and the southwestern USA.

**adolescence** in the human life cycle, the period between the beginning of puberty and adulthood.

**Adonis** (Semitic *Adon*, 'the Lord') in Greek mythology, a beautiful youth loved by the goddess ◊Aphrodite. He was killed while boar-hunting but was allowed to return from the underworld for a period every year to rejoin her. The anemone sprang from his blood.

**adoption** permanent legal transfer of parental rights and duties from one person to another,

usually to provide care for children who would otherwise lack family upbringing.

**adrenal gland** or *suprarenal gland*, triangular gland situated on top of the ◊kidney. The adrenals are soft and yellow, and consist of two parts: the cortex and medulla. The *cortex* (outer part) secretes various steroid hormones and other hormones that control salt and water metabolism and regulate the use of carbohydrates, proteins, and fats. The *medulla* (inner part) secretes the hormones adrenaline and noradrenaline which, during times of stress, cause the heart to beat faster and harder, increase blood flow to the heart and muscle cells, and dilate airways in the lungs, thereby delivering more oxygen to cells throughout the body and in general preparing the body for 'fight or flight'.

**adrenaline** or *epinephrine*, hormone secreted by the medulla of the ◊adrenal glands. Adrenaline is synthesized from a closely related substance, noradrenaline, and the two hormones are released into the bloodstream in situations of fear or stress.

**Adrian IV** Nicholas Breakspear (*c.* 1100–1159) Pope 1154–59, the only English pope. He secured the execution of Arnold of Brescia and crowned Frederick I Barbarossa as German emperor. When he died, Adrian IV was at the height of a quarrel with Barbarossa over papal supremacy. He allegedly issued the controversial bull giving Ireland to Henry II of England in 1154. He was attacked for false representation, and the bull was subsequently refuted.

**Adriatic Sea** large arm of the Mediterranean Sea, lying northwest to southeast between the Italian and the Balkan peninsulas. The western shore is Italian; the eastern includes Croatia, Montenegro, and Albania, with two small strips of coastline owned by Slovenia and Bosnia Herzogovina. The Strait of Otranto, between Italy and Albania, links the Adriatic with the Ionian Sea to the south. The chief ports are Venice, Brindisi, Trieste, Ancona, and Bari in Italy, and Rijeka in Croatia. The sea is about 805 km/500 mi long; area 135,250 sq km/52,220 sq mi.

**adsorption** taking up of a gas or liquid at the surface of another substance, most commonly a solid (for example, activated charcoal adsorbs gases). It involves molecular attraction at the surface, and should be distinguished from ◊absorption (in which a uniform solution results from a gas or liquid being incorporated into the bulk structure of a liquid or solid).

**adultery** voluntary sexual intercourse between a married person and someone other than his or her legal partner.

**Adventist** person who believes that Jesus will return to make a second appearance on Earth. Expectation of the Second Coming of Christ is found in New Testament writings generally. Adventist views are held in particular by the Seventh-Day Adventists church (with 4 million members in 200 countries), the Christadelphians, the ◊Jehovah's Witnesses, the Four

Square Gospel Alliance, the Advent Christian church, and the Evangelical Adventist church.

**advertising** any of various methods used by a company to increase the sales of its products or services or to promote a brand name. Advertising is also used by organizations and individuals to communicate an idea or image, to recruit staff, to publicize an event, or to locate an item or commodity.

**Aegean Islands** region of Greece comprising the Dodecanese islands, the Cyclades islands, Lesvos, Samos, and Chios; area 9,122 sq km/3,523 sq mi; population (1991) 460,800.

**Aegean Sea** branch of the Mediterranean between Greece and Turkey, extending as far south as Crete; the Dardanelles connect it with the Sea of Marmara, in turn linked with the Black Sea via the Bosporus. It is about 600 km/372 mi long and 290 km/180 mi wide, and covers some 214,000 sq km/82,625 sq mi, with a maximum depth of 3,540 m/11,600 ft. Tides are minimal, with a range of only about 40 cm/15 in. The numerous islands in the Aegean Sea include Crete, the Cyclades, the Sporades, and the Dodecanese. There is political tension between Greece and Turkey over sea limits claimed by Greece around such islands as Lesvos, Chios, Samos, and Kos.

**Aeneas** in classical mythology, a Trojan prince who became the ancestral hero of the Romans. According to ◊Homer, he was the son of Anchises and the goddess Aphrodite. During the Trojan War he owed his life to the frequent intervention of the gods. The legend on which Virgil's epic poem the *Aeneid* is based describes his escape from Troy and his eventual settlement in Latium, on the Italian peninsula.

**Aeolian Islands** another name for the Lipari Islands.

**aerial** or *antenna,* in radio and television broadcasting, a conducting device that radiates or receives electromagnetic waves. The design of an aerial depends principally on the wavelength of the signal. Long waves (hundreds of metres in wavelength) may employ long wire aerials; short waves (several centimetres in wavelength) may employ rods and dipoles; microwaves may also use dipoles – often with reflectors arranged like a toast rack – or highly directional parabolic dish aerials. Because microwaves travel in straight lines, requiring line-of-sight communication, microwave aerials are usually located at the tops of tall masts or towers.

**aerobic** in biology, term used to describe those organisms that require oxygen (usually dissolved in water) for the efficient release of energy contained in food molecules, such as glucose. They include almost all organisms (plants as well as animals) with the exception of certain bacteria, yeasts, and internal parasites.

**aerobics** (Greek 'air' and 'life') exercises to improve the performance of the heart and lungs, involving strenuous application of movement to raise the heart rate to 120 beats per minute or more for sessions of 5–20 minutes' duration, 3–5 times per week.

**aerodynamics** branch of fluid physics that studies the forces exerted by air or other gases in motion. Examples include the airflow around bodies moving at speed through the atmosphere (such as land vehicles, bullets, rockets, and aircraft), the behaviour of gas in engines and furnaces, air conditioning of buildings, the deposition of snow, the operation of air-cushion vehicles (hovercraft), wind loads on buildings and bridges, bird and insect flight, musical wind instruments, and meteorology. For maximum efficiency, the aim is usually to design the shape of an object to produce a streamlined flow, with a minimum of turbulence in the moving air. The behaviour of aerosols or the pollution of the atmosphere by foreign particles are other aspects of aerodynamics.

**aeronautics** science of travel through the Earth's atmosphere, including aerodynamics, aircraft structures, jet and rocket propulsion, and aerial navigation.

**aeroplane** US airplane, powered heavier-than-air craft supported in flight by fixed wings. Aeroplanes are propelled by the thrust of a jet engine, a rocket engine, or airscrew (propeller), as well as combinations of these. They must be designed aerodynamically, since streamlining ensures maximum flight efficiency. The Wright brothers flew the first powered plane (a biplane) in Kitty Hawk, North Carolina, USA, in 1903. For the history of aircraft and aviation, see ◊flight.

**aerosol** particles of liquid or solid suspended in a gas. Fog is a common natural example. Aerosol cans contain a substance such as scent or cleaner packed under pressure with a device for releasing it as a fine spray. Most aerosols used chlorofluorocarbons (CFCs) as propellants until these were found to cause destruction of the ◊ozone layer in the stratosphere.

**Aeschylus** (*c.* 525– *c.* 456 BC) Athenian dramatist. He developed Greek tragedy by introducing the second actor, thus enabling true dialogue and dramatic action to occur independently of the chorus. Ranked with ◊Euripides and ◊Sophocles as one of the three great tragedians, Aeschylus composed some 90 plays between 500 and 456 BC, of which seven complete tragedies survive in his name: *Persians* 472 BC, *Seven Against Thebes* 467, *Suppliants* 463, the *Oresteia* trilogy (*Agamemnon, Libation-Bearers,* and *Eumenides*) 458, and *Prometheus Bound* (the last, although attributed to him, is of uncertain date and authorship).

**Aesop** by tradition, a writer of Greek fables. According to the historian Herodotus, he lived in the mid-6th century BC and was a slave. The fables that are ascribed to him were collected at a later date and are anecdotal stories using animal characters to illustrate moral or satirical points.

**Aesthetic Movement** English artistic movement of the late 19th century, dedicated to the doctrine of 'art for art's sake' – that is, art as a self-sufficient entity concerned solely with beauty and not with any moral or social purpose. Associated with the movement were the artists Aubrey ◊Beardsley and James McNeill ◊Whistler and writers Walter Pater and Oscar ◊Wilde.

**aesthetics** branch of philosophy that deals with the nature of beauty, especially in art. It emerged as a distinct branch of enquiry in the mid-18th century.

**aestivation** in zoology, a state of inactivity and reduced metabolic activity, similar to ◊hibernation, that occurs during the dry season in species such as lungfish and snails. In botany, the term is used to describe the way in which flower petals and sepals are folded in the buds. It is an important feature in ◊plant classification.

**affidavit** legal document, used in court applications and proceedings, in which a person swears that certain facts are true.

**affinity** in chemistry, the force of attraction (see ◊bond) between atoms that helps to keep them in combination in a molecule. The term is also applied to attraction between molecules, such as those of biochemical significance (for example, between ◊enzymes and substrate molecules). This is the basis for affinity ◊chromatography, by which biologically important compounds are separated.

**affinity** in law, relationship by marriage not blood (for example, between a husband and his wife's blood relatives, between a wife and her husband's blood relatives, or between stepparent and stepchild), which may legally preclude their marriage. It is distinguished from consanguinity or blood relationship.

**affirmative action** government policy of positive discrimination by the use of legal measures and moral persuasion that favours women and members of minority ethnic groups in such areas as employment and education. It is designed to counter the effects of long-term discrimination against these groups, and in Europe, Sweden, Belgium, the Netherlands, and Italy actively promote affirmative action through legal and financial incentives.

**Afghan hound** breed of fast hunting dog resembling the ◊saluki in build, though slightly smaller.

**Afghan Wars** three wars waged between Britain and Afghanistan to counter the threat to British India from expanding Russian influence in Afghanistan.
*First Afghan War* 1838–42, when the British garrison at Kabul was wiped out.
*Second Afghan War* 1878–80, when General Roberts captured Kabul and relieved Kandahar.
*Third Afghan War* 1919, when peace followed the dispatch by the UK of the first aeroplane ever seen in Kabul.

**Afghanistan** Republic of
*national name Islamic Emirate of Afghanistan*
*area* 652,090 sq km/251,771 sq mi
*capital* Kabul
*major towns/cities* Kandahar, Herat, Mazar-i-Sharif, Jalalabad
*physical features* mountainous in centre and northeast (Hindu Kush mountain range; Khyber and Salang passes, Wakhan salient, and Panjshir

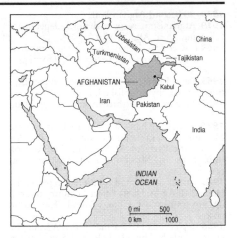

Valley), plains in north and southwest, Amu Darya (Oxus) River, Helmand River, Lake Saberi
*head of state and government* Mohammad Rabbani from 1996
*political system* transitional
*political parties* Hezb-i-Islami, Islamic fundamentalist Mujahedin, anti-Western; Jamiat-i-Islami, Islamic fundamentalist Mujahedin; National Liberation Front, moderate Mujahedin
*currency* afgháni
*GNP per capita (PPP)* (US$) 819 (1992)
*exports* fruit and nuts, carpets, wool, karakul skins, cotton, natural gas. Principal market: Kyrgyzstan 37.3% (1995)
*population* 21,923,000 (1999 est)
*language* Pushtu, Dari (Persian), Uzbek, Turkoman, Kirgiz
*religion* Muslim (85% Sunni, 15% Shiite)
*life expectancy* 45 (men); 46 (women) (1995–2000)
*Chronology*
*6th century BC* Part of Persian Empire under Cyrus II and Darius I.
*329 BC* Conquered by Alexander the Great.
*323 BC* Fell to the Seleucids, who ruled from Babylon.
*304 BC* Ruled by Mauryan dynasty in south and independent Bactria in north.
*135 BC* Central Asian tribes established Kusana dynasty.
*3rd–7th centuries AD* Decline of Kusana dynasty. Emergence of Sassanids as ruling power with Hepthalites (central Asian nomads) and western Turks also fighting for control.
*642–11th century* First Muslim invasion followed by a succession of Muslim dynasties, including Mahmud of Ghazni in 998.
*1219–14th century* Mongol invasions led by Genghis Khan and Tamerlane.
*16th–18th centuries* Much of Afghanistan came under the rule of the Mogul Empire under Babur (Zahir) and Nadir Shah.
*1747* Afghanistan became an independent emirate under Dost Muhammad.
*1838–42* First Afghan War, instigated by Britain to counter the threat to British India from expanding Russian influence in Afghanistan.

*1878–80* Second Afghan War.

*1919* Afghanistan recovered full independence following Third Afghan War.

*1953* Lt-Gen Daud Khan became prime minister and introduced social and economic reform programme.

*1963* Daud Khan forced to resign and constitutional monarchy established.

*1973* Monarchy overthrown in coup by Daud Khan.

*1978* Daud Khan assassinated in coup; Muhammad Taraki and the communist People's Democratic Party of Afghanistan (PDPA) took over. Start of Muslim guerrilla (Mujahedin) resistance.

*1979* Taraki ousted and murdered; replaced by Hafizullah Amin. USSR entered country to prop up government, installing Babrak Karmal in power.

*1986* Replacement of Karmal as PDPA leader by Dr Najibullah Ahmadzai. Partial Soviet troop withdrawal.

*1988* New non-Marxist constitution adopted.

*1989* Withdrawal of Soviet troops; Mujahedin continued resistance to PDPA regime and the civil war intensified.

*1991* US and Soviet military aid withdrawn. Mujahedin began talks with the Russians and Kabul government.

*1992* The Najibullah government overthrown. Mujahedin leader Burhanuddin Rabbani was elected president.

*1993* Intensive fighting around Kabul. A peace agreement between Rabbani and dissident Hezb-i-Islami leader Gulbuddin Hekmatyar made Hekmatyar prime minister.

*1994* Continuing rebel attacks on Kabul quelled. Hekmatyar was dismissed from office.

*1995* Talibaan Islamic fundamentalist army claimed the town of Herat and advanced on Kabul.

*1996* The Talibaan controlled two-thirds of the country, including Kabul; the country was split between the Talibaan-controlled fundamentalist south and the more liberal north; an interim council of clerics was installed, headed by Mohamad Rabbani; strict Islamic law imposed.

*1997* The Talibaan recognized as the legitimate government of Afghanistan by Pakistan and Saudi Arabia.

*1998* Two earthquakes in the north killed over 8,000 people. The USA launched a missile attack on a suspected terrorist site in retaliation for bombings of US embassies in Nairobi and Dar es Salaam. Talibaan extended its control in the north, massacring 6,000 people at Mazar-I-Sharif.

*1999* Fighting resumed in northern Afghanistan after a four-month lull.

**Africa** second largest of the five continents. Africa is connected with Asia by the isthmus of Suez, and separated from Europe by the Mediterranean Sea. The name Africa was first given by the Romans to their African provinces with the city of Carthage, and it has since been extended to the whole continent.

**area** 30,097,000 sq km/11,620,451 sq mi (three times the area of Europe)

**largest cities** (population over 1 million) Cairo, Algiers, Lagos, Kinshasa, Abidjan, Cape Town, Nairobi, Casablanca, El Gîza, Addis Ababa, Luanda, Dar es Salaam, Ibadan, Mogadishu, Maputo, Johannesburg, Harare, Alexandria, Antananarivo, Rabat, Dakar, Durban, East Rand, Pretoria, Tunis

**features** Great Rift Valley, containing most of the great lakes of East Africa (except Lake Victoria); Atlas Mountains in the northwest; Drakensberg mountain range in the southeast; Sahara Desert (world's largest desert) in the north; Namib, Kalahari, and Great Karoo deserts in the south; Nile, Congo-Zaire, Niger, Zambezi, Limpopo, Volta, and Orange rivers

**physical** dominated by a uniform central plateau comprising a southern tableland with a mean altitude of 1,070 m/3,000 ft that falls northwards to a lower elevated plain with a mean altitude of 400 m/1,300 ft. Although there are no great alpine regions or extensive coastal plains, Africa has a mean altitude of 610 m/2,000 ft, two times greater than Europe. The highest points are Mount Kilimanjaro 5,900 m/19,364 ft, and Mount Kenya 5,200 m/17,058 ft; the lowest point is Lac Assal in Djibouti –144 m/–471 ft. Compared with other continents, Africa has few broad estuaries or inlets and therefore has proportionately the shortest coastline (24,000 km/15,000 mi). The geographical extremities of the continental mainland are Cape Hafun in the east, Cape Almadies in the west, Ras Ben Sekka in the north, and Cape Agulhas in the south. The Sahel is a narrow belt of savanna and scrub forest which covers 700 million hectares/1.7 billion acres of west and central Africa; 75% of the continent lies within the tropics.

**African National Congress** (ANC), South African political party, founded 1912 as a multiracial nationalist organization with the aim of extending the franchise to the whole population and ending all racial discrimination. Its president from 1997 is Thabo Mbeki.

The ANC was banned by the government from 1960 to January 1990. Talks between the ANC and the South African government began December 1991 and culminated in the adoption of a nonracial constitution 1993 and the ANC's agreement to participate in a power-sharing administration, as a prelude to full majority rule. In the country's first universal suffrage elections in April 1994, the ANC won a sweeping victory, capturing 62% of the vote, and Mandela was elected president. The ANC also won a majority in South Africa's first democratic local government elections in November 1995, when it won 66.3% of the vote.

**African violet** herbaceous plant from tropical central and East Africa, with velvety green leaves and scentless purple flowers. Different colours and double-flowered varieties have been bred. (*Saintpaulia ionantha*, family Gesneriaceae.)

**Africa, the scramble for** drive by European nations to establish colonies in Africa. It began in the 1880s, and by 1914 only two African countries remained completely independent.

They were Ethiopia, which had been a kingdom for about 2,000 years, and Liberia, established in 1822 as a homeland for freed black slaves. The rest were under the control of seven European powers: Belgium, Britain, France, Germany, Italy, Portugal, and Spain. Britain and France had the most colonies. All these colonies were short-lived, and the majority attained their independence in the 1960s and 1970s.

**Afrikaans language** official language (with English) of the Republic of South Africa and Namibia. Spoken mainly by the Afrikaners – descendants of Dutch and other 17th-century colonists – it is a variety of the Dutch language, modified by circumstance and the influence of German, French, and other immigrant as well as local languages. It became a standardized written language about 1875.

**Afrikaner** formerly known as *Boer,* inhabitants of South Africa descended from the original Dutch, Flemish, and ◊Huguenot settlers of the 17th century. Comprising approximately 60% of the white population in South Africa, they were originally farmers but have now become mainly urbanized. Their language is Afrikaans.

**Afro-Asiatic language** any of a family of languages spoken throughout the world. There are two main branches, the languages of North Africa and the languages originating in Syria, Mesopotamia, Palestine, and Arabia, but now found from Morocco in the west to the Persian Gulf in the east.

**afterbirth** in mammals, the placenta, umbilical cord, and ruptured membranes, which become detached from the uterus and expelled soon after birth.

**afterimage** persistence of an image on the retina of the eye after the object producing it has been removed. This leads to persistence of vision, a necessary phenomenon for the illusion of continuous movement in films and television. The term is also used for the persistence of sensations other than vision.

**Agamemnon** in Greek mythology, a Greek hero of the Trojan wars, son of Atreus, king of Mycenae, and brother of Menelaus. He sacrificed his daughter Iphigenia in order to secure favourable winds for the Greek expedition against Troy and after a ten-year siege sacked the city, receiving Priam's daughter ◊Cassandra as a prize. On his return home, he and Cassandra were murdered by his wife ◊Clytemnestra and her lover Aegisthus.

**agamid** lizard in the family Agamidae, containing about 300 species.

**agaric** any of a group of fungi (see ◊fungus) of typical mushroom shape. Agarics include the field mushroom *Agaricus campestris* and the cultivated edible mushroom *A. brunnesiens.* Closely related is the often poisonous *Amanita,* which includes the fly agaric *A. muscaria.* (Genus *Agaricus,* family Agaricaceae.)

**Agassiz, (Jean) Louis Rodolphe** (1807– 1873) Swiss-born US palaeontologist and geologist who developed the idea of the ice age. He established his name through his work on the classification of fossil fishes. Unlike Charles Darwin, he did not believe that individual species themselves changed, but that new species were created from time to time.

**agate** cryptocrystalline (with crystals too small to be seen with an optical microscope) silica, $SiO_2$, composed of cloudy and banded ◊chalcedony, sometimes mixed with ◊opal, that forms in rock cavities.

**agave** any of several related plants with stiff, sword-shaped, spiny leaves arranged in a rosette. All species come from the warmer parts of the New World. They include *Agave sisalina,* whose fibres are used for rope making, and the Mexican century plant *A. americana,* which may take many years to mature (hence its common name). Alcoholic drinks such as ◊tequila and pulque are made from the sap of agave plants. (Genus *Agave,* family Agavaceae.)

**Agincourt, Battle of** battle fought on 25 October 1415 at Agincourt during the Hundred Years' War, between Henry V of England and a much larger force of French under a divided command. Henry decimated the French and enabled the English conquest of Normandy. Some 6,000 French died and hundreds, including the richest nobles, were taken prisoner. Henry gained France and the French princess Catherine of Valois as his wife. The village of Agincourt (modern *Azincourt*) is south of Calais, in northern France.

**agnosticism** belief that the existence of God cannot be proven; that in the nature of things the individual cannot know anything of what lies behind or beyond the world of natural phenomena. The term was coined 1869 by T H ◊Huxley.

**agoraphobia** ◊phobia involving fear of open spaces and public places. The anxiety produced can be so severe that some sufferers are unable to leave their homes for many years.

**agouti** small rodent of the genus *Dasyprocta,* family Dasyproctidae. It is found in the forests of Central and South America. The agouti is herbivorous, swift-running, and about the size of a rabbit.

**Agra** city in Uttar Pradesh, northern India, on the River Jumna (or Yamuna), 160 km/100 mi southeast of Delhi; population (1991) 892,000. It is a centre for commerce, tourism and industry. There are many small-scale engineering plants, and carpets, leather goods, gold and silver embroidery, and engraved marble are produced. The capital of the Mogul empire from 1566–69 and 1601–1658, it is the site of the ◊Taj Mahal, built during the latter period. Other notable buildings include the Moti Masjid (Pearl Mosque), the Jama Masjid (Great Mosque), and the Red Fort, with red sandstone walls over 20 m/65 ft high and 2.5 km/1.5 mi long. It has a university (1927).

**Agricola, Gnaeus Julius** (AD 40–93) Roman general and politician. Born at Forum Julii (Fréjus) in Provence, he became consul in AD 77, and then governor of Britain 78–85. He extended Roman rule to the Firth of Forth in Scotland and in 84 won the Battle of Mons Graupius. His fleet sailed round the north of Scotland and proved Britain an island.

**agricultural revolution** sweeping changes that took place in British agriculture over the period 1750–1850. The changes were a response to the increased demand for food from a rapidly expanding population. Major events included the ◊enclosure of open fields; the development of improved breeds of livestock; the introduction of four-course crop rotation; and the use of new crops such as turnips as animal fodder.

Recent research has shown that these changes were only part of a much larger, ongoing process of development: many were in fact underway before 1750, and other breakthroughs, such as farm mechanization, did not occur until after 1859.

**agriculture** (Latin *ager* 'field', *colere* 'to cultivate') the practice of farming, including the cultivation of the soil (for raising crops) and the raising of domesticated animals. The units for managing agricultural production vary from smallholdings and individually owned farms to corporate-run farms and collective farms run by entire communities.

*Crops* are for human or animal food, or commodities such as cotton and sisal. For successful production, the land must be prepared (ploughed, cultivated, harrowed, and rolled). Seed must be planted and the growing plants nurtured. This may involve ◊fertilizers, ◊irrigation, pest control by chemicals, and monitoring of acidity or nutrients. When the crop has grown, it must be harvested and, depending on the crop, processed in a variety of ways before it is stored or sold.

Greenhouses allow cultivation of plants that would otherwise find the climate too harsh. ◊Hydroponics allows commercial cultivation of crops using nutrient-enriched solutions instead of soil. Special methods, such as terracing, may be adopted to allow cultivation in hostile terrain and to retain topsoil in mountainous areas with heavy rainfall.

*Animals* are raised for wool, milk, leather, dung (as fuel), or meat. They may be semi-domesticated, such as reindeer, or fully domesticated but nomadic (where naturally growing or cultivated food supplies are sparse), or kept in one location. Animal farming involves accommodation (buildings, fencing, or pasture), feeding, breeding, gathering the produce (eggs, milk, or wool), slaughtering, and further processing such as tanning.

**agronomy** study of crops and soils, a branch of agricultural science. Agronomy includes such topics as selective breeding (of plants and animals), irrigation, pest control, and soil analysis and modification.

**AH** in the Muslim calendar, abbreviation for ◊*anno hegirae.*

**Ahern, Bertie** (1951– ) Irish politician, Taoiseach (prime minister) from 1997, leader of Fianna Fáil from 1994. After the May 1997 election he formed a minority government as Ireland's youngest Taoiseach. His promotion of peace negotiations culminated in the 1998 Good Friday Agreement between Northern Ireland's contending parties, which received 94% backing in a referendum in the Irish Republic in May 1998.

**Ahmadabad** or *Ahmedabad,* city in Gujarat, India, situated on the Sabarmati River, 430 km/ 260 mi north of Mumbai; population (1991) 3,298,000. The former state capital and Gujarat's largest city, it is a major industrial centre specializing in cotton manufacturing. It has many sacred buildings of the Hindu, Muslim, and Jain faiths, as well as buildings designed by 20th-century architects, such as Le Corbusier, reflecting commercial success.

**Ahriman** in Zoroastrianism, the supreme evil spirit, lord of the darkness and death, waging war with his counterpart Ahura Mazda (Ormuzd) until a time when human beings choose to lead good lives and Ahriman is finally destroyed.

**Ahura Mazda** or *Ormuzd,* in Zoroastrianism, the spirit of supreme good. As god of life and light he will finally prevail over his enemy, Ahriman.

**Ahvaz** or *Ahwaz,* capital of ◊Khuzestan province, southwest Iran; population (1991) 724,700. Situated on the River Karun, the city is an important administrative and supply centre for the southwestern Iranian oilfields, and is connected by rail to Tehran and the Gulf. There are also textile and petrochemical industries. Ahvaz was badly damaged during the Iran–Iraq war (1980–88).

**AI** abbreviation for ◊artificial intelligence.

**aid, development** money given or lent on concessional terms to developing countries or spent on maintaining agencies for this purpose. In 1970, all industrialized United Nations (UN) member countries committed to giving at least 0.7% of GNP to aid. All the Scandinavian countries have met or exceeded this target, whereas the UK and the USA have not achieved it; in 1995, the UK aid budget was only 0.28% and the US figure only 0.15% of GNP. Each country spends more than half its contribution on direct bilateral assistance to countries with which they have historical or military links or hope to encourage trade. The rest goes to international organizations such as UN and ◊World Bank agencies, which distribute aid multilaterally.

**aid, foreign** financial and other assistance given by richer, usually industrialized, countries to war-damaged or developing states. See ◊aid, development

**AIDS** acronym for *acquired immune deficiency syndrome,* the gravest of the sexually transmitted diseases, or ◊STDs. It is caused by the human immunodeficiency virus (◊HIV), now known to be a ◊retrovirus, an organism first identified in 1983. HIV is transmitted in body fluids, mainly blood and genital secretions.

**ailanthus** any of several trees or shrubs with compound leaves made up of pointed leaflets and clusters of small greenish flowers with an unpleasant smell. The tree of heaven (*Ailanthus altissima*), native to East Asia, is grown worldwide as an ornamental; it can grow to 30 m/ 100 ft in height and the trunk can reach 1 m/3 ft in diameter. (Genus *Ailanthus*, family Simaroubaceae.)

**air** the mixture of gases making up the Earth's ◊atmosphere.

**aircraft** any aeronautical vehicle capable of flying through the air. It may be lighter than air (supported by buoyancy) or heavier than air (supported by the dynamic action of air on its surfaces). ◊Balloons and ◊airships are lighter-than-air craft. Heavier-than-air craft include the ◊aeroplane, glider, autogiro, and helicopter.

**aircraft carrier** ocean-going naval vessel with a broad, flat-topped deck for launching and landing military aircraft; a floating military base for warplanes too far from home for refuelling, repairing, reconnaissance, escorting, and attack and defence operations. Aircraft are catapult-launched or take off and land on the flight-deck, a large expanse of unobstructed deck, often fitted with barriers and restraining devices to halt the landing aircraft.

**Airedale terrier** breed of large terrier, about 60 cm/24 in tall, with a wiry red-brown coat and black saddle patch. It originated about 1850 in England, as a cross between the otterhound and Irish and Welsh terriers.

**airlock** airtight chamber that allows people to pass between areas of different pressure; also an air bubble in a pipe that impedes fluid flow. An airlock may connect an environment at ordinary pressure and an environment that has high air pressure (such as a submerged caisson used for tunnelling or building dams or bridge foundations).

**air sac** in birds, a thin-walled extension of the lungs. There are nine of these and they extend into the abdomen and bones, effectively increasing lung capacity. In mammals, it is another name for the alveoli in the lungs, and in some insects, for widenings of the trachea.

**airship** or *dirigible*, any aircraft that is lighter than air and power-driven, consisting of an ellipsoidal balloon that forms the streamlined envelope or hull and has below it the propulsion system (propellers), steering mechanism, and space for crew, passengers, and/or cargo. The balloon section is filled with lighter-than-air gas, either the nonflammable helium or, before helium was industrially available in large enough quantities, the easily ignited and flammable hydrogen. The envelope's form is maintained by internal pressure in the nonrigid (blimp) and semirigid (in which the nose and tail sections have a metal framework connected by a rigid keel) types. The rigid type (zeppelin) maintains its form using an internal metal framework. Airships have been used for luxury travel, polar exploration, warfare, and advertising.

**Aix-en-Provence** city and spa in the *département* of Bouches-du-Rhône, southeast France, 29 km/18 mi north of Marseille; population (1990) 126,800. The town dates from Roman times and was the capital of the former province of Provence. The hot springs are still used for the treatment of rheumatic and vascular diseases. As well as being a tourist resort, the city trades in olives, almonds, and wines, and has manufacturing industries including textiles, leather, and processed foods.

**Aix-la-Chapelle** French name of ◊Aachen, an ancient city in Germany.

**Ajax** Greek hero in Homer's *Iliad*. Son of Telamon, King of Salamis, he was second only to Achilles among the Greek heroes in the Trojan War. He fought ◊Hector single-handed, defended the ships, and killed many Trojans. According to subsequent Greek legends, Ajax went mad with jealousy when ◊Agamemnon awarded the armour of the dead Achilles to ◊Odysseus. He later committed suicide in shame.

**Ajman** smallest of the seven states making up the United Arab Emirates; area 250 sq km/96 sq mi; population (1995) 118,800.

**ajolote** Mexican reptile of the genus *Bipes*. It and several other tropical burrowing species are placed in the Amphisbaenia, a group separate from lizards and snakes among the Squamata. Unlike the others, however, which have no legs, it has a pair of short but well-developed front legs. In line with its burrowing habits, the skull is very solid, the eyes small, and external ears absent.

The scales are arranged in rings, giving the body a wormlike appearance.

**Akbar, Jalal ud-Din Muhammad** (1542–1605) Mogul emperor of North India from 1556, when he succeeded his father Humayun. He gradually established his rule throughout North India. He is considered the greatest of the Mogul emperors, and the firmness and wisdom of his rule won him the title 'Guardian of Mankind'; he was a patron of the arts.

**Akhenaton** or *Ikhnaton*, King (pharaoh) of ancient Egypt of the 18th dynasty (*c.* 1353–1335 BC), who may have ruled jointly for a time with his father Amenhotep III. He developed the cult of the Sun, Aton, rather than the rival cult of Amen, and removed his capital to Akhetaton.

**Akihito** (1933– ) Emperor of Japan from 1989, succeeding his father Hirohito (Shōwa). His reign is called the Heisei ('achievement of universal peace') era.

**Akkad** northern Semitic people who conquered the Sumerians 2350 BC and ruled Mesopotamia. Their language was Simitic (old Akkadian). Akkad was also the northern of the two provinces into which Babylonia was divided. The ancient city of Akkad in central Mesopotamia, founded by Sargon I, was an imperial centre in the late 3rd millennium BC; the site is unidentified, but it was on the River Euphrates somewhere near Babylon.

**Akron** (Greek 'summit') city in northeastern Ohio, USA, on the Cuyahoga River, 56 km/35 mi southeast of Cleveland; population (1994 est) 221,900. Industries include chemical, plastic, and aerospace products. Known as the 'Rubber

Capital of the World', it is home to the head-quarters of several tyre and rubber companies, although production had ended here by 1982.

**Aksum** or *Axum,* ancient Greek-influenced Semitic kingdom that flourished in the 1st–6th centuries AD and covered a large part of modern Ethiopia as well as the Sudan. The ruins of its capital, also called Aksum, lie northwest of Ãdwa, but the site has been developed as a modern city.

**al-** for Arabic names beginning *al-,* see rest of name; for example, for 'al-Fatah', see ◊Fatah, al-.

**Alabama** state in southern USA. It is nick-named Heart of Dixie or the Camellia State. Alabama was admitted to the Union in 1819 as the 22nd US state. Historically it was a planta-tion state associated with slavery and, in the 20th century, the civil-rights movement. It is bordered to the east by Georgia, with the Chattahoochee River forming the lower half of the boundary, to the north by Tennessee, and to the west by Mississippi, with the Tennessee River forming a small part of the boundary in the northwest. To the south is the Florida pan-handle and a 100 km/60 mi-long stretch of coast on the Gulf of Mexico, bisected by Mobile Bay
**population** (1996 est) 4,273,100
**area** 134,700 sq km/51,994 sq mi
**capital** Montgomery
**towns and cities** Birmingham, Mobile, Huntsville, Tuscaloosa
**industries and products** cotton (still impor-tant though no longer prime crop), soybeans, peanuts, wood products, marble, coal, oil, natu-ral gas, livestock, poultry, fishing, iron, steel, aluminium, chemicals, textiles, paper, power generation, aerospace industry

**alabaster** naturally occurring fine-grained white or light-coloured translucent form of gyp-sum, often streaked or mottled. A soft material, it is easily carved, but seldom used for outdoor sculpture.

**Alamein, El, Battles of** two decisive battles of World War II in the western desert of north-ern Egypt. In the first (1–27 July 1942), the British 8th Army under Auchinleck held off the German and Italian forces under ◊Rommel; in the second (23 October–4 November 1942), ◊Montgomery defeated Rommel.

**Alaric** (*c.* 370–410) Visigothic king 395–410 who campaigned against the Romans in the Balkans and Italy. On 24 August 410 he cap-tured and sacked Rome. After three days he led the Goths south, intending to invade Sicily and then Africa, but died of a sudden illness. Alaric was buried in the bed of the river Busento in southern Italy. The river was diverted to allow him to be buried, then redirected to flow over the grave. Those who worked on the burial were killed so that his final resting place would never be known.

**Alaska** largest state of the USA, located on the northwest extremity of North America, and sep-arated from the lower 48 states by British Columbia. It is nicknamed Last Frontier. Alaska was admitted to the Union in 1959 as the 49th US state. Historically and commercially the state has been associated with mineral exploitation. It is bordered to the east by the Yukon Territory, Canada, and to the southeast, along its pan-handle, by the Yukon Territory and British Columbia, Canada. Northern Alaska lies on the Beaufort Sea, part of the Arctic Ocean. To the northwest is the Chukchi Sea, narrowing to about 80 km/50 mi at the Bering Strait, which separates the Alaskan Seward Peninsula from Russian East Asia. The Bering Sea is bounded to the south by Alaska's long ◊Aleutian Island chain, extending in an east–west arc across the North Pacific Ocean from the Alaska Peninsula. To the peninsula's east is the Gulf of Alaska
**population** (1996 est) 607,000; including 15% American Indians, Aleuts, and Inuit
**total area** 1,530,700 sq km/591,004 sq mi
**land area** 1,478,457 sq km/570,833 sq mi
**capital** Juneau
**towns and cities** Anchorage, Fairbanks, Fort Yukon, Holy Cross, Nome, College, Sitka
**industries and products** oil, natural gas, coal, copper, iron, gold, tin, fur, salmon fisheries and canneries, lumber; tourism is a large and growing industry (tourists outnumber residents each year).

**Alba** Gaelic name for ◊Scotland; also an alter-native spelling for ◊Alva, Ferdinand Alvarez de Toledo, Duke of Alva, Spanish politician and general.

**Albania** Republic of
**national name** *Republika e Shqipërisë*

**area** 28,748 sq km/11,099 sq mi
**capital** Tiranë (Tirana)
**major towns/cities** Durrës, Shkodër, Elbasan, Vlorë, Korçë
**major ports** Durrës
**physical features** mainly mountainous, with rivers flowing east–west, and a narrow coastal plain

**head of state** Rexhep Mejdani from 1998
**head of government** Pandeli Majko from 1998
**political system** emergent democracy
**political parties** Democratic Party of Albania (PDS; formerly the Democratic Party: DP), moderate, market-oriented; Socialist Party of Albania (PSS), ex-communist; Human Rights Union (HMU), Greek minority party
**currency** lek
**GNP per capita (PPP)** (US$) 3,200 (1998 est)
**exports** chromium and chrome products, processed foodstuffs, textiles and footwear, base metals, machinery and equipment, bitumen, tobacco. Principal market: Italy 49.1% (1997)
**population** 3,113,000 (1999 est)
**language** Albanian, Greek
**religion** Muslim, Orthodox, Roman Catholic
**life expectancy** 70 (men); 76 (women) (1995–2000)
**Chronology**
**2000 BC** Part of Illyria.
**168 BC** Illyria conquered by Romans.
**AD 395** Became part of Byzantine Empire.
**6th–14th centuries** Byzantine decline exploited by Serbs, Normans, Slavs, Bulgarians, and Venetians.
**1381** Ottoman invasion of Albania followed by years of resistance to Turkish rule.
**1468** Resistance led by national hero Skanderbeg (George Kastrioti) largely collapsed, and Albania passed to Ottoman Empire.
**15th–16th centuries** Thousands fled to southern Italy to escape Ottoman rule; over half of the rest of the population converted to Islam.
**1878** Foundation of Albanian League promoted emergence of nationalism.
**1912** Achieved independence from Turkey as a result of First Balkan War and end of Ottoman Empire in Europe.
**1914–20** Occupied by Italy.
**1925** Declared itself a republic.
**1928–39** Monarchy of King Zog.
**1939** Italian occupation led by Benito Mussolini.
**1943–44** Under German rule following Italian surrender.
**1946** Proclaimed Communist People's Republic of Albania, with Enver Hoxha as premier.
**1949** Developed close links with Joseph Stalin in USSR and entered Comecon (Council for Mutual Economic Assistance).
**1961** Broke with USSR in wake of Nikita Khrushchev's denunciation of Stalin, and withdrew from Comecon.
**1978** Severed diplomatic links with China, choosing isolationism and neutrality.
**1982** Hoxha made Ramiz Alia head of state.
**1985** Death of Hoxha. Alia became head of the Party of Labour of Albania (PLA).
**1987** Normal diplomatic relations restored with Canada, Greece, and West Germany.
**1988** Albania attended a conference of Balkan states for the first time since the 1930s.
**1990** The one-party system was abandoned in the face of popular protest; the first opposition party was formed.
**1991** The communist PLA won the first multiparty elections; Alia was re-elected president. The PLA was renamed the PSS.

**1992** Presidential elections were won by Sali Berisha of the Democratic Party (DP). Alia and other former communist officials were charged with corruption and abuse of power. Totalitarian and communist parties were banned.
**1993** Open conflict began between ethnic Greeks and Albanians, followed by a purge of ethnic Greeks from senior positions in the civil service and army. Alia was sentenced to eight years' imprisonment. The DP was renamed the PDS.
**1995** Alia was released from prison following an appeal court ruling. Communist-era MPs and Communist Party officials were banned from national and local elections until 2002.
**1996** The ruling PDS was accused of ballot-rigging following overwhelming victory in elections.
**1997** Antigovernment riots followed the collapse of bogus 'investment' schemes; police killed demonstrators in the southern port of Vlorê. Southern Albania fell under rebel control. A general election was won by PSS; Rexhep Mejdani was elected president; ex-communist Fatos Nano became prime minister at the head of a coalition. Convictions of communist-era leaders were overturned. The government signed a World Bank and IMF rescue package to salvage the economy.
**1998** There was sporadic violence in the north. Nano resigned as prime minister, and was replaced by Pandeli Majko. A new constitution was approved in a national referendum. Albania's constitution came into effect.

**albatross** large seabird, genus *Diomedea*, with long narrow wings adapted for gliding and a wingspan of up to 3 m/10 ft, mainly found in the southern hemisphere. It belongs to the family Diomedeidae, order Procellariiformes, the same group as petrels and shearwaters. The external nostrils of birds in this order are more or less tubular, and the bills are hooked.

**Albert, Prince Consort** (1819–1861) Husband of British Queen ◊Victoria from 1840. A patron of the arts, science, and industry, Albert was the second son of the Duke of Saxe Coburg-Gotha and first cousin to Queen Victoria, whose chief adviser he became. He planned the Great Exhibition of 1851, the profits from which were used to buy the sites in London of all the South Kensington museums and colleges and the Royal Albert Hall, built in 1871. He died of typhoid. The Queen never fully recovered from his premature death, and remained in mourning for him for the rest of her life.

**Alberta** province of western Canada. The most westerly of the Prairie provinces, it is bordered by Saskatchewan on the east and British Columbia on the west (with the Continental Divide in the Canadian Rocky Mountains forming much of the boundary). To the south of Alberta, below the 49th Parallel, lies the US state of Montana, while to its north, above the 60th Parallel, are the Northwest Territories
**area** 661,200 sq km/255,223 sq mi
**capital** Edmonton

***towns and cities*** Calgary, Lethbridge, Medicine Hat, Red Deer
***population*** (1996 est) 2,697,000
***physical*** Rocky Mountains; Lesser Slave Lake; North Saskatchewan and Athabasca rivers
***industries*** oil and natural-gas extraction (Alberta accounts for most of the country's oil production), coal-mining (the largest coal reserves in Canada); agriculture, including cultivation of wheat, barley, oats, and sugar beet (in the south), plus extensive cattle-ranching.

**Alberti, Leon Battista** (1404–1472) Italian Renaissance architect and theorist. He set out the principles of Classical architecture, and covered their modification for Renaissance practice, in *De re aedificatoria/On Architecture*, which he started in 1452 and worked on until his death (published 1485; translated as *Ten Books on Architecture* 1955).

**Albert, Lake** lake on the border of Uganda and the Democratic Republic of Congo in the Great ◊Rift Valley; area 5,600 sq km/2,162 sq mi. The first European to see it was the British explorer Samuel Baker, who named it Lake Albert after the Prince Consort. It was renamed in 1973 by the former Zaire's President Mobutu after himself.

**albinism** rare hereditary condition in which the body has no tyrosinase, one of the enzymes that form the pigment ◊melanin, normally found in the skin, hair, and eyes. As a result, the hair is white and the skin and eyes are pink. The skin and eyes are abnormally sensitive to light, and vision is often impaired. The condition occurs among all human and animal groups.

**Albion** name for Britain used by the ancient Greeks and Romans. It was mentioned by Pytheas of Massilia (4th century BC), and is probably of Celtic origin, but the Romans, having in mind the white cliffs of Dover, assumed it to be derived from the word *albus* (white).

**Ålborg** port in Denmark 32 km/20 mi inland from the Kattegat, on the south shore of the Limfjord; population (1995) 159,000. One of Denmark's oldest cities, it has a castle and the Budolfi cathedral (named after the English St Botolph), dating mainly from about 1400. It is the capital of Nordjylland county in Jylland (Jutland); the port is linked to Nørresundby on the north side of the fjord by a tunnel built 1969. Major industries include shipbuilding, cement, and textiles.

**albumin** any of a group of sulphur-containing ◊proteins. The best known is in the form of egg white (albumen); others occur in milk, and as a major component of serum. Many vegetables and fluids also contain albumins. They are soluble in water and dilute salt solutions, and are coagulated by heat.

**Albuquerque** largest city of New Mexico, USA, situated east of the Rio Grande, in the Pueblo district; seat of Bernalillo County; population (1994 est) 412,000. Albuquerque is a resort and industrial centre specializing in electronic products and aerospace equipment, and is a centre for livestock rearing. Founded in 1706, it was named after the viceroy of New Spain, Afonso de Albuquerque, and was incorporated as a city in 1891.

**alchemy** (Arabic *al-Kimya*) supposed technique of transmuting base metals, such as lead and mercury, into silver and gold by the philosopher's stone, a hypothetical substance, to which was also attributed the power to give eternal life.

**Alcibiades** (451/0–404/3 BC) Athenian politician and general during the Peloponnesian War. In 415 BC Alcibiades was appointed one of the commanders of an Athenian expedition against Sicily, but was recalled to answer charges of sacrilege and fled to Sparta. Further scandal led to his flight to Persia, but he rehabilitated himself with the Athenians and played a leading part at Cyzicus in 410. He was given command of Athenian forces in Asia Minor but was replaced after his lieutenant's defeat off Notium in 407. He was murdered shortly after the war.

**alcohol** any member of a group of organic chemical compounds characterized by the presence of one or more aliphatic OH (hydroxyl) groups in the molecule, and which form ◊esters with acids. The main uses of alcohols are as solvents for gums, resins, lacquers, and varnishes; in the making of dyes; for essential oils in perfumery; and for medical substances in pharmacy. The alcohol produced naturally in the ◊fermentation process and consumed as part of alcoholic beverages is called ◊ethanol.

**alcoholic beverage** any drink containing alcohol, often used for its intoxicating effects. ◊Ethanol (ethyl alcohol), a colourless liquid ($C_2H_5OH$), is the basis of all common intoxicants. Foods rich in sugars, such as grapes, produce this alcohol as a natural product of decay, called fermentation.

**Alcuin** Flaccus Albinus Alcuinus (735–804) English scholar. Born in York, he went to Rome in 780, and in 782 took up residence at Charlemagne's court in Aachen. From 796 he was abbot at St Martin's in Tours. He disseminated Anglo-Saxon scholarship. Alcuin organized education and learning in the Frankish empire and was a prominent member of Charlemagne's academy, providing a strong impulse to the Carolingian Renaissance.

**Aldebaran** or *Alpha Tauri,* brightest star in the constellation Taurus and the 14th-brightest star in the night sky; it marks the eye of the 'bull'. Aldebaran is a red giant 60 light years away from the Sun, shining with a true luminosity of about 100 times that of the Sun.

**aldehyde** any of a group of organic chemical compounds prepared by oxidation of primary alcohols, so that the OH (hydroxyl) group loses its hydrogen to give an oxygen joined by a double bond to a carbon atom (the aldehyde group, with the formula CHO).

**alder** any of a group of trees or shrubs belonging to the birch family, found mainly in cooler parts of the northern hemisphere and characterized by toothed leaves and catkins. (Genus *Alnus,* family Betulaceae.)

**Aleppo** Arabic *Halab,* ancient city in northwest Syria, situated on the River Kuweik on the edge of the Syrian Desert; population (1993) 1,494,000. It is the administrative centre of the governorate of Aleppo (population (1996 est) 3,694,000). Silk and cotton goods, leather, grain, carpets, tobacco, and metalwork are produced. Chief industries are cotton and wool textile manufacturing. There has been a settlement on the site for at least 4,000 years.

**Aleutian Islands** volcanic island chain in the North Pacific, stretching 1,900 km/1,200 mi southwest of Alaska, of which it forms part, towards Kamchatka; population 6,000 Aleuts (most of whom belong to the Orthodox Church), plus a large US military establishment. There are 14 large and more than 100 small islands running along the Aleutian Trench; the largest island is Unimak (with an area of 3,500 sq km/1,360 sq mi), which contains two active volcanoes. The islands are mountainous, barren, and treeless; they are ice-free all year but are often foggy, with only about 25 days of sunshine recorded annually. The only industries are fishing, seal hunting, and sheep farming; the main exports are fish and furs. Unalaska is the chief island for trade as it has a good harbour.

**A level** or *Advanced level,* in England, Wales, and Northern Ireland, examinations taken by students usually at the age of 18, after two years' study, in no more than four subjects at one time. Two A-level passes are normally required for entry to a university degree course. Scottish students sit Highers.

**Alexander** eight popes, including:

**Alexander III** Orlando Bandinelli (died 1181) Pope 1159–81. His authority was opposed by Frederick I Barbarossa, but Alexander eventually compelled him to render homage 1178. He held the third Lateran Council 1179. He supported Henry II of England in his invasion of Ireland, but imposed penance on him after the murder of Thomas à ◊Becket.

**Alexander VI** born Rodrigo Borgia or Borja (1430 or 1432–1503) Pope 1492–1503. Of Spanish origin, he bribed his way to the papacy, where he furthered the advancement of his illegitimate children, who included Cesare and Lucrezia ◊Borgia. When ◊Savonarola preached against his corrupt practices Alexander had him executed.

**Alexander** three tsars of Russia:

**Alexander I** (1777–1825) Tsar of Russia from 1801. Defeated by Napoleon at Austerlitz 1805, he made peace at Tilsit 1807, but economic crisis led to a break with Napoleon's Continental System and the opening of Russian ports to British trade; this led to Napoleon's ill-fated invasion of Russia 1812. After the Congress of Vienna 1815, Alexander hoped through the Holy Alliance with Austria and Prussia to establish a new Christian order in Europe.

**Alexander II** (1818–1881) Tsar of Russia from 1855. He embarked on reforms of the army, the government, and education, and is remembered as 'the Liberator' for his emancipation of the serfs

1861, but he lacked the personnel to implement his reforms. However, the revolutionary element remained unsatisfied, and Alexander became increasingly autocratic and reactionary. He was assassinated by an anarchistic terrorist group, the ◊Nihilists.

**Alexander III** (1845–1894) Tsar of Russia from 1881, when he succeeded his father, Alexander II. He pursued a reactionary policy, promoting Russification and persecuting the Jews. He married Dagmar (1847–1928), daughter of Christian IX of Denmark and sister of Queen Alexandra of Britain, 1866.

**Alexander** three kings of Scotland:

**Alexander I** (*c.* 1078–1124) King of Scotland from 1107, known as *the Fierce.* He ruled over the area to the north of the rivers Forth and Clyde, while his brother and successor ◊David ruled over the area to the south. He assisted Henry I of England in his campaign against Wales in 1114, but defended the independence of the church in Scotland. Several monasteries, including the abbeys of Inchcolm and Scone, were established by him.

**Alexander II** (1198–1249) King of Scotland from 1214, when he succeeded his father, William the Lion. Alexander supported the English barons in their struggle with King John after ◊Magna Carta. The accession of Henry III of England allowed a rapprochement between the two countries, and the boundaries between England and Scotland were agreed by the Treaty of York in 1237. By the treaty of Newcastle in 1244 he pledged allegiance to Henry III. Alexander consolidated royal authority in Scotland and was a generous patron of the church.

**Alexander III** (1241–1286) King of Scotland from 1249, son of Alexander II. After defeating the Norwegian forces in 1263, he was able to extend his authority over the Western Isles, which had been dependent on Norway. The later period of his reign was devoted to administrative reforms, which limited the power of the barons and brought a period of peace and prosperity to Scotland.

**Alexander I, Karageorgevich** (1888– 1934) Regent of Serbia 1912–21 and king of Yugoslavia 1921–34, as dictator from 1929. The second son of Peter I, King of Serbia, he was declared regent for his father in 1912 and on his father's death became king of the state of South Slavs – Yugoslavia – that had come into being 1918.

**Alexander Nevski, St** (1220–1263) Russian military leader, ruler of Novgorod in 1236, and Grand Prince of Vladimir in 1252. He survived Mongol attacks in 1237–40, which enabled him to defeat the Swedes in 1240 and the Germans in 1242.

**Alexander technique** in alternative medicine, a method of correcting bad habits of posture, breathing, and muscular tension, which Australian therapist F M Alexander maintained cause many ailments. The technique is also used to promote general health and relaxation and enhance vitality.

**Alexander (III) the Great** (356–323 BC) King of Macedon 336–323 BC and conqueror of the Persian Empire. As commander of the powerful Macedonian army he conquered Greece in 336, defeated the Persian king Darius III in Asia Minor in 333, then moved on to Egypt where he founded Alexandria. He defeated the Persians again in Assyria in 331, then advanced further east, invading India in 327. He conquered the Punjab before mutinous troops forced his retreat.

**Alexandria** or *Al Iskandariya,* city, chief port, and second-largest city of Egypt, situated between the Mediterranean and Lake Maryut; population (1992) 3,380,000. It is linked by canal with the Nile. There is oil refining, gas processing, and trade in cotton and grain. Founded in 331 BC by Alexander the Great, Alexandria was the capital of Egypt for over 1,000 years.

**Alexandria, Library of** the world's first state-funded scientific institution, founded 330 BC in Alexandria, Egypt, by Ptolemy I and further expanded by Ptolemy II. It comprised a museum, teaching facilities, and a library that contained up to 700,000 scrolls, including much ancient Greek literature. It sustained significant damage AD 391, when the Roman emperor Theodosius I ordered its destruction. It was burned down 640 at the time of the Arab conquest.

**Alexandria, school of** group of writers and scholars of Alexandria, Egypt, who made the city the chief centre of culture in the Western world from about 331 BC to AD 642. They include the poets Callimachus, Apollonius of Rhodes, and Theocritus; ◊Euclid, pioneer of geometry; Eratosthenes, a geographer; Hipparchus, who developed a system of trigonometry; Ptolemy, whose system of astronomy endured for over 1,000 years; and the Jewish philosopher Philo. The Gnostics and Neo-Platonists also flourished in Alexandria.

**Alexius** five emperors of Byzantium, including:

**Alexius I, Comnenus** (1048–1118) Byzantine emperor 1081–1118. With meagre resources, he dealt successfully with internal dissent and a series of external threats from the Turks and Normans. He managed the difficult passage of the First Crusade through Byzantine territory on its way to Jerusalem, and by the end of his reign he had, with the help of the Crusaders, restored much of Byzantine control over Anatolia. His daughter Anna Comnena chronicled his reign.

**Alexius IV, (Angelos)** (1182–1204) Byzantine emperor from 1203, when, with the aid of the army of the Fourth Crusade, he deposed his uncle Alexius III. He soon lost the support of the Crusaders (by that time occupying Constantinople), and was overthrown and murdered by another Alexius, Alexius Mourtzouphlus (son-in-law of Alexius III) in 1204, an act which the Crusaders used as a pretext to sack the city the same year.

**alfalfa** or *lucerne,* perennial tall herbaceous plant belonging to the pea family. It is native to Europe and Asia and has spikes of small purple flowers in late summer. It is now a major fodder crop, commonly processed into hay, meal, or silage. Alfalfa sprouts, the sprouted seeds, have become a popular salad ingredient. (*Medicago sativa,* family Leguminosae.)

**Alfonso** thirteen kings of León, Castile, and Spain, including:

**Alfonso (X),** *the Wise* (1221–1284) King of Castile from 1252. His reign was politically unsuccessful but he contributed to learning: he made Castilian the official language of the country and commissioned a history of Spain and an encyclopedia, as well as several translations from Arabic concerning, among other subjects, astronomy and games.

**Alfonso XIII** (1886–1941) King of Spain 1886–1931. He assumed power 1906 and married Princess Ena, granddaughter of Queen Victoria of the United Kingdom, in the same year. He abdicated 1931 soon after the fall of the Primo de Rivera dictatorship 1923–30 (which he supported), and Spain became a republic. His assassination was attempted several times.

**Alfred the Great** (*c.* 849–*c.* 901) Anglo-Saxon king 871–899 who defended England against Danish invasion and founded the first English navy. He succeeded his brother Aethelred to the throne of Wessex in 871, and a new legal code came into force during his reign. He encouraged the translation of scholarly works from Latin (some he translated himself), and promoted the development of the ◊Anglo-Saxon Chronicle.

**algae** singular *alga,* highly varied group of plants, ranging from single-celled forms to large and complex seaweeds. They live in both fresh and salt water, and in damp soil. Algae do not have true roots, stems, or leaves.

Marine algae help combat ◊global warming by removing carbon dioxide from the atmosphere during ◊photosynthesis.

**Algarve** (Arabic *al-gharb* 'the west') ancient kingdom in southern Portugal, bordered on the east by Spain, and on the west and south by the Atlantic Ocean; it is co-extensive with the modern district of Faro; area 5,071 sq km/1,958 sq mi; population (1991) 341,400. Industries include agriculture, fishing, wine production, mining, and tourism. The Algarve region includes Cape St Vincent, the southwest extremity of Europe, where the British fleet defeated the Spanish in 1797.

**algebra** branch of mathematics in which the general properties of numbers are studied by using symbols, usually letters, to represent variables and unknown quantities. For example, the algebraic statement $(x + y)^2 = x^2 + 2xy + y^2$ is true for all values of $x$ and $y$. If $x = 7$ and $y = 3$, for instance:

$$(7 + 3)^2 = 7^2 + 2(7 \times 3) + 3^2 = 100$$

An algebraic expression that has one or more variables (denoted by letters) is a polynomial equation. Algebra is used in many areas of mathematics – for example, matrix algebra and

Boolean algebra (the latter is used in working out the logic for computers).

**Algeria** Democratic and Popular Republic of
*national name* al-Jumhuriya al-Jazairiya ad-Dimuqratiya ash-Shabiya

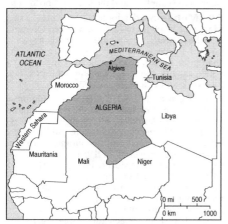

*area* 2,381,741 sq km/919,590 sq mi
*capital* Algiers (al-Jaza'ir)
*major towns/cities* Oran, Annaba, Blida, Sétif, Constantine (Qacentina)
*major ports* Oran (Ouahran), Annaba (Bône)
*physical features* coastal plains backed by mountains in north, Sahara desert in south; Atlas mountains, Barbary Coast, Chott Melrhir depression, Hoggar mountains
*head of state* Abdel Aziz Bouteflika from 1999
*head of government* Ismail Hamdani from 1998
*political system* military rule
*political parties* National Liberation Front (FLN), nationalist, socialist; Socialist Forces Front (FSS), Berber-based, left of centre; Islamic Front for Salvation (FIS), Islamic fundamentalist (banned from 1992); National Democratic Rally (RND), left of centre
*currency* Algerian dinar
*GNP per capita (PPP)* (US$) 4,380 (1998 est)
*exports* crude oil, gas, vegetables, tobacco, hides, dates. Principal market: Italy 19.8% (1997)
*population* 30,774,000 (1999 est)
*language* Arabic (official); Berber, French
*religion* Sunni Muslim (state religion)
*life expectancy* 68 (men); 70 (women) (1995–2000)
**Chronology**
*9th century BC* Part of Carthaginian Empire, centred on Tunisia to the east, with Annaba, Algiers, and Skikda emerging as important trading posts en route to Spain.
*146 BC* Conquered by Romans, who called the area Numidia.
*AD 396* St Augustine, one of the great early Christian leaders, became Bishop of Hippo, modern Annaba.
*6th century* Part of the Byzantine Empire.
*late 7th century* Conquered by Muslim Arabs, who spread Islam as the basis of a new Berberized Arab-Islamic civilization.

*1516* Ottoman Turks expelled recent Christian Spanish invaders. Under Ottoman rule much influence was left to local Arab tribes, Berbers, Barbary pirates, and deys, administrative officers who were elected for life.
*1816* Anglo-Dutch forces bombarded Algiers as a reprisal against the Barbary pirates' attacks on Mediterranean shipping.
*1830–47* French occupation of Algiers, followed by extension of control to the north, overcoming fierce resistance from Amir Abd al-Qadir, a champion of Arab Algerian nationalism, and from Morocco.
*1850–70* Mountainous inland region, inhabited by the Kabyles, occupied by French.
*1871* Major rebellion against French rule as French settlers began to immigrate and take over the best agricultural land.
*1900–09* Sahara region subdued by France, who kept it under military rule.
*1937* Algerian People's Party (PPA) formed by the charismatic separatist Messali Hadj.
*1940* Following France's defeat by Nazi Germany, Algeria became allied to the pro-Nazi Vichy regime during World War II.
*1945* 8,000 died following the ruthless suppression of an abortive PPA-supported uprising against French rule.
*1954–62* Battle of Algiers: bitter war of independence fought between the National Liberation Front (FLN) and the French colonial army.
*1958* French inability to resolve the escalating civil war in Algeria, where French settlers had risen in favour of integration with France, toppled the Fourth Republic and brought to power, in Paris, Gen Charles de Gaulle, who accepted the principle of national self-determination.
*1962* Independence achieved from France. Republic declared. Ahmed Ben Bella of the FLN elected prime minister; many French settlers fled.
*1963* Ben Bella elected Algeria's first president and one-party state established.
*1965* Ben Bella deposed by military, led by Col Houari Boumédienne (FLN).
*1971* Oil and gas industry nationalized.
*1976* New Islamic-socialist constitution approved.
*1978* Death of Boumédienne.
*1979* Benjedid Chadli (FLN) elected president. Ben Bella freed after 14 years of house arrest.
*1981* Algeria helped secure release of US hostages in Iran.
*1988* Riots in protest at austerity policies; 170 killed. Reform programme introduced. Diplomatic relations restored with Morocco after 12-year break.
*1989* Constitutional changes introduced limited political pluralism.
*1991* Elections were cancelled after Islamic fundamentalist Islamic Salvation Front (FIS) won the first round of multiparty elections.
*1992* Chadli resigned; the military took control of the government; Muhammad Boudiaf became president. A state of emergency was declared and the FIS ordered to disband. Boudiaf was assassinated, allegedly by fundamentalists; he was replaced by Ali Kafi.

**1993** The civil strife worsened, with assassinations of politicians and other public figures.

**1994** Gen Lamine Zeroual replaced Kafi as president. The fundamentalists' campaign of violence intensified.

**1995** Zeroual won presidential elections.

**1996** The constitution was amended to increase the president's powers and counter religious fundamentalism. Arabic was declared the official public language.

**1997** Many civilians were killed by Armed Islamic Group (GIA). The RND-FLN won National Assembly elections. Ahmed Ouyuahia was reappointed prime minister. The FIS urged a 'national conference of reconciliation'.

**1998** The violence continued. President Zeroual announced his retirement, planned for 1999. Prime Minister Ahmed Ouyahia resigned and was replaced by Ismail Hamdani.

**1999** Former Prime Minister Ahmed Ouyahia was elected secretary-general of the ruling National Democratic Rally (RND). April: Abdel Aziz Bouteflika elected president amid claims of a fraudulent election. June: FIS ended fighting. President promised an amnesty for men of violence.

**Algiers** Arabic *al-Jazair;* French *Alger,* capital of Algeria, situated on the narrow coastal plain between the Atlas Mountains and the Mediterranean; population (1995) 2,168,000. It distributes grain, iron, phosphates, wines, and oil from central Algeria. The main industries are oil refining, petrochemicals, and metal working. The city is a popular winter resort.

**Algiers, Battle of** bitter conflict in Algiers 1954–62 between the Algerian nationalist population and the French colonial army and French settlers. The conflict ended with Algerian independence 1962.

**ALGOL** acronym for *algorithmic language*, in computing, an early high-level programming language, developed in the 1950s and 1960s for scientific applications. A general-purpose language, ALGOL is best suited to mathematical work and has an algebraic style. Although no longer in common use, it has greatly influenced more recent languages, such as Ada and Pascal.

**Algonquin** the Algonquian-speaking hunting and fishing people who once lived around the Ottawa River in eastern Canada. Many now live on reservations in northeastern USA, eastern Ontario, and western Québec; others have chosen to live among the general populations of Canada and the USA.

**algorithm** procedure or series of steps that can be used to solve a problem.

In computer science, it describes the logical sequence of operations to be performed by a program. A ◊flow chart is a visual representation of an algorithm.

**Ali** (*c.* 598–661) 4th ◊caliph of ◊Islam. He was born in Mecca, the son of Abu Talib, and was the cousin and close friend and supporter of the prophet Muhammad, who gave him his daughter Fatima in marriage. He was one of the first to believe in Islam. On Muhammad's death 632, Ali had a claim to succeed him, but this was not conceded until 656, following the murder of the third caliph, Uthman. After a brief and stormy reign, Ali was assassinated. Controversy has raged around Ali's name between the Sunni Muslims and the Shiites, the former denying his right to the caliphate and the latter supporting it.

**Ali, Muhammad** adopted name of Cassius Marcellus Clay, Jr (1942–   ) US boxer. Olympic light-heavyweight champion in 1960, he went on to become world professional heavyweight champion in 1964, and was the only man to regain the title twice. He was known for his fast footwork and extrovert nature.

**Alia, Ramiz** (1925–   ) Albanian communist politician, head of state 1982–92. He gradually relaxed the isolationist policies of his predecessor, Enver Hoxha, and following public unrest introduced political and economic reforms, including free elections in 1991, when he was elected executive president. In September 1994 Alia was convicted of abuse of power while in office and sentenced to eight years' imprisonment, but was released in July 1995 following an appeal court ruling. In October 1997 the Albanian prosecutor general dropped genocide charges against Alia.

**alibi** (Latin 'elsewhere') in law, a provable assertion that the accused was at some other place when a crime was committed.

**alienation** sense of isolation, powerlessness, and therefore frustration; a feeling of loss of control over one's life; a sense of estrangement from society or even from oneself. As a concept it was developed by German philosophers G W F Hegel and Karl Marx; the latter used it as a description and criticism of the condition that developed among workers in capitalist society.

**alimentary canal** in animals, the tube through which food passes; it extends from the mouth to the anus. It is a complex organ, adapted for ◊digestion. In human adults, it is about 9 m/30 ft long, consisting of the mouth cavity, pharynx, oesophagus, stomach, and the small and large intestines.

**aliphatic compound** any organic chemical compound in which the carbon atoms are joined in straight chains, as in hexane ($C_6H_{14}$), or in branched chains, as in 2-methylpentane ($CH_3CH(CH_3)CH_2CH_2CH_3$).

**alkali** in chemistry, a ◊base that is soluble in water. Alkalis neutralize acids and are soapy to the touch. The strength of an alkali is measured by its hydrogen-ion concentration, indicated by the ◊pH value. They may be divided into strong and weak alkalis: a strong alkali (for example, potassium hydroxide, KOH) ionizes completely when disssolved in water, whereas a weak alkali (for example, ammonium hydroxide, $NH_4OH$) exists in a partially ionized state in solution. All alkalis have a pH above 7.0.

The hydroxides of metals are alkalis. Those of sodium and potassium are chemically powerful; both were historically derived from the ashes of plants.

**alkali metal** any of a group of six metallic elements with similar chemical properties: lithium, sodium, potassium, rubidium, caesium, and francium. They form a linked group (Group One) in the ◊periodic table of the elements. They are univalent (have a valency of one) and of very low density (lithium, sodium, and potassium float on water); in general they are reactive, soft, low-melting-point metals. Because of their reactivity they are only found as compounds in nature.

**alkaline-earth metal** any of a group of six metallic elements with similar bonding properties: beryllium, magnesium, calcium, strontium, barium, and radium. They form a linked group in the ◊periodic table of the elements. They are strongly basic, bivalent (have a valency of two), and occur in nature only in compounds.

**alkaloid** any of a number of physiologically active and frequently poisonous substances contained in some plants. They are usually organic bases and contain nitrogen. They form salts with acids and, when soluble, give alkaline solutions.

**alkane** member of a group of ◊hydrocarbons having the general formula $C_nH_{2n+2}$, commonly known as *paraffins*. As they contain only single ◊covalent bonds, alkanes are said to be saturated. Lighter alkanes, such as methane, ethane, propane, and butane, are colourless gases; heavier ones are liquids or solids. In nature they are found in natural gas and petroleum.

**alkene** member of the group of ◊hydrocarbons having the general formula $C_nH_{2n}$, formerly known as *olefins*. Alkenes are unsaturated compounds, characterized by one or more double bonds between adjacent carbon atoms. Lighter alkenes, such as ethene and propene, are gases, obtained from the cracking of oil fractions. Alkenes react by addition, and many useful compounds, such as poly(ethene) and bromoethane, are made from them.

**alkyne** member of the group of ◊hydrocarbons with the general formula $C_nH_{2n-2}$, formerly known as the *acetylenes*. They are unsaturated compounds, characterized by one or more triple bonds between adjacent carbon atoms. Lighter alkynes, such as ethyne, are gases; heavier ones are liquids or solids.

**Allah** (Arabic *al-Ilah* 'the God') Islamic name for God.

**Allahabad** ('city of god') historic city in Uttar Pradesh state, India, 580 km/360 mi southeast of Delhi, on the Yamuna River where it meets the Ganges and the mythical underground Seraswati River; population (1991) 806,000. A growing commercial centre, its main industries are textiles and food processing. A Hindu religious event, the festival of the jar of nectar of immortality (Kumbh Mela), is held here every 12 years with the participants washing away sin and sickness by bathing in the rivers; in 1989 15 million pilgrims attended. It is also the site of the Asoka Pillar, dating from 232 BC, on which are carved edicts of the Emperor ◊Asoka.

**Allegheny Mountains** or *the Alleghenies,* mountain range over 800 km/500 mi long extending from Pennsylvania to Virginia, rising to more than 1,500 m/4,900 ft and averaging 750 m/2,500 ft. The Alleghenies are rich in hardwood timber and bituminous coal, and also contain iron ore, natural gas, clay, and petroleum. The mountains initially hindered western migration, with the first settlement to the west being Marietta in 1788.

**allegory** in literature, the description or illustration of one thing in terms of another, or the personification of abstract ideas. The term is also used for a work of poetry or prose in the form of an extended metaphor or parable that makes use of symbolic fictional characters.

**allegro** (Italian 'merry, lively') in music, a lively or quick passage, movement, or composition.

**allele** one of two or more alternative forms of a ◊gene at a given position (locus) on a chromosome, caused by a difference in the ◊DNA. Blue and brown eyes in humans are determined by different alleles of the gene for eye colour.

**Allen, Woody** adopted name of Allen Stewart Konigsberg (1935–  ) US film writer, director, and actor. One of the true auteurs of contemporary American cinema, Allen has written, directed, and frequently acted in a number of comic and dramatic works which are informed by his personal aesthetic, religious, and sexual preoccupations. Allen's filmography includes such critically acclaimed works as *Annie Hall* (1977), which won an Academy Award in 1977 for Best Picture, *Manhattan* (1979), *Hannah and Her Sisters* (1986), *Radio Days* (1987), *Crimes and Misdemeanours* (1989), *Bullets Over Broadway* (1994), and *Deconstructing Harry* (1997). In 1998 he wrote and directed *Celebrity.*

**Allende (Gossens), Salvador** (1908– 1973) Chilean left-wing politician, president 1970–73. Elected president as the candidate of the Popular Front alliance, Allende never succeeded in keeping the electoral alliance together in government. His failure to solve the country's economic problems or to deal with political subversion allowed the army, backed by the Central Intelligence Agency (CIA), to stage the 1973 coup that brought about the death of Allende and many of his supporters.

**allergy** special sensitivity of the body that makes it react with an exaggerated response of the natural immune defence mechanism to the introduction of an otherwise harmless foreign substance (*allergen*).

**Allies, the** in World War I, the 23 countries allied against the Central Powers (Germany, Austro-Hungary, Turkey, and Bulgaria), including France, Italy, Russia, the UK, Australia and other Commonwealth nations, and, in the latter part of the war, the USA. In World War II they were the 49 countries allied against the ◊Axis Powers (Germany, Italy, and Japan), including France, the UK, Australia and other Commonwealth nations, the USA, and the former Soviet Union.

**alligator** (Spanish *el lagarto* 'the lizard') reptile of the genus *Alligator,* related to the crocodile. There are only two living species: *A. mississipiensis,* the Mississippi alligator of the southern states of the USA, and *A. sinensis* from the swamps of the lower Chang Jiang River in China. The former grows to about 4 m/12 ft, but the latter only to 1.5 m/5 ft. Alligators lay their eggs in waterside nests of mud and vegetation and are good mothers. They swim well with lashing movements of the tail and feed on fish and mammals but seldom attack people.

**alliteration** in poetry and prose, the use, within a line or phrase, of words beginning with the same sound, as in 'Two tired toads trotting to Tewkesbury'. It was a common device in Old English poetry, and its use survives in many traditional phrases, such as *dead as a doornail* and *pretty as a picture.*

**allopathy** (Greek *allos* 'other', *pathos* 'suffering') in ◊homeopathy, a term used for orthodox medicine, using therapies designed to counteract the manifestations of the disease. In strict usage, allopathy is the opposite of homeopathy.

**allotropy** property whereby an element can exist in two or more forms (allotropes), each possessing different physical properties but the same state of matter (gas, liquid, or solid). The allotropes of carbon are diamond, fullerene, and graphite. Sulphur has several allotropes (flowers of sulphur, plastic, rhombic, and monoclinic). These solids have different crystal structures, as do the white and grey forms of tin and the black, red, and white forms of phosphorus.

**alloy** metal blended with some other metallic or nonmetallic substance to give it special qualities, such as resistance to corrosion, greater hardness, or tensile strength. Useful alloys include bronze, brass, cupronickel, duralumin, German silver, gunmetal, pewter, solder, steel, and stainless steel.

**alluvial deposit** layer of broken rocky matter, or sediment, formed from material that has been carried in suspension by a river or stream

and dropped as the velocity of the current decreases. River plains and deltas are made entirely of alluvial deposits, but smaller pockets can be found in the beds of upland torrents.

**Al Manamah** capital and free trade port of Bahrain, on Bahrain Island; population (1991) 137,000. It handles oil and entrepôt trade.

**Almaty** formerly (1854–1921) *Vernyi*, (1921–94) *Alma-Ata*, former capital of Kazakhstan to 1998, in the southeast of the country on the Almaatinka River, and capital of Almaty oblast (region); population (1996) 1,500,000. Its industries include engineering, printing, tobacco processing, textile manufacturing, and the production of leather goods. The city is at the centre of a large fruit-growing region, and food processing (meat packing, flour milling, wine bottling) is also a major source of employment in the city.

**Almohad** Berber dynasty 1130–1269 founded by the Berber prophet Muhammad ibn Tumart (*c.* 1080–1130). The Almohads ruled much of Morocco and Spain, which they took by defeating the ◊Almoravids; they later took the area that today forms Algeria and Tunis. Their policy of religious 'purity' involved the forced conversion and massacre of the Jewish population of Spain. The Almohads were themselves defeated by the Christian kings of Spain 1212, and in Morocco 1269.

**almond** tree related to the peach and apricot. Dessert almonds are the kernels of the fruit of the sweet variety *Prunus amygdalus dulcis*, which is also used to produce a low-cholesterol cooking oil. Oil of bitter almonds, from the variety *P. amygdalus amara*, is used in flavouring. Almond oil is also used for cosmetics, perfumes, and fine lubricants. (*Prunus amygdalus*, family Rosaceae.)

**Almoravid** Berber dynasty 1056–1147 founded by the prophet Abdullah ibn Tashfin,

## COMMON ALLOYS

| Name | Approximate composition | Uses |
|---|---|---|
| brass | 35–10% zinc, 65–90% copper | decorative metalwork, plumbing fittings, industrial tubing |
| bronze – common | 2% zinc, 6% tin, 92% copper | machinery, decorative work |
| bronze – aluminium | 10% aluminium, 90% copper | machinery castings |
| bronze – coinage | 1% zinc, 4% tin, 95% copper | coins |
| cast iron | 2–4% carbon, 96–98% iron | decorative metalwork, engine blocks, industrial machinery |
| dentist's amalgam | 30% copper, 70% mercury | dental fillings |
| duralumin | 0.5 % magnesium, 0.5% manganese, 5% copper, 95% aluminium | framework of aircraft |
| gold – coinage | 10% copper, 90% gold | coins |
| gold – dental | 14–28% silver, 14–28% copper, 58% gold | dental fillings |
| lead battery plate | 6% antimony, 94% lead | car batteries |
| manganin | 1.5% nickel, 16% manganese, 82.5% copper | resistance wire |
| nichrome | 20% chromium, 80% nickel | heating elements |
| pewter | 20% lead, 80% tin | utensils |
| silver – coinage | 10% copper, 90% silver | coins |
| solder | 50% tin, 50% lead | joining iron surfaces |
| steel – stainless | 8–20% nickel, 10–20% chromium, 60–80% iron | kitchen utensils |
| steel – armour | 1–4% nickel, 0.5–2% chromium, 95–98% iron | armour plating |
| steel – tool | 2–4% chromium, 6–7% molybdenum, 90–95% iron | tools |

ruling much of Morocco and Spain in the 11th–12th centuries. The Almoravids came from the Sahara and in the 11th century began laying the foundations of an empire covering the whole of Morocco and parts of Algeria; their capital was the newly founded Marrakesh. In 1086 they defeated Alfonso VI of Castile to gain much of Spain. They were later overthrown by the ◊Almohads.

**Al Mukalla** seaport capital of the Hadhramaut coastal region of Yemen, on the Gulf of Aden 480 km/300 mi east of Aden; population (1995 est) 154,400.

**aloe** one of a group of plants native to southern Africa, with long, fleshy, spiny-edged leaves. The drug usually referred to as 'bitter aloes' is a powerful purgative (agent that causes the body to expel impurities) prepared from the juice of the leaves of several of the species. (Genus *Aloe,* family Liliaceae.)

**alpaca** domesticated South American hoofed mammal *Lama pacos* of the camel family, found in Chile, Peru, and Bolivia, and herded at high elevations in the Andes. It is bred mainly for its long, fine, silky wool, and stands about 1 m/3 ft tall at the shoulder with neck and head another 60 cm/2 ft.

**alphabet** set of conventional symbols used for writing, based on a correlation between individual symbols and spoken sounds, so called from *alpha* (α) and *beta* (ß), the names of the first two letters of the classical Greek alphabet. The earliest known alphabet is from Palestine, about 1700 BC. Alphabetic writing now takes many forms – for example, the Hebrew *aleph-beth* and the Arabic script, both written from right to left; the Devanagari script of the Hindus, in which the symbols 'hang' from a line common to all the symbols; and the Greek alphabet, with the first clearly delineated vowel symbols.

**Alpha Centauri** or *Rigil Kent,* brightest star in the constellation Centaurus and the third-brightest star in the night sky. It is actually a triple star (see ◊binary star); the two brighter stars orbit each other every 80 years, and the third, Proxima Centauri, is the closest star to the Sun, 4.2 light years away, 0.1 light years closer than the other two.

**alpha particle** positively charged, high-energy particle emitted from the nucleus of a radioactive atom. It is one of the products of the spontaneous disintegration of radioactive elements (see ◊radioactivity) such as radium and thorium, and is identical with the nucleus of a helium atom – that is, it consists of two protons and two neutrons. The process of emission, *alpha decay,* transforms one element into another, decreasing the atomic (or proton) number by two and the atomic mass (or nucleon number) by four.

**Alps** the highest and most extensive mountain range in Europe. The Alps run in an arc from the Mediterranean coast of France in the west through northern Italy, Switzerland, southern Germany, and Austria to the outskirts of Vienna and the River Danube in the east – a total distance of some 960 km/597 mi. Alpine ranges

also extend down the Adriatic coast into Slovenia and Croatia. The Alps form a natural frontier between several countries in south-central Europe. The highest peak, at 4,808 m/15,774 ft, is ◊Mont Blanc, on the Franco-Italian border. The Alps are the source of many of Europe's major rivers – or their tributaries – including the Rhine, the Rhône, the Po, and the Danube. As well as agriculture, an important economic activity in the Alps is tourism: winter visitors come for the skiing offered at numerous resorts; summer tourism centres on sightseeing and walking in this area of outstanding natural beauty. The Alps are also a widely exploited source of hydroelectric power. Much Alpine woodland has been severely damaged by acid rain.

**Alsace** region of France; area 8,300 sq km/3,204 sq mi; population (1990) 1,624,400. It consists of the *départements* of Bas-Rhin and Haut-Rhin; its administrative centre is ◊Strasbourg. Alsace has much rich agricultural land, and is noted for its white wines.

**Alsace-Lorraine** area of northeast France, lying west of the River Rhine. It forms the French regions of ◊Alsace and ◊Lorraine. The former iron and steel industries are being replaced by electronics, chemicals, and precision engineering. The German dialect spoken does not have equal rights with French, and there is autonomist sentiment.

**Alsatian** another name for the ◊German shepherd dog.

**Altair** or *Alpha Aquilae,* brightest star in the constellation Aquila and the 13th-brightest star in the night sky. It is a white star 16 light years away from the Sun and forms the Summer Triangle with the stars Deneb (in the constellation Cygnus) and Vega (in Lyra).

**altarpiece** a painting (more rarely a sculpture) placed on, behind, or above an altar in a Christian church. Altarpieces vary greatly in size, construction, and number of images (diptych, triptych, and polyptych). Some are small and portable; some (known as a *retable* or *reredos* – there is no clear distinction) are fixed.

**Altdorfer, Albrecht** (c. 1480–1538) German painter, architect, and printmaker. He was active in Regensburg, Bavaria. He is best known for his vast panoramic battle scenes in which his use of light creates movement and drama. On a smaller scale, he also painted some of the first true landscapes.

**alternating current** (AC) electric current that flows for an interval of time in one direction and then in the opposite direction, that is, a current that flows in alternately reversed directions through or around a circuit. Electric energy is usually generated as alternating current in a power station, and alternating currents may be used for both power and lighting.

**alternation of generations** typical life cycle of terrestrial plants and some seaweeds, in which there are two distinct forms occurring alternately: *diploid* (having two sets of chromosomes) and *haploid* (one set of chromosomes).

The diploid generation produces haploid spores by ◊meiosis, and is called the sporophyte, while the haploid generation produces gametes (sex cells), and is called the gametophyte. The gametes fuse to form a diploid ◊zygote which develops into a new sporophyte; thus the sporophyte and gametophyte alternate.

**alternative medicine** see ◊medicine, alternative.

**alternator** electricity generator that produces an alternating current.

**Althing** parliament of Iceland, established about 930, the oldest in the world. It was dissolved 1800, revived 1843 as an advisory body, and became a legislative body again 1874. It has 63 members who serve a four-year term.

**altimeter** instrument used in aircraft that measures altitude, or height above sea level. The common type is a form of aneroid ◊barometer, which works by sensing the differences in air pressure at different altitudes. This must continually be recalibrated because of the change in air pressure with changing weather conditions. The ◊radar altimeter measures the height of the aircraft above the ground, measuring the time it takes for radio pulses emitted by the aircraft to be reflected. Radar altimeters are essential features of automatic and blind-landing systems.

**Altiplano** sparsely populated upland plateau of the Andes of South America, stretching from southern Peru to northwestern Argentina. The height of the Altiplano is 3,000–4,000 m/ 10,000–13,000 ft.

**alto** (Italian 'high') voice or musical instrument between tenor and soprano, of approximate range G3–D5. As a prefix to the name of an instrument, for example alto saxophone, it denotes a size larger than soprano.

**altruism** in biology, helping another individual of the same species to reproduce more effectively, as a direct result of which the altruist may leave fewer offspring itself. Female honey bees (workers) behave altruistically by rearing sisters in order to help their mother, the queen bee, reproduce, and forgo any possibility of reproducing themselves.

**alumina** or *corundum,* Al$_2$O$_3$ oxide of aluminium, widely distributed in clays, slates, and shales. It is formed by the decomposition of the feldspars in granite and used as an abrasive. Typically it is a white powder, soluble in most strong acids or caustic alkalis but not in water. Impure alumina is called 'emery'. Rubies, sapphires, and topaz are corundum gemstones.

**aluminium** lightweight, silver-white, ductile and malleable, metallic element, symbol Al, atomic number 13, relative atomic mass 26.9815, melting point 658°C/1,216°F. It is the third most abundant element (and the most abundant metal) in the Earth's crust, of which it makes up about 8.1% by mass. It is non-magnetic, an excellent conductor of electricity, and oxidizes easily, the layer of oxide on its surface making it highly resistant to tarnish.

**Alva, Ferdinand Alvarez de Toledo** *Duke of Alva* or *Alba* (1508–1582) Spanish politician and general. He successfully commanded the Spanish armies of the Holy Roman Emperor Charles V and his son Philip II of Spain. In 1567 he was appointed governor of the Netherlands, where he set up a reign of terror to suppress Protestantism and the revolt of the Netherlands. In 1573 he was recalled at his own request. He later led a successful expedition against Portugal 1580–81.

**Alzheimer's disease** common manifestation of ◊dementia, thought to afflict one in 20 people over 65. After heart disease, cancer, and strokes it is the most common cause of death in the Western world. Attacking the brain's 'grey matter', it is a disease of mental processes rather than physical function, characterized by memory loss and progressive intellectual impairment. It was first described by Alois Alzheimer 1906. It affects up to 4 million people in the USA and around 600,000 in Britain.

**Amal** radical Lebanese ◊Shiite military force, established by Musa Sadr in the 1970s; its headquarters are in Borj al-Barajneh. The movement split into extremist and moderate groups 1982, but both sides agreed on the aim of increasing Shiite political representation in Lebanon.

**amalgam** any alloy of mercury with other metals. Most metals will form amalgams, except iron and platinum. Amalgam is used in dentistry for filling teeth, and usually contains copper, silver, and zinc as the main alloying ingredients. This amalgam is pliable when first mixed and then sets hard, but the mercury leaches out and may cause a type of heavy-metal poisoning.

**Amazon** Portuguese and Spanish *Rio Amazonas* (Indian *Amossona* 'destroyer of boats'), river in South America, the second longest in the world; length 6,516 km/4,050 mi. The Amazon ranks as the largest river in the world in terms of the volume of water it discharges (between 34 million and 121 million l/ 7.5 million and 27 million gal), its number of tributaries (over 500), and the total basin area that it drains (7 million sq km/2.7 million sq mi – almost half the landmass of South America). It has 48,280 km/30,000 mi of navigable waterways. The river empties into the Atlantic Ocean on the Equator, through an estuary 80 km/50 mi wide. Over 5 million sq km/2 million sq mi of the Amazon basin is virgin rainforest, containing 30% of all known plant and animal species. This is the wettest region on Earth, with an average annual rainfall of 2.54 m/8.3 ft.

**Amazon** in Greek mythology, a member of a group of female warriors living near the Black Sea, who cut off their right breasts to use the bow more easily. Their queen Penthesilea was killed by ◊Achilles at the siege of Troy. The term Amazon has come to mean a large, strong woman.

**Amazonia** those regions of Brazil, Colombia, Ecuador, Peru, and Bolivia lying within the basin of the Amazon River.

**amber** fossilized ◊resin from coniferous trees of the Middle ◊Tertiary period. It is often washed ashore on the Baltic coast with plant and animal specimens preserved in it; many extinct species have been found preserved in this way. It ranges in colour from red to yellow, and is used to make jewellery.

**ambergris** fatty substance, resembling wax, found in the stomach and intestines of the sperm ◊whale. It is found floating in warm seas, and is used in perfumery as a fixative.

**Ambrose, Curtly Elconn Lynwall** (1963– ) West Indies cricketer, born in Antigua. He is a very tall right-arm opening bowler, whose ability to bowl fast and accurately whilst extracting bounce and movement from even the most benign pitches made him the world's most feared pace bowler in the 1990s. In 1997 he became only the eleventh player to take 300 or more Test wickets. He played county cricket for Northamptonshire between 1989 and 1996.

*career highlights*
*Test cricket* matches: 88; overs: 3,306 ; runs: 7,865; wickets: 369; average: 21.31; best: 8–45; batting: 1,297 runs (average 12.71)
*One-day internationals* matches: 165; overs: 1,470.5; runs: 5,210; wickets: 220; average: 23.68; best: 5–17; batting: 617 runs (average 11.01)

**Amenhotep III** (1391–1353 BC) King (pharaoh) of ancient Egypt. He built great monuments at Thebes, including the temples at Luxor. Two portrait statues at his mortuary temple were known to the Greeks as the colossi of Memnon; one was cracked, and when the temperature changed at dawn it gave out an eerie sound, then thought supernatural. His son *Amenhotep IV* changed his name to ◊Akhenaton.

**America** western hemisphere of the Earth, containing the continents of ◊North America and ◊South America, with ◊Central America in between. This great landmass extends from the Arctic to the Antarctic, from beyond 75° N to past 55° S. The area is about 42,000,000 sq km/16,000,000 sq mi, and the estimated population is over 500 million. Politically, it consists of 36 nations and US, British, French, and Dutch dependencies.

**American Civil War** 1861–65; see ◊Civil War, American.

**American football** see ◊football, American.

**American Independence, War of** alternative name of the ◊American Revolution, the revolt 1775–83 of the British North American colonies that resulted in the establishment of the United States of America.

**American Indian** or *Native American,* member of one of the aboriginal peoples of the Americas; the Arctic peoples (Inuit and Aleut) are often included, especially by the Bureau of Indian Affairs (BIA) of the US Department of the Interior, responsible for overseeing policy on US American Indian life, their reservations, education, and social welfare. The first American Indians arrived during the last ice age, approximately 20,000–30,000 years ago, passing from northeastern Siberia into Alaska over a land-bridge across the Bering Strait. The

earliest well-dated archaeological sites in North America are about 13,000–14,000 years old. In South America they are generally dated at about 12,000–13,000 years old, but discoveries made in 1989 suggest an even earlier date, perhaps 35,000–40,000 years ago. There are about 1.9 million (1995) American Indians in the USA and Canada.

**American Revolution** revolt 1775–83 of the British North American colonies, resulting in the establishment of the United States of America. It was caused by colonial opposition to British economic exploitation and by the unwillingness of the colonists to pay for a standing army. It was also fuelled by the colonists' antimonarchist sentiment and their desire to participate in the policies affecting them.

**American Samoa** see ◊Samoa, American.

**americium** radioactive metallic element of the ◊actinide series, symbol Am, atomic number 95, relative atomic mass 243.13; it was first synthesized 1944. It occurs in nature in minute quantities in ◊pitchblende and other uranium ores, where it is produced from the decay of neutron-bombarded plutonium, and is the element with the highest atomic number that occurs in nature. It is synthesized in quantity only in nuclear reactors by the bombardment of plutonium with neutrons. Its longest-lived isotope is Am-243, with a half-life of 7,650 years.

**amethyst** variety of ◊quartz, $SiO_2$, coloured violet by the presence of small quantities of impurities such as manganese or iron; used as a semiprecious stone. Amethysts are found chiefly in the Ural Mountains, India, the USA, Uruguay, and Brazil.

**Amhara** an ethnic group comprising approximately 25% of the population of Ethiopia; 13 million (1987). The Amhara are traditionally farmers. They speak Amharic, a language of the Semitic branch of the Hamito-Semitic (Afro-Asiatic) family. Most are members of the Ethiopian Christian Church.

**amide** any organic chemical derived from a fatty acid by the replacement of the hydroxyl group (–OH) by an amino group (–$NH_2$).
  One of the simplest amides is acetamide ($CH_3CONH_2$), which has a strong mousy odour.

**Amin (Dada), Idi** (1925– ) Ugandan politician, president 1971–79. He led the coup that deposed Milton Obote in 1971, expelled the Asian community in 1972, and exercised a reign of terror over his people during which an estimated 300,000 people were killed. After he invaded Tanzania in 1978, the Tanzanian army combined with dissident Ugandans to counter-attack. Despite assistance from Libya, Amin's forces collapsed and he fled in 1979. He now lives in Saudi Arabia.

**amine** any of a class of organic chemical compounds in which one or more of the hydrogen atoms of ammonia ($NH_3$) have been replaced by other groups of atoms.

**amino acid** water-soluble organic ◊molecule, mainly composed of carbon, oxygen, hydrogen,

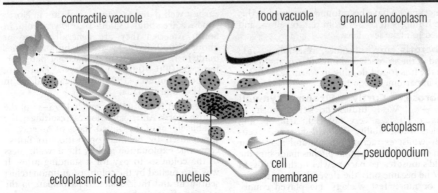

contractile vacuole | food vacuole | granular endoplasm

ectoplasm

pseudopodium

ectoplasmic ridge | nucleus | cell membrane

**amoeba** *The amoebae are among the simplest living organisms, consisting of a single cell. Within the cell, there is a nucleus, which controls cell activity, and many other microscopic bodies and vacuoles (fluid-filled spaces surrounded by a membrane) with specialized functions. Amoebae eat by flowing around food particles, engulfing the particle, a process called phagocytosis.*

and nitrogen, containing both a basic amino group ($NH_2$) and an acidic carboxyl (COOH) group. They are small molecules able to pass through membranes. When two or more amino acids are joined together, they are known as ◊peptides; ◊proteins are made up of peptide chains folded or twisted in characteristic shapes.

**Amis, Kingsley William** (1922–1995) English novelist and poet. He was associated early on with the Angry Young Men group of writers. His sharply ironic works include the best-selling *Lucky Jim* (1954; his first novel), a comic portrayal of life at a provincial university. His later novels include the satiric comedy *The Old Devils* (1986), for which he won the Booker Prize.

**Amis, Martin Louis** (1949–  ) English novelist and journalist, the son of novelist and poet Kingsley Amis. His works are characterized by their acerbic black humour and include *The Rachel Papers* (1973), a memoir of adolescence told through flashbacks, *Dead Babies* (1975), which addresses decadence and sadism, *Money* (1984), *London Fields* (1989), and *Time's Arrow* (1991). Later works include *Night Train* (1997), a novella-length thriller, and *Heavy Water and Other Stories* (1998).

**Amman** capital and chief industrial centre of Jordan, 80 km/50 mi northeast of Jerusalem; population (1994 est) 1,300,000. It is a major communications centre, linking historic trade routes across the Middle East.

**ammeter** instrument that measures electric current (flow of charge per unit time), usually in ◊amperes, through a conductor. It should not to be confused with a voltmeter, which measures potential difference between two points in a circuit. The ammeter is placed in series with the component through which current is to be measured, and is constructed with a low internal resistance in order to prevent the reduction of that current as it flows through the instrument itself. A common type is the moving-coil meter, which measures direct current (DC), but can, in the presence of a rectifier, measure alternating current (AC) also. Hot-wire, moving-iron and

dynamometer ammeters can be used for both DC and AC.

**Ammon** Amen or Amun, in Egyptian mythology, king of the gods; the equivalent of the Greek Zeus (Roman *Jupiter*). The Egyptian pharoahs identified themselves with his supremacy, adopting his name as in Tutankhamen. In art he is represented as a ram or goose, as a man with a ram's head, or as a man crowned with two tall feathers. He had temples at Siwa oasis, Libya, and at Napata and ◊Thebes, Egypt; his oracle at Siwa was patronized by the classical Greeks.

**ammonia** $NH_3$ colourless pungent-smelling gas, lighter than air and very soluble in water. It is made on an industrial scale by the Haber (or Haber–Bosch) process, and used mainly to produce nitrogenous fertilizers, nitric acid, and some explosives.

**ammonite** extinct marine ◊cephalopod mollusc of the order Ammonoidea, related to the modern nautilus. The shell was curled in a plane spiral and made up of numerous gas-filled chambers, the outermost containing the body of the animal. Many species flourished between 200 million and 65 million years ago, ranging in size from that of a small coin to 2 m/6 ft across.

**amnesia** loss or impairment of memory. As a clinical condition it may be caused by disease or injury to the brain, by some drugs, or by shock; in some cases it may be a symptom of an emotional disorder.

**amnesty** act of state granted by a government by which pardon of certain past offences is accorded. This may be in the form of the release of political prisoners under a general pardon, or of the release of a person or group of people from criminal liability for a particular action. In addition, there are occasional amnesties for those who surrender firearms or other items that they hold illegally.

**Amnesty International** human-rights organization established in the UK in 1961 to campaign for the release of prisoners of conscience worldwide; fair trials for all political prisoners; an end to the death penalty, torture, and other inhuman treatment of all prisoners; and the cessation of extrajudicial executions and 'disappearances'. It is politically and economically unaligned. Amnesty International has over a million members in more than 100 countries, and section offices in 54 countries. The organization was awarded the Nobel Prize for Peace in 1978. It is based in London.

**amniocentesis** sampling the amniotic fluid surrounding a fetus in the womb for diagnostic purposes. It is used to detect Down's syndrome and other genetic abnormalities. The procedure carries a 1 in 200 risk of miscarriage.

**amoeba** plural *amoebae*, one of the simplest living animals, consisting of a single cell and belonging to the ◊protozoa group. The body consists of colourless protoplasm. Its activities are controlled by the nucleus, and it feeds by flowing round and engulfing organic debris. It reproduces by ◊binary fission. Some species of amoeba are harmful parasites.

**ampere** SI unit (symbol A) of electrical current. Electrical current is measured in a similar way to water current, in terms of an amount per unit time; one ampere represents a flow of about $6.28 \times 10^{18}$ ◊electrons per second, or a rate of flow of charge of one coulomb per second.

**amphetamine** or *speed*, powerful synthetic ◊stimulant. Benzedrine was the earliest amphetamine marketed, used as a 'pep pill' in World War II to help soldiers overcome fatigue, and until the 1970s amphetamines were prescribed by doctors as an appetite suppressant for weight loss; as an antidepressant, to induce euphoria; and as a stimulant, to increase alertness.

Indications for its use today are very restricted because of severe side effects, including addiction. It is a sulphate or phosphate form of $C_9H_{13}N$.

**amphibian** (Greek 'double life') member of the vertebrate class Amphibia, which generally spend their larval (tadpole) stage in fresh water, transferring to land at maturity (after ◊metamorphosis) and generally returning to water to breed. Like fish and reptiles, they continue to grow throughout life, and cannot maintain a temperature greatly differing from that of their environment. The class contains 4,553 known species, 4,000 of which are frogs and toads, 390 salamanders, and 163 caecilians (wormlike in appearance).

**amphitheatre** (Greek *amphi* 'around') large oval or circular building used by the Romans for gladiatorial contests, fights of wild animals, and other similar events. It is an open structure with a central arena surrounded by rising rows of seats. The ◊Colosseum in Rome, completed AD 80, held 50,000 spectators.

**amplifier** electronic device that magnifies the strength of a signal, such as a radio signal. The ratio of output signal strength to input signal strength is called the *gain* of the amplifier. As well as achieving high gain, an amplifier should be free from distortion and able to operate over a range of frequencies. Practical amplifiers are usually complex circuits, although simple amplifiers can be built from single transistors or valves.

**amplitude** maximum displacement of an oscillation from the equilibrium position. For a transverse wave motion, as in electromagnetic waves, it is the height of a crest (or the depth of a trough). For a longitudinal wave, such as a sound wave, amplitude is the maximum distance a particle is pushed (due to compression) or pulled (due to rarefaction) from its resting position and corresponds to the intensity (loudness) of the sound. Amplitude is generally denoted by *a*.

**amplitude modulation** (AM), method by which radio waves are altered for the transmission of broadcasting signals. AM waves are constant in frequency, but the amplitude of the transmitting wave varies in accordance with the signal being broadcast.

**Amritsar** industrial city in the Punjab, India; population (1991) 709,000. It is the holy city of ◊Sikhism, with the Guru Nanak University (named after the first Sikh guru), and the Golden Temple, surrounded by the sacred pool Amrita Saras. The Jallianwala Bagh area of the city was the scene of the Amritsar Massacre in 1919, when the British Gen Dyer ordered troops to fire on a crowd agitating for self-government; 379 were killed and 1,200 wounded. In 1984, armed Sikh demonstrators were evicted from the Golden Temple by the Indian army, in Operation Bluestar, led by Gen Dayal. Over 300 were killed. Later in 1984, Indian prime minister Indira Gandhi was assassinated in reprisal by Sikh extremists wanting an independent Sikh state in Punjab. The whole of Punjab was put under presidential control in 1987 following riots. Rajiv Gandhi ordered further attacks on the Golden Temple in 1988.

**Amsterdam** capital of the Netherlands; population (1997) 715,100. The Netherlands' second most important port after Rotterdam, Amsterdam is connected to the North Sea by the North Sea Canal, completed in 1876. A new canal leading to the River Waal, south of Utrecht, was completed in 1952 to improve the connection between Amsterdam and the River Rhine. Industries include diamond cutting and polishing, sugar refining, clothes manufacture, printing, chemicals, shipbuilding, brewing, and distilling. Amsterdam is also an international centre of banking and insurance.

**Amu Darya** formerly *Oxus*, river in central Asia, flowing 2,530 km/1,578 mi from the ◊Pamirs to the ◊Aral Sea.

**Amundsen, Roald Engelbrecht Gravning** (1872–1928) Norwegian explorer who in 1903–06 became the first person to navigate the ◊Northwest Passage. Beaten to the North Pole by US explorer Robert Peary 1910, he reached the South Pole ahead of Captain Scott 1911.

**amylase** one of a group of ◊enzymes that break down starches into their component molecules (sugars) for use in the body. It occurs widely in both plants and animals. In humans, it is found in saliva and in pancreatic juices.

**Anabaptist** (Greek 'baptize again') member of any of various 16th-century radical Protestant sects. They believed in adult rather than child baptism, and sought to establish utopian communities. Anabaptist groups spread rapidly in northern Europe, particularly in Germany, and were widely persecuted.

**anabolic steroid** any ◊hormone of the ◊steroid group that stimulates tissue growth. Its use in medicine is limited to the treatment of some anaemias and breast cancers; it may help to break up blood clots. Side effects include aggressive behaviour, masculinization in women, and, in children, reduced height.

**anaconda** South American snake *Eunectes murinus*, a member of the python and boa family, the Boidae. One of the largest snakes, growing to 9 m/30 ft or more, it is found in and near water, where it lies in wait for the birds and animals on which it feeds. The anaconda is not venomous, but kills its prey by coiling round it and squeezing until the creature suffocates.

**anaemia** condition caused by a shortage of haemoglobin, the oxygen-carrying component of red blood cells. The main symptoms are fatigue, pallor, breathlessness, palpitations, and poor resistance to infection. Treatment depends on the cause.

**anaerobic** (of living organisms) not requiring oxygen for the release of energy from food molecules such as glucose. Anaerobic organisms include many bacteria, yeasts, and internal parasites.

**anaesthetic** drug that produces loss of sensation or consciousness; the resulting state is *anaesthesia*, in which the patient is insensitive to stimuli. Anaesthesia may also happen as a result of nerve disorder.

**analgesic** agent for relieving ◊pain. Opiates alter the perception or appreciation of pain and are effective in controlling 'deep' visceral (internal) pain. Non opiates, such as ◊aspirin, ◊paracetamol, and NSAIDs (nonsteroidal antiinflammatory drugs), relieve musculoskeletal pain and reduce inflammation in soft tissues.

**analogue** (of a quantity or device) changing continuously; by contrast a digital quantity or device varies in series of distinct steps. For example, an analogue clock measures time by means of a continuous movement of hands around a dial, whereas a digital clock measures time with a numerical display that changes in a series of discrete steps.

**analogue computer** computing device that performs calculations through the interaction of continuously varying physical quantities, such as voltages (as distinct from the more common digital computer, which works with discrete quantities). An analogue computer is said to operate in real time (corresponding to time in the real world), and can therefore be used to monitor and control other events as they happen.

**analytical chemistry** branch of chemistry that deals with the determination of the chemical composition of substances. *Qualitative analysis* determines the identities of the substances in a given sample; *quantitative analysis* determines how much of a particular substance is present.

**anarchism** (Greek *anarkhos* 'without ruler') political belief that society should have no government, laws, police, or other authority, but should be a free association of all its members. It does not mean 'without order'; most theories of anarchism imply an order of a very strict and symmetrical kind, but they maintain that such order can be achieved by cooperation. Anarchism must not be confused with ◊nihilism (a purely negative and destructive activity directed against society); anarchism is essentially a pacifist movement.

**Anatolia** Turkish *Anadolu,* Asian part of Turkey, consisting of a mountainous peninsula with the Black Sea to the north, the Aegean Sea to the west, and the Mediterranean Sea to the south.

**anatomy** study of the structure of the body and its component parts, especially the human body, as distinguished from physiology, which is the study of bodily functions.

**ANC** abbreviation for ◊*African National Congress,* a South African political party and former nationalist organization.

**ancestor worship** religious rituals and beliefs oriented towards deceased members of a family or group as a symbolic expression of values or in the belief that the souls of the dead remain involved in this world and are capable of influencing current events.

**Anchorage** port and largest city in Alaska, USA, at the head of Cook Inlet; population (1994 est) 253,600. It is an important centre of administration, communication, and commerce for much of central and western Alaska. Local industries include oil and gas extraction, tourism, and fish canning.

**anchovy** small fish *Engraulis encrasicholus* of the ◊herring family. It is fished extensively, being abundant in the Mediterranean, and is also found on the Atlantic coast of Europe and in the Black Sea. It grows to 20 cm/8 in.

**Andalusia** Spanish *Andalucía,* autonomous community of southern Spain, including the provinces of Almería, Cádiz, Córdoba, Granada, Huelva, Jaén, Málaga, and Seville; area 87,300 sq km/33,698 sq mi; population (1991) 6,940,500. The Guadalquivir River flows through Andalusia, which is bounded on the north by the Sierra Morena mountain range. The region is fertile, and produces oranges and wine (especially sherry); horses are bred here also, and copper is mined at Rio Tinto. ◊Seville, an inland port, is the administrative capital and the largest industrial centre; Málaga, Cádiz, and Algeciras are the chief ports and also important industrial centres. The *Costa del Sol* on the south coast has many tourist resorts, including Marbella and Torremolinos; the Sierra Nevada mountain range in the southeast is a winter ski destination.

**Andaman and Nicobar Islands** two groups of islands in the Bay of Bengal, 1,200 km/745 mi off the east coast of India, forming a Union

Territory of the Republic of India; capital Port Blair; area 8,300 sq km/3,204 sq mi; population (1994 est) 322,000. Much of the islands is densely forested and the economy is based on fishing, timber, rubber, fruit, nuts, coffee, and rice.

**Andaman Islands** group of Indian islands, part of the Union Territory of ◊Andaman and Nicobar Islands.

**Andersen, Hans Christian** (1805–1875) Danish writer of fairy tales. Examples include 'The Ugly Duckling', 'The Snow Queen', 'The Little Mermaid', and 'The Emperor's New Clothes'. Their inventiveness, sensitivity, and strong sense of wonder have given these stories perennial and universal appeal; they have been translated into many languages. He also wrote adult novels and travel books.

**Andes** great mountain system or *cordillera* that forms the western fringe of South America, extending through some 67° of latitude and the republics of Colombia, Venezuela, Ecuador, Peru, Bolivia, Chile, and Argentina. It is the longest mountain range in the world, 8,000 km/5,000 mi, and its peaks exceed 3,600 m/12,000 ft in height for half that length.

**andesite** volcanic igneous rock, intermediate in silica content between rhyolite and basalt. It is characterized by a large quantity of feldspar ◊minerals, giving it a light colour. Andesite erupts from volcanoes at destructive plate margins (where one plate of the Earth's surface moves beneath another; see ◊plate tectonics), including the Andes, from which it gets its name.

**Andhra Pradesh** state in east central India
**area** 275,100 sq km/106,216 sq mi
**capital** ◊Hyderabad
**towns and cities** Secunderabad, Visakhapatnam, Vijayawada, Kakinda, Guntur, Nellore
**physical** coastal plains with extensive river valleys (Krishna and Godavari) reaching into the Eastern Ghats; smaller rivers Pennar and Cheyyar; Deccan plateau inland
**industries** mica, coal, iron ore, oil refining, shipbuilding, fertilizers
**agriculture** rice, millet, sugar cane, tobacco, groundnuts, sorghum, cotton
**population** (1994 est) 71,800,000
**language** Telugu, Urdu, Tamil
**history** formed in 1953 from the ◊Telugu-speaking areas of Madras, and enlarged on a similar linguistic basis in 1956 with parts of the former Hyderabad state.

**Andorra** Principality of
**national name** *Principat d'Andorra*
**area** 468 sq km/181 sq mi
**capital** Andorra-la-Vella
**major towns/cities** Les Escaldes, Escaldes-Engordany (suburb of capital)
**physical features** mountainous, with narrow valleys; the eastern Pyrenees, Valira River
**heads of state** Joan Marti i Alanis (bishop of Urgel, Spain) and Jacques Chirac (president of France)
**head of government** Marc Forne from 1994
**political system** co-principality

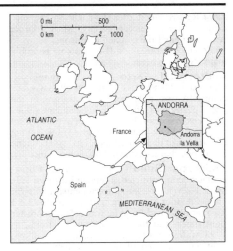

**political parties** National Democratic Grouping (AND; formerly the Democratic Party of Andorra: PDA) moderate, centrist; National Democratic Initiative (IND), left of centre; New Democracy Party (ND), centrist; National Andorran Coalition (CNA), centrist; Liberal Union (UL), right of centre
**currency** French franc and Spanish peseta
**GNP per capita (PPP)** (US$) 16,630 (1995 est)
**exports** cigars and cigarettes, furniture, electricity. Principal market: Spain 47.5% (1997)
**population** 66,000 (1999 est)
**language** Catalan (official); Spanish, French
**religion** Roman Catholic
**life expectancy** 70 (men); 73 (women) (1994 est)
**Chronology**
**AD 803** Holy Roman Emperor Charlemagne liberated Andorra from Muslim control.
**819** Louis I, 'the Pious', the son of Charlemagne, granted control over the area to the Spanish bishop of Urgel.
**1278** Treaty signed making Spanish bishop and French count joint rulers of Andorra (through marriage the king of France later inherited the count's right).
**1806** After temporary suspension during the French Revolution, from 1789 the feudal arrangement of dual allegiance to the co-princes (French and Spanish rulers) was re-established by the French emperor Napoleon Bonaparte.
**1970** Extension of franchise to third-generation female and second-generation male Andorrans.
**1976** First political organization, Democratic Party of Andorra, formed.
**1977** The franchise was extended to first-generation Andorrans.
**1981** The first prime minister was appointed by General Council.
**1991** Links with the European Community (EC) were formalized.
**1993** A new constitution legalized political parties and introduced the first direct elections, leading to a coalition government being formed under the acting prime minister, Oscar Ribas Reig. Andorra became a member of the United Nations (UN).

*1994* Reig resigned after the coalition lost support and was succeeded by Marc Forne; Andorra joined the Council of Europe.
*1997* The Liberal Union (UL) won an assembly majority in a general election.

**Andrea del Sarto** Andrea d'Agnolo di Francesco (1486–1530) Italian Renaissance painter. Active in Florence, he was one of the finest portraitists and religious painters of his time. His frescoes in Florence, such as the *Birth of the Virgin* 1514 (Sta Annunziata), rank among the greatest of the Renaissance. His style is serene and noble, characteristic of High Renaissance art.

**Andreotti, Giulio** (1919–  ) Italian Christian Democrat politician, a fervent European. He headed seven postwar governments: 1972–73, 1976–79 (four successive terms), and 1989–92 (two terms). In addition he was defence minister eight times, and foreign minister five times. In 1993 Andreotti was among several high-ranking politicians accused of possible involvement in Italy's corruption network; he went on trial in 1995 charged with ordering the murder of a journalist and using his influence to protect Mafia leaders in exchange for political support. He was acquitted in September 1999.

**Andrew, (Andrew Albert Christian Edward)** (1960–  ) Prince of the UK, Duke of York, second son of Queen Elizabeth II. He married Sarah Ferguson in 1986; their first daughter, Princess Beatrice, was born in 1988, and their second daughter, Princess Eugenie, was born in 1990. The couple separated in 1992 and were officially divorced in May 1996. Prince Andrew was a naval helicopter pilot, and in 1998 accepted a naval post in international relations.

**Andrew, Rob (Christopher Robert)** (1963–  ) English rugby union player. He is England's record points scorer with 396 points in 71 internationals between 1985 and 1997. He also played five times for the British Lions, and is the most capped fly-half in international rugby. Renowned for his all-round kicking skills, his 23 drop goals are an international record. He retired as a player in September 1999.

**Andrew, St** (lived 1st century AD) New Testament apostle and patron saint of Scotland and Greece. According to tradition, he went with John to Ephesus, preached in Scythia, and was martyred at Patrai in Greece on an X-shaped cross (*St Andrew's cross*). Feast day 30 November.

**androgen** general name for any male sex hormone, of which ◊testosterone is the most important.
  They are all ◊steroids and are principally involved in the production of male secondary sexual characteristics ( such as beard growth).

**Andromeda** major constellation of the northern hemisphere, visible in autumn. Its main feature is the Andromeda galaxy. The star Alpha Andromedae forms one corner of the Square of Pegasus. It is named after the princess of Greek mythology.

**Andromeda galaxy** galaxy 2.2 million light years away from Earth in the constellation Andromeda, and the most distant object visible to the naked eye. It is the largest member of the Local Group of galaxies.
  Like the Milky Way, it is a spiral orbited by several companion galaxies but contains about twice as many stars. It is about 200,000 light years across.

**anemometer** device for measuring wind speed and liquid flow. The most basic form, the *cup-type anemometer,* consists of cups at the ends of arms, which rotate when the wind blows. The speed of rotation indicates the wind speed.

**anemone** flowering plant belonging to the buttercup family, found in northern temperate regions, mainly in woodland. It has ◊sepals which are coloured to attract insects. (Genus *Anemone,* family Ranunculaceae.)

**aneroid barometer** kind of ◊barometer.

**aneurysm** weakening in the wall of an artery, causing it to balloon outwards with the risk of rupture and serious, often fatal, blood loss. If detected in time, some accessible aneurysms can be repaired by bypass surgery, but such major surgery carries a high risk for patients in poor health.

**angel** (Greek *angelos* 'messenger') in Jewish, Christian, and Muslim belief, a supernatural being intermediate between God and humans. The Christian hierarchy has nine orders, from the top down: *Seraphim, Cherubim, Thrones* (who contemplate God and reflect his glory), *Dominations, Virtues, Powers* (who regulate the stars and the universe), *Principalities, Archangels,* and *Angels* (who minister to humanity). In traditional Catholic belief every human being has a guardian angel. The existence of angels was reasserted by Pope John Paul II 1986.

**Angel Falls** waterfall on the River Caroní in the tropical rainforest of Bolívar Region, southeast Venezuela. It is the highest cataract in the world with a total height of 978 m/3,210 ft. The falls plunge from the lip of the Auyán–Tepúplateau (Guinana Highlands). They were named after the aviator and prospector James Angel who flew over the falls and crash-landed nearby in 1935.

**angelfish** any of a number of unrelated fishes. The freshwater *angelfish,* genus *Pterophyllum,* of South America, is a tall, side-to-side flattened fish with a striped body, up to 26 cm/10 in long, but usually smaller in captivity. The *angelfish* or *monkfish* of the genus *Squatina* is a bottom-living shark up to 1.8 m/6 ft long with a body flattened from top to bottom. The *marine angelfishes, Pomacanthus* and others, are long narrow-bodied fish with spiny fins, often brilliantly coloured, up to 60 cm/2 ft long, living around coral reefs in the tropics.

**Angelico, Fra** *Guido di Pietro* (*c.* 1400–1455) Italian painter. He was a monk, active in Florence, and painted religious scenes. His series of frescoes at the monastery of San Marco, Florence, was begun after 1436. He also produced several altarpieces in a style characterized by a delicacy of line and colour.

**Angevin** term used to describe the English kings Henry II and Richard I (also known, with the later English kings up to Richard III, as the *Plantagenets*). Angevin derives from Anjou, a region in northwestern France. The *Angevin Empire* comprised the territories (including England) that belonged to the Anjou dynasty.

**angina** or *angina pectoris,* severe pain in the chest due to impaired blood supply to the heart muscle because a coronary artery is narrowed. Faintness and difficulty in breathing accompany the pain. Treatment is by drugs or bypass surgery.

**angiosperm** flowering plant in which the seeds are enclosed within an ovary, which ripens into a fruit. Angiosperms are divided into ◊monocotyledons (single seed leaf in the embryo) and ◊dicotyledons (two seed leaves in the embryo). They include the majority of flowers, herbs, grasses, and trees except conifers.

**Angkor** site of the ancient capital of the Khmer Empire in northwestern Cambodia, north of Tonle Sap. The remains date mainly from the 10th–12th centuries AD, and comprise temples originally dedicated to the Hindu gods, shrines associated with Theravāda Buddhism, and royal palaces. Many are grouped within the enclosure called *Angkor Thom,* but the great temple of *Angkor Wat* (early 12th century) lies outside.

**Angle** member of the Germanic tribe that occupied the Schleswig-Holstein district of North Germany known as Angeln. The Angles, or Angli, invaded Britain after the Roman withdrawal in the 5th century and settled in East Anglia, Mercia, and Northumbria. The name 'England' (Angleland) is derived from this tribe. See ◊Anglo-Saxon.

**angle** in mathematics, the amount of turn or rotation; it may be defined by a pair of rays (half-lines) that share a common endpoint but do not lie on the same line. Angles are measured in ◊degrees (°) or ◊radians (rads) – a complete turn or circle being 360° or 2π rads.

Angles are classified generally by their degree measures: *acute angles* are less than 90°; *right angles* are exactly 90° (a quarter turn); *obtuse angles* are greater than 90° but less than 180°(a straight line); *reflex angles* are greater than 180° but less than 360°. Angles that add up to 180° are called *supplementary angles.*

**angler** any of an order of fishes Lophiiformes, with flattened body and broad head and jaws. Many species have small, plantlike tufts on their skin. These act as camouflage for the fish as it waits, either floating among seaweed or lying on the sea bottom, twitching the enlarged tip of the threadlike first ray of its dorsal fin to entice prey.

**Anglesey** Welsh *Ynys Môn* – island; *Sir Ynys Môn* – authority, island and unitary authority off the northwest coast of Wales
*area* 720 sq km/278 sq mi (34 km/21 mi long and 31 km/19 mi broad)
*towns* Llangefni (administrative headquarters), Holyhead, Beaumaris, Amlwch
*features* separated from the mainland by the Menai Strait, which is crossed by the Britannia tubular railway bridge and Telford's suspension

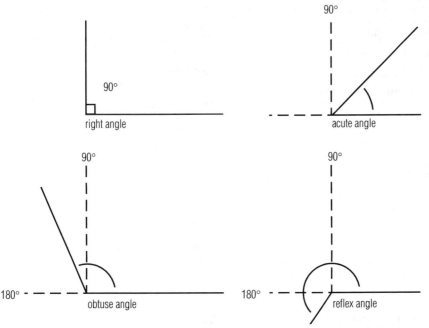

**angle** The four types of angle, as classified by their degree measures. No angle is classified as having a measure of 180°, as by definition such an 'angle' is actually a straight line.

bridge, originally built between 1819 and 1826 but rebuilt since; rich fauna, notably bird life, and flora; many buildings and relics of historic interest
**industries** manufacture of toys and electrical goods; bromine extraction from the sea
**agriculture** sheep farming, varied agriculture
**population** (1996) 71,100.

**Anglican Communion** family of Christian churches including the ◊Church of England, the US Episcopal Church, and those holding the same essential doctrines, that is the Lambeth Quadrilateral 1888 Holy Scripture as the basis of all doctrine, the Nicene and Apostles' Creeds, Holy Baptism and Holy Communion, and the historic episcopate.

**angling** fishing with rod and line. It is widespread and ancient in origin, fish hooks having been found in prehistoric cave dwellings. Competition angling exists and world championships take place for most branches of the sport.

The oldest is the World Freshwater Championship, inaugurated 1957.

**Anglo-American War** war between the USA and Britain 1812–1814; see ◊War of 1812.

**Anglo-Irish Agreement** or *Hillsborough Agreement,* concord reached in 1985 between the UK premier Margaret Thatcher and Irish premier Garret FitzGerald. One sign of the improved relations between the two countries was increased cooperation between police and security forces across the border between Northern Ireland and the Republic of Ireland.

**Anglo-Saxon** one of several groups of Germanic invaders (including Angles, Saxons, and Jutes) that conquered much of Britain between the 5th and 7th centuries. Initially they established conquest kingdoms, commonly referred to as the *Heptarchy;* these were united in the early 9th century under the overlordship of Wessex. The Norman invasion in 1066 brought Anglo-Saxon rule to an end.

**Anglo-Saxon Chronicle** a history of England from the Roman invasion to the 11th century, consisting of a series of chronicles written in Old English by monks, begun in the 9th century (during the reign of King Alfred), and continuing until 1154.

**Angola** People's Republic of
**national name** *República Popular de Angola*
**area** 1,246,700 sq km/481,350 sq mi
**capital** Luanda (and chief port)
**major towns/cities** Lobito, Benguela, Huambo, Lubango, Malange, Namibe (formerly Moçâmedes)
**major ports** Huambo, Lubango, Malange
**physical features** narrow coastal plain rises to vast interior plateau with rainforest in northwest; desert in south; Cuanza, Cuito, Cubango, and Cunene rivers
**head of state** José Eduardo dos Santos from 1979
**head of government** Fernando Franca van Dunem from 1996
**political system** emergent democracy

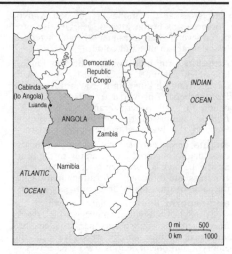

**political parties** People's Movement for the Liberation of Angola–Workers' Party (MPLA–PT), Marxist-Leninist; National Union for the Total Independence of Angola (UNITA); National Front for the Liberation of Angola (FNLA)
**currency** kwanza
**GNP per capita (PPP)** (US$) 840 (1998 est)
**exports** petroleum and petroleum products, diamonds, gas. Principal market: USA 65% (1997)
**population** 12,478,000 (1999 est)
**language** Portuguese (official); Bantu dialects
**religion** Roman Catholic 68%, Protestant 20%, animist 12%
**life expectancy** 45 (men); 48 (women) (1995–2000)
**Chronology**
**14th century** Under Wene, the powerful Kongo kingdom extended control over much of northern Angola.
**early 16th century** The Kongo ruler King Afonso I adopted Christianity and sought constructive relations with Portuguese traders.
**1575 and 1617** Portugal secured control over the ports of Luanda and Benguela and began to penetrate inland, meeting resistance from Queen Nzinga, the Ndonga ruler.
**17th–18th centuries** Inland, the Lunda peoples established powerful kingdoms which stretched into southern Congo; the Portuguese made Angola a key centre for the export of slaves; over 1 million were shipped to Brazil 1580–1680.
**1836** Slave trade officially abolished.
**1885–1915** Military campaigns waged by Portugal to conquer the interior.
**1926** Modern borders delineated.
**1951** Angola became an overseas territory of Portugal.
**1956** Formation of People's Movement for the Liberation of Angola (MPLA), a socialist guerrilla independence movement based in the Congo to the north.
**1961** 50,000 massacred in rebellion on coffee plantations; forced labour abolished, but armed struggle for independence now waged.

**1962** Second nationalist guerrilla movement formed, the National Front for the Liberation of Angola (FNLA), based in north.

**1966** National Union for the Total Independence of Angola (UNITA) formed in southeast Angola as a breakaway from the FNLA.

**1975** Independence achieved from Portugal. MPLA (backed mainly by Cuba) proclaimed People's Republic of Angola under the presidency of Dr Agostinho Neto. FNLA and UNITA (backed by South Africa and the USA) proclaimed People's Democratic Republic of Angola.

**1976** MPLA gained control of most of the country. South African troops withdrew, but Cuban units remained as civil war continued.

**1979** Neto died and was succeeded by José Eduardo dos Santos.

**1980** UNITA guerrillas, aided by South Africa, continued raids against the Luanda government and bases of the Namibian South West Africa People's Organization (SWAPO) in Angola.

**1988** A peace treaty providing for the withdrawal of all foreign troops was signed with South Africa and Cuba.

**1989** A ceasefire agreed with UNITA broke down and guerrilla activity resumed.

**1991** A peace agreement ended the civil war. An amnesty was declared for all political prisoners, and there was a new multiparty constitution.

**1992** MPLA general election victory, led by dos Santos, was fiercely disputed by UNITA, and plunged the country into renewed civil war.

**1993** MPLA government was recognized by the USA. United Nations (UN) sanctions were imposed against UNITA.

**1994** A peace treaty was signed by the government and UNITA representatives.

**1995** UN peacekeepers were drafted in.

**1996** UNITA leader Jonas Savimbi rejected an offer of the vice presidency.

**1997** After some delay a national unity government was eventually sworn in but was boycotted by Savimbi.

**1998** A new agreement led to the demilitarization of UNITA and its transformation into a political party. UNITA was accused of massacres. UNITA ministers were suspended and the peace process threatened. Government forces clashed with UNITA.

**1999** Clashes with the government continued. In April, UNITA sought total control of the country.

**angstrom** unit (symbol Å) of length equal to $10^{-10}$ metres or one-ten-millionth of a millimetre, used for atomic measurements and the wavelengths of electromagnetic radiation.

It is named after the Swedish scientist A J Ångström.

**Anguilla** island in the eastern Caribbean
**area** 160 sq km/62 sq mi
**capital** The Valley
**features** white coral-sand beaches; 80% of its coral reef has been lost through tourism (pollution and souvenir sales)
**exports** lobster, salt
**currency** Eastern Caribbean dollar
**population** (1992) 8,960

**language** English, Creole
**government** from 1982, governor, executive council, and legislative house of assembly
**history** a British colony from 1650, Anguilla was long associated with St Christopher–Nevis but revolted against alleged domination by the larger island and seceded in 1967. A small British force restored order in 1969, and Anguilla retained a special position at its own request; since 1980 it has been a separate dependency of the UK.

**Anhui** or *Anhwei,* province of eastern China, bounded to the north by Shandong, to the east by Jiangsu, to the southeast by Zhejiang, to the south by Jiangxi, to the southwest by Hubei, and to the northwest by Henan provinces
**area** 139,900 sq km/54,000 sq mi
**capital** ◊Hefei
**towns and cities** Anqing, Bengbu, Huainan, Wuhu
**physical** North China Plain; Huangshan Mountains; Chang Jiang and Huai He rivers
**industries** iron, steel, copper, coal, food-processing, domestic appliances
**agriculture** cereals, cotton in the north; rice, tea in the south
**population** (1996) 60,700,000

**anhydride** chemical compound obtained by the removal of water from another compound; usually a dehydrated acid. For example, sulphur(VI) oxide (sulphur trioxide, $SO_3$) is the anhydride of sulphuric acid ($H_2SO_4$).

**aniline** (Portuguese *anil* 'indigo') $C_6H_5NH_2$ or phenylamine one of the simplest aromatic chemicals (a substance related to benzene, with its carbon atoms joined in a ring). When pure, it is a colourless oily liquid; it has a characteristic odour, and turns brown on contact with air. It occurs in coal tar, and is used in the rubber industry and to make drugs and dyes.

It is highly poisonous.

**animal** or *metazoan,* (Latin *anima* 'breath', 'life') member of the ◊kingdom Animalia, one of the major categories of living things, the science of which is *zoology*. Animals are all ◊heterotrophs (they obtain their energy from organic substances produced by other organisms); they have eukaryotic cells (the genetic material is contained within a distinct nucleus) bounded by a thin cell membrane rather than the thick cell wall of plants. Most animals are capable of moving around for at least part of their life cycle.

**animism** in anthropology, the belief that everything, whether animate or inanimate, possesses a soul or spirit. It is a fundamental system of belief in certain religions, particularly those of some pre-industrial societies. Linked with this is the worship of natural objects such as stones and trees, thought to harbour spirits (naturism); fetishism; and ancestor worship.

**anion** ion carrying a negative charge. During electrolysis, anions in the electrolyte move towards the anode (positive electrode).

**Anjou** former province of northern France. Its capital was Angers, and it is now covered by the *département* of Maine-et-Loire and parts of Indre-et-Loire, Mayenne, and Sarthe. In 1154 the count of Anjou became king of England as Henry II, but in 1204 the territory was lost by King John to Philip Augustus of France. In 1480 Anjou was annexed to the French crown. The people are called ◊Angevins, a name also applied by the English to the first three ◊Plantagenet kings.

**Ankara** formerly *Angora,* capital of Turkey; population (1990) 2,559,500. Industries include cement, textiles, and leather products. It replaced Istanbul (then in Allied occupation) as capital 1923.

**Annamese** the majority ethnic group in Vietnam, comprising 90% of the population. The Annamese language is distinct from Vietnamese, though it has been influenced by Chinese and has loan words from Khmer. Their religion combines elements of Buddhism, Confucianism, and Taoism, as well as ancestor worship.

**Annapurna** mountain 8,075 m/26,502 ft in the Himalayas, Nepal. The north face was first climbed by a French expedition (Maurice Herzog) 1950 and the south by a British team 1970.

**Anne** (1665–1714) Queen of Great Britain and Ireland 1702–14. She was the second daughter of James, Duke of York, who became James II, and his first wife, Anne Hyde, daughter of Edward Hyde, Earl of Clarendon. She succeeded William III in 1702. Events of her reign include the War of the Spanish Succession, Marlborough's victories at Blenheim, Ramillies, Oudenarde, and Malplaquet, and the union of the English and Scottish parliaments in 1707.

**Anne, (Anne Elizabeth Alice Louise)** (1950–  ) Princess of the UK, second child of Queen Elizabeth II, declared Princess Royal in 1987. She is actively involved in global charity work, especially for children. An excellent horsewoman, she won silver medals in both individual and team events in the 1975 European Championships, and competed in the 1976 Olympics.

**annealing** controlled cooling of a material to increase ductility and strength. The process involves first heating a material (usually glass or metal) for a given time at a given temperature, followed by slow cooling. It is a common form of ◊heat treatment.

**annelid** any segmented worm of the phylum Annelida. Annelids include earthworms, leeches, and marine worms such as lugworms.

**Anne of Austria** (1601–1666) Queen of France from 1615 and regent 1643–61. Daughter of Philip III of Spain, she married Louis XIII of France (whose chief minister, Cardinal Richelieu, worked against her). On her husband's death she became regent for their son, Louis XIV, until his majority.

**anno hegirae** (Latin 'year of the flight') first year of the Muslim calendar, the year of the flight of Muhammad from Mecca to Medina AD 622. In dates it is often abbreviated to AH.

**annual percentage rate** (APR), the true annual rate of ◊interest charged for a loan. Lenders usually increase the return on their money by compounding the interest payable on a loan to that loan on a monthly or even daily basis. This means that each time that interest is payable on a loan it is charged not only on the initial sum (principal) but also on the interest previously added to that principal. As a result, APR is usually approximately double the flat rate of interest, or simple interest.

**annual plant** plant that completes its life cycle within one year, during which time it germinates, grows to maturity, bears flowers, produces seed, and then dies.

**annual rings** or *growth rings,* concentric rings visible on the wood of a cut tree trunk or other woody stem. Each ring represents a period of growth when new ◊xylem is laid down to replace tissue being converted into wood (secondary xylem). The wood formed from xylem produced in the spring and early summer has larger and more numerous vessels than the wood formed from xylem produced in autumn when growth is slowing down. The result is a clear boundary between the pale spring wood and the denser, darker autumn wood. Annual rings may be used to estimate the age of the plant (see ◊dendrochronology), although occasionally more than one growth ring is produced in a given year.

**Annunciation** in the New Testament, the announcement to Mary by the archangel Gabriel that she is to be the mother of Christ; the feast of the Annunciation is 25 March (also known as Lady Day).

**anode** in chemistry, the positive electrode of an electrolytic ◊cell, towards which negative particles (anions), usually in solution, are attracted. See ◊electrolysis.

**anodizing** process that increases the resistance to ◊corrosion of a metal, such as aluminium, by building up a protective oxide layer on the surface. The natural corrosion resistance of aluminium is provided by a thin film of aluminium oxide; anodizing increases the thickness of this film and thus the corrosion protection.

**anorexia** lack of desire to eat, or refusal to eat, especially the pathological condition of *anorexia nervosa,* most often found in adolescent girls and young women. Compulsive eating, or ◊bulimia, distortions of body image, and depression often accompany anorexia.

**Anselm, St** (*c.* 1033–1109) Italian priest and philosopher. He was born in Piedmont and educated at the abbey of Bec in Normandy, which, as abbot from 1078, he made a centre of scholarship in Europe. He was appointed archbishop of Canterbury by William II of England 1093, but was later forced into exile. He holds an important place in the development of ◊scholasticism. Feast day 21 April.

**ant** insect belonging to the family Formicidae, and to the same order (Hymenoptera) as bees and wasps. Ants are characterized by a conspicuous waist and elbowed antennae. About

10,000 different species are known; all are social in habit, and all construct nests of various kinds. Ants are found in all parts of the world, except the polar regions. It is estimated that there are about 10 million billion ants.

**antacid** any substance that neutralizes stomach acid, such as sodium bicarbonate or magnesium hydroxide ('milk of magnesia'). Antacids are weak ◊bases, swallowed as solids or emulsions. They may be taken between meals to relieve symptoms of hyperacidity, such as pain, bloating, nausea, and 'heartburn'. Excessive or prolonged need for antacids should be investigated medically.

**Antall, József** (1932–1993) Hungarian politician, prime minister 1990–93. He led the centre-right Hungarian Democratic Forum (MDF) to electoral victory in April 1990, becoming Hungary's first post-communist prime minister. He promoted gradual, and successful, privatization and encouraged inward foreign investment.

**Antananarivo** formerly *Tananarive,* capital and administrative centre of Madagascar, on the interior plateau, with a rail link to Tamatave; population (1993) 1,052,800. Industries include food processing, leather goods, clothing, wood pulp and paper manufacturing, and brewing.

**Antarctica** continent surrounding the South Pole, arbitrarily defined as the region lying south of the Antarctic Circle. Occupying 10% of the world's surface, it is almost 1.5 times the size of the USA. Antarctica contains 90% of the world's ice, representing nearly three-quarters of its fresh water. It is thought that if all the ice suddenly melted, the world sea level would rise by 60 m/197 ft
*area* 13,000,000 sq km/5,019,300 sq mi; ice shelves which fill the surrounding seas add a further 1,300,000 sq km/501,930 sq mi to this figure
*features* Mount Erebus on Ross Island is the world's southernmost active volcano; the Ross Ice Shelf is formed by several glaciers coalescing in the Ross Sea
*physical* Antarctica can be divided into two regions, separated by the Transantarctic Mountains, which extend for 3,500 km/2,175 mi and whose peaks, many of them exceeding 3,000 m/9,850 ft in height, protrude through the ice. The larger region, known as Greater or east Antarctica, is comprised of ancient rocks lying mostly at sea level, which are approximately 3,800 million years old. In contrast, Lesser or west Antarctica is 150–200 million years old and has mountain ranges buried under the ice. These include the Antarctic Peninsular and the Ellsworth Mountains, in which the highest peak in Antarctica, the Vinson Massif, is located; height 5,140 m/16,863 ft. The few peaks that are visible above the ice are known as *nunataks.* Two vast seas, the Ross Sea and the Weddell Sea, cut into the continent. Between them lies the mountainous Antarctic Peninsula, which was originally connected to South America before continental drift.

**Antarctic Circle** imaginary line that encircles the South Pole at latitude 66° 32' S. The line encompasses the continent of Antarctica and the Antarctic Ocean.

**Antarctic Ocean** popular name for the reaches of the Atlantic, Indian, and Pacific oceans extending south of the Antarctic Circle (66° 32' S). The term is not used by the International Hydrographic Bureau.

**Australian Antarctic Territory** islands and territories south of 60° south, between 160° and 45° east longitude, excluding Adélie Land; area 6,044,000 sq km/2,332,984 sq mi of land and 75,800 sq km/29,259 sq mi of ice shelf. The population on the Antarctic continent is limited to scientific personnel.

**Antarctic Territory, British** British dependent territory created in 1961 and comprising all British territories south of latitude 60° south and between 20° and 80° west longitude, including the South Orkney Islands, the South Shetland Islands, the Antarctic Peninsula and all adjacent lands, and Coats Land, extending to the South Pole; total land area 1,810,000 sq km/700,000 sq mi; population (exclusively scientific personnel) approximately 300.

**Antares** or *Alpha Scorpii,* brightest star in the constellation Scorpius and the 15th-brightest star in the night sky. It is a red supergiant several hundred times larger than the Sun and perhaps 10,000 times as luminous. It lies about 300 light years away from the Sun, and varies in brightness.

**anteater** mammal of the family Myrmecophagidae, order Edentata, native to Mexico, Central America, and tropical South America. The anteater lives almost entirely on ants and termites. It has toothless jaws, an extensile tongue, and claws for breaking into the nests of its prey.

**antelope** any of numerous kinds of even-toed, hoofed mammals belonging to the cow family, Bovidae. Most antelopes are lightly built and good runners. They are grazers or browsers, and chew the cud. They range in size from the dik-diks and duikers, only 30 cm/1 ft high, to the eland, which can be 1.8 m/6 ft at the shoulder.

**antenatal** in medicine, before birth. Antenatal care refers to health services provided to ensure the health of pregnant women and their babies.

**antenna** in radio and television, another name for ◊aerial.

**antenna** in zoology, an appendage ('feeler') on the head. Insects, centipedes, and millipedes each have one pair of antennae but there are two pairs in crustaceans, such as shrimps. In insects, the antennae are involved with the senses of smell and touch; they are frequently complex structures with large surface areas that increase the ability to detect scents.

**anthem** in music, a short, usually elaborate, religious choral composition, sometimes accompanied by the organ; also a song of loyalty and devotion.

**anther** in a flower, the terminal part of a stamen in which the ◊pollen grains are produced. It is usually borne on a slender stalk or filament, and has two lobes, each containing two chambers, or pollen sacs, within which the pollen is formed.

**Anthony, St** or *Anthony of Thebes* (*c.* 251–356) Egyptian founder of Christian monasticism. At the age of 20, he renounced all his possessions and began a hermetic life of study and prayer, later seeking further solitude in a cave in the desert.

**anthracite** (from Greek *anthrax*, 'coal') hard, dense, shiny variety of ◊coal, containing over 90% carbon and a low percentage of ash and impurities, which causes it to burn without flame, smoke, or smell. Because of its purity, anthracite gives off relatively little sulphur dioxide when burnt.

**anthrax** disease of livestock, occasionally transmitted to humans, usually via infected hides and fleeces. It may develop as black skin pustules or severe pneumonia. Treatment is with antibiotics. Vaccination is effective.

**anthropology** (Greek *anthropos* 'man', *logos* 'discourse') the study of humankind. It investigates the cultural, social, and physical diversity of the human species, both past and present. It is divided into two broad categories: biological or physical anthropology, which attempts to explain human biological variation from an evolutionary perspective; and the larger field of social or cultural anthropology, which attempts to explain the variety of human cultures. This differs from sociology in that anthropologists are concerned with cultures and societies other than their own.

**anthropomorphism** (Greek *anthropos* 'man', *morphe* 'shape') the attribution of human characteristics to animals, inanimate objects, or deities. It appears in the mythologies of many cultures and as a literary device in fables and allegories.

**antibiotic** drug that kills or inhibits the growth of bacteria and fungi. It is derived from living organisms such as fungi or bacteria, which distinguishes it from synthetic antimicrobials.

**antibody** protein molecule produced in the blood by ◊lymphocytes in response to the presence of foreign or invading substances (◊antigens); such substances include the proteins carried on the surface of infecting microorganisms. Antibody production is only one aspect of ◊immunity in vertebrates.

**Antichrist** in Christian theology, the opponent of Christ. The appearance of the Antichrist was believed to signal the Second Coming, at which Christ would conquer his opponent. The concept may stem from the idea of conflict between Light and Darkness, present in Persian, Babylonian, and Jewish literature, which influenced early Christian thought.

**Anti-Corn Law League** an extra-parliamentary pressure group formed in September 1838 by Manchester industrialists, and led by Liberals Richard Cobden and John ◊Bright. It argued for free trade and campaigned successfully against duties on the import of foreign corn to Britain imposed by the ◊Corn Laws, which were repealed in 1846.

**anticyclone** area of high atmospheric pressure caused by descending air, which becomes warm and dry. Winds radiate from a calm centre, taking a clockwise direction in the northern hemisphere and an anticlockwise direction in the southern hemisphere. Anticyclones are characterized by clear weather and the absence of rain and violent winds. In summer they bring hot, sunny days and in winter they bring fine, frosty spells, although fog and low cloud are not uncommon in the UK. *Blocking anticyclones,* which prevent the normal air circulation of an area, can cause summer droughts and severe winters.

**antigen** any substance that causes the production of ◊antibodies by the body's immune system. Common antigens include the proteins carried on the surface of bacteria, viruses, and pollen grains. The proteins of incompatible blood groups or tissues also act as antigens, which has to be taken into account in medical procedures such as blood transfusions and organ transplants.

**Antigua and Barbuda** State of

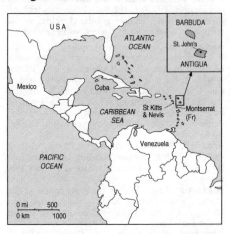

*area* Antigua 280 sq km/108 sq mi, Barbuda 161 sq km/62 sq mi, plus Redonda 1 sq km/0.4 sq mi (440 sq km/169 sq mi altogether)
*capital* St John's (on Antigua) (and chief port)
*major towns/cities* Codrington (on Barbuda)
*physical features* low-lying tropical islands of limestone and coral with some higher volcanic outcrops; no rivers and low rainfall result in frequent droughts and deforestation. Antigua is the largest of the Leeward Islands; Redonda is an uninhabited island of volcanic rock rising to 305 m/1,000 ft
*head of state* Elizabeth II from 1981, represented by governor general James B Carlisle from 1993
*head of government* Lester Bird from 1994
*political system* liberal democracy
*political parties* Antigua Labour Party (ALP), moderate left of centre; United Progressive Party (UPP), centrist; Barbuda People's Movement (BPM), left of centre
*currency* Eastern Caribbean dollar

*GNP per capita (PPP)* (US$) 9,440 (1998)
*exports* petroleum products, food, manufactures, machinery and transport equipment. Principal market: USA (mainly re-exports)
*population* 69,000 (1999 est)
*language* English
*religion* Christian (mostly Anglican)
*life expectancy* 72 (men); 76 (women) (1998 est)
*Chronology*
*1493* Antigua, then peopled by American Indian Caribs, visited by Christopher Columbus; he named it after a painting in the Church of Sante Maria la Antigua, in Seville.
*1632* Antigua colonized by British settlers from St Kitts.
*1667* Treaty of Breda formally ceded Antigua to Britain, ending French claim.
*1674* Christopher Codrington, a sugar planter from Barbados, established sugar plantations and acquired Barbuda island on lease from the British monarch in 1685; Africans brought in as slaves.
*1834* Antigua's slaves were freed.
*1860* Annexation of Barbuda.
*1871–1956* Antigua and Barbuda administered as part of the Leeward Islands federation.
*1946* Antigua Labour Party (ALP) formed by Vere Bird.
*1958–62* Part of West Indies Federation.
*1967* Antigua and Barbuda became an associated state within the Commonwealth, with full internal independence, but Britain responsible for defence and foreign affairs.
*1969* Separatist movement developed on Barbuda.
*1971* The Progressive Labour Movement (PLM) won a general election, defeating the ALP, and George Walter replaced Bird as prime minister.
*1976* The PLM called for early independence, but the ALP urged caution. The ALP, led by Bird, won the general election.
*1981* Independence from Britain was achieved.
*1983* Antigua and Barbuda assisted in the US invasion of Grenada, despite a policy of non-alignment.
*1991* Bird remained in power despite calls for his resignation.
*1993* Lester Bird succeeded his father as ALP leader.
*1999* Vere Bird, founder of the Antigua Labour Party (ALP), died on 28 June.

**antihistamine** any substance that counteracts the effects of ◊histamine. Antihistamines may occur naturally or they may be synthesized.

**Antilles** group of West Indian islands, divided north–south into the *Greater Antilles* (Cuba, Jamaica, Haiti–Dominican Republic, Puerto Rico) and *Lesser Antilles,* subdivided into the Leeward Islands (Virgin Islands, St Christopher–Nevis, Antigua and Barbuda, Anguilla, Montserrat, and Guadeloupe) and the Windward Islands (Dominica, Martinique, St Lucia, St Vincent and the Grenadines, Barbados, and Grenada).

**antimatter** in physics, a form of matter in which most of the attributes (such as electrical charge, magnetic moment, and spin) of ◊elementary particles are reversed. Such particles (◊antiparticles) can be created in particle accelerators, such as those at CERN in Geneva, Switzerland, and at Fermilab in the USA. In 1996 physicists at CERN created the first atoms of antimatter: nine atoms of antihydrogen survived for 40 nanoseconds.

**antimony** silver-white, brittle, semimetallic element (a metalloid), symbol Sb (from Latin *stibium*), atomic number 51, relative atomic mass 121.75. It occurs chiefly as the ore stibnite and is used to make alloys harder; it is also used in photosensitive substances in colour photography, optical electronics, fireproofing, pigment, and medicine. It was employed by the ancient Egyptians in a mixture to protect the eyes from flies.

**Antioch** ancient capital of the Greek kingdom of Syria, founded 300 BC by Seleucus I in memory of his father Antiochus, and famed for its splendour and luxury. Under the Romans it was an early centre of Christianity. St Paul set off on his missionary journeys from here. It was captured by the Arabs 637. After a five-month siege 1098 Antioch was taken by the crusaders, who held it until 1268. The site is now occupied by the Turkish town of Antakya.

**Antiochus (III) the Great** (*c.* 241–187 BC) king of Syria 223–187 BC. He earned his title 'the Great' by restoring the Seleucid empire in 25 years of continuous campaigning from western Asia Minor to Afghanistan. He also finally wrested the Lebanon and Palestine from Egypt, despite defeat at Raphia in 201 BC.

**Antiochus** thirteen kings of Syria of the Seleucid dynasty, including:

**Antiochus IV** (*c.* 215–164 BC) King of Syria from 175 BC, known as Antiochus Epiphanes, the Illustrious, son of Antiochus III. He occupied Jerusalem about 170, seizing much of the Temple treasure, and instituted worship of the Greek type in the Temple in an attempt to eradicate Judaism. This produced the revolt of the Hebrews under the Maccabees; Antiochus died before he could suppress it.

**Antiochus VII** (*c.* 159–129 BC) King of Syria from 138 BC. The last strong ruler of the Seleucid dynasty, he took Jerusalem 134, reducing the Maccabees to subjection. He was defeated and killed in battle against the ◊Parthians.

**antioxidant** any substance that prevents deterioration of fats, oils, paints, plastics, and rubbers by oxidation. When used as food ◊additives, antioxidants prevent fats and oils from becoming rancid when exposed to air, and thus extend their shelf life.

**antiparticle** in nuclear physics, a particle corresponding in mass and properties to a given ◊elementary particle but with the opposite electrical charge, magnetic properties, or coupling to other fundamental forces. For example, an electron carries a negative charge whereas its antiparticle, the positron, carries a positive one. When a particle and its antiparticle collide, they destroy each other, in the process called 'annihilation', their total energy being converted to lighter particles and/or photons. A substance consisting entirely of antiparticles is known as ◊antimatter.

**antipodes** (Greek 'opposite feet') places at opposite points on the globe.

**antipope** rival claimant to the elected pope for the leadership of the Roman Catholic Church, for instance in the Great Schism 1378–1417 when there were rival popes in Rome and Avignon.

**anti-Semitism** prejudice or discrimination against, and persecution of, the Jews as an ethnic group. Historically this has been practised for almost 2,000 years by European Christians. Anti-Semitism was a tenet of Nazi Germany, and in the ◊Holocaust 1933–45 about 6 million Jews died in concentration camps and in local extermination ◊pogroms, such as the siege of the Warsaw ghetto. In eastern Europe, as well as in Islamic nations, anti-Semitism exists and is promulgated by neofascist groups. It is a form of ◊racism.

**antiseptic** any substance that kills or inhibits the growth of micro-organisms. The use of antiseptics was pioneered by Joseph ◊Lister. He used carbolic acid (◊phenol), which is a weak antiseptic; antiseptics such as TCP are derived from this.

**antler** 'horn' of a deer, often branched, and made of bone rather than horn. Antlers, unlike true horns, are shed and regrown each year. Reindeer of both sexes grow them, but in all other types of deer, only the males have antlers.

**Antonello da Messina** (c. 1430–1479) Italian painter. He was a pioneer in his country of the technique of oil painting developed by Flemish artists; he acquired his knowledge of it in Naples, or, if Vasari is to be believed, he may have learnt it from Jan van ◊Eyck himself. Flemish influence is reflected in his brushwork, his use of light, and sometimes in his imagery. Surviving works include bust-length portraits and sombre religious paintings.

**Antonine Wall** Roman line of fortification built in AD 142 in the reign of Antoninus Pius (ruled AD 138–61). It was the Roman empire's furthest northwest frontier, between the Clyde and Forth rivers in Scotland. It was defended until about 200, after which the frontier returned to ◊Hadrian's Wall.

**Antoninus Pius, (Titus Aurelius Fulvus)** (AD 86–161) Roman emperor. He was adopted 138 as Hadrian's heir, and succeeded him later that year. He enjoyed a prosperous reign, during which the ◊Antonine Wall was built. His daughter Faustina the Younger married his successor ◊Marcus Aurelius.

**Antonioni, Michelangelo** (1912– ) Italian film director. He specialized in subtle presentations of neuroses and personal relationships among the leisured classes, with an elliptical approach to film narrative. His directorial credits include *L'Avventura* 1960, *L'Eclisse/Eclipse* 1962, *Il Deserto Rosso/Red Desert* 1964, and *Blow-Up* 1966.

**Antrim** county of Northern Ireland
*area* 2,830 sq km/1,092 sq mi
*towns and cities* ◊Belfast (county town), Larne (port), Antrim, Ballymena, Lisburn, Carrickfergus
*physical* peat bogs; Antrim borders Lough Neagh, and is separated from Scotland by the North Channel, which is only 21 km/13 mi wide at Torr Head, the narrowest point; the main rivers are the Bann and the Lagan
*features* Giant's Causeway, a World Heritage Site, consisting of natural hexagonal and pentagonal basalt columns on the coast; Antrim Mountains (highest point Trostan 554 m/1,817 ft) and the Glen of Antrim; Kebble National Nature Reserve, on Rathlin Island, off the coast near Ballycastle; Bushmills Distillery, in the village of Bushmills, has the oldest known licence for distilling whiskey; there are a number of early fortifications, castles, and medieval ecclesiastical remains in the county; the village of Cushendun was built by Clough Williams-Ellis; Gobbins Cliff Path (19th century), to be restored as a millennium project
*industries* shipbuilding; traditional linen production largely replaced by the manufacture of artificial fibres, whiskey, agriculture (the Bann Valley is particularly fertile)
*agriculture* potatoes, oats, flax
*population* (1981) 642,000.

**Antwerp** Flemish *Antwerpen*, French *Anvers*, port in Belgium on the River Schelde, capital of the province of Antwerp, 43 km/27 mi north of Brussels; population (1997) 453,000. One of the world's busiest ports, it has shipbuilding, oil refining, petrochemical, textile, and diamond cutting industries. The home of the artist Rubens is preserved, and several of his works are in the Gothic cathedral.

**Anubis** in Egyptian mythology, the jackal-headed god of the dead, son of Osiris. Anubis presided over the funeral cult, including the weighing of the heart and embalming, and led the dead to judgement.

**anxiety** unpleasant, distressing emotion usually to be distinguished from fear. Fear is aroused by the perception of actual or threatened danger; anxiety arises when the danger is imagined or cannot be identified or clearly perceived. It is a normal response in stressful situations, but is frequently experienced in many mental disorders.

**Aoraki** formerly *Mount Cook,* highest point, 3,764 m/12,353 ft, of the Southern Alps, a range of mountains running through New Zealand.

**Aouita, Said** (1960– ) Moroccan runner. Outstanding at middle and long distances, he won the 1984 Olympic and 1987 World Championship 5,000-metres title, and has set many world records.
*career highlights*
*Olympic Games* gold 5,000 metres 1984
*world records* 1,500 metres 1985; 2,000 metres 1987; 3,000 metres 1987, 1989; 5,000 metres 1985, 1987
*world championships* gold 5,000 metres 1987
*world best* 2 miles 1987

**Apache** (Apache 'fighting men') member of an ◊American Indian people numbering about 50,000 (1990) and who traditionally lived by hunting bison, gathering wild plant foods, farming maize, and raiding other tribes in what is now Arizona, and parts of Colorado, New Mexico, Texas, and north Mexico. Culturally divided into the Western and Eastern Apache, they and their neighbours the ◊Navajo are descendants of Athabaskan-speaking Indians who migrated to the southwest from Canada about AD 1000. They were known as fierce raiders and horse warriors in the 18th and 19th centuries. They now live on reservations in Arizona, southwest Oklahoma, and New Mexico. Apache also refers to any of several southern Athabaskan languages and dialects spoken by these people.

**apartheid** (Afrikaans 'apartness') racial-segregation policy of the government of South Africa from 1948 to 1994. Under the apartheid system, nonwhites – classified as Bantu (black), coloured (mixed), or Indian – did not share full rights of citizenship with the white minority. For example, black people could not vote in parliamentary elections, and until 1990 many public facilities and institutions were restricted to the use of one race only. The establishment of ◊Black National States was another manifestation of apartheid. In 1991, after years of internal dissent and violence and the imposition of international trade sanctions by the United Nations (UN) and other organizations, President F W de Klerk repealed the key elements of apartheid legislation and by 1994 apartheid had ceased to exist.

The term apartheid has also been loosely applied to similar movements and other forms of racial separation, for example social or educational, in other parts of the world.

**apatosaurus** large plant-eating dinosaur, formerly called *brontosaurus,* which flourished about 145 million years ago. Up to 21 m/69 ft long and 30 tonnes in weight, it stood on four elephantlike legs and had a long tail, long neck, and small head. It probably snipped off low-growing vegetation with peglike front teeth, and swallowed it whole to be ground by pebbles in the stomach.

**ape** ◊primate of the family Pongidae, closely related to humans, including gibbon, orangutan, chimpanzee, and gorilla.

**Apennines** chain of mountains stretching the length of the Italian peninsula. An older and more weathered continuation of the Maritime Alps, from Genoa the Apennines swing across the peninsula to Ancona on the east coast, and then back to the west coast and into the 'toe' of Italy. The system is continued over the Strait of Messina along the north Sicilian coast, then across the Mediterranean Sea in a series of islands to the Atlas Mountains of North Africa. The highest peak is Monte Corno in Gran Sasso d'Italia at 2,914 m/9,560 ft.

**aperture** in photography, an opening in the camera that allows light to pass through the lens to strike the film. Controlled by the iris diaphragm, it can be set mechanically or electronically at various diameters.

**aphid** any of the family of small insects, Aphididae, in the order Hemiptera, suborder Homoptera, that live by sucking sap from plants. There are many species, often adapted to particular plants; some are agricultural pests.

**aphorism** (Greek *apo* 'from', *horos* 'limit') short, sharp, witty saying, usually making a general observation. 'Experience is the name everyone gives to their mistakes' is one of many aphorisms by Irish playwright Oscar Wilde. The term derives from the *Aphorisms* ascribed to Greek writer Hippocrates. An aphorism which has become universally accepted is a proverb.

**Aphrodite** in Greek mythology, the goddess of love (Roman Venus, Phoenician Astarte, Babylonian Ishtar). She is said to be either a daughter of ◊Zeus (in Homer) or sprung from the foam of the sea (in Hesiod). She was the unfaithful wife of Hephaestus, the god of fire, and the mother of Eros.

**Apocrypha** (Greek *apokryptein* 'to hide away') appendix to the Old Testament of the Bible, 14 books not included in the final Hebrew canon but recognized by Roman Catholics. There are also disputed New Testament texts known as Apocrypha.

**Apollinaire, Guillaume** pen-name of Guillaume Apollinaire de Kostrowitsky (1880–1918) French poet of aristocratic Polish descent. He was a leader of the avant-garde in Parisian literary and artistic circles. His novel *Le Poète assassiné/The Poet Assassinated* 1916, followed by the experimental poems *Alcools/Alcohols* 1913 and *Calligrammes/Word Pictures* 1918, show him as a representative of the Cubist and Futurist movements.

**Apollo** in Greek and Roman mythology, the god of sun, music, poetry, prophecy, agriculture, and pastoral life, and leader of the Muses. He was the twin child (with ◊Artemis) of Zeus and Leto. Ancient statues show Apollo as the embodiment of the Greek ideal of male beauty. His chief cult centres were his supposed birthplace on the island of Delos, in the Cyclades, and Delphi.

**Apollo asteroid** member of a group of ◊asteroids whose orbits cross that of the Earth. They are named after the first of their kind, Apollo, discovered in 1932 and then lost until 1973. Apollo asteroids are so small and faint that they are difficult to see except when close to Earth (Apollo is about 2 km/1.2 mi across).

**Apollo project** US space project to land a person on the Moon, achieved 20 July 1969, when Neil ◊Armstrong was the first to set foot there. He was accompanied on the Moon's surface by 'Buzz' Aldrin; Michael Collins remained in the orbiting command module.

**Apo, Mount** active volcano and highest peak in the Philippines, rising to 2,954 m/9,692 ft on the island of Mindanao.

**apostle** (Greek 'messenger') in the New Testament, any of the chosen 12 disciples sent out by Jesus after his resurrection to preach the Gospel.

In the earliest days of Christianity the term was extended to include some who had never known Jesus in the flesh, notably St Paul.

**Appalachian Mountains** mountain system in eastern North America, stretching about 2,400 km/1,500 mi from Alabama to Québec. The chain, composed of ancient eroded rocks and rounded peaks, includes the Allegheny, Catskill, and Blue Ridge Mountains. Its width in some parts reaches 500 km/311 mi. Mount Mitchell, in the Blue Ridge Mountains, is the highest peak at 2,045 m/6,712 ft. The eastern edge has a fall line to the coastal plain where Philadelphia, Baltimore, and Washington stand. The Appalachians are heavily forested and have deposits of coal and other minerals.

**appeal** in law, an application for a rehearing of all or part of an issue that has already been dealt with by a lower court or tribunal.

The outcome can be a new decision on all or part of the points raised, or the previous decision may be upheld. In criminal cases, an appeal may be against conviction and either the prosecution or the defence may appeal against sentence.

**appendicitis** inflammation of the appendix, a small, blind extension of the bowel in the lower right abdomen. In an acute attack, the pus-filled appendix may burst, causing a potentially lethal spread of infection. Treatment is by removal (appendicectomy).

**appendix** a short, blind-ended tube attached to the caecum. It has no known function in humans, but in herbivores it may be large, containing millions of bacteria that secrete enzymes to digest grass (as no vertebrate can secrete enzymes that will digest cellulose, the main constituent of plant cell walls).

**apple** fruit of several species of apple tree. There are several hundred varieties of cultivated apples, grown all over the world, which may be divided into eating, cooking, and cider apples. All are derived from the wild ◊crab apple. (Genus *Malus,* family Rosaceae.)

**Appleton layer** or *F layer,* band containing ionized gases in the Earth's upper atmosphere, at a height of 150–1,000 km/94–625 mi, above the E layer (formerly the Kennelly–Heaviside layer). It acts as a dependable reflector of radio signals as it is not affected by atmospheric conditions, although its ionic composition varies with the sunspot cycle.

**application** in computing, program or job designed for the benefit of the end user. Examples of *general purpose* application programs include word processors, ◊desktop publishing programs, ◊databases, ◊spreadsheet packages, and graphics programs (see ◊CAD and ◊CAM). *Application-specific* programs include payroll and stock control systems. Applications may also be *custom designed* to solve a specific problem, not catered for in other types of application.

The term is used to distinguish such programs from those that control the computer (systems programs) or assist the programmer, such as a ◊compiler.

**Appomattox Court House** former village in Virginia, USA, scene of the surrender 9 April 1865 of the Confederate army under Robert E Lee to the Union army under Ulysses S Grant, which ended the American Civil War.

**apricot** yellow-fleshed fruit of the apricot tree, which is closely related to the almond, peach, plum, and cherry. Although native to the Far East, it has long been cultivated in Armenia, from where it was introduced into Europe and the USA. (Genus *Prunus armeniaca,* family Rosaceae.)

**Apulia** Italian *Puglia,* region of Italy, the southeast 'heel', comprising the provinces of Bari, Brindisi, Foggia, Lecce, and Taranto; area 19,300 sq km/7,450 sq mi; population (1992 est) 4,050,000. The capital is ◊Bari, and the main industrial centre Taranto. Products include wheat, grapes, almonds, olives, figs, and vegetables.

**Aqaba, Gulf of** gulf extending northwards from the Red Sea for 160 km/100 mi to the Negev; its coastline is uninhabited except at its head, where the frontiers of Israel, Egypt, Jordan, and Saudi Arabia converge. The two ports of Elat (Israeli *Elath*) and Aqaba, Jordan's only port, are situated here. A border crossing near the two ports was opened 1994, for non-Israelis and non-Jordanians, to encourage the eastern Mediterranean tourist industry.

**aquaculture** the cultivation of fish and shellfish for human consumption; see ◊fish farming.

**aqualung** or *scuba,* underwater breathing apparatus worn by divers, developed in the early 1940s by French diver Jacques Cousteau. Compressed-air cylinders strapped to the diver's back are regulated by a valve system and by a mouth tube to provide air to the diver at the same pressure as that of the surrounding water (which increases with the depth).

**aquamarine** blue variety of the mineral ◊beryl. A semiprecious gemstone, it is used in jewellery.

**aquaplaning** phenomenon in which the tyres of a road vehicle cease to make direct contact with the road surface, owing to the presence of a thin film of water. As a result, the vehicle can go out of control (particularly if the steered wheels are involved).

**Aquarius** zodiacal constellation a little south of the celestial equator near Pegasus. Aquarius is represented as a figure pouring water from a jar. The Sun passes through Aquarius from late February to early March. In astrology, the dates for Aquarius, the 11th sign of the zodiac, are between about 20 January and 18 February (see ◊precession).

**aquatint** printmaking technique. When combined with ◊etching it produces areas of subtle tone as well as more precisely etched lines. Aquatint became common in the late 18th century.

**aqueduct** any artificial channel or conduit for water, originally applied to water supply tunnels, but later used to refer to elevated structures of stone, wood, or ironcarrying navigable canals across valleys. One of the first great aqueducts was built in 691 BC, carrying water for 80 km/50 mi to Ninevah, capital of the ancient Assyrian Empire. Many Roman aqueducts are still standing, for example the one carried by the Pont du Gard at Nîmes in southern France, built about 8 BC (48 m/160 ft high).

**aqueous humour** watery fluid found in the chamber between the cornea and lens of the vertebrate eye. Similar to blood serum in composition, it is constantly renewed.

**aquifer** a body of rock through which appreciable amounts of water can flow. The rock of an aquifer must be porous and permeable (full of interconnected holes) so that it can conduct water. Aquifers are an important source of fresh water, for example, for drinking and irrigation, in many arid areas of the world, and are exploited by the use of ◊artesian wells.

**Aquinas, St Thomas** (1225–1274) Italian philosopher and theologian, the greatest figure of the school of ◊scholasticism. He was a Dominican monk, known as the 'Angelic Doctor'. In 1879 his works were recognized as the basis of Catholic theology. His *Summa contra Gentiles/Against the Errors of the Infidels* 1259–64 argues that reason and faith are compatible. He assimilated the philosophy of Aristotle into Christian doctrine. He was canonized 1323.

**Aquino, (Maria) Corazon ('Cory')** born Cojuangco (1933– ) Filipino centrist politician, president 1986–92. She was instrumental in the nonviolent overthrow of President Ferdinand ◊Marcos in 1986. As president, she sought to rule in a conciliatory manner, but encountered opposition from the left (communist guerrillas) and the right (army coup attempts), and her land reforms were seen as inadequate.

**Aquitaine** region of southwest France; administrative capital ◊Bordeaux; area 41,300 sq km/15,942 sq mi; population (1990) 2,795,800. It comprises the *départements* of Dordogne, Gironde, Landes, Lot-et-Garonne, and Pyrénées-Atlantiques. Red wines (Margaux, St Julien) are produced in the Médoc district, bordering the Gironde. Aquitaine was an English possession 1152–1453.

**Arab** any of the Semitic (see ◊Semite) people native to the Arabian peninsula, but now settled throughout North Africa and the nations of the Middle East.

**arabesque** in ballet, a pose in which the dancer stands on one leg, straight or bent, with the other leg raised behind, fully extended. The arms are held in a harmonious position to give the longest possible line from fingertips to toes. It is one of the fundamental positions in ballet.

**arabesque** in the visual arts, a linear decoration based on plant forms. It is a feature of ancient Greek and Roman art and is particularly common in Islamic art (hence the term).

**Arabia** Arabian Peninsula, (Arabic *Jazirat al-Arab*, the 'peninsula of the Arabs') peninsula between the Gulf and the Red Sea, in southwest Asia; area 2,600,000 sq km/1,000,000 sq mi. The length from north to south is about 2,400 km/1,490 mi and the greatest width about 1,600 km/994 mi. The peninsula contains the world's richest gas reserves and half the world's oil reserves. It comprises the states of Bahrain, Kuwait, Oman, Qatar, Saudi Arabia, the United Arab Emirates, and Yemen.

**Arabian Sea** northwestern branch of the ◊Indian Ocean, covering 3,859,000 sq km/1,489,960 sq mi, with India to the east, Pakistan and Iran to the north, and the Arabian Peninsula and Somalia to the west. It is linked with the Red Sea via the Gulf of Aden, and with the Persian Gulf via the Gulf of Oman. Its mean depth is 2,730 m/8,956 ft. The chief river flowing into the Arabian Sea is the Indus, which is linked with a large submarine canyon in the continental shelf. The sea is rich in fish.

**Arabic language** major Semitic language of the Hamito-Semitic family of West Asia and North Africa, originating among the Arabs of the Arabian peninsula. It is spoken today by about 120 million people in the Middle East and North Africa. Arabic script is written from right to left.

**Arab–Israeli Conflict** series of wars and territorial conflicts between Israel and various Arab states in the Middle East since the founding of the state of Israel in May 1948. These include the war of 1948–49; the 1956 Suez War between Israel and Egypt; the Six-Day War of 1967, in which Israel captured territory from Syria and Jordan; the October War of 1973; and the 1982–85 war between Israel and Lebanon. In the times between the wars tension has remained high in the area, and has resulted in skirmishes and terrorist activity taking place on both sides.

**Arab League** League of Arab States, organization of Arab states established in Cairo in 1945 to promote Arab unity, primarily in opposition to Israel. The original members were Egypt, Syria, Iraq, Lebanon, Transjordan (Jordan 1949), Saudi Arabia, and Yemen. They were later joined by Algeria, Bahrain, Comoros, Djibouti, Kuwait, Libya, Mauritania, Morocco, Oman, Palestine, the PLO, Qatar, Somalia, Sudan, Tunisia, and the United Arab Emirates. In 1979 Egypt was suspended and the league's headquarters transferred to Tunis in protest against the Egypt–Israeli peace, but Egypt was readmitted as a full member in May 1989, and in March 1990 its headquarters returned to Cairo. Despite the strains imposed on it by the 1990–91 Gulf War, the alliance survived.

**arable farming** cultivation of crops, as opposed to the keeping of animals. Crops may be ◊cereals, vegetables, or plants for producing oils or cloth. Arable farming generally requires less attention than livestock farming. In a mixed farming system, crops may therefore be found farther from the farm centre than animals.

**arachnid** or *arachnoid,* type of arthropod of the class Arachnida, including spiders, scorpions, ticks, and mites. They differ from insects in possessing only two main body regions, the cephalothorax and the abdomen, and in having eight legs.

**Arafat, Yassir** born Muhammad Abed Ar'ouf Arafat (1929– ) Palestinian nationalist politician, cofounder of al-◊Fatah in 1957, president of the Palestinian Authority, and leader of the ◊Palestine Liberation Organization (PLO) from 1969. His support for Saddam Hussein after Iraq's invasion of Kuwait in1990 weakened his international standing, but he was subsequently influential in the Middle East peace talks and in 1993 reached a historic peace accord of mutual recognition with Israel, under which the Gaza Strip and Jericho were transferred to PLO control. He returned to the former occupied territories in 1994 as head of an embryonic Palestinian state, and in 1994 Arafat was awarded the Nobel Prize for Peace jointly with Rabin and Israeli foreign minister Shimon Peres. In 1995 an agreement was reached on further Israeli troop withdrawals from areas in the West Bank, and Arafat took the unprecedented step in October 1995 of inviting the terrorist organization Hamas to talks on Palestinian self-rule.

In November 1995 the Israeli prime minister, Yitzhak ◊Rabin, was assassinated by an Israeli extremist and the peace process appeared to be threatened. Rabin was suceeded by the moderate Shimon ◊Peres but he lost the 1996 general election and was replaced by the hard-line Likud leader Binjamin Netanyahu. Despite this, Arafat continued his efforts for a lasting peace. He was elected president, with almost 90% of the popular vote, of the self-governing Palestinian National Council in 1996. In October 1998, the 'Wye agreement' was signed, providing for a further 13% withdrawal of Israeli forces from the West Bank.

In May 1999 Labour candidate Ehud Barak was elected as Israel's prime minister, and Arafat announced that an independent Palestine state would be declared by the end of the year. Later that month Arafat met with King Abdullah of Jordan prior to the reopening of peace talks with Israel.

**Aragón** autonomous community and former kingdom of northeast Spain, including the provinces of Huesca, Teruel, and Zaragoza; area 47,700 sq km/18,412 sq mi; population (1991) 1,188,800. Products include cereals, rice, olive oil, almonds, figs, grapes, and olives; merino wool is a major export. The principal river of Aragón is the Ebro, which receives numerous tributaries both from the mountains of the south and from the Pyrenees in the north. Aragón was an independent kingdom from 1035 to 1479. The capital of modern Aragón is ◊Zaragoza.

**Aral Sea** Russian *Aralskoye More,* inland sea divided between Kazakhstan and Uzbekistan, the world's fourth-largest lake; former area 62,000 sq km/24,000 sq mi, but decreasing. Water from its tributaries, the Amu Darya and Syr Darya, has been diverted for irrigation and city use, and the sea is disappearing, with long-term consequences for the climate.

**Aramaic language** Semitic language of the Hamito-Semitic family of western Asia, the everyday language of Palestine 2,000 years ago, during the Roman occupation and the time of Jesus.

**Aran Islands** group of three rocky islands in the mouth of Galway Bay, which is about 32 km/20 mi wide. They lie 48 km/30 mi from Galway, on the west coast of the Republic of Ireland; the principal town is Kilronan on Inishmore. The islands form a natural breakwater, and comprise Inishmore (Irish *Inis Mór*), area 3,092 ha/7,637 acres, population (1991) 836; Inishmaan (Irish *Inis Meáin*), area 912 ha/2,253 acres, population (1991) 216; and Inisheer (Irish *Inid Oírr*), area 567 ha/1,400 acres, population (1991) 270. The chief industries are tourism, fishing, and agriculture. J M ◊Synge wrote about the customs and life of the islanders in his plays.

**Ararat, Mount** double-peaked mountain in Turkey near the Iranian border; Great Ararat, at 5,137 m/16,854 ft, is the highest mountain in Turkey. It was the reputed resting place of Noah's Ark after the Flood.

**araucaria** coniferous tree related to the firs, with flat, scalelike needles. Once widespread, it is now native only to the southern hemisphere. Some grow to gigantic size. Araucarias include the monkey-puzzle tree (*Araucaria araucana*), the Australian bunya bunya pine (*A. bidwillii*), and the Norfolk Island pine (*A. heterophylla*). (Genus *Araucaria,* family Araucariaceae.)

**Arawak** indigenous American people of the Caribbean and northeastern Amazon Basin. Arawaks lived mainly by shifting cultivation in tropical forests. They were driven out of many West Indian islands by another American Indian people, the Caribs, shortly before the arrival of the Spanish in the 16th century. Subsequently, their numbers on ◊Hispaniola declined from some 4 million in 1492 to a few thousand after their exploitation by the Spanish in their search for gold; the remaining few were eradicated by disease (smallpox was introduced 1518). Arawakan languages belong to the Andean-Equatorial group.

**arbitrageur** in finance, a person who buys securities (such as currency or commodities) in one country or market for immediate resale in another market, to take advantage of different prices.

**arbitration** submission of a dispute to a third, unbiased party for settlement. It may be personal litigation, a trade-union issue, or an international dispute.

**arc** in geometry, a section of a curved line or circle. A circle has three types of arc: a *semicircle,* which is exactly half of the circle; *minor arcs,* which are less than the semicircle; and *major arcs,* which are greater than the semicircle.

**arch** in masonry, a curved structure that supports the weight of material over an open space, as in a bridge or doorway. The first arches consisted of several wedge-shaped stones supported by their mutual pressure. The term is also applied to any curved structure that is an arch in form only, such as the Arc de Triomphe, Paris, 1806–36.

**Archaea** group of micro-organisms that are without a nucleus and have a single chromosome. All are strict anaerobes, that is, they are killed by oxygen. This is thought to be a primitive condition and to indicate that Archaea are related to the earliest life forms, which appeared about 4 billion years ago, when there was little oxygen in the Earth's atmosphere. They are found in undersea vents, hot springs, the Dead Sea, and salt pans, and have even adapted to refuse tips.

**Archaean** or *Archaeozoic,* widely used term for the earliest era of geological time; the first part of the Precambrian *Eon,* spanning the interval from the formation of Earth to about 2,500 million years ago.

**archaeology** (Greek *archaia* 'ancient things', *logos* 'study') study of prehistory and history, based on the examination of physical remains. Principal activities include preliminary field (or site) surveys, ◊excavation (where necessary), and the classification, ◊dating, and interpretation of finds.

**archaeopteryx** (Greek *archaios* 'ancient', *pterux* 'wing') extinct primitive bird, known from fossilized remains, about 160 million years old, found in limestone deposits in Bavaria, Germany. It is popularly known as 'the first bird', although some earlier bird ancestors are now known. It was about the size of a crow and had feathers and wings, with three clawlike digits at the end of each wing, but in many respects its skeleton is reptilian (teeth and a long, bony tail) and very like some small meat-eating dinosaurs of the time.

**archery** use of the bow and arrow, originally in hunting and warfare, now as a competitive sport. The world governing body is the Fédération Internationale de Tir à l'Arc (FITA) founded 1931. In competitions, results are based on double FITA rounds; that is, 72 arrows at each of four targets at 90, 70, 50, and 30 metres (70, 60, 50, and 30 for women). The best possible score is 2,880. Archery was reintroduced to the Olympic Games 1972.

**Archimedes** (*c.* 287–212 BC) Greek mathematician who made major discoveries in geometry, hydrostatics, and mechanics, and established the sciences of statics and hydrostatics. He formulated a law of fluid displacement (Archimedes' principle), and is credited with the invention of the Archimedes screw, a cylindrical device for raising water. His method of finding mathematical proof to substantiate experiment and observation became the method of modern science in the High Renaissance.

**Archimedes' principle** in physics, the principle that the weight of the liquid displaced by a floating body is equal to the weight of the body. The principle is often stated in the form: 'an object totally or partially submerged in a fluid displaces a volume of fluid that weighs the same as the apparent loss in weight of the object (which, in turn, equals the upwards force, or upthrust, experienced by that object).' It was discovered by the Greek mathematician Archimedes.

**Archimedes screw** one of the earliest kinds of pump, associated with the Greek mathematician Archimedes. It consists of an enormous spiral screw revolving inside a close-fitting cylinder. It is used, for example, to raise water for irrigation.

**archipelago** group of islands, or an area of sea containing a group of islands. The islands of an archipelago are usually volcanic in origin, and they sometimes represent the tops of peaks in areas around continental margins flooded by the sea.

**architecture** art of designing structures. The term covers the design of the visual appearance of structures; their internal arrangements of space; selection of external and internal building materials; design or selection of natural and artificial lighting systems, as well as mechanical, electrical, and plumbing systems; and design or selection of decorations and furnishings. Architectural style may emerge from evolution of techniques and styles particular to a culture in a given time period with or without identifiable individuals as architects, or may be attributed to specific individuals or groups of architects working together on a project.

**arc lamp** or *arc light,* electric light that uses the illumination of an electric arc maintained between two electrodes. The English chemist Humphry Davy demonstrated the electric arc in 1802 and electric arc lighting was first introduced by English electrical engineer W E Staite (1809–1854) in 1846. The lamp consists of two carbon electrodes, between which a very high voltage is maintained. Electric current arcs (jumps) between the two electrolytes, creating a brilliant light. Its main use in recent years has been in cinema projectors.

**arc minute, arc second** units for measuring small angles, used in geometry, surveying, map-making, and astronomy. An arc minute (symbol ′) is one-sixtieth of a degree, and an arc second (symbol ″) is one-sixtieth of an arc minute. Small distances in the sky, as between two close stars or the apparent width of a planet's disc, are expressed in minutes and seconds of arc.

**Arctic, the** that part of the northern hemisphere surrounding the North Pole; arbitrarily defined as the region lying north of the Arctic Circle (66° 32′N) or north of the tree line. There is no Arctic continent; the greater part of the region comprises the Arctic Ocean, which is the world's smallest ocean. Arctic climate, fauna, and flora extend over the islands and northern edges of continental land masses that surround the Arctic Ocean (Svalbard, Iceland, Greenland, Siberia, Scandinavia, Alaska, and Canada) *area* 36,000,000 sq km/14,000,000 sq mi *physical* pack-ice floating on the Arctic Ocean occupies almost the entire region between the North Pole and the coasts of North America and

Eurasia, covering an area that ranges in diameter from 3,000 km/1,900 mi to 4,000 km/2,500 mi. The pack-ice reaches a maximum extent in February when its outer limit (influenced by the cold Labrador Current and the warm Gulf Stream) varies from 50°N along the coast of Labrador to 75°N in the Barents Sea north of Scandinavia. In spring the pack-ice begins to break up into ice floes which are carried by the south-flowing Greenland Current to the Atlantic Ocean. Arctic ice is at its minimum area in August. The greatest concentration of icebergs in Arctic regions is found in Baffin Bay. They are derived from the glaciers of western Greenland, then carried along Baffin Bay and down into the North Atlantic where they melt off Labrador and Newfoundland.

**Arctic Circle** imaginary line that encircles the North Pole at latitude 66° 33′ north. Within this line there is at least one day in the summer during which the Sun never sets, and at least one day in the winter during which the Sun never rises.

**Arctic Ocean** ocean surrounding the North Pole; area 14,000,000 sq km/5,405,400 sq mi. Because of the Siberian and North American rivers flowing into it, it has comparatively low salinity and freezes readily.

**Arcturus** or *Alpha Boötis,* brightest star in the constellation Boötes and the fourth-brightest star in the night sky. Arcturus is a red giant about 28 times larger than the Sun and 70 times more luminous, 36 light years away from the Sun.

**Ardennes** hilly, wooded plateau in northeast France, southeast Belgium, and northern Luxembourg, cut through by the River Meuse. The area gives its name to the region of ◊Champagne-Ardenne and the *département* of the Ardennes in France. The highest hills are about 590 m/1,936 ft. Cattle and sheep are raised and the area is rich in timber and minerals. There was heavy fighting here in both world wars, notably in the Battle of the ◊Bulge (1944–1945, also known as the Ardennes offensive). In World War I it was the route of the main German advance in 1914.

**Arequipa** capital of Arequipa department in the western Andes of southern Peru; it stands at a height of 2,363 m/7,753 ft in a fertile valley at the base of the dormant volcano El Misti (5,822 m/19,100 ft); industries include textiles, soap, and leather goods; population (1993) 619,200. It is the second-largest city of Peru and the cultural focus of southern Peru. Arequipa was founded by Pizarro in 1540 on the site of an ancient Inca city, and has a cathedral, founded in 1621, and a university.

**Ares** in Greek mythology, the god of war, equivalent to the Roman ◊Mars. The son of Zeus and Hera, he was worshipped chiefly in Thrace.

**Argentina** Republic of
*national name* *República Argentina*
*area* 2,780,092 sq km/1,073,393 sq mi
*capital* Buenos Aires

*major towns/cities* Rosario, Córdoba, San Miguel de Tucumán, Mendoza, Santa Fé, La Plata
*major ports* La Plata and Bahía Blanca
*physical features* mountains in west, forest and savanna in north, pampas (treeless plains) in east-central area, Patagonian plateau in south; rivers Colorado, Salado, Paraná, Uruguay, Río de La Plata estuary; Andes mountains, with Aconcagua the highest peak in western hemisphere; Iguaçu Falls
*territories* claims Falkland Islands (*Islas Malvinas*), South Georgia, the South Sandwich Islands, and part of Antarctica
*head of state and government* Carlos Menem from 1989
*political system* democratic federal republic
*political parties* Radical Civic Union Party (UCR), moderate centrist; Justicialist Party (PJ), right-wing Perónist; Movement for Dignity and Independence (Modin), right-wing; Front for a Country in Solidarity (Frepaso), centre left
*currency* peso = 10,000 australs (which it replaced in 1992)
*GNP per capita (PPP)* (US$) 10,200 (1998)
*exports* meat and meat products, prepared animal fodder, cereals, petroleum and petroleum products, soybeans, vegetable oils and fats. Principal market: Brazil 30.4% (1997)
*population* 36,577,000 (1999 est)
*language* Spanish 95% (official); Italian 3%
*religion* Roman Catholic (state-supported)
*life expectancy* 70 (men); 77 (women) (1995–2000)
*Chronology*
*1516* Spanish navigator Juan Diaz de Solis discovered Río de La Plata.
*1536* Buenos Aires founded, but soon abandoned because of attacks by American Indians.
*1580* Buenos Aires re-established as part of Spanish province of Asunción.
*1617* Buenos Aires became a separate province within Spanish viceroyalty of Lima.
*1776* Spanish South American Empire reorganized: Atlantic regions became viceroyalty of La

Plata, with Buenos Aires as capital.

**1810** After French conquest of Spain, Buenos Aires junta took over government of viceroyalty.

**1816** Independence proclaimed as United Provinces of Río de La Plata, but Bolivia and Uruguay soon seceded; civil war followed between federalists and those who wanted a unitary state.

**1835–52** Dictatorship of Gen Juan Manuel Rosas.

**1853** Adoption of federal constitution based on US model; Buenos Aires refused to join confederation.

**1861** Buenos Aires incorporated into Argentine confederation by force.

**1865–70** Argentina took part in War of Triple Alliance against Paraguay.

**late 19th century** Large-scale European immigration and rapid economic development; Argentina became a major world supplier of meat and grain.

**1880** Buenos Aires became a special federal district and national capital.

**1880–1916** Government dominated by oligarchy of conservative landowners; each president effectively chose his own successor.

**1916** Following introduction of secret ballot, Radical Party of Hipólito Irigoyen won election victory, beginning a period of 14 years in government.

**1930** Military coup ushered in a series of conservative governments sustained by violence and fraud.

**1943** Group of pro-German army officers seized power; Col Juan Perón emerged as a leading figure.

**1946** Perón won free presidential election; he secured working-class support through welfare measures, trade unionism, and the popularity of his wife, Eva Perón (Evita).

**1949** New constitution abolished federalism and increased powers of president.

**1952** Death of Evita. Support for Perón began to decline.

**1955** Perón overthrown; constitution of 1853 restored.

**1966–70** Dictatorship of Gen Juan Carlos Ongania.

**1973** Perónist Party won free elections; Perón returned from exile in Spain to become president.

**1974** Perón died; succeeded by his third wife, Isabel Perón.

**1976** Coup resulted in rule by military junta headed by Lt-Gen Jorge Videla (until 1978; succeeded by Gen Roberto Viola 1978–81 and Gen Leopoldo Galtieri 1981–82).

**1976–83** Military regime conducted murderous campaign ('Dirty War') against left-wing elements.

**1982** Invasion of Falkland Islands by Argentina. Intervention and defeat by UK; Galtieri replaced by Gen Reynaldo Bignone.

**1983** Return to civilian rule under President Raúl Alfonsín; investigation launched into 'disappearance' of more than 8,000 people during 'Dirty War'.

**1985** Economic austerity programme failed to halt hyperinflation.

**1989** Perónist candidate Carlos Menem won presidential election. Annual inflation reached 12,000%.

**1990** Full diplomatic relations with the UK were restored.

**1995** President Menem was re-elected.

**1997** The PJ lost its assembly majority.

**argon** (Greek *argos* 'idle') colourless, odourless, nonmetallic, gaseous element, symbol Ar, atomic number 18, relative atomic mass 39.948. It is grouped with the ◊inert gases, since it was long believed not to react with other substances, but observations now indicate that it can be made to combine with boron fluoride to form compounds. It constitutes almost 1% of the Earth's atmosphere, and was discovered in 1894 by British chemists John Rayleigh (1842–1919) and William Ramsay (1852–1916) after all oxygen and nitrogen had been removed chemically from a sample of air. It is used in electric discharge tubes and argon lasers.

**Argonauts** in Greek mythology, the band of heroes who accompanied ◊Jason when he set sail in the *Argo* to find the ◊Golden Fleece.

**Argus** in Greek mythology, a giant with 100 eyes. When he was killed by Hermes, Hera transplanted his eyes into the tail of her favourite bird, the peacock.

**Argyll and Bute** unitary authority in western Scotland, created in 1996 from the district of the same name and part of Dumbarton district, which were both parts of Strathclyde region; it includes the islands of Gigha, Bute, Mull, Islay, Jura, Tiree, Coll, Colonsay, Iona, and Staffa

*area* 7,016 sq km/2,709 sq mi

*towns* Campbeltown, Dunoon, Helensburgh, Inveraray, Lochgilphead (administrative headquarters), Oban, Rothesay

*physical* rural area consisting of mainland and islands; the coast is heavily indented. Inland the area is mountainous; highest peak, Ben Cruachan (1,126 m/3,693 ft). Lochs Fyne and Long are the largest sea lochs; freshwater lochs include Loch Awe and Loch Lomond; Fingal's Cave (Staffa); Corryvrekan Whirlpool (Jura-Scarba); Ben Arthur (The Cobbler), 884 m/ 2,900 ft

*features* Bronze, Stone, and Iron Age remains

*industries* limited manufacture, seaweed processing, fish, timber harvesting

*agriculture* sheep, forestry

*population* (1996) 89,300.

**Århus** or *Aarhus,* second-largest city of Denmark, on the east coast overlooking the Kattegat; population (1995) 277,500. It is the capital of Århus county in Jylland (Jutland) and a shipping and commercial centre.

**aria** (Italian 'air') melodic solo song of reflective character, often with a contrasting middle section, expressing a moment of truth in the action of an opera or oratorio. Already to be found in Peri's *Euridice* (1600) and Monteverdi's *Orfeo* (1607), it reached its more elaborate form in the work of Alessandro Scarlatti and Handel, becoming a set piece for virtuoso opera singers. An example is Handel's 'Where'er you walk' from the secular oratorio

*Semele* (1744) to words by William Congreve. As an instrumental character piece, an aria is melodious and imitative of a vocal line.

**Ariadne** in Greek mythology, the daughter of Minos, King of Crete. When ◊Theseus came from Athens as one of the sacrificial victims offered to the ◊Minotaur, she fell in love with him and gave him a ball of thread, which enabled him to find his way out of the labyrinth. When Theseus abandoned her on the island of Náxos, she married ◊Dionysus.

**Aries** zodiacal constellation in the northern hemisphere between Pisces and Taurus, near Auriga, represented as the legendary ram whose golden fleece was sought by Jason and the Argonauts.

Its most distinctive feature is a curve of three stars of decreasing brightness. The brightest of these is Hamal or Alpha Arietis, 65 light years from Earth. In astrology Aries lies between 21 March and 19 April.

**Ariosto, Ludovico** (1474–1533) Italian poet. He wrote Latin poems and comedies on Classical lines. His major work is the poem *Orlando furioso* (1516, published 1532), an epic treatment of the ◊Roland story, the perfect poetic expression of the Italian Renaissance.

**Aristarchus of Samos** (*c.* 320–*c.* 250 BC) Greek astronomer. The first to argue that the Earth moves around the Sun, he was ridiculed for his beliefs. He was also the first astronomer to estimate (quite inaccurately) the sizes of the Sun and Moon and their distances from the Earth.

**Aristide, Jean-Bertrand** (1953–  ) President of Haiti 1990–91 and 1994–95. A left-wing Catholic priest opposed to the right-wing regime of the Duvalier family, he relinquished his priesthood to concentrate on the presidency. He campaigned for the National Front for Change and Democracy, representing a loose coalition of peasants, trade unionists, and clerics, and won 70% of the vote. He was deposed by the military in September 1991 and took refuge in the USA. In September 1994, under an agreement brokered by former US president Jimmy Carter, the military stepped down and allowed Aristide to return. Constitutionally barred from seeking a second term in December 1995, he was succeeded by his preferred candidate René Préval.

**Aristides** (*c.* 530–468 BC) Athenian politician. He was one of the ten Athenian generals at the Battle of ◊Marathon 490 BC and was elected chief archon, or magistrate. Later he came into conflict with the democratic leader Themistocles, and was exiled about 483 BC. He returned to fight against the Persians at Salamis 480 BC and in the following year commanded the Athenians at Plataea. As commander of the Athenian fleet he established the alliance of Ionian states known as the Delian League.

**aristocracy** (Greek *aristos* 'best', *kratos* 'power') social elite or system of political power associated with landed wealth, as in western Europe; with monetary wealth, as in Carthage and Venice; or with religious superiority, as were the Brahmans in India. Aristocracies are also usually associated with monarchy but have frequently been in conflict with the sovereign over their respective rights and privileges. In Europe, their economic base was undermined during the 19th century by inflation and falling agricultural prices, leading to their demise as a political force after 1914.

**Aristophanes** (*c.* 445–*c.* 380 BC) Greek comedy dramatist. Of his 11 extant plays (of a total of over 40), the early comedies are remarkable for the violent satire with which he ridiculed the democratic war leaders. He also satirized contemporary issues such as the new learning of Socrates in *The Clouds* 423 BC and the obsession with war, with the sex-strike of women in *Lysistrata* 411 BC. The chorus plays a prominent role, frequently giving the play its title, as in *The Wasps* 422 BC, *The Birds* 414 BC, and *The Frogs* 405 BC.

**Aristotle** (384–322 BC) Greek philosopher who advocated reason and moderation. He maintained that sense experience is our only source of knowledge, and that by reasoning we can discover the essences of things, that is, their distinguishing qualities. In his works on ethics and politics, he suggested that human happiness consists in living in conformity with nature. He derived his political theory from the recognition that mutual aid is natural to humankind, and refused to set up any one constitution as universally ideal. Of Aristotle's works, around 22 treatises survive, dealing with logic, metaphysics, physics, astronomy, meteorology, biology, psychology, ethics, politics, and literary criticism.

**arithmetic** branch of mathematics concerned with the study of numbers and their properties. The fundamental operations of arithmetic are addition, subtraction, multiplication, and division. Raising to powers (for example, squaring or cubing a number), the extraction of roots (for example, square roots), percentages, fractions, and ratios are developed from these operations.

**arithmetic mean** the average of a set of $n$ numbers, obtained by adding the numbers and dividing by $n$. For example, the arithmetic mean of the set of 5 numbers 1, 3, 6, 8, and 12 is $(1 + 3 + 6 + 8 + 12)/5 = 30/5 = 6$.

**arithmetic progression** or *arithmetic sequence,* sequence of numbers or terms that have a common difference between any one term and the next in the sequence. For example, 2, 7, 12, 17, 22, 27, ... is an arithmetic sequence with a common difference of 5.

**Arizona** state in southwestern USA. It is nicknamed Grand Canyon State. Arizona was admitted to the Union in 1912 as the 48th US state. The state is renowned for its natural wonders, including Monument Valley and the Grand Canyon, and is strongly associated with such indigenous peoples as the Navajo and Hopi. It is bordered to the east by New Mexico, to the south by the Mexican state of Sonora, to the west by the Mexican state of Baja California and the US states of California and Nevada, and to the north by Utah and, at the 'Four Corners' to the northeast, Colorado

*population* (1996 est) 4,428,100; including

5.6% American Indians (Navajo, Hopi, Apache), who by treaty own 25% of the state
**area** 294,100 sq km/113,500 sq mi
**capital** Phoenix
**towns and cities** Tucson, Scottsdale, Tempe, Mesa, Glendale, Flagstaff
**industries and products** cotton under irrigation, livestock ranching, copper (more than half of US annual output), silver, uranium mining, molybdenum, electronics, aircraft.

**Arjan** Indian religious leader, fifth guru (teacher) of Sikhism 1581–1606. He built the Golden Temple in ◊Amritsar and compiled the *Adi Granth*, the first volume of Sikh scriptures. He died in Muslim custody.

**Arkansas** state in southern central USA. It is nicknamed Land of Opportunity. Arkansas was admitted to the Union in 1836 as the 25th US state. Historically it was a cotton plantation state, dependent on slavery. It was the site of civil-rights struggles in the 1950s and 1960s and became closely associated with the political intrigues surrounding Bill Clinton during his presidential tenure in the 1990s. Arkansas is bordered to the south by Louisiana, to the southwest by Texas, to the west by Oklahoma, to the north by Missouri, and to the east by Tennessee and Mississippi; the Red, St Francis, and Mississippi rivers form part of its natural borders
**population** (1996 est) 2,510,000
**area** 137,800 sq km/53,191 sq mi
**capital** Little Rock
**towns and cities** Fort Smith, Pine Bluff, Fayetteville, North Little Rock
**industries and products** cotton, soybeans, rice, oil, natural gas, timber, processed foods, electronics, financial sector, military bases.

**Arkwright, Richard** (1732–1792) English inventor and manufacturing pioneer who in 1768 developed a machine for spinning cotton (he called it a 'water frame'). In 1771 he set up a water-powered spinning factory and in 1790 he installed steam power in a Nottingham factory. Knighted 1786.

**Arles** town in Bouches-du-Rhône *département*, southwest France, on the Arles canal and the left bank of the Rhône, at the head of the Camargue delta; population (1990) 52,600. Its main economic activities are tourism and agriculture, and it is in an important fruit- and vine-growing district. Roman relics include an aqueduct, baths, and a 21,000-spectator amphitheatre now used for bullfighting and plays. The Romanesque-Provençal church of St-Trophime, formerly an archiepiscopal cathedral, has fine cloisters and a notable 12th-century portal. The painter Vincent ◊van Gogh lived here 1888–89, during which time he painted some of his major works.

**Armada** fleet sent by Philip II of Spain against England in 1588. See ◊Spanish Armada.

**armadillo** mammal of the family Dasypodidae, with an armour of bony plates along its back or, in some species, almost covering the entire body. Around 20 species live between Texas and Patagonia and range in size from the fairy armadillo, or pichiciego, *Chlamyphorus*

*truncatus*, at 13 cm/5 in, to the giant armadillo *Priodontes giganteus*, 1.5 m/4.5 ft long. Armadillos feed on insects, snakes, fruit, and carrion. Some can roll into an armoured ball if attacked; others defend themselves with their claws or rely on rapid burrowing for protection.

**Armageddon** in the New Testament (Revelation 16:16), the site of the final battle between the nations that will end the world; it has been identified with Megiddo in Israel.

**Armagh** (Irish *Ard Mhacha* 'the height of Mhacha' (a legendary queen) county of Northern Ireland
**area** 1,250 sq km/483 sq mi
**towns and cities** Armagh (county town), Lurgan and Portadown (merged to form Craigavon), Keady
**physical** smallest county of Northern Ireland; flat in the north, with many bogs and mounds formed from glacial deposits; low hills in the south, the highest of which is Slieve Gullion (577 m/1,893 ft); principal rivers are the Bann, the Blackwater and its tributary, the Callan
**agriculture** good farmland (apart from the marshy areas by Lough Neagh) with apple orchards; potatoes; flax; emphasis on livestock rearing in the south; fruit-growing and market gardening in the north
**industries** linen manufacture (Portadown and Lurgan were the principal centres of the linen industry); milling; light engineering; concrete; potato crisps
**population** (1981) 119,000

**armature** in a motor or generator, the wire-wound coil that carries the current and rotates in a magnetic field. (In alternating-current machines, the armature is sometimes stationary.) The pole piece of a permanent magnet or electromagnet and the moving, iron part of a ◊solenoid, especially if the latter acts as a switch, may also be referred to as armatures.

**Armenia** Republic of
**national name** *Haikakan Hanrapetoutioun*

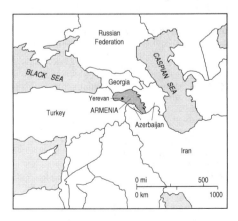

**area** 29,800 sq km/11,505 sq mi
**capital** Yerevan
**major towns/cities** Gyumri (formerly Leninakan), Vanadzor (formerly Kirovakan)

*physical features* mainly mountainous (including Mount Ararat), wooded
*head of state* Robert Kocharyan from 1998
*head of government* Vazgen Sarkisyan from 1999
*political system* authoritarian nationalist
*political parties* Armenian Pan-National Movement (APM), nationalist, left of centre; Armenian Revolutionary Federation (ARF), centrist (banned in 1994); Communist Party of Armenia (banned 1991–92); National Unity, opposition coalition
*currency* dram (replaced Russian rouble in 1993)
*GNP per capita (PPP)* (US$) 2,180 (1998 est)
*exports* machinery and metalworking products, chemical and petroleum products. Principal market: CIS 36.3% (1998)
*population* 3,525,000 (1999 est)
*language* Armenian
*religion* Armenian Christian
*life expectancy* 67 (men); 74 (women) (1995–2000)

*Chronology*
*6th century BC* Armenian peoples moved into the area, which was then part of the Persian Empire.
*c. 94–56 BC* Under King Tigranes II 'the Great', Armenia reached height of its power, expanding southwards to become the strongest state in the eastern Roman empire, controlling an area from the Caucasus to the Mediterranean.
*c. AD 300* Christianity became the state religion when the local ruler was converted by St Gregory the Illuminator.
*c. AD 390* Divided between Byzantine Armenia, which became part of Byzantine Empire, and Persarmenia, under Persian control.
*886–1045* Independent under the Bagratid monarchy.
*13th century* After being overrun by the Mongols, a substantially independent Little Armenia survived until 1375.
*early 16th century* Conquered by Muslim Ottoman Turks.
*1813–28* Russia took control of eastern Armenia.
*late 19th century* Revival in Armenian culture and national spirit, provoking Ottoman backlash in western Armenia and international concern at Armenian maltreatment: the 'Armenian Question'.
*1894–96* Massacre of Armenians by Turkish soldiers to suppress unrest.
*1915* Suspected of pro-Russian sympathies, two-thirds of Armenia's population of 2 million were deported to Syria and Palestine. Around 600,000–1 million died en route: the survivors contributed towards an Armenian diaspora in Europe and North America.
*1916* Conquered by tsarist Russia and became part of a brief 'Transcaucasian Alliance' with Georgia and Azerbaijan.
*1918* Became an independent republic.
*1920* Occupied by Red Army of Soviet Union (USSR), but western Armenia remained part of Turkey and northwest Iran.
*1936* Became constituent republic of USSR; rapid industrial development.

*late 1980s* Armenian 'national reawakening', encouraged by *glasnost* (openness) initiative of Soviet leader Mikhail Gorbachev.
*1988* Earthquake – around 20,000 people died.
*1989* Strife-torn Nagorno-Karabakh placed under direct rule from Moscow; civil war erupted with Azerbaijan over Nagorno-Karabakh and Nakhichevan, an Azerbaijani-peopled enclave in Armenia.
*1990* Nationalists secured control of the Armenian parliament in elections; the former dissident Ter-Petrossian was indirectly elected president; independence was declared, but ignored by Moscow and the international community.
*1991* After the collapse of the USSR, Armenia joined the new Commonwealth of Independent States. Ter-Petrossian was directly elected president. Nagorno-Karabakh declared its independence.
*1992* Armenia was recognized as an independent state by the USA and admitted into the United Nations (UN).
*1993* Armenian forces gained control of more than a fifth of Azerbaijan, including much of Nagorno-Karabakh.
*1994* A Nagorno-Karabakh ceasefire ended the conflict.
*1995* A privatization and price liberalization programme was launched. The ruling APM was re-elected.
*1996* Ter-Petrossian was re-elected president. Hrand Bagratian was replaced as prime minister by Armen Sarkissian.
*1997* Sarkissian resigned for health reasons and was replaced by Robert Kocharyan. There was border fighting with Azerbaijan. Arkady Gukasyan was elected president of Nagorno-Karabakh.
*1998* Ter-Petrossian resigned following opposition within his party to his moderate approach to resolving the dispute with Azerbaijan over Nagorno-Karabakh. Prime minister Robert Kocharyan, a hardliner, was elected president. The formerly banned ARF was brought into the cabinet. A commission was set up to recommend reductions in the president's powers. A new election law was approved. The deputy defence minister, Vagram Khorkoruni, was shot dead in Yerevan.

**Armenian** member of the largest ethnic group inhabiting Armenia. There are Armenian minorities in Azerbaijan (see ◊Nagorno-Karabakh), as well as in Syria, Lebanon, Turkey, and Iran. Christianity was introduced to the ancient Armenian kingdom in the 3rd century. There are 4–5 million speakers of Armenian, which belongs to the Indo-European family of languages.

**Armenian massacres** series of massacres of Armenians by Turkish soldiers between 1895 and 1915. In 1894–96 demands for better treatment led to massacres of Armenians in eastern Asia Minor. Over 50,000 Armenians were killed by Kurdish irregulars and Ottoman troops. The killing was stopped by the major European powers, but in 1915 Ottoman suspicions of Armenian loyalty led to further massacres and deportations. The Turks deported 1.25 million

Armenians to Syria and Palestine; over 600,000 were either killed or died of starvation during the journey.

**armistice** cessation of hostilities while awaiting a peace settlement. *The Armistice* refers specifically to the end of World War I between Germany and the Allies on 11 November 1918. On 22 June 1940, following the German invasion of France, French representatives signed an armistice with Germany in the same railway carriage at Compiègne as in 1918. No armistice was signed with either Germany or Japan in 1945; both nations surrendered and there was no provision for the suspension of fighting. The Korean armistice, signed at Panmunjom on 27 July 1953, terminated the Korean War 1950–53.

**Armistice Day** anniversary of the armistice signed 11 November 1918, ending World War I.

**armour** body protection worn in battle. Body armour is depicted in Greek and Roman art. Chain mail was developed in the Middle Ages but the craft of the armourer in Europe reached its height in design in the 15th century, when knights were completely encased in plate armour that still allowed freedom of movement. Medieval Japanese armour was articulated, made of iron, gilded metal, leather, and silk. Contemporary bulletproof vests and riot gear are forms of armour. The term is used in a modern context to refer to a mechanized armoured vehicle, such as a tank.

**arms control** attempts to limit the arms race between the superpowers by reaching agreements to restrict the production of certain weapons; see ¢disarmament.

**arms trade** sale of weapons from a manufacturing country to another nation. Nearly 56% of the world's arms exports end up in Third World countries. Iraq, for instance, was armed in the years leading up to the 1991 Gulf War mainly by the USSR but also by France, Brazil, and South Africa.

**Armstrong, Louis** or *Satchmo* (1901–1971) US jazz cornet and trumpet player and singer. His Chicago recordings in the 1920s with the Hot Five and Hot Seven brought him recognition for his warm and pure trumpet tone, his skill at improvisation, and his quirky, gravelly voice. From the 1930s he also appeared in films.

**Armstrong, Neil Alden** (1930–  ) US astronaut. In 1969, he became the first person to set foot on the Moon, and said, 'That's one small step for a man, one giant leap for mankind.' The Moon landing was part of the ¢Apollo project.

**Arnhem, Battle of** in World War II, airborne operation by the Allies, 17–26 September 1944, to secure a bridgehead over the Rhine, thereby opening the way for a thrust towards the Ruhr and a possible early end to the war. It was only partially successful, with 7,600 casualties.

**Arnhem Land** plateau of the central peninsula in northeast Northern Territory, Australia, west of the Gulf of Carpentaria; approximate area 80,776 sq km/31,188 sq mi. Arnhem Land was named after a Dutch ship which dropped anchor here 1618. The chief town is Nhulunbuy

(population (1996) 3,695). It is the largest of the Aboriginal reserves, and was declared Aboriginal land in 1976. Many of the inhabitants live in small settlements and maintain a traditional way of life. Bauxite and uranium mining and the supporting industries provide the main economic base of the area.

**Arnold, Matthew** (1822–1888) English poet and critic. His poem 'Dover Beach' (1867) was widely regarded as one of the most eloquent expressions of the spiritual anxieties of Victorian England. In his highly influential critical essays collected in *Culture and Anarchy* (1869), he attacked the smugness and philistinism of the Victorian middle classes, and argued for a new culture based on the pursuit of artistic and intellectual values. He was the son of Thomas Arnold, headmaster of Rugby school.

**aromatherapy** in alternative medicine, use of oils and essences derived from plants, flowers, and wood resins. Bactericidal properties and beneficial effects upon physiological functions are attributed to the oils, which are inhaled and massaged into the skin.

**aromatic compound** organic chemical compound in which some of the bonding electrons are delocalized (shared among several atoms within the molecule and not localized in the vicinity of the atoms involved in bonding). The commonest aromatic compounds have ring structures, the atoms comprising the ring being either all carbon or containing one or more different atoms (usually nitrogen, sulphur, or oxygen). Typical examples are benzene ($C_6H_6$) and pyridine ($C_5H_5N$).

**Arp, Hans** or *Jean* (1887–1966) French abstract painter, sculptor, and poet. He was one of the founders of the ¢Dada movement 1916, and was later associated with the Surrealists. Using chance and automatism, Arp developed an abstract sculpture whose sensuous shapes suggest organic forms. In many of his works, in particular his early collages, he collaborated with his wife *Sophie Taeuber-Arp* (1889–1943).

**arrest** apprehension and detention of a person suspected of a crime. In Britain, an arrest may be made on a magistrate's warrant, but a police constable is empowered to arrest without warrant in all cases where he or she has reasonable ground for thinking a serious offence has been committed.

**Arrhenius, Svante August** (1859–1927) Swedish scientist, the founder of physical chemistry. For his study of electrolysis, he received the Nobel Prize for Chemistry 1903. In 1905 he predicted global warming as a result of carbon dioxide emission from burning fossil fuels.

**arrhythmia** disturbance of the normal rhythm of the heart. There are various kinds of arrhythmia, some benign, some indicative of heart disease. In extreme cases, the heart may beat so fast as to be potentially lethal and surgery may be used to correct the condition.

**arrowroot** starchy substance used as a thickener in cooking, produced from the clumpy roots of various tropical plants. The true arrowroot (*Maranta arundinacea*) was used by native

South Americans as an antidote against the effects of poisoned arrows.

**arsenic** brittle, greyish-white, semimetallic element (a metalloid), symbol As, atomic number 33, relative atomic mass 74.92. It occurs in many ores and occasionally in its elemental state, and is widely distributed, being present in minute quantities in the soil, the sea, and the human body. In larger quantities, it is poisonous. The chief source of arsenic compounds is as a by-product from metallurgical processes. It is used in making semiconductors, alloys, and solders.

**arson** malicious and wilful setting fire to property.

**art** in the broadest sense, all the processes and products of human skill, imagination, and invention; the opposite of nature. In contemporary usage, definitions of art usually reflect aesthetic criteria, and the term may encompass literature, music, drama, painting, and sculpture. Popularly, the term is most commonly used to refer to the visual arts. In Western culture, aesthetic criteria introduced by the ancient Greeks still influence our perceptions and judgements of art.

**Art Deco** style in the decorative arts which influenced design and architecture. It emerged in Europe in the 1920s and continued through the 1930s, becoming particularly popular in the USA and France. A self-consciously modern style, originally called 'Jazz Modern', it is characterized by angular, geometrical patterns and bright colours, and by the use of materials such as enamel, chrome, glass, and plastic. The graphic artist Erté was a fashionable exponent.

**Artemis** in Greek mythology, the goddess of chastity, all young creatures, the Moon, and the hunt (Roman *Diana*). She was the daughter of Zeus and the Titaness Leto, and the twin sister of ◊Apollo. She was worshipped at cult centres throughout the Greek world; one of the largest was at Ephesus where her great temple, reconstructed several times in antiquity, was one of the ◊Seven Wonders of the World.

**arteriosclerosis** hardening of the arteries, with thickening and loss of elasticity. It is associated with smoking, ageing, and a diet high in saturated fats. The term is used loosely as a synonym for ◊atherosclerosis.

**artery** vessel that carries blood from the heart to the rest of the body. It is built to withstand considerable pressure, having thick walls which contain smooth muscle fibres. During contraction of the heart muscle, arteries expand in diameter to allow for the sudden increase in pressure that occurs; the resulting ◊pulse or pressure wave can be felt at the wrist. Not all arteries carry oxygenated (oxygen-rich) blood; the pulmonary arteries convey deoxygenated (oxygen-poor) blood from the heart to the lungs.

**artesian well** well that is supplied with water rising naturally from an underground water-saturated rock layer (◊aquifer). The water rises from the aquifer under its own pressure. Such a well may be drilled into an aquifer that is confined by impermeable rocks both above and below. If the water table (the top of the region of water saturation) in that aquifer is above the level of the well head, hydrostatic pressure will force the water to the surface.

**art for art's sake** artistic theory.

**arthritis** inflammation of the joints, with pain, swelling, and restricted motion. Many conditions may cause arthritis, including gout, infection, and trauma to the joint. There are three main forms of arthritis: rheumatoid arthritis; osteoarthritis; and septic arthritis.

**arthropod** member of the phylum Arthropoda; an invertebrate animal with jointed legs and a segmented body with a horny or chitinous casing (exoskeleton), which is shed periodically and replaced as the animal grows. Included are arachnids such as spiders and mites, crustaceans such as lobsters and woodlice, millipedes, centipedes, and insects.

**Arthur** (lived 6th century) semi-legendary Romano-British warleader who led British resistance against the Saxons, Picts, and Scots in the first half of the 6th century. He was probably a warlord rather than a king. He operated throughout Britain, commanding a small force of mobile warriors, reminiscent of the late Roman *comitatenses* (line units). Arthur is credited with a great victory over the Saxons at Mount Badon, possibly in Dorset.

**artichoke** either of two plants belonging to the sunflower family, parts of which are eaten as vegetables. The *common* or *globe artichoke* (*Cynara scolymus*) is a form of thistle native to the Mediterranean. It is tall, with purplish-blue flowers; the leaflike structures (bracts) around the unopened flower are eaten. The *Jerusalem artichoke* (*Helianthus tuberosus*), which has edible tubers, is a native of North America (its common name is a corruption of the Italian for sunflower, *girasole*). (Family Compositae.)

**artificial insemination** (AI), introduction by instrument of semen from a sperm bank or donor into the female reproductive tract to bring about fertilization. Originally used by animal breeders to improve stock with sperm from high-quality males, in the 20th century it has been developed for use in humans, to help the infertile. See ◊in vitro fertilization.

**artificial intelligence** (AI), branch of science concerned with creating computer programs that can perform actions comparable with those of an intelligent human. Current AI research covers such areas as planning (for robot behaviour), language understanding, pattern recognition, and knowledge representation.

**artificial respiration** emergency procedure to restart breathing once it has stopped; in cases of electric shock or apparent drowning, for example, the first choice is the expired-air method, the *kiss of life* by mouth-to-mouth breathing until natural breathing is restored.

**artificial selection** in biology, selective breeding of individuals that exhibit the particular characteristics that a plant or animal breeder wishes to develop. In plants, desirable features might include resistance to disease, high yield (in crop plants), or attractive appearance. In animal breeding, selection has led to the development of particular breeds of cattle for improved meat production (such as the Aberdeen Angus) or milk production (such as Jerseys).

**artillery** collective term for military ◊firearms too heavy to be carried. Artillery can be mounted on tracks, wheels, ships, or aeroplanes and includes cannons and rocket launchers.

**Art Nouveau** in the visual arts, interior design, and architecture, a decorative style flourishing from 1890 to 1910 and characterized by organic, sinuous patterns and ornamentations based on plant forms. In England, it appears in the illustrations of Aubrey Beardsley; in Scotland, in the interior and exterior designs of Charles Rennie Mackintosh; in France, in the glass of René Lalique and the posters of Alphonse Mucha; and in the USA, in the lamps and metalwork of Louis Comfort Tiffany. It was known as *Jugendstil* in Germany and *Stile Liberty* in Italy, after a fashionable London department store.

**Arts and Crafts movement** English social and aesthetic movement of the late 19th century which stressed the importance of manual skills and the dignity of labour. It expressed a rejection of Victorian industrialization and mass production, and a nostalgic desire to return to a medieval way of life. The movement influenced Art Nouveau and, less directly, the Bauhaus school of design.

**Aruba** island in the Caribbean, the westernmost of the Lesser Antilles, 30 km/19 mi north of the Paraguana Peninsula in Venezuela; an overseas territory of the Netherlands
*area* 193 sq km/75 sq mi
*chief town* Oranjestad
*population* (1996) 66,687 (half of Indian descent)
*language* Dutch (official), Papiamento (a Creole language)
*economy* the economy is based largely on tourism (attracted by duty-free shopping and legalized gambling) and oil refining. A chemical industry has also been developed, including an ammonia plant, nitric acid and urea production, and fertilizer manufacture. There is cigarette and beverage production, in addition to some rum distilling.
*history* First inhabited by Arawak peoples, a number of colonial powers gained hold of Aruba. In 1494, the Spanish arrived on the island, claiming it as Spanish territory in 1499. The Dutch gained control in 1636 and the British occupied the island 1805–16 during the Napoleonic Wars. Part of the Dutch West Indies from 1828, and part of the Netherlands Antilles from 1845, Aruba obtained separate status from the other Netherlands Antilles in 1986 and has full internal autonomy under a political arrangement called 'status aparte'. It was due to become fully independent in 1996, but a 1990 agreement deleted references to eventual independence.

**arum** any of a group of mainly European plants with narrow leaves and a single, usually white, special leaf (spathe) surrounding the spike of tiny flowers. The ornamental arum called the trumpet lily (*Zantedeschia aethiopica*) is a native of South Africa. (Genus *Arum,* family Araceae.)

**Arunachal Pradesh** state of India, in the Himalayas on the borders of Tibet and Myanmar
*area* 83,700 sq km/32,316 sq mi
*capital* Itanagar
*towns* Bomdila, Ziro
*physical* stretches from the foothills of the Himalayas to their peaks; largely forested, ranging from Alpine to sub-tropical conditions: Parasuram Kund, a lake visited by pilgrims; Brahmaputra (or Siang) River flows north–south in a deeply cut valley
*features* Tawang Monastery; Namdapha National Park
*industries* timber, coal mining
*agriculture* rice, coffee, spices, fruit, rubber
*population* (1994 est) 965,000; over 80 ethnic groups
*language* 50 different dialects
*history* formerly part of the state of Assam, it became a state of India in 1987.

**Aryan languages** 19th-century name for the ◊Indo-European languages; the languages of the Aryan peoples of India. The name Aryan is no longer used by language scholars because of its association with the Nazi concept of white supremacy.

**asbestos** any of several related minerals of fibrous structure that offer great heat resistance because of their nonflammability and poor conductivity. Commercial asbestos is generally either made from serpentine ('white' asbestos) or from sodium iron silicate ('blue' asbestos). The fibres are woven together or bound by an inert material. Over time the fibres can work loose and, because they are small enough to float freely in the air or be inhaled, asbestos usage is now strictly controlled; exposure to its dust can cause cancer.

**Ascension** British island of volcanic origin in the South Atlantic, a dependency of ◊St Helena since 1922; area 88 sq km/34 sq mi; population (1993) 1,117 (excluding military personnel). The chief settlement is Georgetown.

**ASCII** acronym for *American standard code for information interchange,* in computing, coding system in which numbers are assigned to letters, digits, and punctuation symbols. Although computers work in code based on the ◊binary number system, ASCII numbers are usually quoted as decimal or ◊hexadecimal numbers. For example, the decimal number 45 (binary 0101101) represents a hyphen, and 65 (binary 1000001) a capital A. The first 32 codes are used for control functions, such as carriage return and backspace.

**ascorbic acid** $C_6H_8O_6$ or *vitamin C,* a relatively simple organic acid found in citrus fruits and vegetables. It is soluble in water and destroyed by prolonged boiling, so soaking or overcooking of vegetables reduces their vitamin C content. Lack of ascorbic acid results in scurvy.

**ASEAN** acronym for ◊*Association of South East Asian Nations.*

**asepsis** practice of ensuring that bacteria are excluded from open sites during surgery, wound dressing, blood sampling, and other medical procedures. Aseptic technique is a first line of defence against infection.

**asexual reproduction** in biology, reproduction that does not involve the manufacture and fusion of sex cells, nor the necessity for two parents. The process carries a clear advantage in that there is no need to search for a mate nor to develop complex pollinating mechanisms; every asexual organism can reproduce on its own. Asexual reproduction can therefore lead to a rapid population build-up.

**ash** any tree of a worldwide group belonging to the olive family, with winged fruits. The ◊*mountain ash* or *rowan,* which resembles the ash, belongs to the family Rosaceae. (Genus *Fraxinus,* family Oleaceae.)

**Ashanti** or *Asante,* region of Ghana, western Africa; area 25,100 sq km/9,700 sq mi; population (1984) 2,090,200. Kumasi is the capital. Most Ashanti are cultivators and the main crop is cocoa, but the region is also noted for its metalwork and textiles. For more than 200 years Ashanti was an independent kingdom.

**Ashcroft, Peggy** (1907–1991) English actress. Her Shakespearean roles included Desdemona in *Othello* (with Paul Robeson) and Juliet in *Romeo and Juliet* (1935) (with Laurence Olivier and John Gielgud), and she appeared in the British TV play *Caught on a Train* (1980) (BAFTA award), the series *The Jewel in the Crown* (1984), and the film *A Passage to India* (1984).

**Ashdown, Paddy (Jeremy John Durham)** (1941– ) British politician, leader of the merged Social and Liberal Democrats 1988–99. His party significantly increased its seat holding in the 1997 general election, winning more seats than it had had since the 1920s, and cooperated in areas such as constitutional reform with the new Labour government of Tony Blair. From 1997 Ashdown sat with Blair on a joint cabinet committee, whose scope was extended from constitutional issues in November 1998 to cover areas such as health, education, and Europe. Ashdown announced in late January 1999 that he would stand down as Liberal Democrat leader in the summer of that year after holding the position for 11 years.

**Ashe, Arthur (Robert, Jr)** (1943–1993) US tennis player and coach. He won the US national men's singles title at Forest Hills and the first US Open 1968. Known for his exceptionally strong serve, Ashe turned professional 1969. He won the Australian men's title 1970 and Wimbledon 1975. Cardiac problems ended his playing career 1979, but he continued his involvement with the sport as captain of the US Davis Cup team. In 1992 he launched a fund-raising campaign to combat AIDS.

**Ashes, the** cricket trophy theoretically held by the winning team in the England–Australia test series.

**Ashgabat** formerly (1919–27) *Poltoratsk;* (1927–92) *Ashkhabad,* capital of Turkmenistan; population (1996) 450,000. Industries include the manufacture of glass, carpets (handwoven 'Bukhara' carpets and rugs are made here), and cotton. The city is in a spectacular natural setting, between the Kara-Kum Desert and the Kopet-Dag mountain range.

**Ashkenazi** plural *Ashkenazim,* any Jew of German or Eastern European descent, as opposed to a Sephardi, of Spanish, Portuguese, or North African descent.

**Ashkenazy, Vladimir** (1937– ) Russian-born pianist and conductor. He was music director of the Royal Philharmonic, London, from 1987 and of the Berlin Radio Symphony Orchestra from 1989. He excels in Rachmaninov, Prokofiev, and Liszt.

**Ashkhabad** former name (to 1992) of ◊Ashgabat.

**Ashley, Laura** born Mountney (1925–1985) Welsh designer. She established and gave her name to a Neo-Victorian country style in clothes and furnishings manufactured by her company from 1953. She founded a highly successful international chain of shops.

**Ashton, Frederick William Mallandaine** (1904–1988) English choreographer and dancer. He was director of the Royal Ballet, London 1963–70. He studied with Marie Rambert before joining the Sadler's Wells (now Royal) Ballet in 1935 as chief choreographer. His choreography is marked by a soft, pliant, classical lyricism. His many works and long association with Margot Fonteyn, for whom he created her most famous roles, contributed to the world-wide reputation of British ballet and to the popularity of ballet in the mid-20th century. He was knighted in 1962.

**Ash Wednesday** first day of Lent, the period in the Christian calendar leading up to Easter; in the Roman Catholic Church the foreheads of the congregation are marked with a cross in ash, as a sign of penitence.

**Asia** largest of the continents, occupying one-third of the total land surface of the world. The origin of the name is unknown, though it seems probable that it was at first used with a restricted local application, gradually extended to the whole continent.
*area* 44,000,000 sq km/17,000,000 sq mi
*largest cities* (population over 5 million) Tokyo, Shanghai, Osaka, Beijing, Seoul, Calcutta, Bombay, Jakarta, Bangkok, Tehran, Hong Kong, Delhi, Tianjin, Karachi
*features* Mount Everest, at 8,872 m/29,118 ft is the world's highest mountain; the Dead Sea at –394 m/–1,293 ft is the world's lowest point below sea level; rivers (over 3,200 km/2,000 mi) include Chang Jiang (Yangtze), Huang He (Yellow River), Ob-Irtysh, Amur, Lena,

Mekong, Yenisey; lakes (over 18,000 sq km/ 7,000 sq mi) include the Caspian Sea (the largest lake in the world), the Aral Sea, Lake Baikal (largest freshwater lake in Eurasia), Balkhash; deserts include the Gobi, Takla Makan, Syrian Desert, Arabian Desert, Negev

*physical* lying in the eastern hemisphere, Asia extends from the Arctic Circle to just over 10° south of the Equator. The Asian mainland, which forms the greater part of the Eurasian continent, lies entirely in the northern hemisphere and stretches from Cape Chelyubinsk at its northern extremity to Cape Piai at the southern tip of the Malay Peninsula. From Dezhneva Cape in the east, the mainland extends west over more than 165° longitude to Cape Baba in Turkey.

**Asia Minor** historical name for ◊Anatolia, the Asian part of Turkey.

**AS level** General Certificate of Education, or *Advanced Supplementary level;* examinations introduced in the UK in 1988 as the equivalent to 'half an ◊A level' as a means of broadening the sixth-form (age 16–18) curriculum and including more students in the examination system.

**Asmara** or *Asmera,* capital of Eritrea, 64 km/ 40 mi southwest of Massawa on the Red Sea and 2,300 m/7,546 ft above sea level; population (1991) 367,300. Products include beer, clothes, and textiles. The University of Asmara is here, together with a naval school, a cathedral and many modern buildings. The population is half Christian and half Muslim.

**Asoka** (lived *c.* 272–228 BC) Mauryan emperor of India *c.* 268–232 BC, the greatest of the Mauryan rulers. He inherited an empire covering most of north and south-central India which, at its height, had a population of at least 30 million, with its capital at Pataliputra. A devout Buddhist, he renounced militarism and concentrated on establishing an efficient administration with a large standing army and a secret police.

**asp** any of several venomous snakes, including *Vipera aspis* of southern Europe, allied to the adder, and the Egyptian cobra *Naja haje,* reputed to have been used by the Egyptian queen Cleopatra for her suicide.

**asparagus** any of a group of plants with small scalelike leaves and many fine, feathery branches. Native to Europe and Asia, *Asparagus officinalis* is cultivated and the tender young shoots (spears) are greatly prized as a vegetable. (Genus *Asparagus,* family Liliaceae.)

**aspartame** noncarbohydrate sweetener used in foods under the tradename Nutrasweet. It is about 200 times as sweet as sugar and, unlike saccharine, has no aftertaste.

**aspen** any of several species of ◊poplar tree. The European quaking aspen (*Populus tremula*) has flattened leafstalks that cause the leaves to flutter in the slightest breeze. The soft, light-coloured wood is used for matches and paper pulp. (Genus *Populus.*)

**asphalt** mineral mixture containing semisolid brown or black ◊bitumen, used in the construction industry. Asphalt is mixed with rock chips to form paving material, and the purer varieties are used for insulating material and for waterproofing masonry. It can be produced artificially by the distillation of ◊petroleum.

**asphodel** either of two related Old World plants of the lily family. The white asphodel or king's spear (*Asphodelus albus*) is found in Italy and Greece, sometimes covering large areas, and providing grazing for sheep. The other asphodel is the yellow asphodel (*Asphodeline lutea*). (Genera *Asphodelus* and *Asphodeline,* family Liliaceae.)

**asphyxia** suffocation; a lack of oxygen that produces a potentially lethal build-up of carbon dioxide waste in the tissues.

**aspidistra** any of several Asiatic plants of the lily family. The Chinese *Aspidistra elatior* has broad leaves which taper to a point and, like all aspidistras, grows well in warm indoor conditions. (Genus *Aspidistra,* family Liliaceae.)

**aspirin** acetylsalicylic acid, a popular pain-relieving drug (◊analgesic) developed in the late 19th century as a household remedy for aches and pains. It relieves pain and reduces inflammation and fever. It is derived from the white willow tree *Salix alba,* and is the world's most widely used drug.

**Asquith, Herbert Henry** 1st Earl of Oxford and Asquith (1852–1928) British Liberal politician, prime minister 1908–16. As chancellor of the Exchequer, he introduced old-age pensions in 1908. He limited the powers of the House of Lords and attempted to give Ireland ◊Home Rule.

**ass** any of several horselike, odd-toed, hoofed mammals of the genus *Equus,* family Equidae. Species include the African wild ass *E. asinus,* and the Asian wild ass *E. hemionus.* They differ from horses in their smaller size, larger ears, tufted tail, and characteristic bray. Donkeys and burros are domesticated asses.

**Assad, Hafez al** (1930– ) Syrian Ba'athist politician, president from 1971. He became prime minister after a bloodless military coup in 1970, and the following year was the first president to be elected by popular vote. Having suppressed dissent, he was re-elected in 1978, 1985, and 1991. He is a Shia (Alawite) Muslim.

**Assam** state of northeast India
*area* 78,400 sq km/30,262 sq mi
*capital* Dispur (a suburb of Guwahati)
*towns and cities* Guwahati, Dibrugarh, Silchar
*industries* half of India's oil produced here; coal, petrochemicals, paper, cement
*agriculture* half of India's tea grown here; rice, jute, sugar, cotton
*population* (1994 est) 24,200,000, including 12 million Assamese (Hindus), 5 million Bengalis (chiefly Muslim immigrants from Bangladesh), Nepalis, and 2 million indigenous people (Christian and traditional religions)
*language* Assamese
*history* a thriving region from 1000 BC; Assam migrants came from China and Myanmar (Burma). After Burmese invasion in 1826,

Britain took control and made Assam a separate province in 1874; it was included in the Dominion of India, except for most of the Muslim district of Silhet, which went to Pakistan in 1947. Ethnic unrest started in the 1960s when Assamese was declared the official language. After protests, the Garo, Khasi, and Jaintia tribal hill districts became the state of Meghalaya in 1971; the Mizo hill district became the Union Territory of Mizoram in 1972. There were massacres of Muslim Bengalis by Hindus in 1983. In 1987 members of the Bodo ethnic group began fighting for a separate homeland. In the early 1990s the Marxist-militant United Liberation Front of Assam (ULFA), which had extorted payments from tea-exporting companies, spearheaded a campaign of separatist terrorist violence. Between November 1990 and March 1991 the ULFA was reportedly involved in 97 killings, mainly of Congress (I) politicians.

**assassination** murder, usually of a political, royal, or public person. The term derives from the order of the Assassins, a Muslim sect that, in the 11th and 12th centuries, murdered officials to further its political ends.

**assassin bug** member of a family of blood-sucking bugs that contains about 4,000 species. Assassin bugs are mainly predators, feeding on other insects, but some species feed on birds and mammals, including humans. They are found, mainly in tropical regions, although some have established themselves in Europe and North America.

*classification* Assassin bugs are in family Reduviidae, suborder Heteroptera, order Hemiptera (true bugs), class Insecta, phylum Arthropoda.

**assault** intentional act or threat of physical violence against a person. In English law it is both a crime and a ◊tort (a civil wrong). The kinds of criminal assault are common (ordinary); aggravated (more serious, such as causing actual bodily harm); or indecent (of a sexual nature).

**assay** in chemistry, the determination of the quantity of a given substance present in a sample. Usually it refers to determining the purity of precious metals.

**assembly language** low-level computer-programming language closely related to a computer's internal codes. It consists chiefly of a set of short sequences of letters (mnemonics), which are translated, by a program called an assembler, into machine code for the computer's ◊central processing unit (CPU) to follow directly. In assembly language, for example, 'JMP' means 'jump' and 'LDA' means 'load accumulator'. Assembly code is used by programmers who need to write very fast or efficient programs.

**asset** in accounting, anything owned by or owed to the company that is either cash or can be turned into cash. The term covers physical assets such as land or property of a company or individual, as well as financial assets such as cash, payments due from bills, and investments.

Assets are divided into fixed assets and current assets. On a company's balance sheet, total assets must be equal to total liabilities (money and services owed).

**asset stripping** sale or exploitation by other means of the assets of a business, often one that has been taken over for that very purpose. The parts of the business may be potentially more valuable separately than together. Asset stripping is a major force for the more efficient use of assets.

**assize** in medieval Europe, the passing of laws, either by the king with the consent of nobles, as in the Constitutions of Clarendon passed by Henry II of England in 1164; or as a complete system, such as the *Assizes of Jerusalem*, a compilation of the law of the feudal kingdom of Jerusalem in the 13th century.

**Association of South East Asian Nations** (ASEAN), regional alliance formed in Bangkok in 1967; it took over the nonmilitary role of the Southeast Asia Treaty Organization in 1975. Its members are Indonesia, Malaysia, the Philippines, Singapore, Thailand, (from 1984) Brunei, (from 1995) Vietnam, and (from 1997) Laos and Myanmar; its headquarters are in Jakarta, Indonesia.

**assonance** the matching of vowel (or, sometimes, consonant) sounds in a line, generally in poetry. 'Load' and 'moat', 'farther' and 'harder' are examples of assonance, since they match in vowel sounds and stress pattern, but do not rhyme.

**assortative mating** in population genetics, selective mating in a population between individuals that are genetically related or have similar characteristics. If sufficiently consistent, assortative mating can theoretically result in the evolution of new species without geographical isolation (see ◊speciation).

**assurance** form of long-term saving where individuals pay monthly premiums, typically over 10 or 25 years, and at the end receive a large lump sum. For example, a person may save £50 a month and at the end of 25 years receive a lump sum of £40,000. Assurance policies are offered by assurance companies which invest savers' monthly premiums, typically in stocks, shares, and property.

**Assyria** empire in the Middle East *c.* 2500–612 BC, in northern Mesopotamia (now Iraq); early capital Ashur, later Nineveh. It was initially subject to Sumer and intermittently to Babylon. The Assyrians adopted largely the Sumerian religion and structure of society. At its greatest extent the empire included Egypt and stretched from the eastern Mediterranean coast to the head of the Persian Gulf.

**Astaire, Fred** adopted name of Frederick Austerlitz (1899–1987) US dancer, actor, singer, and choreographer. The greatest popular dancer of his time, he starred in numerous films, including *Top Hat* 1935, *Easter Parade* 1948, and *Funny Face* 1957, many containing inventive sequences which he designed and choreographed himself. He made ten classic films with the most popular of his dancing partners, Ginger Rogers.

**astatine** (Greek *astatos* 'unstable') nonmetallic, radioactive element, symbol At, atomic number 85, relative atomic mass 210. It is a member of the ◊halogen group, and is very rare in nature. Astatine is highly unstable, with at least 19 isotopes; the longest lived has a half-life of about eight hours.

**aster** any plant of a large group belonging to the same subfamily as the daisy. All asters have starlike flowers with yellow centres and outer rays (not petals) varying from blue and purple to white. Asters come in many sizes. Many are cultivated as garden flowers, including the Michaelmas daisy (*Aster nova-belgii*). (Genus *Aster,* family Compositae.)

**asteroid** or *minor planet,* any of many thousands of small bodies, composed of rock and iron, that orbit the Sun. Most lie in a belt between the orbits of Mars and Jupiter, and are thought to be fragments left over from the formation of the ◊Solar System. About 100,000 may exist, but their total mass is only a few hundredths the mass of the Moon.

**asthma** chronic condition characterized by difficulty in breathing due to spasm of the bronchi (air passages) in the lungs. Attacks may be provoked by allergy, infection, and stress. The incidence of asthma may be increasing as a result of air pollution and occupational hazard. Treatment is with bronchodilators to relax the bronchial muscles and thereby ease the breathing, and in severe cases by inhaled ◊steroids that reduce inflammation of the bronchi.

**astigmatism** aberration occurring in the lens of the eye. It results when the curvature of the lens differs in two perpendicular planes, so that rays in one plane may be in focus while rays in the other are not. With astigmatic eyesight, the vertical and horizontal cannot be in focus at the same time; correction is by the use of a cylindrical lens that reduces the overall focal length of one plane so that both planes are seen in sharp focus.

**Astor** prominent US and British family. *John Jacob Astor* (1763–1848) emigrated from Germany to the USA in 1884, and became a millionaire. His great-grandson *Waldorf Astor,* 2nd Viscount Astor (1879–1952), was a British politician, and served as Conservative member of Parliament for Plymouth from 1910 to 1919, when he succeeded to the peerage. His US-born wife Nancy Witcher Langhorne (1879–1964), *Lady Astor,* was the first woman member of Parliament to take a seat in the House of Commons, when she succeeded her husband in the constituency of Plymouth in November 1919. She remained in parliament until 1945, as an active champion of women's rights, educational issues, and temperance.

**Astrakhan** capital city, economic and cultural centre of Astrakhan oblast (region), southwestern Russian Federation; population (1996 est) 488,000. Astrakhan is sited in the Volga delta on the northeastern shore of the Caspian Sea. It is one of the Russian Federation's principal ports, which developed rapidly in the 1870s with the growth of the oil industry at Baku (now in Azerbaijan). There is a major fishing and canning industry here, together with shipbuilding and cotton manufacturing.

**astrology** (Greek *astron* 'star', *logos* 'study') study of the relative position of the planets and stars in the belief that they influence events on Earth. The astrologer casts a horoscope based on the time and place of the subject's birth. Astrology has no proven scientific basis, but has been widespread since ancient times.

Western astrology is based on the 12 signs of the zodiac; Chinese astrology is based on a 60-year cycle and lunar calendar.

**astronomical unit** unit (symbol AU) equal to the mean distance of the Earth from the Sun: 149,597,870 km/92,955,800 mi. It is used to describe planetary distances. Light travels this distance in approximately 8.3 minutes.

**astronomy** science of the celestial bodies: the Sun, the Moon, and the planets; the stars and galaxies; and all other objects in the universe. It is concerned with their positions, motions, distances, and physical conditions and with their origins and evolution. Astronomy thus divides into fields such as astrophysics, celestial mechanics, and ◊cosmology. See also ◊gamma-ray astronomy, ◊infrared astronomy, ◊radio astronomy, and ◊X-ray astronomy.

**astrophysics** study of the physical nature of stars, galaxies, and the universe. It began with the development of spectroscopy in the 19th century, which allowed astronomers to analyse the composition of stars from their light. Astrophysicists view the universe as a vast natural laboratory in which they can study matter under conditions of temperature, pressure, and density that are unattainable on Earth.

**Asturias** autonomous community of northern Spain; area 10,600 sq km/4,092 sq mi; population (1991) 1,091,100. Agricultural products include maize, fruit, cider, and dairy products, and sheep and other livestock are reared. In the past Asturias produced half of Spain's coal; most of the coal mines have since closed down. Oviedo (the capital) and Gijón are the main industrial towns.

**Asunción** capital and chief port of Paraguay, situated on the east bank of the Paraguay River, near its confluence with the River Pilcomayo; population (1992) 502,400 (metropolitan area 637,700); there are textile, footwear, and food processing industries. The climate is subtropical, and cattle are raised in the surrounding area, and maize, cotton, sugar, fruit, and tobacco are grown.

**asylum, political** in international law, refuge granted in another country to a person who, for political reasons, cannot return to his or her own country without putting himself or herself in danger. A person seeking asylum is a type of ◊refugee.

**asymptote** in ◊coordinate geometry, a straight line that a curve approaches progressively more closely but never reaches. The *x* and *y* axes are asymptotes to the graph of *xy* = constant (a rectangular ◊hyperbola).

**Atacama Desert** arid coastal region of northern Chile, with an area of about 80,000 sq km/ 31,000 sq mi, and extending south from the Peruvian border for 965 km/600 mi. It consists of a series of salt pans within a plateau region. Its rainless condition is caused by the ◊Peru Current offshore; any moist airstreams from the Amazon basin are blocked by the Andean Mountains. The desert has silver and copper mines, and extensive nitrate and iodine deposits. The main population centres are the ports of Antofagasta and Iquique.

**Atahualpa** (*c.* 1502–1533) Last emperor of the Incas of Peru. He was taken prisoner in 1532 when the Spaniards arrived and agreed to pay a substantial ransom, but he was accused of plotting against the conquistador Pizarro and was sentenced to be burned. On his consenting to Christian baptism, the sentence was commuted to strangulation.

**Atatürk, Mustafa Kemal** name assumed in 1934 by Mustafa Kemal Pasha Turkish 'Father of the Turks' (1881–1938) Turkish politician and general, first president of Turkey from 1923. After World War I he established a provisional rebel government and in 1921–22 the Turkish armies under his leadership expelled the Greeks who were occupying Turkey. He was the founder of the modern republic, which he ruled as a virtual dictator, with a policy of consistent and radical westernization.

**atavism** (Latin *atavus* 'ancestor'), in genetics, the reappearance of a characteristic not apparent in the immediately preceding generations; in psychology, the manifestation of primitive forms of behaviour.

**Athanasian creed** one of the three ancient ◊creeds of the Christian church. Mainly a definition of the Trinity and Incarnation, it was written many years after the death of Athanasius, but was attributed to him as the chief upholder of Trinitarian doctrine.

**atheism** nonbelief in, or the positive denial of, the existence of a God or gods. A related concept is ◊agnosticism. Like theism, its opposite, atheism cannot be proved or disproved conclusively.

**Athelstan** (895–939) king of England 924–39. The son of ◊Edward the Elder, Athelstan brought about English unity by ruling both Mercia and Wessex. He defeated an invasion by Scots, Irish, and the men of Strathclyde at Brunanburh in 937. He overcame the Scandinavian kingdom based in York and increased English power on the Welsh and Scottish borders.

**Athena** or *Athene or Pallas Athena*, in Greek mythology, the goddess of war, wisdom, and the arts and crafts (Roman *Minerva)*. She was reputed to have sprung fully-armed and grown from the head of Zeus, after he had swallowed her mother Metis, the Titaness of wisdom. In Homer's *Odyssey,* Athena is the protector of ◊Odysseus and his son Telemachus. Her chief cult centre was the Parthenon in Athens, and her principal festival was the Panathenaea, held every fourth year in August.

**Athens** Greek *Athinai,* capital city of Greece and of ancient Attica; population (1991) 784,100, metropolitan area (1991) 3,096,800. Situated 8 km/5 mi northeast of its port of Piraeus on the Gulf of Aegina, it is built around the rocky hills of the Acropolis 169 m/555 ft and the Areopagus 112 m/368 ft, and is overlooked from the northeast by the hill of Lycabettus, 277 m/909 ft high. It lies in the south of the central plain of Attica, watered by the mountain streams of Cephissus and Ilissus. It has less green space than any other European capital (4%) and severe air and noise pollution.

**atherosclerosis** thickening and hardening of the walls of the arteries, associated with atheroma.

**Atherton, Michael Andrew** (1968– ) English cricketer. A right-handed opening batsman from Lancashire who captained England in a record 52 Tests from 1993 to 1998. He made his Test debut in 1989.
*career highlights*
*Test cricket* matches: 90; innings: 167; not out: 6; runs: 6,178; average: 38.37; highest score: 185 not out; hundreds: 12; catches: 59
*One-Day Internationals (1990– )* matches: 54; innings: 54; not out: 3; runs: 1,791; hundreds: 2; best: 127

**athletics** competitive track and field events consisting of running, throwing, and jumping disciplines. *Running events* range from sprint races (100 metres) and hurdles to cross-country running and the ◊marathon (26 miles 385 yards). *Jumping events* are the high jump, long jump, triple jump, and pole vault. *Throwing events* are javelin, discus, shot put, and hammer throw.

**Atlanta** capital and largest city of ◊Georgia, USA, situated 300 m/984 ft above sea level in the foothills of the Blue Ridge Mountains; seat of Fulton County; population (1994 est) 396,100, metropolitan area (1992) 3,143,000. It is the headquarters of Coca-Cola, and there are Ford and Lockheed motor-vehicle and aircraft assembly plants. The CNN Center, headquarters of Cable News Network, is located here. Atlanta hosted the 1996 Olympic Games.

**Atlantic, Battle of the** German campaign during World War I to prevent merchant shipping from delivering food supplies from the USA to the Allies, chiefly the UK. By 1917, some 875,000 tons of shipping had been lost. The odds were only turned by the belated use of naval *convoys* and *depth charges* to deter submarine attack.

**Atlantic, Battle of the** during World War II, continuous battle fought in the Atlantic Ocean by the sea and air forces of the Allies and Germany, to control the supply routes to the UK. The Allies destroyed nearly 800 U-boats during the war and at least 2,200 convoys of 75,000 merchant ships crossed the Atlantic, protected by US naval forces.

**Atlantic Ocean** ocean lying between Europe and Africa to the east and the Americas to the west; area of basin 81,500,000 sq km/31,500,000 sq mi; including the Arctic Ocean and Antarctic seas, 106,200,000 sq km/41,000,000 sq mi. It is generally divided by the equator into the North Atlantic and South Atlantic. It was probably named after the legendary island continent of ◊Atlantis. The average depth is 3 km/2 mi; greatest depth is at the Milwaukee Depth in the Puerto Rico Trench 8,648 m/28,374 ft. The Mid-Atlantic Ridge, of which the Azores, Ascension, St Helena, and Tristan da Cunha form part, divides it from north to south. Lava welling up from this central area annually increases the distance between South America and Africa. The North Atlantic is the saltiest of the main oceans and has the largest tidal range.

**Atlantis** in Greek mythology, an island continent west of the Straits of Gibraltar, said to have sunk following an earthquake. Although the Atlantic Ocean is probably named after it, the structure of the sea bed rules out its former existence in the Atlantic region. Derived from an Egyptian priest's account, the Greek philosopher Plato created an imaginary early history for the island in *Timaeus and Critias*, describing it as a utopia (perfect place) submerged 9,000 years previously as punishment for waging war against Athens; an act deemed impious.

**Atlas** in Greek mythology, one of the ◊Titans who revolted against the gods; as punishment, he was compelled to support the heavens on his head and shoulders. Growing weary, he asked Perseus to turn him into stone by showing him the ◊Medusa's head, and was transformed into Mount Atlas.

**Atlas Mountains** mountain system of northwest Africa, stretching 2,400 km/1,500 mi from the Atlantic coast of Morocco to the Gulf of Gabes, Tunisia, and lying between the Mediterranean on the north and the Sahara on the south. The highest peak is Mount Toubkal 4,165 m/13,665 ft.

**atmosphere** mixture of gases surrounding a planet. Planetary atmospheres are prevented from escaping by the pull of gravity. On Earth, atmospheric pressure decreases with altitude. In its lowest layer, the atmosphere consists of nitrogen (78%) and oxygen (21%), both in molecular form (two atoms bonded together) and 1% argon. Small quantities of other gases are important to the chemistry and physics of the Earth's atmosphere, including water and carbon dioxide. The atmosphere plays a major part in the various cycles of nature (the ◊water cycle, the ◊carbon cycle, and the ◊nitrogen cycle). It is the principal industrial source of nitrogen, oxygen, and argon, which are obtained by fractional distillation of liquid air.

**atmosphere** or *standard atmosphere,* in physics, a unit (symbol atm) of pressure equal to 760 torr, 1013.25 millibars, or $1.01325 \times 10^5$ newtons per square metre. The actual pressure exerted by the atmosphere fluctuates around this value, which is assumed to be standard at sea level and 0°C/32°F, and is used when dealing with very high pressures.

**atoll** continuous or broken circle of ◊coral reef and low coral islands surrounding a lagoon.

**atom** (Greek *atomos* 'undivided') smallest unit of matter that can take part in a chemical reaction, and which cannot be broken down chemically into anything simpler. An atom is made up of protons and neutrons in a central nucleus surrounded by electrons (see ◊atomic structure). The atoms of the various elements differ in atomic number, relative atomic mass, and chemical behaviour.

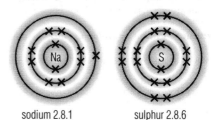

sodium 2.8.1          sulphur 2.8.6

**atom, electronic structure** *The arrangement of electrons in a sodium atom and a sulphur atom. The number of electrons in a neutral atom gives that atom its atomic number: sodium has an atomic number of 11 and sulphur has an atomic number of 16.*

### ATMOSPHERE: COMPOSITION

| Gas | Symbol | Volume (%) | Role |
| --- | --- | --- | --- |
| nitrogen | $N_2$ | 78.08 | cycled through human activities and through the action of micro-organisms on animal and plant waste |
| oxygen | $O_2$ | 20.94 | cycled mainly through the respiration of animals and plants and through the action of photosynthesis |
| carbon dioxide | $CO_2$ | 0.03 | cycled through respiration and photosynthesis in exchange reactions with oxygen. It is also a product of burning fossil fuels |
| argon | Ar | 0.93 | chemically inert and with only a few industrial uses |
| neon | Ne | 0.0018 | as argon |
| helium | He | 0.0005 | as argon |
| krypton | Kr | trace | as argon |
| xenon | Xe | trace | as argon |
| ozone | $O_3$ | 0.00006 | a product of oxygen molecules split into single atoms by the Sun's radiation and unaltered oxygen molecules |
| hydrogen | $H_2$ | 0.00005 | unimportant |

**atom, electronic structure of** the arrangement of electrons around the nucleus of an atom, in distinct energy levels, also called orbitals or shells. These shells can be regarded as a series of concentric spheres, each of which can contain a certain maximum number of electrons; the noble gases have an arrangement in which every shell contains this number. The energy levels are usually numbered beginning with the shell nearest to the nucleus. The outermost shell is known as the ◊valency shell as it contains the valence electrons.

**atomic bomb** or *atom bomb*, bomb deriving its explosive force from nuclear fission (see ◊nuclear energy) as a result of a neutron chain reaction, developed in the 1940s in the USA into a usable weapon.

**atomic clock** timekeeping device regulated by various periodic processes occurring in atoms and molecules, such as atomic vibration or the frequency of absorbed or emitted radiation.

**atomic energy** another name for ◊nuclear energy.

**atomic mass** see ◊relative atomic mass.

**atomic mass unit** or *dalton unit*, (symbol amu or u) unit of mass that is used to measure the relative mass of atoms and molecules. It is equal to one-twelfth of the mass of a carbon-12 atom, which is equivalent to the mass of a proton or $1.66 \times 10^{-27}$ kg. The ◊relative atomic mass of an atom has no units; thus oxygen-16 has an atomic mass of 16 daltons but a relative atomic mass of 16.

**atomic number** or *proton number,* the number (symbol $Z$) of protons in the nucleus of an atom. It is equal to the positive charge on the nucleus.

In a neutral atom, it is also equal to the number of electrons surrounding the nucleus. The chemical elements are arranged in the ◊periodic table of the elements according to their atomic number.

**atomic radiation** energy given out by disintegrating atoms during ◊radioactive decay, whether natural or synthesized. The energy may be in the form of fast-moving particles, known as ◊alpha particles and ◊beta particles, or in the form of high-energy electromagnetic waves known as ◊gamma radiation. Overlong exposure to atomic radiation can lead to ◊radiation sickness.

**atomic structure** internal structure of an ◊atom.

*the nucleus* The core of the atom is the *nucleus,* a dense body only one ten-thousandth the diameter of the atom itself. The simplest nucleus, that of hydrogen, comprises a single stable positively charged particle, the *proton*. Nuclei of other elements contain more protons and additional particles, called *neutrons,* of about the same mass as the proton but with no electrical charge. Each element has its own characteristic nucleus with a unique number of protons, the atomic number. The number of neutrons may vary. Where atoms of a single element have different numbers of neutrons, they are called ◊isotopes. Although some isotopes tend to be unstable and exhibit ◊radioactivity, they all have identical chemical properties.

*electrons* The nucleus is surrounded by a number of moving *electrons,* each of which has a negative charge equal to the positive charge on a proton, but which weighs only 1/1,839 times as much. In a neutral atom, the nucleus is surrounded by the same number of electrons as it contains protons. According to ◊quantum theory, the position of an electron is uncertain; it may be found at any point. However, it is more likely to be found in some places than others. The region of space in which an electron is most likely to be found is called an orbital. The chemical properties of an element are determined by the ease with which its atoms can gain or lose electrons from its outer orbitals.

**atonality** music in which the sense of ◊tonality is distorted or obscured; music of no apparent key. It is used by film and television composers for situations of mystery or horror, exploiting dissonance for its power to disturb.

**atonement** in Christian theology, the doctrine that Jesus suffered on the cross to bring about reconciliation and forgiveness between God and humanity.

**Atonement, Day of** Jewish holy day (*Yom Kippur*) held on the tenth day of Tishri (Sept–Oct), the first month of the Jewish year. It is a day of fasting, penitence, and cleansing from sin, ending the Ten Days of Penitence that follow *Rosh Hashanah,* the Jewish New Year.

**ATP** or *adenosine triphosphate,* abbreviation for a nucleotide molecule found in all cells. It can yield large amounts of energy, and is used to drive the thousands of biological processes needed to sustain life, growth, movement, and reproduction. Green plants use light energy to manufacture ATP as part of the process of ◊photosynthesis. In animals, ATP is formed by the breakdown of glucose molecules, usually obtained from the carbohydrate component of a diet, in a series of reactions termed ◊respiration. It is the driving force behind muscle contraction and the synthesis of complex molecules needed by individual cells.

**atrium** in architecture, an open inner courtyard. An atrium was originally the central court or main room of an ancient Roman house, open to the sky, often with a shallow pool to catch rainwater.

**Attenborough, Richard (Samuel)** Baron Attenborough (1923– ) English director, actor, and producer. He appeared in such films as *Brighton Rock* (1947) and *10 Rillington Place* (1971), and directed *Oh! What a Lovely War* (1969), and such biopics as *Gandhi* (which won eight Academy Awards) (1982) and *Cry Freedom* (1987).

**attention-deficit hyperactivity disorder** (ADHD), psychiatric condition occurring in young children characterized by impaired attention and hyperactivity. The disorder, associated with disruptive behaviour, learning difficulties, and under-achievement, is more common in boys.

It is treated with methylphenidate (Ritalin). There was a 50% increase in the use of the drug in the USA 1994–96, with an estimated 5% of school-age boys diagnosed as suffering from ADHD. In 1998 the number of children and adults in the USA taking medication for ADHD (mostly Ritalin) was approximately 4 million. In the UK the prescription of Ritalin doubles each year.

**Attica** Greek *Attiki,* region of Greece comprising Athens and the district around it; area 3,381 sq km/1,305 sq mi; population (1991) 3,522,800. It is renowned for its language, art, and philosophical thought in Classical times. It is a prefecture of modern Greece with Athens as its capital.

**Attila** (*c.* 406–453) King of the Huns in an area from the Alps to the Caspian Sea from 434, known to later Christian history as the 'Scourge of God'. He twice attacked the Eastern Roman Empire to increase the quantity of tribute paid to him, 441–443 and 447–449, and then attacked the Western Roman Empire 450–452.

**Attlee, Clement Richard** 1st Earl Attlee (1883–1967) British Labour politician. In the coalition government during World War II he was Lord Privy Seal 1940–42, dominions secretary 1942–43, and Lord President of the Council 1943–45, as well as deputy prime minister from 1942. As prime minister 1945–51 he introduced a sweeping programme of nationalization and a whole new system of social services.

**Attorney General** in the UK, principal law officer of the crown and head of the English Bar; the post is one of great political importance. In the USA, it is the chief law officer of the government and head of the Department of Justice.

**aubergine** or *eggplant,* plant belonging to the nightshade family, native to tropical Asia. Its purple-skinned, sometimes white, fruits are eaten as a vegetable. (*Solanum melongena,* family Solanaceae.)

**Auckland** largest city of North Island, New Zealand, in the north of the island, in an area of impressive volcanic scenery; population (1996) 997,900. It fills the isthmus that separates its two harbours (Waitemata and Manukau), and its suburbs spread north across the Harbour Bridge. It is the country's chief port and leading industrial centre, having iron and steel plants, engineering, car assembly, textiles, food processing, sugar refining, and brewing. Auckland was officially founded as New Zealand's capital in 1840, remaining so until 1865.

**Auden, W(ystan) H(ugh)** (1907–1973) English-born US poet. He wrote some of his most original poetry, such as *Look, Stranger!* (1936), in the 1930s when he led the influential left-wing literary group that included Louis MacNeice, Stephen Spender, and C Day-Lewis. He moved to the USA in 1939, became a US citizen in 1946, and adopted a more conservative and Christian viewpoint, for example in *The Age of Anxiety* (1947).

**audit** official inspection of a company's accounts by a qualified accountant as required by law each year to ensure that the company balance sheet reflects the true state of its affairs.

**Augean stables** in Greek mythology, the stables of Augeas, king of Elis in southern Greece. The yards, containing 3,000 cattle, had not been swept for 30 years. ♦Heracles had to clean them as one of 12 labours set by Eurystheus, king of Argos; a feat accomplished in one day by diverting the rivers Peneius and Alpheus.

**Augustan Age** golden age of the Roman emperor ♦Augustus (31 BC–AD 14), during which art and literature flourished. The term is also applied to later periods in which writers used Classical ideals, such as in the reign of Queen Anne in England (1702–14).

**Augustine of Hippo, St, (Aurelius Augustinus)** (354–430) One of the early Christian leaders and writers known as the Fathers of the Church. He was converted to Christianity by Ambrose in Milan and became bishop of Hippo (modern Annaba, Algeria) 396. Among Augustine's many writings are his *Confessions,* a spiritual autobiography, and *De Civitate Dei/The City of God,* vindicating the Christian church and divine providence in 22 books.

**Augustine, St** (died 605) First archbishop of Canterbury, England. He was sent from Rome to convert England to Christianity by Pope Gregory I. He landed at Ebbsfleet in Kent in 597 and soon after baptized Ethelbert, King of Kent, along with many of his subjects. He was consecrated bishop of the English at Arles in the same year, and appointed archbishop in 601, establishing his see at Canterbury. Feast day 26 May.

**Augustus** (63 BC–AD 14) title of Octavian (born Gaius Octavius), first Roman emperor 31 BC–AD 14. He joined forces with ♦Mark Antony and Lepidus in the Second Triumvirate. Following Mark Antony's liaison with the Egyptian queen ♦Cleopatra, Augustus defeated her troops at Actium 31 BC. As emperor he reformed the government of the empire, the army, and Rome's public services, and was a patron of the arts. The period of his rule is known as the ♦Augustan Age.

**auk** oceanic bird belonging to the family Alcidae, order Charadriiformes, consisting of 22 species of marine diving birds including razorbills, puffins, murres, and guillemots. Confined to the northern hemisphere, their range extends from well inside the Arctic Circle to the lower temperate regions. They feed on fish, and use their wings to 'fly' underwater in pursuit.

**Aung San** (1916–1947) Burmese (Myanmar) politician. He was a founder and leader of the Anti-Fascist People's Freedom League, which led Burma's fight for independence from the UK. During World War II he collaborated first with Japan and then with the UK. In 1947 he became head of Burma's provisional government but was assassinated the same year by political opponents. His daughter ♦Suu Kyi spearheaded a nonviolent pro-democracy movement in Myanmar from 1988.

**Aurangzeb** or *Aurungzebe* (1618–1707) Mogul emperor of northern India from 1658. Third son of ♦Shah Jahan, he made himself master of the court by a palace revolution. His reign was the most brilliant period of the Mogul dynasty, but his despotic tendencies and Muslim fanaticism aroused much opposition. His latter years were spent in war with the princes of Rajputana and the Marathas and Sikhs. His drive south into the Deccan overextended Mogul resources.

**Aurelian** Lucius Domitius Aurelianus (*c.* AD 215–275) Roman emperor 270–75. A successful soldier, he was proclaimed emperor by his troops on the death of Claudius II. He campaigned on the Danube and then defeated a large raid into Italy mounted by the Alamanni and Juthungi. He moved east and captured Queen Zenobia of Palmyra (now Tadmur, Syria) by the end of 272, destroying Palmyra itself in 273. He was planning a campaign against the Persians when he was murdered by a group of his own officers.

**Aurelius, Marcus** Roman emperor; see ◊Marcus Aurelius Antoninus.

**Auriga** constellation of the northern hemisphere, represented as a charioteer. Its brightest star is the first-magnitude ◊Capella, about 45 light years from Earth; Epsilon Aurigae is an ◊eclipsing binary star with a period of 27 years, the longest of its kind (last eclipse 1983).

**aurochs** plural *aurochs,* extinct species of long-horned wild cattle *Bos primigenius* that formerly roamed Europe, southwestern Asia, and North Africa. It survived in Poland until 1627. Black to reddish or grey, it was up to 1.8 m/ 6 ft at the shoulder. It is depicted in many cave paintings, and is considered the ancestor of domestic cattle.

**aurora** coloured light in the night sky near the Earth's magnetic poles, called *aurora borealis* ('northern lights') in the northern hemisphere and *aurora australis* in the southern hemisphere. Although aurorae are usually restricted to the polar skies, fluctuations in the ◊solar wind occasionally cause them to be visible at lower latitudes. An aurora is usually in the form of a luminous arch with its apex towards the magnetic pole followed by arcs, bands, rays, curtains, and coronas, usually green but often showing shades of blue and red, and sometimes yellow or white. Aurorae are caused at heights of over 100 km/60 mi by a fast stream of charged particles from solar flares and low-density 'holes' in the Sun's corona.

These are guided by the Earth's magnetic field towards the north and south magnetic poles, where they enter the upper atmosphere and bombard the gases in the atmosphere, causing them to emit visible light.

**Auschwitz** Polish *Oświęcim,* town near Kraków in Poland, the site of a notorious ◊concentration camp used by the Nazis in World War II to exterminate Jews and other political and social minorities, as part of the 'final solution'. Each of the four gas chambers could hold 6,000 people.

**Austen, Jane** (1775–1817) English novelist. She described her raw material as 'three or four families in a Country Village'. *Sense and Sensibility* was published in 1811, *Pride and Prejudice* in 1813, *Mansfield Park* in 1814, *Emma* in 1816, and *Northanger Abbey* and *Persuasion* together in 1818, all anonymously. She observed speech and manners with wit and precision, and her penetrating observation of human behaviour results in insights that transcend period. Many of her works have been successfully adapted for film and television.

**Austerlitz, Battle of** battle on 2 December 1805, in which the French forces of Emperor Napoleon Bonaparte defeated those of Alexander I of Russia and Francis II of Austria at a small town in the Czech Republic (formerly in Austria), 19 km/12 mi east of Brno. The battle was one of Napoleon's greatest victories, resulting in the end of the coalition against France – the Austrians signed the Treaty of Pressburg and the Russians retired to their own territory.

**Australia** Commonwealth of

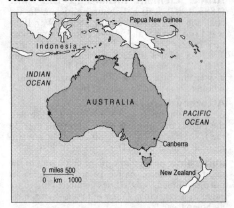

**area** 7,682,300 sq km/2,966,136 sq mi
**capital** Canberra
**major towns/cities** Adelaide, Alice Springs, Brisbane, Darwin, Melbourne, Perth, Sydney, Hobart, Geelong, Newcastle, Townsville, Wollongong
**physical features** Ayers Rock; Arnhem Land; Gulf of Carpentaria; Cape York Peninsula; Great Australian Bight; Great Sandy Desert; Gibson Desert; Great Victoria Desert; Simpson Desert; the Great Barrier Reef; Great Dividing Range and Australian Alps in the east (Mount Kosciusko, 2,229 m/7,136 ft, Australia's highest peak). The fertile southeast region is watered by the Darling, Lachlan, Murrumbridgee, and Murray rivers. Lake Eyre basin and Nullarbor Plain in the south
**territories** Norfolk Island, Christmas Island, Cocos (Keeling) Islands, Ashmore and Cartier Islands, Coral Sea Islands, Heard Island and McDonald Islands, Australian Antarctic Territory
**head of state** Elizabeth II from 1952, represented by governor general William George Hayden from 1989
**head of government** John Howard from 1996

*political system* federal constitutional monarchy

*political parties* Australian Labor Party, moderate left of centre; Liberal Party of Australia, moderate, liberal, free enterprise; National Party of Australia (formerly Country Party), centrist non-metropolitan

*currency* Australian dollar

*GNP per capita (PPP)* (US$) 20,130 (1998)

*exports* major world producer of raw materials: iron ore, aluminium, coal, nickel, zinc, lead, gold, tin, tungsten, uranium, crude oil; wool, meat, cereals, fruit, sugar, wine. Principal markets: Japan 19.6% (1998)

*population* 18,705,000 (1999 est)

*language* English, Aboriginal languages

*religion* Anglican 26%, other Protestant 17%, Roman Catholic 26%

*life expectancy* 76 (men); 81 (women) (1995–2000)

*Chronology*

*c. 40,000 BC* Aboriginal immigration from southern India, Sri Lanka, and Southeast Asia.

*AD 1606* First recorded sightings of Australia by Europeans including discovery of Cape York by Dutch explorer Willem Jansz in *Duyfken*.

*1770* Capt James Cook claimed New South Wales for Britain.

*1788* Sydney founded as British penal colony.

*late 18th–19th centuries* Great age of exploration: coastal surveys by George Bass and Matthew Flinders; interior by Charles Sturt, Edward Eyre, Robert Burke and William Wills, John McDouall Stuart, and John Forrest. Overlanders and squatters also opened up new territory, as did bushrangers, including Ned Kelly.

*1804* Castle Hill Rising by Irish convicts in New South Wales.

*1813* Crossing of Blue Mountains removed major barrier to exploration of interior.

*1825* Tasmania seceded from New South Wales.

*1829* Western Australia colonized.

*1836* South Australia colonized.

*1840–68* End of convict transportation.

*1850* British Act of Parliament permitted Australian colonies to draft their own constitutions and achieve virtual self-government.

*1851–61* Gold rushes contributed to exploration and economic growth.

*1851* Victoria seceded from New South Wales.

*1855* Victoria achieved self-government.

*1856* New South Wales, South Australia, and Tasmania achieved self-government.

*1859* Queensland formed from New South Wales and achieved self-government.

*1860* (National) Country Party founded.

*1890* Western Australia achieved self-government.

*1891* Depression gave rise to Australian Labor Party.

*1899–1900* South African War – forces offered by individual colonies.

*1901* Creation of Commonwealth of Australia.

*1902* Immigration Restriction Act introduced language tests for potential settlers; women gained right to vote.

*1914–18* World War I: over 300,000 Australian volunteers fought in Middle East and on western front.

*1919* Australia given mandates over Papua New Guinea and Solomon Islands.

*1927* Seat of federal government moved to Canberra.

*1931* Statute of Westminster confirmed Australian independence.

*1933* Western Australia's vote to secede was overruled.

*1939–45* World War II: Australian troops fought in Greece, North Africa, and the southwest Pacific.

*1941* Curtin's appeal to USA for military help marked shift away from exclusive relationship with Britain.

*1944* Liberal Party founded by Menzies.

*1948–75* Influx of around 2 million new immigrants, chiefly from continental Europe.

*1950–53* Australia contributed troops to United Nations (UN) forces in Korean War.

*1951* Australia joined USA and New Zealand in ANZUS Pacific security alliance.

*1965–72* Australian troops participated in Vietnam War.

*1967* Referendum gave Australian Aborigines full citizenship rights. Australia became a member of the Association of South East Asian Nations (ASEAN).

*1973* Britain entered European Economic Community (EEC), and in 1970s Japan became Australia's chief trading partner.

*1974* 'White Australia' immigration restrictions abolished.

*1975* Constitutional crisis: Governor General John Kerr dismissed Prime Minister Gough Whitlam after senate blocked financial legislation. Papua New Guinea became independent.

*1978* Northern Territory achieved self-government.

*1983* Labor Party returned to power under Bob Hawke.

*1986* Australia Act passed by British Parliament eliminating last vestiges of British legal authority in Australia.

*1988* A Free Trade Agreement was signed with New Zealand.

*1992* The Citizenship Act removed the oath of allegiance to the British crown.

*1993* The Labor Party won its record fifth election victory.

*1996* A Liberal–National coalition, headed by John Howard, won the general election.

*1997* The Democrat Party leader switched to the Labor Party.

*1998* Howard's Liberal–National coalition government was narrowly re-elected.

**Australian Aborigine** member of any of the 500 groups of indigenous inhabitants of the continent of Australia, who migrated to this region from South Asia about 40,000 years ago. Traditionally hunters and gatherers, they are found throughout the continent and their languages probably belong to more than one linguistic family. They are dark-skinned, with fair hair in childhood and heavy dark beards and body hair in adult males. There are about 228,000 Aborigines in Australia, making up about 1.5% of the population of 16 million. The Aborigine rights movement campaigns against racial discrimination in housing, education, wages, and medical facilities.

**Australian Capital Territory** federal territory of southeastern Austrlia, an enclave in the state of New South Wales; it includes Jervis Bay Territory (the site of Canberra's port on the coast) for administrative purposes
**area** 2,400 sq km/926 sq mi (Jervis Bay 73 sq km/28 sq mi)
**cities** ◊Canberra
**features** Parliament House (1988), Lake Burley Griffin, High Court of Australia, Australian War Memorial, Australian National Gallery, the National Library, Australian National Botanic Gardens, Black Mountain
**industries** government administration and defence employs almost half of the population of Australian Capital Territory; retail, property, and business services are also important
**population** (1996) 297,000
**history** site of capital chosen in 1908; territory ceded to the Commonwealth of Australia by New South Wales in 1911; Jervis Bay area, on the New South Wales south coast, ceded in 1915 to provide site for the port of Canberra; seat of Australian Government moved from Melbourne to Canberra in 1927.

**Austria** Republic of
**national name** *Republik Österreich*

**area** 83,500 sq km/32,239 sq mi
**capital** Vienna
**major towns/cities** Graz, Linz, Salzburg, Innsbruck, Klagenfurt
**physical features** landlocked mountainous state, with Alps in west and south (Austrian Alps, including Grossglockner and Brenner and Semmering passes, Lechtaler and Allgauer Alps north of River Inn, Carnic Alps on Italian border) and low relief in east where most of the population is concentrated; River Danube
**head of state** Thomas Klestil from 1992
**head of government** Viktor Klima from 28 January 1997
**political system** democratic federal republic

**political parties** Social Democratic Party of Austria (SPÖ), democratic socialist; Austrian People's Party (ÖVP), progressive centrist; Freedom (formerly Freedom Party of Austria: FPÖ), right wing; United Green Party of Austria (VGÖ), conservative ecological; Green Alternative Party (ALV), radical ecological
**currency** schilling
**GNP per capita (PPP)** (US$) 22,740 (1998)
**exports** dairy products, food products, wood and paper products, machinery and transport equipment, metal and metal products, chemical products. Principal market for exports: Germany 35.1% (1997)
**population** 8,177,000 (1999 est)
**language** German
**religion** Roman Catholic 78%, Protestant 5%
**life expectancy** 74 (men); 80 (women) (1995–2000)
**Chronology**
**14 BC** Country south of River Danube conquered by Romans.
**5th century AD** Region occupied by Vandals, Huns, Goths, Lombards, and Avars.
**791** Charlemagne conquered Avars and established East Mark, nucleus of future Austrian Empire.
**976** Holy Roman Emperor Otto II granted East Mark to House of Babenburg, which ruled until 1246.
**1156** Margrave of Austria raised to duke.
**1282** Holy Roman Emperor Rudolf of Habsburg seized Austria and invested his son as its duke; for over 500 years most rulers of Austria were elected Holy Roman Emperor.
**1453** Austria became an archduchy.
**1519–56** Emperor Charles V was both archduke of Austria and king of Spain; Habsburgs dominant in Europe.
**1526** Bohemia came under Habsburg rule.
**1529** Vienna besieged by the Ottoman Turks.
**1618–48** Thirty Years' War: Habsburgs weakened by failure to secure control over Germany.
**1683** Polish-Austrian force led by Jan Sobieski defeated the Turks at Vienna.
**1699** Treaty of Karlowitz: Austrians expelled the Turks from Hungary, which came under Habsburg rule.
**1713** By the Treaty of Utrecht, Austria obtained the Spanish Netherlands (Belgium) and political control over most of Italy.
**1740–48** War of Austrian Succession: Prussia (supported by France and Spain) attacked Austria (supported by Holland and England) on the pretext of disputing rights of Maria Theresa; Austria lost Silesia to Prussia.
**1772** Austria joined in partition of Poland, annexing Galicia.
**1780–90** 'Enlightened despotism': Joseph II tried to impose radical reforms.
**1792** Austria went to war with revolutionary France.
**1804** Francis II took the title Emperor of Austria.
**1806** Holy Roman Empire abolished.
**1809–48** Guided by foreign minister Prince Klemens von Metternich, Austria took a leading role in resisting liberalism and nationalism throughout Europe.

**1815** After the Napoleonic Wars, Austria lost its Netherlands but received Lombardy and Venetia.

**1848** Outbreak of liberal-nationalist revolts throughout the Austrian Empire; Ferdinand I abdicated in favour of Franz Joseph; revolutions suppressed with difficulty.

**1859** France and Sardinia expelled Austrians from Lombardy by force.

**1866** Seven Weeks' War: Prussia defeated Austria, which ceded Venetia to Italy.

**1867** Austria conceded equality to Hungary within the dual monarchy of Austria-Hungary.

**1878** Treaty of Berlin: Austria-Hungary occupied Bosnia-Herzegovina; annexed in 1908.

**1914** Archduke Franz Ferdinand, the heir to the throne, assassinated by a Serbian nationalist; Austria-Hungary invaded Serbia, precipitating World War I.

**1916** Death of Franz Joseph; succeeded by Karl I.

**1918** Austria-Hungary collapsed in military defeat; empire dissolved; republic proclaimed.

**1919** Treaty of St Germain reduced Austria to its present boundaries and prohibited union with Germany.

**1934** Political instability culminated in brief civil war; right-wingers defeated socialists.

**1938** The *Anschluss:* Nazi Germany incorporated Austria into the Third Reich.

**1945** Following World War II, the victorious Allies divided Austria into four zones of occupation (US, British, French, and Soviet); Second Republic established under Karl Renner.

**1955** Austrian State Treaty ended occupation; Austria regained independence on condition of neutrality.

**1960–70s** Austria experienced rapid industrialization and prosperity under governments dominated by moderate socialists and centrists.

**1986** Kurt Waldheim was elected president, despite allegations of war crimes during World War II. This led to a measure of diplomatic isolation until Waldheim's replacement in 1992.

**1992** Thomas Klestil was elected president.

**1995** Austria became a full member of the European Union (EU).

**1998** NATO membership was ruled out. President Klestil was re-elected.

**Austrian Succession, War of the** war 1740–48 between Austria (supported by England and Holland) and Prussia (supported by France and Spain). The Holy Roman Emperor Charles VI died in 1740 and the succession of his daughter Maria Theresa was disputed by a number of European powers. Frederick the Great of Prussia seized Silesia from Austria. At Dettingen in 1743 an army of British, Austrians, and Hanoverians under the command of George II was victorious over the French. In 1745 an Austro-English army was defeated at Fontenoy but British naval superiority was confirmed, and there were gains in the Americas and India. The war was ended in 1748 by the Treaty of Aix-la-Chapelle.

**Austro-Hungarian Empire** Dual Monarchy established by the Habsburg Franz Joseph in 1867 between his empire of Austria and his kingdom of Hungary (including territory that became Czechoslovakia as well as parts of Poland, the Ukraine, Romania, Yugoslavia, and Italy).

It collapsed in the autumn of 1918 with the end of World War I. Only two king-emperors ruled: Franz Joseph (1867–1916) and Charles (1916–18).

**Austronesian languages** (also known as *Malayo-Polynesian)* family of languages spoken in Malaysia, the Indonesian archipelago, parts of the region that was formerly Indochina, Taiwan, Madagascar, Melanesia, and Polynesia (excluding Australia and most of New Guinea). The group contains some 500 distinct languages, including Malay in Malaysia, Bahasa in Indonesia, Fijian, Hawaiian, and Maori.

**authoritarianism** rule of a country by a dominant elite who repress opponents and the press to maintain their own wealth and power. They are frequently indifferent to activities not affecting their security, and rival power centres, such as trade unions and political parties, are often allowed to exist, although under tight control. An extreme form is ◊totalitarianism.

**autism, infantile** rare disorder, generally present from birth, characterized by a withdrawn state and a failure to develop normally in language or social behaviour. Although the autistic child may, rarely, show signs of high intelligence (in music or with numbers, for example), many have impaired intellect. The cause is unknown, but is thought to involve a number of factors, possibly including an inherent abnormality of the child's brain. Special education may bring about some improvement.

**autochrome** in photography, a single-plate additive colour process devised by the ◊Lumière brothers in 1903. It was the first commercially available process, in use 1907–35.

**autocracy** form of government in which one person holds absolute power. The autocrat has uncontrolled and undisputed authority. Russian government under the tsars was an autocracy extending from the mid-16th century to the early 20th century. The title *Autocratix* (a female autocrat) was assumed by Catherine II of Russia in the 18th century.

**auto-da-fé** (Portuguese 'act of faith') religious ceremony, including a procession, solemn mass, and sermon, which accompanied the sentencing of heretics by the Spanish Inquisition before they were handed over to the secular authorities for punishment, usually burning.

**autogiro** or *autogyro,* heavier-than-air craft that supports itself in the air with a rotary wing, or rotor. The Spanish aviator Juan de la Cierva designed the first successful autogiro in 1923. The autogiro's rotor provides only lift and not propulsion; it has been superseded by the helicopter, in which the rotor provides both. The autogiro is propelled by an orthodox propeller.

**autoimmunity** in medicine, condition where the body's immune responses are mobilized not against 'foreign' matter, such as invading germs, but against the body itself. Diseases considered to be of autoimmune origin include myasthenia gravis, rheumatoid arthritis, and ◊lupus erythematous.

**automatic pilot** control device that keeps an aeroplane flying automatically on a given course at a given height and speed.

**automation** widespread use of self-regulating machines in industry. Automation involves the addition of control devices, using electronic sensing and computing techniques, which often follow the pattern of human nervous and brain functions, to already mechanized physical processes of production and distribution; for example, steel processing, mining, chemical production, and road, rail, and air control.

**autonomic nervous system** in mammals, the part of the nervous system that controls those functions not controlled voluntarily, including the heart rate, activity of the intestines, and the production of sweat.

There are two divisions of the autonomic nervous system. The *sympathetic* system responds to stress, when it speeds the heart rate, increases blood pressure, and generally prepares the body for action. The *parasympathetic* system is more important when the body is at rest, since it slows the heart rate, decreases blood pressure, and stimulates the digestive system.

**autonomy** in politics, a term used to describe political self-government of a state or, more commonly, a subdivision of a state. Autonomy may be based upon cultural or ethnic differences and often leads eventually to independence.

**autopsy** or *postmortem*, examination of the internal organs and tissues of a dead body, performed to try to establish the cause of death.

**autosome** any ◊chromosome in the cell other than a sex chromosome. Autosomes are of the same number and kind in both males and females of a given species.

**autosuggestion** conscious or unconscious acceptance of an idea as true, without demanding rational proof, but with potential subsequent effect for good or ill. Pioneered by French psychotherapist Emile Coué (1857–1926) in healing, it is sometimes used in modern psychotherapy to conquer nervous habits and dependence on addictive substances such as tobacco and alcohol.

**autotroph** any living organism that synthesizes organic substances from inorganic molecules by using light or chemical energy. Autotrophs are the *primary producers* in all food chains since the materials they synthesize and store are the energy sources of all other organisms. All green plants and many planktonic organisms are autotrophs, using sunlight to convert carbon dioxide and water into sugars by ◊photosynthesis.

**autumn crocus** any of a group of late-flowering plants belonging to the lily family. The mauve *meadow saffron* (*Colchicum autumnale*) yields *colchicine*, which is used in treating gout and in plant breeding. (Genus *Colchicum*, family Liliaceae.)

**Auvergne** ancient province of central France and modern region comprising the *départements* of Allier, Cantal, Haute-Loire, and Puy-de-Dôme; administrative centre Clermont-Ferrand; area 26,000 sq km/10,036 sq mi; population (1990) 1,321,200. It is a mountainous area, composed chiefly of volcanic rocks in several masses. Products include cattle, sheep, tyres, and metal goods.

**auxin** plant ◊hormone that promotes stem and root growth in plants. Auxins influence many aspects of plant growth and development, including cell enlargement, inhibition of development of axillary buds, ◊tropisms, and the initiation of roots. *Synthetic auxins* are used in rooting powders for cuttings, and in some weed-killers, where high auxin concentrations cause such rapid growth that the plants die. They are also used to prevent premature fruitdrop in orchards. The most common naturally occurring auxin is known as indoleacetic acid, or IAA. It is produced in the shoot apex and transported to other parts of the plant.

**avalanche** (from French *avaler* 'to swallow') fall or flow of a mass of snow and ice down a steep slope under the force of gravity. Avalanches occur because of the unstable nature of snow masses in mountain areas.

**Avalokiteśvara** in Mahāyāna Buddhism, one of the most important ◊bodhisattvas, seen as embodying compassion. He is an emanation of Amida Buddha. In China, as *Kuan Yin*, and Japan, as *Kannon*, he is confused with his female consort, becoming the popular goddess of mercy.

**avant-garde** (French 'forward guard') in the arts, those artists or works that are in the forefront of new developments in their media. The term was introduced (as was 'reactionary') after the French Revolution, when it was used to describe any socialist political movement.

**avatar** in Hindu mythology, the descent of a deity to Earth in a visible form, for example the ten avatars of ◊Vishnu.

**Avebury** Europe's largest stone circle (diameter 412 m/1,350 ft), in Wiltshire, England. This megalithic henge monument is thought to be part of a ritual complex, and contains 650 massive blocks of stone arranged in circles and avenues. It was probably constructed around 3,500 years ago, and is linked with nearby Silbury Hill.

**Avedon, Richard** (1923– ) US photographer. A fashion photographer with *Harper's Bazaar* magazine in New York from the mid-1940s, he moved to *Vogue* 1965. He later became the highest-paid fashion and advertising photographer in the world. He became associated with the *New Yorker* 1993. Using large-format cameras, his work consists of intensely realistic images, chiefly portraits.

**average** in statistics, a term used inexactly to indicate the typical member of a set of data. It usually refers to the ◊arithmetic mean. The term is also used to refer to the middle member of the set when it is sorted in ascending or descending order (the ◊median), and the most commonly occurring item of data (the ◊mode), as in 'the average family'.

**Averroës** Arabic *Ibn Rushd* (1126–1198) Arabian philosopher who argued for the eternity of matter and against the immortality of the individual soul. His philosophical writings, including commentaries on Aristotle and on Plato's *Republic*, became known to the West through Latin translations. He influenced Christian and Jewish writers into the Renaissance, and reconciled Islamic and Greek thought in asserting that philosophic truth comes through reason. St Thomas Aquinas opposed this position.

**Avicenna** Arabic *Ibn Sina* (979–1037) Iranian philosopher and physician. He was the most renowned philosopher of medieval Islam. His *Canon Medicinae* was a standard work for many centuries. His philosophical writings were influenced by al-Farabi, Aristotle, and the neo-Platonists, and in turn influenced the scholastics of the 13th century.

**Avignon** city in Provence, France, administrative centre of Vaucluse *département,* on the River Rhône, 80 km/50 mi northwest of Marseille; population (1990) 89,400, conurbation 180,000. Tourism and food processing are important; other industries include the manufacture of leather, textiles, soaps, machinery, and chemicals. Avignon has a significant trade in wine. There is an atomic plant at Marcoule nearby. An important Gallic and Roman city, it has a 12th-century bridge (only half of which still stands), a 13th-century cathedral, 14th-century walls, and the Palais des Papes, the enormous fortress-palace of the popes, one of the most magnificent Gothic buildings of the 14th century.

**avocado** tree belonging to the laurel family, native to Central America. Its dark-green, thick-skinned, pear-shaped fruit has buttery-textured flesh and is used in salads. (*Persea americana,* family Lauraceae.)

**avocet** wading bird, with a characteristic long, narrow, upturned bill, which it uses to sift water as it feeds in the shallows. It is about 45 cm/18 in long, has long legs, partly webbed feet, and black and white plumage. There are four species of avocet, genus *Recurvirostra,* family Recurvirostridae, order Charadriiformes. They are found in Europe, Africa, and central and southern Asia. Stilts belong to the same family.

**Avogadro's hypothesis** in chemistry, the law stating that equal volumes of all gases, when at the same temperature and pressure, have the same numbers of molecules. It was first propounded by Amedeo Avogadro.

**Avogadro's number** or *Avogadro's constant,* the number of carbon atoms in 12 g of the carbon-12 isotope ($6.022045 \times 10^{23}$). The relative atomic mass of any element, expressed in grams, contains this number of atoms. It is named after Amedeo Avogadro.

**avoirdupois** system of units of mass based on the pound (0.45 kg), which consists of 16 ounces (each of 16 drams) or 7,000 grains (each equal to 65 mg).

**Avon** *Upper Avon* or *Warwickshire Avon,* (Celtic *afon* 'river') river in southern England; length 154 km/96 mi. It rises in the Northamptonshire uplands near Naseby and flows southwest through Warwick, Stratford-upon-Avon, and Evesham, before joining the River Severn near Tewkesbury, Gloucestershire.

**axiom** in mathematics, a statement that is assumed to be true and upon which theorems are proved by using logical deduction; for example, two straight lines cannot enclose a space. The Greek mathematician Euclid used a series of axioms that he considered could not be demonstrated in terms of simpler concepts to prove his geometrical theorems.

**axis** plural axes, in geometry, one of the reference lines by which a point on a graph may be located. The horizontal axis is usually referred to as the $x$-axis, and the vertical axis as the $y$-axis. The term is also used to refer to the imaginary line about which an object may be said to be symmetrical (*axis of symmetry*) – for example, the diagonal of a square – or the line about which an object may revolve (*axis of rotation).*

**Axis** alliance of Nazi Germany and Fascist Italy before and during World War II. The *Rome–Berlin Axis* was formed 1936, when Italy was being threatened with sanctions because of its invasion of Ethiopia (Abyssinia). It became a full military and political alliance May 1939. A ten-year alliance between Germany, Italy, and Japan (*Rome–Berlin–Tokyo Axis)* was signed September 1940 and was subsequently joined by Hungary, Bulgaria, Romania, and the puppet states of Slovakia and Croatia. The Axis collapsed with the fall of Mussolini and the surrender of Italy 1943 and Germany and Japan 1945.

**axolotl** (Aztec 'water monster') aquatic larval form ('tadpole') of the Mexican salamander *Ambystoma mexicanum,* belonging to the family Ambystomatidae. Axolotls may be up to 30 cm/12 in long. They are remarkable because they can breed without changing to the adult form, and will metamorphose into adults only in response to the drying-up of their ponds. The adults then migrate to another pond.

**axon** long threadlike extension of a ◊nerve cell that conducts electrochemical impulses away from the cell body towards other nerve cells, or towards an effector organ such as a muscle. Axons terminate in ◊synapses, junctions with other nerve cells, muscles, or glands.

**ayatollah** (Arabic 'sign of God') honorific title awarded to Shiite Muslims in Iran by popular consent, as, for example, to Ayatollah Ruhollah ◊Khomeini.

**Ayckbourn, Alan** (1939– ) English playwright and artistic director of the Stephen Joseph Theatre, Scarborough, North Yorkshire, from 1970. His prolific output, characterized by comic dialogue and teasing experiments in dramatic structure, includes *Relatively Speaking* (1967), *Absurd Person Singular* (1972), a trilogy *The Norman Conquests* (1974), *Intimate Exchanges* (1982), *A Woman in Mind* (1986), *Haunting Julia* (1994), and *Things We Do For Love*. He has also written a number of plays for children, including *Invisible Friends* (1989) and *This Is Where We Came In* (1990).

**aye-aye** nocturnal tree-climbing prosimian *Daubentonia madagascariensis* of Madagascar, related to the lemurs. It is just over 1 m/3 ft long, including a tail 50 cm/20 in long.

**Ayer, A(lfred) J(ules)** (1910–1989) English philosopher. He wrote *Language, Truth and Logic* (1936), an exposition of the theory of 'logical positivism', presenting a criterion by which meaningful statements (essentially truths of logic, as well as statements derived from experience) could be distinguished from meaningless metaphysical utterances (for example, claims that there is a God or that the world external to our own minds is illusory). Knighted 1970.

**Ayers Rock** (Aboriginal *Uluru*) vast ovate mass of pinkish rock in Northern Territory, Australia; 335 m/1,110 ft high and 9 km/6 mi around. For the Aboriginals, whose paintings decorate its caves, it has magical significance.

**Aymara** the American Indian people of Bolivia and Peru, builders of a great culture, who were conquered first by the Incas and then by the Spaniards. Today 1.4 million Aymara farm and herd llamas and alpacas in the highlands; their language, belonging to the Andean-Equatorial language family, survives, and their Roman Catholicism incorporates elements of their old beliefs.

**azalea** any of a group of deciduous flowering shrubs belonging to the heath family. Several species are native to Asia and North America, and many cultivated varieties have been derived from these. Azaleas are closely related to the mostly evergreen ◊rhododendrons. (Genus *Rhododendron*, family Ericaceae.)

**Azerbaijan, Iranian** ancient *Atropatene,* two provinces of northwest Iran: *Eastern Azerbaijan* (population (1991) 3,278,700, capital Tabriz); and *Western Azerbaijan* (population (1991) 2,284,200, capital Orumiyeh). Azerbaijanis in Iran, as in the Republic of Azerbaijan, are mainly Shiite Muslim ethnic Turks, descendants of followers of the Khans from the Mongol Empire.

**Azerbaijan** Republic of
**national name** *Azarbaijchan Respublikasy*

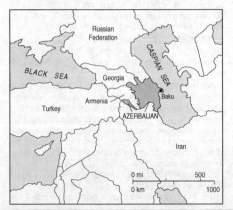

**area** 86,600 sq km/33,436 sq mi
**capital** Baku
**major towns/cities** Gyandzha (formerly Kirovabad), Sumgait, Nakhichevan, Stepanakert
**physical features** Caspian Sea with rich oil reserves; the country ranges from semidesert to the Caucasus Mountains
**head of state** Geidar Aliyev from 1993
**head of government** Artur Rasizade from 1996
**political system** authoritarian nationalist
**political parties** Popular Front of Azerbaijan (FPA), democratic nationalist; New Azerbaijan, ex-communist; Communist Party of Azerbaijan (banned 1991–93); Muslim Democratic Party (Musavat), Islamic, pro-Turkic unity
**currency** manat (left rouble zone in 1993)
**GNP per capita (PPP)** (US$) 1,820 (1998)
**exports** refined petroleum products, machinery, food products, textiles. Principal market: Turkey 22.4% (1998)
**population** 7,697,000 (1999 est)
**language** Azeri
**religion** Shiite Muslim 62%, Sunni Muslim 26%, Orthodox Christian 12%
**life expectancy** 66 (men); 74 (women) (1995–2000)
**Chronology**
**4th century BC** Established as an independent state for the first time by Atrophates, a vassal of Alexander III of Macedon.
**7th century** Spread of Islam.
**11th century** Immigration by Oghuz Seljuk peoples, from the steppes to the northeast.
**13th–14th centuries** Incorporated within Mongol Empire; the Mongol ruler Tamerlane had his capital at Samarkand.
**16th century** Baku besieged and incorporated within Ottoman Empire, before falling under Persian dominance.
**1805** Khanates (chieftaincies), including Karabakh and Shirvan, which had won independence from Persia, gradually became Russian protectorates, being confirmed by the Treaty of Gulistan, which concluded the 1804–13 First Russo-Iranian War.
**1828** Under Treaty of Turkmenchai, which concluded the Second Russo-Iranian War begun in 1826, Persia was granted control over southern and Russia over northern Azerbaijan.
**late 19th century** Petroleum industry developed, resulting in large influx of Slav immigrants to Baku, which supplied half of Russia's oil needs by 1901.
**1906** Himmat ('Effort') Party, linked to the Russian Social-Democrat Labour Party (Bolshevik), founded in Baku.
**1912** Himmat Party banned; Islamic nationalist Musavat ('Equality') Party formed in Baku.
**1917–18** Member of anti-Bolshevik Transcaucasian Federation.
**1918** Became an independent republic.
**1920** Occupied by Red Army and subsequently forcibly secularized.
**1922–36** Became part of the Transcaucasian Federal Republic with Georgia and Armenia.
**early 1930s** Peasant uprisings against agricultural collectivization and Stalinist purges of the local Communist Party.

**1936** Became a constituent republic of the USSR.

**late 1980s** Growth in nationalist sentiment, taking advantage of the *glasnost* initiative of the reformist Soviet leader Mikhail Gorbachev.

**1988** Riots followed the request of Nagorno-Karabakh, an Armenian-peopled enclave within Azerbaijan, for transfer to Armenia.

**1989** Nagorno-Karabakh was placed under direct rule from Moscow; civil war broke out with Armenia over Nagorno-Karabakh.

**1990** Soviet troops were dispatched to Baku to restore order amid Azeri calls for secession from USSR.

**1991** Independence was declared after the collapse of an anti-Gorbachev coup in Moscow, which had been supported by Azeri communist leadership. Azerbaijan joined the new Commonwealth of Independent States (CIS); Nagorno-Karabakh declared independence.

**1992** Azerbaijan was admitted into the United Nations (UN) and accorded diplomatic recognition by the USA; Albulfaz Elchibey, leader of the nationalist Popular Front, was elected president; there was a renewed campaign to capture Nagorno-Karabakh.

**1993** Elchibey fled a military revolt, and was replaced in a coup by former Communist Party leader Geidar Aliyev, who was later elected president. Rebel military leader Surat Huseynov was appointed prime minister. Nagorno-Karabakh was overtaken by Armenian forces.

**1994** A Nagorno-Karabakh ceasefire was agreed. After a coup attempt, Huseynov was replaced as premier by Fuad Kuliyev. A state of emergency was imposed.

**1995** An attempted coup was foiled. Pro-Aliyev legislature was elected and a market-centred economic reform programme was introduced.

**1996** Kuliyev was replaced by Artur Rasizade.

**1997** There was border fighting with Armenia. Arkady Gukasyan was elected president of Nagorno-Karabakh. Former president Elchibey returned from exile to lead an opposition coalition.

**1998** A new pro-government grouping, Democratic Azerbaijan, was formed. Aliyev was re-elected president in a disputed poll. A Nagorno-Karabakh peace plan was rejected.

**Azeri** or *Azerbaijani,* native of the Azerbaijan region of Iran (population 5,500,000) or of the Republic of Azerbaijan (formerly a Soviet republic) (population 7,145,600). Azeri is a Turkic language belonging to the Altaic family. Of the total population of Azeris, 70% are Shiite Muslims and 30% Sunni Muslims.

**Azores** group of nine islands in the north Atlantic, forming an autonomous region belonging to Portugal; area 2,247 sq km/867 sq mi; population (1991) 237,800. The islands are outlying peaks of the Mid-Atlantic Ridge and are volcanic in origin. Products include sugar cane, coffee, tobacco, and fruit, and wine. There are many hot springs, and the countryside is mountainous and rugged. The climate is moist but mild, and some of the islands are used as winter resorts. The administrative capital is Ponta Delgada on the main island, São Miguel; the other islands are Santa Maria, Terceira, Graciosa, São Jorge, Pico, Faial, Flores, and Corvo.

**Azov, Sea of** (Russian *Azovskoye More,* Latin *Palus Maeotis*), inland sea between Ukraine and Russia, forming a gulf in the northeast of the Black Sea, to which it is connected by the narrow Kerch' Strait. It has an area of 37,555 sq km/14,500 sq mi, and is extremely shallow, with an average depth of only 8 m/26 ft, and nowhere exceeeding 16 m/52 ft. The sea is frozen for four to six months every year. Principal ports include Rostov-na-Donu, Mariupol, Kerch', and Taganrog. The main rivers flowing into the Sea of Azov are the ◊Don, and the Kuban.

**AZT** drug used in the treatment of AIDS; see ◊zidovudine.

**Aztec** member of an American Indian people who migrated south into the valley of Mexico in the AD 1100s, and in 1325 began reclaiming lake marshland to build their capital, Tenochtitlán, on the site now occupied by Mexico City. Under their emperor Montezuma I, who reigned from 1440, the Aztecs created an empire in central Mexico.

After the Spanish conquistador Hernán ◊Cortés landed in 1519, ◊Montezuma II, who reigned from 1502, was killed and Tenochtitlán was destroyed. Nahuatl is the Aztec language; it belongs to the Uto-Aztecan family of languages, and is still spoken by some Mexicans.

# B

**BA** in education, abbreviation for the degree of *Bachelor of Arts*.

**Baader–Meinhof gang** popular name for the West German left-wing guerrilla group the *Rote Armee Fraktion/Red Army Faction*, active from 1968 against what it perceived as US imperialism. The three main founding members were Andreas Baader (1943–1977), Gudrun Ensslin, and Ulrike Meinhof (1934–1976).

**Baal** (Semitic 'lord' or 'owner') divine title given to their chief male gods by the Phoenicians, or Canaanites, of the eastern Mediterranean coast about 1200–332 BC. Their worship as fertility gods, often orgiastic and of a phallic character, was strongly denounced by the Hebrew prophets.

**Babangida, Ibrahim** (1941–   ) Nigerian politician and soldier, president 1985–93. He became head of the Nigerian army in 1983, and in 1985 led a coup against President Muhammadu Buhari, assuming the presidency himself. From 1992 he promised a return to civilian rule but resigned in 1993, his commitment to democracy increasingly in doubt.

**Babbage, Charles** (1792–1871) English mathematician who devised a precursor of the computer. He designed an analytical engine, a general-purpose mechanical computing device for performing different calculations according to a program input on punched cards (an idea borrowed from the ◊Jacquard loom). This device was never built, but it embodied many of the principles on which digital computers are based.

**babbler** bird of the thrush family Muscicapidae with a loud babbling cry. Babblers, subfamily Timaliinae, are found in the Old World, and there are some 250 species in the group.

**Babel** Hebrew name for the city of ◊Babylon, chiefly associated with the *Tower of Babel* which, in the Genesis story in the Old Testament, was erected in the plain of Shinar by the descendants of Noah. It was a ziggurat, or staged temple, seven storeys high (100 m/328 ft) with a shrine of Marduk on the summit. It was built by Nabopolassar, father of Nebuchadnezzar, and was destroyed when Sennacherib sacked the city 689 BC.

**Babi faith** faith from which the ◊Baha'i faith grew.

**babirusa** wild pig *Babirousa babyrussa*, becoming increasingly rare, found in the moist forests and by the water of Sulawesi, Buru, and nearby Indonesian islands. The male has large upper tusks which grow upwards through the skin of the snout and curve back towards the forehead. The babirusa is up to 80 cm/2.5 ft at the shoulder. It is nocturnal, and swims well.

**Babi Yar** ravine near Kiev, Ukraine, where more than 100,000 people (80,000 of whom were Jews, the remainder being Poles, Russians, and Ukrainians) were murdered by the Nazis in 1941. The site was ignored until the Soviet poet Yevgeny ◊Yevtushenko wrote a poem called 'Babi Yar' (1961) in protest at plans for a sports centre on the site.

**baboon** large monkey of the genus *Papio*, with a long doglike muzzle and large canine teeth, spending much of its time on the ground in open country. Males, with head and body up to 1.1 m/3.5 ft long, are larger than females, and dominant males rule the 'troops' in which baboons live. They inhabit Africa and southwestern Arabia.

**Babur** or *Zahir ud-Din Muhammad*, (Arabic 'lion') (1483–1530) first Great Mogul of India from 1526. He was the great-grandson of the Mogul conqueror Tamerlane and, at the age of 11, succeeded his father, Omar Sheikh Mirza, as ruler of Ferghana (Turkestan). In 1526 he defeated the emperor of Delhi at Panipat in the Punjab, captured Delhi and ◊Agra (the site of the Taj Mahal), and established a dynasty that lasted until 1858.

**Babylon** capital of ancient Babylonia, on the bank of the lower Euphrates River. The site is now in Iraq, 88 km/55 mi south of Baghdad and 8 km/5 mi north of Hilla, which is built chiefly of bricks from the ruins of Babylon. The Hanging Gardens of Babylon, one of the ◊Seven Wonders of the World, were probably erected on a vaulted stone base, the only stone construction in the mud-brick city. They formed a series of terraces, irrigated by a hydraulic system.

**Bacall, Lauren** stage name of Betty Joan Perske (1924–   ) US actress. She became an overnight star when cast by Howard Hawks opposite Humphrey Bogart in *To Have and Have Not* (1944). She and Bogart went on to star together in *The Big Sleep* (1946), *The Dark Passage* (1947), and *Key Largo* (1948).

**Bacchus** in Greek and Roman mythology, the god of fertility (see ◊Dionysus) and of wine; his rites (the *Bacchanalia*) were orgiastic.

**Bach, Carl Philip Emanuel** (1714–1788) German composer. He was the third son of Johann Sebastian Bach. He introduced a new 'homophonic' style, light and easy to follow, which influenced Mozart, Haydn, and Beethoven.

**Bach, Johann Christian** (1735–1782) German composer. The eleventh son of J S Bach, he became celebrated in Italy as a composer of operas. In 1762 he was invited to London, where he became music master to the royal family. He remained in England until his death; his great popularity both as a composer and a performer declined in his last years for political and medical reasons.

**Bach, Johann Sebastian** (1685–1750) German composer. A master of ◊counterpoint, his music epitomizes the Baroque polyphonic style. His orchestral music includes the six *Brandenburg Concertos* (1721), other concertos for keyboard instrument and violin, four orchestral suites, sonatas for various instruments, three partitas and three sonatas for violin solo, and six unaccompanied cello suites. Bach's keyboard music, for clavier and organ, his fugues, and his choral music are of equal importance. He also wrote chamber music and songs.

**bacille Calmette-Guérin** tuberculosis vaccine ◊BCG.

**bacillus** member of a group of rodlike ◊bacteria that occur everywhere in the soil and air. Some are responsible for diseases such as ◊anthrax or for causing food spoilage.

**backgammon** board game for two players, often used in gambling. It was known in Mesopotamia, Greece, and Rome and in medieval England.

**background radiation** radiation that is always present in the environment. By far the greater proportion (87%) of it is emitted from natural sources. Alpha and beta particles, and gamma radiation are radiated by the traces of radioactive minerals that occur naturally in the environment and even in the human body, and by radioactive gases such as ◊radon and thoron, which are found in soil and may seep upwards into buildings. Radiation from space (◊cosmic radiation) also contributes to the background level.

**backswimmer** or *water boatman,* aquatic predatory bug living mostly in fresh water. The adults are about 15 mm/0.5 in long and rest upside down at the water surface to breathe. When disturbed they dive, carrying with them a supply of air trapped under the wings. They have piercing beaks, used in feeding on tadpoles and small fish.
*classification* Backswimmers belong to the genus *Notonecta,* family Notonectidae in suborder Heteroptera, order Hemiptera (true bugs), class Insecta, phylum Arthropoda.

**Bacon, Francis** (1909–1992) Irish painter. Self-taught, he practised abstract art, then developed a stark Expressionist style characterized by distorted, blurred figures enclosed in loosely defined space. He aimed to 'bring the figurative thing up onto the nervous system more violently and more poignantly'. One of his best-known works is *Study after Velázquez's Portrait of Pope Innocent X* (1953; Museum of Modern Art, New York).

**Bacon, Francis,** 1st Baron Verulam and Viscount St Albans (1561–1626) English philosopher, politician, and writer, a founder of modern scientific research. His works include *Essays* (1597, revised and augmented 1612 and 1625), characterized by pith and brevity; *The Advancement of Learning* (1605), a seminal work discussing scientific method; *Novum Organum* (1620), in which he redefined the task of natural science, seeing it as a means of empirical discovery and a method of increasing human power over nature; and *The New Atlantis* (1626), describing a utopian state in which scientific knowledge is systematically sought and exploited. He was briefly Lord Chancellor in 1618 but lost his post through corruption.

**Bacon, Roger** (*c.* 1214–1294) English philosopher and scientist. He was interested in alchemy, the biological and physical sciences, and magic. Many discoveries have been credited to him, including the magnifying lens. He foresaw the extensive use of gunpowder and mechanical cars, boats, and planes. Bacon was known as *Doctor Mirabilis* (Wonderful Teacher).

**bacteria** singular bacterium, microscopic single-celled organisms lacking a nucleus. Bacteria are widespread, present in soil, air, and water, and as parasites on and in other living things. Some parasitic bacteria cause disease by producing toxins, but others are harmless and may even benefit their hosts. Bacteria usually reproduce by ◊binary fission (dividing into two equal parts), and this may occur approximately every 20 minutes. Only 4,000 species of bacteria are known (in 1998); bacteriologists believe that around 3 million species may actually exist.

**bacteriophage** virus that attacks ◊bacteria. Such viruses are now of use in genetic engineering.

**Baden** former state of southwestern Germany, which had Karlsruhe as its capital. Baden was captured from the Romans 282 by the Alemanni; later it became a margravate and, in 1806, a grand duchy. A state of the German empire 1871–1918, then a republic, and under Hitler a *Gau* (province), it was divided between the *Länder* of Württemberg-Baden and Baden 1945 and in 1952 made part of ◊Baden-Württemberg.

**Baden-Powell, Robert Stephenson Smyth** 1st Baron Baden-Powell (1857–1941) British general, founder of the ◊Scout Association. He was commander of the garrison during the 217-day siege of Mafeking (now Mafikeng) in the Second South African War (1899–1900). After 1907 he devoted his time to developing the Scout movement, which rapidly spread throughout the world.

**Baden-Württemberg** administrative region (German *Land*) of Germany, bounded to the west by France, to the south by Switzerland, to the east by Bavaria, and to the west by the Rhine valley
*area* 35,800 sq km/13,819 sq mi
*capital* ◊Stuttgart
*towns and cities* Mannheim, Karlsruhe, Freiburg im Breisgau, Heidelberg, Heilbronn, Pforzheim, Ulm
*physical* Black Forest; Rhine boundary south and west; source of the River Danube at Donaueschingen; see also ◊Swabia
*industries* luxury motor vehicles, jewellery, watches, clocks, musical instruments, textiles, chemicals, iron, steel, electrical equipment, surgical instruments, precision engineering

**agriculture** wine production, animal husbandry, fruit growing
**population** (1995) 10,350,000
**history** formed in 1952 (following a plebiscite) by the merger of the *Länder* Baden, Württemberg-Baden, and Württemberg-Hohenzollern.

**badger** large mammal of the weasel family with molar teeth of a crushing type adapted to a partly vegetable diet, and short strong legs with long claws suitable for digging. The Eurasian *common badger Meles meles* is about 1 m/3 ft long, with long, coarse, greyish hair on the back, and a white face with a broad black stripe along each side. Mainly a woodland animal, it is harmless and nocturnal, and spends the day in a system of burrows called a 'sett'. It feeds on roots, a variety of fruits and nuts, insects, worms, mice, and young rabbits.

**badlands** barren landscape cut by erosion into a maze of ravines, pinnacles, gullies and sharp-edged ridges. Areas in South Dakota and Nebraska, USA, are examples.

**badminton** racket game similar to lawn ◊tennis but played on a smaller court and with a shuttlecock (a half sphere of cork or plastic with a feather or nylon skirt) instead of a ball. The object of the game is to prevent the opponent from being able to return the shuttlecock.

**Baffin, William** (1584–1622) English explorer and navigator. In 1616 he and Robert Bylot explored Baffin Bay, northeastern Canada, and reached latitude 77° 45′ N, which for 236 years remained the 'furthest north'.

**Baffin Island** island in Northwest Territories, Canada, situated across the entrance to ◊Hudson Bay; area 507,450 sq km/195,875 sq mi.
**features** Baffin Island is the largest island in the Canadian Arctic; the mountains here rise above 2,000 m/6,000 ft, and there are several large lakes. The northernmost part of the strait separating Baffin Island from Greenland forms Baffin Bay; the southern end is Davis Strait. The predominantly Inuit population is settled mainly around Lake Harbour and Frobisher Bay in the south.

It is named after William Baffin, who carried out research here in 1616 during his search for the ◊Northwest Passage. Sir Martin Frobisher, who landed here in 1576, discovered gold, and there are coal and iron-ore deposits.

**Baghdad** historic city and capital of Iraq, on the River Tigris; population (1987) 3,841,300. Industries include oil refining, distilling, tanning, tobacco processing, and the manufacture of textiles and cement. Founded in 762, it became Iraq's capital in 1921. During the Gulf War of 1991, the UN coalition forces bombed it in repeated air raids.

**bagpipes** any of an ancient family of double-reed folk woodwind instruments employing a bladder filled by the player through a mouthpiece, or bellows as an air reservoir to a 'chanter' or fingered melody pipe, and two or three optional drone pipes providing a continuous accompanying harmony.

**Baha'i Faith** religion founded in the 19th century from a Muslim splinter group, Babism, by the Persian Baha'u'llah. His message in essence was that all great religious leaders are manifestations of the unknowable God and all scriptures are sacred. There is no priesthood: all Baha'is are expected to teach, and to work towards world unification. There are about 6 million Baha'is worldwide.

**Bahamas** Commonwealth of the

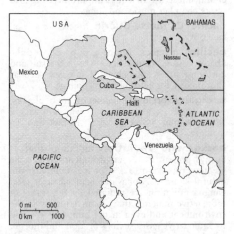

**area** 13,864 sq km/5,352 sq mi
**capital** Nassau (on New Providence Island)
**major towns/cities** Freeport (on Grand Bahama)
**physical features** comprises 700 tropical coral islands and about 1,000 cays; the Exumas are a narrow spine of 365 islands; only 30 of the desert islands are inhabited; Blue Holes of Andros, the world's longest and deepest submarine caves
**principal islands** Andros, Grand Bahama, Abaco, Eleuthera, New Providence, Berry Islands, Bimini Islands, Great Inagua, Acklins Island, Exuma Islands, Mayguana, Crooked Island, Long Island, Cat Islands, Rum Cay, Watling (San Salvador) Island, Inagua Islands
**head of state** Elizabeth II from 1973, represented by governor general Orville Turnquest from 1995
**head of government** Hubert Ingraham from 1992
**political system** constitutional monarchy
**political parties** Progressive Liberal Party (PLP), centrist; Free National Movement (FNM), centre left
**currency** Bahamian dollar
**GNP per capita (PPP)** (US$) 10,460 (1998)
**exports** foodstuffs (fish), oil products and transhipments, chemicals, rum, salt. Principal market: USA 24.5% (1997)
**population** 301,000 (1999 est)
**language** English and some Creole
**religion** Christian 94% (Roman Catholic 26%, Anglican 21%, other Protestant 48%)
**life expectancy** 71 (men); 77 (women) (1995–2000)

## Chronology
**8th–9th centuries AD** Arawak Indians driven northwards to the islands by the Caribs.
**1492** First visited by Christopher Columbus; Arawaks deported to provide cheap labour for the gold and silver mines of Cuba and Hispaniola (Haiti).
**1629** English king Charles I granted the islands to Robert Heath.
**1666** Colonization of New Providence island began.
**1783** Recovered after brief Spanish occupation and became a British colony, being settled during the American War of Independence by American loyalists, who brought with them black slaves.
**1838** Slaves were emancipated.
**1940–45** The Duke of Windsor, the former King Edward VIII, was governor of Bahamas.
**from 1950s** Major development of the tourist trade, especially from the USA.
**1964** Became internally self-governing.
**1967** First national assembly elections; Lynden Pindling, of the centrist Progressive Liberal Party (PLP), became prime minister.
**1973** Full independence was achieved within the British Commonwealth.
**1983** Allegations of drug trafficking were made against government ministers.
**1984** The deputy prime minister and two cabinet ministers resigned. Pindling denied any personal involvement and was endorsed as party leader.
**1992** A centre-left Free National Movement (FNM) led by Hubert Ingraham won an absolute majority in assembly elections, ending 25 years of rule by Pindling.

**Bahawalpur** city in Punjab, Pakistan, situated on the Sutlej River 350 km/220 mi southwest of Lahore; population (1981) 178,000. Once the capital of the former Indian princely state of Bahawalpur, it is now an industrial city producing textiles and soap. The university was established in 1975.

**Bahrain** State of
*national name Dawlat al Bahrayn*

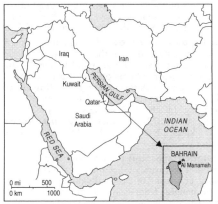

**area** 688 sq km/266 sq mi
**capital** Al Manamah on the largest island (also called Bahrain)

**major towns/cities** Muharraq, Jiddhafs, Isa Town, Hidd, Rifa'a, Sitra
**major ports** Mina Sulman
**physical features** archipelago of 35 islands in Arabian Gulf, composed largely of sand-covered limestone; generally poor and infertile soil; flat and hot; causeway linking Bahrain to mainland Saudi Arabia
**head of state** Sheikh Hamad bin Isa al-Khalifa from 1999
**head of government** Sheikh Khalifa bin Salman al-Khalifa from 1970
**political system** absolute emirate
**political parties** none
**currency** Bahraini dinar
**GNP per capita (PPP)** (US$) 13,700 (1998 est)
**exports** petroleum and petroleum products, aluminium, chemicals (1996). Principal market: India 14% (1997)
**population** 607,000 (1999 est)
**language** Arabic (official); Farsi, English, Urdu
**religion** 85% Muslim (Shiite 60%, Sunni 40%), Christian; Islam is the state religion
**life expectancy** 71 (men); 75 (women) (1995–2000)

## Chronology
**4th century AD** Became part of Persian (Iranian) Sassanian Empire.
**7th century** Adopted Islam.
**8th century** Came under Arab Abbasid control.
**1521** Seized by Portugal and held for eight decades, despite local unrest.
**1602** Fell under the control of a Persian Shiite dynasty.
**1783** Overthrew Persian rule and became a sheikdom under the Sunni Muslim al-Khalifa dynasty, which originated from the same tribal federation, the Anaza, as the al-Saud family, who now rule Saudi Arabia.
**1816–20** Friendship and peace treaties signed with Britain, which sought to end piracy in the Gulf.
**1861** Became British protectorate, government shared between the ruling sheikh (Arab leader) and a British adviser.
**1923** British influence increased when Sheikh Isa al-Khalifa was deposed and Charles Belgrave was appointed as the dominating 'adviser' to the new ruler.
**1928** Sovereignty claimed by Persia (Iran).
**1930s** Oil discovered, providing backbone for country's wealth.
**1953–56** Council for National Unity was formed by Arab nationalists, but suppressed after large demonstrations against British participation in the Suez War.
**1961** Sheikh Isa bin Sulman al-Khalifa succeeded his father, Sheikh Sulman, as head of state.
**1968** Britain announced its intention to withdraw its forces. Bahrain formed, with Qatar and the Trucial States of the United Arab Emirates, the Federation of Arab Emirates.
**1970** Iran accepted a United Nations (UN) report showing that Bahrain's inhabitants preferred independence to Iranian control.
**1971** Qatar and the Trucial States withdrew from the federation; Bahrain became an

independent state under Sheikh Isa bin Sulman al-Khalifa, who assumed the title of Emir.

**1973** New constitution adopted, with an elected national assembly dominated by left-nationalist Bahrain National Liberation Front (BNLF).

**1975** Prime minister Sheikh al-Khalifa, the Emir's brother, resigned; national assembly dissolved and political activists driven underground. Emir and his family assumed virtually absolute power.

**early 1980s** Tensions between the Sunni and Shiite Muslim communities heightened by Iranian Shiite Revolution of 1979.

**1986** Gulf University established in Bahrain. Causeway opened linking the island with Saudi Arabia.

**1991** Bahrain joined a UN coalition that ousted Iraq from its occupation of Kuwait, and signed a defence cooperation agreement with the USA.

**1994** There were antimonarchy protests by the Shiite Muslim majority community.

**1995** Sheikh al-Khalifa was reappointed prime minister. Prodemocracy demonstrations were violently suppressed, with 11 deaths.

**1999** Sheikh Isa bin Sulman al-Khalifa died. Sheikh Hamad succeeded his father as Emir and head of state.

**Baikal, Lake** Russian *Baykal Ozero,* freshwater lake in southern Siberia, Russia, the largest in Asia, and the eighth largest in the world (area 31,500 sq km/12,150 sq mi). Lake Baikal is also the world's deepest lake (up to 1,640 m/5,700 ft) and its oldest, having existed for over 25 million years. It extends for some 636 km/395 mi, and has an average width of 48 km/30 mi. Fed by more than 300 rivers, the main one of which is the Selenga, it is drained only by the Lower Angara. Lake Baikal is famous for its great clarity and the diversity of its fauna.

**bail** the temporary setting at liberty of a person in legal custody on an undertaking (usually backed by some security, bonds or money, given either by that person or by someone else) to attend at a court at a stated time and place. If the person does not attend, the bail may be forfeited.

**Baird, John Logie** (1888–1946) Scottish electrical engineer who pioneered television. In 1925 he gave the first public demonstration of television, transmitting an image of a recognizable human face. The following year, he gave the world's first demonstration of true television before an audience of about 50 scientists at the Royal Institution, London. By 1928 Baird had succeeded in demonstrating colour television.

**Baja California** mountainous peninsula that forms the twin northwestern states of Lower (Spanish *baja*) California, Mexico; Baja California Norte in the north, and Baja California Sur in the south.

**Bakelite** first synthetic ◊plastic, created by Leo Baekeland in 1909. Bakelite is hard, tough, and heatproof, and is used as an electrical insulator. It is made by the reaction of phenol with formaldehyde, producing a powdery resin that sets solid when heated. Objects are made by subjecting the resin to compression moulding (simultaneous heat and pressure in a mould).

**Baker, James Addison III** (1930– ) US Republican politician. Under President Ronald Reagan, he was White House chief of staff 1981–85 and treasury secretary 1985–88. After managing George Bush's successful presidential campaign, Baker was appointed secretary of state in 1989 and played a prominent role in the 1990–91 Gulf crisis and the subsequent search for a lasting Middle East peace settlement. In 1992 he left the state department to become White House chief of staff and to oversee Bush's unsuccessful re-election campaign. In 1997 he served as a UN special envoy to try and broker a peace settlement for the disrupted territory of Western Sahara.

**Baker, Kenneth Wilfrid** (1934– ) British Conservative politician, home secretary 1990–92. He was environment secretary 1985–86, education secretary 1986–89, and chair of the Conservative Party 1989–90, retaining his cabinet seat, before becoming home secretary in John Major's government. After his dismissal in 1992, he became a frequent government critic. He retired from Parliament in 1997.

**Baker, Norma Jean** US film actress; see Marilyn ◊Monroe.

**Baku** capital city of the republic of Azerbaijan, located on the Apsheron Peninsula on the western shore of the Caspian Sea. Baku is an important industrial city and port. It has been a major centre of oil extraction and refining since the 1870s; the oilfields here are linked by pipelines with the Georgian Black Sea port of Batumi, while petroleum exports to Russia are shipped across the Caspian to Astrakhan. Heavy engineering enterprises in the city produce equipment for the oil industry and ships; light industries include leather tanning and food processing. Baku has a hot climate and is subject to strong northwest winds.

**Bakunin, Mikhail** (1814–1876) Russian anarchist, active in Europe. In 1848 he was expelled from France as a revolutionary agitator. In Switzerland in the 1860s he became recognized as the leader of the anarchist movement. In 1869 he joined the First International (a co-ordinating socialist body) but, after stormy conflicts with Karl Marx, was expelled 1872.

**Balaclava, Battle of** a Russian attack on 25 October 1854, during the Crimean War, on British positions, near a town in Ukraine, 10 km/6 mi southeast of Sevastopol. It was the scene of the ill-timed *Charge of the Light Brigade* of British cavalry against the Russian entrenched artillery. Of the 673 soldiers who took part, there were 272 casualties. *Balaclava helmets* were knitted hoods worn here by soldiers in the bitter weather.

**balance** apparatus for weighing or measuring mass. The various types include the *beam balance,* consisting of a centrally pivoted lever with pans hanging from each end, and the *spring balance,* in which the object to be weighed stretches (or compresses) a vertical coil spring fitted with a pointer that indicates the weight on a scale. Kitchen and bathroom scales are balances.

**balance of nature** in ecology, the idea that there is an inherent equilibrium in most ecosystems, with plants and animals interacting so as to produce a stable, continuing system of life on Earth. The activities of human beings can, and frequently do, disrupt the balance of nature.

**balance of payments** in economics, an account of a country's debit and credit transactions with other countries. Items are divided into the *current account*, which includes both visible trade (imports and exports of goods) and invisible trade (services such as transport, tourism, interest, and dividends), and the *capital account*, which includes investment in and out of the country, international grants, and loans. Deficits or surpluses on these accounts are brought into balance by buying and selling reserves of foreign currencies.

**balance of power** in politics, the theory that the best way of ensuring international order is to have power so distributed among states that no single state is able to achieve a dominant position. The term, which may also refer more simply to the actual distribution of power, is one of the most enduring concepts in international relations. Since the development of nuclear weapons, it has been asserted that the balance of power has been replaced by a 'balance of terror'.

**Balanchine, George** born Georgi Melitonovich Balanchivadze (1904–1983) Russian-born US choreographer. After leaving the USSR 1924, he worked with ◊Diaghilev in France. Moving to the USA 1933, he became a major influence on dance, starting the New York City Ballet 1948. He was the most influential 20th-century choreographer of ballet in the USA. He developed an 'American Neo-Classic' dance style and made the New York City Ballet one of the world's great companies. His ballets are usually plotless and are performed in practice clothes to modern music. He also choreographed dances for five Hollywood films.

**Balboa, Vasco Núñez de** (1475–1519) Spanish ◊conquistador. He founded a settlement at Darien (now Panama) 1511 and crossed the Isthmus in search of gold, reaching the Pacific Ocean (which he called the South Sea) on 25 September 1513, after a 25-day expedition. He was made admiral of the Pacific and governor of Panama but was removed by Spanish court intrigue, imprisoned, and executed.

**Baldwin, James Arthur** (1924–1987) US writer and civil-rights activist. He portrayed with vivid intensity the suffering and despair of African-Americans in contemporary society. After his first novel, *Go Tell it on the Mountain* (1953), set in Harlem, and *Giovanni's Room* (1956), about a homosexual relationship in Paris, his writing became more politically indignant with *Another Country* (1962) and *The Fire Next Time* (1963), a collection of essays.

**Baldwin, Stanley** 1st Earl Baldwin of Bewdley (1867–1947) British Conservative politician, prime minister 1923–24, 1924–29, and 1935–37. He weathered the general strike of 1926, secured complete adult suffrage in 1928, and handled the ◊abdication crisis of

Edward VIII in 1936, but failed to prepare Britain for World War II.

**Balearic Islands** Spanish *Baleares,* group of Mediterranean islands forming an autonomous region of Spain; including ◊Mallorca, ◊Menorca, ◊Ibiza, Cabrera, and Formentera
*area* 5,014 sq km/1,936 sq mi
*capital* Palma de Mallorca
*industries* figs, olives, oranges, wine, brandy, coal, iron, slate; tourism is crucial
*population* (1991) 709,100
*history* held successively by Greeks and Carthaginians, the islands became a Roman colony from 123 BC, and an independent Moorish kingdom from 1009 until 1232; they were incorporated into the Christian Spanish kingdom of Aragón in 1349.

**Balfour, Arthur James** 1st Earl of Balfour (1848–1930) British Conservative politician, born in Scotland, prime minister 1902–05, and foreign secretary 1916–19. He issued the Balfour Declaration 1917 and was involved in peace negotiations after World War I, signing the Treaty of Versailles.

**Balfour Declaration** letter, dated 2 November 1917, from British foreign secretary A J Balfour to Lord Rothschild (chair, British Zionist Federation) stating: 'HM government view with favour the establishment in Palestine of a national home for the Jewish people.' It helped form the basis for the foundation of Israel in 1948.

**Bali** island of Indonesia, east of Java, one of the Sunda Islands; area 5,800 sq km/2,240 sq mi; population (1990) 2,777,800. The capital is Denpasar. The island features volcanic mountains. Industries include gold and silver work, woodcarving, weaving, copra, salt, coffee, and tourism, with 1 million tourists a year (1990); arts include Balinese dancing, music, and drama. Bali's Hindu culture goes back to the 7th century; the Dutch gained control of the island by 1908.

**Baliol, John de** or *Balliol* (c. 1249–1315) King of Scotland 1292–96. As an heir to the Scottish throne on the death of Margaret, the Maid of Norway, he had the support of the English king, Edward I, against 12 other claimants. Baliol was proclaimed king, having paid homage to Edward. When English forces attacked Scotland, Baliol rebelled against England and gave up the kingdom.

**Balkans** (Turkish 'mountains') peninsula of southeastern Europe, stretching into Slovenia between the Adriatic and Aegean seas, comprising Albania, Bosnia-Herzegovina, Bulgaria, Croatia, Greece, Romania, the part of Turkey in Europe, and Yugoslavia. It is joined to the rest of Europe by an isthmus 1,200 km/750 mi wide between Rijeka on the west and the mouth of the Danube on the Black Sea to the east.

**Balkan Wars** two wars 1912–13 and 1913 (preceding World War I) which resulted in the expulsion by the Balkan states of Ottoman Turkey from Europe, except for a small area around Istanbul.

**Balkhash, Lake** lake in eastern Kazakhstan, the eastern half of which is salty, and the western half fresh; area 17,400 sq km/6,715 sq mi. Lake Balkhash is 600 km/375 mi long and is fed by several rivers, including the Karatal, Lepsy and Ili, but has no outlet. It is very shallow, especially in the east, and is frozen throughout the winter (November–mid-April).

**Ball, John** (died c. 1381) English priest. He was one of the leaders of the ◊Peasants' Revolt of 1381, known as 'the mad priest of Kent'. A follower of John ◊Wycliffe and a believer in social equality, he was imprisoned for disagreeing with the archbishop of Canterbury. During the revolt he was released from prison, and when in Blackheath, London, incited people against the ruling classes by preaching from the text 'When Adam delved and Eve span, who was then the gentleman?' When the revolt collapsed he escaped but was captured near Coventry and executed.

**ballad** (Latin *ballare* 'to dance') form of traditional narrative poetry, widespread in Europe and the USA. Ballads are metrically simple, sometimes (as in Russia) unstrophic and unrhymed or (as in Denmark) dependent on assonance. Concerned with some strongly emotional event, the ballad is halfway between the lyric and the epic. Most English ballads date from the 15th century but may describe earlier events. Poets of the Romantic movement both in England and in Germany were greatly influenced by the ballad revival, as seen in, for example, the *Lyrical Ballads* (1798) of ◊Wordsworth and ◊Coleridge. *Des Knaben Wunderhorn/The Boy's Magic Horn* (1805–08), a collection edited by Clemens Brentano and Achim von Arnim, was a major influence on 19th-century German poetry. The ballad form was adapted in 'broadsheets', with a satirical or political motive, and in the 'hanging' ballads purporting to come from condemned criminals.

**ballade** in literature, a poetic form developed in France in the later Middle Ages from the ballad, generally consisting of one or more groups of three stanzas of seven or eight lines each, followed by a shorter stanza or envoy, the last line being repeated as a chorus. In music, a ballade is an instrumental piece based on a story; a form used in piano works by Chopin and Liszt.

**Balladur, Edouard** (1929– ) French Conservative politician, prime minister 1993–95. During his first year of 'co-habitation' with socialist president François Mitterrand he demonstrated the sureness of his political touch, retaining popular support despite active opposition to some of his more right-wing policies. He unsuccessfully contested the presidency 1995. He is a supporter of the European Union and of the maintainance of close relations between France and Germany.

**ball-and-socket joint** joint allowing considerable movement in three dimensions, for instance the joint between the pelvis and the femur. To facilitate movement, such joints are rimmed with cartilage and lubricated by synovial fluid. The bones are kept in place by ligaments and moved by muscles.

**Ballesteros, Seve(riano)** (1957– ) Spanish golfer. He came to prominence 1976 and has won several leading tournaments in the USA, including the Masters Tournament 1980 and 1983. He has also won the British Open three times: in 1979, 1984, and 1988.

*career highlights*
*British Open* 1979, 1984, 1988
*Ryder Cup* individual: 1979, 1983, 1985, 1987, 1989, 1991, 1993, 1995; team: 1985, 1987, tie 1989, 1995
*PGA Championship* 1983, 1991
*US Masters* 1980, 1983
*World Match-Play Championship* 1981–82, 1984–85, 1991, captain of 1997 Europe *Ryder Cup* team

**ballet** (Italian *balletto* 'a little dance') theatrical representation in ◊dance form in which music also plays a major part in telling a story or conveying a mood. Some such form of entertainment existed in ancient Greece, but Western ballet as we know it today first appeared in Renaissance Italy, where it was a court entertainment. From there it was brought by Catherine de' Medici to France in the form of a spectacle combining singing, dancing, and declamation. During the 18th century, there were major developments in technique and ballet gradually became divorced from opera, emerging as an art form in its own right.

In the 20th century Russian ballet has had a vital influence on the classical tradition in the West, and ballet developed further in the USA through the work of George Balanchine and the American Ballet Theater, and in the UK through the influence of Marie Rambert.

◊Modern dance is a separate development.

**ballistics** study of the motion and impact of projectiles such as bullets, bombs, and missiles. For projectiles from a gun, relevant exterior factors include temperature, barometric pressure, and wind strength; and for nuclear missiles these extend to such factors as the speed at which the Earth turns.

**balloon** lighter-than-air craft that consists of a gasbag filled with gas lighter than the surrounding air and an attached basket, or gondola, for carrying passengers and/or instruments. In 1783, the first successful human ascent was in Paris, in a hot-air balloon designed by the ◊Montgolfier brothers Joseph Michel and Jacques Etienne. In 1785, a hydrogen-filled balloon designed by French physicist Jacques Charles travelled across the English Channel.

**ballot** (Italian *ballotta*, diminutive of *balla*, 'a ball') the process of voting in an election. In political elections in democracies ballots are usually secret: voters indicate their choice of candidate on a voting slip that is placed in a sealed ballot box. *Ballot rigging* is a term used to describe elections that are fraudulent because of interference with the voting process or the counting of ◊votes.

**ballroom dancing** collective term for social dances such as the ◊foxtrot, quickstep, ◊tango, and ◊waltz.

**ball valve** valve that works by the action of external pressure raising a ball and thereby opening a hole.

**balm, lemon** garden herb, see ◊lemon balm.

**balsam** any of various garden plants belonging to the balsam family. They are usually annuals with spurred red or white flowers and pods that burst and scatter their seeds when ripe. (Genus *Impatiens*, family Balsaminaceae.)

In medicine and perfumery, balsam refers to various oily or gummy aromatic plant ◊resins, such as balsam of Peru from the Central American tree *Myroxylon pereirae*.

**Baltic Sea** shallow sea, extending northeast from the narrow Skagerrak and Kattegat, between Sweden and Denmark, to the Gulf of Bothnia between Sweden and Finland. Its coastline is 8,000 km/5,000 mi long; the sea is 1,500 km/930 mi long and 650 km/404 mi wide, and its area, including the gulfs of Riga, Finland, and Bothnia, is 422,300 sq km/163,000 sq mi. Its average depth is 65 m/213 ft, but is 460 m/1,500 ft at its deepest.

Its shoreline is shared by Denmark, Germany, Poland, the Baltic States, Russia, Finland, and Sweden.

**Baltic States** collective name for the states of Estonia, Latvia, and Lithuania. They were formed as independent states after World War I out of former territories of the Russian Empire. The government of the USSR recognized their independence in peace treaties signed in 1920, but in 1939 forced them to allow occupation of important military bases by Soviet troops. In the following year, the Baltic states were absorbed into the Soviet Union as constituent republics. They regained their independence in September 1991 after the collapse of the Soviet Union.

**Baltimore** industrial port and largest city in Maryland, USA, on the western shore of Chesapeake Bay, 50 km/31 mi northeast of Washington, DC; population (1994 est) 703,000; metropolitan area (1992) 2,434,000. Industries include shipbuilding, oil refining, food processing, and the manufacture of steel, chemicals, and aerospace equipment. The city was named after the founder of Maryland, Lord Baltimore (1579–1632). Baltimore dates from 1729 and was incorporated as a city in 1797.

**Baltistan** region in the ◊Karakoram range of northeast Kashmir, western Ladakh, held by Pakistan since 1949. The region lies to the south of K2, the world's second highest mountain (8611 m/28,2161 ft); the average elevation is 3,350 m/11,000 ft. It contains the upper reaches of the Indus River. It is the home of Balti Muslims of Tibetan origin.

**Baluchistan** mountainous desert area, comprising a province of Pakistan, part of the Iranian province of Sistán and Balúchestan, and a small area of Afghanistan. The Pakistani province has an area of 347,200 sq km/134,019 sq mi and a population (1993 est) of 6,520,000; its capital is Quetta. Sistán and Balúchestan has an area of 181,600 sq km/70,098 sq mi and a population (1986) of 1,197,000; its capital is Zahedan. The Quetta region has become important for fruitgrowing. Coal, natural gas, chrome and other minerals have been discovered and exploited. The 1,600 km/1,000 mi rail network has strategic as well as economic significance.

**Balzac, Honoré de** (1799–1850) French writer. He was one of the major novelists of the 19th century. His first success was *Les Chouans/The Chouans,* inspired by Walter Scott. This was the beginning of the long series of novels *La Comédie humaine/The Human Comedy* which includes *Eugénie Grandet* 1833, *Le Père Goriot* 1834, and *Cousine Bette* 1846. He also wrote the Rabelaisian *Contes drolatiques/Ribald Tales* 1833.

**Bamako** capital and port of Mali on the River Niger; population (1992) 746,000. It produces pharmaceuticals, chemicals, textiles, food products, beer, tobacco, and metal products. The Grand Mosque, Malian Museum, and BCEAO Tower are situated here.

**bamboo** any of a large group of giant grass plants, found mainly in tropical and subtropical regions. Some species grow as tall as 36 m/120 ft. The stems are hollow and jointed and can be used in furniture, house, and boat construction. The young shoots are edible; paper is made from the stems. (Genus *Bambusa,* family Gramineae.)

**banana** any of several treelike tropical plants which grow up to 8 m/25 ft high. The edible banana is the fruit of a sterile hybrid form. (Genus *Musa,* family Musaceae.)

**Banda, Hastings Kamuzu** (1905–1997) Malawi politician, physician, and president (1966–94). He led his country's independence movement and was prime minister of Nyasaland (the former name of Malawi) from 1964. He became Malawi's first president in 1966 and was named president for life in 1971; his rule was authoritarian. Having bowed to opposition pressure and opened the way for a pluralist system, Banda stood in the first free presidential elections for 30 years in 1994, but was defeated by Bakili Muluzi. In January 1996 he and his former aide, John Tembo, were acquitted of the murders of three senior politicians and a lawyer in 1983.

**Bandaranaike, Sirimavo** born Ratwatte (1916–    ) Sri Lankan politician, prime minister from 1994. She succeeded her husband Solomon Bandaranaike to become the world's first female prime minister, 1960–65 and 1970–77, but was expelled from parliament in 1980 for abuse of her powers while in office. Her daughter Chandrika Bandaranaike Kumaratunga was elected president in 1994.

**Bandar Seri Begawan** formerly (until 1970) *Brunei Town,* capital and largest town of ◊Brunei, 14 km/9 mi from the mouth of the Brunei River; population (1992) 55,000. Industries include oil refining and construction.

**bandicoot** small marsupial mammal inhabiting Australia and New Guinea. There are about

11 species, family Peramelidae, rat- or rabbit-sized, and living in burrows. They have long snouts, eat insects, and are nocturnal. A related group, the rabbit bandicoots or bilbies, is reduced to a single species that is now endangered and protected by law.

**banding** in UK education, the division of school pupils into broad streams by ability. Banding is used by some local authorities to ensure that comprehensive schools receive an intake of children spread right across the ability range. It is used internally by some schools as a means of avoiding groups of widely mixed ability.

**Bandung** commercial city and capital of Jawa Barat (West Java) province on the island of Java, Indonesia; population (1990) 2,026,900. Bandung is the third-largest city in Indonesia and was the administrative centre when the country was the Netherlands East Indies.

**Bangalore** capital of ◊Karnataka state, southern India, lying 950 m/3,000 ft above sea-level; population (1991) 4,087,000. Industries include electronics, aircraft and machine-tools construction, and coffee. Bangalore University and the University of Agriculture Sciences were founded in 1964, and the National Aeronautical Institute in 1960.

**Bangkok** (Thai *Krung Thep* 'City of Angels') capital and port of Thailand, on the River Chao Phraya; population (1993) 5,572,700. Products include paper, ceramics, cement, textiles, aircraft, and silk. It is the headquarters of the Southeast Asia Treaty Organization (SEATO).

**Bangladesh** People's Republic of (formerly *East Pakistan*)
*national name* Gana Prajatantri Bangladesh

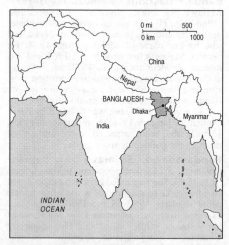

*area* 144,000 sq km/55,598 sq mi
*capital* Dhaka (formerly Dacca)
*major towns/cities* Rajshahi, Khulna, Chittagong, Comilla, Barisal, Sylhet
*major ports* Chittagong, Khulna
*physical features* flat delta of rivers Ganges (Padma) and Brahmaputra (Jamuna), the largest estuarine delta in the world; annual rainfall of 2,540 mm/100 in; some 75% of the land is less than 3 m/10 ft above sea level; hilly in extreme southeast and northeast
*head of state* Abdur Rahman Biswas from 1991
*head of government* Sheikh Hasina Wazed from 1996
*holitical system* emergent democracy
*holitical parties* Bangladesh Nationalist Party (BNP), Islamic, right of centre; Awami League (AL), secular, moderate socialist; Jatiya Dal (National Party), Islamic nationalist
*currency* taka
*GNP per capita (PPP)* (US$) 1,100 (1998)
*exports* raw jute and jute goods, tea, clothing, leather and leather products, shrimps and frogs' legs. Principal market: USA 33.3% (1997)
*population* 126,948,000 (1999 est)
*language* Bengali (official); English
*religion* Sunni Muslim 85%, Hindu 12%; Islam is the state religion
*life expectancy* 58 (men); 58 (women) (1995–2000)
*Chronology*
*c. 1000 BC* Arrival of Bang tribe in lower Ganges valley, establishing the kingdom of Banga (Bengal).
*8th–12th centuries AD* Bengal ruled successively by the Buddhist Pala and Hindu Senha dynasties.
*1199* Bengal was invaded and briefly ruled by the Muslim Khiljis from Central Asia.
*1517* Portuguese merchants arrived in Chittagong.
*1576* Bengal conquered by Muslim Mogul emperor Akbar.
*1651* British East India Company established a commercial factory in Bengal.
*1757* Bengal came under de facto British rule after Robert Clive defeated the nawab (ruler) of Bengal at Battle of Plassey.
*1905–12* Bengal briefly partitioned by the British Raj between a Muslim-dominated east and Hindu-dominated west.
*1906* Muslim League (ML) founded in Dhaka.
*1947* Bengal formed into eastern province of Pakistan on partition of British India, with ML administration in power.
*1952* 12 students killed by troops in anti-Urdu and pro-Bengali language riots in Dhaka.
*1954* The opposition United Front, dominated by the Awami League (AL) and campaigning for East Bengal's autonomy, trounced ML in elections.
*1955* East Bengal renamed East Pakistan.
*1966* Sheikh Mujibur Rahman of AL announced a Six-Point Programme of autonomy for East Pakistan.
*1970* 500,000 people killed in cyclone. Pro-autonomy AL secured crushing electoral victory in East Pakistan.
*1971* Bangladesh ('land of the Bangla speakers') emerged as independent nation, under leadership of Sheikh Mujibur Rahman, after bloody civil war with Indian military intervention on the side of East Pakistan; 10 million refugees fled to India.
*1974* Hundreds of thousands died in famine; state of emergency declared.

**1975** Mujibur Rahman assassinated. Martial law imposed.
**1976–77** Maj-Gen Zia ur-Rahman assumed power as president.
**1978–79** Elections held and civilian rule restored with clear victory for Zia's BNP.
**1981** Maj-Gen Zia assassinated during attempted military coup. Abdul Sattar (BNP) elected president.
**1982** Lt-Gen Hussain Mohammed Ershad assumed power in army coup. Martial law re-imposed; market-oriented economic programme adopted.
**1986** Elections held but disputed and boycotted by BNP. Martial law ended.
**1987** State of emergency declared in response to opposition demonstrations and violent strikes.
**1988** Assembly elections boycotted by main opposition parties. State of emergency lifted. Islam made state religion. Monsoon floods left 30 million homeless and thousands dead.
**1989** Power devolved to Chittagong Hill Tracts to end 14-year conflict between local people and army-protected settlers.
**1990** Following mass antigovernment protests, President Ershad resigned; chief justice Shahabuddin Ahmad became interim president.
**1991** Former president Ershad was jailed for corruption and illegal possession of arms. A cyclone killed around 139,000 people and left up to 10 million homeless. Parliamentary government was restored, with Abdur Rahman Biswas president and Begum Khaleda Zia prime minister.
**1994–95** The opposition boycotted parliament, charging the government with fraud.
**1996** Zia handed power to a neutral caretaker government. A general election was won by the AL, led by Sheika Hasina Wazed, daughter of Sheikh Mujibur Rahman. The BNP boycotted parliament. An agreement was made with India on the sharing of River Ganges water.
**1997** Former president Ershad was released from prison. The BNP boycotted parliament in protest against government 'repression'.
**1998** The BNP ended its boycott of parliament. Two-thirds of Bangladesh was devastated by floods; 1,300 people were killed; damages reached $900 million. Corruption charges were filed against ex-premier Begum Khaleda Zia. Opposition-supported general strikes sought the removal of Sheikh Hasina's government. Fifteen former army officers were sentenced to death for the 1975 assassination of President Sheikh Mujibur Rahman.

**Bangui** capital and main river port of the Central African Republic, on the River Ubangi; population (1988) 597,000. The city is the centre for the country's light industries, including beer, cigarettes, office machinery, and timber and metal products. Bangui also contains the main depot for the storage and transportation of imported petroleum products.

**banjo** resonant stringed musical instrument with a long fretted neck and circular drum-type soundbox covered on the topside only by stretched skin (now usually plastic). It is played with a plectrum. Modern banjos normally have five strings.

**Banjul** capital and chief port of Gambia, on an island at the mouth of the River Gambia; population of urban area (1986) 150,000; city 42,300 (1993). Established 1816 as a settlement for freed slaves, it was known as Bathurst until 1973. Industries include peanut processing and exporting, brewing, and tourism (centred at the nearby resorts of Bakau, Fajara, Kotu, and Kololi).

**bank** financial institution that uses funds deposited with it to lend money to companies or individuals, and also provides financial services to its customers. The first banks opened in Italy and Cataluña around 1400.

**Bank of Commerce and Credit International** (BCCI) international bank, founded 1972. By 1990 BCCI had offices in 69 countries, $15 billion in deposits, and $20 billion in assets. In July 1991 evidence of widespread systematic fraud at BCCI led regulators in seven countries to seize the bank's assets, and its operations in the remaining 62 countries were gradually also shut down. A subsequent investigation resulted in a New York criminal indictment of the institution and four of its units, and the arrest of some 20 BCCI officials in Abu Dhabi for alleged fraud.

**Bank of England** UK central bank founded by act of Parliament in 1694. It was entrusted with issuing bank notes in 1844 and nationalized in 1946. It is banker to the clearing banks and the UK government.

**bankruptcy** process by which the property of a person (in legal terms, an individual or corporation) unable to pay debts is taken away under a court order and divided fairly among the person's creditors, after preferential payments such as taxes and wages. Proceedings may be instituted either by the debtor (voluntary bankruptcy) or by any creditor for a substantial sum (involuntary bankruptcy). Until 'discharged', a bankrupt is severely restricted in financial activities.

**banksia** any shrub or tree of a group native to Australia, including the honeysuckle tree. They are named after the British naturalist and explorer Joseph Banks. (Genus *Banksia*, family Proteaceae.)

**Bannister, Roger Gilbert** (1929– ) English track and field athlete. He was the first person to run a mile in under four minutes. He achieved this feat at Oxford, England, on 6 May 1954, in a time of 3 min 59.4 sec.
*career highlights*
*world records* 4 x 1 mile relay (member of GB & NI squad) 1953; 1 mile 1954
*Commonwealth Games* gold 1 mile 1954
*European championship* silver 800 metres 1950; gold 1,500 metres 1954

**Bannockburn, Battle of** battle fought on 24 June 1314 at Bannockburn, Scotland, between Robert (I) the Bruce, King of Scotland, and Edward II of England. The defeat of the English led to the independence of Scotland.

**bantam** small ornamental variety of domestic chicken weighing about 0.5–1 kg/1–2 lb. Bantams can either be a small version of one of the larger breeds, or a separate type. Some are prolific egg layers. Bantam cocks have a reputation as spirited fighters.

**Banting, Frederick Grant** (1891–1941) Canadian physician. He discovered a technique for isolating the hormone insulin 1921 when he and his colleague Charles ◊Best tied off the ducts of the ◊pancreas to determine the function of the cells known as the islets of Langerhans. This made possible the treatment of diabetes. Banting and John J R Macleod (1876–1935), his mentor, shared the 1923 Nobel Prize for Physiology or Medicine, and Banting divided his prize with Best.

**Bantu languages** group of related languages belonging to the Niger-Congo family, spoken widely over the greater part of Africa south of the Sahara, including Swahili, Xhosa, and Zulu. Meaning 'people' in Zulu, the word Bantu itself illustrates a characteristic use of prefixes: *mu-ntu* 'man', *ba-ntu* 'people'.

**Bantustan** or *homeland*, name until 1978 for a ◊Black National State in the Republic of South Africa.

**banyan** tropical Asian fig tree. It produces aerial roots that grow down from its spreading branches, forming supporting pillars that look like separate trunks. (*Ficus benghalensis,* family Moraceae.)

**baobab** tree with rootlike branches, hence the nickname 'upside-down tree', and a disproportionately thick girth, up to 9 m/30 ft in diameter. The pulp of its fruit is edible and is known as monkey bread. (Genus *Adansonia,* family Bombacaceae.)

**baptism** (Greek 'to dip') immersion in or sprinkling with water as a religious rite of initiation. It was practised long before the beginning of Christianity. In the Christian baptism ceremony, sponsors or godparents make vows on behalf of the child, which are renewed by the child at confirmation. It is one of the seven sacraments. The *amrit* ceremony in Sikhism is sometimes referred to as baptism.

**Baptist** member of any of several Protestant and evangelical Christian sects that practise baptism by immersion only upon profession of faith. Baptists seek their authority in the Bible. They originated among English Dissenters who took refuge in the Netherlands in the early 17th century, and spread by emigration and, later, missionary activity. Of the world total of approximately 31 million, some 26.5 million are in the USA and 265,000 in the UK.

**barb** general name for fish of the genus *Barbus* and some related genera of the family Cyprinidae. As well as the ◊barbel, barbs include many small tropical Old World species, some of which are familiar aquarium species. They are active egg-laying species, usually of 'typical' fish shape and with barbels at the corner of the mouth.

**Barbados**

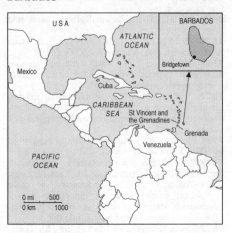

**area** 430 sq km/166 sq mi
**capital** Bridgetown
**major towns/cities** Speightstown, Holetown, Oistins
**physical features** most easterly island of the West Indies; surrounded by coral reefs; subject to hurricanes June–November; highest point Mount Hillaby 340 m/1,115 ft
**head of state** Elizabeth II from 1966, represented by Denys Williams from 1995
**head of government** Owen Arthur from 1994
**political system** constitutional monarchy
**political parties** Barbados Labour Party (BLP), moderate left of centre; Democratic Labour Party (DLP), moderate left of centre; National Democratic Party (NDP), centrist
**currency** Barbados dollar
**GNP per capita (PPP)** (US$) 12,260 (1998)
**exports** sugar, molasses, syrup-rum, chemicals, electrical components. Principal market: USA 17.7% (1997)
**population** 269,000 (1999 est)
**language** English and Bajan (Barbadian English dialect)
**religion** 33% Anglican, 13% Pentecostalist, 6% Methodist, 4% Roman Catholic
**life expectancy** 74 (men); 79 (women) (1995–2000)
*Chronology*
**1536** Visited by Portuguese explorer Pedro a Campos and the name Los Barbados ('The Bearded Ones') given in reference to its 'bearded' fig trees. Indigenous Arawak people were virtually wiped out, via epidemics, after contact with Europeans.
**1627** British colony established; developed as a sugar-plantation economy, initially on basis of black slaves brought in from West Africa.
**1639** Island's first parliament, the House of Assembly, established.
**1816** Last and largest-ever revolt by slaves led by Bussa.
**1834** Slaves freed.
**1937** Outbreak of riots, followed by establishment of the Barbados Labour Party (BLP) by Grantley Adams, and moves towards a more independent political system.

**1951** Universal adult suffrage introduced. BLP won general election.
**1954** Ministerial government established, with BLP leader Adams as first prime minister.
**1955** A group broke away from the BLP and formed the Democratic Labour Party (DLP).
**1961** Independence achieved from Britain. DLP, led by Errol Barrow, in power.
**1966** Barbados achieved full independence within Commonwealth, with Barrow as prime minister.
**1967** Became a member of the United Nations.
**1972** Diplomatic relations with Cuba established.
**1976** The BLP, led by Tom Adams, the son of Grantley Adams, returned to power.
**1983** Barbados supported the US invasion of Grenada.
**1985** Adams died; Bernard St John became prime minister.
**1986** The DLP, led by Barrow, returned to power.
**1987** Barrow died; Erskine Lloyd Sandiford became prime minister.
**1994** The BLP, led by Owen Arthur, won a decisive election victory.
**1999** The BLP gained a landslide victory in general elections, securing 26 of the 28 House of Assembly seats.

**Barbary ape** tailless, yellowish-brown macaque monkey *Macaca sylvanus*, 55–75 cm/ 20–30 in long. Barbary apes are found in the mountains and wilds of Algeria and Morocco, especially in the forests of the Atlas Mountains. They were introduced to Gibraltar, where legend has it that the British will leave if the ape colony dies out.

**barbastelle** insect-eating bat *Barbastella barbastellus* with hairy cheeks and lips, 'frosted' black fur, and a wingspan of about 25 cm/10 in. It lives in hollow trees and under roofs, and is occasionally found in the UK but more commonly in Europe.

**barbel** freshwater fish *Barbus barbus* found in fast-flowing rivers with sand or gravel bottoms in Britain and Europe. Long-bodied, and up to 1 m/3 ft long in total, the barbel has four *barbels* ('little beards' – sensory fleshy filaments) near the mouth.

**barbet** (Latin *barbatus*, 'bearded') small, tropical bird, often brightly coloured. There are about 78 species of barbet in the family Capitonidae, order Piciformes, common to tropical Africa, Asia, and America. Barbets eat insects and fruit and, being distant relations of woodpeckers, drill nest holes with their beaks. The name comes from the 'little beard' of bristles about the mouth that assists them in catching insects.

**Barbie, Klaus** (1913–1991) German Nazi, a member of the ◊SS paramilitary organization from 1936. During World War II he was involved in the deportation of Jews from the occupied Netherlands 1940–42 and in tracking down Jews and Resistance workers in France 1942–45. He was arrested in 1983 and convicted of crimes against humanity in France in 1987.

**barbiturate** hypnosedative drug, commonly known as a 'sleeping pill', consisting of any salt or ester of barbituric acid $C_4H_4O_3N_2$. It works by depressing brain activity. Most barbiturates, being highly addictive, are no longer prescribed and are listed as controlled substances.

**Barbizon School** French school of landscape painters of the mid-19th century, based at Barbizon in the forest of Fontainebleau. They aimed to paint fresh, realistic scenes, sketching and painting their subjects in the open air. Members included Jean François Millet, Théodore Rousseau, and Charles Daubigny (1817–1878).

**Barbour, John** (c. 1320–1395) Scottish poet. His epic 13,000-line poem *The Brus* (written 1374–75, printed 1571) chronicles the war of Scottish independence and includes a vivid account of Robert Bruce's victory over the English at Bannockburn 1314. It is among the earliest known works of Scottish poetry.

**Barbuda** one of the islands that form the state of Antigua and Barbuda.

**Barcelona** port and capital of Barcelona province and of the autonomous community of ◊Cataluña, northeast Spain; population (1994) 1,631,000. Industries include textiles, engineering, and chemicals. As the chief centre of Catalan nationalism, Barcelona was prominent in the overthrow of the monarchy in 1931 and was the last city of the republic to surrender to Franco in 1939. The city hosted the Summer Olympics in 1992.

**bar code** pattern of bars and spaces that can be read by a computer. Bar codes are widely used in retailing, industrial distribution, and libraries. The code is read by a scanning device; the computer determines the code from the widths of the bars and spaces.

**Bardeen, John** (1908–1991) US physicist. He won a Nobel prize in 1956, with Walter Brattain and William Shockley, for the development of the ◊transistor in 1948. In 1972 he became the first double winner of a Nobel prize in the same subject (with Leon Cooper and Robert Schrieffer) for his work on ◊superconductivity.

**Bardot, Brigitte** adopted name of Camille Javal (1934– ) French film actress. A celebrated sex symbol of the 1950s and 1960s, she did much to popularize French cinema internationally. Her films include *Et Dieu créa la femme/And God Created Woman* 1956 directed by Roger Vadim (1928– ), Jean-Luc Godard's *Le Mépris* 1963, Louis Malle's *Viva Maria!* 1965, and *Shalako* 1968.

**Barebones Parliament** English assembly called by Oliver ◊Cromwell to replace the 'Rump Parliament' in July 1653. Although its members attempted to pass sensible legislation (civil marriage; registration of births, deaths, and marriages; custody of lunatics), their attempts to abolish tithes, patronage, and the court of chancery, and to codify the law, led to the resignation of the moderates and its dissolution in December 1653.

**Bari** ancient *Barium,* capital of Apulia region, southern Italy, and industrial and ferry port on the Adriatic Sea; population (1992) 342,100. It is the site of Italy's first nuclear power station. Part of the town is known as Tecnopolis, the Italian equivalent of ◊Silicon Valley.

**baritone** male voice pitched between bass and tenor, of approximate range G2–F4. As a prefix to the name of an instrument, for example baritone saxophone, it indicates that the instrument sounds in approximately the same range.

**barium** (Greek *barytes* 'heavy') soft, silver-white, metallic element, symbol Ba, atomic number 56, relative atomic mass 137.33. It is one of the alkaline-earth metals, found in nature as barium carbonate and barium sulphate. As the sulphate it is used in medicine: taken as a suspension (a 'barium meal'), its movement along the gut is followed using X-rays. The barium sulphate, which is opaque to X-rays, shows the shape of the gut, revealing any abnormalities of the alimentary canal. Barium is also used in alloys, pigments, and safety matches and, with strontium, forms the emissive surface in cathode-ray tubes. It was first discovered in barytes or heavy spar.

**bark** protective outer layer on the stems and roots of woody plants, composed mainly of dead cells. To allow for expansion of the stem, the bark is continually added to from within, and the outer surface often becomes cracked or is shed as scales. Trees deposit a variety of chemicals in their bark, including poisons. Many of these chemical substances have economic value because they can be used in the manufacture of drugs. Quinine, derived from the bark of the *Cinchona* tree, is used to fight malarial infections; curare, an anaesthetic used in medicine, comes from the *Strychnus toxifera* tree in the Amazonian rainforest.

**bark beetle** any one of a number of species of mainly wood-boring beetles. Bark beetles are cylindrical, brown or black, and 1–9 mm/ 0.04–0.4 in long. Some live just under the bark and others bore deeper into the hardwood. The detailed tunnelling pattern that they make within the trunk varies with the species concerned, and is used for identification.

**barley** cereal belonging to a family of grasses. It resembles wheat but is more tolerant of cold and draughts. Cultivated barley (*Hordeum vulgare*) comes in three main varieties – six-rowed, four-rowed, and two-rowed. (Family Gramineae.)

**bar mitzvah** (Hebrew 'son of the commandment') in Judaism, initiation of a boy, which takes place at the age of 13, into the adult Jewish community; less common is the *bat mitzvah* or *bat* for girls aged 12. The child reads a passage from the Torah in the synagogue on the Sabbath and is subsequently regarded as a full member of the congregation.

**barnacle** marine crustacean of the subclass Cirripedia. The larval form is free-swimming, but when mature, it fixes itself by the head to rock or floating wood. The animal then remains attached, enclosed in a shell through which the cirri (modified legs) protrude to sweep food into the mouth. Barnacles include the stalked *goose barnacle Lepas anatifera* found on ships' bottoms, and the *acorn barnacles,* such as *Balanus balanoides,* common on rocks.

**Barnardo, Thomas John** (1845–1905) British philanthropist. He was known as Dr Barnardo, although he was not medically qualified. He opened the first of a series of homes for destitute children 1867 in Stepney, East London.

**barometer** instrument that measures atmospheric pressure as an indication of weather. Most often used are the *mercury barometer* and the *aneroid barometer.*

**Barons' Wars** civil wars in England:
*1215–17* between King ◊John and his barons, over his failure to honour ◊Magna Carta; *1264–67* between ◊Henry III (and the future Edward I) and his barons (led by Simon de ◊Montfort); *1264* 14 May Battle of Lewes at which Henry III was defeated and captured; *1265* 4 August Simon de Montfort was defeated by Edward at Evesham and killed.

**Baroque** in the visual arts, architecture, and music, a style flourishing in Europe 1600–1750, broadly characterized as expressive, flamboyant, and dynamic. Playing a central role in the crusading work of the Catholic Counter-Reformation, the Baroque used elaborate effects to appeal directly to the emotions. In some of its most characteristic works – such as Giovanni Bernini's Cornaro Chapel (Sta Maria della Vittoria, Rome), containing his sculpture *Ecstasy of St Theresa* (1645–52) – painting, sculpture, decoration, and architecture were designed to create a single, dramatic effect. Many masterpieces of the Baroque emerged in churches and palaces in Rome, but the style soon spread throughout Europe, changing in character as it did so. The term Baroque has also by extension been used to describe the music and literature of the period, but it has a much less clear meaning in these fields, and is more a convenient label than a stylistic description.

**barracuda** large predatory fish *Sphyraena barracuda* found in the warmer seas of the world. It can grow over 2 m/6 ft long and has a superficial resemblance to a pike. Young fish shoal, but the older ones are solitary. The barracuda has very sharp shearing teeth and may attack people.

**Barranquilla** major port and capital of Atlántico department on the Caribbean coast of northern Colombia, founded in 1629, on the western bank of the Magdalena River; population (1994) 1,049,000. Industries include chemicals, tobacco, food-processing, textiles, furniture, and footwear. Coffee, coal, oil and nickel are exported. It is a commercial centre and a terminal for river traffic.

**Barras, Paul François Jean Nicolas, Count** (1755–1829) French revolutionary. He was elected to the National Convention 1792 and helped to overthrow Robespierre 1794. In 1795 he became a member of the ruling Directory (see ◊French Revolution). In 1796 he

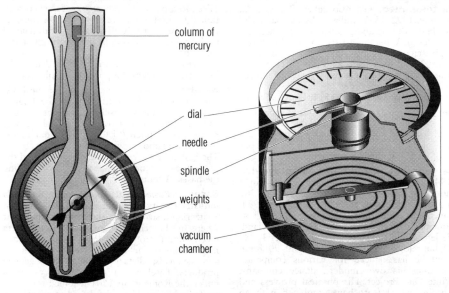

mercury barometer                     aneroid barometer

**barometer** *The mercury barometer (left) and the aneroid barometer (right). In the mercury barometer, the weight of the column of mercury is balanced by the pressure of the atmosphere on the lower end. A change in height of the column indicates a change in atmospheric pressure. In the aneroid barometer, any change of atmospheric pressure causes the metal box which contains the vacuum to be squeezed or to expand slightly. The movements of the box sides are transferred to a pointer and scale via a chain of levers.*

brought about the marriage of his former mistress, Joséphine de Beauharnais, with Napoleon and assumed dictatorial powers. After Napoleon's coup d'état 19 November 1799, Barras fell into disgrace.

**Barrett Browning, Elizabeth** English poet; see ◊Browning, Elizabeth Barrett.

**Barrie, J(ames) M(atthew)** (1860–1937) Scottish dramatist and novelist. His work includes *The Admirable Crichton* (1902) and the children's fantasy *Peter Pan* (1904).

**barrier reef** ◊coral reef that lies offshore, separated from the mainland by a shallow lagoon.

**Barrios de Chamorro, Violeta** (*c.* 1939–  ) Nicaraguan newspaper publisher and politician, president 1990–96. With strong US support, she was elected to be the candidate for the National Opposition Union (UNO) in 1989, winning the presidency from David ◊Ortega Saavedra in February 1990 and thus ending the period of ◊Sandinista rule and the decade-long ◊Contra war. She did not contest the 1996 presidential election.

**barrister** in the UK, a lawyer qualified by study at the ◊Inns of Court to plead for a client in court. In Scotland such lawyers are called advocates. Barristers also undertake the writing of opinions on the prospects of a case before trial. They act for clients through the intermediary of ◊solicitors. In the USA an attorney may serve the functions of barrister and solicitor.

**barrow** (Old English *beorgh* 'hill or mound') burial mound, usually composed of earth but sometimes of stones. Examples are found in many parts of the world. The two main types are *long,* dating from the Neolithic period (New Stone Age), and *round,* dating from the Mesolithic period (early Bronze Age). Barrows made entirely of stones are known as cairns.

**Barry, Charles** (1795–1860) English architect. He designed the Neo-Gothic new Palace of Westminster, London (the Houses of Parliament; 1840–60), in collaboration with A W N ◊Pugin. His early designs for the Travellers Club (1829–23) and for the Reform Club (1837), both in London, were in Renaissance style.

**Barthes, Roland** (1915–1980) French critic and theorist of ◊semiology, the science of signs and symbols. One of the French 'new critics' and an exponent of ◊structuralism, he attacked traditional literary criticism in his first collection of essays, *Le Degré zéro de l'écriture/Writing Degree Zero* 1953.

**Bartók, Béla** (1881–1945) Hungarian composer. His works combine folk elements with mathematical concepts of tonal and rhythmic proportion. His large output includes six string quartets, a *Divertimento* for string orchestra (1939), concertos for piano, violin, and viola, the *Concerto for Orchestra* (1942–45), a one-act opera *Duke Bluebeard's Castle* (1918), and graded teaching pieces for piano.

**Bartolommeo, Fra** also called *Baccio della Porta* (*c.* 1472–1517) Italian religious painter of the High Renaissance, active in Florence. He introduced Venetian artists to the Florentine High Renaissance style during a visit to Venice in 1508, and took back with him to Florence a Venetian sense of colour. His style is one of classic simplicity and order, as in *The Mystical Marriage of St Catherine* (1511, Louvre, Paris).

**baryon** in nuclear physics, a heavy subatomic particle made up of three indivisible elementary particles called quarks. The baryons form a subclass of the ◊hadrons and comprise the nucleons (protons and neutrons) and hyperons.

**Baryshnikov, Mikhail Nikolayevich** (1948– ) Latvian-born dancer, now based in the USA. He joined the Kirov Ballet in 1967 and, after defecting from the USSR in 1974, joined the American Ballet Theater (ABT) as principal dancer, partnering Gelsey Kirkland. He left to join the New York City Ballet 1978–80, but rejoined ABT as director 1980–90. From 1990 he has danced for various companies including his own modern dance company, White Oak Project. His physical prowess and amazing aerial feats have combined with an impish sense of humour and dash to make him one of the most accessible of dancers.

**basal metabolic rate** (BMR) minimum amount of energy needed by the body to maintain life. It is measured when the subject is awake but resting, and includes the energy required to keep the heart beating, sustain breathing, repair tissues, and keep the brain and nerves functioning. Measuring the subject's consumption of oxygen gives an accurate value for BMR, because oxygen is needed to release energy from food.

**basalt** commonest volcanic ◊igneous rock in the Solar System. Much of the surfaces of the terrestrial planets Mercury, Venus, Earth, and Mars, as well as the Moon, are composed of basalt. Earth's ocean floor is virtually entirely made of basalt. Basalt is mafic, that is, it contains relatively little ◊silica: about 50% by weight. It is usually dark grey but can also be green, brown, or black. Its essential constituent minerals are calcium-rich ◊feldspar and calcium and magnesium-rich pyroxene.

**base** in chemistry, a substance that accepts protons. Bases can contain negative ions such as the hydroxide ion (OH⁻), which is the strongest base, or be molecules such as ammonia (NH₃). Ammonia is a weak base, as only some of its molecules accept protons.

$$OH^- + H^+_{(aq)} \rightarrow H_2O_{(l)} NH_3$$
$$+ H_2O \neq NH_4^+ + OH^-$$

Bases that dissolve in water are called alkalis.

**base** in mathematics, the number of different single-digit symbols used in a particular number system. In our usual (decimal) counting system of numbers (with symbols 0, 1, 2, 3, 4, 5, 6, 7, 8, 9) the base is 10. In the ◊binary number system, which has only the symbols 1 and 0, the base is two. A base is also a number that, when raised to a particular power (that is, when multiplied by itself a particular number of times as in $10^2 = 10 \times 10 = 100$), has a ◊logarithm equal to the power. For example, the logarithm of 100 to the base ten is 2.

In geometry, the term is used to denote the line or area on which a polygon or solid stands.

**baseball** national summer game of the USA, derived in the 19th century from the English game of rounders. Baseball is a bat-and-ball game played between two teams, each of nine players, on a pitch ('field') marked out in the form of a diamond, with a base at each corner. The ball is struck with a cylindrical bat, and the players try to score ('make a run') by circuiting the bases. A 'home run' is a circuit on one hit.

**Basel** or *Basle,* French *Bâle,* commercial and industrial city, capital of Basel canton, Switzerland, situated on the Rhine at the point where the French, German, and Swiss borders meet; population (1994) 179,600. Manufactured goods include dyes, textiles, vitamins, agrochemicals, dietary products, and genetic products. Basel was a strong military station under the Romans. In 1501 it joined the Swiss confederation and later developed as a centre for the Reformation.

**basenji** breed of dog originating in Central Africa, where it is used for hunting. About 41 cm/16 in tall, it has pointed ears, curled tail, and short glossy coat of black or red, often with white markings. It is remarkable because it has no true bark.

**base pair** in biochemistry, the linkage of two base (purine or pyrimidine) molecules in ◊DNA. They are found in nucleotides and form the basis of the genetic code.

**base rate** in economics, the rate of interest to which most bank lending is linked, the actual rate depending on the status of the borrower. A prestigious company might command a rate only 1% above base rate, while an individual would be charged several points above.

**Bashō** pen-name of Matsuo Munefusa (1644–1694) Japanese poet. He was a master of the *haiku,* a 17-syllable poetic form with lines of 5, 7, and 5 syllables, which he infused with subtle allusiveness. His *Oku-no-hosomichi/The Narrow Road to the Deep North* 1694, an account of a visit to northern and western Honshū, consists of haiku interspersed with prose passages.

**BASIC** acronym for *beginner's all-purpose symbolic instruction code,* high-level computer-programming language, developed in 1964, originally designed to take advantage of multi-user systems (which can be used by many people at the same time). The language is relatively easy to learn and is popular among microcomputer users.

**basic–oxygen process** most widely used method of steelmaking, involving the blasting of oxygen at supersonic speed into molten pig iron.

**Basie, Count (William)** (1904–1984) US jazz band leader and pianist. He developed the big-band sound and a simplified, swinging style of music. He led impressive groups of musicians in a career spanning more than 50 years. Basie's compositions include 'One O'Clock Jump' and 'Jumpin' at the Woodside'.

**basil** or *sweet basil,* plant with aromatic leaves, belonging to the mint family. A native of the tropics, it is cultivated in Europe as a herb and used to flavour food. Its small white flowers appear on spikes. (Genus *Ocimum basilicum,* family Labiatae.)

**Basil II** (*c.* 958–1025) Byzantine emperor 976–1025. He completed the work of his predecessors Nicephorus (II) Phocas and John Zimisces and expanded the borders of the Byzantine Empire to their greatest extent since the 5th century. He eliminated political rivals, drove the Muslims from Syria, and destroyed the power of the Bulgars.

**basilica** Roman public building; a large roofed hall flanked by columns, generally with an aisle on each side, used for judicial or other public business. The earliest known basilica, at Pompeii, dates from the 2nd century BC. This architectural form was adopted by the early Christians for their churches.

**Basilicata** Roman *Lucania,* mountainous region of southern Italy, comprising the provinces of Potenza and Matera; area 10,000 sq km/3,860 sq mi; population (1992 est) 610,800. Its capital is Potenza. Agriculture is important; durum wheat, olives, and grapes are cultivated, and sheep and goats raised.

**basilisk** Central and South American lizard, genus *Basiliscus.* It is about 50 cm/20 in long and weighs about 90 g/0.2 lb. Its rapid speed (more than 2 m/6.6 ft per second) and the formation of air pockets around the feet enable it to run short distances across the surface of water. The male has a well-developed crest on the head, body, and tail.

**basketball** ball game between two teams of five players on an indoor enclosed court. The object is, via a series of passing moves, to throw the large inflated ball through a circular hoop and net positioned at each end of the court, 3.05 m/10 ft above the ground. The first world championship for men was held in 1950, and 1953 for women. They are now held every four years.

**Basle** alternative form of ◊Basel, a city in Switzerland.

**Basque** the people inhabiting the ◊Basque Country of central northern Spain and the extreme southwest of France. The Basques are a pre-Indo-European people whose language (*Euskara*) is unrelated to any other language. Although both the Romans and, later, the Visigoths conquered them, they largely maintained their independence until the 19th century. During the Spanish Civil War 1936–39, they were on the republican side defeated by Franco. The Basque separatist movement Euskadi ta Askatasuna (ETA; 'Basque Nation and Liberty') and the French organization Iparretarrak ('ETA fighters from the North Side') have engaged in guerrilla activity from 1968 in an attempt to secure a united Basque state.

**Basque Country** Basque *Euskal Herria,* homeland of the ◊Basque people in the western Pyrenees, divided by the Franco-Spanish border. The Spanish Basque Country (Spanish *País Vasco*) is an autonomous region (created in 1979) of central northern Spain, comprising the provinces of Vizcaya, Alava, and Guipúzcoa (Basque *Bizkaia, Araba,* and *Gipuzkoa*); area 7,300 sq km/2,818 sq mi; population (1991) 2,104,000. The French Basque Country (French *Pays Basque*) is the area occupied by Basques in the *département* of Pyrénées-Atlantiques. It is estimated that there are about 170,000 Basques in France.

**Basra** Arabic *al-Basrah,* principal city in southeast Iraq, 97 km/60 mi from the Gulf; population (1991) 850,000. Founded in the 7th century and now Iraq's main port on the Shatt-al-Arab River, exports include wool, oil, cereal, and dates. Aerial bombing during the 1991 Gulf War destroyed bridges, factories, power stations, water-treatment plants, sewage-treatment plants, and the port. A Shiite rebellion in March 1991 was crushed by the Iraqi army, causing further death and destruction.

**bas relief** see ◊relief.

**bass** long-bodied scaly sea fish *Morone labrax* found in the North Atlantic and Mediterranean. They grow to 1 m/3 ft, and are often seen in shoals.

**bass** lowest male voice, of approximate range C2–D4. As the prefix to the name of an instrument, it indicates that the instrument sounds in approximately the same range.

**Basse-Normandie** English *Lower Normandy,* coastal region of northwest France lying between Haute-Normandie and Brittany (Bretagne). It includes the *départements* of Calvados, Manche, and Orne; area 17,600 sq km/6,794 sq mi; population (1990) 1,391,300. Its administrative centre is Caen. Apart from stock farming, dairy farming, and textiles, the area produces apples, cider, and Calvados apple brandy. Tourism is important.

**basset** any of several breeds of hound with a long low body and long pendulous ears, of a type originally bred in France for hunting hares by scent.

**Basseterre** capital and port of St Christopher–Nevis, in the Leeward Islands; population (1990 est) 15,000. Industries include data processing, rum, clothes, and electrical components.

**basset horn** musical woodwind instrument, a wide-bore alto clarinet pitched in F, invented about 1765 and used by Mozart in his *Masonic Funeral Music* (1785), for example, and by Richard Strauss. It was revived in 1981 by Karlheinz Stockhausen and features prominently as a solo in the opera cycle *Licht.* Performers include Alan Hacker and Suzanne Stephens.

**bassoon** double-reed woodwind instrument in C, the bass of the oboe family. It doubles back on itself in a tube about 2.5 m/7.5 ft long and has a rich and deep tone. The bassoon concert repertoire extends from the early Baroque via Vivaldi, Mozart, and Dukas to Stockhausen.

**Bass Strait** sea channel separating the mainland of Australia from Tasmania. The strait is 322 km/200 mi long, with an average width of 255 km/158 mi. Oil was discovered here in 1965 and first extracted in 1969. The region now has 18 oil and gas fields.

**Bastille** castle of St Antoine, built about 1370 as part of the fortifications of Paris. It was made a state prison by Cardinal ◊Richelieu and was stormed by the mob that set the French Revolution in motion 14 July 1789. Only seven prisoners were found in the castle when it was stormed; the governor and most of the garrison were killed, and the Bastille was razed.

**bat** any mammal of the order Chiroptera, related to the Insectivora (hedgehogs and shrews), but differing from them in being able to fly. Bats are the only true flying mammals. Their forelimbs are developed as wings capable of rapid and sustained flight. There are two main groups of bats: *megabats,* which eat fruit, and *microbats,* which mainly eat insects. Although by no means blind, many microbats rely largely on ◊echolocation for navigation and finding prey, sending out pulses of high-pitched sound and listening for the echo. Bats are nocturnal, and those native to temperate countries hibernate in winter. There are about 977 species forming the order Chiroptera, making this the second-largest mammalian order; bats make up nearly one-quarter of the world's mammals. Although bats are widely distributed, populations have declined alarmingly and many species are now endangered.

**Bataan** peninsula in Luzon, the Philippines, which was defended against the Japanese in World War II by US and Filipino troops under General MacArthur 1 Jan–9 April 1942. MacArthur was evacuated, but some 67,000 Allied prisoners died on the *Bataan Death March* to camps in the interior.

**Bates, H(enry) W(alter)** (1825–1892) English naturalist and explorer. He spent 11 years collecting animals and plants in South America and identified 8,000 new species of insects. He made a special study of ◊camouflage in animals, and his observation of insect imitation of species that are unpleasant to predators is known as 'Batesian mimicry'.

**Bath** historic city and administrative headquarters of ◊Bath and North East Somerset unitary authority, southwest England, 171 km/106 mi west of London; population (1991) 78,700. Industries include printing, plastics, engineering, and tourism. Bath was the site of the Roman town of *Aquae Sulis,* and in the 18th century flourished as a fashionable spa, with the only naturally occurring hot mineral springs in Britain. Although the baths were closed to the public in 1977, a Millennium Spa Project is intended to bring back public bathing to Bath's hot springs.

**Bath and North East Somerset** unitary authority in southwest England created in 1996 from part of the former county of Avon

*area* 351 sq km/136 sq mi
*towns and cities* ◊Bath (administrative headquarters), Keynsham, Chew Magna, Paulton, Radstock, Peasedown St John, Midsomer Norton
*features* River Avon and tributaries; Chew Valley Lake; Beckford's Tower (Bath) built in 1827 for William Beckford; Roman baths with hot springs (Bath); Regency architecture including Royal Crescent, The Circus, and Assembly Rooms designed by John Wood (1700–1854) and his son John Wood; Pulteney Bridge, 18th century shop-lined Italianate bridge designed by Robert Adam; Stanton Drew bronze age stone circles including second largest in Great Britain.
*industries* tourism, central government administration, clothing manufacture
*population* (1996) 158,700
*famous people* Thomas Bowdler, John Wood.

**batholith** large, irregular, deep-seated mass of intrusive ◊igneous rock, usually granite, with an exposed surface of more than 100 sq km/40 sq mi. The mass forms by the intrusion or upswelling of magma (molten rock) through the surrounding rock. Batholiths form the core of some large mountain ranges like the Sierra Nevada of western North America.

**Batista, Fulgencio** Colonel Batista y Zaldívar (1901–1973) Cuban right-wing dictator, dictator-president 1934–44 and 1952–59. Having led the September 1933 coup to install Ramón Grau San Martín in power, he forced Grau's resignation in 1934 to become Cuba's effective ruler, as formal president from 1940. Exiled in the USA 1944–49, he ousted President Carlos Prío Socarrás in a military coup in 1952. His authoritarian methods enabled him to jail his opponents and amass a large personal fortune. He was overthrown by rebel forces led by Fidel ◊Castro in 1959. Batista fled to the Dominican Republic and later to Portugal. He died in Spain.

**battery** any energy-storage device allowing release of electricity on demand. It is made up of one or more electrical ◊cells. Primary-cell batteries are disposable; secondary-cell batteries, or ◊accumulators, are rechargeable. Primary-cell batteries are an extremely uneconomical form of energy, since they produce only 2% of the power used in their manufacture. It is dangerous to try to recharge a primary-cell battery.

**baud** in engineering, a unit of electrical signalling speed equal to one pulse per second, measuring the rate at which signals are sent between electronic devices such as telegraphs and computers; 300 baud is about 300 words a minute.

**Baudelaire, Charles Pierre** (1821–1867) French poet. His immensely influential work combined rhythmical and musical perfection with a morbid romanticism and eroticism, finding beauty in decadence and evil. His first and best-known book of verse was *Les Fleurs du mal/Flowers of Evil* 1857. He was one of the main figures in the development of ◊Symbolism.

**Baudouin** (1930–1993) King of the Belgians 1951–93. In 1950 his father, ◊Leopold III, abdicated and Baudouin was known until his succession 1951 as *Le Prince Royal.* During his reign he succeeded in holding together a country divided by religion and language, while presiding over the dismemberment of Belgium's imperial past. In 1960 he married Fabiola de Mora y Aragón (1928– ), member of a Spanish noble family. They were unable to have any children, and he was succeeded by his brother, Albert, 1993.

**Bauhaus** German school of art and design founded in 1919 in Weimar by the architect Walter ◊Gropius in an attempt to fuse art, design, architecture, and crafts into a unified whole. In 1925, under political pressure, it moved to Dessau (where it was housed in a building designed by Gropius), and in 1932 it made another forced move to Berlin, where it was closed to the Nazis the following year. In spite of its short life and troubled existence, the Bauhaus is regarded as the most important art school of the 20th century, and it exercised a huge influence on the world of design and methods of art education. The teachers at the school included some of the outstanding artists of the time, among them the painters Paul Klee and Wassily Kandinsky and the architect Ludwig Mies van der Rohe.

**Baum, L(yman) Frank** (1856–1919) US writer. He was the author of the children's fantasy *The Wonderful Wizard of Oz* (1900) and its 13 sequels.

The series was continued by another author after his death. The film *The Wizard of Oz* (1939) with Judy ◊Garland became a US classic.

**bauxite** principal ore of ◊aluminium, consisting of a mixture of hydrated aluminium oxides and hydroxides, generally contaminated with compounds of iron, which give it a red colour. It is formed by the chemical weathering of rocks in tropical climates. Chief producers of bauxite are Australia, Guinea, Jamaica, Russia, Kazakhstan, Suriname, and Brazil.

**Bavaria** German *Bayern,* administrative region (German *Land*) in southeast Germany; bordered on the west by Hesse and Baden Württemberg, on the north by Thuringia and Saxony, on the northeast by the Czech Republic, and on the south and southeast by Austria
*area* 70,600 sq km/27,252 sq mi
*capital* ◊Munich
*towns and cities* Nuremberg, Augsburg, Würzburg, Regensburg, Passau, Fürth, Ingolstadt
*physical* largest of the German *Länder;* forms the Danube and Main basins; around one-third of the state is woodland, the principal forests being the Frankenwald in the north and the Bavarian Forest, or Bohemian Forest (Böhmerwald), in the northeast; Bavarian Alps in the south
*features* festivals at Bayreuth (Wagner), Oberammergau (Passion Play), Ansbach (Bach), Augsburg (Mozart), Munich (opera), Nuremberg (organ), Würzburg (Mozart); the Oktoberfest, an internationally known beer festival, is held annually in Munich; ski resorts in the Bavarian Alps attract many visitors; the state includes 11 universities
*industries* electronics, electrical engineering, optics, automobile assembly (BMW cars are manufactured at the Bayerische Motoren Werke), aerospace, brewing, chemicals, plastics, oil refining, textiles, glass, toys; post-war industrial dynamism has attracted many immigrants, and research and development and other producer services have developed alongside other industries
*agriculture* wheat, rye, barley, oats, potatoes, and sugar beet; livestock farming; forestry
*population* (1995) 12,100,000
*famous people* Lucas Cranach, Richard Strauss, Bertolt Brecht, Hermann Goering, Heinrich Himmler, Franz Josef Strauss
*religion* 70% Roman Catholic, 26% Protestant
*history* settled by Germanic tribes in the 5th century; part of the Holy Roman Empire; ruled for most of its history by the Wittelsbach dynasty; bastion of Roman Catholicism; became a kingdom under Napoleon Bonaparte; last king of Bavaria, Ludwig III, abdicated in 1918; birthplace of National Socialist movement.

**bay** any of various species of ◊laurel tree. The aromatic evergreen leaves are used for flavouring in cookery. There is also a golden-leaved variety. (Genus *Laurus,* family Lauraceae.)

**Bayeux** town in the *département* of Calvados, northern France, on the River Aure, 27 km/17 mi northwest of Caen; population (1990) 14,700. The town has an agricultural market, and industries include the production of pottery, lace, and processed foods. Its museum houses the 11th-century ◊Bayeux Tapestry. There is a 13th-century Gothic cathedral.

**Bayeux Tapestry** linen hanging made about 1067–70 which gives a vivid pictorial record of the invasion of England by William I (the Conqueror) in 1066. It is an embroidery rather than a true tapestry, sewn with woollen threads in blue, green, red, and yellow, 70 m/231 ft long and 50 cm/20 in wide, and containing 72 separate scenes with descriptive wording in Latin. It is exhibited at the museum of Bayeux in Normandy, France.

**bayonet** short sword attached to the muzzle of a firearm. The bayonet was placed inside the barrel of the muzzleloading muskets of the late 17th century. The *sock* or ring bayonet, invented 1700, allowed a weapon to be fired without interruption, leading to the demise of the pike.

**BBC** abbreviation for ◊*British Broadcasting Corporation.*

**BC** in the Christian calendar, abbreviation for *before Christ,* used with dates.

**BCG** abbreviation for *bacille Calmette-Guérin,* bacillus injected as a vaccine to confer active immunity to ◊tuberculosis (TB).

**Beach Boys, the** US pop group. Their first hit was 'Surfin' USA' (1963); this was followed by 'I Get Around' (1964), and 'California Girls' (1965).

**beak** horn-covered projecting jaws of a bird (see ◊bill), or other horny jaws such as those of the octopus, platypus, or tortoise.

**Beaker people** prehistoric people thought to have been of Iberian origin, who spread out over Europe from the 3rd millennium BC. They were skilled in metalworking, and are associated with distinctive earthenware drinking vessels with various designs, in particular, a type of beaker with a bell-shaped profile, widely distributed throughout Europe.

**bean** seed of a large number of leguminous plants (see ◊legume). Beans are rich in nitrogen compounds and proteins and are grown both for human consumption and as food for cattle and horses. Varieties of bean are grown throughout Europe, the USA, South America, China, Japan, Southeast Asia, and Australia.

**bear** in business, a speculator who sells stocks or shares on the stock exchange expecting a fall in the price in order to buy them back at a profit, the opposite of a ◊bull.

In a bear market, prices fall, and bears prosper.

**bear** large mammal with a heavily built body, short powerful limbs, and a very short tail. Bears breed once a year, producing one to four cubs. In northern regions they hibernate, and the young are born in the winter den. They are found mainly in North America and northern Asia. The skin of the polar bear is black to conserve 80–90% of the solar energy trapped and channelled down the hollow hairs of its fur.

**Beardsley, Aubrey Vincent** (1872–1898) English illustrator and leading member of the ◊Aesthetic Movement. His meticulously executed black-and-white drawings show the influence of Japanese prints and French Rococo, and also display the sinuous line, asymmetry, and decorative mannerisms of Art Nouveau. His work was often charged with being grotesque and decadent.

**Bear, Great and Little** common names (and translations of the Latin) for the constellations ◊Ursa Major and ◊Ursa Minor respectively.

**bearing** device used in a machine to allow free movement between two parts, typically the rotation of a shaft in a housing. *Ball bearings* consist of two rings, one fixed to a housing, one to the rotating shaft. Between them is a set, or race, of steel balls. They are widely used to support shafts, as in the spindle in the hub of a bicycle wheel.

**bearing** the direction of a fixed point, or the path of a moving object, from a point of observation on the Earth's surface, expressed as an angle from the north. Bearings are taken by ◊compass and are measured in degrees (°), given as three-digit numbers increasing clockwise. For instance, north is 000°, northeast is 045°, south is 180°, and southwest is 225°.

**beat frequency** in musical acoustics, fluctuation produced when two notes of nearly equal pitch or ◊frequency are heard together. Beats result from the ◊interference between the sound waves of the notes. The frequency of the beats equals the difference in frequency of the notes.

**Beat Generation** or *Beat movement,* US social and literary movement of the 1950s and early 1960s. Members of the Beat Generation, called *beatniks,* responded to the conformist materialism of the period by adopting lifestyles derived from Henry David Thoreau's social disobedience and Walt Whitman's poetry of the open road. The most influential writers were Jack ◊Kerouac (who is credited with coining the term), Allen ◊Ginsberg, and William ◊Burroughs.

**Beatles, the** English pop group 1960–70. The members, all born in Liverpool, were John ◊Lennon (1940–1980, rhythm guitar, vocals), Paul ◊McCartney (1942– , bass, vocals), George Harrison (1943– , lead guitar, vocals), and Ringo Starr (formerly Richard Starkey, 1940– , drums). Using songs written largely by Lennon and McCartney, the Beatles dominated rock music and pop culture in the 1960s.

**Beaton, Cecil Walter Hardy** (1904–1980) English photographer. His elegant and sophisticated fashion pictures and society portraits often employed exotic props and settings. He adopted a more simple style for his wartime photographs of bomb-damaged London. He also worked as a stage and film designer, notably for the musicals *Gigi* (1959) and *My Fair Lady* (1965). He was knighted in 1972.

**Beatrix, (Wilhelmina Armgard)** (1938– ) Queen of the Netherlands. The eldest daughter of Queen Juliana, she succeeded to the throne on her mother's abdication in 1980. In 1966 she married West German diplomat Claus von Amsberg (1926– ), who was created Prince of the Netherlands. Her heir is Prince Willem Alexander (1967– ).

**Beaufort scale** system of recording wind velocity (speed), devised by Francis Beaufort in 1806. It is a numerical scale ranging from 0 to 17, calm being indicated by 0 and a hurricane by 12; 13–17 indicate degrees of hurricane force.

**Beaufort Sea** section of the Arctic Ocean off Alaska and Canada, named after the British admiral Francis Beaufort. Oil drilling is allowed only in the winter months because the sea is the breeding and migration route of bowhead whales, the staple diet of the local Inuit people.

**Beauvoir, Simone de** (1908–1986) French socialist, feminist, and writer. She played a large role in French intellectual life from the 1940s to the 1980s. Her book *Le Deuxième Sexe/The Second Sex* (1949), one of the first major feminist texts, is an encyclopedic study of the role of women in society, drawing on literature, myth, and history. In this work she argues that the subservient position of women is the result of their systematic repression by a male-dominated society that denies their independence, identity, and sexuality.

**beaver** aquatic rodent with webbed hind feet, a broad flat scaly tail, and thick waterproof fur. It has very large incisor teeth and fells trees to feed on the bark and to use the logs to construct the 'lodge', in which the young are reared, food is stored, and much of the winter

## BEAUFORT SCALE

The Beaufort scale is a system of recording wind velocity (speed) devised in 1806 by Francis Beaufort (1774–1857). It is a numerical scale ranging from 0 for calm to 12 for a hurricane.

| Number and description | Features | Air speed | |
|---|---|---|---|
| | | kph | mph |
| 0 calm | smoke rises vertically; water smooth | 0–2 | 0–1 |
| 1 light air | smoke shows wind direction; water ruffled | 2–5 | 1–3 |
| 2 light breeze | leaves rustle; wind felt on face | 6–11 | 4–7 |
| 3 gentle breeze | loose paper blows around | 12–19 | 8–12 |
| 4 moderate breeze | branches sway | 20–29 | 13–18 |
| 5 fresh breeze | small trees sway, leaves blown off | 30–39 | 19–24 |
| 6 strong breeze | whistling in telephone wires; sea spray from waves | 40–50 | 25–31 |
| 7 near gale | large trees sway | 51–61 | 32–38 |
| 8 gale | twigs break from trees | 62–74 | 39–46 |
| 9 strong gale | branches break from trees | 75–87 | 47–54 |
| 10 storm | trees uprooted; weak buildings collapse | 88–101 | 55–63 |
| 11 violent storm | widespread damage | 102–117 | 64–73 |
| 12 hurricane | widespread structural damage | above 118 | above 74 |

is spent. There are two species, the Canadian *Castor canadensis* and the European *C. fiber*. They grow up to 1.4 m/4.6 ft in length and weigh about 20 kg/44 lb.

**Beaverbrook, (William) Max(well) Aitken** 1st Baron Beaverbrook (1879– 1964) Canadian-born British financier, newspaper proprietor, and politician. He bought a majority interest in the *Daily Express* in 1919, founded the *Sunday Express* in 1921, and bought the London *Evening Standard* in 1923. He served in David Lloyd George's World War I cabinet and Winston Churchill's World War II cabinet.

**bebop** or *bop*, hot jazz style, rhythmically complex, virtuosic, and highly improvisational. It was developed in New York in the 1940s and 1950s by Charlie Parker, Dizzy Gillespie, Thelonius Monk, and other black musicians reacting against ◊swing music.

**Bechuanaland** former name (to 1966) of Botswana.

**Becker, Boris** (1967– ) German tennis player. In 1985, at the age of 17, he became the youngest winner of a singles title at Wimbledon. He has won the title three times and helped West Germany to win the Davis Cup 1988 and 1989. He also won the US Open 1989 and the Grand Prix Masters/ATP Tour World Championship in 1992.
*career highlights*
*Wimbledon* singles: 1985, 1986, 1989
*US Open* singles: 1989
*Australian Open* singles: 1991, 1996
*Grand Prix Masters/ATP Tour World Championship* 1988, 1992

**Becket, St Thomas à** (1118–1170) English priest and politician. He was chancellor to Henry II 1155–62, when he was appointed archbishop of Canterbury. The interests of the church soon conflicted with those of the crown and Becket was assassinated; he was canonized in 1172.

**Beckett, Samuel (Barclay)** (1906–1989) Irish dramatist and novelist. He wrote in both French and English. His play *En attendant Godot* – first performed in Paris 1952, and then

in his own translation as *Waiting for Godot* (1955) in London, 1956 in New York – is possibly the best-known example of Theatre of the ◊Absurd, in which life is taken to be meaningless. This genre is taken to further extremes in *Fin de partie/Endgame* (1957) and *Happy Days* (1961). Nobel Prize for Literature 1969.

**Beckham, David Robert Joseph** (1975– ) English footballer, born in Leytonstone, London. A midfielder with great passing ability, he was a member of the Manchester United sides that won the FA Premier League in the 1995–96, 1996–97, and 1998–99 seasons, and also won an FA Cup-winner's medal with Manchester United in 1996. Beckham was the Professional Footballers' Association Young Player of the Year in 1996–97. As of October 1999 he had made 25 international appearances for England (scoring one goal).
*career highlights*
*international appearances* 25 times for England (1 goal).
*League appearances* Manchester United: 100 (23 goals); Preston North End: 5 (2 goals)
*Honours (with Manchester United)* European Cup: 1999 FA Premier League: 1995–96, 1996–97, 1998–99; FA Cup: 1996, 1999

**becquerel** SI unit (symbol Bq) of ◊radioactivity, equal to one radioactive disintegration (change in the nucleus of an atom when a particle or ray is given off) per second.

**Becquerel, (Antoine) Henri** (1852–1908) French physicist. He discovered penetrating radiation coming from uranium salts, the first indication of ◊radioactivity, and shared a Nobel prize with Marie and Pierre ◊Curie in 1903.

**bed** in geology, a single ◊sedimentary rock unit with a distinct set of physical characteristics or contained fossils, readily distinguishable from those of beds above and below. Well-defined partings called *bedding planes* separate successive beds or strata.

**bedbug** flattened wingless red-brown insect *Cimex lectularius* with piercing mouthparts. Bed bugs live in bedlinen crevices during the day and feed on human blood at night. They lay their eggs in the crevices and these hatch in a few days into nymphs (miniature versions of the adults) that take ten weeks and five skin moults to reach adult size. Adults can live for several years if undisturbed.

**Bede** (c. 673–735) English theologian and historian, known as *the Venerable Bede*. Active in Durham and Northumbria, he wrote many scientific, theological, and historical works. His *Historia Ecclesiastica Gentis Anglorum/ Ecclesiastical History of the English People* of 731 is a primary source for early English history, and was translated into the vernacular by King Alfred.

**Bedfordshire** county of south central England (since April 1997 Luton has been a separate unitary authority)
*area* 1,192 sq km/460 sq mi
*towns and cities* Bedford (administrative headquarters), Dunstable
*physical* the Great Ouse River and its tributary, the Ivel; the county is low lying with the Chiltern Hills in the southwest
*features* Whipsnade Wild Animal Park, near Dunstable (200 ha/494 acres), belonging to the London Zoological Society; Woburn Abbey, seat of the duke of Bedford; Cranfield Institute of Technology
*agriculture* cereals (especially wheat and barley); vegetables
*industries* agricultural machinery; cement manufacture (using local chalk); clay; electrical goods; gravel; motor vehicles and parts; packaging; sand; brickworks at Stewartby
*population* (1996) 548,800
*famous people* John Bunyan, John Howard, Joseph Paxton

**Bedouin** (Arabic 'desert dweller') member of any of the nomadic, Arabic-speaking peoples occupying the desert regions of Arabia and North Africa. Originating in Arabia, they spread to Syria and Mesopotamia, and later to Egypt and Tunisia.

**bee** four-winged insect of the superfamily Apoidea in the order Hymenoptera, usually with a sting. There are over 12,000 species, of which fewer than 1 in 20 are social in habit. The *hive bee* or *honeybee Apis mellifera* establishes perennial colonies of about 80,000, the majority being infertile females (workers), with a few larger fertile males (drones), and a single very large fertile female (the queen). Worker bees live for no more than a few weeks, while a drone may live a few months, and a queen several years. Queen honeybees lay two kinds of eggs: fertilized, female eggs, which have two sets of chromosomes and develop into workers or queens, and unfertilized, male eggs, which have only one set of chromosomes and develop into drones.

**beech** one of several European hardwood trees or related trees growing in Australasia and South America. The common beech (*Fagus sylvaticus*), found in European forests, has a smooth grey trunk and edible nuts, or 'mast', which are used as animal feed or processed for oil. The timber is used in furniture. (Genera *Fagus* and *Nothofagus*, family Fagaceae.)

**Beecham, Thomas** (1879–1961) English conductor and impresario. He established the Royal Philharmonic Orchestra in 1946 and fostered the works of composers such as Delius, Sibelius, and Richard Strauss. He was knighted and succeeded to the baronetcy in 1916.

**Beeching Report** 1963 official report on the railway network of Britain, which recommended the closure of loss-making lines and the improvement of money-making routes. Hundreds of lines and several thousand stations were closed as a result.

**bee-eater** brightly-coloured bird *Merops apiaster*, family Meropidae, order Coraciiformes, found in Africa, southern Europe, and Asia. Bee-eaters are slender, with chestnut, yellow, and blue-green plumage, a long bill and pointed wings, and a flight like that of the swallow, which they resemble in shape. They feed on bees, wasps, and other insects, and nest in colonies in holes dug out with their long bills in sandy river banks.

**Beelzebub** (Hebrew 'lord of the flies') in the New Testament, the leader of the devils, sometimes identified with Satan and sometimes with his chief assistant (see ♦devil). In the Old Testament Beelzebub was a fertility god worshipped by the Philistines and other Semitic groups (♦Baal).

**beer** alcoholic drink made from water and malt (fermented barley or other grain), flavoured with hops. Beer contains between 1% and 6% alcohol. One of the oldest alcoholic drinks, it was brewed in ancient China, Egypt, and Babylon.

**Beersheba** Arabic *Bir-es-Saba*, 'seven wells', industrial city in the south of Israel, 80 km/50 mi from Jerusalem; population (1995) 152,600. It is the chief centre of the Negev Desert and has been a settlement from the Stone Age.

**beet** any of several plants belonging to the goosefoot family, used as food crops. One variety of the common beet (*Beta vulgaris*) is used to produce sugar and another, the mangelwurzel, is grown as a cattle feed. The beetroot, or red beet (*B. rubra*), is a salad plant. (Genus *Beta*, family Chenopodiaceae.)

**Beethoven, Ludwig van** (1770–1827) German composer and pianist. His mastery of musical expression in every genre made him the dominant influence on 19th-century music. Beethoven's repertoire includes concert overtures; the opera *Fidelio* (1805, revised 1814); 5 piano concertos and 2 for violin (one unfinished); 32 piano sonatas, including the *Moonlight* (1801) and *Appassionata* (1804–05); 17 string quartets; the Mass in D (*Missa solemnis*) (1824); and 9 symphonies, as well as many youthful works. He usually played his own piano pieces and conducted his orchestral works until he was hampered by deafness in 1801; nevertheless he continued to compose.

**beetle** common name of insects in the order Coleoptera (Greek 'sheath-winged') with leathery forewings folding down in a protective sheath over the membranous hindwings, which are those used for flight. They pass through a complete metamorphosis. They include some of the largest and smallest of all insects: the largest is the *Hercules beetle Dynastes hercules* of the South American rainforests, 15 cm/6 in long; the smallest is only 0.05 cm/0.02 in long. Comprising more than 50% of the animal kingdom, beetles number some 370,000 named species, with many not yet described.

**Begin, Menachem** (1913–1992) Israeli politician. He was leader of the extremist Irgun Zvai Leumi organization in Palestine from 1942 and prime minister of Israel 1977–83, as head of the right-wing Likud party. Following strong encouragement from US president Jimmy ◊Carter, he entered into negotiations with President Anwar ◊Sadat of Egypt, which resulted in the Camp David Agreements. In 1978 he and Sadat were jointly awarded the Nobel Peace Prize. In 1981 Begin won a new term of office but his health was failing. He retired in September 1983, and spent the rest of his life as a virtual recluse.

**begonia** any of a group of tropical and subtropical plants. They have fleshy and succulent leaves, and some have large, brilliant flowers. There are numerous species in the tropics, especially in South America and India. (Genus *Begonia*, family Begoniaceae.)

**Behan, Brendan Francis** (1923–1964) Irish dramatist. His early experience of prison and knowledge of the workings of the ◊IRA (recounted in his autobiography *Borstal Boy* 1958) provided him with two recurrent themes in his plays. *The Quare Fellow* 1954 was followed by the tragicomedy *The Hostage* 1958, first written in Gaelic.

**behaviourism** school of psychology originating in the USA, of which the leading exponent was John B Watson.

Behaviourists maintain that all human activity can ultimately be explained in terms of conditioned reactions or reflexes and habits formed in consequence. Leading behaviourists include Ivan ◊Pavlov and B F ◊Skinner.

**behaviour therapy** in psychology, the application of behavioural principles, derived from learning theories, to the treatment of clinical conditions such as ◊phobias, ◊obsessions, and sexual and interpersonal problems.

**Behn, Aphra** (1640–1689) English novelist and dramatist. She was the first woman in England to earn her living as a writer. Her works were criticized for their explicitness; they frequently present events from a woman's point of view. Her novel *Oroonoko* (1688), based on her visit to Suriname, is an attack on slavery.

**Behrens, Peter** (1868–1940) German architect. A pioneer of the ◊Modern Movement and of the adaptation of architecture to industry. He designed the AEG turbine factory in Berlin (1909), a landmark in industrial architecture, and taught Le Corbusier, Walter Gropius, and Mies van der Rohe.

**Behring, Emil von** (1854–1917) German physician. He discovered that the body produces antitoxins, substances able to counteract poisons released by bacteria. Using this knowledge, he developed new treatments for such diseases as ◊diphtheria. He won the first Nobel Prize for Physiology or Medicine, 1901.

**Beiderbecke, Bix (Leon Bismarck)** (1903–1931) US jazz cornetist, composer, and pianist. A romantic soloist with the bands of King Oliver, Louis Armstrong, and Paul Whiteman, Beiderbecke was the first acknowledged white jazz innovator. He was influenced by the classical composers Debussy, Ravel, and Stravinsky.

**Beijing** or *Peking,* ('northern capital') capital of China; parts of the northeast municipal boundary coincide with sections of the ◊Great Wall of China; population (1994) 7,084,000. The municipality of Beijing has an area of 17,800 sq km/6,871 sq mi and a population (1996) of 12,590,000. Industries include engineering and the production of steel, vehicles, textiles, and petrochemicals.

**Beirut** or *Beyrouth,* capital and port of Lebanon, 90 km/60 mi northwest of Damascus, situated on a promontory into the eastern Mediterranean with the Lebanon Mountains behind it; population (1993) 1,200,000. It was devastated by civil war in the 1970s and 1980s. The city dates back to at least 1400 BC.

**Bekaa, the** or *El Beqa'a,* valley in central Lebanon, situated between the Lebanon and Anti-Lebanon mountain ranges; length 130 km/80 mi, width 20 km/12 mi. It is also a governorate, its main population centres being the city of Zahle and the ancient town of Baalbek. The Orontes and Litani rivers rise in the Bekaa. The southern part of the valley is particularly fertile with significant production of wheat, maize, cotton, fruit, and, in recent years, hashish and opium. Of strategic importance, the Bekaa was occupied by Syrian troops following the outbreak of the Lebanese civil war in the mid-1970s and has been a centre of operations for the radical Islamic Hezbollah organization.

**Belarus** Republic of
*national name Respublika Belarus*

*area* 207,600 sq km/80,154 sq mi
*capital* Minsk (Mensk)
*major towns/cities* Gomel, Vitebsk, Mogilev, Bobruisk, Hrodna, Brest
*physical features* more than 25% forested; rivers Dvina, Dnieper and its tributaries, including the Pripet and Beresina; the Pripet Marshes in the east; mild and damp climate
*head of state* Alexandr Lukashenko from 1994
*head of government* Syargey Ling from 1996
*political system* emergent democracy
*political parties* Belarus Communist Party (BCP, banned 1991–92); Belarus Patriotic Movement (BPM), populist; Belorussian Popular Front (BPF; Adradzhenne), moderate nationalist; Christian Democratic Union of Belarus, centrist; Socialist Party of Belarus, left of centre
*currency* rouble and zaichik
*GNP per capita (PPP)* (US$) 4,100 (1998 est)
*exports* machinery, chemicals and petrochemicals, iron and steel, light industrial goods. Principal market: Russia 65.5% (1998)
*population* 10,275,000 (1999 est)
*language* Belorussian (official); Russian, Polish
*religion* Russian Orthodox, Roman Catholic; Baptist, Muslim, and Jewish minorities
*life expectancy* 62 (men); 74 (women) (1995–2000)
*Chronology*
*5th–8th centuries* Settled by East Slavic tribes, ancestors of present-day Belorussians.
*11th century* Minsk founded.
*12th century* Part of Kievan Russia, to the south, with independent Belarus state developing around Polotsk, on River Dvina.
*14th century* Incorporated within Slavonic Grand Duchy of Lithuania, to the west.
*1569* Union with Poland.
*late 18th century* Came under control of tsarist Russia as Belarussia ('White Russia'), following three partitions of Poland in 1772, 1793, and 1795.
*1812* Minsk destroyed by French emperor Napoleon Bonaparte during his military campaign against Russia.
*1839* Belorussian Catholic Church forcibly abolished.
*1914–18* Belarus was the site of fierce fighting between Germany and Russia during World War I.
*1918–19* Briefly independent from Russia.
*1919–20* Wars between Poland and Soviet Russia over control of Belarus.
*1921* West Belarus ruled by Poland; East Belarus became a Soviet republic.
*1930s* Agriculture collectivized despite peasant resistance; more than 100,000 people, chiefly writers and intellectuals, shot in mass executions ordered by Soviet dictator Joseph Stalin.
*1939* West Belarus occupied by Soviet troops.
*1941–44* Nazi occupation resulted in death of 1.3 million people, including many Jews; Minsk destroyed.
*1945* Became founding member of United Nations; much of West Belarus incorporated into Soviet republic.

*1950s–60s* Large-scale immigration of ethnic Russians and 'Russification'.
*1986* Fallout from the nearby Chernobyl nuclear reactor in Ukraine rendered 20% of agricultural land unusable.
*1989* The Belorussian Popular Front was established as national identity was revived under the *glasnost* initiative of Soviet leader Mikhail Gorbachev.
*1990* Belorussian was established as the state language and republican sovereignty declared.
*1991* Strikes and unrest in Minsk; the BCP was suspended following an attempted coup against Gorbachev in Moscow; the moderate nationalist Stanislav Shushkevich was elected president. Independence was recognized by the USA; the Commonwealth of Independent States (CIS) was formed in Minsk.
*1993* The BCP was re-established.
*1994* President Shushkevich was ousted; Alexandr Lukashenko, a pro-Russian populist, was elected president.
*1995* A friendship and cooperation pact was signed with Russia.
*1996* An agreement on economic union was signed with Russia. Prime Minister Mikhas Chygir was replaced by Syargey Ling.
*1997* Belarus's observer status in Council of Europe was suspended. The treaty with Russia was ratified. The Council of Republic rejected the president's proposals to curb the media. There were prodemocracy demonstrations.
*1998* The Belarus rouble was devalued. A new left-wing and centrist political coalition was created. Food rationing was imposed as the economy deteriorated. Belarus signed a common policy with Russia on economic, foreign, and military matters.

**Belau** former name for the Republic of Palau.

**Belfast** (Gaelic *Beal Feirste* 'the mouth of the Farset') city and industrial port in County Antrim and County Down, Northern Ireland, at the mouth of the River Lagan on Belfast Lough; county town of County ◊Antrim, and capital of Northern Ireland since 1920.
*population* (1994 est) 290,000 (Protestants form the majority in east Belfast, Catholics in the west)
*industries* aircraft and aircraft components, engineering, electronics, fertilizers, food processing, rope, textiles, tobacco; linen and shipbuilding have declined in importance since the 19th century, although some attempt is being made to revive these industries. The city is currently undergoing major redevelopment, both in terms of physical infrastructure (particularly along the River Lagan) and industrial investment, which is partly funded by the EU
*features* City Hall (1906); Stormont (the former parliament buildings and from 1998 the seat of the Northern Ireland Assembly); Waterfront Hall, opened in 1997; the Linen Hall Library (1788); Belfast Castle (built 1870; former home of the Donegall family); Queen's University (1909)

**Belgian Congo** former name (1908–60) of the Democratic Republic of Congo; known 1960–97 as Zaire.

**Belgium** Kingdom of
**national name** French *Royaume de Belgique,*
Flemish *Koninkrijk België*

**area** 30,510 sq km/11,779 sq mi
**capital** Brussels
**major towns/cities** Antwerp, Ghent, Liège,
Charleroi, Bruges, Mons, Namur, Leuven
**major ports** Antwerp, Ostend, Zeebrugge
**physical features** fertile coastal plain in northwest, central rolling hills rise eastwards, hills
and forest in southeast; Ardennes Forest; rivers
Schelde and Meuse
**head of state** King Albert from 1993
**head of government** Guy Verhofstadt from
1999
**political system** federal constitutional monarchy
**political parties** Flemish Christian Social Party
(CVP), centre left; French Social Christian Party
(PSC), centre left; Flemish Socialist Party (SP),
left of centre; French Socialist Party (PS), left of
centre; Flemish Liberal Party (PVV), moderate
centrist; French Liberal Reform Party (PRL),
moderate centrist; Flemish People's Party (VU),
federalist; Flemish Vlaams Blok, right wing;
Flemish Green Party (Agalev); French Green
Party (Ecolo)
**currency** Belgian franc
**GNP per capita (PPP)** (US$) 23,480 (1998)
**exports** food, livestock and livestock products,
gem diamonds, iron and steel manufacturers,
machinery and transport equipment, chemicals
and related products. Principal market:
Germany 19% (1998)
**population** 10,152,000 (1999 est)
**language** in the north (Flanders) Flemish (a
Dutch dialect, known as *Vlaams*) 55%; in the
south (Wallonia) Walloon (a French dialect)
32%; bilingual 11%; German (eastern border)
0.6%. Dutch is official in the north, French in
the south; Brussels is officially bilingual
**religion** Roman Catholic 75%, various
Protestant denominations
**life expectancy** 74 (men); 81 (women)
(1995–2000)

*Chronology*
**57 BC** Romans conquered the Belgae (the indigenous Celtic people), and formed province of
Belgica.
**3rd–4th centuries AD** Region overrun by
Franks and Saxons.
**8th–9th centuries** Part of Frankish Empire;
peace and order fostered growth of Ghent,
Bruges, and Brussels.
**843** Division of Holy Roman Empire; became
part of Lotharingia, but frequent repartitioning
followed.
**10th–11th centuries** Seven feudal states
emerged: Flanders, Hainaut, Namur, Brabant,
Limburg, and Luxembourg, all nominally subject to French king or Holy Roman Emperor, but
in practice independent.
**12th century** Economy began to flourish: textiles in Bruges, Ghent, and Ypres; copper and tin
in Dinant and Liège.
**15th century** One by one, states came under
rule of dukes of Burgundy.
**1477** Passed into Habsburg dominions through
marriage of Mary of Burgundy to Maximilian,
archduke of Austria.
**1555** Division of Habsburg dominions; Low
Countries allotted to Spain.
**1648** Independence of Dutch Republic recognized; south retained by Spain.
**1713** Treaty of Utrecht transferred Spanish
Netherlands to Austrian rule.
**1792–97** Austrian Netherlands invaded by revolutionary France and finally annexed.
**1815** Congress of Vienna reunited north and
south Netherlands as one kingdom under House
of Orange.
**1830** Largely French-speaking people in south
rebelled against union with Holland and
declared Belgian independence.
**1831** Leopold of Saxe-Coburg-Gotha became
first king of Belgium.
**1839** Treaty of London recognized independence of Belgium and guaranteed its neutrality.
**1847–70** Government dominated by Liberals;
growth of heavy industry.
**1870–1914** Catholic Party predominant.
**1914–18** Invaded and occupied by Germany.
Belgian forces under King Albert I fought in conjunction with Allies.
**1919** Acquired Eupen-Malmédy region from
Germany.
**1940** Second invasion by Germany; King
Leopold III ordered Belgian army to capitulate.
**1944–45** Belgium liberated.
**1948** Belgium formed Benelux customs union
with Luxembourg and the Netherlands.
**1949** Belgium was a founding member of North
Atlantic Treaty Organization (NATO).
**1951** Leopold III abdicated in favour of his son
Baudouin.
**1958** Belgium was a founding member of
European Economic Community (EEC), which
made Brussels its headquarters.
**1967** NATO made Brussels its headquarters.
**1971** Constitution amended to safeguard cultural rights of Flemish- (in Flanders in north)
and French-speaking communities (Walloons in
southeast) in an effort to ease linguistic dispute.

**1974** Separate regional councils and ministerial committees established for Flemings and Walloons.
**1980** There was violence over language divisions; regional assemblies for Flanders and Wallonia and three-member executive for Brussels were created.
**1993** A federal system was adopted, based on Flanders, Wallonia, and Brussels. King Baudouin died and was succeeded by his brother Albert.
**1995** A Dehaene-led coalition was re-elected.
**1998** A high-profile campaign was run to retain the country's unity.

**Belgrade** Serbo-Croat *Beograd*, 'white fortress', port and capital of the Federal Republic of Yugoslavia, and of its constituent republic of Serbia, at the confluence of the Danube and Sava rivers: population (1991) 1,168,500. It is linked to the port of Bar on the Adriatic Sea. Industries include light engineering, food processing, textiles, pharmaceuticals, and electrical goods.

**Belisarius** (*c.* 505–565) East Roman general who led Rome's reconquest of the West. Though given inadequate resources by the jealous emperor Justinian I, Belisarius achieved notable victories against the Persians, Huns, Vandals, and Goths.

**Belize** (formerly *British Honduras)*

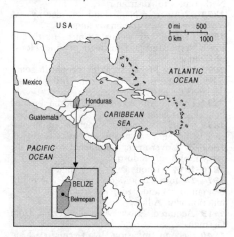

**area** 22,963 sq km/8,866 sq mi
**capital** Belmopan
**major towns/cities** Belize City, Dangriga, Orange Walk, Corozal
**major ports** Belize City, Dangriga, Punta Gorda
**physical features** tropical swampy coastal plain, Maya Mountains in south; over 90% forested
**head of state** Elizabeth II from 1981, represented by governor general Dr Norbert Colville Young from 1993
**head of government** Manuel Esquivel from 1993
**political system** constitutional monarchy
**political parties** People's United Party (PUP), left of centre; United Democratic Party (UDP), moderate conservative

**currency** Belize dollar
**GNP per capita (PPP)** (US$) 3,940 (1998)
**exports** sugar, clothes, citrus products, forestry and fish products, bananas. Principal market: UK 45.5% (1997)
**population** 235,000 (1999 est)
**language** English (official); Spanish (widely spoken), Creole dialects
**religion** Roman Catholic 60%, Protestant 35%
**life expectancy** 73 (men); 76 (women) (1995–2000)
**Chronology**
**325–925 AD** Part of American Indian Maya civilization.
**1600s** Colonized by British buccaneers and logcutters
**1862** Formally declared a British colony, known as British Honduras.
**1893** Mexico renounced its long-standing claim to the territory.
**1954** Constitution adopted, providing for limited internal self-government. General election won by PUP led by George Price.
**1964** Self-government achieved from the UK. Universal adult suffrage and a two-chamber legislature introduced.
**1970** Capital moved from Belize City to new town of Belmopan.
**1973** Name changed to Belize.
**1975** British troops sent to defend the long-disputed frontier with Guatemala.
**1980** The United Nations (UN) called for full independence.
**1981** Full independence was achieved, with Price as prime minister.
**1984** Price was defeated in a general election. Manuel Esquivel of the right-of-centre United Democratic Party (UDP) formed a government. The UK reaffirmed its undertaking to defend the frontier.
**1989** Price and the PUP won a general election.
**1991** Diplomatic relations were re-established with Guatemala, which finally recognized Belize's sovereignty.
**1993** The UDP defeated the PUP in a general election; Esquivel returned as prime minister. The UK announced its intention to withdraw troops following the resolution of the border dispute with Guatemala.
**1998** The PUP won a sweeping victory in assembly elections.

**Belize City** former capital (until 1970) and chief port of Belize, situated at the mouth of the Belize River on the Caribbean coast; population (1991) 44,000. It is Belize's largest city and capital of Belize district. Exports include sugar, timber, citrus fruits, coconuts, and maize. The port also serves parts of Mexico. The city was severely damaged by hurricanes in September 1931 and in October 1961, after which it was decided to move the capital inland, to Belmopan.

**Bell, Alexander Graham** (1847–1922) Scottish-born US scientist and inventor. He was the first person ever to transmit speech from one point to another by electrical means. This invention – the telephone – was made in 1876. Later Bell experimented with a type of phonograph and, in aeronautics, invented the tricycle under-carriage.

**belladonna** or *deadly nightshade,* poisonous plant *Atropa belladonna* belonging to the night-shade family, found in Europe and Asia. It grows to 1.5 m/5 ft in height, with dull green leaves growing in unequal pairs, up to 20 cm/8 in long, and single purplish flowers that produce deadly black berries. Drugs are made from the leaves. (Genus *Atropa,* family Solanaceae.)

**bellflower** general name for many plants with bell-shaped flowers. The ◊harebell (*Campanula rotundifolia*) is a wild bellflower. The Canterbury bell (*C. medium*) is the garden vari-ety, originally from southern Europe. (Genus *Campanula,* family Campanulaceae.)

**Bellini** Venetian family of artists, founders of the Venetian School in the 15th and early 16th centuries. *Jacopo Bellini* (*c.* 1400–1470/71) worked in Venice, Padua, Verona, and Ferrara. *Gentile Bellini* (*c.* 1429–1507) was probably the elder son of Jacopo and was trained by him. Although now overshadowed by his brother, he was no less famous in his own day. *Giovanni Bellini* (*c.* 1430–1516) contributed more than any other painter of his time to the creation of the great Venetian School.

**Bellini, Vincenzo** (1801–1835) Italian com-poser of operas. He collaborated with the tenor Giovanni Battista Rubini (1794–1854) to develop a new simplicity of melodic expression in romantic evocations of classic themes, as in *La Sonnambula/The Sleepwalker* and *Norma,* both 1831. In *I Puritani/The Puritans* 1835, his last work, he discovered a new boldness and vigour of orchestral effect.

**Bellow, Saul** (1915–  ) Canadian-born US novelist. From his first novel, *Dangling Man* (1944), Bellow has typically set his naturalistic narratives in Chicago and made his central char-acter an anxious, Jewish-American intellectual. In *The Adventures of Augie March* (1953) and *Henderson the Rain King* (1959), he created confident and comic picaresque heroes, before *Herzog* (1964), which pitches a comic but dis-tressed scholar into a world of darkening humanism. Later works, developing Bellow's depiction of an age of urban disorder and indif-ference, include the near-apocalyptic *Mr Sammler's Planet* (1970), *Humboldt's Gift* (1975), *The Dean's December* (1982), *More Die of Heartbreak* (1987), and the novella *A Theft* (1989). His finely styled works and skilled char-acterizations won him the Nobel Prize for Literature in 1976. Other works include *Him with His Foot in His Mouth* (1984), *Something to Remember Me By* (1992), and *The Actual* (1997).

**Belmopan** capital of Belize from 1970; situ-ated in central Belize, 80 km/50 mi southwest of Belize City, near the junction of the Western Highway and the Hummingbird Highway to Dangriga; population (1990) 5,300. Principal exports from the region are sugar cane, citrus fruits, bananas, and coconuts. Belmopan was established in 1970 in the mountainous interior

to replace Belize City as the administrative cen-tre of the country following hurricane damage to the latter in 1961. The traditional Maya-style architecture prevails.

**Belorussian** (Byelorussian 'White Russian') member of an eastern Slav people closely related to the Russians (Great Russians) and Ukrainians, who live in Belarus and the sur-rounding area. Belorussian, a Balto-Slavic lan-guage belonging to the Indo-European family, is spoken by about 10 million people, including some in Poland. It is written in the Cyrillic script. Belorussian literature dates from the 11th century AD.

**Ben Ali, Zine el Abidine** (1936–  ) Tunisian politician, president from 1987. After training in France and the USA, he returned to Tunisia and became director general of national security. He was made minister of the interior and then prime minister under the ageing president for life Habib ◊Bourguiba, whom he deposed in 1987 in a bloodless coup with the aid of ministerial col-leagues. He ended the personality cult established by Bourguiba and moved towards a pluralist political system. He was re-elected in 1994, with 99% of the popular vote.

**Benares** alternative transliteration of ◊Varanasi, a holy Hindu city in Uttar Pradesh, India.

**Ben Bella, Muhammad Ahmed** (1916–  ) Algerian politician. He was among the leaders of the Front de Libération Nationale (FLN), the first prime minister of independent Algeria 1962–63, and its first president 1963–65. His centralization of power and systematic purges were among the reasons behind his overthrow in 1965 by Houari ◊Boumédienne. He was detained until 1979. In 1985 he founded a new party, Mouvement pour la Démocratie en Algérie (MDA), and returned to Algeria in 1990 after nine years in exile. The cancellation of the 1991 legislative elections led to his exile for the second time, and his party was banned in 1997.

**bends** or *compressed-air sickness* or *caisson disease,* popular name for a syndrome seen in deep-sea divers, arising from too rapid a release of nitrogen from solution in their blood. If a diver surfaces too quickly, nitrogen that had dis-solved in the blood under increasing water pres-sure is suddenly released, forming bubbles in the bloodstream and causing pain (the 'bends') and paralysis. Immediate treatment is gradual decompression in a decompression chamber, whilst breathing pure oxygen.

**Benedict, St** (*c.* 480–*c.* 547) Founder of Christian monasticism in the West and of the Benedictine order. He founded the monastery of Monte Cassino and others in Italy. His feast day is 11 July.

**Benelux** acronym for *Belgium, the Nether-lands, and Luxembourg,* customs union of Belgium, the Netherlands, and Luxembourg, an agreement for which was signed in London by the three governments in exile in 1944, and rat-ified in 1947. It came into force in 1948 and was further extended and strengthened by the

Benelux Economic Union Treaty in 1958. The full economic union between the three countries came into operation in 1960. The three Benelux countries were founder-members of the European Economic Community (now the ◊European Union), for which the Benelux union was an important stimulus.

**Beneš, Edvard** (1884–1948) Czechoslovak politician. He worked with Tomáš ◊Masaryk towards Czechoslovak nationalism from 1918 and was foreign minister and representative at the League of Nations. He was president of the republic from 1935 until forced to resign by the Germans and headed a government in exile in London during World War II. He personally gave the order for the assassination of Reinhard Heydrich in Prague in 1942. Having signed an agreement with Joseph Stalin, he returned home as president in 1945 but resigned again after the communist coup in 1948.

**Bengal** former province of British India, in the northeast of the subcontinent. It was the first major part of India to come under the control of the British ◊East India Company (the 'Bengal Presidency'). When India gained independence in 1947, Bengal was divided into ◊West Bengal, a state of India, and East Bengal, which from 1972 onwards became part of the newly independent state of Bangladesh.

**Bengal, Bay of** part of the Indian Ocean lying between the east coast of India and the west coast of Myanmar (Burma) and the Malay Peninsula.

The Irrawaddy, Ganges, and Brahmaputra rivers flow into the bay. The principal islands are to be found in the Andaman and Nicobar groups.

**Bengali** people of Bengali culture from Bangladesh and India (West Bengal, Tripura). There are 80–150 million speakers of Bengali, an Indo-Iranian language belonging to the Indo-European family. It is the official language of Bangladesh and of the state of Bengal and is also used by emigrant Bangladeshi and Bengali communities in such countries as the UK and the USA. Bengalis in Bangladesh are predominantly Muslim, whereas those in India are mainly Hindu.

**Benghazi** or *Banghazi*, historic city and industrial port in northern Libya on the Gulf of Sirte; population (1984) 485,000. It was controlled by Turkey between the 16th century and 1911, and by Italy 1911–42; it was a major naval supply base during World War II.

**Ben-Gurion, David** adopted name of David Gruen (1886–1973) Israeli statesman and socialist politician. He was one of the founders of the state of Israel, the country's first prime minister 1948–53, and again 1955–63. He retired from politics in 1970, but remained a lasting symbol of the Israeli state.

**Benin** former African kingdom 1200–1897, now a province of Nigeria. It reached the height of its power in the 14th–17th centuries when it ruled the area between the Niger Delta and Lagos. The province trades in timber and rubber.

**Benin** People's Republic of (formerly known as *Dahomey* 1904–75)
*national name* République Populaire du Bénin

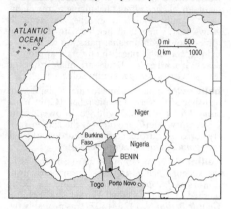

*area* 112,622 sq km/43,483 sq mi
*capital* Porto-Novo (official), Cotonou (de facto)
*major towns/cities* Abomey, Natitingou, Parakou, Kandi, Ouidah, Djougou, Bohicou
*major ports* Cotonou
*physical features* flat to undulating terrain; hot and humid in south; semiarid in north; coastal lagoons with fishing villages on stilts; Niger River in northeast
*head of state* Mathieu Kerekou from 1996
*head of government* vacant from 1998
*political system* socialist pluralist republic
*political parties* Union for the Triumph of Democratic Renewal (UTDR); National Party for Democracy and Development (PNDD); Party for Democratic Renewal (PRD); Social Democratic Party (PSD); National Union for Solidarity and Progress (UNSP); National Democratic Rally (RND). The general orientation of most parties is left of centre
*currency* franc CFA
*GNP per capita (PPP)* (US$) 1,250 (1998)
*exports* cotton, crude petroleum, palm oil and other palm products. Principal market: Brazil 18.2% (1997)
*population* 5,937,000 (1999 est)
*language* French (official); Fon 47% and Yoruba 9% in south; six major tribal languages in north
*religion* animist 60%, Muslim, Roman Catholic
*life expectancy* 52 (men); 55 (women) (1995–2000)
*Chronology*
*12th–13th centuries* Settled by Ewe-speaking people, called the Aja, who mixed with local peoples and gradually formed the Fon ethnic group.
*16th century* Aja kingdom, called Great Ardha, at its peak.
*early 17th century* Kingdom of Dahomey established in south by Fon peoples, who defeated the neighbouring Dan; following contact with European traders, the kingdom became became an intermediary in the slave trade, which was particularly active along the

Bight (Bay) of Benin, between Ghana and Nigeria, during the 16th–19th centuries.

**1800–50** King Dezo of Dahomey raised regiments of female soldiers to attack the Yoruba ('land of the big cities') kingdom of eastern Benin and southwest Nigeria to obtain slaves; palm-oil trade developed.

**1857** French base established at Grand-Popo.

**1892–94** War between the French and Dahomey, after which the victorious French established a protectorate.

**1899** Incorporated in federation of French West Africa as Dahomey.

**1914** French troops from Dahomey participated in conquest of German-ruled Togoland to west, during World War I.

**1940–44** Along with the rest of French West Africa, supported the 'Free French' anti-Nazi resistance cause during World War II.

**1960** Independence achieved from France.

**1960–72** Acute political instability, with frequent switches from civilian to military rule, and regional ethnic disputes.

**1972** Military regime established by Major Mathieu Kerekou.

**1974** Kerekou announced that country would follow a path of 'scientific socialism'.

**1975** Name of country changed from Dahomey to Benin.

**1977** Return to civilian rule under new constitution, but with Kerekou as president.

**1989** The army was deployed against antigovernment strikers and protesters, inspired by Eastern European revolutions; Marxist-Leninism was dropped as the official ideology and a market-centred economic reform programme adopted.

**1990** A referendum backed the establishment of multiparty politics.

**1991** In multiparty elections, President Kerekou was replaced by the leader of the new Benin Renaissance Party (PRB), Nicéphore Soglo, who formed a ten-party coalition government.

**1996** Kerekou defeated Soglo in a presidential election run-off despite opposition claims of fraud.

**1998** Prime Minister Adrien Houngbedji resigned; no immediate successor was appointed.

**Benn, Tony (Anthony Neil Wedgwood)** (1925– ) British Labour politician, formerly the leading figure on the party's left wing. He was minister of technology 1966–70 and secretary of state for industry 1974–75, but his campaign against entry into the European Community (EC; now the European Union) led to his transfer to the Department of Energy 1975–79. A skilled parliamentary orator, he twice unsuccessfully contested the Labour Party leadership. Benn announced in June 1999 that he would stand down as an MP after nearly half a century in Parliament. He would, however, continue to be politically active.

**Bennett, (Enoch) Arnold** (1867–1931) English novelist, playwright, and journalist. His major works are set in the industrial 'five towns' of the Potteries in Staffordshire (now Stoke-on-Trent) and are concerned with the manner in which the environment dictates the pattern of his characters' lives. They include *Anna of the Five Towns* (1902), *The Old Wives' Tale* (1908), and the trilogy *Clayhanger, Hilda Lessways,* and *These Twain* (1910–15).

**Bennett, Alan** (1934– ) English dramatist and screenwriter. His works (often set in his native north of England) treat such subjects as class, senility, illness, and death with macabre comedy. They include the series of monologues for television *Talking Heads* (1988) and *Talking Heads 2* (1998), and the play *The Madness of George III* (1991), made into the critically acclaimed film *The Madness of King George* (1995) (Academy Award for best adapted screenplay).

**Ben Nevis** highest mountain in the British Isles (1,344 m/4,409 ft), 7 km/4 mi southeast of Fort William, Scotland.

**bent** or *bent grass,* any of a group of grasses. Creeping bent grass (*Agrostis stolonifera*), also known as fiorin, is common in northern North America, Europe, and Asia, including lowland Britain. It spreads by ◊runners and has large attractive clusters (panicles) of yellow or purple flowers on thin stalks, like oats. It is often used on lawns and golf courses. (Genus *Agrostris,* family Gramineae.)

**Bentham, Jeremy** (1748–1832) English philosopher, legal and social reformer, and founder of ◊utilitarianism. The essence of his moral philosophy is found in the pronouncement of his *Principles of Morals and Legislation* (written in 1780, published in 1789): that the object of all legislation should be 'the greatest happiness for the greatest number'.

**Benz, Karl Friedrich** (1844–1929) German automobile engineer. He produced the world's first petrol-driven motor vehicle. He built his first model engine 1878 and the petrol-driven car 1885.

**Benzedrine** trade name for ◊amphetamine, a stimulant drug.

**benzene** $C_6H_6$ clear liquid hydrocarbon of characteristic odour, occurring in coal tar. It is used as a solvent and in the synthesis of many chemicals.

**benzodiazepine** any of a group of mood-altering drugs (tranquillizers), for example Librium and Valium. They are addictive and interfere with the process by which information is transmitted between brain cells, and various side effects arise from continued use. They were originally developed as muscle relaxants, and then excessively prescribed in the West as anxiety-relieving drugs.

**Beowulf** Old English poem of 3,182 lines, thought to have been composed in the first half of the 8th century. It is the only complete surviving example of Germanic folk epic and exists in a single manuscript copied in England about 1000 and now housed in the Cottonian collection of the British Museum, London.

**Berber** the non-Semitic Caucasoid people of North Africa who since prehistoric times have inhabited Barbary – the Mediterranean coastlands from Egypt to the Atlantic. Their language, present-day Berber (a member of the Hamito-Semitic or Afro-Asiatic language family), is written in both Arabic and Berber characters and is spoken by about 10 million people: about one-third of Algerians and nearly two-thirds of Moroccans. Berbers are mainly agricultural, but some are still nomadic.

**Bérégovoy, Pierre (Eugène)** (1925–1993) French socialist politician, prime minister 1992–93. A close ally of François ◊Mitterrand, he was named chief of staff in 1981 after managing the successful presidential campaign. He was social affairs minister 1982–84 and finance minister 1984–86 and 1988–92. He resigned as premier after the Socialists' defeat in the March 1993 general election, and shortly afterwards committed suicide.

**Berengaria of Navarre** (1165–c. 1230) Queen of England. The only English queen never to set foot in England, she was the daughter of King Sancho VI of Navarre. She married Richard I of England in Cyprus 1191, and accompanied him on his crusade to the Holy Land.

**Berg, Alban** (1885–1935) Austrian composer. He studied under Arnold Schoenberg and developed a personal 12-tone idiom of great emotional and stylistic versatility. His relatively small output includes two operas: *Wozzeck* (1920), a grim story of working-class life, and the unfinished *Lulu* (1929–35), and chamber music incorporating coded references to friends and family.

**Berg, Paul** (1926– ) US molecular biologist. In 1972, using gene-splicing techniques developed by others, Berg spliced and combined into a single hybrid the ◊DNA from an animal tumour virus (SV40) and the DNA from a bacterial virus. For his work on recombinant DNA, he shared the 1980 Nobel Prize for Chemistry.

**bergamot** small evergreen tree belonging to the rue family. A fragrant citrus-scented essence is obtained from the rind of its fruit and used as a perfume and food flavouring, for example in Earl Grey tea. The sole source of supply is southern Calabria, Italy, but the name comes from the town of Bergamo, in Lombardy. (*Citrus bergamia,* family Rutaceae.)

**Bergen** industrial port and capital of Hordaland county on the southwest coast of Norway; population (1994) 195,000. Industries include shipbuilding, engineering, and fishing. Often called the 'gateway to the fjords', Bergen is a major centre for tours of the fjords of Norway's west coast. Founded in 1070, Bergen was a member of the ◊Hanseatic League.

**Bergman, (Ernst) Ingmar** (1918– ) Swedish stage and film director. He is regarded by many as a unique auteur and one of the masters of modern cinema. His work deals with complex moral, psychological, and metaphysical problems and is often strongly pessimistic. Bergman gained an international reputation with *Det sjunde inseglet/The Seventh Seal* and

*Smultronstället/Wild Strawberries,* both 1957. He has also directed *Junfrukällan/The Virgin Spring* (1959), *Tystnaden/The Silence* (1963), *Persona* (1966), *Viskningar och rop/Cries and Whispers* (1972), and *Fanny och Alexander/ Fanny and Alexander* (1982).

**Bergman, Ingrid** (1915–1982) Swedish-born actress. Having moved to the USA 1939 to appear in David O Selznick's remake of the Swedish film *Intermezzo* (1936) in which she had first come to prominence, she went on to appear in such Hollywood classics as *Casablanca* (1942), *For Whom the Bell Tolls* (1943), *Gaslight* (1944) (for which she won an Academy Award), and *Notorious* (1946). On screen she projected a combination of radiance, refined beauty, and fortitude.

**Bergson, Henri Louis** (1859–1941) French philosopher. He believed that time, change, and development were the essence of reality. He thought that time was a continuous process in which one period merged imperceptibly into the next. In *Creative Evolution* (1907) he attempted to prove that all evolution and progress are due to the working of the *élan vital,* or life force. Nobel Prize for Literature 1928.

**beriberi** nutritional disorder occurring mostly in the tropics and resulting from a deficiency of vitamin $B_1$ (◊thiamine). The disease takes two forms: in one ◊oedema (waterlogging of the tissues) occurs; in the other there is severe emaciation. There is nerve degeneration in both forms and many victims succumb to heart failure.

**Bering, Vitus Jonassen** (1681–1741) Danish explorer. He was the first European to sight Alaska. He died on Bering Island in the Bering Sea, both named after him, as is the Bering Strait, which separates Asia (Russia) from North America (Alaska).

**Bering Sea** section of the Pacific Ocean north of the Aleutian Islands, between Siberia and Alaska; area 2.28 million sq km/880,000 sq mi. It connects with the Chukchi Sea, to the north, via the Bering Strait, extending for 87 km/54 mi from east–west, between the Chukchi Peninsula of Siberia and the Seward Peninsula of Alaska. It is named after the Danish explorer Vitus ◊Bering, who explored the Bering Strait.

**Bering Strait** strait between Alaska and Siberia, linking the North Pacific and Arctic oceans.

**Berio, Luciano** (1925– ) Italian composer. His work combines serial techniques with commedia dell'arte and antiphonal practices, as in *Alleluiah II* (1958), for five instrumental groups. His prolific output includes nine *Sequenzas/ Sequences* (1957–75) for various solo instruments or voice, *Sinfonia* (1969) for voices and orchestra, *Formazioni/Formations* (1987) for orchestra, and the opera *Un re in ascolto/A King Listens* (1984).

**Berkeley, Busby** stage name of William Berkeley Enos (1895–1976) US choreographer and film director. He used ingenious and extravagant sets and teams of female dancers to create song and dance sequences that formed large-scale kaleidoscopic patterns when filmed from above, as in *Gold Diggers of 1933* and *Footlight Parade* (1933).

**berkelium** synthesized, radioactive, metallic element of the actinide series, symbol Bk, atomic number 97, relative atomic mass 247.

It was first produced in 1949 by Glenn Seaborg and his team, at the University of California at Berkeley, USA, after which it is named.

**Berkshire** or *Royal Berkshire,* former county of south-central England; from April 1998 split into six unitary authorities: ◊West Berkshire, ◊Reading, ◊Slough, ◊Windsor and Maidenhead, ◊Wokingham and ◊Bracknell Forest.

**Berlin** industrial city and capital of the Federal Republic of Germany, lying on the River Spree; population (1995) 3,470,200. Products include machine tools, engineering goods (including cars), electrical goods, paper, food and drink, and printed works. After the division of Germany in 1949, East Berlin became the capital of East Germany and Bonn was made the provisional capital of West Germany. The ◊Berlin Wall divided the city from 1961 until it was dismantled in 1989. Following the reunification of Germany on 3rd October 1990, East and West Berlin were once more reunited as the 16th *Land* (state) of the Federal Republic.

**Berlin, Irving** adopted name of Israel Baline (1888–1989) Russian-born US songwriter. His songs include hits such as 'Alexander's Ragtime Band' (1911), 'Always' (1925), 'God Bless America' (1917, published 1939), and 'White Christmas' (1942), and the musicals *Top Hat* (1935), *Annie Get Your Gun* (1946), and *Call Me Madam* (1950). He also provided songs for films like *Blue Skies* (1946) and *Easter Parade* (1948). His 'White Christmas' has been the most performed Christmas song in history, with more than 500 versions recorded.

**Berlin blockade** the closing of entry to Berlin from the west by Soviet forces June 1948–May 1949. It was an attempt to prevent the other Allies (the USA, France, and the UK) unifying the western part of Germany. The British and US forces responded by sending supplies to the city by air for over a year (the *Berlin airlift*). In May 1949 the blockade was lifted; the airlift continued until September. The blockade marked the formal division of the city into Eastern and Western sectors.

**Berlin Wall** dividing barrier between East and West Berlin from 1961 to 1989, erected by East Germany to prevent East Germans from leaving for West Germany. Escapers were shot on sight.

**Berlioz, (Louis) Hector** (1803–1869) French Romantic composer. He is noted as the founder of modern orchestration. Much of his music was inspired by drama and literature and has a theatrical quality. He wrote symphonic works, such as *Symphonie fantastique* (1830–31) and *Roméo et Juliette* (1839); dramatic cantatas including *La Damnation de Faust* (1846) and *L'Enfance du Christ* (1854); sacred music; and three operas: *Benvenuto Cellini* (1838), *Les*

*Troyens* (1856–58), and *Béatrice et Bénédict* (1862).

**Bermuda** British colony in the Northwest Atlantic Ocean

*area* 54 sq km/21 sq mi

*capital* and chief port Hamilton

*features* consists of about 150 small islands, of which 20 are inhabited, linked by bridges and causeways; Britain's oldest colony

*industries* Easter lilies, pharmaceuticals; tourism, banking, and insurance are important

*currency* Bermuda dollar

*population* (1994) 60,500

*language* English

*religion* Christian

*government* under the constitution of 1968, Bermuda is a fully self-governing British colony, with a governor (Lord Waddington from 1992), senate, and elected House of Assembly (premier from 1997 Pamela Gordon, United Bermuda Party)

*history* the islands were named after Juan de Bermudez, who visited them in 1515, and were settled by British colonists in 1609. It is Britain's oldest colony, officially taken by the crown in 1684. Indian and African slaves were transported from 1616 and soon outnumbered the white settlers. Racial violence in 1977 led to intervention, at the request of the government, by British troops. A 1995 referendum rejected independence. The British Labour Party (BLP) won a general election in November 1998.

**Bern** French *Berne,* capital of Switzerland and of Bern canton, in the west of the country on the River Aare; population (1994) 134,100. Industries include the manufacture of textiles, chocolate, pharmaceuticals, and light metal and electrical goods. There is a magnificent Gothic cathedral, dating from the 15th century. Bern joined the Swiss confederation in 1353 as its eighth member, and became the capital in 1848.

**Bernard, Claude** (1813–1878) French physiologist and founder of experimental medicine. Bernard first demonstrated that digestion is not restricted to the stomach, but takes place throughout the small intestine. He discovered the digestive input of the pancreas, several functions of the liver, and the vasomotor nerves which dilate and contract the blood vessels and thus regulate body temperature. This led him to the concept of the *milieu intérieur* ('internal environment') whose stability is essential to good health.

**Bernese Alps** mountainous area in the south of Bern canton. It includes the Jungfrau, Eiger, and Finsteraarhorn peaks. Interlaken is the chief town.

**Bernhardt, Sarah** stage name of Henriette Rosine Bernard (1844–1923) French actress. She dominated the stage in her day, frequently performing at the Comédie Française in Paris. She excelled in tragic roles, including Cordelia in Shakespeare's *King Lear,* the title role in Racine's *Phèdre,* and the male roles of Hamlet and of Napoleon's son in Edmond Rostand's *L'Aiglon.*

**Bernini, Gianlorenzo (Giovanni Lorenzo)** (1598–1680) Italian sculptor, architect, and painter. He was a leading figure in the development of the ◊Baroque style. His work in Rome includes the colonnaded piazza in front of St Peter's Basilica (1656), fountains (as in the Piazza Navona), and papal monuments. His sculpture includes *The Ecstasy of St Theresa* (1645–52; Santa Maria della Vittoria, Rome), and numerous portrait busts.

**Bernoulli's principle** law stating that the pressure of a fluid varies inversely with speed, an increase in speed producing a decrease in pressure (such as a drop in hydraulic pressure as the fluid speeds up flowing through a constriction in a pipe) and vice versa. The principle also explains the pressure differences on each surface of an aerofoil, which gives lift to the wing of an aircraft. The principle was named after Swiss mathematician and physicist Daniel Bernoulli.

**Bernstein, Leonard** (1918–1990) US composer, conductor, and pianist. He is one of the most energetic and versatile 20th-century US musicians. His works, which established a vogue for realistic, contemporary themes, include symphonies such as *The Age of Anxiety* (1949), ballets such as *Fancy Free* (1944), and scores for musicals, including *Wonderful Town* (1953), *West Side Story* (1957), and *Mass* (1971) in memory of President J F Kennedy.

**berry** fleshy, many-seeded ◊fruit that does not split open to release the seeds. The outer layer of tissue, the exocarp, forms an outer skin that is often brightly coloured to attract birds to eat the fruit and thus disperse the seeds. Examples of berries are the tomato and the grape.

**Berry, Chuck (Charles Edward Anderson)** (1926– ) US rock-and-roll singer, songwriter, and guitarist. His characteristic guitar riffs became staples of rock music, and his humorous storytelling lyrics were also emulated. He had a string of hits in the 1950s and 1960s beginning with 'Maybellene' (1955), which became an early rock-and-roll classic. He enjoyed a revival of popularity in the 1970s and 1980s.

**Bertolucci, Bernardo** (1940– ) Italian film director. His work combines political and historical perspectives with an elegant and lyrical visual appeal. Such films as *Strategia del ragno/The Spider's Stratagem* (1970), *Il conformista/The Conformist* (1970), and *The Last Emperor* (1987) (which won nine Academy Awards) have demonstrated his philosophical complexity and visual sophistication.

**beryl** mineral, beryllium aluminium silicate, $Be_3Al_2Si_6O_{18}$, which forms crystals chiefly in granite. It is the chief ore of beryllium. Two of its gem forms are aquamarine (light-blue crystals) and emerald (dark-green crystals).

**Berzelius, Jöns Jakob** (1779–1848) Swedish chemist. He accurately determined more than 2,000 relative atomic and molecular masses. In 1813–14, he devised the system of chemical symbols and formulae now in use and proposed oxygen as a reference standard for atomic masses. His discoveries include the elements cerium 1804, selenium 1817, and thorium 1828;

he was the first to prepare silicon in its amorphous form and to isolate zirconium. The words 'isomerism', 'allotropy', and 'protein' were coined by him.

**Bessarabia** former region in southeastern Europe, bordering on the Black Sea and standing between the Prut and Dniester rivers. Its capital was at Kishinev. The region is now divided between the states of Moldova and Ukraine.

**Bessemer process** the first cheap method of making ◊steel, invented by Henry Bessemer in England 1856. It has since been superseded by more efficient steel-making processes, such as the ◊basic–oxygen process. In the Bessemer process compressed air is blown into the bottom of a converter, a furnace shaped like a cement mixer, containing molten pig iron. The excess carbon in the iron burns out, other impurities form a slag, and the furnace is emptied by tilting.

**Best, Charles H(erbert)** (1899–1978) Canadian physiologist. He was one of the team of Canadian scientists including Frederick ◊Banting whose research resulted 1922 in the discovery of insulin as a treatment for diabetes.

**Best, George** (1946– ) Northern Irish footballer. One of football's greatest talents, he was a vital member of the great Manchester United side which won the league championship in 1965 and 1967, and the European Cup in 1968, when he was voted both English and European footballer of the year. A goal provider as much as a goal scorer, he scored 134 goals in his 349 appearances for the club 1963–73.

*career highlights*
*Football League* appearances: 411; goals: 147
*League championship* 1965, 1967
*Footballer of the Year* 1968
*international appearances* 37; goals: 9
*European Cup* 1968
*European Footballer of the Year* 1968

**bestiary** in medieval times, a book with stories and illustrations which depicted real and mythical animals or plants to illustrate a (usually Christian) moral. The stories were initially derived from the Greek *Physiologus,* a collection of 48 such stories, written in Alexandria around the 2nd century AD.

**beta-blocker** any of a class of drugs that block impulses that stimulate certain nerve endings (beta receptors) serving the heart muscle. This reduces the heart rate and the force of contraction, which in turn reduces the amount of oxygen (and therefore the blood supply) required by the heart. Beta-blockers may be useful in the treatment of angina, arrhythmia (abnormal heart rhythms), and raised blood pressure, and following heart attacks. They must be withdrawn from use gradually.

**beta decay** the disintegration of the nucleus of an atom to produce a beta particle, or high-speed electron, and an electron antineutrino. During beta decay, a neutron in the nucleus changes into a proton, thereby increasing the atomic number by one while the mass number stays the same. The mass lost in the change is converted into kinetic (movement) energy of the beta particle.

Beta decay is caused by the weak nuclear force, one of the fundamental ◊forces of nature operating inside the nucleus.

**beta particle** electron ejected with great velocity from a radioactive atom that is undergoing spontaneous disintegration. Beta particles do not exist in the nucleus but are created on disintegration, beta decay, when a neutron converts to a proton to emit an electron.

**Betelgeuse** or *Alpha Orionis,* red supergiant star in the constellation of ◊Orion. It is the tenth-brightest star in the night sky, although its brightness varies. It is 1,100 million km/700 million mi across, about 800 times larger than the Sun, roughly the same size as the orbit of Mars. It is over 10,000 times as luminous as the Sun, and lies 650 light years from the Sun. Light takes 60 minutes to travel across the giant star.

**betel nut** fruit of the areca palm (*Areca catechu*), which is chewed together with lime and betel pepper as a stimulant by peoples of the East and Papua New Guinea. Chewing it blackens the teeth and stains the mouth deep red.

**Bethlehem** Arabic *Beit-Lahm,* city on the west bank of the River Jordan, 8 km/5 mi south of Jerusalem; population (1997 est) 135,000. It was occupied by Israel in 1967 and came under control of the Palestinian Authority in December 1995. In the Bible it is mentioned as the birthplace of King David and Jesus, and in 326 AD the Church of the Nativity was built over the grotto said to be the birthplace of Jesus.

**Betjeman, John** (1906–1984) English poet and essayist. He was the originator of a peculiarly English light verse, nostalgic, and delighting in Victorian and Edwardian architecture. He also wrote prose works on architecture and social history which reflect his interest in the Gothic Revival. His *Collected Poems* appeared in 1958 and a verse autobiography, *Summoned by Bells,* in 1960.

**betting** wagering money on the outcome of a game, race, or other event, not necessarily a sporting event.

**Beuys, Joseph** (1921–1986) German sculptor and performance artist. He was one of the leaders of the European avant-garde during the 1970s and 1980s. An exponent of Arte Povera, he made use of so-called 'worthless', unusual materials such as felt and fat. His best-known performance was *How to Explain Pictures to a Dead Hare* 1965. He was also an influential exponent of video art, for example, *Felt TV* 1968.

**Bevan, Aneurin (Nye)** (1897–1960) British Labour politician. Son of a Welsh miner, and himself a miner at 13, he was member of Parliament for Ebbw Vale 1929–60. As minister of health 1945–51, he inaugurated the National Health Service (NHS); he was minister of labour from January to April 1951, when he resigned (with Harold Wilson) on the introduction of NHS charges and led a Bevanite faction against the government. In 1956 he became chief

Labour spokesperson on foreign affairs, and deputy leader of the Labour party in 1959. He was an outstanding speaker.

**Bevin, Ernest** (1881–1951) British Labour politician. Chief creator of the Transport and General Workers' Union, he was its general secretary 1921–40. He served as minister of labour and national service 1940–45 in Winston Churchill's wartime coalition government, and organized the 'Bevin boys', chosen by ballot to work in the coalmines as war service. As foreign secretary in the Labour government 1945–51, he played a leading part in the creation of NATO.

**Bhagavad-Gītā** (Hindi 'the Song of the Blessed') religious and philosophical Sanskrit poem, dating from around 300 BC, forming an episode in the sixth book of the *Mahābhārata,* one of the two great Hindu epics. It is the supreme religious work of Hinduism.

**Bhopal** industrial city and capital of ◊Madhya Pradesh, central India, 525 km/326 mi southwest of Allahabad; population (1991) 1,064,000. Textiles, chemicals, electrical goods, and jewellery are manufactured. Nearby Bhimbetka Caves, discovered in 1973, have the world's largest collection of prehistoric paintings, about 10,000 years old. In 1984 some 2,600 people died from an escape of the poisonous gas methyl isocyanate from a factory owned by US company Union Carbide; another 300,000 suffer from long-term health problems.

**Bhumibol Adulyadej** (1927– ) King of Thailand from 1946. Born in the USA and educated in Bangkok and Switzerland, he succeeded to the throne on the assassination of his brother. In 1973 he was active, with popular support, in overthrowing the military government of Marshal Thanom Kittikachorn and thus ended a sequence of army-dominated regimes in power from 1932.

**Bhutan** Kingdom of
**national name** *Druk-yul*
**area** 46,500 sq km/17,953 sq mi

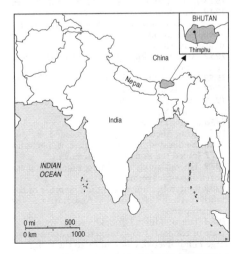

*capital* Thimphu (Thimbu)
*major towns/cities* Paro, Punakha, Mongar, P'sholing, W'phodrang, Bumthang
*physical features* occupies southern slopes of the Himalayas; Gangkar Punsum (7,529 m/24,700 ft) is one of the world's highest unclimbed peaks; cut by valleys formed by tributaries of the Brahmaputra; thick forests in south
*head of state* Jigme Singye Wangchuk from 1972
*head of government* Lyonpo Jigme Thimley from 1998
*political system* absolute monarchy to 1998, when the king conceded political powers to the National Assembly
*political parties* none officially; illegal Bhutan People's Party (BPP) and Bhutan National Democratic Party (BNDP), both ethnic Nepali
*currency* ngultrum; also Indian currency
*GNP per capita (PPP)* (US$) 1,180 (1997 est)
*exports* cardamom, cement, timber, fruit, electricity (to India), precious stones, spices. Principal market: India 90.7% (1997)
*population* 2,064,000 (1999 est)
*language* Dzongkha (official, a Tibetan dialect), Sharchop, Bumthap, Nepali, and English
*religion* 70% Mahayana Buddhist (state religion), 25% Hindu
*life expectancy* 60 (men); 62 (women) (1995–2000)
*Chronology*
*to 8th century* Under effective Indian control.
*16th century* Came under Tibetan rule.
*1616–51* Unified by Ngawang Namgyal, leader of the Drukpa Kagyu (Thunder Dragon) Tibetan Buddhist branch.
*1720* Came under Chinese rule.
*1774* Treaty signed with East India Company.
*1865* Trade treaty with Britain signed after invasion.
*1907* Ugyen Wangchuk, the governor of Tongsa, became Bhutan's first hereditary monarch.
*1910* Anglo-Bhutanese Treaty signed, placing foreign relations under the 'guidance' of the British government in India.
*1926* Jigme Wangchuk succeeded to the throne.
*1949* Indo-Bhutan Treaty of Friendship signed, giving India continued influence over Bhutan's foreign relations, but returning territory annexed in 1865.
*1952* Reformist king Jigme Dorji Wangchuk came to power.
*1953* National assembly (Tshogdu) established.
*1958* Slavery abolished.
*1959* 4,000 Tibetan refugees given asylum after Chinese annexation of Tibet.
*1968* King established first cabinet.
*1972* King died and was succeeded by his Western-educated son Jigme Singye Wangchuk.
*1973* Joined the nonaligned movement.
*1979* Tibetan refugees told to take Bhutanese citizenship or leave; most stayed.
*1983* Bhutan became a founding member of the South Asian Regional Association for Cooperation.
*1988* The Buddhist Dzongkha king imposed a 'code of conduct' suppressing the customs of the large Hindu-Nepali community in the south.

*1990* Hundreds of people were allegedly killed during prodemocracy demonstrations.
*1993* The leader of the banned Bhutan People's Party (BPP) was sentenced to life imprisonment for 'antinational activities'.
*1998* King conceded political powers to the National Assembly. Lyonpo Jigme Thimley became prime minister.

**Bhutto, Benazir** (1953– ) Pakistani politician. She was leader of the Pakistan People's Party (PPP) from 1984, a position she held in exile until 1986. Bhutto became prime minister of Pakistan from 1988–90, when the opposition manoeuvred her from office and charged her with corruption. She again rose to the office of prime minister (1993–96), only to be removed for a second time under suspicion of corruption, an offence for which she was charged late in 1998.

**Bhutto, Zulfikar Ali** (1928–1979) Pakistani politician, president 1971–73, and prime minister from 1973 until the 1977 military coup led by General Zia ul-Haq. In 1978 Bhutto was sentenced to death for conspiring to murder a political opponent and was hanged the following year. He was the father of Benazir Bhutto.

**Biafra, Bight of** or *Bonny, Bight of,* area of sea off the coasts of Nigeria and Cameroon.

**Biafra, Republic of** African state proclaimed 1967 when fears that Nigerian central government was increasingly in the hands of the rival Hausa tribe led the predominantly Ibo Eastern Region of Nigeria to secede under Lt-Col Odumegwu Ojukwu. On the proclamation of Biafra, civil war ensued with the rest of the federation. In a bitterly fought campaign federal forces confined the Biafrans to a shrinking area of the interior by 1968, and by 1970 Biafra ceased to exist.

**Bible** (Greek *ta biblia* 'the books') the sacred book of the Jewish and Christian religions. The Hebrew Bible, recognized by both Jews and Christians, is called the ◊*Old Testament* by Christians. The ◊*New Testament* comprises books recognized by the Christian church from the 4th century as canonical. The Roman Catholic Bible also includes the ◊*Apocrypha.*

**bicycle** pedal-driven two-wheeled vehicle used in ◊cycling. It consists of a metal frame mounted on two large wire-spoked wheels, with handlebars in front and a seat between the front and back wheels. The bicycle is an energy-efficient, nonpolluting form of transport, and it is estimated that 800 million bicycles are in use throughout the world – outnumbering cars three to one. China, India, Denmark, and the Netherlands are countries with a high use of bicycles. More than 10% of road spending in the Netherlands is on cycleways and bicycle parking.

**biennial plant** plant that completes its life cycle in two years. During the first year it grows vegetatively and the surplus food produced is stored in its ◊perennating organ, usually the root. In the following year these food reserves are used for the production of leaves, flowers, and seeds, after which the plant dies. Many root vegetables are biennials, including the carrot *Daucus carota* and parsnip *Pastinaca sativa*. Some garden plants that are grown as biennials are actually perennials, for example, the wall-flower *Cheiranthus cheiri*.

**big-band jazz** ◊swing music created in the late 1930s and 1940s by bands of 13 or more players, such as those of Duke ◊Ellington and Benny Goodman. Big-band jazz relied on fixed arrangements, where there is more than one instrument to some of the parts, rather than improvisation. Big bands were mainly dance bands, and they ceased to be economically viable in the 1950s.

**Big Bang** in astronomy, the hypothetical 'explosive' event that marked the origin of the universe as we know it. At the time of the Big Bang, the entire universe was squeezed into a hot, superdense state. The Big Bang explosion threw this compact material outwards, producing the expanding universe (see ◊red shift). The cause of the Big Bang is unknown; observations of the current rate of expansion of the universe suggest that it took place about 10–20 billion years ago. The Big Bang theory began modern ◊cosmology.

**Big Bang** in economics, popular term for the changes instituted in late 1986 to the organization and practices of the City of London as Britain's financial centre, including the liberalization of the London ◊stock exchange. This involved merging the functions of jobber (dealer in stocks and shares) and broker (who mediates between the jobber and the public), introducing negotiated commission rates, and allowing foreign banks and financial companies to own British brokers/jobbers, or themselves to join the London Stock Exchange.

**Bihar** or *Behar,* state of northeast India
**area** 173,900 sq km/67,125 sq mi
**capital** Patna
**physical** River Ganges runs west–east in the north, through intensely cultivated alluvial plains, prone to drought and floods; Rajmahal Hills, Chota Nagpur plateau in the south, much of which is forested
**industries** copper, iron, coal; 40% of India's mineral production
**agriculture** rice, jute, sugar cane, cereals, oilseed, tobacco, potatoes
**language** Hindi, Bihari
**population** (1994 est) 93,080,000, 75% living in northern plains
**famous people** Chandragupta Maurya, Asoka
**history** the ancient kingdom of Magadha roughly corresponded to central and south Bihar. Many Bihari people were massacred as a result of their protest at the establishment of Bangladesh in 1971. Elections were postponed and direct rule imposed after public disturbances in 1995.

**Bihari** a northern Indian people, also living in Bangladesh, Nepal, and Pakistan, and numbering over 40 million. The Bihari are mainly Muslim. The Bihari language is related to Hindi

and has several widely varying dialects. It belongs to the Indic branch of the Indo-European family. Many Bihari were massacred during the formation of Bangladesh, which they opposed.

**Bikini Atoll** atoll in the Marshall Islands, western Pacific, where the USA carried out 23 atomic- and hydrogen-bomb tests (some underwater) 1946–58.

**Biko, Steve (Stephen)** (1946–1977) South African civil-rights leader. An active opponent of ◊apartheid, he was arrested in September 1977; he died in detention six days later. Following his death in the custody of South African police, he became a symbol of the anti-apartheid movement. An inquest in the late 1980s found no-one was to blame for Biko's death.

Five former security policemen confessed to being involved in Biko's murder in January 1997. They applied for an amnesty to the Truth and Reconciliation Commission (TRC), the body charged with healing South Africa by exposing its past and laying foundations for a more peaceful future. The amnesty application angered Biko's family, and his widow challenged the legitimacy of the TRC in the Constitutional Court.

**Bilbao** industrial port and capital of Vizcaya province in the Basque Country, northern Spain; it is surrounded by mountains, and situated on an inlet of the Bay of Biscay, and on the Nervión River; population (1994) 372,000. Bilbao is a commercial centre and one of the chief ports in Spain; industries include iron and steel production, shipbuilding, chemicals, cement, and food-processing.

**bilberry** any of several shrubs belonging to the heath family, closely related to North American blueberries. They have blue or black edible berries. (Genus *Vaccinium,* family Ericaceae.)

**bile** brownish alkaline fluid produced by the liver. Bile is stored in the gall bladder and is intermittently released into the duodenum (small intestine) to aid digestion. Bile consists of bile salts, bile pigments, cholesterol, and lecithin. *Bile salts* assist in the breakdown and absorption of fats; *bile pigments* are the breakdown products of old red blood cells that are passed into the gut to be eliminated with the faeces.

**bilharzia** or *schistosomiasis,* disease that causes anaemia, inflammation, formation of scar tissue, dysentery, enlargement of the spleen and liver, cancer of the bladder, and cirrhosis of the liver. It is contracted by bathing in water contaminated with human sewage. Some 200 million people are thought to suffer from this disease in the tropics, and 750,000 people a year die.

**bill** in birds, the projection of the skull bones covered with a horny sheath. It is not normally sensitive, except in some aquatic birds, rooks, and woodpeckers, where the bill is used to locate food that is not visible. The bills of birds are adapted by shape and size to specific diets, for example, shovellers use their bills to sieve mud in order to extract food; birds of prey have hooked bills adapted to tearing flesh; the bills of the avocet, and the curlew are long and narrow for picking tiny invertebrates out of the mud; and those of woodpeckers are sharp for pecking holes in trees and plucking out insects. The bill is also used by birds for preening, fighting, display, and nest-building.

**billiards** indoor game played, normally by two players, with tapered poles (cues) and composition balls (one red, two white) on a rectangular table covered with a green, feltlike cloth (baize). The table has six pockets, one at each corner and in each of the long sides at the middle. Scoring strokes are made by potting the red ball, potting the opponent's ball, or potting another ball off one of these two. The cannon (when the cue ball hits the two other balls on the table) is another scoring stroke. In 1998 billiards received recognition from the International Olympic Committee as an Olympic sport, along with snooker, pool, and carom (or French) billiards.

**bill of exchange** form of commercial credit instrument, or IOU, used in international trade. In Britain, a bill of exchange is defined by the Bills of Exchange Act 1882 as an unconditional order in writing addressed by one person to another, signed by the person giving it, requiring the person to whom it is addressed to pay on demand or at a fixed or determinable future time a certain sum in money to or to the order of a specified person, or to the bearer.

**bill of lading** document giving proof of particular goods having been loaded on a ship. The person to whom the goods are being sent normally needs to show the bill of lading in order to obtain the release of the goods. For air freight, there is an *airway bill*.

**Bill of Rights** in the USA, the first ten amendments to the US ◊Constitution, incorporated in 1791:
*1* guarantees freedom of worship, of speech, of the press, of assembly, and to petition the government; *2* grants the right to keep and bear arms; *3* prohibits billeting of soldiers in private homes in peacetime; *4* forbids unreasonable search and seizure; *5* guarantees none be 'deprived of life, liberty or property without due process of law' or compelled in any criminal case to be a witness against himself or herself; *6* grants the right to speedy trial, to call witnesses, and to have defence counsel; *7* grants the right to trial by jury of one's peers; *8* prevents the infliction of excessive bail or fines, or 'cruel and unusual punishment'; *9, 10* provide a safeguard to the states and people for all rights not specifically delegated to the central government.

**Bill of Rights** in Britain, an act of Parliament of 1689 which established Parliament as the primary governing body of the country. It made provisions limiting ◊royal prerogative with respect to legislation, executive power, money levies, courts, and the army, and stipulated Parliament's consent to many government functions.

**Billy the Kid** nickname of William H Bonney (1859–1881) US outlaw. A leader in the 1878 Lincoln County cattle war in New Mexico, he allegedly killed his first victim at 12 and was reputed to have killed 21 men by age 22, when he died.

**binary fission** in biology, a form of ◊asexual reproduction, whereby a single-celled organism, such as the amoeba, divides into two smaller 'daughter' cells. It can also occur in a few simple multicellular organisms, such as sea anemones, producing two smaller sea anemones of equal size.

**binary number system** system of numbers to ◊base two, using combinations of the digits 1 and 0. Codes based on binary numbers are used to represent instructions and data in all modern digital computers, the values of the binary digits (contracted to 'bits') being stored or transmitted as, for example, open/closed switches, magnetized/unmagnetized disks and tapes, and high/low voltages in circuits.

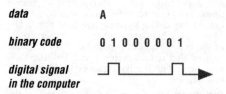

**binary number system** *The capital letter A represented in binary form.*

**binary star** pair of stars moving in orbit around their common centre of mass. Observations show that most stars are binary, or even multiple – for example, the nearest star system to the Sun, ◊Alpha Centauri.

**binary weapon** in chemical warfare, weapon consisting of two substances that in isolation are harmless but when mixed together form a poisonous nerve gas. They are loaded into the delivery system separately and combine after launch.

**binding energy** in physics, the amount of energy needed to break the nucleus of an atom into the neutrons and protons of which it is made.

**bind over** in law, a UK court order that requires a person to carry out some act, usually by an order given in a magistrates' court. A person may be bound over to appear in court at a particular time if bail has been granted or, most commonly, be bound over not to commit some offence; for example, causing a breach of the peace.

**binoculars** optical instrument for viewing an object in magnification with both eyes; for example, field glasses and opera glasses. Binoculars consist of two telescopes containing lenses and prisms, which produce a stereoscopic effect as well as magnifying the image.
   Use of prisms has the effect of 'folding' the light path, allowing for a compact design.

**binomial** in mathematics, an expression consisting of two terms, such as $a + b$ or $a - b$.

**binomial system of nomenclature** in biology, the system in which all organisms are identified by a two-part Latinized name. Devised by the biologist ◊Linnaeus, it is also known as the Linnaean system. The first name is capitalized and identifies the ◊genus; the second identifies the ◊species within that genus.

**binturong** shaggy-coated mammal *Arctitis binturong*, the largest member of the mongoose family, nearly 1 m/3 ft long excluding a long muscular tail with a prehensile tip. Mainly nocturnal and tree-dwelling, the binturong is found in the forests of Southeast Asia, feeding on fruit, eggs, and small animals.

**biochemistry** science concerned with the chemistry of living organisms: the structure and reactions of proteins (such as enzymes), nucleic acids, carbohydrates, and lipids.

**biodegradable** capable of being broken down by living organisms, principally bacteria and fungi. In biodegradable substances, such as food and sewage, the natural processes of decay lead to compaction and liquefaction, and to the release of nutrients that are then recycled by the ecosystem.

**biodiversity** contraction of *biological diversity*, measure of the variety of the Earth's animal, plant, and microbial species; of genetic differences within species; and of the ecosystems that support those species. Its maintenance is important for ecological stability and as a resource for research into, for example, new drugs and crops. In the 20th century, the destruction of habitats is believed to have resulted in the most severe and rapid loss of biodiversity in the history of the planet.

**biodynamic farming** agricultural practice based on the principle of ◊homeopathy: tiny quantities of a substance are applied to transmit vital qualities to the soil. It is a form of ◊organic farming, and was developed by the Austrian holistic mystic Rudolf ◊Steiner and Ehrenfried Pfiffer.

**bioengineering** the application of engineering to biology and medicine. Common applications include the design and use of artificial limbs, joints, and organs, including hip joints and heart valves.

**biological control** control of pests such as insects and fungi through biological means, rather than the use of chemicals. This can include breeding resistant crop strains; inducing sterility in the pest; infecting the pest species with disease organisms; or introducing the pest's natural predator. Biological control tends to be naturally self-regulating, but as ecosystems are so complex, it is difficult to predict all the consequences of introducing a biological controlling agent.

**biological warfare** the use of living organisms, or of infectious material derived from them, to bring about death or disease in humans, animals, or plants. At least ten countries have this capability.

**biology** (Greek *bios* 'life', *logos* 'discourse') science of life. Biology includes all the life sciences – for example, anatomy and physiology (the study of the structure and function of living things), cytology (the study of cells), zoology (the study of animals) and botany (the study of plants), ecology (the study of habitats and the interaction of living species), animal behaviour, embryology, taxonomy, and plant breeding. Increasingly in the 20th century biologists have concentrated on molecular structures: biochemistry, biophysics, and genetics (the study of inheritance and variation).

**bioluminescence** production of light by living organisms. It is a feature of many deep-sea fishes, crustaceans, and other marine animals. On land, bioluminescence is seen in some nocturnal insects such as glow-worms and fireflies, and in certain bacteria and fungi. Light is usually produced by the oxidation of luciferin, a reaction catalysed by the ◊enzyme luciferase. This reaction is unique, being the only known biological oxidation that does not produce heat. Animal luminescence is involved in communication, camouflage, or the luring of prey, but its function in other organisms is unclear.

**biomass** the total mass of living organisms present in a given area. It may be specified for a particular species (such as earthworm biomass) or for a general category (such as herbivore biomass). Estimates also exist for the entire global plant biomass. Measurements of biomass can be used to study interactions between organisms, the stability of those interactions, and variations in population numbers. Where dry biomass is measured, the material is dried to remove all water before weighing.

**biome** broad natural assemblage of plants and animals shaped by common patterns of vegetation and climate. Examples include the tundra biome and the desert biome.

**bionics** (from 'biological electronics') design and development of electronic or mechanical artificial systems that imitate those of living things. The bionic arm, for example, is an artificial limb (◊prosthesis) that uses electronics to amplify minute electrical signals generated in body muscles to work electric motors, which operate the joints of the fingers and wrist.

**biopsy** removal of a living tissue sample from the body for diagnostic examination.

**biosphere** the narrow zone that supports life on our planet. It is limited to the waters of the Earth, a fraction of its crust, and the lower regions of the atmosphere. The biosphere is made up of all the Earth's ecosystems. It is affected by external forces such as the Sun's rays, which provide energy, the gravitational effects of the Sun and Moon, and cosmic radiations.

**biosynthesis** synthesis of organic chemicals from simple inorganic ones by living cells – for example, the conversion of carbon dioxide and water to glucose by plants during ◊photosynthesis.

Other biosynthetic reactions produce cell constituents including proteins and fats.

**biotechnology** industrial use of living organisms to manufacture food, drugs, or other products. The brewing and baking industries have long relied on the yeast micro-organism for ◊fermentation purposes, while the dairy industry employs a range of bacteria and fungi to convert milk into cheeses and yoghurts. ◊Enzymes, whether extracted from cells or produced artificially, are central to most biotechnological applications.

**birch** any of a group of slender trees with small leaves and fine, peeling bark. About 40 species are found in cool temperate parts of the northern hemisphere. Birches grow rapidly, and their hard, beautiful wood is used for veneers and cabinet work. (Genus *Betula,* family Betulaceae.)

**bird** backboned animal of the class Aves, the biggest group of land vertebrates, characterized by warm blood, feathers, wings, breathing through lungs, and egg-laying by the female. Birds are bipedal; feet are usually adapted for perching and never have more than four toes. Hearing and eyesight are well developed, but the sense of smell is usually poor. No existing species of bird possesses teeth.

Most birds fly, but some groups (such as ostriches) are flightless, and others include flightless members. Many communicate by sounds (nearly half of all known species are songbirds) or by visual displays, in connection with which many species are brightly coloured, usually the males. Birds have highly developed patterns of instinctive behaviour. There are nearly 8,500 species of birds.

**bird of paradise** one of 40 species of crow-like birds in the family Paradiseidae, native to New Guinea and neighbouring islands. Females are generally drably coloured, but the males have bright and elaborate plumage used in courtship display. Hunted almost to extinction for their plumage, they are now subject to conservation.

**Birendra, Bir Bikram Shah Dev** (1945–  ) King of Nepal from 1972, when he succeeded his father Mahendra; he was formally crowned in 1975. King Birendra oversaw Nepal's return to multiparty politics and introduced a new constitution in 1990.

**Birmingham** industrial city and administrative headquarters of ◊West Midlands metropolitan county, central England, second-largest city in the UK, 177 km/110 mi northwest of London; population (1994 est) 1,220,000, metropolitan area 2,632,000. It is a major manufacturing, engineering, commercial, and service centre. The city's concert halls, theatres, and three universities also make it an important cultural and educational centre. Its chief products are motor vehicles, vehicle components and accessories, machine tools, aerospace control systems, electrical equipment, plastics, chemicals, food, chocolate (Cadbury), jewellery, tyres, glass, cars, and guns.

**Birmingham** city in north-central Alabama, USA, situated in the Jones Valley, at the southern end of the Appalachian Mountains; seat of Jefferson County; population (1994 est) 265,000. It is the largest city in ◊Alabama and is an industrial centre for iron, steel (Birmingham

was once the steelmaking centre of the South), chemicals, building materials, railroad and aircraft equipment, computers, and cotton textiles; its port is connected to the Gulf of Mexico via the Black Warrior River.

**birth** act of producing live young from within the body of female animals. Both viviparous and ovoviviparous animals give birth to young. In viviparous animals, embryos obtain nourishment from the mother via a ◊placenta or other means.

In ovoviviparous animals, fertilized eggs develop and hatch in the oviduct of the mother and gain little or no nourishment from maternal tissues. See also ◊pregnancy.

**birth control** another name for ◊family planning; see also ◊contraceptive.

**birth rate** the number of live births per thousand of the population over a period of time, usually a year (sometimes it is also expressed as a percentage). For example, a birth rate of 20 per thousand (or 2%) would mean that 20 babies were being born per thousand of the population. It is sometimes called *crude birth rate* because it takes in the whole population, including men and women who are too old to bear children.

**Biscay, Bay of** bay of the Atlantic Ocean between northern Spain and western France, known for rough seas and high tides. It is traditionally a rich fishing area.

**Bishkek** formerly (1878–1926) *Pishpek;* (1926–92) *Frunze,* capital of Kyrgyzstan; population (1996) 670,000. Bishkek is situated in the valley of the River Chu north of the Kyrgyz Alatau mountain range, 180 km/112 mi west of Almaty in Kazakhstan. Among the goods produced here are textiles, agricultural machinery, and electrical goods. Food industries include meat-packing and tobacco production.

**Bismarck, Otto Eduard Leopold von** (1815–1898) German politician, prime minister of Prussia 1862–90 and chancellor of the German Empire 1871–90. He pursued an aggressively expansionist policy, waging wars against Denmark 1863–64, Austria 1866, and France 1870–71, which brought about the unification of Germany. He became Prince 1871.

**Bismarck Archipelago** group of over 200 islands in the southwest Pacific Ocean, part of Papua New Guinea; area 49,660 sq km/19,200 sq mi. The largest island is New Britain. Coconut fibre, copra, cotton, rubber, coffee, tortoiseshell, trepang (sea cucumbers), mother-of-pearl, and fruit are the chief products. The population is mostly Papuan.

**bismuth** hard, brittle, pinkish-white, metallic element, symbol Bi, atomic number 83, relative atomic mass 208.98. It has the highest atomic number of all the stable elements (the elements from atomic number 84 up are radioactive). Bismuth occurs in ores and occasionally as a free metal (native metal). It is a poor conductor of heat and electricity, and is used in alloys of low melting point and in medical compounds to soothe gastric ulcers. The name comes from the

Latin *besemutum,* from the earlier German *Wismut.*

**bison** large, hoofed mammal of the bovine family. There are two species, both brown. The *European bison* or **wisent** *Bison bonasus,* of which only a few protected herds survive, is about 2 m/7 ft high and weighs up to 1,100 kg/2,500 lb. The *North American bison* (often known as 'buffalo') *Bison bison* is slightly smaller, with a heavier mane and more sloping hindquarters. Formerly roaming the prairies in vast numbers, it was almost exterminated in the 19th century, but survives in protected areas. There were about 14,000 bison in North American reserves in 1994.

**Bissau** capital and chief port of Guinea-Bissau, on an island at the mouth of the Geba River; population (1992) 145,000. Originally a Portuguese fortified slave-trading centre (1687), Bissau became a free port in 1869. Industries include agricultural processing, fishing, textiles, and crafts. There are refrigeration units at the port, and there is an international airport and a university. Bissau replaced Bolama as the capital in 1941.

**bit** contraction of binary digit, in computing, a single binary digit, either 0 or 1. A bit is the smallest unit of data stored in a computer; all other data must be coded into a pattern of individual bits. A ◊byte represents sufficient computer memory to store a single character of data, and usually contains eight bits. For example, in the ◊ASCII code system used by most microcomputers the capital letter A would be stored in a single byte of memory as the bit pattern 01000001.

**bittern** any of several species of small herons, in particular the common bittern *Botaurus stellaris* of Europe and Asia. It is shy, stoutly built, buff-coloured, speckled with black and tawny brown, with a long bill and a loud, booming call. Its habit of holding its neck and bill in a vertical position conceals it among the reeds, where it rests by day, hunting for frogs, reptiles, and fish towards nightfall. An inhabitant of marshy country, it is now quite rare in Britain.

**bittersweet** alternative name for the woody ◊nightshade plant.

**bitumen** impure mixture of hydrocarbons, including such deposits as petroleum, asphalt, and natural gas, although sometimes the term is restricted to a soft kind of pitch resembling asphalt.

**bivalve** marine or freshwater mollusc whose body is enclosed between two shells hinged together by a ligament on the dorsal side of the body.

**Bizet, Georges (Alexandre César Léopold)** (1838–1875) French composer of operas. Among his works are *Les Pêcheurs de perles/The Pearl Fishers* (1863) and *La Jolie Fille de Perth/The Fair Maid of Perth* (1866). He also wrote the concert overture *Patrie* and incidental music to Alphonse Daudet's play *L'Arlésienne* (1872), which has remained a standard work in the form of two suites for orchestra. His operatic masterpiece *Carmen* was produced a few months before his death in 1875. His Symphony in C, written when he was 17, is now frequently performed.

**black** English term first used in 1625 to describe West Africans, now used to refer to Africans south of the Sahara and to people of African descent living outside Africa. In some countries such as the UK (but not in North America) the term is sometimes also used for people originally from the Indian subcontinent, for Australian Aborigines, and peoples of Melanesia.

**Black and Tans** nickname for a special auxiliary force of the Royal Irish Constabulary employed by the British 1920–21 to combat the Sinn Feiners (Irish nationalists) in Ireland; the name derives from the colours of the uniforms, khaki with black hats and belts.

**black beetle** another name for ◊cockroach, although cockroaches belong to an entirely different order of insects (Dictyoptera) from the beetles (Coleoptera).

**blackberry** prickly shrub, closely related to raspberries and dewberries. Native to northern parts of Europe, it produces pink or white blossom and edible black compound fruits. (*Rubus fruticosus,* family Rosaceae.)

**blackbird** bird *Turdus merula* of the thrush family, Muscicapidae, order Passeriformes, about 25 cm/10 in long. The male is black with a yellow bill and eyelids, the female dark brown with a dark beak. It lays three to five blue-green eggs with brown spots in a nest of grass and moss, plastered with mud, built in thickets or creeper-clad trees. The blackbird feeds on fruit, seeds, worms, grubs, and snails. Its song is rich and flutelike.

**Blackburn with Darwen** unitary authority (borough status) in northwest England created in 1998, formerly part of Lancashire
*area* 136 sq km2/53 sq mi
*towns and cities* Blackburn (administrative headquarters), Darwen
*features* Leeds–Liverpool canal; River Darwen; Darwen Hill and Tower (372 m/1,220 ft); western foothills of Rossendale uplands; Lewis Textile Museum (Blackburn) includes working model of spinning jenny; Blackburn Museum and Art Gallery has largest display of European icons in Britain
*industries* engineering, brewing, chemicals, high technology industries, textiles, leather, electronics, paint, paper, carpets, compact discs
*population* (1996) 139,400
*famous people* James Hargreaves.

**blackcurrant** variety of ◊currant.

**Black Death** great epidemic of bubonic ◊plague that ravaged Europe in the mid-14th century, killing between one-third and half of the population (about 75 million people). The cause of the plague was the bacterium *Yersinia pestis,* transmitted by fleas borne by migrating Asian black rats. The name Black Death was first used in England in the early 19th century.

**black earth** exceedingly fertile soil that covers a belt of land in northeastern North America, Europe, and Asia.

**blackfly** plant-sucking insect, a type of ◊aphid.

**Black Forest** German *Schwarzwald,* mountainous region of coniferous forest in Baden-Württemberg, western Germany; length 160 km/100 mi, greatest breadth 57 km/35 mi. Bounded to the west and south by the Rhine, which separates it from the Vosges, it rises to 1,493 m/4,898 ft in the Feldberg. It extends to the Swiss border in the south and to the Neckar valley in the north. Parts of the forest have recently been affected by ◊acid rain. The region is a popular tourist destination and lumbering is an important industry.

**black hole** object in space whose gravity is so great that nothing can escape from it, not even light. Thought to form when massive stars shrink at the end of their lives, a black hole sucks in more matter, including other stars, from the space around it. Matter that falls into a black hole is squeezed to infinite density at the centre of the hole. Black holes can be detected because gas falling towards them becomes so hot that it emits X-rays.

**blackmail** criminal offence of extorting money with menaces or threats of detrimental action, such as exposure of some misconduct on the part of the victim.

**black nationalism** movement towards black separatism in the USA during the 1960s; see ◊Black Power.

**Black National State** area in the Republic of South Africa set aside 1971–94 for development towards self-government by black Africans, in accordance with ◊apartheid. Before 1980 these areas were known as *black homelands* or *bantustans.* Making up less than 14% of the country, they tended to be situated in arid areas (though some had mineral wealth), often in scattered blocks. Those that achieved nominal independence were Transkei in 1976, Bophuthatswana in 1977, Venda in 1979, and Ciskei in 1981. They were not recognized outside South Africa because of their racial basis.

**Blackpool** seaside resort and unitary authority in northwest England, 45 km/28 mi north of Liverpool; part of the county of Lancashire until April 1998
*area* 35 sq km/14 sq mi
*physical* with its neighbours Lytham St Annes to the south and Fleetwood to the north, Blackpool is part of an urban ribbon between the Ribble estuary and Morecambe Bay
*features* 11 km/7 mi of promenades, known for their autumn 'illuminations' of coloured lights; Blackpool Tower (built in 1894 and modelled on the Eiffel Tower in Paris), 157 m/518 ft high; the Pleasure Beach, an amusement park that includes Europe's largest and fastest roller-coaster, 75 m/235 ft high and 1.5 km/1 mi long (opened in 1994); three 19th-century piers; the Winter-gardens, Grand Theatre, and Sealife Centre; a tram, which first operated in 1885,

transports visitors along the promenade
*industries* Blackpool is the largest holiday resort in northern England, and provides important conference business facilities. Other industries include light engineering and the production of confectionery and biscuits
*population* (1997) 151,200; Blackpool urban area (1991) 261,400.

**Black Power** movement towards black separatism in the USA during the 1960s, embodied in the *Black Panther Party* founded 1966 by Huey Newton and Bobby Seale. Its declared aim was the creation of a separate black state in the USA to be established by a black plebiscite under the aegis of the United Nations. Following a National Black Political Convention 1972, a National Black Assembly was established to exercise pressure on the Democratic and Republican parties.

**Black Prince** nickname of ◊Edward, Prince of Wales, eldest son of Edward III of England.

**Black Sea** Russian *Chernoye More,* inland sea in southeast Europe, linked with the seas of Azov and Marmara, and via the Dardanelles strait with the Mediterranean; area 423,000 sq km/163,320 sq mi; maximum depth 2,245 m/7,365 ft, decreasing in the Sea of Azov to only 13.5 m/44 ft. It is bounded by Ukraine, Russia, Georgia, Turkey, Bulgaria, and Romania, and the rivers Danube, Volga, Bug, Dniester and Dnieper flow into it, keeping salinity levels low. Uranium deposits beneath it are among the world's largest. About 90% of the water is polluted, mainly by agricultural fertilizers.

**Blackshirts** term widely used to describe fascist paramilitary organizations. Originating with Mussolini's fascist Squadristi in the 1920s, it was also applied to the Nazi SS (*Schutzstaffel*) and to the followers of Oswald Mosley's British Union of Fascists.

**blacksnake** any of several species of snake. The blacksnake *Pseudechis porphyriacus* is a venomous snake of the cobra family found in damp forests and swamps in eastern Australia. The blacksnake, *Coluber constrictor* from the eastern USA, is a relative of the European grass snake, growing up to 1.2 m/4 ft long, and without venom.

**blackthorn** densely branched spiny European bush. It produces white blossom on bare black branches in early spring. Its sour plumlike blue-black fruit, the sloe, is used to make sloe gin. (*Prunus spinosa,* family Rosaceae.)

**black widow** North American spider *Latrodectus mactans.* The male is small and harmless, but the female is 1.3 cm/0.5 in long with a red patch below the abdomen and a powerful venomous bite. The bite causes pain and fever in human victims, but they usually recover.

**bladder** hollow elastic-walled organ which stores the urine produced in the kidneys. It is present in the ◊urinary systems of some fishes, most amphibians, some reptiles, and all mammals. Urine enters the bladder through two ureters, one leading from each kidney, and leaves it through the urethra.

**bladderwort** any of a large group of carnivorous aquatic plants. They have leaves with bladders (hollow sacs) that trap small animals living in the water. (Genus *Utricularia,* family Lentibulariaceae.)

**Blaenau Gwent** unitary authority in south Wales, created in 1996 from part of the former county of Gwent
*area* 109 sq km/42 sq mi
*towns* Ebbw Vale (administrative headquarters), Tredegar, Abertillery
*features* Mynydd Carn-y-Cefn (550 m/1,800 ft); rivers Sirhowy and Ebbw; part of the Brecon Beacons National Park is here
*population* (1996) 73,000.

**Blair, Tony (Anthony Charles Lynton)** (1953– ) British politician, born in Edinburgh, Scotland, leader of the Labour Party from 1994, prime minister from 1997. A centrist in the manner of his predecessor John Smith, he became Labour's youngest leader by a large majority in the first fully democratic elections to the post in July 1994. In 1995 he won approval of a new Labour Party charter, intended to distance the party from its traditional socialist base and promote 'social market' values. He and his party secured a landslide victory in the 1997 general election with a 179-seat majority. He retained a high public approval rating of 60% in February 1998.

**Blake, William** (1757–1827) English poet, artist, engraver, and visionary, and one of the most important figures of English ◊Romanticism. His lyrics, often written with a childlike simplicity, as in *Songs of Innocence* (1789) and *Songs of Experience* (1794), express a unique spiritual vision. In his 'prophetic books', including *The Marriage of Heaven and Hell* (1790), he created a vast personal mythology. He illustrated his own works with hand-coloured engravings.

**blank verse** in literature, the unrhymed iambic pentameter or ten-syllable line of five stresses. First used by the Italian Gian Giorgio Trissino in his tragedy *Sofonisba* (1514–15), it was introduced to England about 1540 by the Earl of Surrey, who used it in his translation of Virgil's *Aeneid*. It was developed by Christopher Marlowe and Shakespeare, quickly becoming the distinctive verse form of Elizabethan and Jacobean drama. It was later used by Milton in *Paradise Lost* (1667) and by Wordsworth in *The Prelude* (1805). More recent exponents of blank verse in English include Thomas Hardy, T S Eliot, and Robert Frost.

**Blantyre** chief industrial and commercial centre of Malawi, in the Shire highlands at the foot of Mchiru Mountain; population (1993) 399,000. The largest city in Malawi, it produces tea, coffee, rubber, tobacco, textiles, and wood products.

**blasphemy** (Greek 'evil-speaking') written or spoken insult directed against religious belief or sacred things with deliberate intent to outrage believers.

**blast furnace** smelting furnace used to extract metals from their ores, chiefly pig iron from iron ore. The temperature is raised by the injection of an air blast.

**blastomere** in biology, a cell formed in the first stages of embryonic development, after the splitting of the fertilized ovum, but before the formation of the blastula or blastocyst.

**Blaue Reiter, der** German 'the Blue Rider', loose association of German Expressionist painters formed 1911 in Munich. They were united by an interest in the expressive qualities of colour, in primitive and folk art, and in the necessity of painting 'the inner, spiritual side of nature', though their individual styles varied greatly. Two central figures were ◊Kandinsky and Franz ◊Marc.

**bleaching** decolorization of coloured materials. The two main types of bleaching agent are the *oxidizing bleaches,* which bring about the ◊oxidation of pigments and include the ultraviolet rays in sunshine, hydrogen peroxide, and chlorine in household bleaches, and the *reducing bleaches,* which bring about ◊reduction and include sulphur dioxide.

**bleeding** loss of blood from the circulation; see ◊haemorrhage.

**blenny** any fish of the family Blenniidae, mostly small fishes found near rocky shores, with elongated slimy bodies tapering from head to tail, no scales, and long pelvic fins set far forward.

**Blériot, Louis** (1872–1936) French aviator. In a 24-horsepower monoplane of his own construction, he made the first flight across the English Channel 25 July 1909.

**Bligh, William** (1754–1817) English sailor. He accompanied Captain James ◊Cook on his second voyage around the world (1772–74), and in 1787 commanded HMS *Bounty* on an expedition to the Pacific. On the return voyage, in protest against harsh treatment, the crew mutinied. Bligh was sent to Australia as governor of New South Wales in 1805, where his discipline again provoked a mutiny 1808 (the Rum Rebellion).

**blind spot** area where the optic nerve and blood vessels pass through the retina of the ◊eye. No visual image can be formed as there are no light-sensitive cells in this part of the retina.

Thus the organism is blind to objects that fall in this part of the visual field.

**Blitzkrieg** (German 'lightning war') swift military campaign, as used by Germany at the beginning of World War II 1939–41. It was characterized by rapid movement by mechanized forces, supported by tactical air forces acting as 'flying artillery' and is best exemplified by the campaigns in Poland 1939 and France 1940.

**Blixen, Karen (Christentze)** Baroness Blixen born Dinesen (1885–1962) Danish writer. She wrote mainly in English and is best known for her short stories, Gothic fantasies with a haunting, often mythic quality, published in such collections as *Seven Gothic Tales* (1934) and *Winter's Tales* (1942) under the pen-name *Isak Dinesen*. Her autobiography *Out of Africa* (1937) (filmed 1985) is based on her experience of running a coffee plantation in Kenya.

**Bloemfontein** (Afrikaans 'fountain of flowers') capital of the ◊Free State (formerly Orange Free State) and judicial capital of the Republic of South Africa; population (1991) 300,150. Founded in 1846 and declared a municipality in 1880, the city produces canned fruit, glassware, furniture, plastics, and railway engineering. The city's climate makes it a popular health resort.

**blood** fluid circulating in the arteries, veins, and capillaries of vertebrate animals; the term also refers to the corresponding fluid in those invertebrates that possess a closed ◊circulatory system. Blood carries nutrients and oxygen to each body cell and removes waste products, such as carbon dioxide. It is also important in the immune response and, in many animals, in the distribution of heat throughout the body.

**blood clotting** complex series of events (known as the blood clotting cascade) that prevents excessive bleeding after injury. The result is the formation of a meshwork of protein fibres (fibrin) and trapped blood cells over the cut blood vessels.

**blood group** any of the types into which blood is classified according to the presence or otherwise of certain ◊antigens on the surface of its red cells. Red blood cells of one individual may carry molecules on their surface that act as antigens in another individual whose red blood cells lack these molecules. The two main antigens are designated A and B. These give rise to four blood groups: having A only (A), having B only (B), having both (AB), and having neither (O). Each of these groups may or may not contain the ◊rhesus factor. Correct typing of blood groups is vital in transfusion, since incompatible types of donor and recipient blood will result in coagulation, with possible death of the recipient.

**blood poisoning** presence in the bloodstream of quantities of bacteria or bacterial toxins sufficient to cause serious illness.

**blood pressure** pressure, or tension, of the blood against the inner walls of blood vessels, especially the arteries, due to the muscular pumping activity of the heart. Abnormally high blood pressure (◊hypertension) may be associated with various conditions or arise with no obvious cause; abnormally low blood pressure (hypotension) occurs in ◊shock and after excessive fluid or blood loss from any cause.

**blood test** laboratory evaluation of a blood sample. There are numerous blood tests, from simple typing to establish the ◊blood group to sophisticated biochemical assays of substances, such as hormones, present in the blood only in minute quantities.

**blood transfusion** see ◊transfusion.

**Bloomsbury Group** intellectual circle of writers and artists based in Bloomsbury, London, which flourished in the 1920s. It centred on the house of publisher Leonard Woolf

(1880–1969) and his wife, novelist Virginia ◊Woolf. Typically Modernist, their innovative artistic contributions represented an important section of the English avant-garde.

**blowfly** any fly of the genus *Calliphora*, also known as bluebottle, or of the related genus *Lucilia*, when it is greenbottle. It lays its eggs in dead flesh, on which the maggots feed.

**Blücher, Gebhard Leberecht von** (1742–1819) Prussian general and field marshal, popularly known as 'Marshal Forward'. He took an active part in the patriotic movement, and in the War of German Liberation defeated the French as commander in chief at Leipzig 1813, crossed the Rhine to Paris 1814, and was made prince of Wahlstadt (Silesia).

**bluebell** name given in Scotland to the ◊harebell (*Campanula rotundifolia*), and in England to the wild hyacinth (*Endymion nonscriptus*), belonging to the lily family (Liliaceae).

**blueberry** any of various North American shrubs belonging to the heath family, growing in acid soil. The genus also includes huckleberries, bilberries, deerberries, and cranberries, many of which resemble each other and are difficult to tell apart from blueberries. All have small oval short-stalked leaves, slender green or reddish twigs, and whitish bell-like blossoms. Only true blueberries, however, have tiny granular speckles on their twigs. Blueberries have black or blue edible fruits, often covered with a white bloom. (Genus *Vaccinium*, family Ericaceae.)

**bluebird** or *blue robin* or *blue warbler,* three species of a North American bird, genus *Sialia,* belonging to the thrush subfamily, Turdinae, order Passeriformes. The eastern bluebird *Sialia sialis* is regarded as the herald of spring as it returns from migration. About 18 cm/7 in long, it has a reddish breast, the upper plumage being sky-blue, and a distinctive song. It lays about six pale-blue eggs.

**bluebottle** another name for ◊blowfly.

**bluebuck** any of several species of antelope, including the blue ◊duiker *Cephalophus monticola* of South Africa, about 33 cm/13 in high. The male of the Indian nilgai antelope is also known as the bluebuck.

**blue chip** in business and finance, a stock that is considered strong and reliable in terms of the dividend yield and capital value. Blue-chip companies are favoured by stock-market investors more interested in security than risk taking.

**bluegrass** dense spreading grass, which is blue-tinted and grows in clumps. Various species are known from the northern hemisphere. Kentucky bluegrass (*Poa pratensis*), introduced to the USA from Europe, provides pasture for horses. (Genus *Poa,* family Gramineae.)

**blue-green algae** or *cyanobacteria,* single-celled, primitive organisms that resemble bacteria in their internal cell organization, sometimes joined together in colonies or filaments. Blue-green algae are among the oldest known living organisms and, with bacteria, belong to the kingdom Monera; remains have been found in rocks up to 3.5 billion years old. They are widely distributed in aquatic habitats, on the damp surfaces of rocks and trees, and in the soil.

**blue gum** either of two Australian trees: Tasmanian blue gum (*Eucalyptus globulus*) of the myrtle family, with bluish bark, a chief source of eucalyptus oil; or the tall, straight Sydney blue gum (*E. saligna*). The former is widely cultivated in California and has also been planted in South America, India, parts of Africa, and southern Europe.

**Blue Mountains** part of the ◊Great Dividing Range, New South Wales, Australia, running almost parallel with the coast, 80–100 km/ 50–62 mi west of Sydney. The highest peak is Mount Beemarang (1,247 m/4,091 ft). The mountains are popular with tourists, attracted by the fine scenery.

**Blue Nile** Arabic *Al Bahr al-Azraq,* river rising at a spring site upstream of Lake Tana in Ethiopia, 2,150 m/7,054 ft above sea level. Flowing west then north for 1,460 km/907 mi, it eventually meets the White Nile at Khartoum. A length of 800 km/500 mi is navigable at high water. Some 80% of Sudan's electricity is provided by hydroelectric schemes at Roseires and Sennar, and these dams provide irrigation water for over 10,000 sq km/3,860 sq mi of the Gezira Plain.

**Blue Ridge Mountains** mountain range in southeastern USA, and part of the ◊Appalachian Mountains system. The Blue Ridge Mountains run from northwest Georgia to West Virginia. The highest summit (and also the highest point in eastern USA) is Mount Mitchell; height 2,037 m/6,684 ft.

**blues** African-American music that originated in the work songs and Negro spirituals of the rural American South in the late 19th century. It is characterized by a 12-bar, or occasionally 16-bar, construction and melancholy lyrics which relate tales of woe or unhappy love. The guitar has been the dominant instrument; harmonica and piano are also common. Blues guitar and vocal styles have played a vital part in the development of jazz, rock, and pop music in general.

**blue shift** in astronomy, a manifestation of the ◊Doppler effect in which an object appears bluer when it is moving towards the observer or the observer is moving towards it (blue light is of a higher frequency than other colours in the spectrum). The blue shift is the opposite of the ◊red shift.

**Blunt, Anthony Frederick** (1907–1983) English art historian and double agent. As a Cambridge lecturer, he recruited for the Soviet secret service and, as a member of the British Secret Service 1940–45, passed information to the USSR. In 1951 he assisted the defection to the USSR of the British agents Guy Burgess and Donald Maclean (1913–1983). He was the author of many respected works on Italian and French art, including a study of Poussin (1966–67). Unmasked in 1964, he was given immunity after his confession.

**Blyton, Enid Mary** (1897–1968) English writer of children's books. She used her abilities as a trained teacher of young children and a journalist, coupled with her ability to think like a child, to produce books at all levels which, though criticized for their predictability and lack of characterization, and more recently for social, racial, and sexual stereotyping, satisfy the reader's need for security. Her best-selling series were, the 'Famous Five' series, the 'Secret Seven', and 'Noddy'.

**boa** any of various nonvenomous snakes of the family Boidae, found mainly in tropical and subtropical parts of the New World. Boas feed mainly on small mammals and birds. They catch these in their teeth or kill them by constriction (crushing the creature within their coils until it suffocates). The boa constrictor *Constrictor constrictor* can grow up to 5.5 m/18.5 ft long, but rarely reaches more than 4 m/12 ft. Other boas include the anaconda and the emerald tree boa *Boa canina,* about 2 m/6 ft long and bright green.

**Boadicea** alternative (Latin) spelling of British queen ◊Boudicca.

**boar** wild member of the pig family, such as the Eurasian wild boar *Sus scrofa,* from which domestic pig breeds derive. The wild boar is sturdily built, being 1.5 m/4.5 ft long and 1 m/3 ft high, and possesses formidable tusks. Of gregarious nature and mainly woodland-dwelling, it feeds on roots, nuts, insects, and some carrion.

**boat people** illegal emigrants travelling by sea, especially those Vietnamese who left their country after the takeover of South Vietnam in 1975 by North Vietnam. In 1979, almost 69,000 boat people landed in Hong Kong in a single year. By 1988, it was decided to treat all boat people as illegal immigrants unless they could prove they qualified for refugee status. In all, some 160,000 Vietnamese fled to Hong Kong, many being attacked at sea by Thai pirates, and in 1989 50,000 remained there in cramped, squalid refugee camps. The UK government began forced repatriation 1989–90, leaving only 18,000 in Hong Kong by 1996. Before taking over Hong Kong in 1997, the Chinese authorities made it clear that they wanted all the Vietnamese cleared out of the territory. At the end of 1997, 3,364 refugees were still living in Hong Kong. In January 1998 the Hong Kong Executive Council ended the policy of granting asylum to the boat people. A UN-backed plan to accelerate the repatriation of around 38,000 boat people living in Southeast Asia was announced January 1996.

**Boat Race, the** annual UK ◊rowing race between the crews of Oxford and Cambridge universities. It is held during the Easter vacation over a 6.8 km/4.25 mi course on the River Thames between Putney and Mortlake, southwest London.

**bobcat** wild cat *Lynx rufus* living in a variety of habitats from southern Canada through to southern Mexico. It is similar to the lynx, but only 75 cm/2.5 ft long, with reddish fur and less well-developed ear tufts.

**bobsleighing** or *bobsledding,* sport of racing steel-bodied, steerable toboggans, crewed by two or four people, down mountain ice chutes at speeds of up to 130 kph/80 mph. It was introduced as an Olympic event in 1924 and world championships have been held every year since 1931. Included among the major bobsleighing events are the Olympic Championships (the four-crew event was introduced at the 1924 Winter Olympics and the two-crew in 1932) and the World Championships, the four-crew championship introduced in 1924 and the two-crew in 1931. In Olympic years winners automatically become world champions.

**Boccaccio, Giovanni** (1313–1375) Italian writer and poet. He is chiefly known for the collection of tales called the *Decameron* (1348–53). Equally at home with tragic and comic narrative, he laid the foundations for the humanism of the Renaissance and raised vernacular literature to the status enjoyed by the ancient classics.

**Bodhidharma** (lived 6th century AD) Indian Buddhist and teacher. He entered China from southern India about 520 and was the founder of the Ch'an school. Ch'an focuses on contemplation leading to intuitive meditation, a direct pointing to and stilling of the human mind. In the 20th century, the Japanese variation, ◊Zen, has attracted many followers in the West.

**bodhisattva** in Mahāyāna Buddhism, someone who seeks ◊enlightenment in order to help other living beings. A bodhisattva is free to enter ◊nirvana but voluntarily chooses to be reborn until all other beings have attained that state. Bodhisattvas are seen as intercessors to whom believers may pray for help.

**Boeing** US military and commercial aircraft manufacturer. Among the models Boeing has produced are the B-17 Flying Fortress, 1935; the B-52 Stratofortress, 1952; the Chinook helicopter, 1961; the first jetliner, the Boeing 707, 1957; the ◊jumbo jet or Boeing 747, 1969; the ◊jetfoil, 1975; and the 777-300 jetliner, 1997.

**Boeotia** ancient and modern district of central Greece, of which ◊Thebes was and remains the chief city. The *Boeotian League* (formed by ten city-states in the 6th century BC) was brought under strong central Theban control in the later 5th century BC. It superseded ◊Sparta as the leading military power in Greece in the 4th century BC until the rise of ◊Philip II of Macedon.

**Boer** Dutch settler or descendant of Dutch and Huguenot settlers in South Africa; see also ◊Afrikaner.

**Boer War** the second of the ◊South African Wars 1899–1902, waged between Dutch settlers in South Africa and the British.

**Boethius, Anicius Manlius Severinus** (AD 480–524) Roman philosopher. He wrote treatises on music and mathematics and *De Consolatione Philosophiae/The Consolation of Philosophy,* a dialogue in prose. It was translated into European languages during the Middle Ages.

**bog** type of wetland where decomposition is slowed down and dead plant matter accumulates as ◊peat. Bogs develop under conditions of low temperature, high acidity, low nutrient supply, stagnant water, and oxygen deficiency. Typical bog plants are sphagnum moss, rushes, and cotton grass; insectivorous plants such as sundews and bladderworts are common in bogs (insect prey make up for the lack of nutrients).

**Bogarde, Dirk** stage name of Derek Niven van den Bogaerde (1921–1999) English actor. He appeared in comedies and adventure films such as *Doctor in the House* (1954) and *Campbell's Kingdom* (1957), before acquiring international recognition for complex roles in Joseph Losey's *The Servant* (1963) and *Accident* (1967), and Luchino Visconti's *Death in Venice* (1971). He was knighted in 1992.

**Bogart, Humphrey (DeForest)** (1899–1957) US film actor. He became an international cult figure through roles as a tough, romantic loner in such films as *High Sierra* (1941), *The Maltese Falcon* (1941), *Casablanca* (1942), *To Have and Have Not* (1944), *The Big Sleep* (1946), and *In a Lonely Place* (1950). He won an Academy Award for his role in *The African Queen* (1952).

**Bogotá** originally *Santa Fé de Bogotá,* capital of Colombia, and of Cundinamarca department, situated at 2,640 m/8,660 ft above sea level, on the edge of the Eastern Cordillera plateau of the Andes; population (1994) 5,132,000. Main industries include textiles, chemicals, food processing, and tobacco. Bogotá is Colombia's largest city, and the financial, commercial, and cultural centre of the country. It has several universities and museums.

**Bohemia** area of the Czech Republic, a fertile plateau drained by the Elbe and Vltava rivers. It is rich in mineral resources, including uranium, coal, lignite, iron ore, silver, and graphite. The main cities are Prague and Plzeň. The name Bohemia derives from the Celtic Boii, its earliest known inhabitants.

**Bohr, Niels Henrik David** (1885–1962) Danish physicist whose theoretical work established the structure of the atom and the validity of ◊quantum theory by showing that the nuclei of atoms are surrounded by shells of electrons, each assigned particular sets of quantum numbers according to their orbits. For this work he was awarded the Nobel Prize for Physics in 1922. He explained the structure and behaviour of the nucleus, as well as the process of nuclear ◊fission. Bohr also proposed the doctrine of *complementarity,* the theory that a fundamental particle is neither a wave nor a particle, because these are complementary modes of description.

**bohrium** synthesized, radioactive element of the ◊transactinide series, symbol Bh, atomic number 107, relative atomic mass 262. It was first synthesized by the Joint Institute for Nuclear Research in Dubna, Russia in 1976; in 1981 the Laboratory for Heavy Ion Research in Darmstadt, Germany, confirmed its existence. It was named in 1997 after Danish physicist Niels ◊Bohr. Its temporary name was unnilseptium.

**boiler** any vessel that converts water into steam. Boilers are used in conventional power stations to generate steam to feed steam ◊turbines, which drive the electricity generators. They are also used in steamships, which are propelled by steam turbines, and in steam locomotives. Every boiler has a furnace in which fuel (coal, oil, or gas) is burned to produce hot gases, and a system of tubes in which heat is transferred from the gases to the water.

**boiling point** for any given liquid, the temperature at which the application of heat raises the temperature of the liquid no further, but converts it into vapour.

**Bokassa, Jean-Bédel** (1921–1996) Central African Republic president 1966–79 and self-proclaimed emperor 1977–79. Commander in chief from 1963, in December 1965 he led the military coup that gave him the presidency. On 4 December 1976 he proclaimed the Central African Empire and one year later crowned himself emperor for life.

His regime was characterized by arbitrary state violence and cruelty. Overthrown in 1979, Bokassa was in exile in the Côte d'Ivoire until 1986. Upon his return he was sentenced to death, but this was commuted to life imprisonment in 1988.

**bolero** Spanish dance in moderate triple time (3/4), invented in the late 18th century. It is performed by a solo dancer or a couple, usually with castanet accompaniment, and is still a contemporary form of dance in Caribbean countries. In music, Ravel's one-act ballet score *Boléro* (1928) is the most famous example, consisting of a theme which is constantly repeated and varied instrumentally, building to a powerful climax. The ballet was choreographed by Nijinsky for Ida Rubinstein 1928.

**boletus** any of several fleshy fungi (see ◊fungus) with thick stems and caps of various colours. The European *Boletus edulis* is edible, but some species are poisonous. (Genus *Boletus*, class Basidiomycetes.)

**Boleyn, Anne** (*c.* 1507–1536) Queen of England 1533–36 as the second wife of Henry VIII. She gave birth to the future Queen Elizabeth I in 1533, but was unable to produce a male heir to the throne, and was executed on a false charge.

**Bolger, Jim (James Brendan)** (1935– ) New Zealand National Party centre-right politician, prime minister 1990–97. His government improved relations with the USA, which had deteriorated sharply when the preceding Labour governments had banned nuclear-powered and nuclear-armed ships from entering New Zealand's harbours. It also oversaw an upturn in the economy. However, the failure to honour election pledges, particularly in the welfare area, where there were cuts in provision, meant that National Party support slipped in the November 1993 general election and the government was only re-elected with a majority of one. The

October 1996 general election, held for the first time under a mixed-member system of proportional representation, was inconclusive and Bolger was forced to form a coalition government, with the New Zealand First Party leader, Winston Peters, as his deputy. In November 1997 he resigned and was replaced as prime minister by his transport minister, Jenny ◊Shipley, who had led a right-wing revolt against his leadership.

**Bolingbroke** title of Henry of Bolingbroke, ◊Henry IV of England.

**Bolingbroke, Henry St John** 1st Viscount Bolingbroke (1678–1751) British Tory politician and political philosopher. He was foreign secretary 1710–14 and a Jacobite conspirator. His books, such as *Idea of a Patriot King* (1738) and *The Dissertation upon Parties* (1735), laid the foundations for 19th-century Toryism.

**Bolívar, Simón** (1783–1830) South American nationalist, leader of revolutionary armies, known as **the Liberator**. He fought the Spanish colonial forces in several uprisings and eventually liberated Colombia 1819, his native Venezuela 1821, Ecuador 1822, Peru 1824, and Bolivia (a new state named after him, formerly Upper Peru) 1825.

**Bolivia** Republic of
*national name Repúb_lica de Bolivia*

**area** 1,098,581 sq km/424,162 sq mi
**capital** La Paz (seat of government), Sucre (legal capital and seat of judiciary)
**major towns/cities** Santa Cruz, Cochabamba, Oruro, El Alto, Potosí
**physical features** high plateau (Altiplano) between mountain ridges (cordilleras); forest and lowlands (llano) in east; Andes; lakes Titicaca (the world's highest navigable lake, 3,800 m/12,500 ft) and Poopó
**head of state and government** Hugo Banzer Suarez from 1997

*political system* emergent democracy

*political parties* National Revolutionary Movement (MNR), centre right; Movement of the Revolutionary Left (MIR), left of centre; Nationalist Democratic Action Party (ADN), right wing; Solidarity and Civic Union (UCS), populist, free market

*currency* boliviano

*GNP per capita (PPP)* (US$) 2,820 (1998)

*exports* metallic minerals, natural gas, jewellery, soybeans, wood. Principal market: UK 16.1% (1998). Illegal trade in coca and its derivatives (mainly cocaine) was worth approximately $600 million in 1990 – almost equal to annual earnings from official exports.

*population* 8,142,000 (1999 est)

*language* Spanish (official); Aymara, Quechua

*religion* Roman Catholic 95% (state-recognized)

*life expectancy* 60 (men); 63 (women) (1995–2000)

*Chronology*

**c. AD 600** Development of sophisticated civilization at Tiahuanaco, south of Lake Titicaca.

**c. 1200** Tiahuanaco culture was succeeded by smaller Aymara-speaking kingdoms.

**16th century** Became incorporated within westerly Quechua-speaking Inca civilization, centred in Peru.

**1538** Conquered by Spanish and, known as 'Upper Peru', became part of the Viceroyalty of Peru, whose capital was at Lima (Peru); Charcas (now Sucre) became the local capital.

**1545** Silver discovered at Potosí in the southwest, which developed into chief silver-mining town and most important city in South America in the 17th and 18th centuries.

**1776** Transferred to the Viceroyalty of La Plata, with its capital in Buenos Aires.

**late 18th century** Increasing resistance of American Indians and Mestizos to Spanish rule; silver production slumped.

**1825** Liberated from Spanish rule by the Venezuelan freedom fighter Simón Bolívar, after whom the country was named, and his general, Antonio José de Sucre, after battle of Tumulsa; Sucre became Bolivia's first president.

**1836–39** Part of a federation with Peru, headed by Bolivian president Andres Santa Cruz, but it dissolved following defeat in war with Chile.

**1879–84** Lost coastal territory in the Atacama, containing valuable minerals, after defeat in war with Chile.

**1880** Start of a period of civilian rule which lasted until 1936.

**1903** Lost territory to Brazil.

**1932–35** Lost further territory after defeated by Paraguay in the Chaco War, fought over control of the Chaco Boreal.

**1952** After military regime overthrown by peasants and mineworkers in the Bolivian National Revolution, the formerly exiled Dr Victor Paz Estenssoro of the centrist National Revolutionary Movement (MNR) became president and introduced social and economic reforms, including universal suffrage, nationalization of tin mines, and land redistribution.

**1956** Dr Hernán Siles Zuazo (MNR) became president, defeating Paz.

**1960** Paz returned to power.

**1964** Army coup led by Vice-president Gen René Barrientos.

**1967** Peasant uprising, led by Ernesto 'Che' Guevara, put down with US help; Guevara was killed.

**1969** Barrientos killed in plane crash, replaced by Vice President Siles Salinas, who was soon deposed in army coup.

**1971** Col Hugo Banzer Suárez came to power after further military coup.

**1974** Attempted coup prompted Banzer to postpone promised elections and ban political and trade-union activity.

**1980** Inconclusive elections were followed by the country's 189th coup, led by Gen Luis García. Allegations of corruption and drug trafficking led to cancellation of US and European Community (EC) aid.

**1981** García forced to resign. Replaced by Gen Celso Torrelio Villa.

**1982** Torrelio resigned and, with economy worsening, junta handed power over to civilian administration headed by Siles Zuazo.

**1983** US and EC economic aid resumed as austerity measures introduced.

**1985** President Siles resigned after a general strike and an attempted coup. Election results were inconclusive; veteran Dr Paz Estenssoro (MNR) was chosen by congress as president. The inflation rate was 23,000%.

**1989** Jaime Paz Zamora of the left-wing Movement of Revolutionary Left (MIR) was chosen as president in a power-sharing arrangement with Banzer.

**1993** Gonzalo Sanchez de Lozada (MNR) was elected president after Banzer withdrew his candidacy. Foreign investment was encouraged as inflation fell to single figures.

**1997** Banzer was elected president.

**Bolkiah, Hassanal** (1946– ) Sultan of Brunei from 1967, following the abdication of his father, Omar Ali Saifuddin (1916–1986). As absolute ruler, Bolkiah also assumed the posts of prime minister and defence minister on independence in 1984.

**Böll, Heinrich (Theodor)** (1917–1985) German novelist. A radical Catholic and anti-Nazi, he attacked Germany's political past and the materialism of its contemporary society. His many publications include poems, short stories, and novels which satirized West German society, for example *Billard um Halbzehn/Billiards at Half-Past Nine* 1959 and *Gruppenbild mit Dame/Group Portrait with Lady* 1971. Nobel Prize for Literature 1972.

**boll weevil** small American beetle *Anthonomus grandis* of the weevil group. The female lays her eggs in the unripe pods or 'bolls' of the cotton plant, and on these the larvae feed, causing great destruction.

**Bologna** Etruscan *Felsina;* Roman *Bononia,* industrial town and capital of Emilia-Romagna, Italy, at the foot of the Apennines, 80 km/50 mi north of Florence; population (1992) 401,300. It is a major rail hub. Industries include engineering, food-processing, and the manufacture of electrical components and chemicals. An important venue for specialist trade fairs (perfume, camping), it also hosts an annual international children's book fair.

**Bolshevik** (from Russian *bolshinstvo* 'a majority') member of the majority of the Russian Social Democratic Party who split from the ◊Mensheviks in 1903. The Bolsheviks, under ◊Lenin, advocated the destruction of capitalist political and economic institutions, and the setting-up of a socialist state with power in the hands of the workers. The Bolsheviks set the ◊Russian Revolution 1917 in motion.

They changed their name to the Russian Communist Party 1918.

**Boltzmann constant** in physics, the constant (symbol $k$) that relates the kinetic energy (energy of motion) of a gas atom or molecule to temperature. Its value is $1.38066 \times 10^{-23}$ joules per kelvin. It is equal to the gas constant $R$, divided by ◊Avogadro's number.

**bomb** container filled with explosive or chemical material and generally used in warfare. There are also ◊incendiary bombs and nuclear bombs and missiles (see ◊nuclear warfare). Any object designed to cause damage by explosion can be called a bomb (car bombs, letter bombs). Initially dropped from aeroplanes (from World War I), bombs were also launched by rocket (V1, V2) in World War II. The 1960s saw the development of missiles that could be launched from aircraft, land sites, or submarines. In the 1970s laser guidance systems were developed to hit small targets with accuracy.

**bombardier beetle** beetle that emits an evil-smelling fluid from its abdomen, as a defence mechanism. This fluid rapidly evaporates into a gas, which appears like a minute jet of smoke when in contact with air, and blinds the predator about to attack.

*classification* Bombardier beetles in genus *Brachinus*, family Carabidae, order Coleoptera, class Insecta, phylum Arthropoda.

**Bombay duck** or *bummalow*, small fish *Harpodon nehereus* found in the Indian Ocean. It has a thin body, up to 40 cm/16 in long, and sharp, pointed teeth. It feeds on shellfish and other small fish. It is valuable as a food fish, and is eaten, salted and dried, with dishes such as curry.

**Bonaparte** Corsican family of Italian origin that gave rise to the Napoleonic dynasty: see ◊Napoleon I, ◊Napoleon II, and ◊Napoleon III. Others were the brothers and sister of Napoleon I: *Joseph* (1768–1844) whom Napoleon made king of Naples 1806 and Spain 1808; *Lucien* (1775–1840) whose handling of the Council of Five Hundred on 10 November 1799 ensured Napoleon's future; *Louis* (1778–1846) the father of Napoleon III, who was made king of Holland 1806–10; also called (from 1810) comte de Saint Leu; *Caroline* (1782–1839) who married Joachim Murat 1800; full name Maria Annunciata Caroline; *Jerome* (1784–1860) made king of Westphalia 1807.

**Bonar Law** British Conservative politician; see ◊Law, Andrew Bonar.

**bond** in chemistry, the result of the forces of attraction that hold together atoms of an element or elements to form a molecule. The principal types of bonding are ◊ionic, ◊covalent, ◊metallic, and intermolecular (such as hydrogen bonding).

**bond** in commerce, a security issued by a government, local authority, company, bank, or other institution on fixed interest. Usually a long-term security, a bond may be irredeemable (with no date of redemption), secured (giving the investor a claim on the company's property or on a part of its assets), or unsecured (not protected by a lien). Property bonds are nonfixed securities with the yield fixed to property investment. See also ◊Eurobond.

**Bond, Edward** (1934– ) English dramatist. His early work aroused controversy because of the savagery of some of his imagery, for example, the brutal stoning of a baby by bored youths in *Saved* (1965). Other works include *Early Morning* (1968); *Lear* (1972), a reworking of Shakespeare's play; *Bingo* (1973), an account of Shakespeare's last days; *The War Plays* (1985); and *Jackets 2/Sugawara* and *In the Company of Men* (both 1990).

**bone** hard connective tissue comprising the ◊skeleton of most vertebrates. Bone is composed of a network of collagen fibres impregnated with mineral salts (largely calcium phosphate and calcium carbonate), a combination that gives it great density and strength, comparable in some cases with that of reinforced concrete. Enclosed within this solid matrix are bone cells, blood vessels, and nerves. The interior of the long bones of the limbs consists of a spongy matrix filled with a soft marrow that produces blood cells. *See illustration on page 116.*

**bone marrow** substance found inside the cavity of bones. In early life it produces red blood cells but later on lipids (fat) accumulate and its colour changes from red to yellow.

**bongo** Central African antelope *Boocercus eurycerus*, living in dense humid forests. Up to 1.4 m/4.5 ft at the shoulder, it has spiral horns which may be 80 cm/2.6 ft or more in length. The body is rich chestnut, with narrow white stripes running vertically down the sides, and a black belly.

**bonito** any of various species of medium-sized tuna, predatory fish of the genus *Sarda*, in the mackerel family. The ocean bonito *Katsuwonus pelamis* grows to 1 m/3 ft and is common in tropical seas. The Atlantic bonito *Sarda sarda* is found in the Mediterranean and tropical Atlantic and grows to the same length but has a narrower body.

**Bonn** industrial city in North Rhine-Westphalia, Germany, 18 km/15 mi southeast of Cologne, on the left bank of the Rhine; population (1995) 291,700. Industries include the manufacture of chemicals, textiles, plastics, and aluminium. Bonn was the seat of government of West Germany 1949–90 and of the Federal Republic of Germany from 1990. In 1991 the Bundestag voted to move the capital to Berlin.

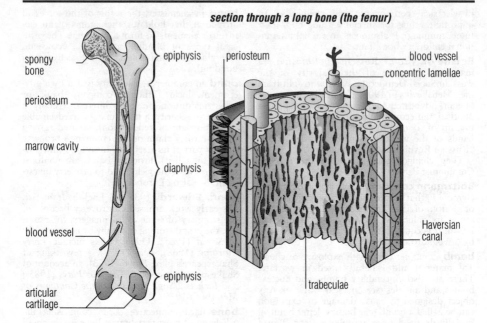

**section through a long bone (the femur)**

spongy bone — epiphysis   periosteum   blood vessel / concentric lamellae

periosteum

marrow cavity

diaphysis

blood vessel

Haversian canal

epiphysis   trabeculae

articular cartilage

**bone** *Bone is a network of fibrous material impregnated with mineral salts and as strong as reinforced concrete. The upper end of the thighbone or femur is made up of spongy bone, which has a fine lacework structure designed to transmit the weight of the body. The shaft of the femur consists of hard compact bone designed to resist bending. Fine channels carrying blood vessels, nerves, and lymphatics interweave even the densest bone.*

This has taken place in phases, with the major phase in 1998.

**Bonnard, Pierre** (1867–1947) French painter, designer, and graphic artist. Influenced by Gauguin and Japanese prints, he specialized in intimate domestic scenes and landscapes, his paintings shimmering with colour and light. With other members of *les Nabis,* he explored the decorative arts (posters, stained glass, furniture), but is most widely known for his series of nudes, for example, *Nude in the Bath* (1938) (Petit Palais, Paris).

**Bonnie Prince Charlie** Scottish name for ◊Charles Edward Stuart, pretender to the throne.

**bonsai** (Japanese 'bowl cultivation') art of producing miniature trees by selective pruning. It originated in China many centuries ago and later spread to Japan. Some specimens in China are about 1,000 years old and some in the imperial Japanese collection are more than 300 years old.

**bony fish** fish of the class Osteichthyes, the largest and most important class of fish. The head covering and the scales are based on bone. Bony fish have a swimbladder, which may be modified into lungs and the gills are covered by a flap, the operculum.

**booby** tropical seabird of the genus *Sula,* in the same family, Sulidae, as the northern ◊gannet, order Pelicaniformes. There are six

species, including the circumtropical brown booby *S. leucogaster.* Plumage is white and black or brown, with no feathers on the throat and lower jaw. They inhabit coastal waters, and dive to catch fish. The name was given by sailors who saw the bird's tameness as stupidity.

**booklouse** any of numerous species of tiny wingless insects of the order Psocoptera, especially *Atropus pulsatoria,* which lives in books and papers, feeding on starches and moulds.

**Boole, George** (1815–1864) English mathematician. His work *The Mathematical Analysis of Logic* (1847) established the basis of modern mathematical logic, and his *Boolean algebra* can be used in designing computers.

**boomslang** rear-fanged venomous African snake *Dispholidus typus,* often green but sometimes brown or blackish, and growing to a length of 2 m/6 ft. It lives in trees, and feeds on tree-dwelling lizards such as chameleons. Its venom can be fatal to humans; however, boomslangs rarely attack people.

**Boone, Daniel** (1734–1820) US pioneer. He cleared a forest path called the Wilderness Road (East Virginia–Kentucky) in 1775 for the first westward migration of settlers.

**boot** or *bootstrap,* in computing, the process of starting up a computer. Most computers have a small, built-in boot program that starts automatically when the computer is switched on – its only task is to load a slightly larger program, usually from a hard disk, which in turn loads the main ◊operating system.

In microcomputers the operating system is often held in the permanent ◊ROM memory and the boot program simply triggers its operation.

**Boötes** constellation of the northern hemisphere represented by a herdsman driving a bear (◊Ursa Major) around the pole. Its brightest star is ◊Arcturus (or Alpha Boötis), which is about 37 light years from Earth. The herdsman is assisted by the neighbouring Canes Venatici, 'the Hunting Dogs'.

**Booth, William** (1829–1912) British founder of the ◊Salvation Army (1878), and its first 'general'.

**bootlegging** illegal manufacture, distribution, or sale of a product. The term originated in the USA, when the sale of alcohol to American Indians was illegal and bottles were hidden for sale in the legs of the jackboots of unscrupulous traders. The term was later used for all illegal liquor sales during the period of ◊Prohibition in the USA 1919–33. More recently it has been applied to unauthorized commercial tape recordings and the copying of computer software.

**Bophuthatswana** Republic of, former ◊Black National State within South Africa, independent from 1977 (although not recognized by the United Nations) until 1994 when it was re-integrated into South Africa (in North West Province, Free State (formerly Orange Free State), and Mpumalanga (formerly Eastern Transvaal)) after rioting broke out in the run-up to the first multiracial elections.

**borage** plant native to southern Europe, used in salads and in medicine. It has small blue flowers and hairy leaves. (*Borago officinalis*, family Boraginaceae.)

**Bordeaux** administrative centre of the *département* of Gironde and of the ◊Aquitaine region, southwest France, situated on the River Garonne, 100 km/62 mi from the Atlantic; population (1990) 213,300, conurbation 685,000. Bordeaux is accessible to seagoing ships and is a major port; it is a centre for the wine trade, oil refining, chemicals, and the aircraft and aeronautics industries. Other industries include shipbuilding, sugar refining, and the manufacture of electrical goods, motor vehicles, and processed foods. Bordeaux was under the English crown for three centuries until 1453. In 1870, 1914, and 1940 the French government was moved here because of German invasions.

**Border, Allan Robert** (1955– ) Australian cricketer, left-handed batsman, and captain of Australia 1985–94. He retired from international cricket in 1994 as holder of world records for most test runs (11,174), most test matches as captain (93), most appearances in test matches (156), most consecutive appearances in test matches (153), most catches in test matches by an outfielder (156), and most appearances in one-day internationals (263). Border played for Queensland after starting his career with New South Wales and has played in England for Gloucestershire and Essex.

*career highlights*
*Test cricket (1978–94)* matches: 156; not out: 44; innings: 265; runs: 11,174; average: 50.56; hundreds: 27; best: 205 not out v. New Zealand 1987–88; bowling: wickets: 39; average: 39.10; best: 7 for 46 v. West Indies 1988–89 ; catches: 156
*One-day internationals* matches: 273; innings: 252 ; not out: 39; runs: 6,524; average: 30.62; hundreds: 3; best: 127 not out; bowling; wickets: 73; average: 28.36

**Borg, Björn Rune** (1956– ) Swedish tennis player. He won the men's singles title at Wimbledon five times 1976–80, a record since the abolition of the challenge system in 1922. He also won six French Open singles titles 1974–75 and 1978–81 inclusive. In 1990 Borg announced plans to return to professional tennis, but he enjoyed little competitive success 1991–92.
*career highlights*
*Wimbledon* singles: 1976–80
*French Open* singles: 1974–75, 1978–81
*Davis Cup* 1975 (member of winning Sweden team)
*Grand Prix Masters* 1980–81
*WCT Champion* 1976
*ITF World Champion* 1978–80

**Borges, Jorge Luis** (1899–1986) Argentine poet and short-story writer. He was an exponent of ◊magic realism. In 1961 he became director of the National Library, Buenos Aires, and was professor of English literature at the university there. He is known for his fantastic and paradoxical work *Ficciones/Fictions* 1944. He became blind in later life, but continued to write.

**Borgia, Cesare** (*c.* 1475–1507) Italian general, illegitimate son of Pope ◊Alexander VI. Made a cardinal at 17 by his father, he resigned to become captain-general of the papacy, campaigning successfully against the city republics of Italy. Ruthless and treacherous in war, he was an able ruler (a model for Machiavelli's *The Prince*), but his power crumbled on the death of his father. He was a patron of artists, including Leonardo da Vinci.

**Borgia, Lucrezia** (1480–1519) Duchess of Ferrara from 1501. She was the illegitimate daughter of Pope ◊Alexander VI and sister of Cesare ◊Borgia. She was married at 12 and again at 13 to further her father's ambitions, both marriages being annulled by him. At 18 she was married again, but her husband was murdered in 1500 on the order of her brother, with whom (as well as with her father) she was said to have committed incest. Her final marriage was to the Alfonso d'Este, the heir to the duchy of Ferrara. She made the court a centre of culture and was a patron of authors and artists such as Ariosto and Titian.

**boric acid** or *boracic acid*, $B(OH)_3$ acid formed by the combination of hydrogen and oxygen with nonmetallic boron. It is a weak antiseptic and is used in the manufacture of glass and enamels. It is also an efficient insecticide against ants and cockroaches.

**Boris Godunov** (1552–1605) tsar of Russia from 1598; see Boris ◊Godunov.

**Born, Max** (1882–1970) German-born British physicist. He received a Nobel prize 1954 for fundamental work on the ◊quantum theory, especially his 1926 discovery that the wave function of an electron is linked to the probability that the electron is to be found at any point.

**Borneo** third-largest island in the world, one of the Sunda Islands in the West Pacific; area 754,000 sq km/290,000 sq mi. It comprises the Malaysian territories of ◊*Sabah* and ◊*Sarawak; Brunei;* and, occupying by far the largest part, the Indonesian territory of ◊*Kalimantan*. It is mountainous and densely forested. A forest fire in early 1998 destroyed 30,000 sq km/11,583 sq mi of forest.

In coastal areas the people of Borneo are mainly of Malaysian origin, with a few Chinese, and the interior is inhabited by the indigenous Dyaks. It was formerly under both Dutch and British colonial influence until Sarawak was formed 1841.

**Bornu** kingdom of the 9th–19th centuries to the west and south of Lake Chad, western central Africa. Converted to Islam in the 11th century, Bornu reached its greatest strength in the 15th–18th centuries. From 1901 it was absorbed in the British, French, and German colonies in this area, which became the states of Niger, Cameroon, and Nigeria. The largest section of ancient Bornu is now the *state of Bornu* in Nigeria.

**boron** nonmetallic element, symbol B, atomic number 5, relative atomic mass 10.811. In nature it is found only in compounds, as with sodium and oxygen in borax. It exists in two allotropic forms (see ◊allotropy): brown amorphous powder and very hard, brilliant crystals. Its compounds are used in the preparation of boric acid, water softeners, soaps, enamels, glass, and pottery glazes. In alloys it is used to harden steel. Because it absorbs slow neutrons, it is used to make boron carbide control rods for nuclear reactors. It is a necessary trace element in the human diet. The element was named by Humphry Davy, who isolated it in 1808, from *bor*ax + -on, as in carb*on*.

**borough** (Old English *burg* 'a walled or fortified place') urban-based unit of local government in the UK and USA. It existed in the UK from the 8th century until 1974, when it continued as an honorary status granted by royal charter to a district council, entitling its leader to the title of mayor. In England in 1998 there were 32 London borough councils and 36 metropolitan borough councils. The name is sometimes encountered in the USA: New York City has five administrative boroughs, Alaska has local government boroughs, and in other states some smaller towns use the name.

**Borromini, Francesco,** originally Francesco Castelli (1599–1667) Swiss-born Italian Baroque architect. He was one of the two most important architects (with ◊Bernini, his main rival) in 17th-century Rome. Whereas Bernini designed in a florid, expansive style, his pupil

Borromini developed a highly idiosyncratic and austere use of the Classical language of architecture. His genius may be seen in the cathedrals of San Carlo alle Quattro Fontane (1637–41), Sant' Ivo alla Sapienza (1643–60), and the Oratory of San Filippo Neri (1638–50).

**borstal** in the UK, formerly a place of detention for offenders aged 15–21, first introduced 1908. From 1983 borstal institutions were officially known as youth custody centres, and have been replaced by *young offender institutions*.

**borzoi** (Russian 'swift') breed of large dog originating in Russia. It is of the greyhound type, white with darker markings, with a thick, silky coat, and stands 75 cm/30 in or more at the shoulder.

**Bosch, Hieronymus** Jerome van Aken (*c.* 1460 –1516) Early Dutch painter. His fantastic visions, often filled with bizarre and cruel images, depict a sinful world in which people are tormented by demons and weird creatures, as in *Hell*, a panel from the triptych *The Garden of Earthly Delights* (about 1505–10, Prado, Madrid). In their richness, complexity, and sheer strangeness, his pictures foreshadow Surrealism.

**Bosnia-Herzegovina** Republic of
*national name Republika Bosna i Hercegovina*

*area* 51,129 sq km/19,740 sq mi
*capital* Sarajevo
*major towns/cities* Banja Luka, Mostar, Prijedor, Tuzla, Zenica
*physical features* barren, mountainous country, part of the Dinaric Alps; limestone gorges; 20 km/12 mi of coastline with no harbour
*heads of state* Rotating chairman of the collective presidency, Ante Jelavic from 1999
*heads of government* Co-prime ministers Haris Silajdzic (from 1997) and Svetozar Mihajlovic (from 1998)
*political system* emergent democracy
*political parties* Party of Democratic Action (PDA), Muslim-oriented; Serbian Renaissance Movement (SPO), Serbian nationalist; Croatian Christian Democratic Union of Bosnia-

Herzegovina (CDU), Croatian nationalist; League of Communists (LC) and Socialist Alliance (SA), left wing
**currency** dinar
**GNP per capita (PPP)** (US$) 450 (1996 est)
**exports** coal, domestic appliances (industrial production and mining remain low). Principal market: Croatia 34.3% (1997)
**population** 3,838,000 (1999 est)
**language** Serbian variant of Serbo-Croatian
**religion** Sunni Muslim, Serbian Orthodox, Roman Catholic
**life expectancy** 71 (men); 76 (women) (1995–2000)

**Chronology**
**1st century** AD Part of Roman province of Illyricum.
**395** On division of Roman Empire, stayed in west, along with Croatia and Slovenia, whereas Serbia to the east became part of the Byzantine Empire.
**7th century** Settled by Slav tribes.
**12–15th centuries** Independent state.
**1463 and 1482** Bosnia and Herzegovina, in south, successively conquered by Ottoman Turks; many Slavs were converted to Sunni Islam.
**1878** Became an Austrian protectorate, following Bosnian revolt against Turkish rule in 1875–76.
**1908** Annexed by Austrian Habsburgs in wake of Turkish Revolution.
**1914** Archduke Franz Ferdinand, the Habsburg heir, assassinated in Sarajevo by a Bosnian-Serb extremist, precipitating World War I.
**1918** On collapse of Habsburg Empire, became part of Serb-dominated 'Kingdom of Serbs, Croats, and Slovenes', known as Yugoslavia from 1929.
**1941** Occupied by Nazi Germany and became 'Greater Croatia' fascist puppet state and scene of fierce fighting.
**1943–44** Bosnia was liberated by the communist Partisans, led by Marshal Tito.
**1945** The region became a republic within Yugoslav Socialist Federation.
**1980** There was an upsurge in Islamic nationalism.
**1990** Ethnic violence erupted between Muslims and Serbs. Communists were defeated in multi-party elections; a coalition was formed by Serb, Muslim, and Croatian parties, with a nationalist Muslim, Alija Izetbegovic, as president.
**1991** The Serb–Croat civil war in Croatia spread disorder into Bosnia. Fears that Serbia aimed to annex Serb-dominated parts of the republic led to a 'sovereignty' declaration by parliament. Serbs within Bosnia established autonomous enclaves.
**1992** In a Serb-boycotted referendum, Bosnian Muslims and Croats voted for independence, which was recognized by the USA and the European Community (EC); Bosnia was admitted into the United Nations (UN). Violent civil war broke out, as independent 'Serbian Republic of Bosnia-Herzegovina', comprising parts of east and west, was proclaimed by Bosnian-Serb militia leader Radovan Karadzic, with Serbian backing. UN forces were drafted

into Sarajevo to break the Serb siege of the city; Bosnian Serbs were accused of 'ethnic cleansing', particularly of Muslims.
**1993** A UN–EC peace plan failed. The USA began airdrops of food and medical supplies. Six UN 'safe areas' were created (Srebrenica, Tuzla, Zepa, Gorazde, Bihac, and Sarajevo), intended as havens for Muslim civilians. A Croat–Serb partition plan was rejected by Muslims.
**1994** The Serb siege of Sarajevo was lifted after a UN–NATO ultimatum and Russian diplomatic intervention. A Croat–Muslim federation was formed after a ceasefire in the north.
**1995** Hostilities resumed; the 'safe areas' of Srebrenica (where more than 4,000 Muslims were massacred) and Zepa were overrun before the Serbs were halted by Croatians near Bihac. A US-sponsored peace accord, providing for two sovereign states (a Muslim–Croat federation and a Bosnian Serb Republic, the Republika Srpska) as well as a central legislature (House of Representatives, House of Peoples, and three-person presidency), was agreed at Dayton, Ohio, USA. A 60,000-strong NATO peacekeeping force was deployed.
**1996** An International Criminal Tribunal for Former Yugoslavia began in the Hague and an arms-control accord was signed. Full diplomatic relations were established with Yugoslavia. The collective presidency was elected, consisting of Alija Izetbegovic (Muslim), Momcilo Krajisnik (Serb), and Kresimir Zubak (Croat); Izetbegovic was elected overall president. Biljana Plavsic was elected president of the Serb Republic and Gojko Klickovic its prime minister. Edhem Bicakcic became prime minister of the Muslim–Croat Federation.
**1997** Haris Silajdzic (Muslim), and Boro Bosic (Serb), were appointed co-chairs of the central Council of Ministers (cabinet). The Serb part of Bosnia signed a joint customs agreement with Yugoslavia. Vladimir Soljic was elected president of the Muslim–Croat Federation. Municipal elections were held, in which nationalist parties were successful. The three-person presidency agreed a common passport and citizenship law.
**1998** The first Muslims and Croats were convicted in The Hague for war crimes during 1992. Zivko Radisic became the first Bosnian Serb to hold power as rotating federal president. Edhem Bicakcic became prime minister of the Bosnian Muslim–Croat state, with Ejup Ganic (a Bosnian Muslim) as president. In January a moderate, pro-western government was formed in the Bosnian Serb republic, headed by Milorad Dodik; Nikola Poplasen became president. In December the moderate Brane Miljus took Dodik's place as prime minister. Haris Silajdzic (a Bosnian Muslim) and Svetozar Mihajlovic (a Bosnian Serb moderate) were nominated as co-chairs of the federation.

**boson** in physics, an elementary particle whose spin can only take values that are whole numbers or zero. Bosons may be classified as ◊gauge bosons (carriers of the four fundamental forces) or ◊mesons. All elementary particles are either bosons or ◊fermions.

**Bosporus** Turkish *Karadeniz Boğazi,* strait 27 km/17 mi long, joining the Black Sea with the Sea of Marmara and forming part of the water division between Europe and Asia; its name may be derived from the Greek legend of Io. Istanbul stands on its west side. The *Bosporus Bridge* 1973, 1,621 m/5,320 ft, links Istanbul and Anatolia (the Asian part of Turkey). In 1988 a second bridge across the straits was opened, linking Asia and Europe.

**Boston** industrial port and commercial centre, capital of Massachusetts, USA, on Massachusetts Bay; population (1992) 551,700; metropolitan area (1992) 5,439,000. Its economy is dominated by financial and health services and government. It is also a publishing and academic centre. The subway system (begun 1897) was the first in the USA. Boston's baseball team, the Red Sox, is based at Fenway Park. Boston was founded by Puritans in 1630 and has played an important role in American history.

**Boston Tea Party** protest 1773 by colonists in Massachusetts, USA, against the tea tax imposed on them by the British government before the ◊American Revolution.

**Boswell, James** (1740–1795) Scottish biographer and diarist. He was a member of Samuel ◊Johnson's Literary Club and the two men travelled to Scotland together in 1773, as recorded in Boswell's *Journal of a Tour to the Hebrides* (1785). His *Life of Samuel Johnson* was published in 1791. Boswell's ability to record Johnson's pithy conversation verbatim makes this a classic of English biography.

**Bosworth, Battle of** battle fought on 22 August 1485, during the English Wars of the Roses (see ◊Roses, Wars of the). Richard III, the Yorkist king, was defeated and killed by Henry Tudor, who became Henry VII. The battlefield is near the village of Market Bosworth, 19 km/12 mi west of Leicester, England.

**botany** (Greek *botane* 'herb') the study of living and fossil ◊plants, including form, function, interaction with the environment, and classification.

**Botany Bay** inlet on the east coast of New South Wales, Australia, 8 km/5 mi south of Sydney. It is the outlet of the River Georges. The English explorer Captain James ◊Cook landed here in 1770. In 1787 the bay was chosen as the site for a British penal colony, but proved unsuitable, and the colony was located at Port Jackson.

**botfly** any fly of the family Oestridae. The larvae are parasites that feed on the skin (warblefly of cattle) or in the nasal cavity (nostrilflies of sheep and deer). The horse botfly belongs to another family, the Gasterophilidae. It has a parasitic larva that feeds in the horse's stomach.

**Botha, Louis** (1862–1919) South African soldier and politician. He was a commander in the Second South African War (Boer War). In 1907 he became premier of the Transvaal and in 1910 of the first Union South African government. On the outbreak of World War I in 1914 he rallied South Africa to the Commonwealth, suppressed a Boer revolt, and conquered German South West Africa.

**Botha, P(ieter) W(illem)** (1916– ) South African politician, prime minister 1978–89. He initiated a modification of ◊apartheid, which later slowed down in the face of Afrikaner (Boer) opposition, and made use of force both inside and outside South Africa to stifle African National Congress (ANC) party activity. In 1984 he became the first executive state president. After suffering a stroke in 1989, he unwillingly resigned both party leadership and presidency and was succeeded by F W de Klerk.

**Botham, Ian Terence** (1955– ) English cricketer. One of the world's greatest all-rounders, in 102 Tests for England between 1977 and 1992 he scored 5,200 runs and took 383 wickets to become the first player in Test cricket to score over 5,000 runs as well as take over 300 wickets. He played county cricket for Somerset, Worcestershire, and Durham, and briefly represented Queensland in the Sheffield Shield.

*career highlights*
*all first-class cricket* runs: 19,399; average: 33.97; best: 228 (Somerset v. Gloucestershire 1980); wickets: 1,172; average: 27.21; best: 8 for 34 (England v. Pakistan 1978)
*Test cricket* (1977–92) appearances: 102; runs: 5,200; average: 33.54; best: 208 (England v. India 1982); wickets: 383; average: 28.40; best: 8 for 34 (England v. Pakistan 1978); catches: 120

**Bothwell, James Hepburn** 4th Earl of Bothwell (*c.* 1536–1578) Scottish nobleman. The third husband of ◊Mary Queen of Scots, 1567–70, he was alleged to have arranged the explosion that killed Darnley, her previous husband, in 1567. He succeeded as Earl in 1556 and became Duke in 1567.

**bo tree** or *peepul,* Indian ◊fig tree, said to be the tree under which the Buddha became enlightened. (*Ficus religiosa,* family Moraceae.)

**Botswana** Republic of
*area* 582,000 sq km/224,710 sq mi

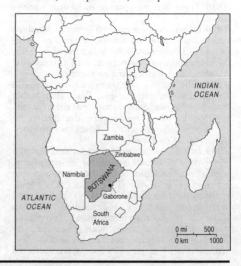

*capital* Gaborone

*major towns/cities* Mahalapye, Serowe, Tutume, Bobonong Francistown, Selebi-Phikwe, Lobatse, Molepolol, Kange

*physical features* Kalahari Desert in southwest (70–80% of national territory is desert), plains (Makgadikgadi salt pans) in east, fertile lands and Okavango Delta in north

*head of state and government* Festus Mogae from 1998

*political system* democracy

*political parties* Botswana Democratic Party (BDP), moderate centrist; Botswana National Front (BNF), moderate left of centre

*currency* franc CFA

*GNP per capita (PPP)* (US$) 8,310 (1998)

*exports* diamonds, copper and nickel, beef. Principal market: EU 79.7% (1997)

*population* 1,597,000 (1999 est)

*language* English (official), Setswana (national)

*religion* Christian 50%, animist, Baha'i, Muslim, Hindu

*life expectancy* 46 (men); 48 (women) (1995–2000)

*Chronology*

*18th century* Formerly inhabited by nomadic hunter-gatherer groups, including the Kung, the area was settled by the Tswana people, from whose eight branches the majority of the people are descended.

*1872* Khama III the Great, a converted Christian, became chief of the Bamangwato, the largest Tswana group. He developed a strong army and greater unity among the Botswana peoples.

*1885* Became the British protectorate of Bechuanaland at the request of Chief Khama, who feared invasion by Boers from the Transvaal (South Africa) following the discovery of gold.

*1895* The southern part of the Bechuanaland Protectorate was annexed by Cape Colony (South Africa).

*1960* New constitution created a legislative council controlled (until 1963) by a British High Commissioner.

*1965* Capital transferred from Mafeking to Gaborone. Internal self-government achieved, with Seretse Khama, the grandson of Khama III and leader of the centrist Democratic Party (BDP), elected head of government.

*1966* Independence achieved from Britain. Name changed to Botswana; Seretse Khama elected president under new presidentialist constitution.

*mid-1970s* The economy grew rapidly as diamond mining expanded.

*1980* Seretse Khama died, and was succeeded by Vice President Quett Masire (BDP).

*1985* South African raid on Gaborone, allegedly in search of African National Congress (ANC) guerrillas.

*1993* Relations with South Africa were fully normalized following the end of apartheid and the establishment of a multiracial government.

*1997* Major constitutional changes reduced the voting age to 18.

*1998* Festus Mogae (BDP) succeeded President Masire, who retired.

**Botticelli, Sandro, born Alessandro Filipepi** (1445–1510) Florentine painter. He depicted religious and mythological subjects. He was patronized by the ruling ♦Medici family and was deeply influenced by their Neo-Platonic circle. It was for the Medicis that he painted *Primavera* (1478) and *The Birth of Venus* (about 1482–84). From the 1490s he was influenced by the religious fanatic ♦Savonarola, and developed a harshly expressive and emotional style, as seen in his *Mystic Nativity* (1500).

**botulism** rare, often fatal type of ♦food poisoning. Symptoms include vomiting, diarrhoea, muscular paralysis, breathing difficulties and disturbed vision.

It is caused by a toxin produced by the bacterium *Clostridium botulinum,* found in soil and sometimes in improperly canned foods.

**Boudicca** (died AD 61) Queen of the Iceni (native Britons), often referred to by the Latin form of her name, *Boadicea.* Her husband, King Prasutagus, had been a tributary of the Romans, but on his death AD 60 the territory of the Iceni was violently annexed. Boudicca was scourged and her daughters raped. Boudicca raised the whole of southeastern England in revolt, and before the main Roman armies could return from campaigning in Wales she burned Londinium (London), Verulamium (St Albans), and Camulodunum (Colchester). Later the Romans under governor Suetonius Paulinus defeated the British between London and Chester; they were virtually annihilated and Boudicca poisoned herself.

**bougainvillea** any plant of a group of South American tropical vines of the four o'clock family, now cultivated in warm countries around the world for the colourful red and purple bracts (leaflike structures) that cover the flowers. They are named after the French navigator Louis de Bougainville. (Genus *Bougainvillea,* family Nyctaginaceae.)

**Boulez, Pierre** (1925– ) French composer and conductor. He is the founder and director of IRCAM, a music research studio in Paris opened in 1977. His music, strictly serial and expressionistic in style, includes the cantatas *Le Visage Nuptial* (1946–52) and *Le Marteau sans maître* (1955), both to texts by René Char; *Pli selon pli* (1962) for soprano and orchestra; and *Répons* (1981) for soloists, orchestra, tapes, and computer-generated sounds.

**Boumédienne, Houari** adopted name of Muhammad Boukharouba (1925–1978) Algerian politician who brought the nationalist leader Mohammed ♦Ben Bella to power by a revolt in 1962 and superseded him as president in 1965 by a further coup. During his 13 years in office, he presided over an ambitious programme of economic development and promoted Algeria as an active champion of the Third World cause. In late 1978 he died of a rare blood disease.

**Boundary Peak** mountain in Esmeralda County, southwest Nevada; height 4,006 m/ 13,143 ft. It is located 105 km/65 mi north-

northwest of Tonopah, in the Toiyabe National Forest. The northernmost peak of the White Mountains, it is the highest point in Nevada and lies immediately northeast of the California–Nevada border.

**Bourbon dynasty** French royal house (succeeding that of Valois), beginning with Henry IV and ending with Louis XVI, with a brief revival under Louis XVIII, Charles X, and Louis Philippe. The Bourbons also ruled Spain almost uninterruptedly from Philip V to Alfonso XIII and were restored 1975 (◊Juan Carlos); at one point they also ruled Naples and several Italian duchies. The Grand Duke of Luxembourg is also a Bourbon by male descent.

**Bourdon gauge** instrument for measuring pressure, patented by French watchmaker Eugène Bourdon in 1849. The gauge contains a C-shaped tube, closed at one end. When the pressure inside the tube increases, the tube uncurls slightly causing a small movement at its closed end. A system of levers and gears magnifies this movement and turns a pointer, which indicates the pressure on a circular scale. Bourdon gauges are often fitted to cylinders of compressed gas used in industry and hospitals.

**Bourgogne** French name of ◊Burgundy, a region of eastern France.

**Bourguiba, Habib ben Ali** (1903– ) Tunisian politician, first president of Tunisia 1957–87. He became prime minister in 1956 and president (for life from 1975) and prime minister of the Tunisian republic in 1957; he was overthrown in a bloodless coup in 1987.

**Bournemouth** seaside resort and unitary authority in southern England. The town lies on Poole Bay, 40 km/25 mi southwest of Southampton, and was part of the county of Dorset until 1997
*area* 46 sq km/18 sq mi
*features* a 10 km/6 mi stretch of sands, as well as parks, winter gardens, and two piers, one of which is 305 m/1,000 ft long. The Bourne stream, bordered by gardens, runs through the town centre. The Russell-Cotes Museum and Art Gallery houses a collection of Japanese art and 17th–20th century paintings. The Pavilion, opened in 1929, includes a theatre and dance hall. Bournemouth University was founded in 1992 (formerly Bournemouth Polytechnic). Bournemouth Airport is at Hurn to the north of the town.
*industries* tourism, the provision of insurance, banking, and financial services, and the manufacture of communications systems (Siemens); an International Conference Centre is situated here
*population* (1997) 161,500
*famous people* Charles Parry, Mary Shelley, Percy Bysshe Shelley, Robert Louis Stevenson.

**Boutros-Ghali, Boutros** (1922– ) Egyptian diplomat and politician, deputy prime minister 1991–92, secretary general of the United Nations (UN) 1992–96. He worked towards peace in the Middle East in the foreign ministry posts he held 1977–91. After taking office at the UN he encountered a succession of challenges

regarding the organization's role in conflict areas such as Bosnia-Herzegovina, Somalia, Haiti, and Rwanda, with which he dealt with varying degrees of success. In June 1996 the US government signified its intention to veto his re-election for a second term, and in December 1996 he was replaced by Kofi Annan.

**bovine somatotropin** (BST), hormone that increases an injected cow's milk yield by 10–40%. It is a protein naturally occurring in milk and breaks down within the human digestive tract into harmless amino acids. However, doubts have arisen recently as to whether such a degree of protein addition could in the long term be guaranteed harmless either to cattle or to humans.

**bovine spongiform encephalopathy** BSE or *mad cow disease*, disease of cattle, related to ◊scrapie in sheep, which attacks the nervous system, causing aggression, lack of coordination, and collapse. First identified in 1985, it is almost entirely confined to the UK. By 1996 it had claimed 158,000 British cattle.

**Bow Bells** the bells of St Mary-le-Bow church, Cheapside, London; a person born within the sound of Bow Bells is traditionally considered a true Cockney. The bells also feature in the legend of Dick Whittington.

**bower bird** New Guinean and northern Australian bird of the family Ptilonorhynchidae, order Passeriformes, related to the ◊bird of paradise. The males are dull-coloured, and build elaborate bowers of sticks and grass, decorated with shells, feathers, or flowers, and even painted with the juice of berries, to attract the females. There are 17 species.

**Bowie, David** Stage name of David Robert Jones (1947– ) English pop singer, songwriter, and actor. His career has been a series of image changes. His hits include 'Jean Genie' (1973), 'Rebel, Rebel' (1974), 'Golden Years' (1975), and 'Underground' (1986). He has acted in plays and films, including Nicolas Roeg's *The Man Who Fell to Earth* (1976).

**bowling** indoor sport; see ◊tenpin bowling.

**bowls** outdoor and indoor game popular in Commonwealth countries. It has been played in Britain since the 13th century and was popularized by Francis Drake, who is reputed to have played bowls on Plymouth Hoe as the Spanish Armada approached in 1588.

**box** any of several small evergreen trees and shrubs, with small, leathery leaves. Some species are used as hedging plants and for shaping into garden ornaments. (Genus *Buxus,* family Buxaceae.)

**boxer** breed of dog, about 60 cm/24 in tall, with a smooth coat and a set-back nose. The tail is usually docked. A boxer is usually brown, often with white markings, but may be fawn or brindled.

**Boxer** member of the *I ho ch'üan* ('Righteous Harmonious Fists'), a society of Chinese nationalists dedicated to fighting European influence. The *Boxer Rebellion* or *Uprising* 1900 was instigated by the empress ◊Zi Xi. European and US legations in Beijing were besieged and thousands of Chinese Christian converts and missionaries murdered. An international punitive force was dispatched, Beijing was captured 14 August 1900, and China agreed to pay a large indemnity.

**boxing** fighting with gloved fists, almost entirely a male sport. The sport dates from the 18th century, when fights were fought with bare knuckles and untimed rounds. Each round ended with a knockdown. Fighting with gloves became the accepted form in the latter part of the 19th century after the formulation of the Queensberry Rules in 1867.

**Boycott, Geoffrey** (1940–  ) English cricketer. A prolific right-handed opening batsman for Yorkshire and England, he made 8,114 Test runs in 108 matches between 1964 and 1982 at an average of 47.72. In all first class cricket he made 48,426 runs at an average of 56.83 between 1962 and 1986. He is one of only five players to have hit over 150 first-class centuries.
*career highlights*
*all first-class cricket* runs: 48,426; average: 56.83; best: 261 not out (MCC v. WIBC President's XI 1973–74)
*Test cricket* runs: 8,114 average: 47.72; best: 246 not out (England v. India 1967)

**Boyle's law** law stating that the volume of a given mass of gas at a constant temperature is inversely proportional to its pressure. For example, if the pressure of a gas doubles, its volume will be reduced by a half, and vice versa. The law was discovered in 1662 by Irish physicist and chemist Robert Boyle. See also ◊gas laws.

**Boyne** river in the Republic of Ireland, rising in the Bog of Allen in County Kildare, and flowing 110 km/69 mi northeastwards through Trim, Navan, and Drogheda to the Irish Sea. An obelisk marks the site of the ◊Battle of the Boyne, fought at Oldbridge near the mouth of the river on 1 July 1690.

**Boyne, Battle of the** battle fought on 1 July 1690 in eastern Ireland, in which the exiled king James II was defeated by William III and fled to France. It was the decisive battle of the War of English Succession, confirming a Protestant monarch. It took its name from the River Boyne which rises in County Kildare and flows 110 km/69 mi northeast to the Irish Sea.

**Brabant** Flemish *Braband,* former duchy of western Europe, comprising the Dutch province of ◊North Brabant and the Belgian provinces of Brabant and Antwerp. They were divided when Belgium became independent in 1830. The present-day Belgian Brabant comprises two provinces: Flemish Brabant (area 2,106 sq km/813 sq mi; population (1997) 1,004,700) and Walloon Brabant (area 1,091 sq km/421 sq mi; population (1997) 341,600). Belgian Brabant is very densely populated, and rich both in agriculture and industry. The principal towns are Louvain in Flemish Brabant, Nivelles in Walloon Brabant, and the Belgian capital, Brussels.

**brachiopod** or *lamp shell,* any member of the phylum Brachiopoda, marine invertebrates with two shells, resembling but totally unrelated to bivalves.

There are about 300 living species; they were much more numerous in past geological ages. They are suspension feeders, ingesting minute food particles from water. A single internal organ, the lophophore, handles feeding, aspiration, and excretion.

**bracken** any of several large ferns (especially *Pteridium aquilinum*) which grow abundantly in the northern hemisphere. The rootstock produces coarse fronds each year, which die down in autumn.

**Bracknell Forest** unitary authority (borough status) in central south England, created in 1998 from part of the former county of Berkshire
*area* 109 sq km/42 sq mi
*towns* Bracknell (administrative headquarters), Sandhurst, Crowthorne
*features* Royal Military Academy at Sandhurst (established in 1799 for officer training); the Meteorological Office at Bracknell (one of two global forecasting centres for the world's airlines); Transport Research Laboratory
*industries* high technology industries, engineering, electronics, manufacture of clothing and furniture, bakery products
*population* (1997) 109,600.

**Bradbury, Malcolm Stanley** (1932–  ) English novelist and critic. His fiction includes comic and satiric portrayals of provincial British and US campus life: *Eating People is Wrong* (1959) (his first novel), *Stepping Westward* (1965), and *The History Man* (1975). *Dr Criminale* (1992) is an academic satire with a 1990s setting. His critical works include *The Modern American Novel* (1983, 2nd edition 1992) and *The Modern British Novel* (1993).

**Bradford** industrial city and metropolitan borough in West Yorkshire, England, 14 km/9 mi west of Leeds; population (1994 est) 357,000. The manufacture of wool textiles, traditionally the base of Bradford's prosperity, declined in the 1970s but remains important. Other principal industries now include printing, precision and construction engineering, and the manufacture of chemicals and electronics. Stone-quarrying, brewing, photo-engraving, and publishing make a notable contribution to the city's economy. Bradford is also a major centre for financial services.

**Bradman, Don(ald) George** (1908–  ) Australian Test cricketer. From 52 Test matches he averaged 99.94 runs per innings, the highest average in Test history. He only needed four runs from his final Test innings to average 100 but was dismissed second ball.
*career highlights*
*all first-class cricket* runs: 28,067; average: 95.14; best: 452 not out (New South Wales v. Queensland 1930)
*Test cricket* runs: 6,996; average: 99.94; best: 334 (Australia v. England 1930)

**Braganza** the royal house of Portugal whose members reigned 1640–1910; members of another branch were emperors of Brazil 1822–89.

**Brahe, Tycho** (1546–1601) Danish astronomer. His accurate observations of the planets enabled German astronomer and mathematician Johannes ◊Kepler to prove that planets orbit the Sun in ellipses. Brahe's discovery and report of the 1572 supernova brought him recognition, and his observations of the comet of 1577 proved that it moved in an orbit among the planets, thus disproving Aristotle's view that comets were in the Earth's atmosphere.

**Brahma** in Hinduism, the creator of the cosmos, who forms with Vishnu and Siva the Trimurti, or three aspects of the absolute spirit.

**Brahman** in Hinduism, the supreme being, an abstract, impersonal world soul into whom the *atman*, or individual soul, will eventually be absorbed when its cycle of rebirth is ended.

**Brahmaputra** river in Asia 2,900 km/1,800 mi long, a tributary of the ◊Ganges, rising in the ◊Himalaya range, and flowing through Tibet, India, and Bangladesh.

**Brahms, Johannes** (1833–1897) German composer, pianist, and conductor. He is considered one of the greatest composers of symphonic music and of songs. His works include four symphonies, lieder (songs), concertos for piano and for violin, chamber music, sonatas, and the choral *Ein Deutsches Requiem/A German Requiem* (1868). He performed and conducted his own works.

**brain** in higher animals, a mass of interconnected ◊nerve cells forming the anterior part of the ◊central nervous system, whose activities it coordinates and controls. In ◊vertebrates, the brain is contained by the skull. At the base of the ◊brainstem, the *medulla oblongata* contains centres for the control of respiration, heartbeat rate and strength, and blood pressure. Overlying this is the *cerebellum,* which is concerned with coordinating complex muscular processes such as maintaining posture and moving limbs.

The cerebral hemispheres (*cerebrum*) are paired outgrowths of the front end of the forebrain, in early vertebrates mainly concerned

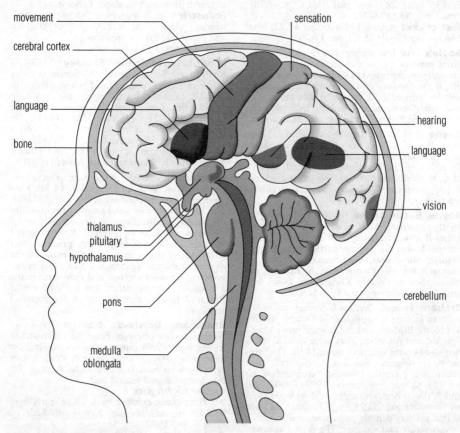

**brain** The structure of the human brain. At the back of the skull lies the cerebellum, which coordinates reflex actions that control muscular activity. The medulla controls respiration, heartbeat, and blood pressure. The hypothalamus is concerned with instinctive drives and emotions. The thalamus relays signals to and from various parts of the brain. The pituitary gland controls the body's hormones. Distinct areas of the large convoluted cerebral hemispheres that fill most of the skull are linked to sensations, such as hearing and sight, and voluntary activities, such as movement.

with the senses, but in higher vertebrates greatly developed and involved in the integration of all sensory input and motor output, and in thought, emotions, memory, and behaviour.

**brainstem** region where the top of the spinal cord merges with the undersurface of the brain, consisting largely of the medulla oblongata and midbrain.

**brake** device used to slow down or stop the movement of a moving body or vehicle. The mechanically applied calliper brake used on bicycles uses a scissor action to press hard rubber blocks against the wheel rim. The main braking system of a car works hydraulically: when the driver depresses the brake pedal, liquid pressure forces pistons to apply brakes on each wheel.

**Bramante** adopted name of *Donato di Pascuccio* (1444–1514) Italian High Renaissance architect and artist. Inspired by classical designs and by the work of Leonardo da Vinci, he was employed by Pope Julius II in rebuilding part of the Vatican and St Peter's in Rome. The circular Tempietto of San Pietro in Montorio, Rome (commissioned in 1502, built about 1510), is possibly his most important completed work. Though small in size, this circular colonnaded building possesses much of the grandeur of ancient Roman buildings.

**bramble** any of a group of prickly bushes belonging to the rose family. Examples are ◊blackberry, raspberry, and dewberry. (Genus *Rubus,* family Rosaceae.)

**Branagh, Kenneth Charles** (1960– ) Northern Irish stage and film actor, director, and producer. He co-founded the Renaissance Theatre Company in 1987. His first film as both actor and director was *Henry V* (1989); he returned to Shakespeare with lavish film versions of *Much Ado About Nothing* (1993) and *Hamlet* (1996).

**Brancusi, Constantin** (1876–1957) Romanian sculptor. One of the main figures of 20th-century art, he revolutionized modern sculpture. Active in Paris from 1904, he was a pioneer of abstract sculpture, reducing a few basic themes such as birds, fishes, and the human head to simple essential forms appropriate to the special quality of his material, whether stone, bronze, or wood. His works include *Sleeping Muse* 1910 (Musée National d'Art Moderne, Paris) and *Bird in Space* 1928 (Museum of Modern Art, New York).

**Brandenburg** administrative *Land* (state) of Germany
*area* 25,000 sq km/10,000 sq mi
*capital* Potsdam
*towns and cities* Cottbus, Brandenburg, Frankfurt-an-der-Oder
*industries* iron and steel, paper, pulp, metal products, semiconductors
*population* (1995) 2,500,000
*history* The Hohenzollern rulers who took control of Brandenburg in 1415 later acquired the powerful duchy of Prussia and became emperors of Germany. At the end of World War II,

Brandenburg lost over 12,950 sq km/5,000 sq mi of territory when Poland advanced its frontier to the line of the Oder and Neisse rivers. The remainder, which became a region of East Germany, was divided in 1952 into the districts of Frankfurt-an-der-Oder, Potsdam, and Cottbus. When Germany was reunited in 1990, Brandenburg reappeared as a *Land* of the Federal Republic. In 1997 the citizens of Brandenburg voted against an amalgamation with Berlin to create a new *Land.*

**Brando, Marlon** (1924– ) US actor. One of the great exponents of method acting, he cultivated a mumbling speech and had a powerful presence on both stage and screen. He won best actor Academy Awards for *On the Waterfront* (1954) and *The Godfather* (1972), although he declined the second award to protest against the way Hollywood portrayed American Indians. Brando directed one film, the camp psychological western *One Eyed Jacks* (1961).

**Brandt, Willy** adopted name of Karl Herbert Frahm (1913–1992) German socialist politician, federal chancellor (premier) of West Germany 1969–74. He played a key role in the remoulding of the Social Democratic Party (SPD) as a moderate socialist force (leader 1964–87). As mayor of West Berlin 1957–66, Brandt became internationally known during the Berlin Wall crisis of 1961. He was awarded the Nobel Peace Prize in 1971.

**brandy** (Dutch *brandewijn* 'burnt wine') alcoholic drink distilled from fermented grape juice (wine). The best-known examples are produced in France, notably Armagnac and Cognac. Brandy can also be prepared from other fruits, for example, apples (Calvados) and cherries (Kirschwasser). Brandies contain up to 55% alcohol.

**Braque, Georges** (1882–1963) French painter. With Picasso, he played a decisive role in the development of Cubism 1907–10. It was during this period that he began to experiment with collage and invented the technique of gluing paper, wood, and other materials to canvas.

**Brasília** capital of Brazil from 1960, situated on the central plateau 1,150 m/3,773 ft above sea level; population (1991) 1,601,100. The main area of employment is in government service; only light industry is allowed within the city. Brasília is also capital of the Federal District, which has an area of 5,794 sq km/2,317 sq mi. The city was originally designed to accommodate up to 500,000 people, which has now been exceeded, and many people live in shanty towns located outside the main city.

**brass** metal ◊alloy of copper and zinc, with not more than 5% or 6% of other metals. The zinc content ranges from 20% to 45%, and the colour of brass varies accordingly from coppery to whitish yellow. Brasses are characterized by the ease with which they may be shaped and machined; they are strong and ductile, resist many forms of corrosion, and are used for electrical fittings, ammunition cases, screws, household fittings, and ornaments.

**brassica** any of a group of plants, many of which are cultivated as vegetables. The most familiar is the common cabbage (*Brassica oleracea*), with its varieties broccoli, cauliflower, kale, and Brussels sprouts. (Genus *Brassica*, family Cruciferae.)

**brass instrument** any of a class of musical instruments made of brass or other metal, including trumpets, bugles, trombones, and horns. The function of a reed is served by the lips, shaped and tensed by the mouthpiece, acting as a valve releasing periodic pulses of pressurised air into the tube. Orchestral brass instruments are derived from signalling instruments that in their natural or valveless form produce a directionally focused range of tones from the harmonic series by overblowing to as high as the 16th harmonic. They are powerful and efficient generators, and produce tones of great depth and resonance.

**Bratislava** German *Pressburg,* industrial port (engineering, chemicals, oil refining) and capital of the Slovak Republic, on the River Danube; population (1991) 441,500. It was the capital of Hungary 1526–1784 and capital of Slovakia (within Czechoslovakia) until 1993.

**Braunschweig** German form of ◊Brunswick, a city in Lower Saxony, Germany.

**Brazil** Federative Republic of
*national name República Federativa do Brasil*

0 mi   500
0 km   1000

*area* 8,511,965 sq km/3,286,469 sq mi
*capital* Brasília
*major towns/cities* São Paulo, Belo Horizonte, Nova Iguaçu, Rio de Janeiro, Belém, Recife, Pôrto Alegre, Salvador, Curitiba, Manaus, Fortaleza
*major ports* Rio de Janeiro, Belém, Recife, Pôrto Alegre, Salvador
*physical features* the densely forested Amazon basin covers the northern half of the country with a network of rivers; south is fertile; enormous energy resources, both hydroelectric

(Itaipú Reservoir on the Paraná, and Tucuruí on the Tocantins) and nuclear (uranium ores); mostly tropical climate
*head of state and government* Fernando Henrique Cardoso from 1994
*political system* democratic federal republic
*political parties* Workers' Party (PT), left of centre; Social Democratic Party (PSDB), moderate, left of centre; Brazilian Democratic Movement Party (PMDB), centre left; Liberal Front Party (PFL), right wing; National Reconstruction Party (PRN), centre right
*currency* real
*GNP per capita (PPP)* (US$) 6,160 (1998)
*exports* steel products, transport equipment, coffee, iron ore and concentrates, aluminium, iron, tin, soybeans, orange juice (85% of world's concentrates), tobacco, leather footwear, sugar, beef, textiles. Principal market: USA 17.8% (1998)
*population* 167,988,000 (1998 est)
*language* Portuguese (official); 120 Indian languages
*religion* Roman Catholic 89%; Indian faiths
*life expectancy* 63 (men); 71 (women) (1995–2000)
*Chronology*
*1500* Originally inhabited by South American Indians. Portuguese explorer Pedro Alvares Cabral sighted and claimed Brazil for Portugal.
*1530* Start of Portuguese colonization; Portugal monopolized trade but colonial government was decentralized.
*1580–1640* Brazil, with Portugal, came under Spanish rule.
*17th century* Huge sugar-cane plantations established with slave labour in coastal regions, making Brazil world's largest supplier of sugar; cattle ranching developed inland.
*1695* Discovery of gold in central highlands.
*1763* Colonial capital moved from Bahía to Rio de Janeiro.
*1770* Brazil's first coffee plantations established in Rio de Janeiro.
*18th century* Population in 1798 totalled 3.3 million, of which around 1.9 million were slaves, mainly of African origin; significant growth of gold-mining industry.
*19th century* Rapid expansion in coffee growing.
*1808* Following Napoleon's invasion of Portugal, the Portuguese regent, Prince John, arrived in Brazil and established his court at Rio de Janeiro; Brazilian trade opened to foreign merchants.
*1815* United Kingdom of Portugal, Brazil, and Algarve made Brazil co-equal with Portugal and Rio de Janeiro as capital.
*1821* Political disorder in Portugal forced King John VI to return to Europe, leaving government of Brazil to his son, Crown Prince Pedro.
*1822* Pedro defied orders from Portuguese parliament to return to Portugal; he declared Brazil's independence to avoid reversion to colonial status.
*1825* King John VI recognized his son as Emperor Pedro I of Brazil.
*1831* Pedro I abdicated in favour of his infant son, Pedro II; regency (to 1840) dominated by Brazilian politicians.

**1847** First prime minister appointed, but emperor retained wide-ranging powers.

**1865–70** Brazilian efforts to control Uruguay led to War of the Triple Alliance with Paraguay.

**1888** Abolition of slavery in Brazil.

**1889** Monarch overthrown by liberal revolt; federal republic established with central government controlled by coffee planters; by 1902 Brazil produced 65% of world's coffee.

**1915–19** Lack of European imports during World War I led to rapid industrialization, especially in state of São Paulo.

**1930** Revolution against planter oligarchy placed Getúlio Vargas in power; he introduced social reforms and economic planning.

**1937** Vargas established authoritarian corporate state.

**1942** Brazil entered World War II as ally of USA; small fighting force sent to Italy in 1944.

**1945** Vargas ousted by military coup, but Gen Eurico Gaspar Dutra soon forced to abandon free-market policies.

**1951** Vargas elected president; continued to extend state control of economy.

**1954** Vargas committed suicide.

**1956–61** Juscelino Kubitschek became president, pursuing measures geared towards rapid economic growth.

**1960** Capital moved to Brasília.

**1961** Janio Quadros elected president, introducing controversial programme for radical reform; resigned after seven months; succeeded by Vice-president João Goulart.

**1964** Bloodless coup established technocratic military regime; free political parties abolished; intense concentration on industrial growth aided by foreign investment and loans.

**1970s** Economic recession and inflation undermined public support for military regime.

**1985** After gradual democratization from 1979, Tancredo Neves became first civilian president in 21 years; on Neves's death, Vice President José Sarney took office.

**1988** New constitution reduced powers of president.

**1989** Fernando Collor (PRN) was elected president, promising economic deregulation; Brazil suspended foreign debt payments.

**1992** Collor was charged with corruption and replaced by Vice-president Itamar Franco.

**1994** A new currency was introduced (the third in eight years). Fernando Henrique Cardoso (PSDB) was elected president. Collor was cleared of corruption charges.

**1997** The constitution was amended to allow the president to seek a second term of office.

**1998** Former president Collor was acquitted on charges of illegal enrichment. President Cardoso was re-elected. An IMF rescue package was announced.

**Brazil nut** gigantic South American tree; also its seed, which is rich in oil and highly nutritious. The seeds (nuts) are enclosed in a hard outer casing, each fruit containing 10–20 seeds arranged like the segments of an orange. The timber of the tree is also valuable. (*Bertholletia excelsa*, family Lecythidaceae.)

**Brazzaville** river port and capital of the Republic of the Congo (Congo-Brazzaville), on the west bank of the Congo-Zaire River, opposite Kinshasa; population (1995 est) 937,600. Industries include foundries, railway repairs, shipbuilding, beverages, textiles, food processing, shoes, soap, furniture, and bricks. Tourism is important, with arts and crafts markets in the Plateau district of the city. There is a cathedral built in 1892 and the Pasteur Institute founded in 1908. The city stands on Malebo Pool (Stanley Pool).

**breadfruit** fruit of two tropical trees belonging to the mulberry family. It is highly nutritious and when baked is said to taste like bread. It is native to many South Pacific islands. (*Artocarpus communis* and *A. altilis*, family Moraceae.)

**Breakspear, Nicholas** Original name of ◊Adrian IV, the only English pope.

**bream** deep-bodied, flattened fish *Abramis brama* of the carp family, growing to about 50 cm/1.6 ft, typically found in lowland rivers across Europe.

**breast** one of a pair of organs on the chest of the human female, also known as a ◊mammary gland. Each of the two breasts contains milk-producing cells and a network of tubes or ducts that lead to openings in the nipple.

**breast screening** in medicine, examination of the breast to detect the presence of breast cancer at an early stage. Screening methods include self-screening by monthly examination of the breasts and formal programmes of screening by palpation (physical examination) and mammography in special clinics. Screening may be offered to older women on a routine basis and it is important in women with a family history of breast cancer.

**breathing** in terrestrial animals, the muscular movements whereby air is taken into the lungs and then expelled, a form of gas exchange. Breathing is sometimes referred to as external respiration, for true respiration is a cellular (internal) process.

**Brecht, Bertolt (Eugen Berthold Friedrich)** (1898–1956) German dramatist and poet. He was one of the most influential figures in 20th-century theatre. A committed Marxist, he sought to develop an 'epic theatre' which aimed to destroy the 'suspension of disbelief' usual in the theatre and so encourage audiences to develop an active and critical attitude to a play's subject. He adapted John Gay's *The Beggar's Opera* as *Die Dreigroschenoper/The Threepenny Opera* 1928, set to music by Kurt Weill. Later plays include *Mutter Courage und ihre Kinder/Mother Courage and her Children* 1941, set during the Thirty Years' War, and *Der kaukasische Kreidekreis/The Caucasian Chalk Circle* 1945.

**breed** recognizable group of domestic animals, within a species, with distinctive characteristics that have been produced by ◊artificial selection.

**breeder reactor** or *fast breeder*, alternative names for ◊fast reactor, a type of nuclear reactor.

**Bremen** industrial port and capital of the *Land* (state) of ◊Bremen, Germany, on the River Weser 69 km/43 mi from the open sea; population (1995) 549,000. Industries include iron, steel, oil refining, the manufacture of chemicals, aircraft, and cars, ship repairing, marine engineering, and electronics. The Bremer Vulkan Shipyards closed in 1996. Nearby Bremerhaven serves as an outport.

**Bremen** administrative region (German *Land*) of Germany, consisting of the cities of Bremen and Bremerhaven; area 400 sq km/154 sq mi; population (1994 est) 683,000.

**Brenner Pass** lowest of the Alpine passes, 1,370 m/4,495 ft; it leads from Trentino–Alto Adige, Italy, to the Austrian Tirol, and is 19 km/12 mi long.

**Brescia** ancient *Brixia*, town in Lombardy, northern Italy, 84 km/52 mi east of Milan; population (1992) 192,900. Industries include precision engineering, brewing, and the manufacture of iron, steel, machine tools, transport equipment, firearms, metal products, and textiles. It has medieval walls and two cathedrals (12th and 17th century).

**Breslau** German name of ◊Wrocław, a city in Poland.

**Brest** naval base and industrial port in the *département* of Finistère, situated on two hills separated by the River Penfeld at *Rade de Brest* (Brest Roads), a great bay whose only entrance is a narrow channel, at the western extremity of Brittany in northwest France; population (1990) 201,500. The town has a naval academy, several schools of nautical science, a university and an oceanographic research centre. Industries include electronics, shipbuilding and the manufacture of chemicals and paper. Occupied as a U-boat base by the Germans 1940–44, part of the old city was destroyed by Allied bombing and the retreating Germans.

**Breton, André** (1896–1966) French writer and poet. He was among the leaders of the ◊Dada art movement and was also a founder of Surrealism, publishing *Le Manifeste de surréalisme/Surrealist Manifesto* 1924.

**Bretton Woods** township in New Hampshire, USA, where the United Nations Monetary and Financial Conference was held 1944 to discuss post-war international payments problems. The agreements reached on financial assistance and measures to stabilize exchange rates led to the creation of the International Bank for Reconstruction and Development 1945 and the International Monetary Fund (IMF).

**Breuer, Marcel Lajos** (1902–1981) Hungarian-born architect and designer. He studied and taught at the ◊Bauhaus school in Germany. His tubular steel chair (1925) was the first of its kind. He moved to England, then to the USA, where he was in partnership with Walter ◊Gropius 1937–40. His buildings show an affinity with natural materials, as exemplified in the Bijenkorf, Rotterdam, the Netherlands (with Elzas; 1953).

**brewing** making of beer, ale, or other alcoholic beverage, from ◊malt and ◊barley by steeping (mashing), boiling, and fermenting.

Mashing the barley releases its sugars. Yeast is then added, which contains the enzymes needed to convert the sugars into ethanol (alcohol) and carbon dioxide. Hops are added to give a bitter taste.

**Brezhnev, Leonid Ilyich** (1906–1982) Soviet leader. A protégé of Joseph Stalin and Nikita Khrushchev, he came to power (after he and Aleksei ◊Kosygin forced Khrushchev to resign) as general secretary of the Communist Party of the Soviet Union (CPSU) 1964–82 and was president 1977–82. Domestically he was conservative; abroad the USSR was established as a military and political superpower during the Brezhnev era, extending its influence in Africa and Asia.

**Brian Boruma** (*c.* 941–1014) king of Munster from 976 and high king of Ireland from 999. His campaigns represent the rise of Munster as a power in Ireland, symbolized by his victory over Leinster and the Dublin Norse at Glen Mama in 999. He was renowned as a builder of forts, and this may have been his most significant military legacy. He died in victory over the Vikings at Clontarf in Dublin.

**bribery** corruptly receiving or agreeing to receive, giving or promising to give, any gift, loan, fee, reward, or advantage as an inducement or reward to persons in certain positions of trust. For example, it is an offence to improperly influence in this way judges or other judicial officers, members and officers of public bodies, or voters at public elections.

**brick** common block-shaped building material, with all opposite sides parallel. It is made of clay that has been fired in a kiln. Bricks are made by kneading a mixture of crushed clay and other materials into a stiff mud and extruding it into a ribbon. The ribbon is cut into individual bricks, which are fired at a temperature of up to about 1,000°C/1,800°F. Bricks may alternatively be pressed into shape in moulds.

**bridge** structure that provides a continuous path or road over water, valleys, ravines, or above other roads. The basic designs and composites of these are based on the way they bear the weight of the structure and its load. *Beam,* or *girder,* bridges are supported at each end by the ground with the weight thrusting downwards. *Cantilever* bridges are a complex form of girder in which only one end is supported. *Arch* bridges thrust outwards and downwards at their ends. *Suspension* bridges use cables under tension to pull inwards against anchorages on either side of the span, so that the roadway hangs from the main cables by the network of vertical cables. The *cable-stayed* bridge relies on diagonal cables connected directly between the bridge deck and supporting towers at each end. Some bridges are too low to allow traffic to pass beneath easily, so they are designed with movable parts, like swing and draw bridges.

**bridge** card game derived from whist. First played among members of the Indian Civil Service about 1900, bridge was brought to England 1903 and played at the Portland Club 1908. It is played in two forms: auction bridge and contract bridge.

**Bridgend** unitary authority in south Wales created in 1996 from part of the former county of Mid Glamorgan
*area* 40 sq km/15 sq mi
*towns* Bridgend (administrative headquarters), Porthcawl (resort and residential area), Maesteg
*physical* most of the authority consists of the western end of a lowland plateau, Bro Morgannwg, a rich agricultural area of mixed farming and large villages; in the north is the Cymer Forest and Mynydd Caerau (556 m/ 1,824 ft)
*industries* civil engineering; chocolate manufacture
*population* (1996) 128,300.

**Bridgetown** port and capital of Barbados; population (1990) 6,700. Sugar is exported through the nearby deep-water port. Bridgetown was founded 1628.

**Bridgewater, Francis Egerton**, 3rd Duke of Bridgewater (1736–1803) pioneer of British inland navigation. With James Brindley as his engineer, he constructed 1762–72 the Bridgewater Canal from Worsley to Manchester and on to the Mersey, a distance of 67.5 km/ 42 mi. Initially built to carry coal, the canal crosses the Irwell Valley on an aqueduct. Succeeded as Duke 1748.

**Bright, John** (1811–1889) British Liberal politician. He was a campaigner for free trade, peace, and social reform. A Quaker millowner, he was among the founders of the Anti-Corn Law League in 1839, and was largely instrumental in securing the passage of the Reform Bill of 1867.

He sat in Gladstone's cabinets as president of the Board of Trade 1868–70 and chancellor of the Duchy of Lancaster 1873–74 and 1880–82, but broke with him over the Irish Home Rule Bill.

**Brighton** seaside resort in ◊Brighton and Hove unitary authority, on the south coast of England; population (1994 est) 155,000. The town was part of the county of East Sussex until 1997. It is an education and service centre with two universities, language schools, and tourist and conference business facilities.

**Brighton and Hove** unitary authority in southern England, created in 1997
*area* 84 sq km/32 sq mi
*towns* Brighton, Hove (administrative headquarters), Woodingdean, Rottingdean, Portslade-by-Sea
*features* English Channel; South Downs; Royal Pavilion (Brighton) redesigned and enlarged by John Nash in the 19th century; Palace Pier and West Pier (Brighton); Hollingbury Castle fort; Booth Museum of Natural History (Brighton); British Engineerium (Hove)

*industries* financial services (including American Express), tourism, conference facilities, language schools
*population* (1996) 248,000.
*famous people* Martin Ryle.

**brill** flatfish *Scophthalmus laevis*, living in shallow water over sandy bottoms in the northeastern Atlantic and Mediterranean. It is a freckled sandy brown, and grows to 60 cm/2 ft.

**Brisbane** capital and chief port of the state of ◊Queensland, Australia; population (1996) 1,291,157. Brisbane is situated on the east coast of Australia, 14 km/9 mi inland of the mouth of the River Brisbane, about 29 km/18 mi south of Moreton Bay. It is the third-largest city in Australia, and the financial and commercial centre for Queensland; it has diverse industries including shipbuilding, engineering, brewing, food processing, tobacco production, tanning, the manufacture of agricultural machinery, shoes, and clothing. Tourism is also important. A pipeline from Moonie carries oil for refining. Brisbane has three universities, Queensland University (1909), Griffith University (1975), and Queensland University of Technology (1989).

**bristletail** primitive wingless insect of the order Thysanura. Up to 2 cm/0.8 in long, bristletails have a body tapering from front to back, two long antennae, and three 'tails' at the rear end. They include the *silverfish Lepisma saccharina* and the *firebrat Thermobia domestica*. Two-tailed bristletails constitute another insect order, the Diplura. They live under stones and fallen branches, feeding on decaying material.

**Bristol** industrial port and unitary authority in southwest England, at the junction of the rivers Avon and Frome; it was part of the former county of Avon to 1996
*area* 109 sq km/42 sq mi
*features* new city centre, with British engineer and inventor Isambard Kingdom ◊Brunel's Temple Meads railway station as its focus; old docks have been redeveloped for housing and industry; there is a 12th-century cathedral and 13th–14th-century St Mary Redcliffe church; National Lifeboat Museum; Clifton Suspension Bridge (completed in 1864), designed by Brunel; aerospace complex in the suburb of Filton; University of Bristol (founded in 1909) and University of the West of England (established in 1992), formerly the Bristol Polytechnic; Ashton Court mansion, which hosts the annual International Balloon Fiesta and North Somerset show; Bristol 2000, a Millennium Commission Landmark Project in the city's harbour area, includes Wildscreen World, the world's first electronic zoo
*industries* engineering, microelectronics, tobacco, printing, metal refining, banking, insurance, sugar refining, and the manufacture of aircraft engines, chemicals, paper, soap, Bristol 'blue' glass, and chocolate
*population* (1996) 374,300, urban area (1991) 516,500
*famous people* Thomas Chatterton, W G Grace, Cary Grant.

**Britain** island off the northwest coast of
Europe, one of the British Isles. It comprises
England, Scotland, and Wales (together officially known as ◊Great Britain), and is part of
the United Kingdom. The name is also sometimes used loosely to denote the United
Kingdom. It is derived from the Roman name
for the island *Britannia*, which in turn is derived
from the ancient Celtic name for the inhabitants,
*Bryttas*.

**Britain, ancient** period in the British Isles
(excluding Ireland) extending through prehistory to the Roman occupation (1st century AD).
Settled agricultural life evolved in Britain during
the 3rd millennium BC. A peak was reached in
Neolithic society in southern England early in
the 2nd millennium BC, with the construction of
the great stone circles of Avebury and
Stonehenge. It was succeeded in central southern
Britain by the Early Bronze Age Wessex culture,
with strong trade links across Europe. The Iron
Age culture of the Celts was predominant in the
last few centuries BC, and the Belgae (of mixed
Germanic and Celtic stock) were partially
Romanized in the century between the first
Roman invasion of Britain under Julius Caesar
(54 BC) and the Roman conquest (AD 43). For
later history, see ◊Roman Britain.

**Britain, Battle of** World War II air battle
between German and British air forces over
Britain 10 July–31 October 1940.

**British Broadcasting Corporation** (BBC),
the UK state-owned broadcasting network. It
operates television and national and local radio
stations, and is financed by the sale of television
(originally radio) licences. It is not permitted to
carry advertisements but it has an additional
source of income through its publishing interests
and the sales of its programmes. The BBC is controlled by a board of governors, each appointed
by the government for five years. The BBC was
converted from a private company (established
1922) to a public corporation under royal charter 1927. Under the Charter, news programmes
were required to be politically impartial. The
first director-general was John Reith 1922–38.

**British Columbia** most westerly, and only
Pacific, province of Canada. It is bordered on
the east by Alberta, with the Continental Divide
in the Rocky Mountains forming its southeastern boundary. To the south, it has a frontier
along the 49th Parallel with the US states of
Montana, Idaho, and Washington. To the north,
along the 60th Parallel, lie the Northwest
Territories and Yukon Territory. British
Columbia borders in the northwest on the panhandle of Alaska for about half its length (the
other half forming the frontier with Yukon
Territory)
*area* 947,800 sq km/365,851 sq mi
*capital* Victoria
*towns and cities* Vancouver, Prince George,
Kamloops, Kelowna, Surrey, Richmond,
Nanaimo
*population* (1996) 3,724,500
*physical* Rocky Mountains, Coast Mountains,
and Coast Range; deeply indented coastline;

rivers include the Fraser and Columbia; over 80
major lakes; more than half the land is forested
*industries* lumbering and manufacture of finished wood products; fishing; mining (coal, copper, iron, lead); extraction of oil and natural gas;
hydroelectric power generation; fruit and vegetable growing.

**British Council** semi-official organization set
up in 1934 (royal charter 1940) to promote a
wider knowledge of the UK, excluding politics
and commerce, and to develop cultural relations
with other countries. It employs more than
6,000 people and is represented in 109 countries, running libraries, English-teaching operations, and resource centres.

**British East India Company** commercial
company (1600–1858) chartered by Queen
Elizabeth I and given a monopoly of trade
between England and the Far East. In the 18th
century, the company became, in effect, the ruler
of a large part of India, and a form of dual control by the company and a committee responsible to Parliament in London was introduced by
Pitt's India Act 1784. The end of the monopoly
of China trade came in 1834, and after the
◊Indian Mutiny of 1857–58 the crown took
complete control of the government of British
India. The India Act 1858 abolished the
company.

**British Empire** empire covering, at its height
in the 1920s, about a sixth of the landmass of
the Earth, all of its lands recognizing the United
Kingdom (UK) as their leader. It consisted of the
Empire of India, four self-governing countries
known as dominions, and dozens of colonies
and territories. After World War II it began to
dissolve as colony after colony became independent, and today the UK has only 13 small
dependent territories. With 52 other independent countries, it forms the ◊Commonwealth.
Although Britain's monarch is accepted as head
of the Commonwealth, most of its member
states are republics.

**British Honduras** former name (to 1973) of
Belize.

**British Indian Ocean Territory** British
colony in the Indian Ocean directly administered by the Foreign and Commonwealth Office.
It consists of the Chagos Archipelago some
1,900 km/1,200 mi northeast of Mauritius
*area* 60 sq km/23 sq mi
*features* lagoons; US naval and air base on
Diego Garcia
*industries* copra, salt fish, tortoiseshell
*population* There is no permanent population.
*history* purchased in 1965 for $3 million by
Britain from Mauritius to provide a joint US/UK
base. The islands of Aldabra, Farquhar, and
Desroches, some 485 km/300 mi north of
Madagascar, originally formed part of the
British Indian Ocean Territory but were
returned to the administration of the Seychelles
in 1976.

**British Isles** group of islands off the northwest coast of Europe, consisting of Great Britain

(England, Wales, and Scotland), Ireland, the Channel Islands, the Orkney and Shetland islands, the Isle of Man, and many other islands that are included in various counties, such as the Isle of Wight, Scilly Isles, Lundy Island, and the Inner and Outer Hebrides. The islands are divided from Europe by the North Sea, Strait of Dover, and the English Channel, and face the Atlantic to the west.

**British Petroleum** (BP), one of the world's largest oil concerns, with more than 128,000 employees in 70 countries. It was formed as the Anglo-Persian Oil Company in 1909 and acquired the chemical interests of the Distillers Company in 1967.

**British Somaliland** British protectorate comprising over 176,000 sq km/67,980 sq mi of territory on the Somali coast of East Africa from 1884 until the independence of Somalia 1960. British authorities were harassed by Somali nationalists under the leadership of Muhammad bin Abdullah Hassan.

**British Virgin Islands** part of the ◊Virgin Islands group in the West Indies.

**Brittany** French *Bretagne,* Breton *Breiz,* modern region of northwest France and former province, on the Breton peninsula between the Bay of Biscay and the English Channel; area 27,200 sq km/10,499 sq mi; population (1990) 2,795,600. A farming region, it includes the *départements* of Côtes-d'Armor, Finistère, Ille-et-Vilaine, and Morbihan. The administrative centre is Rennes, and other towns include Brest, Lorient, Nantes, St-Brieuc, Vannes, and Quimper.

**Britten, (Edward) Benjamin** Baron Britten (1913–1976) English composer. He often wrote for the individual voice; for example, the role in the opera *Peter Grimes* (1945), based on verses by George Crabbe, was written for his life companion, the tenor Peter Pears. Among his many works are the *Young Person's Guide to the Orchestra* (1946); the chamber opera *The Rape of Lucretia* (1946); *Billy Budd* (1951); *A Midsummer Night's Dream* (Shakespeare) (1960); and *Death in Venice* (after Thomas Mann) (1973).

**brittle-star** any member of the echinoderm class Ophiuroidea. A brittle-star resembles a starfish, and has a small, central, rounded body and long, flexible, spiny arms used for walking. The small brittle-star *Amphipholis squamata* is greyish, about 4.5 cm/2 in across, and found on sea bottoms worldwide. It broods its young, and its arms can be luminous.

**BRM** abbreviation for *British Racing Motors,* a racing-car manufacturer founded in 1949 by Raymond Mays (1899–1980). Their first Grand Prix win was in 1959, and in the next 18 years they won 17 Grands Prix. Their world champions include Graham Hill.

**Brno** industrial city (chemicals, arms, textiles, machinery) in the Czech Republic; population (1993) 390,000. Now the second-largest city in the Czech Republic, Brno was formerly the capital of the Austrian crown land of Moravia.

**broadbill** primitive perching bird of the family Eurylaimidae, found in Africa and South Asia. Broadbills are forest birds and are often found near water. They are gregarious and noisy, have brilliant coloration and wide bills, and feed largely on insects.

**broadcasting** the transmission of sound and vision programmes by ◊radio and ◊television. Broadcasting may be organized under private enterprise, as in the USA, or may operate under a compromise system, as in Britain, where a television and radio service controlled by the state-regulated ◊British Broadcasting Corporation (BBC) operates alongside commercial channels operating under franchises granted by the Independent Television Commission (known as the Independent Broadcasting Authority before 1991) and the Radio Authority.

**broad-leaved tree** another name for a tree belonging to the ◊angiosperms, such as ash, beech, oak, maple, or birch. The leaves are generally broad and flat, in contrast to the needle-like leaves of most ◊conifers. See also ◊deciduous tree.

**Broads, Norfolk** area of navigable lakes and rivers in England; see ◊Norfolk Broads.

**Broadway** major avenue in New York running northwest from the tip of Manhattan and crossing Times Square at 42nd Street, at the heart of the theatre district, where Broadway is known as 'the Great White Way'. New York theatres situated outside this area are described as *off-Broadway;* those even smaller and farther away are *off-off-Broadway,* the home of avant-garde and experimental works.

**broccoli** variety of ◊cabbage. It contains high levels of the glucosinolate compound glucoraphanin. A breakdown product of this was found to neutralize damage to cells and so help to prevent cancer.

**Brodsky, Joseph Alexandrovich** (1940–1996) Russian poet. He emigrated to the USA 1972. His work, often dealing with themes of exile, is admired for its wit and economy of language, particularly in its use of understatement. Many of his poems, written in Russian, have been translated into English (*A Part of Speech* 1980). More recently he has also written in English. He was awarded the Nobel Prize for Literature 1987 and became US poet laureate 1991.

**Broglie, Louis Victor Pierre Raymond de** 7th duc de Broglie (1892–1987) French theoretical physicist. He established that all subatomic particles can be described either by particle equations or by wave equations, thus laying the foundations of wave mechanics. He was awarded the 1929 Nobel Prize for Physics. Succeeded as Duke 1960.

**brome grass** any of several annual grasses found in temperate regions; some are used as food for horses and cattle, but many are weeds. (Genus *Bromus,* family Gramineae.)

**bromeliad** any tropical or subtropical plant belonging to the pineapple family, usually with stiff leathery leaves, which are often coloured and patterned, and bright, attractive flower spikes. There are about 1,400 species in tropical America; several are cultivated as greenhouse plants. (Family Bromeliaceae.)

**bromine** (Greek *bromos* 'stench') dark, reddish-brown, nonmetallic element, a volatile liquid at room temperature, symbol Br, atomic number 35, relative atomic mass 79.904. It is a member of the ◊halogen group, has an unpleasant odour, and is very irritating to mucous membranes. Its salts are known as bromides.

**bronchitis** inflammation of the bronchi (air passages) of the lungs, usually caused initially by a viral infection, such as a cold or flu. It is aggravated by environmental pollutants, especially smoking, and results in a persistent cough, irritated mucus-secreting glands, and large amounts of sputum.

**Brontë** three English novelists, daughters of a Yorkshire parson. *Charlotte* (1816–1855), notably with *Jane Eyre* (1847) and *Villette* (1853), reshaped autobiographical material into vivid narrative. *Emily* (1818–1848) in *Wuthering Heights* (1847) expressed the intensity and nature mysticism which also pervades her poetry (*Poems*, 1846). The more modest talent of *Anne* (1820–1849) produced *Agnes Grey* (1847) and *The Tenant of Wildfell Hall* (1848).

**brontosaurus** former name of a type of large, plant-eating dinosaur, now better known as ◊apatosaurus.

**bronze** alloy of copper and tin, yellow or brown in colour. It is harder than pure copper, more suitable for casting, and also resists ◊corrosion. Bronze may contain as much as 25% tin, together with small amounts of other metals, mainly lead.

**Bronze Age** stage of prehistory and early history when copper and bronze (an alloy of tin and copper) became the first metals worked extensively and used for tools and weapons. One of the classifications of the Danish archaeologist Christian Thomsen's Three Age System, it developed out of the Stone Age and generally preceded the Iron Age. It first began in the Far East and may be dated 5000–1200 BC in the Middle East and about 2000–500 BC in Europe.

**Brook, Peter Stephen Paul** (1925– ) English theatre director with a particularly innovative style. His work with the Royal Shakespeare Company (which he joined in 1962) included a production of Shakespeare's *A Midsummer Night's Dream* (1970), set in a white gymnasium and combining elements of circus and commedia dell'arte. In the same year he founded an independent initiative, Le Centre International de Créations Théâtrales/The International Centre for Theatre Research in Paris. Brook's later productions aim to combine elements from different cultures and include *The Conference of the Birds* (1973), based on a Persian story, and *The Mahabarata* (1985–88), a cycle of three plays based on the Hindu epic.

**Brooke, Rupert Chawner** (1887–1915) English poet. He stands as a symbol of the World War I 'lost generation'. His five war

sonnets, including 'The Soldier', were published posthumously. Other notable poems are 'Grantchester' (1912) and 'The Great Lover', written in 1914.

**broom** any of a group of shrubs (especially species of *Cytisus* and *Spartium*), often cultivated for their bright yellow flowers. (Family Leguminosae.)

**Brown, Capability Lancelot** (1716–1783) English landscape gardener and architect. He acquired his nickname because of his continual enthusiasm for the 'capabilities' of natural landscapes. He worked on or improved the gardens of many great houses and estates, including Hampton Court; Kew; Blenheim, Oxfordshire; Stowe, Buckinghamshire; and Petworth, West Sussex, occasionally contributing to the architectural designs.

**Brown, Ford Madox** (1821–1893) English painter, associated with the ◊Pre-Raphaelite Brotherhood through his pupil Dante Gabriel Rossetti. His pictures, which include *The Last of England* (1855; City Art Gallery, Birmingham) and *Work* (1852–65; City Art Gallery, Manchester), are characterized by elaborate symbolism and abundance of realistic detail.

**Brown, John** (1800–1859) US slavery abolitionist. With 18 men, on the night of 16 October 1859, he seized the government arsenal at Harper's Ferry in West Virginia, apparently intending to distribute weapons to runaway slaves who would then defend a mountain stronghold, which Brown hoped would become a republic of former slaves. On 18 October the arsenal was stormed by US Marines under Col Robert E ◊Lee. Brown was tried and hanged at Charlestown on 2 December, becoming a martyr and the hero of the popular song 'John Brown's Body'.

**brown dwarf** in astronomy, an object less massive than a star, but heavier than a planet. Brown dwarfs do not have enough mass to ignite nuclear reactions at their centres, but shine by heat released during their contraction from a gas cloud. Some astronomers believe that vast numbers of brown dwarfs exist throughout the Galaxy.

**Browne, Thomas** (1605–1682) English writer and physician. His works display a richness of style and an enquiring mind. They include *Religio medici/The Religion of a Doctor* (1643), a justification of his profession; 'Vulgar Errors' (1646), an examination of popular legend and superstition; and *Urn Burial* and *The Garden of Cyrus* both 1658.

**Browning, Elizabeth (Moulton) Barrett** (1806–1861) English poet. In 1844 she published *Poems* (including 'The Cry of the Children'), which led to her friendship with and secret marriage to Robert ◊Browning in 1846. She wrote *Sonnets from the Portuguese* (1850), a collection of love lyrics, during their courtship. She wrote strong verse about social injustice and oppression in Victorian England, and she was a learned, fiery, and metrically experimental poet.

**Browning, Robert** (1812–1889) English poet. His work is characterized by the accomplished use of dramatic monologue (in which a single imaginary speaker reveals his or her character, thoughts, and situation) and an interest in obscure literary and historical figures. It includes *Pippa Passes* (1841) (written in dramatic form) and the poems 'The Pied Piper of Hamelin' (1842), 'My Last Duchess' (1842), 'Home Thoughts from Abroad' (1845), and 'Rabbi Ben Ezra' (1864). He was married to Elizabeth Barrett ◊Browning.

**Brownshirts** the SA (*Sturmabteilung*) or Storm Troops, the private army of the German Nazi party, who derived their name from the colour of their uniform.

**Bruce** one of the chief Scottish noble houses. ◊Robert (I) the Bruce and his son, David II, were both kings of Scotland descended from Robert de Bruis (died 1094), a Norman knight who arrived in England with William the Conqueror in 1066.

**Bruce, Robert** King of Scotland; see ◊Robert (I) the Bruce.

**Brücke, die** (German 'the bridge') group of German Expressionist artists (see ◊Expressionism) active from 1905 to 1913, originally in Dresden, and later in Berlin. The members chose the name because they wanted to create a bridge to a new, creative future, and their work represented a rebellion against middle-class conventions and an attempt to create art that was in tune with modern life. They formed the first conscious modern movement in German art and were very influential.

**Brueghel** or *Bruegel*, family of Flemish painters. *Pieter Brueghel the Elder* (c. 1525–1569) was one of the greatest artists of his time. His pictures of peasant life helped to establish genre painting, and he also popularized works illustrating proverbs, such as *The Blind Leading the Blind* (1568, Museo di Capodimonte, Naples). A contemporary taste for the macabre can be seen in *The Triumph of Death* (1562, Prado, Madrid), which clearly shows the influence of Hieronymus Bosch. One of his best-known works is *Hunters in the Snow* (1565, Kunsthistorisches Museum, Vienna).

**Bruges** Flemish *Brugge*, historic city in northwest Belgium; capital of West Flanders province, about 96 km/60 mi northwest of Brussels and 16 km/10 mi from the North Sea, to which it is connected by canal; population (1997) 115,500. The port handles coal, iron ore, oil, and fish; local industries include lace, textiles, paint, steel, beer, furniture, motors, and tourism. Bruges was the capital of medieval ◊Flanders and was mainland Europe's major wool producing town as well as its chief market town.

**Brundtland, Gro Harlem** (1939– ) Norwegian Labour politician, head of the World Health Organization (WHO) from 1998. Environment minister 1974–76, she briefly took over as prime minister in 1981, a post to which she was re-elected in 1986, 1990, and again held 1993–96, when she resigned. Leader of the Norwegian Labour Party from 1981, she resigned the post in 1992 but continued as prime

minister. Retaining her seat count in the 1993 general election, she led a minority Labour government committed to European Union membership, but failed to secure backing for the membership application in a 1994 national referendum. She was chosen as the new leader of the WHO in 1998.

**Brunei** State of
*national name Negara Brunei Darussalam*

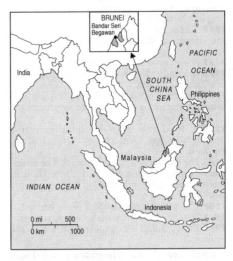

*area* 5,765 sq km/2,225 sq mi
*capital* Bandar Seri Begawan
*major towns/cities* Seria, Kuala Belait, Bangar
*physical features* flat coastal plain with hilly lowland in west and mountains in east (Mount Pagon 1,850 m/6,070 ft); 75% of the area is forested; the Limbang valley splits Brunei in two, and its cession to Sarawak in 1890 is disputed by Brunei; tropical climate; Temburong, Tutong, and Belait rivers
*head of state and government* HM Muda Hassanal Bolkiah Mu'izzaddin Waddaulah, Sultan of Brunei, from 1967
*political system* absolute monarchy
*political parties* Brunei National Democratic Party (BNDP) and Brunei National United Party (BNUP) (both banned since 1988); Brunei People's Party (BPP) (banned since 1962)
*currency* Brunei dollar (ringgit)
*GNP per capita (PPP)* (US$) 25,500 (1998 est)
*exports* crude petroleum, natural gas and refined products. Principal market: Japan 50.9% (1998)
*population* 321,000 (1999 est)
*language* Malay (official), Chinese (Hokkien), English
*religion* Muslim 66%, Buddhist 14%, Christian 10%
*life expectancy* 73 (men); 78 (women) (1995–2000)
*Chronology*
*15th century* Islamic monarchy established, ruling Brunei and north Borneo, including Sabah and Sarawak states of Malaysia.
*1841* Lost control of Sarawak.

**1888** Brunei became a British protectorate.
**1906** Became a dependency when British resident was appointed adviser to the sultan.
**1929** Oil was discovered.
**1941–45** Occupied by Japan.
**1950** Sir Omar became the 28th sultan.
**1959** Written constitution made Britain responsible for defence and external affairs.
**1962** Sultan began rule by decree after plan to join Federation of Malaysia was opposed by a week-long rebellion organized by the Brunei People's Party (BPP).
**1967** Sultan Omar abdicated in favour of his son Hassanal Bolkiah, but remained chief adviser.
**1971** Brunei given full internal self-government.
**1975** United Nations resolution called for independence for Brunei.
**1984** Independence achieved from Britain, with Britain maintaining a small force to protect the oil and gas fields.
**1985** A 'loyal and reliable' political party, the Brunei National Democratic Party (BNDP), legalized.
**1986** The former sultan, Omar, died. The multiethnic Brunei National United Party (BNUP) was formed; nonroyals were given key cabinet posts for the first time.
**1988** The BNDP and the BNUP were banned.
**1991** Brunei joined the nonaligned movement.
**1998** Prince Billah was proclaimed heir to the throne.

**Brunel, Isambard Kingdom** (1806–1859) English engineer and inventor. In 1833 he became engineer to the Great Western Railway, which adopted the 2.1-m/7-ft gauge on his advice. He built the Clifton Suspension Bridge over the River Avon at Bristol and the Saltash Bridge over the River Tamar near Plymouth. His shipbuilding designs include the *Great Western* (1837), the first steamship to cross the Atlantic regularly; the *Great Britain* (1843), the first large iron ship to have a screw propeller; and the *Great Eastern* (1858), which laid the first transatlantic telegraph cable.

**Brunel, Marc Isambard** (1769–1849) French-born British engineer and inventor, father of Isambard Kingdom Brunel. He constructed the tunnel under the River Thames in London from Wapping to Rotherhithe 1825–43. Knighted 1841.

**Brunelleschi, Filippo** (1377–1446) Italian Renaissance architect. The first and one of the greatest of the Renaissance architects, he pioneered the scientific use of perspective. He was responsible for the construction of the dome of Florence Cathedral (completed 1436), a feat deemed impossible by many of his contemporaries.

**Brunswick** German *Braunschweig,* industrial city in Lower Saxony, Germany, on the River Oker, 56 km/35 mi southeast of Hannover; population (1995) 253,600. Industries include chemical engineering, precision engineering, food processing, and the manufacture of motor vehicles, photographic equipment, and musical instruments. It was one of the chief cities of north Germany in the Middle Ages and an important trading city in the ◊Hanseatic League trade federation. It was capital of the duchy of Brunswick from 1671. The city's rich architectural heritage includes a Romanesque cathedral (1173–1195).

**Brussels** Flemish *Brussel,* French *Bruxelles,* city and capital of Belgium and the province of Brabant, situated almost in the centre of the country in the Senne river valley; city population (1997) 133,800; metropolitan/capital region population (1997) 950,600. Industries include lace, textiles, machinery, and chemicals. It is the headquarters of the European Union (EU) and, since 1967, of the international secretariat of ◊NATO. It contains the Belgian royal seat, the chief courts, the chamber of commerce, and is the centre of the principal banks of the country. Founded on an island in the River Senne *c.* 580, Brussels became a city in 1312, and was declared capital of the Spanish Netherlands in 1530 and of Belgium in 1830.

**Brussels sprout** one of the small edible buds along the stem of a variety of ◊cabbage. (*Brassica oleracea* var. *gemmifera.*) They are high in the glucosinolate compound sinigrin. Sinigrin was found to destroy precancerous cells in laboratory rats in 1996.

**Brussels, Treaty of** pact of economic, political, cultural, and military alliance established in 17 March 1948, for 50 years, by the UK, France, and the Benelux countries, joined by West Germany and Italy in 1955. It was the forerunner of the North Atlantic Treaty Organization and the European Community (now the European Union).

**Brutalism** architectural style of the 1950s and 1960s that evolved from the work of Le Corbusier and Mies van der Rohe. Uncompromising in its approach, it stresses functionalism and honesty to materials; steel and concrete are favoured.

**Bruton, John** (1947–  ) Irish politician, leader of Fine Gael (United Ireland Party) from 1990 and prime minister 1994–97. The collapse of Albert ◊Reynolds's Fianna Fáil–Labour government in November 1994 thrust Bruton, as a leader of a new coalition with Labour, into the prime ministerial vacancy. He pledged himself to the continuation of the Anglo-Irish peace process as pursued by his predecessor; in 1995 he pressed with greater urgency in negotiations for a permanent peace agreement. However, his alleged over-willingness to support the British government's cautious approach to the peace process produced strong criticism in April 1995 from the Sinn Fein leader, Gerry Adams.

**Brutus, Marcus Junius** (*c.* 85–42 BC) Roman senator and general who conspired with ◊Cassius to assassinate Julius ◊Caesar in order to restore the purity of the Republic. He and Cassius were defeated by the united forces of ◊Mark Antony and Octavian at Philippi 42 BC, and Brutus committed suicide.

**Bruxelles** French form of ◊Brussels, the capital of Belgium.

**bryophyte** member of the Bryophyta, a division of the plant kingdom containing three classes: the Hepaticae (◊liverwort), Musci (◊moss), and Anthocerotae (◊hornwort). Bryophytes are generally small, low-growing, terrestrial plants with no vascular (water-conducting) system as in higher plants. Their life cycle shows a marked ◊alternation of generations. Bryophytes chiefly occur in damp habitats and require water for the dispersal of the male gametes (antherozoids).

**bubonic plague** epidemic disease of the Middle Ages; see ◊plague and ◊Black Death.

**Bucharest** Romanian *Bucureşti*, capital and largest city of Romania; population (1993) 2,343,800. The conurbation of Bucharest district has an area of 1,520 sq km/587 sq mi. It was originally a citadel built by Vlad the Impaler (see ◊Dracula) to stop the advance of the Ottoman invasion in the 14th century. Bucharest became the capital of the princes of Wallachia 1698 and of Romania 1861. Savage fighting took place in the city during Romania's 1989 revolution.

**Buchenwald** site of a Nazi ◊concentration camp 1937–45 at a village northeast of Weimar, eastern Germany.

**Buckingham, George Villiers** 1st Duke of Buckingham (1592–1628) English courtier, adviser to James I and later Charles I. After Charles's accession, Buckingham attempted to form a Protestant coalition in Europe, which led to war with France; however, he failed to relieve the Protestants (◊Huguenots) besieged in La Rochelle in 1627. His policy on the French Protestants was attacked in Parliament, and when about to sail for La Rochelle for a second time, he was assassinated in Portsmouth.

**Buckingham, George Villiers** 2nd Duke of Buckingham (1628–1687) English politician, a member of the Cabal under Charles II. A dissolute son of the first duke, he was brought up with the royal children. His play *The Rehearsal* satirized the style of the poet Dryden, who portrayed him as Zimri in *Absalom and Achitophel*. He succeeded to the dukedom in 1628.

**Buckinghamshire** county of southeast central England
*area* 1,565 sq km/604 sq mi
*towns* Aylesbury (administrative headquarters), Beaconsfield, Buckingham, High Wycombe, Olney
*physical* Chiltern Hills; Vale of Aylesbury
*features* Chequers (country seat of the prime minister); Burnham Beeches; the church of the poet Gray's 'Elegy' at Stoke Poges; Cliveden, a country house designed by Charles Barry (now a hotel; it was once the home of Nancy, Lady Astor); Bletchley Park, home of World War II code-breaking activities, now used as a training post for GCHQ (Britain's electronic surveillance centre); homes of the poets William Cowper at Olney and John Milton at Chalfont St Giles; homes of the Tory prime minister Disraeli at Hughenden; grave of William Penn, Quaker founder of Pennsylvania, at Jordans, near Chalfont St Giles; Stowe landscape gardens

*industries* engineering; furniture (chiefly beech); paper; printing; railway workshops; motor cars
*agriculture* about 75 % of the land under cultivation, fertile soil; cereals (barley, wheat, oats); cattle, pigs, poultry, sheep
*population* (1996) 671,700
*famous people* John Hampden, William Herschel, Ben Nicholson, George Gilbert Scott, Edmund Waller.

**buckminsterfullerene** form of carbon, made up of molecules (buckyballs) consisting of 60 carbon atoms arranged in 12 pentagons and 20 hexagons to form a perfect sphere. It was named after the US architect and engineer Richard Buckminster Fuller because of its structural similarity to the geodesic dome that he designed. See ◊fullerene.

**buckthorn** any of several thorny shrubs. The buckthorn (*Rhamnus catharticus*) is native to Britain, but is also found throughout Europe, West Asia, and North Africa. Its berries were formerly used in medicine as a purgative, to clean out the bowels. (Genus *Rhamnus*, family Rhamnaceae.)

**buckwheat** any of a group of cereal plants. The name usually refers to *Fagopyrum esculentum*, which reaches about 1 m/3 ft in height and can grow on poor soil in a short summer. The highly nutritious black triangular seeds (groats) are eaten by both animals and humans. They can be cooked and eaten whole or as a cracked meal (kasha), or ground into flour, often made into pancakes. (Genus *Fagopyrum*, family Polygonaceae.)

**buckyballs** popular name for molecules of ◊buckminsterfullerene.

**bud** undeveloped shoot usually enclosed by protective scales; inside is a very short stem and numerous undeveloped leaves, or flower parts, or both. Terminal buds are found at the tips of shoots, while axillary buds develop in the axils of the leaves, often remaining dormant unless the terminal bud is removed or damaged. Adventitious buds may be produced anywhere on the plant, their formation sometimes stimulated by an injury, such as that caused by pruning.

**Budapest** capital of Hungary, industrial city (chemicals, textiles) on the River Danube; population (1993 est) 2,009,000. Buda, on the right bank of the Danube, became the Hungarian capital 1867 and was joined with Pest, on the left bank, 1872.

**Buddha** (c. 563–483 BC) 'enlightened one', title of Prince *Gautama Siddhārtha*, religious leader, founder of ◊Buddhism, born at Lumbini in Nepal. At the age of 29 he left his wife and son and a life of luxury, to resolve the problems of existence. After six years of austerity he realized that asceticism, like overindulgence, was futile, and chose the middle way of meditation. He became enlightened under a bo, or bodhi, tree near Buddh Gaya in Bihar, India. He began teaching at Varanasi, and founded the Sangha, or order of monks. He spent the rest of his life travelling around northern India, and died at Kusinagara in Uttar Pradesh. He is not a god.

**Buddhism** one of the great world religions, which originated in India in the 5th century BC. It derives from the teaching of the ◊Buddha, who is regarded as one of a series of such enlightened beings. The chief doctrine is that all phenomena share three characteristics: they are impermanent, unsatisfactory, and lack a permanent essence (such as a soul). All beings, including gods, are subject to these characteristics, but can achieve freedom through enlightenment. The main forms of Buddhism are *Theravāda* (or Hīnayāna) in Southeast Asia and *Mahāyāna* in North and East Asia; *Lamaism* in Tibet and *Zen* in Japan are among the many Mahāyāna forms of Buddhism. There are over 300 million Buddhists worldwide (1994).

**buddleia** any of a group of ornamental shrubs or trees with spikes of fragrant flowers. The purple or white flower heads of the butterfly bush (*Buddleia davidii*) attract large numbers of butterflies. (Genus *Buddleia*, family Buddleiaceae.)

**budgerigar** small Australian parakeet *Melopsittacus undulatus* of the parrot family, Psittacidae, order Psittaciformes, that feeds mainly on grass seeds. In the wild, it has a bright green body and a blue tail with yellow flares; yellow, white, blue, and mauve varieties have been bred for the pet market. Budgerigars breed freely in captivity.

**Buenos Aires** industrial city, chief port, and capital of Argentina, situated in the 'Capital Federal' – a separate federal district, on the south bank of the Río de la Plata, at its estuary; population (1992 est) 11,662,050. Industries include motor vehicles, engineering, oil, chemicals, textiles, paper, and food processing. Main exports are grain, beef, and wool, which are produced in the surrounding pampas. The administrative Federal District of Buenos Aires has an area of 200 sq km/77 sq mi, with a population of (1991) 2,960,976. Buenos Aires is the financial and cultural centre of Argentina, and has many museums and libraries. It is a major railway terminus, and has an international airport 35 km/22 mi southwest of the city centre

**buffalo** either of two species of wild cattle. The Asiatic water buffalo *Bubalis bubalis* is found domesticated throughout South Asia and wild in parts of India and Nepal. It likes moist conditions. Usually grey or black, up to 1.8 m/ 6 ft high, both sexes carry large horns. The African buffalo *Syncerus caffer* is found in Africa, south of the Sahara, where there is grass, water, and cover in which to retreat. There are a number of subspecies, the biggest up to 1.6 m/ 5 ft high, and black, with massive horns set close together over the head. The name is also commonly applied to the American ◊bison.

**bug** in computing, an ◊error in a program. It can be an error in the logical structure of a program or a syntax error, such as a spelling mistake. Some bugs cause a program to fail immediately; others remain dormant, causing problems only when a particular combination of events occurs. The process of finding and removing errors from a program is called *debugging*.

**bug** in entomology, an insect belonging to the order Hemiptera. All these have two pairs of wings with forewings partly thickened.

They also have piercing mouthparts adapted for sucking the juices of plants or animals, the 'beak' being tucked under the body when not in use.

**Bugatti** racing and sports-car company, founded by the Italian Ettore Bugatti (1881– 1947). The first car was produced 1908, but it was not until 1924 that one of the great Bugattis, the Type 35, was produced. Bugatti cars are credited with more race wins than any others. The company was taken over by Hispano Suiza after Bugatti's death.

**bugle** compact valveless treble brass instrument with a shorter tube and less flared bell than the trumpet. Constructed of copper plated with brass, it has long been used as a military instrument for giving a range of signals based on the tones of a harmonic series. The bugle has a conical bore whereas the trumpet is cylindrical.

**Bujumbura** formerly (until 1962) *Usumbura,* capital of Burundi, located at the northeastern end of Lake Tanganyika; population (1996 est) 300,000. Bujumbura is the main banking and financial centre of Burundi; industries include food processing and paint manufacture. It was founded in 1899 by German colonists, and a university was established in 1960.

**Bukhara** or *Bokhara* or *Bukhoro,* city in south-central Uzbekistan, on the Zerevshan River 220 km/137 mi east of Samarkand; population (1995) 250,000. A historic city with over 140 protected buildings, it was once the heart of Muslim Central Asia, and second only to Mecca as an Islamic holy site. It is the capital of the Bukhara region of Turkestan, which has given its name to a type of handwoven carpet. Textiles, including rugs and carpets, are manufactured here (though 'Bukhara' carpets are now principally made in ◊Ashgabat, in Turkmenistan). Natural gas is extracted in the surrounding region, and cotton is grown extensively.

**Bukharin, Nikolai Ivanovich** (1888–1938) Soviet politician and theorist. A moderate, he was the chief Bolshevik thinker after Lenin. Executed on Stalin's orders for treason in 1938, he was posthumously rehabilitated in 1988.

**Bulawayo** (Ndebele 'place of slaughter') industrial city and railway junction in Zimbabwe; population (1992) 620,900. The city lies at an altitude of 1,355 m/4,450 ft on the River Matsheumlope, a tributary of the Zambezi, and was founded on the site of the kraal (enclosed village), burned down in 1893, of the Matabele chief Lobengula. It produces cement and agricultural and electrical equipment. The former capital of Matabeleland, Bulawayo developed with the exploitation of gold mines in the neighbourhood. It is the second-largest city in Zimbabwe.

**bulb** underground bud with fleshy leaves containing a reserve food supply and with roots growing from its base. Bulbs function in vegetative reproduction and are characteristic of many monocotyledonous plants such as the daffodil, snowdrop, and onion. Bulbs are grown on a commercial scale in temperate countries, such as England and the Netherlands.

**bulbul** fruit-eating bird of the family Pycnonotidae, order Passeriformes, that ranges in size from that of a sparrow to a blackbird. They are mostly rather dull coloured and very secretive, living in dense forests. They are widely distributed throughout Africa and Asia; there are about 120 species.

**Bulganin, Nikolai Aleksandrovich** (1895–1975) Soviet politician and military leader. His career began in 1918 when he joined the Cheka, the Soviet secret police. He helped to organize Moscow's defences in World War II, became a marshal of the USSR in 1947, and was minister of defence 1947–49 and 1953–55. On the fall of Georgi Malenkov he became prime minister (chair of the council of ministers) 1955–58 until ousted by Nikita Khrushchev.

**Bulgaria** Republic of
*national name* *Republika Bulgaria*

*area* 110,912 sq km/42,823 sq mi
*capital* Sofia
*major towns/cities* Plovdiv, Varna, Ruse, Burgas, Stara Zagora
*major ports* Black Sea ports Burgas and Varna
*physical features* lowland plains in north and southeast separated by mountains (Balkan and Rhodope) that cover three-quarters of the country; River Danube in north
*head of state* Petar Stoyanov from 1997
*head of government* Ivan Kostov from 1997
*political system* emergent democracy
*political parties* Union of Democratic Forces (UDF), right of centre; Bulgarian Socialist Party (BSP), left wing, ex-communist; Movement for Rights and Freedoms (MRF), Turkish-oriented, centrist; Civic Alliances for the Republic (CAR), left of centre; Real Reform Movement (DESIR)
*currency* lev

*GNP per capita (PPP)* (US$) 3,920 (1998 est)
*exports* base metals, chemical and rubber products, processed food, beverages, tobacco, chemicals, textiles, footwear. Principal market: Italy 12.7% (1998)
*population* 8,280,000 (1999 est)
*language* Bulgarian, Turkish
*religion* Eastern Orthodox Christian, Muslim, Roman Catholic, Protestant
*life expectancy* 68 (men); 75 (women) (1995–2000)
*Chronology*
*c. 3500 BC onwards* Settlement of semi-nomadic pastoralists from central Asian steppes, who formed the Thracian community.
*mid-5th century BC* Thracian state formed, which was to extend over Bulgaria, northern Greece, and northern Turkey.
*4th century BC* Phillip II and Alexander the Great of Macedonia, to the southwest, waged largely unsuccessful campaigns against the Thracian Empire.
*AD 50* Thracians subdued and incorporated within Roman Empire as province of Moesia Inferior.
*3rd–6th centuries* Successively invaded from north and devastated by the Goths, Huns, Bulgars, and Avars.
*681* The Bulgars, an originally Turkic group that had merged with earlier Slav settlers, revolted against the Avars and established, south of River Danube, the first Bulgarian kingdom, with its capital at Pliska, in the Balkans.
*864* Orthodox Christianity adopted by Boris I.
*1018* Subjugated by the Byzantines, whose empire had its capital at Constantinople; led to Bulgarian Church breaking with Rome in 1054.
*1185* Second independent Bulgarian Kingdom formed.
*mid-13th century* Bulgarian state destroyed by Mongol incursions.
*1396* Bulgaria became first European state to be absorbed into Turkish Ottoman Empire; the imposition of harsh feudal system and sacking of monasteries followed.
*1859* Bulgarian Catholic Church re-established links with Rome.
*1876* Bulgarian nationalist revolt against Ottoman rule crushed brutally by Ottomans, with 15,000 massacred at Plovdiv ('Bulgarian Atrocities').
*1878* At the Congress of Berlin, concluding a Russo-Turkish war in which Bulgarian volunteers had fought alongside the Russians, the area south of the Balkans, Eastern Rumelia, remained an Ottoman province, but the area to the north became the autonomous Principality of Bulgaria, with a liberal constitution and Alexander Battenberg as prince.
*1885* Eastern Rumelia annexed by the Principality; Serbia defeated in war.
*1908* Full independence proclaimed from Turkish rule, with Ferdinand I as tsar.
*1913* Following defeat in the Second Balkan War, King Ferdinand I abdicated and was replaced by his son Boris III.
*1919* Bulgarian Agrarian Union government, led by Alexander Stamboliiski, came to power and redistributed land to poor peasants.

**1923** Agrarian government overthrown in right-wing coup and Stamboliiski murdered.

**1934** Semifascist dictatorship established by King Boris III, who sided with Germany during World War II, but died mysteriously in 1943 after a visit to Adolf Hitler.

**1944** Soviet invasion of German-occupied Bulgaria.

**1946** Monarchy abolished and communist-dominated people's republic proclaimed following plebiscite.

**1947** Gained South Dobruja in the northeast, along the Black Sea, from Romania; Soviet-style constitution established a one-party state; industries and financial institutions nationalized and cooperative farming introduced.

**1949** Death of Georgi Dimitrov, the communist government leader; replaced by Vulko Chervenkov.

**1954** Election of Todor Zhivkov as Bulgarian Communist Party (BCP) general secretary; Bulgaria became a loyal and cautious satellite of the USSR.

**1968** Participated in the Soviet-led invasion of Czechoslovakia.

**1971** Zhivkov became president, under new constitution.

**1985–89** Haphazard administrative and economic reforms, known as *preustroistvo* ('restructuring'), introduced under stimulus of reformist Soviet leader Mikhail Gorbachev.

**1989** A programme of enforced 'Bulgarianization' resulted in a mass exodus of ethnic Turks to Turkey. Zhivkov was ousted by the foreign minister Petar Mladenov. Opposition parties were tolerated.

**1990** The BCP reformed under the new name the Bulgarian Socialist Party (BSP). Zhelyu Zhelev of the centre-right Union of Democratic Forces (UDF) was indirectly elected president. Following mass demonstrations and general strike, the BSP government was replaced by a coalition.

**1991** A new liberal-democratic constitution was adopted. The UDF beat the BSP in a general election; the first noncommunist, UDF-minority government was formed.

**1992** Zhelev became Bulgaria's first directly elected president. Following industrial unrest, Lyuben Berov became head of a nonparty government. Zhivkov was sentenced to seven years' imprisonment for corruption while in government.

**1993** A voucher-based 'mass privatization' programme was launched.

**1994** Berov resigned; a general election was won by the BSP.

**1995** Zhan Videnov (BSP) became prime minister.

**1996** Radical economic and industrial reforms were imposed. Petar Stoyanov replaced Zhelev as president. There was mounting inflation and public protest at the state of the economy.

**1997** A general strike was held. An interim government was led by Stefan Sofiyanski. The UDF leader Ivan Kostov became prime minister. The former communist leader Zhivkov was released from house arrest. The Bulgarian currency was pegged to the Deutschmark in return for support from the International Monetary Fund. A new political group, the Real Reform Movement (DESIR), was formed.

**1999** Bulgaria joined the Central European Free Trade Agreement (CEFTA).

**Bulgarian** an ethnic group living mainly in Bulgaria. There are 8–8.5 million speakers of Bulgarian, a Slavic language belonging to the Indo-European family. The Bulgarians use the Cyrillic alphabet.

**Bulge, Battle of the** or *Ardennes offensive*, in World War II, Hitler's plan (code-named 'Watch on the Rhine') for a breakthrough by his field marshal Gerd von ◊Rundstedt, aimed at the US line in the Ardennes 16 December 1944–28 January 1945. Hitler aimed to isolate the Allied forces north of the corridor which would be created by a drive through the Ardennes, creating a German salient (prominent part of a line of attack, also known as a 'bulge'). There were 77,000 Allied casualties and 130,000 German, including Hitler's last powerful reserve of elite Panzer units. Although US troops were encircled for some weeks at Bastogne, the German counteroffensive failed.

**bulimia** (Greek 'ox hunger') eating disorder in which large amounts of food are consumed in a short time ('binge'), usually followed by depression and self-criticism. The term is often used for *bulimia nervosa*, an emotional disorder in which eating is followed by deliberate vomiting and purging. This may be a chronic stage in ◊anorexia nervosa.

**bull** speculator who buys stocks or shares on the stock exchange expecting a rise in the price in order to sell them later at a profit, the opposite of a ◊bear. In a bull market, prices rise and bulls profit.

**Bull, John** imaginary figure personifying England; see ◊John Bull.

**bulldog** British breed of dog of ancient but uncertain origin, formerly bred for bull-baiting. The head is broad and square, with deeply wrinkled cheeks, small folded ears, very short muzzle, and massive jaws, the peculiar set of the lower jaw making it difficult for the dog to release its grip. Thickset in build, the bulldog grows to about 45 cm/18 in and has a smooth beige, tawny, or brindle coat. The French bulldog is much lighter in build and has large upright ears.

**bullfighting** the national sport of Spain (where there are more than 400 bullrings), which is also popular in Mexico, Portugal, and much of Latin America. It involves the ritualized taunting of a bull in a circular ring, until its eventual death at the hands of the matador. Originally popular in Greece and Rome, it was introduced into Spain by the Moors in the 11th century.

**bullfinch** Eurasian finch with a thick head and neck, and short heavy bill, genus *Pyrrhula pyrrhula*, family Fringillidae, order Passeriformes. It is small and blue-grey or black in colour, the males being reddish and the females brown on the breast. Bullfinches are 15 cm/6 in long, and usually seen in pairs. They feed on tree buds as well as seeds and berries, and are usually seen in woodland. They also live in the Aleutians and on the Alaska mainland.

**bulrush** either of two plants: the great reed mace or cat's tail (*Typha latifolia*) with velvety chocolate-brown spikes of tightly packed flowers reaching up to 15 cm/6 in long; and a type of sedge (*Scirpus lacustris*) with tufts of reddish-brown flowers at the top of a rounded, rushlike stem.

**Bunker Hill, Battle of** the first significant engagement in the ◊American Revolution, 17 June 1775, near a small hill in Charlestown (now part of Boston), Massachusetts; the battle actually took place on Breed's Hill, but is named after Bunker Hill as this was the more significant of the two. Although the colonists were defeated, they were able to retreat to Boston in good order.

**Bunsen burner** gas burner used in laboratories, consisting of a vertical metal tube through which a fine jet of fuel gas is directed. Air is drawn in through airholes near the base of the tube and the mixture is ignited and burns at the tube's upper opening.

**bunting** any of a number of sturdy, finchlike birds with short, thick bills, of the family Emberizidae, order Passeriformes, especially the genera *Passerim* and *Emberiza*. Most of these brightly coloured birds are native to the New World.

**Buñuel, Luis** (1900–1983) Spanish-born film director. He is widely considered one of the giants of European art cinema, responsible for such enduring classics as *Los Olvidados/The Young and the Damned* (1950), *Viridiana* (1961), *Belle de Jour* (1966), and *Le Charme discret de la bourgeoisie/The Discreet Charm of the Bourgeoisie* (1972).

**Bunyan, John** (1628–1688) English writer, author of *The Pilgrim's Progress* (first part 1678, second part 1684), one of the best-known religious allegories in English. A Baptist, he was imprisoned in Bedford 1660–72 for unlicensed preaching and wrote *Grace Abounding* in 1666, which describes his early spiritual life. He started to write *The Pilgrim's Progress* during a second jail sentence in 1676–77. Written in straightforward language with fervour and imagination, it achieved immediate popularity and was highly influential.

**bur** or *burr*, in botany, a type of 'false fruit' or ◊pseudocarp, surrounded by numerous hooks; for instance, that of burdock *Arctium*, where the hooks are formed from bracts surrounding the flowerhead. Burs catch in the feathers or fur of passing animals, and thus may be dispersed over considerable distances.

**burdock** any of several bushy herbs characterized by hairy leaves and ripe fruit enclosed in ◊burs with strong hooks. (Genus *Arctium*, family Compositae.)

**bureaucracy** organization whose structure and operations are governed to a high degree by written rules and a hierarchy of offices; in its broadest sense, all forms of administration, and in its narrowest, rule by officials.

**Burgenland** federal state of southeast Austria, extending south from the Danube along the western border of the Hungarian plain; area 4,000 sq km/1,544 sq mi; population (1994) 273,600. It is a largely agricultural region adjoining the Neusiedler See, and produces timber, fruit, sugar, wine, lignite, antimony, and limestone. Its capital is Eisenstadt. In the north it is generally flat, but in the south are spurs of the Alps, with the valleys of the River Raab and its tributaries.

**Burgess, Anthony** pen-name of *John Anthony Burgess Wilson* (1917–1993) English novelist, critic, and composer. A prolific and versatile writer, Burgess wrote about 60 books as well as screenplays, television scripts, and reviews. His work includes *A Clockwork Orange* (1962) (made into a film by Stanley Kubrick in 1971), a despairing depiction of high technology and violence set in a future London terrorized by teenage gangs, and the panoramic *Earthly Powers* (1980).

**burgh** burh or borough, archaic form of ◊borough.

**burgh** former unit of Scottish local government, referring to a town enjoying a degree of self-government. Burghs were abolished in 1975; the terms *burgh* and *royal burgh* once gave mercantile privilege but are now only an honorary distinction.

**Burghley, William Cecil** 1st Baron Burghley (1520–1598) English politician, chief adviser to Elizabeth I as secretary of state from 1558 and Lord High Treasurer from 1572. He was largely responsible for the religious settlement of 1559, and took a leading role in the events preceding the execution of Mary Queen of Scots in 1587.

**burglary** offence committed when a trespasser enters a building intending to steal, do damage to property, grievously harm any person, or rape a woman. Entry needs only be effective so, for example, a person who puts their hand through a broken shop window to steal something may be guilty of burglary.

**Burgundy** ancient kingdom in the valleys of the rivers Rhône and Saône in eastern France and southwestern Germany, partly corresponding with modern-day Burgundy. Settled by the Teutonic Burgundi around AD 443, and brought under Frankish control 534, Burgundy played a central role in the medieval history of northwestern Europe.

**Burgundy** French *Bourgogne*, modern region and former duchy of east-central France that includes the *départements* of Ain, Côte-d'Or, Nièvre, Saône-et-Loire, and Yonne; area 31,600 sq km/12,198 sq mi; population (1990) 1,609,700. Its administrative centre is Dijon.

**Burke, Edmund** (1729–1797) British Whig politician and political theorist, born in Dublin, Ireland. During a parliamentary career spanning more than 30 years, he was famous for opposing the government's attempts to coerce the American colonists, for example in *Thoughts on the Present Discontents* (1770), and for supporting the emancipation of Ireland. However, he was a vehement opponent of the French Revolution, which he denounced in *Reflections on the Revolution in France* (1790), and attacked the suggestion of peace with France in *Letters on a Regicide Peace* (1795–97).

**Burkina Faso** The People's Democratic Republic of (formerly *Upper Volta*)
*national name* *République Démocratique Populaire de Burkina Faso*

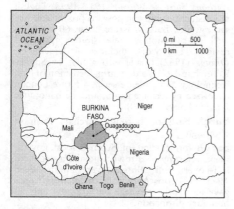

**area** 274,122 sq km/105,838 sq mi
**capital** Ouagadougou
**major towns/cities** Bobo-Dioulasso, Koudougou
**physical features** landlocked plateau with hills in west and southeast; headwaters of the River Volta; semiarid in north, forest and farmland in south; linked by rail to Abidjan in Côte d'Ivoire, Burkina Faso's only outlet to the sea
**head of state** Blaise Compaoré from 1987
**head of government** Kadre Desire Ouedraogo from 1996
**political system** emergent democracy
**political parties** Popular Front (FP), centre-left coalition grouping; National Convention of Progressive Patriots–Democratic Socialist Party (CNPP–PSD), left of centre
**currency** franc CFA
**GNP per capita (PPP)** (US$) 1,020 (1998 est)
**exports** cotton, gold, livestock and livestock products. Principal market: Côte d'Ivoire 12.7% (1997)
**population** 11,616,000 (1999 est)
**language** French (official); about 50 Sudanic languages spoken by 90% of population
**religion** animist 53%, Sunni Muslim 36%, Roman Catholic 11%
**life expectancy** 44 (men); 45 (women) (1995–2000)
**Chronology**
**13th–14th centuries** Formerly settled by Bobo, Lobi, and Gurunsi peoples, east and centre were conquered by Mossi and Gurma peoples, who established powerful warrior kingdoms, some of which survived until late 19th century.
**1895–1903** France secured protectorates over the Mossi kingdom of Yatenga and the Gurma region, and annexed the Bobo and Lobi lands, meeting armed resistance.
**1904** The French-controlled region, known as Upper Volta, was attached administratively to French Sudan; tribal chiefs were maintained in their traditional seats and the region was to serve as a labour reservoir for more developed colonies to south.
**1919** Made a separate French colony.
**1932** Partitioned between French Sudan, the Côte d'Ivoire, and Niger.
**1947** Became a French overseas territory.
**1960** Independence achieved, with Maurice Yaméogo as the first president.
**1966** Military coup led by Lt-Col Sangoulé Lamizana, and a supreme council of the armed forces established.
**1977** Ban on political activities removed. Referendum approved a new constitution based on civilian rule.
**1978** Lamizana elected president.
**1980** Lamizana overthrown in bloodless coup led by Col Saye Zerbo as economy deteriorated.
**1982** Zerbo ousted in a coup by junior officers: Maj Jean-Baptiste Ouedraogo became president and Capt Thomas Sankara prime minister.
**1983** Sankara seized complete power.
**1984** Upper Volta was renamed Burkina Faso ('land of upright men') to signify a break with the colonial past; literacy and afforestation campaigns were instigated by the radical Sankara, who established links with Libya, Benin, and Ghana.
**1987** Sankara was killed in a coup led by Capt Blaise Compaoré.
**1991** A new constitution was approved. Compaoré was re-elected president.
**1992** Multiparty elections were won by the pro-Compaoré Popular Front (FP), despite opposition claims of ballot-rigging.
**1996** Kadre Desire Ouedraogo was appointed prime minister.
**1997** The CDP won assembly elections. Ouedraogo was reappointed prime minister.
**1998** President Blaise Compaoré was re-elected with an overwhelming majority.

**Burlington, Richard Boyle** 3rd Earl of Burlington (1695–1753) Anglo-Irish architectural patron and architect. He was one of the premier exponents of the Palladian style in Britain. His buildings are characterized by absolute adherence to the Classical rules. William ◊Kent was his major protégé.

**Burman** the largest ethnic group in Myanmar (formerly Burma). The Burmans, speakers of a Sino-Tibetan language, migrated from the hills of Tibet, settling in the areas around Mandalay by the 11th century AD.

**burn** in medicine, destruction of body tissue by extremes of temperature, corrosive chemicals, electricity, or radiation. *First-degree burns* may cause reddening; *second-degree burns* cause blistering and irritation but usually heal sponta-neously; *third-degree burns* are disfiguring and may be life-threatening.

**Burne-Jones, Edward Coley** (1833–1898) English painter. In 1856 he was apprenticed to the Pre-Raphaelite painter and poet Dante Gabriel ◊Rossetti, who remained a dominant influence. His paintings, inspired by legend and myth, were characterized by elongated forms and subdued tones, as in *King Cophetua and the Beggar Maid* (1880–84; Tate Gallery, London). He also collaborated with William ◊Morris in designing stained-glass windows, tapestries, and book decorations for the Kelmscott Press. His work influenced both ◊Symbolism and ◊Art Nouveau. He was created a baronet in 1894.

**Burney, Fanny (Frances)** (1752–1840) English novelist and diarist. She achieved success with *Evelina*, an epistolary novel published in 1778, became a member of Samuel ◊Johnson's circle, and received a post at court from Queen Charlotte. She published three further novels, *Cecilia* (1782), *Camilla* (1796), and *The Wanderer* (1814).

**Burnham, (Linden) Forbes (Sampson)** (1923–1985) Guyanese Marxist-Leninist politician. He was prime minister 1964–80 in a coalition government, leading the country to independence in 1966 and declaring it the world's first cooperative republic in 1970. He was executive president 1980–85. Resistance to the US landing in Grenada 1983 was said to be due to his forewarning the Grenadans of the attack.

**Burns, Robert** (1759–1796) Scottish poet. He used a form of Scots dialect at a time when it was not considered suitably 'elevated' for literature. Burns's first volume, *Poems, Chiefly in the Scottish Dialect*, appeared in 1786. In addition to his poetry (such as 'To a Mouse'), Burns wrote or adapted many songs, including 'Auld Lang Syne'. *Burns Night* is celebrated on 25 January, his birthday.

**Burroughs, Edgar Rice** (1875–1950) US novelist. He wrote *Tarzan of the Apes* 1914, the story of an aristocratic child lost in the jungle and reared by apes, and followed it with over 20 more books about the Tarzan character. He also wrote a series of novels about life on Mars, including *A Princess of Mars* 1917 and *Synthetic Men of Mars* 1940.

**Burroughs, William S(eward)** (1914–1997) US author. One of the most culturally influential post-war writers, his work is noted for its experimental methods, black humour, explicit homo-eroticism, and apocalyptic vision. In 1944 he met Allen Ginsberg and Jack Kerouac, all three becoming leading members of the ◊Beat Generation. His first novel, *Junkie* (1953), documented his heroin addiction and expatriation to Mexico, where in 1951 he accidentally killed his common-law wife. He settled in Tangier in 1954 and wrote his celebrated anti-novel *Naked Lunch* (1959). A landmark federal court case deemed *Naked Lunch* not obscene; this broke the ground for other books, helping to eliminate censorship of the printed word in the USA.

**Bursa** city in northwestern Turkey, with a port at Mudania; population (1990) 834,600. It was the capital of the Ottoman Empire 1326–1423.

**Burton, Richard** stage name of *Richard Walter Jenkins* (1925–1984) Welsh stage and screen actor. He had a rich, dramatic voice but his career was dogged by personal problems and an often poor choice of roles. Films in which he appeared with his wife Elizabeth Taylor include *Cleopatra* (1963) and *Who's Afraid of Virginia Woolf?* (1966). Among his later films are *Equus* (1977) and *Nineteen Eighty-Four* (1984).

**Burton, Richard Francis** (1821–1890) English explorer and translator (he knew 35 oriental languages). He travelled mainly in the Middle East and northeast Africa, often disguised as a Muslim. He made two attempts to find the source of the White Nile, in 1855 and 1857–58 (on the second, with John Speke, he reached Lake Tanganyika), and wrote many travel books. He translated oriental erotica and the *Arabian Nights* (1885–88).

**Burundi** Republic of
*national name Republika y'Uburundi*

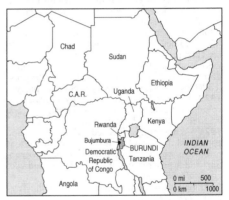

**area** 27,834 sq km/10,746 sq mi
**capital** Bujumbura
**major towns/cities** Kitega, Bururi, Ngozi, Muhinga, Muramuya
**physical features** landlocked grassy highland straddling watershed of Nile and Congo; Lake Tanganyika, Great Rift Valley
**head of state** Pierre Buyoya from 1996
**head of government** Pascal-Firmin Ndimira from 1996
**political system** authoritarian nationalist
**political parties** Front for Democracy in Burundi (FRODEBU), left of centre; Union for National Progress (UPRONA), nationalist socialist
**currency** Burundi franc
**GNP per capita (PPP)** (US$) 620 (1998 est)
**exports** coffee, tea, glass products, hides and skins. Principal market: UK 29.1% (1997)
**population** 6,565,000 (1999 est)
**language** Kirundi (a Bantu language) and French (both official), Kiswahili
**religion** Roman Catholic 62%, Pentecostalist 5%, Anglican 1%, Muslim 1%, animist

*life expectancy* 41 (men); 44 (women) (1995–2000)

*Chronology*

**10th century** Originally inhabited by the hunter-gatherer Twa Pygmies. Hutu peoples settled in the region and became peasant farmers.

**13th century** Taken over by Banu Hutus.

**15th–17th centuries** The majority Hutu community came under the dominance of the cattle-owning Tutsi peoples, immigrants from the east, who became a semi-aristocracy; the minority Tutsis developed a feudalistic political system, organized around a nominal king, with royal princes in control of local areas.

**1890** Known as Urundi, the Tutsi kingdom, along with neighbouring Rwanda, came under nominal German control as Ruanda-Urundi.

**1916** Occupied by Belgium during World War I.

**1923** Belgium was granted a League of Nations mandate to administer Ruanda-Urundi; it was to rule 'indirectly' through the Tutsi chiefs.

**1962** Separated from Ruanda-Urundi, as Burundi, and given independence as a monarchy under Tutsi King Mwambutsa IV.

**1965** King refused to appoint a Hutu prime minister after an election in which Hutu candidates were victorious; attempted coup by Hutu brutally suppressed.

**1966** King deposed by his teenage son Charles, who became Ntare V; he was in turn deposed by his Tutsi prime minister Col Michel Micombero, who declared Burundi a republic; the Tutsi-dominated Union for National Progress (UPRONA) declared only legal political party.

**1972** Ntare V killed, allegedly by Hutus, provoking a massacre of 150,000 Hutus by Tutsi soldiers; 100,000 Hutus fled to Tanzania.

**1976** Army coup deposed Micombero and appointed the Tutsi Col Jean-Baptiste Bagaza as president, who launched a drive against corruption and a programme of land reforms and economic development.

**1987** Bagaza was deposed in a coup by the Tutsi Maj Pierre Buyoya.

**1988** About 24,000 Hutus were killed by Tutsis and 60,000 fled as refugees to Rwanda.

**1992** A new multiparty constitution was adopted following a referendum.

**1993** Melchior Ndadaye, a Hutu, was elected president in the first-ever democratic contest, but was killed in a coup by the Tutsi-dominated army; 100,000 people died in the massacres that followed.

**1994** Cyprien Ntaryamira, a Hutu, became president but was later killed in an air crash along with the Rwandan president Juvenal Habyarimana. There was an eruption of ethnic violence; 750,000 Hutus fled to Rwanda. Hutu Sylvestre Ntibantunganya became head of state, serving with a Tutsi prime minister, as part of a four-year power-sharing agreement between the main political parties.

**1995** Renewed ethnic violence erupted in the capital, Bujumbura, following a massacre of Hutu refugees.

**1996** The former Tutsi president Pierre Buyoya seized power amid renewed ethnic violence; the coup provoked economic sanctions by other African countries. A 'government of national unity' was appointed, with Pascal-Firmin Ndimira as premier. Bujumbura was shelled by Hutu rebels.

**1998** There was renewed fighting between Tutsi-led army and Hutu rebels. A ceasefire was agreed between the warring political factions.

**1999** Seven African countries lifted economic sanctions to encourage peace negotiations but violence continued.

**Bush, George Herbert Walker** (1924– ) 41st president of the USA 1989–93, a Republican. He was director of the Central Intelligence Agency (CIA) 1976–81 and US vice-president 1981–89. As president, his response to the Soviet leader Mikhail Gorbachev's diplomatic initiatives were initially criticized as inadequate, but his sending of US troops to depose his former ally, General Manuel ◊Noriega of Panama, proved a popular move at home. Success in the 1991 Gulf War against Iraq further raised his standing. Domestic economic problems 1991–92 were followed by his defeat in the 1992 presidential elections by the Democrat Bill Clinton.

**bushbaby** small nocturnal African prosimian with long feet, long, bushy tail, and large ears. Bushbabies are active tree dwellers and feed on fruit, insects, eggs, and small birds.

**bushbuck** antelope *Tragelaphus scriptus* found over most of Africa south of the Sahara. Up to 1 m/3 ft high, the males have keeled horns twisted into spirals, and are brown to blackish. The females are generally hornless, lighter, and redder. All have white markings, including stripes or vertical rows of dots down the sides. Rarely far from water, bushbuck live in woods and thick brush.

**bushman's rabbit** or *riverine rabbit,* a wild rodent *Bunolagus monticularis* found in dense riverine bush in South Africa. It lives in small populations, and individuals are only seen very occasionally; it is now at extreme risk of extinction owing to loss of habitat to agriculture. Very little is known about its life or habits.

**bushmaster** large snake *Lachesis muta.* It is a type of pit viper, and is related to the rattlesnakes. Up to 4 m/12 ft long, it is found in wooded areas of South and Central America, and is the largest venomous snake in the New World. When alarmed, it produces a noise by vibrating its tail among dry leaves.

**bustard** bird of the family Otididae, order Gruiformes, related to ◊cranes but with a rounder body, thicker neck, and a relatively short beak. Bustards are found on the ground on open plains and fields.

**butane** $C_4H_{10}$ one of two gaseous alkanes (paraffin hydrocarbons) having the same formula but differing in structure. Normal butane is derived from natural gas; isobutane is a by-product of petroleum manufacture. Liquefied under pressure, it is used as a fuel for industrial and domestic purposes (for example, in portable cookers).

**Buthelezi, Chief Mangosuthu Gatsha** (1928– ) South African Zulu leader and politician, president of the Zulu-based ◊Inkatha Freedom Party (IFP), which he founded as a paramilitary organization for attaining a non-racial democratic society in 1975. Buthelezi's threatened boycott of South Africa's first multi-racial elections led to a dramatic escalation in politically motivated violence, but he eventually agreed to register his party and in May 1994 was appointed home affairs minister in the country's first post-apartheid government. In December 1995 there were unsubstantiated claims that he had colluded with the security service during the apartheid period. In June 1999 Buthelezi was offered the post of deputy president of South Africa by the new president Thabo Mbeki. Buthelezi refused the post.

**Butler, Samuel** (1835–1902) English writer. He made his name in 1872 with a satiric attack on contemporary utopianism, *Erewhon* (an ana-gram of *nowhere*). He is now remembered for his unfinished, semi-autobiographical discursive novel, *The Way of All Flesh*, a study of Victorian conventions, the causes and effects of the clash between generations, and religious hypocrisy (written and frequently revised 1873–84 and posthumously published in 1903).

**buttercup** any plant of the buttercup family with divided leaves and yellow flowers. (Genus *Ranunculus*, family Ranunculaceae.)

**butterfly** insect belonging, like moths, to the order Lepidoptera, in which the wings are cov-ered with tiny scales, often brightly coloured. There are some 15,000 species of butterfly, many of which are under threat throughout the world because of the destruction of habitat.

**butterfly fish** any of several fishes, not all related. They include the freshwater butterfly fish *Pantodon buchholzi* of western Africa and the tropical marine butterfly fishes in family Chaetodontidae.

**butterwort** insectivorous plant belonging to the bladderwort family, with purplish flowers and a rosette of flat leaves covered with a sticky substance that traps insects. (Genus *Pinguicula*, family Lentibulariaceae.)

**buzzard** species of medium-sized hawk with broad wings, often seen soaring. Buzzards are in the falcon family, Falconidae, order Falcon-iformes. The *common buzzard Buteo buteo* of Europe and Asia is about 55 cm/1.8 ft long with a wingspan of over 1.2 m/4 ft. It preys on a variety of small animals up to the size of a rabbit.

**Byatt, A(ntonia) S(usan)** (1936– ) English novelist and critic. Her fifth novel, *Possession*, won the 1990 Booker Prize. *The Virgin in the Garden* (1978) is a confident, zestfully handled account of a varied group of characters putting on a school play during the coronation year of 1953. It has a sequel, *Still Life* (1985). The third part of this projected quartet is *Babel Tower* (1996), set in the 1960s. *Angels and Insects* (1992) has twin themes of entomology and spir-itualism.

**Byrd, Richard Evelyn** (1888–1957) US avia-tor and explorer. The first to fly over the North Pole (1926), he also flew over the South Pole (1929) and led five overland expeditions in Antarctica.

**Byrd, William** (1543–1623) English com-poser. His sacred and secular choral music, including over 200 motets and Masses for three, four, and five voices, exemplifies the English polyphonic style.

**Byron, George Gordon** 6th Baron Byron (1788–1824) English poet. He became the sym-bol of ◊Romanticism and political liberalism throughout Europe in the 19th century. His rep-utation was established with the first two cantos of *Childe Harold* (1812). Later works include *The Prisoner of Chillon* (1816), *Beppo* (1818), *Mazeppa* (1819), and, most notably, the satirical *Don Juan* (1819–24). He left England in 1816 and spent most of his later life in Italy.

**byte** sufficient computer memory to store a single character of data. The character is stored in the byte of memory as a pattern of ◊bits (binary digits), using a code such as ◊ASCII. A byte usually contains eight bits – for example, the capital letter F can be stored as the bit pat-tern 01000110.

**Byzantine Empire** the *Eastern Roman Empire* 395–1453, with its capital at Constan-tinople (formerly Byzantium, modern Istanbul). It was the direct continuation of the Roman Empire in the East, and inherited many of its tra-ditions and institutions.

**Byzantine style** style in the visual arts and architecture that originated in the 4th–5th cen-turies in Byzantium (the capital of the Eastern Roman Empire) and spread to Italy, throughout the Balkans, and to Russia, where it survived for many centuries. It is characterized by heavy styl-ization, strong linear emphasis, the use of rigid artistic stereotypes, and rich colours such as gold. Byzantine artists excelled in mosaic work, manuscript painting, and religious ◊icon paint-ing. In architecture, the dome supported on pen-dentives was in widespread use.

**Byzantium** (modern Istanbul) ancient Greek city on the Bosporus, founded as a colony of the Greek city of Megara on an important strategic site at the entrance to the Black Sea about 660 BC. In AD 330 the capital of the Roman Empire was transferred there by Constantine the Great, who renamed it Constantinople and it became the capital of the ◊Byzantine Empire to which it gave its name.

**c.** abbreviation for *circa* (Latin 'about'), used with dates that are uncertain.

**°C** symbol for degrees ◊Celsius, sometimes called centigrade.

**C** in computing, a high-level, general-purpose programming language popular on minicomputers and microcomputers. Developed in the early 1970s from an earlier language called BCPL, C was first used as the language of the operating system ◊UNIX, though it has since become widespread beyond UNIX. It is useful for writing fast and efficient systems programs, such as operating systems (which control the operations of the computer).

**cabbage** vegetable plant related to the turnip and wild mustard, or charlock. It was cultivated as early as 2000 BC, and the many commercial varieties include kale, Brussels sprouts, common cabbage, savoy, cauliflower, sprouting broccoli, and kohlrabi. (*Brassica oleracea,* family Cruciferae.)

**cabinet** ('a small room, implying secrecy') in politics, the group of ministers holding a country's highest executive offices who decide government policy. In Britain the cabinet system originated under the Stuarts. Under William III it became customary for the king to select his ministers from the party with a parliamentary majority. The US cabinet, unlike the British, does not initiate legislation, and its members, appointed by the president, must not be members of Congress. The term was used in the USA from 1793.

**cable television** distribution of broadcast signals through cable relay systems.

Narrow-band systems were originally used to deliver services to areas with poor regular reception; systems with wider bands, using coaxial and fibreoptic cable, are increasingly used for distribution and development of home-based interactive services, typically telephones.

**Caboto, Giovanni** or *John Cabot* (*c.* 1450– *c.* 1498) Italian navigator. Commissioned, with his three sons, by Henry VII of England to discover unknown lands, he arrived at Cape Breton Island on 24 June 1497, thus becoming the first European to reach the North American mainland (he thought he was in northeast Asia). In 1498 he sailed again, touching Greenland, and probably died on the voyage.

**cacao** tropical American evergreen tree, now also cultivated in West Africa and Sri Lanka. Its seeds are cocoa beans, from which ◊cocoa and chocolate are prepared. (*Theobroma cacao,* family Sterculiaceae.)

**cactus** plural *cacti,* strictly, any plant of the family Cactaceae, although the word is commonly used to describe many different succulent and prickly plants. True cacti have a woody axis (central core) surrounded by a large fleshy stem, which takes various forms and is usually covered with spines (actually reduced leaves). They are all specially adapted to growing in dry areas.

**CAD** acronym for computer-aided design, use of computers in creating and editing design drawings. CAD also allows such things as automatic testing of designs and multiple or animated three-dimensional views of designs. CAD systems are widely used in architecture, electronics, and engineering, for example in the motor-vehicle industry, where cars designed with the assistance of computers are now commonplace. With a CAD system, picture components are accurately positioned using grid lines. Pictures can be resized, rotated, or mirrored without loss of quality or proportion.

A related development is ◊CAM (computer-assisted manufacturing).

**caddis fly** insect of the order Trichoptera. Adults are generally dull brown, mothlike, with wings covered in tiny hairs. Mouthparts are poorly developed, and many caddis flies do not feed as adults. They are usually found near water.

**Cádiz** Spanish city and naval base, capital and seaport of the province of Cádiz, sited on a peninsula on the south side of Cádiz Bay, an inlet of the Atlantic Ocean, 103 km/64 mi south of Seville; population (1991) 153,600. There are ferries to the Canary Islands and Casablanca, and shipbuilding and repairs are important, as are fishing and tourism. After the discovery of the Americas in 1492, Cádiz became one of Europe's most vital trade ports. The English adventurer Francis ◊Drake burned a Spanish fleet here in 1587 to prevent the sailing of the ◊Armada. The city has an 18th-century cathedral.

**cadmium** soft, silver-white, ductile, and malleable metallic element, symbol Cd, atomic number 48, relative atomic mass 112.40. Cadmium occurs in nature as a sulphide or carbonate in zinc ores. It is a toxic metal that, because of industrial dumping, has become an environmental pollutant. It is used in batteries, electroplating, and as a constituent of alloys used for bearings with low coefficients of friction; it is also a constituent of an alloy with a very low melting point.

**caecilian** tropical amphibian of wormlike appearance. There are about 170 species known in the family Caeciliidae, forming the amphibian order Apoda (also known as Caecilia or Gymnophiona). Caecilians have a grooved skin that gives a 'segmented' appearance; they have no trace of limbs or pelvis. The body is 20–130 cm/8–50 in long, beige to black in colour. The eyes are very small and weak or blind. They eat insects and small worms. Some species bear live young, others lay eggs.

Caecilians live in burrows in damp ground in the tropical Americas, Africa, Asia, and the Seychelles Islands.

**Caedmon** (lived c. 660–670) earliest known English Christian poet. According to the Northumbrian historian Bede, when Caedmon was a cowherd at the monastery of Whitby, he was commanded to sing by a stranger in a dream, and on waking produced a hymn on the Creation. The poem is preserved in some manuscripts. Caedmon became a monk and may have composed other religious poems.

**Caerphilly** unitary authority in south Wales, created in 1996 from parts of the former counties of Mid Glamorgan and Gwent
**area** 270 sq km/104 sq mi
**towns** Hengoed (administrative headquarters), Caerphilly, Bargoed, Newbridge, Rhymney
**physical** rivers Rhymney and Sirhowy
**industries** iron and steel production and coal mining have been replaced by a wide range of light industries
**population** (1996) 172,000.

**Caesar** family name of Julius Caesar and later an imperial title. Julius Caesar's grand-nephew and adopted son Octavius became Gaius Julius Caesar Octavianus (the future emperor ◊Augustus). From his day onwards, 'Caesar' became the family name of the reigning emperor and his heirs. When the emperor ◊Nero, the last of the Julio-Claudian line, died, all his successors from Galba onwards were called 'Caesar'. What had been a family name thus became a title.

**Caesar, Gaius Julius** (100–44 BC) Roman general and dictator, considered Rome's most successful military commander. He formed with Pompey the Great and Marcus Licinius ◊Crassus (the Elder) the First Triumvirate in 60 BC. He conquered Gaul in 58–50 and invaded Britain in 55–54. By leading his army across the river Rubicon into Italy in 49, an act of treason, he provoked a civil war which ended in 45 with the defeat of Pompey and his supporters. He was voted dictator for life, but was assassinated by conspirators on 15 March 44 BC. Caesar was a skilled historian whose *Commentarii*, recounting his campaigns, has had a major impact on the way military history is written up to the present day.

**Caesarean section** surgical operation to deliver a baby by way of an incision in the mother's abdominal and uterine walls. It may be recommended for almost any obstetric complication implying a threat to mother or baby.

**caesium** (Latin *caesius* 'bluish-grey') soft, silvery-white, ductile metallic element, symbol Cs, atomic number 55, relative atomic mass 132.905. It is one of the ◊alkali metals, and is the most electropositive of all the elements. In air it ignites spontaneously, and it reacts vigorously with water. It is used in the manufacture of photocells.

**caffeine** ◊alkaloid organic substance found in tea, coffee, and kola nuts; it stimulates the heart and central nervous system. When isolated, it is a bitter crystalline compound, $C_8H_{10}N_4O_2$. Too much caffeine (more than six average cups of tea or coffee a day) can be detrimental to health.

**Cage, John** (1912–1992) US composer. His interest in Indian classical music led him to the view that the purpose of music was to change the way people listen. From 1948 he experimented with instruments, graphics, and methods of random selection in an effort to generate a music of pure incident. For example, he used 24 radios, tuned to random stations, in *Imaginary Landscape No 4* (1951). His ideas profoundly influenced late 20th-century aesthetics.

**caiman** or *cayman*, large reptile, related to the ◊alligator.

**cairn** Scottish breed of ◊terrier. Shaggy, short-legged, and compact, it can be sandy, greyish brindle, or red. It was formerly used for flushing out foxes and badgers.

**Cairo** Arabic *El Qahira*, ('the victorious') capital of Egypt, and the largest city in Africa and in the Middle East, situated on the east bank of the River Nile 13 km/8 mi above the apex of the delta and 160 km/100 mi from the Mediterranean; population (1995 est) 6,955,000. Industries include the manufacture of textiles, cement, vegetable oils, tourism and steel. At Helwan, 24 km/15 mi to the south, an industrial centre is powered by electricity from the Aswan High Dam.

**CAL** acronym for computer-assisted learning, use of computers in education and training: the computer displays instructional material to a student and asks questions about the information given; the student's answers determine the sequence of the lessons.

**Calabria** mountainous region occupying the 'toe' of Italy, comprising the provinces of Catanzaro, Cosenza, and Reggio di Calabria; area 15,100 sq km/5,829 sq mi; population (1992) 2,074,800. Its capital is Catanzaro and the principal towns are Crotone and Reggio di Calabria.

**calceolaria** plant with brilliantly coloured slipper-shaped flowers. Native to South America, calceolarias were introduced to Europe and the USA in the 1830s. (Genus *Calceolaria*, family Scrophulariaceae.)

**calcite** colourless, white, or light-coloured common rock-forming mineral, calcium carbonate, $CaCO_3$. It is the main constituent of ◊limestone and marble and forms many types of invertebrate shell.

**calcium** (Latin *calcis* 'lime') soft, silvery-white metallic element, symbol Ca, atomic number 20, relative atomic mass 40.08. It is one of the ◊alkaline-earth metals. It is the fifth most abundant element (the third most abundant metal) in the Earth's crust. It is found mainly as its carbonate $CaCO_3$ which occurs in a fairly pure condition as chalk and limestone (see ◊calcite). Calcium is an essential component of bones, teeth, shells, milk, and leaves, and it forms 1.5% of the human body by mass.

**calcium carbonate** ($CaCO_3$) white solid, found in nature as limestone, marble, and chalk. It is a valuable resource, used in the making of iron, steel, cement, glass, slaked lime, bleaching powder, sodium carbonate and bicarbonate, and many other industrially useful substances.

**calcium hydroxide** or *slaked lime,* $Ca(OH)_2$ white solid, slightly soluble in water. A solution of calcium hydroxide is called limewater and is used in the laboratory to test for the presence of carbon dioxide.

**calculus** (Latin 'pebble') branch of mathematics which uses the concept of a derivative to analyse the way in which the values of a ◊function vary. Calculus is probably the most widely used part of mathematics. Many real-life problems are analysed by expressing one quantity as a function of another – position of a moving object as a function of time, temperature of an object as a function of distance from a heat source, force on an object as a function of distance from the source of the force, and so on – and calculus is concerned with such functions.

**Calcutta** city in India, on the River Hooghly, the westernmost mouth of the River Ganges, some 130 km/80 mi north of the Bay of Bengal; population (1994) 11,500,000. The capital of West Bengal, it is chiefly a commercial and industrial centre, its industries including engineering, shipbuilding, jute, and other textiles. It was the seat of government of British India 1773–1912. There is severe air pollution.

**calendar** division of the year into months, weeks, and days and the method of ordering the years. From year one, an assumed date of the birth of Jesus, dates are calculated backwards (BC 'before Christ' or BCE 'before common era') and forwards (AD, Latin *anno Domini* 'in the year of the Lord', or CE 'common era'). The *lunar month* (period between one new moon and the next) naturally averages 29.5 days, but the Western calendar uses for convenience a *calendar month* with a complete number of days, 30 or 31 (February has 28). For adjustments, since there are slightly fewer than six extra hours a year left over, they are added to February as a 29th day every fourth year (*leap year*), century years being excepted unless they are divisible by 400. For example, 1896 was a leap year; 1900 was not.

**California** western state of the USA. It is nicknamed the Golden State, originally because of its gold mines, and more recently because of its orange groves and sunshine. California was admitted to the Union in 1850 as the 31st US state. It is bordered to the south by the Mexican state of Baja California, to the east by Arizona and Nevada, to the north by Oregon, and to the west by the Pacific Ocean.
*population* (1996 est) 31,878,000, the most populous state of the USA (69.9% white; 25.8% Hispanic; 9.6% Asian and Pacific islander, including many Vietnamese, 7.4% African-American; 0.8% American Indian)

*area* 411,100 sq km/158,685 sq mi
*capital* Sacramento
*towns and cities* Los Angeles, San Diego, San Francisco, San Jose, Fresno
*industries and products* leading agricultural state with fruit (peaches, citrus, grapes in the valley of the San Joaquin and Sacramento rivers), nuts, wheat, vegetables, cotton, and rice, all mostly grown by irrigation, the water being carried by concrete-lined canals to the Central and Imperial valleys; beef cattle; timber; fish; oil; natural gas; aerospace technology; electronics (Silicon Valley); financial sector; food processing; films and television programmes; tourism; leisure industry; great reserves of energy (geothermal) in the hot water that lies beneath much of the state.

**californium** synthesized, radioactive, metallic element of the actinide series, symbol Cf, atomic number 98, relative atomic mass 251. It is produced in very small quantities and used in nuclear reactors as a neutron source. The longest-lived isotope, Cf-251, has a half-life of 800 years.

**Caligula** Gaius Julius Caesar Germanicus (AD 12–41) Roman emperor AD 37–41, son of Germanicus and Agrippina the Elder, and successor to ◊Tiberius. Caligula was a cruel tyrant and was assassinated by an officer of his guard. He appears to have been mentally unstable.

**caliph** title of civic and religious heads of the world of Islam. The first caliph was ◊Abu Bakr. Nominally elective, the office became hereditary, held by the Umayyad dynasty 661–750 and then by the ◊Abbasid dynasty. After the death of the last Abbasid (1258), the title was claimed by a number of Muslim chieftains in Egypt, Turkey, and India. The most powerful of these were the Turkish sultans of the Ottoman Empire.

**Callaghan, (Leonard) James** Baron Callaghan of Cardiff (1912–  ) British Labour politician. He was home secretary 1967–70 and prime minister 1976–79 in a period of increasing economic stress. As chancellor of the Exchequer 1964–67, he introduced corporation tax, capital gains tax, and selective employment tax, and resigned following devaluation.

**Callas, Maria** adopted name of Maria Kalogeropoulos (1923–1977) US lyric soprano. She was born in New York of Greek parents. With a voice of fine range and a gift for dramatic expression, she excelled in operas including *Norma, La Sonnambula, Madame Butterfly, Aïda, Tosca,* and *Medea.*

**calligraphy** art of handwriting, regarded in China and Japan as the greatest of the visual arts, and playing a large part in Islamic art because the depiction of the human and animal form is forbidden.

**calorie** c.g.s. unit of heat, now replaced by the ◊joule (one calorie is approximately 4.2 joules). It is the heat required to raise the temperature of one gram of water by 1°C. In dietetics, the Calorie or kilocalorie is equal to 1,000 calories.

**calotype** paper-based photograph using a wax paper negative, the first example of the ◊negative/positive process invented by the English photographer Fox Talbot around 1834.

**Calvin, John** also known as *Cauvin* or *Chauvin* (1509–1564) French-born Swiss Protestant church reformer and theologian. He was a leader of the Reformation in Geneva and set up a strict religious community there. His theological system is known as Calvinism, and his church government as ◊Presbyterianism. Calvin wrote (in Latin) *Institutes of the Christian Religion* (1536) and commentaries on the New Testament and much of the Old Testament.

**Calvinism** Christian doctrine as interpreted by John Calvin and adopted in Scotland, parts of Switzerland, and the Netherlands; by the ◊Puritans in England and New England, USA; and by the subsequent Congregational and Presbyter-ian churches in the USA. Its central doctrine is predestination, under which certain souls (the elect) are predestined by God through the sacrifice of Jesus to salvation, and the rest to damnation. Although Calvinism is rarely accepted today in its strictest interpretation, the 20th century has seen a neo-Calvinist revival through the work of Karl Barth.

**calypso** West Indian satirical ballad with a syncopated beat. Calypso is a traditional song form of Trinidad, a feature of its annual carnival, with roots in West African praise-singing. It was first popularized in the USA by Harry Belafonte (1927– ) in 1956. Mighty Sparrow (1935– ) is Trinidad's best-known calypso singer.

**calyx** collective term for the ◊sepals of a flower, forming the outermost whorl of the perianth. It surrounds the other flower parts and protects them while in bud. In some flowers, for example, the campions *Silene*, the sepals are fused along their sides, forming a tubular calyx.

**CAM** acronym for computer-aided manufacturing, use of computers to control production processes; in particular, the control of machine tools and ◊robots in factories. In some factories, the whole design and production system has been automated by linking ◊CAD (computer-aided design) to CAM.

**cam** part of a machine that converts circular motion to linear motion or vice versa. The *edge cam* in a car engine is in the form of a rounded projection on a shaft, the camshaft. When the camshaft turns, the cams press against linkages (plungers or followers) that open the valves in the cylinders.

**cambium** in botany, a layer of actively dividing cells (lateral ◊meristem), found within stems and roots, that gives rise to secondary growth in perennial plants, causing an increase in girth. There are two main types of cambium: *vascular cambium,* which gives rise to secondary ◊xylem and ◊phloem tissues, and *cork cambium* (or phellogen), which gives rise to secondary cortex and cork tissues (see ◊bark).

**Cambodia** State of (Khmer Republic 1970–76, Democratic Kampuchea 1976–79, People's Republic of Kampuchea 1979–89)
*National name* Roat Kampuchea

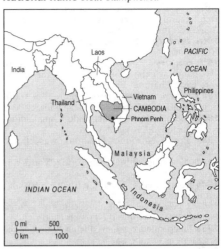

*area* 181,035 sq km/69,897 sq mi
*capital* Phnom Penh
*major towns/cities* Battambang, Kompong Cham
*major ports* Kompong Cham
*physical features* mostly flat, forested plains with mountains in southwest and north; Mekong River runs north–south; Lake Tonle Sap
*head of state* Prince Norodom Sihanouk from 1991
*head of government* joint prime ministers Ung Huot and Hun Sen from 1998
*political system* limited constitutional monarchy
*political parties* United Front for an Independent, Neutral, Peaceful, and Cooperative Cambodia (FUNCINPEC), nationalist, monarchist; Liberal Democratic Party (BLDP), republican, anticommunist (formerly the Khmer People's National Liberation Front (KPNLF)); Cambodian People's Party (CPP), reform socialist (formerly the communist Kampuchean People's Revolutionary Party (KPRP)); Cambodian National Unity Party (CNUP) (political wing of the Khmer Rouge), ultranationalist communist
*currency* Cambodian riel
*GNP per capita (PPP)* (US$) 1,240 (1998)
*exports* timber, rubber, fishery products, garments. Principal market: Vietnam 18% (1997)
*population* 10,946,000 (1999 est)
*language* Khmer (official), French
*religion* Theravāda Buddhist 95%, Muslim, Roman Catholic
*life expectancy* 52 (men); 55 (women) (1995–2000)
*Chronology*
*1st century AD* Part of the kingdom of Hindu-Buddhist Funan (Fou Nan), centred on Mekong delta region.

**6th century** Conquered by the Chenla kingdom.

**9th century** Establishment by Jayavarman II of extensive and sophisticated Khmer Empire, supported by an advanced irrigation system and architectural achievements, with a capital at Angkor in the northwest.

**14th century** Theravāda Buddhism replaced Hinduism.

**15th century** Came under the control of Siam (Thailand), which made Phnom Penh the capital and, later, Champa (Vietnam).

**1863** Became a French protectorate, but traditional political structures left largely intact.

**1887** Became part of French Indo-China Union, which included Laos and Vietnam.

**1941** Prince Norodom Sihanouk was elected king.

**1941–45** Occupied by Japan during World War II.

**1946** Recaptured by France; parliamentary constitution adopted.

**1949** Guerrilla war for independence secured semi-autonomy within the French Union.

**1953** Independence achieved from France as the Kingdom of Cambodia.

**1955** Norodom Sihanouk abdicated as king and became prime minister, representing the Popular Socialist Community mass movement.

**1960** On the death of his father, Norodom Sihanouk became head of state.

**later 1960s** Mounting guerrilla insurgency, led by the communist Khmer Rouge, and civil war in neighbouring Vietnam.

**1970** Sihanouk was overthrown by US-backed Lt-Gen Lon Nol in a right-wing coup; the new name of Khmer Republic was adopted; Sihanouk, exiled in China, formed own guerrilla movement.

**1975** Lon Nol overthrown by Khmer Rouge, which was backed by North Vietnam and China; Sihanouk became head of state.

**1976** The Khmer Republic was renamed Democratic Kampuchea.

**1976–78** The Khmer Rouge, led by Pol Pot, introduced an extreme Maoist communist programme, forcing urban groups into rural areas and resulting in over 2.5 million deaths from famine, disease, and maltreatment; Sihanouk was removed from power.

**1978–79** Vietnam invaded and installed a government headed by Heng Samrin, an anti-Pol Pot communist.

**1979** Democratic Kampuchea was renamed the People's Republic of Kampuchea.

**1980–82** Faced by guerrilla resistance from Pol Pot's Chinese-backed Khmer Rouge and Sihanouk's ASEAN and US-backed nationalists, more than 300,000 Cambodians fled to refugee camps in Thailand and thousands of soldiers were killed.

**1985** Reformist Hun Sen was appointed prime minister and more moderate economic and cultural policies were pursued.

**1987–89** Vietnamese troops were withdrawn.

**1989** The People's Republic of Kampuchea was renamed the State of Cambodia and Buddhism was re-established as the state religion.

**1991** A peace agreement signed in Paris provided for a ceasefire and a United Nations Transitional Authority in Cambodia (UNTAC) to administer the country in conjunction with an all-party Supreme National Council; communism was abandoned. Sihanouk returned as head of state.

**1992** Political prisoners were released; refugees were resettled; freedom of speech and party formation were restored. The Khmer Rouge refused to disarm in accordance with peace process.

**1993** Free general elections were held (and boycotted by the Khmer Rouge), resulting in a win by FUNCINPEC; a new constitution was adopted. Sihanouk was reinstated as constitutional monarch; Prince Norodom Ranariddh, FUNCINPEC leader, was appointed executive prime minister, with reform-socialist CPP leader Hun Sen deputy premier. The Khmer Rouge continued fighting.

**1994** An antigovernment coup was foiled. Seven thousand guerrillas of the outlawed Khmer Rouge surrendered in response to a government amnesty.

**1995** Prince Norodom Sirivudh, FUNCINPEC leader and half-brother of King Sihanouk, was exiled for allegedly plotting to assassinate Hun Sen and topple the government.

**1996** There were heightened tensions between Hun Sen's CPP and the royalist FUNCINPEC.

**1997** Sixteen people were killed in street demonstration; the opposition blamed supporters of Hun Sen. Pol Pot was sentenced to life imprisonment after a trial by the Khmer Rouge. FUNCINPEC troops were routed by the CPP, led by Hun Sen. Prime Minister Prince Norodom Ranariddh was deposed and replaced by Ung Huot. King Sihanouk underwent medical treatment in China. There was fighting between supporters of Hun Sen and Ranariddh.

**1998** Ranariddh was tried in absentia and found guilty of arms smuggling and colluding with the Khmer Rouge. However, as part of a Japanese-brokered peace deal, he was pardoned by the king and returned home to prepare for a July general election. Pol Pot died and and thousands of Khmer Rouge guerrillas defected. The CPP won National Assembly elections. Political unrest followed the poll. A new CPP–FUNCINPEC coalition was formed, with Hun Sen (CPP) as sole prime minister and Prince Norodom Ranariddh as president of the National Assembly. FUNCINPEC troops re-integrated into the government army. Cambodia re-occupied its vacated UN seat.

**Cambrian** period of geological time 570–510 million years ago; the first period of the Palaeozoic era. All invertebrate animal life appeared, and marine algae were widespread. The *Cambrian Explosion* 530–520 million years ago saw the first appearance in the fossil record of all modern animal phyla; the earliest fossils with hard shells, such as trilobites, date from this period.

**Cambrian Mountains** region of hills, plateaux, and deep valleys in Wales, 175 km/110 mi long, linking Snowdonia in the northwest and the Brecon Beacons and Black Mountains in the south.

**Cambridge** city and administrative headquarters of ◊Cambridgeshire, eastern England, on the River Cam, 80 km/50 mi north of London; population (1994 est) 117,000. It is the seat of Cambridge University (founded in the 13th century). Industries include the manufacture of computers and electronic products, scientific instruments, and paper, printing, publishing, financial services, and insurance.

**Cambridgeshire** county of eastern England, which has contained the unitary authority Peterborough since April 1998
*area* 3,410 sq km/1,316 sq mi
*towns and cities* ◊Cambridge (administrative headquarters), Ely, Huntingdon, March, Wisbech, St Neots, Whittlesey
*physical* county is flat with fens, whose soil is very fertile; Bedford Level (a peaty area of the fens); rivers: Nene, Ouse (with tributaries Cam, Lark, and Little Ouse), Welland
*features* Cambridge University
*agriculture* the county is one of the chief cereal and sugar-beet producing districts of England; fruit and vegetables are grown; there is also dairy farming and sheep-rearing
*industries* brewing, paper, electronics, food processing, mechanical engineering; there are scientific and pharmaceutical research establishments
*population* (1996) 703,100
*famous people* Oliver Cromwell, Octavia Hill, John Maynard Keynes.

**Camden Town Group** school of British painters (1911–13), based in Camden, London, led by Walter ◊Sickert. The work of Spencer Gore (1878–1914) and Harold Gilman (1876–1919) is typical of the group, rendering everyday town scenes in Post-Impressionist style. In 1913 they merged with another group to form the London Group.

**camel** large cud-chewing mammal of the even-toed hoofed order Artiodactyla. Unlike typical ruminants, it has a three-chambered stomach. It has two toes which have broad soft soles for walking on sand, and hooves resembling nails. There are two species, the single-humped *Arabian camel Camelus dromedarius* and the twin-humped *Bactrian camel C. bactrianus* from Asia. They carry a food reserve of fatty tissue in the hump, can go without drinking for long periods, can feed on salty vegetation, and withstand extremes of heat and cold, thus being well adapted to desert conditions.

**camellia** any oriental evergreen shrub with roselike flowers belonging to the tea family. Many species, including *Camellia japonica* and *C. reticulata*, have been introduced into Europe, the USA, and Australia; they are widely cultivated as ornamental shrubs. (Genus *Camellia*, family Theaceae.)

**Camelot** in medieval romance, legendary seat of King Arthur.

**camera** apparatus used in ◊photography, consisting of a lens system set in a light-proof box inside of which a sensitized film or plate can be placed. The lens collects rays of light reflected from the subject and brings them together as a sharp image on the film. The opening or hole at the front of the camera, through which light enters, is called an ◊aperture. The aperture size controls the amount of light that can enter. A shutter controls the amount of time light has to affect the film. There are small-, medium-, and large-format cameras; the format refers to the size of recorded image and the dimensions of the image obtained.

**camera obscura** darkened box with a tiny hole for projecting the inverted image of the scene outside on to a screen inside. For its development as a device for producing photographs, see ◊photography.

**Cameroon** Republic of
*national name* *République du Cameroun*

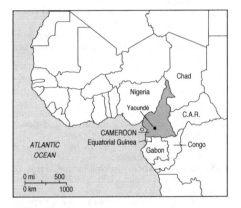

*area* 475,440 sq km/183,567 sq mi
*capital* Yaoundé
*major towns/cities* Garoua, Douala, Nkongsamba, Maroua, Bamenda, Bafoussam
*major ports* Douala
*physical features* desert in far north in the Lake Chad basin, mountains in west, dry savanna plateau in the intermediate area, and dense tropical rainforest in south; Mount Cameroon 4,070 m/13,358 ft, an active volcano on the coast, west of the Adamawa Mountains
*head of state* Paul Biya from 1982
*head of government* Simon Achidi Achu from 1992
*political system* emergent democracy
*political parties* Cameroon People's Democratic Movement (RDPC), nationalist, left of centre; Front of Allies for Change (FAC), centre left
*currency* franc CFA
*GNP per capita (PPP)* (US$) 1,810 (1998)
*exports* crude petroleum and petroleum products, timber and timber products, coffee, aluminium, cotton, bananas. Principal market: Italy 25.4% (1997)
*population* 14,710,000 (1999 est)
*language* French and English in pidgin variations (official); there has been some discontent with the emphasis on French – there are 163 indigenous peoples with their own African

languages (Sudanic languages in north, Bantu languages elsewhere)

**religion** Roman Catholic 35%, animist 25%, Muslim 22%, Protestant 18%

**life expectancy** 53 (men); 56 (women) (1995–2000)

**Chronology**

**1472** First visited by the Portuguese, who named it the Rio dos Camaroes ('River of Prawns') after the giant shrimps they found in the Wouri River estuary, and later introduced slave trading.

**early 17th century** The Douala people migrated to the coastal region from the east and came to serve as intermediaries between Portuguese, Dutch, and English traders and interior tribes.

**1809–48** Northern savannas conquered by the Fulani, Muslim pastoral nomads from the southern Sahara, forcing forest and upland peoples southwards.

**1856** Douala chiefs signed a commercial treaty with Britain and invited British protection.

**1884** Treaty signed establishing German rule as the protectorate of Kamerun; cocoa, coffee, and banana plantations developed.

**1916** Captured by Allied forces in World War I.

**1919** Divided under League of Nations' mandates between Britain, which administered the southwest and north, adjoining Nigeria, and France, which administered the east and south (comprising four-fifths of the area), and developed palm oil and cocoa plantations.

**1946** French Cameroon and British Cameroon made UN trust territories.

**1955** French crushed a revolt by the Union of the Cameroon Peoples (UPC), southern-based radical nationalists.

**1960** French Cameroon became the independent Republic of Cameroon, with Ahmadou Ahidjo, a Muslim from the north, elected president; UPC rebellion in southwest crushed, and a state of emergency declared.

**1961** Following a UN plebiscite, northern part of British Cameroon merged with Nigeria and southern part joined the Republic of Cameroon to become the Federal Republic of Cameroon, with French and English as official languages.

**1966** Autocratic one-party regime introduced; government and opposition parties merged to form Cameroon National Union (UNC).

**1970s** Petroleum exports made possible successful investment in education and agriculture.

**1972** New constitution made Cameroon a unitary state.

**1982** President Ahidjo resigned; succeeded by his prime minister Paul Biya, a Christian from the south.

**1983** Biya began to remove the northern Muslim political 'barons' close to Ahidjo, who went into exile in France.

**1984** Biya defeated a plot by Muslim officers from the north to overthrow him.

**1985** UNC adopted the name RDPC.

**1990** There was widespread public disorder as living standards declined; Biya granted an amnesty to political prisoners.

**1992** The ruling RDPC won the first multiparty elections in 28 years. Biya's presidential victory was challenged by opposition, who claimed ballot-rigging.

**1995** Cameroon was admitted to the Commonwealth.

**1997** RDPC won assembly elections; President Biya was re-elected.

**camouflage** colours or structures that allow an animal to blend with its surroundings to avoid detection by other animals. Camouflage can take the form of matching the background colour, of countershading (darker on top, lighter below, to counteract natural shadows), or of irregular patterns that break up the outline of the animal's body. More elaborate camouflage involves closely resembling a feature of the natural environment, as with the stick insect; this is closely akin to mimicry. Camouflage is also important as a military technique, disguising either equipment, troops, or a position in order to conceal them from an enemy.

**Campania** region of southern Italy, comprising the provinces of Avellino, Benevento, Caserta, Naples, and Salerno; area 13,600 sq km/5,250 sq mi; population (1992) 5,668,900. The administrative capital is ◊Naples; industrial centres include Benevento, Caserta, and Salerno. Agriculture is important; wheat, citrus fruits, wine, vegetables, tobacco, and hemp are produced. The volcano ◊Vesuvius is near Naples, and there are ancient sites at Pompeii, Herculaneum, and Paestum.

**Campbell, Donald Malcolm** (1921–1967) British car and speedboat enthusiast, son of Malcolm Campbell, who simultaneously held the land-speed and water-speed records. In 1964 he set the world water-speed record of 444.57 kph/276.3 mph on Lake Dumbleyung, Australia, with the turbojet hydroplane *Bluebird*, and achieved the land-speed record of 648.7 kph/403.1 mph at Lake Eyre salt flats, Australia. He was killed in an attempt to raise his water-speed record on Coniston Water, England.

**Campbell, Malcolm** (1885–1948) British racing driver who once held both land- and water-speed records. He set the land-speed record nine times, pushing it up to 484.8 kph/301.1 mph at Bonneville Flats, Utah, USA, 1935, and broke the water-speed record three times, the best being 228.2 kph/141.74 mph on Coniston Water, England, 1939. His car and boat were both called *Bluebird*.

**Campbell-Bannerman, Henry** (1836– 1908) British Liberal politician, prime minister 1905–08, leader of the Liberal party 1898–1908. The Entente Cordiale was broadened to embrace Russia during his premiership, which also saw the granting of 'responsible government' to the Boer republics in southern Africa. He was succeeded as prime minister and Liberal leader by H H ◊Asquith, who had effectively led the House during Campbell-Bannermann's premiership, as the latter was dogged by ill health.

**Camp David Agreements** two framework accords agreed in 1978 and officially signed in

March 1979 by Israeli prime minister Begin and Egyptian president Sadat at Camp David, Maryland, USA, under the guidance of US president Carter. They cover an Egypt–Israel peace treaty and phased withdrawal of Israel from Sinai, which was completed in 1982, and an overall Middle East settlement including the election by the West Bank and Gaza Strip Palestinians of a 'self-governing authority'. The latter issue has stalled repeatedly over questions of who should represent the Palestinians and what form the self-governing body should take.

**camphor** ($C_{10}H_{16}O$) volatile, aromatic ◊ketone substance obtained from the camphor tree *Cinnamomum camphora*. It is distilled from chips of the wood, and is used in insect repellents and medicinal inhalants and liniments, and in the manufacture of celluloid.

**Camus, Albert** (1913–1960) Algerian-born French writer. His works, such as the novels *L'Etranger/The Outsider* (1942) and *La Peste/ The Plague* (1948), owe much to ◊existentialism in their emphasis on the absurdity and arbitrariness of life. Other works include *Le Mythe de Sisyphe/The Myth of Sisyphus* (1943) and *L'Homme révolté/The Rebel* (1951). Camus's criticism of communism in the latter book led to a protracted quarrel with the philosopher Jean-Paul Sartre. Nobel Prize for Literature (1957).

**Canaan** ancient region between the Mediterranean and the Dead Sea, called in the Bible the 'Promised Land' of the Israelites. It was occupied as early as the 3rd millennium BC by the Canaanites, a Semitic-speaking people who were known to the Greeks of the 1st millennium BC as Phoenicians. The capital was Ebla (now Tell Mardikh, Syria).

**Canada**

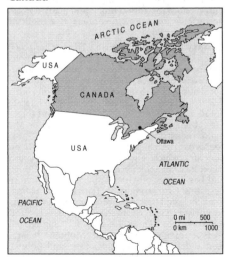

**area** 9,970,610 sq km/3,849,652 sq mi
**capital** Ottawa
**major towns/cities** Toronto, Montréal, Vancouver, Edmonton, Calgary, Winnipeg, Québec, Hamilton, Saskatoon, Halifax, Regina, Windsor, Oshawa, London, Kitchener

**physical features** mountains in west, with low-lying plains in interior and rolling hills in east; St Lawrence Seaway, Mackenzie River; Great Lakes; Arctic Archipelago; Rocky Mountains; Great Plains or Prairies; Canadian Shield; Niagara Falls; climate varies from temperate in south to arctic in north; 45% of country forested
**head of state** Elizabeth II from 1952, represented by governor general Roméo A LeBlanc from 1995
**head of government** Jean Chrétien from 1993
**political system** federal constitutional monarchy
**political parties** Liberal Party, nationalist, centrist; Bloc Québécois, Québec-based, separatist; Reform Party, populist, right wing; New Democratic Party (NDP), moderate left of centre; Progressive Conservative Party (PCP), free enterprise, right of centre
**currency** Canadian dollar
**GNP per capita (PPP)** (US$) 24,050 (1998)
**exports** motor vehicles and parts, lumber, wood pulp, paper and newsprint, crude petroleum, natural gas, aluminium and alloys, petroleum and coal products. Principal market: USA 83.7% (1998)
**population** 30,857,000 (1999 est)
**language** English, French (both official; 60% English mother tongue, 24% French mother tongue); there are also American Indian languages and the Inuit Inuktitut
**religion** Roman Catholic, various Protestant denominations
**life expectancy** 76 (men); 82 (women) (1995–2000)
**Chronology**
**35,000 BC** First evidence of people reaching North America from Asia by way of Beringia.
**c. 2000 BC** Inuit (Eskimos) began settling Arctic coast from Siberia eastwards to Greenland.
**c. 1000 AD** Vikings, including Leif Ericsson, established Vinland, a settlement in northeast America that did not survive.
**1497** John Cabot, an Italian navigator in the service of English king Henry VII, landed on Cape Breton Island and claimed the area for England.
**1534** French navigator Jacques Cartier reached the Gulf of St Lawrence and claimed the region for France.
**1608** Samuel de Champlain, a French explorer, founded Québec; French settlers developed fur trade and fisheries.
**1663** French settlements in Canada formed the colony of New France, which expanded southwards.
**1670** Hudson's Bay Company established trading posts north of New France, leading to Anglo-French rivalry.
**1689–97** King William's War: Anglo-French conflict in North America arising from the 'Glorious Revolution' in Europe.
**1702–13** Queen Anne's War: Anglo-French conflict in North America arising from the War of the Spanish Succession in Europe; Britain gained Newfoundland.
**1744–48** King George's War: Anglo-French conflict in North America arising from the War of Austrian Succession in Europe.

**1756–63** Seven Years' War: James Wolfe captured Québec in 1759; France ceded Canada to Britain by the Treaty of Paris.

**1775–83** American Revolution caused influx of 40,000 United Empire Loyalists, who formed New Brunswick in 1784.

**1791** Canada divided into Upper Canada (much of modern Ontario) and Lower Canada (much of modern Québec).

**1793** British explorer Alexander Mackenzie crossed the Rocky Mountains to reach the Pacific coast.

**1812–14** War of 1812 between Britain and USA; US invasions repelled by both provinces.

**1820s** Start of large-scale immigration from British Isles caused resentment among French Canadians.

**1837** Rebellions led by Louis Joseph Papineau in Lower Canada and William Lyon Mackenzie in Upper Canada.

**1841** Upper and Lower Canada united as Province of Canada; achieved internal self-government in 1848.

**1867** British North America Act united Ontario, Québec, Nova Scotia, and New Brunswick in Dominion of Canada.

**1869** Red River Rebellion of Métis (people of mixed French and American Indian descent), led by Louis Riel, against British settlers in Rupert's Land.

**1870** Manitoba (part of Rupert's Land) formed the fifth province of Canada; British Columbia became the sixth in 1871, and Prince Edward Island became the seventh in 1873.

**late 19th century** Growth of large-scale wheat farming, mining, and railways.

**1885** Northwest Rebellion crushed and Riel hanged. Canadian Pacific Railway completed.

**1896** Wilfred Laurier was the first French Canadian to become prime minister.

**1905** Alberta and Saskatchewan formed from Northwest Territories and became provinces of Canada.

**1914–18** Half a million Canadian troops fought for the British Empire on the western front in World War I.

**1931** Statute of Westminster affirmed equality of status between Britain and Dominions.

**1939–45** World War II: Canadian participation in all theatres.

**1949** Newfoundland became the tenth province of Canada; Canada was a founding member of the North Atlantic Treaty Organization (NATO).

**1950s** Post-war boom caused rapid expansion of industry.

**1957** Progressive Conservatives returned to power after 22 years in opposition.

**1960** Québec Liberal Party of Jean Lesage launched 'Quiet Revolution' to re-assert French–Canadian identity.

**1970** Pierre Trudeau invoked War Measures Act to suppress separatist terrorists of the Front de Libération du Québec.

**1976** Parti Québécois won control of Québec provincial government; referendum rejected independence 1980.

**1982** 'Patriation' of constitution removed Britain's last legal control over Canada.

**1987** Meech Lake Accord: constitutional amendment proposed to increase provincial powers (to satisfy Québec); failed to be ratified in 1990.

**1989** Canada and USA agreed to establish free trade by 1999.

**1992** A self-governing homeland for Inuit was approved; a constitutional reform package, the Charlottetown Accord, was rejected in a national referendum.

**1993** The Progressive Conservatives were reduced to two seats in a crushing election defeat.

**1994** Canada formed the North American Free Trade Area with USA and Mexico.

**1995** A Québec referendum narrowly rejected a sovereignty proposal.

**1997** The Liberals were re-elected by a narrow margin.

**canal** artificial waterway constructed for drainage, irrigation, or navigation. *Irrigation canals* carry water for irrigation from rivers, reservoirs, or wells, and are designed to maintain an even flow of water over the whole length. *Navigation and ship canals* are constructed at one level between ◊locks, and frequently link with rivers or sea inlets to form a waterway system. The Suez Canal in 1869 and the Panama Canal in 1914 eliminated long trips around continents and dramatically shortened shipping routes.

**canary** bird *Serinus canaria* of the finch family Fringillidae, found wild in the Canary Islands and Madeira. In its wild state the plumage is green, sometimes streaked with brown. The wild canary builds its nest of moss, feathers, and hair in thick high shrubs or trees, and produces two to four broods in a season.

Canaries have been bred as cage birds in Europe since the 15th century, and many domestic varieties are yellow or orange as a result of artificial selection.

**Canary Islands** Spanish *Islas Canarias,* group of volcanic islands and autonomous Spanish community 100 km/60 mi off the northwest coast of Africa, comprising the provinces of Las Palmas and Santa Cruz de Tenerife; area 7,300 sq km/2,818 sq mi; population (1991) 1,456,500. Products include bananas and tomatoes, both grown for export. Tourism is the major industry.

*features* The chief centres are Santa Cruz on Tenerife (which also has the highest Spanish peak, Pico de Teide; height 3,718 m/12,198 ft), and Las Palmas on Gran Canaria. The province of Santa Cruz comprises Tenerife, La Palma, Gomera, and Hierro; the province of Las Palmas comprises Gran Canaria, Lanzarote, and Fuerteventura. There are also six uninhabited islets (Graciosa, Alegranza, Montaña Clara, Roque del Oeste, Roque del Este, and Lobos). The Northern Hemisphere Astronomical Observatory (1981) is on the island of La Palma. Observation conditions are exceptionally good here because there is little moisture, no artificial-light pollution, and little natural airglow.

The aboriginal inhabitants of the Canary Islands were called Guanches, and the

Organization of African Unity (OAU) supports the creation of an independent state, the Guanch Republic, and the revival of the Guanch language.

**Canberra** capital of Australia and seat of the federal government, situated in the ◊Australian Capital Territory in southeast Australia; population (1996) 299,243. Canberra is enclosed within the state of New South Wales, 289 km/180 mi southwest of Sydney and 655 km/407 mi northeast of Melbourne, on the River Molonglo, a tributary of the Murrumbidgee. It succeeded Melbourne as capital of Australia in 1927. It is an administrative, cultural, and tourist centre. The new Parliament House (1988) is located here, as well as government offices, foreign embassies, and many buildings of national importance.

**cancer** group of diseases characterized by abnormal proliferation of cells. Cancer (malignant) cells are usually degenerate, capable only of reproducing themselves (tumour formation). Malignant cells tend to spread from their site of origin by travelling through the bloodstream or lymphatic system. Cancer kills about 6 million people a year worldwide.

**Cancer** faintest of the zodiacal constellations (its brightest stars are fourth magnitude). It lies in the northern hemisphere between ◊Leo and ◊Gemini, and is represented as a crab. The Sun passes through the constellation during late July and early August. In astrology, the dates for Cancer are between about 22 June and 22 July (see ◊precession).

**candela** SI unit (symbol cd) of luminous intensity, which replaced the old units of candle and standard candle. It measures the brightness of a light itself rather than the amount of light falling on an object, which is called *illuminance* and measured in ◊lux.

**cane** reedlike stem of various plants such as the sugar cane, bamboo, and, in particular, the group of palms called rattans, consisting of the genus *Calamus* and its allies. Their slender stems are dried and used for making walking sticks, baskets, and furniture.

**cane toad** toad of the genus *Bufo marinus,* family Bufonidae. Also known as the giant or marine toad, the cane toad is the largest in the world. It acquired its name after being introduced to Australia during the 1930s to eradicate the cane beetle, which had become a serious pest there. However, having few natural enemies, the cane toad itself has now become a pest in Australia.

**Canetti, Elias** (1905–1994) Bulgarian-born writer. He was exiled from Austria 1937 and settled in England 1939. His books, written in German, include *Die Blendung/Auto da Fé* (1935). He was concerned with crowd behaviour and the psychology of power, and wrote the anthropological study *Masse und Macht/Crowds and Power* (1960). Nobel Prize for Literature 1981.

**Canis Major** brilliant constellation of the southern hemisphere, represented (with Canis Minor) as one of the two dogs following at the heel of ◊Orion. Its main star, ◊Sirius, is the brightest star in the night sky.

**Canis Minor** small constellation along the celestial equator (see ◊celestial sphere), represented as the smaller of the two dogs of ◊Orion (the other dog being ◊Canis Major). Its brightest star is the first magnitude ◊Procyon.

**cannabis** dried leaves and female flowers (marijuana) and ◊resin (hashish) of certain varieties of ◊hemp, which are smoked or swallowed to produce a range of effects, including feelings of great happiness and altered perception. (*Cannabis sativa,* family Cannabaceae.)

**Cannes** resort in Alpes-Maritimes *département* of southern France, on the Mediterranean coast and 21 km/13 mi southwest of Nice; population (1990) 69,400, Grasse-Cannes-Antibes conurbation 335,000. Formerly a small fishing village and seaport, in 1834 Cannes attracted the patronage of the English Lord Brougham and other distinguished visitors and soon grew into a popular winter and summer holiday resort on the French ◊Riviera. The prestigious Cannes Film Festival is held here annually. The city has textile and aircraft industries, and a strong trade in olive oil, soap, fish, fruit, and flowers.

**canning** food preservation in hermetically sealed containers by the application of heat. Originated by Nicolas Appert in France 1809 with glass containers, it was developed by Peter Durand in England in 1810 with cans made of sheet steel thinly coated with tin to delay corrosion. Cans for beer and soft drinks are now generally made of aluminium.

**Canning, George** (1770–1827) British Tory politician, foreign secretary 1807–10 and 1822–27, and prime minister in 1827 in coalition with the Whigs. He was largely responsible, during the ◊Napoleonic Wars, for the seizure of the Danish fleet and British intervention in the Spanish peninsula.

**canoeing** sport of propelling a lightweight, shallow boat, pointed at both ends, by paddles or sails. Present-day canoes are made from fibreglass, but original boats were of wooden construction covered in bark or skin. Canoeing was popularized as a sport in the 19th century.

**canon law** rules and regulations of the Christian church, especially the Greek Orthodox, Roman Catholic, and Anglican churches. Its origin is sought in the declarations of Jesus and the apostles. In 1983 Pope John Paul II issued a new canon law code reducing offences carrying automatic excommunication, extending the grounds for annulment of marriage, removing the ban on marriage with non-Catholics, and banning trade-union and political activity by priests.

**Canopus** or *Alpha Carinae,* second-brightest star in the night sky (after Sirius), lying in the southern constellation Carina. It is a yellow-white supergiant about 120 light years from the Sun, and thousands of times more luminous.

**Canova, Antonio** Marquese d'Ischia (1757–1822) Italian Neo-Classical sculptor. He was based in Rome from 1781. He received commissions from popes, kings, and emperors for his highly finished marble portrait busts and groups of figures. He made several portraits of Napoleon.

**Cantabria** autonomous community of northern Spain; area 5,300 sq km/2,046 sq mi; population (1991) 527,300. From the coastline on the Bay of Biscay it rises to the Cantabrian Mountains. There is some mining here, as well as engineering and food industries, particularly dairy products. The capital is Santander.

**cantata** in music, an extended work for voices, from the Italian, meaning 'sung', as opposed to ◊sonata ('sounded') for instruments. A cantata can be sacred or secular, sometimes uses solo voices, and usually has orchestral accompaniment. The first printed collection of sacred cantata texts dates from 1670.

**Canterbury** (Old English *Cantwarabyrig* 'fortress of the men of Kent') historic cathedral city in Kent, southeast England, on the River Stour, 100 km/62 mi southeast of London; population (1991) 36,500. The city is the metropolis of the Anglican Communion and seat of the archbishop of Canterbury. It is a popular tourist destination. Paper, paper products, and electrical goods are manufactured.

**Canterbury, archbishop of** archbishop of the Church of England (Anglican), the primate (archbishop) of all England, and first peer of the realm, ranking next to royalty. He crowns the sovereign, has a seat in the House of Lords, and is a member of the Privy Council. He is appointed by the prime minister.

**cantilever** beam or structure that is fixed at one end only, though it may be supported at some point along its length; for example, a diving board. The cantilever principle, widely used in construction engineering, eliminates the need for a second main support at the free end of the beam, allowing for more elegant structures and reducing the amount of materials required. Many large-span bridges have been built on the cantilever principle.

**Canton** alternative spelling of ◊Guangzhou or Kwangchow, capital of Guangdong province in China.

**Canute** also known as Cnut the Great (*c.* 995–1035) king of England from 1016, Denmark from 1018, and Norway from 1028. Having invaded England in 1013 with his father, Sweyn, king of Denmark, he was acclaimed king on Sweyn's death in 1014 by his ◊Viking army. Canute defeated Edmund (II) Ironside at Assandun, Essex, in 1016, and became king of all England on Edmund's death. He succeeded his brother Harold as king of Denmark in 1018, compelled King Malcolm to pay homage by invading Scotland in about 1027, and conquered Norway in 1028. He was succeeded by his illegitimate son Harold I.

**capacitor** or *condenser,* device for storing electric charge, used in electronic circuits; it consists of two or more metal plates separated by an insulating layer called a dielectric.

**Cape Canaveral** promontory on the Atlantic coast of Florida, USA, 367 km/228 mi north of Miami, used as a rocket launch site by ◊NASA.

**Cape Cod** hook-shaped peninsula in southeastern Massachusetts, USA, separated from the rest of the state by the Cape Cod Canal; length 100 km/62 mi; width 1.6–32 km/1–20 mi. Its beaches and woods make it a popular tourist area. The islands of Martha's Vineyard and ◊Nantucket are just south of the cape.

**Capella** or *Alpha Aurigae,* brightest star in the constellation ◊Auriga and the sixth-brightest star in the night sky. It is a visual and spectroscopic binary that consists of a pair of yellow-giant stars 45 light years from the Sun, orbiting each other every 104 days.

**Cape Province** Afrikaans *Kaapprovinsie,* former province of the Republic of South Africa to 1994, now divided into Western, Eastern, and Northern Cape Provinces. It was named after the Cape of Good Hope. Dutch traders (the Dutch East India Company) established the first European settlement on the Cape in 1652, but it was taken by the British in 1795, after the French Revolutionary armies had occupied the Netherlands, and was sold to Britain for £6 million in 1814. The Cape achieved self-government in 1872. It was an original province of the Union of 1910.

**capercaillie** or *wood-grouse* or *cock of the wood,* (Gaelic *capull coille,* 'cock of the wood') large bird *Tetrao urogallus* of the ◊grouse type, family Tetraonidae, order Galliformes. Found in coniferous woodland in Europe and northern Asia, it is about the size of the turkey and resembles the blackcock in appearance and polygamous habit. The general colour of the male is blackish-grey above, black below, with a dark green chest, and rounded tail which is fanned out in courtship. The female is smaller, mottled, and has a reddish breast barred with black. The feathers on the legs and feet are longest in winter time, and the toes are naked. The capercaillie feeds on insects, worms, berries, and young pine-shoots. At nearly 1 m/3 ft long, the male is the biggest gamebird in Europe. The female is about 60 cm/2 ft long.

**Capet, Hugh** (938–996) King of France from 987, when he claimed the throne on the death of Louis V. He founded the *Capetian dynasty,* of which various branches continued to reign until the French Revolution, for example, Valois and ◊Bourbon.

**Cape Town** Afrikaans *Kaapstad,* port and oldest city (founded 1652) in South Africa, situated at the northern end of the Cape Peninsula, on Table Bay; population (1991) 854, 616 (urban area); (1991) 2,350,200 (peninsula). Industries include horticulture and trade in wool, wine, fruit, grain, and oil. Tourism is important. It is the legislative capital of the Republic of South Africa and capital of ◊Western Cape province.

**Cape Verde** Republic of
*national name Repúbica de Cabo Verde*
*area* 4,033 sq km/1,557 sq mi

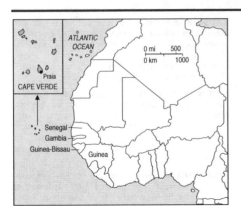

**capital** Praia
**major towns/cities** Mindelo
**major ports** Mindelo
**physical features** archipelago of ten volcanic islands 565 km/350 mi west of Senegal; the windward (Barlavento) group includes Santo Antão, São Vicente, Santa Luzia, São Nicolau, Sal, and Boa Vista; the leeward (Sotovento) group comprises Maio, São Tiago, Fogo, and Brava; all but Santa Luzia are inhabited
**head of state** Monteiro Mascarenhas from 1991
**head of government** Carlos Viega from 1991
**political system** emergent democracy
**political parties** African Party for the Independence of Cape Verde (PAICV), African nationalist; Movement for Democracy (MPD), moderate, centrist
**currency** Cape Verde escudo
**GNP per capita (PPP)** (US$) 2,950 (1998)
**exports** fish, shellfish and fish products, salt, bananas. Principal market: Portugal 45% (1997)
**population** 418,000 (1999 est)
**language** Portuguese (official), Creole
**religion** Roman Catholic 93%, Protestant (Nazarene Church)
**life expectancy** 66 (men); 71 (women) (1995–2000)
**Chronology**
**1462** Originally uninhabited; settled by Portuguese, who brought in slave labour from West Africa.
**later 19th century** There was a decline in prosperity as slave trade ended.
**1950s** A liberation movement developed on the islands and the Portuguese African mainland colony of Guinea-Bissau.
**1951** Cape Verde became an overseas territory of Portugal.
**1975** Independence was achieved and a national people's assembly elected, with Aristides of the PAICV as the first executive president; a policy of nonalignment followed.
**1981** The goal of union with Guinea-Bissau was abandoned; Cape Verde became a one-party state.
**1988** There was rising unrest and demand for political reforms.
**1991** In the first multiparty elections, the new MPD won a majority and Monteiro

Mascarenhas became president; market-centred economic reforms were introduced.

**capillarity** spontaneous movement of liquids up or down narrow tubes, or capillaries. The movement is due to unbalanced molecular attraction at the boundary between the liquid and the tube. If liquid molecules near the boundary are more strongly attracted to molecules in the material of the tube than to other nearby liquid molecules, the liquid will rise in the tube. If liquid molecules are less attracted to the material of the tube than to other liquid molecules, the liquid will fall.

**capillary** narrowest blood vessel in vertebrates, 0.008–0.02 mm in diameter, barely wider than a red blood cell. Capillaries are distributed as *beds,* complex networks connecting arteries and veins. Capillary walls are extremely thin, consisting of a single layer of cells, and so nutrients, dissolved gases, and waste products can easily pass through them. This makes the capillaries the main area of exchange between the fluid (◊lymph) bathing body tissues and the blood. They provide a large surface area in order to maximize ◊diffusion.

**capital** in architecture, a stone placed on the top of a column, pier, or pilaster, and usually wider on the upper surface than the diameter of the supporting shaft. A capital consists of three parts: the top member, called the *abacus,* a block that acts as the supporting surface to the superstructure; the middle portion, known as the bell or *echinus;* and the lower part, called the necking or *astragal.*

**capital** in economics, the stock of goods used in the production of other goods. *Financial capital* is accumulated or inherited wealth held in the form of assets, such as stocks and shares, property, and bank deposits.

**capital bond** in economics, an investment bond that is purchased by a single payment, set up for a fixed period, and offered for sale by a life insurance company. The emphasis is on capital growth of the lump sum invested rather than on income.

**capitalism** economic system in which the principal means of production, distribution, and exchange are in private (individual or corporate) hands and competitively operated for profit. A *mixed economy* combines the private enterprise of capitalism and a degree of state monopoly, as in nationalized industries and welfare services.

**capital punishment** punishment by death. Capital punishment is retained in 92 countries and territories (1990), including the USA (38 states), China, and Islamic countries. It was abolished in the UK in 1965 for all crimes except treason. Methods of execution include electrocution, lethal gas, hanging, shooting, lethal injection, garrotting, and decapitation.

**Capote, Truman** pen-name of Truman Streckfus Persons (1924–1984) US novelist, journalist, and playwright. After achieving early success as a writer of sparkling prose in the stories of *Other Voices, Other Rooms* (1948) and the novel *Breakfast at Tiffany's* (1958), Capote's career flagged until the sensational 'nonfiction novel' *In Cold Blood* (1965) made him a celebrity.

**Cappadocia** ancient region of Asia Minor, in eastern central Turkey. It was conquered by the Persians 584 BC but in the 3rd century BC became an independent kingdom. The region was annexed as a province of the Roman empire AD 17.

**Capricornus** zodiacal constellation in the southern hemisphere next to ◊Sagittarius. It is represented as a fish-tailed goat, and its brightest stars are third magnitude. The Sun passes through it late January to mid-February. In astrology, the dates for Capricornus (popularly known as Capricorn) are between about 22 December and 19 January(see ◊precession).

**capsicum** any of a group of pepper plants belonging to the nightshade family, native to Central and South America. The different species produce green to red fruits that vary in size. The small ones are used whole to give the hot flavour of chilli, or ground to produce cayenne or red pepper; the large pointed or squarish pods, known as sweet peppers or pimientos (green, red, or yellow peppers), are mild-flavoured and used as a vegetable. (Genus *Capsicum*, family Solanaceae.)

**capsule** in botany, a dry, usually many-seeded fruit formed from an ovary composed of two or more fused ◊carpels, which splits open to release the seeds. The same term is used for the spore-containing structure of mosses and liverworts; this is borne at the top of a long stalk or seta.

**capuchin** monkey of the genus *Cebus* found in Central and South America, so called because the hairs on the head resemble the cowl of a Capuchin monk. Capuchins live in small groups, feed on fruit and insects, and have a long tail that is semiprehensile and can give support when climbing through the trees.

**capybara** world's largest rodent *Hydrochoerus hydrochaeris*, up to 1.3 m/4 ft long and 50 kg/110 lb in weight. It is found in South America, and belongs to the guinea-pig family. The capybara inhabits marshes and dense vegetation around water. It has thin, yellowish hair, swims well, and can rest underwater with just eyes, ears, and nose above the surface.

**car** small, driver-guided, passenger-carrying motor vehicle; originally the automated version of the horse-drawn carriage, meant to convey people and their goods over streets and roads.

Over 50 million motor cars are produced each year worldwide. The number of cars in the

---

## CAR: CHRONOLOGY

**1769** Nicholas-Joseph Cugnot in France builds a steam tractor.
**1801** Richard Trevithick builds a steam coach.
**1860** Jean Etienne Lenoir builds a gas-fuelled internal-combustion engine.
**1865** The British government passes the Red Flag Act, requiring a person to precede a 'horseless carriage' with a red flag.
**1876** Nikolaus August Otto improves the gas engine, making it a practical power source.
**1885** Gottlieb Daimler develops a successful lightweight petrol engine and fits it to a bicycle to create the prototype of the present-day motorcycle; Karl Benz fits his lightweight petrol engine to a three-wheeled carriage to pioneer the motorcar.
**1886** Gottlieb Daimler fits his engine to a four-wheeled carriage to produce a four-wheeled motorcar.
**1891** René Panhard and Emile Levassor establish the present design of cars by putting the engine in front.
**1896** Frederick Lanchester introduces epicyclic gearing, which foreshadows automatic transmission.
**1899** C Jenatzy breaks the 100-kph barrier in an electric car *La Jamais Contente* at Achères, France, reaching 105.85 kph/65.60 mph.
**1901** The first Mercedes takes to the roads; it is the direct ancestor of the present car. Ransome Olds in the USA introduces mass production on an assembly line.
**1904** Louis Rigolly breaks the 100 mph barrier, reaching 166.61 kph/103.55 mph in a Gobron-Brillé at Nice, France.
**1906** Rolls-Royce introduces the Silver Ghost, which establishes the company's reputation for superlatively engineered cars.

**1908** Henry Ford also uses assembly-line production to manufacture his celebrated Model T, nicknamed the Tin Lizzie because it uses lightweight steel sheet for the body.
**1911** Cadillac introduces the electric starter and dynamo lighting.
**1913** Ford introduces the moving conveyor belt to the assembly line, further accelerating production of the Model T.
**1920** Duesenberg begins fitting four-wheel hydraulic brakes.
**1922** The Lancia Lambda features unitary (all-in-one) construction and independent front suspension.
**1927** Henry Segrave breaks the 200 mph barrier in a Sunbeam, reaching 327.89 kph/203.79 mph.
**1928** Cadillac introduces the synchromesh gearbox, greatly facilitating gear changing.
**1934** Citroën pioneers front-wheel drive in their 7CV model.
**1936** Fiat introduces their baby car, the Topolino, 500 cc.
**1938** Germany produces its 'people's car', the Volkswagen Beetle.
**1948** Jaguar launches the XK120 sports car; Michelin introduced the radial-ply tyre; Goodrich produces the tubeless tyre.
**1950** Dunlop announces the disc brake.
**1951** Buick and Chrysler introduce power steering.
**1952** Rover's gas-turbine car sets a speed record of 243 kph/152 mph.
**1954** Carl Bosch introduces fuel injection for cars.
**1955** Citroën produces the advanced DS-19 'shark-front' car with hydropneumatic suspension.

world in 1997 exceeded 500 million. Most are four-wheeled and have water-cooled, piston-type internal-combustion engines fuelled by petrol or diesel. Variations have existed for decades that use ingenious and often nonpolluting power plants, but the motor industry long ago settled on this general formula for the consumer market. Experimental and sports models are streamlined, energy-efficient, and hand-built.

**carat** (Arabic *quirrat* 'seed') unit for measuring the mass of precious stones; it is equal to 0.2 g/ 0.00705 oz, and is part of the troy system of weights. It is also the unit of purity in gold (US 'karat'). Pure gold is 24-carat; 22-carat (the purest used in jewellery) is 22 parts gold and two parts alloy (to give greater strength); 18-carat is 75% gold.

**Caravaggio, Michelangelo Merisi da** (1573–1610) Italian early Baroque painter. He was active in Rome 1592–1606, then in Naples, and finally in Malta. He created a forceful style, using contrasts of light and shade, dramatic foreshortening, and a meticulous attention to detail. His life was as dramatic as his art (he had to leave Rome after killing a man in a brawl).

**caraway** herb belonging to the carrot family. Native to northern temperate regions of Europe and Asia, it is grown for its spicy, aromatic seeds, which are used in cookery, medicine, and perfumery. (*Carum carvi*, family Umbelliferae.)

**carbide** compound of carbon and one other chemical element, usually a metal, silicon, or boron.

**carbohydrate** chemical compound composed of carbon, hydrogen, and oxygen, with the basic formula $C_m(H_2O)_n$, and related compounds with the same basic structure but modified ◊functional groups. As sugar and starch, carbohydrates are an important part of a balanced human diet, providing energy for life processes including growth and movement. Excess carbohydrate intake can be converted into fat and stored in the body.

**carbon** (Latin *carbo*, *carbonaris* 'coal') non-metallic element, symbol C, atomic number 6, relative atomic mass 12.011. It occurs on its own as diamond, graphite, and as fullerenes (the allotropes), as compounds in carbonaceous rocks such as chalk and limestone, as carbon dioxide in the atmosphere, as hydrocarbons in petroleum, coal, and natural gas, and as a constituent of all organic substances.

---

## CAR: CHRONOLOGY (continued)

**1957** Felix Wankel builds his first rotary petrol engine.

**1959** BMC (now Rover) introduces the Issigonis-designed Mini, with front-wheel drive, transverse engine, and independent rubber suspension.

**1965** US car manufacturers are forced to add safety features after the publication of Ralph Nader's *Unsafe at Any Speed*.

**1966** California introduces legislation regarding air pollution by cars.

**1970** American Gary Gabelich drives a rocket-powered, *Blue Flame*, to a new record speed of 1,001.473 kph/622.287 mph.

**1972** Dunlop introduces safety tyres, which seal themselves after a puncture.

**1979** American Sam Barrett exceeds the speed of sound in the rocket-engined *Budweiser Rocket,* reaching 1,190.377 kph/ 739.666 mph, a speed not officially recognized as a record because of timing difficulties.

**1980** The first mass-produced car with four-wheel drive, the Audi Quattro, is introduced; Japanese car production overtakes that of the USA.

**1981** BMW introduces the on-board computer, which monitors engine performance and indicates to the driver when a service is required.

**1983** British driver Richard Noble sets an official speed record in the jet-engined *Thrust 2* of 1,019.4 kph/633.5 mph; Austin Rover introduces the Maestro, the first car with a 'talking dashboard' that alerts the driver to problems.

**1987** The solar-powered *Sunraycer* travels 3,000 km/1,864 mi from Darwin to Adelaide,

Australia, in six days. Toyota Corona production tops 6 million in 29 years.

**1988** California introduces stringent controls on car emissions, aiming for widespread use of zero emission vehicles by 1998.

**1989** The first mass-produced car with four-wheel steering, the Mitsubishi Galant, is launched.

**1990** Fiat of Italy and Peugeot of France launch electric passenger cars on the market.

**1991** Satellite-based car navigation systems are launched in Japan. European Parliament votes to adopt stringent control of car emissions.

**1992** Mazda and NEC of Japan develop an image-processing system for cars, which views the road ahead through a video camera, identifies road signs and markings, and helps the driver to avoid obstacles.

**1993** A Japanese electric car, the *IZA*, built by the Tokyo Electric Power Company, reaches a speed of 176 kph/109 mph (10 kph/6 mph faster than the previous record for an electric car).

**1995** Greenpeace designs its own environmentally friendly car to show the industry how 'it could be done'. It produces a modified Renault Twingo with 30% less wind resistance, capable of doing 67–78 mi to the gallon (100 km per 3–3.5 litres).

**1996** Daimler–Benz unveils the first fuel-cell-powered car. It is virtually pollution-free.

**1997** RAF fighter pilot Andy Green breaks the sound barrier in *Thrust SCC,* a car with two Rolls-Royce Spey engines (the same kind used in RAF Phantom jets), setting a speed of 1,149.3 kph/714.1 mph.

**carbonate** ($CO_3^{2-}$), ion formed when carbon dioxide dissolves in water; any salt formed by this ion and another chemical element, usually a metal.

**carbon cycle** sequence by which ◊carbon circulates and is recycled through the natural world. Carbon dioxide is released into the atmosphere by living things as a result of ◊respiration. The $CO_2$ is taken up and converted into carbohydrates during ◊photosynthesis by plants and by organisms such as diatoms and dinoflagellates in the oceanic ◊plankton; the oxygen component is released back into the atmosphere. The carbon they accumulate is later released back into circulation in various ways. The simplest occurs when an animal eats a plant and carbon is transferred from, say, a leaf cell to the animal body. Carbon is also released through the ◊decomposition of decaying plant matter, and the burning of fossil fuels such as ◊coal (fossilized plants). The oceans absorb 25–40% of all carbon dioxide released into the atmosphere.

**carbon dating** alternative name for ◊radiocarbon dating.

**carbon dioxide** ($CO_2$), colourless, odourless gas, slightly soluble in water and denser than air.

It is formed by the complete oxidation of carbon.

**carbon fibre** fine, black, silky filament of pure carbon produced by heat treatment from a special grade of Courtelle acrylic fibre and used for reinforcing plastics. The resulting composite is very stiff and, weight for weight, has four times the strength of high-tensile steel. It is used in the aerospace industry, cars, and electrical and sports equipment.

**Carboniferous** period of geological time 362.5–290 million years ago, the fifth period of the Palaeozoic era. In the USA it is divided into two periods: the Mississippian (lower) and the Pennsylvanian (upper).

Typical of the lower-Carboniferous rocks are shallow-water ◊limestones, while upper-Carboniferous rocks have ◊delta deposits with ◊coal (hence the name). Amphibians were abundant, and reptiles evolved during this period.

**carbon monoxide** (CO), colourless, odourless gas formed when carbon is oxidized in a limited supply of air. It is a poisonous constituent of car exhaust fumes, forming a stable compound with haemoglobin in the blood, thus preventing the haemoglobin from transporting oxygen to the body tissues.

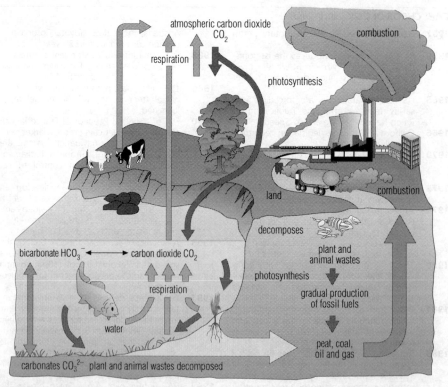

**carbon cycle** *The carbon cycle is necessary for the continuation of life. Since there is only a limited amount of carbon in the Earth and its atmosphere, carbon must be continuously recycled if life is to continue. Other chemicals necessary for life – nitrogen, sulphur, and phosphorus, for example – also circulate in natural cycles.*

**carburation** any process involving chemical combination with carbon, especially the mixing or charging of a gas, such as air, with volatile compounds of carbon (petrol, kerosene, or fuel oil) in order to increase potential heat energy during combustion. Carburation applies to combustion in the cylinders of reciprocating petrol engines of the types used in aircraft, road vehicles, or marine vessels. The device by which the liquid fuel is atomized and mixed with air is called a *carburettor.*

**carcinogen** any agent that increases the chance of a cell becoming cancerous (see ◊cancer), including various chemical compounds, some viruses, X-rays, and other forms of ionizing radiation. The term is often used more narrowly to mean chemical carcinogens only.

**carcinoma** malignant ◊tumour arising from the skin, the glandular tissues, or the mucous membranes that line the gut and lungs.

**Cardiff** unitary authority in south Wales, created in 1996 from part of the former county of South Glamorgan; administrative headquarters is ◊Cardiff
*area* 139 sq km/54 sq mi
*population* (1996) 306,500.

**Cardiff** Welsh *Caerdydd,* seaport, capital of Wales (from 1955), and administrative centre of ◊Cardiff unitary authority, situated at the mouth of the Taff, Rhymney, and Ely rivers; population (1994 est) 290,000. Industries include car components, flour milling, ship repairs, electrical goods, paper, and cigars; there are also high-tech industries.

**Cardin, Pierre** (1922– ) French pioneering fashion designer. He was the first to launch menswear (1960) and designer ready-to-wear collections (1963) and has given his name to a perfume. Cardin has franchised his name for labelling many different accessories and household products.

**cardinal** in the Roman Catholic church, the highest rank next to the pope. Cardinals act as an advisory body to the pope and elect him. Their red hat is the badge of office. The number of cardinals has varied; there were 151 in 1989.

**cardinal number** in mathematics, one of the series of numbers 0, 1, 2, 3, 4, ... . Cardinal numbers relate to quantity, whereas ordinal numbers (first, second, third, fourth, ... .) relate to order.

**cardioid** heart-shaped curve traced out by a point on the circumference of a circle, resulting from the circle rolling around the edge of another circle of the same diameter.

**Carey, George Leonard** (1935– ) 103rd archbishop of Canterbury from 1991. A product of a liberal evangelical background, he was appointed bishop of Bath and Wells in 1987.

**cargo cult** one of a number of religious movements, chiefly in Melanesia, that first appeared in the late 19th century but were particularly prevalent during and after World War II with the apparently miraculous dropping of supplies from aeroplanes. Adherents believe in the imminent arrival of European material goods, or 'cargo', by supernatural agents such as tribal gods or ancestral spirits. In anticipation, landing strips, wharves, warehouses, and other elaborate preparations for receiving the cargo are often made, and normal activities such as gardening cease, stocks of food are destroyed, and current customs abandoned. These preparations herald the end of the old order and the arrival of a new age of freedom and plenty.

**Caribbean Sea** western part of the Atlantic Ocean between Cuba to the north and the northern coasts of South America to the south. Central America is to the west and to the east are the West Indies. The sea is about 2,740 km/1,700 mi long and 650–1,500 km/400–900 mi wide; area 2,640,000 sq km/1,019,304 sq mi. It is linked with the Gulf of Mexico via the Yucatan Strait. It is from here that the ◊Gulf Stream turns towards Europe.

**caribou** the ◊reindeer of North America.

**caricature** in the arts or literature, an exaggerated portrayal of an individual or type, aiming to ridicule or otherwise expose the subject. Classical and medieval examples of pictorial caricatures survive. Artists of the 18th, 19th, and 20th centuries have often used caricature as a way of satirizing society and politics. Notable exponents include the French artist Honoré Daumier and the German George ◊Grosz. In literature, caricatures have appeared since the comedies of Aristophanes in ancient Greece. Shakespeare and Dickens were adept at creating caricatures.

**caries** decay and disintegration, usually of the substance of teeth (cavity) or bone, caused by acids produced when the bacteria that live in the mouth break down sugars in the food. Fluoride, a low sugar intake, and regular brushing are all protective. Caries form mainly in the 45 minutes following consumption of sugary food.

**Carinthia** German *Kärnten,* federal state of alpine southeast Austria, bordering Italy and Slovenia in the south; area 9,500 sq km/3,667 sq mi; population (1994) 559,700. The capital is Klagenfurt. Mining, stock raising and forestry are important. It was an independent duchy from 976 and a possession of the Habsburg dynasty from 1276–1918.

**Carlisle** city and administrative headquarters of ◊Cumbria, northwest England, on the River Eden at the western end of Hadrian's Wall, 14 km/9 mi south of the Scottish border; population (1991) 72,400. It is a leading railway and service centre. Industries include engineering and brewing (Scottish and Newcastle), and the manufacture of textiles, agricultural machinery, metal goods, confectionery, and processed foods. Carlisle was the Roman settlement of *Luguvalium.* There is a Norman cathedral and a restored castle dating from 1092.

**Carlow** second-smallest county in the Republic of Ireland, in the province of Leinster; county town Carlow; area 900 sq km/347 sq mi; population (1991) 40,900. The land is mostly flat except for the Blackstairs mountains in the south (rising to 796 m/2,612 ft in Mount Leinster). The land in the west is fertile and well suited to dairy farming. Products include barley, wheat, and sugar beet.

**Carlyle, Thomas** (1795–1881) Scottish essayist and social historian. His works include the partly autobiographical *Sartor Resartus/The Tailor Retailored* (1833–34), reflecting his loss of Christian belief; *The French Revolution* (1837); and the long essay 'Chartism' (1839), attacking the doctrine of *laissez faire*. His prose style was idiosyncratic, encompassing grand, thunderous rhetoric and deliberate obscurity.

**Carmarthenshire** Welsh *Sir Gaerfyrddin*, unitary authority in south Wales; a former county, it was part of Dyfed between 1975 and 1996
*area* 2,390 sq km/923 sq mi
*towns* Carmarthen (administrative headquarters), Llanelli
*physical* rivers Tywi, Taf, Teifi; Black Mountain range in the east, southern spur of the Cambrian Mountains in the north, including Mynydd Mallaen (459 m/1,506 ft); along the coast are extensive sands and marshes. Carmarthenshire is dominated by the Vale of Tywi, but there are numerous grassy hills, mostly under 300 m/1,000 ft; the valleys are fertile and the hillsides afford good pasturage
*features* Brecon Beacons National Park on the eastern border; Museum of the Woollen Industry at DreFach-Felindre; home of Dylan ◊Thomas in the village of Laugharne, 6 km/3.7 mi southeast of St Clears
*agriculture* dairy farming, stock-raising
*population* (1996) 68,900.

**carnation** any of a large number of double-flowered cultivated varieties of a plant belonging to the ◊pink family. The flowers smell like cloves; they are divided into flake, bizarre, and picotees, according to whether the petals have one or more colours on their white base, have the colour appearing in strips, or have a coloured border to the petals. (*Dianthus caryophyllus,* family Carophyllaceae.)

**Carnegie, Andrew** (1835–1919) US industrialist and philanthropist, born in Scotland, who developed the Pittsburgh iron and steel industries, making the USA the world's leading producer. He endowed public libraries, education, and various research trusts.

**carnivore** in zoology, mammal of the order Carnivora. Although its name describes the flesh-eating ancestry of the order, it includes pandas, which are herbivorous, and civet cats, which eat fruit.

**Carnot, Lazare Nicolas Marguerite** (1753–1823) French general and politician. A member of the National Convention in the French Revolution, he organized the armies of the republic. He was war minister 1800–01 and minister of the interior 1815 under Napoleon. His work on fortification, *De la Défense de places fortes* (1810), became a military textbook. Minister of the interior during the hundred days, he was proscribed at the restoration of the monarchy and retired to Germany.

**Carnot cycle** series of changes in the physical condition of a gas in a reversible heat engine, necessarily in the following order: (1) isothermal expansion (without change of temperature), (2) adiabatic expansion (without change of heat content), (3) isothermal compression, and (4) adiabatic compression.

**carob** small Mediterranean tree belonging to the ◊legume family. Its pods, 20 cm/8 in long, are used as an animal feed; they are also the source of a chocolate substitute. (*Ceratonia siliqua,* family Leguminosae.)

**Carolina** either of two separate states of the USA; see ◊North Carolina and ◊South Carolina.

**Caroline Islands** scattered archipelago in Micronesia, Pacific Ocean, consisting of over 500 coral islets; area 1,200 sq km/463 sq mi. The chief islands are Ponape, Kusai, and Truk in the eastern group, and Yap and Palau in the western group.

**Caroline of Brunswick** (1768–1821) Queen consort of George IV of Great Britain. King George attempted to divorce her, unsuccessfully, on his accession to the throne in 1820.

**carp** fish *Cyprinus carpio* found all over the world. It commonly grows to 50 cm/1.8 ft and 3 kg/7 lb, but may be even larger. It lives in lakes, ponds, and slow rivers. The wild form is drab, but cultivated forms may be golden, or may have few large scales (mirror carp) or be scaleless (leather carp). *Koi* carp are highly prized and can grow up to 1 m/3 ft long with a distinctive pink, red, white, or black colouring.

**Carpathian Mountains** central European mountain system, forming a semicircle through Slovakia–Poland–Ukraine–Moldova–Romania, 1,450 km/900 mi long. The central *Tatra Mountains* on the Slovak–Polish frontier include the highest peak, Gerlachovka, 2,663 m/8,737 ft.

**carpel** female reproductive unit in flowering plants (◊angiosperms). It usually comprises an ◊ovary containing one or more ovules, the stalk or style, and a ◊stigma at its top which receives the pollen. A flower may have one or more carpels, and they may be separate or fused together. Collectively the carpels of a flower are known as the ◊gynoecium.

**Carreras, José Maria** (1947–  ) Spanish operatic tenor. His comprehensive repertoire includes Handel's Samson and his recordings include *West Side Story* (1984) under Leonard Bernstein. His vocal presence, charmingly insinuating rather than forceful, is favoured for Italian and French romantic roles.

**carrier** in medicine, anyone who harbours an infectious organism without ill effects but can pass the infection to others. The term is also applied to those who carry a recessive gene for a disease or defect without manifesting the condition.

**Carroll, Lewis** pen-name of Charles Lutwidge Dodgson (1832–1898) English author of the children's classics *Alice's Adventures in Wonderland* (1865) and its sequel *Through the*

*Looking-Glass, and What Alice Found There* (1872). Among later works was the mock-heroic narrative poem *The Hunting of the Snark* (1876). He was a lecturer in mathematics at Oxford University from 1855–81 and also published mathematical works.

**carrot** hardy European biennial plant with feathery leaves and an orange tapering root that is eaten as a vegetable. It has been cultivated since the 16th century. The root has a high sugar content and also contains carotene, which is converted into vitamin A by the human liver. (*Daucus carota*, family Umbelliferae.)

**Cartagena** or *Cartagena de los Indes*, historic port, industrial centre, and capital of Bolívar department, on the Caribbean coast of northwest Colombia; population (1994) 726,000. There are petrochemical, textile, and pharmaceutical industries; oil and coffee are exported. The city is also a fashionable tourist resort, with beaches, lakes, and inland lagoons. There is a 16th-century cathedral, and several 16–17th-century churches, and a state university, founded in 1827. The fortress 'Castillo de San Felipe de Barajas' was constructed over a period of 150 years, commencing in 1639.

**cartel** (German *Kartell* 'a group') agreement among national or international firms to fix prices for their products. A cartel may restrict supply (output) to raise prices in order to increase member profits. It therefore represents a form of oligopoly. ◊OPEC, for example, is an oil cartel.

**Carter, Jimmy** James Earl (1924– ) 39th president of the USA 1977–81, a Democrat. Features of his presidency were the return of the Panama Canal Zone to Panama, the introduction of an amnesty programme for deserters and draft dodgers of the Vietnam War, and the Camp David Agreements for peace in the Middle East. He was defeated by Ronald Reagan 1980. During the 1990s he emerged as a mediator and peace negotiator, securing President Aristide's safe return to Haiti October 1994. In August 1999 he was awarded the Presidential Medal of Freedom.

**Cartesian coordinates** in ◊coordinate geometry, components used to define the position of a point by its perpendicular distance from a set of two or more axes, or reference lines. For a two-dimensional area defined by two axes at right angles (a horizontal $x$-axis and a vertical $y$-axis), the coordinates of a point are given by its perpendicular distances from the $y$-axis and $x$-axis, written in the form $(x, y)$. For example, a point P that lies three units from the $y$-axis and four units from the $x$-axis has Cartesian coordinates (3,4) (see ◊abscissa).

**Carthage** ancient Phoenician port in North Africa founded by colonists from Tyre in the late 9th century BC; it lay 16 km/10 mi north of Tunis, Tunisia. A leading trading centre, it was in conflict with Greece from the 6th century BC, and then with Rome, and was destroyed by Roman forces 146 BC at the end of the ◊*Punic Wars*. About 45 BC, Roman colonists settled in Carthage, and it became the wealthy capital of

the province of Africa. After its capture by the Vandals AD 439 it was little more than a pirate stronghold. From 533 it formed part of the Byzantine Empire until its final destruction by Arabs 698, during their conquest in the name of Islam.

**Cartier, Jacques** (1491–1557) French navigator who, while seeking a northwest passage to China and Japan in 1535, was the first European to sail up the St Lawrence River, Canada. On this expedition, he named the site of Montréal.

**Cartier-Bresson, Henri** (1908– ) French photographer. He is considered one of the greatest photographic artists. His documentary work was shot in black and white, using a small-format Leica camera. His work is remarkable for its tightly structured composition and his ability to capture the decisive moment. He was a founder member of the Magnum photographic agency.

**cartilage** flexible bluish-white ◊connective tissue made up of the protein collagen. In cartilaginous fish it forms the skeleton; in other vertebrates it forms the greater part of the embryonic skeleton, and is replaced by ◊bone in the course of development, except in areas of wear such as bone endings, and the discs between the backbones. It also forms structural tissue in the larynx, nose, and external ear of mammals.

**cartilaginous fish** fish in which the skeleton is made of cartilage. Sharks, rays, and skates are cartilaginous. Their scales are placoid (isolated structures made of dentine resembling simple teeth) that are present all over the body surface. The scales do not continue to grow once fully formed, but are replaced by new scales as they wear out. The notochord (primitive skeletal rod) is reduced and replaced to varying degrees by cartilage.

**cartography** art and practice of drawing ◊maps.

**cartoon** humorous or satirical drawing or ◊caricature; a strip cartoon or comic strip; traditionally, the base design for a large fresco, mosaic, or tapestry, transferred to a wall or canvas by tracing or pricking out the design on the cartoon and then dabbing with powdered charcoal to create a faint reproduction. Surviving examples include Leonardo da Vinci's *Virgin and St Anne* (National Gallery, London).

**Cartwright, Edmund** (1743–1823) English inventor. He patented the power loom (1785), built a weaving mill (1787), and patented a wool-combing machine (1789).

**Caruso, Enrico** (1873–1921) Italian operatic tenor. His voice was dark, with full-bodied tone and remarkable dynamic range. In 1902 he starred, with Australian soprano Nellie Melba, in Puccini's *La Bohème/Bohemian Life*. He was among the first opera singers to achieve lasting fame through gramophone recordings.

**Casablanca** Arabic *Dar el-Beida*, port, commercial, and industrial centre on the Atlantic coast of Morocco; population (1993) 2,943,000. Casablanca is one of the major ports of Africa, and the industrial centre of Morocco. It trades in fish, phosphates, and manganese. The Great Hassan II Mosque, completed in 1989, is the world's largest; it is built on a platform (40,000 sq m/430,000 sq ft) jutting out over the Atlantic, with walls 60 m/200 ft high, topped by a hydraulic sliding roof, and a minaret 175 m/574 ft high.

**Casals, Pablo (Paul)** (1876–1973) Catalan cellist, composer, and conductor. He was largely self-taught. As a cellist, he was celebrated for his interpretations of Johann Sebastian Bach's unaccompanied suites. He wrote instrumental and choral works, including the Christmas oratorio *The Manger.*

He was an outspoken critic of fascism who openly defied Franco, and a tireless crusader for peace.

**Casanova de Seingalt, Giovanni Giacomo** (1725–1798) Italian adventurer, spy, violinist, librarian, and, according to his *Memoires* (published 1826–38, although the complete text did not appear until 1960–61), one of the world's great lovers. From 1774 he was a spy in the Venetian police service. In 1782 a libel got him into trouble, and after more wanderings he was in 1785 appointed librarian to Count Waldstein at his castle of Dûx in Bohemia. It was here that Casanova wrote his *Memoires.*

**casein** main protein of milk, from which it can be separated by the action of acid, the enzyme rennin, or bacteria (souring); it is also the main protein in cheese. Casein is used as a protein supplement in the treatment of malnutrition. It is used commercially in cosmetics, glues, and as a sizing for coating paper.

**cash crop** crop grown solely for sale rather than for the farmer's own use, for example, coffee, cotton, or sugar beet. Many Third World countries grow cash crops to meet their debt repayments rather than grow food for their own people. The price for these crops depends on financial interests, such as those of the multinational companies and the International Monetary Fund.

**cashew** tropical American tree. Widely cultivated in India and Africa, it produces poisonous kidney-shaped nuts that become edible after being roasted. (*Anacardium occidentale,* family Anacardiaceae.)

**cash flow** input of cash required to cover all expenses of a business, whether revenue or capital. Alternatively, the actual or prospective balance between the various outgoing and incoming movements which are designated in total. Cash flow is positive if receipts are greater than payments; negative if payments are greater than receipts.

**Caspian Sea** world's largest inland sea, on the border between Europe and Asia east of the Black Sea, divided between Iran, Azerbaijan, Russia, Kazakhstan, and Turkmenistan. It extends north–south for 1,200 km/745 mi, and its average width is 300 km/186 mi; area about 400,000 sq km/155,000 sq mi, with a maximum depth of 1,000 m/3,250 ft. An underwater ridge divides it into two halves, of which the shallow northern half is almost salt-free. There are no tides, but violent storms make navigation hazardous. The chief ports are Astrakhan (Russia), Baku (Ajerbaijan), and Bandar Shah (Iran). The River Volga supplies 80% of freshwater inflow; the Ural, Emba, Terek, Kura, and Atrek rivers also flow into the Caspian Sea. Prolonged drought, drainage in the north, and regulation of the Volga and Kura rivers reduced the area from 430,000 sq km/166,000 sq mi in 1930 to 382,000 sq km/147,000 sq mi in 1957, and left the sea approximately 28 m/90 ft below sea level. In June 1991 opening of sluices in the dams caused the water level to rise dramatically, threatening towns and industrial areas.

**Cassandra** in Greek mythology, Trojan daughter of Priam and Hecuba. Loved by the god ◊Apollo, she was promised the gift of prophecy in return for her favours, but rejected his advances after receiving her powers. Her thwarted lover cursed her prophecies with disbelief, including that of the fall of Troy.

**cassava** or *manioc,* plant belonging to the spurge family. Native to South America, it is now widely grown throughout the tropics for its starch-containing roots, from which tapioca and bread are made. (*Manihot utilissima,* family Euphorbiaceae.)

**Cassiopeia** prominent constellation of the northern hemisphere, named after the mother of Andromeda. It has a distinctive W-shape, and contains one of the most powerful radio sources in the sky, Cassiopeia A. This is the remains of a ◊supernova (star explosion) that occurred *c.* AD 1702, too far away to be seen from Earth.

**Cassius** (*c.* 85 BC–42 BC) Gaius Cassius Longinus, Roman general and politician, one of Julius ◊Caesar's assassins. He fought with Marcus Licinius ◊Crassus (the Elder) against the Parthians in 53 BC and distinguished himself after Carrhae by defending the province of Syria. He sided with Pompey against Julius Caesar on the outbreak of the civil war in 49, but was pardoned after the battle of Pharsalus in 48. Nevertheless, he became a leader in the conspiracy against Caesar which resulted in his murder in 44.

**cassowary** large flightless bird, genus *Casuarius,* of the family Casuariidae, order Casuariiformes, found in New Guinea and northern Australia, usually in forests. Related to the emu, the cassowary has a bare head with a horny casque, or helmet, on top, and brightly-coloured skin on the neck. Its loose plumage is black and its wings tiny, but it can run and leap well and defends itself by kicking. Cassowaries stand up to 1.5 m/5 ft tall. They live in pairs and the male usually incubates the eggs, about six in number, which the female lays in a nest of leaves and grass.

**caste** (Portuguese *casta* 'race') a system of stratifying a society into ranked groups defined by marriage, descent, and occupation. Most common in South Asia, caste systems are also found in other societies such as in Mali and

Rwanda, and in the past, in Japan, in South Africa under apartheid, and among the Natchez.

The system in Hindu society dates from ancient times and there are over 3,000 castes, known as 'jatis', which are loosely ranked into four classes known as 'varnas': *Brahmans* (priests), *Kshatriyas* (nobles and warriors), *Vaisyas* (traders and farmers), and *Sudras* (servants); plus a fifth group, *Harijan* (untouchables).

**Castile** kingdom founded in the 10th century, occupying the central plateau of Spain. Its union with ◊Aragón 1479, based on the marriage of Ferdinand and Isabella, effected the foundation of the Spanish state, which at the time was occupied and ruled by the ◊Moors. Castile comprised the two great basins separated by the Sierra de Gredos and the Sierra de Guadarrama, known traditionally as Old and New Castile. The area now forms the regions of ◊Castilla–León and ◊Castilla–La Mancha.

**Castilian language** member of the Romance branch of the Indo-European language family, originating in northwestern Spain, in the provinces of Old and New Castile. It is the basis of present-day standard Spanish (see ◊Spanish language) and is often seen as the same language, the terms *castellano* and *español* being used interchangeably in both Spain and the Spanish-speaking countries of the Americas.

**Castilla–La Mancha** autonomous community of central Spain; area 79,200 sq km/30,571 sq mi; population (1991) 1,658,400. It includes the provinces of Albacete, Ciudad Real, Cuenca, Guadalajara, and Toledo. Irrigated land produces mainly cereals and vines, especially in the Valdepeñas region, and merino sheep are raised. The capital is ◊Toledo.

**Castilla–León** autonomous community of central Spain; area 94,100 sq km/36,323 sq mi; population (1991) 2,545,900. It includes the provinces of Avila, Burgos, León, Palencia, Salamanca, Segovia, Soria, Valladolid, and Zamora. Irrigated land produces wheat and rye; cattle, sheep, and fighting bulls are bred in the uplands. There are important food industries in Burgos, Palencia, and Segovia provinces. The capital is ◊Valladolid, which is the main manufacturing centre, particularly for engineering and the production of motor vehicles.

**cast iron** cheap but invaluable constructional material, most commonly used for car engine blocks. Cast iron is partly refined pig (crude) ◊iron, which is very fluid when molten and highly suitable for shaping by casting; it contains too many impurities (for example, carbon) to be readily shaped in any other way. Solid cast iron is heavy and can absorb great shock but is very brittle.

**castle** fortified building or group of buildings, characteristic of medieval Europe. The castle underwent many changes, its size, design, and construction being largely determined by changes in siege tactics and the development of artillery. Outstanding examples are the 12th-century Krak des Chevaliers, Syria (built by crusaders); 13th-century Caernarfon Castle, Wales; and 15th-century Manzanares el Real, Spain.

**Castlereagh, Robert Stewart** Viscount Castlereagh (1769–1822) British Tory politician. As chief secretary for Ireland 1797–1801, he suppressed the rebellion of 1798 and helped the younger Pitt secure the union of England, Scotland, and Ireland in 1801. As foreign secretary 1812–22, he coordinated European opposition to Napoleon and represented Britain at the Congress of Vienna 1814–15.

**castor-oil plant** tall tropical and subtropical shrub belonging to the spurge family. The seeds, called 'castor beans' in North America, yield the purgative castor oil (which cleans out the bowels) and also ricin, one of the most powerful poisons known. Ricin can be used to destroy cancer cells, leaving normal cells untouched. (*Ricinus communis*, family Euphorbiaceae.)

**castration** removal of the sex glands (either ovaries or testes). Male domestic animals may be castrated to prevent reproduction, to make them larger or more docile, or to eradicate disease.

**Castries** port and capital of St Lucia, on the northwest coast of the island in the Caribbean; population (1992) 53,900. It produces textiles, chemicals, tobacco, and wood and rubber products.

**Castro (Ruz), Fidel** (1927– ) Cuban communist politician, prime minister 1959–76, and president from 1976. He led two unsuccessful coups against the right-wing regime of Fulgencio ◊Batista, and led the revolution that overthrew the dictator 1959. He raised the standard of living for most Cubans but dealt harshly with dissenters. From 1990, deprived of the support of the USSR and experiencing the long-term effects of a US trade embargo, Castro faced increasing pressure for reform; in September 1995 he moved towards greater economic flexibility by permitting foreign ownership in major areas of commerce and industry. In January 1996 the *rapprochement* between Cuba and the USA appeared to have progressed after a visit by Democratic members of the House of Representatives, although the US embargo was not lifted. In 1998 he invited the Pope to make an unprecedented visit to Cuba. In February 1998 Castro was elected president.

**cat** small, domesticated, carnivorous mammal *Felis catus*, often kept as a pet or for catching small pests such as rodents. Found in many colour variants, it may have short, long, or no hair, but the general shape and size is constant. Cats have short muzzles, strong limbs, and flexible spines which enable them to jump and climb. All walk on the pads of their toes (*digitigrade*) and have retractile claws, so are able to stalk their prey silently. They have large eyes and an acute sense of hearing. The canine teeth are long and well-developed, as are the shearing teeth in the side of the mouth.

**catabolism** in biology, the destructive part of ◊metabolism where living tissue is changed into energy and waste products.

It is the opposite of anabolism. It occurs continuously in the body, but is accelerated during many disease processes, such as fever, and in starvation.

**Catalan language** member of the Romance branch of the Indo-European language family, an Iberian language closely related to Provençal in France.

It is spoken in Cataluña in northeastern Spain, the Balearic Islands, Andorra, and a corner of southwestern France.

**Catalonia** alternative spelling for ◊Cataluña.

**Cataluña** or *Catalonia* (Catalan *Catalunya*), autonomous community of northeast Spain; area 31,900 sq km/12,313 sq mi; population (1991) 6,059,500. It includes the provinces of Barcelona, Girona (formerly Gerona), Lleida (formerly Lérida), and Tarragona. Olives, vines, cereals, and nuts are grown, and some livestock is raised. Cataluña is the main industrial region of Spain. Originally based on the textile industry, the region has diversified into engineering, chemicals, paper, publishing, and many service industries; hydroelectric power is also produced. The capital is ◊Barcelona.

**catalyst** substance that alters the speed of, or makes possible, a chemical or biochemical reaction but remains unchanged at the end of the reaction. ◊Enzymes are natural biochemical catalysts. In practice most catalysts are used to speed up reactions.

**catalytic converter** device fitted to the exhaust system of a motor vehicle in order to reduce toxic emissions from the engine. It converts harmful exhaust products to relatively harmless ones by passing the exhaust gases over a mixture of catalysts coated on a metal or ceramic honeycomb (a structure that increases the surface area and therefore the amount of active catalyst with which the exhaust gases will come into contact). *Oxidation catalysts* (small amounts of precious palladium and platinum metals) convert hydrocarbons (unburnt fuel) and carbon monoxide into carbon dioxide and water, but do not affect nitrogen oxide emissions. *Three-way catalysts* (platinum and rhodium metals) convert nitrogen oxide gases into nitrogen and oxygen.

**catamaran** (Tamil 'tied log') twin-hulled sailing vessel, based on the native craft of South America and the Indies, made of logs lashed together, with an outrigger. A similar vessel with three hulls is known as a trimaran. Car ferries with a wave-piercing catamaran design are also in use in parts of Europe and North America. They have a pointed main hull and two outriggers and travel at a speed of 35 knots (84.5 kph/52.5 mph).

**cataract** eye disease in which the crystalline lens or its capsule becomes cloudy, causing blindness. Fluid accumulates between the fibres of the lens and gives place to deposits of ◊albumin. These coalesce into rounded bodies, the lens fibres break down, and areas of the lens or the lens capsule become filled with opaque products of degeneration. The condition is estimated to have blinded more than 25 million people worldwide, and 150,000 in the UK.

**catarrh** inflammation of any mucous membrane, especially of the nose and throat, with increased production of mucus.

**catastrophe theory** mathematical theory developed by René Thom 1972, in which he showed that the growth of an organism proceeds by a series of gradual changes that are triggered by, and in turn trigger, large-scale changes or 'catastrophic' jumps. It also has applications in engineering – for example, the gradual strain on the structure of a bridge that can eventually result in a sudden collapse – and has been extended to economic and psychological events.

**catechism** teaching by question and answer on the Socratic method, but chiefly as a means of instructing children in the basics of the Christian creed. A person being instructed in this way in preparation for baptism or confirmation is called a *catechumen.*

**category** in philosophy, a fundamental concept applied to a being that cannot be reduced to anything more elementary. Aristotle listed ten categories: substance, quantity, quality, relation, place, time, position, state, action, and passion.

**caterpillar** larval stage of a ◊butterfly or ◊moth. Wormlike in form, the body is segmented, may be hairy, and often has scent glands. The head has strong biting mandibles, silk glands, and a spinneret.

**catfish** fish belonging to the order Siluriformes, in which barbels (feelers) on the head are well-developed, so giving a resemblance to the whiskers of a cat. Catfishes are found worldwide, mainly but not exclusively in fresh water, and are plentiful in South America.

**cathedral** (Latin *cathedra* 'seat' or 'throne') principal Christian church of a bishop or archbishop, containing his throne, which is usually situated on the south side of the choir. A cathedral is governed by a dean and chapter.

**Catherine (II) the Great** (1729–1796) Empress of Russia from 1762, and daughter of the German prince of Anhalt-Zerbst. In 1745, she married the Russian grand duke Peter. Catherine dominated her husband; six months after he became Tsar Peter III in 1762, he was murdered in a coup and Catherine ruled alone. During her reign Russia extended its boundaries to include territory from wars with the Turks 1768–74, 1787–92, and from the partitions of Poland 1772, 1793, and 1795, as well as establishing hegemony over the Black Sea.

**Catherine de' Medici** (1519–1589) French queen consort of Henry II, whom she married in 1533; daughter of Lorenzo de' Medici, Duke of Urbino; and mother of Francis II, Charles IX, and Henry III. At first outshone by Henry's mistress Diane de Poitiers (1490–1566), she became regent 1560–63 for Charles IX and remained in power until his death in 1574.

**Catherine of Aragón** (1485–1536) First queen of Henry VIII of England, 1509–33, and mother of Mary I. Catherine had married Henry's elder brother Prince Arthur in 1501 and on his death in 1502 was betrothed to Henry, marrying him on his accession. She failed to produce a male heir and Henry divorced her without papal approval, thus creating the basis for the English ◊Reformation.

**cathode** in chemistry, the negative electrode of an electrolytic ◊cell, towards which positive particles (cations), usually in solution, are attracted. See ◊electrolysis.

**cathode** in electronics, the part of an electronic device in which electrons are generated. In a thermionic valve, electrons are produced by the heating effect of an applied current; in a photocell, they are produced by the interaction of light and a semiconducting material. The cathode is kept at a negative potential relative to the device's other electrodes (anodes) in order to ensure that the liberated electrons stream away from the cathode and towards the anodes.

**cathode ray** stream of fast-moving electrons that travel from a cathode (negative electrode) towards an anode (positive electrode) in a vacuum tube. They carry a negative charge and can be deflected by electric and magnetic fields. Cathode rays focused into fine beams of fast electrons are used in cathode-ray tubes, the electrons' ◊kinetic energy being converted into light energy as they collide with the tube's fluorescent screen.

**cathode-ray oscilloscope** (CRO), instrument used to measure electrical potentials or voltages that vary over time and to display the waveforms of electrical oscillations or signals. Readings are displayed graphically on the screen of a ◊cathode-ray tube.

**cathode-ray tube** (CRT), vacuum tube in which a beam of electrons is produced and focused onto a fluorescent screen. The electrons' kinetic energy is converted into light energy as they collide with the screen. It is an essential component of television receivers, computer visual display units, and ◊oscilloscopes.

**Catholic church** the whole body of the Christian church, though usually referring to the Roman Catholic Church (see ◊Roman Catholicism).

**Catholic Emancipation** in British history, acts of Parliament passed 1780–1829 to relieve Roman Catholics of civil and political restrictions imposed from the time of Henry VIII and the Reformation.

**cation** ◊ion carrying a positive charge. During electrolysis, cations in the electrolyte move to the cathode (negative electrode).

**catkin** in flowering plants (◊angiosperms), a pendulous inflorescence, bearing numerous small, usually unisexual flowers. The tiny flowers are stalkless and the petals and sepals are usually absent or much reduced in size. Many types of trees bear catkins, including willows, poplars, and birches. Most plants with catkins are wind-pollinated, so the male catkins produce large quantities of pollen. Some ◊gymnosperms also have catkin-like structures that produce pollen, for example, the swamp cypress *Taxodium*.

**CAT scan** or *CT scan*, (acronym for *computerized axial tomography scan*) sophisticated method of X-ray imaging. Quick and noninvasive, CAT scanning is used in medicine as an aid to diagnosis, helping to pinpoint problem areas without the need for exploratory surgery. It is also used in archaeology to investigate mummies.

**cattle** any large, ruminant, even-toed, hoofed mammal of the genus *Bos*, family Bovidae, including wild species such as the yak, gaur, gayal, banteng, and kouprey, as well as domestic breeds. Asiatic water buffaloes *Bubalus*, African buffaloes *Syncerus*, and American bison *Bison* are not considered true cattle. Cattle are bred for meat (beef cattle) or milk (dairy cattle).

**Catullus, Gaius Valerius** (*c.* 84–54 BC) Roman lyric poet. He wrote in a variety of metres and forms, from short narratives and hymns to epigrams. He moved with ease through the literary and political society of late republican Rome. His love affair with the woman he called 'Lesbia' provided the inspiration for many of his poems.

**Caucasus** mountain range extending from the Taman Peninsula on the Black Sea to the Apsheron Peninsula on the Caspian Sea, a total length of 1,200 km/750 mi. The Caucasus, which form the boundary between Europe and Asia, is divided into the **Greater Caucasus** (northern) and **Little Caucasus** (southern) chains. The range crosses the territory of the Russian Federation, Georgia, Armenia, and Azerbaijan. At 5,642 m/18,510 ft, Elbrus (in the Greater Caucasus) is the highest peak in Europe. The northern Caucasus region is home to some 40 different ethnic groups.

**cauliflower** variety of ◊cabbage, with a large edible head of fleshy, cream-coloured flowers which do not fully mature. It is similar to broccoli but less hardy. (*Brassica oleracea botrytis*, family Cruciferae.)

**cauterization** in medicine, the use of special instruments to burn or fuse small areas of body tissue to destroy dead cells, prevent the spread of infection, or seal tiny blood vessels to minimize blood loss during surgery.

**caution** legal term for a warning given by police questioning a suspect, which in the UK must be couched in the following terms: 'You do not have to say anything unless you wish to do so, but what you say may be given in evidence.' Persons not under arrest must also be told that they do not have to remain at the police station or with the police officer but that if they do, they may obtain legal advice if they wish. A suspect should be cautioned again after a break in questioning and upon arrest.

**Cavaco Silva, Anibal** (1939– ) Portuguese politician, finance minister 1980–81, and prime minister and Social Democratic Party (PSD) leader 1985–95. Under his leadership Portugal joined the European Community in 1985 and the Western European Union in 1988.

**cavalier** horseman of noble birth, but mainly used as a derogatory nickname to describe a male supporter of Charles I in the English Civil War (Cavalier), typically with courtly dress and long hair (as distinct from a Roundhead); also a supporter of Charles II after the Restoration.

**Cavalier poets** poets of Charles I's court, including Thomas Carew, Robert ◊Herrick,

Richard Lovelace, and John Suckling. They wrote witty, lighthearted lyrics about love and loyalty to the monarch.

**Cavan** county of the Republic of Ireland, in the province of Ulster; county town Cavan; area 1,890 sq km/730 sq mi; population (1991) 52,800. The chief rivers are the Woodford, the Shannon (rising on the south slopes of Cuilcagh mountain; 667 m/2,188 ft), and the Erne, which divides Cavan into two parts: a narrow, mostly low-lying peninsula, 30 km/19 mi long, between Leitrim and Fermanagh; and an eastern section of wild and bare hill country. The chief towns are Cavan, population (1991) 3,300, and Kilmore, seat of Roman Catholic and Protestant bishoprics. The soil is generally poor and the climate moist and cold.

**cave** roofed-over cavity in the Earth's crust usually produced by the action of underground water or by waves on a seacoast. Caves of the former type commonly occur in areas underlain by limestone, such as Kentucky and many Balkan regions, where the rocks are soluble in water. A *pothole* is a vertical hole in rock caused by water descending a crack; it is thus open to the sky.

**Cavendish, Henry** (1731–1810) English physicist and chemist. He discovered hydrogen (which he called 'inflammable air') in 1766, and determined the compositions of water and of nitric acid. The Cavendish experiment (1798) enabled him to discover the mass and density of the Earth.

**caviar** salted roe (eggs) of sturgeon, salmon, and other fishes. Caviar is prepared by beating and straining the egg sacs until the eggs are free from fats and then adding salt. Russia and Iran are the main exporters of the most prized variety of caviar, derived from Caspian Sea sturgeon. Iceland produces various high-quality, lower-priced caviars.

**Cavour, Camillo Benso di, Count** (1810–1861) Italian nationalist politician, a leading figure in the Italian ◊*Risorgimento*. As prime minister of Piedmont 1852–59 and 1860–61, he enlisted the support of Britain and France for the concept of a united Italy, achieved 1861; after expelling the Austrians 1859, he assisted Garibaldi in liberating southern Italy 1860.

**cavy** short-tailed South American rodent, family Caviidae, of which the guinea-pig *Cavia porcellus* is an example. Wild cavies are greyish or brownish with rather coarse hair. They live in small groups in burrows, and have been kept for food since ancient times.

**Caxton, William** (c. 1422–1491) English printer. He learned the art of ◊printing in Cologne, Germany, in 1471 and set up a press in Belgium where he produced the first book printed in English, his own version of a French romance, *Recuyell of the Historyes of Troye* (1474). Returning to England in 1476, he established himself in London, where he produced the first book printed in England, *Dictes or Sayengis of the Philosophres* (1477).

**Cayenne** capital and chief port of the overseas *département* of ◊French Guiana in South America; situated on Cayenne Island on the Atlantic coast at the mouth of the River Cayenne; population (1990) 41,700. The main occupation is fishing, of which fresh and processed shrimp constitute nearly 75% of total exports by value. Rum, pineapples, and hardwoods are also exported. Many imports pass through the port as the country is very much import-dependent. A thermal power station provides electricity to the area. There are some unexploited reserves of bauxite in the surrounding region which may become a future export product. There is an international airport 16 km/10 mi south of Cayenne.

**cayman** another name for ◊caiman.

**Cayman Islands** British island group in the West Indies

*area* 260 sq km/100 sq mi

*capital* George Town (on Grand Cayman)

*features* comprises three low-lying islands: Grand Cayman, Cayman Brac, and Little Cayman

*government* governor, executive council, and legislative assembly

*exports* seawhip coral, a source of ◊prostaglandins; shrimps; honey; jewellery

*currency* Cayman Island dollar

*population* (1993 est) 31,150 (mostly on Grand Cayman)

*language* English

*history* first reached by Christopher Columbus in 1503; acquired by Britain following the Treaty of Madrid in 1670; became a dependency of Jamaica in 1863. In 1959 the islands became a separate crown colony, although the inhabitants chose to remain British. From that date, changes in legislation attracted foreign banks and the Caymans are now an international financial centre and tax haven as well as a tourist resort, with emphasis on scuba diving.

**CD** abbreviation for ◊*compact disc; Corps Diplomatique* (French 'Diplomatic Corps'); *certificate of deposit.*

**CD-ROM** abbreviation for compact-disc read-only memory, computer storage device developed from the technology of the audio ◊compact disc. It consists of a plastic-coated metal disk, on which binary digital information is etched in the form of microscopic pits. This can then be read optically by passing a laser beam over the disk. CD-ROMs typically hold about 650 megabytes of data, and are used in distributing large amounts of text, graphics, audio, and video, such as encyclopedias, catalogues, technical manuals, and games.

**Ceauşescu, Nicolae** (1918–1989) Romanian politician, leader of the Romanian Communist Party (RCP), in power 1965–89. He pursued a policy line independent of and critical of the USSR. He appointed family members, including his wife Elena Ceauşescu (1919– 1989), to senior state and party posts, and governed in an increasingly repressive manner, zealously implementing schemes that impoverished the nation. The Ceauşescus were overthrown in a bloody revolutionary coup in December 1989 and executed on Christmas Day that year.

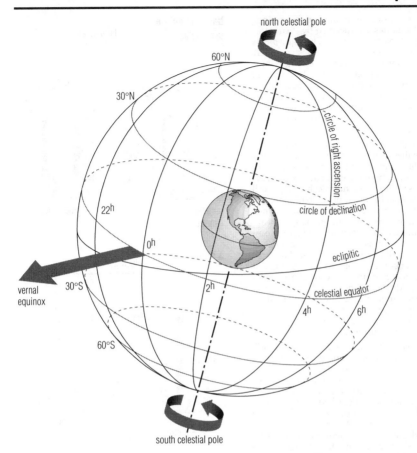

north celestial pole

60°N

30°N

circle of right ascension

circle of declination

22h

0h

ecliptic

vernal
equinox

30°S

2h

celestial equator

4h 6h

60°S

south celestial pole

***celestial sphere*** *The main features of the celestial sphere. The equivalents of latitude and longitude on the celestial sphere are declination and right ascension. Declination runs from 0° at the celestial equator to 90° at the celestial poles. Right ascension is measured in hours eastwards from the vernal equinox, one hour corresponding to 15° of longitude.*

**Cebu** chief city and port of the island of Cebu in the Philippines; population (1990) 610,400; area of the island 5,086 sq km/1,964 sq mi. The oldest city of the Philippines, Cebu was founded as San Miguel 1565 and became the capital of the Spanish Philippines.

**Cecil, Robert** 1st Earl of Salisbury (1563–1612) Secretary of state to Elizabeth I of England, succeeding his father, Lord Burghley; he was afterwards chief minister to James I (James VI of Scotland) whose accession to the English throne he secured. He discovered the ◊Gunpowder Plot, the conspiracy to blow up the king and Parliament in 1605. James I created him Earl of Salisbury in 1605. He was knighted in 1591, and made a baron in 1603 and viscount in 1604.

**cedar** any of an Old World group of coniferous trees belonging to the pine family. The cedar of Lebanon (*Cedrus libani*) grows to great height and age in the mountains of Syria and Asia Minor. Of the historic forests on Mount Lebanon itself, only a few groups of trees remain. (Genus *Cedrus*, family Pinaceae.)

**celandine** either of two plants belonging to different families, the only similarity being their bright yellow flowers. The *greater celandine* (*Chelidonium majus*) belongs to the poppy family and is common in hedgerows. The *lesser celandine* (*Ranunculus ficaria*) is a member of the buttercup family and is a common wayside and meadow plant in Europe.

**celery** Old World plant belonging to the carrot family. It grows wild in ditches and salt marshes and has a coarse texture and sharp taste. Cultivated varieties of celery are grown under cover to make the edible stalks less bitter. (*Apium graveolens*, family Umbelliferae.)

**celestial mechanics** branch of astronomy that deals with the calculation of the orbits of celestial bodies, their gravitational attractions (such as those that produce the Earth's tides), and also the orbits of artificial satellites and space probes. It is based on the laws of motion and gravity laid down by Isaac ◊Newton.

**celestial sphere** imaginary sphere surrounding the Earth, on which the celestial bodies seem to lie. The positions of bodies such as stars, planets, and galaxies are specified by their coordinates on the celestial sphere. The equivalents of latitude and longitude on the celestial sphere are called declination and right ascension (which is measured in hours from 0 to 24). The *celestial poles* lie directly above the Earth's poles, and the *celestial equator* lies over the Earth's Equator. The celestial sphere appears to rotate once around the Earth each day, actually a result of the rotation of the Earth on its axis.

**cell** in biology, the basic structural unit of life. It is the smallest unit capable of independent existence which can reproduce itself exactly. All living organisms – with the exception of ◊viruses – are composed of one or more cells. Single cell organisms such as bacteria, protozoa, and other micro-organisms are termed *unicellular,* while plants and animals which contain many cells are termed *multicellular* organisms. Highly complex organisms such as human beings consist of billions of cells, all of which are adapted to carry out specific functions – for instance, groups of these specialized cells are organized into tissues and organs. Although these cells may differ widely in size, appearance, and function, their essential features are similar.

Cells divide by ◊mitosis, or by ◊meiosis when ◊gametes are being formed.

**cell, electrical** or *voltaic cell* or *galvanic cell,* device in which chemical energy is converted into electrical energy; the popular name is ◊'battery', but this actually refers to a collection of cells in one unit. The reactive chemicals of a *primary cell* cannot be replenished, whereas *secondary cells* – such as storage batteries – are rechargeable: their chemical reactions can be reversed and the original condition restored by applying an electric current. It is dangerous to attempt to recharge a primary cell.

**cell, electrolytic** device to which electrical energy is applied in order to bring about a chemical reaction; see ◊electrolysis.

**Cellini, Benvenuto** (1500–1571) Italian Mannerist sculptor and goldsmith. Among his works are a graceful bronze *Perseus* (1545–54, Loggia dei Lanzi, Florence) and a gold salt cellar made for Francis I of France (1540–43, Kunsthistorisches Museum, Vienna), topped by nude reclining figures. He wrote a frank autobiography (begun 1558), which gives a vivid picture both of him and his age.

**cello** common abbreviation for *violoncello,* bass member of the violin family and lowest-pitched member of the string quartet. Its four strings are tuned C2, G2, D3, and A4. In the 17th and 18th centuries a version was made with a fifth string tuned E4. Its solo potential was recognized by Johann Sebastian Bach, and a concerto repertoire extends from Haydn (who also gave the cello a leading role in his string quartets), and Boccherini to Dvořák, Elgar, Britten, Ligeti, and Lukas Foss. The *Bachianas Brasilieras 1* by Villa-Lobos is scored for eight cellos, and Boulez's *Messagesquisse* 1977 for seven cellos.

**cellophane** transparent wrapping film made from wood ◊cellulose, widely used for packag-

## basic principles

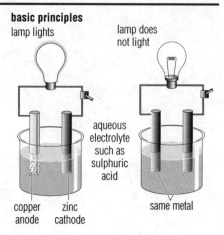

lamp lights

lamp does not light

aqueous electrolyte such as sulphuric acid

copper anode    zinc cathode

same metal

## a simple cell

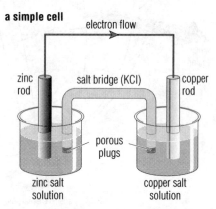

electron flow

zinc rod    salt bridge (KCl)    copper rod

porous plugs

zinc salt solution    copper salt solution

**cell, electrical** *When electrical energy is produced from chemical energy using two metals acting as electrodes in an aqueous solution, it is sometimes known as a galvanic cell or voltaic cell. Here the two metals copper (+) and zinc (–) are immersed in dilute sulphuric acid, which acts as an electrolyte. If a light bulb is connected between the two, an electric current will flow with bubbles of gas being deposited on the electrodes in a process known as polarization.*

ing, first produced by Swiss chemist Jacques Edwin Brandenberger in 1908.

**cellular phone** or *cellphone,* mobile radio telephone, one of a network connected to the telephone system by a computer-controlled communication system. Service areas are divided into small 'cells', about 5 km/3 mi across, each with a separate low-power transmitter.

**cellulite** fatty compound alleged by some dietitians to be produced in the body by liver disorder and to cause lumpy deposits on the hips and thighs. Medical opinion generally denies its existence, attributing the lumpy appearance to a type of subcutaneous fat deposit.

**celluloid** transparent or translucent, highly flammable, plastic material (a thermoplastic) made from cellulose nitrate and camphor. It was once used for toilet articles, novelties, and photographic film, but has now been replaced by the nonflammable substance cellulose acetate.

**cellulose** complex ◊carbohydrate composed of long chains of glucose units, joined by chemical bonds called glycosidic links. It is the principal constituent of the cell wall of higher plants, and a vital ingredient in the diet of many ◊herbivores. Molecules of cellulose are organized into long, unbranched microfibrils that give support to the cell wall. No mammal produces the enzyme cellulase, necessary for digesting cellulose; mammals such as rabbits and cows are only able to digest grass because the bacteria present in their gut can manufacture it.

**cell wall** in plants, the tough outer surface of the cell. It is constructed from a mesh of ◊cellulose and is very strong and relatively inelastic. Most living cells are turgid (swollen with water) and develop an internal hydrostatic pressure (wall pressure) that acts against the cellulose wall. The result of this turgor pressure is to give the cell, and therefore the plant, rigidity. Plants that are not woody are particularly reliant on this form of support.

**Celsius** scale of temperature, previously called centigrade, in which the range from freezing to boiling of water is divided into 100 degrees, freezing point being 0 degrees and boiling point 100 degrees.

**Celt** (Greek *Keltoi*) Indo-European people that originated in Alpine Europe and spread to the Iberian peninsula and beyond. They were ironworkers and farmers. In the 1st century BC they were defeated by the Roman Empire and by Germanic tribes and confined largely to Britain, Ireland, and northern France.

**Celtic languages** branch of the Indo-European family, divided into two groups: the *Brythonic* or *P-Celtic* (◊Welsh language, Cornish, Breton, and Gaulish) and the *Goidelic* or *Q-Celtic* (Irish, Scottish, and Manx ◊Gaelic languages). Celtic languages once stretched from the Black Sea to Britain, but have been in decline for centuries, limited to the so-called 'Celtic fringe' of western Europe.

**cement** any bonding agent used to unite particles in a single mass or to cause one surface to adhere to another. *Portland cement* is a powder which when mixed with water and sand or gravel turns into mortar or concrete.

In geology, cement refers to a chemically precipitated material such as carbonate that occupies the interstices of clastic rocks.

**Cenozoic** or *Caenozoic,* era of geological time that began 65 million years ago and continues to the present day. It is divided into the Tertiary and Quaternary periods. The Cenozoic marks the emergence of mammals as a dominant group, including humans, and the formation of the mountain chains of the Himalayas and the Alps.

**censorship** suppression by authority of material considered immoral, heretical, subversive, libellous, damaging to state security, or otherwise offensive. It is generally more stringent under totalitarian or strongly religious regimes and in wartime. Concerns over the ready availability of material such as bomb recipes and pornography have led a number of countries to pass laws attempting to censor the Internet, such as the US Communications Decency Act of 1996.

**census** official count of the population of a country, originally for military call-up and taxation, later for assessment of social trends as other information regarding age, sex, and occupation of each individual was included. They may become unnecessary as computerized databanks are developed. The data collected are used by government departments in planning for the future in such areas as health, education, transport, and housing.

**centaur** in Greek mythology, a creature half human and half horse, wild and lawless. Chiron, the mentor of the hero Heracles and tutor of the god of medicine Asclepius, was an exception. Their home was said to be on Mount Pelion, Thessaly.

**centigrade** former name for the ◊Celsius temperature scale.

**centipede** jointed-legged animal of the group Chilopoda, members of which have a distinct head and a single pair of long antennae. Their bodies are composed of segments (which may number nearly 200), each of similar form and bearing a single pair of legs. Most are small, but the tropical *Scolopendra gigantea* may reach 30 cm/1 ft in length. *Millipedes,* class Diplopoda, have fewer segments (up to 100), but have two pairs of legs on each.

## Central African Republic
*national name* *République Centrafricaine*

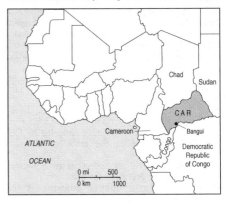

*area* 622,436 sq km/240,322 sq mi
*capital* Bangui
*major towns/cities* Berbérati, Bouar, Bambari, Bossangoa, Carnot
*physical features* landlocked flat plateau, with rivers flowing north and south, and hills in northeast and southwest; dry in north, rainforest in southwest; mostly wooded; Kotto and Mbali river falls; the Oubangui River rises 6 m/20 ft at Bangui during the wet season (June–November)

**head of state** Anicet Georges Dologuele from 1998
**head of government** Gabriel Koyambounou from 1995
**political system** emergent democracy
**political parties** Central African People's Liberation Party (MPLC), left of centre; Central African Democratic Rally (RDC), nationalist, right of centre
**currency** franc CFA
**GNP per capita (PPP)** (US$) 1,290 (1998 est)
**exports** diamonds, coffee, timber, cotton. Principal market: Belgium – Luxembourg 36.2% (1997)
**population** 3,594,000 (1999 est)
**language** French (official), Sangho (national), Arabic, Hunsa, and Swahili
**religion** Protestant, Roman Catholic, Muslim, animist
**life expectancy** 43 (men); 47 (women) (1995–2000)
**Chronology**
**10th century** Immigration by peoples from Sudan to the east and Cameroon to the west.
**16th century** Part of the Gaoga Empire.
**16th–18th centuries** Population reduced greatly by slave raids both by coastal traders and Arab empires in Sudan and Chad.
**19th century** The Zande nation of the Bandia peoples became powerful in the east. Bantu speakers immigrated from Zaire and the Baya from northern Cameroon.
**1889–1903** The French established control over the area, quelling insurrections; a French colony known as Oubangi-Chari was formed and partitioned among commercial concessionaries.
**1920–30** Series of rebellions against forced labour on coffee and cotton plantations savagely repressed by French.
**1946** Given a territorial assembly and representation in French parliament.
**1958** Achieved self-government within French Equatorial Africa, with Barthélémy Boganda, founder of the pro-independence Movement for the Social Evolution of Black Africa (MESAN) prime minister.
**1960** Achieved independence as Central African Republic; David Dacko, nephew of the late Boganda, elected president.
**1962** The republic made a one-party state, dominated by MESAN and loyal to the French interest.
**1965** Dacko ousted in military coup led by Col Jean-Bedel Bokassa as the economy deteriorated.
**1972** Bokassa, a violent and eccentric autocrat, declared himself president for life.
**1977** Bokassa made himself emperor of the 'Central African Empire'.
**1979** Bokassa deposed by Dacko in French-backed bloodless coup, following violent repressive measures including the massacre of 100 children by the emperor, who went into exile.
**1981** Dacko deposed in a bloodless coup, led by Gen André Kolingba, and military government established.
**1983** Clandestine opposition movement formed.
**1984** Amnesty for all political party leaders announced. President Mitterrand of France paid a state visit.

**1988** Bokassa, who had returned from exile, found guilty of murder and embezzlement; he received death sentence, later commuted to life imprisonment.
**1991** Opposition parties were allowed to form.
**1992** Multiparty elections were promised, but cancelled with Kolingba in last place.
**1993** Kolingba released thousands of prisoners, including Bokassa. Ange-Félix Patasse of the leftist African People's Labour Party (MLPC) was elected president, ending 12 years of military dictatorship.
**1996** There was an army revolt over pay; Patasse was forced into hiding.
**1998** Anicet Georges Dologuele was appointed prime minister.

**Central America** the part of the Americas that links Mexico with the Isthmus of Panama, comprising Belize and the republics of Costa Rica, El Salvador, Guatemala, Honduras, Nicaragua, and Panama.

It is also an isthmus, crossed by mountains that form part of the Cordilleras, rising to a maximum height of 4,220 m/13,845 ft. There are numerous active volcanoes. The principal river is the Usumacinta, which rises in Guatemala and flows north for 965 km/600 mi, crossing Mexico, and empties into the Bay of Campeche in the Gulf of Mexico. Central America has an area of about 523,000 sq km/200,000 sq mi, and a population estimated (1995) at 33,132,000, comprising mostly Indians or mestizos (of mixed white–Indian ancestry), with the exception of Costa Rica, which has a predominantly white population. Tropical agricultural products, raw materials, and other basic commodities are exported.

**Central Asian Republics** geographical region covering the territory of five nation-states: Kazakhstan, Kyrgyzstan, Tajikistan, Turkmenistan, and Uzbekistan. These republics were part of the Soviet Union before gaining their independence in 1991. Central Asia is bordered on the north by the Russian Federation, on the south by Iran and Afghanistan, and on the east by the Chinese region of Xinjiang Uygur. The western boundary of Central Asia is marked by the Caspian Sea. The topography of the region is characterized by several major mountain ranges, including the Tien Shan range and the ◊Pamirs, and extensive deserts, principally the Kara-Kum and Kyzyl-Kum. The people of Central Asia are predominantly Muslim.

**central dogma** in genetics and evolution, the fundamental belief that ◊genes can affect the nature of the physical body, but that changes in the body (◊acquired character, for example, through use or accident) cannot be translated into changes in the genes.

**Central Intelligence Agency** (CIA), US intelligence organization established in 1947. It has actively intervened overseas, generally to undermine left-wing regimes or to protect US financial interests; for example, in the Democratic Republic of Congo (formerly Zaire) and Nicaragua. From 1980 all covert activity by the CIA had by law to be reported to Congress,

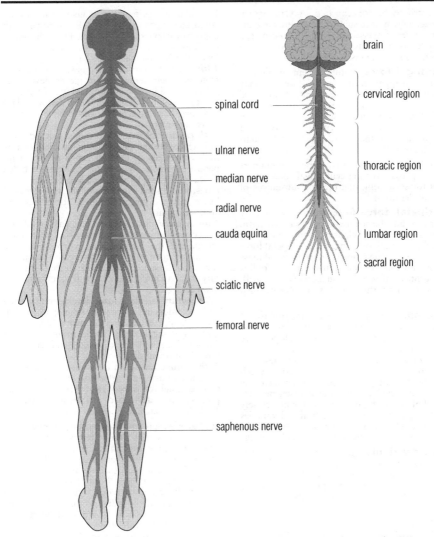

brain

cervical region

spinal cord

thoracic region

ulnar nerve

median nerve

radial nerve

cauda equina

lumbar region

sacral region

sciatic nerve

femoral nerve

saphenous nerve

**central nervous system** *The central nervous system (CNS) with its associated nerves. The CNS controls and integrates body functions. In humans and other vertebrates it consists of a brain and a spinal cord, which are linked to the body's muscles and organs by means of the peripheral nervous system.*

preferably beforehand, and to be authorized by the president. In 1994 the CIA's estimated budget was around $3.1 billion. John M Deutsch became CIA director in 1995 after the Agency's standing was diminished by a scandal involving Aldrich Arnes, a CIA agent who had been a longtime mole for the KGB. George Tenate became director in 1997.

**Central Lowlands** one of the three geographical divisions of Scotland, being the fertile and densely populated plain that lies between two geological fault lines, which run nearly parallel northeast–southwest across Scotland from Stonehaven to Dumbarton and from Dunbar to Girvan.

**central nervous system** (CNS) the brain and spinal cord, as distinct from other compo-

nents of the ⟩nervous system. The CNS integrates all nervous function.

**central processing unit** (CPU), main component of a computer, the part that executes individual program instructions and controls the operation of other parts. It is sometimes called the central processor or, when contained on a single integrated circuit, a microprocessor.

**Centre** region of north-central France; area 39,150 sq km/15,116 sq mi; population (1990) 2,371,000. Centre includes the *départements* of Cher, Eure-et-Loir, Indre, Indre-et-Loire, Loire-et-Cher, and Loiret. The administrative centre is ⟩Orléans.

**centre of mass** point in or near an object at which the whole mass of the object may be considered to be concentrated. A symmetrical homogeneous object such as a sphere or cube has its centre of mass at its geometrical centre; a hollow object (such as a cup) may have its centre of mass in space inside the hollow.

**centrifugal force** useful concept in physics, based on an apparent (but not real) force. It may be regarded as a force that acts radially outward from a spinning or orbiting object, thus balancing the ◊centripetal force (which is real). For an object of mass $m$ moving with a velocity $v$ in a circle of radius $r$, the centrifugal force $F$ equals $mv^2/r$ (outward).

**centrifuge** apparatus that rotates containers at high speeds, creating centrifugal forces. One use is for separating mixtures of substances of different densities.

**centripetal force** force that acts radially inward on an object moving in a curved path. For example, with a weight whirled in a circle at the end of a length of string, the centripetal force is the tension in the string. For an object of mass $m$ moving with a velocity $v$ in a circle of radius $r$, the centripetal force $F$ equals $mv^2/r$ (inward). The reaction to this force is the ◊centrifugal force.

**cephalopod** any predatory marine mollusc of the class Cephalopoda, with the mouth and head surrounded by tentacles. Cephalopods are the most intelligent, the fastest-moving, and the largest of all animals without backbones, and there are remarkable luminescent forms which swim or drift at great depths. They have the most highly developed nervous and sensory systems of all invertebrates, the eye in some closely paralleling that found in vertebrates. Examples include squid, ◊octopus, and ◊cuttlefish. Shells are rudimentary or absent in most cephalopods.

**Cepheid variable** yellow supergiant star that varies regularly in brightness every few days or weeks as a result of pulsations. The time that a Cepheid variable takes to pulsate is directly related to its average brightness; the longer the pulsation period, the brighter the star.

**ceramics** objects made from clay, hardened into a permanent form by baking (firing) at very high temperatures in a kiln. Ceramics are used for building construction and decoration (bricks, tiles), for specialist industrial uses (linings for furnaces used to manufacture steel, fuel elements in nuclear reactors, and so on), and for plates and vessels used in the home. Different types of clay and different methods and temperatures of firing create a variety of results. Ceramics may be cast in a mould or hand-built out of slabs of clay, coiled, or thrown on a wheel. Technically, the main categories are earthenware, stoneware, and hard- and soft-paste porcelain (see under ◊pottery and porcelain).

*ceramics: examples through Western history*
*Roman period* potter's wheel; lead glazing; decorative use of slip (watered-down clay)
*medieval period* sgraffito (scratched) tiles and other products (earthenware decorated with slip of a contrasting colour, which is then scratched through) such as those made in Bologna, Italy.

Lead-glazed jugs made in England and France, coloured bright green or yellow-brown with copper or iron oxides. Tin-glazed ware in southern Italy and Spain by 13th century, influenced by established Islamic techniques
*14th-century Germany* stoneware developed from hard earthenwares; tin glazes developed; colour added by thin slips mixed with high-temperature colours. Later, mottled brown glaze recognized as characteristic of Cologne, referred to as 'tigerware' in Britain
*15th century* Hispano-Moresque painted ware imitated by Italians, developing into majolica by mid-century, using the full range of high-temperature colours; centres of the craft included Tuscany, Faenza, Urbino, and Venice. Some potteries, such as that at Gubbio, additionally used lustre glazes. Typical products are dishes and apothecary jars
*16th century* potters from Faenza spread tin-glazed earthenware (majolica) skills to France, Spain, and the Netherlands, where it became known as faience; from Antwerp the technique spread to England. The English in the 17th century named Dutch faience 'Delftware', after the main centre of production
*17th century* faience centres developed at Rouen and Moustiers in France, Alcora in Spain, and in Switzerland, Austria, and Germany. Blue underglaze was increasingly used, in imitation of Chinese blue and white designs, reflecting the growth of orientalism
*18th century* European developments in porcelain, also in using a rich palette of low-temperature enamel colours. The vitreous enamel process, first developed at Strasbourg about 1750, spread around northern Europe.

**cereal** grass grown for its edible, nutrient-rich, starchy seeds. The term refers primarily to wheat, oats, rye, and barley, but may also refer to maize (corn), millet, and rice. Cereals contain about 75% complex carbohydrates and 10% protein, plus fats and fibre (roughage). They store well. If all the world's cereal crop were consumed as whole-grain products directly by humans, everyone could obtain adequate protein and carbohydrate; however, a large proportion of cereal production in affluent nations is used as animal feed to boost the production of meat, dairy products, and eggs.

**cerebral haemorrhage** or *apoplectic fit,* in medicine, a form of ◊stroke in which there is bleeding from a cerebral blood vessel into the surrounding brain tissue. It is generally caused by degenerative disease of the arteries and high blood pressure. Depending on the site and extent of bleeding, the symptoms vary from transient weakness and numbness to deep coma and death. Damage to the brain is permanent, though some recovery can be made. Strokes are likely to recur.

**cerebral palsy** any nonprogressive abnormality of the brain occurring during or shortly after birth. It is caused by oxygen deprivation, injury during birth, haemorrhage, meningitis, viral infection, or faulty development. Premature babies are at greater risk of being born with cerebral palsy, and in 1996 US researchers linked this to low levels of the thyroid hormone thyroxine. The condition is characterized by muscle spasm, weakness, lack of coordination, and impaired movement; or there may be spastic paralysis, with fixed deformities of the limbs. Intelligence is not always affected.

**Ceredigion** unitary authority in southwest Wales, created in 1996 from part of the former county of Dyfed, of which it was a district
*area* 1,793 sq km/ 692 sq mi
*towns* Aberaeron (administrative headquarters), Aberystwyth, Cardigan, Lampeter, Llandyssul, Tregaron
*physical* part of the Cambrian Mountains, including Plynlimon Fawr (752 m/2,468 ft); rivers Teifi, Rheidol, Ystwyth, Aeron, and Tywi
*features* remains of Roman roads and military stations, and inscribed stones; ruins of 12th-century Strata Florida Abbey southeast of Aberystwyth; Devil's Bridge) (spanning the Rheidol Falls)
*industries* tourism, woollens production
*agriculture* sheep-rearing, dairy production
*population* (1996) 68,900.

**Ceres** largest asteroid, 940 km/584 mi in diameter, and the first to be discovered (by Italian astronomer Giuseppe Piazzi 1801). Ceres orbits the Sun every 4.6 years at an average distance of 414 million km/257 million mi. Its mass is about one-seventieth of that of the Moon.

**Ceres** in Roman mythology, the goddess of corn, representing the fertility of the earth as its producer; patron of the corn trade. Her cult was established in Rome by 496 BC, and showed early identification with the Greek ◊Demeter.

**cerium** malleable and ductile, grey, metallic element, symbol Ce, atomic number 58, relative atomic mass 140.12. It is the most abundant member of the lanthanide series, and is used in alloys, electronic components, nuclear fuels, and lighter flints. It was discovered 1804 by the Swedish chemists Jöns Berzelius and Wilhelm Hisinger (1766–1852), and, independently, by Martin Klaproth. The element was named after the then recently discovered asteroid Ceres.

**Cervantes, Saavedra, Miguel de** (1547–1616) Spanish novelist, dramatist, and poet. His masterpiece *Don Quixote de la Mancha* (in full *El ingenioso hidalgo Don Quixote de la Mancha*) was published in 1605. In 1613 his *Novelas ejemplares/Exemplary Novels* appeared, followed by *Viaje del Parnaso/The Voyage to Parnassus* (1614). A spurious second part of *Don Quixote* prompted Cervantes to bring out his own second part in 1615, often considered superior to the first in construction and characterization.

**cervical cancer** in medicine, ◊cancer of the cervix (neck of the womb).

**cervical smear** in medicine, removal of a small sample of tissue from the cervix (neck of the womb) to screen for changes implying a likelihood of cancer. The procedure is also known as the *Pap test* after its originator, George Papanicolau.

**Ceylon** former name (to 1972) of Sri Lanka.

**Cézanne, Paul** (1839–1906) French Post-Impressionist painter. He was a leading figure in the development of modern art. He broke away from the Impressionists' concern with the ever-changing effects of light to develop a style that tried to capture the structure of natural forms, whether in landscapes, still lifes, or portraits. *Joueurs de Cartes/Cardplayers* (about 1890–95; Louvre, Paris) is typical of his work.

**CFC** abbreviation for ◊chlorofluorocarbon.

**c.g.s. system** system of units based on the centimetre, gram, and second, as units of length, mass, and time, respectively. It has been replaced for scientific work by the ◊SI units to avoid inconsistencies in definition of the thermal calorie and electrical quantities.

**Chaco** province of northeast Argentina; area 99,633 sq km/38,458 sq mi; population (1991) 838,300; its capital is Resistencia, in the southeast. The province forms part of the Gran Chaco area of South America, which extends into Bolivia and Paraguay, and consists of a flat savanna lowland, mainly covered with scrub, and has many lakes and swamps. The eastern parts of the province are heavily forested, producing timber and the quebracho tree, from which tannin extract is made. The chief crop is cotton, and there is cattle-raising.

**Chad** Republic of
*national name* *République du Tchad*

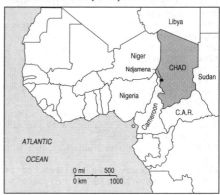

*area* 1,284,000 sq km/495,752 sq mi
*capital* N'djaména (formerly Fort Lamy)
*major towns/cities* Sarh, Moundou, Abéché, Bongor, Doba
*physical features* landlocked state with mountains (Tibetsi) and part of Sahara Desert in north; moist savanna in south; rivers in south flow northwest to Lake Chad
*head of state* Idriss Deby from 1990
*head of government* Nassour Ouaidou Guelendouksia from 1997
*political system* emergent democracy
*political parties* Patriotic Salvation Movement (MPS), centre left; Alliance for Democracy and Progress (RDP), centre left; Union for Democracy and Progress (UPDT), centre left; Action for Unity and Socialism (ACTUS), centre left; Union for Democracy and the Republic (UDR), centre left

**currency** franc CFA
**GNP per capita (PPP)** (US$) 1,020 (1998 est)
**exports** cotton, live cattle, meat, hides and skins. Principal market: Portugal 29.8% (1997)
**population** 7,458,000 (1999 est)
**language** French, Arabic (both official), over 100 African languages spoken
**religion** Muslim, Christian, animist
**life expectancy** 46 (men); 49 (women) (1995–2000)
**Chronology**
**7th–9th centuries** Berber pastoral nomads, the Zaghawa, immigrated from north and became ruling aristocracy, dominating the Sao people, sedentary black farmers, and established Kanem state.
**9th–19th centuries** The Zaghawa's Saifi dynasty formed the kingdom of Bornu, which stretched to the west and south of Lake Chad, and converted to Islam in the 11th century. At its height between the 15th and 18th centuries, it raided the south for slaves, and faced rivalry from the 16th century from the Baguirmi and Ouadai Arab kingdoms.
**1820s** Visited by British explorers.
**1890s–1901** Conquered by France, who ended slave raiding by Arab kingdoms.
**1910** Became a colony in French Equatorial Africa and cotton production expanded in the south.
**1944** The pro-Nazi Vichy government signed agreement giving Libya rights to the Aouzou Strip in northern Chad.
**1946** Became overseas territory of French Republic, with its own territorial assembly and representation in the French parliament.
**1960** Independence achieved, with François Tombalbaye of the Chadian Progressive Party (CPT), dominated by Sara Christians from the south, as president.
**1963** Violent opposition in the Muslim north, led by the Chadian National Liberation Front (Frolinat), backed by Libya following the banning of opposition parties.
**1968** Revolt of northern militias quelled with France's help.
**1973** Africanization campaign launched by Tombalbaye, who changed his first name to Ngarta.
**1975** Tombalbaye killed in military coup led by southerner Gen Félix Malloum. Frolinat continued its resistance.
**1978** Malloum tried to find a political solution by forming a coalition government with former Frolinat leader Hissène Habré, but it soon broke down.
**1979** Malloum forced to leave the country; interim government set up under Gen Goukouni Oueddei (Frolinat). Habré continued his opposition with his Army of the North (FAN), and Libya provided support for Goukouni.
**1981–82** Habré gained control of half the country. Goukouni fled and set up a 'government in exile'.
**1983** Habré's regime recognized by the Organization of African Unity (OAU) and France, but in the north, Goukouni's supporters, with Libya's help, fought on. Eventually a

ceasefire was agreed, with latitude 16°north dividing the country.
**1987** Chad, France, and Libya agreed on OAU ceasefire to end the civil war between the Muslim Arab north and Christian and animist black African south.
**1988** Libya relinquished its claims to the Aozou Strip.
**1990** President Habré was ousted after the army was defeated by Libyan-backed Patriotic Salvation Movement (MPS) rebel troops based in the Sudan and led by Habré's former ally Idriss Deby.
**1991–92** Several antigovernment coups were foiled.
**1993** A transitional charter was adopted, as a prelude to full democracy at a later date.
**1997** Nassour Ouaidou Guelendouksia was appointed prime minister. A reconciliation agreement was signed with rebel forces.

**Chad, Lake** lake on the northeastern boundary of Nigeria and the eastern boundary of Chad. It once varied in extent between rainy and dry seasons from 50,000 sq km/20,000 sq mi to 20,000 sq km/7,000 sq mi, but a series of droughts 1979–89 reduced its area to 2,500 sq km/965 sq mi in 1993. It is a shallow lake (depth does not exceed 5–8 m/16–26 ft), with the northern part being completely dry and the southern area being densely vegetated, with swamps and open pools. The lake was first seen by European explorers in 1823.

**chafer** beetle of the family Scarabeidae. The adults eat foliage or flowers, and the underground larvae feed on roots, chiefly those of grasses and cereals, and can be very destructive. Examples are the ◊*cockchafer* and the *rose chafer* Cetonia aurata, about 2 cm/0.8 in long and bright green.

**chaffinch** bird *Fringilla coelebs* of the finch family, common throughout much of Europe and West Asia. About 15 cm/6 in long, the male is olive-brown above, with a bright chestnut breast, a bluish-grey cap, and two white bands on the upper part of the wing; the female is duller. During winter they form single-sex flocks.

**Chagall, Marc** (1887–1985) Belorussian-born French painter and designer. Much of his highly coloured, fantastic imagery was inspired by the village life of his boyhood and by Jewish and Russian folk traditions. He was an original figure, often seen as a precursor of Surrealism. *I and the Village* (1911; Museum of Modern Art, New York) is characteristic.

**Chagas's disease** disease common in Central and South America, infecting approximately 18 million people worldwide. It is caused by a trypanosome parasite, *Trypanosoma cruzi*, transmitted by several species of blood-sucking insect; it results in incurable damage to the heart, intestines, and brain. It is named after Brazilian doctor Carlos Chagas (1879–1934).

**chain reaction** in chemistry, a succession of reactions, usually involving ◊free radicals, where the products of one stage are the reactants of the next. A chain reaction is characterized by the continual generation of reactive substances.

**chain reaction** in nuclear physics, a fission reaction that is maintained because neutrons released by the splitting of some atomic nuclei themselves go on to split others, releasing even more neutrons. Such a reaction can be controlled (as in a nuclear reactor) by using moderators to absorb excess neutrons. Uncontrolled, a chain reaction produces a nuclear explosion (as in an atom bomb).

**chalcedony** form of the mineral quartz, $SiO_2$, in which the crystals are so fine-grained that they are impossible to distinguish with a microscope (cryptocrystalline). Agate, onyx, and carnelian are ◊gem varieties of chalcedony.

**chalk** soft, fine-grained, whitish sedimentary rock composed of calcium carbonate, $CaCO_3$, extensively quarried for use in cement, lime, and mortar, and in the manufacture of cosmetics and toothpaste. *Blackboard chalk* in fact consists of gypsum (calcium sulphate, $CaSO_4.2H_2O$).

**Chamberlain, (Arthur) Neville** (1869–1940) British Conservative politician, son of Joseph ◊Chamberlain. He was prime minister 1937–40; his policy of appeasement toward the Italian fascist dictator Benito Mussolini and German Nazi Adolf Hitler (with whom he concluded the ◊Munich Agreement in 1938) failed to prevent the outbreak of World War II. He resigned in 1940 following the defeat of the British forces in Norway.

**Chamberlain, (Joseph) Austen** (1863–1937) British Conservative politician, elder son of Joseph ◊Chamberlain; as foreign secretary 1924–29 he negotiated and signed the Pact of ◊Locarno, which fixed the boundaries of Germany; for this he won the Nobel Peace Prize in 1925. In 1928 he also signed the Kellogg–Briand pact to outlaw war and provide for peaceful settlement of disputes.

**Chamberlain, Joseph** (1836–1914) British politician, reformist mayor of and member of Parliament for Birmingham. In 1886 he resigned from the cabinet over William Gladstone's policy of Home Rule for Ireland, and led the revolt of the Liberal-Unionists that saw them merge with the Conservative Party.

**chamber music** music intended for performance in a small room or chamber, rather than in the concert hall, and usually written for instrumental combinations, played with one instrument to a part, as in the ◊string quartet.

**chameleon** any of 80 or so species of lizard of the family Chameleontidae. Some species have highly developed colour-changing abilities, caused by stress and changes in the intensity of light and temperature, which alter the dispersal of pigment granules in the layers of cells beneath the outer skin.

**chamois** goatlike mammal *Rupicapra rupicapra* found in mountain ranges of southern Europe and Asia Minor. It is brown, with dark patches running through the eyes, and can be up to 80 cm/2.6 ft high. Chamois are very sure-footed, and live in herds of up to 30 members.

**Chamorro, Barrios de, Violeta** president of Nicaragua from 1990; see ◊Barrios de Chamorro.

**champagne** sparkling white wine invented by Dom Pérignon, a Benedictine monk, 1668. It is made from a blend of grapes (*pinot noir* and *chardonnay*) grown in the Marne River region around Reims and Epernay, in Champagne, northeastern France. After a first fermentation, sugar and yeast are added to the still wine, which, when bottled, undergoes a second fermentation to produce the sparkle. Sugar syrup may be added to make the wine sweet (*sec*) or dry (*brut*).

**Champagne-Ardenne** region of northeast France; area 25,600 sq km/9,882 sq mi; population (1990) 1,347,800. Its largest town is ◊Reims, but its administrative centre is Châlons-sur-Marne. It comprises the *départements* of Ardennes, Aube, Marne, and Haute-Marne. The land is fertile in the west and supports sheep and dairy farming; its vineyards produce the famous ◊champagne wines. The region also includes part of the ◊Ardennes forest.

**champignon** any of a number of edible fungi (see ◊fungus). The fairy ring champignon (*Marasmius oreades*) has this name because its fruiting bodies (mushrooms) grow in rings around the outer edge of the underground mycelium (threadlike body) of the fungus. (Family Agaricaceae.)

**Champlain, Samuel de** (1567–1635) French pioneer, soldier, and explorer in Canada. Having served in the army of Henry IV and on an expedition to the West Indies, he began his exploration of Canada in 1603. In a third expedition in 1608 he founded and named Québec, and was appointed lieutenant governor of French Canada in 1612.

**Champlain, Lake** lake in northeastern USA (extending some 10 km/6 mi into Canada) on the New York–Vermont border, west of the Green Mountains and east of the Adirondacks; length 201 km/125 mi; area 1,116 sq km/430 sq mi. Lake Champlain is linked to the St Lawrence River via the Richelieu River, and to the Hudson River by canal; it is the fourth-largest freshwater lake in the USA.

**chance** likelihood, or ◊probability, of an event taking place, expressed as a fraction or percentage. For example, the chance that a tossed coin will land heads up is 50%.

**chancellor of the Exchequer** in the UK, senior cabinet minister responsible for the national economy. The office, established under Henry III, originally entailed keeping the Exchequer seal. The current chancellor of the Exchequer from 1997 is Gordon Brown.

**Chancery** in the UK, a division of the High Court that deals with such matters as the administration of the estates of deceased persons, the execution of trusts, the enforcement of sales of land, and ◊foreclosure of mortgages. Before reorganization of the court system in 1875, it administered the rules of ◊equity as distinct from ◊common law.

**Chandigarh** city of north India, in the foothills of the Himalayas; population (1991) 511,000. It is also a Union Territory; area 114 sq km/44 sq mi; population (1991) 640,725. Planned by the architect ◊Le Corbusier, the city was inaugurated in 1953 to replace Lahore (capital of British Punjab), which went to Pakistan at partition in 1947. Since 1966, when Chandigarh became a Union Territory, it has been the capital city of the states of both Haryana and Punjab, pending the construction of a new capital for the former.

**Chandler, Raymond Thornton** (1888–1959) US novelist. He turned the pulp detective mystery form into a successful genre of literature and created the quintessential private eye in the tough but chivalric loner, Philip Marlowe. Marlowe is the narrator of such books as *The Big Sleep* (1939; filmed 1946), *Farewell My Lovely* (1940; filmed 1944), *The Lady in the Lake* (1943; filmed 1947), and *The Long Goodbye* (1954; filmed 1975). He also wrote numerous screenplays, notably *Double Indemnity* (1944), *Blue Dahlia* (1946), and *Strangers on a Train* (1951).

**Chandragupta Maurya** (died *c.* 297 BC) ruler of northern India and first Indian emperor *c.* 325–296 BC, founder of the Mauryan dynasty. He overthrew the Nanda dynasty of Magadha in 325 BC and then conquered the Punjab in 322 BC after the death of ◊Alexander (III) the Great, expanding his empire west to Iran. He is credited with having united most of India.

**Chanel, Coco (Gabrielle)** (1883–1971) French fashion designer. She was renowned as a trendsetter and her designs have been copied worldwide. She created the 'little black dress', the informal cardigan suit, costume jewellery, and perfumes.

**Changchun** industrial city and capital of ◊Jilin province, northeast China; population (1994) 2,237,000. It is the centre of an agricultural district, and manufactures machinery, vehicles, and railway equipment.

**change of state** in science, a change in the physical state (solid, liquid, or gas) of a material. For instance, melting, boiling, evaporation, and their opposites, solidification and condensation, are changes of state. The former set of changes are brought about by heating or decreased pressure; the latter by cooling or increased pressure.

**Chang Jiang** or *Yangtze Kiang,* ('long river') longest river of China and third longest in the world, flowing about 6,300 km/3,900 mi from Qinghai to the Yellow Sea. It is a major commercial waterway. Work began on the Three Gorges Dam on the river in December 1994.

**Channel, English** see ◊English Channel.

**Channel 4** Britain's fourth national television channel, launched on 2 November 1982 as a wholly-owned subsidiary of the IBA (Independent Broadcasting Authority; now known as the ITC or Independent Television Commission). Its brief was to serve minority interests, encourage innovation through the use of independent producers, and develop a character distinct from the other channels.

**Channel 5** Britain's fifth television channel. Launched on 30 March 1997, it was set up by the 1990 Broadcasting Act, under which the Independent Television Commission (ITC) was required to create a fifth national channel. It was awarded by competitive tender in 1995 to Channel 5 Broadcasting Ltd, a consortium of companies including Pearson, owners of the *Financial Times,* and United News and Media, owners of the *Daily Express* and Anglia Television.

**Channel Islands** group of islands in the English Channel, off the northwest coast of France; they are a possession of the British crown. They comprise the islands of Jersey,

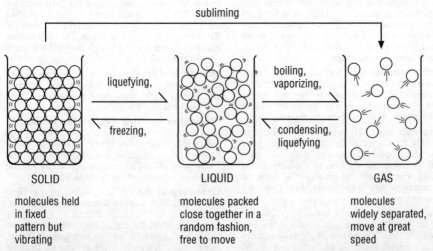

**SOLID**
molecules held in fixed pattern but vibrating

**LIQUID**
molecules packed close together in a random fashion, free to move

**GAS**
molecules widely separated, move at great speed

*change of state* The state (solid, liquid, or gas) of any substance is not fixed but varies with changes in temperature and pressure.

Guernsey, Alderney, Great and Little Sark, with the lesser Herm, Brechou, Jethou, and Lihou.

**Channel Tunnel** tunnel built beneath the ◊English Channel, linking Britain with mainland Europe. It comprises twin rail tunnels, 50 km/31 mi long and 7.3 m/24 ft in diameter, located 40 m/130 ft beneath the seabed. Construction began in 1987, and the French and English sections were linked in December 1990. It was officially opened on 6 May 1994. The shuttle train service, Le Shuttle, opened to lorries in May 1994 and to cars in December 1994. The tunnel's high-speed train service, Eurostar, linking London to Paris and Brussels, opened in November 1994.

The estimated cost of the tunnel has continually been revised upwards to a figure of £8 billion (1995). In 1995 Eurotunnel plc, the Anglo-French company that built the tunnel, made a loss of £925 million.

*chanson de geste* (medieval French 'song of (great) deeds') one of a genre of epic poems of medieval Europe, based on a legendary Carolingian past and dealing with matters of importance to the military classes – loyalty, lineage, courage, fighting skills, and battle tactics – often against an imaginary 'Saracen' foe. It probably developed from oral poetry recited in royal or princely courts.

**chant** ritual incantation by an individual or group, for confidence or mutual support. Chants can be secular (as, for example, sports supporters' chants) or religious, both Eastern and Western. Ambrosian and ◊Gregorian chants are forms of plainsong.

**chaos theory** or *chaology* or *complexity theory,* branch of mathematics that attempts to describe irregular, unpredictable systems – that is, systems whose behaviour is difficult to predict because there are so many variable or unknown factors. Weather is an example of a chaotic system.

**chapel** (from Latin *capella,* diminutive of *cappa* 'a cloak') a small or subordinate place of Christian worship other than a parish or cathedral church; also a church subordinate to and dependent on the principal parish church, to which it is in some way supplementary. The term can also refer to a building or part of a building or institution (for example, a palace, college, convent, hospital, or prison) erected for private devotion and often for private or semipublic religious services; also a recess in a church containing an altar that has been separately dedicated. In England the word 'chapel' is commonly applied to places of Nonconformist worship, as distinct from those of the Anglican and Roman Catholic churches.

**Chaplin, Charlie (Charles Spencer)** (1889–1977) English film actor and director. One of cinema's most popular stars, he made his reputation as a tramp with a smudge moustache, bowler hat, and twirling cane in silent comedies, including *The Rink* (1916), *The Kid* (1921), and *The Gold Rush* (1925). His work combines buffoonery with pathos, as in *The Great Dictator* (1940) and *Limelight* (1952).

**char** or *charr,* fish *Salvelinus alpinus* related to the trout, living in the Arctic coastal waters, and also in Europe and North America in some upland lakes. It is one of Britain's rarest fish, and is at risk from growing acidification.

**characin** freshwater fish belonging to the family Characidae. There are over 1,300 species, mostly in South and Central America, but also in Africa. Most are carnivores. In typical characins, unlike the somewhat similar carp family, the mouth is toothed, and there is a small dorsal adipose fin just in front of the tail.

**charcoal** black, porous form of ◊carbon, produced by heating wood or other organic materials in the absence of air. It is used as a fuel in the smelting of metals such as copper and zinc, and by artists for making black line drawings. *Activated charcoal* has been powdered and dried so that it presents a much increased surface area for adsorption; it is used for filtering and purifying liquids and gases – for example, in drinking-water filters and gas masks.

**Chardin, Jean-Baptiste-Siméon** (1699–1779) French painter. He took as his subjects naturalistic still lifes and quiet domestic scenes that recall the Dutch tradition. His work is a complete contrast to that of his contemporaries, the Rococo painters. He developed his own technique, using successive layers of paint to achieve depth of tone, and is generally considered one of the finest exponents of genre painting.

**charge** see ◊electric charge.

**charge-coupled device** (CCD), device for forming images electronically, using a layer of silicon that releases electrons when struck by incoming light. The electrons are stored in ◊pixels and read off into a computer at the end of the exposure. CCDs are used in digital cameras, and have now almost entirely replaced photographic film for applications such as astrophotography where extreme sensitivity to light is paramount.

**Charge of the Light Brigade** disastrous attack by the British Light Brigade of cavalry against the Russian entrenched artillery on 25 October 1854 during the Crimean War at the Battle of ◊Balaclava. Of the 673 soldiers who took part, there were 272 casualties.

**chariot** ancient two-wheeled carriage, used both in peace and war by the Egyptians, Assyrians, Babylonians, Greeks, Romans, ancient Britons, and others.

**charismatic movement** late 20th-century movement within the Christian church that emphasizes the role of the Holy Spirit in the life of the individual believer and in the life of the church. See ◊Pentecostal movement.

**Charlemagne, Charles I the Great** (742–814) king of the Franks from 768 and Holy Roman Emperor from 800. By inheritance (his father was ◊Pepin the Short) and extensive campaigns of conquest, he united most of western Europe by 804, when after 30 years of war the Saxons came under his control.

**Charles, (Mary) Eugenia** (1919– ) Dominican centre-right politician, prime minister

1980–95; cofounder and first leader of the cente-right Dominica Freedom Party (DFP). Two years after Dominica's independence the DFP won the 1980 general election and Charles became the Caribbean's first female prime minister. In 1993 she resigned the leadership of the DFP, but remained as prime minister until the 1995 elections, which were won by the opposition United Workers' Party (UNP). She then announced her retirement from politics.

**Charles, Jacques Alexandre César** (1746–1823) French physicist who studied gases and made the first ascent in a hydrogen-filled balloon in 1783. His work on the expansion of gases led to the formulation of ◊Charles's law.

**Charles** two kings of Great Britain and Ireland:

**Charles I** (1600–1649) King of Great Britain and Ireland from 1625, son of James I of England (James VI of Scotland). He accepted the petition of right in 1628 but then dissolved Parliament and ruled without a parliament 1629–40. His advisers were ◊Strafford and ◊Laud, who persecuted the Puritans and provoked the Scots to revolt. The ◊Short Parliament, summoned in 1640, refused funds, and the ◊Long Parliament later that year rebelled. Charles declared war on Parliament in 1642 but surrendered in 1646 and was beheaded in 1649. He was the father of Charles II.

**Charles II** (1630–1685) King of Great Britain and Ireland from 1660, when Parliament accepted the restoration of the monarchy after the collapse of Oliver Cromwell's Commonwealth; son of Charles I. His chief minister Edward Clarendon, who arranged Charles marriage in 1662 with Catherine of Braganza, was replaced in 1667 with the Cabal of advisers. His plans to restore Catholicism in Britain led to war with the Netherlands 1672–74 in support of Louis XIV of France and a break with Parliament, which he dissolved in 1681. He was succeeded by James II.

**Charles, (Charles Philip Arthur George)** (1948–   ) Prince of the UK, heir to the British throne, and Prince of Wales since 1958 (invested 1969). He is the first-born child of Queen Elizabeth II and the Duke of Edinburgh. He studied at Trinity College, Cambridge, 1967–70, before serving in the Royal Air Force and Royal Navy. The first royal heir since 1660 to have an English wife, he married Diana, Princess of Wales (then Lady Diana Spencer), daughter of the 8th Earl Spencer, in 1981. There are two sons and heirs, William (1982–   ) and Henry (1984–   ). Amid much publicity, Charles and Diana separated in 1992 and were divorced in 1996. Following the death of Diana, Princess of Wales in 1997 his popularity with the British public seemed in some doubt; however opinion polls in 1998 indicated that public feeling had warmed towards him and to his long-standing relationship with Camilla Parker Bowles (1946–   ).

**Charles** ten kings of France, including:

**Charles I** king of France, better known as the Holy Roman Emperor ◊Charlemagne.

**Charles (V) the Wise** (1337–1380) king of France 1364–80. He was regent during the captivity of his father John II in England from 1356 to 1360, and became king upon John's death. He reconquered nearly all of France from England in 1369–80, and diminished the power of mercenary companies in France.

**Charles (VI) the Mad** or *the Well-Beloved* (1368–1422) King of France from 1380, succeeding his father Charles V; he was under the regency of his uncles until 1388. He became mentally unstable in 1392, and civil war broke out between the dukes of Orléans and Burgundy. Henry V of England invaded France in 1415, conquering Normandy, and in 1420 forced Charles to sign the Treaty of Troyes, recognizing Henry as his successor.

**Charles VII** (1403–1461) King of France from 1429. Son of Charles VI, he was excluded from the succession by the Treaty of Troyes, but recognized by the south of France. In 1429 Joan of Arc raised the siege of Orléans and had him crowned at Reims. He organized France's first standing army and by 1453 had expelled the English from all of France except Calais.

**Charles IX** (1550–1574) King of France from 1560. Second son of Henry II and Catherine de' Medici, he succeeded his brother Francis II at the age of ten but remained under the domination of his mother's regency for ten years while France was torn by religious wars. In 1570 he fell under the influence of the ◊Huguenot leader Gaspard de Coligny; alarmed by this, Catherine instigated his order for the Massacre of ◊St Bartholomew, which led to a new religious war.

**Charles X** (1757–1836) King of France from 1824. Grandson of Louis XV and brother of Louis XVI and Louis XVIII, he was known as the comte d'Artois before his accession. He fled to England at the beginning of the French Revolution, and when he came to the throne on the death of Louis XVIII, he attempted to reverse the achievements of the Revolution. A revolt ensued 1830, and he again fled to England.

**Charles** seven rulers of the Holy Roman Empire, including:

**Charles (III) the Fat** (839–888) Holy Roman Emperor 881–87; he became king of the West Franks 885, thus uniting for the last time the whole of Charlemagne's dominions, but was deposed.

**Charles IV** (1316–1378) Holy Roman Emperor from 1355 and king of Bohemia from 1346. Son of John of Luxembourg, King of Bohemia, he was elected king of Germany in 1346 and ruled all Germany from 1347. He was the founder of the first German university in Prague in 1348.

**Charles V** (1500–1558) Holy Roman Emperor 1519–56. Son of Philip of Burgundy and Joanna of Castile, he inherited vast possessions, which led to rivalry from Francis I of France, whose alliance with the Ottoman Empire brought Vienna under siege in 1529 and 1532. Charles was also in conflict with the Protestants in

Germany until the Treaty of Passau of 1552, which allowed the Lutherans religious liberty.

**Charles VI** (1685–1740) Holy Roman Emperor from 1711, father of ◊Maria Theresa, whose succession to his Austrian dominions he tried to ensure, and himself claimant to the Spanish throne 1700, thus causing the War of the ◊Spanish Succession.

**Charles, (Karl Franz Josef)** (1887–1922) Emperor of Austria and king of Hungary from 1916, the last of the Habsburg emperors. He succeeded his great-uncle Franz Josef 1916 but was forced to withdraw to Switzerland 1918, although he refused to abdicate. In 1921 he attempted unsuccessfully to regain the crown of Hungary and was deported to Madeira, where he died.

**Charles, (Spanish** *Carlos)* four kings of Spain, including:

**Charles II** (1661–1700) King of Spain from 1665. The second son of Philip IV, he was the last of the Spanish Habsburg kings. Mentally disabled from birth, he bequeathed his dominions to Philip of Anjou, grandson of Louis XIV, which led to the War of the ◊Spanish Succession.

**Charles III** (1716–1788) King of Spain from 1759. Son of Philip V, he became duke of Parma 1732 and conquered Naples and Sicily 1734. On the death of his half-brother Ferdinand VI (1713–1759), he became king of Spain, handing over Naples and Sicily to his son Ferdinand (1751–1825). At home, he reformed state finances, strengthened the armed forces, and expelled the Jesuits. During his reign, Spain was involved in the Seven Years' War with France against England. This led to the loss of Florida 1763, which was only regained when Spain and France supported the colonists during the American Revolution.

**Charles IV** (1748–1819) King of Spain from 1788, when he succeeded his father, Charles III; he left the government in the hands of his wife and her lover, the minister Manuel de Godoy (1767–1851). In 1808 Charles was induced to abdicate by Napoleon's machinations in favour of his son Ferdinand VII (1784–1833), who was subsequently deposed by Napoleon's brother Joseph. Charles was awarded a pension by Napoleon and died in Rome.

**Charles, (Swedish** *Carl)* fifteen kings of Sweden (the first six were local chieftains), including:

**Charles X** (1622–1660) King of Sweden from 1654, when he succeeded his cousin Christina. He waged war with Poland and Denmark and in 1657 invaded Denmark by leading his army over the frozen sea.

**Charles XII** (1682–1718) King of Sweden from 1697, when he succeeded his father, Charles XI. From 1700 he was involved in wars with Denmark, Poland, and Russia.

He won a succession of victories until, in 1709 while invading Russia, he was defeated at Poltava in the Ukraine, and forced to take refuge in Turkey until 1714. He was killed while besieging Fredrikshall, Norway, although it was not known whether he was murdered by his own side or by the enemy.

**Charles XIV** Jean Baptiste Jules Bernadotte (1763–1844) King of Sweden and Norway from 1818. A former marshal in the French army, in 1810 he was elected crown prince of Sweden under the name of Charles John (Carl Johan). Loyal to his adopted country, he brought Sweden into the alliance against Napoleon 1813, as a reward for which Sweden received Norway. He was the founder of the present dynasty.

**Charles Edward Stuart** the *Young Pretender* or *Bonnie Prince Charlie* (1720–1788) British prince, grandson of James II and son of James, the Old Pretender. In the Jacobite rebellion of 1745 Charles won the support of the Scottish Highlanders; his army invaded England to claim the throne but was beaten back by the duke of Cumberland and routed at ◊Culloden on 16 April 1746. Charles fled; for five months he wandered through the Highlands with a price of £30,000 on his head before escaping to France. He visited England secretly in 1750, and may have made other visits. In later life he degenerated into a friendless drunkard. He settled in Italy in 1766.

**Charles Martel** (*c.* 688–741) Frankish ruler (Mayor of the Palace) of the eastern Frankish kingdom from 717 and the whole kingdom from 731. His victory against the Moors at Moussais-la-Bataille near Tours 732 earned him his nickname of Martel, 'the Hammer', because he halted the Islamic advance by the ◊Moors into Europe.

**Charles's law** law stating that the volume of a given mass of gas at constant pressure is directly proportional to its absolute temperature (temperature in kelvin). It was discovered by French physicist Jacques Charles 1787, and independently by French chemist Joseph Gay-Lussac in 1802.

**Charles (II) the Bald** (823–877) Holy Roman Emperor from 875 and (as Charles II) king of West Francia from 843. He was the younger son of Louis (I) 'the Pious' (778–840) and warred against his brother the emperor Lothair I (*c.* 795–855). The Treaty of Verdun in 843 made him king of the West Frankish Kingdom (now France and the Spanish Marches). He entered Italy in 875 and was crowned emperor.

**Charles the Bold, Duke of Burgundy** (1433–1477) Duke of Burgundy from 1463 who fought in the French civil war at Montlhéry in 1465, then crushed Liège in 1464–68. He reformed his army before engaging in an ambitious campaign for conquest, unsuccessfully besieging the imperial town of Neuss in 1474–75 before being defeated in his attack on the Swiss Federation in 1476–77. He died in battle near Nancy, in Lorraine.

**Charleston** back-kicking dance of the 1920s that originated in Charleston, South Carolina, and became an American craze following the musical *Runnin' Wild* (1923).

**Charlotte Amalie** capital, tourist resort, and free port of the US Virgin Islands, on the island of St Thomas; population (1990) 12,331. Boatbuilding and rum distilling are among the economic activities. It was founded 1672 by the Danish West India Company.

**Charlton, Bobby (Robert)** (1937– ) English footballer who between 1958 and 1970 scored a record 49 goals for England in 106 appearances. An elegant attacking midfield player who specialized in fierce long-range shots, he spent most of his playing career with Manchester United and played in the England team that won the World Cup 1966. He is the younger brother of Jack ♢Charlton and the nephew of the Newcastle and England forward Jackie Milburn. Knighted in 1994.

*career highlights*
*Football League* appearances: 644; goals: 206
*international appearances* 106; goals: 49
*World Cup* 1966
*Football League* 1965, 1967
*FA Cup* 1963
*Footballer of the Year* 1966
*European Footballer of the Year* 1966
*European Cup* 1968.

**Charlton, Jack (John)** (1935– ) English footballer. A tall commanding centre-half he spent all his playing career with Leeds United and played more than 750 games for them. He appeared in the England team that won the World Cup in 1966. He is the older brother of Robert (Bobby) ♢Charlton and the nephew of the Newcastle and England forward Jackie Milburn.

*career highlights*
*World Cup* 1966
*Footballer of the Year* 1967
*Football League Cup* 1968
*Fairs Cup* 1968, 1971
*Football League* 1969
*FA Cup* 1972.

**Charon** in Greek mythology, the boatman who ferried the dead (shades) over the rivers Acheron and Styx to ♢Hades, the underworld. An *obolus* (coin) placed on the tongue of the dead paid for their passage.

**Chartism** radical British democratic movement, mainly of the working classes, which flourished around 1838–48. It derived its name from the People's Charter, a six-point programme comprising universal male suffrage, equal electoral districts, secret ballot, annual parliaments, and abolition of the property qualification for, and payment of, members of Parliament.

**Charybdis** in Greek mythology, a monster and the whirlpool it forms, on the Sicilian side of the northern end of the narrow Straits of Messina, opposite the sea monster Scylla.

**château** country house or important residence in France. The term originally applied to a French medieval castle. The château was first used as a domestic building in the late 15th century. By the reign of Louis XIII (1610–43) fortifications such as moats and keeps were no longer used for defensive purposes, but merely as decorative features. The Loire valley contains some fine examples of châteaux.

**Chateaubriand, François Auguste René, vicomte de** (1768–1848) French writer. He was a founder of Romanticism. Having lived in exile from the French Revolution 1794–1800, he wrote *Atala* 1801 (based on his encounters with North American Indians), *Le Génie du christianisme/The Genius of Christianity* (1802) – a defence of the Christian faith in terms of social, cultural, and spiritual benefits – and the autobiographical *René* (1805).

**Chatterton, Thomas** (1752–1770) English poet. His medieval-style poems and brief life were to inspire English Romanticism. Having studied ancient documents, he composed poems he ascribed to a 15th-century monk, 'Thomas Rowley', and these were at first accepted as genuine. He committed suicide after becoming destitute.

**Chaucer, Geoffrey** (*c.* 1340–1400) English poet. *The Canterbury Tales,* a collection of stories told by a group of pilgrims on their way to Canterbury, reveals his knowledge of human nature and his stylistic variety, from urbane and ironic to simple and bawdy. His early work shows formal French influence, as in the dream-poem *The Book of the Duchess* and his adaptation of the French allegorical poem on courtly love, *The Romaunt of the Rose.* More mature works reflect the influence of Italian realism, as in *Troilus and Criseyde,* a substantial narrative poem about the tragic betrayal of an idealized courtly love, adapted from ♢Boccaccio. In *The Canterbury Tales* he shows his own genius for metre and characterization. Chaucer was the most influential English poet of the Middle Ages.

**cheese** food made from the *curds* (solids) of soured milk from cows, sheep, or goats, separated from the *whey* (liquid), then salted, put into moulds, and pressed into firm blocks. Cheese is ripened with bacteria or surface fungi, and kept for a time to mature before eating.

**cheetah** large wild cat *Acinonyx jubatus* native to Africa, Arabia, and southwestern Asia, but now rare in some areas. Yellowish with black spots, it has a slim lithe build. It is up to 1 m/3 ft tall at the shoulder, and up to 1.5 m/5 ft long. It can reach 103 kph/64 mph, but tires after about 400 yards. Cheetahs live in open country where they hunt small antelopes, hares, and birds.

**Chekhov, Anton Pavlovich** (1860–1904) Russian dramatist and writer of short stories. His plays concentrate on the creation of atmosphere and delineation of internal development, rather than external action. His first play, *Ivanov* (1887), was a failure, as was *The Seagull* (1896) until revived by Stanislavsky 1898 at the Moscow Art Theatre, for which Chekhov went on to write his finest plays: *Uncle Vanya* 1897, *The Three Sisters* (1901), and *The Cherry Orchard* (1904).

**chelate** chemical compound whose molecules consist of one or more metal atoms or charged ions joined to chains of organic residues by coordinate (or dative covalent) chemical ◊bonds.

**Chelyabinsk** capital city, economic and cultural centre of Chelyabinsk oblast (region), Russian Federation, 240 km/150 mi south of Yekaterinburg on the Miass River; population (1996 est) 1,083,000. Chelyabinsk is a major industrial centre in the Urals and an important rail centre. The main branches of industry are engineering (tractors, aircraft, machine tools), and metallurgy (steel, ferro-alloys, zinc). There is a large lignite-fired power station nearby. The important Chelyabinsk coal basin (first exploited in 1906) lies 15 km/9 mi to the east of the city. Waste from the city's plutonium plant makes it possibly the most radioactive place in the world.

**chemical change** change that occurs when two or more substances (reactants) interact with each other, resulting in the production of different substances (products) with different chemical compositions. A simple example of chemical change is the burning of carbon in oxygen to produce carbon dioxide (◊combustion). Other types of chemical change include ◊decomposition, ◊oxidation, and ◊reduction.

**chemical element** alternative name for ◊element.

**chemical equation** method of indicating the reactants and products of a chemical reaction by using chemical symbols and formulae. A chemical equation gives two basic pieces of information: (1) the reactants (on the left-hand side) and products (right-hand side); and (2) the reacting proportions (stoichiometry) – that is, how many units of each reactant and product are involved. The equation must balance; that is, the total number of atoms of a particular element on the left-hand side must be the same as the number of atoms of that element on the right-hand side.

**chemical equilibrium** condition in which the products of a reversible chemical reaction ◊reversible reaction are formed at the same rate at which they decompose back into the reactants, so that the concentration of each reactant and product remains constant.

**chemical warfare** use in war of gaseous, liquid, or solid substances intended to have a toxic effect on humans, animals, or plants. Together with ◊biological warfare, it was banned by the Geneva Protocol in 1925, and the United Nations in 1989 also voted for a ban. In June 1990, the USA and USSR agreed bilaterally to reduce their stockpile to 5,000 tonnes each by 2002. The USA began replacing its stocks with new nerve-gas ◊binary weapons. In 1993, over 120 nations, including the USA and Russia, signed a treaty outlawing the manufacture, stockpiling, and use of chemical weapons. However, it was not until 1997 that the Russian parliament ratified the treaty.

**chemisorption** the attachment, by chemical means, of a single layer of molecules, atoms, or ions of gas to the surface of a solid or, less frequently, a liquid. It is the basis of catalysis (see ◊catalyst) and is of great industrial importance.

**chemistry** branch of science concerned with the study of the structure and composition of the different kinds of matter, the changes which matter may undergo and the phenomena which occur in the course of these changes.

*Organic chemistry* is the branch of chemistry that deals with carbon compounds. *Inorganic chemistry* deals with the description, properties, reactions, and preparation of all the elements and their compounds, with the exception of carbon compounds. *Physical chemistry* is concerned with the quantitative explanation of chemical phenomena and reactions, and the measurement of data required for such explanations. This branch studies in particular the movement of molecules and the effects of temperature and pressure, often with regard to gases and liquids.

**chemosynthesis** method of making ◊protoplasm (contents of a cell) using the energy from chemical reactions, in contrast to the use of light energy employed for the same purpose in ◊photosynthesis. The process is used by certain bacteria, which can synthesize organic compounds from carbon dioxide and water using the energy from special methods of ◊respiration.

**chemotherapy** any medical treatment with chemicals. It usually refers to treatment of cancer with cytotoxic and other drugs. The term was coined by the German bacteriologist Paul Ehrlich for the use of synthetic chemicals against infectious diseases.

**chemotropism** movement by part of a plant in response to a chemical stimulus. The response by the plant is termed 'positive' if the growth is towards the stimulus or 'negative' if the growth is away from the stimulus.

**Chengdu** or *Chengtu,* ancient city and capital of ◊Sichuan province, China; population (1994) 3,016,000. It is a busy rail junction and has railway workshops. Industries include food-processing, engineering, electronics, and the manufacture of textiles and petrochemicals. There are well-preserved temples of the 8th-century poet Tu Fu and other historical figures.

**Chennai** formerly, to 1996, *Madras,* industrial port and capital of Tamil Nadu, India, on the Bay of Bengal; population (1991) 5,361,000. An all-weather artificial harbour handles cotton goods, oilseeds, hides and skins, and industrial raw materials. Main industries include cotton, cement, chemicals, railway, car and bicycle manufacture, oil refining, iron, and steel. Fort St George (1639) remains from the East India Company when Chennai was the chief port on the east coast; the fort now contains government offices and St Mary's Church, the first English church built in India (1680). Chennai was occupied by the French 1746–48 and shelled by the German ship *Emden* in 1914, the only place in India attacked in World War I. The University of Madras was founded in 1857, and there is a technical institute (1959).

**Cherenkov, Pavel Alexeevich** (1904–1990) Soviet physicist. In 1934 he discovered *Cherenkov radiation;* this occurs as a bluish light when charged atomic particles pass through water or other media at a speed in excess of that of light. He shared a Nobel prize in 1958 with his colleagues Ilya Frank and Igor Tamm for work resulting in a cosmic-ray counter.

**Chernobyl** town in northern Ukraine, 100 km/ 62 mi north of Kiev; site of a nuclear power station. On 26 April 1986, two huge explosions occurred at the plant, destroying a central reactor and breaching its 1,000-tonne roof. In the immediate vicinity of Chernobyl, 31 people died (all firemen or workers at the plant) and 135,000 were permanently evacuated. It has been estimated that there will be an additional 20–40,000 deaths from cancer in the following 60 years; 600,000 are officially classified as at risk. According to WHO figures of 1995, the incidence of thyroid cancer in children has increased 200-fold in Belarus as a result of fallout from the disaster.

**cherry** any of a group of fruit-bearing trees distinguished from plums and apricots by their fruits, which are round and smooth and not covered with a bloom. They are cultivated in temperate regions with warm summers and grow best in deep fertile soil. (Genus *Prunus,* family Rosaceae.)

**chervil** any of several plants belonging to the carrot family. The garden chervil (*Anthriscus cerefolium*) has leaves with a sweetish smell, similar to parsley. It is used as a garnish and in soups. Chervil originated on the borders of Europe and Asia and was introduced to Western Europe by the Romans. (Genus *Anthriscus,* family Umbelliferae.)

**Chesapeake Bay** largest of the inlets on the Atlantic coast of the USA, bordered by eastern Maryland and eastern Virginia. Chesapeake Bay extends southwards from Havre de Grace in northeast Maryland, and enters the Atlantic between Cape Charles and Cape Henry in Virginia; it is about 320 km/200 mi in length and 6–64 km/4–40 mi in width. There are several deep-water ports located on the bay: Newport News, Norfolk, Portsmouth, and Baltimore.

**Cheshire** county of northwest England, which has contained the unitary authorities Halton and Warrington since April 1998
*area* 2,320 sq km/896 sq mi
*towns and cities* Chester (administrative headquarters), Crewe, Congleton, Macclesfield
*physical* chiefly a fertile plain, with the Pennines in the east; rivers: Mersey, Dee, Weaver; a sandstone ridge extending south through central Cheshire together with Delamere Forest constitute a woodland and heath landscape
*features* salt mines and geologically rich former copper workings at Alderley Edge (in use from Roman times until the 1920s); Little Moreton Hall; discovery of Lindow Man, the first 'bogman' to be found in mainland Britain, dating from around 500 BC; Museum of the Chemical Industry on Spike Island; Quarry Bank Mill at Styal is a cotton-industry museum
*agriculture* arable farming in the north; cheese

(at one time produced entirely in farmhouses) and dairy products in the centre and south of the county
*industries* aerospace industry, chemicals, pharmaceuticals, salt, silk and textiles (at Congleton and Macclesfield), vehicles
*famous people* Charles Dodgson (Lewis Carroll), Elizabeth Gaskell
*population* (1996) 980,000.

**chess** board game originating as early as the 2nd century AD. Two players use 16 pieces each, on a board of 64 squares of alternating colour, to try to force the opponent into a position where the main piece (the king) is threatened and cannot move to another position without remaining threatened.

**Chesterton, G(ilbert) K(eith)** (1874– 1936) English novelist, essayist, and poet. He wrote numerous short stories featuring a Catholic priest, Father Brown, who solves crimes by drawing on his knowledge of human nature. Other novels include the fantasy *The Napoleon of Notting Hill* (1904) and *The Man Who Was Thursday* (1908), a deeply emotional allegory about the problem of evil.

**chestnut** any of a group of trees belonging to the beech family. The Spanish or sweet chestnut (*Castanea sativa*) produces edible nuts inside husks; its timber is also valuable. ◊Horse chestnuts are quite distinct, belonging to the genus *Aesculus,* family Hippocastanaceae. (True chestnut genus *Castanea,* family Fagaceae.)

**Chetnik** member of a Serbian nationalist group that operated underground during the German occupation of Yugoslavia in World War II. Led by Col Draza Mihailovič, the Chetniks initially received aid from the Allies, but this was later transferred to the communist partisans led by Tito. The term was also popularly applied to Serb militia forces in the 1991–92 Yugoslav civil war.

**Chiang Kai-shek** Wade-Giles transliteration of ◊Jiang Jie Shi.

**Chicago** (Ojibway 'wild onion place') financial and industrial city in Illinois, USA, on Lake Michigan. It is the third-largest US city; population (1992) 2,768,500; metropolitan area (1992) 8,410,000. Industries include iron, steel, chemicals, electrical goods, machinery, meatpacking and food processing, publishing, and fabricated metals. The once famous stockyards are now closed. Chicago grew from a village in the mid-19th century. The world's first skyscraper was built here 1885 and some of the world's tallest skyscrapers, including the tallest, the Sears Tower at 443 m/1,454 ft, are in Chicago.

**chicken** domestic fowl; see under ◊poultry.

**chickenpox** or *varicella,* common, usually mild disease, caused by a virus of the ◊herpes group and transmitted by airborne droplets. Chickenpox chiefly attacks children under the age of ten. The incubation period is two to three weeks. One attack normally gives immunity for life.

**chickpea** annual leguminous plant (see ◊legume), grown for food in India and the Middle East. Its short hairy pods contain edible seeds similar to peas. (*Cicer arietinum,* family Leguminosae.)

**chicory** plant native to Europe and West Asia, with large, usually blue, flowers. Its long taproot is used dried and roasted as a coffee substitute. As a garden vegetable, grown under cover, its blanched leaves are used in salads. It is related to ◊endive. (*Cichorium intybus,* family Compositae.)

**chiffchaff** small songbird *Phylloscopus collybita* of the warbler family, Muscicapidae, order Passeriformes. It is found in woodlands and thickets in Europe and northern Asia during the summer, migrating south for winter. About 11 cm/4.3 in long, olive above, greyish below, with yellow-white nether parts, an eyestripe, and usually dark legs, it looks similar to a willow warbler but has a distinctive song.

**chihuahua** smallest breed of dog, 15 cm/10 in high, developed in the USA from Mexican origins. It may weigh only 1 kg/2.2 lb. The domed head and wide-set ears are characteristic, and the skull is large compared to the body. It can be almost any colour, and occurs in both smooth (or even hairless) and long-coated varieties.

**Chihuahua** capital of Chihuahua state, Mexico, 1,285 km/800 mi northwest of Mexico City; population (1990) 530,800. It was founded 1707. It is the centre of a mining district and has textile mills.

**chilblain** painful inflammation of the skin of the feet, hands, or ears, due to cold. The parts turn red, swell, itch violently, and are very tender. In bad cases, the skin cracks, blisters, or ulcerates.

**Chile** Republic of
**national name** *República de Chile*

**area** 756,950 sq km/292,258 sq mi
**capital** Santiago
**major towns/cities** Concepción, Viña del Mar, Valparaiso, Talcahuano, San Bernardo, Puente Alto, Chillán, Rancagua, Talca, Temuco
**major ports** Valparaíso, Antofagasta, Arica, Iquique, Punta Arenas
**physical features** Andes mountains along eastern border, Atacama Desert in north, fertile central valley, grazing land and forest in south
**territories** Easter Island, Juan Fernández Islands, part of Tierra del Fuego, claim to part of Antarctica
**head of state** Eduardo Frei from 1993
**head of government** Dante Cordova from 1995
**political system** emergent democracy
**political parties** Christian Democratic Party (PDC), moderate centrist; National Renewal Party (RN), right wing; Socialist Party of Chile (PS), left wing; Independent Democratic Union (UDI), right wing; Party for Democracy (PPD), left of centre; Union of the Centre-Centre (UCC), right wing; Radical Party (PR), left of centre
**currency** Chilean peso
**GNP per capita (PPP)** (US$) 12,890 (1998)
**exports** copper, fruits, timber products, fishmeal, vegetables, manufactured foodstuffs and beverages. Principal market: USA 17.7% (1998)
**population** 15,019,000 (1999 est)
**language** Spanish
**religion** Roman Catholic
**life expectancy** 72 (men); 78 (women) (1995–2000)
**Chronology**
**1535** First Spanish invasion of Chile abandoned in face of fierce resistance from indigenous Araucanian Indians.
**1541** Pedro de Valdivia began Spanish conquest and founded Santiago.
**1553** Valdivia captured and killed by Araucanian Indians led by Chief Lautaro.
**17th century** Spanish developed small agricultural settlements ruled by government subordinate to viceroy in Lima, Peru.
**1778** King of Spain appointed a separate captain-general to govern Chile.
**1810** Santiago junta proclaimed Chilean autonomy after Napoleon dethroned King of Spain.
**1814** Spanish viceroy regained control of Chile.
**1817** Army of the Andes, led by José de San Martín and Bernardo O'Higgins, defeated the Spanish.
**1818** Achieved independence from Spain with O'Higgins as supreme director.
**1823–30** O'Higgins forced to resign; civil war between conservative centralists and liberal federalists ended with conservative victory.
**1833** Autocratic republican constitution created unitary Roman Catholic state with strong president and limited franchise.
**1851–61** President Manuel Montt bowed to pressure to liberalize constitution and reduce privileges of landowners and church.
**1879–84** Chile defeated Peru and Bolivia in War of the Pacific and increased its territory by a third.
**late 19th century** Mining of nitrate and copper became major industry; large-scale European immigration followed 'pacification' of Araucanian Indians.

**1891** Constitutional dispute between president and congress led to civil war; congressional victory reduced president to figurehead status.
**1920** Election of liberal president Arturo Alessandri Palma; congress blocked his social reform programme.
**1925** New constitution increased presidential powers, separated church and state, and made primary education compulsory.
**1927** Military coup led to dictatorship of Gen Carlos Ibáñez del Campo.
**1931** Sharp fall in price of copper and nitrate caused dramatic economic and political collapse.
**1932** Re-election of President Alessandri, who restored order by harsh measures.
**1938** Popular Front of Radicals, Socialists, and Communists took power under Pedro Aguirre Cedra, who introduced economic policies based on US New Deal.
**1947** Communists organized violent strikes to exploit discontent over high inflation.
**1948–58** Communist Party banned.
**1952** Gen Ibáñez elected president on law-and-order platform; austerity policies reduced inflation to 20%.
**1958** Jorge Alessandri (son of former president) succeeded Ibáñez as head of Liberal-Conservative coalition.
**1964** Christian Democrat Eduardo Frei Montalva became president; he introduced cautious 'communitarian' social reforms, but failed to combat inflation.
**1970** Salvador Allende, leader of Popular Unity coalition, became world's first democratically elected Marxist president; he embarked on an extensive programme of nationalization and radical social reform.
**1973** Allende killed in CIA-backed military coup; Gen Augusto Pinochet established dictatorship combining severe political repression with free-market economics.
**1981** Pinochet began eight-year term as president under new constitution described as 'transition to democracy'.
**1983** Economic recession provoked growing opposition to regime from all sides.
**1988** Referendum on whether Pinochet should serve a further term resulted in a clear 'No' vote; he agreed to hold elections in following year.
**1990** The end of the military regime; Christian Democrat Patricio Aylwin became president, with Pinochet as commander in chief of the army; an investigation was launched into over 2,000 political executions during the military regime.
**1994** Eduardo Frei (son of former president) succeeded Aylwin as president.
**1995** Frei introduced measures to reduce military influence in government.
**1998** Pinochet retired from the army and was made life senator. The state of the economy worsened. Pinochet was placed under arrest in the UK; proceedings began to extradite him to Spain on murder charges.
**1999** The UK government ruled that Pinochet would be extradited to Spain for crimes including torture.

**chilli** pod, or powder made from the pod, of a variety of ⟨capsicum (*Capsicum frutescens*), a small, hot, red pepper. It is widely used in cooking. The hot ingredient of chilli is capsaicin. It causes a burning sensation in the mouth by triggering nerve branches in the eyes, nose, tongue, and mouth.
Capsaicin does not activate the taste buds and therefore has no flavour. It is claimed that people can become physically addicted to it.

**chimera** or *chimaera*, in Greek mythology, a fire-breathing animal with a lion's head and foreparts, a goat's middle, a dragon's rear, and a tail in the form of a snake; hence any apparent hybrid of two or more creatures. The chimera was killed by the hero Bellerophon on the winged horse Pegasus.

**chimpanzee** highly intelligent African ape *Pan troglodytes* that lives mainly in rain forests but sometimes in wooded savanna. Chimpanzees are covered in thin but long black body hair, except for the face, hands, and feet, which may have pink or black skin. They normally walk on all fours, supporting the front of the body on the knuckles of the fingers, but can stand or walk upright for a short distance. They can grow to 1.4 m/4.5 ft tall, and weigh up to 50 kg/110 lb. They are strong and climb well, but spend time on the ground, living in loose social groups. The bulk of the diet is fruit, with some leaves, insects, and occasional meat. Females reach sexual maturity at 8–12 years of age, males at 17–18. Chimpanzees give birth to a single infant approximately every five years. Chimpanzees can use 'tools', fashioning twigs to extract termites from their nests. According to a 1998 estimate by the Worldwide Fund for Nature, the world population of chimpanzees stands at 200,000.
The *bonobo* or pygmy chimpanzee, *Pan paniscus* is found only in a small area of rainforest in the Democratic Republic of Congo (formerly Zaire). Bonobos are a distinct species about the same height as 'common' chimpanzees, but they are of a slighter build, with less hair, and stand upright more frequently. In 1999 there were believed to be fewer than 15,000 bonobos left and these were threatened by the civil war in the Democratic Republic of Congo.

**China** People's Republic of
***national name*** *Zhonghua Renmin Gonghe Guo*
***area*** 9,572,900 sq km/3,696,000 sq mi
***capital*** Beijing (Peking)
***major towns/cities*** Shanghai, Hong Kong, Chongqing (Chungking), Tianjin, Guangzhou (Canton), Shenyang (Mukden), Wuhan, Nanjing (Nanking), Harbin, Chengdu, Xi'an, Zibo
***major ports*** Tianjin (Tientsin), Shanghai, Hong Kong, Qingdao (Tsingtao), Guangzhou (Canton)
***physical features*** two-thirds of China is mountains or desert (north and west); the low-lying east is irrigated by rivers Huang He (Yellow River), Chang Jiang (Yangtze-Kiang), Xi Jiang (Si Kiang)

**head of state** Jiang Zemin from 1993
**head of government** Zhu Rongji from 1998
**political system** communist republic
**political party** Chinese Communist Party
(CCP), Marxist-Leninist-Maoist
**currency** yuan
**GNP per capita (PPP)** (US$) 3,220 (1998)
**exports** basic manufactures, miscellaneous
manufactured articles (particularly clothing and
toys), crude petroleum, machinery and transport
equipment, fishery products, cereals, canned
food, tea, raw silk, cotton cloth. Principal market: Hong Kong 21.1% (1998)
**population** 1,273,639,000 (1999 est)
**language** Chinese, including Mandarin (official), Cantonese, Wu, and other dialects
**religion** Taoist, Confucianist, and Buddhist;
Muslim 20 million; Catholic 3–6 million
(divided between the 'patriotic' church established in 1958 and the 'loyal' church subject to
Rome); Protestant 3 million
**life expectancy** 68 (men); 72 (women) (1995–
2000)
**Chronology**
**c. 3000 BC** Yangshao culture reached its peak in
the Huang He Valley; displaced by Longshan
culture in eastern China.
**c. 1766– c. 1122 BC** First major dynasty, the
Shang, arose from Longshan culture; writing
and calendar developed.
**c. 1122–256 BC** Zhou people of western China
overthrew Shang and set up new dynasty; development of money and written laws.
**c. 500 BC** Confucius expounded philosophy
which guided Chinese government and society
for the next 2,000 years.
**403–221 BC** 'Warring States Period': Zhou
Empire broke up into small kingdoms.
**221–206 BC** Qin kingdom defeated all rivals and
established first empire with strong central government; emperor Shi Huangdi built Great Wall
of China.
**202 BC–AD 220** Han dynasty expanded empire
into central Asia; first overland trade with
Europe; art and literature flourished; Buddhism
introduced from India.
**220–581** Large-scale rebellion destroyed Han
dynasty; empire split into three competing king-

doms; several short-lived dynasties ruled parts
of China.
**581–618** Sui dynasty reunified China and
repelled Tatar invaders.
**618–907** Tang dynasty enlarged and strengthened the empire; great revival of culture; major
rebellion 875–84.
**907–60** 'Five Dynasties and Ten Kingdoms': disintegration of empire amid war and economic
decline; development of printing.
**960–1279** Song dynasty reunified China and
restored order; civil service examinations introduced; population reached 100 million;
Manchurians occupied northern China in 1127.
**1279** Mongols conquered all China, which
became part of the vast empire of Kublai Khan,
founder of the Yuan dynasty; Venetian traveller
Marco Polo visited China 1275–92.
**1368** Rebellions drove out the Mongols; Ming
dynasty expanded empire; architecture flourished in new capital of Beijing; dislike of
Mongols led to contempt for all things foreign.
**1516** Portuguese explorers reached Macau;
other European traders followed; first Chinese
porcelain arrived in Europe 1580.
**1644** Manchurian invasion established the Qing
(or Manchu) dynasty; Manchurians assimilated
and Chinese trade and culture continued to
thrive.
**1796–1804** Anti-Manchu revolt weakened Qing
dynasty; population increase in excess of food
supplies led to falling living standards and cultural decline.
**1839–42** First Opium War; Britain forced China
to cede Hong Kong and open five ports to
European trade; Second Opium War extracted
further trade concessions 1856–60.
**1850–64** Millions died in Taiping Rebellion;
Taipings combined Christian and Chinese beliefs
and demanded land reform.
**1894–95** Sino-Japanese War: Chinese driven out
of Korea.
**1897–98** Germany, Russia, France, and Britain
leased ports in China; conquest by European
empires seemed likely.
**1898** Hong Kong was secured by Britain on a
99-year lease.
**1900** Anti-Western Boxer Rebellion crushed by
foreign intervention; jealousy between Great
Powers prevented partition.
**1911** Revolution broke out; Republic of China
proclaimed by Sun Zhong Shan (Sun Yat-sen) of
Guomindang (National People's Party).
**1912** Abdication of infant emperor Pu-i; Gen
Yuan Shih-K'ai became dictator.
**1916** Power of central government collapsed on
death of Yuan Shih-K'ai; northern China dominated by local warlords.
**1919** Beijing students formed 4th May movement to protest at transfer of German possessions in China to Japan.
**1921** Sun Zhong Shan elected president of nominal national government; Chinese Communist
Party founded; communists worked with
Guomindang to reunite China from 1923.
**1925** Death of Sun Zhong Shan; leadership of
Guomindang gradually passed to military
commander Jiang Jie Shi (Chiang Kai-shek).

**1926–28** Revolutionary Army of Jiang Jie Shi reunified China; Guomindang broke with communists and tried to suppress them in civil war.
**1932** Japan invaded Manchuria and established puppet state of Manchukuo.
**1934–35** Communists undertook Long March from Jiangxi and Fujian in south to Yan'an in north to escape encirclement by Guomindang.
**1937–45** Japan renewed invasion of China; Chiang Kai-shek received help from USA and Britain from 1941.
**1946** Civil war resumed between Guomindang and communists led by Mao Zedong.
**1949** Victorious communists proclaimed People's Republic of China under Chairman Mao; Guomindang fled to Taiwan.
**1950–53** China intervened heavily in Korean War.
**1958** 'Great Leap Forward': extremist five-year plan to accelerate output severely weakened economy.
**1960** Sino-Soviet split: China accused USSR of betraying communism; USSR withdrew technical advisers; border clashes on Ussuri River in 1969.
**1962** Economic recovery programme under Liu Shaoqi caused divisions between 'rightists' and 'leftists'; brief border war with India.
**1966–69** 'Great Proletarian Cultural Revolution'; leftists overthrew Liu Shaoqi with support of Mao; Red Guards disrupted education, government, and daily life in attempt to enforce revolutionary principles.
**1970** Mao supported efforts of Prime Minister Zhou Enlai to restore order.
**1971** People's Republic of China admitted to United Nations; full diplomatic relations with USA established in 1979.
**1976** Deaths of Zhou Enlai and Mao Zedong led to power struggle between rightists and leftists; Hua Guofeng became leader and arrested leftist 'Gang of Four'.
**1977–81** Rightist Deng Xiaoping emerged as supreme leader; pragmatic economic policies introduced market incentives and encouraged foreign trade.
**1987** Deng Xiaoping retired from Politburo but remained a dominant figure.
**1989** Over 2,000 people were killed when the army crushed prodemocracy student demonstrations in Tiananmen Square, Beijing; international sanctions were imposed.
**1991** China and the USSR reached an agreement on their disputed border.
**1996** Reunification with Taiwan was declared a priority.
**1997** Deng Xiaoping died aged 92. A border agreement was signed with Russia. Hong Kong was returned to Chinese sovereignty.
**1998** Zhu Rongji became the new prime minister. The Yangtze in Hubei province flooded, causing widespread devastation. Former Communist leader Chen Xitong was sentenced to 16 years' imprisonment. Dissident Xu Wenli was jailed for trying to set up an opposition party.
**1999** Jiang Zemin made a state visit to the USA.

**China Sea** area of the Pacific Ocean bordered by China, Vietnam, Borneo, the Philippines, and Japan. Various groups of small islands and shoals, including the Paracels, 500 km/300 mi east of Vietnam, have been disputed by China and other powers because they lie in oil-rich areas. The chief rivers which flow into the South China Sea are the Red River and Mekong; the main ports include Canton, Hong Kong, Manila, Bangkok, Singapore, and Ho Chi Minh City.

**chinchilla** South American rodent *Chinchilla laniger* found in high, rather barren areas of the Andes in Bolivia and Chile. About the size of a small rabbit, it has long ears and a long bushy tail, and shelters in rock crevices. These gregarious animals have thick, soft, silver-grey fur, and were hunted almost to extinction for it. They are now farmed and protected in the wild.

**Chinese** the native groups or inhabitants of China and Taiwan, and those people of Chinese descent. The Chinese comprise more than 25% of the world's population, and the Chinese language (Mandarin) is the largest member of the Sino-Tibetan family.

**Chinese language** language or group of languages of the Sino-Tibetan family, spoken in China, Taiwan, Hong Kong, Singapore, and Chinese communities throughout the world. Varieties of spoken Chinese differ greatly, but all share a written form using thousands of ideographic symbols – characters – which have changed little in 2,000 years. Nowadays, *putonghua* ('common speech'), based on the educated Beijing dialect known as Mandarin Chinese, is promoted throughout China as the national spoken and written language.

**Chinese Revolution** series of great political upheavals in China between 1911 and 1949 which eventually led to Communist Party rule and the establishment of the People's Republic of China. In 1912 a nationalist revolt overthrew the imperial Manchu dynasty. Under the leaders Sun Zhong Shan (Sun Yat-sen) (1923–25) and Jiang Jie Shi (Chiang Kai-shek) (1925–49), the nationalists, or Guomindang, were increasingly challenged by the growing communist movement. The 10,000-km/6,000-mi ◊Long March to the northwest, undertaken by the communists in 1934–35 to escape Guomindang harassment, resulted in the emergence of ◊Mao Zedong as a communist leader. During World War II the various Chinese political groups pooled military resources against the Japanese invaders, but in 1946 the conflict reignited into open civil war. In 1949 the Guomindang were defeated at Nanjing and forced to flee to Taiwan. Communist rule was established in the People's Republic of China under the leadership of Mao Zedong.

**chip** or *silicon chip,* another name for an ◊*integrated circuit,* a complete electronic circuit on a slice of silicon (or other semiconductor) crystal only a few millimetres square.

**chipmunk** any of several species of small ground squirrel with characteristic stripes along its side. Chipmunks live in North America and East Asia, in a variety of habitats, usually wooded, and take shelter in burrows. They have pouches in their cheeks for carrying food. They climb well but spend most of their time on or near the ground.

**Chippendale, Thomas** (1718–1779) English furniture designer. He set up his workshop in St Martin's Lane, London, in 1753. His trade catalogue *The Gentleman and Cabinet Maker's Director* (1754), was a significant contribution to furniture design, and the first of its type to be published. Although many of his most characteristic designs are ◊Rococo, he also employed Louis XVI, Chinese, Gothic, and Neo-Classical styles. He worked mainly in mahogany, newly introduced from South America.

**Chirac, Jacques René** (1932– ) French Gaullist politician and head of state, president from 1995 and twice prime minister 1974–76 and 1986–88, 'co-habiting' on the second occasion with the socialist president François ◊Mitterrand. Chirac led the Gaullist party 1974–95, refounding it in 1976 as the Rassemblement pour la République (RPR). He also served as the first elected mayor of Paris 1977–95.

**Chirico, Giorgio de** (1888–1978) Greek-born Italian painter. He founded the school of Metaphysical Painting, which in its enigmatic imagery and haunted, dreamlike settings presaged Surrealism, as in *Nostalgia of the Infinite* (1911; Museum of Modern Art, New York).

**chiropractic** in alternative medicine, technique of manipulation of the spine and other parts of the body, based on the principle that physical disorders are attributable to aberrations in the functioning of the nervous system, which manipulation can correct.

**Chisinău** Russian *Kishinev,* capital of Moldova, situated in a rich agricultural area; population (1990) 676,000. It is a commercial and cultural centre; industries include cement, food processing, tobacco, and textiles.

**Chissano, Joaquim** (1939– ) Mozambique nationalist politician, president from 1986; foreign minister 1975–86. In October 1992 he signed a peace accord with the leader of the rebel Mozambique National Resistance (MNR) party, bringing to an end 16 years of civil war, and in 1994 won the first free presidential elections.

**chitin** complex long-chain compound, or ◊polymer; a nitrogenous derivative of glucose. Chitin is widely found in invertebrates. It forms the ◊exoskeleton of insects and other arthropods. It combines with protein to form a covering that can be hard and tough, as in beetles, or soft and flexible, as in caterpillars and other insect larvae. It is insoluble in water and resistant to acids, alkalis, and many organic solvents. In crustaceans such as crabs, it is impregnated with calcium carbonate for extra strength.

**Chittagong** city and port in Bangladesh, 16 km/10 mi from the mouth of the Karnaphuli River, on the Bay of Bengal; population (1991) 1,364,000. Industries include steel, engineering, chemicals, and textiles.

**chivalry** code of gallantry and honour that medieval knights were pledged to observe. Its principal virtues were piety, honour, valour, courtesy, chastity, and loyalty. The word originally meant the knightly class of the feudal Middle Ages. Modern orders of chivalry such as the Order of the Garter are awarded as a mark of royal favour or as a reward for public services; see ◊knighthood, order of.

**chive** or *chives,* perennial European plant belonging to the lily family, related to onions and leeks. It has an underground bulb, long hollow tubular leaves, and globe-shaped purple flower heads. The leaves are used as a garnish for salads. (*Allium schoenoprasum,* family Liliaceae.)

**chlamydia** viruslike bacteria which live parasitically in animal cells, and cause disease in humans and birds. Chlamydiae are thought to be descendants of bacteria that have lost certain metabolic processes. In humans, a strain of chlamydia causes ◊trachoma, a disease found mainly in the tropics (a leading cause of blindness); venereally transmitted chlamydiae cause genital and urinary infections.

**chloride** Cl⁻ negative ion formed when hydrogen chloride dissolves in water, and any salt containing this ion, commonly formed by the action of hydrochloric acid (HCl) on various metals or by direct combination of a metal and chlorine. Sodium chloride (NaCl) is common table salt.

**chlorine** (Greek *chloros* 'green') greenish-yellow, gaseous, nonmetallic element with a pungent odour, symbol Cl, atomic number 17, relative atomic mass 35.453. It is a member of the ◊halogen group and is widely distributed, in combination with the ◊alkali metals, as chlorates or chlorides.

**chlorofluorocarbon** (CFC), a class of synthetic chemicals that are odourless, nontoxic, nonflammable, and chemically inert. The first CFC was synthesized in 1892, but no use was found for it until the 1920s. Since then their stability and apparently harmless properties have made CFCs popular as propellants in ◊aerosol cans, as refrigerants in refrigerators and air conditioners, as degreasing agents, and in the manufacture of foam packaging. They are partly responsible for the destruction of the ◊ozone layer. In June 1990 representatives of 93 nations, including the UK and the USA, agreed to phase out production of CFCs and various other ozone-depleting chemicals by the end of the 20th century.

**chloroform** technical name *trichloromethane,* CHCl₃ clear, colourless, toxic, carcinogenic liquid with a characteristic pungent, sickly sweet smell and taste, formerly used as an anaesthetic (now superseded by less harmful substances).

It is used as a solvent and in the synthesis of organic chemical compounds.

**chlorophyll** green pigment present in most plants; it is responsible for the absorption of light energy during ◊photosynthesis.

The pigment absorbs the red and blue-violet parts of sunlight but reflects the green, thus giving plants their characteristic colour.

**chloroplast** structure (◊organelle) within a plant cell containing the green pigment

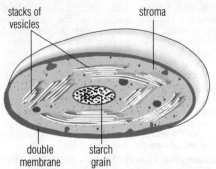

stacks of vesicles

stroma

double membrane

starch grain

***chloroplast*** *Green chlorophyll molecules on the membranes of the vesicle stacks capture light energy to produce food by photosynthesis.*

chlorophyll. Chloroplasts occur in most cells of the green plant that are exposed to light, often in large numbers. Typically, they are flattened and disclike, with a double membrane enclosing the stroma, a gel-like matrix. Within the stroma are stacks of fluid-containing cavities, or vesicles, where ◊photosynthesis occurs.

**chlorosis** abnormal condition of green plants in which the stems and leaves turn pale green or yellow. The yellowing is due to a reduction in the levels of the green chlorophyll pigments. It may be caused by a deficiency in essential elements (such as magnesium, iron, or manganese), a lack of light, genetic factors, or viral infection.

**chocolate** powder, syrup, confectionery, or beverage derived from cacao seeds. See ◊cocoa and chocolate.

**choir** body of singers, usually of sacred music, of more than one voice to a part, whose members are able to sight read music and hold a melody. A traditional cathedral choir of male voices is required to sing responses, hymns, and psalms appropriate to the church calendar.

**cholera** disease caused by infection with various strains of the bacillus *Vibrio cholerae,* transmitted in contaminated water and characterized by violent diarrhoea and vomiting. It is prevalent in many tropical areas.

**cholesterol** white, crystalline ◊sterol found throughout the body, especially in fats, blood, nerve tissue, and bile; it is also provided in the diet by foods such as eggs, meat, and butter. A high level of cholesterol in the blood is thought to contribute to atherosclerosis (hardening of the arteries).

**Chomsky, (Avram) Noam** (1928–  ) US professor of linguistics and political commentator. He proposed a theory of transformational generative grammar, which attracted widespread interest because of the claims it made about the relationship between language and the mind and the universality of an underlying language structure. He has been a leading critic of the imperialist tendencies of the US government.

**Chongqing** or *Chungking; also Pahsien,* city in Sichuan province, China, at the confluence of the Chang Jiang and Jialing Jiang rivers; population (1994) 5,408,000. It is the largest of China's four municipalities directly under the central government, with an area of 82,000 sq km/31,600 sq mi and population (1996) of 30,000,000. Industries include coalmining, food processing, and the manufacture of iron, steel, chemicals, synthetic rubber, automobiles, electrical equipment, and textiles.

**Chopin, Frédéric François** (1810–1849) Polish composer and pianist. He made his debut as a pianist at the age of eight. As a performer, Chopin revolutionized the technique of pianoforte-playing, turning the hands outward and favouring a light, responsive touch. His compositions for piano, which include two concertos and other works with orchestra, are characterized by great volatility of mood, and rhythmic fluidity.

**chord** in geometry, a straight line joining any two points on a curve. The chord that passes through the centre of a circle (its longest chord) is the diameter. The longest and shortest chords of an ellipse (a regular oval) are called the major and minor axes, respectively.

**chord** in music, a group of three or more notes sounded together. The resulting combination of tones may be either harmonious or dissonant.

**chordate** animal belonging to the phylum Chordata, which includes vertebrates, sea squirts, amphioxi, and others. All these animals, at some stage of their lives, have a supporting rod of tissue (notochord or backbone) running down their bodies.

**choreography** the art of creating and arranging ballet and dance for performance; originally, in the 18th century, dance notation.

**Chou En-lai** alternative transliteration of ◊Zhou Enlai.

**Chrétien, (Joseph Jacques) Jean** (1934–  ) French-Canadian politician, prime minister from 1993. He won the leadership of the Liberal Party in 1990 and defeated Kim Campbell in the October 1993 election. He was a vigorous advocate of national unity and, although himself a Québecois, consistently opposed the province's separatist ambitions. His Liberal Party won the Canadian election in June 1997 to gain its first back-to-back win in 44 years.

**Chrétien de Troyes** (died *c.* 1183) French poet. His epics, which introduced the concept of the ◊Holy Grail, include *Lancelot, ou le chevalier de la charrette* (about 1178), written for Marie, Countess of Champagne; *Perceval, ou le conte du Graal* (about 1182), written for Philip, Count of Flanders; *Erec* (about 1170); *Yvain, ou le chevalier au Lion* (about 1178); and other Arthurian romances.

**Christ** (Greek *khristos* 'anointed one') the ◊Messiah as prophesied in the Hebrew Bible, or Old Testament.

**Christchurch** city on South Island, New Zealand, 11 km/7 mi from the mouth of the Avon River; population (1996) 331,400. It is the principal commercial centre of the Canterbury

Plains and the seat of the University of Canterbury. Industries include fertilizers, chemicals, canning, meat processing, rail workshops, and shoes.

**Christian** ten kings of Denmark and Norway, including:

**Christian IV** (1577–1648) King of Denmark and Norway from 1588. He sided with the Protestants in the Thirty Years' War (1618–48), and founded Christiania (now Oslo, capital of Norway). He was succeeded by Frederick II 1648.

**Christianity** world religion derived from the teaching of Jesus, as found in the ◊New Testament, during the first third of the 1st century. It has a present-day membership of about 1 billion, and is divided into groups or denominations that differ in some areas of belief and practice. Its main divisions are the ◊Roman Catholic, ◊Eastern Orthodox, and ◊Protestant churches.

*beliefs* Christians believe in one God with three aspects: God the Father, God the Son (Jesus), and God the Holy Spirit, who is the power of God working in the world. God created everything that exists and showed his love for the world by coming to Earth as Jesus, and suffering and dying in order to reconcile humanity to himself. Christians believe that three days after his death by crucifixion Jesus was raised to life by God's power, appearing many times in bodily form to his followers, and that he is now alive in the world through the Holy Spirit. Christians speak of the sufferings they may have to endure because of their faith, and the reward of everlasting life in God's presence, which is promised to those who have faith in Jesus Christ and who live according to his teaching.

**Christian Science** or *the Church of Christ, Scientist,* sect established in the USA by Mary Baker Eddy 1879. Christian Scientists believe that since God is good and is a spirit, matter and evil are not ultimately real. Consequently they refuse all medical treatment. The church publishes a daily newspaper, the *Christian Science Monitor,* which reports on international news.

**Christie, Agatha (Mary Clarissa)** born Miller (1890–1976) English detective novelist. She is best known for her ingenious plots and for the creation of the characters Hercule Poirot and Miss Jane Marple. She wrote more than 70 novels, including *The Murder of Roger Ackroyd* (1926) and *The Body in the Library* (1942). Her play *The Mousetrap,* which opened in London in 1952, is the longest continuously running show in the world.

**Christie, Linford** (1960– ) Jamaican-born English sprinter who, with his win in the 1993 world championships, became the first track athlete ever to hold World, Olympic, European, and Commonwealth 100-metres titles simultaneously.

*career highlights*
*Olympic Games*: silver 100 metres 1988; silver 4 x 100 metres relay 1988; gold 100 metres 1992

*Commonwealth Games* gold 100 metres 1990; gold 4 x 100 metres relay 1990; gold 100 metres 1994
*European championships* gold 100 metres 1986; gold 100 metres 1990; gold 100 metres 1994
*World Cup* gold 100 metres 1989; gold 100 metres 1992; gold 100 metres 1994
*World Athletics Championships* gold 100 metres 1993
*European Cup* gold 100 metres 1997.

**Christina** (1626–1689) Queen of Sweden 1632–54. Succeeding her father Gustavus Adolphus at the age of six, she assumed power 1644, but disagreed with the former regent Oxenstjerna. Refusing to marry, she eventually nominated her cousin Charles Gustavus (Charles X) as her successor. As a secret convert to Roman Catholicism, which was then illegal in Sweden, she had to abdicate 1654, and went to live in Rome, twice returning to Sweden unsuccessfully to claim the throne.

**Christmas** Christian religious holiday, observed throughout the Western world on December 25 and traditionally marked by feasting and gift-giving. In the Christian church, it is the day on which the birth of Jesus is celebrated, although his actual birth date is unknown. Many of its customs have a non-Christian origin and were adapted from celebrations of the winter ◊solstice.

**Christopher, St** patron saint of travellers. His feast day, 25 July, was dropped from the Roman Catholic liturgical calendar in 1969.

**chromatic scale** musical scale proceeding by semitones. In theory the inclusion of all 12 notes makes it a neutral scale without the focus provided by the seven-tone diatonic major or minor scale; in practice however, owing to small deviations from equal temperament, it is possible for a trained ear to identify the starting point of a randomly chosen chromatic scale.

**chromatography** (Greek *chromos* 'colour') technique for separating or analysing a mixture of gases, liquids, or dissolved substances. This is brought about by means of two immiscible substances, one of which (*the mobile phase*) transports the sample mixture through the other (*the stationary phase*). The mobile phase may be a gas or a liquid; the stationary phase may be a liquid or a solid, and may be in a column, on paper, or in a thin layer on a glass or plastic support. The components of the mixture are absorbed or impeded by the stationary phase to different extents and therefore become separated. The technique is used for both qualitative and quantitative analyses in biology and chemistry.

**chromite** ($FeCr_2O_4$), iron chromium oxide, the main chromium ore. It is one of the spinel group of minerals, and crystallizes in dark-coloured octahedra of the cubic system. Chromite is usually found in association with ultrabasic and basic rocks; in Cyprus, for example, it occurs with serpentine, and in South Africa it forms continuous layers in a layered ◊intrusion.

**chromium** (Greek *chromos* 'colour') hard, brittle, grey-white, metallic element, symbol Cr, atomic number 24, relative atomic mass 51.996. It takes a high polish, has a high melting point, and is very resistant to corrosion. It is used in chromium electroplating, in the manufacture of stainless steel and other alloys, and as a catalyst. Its compounds are used for tanning leather and for alums. In human nutrition it is a vital trace element. In nature, it occurs chiefly as chrome iron ore or chromite ($FeCr_2O_4$). Kazakhstan, Zimbabwe, and Brazil are sources.

**chromosome** structure in a cell nucleus that carries the ◊genes. Each chromosome consists of one very long strand of DNA, coiled and folded to produce a compact body. The point on a chromosome where a particular gene occurs is known as its locus. Most higher organisms have two copies of each chromosome, together known as a *homologous pair* (they are ◊diploid) but some have only one (they are ◊haploid). There are 46 chromosomes in a normal human cell. See also ◊mitosis and ◊meiosis.

XY
**chromosome** The 23 pairs of chromosomes of a normal human male.

**chromosphere** (Greek 'colour' and 'sphere') layer of mostly hydrogen gas about 10,000 km/6,000 mi deep above the visible surface of the Sun (the photosphere). It appears pinkish red during ◊eclipses of the Sun.

**chronic** in medicine, term used to describe a condition that is of slow onset and then runs a prolonged course, such as rheumatoid arthritis or chronic bronchitis. In contrast, an *acute* condition develops quickly and may be of relatively short duration.

**chronic fatigue syndrome** a common debilitating condition also known as myalgic encephalomyelitis (ME), postviral fatigue syndrome, or 'yuppie flu'. It is characterized by a diffuse range of symptoms present for at least six months including extreme fatigue, muscular pain, weakness, depression, poor balance and coordination, joint pains, and gastric upset. It is usually diagnosed after exclusion of other diseases and frequently follows a flulike illness.

**chrysalis** pupa of an insect, but especially that of a ◊butterfly or ◊moth. It is essentially a static stage of the creature's life, when the adult insect, benefiting from the large amounts of food laid down by the actively feeding larva, is built up from the disintegrating larval tissues. The chrysalis may be exposed or within a cocoon.

**chrysanthemum** any of a large group of plants with colourful, showy flowers, containing about 200 species. There are hundreds of cultivated varieties, whose exact wild ancestry is uncertain. In the Far East the common chrysanthemum has been cultivated for more than 2,000 years and is the imperial emblem of Japan. Chrysanthemums can be grown from seed, but new plants are more commonly produced from cuttings or by dividing up established plants. (Genus *Chrysanthemum*, family Compositae.)

**Chuang** the largest minority group in China, numbering about 15 million. They live in southern China, where they cultivate rice fields. Their religion includes elements of ancestor worship. The Chuang language belongs to the Tai family.

**chub** freshwater fish *Leuciscus cephalus* of the carp family. Thickset and cylindrical, it grows up to 60 cm/2 ft, is dark greenish or grey on the back, silvery yellow below, with metallic flashes on the flanks. It lives generally in clean rivers throughout Europe.

**Chubu** mountainous coastal region of central Honshu island, Japan, area 66,774 sq km /25,781 sq mi; population (1992) 21,162,000. The chief city is ◊Nagoya. The region, which produces tea, fruits, and fish, contains the Niigata plain, one of the country's largest rice-producing areas. Mount Fuji and several of Japan's longest rivers can also be found in the region.

**Chugoku** southwest region of Honshu island, Japan, area 31,881 sq km/12,309 sq mi; population (1992) 7,754,000. The chief city is ◊Hiroshima. Citrus and grapes are grown in the region. Formerly rich fishing grounds have been damaged by industrial pollution.

**church** (from Greek *kuriakon*, 'belonging to the lord') in architecture, a building designed as a Christian place of worship; also the Christian community generally, or a subdivision or denomination of it, such as the Protestant

Episcopal Church. Churches were first built in the 3rd century, when persecution ceased under the Roman emperor Constantine.

**Churchill, Lord Randolph Henry Spencer** (1849–1895) British Conservative politician, chancellor of the Exchequer and leader of the House of Commons in 1886; father of Winston Churchill.

**Churchill, Winston (Leonard Spencer)** (1874–1965) British Conservative politician, prime minister 1940–45 and 1951–55. In Parliament from 1900, as a Liberal until 1923, he held a number of ministerial offices, including First Lord of the Admiralty 1911–15 and chancellor of the Exchequer 1924–29. Absent from the cabinet in the 1930s, he returned in September 1939 to lead a coalition government 1940–45, negotiating with Allied leaders in World War II to achieve the unconditional surrender of Germany in 1945. He led a Conservative government 1951–55. He received the Nobel Prize for Literature in 1953.

**Church of England** established form of Christianity in England, a member of the Anglican Communion. It was dissociated from the Roman Catholic Church in 1534 under Henry VIII; the British monarch is still the supreme head of the Church of England today. The service book is the Book of Common Prayer.

**Church of Scotland** established form of Christianity in Scotland, first recognized by the state in 1560. It is based on the Protestant doctrines of the reformer ◊Calvin and governed on Presbyterian lines. The church went through several periods of episcopacy (government by bishops) in the 17th century, and those who adhered to episcopacy after 1690 formed the Episcopal Church of Scotland, an autonomous church in communion with the Church of England. In 1843 there was a split in the Church of Scotland (the Disruption), in which almost a third of its ministers and members left and formed the ◊Free Church of Scotland. By an Act of Union of 3 October 1929 the Church of Scotland was united with the United Free Church of Scotland to form the United Church of Scotland. There are over 680,000 members of the Church of Scotland (1998).

**CIA** abbreviation for the US ◊*Central Intelligence Agency.*

**cicada** any of several insects of the family Cicadidae. Most species are tropical, but a few occur in Europe and North America. The adults live on trees, whose juices they suck. The males produce a loud, almost continuous, chirping by vibrating membranes in resonating cavities in the abdomen.

Cicadas with a periodic life cycle, such as the 13-year cicada and the *17-year cicada,* are found only in the USA. These species spend most of their lives as larvae underground, synchronizing their emergence every 13 or 17 years depending on species.

**Cicero, Marcus Tullius** (106–43 BC) Roman orator, writer, and politician. His speeches and philosophical and rhetorical works are models of Latin prose, and his letters provide a picture of contemporary Roman life. As consul 63 BC he exposed the Roman politician Catiline's conspiracy in four major orations.

**cichlid** any freshwater fish of the family Cichlidae. Cichlids are somewhat perchlike, but have a single nostril on each side instead of two. They are mostly predatory, and have deep, colourful bodies, flattened from side to side so that some are almost disc-shaped. Many are territorial in the breeding season and may show care of the young. There are more than 1,000 species found in South and Central America, Africa, and India.

**Cid, El, Rodrigo Díaz de Vivar** (c. 1043–1099) Spanish soldier, nicknamed *El Cid* ('the lord') by the ◊Moors. Born in Castile of a noble family, he fought against the king of Navarre and won his nickname *el Campeador* ('the Champion') by killing the Navarrese champion in single combat. Essentially a mercenary, fighting both with and against the Moors, he died while defending Valencia against them, and in subsequent romances became Spain's national hero.

**cider** in the UK, a fermented drink made from the juice of the apple; in the USA, the term cider usually refers to unfermented (nonalcoholic) apple juice. Cider has been made for more than 2,000 years, and for many centuries has been a popular drink in France and England, which are now its main centres of production.

**cilia** singular *cilium,* small hairlike organs on the surface of some cells, particularly the cells lining the upper respiratory tract. Their wave-like movements waft particles of dust and debris towards the exterior. Some single-celled organisms move by means of cilia. In multicellular animals, they keep lubricated surfaces clear of debris. They also move food in the digestive tracts of some invertebrates.

**Cilicia** ancient region of Asia Minor, now forming part of Turkey, situated between the Taurus Mountains and the Mediterranean. Access from the north across the Taurus range is through the *Cilician Gates,* a strategic pass that has been used for centuries as part of a trade route linking Europe and the Middle East.

**Cimabue, Giovanni** Cenni di Peppi (c. 1240–1302) Italian painter. Active in Florence, he is traditionally styled the 'father of Italian painting'. His paintings retain the golden background of Byzantine art but the figures have a new naturalism. Among the works attributed to him are *Maestà* (about 1280; Uffizi, Florence), a huge Gothic image of the Virgin, with a novel softness and solidity that points forwards to Giotto.

**cinchona** any of a group of tropical American shrubs or trees belonging to the madder family. The drug ◊quinine is produced from the bark of some species, and these are now cultivated in India, Sri Lanka, the Philippines, and Indonesia. (Genus *Chinchona,* family Rubiaceae.)

**cine camera** camera that takes a rapid sequence of still photographs called frames. When the frames are projected one after the other on to a screen, they appear to show movement, because our eyes hold on to the image of one picture until the next one appears.

**cinema** (Greek *kinema* 'movement') form of art and entertainment consisting of moving pictures, in either black and white or colour, projected on a screen. Cinema draws on other arts, such as literature, drama, and music. Its development, beginning in the 1890s, has been closely linked to technological advances, including action and colour ◊photography, sound reproduction, and film processing and printing. The first sound films were released in 1926–27.

**cinnabar** mercuric sulphide mineral, HgS, the only commercially useful ore of mercury. It is deposited in veins and impregnations near recent volcanic rocks and hot springs. The mineral itself is used as a red pigment, commonly known as *vermilion*. Cinnabar is found in the USA (California), Spain (Almadén), Peru, Italy, and Slovenia.

**cinnamon** dried inner bark of a tree belonging to the laurel family, grown in India and Sri Lanka. The bark is ground to make the spice used in curries and confectionery. Oil of cinnamon is obtained from waste bark and is used as flavouring in food and medicine. (*Cinnamomum zeylanicum*, family Lauraceae.)

**cinquefoil** any of a group of plants that usually have five-lobed leaves and brightly coloured flowers. They are widespread in northern temperate regions. (Genus *Potentilla*, family Rosaceae.)

**Cinque Ports** group of ports in southern England, originally five, Sandwich, Dover, Hythe, Romney, and Hastings, later including Rye, Winchelsea, and others. Probably founded in Roman times, they rose to importance after the Norman conquest and until the end of the 15th century were bound to supply the ships and men necessary against invasion. Their importance declined in the 16th and 17th centuries with the development of a standing navy.

**circadian rhythm** metabolic rhythm found in most organisms, which generally coincides with the 24-hour day. Its most obvious manifestation is the regular cycle of sleeping and waking, but body temperature and the concentration of ◊hormones that influence mood and behaviour also vary over the day. In humans, alteration of habits (such as rapid air travel round the world) may result in the circadian rhythm being out of phase with actual activity patterns, causing malaise until it has had time to adjust.

**circle** perfectly round shape, the path of a point that moves so as to keep a constant distance from a fixed point (the centre). Each circle has a *radius* (the distance from any point on the circle to the centre), a *circumference* (the boundary of the circle, part of which is called an arc), *diameters* (straight lines crossing the circle through the centre), *chords* (lines joining two points on the circumference), *tangents* (lines that touch the circumference at one point only),

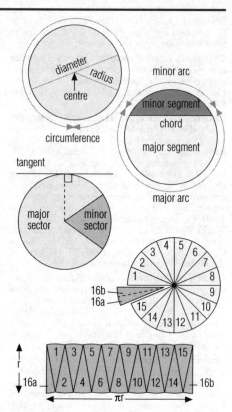

*circle* Technical terms used in the geometry of the circle; the area of a circle can be seen to equal $\pi r^2$ by dividing the circle into segments which form a rectangle.

*sectors* (regions inside the circle between two radii), and *segments* (regions between a chord and the circumference).

**circuit** in physics or electrical engineering, an arrangement of electrical components through which a current can flow. There are two basic circuits, series and parallel. In a series circuit, the components are connected end to end so that the current flows through all components one after the other. In a parallel circuit, components are connected side by side so that part of the current passes through each component. A circuit diagram shows in graphical form how components are connected together, using standard symbols for the components.

**circulatory system** system of vessels in an animal's body that transports essential substances (◊blood or other circulatory fluid) to and from the different parts of the body. It was first discovered and described by English physician, William ◊Harvey. All animals except for the simplest kinds – such as sponges, jellyfish, sea anemones, and corals – have some type of circulatory system. Some invertebrates (animals without a backbone), such as insects, spiders, and most shellfish, have an 'open' circulatory system which consists of a simple network of tubes and

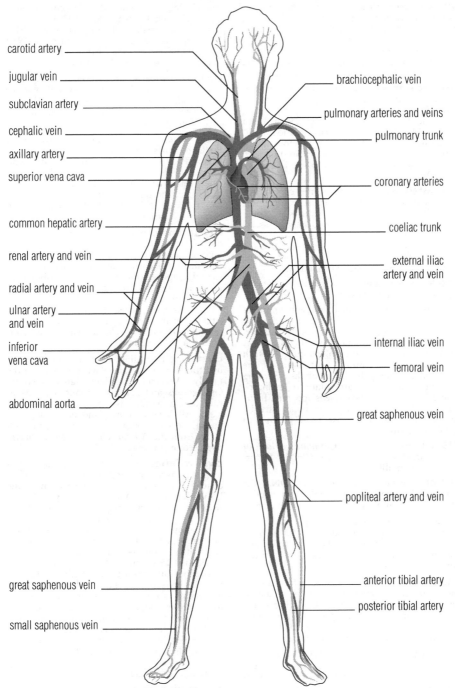

carotid artery

jugular vein

subclavian artery

cephalic vein

axillary artery

superior vena cava

common hepatic artery

renal artery and vein

radial artery and vein

ulnar artery and vein

inferior vena cava

abdominal aorta

great saphenous vein

small saphenous vein

brachiocephalic vein

pulmonary arteries and veins

pulmonary trunk

coronary arteries

coeliac trunk

external iliac artery and vein

internal iliac vein

femoral vein

great saphenous vein

popliteal artery and vein

anterior tibial artery

posterior tibial artery

**circulatory system** Blood flows through 96,500 km/60,000 mi of arteries and veins, supplying oxygen and nutrients to organs and limbs. Oxygen-poor blood (dark shading) circulates from the heart to the lungs where oxygen is absorbed. Oxygen-rich blood (light shading) flows back to the heart and is then pumped round the body through the aorta, the largest artery, to smaller arteries and capillaries. Here oxygen and nutrients are exchanged with carbon dioxide and waste products and the blood returns to the heart via the veins. Waste products are filtered by the liver, spleen, and kidneys, and nutrients are absorbed from the stomach and small intestine.

hollow spaces. Other invertebrates have pump-like structures that send blood through a system of blood vessels. All vertebrates (animals with a backbone), including human beings, have a 'closed' circulatory system which principally consists of a pumping organ – the ◊heart – and a network of blood vessels.

**circumcision** surgical removal of all or part of the foreskin (prepuce) of the penis, usually performed on the newborn; it is practised among Jews and Muslims. In some societies in Africa and the Middle East, female circumcision or clitoridectomy (removal of the labia minora and/or clitoris; see ◊female genital mutilation) is practised on adolescents as well as babies; it is illegal in the West.

**circumference** in geometry, the curved line that encloses a curved plane figure, for example a ◊circle or an ellipse. Its length varies according to the nature of the curve, and may be ascertained by the appropriate formula. The circumference of a circle is $\pi d$ or $2\pi r$, where $d$ is the diameter of the circle, $r$ is its radius, and $\pi$ is the constant pi, approximately equal to 3.1416.

**cirque** French name for a corrie, a steep-sided hollow in a mountainside.

**cirrhosis** any degenerative disease in an organ of the body, especially the liver, characterized by excessive development of connective tissue, causing scarring and painful swelling. Cirrhosis of the liver may be caused by an infection such as viral hepatitis, chronic obstruction of the common bile duct, chronic alcoholism or drug use, blood disorder, heart failure, or malnutrition. However, often no cause is apparent. If cirrhosis is diagnosed early, it can be arrested by treating the cause; otherwise it will progress to coma and death.

**CIS** abbreviation for ◊*Commonwealth of Independent States,* established 1992 by 11 former Soviet republics.

**cistron** in genetics, the segment of ◊DNA that is required to synthesize a complete polypeptide chain. It is the molecular equivalent of a ◊gene.

**citizens' band** (CB), short-range radio communication facility (around 27 MHz) used by members of the public in the USA and many European countries to talk to one another or call for emergency assistance.

**citizenship** status as a member of a state. In most countries citizenship may be acquired either by birth or by naturalization. The status confers rights such as voting and the protection of the law and also imposes responsibilities such as military service, in some countries.

**citric acid** ($HOOCCH_2C(OH)(COOH)CH_2COOH$), organic acid widely distributed in the plant kingdom; it is found in high concentrations in citrus fruits and has a sharp, sour taste. At one time it was commercially prepared from concentrated lemon juice, but now the main source is the fermentation of sugar with certain moulds.

**Citroën** French motor company founded 1913, acquired by ◊Peugeot 1974. Originally a gear-cutting firm founded by motor engineer André-Gustave Citroën (1878–1935), the company began making low-priced cars 1919, becoming France's first mass-producer. In 1934 Citroën made motoring history when it introduced cars with front-wheel drive.

**citrus** any of a group of evergreen and aromatic trees or shrubs, found in warm parts of the world. Several species – the orange, lemon, lime, citron, and grapefruit – are cultivated for their fruit. (Genus *Citrus,* family Rutaceae.)

**City, the** financial centre of ◊London, England. It is situated on the north bank of the River Thames, between Tower Bridge and London Bridge, in the oldest part of the capital. The ◊Bank of England, Lloyd's, the Royal Exchange, and the head offices of the 'big four' banks (Barclays, Lloyds, HSBC (Midland), and National Westminster) are in the City.

**city technology college** (CTC), in the UK, one of a network of some 20 proposed schools, financed jointly by government and industry, designed to teach the national curriculum with special emphasis on technological subjects in inner-city areas to students aged 11 to 18. The first school was opened in 1988. By 1994 only 15 schools had opened in England and Wales (still 15 in mid-1998), industry having proved reluctant to fund the scheme, which was abandoned in its original form.

**civet** small to medium-sized carnivorous mammal found in Africa and Asia, belonging to the family Viverridae, which also includes ◊mongooses and ◊genets. Distant relations of cats, they generally have longer jaws and more teeth. All have a scent gland in the inguinal (groin) region. Extracts from this gland are taken from the *African civet Civettictis civetta* and used in perfumery.

**civil aviation** operation of passenger and freight transport by air. With increasing traffic, control of air space is a major problem. In the USA, the Federal Aviation Agency (FAA) is responsible for regulating development of aircraft, air navigation, traffic control, and communications and the Civil Aeronautics Board prescribes safety regulations and investigates accidents. In Europe, Eurocontrol was established in 1963 by Belgium, France, West Germany, Luxembourg, the Netherlands, and the UK to supervise both military and civil movement in the air space over member countries. Close cooperation is maintained with authorities in other countries, and there is also a tendency to coordinate services and other facilities between national airlines; for example, the establishment of Air Union in 1963 by France (Air France), West Germany (Lufthansa), Italy (Alitalia), and Belgium (Sabena).

**civil engineering** branch of engineering that is concerned with the construction of roads, bridges, airports, aqueducts, waterworks, tunnels, canals, irrigation works, and harbours.

**civil law** legal system based on ◊Roman law. It is one of the two main European legal systems, ◊English (common) law being the other. Civil law may also mean the law relating to matters other than criminal law, such as ◊contract and ◊tort.

**civil rights** rights of the individual citizen. In many countries they are specified (as in the Bill of Rights of the US constitution) and guaranteed by law to ensure equal treatment for all citizens. In the USA, the struggle to obtain civil rights for former slaves and their descendants, both through legislation and in practice, has been a major theme since the Civil War. See *history* under ◊black.

**civil-rights movement** general term for efforts by African-American people to affirm their constitutional rights and improve their status in society after World War II. Having made a significant contribution to the national effort in wartime, they began a sustained campaign for full civil rights which challenged racial discrimination and segregation; the Civil Rights Commission was created by the Civil Rights Act of 1957.

Further favourable legislation followed, such as the Civil Rights Act 1964 and the 1965 Voting Rights Act. See also *history* under ◊black. Other civil-rights movements have included women (see ◊women's movement) and homosexuals (see ◊homosexuality).

**civil service** body of administrative staff appointed to carry out the policy of a government. In the USA, federal employees are restricted in the role they may play in political activity, and they retain their posts (except at senior levels) when there is a change in administration. Members of the UK civil service may not take an active part in politics, and do not change with the government.

**Civil War, American** also called the *War Between the States*, war 1861–65 between the Southern or Confederate States of America (see ◊Confederacy) and the Northern or Union states. The former wished to maintain certain

---

## CIVIL WAR, AMERICAN: CHRONOLOGY

| | |
|---|---|
| **1861** **February** | Having seceded from the Union, seven southern states (South Carolina, Mississippi, Florida, Alabama, Georgia, Louisiana, and Texas) send representatives to Montgomery, Alabama, to form the rebel Confederate States of America under the presidency of Jefferson Davis. Their constitution legalizes slavery. |
| **April** | Rebel forces attack a Federal garrison at Fort Sumter, Charleston, South Carolina, capturing it 14 April. President Lincoln proclaims a blockade of southern ports. |
| **April– May** | Four more states secede from the Union: Virginia (part remaining loyal, eventually becoming West Virginia), Arkansas, Tennessee, and North Carolina. |
| **July** | Battle of Bull Run is the first major military engagement of the war, near Manassas Junction, Virginia; Confederate army under generals P G T Beauregard and Thomas 'Stonewall' Jackson forces Union army to retreat to Washington DC. |
| **1862** **February** | Union general Ulysses S Grant captures strategically located forts Henry and Donelson in Tennessee. |
| **April** | Battle of Shiloh, the bloodiest Americans had yet fought, when at terrible cost Grant's army forces rebel troops to withdraw. Confederate government introduces conscription of male white citizens aged 18–35. |
| **June–July** | Seven Days' battles in Virginia between Union army under George B McClellan and Confederate forces under generals Jackson and Robert E Lee; McClellan withdraws, but continues to threaten the Confederate capital at Richmond, Virginia. |
| **August** | At second Battle of Bull Run, Lee's troops force Union army to fall back again to Washington DC. |
| **September** | At Battle of Antietam, near Sharpsburg, Maryland, McClellan forces Lee to give up his offensive, but fails to pursue the enemy. Lincoln removes him from his command. |
| **December** | Lee inflicts heavy losses on Federal forces attacking his position at Battle of Fredericksburg, Virginia. |

| | |
|---|---|
| **1863** **January** | Lincoln's Emancipation Proclamation comes into effect, freeing slaves in the Confederate states (but not those in border states which have remained loyal to the Union). Some 200,000 blacks eventually serve in Union armies. |
| **March** | Federal government introduces conscription. |
| **May** | Battle of Chancellorsville, Virginia; Lee and Jackson rout Union forces. |
| **July** | Lee fails to break through Union lines at decisive Battle of Gettysburg, Pennsylvania, while Grant captures Vicksburg and the west and takes control of the Mississippi, cutting the Confederacy in two. |
| **November** | Grant's victory at Chattanooga, Tennessee, leads to his appointment as general in chief by Lincoln (March 1864). Lincoln's Gettysburg Address. |
| **1864 May** | Battle of the Wilderness, Virginia. Lee inflicts heavy casualties on Union forces, but Grant continues to move south through Virginia. They clash again at Battle of Spotsylvania. |
| **June** | Battle of Cold Harbor claims 12,000 casualties in a few hours. Grant writes: 'i propose to fight it out along this line if it takes all summer'. |
| **September** | Union general William T Sherman occupies Atlanta, Georgia, and marches through the state to the sea, cutting a wide swathe of destruction. |
| **November** | Lincoln is re-elected president. |
| **December** | Sherman marches into Savannah, Georgia, continuing over the next three months into South and North Carolina. |
| **1865** **March** | Lee fails to break through Union lines at Battle of Petersburg, Virginia. |
| **April** | Lee abandons Confederate capital at Richmond, Virginia, and surrenders to Grant at Appomattox courthouse, Virginia. John Wilkes Booth assassinates President Lincoln at Ford's Theatre, Washington DC. |
| **May** | Last Confederate soldiers lay down their arms. The war has taken the lives of 359,528 Union troops and 258,000 Confederates, and cost $20 billion. |

'states' rights', in particular the right to determine state law on the institution of slavery, and claimed the right to secede from the Union; the latter fought primarily to maintain the Union, with slave emancipation (proclaimed 1863) a secondary issue.

**Civil War, English** conflict between King Charles I and the Royalists (also called Cavaliers) on one side and the Parliamentarians (also called Roundheads) under Oliver ◊Cromwell on the other. Their differences centred initially on the king's unconstitutional acts, but later became a

---

## CIVIL WAR, ENGLISH: CHRONOLOGY

| | |
|---|---|
| **1625** | James I dies, and is succeeded by Charles I, whose first parliament is dissolved after refusing to grant him tonnage and poundage (taxation revenues) for life. |
| **1627** | 'Five Knights' case in which men who refuse to pay a forced loan are imprisoned. |
| **1628** | Coke, Wentworth, and Eliot present the Petition of Right, requesting the king not to tax without parliamentary consent, not to billet soldiers in private homes, and not to impose martial law on civilians. Charles accepts this as the price of parliamentary taxation to pay for war with Spain and France. The Duke of Buckingham is assassinated. |
| **1629** | Parliament is dissolved following disagreement over religious policy, tonnage and poundage, beginning Charles' 'Eleven Years' Tyranny'. War with France ends. |
| **1630** | War with Spain ends. |
| **1632** | Strafford is made lord deputy in Ireland. |
| **1633** | Laud becomes archbishop of Canterbury. Savage punishment of puritan William Prynne for his satirical pamphlet 'Histriomastix'. |
| **1634** | Ship money is first collected in London. |
| **1634–37** | Laud attempts to enforce ecclesiastical discipline by metropolitan visits. |
| **1637** | The conviction of John Hampden for refusal to pay ship money infringes the Petition of Right. |
| **1638** | Covenanters in Scotland protest at the introduction of the Laudian Prayer Book into the Kirk. |
| **1639** | First Bishops' War. Charles sends army to Scotland after its renunciation of episcopacy. Agreement is reached without fighting. |
| **1640** | Short Parliament April–May votes for taxes for the suppression of the Scots, but dissolves to forestall petition against Scottish war. Second Bishops' War ends in defeat for English at Newburn-on-Tyne. Scots receive pension and hold Northumberland and Durham in Treaty of Ripon. Long Parliament is called, passing the Triennial Act and abolishing the Star Chamber. High Commission and Councils of the North and of Wales is set up. |
| **1641** | Strafford is executed. English and Scots are massacred at Ulster. Grand Remonstrance is passed appealing to mass opinion against episcopacy and the royal prerogative. Irish Catholic nobles are massacred. |
| **1642 January** | Charles leaves Westminster after an unsuccessful attempt to arrest five members of the Commons unites both Houses of Parliament and the City against him. |
| **February** | Bishop's Exclusion Bill is passed, barring clergy from secular office and the Lords. |
| **May–** | Irish rebels establish supreme council. |
| **June** | Militia Ordinance is passed, assuming sovereign powers for parliament. Nineteen Propositions are rejected by Charles. |
| **August** | Charles raises his standard at Nottingham. Outbreak of first Civil War. |
| **October** | General Assembly of the Confederate Catholics meets at Kilkenny. Battle of Edgehill inconclusive. |
| **1643** | Irish truce leaves rebels in control of more of Ireland. Solemn League and Covenant, alliance between English Parliamentarians and Scots, pledges to establish Presbyterianism in England and Ireland, and to provide a Scottish army. Scots intervene in Civil War. |
| **1643–49** | Westminster Assembly attempts to draw up Calvinist religious settlement. |
| **1644** | Committee of Both Kingdoms to coordinate Scottish and Parliamentarians' military activities is established. Royalists are decisively beaten at Marston Moor. |
| **1645** | Laud is executed. The New Model Army is created. Charles pulls out of Uxbridge negotiations on a new constitutional position. Cromwell and the New Model Army destroy Royalist forces at Naseby. |
| **1646** | Charles flees to Scotland. Oxford surrenders to Parliament. End of first Civil War. |
| **1647 May** | Charles agrees with Parliament to accept Presbyterianism and to surrender control of the militia. |
| **June–August** | Army seized Charles and resolves not to disband without satisfactory terms. Army presents Heads of Proposals to Charles. |
| **October–December** | Army debates Levellers' Agreement of the People at Putney. Charles escapes to the Isle of Wight, and reaches agreement with the Scots by Treaty of Newport. |
| **1648 January** | Vote of No Addresses passed by Long Parliament declares an end to negotiations with Charles. |
| **August** | Cromwell defeats Scots at Preston. Second Civil War begins. |
| **November –December** | Army demands trial of Charles I. Pride's Purge of Parliament transfers power to the Rump of independent MPs. |
| **1649 January–February** | Charles is tried and executed. Rump elects Council of State as its executive. |
| **May** | Rump declares England a Commonwealth. Cromwell lands in Dublin. |
| **September –October** | Massacres of garrisons at Drogheda and Wexford by Cromwell. Large numbers of native Irish were transplanted. |
| **1650 September** | Cromwell defeated Scots under Leslie at Dunbar. |
| **1651** | Scots under Charles II invaded England, but were decisively defeated at Worcester (3 September) by Cromwell. Charles fled to the Continent and lived in exile for nine years. |

struggle over the relative powers of crown and Parliament. Hostilities began in 1642 and a series of Royalist defeats (at Marston Moor in 1644, and then at Naseby in 1645) culminated in Charles's capture in 1647, and execution in 1649. The war continued until the final defeat of Royalist forces at Worcester in 1651. Cromwell then became Protector (ruler) from 1653 until his death in 1658.

**Civil War, Spanish** war 1936–39 precipitated by a military revolt led by General Franco against the Republican government. Inferior military capability led to the gradual defeat of the Republicans by 1939, and the establishment of Franco's dictatorship.

**cladistics** method of biological classification that uses a formal step-by-step procedure for objectively assessing the extent to which organisms share particular characteristics, and for assigning them to taxonomic groups called *clades.* Clades comprise all the species descended from a known or inferred common ancestor plus the ancestor itself, and may be large – consisting of a hierarchy of other clades.

**clam** common name for a ◊bivalve mollusc. The giant clam *Tridacna gigas* of the Indopacific can grow to 1 m/3 ft across in 50 years and weigh, with the shell, 500 kg/1,100 lb.
A giant clam produces a billion eggs in a single spawning.

**clan** (Gaelic *clann* 'children') social grouping based on ◊kinship. Some traditional societies are organized by clans, which are either matrilineal or patrilineal, and whose members must marry into another clan in order to avoid in-breeding.

**Clapton, Eric** (1945– ) English blues and rock guitarist, singer, and songwriter. Originally a blues purist, then one of the pioneers of heavy rock with Cream 1966–68, he returned to the blues after making the landmark album *Layla and Other Assorted Love Songs* (1970) by Derek and the Dominos. Solo albums include *Journeyman* (1989) and the acoustic *Unplugged* (1992), for which he received six Grammy awards (1993). He won a Grammy award for Record of the Year with 'Change the World' in 1997.

**Clare** county on the west coast of the Republic of Ireland, in the province of Munster, situated between Galway Bay in the north and the Shannon estuary in the south; county town Ennis; area 3,190 sq km/1,231 sq mi; population (1991) 90,800. Other towns include Kilrush, Kilkee, and Shannon, an important 'new' town noted for its light industry, and electronics and aerospace industries. Dairying and cattle rearing are the principal farming activities; there are also important salmon fisheries and extensive oyster beds. Slate and black marble are quarried and worked; lead is also found. The Shannon is a source of hydroelectricity: there is a power station at Ardnachusha, 5 km/3 mi north of Limerick.

**clarinet** any of a family of single-reed woodwind instruments of cylindrical bore. The clarinet did not establish itself in the orchestra until after the middle of the 18th century. In their concertos for clarinet, Mozart and Weber exploited the instrument's range of tone from the dark low register rising to brilliance, and its capacity for sustained dynamic control. The ability of the clarinet both to blend and to contrast with other instruments makes it popular for chamber music and as a solo instrument. It is also heard in military and concert bands and as a jazz instrument.

**Clarke, Arthur C(harles)** (1917– ) English science-fiction and nonfiction writer. He originated the plan for a system of communications satellites in geostationary orbit in 1945. His works include the short story 'The Sentinel' (1951) (filmed in 1968 by Stanley Kubrick as *2001: A Space Odyssey*), and the novels *Childhood's End* (1953), *2010: Odyssey Two* (1982), *3001: The Final Odyssey* (1997), *Rendezvous with Rama* (1997), and *A Fall of Moondust* (1998).

**Clarke, Kenneth Harry** (1940– ) British Conservative politician. A cabinet minister 1985–97, he held the posts of education secretary 1990–92 and home secretary 1992–93. He succeeded Norman Lamont as chancellor of the Exchequer in May 1993, bringing to the office a more open and combative approach. Along with his colleagues Malcolm Rifkind, Tony Newton, and Patrick Mayhew, in 1996 he became the longest continuously serving minister since Lord Palmerston in the early 19th century.

**class** in biological classification, a group of related ◊orders. For example, all mammals belong to the class Mammalia and all birds to the class Aves. Among plants, all class names end in 'idae' (such as Asteridae) and among fungi in 'mycetes'; there are no equivalent conventions among animals. Related classes are grouped together in a ◊phylum.

**class** in sociology, the main grouping of social stratification in industrial societies, based primarily on economic and occupational factors, but also referring to people's style of living or sense of group identity.

**Classicism** term used in art, music, and literature, to characterize work that emphasizes the qualities traditionally associated with ancient Greek and Roman art, that is, reason, balance, objectivity, and restraint, as opposed to the individuality of expression typical of Romanticism. Classicism and Romanticism are often considered as opposite poles of art, but in fact many artists show elements of both in their work. At certain times, however, Classicism has been a dominant trend, notably during the Renaissance and the Neo-Classical periods. At both these times ancient art exercised a strong direct influence, but this is not an essential component of Classicism. The word is often used imprecisely and sometimes conveys no more than an idea of clarity or conservatism.

**classification** in biology, the arrangement of organisms into a hierarchy of groups on the basis of their similarities. The basic grouping is a ◊species, several of which may constitute a ◊genus, which in turn are grouped into families, and so on up through orders, classes, phyla (in plants, sometimes called divisions), to kingdoms.

**Claude Lorrain, (Claude Gellée)** (1600–1682) French painter who worked in Rome. One of the leading Classical painters of the 17th century, he painted landscapes in a distinctive, luminous style that had a great impact on late 17th- and 18th-century taste. In his paintings insignificant figures (mostly mythological or historical) are typically lost in great expanses of poetic scenery, as in *The Enchanted Castle* (1664; National Gallery, London).

**Claudius I** Tiberius Claudius Drusus Nero Germanicus (10 BC–AD 54) nephew of ◊Tiberius, and son of Drusus Nero, made Roman emperor by the Praetorian Guard AD 41, after the murder of his nephew ◊Caligula. Claudius was a scholar and historian. During his reign the Roman empire was considerably extended, and in 43 he took part in the invasion of Britain.

**Clausewitz, Carl Philipp Gottlieb von** (1780–1831) Prussian officer whose book *Vom Kriege/On War* (1833) exerted a powerful influence on military strategists well into the 20th century. Although he advocated the total destruction of an enemy's forces as one of the strategic targets of warfare, his most important idea was to see war as an extension of political policy and not as an end in itself.

**clausius** in engineering, a unit of ◊entropy (the loss of energy as heat in any physical process). It is defined as the ratio of energy to temperature above absolute zero.

**claustrophobia** ◊phobia involving fear of enclosed spaces.

**clavichord** small domestic keyboard instrument. Of delicate tone, the clavichord was developed in the 16th century on the principle of the monochord. Notes are sounded by a metal blade striking the string. The sound is clear and precise, and a form of vibrato (bebung) is possible by varying finger pressure on the key. It was superseded in the 18th century by the fortepiano.

**clay** very fine-grained ◊sedimentary deposit that has undergone a greater or lesser degree of consolidation. When moistened it is plastic, and it hardens on heating, which renders it impermeable. It may be white, grey, red, yellow, blue, or black, depending on its composition. Clay minerals consist largely of hydrous silicates of aluminium and magnesium together with iron, potassium, sodium, and organic substances. The crystals of clay minerals have a layered structure, capable of holding water, and are responsible for its plastic properties. According to international classification, in mechanical analysis of soil, clay has a grain size of less than 0.002 mm/0.00008 in.

**Clay, Cassius Marcellus, Jr** original name of boxer Muhammad ◊Ali.

**clay mineral** one of a group of hydrous silicate minerals that form most of the fine-grained particles in clays. Clay minerals are normally formed by weathering or alteration of other silicate minerals. Virtually all have sheet silicate structures similar to the ◊micas. They exhibit the following useful properties: loss of water on heating; swelling and shrinking in different conditions;, cation exchange with other media; and plasticity when wet. Examples are kaolinite, illite, and montmorillonite.

**Cleese, John (Marwood)** (1939–  ) English actor and comedian. He has written for and appeared in both television programmes and films, and has worked in television advertising. On British television, he is particularly associated with the comedy series *Monty Python's Flying Circus* and *Fawlty Towers* (1975–79). His films include *Monty Python and the Holy Grail* (1974), *The Life of Brian* (1979), and *A Fish Called Wanda* (1988).

**clef** in music, a symbol prefixed to a five-line stave indicating the pitch range to which the written notes apply. Introduced as a visual aid in plainchant notation, it is based on the letter G (treble clef), establishing middle C (C4) as a prime reference pitch, G4 a fifth higher for higher voices, and F3 a fifth lower for lower voices.

**cleg** another name for ◊horsefly.

**Cleisthenes** (born *c.* 570) Athenian statesman, later celebrated as the founder of Athenian democracy. Although an early collaborator of the Pisistratids, the Athenian tyrants, he was later exiled with his family, the Alcmaeonidae, and intrigued and campaigned against Hippias and Hipparchus. After their removal 510 BC, in 508/7 he won over the people by offering to place the constitution on a more democratic basis. His democracy was established by his reforms over the next few years.

**clematis** any of a group of temperate woody climbing plants with colourful showy flowers. They belong to the buttercup family. (Genus *Clematis,* family Ranunculaceae.)

**Cleopatra** (*c.* 68–30 BC) Queen of Egypt 51–48 and 47–30 BC. When the Roman general Julius Caesar arrived in Egypt, he restored Cleopatra to the throne from which she had been ousted. Cleopatra and Caesar became lovers and she went with him to Rome. After Caesar's assassination 44 BC she returned to Alexandria and resumed her position as queen of Egypt. In 41 BC she was joined there by Mark Antony, one of Rome's rulers. In 31 BC Rome declared war on Egypt and scored a decisive victory in the naval Battle of Actium off the west coast of Greece. Cleopatra fled with her 60 ships to Egypt; Antony abandoned the struggle and followed her. Both he and Cleopatra committed suicide.

**client–server architecture** in computing, a system in which the mechanics of looking after data are separated from the programs that use the data. For example, the 'server' might be a central database, typically located on a large computer that is reserved for this purpose. The 'client' would be an ordinary program that requests data from the server as needed.

**climate** combination of weather conditions at a particular place over a period of time – usually a minimum of 30 years. A classification of climate encompasses the averages, extremes, and frequencies of all meteorological elements such as temperature, atmospheric pressure, precipitation, wind, humidity, and sunshine, together with the factors that influence them. The primary factors involved are: the Earth's rotation and latitudinal effects; ocean currents; large-scale movements of wind belts and air masses over the Earth's surface; temperature differences between land and sea surfaces; and topography. Climatology, the scientific study of climate, includes the construction of computer-generated models, and considers not only present-day climates, their effects and their classification, but also long-term climate changes, covering both past climates (paleoclimates) and future predictions. Climatologists are especially concerned with the influence of human activity on climate change, among the most important of which, at both a local and global level, are those currently linked with ⟡ozone depleters and the ⟡greenhouse effect.

**climax community** assemblage of plants and animals that is relatively stable in its environment. It is brought about by ecological ⟡succession, and represents the point at which succession ceases to occur.

**clinical psychology** branch of psychology dealing with the understanding and treatment of health problems, particularly mental disorders. The main problems dealt with include anxiety, phobias, depression, obsessions, sexual and marital problems, drug and alcohol dependence, childhood behavioural problems, psychoses (such as schizophrenia), mental disability, and brain disease (such as dementia) and damage. Other areas of work include forensic psychology (concerned with criminal behaviour) and health psychology.

**Clinton, Bill (William Jefferson)** (1946– ) 42nd president of the USA from 1993, a Democrat. He served as governor of Arkansas 1979–81 and 1983–93, establishing a liberal and progressive reputation. As president, he sought to implement a *New Democrat* programme, combining social reform with economic conservatism as a means of bringing the country out of reces-

sion. He introduced legislation to reduce the federal deficit and cut crime, but the loss of both houses of Congress to the Republicans in 1994 presented a serious obstacle to further social reform. However, he successfully repositioned himself on the centre-right to become the first Democrat since F D Roosevelt to be elected for a second term in 1996. Following accusations of perjury and obstruction of justice, concerning mainly his improper relationship with a White House intern, Clinton underwent an impeachment trial in early 1999 and was acquitted.

**Clinton, Hillary Diane Rodham** (1947– ) US lawyer and first lady. In 1993 President Bill Clinton appointed her to head his task force on the reform of the national health-care system, but her proposal of health insurance for all US citizens was blocked by Congress in 1994. In the same year the Justice Department appointed a special prosecutor to investigate the Whitewater affair relating to alleged irregularities in property deals made by the Clintons in Arkansas. A formidable, polarizing figure, Hillary Clinton became the first ever first lady to be subpoenaed to appear before a Federal Grand Jury. In 1999 she moved out of the White House to begin her own campaign for the vacant Senate seat in New York in 2000.

**clitoris** (Greek *kleitoris* 'little hill') in anatomy, part of the female reproductive system. The glans of the clitoris is visible externally. It connects to a pyramid-shaped pad of erectile tissue. Attached to this are two 'arms' that extend backwards into the body towards the anus and are approximately 9 cm/3.5 in in length. Between these arms are the clitoral bulbs, lying one on each side of the vaginal cavity.

**Clive, Robert** 1st Baron Clive (1725–1774) British soldier and administrator who established British rule in India by victories over French troops at Arcot and over the nawab of Bengal at Plassey in 1757. This victory secured

---

## CLONING CHRONOLOGY

**1975** British scientist Derek Brownhall produces the first clone of a rabbit, in Oxford, England.

**1981** Chinese scientists make the first clone of a fish (a golden carp).

**1984** Allan Wilson and Russell Higuchi of the University of California, Berkeley, USA, clone genes from an extinct animal, the quagga.

**1984** Sheep are successfully cloned.

**1988** The first dairy cattle are produced by cloning embryos.

**1996** US geneticists clone two rhesus monkeys from embryo cells.

**1997** British geneticists clone an adult sheep. A cell is taken from the udder of the mother sheep and its DNA (deoxyribonucleic acid) is combined with an unfertilized egg that has had its DNA removed. The fused cells are grown in the laboratory and then implanted into the uterus of a surrogate mother sheep. The resulting lamb, Dolly, comes from an animal that is six years old. This is the first time cloning has been achieved using cells other than reproductive cells. The news is met with international calls to prevent the cloning of humans.

**1997** US president Bill Clinton announces a ban on using federal funds to support human cloning research, and calls for a moratorium on this type of scientific research. He also asks the National Bioethics Advisory Commission to review and issue a report on the ramifications that cloning will have on humans.

**1997** US genetic scientist Don Wolf announces the production of monkeys cloned from embryos. It is a step closer to cloning humans and raises acute philosophical issues.

**1998** Doctors meeting at the World Medical Association's conference in Hamburg, Germany, call for a worldwide ban on human cloning. US president Clinton calls for legislation banning cloning the following day.

**1998** Dolly, the sheep who was cloned in 1997, gives birth to a female lamb at the Roslin Institute in Edinburgh, Scotland.

**1999** Dolly is revealed to be not an exact clone when her mitochondria are discovered to have come mainly from the egg rather than the udder cell.

Bengal for the East india Company, and Clive was appointed governor of the province from 1757. He returned to Britain on account of ill health in 1760, but was governor for a further year in 1765–6. On his return to Britain in 1766, his wealth led to allegations that he had abused his power. Although acquitted by a Parliamentary enquiry, he committed suicide.

**clone** an exact replica. In genetics, any one of a group of genetically identical cells or organisms. An identical ♢twin is a clone; so, too, are bacteria living in the same colony. The term 'clone' has also been adopted by computer technology to describe a (nonexistent) device that mimics an actual one to enable certain software programs to run correctly. *See chronology on page 199.*

**closed shop** any place of work, such as a factory or an office, where all workers within a section must belong to a single, officially recognized trade union.

**clothes moth** moth whose larvae feed on clothes, upholstery, and carpets. The adults are small golden or silvery moths. The natural habitat of the larvae is in the nests of animals, feeding on remains of hair and feathers, but they have adapted to human households and can cause considerable damage, for example, the common clothes moth *Tineola bisselliella.*

**cloud** water vapour condensed into minute water particles that float in masses in the atmosphere. Clouds, like fogs or mists, which occur at lower levels, are formed by the cooling of air containing water vapour, which generally condenses around tiny dust particles.

**cloud chamber** apparatus for tracking ionized particles. It consists of a vessel fitted with a piston and filled with air or other gas, saturated with water vapour. When the volume of the vessel is suddenly expanded by moving the piston outwards, the vapour cools and a cloud of tiny droplets forms on any nuclei, dust, or ions present. As fast-moving ionizing particles collide with the air or gas molecules, they show as visible tracks.

**clove** dried, unopened flower bud of the clove tree. A member of the myrtle family, the tree is a native of the Maluku Islands, Indonesia. Cloves are used for flavouring in cookery and confectionery. Oil of cloves, which has tonic qualities and relieves wind, is used in medicine. The aroma of cloves is also shared by the leaves, bark, and fruit of the tree. (*Eugenia caryophyllus,* family Myrtaceae.)

**clover** any of an Old World group of low-growing leguminous plants (see ♢legume), usually with leaves consisting of three leaflets and small flowers in dense heads. Sweet clover refers to various species belonging to the related genus *Melilotus.* (True clover genus *Trifolium,* family Leguminosae.)

**Clovis** also known as Chlodovech (465–511) Merovingian king of the Franks 481–511, who extended his realm from a small area around Tournai to encompass most of modern France and parts of modern Germany. He succeeded his father Childeric I as king of the Salian (western) Franks; defeated the Gallo-Romans (Romanized Gauls) near Soissons; and defeated the Alemanni, a confederation of Germanic tribes, near Cologne. He embraced Christianity and subsequently proved a powerful defender of orthodoxy against the Arian Visigoths, whom he defeated at Poitiers. He made Paris his capital.

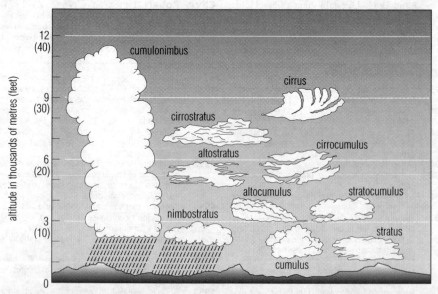

*cloud* Standard types of cloud. The height and nature of a cloud can be deduced from its name. Cirrus clouds are at high levels and have a wispy appearance. Stratus clouds form at low level and are layered. Middle-level clouds have names beginning with 'alto'. Cumulus clouds, ball or cottonwool clouds, occur over a range of height.

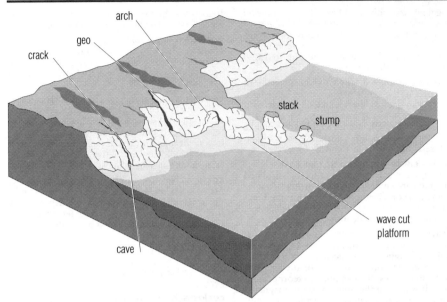

**coastal erosion** *Typical features of coastal erosion: from the initial cracks in less resistant rock through to arches, stacks, and stumps that can occur as erosion progresses.*

**club moss** or *lycopod,* any of a group of mosslike plants that do not produce seeds but reproduce by ◊spores. They are related to the ferns and horsetails. (Order Lycopodiales, family Pteridophyta.)

**clutch** any device for disconnecting rotating shafts, used especially in a car's transmission system. In a car with a manual gearbox, the driver depresses the clutch when changing gear, thus disconnecting the engine from the gearbox.

**Clwyd** former county of north Wales, created in 1974 and, in 1996, divided between ◊Conwy, ◊Denbighshire, ◊Flintshire, ◊Powys, and ◊Wrexham unitary authorities.

**Clyde** third longest river and firth in Scotland, and longest in southern Scotland; 171 km/106 mi long. Formerly one of the world's great industrial waterways, and famed for its shipbuilding, its industrial base has declined in recent years and the capacity of the ports on the Clyde has reduced.

**Clytemnestra** in Greek mythology, the daughter of King Tyndareus of Sparta and ◊Leda, half-sister of ◊Helen, and wife of ◊Agamemnon, king of Mycenae. After killing her first husband in battle, Agamemnon had married her by force, and later sacrificed their daugher Iphegenia to secure fair winds for the Greek expedition to Troy. With the help of her lover Aegisthus, she murdered her husband and the seer ◊Cassandra, whom he brought back from the Trojan War, but was killed in turn by her son ◊Orestes, aided by her daughter Electra.

**cm** symbol for *centimetre.*

**CND** in Britain, abbreviation for *Campaign for Nuclear Disarmament.*

**Cnut** alternative spelling of ◊Canute.

**coal** black or blackish mineral substance formed from the compaction of ancient plant matter in tropical swamp conditions. It is used as a fuel and in the chemical industry. Coal is classified according to the proportion of carbon it contains. The main types are ◊*anthracite* (shiny, with about 90% carbon), *bituminous coal* (shiny and dull patches, about 75% carbon), and *lignite* (woody, grading into peat, about 50% carbon). Coal burning is one of the main causes of ◊acid rain.

**coal gas** gas produced when coal is destructively distilled or heated out of contact with the air. Its main constituents are methane, hydrogen, and carbon monoxide. Coal gas has been superseded by ◊natural gas for domestic purposes.

**coal mining** extraction of coal from the Earth's crust. Coal mines may be opencast adit, or deepcast. The least expensive is opencast but this may result in scars on the landscape.

**coastal erosion** the erosion of the land by the constant battering of the sea's waves, primarily by the processes of hydraulic action, corrasion, attrition, and corrosion. Hydraulic action occurs when the force of the waves compresses air pockets in coastal rocks and cliffs. The air expands explosively, breaking the rocks apart. Rocks and pebbles flung by waves against the cliff face wear it away by the process of corrasion. Chalk and limestone coasts are often broken down by ◊solution (also called corrosion). Attrition is the process by which the eroded rock particles themselves are worn down, becoming smaller and more rounded.

**coastguard** governmental organization whose members patrol a nation's seacoast to prevent smuggling, assist distressed vessels, watch for oil slicks, and so on. In 1994 the Coastguard became an Executive Agency and is responsible for all civil maritime search and rescue operations around the UK coastline and up to 1,000 mi into the North Atlantic.

**coati** or *coatimundi*, any of several species of carnivores of the genus *Nasua*, in the same family, Procyonidae, as the raccoons. A coati is a good climber and has long claws, a long tail, a good sense of smell, and a long, flexible piglike snout used for digging. Coatis live in packs in the forests of South and Central America.

**coaxial cable** electric cable that consists of a solid or stranded central conductor insulated from and surrounded by a solid or braided conducting tube or sheath. It can transmit the high-frequency signals used in television, telephone, and other telecommunications transmissions.

**cobalt** (German *Kobalt* 'evil spirit') hard, lustrous, grey, metallic element, symbol Co, atomic number 27, relative atomic mass 58.933. It is found in various ores and occasionally as a free metal, sometimes in metallic meteorite fragments. It is used in the preparation of magnetic, wear-resistant, and high-strength alloys; its compounds are used in inks, paints, and varnishes.

**Cobb, Ty(rus Raymond)** nicknamed 'the Georgia Peach' (1886–1961) US baseball player, one of the greatest batters and base runners of all time. He played for Detroit and Philadelphia 1905–28, and won the American League batting average championship 12 times. He holds the record for runs scored (2,254) and lifetime batting average (367). He had 4,191 hits in his career – a record that stood for almost 60 years.

**cobra** any of several poisonous snakes, especially the genus *Naja*, of the family Elapidae, found in Africa and southern Asia, species of which can grow from 1 m/3 ft to over 4.3 m/14 ft. The neck stretches into a hood when the snake is alarmed. Cobra venom contains nerve toxins powerful enough to kill humans.

**coca** South American shrub belonging to the coca family, whose dried leaves are the source of the drug cocaine. It was used as a holy drug by the Andean Indians. (*Erythroxylon coca*, family Erythroxylaceae.)

**cocaine** alkaloid $C_{17}H_{21}NO_4$ extracted from the leaves of the coca tree. It has limited medical application, mainly as a local anaesthetic agent that is readily absorbed by mucous membranes (lining tissues) of the nose and throat. It is both toxic and addictive. Its use as a stimulant is illegal. Crack is a derivative of cocaine.

**coccus** plural *cocci*, member of a group of globular bacteria, some of which are harmful to humans. The cocci contain the subgroups *streptococci*, where the bacteria associate in straight chains, and *staphylococci*, where the bacteria associate in branched chains.

**Cochin-China** region of Southeast Asia. With Cambodia it formed part of the ancient Khmer empire. In the 17th–18th centuries it was conquered by Annam. Together with Cambodia it became, 1863–67, the first part of the Indochinese peninsula to be occupied by France. Since 1949 it has been part of Vietnam.

**cockatiel** Australian parrot *Nymphicus hollandicus*, about 20 cm/8 in long, with greyish or yellow plumage, yellow cheeks, a long tail, and a crest like a cockatoo. Cockatiels are popular as pets and aviary birds.

**cockatoo** any of several crested parrots, especially of the genus *Cacatua*, family Psittacidae, of the order Psittaciformes. They usually have light-coloured plumage with tinges of red, yellow, or orange on the face, and an erectile crest on the head. They are native to Australia, New Guinea, and nearby islands.

**cockchafer** or *maybug*, European beetle *Melolontha melolontha*, of the scarab family, up to 3 cm/1.2 in long, with clumsy, buzzing flight, seen on early summer evenings. Cockchafers damage trees by feeding on the foliage and flowers.

**cockle** any of over 200 species of bivalve mollusc with ribbed, heart-shaped shells. Some are edible and are sold in Western European markets.

**cockroach** any of numerous insects of the family Blattidae, distantly related to mantises and grasshoppers. There are 3,500 species, mainly in the tropics. They have long antennae and biting mouthparts. They can fly, but rarely do so.

**cocoa and chocolate** (Aztec *xocolatl*) food products made from the ◊cacao (or cocoa) bean, fruit of a tropical tree *Theobroma cacao*, now cultivated mainly in Africa. Chocolate as a drink was introduced to Europe from the New World by the Spanish in the 16th century; eating-chocolate was first produced in the late 18th century. Cocoa and chocolate are widely used in confectionery and drinks. More than 30 different pesticides are commonly used on cocoa crops, and traces of some have been detected in chocolate.

**coconut** fruit of the coconut palm, which grows throughout the lowland tropics. The fruit has a large outer husk of fibres, which is removed and used to make coconut matting and ropes. Inside this is the nut which is exported to temperate countries. Its hard shell contains white flesh and clear coconut milk, both of which are tasty and nourishing. (*Cocos nucifera*, family Arecaceae.)

**cocoon** pupa-case of many insects, especially of ◊moths and ◊silkworms. This outer web or ball is spun from the mouth by caterpillars before they pass into the ◊chrysalis state.

**Cocos Islands** or *Keeling Islands*, group of 27 small coral islands in the Indian Ocean, about 2,700 km/1,678 mi northwest of Perth, Australia; area 14 sq km/5.5 sq mi; population (1996) 655. An Australian external territory since 1955, the islanders voted to become part of Australia in 1984, and in 1992 they became subject to the laws of Western Australia. The main product is copra (dried kernels of coconut, used to make coconut oil), and the islands are a site for ecotourism.

**Cocteau, Jean** (1889–1963) French poet, dramatist, and film director. A leading figure in European Modernism, he worked with the artist ◊Picasso, the choreographer ◊Diaghilev, and the composer ◊Stravinsky. He produced many volumes of poetry, ballets such as *Le Boeuf sur le toit/The Ox on the Roof* (1920), plays like *Orphée/Orpheus* (1926), and a mature novel of bourgeois French life, *Les Enfants Terribles* (1929), which he filmed 1948.

**cod** any fish of the family Gadidae, especially the Atlantic cod, *Gadus morhua* found in the North Atlantic and Baltic. It is brown to grey with spots, white below, and can grow to 1.5 m/5 ft.

**codeine** opium derivative that provides ◊analgesia in mild to moderate pain. It also suppresses the cough centre of the brain. It is an alkaloid, derived from morphine but less toxic and addictive.

**Cody, William Frederick** 'Buffalo Bill' (1846–1917) US scout and performer. From 1883 he toured the USA and Europe with a Wild West show which featured the recreation of Indian attacks and, for a time, the cast included Chief ◊Sitting Bull as well as Annie Oakley. His nickname derives from a time when he had a contract to supply buffalo carcasses to railway labourers (over 4,000 in 18 months).

**Coe, Sebastian Newbold** (1956– ) English middle-distance runner, Olympic 1,500-metres champion in 1980 and 1984. He became UK's most prolific world-record breaker with eight outdoor world records and three indoor world records (1979–81).
*career highlights*
**Olympic Games** gold 1,500 metres 1980; silver 800 metres 1980; gold 1,500 metres 1984; silver 800 metres 1984
**world records** 800 metres: 1979, 1981; 1,000 metres: 1980, 1981; one mile: 1979, 1981 (twice); 1,500 metres: 1979; 4 x 800 metres relay: 1982.

**coefficient** the number part in front of an algebraic term, signifying multiplication. For example, in the expression $4x^2 + 2xy - x$, the coefficient of $x^2$ is 4 (because $4x^2$ means $4 \times x^2$), that of $xy$ is 2, and that of $x$ is –1 (because $-1 \times x = -x$).

**coelacanth** large dark brown to blue-grey fish that lives in the deep waters (200 m/650 ft) of the western Indian Ocean around the Comoros Islands and also off Sulawesi, Indonesia. They can grow to about 2 m/6 ft in length, and weigh up to 90 kg/200 lb. They have bony, overlapping scales, and muscular lobe (limblike) fins sometimes used like oars when swimming and for balance while resting on the sea floor. They feed on other fish, and give birth to live young rather than shedding eggs as most fish do. Coelacanth fossils exist dating back over 400 million years and coelacanth were believed to be extinct until one was caught in 1938 off the coast of South Africa. For this reason they are sometimes referred to as 'living fossils'.

*coelacanth* The coelacanth is the sole survivor of an ancient group of fishes and is found only in deep trenches of the tropical W Indian Ocean. It is a heavy-bodied fish with fleshy fin lobes and small scales. It grows to a weight of 90 kg/200 lb and is dark brown to blue in colour.

**coelenterate** any freshwater or marine organism of the phylum Coelenterata, having a body wall composed of two layers of cells. They also possess stinging cells. Examples are jellyfish, hydra, and coral.

**coffee** drink made from the roasted and ground beanlike seeds found inside the red berries of any of several species of shrubs, originally native to Ethiopia and now cultivated throughout the tropics. It contains a stimulant, ◊caffeine. (Genus *Coffea*, family Rubiaceae.)

**cogito, ergo sum** (Latin) 'I think, therefore I am'; quotation from French philosopher René Descartes. The concept formed the basis of the philosophical doctrine of ◊dualism.

**cognition** in psychology, a general term covering the functions involved in synthesizing information – for example, perception (seeing, hearing, and so on), attention, memory, and reasoning.

**cohesion** in physics, a phenomenon in which interaction between two surfaces of the same material in contact makes them cling together (with two different materials the similar phenomenon is called adhesion). According to kinetic theory, cohesion is caused by attraction between particles at the atomic or molecular level. ◊Surface tension, which causes liquids to form spherical droplets, is caused by cohesion.

**coil** in medicine, another name for an ◊intrauterine device.

**coke** clean, light fuel produced, along with town gas, when coal is strongly heated in an airtight oven. Coke contains 90% carbon and makes a useful domestic and industrial fuel (used, for example in the iron and steel industries).

**Coke, Edward** (1552–1634) Lord Chief Justice of England 1613–17. He was a defender of common law against royal prerogative;

against Charles I he drew up the petition of right in 1628, which defines and protects Parliament's liberties.

**cola** or *kola,* any of several tropical trees, especially *Cola acuminata.* In West Africa the nuts are chewed for their high ◊caffeine content, and in the West they are used to flavour soft drinks. (Genus *Cola,* family Sterculiaceae.)

**cold, common** minor disease of the upper respiratory tract, caused by a variety of viruses. Symptoms are headache, chill, nasal discharge, sore throat, and occasionally cough. Research indicates that the virulence of a cold depends on psychological factors and either a reduction or an increase of social or work activity, as a result of stress, in the previous six months.

**cold-blooded** of animals, dependent on the surrounding temperature; see ◊*poikilothermy.*

**cold fusion** in nuclear physics, the fusion of atomic nuclei at room temperature. If cold fusion were possible it would provide a limitless, cheap, and pollution-free source of energy, and it has therefore been the subject of research around the world.

**Colditz** castle in eastern Germany, near Leipzig, used as a high-security prisoner-of-war camp (Oflag IVC) in World War II. Among daring escapes was that of British Captain Patrick Reid (1910–1990) and others in October 1942, whose story contributed much to its fame. It became a museum in 1989. A highly successful British TV drama series called *Colditz* (1972) was based on prisoners' experiences.

**Cold War** ideological, political, and economic tensions 1945–89 between the USSR and Eastern Europe on the one hand and the USA and Western Europe on the other. The Cold War was fuelled by propaganda, undercover activity by intelligence agencies, and economic sanctions; and was intensified by signs of conflict anywhere in the world. Arms-reduction agreements between the USA and USSR in the late 1980s, and a reduction of Soviet influence in Eastern Europe, led to a reassessment of positions, and the 'war' was officially ended in December 1989.

The term 'Cold War' was first used by Bernard Baruch, advisor to US President Truman's, in a speech made in April 1947. He spoke about Truman's intent for the USA to 'support free peoples who are resisting attempted subjugation by armed minorities or by outside pressures'.

**coleoptile** the protective sheath that surrounds the young shoot tip of a grass during its passage through the soil to the surface. Although of relatively simple structure, most coleoptiles are very sensitive to light, ensuring that seedlings grow upwards.

**Coleridge, Samuel Taylor** (1772–1834) English poet, critic, and philosopher. A friend of the poets Robert Southey and William ◊Wordsworth, he collaborated with the latter on the highly influential collection *Lyrical Ballads* (1798), which expressed their theory of poetic sensation and was the spearhead of the English Romantic Movement. His poems include 'The Rime of the Ancient Mariner', 'Christabel', and 'Kubla Khan' (all written 1797–98); his critical works include *Biographia Literaria* (1817).

**Colette, Sidonie-Gabrielle** (1873–1954) French writer. Her best novels reveal an exquisite sensitivity, largely centred on the joys and sorrows of love, and include *Chéri* (1920), *La Fin de Chéri*/*The End of Chéri* (1926), and *Gigi* (1944).

**colic** spasmodic attack of pain in the abdomen, usually coming in waves. Colicky pains are caused by the painful muscular contraction and subsequent distension of a hollow organ; for example, the bowels, gall bladder (biliary colic), or ureter (renal colic).

**colitis** inflammation of the colon (large intestine) with diarrhoea (often bloody). It is usually due to infection or some types of bacterial dysentery.

**collage** (French 'sticking', 'pasting', or 'paperhanging') in art, the use of various materials, such as pieces of newspaper, fabric, and wallpaper, to create a picture or design by sticking them on canvas or other suitable surface, often in combination with painted or drawn features. The technique was used in scrapbooks in the 19th century and was first seriously adopted by artists in the early 20th century. Georges Braque and Pablo Picasso became the first major exponents in 1912, and it soon became a distinctive feature of ◊Cubism. Subsequently it has featured prominently in several movements, particularly ◊Dada and ◊Surrealism, in which the technique was extended to encompass an assortment of three-dimensional objects. Among Dadaists, the best-known exponent of collage was Kurt Schwitters, who made it his life's work, creating a personal variant he called Merz, using refuse such as used bus tickets and pieces of string. Among the Surrealists, the most distinctive exponent was probably Max Ernst, who fitted together cuttings from banal 19th-century engravings to form incongruous images that he arranged in 'collage novels'. Among later artists, one of the most original exponents was the Italian Alberto Burri, whose work often features pieces of sacking.

**collagen** protein that is the main constituent of ◊connective tissue. Collagen is present in skin, cartilage, tendons, and ligaments. Bones are made up of collagen, with the mineral calcium phosphate providing increased rigidity.

**collective security** system for achieving international stability by an agreement among all states to unite against any aggressor. Such a commitment was embodied in the post–World War I ◊League of Nations and also in the ◊United Nations (UN), although the League was not able to live up to the ideals of its founders, nor has the UN been able to do so.

**collectivism** in politics, a position in which the collective (such as the state) has priority over its individual members. It is the opposite of ◊individualism, which is itself a variant of anarchy.

**collie** any of several breeds of sheepdog originally bred in Britain. They include the border collie, the bearded collie, and the rough collie and its smooth-haired counterpart.

**Collier, Lesley Faye** (1947– ) English ballerina. She became a principal dancer of the Royal Ballet 1972. She created roles in Kenneth MacMillan's *Anastasia* (1971) and *Four Seasons* (1975), Hans van Manen's *Four Schumann Pieces* (1975), Frederick Ashton's *Rhapsody* (1980), and Glen Tetley's *Dance of Albiar* (1980).

**Collins, Michael** (1890–1922) Irish nationalist. He was a ◊Sinn Fein leader, a founder and director of intelligence of the ◊Irish Republican Army in 1919, minister for finance in the provisional government of the Irish Free State in 1922, commander of the Free State forces in the civil war, and for ten days head of state before being killed by Irishmen opposed to the partition treaty with Britain.

**Collins, Phil(lip) David Charles** (1951– ) English pop singer, drummer, and actor. A member of the group Genesis from 1970, he has also pursued a successful middle-of-the-road solo career since 1981, with hits (often new versions of old songs) including 'In the Air Tonight' (1981), 'Groovy Kind of Love' (1988), 'Another Day in Paradise' (1989), 'I Wish it Would Rain' (1990), and 'Both Sides of the Story' (1993). He starred as the train robber Buster Edwards in the film *Buster* (1988).

**Collins, (William) Wilkie** (1824–1889) English author of mystery and suspense novels. He wrote *The Woman in White* (1860) (with its fat villain Count Fosco), often called the first English detective novel, and *The Moonstone* (1868) (with Sergeant Cuff, one of the first detectives in English literature).

**colloid** substance composed of extremely small particles of one material (the dispersed phase) evenly and stably distributed in another material (the continuous phase). The size of the dispersed particles (1–1,000 nanometres across) is less than that of particles in suspension but greater than that of molecules in true solution. Colloids involving gases include *aerosols* (dispersions of liquid or solid particles in a gas, as in fog or smoke) and *foams* (dispersions of gases in liquids).

Those involving liquids include *emulsions* (in which both the dispersed and the continuous phases are liquids) and *sols* (solid particles dispersed in a liquid). Sols in which both phases contribute to a molecular three-dimensional network have a jellylike form and are known as *gels;* gelatin, starch 'solution', and silica gel are common examples.

**Cologne** German *Köln*, industrial and commercial port in North Rhine-Westphalia, Germany, on the left bank of the Rhine, 35 km/ 22 mi southeast of Düsseldorf; population (1995) 964,200. Cologne is an important transhipment centre, and a major industrial centre for the manufacture of cars (Ford), machinery, electrical goods, chemicals, clothing, and food; other industries include environmental and chemical engineering, and waste management.

**Colombia** Republic of
*national name Repúblíca de Colombia*

**area** 1,141,748 sq km/440,828 sq mi
**capital** Bogotá
**major towns/cities** Medellín, Cali, Barranquilla, Cartagena, Bucaramanga, Buenaventura
**major ports** Barranquilla, Cartagena, Buenaventura
**physical features** the Andes mountains run north–south; flat coastland in west and plains (llanos) in east; Magdalena River runs north to Caribbean Sea; includes islands of Providencia, San Andrés, and Mapelo; almost half the country is forested
**head of state and government** Andres Pastrana from 1998
**political system** democracy
**political parties** Liberal Party (PL), centrist; Conservative Party (PSC), right of centre; M-19 Democratic Alliance (ADM-19), left of centre; National Salvation Movement (MSN), right-of-centre coalition grouping
**currency** Colombian peso
**GNP per capita (PPP)** (US$) 7,500 (1998)
**exports** coffee, petroleum and petroleum products, coal, gold, bananas, cut flowers, cotton, chemicals, textiles, paper. Principal market: USA 36% (1998). Illegal trade in cocaine in 1995; it was estimated that approximately $3.5 billion (equivalent to about 4% of GDP) was entering Colombia as the proceeds of drug-trafficking
**population** 41,564,000 (1999 est)
**language** Spanish
**religion** Roman Catholic
**life expectancy** 67 (men); 74 (women) (1995–2000)
**Chronology**
**late 15th century** Southern Colombia became part of Inca Empire, whose core lay in Peru.
**1522** Spanish conquistador Pascual de Andagoya reached San Juan River.
**1536–38** Spanish conquest by Jimenez de Quesada overcame powerful Chibcha Indian chiefdom, which had its capital in the uplands at Bogotá and was renowned for its gold crafts; became part of Spanish Viceroyalty of Peru, which covered much of South America.
**1717** Bogotá became capital of new Spanish Viceroyalty of Nueva (New) Granada, which also ruled Ecuador and Venezuela.
**1809** Struggle for independence from Spain began.

**1819** Venezuelan freedom fighter Simón Bolívar, 'The Liberator', who had withdrawn to Colombia 1814, raised a force of 5,000 British mercenaries and defeated Spanish at the battle of Boyaca, establishing Colombia's independence; Gran Colombia formed, also comprising Ecuador, Panama, and Venezuela.

**1830** Became separate state, which included Panama, on dissolution of Republic of Gran Colombia.

**1863** Became major coffee exporter. Federalizing, anti-clerical Liberals came to power, with country divided into nine largely autonomous 'sovereign' states; church disestablished.

**1885** Conservatives came to power, beginning 45 years of political dominance; power was recentralized and church restored to influence.

**1899–1903** Civil war between Liberals and Conservatives, ended with Panama's separation as an independent state.

**1930** Liberals returned to power at the time of the economic depression; social legislation introduced and labour movement encouraged.

**1946** Conservatives returned to power after Liberal vote divided between rival candidates.

**1948** Left-wing mayor of Bogotá assassinated; widespread outcry.

**1949** Start of civil war, 'La Violencia', during which over 250,000 people died.

**1957** Hoping to halt violence, Conservatives and Liberals agreed to form National Front, sharing the presidency.

**1970** National Popular Alliance (ANAPO) formed as left-wing opposition to National Front.

**1974** National Front accord temporarily ended.

**1975** Civil unrest due to disillusionment with government.

**1978** Liberals, under Julio Turbay, revived the accord and began an intensive fight against drug dealers.

**1982** The Liberals maintained their control of congress but lost the presidency. Conservative president Belisario Betancur granted guerrillas an amnesty and freed political prisoners.

**1984** The minister of justice was assassinated by drug dealers; the campaign against them was stepped up.

**1986** Virgilio Barco Vargas, Liberal, was elected president by a record margin.

**1989** A drug cartel assassinated the leading presidential candidate; Vargas declared an antidrug war; a bombing campaign by drug traffickers killed hundreds; the police killed José Rodríguez Gacha, one of the most wanted cartel leaders.

**1990** Cesar Gaviria Trujillo was elected president. The Liberals maintained their control of congress.

**1991** A new constitution prohibited the extradition of Colombians wanted for trial in other countries. Several leading drug traffickers were arrested. Many guerrillas abandoned the armed struggle, but the Colombian Revolutionary Armed Forces (FARC) and the National Liberation Army remained active. The Liberals won a general election.

**1993** Medellín drug-cartel leader Pablo Escobar was shot while attempting to avoid arrest.

**1994** The Liberals returned to power, with a reduced majority. Ernesto Samper Pizano, Liberal, was elected president.

**1995** Samper was under pressure to resign over corruption allegations; a state of emergency was declared. Leaders of the Cali drug cartel were imprisoned.

**1998** There were clashes between the army and left-wing guerrillas. The Liberal Party secured an assembly majority. Andres Pastrama won presidential elections. Peace talks were held with rebels.

**1999** In May, formal peace talks began between the government and the leading rebel group, the Revolutionary Armed Forces of Colombia.

**Colombo** capital and principal seaport of Sri Lanka, on the west coast near the mouth of the Kelani River; population (1993) 2,026,000. It trades in tea, rubber, and cacao. It has iron- and steelworks and an oil refinery.

**Colón** chief port and second-largest city of Panama, built on Manzanillo Island at the Caribbean entrance of the Panama Canal, 80 km/50 mi northwest of Panamá; population (1990) 140,900. It is a major commercial centre and has an oil refining industry. Its free trade zone, created in 1948, is the second-largest in the world. The zone has a pivotal role in bolstering the Panamanian economy.

**colonialism** another name for ⋄*imperialism*.

**Colorado** river in southwestern USA and northwestern Mexico, rising in the Rocky Mountains and flowing 2,333 km/1,447 mi to the Gulf of California through Colorado, Utah, Arizona (including the Grand Canyon), and extending into northern Mexico. The many dams along its course, including Hoover Dam and Glen Canyon Dam, provide hydroelectric power and irrigation water, but have destroyed wildlife and scenery; they have also created a series of lakes including Lake Powell, Lake Mead, and Lake Havasu.

To the west of the river in southeastern California is the **Colorado Desert,** an arid area of some 5,000 sq km/1,931 sq mi.

**Colorado** state of the western central USA. It is nicknamed the Centennial State. Colorado was admitted to the Union in 1876 as the 38th US state. Its expansion from World War II onwards has been closely associated with the US's military-industrial surge, with the state serving as the home of numerous military facilities and weapons plants. Colorado is bordered to the east by Kansas and Nebraska, to the north by Nebraska and Wyoming, and to the west by Utah. To the southwest, at the 'Four Corners', it meets Utah, Arizona, and New Mexico. New Mexico extends east along its southern border, which in the southeast also adjoins part of the Oklahoma panhandle

**population** (1996 est) 3,823,000

**area** 269,700 sq km/104,104 sq mi

**capital** Denver

**towns and cities** Colorado Springs, Aurora, Lakewood, Fort Collins, Greeley, Pueblo, Boulder, Arvada

**industries and products** cereals, meat and dairy products, oil, coal, molybdenum, uranium, iron, steel, scientific instruments, machinery.

**Colorado beetle** or *potato beetle,* North American black and yellow striped beetle that is a pest on potato crops. Although it was once a serious pest, it can now usually be controlled by using insecticides. It has also colonized many European countries.

Colarado beetles *Leptinotarsa decemlineata* are in the family Chrysomelidae, order Coleoptera, class Insecta, phylum Arthropoda.

**coloratura** in music, a rapid ornamental vocal passage with runs and trills. A *coloratura soprano* is a light, high voice suited to such music.

**Colosseum** amphitheatre in ancient Rome, begun by the emperor Vespasian to replace the one destroyed by fire during the reign of Nero, and completed by his son Titus AD 80. It was 187 m/615 ft long and 49 m/160 ft high, and seated 50,000 people. Early Christians were martyred there by lions and gladiators. It could be flooded for mock sea battles.

**colour** in art, the quality or ◊wavelength of light emitted or reflected from an object. Colours may be produced by the use of pigment (paint or dye), by the choice of naturally coloured objects, or (in installation art) by the use of lights or television screens.

**colour** quality or wavelength of light emitted or reflected from an object. Visible white light consists of electromagnetic radiation of various wavelengths, and if a beam is refracted through a prism, it can be spread out into a spectrum, in which the various colours correspond to different wavelengths. From long to short wavelengths (from about 700 to 400 nanometres) the colours are red, orange, yellow, green, blue, indigo, and violet.

**colour blindness** hereditary defect of vision that reduces the ability to discriminate certain colours, usually red and green. The condition is sex-linked, affecting men more than women.

**Coltrane, John William** (1926–1967) US jazz saxophonist. He first came to prominence 1955 with the Miles ◊Davis quintet, later playing with Thelonious Monk 1957. He was a powerful and individual artist, whose performances featured much experimentation. His 1960s quartet was highly regarded for its innovations in melody and harmony.

**colugo** or *flying lemur,* Southeast Asian climbing mammal of the genus *Cynocephalus,* order Dermoptera, about 60 cm/2 ft long including the tail. It glides between forest trees using a flap of skin that extends from head to forelimb to hindlimb to tail. It may glide 130 m/425 ft or more, losing little height. It feeds largely on buds and leaves, and rests hanging upside down under branches.

**Columba, St** (Latin form of *Colum-cille,* 'Colum of the cell') (521–597) Irish Christian abbot, missionary to Scotland. He was born in County Donegal of royal descent, and founded monasteries and churches in Ireland. In 563 he

sailed with 12 companions to Iona, and built a monastery there that was to play a leading part in the conversion of Britain. Feast day 9 June.

**Columbia** river in western North America; length over 2,005 km/1,245 mi. It rises in Columbia Lake on the western slope of the Rocky Mountains in British Columbia, Canada, 130 km/81 mi north of the USA border. It flows through Washington State along the northern border of Oregon, until it reaches the Pacific below Astoria; its estuary is about 55 km/34 mi long and 5–11 km/3–7 mi wide, and its mouth is the only deep-water harbour between San Francisco and Cape Flattery.

**Columbia, District of** federal district of the USA, see ◊District of Columbia and ◊Washington, DC.

**columbine** any of a group of plants belonging to the buttercup family. All are perennial herbs with divided leaves and hanging flower heads with spurred petals. (Genus *Aquilegia,* family Ranunculaceae.)

**Columbus** capital of ◊Ohio, USA, on the Scioto and Olentangy rivers; seat of Franklin County; population (1994 est) 636,000; metropolitan area (1992) 1,394,000. There are coalfields and natural gas resources nearby, and local industries include the manufacture of cars, aircraft, space equipment, missiles, and electrical goods; it is also a centre for government, banking and insurance. Columbus was founded in 1812, became the state capital in 1816, and was incorporated as a city in 1834.

**Columbus, Christopher** Spanish *Cristóbal Colón* (1451–1506) Italian navigator and explorer who made four voyages to the New World: 1492 to San Salvador Island, Cuba, and Haiti; 1493–96 to Guadaloupe, Montserrat, Antigua, Puerto Rico, and Jamaica; 1498 to Trinidad and the mainland of South America; 1502–04 to Honduras and Nicaragua.

Believing that Asia could be reached by sailing westwards, he eventually won the support of King Ferdinand and Queen Isabella of Spain and set off on his first voyage from Palos on 3 August 1492 with three small ships, the *Niña,* the *Pinta,* and his flagship the *Santa Maria.* Land was sighted on 12 October, probably Watling Island (now San Salvador Island), and within a few weeks he reached Cuba and Haiti, returning to Spain in March 1493.

**column** in architecture, a structure, round or polygonal in plan, erected vertically as a support for some part of a building. Cretan paintings reveal the existence of wooden columns in Aegean architecture about 1500 BC. The Hittites, Assyrians, and Egyptians also used wooden columns, and they are a feature of the monumental architecture of China and Japan. In Classical architecture there are five principal types of column; see ◊order.

**coma** in medicine, a state of deep unconsciousness from which the subject cannot be roused. Possible causes include head injury, brain disease, liver failure, cerebral haemorrhage, and drug overdose.

**Comaneci, Nadia** (1961–  ) Romanian gymnast. She won three gold medals at the 1976 Olympics at the age of 14, and was the first gymnast to record a perfect score of 10 in international competition. Upon retirement she became a coach of the Romanian team, but defected to Canada in 1989.
*career highlights*
*Olympic Games* gold: beam, vault, floor exercise 1976; gold: beam, parallel bars 1980.

**Combination Acts** laws passed in Britain in 1799 and 1800 making trade unionism illegal. They were introduced after the French Revolution for fear that the unions would become centres of political agitation. The unions continued to exist, but claimed to be friendly societies or went underground, until the acts were repealed in 1824, largely owing to the radical Francis Place.

**combine harvester** or *combine,* machine used for harvesting cereals and other crops, so called because it combines the actions of reaping (cutting the crop) and threshing (beating the ears so that the grain separates).

**combustion** burning, defined in chemical terms as the rapid combination of a substance with oxygen, accompanied by the evolution of heat and usually light. A slow-burning candle flame and the explosion of a mixture of petrol vapour and air are extreme examples of combustion. Combustion is an exothermic reaction as heat energy is given out.

**Comecon** (acronym for *Council for Mutual Economic Assistance,* or *CMEA)* economic organization 1949–91, linking the USSR with Bulgaria, Czechoslovakia, Hungary, Poland, Romania, East Germany (1950–90), Mongolia (from 1962), Cuba (from 1972), and Vietnam (from 1978), with Yugoslavia as an associated member. Albania also belonged 1949–61. Its establishment was prompted by the ◊Marshall Plan. Comecon was formally disbanded June 1991.

**Comédie Française** French national theatre (for both comedy and tragedy) in Paris, founded 1680 by Louis XIV. Its base is the Salle Richelieu on the right bank of the River Seine, and the Théâtre de l'Odéon, on the left bank, is a testing ground for avant-garde ideas.

**comedy** drama that aims to make its audience laugh, usually with a happy or amusing ending, as opposed to ◊tragedy. The comic tradition has undergone many changes since its Greek roots; the earliest comedy developed in ancient Greece, in the topical and fantastic satires of Aristophanes. Great comic dramatists include William Shakespeare, Molière, Carlo Goldoni, Pierre de Marivaux, George Bernard Shaw, and Oscar Wilde. Genres of comedy include pantomime, satire, farce, black comedy, and ◊commedia dell'arte.

**comet** small, icy body orbiting the Sun, usually on a highly elliptical path. A comet consists of a central nucleus a few kilometres across, and has been likened to a dirty snowball because it consists mostly of ice mixed with dust. As a comet approaches the Sun its nucleus heats up, releasing gas and dust which form a tenuous

### SOME MAJOR COMETS

| Name | First recorded sighting | Orbital period (yrs) | Interesting facts |
|---|---|---|---|
| Halley's comet | 240 BC | 76 | parent of Eta Aquarid and Orionid meteor showers |
| Comet Tempel-Tuttle | AD 1366 | 33 | parent of Leonid meteors |
| Biela's comet | 1772 | 6.6 | broke in half in 1846; not seen since 1852 |
| Encke's comet | 1786 | 3.3 | parent of Taurid meteors |
| Comet Swift-Tuttle | 1862 | 130 | parent of Perseid meteors; reappeared 1992 |
| Comet Ikeya-Seki | 1965 | 880 | so-called 'Sun-grazing' comet, passed 500,000 km/300,000 mi above surface of the Sun on 21 October 1965 |
| Comet Kohoutek | 1973 | – | observed from space by *Skylab* astronauts |
| Comet West | 1975 | 500,000 | nucleus broke into four parts |
| Comet Bowell | 1980 | – | ejected from Solar System after close encounter with Jupiter |
| Comet IRAS-Araki-Alcock | 1983 | – | passed only 4.5 million km/2.8 million mi from the Earth on 11 May 1983 |
| Comet Austin | 1989 | – | passed 32 million km/20 million mi from the Earth in 1990 |
| Comet Shoemaker-Levy 9 | 1993 | – | made up of 21 fragments; crashed into Jupiter in July 1994 |
| Comet Hale-Bopp | 1995 | 1,000 | spitting out of gas and debris produced a coma, a surrounding hazy cloud of gas and dust, of greater volume than the Sun; the bright coma is due to an outgassing of carbon monoxide; clearly visible with the naked eye in March 1997 |
| Comet Hyakutake | 1996 | – | passed 15 million km/9.3 million mi from the Earth in 1996 |

coma, up to 100,000 km/60,000 mi wide, around the nucleus. Gas and dust stream away from the coma to form one or more tails, which may extend for millions of kilometres. US astronomers concluded in 1996 that there are two distinct types of comet: one rich in methanol and one low in methanol. Evidence for this comes in part from observations of the spectrum of Comet Hyakutake.

**Comet Hale-Bopp** C/1995 01, large and exceptionally active comet, which in March 1997 made its closest flyby to Earth since 2000 BC, coming within 190 million km/118 million mi. It has a diameter of approximately 40 km/25 mi and an extensive gas coma (when close to the Sun Hale-Bopp released 10 tonnes of gas every second). Unusually, Hale-Bopp has three tails: one consisting of dust particles, one of charged particles, and a third of sodium particles.

Comet Hale-Bopp was discovered independently in July 1995 by two amateur US astronomers, Alan Hale and Thomas Bopp.

**comfrey** any of a group of plants belonging to the borage family, with rough, hairy leaves and small bell-shaped flowers (blue, purple-pink, or white). They are found in Europe and western Asia. (Genus *Symphytum*, family Boraginaceae.)

**Comintern** acronym for *Communist ◊International.*

**command language** in computing, a set of commands and the rules governing their use, by which users control a program. For example, an ◊operating system may have commands such as SAVE and DELETE, or a payroll program may have commands for adding and amending staff records.

**commando** member of a specially trained, highly mobile military unit. The term originated in South Africa in the 19th century, where it referred to Boer military reprisal raids against Africans and, in the South African Wars, against the British. Commando units have often carried out operations behind enemy lines.

**commedia dell'arte** popular form of Italian improvised comic drama in the 16th and 17th centuries, performed by trained troupes of actors and involving stock characters and situations. It exerted considerable influence on writers such as Molière and Carlo Goldoni, and on the genres of ◊pantomime, harlequinade, and the Punch and Judy show. It laid the foundation for a tradition of mime, strong in France, that has continued with the modern mime of Jean-Louis Barrault and Marcel Marceau.

**commensalism** in biology, a relationship between two ◊species whereby one (the commensal) benefits from the association, whereas the other neither benefits nor suffers. For example, certain species of millipede and silverfish inhabit the nests of army ants and live by scavenging on the refuse of their hosts, but without affecting the ants.

**commodity** something produced for sale. Commodities may be consumer goods, such as radios, or producer goods, such as copper bars. *Commodity markets* deal in raw or semi-raw

materials that are amenable to grading and that can be stored for considerable periods without deterioration.

**common land** unenclosed wasteland, forest, and pasture used in common by the community at large. Poor people have throughout history gathered fruit, nuts, wood, reeds, roots, game, and so on from common land; in dry regions of India, for example, the landless derive 20% of their annual income in this way, together with much of their food and fuel. Codes of conduct evolved to ensure that common resources were not depleted. But in the 20th century, in the Third World as elsewhere, much common land has been privatized or appropriated by the state, and what remains is overburdened by those dependent on it.

**common law** that part of the English law not embodied in legislation. It consists of rules of law based on common custom and usage and on judicial decisions. English common law became the basis of law in the USA and many other English-speaking countries.

**Common Market** popular name for the *European Economic Community;* see ◊European Union.

**Commons, House of** lower chamber of the UK ◊Parliament. It consists of 659 elected members of Parliament, each of whom represents a constituency. Its functions are to debate, legislate, and to scrutinize the activities of government. Constituencies are kept under continuous review by the Parliamentary Boundary Commissions 1944. The House of Commons is presided over by the Speaker. Proceedings in the House of Commons began to be televised from November 1989. After the 1997 election, the Commons included a record 120 women members, including 101 female Labour MPs.

**commonwealth** body politic founded on law for the common 'weal' or good. Political philosophers of the 17th century, such as Thomas Hobbes and John Locke, used the term to mean an organized political community. In Britain it was specifically applied to the regime (*the Commonwealth*) of Oliver ◊Cromwell 1649–60.

**Commonwealth Games** multisport gathering of competitors from British Commonwealth countries, held every four years. The first meeting (known as the British Empire Games) was in Hamilton, Canada, in August 1930. It has been held in Britain on four occasions: London in 1934; Cardiff in 1958; Edinburgh in 1970 and 1986. Manchester will host the 2002 games.

**Commonwealth of Independent States** (CIS), successor body to the Union of Soviet Socialist Republics, initially formed as a new commonwealth of Slav republics on 8 December 1991 by the presidents of the Russian Federation, Belarus, and Ukraine. On 21 December, eight of the nine remaining non-Slav republics – Moldova, Tajikistan, Armenia, Azerbaijan, Turkmenistan, Kazakhstan, Kyrgyzstan, and Uzbekistan – joined the CIS at a meeting held in Kazakhstan's former capital,

Alma-Ata (now Almaty). The CIS formally came into existence January 1992 when President Gorbachev resigned and the Soviet government voted itself out of existence. It has no real, formal political institutions and its role is uncertain. Georgia joined in 1994. There is a 2,000-strong CIS bureaucracy in Moscow.

**Commonwealth, the (British)** voluntary association of 54 sovereign countries and their dependencies, the majority of which once formed part of the ◊British Empire and are now independent sovereign states. They are all regarded as 'full members of the Commonwealth'; the newest member being Mozambique, which was admitted in November 1995. Additionally, there are some 20 territories that are not completely sovereign and remain dependencies of the UK or one of the other fully sovereign members, and are regarded as 'Commonwealth countries'. Heads of government meet every two years, apart from those of Nauru and Tuvalu; however, Nauru and Tuvalu have the right to participate in all functional activities. The Commonwealth, which was founded in 1931, has no charter or constitution, and is founded more on tradition and sentiment than on political or economic factors. However, it can make political statements by withdrawing membership; a recent example was Nigeria's suspension in November 1995 because of human-rights abuses. Fiji Islands was readmitted in October 1997, ten years after its membership had been suspended as a result of discrimination against its ethnic Indian community.

**commune** group of people or families living together, sharing resources and responsibilities. There have been various kinds of commune through the ages, including a body of burghers or burgesses in medieval times, a religious community in America, and a communal division in communist China.

**Commune, Paris** two separate periods in the history of Paris 1789–94 and March–May 1871; see ◊Paris Commune.

**communication** in biology, the signalling of information by one organism to another, usually with the intention of altering the recipient's behaviour. Signals used in communication may be *visual* (such as the human smile or the display of colourful plumage in birds), *auditory* (for example, the whines or barks of a dog), *olfactory* (such as the odours released by the scent glands of a deer), *electrical* (as in the pulses emitted by electric fish), or *tactile* (for example, the nuzzling of male and female elephants).

**communications satellite** relay station in space for sending telephone, television, telex, and other messages around the world. Messages are sent to and from the satellites via ground stations. Most communications satellites are in ◊geostationary orbit, appearing to hang fixed over one point on the Earth's surface.

**Communion, Holy** in the Christian church, another name for the ◊Eucharist.

**communism** (French *commun* 'common, general') revolutionary socialism based on the theories of the political philosophers Karl ◊Marx and Friedrich ◊Engels, emphasizing common ownership of the means of production and a planned economy. The principle held is that each should work according to his or her capacity and receive according to his or her needs. Politically, it seeks the overthrow of capitalism through a proletarian revolution. The first communist state was the USSR after the revolution of 1917. Revolutionary socialist parties and groups united to form communist parties in other countries during the interwar years. After World War II, communism was enforced in those countries that came under Soviet occupation.

China emerged after 1961 as a rival to the USSR in world communist leadership, and other countries attempted to adapt communism to their own needs. The late 1980s saw a movement for more individual freedoms in many communist countries, culminating in the abolition or overthrow of communist rule in Eastern European countries and Mongolia, and further state repression in China. The failed hard-line coup in the USSR against President Gorbachev in 1991 resulted in the abandonment of communism there. However, in December 1995 the communists polled strongly in Russian parliamentary elections, with the party's leader, Gennady Zyuganov, running high in the opinion polls. Reform communist parties have also recovered some strength in other states in central and Eastern Europe, forming governments in Hungary, Lithuania, and Poland from 1993 and remaining the largest parliamentary forces in Moldova and the Ukraine.

Communism as the ideology of a nation state survives in only a few countries, notably China, Cuba, North Korea, Laos, and Vietnam, where market forces are being encouraged in the economic sphere.

**Communism Peak** alternative form of Pik ◊Kommunizma, the highest mountain in the ◊Pamirs.

**community** in the social sciences, the sense of identity, purpose, and companionship that comes from belonging to a particular place, organization, or social group. The concept dominated sociological thinking in the first half of the 20th century, and inspired the academic discipline of *community studies*.

**community council** in Wales, name for a parish council.

**community service** in the penal systems of the UK and the USA, unpaid work in the service of the community (aiding children, the elderly, or the disabled), performed by a convicted person by order of the court as an alternative to prison.

**Comoros** Federal Islamic Republic of
*national name Jumhurīyat al-Qumur al-Itthādīyah al-Islāmīyah* or *République Fédérale Islamique des Comoros*
*area* 1,862 sq km/718 sq mi
*capital* Moroni
*major towns/cities* Mutsamudu, Domoni, Fomboni, Dzaoudzi

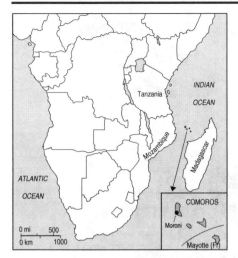

**physical features** comprises the volcanic islands of Njazídja, Nzwani, and Mwali (formerly Grande Comore, Anjouan, Moheli); at northern end of Mozambique Channel in Indian Ocean between Madagascar and coast of Africa
**head of state and government** Azali Assoumani from 1999
**political system** transitional
**political parties** National Union for Democracy in the Comoros (UNDC), Islamic, nationalist; Rally for Democracy and Renewal (RDR), left of centre
**currency** Comorian franc
**GNP per capita (PPP)** (US$) 1,480 (1998)
**exports** vanilla, cloves, ylang-ylang, essences, copra, coffee. Principal market: France 42.9% (1997)
**population** 676,000 (1999 est)
**language** Arabic (official), Comorian (Swahili and Arabic dialect), Makua, French
**religion** Muslim; Islam is the state religion
**life expectancy** 57 (men); 60 (women) (1995–2000)
**Chronology**
**5th century** AD First settled by Malay-Polynesian immigrants.
**7th century** Converted to Islam by Arab seafarers and fell under the rule of local sultans.
**late 16th century** First visited by European navigators.
**1886** Moheli island in south became a French protectorate.
**1904** Slave trade abolished, ending influx of Africans.
**1912** Grande Comore and Anjouan, the main islands, joined Moheli to become a French colony, which was attached to Madagascar from 1914.
**1947** Became a French Overseas Territory separate from Madagascar.
**1961** Internal self-government achieved.
**1975** Independence achieved from France, but island of Mayotte to the southeast voted to remain part of France. Joined the United Nations.
**1976** President Ahmed Abdallah overthrown in a coup by Ali Soilih; relations deteriorated with France as a Maoist-Islamic socialist programme

was pursued.
**1978** Soilih killed by French mercenaries led by Bob Denard. Federal Islamic republic proclaimed, with exiled Abdallah restored as president; diplomatic relations re-established with France.
**1979** The Comoros became a one-party state; powers of the federal government increased.
**1989** Abdallah killed by French mercenaries who, under French and South African pressure, turned authority over to French administration; Said Muhammad Djohar became president in a multiparty democracy.
**1990–92** Antigovernment coups were foiled.
**1993** Djohar's supporters won an overall majority in assembly elections.
**1995** Djohar was overthrown in a coup led by Col Denard, who was persuaded to withdraw by French troops.
**1996** Djohar was allowed to return from exile in a nonpolitical capacity and Muhammad Taki Abdoulkarim was elected president. The National Rally for Development (RND) was virtually unopposed in assembly elections. Ahmed Abdou was appointed prime minister.
**1997** Secessionist rebels took control of the island of Anjouan.
**1998** President Muhammad Taki Abdoulkarim died and was succeeded by Tajiddine Ben Said Massounde.
**1999** Government overthrown by army coup, after government had granted greater autonomy to the islands of Anjouan and Moheli.

**compact disc** or **CD,** disk for storing digital information, about 12 cm/4.5 in across, mainly used for music, when it can have over an hour's playing time. A laser beam etches the compact disc with microscopic pits that carry a digital code representing the sounds; the pitted surface is then coated with aluminium. During playback, a laser beam reads the code and produces signals that are changed into near-exact replicas of the original sounds. *See illustration on page 212.*

**company** in economics, a number of people grouped together as a business enterprise. Types of company include public limited companies, partnerships, joint ventures, sole proprietorships, and branches of foreign companies. Most companies are private and, unlike public companies, cannot offer their shares to the general public.

**compass** any instrument for finding direction. The most commonly used is a magnetic compass, consisting of a thin piece of magnetic material with the north-seeking pole indicated, free to rotate on a pivot and mounted on a compass card on which the points of the compass are marked. When the compass is properly adjusted and used, the north-seeking pole will point to the magnetic north, from which true north can be found from tables of magnetic corrections.

**competition** in ecology, the interaction between two or more organisms, or groups of organisms (for example, species), that use a common resource which is in short supply. Competition invariably results in a reduction in the numbers of one or both competitors, and in ◊evolution contributes both to the decline of

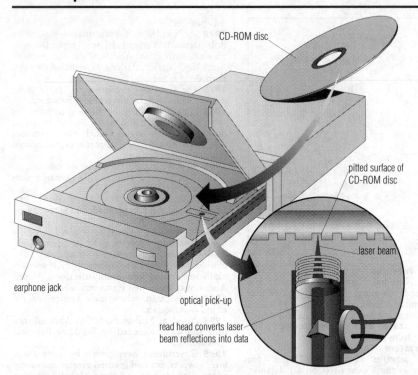

CD-ROM disc

pitted surface of
CD-ROM disc

laser beam

earphone jack

optical pick-up

read head converts laser
beam reflections into data

**compact disc** *The compact disc is a digital storage device; music is recorded as a series of etched pits representing numbers in digital code. During playing, a laser scans the pits and the pattern of reflected light reveals the numbers representing the sound recorded. The optical signal is converted to electrical form by a photocell and sent to the amplifiers and loudspeakers.*

certain species and to the evolution of ◊adaptations.

**compiler** computer program that translates programs written in a high-level language into machine code (the form in which they can be run by the computer). The compiler translates each high-level instruction into several machine-code instructions – in a process called *compilation* – and produces a complete independent program that can be run by the computer as often as required, without the original source program being present.

**complementary medicine** in medicine, systems of care based on methods of treatment or theories of disease that differ from those taught in most western medical schools. See ◊medicine, alternative.

**complex** in psychology, a group of ideas and feelings that have become repressed because they are distasteful to the person in whose mind they arose, but are still active in the depths of the person's unconscious mind, continuing to affect his or her life and actions, even though he or she is no longer fully aware of their existence. Typical examples include the ◊Oedipus complex and the ◊inferiority complex.

**complex number** in mathematics, a number written in the form $a + ib$, where $a$ and $b$ are ◊real numbers and i is the square root of $-1$ (that is, $i^2 = -1$); i used to be known as the 'imaginary'

part of the complex number. Some equations in algebra, such as those of the form $x^2 + 5 = 0$ cannot be solved without recourse to complex numbers, because the real numbers do not include square roots of negative numbers.

**Compositae** daisy family, comprising dicotyledonous flowering plants characterized by flowers borne in composite heads. It is the largest family of flowering plants, the majority being herbaceous. Birds seem to favour the family for use in nest 'decoration', possibly because many species either repel or kill insects (see ◊pyrethrum). Species include the daisy and dandelion; food plants such as the artichoke, lettuce, and safflower; and the garden varieties of chrysanthemum, dahlia, and zinnia.

**compost** organic material decomposed by bacteria under controlled conditions to make a nutrient-rich natural fertilizer for use in gardening or farming. A well-made compost heap reaches a high temperature during the composting process, killing most weed seeds that might be present.

**compound** chemical substance made up of two or more ◊elements bonded together, so that they cannot be separated by physical means. Compounds are held together by ionic or covalent bonds.

**compound interest** interest calculated by computing the rate against the original capital plus reinvested interest each time the interest becomes due. When simple interest is calculated, only the interest on the original capital is added.

**comprehensive school** secondary school that admits pupils of all abilities, and therefore without any academic selection procedure. In England 86.8% of all pupils attend a comprehensive school. Other state secondary schools are middle, deemed secondary (5.2%), secondary modern (2.6%), secondary grammar (4.2%), and technical (0.1%). There were 4,462 state secondary schools in 1995–96, with 3,675,600 pupils.

**Compton, Denis Charles Scott** (1918–1997) English cricketer and football player. He played for Middlesex and England, and was a right-handed batsman of prodigious talent and great style, who in 78 tests between 1937 and 1957 scored 5,807 runs at an average of 50.06. In the 1947 English season he scored 3,816 runs (at an average of 90.85) and 18 hundreds, records which are unlikely ever to be surpassed. As a footballer he won Football League and FA Cup winners' medals with Arsenal and played in 12 wartime internationals for England.

*career highlights*
*all first-class cricket* matches: 515
*Test cricket* runs: 5,807; average: 50.06; hundreds: 17; highest score: 278 (v. Pakistan, Nottingham 1954)
*batting* innings: 839; runs: 38,942; average: 51.85; hundreds: 123
*bowling* wickets: 622; average: 32.27.

**Compton-Burnett, Ivy** (1884–1969) English novelist. She used dialogue to show reactions of small groups of characters dominated by the tyranny of family relationships. Her novels, set at the turn of the century, include *Pastors and Masters* (1925), *More Women than Men* (1933), and *Mother and Son* (1955).

**computer** programmable electronic device that processes data and performs calculations and other symbol-manipulation tasks. There are three types: the *digital computer,* which manipulates information coded as binary numbers (see ◊binary number system); the *analogue computer,* which works with continuously varying quantities; and the *hybrid computer,* which has characteristics of both analogue and digital computers.

**computer-aided design** use of computers to create and modify design drawings; see ◊CAD.

**computer-aided manufacturing** use of computers to regulate production processes in industry; see ◊CAM.

**computer-assisted learning** use of computers in education and training; see ◊CAL.

**computer game** or *video game,* any computer-controlled game in which the computer (sometimes) opposes the human player. Computer games typically employ fast, animated graphics on a ◊VDU (visual display unit) and synthesized sound.

**computer graphics** use of computers to display and manipulate information in pictorial

**3-D design created with CAD software**
3-D model    shape menu

graphics and text combined in illustration program

tools    colour palette

**simple pie chart generated by spreadsheet program**

*computer graphics* Some examples of the kinds of graphic design that can be achieved using computers. Text and graphics may be combined within an illustration package, and sophisticated three-dimensional drawings can be created using a computer-aided design (CAD) system.

form. Input may be achieved by scanning an image, by drawing with a mouse or stylus on a graphics tablet, or by drawing directly on the screen with a light pen.

**computerized axial tomography** medical technique, usually known as ◊CAT scan, for noninvasive investigation of disease or injury.

**computer program** coded instructions for a computer; see ◊program.

**computer simulation** representation of a real-life situation in a computer program. For example, the program might simulate the flow of customers arriving at a bank. The user can alter variables, such as the number of cashiers on duty, and see the effect.

**Comte, (Isidore) Auguste (Marie François Xavier)** (1798–1857) French philo-sopher regarded as the founder of sociology, a term he coined 1830. He sought to establish sociology as an intellectual discipline, using a scientific approach ('positivism') as the basis of a new science of social order and social development.

**Conakry** capital and chief port of the Republic of Guinea; population (1992) 950,000. It is on the island of Tumbo, and is linked with the Kaloum Peninsula by a causeway and (from 1914) by rail with Kankan, 480 km/300 mi to the northeast. One of the major exports is alumina (treated bauxite), which is mined at Fria; iron ore is mined on the nearby Kaloum Peninsula. Other industries include plastics, fisheries, motor vehicle assembly, and tourism. Agricultural products include bananas, oranges, pineapples, palm products, and coffee.

**concave** of a surface, curving inwards, or away from the eye. For example, a bowl appears concave when viewed from above. In geometry, a concave polygon is one that has an interior angle greater than 180°. Concave is the opposite of ◊convex.

**concave lens** lens that possesses at least one surface that curves inwards. It is a diverging lens, spreading out those light rays that have been refracted through it. A concave lens is thinner at its centre than at its edges, and is used to correct short-sightedness.

**concentration** in chemistry, the amount of a substance (◊solute) present in a specified amount of a solution. Either amount may be specified as a mass or a volume (liquids only). Common units used are ◊moles per cubic decimetre, grams per cubic decimetre, grams per 100 cubic centimetres, and grams per 100 grams.

**concentration camp** prison camp for civilians in wartime or under totalitarian rule. The first concentration camps were devised by the British during the Second Boer War in South Africa in 1899 for the detention of Afrikaner women and children (with the subsequent deaths of more than 20,000 people). A system of hundreds of concentration camps was developed by the Nazis in Germany and occupied Europe (1933–45) to imprison Jews and political and ideological opponents after Adolf ◊Hitler became chancellor in January 1933. The most

infamous camps in World War II were the extermination camps of ◊Auschwitz, Belsen, ◊Dachau, Maidanek, Sobibor, and Treblinka. The total number of people who died at the camps exceeded 6 million, and some inmates were subjected to medical experimentation before being killed.

**concerto** composition, usually in three movements, for solo instrument (or instruments) and orchestra. It developed during the 18th century from the *concerto grosso* form for string orchestra, in which a group of solo instruments (concerto) is contrasted with a full orchestra (ripieno).

**Concorde** the only supersonic airliner, which cruises at Mach 2, or twice the speed of sound, about 2,170 kph/1,350 mph. Concorde, the result of Anglo-French cooperation, made its first flight in 1969 and entered commercial service seven years later. It is 62 m/202 ft long and has a wing span of nearly 26 m/84 ft. Developing Concorde cost French and British taxpayers £2 billion.

**concrete** building material composed of cement, stone, sand, and water. It has been used since Egyptian and Roman times. Since the late 19th century, it has been increasingly employed as an economical alternative to materials such as brick and wood, and has been combined with steel to increase its tension capacity.

**concussion** temporary unconsciousness resulting from a blow to the head. It is often followed by amnesia for events immediately preceding the blow.

**condensation** conversion of a vapour to a liquid. This is frequently achieved by letting the vapour come into contact with a cold surface. It is the process by which water vapour turns into fine water droplets to form ◊cloud.

**condensation polymerization** polymerization reaction in which one or more monomers, with more than one reactive functional group, combine to form a polymer with the elimination of water or another small molecule.

**condenser** laboratory apparatus used to condense vapours back to liquid so that the liquid can be recovered. It is used in distillation and in reactions where the liquid mixture can be kept boiling without the loss of solvent.

**conditioning** in psychology, two major principles of behaviour modification.

In *classical conditioning,* described by Russian psychologist Ivan Pavlov, a new stimulus can evoke an automatic response by being repeatedly associated with a stimulus that naturally provokes that response. For example, the sound of a bell repeatedly associated with food will eventually trigger salivation, even if sounded without food being presented. In *operant conditioning,* described by US psychologists Edward Lee Thorndike (1874–1949) and B F Skinner, the frequency of a voluntary response can be increased by following it with a reinforcer or reward.

**condom** or *sheath* or *prophylactic,* barrier contraceptive, made of rubber, which fits over an erect penis and holds in the sperm produced by ejaculation. It is an effective means of preventing pregnancy if used carefully, preferably with a ◊spermicide. A condom with spermicide is 97% effective; one without spermicide is 85% effective as a contraceptive. Condoms can also give some protection against sexually transmitted diseases, including AIDS.

**condor** name given to two species of birds in separate genera. The *Andean condor Vultur gryphus*, has a wingspan up to 3 m/10 ft, weighs up to 13 kg/28 lb, and can reach up to 1.2 m/3.8 ft in length. It is black, with some white on the wings and a white frill at the base of the neck. It lives in the Andes at heights of up to 4,500 m/14,760 ft, and along the South American coast, and feeds mainly on carrion. The *Californian condor Gymnogyps californianus* is a similar bird, with a wingspan of about 3 m/10 ft. It feeds entirely on carrion, and is on the verge of extinction.

**conductance** ability of a material to carry an electrical current, usually given the symbol $G$. For a direct current, it is the reciprocal of ◊resistance: a conductor of resistance $R$ has a conductance of $1/R$. For an alternating current, conductance is the resistance $R$ divided by the impedance $Z$: $G = R/Z$. Conductance was formerly expressed in reciprocal ohms (or mhos); the SI unit is the ◊siemens (S).

**conduction, electrical** flow of charged particles through a material giving rise to electric current. Conduction in metals involves the flow of negatively charged free ◊electrons. Conduction in gases and some liquids involves the flow of ◊ions that carry positive charges in one direction and negative charges in the other. Conduction in a ◊semiconductor such as silicon involves the flow of electrons and positive holes.

**conduction, heat** flow of heat energy through a material without the movement of any part of the material itself (compare ◊conduction, electrical). Heat energy is present in all materials in the form of the kinetic energy of their vibrating molecules, and may be conducted from one molecule to the next in the form of this mechanical vibration. In the case of metals, which are particularly good conductors of heat, the free electrons within the material carry heat around very quickly.

**conductor** any material that conducts heat or electricity (as opposed to an insulator, or nonconductor). A good conductor has a high electrical or heat conductivity, and is generally a substance rich in free electrons such as a metal. A poor conductor (such as the nonmetals, glass and porcelain) has few free electrons. ◊Carbon is exceptional in being nonmetallic and yet (in some of its forms) a relatively good conductor of heat and electricity. Substances such as ◊silicon and ◊germanium, with intermediate conductivities that are improved by heat, light, or impurities, are known as ◊semiconductors.

**cone** in botany, the reproductive structure of the conifers and cycads; also known as a strobilus. It consists of a central axis surrounded by numerous, overlapping, scalelike, modified leaves (sporophylls) that bear the reproductive organs. Usually there are separate male and female cones, the former bearing pollen sacs containing pollen grains, and the larger female cones bearing the ovules that contain the ova or egg cells. The pollen is carried from male to female cones by the wind (anemophily). The seeds develop within the female cone and are released as the scales open in dry atmospheric conditions, which favour seed dispersal.

**cone** in geometry, a solid or surface consisting of the set of all straight lines passing through a fixed point (the vertex) and the points of a circle or ellipse whose plane does not contain the vertex.

**Confederacy** in US history, popular name for the *Confederate States of America*, the government established by 7 (later 11) Southern states in February 1861 when they seceded from the Union, precipitating the American ◊Civil War. Richmond, Virginia, was the capital, and Jefferson Davis the president. The Confederacy fell after its army was defeated 1865 and General Robert E ◊Lee surrendered.

**Confederation, Articles of** in US history, the initial means by which the 13 former British colonies created a form of national government. Ratified 1781, the articles established a unicameral legislature, Congress, with limited powers of raising revenue, regulating currency, and conducting foreign affairs. But because the individual states retained significant autonomy, the confederation was unmanageable. The articles were superseded by the US Constitution 1788.

**Confederation of British Industry** (CBI), UK organization of employers, established in 1965, combining the former Federation of British Industries (founded in 1916), British Employers' Confederation, and National Association of British Manufacturers. It acts as a pressure group for businesses, promoting their interests to government, overseas, and to workers.

**confession** in law, a criminal's admission of guilt. Since false confessions may be elicited by intimidation or ill treatment of the accused, the validity of confession in a court of law varies from one legal system to another. For example, in England and Wales a confession, without confirmatory evidence, is sufficient to convict; in Scotland it is not. In the USA a confession that is shown to be coerced does not void a conviction as long as it is supported by independent evidence.

**confession** in religion, the confession of sins practised in Roman Catholic, Orthodox, and most Far Eastern Christian churches, and since the early 19th century revived in Anglican and Lutheran churches. The Lateran Council of 1215 made auricular confession (self-accusation by the penitent to a priest, who in Catholic doctrine is divinely invested with authority to give absolution) obligatory once a year.

**confidence vote** in politics, a test of support for the government in the legislature. In political systems modelled on that of the UK, the survival of a government depends on assembly support. The opposition may move a vote of 'no confidence'; if the vote is carried, it requires the government, by convention, to resign.

**confirmation** rite practised by a number of Christian denominations, including Roman Catholic, Anglican, and Orthodox, in which a previously baptized person is admitted to full membership of the church. In Reform Judaism there is often a confirmation service several years after the bar or bat mitzvah (initiation into the congregation).

**Confucianism** body of beliefs and practices based on the Chinese classics and supported by the authority of the philosopher Confucius. The origin of things is seen in the union of *yin* and *yang,* the passive and active principles. Human relationships follow the patriarchal pattern. For more than 2,000 years Chinese political government, social organization, and individual conduct was shaped by Confucian principles. In 1912, Confucian philosophy, as a basis for government, was dropped by the state.

**Confucius** (551–479 BC) Latinized form of *Kong Zi* or *K'ung Fu Tzu,* 'Kong the master', Chinese sage whose name is given to the ethical system of Confucianism. He placed emphasis on moral order and observance of the established patriarchal family and social relationships of authority, obedience, and mutual respect. His emphasis on tradition and ethics attracted a growing number of pupils during his lifetime. *The Analects of Confucius,* a compilation of his teachings, was published after his death.

**conga** Latin American dance, originally from Cuba, in which the participants form a winding line, take three steps forwards or backwards, and then kick.

**congenital disease** in medicine, a disease that is present at birth. It is not necessarily genetic in origin; for example, congenital herpes may be acquired by the baby as it passes through the mother's birth canal.

**conger** any large marine eel of the family Congridae, especially the genus *Conger.* Conger eels live in shallow water, hiding in crevices during the day and active by night, feeding on fish and crabs. They are valued for food and angling.

**Congo, Democratic Republic of** formerly *Zaire*
**national name** *République Démocratique du Congo*
**area** 2,344,900 sq km/905,366 sq mi
**capital** Kinshasa
**major towns/cities** Lubumbashi, Kananga, Mbuji-Mayi, Kisangani, Bukavu, Kikwit, Matadi
**major ports** Matadi, Kalemie
**physical features** Zaïre/Congo River basin has tropical rainforest (second-largest remaining in world) and savanna; mountains in east and west; lakes Tanganyika, Albert, Edward; Ruwenzori Range; Victoria Falls
**head of state and government** Laurent Kabila from 1997
**political system** transitional

**political parties** Popular Movement of the Revolution (MPR), African socialist; Democratic Forces of Congo–Kinshasa (formerly Sacred Union, an alliance of some 130 opposition groups), moderate, centrist; Union for Democracy and Social Progress (UPDS), left of centre; Congolese National Movement–Lumumba (MNC), left of centre
**currency** zaïre
**GNP per capita (PPP)** (US$) 750 (1998 est)
**exports** mineral products (mainly copper, cobalt, industrial diamonds, and petroleum), agricultural products (chiefly coffee). Principal market: Belgium – Luxembourg 42.7% (1997)
**population** 50,336,000 (1999 est)
**language** French (official); Swahili, Lingala, Kikongo, and Tshiluba are recognized as national languages; over 200 other languages
**religion** Roman Catholic, Protestant, Kimbanguist; also half a million Muslims
**life expectancy** 50 (men); 52 (women) (1995–2000)
**Chronology**
**13th century** Rise of Kongo Empire, centred on banks of Zaïre/Congo River.
**1483** First visited by Portuguese, who named the area Zaire (from Zadi, 'big water') and converted local rulers to Christianity.
**16th–17th centuries** Great development of slave trade by Portuguese, Dutch, British, and French merchants, initially supplied by Kongo intermediaries.
**18th century** Rise of Luba state, in southern copper belt of north Katanga, and Lunda, in Kasai region in central south.
**mid-19th century** Eastern Zaire invaded by Arab slave traders from East Africa.
**1874–77** British explorer Henry Morton Stanley navigated Congo River to Atlantic Ocean.
**1879–87** Stanley engaged by King Leopold II of Belgium to sign protection treaties with local chiefs and 'Congo Free State' awarded to Leopold by 1884–85 Berlin Conference; great expansion in rubber export, using forced labour.
**1908** Leopold forced to relinquish personal control of Congo Free State, after international

condemnation of human-rights abuses. Became colony of Belgian Congo and important exporter of minerals.

**1959** Riots in Kinshasa (Leopoldville) persuaded Belgium to decolonize rapidly.

**1960** Independence achieved as Republic of the Congo. Civil war broke out between central government based in Kinshasa (Leopoldville) with Joseph Kasavubu as president, and rich mining province of Katanga.

**1961** Former prime minister Patrice Lumumba murdered in Katanga; fighting between mercenaries engaged by Katanga secessionist leader Moise Tshombe, and United Nations troops; Kasai and Kivu provinces also sought (briefly) to secede.

**1963** Katanga secessionist war ended; Tshombe forced into exile.

**1964** Tshombe returned from exile to become prime minister; pro-Marxist groups took control of eastern Zaire.

**1965** Western-backed Col Sese Seko Mobutu seized power in coup, ousting Kasavubu and Tshombe.

**1971** Country renamed Republic of Zaire, with Mobutu as president as *authenticité* (Africanization) policy launched.

**1972** Mobutu's Popular Movement of the Revolution (MPR) became only legal political party. Katanga province renamed Shaba.

**1974** Foreign-owned businesses and plantations seized by Mobutu and given to his political allies.

**1977** Original owners of confiscated properties invited back. Zairean guerrillas, chiefly Lundas, invaded Shaba province from Angola, but were repulsed by Moroccan, French, and Belgian paratroopers.

**1980s** International creditors forced a series of austerity programmes, after the level of foreign indebtedness had mounted with the collapse in world copper prices.

**1991** After antigovernment riots, Mobutu agreed to end the ban on multiparty politics and share power with the opposition; Etienne Tshisekedi was appointed premier, but was soon dismissed.

**1992** Tshisekedi was reinstated against Mobutu's wishes after renewed rioting.

**1993** Rival pro- and anti-Mobutu governments were created.

**1994** Kengo Wa Dondo was elected prime minister by an interim parliament, with Mobutu's agreement. There was an influx of Rwandan refugees.

**1995** There was secessionist activity in Shaba and Kasai provinces and interethnic warfare in Kivu, adjoining Rwanda in the east.

**1996** Thousands of refugees were allowed to return to Rwanda.

**1997** Mobutu was ousted by the rebel forces of Laurent Kabila, who declared himself president and renamed Zaire the Democratic Republic of the Congo. There was fighting between army factions.

**1998** There was a rebellion by Tutsi-led forces, backed by Rwanda and Uganda, against President Kabila; government troops aided by Angola and Zimbabwe put down the rebellion.

A constituent assembly was appointed prior to a general election. UN-urged peace talks failed. A ceasefire agreed by rebel forces also failed.

## Congo, Republic of
*national name* *République du Congo*

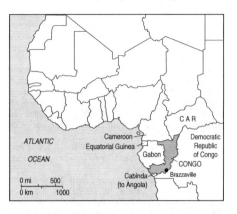

**area** 342,000 sq km/132,046 sq mi
**capital** Brazzaville
**major towns/cities** Pool, Pointe-Noire, Nkayi, Loubomo, Bouenza, Cuvette, Niari, Plateaux
**major ports** Pointe-Noire
**physical features** narrow coastal plain rises to central plateau, then falls into northern basin; Congo River on the border with the Democratic Republic of Congo; half the country is rainforest
**head of state** Denis Sassou-Nguessou from 1997
**head of government** Charles David Ganao from 1996
**political system** emergent democracy
**political parties** Pan-African Union for Social Democracy (UPADS), moderate, left of centre; Congolese Movement for Democracy and Integral Development (MCDDI), moderate, left of centre; Congolese Labour Party (PCT), left wing
**currency** franc CFA
**GNP per capita (PPP)** (US$) 1,430 (1998)
**exports** petroleum and petroleum products, saw logs and veneer logs, veneer sheets. Principal market: USA 36.9% (1997)
**population** 2,864,000 (1999 est)
**language** French (official); Kongo languages; local patois Monokutuba and Lingala
**religion** animist, Christian, Muslim
**life expectancy** 48 (men); 51 (women) (1995–2000)
*Chronology*
**late 15th century** First visited by Portuguese explorers, at which time the Bakongo (a six-state confederation centred south of the Congo River in Angola) and Bateke, both Bantu groups, were the chief kingdoms.
**16th century** Portuguese, in collaboration with coastal peoples, exported slaves from the interior to plantations in Brazil and São Tomé; missionaries spread Roman Catholicism.

**1880** French explorer Pierre Savorgnan de Brazza established French claims to coastal region, with the makoko (king) of the Bateke accepting French protection.

**1905** International outrage at revelations of the brutalities of forced labour, which decimated the population, as ivory and rubber resources were ruthlessly exploited by private concessionaries.

**1910** As Moyen-Congo, became part of French Equatorial Africa, which also comprised Gabon and the Central African Republic, with the capital at Brazzaville.

**1920s** More than 17,000 were killed as forced labour used to build the Congo-Ocean railroad; first Bakongo political organization founded.

**1940–44** Supported the 'Free French' anti-Nazi resistance cause during World War II, Brazzaville serving as capital for Gen Charles de Gaulle's forces.

**1946** Became autonomous, with a territorial assembly and representation in French parliament.

**1960** Achieved independence from France, with Abbé Fulbert Youlou, a moderate Catholic Bakongo priest, as the first president.

**1963** Youlou forced to resign after labour unrest. Alphonse Massamba-Débat became president with Pascal Lissouba as prime minister, and a single-party state was established under the socialist National Revolutionary Movement (MNR).

**1968** Military coup, led by Capt Marien Ngouabi, ousted Massamba-Débat.

**1970** A Marxist People's Republic declared, with Ngouabi's PCT the only legal party.

**1977** Ngouabi assassinated in a plot by Massamba-Débat, who was executed; Col Joachim Yhombi-Opango became president.

**1979** Yhombi-Opango handed over the presidency to the PCT, who chose Col Denis Sassou-Nguessou as his successor.

**early 1980s** Petroleum production increased fivefold.

**1990** With the collapse of Eastern European communism, the PCT abandoned Marxist-Leninism and promised multiparty politics and market-centred reforms in an economy crippled by foreign debt.

**1992** Multiparty elections gave the coalition dominated by the Pan-African Union for Social Democracy (UPADS) an assembly majority, with Pascal Lissouba elected president.

**1993** Yhombi-Opango was appointed prime minister; there was unrest after the opposition disputed the election results.

**1994** An international panel was appointed to investigate the election results; a UPADS-dominated coalition was declared the winner.

**1995** A new broad-based government was formed, including opposition groups; market-centred economic reforms were instigated, including privatization.

**1996** Charles David Ganao was appointed prime minister.

**1997** Violence between factions continued despite the unity government. Sassou-Nguesso took over the presidency.

**Congo-Zaire River** second-longest river in Africa, rising near the Zambia–Democratic Republic of Congo border (and known as the *Lualaba River* in the upper reaches) and flowing 4,500 km/2,800 mi to the Atlantic Ocean, running in a great curve that crosses the equator twice, and discharging a volume of water second only to the River Amazon. The chief tributaries are the Ubangi, Sangha, and Kasai.

**Congress** national legislature of the USA, consisting of the House of Representatives (435 members, apportioned to the states of the Union on the basis of population, and elected for two-year terms) and the Senate (100 senators, two for each state, elected for six years, one-third elected every two years). Both representatives and senators are elected by direct popular vote. Congress meets in Washington DC, in the Capitol Building. An ◊act of Congress is a bill passed by both houses.

**Congreve, William** (1670–1729) English dramatist and poet. His first success was the comedy *The Old Bachelor* (1693), followed by *The Double Dealer* (1694), *Love for Love* (1695), the tragedy *The Mourning Bride* (1697), and *The Way of the World* (1700). His plays, which satirize the social affectations of the time, are characterized by elegant wit and wordplay, and complex plots.

**congruent** in geometry, having the same shape and size, as applied to two-dimensional or solid figures. With plane congruent figures, one figure will fit on top of the other exactly, though this may first require rotation and/or rotation of one of the figures.

**conic section** curve obtained when a conical surface is intersected by a plane. If the intersecting plane cuts both extensions of the cone, it yields a ◊hyperbola; if it is parallel to the side of the cone, it produces a ◊parabola. Other intersecting planes produce ◊circles or ellipses.

**conifer** any of a large number of cone-bearing trees or shrubs. They are often pyramid-shaped, with leaves that are either scaled or needle-shaped; most are evergreen. Conifers include pines, spruces, firs, yews, junipers, monkey puzzles, and larches. (Order Coniferales.)

**conjugation** in biology, the bacterial equivalent of sexual reproduction. A fragment of the ◊DNA from one bacterium is passed along a thin tube, the pilus, into another bacterium.

**conjunction** in astronomy, the alignment of two celestial bodies as seen from Earth. A superior planet (or other object) is in conjunction when it lies behind the Sun. An inferior planet (or other object) comes to *inferior conjunction* when it passes between the Earth and the Sun; it is at *superior conjunction* when it passes behind the Sun.
*Planetary conjunction* takes place when a planet is closely aligned with another celestial object, such as the Moon, a star, or another planet.

**conjunctivitis** inflammation of the conjunctiva, the delicate membrane that lines the inside of the eyelids and covers the front of the eye. Symptoms include redness, swelling, and a watery or pus-filled discharge. It may be caused by infection, allergy, or other irritant.

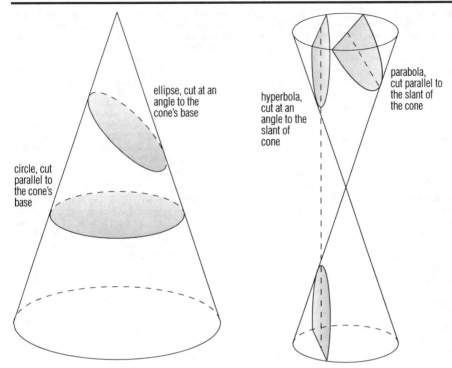

**conic section** *The four types of curve that may be obtained by cutting a single or double right-circular cone with a plane (two-dimensional surface).*

**Connacht** or *Connaught,* historic province of the Republic of Ireland, comprising the counties of Galway, Leitrim, Mayo, Roscommon, and Sligo; area 17,130 sq km/6,612 sq mi; population (1991) 422,900. The chief towns are Galway, Roscommon, Castlebar, Sligo, and Carrick-on-Shannon. Mainly lowland, it is agricultural and stock-raising country, with poor land in the west.

**Connecticut** state in New England, USA. It is nicknamed Constitution State or the Nutmeg State. Connecticut ratified the US Constitution in 1788, becoming the 5th state in the Union. It is bordered to the north by Massachusetts, to the east by Rhode Island, with the Pawcatuck River forming part of the boundary, to the west and southwest by New York, and to the south by the Long Island Sound, across which are New York's Long and Fishers islands.
**population** (1996 est) 3,274,000
**area** 13,000 sq km/5,018 sq mi
**capital** Hartford
**towns and cities** Bridgeport, New Haven, Waterbury, Stamford
**industries and products** dairy, poultry, and market-garden products; tobacco, watches, clocks, silverware, helicopters, jet engines, nuclear submarines, hardware and locks, electrical and electronic equipment, guns and ammunition, optical instruments. Hartford is the centre of the nation's insurance industry.

**connective tissue** in animals, tissue made up of a noncellular substance, the extracellular matrix, in which some cells are embedded. Skin, bones, tendons, cartilage, and adipose tissue (fat) are the main connective tissues. There are also small amounts of connective tissue in organs such as the brain and liver, where they maintain shape and structure.

**Connery, Sean (Thomas)** (1930– ) Scottish film actor. He was the first interpreter of James Bond in several films based on the spy thrillers of Ian Fleming. He has since enjoyed success as a mature actor in such films as *The Name of the Rose* (1986), *Highlander* (1986), and *Indiana Jones and the Last Crusade* (1989). He won an Academy Award for his supporting performance in the crime thriller *The Untouchables* (1987).

**Connors, Jimmy (James Scott)** (1952– ) US tennis player who won the Wimbledon title in 1974 and 1982, and subsequently won ten Grand Slam events. He was one of the first players to popularize the two-handed backhand, and won a record 109 tournaments.
**career highlights**
**Wimbledon** singles: 1974, 1982; doubles: 1973
**US Open** singles: 1974, 1976, 1978, 1982–83; doubles: 1975
**Australian Open** singles: 1974
**Grand Prix Masters** 1978

**conquistador** (Spanish 'conqueror') any of the early Spanish conquerors in the Americas. The title is applied in particular to those leaders who overthrew the indigenous empires of Peru and Mexico, and other parts of Central and South America. They include Hernán ◊Cortés, who subjugated Mexico; Francisco ◊Pizarro, conqueror of Peru with Diego de Almagro; and Juan ◊Ponce de León.

**Conrad, Joseph** pen-name of Teodor Józef Konrad Nałęcz Korzeniowski (1857–1924) British novelist, born in Ukraine of Polish parents. His greatest works include the novels *Lord Jim* (1900), *Nostromo* (1904), *The Secret Agent* (1907), and *Under Western Eyes* (1911); the short story 'Heart of Darkness' (1902); and the short novel *The Shadow Line* (1917). These combine a vivid and sensuous evocation of various lands and seas with a rigorous, humane scrutiny of moral dilemmas, pitfalls, and desperation.

**conscientious objector** person refusing compulsory service, usually military, on moral, religious, or political grounds.

**conscription** legislation for all able-bodied male citizens (and female in some countries, such as Israel) to serve with the armed forces. It originated in France in 1792, and in the 19th and 20th centuries became the established practice in almost all European states. Modern conscription systems often permit alternative national service for conscientious objectors.

**conservation** in the life sciences, action taken to protect and preserve the natural world, usually from pollution, overexploitation, and other harmful features of human activity. The late 1980s saw a great increase in public concern for the environment, with membership of conservation groups, such as ◊Friends of the Earth, ◊Greenpeace, and the US Sierra Club, rising sharply. Globally the most important issues include the depletion of atmospheric ozone by the action of ◊chlorofluorocarbons (CFCs), the build-up of carbon dioxide in the atmosphere (thought to contribute to an intensification of the ◊greenhouse effect), and ◊deforestation.

**conservation of mass** in chemistry, the principle that states that in a chemical reaction the sum of all the masses of the substances involved in the reaction (reactants) is equal to the sum of all of the masses of the substances produced by the reaction (products) – that is, no matter is gained or lost.

**conservatism** approach to government favouring the maintenance of existing institutions and identified with a number of Western political parties, such as the British Conservative, US Republican, German Christian Democratic, and Australian Liberal parties. It tends to be explicitly nondoctrinaire and pragmatic but generally emphasizes free-enterprise capitalism, minimal government intervention in the economy, rigid law and order, and the importance of national traditions. In the UK, modern conservatism, under the ideological influence of ◊Thatcherism, has become increasingly radical, attacking entrenched institutions and promoting free-market economies.

**Conservative Party** UK political party, one of the two historic British parties; the name replaced *Tory* in general use from 1830

onwards. Traditionally the party of landed interests, it broadened its political base under Benjamin Disraeli's leadership in the 19th century. The present Conservative Party's free-market capitalism is supported by the world of finance and the management of industry. In recent history, the Conservative Party was in power under Margaret Thatcher (1979–90) and John Major (1990–97). After the party's defeat in the 1997 general election, John Major resigned and was succeeded by William Hague. The party's Central Office is located in Smith Square, London, and the current party chairman is Cecil Parkinson.

**conspiracy** in law, an agreement between two or more people to do something unlawful.

**Constable, John** (1776–1837) English artist; one of the greatest landscape painters of the 19th century. He painted scenes of his native Suffolk, including *The Haywain* (1821; National Gallery, London), as well as castles, cathedrals, landscapes, and coastal scenes in other parts of Britain. Constable inherited the Dutch tradition of sombre Realism, in particular the style of Jacob ◊Ruisdael. He aimed to capture the momentary changes of the weather as well as to create monumental images of British scenery, as in *The White Horse* (1819; Frick Collection, New York) and *Salisbury Cathedral from the Bishop's Grounds* (1827; Victoria and Albert Museum, London).

**constant** in mathematics, a fixed quantity or one that does not change its value in relation to ◊variables. For example, in the algebraic expression $y^2 = 5x - 3$, the numbers 3 and 5 are constants. In physics, certain quantities are regarded as universal constants, such as the speed of light in a vacuum.

**Constantine the Great** (*c.* AD 285–337) First Christian emperor of Rome and founder of Constantinople. He defeated Maxentius, joint emperor of Rome AD 312, and in 313 formally recognized Christianity. As sole emperor of the west of the empire, he defeated Licinius, emperor of the east, to become ruler of the Roman world 324. He presided over the church's first council at Nicaea 325. Constantine moved his capital to Byzantium on the Bosporus 330, renaming it Constantinople (now Istanbul).

**Constantinople** ancient city founded by the Greeks as Byzantium about 660 BC and refounded by the Roman emperor Constantine (I) the Great in AD 330 as the capital of the Eastern Roman Empire. Constantinople (modern Istanbul, Turkey) was the impregnable bastion of the Eastern Roman Empire and the Byzantine Empire, its successor, until it fell to the Turks on 29 May 1453 after nearly a year's siege and became the capital of the Ottoman Empire.

**constellation** one of the 88 areas into which the sky is divided for the purposes of identifying and naming celestial objects. The first constellations were simple, arbitrary patterns of stars in which early civilizations visualized gods, sacred beasts, and mythical heroes.

## CONSTELLATIONS

| Constellation | Abbreviation | Popular name | Constellation | Abbreviation | Popular name |
| --- | --- | --- | --- | --- | --- |
| Andromeda | And | – | Indus | Ind | American |
| Antlia | Ant | Airpump | | | Indian |
| Apus | Aps | Bird of Paradise | Lacerta | Lac | Lizard |
| Aquarius | Aqr | Water-bearer | Leo | Leo | Lion |
| Aquila | Aqi | Eagle | Leo Minor | LMi | Little Lion |
| Ara | Ara | Altar | Lepus | Lep | Hare |
| Aries | Ari | Ram | Libra | Lib | Balance |
| Auriga | Aur | Charioteer | Lupus | Lup | Wolf |
| Boötes | Boo | Herdsman | Lynx | Lyn | – |
| Caelum | Cae | Chisel | Lyra | Lyr | Harp |
| Camelopardalis | Cam | Giraffe | Mensa | Men | Table |
| Cancer | Cnc | Crab | Microscopium | Mic | Microscope |
| Canes Venatici | CVn | Hunting Dogs | Monoceros | Mon | Unicorn |
| Canis Major | CMa | Great Dog | Musca | Mus | Fly |
| Canis Minor | CMi | Little Dog | Norma | Nor | Level, Square |
| Capricornus | Cap | Goat | Octans | Oct | Octant |
| Carina | Car | Keel | Ophiuchus | Oph | Serpent-bearer |
| Cassiopeia | Cas | – | Orion | Ori | – |
| Centaurus | Cen | Centaur | Pavo | Pav | Peacock |
| Cepheus | Cep | – | Pegasus | Peg | Flying Horse |
| Cetus | Cet | Sea Monster, | Perseus | Per | – |
| | | Whale | Phoenix | Phe | – |
| Chamaeleon | Cha | Chameleon | Pictor | Pic | Painter |
| Circinus | Cir | Compasses | Pisces | Psc | Fishes |
| Columba | Col | Dove | Piscis Austrinus | PsA | Southern Fish |
| Coma Berenices | Com | Berenice's Hair | Puppis | Pup | Poop, Stern |
| Corona Australis | CrA | Southern | Pyxis | Pyx | Compass |
| | | Crown | Reticulum | Ret | Net |
| Corona Borealis | CrB | Northern | Sagitta | Sge | Arrow |
| | | Crown | Sagittarius | Sgr | Archer |
| Corvus | Crv | Crow | Scorpius | Sco | Scorpion |
| Crater | Crt | Cup | Sculptor | Scl | Sculptor's Tools |
| Crux | Cru | Southern Cross | Scutum | Sct | Shield |
| Cygnus | Cyn | Swan | Serpens | Ser | Serpent |
| Delphinus | Del | Dolphin | Sextans | Sex | Sextant |
| Dorado | Dor | Goldfish | Taurus | Tau | Bull |
| Draco | Dra | Dragon | Telescopium | Tel | Telescope |
| Equuleus | Equ | Foal | Triangulum | Tri | Triangle |
| Eridanus | Eri | River | Triangulum | TrA | Southern |
| Fornax | For | Furnace | Australe | | Triangle |
| Gemini | Gem | Twins | Tucana | Tuc | Toucan |
| Grus | Gru | Crane | Ursa Major | UMa | Great Bear |
| Hercules | Her | – | Ursa Minor | UMi | Little Bear |
| Horologium | Hor | Clock | Vela | Vel | Sails |
| Hydra | Hya | Watersnake | Virgo | Vir | Virgin |
| Hydrus | Hyi | Little Snake | Volans | Vol | Flying Fish |
| | | | Vulpecula | Vul | Fox |

**constitution** body of fundamental laws of a state, laying down the system of government and defining the relations of the legislature, executive, and judiciary to each other and to the citizens. Since the French Revolution (1789–1799) almost all countries (the UK is an exception) have adopted written constitutions; that of the USA (1787) is the oldest. Of all the world's states, 69 have adopted their current constitutions in the period since 1989.

**Constructivism** abstract art movement that originated in Russia in about 1914 and subsequently had great influence on Western art. Constructivism usually involves industrial materials such as glass, steel, and plastic in clearly defined arrangements, but the term is difficult to define precisely, as the meaning attached to it has varied according to place and time. Some art historians distinguish between Russian (or Soviet) Constructivism and the more diffuse European (or International) Constructivism.

**consul** chief magistrate of the ancient Roman Republic, after the expulsion of the last king in 510 BC. Two consuls were elected annually by the *comitia centuriata* (assembly of the Roman people), and their names were used to date the year. With equal power they shared the full civil authority in Rome and the chief military command in the field. After the establishment of the Roman empire the office became far less important.

**consumption** in economics, the purchase of goods and services for final use, as opposed to spending by firms on capital goods, known as capital formation.

**contact lens** lens, made of soft or hard plastic, that is worn in contact with the cornea and conjunctiva of the eye, beneath the eyelid, to correct defective vision. In special circumstances, contact lenses may be used as protective shells or for cosmetic purposes, such as changing eye colour.

**contempt of court** behaviour that shows lack of respect for the authority of a court of law, such as disobeying a court order, breach of an injunction, or improper use of legal documents. Behaviour that disrupts, prejudices, or interferes with court proceedings either inside or outside the courtroom may also be contempt. The court may punish contempt with a fine or imprisonment.

**continent** any one of the seven large land masses of the Earth, as distinct from the oceans. They are Asia, Africa, North America, South America, Europe, Australia, and Antarctica. Continents are constantly moving and evolving (see ◊plate tectonics). A continent does not end at the coastline; its boundary is the edge of the shallow continental shelf, which may extend several hundred kilometres out to sea.

**Continental Congress** in US history, the federal legislature of the original 13 states, acting as a provisional government during the ◊American Revolution. It convened in Philadelphia from 1774 to 1789, when the US Constitution was adopted. The Second Continental Congress, convened in May 1775, was responsible for drawing up the ◊Declaration of Independence and, in 1777, the ◊Articles of Confederation.

**continental drift** in geology, the theory that, about 250–200 million years ago, the Earth consisted of a single large continent (Pangaea), which subsequently broke apart to form the continents known today. The theory was proposed in 1912 by German meteorologist Alfred Wegener, but vast continental movements could not be satisfactorily explained until the study of ◊plate tectonics in the 1960s.

**continuous data** data that can take any of an infinite number of values between whole numbers and so may not be measured completely accurately. This type of data contrasts with discrete data, in which the variable can only take one of a finite set of values. For example, the sizes of apples on a tree form continuous data, whereas the numbers of apples form discrete data.

**Contra** member of a Central American right-wing guerrilla force attempting to overthrow the democratically elected Nicaraguan Sandinista government 1979–90. The Contras, many of them mercenaries or former members of the deposed dictator Somoza's guard, operated mainly from bases outside Nicaragua, mostly in Honduras, with covert US funding, as revealed by the ◊Irangate hearings 1986–87.

**contraceptive** any drug, device, or technique that prevents pregnancy. The contraceptive pill (the ◊Pill) contains female hormones that interfere with egg production or the first stage of pregnancy. The 'morning-after' pill can be taken up to 72 hours after unprotected intercourse. Barrier contraceptives include ◊condoms (sheaths) and ◊diaphragms, also called caps or Dutch caps; they prevent the sperm entering the

Upper Carboniferous period

Eocene

Lower Quaternary

**continental drift** *The continents are slowly shifting their positions, driven by fluid motion beneath the Earth's crust. Over 200 million years ago, there was a single large continent called Pangaea. By 200 million years ago, the continents had started to move apart. By 50 million years ago, the continents were approaching their present positions.*

cervix (neck of the womb).

◊Intrauterine devices, also known as IUDs or coils, cause a slight inflammation of the lining of the womb; this prevents the fertilized egg from becoming implanted. See also ◊family planning.

**contract** legal agreement between two or more parties, where each party agrees to do something. For example, a contract of employment is a legal agreement between an employer and an employee and lays out the conditions of employment. Contracts need not necessarily be written; they can be verbal contracts. In consumer law, for example, a contract is established when a good is sold.

**contractile root** in botany, a thickened root at the base of a corm, bulb, or other organ that helps position it at an appropriate level in the ground. Contractile roots are found, for example, on the corms of plants of the genus *Crocus*. After they have become anchored in the soil, the upper portion contracts, pulling the plant deeper into the ground.

**contralto** low-register female voice, a high (falsetto) male voice, or a low boy's voice; also called an ◊*alto*.

**convection** heat energy transfer that involves the movement of a fluid (gas or liquid). Fluid in contact with the source of heat expands and tends to rise within the bulk of the fluid. Cooler fluid sinks to take its place, setting up a convection current. This is the principle of natural convection in many domestic hot-water systems and space heaters.

**convection current** current caused by the expansion of a liquid or gas as its temperature rises. The expanded material, being less dense, rises above colder and therefore denser material. Convection currents arise in the atmosphere above warm land masses or seas, giving rise to sea breezes and land breezes, respectively. In some heating systems, convection currents are used to carry hot water upwards in pipes.

**convex** of a surface, curving outwards, or towards the eye. For example, the outer surface of a ball appears convex. In geometry, the term is used to describe any polygon possessing no interior angle greater than 180°. Convex is the opposite of ◊concave.

**conveyancing** administrative process involved in transferring title to land, usually on its sale or purchase.

**convolvulus** or *bindweed,* any of a group of plants belonging to the morning-glory family. They are characterized by their twining stems and by their petals, which are joined into a funnel-shaped tube. (Genus *Convolvulus,* family Convolvulaceae.)

**convulsion** series of violent contractions of the muscles over which the patient has no control. It may be associated with loss of consciousness. Convulsions may arise from any one of a number of causes, including brain disease (such as ◊epilepsy), injury, high fever, poisoning, and electrocution.

**Conwy** unitary authority in north Wales, created in 1996 from parts of the former counties of Clwyd and Gwynedd
*area* 1,107 sq km/427 sq mi
*towns* Conwy (administrative headquarters), Abergele, Llandudno, Llanrwst
*physical* rivers Conwy and Elwy
*features* Snowdonia National Park; coastline of sandy beaches, including the seaside resort of Colwyn Bay
*industries* tourism
*population* (1996) 113,000.

**Cook, James** (1728–1779) English naval explorer. After surveying the St Lawrence River in North America in 1759, he made three voyages: 1768–71 to Tahiti, New Zealand, and Australia; 1772–75 to the South Pacific; and 1776–79 to the South and North Pacific, attempting to find the Northwest Passage and charting the Siberian coast. He was largely responsible for Britain's initial interest in acquiring colonies in Australasia. He was killed in Hawaii early in 1779 in a scuffle with islanders.

**Cook, Robin (Robert Finlayson)** (1946–  ) British Labour politician, foreign secretary from 1997, born in Scotland. A member of the moderate-left Tribune Group, he entered Parliament in 1974 and became a leading member of Labour's shadow cabinet, specializing in health matters. When John Smith assumed the party leadership in July 1992, Cook remained in the shadow cabinet as spokesperson for trade and industry. He became shadow foreign secretary under Smith's successor, Tony ◊Blair, in October 1994. As foreign secretary, he placed a new emphasis on human rights as part of an ethical foreign policy.

**cooking** heat treatment of food to make it more palatable, digestible, and safe. It breaks down connective tissue in meat, making it tender, and softens the cellulose in plant tissue. Some nutrients may be lost in the process, but this does not affect the overall nutritional value of a balanced diet.

**Cook Islands** group of six large and a number of smaller Polynesian islands 2,600 km/1,600 mi northeast of Auckland, New Zealand; area 290 sq km/112 sq mi; population (1994) 17,400. Their main products include citrus fruit, copra, bananas, pearl-shell, cultivated (black) pearls, and crafts. The islands became a self-governing overseas territory of New Zealand in 1965.

**Cook Strait** strait dividing North Island and South Island, New Zealand, about 30 km/19 mi in width at its narrowest point. A submarine cable carries electricity from South to North Island.

**Coolidge, (John) Calvin** (1872–1933) 30th president of the USA 1923–29, a Republican. As governor of Massachusetts in 1919, he was responsible for crushing a Boston police strike. As Warren ◊Harding's vice-president 1921–23, he succeeded to the presidency on Harding's death. He won the 1924 presidential election, and his period of office was marked by economic growth.

**Cooper, Gary (Frank James)** (1901–1961) US film actor. One of the great stars of the classical Hollywood era, who created a screen persona of quiet dignity, moral rectititude, and powerful action. He won Academy Awards for his performances in *Sergeant York* (1941) and *High Noon* (1952).

**cooperative** business organization with limited liability where each shareholder has only one vote however many shares they own. In a worker cooperative, it is the workers who are the shareholders and own the company. The workers decide on how the company is to be run. In a consumer cooperative, consumers control the company.

**cooperative movement** the banding together of groups of people for mutual assistance in trade, manufacture, the supply of credit, housing, or other services. The original principles of the cooperative movement were laid down 1844 by the Rochdale Pioneers, under the influence of Robert Owen, and by Charles Fourier in France.

**coordinate** in geometry, a number that defines the position of a point relative to a point or axis (reference line). ◊Cartesian coordinates define a point by its perpendicular distances from two or more axes drawn through a fixed

*Cartesian coordinates*

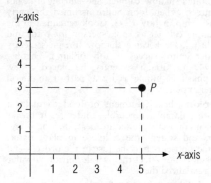

the Cartesian coordinates of *P* are (5,3)

*Polar coordinates*

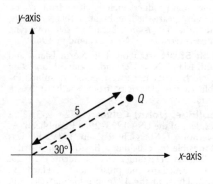

the Polar coordinates of *Q* are (5,30°)

**coordinate** *Coordinates are numbers that define the position of points in a plane or in space. In the Cartesian coordinate system, a point in a plane is charted based upon its location along intersecting horizontal and vertical axes. In the polar coordinate system, a point in a plane is defined by its distance from a fixed point and direction from a fixed line.*

point mutually at right angles to each other. Polar coordinates define a point in a plane by its distance from a fixed point and direction from a fixed line.

**coordinate geometry** or *analytical geometry,* system of geometry in which points, lines, shapes, and surfaces are represented by algebraic expressions. In plane (two-dimensional) coordinate geometry, the plane is usually defined by two axes at right angles to each other, the horizontal *x*-axis and the vertical *y*-axis, meeting at O, the origin. A point on the plane can be represented by a pair of ◊Cartesian coordinates, which define its position in terms of its distance along the *x*-axis and along the *y*-axis from O. These distances are respectively the *x* and *y* coordinates of the point.

**coot** freshwater bird of the genus *Fulica* in the rail family, order Gruiformes. Coots are about

38 cm/1.2 ft long, and mainly black. They have a white bill, extending up the forehead in a plate, and big feet with four lobed toes. Coots are omnivores, but feed mainly on water weed, except as chicks, when they feed on insects and other invertebrates.

**Copenhagen** Danish *København,* capital of Denmark, on the islands of Zealand and Amager; population (1995) 1,353,300 (including suburbs).

**Copenhagen, Battle of** naval victory on 2 April 1801 by a British fleet under Sir Hyde Parker (1739–1807) and ◊Nelson over the Danish fleet. Nelson put his telescope to his blind eye and refused to see Parker's signal for withdrawal.

**Copernicus, Nicolaus** Latinized form of *Mikolaj Kopernik* (1473–1543) Polish astronomer who believed that the Sun, not the Earth, is at the centre of the Solar System, thus defying the Christian church doctrine of the time. For 30 years, he worked on the hypothesis that the rotation and the orbital motion of the Earth are responsible for the apparent movement of the heavenly bodies. His great work *De Revolutionibus Orbium Coelestium/On the Revolutions of the Heavenly Spheres* was the important first step to the more accurate picture of the Solar System built up by Tycho ◊Brahe, ◊Kepler, ◊Galileo, and later astronomers.

**Copland, Aaron** (1900–1990) US composer. His early works, such as his piano concerto 1926, were in the jazz idiom but he gradually developed a gentler style with a regional flavour drawn from American folk music. Among his works are the ballets *Billy the Kid* (1939), *Rodeo* (1942), and *Appalachian Spring* (1944; based on a poem by Hart Crane). Among his orchestral works is *Inscape* (1967).

**copper** orange-pink, very malleable and ductile, metallic element, symbol Cu (from Latin *cuprum*), atomic number 29, relative atomic mass 63.546. It is used for its durability, pliability, high thermal and electrical conductivity, and resistance to corrosion.

**coppicing** woodland management practice of severe pruning where trees are cut down to near ground level at regular intervals, typically every 3–20 years, to promote the growth of numerous shoots from the base.

**Coppola, Francis (Ford)** (1939–  ) US film director and screenwriter. He directed *The Godfather* (1972), which became one of the biggest moneymaking films of all time, and its sequels *The Godfather Part II* (1974), which won seven Academy Awards, and *The Godfather Part III* (1990). His other films include *Apocalypse Now* (1979), and *Rumblefish* (1983).

**copra** dried meat from the kernel of the ◊coconut, used to make coconut oil.

**Copt** descendant of those ancient Egyptians who adopted Christianity in the 1st century and refused to convert to Islam after the Arab conquest. They now form a small minority (about 5%) of Egypt's population. *Coptic* is a member of the Hamito-Semitic language family. It is descended from the language of the ancient Egyptians and is the ritual language of the Coptic Christian church. It is written in the Greek alphabet with some additional characters derived from ◊demotic script.

**copulation** act of mating in animals with internal ◊fertilization. Male mammals have a ◊penis or other organ that is used to introduce spermatozoa into the reproductive tract of the female. Most birds transfer sperm by pressing their cloacas (the openings of their reproductive tracts) together.

**copyright** law applying to literary, musical, and artistic works (including plays, recordings, films, photographs, radio and television broadcasts, and, in the USA and the UK, computer programs), which prevents the reproduction of the work, in whole or in part, without the author's consent.

**coral** marine invertebrate of the class Anthozoa in the phylum Cnidaria, which also includes sea anemones and jellyfish. It has a skeleton of lime (calcium carbonate) extracted from the surrounding water. Corals exist in warm seas, at moderate depths with sufficient light. Some coral is valued for decoration or jewellery, for example, Mediterranean red coral *Corallum rubrum.*

**Coral Sea** or *Solomon Sea,* part of the ◊Pacific Ocean bounded by northeastern Australia, New Guinea, the Solomon Islands, Vanuatu, and New Caledonia; area 4,790,000 sq km/ 1,849,000 sq mi, with an average depth of 2,400 m/7,870 ft, with three deep trenches on its eastern edge. It contains numerous coral islands and reefs. The Coral Sea Islands are a territory of Australia; they comprise scattered reefs and islands over an area of about 1,000,000 sq km/386,000 sq mi. They are uninhabited except for a meteorological station on Willis Island. The ◊Great Barrier Reef lies along its western edge, just off the east coast of Australia.

**cor anglais** or *English horn,* musical instrument, an alto ◊oboe, pitched a fifth lower than the oboe in F, with a distinctive tulip-shaped bell and warm nasal tone. It is heard to pastoral effect in Rossini's overture to *William Tell* (1829), and portraying a plaintive Sasha the duck in Prokofiev's *Peter and the Wolf* (1936).

**Corbusier, Le** French architect; see ◊Le Corbusier.

**Cordilleras, The** mountainous western section of North America, with the Rocky Mountains and the coastal ranges parallel to the contact between the North American and the Pacific plates.

**Córdoba** industrial city and capital of Córdoba province, central Argentina, situated on the Primero (or Suquiá)River, 400 m/1,310 ft above sea level at the foot of the Sierra Chica, between the pampas on the east and the Andes on the west; population (1992 est) 1,179,400. Main industries include cement, glass, textiles, and motor vehicles. The city's water and electric

power come from the lake created by the San Roque Dam on the River Primero.

**Córdoba** capital of Córdoba province, southern Spain, on the River Guadalquivir; population (1991) 300,200. Paper, textiles, silverware, and copper products are manufactured, and there is a large trade in agricultural produce, wine, olive oil, and lead. It has many Moorish remains, including the mosque, now a cathedral, founded by 'Abd-ar-Rahman I in 785, which is one of the largest Christian churches in the world. Córdoba was probably founded by the Carthaginians; it was held by the Moors from 711 to 1236.

**Corfu** Greek *Kérkyra,* northernmost and second largest of the Ionian islands of Greece, off the coast of Epirus in the Ionian Sea; area 1,072 sq km/414 sq mi; population (1991) 105,000. Its businesses include tourism, fruit, olive oil, and textiles. Its largest town is the port of Corfu (Kérkyra), population (1991) 36,900. Corfu was colonized by the Corinthians about 700 BC. Venice held it 1386–1797, Britain 1815–64.

**coriander** pungent fresh herb belonging to the parsley family, native to Europe and Asia; also a spice made from its dried ripe seeds. The spice is used commercially as a flavouring in meat products, bakery goods, tobacco, gin, liqueurs, chilli, and curry powder. Both are commonly used in cooking in the Middle East, India, Mexico, and China. (*Coriandrum sativum,* family Umbelliferae.)

**Corinth** Greek *Kórinthos,* port in Greece, on the isthmus connecting the Peloponnese with the mainland; population (1981) 22,650. The rocky isthmus is bisected by the 6.5 km/4 mi Corinth canal, opened 1893. The site of the ancient city-state of Corinth lies 7 km/4.5 mi southwest of the port.

**Coriolis effect** the effect of the Earth's rotation on the atmosphere and on all objects on the Earth's surface. In the northern hemisphere it causes moving objects and currents to be deflected to the right; in the southern hemisphere it causes deflection to the left. The effect is named after its discoverer, French mathematician Gaspard de Coriolis (1792–1843).

**cork** light, waterproof outer layers of the bark covering the branches and roots of almost all trees and shrubs. The cork oak (*Quercus suber*), a native of southern Europe and North Africa, is cultivated in Spain and Portugal; the exceptionally thick outer layers of its bark provide the cork that is used commercially.

**Cork** largest county of the Republic of Ireland, in the province of Munster; county town ◊Cork; area 7,460 sq km/2,880 sq mi; population (1991) 410,400. Cork is mainly agricultural, but there is some copper and manganese mining, marble quarrying, salmon farming, and river and sea fishing; industries include chemical, and computer hardware and software. There are natural gas and oil fields off the south coast at Kinsale. Angling is a popular sport, and tourism is concentrated in Kinsale, Bantry, Glengarriff, and Youghal. Cork is rich in Christian and pre-Christian antiquities.

**Cork** third-largest city in Ireland; port and county town of County ◊Cork, important industrial and trading centre on the River Lee, at the head of the long inlet of Cork harbour, 21 km/13 mi from the sea; population (1991) 127,000. The lower harbour, at Cobh, can berth liners. The city has breweries, distilleries, container ports, and iron foundries. Other industries include cars, chemicals, food processing, oil refining, pharmaceuticals, pottery, steel, and tanning; manufacturing includes rubber and metal products, and computer hardware and software. St Finbarr founded a school and an abbey here in the 7th century. The area was subsequently settled by Danes, who were in turn dispossessed by the Normans in 1172.

**corm** short, swollen, underground plant stem, surrounded by protective scale leaves, as seen in the genus *Crocus*. It stores food, provides a means of ◊vegetative reproduction, and acts as a ◊perennating organ.

**cormorant** any of various diving seabirds, mainly of the genus *Phalacrocorax,* order Pelecaniformes, about 90 cm/3 ft long, with webbed feet, a long neck, hooked beak, and glossy black plumage. Cormorants generally feed on fish and shellfish, which they catch by swimming and diving under water, sometimes to a considerable depth. They collect the food in a pouch formed by the dilatable skin at the front of the throat. Some species breed on inland lakes and rivers.

**corn** general term for the main ◊cereal crop of a region – for example, wheat in the UK, oats in Scotland and Ireland, maize in the USA. Also, another word for ◊maize.

**corncrake** or *landrail,* bird *Crex crex* of the rail family Rallidae, order Gruiformes. About 25 cm/10 in long, the bill and tail are short, the legs long and powerful, and the toes have sharp claws. It is drably coloured, shy, and has a persistent rasping call. The corncrake can swim and run easily, but its flight is heavy. It lives in meadows and crops in temperate regions, but has become rare where mechanical methods of cutting corn are used.

**cornea** transparent front section of the vertebrate ◊eye. The cornea is curved and behaves as a fixed lens, so that light entering the eye is partly focused before it reaches the lens.

**Corneille, Pierre** (1606–1684) French dramatist. His tragedies, such as *Horace* (1640), *Cinna* (1641), and *Oedipe* (1659), glorify the strength of will governed by reason, and established the French classical dramatic tradition. His first comedy, *Mélite*, was performed in 1629, followed by others that gained him a brief period of favour with Cardinal Richelieu. His early masterpiece, *Le Cid* (1636), was attacked by the Academicians, although it received public acclaim, and was produced in the same year as *L'Illusion comique/The Comic Illusion*.

**cornet** three-valved brass-band instrument, soprano member (usually in B-flat) of a group of valved horns developed from the coiled posthorn in Austria and Germany about 1820–50 for military band use. Of cylindrical bore, its compact shape and deeper conical bell allow greater speed and agility of intonation than the trumpet, at the expense of less tonal precision and brilliance. A small E-flat cornet is standard in brass bands alongside a B-flat cornet section.

**cornflower** native European and Asian plant belonging to the same genus as the ◊knapweeds but distinguished from them by its deep azure-blue flowers. Formerly a common weed in northern European wheat fields, it is now widely grown in gardens as a herbaceous plant with flower colours ranging from blue through shades of pink and purple to white. (*Centaurea cyanus*, family Compositae.)

**Cornish language** extinct member of the ◊Celtic languages, a branch of the Indo-European language family, spoken in Cornwall, England, until 1777. In recent years the language has been revived in a somewhat reconstructed form by people interested in their Cornish heritage.

**Corn Laws** in Britain until 1846, laws used to regulate the export or import of cereals in order to maintain an adequate supply for consumers and a secure price for producers. For centuries the Corn Laws formed an integral part of the mercantile system in England; they were repealed because they became an unwarranted tax on food and a hindrance to British exports.

**cornucopia** (Latin 'horn of plenty') in Greek mythology, one of the horns of the goat Amalthaea, which Zeus caused to refill perpetually with food and drink. As an artistic symbol it denotes prosperity. In paintings, the cornucopia is depicted as a horn-shaped container spilling over with fruit and flowers.

**Cornwall** county in southwest England including the Isles of ◊Scilly (Scillies)
**area** (excluding Scillies) 3,550 sq km/1,370 sq mi
**towns and cities** Truro (administrative headquarters), Camborne, Launceston; Bude, Falmouth, Newquay, Penzance, St Ives (resorts)
**physical** Bodmin Moor (including Brown Willy 419 m/1,375 ft); Land's End peninsula; rivers Camel, Fal, Fowey, Tamar
**features** St Michael's Mount; Poldhu, site of first transatlantic radio signal (1901); the Stannary or Tinners' Parliament; Tate Gallery, St Ives; the Mineral Tramways Project, which aims to preserve the mining landscape, once the centre of the world's hard-rock mining industry; Eden Project, two 'biomes' (tropical rainforest and Mediterranean) being built in disused china-clay pit near St Austell, scheduled to open in 2000 as a Millennium Commission Landmark Project; the 'Lost' Gardens of Heligan
**agriculture** crops are early in some places: fruit, oats, and vegetables, including swedes, turnips, and mangolds (a root vegetable used as cattle fodder); spring flowers; cattle and sheep rearing; dairy farming; fishing (Mevagissey, Newlyn, and St Ives are the principal fishing ports)

*industries* tourism; electronics; kaolin (a white clay used in the manufacture of porcelain; St Austell is the main centre for production)
*population* (1996) 483,300
*famous people* John Betjeman, Humphry Davy, Daphne Du Maurier, William Golding.

**Cornwallis, Charles** 1st Marquis and 2nd Earl (1738–1805) British general in the ◊American Revolution until 1781, when his defeat at Yorktown led to final surrender and ended the war. He then served twice as governor-general of India and once as viceroy of Ireland. He succeeded to the earldom in 1762, and was made a marquis in 1792.

**corona** faint halo of hot (about 2,000,000°C/3,600,000°F) and tenuous gas around the Sun, which boils from the surface. It is visible at solar ◊eclipses or through a *coronagraph,* an instrument that blocks light from the Sun's brilliant disc. Gas flows away from the corona to form the ◊solar wind.

**coronary artery disease** (Latin *corona* 'crown', from the arteries encircling the heart) condition in which the fatty deposits of ◊atherosclerosis form in the coronary arteries that supply the heart muscle, narrowing them and restricting the blood flow.

**coroner** official who investigates the deaths of persons who have died suddenly by acts of violence or under suspicious circumstances, by holding an inquest or ordering a postmortem examination (autopsy).

**Corot, Jean-Baptiste Camille** (1796–1875) French painter. He created a distinctive landscape style using a soft focus and a low-key palette of browns, ochres, and greens. His early work, including Italian scenes of the 1820s, influenced the ◊Barbizon School of painters. Like them, Corot worked outdoors, but he also continued a conventional academic tradition with his romanticized paintings of women.

**corporal punishment** physical punishment of wrongdoers – for example, by whipping. It is still used as a punishment for criminals in many countries, especially under Islamic law. Corporal punishment of children by parents is illegal in some countries, including Sweden, Finland, Denmark, and Norway.

**corporatism** belief that the state in capitalist democracies should intervene to a large extent in the economy to ensure social harmony. In Austria, for example, corporatism results in political decisions often being taken after discussions between chambers of commerce, trade unions, and the government.

**corpus luteum** glandular tissue formed in the mammalian ◊ovary after ovulation from the Graafian follicle, a group of cells associated with bringing the egg to maturity. It secretes the hormone progesterone in anticipation of pregnancy.

**Correggio** assumed name of Antonio Allegri (c. 1494–1534) Italian painter of the High Renaissance. His style followed the Classical grandeur of ◊Leonardo da Vinci and ◊Titian, but anticipated the ◊Baroque in its emphasis on movement, softer forms, and contrasts of light and shade.

**correlation** the degree of relationship between two sets of information. If one set of data increases at the same time as the other, the relationship is said to be positive or direct. If one set of data increases as the other decreases, the relationship is negative or inverse. Correlation can be shown by plotting a best-fit line on a scatter diagram.

**corrosion** in earth science, an alternative name for ◊solution, the process by which water dissolves rocks such as limestone.

**corrosion** the eating away and eventual destruction of metals and alloys by chemical attack. The rusting of ordinary iron and steel is the most common form of corrosion. Rusting takes place in moist air, when the iron combines with oxygen and water to form a brown-orange deposit of ◊rust (hydrated iron oxide). The rate of corrosion is increased where the atmosphere is polluted with sulphur dioxide. Salty road and air conditions accelerate the rusting of car bodies.

**Corsica** French *Corse,* island region of France, in the Mediterranean off the west coast of Italy, north of Sardinia; it comprises the *départements* of Haute Corse and Corse du Sud. Corsica's mountain bandits were eradicated 1931, but the tradition of the vendetta or blood feud lingers. The island is the main base of the Foreign Legion
*area* 8,700 sq km/3,358 sq mi
*capital* Ajaccio (port)
*physical* mountainous; maquis vegetation (drought-tolerant shrubs such as cork oak and myrtle)
*government* its special status involves a 61-member regional parliament with the power to scrutinize French National Assembly bills applicable to the island and propose amendments
*products* wine, olive oil
*population* (1990) 250,400, including just under 50% native Corsicans. There are about 400,000 *émigrés,* mostly in Mexico and Central America, who return to retire
*language* French (official); the majority speak Corsican, an Italian dialect
*famous people* Napoleon

**Cortés, Hernán Ferdinand** (1485–1547) Spanish conquistador. He conquered the Aztec empire 1519–21, and secured Mexico for Spain.

**corticosteroid** any of several steroid hormones secreted by the cortex of the ◊adrenal glands; also synthetic forms with similar properties. Corticosteroids have anti-inflammatory and immunosuppressive effects and may be used to treat a number of conditions, including rheumatoid arthritis, severe allergies, asthma, some skin diseases, and some cancers. Side effects can be serious, and therapy must be withdrawn very gradually.

**cortisone** natural corticosteroid produced by the ◊adrenal gland, now synthesized for its anti-inflammatory qualities and used in the treatment of rheumatoid arthritis.

**Cortona, Pietro da** Italian Baroque painter; see ◊Pietro da Cortona.

**corundum** native aluminium oxide, $Al_2O_3$, the hardest naturally occurring mineral known apart from diamond (corundum rates 9 on the Mohs scale of hardness); lack of cleavage also increases its durability. Its crystals are barrel-shaped prisms of the trigonal system. Varieties of gem-quality corundum are *ruby* (red) and *sapphire* (any colour other than red, usually blue). Poorer-quality and synthetic corundum is used in industry, for example as an ◊abrasive.

**Cosgrave, William Thomas** (1880–1965) Irish revolutionary and politician; president of the executive council (prime minister) 1922–32, leader of Cumann na nGaedheal 1923–33, leader of Fine Gael 1935–44.

**cosine** in trigonometry, a ◊function of an angle in a right-angled triangle found by dividing the length of the side adjacent to the angle by the length of the hypotenuse (the longest side). It is usually shortened to *cos.*

**cosmic background radiation** or *3° radiation,* electromagnetic radiation left over from the original formation of the universe in the Big Bang around 15 billion years ago. It corresponds to an overall background temperature of 3K (–270°C/–454°F), or 3°C above absolute zero. In 1992 the Cosmic Background Explorer satellite, COBE, detected slight 'ripples' in the strength of the background radiation that are believed to mark the first stage in the formation of galaxies.

**cosmic radiation** streams of high-energy particles from outer space, consisting of protons, alpha particles, and light nuclei, which collide with atomic nuclei in the Earth's atmosphere, and produce secondary nuclear particles (chiefly ◊mesons, such as pions and muons) that shower the Earth.

**cosmology** branch of astronomy that deals with the structure and evolution of the universe as an ordered whole. Its method is to construct 'model universes' mathematically and compare their large-scale properties with those of the observed universe.

**Cossack** people of southern and southwestern Russia, Ukraine, and Poland, predominantly of Russian or Ukrainian origin, who took in escaped serfs and lived in independent communal settlements (military brotherhoods) from the 15th to the 19th century. Later they held land in return for military service in the cavalry under Russian and Polish rulers. After 1917, the various Cossack communities were incorporated into the Soviet administrative and collective system.

**Costa Brava** (Spanish 'Wild Coast') Mediterranean coastline of northeast Spain, stretching from Port-Bou on the French border southwards to Blanes, northeast of Barcelona. It is noted for its irregular rocky coastline, small fishing villages, and resorts such as Puerto de la Selva, Palafrugell, Playa de Aro, and Lloret del Mar.

**Costa del Sol** (Spanish 'Coast of the Sun')

Mediterranean coastline of Andalusia, southern Spain, stretching for nearly 300 km/190 mi from Gibraltar to Almería. Málaga is the principal port and Marbella, Torremolinos, and Nerja are the chief tourist resorts.

**Costa Rica** Republic of

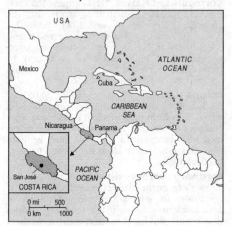

*national name* *República de Costa Rica*
*area* 51,100 sq km/19,729 sq mi
*capital* San José
*major towns/cities* Alajuela, Cartago, Limón, Puntarenas
*major ports* Limón, Puntarenas
*physical features* high central plateau and tropical coasts; Costa Rica was once entirely forested, containing an estimated 5% of the Earth's flora and fauna
*head of state and government* Miguel Angel Rodriguez Echeverria, from 1998
*political system* liberal democracy
*political parties* National Liberation Party (PLN), left of centre; Christian Socialist Unity Party (PUSC), centrist coalition; ten minor parties
*currency* colón
*GNP per capita (PPP)* (US$) 6,620 (1997)
*exports* bananas, coffee, sugar, cocoa, textiles, seafood, meat, tropical fruit. Principal market: USA 52.5% (1998)
*population* 3,933,000 (1999 est)
*language* Spanish (official)
*Religion* Roman Catholic 90%
*life expectancy* 74 (men); 79 (women) (1995–2000)
*Chronology*
*1502* Visited by Christopher Columbus, who named the area Costa Rica (the rich coast), observing the gold decorations worn by the American Indian Guaymi.
*1506* Colonized by Spain, but fierce guerrilla resistance was mounted by the indigenous population, although many later died from exposure to European diseases.
*18th century* Settlements began to be established in the fertile central highlands, including San José and Alajuela.
*1808* Coffee was introduced from Cuba and soon became the staple crop.
*1821* Independence achieved from Spain, and

was joined initially with Mexico.

**1824** Became part of United Provinces (Federation) of Central America, also embracing El Salvador, Guatemala, Honduras, and Nicaragua.

**1838** Became fully independent when it seceded from the Federation.

**1849–59** Under presidency of Juan Rafael Mora.

**1870–82** Period of military dictatorship.

**later 19th century** Immigration by Europeans to run and work small coffee farms.

**1917–19** Brief dictatorship by Frederico Tinoco.

**1940–44** Liberal reforms, including recognition of workers' rights and minimum wages, introduced by President Rafael Angel Calderón Guradia, founder of the United Christian Socialist Party (PUSC).

**1948** Brief civil war following a disputed presidential election.

**1949** New constitution adopted, giving women and blacks the vote. National army abolished and replaced by civil guard. José Figueres Ferrer, cofounder of the PLN, elected president; he embarked on ambitious socialist programme, nationalizing the banks and introducing a social security system.

**1958–73** Mainly conservative administrations.

**1974** PLN regained the presidency under Daniel Oduber and returned to socialist policies.

**1978** Rodrigo Carazo, conservative, elected president. Sharp deterioration in the state of the economy.

**1982** Luis Alberto Monge (PLN) elected president. Harsh austerity programme introduced. Pressure from the USA to abandon neutral stance and condemn Sandinista regime in Nicaragua.

**1985** Following border clashes with Nicaraguan Sandinista forces, a US-trained antiguerrilla guard formed.

**1986** Oscar Arias Sanchez (PLN) won the presidency on a neutralist platform.

**1987** Arias won the Nobel Prize for Peace for devising a Central American peace plan signed by the leaders of Nicaragua, El Salvador, Guatemala, and Honduras.

**1990** Rafael Calderón of the centrist PUSC was elected president as the economy deteriorated.

**1994** José Maria Figueres Olsen (PLN), son of José Figueres Ferrer, was elected president.

**1998** Miguel Angel Rodriguez (PUSC) was elected president.

**Costner, Kevin** (1955– ) US film actor. He emerged as a star in the late 1980s, with roles in *The Untouchables* (1987), *Bull Durham* (1988), and *Field of Dreams* (1989). Increasingly identified with the embodiment of idealism and high principle, Costner went on to direct and star in *Dances with Wolves* (1990), a western sympathetic to the American Indians, which won several Academy Awards.

**cot death** or *sudden infant death syndrome* (SIDS) death of an apparently healthy baby, almost always during sleep. It is most common in the winter months, and strikes more boys than girls. The cause is not known but risk factors that have been identified include prematu-rity, respiratory infection, overheating, and sleeping position.

**Côte d'Ivoire** Republic of

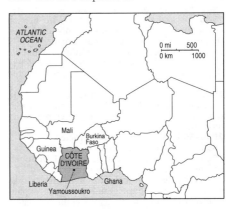

**national name** *République de la Côte d'Ivoire*
**area** 322,463 sq km/124,502 sq mi
**capital** Yamoussoukro
**major towns/cities** Abidjan, Bouaké, Daloa, Man, Korhogo
**major ports** Abidjan, San Pedro
**physical features** tropical rainforest (diminishing as exploited) in south; savanna and low mountains in north; coastal plain; Vridi canal, Kossou dam, Monts du Toura
**head of state** Henri Konan Bedie from 1993
**head of government** Kablan Daniel Duncan from 1993
**political system** emergent democracy
**political parties** Democratic Party of Côte d'Ivoire (PDCI), nationalist, free enterprise; Rally of Republicans (RDR), nationalist; Ivorian Popular Front (FPI), left of centre; Ivorian Labour Party (PIT), left of centre
**currency** franc CFA
**GNP per capita (PPP)** (US$) 1,730 (1998)
**exports** cocoa beans and products, petroleum products, timber, coffee, cotton, tinned tuna. Principal market: Netherlands 16.6% (1997)
**population** 14,527,000 (1999 est)
**language** French (official); over 60 local languages
**religion** animist, Muslim (mainly in north), Christian (mainly Roman Catholic in south)
**life expectancy** 46 (men); 47 (women) (1995–2000)
**Chronology**
**1460s** Portuguese navigators arrived.
**16th century** Ivory export trade developed by Europeans and slave trade, though to a lesser extent than neighbouring areas; Krou people migrated from Liberia to the west and Senoufo and Lubi from the north.
**late 17th century** French coastal trading posts established at Assini and Grand Bassam.
**18th–19th centuries** Akan peoples, including the Baoulé, immigrated from the east and Malinke from the northwest.
**1840s** French began to conclude commercial treaties with local rulers.
**1893** Colony of Côte d'Ivoire created by French,

after war with Mandinkas; Baoulé resistance continued until 1917.

**1904** Became part of French West Africa; cocoa production encouraged.

**1940–42** Under pro-Nazi French Vichy regime.

**1946** Became overseas territory in French Union, with own territorial assembly and representation in French parliament: Felix Houphoüet-Boigny, a Western-educated Baoulé chief who had formed the Democratic Party (PDCI) to campaign for autonomy, was elected to the French assembly.

**1947** A French-controlled area to the north, which had been added to Côte d'Ivoire in 1932, separated to create new state of Upper Volta (now Burkina Faso).

**1950–54** Port of Abidjan constructed.

**1958** Achieved internal self-government.

**1960** Independence secured, with Houphouët-Boigny as president of a one-party state.

**1960s–1980s** Political stability, close links maintained with France and economic expansion of 10% per annum, as the country became one of the world's largest coffee producers.

**1986** The country's name was officially changed from Ivory Coast to Côte d'Ivoire.

**1987–93** Per capita incomes fell by 25% owing to an austerity programme promoted by the International Monetary Fund.

**1990** There were strikes and student unrest. Houphouët-Boigny was re-elected in a contested presidential election, as multiparty politics were re-established.

**1993** Houphouët-Boigny died and was succeeded by parliamentary speaker and Baoulé Henri Konan Bedie.

**1995** Bedie and the PDCI were re-elected in a contest boycotted by the opposition.

**cotoneaster** any of a group of shrubs or trees found in Europe and Asia, belonging to the rose family and closely related to the hawthorn and medlar. The fruits, though small and unpalatable, are usually bright red and conspicuous, often surviving through the winter. Some of the shrubs are cultivated for their attractive appearance. (Genus *Cotoneaster*, family Rosaceae.)

**Cotonou** chief port and largest city of Benin, on the Bight of Benin; population (1994) 537,000. Palm products and timber are exported, and textiles are manufactured. Although not the official capital, it is the seat of the president, and the main centre of commerce and politics.

**Cotopaxi** active Andean volcano in north-central Ecuador on the border of the Cotopaxi, Napo, and Pichincha provinces. It is located 48 km/30 mi south of ◊Quito at an altitude of 5,896 m/19,344 ft above sea level. It is the highest active volcano in the world. It is now contained within a 340 sq km/131 sq mi national park, established in 1975.

**cotton** tropical and subtropical herbaceous plant belonging to the mallow family. Fibres surround the seeds inside the ripened fruits, or bolls, and these are spun into yarn for cloth. (Genus *Gossypium*, family Malvaceae.)

**cotyledon** structure in the embryo of a seed plant that may form a 'leaf' after germination and is commonly known as a seed leaf. The number of cotyledons present in an embryo is an important character in the classification of flowering plants (◊angiosperms).

**couch grass** European grass that spreads rapidly by underground stems. It is considered a troublesome weed in North America, where it has been introduced. (*Agropyron repens,* family Gramineae.)

**cougar** another name for the ◊puma, a large North American cat.

**coulomb** SI unit (symbol C) of electrical charge. One coulomb is the quantity of electricity conveyed by a current of one ◊ampere in one second.

**council** in local government in England and Wales, a popularly elected local assembly charged with the government of the area within its boundaries. Under the Local Government Act 1972, they comprise three types: ◊county councils, ◊district councils, and parish councils. Many city councils exist in the USA.

**Council of Europe** body constituted in 1949 to achieve greater unity between European countries, to facilitate their economic and social progress, and to uphold the principles of parliamentary democracy and respect for human rights. It has a *Committee* of foreign ministers, a *Consultative Assembly,* a *Parliamentary Assembly* (with members from national parliaments), and, to fulfil one of its main functions, a *European Commission on Human Rights,* which examines complaints about human-rights abuses. If the commission is unable to achieve a friendly settlement after examining alleged violations, the case may be taken to the European Court of Human Rights for adjudication. Its headquarters are in Strasbourg, France.

**council tax** method of raising revenue for local government in Britain. It replaced the community charge, or ◊poll tax, from April 1993. The tax is based on property values at April 1991, but takes some account of the number of people occupying each property.

**counterpoint** in music, the art of combining different forms of an original melody with apparent freedom while preserving a harmonious effect. Giovanni Palestrina and Johann Sebastian Bach were masters of counterpoint.

**Counter-Reformation** movement initiated by the Catholic church at the Council of Trent (1545–63) to counter the spread of the ◊Reformation. Extending into the 17th century, its dominant forces included the rise of the Jesuits as an educating and missionary group and the deployment of the Spanish Inquisition in Europe and the Americas. See also Germany: history 1519–1815, *impact of the Counter-Reformation, reign of Philip II.*

**countertenor** the highest natural male voice, as opposed to the falsetto of the male ◊alto. It was favoured by the Elizabethans for its heroic brilliance of tone.

**country** or *country and western,* popular music of the white US South and West; it evolved from the folk music of the English, Irish, and Scottish settlers and has a strong blues influence. Characteristic instruments are slide guitar, mandolin, and fiddle. Lyrics typically extol family values and traditional sex roles, and often have a strong narrative element. Country music encompasses a variety of regional styles, and ranges from mournful ballads to fast and intricate dance music.

**county** (Latin *comitatus* through French *comté*) administrative unit of a country or state. It was the name given by the Normans to Anglo-Saxon 'shires', and the boundaries of many present-day English counties date back to Saxon times. There are currently 34 English administrative non-metropolitan counties and 6 metropolitan counties, in addition to 34 unitary authorities. Welsh and Scottish counties were abolished in 1996 in a reorganization of local government throughout the UK, and replaced by 22 and 33 unitary authorities respectively. Northern Ireland has 6 geographical counties, although administration is through 26 district councils. In the USA a county is a subdivision of a state; the power of counties differs widely among states.

**county council** in England, a unit of local government whose responsibilities include broad planning policy, highways, education, personal social services, and libraries; police, fire, and traffic control; and refuse disposal. The tier below the county council has traditionally been the district council, but with local government reorganization from 1996, there has been a shift towards unitary authorities (based on a unit smaller than the county) replacing both. By 1998 there were 34 two-tier non-metropolitan county councils under which there were 274 district councils. (See also ◊local government.)

**county palatine** in medieval England, a county whose lord held particular rights, in lieu of the king, such as pardoning treasons and murders. Under William I there were four counties palatine: Chester, Durham, Kent, and Shropshire.

**coup d'état** or *coup,* (French 'stroke of state') forcible takeover of the government of a country by elements from within that country, generally carried out by violent and illegal means. It differs from a revolution in typically being carried out by a small group (for example, of army officers or opposition politicians) to install its leader as head of government, rather than being a mass uprising by the people.

**Courbet, Gustave** (1819–1877) French artist. He was a portrait, genre, and landscape painter. Reacting against academic trends, both Classicist and Romantic, he became a major exponent of ◊Realism, depicting contemporary life with an unflattering frankness. His *Burial at Ornans* 1850 (Musée d'Orsay, Paris), showing ordinary working people gathered around a village grave, shocked the public and the critics with its 'vulgarity'.

**courgette** small variety of ◊marrow, belonging to the gourd family. It is cultivated as a vegetable and harvested before it is fully mature, at 15–20 cm/6–8 in. In the USA and Canada it is known as a zucchini. (*Cucurbita pepo,* family Cucurbitaceae.)

**Court, Margaret** born Smith (1942–  ) Australian tennis player. The most prolific winner in the women's game, she won a record 64 Grand Slam titles, including 25 at singles.
*career highlights*
***Wimbledon*** singles: 1963, 1965, 1970; doubles: 1964, 1969; mixed: 1963, 1965–66, 1968, 1975
***US Open*** singles: 1962, 1965, 1968–70, 1973; doubles: 1963, 1968–70, 1973, 1975; mixed: 1961–65, 1969–70, 1972
***French Open*** singles: 1962, 1964, 1969–70, 1973; doubles: 1964–66, 1973; mixed: 1963–65, 1969
***Australian Open*** singles: 1960–66, 1969–71, 1973; doubles: 1961–63, 1965, 1969–71, 1973; mixed: 1963–64.

**Cousteau, Jacques Yves** (1910–1997) French oceanographer. He pioneered the invention of the aqualung in 1943, as well as techniques in underwater filming. In 1951 he began the first of many research voyages in the ship *Calypso*. His film and television documentaries and books established him as a household name.

**covalent bond** chemical ◊bond produced when two atoms share one or more pairs of electrons (usually each atom contributes an electron). The bond is often represented by a single line drawn between the two atoms. Covalently bonded substances include hydrogen ($H_2$), water ($H_2O$), and most organic substances.

**Covenanter** in Scottish history, one of the Presbyterian Christians who swore to uphold their forms of worship in a National Covenant, signed 28 February 1638, when Charles I attempted to introduce a liturgy on the English model into Scotland.

**Coventry** industrial city in the West Midlands, England, on the River Sherbourne, 29 km/18 mi southeast of Birmingham; population (1994 est) 303,000. Principal industries are engineering and the manufacture of electronic equipment, machine tools, agricultural machinery, man-made fibres, aerospace components, telecommunications equipment, and vehicles, including London taxis and Massey Ferguson tractors.

**Coward, Noël Peirce** (1899–1973) English dramatist, actor, revue-writer, director, and composer. He epitomized the witty and sophisticated man of the theatre. From his first success with *The Young Idea* (1923), he wrote and appeared in plays and comedies on both sides of the Atlantic such as *Hay Fever* (1925), *Private Lives* (1930) with Gertrude Lawrence, *Design for Living* (1933), *Blithe Spirit* (1941), and *A Song at Twilight* (1966). His revues and musicals included *On With the Dance* (1925) and *Bitter Sweet* (1929).

**cow parsley** or *keck,* tall perennial plant belonging to the carrot family, found in Europe, northern Asia, and North Africa. It grows up to 1 m/3 ft tall and has pinnate leaves (leaflets growing on either side of a stem), hollow furrowed stems, and heads of delicate white flowers. (*Anthriscus sylvestris,* family Umbelliferae.)

**cowrie** marine snail of the family Cypreidae, in which the interior spiral form is concealed by a double outer lip. The shells are hard, shiny, and often coloured. Most cowries are shallow-water forms, and are found in many parts of the world, particularly the tropical Indo-Pacific. Cowries have been used as ornaments and fertility charms, and also as currency, for example the Pacific money cowrie *Cypraea moneta*.

**cowslip** European plant related to the primrose, with several small deep-yellow fragrant flowers growing from a single stem. It is native to temperate regions of the Old World. The oxlip (*Primula elatior*) is also closely related. (*Primula veris,* family Primulaceae.)

**coyote** wild dog *Canis latrans,* in appearance like a small wolf, living in North and Central America. Its head and body are about 90 cm/3 ft long and brown, flecked with grey or black. Coyotes live in open country and can run at 65 kph/40 mph. Their main foods are rabbits and rodents. Although persecuted by humans for over a century, the species is very successful.

**coypu** South American water rodent *Myocastor coypus,* about 60 cm/2 ft long and weighing up to 9 kg/20 lb. It has a scaly, ratlike tail, webbed hind feet, a blunt-muzzled head, and large orange incisors. The fur ('nutria') is reddish brown. It feeds on vegetation, and lives in burrows in rivers and lake banks.

**CPU** in computing, abbreviation for ◊central processing unit.

**CPVE** abbreviation for *Certificate of Pre-Vocational Education,* in the UK, an educational qualification introduced in 1986 for students over 16 in schools and colleges who want a one-year course of preparation for work or further vocational study.

**crab** any decapod (ten-legged) crustacean of the division Brachyura, with a broad, rather round, upper body shell (carapace) and a small ◊abdomen tucked beneath the body. Crabs are related to lobsters and crayfish. Mainly marine, some crabs live in fresh water or on land. They are alert carnivores and scavengers. They have a typical sideways walk, and strong pincers on the first pair of legs, the other four pairs being used for walking. Periodically, the outer shell is cast to allow for growth. The name 'crab' is sometimes used for similar arthropods, such as the horseshoe crab, which is neither a true crab nor a crustacean.

**crab apple** any of 25 species of wild apple trees, native to temperate regions of the northern hemisphere. Numerous varieties of cultivated apples have been derived from *Malus pumila,* the common native crab apple of southeastern Europe and central Asia. The fruit of native species is smaller and more bitter than that of cultivated varieties and is used in crab-apple jelly. (Genus *Malus,* family Rosaceae.)

**Crab nebula** cloud of gas 6,000 light years from Earth, in the constellation ◊Taurus. It is the remains of a star that according to Chinese records, exploded as a ◊supernova observed as a brilliant point of light on 4 July 1054. At its centre is a ◊pulsar that flashes 30 times a second. It was named by Lord Rosse after its crablike shape.

**Cracow** alternative form of ◊Kraków, a Polish city.

**crag** in previously glaciated areas, a large lump of rock that a glacier has been unable to wear away. As the glacier passed up and over the crag, weaker rock on the far side was largely protected from erosion and formed a tapering ridge, or *tail,* of debris.

**Craig, James** 1st Viscount Craigavon (1871–1940) Ulster Unionist politician, the first prime minister of Northern Ireland 1921–40. Craig became a member of Parliament in 1906, and was a highly effective organizer of Unionist resistance to Home Rule. As prime minister he carried out systematic discrimination against the Catholic minority, abolishing proportional representation in 1929 and redrawing constituency boundaries to ensure Protestant majorities. Viscount 1927.

**Cranach, Lucas** *the Elder* originally *Lucas Müller* (1472–1553) German painter, etcher, and woodcut artist. A leading figure in the German Renaissance, he painted religious scenes, allegories (many featuring full-length nudes), and precise and polished portraits, such as *Martin Luther* (1521; Uffizi, Florence).

**cranberry** any of several trailing evergreen plants belonging to the heath family, related to bilberries and blueberries. They grow in marshy places and bear small, acid, crimson berries, high in vitamin C content, used for making sauce and jelly. (Genus *Vaccinium,* family Ericaceae.)

**crane** in zoology, a large, wading bird of the family Gruidae, order Gruiformes, with long legs and neck, short powerful wings, a naked or tufted head, and unwebbed feet. The hind toe is greatly elevated, and has a sharp claw. Cranes are marsh- and plains-dwelling birds, feeding on plants as well as insects and small animals. They fly well and are usually migratory. Their courtship includes frenzied, leaping dances. They are found in all parts of the world except South America.

**crane fly** or *daddy-long-legs,* any fly of the family Tipulidae, with long, slender, fragile legs. They look like giant mosquitoes, but the adults are quite harmless. The larvae live in soil or water. Females have a pointed abdomen; males have a club-shaped one.

**cranesbill** any of a group of plants containing about 400 species. The plants are named after the long beaklike protrusion attached to the seed vessels. When ripe, this splits into coiling spirals which jerk the seeds out, helping to scatter them. (Genus *Geranium,* family Geraniaceae.)

**cranium** the dome-shaped area of the vertebrate skull that protects the brain. It consists of eight bony plates fused together by sutures (immovable joints). Fossil remains of the human cranium have aided the development of theories concerning human evolution.

**crankshaft** essential component of piston engines that converts the up-and-down (reciprocating) motion of the pistons into useful rotary motion. The car crankshaft carries a number of cranks. The pistons are connected to the cranks by connecting rods and ◊bearings; when the pistons move up and down, the connecting rods force the offset crank pins to describe a circle, thereby rotating the crankshaft.

**Cranmer, Thomas** (1489–1556) English cleric, archbishop of Canterbury from 1533. A Protestant convert, he helped to shape the doctrines of the Church of England under Edward VI. He was responsible for the issue of the Prayer Books of 1549 and 1552, and supported the succession of Lady Jane Grey in 1553.

**Crassus the Elder, Marcus Licinius** (115–53 BC) Roman general who crushed the Spartacus Revolt in 71 BC and became consul in 70 BC. In 60 BC he joined with Julius Caesar and Pompey the Great in the First Triumvirate and obtained a command in the east in 55 BC. Eager to gain his own reputation for military glory, he invaded Parthia (Mesopotamia and Persia), but was defeated by the Parthians at Carrhae, captured, and put to death.

**Crassus the Younger, Marcus Licinius** Roman general, grandson of the triumvir Marcus Licinius Crassus the Elder. He fought first with Sextus Pompeius and Mark Antony before defecting to Octavian (later the emperor Augustus). In 29 BC he defeated the Bastarnae of modern Romania and Bulgaria, killing their king, Deldo, in single combat.

**crater** bowl-shaped depression in the ground, usually round and with steep sides. Craters are formed by explosive events such as the eruption of a volcano, the explosion of bomb, or the impact of a meteorite.

**Crawford, Joan** stage name of Lucille Le Sueur (1908–1977) US film actress. She became a star with her performance as a flapper in *Our Dancing Daughters* (1928). Later she appeared as a sultry, often suffering, mature woman. She won an Academy Award for *Mildred Pierce* (1945).

**Craxi, Bettino (Benedetto)** (1934– ) Italian socialist politician, leader of the Italian Socialist Party (PSI) 1976–93, prime minister 1983–87. In 1993 he was one of many politicians suspected of involvement in Italy's corruption network; in 1994 he was sentenced in absentia to eight and a half years in prison for accepting bribes, and in 1995 he received a further four-year sentence for corruption. In April 1996, with other former ministers, he was found guilty of further corruption charges, and received a prison sentence of eight years and three months.

**crayfish** freshwater decapod (ten-limbed) crustacean belonging to several families structurally similar to, but smaller than, the lobster. Crayfish are brownish-green scavengers and are found in all parts of the world except Africa. They are edible, and some species are farmed.

**creationism** theory concerned with the origins of matter and life, claiming, as does the Bible in Genesis, that the world and humanity were created by a supernatural Creator, not more than 6,000 years ago. It was developed in response to Darwin's theory of ◊evolution; it is not recognized by most scientists as having a factual basis.

**Crécy, Battle of** first major battle of the Hundred Years' War, fought on 26 August 1346. Philip VI of France was defeated by ◊Edward III of England at the village of Crécy-en-Ponthieu, now in Somme *département*, France, 18 km/11 mi northeast of Abbeville. The English archers played a crucial role in Edward's victory, which allowed him to besiege and take Calais.

**credit** in economics, a means by which goods or services are obtained without immediate payment, usually by agreeing to pay interest. The three main forms are *consumer credit* (usually extended to individuals by retailers), *bank credit* (such as overdrafts or personal loans), and *trade credit* (common in the commercial world both within countries and internationally).

**creed** in general, any system of belief; in the Christian church the verbal confessions of faith expressing the accepted doctrines of the church. The different forms are the Apostles' Creed, the ◊Nicene Creed, and the ◊Athanasian Creed. The only creed recognized by the Orthodox Church is the Nicene Creed.

**creeper** any small, short-legged passerine bird of the family Certhidae. They spiral with a mouselike movement up tree trunks, searching for insects and larvae with their thin, down-curved beaks.

**crème de la crème** (French 'the cream of the cream') the elite, the very best.

**Creole** (Spanish *criar* 'to create') in the West Indies and Spanish America, originally someone of European descent born in the New World; later someone of mixed European and African descent. In Louisiana and other states on the Gulf of Mexico, it applies either to someone of French or Spanish descent or (popularly) to someone of mixed French or Spanish and African descent.

**creole language** any ◊pidgin language that has ceased to be simply a trade jargon in ports and markets and has become the mother tongue of a particular community, such as the French dialects of the New Orleans area. Many creoles have developed into distinct languages with literatures of their own; for example, Jamaican Creole, Haitian Creole, Krio in Sierra Leone, and Tok Pisin, now the official language of Papua New Guinea.

**cress** any of several plants of the cress family, characterized by a pungent taste. The common European garden cress (*Lepidium sativum*) is cultivated worldwide. (Genera include *Lepidium, Cardamine,* and *Arabis;* family Cruciferae.)

**Cretaceous** (Latin *creta* 'chalk') period of geological time approximately 144.2–65 million years ago. It is the last period of the Mesozoic era, during which angiosperm (seed-bearing) plants evolved, and dinosaurs reached a peak before their extinction at the end of the period. The north European chalk, which forms the white cliffs of Dover, was deposited during the latter half of the Cretaceous.

**Crete** Greek *Kríti,* largest Greek island in the eastern Mediterranean Sea, 100 km/62 mi southeast of mainland Greece
**area** 8,378 sq km/3,234 sq mi
**capital** Irákleion (Heraklion)
**towns and cities** Khaniá (Canea), Rethymnon, Aghios Nikolaos
**products** citrus fruit, olives, wine
**population** (1991) 536,900
**language** Cretan dialect of Greek
**history** it has remains of the Minoan civilization 3000–1400 BC (see ◊Knossos), and was successively under Roman, Byzantine, Venetian, and Turkish rule. The island was annexed by Greece 1913.

**crevasse** deep crack in the surface of a glacier; it can reach several metres in depth. Crevasses often occur where a glacier flows over the break of a slope, because the upper layers of ice are unable to stretch and cracks result. Crevasses may also form at the edges of glaciers owing to friction with the bedrock.

**Crick, Francis Harry Compton** (1916–  ) English molecular biologist. From 1949 he researched the molecular structure of ◊DNA, and the means whereby characteristics are transmitted from one generation to another. For this work he was awarded a Nobel prize (with Maurice ◊Wilkins and James ◊Watson) in 1962.

**cricket** in zoology, an insect belonging to any of various families, especially the Gryllidae, of the order Orthoptera. Crickets are related to grasshoppers. They have somewhat flattened bodies and long antennae. The males make a chirping noise by rubbing together special areas on the forewings. The females have a long needlelike egglaying organ (ovipositor). There are around 900 species known worldwide.

**cricket** bat-and-ball game between two teams of 11 players each. It is played with a small solid ball and long flat-sided wooden bats, on a round or oval field, at the centre of which is a finely mown pitch, 20 m/22 yd long. At each end of the pitch is a wicket made up of three upright wooden sticks (stumps), surmounted by two smaller sticks (bails). The object of the game is to score more runs than the opposing team. A run is normally scored by the batsman striking the ball and exchanging ends with his or her partner until the ball is returned by a fielder, or by hitting the ball to the boundary line for an automatic four or six runs.

**Crimea** northern peninsula on the Black Sea, an autonomous republic of Ukraine; formerly a region (oblast) of the Soviet Union (1954–91)
**area** 27,000 sq km/10,425 sq mi
**capital** Simferopol
**towns and cities** Sevastopol, Yalta
**features** mainly steppe, but south coast is a holiday resort; home of the Black Sea fleet (ownership of which has been the source of a dispute between Russia and Ukraine)

**products** iron and steel, oil, fruit- and vine-growing
**population** (1989) 2,456,000
**history** After successive occupation from the 8th century BC onwards by Scythians, Greeks, Goths, Huns, and Khazars, Crimea became a Tatar khanate in the 13th century. The Genoese trading port of Kaffa (modern Feodosiya) in eastern Crimea was the place from which the ◊Black Death spread from Asia to western Europe in 1346. Crimea was part of the Ottoman empire 1475–1774. A subsequent brief independence as the Khanate of Crimea was ended by Russian annexation in 1783. It was the scene of conflict between Russia and a coalition of Britain, France, Turkey, and Sardinia in the ◊Crimean War (1853–56). The resort of Yalta was the scene of an important conference of the Allied leaders during World War II.

**Crimean War** war 1853–56 between Russia and the allied powers of England, France, Turkey, and Sardinia. The war arose from British and French mistrust of Russia's ambitions in the Balkans. It began with an allied Anglo-French expedition to the Crimea to attack the Russian Black Sea city of Sevastopol. The battles of the River Alma, Balaclava (including the charge of the Light Brigade), and Inkerman 1854 led to a siege which, owing to military mismanagement, lasted for a year until September 1855. The war was ended by the Treaty of Paris in 1856. The scandal surrounding French and British losses through disease led to the organization of proper military nursing services by Florence Nightingale.

**criminal law** body of law that defines the public wrongs (crimes) that are punishable by the state and establishes methods of prosecution and punishment. It is distinct from ◊civil law, which deals with legal relationships between individuals (including organizations), such as contract law.

**critical mass** in nuclear physics, the minimum mass of fissile material that can undergo a continuous ◊chain reaction. Below this mass, too many ◊neutrons escape from the surface for a chain reaction to carry on; above the critical mass, the reaction may accelerate into a nuclear explosion.

**Croagh Patrick** holy mountain rising to 765 m/2,510 ft in County Mayo, western Republic of Ireland, a national place of pilgrimage. An annual pilgrimage on the last Sunday of July commemorates St Patrick, who fasted there for the 40 days of Lent in 441 AD.

**Croatia** Republic of
**national name** *Republika Hrvatska*
**area** 56,538 sq km/21,829 sq mi
**capital** Zagreb
**major towns/cities** Osijek, Split, Dubrovnik, Rijeka, Zadar, Pula
**major ports** chief port: Rijeka (Fiume); other ports: Zadar, Sibenik, Split, Dubrovnik
**physical features** Adriatic coastline with large islands; very mountainous, with part of the

Karst region and the Julian and Styrian Alps; some marshland
**head of state** Franjo Tudjman from 1990
**head of government** Zlatko Matesa from 1995
**political system** emergent democracy
**political parties** Croatian Democratic Union (CDU), Christian Democrat, right of centre, nationalist; Croatian Social-Liberal Party (CSLP), centrist; Social Democratic Party of Change (SDP), reform socialist; Croatian Party of Rights (HSP), Croat-oriented, ultranationalist; Croatian Peasant Party (HSS), rural-based; Serbian National Party (SNS), Serb-oriented
**currency** kuna
**GNP per capita (PPP)** (US$) 7,100 (1998 est)
**exports** machinery and transport equipment, chemicals, foodstuffs, miscellaneous manufactured items (mainly clothing). Principal market: Italy 17.7% (1998)
**population** 4,477,000 (1999 est)
**language** Croatian variant of Serbo-Croatian (official); Serbian variant of Serbo-Croatian also widely spoken, particularly in border areas in east
**religion** Roman Catholic (Croats); Orthodox Christian (Serbs)
**life expectancy** 69 (men); 77 (women) (1995–2000)
**Chronology**
**early centuries** AD Part of Roman region of Pannonia.
**AD 395** On division of Roman Empire, stayed in western half, along with Slovenia and Bosnia.
**7th century** Settled by Carpathian Croats, from northeast; Christianity adopted.
**924** Formed by Tomislav into independent kingdom, which incorporated Bosnia from 10th century.
**12th–19th centuries** Enjoyed autonomy under Hungarian crown, following dynastic union in 1102.
**1526–1699** Slavonia, in east, held by Ottoman Turks, while Serbs were invited by Austria to settle along the border with Ottoman-ruled Bosnia, in Vojna Krajina (military frontier).
**1797–1815** Dalmatia, in west, ruled by France.
**19th century** Part of Austro-Hungarian Habsburg Empire.
**1918** On dissolution of Habsburg Empire, joined Serbia, Slovenia, and Montenegro in 'Kingdom of Serbs, Croats, and Slovenes', under Serbian Karageorgevic dynasty.
**1929** The Kingdom became Yugoslavia. Croatia continued its campaign for autonomy.
**1930s** Ustasa, a Croat terrorist organization, began a campaign against dominance of Yugoslavia by the non-Catholic Serbs.
**1941–44** Following German invasion, a 'Greater Croatia' Nazi puppet state, including most of Bosnia and western Serbia, formed under Ustasa leader, Ante Pavelic; more than half a million Serbs, Jews, and members of the Romany community were massacred in extermination camps.
**1945** Became constituent republic of Yugoslavia Socialist Federation after communist partisans, led by Croat Marshal Tito, overthrew Pavelic.
**1970s** Separatist demands resurfaced, provoking a crackdown.

**late 1980s** Spiralling inflation and a deterioration in living standards sparked industrial unrest and a rise in nationalist sentiment, which affected the local communist party.
**1989** The formation of opposition parties was permitted.
**1990** The communists were defeated by the conservative nationalist CDU led by ex-Partisan Franjo Tudjman in the first free election since 1938. Sovereignty was declared.
**1991** The Serb-dominated region of Krajina in the southwest announced its secession from Croatia. Croatia declared independence, leading to military conflict with Serbia, and civil war ensued.
**1992** A United Nations (UN) peace accord was accepted; independence was recognized by the European Community (EC) and the USA; Croatia joined the UN. A UN peacekeeping force was stationed in Croatia. Tudjman was elected president.
**1993** A government offensive was launched to retake parts of Serb-held Krajina, violating the 1992 UN peace accord.
**1994** There was an accord with Muslims and ethnic Croats within Bosnia, to the east, to link the recently formed Muslim–Croat federation with Croatia.
**1995** Serb-held western Slavonia and Krajina were captured by government forces; there was an exodus of Croatian Serbs. The offensive extended into Bosnia-Herzegovina to halt a Bosnian Serb assault on Bihac in western Bosnia. Serbia agreed to cede control of eastern Slavonia to Croatia over a two-year period.
**1996** Diplomatic relations between Croatia and Yugoslavia were restored. Croatia entered the Council of Europe.
**1997** The opposition was successful in local elections. Tudjman was re-elected despite failing health. The Serb enclave in eastern Slavonia was reintegrated into Croatia. The constitution was amended to prevent the weakening of Croatia's national sovereignty.
**1998** Croatia resumed control over East Slavonia.

**crocodile** large scaly-skinned ◊reptile with a long, low cigar-shaped body and short legs. Crocodiles can grow up to 7 m/23 ft in length, and have long, powerful tails that propel them when swimming. They are found near swamps, lakes, and rivers in Asia, Africa, Australia, and Central America, where they are often seen floating in the water like logs, with only their nostrils, eyes, and ears above the surface. They are fierce hunters and active mainly at night. Young crocodiles eat worms and insects, but as they mature they add frogs and small fish to their diet. Adult crocodiles will attack animals the size of antelopes and even, occasionally, people. They can live up to 100 years and are related to the ◊alligator and the smaller cayman.

**crocus** any of a group of plants belonging to the iris family, with single yellow, purple, or white flowers and narrow, pointed leaves. They are native to northern parts of the Old World, especially southern Europe and Asia Minor. (Genus *Crocus*, family Iridaceae.)

**Croesus** (died 547 BC) last king of Lydia (in western Asia Minor) 560–547 BC. Famed for his wealth, he expanded Lydian power to its greatest extent, conquering all Anatolia west of the river Halys and entering alliances with Media, Egypt, and Sparta. He invaded Persia but was defeated by ◊Cyrus (II) the Great. Lydia was subsequently absorbed into the Persian Empire.

**croft** small farm in the Highlands of Scotland, traditionally the farming of common land cooperatively; the 1886 Crofters Act gave security of tenure to crofters. Today, although grazing land is still shared, arable land is typically enclosed. Crofting is the only form of subsistence farming found in the UK.

**Crohn's disease** or *regional ileitis,* chronic inflammatory bowel disease. It tends to flare up for a few days at a time, causing diarrhoea, abdominal cramps, loss of appetite, weight loss, and mild fever. The cause of Crohn's disease is unknown, although stress may be a factor.

**Cro-Magnon** prehistoric human *Homo sapiens sapiens* believed to be ancestral to Europeans, the first skeletons of which were found 1868 in the Cro-Magnon cave near Les Eyzies, in the Dordogne region of France. They are thought to have superseded the Neanderthals in the Middle East, Africa, Europe, and Asia about 40,000 years ago. Although modern in skeletal form, they were more robust in build than some present-day humans. They hunted bison, reindeer, and horses, and are associated with Upper Palaeolithic cultures, which produced fine flint and bone tools, jewellery, and naturalistic cave paintings.

**Cromwell, Oliver** (1599–1658) English general and politician, Puritan leader of the Parliamentary side in the ◊Civil War. He raised cavalry forces (later called *Ironsides)* which aided the victories at Edgehill in 1642 and ◊Marston Moor in 1644, and organized the New Model Army, which he led (with General Fairfax) to victory at Naseby in 1645. He declared Britain a republic ('the Commonwealth') in 1649, following the execution of Charles I. As Lord Protector (ruler) from 1653, Cromwell established religious toleration and raised Britain's prestige in Europe on the basis of an alliance with France against Spain.

**Cromwell, Thomas** Earl of Essex (c. 1485–1540) English politician who drafted the legislation that made the Church of England independent of Rome. Originally in Lord Chancellor Wolsey's service, he became secretary to ◊Henry VIII in 1534 and the real director of government policy; he was executed for treason. He was created a baron in 1536.

**Cronus** or *Kronos,* in Greek mythology, the youngest of the ◊Titans; ruler of the world under his father ◊Uranus, the sky; and son of ◊Gaia, mother of the Earth. He was eventually overthrown by his son ◊Zeus.

**crop** in birds, the thin-walled enlargement of the digestive tract between the oesophagus and stomach. It is an effective storage organ especially in seed-eating birds; a pigeon's crop can hold about 500 cereal grains. Digestion begins in the crop, by the moisturizing of food. A crop also occurs in insects and annelid worms.

**crop rotation** system of regularly changing the crops grown on a piece of land. The crops are grown in a particular order to utilize and add to the nutrients in the soil and to prevent the build-up of insect and fungal pests. Including a legume crop, such as peas or beans, in the rotation helps build up nitrate in the soil, because the roots contain bacteria capable of fixing nitrogen from the air.

**croquet** outdoor game played with mallets and balls on a level hooped lawn measuring 27 m/90 ft by 18 m/60 ft. Played in France in the 16th and 17th centuries, it gained popularity in the USA and England in the 1850s.

**Crosby, Bing (Harry Lillis)** (1904–1977) US film actor and singer. He achieved world success with his distinctive style of crooning in such songs as 'Pennies from Heaven' (1936; featured in a film of the same name) and 'White Christmas' (1942). He won an Academy Award for his acting in *Going My Way* (1944).

**croup** inflammation of the larynx in small children, with harsh, difficult breathing and hoarse coughing. Croup is most often associated with viral infection of the respiratory tract.

**crow** any of 35 species of omnivorous birds in the genus *Corvus,* family Corvidae, order Passeriformes, which also includes choughs, jays, and magpies. Crows are usually about 45 cm/1.5 ft long, black, with a strong bill feathered at the base. The tail is long and graduated, and the wings are long and pointed, except in the jays and magpies, where they are shorter. Crows are considered to be very intelligent. The family is distributed throughout the world, though there are very few species in eastern Australia or South America. The common crows are *C. brachyrhynchos* in North America, and *C. corone* in Europe and Asia.

**Crown colony** any British colony that is under the direct legislative control of the Crown and does not possess its own system of representative government. Crown colonies are administered by a crown-appointed governor or by elected or nominated legislative and executive councils with an official majority. Usually the Crown retains rights of veto and of direct legislation by orders in council.

**crown court** in England and Wales, any of several courts that hear serious criminal cases referred from magistrates' courts after committal proceedings. They replaced quarter sessions and assizes, which were abolished in 1971. Appeals against conviction or sentence at magistrates' courts may be heard in crown courts. Appeal from a crown court is to the Court of Appeal.

**Crown Prosecution Service** body established by the Prosecution of Offences Act 1985, responsible for prosecuting all criminal offences in England and Wales. It is headed by the Director of Public Prosecutions (DPP), and brought England and Wales in line with Scotland (which has a procurator fiscal) in

## CRUSADES: CHRONOLOGY

**1076**  Seljuk Turks capture Jerusalem and begin to restrict access of Christian pilgrims to the holy places.

**1095**  Byzantine emperor Alexius Comnenus, threatened by Muslim advances in Anatolia, appeals to the pope for help against the Seljuk Turks. Pope Urban II proclaims a holy war.

**1096–99**  First Crusade, led by Baldwin of Boulogne, Godfrey of Bouillon, and Peter the Hermit. Motivated by occupation of Anatolia and Jerusalem by Seljuk Turks.

**1099**  Capture of Jerusalem by the crusaders, accompanied by looting and massacre. A number of small crusader states established on the Syrian coast.

**1147–49**  Second Crusade, led by Louis VII of France and Emperor Conrad III, fails to capture Damascus and Edessa.

**1187**  Jerusalem seized by Saladin, sultan of Egypt and Syria and leader of the Muslims against the crusaders.

**1189–92**  Third Crusade, led by Philip II Augustus of France and Richard I the Lion-Heart of England, fails to recapture Jerusalem.

**1202–04**  Fourth Crusade, led by William of Montferrata and Baldwin of Hainault. Originally intended to recover the holy places, it is diverted by its Venetian financial backers to sack and divide Constantinople.

**1212**  Children's Crusade. Thousands of children cross Europe on their way to Palestine but many are sold into slavery in Marseille, or die of disease and hunger.

**1218–21**  Fifth Crusade, led by King Andrew of Hungary, Cardinal Pelagius, King John of Jerusalem, and King Hugh of Cyprus. Captures and then loses Damietta, Egypt.

**1228–29**  Sixth Crusade, led by the Holy Roman Emperor Frederick II. Jerusalem recovered by negotiation with the sultan of Egypt.

**1244**  Jerusalem finally lost, to remain in Turkish hands until liberated by the British general Allenby in 1917.

**1249–54**  Seventh Crusade led by Louis IX of France.

**1270–72**  Eighth Crusade, also led by Louis IX of France.

**1291**  Acre, the last Christian fortress in Syria, falls to the Turks.

having a prosecution service independent of the police.

**crucifixion** death by fastening to a cross, a form of capital punishment used by the ancient Romans, Persians, and Carthaginians, and abolished by the Roman emperor Constantine. Specifically, *the Crucifixion* refers to the execution by the Romans of ◊Jesus in this manner.

**cruise missile** long-range guided missile that has a terrain-seeking radar system and flies at moderate speed and low altitude. It is descended from the German V1 of World War II. Initial trials in the 1950s demonstrated the limitations of cruise missiles, which included high fuel consumption and relatively slow speeds (when compared to intercontinental ballistic missiles – ICBMs) as well as inaccuracy and a small warhead. Improvements to guidance systems by the use of terrain-contour matching (TERCOM) ensured pinpoint accuracy on low-level flights after launch from a mobile ground launcher (ground-launched cruise missile – GLCM), from an aircraft (air-launched cruise missile – ALCM), or from a submarine or ship (sealaunched cruise missile – SLCM).

**crusade** (French *croisade*) European war against non-Christians and heretics, sanctioned by the pope; in particular, the Crusades, a series of wars undertaken 1096–1291 by European rulers to recover Palestine from the Muslims. Motivated by religious zeal, the desire for land, and the trading ambitions of the major Italian cities, the Crusades were varied in their aims and effects.

**crustacean** one of the class of arthropods that includes crabs, lobsters, shrimps, woodlice, and barnacles. The external skeleton is made of protein and chitin hardened with lime. Each segment bears a pair of appendages that may be modified as sensory feelers (antennae), as mouthparts, or as swimming, walking, or grasping structures.

**cryogenics** science of very low temperatures (approaching ◊absolute zero), including the production of very low temperatures and the exploitation of special properties associated with them, such as the disappearance of electrical resistance (◊superconductivity).

**crystal** substance with an orderly three-dimensional arrangement of its atoms or molecules, thereby creating an external surface of clearly defined smooth faces having characteristic angles between them. Examples are table salt and quartz. *See illustration on page 238.*

**crystallography** the scientific study of crystals. In 1912 it was found that the shape and size of the repeating atomic patterns (unit cells) in a crystal could be determined by passing X-rays through a sample. This method, known as ◊X-ray diffraction, opened up an entirely new way of 'seeing' atoms. It has been found that many substances have a unit cell that exhibits all the symmetry of the whole crystal; in table salt (sodium chloride, NaCl), for instance, the unit cell is an exact cube.

**CSE** abbreviation for *Certificate of Secondary Education,* in the UK, the examinations taken by the majority of secondary school pupils who were not regarded as academically capable of GCE O level, until the introduction of the common secondary examination system, ◊GCSE, in 1988.

**CT scanner** medical device used to obtain detailed X-ray pictures of the inside of a patient's body. See ◊CAT scan.

*sodium chloride*

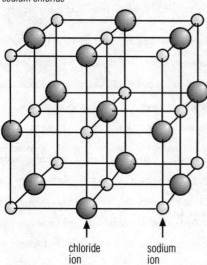

chloride     sodium
ion          ion

**crystal** *The sodium chloride, or common salt, crystal is a regular cubic array of charged atoms (ions) – positive sodium atoms and negative chlorine atoms. Repetition of this structure builds up into cubic salt crystals.*

**Cuba** Republic of
**National name** *República de Cuba*

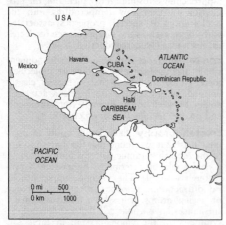

**area** 110,860 sq km/42,803 sq mi
**capital** Havana
**major towns/cities** Santiago de Cuba, Camagüey, Holguín, Guantánamo, Santa Clara, Bayamo, Cienfuegos
**physical features** comprises Cuba and smaller islands including Isle of Youth; low hills; Sierra Maestra mountains in southeast; Cuba has 3,380 km/2,100 mi of coastline, with deep bays, sandy beaches, coral islands and reefs
**head of state and government** Fidel Castro Ruz from 1959
**political system** communist republic

**political party** Communist Party of Cuba (PCC), Marxist-Leninist
**currency** Cuban peso
**GNP per capita (PPP)** (US$) 3,520 (1997 est)
**exports** sugar, minerals, tobacco, citrus fruits, fish products. Principal market: Russia 17.6% (1997)
**population** 11,160,000 (1999 est)
**language** Spanish
**religion** Roman Catholic; also Episcopalians and Methodists
**life expectancy** 74 (men); 78 (women) (1995–2000)
**Chronology**
**3rd century** AD The Ciboney, Cuba's earliest known inhabitants, were dislodged by the immigration of Taino, Arawak Indians from Venezuela.
**1492** Christopher Columbus landed in Cuba and claimed it for Spain.
**1511** Spanish settlement established at Baracoa by Diego Velazquez.
**1523** Decline of American Indian population and rise of sugar plantations led to import of slaves from Africa.
**mid-19th century** Cuba produced one-third of the world's sugar.
**1868–78** Unsuccessful first war for independence from Spain.
**1886** Slavery was abolished.
**1895–98** Further uprising against Spanish rule, led by José Martí, who died in combat; 200,000 soldiers deployed by Spain.
**1898** USA defeated Spain in Spanish-American War; Spain gave up all claims to Cuba, which was ceded to the USA.
**1901** Cuba achieved independence; Tomás Estrada Palma became first president of the Republic of Cuba.
**1906–09** Brief period of US administration after Estrada resigned in the face of an armed rebellion by political opponents.
**1909** The liberal, José Miguel Gomez became president, but soon became tarred by corruption.
**1924** Gerado Machado, an admirer of the Italian fascist leader Benito Mussolini, established a brutal dictatorship which lasted nine years.
**1925** Socialist Party founded, from which the Communist Party later developed.
**1933** Army sergeant Fulgencio Batista seized power.
**1934** USA abandoned its right to intervene in Cuba's internal affairs.
**1944** Batista retired and was succeeded by the civilian Ramon Gray San Martin.
**1952** Batista seized power again to begin an oppressive and corrupt regime.
**1953** Fidel Castro Ruz led an unsuccessful coup against Batista on the 100th anniversary of the birth of Martí.
**1956** Second unsuccessful coup by Castro.
**1959** Batista overthrown by Castro and his 9,000-strong guerrilla army. Constitution of 1940 replaced by a 'Fundamental Law', making Castro prime minister, his brother Raúl Castro his deputy, and Argentine-born Ernesto 'Che' Guevara third in command.

**1960** All US businesses in Cuba appropriated without compensation; USA broke off diplomatic relations.

**1961** USA sponsored an unsuccessful invasion by Cuban exiles at the Bay of Pigs. Castro announced that Cuba had become a communist state, with a Marxist-Leninist programme of economic development, and became allied with the USSR.

**1962** Cuban missile crisis: Cuba was expelled from the Organization of American States. Castro responded by tightening relations with the USSR, which installed nuclear missiles in Cuba (subsequently removed at US insistence). US trade embargo imposed.

**1965** Cuba's sole political party renamed Cuban Communist Party (PCC). With Soviet help, Cuba began to make considerable economic and social progress.

**1972** Cuba became a full member of the Moscow-based Council for Mutual Economic Assistance (COMECON).

**1976** New socialist constitution approved; Castro elected president.

**1976–81** Castro became involved in extensive international commitments, sending troops as Soviet surrogates, particularly to Africa.

**1982** Cuba joined other Latin American countries in giving moral support to Argentina in its dispute with Britain over the Falklands.

**1984** Castro tried to improve US-Cuban relations by discussing exchange of US prisoners in Cuba for Cuban 'undesirables' in the USA.

**1988** A peace accord with South Africa was signed, agreeing to the withdrawal of Cuban troops from Angola, as part of a reduction in Cuba's overseas military activities.

**1991** Soviet troops were withdrawn with the collapse of the USSR.

**1993** The US trade embargo was tightened; market-oriented reforms were introduced in the face of a deteriorating economy.

**1994** There was a refugee exodus; US policy on Cuban asylum seekers was revised.

**1998** Castro was confirmed as president for a further five-year term. The UN declined to condemn Cuba's human-rights record.

**Cuban missile crisis** confrontation in international relations October 1962 when Soviet rockets were installed in Cuba and US president Kennedy compelled Soviet leader Khrushchev, by military threats and negotiation, to remove them. This event prompted an unsuccessful drive by the USSR to match the USA in nuclear weaponry.

**cube** in geometry, a regular solid figure whose faces are all squares. It has 6 equal-area faces and 12 equal-length edges.

**cube** to multiply a number by itself and then by itself again. For example, 5 cubed = $5^3$ = 5 × 5 × 5 = 125. The term also refers to a number formed by cubing; for example, 1, 8, 27, 64 are the first four cubes.

**Cubism** revolutionary style of painting created by Georges Braque and Pablo Picasso in Paris in 1907–14. It was the most radical of the developments that revolutionized art in the years of unprecedented experimentation leading up to

World War I, and it changed the course of painting by introducing a new way of seeing and depicting the world. To the Cubists, a painting was first and foremost a flat object that existed in its own right, rather than a kind of window through which a representation of the world is seen. Cubism also had a marked, though less fundamental, effect on sculpture, and even influenced architecture and the decorative arts.

**Cuchulain** (lived 1st century AD) or *Cu Chulainn,* legendary Celtic hero, chief figure in a cycle of Irish tales associated with his uncle Conchobar mac Nessa, king of Ulster. His most famous exploits are described in the central story of the cycle, *Taín Bó Cuailnge/The Cattle Raid of Cooley.*

**cuckoo** species of bird, any of about 200 members of the family Cuculidae, order Cuculiformes, especially the Eurasian cuckoo *Cuculus canorus,* whose name derives from its characteristic call. Somewhat hawklike, it is about 33 cm/1.1 ft long, bluish-grey and barred beneath (females are sometimes reddish), and typically has a long, rounded tail. Cuckoos feed on insects, including hairy caterpillars that are distasteful to most birds. It is a 'brood parasite', laying its eggs singly, at intervals of about 48 hours, in the nests of small insectivorous birds. As soon as the young cuckoo hatches, it ejects all other young birds or eggs from the nest and is tended by its 'foster parents' until fledging. American species of cuckoo hatch and rear their own young.

**cucumber** trailing annual plant belonging to the gourd family, producing long, green-skinned fruit with crisp, translucent, edible flesh. Small cucumbers, called gherkins, usually the fruit of *Cucumis anguria,* are often pickled. (*Cucumis sativus,* family Cucurbitaceae.)

**Culloden, Battle of** defeat in 1746 of the ◊Jacobite rebel army of the British prince ◊Charles Edward Stuart (the 'Young Pretender') by the Duke of Cumberland on a stretch of moorland in Inverness-shire, Scotland. This battle effectively ended the military challenge of the Jacobite rebellion.

**Cultural Revolution** Chinese mass movement from 1966 to 1969 begun by Communist Party leader ◊Mao Zedong, directed against the upper middle class – bureaucrats, artists, and academics – who were killed, imprisoned, humiliated, or 'resettled'. Intended to 'purify' Chinese communism, it was also an attempt by Mao to renew his political and ideological pre-eminence inside China. Half a million people are estimated to have been killed.

**culture** in sociology and anthropology, the way of life of a particular society or group of people, including patterns of thought, beliefs, behaviour, customs, traditions, rituals, dress, and language, as well as art, music, and literature. Archaeologists use the word to mean the surviving objects or artefacts that provide evidence of a social grouping.

**Cumbria** county of northwest England, created in 1974 from Cumberland, Westmorland,

the Furness district of northwest Lancashire, and the Sedbergh district of northwest Yorkshire
**area** 6,810 sq km/2,629 sq mi
**towns and cities** ◊Carlisle (administrative headquarters), Barrow, Kendal, Penrith, Whitehaven, Workington
**physical** Scafell Pike (978 m/3,210 ft), the highest mountain in England, Helvellyn (950 m/3,118 ft); Lake Windermere, the largest lake in England (17 km/10.5 mi long, 1.6 km/1 mi wide), and other lakes (Derwentwater, Grasmere, Haweswater, Ullswater); the rivers Eden and Derwent; the M6 motorway runs north to south through the centre of the county
**features** Lake District National Park; Grizedale Forest sculpture project; Furness peninsula; western part of Hadrian's Wall
**agriculture** in the north and east there is dairy farming; sheep are also reared; the West Cumberland Farmers is England's largest agricultural cooperative
**industries** the traditional coal, iron, and steel industries of the coast towns have been replaced by newer industries including chemicals, plastics, marine engineering, electronics, and shipbuilding (at Barrow-in-Furness, nuclear submarines and warships), tourism, salmon fishing
**population** (1996) 490,600
**famous people** Samuel Taylor Coleridge, Stan Laurel, Beatrix Potter, Thomas de Quincey, John Ruskin, Robert Southey, William Wordsworth.

**cumin** seedlike fruit of the herb cumin, which belongs to the carrot family. It has a bitter flavour and is used as a spice in cooking. (*Cuminum cyminum,* family Umbelliferae.)

**cuneiform** ancient writing system formed of combinations of wedge-shaped strokes, usually impressed on clay. It was probably invented by the Sumerians, and was in use in Mesopotamia as early as the middle of the 4th millennium BC.

**Cunningham, Merce** (1919–   ) US choreographer and dancer. He is recognized as the father of postmodernist, or experimental, dance. He liberated dance from its relationship with music, allowing it to obey its own dynamics.

Along with his friend and collaborator, composer John ◊Cage, he introduced chance into the creative process, such as tossing coins to determine options. Influenced by Martha ◊Graham, with whose company he was soloist 1939–45, he formed his own avant-garde dance company and school in New York 1953. His works include *The Seasons* (1947), *Antic Meet* (1958), *Squaregame* (1976), and *Arcade* (1985).

**Cupid** or Amor, (Latin *cupido* 'desire') in Roman mythology, the god of love (Greek Eros); son of the goddess of love, ◊Venus, and either ◊Mars, ◊Jupiter, or ◊Mercury. Joyous and mischievous, he is generally represented as a winged, naked boy with a bow and arrow, sometimes with a blindfold, torch, or quiver. According to the Roman poet Ovid, his golden arrows inspired love, while those of lead put love to flight.

**cupronickel** copper alloy (75% copper and 25% nickel), used in hardware products and for coinage.

**Curaçao** island in the West Indies, one of the ◊Netherlands Antilles; area 444 sq km/171 sq mi; population (1993 est) 146,800. The principal industry, dating from 1918, is the refining of Venezuelan petroleum. Curaçao was colonized by Spain 1527, annexed by the Dutch West India Company 1634, and gave its name from 1924 to the group of islands renamed the Netherlands Antilles 1948. Its capital is the port of Willemstad.

**curare** black, resinous poison extracted from the bark and juices of various South American trees and plants. Originally used on arrowheads by Amazonian hunters to paralyse prey, it blocks nerve stimulation of the muscles. Alkaloid derivatives (called curarines) are used in medicine as muscle relaxants during surgery.

**Curie, Marie** born Manya Sklodowska (1867–1934) Polish scientist who, with husband Pierre Curie, discovered in 1898 two new radioactive elements in pitchblende ores: polonium and radium. They isolated the pure elements in 1902. Both scientists refused to take out a patent on their discovery and were jointly awarded the Nobel Prize for Physics 1903, with Henri ◊Becquerel. Marie Curie was also awarded the Nobel Prize for Chemistry 1911.

**curium** synthesized, radioactive, metallic element of the *actinide* series, symbol Cm, atomic number 96, relative atomic mass 247. It is produced by bombarding plutonium or americium with neutrons. Its longest-lived isotope has a half-life of $1.7 \times 10^7$ years.

**curlew** wading bird of the genus *Numenius* of the sandpiper family, Scolopacidae, order Charadriiformes. The curlew is between 36 cm/14 in and 55 cm/1.8 ft long, and has pale brown plumage with dark bars and mainly white underparts, long legs, and a long, thin, downcurved bill. It feeds on a variety of insects and other invertebrates. Several species live in northern Europe, Asia, and North America. The name derives from its haunting flutelike call.

**currant** berry of a small seedless variety of cultivated grape (*Vitis vinifera*). Currants are grown on a large scale in Greece and California and are dried for use in cooking and baking. Because of the similarity of the fruit, the name 'currant' is also given to several species of shrubs (genus *Ribes,* family Grossulariaceae).

**current** flow of a body of water or air, or of heat, moving in a definite direction. Ocean currents are fast-flowing currents of seawater generated by the wind or by variations in water density between two areas. They are partly responsible for transferring heat from the Equator to the poles and thereby evening out the global heat imbalance. There are three basic types of ocean current: *drift currents* are broad and slow-moving; *stream currents* are narrow and swift-moving; and *upwelling currents* bring cold, nutrient-rich water from the ocean bottom.

**curry** (Tamil *kari* 'sauce') traditional Indian mixture of spices used to flavour a dish of rice, meat, and/or vegetables. Spices include turmeric, fenugreek, cloves, chillies, cumin, cinnamon, ginger, black and cayenne pepper, coriander, and caraway.

**custard apple** any of several large edible heart-shaped fruits produced by a group of tropical trees and shrubs which are often cultivated. Bullock's heart (*Annona reticulata*) produces a large dark-brown fruit containing a sweet reddish-yellow pulp; it is a native of the West Indies. (Family Annonaceae.)

**Custer, George Armstrong** (1839–1876) US Civil War general, who became the Union's youngest brigadier general 1863 as a result of a brilliant war record. He was made a major general 1865, but following the end of the Civil War, his rank was reduced to captain. He took part in an expedition against the Cheyennes 1867–68, and several times defeated other American Indian groups in the West. He campaigned against the Sioux from 1874, and was killed with a detachment of his troops by the forces of Sioux chief Sitting Bull in the Battle of Little Bighorn, Montana, also known as *Custer's last stand,* 25 June 1876.

**Customs and Excise** government department responsible for taxes levied on imports (customs duty). Excise duties are levied on goods produced domestically or on licences to carry on certain trades (such as sale of wines and spirits) or other activities (theatrical entertainments, betting, and so on) within a country.

**cuttlefish** any of a family, Sepiidae, of squidlike cephalopods with an internal calcareous shell (cuttlebone). The common cuttle *Sepia officinalis* of the Atlantic and Mediterranean is up to 30 cm/1 ft long. It swims actively by means of the fins into which the sides of its oval, flattened body are expanded, and jerks itself backwards by shooting a jet of water from its 'siphon'.

**cyanide** CN⁻ ion derived from hydrogen cyanide (HCN), and any salt containing this ion (produced when hydrogen cyanide is neutralized by alkalis), such as potassium cyanide (KCN). The principal cyanides are potassium, sodium, calcium, mercury, gold, and copper. Certain cyanides are poisons.

**cyanocobalamin** chemical name for vitamin $B_{12}$, which is normally produced by microorganisms in the gut. The richest sources are liver, fish, and eggs. It is essential to the replacement of cells, the maintenance of the myelin sheath which insulates nerve fibres, and the efficient use of folic acid, another vitamin in the B complex. Deficiency can result in pernicious anaemia (defective production of red blood cells), and possible degeneration of the nervous system.

**cybernetics** (Greek *kubernan* 'to steer') science concerned with how systems organize, regulate, and reproduce themselves, and also how they evolve and learn. In the laboratory, inanimate objects are created that behave like living systems. Applications range from the creation of electronic artificial limbs to the running of the fully automated factory where decisionmaking machines operate up to managerial level.

**cycad** any of a group of plants belonging to the ◊gymnosperms, whose seeds develop in cones. Some are superficially similar to palms, others to ferns. Their large cones (up to 0.5 m/1.6 ft in length) contain fleshy seeds. There are ten genera and about 80–100 species, native to tropical and subtropical countries. Cycads were widespread during the Mesozoic era (245–65 million years ago). (Order Cycadales.)

**cyclamen** any of a group of perennial plants belonging to the primrose family, with heart-shaped leaves and petals that are twisted at the base and bent back, away from the centre of the downward-facing flower. The flowers are usually white or pink, and several species are cultivated. (Genus *Cyclamen,* family Primulaceae.)

**cycle** in physics, a sequence of changes that moves a system away from, and then back to, its original state. An example is a vibration that moves a particle first in one direction and then in the opposite direction, with the particle returning to its original position at the end of the vibration.

**cycling** riding a ◊bicycle for sport, pleasure, or transport. Cycle racing can take place on oval artificial tracks, on the road, or across country (cyclocross and mountain biking).

**cyclone** alternative name for a ◊depression, an area of low atmospheric pressure. A severe cyclone that forms in the tropics is called a tropical cyclone or ◊hurricane.

**Cyclops** (Greek 'circle-eyed') in Greek mythology, one of a race of Sicilian giants with one eye in the middle of their foreheads. According to Homer, they lived as shepherds. ◊Odysseus blinded the Cyclops Polyphemus in Homer's *Odyssey.*

**cylinder** in geometry, a tubular solid figure with a circular base. In everyday use, the term applies to a *right cylinder,* the curved surface of which is at right angles to the base.

**cymbal** ancient percussion instrument of indefinite pitch, consisting of a shallow circular brass dish suspended at the centre; either used in pairs clashed together or singly, struck with a beater. Smaller finger cymbals or *crotala,* of ancient origin but used in the 20th century by Debussy and Stockhausen, are precise in pitch. Turkish or 'buzz' cymbals incorporate loose rivets to extend the sound.

**Cymbeline** (lived 1st century AD) or *Cunobelin,* King of the Catuvellauni AD 5–40, who fought unsuccessfully against the Roman invasion of Britain. His capital was at Colchester.

**Cymru** Welsh name for ◊Wales.

**cynic** member of a school of Greek philosophy (cynicism), founded in Athens about 400 BC by Antisthenes, a disciple of Socrates, who advocated a stern and simple morality and a complete disregard of pleasure and comfort.

**cypress** any of a group of coniferous trees or shrubs containing about 20 species, originating from temperate regions of the northern hemisphere. They have tiny scalelike leaves and cones made up of woody, wedge-shaped scales containing an aromatic ◊resin. (Genera *Cupressus* and *Chamaecyparis,* family Cupressaceae.)

**Cyrano de Bergerac, Savinien** (1619–1655) French writer. Joining a corps of guards at the age of 19, he performed heroic feats. He is the hero of a classic play by Edmond Rostand, in which his excessively long nose is used as a counterpoint to his chivalrous character.

**Cyrenaic** member of a school of Greek ◊hedonistic philosophy founded about 400 BC by Aristippus of Cyrene. He regarded pleasure as the only absolutely worthwhile thing in life but taught that self-control and intelligence were necessary to choose the best pleasures.

**Cyrus (II) the Great** (died 530 BC) king of Persia 559–530 BC and founder of the Achaemenid Persian Empire. The son of the vassal king of Persia and of a daughter of his Median overlord Astyages, Cyrus rebelled in about 550 BC with the help of mutiny in the Median army and replaced the Median Empire with a Persian one. In 547 he defeated ◊Croesus of Lydia at Pteria and Sardis, conquering Asia Minor. In 539 he captured Babylon from Nabu-naid (Nabonidus) the Chaldaean, formerly his ally against the Medes, and extended his frontiers to the borders of Egypt. He was killed while campaigning in Central Asia, and was succeeded by his son Cambyses II.

**Cyprus** *Greek Republic of Cyprus* in south, and *Turkish Republic of Northern Cyprus* in north

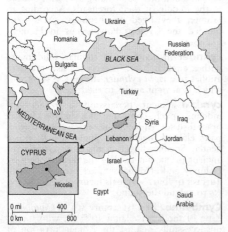

**national name** *Kypriakí Dimokratía* (south), and *Kibris Cumhuriyeti* (north)
**area** 9,251 sq km/3,571 sq mi (3,335 sq km/1,287 sq mi is Turkish-occupied)
**capital** Nicosia (divided between Greek and Turkish Cypriots)
**major towns/cities** Morphou, Limassol, Larnaca, Famagusta, Paphos
**major ports** Limassol, Larnaca, and Paphos (Greek); Kyrenia and Famagusta (Turkish)
**physical features** central plain between two east–west mountain ranges

**head of state and government** Glafkos Clerides (Greek) from 1993, Rauf Denktaş (Turkish) from 1976
**political system** democratic divided republic
**political parties** *Greek zone*: Democratic Party (DEKO), federalist, centre left; Progressive Party of the Working People (AKEL), socialist; Democratic Rally (DISY), centrist; Socialist Party–National Democratic Union of Cyprus (SK–EDEK), socialist; *Turkish zone*: National Unity Party (NUP), Communal Liberation Party (CLP), Republican Turkish Party (RTP), New British Party (NBP)
**currency** Cyprus pound and Turkish lira
**GNP per capita (PPP)** (US\$) 14,090 (1997 est)
**exports** clothing, potatoes, pharmaceutical products, manufactured foods, minerals, citrus fruits, industrial products. Principal market: UK 15.5% (1998)
**population** 779,000 (1999 est)
**language** Greek and Turkish (official), English
**religion** Greek Orthodox, Sunni Muslim
**life expectancy** 76 (men); 80 (women) (1995–2000)
*Chronology*
**14th–11th centuries BC** Colonized by Myceneans and Achaeans from Greece.
**9th century BC** Phoenicans settled in Cyprus.
**7th century BC** Several Cypriot kingdoms flourished under Assyrian influence.
**414–374 BC** Under Evagoras of Salamis (in eastern Cyprus) the island's ten city kingdoms were united into one state and Greek culture, including the Greek alphabet, was promoted.
**333–58 BC** Became part of the Greek Hellenistic and then, from 294 BC, the Egypt-based Ptolemaic empire.
**58 BC** Cyprus was annexed by the Roman Empire.
**AD 45** Christianity introduced.
**AD 395** When the Roman Empire divided, Cyprus was allotted to the Byzantine Empire.
**7th–10th centuries** Byzantines and Muslim Arabs fought for control of Cyprus.
**1191** Richard I of England, 'the Lionheart', conquered Cyprus as a base for Crusades; he later sold it to a French noble, Guy de Lusignan, who established a feudal monarchy which ruled for three centuries.
**1498** Venetian Republic took control of Cyprus.
**1571** Conquered by Ottoman Turks, who introduced Turkish Muslim settlers, but permitted Christianity to continue in rural areas.
**1821–33** Period of unrest, following execution of popular Greek Orthodox Archbishop Kyprianos.
**1878** Anglo-Turkish Convention: Turkey ceded Cyprus to British administration in return for defensive alliance.
**1914** Formally annexed by Britain after Turkey entered World War I as a Central Power.
**1915** Greece rejected an offer of Cyprus in return for entry into World War I on Allied side.
**1925** Cyprus became a crown colony.
**1931** Greek Cypriots rioted in support of demand for union with Greece (*enosis*); legislative council suspended.
**1948** Greek Cypriots rejected new constitution because it did not offer links with Greece.

**1951** Britain rejected Greek proposals for *enosis*.
**1955** National Organization of Cypriot Fighters (EOKA), led by George Grivas, began terrorist campaign for *enosis*.
**1956** British authorities deported Archbishop Makarios, head of the Cypriot Orthodox Church, for encouraging EOKA.
**1958** Britain proposed autonomy for Greek and Turkish Cypriot communities under British sovereignty; plan accepted by Turks, rejected by Greeks; violence increased.
**1959** Britain, Greece, and Turkey agreed to Cypriot independence, with partition and *enosis* both ruled out.
**1960** Cyprus became an independent republic with Archbishop Makarios as president; Britain retained two military bases.
**1963** Makarios proposed major constitutional reforms; Turkish Cypriots withdrew from government and formed separate enclaves; communal fighting broke out.
**1964** United Nations (UN) peacekeeping force installed.
**1968** Intercommunal talks made no progress; Turkish Cypriots demanded federalism; Greek Cypriots insisted on unitary state.
**1974** Coup by Greek officers in Cypriot National Guard installed Nikos Sampson as president; Turkey, fearing *enosis*, invaded northern Cyprus; Greek Cypriot military regime collapsed; President Makarios restored.
**1975** Northern Cyprus declared itself the Turkish Federated State of Cyprus, with Rauf Denktaş as president.
**1977** Makarios died; succeeded by Spyros Kyprianou.
**1983** Denktaş proclaimed independent Turkish Republic of Cyprus; recognized only by Turkey.
**1985** Summit meeting between Kyprianou and Denktaş failed to reach agreement; further peace talks failed in 1989 and 1992.
**1988** Kyprianou was succeeded as Greek Cypriot president by Georgios Vassiliou.
**1993** Glafkos Clerides (DISY) replaced Vassiliou.
**1994** The European Court of Justice declared trade with northern Cyprus illegal.
**1996** Further peace talks were jeopardized by the boundary killing of a Turkish Cypriot soldier; there was mounting tension between north and south.
**1997** The decision to purchase Russian anti-aircraft missiles created tension. UN-mediated peace talks between Clerides and Denktaş collapsed.
**1998** President Clerides was re-elected. Denktaş refused to meet a British envoy. US mediation failed. Full EU membership negotiations commenced. Greek Cyprus rejected Denktaş's confederation proposals.

**cystic fibrosis** hereditary disease involving defects of various tissues, including the sweat glands, the mucous glands of the bronchi (air passages), and the pancreas. The sufferer experiences repeated chest infections and digestive disorders and generally fails to thrive. In 1989 a gene for cystic fibrosis was identified by teams of researchers in Michigan, USA, and Toronto, Canada. This discovery enabled the development of a screening test for carriers; the disease can also be detected in the unborn child.

**cystitis** inflammation of the bladder, usually caused by bacterial infection, and resulting in frequent and painful urination. It is more common in women. Treatment is by antibiotics and copious fluids with vitamin C.

**cytology** the study of ◊cells and their functions. Major advances have been made possible in this field by the development of ◊electron microscopes.

**cytoplasm** the part of the cell outside the ◊nucleus. Strictly speaking, this includes all the ◊organelles (mitochondria, chloroplasts, and so on), but often cytoplasm refers to the jellylike matter in which the organelles are embedded (correctly termed the cytosol). The cytoplasm is the site of protein synthesis.

**Czech Republic**
*national name* Česká Republika

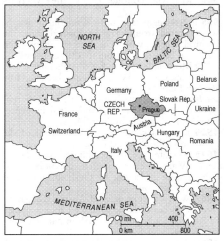

*area* 78,864 sq km/30,449 sq mi
*capital* Prague
*major towns/cities* Brno, Ostrava, Olomouc, Liberec, Plzeň, Ustí nad Labem, Hradec Králové
*physical features* mountainous; rivers: Morava, Labe (Elbe), Vltava (Moldau)
*head of state* Václav Havel from 1993
*head of government* Miloš Zeman from 1998
*political system* emergent democracy
*political parties* Civic Democratic Party (CDP), right of centre, free-market; Civic Democratic Alliance (CDA), right of centre, free-market; Civic Movement (CM), liberal, left of centre; Communist Party of Bohemia and Moravia (KSCM), reform socialist; Agrarian Party, centrist, rural-based; Liberal National Social Party (LNSP; formerly the Czech Socialist Party (SP)), reform socialist; Czech Social Democratic Party (CSDP), moderate left of centre; Christian Democratic Union–Czech People's Party (CDU–CPP), centre right; Movement for Autonomous Democracy of Moravia and Silesia (MADMS), Moravian and Silesian-based, separatist; Czech Republican Party, far right

*currency* koruna (based on Czechoslovak koruna)
*GNP per capita (PPP)* (US$) 11,640 (1998 est)
*exports* basic manufactures, machinery and transport equipment, miscellaneous manufactured articles, chemicals, beer. Principal market: Germany 35.6% (1998)
*population* 10,263,000 (1999 est)
*language* Czech (official)
*religion* Roman Catholic, Hussite, Presbyterian Evangelical Church of Czech Brethren, Orthodox
*life expectancy* 70 (men); 77 (women) (1995–2000)

**Chronology**

**5th century** Settled by West Slavs.
**8th century** Part of Charlemagne's Holy Roman Empire.
**9th century** Kingdom of Greater Moravia, centred around the eastern part of what is now the Czech Republic, founded by the Slavic prince Sviatopluk; Christianity adopted.
**906** Moravia conquered by the Magyars (Hungarians).
**995** Independent state of Bohemia in the northwest, centred around Prague, formed under the Premysl rulers, who had broken away from Moravia; became kingdom in 12th century.
**1029** Moravia became a fief of Bohemia.
**1355** King Charles IV of Bohemia became Holy Roman Emperor.
**early 15th century** Nationalistic Hussite religion, opposed to German and papal influence, founded in Bohemia by John Huss.
**1526** Bohemia came under the control of the Austrian Catholic Habsburgs.
**1618** Hussite revolt precipitated the Thirty Years' War, which resulted in the Bohemians' defeat, more direct rule by the Habsburgs, and re-Catholicization.
**1867** With creation of dual Austro-Hungarian monarchy, Bohemia was reduced to a province of Austria, leading to a growth in national consciousness.
**1918** Austro-Hungarian Empire dismembered; Czechs joined Slovaks in forming Czechoslovakia as independent democratic nation, with Tomas Masaryk president.
**1938** Under the Munich Agreement, Czechoslovakia was forced to surrender the Sudeten German districts in the north to Germany.
**1939** The remainder of Czechoslovakia annexed by Germany, Bohemia-Moravia being administered as a 'protectorate'; President Eduard Beneš set up a government-in-exile in London; liquidation campaigns against intelligentsia.
**1945** Liberated by Soviet and US troops; communist-dominated government of national unity formed under Beneš; 2 million Sudeten Germans expelled.
**1948** Beneš ousted; communists assumed full control under a Soviet-style single-party constitution.
**1950s** Political opponents purged; nationalization of industries.

**1968** 'Prague Spring' political liberalization programme, instituted by Communist Party leader Alexander Dubček, crushed by invasion of Warsaw Pact forces to restore the 'orthodox line'.
**1969** New federal constitution, creating a separate Czech Socialist Republic; Gustáv Husák became Communist Party leader.
**1977** Formation of the 'Charter '77' human-rights group by intellectuals, including the playwright Václav Havel, encouraged a crackdown against dissidents.
**1987** Reformist Miloš Jakeš replaced Husák as communist leader, and introduced a *prestvaba* ('restructuring') reform programme on the Soviet leader Mikhail Gorbachev's *perestroika* model.
**1989** Major prodemocracy demonstrations in Prague; new political parties formed and legalized, including Czech-based Civic Forum under Havel; Communist Party stripped of powers. New 'grand coalition' government formed; Havel appointed state president. Amnesty granted to 22,000 prisoners.
**1990** Multiparty elections were won by the Civic Forum.
**1991** The Civic Forum split into the centre-right Civic Democratic Party (CDP) and the centre-left Civic Movement (CM), evidence of increasing Czech and Slovak separatism.
**1992** Václav Klaus, leader of the Czech-based CDP, became prime minister; Havel resigned as president following nationalist Slovak gains in assembly elections. The creation of separate Czech and Slovak states and a customs union were agreed. A market-centred economic-reform programme was launched, including mass privatizations.
**1993** The Czech Republic became a sovereign state within the United Nations (UN), with Klaus as prime minister. Havel was elected president.
**1994** The Czech Republic joined NATO's 'partnership for peace' programme. Strong economic growth was registered.
**1996** The Czech Republic applied for European Union (EU) membership. The Klaus-led coalition lost its parliamentary majority after elections but remained in power. The ruling coalition was successful in upper-house elections.
**1997** The former communist leader Miloš Jakeš was charged with treason. The ruling coalition survived a currency crisis. The Czech Republic was invited to join NATO and to begin EU membership negotiations. Klaus resigned after allegations of misconduct.
**1998** Havel was re-elected president. The centre-left Social Democrats won a general election and a minority government was formed by Milos Zeman, including communist ministers and supported from outside by Vacláv Klaus. Full EU membership negotiations commenced.
**1999** The Czech Republic became a full member of NATO.

**dab** small marine flatfish of the flounder family, especially the genus *Limanda*. Dabs live in the North Atlantic and around the coasts of Britain and Scandinavia.

**Dacca** alternative name for ◊Dhaka, the capital of Bangladesh.

**dace** freshwater fish *Leuciscus leuciscus* of the carp family. Common in England and mainland Europe, it is silvery and grows up to 30 cm/1 ft.

**Dachau** site of a Nazi ◊concentration camp during World War II, in Bavaria, Germany. The first such camp to be set up, it opened early 1933 and functioned as a detention and forced labour camp until liberated 1945.

**dachshund** (German 'badger-dog') small dog of German origin, bred originally for digging out badgers. It has a long body and short legs. Several varieties are bred: standard size (up to 10 kg/22 lb), miniature (5 kg/11 lb or less), long-haired, smooth-haired, and wire-haired.

**Dacia** ancient region covering much of modern Romania. The various Dacian tribes were united around 60 BC, and for many years posed a threat to the Roman empire; they were finally conquered by the Roman emperor Trajan AD 101–07, and the region became a province of the same name. It was abandoned by the emperor Aurelian to the invading Goths about 270.

**Dada** or *Dadaism*, artistic and literary movement founded in 1915 in a spirit of rebellion and disillusionment during World War I and lasting until about 1922. Although the movement had a fairly short life and was concentrated in only a few centres (New York being the only non-European one), Dada was highly influential, establishing the tendency for avant-garde art movements to question traditional artistic conventions and values. There are several accounts of how the name Dada (French for hobby horse) originated; the most often quoted is that it was chosen at random by inserting a penknife into a dictionary, symbolizing the antirational nature of the movement.

**daddy-long-legs** popular name for a ◊crane fly.

**Dadra and Nagar Haveli** since 1961, a Union Territory of west India, between Gujarat and Maharashtra states; area 490 sq km/189 sq mi; population (1991) 138,500. The capital is Silvassa. Until 1954 it was part of Portuguese Daman. It produces rice, wheat, and millet. 40% of the total area is forest.

**Daedalus** in Greek mythology, a talented Athenian artisan. He made a wooden cow to disguise Pasiphae, wife of King Minos of Crete, when she wished to mate with a bull, and then constructed a ◊Labyrinth to house the creature of their union, the ◊Minotaur. Having incurred the displeasure of Minos, Daedalus fled from Crete with his son ◊Icarus, using wings made from feathers fastened with wax.

**daffodil** any of several Old World species of bulbous plants belonging to the amaryllis family, characterized by their trumpet-shaped yellow flowers which appear in spring. The common daffodil of northern Europe (*Narcissus pseudonarcissus*) has large yellow flowers and grows from a large bulb. There are numerous cultivated forms in which the colours range from white to deep orange. (Genus *Narcissus*, family Amaryllidaceae.)

**Daguerre, Louis Jacques Mandé** (1787–1851) French pioneer of photography. Together with Joseph Niépce, he is credited with the invention of photography (though others were reaching the same point simultaneously). In 1838 he invented the ◊daguerreotype, a single image process superseded ten years later by Fox Talbot's negative/positive process.

**daguerreotype** in photography, a single-image process using mercury vapour and an iodine-sensitized silvered plate; it was invented by Louis Daguerre 1838.

**Dahl, Roald** (1916–1990) British writer, of Norwegian ancestry. He is celebrated for short stories with a twist, such as *Tales of the Unexpected* (1979), and for his children's books, including *James and the Giant Peach* (1961), *Charlie and the Chocolate Factory* (1964), *The BFG* (1982), and *Matilda* (1988). Many of his works have been successfully adapted for television or film. He also wrote the screenplay for the James Bond film *You Only Live Twice* (1967), and the script for *Chitty Chitty Bang Bang* (1968).

**dahlia** any of a group of perennial plants belonging to the daisy family, comprising 20 species and many cultivated forms. Dahlias are stocky plants with tuberous roots and showy flowers that come in a wide range of colours. They are native to Mexico and Central America. (Genus *Dahlia*, family Compositae.)

**Dahomey** former name (until 1975) of the People's Republic of Benin.

**Dáil Éireann** lower house of the legislature of the Republic of Ireland (Oireachtas). It consists of 166 members elected by adult suffrage through the single transferable vote system of proportional representation, for a five-year term.

**Daimler, Gottlieb Wilhelm** (1834–1900) German engineer who pioneered the car and the internal-combustion engine together with Wilhelm Maybach. In 1885 he produced a motor bicycle and in 1889 his first four-wheeled motor vehicle. He combined the vaporization of fuel with the high-speed four-stroke petrol engine.

**daisy** any of numerous species of perennial plants belonging to the daisy family, especially the field daisy of Europe and North America (*Chrysanthemum leucanthemum*) and the English common daisy (*Bellis perennis*), with a single white or pink flower rising from a rosette of leaves. (Family Compositae.)

**Dakar** capital, chief port (with artificial harbour), and administrative centre of Senegal; population (1992) 1,729,800. It is situated at the tip of the Cape Verde peninsula, the westernmost point of Africa. It is a major industrial centre, with industries including crude-oil refining, engineering, chemicals, brewing, and tobacco and food processing. Dakar contains the Grand Mosque, National Museum, and a university (established in 1949).

**Dakota** see ◊North Dakota and ◊South Dakota.

**Dalai Lama** title of Tenzin Gyatso, (Tibetan 'oceanic guru') (1935– ) Tibetan Buddhist monk, political ruler of Tibet from 1940 until 1959, when he went into exile in protest against Chinese annexation and oppression. He has continued to campaign for self-government, and was awarded Nobel Peace Prize in 1989. Tibetan Buddhists believe that each Dalai Lama is a reincarnation of his predecessor and also of ◊Avalokiteśvara. His deputy is called the Panchen Lama.

**Dalglish, Kenny (Kenneth Mathieson)** (1951– ) Scottish footballer and football manager. A prolific goalscorer for Glasgow Celtic and then Liverpool, he was the first player to score 100 goals in both the English and Scottish first divisions. He won nine trophies as a player with Celtic and 12 with Liverpool including three European Cups. As a manager he won the league championship with Liverpool 1986, 1988, and 1990, and with Blackburn Rovers 1995. Overall, Dalglish made a record 102 international appearances for Scotland and equalled Denis Law's record of 30 goals.

**Dalí, Salvador Felippe Jacinto** (1904– 1989) Spanish painter and designer. In 1929 he joined the Surrealists (see ◊Surrealism) and became notorious for his flamboyant eccentricity. Influenced by the psychoanalytic theories of Sigmund ◊Freud, he developed a repertoire of striking, hallucinatory images – distorted human figures, limp pocket watches, and burning giraffes – in superbly executed works, which he termed 'hand-painted dream photographs'. *The Persistence of Memory* (1931; Museum of Modern Art, New York) is typical. By the late 1930s he had developed a more conventional style – this, and his apparent fascist sympathies, led to his expulsion from the Surrealist movement 1938. It was in this more traditional though still highly inventive and idiosyncratic style that he painted such celebrated religious works as *The Crucifixion* (1951; Glasgow Art School). He also painted portraits of his wife Gala.

**Dalian** *Talien* or *Dairen*, port in Liaoning province, China, on the Liaodong Peninsula, facing the Yellow Sea; population (1994) 2,638,300. Industries include engineering, oil-refining, shipbuilding, food processing (soybeans), and the manufacture of chemicals, textiles, railway locomotives, and fertilizers. It has ice-free, deep water facilities, and comprises the naval base of Lüshun (known under 19th-century Russian occupation as Port Arthur) and the commercial port of Dalian, together formerly known as Lüda.

**Dallas** commercial city in northeastern Texas, USA, on the Trinity River; seat of Dallas County; population (1994 est) 1,023,000, metropolitan area (with Fort Worth) (1994 est) 4,362,000. The second-largest city in Texas (Houston is the largest), Dallas is the hub of a rich cotton-farming and oil-producing region, and is one of the leading cultural and manufacturing centres in the Southwest; its industries include banking, insurance, oil, aviation, aerospace, and electronics. Dallas was founded in 1841, and was incorporated as a city in 1871.

**Dalmatia** region divided between Croatia, Montenegro in Yugoslavia, and Bosnia-Herzegovina. The capital is Split. It lies along the eastern shore of the Adriatic Sea and includes a number of islands. The interior is mountainous. Important products are wine, olives, and fish. Notable towns in addition to the capital are Zadar, Sibenik, and Dubrovnik.

*history* Dalmatia became Austrian 1815 and by the treaty of Rapallo 1920 became part of the kingdom of the Serbs, Croats, and Slovenes (Yugoslavia from 1931), except for the town of Zadar (Zara) and the island of Lastovo (Lagosta), which, with neighbouring islets, were given to Italy until transferred to Yugoslavia 1947.

**Dalton, John** (1766–1844) English chemist who proposed the theory of atoms, which he considered to be the smallest parts of matter. He produced the first list of relative atomic masses in 'Absorption of Gases' in 1805 and put forward the law of partial pressures of gases (*Dalton's law*).

**dam** structure built to hold back water in order to prevent flooding, to provide water for irrigation and storage, and to provide hydroelectric power. The biggest dams are of the earth- and rock-fill type, also called *embankment dams*. Early dams in Britain, built before and about 1800, had a core made from puddled clay (clay which has been mixed with water to make it impermeable). Such dams are generally built on broad valley sites. Deep, narrow gorges dictate a *concrete dam*, where the strength of reinforced concrete can withstand the water pressures involved.

**damages** in law, compensation for a ◊tort (such as personal injuries caused by negligence) or breach of contract.

In the case of breach of contract the complainant can claim all the financial loss he or she has suffered. Damages for personal injuries include compensation for loss of earnings, as well as for the injury itself. The court might reduce the damages if the claimant was partly to blame. In the majority of cases, the parties involved reach an out-of-court settlement (a compromise without going to court).

**Daman and Diu** Union Territory of west India; area 112 sq km/43 sq mi; capital Daman; population (1991) 101,400. *Daman* has an area of 72 sq km/28 sq mi. The port and capital, Daman, is on the west coast, 160 km/100 mi north of Mumbai, on the estuary of the Daman Ganga River flowing in the Gulf of Khambhat. The economy is based on tourism and fishing. *Diu* is an island off the Kathiawar peninsula with an area of 40 sq km/15 sq mi. The main town is also called Diu. The economy is based on tourism, coconuts, pearl millet, and salt.

*history* Daman was seized by Portugal in 1531 and ceded to Portugal by the Shah of Gujarat in 1539; Diu was captured by the Portuguese in 1534. Both areas were annexed by India in 1961 and were part of the Union Territory of ♭Goa, Daman, and Diu until Goa became a separate state in 1987.

**Damascus** Arabic *Dimashq* or *ash-Sham,* capital of Syria, on the River Barada, 100 km/62 mi southeast of Beirut; population (1993) 1,497,000. It produces silk, wood products, textiles, brass, and copperware. Said to be the oldest continuously inhabited city in the world, Damascus was an ancient city even in Old Testament times.

**damson** cultivated variety of plum tree, distinguished by its small oval edible fruits, which are dark purple or blue-black in colour. (*Prunus domestica* var. *institia.*)

**dance** rhythmic movement of the body, usually performed in time to music. Its primary purpose may be religious, magical, martial, social, or artistic – the last two being characteristic of non-traditional societies. The pre-Christian era had a strong tradition of ritual dance, and ancient Greek dance still exerts an influence on dance movement today. Although Western folk and social dances have a long history, the Eastern dance tradition long predates the Western. The European classical tradition dates from the 15th century in Italy, the first printed dance text from 16th-century France, and the first dance school in Paris from the 17th century. The 18th century saw the development of European classical ballet as we know it today, and the 19th century saw the rise of Romantic ballet. In the 20th century ♭modern dance firmly established itself as a separate dance idiom, not based on classical ballet, and many divergent styles and ideas have grown from a willingness to explore a variety of techniques and amalgamate different traditions.

**dandelion** common plant throughout Europe and Asia, belonging to the same family as the daisy. The stalk rises from a rosette of leaves that are deeply indented like a lion's teeth, hence the name (from French *dent de lion*). The flower heads are bright yellow, and the fruit is covered with fine hairs, known as the dandelion 'clock'. (*Taraxacum officinale,* family Compositae.)

**Dane** people of Danish culture from Denmark and northern Germany. There are approximately 5 million speakers of Danish (including some in the USA), a Germanic language belonging to the Indo-European family. The Danes are known for their seafaring culture, which dates back to the Viking age of expansion between the 8th and 10th centuries.

**danegeld** in English history, a tax imposed from 991 onwards by Anglo-Saxon kings to pay tribute to the Vikings. After the Norman Conquest (1066), the tax was revived and was levied until 1162; the Normans used it to finance military operations.

**Danelaw** 11th-century name for the area of northern and eastern England settled by the Vikings in the 9th century. It occupied about half of England, from the River Tees to the River Thames. Within its bounds, Danish law, customs, and language prevailed, rather than West Saxon or Mercian law. Its linguistic influence is still apparent in place names in this area.

**Danish language** member of the North Germanic group of the Indo-European language family, spoken in Denmark and Greenland and related to Icelandic, Faroese, Norwegian, and Swedish. It has had a particularly strong influence on Norwegian. As one of the languages of the Vikings, who invaded and settled in parts of Britain during the 9th to 11th centuries, Old Danish had a strong influence on English.

**Dante Alighieri** (1265–1321) Italian poet. His masterpiece *La divina commedia/The Divine Comedy* (1307–21) is an epic account in three parts of his journey through Hell, Purgatory, and Paradise, during which he is guided part of the way by the poet Virgil; on a metaphorical level, the journey is also one of Dante's own spiritual development. Other works include *De vulgari eloquentia/Concerning the Vulgar Tongue* (1304–06), an original Latin work on Italian, its dialects, and kindred languages; the philosophical prose treatise *Convivio/The Banquet* (1306–08), the first major work of its kind to be written in Italian rather than Latin; *De monarchia/On World Government* (1310–13), expounding his political theories; and *Canzoniere/Lyrics.*

**Danton, Georges Jacques** (1759–1794) French revolutionary. Originally a lawyer, during the early years of the Revolution he was one of the most influential people in Paris. He organized the uprising 10 August 1792 that overthrew Louis XVI and the monarchy, roused the country to expel the Prussian invaders, and in April 1793 formed the revolutionary tribunal and the ***Committee of Public Safety,*** of which he was the leader until July of that year.

Thereafter he lost power to the ♭Jacobins, and, when he attempted to recover it, was arrested and guillotined.

**Danube** German *Donau,* second longest of European rivers, rising on the eastern slopes of the Black Forest, and flowing 2,858 km/1,776 mi across Europe to enter the Black Sea in Romania by a swampy delta.

**Danzig** German name for the Polish port of ◊Gdańsk.

**Daphne** in Greek mythology, a river ◊nymph who was changed by her mother, the earth goddess ◊Gaia, into a laurel tree to escape ◊Apollo's amorous pursuit. Determined to possess her, Apollo fashioned her branches and leaves into a crown and decorated his lyre and quiver with her foliage.

**Dardanelles** (ancient name *Hellespont,* Turkish name *Canakkale Boğazi)* Turkish strait connecting the Sea of Marmara with the Aegean Sea; its shores are formed by the ◊Gallipoli peninsula on the northwest and the mainland of Anatolia on the southeast. It is 75 km/47 mi long and 5–6 km/3–4 mi wide.

**Dar es Salaam** (Arabic 'haven of peace') chief seaport in Tanzania, on the Indian Ocean, and capital of Tanzania until its replacement by ◊Dodoma in 1974; population (1988) 1,360,900. Industries include food processing, textiles, clothing, footwear, petroleum refining, and metal working. Exports include copper, coffee, sisal, and cotton.

**dark matter** matter that, according to current theories of ◊cosmology, makes up 90–99% of the mass of the universe but so far remains undetected. Dark matter, if shown to exist, would explain many currently unexplained gravitational effects in the movement of galaxies.

**Darlington** unitary authority (borough status) in northeast England, created in 1997
*area* 197 sq km/76 sq mi
*towns and cities* Darlington (administrative headquarters); villages of Hurworth on Tees, Middleton St George, Heighington, Hurworth Place
*features* River Skerne flows through Darlington, River Tees forms southern boundary of authority; Darlington Railway Centre and Museum houses English engineer George Stephenson's locomotion engine
*industries* heavy engineering, iron and steel, vehicle components, bridge building, telecommunications, fitted furniture, textiles, knitting wool, agriculture
*population* (1996) 100,600
*famous people* Joseph Dent, Ralph Hodgson.

**Darwin** port and capital of ◊Northern Territory, Australia; population (1996) 70,251. Darwin is situated on the centre of Australia's north coast, in the northwest of Arnhem Land. It is a service centre for the northern part of Northern Territory, and industries include mining (uranium and copper), horticulture, fruit growing, and tourism. Darwin was destroyed in 1974 by Cyclone Tracy, and rebuilt on the same site. It is a base for tourists visiting Kakadu National Park, Bathurst Island, and Melville Island.

**Darwin, Charles Robert** (1809–1882) English naturalist who developed the modern theory of ◊evolution and proposed, with Alfred Russel Wallace, the principle of ◊natural selection.

**DAT** abbreviation for ◊*digital audio tape.*

**data** singular datum, facts, figures, and symbols, especially as stored in computers. The term is often used to mean raw, unprocessed facts, as distinct from information, to which a meaning or interpretation has been applied.
*Continuous data* is data that can take any of an infinite number of values between whole numbers and so may not be measured completely accurately. This type of data contrasts with *discrete data,* in which the variable can only take one of a finite set of values. For example, the sizes of apples on a tree form continuous data, whereas the numbers of apples form discrete data.

**database** in computing, a structured collection of data, which may be manipulated to select and sort desired items of information. For example, an accounting system might be built around a database containing details of customers and suppliers. In larger computers, the database makes data available to the various programs that need it, without the need for those programs to be aware of how the data are stored. The term is also sometimes used for simple record-keeping systems, such as mailing lists, in which there are facilities for searching, sorting, and producing records.

**data protection** safeguarding of information about individuals stored on computers, to protect privacy.

**date** palm tree, also known as the date palm. The female tree produces the brown oblong fruit, dates, in bunches weighing 9–11 kg/20–25 lb. Dates are an important source of food in the Middle East, being rich in sugar; they are dried for export. The tree also supplies timber and materials for baskets, rope, and animal feed. (Genus *Phoenix.)*

**dating** science of determining the age of geological structures, rocks, and fossils, and placing them in the context of geological time. The techniques are of two types: relative dating and absolute dating.
*Relative dating* can be carried out by identifying fossils of creatures that lived only at certain times (marker fossils), and by looking at the physical relationships of rocks to other rocks of a known age. *Absolute dating* is achieved by measuring how much of a rock's radioactive elements have changed since the rock was formed, using the process of radiometric dating.

**dauphin** title of the eldest son of the kings of France, derived from the personal name of a count, whose lands, known as the *Dauphiné,* traditionally passed to the heir to the throne from 1349 to 1830.

**David** king of the Hebrews 1004–965 BC. He became king of Judah on the death of King Saul at Mount Gilboa in 1004 BC, then king of Israel in 997 BC. He united the tribes against the Philistines, conquering their cities (such as Ekron), and extending his kingdom over Moab and other surrounding lands. He captured Jerusalem to make it the City of David, capital of the united tribes of Israel and Judah. He was succeeded by his son Solomon, and the Davidic line ruled in Jerusalem until 586 BC when the city was destroyed by ◊Nebuchadnezzar.

**David, Jacques-Louis** (1748–1825) French painter. One of the greatest of the Neo-Classicists, he sought to give his art a direct political significance. He was an active supporter of the republic during the French Revolution, and was imprisoned 1794–95. In his *Death of Marat* (1793; Musées Royaux, Brussels), he turned political murder into Classical tragedy. Later he devoted himself to the newly created empire in grandiose paintings such as *The Coronation of Napoleon* (1805–07; Louvre, Paris).

**David** two kings of Scotland:

**David I** (1084–1153) King of Scotland from 1124. The youngest son of Malcolm III Canmore and St ◊Margaret, he was brought up in the English court of Henry I, and in 1113 married ◊Matilda, widow of the 1st earl of Northampton.

He invaded England in 1138 in support of Queen Matilda, but was defeated at Northallerton in the Battle of the Standard, and again in 1141.

**David II** (1324–1371) King of Scotland from 1329, son of ◊Robert (I) the Bruce. David was married at the age of four to Joanna, daughter of Edward II of England. In 1346 David invaded England, was captured at the battle of Neville's Cross, and imprisoned for 11 years.

**David, St** (lived 5th–6th century) or *Dewi,* Patron saint of Wales, Christian abbot and bishop. According to legend he was the son of a prince of Dyfed and uncle of King Arthur. He was responsible for the adoption of the leek as the national emblem of Wales, but his own emblem is a dove. Feast day 1 March.

**da Vinci** Italian painter, sculptor, architect, engineer, and scientist; see ◊Leonardo da Vinci.

**Davis, Bette (Ruth Elizabeth)** (1908–1989) US actress. She entered films 1930, and established a reputation as a forceful dramatic actress with *Of Human Bondage* (1934). Later films include *Jezebel* (1938; Academy Award), *Now, Voyager* (1942), *All About Eve* (1950), and *The Whales of August* (1987), in which she co-starred with Lillian Gish.

**Davis, Jefferson** (1808–1889) US politician, president of the short-lived Confederate States of America 1861–65. He was a leader of the Southern Democrats in the US Senate from 1857, and a defender of 'humane' slavery; in 1860 he issued a declaration in favour of secession from the USA. During the Civil War he assumed strong political leadership, but often disagreed with military policy. He was imprisoned for two years after the war, one of the few cases of judicial retribution against Confederate leaders.

**Davis, Miles Dewey, Jr** (1926–1991) US jazz trumpeter, composer, and bandleader. He was one of the most influential and innovative figures in jazz. He pioneered bebop with Charlie Parker 1945, cool jazz in the 1950s, and jazz-rock fusion from the late 1960s. His albums include *Birth of the Cool* (1957; recorded 1949 and 1950), *Sketches of Spain* (1959), *Bitches Brew* (1970), and *Tutu* (1985).

**Davis, Steve** (1957– ) English snooker player who has won every major honour in the game since turning professional in 1978. He has been world champion six times.

*career highlights*
**World Professional Champion** 1981, 1983–84, 1987–89
**Rothmans Grand Prix** 1985, 1988–89
**World Pairs Championship** (with Tony Meo) 1982–83, 1985–86
**World Team Championship** 1981, 1983, 1988–89
**Benson & Hedges Masters** 1982, 1988, 1997
**UK Open/Championship** 1980–81, 1984–87
**British Open** 1981–82, 1984, 1986, 1993.

**Davis Cup** annual lawn tennis tournament for men's international teams, first held 1900 after Dwight Filley Davis (1879–1945) donated the trophy.

**Davison, Emily Wilding** (1872–1913) English militant ◊suffragette who died after throwing herself under the king's horse at the Derby at Epsom (she was trampled by the horse). She joined the Women's Social and Political Union in 1906 and served several prison sentences for militant action such as stone throwing, setting fire to pillar boxes, and bombing Lloyd George's country house.

**Davy, Humphry** (1778–1829) English chemist. He discovered, by electrolysis, the metallic elements sodium and potassium in 1807, and calcium, boron, magnesium, strontium, and barium in 1808. In addition, he established that chlorine is an element and proposed that hydrogen is present in all acids. He invented the safety lamp for use in mines where methane was present, enabling miners to work in previously unsafe conditions. Knighted 1812, baronet 1818.

**Dayan, Moshe** (1915–1981) Israeli general and politician. As minister of defence 1967 and 1969–74, he was largely responsible for the victory over neighbouring Arab states in the 1967 Six-Day War, but he was criticized for Israel's alleged unpreparedness in the 1973 October War and resigned along with Prime Minister Golda ◊Meir.

**Day-Lewis, Cecil** (1904–1972) Irish poet who wrote under the name *C Day Lewis.* With W H Auden and Stephen Spender, he was one of the influential left-wing poets of the 1930s. His later poetry moved from political concerns to a more traditional personal lyricism. He also wrote detective novels under the pseudonym *Nicholas Blake.* He was British poet laureate from 1968 to 1972.

**Day-Lewis, Daniel** (1958– ) English actor. He first came to prominence in *My Beautiful Laundrette* and *A Room With a View* (both 1985). He won an Academy Award for his performance as a painter suffering from cerebral palsy in *My Left Foot* (1989).

**DCC** abbreviation for ◊*digital compact cassette.*

**D-day** 6 June 1944, the day of the Allied invasion of Normandy under the command of General Eisenhower to commence Operation Overlord, the liberation of Western Europe from German occupation. The Anglo-US invasion fleet landed on the Normandy beaches on the stretch of coast between the Orne River and St Marcouf. Artificial harbours known as 'Mulberries' were constructed and towed across the Channel so that equipment and armaments could be unloaded on to the beaches. After overcoming fierce resistance the allies broke through the German defences; Paris was liberated on 25 August, and Brussels on 2 September. D-day is also military jargon for any day on which a crucial operation is planned. D+1 indicates the day after the start of the operation.

**DDT** abbreviation for *dichloro-diphenyl-trichloroethane*, $(ClC_6H_{52}CHC(HCl_2)$ insecticide discovered in 1939 by Swiss chemist Paul Müller. It is useful in the control of insects that spread malaria, but resistant strains develop. DDT is highly toxic and persists in the environment and in living tissue. Its use is now banned in most countries, but it continues to be used on food plants in Latin America.

**deadly nightshade** another name for ◊belladonna, a poisonous plant.

**Dead Sea** large lake, partly in Israel and partly in Jordan, lying 394 m/1,293 ft below sea level; it is the lowest surface point on earth; area 1,020 sq km/394 sq mi. The chief river entering it is the Jordan; it has no outlet and the water is very salty (340 g of salt per litre of water). The sea is not, however, completely dead. *Dunaliella parva*, a single-celled green alga, and a group of halophilic (salt-loving) ◊Archaea are found here. In 1998, three species of fungi were discovered to be living in the Dead Sea. One of the species is new to science and cannot survive without salt.

**Dead Sea Scrolls** collection of ancient scrolls (rolls of writing) and fragments of scrolls found 1947–56 in caves on the western side of the Jordan, at Qumran. They include copies of Old Testament books a thousand years older than those previously known to be extant. The documents date mainly from about 150 BC–AD 68, when the monastic community that owned them, the Essenes, was destroyed by the Romans because of its support for a revolt against their rule.

**Dean, James (Byron)** (1931–1955) US actor. A stage performer who had appeared in a small number of minor film roles, Dean was killed in a car accident soon after the public showing of the first film in which he starred, Elia Kazan's *East of Eden* (1955). He posthumously became a cult hero with *Rebel Without a Cause* (1955) and *Giant* (1956). Since his death, his image has endured as the classic icon of teenage rebellion.

**death** cessation of all life functions, so that the molecules and structures associated with living things become disorganized and indistinguishable from similar molecules found in nonliving things. In medicine, a person is pronounced dead when the brain ceases to control the vital functions, even if breathing and heartbeat are maintained artificially.

**death cap** fungus of the amanita group, the most poisonous mushroom known. The fruiting body, or mushroom, has a scaly white cap and a collarlike structure (volva) near the base of the stalk. (*Amanita phalloides,* family Agaricaceae.)

**death penalty** another name for ◊capital punishment.

**death's-head moth** largest British ◊hawk moth with downy wings measuring 13 cm/5 in from tip to tip, and its thorax is marked as though with a skull.

**Death Valley** desert depression in southeastern California, USA; 225 km/140 mi long and 6–26 km/4–16 mi wide; area 8,368 sq km/3,231 sq mi. At 85 m/280 ft below sea level, Death Valley is the lowest point in North America. It is one of the world's hottest and driest places, with summer temperatures sometimes exceeding 51.7°C/125°F and an annual rainfall of less than 5 cm/2 in. Borax, iron ore, tungsten, gypsum, and salts are extracted here.

**deathwatch beetle** any wood-boring beetle of the family Anobiidae, especially *Xestobium rufovillosum*. The larvae live in oaks and willows, and sometimes cause damage by boring in old furniture or structural timbers. To attract the female, the male beetle produces a ticking sound by striking his head on a wooden surface, and this is taken by the superstitious as a warning of approaching death.

**Debrecen** second-largest city in Hungary, 193 km/120 mi east of Budapest, in the Great Plain (*Alföld*) region; population (1995) 211,000. It produces tobacco, agricultural machinery, and pharmaceuticals. Lajos ◊Kossuth declared Hungary independent of the ◊Habsburgs here 1849. It is a commercial centre and has a university founded 1912.

**de Broglie** Maurice and Louis. French physicists; see ◊Broglie.

**debt** something that is owed by a person, organization, or country, usually money, goods, or services. Debt usually occurs as a result of borrowing ◊credit. *Debt servicing* is the payment of interest on a debt. The *national debt* of a country is the total money owed by the national government to private individuals, banks, and so on; *international debt,* the money owed by one country to another, began on a large scale with the investment in foreign countries by newly industrialized countries in the late 19th to early 20th centuries. International debt became a global problem as a result of the oil crisis of the 1970s.

**debt-for-nature swap** agreement under which a proportion of a country's debts are written off in exchange for a commitment by the debtor country to undertake projects for environmental protection. Debt-for-nature swaps were set up by environment groups in the 1980s in an attempt to reduce the debt problem of poor countries, while simultaneously promoting conservation.

**Debussy, (Achille-) Claude** (1862–1918) French composer. He broke with German Romanticism and introduced new qualities of melody and harmony based on the whole-tone scale, evoking oriental music. His work includes *Prélude à l'après-midi d'un faune/Prelude to the Afternoon of a Faun* (1894), illustrating a poem by Mallarmé, and the opera *Pelléas et Mélisande* (1902).

**decathlon** two-day athletic competition for men consisting of ten events: 100 metres, long jump, shot put, high jump, 400 metres (day one); 110 metres hurdles, discus, pole vault, javelin, 1,500 metres (day two). Points are awarded for performances, and the winner is the athlete with the greatest aggregate score. The decathlon is an Olympic event.

**decay, radioactive** see ◊radioactive decay.

**decibel** unit (symbol dB) of measure used originally to compare sound intensities and subsequently electrical or electronic power outputs; now also used to compare voltages. An increase of 10 dB is equivalent to a 10-fold increase in intensity or power, and a 20-fold increase in voltage. The decibel scale is used for audibility measurements, as one decibel, representing an increase of about 25%, is about the smallest change the human ear can detect. A whisper has an intensity of 20 dB; 140 dB (a jet aircraft taking off nearby) is the threshold of pain.

**deciduous** of trees and shrubs, that shed their leaves at the end of the growing season or during a dry season to reduce ◊transpiration (the loss of water by evaporation).

**decimal fraction** in mathematics, ◊fraction in which the denominator is any higher power of 10. Thus $\frac{3}{10}$, $\frac{51}{100}$, and $\frac{23}{1,000}$ are decimal fractions and are normally expressed as 0.3, 0.51, and 0.023. The use of decimals greatly simplifies addition and multiplication of fractions, though not all fractions can be expressed exactly as decimal fractions.

**decimal number system** or *denary number system,* most commonly used number system, to the base ten. Decimal numbers do not necessarily contain a decimal point; 563, 5.63, and −563 are all decimal numbers. Other systems are mainly used in computing and include the ◊binary number system, octal number system, and ◊hexadecimal number system.

**Declaration of Independence** historic US document stating the theory of government on which the USA was founded, based on the right 'to life, liberty, and the pursuit of happiness'. The statement was issued by the ◊Continental Congress 4 July 1776, renouncing all allegiance to the British crown and ending the political connection with Britain.

**Declaration of Rights** in Britain, the statement issued by the Convention Parliament in February 1689, laying down the conditions under which the crown was to be offered to William III and Mary. Its clauses were later incorporated in the ◊Bill of Rights.

**decomposition** process whereby a chemical compound is reduced to its component substances. In biology, it is the destruction of dead organisms either by chemical reduction or by the action of decomposers, such as bacteria and fungi.

**Deconstructionism** in architecture, a style that fragments forms and space by taking the usual building elements of floors, walls, and ceilings and sliding them apart to create a sense of disorientation and movement.

**Dee** river which flows through Aberdeenshire, Scotland and the city of Aberdeen; length 137 km/85 mi. From its source in the Cairngorm Mountains, it flows east into the North Sea at Aberdeen (by an artificial channel in this latter stage). Near Braemar the river passes through a rock gorge, the **Linn of Dee**. Balmoral Castle is on its banks. It is noted for salmon fishing and is the fifth longest river in Scotland.

**Dee** river that flows through Wales and England; length 112 km/70 mi. Rising in Bala Lake, Gwynedd, it flows into the Irish Sea west of Chester.

**deed** legal document that passes an interest in property or binds a person to perform or abstain from some action. Deeds are of two kinds: indenture and deed poll. *Indentures* bind two or more parties in mutual obligations. A *deed poll* is made by one party only, such as when a person changes his or her name.

**deep-sea trench** another term for ◊ocean trench.

**deer** any of various ruminant, even-toed, hoofed mammals belonging to the family Cervidae. The male typically has a pair of antlers, shed and regrown each year. Most species of deer are forest-dwellers and are distributed throughout Eurasia and North America, but are absent from Australia and Africa south of the Sahara.

**deerhound** breed of large, rough-coated dog, formerly used in Scotland for hunting and killing deer. Slim and long-legged, it grows to 75 cm/30 in or more, usually with a bluish-grey coat.

**de Falla, Manuel** Spanish composer; see ◊Falla, Manuel de.

**Defender of the Faith** one of the titles of the English sovereign, conferred on Henry VIII in 1521 by Pope Leo X in recognition of the king's treatise against the Protestant Martin Luther. It appears on coins in the abbreviated form *F.D.* (Latin *Fidei Defensor*).

**deflation** in economics, a reduction in the level of economic activity, usually caused by an increase in interest rates and reduction in the money supply, increased taxation, or a decline in government expenditure.

**Defoe, Daniel** (1660–1731) English writer. His *Robinson Crusoe* (1719), though purporting to be a factual account of shipwreck and solitary survival, was influential in the development of the novel. The fictional *Moll Flanders* (1722) and the partly factual *A Journal of the Plague Year* (1722) are still read for their concrete realism. A prolific journalist and pamphleteer, he was imprisoned in 1703 for the ironic *The Shortest Way with Dissenters* (1702).

**deforestation** destruction of forest for timber, fuel, charcoal burning, and clearing for agriculture and extractive industries, such as mining, without planting new trees to replace those lost (reafforestation) or working on a cycle that allows the natural forest to regenerate. Deforestation causes fertile soil to be blown away or washed into rivers, leading to ◊soil erosion, drought, flooding, and loss of wildlife. It may also increase the carbon dioxide content of the atmosphere and intensify the ◊greenhouse effect, because there are fewer trees absorbing carbon dioxide from the air for photosynthesis.

**Degas, (Hilaire Germain) Edgar** (1834–1917) French Impressionist (see ◊Impressionism) painter and sculptor. He devoted himself to lively, informal studies (often using pastels) of ballet, horse racing, and young women working. From the 1890s he turned increasingly to sculpture, modelling figures in wax in a fluent, naturalistic style.

**de Gaulle, Charles André Joseph Marie** (1890–1970) French general and first president of the Fifth Republic 1958–69. He organized the Free French troops fighting the Nazis 1940–44, was head of the provisional French government 1944–46, and leader of his own Gaullist party. In 1958 the national assembly asked him to form a government during France's economic recovery and to solve the crisis in Algeria. He became president at the end of 1958, having changed the constitution to provide for a presidential system, and served until 1969.

**degree** in mathematics, a unit (symbol °) of measurement of an angle or arc. A circle or complete rotation is divided into 360°. A degree may be subdivided into 60 minutes (symbol '), and each minute may be subdivided in turn into 60 seconds (symbol ').
*Temperature* is also measured in degrees, which are divided on a decimal scale. See also ◊Celsius, and ◊Fahrenheit.

**De Havilland, Geoffrey** (1882–1965) British aircraft designer who designed and whose company produced the Moth biplane, the Mosquito fighter-bomber of World War II, and in 1949 the Comet, the world's first jet-driven airliner to enter commercial service. Knighted 1944.

**Deimos** one of the two moons of Mars. It is irregularly shaped, $15 \times 12 \times 11$ km/$9 \times 7.5 \times 7$ mi, orbits at a height of 24,000 km/15,000 mi every 1.26 days, and is not as heavily cratered as the other moon, Phobos. Deimos was discovered in 1877 by US astronomer Asaph Hall (1829–1907), and is thought to be an asteroid captured by Mars's gravity.

**Deirdre** in Celtic mythology, the beautiful intended bride of Conchobar, king of Ulster. She eloped with Noísi, and died of sorrow when Conchobar killed him and his two brothers.

**deism** (Latin *deus* 'god') belief in a supreme being. The term usually refers to a movement in the 17th and 18th centuries characterized by the belief in a rational 'religion of nature' as opposed to the orthodox beliefs of Christianity. Deists believed that God is the source of natural law but does not intervene directly in the affairs of the world, and that the only religious duty of humanity is to be virtuous.

**de Klerk, F(rederik) W(illem)** (1936–  ) South African National Party politician, president 1989–94. Projecting himself as a pragmatic conservative who sought gradual reform of the apartheid system, he won the September 1989 elections for his party, but with a reduced majority. In February 1990 he ended the ban on the ◊African National Congress (ANC) opposition movement and released its effective leader Nelson ◊Mandela. By June 1991 he had repealed all racially discriminating laws. After a landslide victory for Mandela and the ANC in the first universal suffrage elections in April 1994, de Klerk became second executive deputy president.
   He was awarded the Nobel Prize for Peace jointly with Mandela in 1993.

**Delacroix, (Ferdinand Victor) Eugène** (1798–1863) French Romantic painter. His prolific output included religious and historical subjects and portraits of friends, among them the musicians Paganini and Chopin. Antagonistic to the French academic tradition, he evolved a highly coloured, fluid style, as in *The Death of Sardanapalus* (1829;Louvre, Paris).

**de la Mare, Walter John** (1873–1956) English poet and writer. His works include verse for children, such as *Peacock Pie* (1913), and the novels *The Three Royal Monkeys* (1910) (for children) and *The Memoirs of a Midget* (1921) (for adults). He excelled at creating a sense of eeriness and supernatural mystery.

**Delaunay, Robert** (1885–1941) French painter. He was a pioneer of abstract art. With his wife Sonia Delaunay-Terk, he developed a style known as Orphism, an early variation of Cubism, focusing on the effects of pure colour contrasts.

**Delaware** state in northeastern USA. It is nicknamed the First State or the Diamond State. Delaware ratified the US Constitution in 1787, becoming the first state in the Union, hence its nickname. It is one of the most industrialized states in the USA. It is bordered to the north by Pennsylvania, to the west and south by Maryland, with which it shares the upper part of the Delmarva Peninsula, and to the east by the Atlantic Ocean
*population* (1996 est) 725,000
*area* 5,300 sq km/2,046 sq mi
*capital* Dover
*towns and cities* Wilmington, Newark
*industries and products* dairy, poultry, and market-garden produce; fishing; chemicals, motor vehicles, and textiles.

**de Lesseps, Ferdinand, vicomte** French engineer; see ◊Lesseps, Ferdinand, vicomte de Lesseps.

**Delft** town in South Holland province, the Netherlands, on the Schie Canal, 14 km/9 mi northwest of Rotterdam; population (1997) 94,000. It is known worldwide for its pottery and Delftware porcelain. Other industries include engineering, electronic equipment and cable production, and printing. There is a technical university, founded in 1863. The Dutch nationalist leader William the Silent was murdered here in 1584. It is the birthplace of the artists Jan Vermeer and Michiel van Miereveld.

**Delhi** also *Old Delhi*, city of India, and administrative capital of the Union Territory of ◊Delhi (state); population (1991) 8,375,000. It borders on ◊New Delhi, capital of India, to the south. Manufactured goods include electronic goods, chemicals, and precision instruments, as well as traditional handicrafts such as hand-woven textiles and jewellery. An international airport is 13 km/8 mi away at Palam. The University of Delhi (1922) has over 20,000 students.

**Delhi** Union Territory of India from 1956, capital ◊Delhi; area 1,500 sq km/579 sq mi; population (1994) 9,500,000. It produces grain, sugar cane, fruit, and vegetables.

**delirium** in medicine, a state of acute confusion in which the subject is incoherent, frenzied, and out of touch with reality. It is often accompanied by delusions or hallucinations.

**della Robbia** Italian family of artists; see ◊Robbia, della.

**Delors, Jacques Lucien Jean** (1925–    ) French socialist politician, economy and finance minister 1981–84 under François ◊Mitterrand's presidency, and president of the European Commission, 1985–94, when he oversaw significant budgetary reform, the introduction of the Single European Market, and the negotiation and ratification of the 1992 Maastricht Treaty on European Union.

**Delphi** city of ancient Greece, situated in a rocky valley north of the gulf of Corinth, on the southern slopes of Mount Parnassus, site of a famous ◊oracle in the temple of Apollo. The site was supposed to be the centre of the Earth and was marked by a conical stone, the *omphalos*. Towards the end of the 6th century BC the Athenian family of the Alcmaeonidae helped to rebuild the temple. The oracle was interpreted by priests from the inspired utterances of the Pythian priestess until it was closed down by the Roman emperor Theodosius I AD 390.

**delphinium** any of a group of plants containing about 250 species, including the butterfly or Chinese delphinium (*Delphinium grandiflorum*), an Asian form and one of the ancestors of the garden delphinium. Most species have blue, purple, or white flowers on a long spike. (Genus *Delphinium*, family Ranunculaceae.)

**del Sarto, Andrea** Italian Renaissance painter; see ◊Andrea del Sarto.

**delta** tract of land at a river's mouth, composed of silt deposited as the water slows on entering the sea. Familiar examples of large deltas are those of the Mississippi, Ganges and Brahmaputra, Rhône, Po, Danube, and Nile; the shape of the Nile delta is like the Greek letter *delta* Δ, and thus gave rise to the name.

**dementia** mental deterioration as a result of physical changes in the brain. It may be due to degenerative change, circulatory disease, infection, injury, or chronic poisoning. *Senile dementia*, a progressive loss of mental faculties such as memory and orientation, is typically a disease process of old age, and can be accompanied by ◊depression.

**Demeter** in Greek mythology, the goddess of agriculture, especially corn (Roman *Ceres*); daughter of the Titans Kronos and Rhea; and mother of ◊Persephone by Zeus. Demeter and her daughter were worshipped in a sanctuary at Eleusis, where the Eleusinian Mysteries, one of the foremost ◊mystery religions of Greece, were celebrated.

**democracy** (Greek *demos* 'the community', *kratos* 'sovereign power') government by the people, usually through elected representatives. In the modern world, democracy has developed from the American and French revolutions.

**Democratic Party** one of the two main political parties of the USA. It tends to be the party of the working person, as opposed to the Republicans, the party of big business, but the divisions between the two are not clear cut. Its stronghold since the Civil War has traditionally been industrial urban centres and the Southern states, but conservative Southern Democrats were largely supportive of Republican positions in the 1980s and helped elect President Reagan. Bill Clinton became the first Democrat president for 13 years in 1993. The party lost control of both chambers of Congress to the Republicans November 1994, and increasing numbers of Southern Democrat politicians later defected. However, in November 1996 Clinton became the first Democrat president since F D Roosevelt to be elected for a second term, winning 31 states, chiefly in the northeast and west.

**demography** study of the size, structure, dispersement, and development of human ◊populations to establish reliable statistics on such factors as birth and death rates, marriages and divorces, life expectancy, and migration. Demography is used to calculate life tables, which give the life expectancy of members of the population by sex and age.

**Demosthenes** (c. 384–322 BC) Athenian politician, famed for his oratory. From 351 BC he led the party that advocated resistance to the growing power of ◊Philip of Macedon, and in his *Philippics*, a series of speeches, incited the Athenians to war. This policy resulted in the defeat of Chaeronea 338, and the establishment of Macedonian supremacy. After the death of Alexander he organized a revolt; when it failed, he took poison to avoid capture by the Macedonians.

**Demotic Greek** common or vernacular variety of the modern ◊Greek language.

**demotic script** cursive (joined) writing derived from Egyptian hieratic script, itself a cursive form of ◊hieroglyphic.

Demotic documents are known from the 6th

century BC to about AD 470. It was written horizontally, from right to left.

**Dempsey, Jack (William Harrison)** (1895–1983) US heavyweight boxing champion, nicknamed 'the Manassa Mauler'. He beat Jess Willard in 1919 to win the title and held it until 1926, when he lost it to Gene Tunney. He engaged in the 'Battle of the Long Count' with Tunney 1927.

*career highlights*
*fights* fights total: 79; wins: 64; draws: 9; defeats: 6

**Denbighshire** Welsh *Sir Ddinbych,* unitary authority in north Wales. A former county, between 1974 and 1996 it was largely merged, together with Flint and part of Merioneth, into Clwyd; a small area along the western border was included in Gwynedd
*area* 844 sq km/326 sq mi
*towns* Ruthin (administrative headquarters), Denbigh, Llangollen
*physical* Clwydian range of mountains rises to a height of 555 m/1,820 ft, with ◊Offa's Dyke along the main ridge; rivers Clwyd, Dee, Elwy
*features* Denbigh and Rhuddlan castles; seaside resorts of Rhyl and Prestatyn
*industries* agriculture (chiefly dairy), tourism
*population* (1996) 91,000.

**dendrite** part of a ◊nerve cell or neuron. The dendrites are slender filaments projecting from the cell body. They receive incoming messages from many other nerve cells and pass them on to the cell body.

If the combined effect of these messages is strong enough, the cell body will send an electrical impulse along the axon (the threadlike extension of a nerve cell). The tip of the axon passes its message to the dendrites of other nerve cells.

**dendrochronology** or *tree-ring dating,* analysis of the ◊annual rings of trees to date past events by determining the age of timber. Since annual rings are formed by variations in the water-conducting cells produced by the plant during different seasons of the year, they also provide a means of establishing past climatic conditions in a given area.

**Deneb** or *Alpha Cygni,* brightest star in the constellation Cygnus, and the 20th-brightest star in the night sky. It is one of the greatest supergiant stars known, with a true luminosity of about 60,000 times that of the Sun. Deneb is about 1,800 light years from the Sun.

**Deng Xiaoping** or *Teng Hsiao-ping* (1904–1997) Chinese political leader. A member of the Chinese Communist Party (CCP) from the 1920s, he took part in the ◊Long March (1934–36). He was in the Politburo from 1955 until ousted in the ◊Cultural Revolution (1966–69). Reinstated in the 1970s, he gradually took power and introduced a radical economic modernization programme. He retired from the Politburo in 1987 and from his last official position (as chair of the State Military Commission) in March 1990. He was last seen in public in February 1994. He appointed President Jiang Zemin to succeed him on his death in 1997.

**De Niro, Robert** (1943–   ) US actor. He has frequently appeared in the works of the filmmaker Martin ◊Scorsese; for example, *Taxi Driver* (1976). He won Academy Awards for his performances in *The Godfather Part II* (1974) and *Raging Bull* (1980), in which he played a boxer struggling to control his emotional agression. He is known for his total immersion in his screen roles.

**Denktaş, Rauf R** (1924–   ) Turkish-Cypriot nationalist politician. In 1975 the Turkish Federated State of Cyprus (TFSC) was formed in the northern third of the island, with Denktaş as its head, and in 1983 he became president of the breakaway Turkish Republic of Northern Cyprus (TRNC). He was re-elected in 1995, and survived a heart attack in March 1996.

**Denmark** Kingdom of
*national name Kongeriget Danmark*

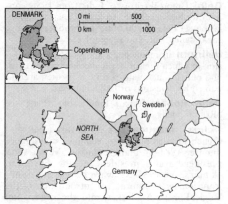

*area* 43,075 sq km/16,631 sq mi
*capital* Copenhagen
*major towns/cities* Århus, Odense, Ålborg, Esbjerg, Randers
*major ports* Århus, Odense, Ålborg, Esbjerg
*physical features* comprises the Jutland peninsula and about 500 islands (100 inhabited) including Bornholm in the Baltic Sea; the land is flat and cultivated; sand dunes and lagoons on the west coast and long inlets on the east; the main island is Sjælland (Zealand), where most of Copenhagen is located (the rest is on the island of Amager)
*territories* the dependencies of Faroe Islands and Greenland
*head of state* Queen Margrethe II from 1972
*head of government* Poul Nyrup Rasmussen from 1993
*political system* liberal democracy
*political parties* Social Democrats (SD), left of centre; Conservative People's Party (KF), moderate centre right; Liberal Party (V), centre left; Socialist People's Party (SF), moderate left wing; Radical Liberals (RV), radical internationalist, left of centre; Centre Democrats (CD), moderate centrist; Progress Party (FP), radical antibureaucratic; Christian People's Party (KrF), interdenominational, family values
*currency* Danish krone

**GNP per capita (PPP)** (US$) 23,830 (1998)
**exports** pig meat and pork products, other food products, fish, industrial machinery, chemicals, transport equipment. Principal market: Germany 21.4% (1998)
**population** 5,283,000 (1999 est)
**language** Danish (official); there is a German-speaking minority
**religion** Lutheran 97%
**life expectancy** 73 (men); 78 (women) (1995–2000)
*Chronology*
**5th–6th centuries** Danes migrated from Sweden.
**8th–10th centuries** Viking raids throughout Europe.
**c. 940–85** Harald Bluetooth unified Kingdom of Denmark and established Christianity.
**1014–35** King Canute I created empire embracing Denmark, Norway, and England; empire collapsed after his death.
**12th century** Denmark re-emerged as dominant Baltic power.
**1340–75** Valdemar IV restored order after period of civil war and anarchy.
**1397** Union of Kalmar: Denmark, Sweden, and Norway (with Iceland) united under a single monarch.
**1449** Sweden broke away from union.
**1460** Christian I secured duchies of Schleswig and Holstein.
**1523** Denmark recognized Sweden's independence.
**1536** Lutheranism established as official religion of Denmark.
**1563–70** Unsuccessful war to recover Sweden.
**1625–29** Denmark sided with Protestants in Thirty Years' War.
**1643–45** Second attempt to reclaim Sweden ended in failure.
**1657–60** Further failed attempt to reclaim Sweden.
**1665** Frederick III made himself absolute monarch.
**1729** Greenland became Danish province.
**1780–81** Denmark, Russia, and Sweden formed 'Armed Neutrality' coalition to protect neutral shipping during War of American Independence.
**1788** Serfdom abolished.
**1800** France persuaded Denmark to revive Armed Neutrality against British blockade.
**1801** First Battle of Copenhagen: much of Danish fleet destroyed by British navy.
**1807** Second Battle of Copenhagen: British seized rebuilt fleet to pre-empt Danish entry into Napoleonic War on French side.
**1814** Treaty of Kiel: Denmark ceded Norway to Sweden as penalty for supporting France in Napoleonic War; Denmark retained Iceland.
**1848–50** Germans of Schleswig-Holstein revolted with Prussian support.
**1849** Liberal pressure compelled Frederick VII to grant democratic constitution.
**1864** Prussia seized Schleswig-Holstein after short war.
**1914–1919** Denmark neutral during World War I.
**1918** Iceland achieved full self-government.
**1919** Denmark recovered northern Schleswig under peace settlement after World War I.
**1929–40** Welfare state established under left-wing coalition government dominated by Social Democrat Party.
**1940–45** German occupation.
**1944** Iceland declared independence.
**1949** Denmark became a founding member of the North Atlantic Treaty Organization (NATO).
**1960** Denmark joined the European Free Trade Association (EFTA).
**1973** Denmark withdrew from EFTA and joined the European Economic Community (EEC).
**1981** Greenland achieved full self-government.
**1992** A referendum rejected the Maastricht Treaty on European union.
**1993** A second referendum approved the Maastricht Treaty after the government negotiated a series of 'opt-out' clauses.
**1996** The Centre Democrats withdrew from the governing coalition.
**1998** The government won a slim majority in assembly elections. A referendum endorsed the Amsterdam European Union (EU) treaty.

**Denpasar** capital town of Bali in the Lesser Sunda Islands of Indonesia; population (urban area, 1990 est) 3,370,000. Industries include food processing, machinery, papermaking and printing, and handicrafts. There is a university (1962) and, housed in the temple and palace, a museum of Balinese art.

**density** measure of the compactness of a substance; it is equal to its mass per unit volume and is measured in kg per cubic metre/lb per cubic foot. Density is a scalar quantity. The average density $D$ of a mass $m$ occupying a volume $V$ is given by the formula:

$$D = \frac{m}{V}$$

Relative density is the ratio of the density of a substance to that of water at 4°C/32.2°F.

**dental caries** in medicine, another name for ◊caries.

**dental formula** way of showing the number of teeth in an animal's mouth. The dental formula consists of eight numbers separated by a line into two rows. The four above the line represent the teeth on one side of the upper jaw, starting at the front. If this reads 2 1 2 3 (as for humans) it means two incisors, one canine, two premolars, and three molars (see ◊tooth). The numbers below the line represent the lower jaw. The total number of teeth can be calculated by adding up all the numbers and multiplying by two.

**dentistry** care and treatment of the teeth and gums. *Orthodontics* deals with the straightening of the teeth for aesthetic and clinical reasons, and *periodontics* with care of the supporting tissue (bone and gums).

**dentition** type and number of teeth in a species. Different kinds of teeth have different functions; a grass-eating animal will have large molars for grinding its food, whereas a meat-eater will need powerful canines for catching

*herbivore (sheep)*

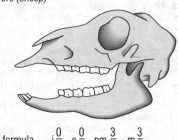

dental formula    $i\dfrac{0}{3}$  $c\dfrac{0}{0}$  $pm\dfrac{3}{3}$  $m\dfrac{3}{3}$

*carnivore (dog)*

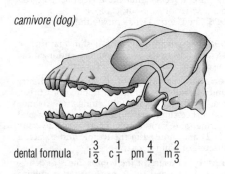

dental formula    $i\dfrac{3}{3}$  $c\dfrac{1}{1}$  $pm\dfrac{4}{4}$  $m\dfrac{2}{3}$

**dentition** *The dentition and dental formulae of a typical herbivore (sheep) and carnivore (dog). The dog has long pointed canines for puncturing and gripping its prey and has modified premolars and molars (carnassials) for shearing flesh. In the sheep, by contrast, there is a wide gap, or diastema, between the incisors, developed for cutting through blades of grass, and the grinding premolars and molars; the canines are absent.*

and killing its prey. The teeth that are less useful to an animal's lifestyle may be reduced in size or missing altogether. An animal's dentition is represented diagramatically by a ◊dental formula.

**Denver** city and capital of ◊Colorado, USA, on the South Platte River, on the western edge of the Great Plains, 24 km/15 mi from the foothills of the Rocky Mountains; population (1994 est) 494,000; Denver–Boulder metropolitan area (1994 est) 2,190,000. At 1,609 m/5,280 ft above sea level, it is known as 'Mile High City'. Denver is the commercial, manufacturing, and transportation centre for the central west region of the USA.

**deoxyribonucleic acid** full name of ◊DNA.

**Depardieu, Gérard** (1948–  ) French actor. His imposing physique and screen presence won him international acclaim as the eponymous hero in *Cyrano de Bergerac* (1990).

**depreciation** in economics, the decline of a currency's value in relation to other currencies. Depreciation also describes the fall in value of an asset (such as factory machinery) resulting

from age, wear and tear, or other circumstances. It is an important factor in assessing company profits and tax liabilities.

**depression** in economics, a period of low output and investment, with high unemployment. Specifically, the term describes two periods of crisis in world economy: 1873–96 and 1929 to the mid-1930s.

**depression** in medicine, an emotional state characterized by sadness, unhappy thoughts, apathy, and dejection. Sadness is a normal response to major losses such as bereavement or unemployment. After childbirth, ◊postnatal depression is common. Clinical depression, which is prolonged or unduly severe, often requires treatment, such as antidepressant medication, cognitive therapy, or, in very rare cases, ◊electroconvulsive therapy (ECT), in which an electrical current is passed through the brain.

**depression** or *cyclone* or *low*, in meteorology, a region of low atmospheric pressure. In mid latitudes a depression forms as warm, moist air from the tropics mixes with cold, dry polar air, producing warm and cold boundaries (◊fronts) and unstable weather – low cloud and drizzle, showers, or fierce storms. The warm air, being less dense, rises above the cold air to produce the area of low pressure on the ground. Air spirals in towards the centre of the depression in an anticlockwise direction in the northern hemisphere, clockwise in the southern hemisphere, generating winds up to gale force. Depressions tend to travel eastwards and can remain active for several days.

**De Quincey, Thomas** (1785–1859) English writer. His works include *Confessions of an English Opium-Eater* (1821) and the essays 'On the Knocking at the Gate in Macbeth' (1825) and 'On Murder Considered as One of the Fine Arts' (in three parts, 1827, 1839, and 1854). He was a friend of the poets William ◊Wordsworth and Samuel Taylor ◊Coleridge, and his work had a powerful influence on Charles Baudelaire and Edgar Allan Poe, among others.

**Derby** English horseracing event, run over 2.4 km/1.5 mi at Epsom Downs, Surrey, every June. It was established in 1780 and named after the 12th Earl of Derby. The USA has an equivalent horse race, the *Kentucky Derby*.

**Derby, Edward (George Geoffrey Smith) Stanley** 14th Earl of Derby (1799–1869) British politician. He was leader of the Conservative Party 1846–68 and prime minister 1852, 1858–59, and 1866–68, each time as head of a minority government. Originally a Whig, he became secretary for the colonies in 1830, and introduced the bill for the abolition of slavery. He joined the Tories in 1834, serving as secretary for war and the colonies in Peel's government. Derby was a protectionist and the split in the Tory party over Peel's free-trade policy gave him the leadership for 20 years. During his third adminstration, the second Reform Act (1867) was passed. He inherited the title of Lord Stanley in 1834, became a peer in 1844, and succeeded to the earldom in 1851.

**Derby City** industrial city and unitary authority in north central England, on the River Derwent, 200 km/124 mi north of London; the city was part of the county of Derbyshire until 1997
*area* 87 sq km/30 sq mi
*features* Derby Cathedral, originally a parish church, was rebuilt in the 18th century but retains its 16th-century tower; the University of Derby was established in 1993
*industries* cars (Rolls-Royce and Toyota), aero engines (Rolls-Royce), chemicals, paper, textiles, plastics, Royal Crown Derby porcelain (Royal Doulton), and electrical, mining, and engineering equipment; financial services; train repair workshops
*population* (1996) 218,800
*famous people* Herbert Spencer, Joseph Wright.

**Derbyshire** county of north central England (since April 1997 Derby City has been a separate unitary authority)
*area* 2,550 sq km/984 sq mi
*towns and cities* Matlock (administrative headquarters), Buxton, Chesterfield, Glossop, Ilkeston, Long Eaton
*physical* Peak District National Park (including Kinder Scout 636 m/2,088 ft); rivers Dane, Derwent, Dove, Goyt, Rother, Trent, Wye; Dove Dale
*features* Chatsworth House, Bakewell (seat of the Duke of Devonshire); Haddon Hall; Hardwick Hall; Kedleston Hall (designed by Robert Adam); well-dressing at Tissington, Wirksworth, Eyam, and other villages; Castleton Caverns
*agriculture* cereals, root crops, and dairy farming (in the south); sheep farming (in the northern hills)
*industries* heavy engineering; manufacturing (cotton, hosiery, lace, porcelain, textiles); mineral and metal working (barytes, gypsum, lead, zinc); quarrying (marble, sandstone, pipeclay); motor cars; limestone
*population* (1996) 962,000
*famous people* Thomas Cook, Marquess Curzon of Kedleston, Samuel Richardson.

**deregulation** action to abolish or reduce government controls and supervision of private economic activities, with the aim of improving competitiveness. In Britain, the major changes in the City of London in 1986 (the ◊Big Bang) were in part deregulation. Another UK example was the Building Societies Act 1985 that enabled building societies to compete in many areas with banks.

**dermatology** medical speciality concerned with the diagnosis and treatment of skin disorders.

**De Roburt, Hammer** (1923–1992) Nauruan politician, president 1968–76, 1978–83, and 1987–89.

**Derwent** river in North Yorkshire, northeast England; length 92 km/57 mi. Rising in the North Yorkshire moors, it flows south through Malton and joins the River Ouse southeast of Selby.

**desalination** removal of salt, usually from sea water, to produce fresh water for irrigation or drinking. Distillation has usually been the method adopted, but in the 1970s a cheaper process, using certain polymer materials that filter the molecules of salt from the water by reverse osmosis, was developed.

**Descartes, René** (1596–1650) French philosopher and mathematician. He believed that commonly accepted knowledge was doubtful because of the subjective nature of the senses, and attempted to rebuild human knowledge using as his foundation the dictum *cogito ergo sum* ('I think, therefore I am'). He also believed that the entire material universe could be explained in terms of mathematical physics, and founded coordinate geometry as a way of defining and manipulating geometrical shapes by means of algebraic expressions. ◊Cartesian coordinates, the means by which points are represented in this system, are named after him. Descartes also established the science of optics, and helped to shape contemporary theories of astronomy and animal behaviour.

**desert** arid area with sparse vegetation (or, in rare cases, almost no vegetation). Soils are poor, and many deserts include areas of shifting sands. Deserts can be either hot or cold. Almost 33% of the Earth's land surface is desert, and this proportion is increasing.

**desertification** spread of deserts by changes in climate, or by human-aided processes. Desertification can sometimes be reversed by special planting (marram grass, trees) and by the use of water-absorbent plastic grains, which, added to the soil, enable crops to be grown. About 30% of land worldwide is affected by desertification (1998), including 1 million hectares in Africa and 1.4 million hectares in Asia.

**desktop publishing** (DTP), use of microcomputers for small-scale typesetting and page makeup. DTP systems are capable of producing camera-ready pages (pages ready for photographing and printing), made up of text and graphics, with text set in different typefaces and sizes. The page can be previewed on the screen before final printing on a laser printer.

**détente** (French) reduction of political tension and the easing of strained relations between nations; for example, the ending of the Cold War 1989–90. The term was first used in the 1970s to describe the easing of East–West relations in the form of trade agreements and cultural exchanges.

**detergent** surface-active cleansing agent. The common detergents are made from ◊fats (hydrocarbons) and sulphuric acid, and their long-chain molecules have a type of structure similar to that of ◊soap molecules: a salt group at one end attached to a long hydrocarbon 'tail'. They have the advantage over soap in that they do not produce scum by forming insoluble salts with the calcium and magnesium ions present in hard water.

**determinant** in mathematics, an array of elements written as a square, and denoted by two vertical lines enclosing the array. For a 2 × 2 matrix, the determinant is given by the difference between the products of the diagonal terms. Determinants are used to solve sets of ◊simultaneous equations by matrix methods.

**determinism** in philosophy, the view that every event is an instance of some scientific law of nature; or that every event has at least one cause; or that nature is uniform. The thesis cannot be proved or disproved. Determinism is also the theory that we do not have free will, because our choices and actions are caused.

**de Tocqueville, Alexis** French politician; see ◊Tocqueville, Alexis de.

**Detroit** industrial city and port in southeastern Michigan, USA, 788 km/489 mi west of New York and 395 km/245 mi east of Chicago, situated on the Detroit River opposite the city of Windsor in Ontario, Canada; seat of Wayne County; area 370 sq km/143 sq mi (excluding neighbouring cities); metropolitan area 10,093 sq km/3,897 sq mi; population (1998) 970,196, metropolitan area 5,246,000. Detroit is the headquarters of Ford, Chrysler, and General Motors, hence its nickname, Motown (from 'motor town'). Other manufactured products include steel, machine tools, chemicals, and pharmaceuticals. It is the seventh-largest city in the USA.

**deuterium** naturally occurring heavy isotope of hydrogen, mass number 2 (one proton and one neutron), discovered by Harold Urey in 1932. It is sometimes given the symbol D. In nature, about one in every 6,500 hydrogen atoms is deuterium. Combined with oxygen, it produces 'heavy water' ($D_2O$), used in the nuclear industry.

**de Valera, Éamon** (1882–1975) Irish nationalist politician, prime minister of the Irish Free State/Eire/Republic of Ireland 1932–48, 1951–54, and 1957–59, and president 1959–73. Repeatedly imprisoned, he participated in the ◊Easter Rising in 1916 and was leader of the nationalist ◊Sinn Fein party 1917–26, when he formed the republican ◊Fianna Fáil party; he directed negotiations with Britain in 1921 but refused to accept the partition of Ireland until 1937.

**de Valois, Ninette** Stage name of Edris Stannus (1898–  ) Irish choreographer, dancer, and teacher. In setting up the Vic-Wells Ballet in 1931 (later the Royal Ballet and Royal Ballet School) she was, along with choreographer Frederick ◊Ashton, one of the architects of British ballet. Among her works are *Job* (1931), *The Rake's Progress* (1935), *Checkmate* (1937), and *The Prospect Before Us* (1940), revived by the Birmingham Royal Ballet in honour of her 100th birthday in June 1998. She is reverentially and affectionately known as 'Madam' in the ballet world.

**devaluation** in economics, the lowering of the official value of a currency against other currencies, so that exports become cheaper and imports more expensive. Used when a country is badly in deficit in its balance of trade, it results in the goods the country produces being cheaper abroad, so that the economy is stimulated by increased foreign demand.

**development** in biology, the process whereby a living thing transforms itself from a single cell into a vastly complicated multicellular organism, with structures, such as limbs, and functions, such as respiration, all able to work correctly in relation to each other. Most of the details of this process remain unknown, although some of the central features are becoming understood.

**developmental psychology** study of development of cognition and behaviour from birth to adulthood.

**devil** in Jewish, Christian, and Muslim theology, the supreme spirit of evil (*Beelzebub, Lucifer, Iblis*), or an evil spirit generally.

**devil ray** any of several large rays of the genera *Manta* and *Mobula,* in which two 'horns' project forwards from the sides of the huge mouth. These flaps of skin guide the plankton, on which the fish feed, into the mouth.

The largest of these rays can be 7 m/23 ft across, and weigh 1,000 kg/2,200 lb. They live in warm seas.

**devil's coach horse** large, black, long-bodied, omnivorous beetle *Ocypus olens,* about 3 cm/1.2 in long. It has powerful jaws and is capable of giving a painful bite. It emits an unpleasant smell when threatened.

**devolution** delegation of authority and duties; in the later 20th century, the movement to decentralize governmental power. In the UK a bill for the creation of Scottish and Welsh assemblies was introduced in 1976 and rejected by referenda in Scotland and Wales in 1979. The Labour government which took office in May 1997 introduced legislation to establish Scottish and Welsh assemblies. The ◊Scottish parliament is located in Edinburgh and the ◊National Assembly for Wales in Cardiff.

**Devon** or *Devonshire,* county of southwest England; Plymouth and Torbay have been separate unitary authorities since April 1998
*area* 6,720 sq km/2,594 sq mi
*towns and cities* Exeter (administrative headquarters); resorts: Barnstaple, Bideford, Exmouth, Ilfracombe, Sidmouth, Teignmouth, Tiverton
*physical* rivers: Dart, Exe, Plym, Tamar (94 km/58 mi), Taw, Teign, Torridge; National Parks: Dartmoor, Exmoor
*features* Lundy bird sanctuary and marine nature reserve in the Bristol Channel
*agriculture* sheep and dairy farming, beef cattle; cider and clotted cream; fishing
*industries* kaolin in the south; lace (at Honiton); Dartington glass; carpets (Axminster); quarrying (granite, limestone, sandstone); minerals (copper, iron, lead, manganese); tourism
*population* (1996) 1,059,300
*famous people* St Boniface, Henry de Bracton, Samuel Taylor Coleridge, John Davis, Francis Drake, Humphrey Gilbert, Richard

Grenville, John Hawkins, Charles Kingsley, Thomas Newcomen, Walter Raleigh, Joshua Reynolds, Robert F Scott, Joanna Southcott.

**Devonian** period of geological time 408–360 million years ago, the fourth period of the Palaeozoic era. Many desert sandstones from North America and Europe date from this time. The first land plants flourished in the Devonian period, corals were abundant in the seas, amphibians evolved from air-breathing fish, and insects developed on land.

**Devonshire, 8th Duke of** British politician; see Spencer Compton Cavendish ◊Hartington.

**dew** precipitation in the form of moisture that collects on the ground. It forms after the temperature of the ground has fallen below the dew point of the air in contact with it. As the temperature falls during the night, the air and its water vapour become chilled, and condensation takes place on the cooled surfaces.

**Dewar, James** (1842–1923) Scottish chemist and physicist who invented the ◊vacuum flask (Thermos) in 1872 during his research into the properties of matter at extremely low temperatures. Knighted 1904.

**Dewey, Melvil** (1851–1931) US librarian. In 1876, he devised the Dewey decimal system of classification for accessing, storing, and retrieving books, widely used in libraries. The system uses the numbers 000 to 999 to designate the major fields of knowledge, then breaks these down into more specific subjects by the use of decimals.

**Dhaka** or *Dacca*, capital of Bangladesh since 1971, in Dhaka region, west of the River Meghna on the ◊Ganges delta; population (1991) 3,397,200. It trades in rice, oilseed, sugar, and tea; industries include jute processing, tanning, and productions of textiles, chemicals, glass, and metal products.

**dhole** wild dog *Cuon alpinus* found in Asia from Siberia to Java. With head and body up to 1 m/39 in long, variable in colour but often reddish above and lighter below, the dhole lives in groups of from 3 to 30 individuals. The species is becoming rare and is protected in some areas.

**diabetes** disease *diabetes mellitus* in which a disorder of the islets of Langerhans in the ◊pancreas prevents the body producing the hormone ◊insulin, so that sugars cannot be used properly.

Treatment is by strict dietary control and oral or injected insulin, depending on the type of diabetes.

**Diaghilev, Sergei Pavlovich** (1872–1929) Russian ballet impresario. In 1909 he founded the Ballets Russes/Russian Ballet (headquarters in Monaco), which he directed for 20 years. Through this company he brought Russian ballet to the West, introducing a dazzling array of dancers, choreographers, composers, and artists, such as Anna Pavlova, Vaslav Nijinsky, Bronislava Nijinksa, Mikhail Fokine, Léonide Massine, George Balanchine, Igor Stravinsky, Sergey Prokofiev, Pablo Picasso, and Henri Matisse.

**dialectic** Greek term, originally associated with the philosopher Socrates' method of argument through dialogue and conversation. *Hegelian dialectic,* named after the German philosopher ◊Hegel, refers to an interpretive method in which the contradiction between a thesis and its antithesis is resolved through synthesis.

**dialectical materialism** political, philosophical, and economic theory of the 19th-century German thinkers Karl Marx and Friedrich Engels, also known as ◊Marxism.

**dialysis** technique for removing waste products from the blood suffering chronic or acute kidney failure. There are two main methods, haemodialysis and peritoneal dialysis.

**diamond** generally colourless, transparent mineral, an ◊allotrope of carbon. It is regarded as a precious gemstone, and is the hardest substance known (10 on the ◊Mohs scale). Industrial diamonds, which may be natural or synthetic, are used for cutting, grinding, and polishing.

**Diana** in Roman mythology, the goddess of chastity, hunting, and the Moon; daughter of Jupiter and twin of ◊Apollo. Her Greek equivalent is the goddess ◊Artemis.

**Diana, Princess of Wales** born Diana Frances Spencer (1961–1997) Daughter of the 8th Earl Spencer, Diana married Prince Charles in St Paul's Cathedral, London, in 1981. She had two sons, William and Harry, before her separation from Charles in 1992. In February 1996 she agreed to a divorce, after which she became known as Diana, Princess of Wales. Her worldwide prominence for charity work contributed to a massive outpouring of public grief after her death in a car crash in Paris, France, on 31 August 1997. Her funeral proved to be the biggest British televised event in history.

**diaphragm** in mammals, a thin muscular sheet separating the thorax from the abdomen. It is attached by way of the ribs at either side and the breastbone and backbone, and a central tendon. Arching upwards against the heart and lungs, the diaphragm is important in the mechanics of breathing. It contracts at each inhalation, moving downwards to increase the volume of the chest cavity, and relaxes at exhalation.

**diaphragm** or *cap* or *Dutch cap,* barrier ◊contraceptive that is passed into the vagina to fit over the cervix (neck of the uterus), preventing sperm from entering the uterus. For a cap to be effective, a ◊spermicide must be used and the diaphragm left in place for six to eight hours after intercourse. This method is 97% effective if practised correctly.

**diarrhoea** frequent or excessive action of the bowels so that the faeces are liquid or semiliquid. It is caused by intestinal irritants (including some drugs and poisons), infection with harmful organisms (as in dysentery, salmonella, or cholera), or allergies.

**diary** informal record of day-to-day events, observations, or reflections, usually not intended for a general readership. One of the earliest diaries extant is that of a Japanese noblewoman, the *Kagerō Nikki* (954–974), and the earliest known diary in English is that of Edward VI (ruled 1547–53). Notable diaries include those of Samuel ◊Pepys and Anne ◊Frank.

**Diaspora** (Greek 'dispersion') dispersal of the Jews, initially from Palestine after the Babylonian conquest 586 BC, and then following the Roman sack of Jerusalem AD 70 and their crushing of the Jewish revolt of 135. The term has come to refer to all the Jews living outside Israel.

**diatom** microscopic ◊alga found in all parts of the world in either fresh or marine waters. Diatoms consist of single cells that secrete a hard cell wall made of ◊silica. There are approximately 10,000 species of diatom. (Division Bacillariophyta.)

**diatonic scale** in music, a scale consisting of the seven notes of any major or minor key.

**Diaz, Bartholomeu** (c. 1450–1500) Portuguese explorer, the first European to reach the Cape of Good Hope, in 1488, and to establish a route around Africa. He drowned during an expedition with Pedro Cabral.

**dichloro-diphenyl-trichloroethane** full name of the insecticide ◊DDT.

**Dickens, Charles (John Huffam)** (1812–1870) English novelist. He is enduringly popular for his memorable characters and his portrayal of the social evils of Victorian England. In 1836 he published the first number of the *Pickwick Papers*, followed by *Oliver Twist* (1837), the first of his 'reforming' novels; *Nicholas Nickleby* (1838); *The Old Curiosity Shop* (1840); *Barnaby Rudge* (1841); and *David Copperfield* (1850). Among his later books are *A Tale of*

*Two Cities* (1859) and *Great Expectations* (1861). All his novels were written as serials.

**Dickinson, Emily Elizabeth** (1830–1886) US poet. She wrote most of her poetry between 1850 and the late 1860s and was particularly prolific during the Civil War years. She experimented with poetic rhythms, rhymes, and forms, as well as language and syntax. Her work is characterized by a wit and boldness that seem to contrast sharply with the reclusive life she led. Very few of her many short, mystical poems were published during her lifetime, and her work became well known only in the 20th century. The first collection of her poetry, *Poems by Emily Dickinson*, was published 1890.

**dicotyledon** major subdivision of the ◊angiosperms, containing the great majority of flowering plants. Dicotyledons are characterized by the presence of two seed leaves, or ◊cotyledons, in the embryo, which is usually surrounded by the endosperm. They generally have broad leaves with netlike veins.

**dictatorship** term or office of an absolute ruler, overriding the constitution. (In ancient Rome a dictator was a magistrate invested with emergency powers for six months.) Although dictatorships were common in Latin America during the 19th century, the only European example during this period was the rule of Napoleon III. The crises following World War I produced many dictatorships, including the regimes of Atatürk and Pilsudski (nationalist); Mussolini, Hitler, Primo de Rivera, Franco, and Salazar (all right-wing); and Stalin (communist). The most notable contemporary dictatorship is that of Saddam ◊Hussein in Iraq.

**Diderot, Denis** (1713–1784) French philosopher. He is closely associated with the

## DICKENS: MAJOR WORKS

| Title | Date | Well-known characters |
|-------|------|----------------------|
| *The Pickwick Papers* | 1836 | Mr Pickwick, Sam Weller, Mr Snodgrass, Mr Jingle, Mr and Mrs Bardell |
| *Oliver Twist* | 1837 | Oliver Twist, Fagin, Mr Bumble, The Artful Dodger |
| *Nicholas Nickleby* | 1838 | Nicholas Nickleby, Wackford Squeers, Madame Mantalini, Smike, Vincent Crummles |
| *The Old Curiosity Shop* | 1840 | Little Nell, Dick Swiveller, Daniel Quilp |
| *Barnaby Rudge* | 1841 | Simon Tappertit (Sim), Miss Miggs, Gashford |
| *A Christmas Carol* | 1843 | Ebenezer Scrooge, Bob Cratchit, Marley's Ghost, Tiny Tim |
| *Martin Chuzzlewit* | 1844 | Martin Chuzzlewit (Junior), Mr Pecksniff, Mrs Gamp, Tom Pinch |
| *Dombey and Son* | 1848 | Dombey, Paul and Florence Dombey, Edith Granger, James Carker, Major Bagstock |
| *David Copperfield* | 1850 | David Copperfield, Mr Micawber, Mr Dick, Uriah Heep, Little Em'ly, Betsey Trotwood |
| *Bleak House* | 1853 | John Jarndyce, Esther Summerson, Harold Skimpole, Lady Dedlock, Mrs Jellyby |
| *Hard Times* | 1854 | Gradgrind, Tom and Louisa Gradgrind, Josiah Bounderby, Bitzer, Cissy Jupe |
| *Little Dorrit* | 1857 | Amy Dorrit, Flora Finching, Mr Merille |
| *A Tale of Two Cities* | 1859 | Dr Manette, Charles Darnay, Sydney Carton, Jerry Cruncher, Madame Defarge |
| *Great Expectations* | 1861 | Pip, Estella, Miss Havisham, Joe Gargery, Wemmick, Magwitch |
| *Our Mutual Friend* | 1865 | Noddy Boffin, Silas Wegg, Mr Podsnap, Betty Higden, Bradley Headstone, Reginald Wilfer |
| *The Mystery of Edwin Drood* (unfinished) | 1870 | Rosa Bud, John Jasper |

Enlightenment, the European intellectual movement for social and scientific progress, and was editor of the enormously influential *Encyclopédie* (1751–80).

**didjeridu** or *didgeridoo,* musical lip-reed wind instrument, made from a hollow eucalyptus branch 1.5 m/4 ft long and blown to produce rhythmic, booming notes of relatively constant pitch. It was first developed and played by Australian Aborigines.

**Dido** or *Elissa,* in Greek mythology, a Phoenician princess and legendary founder of ◊Carthage, northern Africa, in 853 BC. She was the sister of ◊Pygmalion, king of Tyre. According to Carthaginian tradition, Dido committed suicide to avoid a marriage, but in the Latin epic *Aeneid,* Virgil places her 300 years earlier, attributing the suicide to her desertion by ◊Aeneas at the fall of Troy (traditionally 1184 BC).

**Dieppe** channel port and holiday resort at the mouth of the River Arques in Seine-Maritime *département,* northern France, 53 km/33 mi north of Rouen; population (1990) 36,600. There are ferry services from its harbour to Newhaven in England. It is a trading centre for fish and fruit; industries include fishing, shipbuilding, pharmaceuticals, and light manufacturing.

**diesel engine** ◊internal-combustion engine that burns a lightweight fuel oil. The diesel engine operates by compressing air until it becomes sufficiently hot to ignite the fuel. It is a piston-in-cylinder engine, like the ◊petrol engine, but only air (rather than an air-and-fuel mixture) is taken into the cylinder on the first piston stroke (down). The piston moves up and compresses the air until it is at a very high temperature. The fuel oil is then injected into the hot air, where it burns, driving the piston down on its power stroke. For this reason the engine is called a compression-ignition engine.

**diesel oil** lightweight fuel oil used in diesel engines. Like petrol, it is a petroleum product. When used in vehicle engines, it is also known as *derv* (diesel-engine road vehicle).

**diet** range of foods eaten by an animal each day; it is also a particular selection of food, or the total amount and choice of food for a specific person or people. Most animals require seven kinds of food in their diet: proteins, carbohydrates, fats, vitamins, minerals, water, and roughage. A diet that contains all of these things in the correct amounts and proportions is termed a balanced diet. The amounts and proportions required vary with different animals, according to their size, age, and lifestyle. The ◊digestive systems of animals have evolved to meet particular needs; they have also adapted to cope with the foods available in the surroundings in which they live. The necessity of finding and processing an appropriate diet is a very basic drive in animal evolution. *Dietetics* is the science of feeding individuals or groups; a dietition is a specialist in this science.

**Dietrich, Marlene** born Maria Magdalene Dietrich von Losch (1901–1992) German-born US actress and singer. She became a star in *Der Blaue Engel/The Blue Angel* (1930), directed by Josef von Sternberg, with whom she would collaborate throughout the 1930s. Her films include *Morocco* (1930), *Blonde Venus* (1932), *The Devil is a Woman* (1935), *Destry Rides Again* (1939), and *Touch of Evil* (1958). In the 1960s she stopped acting and began a career as a concert singer.

**differential calculus** branch of ◊calculus involving applications such as the determination of maximum and minimum points and rates of change.

**differentiation** in embryology, the process by which cells become increasingly different and specialized, giving rise to more complex structures that have particular functions in the adult organism. For instance, embryonic cells may develop into nerve, muscle, or bone cells.

**diffraction** the spreading out of waves when they pass through a small gap or around a small object, resulting in some change in the direction of the waves. In order for this effect to be observed the size of the object or gap must be comparable to or smaller than the ◊wavelength of the waves. Diffraction occurs with all forms of progressive waves – electromagnetic, sound, and water waves – and explains such

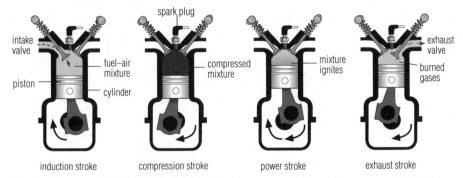

*diesel engine* In a diesel engine, fuel is injected on the power stroke into hot compressed air at the top of the cylinder, where it ignites spontaneously. The four stages are exactly the same as those of the four-stroke or Otto cycle.

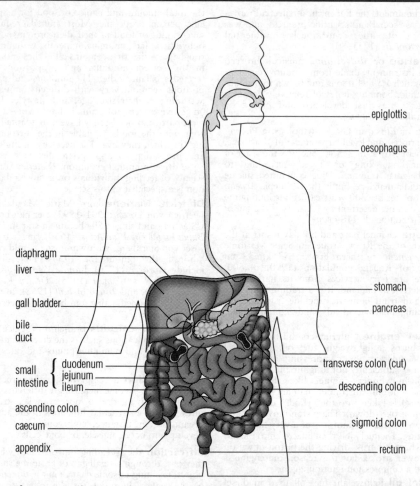

**digestive system** *The human digestive system. When food is swallowed, it is moved down the oesophagus by the action of muscles (peristalsis) into the stomach. Digestion starts in the stomach as the food is mixed with enzymes and strong acid. After several hours, the food passes to the small intestine. Here more enzymes are added and digestion is completed. After all nutrients have been absorbed, the indigestible parts pass into the large intestine and thence to the rectum. The liver has many functions, such as storing minerals and vitamins and making bile, which is stored in the gall bladder until needed for the digestion of fats. The pancreas supplies enzymes. The appendix appears to have no function in human beings.*

phenomena as why long-wave radio waves can bend round hills better than short-wave radio waves.

**diffusion** spontaneous and random movement of molecules or particles in a fluid (gas or liquid) from a region in which they are at a high concentration to a region of lower concentration, until a uniform concentration is achieved throughout. The difference in concentration between two such regions is called the *concentration gradient.* No mechanical mixing or stirring is involved. For instance, if a drop of ink is added to water, its molecules will diffuse until their colour becomes evenly distributed throughout. Diffusion occurs more rapidly across a higher concentration gradient and at higher temperature.

**digestion** process whereby food eaten by an animal is broken down mechanically, and chemically by ⟡enzymes, mostly in the ⟡stomach and ⟡intestines, to make the nutrients available for absorption and cell metabolism.

**digestive system** in the body, all the organs and tissues involved in the digestion of food. In animals, these consist of the mouth, stomach, intestines, and their associated glands. The process of digestion breaks down the food by physical and chemical means into the different elements that are needed by the body for energy and tissue building and repair. Digestion begins in the mouth and is completed in the ⟡stomach; from there most nutrients are absorbed into the small intestine from where they pass through the intestinal wall into the bloodstream; what remains is stored and concentrated into faeces in the large intestine. Birds have two additional digestive organs – the ♢crop and ♢gizzard. In smaller, simpler animals such as jellyfish, the digestive system is simply a cavity (coelenteron or enteric cavity) with a 'mouth' into which food is taken; the digestible portion is dissolved and absorbed in this cavity, and the remains are ejected back through the mouth.

**Digger** or *True Leveller,* member of an English 17th-century radical sect that attempted to seize and share out common land. The Diggers became prominent in April 1649 when, headed by Gerrard Winstanley (*c.* 1609–1660), they set up communal colonies near Cobham, Surrey, and elsewhere. These colonies were attacked by mobs and, being pacifists, the Diggers made no resistance. The support they attracted alarmed the government and they were dispersed in 1650. Their ideas influenced the early ♢Quakers.

**digit** any of the numbers from 0 to 9 in the decimal system. Different bases have different ranges of digits. For example, the ♢hexadecimal system has digits 0 to 9 and A to F, whereas the binary system has two digits (or ♢bits), 0 and 1.

**digital audio tape** (DAT), digitally recorded audio tape produced in cassettes that can carry up to two hours of sound on each side and are about half the size of standard cassettes. DAT players/recorders were developed in 1987. Prerecorded cassettes are copy-protected. The first DAT for computer data was introduced in 1988.

**digital compact cassette** (DCC) digitally recorded audio cassette that is roughly the same size as a standard cassette. It cannot be played on a normal tape recorder, though standard tapes can be played on a DCC machine; this is known as 'backwards compatibility'. The playing time is 90 minutes.

**digitalis** drug that increases the efficiency of the heart by strengthening its muscle contractions and slowing its rate. It is derived from the leaves of the common European woodland plant *Digitalis purpurea* (foxglove).

**digitalis** any of a group of plants belonging to the figwort family, which includes the ♢foxgloves. The leaves of the common foxglove (*Digitalis purpurea*) are the source of the drug *digitalis* used in the treatment of heart disease. (Genus *Digitalis*, family Scrophulariaceae.)

**digital recording** technique whereby the pressure of sound waves is sampled more than 30,000 times a second and the values converted by computer into precise numerical values. These are recorded and, during playback, are reconverted to sound waves.

**digital-to-analogue converter** electronic circuit that converts a digital signal into an ♢analogue (continuously varying) signal. Such a circuit is used to convert the digital output from a computer into the analogue voltage required to produce sound from a conventional loudspeaker.

**dik-dik** any of several species of tiny antelope, genus *Madoqua*, found in Africa south of the Sahara in dry areas with scattered brush. Dik-diks are about 60 cm/2 ft long and 35 cm/1.1 ft tall, and are often seen in pairs. Males have short, pointed horns. The dik-dik is so named because of its alarm call.

**dilatation and curettage** D and C, common gynaecological procedure in which the cervix (neck of the womb) is widened, or dilated, giving access so that the lining of the womb can be scraped away (curettage). It may be carried out to terminate a pregnancy, treat an incomplete miscarriage, discover the cause of heavy menstrual bleeding, or for biopsy.

**dill** herb belonging to the carrot family, whose bitter seeds and aromatic leaves are used in cooking and in medicine. (*Anethum graveolens,* family Umbelliferae.)

**dilution** process of reducing the concentration of a solution by the addition of a solvent.

**dimension** in science, any directly measurable physical quantity such as mass (M), length (L), and time (T), and the derived units obtainable by multiplication or division from such quantities.

For example, acceleration (the rate of change of velocity) has dimensions $(LT^{-2})$, and is expressed in such units as km s$^{-2}$. A quantity that is a ratio, such as relative density or humidity, is dimensionless.

**Dinesen, Isak** (1885–1962) Pen-name of Danish writer Karen ♢Blixen, born Dinesen.

**dingo** wild dog of Australia. Descended from domestic dogs brought from Asia by Aborigines thousands of years ago, it belongs to the same species *Canis familiaris* as other domestic dogs. It is reddish brown with a bushy tail, and often hunts at night. It cannot bark.

**dinitrogen oxide** alternative name for ♢nitrous oxide, or 'laughing gas', one of the nitrogen oxides.

**dinosaur** (Greek *deinos* 'terrible', *sauros* 'lizard') any of a group (sometimes considered as two separate orders) of extinct reptiles living between 205 million and 65 million years ago. Their closest living relations are crocodiles and birds. Many species of dinosaur evolved during the millions of years they were the dominant large land animals. Most were large (up to 27 m/90 ft), but some were as small as chickens. They disappeared 65 million years ago for reasons not fully understood, although many theories exist.

**Diocletian** Gaius Aurelius Valerius Diocletianus (AD 245–313) Roman emperor 284–305 who initiated severe persecution of Christians in 303. He was commander of the *protectores domestici* (Roman staff officers) under the emperor Numerian, and proclaimed emperor by his troops following Numerian's death. He defeated his rival Carinus in 285. In 293 he appointed Maximian (*c.* 240–*c.* 310) as co-ruler and reorganized and subdivided the empire, with two joint and two subordinate emperors. This was known as the Tetrarchic system. In 305 he abdicated in favour of Galerius, living in retirement until his death.

**diode** combination of a cold anode and a heated cathode, or the semiconductor equivalent, which incorporates a *p–n* junction semiconductor diode. Either device allows the passage of direct current in one direction only, and so is commonly used in a ◊rectifier to convert alternating current (AC) to direct current (DC).

**Diogenes** (c. 412–c. 323 BC) Ascetic Greek philosopher of the ◊cynic school. He believed in freedom and self-sufficiency for the individual, and that the virtuous life was the simple life; he did not believe in social mores. His writings do not survive.

**Dionysius** two tyrants of the ancient Greek city of Syracuse in Sicily. *Dionysius the Elder* (c. 430–367 BC) seized power 405 BC. His first two wars with Carthage further extended the power of Syracuse, but in a third (383–378 BC) he was defeated. He was a patron of ◊Plato. He was succeeded by his son, *Dionysius the Younger*, who was driven out of Syracuse by Dion 356; he was tyrant again 353, but in 343 returned to Corinth.

**Dionysus** in Greek mythology, the god of wine, mystic ecstasy, and orgiastic excess; son of princess Semele and Zeus. In his original savage form he was attended by satyrs, lustful, drunken creatures; and *maenads*, women considered capable of tearing animals to pieces with their bare hands when under his influence. Later, as a more benign deity, his rites became less extreme; the Roman ◊Bacchus embodied this form.

**Dior, Christian** (1905–1957) French couturier. He established his own Paris salon 1947 and made an impact with the 'New Look' – long, cinch-waisted, and full-skirted – after wartime austerity.

**Diouf, Abdou** (1935– ) Senegalese left-wing politician, president from 1980. He became prime minister in 1970 under President Leopold Senghor and, on his retirement, succeeded him, being re-elected in 1983, 1988, and 1993. His presidency was characterized by authoritarianism.

**dioxin** any of a family of over 200 organic chemicals, all of which are heterocyclic hydrocarbons.

The term is commonly applied, however, to only one member of the family, 2,3,7,8-tetrachlorodibenzo-*p*-dioxin (2,3,7,8-TCDD), a highly toxic chemical that occurs, for example, as an impurity in the defoliant Agent Orange, used in the Vietnam War, and sometimes in the weedkiller 2,4,5-T. It has been associated with a disfiguring skin complaint (chloracne), birth defects, miscarriages, and cancer.

**diphtheria** acute infectious disease in which a membrane forms in the throat (threatening death by ◊asphyxia), along with the production of a powerful toxin that damages the heart and nerves. The organism responsible is a bacterium (*Corynebacterium diphtheriae*). It is treated with antitoxin and antibiotics.

**diplodocus** plant-eating sauropod dinosaur that lived about 145 million years ago, the fossils of which have been found in the western USA. Up to 27 m/88 ft long, most of which was neck and tail, it weighed about 11 tonnes. It walked on four elephantine legs, had nostrils on top of the skull, and peglike teeth at the front of the mouth.

**diploid** having paired ◊chromosomes in each cell. In sexually reproducing species, one set is derived from each parent, the ◊gametes, or sex cells, of each parent being ◊haploid (having only one set of chromosomes) due to ◊meiosis (reduction cell division).

**diplomacy** process by which states attempt to settle their differences through peaceful means such as negotiation or ◊arbitration.

**dipper** or *water ouzel,* any of various birds of the genus *Cinclus,* family Cinclidae, order Passeriformes, found in hilly and mountainous regions across Eurasia and North America, where there are clear, fast-flowing streams. It can swim, dive, or walk along the bottom, using the pressure of water on its wings and tail to keep it down, while it searches for insect larvae and other small animals. Both wings and tail are short, the beak is fairly short and straight, and the general colour of the bird is brown, the throat and part of the breast being white.

**Dirac, Paul Adrien Maurice** (1902–1984) British physicist who worked out a version of quantum mechanics consistent with special ◊relativity. The existence of antiparticles, such as the positron (positive electron), was one of its predictions. He shared the Nobel Prize for Physics in 1933 with Austrian physicist Erwin ◊Schrödinger.

**direct current** (DC) electric current that flows in one direction, and does not reverse its flow as ◊alternating current does. The electricity produced by a battery is direct current.

**Dire Straits** UK rock group formed in 1977 by guitarist, singer, and songwriter Mark Knopfler (1949– ). Their tasteful musicianship, influenced by American country rock, was tailor-made for the new compact-disc audience, and their 1985 LP *Brothers in Arms* went on to sell 20 million copies. Other albums include *On Every Street* (1991). Knopfler is also much in demand as a producer.

**dirigible** another name for ◊airship.

**Dis** in Roman mythology, the god of the underworld, also known as Orcus; he is equivalent to the Greek god ◊Pluto, ruler of Hades. Dis is also a synonym for the underworld itself.

**disaccharide** ◊sugar made up of two monosaccharides or simple sugars. Sucrose, $C_{12}H_{22}O_{11}$, or table sugar, is a disaccharide.

**disarmament** reduction of a country's weapons of war. Most disarmament talks since World War II have been concerned with nuclear-arms verification and reduction, but biological, chemical, and conventional weapons have also come under discussion at the United Nations and in other forums. Attempts to limit the arms race (initially between the USA and the USSR and since 1992 between the USA and Russia) have included the ◊Strategic Arms Limitation Talks (SALT) of the 1970s and the ◊Strategic Arms Reduction Talks (START) of the 1980s–90s.

**discrimination** distinction made (social, economic, political, legal) between individuals or groups such that one has the power to treat the other unfavourably. *Negative discrimination,* often based on ◊stereotype, includes anti-Semitism, apartheid, caste, racism, sexism, and slavery. *Positive discrimination,* or 'affirmative action', is sometimes practised in an attempt to counteract the effects of previous long-term discrimination. Minorities and, in some cases, majorities have been targets for discrimination.

**discus** circular disc thrown by athletes who rotate the body to gain momentum from within a circle 2.5 m/8 ft in diameter. The men's discus weighs 2 kg/4.4 lb and the women's 1 kg/2.2 lb. Discus throwing was a competition in ancient Greece at gymnastic contests, such as those of the Olympic Games. It is an event in the modern Olympics and athletics meetings.

**disease** condition that disturbs or impairs the normal state of an organism. Diseases can occur in all life forms, and normally affect the functioning of cells, tissues, organs, or systems. Diseases are usually characterized by specific symptoms and signs, and can be mild and short-lasting – such as the common cold – or severe enough to decimate a whole species – such as Dutch elm disease. Diseases can be classified as infectious or noninfectious. Infectious diseases are caused by micro-organisms, such as bacteria and viruses, invading the body; they can be spread across a species, or transmitted between one or more species. All other diseases can be grouped together as noninfectious diseases. These can have many causes: they may be inherited (◊congenital diseases); they may be caused by the ingestion or absorption of harmful substances, such as toxins; they can result from poor nutrition or hygiene; or they may arise from injury or ageing. The causes of some diseases are still unknown.

**disk** in computing, a common medium for storing large volumes of data (an alternative is ◊magnetic tape). A *magnetic disk* is rotated at high speed in a disk-drive unit as a read/write (playback or record) head passes over its sur-

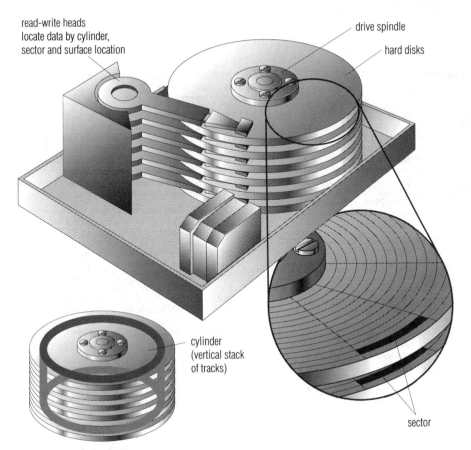

read-write heads locate data by cylinder, sector and surface location

drive spindle

hard disks

cylinder (vertical stack of tracks)

sector

**disk** A hard disk. Data is stored in sectors within cylinders and is read by a head which passes over the spinning surface of each disk.

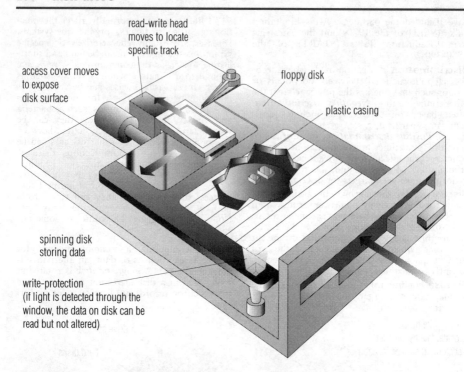

access cover moves
to expose
disk surface

read-write head
moves to locate
specific track

floppy disk

plastic casing

spinning disk
storing data

write-protection
(if light is detected through the
window, the data on disk can be
read but not altered)

**disk drive** *A floppy disk drive. As the disk is inserted into the drive, its surface is exposed to the read-write head, which moves over the spinning disk surface to locate a specific track.*

faces to record or read the magnetic variations that encode the data. Recently, *optical disks,* such as ◊CD-ROM (compact-disc read-only memory) and ◊WORM (write once, read many times), have been used to store computer data. Data are recorded on the disk surface as etched microscopic pits and are read by a laser-scanning device. Optical disks have an enormous capacity – about 550 megabytes (million ◊bytes) on a compact disc, and thousands of megabytes on a full-size optical disk.

**disk drive** mechanical device that reads data from, and writes data to, a magnetic ◊disk.

**Disney, Walt(er Elias)** (1901–1966) US filmmaker and animator, a pioneer of family entertainment. He and his brother established an animation studio in Hollywood in 1923, and his first Mickey Mouse cartoons (*Plane Crazy* (1928), which was silent, and *Steamboat Willie* (1928), which had sound and was also in colour) appeared in 1928.

In addition to short cartoons, the studio later made feature-length animated films, including *Snow White and the Seven Dwarfs* (1938), *Pinocchio* (1940), and *Dumbo* (1941). Disney's cartoon figures, such as Donald Duck, also appeared in comic books worldwide. In 1955, Disney opened the first theme park, Disneyland, in California.

**dispersion** in physics, a particular property of ◊refraction in which the angle and velocity of waves passing through a dispersive medium

depend upon their frequency. In the case of visible light the frequency corresponds to colour. The splitting of white light into a spectrum (see ◊electromagnetic waves) when it passes through a prism occurs because each component frequency of light moves through at a slightly different angle and speed. A rainbow is formed when sunlight is dispersed by raindrops.

**Disraeli, Benjamin** 1st Earl of Beaconsfield (1804–1881) British Conservative politician and novelist. Elected to Parliament in 1837, he was chancellor of the Exchequer under Lord ◊Derby 1852, 1858–59, and 1866–68, and prime minister 1868 and 1874–80. His imperialist policies brought India directly under the crown, and he was personally responsible for purchasing control of the Suez Canal. The central Conservative Party organization is his creation. His popular, political novels reflect an interest in social reform and include *Coningsby* (1844) and *Sybil* (1845).

**dissection** cutting apart of bodies to study their organization, or tissues to gain access to a site in surgery. Postmortem dissection was considered a sin in the Middle Ages. In the UK before 1832, hanged murderers were the only legal source of bodies, supplemented by graverobbing (Burke and Hare were the most notorious grave robbers). The Anatomy Act of 1832 authorized the use of deceased institutionalized paupers unclaimed by next of kin, and by the 1940s bequests of bodies had been introduced.

**Dissenter** in Britain, former name for a Protestant refusing to conform to the established Christian church. For example, Baptists, Presbyterians, and Independents (now known as Congregationalists) were Dissenters.

**distemper** any of several infectious diseases of animals characterized by catarrh, cough, and general weakness. Specifically, it refers to a virus disease in young dogs, also found in wild animals, which can now be prevented by vaccination. In 1988 an allied virus killed over 10,000 common seals in the Baltic and North seas.

**district council** lower unit of local government in England. In 1998 there were 274 district councils under 34 (two-tier) non-metropolitan county councils, and 36 single-tier metropolitan district councils. Their responsibilities cover housing, local planning and development, roads (excluding trunk and classified), bus services, environmental health (refuse collection, clean air, food safety and hygiene, and enforcement of the Offices, Shops and Railway Premises Act), council tax, museums and art galleries, parks and playing fields, swimming baths, cemeteries, and so on.

**District of Columbia** seat of the federal government of the USA, coextensive with the city of Washington, DC, situated on the Potomac and Anacostia rivers; area 178 sq km/69 sq mi; population (1996 est) 543,000. Government agencies are its main source of employment, but tourism and the manufacture of scientific and technical equipment are also important to the economy. The district was ceded by Maryland as the site of the national capital in 1790.

**diuretic** any drug that increases the output of urine by the kidneys. It may be used in the treatment of high blood pressure and to relieve ◊oedema associated with heart, lung, kidney or liver disease, and some endocrine disorders.

**diver** or *loon*, any of four species of marine bird of the order Gaviiformes, specialized for swimming and diving, found in northern regions of the northern hemisphere. The legs are set so far back that walking is almost impossible, but they are powerful swimmers and good flyers, and only come ashore to nest. They have straight bills, short tail-feathers, webbed feet, and long bodies; they feed on fish, crustaceans, and some water plants. During the breeding period they live inland and the female lays two eggs which hatch into down-covered chicks. Of the four species, the largest is the white-billed diver *Gavia adamsii*, an Arctic species 75 cm/2.5 ft long.

**dividend** in business, the amount of money that company directors decide should be taken out of net profits for distribution to shareholders. It is usually declared as a percentage or fixed amount per ◊share.

**divine right of kings** Christian political doctrine that hereditary monarchy is the system approved by God, hereditary right cannot be forfeited, monarchs are accountable to God alone for their actions, and rebellion against the lawful sovereign is therefore blasphemous.

**diving** sport of entering water either from a springboard 1 m/3 ft or 3 m/10 ft above the water, or from a platform, or highboard, 10 m/33 ft above the water. Various differing starts are adopted, facing forwards or backwards, and somersaults, twists, and combinations thereof are performed in midair before entering the water. A minimum pool depth of 5 m/16.5 ft is needed for high or platform diving. Points are awarded and the level of difficulty of each dive is used as a multiplying factor.

**divorce** legal dissolution of a lawful marriage. It is distinct from an annulment, which is a legal declaration that the marriage was invalid. The ease with which a divorce can be obtained in different countries varies considerably and is also affected by different religious practices.

**Diwali** ('garland of lamps') Hindu festival in October/November celebrating Lakshmi, goddess of light and wealth, as well as the New Year and the story of the *Rāmāyana*. It is marked by the lighting of lamps and candles (inviting the goddess into the house), feasting, and the exchange of gifts. For Sikhs, Diwali celebrates Guru Hargobind's release from prison.

**Djibouti** Republic of
*national name Jumhouriyya Djibouti*

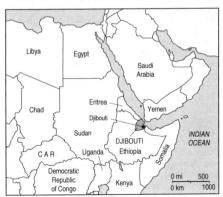

*area* 23,200 sq km/8,957 sq mi
*capital* Djibouti (and chief port)
*major towns/cities* Tadjoura, Obock, Dikhil, Ali-Sabieh
*physical features* mountains divide an inland plateau from a coastal plain; hot and arid
*head of state* Hassan Gouled Aptidon from 1977
*head of government* Barkat Gourad from 1981
*political system* emergent democracy
*political parties* People's Progress Assembly (RPP), nationalist; Democratic Renewal Party (PRD), moderate left of centre
*currency* Djibouti franc
*GNP per capita (PPP)* (US$) 1,100 (1997 est)
*exports* hides, cattle, coffee (exports are largely re-exports). Principal market: Somalia 41% (1997)
*population* 629,000 (1999 est)

*language* French (official), Somali, Afar, Arabic
*religion* Sunni Muslim
*life expectancy* 49 (men); 52 (women) (1995–2000)
*Chronology*
**3rd century BC** The north settled by Able immigrants from Arabia, whose descendants are the Afars (Danakil).
**early Christian era** Somali Issas settled in coastal areas and south, ousting Afars.
**825** Islam introduced by missionaries.
**16th century** Portuguese arrived to challenge trading monopoly of Arabs.
**1862** French acquired a port at Obock.
**1888** Annexed by France as part of French Somaliland.
**1900s** Railroad linked Djibouti port with the Ethiopian hinterland.
**1946** Became overseas territory within French Union, with own assembly and representation in French parliament.
**1958** Voted to become overseas territorial member of French Community.
**1967** French Somaliland renamed the French Territory of the Afars and the Issas.
**early 1970s** Issas (Somali) peoples campaigned for independence, but the minority Afars, of Ethiopian descent, and Europeans sought to remain French.
**1977** Independence was achieved as Djibouti, with Hassan Gouled Aptidon, the leader of the independence movement, elected president.
**1981** A new constitution made the People's Progress Assembly (RPP) the only legal party. Treaties of friendship were signed with Ethiopia, Somalia, Kenya, and Sudan.
**1984** The policy of neutrality was reaffirmed. The economy was undermined by severe drought.
**1992** A new multiparty constitution was adopted; fighting erupted between government forces and Afar Front for Restoration of Unity and Democracy (FRUD) guerrilla movement in the northeast.
**1993** Opposition parties were allowed to operate, but Gouled was re-elected president.
**1994** A peace agreement was reached with Afar FRUD militants, ending the civil war.

**Djibouti** or *Jibuti*, chief port and capital of the Republic of Djibouti, on a peninsula 240 km/149 mi southwest of Aden and 565 km/351 mi northeast of Addis Ababa; population (1995) 383,000. Industries include petroleum refining, textiles, and rail freighting. The city is an important regional bunkering and supply centre for the export trade in petroleum, and is the main export route for Ethiopian coffee.

**DNA** abbreviation for *deoxyribonucleic acid,* complex giant molecule that contains, in chemically coded form, the information needed for a cell to make proteins. DNA is a ladderlike double-stranded ◊nucleic acid which forms the basis of genetic inheritance in all organisms, except for a few viruses that have only ◊RNA. DNA is organized into ◊chromosomes and, in organisms other than bacteria, it is found in the cell nucleus.

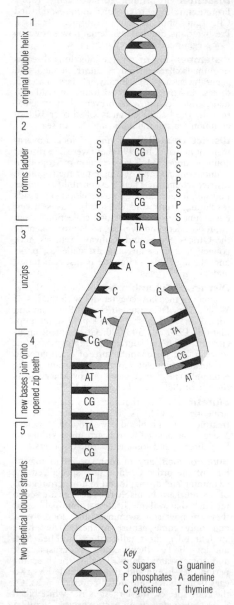

Key
S sugars    G guanine
P phosphates A adenine
C cytosine   T thymine

**DNA** How the DNA molecule divides. The DNA molecule consists of two strands wrapped around each other in a spiral or helix. The main strands consist of alternate sugar (S) and phosphate (P) groups, and attached to each sugar is a nitrogenous base – adenine (A), cytosine (C), guanine (G), or thymine (T). The sequence of bases carries the genetic code which specifies the characteristics of offspring. The strands are held together by weak bonds between the bases, cytosine to guanine, and adenine to thymine. The weak bonds allow the strands to split apart, allowing new bases to attach, forming another double strand.

**DNA finger printing** or *DNA profiling,* another name for ◊genetic fingerprinting.

**Dnieper** or *Dnepr* (Greek *Borysthenes*), river rising in the Valdai Hills west of Moscow, in the Smolensk region of the Russian Federation, and flowing south through Belarus and Ukraine to enter the Black Sea near Kherson; total length 2,250 km/1,400 mi. The Dnieper is the third longest European river (after the Volga and Danube).

**Dnipropetrovsk** city in Ukraine, on the right bank of the River Dnieper and capital of an oblast of the same name; population (1990) 1,200,000. It is the centre of a major industrial region, with iron, steel, chemical, and engineering industries. The city draws much of its power from the Dneproges Dam, 60 km/37 mi downstream.

**Dobermann** or *Dobermann pinscher,* breed of smooth-coated dog with a docked tail, much used as a guard dog. It stands up to 70 cm/27.5 in tall, has a long head with a flat, smooth skull, and is often black with brown markings. It takes its name from the man who bred it in 19th-century Germany.

**dock** or *sorrel,* in botany, any of a number of plants belonging to the buckwheat family. They are tall, annual or perennial herbs, often with lance-shaped leaves and small greenish flowers. Native to temperate regions, there are 30 North American and several British species. (Genus *Rumex,* family Polygonaceae.)

**dodecahedron** regular solid with 12 pentagonal faces and 12 vertices. It is one of the five regular polyhedra, or Platonic solids.

**Dodgson, Charles Lutwidge** Real name of writer Lewis ◊Carroll.

**dodo** extinct flightless bird *Raphus cucullatus,* order Columbiformes, formerly found on the island of Mauritius, but exterminated by early settlers around 1681. Although related to the pigeons, it was larger than a turkey, with a bulky body, rudimentary wings, and short curly tail-feathers. The bill was blackish in colour, forming a horny hook at the end.

**Dodoma** capital (replacing Dar es Salaam in 1974) of Tanzania; 1,132 m/3,713 ft above sea level; population (1988) 203,800. It is a centre of communications, linked by rail with Dar es Salaam and Kigoma on Lake Tanganyika, and by road with Kenya to the north and Zambia and Malawi to the south. Dodoma is a marketplace for locally-grown coffee and peanuts, but has a limited industrial base.

**Doe, Samuel Kanyon** (1950–1990) Liberian politician and soldier, head of state 1980–90. After seizing power in a coup, Doe made himself general and army commander in chief. As chair of the People's Redemption Council (PRC) he was the first Liberian ruler to come from an indigenous Liberian group, ending the political dominance of the US-Liberian elite. He lifted the ban on political parties in 1984 and was elected president in 1985, as leader of the newly formed National Democratic Party of Liberia. Despite alleged electoral fraud, he was sworn in during January 1986. Having successfully put down an uprising in April 1990, Doe was deposed and killed by rebel forces in September 1990. His regime was notable for incompetence and a poor human-rights record.

**dog** any carnivorous mammal of the family Canidae, including wild dogs, wolves, jackals, coyotes, and foxes. Specifically, the domestic dog *Canis familiaris,* the earliest animal descended from the wolf. Dogs were first domesticated around 14,000 years ago, and migrated with humans to all the continents. They have been selectively bred into many different varieties for use as working animals and pets.

**doge** chief magistrate in the ancient constitutions of Venice and Genoa. The first doge of Venice was appointed 697 with absolute power (modified 1297), and from his accession dates Venice's prominence in history. The last Venetian doge, Lodovico Manin, retired 1797 and the last Genoese doge 1804.

**dogfish** any of several small sharks found in the northeast Atlantic, Pacific, and Mediterranean.

**dogwood** any of a group of trees and shrubs belonging to the dogwood family, native to temperate regions of North America, Europe, and Asia. The flowering dogwood (*Cornus florida*) of the eastern USA is often cultivated as an ornamental for its beautiful blooms consisting of clusters of small greenish flowers surrounded by four large white or pink petal-like bracts (specialized leaves). (Genus *Cornus,* family Cornaceae.)

**Doha** Arabic *Ad Dawhah,* capital and chief port of Qatar; population (1992) 243,000. It is the country's only main town and port and is the sultan's residence. Industries include oil refining, refrigeration plants, engineering, and food processing. It has a deep-water port and an international airport. It is the centre of vocational training for all the Gulf states.

**doldrums** area of low atmospheric pressure along the Equator, in the intertropical convergence zone where the northeast and southeast trade winds converge. The doldrums are characterized by calm or very light winds, during which there may be sudden squalls and stormy weather. For this reason the areas are avoided as far as possible by sailing ships.

**dolerite** igneous rock formed below the Earth's surface, a form of basalt, containing relatively little silica (mafic in composition).

**Dollfuss, Engelbert** (1892–1934) Austrian Christian Socialist politician. He was appointed chancellor in 1932, and in 1933 suppressed parliament and ruled by decree. In February 1934 he crushed a protest by the socialist workers by force, and in May Austria was declared a 'corporative' state. The Nazis attempted a coup on 25 July; the Chancellery was seized and Dollfuss murdered.

**dolomite** in mineralogy, white mineral with a rhombohedral structure, calcium magnesium carbonate (CaMg $(CO_3)_2$). Dolomites are common in geological successions of all ages and are often formed when ◊limestone is changed by the replacement of the mineral calcite with the mineral dolomite.

**dolphin** any of various highly intelligent aquatic mammals of the family Delphinidae, which also includes porpoises. There are about 60 species. Most inhabit tropical and temperate oceans, but there are some freshwater forms in rivers in Asia, Africa, and South America. The name 'dolphin' is generally applied to species having a beaklike snout and slender body, whereas the name 'porpoise' is reserved for the smaller species with a blunt snout and stocky body. Dolphins use sound (◊echolocation) to navigate, to find prey, and for communication. The common dolphin *Delphinus delphis* is found in all temperate and tropical seas. It is up to 2.5 m/8 ft long, and is dark above and white below, with bands of grey, white, and yellow on the sides. It has up to 100 teeth in its jaws, which make the 15 cm/6 in 'beak' protrude forward from the rounded head. The corners of its mouth are permanently upturned, giving the appearance of a smile, though dolphins cannot actually smile. Dolphins feed on fish and squid.

**Domesday Book** record of the survey of England carried out in 1086 by officials of William the Conqueror in order to assess land tax and other dues, ascertain the value of the crown lands, and enable the king to estimate the power of his vassal barons. The name is derived from the belief that its judgement was as final as that of Doomsday.

**dominance** in genetics, the masking of one allele (an alternative form of a gene) by another allele. For example, if a heterozygous person has one allele for blue eyes and one for brown eyes, his or her eye colour will be brown. The allele for blue eyes is described as ◊recessive and the allele for brown eyes as dominant.

**dominant** in music, the fifth note of the diatonic scale, for example, G in the C major scale. The chord of the dominant is related to the tonic chord by the dominant note, which corresponds to its third harmonic. Classical modulation involves a harmonic progression from the tonic to the dominant and back. The return may be a symmetrical journey, as in the binary form of a sonata by Scarlatti, or an abrupt resolution of dominant to tonic chords in a 'perfect' cadence.

**Domingo, Placido** (1941– ) Spanish lyric tenor. He specializes in Italian and French 19th-century operatic roles to which he brings a finely-tuned dramatic temperament. As a youth in Mexico, he sang baritone roles in zarzuela (musical theatre), moving up to tenor as a member of the Israel National Opera 1961–64. Since his New York debut in 1965 he has established a world reputation as a sympathetic leading tenor, and has made many films including the 1988 version of Puccini's *Tosca* set in Rome, and the 1990 Zeffirelli production of Leoncavallo's *I Pagliacci/The Strolling Players*. He also sang with José ◊Carreras and Luciano Pavarotti in a recording of operatic hits released to coincide with the World Cup soccer series in Rome in 1990, and again in the USA in 1994. He was named artistic director of the Los Angeles Opera in November 1998, and will assume the post in 2000.

**Dominica** Commonwealth of

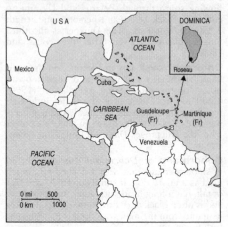

**area** 751 sq km/290 sq mi
**capital** Roseau, with a deepwater port
**major towns/cities** Portsmouth, Berekua, Marigot, Rosalie
**major ports** Roseau, Portsmouth, Berekua, Marigot, Rosalie
**physical features** second-largest of the Windward Islands, mountainous central ridge with tropical rainforest
**head of state** Vernon Shaw from 1998
**head of government** Edison James from 1995
**political system** liberal democracy
**political parties** Dominica Freedom Party (DFP), centrist; Labour Party of Dominica (LPD), left-of-centre coalition; Dominica United Workers' Party (DUWP), left of centre
**currency** Eastern Caribbean dollar; pound sterling; French franc
**GNP per capita (PPP)** (US$) 3,940 (1998)
**exports** bananas, soap, coconuts, grapefruit, galvanized sheets. Principal market: UK 32.8% (1997)
**population** 75,000 (1999 est)
**language** English (official), but the Dominican patois reflects earlier periods of French rule
**religion** Roman Catholic 80%
**life expectancy** 75 (men); 81 (women) (1998 est)
**Chronology**
**1493** Visited by the explorer Christopher Columbus, who named the island Dominica ('Sunday Island').
**1627** Presented by the English King Charles I to the Earl of Carlisle, but initial European attempts at colonization were fiercely resisted by the indigenous Carib community.
**later 18th century** Succession of local British and French conflicts over control of the fertile island.
**1763** British given possession of the island by the Treaty of Paris (ending the Seven Years' War), but France continued to challenge this

militarily until 1805, when there was formal cession in return for the sum of £12,000.

**1834** Slaves, who had been brought in from Africa, were emancipated.

**1870** Became part of the British Leeward Islands federation.

**1940** Transferred to British Windward Islands federation.

**1951** Universal adult suffrage established.

**1958–62** Part of the West Indies Federation.

**1960** Granted separate, semi-independent status, with a legislative council and chief minister.

**1961** Edward leBlanc, leader of newly formed DLP, became chief minister.

**1974** LeBlanc retired; replaced as chief minister by Patrick John (DLP).

**1978** Independence was achieved as a republic within the Commonwealth, with John as prime minister.

**1980** The DFP won a convincing victory in a general election, and Eugenia Charles became the Caribbean's first woman prime minister.

**1981** John was implicated in a plot to overthrow the government, but was subsequently acquitted.

**1983** A small force participated in the US-backed invasion of Grenada.

**1985** John was retried, found guilty, and sentenced to 12 years' imprisonment. The regrouping of left-of-centre parties resulted in the new Labour Party of Dominica (LPD).

**1991** A Windward Islands confederation comprising St Lucia, St Vincent, Grenada, and Dominica was proposed.

**1993** Charles resigned the DFP leadership, but continued as prime minister.

**1995** DUWP won a general election; Edison James was appointed prime minister and Eugenia Charles retired from politics.

**1998** Vernon Shaw elected president.

## Dominican Republic
*national name* República Dominicana

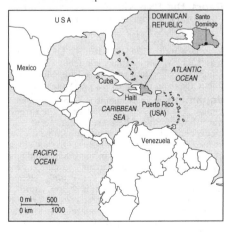

**area** 48,442 sq km/18,703 sq mi
**capital** Santo Domingo
**major towns/cities** Santiago de los Caballeros, La Romana, San Pedro de Macoris, San

Francisco de Macoris, Concepcion de la Vega, San Juan

*physical features* comprises eastern two-thirds of island of Hispaniola; central mountain range with fertile valleys; Pico Duarte 3,174 m/10,417 ft, highest point in Caribbean islands

*head of state and government* Leoned Fernandez from 1996

*political system* democracy

*political parties* Dominican Revolutionary Party (PRD), moderate, left of centre; Christian Social Reform Party (PRSC), independent socialist; Dominican Liberation Party (PLD), nationalist

*currency* Dominican Republic peso

*GNP per capita (PPP)* (US$) 4,700 (1998)

*exports* raw sugar, molasses, coffee, cocoa, tobacco, ferro-nickel, gold, silver. Principal market: USA 44.7% (1997)

*population* 8,365,000 (1999 est)

*language* Spanish (official)

*religion* Roman Catholic

*life expectancy* 69 (men); 73 (women) (1995–2000)

*Chronology*

**14th century** Settled by Carib Indians, who followed an earlier wave of Arawak Indian immigration.

**1492** Visited by Christopher Columbus, who named it Hispaniola ('Little Spain').

**1496** At Santo Domingo, the Spanish established the first European settlement in the western hemisphere, which became capital of all Spanish colonies in America.

**first half of 16th century** One-third of a million Arawaks and Caribs died, as a result of enslavement and exposure to European diseases; black African slaves were consequently brought in to work the island's gold and silver mines, which were swiftly exhausted.

**1697** Divided between France, which held the western third (Haiti), and Spain, which held the east (Dominican Republic, or Santo Domingo).

**1795** Santo Domingo was ceded to France.

**1808** Following a revolt by Spanish Creoles, with British support, Santo Domingo was retaken by Spain.

**1821** Became briefly independent after uprising against Spanish rule, and then fell under the control of Haiti.

**1844** Separated from Haiti to form Dominican Republic.

**1861–65** Under Spanish protection.

**1904** The USA took over the near-bankrupt republic's debts.

**1916–24** Temporarily occupied by US forces.

**1930** Military coup established personal dictatorship of Gen Rafael Trujillo Molina after overthrow of president Horacio Vázquez.

**1937** Army massacred 19,000–20,000 Haitians living in the Dominican provinces adjoining the frontier.

**1961** Trujillo assassinated.

**1962** First democratic elections resulted in Juan Bosch, founder of the left-wing Dominican Revolutionary Party (PRD), becoming president.

**1963** Bosch overthrown in military coup.

**1965** 30,000 US marines intervened to restore

order and protect foreign nationals after Bosch had attempted to seize power.

**1966** New constitution adopted. Joaquín Balaguer, protégé of Trujillo and leader of the centre-right Christian Social Reform Party (PRSC), became president.

**1978** PRD returned to power, with Silvestre Antonio Guzmán as president.

**1982** PRD re-elected, with Jorge Blanco as president.

**1985** Blanco was forced by the International Monetary Fund to adopt austerity measures to save the economy.

**1986** The PRSC returned to power; Balaguer was re-elected president.

**1990** Balaguer was re-elected by a small majority.

**1994** Balaguer was re-elected; the election results were disputed by the opposition but were eventually declared valid on the condition that Balaguer serve a reduced two-year term.

**1996** Leoned Fernandez of the left-wing Dominican Liberation Party (PLD) was elected president.

**1998** The Dominican Revolutionary Party (PRD) won an assembly victory.

**Don** Ancient Greek *Tanais,* navigable river in the western Russian Federation; length 1,870 km/1,162 mi; basin covers 422,000 sq km/162,934 sq mi. The Don rises in the central Russian uplands near the city of Tula, flows southeast towards the Volga near Volgograd, then turns southwest to empty into the northeast of the Sea of Azov. In its lower reaches the Don is 1.5 km/1 mi wide, and for about four months of the year it is closed by ice. It has long been a major traffic artery linking inland European Russia with the Black Sea. Its chief tributaries are the Donets, Voronezh, Khoper, and Medveditsa, and it is linked to the Volga by the Volga–Don Canal. The main port is Rostov-on-Don, which lies near the river's mouth.

**Donatello** Donato di Niccolo Bardi (c. 1386–1466) Italian sculptor of the early Renaissance. He was instrumental in reviving the Classical style, as in his graceful bronze statue of the youthful *David* (about 1433; Bargello, Florence) and his equestrian statue of the general *Gattamelata* (1447–50; Piazza del Santo, Padua). The course of Florentine art in the 15th century was strongly influenced by his work.

**Donau** German name for the River ◊Danube.

**Donegal** mountainous county in the northwest of the Republic of Ireland, surrounded on three sides by the Atlantic Ocean, and bordering the counties of Londonderry, Tyrone, and Fermanagh (Northern Ireland), and Leitrim (Republic of Ireland); area 4,830 sq km/1,864 sq mi; county town Lifford; population (1991) 127,900. Ballyshannon is the largest town, and the market town and port of *Donegal* is at the head of *Donegal Bay* in the southwest. The severe climate renders much of the county barren, although the soil is suitable for potatoes, oats, and barley in places. Commercial activities include sheep and cattle raising, tweed, linen, and carpet manufacture, and some salmon and deep-sea fishing. Tourism is also very important; the county is noted for dramatic scenery and geology as well as archaeological and historic remains. The River Erne hydroelectric project (1952) involved the building of a large artificial lake (405 ha/1,000 acres) and a power station at Ballyshannon.

**Donetsk** city in Ukraine; capital of Donetsk region (oblast), situated in the Donets Basin, a major coal-mining area, 600 km/372 mi southeast of Kiev; population (1996) 1,121,000. Donetsk has blast furnaces, rolling mills, and other heavy industries.

**Donizetti, (Domenico) Gaetano (Maria)** (1797–1848) Italian composer. He created more than 60 operas, including *Lucrezia Borgia* (1833), *Lucia di Lammermoor* (1835), *La Fille du régiment* (1840), *La Favorite* (1840), and *Don Pasquale* (1843). They show the influence of Rossini and Bellini, and are characterized by a flow of expressive melodies.

**Don Juan** Italian *Don Giovanni,* character of Spanish legend, Don Juan Tenorio, supposed to have lived in the 14th century and notorious for his debauchery. Tirso de Molina, Molière, Mozart, Byron, and George Bernard Shaw have featured the legend in their works.

**donkey** another name for ◊ass.

**Donne, John** (1572–1631) English metaphysical poet. His work consists of love poems, religious poems, verse satires, and sermons. His sermons rank him with the century's greatest orators, and his fervent poems of love and hate, violent, tender, or abusive, give him a unique position among English poets. A Roman Catholic in his youth, he converted to the Church of England and finally became dean of St Paul's Cathedral, London.

**Doomsday Book** variant spelling of ◊Domesday Book, the English survey of 1086.

**Doors, the** US psychedelic rock group formed in 1965 in Los Angeles by Jim Morrison (1943–1971, vocals), Ray Manzarek (1935– , keyboards), Robby Krieger (1946– , guitar), and John Densmore (1944– , drums). Their first hit was 'Light My Fire' from their debut album *The Doors* (1967). They were noted for Morrison's poetic lyrics and flamboyant performance.

**dopamine** neurotransmitter, hydroxytyramine $C_8H_{11}NO_2$, an intermediate in the formation of adrenaline. There are special nerve cells (neurons) in the brain that use dopamine for the transmission of nervous impulses. One such area of dopamine neurons lies in the basal ganglia, a region that controls movement. Patients suffering from the tremors of Parkinson's disease show nerve degeneration in this region. Another dopamine area lies in the limbic system, a region closely involved with emotional responses. It has been found that schizophrenic patients respond well to drugs that limit dopamine excess in this area.

**Doppler effect** change in the observed frequency (or wavelength) of waves due to relative motion between the wave source and the observer. The Doppler effect is responsible for the perceived change in pitch of a siren as it approaches and then recedes, and for the ◊red shift of light from distant galaxies. It is named after the Austrian physicist Christian Doppler.

**Dordogne** river in southwest France, rising on the slopes of the Puy de Sancy in the Massif Central, Puy-de-Dôme *département,* and flowing 490 km/300 mi through Souillac, Bergerac, Castillon, Libourne, and Cubzac, to join the River Garonne at Ambes, 23 km/14 mi north of Bordeaux. The river is a major source of hydroelectric power, and the last 180 km/112 mi of its course sees much river traffic. It gives its name to the Dordogne *département.*

**Doré, (Paul) Gustave** (1832–1883) French artist. Chiefly known as a prolific illustrator, he was also active as a painter, etcher, and sculptor. He produced closely worked engravings of scenes from, for example, Rabelais, Dante, Cervantes, the Bible, Milton, and Edgar Allan Poe.

**Dorian** people of ancient Greece. They entered Greece from the north and took most of the Peloponnese from the Achaeans, perhaps destroying the ◊Mycenaean civilization; this invasion appears to have been completed before 1000 BC. Their chief cities were Sparta, Argos, and Corinth.

**dormouse** small rodent, of the family Gliridae, with a hairy tail. There are about ten species, living in Europe, Asia, and Africa. They are arboreal (live in trees) and nocturnal, hibernating during winter in cold regions. They eat berries, nuts, pollen, and insects.

**dorsal** in vertebrates, the surface of the animal closest to the backbone. For most vertebrates and invertebrates this is the upper surface, or the surface furthest from the ground. For bipedal primates such as humans, where the dorsal surface faces backwards, then the word is 'back'.

**Dorset** county of southwest England (since April 1997 Bournemouth and Poole have been separate unitary authorities)
*area* 2,541 sq km/981 sq mi
*towns and cities* Dorchester (administrative headquarters), Shaftesbury, Sherborne; Lyme Regis, Weymouth, Poole (resorts)
*physical* Chesil Beach, a shingle bank along the coast 19 km/11 mi long, connecting Isle of Portland to the mainland; Dorset Downs (chalk); River Stour, and rivers Frome and Piddle (which flow into Poole Harbour); clay beds in the north and west; Canford Heath, the home of some of Britain's rarest breeding birds and reptiles (including the nightjar, Dartford warbler, sand lizard, and smooth snake)
*features* Isle of Purbeck, a peninsula where china clay and Purbeck 'marble' are quarried, and which includes Corfe Castle and the holiday resort of Swanage; Cranborne Chase; Maiden Castle (prehistoric earthwork); Tank Museum at Royal Armoured Corps Centre, Bovington, where the cottage of the soldier and writer T E ◊Lawrence is a museum; Wimborne Minster; abbey church of Sherborne
*agriculture* dairy farming

*industries* Wytch Farm is the largest onshore oilfield in the UK; production at Wareham onshore oilfield started in 1991; quarrying (marble from the Isle of Purbeck, and Portland stone, which has been used for buildings all over the world); manufacturing (rope, twine, and net at Bridport); sand and gravel extraction; tourism
*population* (1996) 681,900
*famous people* Anthony Ashley Cooper, Thomas Hardy, Thomas Love Peacock

**Dortmund** city and industrial centre in the ◊Ruhr, in North Rhine-Westphalia, Germany, 58 km/36 mi northeast of Düsseldorf; population (1995) 600,000. It is the largest mining town of the Westphalian coalfield and the southern terminus of the Dortmund–Ems Canal. The enlargement of the Wesel–Datteln Canal (1989), connecting Dortmund to the Rhine River, allows barges to travel between Dortmund and Rotterdam in the Netherlands. Industries include coal, iron, and steel (headquarters of Hoesch), mechanical engineering, and brewing (output exceeds that of Munich), and high-tech industries are developing. There is also a modern university.

**dory** marine fish *Zeus faber* found in the Mediterranean and Atlantic. It grows up to 60 cm/2 ft, and has nine or ten long spines at the front of the dorsal fin, and four at the front of the anal fin. It is considered to be an excellent food fish and is also known as *John Dory.*

**DOS** acronym for disk operating system, computer ◊operating system specifically designed for use with disk storage; also used as an alternative name for a particular operating system, MS-DOS.

**Dos Santos, José Eduardo** (1942– ) Angolan left-wing politician, president from 1979, a member of the People's Movement for the Liberation of Angola (MPLA). By 1989, he had negotiated the withdrawal of South African and Cuban forces, and in 1991 a peace agreement to end the civil war. In 1992 his victory in multiparty elections was disputed by Jonas Savimbi, leader of the rebel group National Union for the Total Independence of Angola (◊UNITA), and fighting resumed, escalating into full-scale civil war in 1993. Representatives of the two leaders signed a peace agreement in 1994. Dos Santos' proposal to make Savimbi vice-president was declined by the latter in 1996.

**Dostoevsky, Fyodor Mihailovich** (1821–1881) Russian novelist. Remarkable for their profound psychological insight, Dostoevsky's novels have greatly influenced Russian writers, and since the beginning of the 20th century have been increasingly influential abroad. In 1849 he was sentenced to four years' hard labour in Siberia, followed by army service, for printing socialist propaganda. *The House of the Dead* 1861 recalls his prison experiences, followed by his major works *Crime and Punishment* (1866), *The Idiot* (1868–69), and *The Brothers Karamazov* (1879–80).

**dotterel** bird *Eudromias morinellus* of the plover family, in order Charadriiformes, nesting on high moors and tundra in Europe and Asia, and migrating south for the winter. About 23 cm/9 in long, its plumage is patterned with black, brown, and white in summer, duller in winter, but always with white eyebrows and breastband. The female is larger than the male, and mates up to five times with different partners, each time laying her eggs and leaving them in the sole care of the male, who incubates and rears the brood. Three pale-green eggs with brown markings are laid in hollows in the ground.

**Douala** or *Duala,* chief port and industrial centre of Cameroon, on the Wouri River estuary by the Gulf of Guinea; population (1991) 884,000. Industries include aluminium, chemicals, textiles, and pulp. Known as Kamerunstadt until 1907, it was capital of German Cameroon, which became a German protectorate in 1884, 1885–1901.

**double bass** large, bowed four-stringed (sometimes five-stringed) musical instrument, the bass of the violin family. It is descended from the bass viol or violone. Until 1950, after which it was increasingly superseded by the electric bass, it also provided bass support (plucked) for jazz and dance bands. Performers include Domenico Dragonetti, composer of eight concertos, the Russian-born US conductor Serge Koussevitsky (1874–1951), and the jazz player and composer Charles Mingus. The double bass features in the well-loved 'Elephants' solo, No 5 of Saint-Saëns' *Carnival of the Animals* (1897).

**double star** two stars that appear close together. Many stars that appear single to the naked eye appear double when viewed through a telescope. Some double stars attract each other due to gravity, and orbit each other, forming a genuine ◊binary star, but other double stars are at different distances from Earth, and lie in the same line of sight only by chance. Through a telescope both types look the same.

**Douglas** capital of the Isle of Man in the Irish Sea; population (1991) 22,200. It is situated in the southeast of the island, and is a holiday resort and terminus of shipping routes to and from Fleetwood and Liverpool. Banking and financial services are important, and the Manx Parliament, Tynwald meets here.

**Douglas, Kirk** stage name of Issur Danielovitch Demsky (1916–  ) US film actor. Usually cast as a dynamic though ill-fated hero, as in *Spartacus* (1960), he was a major star of the 1950s and 1960s, appearing in such films as *Ace in the Hole* (1951), *The Bad and the Beautiful* (1953), *Lust for Life* (1956), *The Vikings* (1958), *Seven Days in May* (1964), and *The War Wagon* (1967). He received the American Film Institute's life achievement award in 1991 and a lifetime achievement Academy Award in 1995. In March 1999 he received the Screen Actors Guild Life Achievement Award.

**Douglas, Michael (Kirk)** (1944–  ) US film actor and producer. He made his feature-film acting debut in *Hail, Hero!* (1969) and produced the award-winning *One Flew Over the Cuckoo's Nest* (1975). He won an Academy Award for his portrayal of a ruthless entrepreneur in *Wall Street* (1987).

**Douglas fir** any of some six species of coniferous evergreen tree belonging to the pine family. The most common is *Pseudotsuga menziesii,* native to western North America and east Asia. It grows up to 60–90 m/200–300 ft in height, has long, flat, spirally-arranged needles and hanging cones, and produces hard, strong timber. *P. glauca* has shorter, bluish needles and grows to 30 m/100 ft in mountainous areas. (Genus *Pseudotsuga,* family Pinaceae.)

**Douglas-Home, Alec (Alexander Frederick)** Baron Home of the Hirsel (1903–1995) British Conservative politician. He was foreign secretary 1960–63, and succeeded Harold Macmillan as prime minister in 1963. He renounced his peerage (as 14th Earl of Home) and re-entered the Commons after successfully contesting a by-election, but failed to win the 1964 general election, and resigned as party leader in 1965. He was again foreign secretary 1970–74, when he received a life peerage. The playwright William Douglas-Home was his brother. Knighted 1962.

**Doulton, Henry** (1820–1897) English ceramicist. He developed special wares for the chemical, electrical, and building industries, and established the world's first stoneware-drainpipe factory in 1846. From 1870 he created art pottery and domestic tablewares in Lambeth, South London, and Burslem, near Stoke-on-Trent. He was knighted in 1887.

**Dounreay** site of the world's first fast-breeder nuclear reactor (1962) on the north coast of Scotland, in the Highland unitary authority, 12 km/7 mi west of Thurso. It is now a nuclear reprocessing plant.

**Douro** Spanish *Duero,* river in Spain and Portugal, the third largest in the Iberian peninsula; length 775 km/482 mi. It rises in Spain, on the south side of the Peña de Urbión in the province of Soria, and flows west across the plateau of Castile. It follows the Spanish-Portuguese frontier for 105 km/65 mi, and reaches the Atlantic Ocean at São João de Foz, 5 km/3 mi south of ◊Pôrto. Navigation at the river mouth is hindered by sand bars. There are hydroelectric installations along its course.

**dove** person who takes a moderate, sometimes pacifist, view on political issues. The term originated in the US during the Vietnam War. Its counterpart is a hawk. In more general usage today, a dove is equated with liberal policies, and a hawk with conservative ones.

**dove** another name for ◊pigeon.

**Dover** market town and seaport in Kent, southeast England, on the coast of the English Channel; population (1991) 34,200. It is Britain's nearest point to mainland Europe, 34 km/21 mi from Calais, France. Dover is the world's busiest passenger port and England's principal cross-channel port, with ferry, hovercraft, and cross-channel train services. Industries include electronics, paper manufacturing, and light engineering.

**Dover, Strait of** French *Pas-de-Calais,* stretch of water separating England from France, and connecting the English Channel with the North Sea. It is about 35 km/22 mi long and 34 km/21 mi wide at its narrowest part (from Dover pier to Cap Griz-Nez); its greatest depth is 55 m/180 ft. It is one of the world's busiest sea lanes. The main ports are Dover and Folkestone (England), and Calais and Boulogne (France).

**Dowell, Anthony James** (1943– ) English classical ballet dancer. He is known for his elegant poise, accurate finish, and exemplary classical style. He was principal dancer with the Royal Ballet 1966–86, and became artistic director in 1986.

**Dow Jones average** New York Stock Exchange index, the most widely used indicator of US stock market prices. The average (no longer simply an average but today calculated to take into account changes in the constituent companies) is based on prices of 30 major companies, such as IBM and Walt Disney. It was first compiled 1884 by Charles Henry Dow, cofounder of Dow Jones & Co., publishers of the *Wall Street Journal.*

**Dow Jones Index** *Dow Jones Industrial 30 Share Index,* scale for measuring the average share price and percentage change of 30 major US industrial companies. It has been calculated and published since 1897 by the financial news publisher Dow Jones and Co.

**Down** county of southeastern Northern Ireland
*area* 2,470 sq km/953 sq mi
*towns and cities* Downpatrick (county town), Bangor (seaside resort), Newtownards, Newry, and Banbridge; the northern part lies within the commuter belt for Belfast, and includes part of the city of Belfast, east of the River Lagan
*physical* Mourne Mountains; Strangford sea lough
*industries* light manufacturing, plastics, linen, high technology and computer companies, fishing, quarrying
*agriculture* County Down has very fertile land. The principal crops are barley, potatoes, and oats; there is livestock rearing and dairying
*population* (1981) 339,200
*government* the county returns two members to the UK Parliament.

**Downing Street** street in Westminster, London, leading from Whitehall to St James's Park, named after Sir George Downing (died 1684), a diplomat under Cromwell and Charles II. *Number 10* is the official residence of the prime minister and *number 11* is the residence of the chancellor of the Exchequer. *Number 12* is the office of the government whips. After his appointment as prime minister May 1997, Tony Blair chose to use Number 11 to accommodate his family, using Number 10 as his office and for Cabinet meetings. The chancellor of the Exchequer, Gordon Brown, retained his office in Number 11 but used the flat above Number 10 as his residence.

**Down's syndrome** condition caused by a chromosomal abnormality (the presence of an extra copy of chromosome 21), which in humans produces mental retardation; a flattened face; coarse, straight hair; and a fold of skin at the inner edge of the eye (hence the former name 'mongolism'). The condition can be detected by prenatal testing.

**Doyle, Arthur Conan** (1859–1930) Scottish writer. He created the detective Sherlock ◊Holmes and his assistant Dr Watson, who first appeared in *A Study in Scarlet* (1887) and featured in a number of subsequent stories, including *The Hound of the Baskervilles* (1902). Among Doyle's other works is the fantasy adventure *The Lost World* (1912). In his later years he became a spiritualist and wrote a *History of Spiritualism* (1926).

**D'Oyly Carte, Richard** (1844–1901) English producer of the Gilbert and Sullivan operas. They were performed at the Savoy Theatre, London, which he built. The D'Oyly Carte Opera Company, founded in 1876, was disbanded in 1982 following the ending of its monopoly on the Gilbert and Sullivan operas. The present company, founded in 1988, moved to the Alexandra Theatre, Birmingham, in 1991.

**Drabble, Margaret** (1939– ) English writer. Her novels include *The Millstone* (1965), *The Middle Ground* (1980), the trilogy *The Radiant Way* (1987), *A Natural Curiosity* (1989), and *The Gates of Ivory* (1991), and *The Witch of Exmoor* (1996). She portrays contemporary life with toughness and sensitivity, often through the eyes of intelligent modern women.

**Draco** in astronomy, a large but faint constellation represented as a dragon coiled around the north celestial pole. Due to ◊precession the star Alpha Draconis (Thuban) was the pole star 4,800 years ago.

**Draco** (lived 7th century BC) Athenian politician, the first to codify the laws of the Athenian city-state. These were notorious for their severity; hence *draconian,* meaning particularly harsh.

**Dracula** in the novel *Dracula* (1897) by Bram Stoker, the caped count who, as a ◊vampire, drinks the blood of beautiful women. The original of Dracula is thought to have been Vlad Tepes, or Vlad the Impaler, ruler of medieval Wallachia, who used to impale his victims and then mock them.

**dragon** name popularly given to various sorts of lizard. These include the flying dragon *Draco volans* of southeast Asia; the komodo dragon *Varanus komodoensis* of Indonesia, at over 3 m/10 ft the largest living lizard; and some Australian lizards with bizarre spines or frills.

**dragonfly** any of numerous insects of the order Odonata, including the damselfly. They all have long narrow bodies, two pairs of almost equalsized, glassy wings with a network of veins; short, bristlelike antennae; powerful, 'toothed' mouthparts; and very large compound eyes which may have up to 30,000 facets. They can fly at speeds of up to 64–96 kph/40–60 mph.

**Drake, Francis** (c. 1540–1596) English bucca-neer and explorer. Having enriched himself as a pirate against Spanish interests in the Caribbean 1567–72, he was sponsored by Elizabeth I for an expedition to the Pacific, sailing round the world 1577–80 in the *Golden Hind*, robbing Spanish ships as he went. This was the second circum-navigation of the globe (the first was by the Portuguese explorer Ferdinand Magellan). Drake also helped to defeat the ◊Spanish Armada in 1588 as a vice admiral in the *Revenge*.

**drama** (Greek 'action') in theatre, any play composed to be performed by actors for an audience. The term is also used collectively to group plays into historical or stylistic periods – for example, Greek drama, Restoration drama – as well as referring to the whole body of work written by a dramatist for performance. Drama is distinct from literature in that it is a perform-ing art open to infinite interpretation, the prod-uct not merely of the dramatist but also of the collaboration of director, designer, actors, and technical staff. See also ◊theatre, ◊comedy, ◊tragedy, and ◊pantomime.

**dream** series of events or images perceived through the mind during sleep. Their function is unknown, but Sigmund ◊Freud saw them as wish fulfilment (nightmares being failed dreams prompted by fears of 'repressed' impulses). Dreams occur in periods of rapid eye movement (REM) by the sleeper, when the cortex of the brain is approximately as active as in waking hours. Dreams occupy about a fifth of sleeping time.

**Dreamtime** or *Dreaming*, mythical past of the Australian Aborigines, the basis of their reli-gious beliefs and creation stories. In the Dreamtime, spiritual beings shaped the land, the first people were brought into being and set in their proper territories, and laws and rituals were established. Belief in a creative spirit in the form of a huge snake, the Rainbow Serpent, occurs over much of Aboriginal Australia, usu-ally associated with waterholes, rain, and thun-der. A common feature of religions across the continent is the Aborigines' bond with the land.

**Drenthe** low-lying northern province of the Netherlands, south of Groningen and Friesland
*area* 2,660 sq km/1,027 sq mi
*capital* Assen
*cities* Emmen, Hoogeveen
*physical* fenland and moors; well-drained clay and peat soils
*industries* petroleum
*agriculture* livestock, arable crops, horticul-ture
*population* (1997) 460,800
*history* governed in the Middle Ages by provincial nobles and by bishops of Utrecht, Drenthe was eventually acquired by Charles V of Spain in 1536. It developed following land drainage initiated in the mid-18th century and was established as a separate province of the Netherlands in 1796.

**Dresden** capital of the *Land* (state) of ◊Saxony, Germany, lying in a wide basin in the upper Elbe Valley; population (1995) 472,900. Products include chemicals, machinery, glass-ware, and musical instruments; telecommunica-tions and high-tech industries are also important. One of the most beautiful German cities, with a rich architectural and cultural her-itage, it was devastated by Allied bombing in 1945; much rebuilding has since taken place, and the city has become an important tourist destination.

**Dreyfus, Alfred** (1859–1935) French army officer, victim of miscarriage of justice, anti-Semitism, and cover-up. Employed in the War Ministry, in 1894 he was accused of betraying military secrets to Germany, court-martialled, and sent to the penal colony on Devil's Island, French Guiana. When his innocence was discov-ered in 1896 the military establishment tried to conceal it, and the implications of the Dreyfus affair were passionately discussed in the press until he was exonerated in 1906.

**dromedary** variety of Arabian ◊camel. The dromedary or one-humped camel has been domesticated since 400 BC. During a long period without water, it can lose up to one-quarter of its body weight without ill effects.

**drug** any of a range of substances, natural or synthetic, administered to humans and animals as therapeutic agents: to diagnose, prevent, or treat disease, or to assist recovery from injury. Traditionally many drugs were obtained from plants or animals; some minerals also had medicinal value. Today, increasing numbers of drugs are synthesized in the laboratory.

**drug misuse** illegal use of drugs for nonther-apeutic purposes. Under the UK Misuse of Drugs regulations drugs used illegally include: narcotics, such as heroin, morphine, and the synthetic opioids; barbiturates; amphetamines and related substances; ◊benzodiazepine tran-quillizers; cocaine, LSD, and cannabis. *Designer drugs*, for example ecstasy, are usually modifica-tions of the amphetamine molecule, altered in order to evade the law as well as for different effects, and may be many times more powerful and dangerous. Crack, a highly toxic derivative of cocaine, became available to drug users in the 1980s. Some athletes misuse drugs such as ephedrine and ◊anabolic steroids.

In 1998 there were an estimated 100,000 problem drug users in Britain.

**Druidism** religion of the Celtic peoples of the pre-Christian British Isles and Gaul. The word is derived from the Greek *drus* ('oak'), a tree regarded by the Druids as sacred. One of the Druids' chief rites was the cutting of mistletoe from the oak with a golden sickle. They taught the immortality of the soul and a reincarnation doctrine, and were expert in astronomy. The Druids are thought to have offered human sacri-fices.

**drum** any of a class of percussion instruments including *slit drums* made of wood, *steel drums* fabricated from oil containers, and a majority group of *skin drums* consisting of a shell or ves-sel of wood, metal, or earthenware across one or both ends of which is stretched a membrane of hide or plastic. Drums are struck with the hands or with a stick or pair of sticks; they are among the oldest instruments known.

**drupe** fleshy ◊fruit containing one or more seeds which are surrounded by a hard, protective layer – for example cherry, almond, and plum. The wall of the fruit (◊pericarp) is differentiated into the outer skin (exocarp), the fleshy layer of tissues (mesocarp), and the hard layer surrounding the seed (endocarp).

**Druze** or *Druse,* religious sect in the Middle East of some 300,000 people. It began as a branch of Shiite Islam, based on a belief in the divinity of the Fatimid caliph al-Hakim (996–1021) and that he will return at the end of time. Their particular doctrines are kept secret, even from the majority of members. They refer to themselves as the Mowahhidoon, meaning monotheistic. The religion is exclusive, with conversion forbidden, either to or from the sect.

**dryad** (Greek *drys* '(oak) tree') in Greek mythology, a forest ◊nymph or tree spirit, especially of the oak. Each tree had a *hamadryad* who lived and died with it, from the Greek *hama* meaning 'together'.

**Dryden, John** (1631–1700) English poet and dramatist. He is noted for his satirical verse and for his use of the heroic couplet. His poetry includes the verse satire *Absalom and Achitophel* (1681), *Annus Mirabilis* (1667), and 'A Song for St Cecilia's Day' (1687). Plays include the heroic drama *The Conquest of Granada* (1672), the comedy *Marriage à la Mode* (1673), and *All for Love* (1678), a reworking of Shakespeare's *Antony and Cleopatra.*

**dry ice** solid carbon dioxide ($CO_2$), used as a refrigerant. At temperatures above –79°C/ –110.2°F, it sublimes (turns into vapour without passing through a liquid stage) to gaseous carbon dioxide.

**dry rot** infection of timber in damp conditions by fungi (see ◊fungus), such as *Merulius lacrymans,* that form a threadlike surface. Whitish at first, the fungus later reddens as reproductive spores are formed. Tentacles from the fungus also work their way into the timber, making it dry-looking and brittle. Dry rot spreads rapidly through a building.

**DTP** abbreviation for ◊desktop publishing.

**dualism** in philosophy, the belief that reality is essentially dual in nature. The French philosopher René ◊Descartes, for example, referred to thinking and material substance. These entities interact but are fundamentally separate and distinct.

Dualism is contrasted with monism, the theory that reality is made up of only one substance.

**Duarte, José Napoleon** (1925–1990) El Salvadorean politician, president 1980–82 and 1984–88. He was mayor of San Salvador 1964–70, and was elected president in 1972, but was soon exiled by the army for seven years in Venezuela. He returned in 1980, after the assassination of Archbishop Romero had increased support for the Christian Democratic Party (PDC), and became president, with US backing. He lost the 1982 presidential election, but was successful in May 1984. On becoming president again, he sought a negotiated settlement with the left-wing guerrillas in 1986, but resigned in mid-1988, as he had terminal liver cancer.

**Dubai** one of the United Arab Emirates; population (1995) 674,100.

**Dubček, Alexander** (1921–1992) Czechoslovak politician, chair of the federal assembly 1989–92. He was a member of the Slovak ◊resistance movement during World War II, and became first secretary of the Communist Party 1967–69. He launched a liberalization campaign (called the ◊Prague Spring) that was opposed by the USSR and led to the Soviet invasion of Czechoslovakia in 1968. He was arrested by Soviet troops and expelled from the party in 1970. In 1989 he gave speeches at pro-democracy rallies, and after the fall of the hardline regime, he was elected speaker of the National Assembly in Prague, a position to which he was re-elected in 1990. He was fatally injured in a car crash in September 1992.

**Dublin** Gaelic *Baile Atha Cliath* 'the town of the ford of the hurdles', (Gaelic *dubh linn* 'dark pool') city and port on the east coast of Ireland, at the mouth of the River Liffey, facing the Irish Sea; capital of the Republic of Ireland, and county town of County ◊Dublin; population (1991) 478,400; Greater Dublin, including Dún Laoghaire (1986 est) 921,000. Dublin is the site of one of the world's largest breweries (Guinness); other industries include textiles, pharmaceuticals, electrical goods, whisky distilling, glass, food processing, and machine tools. Dublin is also an important cultural centre.

**Dublin** county in the Republic of Ireland, in Leinster province, facing the Irish Sea and bounded by the counties of Meath, Kildare, and Wicklow; county town ◊Dublin; area 920 sq km/355 sq mi; population (1986) 1,021,000. The county is mostly level and low-lying, but rises in the south to 753 m/2,471 ft in Kippure, part of the Wicklow Mountains. The River Liffey enters Dublin Bay. The county is dominated by Ireland's capital city of Dublin and its suburbs, but also contains pastoral and agricultural land. Dún Laoghaire is the other major town and large port.

**dubnium** synthesized, radioactive, metallic element of the ◊transactinide series, symbol Db, atomic number 105, relative atomic mass 261. Six isotopes have been synthesized, each with very short (fractions of a second) half-lives. Two institutions claim to have been the first to produce it: the Joint Institute for Nuclear Research in Dubna, Russia, 1967; and the University of California at Berkeley, USA, who disputed the Soviet claim, 1970. Its temporary name was unnilpentium.

**Duchamp, Marcel** (1887–1968) French-born US artist. He achieved notoriety with his *Nude Descending a Staircase No 2* (1912; Philadelphia Museum of Art), influenced by Cubism and Futurism. An active exponent of ◊Dada, he invented ready-mades, everyday items (for example, a bicycle wheel mounted on a kitchen stool) which he displayed as works of art.

**duck** any of about 50 species of short-legged waterbirds with webbed feet and flattened bills, of the family Anatidae, order Anseriformes, which also includes the larger geese and swans. Ducks were domesticated for eggs, meat, and feathers by the ancient Chinese and the ancient Maya (see ◊poultry). Most ducks live in fresh water, feeding on worms and insects as well as vegetable matter. They are generally divided into dabbling ducks and diving ducks.

**ductless gland** alternative name for an ◊endocrine gland.

**Dufourspitze** second highest of the alpine peaks, 4,634 m/15,203 ft high. It is the highest peak in the Monte Rosa group of the Pennine Alps on the Swiss-Italian frontier.

**Dufy, Raoul** (1877–1953) French painter and designer. Inspired by ◊Fauvism he developed a fluent, brightly coloured style in watercolour and oils, painting scenes of gaiety and leisure, such as horse racing, yachting, and life on the beach. He also designed tapestries, textiles, and ceramics.

**dugong** marine mammal *Dugong dugong* of the order Sirenia (sea cows), found in the Red Sea, the Indian Ocean, and western Pacific. It can grow to 3.6 m/11 ft long, and has a tapering body with a notched tail and two fore-flippers. It has a very long hind gut (30 m/98 ft in adults) which functions similarly to the rumen in ◊ruminants. It is largely herbivorous, feeding mostly on sea grasses and seaweeds, and is thought to have given rise to the mermaid myth.

**duiker** (Afrikaans *diver*) any of several antelopes of the family Bovidae, common in Africa. Duikers are shy and nocturnal, and grow to 30–70 cm/12–28 in tall.

**Duisburg** formerly (until 1934) *Duisburg-Hamborn*, river port and industrial city in North Rhine-Westphalia, Germany, at the confluence of the Rhine and Ruhr rivers, 20 km/12 mi northwest of Düsseldorf; population (1995) 535,200. It is the largest inland river port in Europe. Located at the western end of the Ruhrgebiet (Ruhr District), Duisburg possesses the major Rhine docks at Ruhrort through which raw materials, such as iron ore and petroleum are imported. It has the largest concentration of heavy industry (iron and steelmaking, oil refining, heavy engineering, chemicals, and barge building) in the Ruhr.

**Dukas, Paul Abraham** (1865–1935) French composer and teacher. His scrupulous orchestration and chromatically enriched harmonies were admired by Debussy. His small output includes the opera *Ariane et Barbe-Bleue/Ariane and Bluebeard* (1907), the ballet *La Péri/The Peri* (1912), and the animated orchestral scherzo *L'Apprenti sorcier/The Sorcerer's Apprentice* (1897).

**dulcimer** musical instrument, a form of ◊zither, consisting of a shallow open trapezoidal soundbox across which strings are stretched laterally; they are horizontally struck by lightweight hammers or beaters. It produces clearly-differentiated pitches of consistent quality and is more agile and wide-ranging in pitch than the harp or lyre. In Hungary the dulcimer is known as a cimbalom, and is a national instrument.

**Dumas, Alexandre** (1802–1870) French writer, known as Dumas *père* (the father). His popular historical romances were the reworked output of a 'fiction-factory' of collaborators. They include *Les Trois Mousquetaires/The Three Musketeers* (1844) and its sequels. He is best known for *Le Comte de Monte Cristo/The Count of Monte Cristo*, which appeared in 12 volumes (1845). His play *Henri III et sa cour/ Henry III and His Court* (1829) established French romantic historical drama. Dumas *fils* was his son.

**Dumas, Alexandre** (1824–1895) French author, known as Dumas *fils* (the son of Dumas *père*). He is remembered for the play *La Dame aux camélias/The Lady of the Camellias* (1852), based on his own novel, and the source of Verdi's opera *La Traviata*.

**Du Maurier, Daphne** (1907–1989) English novelist. Her romantic fiction includes *Jamaica Inn* (1936), *Rebecca* (1938), *Frenchman's Creek* (1942), and *My Cousin Rachel* (1951), and is set in Cornwall. Her work, though lacking in depth and original insights, is made compelling by her storytelling gift.

**Dumfries and Galloway** unitary authority in southern Scotland, formed in 1996 from the regional council of the same name (1975–96)
*area* 6,421 sq km/2,479 sq mi
*towns* Annan, Dumfries (administrative headquarters), Kirkcudbright, Stranraer, Castle Douglas, Newton Stewart
*physical* area characterized by an indented coastline, including Luce Bay and Wigtown Bay, backed by a low-lying coastal strip of varying width; intensively forested in the Galloways. Much of the inland area is upland: east to west this includes Eskdalemuir (Hart Fell 808 m/ 2,651 ft), the Lowther Hills (Green Lowther 732 m/2,402 ft) and the Galloway Hills (the Merrick 843 m/2,766 ft)
*features* Wanlockhead (the highest village in Scotland); the oldest working post office in the world at Sanquhar; Glen Trool National Park; Ruthwell Cross, Whithorn archaeological dig
*industries* timber, chemicals, food processing
*agriculture* beef and dairy cattle, sheep, forestry
*population* (1996) 147,800.

**Duncan, Isadora** originally Angela Duncan (1878–1927) US dancer. A pioneer of modern dance, she adopted an emotionally expressive free form, dancing barefoot and wearing a loose tunic, inspired by the ideal of Hellenic beauty. She danced solos accompanied to music by Beethoven and other great composers, believing that the music should fit the grandeur of the dance.

Having made her base in Paris 1908, she toured extensively, often returning to Russia after her initial success there 1904.

**Dundee City** city and unitary authority in eastern Scotland, on the north side of the Firth of Tay
**area** 62 sq km/24 sq mi
**towns** Monifieth, Broughty Ferry, Dundee (administrative headquarters)
**physical** Firth of Tay
**features** Tay Bridges; Scott's ship *Discovery*
**agriculture** fishing
**industries** engineering, textiles, electronics, printing, food processing
**population** (1996) 155,000.

**dune** mound or ridge of wind-drifted sand common on coasts and in deserts. Loose sand is blown and bounced along by the wind, up the windward side of a dune. The sand particles then fall to rest on the lee side, while more are blown up from the windward side. In this way a dune moves gradually downwind.

**Dunfermline** industrial town north of the Firth of Forth in Fife, Scotland; population (1991) 55,100. Industries include engineering, electronics, and textiles. It was the ancient capital of Scotland, with many sites of royal historical significance. Many Scottish kings, including Robert the Bruce and Malcolm Canmore, are buried in *Dunfermline Abbey.*

**dunnock** or *hedge sparrow,* European bird *Prunella modularis* family Prunellidae, similar in size and colouring to the sparrow, but with a slate-grey head and breast, and more slender bill. It is characterized in the field by a hopping gait, with continual twitches of the wings whilst feeding. It nests in bushes and hedges.

**Du Pré, Jacqueline Mary** (1945–1987) English cellist. She was celebrated for her proficient technique and powerful interpretations of the classical cello repertory, particularly of Elgar. She had an international concert career while still in her teens and made many recordings.

**Durban** principal port of KwaZulu-Natal, South Africa, and main harbour of the republic; population (urban area, 1991) 1,137,400. Exports include coal, chemicals, steel, granite, wood products, sugar, fruit, grain, rice, and wool; imports include heavy machinery and mining equipment. Durban is also a holiday resort.

**Dürer, Albrecht** (1471–1528) German artist. He was the leading figure of the northern Renaissance. He was born in Nürnberg and travelled widely in Europe. Highly skilled in drawing and a keen student of nature, he perfected the technique of woodcut and engraving, producing woodcut series such as the *Apocalypse* (1498) and copperplate engravings such as *The Knight, Death, and the Devil* (1513) and *Melancholia* (1514). His paintings include altarpieces and meticulously observed portraits, including many self-portraits.

**Durham** county of northeast England (since April 1997 Darlington has been a separate unitary authority)
**area** 2,232 sq km/862 sq mi
**towns and cities** Durham (administrative headquarters), Newton Aycliffe, Peterlee, Chester-le-Street
**physical** Pennine Hills; rivers Wear and Tees
**features** Beamish open-air industrial museum; site of one of Britain's richest coalfields (pits no longer functioning); Bowes Museum; Barnard Castle; Durham Cathedral; University of Durham (1832), housed in Durham Castle; dales in the west of the county
**agriculture** sheep; dairy produce; hill farming
**industries** clothing; chemicals; iron and steel processing; light engineering industries; quarrying; cement; pharmaceuticals
**population** (1996) 608,100
**famous people** Elizabeth Barrett Browning, Anthony Eden.

**Durkheim, Emile** (1858–1917) French sociologist, one of the founders of modern sociology, who also influenced social anthropology. He worked to establish sociology as a respectable and scientific discipline, capable of diagnosing social ills and recommending possible cures.

**Durrell, Gerald (Malcolm)** (1925–1995) English naturalist, writer, and zoo curator. He became director of Jersey Zoological Park in 1958, and wrote 37 books, including the humorous memoir *My Family and Other Animals* (1956). He was the brother of the writer Lawrence Durrell.

**Durrell, Lawrence (George)** (1912–1990) British novelist and poet. He lived mainly in the eastern Mediterranean, the setting of his novels, including the Alexandria Quartet: *Justine, Balthazar, Mountolive,* and *Clea* (1957–60). He also wrote travel books, including *Bitter Lemons* (1957) about Cyprus. His heady prose and bizarre characters reflect his exotic sources of inspiration. He was the brother of the naturalist Gerald Durrell.

**Durrës** chief port of Albania; population (1991) 86,900. It is a commercial and communications centre, with flour mills, soap and cigarette factories, distilleries, and an electronics plant. It was the capital of Albania 1912–21.

**Dushanbe** formerly (1929–61) *Stalinabad,* capital of Tajikistan, situated in the Gissar Valley 160 km/100 mi north of the Afghan frontier; population (1996) 582,000. Dushanbe is a road, rail, and air centre. Its industries include cotton and silk mills, tanneries, meat-packing factories, and printing works. It is the seat of the Tajik state university.

**Düsseldorf** commercial city and capital of ◊North Rhine-Westphalia, Germany, on the right bank of the River Rhine, 26 km/16 mi northwest of Cologne; population (1995) 571,900. It is a river port and the commercial and financial centre of the Ruhr area, with food processing, brewing, agricultural machinery, textile, and chemical industries.

**Dutch cap** common name for a barrier method of contraception; see ◊diaphragm.

**Dutch East Indies** former Dutch colony, which in 1945 became independent as Indonesia.

**Dutch Guiana** former Dutch colony, which in 1975 became independent as Suriname.

**Dutch language** member of the Germanic branch of the Indo-European language family, often referred to by scholars as Netherlandic and taken to include the standard language and dialects of the Netherlands (excluding Frisian) as well as Flemish (in Belgium and northern France) and, more remotely, its offshoot Afrikaans in South Africa.

**Duvalier, François** (1907–1971) Right-wing president of Haiti 1957–71. Known as *Papa Doc*, he ruled as a dictator, organizing the Tontons Macoutes ('bogeymen') as a private security force to intimidate and assassinate opponents of his regime. He rigged the 1961 elections in order to have his term of office extended until 1967, and in 1964 declared himself president for life. He was excommunicated by the Vatican for harassing the church, and was succeeded on his death by his son Jean-Claude Duvalier.

**Duvalier, Jean-Claude** (1951– ) Right-wing president of Haiti 1971–86. Known as *Baby Doc*, he succeeded his father François Duvalier, becoming, at the age of 19, the youngest president in the world. He continued to receive support from the USA but was pressured into moderating some elements of his father's regime, yet still tolerated no opposition. In 1986, with Haiti's economy stagnating and with increasing civil disorder, Duvalier fled to France, taking much of the Haitian treasury with him.

**Dvořák, Antonín Leopold** (1841–1904) Czech composer. His Romantic music extends the Classical tradition of Beethoven and Brahms and displays the influence of Czech folk music. He wrote nine symphonies; tone poems; operas, including *Rusalka* (1900); large-scale choral works; the *Carnival* (1891–92) and other overtures; violin and cello concertos; chamber music; piano pieces; and songs. International recognition came with two sets of *Slavonic Dances* (1878 and 1886). Works such as his *New World Symphony* (1893) reflect his interest in American folk themes, including black and American Indian music. He was director of the National Conservatory, New York, 1892–95.

**Dyck, Anthony van** (1599–1641) Flemish painter. He was an assistant to Rubens from 1618 to 1620, then worked briefly in England at the court of James I before moving to Italy in 1622. In 1627 he returned to his native Antwerp, where he continued to paint religious works and portraits. From 1632 he lived in England and produced numerous portraits of royalty and aristocrats, such as *Charles I on Horseback* (about 1638; National Gallery, London).

**dye** substance that, applied in solution to fabrics, imparts a colour resistant to washing. *Direct dyes* combine with the material of the fabric, yielding a coloured compound; *indirect dyes* require the presence of another substance (a mordant), with which the fabric must first be treated; *vat dyes* are colourless soluble substances that on exposure to air yield an insoluble coloured compound.

**Dyfed** former county of southwest Wales, created in 1974 and, in 1996, divided between the unitary authorities of ◊Carmarthenshire, ◊Ceredigion, and ◊Pembrokeshire.

**Dylan, Bob** adopted name of Robert Allen Zimmerman (1941– ) US singer and songwriter. His lyrics provided catchphrases for a generation and influenced innumerable songwriters. He began in the folk-music tradition. His early songs, as on his albums *The Freewheelin' Bob Dylan* (1963) and *The Times They Are A-Changin'* (1964), were associated with the US civil-rights movement and antiwar protest. From 1965 he worked in an individualistic rock style, as on the albums *Highway 61 Revisited* (1965) and *Blonde on Blonde* (1966). His 15th album, *Time Out of Mind*, was released in 1997.

**Dynamic HTML** in computing, the fourth version of hypertext markup language (HTML), the language used to create Web pages. It is called Dynamic HTML because it enables dynamic effects to be incorporated in pages without the delays involved in downloading Java applets and without referring back to the server.

**dynamics** or *kinetics*, in mechanics, the mathematical and physical study of the behaviour of bodies under the action of forces that produce changes of motion in them.

**dynamo** in physics, a simple generator or machine for transforming mechanical energy into electrical energy. A dynamo in basic form consists of a powerful field magnet between the poles of which a suitable conductor, usually in the form of a coil (armature), is rotated. The mechanical energy of rotation is thus converted into an electric current in the armature.

**dysentery** infection of the large intestine causing abdominal cramps and painful ◊diarrhoea with blood. There are two kinds of dysentery: *amoebic* (caused by a protozoan), common in the tropics, which may lead to liver damage; and *bacterial*, the kind most often seen in the temperate zones.

**dyslexia** (Greek 'bad', 'pertaining to words') malfunction in the brain's synthesis and interpretation of written information, popularly known as 'word blindness'.

**dysprosium** (Greek *dusprositos* 'difficult to get near') silver-white, metallic element of the ◊lanthanide series, symbol Dy, atomic number 66, relative atomic mass 162.50. It is among the most magnetic of all known substances and has a great capacity to absorb neutrons.

# E

**eagle** any of several genera of large birds of prey of the family Accipitridae, order Falconiformes, including the golden eagle *Aquila chrysaetos* of Eurasia and North America, which has a 2 m/6 ft wingspan. Eagles occur worldwide, usually building eyries or nests in forests or mountains, and all are fierce and powerful birds of prey. The harpy eagle is the largest eagle.

**ear** organ of hearing in animals. It responds to the vibrations that constitute sound, which are translated into nerve signals and passed to the brain. A mammal's ear consists of three parts: outer ear, middle ear, and inner ear. The *outer ear* is a funnel that collects sound, directing it down a tube to the *ear drum* (tympanic membrane), which separates the outer and *middle ears*. Sounds vibrate this membrane, the mechanical movement of which is transferred to a smaller membrane leading to the *inner ear* by three small bones, the auditory ossicles. Vibrations of the inner ear membrane move fluid contained in the snail-shaped cochlea, which vibrates hair cells that stimulate the auditory nerve connected to the brain. There are approximately 30,000 sensory hair cells (*stereocilia*). Exposure to loud noise and the process of ageing damages the stereocilia, resulting in hearing loss. Three fluid-filled canals of the inner ear detect changes of position; this mechanism, with other sensory inputs, is responsible for the sense of balance.

**Earhart, Amelia** (1898–1937) US aviation pioneer and author, who in 1928 became the first woman to fly across the Atlantic. With copilot Frederick Noonan, she attempted a round-the-world flight 1937. Somewhere over the Pacific their plane disappeared.

**Earth** third planet from the Sun. It is almost spherical, flattened slightly at the poles, and is composed of three concentric layers: the core, the mantle, and the crust. About 70% of the surface (including the north and south polar icecaps) is covered with water. The Earth is surrounded by a life-supporting atmosphere and is the only planet on which life is known to exist.

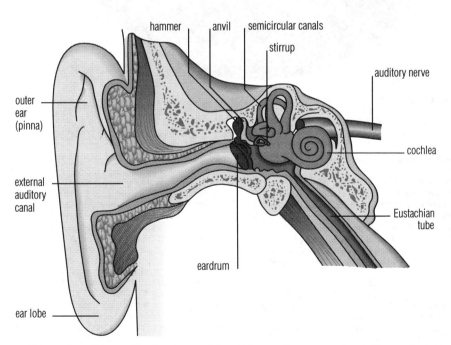

**ear** The structure of the ear. The three bones of the middle ear – hammer, anvil, and stirrup – vibrate in unison and magnify sounds about 20 times. The spiral-shaped cochlea is the organ of hearing. As sound waves pass down the spiral tube, they vibrate fine hairs lining the tube, which activate the auditory nerve connected to the brain. The semicircular canals are the organs of balance, detecting movements of the head.

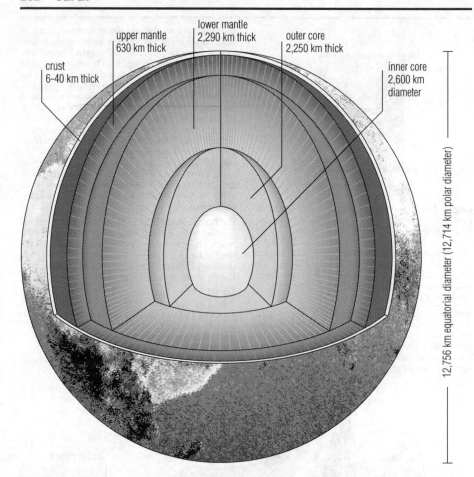

crust
6-40 km thick

upper mantle
630 km thick

lower mantle
2,290 km thick

outer core
2,250 km thick

inner core
2,600 km
diameter

12,756 km equatorial diameter (12,714 km polar diameter)

**Earth** *Inside the Earth. The surface of the Earth is a thin crust about 6 km/4 mi thick under the sea and 40 km/25 mi thick under the continents. Under the crust lies the mantle about 2,900 km/1,800 mi thick and with a temperature of 1,500–3,000°C/2,700–5,400°F. The outer core is about 2,250 km/1,400 mi thick, of molten iron and nickel. The inner core is probably solid iron and nickel at about 5,000°C/9,000°F.*

**mean distance from the Sun** 149,500,000 km/92,860,000 mi
**equatorial diameter** 12,756 km/7,923 mi
**circumference** 40,070 km/24,900 mi
**rotation period** 23 hr 56 min 4.1 sec
**year** (complete orbit, or sidereal period) 365 days 5 hr 48 min 46 sec. Earth's average speed around the Sun is 30 kps/18.5 mps; the plane of its orbit is inclined to its equatorial plane at an angle of 23.5°, the reason for the changing seasons
**atmosphere** nitrogen 78.09%; oxygen 20.95%; argon 0.93%; carbon dioxide 0.03%; and less than 0.0001% neon, helium, krypton, hydrogen, xenon, ozone, radon
**surface** land surface 150,000,000 sq km/ 57,500,000 sq mi (greatest height above sea level 8,872 m/29,118 ft Mount Everest); water surface 361,000,000 sq km/139,400,000 sq mi (greatest depth 11,034 m/36,201 ft ◊Mariana Trench in the Pacific). The interior is thought to

be an inner core about 2,600 km/1,600 mi in diameter, of solid iron and nickel; an outer core about 2,250 km/1,400 mi thick, of molten iron and nickel; and a mantle of mostly solid rock about 2,900 km/1,800 mi thick, separated from the Earth's crust by the Mohorovičić discontinuity. The crust and the topmost layer of the mantle form about twelve major moving plates, some of which carry the continents. The plates are in constant, slow motion, called tectonic drift. US geophysicists announced in 1996 that they had detected a difference in the spinning time of the Earth's core and the rest of the planet; the core is spinning slightly faster.
**satellite** the ◊Moon
**age** 4.6 billion years. The Earth was formed with the rest of the ◊Solar System by consolidation of interstellar dust. Life began 3.5–4 billion years ago.

**earth** electrical connection between an appliance and the ground. In the event of a fault in an electrical appliance, for example, involving connection between the live part of the circuit and the outer casing, the current flows to earth, causing no harm to the user.

**earthquake** abrupt motion that propagates through the Earth and along its surfaces. Earthquakes are caused by the sudden release in rocks of strain accumulated over time as a result of tectonics. The study of earthquakes is called ◊seismology. Most earthquakes occur along ◊faults (fractures or breaks) and Benioff zones. Plate tectonic movements generate the major proportion: as two plates move past each other they can become jammed. When sufficient strain has accumulated, the rock breaks, releasing a series of elastic waves (◊seismic waves) as the plates spring free. The force of earthquakes (magnitude) is measured on the ◊Richter scale, and their effect (intensity) on the ◊Mercalli scale. The point at which an earthquake originates is the *seismic focus* or *hypocentre;* the point on the Earth's surface directly above this is the *epicentre.*

**earth science** scientific study of the planet Earth as a whole. The mining and extraction of minerals and gems, the prediction of weather and earthquakes, the pollution of the atmosphere, and the forces that shape the physical world all fall within its scope of study. The emergence of the discipline reflects scientists' concern that an understanding of the global aspects of the Earth's structure and its past will hold the key to how humans affect its future, ensuring that its resources are used in a sustainable way. It is a synthesis of several traditional subjects such as ◊geology, ◊meteorology, ◊oceanography, geophysics, geochemistry, and ◊palaeontology.

**Earth Summit** official name *United Nations Conference on Environment and Development,* international meetings aiming at drawing measures towards environmental protection of the world. The first summit took place in Rio de Janeiro, Brazil, in June 1992. Treaties were made to combat global warming and protect wildlife ('biodiversity') (the latter was not signed by the USA). The second Earth Summit was held in New York in June 1997 to review progress on the environment. The meeting agreed to work towards a global forest convention in 2000 with the aim of halting the destruction of tropical and old-growth forests.

**earthworm** ◊annelid worm of the class Oligochaeta. Earthworms are hermaphroditic and deposit their eggs in cocoons. They live by burrowing in the soil, feeding on the organic matter it contains. They are vital to the formation of humus, aerating the soil and levelling it by transferring earth from the deeper levels to the surface as castings.

**earwig** nocturnal insect of the order Dermaptera. The forewings are short and leathery and serve to protect the hindwings, which are large and are folded like a fan when at rest. Earwigs seldom fly. They have a pincerlike appendage in the rear. The male is distinguished by curved pincers; those of the female are straight. Earwigs

are regarded as pests because they feed on flowers and fruit, but they also eat other insects, dead or alive. Eggs are laid beneath the soil, and the female cares for the young even after they have hatched. The male dies before the eggs have hatched.

**East Anglia** region of eastern England, formerly a Saxon kingdom, including Norfolk, Suffolk, and parts of Essex and Cambridgeshire. Norwich is the principal city of East Anglia. The Sainsbury Centre for Visual Arts, opened in 1978 at the University of East Anglia, has a collection of ethnographic art and sculpture. East Anglian ports such as Harwich and Felixstowe have greatly developed as trade with the rest of Europe has increased.

**East Ayrshire** unitary authority in southwest Scotland, created in 1996 from two districts of Strathclyde region
*area* 1,269 sq km/490 sq mi
*towns* Kilmarnock (administrative headquarters), Cumnock, Stewarton, Galston, Crosshouse
*physical* predominantly low lying and undulating in the north, mountainous toward the south; Loch Doon; rivers Ayr, Irvine; Blackcraig Hill (700 m/2,298 ft); Loudoun Hill
*features* Burns' House Museum, Mauchline; Loudoun Castle Theme Park; Dunaskin Heritage Museum
*industries* textiles, light engineering, food and drink, printing
*agriculture* dairy farming, sheep, beef cattle
*population* (1996) 124,000
*history* at Loudoun Hill, Robert the Bruce defeated 6,000 of the Earl of Pembroke's men with a force of 600 in 1306.

**East Dunbartonshire** unitary authority in central Scotland, created in 1996 from two districts of Strathclyde region
*area* 175 sq km/67 sq mi
*towns* Kirkintilloch (administrative headquarters), Bearsden, Milngavie
*physical* low-lying lands to the south give way dramatically to the Campsie Fells in the north; Earl's Seat (578 m/1,896 ft); River Kelvin
*features* Forth and Clyde Canal; Antonine Wall
*population* (1996) 110,000.

**Easter** spring feast of the Christian church, commemorating the Resurrection of Jesus. It is a moveable feast, falling on the first Sunday following the full moon after the vernal equinox (21 March); that is, between 22 March and 25 April.

**Easter Island** or *Rapa Nui,* Spanish *Isla de Pascua,* Chilean island in the south Pacific Ocean, part of the Polynesian group, about 3,500 km/2,200 mi west of Chile; area about 166 sq km/64 sq mi; population (1994) 2,800. It was first reached by Europeans on Easter Sunday 1722. On it stand over 800 huge carved statues (*moai*) and the remains of boat-shaped stone houses, the work of Neolithic peoples from Polynesia. The chief centre is Hanga-Roa.

**Eastern Cape** province of the Republic of South Africa from 1994, formerly part of Cape Province

*area* 170,616 sq km/65,875 sq mi
*capital* Bisho
*towns and cities* East London, Port Elizabeth, Grahamstown
*features* includes the former independent homelands of the Transkei and the Ciskei; Little and Great Karoo; Drakensberg mountains; Orange River
*industries* motor manufacturing, textiles, sheep, citrus fruits, grain, and dairy and meat products
*population* (1995 est) 6,481,300
*languages* Xhosa 85%, Afrikaans 9%, English 3%

**Eastern Orthodox Church** see ◊Orthodox Church.

**Easter Rising** or *Easter Rebellion,* in Irish history, a republican insurrection that began on Easter Monday, April 1916, in Dublin. It was inspired by the Irish Republican Brotherhood (IRB) in an unsuccessful attempt to overthrow British rule in Ireland. It was led by Patrick Pearce of the IRB and James Connolly of Sinn Fein.

**East Germany** see ◊Germany, East.

**East India Company, British** commercial company (1600–1858) that had a monopoly of trade between England and the Far East; see ◊British East India Company.

**East India Company (Dutch)** trading monopoly of the 17th and 18th centuries.

**East Lothian** unitary authority in southeast Scotland which was previously a district within Lothian region (1975–96) and a county until 1974
*area* 677 sq km/261 sq mi
*towns* Haddington (administrative headquarters), North Berwick, Dunbar
*physical* area of contrasts, with coastal plains of cliffs, beaches and estuarine marines, broad river valley of the Tyne, volcanic outcrops (Bass Rock, Traprain Law) and gentle slopes of the Lammermuir Hills
*features* Tantallon Castle; Muirfield golf course; Traprain Law fort
*industries* whisky distilling, agricultural-based
*agriculture* arable farming on plains
*population* (1996) 85,500.

**East Renfrewshire** unitary authority in central Scotland, created in 1996 from part of Renfrew district in Strathclyde region
*area* 174 sq km/67 sq mi
*towns* Barrhead, Giffnock (administrative headquarters), Newton Mearns, Clarkston
*physical* low-lying plateau rising from the plain of the River Clyde
*industries* engineering, cotton textiles
*agriculture* sheep, rough grazing, some dairy farming
*population* (1996) 86,800.

**East Riding of Yorkshire** unitary authority in northern England created in 1996 from part of the former county of Humberside
*area* 2,416 sq km/933 sq mi
*towns* Beverley (administrative headquarters), Driffield, Goole, Hornsea, Bridlington

*features* Humber Estuary to south of authority; North Sea to east; Flamborough Head chalk cliffs; Spurn Head – dynamic spit at mouth of estuary; River Hull; River Ouse; Holderness Peninsula; The Wolds; Hornsea Mere; Beverley Minster (13th century); All Saints Tower (34 m/110 ft) at Driffield; Sledmere House – 18th century mansion with grounds laid out by Capability Brown; Rudstone has Britain's tallest standing stone (8 m/25 ft); Sewerby Hall (Bridlington) – Georgian mansion including museum dedicated to the aviator Amy Johnson (1903–1941); Hornsea Pottery; Withernsea Lighthouse (39 m/127 ft) including museum
*industries* chemicals, pottery, agriculture, agricultural machinery and services, passenger vehicle components, bakery products
*population* (1996) 310,000
*famous people* St John of Beverley, William Kent.

**East Sussex** county of southeast England, created in 1974, formerly part of Sussex (since April 1997 Brighton and Hove has been a separate unitary authority)
*area* 1,725 sq km/666 sq mi
*towns* Lewes (administrative headquarters), Newhaven (cross-channel port), Eastbourne, Rye, Winchelsea; Bexhill-on-Sea, Hastings, St Leonards, Seaford (all coastal resorts)
*physical* Beachy Head, highest headland on the south coast (180 m/590 ft), the eastern end of the South Downs; the Weald (including Ashdown Forest); Friston Forest; rivers Cuckmere, Ouse, and East Rother (which flows into the sea near Rye); Romney Marsh
*features* the 'Long Man' chalk hill figure at Wilmington, near Eastbourne; prehistoric earthworks; Iron Age hill fort at Mount Caburn, near Lewes; Roman villas; Herstmonceux, with a 15th-century castle (conference and exhibition centre) and adjacent modern buildings, site of the Greenwich Royal Observatory (1958–90); other castles at Hastings, Lewes, Pevensey, and Bodiam; Bayham Abbey; Battle Abbey and the site of the Battle of Hastings; Michelham Priory; Sheffield Park garden; University of Sussex at Falmer, near Brighton, founded in 1961
*agriculture* cereals; hops; fruit and vegetables; fishing (at Hastings)
*industries* electronics; gypsum; light engineering; timber
*population* (1996) 734,900
*famous people* former homes of Henry James at Rye, Rudyard Kipling at Batemans in Burwash, Thomas Sackville at Buckhurst, Virginia Woolf at Rodmell; Angus Wilson.

**East Timor** disputed territory on the island of ◊Timor in the Malay Archipelago, claimed by Indonesia as the province of Timor Timur; prior to 1975, it was a Portuguese colony for almost 460 years
*area* 14,874 sq km/5,706 sq mi
*capital* Dili
*industries* coffee
*population* (1990) 747,750
*history* Following Portugal's withdrawal in 1975, East Timor was left with a literacy rate of under 10% and no infrastructure. Civil war

broke out and the left-wing Revolutionary Front of Independent East Timor (Fretilin) occupied the capital, calling for independence. In opposition, troops from neighbouring Indonesia invaded the territory, declaring East Timor (*Loro Sae*) the 17th province of Indonesia in July 1976 – a claim not recognized by the United Nations. (It had long been the aim of Indonesian military rulers to absorb the remaining colonial outposts in the East Indies.)

The war and its attendant famine are thought to have caused more than 100,000 deaths, but starvation had been alleviated by the mid-1980s, and the Indonesian government had built schools, roads, and hospitals. Fretilin guerrillas remained active protesting against the 'transmigration' of Indonesian Muslims into the predominantly Christian island. In November 1991 Indonesian troops fired on pro-independence demonstrators, killing 50. Between 100 and 200 unarmed protestors died in ensuing clashes. More than 1,000 Fretilin guerrillas were reported to have surrendered in November 1992 following the capture of their leader, Jose Alexandre 'Xanana' Gusmao. Indonesia announced plans to withdraw most of its troops from East Timor August 1993. The 1996 Nobel Peace Prize was awarded jointly to Bishop Carlos Belo, who had persistently denounced human-rights violations by Indonesian soldiers in East Timor, and Jorge Ramas-Horta, an exiled spokesman for the Fretilin Independence Movement. The campaign for independence was renewed in 1998 after president ◊Suharto of Indonesia had stepped down. On 28 July 1998 Indonesia withdrew 400 troops. A resolution to the 22-year-old dispute over the sovereignty of East Timor seemed a step closer in August 1998 after the governments of Indonesia and Portugal set a tentative end-of-year deadline for reaching a final agreement to grant limited autonomy to the region.

Indonesian government stated in late January 1999 that the parliament might consider independence for East Timor after the general election scheduled for 7 June 1999. In February, 'Xanana' Gusmao, the East Timorese guerrilla commander, was released from prison in Jakarta in the first concrete sign of changes. A referendum for either autonomy within Indonesia or complete separation from it was set for 8 August 1999, in a UN-sanctioned document signed by Indonesia and Portugal. In April, the rival groups in East Timor agreed a ceasefire. In June peace talks opened, but the referendum for autonomy was postponed for at least two weeks to allow UN observers to monitor security more efficiently.

**Eastwood, Clint(on)** (1930– ) US film actor and director. His breakthrough came in the western *A Fistful of Dollars* (1964), after which he proved himself a box-office attraction in such films as *Dirty Harry* (1973), directed by his regular collaborator Don Siegel, and *In the Line of Fire* (1993). In 1971 he started an accomplished directing career with *Play Misty for Me*, and his latter-day western *Unforgiven* (1992) won Academy Awards for best film and direction.

**ebony** any of a group of hardwood trees belonging to the ebony family, especially some tropical ◊persimmons native to Africa and Asia. (Genus chiefly *Diospyros*, family Ebenaceae.)

**EC** abbreviation for *European Community*, former name (to 1993) of the ◊European Union.

**echidna** or *spiny anteater*, toothless, egg-laying, spiny mammal of the order Monotremata, found in Australia and New Guinea. There are two species: *Tachyglossus aculeatus*, the short-nosed echidna, and the rarer *Zaglossus bruijni*, the long-nosed echidna. They feed entirely upon ants and termites, which they dig out with their powerful claws and lick up with their prehensile tongues. When attacked, an echidna rolls itself into a ball, or tries to hide by burrowing in the earth.

**echinoderm** marine invertebrate of the phylum Echinodermata ('spiny-skinned'), characterized by a five-radial symmetry. Echinoderms have a water-vascular system which transports substances around the body. They include starfishes (or sea stars), brittle-stars, sea lilies, sea urchins, and sea cucumbers. The skeleton is external, made of a series of limy plates. Echinoderms generally move by using tube-feet, small water-filled sacs that can be protruded or pulled back to the body.

**echo** repetition of a sound wave, or of a ◊radar or ◊sonar signal, by reflection from a surface. By accurately measuring the time taken for an echo to return to the transmitter, and by knowing the speed of a radar signal (the speed of light) or a sonar signal (the speed of sound in water), it is possible to calculate the range of the object causing the echo (◊echolocation).

**echolocation** or *biosonar*, method used by certain animals, notably bats, whales, and dolphins, to detect the positions of objects by using sound. The animal emits a stream of high-pitched sounds, generally at ultrasonic frequencies (beyond the range of human hearing), and listens for the returning echoes reflected off objects to determine their exact location.

**eclipse** passage of an astronomical body through the shadow of another. The term is usually used for solar and lunar eclipses, which may be either partial or total, but may also refer to other bodies, for example, to an eclipse of one of Jupiter's satellites by Jupiter itself. An eclipse of a star by a body in the Solar System is also called an occultation. *See illustration on page 286.*

**eclipsing binary** binary (double) star in which the two stars periodically pass in front of each other as seen from Earth.

**Eco, Umberto** (1932– ) Italian writer, semiologist, and literary critic. His works include *The Role of the Reader* (1979), the 'philosophical thriller' *The Name of the Rose* (1983), and *Foucault's Pendulum* (1988).

**ecology** (Greek *oikos* 'house') study of the relationship among organisms and the environments in which they live, including all living and nonliving components. The chief environmental factors governing the distribution of plants and

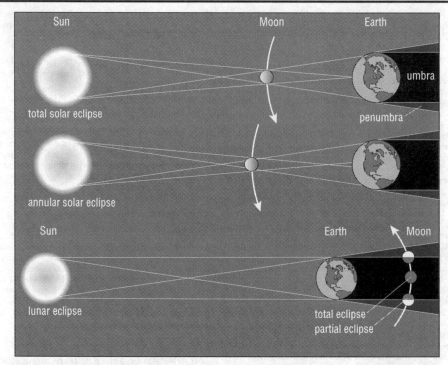

***eclipse*** *The two types of eclipse: lunar and solar. A lunar eclipse occurs when the Moon passes through the shadow of the Earth. A solar eclipse occurs when the Moon passes between the Sun and the Earth, blocking out the Sun's light. During a total solar eclipse, when the Moon completely covers the Sun, the Moon's shadow sweeps across the Earth's surface from west to east at a speed of 3,200kph/2,000mph.*

animals are temperature, humidity, soil, light intensity, daylength, food supply, and interaction with other organisms. The term was coined by the biologist Ernst Haeckel in 1866.

**economics** (Greek 'household management') social science devoted to studying the production, distribution, and consumption of wealth. It consists of the disciplines of *microeconomics*, the study of individual producers, consumers, or markets, and *macroeconomics*, the study of whole economies or systems (in particular, areas such as taxation and public spending).

**ectoparasite** ◊parasite that lives on the outer surface of its host.

**ectopic** in medicine, term applied to an anatomical feature that is displaced or found in an abnormal position. An ectopic pregnancy is one occurring outside the womb, usually in a Fallopian tube.

**ECU** abbreviation for *European Currency Unit,* the official monetary unit of the European Union. It is based on the value of the different currencies used in the ◊European Monetary System (EMS).

**Ecuador** Republic of
*national name República del Ecuador*
*area* 270,670 sq km/104,505 sq mi
*capital* Quito

*major towns/cities* Guayaquil, Cuenca, Machala, Portoviejo, Manta, Ambeto, Esmeraldas
*major ports* Guayaquil
*physical features* coastal plain rises sharply to Andes Mountains, which are divided into a series of cultivated valleys; flat, low-lying

rainforest in the east; Galápagos Islands; Cotopaxi, the world's highest active volcano. Ecuador is crossed by the equator, from which it derives its name

**head of state and government** Jamil Mahuad Witt from 1998

**political system** emergent democracy

**political parties** Social Christian Party (PSC), right wing; Ecuadorean Roldosist Party (PRE), populist, centre left; Popular Democracy (DP), centre right; Democratic Left (ID), moderate socialist; Conservative Party (PCE), right wing

**currency** sucre

**GNP per capita (PPP)** (US$) 4,630 (1998)

**exports** petroleum and petroleum products, bananas, shrimps (a major exporter), coffee, seafood products, cocoa beans and products, cut flowers. Principal market: USA 39.2% (1998)

**population** 12,411,000 (1999 est)

**language** Spanish (official), Quechua, Jivaro, and other indigenous languages

**religion** Roman Catholic

**life expectancy** 67 (men); 73 (women) (1995–2000)

**Chronology**

**1450s** The Caras people, whose kingdom had its capital at Quito, conquered by Incas of Peru.

**1531** Spanish conquistador Francisco Pizarro landed on Ecuadorean coast, en route to Peru, where Incas were defeated.

**1534** Conquered by Spanish. Quito, which had been destroyed by American Indians, was refounded by Sebastian de Belalcazar; the area became part of Spanish Viceroyalty of Peru, which covered much of South America, with its capital at Lima (Peru).

**later 16th century** Spanish established large agrarian estates, owned by Europeans and worked by American Indian peons.

**1739** Became part of new Spanish Viceroyalty of Nueva Granada, which included Colombia and Venezuela, with its capital in Bogotá (Colombia).

**1809** With the Spanish monarchy having been overthrown by Napoleon Bonaparte, creole middle class began to press for independence.

**1822** Spanish Royalists defeated by Field Marshal Antonio José de Sucre, fighting for Simón Bolívar, 'The Liberator', at battle of Pichincha, near Quito; became part of independent Gran Colombia, which also comprised Colombia, Panama, and Venezuela.

**1830** Became fully independent state, after leaving Gran Colombia.

**1845–60** Political instability, with five presidents holding power, increasing tension between conservative Quito and liberal Guayaquil on the coast, and minor wars with Peru and Colombia.

**1860–75** Power held by Gabriel García Moreno, an autocratic theocrat-Conservative who launched education and public-works programmes.

**1895–1912** Dominated by Gen Eloy Alfaro, a radical, anticlerical Liberal from the coastal region, who reduced the power of the church.

**1925–48** Great political instability; no president completed his term of office.

**1941** Lost territory in Amazonia after defeat in war with Peru.

**1948–55** Liberals in power.

**1956** Camilo Ponce became first conservative president in 60 years.

**1960** Liberals in power, with José María Velasco Ibarra returning as president.

**1961** Velasco deposed and replaced by vice president.

**1962** Military junta installed.

**1968** Velasco returned as president.

**1970s** Ecuador emerged as significant oil producer.

**1972** Coup put military back in power.

**1979** New democratic constitution; Liberals in power but opposed by right- and left-wing parties.

**1981** Border dispute with Peru flared up again.

**1982** The deteriorating economy and austerity measures provoked strikes, demonstrations, and a state of emergency.

**1984–85** There was no party with a clear majority in the national congress; León Febres Cordero narrowly won the presidency for the Conservatives.

**1988** Rodrigo Borja Cevallos was elected president for a moderate left-wing coalition and introduced unpopular austerity measures.

**1992** PUR leader Sixto Duran Ballen was elected president; PSC became the largest party in congress. Ecuador withdrew from OPEC to enable it to increase its oil exports.

**1994** There was mounting opposition to Duran's economic liberalization and privatization programme.

**1996** Abdala Bucaram was elected president.

**1997** Bucaram was removed from office and replaced by vice-president Rosalia Arteaga, but a national referendum later ratified Fabian Alarcon as interim president.

**1998** Jamil Mahuad Witt was elected president. A 157-year border dispute was settled with Peru.

**ecumenical movement** movement for reunification of the various branches of the Christian church. It began in the 19th century with the extension of missionary work to Africa and Asia, where the divisions created in Europe were incomprehensible; the movement gathered momentum from the need for unity in the face of growing secularism in Christian countries and of the challenge posed by such faiths as Islam. The *World Council of Churches* was founded 1948.

**eczema** inflammatory skin condition, a form of dermatitis, marked by dryness, rashes, itching, the formation of blisters, and the exudation of fluid. It may be allergic in origin and is sometimes complicated by infection.

**Edberg, Stefan** (1966– ) Swedish tennis player. He won the junior Grand Slam in 1983 and his first Grand Slam title, the Australian Open, in 1985, repeated in 1987. Other Grand Slam singles titles include Wimbledon 1988 and 1990 and the US Open 1991 and 1992. He has now retired from tennis.

**career highlights**

**Wimbledon** singles: 1988, 1990

**Australian Open** singles: 1985, 1987; doubles: 1987

**US Open** singles: 1991, 1992; doubles: 1987
**Grand Prix Masters** 1989

**Eddery, Pat(rick James John)** (1952– )
Irish-born flat-racing jockey who has ridden 13
English classic winners including the Derby winner on three occasions. He won the jockey's
championship in Britain eleven times.
*career highlights*
*champion jockey* 1974–77, 1986, 1988–91,
1993, 1996
*Derby* 1975 (Grundy), 1982 (Golden Fleece),
1990 (Quest for Fame)
*Prix de l'Arc de Triomphe* 1980, 1985–87
*Oaks* 1974,1979
*St Leger* 1986, 1991, 1994, 1997
*1000 Guineas* 1996
*2000 Guineas* 1983, 1984, 1993

**edelweiss** perennial alpine plant belonging to
the daisy family, with a white, woolly, star-
shaped flower, found in the high mountains of
Europe and Asia. (*Leontopodium alpinum*, family Compositae.)

**Eden, (Robert) Anthony** 1st Earl of Avon
(1897–1977) British Conservative politician,
foreign secretary 1935–38, 1940–45, and
1951–55; prime minister 1955–57, when he
resigned after the failure of the Anglo-French
military intervention in the ◊Suez Crisis.

**Edgar the Peaceful** (944–975) King of all
England from 959. He was the younger son of
Edmund I, and strove successfully to unite
English and Danes as fellow subjects.

**Edgehill, Battle of** first battle of the English
Civil War. It took place in 1642, on a ridge in
south Warwickshire, between Royalists under
Charles I and Parliamentarians under the Earl of
Essex. Both sides claimed victory.

**Edinburgh** capital of Scotland and, as *the
City of Edinburgh,* a unitary authority, located
near the southern shores of the Firth of Forth
*area* 263 sq km/122 sq mi
*physical* Water of Leith, Salisbury Crags,
Arthur's Seat
*industries* printing, publishing, banking,
insurance, chemical manufacture, electronics,
distilling, brewing
*population* (1996) 477,600.

**Edinburgh, Duke of** title of Prince ◊Philip of
the UK.

**Edison, Thomas Alva** (1847–1931) US scientist and inventor, whose work in the fields of
communications and electrical power greatly
influenced the world in which we live. With
more than 1,000 patents, Edison produced his
most important inventions in Menlo Park, New
Jersey 1876–87, including the phonograph and
the electric light bulb in 1879. He also constructed a system of electric power distribution
for consumers, the telephone transmitter, and
the megaphone.

**Edmonton** capital of ◊Alberta, Canada, on
the North Saskatchewan River at an altitude of
665 m/2,182 ft; population (1991) 616,700. It is
the centre of an oil and mining area to the north
and is also an agricultural and dairying region.

Manufactured goods include processed foods,
petrochemicals, plastic and metal products, lumber, and clothing. Edmonton is known as the
'gateway to the north': it is situated on the
Alaska Highway, and petroleum pipelines link
the city with Superior in Wisconsin, USA, and
Vancouver in British Columbia.

**Edmund (II) Ironside** (c. 981–1016) king of
England in 1016, the son of Ethelred II 'the
Unready' (c. 968–1016). He led the resistance to
Canute's invasion in 1015, and on Ethelred's
death in 1016 was chosen king by the citizens of
London. Meanwhile, the Witan (the king's council) elected Canute. In the struggle for the
throne, Canute defeated Edmund at Ashingdon
(or Assandun) and they divided the kingdom
between them. When Edmund died the same
year, Canute ruled the whole kingdom.

**Edo** or *Yedo,* former name of ◊Tokyo, Japan,
until 1868.

**education** process, beginning at birth, of
developing intellectual capacity, manual skill,
and social awareness, especially by instruction.
In its more restricted sense, the term refers to the
process of imparting literacy, numeracy, and a
generally accepted body of knowledge.

**Edward, (Charles Edward Antony
Richard Louis)** (1964– ) Prince of the UK,
third son of Queen Elizabeth II. He is seventh in
line to the throne after Charles, Charles's two
sons, Andrew, and Andrew's two daughters. In
1999 he married Sophie Rhys-Jones.

**Edward** called *the Black Prince* (1330–1376)
Prince of Wales, eldest son of Edward III of
England. The epithet (probably posthumous)
may refer to his black armour. During the
Hundred Years' War he fought at the Battle of
Crécy in 1346 and captured the French king at
Poitiers in 1356. He ruled Aquitaine from 1360
to 1371. In 1367 he invaded Castile and
restored to the throne the deposed king, Pedro
the Cruel (1334–69). During the revolt that
eventually ousted him, he caused the massacre
of Limoges in 1370.

**Edward** eight kings of England or Great
Britain:

**Edward I** (1239–1307) king of England from
1272, son of Henry III (1207–72). He led the
royal forces against Simon de Montfort (the
Younger) in the Barons' War of 1264–67, and
was on a crusade when he succeeded to the
throne. He established English rule over all of
Wales in 1282–84, and secured recognition of
his overlordship from the Scottish king,
although the Scots under Sir William Wallace
and Robert (I) the Bruce fiercely resisted actual
conquest. His reign saw Parliament move
towards its modern form with the ◊Model
Parliament of 1295. He married Eleanor of
Castile (1254–90) and in 1299 married
Margaret, daughter of Philip III of France. He
was succeeded by his son Edward II
(1284–1327).

**Edward II** (1284–1327) King of England from
1307, son of Edward I. Born at Caernarfon
Castle, he was created the first Prince of Wales in

1301. Incompetent and frivolous, and unduly influenced by his favourite, Piers Gaveston, Edward struggled throughout his reign with discontented barons, who attempted to restrict his power through the Ordinances of 1311. His invasion of Scotland in 1314 to suppress revolt resulted in defeat at Bannockburn. When he fell under the influence of a new favourite, Hugh le Depenser, he was deposed in 1327 by his wife Isabella (1292–1358), daughter of Philip IV of France, and her lover Roger de ◊Mortimer, and murdered in Berkeley Castle, Gloucestershire. He was succeeded by his son, Edward III.

**Edward III** (1310–1377) king of England from 1327, son of Edward II. He assumed the government in 1330 from his mother, through whom in 1337 he laid claim to the French throne and thus began the Hundred Years' War. Edward was the victor of Halidon Hill in 1333, Sluys in 1340, Crécy in 1346, and at the siege of Calais 1346–47, and created the Order of the Garter. He was succeeded by his grandson Richard II.

**Edward IV** (1442–1483) king of England 1461–70 and from 1471. He was the son of Richard, Duke of York, and succeeded Henry VI in the Wars of the Roses (see Roses, Wars of the), temporarily losing his throne to Henry when Edward fell out with his adviser Richard Neville, Earl of Warwick (Warwick the Kingmaker). Edward was a fine warrior and intelligent strategist, with victories at Mortimer's Cross and Towton in 1461, Empingham in 1470, and Barnet and Tewkesbury in 1471. He was succeeded by his son Edward V.

**Edward V** (1470–1483) King of England 1483. Son of Edward IV, he was deposed three months after his accession in favour of his uncle (◊Richard III), and is traditionally believed to have been murdered (with his brother) in the Tower of London on Richard's orders.

**Edward VI** (1537–1553) King of England from 1547, only son of Henry VIII and his third wife, Jane Seymour. The government was entrusted to his uncle the Duke of Somerset (who fell from power in 1549), and then to the Earl of Warwick, later created Duke of Northumberland. He was succeeded by his sister Mary I.

**Edward VII** (1841–1910) King of Great Britain and Ireland from 1901. As Prince of Wales he was a prominent social figure, but his mother Queen Victoria considered him too frivolous to take part in political life. In 1860 he made the first tour of Canada and the USA ever undertaken by a British prince.

**Edward VIII** (1894–1972) King of Great Britain and Northern Ireland January– December 1936, when he renounced the throne to marry Wallis Warfield ◊Simpson (see ◊abdication crisis). He was created Duke of Windsor and was governor of the Bahamas 1940–45.

**Edward the Confessor** (c. 1003–1066) King of England from 1042, the son of Ethelred II. He lived in Normandy until shortly before his accession. During his reign power was held by Earl Godwin and his son ◊Harold, while the king devoted himself to religion, including the rebuilding of Westminster Abbey (consecrated in 1065), where he is buried. His childlessness led ultimately to the Norman Conquest in 1066. He was canonized in 1161.

**Edward the Elder** (c. 870–924) king of the West Saxons. He succeeded his father Alfred the Great in 899. He reconquered southeast England and the Midlands from the Danes, uniting Wessex and Mercia with the help of his sister Aethelflaed. By the time of his death his kingdom was the most powerful in the British Isles. He was succeeded by his son ◊Athelstan.

**Edward the Martyr** (c. 963–978) King of England from 975. Son of King Edgar, he was murdered at Corfe Castle, Dorset, probably at his stepmother Aelfthryth's instigation (she wished to secure the crown for her son, Ethelred). He was canonized in 1001.

**EEC** abbreviation for *European Economic Community.*

**eel** any fish of the order Anguilliformes. Eels are snakelike, with elongated dorsal and anal fins. They include the freshwater eels of Europe and North America (which breed in the Atlantic), the marine conger eels, and the morays of tropical coral reefs.

**EFTA** acronym for ◊*European Free Trade Association.*

**Egbert** (died 839) King of the West Saxons from 802, the son of Ealhmund, an under-king of Kent. By 829 he had united England for the first time under one king.

**egg** in animals, the ovum, or female ◊gamete (reproductive cell).
   After fertilization by a sperm cell, it begins to divide to form an embryo. Eggs may be deposited by the female (ovipary) or they may develop within her body (◊vivipary and ◊ovovivipary). In the oviparous reptiles and birds, the egg is protected by a shell, and well supplied with nutrients in the form of yolk. *See illustration on page 290.*

**ego** (Latin 'I') in psychology, the processes concerned with the self and a person's conception of himself or herself, encompassing values and attitudes. In Freudian psychology, the term refers specifically to the element of the human mind that represents the conscious processes concerned with reality, in conflict with the ◊id (the instinctual element) and the ◊superego (the ethically aware element).

**egret** any of several ◊herons with long tufts of feathers on the head or neck. They belong to the order Ciconiiformes.

**Egypt** Arab Republic of
*national name Jumhuriyat Misr al-Arabiya*
**area** 1,001,450 sq km/386,659 sq mi
*capital* Cairo
*major towns/cities* El Gîza, Shubra Al Khayma, Alexandria, Port Said, El-Mahalla el-Koubra, Tauta, El-Mansoura
*major ports* Alexandria, Port Said, Suez, Damietta, Shubra Al Khayma

## Section through a fertilized egg

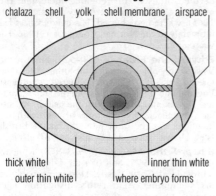

chalaza  shell  yolk  shell membrane  airspace

thick white — inner thin white
outer thin white — where embryo forms

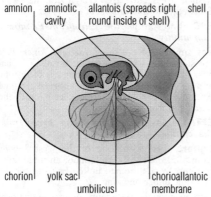

amnion  amniotic  allantois (spreads right  shell
cavity  round inside of shell)

chorion  yolk sac  chorioallantoic
umbilicus  membrane

*egg Section through a fertilized bird egg. Inside a bird's egg is a complex structure of liquids and membranes designed to meet the needs of the growing embryo. The yolk, which is rich in fat, is gradually absorbed by the embryo. The white of the egg provides protein and water. The chalaza is a twisted band of protein which holds the yolk in place and acts as a shock absorber. The airspace allows gases to be exchanged through the shell. The allantois contains many blood vessels which carry gases between the embryo and the outside.*

**physical features** mostly desert; hills in east; fertile land along Nile valley and delta; cultivated and settled area is about 35,500 sq km/13,700 sq mi; Aswan High Dam and Lake Nasser; Sinai
**head of state** Hosni Mubarak from 1981
**head of government** Kamal Ahmed Ganzouri from 1996
**political system** democracy
**political parties** National Democratic Party (NDP), moderate, left of centre; Socialist Labour Party (SLP), right of centre; Liberal Socialist Party, free enterprise; New Wafd Party, nationalist; National Progressive Unionist Party, left wing
**Ccurrency** Egyptian pound
**GNP per capita (PPP)** (US$) 3,130 (1998)
**exports** petroleum and petroleum products, textiles, clothing, food, live animals. Principal

market: EU 32% (1998)
**population** 67,226,000 (1999 est)
**language** Arabic (official); ancient Egyptian survives to some extent in Coptic; English; French
**religion** Sunni Muslim 90%, Coptic Christian 7%
**life expectancy** 65 (men); 68 (women) (1995–2000)
**Chronology**
**1st century BC –7th century AD** Conquered by Augustus in AD 30, Egypt passed under rule of Roman, and later Byzantine, governors.
**AD 639–42** Arabs conquered Egypt, introducing Islam and Arabic; succession of Arab dynasties followed.
**1250** Mamelukes seized power.
**1517** Became part of Turkish Ottoman Empire.
**1798–1801** Invasion by Napoleon followed by period of French occupation.
**1801** Control regained by Turks.
**1869** Opening of Suez Canal made Egypt strategically important.
**1881–82** Nationalist revolt resulted in British occupation.
**1914** Egypt became a British protectorate.
**1922** Achieved nominal independence under King Fuad I.
**1936** Full independence from Britain achieved. King Fuad succeeded by his son Farouk.
**1946** Withdrawal of British troops except from Suez Canal zone.
**1952** Farouk overthrown by army in bloodless coup.
**1953** Egypt declared a republic, with Gen Neguib as president.
**1956** Neguib replaced by Col Gamal Nasser. Nasser announced nationalization of Suez Canal; Egypt attacked by Britain, France, and Israel. Ceasefire agreed following US intervention.
**1958** Short-lived merger of Egypt and Syria as United Arab Republic (UAR).
**1967** Six-Day War with Israel ended in Egypt's defeat and Israeli occupation of Sinai and Gaza Strip.
**1970** Nasser died suddenly; succeeded by Anwar Sadat.
**1973** Attempt to regain territory lost to Israel led to Yom Kippur War; ceasefire arranged by US secretary of state Henry Kissinger.

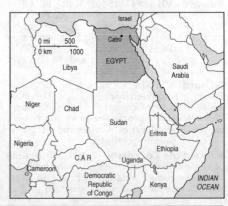

*1978–79* Camp David talks in USA resulted in a peace treaty between Egypt and Israel. Egypt expelled from Arab League.

*1981* Sadat was assassinated by Muslim fundamentalists and succeeded by Hosni Mubarak.

*1983* Relations between Egypt and the Arab world improved; only Libya and Syria maintained a trade boycott.

*1987* Egypt was readmitted to the Arab League.

*1989* Relations with Libya improved; diplomatic relations with Syria were restored.

*1991* Egypt participated in the Gulf War on the US-led side and was a major force in convening a Middle East peace conference in Spain.

*1992* There was violence between Muslims and Christians.

*1994* The government cracked down on Islamic militants.

*1995* An abortive attempt was made to assassinate Mubarak.

*1996* Kamal Ahmed Ganzouri was appointed prime minister.

*1997* Islamic extremists killed and injured tourists at Luxor.

**Egypt, ancient** ancient civilization, based around the River Nile in Egypt, which emerged 5,000 years ago and reached its peak in the 16th century BC. Ancient Egypt was famed for its great power and wealth, due to the highly fertile lands of the Nile delta, which were rich sources of grain for the whole Mediterranean region. Egyptians were advanced in agriculture, engineering, and applied sciences. Many of their monuments, such as the ◊pyramids and the sphinx, survive today.

**Ehrlich, Paul** (1854–1915) German bacteriologist and immunologist who produced the first cure for ◊syphilis. He developed the arsenic compounds, in particular Salvarsan, that were used in the treatment of syphilis before the discovery of antibiotics. He shared the 1908 Nobel Prize for Physiology or Medicine with Ilya Mechnikov, awarded for his work on immunity.

**eider** large marine ◊duck of the genus *Somateria*, family Anatidae, order Anseriformes. They are found on the northern coasts of the Atlantic and Pacific Oceans. The *common eider S. molissima* is highly valued for its soft down, which is used in quilts and cushions for warmth. The adult male has a black cap and belly and a green nape. The rest of the plumage is white with a pink breast and throat, while the female is a mottled brown. The bill is large and flattened and both bill and feet are olive green.

**Eiffel, (Alexandre) Gustave** (1832–1923) French engineer who constructed the *Eiffel Tower* for the 1889 Paris Exhibition. The tower, made of iron, is 320 m/1,050 ft high and stands in the Champ de Mars, Paris. Sightseers may ride to the top for a view.

**Einstein, Albert** (1879–1955) German-born US physicist whose theories of ◊relativity revolutionized our understanding of matter, space, and time. Einstein established that light may have a particle nature and deduced the *photoelectric law,* for which he was awarded the Nobel Prize for Physics in 1921. He also investigated Brownian motion, confirming the existence of atoms. His last conception of the basic laws governing the universe was outlined in his ◊unified field theory, made public in 1953.

**einsteinium** synthesized, radioactive, metallic element of the actinide series, symbol Es, atomic number 99, relative atomic mass 254.09.

## EGYPT, ANCIENT: CHRONOLOGY

| | |
|---|---|
| **5000 BC** | Egyptian culture already well established in the Nile Valley, with Neolithic farming villages. |
| **c. 3050** | Menes unites Lower Egypt (the delta) with his own kingdom of Upper Egypt. |
| **c. 2630** | The architect Imhotep builds the step pyramid at Sakkara. |
| **c. 2550** | **Old Kingdom** reaches the height of its power and the kings of the 4th dynasty build the pyramids at El Gîza. |
| **c. 2040–1640** | **Middle Kingdom,** under which the unity lost towards the end of the Old Kingdom is restored. |
| **c. 1750** | Infiltrating Asian Hyksos people establish their kingdom in the Nile Delta. |
| **c. 1550** | **New Kingdom** established by the 18th dynasty following the eviction of the Hyksos, with its capital at Thebes. The high point of ancient Egyptian civilization under the pharaohs Thothmes, Hatshepsut, Amenhotep, Akhenaton (who moves the capital to Akhetaton), and Tutankhamen. |
| **c. 1307–1196** | 19th dynasty: Major building works by Seti I and Ramses II at Thebes, Abydos and Abu Simbel. |
| **1191** | Ramses III defeats the Indo-European Sea Peoples, but after him there is decline, and power within the country passes from the pharaohs to the priests of Amen. |
| **1070–664** | **Third Intermediate Period** during this period Egypt is often divided between two or more dynasties; the nobles become virtually independent. |
| **8th–7th centuries** | Brief interlude of rule by kings from Nubia. |
| **666** | The Assyrians under Ashurbanipal occupy Thebes. |
| **663–609** | Psammetichus I restores Egypt's independence and unity. |
| **525** | Egypt is conquered by Cambyses and becomes a Persian province. |
| **c. 405–340** | Period of independence. |
| **332** | Conquest by Alexander the Great. On the division of his empire, Egypt goes to one of his generals, Ptolemy I, and his descendants, the Macedonian dynasty. |
| **30** | Death of Cleopatra, last of the Macedonians, and conquest by the Roman emperor Augustus; Egypt becomes a province of the Roman empire. |
| **AD 641** | Conquest by the Arabs; the Christianity of later Roman rule is for the most part replaced by Islam. |

**Eire** former name (1937–48) of Southern Ireland, now the Republic of Ireland. In Gaelic the name Eire is also used to refer to the whole of Ireland.

**Eisenhower, Dwight David ('Ike')** (1890–1969) 34th president of the USA 1953–60, a Republican. A general in World War II, he commanded the Allied forces in Italy 1943, then the Allied invasion of Europe, and from October 1944 all the Allied armies in the West. As president he promoted business interests at home and conducted the ◊Cold War abroad. His vice president was Richard Nixon.

**eland** largest species of ◊antelope, *Taurotragus oryx*. Pale fawn in colour, it is about 2 m/6 ft high, and both sexes have spiral horns about 45 cm/18 in long. It is found in central and southern Africa.

**elasticity** in physics, the ability of a solid to recover its shape once deforming forces (stresses modifying its dimensions or shape) are removed. An elastic material obeys ◊Hooke's law, which states that its deformation is proportional to the applied stress up to a certain point, called the *elastic limit,* beyond which additional stress will deform it permanently. Elastic materials include metals and rubber; however, all materials have some degree of elasticity.

**Elbe** Czech *Labe,* ancient *Albis,* one of the principal rivers of Germany; length 1,166 km/725 mi. It rises on the southern slopes of the Riesengebirge, Czech Republic, and flows northwest across the German plain to the North Sea. It is navigable for ocean-going vessels as far as Hamburg (101 km/62 mi from the mouth), and for smaller boats as far as its junction with the Vltava (845 km/525 mi). The river basin is approximately 145,039 sq km/56,000 sq mi.

**Elbrus** or *Elbruz,* (Persian 'two heads') highest peak in Europe; located in the Caucasus Mountains, Caucasia, in the Russian Federation. Its western summit reaches a height of 5,642 m/18,510 ft, while the eastern summit stands at 5,595 m/18,356 ft.

**elder** in botany, any of a group of small trees or shrubs belonging to the honeysuckle family, native to North America, Europe, Asia, and North Africa. Some are grown as ornamentals for their showy yellow or white flower clusters and their colourful black or scarlet berries. (Genus *Sambucus,* family Caprifoliaceae.)

**El Dorado** fabled city of gold believed by the 16th-century Spanish and other Europeans to exist somewhere in the area of the Orinoco and Amazon rivers.

**Eleanor of Aquitaine** (*c.* 1122–1204) Queen of France 1137–51 as wife of Louis VII, and of England from 1154 as wife of Henry II. Henry imprisoned her 1174–89 for supporting their sons, the future Richard I and King John, in revolt against him.

**Eleanor of Castile** (*c.* 1245–1290) Queen of Edward I of England, the daughter of Ferdinand III of Castile. She married Prince Edward in 1254, and accompanied him on his crusade in 1270. She died at Harby, Nottinghamshire, and Edward erected stone crosses in towns where her body rested on the funeral journey to London. Several *Eleanor Crosses* are still standing, for example, at Northampton.

**election** process of appointing a person to public office or a political party to government by voting. Elections were occasionally held in ancient Greek democracies; Roman tribunes were regularly elected.

**electoral system** see ◊vote and ◊proportional representation.

**electric arc** a continuous electric discharge of high current between two electrodes, giving out a brilliant light and heat. The phenomenon is exploited in the carbon-arc lamp, once widely used in film projectors. In the electric-arc furnace an arc struck between very large carbon electrodes and the metal charge provides the heating. In arc ◊welding an electric arc provides the heat to fuse the metal. The discharges in low-pressure gases, as in neon and sodium lights, can also be broadly considered as electric arcs.

**electric charge** property of some bodies that causes them to exert forces on each other. Two bodies both with positive or both with negative charges repel, each other, whereas bodies with opposite or 'unlike' charges attract each other, since each is in the ◊electric field of the other. In atoms, ◊electrons possess a negative charge, and ◊protons an equal positive charge. The ◊SI unit of electric charge is the coulomb (symbol C).

**electric current** the flow of electrically charged particles through a conducting circuit due to the presence of a ◊potential difference. The current at any point in a circuit is the amount of charge flowing per second; its SI unit is the ampere (coulomb per second).

**electric eel** South American freshwater bony fish. It grows to almost 3 m/10 ft and the electric shock produced, normally for immobilizing prey, is enough to stun an adult human. Electric eels are not true eels. *classification Electrophorus electricus* is in the order Cypriniformes, class Osteichthyes.

**electric field** in physics, a region in which a particle possessing electric charge experiences a force owing to the presence of another electric charge. The strength of an electric field, *E,* is measured in volts per metre (V m$^{-1}$). It is a type of ◊electromagnetic field.

**electricity** all phenomena caused by ◊electric charge, whether static or in motion. Electric charge is caused by an excess or deficit of electrons in the charged substance, and an electric current is the movement of charge through a material. Substances may be electrical conductors, such as metals, that allow the passage of electricity through them readily, or insulators, such as rubber, that are extremely poor conductors. Substances with relatively poor conductivities that can be improved by the addition of heat or light are known as ◊semiconductors.

**electroconvulsive therapy** (ECT) or *electroshock therapy,* treatment mainly for severe ◊depression, given under anaesthesia and with a muscle relaxant. An electric current is passed through one or both sides of the brain to induce alterations in its electrical activity. The treatment can cause distress and loss of concentration and memory, and so there is much controversy about its use and effectiveness.

**electrocution** death caused by electric current. It is used as a method of execution in some US states. The condemned person is strapped into a special chair and a shock of 1,800–2,000 volts is administered. See ◊capital punishment.

**electrode** any terminal by which an electric current passes in or out of a conducting substance; for example, the anode or ◊cathode in a battery or the carbons in an arc lamp. The terminals that emit and collect the flow of electrons in thermionic valves (electron tubes) are also called electrodes: for example, cathodes, plates, and grids.

**electroencephalogram** (EEG) graphic record of the electrical discharges of the brain, as detected by electrodes placed on the scalp. The pattern of electrical activity revealed by electroencephalography is helpful in the diagnosis of some brain disorders, in particular epilepsy.

**electrolysis** in chemistry, the production of chemical changes by passing an electric current through a solution or molten salt (the electrolyte), resulting in the migration of ions to the electrodes: positive ions (cations) to the negative electrode (cathode) and negative ions (anions) to the positive electrode (anode).

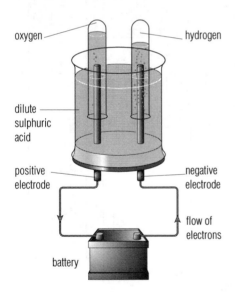

*electrolysis* Passing an electric current through acidified water (such as diluted sulphuric acid) breaks down the water into its constituent elements – hydrogen and oxygen.

**electromagnet** coil of wire wound around a soft iron core that acts as a magnet when an electric current flows through the wire.

Electromagnets have many uses: in switches, electric bells, ◊solenoids, and metal-lifting cranes.

**electromagnetic field** in physics, the region in which a particle with an ◊electric charge experiences a force. If it does so only when moving, it is in a pure *magnetic field;* if it does so when stationary, it is in an *electric field.* Both can be present simultaneously.

**electromagnetic force** one of the four fundamental ◊forces of nature, the other three being the gravitational force or gravity, the weak nuclear force, and the strong nuclear force. The particle that is the carrier for the electromagnetic force is the ◊photon.

**electromagnetic waves** oscillating electric and magnetic fields travelling together through space at a speed of nearly 300,000 km/186,000 mi per second. The (limitless) range of possible wavelengths and ◊frequencies of electromagnetic waves, which can be thought of as making up the *electromagnetic spectrum,* includes radio waves, infrared radiation, visible light, ultraviolet radiation, X-rays, and gamma rays. *See illustration on page 294.*

**electromotive force** (emf), loosely, the voltage produced by an electric battery or generator in an electrical circuit or, more precisely, the energy supplied by a source of electric power in driving a unit charge around the circuit. The unit is the ◊volt.

**electron** stable, negatively charged ◊elementary particle; it is a constituent of all atoms, and a member of the class of particles known as ◊leptons. The electrons in each atom surround the nucleus in groupings called shells; in a neutral atom the number of electrons is equal to the number of protons in the nucleus. This electron structure is responsible for the chemical properties of the atom (see ◊atomic structure).

**electronic mail** or *e-mail,* messages sent electronically from computer to computer via network connections such as Ethernet or the ◊Internet, or via telephone lines to a host system. Messages once sent are stored on the network or by the host system until the recipient picks them up. As well as text, messages may contain enclosed text files, artwork, or multimedia clips. *See illustration on page 295.*

**electronic music** music composed mainly of electronically generated and modified sounds. The term was first used in 1954 to describe music made up of synthesized sounds recorded on tape, to distinguish it from *musique concrète* (concrete music), but later included music for electronic sounds with traditional instruments or voices.

**electronic publishing** distribution of information using computer-based media such as ◊multimedia and ◊hypertext in the creation of electronic 'books'. Critical technologies in the development of electronic publishing were ◊CD-ROM, with its massive yet compact storage capabilities, and the advent of computer networking with its ability to deliver information instantaneously anywhere in the world.

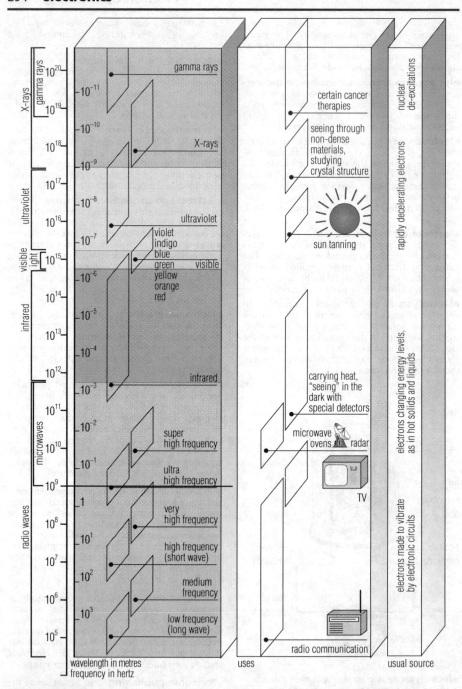

**electromagnetic waves** *Radio waves have the lowest frequency. Infrared radiation, visible light, ultraviolet radiation, X-rays, and gamma rays have progressively higher frequencies.*

**electronics** branch of science that deals with the emission of ◊electrons from conductors and ◊semiconductors, with the subsequent manipulation of these electrons, and with the construction of electronic devices. The first electronic device was the thermionic valve, or vacuum tube, in which electrons moved in a vacuum, and led to such inventions as ◊radio, ◊television, ◊radar, and the digital ◊computer. Replacement of valves with the comparatively tiny and

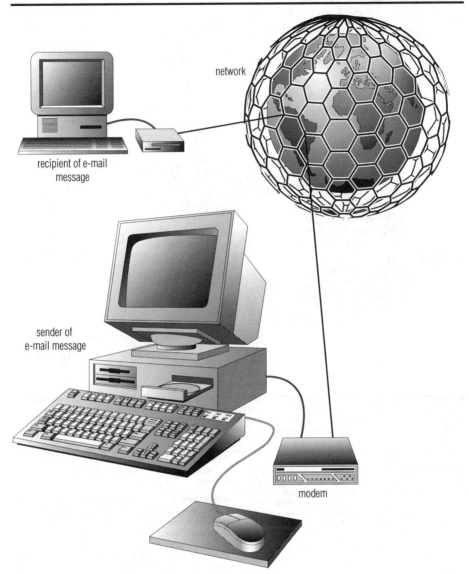

network

recipient of e-mail
message

sender of
e-mail message

modem

***electronic mail*** *The basic structure of an electronic mail system. A message is sent via a telephone line and stored in a central computer. The message remains there until the recipient calls up the central computer and collects the message.*

reliable ◊transistor from 1948 revolutionized electronic development. Modern electronic devices are based on minute ◊integrated circuits (silicon chips), wafer-thin crystal slices holding tens of thousands of electronic components.

**electron microscope** instrument that produces a magnified image by using a beam of ◊electrons instead of light rays, as in an optical ◊microscope. An *electron lens* is an arrangement of electromagnetic coils that control and focus the beam. Electrons are not visible to the eye, so instead of an eyepiece there is a fluorescent screen or a photographic plate on which

the electrons form an image. The wavelength of the electron beam is much shorter than that of light, so much greater magnification and resolution (ability to distinguish detail) can be achieved. The development of the electron microscope has made possible the observation of very minute organisms, viruses, and even large molecules. *See illustration on page 296.*

**electroplating** deposition of metals upon metallic surfaces by electrolysis for decorative and/or protective purposes. It is used in the preparation of printers' blocks, 'master' audio discs, and in many other processes.

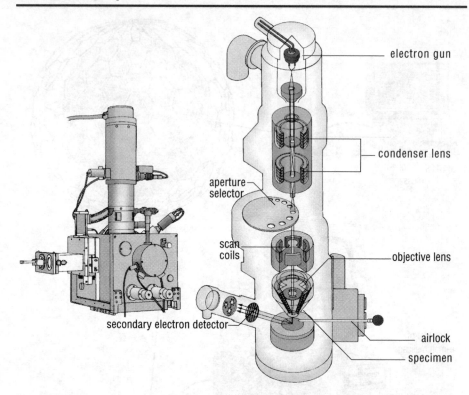

electron gun

condenser lens

aperture selector

scan coils

objective lens

secondary electron detector

airlock

specimen

***electron microscope*** *The scanning electron microscope. Electrons from the electron gun are focused to a fine point on the specimen surface by the lens systems. The beam is moved across the specimen by the scan coils. Secondary electrons are emitted by the specimen surface and pass through the detector, which produces an electrical signal. The signal is passed to an electronic console, and produces an image on a screen.*

**electroscope** apparatus for detecting ⟩electric charge. The simple gold-leaf electroscope consists of a vertical conducting (metal) rod ending in a pair of rectangular pieces of gold foil, mounted inside and insulated from an earthed metal case or glass jar. An electric charge applied to the end of the metal rod makes the gold leaves diverge, because they each receive a similar charge (positive or negative) and so repel each other.

**element** substance that cannot be split chemically into simpler substances. The atoms of a particular element all have the same number of protons in their nuclei (their ⟩atomic number). Elements are classified in the ⟩periodic table of the elements. Of the known elements, 92 are known to occur in nature (those with atomic numbers 1–92). Those elements with atomic numbers above 96 do not occur in nature and are synthesized only, produced in particle accelerators. Of the elements, 81 are stable; all the others, which include atomic numbers 43, 61, and from 84 up, are radioactive.

**elementary particle** in physics, a subatomic particle that is not made up of smaller particles, and so can be considered one of the fundamental units of matter. There are three groups of elementary particles: quarks, leptons, and gauge bosons.

**elephant** large grazing mammal with thick, grey wrinkled skin, large ears, a long flexible trunk, and huge curving tusks. There are finger-like projections at the end of its trunk used for grasping food and carrying it to its mouth. The trunk is also used for carrying water to the mouth. The elephant is herbivorous and, because of its huge size, much of its time must be spent feeding on leaves, shoots, bamboo, reeds, grasses and fruits and, where possible, cultivated crops such as maize and bananas. They are the largest living land animal.

Elephants usually live in herds containing between 20–40 females (cows), led by a mature, experienced cow. Most bull elephants live alone or in small groups; young males remain with the herd until they reach sexual maturity. Elephants have the longest gestation period of any animal (18–23 months between conception and birth) and usually produce one calf, which takes between 10–15 years to reach maturity. Elephants can live up to 60 years in the wild, but those in captivity have been known to reach over 65. There are two species of elephant, the African and the Indian or Asian elephant.

**Elgar, Edward (William)** (1857–1934) English composer. Although his celebrated oratorio *The Dream of Gerontius* (1900), based on the written work by theologian John Henry Newman, was initially unpopular in Britain, its good reception in Düsseldorf in 1902 led to a surge of interest in his earlier works, including the *Pomp and Circumstance Marches* (1901). His *Enigma Variations* (1899) brought him lasting fame.

**Elgin marbles** collection of ancient Greek sculptures, including the famous frieze and other sculptures from the Parthenon at Athens, assembled by the 7th Earl of Elgin. Sent to England 1803–1812, and bought for the nation in 1816 for £35,000, they are now in the British Museum. Greece has repeatedly asked for them to be returned to Athens.

**Elijah** (lived c. mid-9th century BC) In the Old Testament, a Hebrew prophet during the reigns of the Israelite kings Ahab and Ahaziah. He came from Gilead. He defeated the prophets of ◊Baal, and was said to have been carried up to heaven in a fiery chariot in a whirlwind. In Jewish belief, Elijah will return to Earth to herald the coming of the Messiah.

**Eliot, George** pen-name of Mary Ann (later Marian) Evans (1819–1880) English novelist. Her works include the pastoral *Adam Bede* (1859); *The Mill on the Floss* (1860), with its autobiographical elements; *Silas Marner* (1861), containing elements of the folk tale; and *Daniel Deronda* (1876). *Middlemarch,* published serially (1871–72), is considered her greatest novel for its confident handling of numerous characters and central social and moral issues. She developed a subtle psychological presentation of character, and her work is pervaded by a penetrating and compassionate intelligence.

**Eliot, T(homas) S(tearns)** (1888–1965) US-born poet, playwright, and critic, who lived in England from 1915. His first volume of poetry, *Prufrock and Other Observations* (1917), introduced new verse forms and rhythms; subsequent major poems were *The Waste Land* (1922), a long symbolic poem of disillusionment, and 'The Hollow Men' (1925). For children he published *Old Possum's Book of Practical Cats* (1939). Eliot's plays include *Murder in the Cathedral* (1935) and *The Cocktail Party* (1950). His critical works include *The Sacred Wood* (1920), setting out his views on poetic tradition.

**Elizabeth, the Queen Mother** (1900– ), wife of King George VI of England. She was born Lady Elizabeth Angela Marguerite Bowes-Lyon, and on 26 April 1923 she married Albert, Duke of York, who became King George VI in 1936. Their children are Queen Elizabeth II and Princess Margaret.

**Elizabeth** two queens of England or the UK:

**Elizabeth I** (1533–1603) Queen of England (1558–1603), the daughter of Henry VIII and Anne Boleyn. Through her Religious Settlement of 1559 she enforced the Protestant religion by law. She had ◊Mary Queen of Scots executed in 1587. Her conflict with Roman Catholic Spain led to the defeat of the ◊Spanish Armada in 1588. The Elizabethan age was expansionist in commerce and geographical exploration, and arts and literature flourished. The rulers of many European states made unsuccessful bids to marry Elizabeth, and she used these bids to strengthen her power. She was succeeded by James I.

**Elizabeth II** Elizabeth Alexandra Mary (1926– ) Queen of Great Britain and Northern Ireland from 1952, the elder daughter of George VI. She married her third cousin, Philip, Duke of Edinburgh, in 1947. They have four children: Charles, Anne, Andrew, and Edward.

**elk** large deer *Alces alces* inhabiting northern Europe, Asia, Scandinavia, and North America, where it is known as the moose. It is brown in colour, stands about 2 m/6 ft at the shoulders, has very large palmate antlers, a fleshy muzzle, short neck, and long legs. It feeds on leaves and shoots. In North America, the ◊wapiti is called an elk.

**elkhound** Norwegian dog resembling the husky but much smaller. Its coat is thick, with a full undercoat and the tail is bushy. Elkhounds are grey, with a darker shade on the back, and are about 50 cm/20 in high, weighing approximately 22 kg/48 lb.

**Ellesmere Island** island in the extreme northeast of the Arctic Archipelago, Northwest Territories, Canada; area 196,236 sq km/75,767 sq mi; the population is about 100. It is the second-largest island in the Archipelago (Baffin Island is the largest) and is part of the Queen Elizabeth island group, at the northern end of Baffin Bay. Its northern tip, Cape Columbia, is the most northerly point of the North American continent. The island is, for the most part, barren or glacier-covered. It was first sighted in 1616 by William Baffin.

**Ellice Islands** former name of Tuvalu, a group of islands in the western Pacific Ocean.

**Ellington, Duke (Edward Kennedy)** (1899–1974) US pianist. He had an outstanding career as a composer and arranger of jazz. He wrote numerous pieces for his own jazz orchestra, accentuating the strengths of individual virtuoso instrumentalists, and became one of the leading figures in jazz over a 55-year period. Some of his most popular compositions include 'Mood Indigo', 'Sophisticated Lady', 'Solitude', and 'Black and Tan Fantasy'. He was one of the founders of big-band jazz.

**elm** any of a group of trees found in temperate regions of the northern hemisphere and in mountainous parts of the tropics. All have doubly-toothed leaf margins and clusters of small flowers. (Genus *Ulmus,* family Ulmaceae.)

**El Paso** city and administrative headquarters of El Paso County, Texas, at the base of the Franklin Mountains, on the Rio Grande, opposite the Mexican city of Ciudad Juárez; population (1994 est) 579,000. It is the centre of an agricultural and cattle-raising area, and there are electronics, food processing, packing, and leather industries, as well as oil refineries and industries based on local iron and copper mines. There are several military installations in the area. The city is home to the University of Texas at El Paso (formerly Texas Western; founded in 1913).

**El Salvador** Republic of
**national name** *República de El Salvador*

**area** 21,393 sq km/8,259 sq mi
**capital** San Salvador
**major towns/cities** Soyapango, Santa Ana, San Miguel, Nueva San Salvador, Mejicanos
**physical features** narrow coastal plain, rising to mountains in north with central plateau
**head of state and government** Francisco Guillermo Flores Pérez from 1999
**political system** emergent democracy
**political parties** Christian Democrats (PDC), anti-imperialist; Farabundo Martí Liberation Front (FMLN), left wing; National Republican Alliance (ARENA), extreme right wing; National Conciliation Party (PCN), right wing
**currency** Salvadorean colón
**GNP per capita (PPP)** (US$) 2,850 (1998)
**exports** coffee, textiles and garments, sugar, shrimp, footwear, pharmaceuticals. Principal market: USA 59.4 % (1998)
**population** 6,154,000 (1999 est)
**language** Spanish, Nahuatl
**religion** Roman Catholic, Protestant
**life expectancy** 67 (men); 73 (women) (1995–2000)
*Chronology*
**11th century** Pipils, descendants of the Nahuatl-speaking Toltec and Aztec peoples of Mexico, settled in the country and came to dominate El Salvador until the Spanish conquest.
**1524** Conquered by the Spanish adventurer Pedro de Alvarado and made a Spanish colony, with resistance being crushed by 1540.
**1821** Independence achieved from Spain; briefly joined with Mexico.
**1823** Became part of United Provinces (Federation) of Central America, also embracing Costa Rica, Guatemala, Honduras, and Nicaragua.
**1833** Unsuccessful rebellion against Spanish control of land led by Anastasio Aquino.

**1840** Became fully independent when Federation dissolved.
**1859–63** Coffee growing introduced by president Gerardo Barrios.
**1932** Peasant uprising, led by Augustín Farabundo Martí, suppressed by military at a cost of the lives of 30,000, virtually eliminating American Indian Salvadoreans.
**1961** Following a coup, the right-wing National Conciliation Party (PCN) established and in power.
**1969** Brief 'Football War' with Honduras, which El Salvador attacked, at the time of a football competition between the two states, following evictions of thousands of Salvadoran illegal immigrants from Honduras.
**1977** Allegations of human-rights violations; growth of left-wing Farabundo Martí National Liberation Front (FMLN) guerrilla activities. Gen Carlos Romero elected president.
**1979** A coup replaced Romero with a military-civilian junta.
**1980** The archbishop of San Salvador and human-rights champion, Oscar Romero, was assassinated; the country was on the verge of civil war. José Napoleón Duarte (PDC) became the first civilian president since 1931.
**1979–81** 30,000 people were killed by right-wing death squads.
**1981** Mexico and France recognized the FMLN guerrillas as a legitimate political force, but the USA actively assisted the government in its battle against them.
**1982** Assembly elections were boycotted by left-wing parties. Held amid considerable violence, they were won by far-right National Republican Alliance (ARENA).
**1984** Duarte won the presidential election.
**1986** Duarte sought a negotiated settlement with the guerrillas.
**1989** Alfredo Cristiani (ARENA) became president in rigged elections; rebel attacks intensified.
**1991** A peace accord sponsored by the United Nations (UN) was signed by representatives of the government and the socialist guerrilla group, the FMLN, which became a political party.
**1993** A UN-sponsored commission published a report on war atrocities; there was a government amnesty for those implicated; top military leaders officially retired.
**1994** Armando Calderón Sol (ARENA) was elected president.

**Elysium** or **the Elysian Fields**, in Greek mythology, an afterworld or paradise, originally identified with the Islands of the Blessed, for those who found favour with the gods. Later poets depicted Elysium as a region in ◊Hades, the underworld. It was ruled over by Rhadamanthys, a judge of the dead.

**e-mail** abbreviation for ◊electronic mail.

**Emancipation Proclamation** in US history, President Lincoln's Civil War announcement, 22 September 1862, stating that from the beginning of 1863 all black slaves in states still engaged in rebellion against the federal government would be emancipated. Slaves in border states still remaining loyal to the Union were excluded.

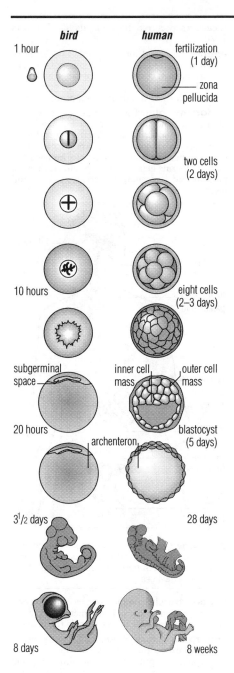

**bird** | **human**

1 hour — fertilization (1 day), zona pellucida

two cells (2 days)

eight cells (2–3 days)

10 hours

subgerminal space

inner cell mass | outer cell mass

20 hours

blastocyst (5 days)

archenteron

3½ days | 28 days

8 days | 8 weeks

**embryo** *The development of a bird and a human embryo. In the human, division of the fertilized egg, or ovum, begins within hours of conception. Within a week, a hollow, fluid-containing ball – a blastocyst – with a mass of cells at one end has developed. After the third week, the embryo has changed from a mass of cells into a recognizable shape. At four weeks, the embryo is 3 mm/0.1 in long, with a large bulge for the heart and small pits for the ears. At six weeks, the embryo is 1.5 cm/0.6 in long with a pulsating heart and ear flaps. By the eighth week, the embryo (now technically a fetus) is 2.5 cm/1 in long and recognizably human, with eyelids and small fingers and toes.*

**embryo** early developmental stage of an animal or a plant following fertilization of an ovum (egg cell), or activation of an ovum by ◊parthenogenesis. In humans, the term embryo describes the fertilized egg during its first seven weeks of existence; from the eighth week onwards it is referred to as a fetus.

**embryology** study of the changes undergone by an organism from its conception as a fertilized ovum (egg) to its emergence into the world at hatching or birth. It is mainly concerned with the changes in cell organization in the embryo and the way in which these lead to the structures and organs of the adult (the process of ◊differentiation).

**emerald** a clear, green gemstone variety of the mineral ◊beryl. It occurs naturally in Colombia, the Ural Mountains in Russia, Zimbabwe, and Australia. The green colour is caused by the presence of the element chromium in the beryl.

**Emerson, Ralph Waldo** (1803–1882) US philosopher, essayist, and poet. He settled in Concord, Massachusetts, which he made a centre of ◊transcendentalism, and wrote *Nature* (1836), which states the movement's main principles emphasizing the value of self-reliance and the godlike nature of human souls. His two volumes of *Essays* (1841, 1844) made his reputation: 'Self-Reliance' and 'Compensation' in the earlier volume are among the best known.

**emery** black to greyish form of impure ◊corundum that also contains the minerals magnetite and haematite. It is used as an ◊abrasive.

**emf** in physics, abbreviation for ◊*electromotive force*.

**Emilia-Romagna** region of northern central Italy, comprising the provinces of Bologna, Ferrara, Forli, Modena, Parma, Piacenza, and Reggio nell'Emilia; area 22,100 sq km/8,531 sq mi; population (1992) 3,920,200. The capital is ◊Bologna; other towns include Reggio nell'Emilia, Rimini, Parma, Ferrara, and Ravenna. Agricultural produce includes fruit, wine, sugar beet, beef, dairy products, rice, and wheat. Oil and natural-gas resources have been developed in the Po Valley.

**Emmental** district in the valley of the Emme River, Bern canton, Switzerland, where a hard cheese of the same name has been made since the mid-15th century. The main town in Emmental is Langnau.

**emphysema** incurable lung condition characterized by disabling breathlessness. Progressive loss of the thin walls dividing the air spaces (alveoli) in the lungs reduces the area available for the exchange of oxygen and carbon dioxide, causing the lung tissue to expand. The term 'emphysema' can also refer to the presence of air in other body tissues.

**empire** collective name for a group of countries under the control of a single country or dynasty. Major empires in Europe have included the ◊Roman Empire and the ◊British Empire, and in Asia the ◊Ottoman Empire and Mogul Empire (see ◊Mogul dynasty).

**Empire State Building** landmark building in New York, USA. It is 443 m/1,454 ft high with 102 floors, and was the highest building in the world until 1972, when it was superseded by the World Trade Center, New York. It was built in 1930 at a cost of over $40,000,000.

**empiricism** (Greek *empeiria* 'experience' or 'experiment') in philosophy, the belief that all knowledge is ultimately derived from sense experience. It is suspicious of metaphysical schemes based on a priori propositions, which are claimed to be true irrespective of experience. It is frequently contrasted with ◊rationalism.

**EMS** abbreviation for ◊*European Monetary System.*

**emu** flightless bird *Dromaius novaehollandiae*, family Dromaiidae, order Casuariidae, native to Australia. It stands about 1.8 m/6 ft high and has coarse brown plumage, small rudimentary wings, short feathers on the head and neck, and powerful legs, which are well adapted for running and kicking.

The female has a curious bag or pouch in the windpipe that enables her to emit a characteristic loud booming note. Emus are monogamous, and the male wholly or partially incubates the eggs.

**EMU** abbreviation for *economic and monetary union*, the ◊European Union (EU) policy for a single currency and common economic policies. In June 1994 EU finance ministers agreed to postpone the lauch of EMU until 1999, after it emerged that most countries would be unable to meet the economic criteria outlined in the ◊Maastricht Treaty by the original target date of 1997.

**emulsion** stable dispersion of a liquid in another liquid – for example, oil and water in some cosmetic lotions.

**enamel** vitrified (glasslike) coating of various colours used for decorative purposes on a metallic or porcelain surface. In *cloisonné* the various sections of the design are separated by thin metal wires or strips. In *champlevé* the enamel is poured into engraved cavities in the metal surface.

**encephalitis** inflammation of the brain, nearly always due to viral infection but it may also occur in bacterial and other infections. It varies widely in severity, from shortlived, relatively slight effects of headache, drowsiness, and fever to paralysis, coma, and death.

**enclosure** in Britain, appropriation of ◊common land as private property, or the changing of open-field systems to enclosed fields (often used for sheep). This process began in the 14th century and became widespread in the 15th and 16th centuries. It caused poverty, homelessness, and rural depopulation, and resulted in revolts in 1536, 1569, and 1607. A further wave of enclosures occurred between about 1760 and 1820.

**endive** cultivated annual plant, the leaves of which are used in salads and cooking. One variety has narrow, curled leaves; another has wide, smooth leaves. It is related to ◊chicory. (*Cichorium endivia*, family Compositae.)

**endocrine gland** gland that secretes hormones into the bloodstream to regulate body processes. Endocrine glands are most highly developed in vertebrates, but are also found in other animals, notably insects. In humans the main endocrine glands are the pituitary, thyroid, parathyroid, adrenal, pancreas, ovary, and testis.

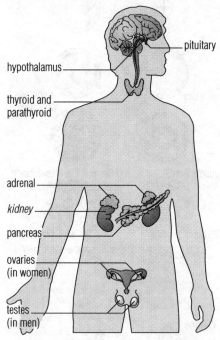

Labels: pituitary, hypothalamus, thyroid and parathyroid, adrenal, kidney, pancreas, ovaries (in women), testes (in men)

**endocrine gland** *The main human endocrine glands. These glands produce hormones – chemical messengers – which travel in the bloodstream to stimulate certain cells.*

**endometriosis** common gynaecological complaint in which patches of endometrium (the lining of the womb) are found outside the uterus.

**endorphin** natural substance (a polypeptide) that modifies the action of nerve cells. Endorphins are produced by the pituitary gland and hypothalamus of vertebrates. They lower the perception of pain by reducing the transmission of signals between nerve cells.

**endoscopy** examination of internal organs or tissues by an instrument allowing direct vision. An endoscope is equipped with an eyepiece, lenses, and its own light source to illuminate the field of vision. The endoscope used to examine the digestive tract is a flexible fibreoptic instrument swallowed by the patient.

**endoskeleton** the internal supporting structure of vertebrates, made up of cartilage or bone. It provides support, and acts as a system of levers to which muscles are attached to provide movement. Certain parts of the skeleton (the skull and ribs) give protection to vital body organs.

**Endymion** in Greek mythology, a beautiful young shepherd or hunter visited each night by ◊Selene, the Moon goddess. She kissed him as he slept in a cave on Mount Latmos in Caria, sending him into an eternal sleep in which he became ageless.

**energy** capacity for doing ◊work. Energy can exist in many different forms. For example, potential energy (PE) is energy deriving from position; thus a stretched spring has elastic PE, and an object raised to a height above the Earth's surface, or the water in an elevated reservoir, has gravitational PE. Moving bodies possess kinetic energy (KE). Energy can be converted from one form to another, but the total quantity in a system stays the same (in accordance with the conservation of energy principle). Energy cannot be created or destroyed. For example, as an apple falls it loses gravitational PE but gains KE.

Although energy is never lost, after a number of conversions it tends to finish up as the kinetic energy of random motion of molecules (of the air, for example) at relatively low temperatures. This is 'degraded' energy that is difficult to convert back to other forms.

**energy, alternative** energy from sources that are renewable and ecologically safe, as opposed to sources that are nonrenewable with toxic by-products, such as coal, oil, or gas (fossil fuels), and uranium (for nuclear power). The most important alternative energy source is flowing water, harnessed as ◊hydroelectric power. Other sources include the oceans' tides and waves (see ◊wave power), ◊wind power (harnessed by windmills and wind turbines), the Sun (◊solar energy), and the heat trapped in the Earth's crust (◊geothermal energy) (see also ◊cold fusion).

**energy of reaction** energy released or absorbed during a chemical reaction, also called *enthalpy of reaction* or *heat of reaction.* In a chemical reaction, the energy stored in the reacting molecules is rarely the same as that stored in the product molecules. Depending on which is the greater, energy is either released (an exothermic reaction) or absorbed (an endothermic reaction) from the surroundings. The amount of energy released or absorbed by the quantities of substances represented by the chemical equation is the energy of reaction.

**Engels, Friedrich** (1820–1895) German social and political philosopher, a friend of, and collaborator with, Karl ◊Marx on *The Communist Manifesto* (1848( and other key works. His later interpretations of Marxism, and his own philosophical and historical studies such as *Origins of the Family, Private Property, and the State* (1884; which linked patriarchy with the development of private property), developed such concepts as historical materialism. His use of

positivism and Darwinian ideas gave Marxism a scientific and deterministic flavour which was to influence Soviet thinking.

**engine** device for converting stored energy into useful work or movement. Most engines use a fuel as their energy store. The fuel is burnt to produce heat energy – hence the name 'heat engine' – which is then converted into movement. Heat engines can be classified according to the fuel they use (◊petrol engine or ◊diesel engine), or according to whether the fuel is burnt inside (◊internal combustion engine) or outside (◊steam engine) the engine, or according to whether they produce a reciprocating or rotary motion (◊turbine or Wankel engine).

**engineering** the application of science to the design, construction, and maintenance of works, machinery, roads, railways, bridges, harbour installations, engines, ships, aircraft and airports, spacecraft and space stations, and the generation, transmission, and use of electrical power. The main divisions of engineering are aerospace, chemical, civil, computer, electrical, electronic, gas, marine, materials, mechanical, mining, production, radio, and structural.

**England** largest division of the United Kingdom.
*area* 130,357 sq km/50,318 sq mi
*capital* London
*towns and cities* Birmingham, Cambridge, Coventry, Leeds, Leicester, Manchester, Newcastle upon Tyne, Nottingham, Oxford, Sheffield, York; ports: Bristol, Dover, Felixstowe, Harwich, Liverpool, Portsmouth, Southampton
*features* variability of climate and diversity of scenery; among European countries, only the Netherlands is more densely populated
*exports* agricultural (cereals, rape, sugar beet, potatoes); meat and meat products; electronic (software) and telecommunications equipment; scientific instruments; textiles and fashion goods; North Sea oil and gas, petrochemicals, pharmaceuticals, fertilizers; beer; china clay, pottery, porcelain, and glass; film and television programmes, and sound recordings. Tourism is important. There are worldwide banking and insurance interests
*currency* pound sterling
*population* (1993 est) 48,500,000
*language* English, with more than 100 minority languages
*religion* Christian, with the Church of England as the established church, 31,500,000; and various Protestant groups, of which the largest is the Methodist 1,400,000; Roman Catholic about 5,000,000; Muslim 900,000; Jewish 410,000; Sikh 175,000; Hindu 140,000
*government* returns 529 members to Parliament; a mixture of 2-tier and unitary local authorities, with 34 non-metropolitan counties, 46 unitary authorities, 6 metropolitan counties (with 36 metropolitan boroughs), 32 London boroughs, and the Corporation of London.

For *government* and *history,* see ◊Britain, ancient.

**English Channel** stretch of water between England and France, leading in the west to the

Atlantic Ocean, and in the east via the Strait of Dover to the North Sea; it is also known as *La Manche* (French 'the sleeve') from its shape. The ◊Channel Tunnel, opened in 1994, runs between Folkestone, Kent, and Sangatte, west of Calais.

**English language** member of the Germanic branch of the Indo-European language family. It is traditionally described as having passed through four major stages over about 1,500 years: *Old English* or *Anglo-Saxon* (*c.* 500–1050), rooted in the dialects of invading settlers (Jutes, Saxons, Angles, and Frisians); *Middle English* (*c.* 1050–1550), influenced by Norman French after the Conquest 1066 and by ecclesiastical Latin; *Early Modern English* (*c.* 1550–1700), including a standardization of the diverse influences of Middle English; and *Late Modern English* (*c.* 1700 onwards), including in particular the development and spread of current Standard English. Through extensive exploration, colonization, and trade, English spread worldwide from the 17th century onwards and remains the most important international language of trade and technology. It is used in many variations, for example, British, American, Canadian, West Indian, Indian, Singaporean, and Nigerian English, and many pidgins and creoles.

**English law** one of the major European legal systems, ◊Roman law being the other. English law has spread to many other countries, including former English colonies such as the USA, Canada, Australia, and New Zealand.

**engraving** art of creating a design by means of inscribing blocks of metal, wood, or some other hard material with a point. With *intaglio printing* the design is cut into the surface of a plate, usually metal. It is these cuts, often very fine, which hold the ink. In *relief printing*, by contrast, it is the areas left when the rest has been cut away which are inked for printing. See ◊printmaking.

**enlightenment** in Buddhism, the term used to translate the Sanskrit *bodhi*, awakening: perceiving the true nature of the world, the unreality of the self, and becoming liberated from suffering (Sanskrit *duhkha*). By experience of *bodhi*, ◊nirvana is attained.

**Enlightenment** European intellectual movement that reached its high point in the 18th century. Enlightenment thinkers were believers in social progress and in the liberating possibilities of rational and scientific knowledge. They were often critical of existing society and were hostile to religion, which they saw as keeping the human mind chained down by superstition.

**Entebbe** city in Uganda, on the northwest shore of Lake Victoria, 20 km/12 mi southwest of Kampala, the capital; 1,136 m/3,728 ft above sea level; population (1991) 41,600. Founded in 1893, it was the administrative centre of Uganda 1894–1962. The international airport of Uganda is here. Industries include tourism and fishing.

**entomology** study of ◊insects.

**entropy** in ◊thermodynamics, a parameter representing the state of disorder of a system at the atomic, ionic, or molecular level; the greater the disorder, the higher the entropy. Thus the fast-moving disordered molecules of water vapour have higher entropy than those of more ordered liquid water, which in turn have more entropy than the molecules in solid crystalline ice.

**Enver Pasha** (1881–1922) Turkish politician and soldier. He led the military revolt of 1908 that resulted in the Young Turks' revolution. He was killed fighting the Bolsheviks in Turkestan.

**environmental audit** another name for ◊green audit, the inspection of a company to assess its environmental impact.

**environmental issues** matters relating to the detrimental effects of human activity on the biosphere, their causes, and the search for possible solutions. Since the Industrial Revolution, the demands made by both the industrialized and developing nations on the Earth's natural resources are increasingly affecting the balance of the Earth's resources. Over a period of time, some of these resources are renewable – trees can be replanted, soil nutrients can be replenished – but many resources, such as fossil fuels and minerals, are non-renewable and in danger of eventual exhaustion. In addition, humans are creating many other problems which may endanger not only their own survival, but also that of other species. For instance, ◊deforestation and air pollution are not only damaging and radically altering many natural environments, they are also affecting the Earth's climate by adding to the ◊greenhouse effect and ◊global warming, while ◊water pollution is seriously affecting aquatic life, including fish populations, as well as human health.

**environment–heredity controversy** see ◊nature–nurture controversy.

**enzyme** biological ◊catalyst produced in cells, and capable of speeding up the chemical reactions necessary for life. They are large, complex ◊proteins, and are highly specific, each chemical reaction requiring its own particular enzyme. The enzyme's specificity arises from its *active site,* an area with a shape corresponding to part of the molecule with which it reacts (the substrate). The enzyme and the substrate slot together forming an enzyme–substrate complex that allows the reaction to take place, after which the enzyme falls away unaltered.

**Eocene** second epoch of the Tertiary period of geological time, 56.5–35.5 million years ago. Originally considered the earliest division of the Tertiary, the name means 'early recent', referring to the early forms of mammals evolving at the time, following the extinction of the dinosaurs.

**Ephesus** ancient Greek seaport in Asia Minor, a centre of the ◊Ionian Greeks, with a temple of Artemis destroyed by the Goths AD 262. Now in Turkey, it is one of the world's largest archaeological sites. St Paul visited the city and addressed a letter (◊epistle) to the Christians there.

**epic** narrative poem or cycle of poems dealing with some great deed – often the founding of a nation or the forging of national unity – and often using religious or cosmological themes. The two main epic poems in the Western tradition are *The Iliad* and *The Odyssey*, attributed to ◊Homer, which were probably intended to be chanted in sections at feasts.

**epicentre** the point on the Earth's surface immediately above the seismic focus of an ◊earthquake. Most damage usually takes place at an earthquake's epicentre. The term sometimes refers to a point directly above or below a nuclear explosion ('at ground zero').

**Epicureanism** system of moral philosophy named after the Greek philosopher Epicurus. He argued that pleasure is the basis of the ethical life, and that the most satisfying form of pleasure is achieved by avoiding pain, mental or physical. This is done by limiting desire as far as possible, and by choosing pleasures of the mind over those of the body.

**epicyclic gear** or *sun-and-planet gear,* gear system that consists of one or more gear wheels moving around another. Epicyclic gears are found in bicycle hub gears and in automatic gearboxes.

**epidemic** outbreak of infectious disease affecting large numbers of people at the same time. A widespread epidemic that sweeps across many countries (such as the ◊Black Death in the late Middle Ages) is known as a *pandemic.*

**epidermis** outermost layer of ◊cells on an organism's body. In plants and many invertebrates such as insects, it consists of a single layer of cells. In vertebrates, it consists of several layers of cells.

**epilepsy** medical disorder characterized by a tendency to develop fits, which are convulsions or abnormal feelings caused by abnormal electrical discharges in the cerebral hemispheres of the ◊brain. Epilepsy can be controlled with a number of anticonvulsant drugs.

**Epiphany** festival of the Christian church, held 6 January, celebrating the coming of the Magi (the three Wise Men) to Bethlehem with gifts for the infant Jesus, and symbolizing the manifestation of Jesus to the world. It is the 12th day after Christmas, and marks the end of the Christmas festivities.

**epiphyte** any plant that grows on another plant or object above the surface of the ground, and has no roots in the soil. An epiphyte does not parasitize the plant it grows on but merely uses it for support. Its nutrients are obtained from rainwater, organic debris such as leaf litter, or from the air.

**Epirus** Greek *Ipiros,* 'mainland', region of northwestern Greece; area 9,200 sq km/3,551 sq mi; population (1991) 339,200. Its capital is Yannina, and it consists of the provinces (nomes) of Arta, Thesprotia, Yannina, and Preveza. There is livestock farming. It was part of an ancient Greek region by the same name: the northern part was in Albania, the remainder in northwest Greece.

**episcopacy** in the Christian church, a system of government in which administrative and spiritual power over a district (diocese) is held by a bishop.

**epistemology** branch of philosophy that examines the nature of knowledge and attempts to determine the limits of human understanding. Central issues include how knowledge is derived and how it is to be validated and tested.

**epistle** in the New Testament, any of the 21 letters to individuals or to the members of various churches written by Christian leaders, including the 13 written by St ◊Paul. The term also describes a letter with a suggestion of pomposity and literary affectation, and a letter addressed to someone in the form of a poem, as in the epistles of ◊Horace and Alexander ◊Pope.

**epoch** subdivision of a geological period in the geological time scale. Epochs are sometimes given their own names (such as the Palaeocene, Eocene, Oligocene, Miocene, and Pliocene epochs comprising the Tertiary period), or they are referred to as the late, early, or middle portions of a given period (as the Late Cretaceous or the Middle Triassic epoch).

**EPROM** acronym for erasable programmable read-only memory, computer memory device in the form of an ◊integrated circuit (chip) that can record data and retain it indefinitely. The data can be erased by exposure to ultraviolet light, and new data recorded. Other kinds of computer memory chips are ◊ROM (read-only memory), ◊PROM (programmable read-only memory), and ◊RAM (random-access memory).

**Epsom salts** $MgSO_4.7H_2O$ hydrated magnesium sulphate, used as a relaxant and laxative and added to baths to soothe the skin. The name is derived from a bitter saline spring at Epsom, Surrey, England, which contains the salt in solution.

**Epstein, Jacob** (1880–1959) US-born British sculptor. Initially influenced by Rodin, he turned to primitive forms after Brancusi and is chiefly known for his controversial muscular nude figures, such as *Genesis* (1931; Whitworth Art Gallery, Manchester). He was better appreciated as a portraitist; his bust of Albert Einstein (1933) demonstrating a characteristic vigorous modelling in clay. In later years he executed several monumental figures, notably the bronze *St Michael and the Devil* (1959; Coventry Cathedral) and *Social Consciousness* (1953; Fairmount Park, Philadelphia).

**equation** in mathematics, expression that represents the equality of two expressions involving constants and/or variables, and thus usually includes an equals (=) sign. For example, the equation $A = \pi r^2$ equates the area $A$ of a circle of radius $r$ to the product $\pi r^2$.

The algebraic equation $y = mx + c$ is the general one in coordinate geometry for a straight line. See also ◊quadratic equation.

**Equator** or *terrestrial equator* the great circle whose plane is perpendicular to the Earth's axis (the line joining the poles). Its length is 40,092 km/24,901.8 mi, divided into 360 degrees of longitude. The Equator encircles the broadest part of the Earth, and represents 0° latitude. It divides the Earth into two halves, called the northern and the southern hemispheres.

**Equatorial Guinea** Republic of
**national name** *República de Guinea Ecuatorial*

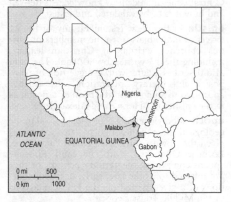

**area** 28,051 sq km/10,830 sq mi
**capital** Malabo
**major towns/cities** Bata, Evinayong, Ebebiyin, Mongomo
**physical features** comprises mainland Río Muni, plus the small islands of Corisco, Elobey Grande and Elobey Chico, and Bioko (formerly Fernando Po) together with Annobón (formerly Pagalu); nearly half the land is forested; volcanic mountains on Bioko
**head of state** Teodoro Obiang Nguema Mbasogo from 1979
**head of government** Angel Serafin Seriche Dougan, from 1996
**political system** emergent democracy
**political parties** Democratic Party of Equatorial Guinea (PDGE), nationalist, right of centre, militarily controlled; People's Social Democratic Convention (CSDP), left of centre; Democratic Socialist Union of Equatorial Guinea (UDSGE), left of centre
**currency** franc CFA
**GNP per capita (PPP)** (US$) 4,400 (1998 est)
**exports** timber, re-exported ships and boats, textile fibres and waste, cocoa, coffee. Principal market: USA 66% (1997)
**population** 442,000 (1999 est)
**language** Spanish (official); pidgin English is widely spoken, and on Annobón (whose people were formerly slaves of the Portuguese) a Portuguese patois; Fang and other African patois spoken on Río Muni
**religion** Roman Catholic, Protestant, animist
**life expectancy** 48 (men); 52 (women) (1995–2000)
**Chronology**
**1472** First visited by Portuguese explorers.
**1778** Bioko (formerly known as Fernando Po) Island ceded to Spain, which established cocoa plantations there in the late 19th century, importing labour from West Africa.

**1885** Mainland territory of Mbini (formerly Rio Muni) came under Spanish rule, the whole colony being known as Spanish Guinea, with the capital at Malabu on Bioko Island.
**1920s** League of Nations special mission sent to investigate the forced, quasi-slave labour conditions on the Bioko cocoa plantations, then the largest in the world.
**1959** Became a Spanish Overseas Province; African population finally granted full citizenship.
**early 1960s** On the mainland, the Fang people spearheaded a nationalist movement directed against Spanish favouritism towards Bioko Island and its controlling Bubi tribe.
**1963** Achieved internal autonomy.
**1968** Independence achieved from Spain. Macias Nguema, a nationalist Fang, became first president, discriminating against the Bubi community.
**1970s** The economy collapsed as Spanish settlers and other minorities fled in the face of intimidation by Nguema's brutal, dictatorial regime, which was marked by the murder, torture, and imprisonment of tens of thousands of political opponents and rivals, as well as the closing of churches.
**1979** Nguema was overthrown, tried, and executed. He was replaced by his nephew, Teodoro Obiang Nguema Mbasogo, who established a military regime, but released political prisoners and imposed restrictions on the Catholic church.
**1992** A new pluralist constitution was approved by referendum.
**1993** Obiang's PDGE won the first multiparty elections on low turnout.
**1996** Obiang was re-elected amid claims of fraud by opponents. Angel Serafin Seriche Dougan became prime minister.
**1998** Angel Serafin Seriche Dougan was re-appointed prime minister.

**equestrianism** skill in horse riding, as practised under International Equestrian Federation rules. An Olympic sport, there are three main branches of equestrianism: showjumping, dressage, and three-day eventing. Three other disciplines are under the authority of the International Equestrian Federation (FEI): carriage driving, endurance riding, and vaulting.

**equilateral** geometrical figure, having all sides of equal length.

**equity** system of law supplementing the ordinary rules of law where the application of these would operate harshly in a particular case; sometimes it is regarded as an attempt to achieve 'natural justice'. So understood, equity appears as an element in most legal systems, and in a number of legal codes judges are instructed to apply both the rules of strict law and the principles of equity in reaching their decisions.

**era** any of the major divisions of geological time, each including several periods, but smaller than an eon. The currently recognized eras all fall within the Phanerozoic eon – or the vast span of time, starting about 570 million years ago, when fossils are found to become abundant. The eras in ascending order are the

Palaeozoic, Mesozoic, and Cenozoic. We are living in the Recent epoch of the Quaternary period of the Cenozoic era.

**Erasmus, Desiderius** (c. 1469–1536) Dutch scholar and leading humanist of the Renaissance era, who taught and studied all over Europe and was a prolific writer. His pioneer translation of the Greek New Testament (with parallel Latin text, 1516) exposed the Vulgate as a second-hand document. Although opposed to dogmatism and abuse of church power, he remained impartial during Martin ◊Luther's conflict with the pope.

**erbium** soft, lustrous, greyish, metallic element of the ◊lanthanide series, symbol Er, atomic number 68, relative atomic mass 167.26. It occurs with the element yttrium or as a minute part of various minerals. It was discovered in 1843 by Carl Mosander (1797–1858), and named after the town of Ytterby, Sweden, near which the lanthanides (rare-earth elements) were first found.

Erbium has been used since 1987 to amplify data pulses in optical fibre, enabling faster transmission. Erbium ions in the fibreglass, charged with infrared light, emit energy by amplifying the data pulse as it moves along the fibre.

**Erebus, Mount** the world's southernmost active volcano, located on Ross Island, Antarctica; height 4,072 m/13,359 ft.

**ergo** (Latin) therefore; hence.

**ergonomics** study of the relationship between people and the furniture, tools, and machinery they use at work. The object is to improve work performance by removing sources of muscular stress and general fatigue: for example, by presenting data and control panels in easy-to-view form, making office furniture comfortable, and creating a generally pleasant environment.

**ergot** any of a group of parasitic fungi (especially of the genus *Claviceps*), whose brown or black grainlike masses replace the kernels of rye or other cereals. *C. purpurea* attacks the rye plant. Ergot poisoning is caused by eating infected bread, resulting in burning pains, gangrene, and convulsions.

**Erhard, Ludwig** (1897–1977) West German economist and Christian Democrat politician, chancellor of the Federal Republic 1963–66. He became known as the 'father of the German economic miracle'. As economics minister 1949–63 he instituted policies driven by his vision of a 'social market economy', in which a capitalist free market would be tempered by an active role for the state in providing a market-friendly social welfare system. His period as chancellor was less distinguished.

**erica** any plant of a large group that includes the heathers. There are about 500 species, distributed mainly in South Africa with some in Europe. (Genus *Erica*, family Ericaceae.)

**Eric the Red** (c. 950–1010) Allegedly the first European to find Greenland. According to a 13th-century saga, he was the son of a Norwegian chieftain, and was banished from Iceland about 982 for murder. He then sailed westward and discovered a land that he called Greenland.

**Eridanus** in astronomy, the sixth-largest constellation, which meanders from the celestial equator (see ◊celestial sphere) deep into the southern hemisphere of the sky. Eridanus is represented as a river. Its brightest star is ◊Achernar, a corruption of the Arabic for 'the end of the river'.

**Erie, Lake** fourth largest of the Great Lakes of North America, connected to Lake Ontario by the Niagara River and bypassed by the Welland Canal; length 388 km/241 mi; width 48–91 km/30–56 mi; area 25,720 sq km/9,930 sq mi. The most southerly of the Great Lakes, it is bounded on the north by Ontario, Canada; on the south and south-east by Ohio, Pennsylvania, and New York; and on the west by Michigan. Lake Erie is an important link in the St Lawrence Seaway.

**Eritrea** State of

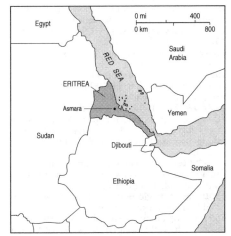

**area** 125,000 sq km/48,262 sq mi
**capital** Asmara
**major towns/cities** Asab, Keren, Massawa
**major ports** Asab, Massawa
**physical features** coastline along the Red Sea 1,000 km/620 mi; narrow coastal plain that rises to an inland plateau; Dahlak Islands
**head of state and government** Issaias Afwerki from 1993
**political system** emergent democracy
**political parties** People's Front for Democracy and Justice (PFDJ) (formerly Eritrean People's Liberation Front: EPLF), left of centre; Eritrean National Pact Alliance (ENPA), moderate, centrist
**currency** Ethiopian birr
**GNP per capita (PPP)** (US$) 950 (1998)
**exports** textiles, leather and leather products, beverages, petroleum products, basic household goods. Principal market: Ethiopia 63.5% (1997)
**population** 3,720,000 (1999 est)
**language** Tigrinya (official), Arabic (official), Afar, Amharic, Bilen, Hidareb, Kunama, Nara, Rashaida, Saho, and Tigre

*religion* Sunni Muslim, Coptic Christian
*life expectancy* 49 (men); 52 (women) (1995–2000)

**Chronology**
**4th–7th centuries AD** Part of Ethiopian Aksum kingdom.
**8th century** Islam introduced to coastal areas by Arabs.
**12th–16th centuries** Under influence of Ethiopian Abyssinian kingdoms.
**mid-16th century** Came under control of Turkish Ottoman Empire.
**1882** Occupied by Italy.
**1889** Italian colony of Eritrea created out of Ottoman areas and coastal districts of Ethiopia.
**1920s** Massawa developed into largest port in East Africa.
**1935–36** Used as base for Italy's conquest of Ethiopia and became part of Italian East Africa.
**1941** Became British protectorate after Italy removed from North Africa.
**1952** Federation formed with Ethiopia by United Nations (UN).
**1958** Eritrean People's Liberation Front (EPLF) formed to fight for independence after general strike brutally suppressed by Ethiopian rulers.
**1962** Annexed by Ethiopia, sparking a secessionist rebellion which was to last 30 years and claim 150,000 lives.
**1974** Ethiopian emperor Haile Selassie was deposed by the military; the EPLF continued the struggle for independence.
**1977–78** The EPLF cleared the territory of Ethiopian forces, but the position was soon reversed by the Soviet-backed Marxist Ethiopian government of Col Mengistu Haile Mariam.
**mid-1980s** There was severe famine in Eritrea and a refugee crisis as the Ethiopian government sought forcible resettlement.
**1990** The strategic port of Massawa was captured by Eritrean rebel forces.
**1991** Ethiopian president Mengistu was overthrown. The EPLF secured the whole of Eritrea and a provisional government was formed under Issaias Afwerki.
**1993** Independence was approved in a regional referendum and recognized by Ethiopia. A transitional government was established, with Afwerki elected president; 500,000 refugees outside Eritrea began to return.
**1997** A new constitution was adopted.
**1998** Border disputes with Ethiopia escalated, with bombing raids from both sides.
**1999** The border dispute with Ethiopia erupted into outright war in February. Peace was agreed the following month, but fighting was renewed.

**ERM** abbreviation for ◊*Exchange Rate Mechanism.*

**ermine** the ◊stoat during winter, when its coat becomes white. In northern latitudes the coat becomes completely white, except for a black tip on the tail, but in warmer regions the back may remain brownish. The fur is used commercially.

**Ernst, Max** (1891–1976) German artist, a major figure in ◊Dada and then ◊Surrealism. He worked in France 1922–38 and in the USA from 1941. He experimented with collage, photomontage, and surreal images, creating some of the most haunting and distinctive images of 20th-century art. His works include *The Elephant Celebes* (1921; Tate Gallery, London) and *The Temptation of St Anthony* (1945; Lehmbruck Museum, Duisburg).

**Eros** in astronomy, an asteroid, discovered in 1898, that can pass 22 million km/14 million mi from the Earth, as observed in 1975. Eros was the first asteroid to be discovered that has an orbit coming within that of Mars. It is elongated, measures about $36 \times 12$ km/$22 \times 7$ mi, rotates around its shortest axis every 5.3 hours, and orbits the Sun every 1.8 years.

**erosion** wearing away of the Earth's surface, caused by the breakdown and transportation of particles of rock or soil (by contrast, ◊weathering does not involve transportation). Agents of erosion include the sea, rivers, glaciers, and wind.

Water, consisting of sea waves and currents, rivers, and rain; ice, in the form of glaciers; and wind, hurling sand fragments against exposed rocks and moving dunes along, are the most potent forces of erosion.

People also contribute to erosion by bad farming practices and the cutting down of forests, which can lead to the formation of dust bowls.

**error** in computing, a fault or mistake, either in the software or on the part of the user, that causes a program to stop running (crash) or produce unexpected results. Program errors, or bugs, are largely eliminated in the course of the programmer's initial testing procedure, but some will remain in most programs. All computer operating systems are designed to produce an *error message* (on the display screen, or in an error file or printout) whenever an error is detected, reporting that an error has taken place and, wherever possible, diagnosing its cause.

**ESA** abbreviation for ◊*European Space Agency.*

**escape velocity** in physics, minimum velocity with which an object must be projected for it to escape from the gravitational pull of a planetary body. In the case of the Earth, the escape velocity is 11.2 kps/6.9 mps; the Moon, 2.4 kps/1.5 mps; Mars, 5 kps/3.1 mps; and Jupiter, 59.6 kps/37 mps.

**escarpment** or *cuesta*, large ridge created by the erosion of dipping sedimentary rocks. It has one steep side (scarp) and one gently sloping side (dip). Escarpments are common features of chalk landscapes, such as the Chiltern Hills and the North Downs in England. Certain features are associated with chalk escarpments, including dry valleys (formed on the dip slope), combes (steep-sided valleys on the scarp slope), and springs.

**Esfahan** or *Isfahan;* formerly *Ispahan,* city in central Iran and capital of the province of the same name; population (1991) 1,127,000. The town lies on the Zayandeh Rud River at an altitude of 1,600 m/5,250 ft, in the centre of a large fertile oasis. Industries include steel, textiles, carpets, and traditional handicrafts. It was the ancient capital (1598–1722) of Abbas I. Its features include the Great Square, where polo was played, the Sheikh Lutfullah Mosque, the Hall of Forty Pillars known as Chihil Sutun, the Ali Qapu gate, the Khaju and Aliverdi Khan bridges, and the Shah Hussain madrasah, a school for dervishes built in 1710.

**Eskimo** Algonquian term for Arctic peoples meaning 'eater of raw meat', now considered offensive. See ◊Inuit.

**ESP** abbreviation for ◊*extrasensory perception.*

**esparto** species of grass native to southern Spain, southern Portugal, and the Balearics, but now widely grown in dry, sandy locations throughout the world. The plant is just over 1 m/3 ft high, producing greyish-green leaves, which are used for making paper, ropes, baskets, mats, and cables. (*Stipa tenacissima.*)

**Esperanto** language devised 1887 by Polish philologist Ludwig L Zamenhof as an international auxiliary language. For its structure and vocabulary it draws on Latin, the Romance languages, English, and German. At its centenary 1987, Esperantists claimed 10–15 million users worldwide.

**essay** short piece of nonfiction, often dealing with a particular subject from a personal point of view. The essay became a recognized genre with the French writer Montaigne's *Essais* (1580) and in English with Francis Bacon's *Essays* (1597). Today the essay is a part of journalism: articles in the broadsheet newspapers are in the essay tradition.

**Essen** city in North Rhine-Westphalia, Germany, 29 km/18 mi northeast of Düsseldorf,; population (1995) 616,400. It is the administrative centre of the ◊Ruhr region, situated between the rivers Emscher and Ruhr. Industries include coalmining, steel, glass-making, chemicals, telecommunications, and electronics. Its 9th–14th-century minster is one of the oldest churches in Germany. Half of the city's buildings were destroyed during World War II.

**Essequibo** longest river in Guyana, South America, draining more than half the total area of the country; length 1,014 km/630 mi; it rises in the Guiana Highlands of southern Guyana and flows north past Bartica to meet the Atlantic at a 32 km/20 mi wide delta. Its course is interrupted by numerous rapids and falls, but its lower course is navigable for large vessels for 80 km/50 mi as far as Bartica. Its major tributaries include the Rupununi, Potaro, Mazaruni, and Cuyuni rivers.

**Essex** (Old English East-Seaxe) county of southeast England, which has contained the unitary authorities Southend and Thurrock since April 1998

*area* 3,670 sq km/1,417 sq mi

*towns and cities* Chelmsford (administrative headquarters), Basildon, Colchester, Harlow, Harwich (port), Clacton-on-Sea (resort)

*physical* flat and marshy near the coast; richly wooded in the southwest; rivers: the Blackwater, Crouch, Colne, Lee, Stour, and Thames

*features* former royal hunting ground of Epping Forest (2300 ha/5680 acres, controlled from 1882 by the City of London); since 1111 at Little Dunmow (and later at Great Dunmow) the Dunmow flitch (side of cured pork) can be claimed every four years by any couple proving to a jury they have not regretted their marriage within the year (winners are few); Stansted, London's third airport; new Roman Catholic cathedral at Brentwood (designed by Quinlan Terry), dedicated in 1991

*agriculture* cereals (wheat), fruit, sugar beet; livestock rearing, dairy products; oysters

*industries* brewing, cars, cement, engineering (at Dagenham, Chelmsford, and Colchester), food processing, oil products (there are large oil refineries at Shellhaven and Canvey)

*population* (1996) 1,586,100

*famous people* William Gilbert, William Harvey, Joseph Lister, Gerard Manley Hopkins, John Ray.

**Essex, Robert Devereux,** 2nd Earl of Essex (1566–1601) English soldier and politician. Having taken part in the Dutch fight against Spain, he became a favourite with Queen Elizabeth I in 1587, but fell from grace because of his policies in Ireland, where he was Lieutenant from 1599, and was executed.

**estate** in law, the rights that a person has in relation to any property. *Real estate* is an interest in any land; *personal estate* is an interest in any other kind of property.

**ester** organic compound formed by the reaction between an alcohol and an acid, with the elimination of water. Unlike ◊salts, esters are covalent compounds.

**Estonia** Republic of
*national name* Eesti Vabariik

*area* 45,000 sq km/17,374 sq mi
*capital* Tallinn
*major towns/cities* Tartu, Narva, Kohtla-Järve, Pärnu
*physical features* lakes and marshes in a partly forested plain; 774 km/481 mi of coastline; mild climate; Lake Peipus and Narva River forming boundary with Russian Federation; Baltic islands, the largest of which is Saaremaa

**head of state** Lennart Meri from 1992
**head of government** Mart Siimann from 1997
**political system** emergent democracy
**political parties** Coalition Party (KMU), ex-communist, left of centre, 'social market'; Isamaa (National Fatherland Party, or Pro Patria), right wing, nationalist, free market; Estonian Reform Party (ERP), freemarket; Centre Party (CP), moderate nationalist (formerly the Estonian Popular Front (EPF; Rahvarinne); Estonian National Independence Party (ENIP), radical nationalist; Communist Party of Estonia (CPE); Our Home is Estonia; Estonian Social Democratic Party (ESDP) (last three draw much of their support from ethnic Russian community)
**currency** kroon
**GNP per capita (PPP)** (US$) 6,120 (1998 est)
**exports** foodstuffs, animal products, textiles, timber products, base metals, mineral products, machinery. Principal market: Finland 22.1% (1998)
**population** 1,412,000 (1999 est)
**language** Estonian (official), Russian
**religion** Lutheran, Russian Orthodox
**life expectancy** 63 (men); 75 (women) (1995–2000)
**Chronology**
**1st century AD** First independent state formed.
**9th century** Invaded by Vikings.
**13th century** Tallinn, in the Danish-controlled north, joined Hanseatic League, a northern European union of commercial towns; Livonia, comprising southern Estonia and Latvia, came under control of German Teutonic Knights and was converted to Christianity.
**1561** Sweden took control of northern Estonia.
**1629** Sweden took control of southern Estonia from Poland.
**1721** Sweden ceded the country to tsarist Russia.
**late 19th century** Estonian nationalist movement developed in opposition to Russian political and cultural repression and German economic control.
**1914** Occupied by German troops.
**1918–19** Estonian nationalists, led by Konstantin Pats, proclaimed and achieved independence, despite efforts by the Russian Red Army to regain control.
**1920s** Land reforms and cultural advances under democratic regime.
**1934** Pats overthrew parliamentary democracy in a quasi-fascist coup at a time of economic depression; Baltic Entente mutual defence pact signed with Latvia and Lithuania.
**1940** Estonia incorporated into Soviet Union (USSR); 100,000 Estonians deported to Siberia or killed.
**1941–44** German occupation during World War II.
**1944** USSR regained control; 'Sovietization' followed, including agricultural collectivization and immigration of ethnic Russians.
**late 1980s** Beginnings of nationalist dissent, encouraged by *glasnost* initiative of reformist Soviet leader Mikhail Gorbachev.

**1988** Popular Front (EPF) established to campaign for democracy. Sovereignty declaration issued by state assembly rejected by USSR as unconstitutional.
**1989** Estonian replaced Russian as the main language.
**1990** The CPE monopoly of power was abolished; pro-independence candidates secured a majority after multiparty elections; a coalition government was formed with EPF leader Edgar Savisaar as prime minister; Arnold Rüütel became president. The prewar constitution was partially restored.
**1991** Independence was achieved after an attempted anti-Gorbachev coup in Moscow; the CPE was outlawed. Estonia joined the United Nations (UN).
**1992** Savisaar resigned over food and energy shortages; Isamaa leader Lennart Meri became president and free-marketer Mart Laar prime minister.
**1993** Estonia joined the Council of Europe and signed a free-trade agreement with Latvia and Lithuania.
**1994** The last Russian troops were withdrawn. A radical economic-reform programme was introduced; a controversial law on 'aliens' was passed, requiring non-ethnic Estonians to apply for residency. Laar resigned.
**1995** Former communists won the largest number of seats in a general election; a left-of-centre coalition was formed under Tiit Vahi.
**1996** President Meri was re-elected. The ruling coalition collapsed; Prime Minister Tiit Vahi continued with a minority government.
**1997** Vahi, accused of corruption, resigned and was replaced by Mart Siimann. Estonia was invited to begin European Union (EU) membership negotiations.
**1998** The legislature voted to ban electoral alliances in future elections.

**Estonian** the largest ethnic group in Estonia. There are 1 million speakers of the Estonian language, a member of the Finno-Ugric branch of the Uralic family. Most live in Estonia.

**etching** printmaking technique in which a metal plate (usually copper or zinc) is covered with a waxy overlayer (ground) and then drawn on with an etching needle. The exposed areas are then 'etched', or bitten into, by a corrosive agent (acid), so that they will hold ink for printing.

**ethanol** common name *ethyl alcohol*, $C_2H_5OH$ alcohol found in beer, wine, cider, spirits, and other alcoholic drinks. When pure, it is a colourless liquid with a pleasant odour, miscible with water or ether; it burns in air with a pale blue flame. The vapour forms an explosive mixture with air and may be used in high-compression internal combustion engines.

It is produced naturally by the fermentation of carbohydrates by yeast cells. Industrially, it can be made by absorption of ethene and subsequent reaction with water, or by the reduction of ethanal in the presence of a catalyst, and is widely used as a solvent.

**Ethelbert** (c. 552–616) King of Kent 560–616. He was defeated by the West Saxons in 568 but later became ruler of England south of the River Humber. Ethelbert received the Christian missionary Augustine in 597 and later converted to become the first Christian ruler of Anglo-Saxon England. He issued the first written code of laws known in England.

**Ethelred (II) the Unready** (968–1016) King of England from 978, following the murder of his half-brother, Edward the Martyr. He was son of King Edgar. Ethelred tried to buy off the Danish raiders by paying Danegeld. In 1002 he ordered the massacre of the Danish settlers, provoking an invasion by Sweyn I of Denmark. War with Sweyn and Sweyn's son, Canute, occupied the rest of Ethelred's reign. His nickname is a corruption of the Old English 'unreed', meaning badly counselled or poorly advised.

**ethene** common name *ethylene,* $C_2H_4$ colourless, flammable gas, the first member of the ◊alkene series of hydrocarbons. It is the most widely used synthetic organic chemical and is used to produce the plastics polythene (polyethylene), polychloroethene, and polyvinyl chloride (PVC). It is obtained from natural gas or coal gas, or by the dehydration of ethanol.

**ether** in chemistry, any of a series of organic chemical compounds having an oxygen atom linking the carbon atoms of two hydrocarbon radical groups (general formula R-O-R); also the common name for ethoxyethane $C_2H_5OC_2H_5$ (also called diethyl ether).

This is used as an anaesthetic and as an external cleansing agent before surgical operations. It is also used as a solvent, and in the extraction of oils, fats, waxes, resins, and alkaloids.

**ethics** or *moral philosophy,* branch of ◊philosophy concerned with the systematic study of human values. It involves the study of theories of conduct and goodness, and of the meanings of moral terms.

**Ethiopia** Federal Democratic Republic of (formerly known as *Abyssinia)*
**national name** *Hebretesebawit Ityopia*

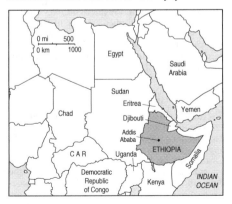

**area** 1,096,900 sq km/423,513 sq mi
**capital** Addis Ababa
**major towns/cities** Jimma, Dire Dawa, Harar, Nazret, Dessie, Gonder, Mek'elē

**physical features** a high plateau with central mountain range divided by Rift Valley; plains in east; source of Blue Nile River; Danakil and Ogaden deserts
**head of state** Negasso Ghidada from 1995
**head of government** Meles Zenawi from 1995
**political system** transition to democratic federal republic
**political parties** Ethiopian People's Revolutionary Democratic Front (EPRDF), nationalist, left of centre; Tigré People's Liberation Front (TPLF); Ethiopian People's Democratic Movement (EPDM); United Oromo Liberation Front, Islamic nationalist
**currency** Ethiopian birr
**GNP per capita (PPP)** (US$) 500 (1998)
**exports** coffee, hides and skins, petroleum products, fruit and vegetables. Principal market: Germany 22.4% (1997)
**population** 61,095,000 (1999 est)
**language** Amharic (official), Tigrinya, Orominga, Arabic
**religion** Sunni Muslim, Christian (Ethiopian Orthodox Church, which has had its own patriarch since 1976) 40%, animist
**life expectancy** 42 (men); 44 (women) (1995–2000)
*Chronology*
*1st–7th centuries* AD Founded by Semitic immigrants from Saudi Arabia, the kingdom of Aksum and its capital, northwest of Adwa, flourished. It reached its peak in the 4th century when Coptic Christianity was introduced from Egypt.
*7th century onwards* Islam was spread by Arab conquerors.
*11th century* Emergence of independent Ethiopian kingdom of Abyssinia, which was to remain dominant for nine centuries.
*late 15th century* Abyssinia visited by Portuguese explorers.
*1889* Abyssinia reunited by Menelik II.
*1896* Invasion by Italy defeated at Adwa by Menelik, who went on to annex Ogaden in the southeast and areas to the west.
*1916* Haile Selassie became regent.
*1930* Haile Selassie became emperor.
*1936* Conquered by Italy and incorporated in Italian East Africa.
*1941* Return of Emperor Selassie after liberation by the British.
*1952* Ethiopia federated with Eritrea.
*1962* Eritrea annexed by Selassie; Eritrean People's Liberation front (EPLF) resistance movement began, a rebellion that was to continue for 30 years.
*1963* First conference of Selassie-promoted Organization of African Unity (OAU) held in Addis Ababa.
*1973–74* Severe famine in northern Ethiopia; 200,000 died in Wallo province.
*1974* Haile Selassie deposed and replaced by a military government led by Gen Teferi Benti.
*1977* Teferi Benti killed and replaced by Col Mengistu Haile Mariam. Somali forces ejected from the Somali-peopled Ogaden in the southeast.

*1977–79* 'Red Terror' period in which Mengistu's single-party Marxist regime killed thousands of people and promoted collective farming; Tigré People's Liberation Front guerrillas began fighting for regional autonomy in the northern highlands.

*1984* The Workers' Party of Ethiopia (WPE) was declared the only legal political party.

*1985* The worst famine in more than a decade; Western aid was sent and forcible internal resettlement programmes undertaken in Eritrea and Tigré in the north.

*1987* Mengistu Mariam was elected president under a new constitution. There was another famine; food aid was hindered by guerrillas.

*1989* A coup attempt against Mengistu was foiled. Peace talks with Eritrean rebels were mediated by the former US president Jimmy Carter.

*1991* Mengistu was overthrown; a transitional government was set up by the opposing Ethiopian People's Revolutionary Democratic Front (EPRDF), headed by Meles Zenawi. The EPLF took control of Eritrea. Famine again gripped the country.

*1993* Eritrean independence was recognized after a referendum; private farming and market sector were encouraged by the EPRDF government.

*1994* A new federal constitution was adopted.

*1995* The ruling EPRDF won a majority in the first multiparty elections to an interim parliament. Negasso Ghidada was chosen as president; Zenawi was appointed premier.

*1998* There was a border dispute with Eritrea.

*1999* The border dispute with Eritrea erupted into outright war. Peace proposals were agreed by Eritrea but fighting continued.

**ethnic cleansing** the forced expulsion of one ethnic group by another to create an homogenous population, for example, of more than 2 million Muslims by Serbs in Bosnia-Herzegovina 1992–95. The term has also been used to describe the killing of Hutus and Tutsis in Rwanda and Burundi 1994, and for earlier mass exiles, as far back as the book of Exodus.

**ethnography** study of living cultures, using anthropological techniques like participant observation (where the anthropologist lives in the society being studied) and a reliance on informants. Ethnography has provided much data of use to archaeologists as analogies.

**ethnology** study of contemporary peoples, concentrating on their geography and culture, as distinct from their social systems. Ethnologists make a comparative analysis of data from different cultures to understand how cultures work and why they change, with a view to deriving general principles about human society.

**ethology** comparative study of animal behaviour in its natural setting. Ethology is concerned with the causal mechanisms (both the stimuli that elicit behaviour and the physiological mechanisms controlling it), as well as the development of behaviour, its function, and its evolutionary history.

**ethyl alcohol** common name for ⟩ethanol.

**ethylene** common name for ⟩ethene.

**ethyne** common name *acetylene*, CHCH, colourless inflammable gas produced by mixing calcium carbide and water. It is the simplest member of the ⟩alkyne series of hydrocarbons. It is used in the manufacture of the synthetic rubber neoprene, and in oxyacetylene welding and cutting.

**etiolation** in botany, a form of growth seen in plants receiving insufficient light. It is characterized by long, weak stems, small leaves, and a pale yellowish colour (⟩chlorosis) owing to a lack of chlorophyll. The rapid increase in height enables a plant that is surrounded by others to quickly reach a source of light, after which a return to normal growth usually occurs.

**Etna, Mount** volcano on the east coast of Sicily, 3,323 m/10,906 ft, the highest in Europe. About 90 eruptions have been recorded since 1800 BC, yet because of the rich soil, the cultivated zone on the lower slopes is densely populated, including the coastal town of Catania. The most recent eruption was in December 1985.

**Etruscan** member of an ancient people inhabiting Etruria, Italy (modern-day Tuscany and part of Umbria) from the 8th to 2nd centuries BC. The Etruscan dynasty of the Tarquins ruled Rome 616–509 BC. At the height of their civilization, in the 6th century BC, the Etruscans achieved great wealth and power from their maritime strength. They were driven out of Rome 509 BC and eventually dominated by the Romans.

**etymology** study of the origin and history of words within and across languages. It has two major aspects: the study of the phonetic and written forms of words, and of the semantics or meanings of those words.

**EU** abbreviation for ⟩*European Union.*

**eucalyptus** any tree of a group belonging to the myrtle family, native to Australia, where they are commonly known as gumtrees. About 90% of Australian timber belongs to the eucalyptus genus, which contains about 500 species. The trees have dark hardwood timber which is used for heavy construction work such as railway and bridge building. They are mostly tall, aromatic, evergreen trees with pendant leaves and white, pink, or red flowers. (Genus *Eucalyptus,* family Myrtaceae.)

**Eucharist** chief Christian sacrament, in which bread is eaten and wine drunk in memory of the death of Jesus. Other names for it are the *Lord's Supper, Holy Communion,* and (among Roman Catholics, who believe that the bread and wine are transubstantiated, that is, converted to the body and blood of Christ) the *Mass.* The doctrine of transubstantiation was rejected by Protestant churches during the Reformation.

**Euclid** (c. 330–c. 260 BC) Greek mathematician who wrote the *Stoicheia/Elements* in 13 books, nine of which deal with plane and solid geometry and four with number theory. His great achievement lay in the systematic arrangement of previous mathematical discoveries and a methodology based on axioms, definitions, and theorems.

**eugenics** (Greek *eugenes* 'well-born') study of ways in which the physical and mental characteristics of the human race may be improved. The eugenic principle was abused by the Nazi Party in Germany during the 1930s and early 1940s to justify the attempted extermination of entire social and ethnic groups and the establishment of selective breeding programmes. Modern eugenics is concerned mainly with the elimination of genetic disease.

**eukaryote** in biology, one of the two major groupings into which all organisms are divided. Included are all organisms, except bacteria and cyanobacteria (◊blue-green algae), which belong to the ◊prokaryote grouping.

**Eumenides** or Semnai, (Greek 'kindly ones') in Greek mythology, an appeasing name for the ◊Furies, used by 458 BC in *Eumenides* by the Greek dramatist ◊Aeschylus. Originally they were worshipped at the foot of the Areopagus in Athens, in Colonus, and outside Attica; their cult was similar to that of ◊Gaia, mother of the Earth.

**eunuch** (Greek *eunoukhos* 'one in charge of a bed') castrated man. Originally eunuchs were bedchamber attendants in harems in the East, but as they were usually castrated to keep them from taking too great an interest in their charges, the term became applied more generally. In China, eunuchs were employed within the imperial harem from some 4,000 years ago and by medieval times wielded considerable political power. Eunuchs often filled high offices of state in India and Persia.

**Euphrates** Turkish *Firat*, Arabic *Al Furat*, river rising in east Turkey and flowing through Syria and Iraq, joining the River Tigris above Basra to form the River ◊Shatt-al-Arab at the head of the Gulf; length 3,600 km/2,240 mi. The ancient cities of Babylon, Eridu, and Ur were situated along its course.

**Eureka Stockade** incident at Ballarat, Australia, when about 150 goldminers, or 'diggers', rebelled against the Victorian state police and military authorities. They took refuge behind a wooden stockade, which was taken in a few minutes by the military on 3 December 1854. Some 30 gold diggers were killed, and a few soldiers killed or wounded, but the majority of the rebels were taken prisoner. Among those who escaped was Peter Lalor, their leader. Of the 13 tried for treason, all were acquitted, thus marking the emergence of Australian democracy.

**Euripides** (c. 485– c. 406 BC) Athenian tragic dramatist. He is ranked with Aeschylus and Sophocles as one of the three great tragedians. His plays deal with the emotions and reactions of ordinary people and social issues rather than with deities and the grandiose themes of his contemporaries. He wrote about 90 plays, of which 18 and some long fragments survive. These include *Alcestis* (438 BC), *Medea* (431),

*Andromache* (about 430), *Hippolytus* (428), the satyr-drama *Cyclops* (about 424–423), *Electra* (417), *Trojan Women* (415), *Iphigenia in Tauris* (413), *Iphigenia in Aulis* (about 414–412), and *The Bacchae* (about 405) (the last two were produced shortly after his death).

**Eurobond** in finance, a bond underwritten by an international syndicate and sold in countries other than the country of the currency in which the issue is denominated. It provides longer-term financing than is possible with loans in Eurodollars.

**Europa** in astronomy, the fourth-largest moon of the planet Jupiter, diameter 3,140 km/1,950 mi, orbiting 671,000 km/417,000 mi from the planet every 3.55 days. It is covered by ice and criss-crossed by thousands of thin cracks, each some 50,000 km/30,000 mi long.

**Europa** in Greek mythology, a princess carried off by Zeus under the guise of a white bull. She was the daughter of the Phoenician king Agenor of Tyre; sister of Cadmus, founder of Thebes; and the personification of the continent of Europe.

**Europe** the second-smallest continent, occupying 8% of the Earth's surface
*area* 10,400,000 sq km/4,000,000 sq mi
*largest cities* (population over 1.5 million) Athens, Barcelona, Berlin, Birmingham, Bucharest, Budapest, Hamburg, Istanbul, Kharkov, Kiev, Lisbon, London, Madrid, Manchester, Milan, Moscow, Paris, Rome, St Petersburg, Vienna, Warsaw
*features* Mount Elbrus 5,642 m/18,517 ft in the Caucasus Mountains is the highest peak in Europe; Mont Blanc 4,807 m/15,772 ft is the highest peak in the Alps; lakes (over 5,100 sq km/2,000 sq mi) include Ladoga, Onega, Vänern; rivers (over 800 km/500 mi) include the Volga, Danube, Dnieper Ural, Don, Pechora, Dniester, Rhine, Loire, Tagus, Ebro, Oder, Prut, Rhône
*physical* conventionally occupying that part of Eurasia to the west of the Ural Mountains, north of the Caucasus Mountains, and north of the Sea of Marmara, Europe lies entirely in the northern hemisphere between 36° N and the Arctic Ocean. About two-thirds of the continent is a great plain which covers the whole of European Russia and spreads westwards through Poland to the Low Countries and the Bay of Biscay. To the north lie the Scandinavian highlands, rising to 2,472 m/8,110 ft at Glittertind in the Jotenheim range of Norway. To the south, a series of mountain ranges stretch east–west (Caucasus, Balkans, Carpathians, Apennines, Alps, Pyrenees, and Sierra Nevada). The most westerly point of the mainland is Cape Roca in Portugal; the most southerly location is Tarifa Point in Spain; the most northerly point on the mainland is Nordkynn in Norway.

**European Community** (EC), former name (to 1993) of the ◊European Union.

**European Court of Justice** the court of the European Union (EU), which is responsible for interpreting Community law and ruling on breaches by member states and others of such law. It sits in Luxembourg with judges from the member states.

**European Economic Area** agreement 1991 between the European Community (now the ◊European Union (EU)) and the ◊European Free Trade Association (EFTA) to create a zone of economic cooperation, allowing their 380 million citizens to transfer money, shares, and bonds across national borders and to live, study, or work in one another's countries. The pact, which took effect January 1994, was seen as a temporary arrangement since most EFTA members hoped, eventually, to join the EU.

**European Free Trade Association** (EFTA), organization established 1960 consisting of Iceland, Norway, Switzerland, and (from 1991) Liechtenstein, previously a nonvoting associate member. There are no import duties between members. Of the original EFTA members, Britain and Denmark left (1972) to join the European Community (EC), as did Portugal (1985); Austria, Finland, and Sweden joined the EC's successor, the European Union (EU) 1995.

**European Monetary System** (EMS), attempt by the European Community (now the European Union) to bring financial cooperation and monetary stability to Europe. It was established in 1979 in the wake of the 1974 oil crisis, which brought growing economic disruption to European economies because of floating exchange rates. Central to the EMS is the ◊*Exchange Rate Mechanism* (ERM), a voluntary system of semi-fixed exchange rates based on the European Currency Unit (ECU).

**European Monetary Union** (EMU), the proposed European Union (EU) policy for a single currency and common economic policies. The proposal was announced by what was then a European Community (EC) committee headed by EC Commission president Jacques Delors April 1989. In May 1998 EU leaders formalized the creation of the euro monetary zone, to take effect from 1 January 1999.

**European Parliament** the parliament of the ◊European Union, which meets in Strasbourg and Brussels to comment on the legislative proposals of the European Commission. Members are elected for a five-year term. The European Parliament has 626 seats, apportioned on the basis of population, of which Germany has 99; the UK, France, and Italy have 87 each; Spain 64; the Netherlands 31; Belgium, Greece, and Portugal 25 each; Sweden 22; Austria 21; Denmark and Finland 16 each; the Republic of Ireland 15; and Luxembourg 6.

**European Space Agency** (ESA), organization of European countries (Austria, Belgium, Denmark, Finland, France, Germany, Ireland, Italy, the Netherlands, Norway, Spain, Sweden, Switzerland, and the UK) that engages in space research and technology. It was founded in 1975, with headquarters in Paris.

**European Union** (EU); formerly (to 1993) European Community, political and economic alliance consisting of the European Coal and Steel Community (1952), the European Economic Community (EEC, popularly called the Common Market, 1957), and the European Atomic Energy Community (Euratom, 1957). The original six members – Belgium, France, West Germany, Italy, Luxembourg, and the Netherlands – were joined by the UK, Denmark, and the Republic of Ireland in 1973, Greece in 1981, and Spain and Portugal in 1986. East Germany was incorporated on German reunification in 1990. Austria, Finland, and Sweden joined in 1995. Association agreements, providing for free trade within ten years and the possibility of full membership, were signed with Czechoslovakia, Hungary, and Poland in 1991, Romania in 1992, and later with Bulgaria and Slovakia. Estonia and Latvia applied for full membership in 1995. A customs pact with Turkey approved in December 1995 was seen as their first step towards full membership; however, the move has been criticized by human-rights activists. Cyprus, Malta, and Slovenia also aspire to membership. In 1995 there were more than 360 million people in the EU countries.

A European Charter of Social Rights was approved at the Maastricht summit in December 1991 by all members except the UK. The same meeting secured agreement on a treaty framework for European union, including political and monetary union, and for a new system of police and military cooperation. After initial rejection by Denmark in a national referendum in June 1992, the ◊Maastricht Treaty on European union came into effect on 1 November 1993 and the new designation European Union was adopted, embracing not only the various bodies of its predecessor, the EC, but also two intergovernmental 'pillars', covering common foreign and security policy (CFSP) and cooperation on justice and home affairs. In September 1995 the EU's member nations stated their commitment to the attainment of monetary union by 1999, and in December of the same year they agreed to call the new currency the euro.

The aims of the EU include the expansion of trade, reduction of competition, the abolition of restrictive trading practices, the encouragement of free movement of capital and labour within the alliance, and the establishment of a closer union among European people. A single market with free movement of goods and capital was established in January 1993. The EU reached agreement on closer economic and political cooperation with 12 Middle Eastern and North African countries in the Barcelona Declaration in November 1995, and an agreement between the USA and the EU to move towards closer economic and political cooperation was signed in December 1995. In May 1998 the leaders of EU governments formalized the creation of the euro monetary zone. Also in May, EU governments agreed on the Union's first ethical arms export policy.

**europium** soft, greyish, metallic element of the ◊lanthanide series, symbol Eu, atomic number 63, relative atomic mass 151.96. It is used in lasers and as the red phosphor in colour televisions; its compounds are used to make control rods for nuclear reactors. It was named in 1901 by French chemist Eugène Demarçay (1852–1904) after the continent of Europe, where it was first found.

**Euskal Herria** Basque name for the ◊Basque Country.

**eusociality** form of social life found in insects such as honey bees and termites, in which the colony is made up of special castes (for example, workers, drones, and reproductives) whose membership is biologically determined. The worker castes do not usually reproduce. Only one mammal, the naked mole rat, has a social organization of this type. A eusocial shrimp was discovered in 1996 living in the coral reefs of Belize. *Synalpheus regalis* lives in colonies of up to 300 individuals, all the offspring of a single reproductive female.

**Eustachian tube** small air-filled canal connecting the middle ◊ear with the back of the throat. It is found in all land vertebrates and equalizes the pressure on both sides of the eardrum.

**euthanasia** in medicine, mercy killing of someone with a severe and incurable condition or illness. Euthanasia is an issue that creates much controversy on medical and ethical grounds. A patient's right to refuse life-prolonging treatment is recognized in several countries.

**eutrophication** excessive enrichment of rivers, lakes, and shallow sea areas, primarily by nitrate fertilizers washed from the soil by rain, by phosphates from fertilizers, and from nutrients in municipal sewage, and by sewage itself. These encourage the growth of algae and bacteria which use up the oxygen in the water, thereby making it uninhabitable for fishes and other animal life.

**evangelicalism** the beliefs of some Protestant Christian movements that stress biblical authority, faith, and the personal commitment of the 'born again' experience.

**evangelist** person travelling to spread the Christian gospel, in particular the authors of the four Gospels in the New Testament: Matthew, Mark, Luke, and John. Proselytizers who appear mainly on television are known as televangelists.

**Evans, Edith (Mary)** (1888–1976) English character actress. She performed on the London stage and on Broadway. Her many imposing performances include the Nurse in *Romeo and Juliet* (first performed in 1926); her film roles include Lady Bracknell in Oscar Wilde's comedy *The Importance of Being Earnest* (1952). Among her other films are *Tom Jones* (1963) and *Crooks and Coronets* (1969). She was made a DBE in 1946.

**evaporation** process in which a liquid turns to a vapour without its temperature reaching boiling point. A liquid left to stand in a saucer eventually evaporates because, at any time, a proportion of its molecules will be fast enough (have enough kinetic energy) to escape through the attractive intermolecular forces at the liquid surface into the atmosphere. The temperature of the liquid tends to fall because the evaporating molecules remove energy from the liquid. The rate of evaporation rises with increased temperature because as the mean kinetic energy of the liquid's molecules rises, so will the number possessing enough energy to escape.

**Eve** in the Old Testament, the first woman, wife of ◊Adam. She was tempted by Satan (in the form of a snake) to eat the fruit of the Tree of Knowledge of Good and Evil, and then tempted Adam to eat of the fruit as well, thus bringing about their expulsion from the Garden of Eden.

**Evelyn, John** (1620–1706) English diarist and author. He was a friend of the diarist Samuel Pepys, and like him remained in London during the Plague and the Great Fire of London. His fascinating diary, covering the years 1641–1706, and first published in 1818, is an important source of information about 17th-century England. He also wrote some 30 books on a wide variety of subjects, including horticulture and the cultivation of trees, history, religion, and the arts. He was one of the founders of the Royal Society.

**evening primrose** any of a group of plants that typically have pale yellow flowers which open in the evening. About 50 species are native to North America, several of which now also grow in Europe. Some are cultivated for their oil, which is rich in gamma-linoleic acid (GLA). The body converts GLA into substances which resemble hormones, and *evening primrose oil* is beneficial in relieving the symptoms of ◊premenstrual tension. It is also used in treating eczema and chronic fatigue syndrome. (Genus *Oenothera*, family Onagraceae.)

**Everest, Mount** Tibetan Qomolungma ('goddess mother of the world'), Nepalese Sagarmatha ('head of the earth'), world's highest mountain above sea level, in the ◊Himalaya range, on the China–Nepal frontier; height 8,848 m/29,028 ft. It was first climbed by New Zealand mountaineer Edmund ◊Hillary and Sherpa Tenzing Norgay in 1953. More than 360 climbers have reached the summit; over 100 have died during the ascent.

**Everglades** subtropical area of swamps, marsh, and lakes in southern Florida, USA; area 7,000 sq km/2,700 sq mi. Formed by the overflow of Lake Okeechobee after heavy rains, it is one of the wildest areas in the USA, with distinctive plant and animal life. The natural vegetation of the swamplands is sawgrass and rushes, with trees such as cypress, palm, and hardwoods where the conditions are slightly drier. Several hundred Seminole, an American Indian people, live here. A national park (established in 1947) covers the southern tip of the Everglades, making up about one-fifth of the Everglades' original area.

**evergreen** in botany, a plant such as pine, spruce, or holly, that bears its leaves all year round. Most ◊conifers are evergreen. Plants that shed their leaves in autumn or during a dry season are described as ◊deciduous.

**Evert, Chris(tine Marie)** (1954–   ) US tennis player. She won her first Wimbledon title in 1974, and has since won 21 Grand Slam titles. She became the first woman tennis player to win $1 million in prize money. She has an outstanding two-handed backhand and is a great exponent of baseline technique. Evert retired from competitive tennis in 1989 and is known for her charity work, raising $7.3 million over nine years.

*career highlights*
*Wimbledon* singles: 1974, 1976, 1981; doubles: 1976
*US Open* singles: 1975–78, 1980, 1982
*French Open* singles: 1974–75, 1979–80, 1983, 1985–86; doubles: 1974–75
*Australian Open* singles: 1982, 1984.

**evolution** the slow, gradual process of change from one form to another, as in the evolution of the universe from its formation to its present state, or in the evolution of life on Earth. In biology, it is the process by which life has developed by stages from single-celled organisms into the multiplicity of animal and plant life, extinct and existing, that inhabit the Earth. The development of the concept of evolution is usually associated with the English naturalist Charles ◊Darwin who attributed the main role in evolutionary change to ◊natural selection acting on randomly occurring variations. However, these variations in species are now known to be ◊adaptations produced by spontaneous changes or ◊mutations in the genetic material of organisms.

**evolutionary stable strategy** (ESS), in ◊sociobiology, an assemblage of behavioural or physical characters (collectively termed a 'strategy') of a population that is resistant to replacement by any forms bearing new traits, because the new traits will not be capable of successful reproduction.

**excavation** or *dig,* in archaeology, the systematic recovery of data through the exposure of buried sites and artefacts. Excavation is destructive, and is therefore accompanied by a comprehensive recording of all material found and its three-dimensional locations (its context). As much material and information as possible must be recovered from any dig. A full record of all the techniques employed in the excavation itself must also be made, so that future archaeologists will be able to evaluate the results of the work accurately.

**exchange rate** the price at which one currency is bought or sold in terms of other currencies, gold, or accounting units such as the special drawing right (SDR) of the ◊International Monetary Fund. Exchange rates may be fixed by international agreement or by government policy; or they may be wholly or partly allowed to 'float' (that is, find their own level) in world currency markets.

**Exchange Rate Mechanism** (ERM), voluntary system for controlling exchange rates within the ◊European Monetary System of the European Union (EU) intended to prepare the way for a single currency. The member currencies of the ERM are fixed against each other within a narrow band of fluctuation based on a central European Currency Unit (ECU) rate, but floating against nonmember countries. If a currency deviates significantly from the central ECU rate, the European Monetary Cooperation Fund and the central banks concerned intervene to stabilize the currency.

**excise duty** indirect tax levied on certain goods produced within a country, such as petrol, alcohol, and tobacco. It is collected by the government's ◊Customs and Excise department.

**excommunication** in religion, exclusion of an offender from the rights and privileges of the Roman Catholic Church. The English monarchs King John, Henry VIII, and Elizabeth I were all excommunicated.

**excretion** in biology, the removal of the waste products of metabolism from living organisms. In plants and simple animals, waste products are removed by ◊diffusion. Plants, for example, excrete $O_2$, a product of photosynthesis. In mammals, waste products are removed by specialized excretory organs, principally the ◊kidneys, which excrete urea. Water and metabolic wastes are also excreted in the faeces and, in humans, through the sweat glands in the skin; carbon dioxide and water are removed via the lungs. The liver excretes bile pigments.

**existentialism** branch of philosophy based on the situation of the individual in an absurd or meaningless universe where humans have free will. Existentialists argue that people are responsible for and the sole judge of their actions as they affect others. The origin of existentialism is usually traced back to the Danish philosopher ◊Kierkegaard; among its proponents were Martin Heidegger in Germany and Jean-Paul ◊Sartre in France.

**exocrine gland** gland that discharges secretions, usually through a tube or a duct, on to a surface. Examples include sweat glands which release sweat on to the skin, and digestive glands which release digestive juices on to the walls of the intestine. Some animals also have ◊endocrine glands (ductless glands) that release hormones directly into the bloodstream.

**exorcism** rite used in a number of religions for the expulsion of evil spirits and ghosts. In Christianity it is employed, for example, in the Roman Catholic and Pentecostal churches.

**exoskeleton** the hardened external skeleton of insects, spiders, crabs, and other arthropods. It provides attachment for muscles and protection for the internal organs, as well as support. To permit growth it is periodically shed in a process called ecdysis.

**exosphere** the uppermost layer of the ◊atmosphere. It is an ill-defined zone above the thermosphere, beginning at about 700 km/435 mi and fading off into the vacuum of space. The gases are extremely thin, with hydrogen as the main constituent.

**expansion** in physics, the increase in size of a constant mass of substance caused by, for example, increasing its temperature (thermal expansion) or its internal pressure. The *expansivity,* or coefficient of thermal expansion, of a material is its expansion (per unit volume, area, or length) per degree rise in temperature.

**experimental psychology** the application of scientific methods to the study of mental processes and behaviour.

**exponent** or *index,* in mathematics, a superscript number that indicates the number of times a term is multiplied by itself; for example $x^2 = x$ x x, $4^3 = 4$ x 4 x 4.

**export** goods or service produced in one country and sold to another. Exports may be visible (goods such as cars physically exported) or invisible (services such as banking and tourism, that are provided in the exporting country but paid for by residents of another country).

**Expressionism** style of painting, sculpture, and literature that expresses inner emotions; in particular, a movement in early 20th-century art in northern and central Europe. Expressionists tended to distort or exaggerate natural appearance in order to create a reflection of an inner world; the Norwegian painter Edvard Munch's *Skriket/The Scream* (1893; National Gallery, Oslo) is perhaps the most celebrated example.

Expressionist writers include August Strindberg and Frank Wedekind.

**extinction** in biology, the complete disappearance of a species or higher taxon. Extinctions occur when an animal becomes unfit for survival in its natural habitat usually to be replaced by another, better-suited animal. An organism becomes ill-suited for survival because its environment is changed or because its relationship to other organisms is altered. For example, a predator's fitness for survival depends upon the availability of its prey.

**extradition** surrender, by one state or country to another, of a person accused of a criminal offence in the state or country to which that person is extradited.

**extrasensory perception** (ESP), any form of perception beyond and distinct from the known sensory processes. The main forms of ESP are clairvoyance (intuitive perception or vision of events and situations without using the senses); precognition (the ability to foresee events); and telepathy or thought transference (communication between people without using any known visible, tangible, or audible medium). Verification by scientific study has yet to be achieved.

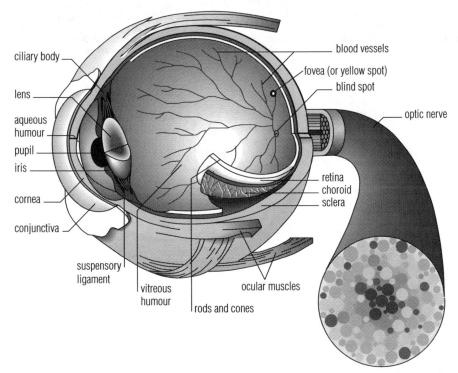

**eye** *The human eye. The retina of the eye contains about 137 million light-sensitive cells in an area of about 650 sq mm/1 sq in. There are 130 million rod cells for black and white vision and 7 million cone cells for colour vision. The optic nerve contains about 1 million nerve fibres. The focusing muscles of the eye adjust about 100,000 times a day. To exercise the leg muscles to the same extent would need an 80 km/50 mi walk.*

**Extremadura** autonomous community of western Spain, comprising the provinces of Badajoz and Cáceres; area 41,600 sq km/16,062 sq mi; population (1991) 1,061,900. Irrigated land is used for growing wheat; the remainder is either oak forest or used for pig or sheep grazing. There are food industries. The capital is Mérida.

**extroversion** or *extraversion,* personality dimension described by the psychologists Carl ◊Jung and, later, Hans Eysenck. The typical extrovert is sociable, impulsive, and carefree. The opposite of extroversion is ◊introversion.

**extrusive rock** or *volcanic rock,* ◊igneous rock formed on the surface of the Earth by volcanic activity. The term includes fine-grained crystalline or glassy rocks formed from hot lava quenched at or near Earth's surface and rocks composed of solid debris, called pyroclastics, deposted by explosive eruptions.

**Eyck, Jan van** (c. 1390–1441) Netherlandish painter, who gained in his lifetime a Europewide reputation. One of the first painters to use oil paint effectively, he is noted for his meticulous detail and his brilliance of colour and finish. He painted religious scenes like the altarpiece, *The Adoration of the Lamb* (1432; St Bavo Cathedral, Ghent), and portraits, including *The Arnolfini Wedding* (1434; National Gallery, London), which records the betrothal of the Bruges-based Lucchese cloth merchant Giovanni Arnolfini to Giovanna Cenami.

**eye** the organ of vision. In the human eye, the light is focused by the combined action of the curved *cornea,* the internal fluids, and the *lens.* The insect eye is compound – made up of many separate facets – known as ommatidia, each of which collects light and directs it separately to a receptor to build up an image. Invertebrates have much simpler eyes, with no lenses. Among molluscs, cephalopods have complex eyes similar to those of vertebrates.

The mantis shrimp's eyes contain ten colour pigments with which to perceive colour; some flies and fishes have five, while the human eye has only three. *See illustration on page 315.*

**Eyre, Richard (Charles Hastings)** (1943– ) English stage and film director. He succeeded Peter Hall as artistic director of the National Theatre, London, 1988–97. His stage productions include *Guys and Dolls* (1982), *Bartholomew Fair* (1988), *Richard III* (1990), which he set in 1930s Britain; *Night of the Iguana* (1992), *Macbeth* (1993), *Skylight* (1995), and *Amy's View* and *King Lear* (both 1997). His films include *The Ploughman's Lunch* (1983), *Laughterhouse* (US *Singleton's Pluck*) (1984), *Tumbledown* (1988, for television), *Suddenly Last Summer* (1992), and *The Absence of War* (1995). He also directed the opera *La Traviata* at Covent Garden, London, in 1994.

**Eyre, Lake** lake in northeast South Australia; area up to 9,000 sq km/3,500 sq mi. It is the largest lake in Australia, and includes Lake Eyre North and Lake Eyre South. Much of the lake remains a dry salt crust, while parts form a salt marsh in dry seasons. It is the continent's lowest point, 16 m/52 ft below sea level.

**Fabergé, Peter Carl** born Karl Gustavovich (1846–1920) Russian goldsmith and jeweller. Among his masterpieces was a series of jewelled Easter eggs, the first of which was commissioned by Alexander III for the tsarina 1884.

**Fabian Society** UK socialist organization for research, discussion, and publication, founded in London in 1884. Its name is derived from the Roman commander Fabius Maximus, and refers to the evolutionary methods by which it hopes to attain socialism by a succession of gradual reforms. Early members included the playwright George Bernard Shaw and Beatrice and Sidney Webb. The society helped to found the Labour Representation Committee in 1900, which became the Labour Party in 1906.

**Fabius, Laurent** (1946– ) French politician, leader of the Socialist Party (PS) 1992–93. As prime minister 1984–86, he introduced a liberal, free-market economic programme, but his career was damaged by the 1985 ◊Greenpeace sabotage scandal.

**fable** story, in either verse or prose, in which animals or inanimate objects are given the mentality and speech of human beings to point out a moral. Fables are common in folklore and children's literature, and range from the short fables of the ancient Greek writer Aesop to the modern novel *Animal Farm* (1945) by George Orwell.

**facsimile transmission** full name for ◊*fax* or *telefax.*

**factor** a number that divides into another number exactly. For example, the factors of 64 are 1, 2, 4, 8, 16, 32, and 64. In algebra, certain kinds of polynomials (expressions consisting of several or many terms) can be factorized. For example, the factors of $x^2 + 3x + 2$ are $x + 1$ and $x + 2$, since $x^2 + 3x + 2 = (x + 1)(x + 2)$. This is called factorization. See also ◊prime number.

**factory farming** intensive rearing of poultry or other animals for food, usually on high-protein foodstuffs in confined quarters. Chickens for eggs and meat, and calves for veal are commonly factory farmed. Some countries restrict the use of antibiotics and growth hormones as aids to factory farming because they can persist in the flesh of the animals after they are slaughtered. The emphasis is on productive yield rather than animal welfare so that conditions for the animals are often very poor. For this reason, many people object to factory farming on moral as well as health grounds.

**FA Cup** abbreviation for *Football Association Challenge Cup,* the major annual soccer knockout competition in England and Wales, open to all member clubs of the English Football Association. First held in 1871–72, it is the oldest football knockout competition.

**Faeroe Islands** or *Faeroes,* alternative spelling of the ◊Faroe Islands, in the North Atlantic.

**Fagatogo** seat of government of American ◊Samoa, situated on Pago Pago Harbour, Tutuila Island; population (1980) 30,124 (no current population figures available).

**Fahd** Ibn Abdul Aziz (1923– ) King of Saudi Arabia from 1982. He encouraged the investment of the country's enormous oil wealth in infrastructure and new activities – such as petrochemical industries – in order to diversify the economy, and also built up the country's military forces. When Iraq invaded neighbouring Kuwait in August 1990, King Fahd joined with the USA and other international forces in 'Operation Desert Storm' in the course of the 1990–91 Gulf War, in which Saudi Arabia was used as the base from which Kuwait was liberated, in February 1991.

Falling oil prices, since the 1980s, led to a gradual reduction in the country's financial reserves, and to some retrenchment and, in the 1990s, gradual privatization. From the early 1990s King Fahd's absolutist regime faced twin pressures from liberals, campaigning for democratic elections, and from fundamentalist Islamic groups, which opposed the monarchy and sought the full imposition of Islamic *sharia* law. In May 1993 a group of Islamic activists, led by Muhammad al-Masari, formed a Committee for the Defence of Legitimate Rights to monitor the regime's adherence to Islamic principles. In response to pro-democracy pressures, in August 1993, the king established an advisory Shura Council, comprising 60 members of the national elite, drawn from outside the royal family, and also established a system of regional government. In November 1995 King Fahd suffered a stroke, and in January 1996 he temporarily ceded power to Crown Prince Abdullah, his legal successor.

**Fahrenheit scale** temperature scale invented in 1714 by Gabriel Fahrenheit which was commonly used in English-speaking countries until the 1970s, after which the ◊Celsius scale was generally adopted, in line with the rest of the world. In the Fahrenheit scale, intervals are measured in degrees (°F); °F = (°C x 9/5) + 32.

**fainting** sudden, temporary loss of consciousness caused by reduced blood supply to the brain. It may be due to emotional shock or physical factors, such as pooling of blood in the legs from standing still for long periods.

**Fairbanks, Douglas, Sr** stage name of Douglas Elton Ulman (1883–1939) US actor. He played acrobatic, swashbuckling heroes in silent films such as *The Mark of Zorro* (1920), *The Three Musketeers* 1921, *Robin Hood* (1922),

*The Thief of Bagdad* (1924), and *Don Quixote* (1925). He was married to the film star Mary Pickford 1920–35. In 1919 they founded United Artists with Charlie Chaplin and D W Griffith.

**Fairbanks, Douglas (Elton Ulman), Jr** (1909–  ) US actor. He initially appeared in the same type of swashbuckling film roles – *Catherine the Great* (1934), *The Prisoner of Zenda* (1937), and *Sinbad the Sailor* (1947) – as his father, Douglas Fairbanks. Later he produced TV films and acted in a variety of productions. He has lived in England since the early 1950s.

**Fairfax, Thomas** 3rd Baron Fairfax (1612–1671) English general, commander in chief of the Parliamentary army in the English ◊Civil War. With Oliver ◊Cromwell he formed the ◊New Model Army and defeated Charles I at Naseby. He opposed the king's execution, resigned in protest against the invasion of Scotland in 1650, and participated in the restoration of Charles II after Cromwell's death. Knighted 1640, succeeded to barony 1648.

**fairy tale** magical story, usually a folk tale in origin. Typically in European fairy tales, a poor, brave, and resourceful hero or heroine goes through testing adventures to eventual good fortune.

**Faisalabad** city in Punjab province, Pakistan, 120 km/75 mi west of Lahore; population (1981) 1,092,000. It trades in grain, cotton, and textiles. Formerly known as Lyallpur, it was founded in 1892 by the British, and laid out in the shape of a Union Jack.

**Faisal Ibn Abd al-Aziz** (1905–1975) King of Saudi Arabia 1964–75. Ruling without a prime minister, he instituted a successful programme of economic modernization, using Saudi Arabia's vast annual oil revenues, which grew from $334 million in 1960 to $22.5 billion in 1974, after the quadrupling of world oil prices in 1973–74. A generous welfare system was established, including free medical care and education to postgraduate level, and subsidized food, water, fuel, electricity, and rents; slavery was outlawed; and financial support was given to other Arab states in their struggle with Israel. In March 1975 Faisal was assassinated by a mentally unstable nephew, Prince Museid, and his half-brother Khalid became king.

**falcon** any bird of prey of the genus *Falco,* family Falconidae, order Falconiformes. Falcons are the smallest of the hawks (15–60 cm/6–24 in). They have short curved beaks with one tooth in the upper mandible; the wings are long and pointed, and the toes prehensile. They nest in high places and kill their prey on the wing by 'stooping' (swooping down at high speed). They include the peregrine and kestrel.

**falconry** the use of specially trained falcons and hawks to capture birds or small mammals. Practised since ancient times in the Middle East, falconry was introduced from continental Europe to Britain in Saxon times.

**Faldo, Nick (Nicholas Alexander)** (1957–  ) English golfer who was the first Briton in 54 years to win three British Open titles, and the only person after Jack Nicklaus to win two successive US Masters titles (1989 and 1990). He is one of only seven golfers to win the Masters and British Open in the same year.
*career highlights*
*British Open* 1987, 1989, 1992
*US Masters* 1989, 1990, 1996
*PGA Championship* 1978, 1980–81, 1989
*Ryder Cup winning team* 1985, 1987, tie 1989, 1991, 1993
*World Match-Play Championship* 1989, 1992

**Falkirk** unitary authority in central Scotland, created from the former district of the same name in 1996 from part of the former Central region
*area* 297 sq km/115 sq mi
*towns* Falkirk (administrative headquarters), Grangemouth
*physical* centrally located between Edinburgh and Glasgow, this low-lying area borders the southern side of the Firth of Forth; River Avon flows through
*features* Forth and Clyde and Union canals; Rough Castle; Antonine Wall
*industries* chemicals and petrochemicals, bus building, soft drinks, toffees
*agriculture* some dairy and arable farming
*population* (1996) 142,500.

**Falkland Islands** Argentine *Islas Malvinas,* British crown colony in the South Atlantic, 300 miles east of the Straits of Magellan
*area* 12,173 sq km/4,700 sq mi, made up of two main islands: East Falkland 6,760 sq km/2,610 sq mi, and West Falkland 5,413 sq km/2,090 sq mi
*capital* Stanley; new port facilities opened in 1984, Mount Pleasant airport in 1985
*features* in addition to the two main islands, there are about 200 small islands, all with wild scenery and rich bird life; Mount Usborne (705 m/2,312 ft); moorland
*industries* wool, alginates (used as dyes and as a food additive) from seaweed beds, fishing (especially squid)
*population* (1991) 2,120.

**Falklands War** war between Argentina and Britain over disputed sovereignty of the Falkland Islands initiated when Argentina invaded and occupied the islands on 2 April 1982. On the following day, the United Nations Security Council passed a resolution calling for Argentina to withdraw. A British task force was immediately dispatched and, after a fierce conflict in which more than 1,000 Argentine and British lives were lost, 12,000 Argentine troops surrendered and the islands were returned to British rule on 14–15 June 1982.

**Falla, Manuel de** full name Manuel Maria de Falla y Matheu (1876–1946) Spanish composer. The folk idiom of southern Spain is an integral part of his compositions. His opera *La vida breve/Brief Life* (1905; performed 1913) was followed by the ballets *El amor brujo/Love the Magician* (1915) and *El sombrero de tres picos/ The Three-Cornered Hat* (1919), and his most ambitious concert work, *Noches en los jardines de España/Nights in the Gardens of Spain* (1916). He also wrote songs and pieces for piano and guitar.

**Fallopian tube** or *oviduct*, in mammals, one of two tubes that carry eggs from the ovary to the uterus. An egg is fertilized by sperm in the Fallopian tubes, which are lined with cells whose ◊cilia move the egg towards the uterus.

**fallout** harmful radioactive material released into the atmosphere in the debris of a nuclear explosion (see ◊nuclear warfare) and descending to the surface of the Earth. Such material can enter the food chain, cause ◊radiation sickness, and last for hundreds or thousands of years (see ◊half-life).

**family** in biological classification, a group of related genera (see ◊genus). Family names are not printed in italic (unlike genus and species names), and by convention they all have the ending -idae (animals) or -aceae (plants and fungi). For example, the genera of hummingbirds are grouped in the hummingbird family, Trochilidae. Related families are grouped together in an ◊order.

**family** group of people related to each other by blood or by marriage. Families are usually described as either *extended* (a large group of relations living together or in close contact with each other) or *nuclear* (a family consisting of two parents and their children).

**family planning** spacing or preventing the birth of children. Access to family-planning services (see ◊contraceptive) is a significant factor in women's health as well as in limiting population growth. If all those women who wished to avoid further childbirth were able to do so, the number of births would be reduced by 27% in Africa, 33% in Asia, and 35% in Latin America; and the number of women who die during pregnancy or childbirth would be reduced by about 50%.

**famine** severe shortage of food affecting a large number of people. Almost 750 million people (equivalent to double the population of Europe) worldwide suffer from hunger and malnutrition. The *food availability deficit* (FAD) theory explains famines as being caused by insufficient food supplies. A more recent theory is that famines arise when one group in a society loses its opportunity to exchange its labour or possessions for food.

**farad** SI unit (symbol F) of electrical capacitance (how much electric charge a ◊capacitor can store for a given voltage). One farad is a capacitance of one ◊coulomb per volt. For practical purposes the microfarad (one millionth of a farad, symbol µF) is more commonly used.

**faraday** unit of electrical charge equal to the charge on one mole of electrons. Its value is $9.648 \times 10^4$ coulombs.

**Faraday, Michael** (1791–1867) English chemist and physicist. In 1821, he began experimenting with electromagnetism, and discovered the induction of electric currents and made the first

dynamo, the first electric motor, and the first transformer. Faraday isolated benzene from gas oils and produced the basic laws of ◊electrolysis in 1834. He also pointed out that the energy of a magnet is in the field around it and not in the magnet itself, extending this basic conception of field theory to electrical and gravitational systems.

**Faraday's constant** constant (symbol $F$) representing the electric charge carried on one mole of electrons. It is found by multiplying Avogadro's constant by the charge carried on a single electron, and is equal to $9.648 \times 10^4$ coulombs per mole.

One *faraday* is this constant used as a unit. The constant is used to calculate the electric charge needed to discharge a particular quantity of ions during ◊electrolysis.

**Faraday's laws** three laws of electromagnetic induction, and two laws of electrolysis, all proposed originally by English scientist Michael Faraday:

*induction* (1) a changing magnetic field induces an electromagnetic force in a conductor; (2) the electromagnetic force is proportional to the rate of change of the field; (3) the direction of the induced electromagnetic force depends on the orientation of the field.

*electrolysis* (1) the amount of chemical change during electrolysis is proportional to the charge passing through the liquid; (2) the amount of chemical change produced in a substance by a given amount of electricity is proportional to the electrochemical equivalent of that substance.

**farce** broad popular comedy involving stereotyped characters in complex, often improbable situations frequently revolving around extramarital relationships (hence the term 'bedroom farce').

**Far East** geographical term for all Asia east of the Indian subcontinent.

**Faroe Islands** or *Faeroe Islands* or *Faeroes* (Danish *Færøerne* 'Sheep Islands'), island group (18 out of 22 inhabited) in the North Atlantic, between the Shetland Islands and Iceland, forming an outlying part of Denmark
*area* 1,399 sq km/540 sq mi; largest islands are Strømø, Østerø, Vagø, Suderø, Sandø, and Bordø
*capital* Thorshavn on Strømø, population (1992) 14,600
*industries* fish, crafted goods
*currency* Danish krone
*population* (1992 est) 46,800
*language* Faeroese, Danish
*government* since 1948 the islands have had full self-government; they do not belong to the European Union
*history* first settled by Norsemen in the 9th century, the Faroes were a Norwegian province 1380–1709. Their parliament was restored 1852. They withdrew from the European Free Trade Association 1972.

**Farouk** (1920–1965) King of Egypt. He succeeded the throne on the death of his father Fuad I. His early popularity was later overshadowed by his somewhat unsuccessful private life, and more importantly by the humiliating defeat of the Egyptian army in 1948. In 1952 a group called the 'Free Officers', led by Muhammad Neguib and Gamal Abdel Nasser, forced him to abdicate, and he was temporarily replaced by his son Ahmad Fuad II. Exiled for the remainder of his life, he died in Rome in 1965.

**Farrell, Terry (Terence)** (1938–  ) English architect. He works in a postmodern idiom, largely for corporate clients seeking an alternative to the rigours of Modernist or High Tech office blocks. His Embankment Place scheme (1991) sits theatrically on top of Charing Cross station in Westminster, London, and has been likened to a giant jukebox. Alban Gate (1992) in the City of London is a continuation of the language but is more towerlike in form.

**Farsi** or *Persian,* language belonging to the Indo-Iranian branch of the Indo-European family, and the official language of Iran (formerly Persia). It is also spoken in Afghanistan, Iraq, and Tajikistan.

**fascism** political ideology that denies all rights to individuals in their relations with the state; specifically, the totalitarian nationalist movement founded in Italy 1919 by ◊Mussolini and followed by Hitler's Germany 1933.

Fascism was essentially a product of the economic and political crisis of the years after World War I. Units called *fasci di combattimento* (combat groups), from the Latin fasces, were originally established to oppose communism. The fascist party, the *Partitio Nazionale Fascista,* controlled Italy 1922–43. Fascism protected the existing social order by forcible suppression of the working-class movement and by providing scapegoats for popular anger such as minority groups: Jews, foreigners, or blacks; it also prepared the citizenry for the economic and psychological mobilization of war.

**Fassbinder, Rainer Werner** (1946–1982) West German film director. He began as a fringe actor and founded his own 'anti-theatre' before moving into films. His works are mainly stylized indictments of contemporary German society. He made more than 40 films, including *Die bitteren Tränen der Petra von Kant/The Bitter Tears of Petra von Kant* (1972), *Angst essen Seele auf/Fear Eats the Soul* (1974), and *Die Ehe von Maria Braun/The Marriage of Maria Braun* (1979).

**fast breeder** or *breeder reactor,* alternative names for ◊fast reactor, a type of nuclear reactor.

**fasting** the practice of voluntarily going without food. It can be undertaken as a religious observance, a sign of mourning, a political protest (hunger strike), or for slimming purposes.

**fast reactor** or *fast breeder reactor,* ◊nuclear reactor that makes use of fast neutrons to bring about fission. Unlike other reactors used by the nuclear-power industry, it has little or no moderator, to slow down neutrons. The reactor core is surrounded by a 'blanket' of uranium carbide. During operation, some of this uranium is converted into plutonium, which can be extracted and later used as fuel.

**fat** in the broadest sense, a mixture of ◊lipids – chiefly triglycerides (lipids containing three ◊fatty acid molecules linked to a molecule of glycerol). More specifically, the term refers to a lipid mixture that is solid at room temperature (20°C); lipid mixtures that are liquid at room temperature are called *oils.* The higher the proportion of saturated fatty acids in a mixture, the harder the fat.

**Fatah, al-** Palestinian nationalist organization, founded 1958 to bring about an independent state of Palestine. It was the first Palestinian resistance group, based 1968–70 in Jordan, then in Lebanon, and from 1982 in Tunisia. Also called the Palestine National Liberation Movement, it is the main component of the ◊Palestine Liberation Organization. Its leader (from 1968) is Yassir ◊Arafat.

**Fates** or *Moirai,* in Greek mythology, three female figures who determined the destiny of human lives; later, the duration of human life. They were envisaged as spinners: Clotho spun the thread of life, Lachesis apportioned the thread, and Atropos cut it off. They are analogous to the Roman *Parcae* or *Fata* and Norse Norns.

**Father Christmas** or *Santa Claus,* popular personification of the spirit of Christmas, derived from the Christian legend of St ◊Nicholas and elements of Scandinavian mythology. He is depicted as a fat, jolly old man with a long white beard, dressed in boots and a red hat and suit trimmed with white fur. He lives with his toy-making elves at the North Pole, and on Christmas Eve he travels in an airborne sleigh, drawn by eight reindeer, to deliver presents to good children, who are fast asleep when he arrives. The most popular legends claim that Father Christmas lands his sleigh on rooftops, secretly entering homes through the chimney.

**Fatimid** dynasty of Muslim Shiite caliphs founded 909 by Obaidallah, who claimed to be a descendant of Fatima (the prophet Muhammad's daughter) and her husband Ali, in North Africa. In 969 the Fatimids conquered Egypt, and the dynasty continued until overthrown by Saladin 1171.

**fatty acid** or *carboxylic acid,* organic compound consisting of a hydrocarbon chain, up to 24 carbon atoms long, with a carboxyl group (–COOH) at one end. The covalent bonds between the carbon atoms may be single or double; where a double bond occurs the carbon atoms concerned carry one instead of two hydrogen atoms. Chains with only single bonds have all the hydrogen they can carry, so they are said to be *saturated* with hydrogen. Chains with one or more double bonds are said to be *unsaturated* (see ◊polyunsaturate). Fatty acids are produced in the small intestine when fat is digested.

**fatwa** in Islamic law, an authoritative legal opinion on a point of doctrine. In 1989 a fatwa calling for the death of British novelist Salman

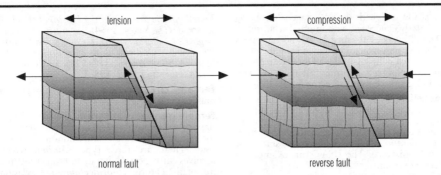

**fault** *Faults are caused by the movement of rock layers, producing such features as block mountains and rift valleys. A normal fault is caused by a tension or stretching force acting in the rock layers. A reverse fault is caused by compression forces. Faults can continue to move for thousands or millions of years.*

◊Rushdie was made by the Ayatollah ◊Khomeini of Iran, following publication of Rushdie's controversial and allegedly blasphemous book *The Satanic Verses* (1988).

**Faulkner, William (Cuthbert)** (1897–1962) US novelist. His works employ difficult narrative styles in their epic mapping of a quasi-imaginary region of the American South. His third novel, *The Sound and the Fury* (1929), deals with the decline of a Southern family, told in four voices, beginning with an especially complex stream-of-consciousness narrative. He was awarded the Nobel Prize for Literature in 1949.

**fault** in geology, a fracture in the Earth either side of which rocks have moved past one another. Faults involve displacements, or offsets, ranging from the microscopic scale to hundreds of kilometres. Large offsets along a fault are the result of the accumulation of smaller movements (metres or less) over long periods of time. Large motions cause detectable ◊earthquakes.

**Faunus** in Roman mythology, one of the oldest Italian deities; god of fertility and prophecy; protector of agriculturists and shepherds. He was later identified with the Greek ◊Pan and represented with goat's ears, horns, tail, and hind legs.

**Faust** legendary magician who sold his soul to the devil. The historical Georg (or Johann) Faust appears to have been a wandering scholar and conjurer in Germany at the start of the 16th century. Christopher Marlowe, J W Goethe, Heinrich Heine, and Thomas Mann all used the legend, and it inspired musical works by Franz Liszt, Hector Berlioz, Charles Gounod, and Richard Wagner.

**Fauvism** (French *fauve*, 'wild beast') movement in modern French painting characterized by the use of very bold, vivid colours. The name is a reference to the fact that the works seemed to many people at the time to be crude and untamed. Although short-lived, lasting only about two years (1905–07), the movement was highly influential. It was the first of the artistic movements that transformed European art between the turn of the century and World War I.

**Fawkes, Guy** (1570–1606) English conspirator in the ◊Gunpowder Plot to blow up King James I and the members of both Houses of Parliament. Fawkes, a Roman Catholic convert, was arrested in the cellar underneath the House of Lords on 4 November 1605, tortured, and executed. The event is still commemorated in Britain and elsewhere every 5 November with bonfires, fireworks, and the burning of the 'guy', an effigy.

**fax** common name for facsimile transmission or telefax, transmission of images over a ◊telecommunications link, usually the telephone network. When placed on a fax machine, the original image is scanned by a transmitting device and converted into coded signals, which travel via the telephone lines to the receiving fax machine, where an image is created that is a copy of the original. Photographs as well as printed text and drawings can be sent. The standard transmission takes place at 4,800 or 9,600 bits of information per second.

**FBI** abbreviation for ◊*Federal Bureau of Investigation,* agency of the US Department of Justice.

**feather** rigid outgrowth of the outer layer of the skin of birds, made of the protein keratin. Feathers provide insulation and facilitate flight. There are several types, including long quill feathers on the wings and tail, fluffy down feathers for retaining body heat, and contour feathers covering the body. The colouring of feathers is often important in camouflage or in courtship and other displays. Feathers are normally replaced at least once a year.

There is an enormous variation between species in the number of feathers, for example a whistling swan has over 25,000 contour feathers, whereas a ruby-throated hummingbird has fewer than 950.

**feather star** any of an unattached, free-swimming group of sea lilies, order Comatulida. The arms are branched into numerous projections (hence 'feather' star), and grow from a small cup-shaped body. Below the body are appendages that can hold on to a surface, but the feather star is not permanently attached.

**Federal Bureau of Investigation** (FBI), agency of the US Department of Justice that investigates violations of federal law not specifically assigned to other agencies, being particularly concerned with internal security.

The FBI was established 1908 and built up a position of powerful autonomy during the autocratic directorship of J Edgar Hoover 1924–72. Louis Joseph Freeh, a former FBI agent and federal prosecutor, became director in 1993.

**federalism** system of government in which two or more separate states unite into a ◊federation under a common central government. A federation should be distinguished from a *confederation,* a looser union of states for mutual assistance. The USA is an example of federal government.

**federation** political entity made up from a number of smaller units or states where the central government has powers over national issues such as foreign policy and defence, while the individual states retain a high degree of regional and local autonomy. A federation should be distinguished from a *confederation,* a looser union of states for mutual assistance. Contemporary examples of federated states established since 1750 include the USA, Canada, Australia, India, the Federal Republic of Germany, Malaysia, and Micronesia.

**feedback** general principle whereby the results produced in an ongoing reaction become factors in modifying or changing the reaction; it is the principle used in self-regulating control systems, from a simple ◊thermostat and steam-engine governor to automatic computer-controlled machine tools. A fully computerized control system, in which there is no operator intervention, is called a *closed-loop feedback* system. A system that also responds to control signals from an operator is called an *open-loop feedback* system.

**feldspar** a group of ◊silicate minerals. Feldspars are the most abundant mineral type in the Earth's crust. They are the chief constituents of ◊igneous rock and are present in most metamorphic and sedimentary rocks. All feldspars contain silicon, aluminium, and oxygen, linked together to form a framework. Spaces within this framework structure are occupied by sodium, potassium, calcium, or occasionally barium, in various proportions. Feldspars form white, grey, or pink crystals and rank 6 on the ◊Mohs scale of hardness.

**feldspathoid** any of a group of silicate minerals resembling feldspars but containing less silica. Examples are nepheline ($NaAlSiO_4$ with a little potassium) and leucite ($KAlSi_2O_6$). Feldspathoids occur in igneous rocks that have relatively high proportions of sodium and potassium. Such rocks may also contain alkali feldspar, but they do not generally contain quartz because any free silica would have combined with the feldspathoid to produce more feldspar instead.

**Fellini, Federico** (1920–1993) Italian film director and screenwriter. His work has been a major influence on modern cinema. Many of his films combine dream and fantasy sequences with satire and autobiographical detail. They include

*I vitelloni/The Young and the Passionate* (1953), *La strada/The Street* (1954), *Le notti di Cabiria/ Nights of Cabiria* (1956), *La dolce vita* (1960), *8½* (1963), *Giulietta degli spiriti/Juliet of the Spirits* (1965), *Amarcord* (1974), and *Ginger e Fred/Ginger and Fred* (1986).

**female circumcision** See ◊female genital mutilation.

**female genital mutilation** (FGM), the partial or total removal of female external genitalia for cultural, religious, or other non-medical reasons. There are three types: *Sunna,* which involves cutting off the hood, and sometimes the tip, of the clitoris; *clitoridectomy,* the excision of the clitoris and removal of parts of the inner and outer labia; *infibulation* (most widely practised in Sudan and Somalia), the removal of the clitoris, the inner and outer labia; and the stitching of the scraped sides of the vulva across the vagina leaving a small hole to allow passage of urine and menstrual blood.

**feminism** active belief in equal rights and opportunities for women; see ◊women's movement.

**fencing** sport of fighting with swords including the *foil,* derived from the light weapon used in practice duels; the *épée,* a heavier weapon derived from the duelling sword proper; and the *sabre,* with a curved handle and narrow V-shaped blade. In sabre fighting, cuts count as well as thrusts. Masks and protective jackets are worn, and hits are registered electronically in competitions. Men's fencing has been part of every Olympic programme since 1896; women's fencing was included from 1924 but only using the foil.

**Fenian movement** Irish-American republican secret society, founded in 1858 and named after the ancient Irish legendary warrior band of the Fianna. The collapse of the movement began when an attempt to establish an independent Irish republic by an uprising in Ireland in 1867 failed, as did raids into Canada in 1866 and 1870, and England in 1867.

**fennec** small nocturnal desert ◊fox *Fennecus zerda* found in North Africa and Arabia. It has a head and body only 40 cm/1.3 ft long, and its enormous ears act as radiators to lose excess heat. It eats insects and small animals.

**fennel** any of several varieties of a perennial plant with feathery green leaves, belonging to the carrot family. Fennels have an aniseed (liquorice) flavour, and the leaves and seeds are used in seasoning. The thickened leafstalks of sweet fennel (*F. vulgare dulce*) are eaten as a vegetable. (*Foeniculum vulgare,* family Umbelliferae.)

**Fens, the** level, low-lying tracts of reclaimed marsh in eastern England, west and south of the Wash, covering an area of around 40,000 sq km/15,500 sq mi, about 115 km/70 mi north–south and 55 km/34 mi east–west. They fall within the counties of Lincolnshire, Cambridgeshire, and Norfolk. Formerly a bay of the North Sea, they are now crossed by numerous drainage canals and form some of the most fertile and productive agricultural land in Britain. The southern peat portion of the Fens is known as the Bedford Level.

**Ferdinand** five kings of Castile, including:

**Ferdinand (I) the Great** (c. 1016–1065) King of Castile from 1035. He began the reconquest of Spain from the Moors and united all northwestern Spain under his and his brothers' rule.

**Ferdinand II** (1452–1516) King-consort of Castile from 1474 (as *Ferdinand V*), King of Aragon from 1479, and *Ferdinand III* of Naples from 1504. In 1469 he married his cousin Isabella I, who succeeded to the throne of Castile in 1474; they were known as *the Catholic Monarchs* because they completed the *reconquista* (reconquest) of the Spanish peninsula from the Muslims by taking the last Moorish kingdom, Granada, in 1492. To celebrate this success they expelled the Jews and financed Christopher ◊Columbus's expedition to the Americas in 1492.

**Ferdinand** three Holy Roman emperors, including:

**Ferdinand II** (1578–1637) Holy Roman Emperor from 1619, when he succeeded his uncle Matthias; king of Bohemia from 1617 and of Hungary from 1618. A zealous Catholic, he provoked the Bohemian revolt that led to the Thirty Years' War. He was a grandson of Ferdinand I.

**Ferguson, Alex(ander)** (1941– ) Scottish football manager. One of British football's most successful managers, he has won nine trophies with Manchester United including four league championship titles. In 1996, under his charge, Manchester United became the first club to achieve the league championship and FA Cup double twice. Earlier, as manager of Aberdeen from 1978 to 1986, he won ten trophies including three Scottish championships and the European Cup Winners' Cup. He was also manager of the Scottish national side 1985–86. Knighted 1999.

Under his management, Manchester United won the European Cup for the first time in 1999, also winning the league championship and the FA Cup. He is the first manager to lead an English team to all three trophies in the same season, and the first to win three English league championship and cup doubles (they previously won the double in 1994 and 1996).

*career highlights*
*with Manchester United*
**European Cup** 1999
**FA Premiership** 1993, 1994, 1996, 1997, 1999
**FA Cup** 1990, 1994, 1996, 1999
**European Cup Winners' Cup** 1991
**League (Rumbelows) Cup** 1992
*with Aberdeen*
**Scottish Premier League** 1980, 1984, 1985
**Scottish Cup** 1982, 1983, 1984, 1986
**League (Skol) Cup** 1986
**European Cup Winners' Cup** 1983
**European Super Cup** 1983

**Fermanagh** county of Northern Ireland
*area* 1,680 sq km/648 sq mi
*towns* Enniskillen (county town), Lisnaskea, Irvinestown
*physical* in the centre is a broad trough of low-lying land, in which lie Upper and Lower Lough Erne
*industries* clothing, tweeds, cotton thread, food processing, light engineering, china, tourism, electronics
*agriculture* small farms, livestock, potatoes
*population* (1991) 50,000.

**Fermat, Pierre de** (1601–1665) French mathematician who, with Blaise ◊Pascal, founded the theory of ◊probability and the modern theory of numbers. Fermat also made contributions to analytical geometry. In 1657, Fermat published a series of problems as challenges to other mathematicians, in the form of theorems to be proved.

**fermentation** breakdown of sugars by bacteria and yeasts using a method of respiration without oxygen (◊anaerobic). Fermentation processes have long been utilized in baking bread, making beer and wine, and producing cheese, yogurt, soy sauce, and many other foodstuffs.

**Fermi, Enrico** (1901–1954) Italian-born US physicist who proved the existence of new radioactive elements produced by bombardment with neutrons, and discovered nuclear reactions produced by low-energy neutrons. This research won him the Nobel Prize for Physics in 1938 and was the basis for studies leading to the atomic bomb and nuclear energy. Fermi built the first nuclear reactor in 1942 at Chicago University and later took part in the Manhattan Project to construct an atom bomb. His theoretical work included the study of the weak nuclear force, one of the fundamental forces of nature, and beta decay.

**fermion** in physics, a subatomic particle whose spin can only take values that are half-integers, such as 1/2 or 3/2. Fermions may be classified as leptons, such as the electron, and baryons, such as the proton and neutron. All elementary particles are either fermions or ◊bosons.

**fermium** synthesized, radioactive, metallic element of the ◊actinide series, symbol Fm, atomic number 100, relative atomic mass 257.10. Ten isotopes are known, the longest-lived of which, Fm-257, has a half-life of 80 days. Fermium has been produced only in minute quantities in particle accelerators.

**fern** any of a group of plants related to horsetails and clubmosses. Ferns are spore-bearing, not flowering, plants and most are perennial, spreading by slow-growing roots. The leaves, known as fronds, vary widely in size and shape. Some taller types, such as tree ferns, grow in the tropics. There are over 7,000 species. (Order Filicales.) *See illustration on page 324.*

**Ferrari, Enzo** (1898–1988) Italian founder of the Ferrari car-manufacturing company, which specializes in Grand Prix racing cars and high-quality sports cars. He was a racing driver for Alfa Romeo in the 1920s, went on to become

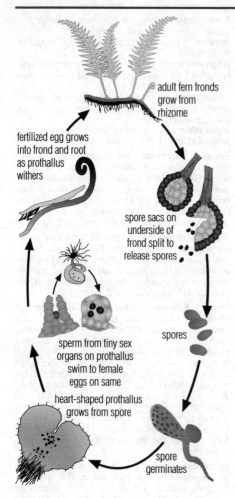

**fern** The life cycle of a fern. Ferns have two distinct forms that alternate during their life cycle. For the main part of its life, a fern consists of a short stem (or rhizome) from which roots and leaves grow. The other part of its life is spent as a small heart-shaped plant called a prothallus.

*Labels in figure:*

adult fern fronds grow from rhizome

fertilized egg grows into frond and root as prothallus withers

spore sacs on underside of frond split to release spores

spores

sperm from tiny sex organs on prothallus swim to female eggs on same

heart-shaped prothallus grows from spore

spore germinates

one of their designers, and took over their racing division 1929. In 1947 the first 'true' Ferrari was seen. The Ferrari car won more world championship Grand Prix than any other car until very recently, when the McLaren Formula 1 team equalled their record.

**Formula 1 highlights**
**Grand Prix** starts 603 victories 119 constructors' titles 8 drivers' titles 9

**ferret** domesticated variety of the Old World ◊polecat.

About 35 cm/1.2 ft long, it usually has yellowish-white fur and pink eyes, but may be the dark brown colour of a wild polecat.

Ferrets may breed with wild polecats. They have been used since ancient times to hunt rabbits and rats.

**ferromagnetism** form of ◊magnetism that can be acquired in an external magnetic field and usually retained in its absence, so that ferromagnetic materials are used to make permanent magnets. A ferromagnetic material may therefore be said to have a high magnetic permeability and susceptibility (which depends upon temperature). Examples are iron, cobalt, nickel, and their alloys.

**fertilization** in ◊sexual reproduction, the union of two ◊gametes (sex cells, often called egg and sperm) to produce a ◊zygote, which combines the genetic material contributed by each parent. In self-fertilization the male and female gametes come from the same plant; in cross-fertilization they come from different plants. Self-fertilization rarely occurs in animals; usually even ◊hermaphrodite animals cross-fertilize each other.

**fertilizer** substance containing some or all of a range of about 20 chemical elements necessary for healthy plant growth, used to compensate for the deficiencies of poor or depleted soil. Fertilizers may be *organic,* for example farmyard manure, composts, bonemeal, blood, and fishmeal; or *inorganic,* in the form of compounds, mainly of nitrogen, phosphate, and potash, which have been used on a very much increased scale since 1945. Compounds of nitrogen and phosphorus are of particular importance.

**Fès** or *Fez,* Arabic *Fas,* former capital of Morocco 808–1062, 1296–1548, and 1662–1912, in the Fès valley north of the Great Atlas Mountains, 160 km/100 mi east of Rabat; population (1993) 564,000. Textiles, carpets, and leather are manufactured, and the *fez,* a brimless hat worn in southern and eastern Mediterranean countries, is traditionally said to have originated here. Qarawiyin Islamic University dates from 859; a second university was founded in 1961.

**fetishism** in anthropology, belief in the supernormal power of some inanimate object that is known as a fetish. Fetishism in some form is common to most cultures, and often has religious or magical significance.

**fetishism** in psychology, the transfer of erotic interest to an object, such as an item of clothing, whose real or fantasized presence is necessary for sexual gratification. The fetish may also be a part of the body not normally considered erogenous, such as the feet.

**fetus** or *foetus,* stage in mammalian ◊embryo development. The human embryo is usually termed a fetus after the eighth week of development, when the limbs and external features of the head are recognizable.

**feudalism** (Latin *feudem* 'fief', coined 1839) the main form of social organization in medieval Europe. A system based primarily on land, it involved a hierarchy of authority, rights, and power that extended from the monarch downwards. An intricate network of duties and obligations linked royalty, nobility, lesser gentry, free tenants, villeins, and serfs. Feudalism was reinforced by a complex legal system and supported by the Christian church. With the growth of commerce and industry from the 13th century, feudalism gradually gave way to the class system as the dominant form of social ranking.

**fever** condition of raised body temperature, usually due to infection.

**Fez** alternative spelling of ◊Fès, a city in Morocco.

**Fianna Fáil** (Gaelic 'Soldiers of Destiny') Republic of Ireland political party, founded by the Irish nationalist Edmund de Valera 1926, and led since 1994 by Bertie Ahern. It was the governing party in the Republic of Ireland 1932–48, 1951–54, 1957–73, 1977–81, 1982, 1987–94 (from 1993 in coalition with Labour), and since 1997. It aims at the establishment of a united and completely independent all-Ireland republic.

**Fibonacci, Leonardo** also known as *Leonardo of Pisa* (c. 1170–c. 1250) Italian mathematician. He published *Liber abaci/The Book of the Calculator* in Pisa (1202), which was instrumental in the introduction of Arabic notation into Europe. From 1960, interest increased in *Fibonacci numbers,* in their simplest form a sequence in which each number is the sum of its two predecessors (1, 1, 2, 3, 5, 8, 13, ...). They have unusual characteristics with possible applications in botany, psychology, and astronomy (for example, a more exact correspondence than is given by Bode's law to the distances between the planets and the Sun).

**fibre, dietary** or *roughage,* plant material that cannot be digested by human digestive enzymes; it consists largely of cellulose, a carbohydrate found in plant cell walls. Fibre adds bulk to the gut contents, assisting the muscular contractions that force food along the intestine. A diet low in fibre causes constipation and is believed to increase the risk of developing diverticulitis, diabetes, gall-bladder disease, and cancer of the large bowel – conditions that are rare in nonindustrialized countries, where the diet contains a high proportion of unrefined cereals.

**fibreglass** glass that has been formed into fine fibres, either as long continuous filaments or as a fluffy, short-fibred glass wool. Fibreglass is heat- and fire-resistant and a good electrical insulator. It has applications in the field of fibre optics and as a strengthener for plastics in GRP (glass-reinforced plastics).

**fibre optics** branch of physics dealing with the transmission of light and images through glass or plastic fibres known as ◊optical fibres.

**fibula** the rear lower bone in the hind leg of a vertebrate. It is paired and often fused with a smaller front bone, the tibia.

**fiction** in literature, any work in which the content is completely or largely invented. The term describes imaginative works of narrative prose (such as the novel or the short story), and is distinguished from *nonfiction* (such as history, biography, or works on practical subjects) and *poetry.*

**field** in physics, a region of space in which an object exerts a force on another separate object because of certain properties they both possess. For example, there is a force of attraction between any two objects that have mass when one is in the gravitational field of the other.

**Fielding, Henry** (1707–1754) English novelist. His greatest work, *The History of Tom Jones, a Foundling* (1749), which he described as 'a comic epic poem in prose', was an early landmark in the development of the English novel, realizing for the first time in English the form's potential for memorable characterization, coherent plotting, and perceptive analysis. The vigour of its comic impetus, descriptions of high and low life in town and country, and its variety of characters made it immediately popular.

**Fields, W C** stage name of William Claude Dukenfield (1880–1946) US actor and screenwriter. His distinctive speech and professed attitudes such as hatred of children and dogs gained him enormous popularity in such films as *David Copperfield* (1935), *My Little Chickadee* (1940) (co-written with Mae West), *The Bank Dick* (1940), and *Never Give a Sucker an Even Break* (1941).

**Fife** unitary authority in eastern Scotland, which was formerly a region of three districts (1975–96) and a county until 1974
*area* 1,321 sq km/510 sq mi
*towns* Cupar, Dunfermline, Glenrothes (administrative headquarters), Kirkcaldy, St Andrews
*physical* coastal area, predominantly low lying, undulating interior with dramatic escarpment at Lomond Hills; rivers Eden and Leven flow through
*features* Rosyth naval base; Old Course, St Andrews
*industries* electronics, petrochemicals, light engineering, oil servicing, paper
*agriculture* potatoes, cereals, sugar beet, fishing (Pittenweem)
*population* (1996) 351,200
*history* Tentsmuir, a coastal sand-dune area in the north, is possibly the earliest settled site in Scotland; the ancient palace of the Stuarts (16th century) was at Falkland; eight Scottish kings buried at Dunfermline.

**fifth-generation computer** anticipated new type of computer based on emerging microelectronic technologies with high computing speeds and ◊parallel processing. The development of very large-scale integration (VLSI) technology, which can put many more circuits on to an integrated circuit (chip) than is currently possible, and developments in computer hardware and software design may produce computers far more powerful than those in current use.

**fig** any of a group of trees belonging to the mulberry family, including the many cultivated varieties of *F. carica,* originally from western Asia. They produce two or three crops of fruit a year. Eaten fresh or dried, figs have a high sugar content and laxative properties. (Genus *Ficus,* family Moraceae.)

**fighting fish** any of a southeast Asian genus

*Betta* of fishes of the gourami family, especially *B. splendens,* about 6 cm/2 in long and a popular aquarium fish. It can breathe air, using an accessory breathing organ above the gill, and can live in poorly oxygenated water. The male has large fins and various colours, including shining greens, reds, and blues. The female is yellowish brown with short fins.

**figwort** any of a group of Old World plants belonging to the figwort family, which also includes foxgloves and snapdragons. Members of the genus have square stems, opposite leaves, and open two-lipped flowers in a cluster at the top of the stem. (Genus *Scrophularia,* family Scrophulariaceae.)

**file** in computing, a collection of data or a program stored in a computer's external memory (for example, on ◊disk). It might include anything from information on a company's employees to a program for an adventure game. *Serial (or sequential) access files* hold information as a sequence of characters, so that, to read any particular item of data, the program must read all those that precede it. *Random-access (or direct access) files* allow the required data to be reached directly. Files are usually located via a directory.

**Fiji Islands** Republic of

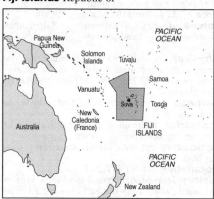

**area** 18,333 sq km/7,078 sq mi
**capital** Suva
**major towns/cities** Lautoka, Nadi, Ba, Labasa
**major ports** Lautoka and Levuka
**physical features** comprises about 844 Melanesian and Polynesian islands and islets (about 100 inhabited), the largest being Viti Levu (10,429 sq km/4,028 sq mi) and Vanua Levu (5,556 sq km/2,146 sq mi); mountainous, volcanic, with tropical rainforest and grasslands; almost all islands surrounded by coral reefs; high volcanic peaks
**head of state** Ratu Sir Kamisese Mara from 1994
**head of government** Prime Minister Mahendra Chaudhry from 1999
**political system** democracy
**political parties** National Federation Party (NFP), moderate left of centre, Indian; Fijian Labour Party (FLP), left of centre, Indian;

United Front, Fijian; Fijian Political Party (FPP), Fijian centrist
**currency** Fiji dollar
**GNP per capita (PPP)** (US$) 3,580 (1998)
**exports** sugar, gold, fish and fish products, clothing, re-exported petroleum products, timber, ginger, molasses. Principal market: Australia 33.1% (1997)
**population** 806,000 (1999 est)
**language** English (official), Fijian, Hindi
**religion** Methodist, Hindu, Muslim, Sikh
**life expectancy** 71 (men); 75 (women) (1995–2000)
**Chronology**
**c. 1500 BC** Peopled by Polynesian and, later, by Melanesian settlers.
**1643** The islands were visited for the first time by a European, the Dutch navigator Abel Tasman.
**1830s** Arrival of Western Christian missionaries.
**1840s–50s** Western Fiji came under dominance of a Christian convert prince, Cakobau, ruler of Bau islet, who proclaimed himself Tui Viti (King of Fiji), while the east was controlled by Ma'afu, a Christian prince from Tonga.
**1857** British consul appointed, encouraging settlers from Australia and New Zealand to set up cotton farms in Fiji.
**1874** Fiji became a British crown colony after deed of cession signed by King Cakobau.
**1875–76** A third of the Fijian population wiped out by a measles epidemic; rebellion against British suppressed with the assitance of Fijian chiefs.
**1877** Fiji became headquarters of the British Western Pacific High Commission (WPHC), which controlled other British protectorates in the Pacific region.
**1879–1916** Indian labourers brought in, on ten-year indentured contracts, to work sugar plantations.
**1904** Legislative Council formed, with elected Europeans and nominated Fijians, to advise the British governor.
**1963** Legislative Council enlarged; women and Fijians were enfranchised. The predominantly Fijian Alliance Party (AP) formed.
**1970** Independence was achieved from Britain; Ratu Sir Kamisese Mara of the AP was elected as the first prime minister.
**1973** Ratu Sir George Cakobau, the great-grandson of the chief who had sworn allegiance to the British in 1874, became governor general.
**1985** The FLP was formed by Timoci Bavadra, with trade-union backing.
**1987** After a general election had brought to power an Indian-dominated coalition led by Bavadra, Lt-Col Sitiveni Rabuka seized power in a military coup, and proclaimed a Fijian-dominated republic outside the Commonwealth.
**1990** A new constitution, favouring indigenous (Melanese) Fijians, was introduced. Civilian rule was re-established, with resignations from the cabinet of military officers, but Rabuka remained as home affairs minister, with Mara as prime minister.
**1992** A general election produced a coalition government with Rabuka of the FPP as prime minister.

**1993** President Ganilau died and was replaced by Ratu Sir Kamisese Mara.

**1994** Rabuka and the FPP were re-elected.

**1997** A nondiscriminatory constitution was introduced. Fiji was re-admitted to the Commonwealth.

**1998** A new three-party governing coalition was formed, led by the Fijian Political Party.

**1999** President Mara's term in office was renewed for an additional five years. May: Mahendra Chaudhry became Fiji's first female prime minister and first prime minister of Indian descent.

**film, photographic** strip of transparent material (usually cellulose acetate) coated with a light-sensitive emulsion, used in cameras to take pictures. The emulsion contains a mixture of light-sensitive silver halide salts (for example, bromide or iodide) in gelatin. When the emulsion is exposed to light, the silver salts are invisibly altered, giving a latent image, which is then made visible by the process of developing. Films differ in their sensitivities to light, this being indicated by their speeds. Colour film consists of several layers of emulsion, each of which records a different colour in the light falling on it.

**filter** in chemistry, a porous substance, such as blotting paper, through which a mixture can be passed to separate out its solid constituents.

**filter** in electronics, a circuit that transmits a signal of some frequencies better than others. A low-pass filter transmits signals of low frequency and direct current; a high-pass filter transmits high-frequency signals; a band-pass filter transmits signals in a band of frequencies.

**filter** in optics, a device that absorbs some parts of the visible ◊spectrum and transmits others. For example, a green filter will absorb or block all colours of the spectrum except green, which it allows to pass through. A yellow filter absorbs only light at the blue and violet end of the spectrum, transmitting red, orange, green, and yellow light.

**filtration** technique by which suspended solid particles in a fluid are removed by passing the mixture through a filter, usually porous paper, plastic, or cloth. The particles are retained by the filter to form a residue and the fluid passes through to make up the filtrate. For example, soot may be filtered from air, and suspended solids from water.

**fin** in aquatic animals, flattened extension from the body that aids balance and propulsion through the water.

**Financial Times Index** (FT Index), indicator measuring the daily movement of 30 major industrial share prices on the London Stock Exchange, issued by the UK *Financial Times* newspaper. Other FT indices cover government securities, fixed-interest securities, gold mine shares, and Stock Exchange activity.

**finch** any of various songbirds of the family Fringillidae, in the order Passeriformes (perching birds). They are seed-eaters with stout conical beaks. The name may also be applied to members of the Emberizidae (buntings), and Estrildidae (weaver-finches).

*fin de siècle* (French 'end of century') the art and literature of the 1890s; decadent.

**Fine Gael** (Gaelic 'United Ireland') Republic of Ireland political party founded 1933 by W J ◊Cosgrave and led by John Bruton from 1990. It is socially liberal but fiscally conservative. From 1994 it formed a coalition government with Labour.

**fingerprint** ridge pattern of the skin on a person's fingertips; this is constant through life and no two are exactly alike. Fingerprinting was first used as a means of identifying crime suspects in India, and was adopted by the English police 1901; it is now widely employed in police and security work.

**Finland** Republic of
*national name* Suomen Tasavalta

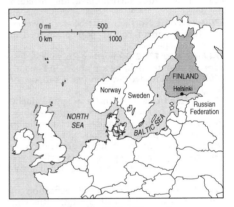

*area* 338,145 sq km/130,557 sq mi
*capital* Helsinki (Helsingfors)
*major towns/cities* Tampere, Turku, Espoo, Vantaa
*major ports* Turku, Oulu
*physical features* most of the country is forest, with low hills and about 60,000 lakes; one-third is within the Arctic Circle; archipelago in south includes Åland Islands; Helsinki is the most northerly national capital on the European continent. At the 70th parallel there is constant daylight for 73 days in summer and 51 days of uninterrupted night in winter.
*head of state* Martti Ahtisaari from 1994
*head of government* Paavo Lipponen from 1995
*political system* democracy
*political parties* Finnish Social Democratic Party (SSDP), moderate left of centre; National Coalition Party (KOK), moderate right of centre; Finnish Centre Party (KESK), radical centrist, rural-oriented; Swedish People's Party (SFP), independent Swedish-oriented; Finnish Rural Party (SMP), farmers and small businesses; Left-Wing Alliance (VL), left wing
*currency* markka
*GNP per capita (PPP)* (US$) 20,270 (1998)
*exports* metal and engineering products, gold, paper and paper products, machinery, ships, wood and pulp, clothing and footwear, chemicals. Principal market: Germany 11.8% (1998)

*population* 5,165,000 (1999 est)
*language* Finnish 93%, Swedish 6% (both official); small Saami- and Russian-speaking minorities
*religion* Lutheran 90%, Orthodox 1%
*life expectancy* 73 (men); 81 (women) (1995–2000)
*Chronology*
*1st century* Occupied by Finnic nomads from Asia who drove out native Saami (Lapps) to the far north.
*12th–13th centuries* Series of Swedish crusades conquered Finns and converted them to Christianity.
*16th–17th centuries* Finland was a semi-autonomous Swedish duchy with Swedish landowners ruling Finnish peasants; Finland allowed relative autonomy, becoming a grand duchy in 1581.
*1634* Finland fully incorporated into Swedish kingdom.
*1700–21* Great Northern War between Sweden and Russia; half of Finnish population died in famine and epidemics.
*1741–43 and 1788–90* Further Russo–Swedish wars; much of the fighting took place in Finland.
*1808* Russia invaded Sweden (with support of Napoleon).
*1809* Finland ceded to Russia as grand duchy with Russian tsar as grand duke; Finns retained their own legal system and Lutheran religion and were exempt from Russian military service.
*1812* Helsinki became capital of grand duchy.
*19th century* Growing prosperity was followed by rise of national feeling among new Finnish middle class.
*1904–05* Policies promoting Russification of Finland provoked national uprising; Russians imposed military rule.
*1917* Finland declared independence.
*1918* Bitter civil war between Reds (supported by Russian Bolsheviks) and Whites (supported by Germany); Baron Carl Gustaf Mannerheim led Whites to victory.
*1919* Republican constitution adopted with Kaarlo Juho Ståhlberg as first president.
*1927* Land reform broke up big estates and created many small peasant farms.
*1939–40* Winter War: USSR invaded Finland after demand for military bases was refused.
*1940* Treaty of Moscow: Finland ceded territory to USSR.
*1941* Finland joined German attack on USSR in hope of regaining lost territory.
*1944* Finland agreed separate armistice with USSR; German troops withdrawn.
*1947* Finno-Soviet peace treaty: Finland forced to cede 12% of its total area and to pay $300 million in reparations.
*1948* Finno-Soviet Pact of Friendship, Cooperation, and Mutual Assistance (YYA treaty): Finland pledged to repel any attack on USSR through its territories.
*1950s* Unstable centre-left coalitions excluded communists from government and adopted strict neutrality in foreign affairs.
*1955* Finland joined the United Nations (UN) and the Nordic Council.

*1956* Urho Kekkonen was elected president. There was a general strike as a result of unemployment and inflation.
*1973* Trade agreements were signed with the European Economic Community (EEC) and Comecon.
*1982* Mauno Koivisto was elected president.
*1987* A new coalition of Social Democrats and conservatives was formed.
*1991* There was a swing towards the Centre Party in a general election.
*1994* Martti Ahtisaari (SSDP) was elected president.
*1995* Finland joined the European Union (EU); the Social Democrats won a general election.
*1999* The Social Democrats narrowly retained power after a general election.

**Finland, Gulf of** eastern arm of the ◊Baltic Sea, separating Finland from Estonia. It is 420 km/260 mi long and 40–150 km/25–90 mi wide. Helsinki and St Petersburg are the main ports.

**Finn Mac Cumhaill** or *Finn McCool*, legendary Irish hero, identified with a general who organized an Irish regular army in the 3rd century. The Scottish writer James Macpherson featured him (as Fingal) and his followers in the verse of his popular epics 1762–63, which were supposedly written by a 3rd-century bard called Ossian.

**Finno-Ugric** group or family of more than 20 languages spoken by some 22 million people in scattered communities from Norway in the west to Siberia in the east and to the Carpathian mountains in the south. Members of the family include Finnish, Lapp, and Hungarian.

**fir** any of a group of ◊conifer trees belonging to the pine family. The true firs include the balsam fir (*A. balsamea*) of northern North America and the silver fir (*A. alba*) of Europe and Asia. Douglas firs of the genus *Pseudotsuga* are native to western North America and the Far East. (True fir genus *Abies*, family Pinaceae.)

**firearm** weapon from which projectiles are discharged by the combustion of an explosive. Firearms are generally divided into two main sections: ◊*artillery* (ordnance or cannon), with a bore greater than 2.54 cm/1 in, and ◊*small arms*, with a bore of less than 2.54 cm/1 in.
    Although gunpowder was known in Europe 60 years previously, the invention of guns dates from 1300 to 1325, and is attributed to Berthold Schwartz, a German monk.

**firedamp** gas that occurs in coal mines and is explosive when mixed with air in certain proportions. It consists chiefly of methane ($CH_4$, natural gas or marsh gas) but always contains small quantities of other gases, such as nitrogen, carbon dioxide, and hydrogen, and sometimes ethane and carbon monoxide.

**Fire of London** fire 2–5 September 1666 that destroyed four fifths of the City of London. It broke out in a bakery in Pudding Lane and spread as far west as the Temple. It destroyed 87 churches, including St Paul's Cathedral, and 13,200 houses, although fewer than 20 people lost their lives.

**First World War** another name for ◊World War I, 1914–18.

**fiscal policy** that part of government policy concerning ◊taxation and other revenues, ◊public spending, and government borrowing (the public sector borrowing requirement).

**fiscal year** a year as defined by a company or government for financial accounting purposes. A company can choose any 12-month period for its accounting year and in exceptional circumstances may determine a longer or shorter period as its fiscal year. It does not necessarily coincide with the calendar year.

**Fischer, Bobby (Robert James)** (1943–  ) World Chess Champion 1972–5, 1992. In 1958, after proving himself in international competition, he became the youngest grand master in history. He was the author of *Games of Chess* (1959), and was also celebrated for his unorthodox psychological tactics.

**fish** aquatic vertebrate that uses gills to obtain oxygen from fresh or sea water. There are three main groups: the bony fishes or Osteichthyes (goldfish, cod, tuna); the cartilaginous fishes or Chondrichthyes (sharks, rays); and the jawless fishes or Agnatha (hagfishes, lampreys).

Fishes of some form are found in virtually every body of water in the world except for the very salty water of the Dead Sea and some of the hot larval springs. Of the 30,000 fish species, approximately 2,500 are freshwater.

**fish farming** or *aquaculture,* raising fish (including molluscs and crustaceans) under controlled conditions in tanks and ponds, sometimes in offshore pens. It has been practised for centuries in the Far East, where Japan today produces some 100,000 tonnes of fish a year; the US, Norway, and Canada are also big producers.

In the 1980s 10% of the world's consumption of fish was farmed, notably carp, catfish, trout, Atlantic salmon, turbot, eel, mussels, clams, oysters, and shrimp.

**fission** in physics, the splitting of a heavy atomic nucleus into two or more major fragments. It is accompanied by the emission of two or three neutrons and the release of large amounts of ◊nuclear energy.

**fit** in medicine, popular term for ◊convulsion.

**Fitzgerald, Ella** (1917–1996) US jazz singer. She is recognized as one of the finest, most lyrical voices in jazz, both in solo work and with big bands. She is celebrated for her smooth interpretations of George and Ira Gershwin and Cole Porter songs.

**Fitzgerald, F(rancis) Scott (Key)** (1896–1940) US novelist and short-story writer. His early autobiographical novel *This Side of Paradise* (1920) made him known in the postwar society of the East Coast, and *The Great Gatsby* (1925) epitomizes the Jazz Age.

**fjord** or *fiord,* narrow sea inlet enclosed by high cliffs. Fjords are found in Norway, New Zealand, and western parts of Scotland. They are formed when an overdeepened U-shaped glacial valley is drowned by a rise in sea-level. At the mouth of the fjord there is a characteristic lip causing a shallowing of the water. This is due to reduced glacial erosion and the deposition of moraine at this point.

**flame test** in chemistry, the use of a flame to identify metal ◊cations present in a solid.

**flamingo** long-legged and long-necked wading bird, family Phoenicopteridae, of the stork order Ciconiiformes. Largest of the family is the greater or roseate flamingo *Phoenicopterus ruber,* found in Africa, the Caribbean, and South

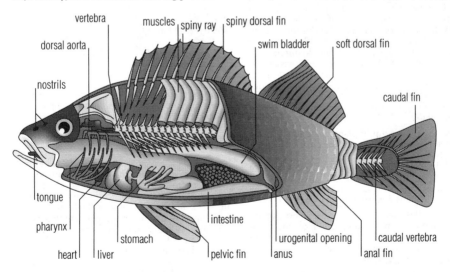

**fish** *The anatomy of a fish. All fishes move through water using their fins for propulsion. The bony fishes, like the specimen shown here, constitute the largest group of fishes with about 20,000 species.*

America, with delicate pink plumage and 1.25 m/4 ft tall. They sift the mud for food with their downbent bills, and build colonies of high, cone-like mud nests, with a little hollow for the eggs at the top.

**Flanders** region of the Low Countries that in the 8th and 9th centuries extended from Calais to the Schelde and is now covered by the Belgian provinces of Oost Vlaanderen and West Vlaanderen (East and West Flanders), the French *département* of Nord, and part of the Dutch province of Zeeland. The language is Flemish. East Flanders, capital Ghent, has an area of 3,000 sq km/1,158 sq mi and a population (1995) of 1,349,400. West Flanders, capital Bruges, has an area of 3,100 sq km/1,197 sq mi and a population (1995) of 1,121,100.

**flare, solar** brilliant eruption on the Sun above a ◊sunspot, thought to be caused by release of magnetic energy. Flares reach maximum brightness within a few minutes, then fade away over about an hour. They eject a burst of atomic particles into space at up to 1,000 kps/600 mps. When these particles reach Earth they can cause radio blackouts, disruptions of the Earth's magnetic field, and ◊aurorae.

**flatfish** bony fishes of the order Pleuronectiformes, having a characteristically flat, asymmetrical body with both eyes (in adults) on the upper side. Species include flounders, turbots, halibuts, plaice, and the European soles.

**flatworm** invertebrate of the phylum Platyhelminthes. Some are free-living, but many are parasitic (for example, tapeworms and flukes). The body is simple and bilaterally symmetrical, with one opening to the intestine. Many are hermaphroditic (with both male and female sex organs) and practise self-fertilization.

**Flaubert, Gustave** (1821–1880) French writer. One of the major novelists of the 19th century, he was the author of *Madame Bovary* (1857), *Salammbô* (1862), *L'Education sentimentale/Sentimental Education* (1869), and *La Tentation de Saint Antoine/The Temptation of St Anthony* (1874). Flaubert also wrote the short stories *Trois Contes/Three Tales* (1877). His dedication to art resulted in a meticulous prose style, realistic detail, and psychological depth, which is often revealed through interior monologue.

**flax** any of a group of plants including the cultivated *L. usitatissimum; linen* is produced from the fibre in its stems. The seeds yield *linseed oil,* used in paints and varnishes. The plant, of almost worldwide distribution, has a stem up to 60 cm/24 in high, small leaves, and bright blue flowers. (Genus *Linum,* family Linaceae.)

**flea** wingless insect of the order Siphonaptera, with blood-sucking mouthparts. Fleas are parasitic on warm-blooded animals. Some fleas can jump 130 times their own height.

**Fleming, Alexander** (1881–1955) Scottish bacteriologist who discovered the first antibiotic drug, ◊penicillin, in 1928. In 1922 he had discovered lysozyme, an antibacterial enzyme present in saliva, nasal secretions, and tears. While studying this, he found an unusual mould growing on a culture dish, which he isolated and grew into a pure culture; this led to his discovery of penicillin. It came into use in 1941. In 1945 he won the Nobel Prize for Physiology or Medicine with Howard W Florey and Ernst B Chain, whose research had brought widespread realization of the value of penicillin.

**Fleming's rules** memory aids used to recall the relative directions of the magnetic field, current, and motion in an electric generator or motor, using one's fingers. The three directions are represented by the thu*m*b (for *m*otion), *f*orefinger (for *f*ield), and se*c*ond finger (for conventional *c*urrent), all held at right angles to each other. The right hand is used for generators and the left for motors.

The rules were devised by the English physicist John Fleming.

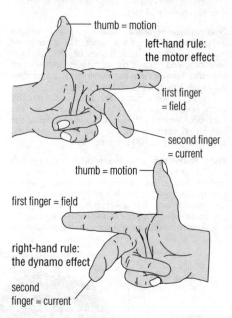

thumb = motion

**left-hand rule:**
**the motor effect**

first finger
= field

second finger
= current

thumb = motion

first finger = field

**right-hand rule:**
**the dynamo effect**

second
finger = current

**Fleming's rules** *Fleming's rules give the direction of the magnetic field, motion, and current in electrical machines. The left hand is used for motors, and the right hand for generators and dynamos.*

**flight** or *aviation,* method of transport in which aircraft carry people and goods through the air. People first took to the air in ◊balloons in 1783 and began powered flight in 1852 in ◊airships, but the history of flying, both for civilian and military use, is dominated by the ◊aeroplane. The earliest planes were designed for ◊gliding; the advent of the petrol engine saw the first powered flight by the ◊Wright brothers in 1903 in the USA. This inspired the development of aircraft throughout Europe. Biplanes were succeeded by monoplanes in the 1930s. The first jet plane was produced in 1939, and after the end of World War II the development of jetliners brought about a continuous expansion in passenger air travel. In 1969 came the supersonic aircraft ◊Concorde.

**flint** compact, hard, brittle mineral (a variety of chert), brown, black, or grey in colour, found as nodules in limestone or shale deposits. It consists of cryptocrystalline (grains too small to be visible even under a light microscope) ◊silica, $SiO_2$, principally in the crystalline form of ◊quartz. Implements fashioned from flint were widely used in prehistory.

**Flintshire** Welsh *Sir y Fflint,* unitary authority in north Wales. A former county, it was part of Clwyd between 1974 and 1996
*area* 437 sq km/167 sq mi
*towns* Mold (administrative headquarters), Flint, Holywell, Buckley, Connah's Quay
*physical* bounded by the Irish Sea in the north, the Dee estuary in the east, and the Clwydian Range, which rises to 555 m/1,820 ft, in the southwest; rivers Dee, Alyn
*industries* artificial silk, chemicals, optical glass
*agriculture* dairy farming, stock-raising
*population* (1996) 144,000.

**Flodden, Battle of** defeat of the Scots by the English under the Earl of Surrey on 9 September 1513, on a site 5 km/3 mi southeast of Coldstream, in Northumberland, England. ◊James IV of Scotland, declaring himself the active ally of France, crossed the border to England with an invading army of 30,000. The Scots were defeated, suffering heavy losses, and James himself was killed.

**floppy disk** in computing, a storage device consisting of a light, flexible disk enclosed in a cardboard or plastic jacket. The disk is placed in a disk drive, where it rotates at high speed. Data are recorded magnetically on one or both surfaces.

**Florence** Italian *Firenze;* Roman *Florentia,* capital of ◊Tuscany, northern Italy, on the River Arno, 88 km/55 mi from the river's mouth; population (1992) 397,400. It has printing, engineering, and optical industries; many crafts, including leather, gold and silver work, and embroidery; and its art and architecture attract large numbers of tourists. Notable medieval and Renaissance citizens included the writers Dante and Boccaccio, and the artists Giotto, Leonardo da Vinci, and Michelangelo.

**Florida** southeasternmost state of the USA. It is nicknamed the Sunshine State. Florida was admitted to the Union in 1845 as the 27th US state. Much of the state is subtropical and is a popular tourist and retirement destination; the Miami region in particular has a thriving cosmopolitan community, serving as a gateway to both the Caribbean and Latin America. Florida is bordered to the north by Georgia and by Alabama. The state consists of a 640 km/400 mi-long peninsula jutting into the Atlantic, which it separates from the Gulf of Mexico, with a 390 km/240 mi-long panhandle to the northwest on the mainland. At the peninsula's southern end, the 220 km/135 mi-long chain of Florida Keys extends to the southwest
*population* (1996 est) 14,400,000, one of the fastest-growing of the states; including 12% Hispanic (especially Cuban) and 13.6% African-American
*area* 152,000 sq km/58,672 sq mi
*capital* Tallahassee
*towns and cities* Miami, Tampa, Jacksonville, Hialeah, Orlando, Fort Lauderdale
*industries and products* tourism, leisure industry, citrus fruits, melons, vegetables, sugar cane, fish, shellfish, phosphates, chemicals, electrical and electronic equipment, aircraft, fabricated metals, finance sector.

**flotation, law of** law stating that a floating object displaces its own weight of the fluid in which it floats. See ◊Archimedes' principle.

**flounder** small flatfish *Platychthys flesus* of the northeastern Atlantic and Mediterranean, although it sometimes lives in estuaries. It is dull in colour and grows to 50 cm/1.6 ft.

**flow chart** diagram, often used in computing, to show the possible paths that data can take through a system or program.

**flower** the reproductive unit of an angiosperm or flowering plant, typically consisting of four whorls of modified leaves: ◊sepals, ◊petals, ◊stamens, and ◊carpels. These are borne on a central axis or ◊receptacle. The many variations in size, colour, number, and arrangement of parts are closely related to the method of pollination. Flowers adapted for wind pollination typically have reduced or absent petals and sepals and long, feathery ◊stigmas that hang outside the flower to trap airborne pollen. In contrast, the petals of insect-pollinated flowers are usually conspicuous and brightly coloured.

**flowering plant** term generally used for ◊angiosperms, which bear flowers with various

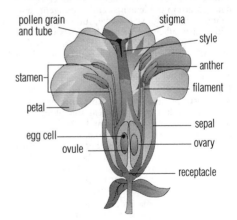

**flower** Cross section of a typical flower showing its basic components: sepals, petals, stamens (anthers and filaments), and carpel (ovary and stigma). Flowers vary greatly in the size, shape, colour, and arrangement of these components.

parts, including sepals, petals, stamens, and carpels.

Sometimes the term is used more broadly, to include both angiosperms and ◊gymnosperms, in which case the ◊cones of conifers and cycads are referred to as 'flowers'. Usually, however, the angiosperms and gymnosperms are referred to collectively as ◊seed plants, or spermatophytes.

**flugelhorn** valved brass instrument of the ◊bugle type. It is made in three sizes: soprano, alto, and tenor, and is used in military and brass bands. In Britain only the alto instrument, in B-flat, is used, normally only in brass bands. The alto flugelhorn has a similar range to the cornet but is of mellower tone.

**fluke** any of various parasitic flatworms of the classes Monogenea and Digenea, that as adults live in and destroy the livers of sheep, cattle, horses, dogs, and humans. Monogenetic flukes can complete their life cycle in one host; digenetic flukes require two or more hosts, for example a snail and a human being, to complete their life cycle.

**fluorescence** short-lived ◊luminescence (a glow not caused by high temperature). ◊Phosphorescence lasts a little longer.

**fluoridation** addition of small amounts of fluoride salts to drinking water by certain water authorities to help prevent tooth decay. Experiments in Britain, the USA, and elsewhere have indicated that a concentration of fluoride of 1 part per million in tap water retards the decay of children's teeth by more than 50%.

**fluoride** negative ion ($F^-$) formed when hydrogen fluoride dissolves in water; compound formed between fluorine and another element in which the fluorine is the more electronegative element (see electronegativity).

**fluorine** pale yellow, gaseous, nonmetallic element, symbol F, atomic number 9, relative atomic mass 19. It is the first member of the halogen group of elements, and is pungent, poisonous, and highly reactive, uniting directly with nearly all the elements. It occurs naturally as the minerals fluorite ($CaF_2$) and cryolite ($Na_3AlF_6$). Hydrogen fluoride is used in etching glass, and the freons, which all contain fluorine, are widely used as refrigerants.

**flute** or *transverse flute*, side-blown woodwind instrument of considerable antiquity. The flute is difficult to master but capable of intricate melodies and expressive tonal shading. The player blows across an end hole, the air current being split by the opposite edge, which causes pressure waves to form within the tube. The fingers are placed over holes in the tube to create different notes. The standard soprano flute has a range of three octaves or more.

**fly** any insect of the order Diptera. A fly has a single pair of wings, antennae, and compound eyes; the hind wings have become modified into knoblike projections (halteres) used to maintain equilibrium in flight. There are over 90,000 species.

**flying fish** any marine bony fishes of the family Exocoetidae, order Beloniformes, best represented in tropical waters. They have wing-like pectoral fins that can be spread to glide over the water.

**flying fox** another name for the fruit bat, a fruit-eating ◊bat of the suborder Megachiroptera.

**flying squirrel** any of 43 known species of squirrel, not closely related to the true squirrels. They are characterized by a membrane along the side of the body from forelimb to hindlimb (in some species running to neck and tail) which allows them to glide through the air. Several genera of flying squirrel are found in the Old World; the New World has the genus *Glaucomys*. Most species are eastern Asian.

**Flynn, Errol** stage name of Leslie Thomson Flynn (1909–1959) Australian-born US film actor. He portrayed swashbuckling heroes in such films as *Captain Blood* (1935), *Robin Hood* (1938), *The Charge of the Light Brigade* (1938), *The Private Lives of Elizabeth and Essex* (1939), *The Sea Hawk* (1940), and *The Master of Ballantrae* (1953).

**focal length** or *focal distance*, the distance from the centre of a lens or curved mirror to the focal point. For a concave mirror or convex lens, it is the distance at which rays of light parallel to the principal axis of the mirror or lens are brought to a focus (for a mirror, this is half the radius of curvature). For a convex mirror or concave lens, it is the distance from the centre to the point from which rays of light parallel to the principal axis of the mirror or lens diverge.

**focus** or *focal point,* in optics, the point at which light rays converge, or from which they appear to diverge. Other electromagnetic rays, such as microwaves, and sound waves may also be brought together at a focus. Rays parallel to the principal axis of a lens or mirror are converged at, or appear to diverge from, the principal focus.

**foetus** stage in mammalian embryo development; see ◊fetus.

**fog** cloud that collects at the surface of the Earth, composed of water vapour that has condensed on particles of dust in the atmosphere. Cloud and fog are both caused by the air temperature falling below dew point. The thickness of fog depends on the number of water particles it contains. Officially, fog refers to a condition when visibility is reduced to 1 km/0.6 mi or less, and mist or haze to that giving a visibility of 1–2 km or about 1 mi.

**fold** in geology, a bend in ◊beds or layers of rock. If the bend is arched up in the middle it is called an *anticline;* if it sags downwards in the middle it is called a *syncline.* The line along which a bed of rock folds is called its axis. The axial plane is the plane joining the axes of successive beds.

**folic acid** a ◊vitamin of the B complex. It is found in liver, legumes and green leafy vegetables, and whole grain foods, and is also synthesized by the intestinal bacteria. It is essential for growth, and plays many other roles in the body.

Lack of folic acid causes anaemia because it is necessary for the synthesis of nucleic acids and the formation of red blood cells.

**folklore** oral traditions and culture of a people, expressed in legends, riddles, songs, tales, and proverbs. The term was coined in 1846 by W J Thoms (1803–1885), but the founder of the systematic study of the subject was Jacob Grimm; see also ◊oral literature.

**folk music** traditional music, especially from rural areas, which is passed on by listening and repeating, and is usually performed by amateurs. The term is used to distinguish it from the classical music of a country, and from urban popular or commercial music. Most folk music exists in the form of songs, or instrumental music to accompany folk dancing, and is usually melodic and rhythmic rather than harmonic in style.

Each country has its own styles of folk music, based on distinctive ◊scales and modes, and often played on instruments associated with that culture alone, such as the Scottish ◊bagpipes, the Russian balalaika, or the Australian ◊didjeridu. A number of composers of classical music have used folk music in their own pieces to give them a particular national character, and in the late 19th century the use of folk tunes was a prominent feature of nationalism in music.

In the 20th century a number of people, such as the composers Zoltán Kodály and Béla ◊Bartók, and the musicologists Cecil Sharp and Alan Lomax, have transcribed and recorded folk music to preserve it for the future. Since World War II, a renewed interest – especially among young people – led to a 'folk revival'. Traditional folk music was performed to a much wider audience, and songwriters such as Pete Seeger, Joan Baez, and Bob ◊Dylan composed popular songs in a folk style.

Elements of folk music have also been combined with rock and pop music, and form an important part of ◊world music.

**follicle** in zoology, a small group of cells that surround and nourish a structure such as a hair (hair follicle) or a cell such as an egg (Graafian follicle; see ◊menstrual cycle).

**Fomalhaut** or *Alpha Piscis Austrini,* brightest star in the southern constellation Piscis Austrinus and the 18th-brightest star in the night sky. It is 22 light years from the Sun, with a true luminosity 13 times that of the Sun.

**Fonda, Henry (Jaynes)** (1905–1982) US actor. His engaging style made him ideal in the role of the American pioneer and honourable man. His many films include *Young Mr Lincoln* (1939), *The Grapes of Wrath* (1940), *My Darling Clementine* (1946), *12 Angry Men* (1957), and *On Golden Pond* (1981), for which he won an Academy Award.

**Fonda, Jane (Seymour)** (1937– ) US actress and producer. She won Academy Awards for her roles in *Klute* (1971) and *Coming Home* (1978). Other films include *Barbarella* (1968) and *They Shoot Horses, Don't They?* (1969).

**font** or *fount,* complete set of printed or display characters of the same typeface, size, and style (bold, italic, underlined, and so on).

**Fonteyn, Margot** stage name of Peggy (Margaret) Hookham (1919–1991) English ballet dancer. She made her debut with the Vic-Wells Ballet in *Nutcracker* (1934) and first appeared as Giselle in 1937, eventually becoming prima ballerina of the Royal Ballet, London. Renowned for her perfect physique, clear line, musicality, and interpretive powers, she created many roles in Frederick ◊Ashton's ballets and formed a legendary partnership with Rudolf ◊Nureyev. She retired from dancing in 1979.

**food** anything eaten by human beings and other animals and absorbed by plants to sustain life and health. The building blocks of food are nutrients, and humans can utilize the following nutrients: *carbohydrates* as starches found in bread, potatoes, and pasta; as simple sugars in sucrose and honey; and as fibres in cereals, fruit, and vegetables; *proteins* as from nuts, fish, meat, eggs, milk, and some vegetables; *fats* as found in most animal products (meat, lard, dairy products, fish), also in margarine, nuts and seeds, olives, and edible oils; *vitamins,* found in a wide variety of foods, except for vitamin $B_{12}$, which is found mainly in foods of animal origin; and *minerals,* found in a wide variety of foods (for example, calcium from milk and broccoli, iodine from seafood, and iron from liver and green vegetables).

**food chain** in ecology, a sequence showing the feeding relationships between organisms in a particular ecosystem. Each organism depends on the next lowest member of the chain for its food. A pyramid of numbers can be used to show the reduction in food energy at each step up the food chain. *See illustration on page 334.*

**food poisoning** any acute illness characterized by vomiting and diarrhoea and caused by eating food contaminated with harmful bacteria (for example, listeriosis), poisonous food (for example, certain mushrooms, puffer fish), or poisoned food (such as lead or arsenic introduced accidentally during processing). A frequent cause of food poisoning is ◊*Salmonella* bacteria. *Salmonella* comes in many forms, and strains are found in cattle, pigs, poultry, and eggs.

**foot** imperial unit of length (symbol ft), equivalent to 0.3048 m, in use in Britain since Anglo-Saxon times. It originally represented the length of a human foot. One foot contains 12 inches and is one-third of a yard.

**Foot, Michael Mackintosh** (1913– ) British Labour politician and writer. A leader of the left-wing Tribune Group, he was secretary of state for employment 1974–76, Lord President of the Council and leader of the House 1976–79, and succeeded James Callaghan as Labour Party leader 1980–83.

**foot-and-mouth disease** contagious eruptive viral disease of cloven-hoofed mammals, characterized by blisters in the mouth and around the hooves. In cattle it causes deterioration of milk yield and abortions. It is an airborne virus, which makes its eradication extremely difficult.

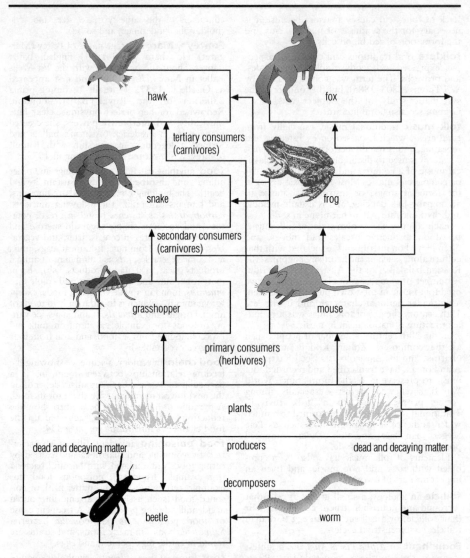

**food chain** *The complex interrelationships between animals and plants in a food web. A food web shows how different food chains are linked in an ecosystem. Note that the arrows indicate movement of energy through the web. For example, an arrow shows that energy moves from plants to the grasshopper, which eats the plants.*

**football, American** contact sport similar to the English game of rugby, played between two teams of 11 players, with an inflated oval ball. Players are well padded for protection and wear protective helmets. The *Super Bowl*, first held in 1967, is now an annual meeting between the winners of the National and American Football Conferences.

**football, association** or *soccer*, form of football originating in the UK, popular throughout the world. The modern game is played in the UK according to the rules laid down by the home countries' football associations. Slight amendments to the rules take effect in certain competitions and international matches as laid down by the sport's world governing body, Fédération Internationale de Football Association (FIFA, 1904). FIFA organizes the competitions for the World Cup, held every four years since 1930.

**football, Australian rules** game that combines aspects of Gaelic football, rugby, and association football; it is played between two teams of 18 players each, with an inflated oval ball. It is unique to Australia.

**football, Gaelic** kicking and catching game played mainly in Ireland. The two teams have 15 players each. The game is played on a field with an inflated spherical ball. The goalposts have a crossbar and a net across the lower half. Goals are scored by kicking the ball into the net (3 points) or over the crossbar (1 point).

**force** any influence that tends to change the state of rest or the uniform motion in a straight line of a body. The action of an unbalanced or resultant force results in the acceleration of a body in the direction of action of the force, or it may, if the body is unable to move freely, result in its deformation (see ◊Hooke's law). Force is a vector quantity, possessing both magnitude and direction; its ◊SI unit is the newton.

**forces, fundamental** in physics, the four fundamental interactions believed to be at work in the physical universe. There are two long-range forces: the *gravitational force,* or *gravity,* which keeps the planets in orbit around the Sun, and acts between all particles that have mass; and the *electromagnetic force,* which stops solids from falling apart, and acts between all particles with ◊electric charge. There are two very short-range forces which operate only inside the atomic nucleus: the *weak nuclear force,* responsible for the reactions that fuel the Sun and for the emission of ◊beta particles from certain nuclei; and the *strong nuclear force,* which binds together the protons and neutrons in the nuclei of atoms. The relative strengths of the four forces are: strong, 1; electromagnetic, $10^{-2}$; weak, $10^{-6}$; gravitational, $10^{-40}$.

**Ford, Henry** (1863–1947) US automobile manufacturer. He built his first car 1896 and founded the Ford Motor Company 1903. His Model T (1908–27) was the first car to be constructed solely by assembly-line methods and to be mass-marketed; 15 million of these cars were sold.

**Ford, John** adopted name of Sean Aloysius O'Feeney (1895–1973) US film director. Active from the silent film era, he became one of the most acclaimed figures of classical Hollywood cinema, winning four Academy Awards for best director. Responsible for a range of impressive westerns such as *The Iron Horse* (1924), *Stagecoach* (1939), *My Darling Clementine* (1946), *She Wore a Yellow Ribbon* (1949), *The Searchers* (1956), and *The Man Who Shot Liberty Valance* (1962), he also directed a range of comedies and dramas, including *The Grapes of Wrath* (1940).

**foreclosure** in law, the transfer of title of a mortgaged property from the mortgagor (borrower, usually a home owner) to the mortgagee (loaner, for example a bank) if the mortgagor is in breach of the mortgage agreement, usually by failing to make a number of payments on the mortgage (loan).

**forensic medicine** in medicine, branch of medicine concerned with the resolution of crimes. Examples of forensic medicine include the determination of the cause of death in suspicious circumstances or the identification of a criminal by examining tissue found at the scene of a crime. Forensic psychology involves the establishment of a psychological profile of a criminal that can assist in identification.

**forensic science** the use of scientific techniques to solve criminal cases. A multidisciplinary field embracing chemistry, physics, botany, zoology, and medicine, forensic science includes the identification of human bodies or traces. Ballistics (the study of projectiles, such as bullets), another traditional forensic field, makes use of such tools as the comparison microscope and the electron microscope.

**forestry** the science of forest management. Recommended forestry practice aims at multipurpose crops, allowing the preservation of varied plant and animal species as well as human uses (lumbering, recreation). Forestry has often been confined to the planting of a single species, such as a rapid-growing conifer providing softwood for paper pulp and construction timber, for which world demand is greatest. In tropical countries, logging contributes to the destruction of ◊rainforests, causing global environmental problems. Small unplanned forests are ◊woodland.

**forget-me-not** any of a group of plants belonging to the borage family, including *M. sylvatica* and *M. scorpioides,* with small bright blue flowers. (Genus *Myosotis,* family Boraginaceae.)

**formaldehyde** common name for ◊methanal.

**formic acid** common name for ◊methanoic acid.

**formula** in chemistry, a representation of a molecule, radical, or ion, in which the component chemical elements are represented by their symbols. An *empirical formula* indicates the simplest ratio of the elements in a compound, without indicating how many of them there are or how they are combined. A *molecular formula* gives the number of each type of element present in one molecule. A *structural formula* shows the relative positions of the atoms and the bonds between them. For example, for ethanoic acid, the empirical formula is $CH_2O$, the molecular formula is $C_2H_4O_2$, and the structural formula is $CH_3COOH$.

**Forster, E(dward) M(organ)** (1879–1970) English novelist, short-story writer, and critic. He was concerned with the interplay of personality and the conflict between convention and instinct. His novels include *A Room with a View* (1908), *Howards End* (1910), and *A Passage to India* (1924). Collections of stories include *The Celestial Omnibus* (1911) and *Collected Short Stories* (1948), and of essays and reviews *Abinger Harvest* (1936). His most lasting critical work is *Aspects of the Novel* (1927).

**forsythia** any of a group of temperate eastern Asian shrubs, which bear yellow bell-shaped flowers in early spring before the leaves appear. (Genus *Forsythia,* family Oleaceae.)

**Fort-de-France** capital, chief commercial centre, and port of Martinique, West Indies, at the mouth of the Madame River; population (1990) 101,500. It trades in sugar, rum, and cacao.

**Forth** river in central Scotland, with its headstreams, Duchray Water and Avondhu, rising on the northeast slopes of Ben Lomond. It flows east approximately 105 km/65 mi to Kincardine where the *Firth of Forth* begins. The Firth is approximately 80 km/50 mi long, and is 26 km/16 mi wide where it joins the North Sea.

**FORTRAN** or *fortran*, contraction of formula translation, high-level computer-programming language suited to mathematical and scientific computations. Developed by John Backus at IBM in 1956, it is one of the earliest computer languages still in use. A recent version, Fortran 90, is now being used on advanced parallel computers. ◊BASIC was strongly influenced by FORTRAN and is similar in many ways.

**fossil** (Latin *fossilis* 'dug up') a cast, impression, or the actual remains of an animal or plant preserved in rock. Fossils were created during periods of rock formation, caused by the gradual accumulation of sediment over millions of years at the bottom of the sea bed or an inland lake. Fossils may include footprints, an internal cast, or external impression. A few fossils are preserved intact, as with ◊mammoths fossilized in Siberian ice, or insects trapped in tree resin that is today amber. The study of fossils is called ◊palaeontology. Palaeontologists are able to deduce much of the geological history of a region from fossil remains.

**fossil fuel** fuel, such as coal, oil, and natural gas, formed from the fossilized remains of plants that lived hundreds of millions of years ago. Fossil fuels are a nonrenewable resource and will eventually run out. Extraction of coal and oil causes considerable environmental pollution, and burning coal contributes to problems of ◊acid rain and the ◊greenhouse effect.

**Foster, Jodie** stage name of Alicia Christian Foster (1962–  ) US film actress and director. She began acting as a child in a great variety of roles. In 1976 she starred in *Taxi Driver* (by Martin Scorsese) and *Bugsy Malone* when only 14. She won Academy Awards for her performances in *The Accused* (1988) and *The Silence of the Lambs* (1991).

**Foster, Norman Robert** (1935–  ) English architect of the High Tech school. His buildings include the Willis Faber & Dumas insurance offices, Ipswich (1975); the Sainsbury Centre for the Visual Arts, Norwich (1977); the headquarters of the Hong Kong and Shanghai Bank, Hong Kong (1986); and Stansted Airport, Essex (1991). In 1999 he won the Pritzker Architecture Prize.

**Foucault, Jean Bernard Léon** (1819–1868) French physicist who used a pendulum to demonstrate the rotation of the Earth on its axis, and invented the ◊gyroscope 1852. In 1862 he made the first accurate determination of the velocity of light.

**Foucault, Michel Paul** (1926–1984) French philosopher who argued that human knowledge and subjectivity are dependent upon specific institutions and practices, and that they change through history. In particular, he was concerned to subvert conventional assumptions about 'social deviants' – the mentally ill, the sick, and the criminal – who, he believed, are oppressed by the approved knowledge of the period in which they live.

**four-colour process** colour ◊printing using four printing plates, based on the principle that any colour is made up of differing proportions of the primary colours blue, red, and green. The first stage in preparing a colour picture for printing is to produce separate films, one each for the blue, red, and green respectively in the picture (colour separations). From these separations three printing plates are made, with a fourth plate for black (for shading or outlines and type). Ink colours complementary to those represented on the plates are used for printing – yellow for the blue plate, cyan for the red, and magenta for the green.

**Four Noble Truths** in Buddhism, a summary of the basic concepts: there is suffering (Sanskrit *duhkha*); suffering has its roots in desire (*tanha*, clinging or grasping); the cessation of desire is the end of suffering, *nirvana;* and this can be reached by the Noble Eightfold Path as taught by the Buddha.

**four-stroke cycle** the engine-operating cycle of most petrol and ◊diesel engines. The 'stroke' is an upward or downward movement of a piston in a cylinder. In a petrol engine the cycle begins with the induction of a fuel mixture as the piston goes down on its first stroke. On the second stroke (up) the piston compresses the mixture in the top of the cylinder. An electric spark then ignites the mixture, and the gases produced force the piston down on its third, power, stroke. On the fourth stroke (up) the piston expels the burned gases from the cylinder into the exhaust.

**fowl** chicken or chickenlike bird. Sometimes the term is also used for ducks and geese. The red jungle fowl *Gallus gallus* is the ancestor of all domestic chickens. It is a forest bird of Asia, without the size or egg-laying ability of many domestic strains. ◊Guinea fowl are of African origin.

**fox** one of the smaller species of wild dog of the family Canidae, which live in Africa, Asia, Europe, North America, and South America. Foxes feed on a wide range of animals from worms to rabbits, scavenge for food, and also eat berries. They are very adaptable, maintaining high populations close to urban areas.

**Fox, Charles James** (1749–1806) English Whig politician, son of the 1st Baron Holland. He entered Parliament in 1769 as a supporter of the court, but went over to the opposition in 1774. As secretary of state in 1782, leader of the opposition to William Pitt the Younger, and foreign secretary in 1806, he welcomed the French Revolution and brought about the abolition of the slave trade.

**foxglove** any of a group of flowering plants found in Europe and the Mediterranean region. They have showy spikes of bell-like flowers, and grow up to 1.5 m/5 ft high. (Genus *Digitalis*, family Scrophulariaceae.)

**fox-hunting** the pursuit of a fox across country on horseback, aided by a pack of foxhounds specially trained to track the fox's scent. The aim is to catch and kill the fox. In *drag-hunting,* hounds pursue a prepared trail rather than a fox.

**foxtrot** ballroom dance originating in the USA about 1914. It is believed to be named after Harry Fox, a US vaudeville comedian who did a distinctive trotting dance to ragtime music.

**fractal** (from Latin *fractus* 'broken') irregular shape or surface produced by a procedure of repeated subdivision. Generated on a computer screen, fractals are used in creating models of geographical or biological processes (for example, the creation of a coastline by erosion or accretion, or the growth of plants).

**fraction** in chemistry, a group of similar compounds, the boiling points of which fall within a particular range and which are separated during fractional distillation (fractionation).

**fraction** (from Latin *fractus* 'broken') in mathematics, a number that indicates one or more equal parts of a whole. Usually, the number of equal parts into which the unit is divided (denominator) is written below a horizontal line, and the number of parts comprising the fraction (numerator) is written above; thus 2/3 or 3/4. Such fractions are called *vulgar* or *simple* fractions. The denominator can never be zero.

**fractionation** or *fractional distillation,* process used to split complex mixtures (such as ◊petroleum) into their components, usually by repeated heating, boiling, and condensation. In the laboratory it is carried out using a fractionating column.

**Fragonard, Jean-Honoré** (1732–1806) French painter. He was the leading exponent of the Rococo style (along with his teacher François Boucher). His light-hearted subjects, often erotic, include *Les heureux Hazards de l'escarpolette/The Swing* (*c.* 1766; Wallace Collection, London). Madame de Pompadour was one of his patrons.

**France** French Republic
*national name* *République Française*
*area* (including Corsica) 543,965 sq km/ 210,024 sq mi
*capital* Paris
*major towns/cities* Lyon, Lille, Bordeaux, Toulouse, Nantes, Strasbourg, Montpellier, Saint-Etienne, Rennes, Reims, Grenoble
*major ports* Marseille, Nice, Le Havre
*physical features* rivers Seine, Loire, Garonne, Rhône; mountain ranges Alps, Massif Central, Pyrenees, Jura, Vosges, Cévennes; Auvergne mountain region; Mont Blanc (4,810 m/15,781 ft); Ardennes forest; Riviera; caves of Dordogne with relics of early humans; the island of Corsica
*territories* Guadeloupe, French Guiana, Martinique, Réunion, St Pierre and Miquelon, Southern and Antarctic Territories, New Caledonia, French Polynesia, Wallis and Futuna, Mayotte
*head of state* Jacques Chirac from 1995

*head of government* Lionel Jospin from 1997
*political system* liberal democracy
*political parties* Rally for the Republic (RPR), neo-Gaullist conservative; Union for French Democracy (UDF), centre right; Socialist Party (PS), left of centre; Left Radical Movement (MRG), centre left; French Communist Party (PCF), Marxist-Leninist; National Front, far right; Greens, fundamentalist-ecologist; Génération Ecologie, pragmatic ecologist; Movement for France, right wing, anti-Maastricht
*currency* franc
*GNP per capita (PPP)* (US$) 22,320 (1997)
*exports* machinery and transport equipment, food and live animals, chemicals, beverages and tobacco, textile yarn, fabrics and other basic manufactures, clothing and accessories, perfumery and cosmetics. Principal market: Germany 15.9% (1998)
*population* 58,886,000 (1999 est)
*language* French (regional languages include Basque, Breton, Catalan, and Provençal)
*religion* Roman Catholic; also Muslim, Protestant, and Jewish minorities
*life expectancy* 74 (men); 82 (women) (1995–2000)
*Chronology*
*5th century* **BC** Celtic peoples invaded the region.
*58–51* **BC** Romans conquered Celts and formed province of Gaul.
*5th century* **AD** Gaul overrun by Franks and other Germanic tribes.
*481–511* Frankish chief Clovis accepted Christianity and formed a kingdom based at Paris; under his successors, the Merovingian dynasty, the kingdom disintegrated.
*751–68* Pepin the Short usurped the Frankish throne, reunified the kingdom, and founded the Carolingian dynasty.
*768–814* Charlemagne conquered much of western Europe and created the Holy Roman Empire.
*843* Treaty of Verdun divided the Holy Roman Empire into three, with the western portion corresponding to modern France.

**9th–10th centuries** Weak central government allowed the great nobles to become virtually independent.

**987** Frankish crown passed to House of Capet; the Capets ruled the district around Paris, but were surrounded by vassals more powerful than themselves.

**1180–1223** Philip II doubled the royal domain and tightened control over the nobles; the power of the Capets gradually extended with support of church and towns.

**1328** When Charles IV died without an heir, Philip VI established the House of Valois.

**1337** Start of the Hundred Years' War: Edward III of England disputed the Valois succession and claimed the throne. English won victories at Crécy in 1346 and Agincourt in 1415.

**1429** Joan of Arc raised the siege of Orléans; Hundred Years' War ended with Charles VII expelling the English 1453.

**1483** France annexed Burgundy and Brittany after Louis XI had restored royal power.

**16th–17th centuries** French kings fought the Habsburgs (of Holy Roman Empire and Spain) for supremacy in western Europe.

**1562–98** Civil wars between nobles were fought under religious slogans, Catholic versus Protestant (or Huguenot).

**1589–1610** Henry IV, first king of Bourbon dynasty, established peace, religious tolerance, and absolute monarchy.

**1634–48** The ministers Richelieu and Mazarin, by intervening in the Thirty Years' War, secured Alsace and made France the leading power in Europe.

**1701–14** War of the Spanish Succession: England, Austria, and allies checked expansionism of France under Louis XIV.

**1756–63** Seven Years' War: France lost most of its colonies in India and Canada to Britain.

**1789** French Revolution abolished absolute monarchy and feudalism; First Republic proclaimed and revolutionary wars began 1792.

**1799** Napoleon Bonaparte seized power in coup; crowned himself emperor in 1804; France conquered much of Europe.

**1814** Defeat of France; restoration of Bourbon monarchy; comeback by Napoleon defeated at Waterloo in 1815.

**1830** Liberal revolution deposed Charles X in favour of his cousin Louis Philippe, the 'Citizen King'.

**1848** Revolution established Second Republic; conflict between liberals and socialists; Louis Napoleon, nephew of Napoleon I, elected president.

**1852** Louis Napoleon proclaimed Second Empire, taking title Napoleon III.

**1870–71** Franco-Prussian War: France lost Alsace-Lorraine; Second Empire abolished; Paris Commune crushed; Third Republic founded.

**late 19th century** France colonized Indochina, much of North Africa, and South Pacific.

**1914–18** France resisted German invasion in World War I; Alsace-Lorraine recovered in 1919.

**1936–37** Left-wing 'Popular Front' government of Léon Blum introduced many social reforms.

**1939** France entered World War II.

**1940** Germany invaded and occupied northern France; Marshal Pétain formed right-wing puppet regime at Vichy; resistance maintained by Maquis and Free French; Germans occupied all France in 1942.

**1944** Allies liberated France; provisional government formed by Gen Charles de Gaulle, leader of Free French.

**1946** Fourth Republic proclaimed.

**1949** Became a member of NATO; withdrew from military command structure in 1966.

**1954** French withdrew from Indochina after eight years of war; start of guerrilla war against French rule in Algeria.

**1957** France was a founder member of the European Economic Community.

**1958** Algerian crisis caused collapse of Fourth Republic; de Gaulle took power, becoming president of the Fifth Republic in 1959.

**1962** Algeria achieved independence.

**1968** Revolutionary students rioted in Paris; there was a general strike throughout France.

**1981** François Mitterrand was elected the Fifth Republic's first socialist president.

**1986–88** There was a socialist president with a conservative prime minister; this occurred again 1993–95.

**1995** Jacques Chirac (RPR) was elected president. There was widespread condemnation of the government's decision to resume nuclear tests in the Pacific region.

**1996** Nuclear testing in the South Pacific came to an end. Spending cuts were agreed to meet European Monetary Union entry criteria. Unemployment was at a post-war high.

**1997** A general election was called by President Chirac, with victory for Socialists; Lionel Jospin (PS) was appointed prime minister.

**1998** There were protests by the unemployed.

**France, Anatole** pen-name of Jacques Anatole François Thibault (1844–1924) French writer. His works are marked by wit, urbanity, and style. His earliest novel was *Le Crime de Sylvestre Bonnard/The Crime of Sylvester Bonnard* (1881); later books include the satiric *L'Ile des pingouins/Penguin Island* (1908). Nobel Prize for Literature 1921.

**Francesca, Piero della** Italian painter; see ◊Piero della Francesca.

**Franche-Comté** region of eastern France; area 16,200 sq km/6,253 sq mi; population (1990) 1,097,300. Its administrative centre is Besançon, and it includes the *départements* of Doubs, Jura, Haute-Saône, and Territoire de Belfort. In the mountainous Jura, there is farming and forestry, and elsewhere there are engineering and plastics industries.

**franchise** in business, the right given by one company to another to manufacture, distribute, or provide its branded products. It is usual for the franchisor to impose minimum quality conditions on its franchisees to make sure that customers receive a fair deal from the franchisee and ensure that the brand image is maintained.

**franchise** in politics, the eligibility, right, or privilege to vote at public elections, especially for the members of a legislative body, or parliament. In the UK adult citizens are eligible to vote from the age of 18, with the exclusion of peers, the insane, and criminals. The voting age for adults in the USA was lowered from 21 to 18 by the 26th Amendment in 1971, and the Voting Rights Act of 1965 eliminated local laws that restricted full participation by minorities.

**Francis** or *François*, two kings of France:

**Francis I** (1494–1547) King of France from 1515. He succeeded his cousin Louis XII, and from 1519 European politics turned on the rivalry between him and the Holy Roman emperor Charles V, which led to war in 1521–29, 1536–38, and 1542–44. In 1525 Francis was defeated and captured at Pavia and released only after signing a humiliating treaty. At home, he developed absolute monarchy.

**Francis II** (1544–1560) King of France from 1559 when he succeeded his father, Henri II. He married Mary Queen of Scots in 1558. He was completely under the influence of his mother, ◊Catherine de' Medici.

**Francis II** (1768–1835) Holy Roman Emperor 1792–1806. He became Francis I, Emperor of Austria 1804, and abandoned the title of Holy Roman Emperor 1806. During his reign Austria was five times involved in war with France, 1792–97, 1798–1801, 1805, 1809, and 1813–14. He succeeded his father, Leopold II.

**Francis Ferdinand** archduke of Austria, also known as ◊Franz Ferdinand.

**Francis Joseph** emperor of Austria-Hungary, also known as ◊Franz Joseph.

**Francis of Assisi, St** born Giovanni Bernadone (1182–1226) Italian founder of the Roman Catholic Franciscan order of friars 1209 and, with St Clare, of the Poor Clares 1212. In 1224 he is said to have undergone a mystical experience during which he received the stigmata (five wounds of Jesus). Many stories are told of his ability to charm wild animals, and he is the patron saint of ecologists. His feast day is 4 October. Canonized 1228.

**francium** radioactive metallic element, symbol Fr, atomic number 87, relative atomic mass 223. It is one of the alkali metals and occurs in nature in small amounts as a decay product of actinium. Its longest-lived isotope has a half-life of only 21 minutes. Francium was discovered and named in 1939 by Marguérite Perey to honour her country.

**Franco, Francisco (Paulino Hermenegildo Teódulo Bahamonde)** (1892–1975) Spanish dictator from 1939. As a general, he led the insurgent Nationalists to victory in the Spanish ◊Civil War 1936–39, supported by Fascist Italy and Nazi Germany, and established a dictatorship. In 1942 Franco reinstated a Cortes (Spanish parliament), which in 1947 passed an act by which he became head of state for life.

**Franco, Itamar** (1931–   ) Brazilian politician and president 1992–94, governor of Minas Gerais state from 1998. During his first months in office he attracted widespread criticism, both from friends (for his working methods and lack of clear policies) and opponents. Franco's greatest achievement was the introduction in 1994 of the Plano Real programme to stabilize the economy. He was defeated by Fernando Henrique Cardoso in the October 1994 presidential election but Cardoso saw the programme implemented.

He also introduced a rapid privatization programme and was bold enough to acknowledge the poverty that afflicted the nation, requesting the middle classes to organize themselves into groups to help the disadvantaged.

**François** French form of ◊Francis, two kings of France.

**Franco-Prussian War** 1870–71. The Prussian chancellor Otto von Bismarck put forward a German candidate for the vacant Spanish throne with the deliberate, and successful, intention of provoking the French emperor Napoleon III into declaring war. The Prussians defeated the French at Sedan, then besieged Paris. The Treaty of Frankfurt May 1871 gave Alsace, Lorraine, and a large French indemnity to Prussia. The war established Prussia, at the head of a newly established German empire, as Europe's leading power.

**frangipani** any of a group of tropical American trees, especially the species *P. rubra,* belonging to the dogbane family. Perfume is made from the strongly scented waxy flowers. (Genus *Plumeria,* family Apocynaceae.)

**Frank** member of a group of Germanic peoples prominent in Europe in the 3rd to 9th centuries. Believed to have originated in Pomerania on the Baltic Sea, they had settled on the Rhine by the 3rd century, spread into the Roman Empire by the 4th century, and gradually conquered most of Gaul, Italy, and Germany under the ◊Merovingian and Carolingian dynasties. The kingdom of the western Franks became France; the kingdom of the eastern Franks became Germany.

**Frank, Anne (Anneliese Marie)** (1929–1945) German diarist. She fled to the Netherlands with her family 1933 to escape Nazi anti-Semitism (the ◊Holocaust).

During the German occupation of Amsterdam, they and two other families remained in a sealed-off room, protected by Dutch sympathizers 1942–44, when betrayal resulted in their deportation and Anne's death in Belsen concentration camp. Her diary of her time in hiding was published in 1947.

**Frankfurt am Main** (German 'ford of the Franks') city in Hessen, Germany, 72 km/45 mi northeast of Mannheim; population (1995) 651,200. It is a commercial and banking centre, with electrical and machine industries, and an inland port on the River Main. The International Book Fair is held here annually in the autumn. It is the site of the Bundesbank (German Central Bank), and the European Central Bank (from 1999).

**frankincense** resin of various African and Asian trees, burned as incense. Costly in ancient times, it is traditionally believed to be one of the three gifts brought by the Magi to the infant Jesus. (Genus *Boswellia,* family Burseraceae.)

**Franklin, Benjamin** (1706–1790) US scientist, statesman, writer, printer, and publisher. He proved that lightning is a form of electricity, distinguished between positive and negative electricity, and invented the lightning conductor. He was the first US ambassador to France 1776–85, and negotiated peace with Britain in 1783. As a delegate to the ◊Continental Congress from Pennsylvania 1785–88, he helped to draft the ◊Declaration of Independence and the US Constitution.

**Franz Ferdinand** or *Francis Ferdinand* (1863–1914) Archduke of Austria. He became heir to Emperor Franz Joseph, his uncle, 1884 but while visiting Sarajevo on 28 June 1914, he and his wife were assassinated by a Serbian nationalist. Austria used the episode to make unreasonable demands on Serbia that ultimately precipitated World War I.

**Franz Joseph** or *Francis Joseph* (1830–1916) Emperor of Austria-Hungary from 1848, when his uncle Ferdinand I abdicated. After the suppression of the 1848 revolution, Franz Joseph tried to establish an absolute monarchy but had to grant Austria a parliamentary constitution in 1861 and Hungary equality with Austria in 1867. He was defeated in the Italian War in 1859 and the Prussian War in 1866. In 1914 he made the assassination of his heir and nephew Franz Ferdinand the excuse for attacking Serbia, thus precipitating World War I.

**fraud** in law, an act of deception resulting in injury to another. To establish fraud it has to be demonstrated that (1) a false representation (for example, a factually untrue statement) has been made, with the intention that it should be acted upon; (2) the person making the representation knows it is false or does not attempt to find out whether it is true or not; and (3) the person to whom the representation is made acts upon it to his or her detriment.

**Frederick** two Holy Roman emperors:

**Frederick (I) Barbarossa** 'red-beard' (*c.* 1123–1190) Holy Roman Emperor from 1152. Originally duke of Swabia, he was elected emperor in 1152, and was engaged in a struggle with Pope Alexander III 1159–77, which ended in his submission; the Lombard cities, headed by Milan, took advantage of this to establish their independence of imperial control. Frederick joined the Third Crusade, and was drowned while crossing a river in Anatolia.

**Frederick II** (1194–1250) Holy Roman Emperor 1212–50, called 'the Wonder of the World'. He was the son of Holy Roman Emperor ◊Henry VI. He led a crusade in 1228–29 that recovered Jerusalem by treaty without fighting. Frederick quarrelled with the pope, who excommunicated him three times, and a feud began that lasted with intervals until the end of his reign. Frederick, who was a religious sceptic, is often considered the most cultured person of his age. His later years were marred by the rebellions of his chief minister and his son.

**Frederick** three kings of Prussia, including:

**Frederick (II) the Great** (1712–1786) King of Prussia from 1740, when he succeeded his father Frederick William I. In that year he started the War of the ◊Austrian Succession by his attack on Austria. In the peace of 1745 he secured Silesia. The struggle was renewed in the ◊Seven Years' War 1756–63. He acquired West Prussia in the first partition of Poland in 1772 and left Prussia as Germany's foremost state. He was an efficient and just ruler in the spirit of the Enlightenment and a patron of the arts.

**Frederick William** four kings of Prussia, including:

**Frederick William I** (1688–1740) King of Prussia from 1713, who developed Prussia's military might and commerce.

**Frederick William III** (1770–1840) King of Prussia from 1797. He was defeated by Napoleon 1806, but contributed to his final overthrow 1813–15 and profited by being allotted territory at the Congress of Vienna.

**Free Church** the Protestant denominations in England and Wales that are not part of the Church of England; for example, the Methodist Church, Baptist Union, and United Reformed Church (Congregational and Presbyterian). These churches joined for common action in the Free Church Federal Council 1940.

**Free Church of Scotland** body of Scottish Presbyterians who seceded from the Established Church of Scotland in the Disruption of 1843. In 1900 all but a small section that retains the old name (known as the *Wee Frees)* combined with the United Presbyterian Church to form the United Free Church of Scotland. Most of this reunited with the Church of Scotland in 1929, although there remains a continuing United Free Church of Scotland. It has 6,000 members, 110 ministers, and 140 churches.

**free enterprise** or *free market,* economic system where private capital is used in business with profits going to private companies and individuals. The term has much the same meaning as ◊capitalism.

**freehold** in England and Wales, ownership of land for an indefinite period. It is contrasted with a *leasehold,* which is always for a fixed period. In practical effect, a freehold is absolute ownership.

**freemasonry** beliefs and practices of a group of linked national organizations open to men over the age of 21, united by a common code of morals and certain traditional 'secrets'. Modern freemasonry began in 18th-century Europe. Freemasons do much charitable work, but have been criticized in recent years for their secrecy, their male exclusivity, and their alleged use of influence within and between organizations (for example, the police or local government) to further each other's interests.

**free port** port or sometimes a zone within a port, where cargo may be accepted for handling, processing, and reshipment without the imposition of tariffs or taxes. Duties and tax become payable only if the products are for consumption in the country to which the free port belongs.

**Free Presbyterian Church of Scotland** body seceded from the ◊Free Church of Scotland 1893. In 1990 a further split created the Associated Presbyterian Churches of Scotland and Canada.

**free radical** in chemistry, an atom or molecule that has an unpaired electron and is therefore highly reactive. Most free radicals are very short-lived. They are by-products of normal cell chemistry and rapidly oxidize other molecules they encounter. Free radicals are thought to do considerable damage. They are neutralized by protective enzymes.

**freesia** any of a South African group of plants belonging to the iris family, commercially grown for their scented, funnel-shaped flowers. (Genus *Freesia*, family Iridaceae.)

**Free State** formerly *Orange Free State*, province of the Republic of South Africa
**area** 127,993 sq km/49,405 sq mi
**capital** Bloemfontein
**towns and cities** Springfontein, Kroonstad, Bethlehem, Harrismith, Koffiefontein
**physical** plain of the High Veld; Lesotho forms an enclave on the KwaZulu-Natal and Eastern Cape Province border; Orange River; Vaal River
**industries** gold, oil from coal, cement, pharmaceuticals
**agriculture** grain, wool, cattle
**population** (1995 est) 2,782,500; 82% ethnic Africans
**languages** Sotho 56%, Afrikaans 14%, Xhosa 9%
**history** original settlements from 1810 were complemented by the ◊Great Trek, and the state was recognized by Britain as independent in 1854. Following the South African, or Boer, War of 1899–1902, it was annexed by Britain as the Orange River Colony until it entered the Union as a province in 1910.

**Freetown** capital of Sierra Leone; population (1992) 505,000. It has a naval station and a harbour. Industries include cement, plastics, footwear, oil refining, food production, and tobacco processing. Platinum, chromite, rutile, diamonds, and gold are traded. Freetown was founded as a settlement for freed slaves in 1787. It was made capital of the independent Sierra Leone in 1961. The beaches of Freetown peninsula attract tourists.

**free trade** economic system where governments do not interfere in the movement of goods between countries; there are thus no taxes on imports. In the modern economy, free trade tends to hold within economic groups such as the European Union (EU), but not generally, despite such treaties as the ◊General Agreement on Tariffs and Trade 1948 and subsequent agreements to reduce tariffs. The opposite of free trade is ◊protectionism.

**free verse** poetry without metrical form. At the beginning of the 20th century, many poets believed that the 19th century had accomplished most of what could be done with regular metre, and rejected it, in much the same spirit as John Milton in the 17th century had rejected rhyme, preferring irregular metres that made it possible to express thought clearly and without distortion.

**free will** the doctrine that human beings are free to control their own actions, and that these actions are not fixed in advance by God or fate. Some Jewish and Christian theologians assert that God gave humanity free will to choose between good and evil; others that God has decided in advance the outcome of all human choices (◊predestination), as in Calvinism.

**freezing** change from liquid to solid state, as when water becomes ice. For a given substance, freezing occurs at a definite temperature, known as the *freezing point*, that is invariable under similar conditions of pressure, and the temperature remains at this point until all the liquid is frozen. The amount of heat per unit mass that has to be removed to freeze a substance is a constant for any given substance, and is known as the latent heat of fusion.

**French Community** former association consisting of France and those overseas territories joined with it by the constitution of the Fifth Republic, following the 1958 referendum. Many of the constituent states withdrew during the 1960s, and it no longer formally exists, but in practice all former French colonies have close economic and cultural as well as linguistic links with France.

**French Guiana** French *Guyane Française,* French overseas *département* from 1946, and administrative region from 1974, on the north coast of South America, bounded west by Suriname and east and south by Brazil
**area** 83,500 sq km/32,230 sq mi
**capital** Cayenne
**towns and cities** St Laurent
**features** Eurospace rocket launch pad at Kourou; Îles du Salut, which include Devil's Island
**industries** timber, shrimps, gold
**currency** franc
**population** (1990) 114,800
**language** 90% Creole, French, American Indian
**famous people** Alfred ◊Dreyfus
**history** first settled by France 1604, the territory became a French possession 1817; penal colonies, including Devil's Island, were established from 1852; by 1945 the shipments of convicts from France ceased.

**French horn** musical brass instrument, a descendant of the natural hunting horn, valved and curved into a circular loop, with a funnel-shaped mouthpiece and wide bell.

**French language** member of the Romance branch of the Indo-European language family, spoken in France, Belgium, Luxembourg, Monaco, and Switzerland in Europe; also in

Canada (principally in the province of Québec), various Caribbean and Pacific Islands (including overseas territories such as Martinique and French Guiana), and certain North and West African countries (for example, Mali and Senegal).

**French Polynesia** French Overseas Territory in the South Pacific, consisting of five archipelagos: Windward Islands, Leeward Islands (the two island groups comprising the ◊Society Islands), Tuamotu Archipelago (including Gambier Islands), Tubuai Islands, and ◊Marquesas Islands
***total area*** 3,940 sq km/1,521 sq mi
***capital*** Papeete on Tahiti
***industries*** cultivated pearls, coconut oil, vanilla; tourism is important
***population*** (1994) 216,600
***languages*** Tahitian (official), French
***government*** the French government is represented by a high commissioner (Paul Roncière). It is administered by a Council of Ministers, with a president elected by the Territorial Assembly from its own members; two deputies are returned to the National Assembly in France and one senator to the Senate
***history*** first visited by Europeans 1595; French protectorate 1843; annexed to France 1880–82; became an Overseas Territory, changing its name from French Oceania 1958; self-governing 1977. Following demands for independence in ◊New Caledonia 1984–85, agitation increased also in Polynesia.

**French Revolution** the period 1789–1799 that saw the end of the monarchy in France. The revolution began as an attempt to create a constitutional monarchy, but by late 1792 demands for long-overdue reforms resulted in the proclamation of the First Republic. The violence of the revolution; attacks by other nations; and bitter factional struggles, riots, and counter-revolutionary uprisings consumed the republic. This helped bring the extremists to power, and the bloody Reign of Terror followed. French armies then succeeded in holding off their foreign enemies and one of the generals, ◊Napoleon, seized power in 1799.

**frequency** in physics, the number of periodic oscillations, vibrations, or waves occurring per unit of time. The SI unit of frequency is the hertz (Hz), one hertz being equivalent to one cycle per second. Frequency is related to wavelength and velocity by the relationship

$$f = \frac{v}{\lambda}$$

where f is frequency, $v$ is velocity and $\lambda$ is wavelength.
Frequency is the reciprocal of the period T:

$$f = \frac{1}{T}.$$

**frequency** in statistics, the number of times an event occurs. For example, when two dice are thrown repeatedly and the two scores added together, each of the numbers 2 to 12 may have a frequency of occurrence. The set of data including the frequencies is called a *frequency distribution*, usually presented in a frequency table or shown diagrammatically, by a frequency polygon.

**frequency modulation** (FM) method by which radio waves are altered for the transmission of broadcasting signals. FM varies the frequency of the carrier wave in accordance with the signal being transmitted. Its advantage over AM (◊amplitude modulation) is its better signal-to-noise ratio. It was invented by the US engineer Edwin Armstrong.

**fresco** mural painting technique using water-based paint on wet plaster that has been freshly applied to the wall (*fresco* is Italian for fresh). The technique is ancient and widespread; some of the earliest examples (*c.* 1750–1400 BC) were found in Knossos, Crete (now preserved in the Archeological Museum in Heraklion). However, fresco reached its finest expression in Italy from the 13th to the 17th centuries.

**Freud, Lucian** (1922–  ) German-born British painter. One of the greatest contemporary figurative artists, he combines meticulous accuracy with a disquieting intensity, painting from unusual angles and emphasizing the physicality of his subjects, whether nudes, still lifes, or interiors. His *Portrait of Francis Bacon* (1952; Tate Gallery, London) is one of his best-known works. He is a grandson of Sigmund Freud.

**Freud, Sigmund** (1856–1939) Austrian physician who pioneered the study of the ◊unconscious mind. He developed the methods of free association and interpretation of dreams that are basic techniques of ◊psychoanalysis. The influence of unconscious forces on people's thoughts and actions was Freud's discovery, as was his controversial theory of the repression of infantile sexuality as the root of neuroses in the adult. His books include *Die Traumdeutung/ The Interpretation of Dreams* (1900), *Jenseits des Lustprinzips/Beyond the Pleasure Principle* (1920), *Das Ich und das Es/The Ego and the Id* (1923), and *Das Unbehagen in der Kultur/ Civilization and its Discontents* (1930). His influence has permeated the world to such an extent that it may be discerned today in almost every branch of thought.

**Freya** or *Freyja* in Norse mythology, goddess of married love and the hearth. She was also the goddess of death, Odin's punishment after her dalliance with four dwarfs to gain the necklace Brisingamen. In this capacity, she caused war between mortals and flew over their battlefields in a chariot drawn by two cats. Half the heroes slain were banqueted in her hall Sessrumnir in Asgard, the others being feasted by Odin. Friday is named after her.

**friction** in physics, the force that opposes the relative motion of two bodies in contact. The *coefficient of friction* is the ratio of the force required to achieve this relative motion to the force pressing the two bodies together.

**Friedman, Milton** (1912–  ) US economist, a pioneer of ◊monetarism. He argued that a country's economy, and hence inflation, can be controlled through its money supply, although most governments lack the 'political will' to cut government spending and thereby increase unemployment. Nobel Prize for Economics 1976.

**Friendly Islands** another name for Tonga, a country in the Pacific.

**Friends of the Earth** (*FoE*), or (*FOE*), largest international network of environmental pressure groups, established in the UK in 1971, that aims to protect the environment and to promote rational and sustainable use of the Earth's resources. It campaigns on such issues as acid rain; air, sea, river, and land pollution; recycling; disposal of toxic wastes; nuclear power and renewable energy; the destruction of rainforests; pesticides; and agriculture. FoE is represented in 52 countries.

**Friends, Society of** or *Quakers,* Christian Protestant sect founded by George Fox in England in the 17th century. They were persecuted for their nonviolent activism, and many emigrated to form communities elsewhere; for example, in Pennsylvania and New England. The worldwide movement had about 219,800 members in 1997. Their worship stresses meditation and the freedom of all to take an active part in the service (called a meeting, held in a meeting house). They have no priests or ministers.

**fritillary** in botany, any of a group of plants belonging to the lily family. The snake's head fritillary (*F. meleagris*) has bell-shaped flowers with purple-chequered markings. (Genus *Fritillaria,* family Liliaceae.)

**fritillary** in zoology, any of a large grouping of butterflies of the family Nymphalidae. Mostly medium-sized, fritillaries are usually orange and reddish with a black criss-cross pattern or spots above and with silvery spots on the underside of the hindwings.

**Friuli-Venezia Giulia** autonomous agricultural and wine-producing region of northeast Italy, bordered to the east by Slovenia, comprising the provinces of Pordenone, Gorizia, Trieste, and Udine; area 7,800 sq km/3,011 sq mi; population (1992) 1,195,100. The most important industrial centres are Udine,which is the region's capital, Gorizia, the ports of ◊Trieste and

Monfalcone (dockyards and chemical industries), and Pordenone.

**frog** any amphibian of the order Anura (Greek 'tailless'). There are about 24 different families of frog, containing more than 3,800 species. There are no clear rules for distinguishing between frogs and ◊toads.

Frogs usually have squat bodies, with hind legs specialized for jumping, and webbed feet for swimming. Most live in or near water, though as adults they are air-breathing. A few live on land or even in trees. Their colour is usually greenish in the genus *Rana,* but other Ranidae are brightly coloured, for instance black and orange or yellow and white. Many use their long, extensible tongues to capture insects. The eyes are large and bulging. Frogs vary in size from the North American little grass frog *Limnaoedus ocularis,* 12 mm/0.5 in long, to the giant aquatic frog *Telmatobius culeus,* 50 cm/20 in long, of Lake Titicaca, South America. Frogs are widespread, inhabiting all continents except Antarctica, and they have adapted to a range of environments including deserts, forests, grasslands, and even high altitudes, with some species in the Andes and Himalayas existing above 5,000 m/19,600 ft.

**Fronde** French revolts 1648–53 against the administration of the chief minister ◊Mazarin during Louis XIV's minority. In 1648–49 the Paris *parlement* attempted to limit the royal power, its leaders were arrested, Paris revolted, and the rising was suppressed by the royal army under Louis II Condé. In 1650 Condé led a new revolt of the nobility, but this was suppressed by 1653. The defeat of the Fronde enabled Louis to establish an absolutist monarchy in the later 17th century.

**front** in meteorology, the boundary between two air masses of different temperature or humidity. A *cold front* marks the line of advance of a cold air mass from below, as it displaces a warm air mass; a *warm front* marks the advance of a warm air mass as it rises up over a cold one. Frontal systems define the weather of the mid-latitudes, where warm tropical air is constantly meeting cold air from the poles.

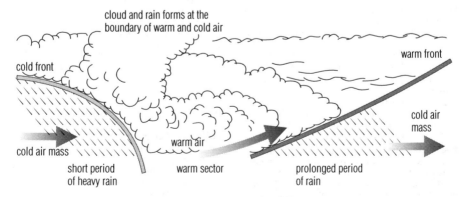

**front** *The boundaries between two air masses of different temperature and humidity. A warm front is when warm air displaces cold air; if cold air replaces warm air, it is a cold front.*

**frost** condition of the weather that occurs when the air temperature is below freezing, 0°C/32°F. Water in the atmosphere is deposited as ice crystals on the ground or exposed objects. As cold air is heavier than warm, ground frost is more common than hoar frost, which is formed by the condensation of water particles in the same way that ◊dew collects.

**Frost, Robert Lee** (1874–1963) US poet. His accessible, colloquial blank verse, often flavoured with New England speech patterns, is written with an individual voice and penetrating vision. His poems include 'Mending Wall' ('Something there is that does not love a wall'), 'The Road Not Taken', and 'Stopping by Woods on a Snowy Evening' and are collected in *Complete Poems* (1951).

**frostbite** the freezing of skin or flesh, with formation of ice crystals leading to tissue damage. The treatment is slow warming of the affected area; for example, by skin-to-skin contact or with lukewarm water. Frostbitten parts are extremely vulnerable to infection, with the risk of gangrene.

**fructose** $C_6H_{12}O_6$ a sugar that occurs naturally in honey, the nectar of flowers, and many sweet fruits; it is commercially prepared from glucose.

**fruit** (from Latin *frui* 'to enjoy') in botany, the ripened ovary in flowering plants that develops from one or more seeds or carpels and encloses one or more seeds. Its function is to protect the seeds during their development and to aid in their dispersal. Fruits are often edible, sweet, juicy, and colourful. When eaten they provide vitamins, minerals, and enzymes, but little protein. Most fruits are borne by perennial plants.

**ft** symbol for ◊*foot*, a measure of distance.

**FT Index** abbreviation for ◊*Financial Times Index*, a list of leading share prices.

**fuchsia** any shrub or herbaceous plant of a group belonging to the evening-primrose family. Species are native to South and Central America and New Zealand, and bear red, purple, or pink bell-shaped flowers that hang downwards. (Genus *Fuchsia*, family Onagraceae.)

**fuel** any source of heat or energy, embracing the entire range of materials that burn in air (combustibles). A *nuclear fuel* is any material that produces energy by nuclear fission in a nuclear reactor. ◊Fossil fuels are formed from the fossilized remains of plants and animals.

**fuel cell** cell converting chemical energy directly to electrical energy.

It works on the same principle as a battery but is continually fed with fuel, usually hydrogen. Fuel cells are silent and reliable (no moving parts) but expensive to produce.

**fuel injection** injecting fuel directly into the cylinders of an internal-combustion engine, instead of by way of a carburettor. It is the standard method used in ◊diesel engines, and is now becoming standard for petrol engines. In the diesel engine, oil is injected into the hot compressed air at the top of the second piston stroke

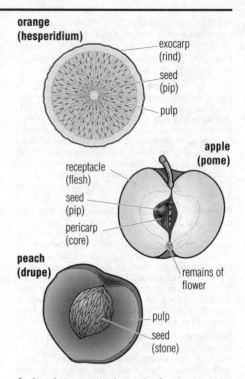

**orange (hesperidium)**
exocarp (rind)
seed (pip)
pulp

**apple (pome)**
receptacle (flesh)
seed (pip)
pericarp (core)
remains of flower

**peach (drupe)**
pulp
seed (stone)

*fruit A fruit contains the seeds of a plant. Its outer wall is the exocarp, or epicarp; its inner layers are the mesocarp and endocarp. The orange is a hesperidium, a berry having a leathery rind and containing many seeds. The peach is a drupe, a fleshy fruit with a hard seed, or 'stone', at the centre. The apple is a pome, a fruit with a fleshy outer layer and a core containing the seeds.*

and explodes to drive the piston down on its power stroke. In the petrol engine, fuel is injected into the cylinder at the start of the first induction stroke of the ◊four-stroke cycle.

**fugue** (Latin 'flight') in music, a contrapuntal form with two or more subjects (principal melodies) for a number of parts, which enter in succession in direct imitation of each other or transposed to a higher or lower key, and may be combined in augmented form (larger note values). It represents the highest form of contrapuntal ingenuity in works such as Johann Sebastian Bach's *Das musikalische Opfer/The Musical Offering* (1747), on a theme of Frederick II of Prussia, and *Die Kunst der Fuge/The Art of the Fugue* (published 1751), and Beethoven's *Grosse Fuge/Great Fugue* for string quartet (1825–26).

**Fujian** or *Fukien*, maritime province of southeast China, bounded to the southwest by Guangdong, to the west and northwest by Jiangxi, to the northeast by Zhejiang, and to the southeast by the Taiwan Strait on the China Sea; opposite Taiwan
*area* 123,100 sq km/47,517 sq mi
*capital* ◊Fuzhou

***cities and towns*** Xiamen, Zhangzhou, Nanping
***physical*** dramatic mountainous coastline
***industries*** steel-rolling, electrical goods, tourism, handicrafts, leather goods
***agriculture*** rice, sweet potatoes, sugar, special aromatic teas, tobacco, timber, citrus fruit
***population*** (1994) 32,610,000.

**Fujimori, Alberto** (1938– ) Peruvian politician, president from 1990. As leader of the newly formed Cambio 90 (Change 90) he campaigned on a promarket reformist ticket and defeated his more experienced Democratic Front opponent. Lacking an assembly majority and faced with increasing opposition to his policies, he closed congress and imposed military rule in early 1992, to fight the Sendero Luminoso (Shining Path) guerrillas and the left-wing Tupac Amaru Revolutionary Movement (MRTA). In 1993 a plebiscite narrowly approved his constitutional reform proposals, allowing him to seek, and achieve, re-election in 1995.

**Fuji, Mount** Japanese volcano and highest peak, on Honshu Island, near Tokyo; height 3,778 m/12,400 ft. Extinct since 1707, it has a ◊Shinto shrine and a weather station on its summit. Fuji has long been revered for its picturesque cone-shaped crater peak, and figures prominently in Japanese art, literature, and religion.

**Fujiyama** another name for Mount Fuji (see ◊Fuji, Mount.

**Fuller, (Richard) Buckminster** (1895–1983) US architect, engineer, and social philosopher. He embarked on an unorthodox career in an attempt to maximize energy resources through improved technology. In 1947 he invented the lightweight geodesic dome, a hemispherical space-frame of triangular components linked by rods, independent of buttress or vault and capable of covering large-span areas. Within 30 years over 50,000 had been built.

**fullerene** form of carbon, discovered in 1985, based on closed cages of carbon atoms. The molecules of the most symmetrical of the fullerenes are called ◊buckminsterfullerenes (or buckyballs). They are perfect spheres made up of 60 carbon atoms linked together in 12 pentagons and 20 hexagons fitted together like those of a spherical football. Other fullerenes, with 28, 32, 50, 70, and 76 carbon atoms, have also been identified.

**fuller's earth** soft, greenish-grey rock resembling clay, but without clay's plasticity. It is formed largely of clay minerals, rich in montmorillonite, but a great deal of silica is also present. Its absorbent properties make it suitable for removing oil and grease, and it was formerly used for cleaning fleeces ('fulling'). It is still used in the textile industry, but its chief application is in the purification of oils. Beds of fuller's earth are found in the southern USA, Germany, Japan, and the UK.

**fulmar** any of several species of petrels of the family Procellariidae, which are similar in size and colour to herring gulls. The northern fulmar *Fulmarus glacialis* is found in the North Atlantic and visits land only to nest, laying a single egg.

**fumitory** any of a group of plants native to Europe and Asia. The common fumitory (*F. officinalis*) grows to 50 cm/20 in and produces pink flowers tipped with blackish red; it has been used in medicine for stomach and liver complaints. (Genus *Fumeria*, family Fumariaceae.)

**function** in computing, a small part of a program that supplies a specific value – for example, the square root of a specified number, or the current date. Most programming languages incorporate a number of built-in functions; some allow programmers to write their own. A function may have one or more arguments (the values on which the function operates). A *function key* on a keyboard is one that, when pressed, performs a designated task, such as ending a program.

**function** in mathematics, a function $f$ is a nonempty set of ordered pairs $(x, f(x))$ of which no two can have the same first element. Hence, if $f(x) = x^2$ two ordered pairs are $(-2,4)$ and $(2,4)$. The set of all first elements in a function's ordered pairs is called the ***domain;*** the set of all second elements is the ***range.*** In the algebraic expression

$$y = 4x^3 + 2$$

the dependent variable $y$ is a function of the independent variable $x$, generally written as $f(x)$.

**functional group** in chemistry, a small number of atoms in an arrangement that determines the chemical properties of the group and of the molecule to which it is attached (for example, the carboxyl group COOH, or the amine group $NH_2$). Organic compounds can be considered as structural skeletons, with a high carbon content, with functional groups attached.

**Functionalism** in architecture and design, the principle of excluding everything that serves no practical purpose. Central to 20th-century ◊Modernism, the Functionalist ethic developed as a reaction against the 19th-century practice of imitating and combining earlier styles. Its finest achievements are in the realms of industrial architecture and office furnishings.

**fundamental constant** physical quantity that is constant in all circumstances throughout the whole universe. Examples are the electric charge of an electron, the speed of light, Planck's constant, and the gravitational constant.

**fundamental forces** see ◊forces, fundamental.

**fundamentalism** in religion, an emphasis on basic principles or articles of faith. *Christian fundamentalism* emerged in the USA just after World War I (as a reaction to theological modernism and the historical criticism of the Bible) and insisted on belief in the literal truth of everything in the Bible. *Islamic fundamentalism* insists on strict observance of Muslim Shari'a law.

**fungus** plural *fungi,* any of a unique group of organisms that includes moulds, yeasts, rusts, smuts, mildews, mushrooms, and toadstools. There are around 70,000 species of fungi known to science (1998), though there may be as many as 1.5 million actually in existence. They are not considered to be plants for three main reasons: they have no leaves or roots; they contain no chlorophyll (green colouring) and are therefore unable to make their own food by ◊photosynthesis; and they reproduce by ◊spores. Some fungi are edible but many are highly poisonous; they often cause damage and sometimes disease to the organic matter they live and feed on, but some fungi are exploited in the production of food and drink (for example, yeasts in baking and brewing) and in medicine (for example, penicillin). (Kingdom Fungi.)

**fur** the ◊hair of certain animals. Fur is an excellent insulating material and so has been used as clothing. This is, however, vociferously criticized by many groups on humane grounds, as the methods of breeding or trapping animals are often cruel. Mink, chinchilla, and sable are among the most valuable, the wild furs being finer than the farmed.

Fur such as mink is made up of a soft, thick, insulating layer called underfur and a top layer of longer, lustrous guard hairs.

**Furies** or *Erinyes,* in Greek mythology, spirits of vengeance, principally of murder within the family but also of other breaches of natural order such as filial disobedience, inhospitality, and oath-breaking; they may have been considered the personifications of curses. The Furies were also associated with fertility, and were appeasingly called the ◊Eumenides 'kindly ones'. Represented as winged maidens with serpents twisted in their hair, they inhabited Hades, the underworld.

**fusion** in physics, the fusing of the nuclei of light elements, such as hydrogen, into those of a heavier element, such as helium. The resultant loss in their combined mass is converted into energy. Stars and thermonuclear weapons are powered by nuclear fusion.

**futures trading** buying and selling commodities (usually cereals and metals) at an agreed price for delivery several months ahead. The notional value of the futures contracts traded annually worldwide is $140,000 bn (1994). The volume of crude oil futures and options traded on the New York Mercantile Exchange amounts to 200 million barrels a day, almost four times the amount actually produced.

**Futurism** avant-garde art movement founded in 1909 that celebrated the dynamism of the modern world. It was chiefly an Italian movement and was mainly expressed in painting, but it also embraced other arts, including literature and music, and it had extensive influence outside Italy, particularly in Russia. In Italy the movement virtually died during World War I, but in Russia it continued to flourish into the 1920s.

**Fuzhou** or *Foochow;* formerly *Minhow,* industrial port and capital of Fujian province, on the Min River in southeast China; population (1994) 1,354,800. It is a centre for shipbuilding and steel production; rice, sugar, tea, and fruit pass through the port. Traditionally renowned for its handicrafts, particularly carving and lacquerware, Fuzhou's industries now include electronics, food processing, and the manufacture of textiles and building materials. There are joint foreign and Chinese factories.

**fuzzy logic** in mathematics and computing, a form of knowledge representation suitable for notions (such as 'hot' or 'loud') that cannot be defined precisely but depend on their context. For example, a jug of water may be described as too hot or too cold, depending on whether it is to be used to wash one's face or to make tea.

**g** symbol for ◊*gram*.

**gabbro** mafic (consisting primarily of dark-coloured crystals) igneous rock formed deep in the Earth's crust. It contains pyroxene and calcium-rich feldspar, and may contain small amounts of olivine and amphibole. Its coarse crystals of dull minerals give it a speckled appearance.

**Gable, (William) Clark** (1901–1960) US actor. A star for more than 30 years, he played a range of hard-boiled, comic, and romantic roles. He won an Academy Award for his performance in Frank Capra's *It Happened One Night* (1934), and starred as Rhett Butler in *Gone With the Wind* (1939).

**Gabo, Naum** Adopted name of Naum Neemia Pevsner (1890–1977) Russian-born US abstract sculptor. One of the leading exponents of Constructivism, he was one of the first artists to make kinetic sculpture. In later works he often used transparent plastics in works that attempt to define space rather than occupy it, as in *Linear Construction* (1942; Tate Gallery, London).

**Gabon** Gabonese Republic
**national name** *République Gabonaise*

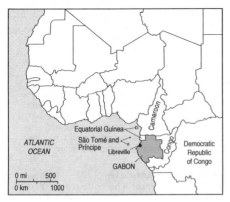

**area** 267,667 sq km/103,346 sq mi
**capital** Libreville
**major towns/cities** Port-Gentil, Masuku (Franceville), Lambaréné, Mouanda
**major ports** Port-Gentil and Owendo
**physical features** virtually the whole country

is tropical rainforest; narrow coastal plain rising to hilly interior with savanna in east and south; Ogooué River flows north–west
**head of state** Omar Bongo from 1964
**head of government** Jean-François Ntoutoume-Emane from 1999
**political system** emergent democracy
**political parties** Gabonese Democratic Party (PDG), nationalist; Gabone Progress Party (PGP), left of centre; National Rally of Woodcutters (RNB), left of centre
**currency** franc CFA
**GNP per capita (PPP)** (US$) 6,660 (1998)
**exports** petroleum and petroleum products, manganese, timber and wood products, uranium. Principal market: USA 67% (1997)
**population** 1,197,000 (1999 est)
**language** French (official), Bantu
**religion** Roman Catholic, also Muslim, animist
**life expectancy** 51 (men); 54 (women) (1995–2000)
**Chronology**
**12th century** Immigration of Bantu speakers into an area previously peopled by Pygmies.
**1472** Gabon Estuary first visited by Portuguese navigators, who named it Gabao ('hooded cloak'), after the shape of the coastal area.
**17th–18th centuries** Fang, from Cameroon in the north, and Omiene peoples colonized the area, attracted by presence in coastal areas of European traders, who developed the ivory and slave trades, which lasted until the mid-19th century.
**1839–42** Mpongwe coastal chiefs agreed to transfer sovereignty to France; Catholic and Protestant missionaries attracted to the area.
**1849** Libreville ('Free Town') formed by slaves from a slave ship liberated by the French.
**1889** Became part of French Congo, with Congo.
**1910** Became part of French Equatorial Africa, which also comprised Congo, Chad, and Central African Republic.
**1890s–1920s** Human and natural resources exploited by private concessionary companies.
**1940–44** Supported the 'Free French' anti-Nazi cause during World War II.
**1946** Became overseas territory within the French Community, with its own assembly.
**1960** Independence achieved; Léon M'ba, a Fang of the pro-French Gabonese Democratic Block (BDG) became the first president.
**1964** Attempted military coup by supporters of rival party foiled with French help.
**1967** M'ba died and was succeeded by his protégé Albert Bernard Bongo, drawn from the Teke community.
**1968** One-party state established, with BDG dissolved and replaced by Gabonese Democratic Party (PDG).
**1973** Bongo converted to Islam and changed his first name to Omar, but continued to follow a pro-Western policy course and exploit rich mineral resources to increase prosperity.
**1989** A coup attempt against Bongo was defeated; the economy deteriorated.
**1990** The PDG won the first multiparty elections since 1964. French troops were sent in to maintain order following antigovernment riots.

*1993* A national unity government was formed, including some opposition members.

*1997* Paulin Obame-Nguema was reappointed prime minister after the ruling Gabonese Democratic Party (PDG) won a large assembly majority.

*1998* A new party, Rassemblement des Gaullois, was recognized. President Bongo was re-elected.

*1999* Jean-François Ntoutoume-Emane was appointed prime minister.

**Gaborone** capital of Botswana, mainly an administrative and government-service centre; population (1991) 133,500. Light industries include motor vehicle assembly, textiles, brewing, printing and publishing, and construction. The University of Botswana (1976) is here. The city developed after 1962 when it replaced Mafikeng as capital in preparation for the country's independence in 1966.

**Gabriel** in the New Testament, the archangel who foretold the birth of John the Baptist to Zacharias and of Jesus to the Virgin Mary. He is also mentioned in the Old Testament in the book of Daniel. In Muslim belief, Gabriel revealed the Koran to Muhammad and escorted him on his Night Journey.

**Gaddafi** alternative form of ◊Khaddhafi, Libyan leader.

**gadolinium** silvery-white metallic element of the lanthanide series, symbol Gd, atomic number 64, relative atomic mass 157.25. It is found in the products of nuclear fission and used in electronic components, alloys, and products needing to withstand high temperatures.

**Gaelic language** member of the Celtic branch of the Indo-European language family, spoken in Ireland, Scotland, and (until 1974) the Isle of Man. Gaelic has been in decline for several centuries, though efforts are being made to keep it alive, for example by means of the government's Gaelic Broadcasting Fund, established in 1993, which subsidises television and radio programmes in Gaelic for transmission in Scotland.

**Gagarin, Yuri (Alexeyevich)** (1934–1968) Soviet cosmonaut who in 1961 became the first human in space aboard the spacecraft *Vostok 1.*

**Gaia** or *Ge,* in Greek mythology, the goddess of the Earth. She sprang from primordial Chaos and herself produced Uranus, by whom she was the mother of the Cyclopes and ◊Titans.

**Gaia hypothesis** theory that the Earth's living and nonliving systems form an inseparable whole that is regulated and kept adapted for life by living organisms themselves. The planet therefore functions as a single organism, or a giant cell. The hypothesis was elaborated by British scientist James Lovelock and first published in 1968.

**gain** in electronics, the ratio of the amplitude of the output signal produced by an amplifier to that of the input signal.

In a voltage amplifier the voltage gain is the ratio of the output voltage to the input voltage; in an inverting operational amplifier (op-amp) it is equal to the ratio of the resistance of the feedback resistor to that of the input resistor.

**Gainsborough, Thomas** (1727–1788) English landscape and portrait painter. In 1760 he settled in Bath, where his elegant and subtly characterized society portraits brought great success. In 1774 he went to London, becoming one of the original members of the Royal Academy and the principal rival of Joshua Reynolds. He was one of the first British artists to follow the Dutch example in painting realistic landscapes rather than imaginative Italianate scenery, as in *Mr and Mrs Andrews* (about 1750; National Gallery, London).

**gal** symbol for ◊*gallon, galileo.*

**Galahad** in Arthurian legend, one of the knights of the Round Table. His virtue allowed him to succeed in the quest for the ◊Holy Grail, and he died in ecstasy, having seen its mystery.

He was the son of Lancelot of the Lake and Elaine, daughter of the Fisher King, whom Lancelot believed to be his beloved ◊Guinevere.

**Galápagos Islands** official name *Archipiélago de Colón,* group of 12 large and several hundred smaller islands in the Pacific about 500 miles from the mainland, belonging to Ecuador; area 7,800 sq km/3,000 sq mi; population (1990) 9,800. The capital is San Cristóbal. The islands are a nature reserve; their unique fauna (including giant tortoises, iguanas, penguins, flightless cormorants, and Darwin's finches, which inspired Charles ◊Darwin to formulate the principle of evolution by natural selection) is under threat from introduced species. The marine ecosystem surrounding the island supports 437 species of fish, 41 of which are unique to the Galápagos. The main industry is tuna and lobster fishing.

**galaxy** congregation of millions or billions of stars, held together by gravity. *Spiral galaxies,* such as the ◊Milky Way, are flattened in shape, with a central bulge of old stars surrounded by a disc of younger stars, arranged in spiral arms like a Catherine wheel.

*Barred spirals* are spiral galaxies that have a straight bar of stars across their centre, from the ends of which the spiral arms emerge. The arms of spiral galaxies contain gas and dust from which new stars are still forming.

*Elliptical galaxies* contain old stars and very little gas. They include the most massive galaxies known, containing a trillion stars. At least some elliptical galaxies are thought to be formed by mergers between spiral galaxies. There are also irregular galaxies. Most galaxies occur in clusters, containing anything from a few to thousands of members.

**Galbraith, John Kenneth** (1908–   ) Canadian-born US economist who criticized the neoclassical view that in the economy market forces were in a state approximating perfect competition. He suggested that the 'affluent society' develops an economic imbalance, devoting too many resources to the production of consumer goods and not enough to public services and infrastructure.

**Galen** (*c.* 129–*c.* 200) Greek physician and anatomist whose ideas dominated Western medicine for almost 1,500 years. Central to his thinking were the theories of humours and the threefold circulation of the blood. He remained the highest medical authority until Andreas ◊Vesalius and William ◊Harvey exposed the fundamental errors of his system.

**galena** mineral consisting of lead sulphide, PbS, the chief ore of lead. It is lead-grey in colour, has a high metallic lustre and breaks into cubes because of its perfect cubic cleavage. It may contain up to 1% silver, and so the ore is sometimes mined for both metals. Galena occurs mainly among limestone deposits in Australia, Mexico, Russia, Kazakhstan, the UK, and the USA.

**Galicia** mountainous but fertile autonomous community of northwest Spain, comprising the provinces of La Coruña, Lugo, Orense, and Pontevedra; area 29,400 sq km/11,348 sq mi; population (1991) 2,731,700. Industries include fishing, and tungsten and tin mining; Galicia has the largest fishing fleet in the European Union. The climate is very wet, and the region is traversed northeast to southwest by the River Miño. The chief harbours are La Coruña, Vigo, and El Ferrol. The Galician language (Gallego) is similar to Portuguese. The capital is Santiago de Compostela.

**Galilee** region of northern Israel (once a Roman province in Palestine) which includes Nazareth and Tiberias, frequently mentioned in the Gospels of the New Testament.

**Galilee, Sea of** alternative name for Lake Tiberias in northern Israel.

**Galileo** properly *Galileo Galilei* (1564–1642) Italian mathematician, astronomer, and physicist. He developed the astronomical telescope and was the first to see sunspots, the four main satellites of Jupiter, and the appearance of Venus going through phases, thus proving it was orbiting the Sun. Galileo discovered that freely falling bodies, heavy or light, have the same, constant acceleration and that this acceleration is due to gravity. He also determined that a body moving on a perfectly smooth horizontal surface would neither speed up nor slow down. He invented a thermometer, a hydrostatic balance, and a compass, and discovered that the path of a projectile is a parabola.

**gall** abnormal outgrowth on a plant that develops as a result of attack by insects or, less commonly, by bacteria, fungi, mites, or nematodes. The attack causes an increase in the number of cells or an enlargement of existing cells in the plant. Gall-forming insects generally pass the early stages of their life inside the gall.

Gall wasps are responsible for the conspicuous bud galls forming on oak trees, 2.5–4 cm/1–1.5 in across, known as 'oak apples'. The organisms that cause galls are host-specific. Thus, for example, gall wasps tend to parasitize oaks, and ◊sawflies willows.

**gall bladder** small muscular sac, part of the digestive system of most, but not all, vertebrates. In humans, it is situated on the underside of the liver and connected to the small intestine by the bile duct. It stores bile from the liver.

**galley** ship powered by oars, and usually also equipped with sails. Galleys typically had a crew of hundreds of rowers arranged in banks. They were used in warfare in the Mediterranean from antiquity until the 18th century.

**Gallic Wars** series of military campaigns 58–51 BC in which Julius Caesar, as proconsul of Gaul, annexed Transalpine Gaul (the territory that formed the geographical basis of modern-day France). His final victory over the Gauls led by Vercingetorix 52 BC left him in control of the land area from the Rhine to the Pyrenees and from the Alps to the Atlantic. The final organization of the provinces followed under Augustus.

**Gallipoli** port in European Turkey, giving its name to the peninsula (ancient name *Chersonesus)* on which it stands. In World War I, at the instigation of Winston Churchill, an unsuccessful attempt was made between February 1915 and January 1916 by Allied troops to force their way through the Dardanelles and link up with Russia. The campaign was fought mainly by Australian and New Zealand (Anzac) forces, who suffered heavy losses. An estimated 36,000 Commonwealth troops died during the nine-month campaign.

**gallium** grey metallic element, symbol Ga, atomic number 31, relative atomic mass 69.72. It is liquid at room temperature. Gallium arsenide (GaAs) crystals are used in microelectronics, since electrons travel a thousand times faster through them than through silicon. The element was discovered in 1875 by Lecoq de Boisbaudran (1838–1912).

**gallon** imperial liquid or dry measure, equal to 4.546 litres, and subdivided into four quarts or eight pints. The US gallon is equivalent to 3.785 litres.

**gallstone** pebblelike, insoluble accretion formed in the human gall bladder or bile ducts from cholesterol or calcium salts present in bile. Gallstones may be symptomless or they may cause pain, indigestion, or jaundice. They can be dissolved with medication or removed, either by means of an endoscope or, along with the gall bladder, in an operation known as cholecystectomy.

**Galsworthy, John** (1867–1933) English novelist and dramatist. His work examines the social issues of the Victorian period. He wrote *The Forsyte Saga* (1906–22) and its sequel, the novels collectively entitled *A Modern Comedy* (1929). His plays include *The Silver Box* (1906). He won the Nobel Prize for Literature in 1932.

**galvanizing** process for rendering iron rustproof, by plunging it into molten zinc (the dipping method), or by electroplating it with zinc.

**Galway** county on the west coast of the Republic of Ireland, in the province of Connacht; county town Galway; area 5,940 sq km/2,293 sq mi; population (1991) 180,300.

Lead is found at Tynagh, and copper, lead, and zinc near Loughrea; marble is quarried and processed at Recess and Inverin. The main farming activity is cattle and sheep grazing. Towns include Salthill, a suburb of *Galway* city and seaside resort, Ballinasloe, Clifden, and Tuam.

**Gama, Vasco da** (*c.* 1469–1524) Portuguese navigator. He commanded an expedition in 1497 to discover the route to India around the Cape of Good Hope (in modern South Africa). On Christmas Day 1497 he reached land, which he named Natal. He then crossed the Indian Ocean, arriving at Calicut (now Kozhikode in Kerala) in May 1498, and returned to Portugal in September 1499.

**Gambia, The** Republic of

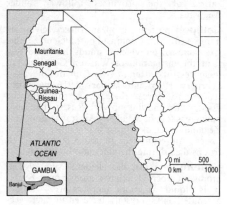

Mauritania
Senegal
Guinea-Bissau
ATLANTIC OCEAN
GAMBIA
Banjul

0 mi 500
0 km 1000

*area* 10,402 sq km/4,016 sq mi
*capital* Banjul
*major towns/cities* Serekunda, Birkama, Bakau, Farafenni, Sukuta, Gunjur, Georgetown
*physical features* consists of narrow strip of land along the River Gambia; river flanked by low hills
*head of state and government* (interim) Yahya Jameh from 1994
*political system* transitional
*political parties* Progressive People's Party (PPP), moderate centrist; National Convention Party (NCP), left of centre
*currency* dalasi
*GNP per capita (PPP)* (US$) 1,430 (1998)
*exports* groundnuts and related products, cotton lint, fish and fish preparations, hides and skins. Principal market: Belgium–Luxembourg 78% (1997 est)
*population* 1,268,000 (1999 est)
*language* English (official), Mandinka, Fula, and other indigenous tongues
*religion* Muslim 90%, with animist and Christian minorities
*life expectancy* 45 (men); 49 (women) (1995–2000)
*Chronology*
*13th century* Wolof, Malinke (Mandingo), and Fulani tribes settled in the region from east and north.
*14th century* Became part of the great Muslim Mali Empire, which, centred to northeast, also

extended across Senegal, Mali, and southern Mauritania.
*1455* The Gambia River was first sighted by the Portuguese.
*1663 and 1681* The British and French established small settlements on the river at Fort James and Albreda.
*1843* The Gambia became a British crown colony, administered with Sierra Leone until 1888.
*1965* Independence was achieved as a constitutional monarchy within the Commonwealth, with Dawda K Jawara of the People's Progressive Party (PPP) as prime minister at the head of a multiparty democracy.
*1970* The Gambia became a republic, with Jawara as president.
*1981* An attempted coup was foiled with the help of Senegal.
*1982* The Gambia formed with Senegal the Confederation of Senegambia, which involved the integration of military forces, economic and monetary union, and coordinated foreign policy.
*1994* Jawara was ousted in a military coup, and fled to Senegal; Yahya Jameh was named acting head of state.
*1995* A counter-coup attempt failed.
*1996* A civilian constitution was adopted.

**gamelan** percussion ensemble consisting largely of tuned knobbed gongs and keyed metallophones found in Indonesia (especially Java and Bali) and Malaysia. Most modern gamelan are tuned to a 5-note or 7-note system. Gamelan music is performed as an accompaniment for dance and theatre.

**gamete** cell that functions in sexual reproduction by merging with another gamete to form a ◊zygote. Examples of gametes include sperm and egg cells. In most organisms, the gametes are haploid (they contain half the number of chromosomes of the parent), owing to reduction division or ◊meiosis.

**game theory** group of mathematical theories, developed in 1944 by Oscar Morgenstern (1902–1977) and Hungarian-born US mathematician John Von Neumann, that seeks to abstract from invented game-playing scenarios and their outcome the essence of situations of conflict and/or cooperation in the real political, business, and social world.

**gametophyte** the ◊haploid generation in the life cycle of a plant that produces gametes; see ◊alternation of generations.

**gamma radiation** very high-frequency electromagnetic radiation, similar in nature to X-rays but of shorter wavelength, emitted by the nuclei of radioactive substances during decay or by the interactions of high-energy electrons with matter. Cosmic gamma rays have been identified as coming from pulsars, radio galaxies, and quasars, although they cannot penetrate the Earth's atmosphere.

**gamma-ray astronomy** study of gamma rays from space. Much of the radiation detected comes from collisions between hydrogen gas and cosmic rays in our Galaxy. Some sources have been identified, including the Crab nebula and the Vela pulsar (the most powerful gamma-ray source detected).

**Gandhi, Indira Priyadarshani** born Nehru (1917–1984) Indian politician, prime minister of India 1966–77 and 1980–84, and leader of the Congress Party 1966–77 and subsequently of the Congress (I) party. She was assassinated in 1984 by members of her Sikh bodyguard, resentful of her use of troops to clear malcontents from the Sikh temple at ◊Amritsar.

**Gandhi, Mahatma** Sanskrit 'Great Soul', Honorific name of Mohandas Karamchand Gandhi (1869–1948) Indian nationalist leader. A pacifist, he led the struggle for Indian independence from the UK by advocating nonviolent noncooperation (*satyagraha*, defence of and by truth) from 1915. He was imprisoned several times by the British authorities and was influential in the nationalist Congress Party and in the independence negotiations in 1947. He was assassinated by a Hindu nationalist in the violence that followed the partition of British India into India and Pakistan.

**Gandhi, Rajiv** (1944–1991) Indian politician, prime minister from 1984 (following his mother Indira Gandhi's assassination) to November 1989. As prime minister, he faced growing discontent with his party's elitism and lack of concern for social issues. He was assassinated at an election rally.

**Ganesh** Hindu god, son of Siva and Parvati; he is represented as elephant-headed and is worshipped as a remover of obstacles.

**Ganges** Hindi *Ganga,* major river of India and Bangladesh; length 2,510 km/1,560 mi. It is the most sacred river for Hindus.

**ganglion** plural *ganglia,* solid cluster of nervous tissue containing many cell bodies and ◊synapses, usually enclosed in a tissue sheath; found in invertebrates and vertebrates.

**Gang of Four** in Chinese history, the chief members of the radical faction that played a key role in directing the ◊Cultural Revolution and tried to seize power after the death of the communist leader Mao Zedong 1976. It included his widow ◊Jiang Qing; the other members were three young Shanghai politicians: Zhang Chunqiao, Wang Hongwen, and Yao Wenyuan. The coup failed and the Gang of Four were arrested. Publicly tried in 1980, they were found guilty of treason.

**gangrene** death and decay of body tissue (often of a limb) due to bacterial action; the affected part gradually turns black and causes blood poisoning.

**gannet** any of three species of North Atlantic seabirds; the largest is *Sula bassana.* When fully grown, it is white with buff colouring on the head and neck; the beak is long and thick and compressed at the point; the wings are black-tipped with a span of 1.7 m/5.6 ft. It breeds on cliffs in nests made of grass and seaweed, laying a single white egg. Gannets feed on fish that swim near the surface, such as herrings and pilchards. (Family Sulidae, order Pelecaniformaes.)

**Gansu** or *Kansu,* province of northwest China, bounded to the north by Mongolia and Inner Mongolia, to the east by Ningxia Hui Autonomous Region and Shaanxi, to the south by Sichuan, and to the west by Qinghai and Xinjiang Uygur Autonomous Region
**area** 530,000 sq km/204,580 sq mi
**capital** Lanzhou
**cities and towns** Yumen, Tianshui, Dunhuang, Jiayuguan
**physical** loess (loamy) soils in the east; mountains in the south and west; Huang He River
**features** Silk Road medieval trade route to central Asia; western end of the Great Wall at Jiayuguan; Buddhist frescoes at Mogao caves near Dunhuang
**industries** coal, oil, hydroelectric power from the Huang He River, mining, metal-processing, tourism
**agriculture** spring wheat, millet, sorghum, flax, fruit, animal rearing
**population** (1996) 24,670,000; including many Muslims.

**Ganymede** in Greek mythology according to Homer, a youth so beautiful he was taken as cupbearer to Zeus, king of the gods. He was deemed responsible for the annual flooding of the Nile, and was later identified with the constellation ◊Aquarius.

**Garbo, Greta** stage name of Greta Lovisa Gustafsson (1905–1990) Swedish-born US film actress. She went to the USA 1925, and her captivating beauty and leading role in *Flesh and the Devil* 1927 made her one of Hollywood's greatest stars. Her later films include *Mata Hari* (1931), *Grand Hotel* (1932), *Queen Christina* (1933), *Anna Karenina* (1935), *Camille* (1936), and *Ninotchka* (1939). Her ethereal qualities and romantic mystery on the screen intermingled with her seclusion in private life. She retired 1941.

**García Lorca, Federico** Spanish poet. See ◊Lorca, Federico García.

**García Márquez, Gabriel (Gabo)** (1928–  ) Colombian novelist. His sweeping novel *Cien años de soledad/One Hundred Years of Solitude* (1967) (which tells the story of a family over a period of six generations) is an example of magic realism, a technique used to heighten the intensity of realistic portrayal of social and political issues by introducing grotesque or fanciful material. Nobel Prize for Literature 1982.

**gardenia** any of a group of subtropical and tropical trees and shrubs found in Africa and Asia, belonging to the madder family, with evergreen foliage and flattened rosettes of fragrant waxen-looking flowers, often white in colour. (Genus *Gardenia,* family Rubiaceae.)

**Garibaldi, Giuseppe** (1807–1882) Italian soldier who played a central role in the unification of Italy by conquering Sicily and Naples 1860. From 1834 a member of the nationalist Mazzini's Young Italy society, he was forced into exile until 1848 and again 1849–54. He fought against Austria 1848–49, 1859, and 1866, and led two unsuccessful expeditions to liberate Rome from papal rule in 1862 and 1867.

**Garland, Judy** stage name of Frances Gumm (1922–1969) US singer and actress. Her performances are marked by a compelling intensity. Her films include *The Wizard of Oz* (1939) (which featured the tune that was to become her theme song, 'Over the Rainbow'), *Babes in Arms* (1939), *Strike Up the Band* (1940), *Meet Me in St Louis* (1944), *Easter Parade* (1948), *A Star is Born* (1954), and *Judgment at Nuremberg* (1961).

**garlic** perennial Asian plant belonging to the lily family, whose strong-smelling and sharp-tasting bulb, made up of several small segments, or cloves, is used in cooking. The plant has white flowers. It is widely cultivated and has been used successfully as a fungicide in the cereal grass ◊sorghum. It also has antibacterial properties. (*Allium sativum*, family Liliaceae.)

**garnet** group of ◊silicate minerals with the formula $X_3Y_3(SiO_4)_3$, where $X$ is calcium, magnesium, iron, or manganese, and $Y$ is usually aluminium or sometimes iron or chromium. Garnets are used as semiprecious gems (usually pink to deep red) and as abrasives. They occur in metamorphic rocks such as gneiss and schist.

**Garrick, David** (1717–1779) English actor and theatre manager. From 1747 he became joint licensee of the Drury Lane Theatre, London, with his own company, and instituted a number of significant theatrical conventions including concealed stage lighting and banishing spectators from the stage. He played Shakespearean characters such as Richard III, King Lear, Hamlet, and Benedick, and collaborated with George Colman (1732–1794) in writing the play *The Clandestine Marriage* (1766). He retired from the stage in 1766, but continued as a manager.

**Garvey, Marcus (Moziah)** (1887–1940) Jamaican political thinker and activist, an early advocate of black nationalism. He led a Back to Africa movement for black Americans to establish a black-governed country in Africa. The Jamaican cult of ◊Rastafarianism is based largely on his ideas.

**gas** in physics, a form of matter, such as air, in which the molecules move randomly in otherwise empty space, filling any size or shape of container into which the gas is put.

**Gascony** ancient province of southwest France. With Guienne it formed the duchy of Aquitaine in the 12th century. Henry II of England gained possession of it through his marriage to Eleanor of Aquitaine in 1152, and it was often in English hands until 1451. Thereafter it was ruled by the king of France until it was united with the French royal domain in 1607 under Henry IV.

**Gaskell, Elizabeth** Cleghorn, born Stevenson (1810–1865) English novelist. Her most popular book, *Cranford* (1853), is the study of a small, close-knit circle in a small town, modelled on Knutsford, Cheshire, where she was brought up.

Her other books, which often deal with social concerns, include *Mary Barton* (1848), *North and South* (1855), *Sylvia's Lovers* (1863–64), and the unfinished *Wives and Daughters* (1866). She wrote a frank and sympathetic biography of her friend Charlotte ◊Brontë (1857).

**gas laws** physical laws concerning the behaviour of gases. They include ◊Boyle's law and ◊Charles's law, which are concerned with the relationships between the pressure, temperature, and volume of an ideal (hypothetical) gas. These two laws can be combined to give the *general* or *universal gas law*, which may be expressed as:

$$\frac{(\text{pressure} \times \text{volume})}{\text{temperature}} = \text{constant}$$

Van der Waals' law includes corrections for the nonideal behaviour of real gases.

**gastroenteritis** inflammation of the stomach and intestines, giving rise to abdominal pain, vomiting, and diarrhoea. It may be caused by food or other poisoning, allergy, or infection. Dehydration may be severe and it is a particular risk in infants.

**gastrolith** stone that was once part of the digestive system of a dinosaur or other extinct animal. Rock fragments were swallowed to assist in the grinding process in the dinosaur digestive tract, much as some birds now swallow grit and pebbles to grind food in their crop. Once the animal has decayed, smooth round stones remain – often the only clue to their past use is the fact that they are geologically different from their surrounding strata.

**gastropod** any member of a very large group of ◊molluscs (soft-bodied invertebrate animals). Gastropods have a single shell (in a spiral or modified spiral form) and eyes on stalks, and they move on a flattened, muscular foot. They have well-developed heads and rough, scraping tongues called radulae. Some are marine, some freshwater, and others land creatures, but they all tend to live in damp places. (Class Gastropoda.)

**gas turbine** engine in which burning fuel supplies hot gas to spin a ◊turbine. The most widespread application of gas turbines has been in aviation. All jet engines are modified gas turbines, and some locomotives and ships also use gas turbines as a power source.

They are also used in industry for generating and pumping purposes.

**GATT** acronym for ◊*General Agreement on Tariffs and Trade.*

**Gaudí, Antonio** (1852–1926) Spanish architect. He is distinguished for his flamboyant ◊Art Nouveau style. Gaudí worked mainly in Barcelona, designing both domestic and industrial buildings. He introduced colour, unusual materials, and audacious technical innovations. His spectacular Church of the Holy Family, Barcelona, begun 1883, is still under construction.

**Gaudier-Brzeska, Henri** born Henri Gaudier (1891–1915) French sculptor, active in London from 1911. He is regarded as one of the outstanding sculptors of his generation. He studied art in Bristol, Nuremberg, and Munich, and became a member of the English Vorticist movement, which sought to reflect the energy of the industrial age through an angular, semi-abstract style. His works include the portrait *Horace Brodsky* (1913; Tate Gallery, London); and *Birds Erect* (1914; Museum of Modern Art, New York).

**gauge boson** or *field particle*, any of the particles that carry the four fundamental forces of nature (see ◊forces, fundamental).

Gauge bosons are ◊elementary particles that cannot be subdivided, and include the photon, the graviton, the gluons, and the weakons.

**Gauguin, (Eugène Henri) Paul** (1848–1903) French Post-Impressionist painter. Going beyond the Impressionists' concern with ever-changing appearances, he developed a heavily symbolic and decorative style characterized by his sensuous use of pure colours. In his search for a more direct and intense experience of life, he moved to islands in the South Pacific, where he created many of his finest works. Among his paintings is *The Yellow Christ* (1889; Albright-Knox Art Gallery, Buffalo, New York State).

**Gaul** the Celtic-speaking peoples who inhabited France and Belgium in Roman times; also their territory. Certain Gauls invaded Italy around 400 BC, sacked Rome 387 BC, and settled between the Alps and the Apennines; this district, known as Cisalpine Gaul, was conquered by Rome in about 225 BC.

**Gaulle, Charles de** French politician, see Charles ◊de Gaulle.

**Gauteng** Sotho 'Place of Gold', province of the Republic of South Africa from 1994, known as Pretoria-Witwatersrand-Vereeniging before 1995, and historically part of the Transvaal
*area* 18,760 sq km/7,243 sq mi
*capital* Johannesburg
*towns and cities* Pretoria, Vereeniging, Krugersdorp, Benoni, Germiston
*features* Vaal River, Magaliesberg Mountains
*industries* gold mining, coal, iron and steel, uranium, chemicals, railway workshops, tobacco, maize
*population* (1995 est) 7,048,300
*languages* Afrikaans 20%, Zulu 18%, English 15%.

**Gaviria (Trujillo), César** (1947– ) Colombian Liberal Party politician, president 1990–94. He was finance minister 1986–87 and minister of government 1987–89. He supported a constitutional amendment that prohibited the extradition of Colombian citizens wanted in the USA for drug-related crimes and sought more US aid in return for stepping up the drug war.

**Gawain** in Arthurian legend, one of the knights of the Round Table who participated in the quest for the ◊Holy Grail. He is the hero of the 14th-century epic poem *Sir Gawayne and the Greene Knight*.

**Gay, John** (1685–1732) English poet and dramatist. He wrote *Trivia* (1716), a verse picture of 18th-century London. His *The Beggar's Opera* (1728), a 'Newgate pastoral' using traditional songs and telling of the love of Polly for highwayman Captain Macheath, was an extraordinarily popular success. Its satiric political touches led to the banning of *Polly*, a sequel. Bertolt Brecht (1898–1956) based his *Threepenny Opera* (1928) on the story of *The Beggar's Opera*.

**gay politics** political activity by homosexuals in pursuit of equal rights and an end to discrimination. A gay political movement first emerged in the late 1960s in New York with the founding of the Gay Liberation Front. It aimed to counter negative and critical attitudes to homosexuality and encouraged pride and solidarity among homosexuals.

**Gaza Strip** strip of land on the Mediterranean sea, 10 km/6 mi wide and 40 km/25 mi long, extending northeast from the Egyptian border; area 363 sq km/140 sq mi; population (1994) 724,500, mainly Palestinians, plus about 2,500 Israeli settlers. It was occupied by Israel from 1967 till 1994, when responsibility for its administration was transferred to the Palestine National Authority. The capital is Gaza; other main centres of population are Khan Yunis and Rafah. Agriculture is the main activity, producing citrus fruit, wheat, and olives. Prior to the great influx of Palestinian refugees in 1948 the area was rural, and is geographically part of the ◊Negev.

**gazelle** any of a number of lightly built, fast-running antelopes found on the open plains of Africa and southern Asia. (Especially species of the genus *Gazella*.)

**GCE** abbreviation for *General Certificate of Education,* in the UK, the public examination formerly taken at the age of 16 at Ordinary level (O level) and still taken at 18 at Advanced level (A level). The GCE O-level examination, aimed at the top 20% of the ability range, was superseded in 1988 by the General Certificate of Secondary Education (◊GCSE).

**GCSE** abbreviation for *General Certificate of Secondary Education,* in the UK, from 1988, the examination for 16-year-old pupils, superseding both GCE O level and CSE, and offering qualifications for up to 60% of school leavers in any particular subject.

**Gdańsk** German *Danzig*, Polish port; population (1993) 466,500. Oil is refined, and textiles, televisions, and fertilizers are produced. In the 1980s there were repeated antigovernment strikes at the Lenin shipyards; many were closed 1996.

**GDP** abbreviation for ◊*gross domestic product.*

**gear** toothed wheel that transmits the turning movement of one shaft to another shaft. Gear wheels may be used in pairs, or in threes if both shafts are to turn in the same direction. The gear ratio – the ratio of the number of teeth on the two wheels – determines the torque ratio, the turning force on the output shaft compared with the turning force on the input shaft. The ratio of the angular velocities of the shafts is the inverse of the gear ratio.

**Gebrselassie, Haile** (1973– ) Ethiopian long-distance runner who won the men's 10,000 metres gold medal at the 1996 Olympics and has also won three consecutive 10,000 metres world titles, 1993–97. Between 1994 and 1997 he broke the 5,000 metres world record three times, the 10,000 metres record twice, and in 1996 set world indoor records at 3,000 and 5,000 metres. On 25 January 1998 in Karlsruhe, Germany, he reduced his own 3,000 metres world record of 7 minutes 30.72 seconds set in Stuttgart on 4 February 1996 by over four and a half seconds with a time of 7 minutes 26.14 seconds. In June 1998 he regained the 5,000 and 10,000 metres world records he lost to the Kenyan runners Daniel Komen and Paul Tergat in 1997. At the World Championships in Seville, Spain, Gebrselassie won a fourth consecutive men's 10,000 metres gold medal.

*career highlights*
*Olympic Games* gold 10,000 metres 1996
*World Championships* 10,000 metres 1993, 1995, 1997, 1999
*Indoor World Championships* 1,500 metres 1999; 3,000 metres 1997, 1999.

**gecko** any of a group of lizards. Geckos are common worldwide in warm climates, and have large heads and short, stout bodies. Many have no eyelids. Their sticky toe pads enable them to climb vertically and walk upside down on smooth surfaces in their search for flies, spiders, and other prey. (Family Gekkonidae.)

**Geddes, Patrick** (1854–1932) Scottish town planner. He established the importance of surveys, research work, and properly planned 'diagnoses before treatment'. His major work is *City Development* (1904). His protégé was Lewis Mumford.

**Geiger counter** any of a number of devices used for detecting nuclear radiation and/or measuring its intensity by counting the number of ionizing particles produced (see ◊radioactivity). It detects the momentary current that passes between ◊electrodes in a suitable gas when a nuclear particle or a radiation pulse causes the ionization of that gas. The electrodes are connected to electronic devices that enable the number of particles passing to be measured. The increased frequency of measured particles indicates the intensity of radiation. The device is named after the German physicist Hans Geiger.

**Geingob, Hage Gottfried** (1941– ) Namibian politician, from 1990 the first prime minister of an independent Namibia. He played a major role in the South West Africa's People's Organization (SWAPO), as its representative in Botswana 1963–34, and as a petitioner to the United Nations 1964–71 to obtain international recognition for SWAPO. In 1975 he was the founding director of the UN Institute for Namibia in Lusaka, educating future administrators for an independent Namibia. In 1989 he returned to Namibia as the head of SWAPO's election campaign and played a leading role in drawing up the post-independence constitution.

**gel** solid produced by the formation of a three-dimensional cage structure, commonly of linked

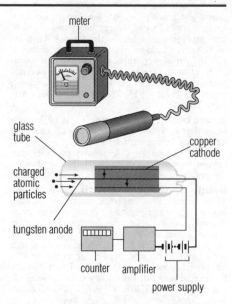

**Geiger counter** *A Geiger–Müller counter detects and measures ionizing radiation (alpha, beta, and gamma particles) emitted by radioactive materials. Any incoming radiation creates ions (charged particles) within the counter, which are accelerated by the anode and cathode to create a measurable electric current.*

large-molecular-mass polymers, in which a liquid is trapped. It is a form of ◊colloid. A gel may be a jellylike mass (pectin, gelatin) or have a more rigid structure (silica gel).

**gelatin** water-soluble protein prepared from boiled hide and bone, used in cookery to set jellies, and in glues and photographic emulsions.

**Gelderland** English *Guelders,* province of the east Netherlands, bounded on the southeast by Germany, on the southwest by the River Maas, and on the northwest by the IJsselmeer
*area* 5,020 sq km/1,938 sq mi
*capital* Arnhem
*towns and cities* Apeldoorn, Nijmegen, Ede
*physical* region of low hills (formed as moraine features of the Ice Age, maximum height about 100 m/328 ft) with heaths and woodlands; fertile lowlands crossed by the rivers Rhine, IJssel, Meuse, and Waal
*features* Veluwe, in the northwest, is a favourite holiday resort
*industries* textiles, electrical goods, paper
*agriculture* livestock, wheat, fruit, and vegetables
*population* (1997) 1,886,100
*history* in the Middle Ages Gelderland was divided into Upper Gelderland (Roermond in North Limburg) and Lower Gelderland (Nijmegen, Arnhem, Zutphen). These territories were inherited by Charles V of Spain in 1506, but when the revolt against Spanish rule reached a climax in 1579, Lower Gelderland joined the United Provinces of the Netherlands. Gelderland

was part of the former duchy of Gelderland, which was a Hapsburg possession but was divided at the beginning of the 19th century between Prussia and the Netherlands.

**gem** mineral valuable by virtue of its durability (hardness), rarity, and beauty, cut and polished for ornamental use, or engraved. Of 120 minerals known to have been used as gemstones, only about 25 are in common use in jewellery today; of these, the diamond, emerald, ruby, and sapphire are classified as precious, and all the others semiprecious; for example, the topaz, amethyst, opal, and aquamarine.

**Gemini** prominent zodiacal constellation in the northern hemisphere represented as the twins Castor and Pollux. Its brightest star is ◊Pollux; Castor is a system of six stars. The Sun passes through Gemini from late June to late July. Each December, the Geminid meteors radiate from Gemini. In astrology, the dates for Gemini are between about 21 May and 21 June (see ◊precession).

**gender** in grammar, one of the categories into which nouns are divided in many languages, such as masculine, feminine, and neuter (as in Latin, German, and Russian), masculine and feminine (as in French, Italian, and Spanish), or animate and inanimate (as in some American Indian languages).

**gene** unit of inherited material, encoded by a strand of ◊DNA and transcribed by ◊RNA. In higher organisms, genes are located on the ◊chromosomes. A gene consistently affects a particular character in an individual – for example, the gene for eye colour. Also termed a Mendelian gene, after Austrian biologist Gregor Mendel, it occurs at a particular point, or locus, on a particular chromosome and may have several variants, or ◊alleles, each specifying a particular form of that character – for example, the alleles for blue or brown eyes. Some alleles show ◊dominance. These mask the effect of other alleles, known as ◊recessive.

**gene bank** collection of seeds or other forms of genetic material, such as tubers, spores, bacterial or yeast cultures, live animals and plants, frozen sperm and eggs, or frozen embryos. These are stored for possible future use in agriculture, plant and animal breeding, or in medicine, genetic engineering, or the restocking of wild habitats where species have become extinct. Gene banks will be increasingly used as the rate of extinction grows, depleting the Earth's genetic variety (biodiversity).

**gene pool** total sum of ◊alleles (variants of ◊genes) possessed by all the members of a given population or species alive at a particular time.

**General Agreement on Tariffs and Trade** (GATT), organization within the United Nations founded in 1948 with the aim of encouraging ◊free trade between nations by reducing tariffs, subsidies, quotas, and regulations that discriminate against imported products. GATT was effectively replaced by the ◊World Trade Organization in January 1995.

**General Motors** the USA's largest company, a vehicle manufacturer founded in 1908 in Flint, Michigan, from a number of small carmakers; it went on to acquire many more companies, including those that produced the Oldsmobile, Pontiac, Cadillac, and Chevrolet. It has headquarters in Detroit, Michigan, and New York.

**general strike** refusal to work by employees in several key industries, with the intention of paralysing the economic life of a country. In British history, the General Strike was a nationwide strike called by the Trade Union Congress (TUC) on 3 May 1926 in support of striking miners. Elsewhere, the general strike was used as a political weapon by anarchists and others (see ◊syndicalism), especially in Spain and Italy. See also ◊strike.

**genet** any of several small, nocturnal, carnivorous mammals belonging to the mongoose and civet family. Most species live in Africa, but the common genet *G. genetta* is also found in Europe and the Middle East. It is about 50 cm/1.6 ft long with a 45 cm/1.5 ft tail, weighs up to 2 kg/4.4 lb, with the male slightly larger than the female, and is greyish yellow in colour with rows of black spots. It is a good climber. Females have up to four young that begin to fend for themselves after about the age of four months. (Genus *Genetta,* family Viverridae.)

**gene therapy** medical technique for curing or alleviating inherited diseases or defects, certain infections, and several kinds of cancer in which affected cells from a sufferer would be removed from the body, the ◊DNA repaired in the laboratory (◊genetic engineering), and the functioning cells reintroduced. In 1990 a genetically engineered gene was used for the first time to treat a patient.

**genetically modified foods** or *GM foods,* foods produced using genetic engineering technology. Individual genes can be copied or transferred from one living organism to another, to incorporate specific characteristics into the organism or remove undesirable characteristics. The technology, developed in the 1980s, may be used, for example, to produce crops with higher yields, enhanced taste, resistance to pests, or a longer growing season. The first genetically modified food, the 'Flavr Savr' tomato, went on sale in the USA in 1994. Genetically modified ingredients appearing in foods on the market today include tomatoes, soya, and maize.

**genetic code** the way in which instructions for building proteins, the basic structural molecules of living matter, are 'written' in the genetic material ◊DNA. This relationship between the sequence of bases (the subunits in a DNA molecule) and the sequence of ◊amino acids (the subunits of a protein molecule) is the basis of heredity. The code employs codons of three bases each; it is the same in almost all organisms, except for a few minor differences recently discovered in some protozoa.

**genetic engineering** deliberate manipulation of genetic material by biochemical techniques. It is often achieved by the introduction of new ◊DNA, usually by means of a virus or ◊plasmid. This can be for pure research, ◊gene therapy, or to breed functionally specific plants, animals, or bacteria. These organisms with a foreign gene added are said to be transgenic. In 1999 the UK Department of the Environment initiated a four-year study to assess the risk to nature from genetically engineered crops.

**genetic fingerprinting** or *genetic profiling*, technique developed in the UK by Professor Alec Jeffreys (1950–    ), and now allowed as a means of legal identification. It determines the pattern of certain parts of the genetic material ◊DNA that is unique to each individual. Like conventional fingerprinting, it can accurately distinguish humans from one another, with the exception of identical siblings from multiple births. It can be applied to as little material as a single cell.

**genetics** branch of biology concerned with the study of ◊heredity and variation; it attempts to explain how characteristics of living organisms are passed on from one generation to the next. The science of genetics is based on the work of Austrian biologist Gregor Mendel whose experiments with the cross-breeding (hybridization) of peas showed that the inheritance of characteristics and traits takes place by means of discrete 'particles' (◊genes). These are present in the cells of all organisms, and are now recognized as being the basic units of heredity. All organisms possess ◊genotypes (sets of variable genes) and ◊phenotypes (characteristics produced by certain genes). Modern geneticists investigate the structure, function, and transmission of genes.

**genetic screening** in medicine, the study of the genetic make-up of an individual to determine if he or she is at risk of developing a hereditary disease later in life. Genetic screening can also be used to determine if an individual is a carrier for a particular genetic disease and, hence, can pass the disease on to any children. Genetic counselling should be undertaken at the same time as genetic screening of affected individuals. Diseases that can be screened for include cystic fibrosis, Huntington's chorea, and certain forms of cancer.

**Geneva** French *Genève*, city in Switzerland, capital of Geneva canton, on the southwestern shore of ◊Lake Geneva; population (1994 est) 174,400. It is a point of convergence of natural routes and is a cultural and commercial centre. Industries include the manufacture of watches, scientific and optical instruments, foodstuffs, jewellery, and musical boxes. CERN, the particle physics research organization, is here, as are the headquarters of the International Red Cross and the World Health Organization. The United Nations has its second-largest office (after New York) in Geneva.

**Geneva Convention** international agreement 1864 regulating the treatment of those wounded in war, and later extended to cover the types of weapons allowed, the treatment of prisoners and the sick, and the protection of civil-ians in wartime. The rules were revised at conventions held 1906, 1929, and 1949, and by the 1977 Additional Protocols.

**Geneva, Lake** French *Lac Léman*, German *Genfersee*, largest of the central European lakes, between Switzerland and France; area 580 sq km/225 sq mi. The main part of the lake lies in western Switzerland. It is in the shape of a crescent 72 km/45 mi long and 13 km/8 mi wide.

**Genghis Khan** also known as Chingiz Khan, (Greek 'World Conqueror') (c. 1155–1227) Mongol conqueror, ruler of all Mongol peoples from 1206. He conquered the empires of northern China 1211–15 and Khwarazm 1219–21, and invaded northern India in 1221, while his lieutenants advanced as far as the Crimea. When he died, his empire ranged from the Yellow Sea to the Black Sea; it continued to expand after his death to extend from Hungary to Korea. Genghis Khan controlled probably a larger area than any other individual in history. He was not only a great military leader, but the creator of a stable political system.

**Genoa** Italian *Genova;* ancient *Genua,* historic city in northwest Italy, capital of Liguria, on the Gulf of Genoa, 400 km/249 mi northwest of Rome; population (1992) 667,600. It is Italy's largest port, with a major container port facility at Voltri, 10 km/6 mi to the west. Industries include oil-refining, chemicals, engineering, and the manufacture of textiles.

**genocide** deliberate and systematic destruction of a national, racial, religious, or ethnic group defined by the exterminators as undesirable. The term is commonly applied to the policies of the Nazis during World War II (what they called the 'final solution' – the extermination of all 'undesirables' in occupied Europe, particularly the Jews). See ◊Holocaust.

**genome** the full complement of ◊genes carried by a single (haploid) set of ◊chromosomes. The term may be applied to the genetic information carried by an individual or to the range of genes found in a given species. The human genome is made up of approximately 100,000 genes (though there may be as many as 140,000 according to a 1999 estimate as a deriving from the ◊Human Genome Project).

**genotype** particular set of ◊alleles (variants of genes) possessed by a given organism. The term is usually used in conjunction with ◊phenotype, which is the product of the genotype and all environmental effects. See also ◊nature–nurture controversy.

**genre** a particular kind of work within an art form, differentiated by its structure, content, or style. For instance, the novel is a literary genre and the historical novel is a genre of the novel. The Western is a genre of film, and the symphonic poem is a musical genre.

**Gentile da Fabriano** born *Niccolo di Giovanni di Massio* (c. 1370–c. 1427) Italian painter of frescoes and altarpieces who worked in a gothic style uninfluenced by the fashions of contemporary Florence. Gentile was active in Venice, Florence, Siena, Orvieto, and Rome and collaborated with the artists Pisanello and Jacopo Bellini. His *Adoration of the Magi* (1423; Uffizi, Florence) painted for the church of Santa Trinità in Florence is typically rich in detail and colour.

**genus** plural *genera,* group of ◊species with many characteristics in common.

Thus all doglike species (including dogs, wolves, and jackals) belong to the genus *Canis* (Latin 'dog').

Species of the same genus are thought to be descended from a common ancestor species. Related genera are grouped into ◊families.

**geochronology** the branch of geology that deals with the dating of the Earth by studying its rocks and contained fossils. The ◊geological time chart is a result of these studies. Absolute dating methods involve the measurement of radioactive decay over time in certain chemical elements found in rocks, whereas relative dating methods establish the sequence of deposition of various rock layers by identifying and comparing their contained fossils.

**Geoffrey of Monmouth** (*c.* 1100–1154) Welsh writer and chronicler. While a canon at Oxford, he wrote *Historia Regum Britanniae/ History of the Kings of Britain* (*c.* 1139), which included accounts of the semi-legendary kings Lear, Cymbeline, and Arthur. He is also thought by some to be the author of *Vita Merlini,* a life of the legendary wizard. He was bishop-elect of St Asaph, North Wales, in 1151 and ordained a priest in 1152.

**geography** the study of the Earth's surface; its topography, climate, and physical conditions, and how these factors affect people and society. It is usually divided into *physical geography,* dealing with landforms and climates, and *human geography,* dealing with the distribution and activities of peoples on Earth.

**geological time** time scale embracing the history of the Earth from its physical origin to the present day. Geological time is traditionally divided into eons (Archaean or Archaeozoic, Proterozoic, and Phanerozoic in ascending chronological order), which in turn are subdivided into eras, periods, epochs, ages, and finally chrons.

**geology** science of the Earth, its origin, composition, structure, and history. It is divided into several branches: *mineralogy* (the minerals of Earth), *petrology* (rocks), *stratigraphy* (the deposition of successive beds of sedimentary rocks), *palaeontology* (fossils), and *tectonics* (the deformation and movement of the Earth's crust).

**geometry** branch of mathematics concerned with the properties of space, usually in terms of plane (two-dimensional) and solid (three-dimensional) figures. The subject is usually divided into *pure geometry,* which embraces roughly the plane and solid geometry dealt with in Greek mathematician ◊Euclid's *Stoicheia/Elements,* and *analytical* or ◊*coordinate geometry,* in which problems are solved using algebraic methods. A third, quite distinct, type includes the non-Euclidean geometries.

**George** six kings of Great Britain:

**George I** (1660–1727) King of Great Britain and Ireland from 1714. He was the son of the first elector of Hanover, Ernest Augustus (1629–1698), and his wife Sophia, and a great-grandson of James I. He succeeded to the electorate in 1698, and became king on the death of Queen Anne. He attached himself to the Whigs, and spent most of his reign in Hanover, never having learned English.

**George II** (1683–1760) King of Great Britain and Ireland from 1727, when he succeeded his father, George I. He was accused, with his minister John Carteret, of favouring Hanover at the expense of Britain's interest in the War of the Austrian Succession; his victory at Dettingen in 1743 was the last battle to be commanded by a British king. He married Caroline of Anspach in 1705, and was succeeded by his grandson, George III.

**George III** (1738–1820) King of Great Britain and Ireland from 1760, when he succeeded his grandfather George II. His rule was marked by intransigence resulting in the loss of the American colonies, for which he shared the blame with his chief minister Lord North, and the emancipation of Catholics in England. Possibly suffering from porphyria, he had repeated attacks of insanity, permanent from 1811. He was succeeded by his son George IV.

**George IV** (1762–1830) King of Great Britain and Ireland from 1820, when he succeeded his father George III, for whom he had been regent during the king's period of insanity 1811–20. In 1785 he secretly married a Catholic widow, Maria Fitzherbert, but in 1795 also married Princess ◊Caroline of Brunswick, in return for payment of his debts. He was a patron of the arts. His prestige was undermined by his treatment of Caroline (they separated in 1796), his dissipation, and his extravagance. He was succeeded by his brother, the duke of Clarence, who became William IV.

**George V** (1865–1936) King of Great Britain and Northern Ireland from 1910, when he succeeded his father Edward VII. He was the second son, and became heir in 1892 on the death of his elder brother Albert, Duke of Clarence. In 1893, he married Princess Victoria Mary of Teck (Queen Mary), formerly engaged to his brother. During World War I he made several visits to the front. In 1917, he abandoned all German titles for himself and his family. The name of the royal house was changed from Saxe-Coburg-Gotha (popularly known as Brunswick or Hanover) to Windsor.

**George VI** (1895–1952) King of Great Britain and Northern Ireland from 1936, when he succeeded after the abdication of his brother Edward VIII, who had succeeded their father George V. Created Duke of York in 1920, he married in 1923 Lady Elizabeth Bowes-Lyon (1900–  ), and their children are Elizabeth II and Princess Margaret. During World War II, he visited the Normandy and Italian battlefields.

**George** two kings of Greece, including:

**George II** (1890–1947) King of Greece 1922–23 and 1935–47. He became king on the expulsion of his father Constantine I 1922 but was himself overthrown 1923. Restored by the military 1935, he set up a dictatorship under Joannis Metaxas, and went into exile during the German occupation 1941–45.

**George, St** (died *c.* 303) Patron saint of England. The story of St George rescuing a woman by slaying a dragon, evidently derived from the Greek Perseus legend, first appears in the 6th century. The cult of St George was introduced into western Europe by the Crusaders. His feast day is 23 April.

**Georgetown** capital and main port of Guyana, situated on the east bank of the Demerara River at its mouth on the Atlantic coast; population (1992) 200,000. There are food processing and shrimp fishing industries. Principal exports include sugar, bauxite, and rice.

**George Town** or *Penang*, chief port of the Federation of Malaysia, and capital of Penang, on the island of Penang; population (1991) 219,000. It produces textiles and toys.

**Georgia** Republic of

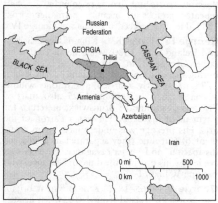

**area** 69,700 sq km/26,911 sq mi
**capital** Tbilisi
**major towns/cities** Kutaisi, Rustavi, Batumi, Sukhumi
**physical features** largely mountainous with a variety of landscape from the subtropical Black Sea shores to the ice and snow of the crest line of the Caucasus; chief rivers are Kura and Rioni
**head of state** Eduard Shevardnadze from 1992
**head of government** Otar Patsatsia from 1993
**political system** transitional
**political parties** Citizens' Union of Georgia (CUG), nationalist, pro-Shevardnadze; National Democratic Party of Georgia (NDPG), nationalist; Round Table/Free Georgia Bloc, nationalist; Georgian Popular Front (GPF), moderate nationalist, prodemocratization; Georgian Communist Party (GCP); National Independence Party (NIP), ultranationalist; Front for the Reinstatement of Legitimate Power

in Georgia, strong nationalist
**currency** lari
**GNP per capita (PPP)** (US$) 2,620 (1998 est)
**exports** metal products, machinery, tea, beverages, food and tobacco products. Principal market: Russia 27.4% (1997)
**population** 5,005,000 (1999 est)
**language** Georgian
**religion** Georgian Orthodox, also Muslim
**life expectancy** 69 (men); 77 (women) (1995–2000)
**Chronology**
**4th century BC** Georgian kingdom founded.
**1st century BC** Part of Roman Empire.
**AD 337** Christianity adopted.
**458** Tbilisi founded by King Vakhtang Gorgasal.
**mid-7th century** Tbilisi brought under Arab rule and renamed Tiflis.
**1121** Tbilisi liberated by King David II the Builder, of the Gagrationi dynasty, which traced its ancestry to the biblical King David. An empire was established across the Caucasus region, remaining powerful until Mongol onslaughts in the 13th and 14th centuries.
**1555** Western Georgia fell to Turkey and Eastern Georgia to Persia (Iran).
**1783** Treaty of Georgievsk established Russian dominance over Georgia.
**1804–13** First Russo-Iranian war fought largely over Georgia.
**late 19th century** Abolition of serfdom and beginnings of industrialization, but Georgian church suppressed.
**1918** Independence established after Russian Revolution.
**1921** Invaded by Red Army; Soviet republic established.
**1922–36** Linked with Armenia and Azerbaijan as the Transcaucasian Federation.
**1930s** Rapid industrial development, but resistance to agricultural collectivization and violent political purges instituted by the Georgian Soviet dictator Joseph Stalin.
**1936** Became separate republic within the USSR.
**early 1940s** 200,000 Meskhetians deported from southern Georgia to Central Asia on Stalin's orders.
**1972** Drive against endemic corruption launched by new Georgian Communist Party (GCP) leader Eduard Shevardnadze.
**1977** Initiative Group for the Defence of Human Rights formed by Zviad Gamsakhurdia, a nationalist intellectual.
**1978** Violent demonstrations by nationalists in Tbilisi.
**1981–88** Increasing demands for autonomy were encouraged from 1986 by the *glasnost* initiative of the reformist Soviet leader Mikhail Gorbachev.
**1989** The formation of the nationalist Georgian Popular Front led the minority Abkhazian and Ossetian communities in northwest and central-north Georgia to demand secession, provoking interethnic clashes. A state of emergency was imposed in Abkhazia; 20 pro-independence demonstrators were killed in Tbilisi by Soviet troops; Georgian sovereignty was declared by parliament.

**1990** A nationalist coalition triumphed in elections and Gamsakhurdia became president. The GCP seceded from the Communist Party of the USSR.

**1991** Independence was declared. The GCP was outlawed and all relations with the USSR severed. Demonstrations were held against the increasingly dictatorial Gamsakhurdia; a state of emergency was declared. Georgia failed to join the new Commonwealth of Independent States (CIS) as civil war raged.

**1992** Gamsakhurdia fled to Armenia; Shevardnadze, with military backing, was appointed interim president. Georgia was admitted into the United Nations (UN). Clashes continued in South Ossetia and Abkhazia, where independence had been declared.

**1993** The conflict with Abkhazi separatists intensified, forcing Shevardnadze to seek Russian military help. A pro-Gamsakhurdia revolt was put down by government forces and Gamsakhurdia died.

**1994** Georgia joined the CIS. A military cooperation pact was signed with Russia. A ceasefire was agreed with the Abkhazi separatists; 2,500 Russian peacekeeping troops were deployed in the region and paramilitary groups disarmed. Inflation exceeded 5,000% per annum.

**1995** Shevardnadze survived an assassination attempt and was re-elected; a privatization programme was launched.

**1996** A cooperation pact with the European Union (EU) was signed as economic growth resumed and monthly inflation fell to below 3%. Elections to the secessionist Abkhazi parliament were declared illegal by the Georgian government.

**1997** A new opposition party, Front for the Reinstatement of Legitimate Power in Georgia, was formed. There were talks between the government and the breakaway Abkhazi government.

**1998** Shevardnadze survived another assassination attempt. There was another outbreak of fighting in Abkhazia.

**Georgia** state in southeastern USA. It is nicknamed the Empire State of the South or the Peach State. Georgia ratified the US Constitution in 1788, becoming the 4th state to join the Union. Historically it was a cotton-producing state associated with slavery; as the birthplace of Martin Luther King, Jr, it also has strong links with the history of the civil-rights movement. Georgia is bordered to the northeast by South Carolina, to the north by North Carolina and Tennessee, to the west by Alabama, and to the south by Florida. In the southeast, Georgia has a coastline some 145 km/90 mi long on the Atlantic, off which are many of the Sea Islands

*population* (1996 est) 7,353,000
*area* 152,600 sq km/58,904 sq mi
*capital* Atlanta
*towns and cities* Columbus, Savannah, Macon, Albany
*industries and products* poultry, livestock, tobacco, maize, peanuts, cotton, soybeans, china clay, crushed granite, marble, clothing and

textiles, carpets, aircraft, paper products, lumber, turpentine, finance sector, tourism.

**Georgian** period of English architecture, furniture making, and decorative art between 1714 and 1830. The architecture is mainly Classical in style, although external details and interiors were often rich in ◊Rococo carving. Furniture was frequently made of mahogany and satinwood, and mass production became increasingly common; designers included Thomas Chippendale, George Hepplewhite, and Thomas Sheraton. The silver of this period is particularly fine, and ranges from the earlier, simple forms to the ornate, and from the Neo-Classical style of Robert Adam to the later, more decorated pre-Victorian taste.

**geostationary orbit** circular path 35,900 km/22,300 mi above the Earth's Equator on which a ◊satellite takes 24 hours, moving from west to east, to complete an orbit, thus appearing to hang stationary over one place on the Earth's surface. Geostationary orbits are used particularly for communications satellites and weather satellites. They were first thought of by the author Arthur C Clarke. A *geosynchronous orbit* lies at the same distance from Earth but is inclined to the Equator.

**geothermal energy** energy extracted for heating and electricity generation from natural steam, hot water, or hot dry rocks in the Earth's crust. Water is pumped down through an injection well where it passes through joints in the hot rocks. It rises to the surface through a recovery well and may be converted to steam or run through a heat exchanger. Dry steam may be directed through turbines to produce electricity. It is an important source of energy in volcanically active areas such as Iceland and New Zealand.

**geranium** any of a group of plants either having divided leaves and white, pink, or purple flowers (geraniums), or having a hairy stem, and white, pink, red, or black-purple flowers (◊pelargoniums). Some geraniums are also called ◊cranesbill. (Genera *Geranium* and *Pelargonium*, family Geraniaceae.)

**gerbil** any of numerous rodents with elongated back legs, good at hopping or jumping. Gerbils range from mouse- to rat-size, and have hairy tails. Many of the 13 genera live in dry, sandy, or sparsely vegetated areas of Africa and Asia. (Family Cricetidae.)

**Géricault, (Jean Louis André) Théodore** (1791–1824) French painter and graphic artist. One of the main figures of the Romantic movement, he brought a new energy and emotional intensity to painting. His subjects included spirited horses, Napoleonic cavalry officers, and portraits, including remarkable studies of the insane, such as *A Kleptomaniac* (1822–23; Musée des Beaux Arts, Ghent). His *The Raft of the Medusa* (1819; Louvre, Paris), a vast history piece, was notorious in its day for its grim depiction of a recent scandal in which shipwrecked sailors had turned to murder and cannibalism in order to survive.

**germ** colloquial term for a micro-organism that causes disease, such as certain ◊bacteria and ◊viruses. Formerly, it was also used to mean something capable of developing into a complete organism (such as a fertilized egg, or the ◊embryo of a seed).

**Germanic languages** branch of the Indo-European language family, divided into *East Germanic* (Gothic, now extinct), *North Germanic* (Danish, Faroese, Icelandic, Norwegian, Swedish), and *West Germanic* (Afrikaans, Dutch, English, Flemish, Frisian, German, Yiddish).

**germanium** brittle, grey-white, weakly metallic (metalloid) element, symbol Ge, atomic number 32, relative atomic mass 72.6. It belongs to the silicon group, and has chemical and physical properties between those of silicon and tin. Germanium is a semiconductor material and is used in the manufacture of transistors and integrated circuits. The oxide is transparent to infrared radiation, and is used in military applications. It was discovered in 1886 by German chemist Clemens Winkler (1838–1904).

**German measles** or *rubella*, mild, communicable virus disease, usually caught by children. It is marked by a sore throat, pinkish rash, and slight fever, and has an incubation period of two to three weeks. If a woman contracts it in the first three months of pregnancy, it may cause serious damage to the unborn child.

**German shepherd** or *Alsatian*, breed of dog. It is about 63 cm/25 in tall and has a wolflike appearance, a thick coat with many varieties of colouring, and a distinctive way of moving. German shepherds are used as police dogs because of their courage and intelligence.

**Germany** Federal Republic of
*national name* *Bundesrepublik Deutschland*

*area* 357,041 sq km/137,853 sq mi
*capital* Berlin (government offices moving in phases from Bonn back to Berlin)
*major towns/cities* Cologne, Hamburg, Munich, Essen, Frankfurt am Main, Dortmund, Stuttgart, Düsseldorf, Leipzig, Dresden, Bremen, Duisburg, Hannover
*major ports* Hamburg, Kiel, Bremerhaven, Rostock
*physical features* flat in north, mountainous in south with Alps; rivers Rhine, Weser, Elbe flow north, Danube flows southeast, Oder and Neisse flow north along Polish frontier; many lakes, including Müritz; Black Forest, Harz Mountains, Erzgebirge (Ore Mountains), Bavarian Alps, Fichtelgebirge, Thüringer Forest
*head of state* Johannes Rau from 1999
*head of government* Gerhard Schroeder from 1998
*political system* liberal democratic federal republic
*political parties* Christian Democratic Union (CDU), right of centre, 'social market'; Christian Social Union (CSU), right of centre; Social Democratic Party (SPD), left of centre; Free Democratic Party (FDP), liberal; Greens, environmentalist; Party of Democratic Socialism (PDS), reform-socialist (formerly Socialist Unity Party: SED); German People's Union (DVU), far-right
*currency* Deutschmark
*GNP per capita (PPP)* (US$) 20,810 (1998)
*exports* road vehicles, electrical machinery, metals and metal products, textiles, chemicals. Principal market: France 11.7% (1998)
*population* 82,177,000 (1999 est)
*language* German
*religion* Protestant (mainly Lutheran) 43%, Roman Catholic 36%
*life expectancy* 74 (men); 80 (women) (1995–2000)
*Chronology*
*c. 1000 BC* Germanic tribes from Scandinavia began to settle the region between the rivers Rhine, Elbe, and Danube.
*AD 9* Romans tried and failed to conquer Germanic tribes.
*5th century* Germanic tribes plundered Rome, overran western Europe, and divided it into tribal kingdoms.
*496* Clovis, King of the Franks, conquered the Alemanni tribe of western Germany.
*772–804* After series of fierce wars, Charlemagne extended Frankish authority over Germany, subjugated Saxons, imposed Christianity, and took title of Holy Roman Emperor.
*843* Treaty of Verdun divided the Holy Roman Empire into three, with eastern portion corresponding to modern Germany; local princes became virtually independent.
*919* Henry the Fowler restored central authority and founded Saxon dynasty.
*962* Otto the Great enlarged the kingdom and revived title of Holy Roman Emperor.
*1024–1254* Emperors of Salian and Hohenstaufen dynasties came into conflict with popes; frequent civil wars allowed German princes to regain independence.
*12th century* German expansion eastwards into lands between rivers Elbe and Oder.
*13th–14th centuries* Hanseatic League of Allied German cities became a great commercial and naval power.

**1438** Title of Holy Roman Emperor became virtually hereditary in the Habsburg family of Austria.

**1517** Martin Luther began the Reformation; Emperor Charles V tried to suppress Protestantism; civil war ensued.

**1555** Peace of Augsburg: Charles V forced to accept that each German prince could choose religion of his own lands.

**1618–48** Thirty Years' War: bitter conflict, partly religious, between certain German princes and emperor, with foreign intervention; the war wrecked the German economy and reduced the Holy Roman Empire to a name.

**1701** Frederick I, Elector of Brandenburg, promoted to King of Prussia.

**1740** Frederick the Great of Prussia seized Silesia from Austria and retained it through war of Austrian Succession (1740–48) and Seven Years' War (1756–63).

**1772–95** Prussia joined Russia and Austria in the partition of Poland.

**1792** Start of French Revolutionary Wars, involving many German states, with much fighting on German soil.

**1806** Holy Roman Empire abolished; France formed puppet Confederation of the Rhine in western Germany and defeated Prussia at Battle of Jena.

**1813–15** National revival enabled Prussia to take part in defeat of Napoleon at Battles of Leipzig and Waterloo.

**1814–15** Congress of Vienna rewarded Prussia with Rhineland, Westphalia, and much of Saxony; loose German Confederation formed by 39 independent states.

**1848–49** Liberal revolutions in many German states; Frankfurt Assembly sought German unity; revolutions suppressed.

**1862** Otto von Bismarck became prime minister of Prussia.

**1866** Seven Weeks' War: Prussia defeated Austria, dissolved German Confederation, and established North German Confederation under Prussian leadership.

**1870–71** Franco-Prussian War; southern German states agreed to German unification; German Empire proclaimed, with King of Prussia as emperor and Bismarck as chancellor.

**1890** Wilhelm II dismissed Bismarck and sought to make Germany a leading power in world politics.

**1914** Germany encouraged Austrian attack on Serbia that started World War I; Germany invaded Belgium and France.

**1918** Germany defeated; revolution overthrew monarchy.

**1919** Treaty of Versailles: Germany lost land to France, Denmark, and Poland; demilitarization and reparations imposed; Weimar Republic proclaimed.

**1922–23** Hyperinflation: in 1922, one dollar was worth 50 marks; in 1923, one dollar was worth 2.5 trillion marks.

**1929** Start of economic slump caused mass unemployment and brought Germany close to revolution.

**1933** Adolf Hitler, leader of Nazi Party, became chancellor.

**1934** Hitler took title of *Führer* (leader), murdered rivals, and created one-party state with militaristic and racist ideology; rearmament reduced unemployment.

**1938** Germany annexed Austria and Sudeten; occupied remainder of Czechoslovakia in 1939.

**1939** German invasion of Poland started World War II; Germany defeated France in 1940, attacked USSR in 1941, and pursued extermination of Jews.

**1945** Germany defeated and deprived of its conquests; eastern lands transferred to Poland; USA, USSR, UK, and France established zones of occupation.

**1948–49** Disputes between Western allies and USSR led to Soviet blockade of West Berlin.

**1949** Partition of Germany: US, French, and British zones in West Germany became Federal Republic of Germany with Konrad Adenauer as chancellor; Soviet zone in East Germany became communist German Democratic Republic led by Walter Ulbricht.

**1953** Uprising in East Berlin suppressed by Soviet troops.

**1955** West Germany became a member of NATO; East Germany joined Warsaw Pact.

**1957** West Germany was a founder member of the European Economic Community.

**1960s** 'Economic miracle': West Germany achieved rapid growth and great prosperity.

**1961** East Germany constructed Berlin Wall to prevent emigration to West Berlin (part of West Germany).

**1969** Willy Brandt, Social Democratic Party chancellor of West Germany, sought better relations with USSR and East Germany.

**1971** Erich Honecker succeeded Ulbricht as Communist Party leader, and became head of state in 1976.

**1972** The Basic Treaty established relations between West Germany and East Germany as between foreign states.

**1982** Helmut Kohl (Christian Democratic Union) became the West German chancellor.

**1989** There was a mass exodus of East Germans to West Germany via Hungary; Honecker was replaced; East Germany opened its frontiers, including the Berlin Wall.

**1990** The communist regime in East Germany collapsed; Germany was reunified with Kohl as chancellor.

**1991** Germany took the lead in pressing for closer European integration in the Maastricht Treaty.

**1995** Unemployment reached 3.8 million.

**1996** There was a public-sector labour dispute over welfare reform plans and the worsening economy. Spending cuts were agreed to meet European Monetary Union entry criteria.

**1997** Unemployment continued to rise. The SPD polled badly in local elections.

**1998** Unemployment reached a post-war high of 12.6%. The CDU–CSU–FDP coalition was defeated in a general election and a 'Red–Green' coalition government was formed by the SPD and the Greens, with Gerhard Schroeder as chancellor. Kohl was replaced as CDU leader by Wolfgang Schäuble.

**1999** A delay was announced in the planned

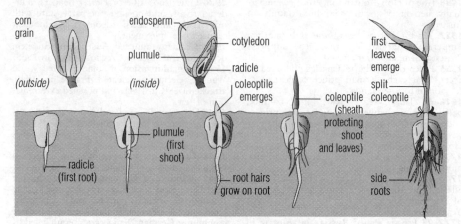

**germination** *The germination of a corn grain. The plumule and radicle emerge from the seed coat and begin to grow into a new plant. The coleoptile protects the emerging bud and the first leaves.*

phasing out of nuclear power. Social Democrat Johannes Rau was elected president.

**Germany, East** German Democratic Republic, GDR, country 1949–90, formed from the Soviet zone of occupation in the partition of Germany following World War II. East Germany became a sovereign state in 1954, and was reunified with West Germany in October 1990.

**Germany, West** Federal Republic of Germany, FRG, country 1949–90, formed from the British, US, and French occupation zones in the partition of Germany following World War II; reunified with East Germany in October 1990.

**germination** in botany, the initial stages of growth in a seed, spore, or pollen grain. Seeds germinate when they are exposed to favourable external conditions of moisture, light, and temperature, and when any factors causing dormancy have been removed.

**Gershwin, George** born Jacob (1898–1937) US composer. His musical comedies, mostly to lyrics by his brother *Ira Gershwin* (1896–1983), were among Broadway's most successful in the 1920s and 1930s, including *Strike up the Band* (1927), *Funny Face* (1927), and *Girl Crazy* (1930). He also wrote concert works including the tone poems *Rhapsody in Blue* (1924) and *An American in Paris* (1928). His opera *Porgy and Bess* (1935) incorporated jazz rhythms and popular song styles in an operatic format.

**Gestapo** (contraction of *Geheime Staatspolizei*) Nazi Germany's secret police, formed 1933, and under the direction of Heinrich ◊Himmler from 1934.

**gestation** in all mammals except the ◊monotremes (platypus and spiny anteaters), the period from the time of implantation of the embryo in the uterus to birth. This period varies among species; in humans it is about 266 days, in elephants 18–22 months, in cats about 60 days, and in some species of marsupial (such as opossum) as short as 12 days.

**Gethsemane** site of the garden where Judas Iscariot, according to the New Testament, betrayed Jesus. It is on the Mount of Olives, in east Jerusalem. When Jerusalem was divided between Israel and Jordan in 1948, Gethsemane fell within Jordanian territory.

**Getty, J(ean) Paul** (1892–1976) US oil billionaire, president of the Getty Oil Company from 1947, and founder of the Getty Museum (housing the world's highest-funded art collections) in Malibu, California.

**Gettysburg** site of one of the decisive battles of the American ◊Civil War: a Confederate defeat by Union forces 1–3 July 1863, at Gettysburg, Pennsylvania, 80 km/50 mi northwest of Baltimore. The site is now a national cemetery, at the dedication of which President Lincoln delivered the *Gettysburg Address* 19 November 1863, a speech in which he reiterated the principles of freedom, equality, and democracy embodied in the US Constitution.

**geyser** natural spring that intermittently discharges an explosive column of steam and hot water into the air due to the build-up of steam in underground chambers. One of the most remarkable geysers is Old Faithful, in Yellowstone National Park, Wyoming, USA. Geysers also occur in New Zealand and Iceland.

**g-force** force that pilots and astronauts experience when their craft accelerate or decelerate rapidly. One *g* is the ordinary pull of gravity.

Early astronauts were subjected to launch and reentry forces of up to six *g* or more; in the space shuttle, more than three *g* is experienced on liftoff. Pilots and astronauts wear *g*-suits that prevent their blood pooling too much under severe *g*-forces, which can lead to unconsciousness.

**Ghana** Republic of (formerly the *Gold Coast*)
*area* 238,305 sq km/92,009 sq mi
*capital* Accra
*major towns/cities* Kumasi, Tamale, Tema, Sekondi-Takoradi, Cape Coast, Sunyani, Koforidua, Ho, Yendi, Tarkwa, Wa, Bolgatanga

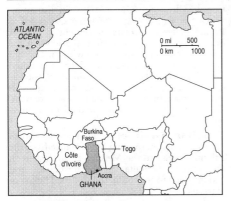

**major ports** Sekondi, Tema
**physical features** mostly tropical lowland plains; bisected by River Volta
**head of state and government** Jerry Rawlings from 1981
**political system** emergent democracy
**political parties** National Democratic Congress (NDC), centrist, progovernment; New Patriotic Party (NPP), left of centre
**currency** cedi
**GNP per capita (PPP)** (US$) 1,610 (1998 est)
**exports** gold, cocoa and related products, timber. Principal market: Togo 13% (1997)
**population** 19,678,000 (1999 est)
**language** English (official) and African languages
**religion** Christian 62%, Muslim 16%, animist
**life expectancy** 58 (men); 62 (women) (1995–2000)
**Chronology**
**5th–12th century** Ghana Empire (from which present-day country's name derives) flourished, with its centre 800 km/500 mi to the northwest, in Mali.
**13th century** In coastal and forest areas Akan peoples founded first states.
**15th century** Gold-seeking Mande traders entered northern Ghana from the northeast, founding Dagomba and Mamprussi states; Portuguese navigators visited coastal region, naming it the 'Gold Coast', building a fort at Elmina, and slave trading began.
**17th century** Gonja kingdom founded in north by Mande speakers; Ga and Ewe states founded in southeast by immigrants from Nigeria; in central Ghana, controlling gold reserves around Kumasi, the Ashanti, a branch of the Akans, founded what became the most powerful state in precolonial Ghana.
**1618** British trading settlement established on Gold Coast.
**18th–19th centuries** Centralized Ashanti kingdom at its height, dominating between Komoe River in the west and Togo Mountains in the east and active in slave trade; Fante state powerful along coast in the south.
**1874** Britain, after ousting the Danes and Dutch and defeating the Ashanti, made the Gold Coast (the southern provinces) a crown colony.
**1898–1901** After three further military campaigns, Britain finally subdued and established

protectorates over Ashanti and the northern territories.
**early 20th century** The colony developed into a major cocoa-exporting region.
**1917** West Togoland, formerly German-ruled, was administered with the Gold Coast as British Togoland.
**1949** Campaign for independence launched by Kwame Nkrumah, who formed Convention People's Party (CPP) and became prime minister in 1952.
**1957** Independence achieved, within the Commonwealth, as Ghana, which included British Togoland; Nkrumah became prime minister. Policy of 'African socialism' and nonalignment pursued.
**1960** Became a republic, with Nkrumah as president.
**1964** Ghana became a one-party state, dominated by the CCP, and developed links with communist bloc.
**1966** Nkrumah deposed in military coup and replaced by Gen Joseph Ankrah; political prisoners released.
**1969** Ankrah was replaced by Gen Akwasi Afrifa, who initiated a return to civilian government.
**1970** Edward Akufo-Addo was elected president.
**1972** Another coup placed Col Ignatius Acheampong at the head of a military government as the economy deteriorated.
**1978** Acheampong was deposed in a bloodless coup led by Frederick Akuffo; another coup put Flight-Lt Jerry Rawlings, a populist soldier who launched a drive against corruption, in power.
**1979** There was a return to civilian rule under Hilla Limann.
**1981** Rawlings seized power again. All political parties were banned.
**1992** A pluralist constitution was approved in a referendum, lifting the ban on political parties. Rawlings won presidential elections.
**1996** Rawlings was re-elected. The New Democratic Congress (NDC) won an assembly majority.

**Ghent** Flemish *Gent*, French *Gand*, port city and capital of East Flanders province, northwest Belgium, situated at the junction of the rivers Lys and Schelde, 55 km/34 mi northwest of Brussels; population (1997) 225,500. Industries include textiles, chemicals, electronics, metallurgy, and motor-vehicle manufacturing. The cathedral of St Bavon (12th–14th centuries) has paintings by van Eyck and Rubens.

**ghetto** (Old Venetian *gèto* 'foundry') any deprived area occupied by a minority group, whether voluntarily or not. Originally a ghetto was the area of a town where Jews were compelled to live, decreed by a law enforced by papal bull 1555. The term came into use 1516 when the Jews of Venice were expelled to an island within the city which contained an iron foundry. Ghettos were abolished, except in Eastern Europe, in the 19th century, but the concept and practice were revived by the Germans and Italians 1940–45.

**Ghiberti, Lorenzo** (1378–1455) Italian sculptor and goldsmith. In 1402 he won the commission for a pair of gilded bronze doors for the baptistry of Florence's cathedral. He produced a second pair (1425–52), the *Gates of Paradise,* one of the masterpieces of the early Italian Renaissance. They show a sophisticated use of composition and perspective, and the influence of classical models. Around 1450 he wrote *Commentarii/Commentaries,* the earliest surviving autobiography of an artist and an important source of information on the art of his time.

**GI** abbreviation for *government issue,* hence (in the USA) a common soldier.

**Giacometti, Alberto** (1901–1966) Swiss sculptor and painter. In the 1940s, he developed a highly original style, creating thin, rough-textured single figures in bronze. These emaciated figures have often been seen as an expression of the acute sense of alienation of people in the modern world. *Man Pointing* (1947) is one of many examples in the Tate Gallery, London.

**gibberellin** plant growth substance (see also ◊auxin) that promotes stem growth and may also affect the breaking of dormancy in certain buds and seeds, and the induction of flowering. Application of gibberellin can stimulate the stems of dwarf plants to additional growth, delay the ageing process in leaves, and promote the production of seedless fruit (parthenocarpy).

**gibbon** any of a group of several small southern Asian apes. The *common* or *lar gibbon* (*H. lar*) is about 60 cm/2 ft tall, with a body that is hairy except for the buttocks, which distinguishes it from other types of apes. Gibbons have long arms and no tail. They spend most of their time in trees and are very agile when swinging from branch to branch. On the ground they walk upright, and are more easily caught by predators. (Genus *Hylobates,* including the subgenus *Symphalangus.*)

**Gibbon, Edward** (1737–1794) English historian. He wrote one major work, arranged in three parts, *The History of the Decline and Fall of the Roman Empire* (1776–88), a continuous narrative from the 2nd century AD to the fall of Constantinople in 1453.

**Gibraltar** (Arabic *Jebel Tariq* 'Mountain of Tariq') British dependency, situated on a narrow rocky promontory at the southern tip of Spain; the *Rock of Gibraltar* formed one of the Pillars of ◊Hercules with Mount Acho, near Ceuta, across the Strait of Gibraltar on the north African coast
*area* 6.5 sq km/2.5 sq mi
*features* strategic naval and air base, with NATO underground headquarters and communications centre; there are numerous caverns and galleries cut out in the rock, the largest of which is 70 m/230 ft long; colony of Barbary apes; the frontier zone is adjoined by the Spanish port of La Línea
*exports* mainly a trading centre for the import and re-export of goods
*population* (1993) 29,000
*history* the fortress was taken by the Moors in 711 who finally ceded it to Spain in 1462.

Captured from Spain in 1704 by English admiral George Rooke (1650–1709), it was ceded to Britain under the Treaty of Utrecht (1713). A referendum in 1967 confirmed the wish of the people to remain in association with the UK, but Spain continues to claim sovereignty and closed the border from 1969 to 1985. In 1989, the UK government announced it would reduce the military garrison by half. Ground troops were withdrawn in 1991, but navy and airforce units remained.

**Gibraltar, Strait of** strait between north Africa and Spain, forming the entrance from the Atlantic Ocean to the Mediterranean Sea, with the Rock of Gibraltar to the north side and Mount Acho to the south, the so-called Pillars of ◊Hercules.

**Gide, André (Paul Guillaume)** (1869–1951) French novelist. His work is largely autobiographical and concerned with the conflict between desire and conventional morality. It includes *Les Nourritures terrestres/Fruits of the Earth* (1897), *L'Immoraliste/The Immoralist* (1902), *La Porte étroite/Strait is the Gate* (1909), *Les Caves du Vatican/The Vatican Cellars* (1914), and *Les Faux-monnayeurs/The Counterfeiters* (1926). He was a cofounder of the influential literary periodical *Nouvelle Revue française* (1908), and kept an almost lifelong *Journal.* Nobel Prize for Literature 1947.

**Gielgud, (Arthur) John** (1904–   ) English actor and director. One of the greatest Shakespearean actors of his time, he made his debut at the Old Vic in 1921 and played Hamlet in 1929. His stage appearances range from roles in works by Anton Chekhov and Richard Sheridan to those of Alan Bennett, Harold Pinter, and David Storey. He won an Academy Award for his role as a butler in the film *Arthur* (1981).

**gigabyte** in computing, a measure of ◊memory capacity, equal to 1,024 megabytes. It is also used, less precisely, to mean 1,000 billion ◊bytes.

**gila monster** lizard native to the southwestern USA and Mexico. It is one of the only two existing venomous lizards, the other being the Mexican beaded lizard of the same genus. It has poison glands in its lower jaw, but its bite is not usually fatal to humans. (Species *Heloderma suspectum.*)

**Gilbert, W(illiam) S(chwenck)** (1836–1911) English humorist and dramatist. He collaborated with composer Arthur ◊Sullivan, providing the libretti for their series of light comic operas from 1871 performed by the ◊D'Oyly Carte Opera Company; they include *HMS Pinafore* (1878), *The Pirates of Penzance* (1879), and *The Mikado* (1885).

**Gilbert and Ellice Islands** former British colony in the Pacific, known since independence 1978 as the countries of Tuvalu and Kiribati.

**Gilgamesh** hero of Sumerian, Hittite, Akkadian, and Assyrian legend, and lord of the Sumerian city of Uruk. The 12 verse books of the *Epic of Gilgamesh* were recorded in a standard version on 12 cuneiform tablets by the Assyrian king Ashurbanipal's scholars in the 7th century BC, and the epic itself is older than Homer's *Iliad* by at least 1,500 years.

**gill** in biology, the main respiratory organ of most fishes and immature amphibians, and of many aquatic invertebrates. In all types, water passes over the gills, and oxygen diffuses across the gill membranes into the circulatory system, while carbon dioxide passes from the system out into the water.

**gill** imperial unit of volume for liquid measure, equal to one-quarter of a pint or five fluid ounces (0.142 litre), traditionally used in selling alcoholic drinks.

**Gillespie, Dizzy (John Birks)** (1917–1993) US jazz trumpeter. With Charlie ◊Parker, he was the chief creator and exponent of the ◊bebop style (*Groovin' High* is a CD re-issue of their seminal 78-rpm recordings). Gillespie influenced many modern jazz trumpeters, including Miles Davis.

**gilt-edged securities** stocks and shares issued and guaranteed by the British government to raise funds and traded on the Stock Exchange. A relatively risk-free investment, gilts bear fixed interest and are usually redeemable on a specified date. The term is now used generally to describe securities of the highest value.

**ginger** southeast Asian reedlike perennial plant; the hot-tasting spicy underground root is used as a food flavouring and in preserves. (*Zingiber officinale*, family Zingiberaceae.)

**Gingrich, Newt (Newton Leroy)** (1943– ) US Republican politician, speaker of the ◊House of Representatives from 1995. A radical-right admirer of Reagan, he was the driving force behind his party's victory in the 1994 congressional elections, when it gained a House majority for the first time since 1954. On taking office, he sought to implement a conservative, populist manifesto – 'Contract with America' – designed to reduce federal powers, balance the budget, tackle crime, and limit congressional terms.

**ginkgo** or *maidenhair tree*, tree belonging to the ◊gymnosperm (or naked-seed-bearing) division of plants. It may reach a height of 30 m/100 ft by the time it is 200 years old. (*Ginkgo biloba*.)

**Ginsberg, (Irwin) Allen** (1926–1997) US poet and political activist. His reputation as a visionary, overtly political poet was established by *Howl* (1956), which expressed and shaped the spirit of the ◊Beat Generation and criticized the materialism of contemporary US society. Ginsberg, like many of his generation of poets, found his authorial voice via experimentation with drugs, alternative religion, and the hippie culture; his poetry drew, for example, on Oriental philosophies and utilized mantric breath meditations.

**ginseng** plant with a thick forked aromatic root used in alternative medicine as a tonic. (*Panax ginseng*, family Araliaceae.)

**Giorgione, da Castelfranco** Giorgio Barbarelli (1475–1510) Italian Renaissance painter. Active in Venice, he created the Renaissance poetic landscape, with its rich colours, soft forms, and gentle sense of intimacy. An example is his *Sleeping Venus* (about 1510; Gemäldegalerie, Dresden), a work that was probably completed by ◊Titian.

**Giotto** di Bondone (c. 1267/77–1337) Italian painter and architect. Widely considered the founder of modern painting, he had a profound influence on the development of European art. He broke away from the conventions of the Byzantine style and introduced a new naturalism, painting saints as real people, solid, lifelike, and expressive. His style gave a greater narrative coherence, dramatic power, and dignity to the depiction of biblical incidents. His main works are cycles of frescoes in churches in Florence and Padua.

**giraffe** world's tallest mammal. It stands over 5.5 m/18 ft tall, the neck accounting for nearly half this amount. The giraffe has two to four small, skin-covered, hornlike structures on its head and a long, tufted tail. The fur has a mottled appearance and is reddish brown and cream. Giraffes are found only in Africa, south of the Sahara Desert. They eat leaves and vegetation that is out of reach of smaller mammals, and are ruminants; that is, they chew the cud. (Species *Giraffa camelopardalis*, family Giraffidae.)

**Girl Guides** female equivalent of the ◊Scout organization, founded in 1910 in the UK by Robert Baden-Powell and his sister Agnes. There are three branches: Brownie Guides (age 7–11); Guides (10–16); Ranger Guides (14–20); they are led by Guiders (adult leaders). The World Association of Girl Guides and Girl Scouts (as they are known in the USA) has some 9 million members (1998).

**giro** system of making payments by direct transfer between one bank or post-office account and another.

**Gironde** navigable estuary 75 km/46 mi long on the southwest coast of France between Bordeaux and the sea, formed by the mouths of the Garonne and ◊Dordogne rivers. It flows into the Bay of Biscay between the Médoc and Côtes vineyards. The estuary has sand banks and strong tides, but is used by ocean-going vessels. The passenger port is Le Verdon-sur-Mer. There are oil refineries at Pauillac and Bec d'Ambès.

**Girondin** or *Girondist, Brissotin,* member of the moderate republican party in the French Revolution, so called because a number of its leaders came from the Gironde region of southwestern France. The Girondins controlled the Legislative Assembly from late 1791 to late 1792, but were ousted by the radical Montagnards under Jean Paul ◊Marat in 1793. Many Girondin leaders were executed during the ◊Reign of Terror.

**Giscard d'Estaing, Valéry** (1926– ) French centre-right politician and head of state, president of France 1974–81. At home he secured divorce and abortion law reforms early on, reduced the voting age to 18, and amended the constitution to enable the parliamentary opposition to refer legislation to the Constitutional Council. In Europe, he helped initiate the new Exchange Rate Mechanism in 1978 and direct elections to the European Parliament from 1979. Faced with increasingly difficult economic circumstances, he brought in Raymond Barre as prime minister to manage a deflationary programme from 1976. Defeated by Mitterrand in 1981, he was re-elected to the National Assembly in 1984, resigning in 1989 in order to sit in the European Parliament.

**Gish, Lillian** stage name of Lillian (Diana) de Guiche (1899–1993) US film and stage actress. She worked with the director D W Griffith, playing virtuous heroines in *The Birth of a Nation* (1915), *Broken Blossoms* (1919), and *Way Down East* (1920). She went on to appear in such silent classics as Victor Sjöström's *The Scarlet Letter* (1926) and *The Wind* (1928). Her career continued well into the 1980s, including performances in *Duel in the Sun* (1947), *Night of the Hunter* (1955), and *The Whales of August* (1987).

**Giza, El** or *al-Jizah,* city and governorate of Egypt, situated on the west bank of the Nile to the southwest of ◊Cairo, of which it forms a suburb of the greater metropolitan area; population of city (1992) 2,144,000, and governorate (1995 est) 4,525,000. It has textile, footwear, brewing, and film industries. It is noted for its archaeological sites; 8 km/5 mi to the southwest are the pyramids of Khufu, Khafre, and Menkure, and the Great Sphinx.

**gizzard** muscular grinding organ of the digestive tract, below the ◊crop of birds, earthworms, and some insects, and forming part of the ◊stomach. The gizzard of birds is lined with a hardened horny layer of the protein keratin, preventing damage to the muscle layer during the grinding process. Most birds swallow sharp grit which aids maceration of food in the gizzard.

**glacier** tongue of ice, originating in mountains in snowfields above the snowline, which moves slowly downhill and is constantly replenished from its source. The geographic features produced by the erosive action of glaciers (glacial erosion) are characteristic and include glacial troughs (U-shaped valleys), corries, and arêtes. In lowlands, the laying down of rocky debris carried by glaciers (glacial deposition) produces a variety of landscape features, such as ◊moraines, eskers, and drumlins.

**gladiator** in ancient Rome, a trained fighter, recruited mainly from slaves, criminals, and prisoners of war, who fought to the death in arenas for the entertainment of spectators. The custom was introduced into Rome from Etruria in 264 BC and continued until the 5th century AD.

**Gladio** code name for the Italian branch of a secret paramilitary network backed by the Central Intelligence Agency and the North Atlantic Treaty Organization (NATO), the Allied Coordination Committee, made public and disbanded 1990. The name Gladio has also been used for the entire network.

**gladiolus** any plant of a group of southern European and African cultivated perennials belonging to the iris family, with brightly coloured funnel-shaped flowers borne on a spike; the swordlike leaves spring from a corm (swollen underground stem). (Genus *Gladiolus,* family Iridaceae.)

**Gladstone, William Ewart** (1809–1898) British Liberal politician, four times prime minister. He entered Parliament as a Tory in 1833 and held ministerial office, but left the party in 1846 and after 1859 identified himself with the Liberals. He was chancellor of the Exchequer 1852–55 and 1859–66, and prime minister 1868–74, 1880–85, 1886, and 1892–94. He introduced elementary education 1870 and vote by secret ballot 1872 and many reforms in Ireland, although he failed in his efforts to get a Home Rule Bill passed.

**Glamorgan** Welsh *Morgannwg,* three counties of south Wales – ◊Mid Glamorgan, ◊South Glamorgan, and ◊West Glamorgan – created in 1974 from the former county of Glamorganshire. All are on the Bristol Channel. In 1996 Mid Glamorgan was divided amongst Rhondda Cynon Taff, Merthyr Tydfil, Bridgend, and Vale of Glamorgan; South Glamorgan was divided amongst Cardiff and Vale of Glamorgan; and West Glamorgan was divided into Neath Port Talbot and Swansea.

**gland** specialized organ of the body that manufactures and secretes enzymes, hormones, or other chemicals. In animals, glands vary in size from small (for example, tear glands) to large (for example, the pancreas), but in plants they are always small, and may consist of a single cell. Some glands discharge their products internally, ◊endocrine glands, and others, externally, ◊exocrine glands. Lymph nodes are sometimes wrongly called glands.

**glandular fever** or *infectious mononucleosis,* viral disease characterized at onset by fever and painfully swollen lymph nodes (in the neck); there may also be digestive upset, sore throat, and skin rashes. Lassitude persists for months and even years, and recovery can be slow. It is caused by the Epstein–Barr virus.

**Glasgow** city and, as *Glasgow City,* unitary authority in west-central Scotland; the unitary authority formed in 1995 from the majority of land from Glasgow District Council of Strathclyde Region
*area* 176 sq km/68 sq mi
*industries* engineering, chemicals, printing, whisky blending, brewing, electronics, textiles, light manufacturing
*population* (1996) 618,400.

**glasnost** (Russian 'openness') Soviet leader Mikhail ◊Gorbachev's policy of liberalizing various aspects of Soviet life, such as introducing greater freedom of expression and information and opening up relations with Western countries. *Glasnost* was introduced and adopted by the Soviet government 1986.

**glass** transparent or translucent substance that is physically neither a solid nor a liquid. Although glass is easily shattered, it is one of the strongest substances known. It is made by fusing certain types of sand (silica); this fusion occurs naturally in volcanic glass (see ◊obsidian).

**Glass, Philip** (1937–  ) US composer. As a student of Nadia Boulanger, he was strongly influenced by Indian music; his work is characterized by repeated rhythmic figures that are continually expanded and modified. His compositions include the operas *Einstein on the Beach* (1976), *Akhnaten* (1984), *The Making of the Representative for Planet 8* (1988), and the *'Low' Symphony* (1992) on themes from David Bowie's *Low* album.

**Glastonbury** market town in Somerset, southwest England, on the River Brue, 8 km/5 mi southwest of Wells; population (1996 est) 8,100. Light industries include injection moulding, and the production of footwear and leather goods. Tourism and warehousing are also important. *Glastonbury Tor,* a hill crowned by a ruined 14th-century church tower, rises to 159 m/522 ft. Glastonbury lake village, occupied from around 150 BC to AD 50, lies 5 km/3 mi to the northwest.

**glaucoma** condition in which pressure inside the eye (intraocular pressure) is raised abnormally as excess fluid accumulates. It occurs when the normal outflow of fluid within the chamber of the eye (aqueous humour) is interrupted. As pressure rises, the optic nerve suffers irreversible damage, leading to a reduction in the field of vision and, ultimately, loss of eyesight.

**Glendower, Owen** also known as Owain Glyndwr (*c.* 1350–1416) Welsh nationalist leader. He led a rebellion against Henry IV of England, taking the title 'Prince of Wales' in 1400, and successfully led the Welsh defence against English invasions in 1400–02, although Wales was reconquered 1405–13. He gained control of most of the country and established an independent Welsh parliament, but from 1405 onwards suffered repeated defeats at the hands of Prince Hal, later ◊Henry V.

**gliding** the art of using air currents to fly unpowered aircraft. Technically, gliding involves the gradual loss of altitude; gliders designed for soaring flight (utilizing air rising up a cliff face or hill, warm air rising as a thermal above sun-heated ground, and so on) are known as sailplanes.

**global warming** an increase in average global temperature of approximately 1°F/0.5°C over the past century. Global temperature has been highly variable in Earth history and many fluctuations in global temperature have occurred in historical times, but this most recent episode of warming coincides with the spread of industrialization, prompting the hypothesis that it is the result of an accelerated ◊greenhouse effect caused by atmospheric pollutants, especially carbon dioxide gas. Recent melting and collapse of the Larsen Ice Shelf, Antarctica, is a consequence of global warming. Melting of ice is expected to raise sea level in the coming decades.

**globefish** another name for the ◊puffer fish.

**Glorious Revolution** in British history, the events surrounding the removal of James II from the throne and his replacement in 1689 by his daughter Mary and William of Orange as joint sovereigns (◊Mary II and ◊William III), bound by the ◊Bill of Rights.

**glottis** in medicine, narrow opening at the upper end of the larynx that contains the vocal cords.

**Gloucestershire** county of southwest England

*area* 2,640 sq km/1,019 sq mi

*towns and cities* Gloucester (administrative headquarters), Cheltenham, Cirencester, Stroud, Tewkesbury

*physical* Cotswold Hills; River Severn and tributaries

*features* Berkeley Castle, where Edward II was murdered; Prinknash Abbey, where pottery is made; Cotswold Farm Park, near Stow-on-the-Wold, which has rare and ancient breeds of farm animals; pre-Norman churches at Cheltenham and Cleeve; Gloucester Cathedral; Tewkesbury Abbey, with early 12th-century nave

*agriculture* cereals (in the Cotswolds), fruit (apples and pears), cider, dairy products ('double Gloucester' cheese was formerly made here), sheep farming

*industries* aerospace industry, light engineering, manufacturing (bricks, carpets, furniture, glass, pins, pottery, tiles, watches), plastics, timber

*population* (1996) 556,300

*famous people* Gustav Holst, Edward Jenner, John Keble.

**glow-worm** wingless female of any of a large number of luminous beetles (fireflies). The luminous organs, situated under the abdomen, at the end of the body, give off a greenish glow at night and attract winged males for mating. There are about 2,000 species of glow-worms, distributed worldwide. (Family Lampyridae.)

**glucose** or *dextrose* or *grape sugar,* $C_6H_{12}O_6$ sugar present in the blood and manufactured by green plants during ◊photosynthesis. The ◊respiration reactions inside cells involve the oxidation of glucose to produce ◊ATP, the 'energy molecule' used to drive many of the body's biochemical reactions.

**glue-sniffing** or *solvent misuse,* inhalation of the fumes from organic solvents of the type found in paints, lighter fuel, and glue, for their hallucinatory effects. As well as being addictive, solvents are dangerous for their effects on the user's liver, heart, and lungs. It is believed that solvents produce hallucinations by dissolving the cell membrane of brain cells, thus altering the way the cells conduct electrical impulses.

**gluon** in physics, a ◊gauge boson that carries the ◊strong nuclear force, responsible for binding quarks together to form the strongly interacting subatomic particles known as ◊hadrons. There are eight kinds of gluon.

**glycerine** another name for ◊glycerol.

**glycerol** or *glycerine* or *propan-1,2,3-triol,* $HOCH_2CH(OH)CH_2OH$ thick, colourless, odourless, sweetish liquid. It is obtained from vegetable and animal oils and fats (by treatment with acid, alkali, superheated steam, or an enzyme), or by fermentation of glucose, and is used in the manufacture of high explosives, in antifreeze solutions, to maintain moist conditions in fruits and tobacco, and in cosmetics.

**gnat** any of a group of small two-winged biting insects belonging to the mosquito family. The eggs are laid in water, where they hatch into wormlike larvae, which pass through a pupal stage (see ◊pupa) to emerge as adults. (Family Culicidae.)

**gneiss** coarse-grained ◊metamorphic rock, formed under conditions of high temperature and pressure, and often occurring in association with schists and granites. It has a foliated, or layered, structure consisting of thin bands of micas and/or amphiboles dark in colour alternating with bands of granular quartz and feldspar that are light in colour. Gneisses are formed during regional ◊metamorphism; *paragneisses* are derived from metamorphism of sedimentary rocks and *orthogneisses* from metamorphism of granite or similar igneous rocks.

**Gnosticism** esoteric cult of divine knowledge (a synthesis of Christianity, Greek philosophy, Hinduism, Buddhism, and the mystery cults of the Mediterranean), which flourished during the 2nd and 3rd centuries and was a rival to, and influence on, early Christianity. The medieval French Cathar heresy and the modern Mandean sect (in southern Iraq) descend from Gnosticism.

**GNP** abbreviation for ◊gross national product.

**gnu** another name for ◊wildebeest.

**Goa** state on the west coast of India, lying 400 km/250 mi south of Mumbai
*area* 3,700 sq km/1,428 sq mi
*capital* Panaji
*population* (1991) 1,169,800
*physical* bounded on the east by the Western Ghats reaching nearly 1,300 m/4,260 ft; rich lowland soils with high mineral content; the Mandovi and Zuari rivers share an estuary at Panaji, which has mangrove forests providing habitats for marine birdlife
*features* Portuguese colonial architecture; Baroque church of Bom Jesus (built 1594–1603) with remains of St Francis Xavier; Salim Ali bird sanctuary on Chorao Island opposite Panaji
*industries* tourism, clothing, footwear, pesticides, iron ore, manganese, fishing nets
*agriculture* rice, pulses, cashew nuts, coconuts, ragi (a cereal)
*history* captured by the Portuguese in 1510; the inland area was added in the 18th century. Goa was incorporated into India as a Union Territory with ◊Daman and Diu in 1961 and became a state in 1987. The long European period has left many legacies, including a large (40%) Christian minority.

**goat** ruminant mammal (it chews the cud), closely related to sheep. Both male and female goats have horns and beards. They are sure-footed animals, and feed on shoots and leaves more than on grass. (Genus *Capra*, family Bovidae.)

**Gobi** vast desert region of Central Asia in the independent state of Mongolia, and Inner Mongolia, China. It covers an area of 1,280,000 sq km/500,000 sq mi (800 km/500 mi north–south and 1,600 km/1,000 mi east–west), and lies on a high plateau 900–1,500 m/2,950–4,920 ft above sea level. It is mainly rocky, with shifting sands and salt marshes at lower levels. The desert is sparsely populated, mainly by nomadic herders. It is rich in the fossil remains of extinct species, and Stone Age implements.

**Gobind Singh** (1666–1708) Indian religious leader, the tenth and last guru (teacher) of Sikhism, 1675–1708, and founder of the Sikh brotherhood known as the ◊Khalsa. On his death, the Sikh holy book, the *Guru Granth Sahib,* replaced the line of human gurus as the teacher and guide of the Sikh community.

**God** the concept of a supreme being, a unique creative entity, basic to several monotheistic religions (for example Judaism, Christianity, Islam); in many polytheistic cultures (for example Norse, Roman, Greek), the term 'god' refers to a supernatural being who personifies the force behind an aspect of life (for example Neptune, Roman god of the sea).

**Godard, Jean-Luc** (1930– ) French film director. A politically motivated, neo-Modernist filmmaker, he was one of the leaders of New Wave cinema. He made his name with *A bout de souffle/Breathless* 1959, in which his challenging, subversive approach to conventional narrative cinema was clear in his handling of a story based on US gangster movies.

**Godiva,** or *Godgifu,* Lady (c. 1040–1080) Wife of Leofric, Earl of Mercia (died 1057). Legend has it that her husband promised to reduce the heavy taxes on the people of Coventry if she rode naked through the streets at noon. The grateful citizens remained indoors as she did so, but 'Peeping Tom' bored a hole in his shutters and was struck blind.

**Godthåb** Greenlandic *Nuuk,* capital and largest town of Greenland; population (1993) 12,200. It is a storage centre for oil and gas, and the chief industry is fish processing.

**Godunov, Boris Fyodorovich** (1552– 1605) Tsar of Russia from 1598, elected after the death of Fyodor I, son of Ivan the Terrible. He was assassinated by a pretender to the throne who professed to be Dmitri, a brother of Fyodor and the rightful heir. The legend that has grown up around this forms the basis of Pushkin's play *Boris Godunov* (1831) and Mussorgsky's opera of the same name (1874).

**Goebbels, (Paul) Joseph** (1897–1945) German Nazi leader. As minister of propaganda from 1933, he brought all cultural and educational activities under Nazi control and built up sympathetic movements abroad to carry on the 'war of nerves' against Hitler's intended victims. On the capture of Berlin by the Allies, he committed suicide.

**Goering, Hermann Wilhelm** (1893–1946) Nazi leader, German field marshal from 1938. He was part of Hitler's inner circle, and with Hitler's rise to power was appointed commissioner for aviation from 1933 and built up the Luftwaffe (airforce). He built a vast economic empire in occupied Europe, but later lost favour and was expelled from the party in 1945. Tried at Nürnberg for war crimes, he poisoned himself before he could be executed.

**Goethe, Johann Wolfgang von** (1749–1832) German poet, novelist, dramatist, and scholar. He is generally considered the founder of modern German literature, and was the leader of the Romantic *Sturm und Drang* movement. His masterpiece is the poetic play *Faust* 1808 and 1832. His other works include the partly autobiographical *Die Leiden des Jungen Werthers/The Sorrows of the Young Werther* (1774); the classical dramas *Iphigenie auf Tauris/Iphigenia in Tauris* (1787), *Egmont* (1788), and *Torquato Tasso* (1790); the *Wilhelm Meister* novels (1795–1829); the short novel *Die Wahlver-wandschaften/Elective Affinities* (1809); and scientific treatises including *Farbenlehre/ Treatise on Colour* (1810).

**Gogh, Vincent (Willem) van** (1853–1890) Dutch Post-Impressionist painter. He began painting in the 1880s, his early works often being sombre depictions of peasant life, such as *The Potato Eaters* (1885; Van Gogh Museum, Amsterdam). Influenced by the Impressionists and by Japanese prints, he developed a freer style characterized by intense colour and expressive brushwork, as seen in his *Sunflowers* series 1888. His influence on modern art, particularly on Expressionism, has been immense.

**Gogol, Nicolai Vasilyevich** (1809–1852) Russian writer. His first success was a collection of stories, *Evenings on a Farm near Dikanka* (1831–32), followed by *Mirgorod* (1835). Later works include *Arabesques* (1835), the comedy play *The Inspector General* (1836), and the picaresque novel *Dead Souls* (1842), which satirizes Russian provincial society.

**Goh Chok Tong** (1941– ) Singaporean politician, prime minister from 1990. A trained economist, Goh became a member of parliament for the ruling People's Action Party in 1976. Rising steadily through the party ranks, he was appointed deputy prime minister in 1985, and subsequently chosen by the cabinet as Lee Kuan Yew's successor, first as prime minister and from 1992 also as party leader.

**goitre** enlargement of the thyroid gland seen as a swelling on the neck. It is most pronounced in simple goitre, which is caused by iodine deficiency. More common is toxic goitre or hyperthyroidism, caused by overactivity of the thyroid gland.

**Golan Heights** Arabic *Jawlan,* plateau on the Syrian border with Israel, bitterly contested in the ◊Arab–Israeli Wars and annexed by Israel on 14 December 1981. In the 1996 peace talks Syria insisted that Israel withdraw from the Golan Heights, following its capture in 1967. Demands for the return of the Golan to Syrian control have stalled negotiations towards normalization of Israeli–Syrian relations.

**gold** heavy, precious, yellow, metallic element; symbol Au (from Latin *aurum,* 'gold'), atomic number 79, relative atomic mass 197.0. It occurs in nature frequently as a free metal and is highly resistant to acids, tarnishing, and corrosion. Pure gold is the most malleable of all metals and is used as gold leaf or powder, where small amounts cover vast surfaces, such as gilded domes and statues.

The elemental form is so soft that it is alloyed for strength with a number of other metals, such as silver, copper, and platinum. Its purity is then measured in ◊carats on a scale of 24 (24 carats is pure gold). It is used mainly for decorative purposes (jewellery, gilding) but also for coinage, dentistry, and conductivity in electronic devices.

**Gold Coast** former name for Ghana, but historically the west coast of Africa from Cape Three Points to the Volta River, where alluvial gold is washed down. Portuguese and French navigators visited this coast in the 14th century, and a British trading settlement developed into the colony of the Gold Coast in 1618. With its dependencies of Ashanti and Northern Territories plus the trusteeship territory of Togoland, it became Ghana in 1957. The name is also used for many coastal resort areas – for example, in Florida, USA.

**Golden Fleece** in Greek legend, the fleece of the winged ram Chrysomallus, which hung on an oak tree at Colchis and was guarded by a dragon. It was stolen by ◊Jason and the Argonauts.

**Golden Horde** the invading Mongol-Tatar army that first terrorized Europe from 1237 under the leadership of Batu Khan, a grandson of Genghis Khan. ◊Tamerlane broke their power 1395, and ◊Ivan III ended Russia's payment of tribute to them 1480.

**golden section** visually satisfying ratio, first constructed by the Greek mathematician ◊Euclid and used in art and architecture. It is found by dividing a line AB at a point O such that the rectangle produced by the whole line and one of the segments is equal to the square drawn on the other segment. The ratio of the two segments is about 8:13 or 1:1.618, and a rectangle whose sides are in this ratio is called a *golden rectangle.* The ratio of consecutive ◊Fibonacci numbers tends to the golden ratio. *See illustration on page 370.*

**goldfish** fish belonging to the ◊carp family, found in East Asia. It is greenish-brown in its natural state, but has been bred by the Chinese for centuries, taking on highly coloured and sometimes freakishly shaped forms. Goldfish can occur in a greater range of colours than any other animal tested. (Species *Carassius auratus,* family Cyprinidae.)

**Golding, William (Gerald)** (1911–1993) English novelist. His work is often principally concerned with the fundamental corruption and

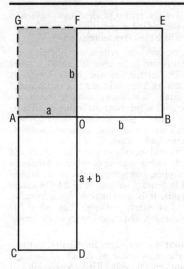

**golden section** *The golden section is the ratio a:b, equal to 8:13. A golden rectangle is one, like that shaded in the picture, that has its length and breadth in this ratio. These rectangles are said to be pleasant to look at and have been used instinctively by artists in their pictures.*

evil inherent in human nature. His first book, *Lord of the Flies* (1954; filmed in 1962), concerns the degeneration into savagery of a group of English schoolboys marooned on a Pacific island after their plane crashes; it is a chilling allegory about the savagery lurking beneath the thin veneer of modern 'civilized' life. *Pincher Martin* (1956) is a study of greed and self-delusion. Later novels include *The Spire* (1964). He was awarded the Nobel Prize for Literature in 1983 and knighted in 1988.

**Goldsmith, Oliver** (1728–1774) Irish playwright, novelist, poet, and essayist. His works include the novel *The Vicar of Wakefield* (1766), an outwardly artless and gentle story which is also social and political satire, and in which rural honesty, kindness, and patience triumph over urban values; it became one of the most popular works of English fiction. Other works include the poem 'The Deserted Village' (1770) and the play *She Stoops to Conquer* (1773). In 1761 Goldsmith met Samuel ◊Johnson and became a member of his circle.

**gold standard** system under which a country's currency is exchangeable for a fixed weight of gold on demand at the central bank. It was almost universally applied 1870–1914, but by 1937 no single country was on the full gold standard. Britain abandoned the gold standard 1931; the USA abandoned it 1971. Holdings of gold are still retained because it is an internationally recognized commodity, which cannot be legislated upon or manipulated by interested countries.

**golf** outdoor game in which a small rubber-cored ball is hit with a wooden- or iron-faced club into a series of holes using the least number of shots. On the first shot for each hole, the ball

is hit from a tee, which elevates the ball slightly off the ground; subsequent strokes are played off the ground. Most courses have 18 holes and are approximately 5,500 m/6,000 yd in length. Golf developed in Scotland in the 15th century.

**gonad** the part of an animal's body that produces the sperm or egg cells (ova) required for sexual reproduction. The sperm-producing gonad is called a ◊testis, and the egg-producing gonad is called an ◊ovary.

**Goncourt, de, Edmond** (1822–1896) **and Jules** (1830–1870) French writers. The brothers collaborated in producing a compendium, *L'Art du XVIIIème siècle/18th-Century Art* (1859–75), historical studies, and a *Journal* published 1887–96 that depicts French literary life of their day. Edmond de Goncourt founded the Académie Goncourt, opened 1903, which awards an annual prize, the Prix Goncourt, to the author of the best French novel of the year.

**gonorrhoea** common sexually transmitted disease arising from infection with the bacterium *Neisseria gonorrhoeae*, which causes inflammation of the genito-urinary tract. After an incubation period of two to ten days, infected men experience pain while urinating and a discharge from the penis; infected women often have no external symptoms.

**González Márquez, Felipe** (1942– ) Spanish socialist politician, leader of the Socialist Workers' Party (PSOE), and prime minister 1982–96. His party was re-elected in 1989 and 1993, but his popularity suffered as a result of economic upheaval and revelations of corruption within his administration. During 1995 he was himself briefly under investigation for alleged involvement with anti-terrorist death squads in the 1980s, and in March 1996, he and his party were narrowly defeated in the general elections.

**Gooch, Graham Alan** (1953– ) English cricketer. An attacking right-handed opening batsman, he is England's leading run-scorer in Test cricket with 8,900 runs in 118 matches, at an average of 42.58 (1975–95). He hit 20 test hundreds with a highest score of 333. He is also England's top scorer in limited overs cricket with 4,295 runs in 125 one-day internationals.

**Good Hope, Cape of** South African headland forming a peninsula between Table Bay and False Bay, Cape Town. The first European to sail around it was Bartolomeu ◊Diaz 1488. Formerly named Cape of Storms, it was given its present name by King John II of Portugal.

**Goodman, Benny** (1909–1986) US clarinettist, composer, and band-leader, nicknamed the 'King of Swing'. He played in various jazz and dance bands from 1921. In 1934 he founded a 12-piece band, which combined the expressive improvisatory style of black jazz with disciplined precision ensemble playing. He is associated with such numbers as 'Blue Skies' and 'Let's Dance'.

**goose** any of several large aquatic birds belonging to the same family as ducks and swans. There are about 12 species, found in

North America, Greenland, Europe, North Africa, and Asia north of the Himalayas. Both sexes are similar in appearance: they have short, webbed feet, placed nearer the front of the body than in other members of the family, and a slightly hooked beak. Geese feed entirely on grass and plants, build nests of grass and twigs on the ground, and lay 5–9 eggs, white or cream-coloured, according to the species. (Genera mainly *Anser* and *Branta,* family Anatidae, order Anseriformes.)

**gooseberry** edible fruit of a low-growing bush (*Ribes uva-crispa*) found in Europe and Asia, related to the ◊currant. It is straggling in its growth, and has straight sharp spines in groups of three and rounded, lobed leaves. The flowers are green and hang on short stalks. The sharp-tasting fruits are round, hairy, and generally green, but there are reddish and white varieties.

**gopher** any of a group of burrowing rodents. Gophers are a kind of ground squirrel represented by some 20 species distributed across western North America, Europe, and Asia. Length ranges from 15 cm/6 in to 90 cm/16 in, excluding the furry tail; colouring ranges from plain yellowish to striped and spotted species. (Genus *Citellus,* family Sciuridae.)

**Gorbachev, Mikhail Sergeyevich** (1931– ) Soviet president, in power 1985–91. He was a member of the Politburo from 1980. As general secretary of the Communist Party (CPSU) 1985–91 and president of the Supreme Soviet 1988–91, he introduced liberal reforms at home (◊*perestroika* and ◊*glasnost*), proposed the introduction of multiparty democracy, and attempted to halt the arms race abroad. He became head of state in 1989. He was awarded the Nobel Peace Prize in 1990.

**Gordimer, Nadine** (1923– ) South African novelist, an opponent of apartheid and censorship. Her finest writing is characterized by beautiful evocations of the rural Transvaal, effective renderings of sexuality, and interacting characters from different racial backgrounds. Her first novel, *The Lying Days,* appeared in 1953; her other works include *The Conservationist* (1974), the volume of short stories *A Soldier's Embrace* (1980), *July's People* (1981), and *Why Haven't You Written?* (1992). Nobel Prize for Literature 1991.

**Gore, Al (Albert Arnold, Jnr)** (1948– ) US politician, vice-president from 1993. A Democrat, he was a member of the House of Representatives 1977–79, and was senator for Tennessee 1985–92. He was on the conservative wing of the party, but held liberal views on such matters as women's rights, environmental issues, and abortion. As vice-president he was unusually active in foreign affairs, and put forward proposals for 'reinventing government' by cutting red tape and improving efficiency. Gore officially started his presidential campaign in Carthage, Tennessee, in June 1999.

**Gorgon** in Greek mythology according to the Greek poet Hesiod, any of three monsters; the sisters *Stheno* and *Euryale,* daughters of the sea god Phorcys and Ceto, and the mortal ◊Medusa. They had wings, claws, enormous teeth, and snakes for hair; direct sight of them turned living creatures to stone. Medusa was slain by Perseus who watched her reflection in his shield, although her head retained its power to transform.

**gorilla** largest of the apes, found in the dense forests of West Africa and mountains of central Africa. The male stands about 1.8 m/6 ft high and weighs about 200 kg/450 lb. Females are about half this size. The body is covered with blackish hair, silvered on the back in older males. Gorillas live in family groups; they are vegetarian, highly intelligent, and will attack only in self-defence. They are dwindling in numbers, being shot for food by some local people, or by poachers taking young for zoos, but protective measures are having some effect. (Species *Gorilla gorilla.*)

**Göring, Hermann** German spelling of ◊Goering, Nazi leader.

**Gorky, Maxim** pen-name of Alexei Maximovich Peshkov (1868–1936) Russian writer. Born in Nizhniy-Novgorod (named Gorky 1932–90 in his honour), he was exiled 1906–13 for his revolutionary principles. His works, which include the play *The Lower Depths* (1902) and the memoir *My Childhood* (1913–14), combine realism with optimistic faith in the potential of the industrial proletariat.

**gorse** or *furze* or *whin,* any of a group of plants native to Europe and Asia, consisting of thorny shrubs with spine-shaped leaves growing thickly along the stems and bright-yellow coconut-scented flowers. (Genus *Ulex,* family Leguminosae.)

**goshawk** or *northern goshawk,* woodland hawk similar in appearance to the peregrine falcon, but with shorter wings and legs. It is native to most of Europe, Asia, and North America, and is used in falconry. The male is much smaller than the female. It is ash grey on the upper part of the body and whitish underneath with brown horizontal stripes; it has a dark head and cheeks with a white stripe above the eye. The tail has dark bands across it. (Species *Accipiter gentilis,* order Falconiformes.)

**Gospel** (Middle English 'good news') in the New Testament generally, the message of Christian salvation; in particular the four written accounts of the life of Jesus by Matthew, Mark, Luke, and John. Although the first three give approximately the same account or synopsis (thus giving rise to the name 'Synoptic Gospels'), their differences from John have raised problems for theologians.

**gospel music** vocal music developed in the 1920s in the black Baptist churches of the US South from spirituals. Outstanding among the early gospel singers was Mahalia Jackson, but from the 1930s to the mid-1950s male harmony groups predominated, among them the Dixie Hummingbirds, the Swan Silvertones, and the Five Blind Boys of Mississippi.

**Göteborg** German *Gothenburg,* port and

industrial city (ships, vehicles, chemicals) on the west coast of Sweden, at the mouth of the Göta River; population (1994 est) 444,600. It is Sweden's second-largest city and is linked with Stockholm by the Göta Canal (built 1832).

**Goth** East Germanic people who settled near the Black Sea around AD 2nd century. There are two branches, the eastern Ostrogoths and the western Visigoths. The *Ostrogoths* were conquered by the Huns 372. They regained their independence 454 and under Theodoric the Great conquered Italy 488–93; they disappeared as a nation after the Byzantine emperor Justinian I reconquered Italy 535–55.

The *Visigoths* migrated to Thrace. Under ◊Alaric they raided Greece and Italy 395–410, sacked Rome, and established a kingdom in southern France. Expelled from there by the Franks, they established a Spanish kingdom which lasted until the Moorish conquest of 711.

**Gothic architecture** style of architecture that flourished in Europe from the mid-12th century to the end of the 15th century. It is characterized by the vertical lines of tall pillars and spires, greater height in interior spaces, the pointed arch, rib vaulting, and the flying buttress.

**gouache** or *body colour,* painting medium in which watercolour is mixed with white pigment. Applied in the same way as watercolour, gouache gives a chalky finish similar to that of ◊tempera painting. It has long been popular in continental Europe, where Dürer and Boucher were both masters of the technique. Poster paints are usually a form of gouache.

**Gounod, Charles François** (1818–1893) French composer and organist. His operas, notably *Faust* (1859) and *Roméo et Juliette* (1867), and church music, including *Messe solennelle/Solemn Mass* (1849), combine graceful melody and elegant harmonization. His *Méditation sur le prélude de Bach/Meditation on Bach's 'Prelude'* (1889) for soprano and instruments, based on Prelude No 1 of Bach's *Well-Tempered Clavier,* achieved popularity as 'Gounod's *Ave Maria'.*

**gourd** any of a group of plants that includes melons and pumpkins. In a narrower sense, the name applies only to the genus *Lagenaria,* of which the bottle gourd or calabash (*L. siceraria*) is best known. (Family Cucurbitaceae.)

**gout** hereditary form of ◊arthritis, marked by an excess of uric acid crystals in the tissues, causing pain and inflammation in one or more joints (usually of the feet or hands). Acute attacks are treated with anti-inflammatories.

**government** any system whereby political authority is exercised. Modern systems of government distinguish between liberal democracies, totalitarian (one-party) states, and autocracies (authoritarian, relying on force rather than ideology). The Greek philosopher Aristotle was the first to attempt a systematic classification of governments. His main distinctions were between government by one person, by few, and by many (monarchy, oligarchy, and democracy), although the characteristics of each may vary between states and each may

degenerate into tyranny (rule by an oppressive elite in the case of oligarchy or by the mob in the case of democracy).

**Gower, David Ivon** (1957–  ) English cricketer. An elegant left-handed batsman who in 117 Tests between 1978 and 1992 scored 8,231 runs at an average of 44.25. He was England's record run scorer in Test cricket from 1992, when he surpassed Geoffrey Boycott's record, until 1993, when his total was overtaken by Graham ◊Gooch. He played county cricket for Leicestershire 1975–89 and for Hampshire 1990–93. He retired in 1993.

*career highlights*
*all first-class cricket* runs: 26,339; average: 40.08; best: 228 (Leicestershire v. Glamorgan 1989)
*Test cricket* appearances: 117; runs: 8,231; average: 44.25; best: 215 (England v. Australia 1985)

**Goya, Francisco José de Goya y Lucientes** (1746–1828) Spanish painter and engraver. One of the major figures of European art, Goya depicted all aspects of Spanish life – portraits, including those of the royal family, religious works, scenes of war and of everyday life. Towards the end of his life, he created strange, nightmarish works, the 'Black Paintings', with such horrific images as *Saturn Devouring One of His Sons* about (1822; Prado, Madrid). His series of etchings include *The Disasters of War* (1810–14), depicting the horrors of the French invasion of Spain.

**Graafian follicle** fluid-filled capsule that surrounds and protects the developing egg cell inside the ovary during the ◊menstrual cycle. After the egg cell has been released, the follicle remains and is known as a corpus luteum.

**Grace, W(illiam) G(ilbert)** (1848–1915) English cricketer. By profession a doctor, he became the most famous sportsman in Victorian England. A right-handed batsman, he began playing first-class cricket at the age of 16, scored 152 runs in his first Test match, and scored the first triple century in 1876. Throughout his career, which lasted nearly 45 years, he scored 54,896 runs and took 2,876 wickets.

*career highlights*
*all first-class cricket* runs: 54,896; average: 39.55; best: 344 (MCC v. Kent 1876); wickets: 2,876; average: 17.92; best: 10–49 (MCC v. Oxford University 1886)
*Test cricket* runs: 1,098; average: 32.29; best: 170 (v. Australia 1886); wickets: 9; average: 26.22; best: 2–12 (v. Australia 1890)

**Graces** in Greek mythology, three goddesses (Aglaia, Euphrosyne, Thalia), daughters of Zeus and Hera, personifications of pleasure, charm, and beauty; the inspirers of the arts and the sciences.

**Graf, Steffi** (1969–  ) German lawn-tennis player who brought Martina ◊Navratilova's long reign as the world's number-one female player to an end. Graf reached the semi-final of the US Open in 1985 at the age of 16, and won five consecutive Grand Slam singles titles

1988–89. In 1994 she became the first defending Wimbledon ladies' singles champion to lose her title in the first round. In June 1999 she won her sixth French Open singles title, and her 22nd Grand Slam singles in total. Only Chris Evert with seven victories has won the women's French Open more times, and only Margaret Court has won more Grand Slam singles titles. In August 1999 Graf announced her retirement from competitive tennis.

*career highlights*
**Wimbledon** singles: 1988–89, 1991, 1992, 1993, 1995, 1996; doubles: 1988
**US Open** singles: 1988–89, 1993, 1995
**French Open** singles: 1987–88, 1993, 1995–96, 1999
**Australian Open** singles: 1988–90, 1994
**Olympics** gold: 1988

**grafting** in medicine, the operation by which an organ or other living tissue is removed from one organism and transplanted into the same or a different organism.

In horticulture, it is a technique widely used for propagating plants, especially woody species. A bud or shoot on one plant, termed the *scion*, is inserted into another, the *stock*, so that they continue growing together, the tissues combining at the point of union. In this way some of the advantages of both plants are obtained.

**Graham, Martha** (1894–1991) US dancer, choreographer, teacher, and director. The greatest exponent of modern dance in the USA, she developed a distinctive vocabulary of movement, the *Graham Technique*, now taught worldwide. Her pioneering technique, designed to express inner emotion and intention through dance forms, represented the first real alternative to classical ballet.

**Grahame, Kenneth** (1859–1932) Scottish-born writer. The early volumes of sketches of childhood, *The Golden Age* (1895) and *Dream Days* (1898), were followed by his masterpiece *The Wind in the Willows* (1908) which became a children's classic. Begun as a bedtime story for his son, it is a charming tale of life on the river bank, with its blend of naturalistic style and fantasy, and its memorable animal characters, the practical Rat, Mole, Badger, and conceited, bombastic Toad. It was dramatized by A A Milne as *Toad of Toad Hall* (1929) and by Alan Bennett (1990).

**gram** metric unit of mass; one-thousandth of a kilogram.

**grammar** (Greek *grammatike tekhne* 'art of letters') the rules for combining words into phrases, clauses, sentences, and paragraphs. The standardizing impact of print has meant that spoken or colloquial language is often perceived as less grammatical than written language, but all forms of a language, standard or otherwise, have their own grammatical systems. People often acquire several overlapping grammatical systems within one language; for example, a formal system for writing and standard communication and a less formal system for everyday and peer-group communication.

**grammar school** in the UK, secondary school catering for children of high academic ability, about 20% of the total, usually measured by the Eleven Plus examination. Most grammar schools have now been replaced by ♭comprehensive schools.

**Gramsci, Antonio** (1891–1937) Italian Marxist who attempted to unify social theory and political practice. He helped to found the Italian Communist Party in 1921 and was elected to parliament in 1924, but was imprisoned by the Fascist leader Mussolini from 1926; his *Quaderni di carcere/Prison Notebooks* were published posthumously in 1947.

**Granada** capital of Granada province in Andalusia, southern Spain, situated to the north of the Sierra Nevada on the River Genil; population (1991) 254,000. Products include textiles, soap, and paper; there are also food industries and tourism. Granada has many palaces and monuments, including the Alhambra, a fortified hilltop palace built in the 13th and 14th centuries by the Moorish kings; a Gothic and Renaissance archiepiscopal cathedral (1523–1703); and a university, founded in 1533.

**Grand Canal** or *Imperial Canal;* Chinese *Da Yunhe,* the world's longest canal, running north from Hangzhou to Tianjin, China; 1,600 km/1,000 mi long and 30–61 m/100–200 ft wide. The earliest section was completed in 486 BC; the central section linking the Chang Jiang and Huang He rivers was built from AD 605 to 610; and the northern section was built between 1282 and 1292 during the reign of Kublai Khan.

**Grand Canyon** gorge in northwestern Arizona, USA, containing the ♭Colorado River. It is 350 km/217 mi long, 6–29 km/4–18 mi wide, and reaches depths of over 1.7 km/1.1 mi. The gorge cuts through a multicoloured series of rocks – mainly limestones, sandstones, and shales, and ranging in age from the Precambrian to the Cretaceous – and various harder strata stand out as steps on its slopes. It is one of the country's most popular national parks and millions of tourists visit here each year.

**Grand National** horse-race held in March or April at Aintree, Liverpool, England. The most famous steeplechase race in the world, it was inaugurated in 1839 as the Grand Liverpool Steeple Chase, adopting its present name in 1847. The current course is 7,242 m/4.5 mi long, with 30 formidable jumps. The highest jump is the Chair at 156 cm/5 ft 2in. Grand National steeplechases based on the Aintree race are held in Scotland, Wales, and Ireland at Ayr, Chepstow, and Fairyhouse respectively.

**Grand Remonstrance** petition passed by the English Parliament in November 1641 that listed all the alleged misdeeds of Charles I and demanded parliamentary approval for the king's ministers and the reform of the church. Charles refused to accept the Grand Remonstrance and countered by trying to arrest five leading members of the House of Commons. The worsening of relations between king and Parliament led to the outbreak of the English Civil War in 1642.

**grand slam** in tennis, the winning of four major tournaments in one season: the Australian Open, the French Open, Wimbledon, and the US Open. In golf, it is also winning the four major tournaments in one season: the US Open, the British Open, the Masters, and the PGA (Professional Golfers Association). In baseball, a grand slam is a home run with runners on all the bases. A grand slam in bridge is when all 13 tricks are won by one team.

**grand unified theory** in physics, a sought-for theory that would combine the theory of the strong nuclear force (called quantum chromodynamics) with the theory of the weak nuclear and electromagnetic forces. The search for the grand unified theory is part of a larger programme seeking a ◊unified field theory, which would combine all the forces of nature (including gravity) within one framework.

**granite** coarse-grained intrusive ◊igneous rock, typically consisting of the minerals quartz, feldspar, and biotite mica. It may be pink or grey, depending on the composition of the feldspar. Granites are chiefly used as building materials.

**Grant, Cary** stage name of Archibald Alexander Leach (1904–1986) English-born actor, a US citizen from 1942. His witty, debonair personality made him a screen favourite for more than three decades. Among his many films are *She Done Him Wrong* (1933), *Bringing Up Baby* (1938), *The Philadelphia Story* (1940), *Notorious* (1946), *To Catch a Thief* (1955), *North by Northwest* (1959), and *Charade* (1963).

**Grant, Ulysses S(impson)** born Hiram Ulysses Grant (1822–1885) US Civil War general in chief for the Union and 18th president of the USA 1869–77. As a Republican president, he

carried through a liberal ◊Reconstruction policy in the South. He failed to suppress extensive political corruption within his own party and cabinet, which tarnished the reputation of his second term.

**grant-maintained school** in the UK, a state school that has voluntarily withdrawn itself from local authority support (an action called *opting out*), and instead is maintained directly by central government. The schools are managed by their own boards of governors. In 1996 there were 1,090 grant-maintained schools, of which 60% were secondary schools.

**grape** fruit of any grape ◊vine, especially *V. vinifera*. (Genus *Vitis,* family Vitaceae.)

**grapefruit** round, yellow, juicy, sharp-tasting fruit of the evergreen grapefruit tree. The tree grows up to 10 m/more than 30 ft and has dark shiny leaves and large white flowers. The large fruits grow in grapelike clusters (hence the name). Grapefruits were first established in the West Indies and subsequently cultivated in Florida by the 1880s; they are now also grown in Israel and South Africa. Some varieties have pink flesh. (*Citrus paradisi,* family Rutaceae.)

**graph** pictorial representation of numerical data, such as statistical data, or a method of showing the mathematical relationship between two or more variables by drawing a diagram.

**graphical user interface** GUI or WIMP, in computing, a type of ◊user interface in which programs and files appear as icons (small pictures), user options are selected from pull-down menus, and data are displayed in windows (rectangular areas), which the operator can manipulate in various ways. The operator uses a pointing device, typically a ◊mouse, to make selections and initiate actions.

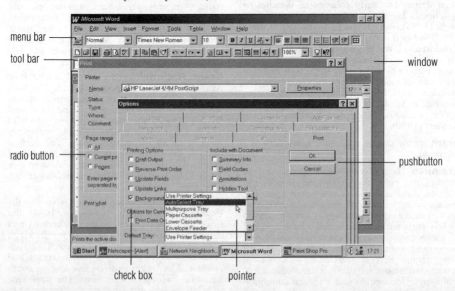

**graphical user interface** *A typical graphical user interface (GUI), where the user moves around the system by clicking on representative buttons or icons using the mouse.*

**graphite** blackish-grey, laminar, crystalline form of ◊carbon. It is used as a lubricant and as the active component of pencil lead.

**graph plotter** alternative name for a plotter.

**grass** any of a very large family of plants, many of which are economically important because they provide grazing for animals and food for humans in the form of cereals. There are about 9,000 species distributed worldwide except in the Arctic regions. Most are perennial, with long, narrow leaves and jointed, hollow stems; flowers with both male and female reproductive organs are borne on spikelets; the fruits are grainlike. Included in the family are bluegrass, wheat, rye, maize, sugarcane, and bamboo. (Family Gramineae.)

**Grass, Günter (Wilhelm)** (1927– ) German writer. The grotesque humour and socialist feeling of his novels *Die Blechtrommel/ The Tin Drum* 1959 and *Der Butt/The Flounder* (1977) are also characteristic of many of his poems. Other works include *Katz und Maus/Cat and Mouse* 1961, *Hundejahre/Dog Years* (1963), and *Ortlich betäubt/Local Anaesthetic* (1969). Deeply committed politically, Grass's works contain a mixture of scurrility, humour, tragedy, satire, and marvellously inventive imagery.

**grasshopper** any of several insects with strongly developed hind legs, enabling them to leap into the air. The hind leg in the male usually has a row of protruding joints that produce the characteristic chirping sound when rubbed against the hard wing veins. ◊Locusts, ◊crickets, and katydids are related to grasshoppers. (Families Acrididae and Tettigoniidae, order Orthoptera.)

**Grateful Dead, the** US psychedelic rock group formed in 1965. Their shows featured long improvisations and subtle ensemble playing, seldom fully captured in recording; albums include *Live Dead* (1969), *Workingman's Dead* (1970), and *Built to Last* (1989). They continued to tour until the death of Jerry Garcia in 1995.

**Graubünden** French *Grisons*, Swiss canton, the largest in Switzerland; area 7,106 sq km/ 2,743 sq mi; population (1995) 173,300. The capital is Chur. The inner valleys are the highest in Europe, and the main sources of the River Rhine rise here. It also includes the resort of Davos and, in the Upper Engadine, St Moritz. Ladin (a form of Romansch) is still widely spoken. Graubünden entered the Swiss Confederation in 1803.

**gravel** coarse ◊sediment consisting of pebbles or small fragments of rock, originating in the beds of lakes and streams or on beaches. Gravel is quarried for use in road building, railway ballast, and for an aggregate in concrete. It is obtained from quarries known as gravel pits, where it is often found mixed with sand or clay.

**Graves, Robert (Ranke)** (1895–1985) English poet and writer. He was severely wounded on the Somme in World War I, and his frank autobiography *Goodbye to All That* (1929) contains outstanding descriptions of the war. *Collected Poems* (1975) contained those verses

he wanted preserved, some of which were influenced by the American poet Laura Riding, with whom he lived for some years. His fiction includes two historical novels of imperial Rome, *I Claudius* and *Claudius the God* (both 1934). His most significant critical work is *The White Goddess: A Historical Grammar of Poetic Myth* (1948, revised edition 1966).

**gravitational force** or *gravity*, one of the four fundamental ◊forces of nature, the other three being the electromagnetic force, the weak nuclear force, and the strong nuclear force. The gravitational force is the weakest of the four forces, but it acts over great distances. The particle that is postulated as the carrier of the gravitational force is the graviton.

**gravity** force of attraction that arises between objects by virtue of their masses. On Earth, gravity is the force of attraction between any object in the Earth's gravitational field and the Earth itself. It is regarded as one of the four fundamental ◊forces of nature, the other three being the ◊electromagnetic force, the ◊strong nuclear force, and the ◊weak nuclear force. The gravitational force is the weakest of the four forces, but it acts over great distances. The particle that is postulated as the carrier of the gravitational force is the graviton.

**gravure** one of the three main ◊printing methods, in which printing is done from a plate etched with a pattern of recessed cells in which the ink is held. The greater the depth of a cell, the greater the strength of the printed ink. Gravure plates are expensive to make, but the process is economical for high-volume printing and reproduces illustrations well.

**gray** SI unit (symbol Gy) of absorbed radiation dose. It replaces the rad (1 Gy equals 100 rad), and is defined as the dose absorbed when one kilogram of matter absorbs one joule of ionizing radiation. Different types of radiation cause different amounts of damage for the same absorbed dose; the SI unit of *dose equivalent* is the ◊sievert.

**Gray, Thomas** (1716–1771) English poet. His *Elegy Written in a Country Churchyard* (1751), a dignified contemplation of death, was instantly acclaimed and is one of the most quoted poems in the English language. Other poems include *Ode on a Distant Prospect of Eton College* (1747), *The Progress of Poesy*, and *The Bard* (both 1757). He is now seen as a forerunner of ◊Romanticism.

**grayling** freshwater fish with a long multirayed dorsal (back) fin and silver to purple body colouring. It is found in northern parts of Europe, Asia, and North America, where it was once common in the Great Lakes. (Species *Thymallus thymallus*, family Salmonidae.)

**Graz** capital of Styria province, and second-largest city in Austria, situated on the River Mur, 150 km/93 mi southwest of Vienna; population (1995) 243,700. Industries include engineering and the manufacture of chemicals, iron, steel, automobiles, precision and optical instruments, paper, textiles, and leather. Tourism is also important. It has a 15th-century cathedral and a university founded in 1586. Lippizaner horses are bred near here.

**Great Barrier Reef** chain of ◊coral reefs and islands about 2,000 km/1,250 mi long, in the Coral Sea, off the east coast of Queensland, Australia, about 16–241 km/10–150 mi off-shore. The Great Barrier Reef is made up of 3,000 individual reefs, and is believed to be the world's largest living organism. Only ten navigable channels break through the reef. The most valuable products of the reef are pearls, pearl shells, trepangs (edible sea slugs), and sponges. The reef is popular with tourists. In 1976 it became a Marine Park and was declared a World Heritage Site by UNESCO in 1981.

**Great Bear** popular name for the constellation ◊Ursa Major.

**Great Bear Lake** freshwater lake in the western Northwest Territories, Canada, on the Arctic Circle; area 31,153 sq km/12,028 sq mi; depth 410 m/1,345 ft.

**Great Britain** official name for ◊England, ◊Scotland, and ◊Wales, and the adjacent islands (except the Channel Islands and the Isle of Man) from 1603, when the English and Scottish crowns were united under James I of England (James VI of Scotland). With Northern Ireland it forms the United Kingdom.

**Great Dane** breed of large, short-haired dog, often fawn or brindle in colour, standing up to 76 cm/30 in tall, and weighing up to 70 kg/154 lb. It has a large head and muzzle, and small, erect ears. It was formerly used in Europe for hunting boar and stags.

**Great Dividing Range** eastern Australian mountain range, extending 3,700 km/2,300 mi N–S from Cape York Peninsula, Queensland, to Victoria. It includes the Carnarvon Range, Queensland, which has many Aboriginal cave paintings, the Blue Mountains in New South Wales, and the Australian Alps.

**Great Exhibition** world fair held in Hyde Park, London, UK, in 1851, proclaimed by its originator Prince Albert as 'the Great Exhibition of the Industries of All Nations'. In practice, it glorified British manufacture: over half the 100,000 exhibits were from Britain or the British Empire. Over 6 million people attended the exhibition. The exhibition hall, popularly known as the *Crystal Palace*, was constructed of glass with a cast-iron frame, and designed by Joseph ◊Paxton.

**Great Lakes** series of five freshwater lakes along the USA–Canadian border: Superior, ◊Michigan, ◊Huron, ◊Erie, and ◊Ontario; total area 245,000 sq km/94,600 sq mi. Interconnected by a network of canals and rivers, the lakes are navigable by large ships, and they are connected with the Atlantic Ocean via the ◊St Lawrence River and by the St Lawrence Seaway (completed in 1959), which is navigable by medium-sized ocean-going ships. In March 1998 a bill was passed through Congress designating Lake ◊Champlain the sixth Great Lake, although controversy over this continues.

**Great Leap Forward** change in the economic policy of the People's Republic of China introduced by ◊Mao Zedong under the second five-year plan of 1958 to 1962. The aim was to achieve rapid and simultaneous agricultural and industrial growth through the creation of large new agro-industrial communes. The inefficient and poorly planned allocation of state resources led to the collapse of the strategy by 1960 and the launch of a 'reactionary programme', involving the use of rural markets and private subsidiary plots. More than 20 million people died in the Great Leap famines of 1959 to 1961.

**Great Patriotic War** 1941–45, war between the USSR and Germany during ◊World War II.

**Great Plains** semi-arid region to the east of the Rocky Mountains, stretching as far as the 100th meridian of longitude through Oklahoma, Kansas, Nebraska, and the Dakotas. The plains, which cover one-fifth of the USA, extend from Texas in the south over 2,400 km/1,500 mi north to Canada. The Great Plains have extensive oil and coal reserves, many of which are actively worked. Ranching and wheat farming have resulted in overuse of water resources to such an extent that available farmland has been reduced by erosion.

**Great Power** any of the major European powers of the 19th century: Russia, Austria (Austria-Hungary), France, Britain, and Prussia.

**Great Red Spot** prominent oval feature, 14,000 km/8,500 mi wide and some 30,000 km/20,000 mi long, in the atmosphere of the planet ◊Jupiter, south of the Equator. It was first observed in the 19th century. Space probes show it to be an anticlockwise vortex of cold clouds, coloured possibly by phosphorus.

**Great Rift Valley** volcanic valley formed 10– 20 million years ago owing to rifting of the Earth's crust and running about 8,000 km/5,000 mi from the Jordan Valley through the Red Sea to central Mozambique in southeast Africa. It is marked by a series of lakes, including Lake Turkana (formerly Lake Rudolf), and volcanoes, such as Mount Kilimanjaro. The rift system associated with the Rift Valley extends into northern Botswana, with geological faults controlling the location of the Okavango Delta.

**Great Schism** in European history, the period 1378–1417 in which rival popes had seats in Rome and in Avignon; it was ended by the election of Martin V during the Council of Constance 1414–17.

**Great Slave Lake** freshwater lake in the Northwest Territories, Canada; area 28,450 sq km/10,980 sq mi. It is about 480 km/298 mi long and 100 km/62 mi wide, and is the deepest lake (615 m/2,020 ft) in North America. The lake forms two large bays, McLeod's Bay in the north and Christie's Bay in the south. It is connected with Artillery Lake, Clinton-Golden Lake, and Aylmer Lake, and the Mackenzie River flows out from it on the west. The Great Slave Lake contains many fish, including salmon and trout, and has major commercial fisheries.

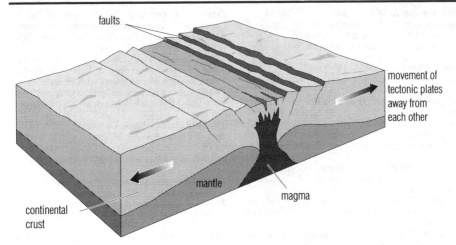

faults

movement of
tectonic plates
away from
each other

mantle

magma

continental
crust

**Great Rift Valley** *The subsidence of rock resulting from two or more parallel rocks moving apart is known as a graben. When this happens on a large scale, with tectonic plates moving apart, a rift valley is created.*

**Great Trek** in South African history, the movement of 12,000–14,000 Boer (Dutch) settlers from Cape Colony 1835 and 1845 to escape British rule. They established republics in Natal and the Transvaal. It is seen by many white South Africans as the main event in the founding of the present republic and was cited as a justification for whites-only rule.

**Great Wall of China** continuous defensive wall stretching from western Gansu to the Gulf of Liaodong (2,250 km/1,450 mi). It was once even longer. It was built under the Qin dynasty from 214 BC to prevent incursions by the Turkish and Mongol peoples and extended westwards by the Han dynasty. Some 8 m/25 ft high, it consists of a brick-faced wall of earth and stone, has a series of square watchtowers, and has been carefully restored. It is so large that it can be seen from space.

**Great War** another name for ◊World War I.

**grebe** any of a group of 19 species of water birds. The *great crested grebe* (*Podiceps cristatus*) is the largest of the Old World grebes. It feeds on fish, and lives on ponds and marshes in Europe, Asia, Africa, and Australia. It grows to 50 cm/20 in long and has a white breast, with chestnut and black feathers on its back and head. Dark ear tufts and a prominent collar or crest of feathers around the base of the head appear during the breeding season; these are lost in winter. (Family Podicipedidae, order Podicipediformes.)

**Greco, El** *Doménikos Theotokopoulos* (1541–1614) Spanish painter called 'the Greek' because he was born in Crete. He studied in Italy, worked in Rome from about 1570, and by 1577 had settled in Toledo. He painted elegant portraits and intensely emotional religious scenes with increasingly distorted figures and unearthly light, such as *The Burial of Count Orgaz* (1586; Church of S Tomé, Toledo).

**Greece** Hellenic Republic
*national name Elliniki Dimokratia*

*area* 131,957 sq km/50,948 sq mi
*capital* Athens
*major towns/cities* Thessaloníki, Piraeus, Patras, Irákleion, Larissa, Volos
*major ports* Piraeus, Thessaloníki, Patras, Irákleion
*physical features* mountainous (Mount Olympus); a large number of islands, notably Crete, Corfu, and Rhodes, and Cyclades and Ionian Islands
*head of state* Costis Stephanopoulos from 1995
*head of government* Costis Simitis from 1996
*political system* democracy
*political parties* Panhellenic Socialist Movement (PASOK), nationalist, democratic socialist; New Democracy Party (ND), centre right; Democratic Renewal (DIANA), centrist; Communist Party (KJKE), left wing; Political Spring, moderate, left of centre
*currency* drachma

**GNP per capita (PPP)** (US$) 13,010 (1998)
**exports** fruit and vegetables, clothing, mineral fuels and lubricants, textiles, iron and steel, aluminium and aluminium alloys. Principal market: Germany 25.2% (1997)
**population** 10,626,000 (1999 est)
**language** Greek (official), Macedonian (100,000–200,000 est)
**religion** Greek Orthodox; also Roman Catholic
**life expectancy** 76 (men); 81 (women) (1995–2000)
**Chronology**
**c. 2000–1200 BC** Mycenaean civilization flourished.
**c. 1500–1100 BC** Central Greece and Peloponnese invaded by tribes of Achaeans, Aeolians, Ionians, and Dorians.
**c. 1000–500 BC** Rise of the Greek city states; Greek colonies established around the shores of the Mediterranean.
**c. 490–404 BC** Ancient Greek culture reached its zenith in the democratic city state of Athens.
**357–338 BC** Philip II of Macedon won supremacy over Greece; cities fought to regain and preserve independence.
**146 BC** Roman Empire defeated Macedon and annexed Greece.
**AD 476** Western Roman Empire ended; Eastern Empire continued as Byzantine Empire, based at Constantinople, with essentially Greek culture.
**1204** Crusaders partitioned Byzantine Empire; Athens, Achaea, and Thessaloniki came under Frankish rulers.
**late 14th century–1461** Ottoman Turks conquered mainland Greece and captured Constantinople in 1453; Greek language and culture preserved by Orthodox Church.
**1685** Venetians captured Peloponnese; regained by Turks in 1715.
**late 18th century** Beginnings of Greek nationalism among émigrés and merchant class.
**1814** *Philike Hetairia* ('Friendly Society') formed by revolutionary Greek nationalists in Odessa.
**1821** *Philike Hetairia* raised Peloponnese brigands in revolt against Turks; War of Independence ensued.
**1827** Battle of Navarino: Britain, France, and Russia intervened to destroy Turkish fleet; Count Ioannis Kapodistrias elected president of Greece.
**1829** Treaty of Adrianople: under Russian pressure, Turkey recognized independence of small Greek state.
**1832** Great Powers elected Otto of Bavaria as king of Greece.
**1843** Coup forced King Otto to grant a constitution.
**1862** Mutiny and rebellion led King Otto to abdicate.
**1863** George of Denmark became king of the Hellenes.
**1864** Britain transferred Ionian islands to Greece.
**1881** Following Treaty of Berlin in 1878, Greece was allowed to annex Thessaly and part of Epirus.

**late 19th century** Politics dominated by Kharilaos Trikoupis, who emphasized economic development, and Theodoros Deliyiannis, who emphasized territorial expansion.
**1897** Greco-Turkish War ended in Greek defeat.
**1908** Cretan Assembly led by Eleutherios Venizelos proclaimed union with Greece.
**1910** Venizelos became prime minister and introduced financial, military, and constitutional reforms.
**1912–13** Balkan Wars: Greece annexed a large area of Epirus and Macedonia.
**1916** 'National Schism': Venizelos formed rebel pro-Allied government while royalists remained neutral.
**1917–18** Greek forces fought on Allied side in World War I.
**1919–22** Greek invasion of Asia Minor; after Turkish victory, a million refugees came to Greece.
**1924** Republic declared amid great political instability.
**1935** Greek monarchy restored with George II.
**1936** Gen Ioannia Metaxas established right-wing dictatorship.
**1940** Greece successfully repelled Italian invasion.
**1941–44** German occupation of Greece; rival monarchist and communist resistance groups operated from 1942.
**1946–49** Civil war: communists defeated by monarchists with military aid from Britain and USA.
**1952** Became a member of NATO.
**1967** 'Greek Colonels' seized power under George Papadopoulos; political activity banned; King Constantine II exiled.
**1973** Republic proclaimed with Papadopoulos as president.
**1974** Cyprus crisis caused downfall of military regime; Constantine Karamanlis returned from exile to form Government of National Salvation and restore democracy.
**1981** Andreas Papandreou was elected Greece's first socialist prime minister; Greece entered the European Community.
**1989–93** The election defeat of Panhellenic Socialist Movement (PASOK) was followed by unstable coalition governments.
**1993** PASOK returned to power.
**1996** Costis Simitis succeeded Papandreou as prime minister. PASOK retained its majority in the general election.
**1997** Direct talks with Turkey resulted in an agreement to settle all future disputes peacefully.

**Greece, ancient** ancient civilization that flourished 2,500 years ago on the shores of the Ionian and Aegean Seas (modern Greece and the west coast of Turkey). Although its population never exceeded 2 million, ancient Greece made great innovations in philosophy, politics, science, architecture, and the arts, and Greek culture forms the basis of western civilization to this day.

**Greek architecture** the architecture of ancient Greece is the base for virtually all architectural developments in Europe. The Greeks

## GREECE, ANCIENT: CHRONOLOGY

| | |
|---|---|
| **c. 1550–1050 BC** | The first Greek civilization, known as Mycenaean, owes much to the Minoan civilization of Crete and may have been produced by the intermarriage of Greek-speaking invaders with the original inhabitants. |
| **c. 1300** | A new wave of invasions begins. The Achaeans overrun Greece and Crete, destroying the Minoan and Mycenaean civilizations and penetrating Asia Minor. |
| **1000** | Aeolians, Ionians and Dorians have settled in the area that is now Greece. Many independent city states, such as Sparta and Athens, have developed. |
| **c. 800–500** | During the Archaic Period, Ionian Greeks lead the development of philosophy, science and lyric poetry. The Greeks become great sea traders, and found colonies around the coasts of the Mediterranean and the Black Sea, from Asia Minor in the east to Spain in the west. |
| **776** | The first Olympic games are held. |
| **594** | The laws of Solon take the first step towards a more democratic society. |
| **c. 560–510** | The so-called 'tyranny' of the Pisistratids in Athens is typical of a pre-democratic stage that many Greek cities pass through after overturning aristocratic rule. |
| **545** | From this date the Ionian cities in Asia Minor fall under the dominion of the Persian Empire. |
| **507** | Cleisthenes, ruler of Athens, is credited with the establishment of democracy. Other cities follow this lead, but Sparta remains unique, a state in which a ruling race, organized on military lines, dominates the surrounding population. |
| **499–494** | The Ionian cities, aided by Athens, revolts unsuccessfully against the Persians. |
| **490** | Darius of Persia invades Greece only to be defeated by the Athenians at Marathon and forced to withdraw. |
| **480** | Another invasion by the Persian emperor Xerxes, after being delayed by the heroic defence of Thermopylae by 300 Spartans, is defeated at sea off Salamis. |
| **480–323** | The Classical Period in ancient Greece. |
| **479** | The Persians are defeated on land at Plataea. |
| **478** | The Ionian cities, now liberated, form a naval alliance with Athens, the Delian League. |
| **455–429** | Under Pericles, the democratic leader of Athens, drama, sculpture, and architecture are at their peak. |
| **433** | The Parthenon in Athens is completed. |
| **431–404** | The Peloponnesian War destroys the political power of Athens, but Athenian thought and culture remain influential. Sparta becomes the leading Greek power. |
| **370** | The philosopher Plato opens his Academy in Athens. |
| **338** | Philip II of Macedon (359–336 BC) takes advantage of the wars between the city states and conquers Greece. |
| **336–323** | Rule of Philip's son, Alexander the Great. Alexander overthrows the Persian Empire, conquers Syria and Egypt, and invades the Punjab. After his death, his empire is divided among his generals, but his conquests have spread Greek culture across the known world. |
| **280** | Achaean League of 12 Greek city states formed in an attempt to maintain their independence against Macedon, Egypt, and Rome. |
| **146** | Destruction of Corinth. Greece becomes part of the Roman Empire. Under Roman rule Greece remains a cultural centre and Hellenistic culture remains influential. |

invented the entablature, which allowed roofs to be hipped (inverted V-shape), and perfected the design of arcades with support columns. There were three styles, or orders, of columns: Doric (with no base), Ionic (with scrolled capitals), and Corinthian (with acanthus-leafed capitals).

**Greek language** member of the Indo-European language family, which has passed through at least five distinct phases since the 2nd millennium BC: *Ancient Greek* 14th–12th centuries BC; *Archaic Greek,* including Homeric epic language, until 800 BC; *Classical Greek* until 400 BC; *Hellenistic Greek,* the common language of Greece, Asia Minor, West Asia, and Egypt to the 4th century AD, and *Byzantine Greek,* used until the 15th century and still the ecclesiastical language of the Greek Orthodox Church. *Modern Greek* is principally divided into the general vernacular (*Demotic Greek)* and the language of education and literature (*Katharevousa).*

**Greek Orthodox Church** see ◊Orthodox Church.

**green audit** inspection of a company to assess the total environmental impact of its activities or of a particular product or process.

### GREEK LANGUAGE: ALPHABET

| | | |
|---|---|---|
| A | α | alpha |
| B | β | beta |
| Γ | γ | gamma |
| Δ | δ | delta |
| E | ε | epsilon |
| Φ | φ | zeta |
| | | eta |
| T | τ | theta |
| I | ι | iota |
| K | κ | kappa |
| Λ | λ | lambda |
| μ | μ | mu |
| N | ν | nu |
| X | χ | xi |
| O | o | omicron |
| Π | π | pi |
| P | ρ | rho |
| Σ | σ | sigma |
| T | τ | tau |
| Θ | θ | upsilon |
| P | ρ | phi |
| Ψ | ψ | chi |
| X | χ | psi |
| Ω | ω | omega |

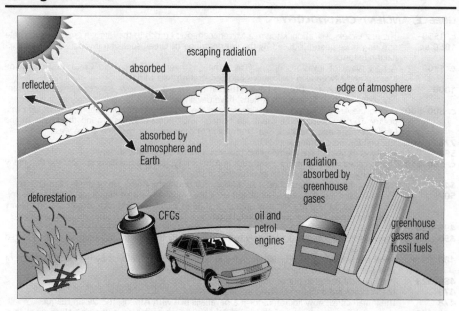

**greenhouse effect** *The warming effect of the Earth's atmosphere is called the greenhouse effect. Radiation from the Sun enters the atmosphere but is prevented from escaping back into space by gases such as carbon dioxide (produced for example, by the burning of fossil fuels), nitrogen oxides (from car exhausts), and CFCs (from aerosols and refrigerators). As these gases build up in the atmosphere, the Earth's average temperature is expected to rise.*

**green belt** area surrounding a large city, officially designated not to be built on but preserved where possible as open space for agricultural and recreational use. In the UK the first green belts were established from 1938 around conurbations such as London in order to prevent urban sprawl. New towns were set up to take the overspill population.

**Greene, (Henry) Graham** (1904–1991) English writer. His novels of guilt, despair, and penitence are set in a world of urban seediness or political corruption in many parts of the world. They include *Brighton Rock* (1938), *The Power and the Glory* (1940), *The Heart of the Matter* (1948), *The Third Man* (1949), *The Honorary Consul* (1973), and *Monsignor Quixote* (1982).

**greenfinch** olive-green songbird common in Europe and North Africa. It has bright-yellow markings on the outer tail feathers and wings; males are much brighter in colour than females. (Species *Carduelis chloris*, family Fringillidae, order Passeriformes.)

**greenfly** plant-sucking insect, a type of ◊aphid.

**greenhouse effect** phenomenon of the Earth's atmosphere by which solar radiation, trapped by the Earth and re-emitted from the surface as infrared radiation, is prevented from escaping by various gases in the air. Greenhouse gases trap heat because they readily absorb infrared radiation. The result is a rise in the Earth's temperature (◊global warming). The main greenhouse gases are carbon dioxide, methane, and ◊chlorofluorocarbons (CFCs) as well as water vapour. Fossil-fuel consumption and forest fires are the principal causes of carbon dioxide build-up; methane is a by-product of agriculture (rice, cattle, sheep).

**Greenland** Greenlandic *Kalaallit Nunaat*, world's largest island, lying between the North Atlantic and Arctic Oceans east of North America
**area** 2,175,600 sq km/840,000 sq mi
**capital** Godthaab (Greenlandic *Nuuk*) on the west coast
**features** the whole of the interior is covered by a vast ice sheet (the remnant of the last glaciation, part of the icecap of the North Pole); the island has an important role strategically and in civil aviation, and shares military responsibilities with the USA; there are lead and cryolite deposits, and offshore oil is being explored
**economy** fishing and fish-processing
**population** (1993) 55,100; Inuit (Ammassalik Eskimoan), Danish, and other European
**language** Greenlandic (Ammassalik Eskimoan)
**history** Greenland was discovered in about 982 by Eric the Red, who founded colonies on the west coast soon after Inuit from the North American Arctic had made their way to Greenland. Christianity was introduced to the Vikings in about 1000. In 1261 the Viking colonies accepted Norwegian sovereignty, but early in the 15th century all communication with Europe ceased, and by the 16th century the

colonies had died out, but the Inuit had moved on to the east coast. It became a Danish colony in the 18th century, and following a referendum in 1979 was granted full internal self-government in 1981.

**Green Man** or *Jack-in-the-Green,* in English folklore, a figure dressed and covered in foliage, associated with festivities celebrating the arrival of spring.

**green movement** collective term for the individuals and organizations involved in efforts to protect the environment. The movement encompasses political parties such as the ◊Green Party and organizations like ◊Friends of the Earth and ◊Greenpeace.

**Green Paper** publication issued by a British government department setting out various aspects of a matter on which legislation is contemplated, and inviting public discussion and suggestions. In due course it may be followed by a White Paper, giving details of proposed legislation. The first Green Paper was published in 1967.

**Green Party** political party aiming to 'preserve the planet and its people', based on the premise that incessant economic growth is unsustainable. The leaderless party structure reflects a general commitment to decentralization. Green parties sprang up in Western Europe in the 1970s and in Eastern Europe from 1988. Parties in different countries are linked to one another but unaffiliated with any pressure group.

**Greenpeace** international environmental pressure group, founded in 1971, with a policy of nonviolent direct action backed by scientific research. During a protest against French atmospheric nuclear testing in the South Pacific in 1985, its ship *Rainbow Warrior* was sunk by French intelligence agents, killing a crew member. In 1995 it played a prominent role in opposing the disposal of waste from an oil rig in the North Sea, and again attempted to disrupt French nuclear tests in the Pacific. In 1997 Greenpeace had a membership in 43 'chapters' worldwide.

**green revolution** in agriculture, the change in methods of arable farming instigated in the 1940s and 1950s in Third World countries. The intent was to provide more and better food for their populations, albeit with a heavy reliance on chemicals and machinery. It was abandoned by some countries in the 1980s. Much of the food produced was exported as ◊cash crops, so that local diet did not always improve.

**greenshank** greyish shorebird of the sandpiper group. It has long olive-green legs and a long, slightly upturned bill, with white underparts and rump and dark grey wings. It breeds in northern Europe and regularly migrates through the Aleutian Islands, southwest of Alaska. (Species *Tringa nebularia,* family Scolopacidae, order Charadriiformes.)

**Greenwich Mean Time** (GMT), local time on the zero line of longitude (the *Greenwich meridian*), which passes through the Old Royal Observatory at Greenwich, London. It was replaced in 1986 by coordinated universal time (UTC), but continued to be used to measure longitudes and the world's standard time zones.

**Greer, Germaine** (1939– ) Australian academic and feminist, author of *The Female Eunuch* (1970). The book is a polemical study of how patriarchy – through the nuclear family and capitalism – subordinates women by forcing them to conform to feminine stereotypes that effectively 'castrate' them. With its publication, Greer became identified as a leading figure of the women's movement.

**Gregorian chant** any of a body of plainsong choral chants associated with Pope Gregory the Great (540–604), which became standard in the Roman Catholic Church.

**Gregory** name of 16 popes, including:

**Gregory (I) the Great** St Gregory (c. 540–604) Pope from 590 who asserted Rome's supremacy and exercised almost imperial powers. In 596 he sent St ◊Augustine to England. He introduced the choral *Gregorian chant* into the liturgy. Feast day 12 March.

**Gregory VII** monastic name *Hildebrand* (c. 1023–1085) Chief minister to several popes before his election to the papacy 1073. In 1077 he forced the Holy Roman Emperor Henry IV to wait in the snow at Canossa for four days, dressed as a penitent, before receiving pardon. He was driven from Rome and died in exile. His feast day is 25 May. Canonized 1606.

**Gregory XIII** (1502–1585) Pope from 1572 who introduced the reformed *Gregorian calendar,* still in use, in which a century year is not a leap year unless it is divisible by 400.

**Grenada**

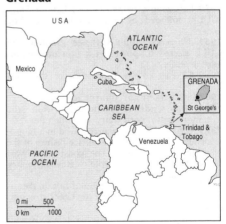

**area** (including the southern Grenadine Islands, notably Carriacou and Petit Martinique) 344 sq km/133 sq mi
**capital** St George's
**major towns/cities** Grenville, Sauteurs, Victoria, Hillsborough (Carriacou)
**physical features** southernmost of the Windward Islands; mountainous; Grand-Anse

beach; Annandale Falls; the Great Pool volcanic crater
**head of state** Elizabeth II from 1974, represented by governor general Reginald Palmer from 1992
**head of government** Keith Mitchell from 1995
**political system** emergent democracy
**political parties** Grenada United Labour Party (GULP), nationalist, left of centre; National Democratic Congress (NDC), centrist; National Party (TNP), centrist
**currency** Eastern Caribbean dollar
**GNP per capita (PPP)** (US$) 4,720 (1998)
**exports** cocoa, bananas, cocoa, mace, fresh fruit. Principal market: UK, USA, France 18.5% each (1995)
**population** 97,000 (1999 est)
**language** English (official); some French-African patois spoken
**religion** Roman Catholic 53%, Anglican, Seventh Day Adventist, Pentecostal
**life expectancy** 69 (men); 74 (women) (1998 est)
**Chronology**
**1498** Sighted by the explorer Christopher Columbus; Spanish named it Grenada since its hills were reminiscent of the Andalusian city.
**1650** Colonized by French settlers from Martinique, who faced resistance from the local Carib Indian community armed with poison arrows, before the defeated Caribs performed a mass suicide.
**1783** Ceded to Britain as a colony by the Treaty of Versailles; black African slaves imported to work cotton, sugar, and tobacco plantations.
**1795** Abortive rebellion against British rule led by Julien Fedon, a black planter inspired by the ideas of the French Revolution.
**1834** Slavery abolished.
**1950** Left-wing Grenada United Labour Party (GULP) founded by trade union leader Eric Gairy.
**1951** Universal adult suffrage granted and GULP elected to power in a nonautonomous local assembly.
**1958–62** Part of the Federation of the West Indies.
**1967** Internal self-government achieved.
**1974** Independence achieved within the Commonwealth, with Gairy as prime minister.
**1979** Autocratic Gairy was removed in a bloodless coup led by left-wing Maurice Bishop of the New Jewel Movement. The constitution was suspended and a People's Revolutionary Government established.
**1982** Relations with the USA and Britain deteriorated as ties with Cuba and the USSR strengthened.
**1983** After attempts to improve relations with the USA, Bishop was overthrown by left-wing opponents, precipitating a military coup by Gen Hudson Austin. Bishop and three colleagues were executed. The USA invaded, accompanied by troops from other eastern Caribbean countries; there were 250 fatalities. Austin was arrested and the 1974 constitution was reinstated.

**1984** Newly formed centre-left New National Party (NNP) won a general election and its leader, Herbert Blaize, became prime minister.
**1989** Blaize was replaced as leader of NNP, but remained as head of government; on his death, he was succeeded by Ben Jones.
**1991** Inconclusive general election; Nicholas Braithwaite of the centrist National Democratic Congress (NDC) became prime minister. Integration of the Windward Islands was proposed.
**1995** Brathwaite retired and was succeeded as prime minister by the new NDC leader, George Brizan. General election was won by the NNP, led by Keith Mitchell. A plague of pink mealy bugs caused damage to crops estimated at $60 million.
**1999** The ruling NNP gained a sweeping general election victory.

**Grenadines** chain of about 600 small islands in the Caribbean Sea, part of the group known as the Windward Islands. They are divided between St Vincent and Grenada.

**Grenville, George** (1712–1770) English Whig politician, prime minister, and chancellor of the Exchequer, whose introduction of the ◊Stamp Act of 1765 to raise revenue from the colonies was one of the causes of the American Revolution. His government was also responsible for prosecuting the radical John Wilkes.

**Grey, Charles** 2nd Earl Grey (1764–1845) British Whig politician. He entered Parliament in 1786, and in 1806 became First Lord of the Admiralty, and foreign secretary soon afterwards. As prime minister 1830–34, he carried the Great Reform Bill of 1832 that reshaped the parliamentary representative system and the act abolishing slavery throughout the British Empire in 1833. He succeeded to earldom in 1807.

**Grey, Lady Jane** (1537–1554) Queen of England for nine days, 10–19 July 1553, the great-granddaughter of Henry VII. She was married in 1553 to Lord Guildford Dudley (died 1554), son of the Duke of Northumberland. Edward VI was persuaded by Northumberland to set aside the claims to the throne of his sisters Mary and Elizabeth. When Edward died on 6 July 1553, Jane reluctantly accepted the crown and was proclaimed queen four days later. Mary, although a Roman Catholic, had the support of the populace, and the Lord Mayor of London announced that she was queen on 19 July. Grey was executed on Tower Green.

**greyhound** ancient breed of dog, with a long narrow head, slight build, and long legs. It stands up to 75 cm/30 in tall. It is renowned for its swiftness, and can exceed 60 kph/40 mph. Greyhounds were bred to hunt by sight, their main quarry being hares. Hunting hares with greyhounds is the basis of the ancient sport of coursing. Track-based greyhound racing is a popular spectator sport.

**Grieg, Edvard (Hagerup)** (1843–1907) Norwegian nationalist composer. Much of his music is small-scale, particularly his songs, dances, sonatas, and piano works, strongly identifying with Norwegian folk music. Among his orchestral works are the *Piano Concerto in A Minor* (1869) and the incidental music for Henrik Ibsen's drama *Peer Gynt* (1876), commissioned by Ibsen and the Norwegian government.

**griffin** mythical monster, the supposed guardian of hidden treasure, with the body, tail, and hind legs of a lion, and the head, forelegs, and wings of an eagle, though in classical times all four legs were those of a lion.

**Griffith, D(avid) W(ark)** (1875–1948) US film director. He was an influential figure in the development of cinema as an art. He made hundreds of one-reelers 1908–13, in which he pioneered the techniques of masking, fade-out, flashback, crosscut, close-up, and long shot. After much experimentation with photography and new techniques, he directed *The Birth of a Nation* (1915), about the aftermath of the Civil War, later criticized as degrading to African-Americans.

**griffon Bruxelloise** breed of terrierlike toy dog originally bred in Belgium. It weighs up to 4.5 kg/10 lb and has a harsh and wiry coat that is red or black in colour. The smooth-haired form of the breed is called the *petit Brabançon.*

**Grimm brothers** Jakob (Ludwig Karl) (1785–1863) and Wilhelm (1786–1859), philologists and collectors of German fairy tales such as 'Hansel and Gretel' and 'Rumpelstiltskin'. Joint compilers of an exhaustive dictionary of German, they saw the study of language and the collecting of folk tales as strands in a single enterprise.

**Gris, Juan** adopted name of José Victoriano Gonzalez (1887–1927) Spanish painter, one of the earliest Cubists. He developed a distinctive geometrical style, often strongly coloured. He experimented with paper collage and made designs for Serge Diaghilev's Ballets Russes 1922–23.

**Gromyko, Andrei Andreyevich** (1909–1989) President of the USSR 1985–88. As ambassador to the USA from 1943, he took part in the Tehran, Yalta, and Potsdam conferences; as United Nations representative 1946–49, he exercised the Soviet veto 26 times. He was foreign minister 1957–85. It was Gromyko who formally nominated Mikhail Gorbachev as Communist Party leader 1985.

**Groningen** most northerly province of the Netherlands, located on the Ems estuary and also including the innermost West Friesian Islands, bounded to the north by the North Sea, to the south by the province of Drenthe, to the east by Germany, and to the west by Friesland
*area* 2,350 sq km/907 sq mi
*capital* Groningen
*towns and cities* Hoogezand-Sappemeer, Stadskanaal, Veendam, Delfzijl, Winschoten
*physical* very low and much reclaimed marshland; fertile soil
*industries* natural gas, textiles, sugar refining, shipbuilding, papermaking
*agriculture* arable farming, livestock farming, dairy produce, tobacco, fishing

*population* (1997) 558,100
*history* under the power of the bishops of Utrecht from 1040, the provincial capital, also called Groningen, became a member of the ◊Hanseatic League in 1284. Taken by Spain in 1580, it was recaptured by Maurice of Nassau in 1594. Its university was founded in 1614.

**Gropius, Walter Adolf** (1883–1969) German architect, in the USA from 1937. He was an early exponent of the ◊International Style, defined by glass curtain walls, cubic blocks, and unsupported corners. A founder director of the ◊Bauhaus school in Weimar 1919–28, he advocated teamwork in design and artistic standards in industrial production. He was responsible for the new Bauhaus premises in Dessau 1925–26.

**gross** a particular figure or price, calculated before the deduction of specific items such as commission, discounts, interest, and taxes. The opposite is ◊net.

**gross domestic product** (GDP), value of the output of all goods and services produced within a nation's borders, normally given as a total for the year. It thus includes the production of foreign-owned firms within the country, but excludes the income from domestically owned firms located abroad. See also ◊gross national product.

**gross national product** (GNP), the most commonly used measurement of the wealth of a country. GNP is defined as the total value of all goods and services produced by firms owned by the country concerned. It is measured as the ◊gross domestic product plus income from abroad, minus income earned during the same period by foreign investors within the country.

**Grosz, George** (1893–1959) German-born US Expressionist painter and graphic artist. He was a founder of the Berlin Dada group in 1918, and excelled in savage satirical drawings criticizing the government and the military establishment. After numerous prosecutions, he fled his native Berlin in 1932 and went to the USA.

**Grotius, Hugo** or *Huig de Groot* (1583–1645) Dutch jurist and politician. His book *De Jure Belli et Pacis/On the Law of War and Peace* (1625) is the foundation of international law.

**groundnut** another name for ◊peanut.

**ground water** water collected underground in porous rock strata and soils; it emerges at the surface as springs and streams. The groundwater's upper level is called the *water table.* Sandy or other kinds of beds that are filled with groundwater are called *aquifers.* Recent estimates are that usable ground water amounts to more than 90% of all the fresh water on Earth; however, keeping such supplies free of pollutants entering the recharge areas is a critical environmental concern.

**group** in chemistry, a vertical column of elements in the ◊periodic table. Elements in a group have similar physical and chemical properties; for example, the group I elements (the ◊alkali metals: lithium, sodium, potassium, rubidium, caesium, and francium) are all highly reactive metals that form univalent ions. There is a gradation of properties down any group: in group I, melting and boiling points decrease, and density and reactivity increase.

**grouper** any of several species of large sea perch (spiny-finned fish), found in warm waters. Some species grow to 2 m/6.5 ft long, and can weigh 300 kg/660 lbs. (Family Serranidae.)

**Group of Seven** (G7), the seven leading industrial nations of the world: the USA, Japan, Germany, France, the UK, Italy, and Canada, which account for more than three-fifths of global GDP. Since 1975 their heads of government have met once a year to discuss economic and, increasingly, political matters; annual summits are also attended by the president of the European Commission and, from 1991, Russia.

**grouse** plump fowl-like game bird belonging to a subfamily of the pheasant family, which also includes the ptarmigan, capercaillie, and prairie chicken. Grouse are native to North America and northern Europe. They spend most of their time on the ground. During the mating season the males undertake elaborate courtship displays in small individual territories (◊leks). (Subfamily Tetraonidae, family Phasianidae, order Galliformes.)

**Grünewald, Matthias** or *Mathis Gothardt-Neithardt* (c. 1475–1528) German painter, architect, and engineer. His altarpiece at Isenheim, southern Alsace, (1515; Unterlinden Museum, Colmar, France), with its grotesquely tortured figure of Jesus and its radiant *Resurrection,* is his most important work.

**Guadalajara** industrial city (textiles, glass, soap, pottery), capital of Jalisco state, western Mexico; population (1990) 2,847,000. It is a key communications centre. It has a 16th–17th-century cathedral, the Governor's Palace, and an orphanage with murals by the Mexican painter José Orozco (1883–1949).

**Guadalcanal Island** largest of the Solomon Islands; area 6,500 sq km/2,510 sq mi; population (1991) 60,700. The principal population centres are ◊Honiara, capital of the Solomon Islands, Aola, and Lunga, all on the north coast. Gold, copra, and rubber are produced. The population are Melanesians (or Papuasians). In 1942, during World War II, it was the scene of a battle for control of the area that was won by US forces after six months of fighting.

**Guatemala** Republic of
***national name*** *República de Guatemala*
***area*** 108,889 sq km/42,042 sq mi
***capital*** Guatemala City
***major towns/cities*** Quezaltenango, Escuintla, Puerto Barrios (naval base), Retalhuleu, Chiquimula
***physical features*** mountainous; narrow coastal plains; limestone tropical plateau in north; frequent earthquakes
***head of state and government*** Alvaro Arzú from 1996
***political system*** democracy

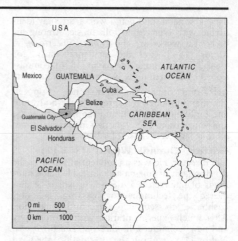

***political parties*** Guatemalan Christian Democratic Party (PDCG), Christian, centre left; Centre Party (UCN), centrist; Revolutionary Party (PR), radical; Movement of National Liberation (MLN), extreme right wing; Democratic Institutional Party (PID), moderate conservative; Solidarity and Action Movement (MAS), right of centre; Guatemalan Republican Front (FRG), right wing; National Advancement Party (PAN), right of centre; Social Democratic Party (PSD), right of centre
***currency*** quetzal
***GNP per capita (PPP)*** (US$) 4,070 (1998)
***exports*** coffee, bananas, sugar, cardamoms, shellfish, tobacco. Principal market: USA 35.8% (1997)
***population*** 11,090,000 (1999 est)
***language*** Spanish (official); 45% speak Mayan languages
***religion*** Roman Catholic 70%, Protestant 30%
***life expectancy*** 61 (men); 67 (women) (1995–2000)
***Chronology***
***c. AD 250–900*** Part of culturally advanced Maya civilization.
***1524*** Conquered by the Spanish adventurer Pedro de Alvarado and became a Spanish colony.
***1821*** Independence achieved from Spain, joining Mexico initially.
***1823*** Became part of United Provinces (Federation) of Central America, also embracing Costa Rica, El Salvador, Honduras, and Nicaragua.
***1839*** Achieved full independence.
***1844–65*** Rafael Carrera held power as president.
***1873–85*** The country was modernized on liberal lines by President Justo Rufino Barrios, the army was built up, and coffee growing introduced.
***1944*** Juan José Arevalo became president, ending a period of rule by dictators. Socialist programme of reform instituted by Arevalo and his successor, from 1951, Col Jacobo Arbenz Guzman, including establishing a social security system and redistributing land expropriated from large estates to landless peasants.

**1954** Col Carlos Castillo Armas became president in US-backed coup, after United Fruit Company plantations had been nationalized by Arbenz. Land reform halted.
**1963** Castillo assassinated and military coup made Col Enrique Peralta president.
**1966** Cesar Méndez elected president as civilian rule restored.
**1970s** More than 50,000 died in a spate of political violence as the military regime sought to liquidate left-wing dissidents.
**1970** Carlos Araña elected president, with military back in power.
**1976** An earthquake killed 27,000 and left more than 1 million homeless.
**1981** Growth of an antigovernment guerrilla movement. Death squads and soldiers killed an estimated 11,000 civilians during the year.
**1982** Right-wing army coup installed Gen Ríos Montt as head of junta and then as president, determined to fight corruption and end violence.
**1983** Montt was removed in a coup led by Gen Mejía Victores, who declared amnesty for the guerrillas.
**1985** A new constitution was adopted; PDCG won the congressional elections; Marco Vinicio Cerezo Arevalo became civilian president.
**1989** A coup attempt against Cerezo was foiled. Over 100,000 people were killed, and 40,000 reported missing, since 1980.
**1991** Jorge Serrano Elías of MAS was elected president. Diplomatic relations established with Belize, which Guatemala had long claimed.
**1993** President Serrano was deposed after attempting to impose an authoritarian regime; Ramiro de Leon Carpio, a human-rights ombudsman, was elected president by the assembly.
**1994** Peace talks were held with Guatemalan Revolutionary National Unity (URNG) rebels. Right-wing parties secured a majority in congress after elections.
**1995** The government was criticized by USA and United Nations for widespread human-rights abuses. There was a ceasefire by rebels, the first in 30 years.
**1996** Alvaro Arzú was elected president. A peace agreement was signed which ended the 36-year war.

**Guadeloupe** island group in the Leeward Islands, West Indies, an overseas *département* of France. The main islands are Basse-Terre and Grande-Terre.
*area* 1,705 sq km/658 sq mi
*chief town* The chief town and seat of government is Basse-Terre (on the island of the same name), population (1988) 14,000.
*population* (1990) 387,000 (77% mulatto, 10% black, and 10% mestizo). The people of St Barthélemy and Les Saintes are mainly descended from 17th century Norman and Breton settlers
*languages* French (official); Creole (the main language)
*industries* sugar refining and rum distilling.

**Guam** largest and southernmost of the ◊Mariana Islands in the West Pacific, an unincorporated territory of the USA

*area* 540 sq km/208 sq mi
*capital* Agana
*towns and cities* Apra (port), Tamuning
*features* major US air and naval base, much used in the Vietnam War; tropical, with much rain
*industries* sweet potatoes, fish; tourism is important
*currency* US dollar
*population* (1992) 140,200
*language* English, Chamorro (basically Malay-Polynesian)
*religion* 96% Roman Catholic
*government* popularly elected governor (the Democrat Carl Gutierrez from 1994) and single-chamber legislature
*physical* largely limestone plateau in the north and volcanic in the south, with much jungle
*history* claimed by Ferdinand Magellan for Spain in 1521; captured by the USA in 1898 in the Spanish-American War; achieved full US citizenship and self-government from 1950. A referendum in 1982 favoured the status of a commonwealth, in association with the USA.

**guanaco** hoofed ruminant (cud-chewing) mammal belonging to the camel family, found in South America on the pampas and mountain plateaux. It grows up to 1.2 m/4 ft at the shoulder, with the head and body measuring about 1.5 m/5 ft in length. It is sandy brown in colour, with a blackish face, and has fine wool. It lives in small herds and is the ancestor of the domestic ◊llama and ◊alpaca. It is also related to the other wild member of the camel family, the ◊vicuna. (Species *Lama guanacoe*, family Camelidae.)

**Guangdong** or *Kwangtung,* province of south China, bounded to the north by Hunan and Jiangxi; to the northeast by Fujian; to the south by the South China Sea, Hong Kong, Macau, and the island province of Hainan; and to the west by Guangxi Zhuang Autonomous Region
*area* 178,000 sq km/69,530 sq mi
*capital* Guangzhou
*cities and towns* Maoming, Shantou, Shenzhen, Zhanjiang
*physical* tropical climate; Leizhou Peninsula; the Pearl River plain
*industries* minerals, electronics, household appliances, textiles
*agriculture* rice, sugar, fruit, tobacco, fish
*population* (1996) 69,610,000
*famous people* Sun Zhong Shan (Sun Yat-sen), the revolutionary leader.

**Guangxi Zhuang Autonomous Region**
*Guangxi* or *Kwangsi Chuang Autonomous Region,* autonomous region in south China, bounded to the north by Guizhou, to the northeast by Hunan, to the east by Guangdong, to the south by the Gulf of Tongking, to the southwest by Vietnam, and to the west by Yunnan
*area* 236,700 sq km/91,400 sq mi
*capital* ◊Nanning
*cities and towns* Guilin, Liuzhou, Wuzhou
*physical* mountainous; unusual limestone formations
*industries* sugar-refining, metallurgy, fishing,

food-processing, tourism
*agriculture* rice, maize, barley, millet, sugar, tropical fruits, timber, tea
*population* (1996) 45,890,000; including the Zhuang people, related to the Thai, who form China's largest ethnic minority.

**Guangzhou** *Kwangchow* or *Canton,* capital of ◊Guangdong province, south China; population (1993) 3,560,000. Industries include shipbuilding, engineering, and the manufacture of automobiles, electronics, chemicals, and textiles.

**guarana** Brazilian woody climbing plant. A drink with a high caffeine content is made from its roasted seeds, and it is the source of the drug known as zoom in the USA. Starch, gum, and several oils are extracted from it for commercial use. (*Paullinia cupana,* family Sapindaceae.)

**Guaraní** member of an American Indian people who formerly inhabited the area that is now Paraguay, southern Brazil, and Bolivia. The Guaraní live mainly in reserves; few retain the traditional ways of hunting in the tropical forest, cultivation, and ritual warfare. About 1 million speak Guaraní, a member of the Tupian language group.

**Guatemala City** capital of Guatemala, situated in the *Guatemalan Highlands* at an altitude of 1,500 m/4,921 ft; population (1990 est) 1,675,600. A group of volcanoes overlooks the city: Acatenango (3,976 m/13,044 ft); Fuego (3,763 m/12,346 ft); Agua (3,760 m/12,336 ft). Industries include textiles, tyres, silverware, footwear, and cement. Half of the industrial output of Guatemala emanates from Guatemala City. It was founded in 1776 as Guatemala's third capital after earthquakes destroyed the earlier capitals of Antigua and Cuidad Vieja in 1773 and 1542 respectively. It was itself severely damaged by subsequent earthquakes in 1917–18, and 1976.

**guava** tropical American tree belonging to the myrtle family; the astringent yellow pear-shaped fruit is used to make guava jelly, or it can be stewed or canned. It has a high vitamin C content. (*Psidium guajava,* family Myrtaceae.)

**Guayaquil** largest city and chief port of Ecuador near the mouth of the Guayas River; population (1990) 1,508,000. The economic centre of Ecuador and the capital of Guayas province, Guayaquil manufactures machinery and consumer goods, processes food, and refines petroleum. It was founded 1537 by the Spanish explorer Francisco de Orellana. The port exports bananas, cacao, and coffee.

**gudgeon** any of an Old World group of freshwater fishes of the carp family, especially the species *G. gobio* found in Europe and northern Asia on the gravel bottoms of streams. It is olive-brown, spotted with black, and up to 20 cm/8 in long, with a distinctive barbel (sensory bristle, or 'whisker') at each side of the mouth. (Genus *Gobio,* family Cyprinidae.)

**Guernsey** second largest of the ◊Channel Islands; area 63 sq km/24.3 sq mi; population (1991) 58,900. The capital is St Peter Port.

Products include electronics, tomatoes, flowers, and butterflies; and since 1975 it has been a major financial centre. Guernsey cattle, which are a distinctive pale fawn colour and give rich, creamy milk, originated here.

**guerrilla** (Spanish 'little war') irregular soldier fighting in a small, unofficial unit, typically against an established or occupying power, and engaging in sabotage, ambush, and the like, rather than pitched battles against an opposing army. Guerrilla tactics have been used both by resistance armies in wartime (for example, the Vietnam War) and in peacetime by national liberation groups and militant political extremists (for example, the Tamil Tigers).

**Guevara, Che (Ernesto)** (1928–1967) Latin American revolutionary. He was born in Resario, Argentina, and trained there as a doctor, but left his homeland in 1953 because of his opposition to the right-wing president Juan Perón. In effecting the Cuban revolution of 1959 against the Cuban dictator Fulgencio Batista, he was second only to Castro and Castro's brother Raúl. Between 1961 and 1965, he served as Cuba's minister of industry. In 1965 he went to the Congo to fight against white mercenaries, and then to Bolivia, where he was killed in an unsuccessful attempt to lead a peasant rising near Vallegrande. He was an orthodox Marxist and renowned for his guerrilla techniques.

**Guiana** Northeastern part of South America that includes ◊French Guiana, Guyana, and Suriname.

**guild** or *gild,* medieval association, particularly of artisans or merchants, formed for mutual aid and protection and the pursuit of a common purpose, religious or economic. Guilds became politically powerful in Europe but after the 16th century their position was undermined by the growth of capitalism.

**guillemot** any of several diving seabirds belonging to the auk family that breed on rocky North Atlantic and Pacific coasts. The *common guillemot* (*U. aalge*) has a long straight beak and short tail and wings; the feet are three-toed and webbed, the feathers are sooty brown and white. It breeds in large colonies on sea cliffs. The *black guillemot* (*C. grylle*) of northern coasts is much smaller and mostly black in summer, with orange legs when breeding. Guillemots build no nest, but lay one large, almost conical egg. (Genera *Uria* and *Cepphus,* family Alcidae, order Charadriiformes.)

**guillotine** beheading device consisting of a metal blade that descends between two posts. It was common in the Middle Ages and was introduced 1791 in an improved design by physician Joseph Ignace Guillotin (1738–1814) in France. It was subsequently used for executions during the French Revolution. It is still in use in some countries.

**Guinea** Republic of
*national name* *République de Guinée*
*area* 245,857 sq km/94,925 sq mi
*capital* Conakry

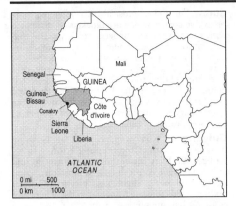

**major towns/cities** Labé, Nzérékoré, Kankan, Kindia

**physical features** flat coastal plain with mountainous interior; sources of rivers Niger, Gambia, and Senegal; forest in southeast; Fouta Djallon, area of sandstone plateaux, cut by deep valleys

**head of state** Lansana Conté from 1984

**head of government** Lamine Sidime from 1999

**political system** emergent democracy

**political parties** Party of Unity and Progress (PUP), centrist; Rally of the Guinean People (RPG), left of centre; Union of the New Republic (UNR), left of centre; Party for Renewal and Progress (PRP), left of centre

**currency** Guinean franc

**GNP per capita (PPP)** (US$) 1,760 (1998)

**exports** bauxite, alumina, diamonds, coffee. Principal market: Russia 16.7% (1997)

**population** 7,359,000 (1999 est)

**language** French (official), African languages (of which eight are official)

**religion** Muslim 95%, Christian

**life expectancy** 46 (men); 47 (women) (1995–2000)

**Chronology**

**c. AD 900** The Susi people, a community related to the Malinke, immigrated from the northeast, pushing the indigenous Baga towards the Atlantic coast.

**13th century** Susi kingdoms established, extending their influence to the coast; northeast Guinea was part of Muslim Mali Empire, centred to northeast.

**mid-15th century** Portuguese traders visited the coast and later developed trade in slaves and ivory.

**1849** French protectorate established over coastal region around Nunez River, which was administered with Senegal.

**1890** Separate Rivières du Sud colony formed.

**1895** Renamed French Guinea, the colony became part of French West Africa.

**1946** French Guinea became an overseas territory of France.

**1958** Full independence from France achieved as Guinea after referendum rejected remaining within French Community; Sékou Touré of the Democratic Party of Guinea (PDG) elected president.

**1960s and 1970s** Touré established socialist one-party state, leading to deterioration in economy as 200,000 fled abroad.

**1979** Strong opposition to Touré's rigid Marxist policies forced him to accept a return to mixed economy and legalize private enterprise.

**1984** Touré died. A bloodless military coup brought Col Lansana Conté to power; the PDG was outlawed and political prisoners released; and there were market-centred economic reforms.

**1985** An attempted coup against Conté while he was out of the country was foiled by loyal troops.

**1991** Antigovernment general strike and mass protests.

**1992** The constitution was amended to allow for multiparty politics.

**1993** Conté was narrowly re-elected in the first direct presidential election.

**1995** Assembly elections were won by Conté's supporters.

**1996** An attempted military coup was thwarted.

**1998** President Conté was re-elected.

**Guinea-Bissau** Republic of (formerly *Portuguese Guinea*)

**national name** *República da Guiné-Bissau*

**area** 36,125 sq km/13,947 sq mi

**capital** Bissau (main port)

**major towns/cities** Mansôa, São Domingos, Bolama/Bijagós, Catio, Buba, Butata, Farim, Cacine

**physical features** flat coastal plain rising to savanna in east

**head of state** Malan Bacai Sanha from 1999

**head of government** Francisco Fadul from 1998

**political system** emergent democracy

**political parties** African Party for the Independence of Portuguese Guinea and Cape Verde (PAIGC), nationalist socialist; Party for Social Renovation (PRS), left of centre; Guinea-Bissau Resistance–Bafata Movement (PRGB-MB), centrist

**currency** Guinean peso

**GNP per capita (PPP)** (US$) 750 (1998)

**exports** cashew nuts, palm kernels, groundnuts, fish and shrimp, timber. Principal market: India 59.1% (1997)

**population** 1,187,000 (1999 est)

**language** Portuguese (official); Crioulo (Cape Verdean dialect of Portuguese), African languages
**religion** animist 65%, Muslim 38%, Christian 5% (mainly Roman Catholic)
**life expectancy** 44 (men); 47 (women) (1995–2000)
**Chronology**
**10th century** Known as Gabu, became a tributary kingdom of the Mali Empire to northeast.
**1446** Portuguese arrived, establishing nominal control over coastal areas and capturing slaves to send to Cape Verde.
**1546** Gabu kingdom became independent of Mali and survived until 1867.
**1879** Portugal, which had formerly administered the area with Cape Verde islands, created the separate colony of Portuguese Guinea.
**by 1915** The interior had been subjugated by the Portuguese.
**1956** African Party for the Independence of Portuguese Guinea and Cape Verde (PAIGC) formed to campaign for independence from Portugal.
**1961** The PAIGC began to wage a guerrilla campaign against Portuguese rule.
**1973** Independence was declared in the two-thirds of the country that had fallen under the control of the PAIGC; heavy losses sustained by Portuguese troops who tried to put down the uprising.
**1974** Independence separately from Cape Verde accepted by Portugal, with Luiz Cabral (PAIGC) president.
**1980** Cabral was deposed, and João Vieira became chair of a council of revolution.
**1981** PAIGC was confirmed as the only legal party, with Vieira as its secretary general; Cape Verde decided not to form a union.
**1984** A new constitution made Vieira head of both government and state.
**1991** Other parties were legalized in response to public pressure.
**1994** PAIGC secured a clear assembly majority and Vieira narrowly won the first multiparty presidential elections.
**1997** Carlos Correia was appointed prime minister.
**1998** Peacekeeping troops were deployed. Francisco Fadul was appointed prime minister.
**1999** President Vieira ousted by the army. Malan Bacai Sanha was appointed acting president, pending elections.

**guinea fowl** any of a group of chickenlike African birds, including the *helmet guinea fowl* (*Numida meleagris*), which has a horny growth on the head, white-spotted feathers, and fleshy cheek wattles (loose folds of skin). It is the ancestor of the domestic guinea fowl. Guinea fowl are mostly gregarious ground-feeders, eating insects, leaves, and snails; at night they roost in trees. (Family Numididae, order Galliformes.)

**guinea pig** species of ◊cavy, a type of rodent.

**Guinevere** Welsh *Gwenhwyfar*, in British legend, the wife of King Arthur. Her adulterous love affair with the knight Lancelot of the Lake led ultimately to Arthur's death.

**guitar** flat-bodied musical instrument with six or twelve strings which are plucked or strummed with the fingers. The fingerboard is usually fretted, although some modern electric guitars are fretless. The Hawaiian guitar is laid across the player's lap, and uses a metal bar to produce a distinctive gliding tone. The solid-bodied electric guitar, developed in the 1950s by Les Paul and Leo Fender, mixes and amplifies vibrations from electromagnetic pickups at different points to produce a range of tone qualities.

**Guiyang** or *Kweiyang*, capital of Guizhou province, south China; population (1994) 1,602,400. It is an important transport and industrial centre, producing aluminium, iron, steel, machinery, chemicals, pharmaceuticals, textiles, and construction materials. There are coal and bauxite mines nearby.

**Guizhou** or *Kweichow*, province of south China, bounded to the north by Sichuan, to the east by Hunan, to the south by Guangxi Zhuang Autonomous Region, and to the west by Yunnan.
**area** 174,000 sq km/67,164 sq mi
**capital** ◊Guiyang
**cities and towns** Zunyi, Anshun, Duyun
**physical** part of the Yunnan–Guizhou Plateau
**industries** nonferrous minerals, machinery, food-processing
**agriculture** rice, maize, tobacco, tea, rapeseed, timber
**population** (1996) 35,550,000; ethnic minorities comprise about 25% of the population

**Gujarat** or *Gujerat*, state of west India, formed from north and west Mumbai state in 1960; bordered to the north by Pakistan and the Rajasthan state, with Madhya Pradesh and Maharashtra states to the east and southeast
**area** 196,000 sq km/75,656 sq mi
**capital** Gandhinagar (founded 1961)
**major towns** ◊Ahmadabad, Vadodara; main port Kandla
**physical** includes most of the arid Rann of Kutch and the peninsula of Kathiawar, a low basalt plateau; the more fertile southwestern plain watered by the Tapti and ◊Narmada rivers, which have contributed to the silting and decline in trading importance of the Gulf of Khambhat; the Gir Forest (the last home of the wild Asian lion)
**features** heavily industrialized; Karjan Dam under construction
**agriculture** wheat, millet, cotton, rice, maize, tobacco, groundnut oil, fishing; irrigation schemes such as the Kakrapara canal have allowed a food surplus to be produced in most areas
**industries** petrochemicals, oil (from Kalol, refined at Koyali near Baroda), gas, textiles, coal, limestone, pharmaceuticals, soda ash; dairy industry using imported and local milk
**language** Gujarati (or Gujerati) (20 million speakers), Hindi
**population** (1994 est) 44,235,000 (90% Hindu)
**history** ◊Indus valley civilization settlements dating from the 3rd and 2nd millennia BC have

been found at Lothal on the Gulf of Khambhat and more recently at Kuntasi near Morvi; subsequently there was a succession of ruling groups until the British took control 1818; after independence the area was part of the former Mumbai state, but demands for a separate Gujarati-speaking state were met in 1960.

**Gujarati** inhabitants of Gujarat on the northwest coast of India. The Gujaratis number approximately 30 million and speak their own Indo-European language, Gujarati, which has a long literary tradition. They are predominantly Hindu (90%), with Muslim (8%) and Jain (2%) minorities.

**Gujarati language** member of the Indo-Iranian branch of the Indo-European language family, spoken in and around the state of Gujarat in western India. It is written in its own script, a variant of the Devanagari script used for Sanskrit and Hindi.

**Gulf States** oil-rich countries sharing the coastline of the ◊Gulf (Bahrain, Iran, Iraq, Kuwait, Oman, Qatar, Saudi Arabia, and the United Arab Emirates). In the USA, the term refers to those states bordering the Gulf of Mexico (Alabama, Florida, Louisiana, Mississippi, and Texas).

**Gulf Stream** warm ocean ◊current that flows north from the warm waters of the Gulf of Mexico along the east coast of America, from which it is separated by a channel of cold water originating in the southerly Labrador current. Off Newfoundland, part of the current is diverted east across the Atlantic, where it is known as the *North Atlantic Drift*, dividing to flow north and south, and warming what would otherwise be a colder climate in the British Isles and northwest Europe.

**Gulf War** war 16 Jan–28 February 1991 between Iraq and a coalition of 28 nations led by the USA. The invasion and annexation of Kuwait by Iraq on 2 August 1990 provoked a build-up of US troops in Saudi Arabia, eventually totalling over 500,000. The UK subsequently deployed 42,000 troops, France 15,000, Egypt 20,000, and other nations smaller contingents.

An air offensive lasting six weeks, in which 'smart' weapons came of age, destroyed about one-third of Iraqi equipment and inflicted massive casualties. A 100-hour ground war followed, which effectively destroyed the remnants of the 500,000-strong Iraqi army in or near Kuwait.

**gull** any of a group of seabirds that are usually 25–75 cm/10–30 in long, white with grey or black on the back and wings, and have large beaks. Immature birds are normally a mottled brown colour. Gulls are sociable, noisy birds and they breed in colonies. (Genus principally *Larus*, subfamily Larinae, family Laridae, order Charadriiformes.)

**gum** in botany, complex polysaccharides (carbohydrates) formed by many plants and trees, particularly by those from dry regions. They form four main groups: plant exudates (gum

arabic); marine plant extracts (agar); seed extracts; and fruit and vegetable extracts. Some are made synthetically.

**Gummer, John Selwyn** (1939– ) British Conservative politician. He was minister of state for employment 1983–84, chair of the party 1983–85, paymaster general 1984–85, minister for agriculture 1985–89, secretary of state for agriculture 1989–93, and secretary of state for the environment 1993–97.

**gun** any kind of firearm or any instrument consisting of a metal tube from which a projectile is discharged; see also ◊artillery, machine gun, and ◊small arms.

**Gunnell, Sally** (1966– ) British hurdler. She won the 1986 Commonwealth 100-metre hurdles gold medal before moving on to 400-metre hurdles. She announced her retirement from competition in 1997.

*career highlights*
*Olympic Games* gold 400-metre hurdles 1992
*world champion* 1993 (world record)
*Commonwealth Games* 1990, 1994
*European champion* 1994

**gunpowder** or *black powder*, the oldest known explosive, a mixture of 75% potassium nitrate (saltpetre), 15% charcoal, and 10% sulphur. Sulphur ignites at a low temperature, charcoal burns readily, and the potassium nitrate provides oxygen for the explosion. As gunpowder produces lots of smoke and burns quite slowly, it has progressively been replaced since the late 19th century by high explosives, although it is still widely used for quarry blasting, fuses, and fireworks. Gunpowder has high activation energy; a gun based on gunpowder alone requires igniting by a flint or a match.

**Gunpowder Plot** in British history, the Catholic conspiracy to blow up James I and his parliament on 5 November 1605. It was discovered through an anonymous letter. Guy ◊Fawkes was found in the cellar beneath the Palace of Westminster, ready to fire a store of explosives. Several of the conspirators were killed as they fled, and Fawkes and seven others were captured and executed.

**Guomindang** or *Kuomintang*, Chinese National People's Party, founded in 1894 by ◊Sun Zhong Shan (Sun Yat-sen), which overthrew the Manchu Empire in 1912. From 1927 the right wing, led by ◊Jiang Jie Shi (Chiang Kai-shek), was in conflict with the left, led by Mao Zedong until the communist victory of 1949 (except for the period of the Japanese invasion from 1937 to 1945). It survives as the dominant political party of Taiwan, where it is still spelled *Kuomintang*. However, in recent years there have been splits between mainland-born hardliners and moderates, led by the president of Taiwan and Kuomintang leader ◊Lee Teng-hui.

**Gupta dynasty** Indian hereditary rulers that reunified and ruled over much of northern and central India 320–550. The dynasty's stronghold lay in the Magadha region of the middle Ganges valley, with the capital Pataliputra. Gupta influence was extended through military conquest east, west, and south by Chandragupta I, Chandragupta II, and Samudragupta. Hun raids in the northwest from the 6th century undermined the Guptas' decentralized administrative structure.

**guru** Hindi *gurū,* Hindu or Sikh leader, or religious teacher.

**Guru Granth Sahib** the holy book of Sikhism, a collection of nearly 6,000 hymns by the first five and the ninth Sikh gurus, but also including the writings of some Hindus and Muslims. It is regarded as a living guru and treated with the respect that this implies.

**Guscott, Jeremey** (1965–  ) English rugby union player for Bath, England, and the British Lions. A fast, elusive centre of prodigious talent, he was a key member of the England side which won three Grand Slams in the Five Nations Championship between 1991 and 1995. He has played on three consecutive British Lions tours since 1989, most memorably in the second Test on the 1997 tour of South Africa when he sealed the series for the Lions with a drop goal. As of 13 April 1999 he had won 60 England caps, scoring 24 tries.
*career highlights*
*international appearances (1989–  )* 60 (including 6 for the British Lions)
*tries* 24
*drop goals* 3.

**Gustavus** or *Gustaf,* six kings of Sweden, including:

**Gustavus Adolphus** *Gustavus II* or *Gustaf II* (1594–1632) King of Sweden from 1611, when he succeeded his father Charles IX. He waged successful wars with Denmark, Russia, and Poland, and in the ◊Thirty Years' War became a champion of the Protestant cause. Landing in Germany 1630, he defeated the German general Wallenstein at Lützen, southwest of Leipzig 6 November 1632, but was killed in the battle. He was known as the 'Lion of the North'.

**Gustavus Vasa** *Gustavus I* or *Gustaf I* (1496–1560) King of Sweden from 1523, when he was elected after leading the Swedish revolt against Danish rule. He united and pacified the country and established Lutheranism as the state religion.

**Gutenberg, Johannes** Gensfleisch (c. 1398–1468) German printer, the inventor of European printing from movable metal type (although Laurens Janszoon Coster has a rival claim).

**Guthrie, Woody** born Woodrow Wilson Guthrie (1912–1967) US folk singer and songwriter. His left-wing protest songs, 'dustbowl ballads', and 'talking blues' influenced, among others, Bob Dylan; they include 'Deportees', 'Hard Travelin'', and 'This Land Is Your Land'.

**Guyana** Cooperative Republic of
*area* 214,969 sq km/82,999 sq mi
*capital* Georgetown (and port)
*major towns/cities* Linden, New Amsterdam, Rose Hall, Corriverton
*major ports* New Amsterdam

*physical features* coastal plain rises into rolling highlands with savanna in south; mostly tropical rainforest; Mount Roraima; Kaietur National Park, including Kaietur Falls on the Potaro (tributary of Essequibo) 250 m/821 ft
*head of state* Janet Jagan from 1997
*head of government* Samuel Hinds from 1992
*political system* democracy
*political parties* People's National Congress (PNC), Afro-Guyanan, nationalist socialist; People's Progressive Party (PPP), Indian-based, left wing
*currency* Guyana dollar
*GNP per capita (PPP)* (US$) 2,680 (1998)
*exports* sugar, bauxite, alumina, rice, gold, rum, timber, molasses, shrimp. Principal market: Canada 24.2% (1997)
*population* 855,000 (1999 est)
*language* English (official), Hindi, American Indian languages
*religion* Hindu 54%, Christian 27%, Sunni Muslim 15%
*life expectancy* 61 (men); 68 (women) (1995–2000)
*Chronology*
*1498* The explorer Christopher Columbus sighted Guyana, whose name, 'land of many waters', was derived from a local American Indian word.
*c. 1620* Settled by Dutch West India Company, who established armed bases and brought in slaves from Africa.
*1814* After period of French rule, Britain occupied Guyana during the Napoleonic Wars and purchased Demerara, Berbice, and Essequibo.
*1831* Became British colony under name of British Guiana.
*1834* Slavery was abolished, resulting in an influx of indentured labourers from India and China to work on sugar plantations.
*1860* Settlement of the Rupununi Savanna commenced.
*1860s* Gold was discovered.
*1899* International arbitration tribunal found in favour of British Guiana in a long-running dispute with Venezuela over lands west of Essequibo River.

**1953** Assembly elections won by left-wing People's Progressive Party (PPP), drawing most support from the Indian community; Britain suspended constitution and installed interim administration, fearing communist takeover.

**1961** Internal self-government granted; Cheddi Jagan (PPP) became prime minister.

**1964** PNC leader Forbes Burnham led PPP–PNC coalition; racial violence between the Asian- and African-descended communities.

**1966** Independence achieved from Britain as Guyana, with Burnham as prime minister.

**1970** Guyana became a republic within the Commonwealth, with Raymond Arthur Chung as president; Burnham remained as prime minister.

**1980** Burnham became the first executive president under the new constitution, which ended the three-year boycott of parliament by the PPP.

**1985** Burnham died; he was succeeded by Desmond Hoyte (PNC), as the economy deteriorated.

**1992** PPP had a decisive victory in the first completely free assembly elections for 20 years; Cheddi Jagan became president; a privatization programme was launched.

**1997** Samuel Hinds became interim president on the death of Cheddi Jagan. Jagan's wife Janet Jagan was elected president.

**1998** Violent antigovernment protests. Government and opposition agreed to an independent audit of elections.

**1999** A constitutional reform commission was appointed.

**Gwent** former county of south Wales, 1974–1996, now divided between ◊Blaenau Gwent, ◊Caerphilly, ◊Monmouthshire, ◊Newport, and ◊Torfaen unitary authorities.

**Gwynedd** unitary authority in northwest Wales, created 1996 from part of the former county of Gwynedd
**area** 2,546 sq km/983 sq mi
**towns** Caernarfon (administrative headquarters)
**physical** area includes the highest mountain in Wales, ◊Snowdon (1,085 m/3,560 ft), and the largest Welsh lake, Llyn Tegid (Bala Lake)
**features** Snowdonia National Park, seaside resorts, Bardsey Island
**industries** gold mining at Dolgellau, textiles, electronics, slate, tourism
**agriculture** cattle and sheep-farming
**population** (1996) 116,000.

**gymnastics** physical exercises, originally for health and training (so called from the way in which men of ancient Greece trained: *gymnos* 'naked'). The *gymnasia* were schools for training competitors for public games.
*Men's gymnastics* includes high bar, parallel bars, horse vault, rings, pommel horse, and floor exercises. *Women's gymnastics* includes asymmetrical bars, side horse vault, balance beam, and floor exercises. Also popular are *sports acrobatics,* performed by gymnasts in pairs, trios, or fours to music, where the emphasis is on dance, balance, and timing, and *rhythmic gymnastics,* choreographed to music and performed by individuals or six-girl teams, with small hand apparatus such as a ribbon, ball, or hoop.

**gymnosperm** (Greek 'naked seed') in botany, any plant whose seeds are exposed, as opposed to the structurally more advanced ◊angiosperms, where they are inside an ovary. The group includes conifers and related plants such as cycads and ginkgos, whose seeds develop in ◊cones. Fossil gymnosperms have been found in rocks about 350 million years old.

**gynaecology** medical speciality concerned with disorders of the female reproductive system.

**gynoecium** or *gynaecium,* collective term for the female reproductive organs of a flower, consisting of one or more ◊carpels, either free or fused together.

**gyroscope** mechanical instrument, used as a stabilizing device and consisting, in its simplest form, of a heavy wheel mounted on an axis fixed in a ring that can be rotated about another axis, which is also fixed in a ring capable of rotation about a third axis. Applications of the gyroscope principle include the gyrocompass, the gyropilot for automatic steering, and gyro-directed torpedoes

**Haakon** seven kings of Norway, including:

**Haakon IV** (1204–1263) King of Norway from 1217, the son of Haakon III. Under his rule, Norway flourished both militarily and culturally; he took control of the Faroe Islands, Greenland 1261, and Iceland 1262–64. His court was famed throughout northern Europe.

**Haakon VII** (1872–1957) King of Norway from 1905. Born Prince Charles, the second son of Frederick VIII of Denmark, he was elected king of Norway on the country's separation from Sweden, and in 1906 he took the name Haakon. On the German invasion in 1940 he refused to accept Vidkun ◊Quisling's collaborationist government, and instead escaped to London and acted as constitutional head of the government-in-exile. He served as a powerful personification of Norwegian nationhood.

**Haarlem** industrial city and capital of the province of North Holland, the Netherlands, 20 km/12 mi west of Amsterdam; population (1997) 147,400. At Velsea, to the north, a road and rail tunnel runs under the North Sea Canal, linking North and South Holland. Industries include chemicals, pharmaceuticals, textiles, and printing. Haarlem is in an area of flowering bulbs and has a 15th–16th-century cathedral and a Frans Hals museum.

**habeas corpus** (Latin 'you may have the body') in law, a writ directed to someone who has custody of a person, ordering him or her to bring the person before the court issuing the writ and to justify why the person is detained in custody.

**Haber, Fritz** (1868–1934) German chemist whose conversion of atmospheric nitrogen to ammonia opened the way for the synthetic fertilizer industry. His study of the combustion of hydrocarbons led to the commercial 'cracking' or fractional distillation of natural oil (petroleum) into its components (for example, diesel, petrol, and paraffin). In electrochemistry, he was the first to demonstrate that oxidation and reduction take place at the electrodes; from this he developed a general electrochemical theory.

**habitat** in ecology, the localized environment in which an organism lives, and which provides for all (or almost all) of its needs. The diversity of habitats found within the Earth's ecosystem is enormous, and they are changing all the time. Many can be considered inorganic or physical;

for example, the Arctic ice cap, a cave, or a cliff face. Others are more complex; for instance, a woodland, or a forest floor. Some habitats are so precise that they are called *microhabitats*, such as the area under a stone where a particular type of insect lives. Most habitats provide a home for many species.

**Habsburg** or *Hapsburg,* European royal family, former imperial house of Austria–Hungary. A Habsburg, Rudolf I, became king of Germany in 1273 and began the family's control of Austria and Styria. They acquired a series of lands and titles, including that of Holy Roman Emperor which they held during 1273–91, 1298–1308, 1438–1740, and 1745–1806. The Habsburgs reached the zenith of their power under the emperor Charles V (1519–1556) who divided his lands, creating an Austrian Habsburg line (which ruled until 1918) and a Spanish line (which ruled to 1700).

**hacking** unauthorized access to a computer, either for fun or for malicious or fraudulent purposes. Hackers generally use microcomputers and telephone lines to obtain access. In computing, the term is used in a wider sense to mean using software for enjoyment or self-education, not necessarily involving unauthorized access. The most destructive form of hacking is the introduction of a computer virus.

**Hadar** or *Beta Centauri*, second-brightest star in the constellation of Centaurus, and the 11th-brightest in the night sky. It is a blue-white giant star of magnitude 0.61, some 320 light years from the Sun. It is a ◊binary star, comprising two stars of magnitudes 0.7 and 3.9.

**haddock** marine fish belonging to the cod family and found off the North Atlantic coastline. It is brown with silvery underparts and black markings above the pectoral fins. It can grow up to 1 m/3 ft in length. Haddock are important food fish; about 45 million kg/100 million lb are taken annually off the New England fishing banks alone. (Species *Melanogrammus aeglefinus,* family Gadidae.)

**Hades** in Greek mythology, the underworld where spirits (shades) went after death, usually depicted as a cavern or pit underneath the Earth, the entrance of which was guarded by the three-headed dog Cerberus. It was presided over by the god ◊Pluto, originally also known as Hades (Roman *Dis).* Pluto was the brother of Zeus and married ◊Persephone, daughter of Demeter and Zeus.

**Hadlee, Richard John** (1951– ) New Zealand cricketer who broke Ian Botham's world record of 373 test wickets and improved the total to 431, a figure then beaten by Kapil Dev in 1994. He played for Canterbury (NZ) and Nottinghamshire (England). In 1990 he retired from test cricket.
*career highlights*
*all first-class cricket* runs: 12,052; average: 31.78; best: 210 not out (Nottinghamshire v. Middlesex 1984); wickets: 1,490; average: 18.11; best: 9 for 52 (New Zealand v. Australia 1985–86)

**Test cricket** appearances: 86; runs: 3,124; average: 27.16; best: 151 not out (New Zealand v. Sri Lanka 1986–87); wickets: 431; average: 22.29; best: 9 for 52 (New Zealand v. Australia 1985–86)

**Hadrian, Publius Aelius Hadrianus** (AD 76–138) Roman emperor 117–138. He was adopted by the emperor Trajan, whom he succeeded. He pursued a policy of non-expansion and consolidation after the vast conquests of Trajan's reign. His defensive policy aimed at fixing the boundaries of the empire, which included the building of Hadrian's Wall in Britain. He travelled more widely than any other emperor, and consolidated both the army and Roman administration.

**Hadrian's Wall** line of fortifications built by the Roman emperor Hadrian (reigned AD 117–38) across northern Britain from the Cumbrian coast on the west to the North Sea on the east. The wall itself ran from Bowness on the Solway Firth to Wallsend on the river Tyne, a distance of 110 km/68 mi. It was defended by 16 forts and smaller intermediate fortifications. It was breached by the Picts on several occasions and finally abandoned in about 383.

**hadron** in physics, a subatomic particle that experiences the strong nuclear force. Each is made up of two or three indivisible particles called ◊quarks. The hadrons are grouped into the ◊baryons (protons, neutrons, and hyperons) and the ◊mesons (particles with masses between those of electrons and protons).

**haematite** principal ore of iron, consisting mainly of iron(III) oxide, $Fe_2O_3$. It occurs as *specular haematite* (dark, metallic lustre), *kidney ore* (reddish radiating fibres terminating in smooth, rounded surfaces), and a red earthy deposit.

**haematology** medical speciality concerned with disorders of the blood.

**haemoglobin** protein used by all vertebrates and some invertebrates for oxygen transport because the two substances combine reversibly. In vertebrates it occurs in red blood cells (erythrocytes), giving them their colour.

**haemophilia** any of several inherited diseases in which normal blood clotting is impaired. The sufferer experiences prolonged bleeding from the slightest wound, as well as painful internal bleeding without apparent cause.

**haemorrhage** loss of blood from the circulatory system. It is 'manifest' when the blood can be seen, as when it flows from a wound, and 'occult' when the bleeding is internal, as from an ulcer or internal injury.

**haemorrhoids** distended blood vessels (◊varicose veins) in the area of the anus, popularly called *piles*.

**haemostasis** natural or surgical stoppage of bleeding. In the natural mechanism, the damaged vessel contracts, restricting the flow, and blood ◊platelets plug the opening, releasing chemicals essential to clotting.

**hafnium** (Latin *Hafnia* 'Copenhagen') silvery, metallic element, symbol Hf, atomic number 72, relative atomic mass 178.49. It occurs in nature in ores of zirconium, the properties of which it resembles. Hafnium absorbs neutrons better than most metals, so it is used in the control rods of nuclear reactors; it is also used for light-bulb filaments.

**Hague, The** Dutch *'s-Gravenhage,* or *Den Haag,* capital of South Holland province, and seat of the Netherlands government, linked by canal to Rotterdam and Amsterdam, 3 km/2 mi from the North Sea; population (1997) 442,200.

**Haifa** chief seaport and industrial centre of Israel, situated in the northeast of the country at the foot of Mount Carmel, about 85 km/53 mi north of Tel Aviv; population (1995) 252,300. Industries include textiles, steel, chemicals, glass, soap, building materials, metal goods, and vehicle assembly. Israel's main naval base is here. It is the capital of a district of the same name.

**Haig, Douglas** 1st Earl Haig (1861–1928) Scottish army officer, commander in chief in World War I, born in Edinburgh, Scotland. His Somme offensive in France in the summer of 1916 made considerable advances only at enormous cost to human life, and his Passchendaele offensive in Belgium from July to November 1917 achieved little at a similar loss. He was created field marshal in 1917 and, after retiring, became first president of the British Legion in 1921.

**haiku** seventeen-syllable Japanese verse form, usually divided into three lines of five, seven, and five syllables. ◊Bashō popularized the form in the 17th century. It evolved from the 31-syllable *tanka* form dominant from the 8th century.

**hail** precipitation in the form of pellets of ice (hailstones). It is caused by the circulation of moisture in strong convection currents, usually within cumulonimbus ◊clouds.

**Haile Selassie, Ras (Prince) Tafari** 'the Lion of Judah' (1892–1975) Emperor of Ethiopia 1930–74. He pleaded unsuccessfully to the League of Nations against the Italian conquest of his country 1935–36, and was then deposed and fled to the UK. He went to Egypt in 1940 and raised an army, which he led into Ethiopia in January 1941 alongside British forces and was restored to the throne on 5 May. He was deposed by a military coup in 1974 and died in captivity the following year. Followers of the Rastafarian religion (see ◊Rastafarianism) believe that he was the Messiah, the incarnation of God (Jah).

**Hainan** island province of south China, in the South China Sea, off the southwest coast of Guangdong province
*area* 34,000 sq km/13,124 sq mi
*capital* Haikou
*towns* Wenchang, Xincun, Tongzha, Sanya
*physical* China's second-largest island; mountains in central and southern parts; plain in the north
*industries* tourism, food-processing
*agriculture* rice, sugar, rubber, pineapples, sugar, betel nuts, animal husbandry
*population* (1996) 7,340,000.

**Hainaut** Flemish *Henegouwen,* industrial province of southwest Belgium, bounded on its south side by France
**area** area 3,800 sq km/1,467 sq mi
**capital** Mons
**towns** Charleroi, Tournai, Soignies
**physical** the rivers Schelde and Sambre; fertile agricultural area in the north; extensive coal-fields in the south
**industries** iron, steel, glass, textiles
**agriculture** the arable land in the north produces wheat, sugar beet, barley, and oil seed rape
**population** (1997) 1,284,300
**history** the old county of Hainaut was united several times with Flanders. In 1433 it came under the rule of Burgundy; in 1477 under Austria; in 1555 under Spain. In the 17th century parts of it were acquired by France. It fell once again under Austrian rule in 1714; was incorporated in the united Netherlands in 1815 and eventually became a Belgian province in 1830.

**hair** fine filament growing from mammalian skin. Each hair grows from a pit-shaped follicle embedded in the second layer of the skin, the dermis. It consists of dead cells impregnated with the protein keratin.

**Haiti** Republic of
**national name** *République d'Haïti*

**area** 27,750 sq km/10,714 sq mi
**capital** Port-au-Prince
**major towns/cities** Cap-Haïtien, Gonaïves, Les Cayes, Port-de-Paix, Jérémie, Jacmée, St Marc
**physical features** mainly mountainous and tropical; occupies western third of Hispaniola Island in Caribbean Sea
**head of state** René Preval from 1995
**head of government** Jacques Edouard Alexis from 1998
**political system** transitional
**political parties** National Front for Change and Democracy (FNCD), left of centre; Lavalas Political Organization, populist
**currency** gourde

**GNP per capita (PPP)** (US$) 1,250 (1998 est)
**exports** manufactured articles, coffee, essential oils, sisal. Principal market: USA 81.4% (1997)
**population** 8,087,000 (1999 est)
**language** French (official, spoken by literate 10% minority), Creole (official)
**religion** Christian 95% (of which 80% are Roman Catholic), voodoo 4%
**life expectancy** 51 (men); 56 (women) (1995–2000)
**Chronology**
**14th century** Settled by Carib Indians, who followed an earlier wave of Arawak Indian immigration.
**1492** The first landing place of the explorer Christopher Columbus in the New World, who named the island Hispaniola ('Little Spain').
**1496** At Santo Domingo, now in the Dominican Republic to the east, the Spanish established the first European settlement in the Western hemisphere, which became capital of all Spanish colonies in America.
**first half of 16th century** A third of a million Arawaks and Caribs died, as a result of enslavement and exposure to European diseases; black African slaves were consequently brought in to work the island's gold and silver mines, which were swiftly exhausted.
**1697** Spain ceded western third of Hispaniola to France, which became known as Haiti, but kept the east, which was known as Santo Domingo (the Dominican Republic).
**1804** Independence achieved after uprising against French colonial rule led by the former slave Toussaint l'Ouverture, who died in prison in 1803, and Jean-Jacques Dessalines.
**1818–43** Ruled by Jean-Pierre Boyer, who excluded the blacks from power.
**1821** Santo Domingo fell under the control of Haiti until 1844.
**1847–59** Blacks reasserted themselves under President Faustin Soulouque.
**1915** Haiti invaded by USA as a result of political instability caused by black-mulatto friction; remained under US control until 1934.
**1956** Dr François Duvalier (Papa Doc), a voodoo physician, seized power in military coup and was elected president one year later.
**1964** Duvalier pronounced himself president for life, establishing a dictatorship based around a personal militia, the Tonton Macoutes.
**1971** Duvalier died, succeeded by his son Jean-Claude (Baby Doc); thousands murdered during Duvalier era.
**1986** Duvalier deposed and fled the country; replaced by Lt-Gen Henri Namphy as head of a governing council.
**1988** Leslie Manigat became president, but was ousted in a military coup by Brig-Gen Prosper Avril, who installed a civilian government under military control.
**1989** A coup attempt against Avril was foiled; US aid was resumed.
**1990** Left-wing Catholic priest Jean-Bertrand Aristide was elected president.
**1991** Aristide was overthrown in a military coup led by Brig-Gen Raoul Cedras. Sanctions were imposed by the Organization of American States (OAS) and the USA.

**1993** United Nations (UN) embargo was imposed. Aristide's return was blocked by the military.

**1994** The threat of a US invasion led to the regime recognizing Aristide as president, under an agreement brokered by the former US president Jimmy Carter. US troops landed peacefully; Cedras relinquished power and withdrew to Panama; and Aristide returned.

**1995** UN peacekeepers were drafted in to replace US troops. Assembly elections were won by Aristide's supporters. René Preval was elected to replace Aristide as president.

**1996** Peaceful handover of power to Preval.

**1997** Prime Minister Smarth resigned, following a series of strikes and protests; he was replaced by Herve Denis.

**1998** Jacques Edouard Alexis was nominated prime minister and endorsed by assembly.

**Haitink, Bernard** (1929– ) Dutch conductor. He was associated with the Concertgebouw Orchestra, Amsterdam, from 1958, and the London Philharmonic Orchestra from 1967; musical director at Glyndebourne 1977–87 and at the Royal Opera House, Covent Garden, London, 1987–98. He is a noted interpreter of Mahler and Shostakovitch.

**hajj** pilgrimage to Mecca that should be undertaken by every Muslim at least once in a lifetime, unless he or she is prevented by financial or health difficulties. A Muslim who has been on hajj may take the additional name Hajji. Many of the pilgrims on hajj also visit Medina, where the prophet Muhammad is buried.

**hake** any of various marine fishes belonging to the cod family, found in northern European, African, and American waters. They have silvery elongated bodies and grow up to 1 m/3 ft in length. They have two dorsal fins and one long anal fin. The silver hake (*M. bilinearis*) is an important food fish. (Genera *Merluccius* and *Urophycis*, family Gadidae.)

**Hakkinen, Mika Pauli** (1968– ) Finnish motor racing driver who won the 1998 Formula 1 World Drivers' Championship. He made his Formula 1 debut in 1991(for Lotus-Judd), a year after winning the British Formula 3 title. Switching to McLaren, he finished fourth in the championship in 1993 and 1994, and fifth in 1996, but it was not until the final race of the 1997 season that he won his first Formula 1 Grand Prix. In 1998, however, he won a further eight Grand Prix to take the drivers' crown and help McLaren-Mercedes to the Constructors' title.

*career highlights*
*total Grand Prix raced* 112
*Grand Prix wins* 9
*World Drivers' champion* 1998

**halal** (Arabic 'lawful') conforming to the rules laid down by Islam. The term can be applied to all aspects of life, but usually refers to food permissible under Muslim dietary laws, including meat from animals that have been slaughtered in the correct ritual fashion.

**Hale, George Ellery** (1868–1938) US astronomer. He made pioneer studies of the Sun and founded three major observatories. In 1889 he invented the spectroheliograph, a device for photographing the Sun at particular wavelengths. In 1917 he established on Mount Wilson, California, a 2.5-m/100-in reflector, the world's largest telescope until superseded 1948 by the 5-m/200-in reflector on Mount Palomar, which Hale had planned just before he died.

**Hale-Bopp, Comet** see ◊Comet Hale-Bopp.

**half-life** during ◊radioactive decay, the time in which the strength of a radioactive source decays to half its original value. In theory, the decay process is never complete and there is always some residual radioactivity. For this reason, the half-life of a radioactive isotope is measured, rather than the total decay time. It may vary from millionths of a second to billions of years.

**halftone process** technique used in printing to reproduce the full range of tones in a photograph or other illustration. The intensity of the printed colour is varied from full strength to the lightest shades, even if one colour of ink is used. The picture to be reproduced is photographed through a screen ruled with a rectangular mesh of fine lines, which breaks up the tones of the original into areas of dots that vary in frequency according to the intensity of the tone. In the darker areas the dots run together; in the lighter areas they have more space between them.

**halibut** any of a group of large flatfishes found in the Atlantic and Pacific oceans. The largest of the flatfishes, they may grow up to 2 m/6 ft in length and weigh 90–135 kg/200–300 lb. They are a very dark mottled brown or green above and pure white on the underside. The Atlantic halibut (*H. hippoglossus*) is caught offshore at depths from 180 m/600 ft to 730 m/2,400 ft. (Genus *Hippoglossus*, family Pleuronectidae.)

**Halifax** capital of ◊Nova Scotia, Canada, on the eastern shore of the province; population of city (1991)114,000; metropolitan area (1991) 321,000. It is the largest and most important city of the Canadian Maritime Provinces (consisting of Nova Scotia, Prince Edward Island, and New Brunswick), and is the main port in eastern Canada; industries include oil refining, food processing, and aerospace. Halifax Harbour is ice-free all year round, due to the warm Gulf Stream current. There are six military bases located here, and the city is a centre for oceanography.

**Hall, Peter (Reginald Frederick)** (1930– ) English theatre, opera, and film director. He was director of the Royal Shakespeare Theatre in Stratford-upon-Avon 1960–68 and developed the Royal Shakespeare Company 1968–73 until appointed director of the National Theatre 1973–88, succeeding Laurence Olivier. He founded the Peter Hall Company in 1988. He was knighted in 1977.

**Haller, Albrecht von** (1708–1777) Swiss physician and scientist, founder of neurology. He studied the muscles and nerves, and concluded that nerves provide the stimulus that triggers muscle contraction. He also showed that it is the nerves, not muscle or skin, that receive sensation.

**Halley, Edmond** (1656–1742) English astronomer. He not only identified the comet that was later to be known by his name, but also compiled a star catalogue, detected the proper motion of stars using historical records, and began a line of research that, after his death, resulted in a reasonably accurate calculation of the astronomical unit.

**Halley's comet** comet that orbits the Sun about every 76 years, named after English astronomer Edmond Halley who calculated its orbit. It is the brightest and most conspicuous of the periodic comets. Recorded sightings go back over 2,000 years. It travels around the Sun in the opposite direction to the planets. Its orbit is inclined at almost 20° to the main plane of the Solar System and ranges between the orbits of Venus and Neptune. It will next reappear 2061.

**hallucinogen** any substance that acts on the ◊central nervous system to produce changes in perception and mood and often hallucinations. Hallucinogens include ◊LSD, ◊peyote, and mescaline. Their effects are unpredictable and they are illegal in most countries.

**halogen** any of a group of five nonmetallic elements with similar chemical bonding properties: fluorine, chlorine, bromine, iodine, and astatine. They form a linked group in the ◊periodic table of the elements, descending from fluorine, the most reactive, to astatine, the least reactive. They combine directly with most metals to form salts, such as common salt (NaCl). Each halogen has seven electrons in its valence shell, which accounts for the chemical similarities displayed by the group.

**halon** organic chemical compound containing one or two carbon atoms, together with ◊bromine and other ◊halogens. The most commonly used are halon 1211 (bromochlorodifluoromethane) and halon 1301 (bromotrifluoromethane). The halons are gases and are widely used in fire extinguishers. As destroyers of the ◊ozone layer, they are up to ten times more effective than ◊chlorofluorocarbons (CFCs), to which they are chemically related.

**halophyte** plant adapted to live where there is a high concentration of salt in the soil, for example, in salt marshes and mud flats.

**Hals, Frans** (*c.* 1581–1666) Flemish-born painter. The pioneer in the Dutch school of free, broad brushwork, he painted directly on to the canvas to create portraits that are spontaneous and full of life. His work includes the famous *Laughing Cavalier* (1624;Wallace Collection, London), and group portraits of military companies, governors of charities, and others.

**Halton** unitary authority in northwest England, created in 1998 from part of Cheshire
*area* 74 sq km/29 sq mi
*towns and cities* Runcorn, Widnes (administrative headquarters), Ditton
*features* River Mersey divides Runcorn from Widnes and Ditton; Manchester Ship Canal and Bridgewater Canal reach Mersey at Runcorn; St Helen's Canal reaches Mersey via a series of locks at Widnes; Catalyst: the Museum of the Chemical Industry is at Widnes; Norton Priory Museum (Runcorn) is on the site of a 12th-century priory
*industries* industrial chemicals, pharmaceuticals, plastics manufacturing and coatings, light engineering, scientific instruments
*population* (1996) 122,300
*famous people* Charles Barkla, Thomas Caine, Robert Mond.

**Hamburg** largest inland port of Europe, in Germany, on the Elbe and Alster rivers, 103 km/ 64 mi from the mouth of the Elbe; population (1995) 1,706,800. Industries include marine engineering, ship-repairing, oil-refining, printing, publishing, and the production of chemicals, electronics, processed foods, and cosmetics. It is the capital of the *Land* of Hamburg, and has been an archbishopric since 834. In alliance with Lübeck, it founded the ◊Hanseatic League. The city suffered extensive bomb damage during World War II.

**Hamburg** administrative region (German *Land*) of Germany, situated between Schleswig-Holstein and Lower Saxony
*area* 760 sq km/293 sq mi
*capital* Hamburg
*physical* comprises the city and surrounding districts; fenland areas are dyked in some parts; sandy heathlands away from the River Elbe
*features* four universities (earliest established in 1919); the Hamburg Schauspielhaus is one of Germany's leading theatres
*industries* refined oil, chemicals, electrical goods, marine engineering, ship-repairing, food-processing, printing, publishing
*agriculture* area is mostly urban, but small parts of fenland are used for dairying and apple orchards
*population* (1995) 1,706,800
*religion* 74% Protestant, 8% Roman Catholic
*history* reputedly founded by Charlemagne in the early 9th century. A trading league formed with Lübeck in 1241 developed into the Hanseatic League, with influence throughout the North Sea and Baltic coastal regions, and along the rivers well into the German lands. In 1510 the Emperor Maximilian I made Hamburg a free imperial city, and in 1871 it became a state of the German Empire.

**Hamed, 'Prince' Naseem** (1974–   ) English boxer. Born in Sheffield of Yemeni extraction and known as 'Prince' Naseem for his showmanship qualities. An exceptionally strong puncher for a featherweight, he is widely regarded as one of British boxing's greatest talents. He made his professional debut in 1992 and by April 1999 he was still unbeaten after 30 fights. He won the European bantamweight title and the WBC International super-bantamweight championship in 1994, before capturing the WBO world featherweight title in September 1995. He won the IBF version of the world featherweight title in February 1997, but relinquished it after a few months. In January 1999 he was awarded an MBE in the New Year Honours List. As of 12 April 1999 his record as a professional fighter listed 32 wins (29 inside the distance) and no defeats.

**Hamilcar Barca** (died 229 BC) Carthaginian general, the father of ◊Hannibal the Great. Hamilcar rose to prominence in 249 BC at the first Battle of Eryx, during the later stages of the First Punic War. He negotiated the peace treaty with the Carthaginians at the end of the war in 241 BC, and suppressed the revolt of Carthage's foreign troops, the Mercenary War (241–237 BC). He then campaigned in Spain until his death, substantially enlarging and enriching the Carthaginian Empire.

**Hamilton** capital (since 1815) of Bermuda, on Bermuda Island; population about (1994) 1,100. It has a deep-sea harbour.

**Hamilton, Alexander** (1757–1804) US politician who influenced the adoption of a constitution with a strong central government and was the first secretary of the Treasury 1789–95. He led the Federalist Party, and incurred the bitter hatred of Aaron Burr when he voted against Burr and in favour of Thomas Jefferson for the presidency 1801. Challenged to a duel by Burr, Hamilton was wounded and died the next day.

**Hamilton, Richard** (1922– ) English artist, a pioneer of Pop art. His collage *Just What Is It That Makes Today's Homes So Different, So Appealing?* (1956; Kunsthalle, Tübingen, Germany) is often cited as the first Pop art work: its 1950s interior, inhabited by the bodybuilder Charles Atlas and a pin-up, is typically humorous, concerned with popular culture and contemporary kitsch.

**Hammarskjöld, Dag (Hjalmar Agne Carl)** (1905–1961) Swedish secretary general of the United Nations 1953–61. He opposed the UK over the ◊Suez Crisis of 1956. His attempts to solve the problem of the Congo (now the Democratic Republic of Congo), where he was killed in a plane crash, were criticized by the USSR. He was awarded the Nobel Peace Prize in 1961.

**hammer** throwing event in track and field athletics. The hammer is a spherical weight attached to a wire with a handle. The competitors spin the hammer over their heads to gain momentum, within the confines of a circle, and throw it as far as they can. The senior men's hammer weighs 7.26 kg/16 lb and may originally have been a blacksmith's hammer. Women and junior men throw lighter implements.

**hammerhead** any of several species of shark found in tropical seas, characterized by having eyes at the ends of flattened hammerlike extensions of the skull. Hammerheads can grow to 4 m/13 ft in length. (Genus *Sphyrna*, family Sphyrnidae.)

**Hammerstein, Oscar, II** (1895–1960) US lyricist and librettist. He collaborated with Richard ◊Rodgers over a period of 16 years on some of the best-known US musicals, including *Oklahoma!* (1943; Pulitzer prize), *Carousel* 1945, *South Pacific* (1949; Pulitzer prize), *The King and I* (1951), and *The Sound of Music* (1959).

**Hammett, (Samuel) Dashiell** (1894–1961) US crime novelist. He introduced the 'hardboiled' detective character into fiction and attracted a host of imitators, with works including *The Maltese Falcon* (1930, filmed 1941), *The Glass Key* (1931, filmed 1942), and his most successful novel, the light-hearted *The Thin Man* (1932, filmed 1934). His Marxist politics were best expressed in *Red Harvest* (1929), which depicts the corruption of capitalism in 'Poisonville'.

**Hampshire** county of south England (since April 1997 Portsmouth and Southampton have been separate unitary authorities)
*area* 3,679 sq km/1,420 sq mi
*towns and cities* ◊Winchester (administrative headquarters), Aldershot, Andover, Basingstoke, Eastleigh, Gosport, Romsey, and Lymington
*physical* New Forest (area 373 sq km/144 sq mi), in the southeast of the county, a Saxon royal hunting ground; rivers Avon, Ichen, and Test (which has trout fishing)
*features* Hampshire Basin, where Britain has onshore and offshore oil; Danebury, 2,500-year-old Celtic hill fort; Beaulieu (including National Motor Museum); Broadlands (home of Lord Mountbatten); Highclere castle (home of the Earl of Carnarvon, with gardens by Capability Brown); Hambledon, where the first cricket club was founded in 1750; site of the Roman town of Silchester; Jane Austen's cottage at Chawton (1809–17), now a museum; Twyford Down section of the M3 motorway was completed in 1994 despite protests
*agriculture* market gardening (watercress)
*industries* aeronautics, brewing, chemicals, electronics, light engineering (at Basingstoke), oil from refineries at Fawley, perfume, pharmaceuticals
*population* (1996) 1,627,400
*famous people* Jane Austen, Charles Dickens, Gilbert White.

**hamster** any of a group of burrowing rodents with a thickset body, short tail, and cheek pouches to carry food. Several genera are found across Asia and in southeastern Europe. Hamsters are often kept as pets. (Genera include *Cricetus* and *Mesocricetus*, family Cricetidae.)

**Han** the majority ethnic group in China, numbering about 990 million. The Hans speak a wide variety of dialects of the same monosyllabic language, a member of the Sino-Tibetan family. Their religion combines Buddhism, Taoism, Confucianism, and ancestor worship.

**hand** unit used in measuring the height of a horse from front hoof to shoulder (withers). One hand equals 10.2 cm/4 in.

**Handel, George Frideric** originally Georg Friedrich Händel (1685–1759) German composer, a British subject from 1726. His first opera, *Almira*, was performed in Hamburg in 1705. In 1710 he was appointed Kapellmeister to the elector of Hanover (the future George I of England). In 1712 he settled in England, where he established his popularity with such works as the *Water Music* (1717), written for George I.

His great choral works include the *Messiah* (1742) and the later oratorios *Samson* (1743), *Belshazzar* (1745), *Judas Maccabaeus* (1747), and *Jephtha* (1752).

**hang-gliding** technique of unpowered flying using air currents, perfected by US engineer Francis Rogallo in the 1970s. The aeronaut is strapped into a carrier, attached to a sail wing of nylon stretched on an aluminium frame like a paper dart, and jumps into the air from a high place, where updraughts of warm air allow soaring on the thermals. See ◊gliding.

**Hangzhou** or *Hangchow,* port and capital of ◊Zhejiang province, China, on the mouth of the Qiantang River, at the southern terminus of the ◊Grand Canal, 175 km/109 mi southwest of Shanghai; population (1994) 1,412,700. Products include jute, steel, machine tools, chemicals, electronics, processed foods, tea, silk and cotton textiles, fans, and gold-embroidered goods. Hangzhou has fine landscaped gardens, and was the capital of China from 1127 to 1278 under the Song dynasty.

**Hannibal** (247–182 BC) 'the Great', Carthaginian general from 221 BC, son of Hamilcar Barca. His siege of Saguntum (now Sagunto, near Valencia) precipitated the Second ◊Punic War with Rome. Following a campaign in Italy (after crossing the Alps in 218), Hannibal was the victor at Trasimene in 217 and Cannae in 216, but he failed to take Rome. In 203 he returned to Carthage to meet a Roman invasion but was defeated at Zama in 202 and exiled in 196 at Rome's insistence.

**Hannover** or *Hanover,* industrial city and capital of Lower Saxony, Germany, on the rivers Leine and Ihme; population (1995) 524,600. Industries include mechanical engineering, telecommunications, and the manufacture of electrical goods, rubber, and textiles. From 1386 it was a member of the ◊Hanseatic League, and from 1692 capital of the electorate of Hannover (created a kingdom in 1815). ◊George I of Great Britain and Ireland was also Elector of Hannover.

**Hanoi** capital of Vietnam, on the Red River; population (1989) 1,088,900. Central Hanoi has one of the highest population densities in the world: 1,300 people per hectare/3,250 per acre. Industries include textiles, paper, and engineering.

**Hansard** official report of the proceedings of the British Houses of Parliament, named after Luke Hansard (1752–1828), printer of the House of Commons *Journal* from 1774. It is published by Her Majesty's Stationery Office. The name *Hansard* was officially adopted in 1943. Hansard can now be consulted on the Internet.

**Hanseatic League** (German *Hanse* 'group, society') confederation of northern European trading cities from the 12th century to 1669. At its height in the late 14th century the Hanseatic League included over 160 cities and towns, among them Lübeck, Hamburg, Cologne, Breslau, and Kraków. The basis of the league's power was its monopoly of the Baltic trade and its relations with Flanders and England. The decline of the Hanseatic League from the 15th century was caused by the closing and moving of trade routes and the development of nation states.

**Hanukkah** or *Hanukah* or *Chanukkah,* in Judaism, an eight-day festival of lights that takes place at the beginning of December. It celebrates the recapture and rededication of the Temple in Jerusalem by Judas Maccabaeus in 164 BC.

**haploid** having a single set of ◊chromosomes in each cell. Most higher organisms are ◊diploid – that is, they have two sets – but their gametes (sex cells) are haploid. Some plants, such as mosses, liverworts, and many seaweeds, are haploid, and male honey bees are haploid because they develop from eggs that have not been fertilized. See also ◊meiosis.

**Hapsburg** alternative form of ◊Habsburg, former imperial house of Austria–Hungary.

**Harare** formerly *Salisbury,* capital of Zimbabwe, in Mashonaland East Province, about 1,525 m/5,000 ft above sea level; population (1992) 1,184,200. It is the centre of a rich farming area producing tobacco and maize. The city's industries include milling, textiles, electrical and mechanical engineering, motor assembly, railway rolling stock, chemicals, furniture, consumer goods, and metallurgical and food processing.

**Harbin** *Haerhpin* or *Pinkiang,* port and capital of ◊Heilongjiang province, northeast China, on the Songhua River; population (1994) 2,887,800. It is a major rail junction. Industries include metallurgy, food processing, and sugar-refining; the manufacture of machinery and paper; and tourism. Harbin was developed by Russian settlers after Russia was granted trading rights here in 1896, and more Russians arrived as refugees after the October Revolution (1917). In World War II, it was the key objective of the Soviet invasion of Manchuria in August 1945.

**hard disk** in computing, a storage device usually consisting of a rigid metal ◊disk coated with a magnetic material. Data are read from and written to the disk by means of a disk drive. The hard disk may be permanently fixed into the drive or in the form of a disk pack that can be removed and exchanged with a different pack. Hard disks vary from large units with capacities of more than 3,000 megabytes, intended for use with mainframe computers, to small units with capacities as low as 20 megabytes, intended for use with microcomputers.

**Hardicanute** (*c.* 1019–1042) King of Denmark from 1028, and of England from 1040; son of Canute. In England he was considered a harsh ruler.

**Hardie, (James) Keir** (1856–1915) Scottish socialist, the first British Labour politician, member of Parliament 1892–95 and 1900–15. He worked in the mines as a boy and in 1886 became secretary of the Scottish Miners' Federation. In 1888 he was the first Labour candidate to stand for Parliament; he entered Parliament independently as a Labour member in 1892, he became chair of the Labour party

1906–08 and 1909–10, and in 1893 was a chief founder of the Independent Labour Party.

**Harding, Warren G(amaliel)** (1865–1923) 29th president of the USA 1921–23, a Republican. As president he concluded the peace treaties of 1921 with Germany, Austria, and Hungary, and in the same year called the Washington Naval Conference to resolve conflicting British, Japanese, and US ambitions in the Pacific. He opposed US membership of the ◊League of Nations. There were charges of corruption among members of his cabinet (the Teapot Dome Scandal), with the secretary of the interior later convicted for taking bribes.

**hardness** physical property of materials that governs their use. Methods of heat treatment can increase the hardness of metals. A scale of hardness was devised by German–Austrian mineralogist Friedrich Mohs in the 1800s, based upon the hardness of certain minerals from soft talc (Mohs hardness 1) to diamond (10), the hardest of all materials.

**hardware** mechanical, electrical, and electronic components of a computer system, as opposed to the various programs, which constitute ◊software.

**hard water** water that does not lather easily with soap, and produces a deposit or 'scale' in kettles. It is caused by the presence of certain salts of calcium and magnesium.

**Hardy, Thomas** (1840–1928) English novelist and poet. His novels, set in rural 'Wessex' (his native West Country), portray intense human relationships played out in a harshly indifferent natural world. They include *Far From the Madding Crowd* (1874), *The Return of the Native* (1878), *The Mayor of Casterbridge* (1886), *The Woodlanders* (1887), *Tess of the d'Urbervilles* (1891), and *Jude the Obscure* (1895). His poetry includes the *Wessex Poems* (1898), the blank-verse epic of the Napoleonic Wars *The Dynasts* (1903–08), and several volumes of lyrics. Many of his books have been successfully dramatized for film and television.

**hare** mammal closely related to the rabbit, similar in appearance but larger. Hares have very long black-tipped ears, long hind legs, and short upturned tails. (Genus *Lepus*, family Leporidae, order Lagomorpha.)

**harebell** perennial plant of the ◊bellflower family, with bell-shaped blue flowers, found on dry grassland and heaths. It is known in Scotland as the bluebell. (*Campanula rotundifolia*, family Campanulaceae.)

**Hare Krishna** popular name for a member of the ◊International Society for Krishna Consciousness, derived from their chant.

**Hargreaves, James** (*c.* 1720–1778) English inventor who co-invented a carding machine for combing wool in 1760. About 1764 he invented his 'spinning jenny' (patented in 1770), which enabled a number of threads to be spun simultaneously by one person.

**Harlow, Jean** stage name of Harlean Carpentier (1911–1937) US film actress. She was the original 'platinum blonde' and the wisecracking sex symbol of the 1930s. Her films include *Hell's Angels* (1930), *Red Dust* (1932), *Platinum Blonde* (1932), *Dinner at Eight* (1933), *China Seas* (1935), and *Saratoga* (1937), during the filming of which she died (her part was completed by a double).

**harmonica** musical instrument, a pocket-sized reed organ blown directly from the mouth, invented by Charles Wheatstone in 1829; see ◊mouth organ.

**harmonium** keyboard reed organ of the 19th century, powered by foot-operated bellows and incorporating lever-action knee swells to influence dynamics. It was invented by Alexandre Debain in Paris about 1842.

**harmony** in music, any simultaneous combination of sounds, as opposed to melody, which is a succession of sounds. Although the term suggests a pleasant or agreeable sound, it is applied to any combination of notes, whether consonant or dissonant. The theory of harmony

---

### HARDY: MAJOR WORKS

| Title | Date | Well-known characters |
|---|---|---|
| *Under the Greenwood Tree* | 1872 | Joseph Bowman, Fancy Day, Dick Dewy, Reuben Dewy, William Dewy, Arthur Maybold, Farmer Fred Shiner |
| *Far From the Madding Crowd* | 1874 | William Boldwood, Bathsheba Everdene, Gabriel Oak, Joseph Poorgrass, Fanny Robin, Lyddy Smallbury, Sergeant Francis Troy |
| *The Return of the Native* | 1878 | Christian Cantle, Grandfer Cantle, Diggory Venn, Clym Yeobright, Mrs Yeobright, Thomasin Yeobright, Damon Wildeve |
| *The Trumpet Major* | 1880 | Festus Derriman, Anne Garland, Mrs Garland, Bob Loveday, John Loveday |
| *The Mayor of Casterbridge* | 1886 | Suke Damson, Donald Farfrae, Elizabeth Jane Henchard, Mrs Henchard, Michael Henchard, Richard Newson, Lucetta Templeman/Le Sueur |
| *The Woodlanders* | 1887 | Felice Charmond, Robert Creedle, Edred Fitzpiers, Grace Melbury, Marty South, Giles Winterbourne |
| *Tess of the d'Urbervilles* | 1891 | Mercy Chant, Angel Clare, Rev James Clare, Dairyman Crick, Car Darch, Izz Huett, Marian, Retty Priddle, Alec d'Urberville, Tess Durbeyfield, John and Joan Durbeyfield |
| *Jude the Obscure* | 1895 | Sue Bridehead, Arabella Donn, Jude Fawley, Little Father Time, Richard Phillotson |

deals with the formation of chords and their interrelation and logical progression.

**harness racing** form of horse racing, also known as trotting or pacing, in which the horses are harnessed, pull a light vehicle (sulky) and compete at either a trotting or pacing gait. If a horse breaks the pace and gallops, the driver must start it again.

**Harold** two kings of England:

**Harold I** (1016–1040) King of England from 1035. The illegitimate son of Canute, known as *Harefoot*, he claimed the crown on the death of his father, when the rightful heir, his half-brother Hardicanute, was in Denmark and unable to ascend the throne. He was elected king in 1037, but died three years later, as Hardicanute was preparing to invade England.

**Harold (II) Godwinson** (*c.* 1020–1066) last Anglo-Saxon king of England, January to October 1066. He was defeated and killed by William of Normandy (◊William (I) the Conqueror) at the Battle of Hastings.

**harp** plucked musical string instrument, with the strings stretched vertically and parallel to one member of a triangular framework. A second member of the triangle is a wood and brass soundbox of triangular shape; the third member locates pegs by means of which the strings are tensioned. The orchestral harp is the largest instrument of its type. It has up to 47 diatonically tuned strings, in the range B0–C7 (seven octaves), and seven double-action pedals to alter pitch. Before the pedals are depressed, the strings sound the diatonic scale of C-flat major, but each note can be raised a semitone or a whole tone by one of the pedals. Thus all the notes of the chromatic scale can be sounded.

**Harper's Ferry** town in Jefferson County, West Virginia, in the Blue Ridge Mountains, where the Potomac and Shenandoah rivers meet; population (1990) 300. It was first settled in 1732 and incorporated as a town in 1763. In 1859 the antislavery leader John ◊Brown seized the federal government's arsenal here, an action that helped precipitate the American Civil War.

**harpsichord** the largest and grandest of 18th-century keyboard string instruments, used in orchestras and as a solo instrument. The strings are plucked by 'jacks' made of leather or quill, and multiple keyboards offering variation in tone are common. However, unlike the piano, the tone cannot be varied by the player's touch. The revival of the harpsichord repertoire in the 20th century owes much to Wanda Landowska and Ralph Kirkpatrick (1911–1984).

**Harpy** (Greek 'snatcher') in early Greek mythology, a wind spirit; in later legend, such as the story of the ◊Argonauts, a female monster with a horrific face, pale with hunger, and the body of a vulture. Often associated with the underworld, harpies were believed to abduct those people who disappeared without trace, and were perceived as an instrument of torment used by the gods.

**Harrier** the only truly successful vertical take-off and landing fixed-wing aircraft, often called the *jump jet*. It was built in Britain and made its first flight in 1966. It has a single jet engine and a set of swivelling nozzles. These deflect the jet exhaust vertically downwards for takeoff and landing, and to the rear for normal flight. Designed to fly from confined spaces with minimal ground support, it refuels in midair.

**harrier** any of a group of birds of prey. Harriers have long wings and legs, a small head with a short beak, an owl-like frill of thickset feathers around the face, and soft plumage. They eat frogs, birds, snakes, and small mammals, and are found mainly in marshy areas throughout the world. (Genus *Circus*, family Accipitridae, order Falconiformes.)

**Harrison, Benjamin** (1833–1901) 23rd president of the USA 1889–93, a Republican. He called the first Pan-American Conference, which led to the establishment of the Pan-American Union, to improve inter-American cooperation and develop commercial ties. In 1948 this became the ◊Organization of American States.

**Harrison, Rex (Reginald Carey)** (1908–1990) English film and theatre actor. He appeared in over 40 films and numerous plays, often portraying sophisticated and somewhat eccentric characters, such as the waspish Professor Higgins in *My Fair Lady* (1964; Academy Award), the musical version of *Pygmalion*. His other films include *Blithe Spirit* (1945), *The Ghost and Mrs Muir* (1947), and *Dr Doolittle* (1967).

**hartebeest** large African antelope with lyre-shaped horns set close on top of the head in both sexes. It can grow to 1.5 m/5 ft tall at the rather humped shoulders and up to 2 m/6 ft long. Although they are clumsy-looking runners, hartebeest can reach speeds of 65 kph/40 mph. (Species *Alcelaphus buselaphus*, family Bovidae.)

**Hartington, Spencer Compton Cavendish,** Marquess of Hartington and 8th Duke of Devonshire (1833–1908) British politician, first leader of the Liberal Unionists 1886–1903. As war minister he opposed devolution for Ireland in cabinet and later led the revolt of the Liberal Unionists that defeated Gladstone's Irish Home Rule bill of 1886. Hartington refused the premiership three times, in 1880, 1886, and 1887, and led the opposition to the Irish Home Rule bill in the House of Lords in 1893.

**Hartlepool** town, port, and, since 1996, unitary authority in northeast England, formed from part of the county of Cleveland
*area* 94 sq km/36 sq mi
*features* redeveloped dock area including the Museum of Hartlepool (opened in 1995); the Gray Art Gallery and Museum; remains of the medieval town walls; Early English church of St Hilda with a Norman doorway
*industries* the local economy depends on metal industries, engineering, support services for the oil industry, fishing, and brewing. A nuclear power station is located 5 km/3 mi southeast of the town at Seaton Carew
*population* (1996) 90,400

**famous people** Christopher Furness, Compton Mackenzie, Edward Mellanby, Kenneth Mellanby.

**Hartz Mountains** range running N–S in Tasmania, Australia, with two remarkable peaks: Hartz Mountain (1,254 m/4,113 ft) and Adamsons Peak (1,224 m/4,017 ft).

**harvestman** small animal (an ◊arachnid) related to spiders with very long, thin legs and a small body. Harvestmen are different from true spiders in that they do not have a waist or narrow part to the oval body. They feed on small insects and spiders, and lay their eggs in autumn, to hatch the following spring or early summer. They are found from the Arctic to the tropics. (Order Opiliones.)

**Harvey, William** (1578–1657) English physician who discovered the circulation of blood. In 1628 he published his book *De motu cordis/On the Motion of the Heart and the Blood in Animals.* He also explored the development of chick and deer embryos.

**Haryana** (Hindi 'God's home') state of northwest India
**area** 44,200 sq km/17,061 sq mi
**capital** ◊Chandigarh (also capital of Punjab state)
**physical** part of the Gangetic plain; drained by the Yamuna River
**features** a centre of Hinduism; the Grand Trunk Road (from Peshawar to Calcutta) runs through it
**industries** textiles, cement, iron ore, agricultural processing
**agriculture** wheat (with Punjab accounting for one-third of India's total production), sugar, cotton, oilseed, rice, pulses
**population** (1994 est) 17,925,000
**language** Hindi
**history** created in 1966 when Punjab state was divided on linguistic grounds into the Hindi-speaking Haryana (mainly Hindu) and the predominantly Sikh Punjab (Punjabi-speaking)(see ◊Sikhism).

**hashish** drug made from the resin contained in the female flowering tops of hemp (◊cannabis).

**Hasidism** or *Hassidism* or *Chasidism* or *Chassidism,* sect of Orthodox Judaism, originating in 18th-century Poland under the leadership of Israel Ba'al Shem Tov (*c.* 1700–1760). Hasidic teachings encourage prayer, piety, and 'serving the Lord with joy'. Many of the Hasidic ideas are based on the ◊kabbala.

**Hassan II** (1929– ) King of Morocco from 1961. He succeeded the throne upon the death of his father Mohamed V. Following riots in Casablanca in 1965, he established a royal dictatorship and survived two coup attempts. The occupation of the former Spanish Western Sahara in 1976 enabled him to rally strong popular support and consolidate his power. He returned to constitutional government in 1984, with a civilian prime minister leading a government of national unity.

**hassium** synthesized, radioactive element of the ◊transactinide series, symbol Hs, atomic number 108, relative atomic mass 265. It was first synthesized in 1984 by the Laboratory for Heavy Ion Research in Darmstadt, Germany. Its temporary name was unniloctium.

**Hastert, Denny** J Dennis (1942– ) US Republican politician, speaker of the House of Representatives from 1999. Known as 'the Coach' for his work as a high-school teacher and wrestling coach 1964–80, Hastert served in the Illinois General Assembly from 1980 until 1986, when he was first elected a representative to Congress for the 14th District of Illinois. He was appointed in 1993 as the House Republican representative on the White House Healthcare Reform Task Force, chaired by Hillary ◊Clinton, and chaired the Speaker's Steering Committee on Health and the Resource Group on Health. He was appointed Chief Deputy Whip for the Republicans in 1995, and was a member of the Commerce Committee and the Committee of Government Reform and Oversight.

**Hastings, Battle of** battle on 14 October 1066 at which William, Duke of Normandy ('the Conqueror') defeated King Harold of England, and himself took the throne. The site is 10 km/6 mi inland from Hastings, at Senlac, Sussex; it is marked by Battle Abbey.

**Haute-Normandie** English *Upper Normandy,* coastal region of northwest France lying between Basse-Normandie and Picardy and bisected by the River Seine; area 12,300 sq km/4,757 sq mi; population (1990) 1,737,200. It comprises the *départements* of Eure and Seine-Maritime; its administrative centre is Rouen. Ports include Le Havre, Dieppe and Fécamp. The area is fertile and has many beech forests. There is dairy-farming and fishing, cars are manufactured, and the region is a petrochemical centre.

**Havana** capital and port of Cuba, on the northwest coast of the island; population (1990) 2,096,100. Products include cigars and tobacco, sugar, coffee, and fruit. The palace of the Spanish governors and the stronghold of La Fuerza (1583) survive.

**Havel, Václav** (1936– ) Czech dramatist and politician, president of Czechoslovakia 1989–92 and of the Czech Republic from 1993. His plays include *The Garden Party* (1963) and *Largo Desolato* (1985), about a dissident intellectual. Havel became widely known as a human-rights activist. He was imprisoned 1979–83 and again 1989 for support of Charter 77, a human-rights manifesto. As president of Czechoslovakia he sought to preserve a united republic, but resigned in recognition of the breakup of the federation 1992. In 1993 he became president of the newly independent Czech Republic. In December 1996 he underwent surgery for lung cancer but was re-elected president, by the Czech parliament, in January 1998.

**Hawaii** Pacific state of the USA. It is nicknamed the Aloha State. Hawaii was admitted to the Union in 1959 as the 50th US state. The only

state not part of North America, Hawaii, variously described as part of Oceania or Polynesia, comprises a west-northwest–east-southeast oriented island chain 2,700km/1,700 mi in length, the east end of which lies some 3,400km/2,100 mi southwest of California. The Tropic of Cancer passes through the islands
**population** (1995) 1,186,800 (34% of European descent, 25% Japanese, 14% Filipino, 12% Hawaiian, 6% Chinese)
**area** 16,800 sq km/6,485 sq mi
**capital** ◊Honolulu on Oahu
**towns and cities** Hilo, Kailua, Kaneohe
**industries and products** tourism is the chief source of income; other industries include sugar, coffee, pineapples, macadamia nuts, orchids and other flowers, livestock, poultry, dairy goods, clothing.

**hawfinch** European ◊finch, about 18 cm/7 in long. It feeds on berries and seeds, and can crack cherry stones with its large, powerful beak. The male bird has brown plumage, a black throat and black wings with a bold white shoulder stripe, a short white-tipped tail, and a broad band of grey at the back of the neck. (Species *Coccothraustes coccothraustes,* family Fringillidae, order Passeriformes.)

**hawk** any of a group of small to medium-sized birds of prey, belonging to the same family as eagles, kites, ospreys, and vultures. Hawks have short, rounded wings and a long tail compared with ◊falcons, and keen eyesight; the ◊sparrowhawk and ◊goshawk are examples. (Especially genera *Accipiter* and *Buteo,* family Accipitridae.)

**Hawking, Stephen (William)** (1942– ) English physicist whose work in general ◊relativity – particularly gravitational field theory – led to a search for a quantum theory of gravity to explain ◊black holes and the ◊Big Bang, singularities that classical relativity theory does not adequately explain. His book *A Brief History of Time* (1988) gives a popular account of cosmology and became an international bestseller. His latest book is *The Nature of Space and Time* (1996), written with Roger Penrose.

**Hawkins, Coleman (Randolph)** (1904–1969) US virtuoso tenor saxophonist. He was, until 1934, a soloist in the swing band led by Fletcher Henderson (1898–1952), and was an influential figure in bringing the jazz saxophone to prominence as a solo instrument.

**hawk moth** any member of a family of ◊moths with more than 1,000 species distributed throughout the world, but found mainly in tropical regions. Some South American hawk moths closely resemble hummingbirds. (Family Sphingidae.)

**Hawks, Howard (Winchester)** (1896–1977) US director, screenwriter, and producer. He made a wide range of classic films in virtually every American genre. Swift-moving and immensely accomplished, his films include the gangster movie *Scarface* (1932), the screwball comedy *Bringing Up Baby* (1938), the *film noir The Big Sleep* (1946), the musical comedy *Gentlemen Prefer Blondes* (1953), and the western *Rio Bravo* (1959).

**Hawksmoor, Nicholas** (1661–1736) English architect. He was assistant to Christopher ◊Wren in designing various London churches and St Paul's Cathedral, and joint architect of Castle Howard and Blenheim Palace with John ◊Vanbrugh. His genius is displayed in a quirky and uncompromising style incorporating elements from both Gothic and Classical sources.

**hawthorn** any of a group of shrubs or trees belonging to the rose family, growing abundantly in eastern North America, and also in Europe and Asia. All have alternate, toothed leaves and bear clusters of showy white, pink, or red flowers. Their small applelike fruits can be red, orange, blue, or black. Hawthorns are popular as ornamentals. (Genus *Crataegus,* family Rosaceae.)

**Haydn, (Franz) Joseph** (1732–1809) Austrian composer. He was a major exponent of the classical sonata form in his numerous chamber and orchestral works (he wrote more than 100 symphonies). He also composed choral music, including the oratorios *The Creation* (1798) and *The Seasons* (1801). He was the first great master of the string quartet, and was a teacher of Mozart and Beethoven.

**Hayes, Rutherford (Birchard)** (1822–1893) 19th president of the USA 1877–81, a Republican. He was a major general on the Union side in the Civil War. During his presidency federal troops were withdrawn from the Southern states (after ◊Reconstruction) and the Civil Service was reformed.

**hay fever** allergic reaction to pollen, causing sneezing, with inflammation of the nasal membranes and conjunctiva of the eyes. Symptoms are due to the release of ◊histamine. Treatment is by antihistamine drugs. An estimated 25% of Britons, 33% of Americans, and 40% of Australians suffer from hayfever.

**hazardous waste** waste substance, usually generated by industry, that represents a hazard to the environment or to people living or working nearby. Examples include radioactive wastes, acidic resins, arsenic residues, residual hardening salts, lead from car exhausts, mercury, nonferrous sludges, organic solvents, asbestos, chlorinated solvents, and pesticides. The cumulative effects of toxic waste can take some time to become apparent (anything from a few hours to many years), and pose a serious threat to the ecological stability of the planet; its economic disposal or recycling is the subject of research.

**hazel** any of a group of shrubs or trees that includes the European common hazel or cob (*C. avellana*), of which the filbert is the cultivated variety. North American species include the American hazel (*C. americana*). (Genus *Corylus,* family Corylaceae.)

**H-bomb** abbreviation for ◊*hydrogen bomb.*

**HDTV** abbreviation for ◊*high-definition television.*

**head louse** parasitic insect that lives in human hair. See ◊louse.

harmful/irritant

toxic

radioactive

explosive

flammable

corrosive

oxidizing/supports fire

biohazardous/infectious

environmentally dangerous

**hazardous waste** *The internationally recognized symbols, warning of the potential dangers of handling certain substances.*

**health, world** the health of people worldwide is monitored by the ◊World Health Organization (WHO). Outside the industrialized world in particular, poverty and degraded environmental conditions mean that easily preventable diseases are widespread: WHO estimated in 1990 that 1 billion people, or 20% of the world's population, were diseased, in poor health, or malnourished. In North Africa and the Middle East, 25% of the population were ill.

**Heaney, Seamus (Justin)** (1939– ) Irish poet and critic. He has written powerful verse about the political situation in Northern Ireland and reflections on Ireland's cultural heritage. Collections include *Death of a Naturalist* (1966), *Field Work* (1979), *The Haw Lantern* (1987), and *The Spirit Level* (1996; Whitbread Book of the Year), *Opened Ground: Poems 1966–1996* (1998). Critical works include *The Redress of Poetry* (1995). In 1999 he published *Beowulf: A New Translation.* He was professor of poetry at Oxford 1989–94 and was awarded the Nobel Prize for Literature in 1995.

**heart** muscular organ that rhythmically contracts to force blood around the body of an animal with a circulatory system. Annelid worms and some other invertebrates have simple hearts consisting of thickened sections of main blood vessels that pulse regularly. An earthworm has ten such hearts. Vertebrates have one heart. A fish heart has two chambers – the thin-walled *atrium* (once called the auricle) that expands to receive blood, and the thick-walled *ventricle* that pumps it out. Amphibians and most reptiles have two atria and one ventricle; birds and mammals have two atria and two ventricles. The beating of the heart is controlled by the autonomic nervous system and an internal control centre or pacemaker, the *sinoatrial node.*

**heart attack** or *myocardial infarction,* sudden onset of gripping central chest pain, often accompanied by sweating and vomiting, caused by death of a portion of the heart muscle following obstruction of a coronary artery by thrombosis (formation of a blood clot). Half of all heart attacks result in death within the first two hours, but in the remainder survival has improved following the widespread use of thrombolytic (clot-buster) drugs.

**heat** form of energy possessed by a substance by virtue of the vibrating movement (kinetic energy) of its molecules or atoms. Heat energy is transferred by conduction, convection, and radiation. It always flows from a region of higher ◊temperature (heat intensity) to one of lower temperature. Its effect on a substance may be simply to raise its temperature, or to cause it to expand, melt (if a solid), vaporize (if a liquid), or increase its pressure (if a confined gas).

**heat capacity** in physics, the quantity of heat required to raise the temperature of an object by one degree. The *specific heat capacity* of a substance is the heat capacity per unit of mass, measured in joules per kilogram per kelvin (J kg$^{-1}$ K$^{-1}$).

**Heath, Edward (Richard George)** (1916– ) British Conservative politician, party leader 1965–75. As prime minister 1970–74 he took the UK into the European Community (EC) but was brought down by economic and industrial-relations crises at home. He was replaced as party leader by Margaret Thatcher in 1975, and became increasingly critical of her policies and her opposition to the UK's full participation in the EC. During John Major's administration, he continued his attacks on 'Eurosceptics' within the party.

**heather** low-growing evergreen shrub of the heath family, common on sandy or acid soil. The common heather (*Calluna vulgaris*) is a carpet-forming shrub, growing up to 60 cm/24 in high and bearing pale pink-purple flowers. It is found over much of Europe and has been introduced to North America.

**heatstroke** or *sunstroke,* rise in body temperature caused by excessive exposure to heat.

Mild heatstroke is experienced as feverish lassitude, sometimes with simple fainting; recovery is prompt following rest and replenishment of salt lost in sweat. Severe heatstroke causes collapse akin to that seen in acute ◊shock, and is potentially lethal without prompt treatment, including cooling the body carefully and giving fluids to relieve dehydration.

**heat treatment** in industry, the subjection of metals and alloys to controlled heating and cooling after fabrication to relieve internal stresses and improve their physical properties. Methods include ◊annealing, quenching, and ◊tempering.

**heaven** in Christianity and some other religions, the abode of God and the destination of the virtuous after death. In Islam, heaven is seen as a paradise of material delights, though such delights are generally accepted as being allegorical.

**heavy metal** in music, a style of rock characterized by histrionic guitar solos and a macho swagger. Heavy metal developed out of the hard rock of the late 1960s and early 1970s, was performed by such groups as ◊Led Zeppelin and Deep Purple (formed in 1968), and enjoyed a resurgence in the late 1980s. Bands include Van Halen (formed 1974), Def Leppard (formed 1977), and Guns n' Roses (formed 1987).

**heavy water** or *deuterium oxide,* D$_2$O water containing the isotope deuterium instead of hydrogen (relative molecular mass 20 as opposed to 18 for ordinary water).

**Hebei** *Hopei, Hopeh,* or *Chihli,* province of north China, bounded to the north by Inner Mongolia, to the northeast by Liaoning, to the east by the Bohai Gulf, to the south by Shandong and Henan, and to the west by Shanxi
*area* 185,900 sq km/71,780 sq mi
*capital* ◊Shijiazhuang
*cities and towns* Baoding, Tangshan, Handan, Zhangjiakou
*physical* part of the North China Plain
*features* includes special municipalities of Beijing and Tianjin
*industries* cereals, textiles, coal, iron, steel, oil
*agriculture* winter wheat, barley, maize, cotton
*population* (1996) 64,840,000.

**Hebrew** member of the Semitic people who lived in Palestine at the time of the Old Testament and who traced their ancestry to ◊Abraham of Ur, a city of Sumer.

**Hebrew Bible** the sacred writings of Judaism (some dating from as early as 1200 BC), called by Christians the ◊Old Testament. It includes the Torah (the first five books, ascribed to Moses), historical and prophetic books, and psalms, originally written in Hebrew and later translated into Greek (Septuagint) and other languages.

**Hebrew language** member of the ◊Afro-Asiatic language family spoken in Southwest Asia by the ancient Hebrews, sustained for many centuries in the ◊Diaspora as the liturgical language of Judaism, and revived by the late-19th-century Haskalah intellectual movement, which spread modern European culture among Jews. The language developed in the 20th century as Israeli Hebrew, the national language of the state of Israel. It is the original language of the Old Testament of the Bible.

**Hebrides** group of more than 500 islands (fewer than 100 inhabited) off the west coast of mainland Scotland; total area 2,900 sq km/1,120 sq mi. The Hebrides were settled by Scandinavians during the 6th–9th centuries and passed under Norwegian rule from about 890 to 1266.

**Hecate** (Greek 'worker from afar') in Greek mythology, the goddess of the underworld and magic arts. Her association with night led to her identification with the Moon goddess ◊Selene and ◊Artemis. She is first mentioned by Hesiod as having universal power to confer wealth and all the blessings of daily life. Ovid depicted her in *Fasti* with three bodies and heads, standing back-to-back to see in three directions.

**hectare** metric unit of area equal to 100 ares or 10,000 square metres (2.47 acres), symbol ha.

**Hector** in Greek mythology, a Trojan prince; son of King Priam and Hecuba, husband of Andromache, and father of Astyanax. He was the foremost warrior in the siege of ◊Troy until killed by the Greek hero ◊Achilles.

**hedgehog** insectivorous mammal native to Europe, Asia, and Africa. The body, including the tail, is 30 cm/1 ft long. It is greyish brown in colour, has a piglike snout, and its back and sides are covered with sharp spines. When threatened it rolls itself into a ball bristling with spines. Hedgehogs feed on insects, slugs, mice, frogs, young birds, and carrion. Long-eared hedgehogs and desert hedgehogs are placed in different genera. (Genus *Erinaceus,* order Insectivora, family Erinaceidae.)

**hedge sparrow** another name for the ◊*dunnock,* a small European bird.

**hedonism** ethical theory that pleasure or happiness is, or should be, the main goal in life. Hedonist sects in ancient Greece were the ◊Cyrenaics, who held that the pleasure of the moment is the only human good, and the ◊Epicureans, who advocated the pursuit of pleasure under the direction of reason. Modern hedonistic philosophies, such as those of the British philosophers Jeremy Bentham and J S Mill, regard the happiness of society, rather than that of the individual, as the aim.

**Hefei** *Hofei* or *Luzhou,* capital of ◊Anhui province, eastern China; population (1994) 1,126,600. Once just a trading hub for agricultural products, especially rice, it is now a centre of heavy industry. Products include textiles, chemicals, steel, electronics, and domestic appliances.

**Hegel, Georg Wilhelm Friedrich** (1770–1831) German philosopher who conceived of mind and nature as two abstractions of one indivisible whole, Spirit. His system, which is a type of ◊idealism, traces the emergence of Spirit in the logical study of concepts and the process of world history.

**hegemony** (Greek *hegemonia* 'authority') political dominance of one power over others in a group in which all are supposedly equal. The term was first used for the dominance of Athens over the other Greek city states, later applied to Prussia within Germany, and, in more recent times, to the USA and the USSR with regard to the rest of the world.

**Hegira** flight of the prophet Muhammad; see ◊Hijrah.

**Heidegger, Martin** (1889–1976) German philosopher, often classed as an existentialist. He believed that Western philosophy had 'forgotten' the fundamental question of the 'meaning of Being', and his work concerns the investigation of what he thought were the different types of being appropriate to people and to things in general.

**Heilongjiang** or *Heilungkiang,* province of northeast China, bordered to the north and east by Russia, to the south by Jilin, and to the northwest by Inner Mongolia
**area** 463,600 sq km/178,950 sq mi
**capital** ◊Harbin
**cities and towns** Qiqihar, Hegang, Jiamusi
**physical** Lesser Hingan Mountains; hills in centre and south, lowlands to east and west
**industries** China's largest oilfield at Daqing, engineering, food processing, wood products, building materials, ice-skates
**agriculture** maize, sugar beet, dairy farming, sheep rearing, timber
**population** (1996) 37,280,000.

**Heine, Heinrich (Christian Johann)** (1797–1856) German Romantic poet and journalist. He wrote *Reisebilder* (1826–31), blending travel writing and satire, and *Das Buch der Lieder/The Book of Songs* (1827). Disillusioned by undercurrents of anti-Semitism and antiliberal censorship, he severed his ties with Germany and from 1831 lived mainly in Paris. His *Neue Gedichte/New Poems* appeared 1844. He excelled in both the Romantic lyric and satire. Franz Schubert and Robert Schumann set many of his lyrics to music.

**Heisenberg, Werner (Karl)** (1901–1976) German physicist who developed ◊quantum theory and formulated the ◊uncertainty principle, which concerns matter, radiation, and their reactions, and places absolute limits on the achievable accuracy of measurement. He was awarded a Nobel prize in 1932 for work he carried out when only 24.

**Hejaz** also *Hedjaz* or *Al Hedjaz,* historic region of Saudi Arabia, on the Red Sea; area about 290,000 sq km/11,970 sq mi. A former independent kingdom, it merged in 1932 with Nejd to form Saudi Arabia. Historically its principal city has been ◊Mecca. The other main cities are ◊Jiddah, on the coast, Taif, a mountain resort at an altitude of 1,800 m/5,905 ft, and ◊Medina.

**Hekmatyar, Gulbuddin** (1949– ) Afghani leader of the Mujaheddin (Islamic fundamentalist guerrillas), prime minister 1993–94 and 1996. Strongly anticommunist and leading the Hezb-i-Islami (Islamic Party) faction, he resisted the takeover of Kabul by moderate Mujaheddin forces in April 1992 and refused to join the interim administration, continuing to bombard the city until being driven out. In June 1993,

under a peace agreement with President Burhanuddin Rabbani, Hekmatyar was readmitted to the city as prime minister, but his forces renewed their attacks on Kabul during 1994. He was subsequently dismissed from the premiership, but returned to Kabul in June 1996, when he became combined prime minister, defence minister, and finance minister. However, in September he was driven out of Kabul by the Taliban (fundamentalist student army) who had seized control of much of Afghanistan.

**Helen** in Greek mythology, the most beautiful of women; daughter of ◊Leda and Zeus (transformed as a swan). She was abducted as a young girl by Theseus, but rescued by her brothers Castor and Pollux (Greek Polydeuces). Helen married Menelaus, king of Sparta, and bore him Hermione, but during his absence was seduced by ◊Paris, prince of Troy; their flight precipitated the Trojan wars.

**Helicon** mountain in central Greece, on which was situated a spring and a sanctuary sacred to the ◊Muses.

**helicopter** powered aircraft that achieves both lift and propulsion by means of a rotary wing, or rotor, on top of the fuselage. It can take off and land vertically, move in any direction, or remain stationary in the air. It can be powered by piston or jet engine. The ◊autogiro was a precursor.

**Helios** Roman *Sol,* in Greek mythology, the god of the Sun; a ◊Titan who drove the Sun's chariot across the sky. He was the father of Phaethon who almost set the Earth alight. From the 5th century BC, Helios was identified with the god ◊Apollo.

**heliotrope** decorative plant belonging to the borage family, with distinctive spikes of blue, lilac, or white flowers, including the Peruvian or cherry pie heliotrope (*H. peruvianum*). (Genus *Heliotropium,* family Boraginaceae.)

**helium** (Greek *helios* 'Sun') colourless, odourless, gaseous, nonmetallic element, symbol He, atomic number 2, relative atomic mass 4.0026. It is grouped with the ◊inert gases, is nonreactive, and forms no compounds. It is the second-most abundant element (after hydrogen) in the universe, and has the lowest boiling (−268.9°C/−452°F) and melting points (−272.2°C/−458°F) of all the elements. It is present in small quantities in the Earth's atmosphere from gases issuing from radioactive elements (from alpha decay) in the Earth's crust; after hydrogen it is the second lightest element.

**hell** in various religions, a place of posthumous punishment. In Hinduism, Buddhism, and Jainism, hell is a transitory stage in the progress of the soul, but in Christianity and Islam it is eternal (◊purgatory is transitory). Judaism does not postulate such punishment.

**hellebore** poisonous European herbaceous plant belonging to the buttercup family. The stinking hellebore (*H. foetidus*) has greenish flowers early in the spring. (Genus *Helleborus,* family Ranunculaceae.)

**helleborine** one of several temperate Old World orchids, including the marsh helleborine (*E. palustris*) and the hellebore orchid (*E. helleborine*) introduced to North America. (Genera *Epipactis* and *Cephalanthera*, family Orchidaceae.)

**Hellenic period** (from *Hellas*, Greek name for Greece) classical period of ancient Greek civilization, from the first Olympic Games 776 BC until the death of Alexander the Great 323 BC.

**Hellenistic period** period in Greek civilization from the death of Alexander 323 BC until the accession of the Roman emperor Augustus 27 BC. Alexandria in Egypt was the centre of culture and commerce during this period, and Greek culture spread throughout the Mediterranean region and the near East.

**Hellespont** former name of the ◊Dardanelles, the strait that separates Europe from Asia.

**Héloïse** (1101–1164) Abbess of Paraclete in Champagne, France, correspondent and lover of ◊Abelard. She became deeply interested in intellectual study in her youth and was impressed by the brilliance of Abelard, her teacher, whom she secretly married.

After her affair with Abelard, and the birth of a son, Astrolabe, she became a nun 1129, and with Abelard's assistance, founded a nunnery at Paraclete. Her letters show her strong and pious character and her devotion to Abelard.

**Helsinki** Swedish *Helsingfors,* capital and port of Finland; population (1994) 516,000. Industries include shipbuilding, engineering, and textiles. The port is kept open by icebreakers in winter.

**Hemingway, Ernest (Miller)** (1899–1961) US writer. War, bullfighting, and fishing are used symbolically in his work to represent honour, dignity, and primitivism – prominent themes in his short stories and novels, which include *A Farewell to Arms* (1929), *For Whom the Bell Tolls* (1941), and *The Old Man and the Sea* (1952) (Pulitzer prize). His deceptively simple writing style attracted many imitators. Nobel Prize for Literature 1954.

**hemlock** plant belonging to the carrot family, native to Europe, western Asia, and North Africa. It grows up to 2 m/6 ft high and produces delicate clusters of small white flowers. The whole plant, especially the root and fruit, is poisonous, causing paralysis of the nervous system. The name 'hemlock' is also given to some North American and Asiatic conifers (genus *Tsuga*) belonging to the pine family. (*Conium maculatum,* family Umbelliferae.)

**hemp** annual plant originally from Asia, now cultivated in most temperate countries for the fibres produced in the outer layer of the stem, which are used in ropes, twines, and, occasionally, in a type of linen or lace. The drug ◊cannabis is obtained from certain varieties of hemp. (*Cannabis sativa,* family Cannabaceae.)

**Henan** or *Honan,* province of east central China, bounded to the north by Hebei, to the east by Shandong and Anhui, to the south by Hubei, and to the west by Shaanxi and Shanxi provinces

*area* 167,000 sq km/64,462 sq mi

*capital* ◊Zhengzhou

*towns and cities* Luoyang, Kaifeng, Anyang

*physical* Huang He River in the north; mountains in the southwest

*features* ruins of Xibo, the 16th-century BC capital of the Shang dynasty

*industries* coal, oil, textiles, cement, glass, fertilizer

*agriculture* cereals, cotton, fruit, tobacco, meat, peanuts

*population* (1996) 91,720,000.

**henbane** poisonous plant belonging to the nightshade family, found on waste ground throughout most of Europe and western Asia. It is a branching plant, up to 80 cm/31 in high, with hairy leaves and a sickening smell. The yellow flowers are bell-shaped. Henbane is used in medicine as a source of the drugs hyoscyamine and scopolamine. (*Hyoscyamus niger,* family Solanaceae.)

**Hendrix, Jimi (James Marshall)** (1942–1970) US rock guitarist, songwriter, and singer. He was legendary for his virtuoso experimental technique and flamboyance. *Are You Experienced?* (1967) was his first album. His performance at the 1969 Woodstock festival included a memorable version of 'The Star-Spangled Banner' and is recorded in the film *Woodstock* (1970). He greatly expanded the vocabulary of the electric guitar and influenced both rock and jazz musicians.

**Hendry, Stephen** (1970– ) Scottish snooker player who in 1990 became the youngest ever world champion at the age of 21 years 106 days. He won the title five years in succession 1991–96, an unprecedented achievement in modern snooker. The world number one from 1990 to 1998, he has won a world record 29 ranking tournaments. In May 1999 he won a record seventh World Professional Championship title. At the end of the 1998–99 season he had amassed over £6 million in career prize money.

*career highlights*
*Embassy World Professional Championship* 1990, 1992–96
*Rothmans Grand Prix* 1987, 1990–91, 1995
*British Open* 1988, 1991
*Benson and Hedges Masters* 1989–93, 1996
*UK Open/Championship (later Royal Liver Assurance UK Championship)* 1989–90, 1994–96.

**henna** small shrub belonging to the loosestrife family, found in Iran, India, Egypt, and North Africa. The leaves and young twigs are ground to a powder, mixed to a paste with hot water, and applied to the fingernails and hair to give an orange-red hue. The colour may then be changed to black by applying a preparation of indigo. (*Lawsonia inermis,* family Lythraceae.)

**Henrietta Maria** (1609–1669) Queen of England 1625–49. The daughter of Henry IV of France, she married Charles I of England in 1625. By encouraging him to aid Roman Catholics and make himself an absolute ruler, she became highly unpopular and was exiled 1644–60. She returned to England at the Restoration but retired to France in 1665.

**henry** SI unit (symbol H) of ◊inductance (the reaction of an electric current against the magnetic field that surrounds it). One henry is the inductance of a circuit that produces an opposing voltage of one volt when the current changes at one ampere per second.

**Henry, (Charles Albert David)** known as *Harry* (1984– ) Prince of the UK; second child of the Prince and Princess of Wales.

**Henry, Joseph** (1797–1878) US physicist, inventor of the electromagnetic motor 1829 and of a telegraphic apparatus. He also discovered the principle of electromagnetic induction, roughly at the same time as Michael ◊Faraday, and the phenomenon of self-induction. The unit of inductance, the *henry*, is named after him.

**Henry** eight kings of England:

**Henry I** (1068–1135) King of England from 1100. Youngest son of William the Conqueror, he succeeded his brother William II. He won the support of the Saxons by granting them a charter and marrying a Saxon princess, Matilda, daughter of Malcolm III of Scotland. An able administrator, he established a professional bureaucracy and a system of travelling judges.

**Henry II** (1133–1189) king of England 1154–89. The son of ◊Matilda and Geoffrey V, Count of Anjou, he succeeded King ◊Stephen (*c.* 1097–1154). He curbed the power of the barons, but his attempt to bring the church courts under control was abandoned after the murder of Thomas à ◊Becket, Archbishop of Canterbury, in 1170. The English conquest of Ireland began during Henry's reign. On several occasions his sons rebelled, notably 1173–74. Henry was succeeded by his son Richard (I) the Lionheart.

**Henry III** (1207–1272) King of England from 1216, when he succeeded John, but the royal powers were exercised by a regency until 1232, and by two French nobles, Peter des Roches and Peter des Rivaux, until the barons forced their expulsion in 1234, marking the start of Henry's personal rule. His financial commitments to the papacy and his foreign favourites antagonized the barons who issued the Provisions of Oxford in 1258, limiting the king's power. Henry's refusal to accept the provisions led to the second Barons' War in 1264, a revolt of nobles led by his brother-in-law Simon de ◊Montfort. Henry was defeated at Lewes, Sussex, and imprisoned, but restored to the throne after the royalist victory at Evesham in 1265. He was succeeded by his son Edward I.

**Henry IV** originally Henry Bolingbroke (1367–1413) king of England from 1399, the son of ◊John of Gaunt. In 1398 he was banished by ◊Richard II but returned in 1399 to head a revolt and be accepted as king by Parliament. He was succeeded by his son Henry V.

**Henry V** (1387–1422) king of England 1413–22, son of Henry IV. Invading Normandy in 1415 (during the Hundred Years' War), he captured Harfleur and defeated the French at ◊Agincourt. He invaded again in 1417–19, capturing Rouen. His military victory forced the French into the Treaty of Troyes in 1420, which gave Henry control of the French government. He married Catherine of Valois in 1420 and gained recognition as heir to the French throne by his father-in-law Charles VI, but died before him. He was succeeded by his son Henry VI.

**Henry VI** (1421–1471) King of England from 1422, son of Henry V. He assumed royal power 1442 and sided with the party opposed to the continuation of the Hundred Years' War with France. After his marriage 1445, he was dominated by his wife, ◊Margaret of Anjou. He was deposed 1461 in the Wars of the ◊Roses; was captured 1465, temporarily restored 1470, but again imprisoned 1471 and then murdered.

**Henry VII** (1457–1509) King of England from 1485, when he overthrew Richard III at the Battle of ◊Bosworth. A descendant of ◊John of Gaunt, Henry, by his marriage to Elizabeth of York 1486, united the houses of York and Lancaster. Yorkist revolts continued until 1497, but Henry restored order after the Wars of the Roses by the ◊Star Chamber and achieved independence from Parliament by amassing a private fortune through confiscations. He was succeeded by his son Henry VIII.

**Henry VIII** (1491–1547) King of England from 1509, when he succeeded his father Henry VII and married Catherine of Aragón, the widow of his brother.

During the period 1513–29 Henry pursued an active foreign policy, largely under the guidance of his Lord Chancellor, Cardinal Wolsey, who shared Henry's desire to make England stronger. Wolsey was replaced by Thomas More in 1529 for failing to persuade the pope to grant Henry a divorce. After 1532 Henry broke with papal authority, proclaimed himself head of the church in England, dissolved the monasteries, and divorced Catherine. His subsequent wives were Anne Boleyn, Jane Seymour, Anne of Cleves, Catherine Howard, and Catherine Parr.

He was succeeded by his son Edward VI.

**Henry** four kings of France, including:

**Henry III** (1551–1589) King of France from 1574. He fought both the ◊Huguenots (headed by his successor, Henry of Navarre) and the Catholic League (headed by the third Duke of Guise). Guise expelled Henry from Paris in 1588 but was assassinated. Henry allied with the Huguenots under Henry of Navarre to besiege the city, but was assassinated by a monk.

**Henry IV** (1553–1610) King of France from 1589. Son of Antoine de Bourbon and Jeanne, Queen of Navarre, he was brought up as a Protestant and from 1576 led the ◊Huguenots. On his accession he settled the religious question by adopting Catholicism while tolerating Protestantism. He restored peace and strong government to France and brought back prosperity by measures for the promotion of industry and agriculture and the improvement of communications. He was assassinated by a Catholic extremist.

**Henry** seven Holy Roman emperors, including:

**Henry (III) the Black** (1017–1056) King of Germany from 1028, Holy Roman Emperor from 1039 (crowned 1046). He raised the empire to the height of its power, and extended its authority over Poland, Bohemia, and Hungary.

**Henry IV** (1050–1106) Holy Roman Emperor from 1056. He was involved from 1075 in a struggle with the papacy. Excommunicated twice (1076 and 1080), Henry deposed ◊Gregory VII and set up the antipope Clement III (died 1191) by whom he was crowned Holy Roman Emperor 1084.

**Henry VI** (1165–1197) Holy Roman Emperor 1191–97. He conquered the Norman Kingdom of Sicily in the name of his wife, Constance, aunt and heiress of William II of Sicily, and was crowned at Palermo, Sicily, on Christmas Day 1194. As part of his plan for making the empire universal, he captured and imprisoned Richard I of England and compelled him to do homage.

**Henry the Navigator** (1394–1460) Portuguese prince, the fourth son of John I. He is credited with setting up a school for navigators in 1419 and under his patronage Portuguese sailors explored and colonized Madeira, the Cape Verde Islands, and the Azores; they sailed down the African coast almost to Sierra Leone.

**Henson, Jim (James Maury)** (1936–1990) US puppeteer who created the television Muppet characters, including Kermit the Frog, Miss Piggy, and Fozzie Bear. The Muppets became popular on the children's educational TV series *Sesame Street,* which first appeared in 1969 and soon became regular viewing in over 80 countries. In 1976 Henson created *The Muppet Show,* which ran for five years and became one of the world's most widely seen TV programmes, reaching 235 million viewers in 100 countries. Several Muppet movies followed.

**hepatitis** any inflammatory disease of the liver, usually caused by a virus. Other causes include alcohol, drugs, gallstones, ◊lupus erythematous, and amoebic ◊dysentery. Symptoms include weakness, nausea, and jaundice.

**Hepburn, Audrey** born Hepburn-Ruston (1929–1993) English actress. She often played innocent, childlike characters. Slender and doe-eyed, she set a different style from the more ample women stars of the 1950s. After playing minor parts in British films in the early 1950s, she became a Hollywood star in *Roman Holiday* (1951), for which she won an Academy Award, and later starred in such films as *Funny Face* (1957) and *My Fair Lady* (1964).

**Hepburn, Katharine** (1909–  ) US actress. An acclaimed actress of the classical Hollywood era, Hepburn has won four Academy Awards and been nominated on 12 separate occasions. Feisty self-assurance was her trademark in both comic and dramatic roles. She was a frequent collaborator with the director George Cukor, and appeared in several films with her off-screen partner Spencer Tracy, including *Woman of the Year* (1942) and *Pat and Mike* (1952).

**Hephaestus** in Greek mythology, the god of fire and metalcraft (Roman *Vulcan*); the lame son of Zeus and Hera; and in Homer's *Odyssey,* husband of Aphrodite, goddess of love. He created armour for the Greek hero ◊Achilles, Harmonia's magic necklace, and other objects famed in legend.

**Hepworth, (Jocelyn) Barbara** (1903–1975) English sculptor. She developed a distinctive abstract style, creating slender upright forms reminiscent of standing stones or totems; and round, hollowed forms with spaces bridged by wires or strings, as in *Pelagos* (1946; Tate Gallery, London). Her preferred medium was stone, but she also worked in concrete, wood, and aluminium, and many of her later works were in bronze.

**Hera** (Greek 'lady') in Greek mythology, the goddess of women and marriage (Roman *Juno*); sister and consort of Zeus; and mother of ◊Hephaestus, god of fire and metalcraft, the war god Ares, and Hebe, the original cupbearer to the gods. The peacock was sacred to her; the eyes in its tail were transplanted from her servant, the 100-eyed Argus, who had watched over Zeus' lover Io.

**Heracles** or *Alcides,* in Greek mythology, an immortalized hero (Roman *Hercules*); son of Zeus and Alcmene; and famed for his strength. While serving Eurystheus, king of Argos, he performed 12 labours, including the cleansing of the ◊Augean stables. Driven mad by the goddess ◊Hera, he murdered his children by Megara, his first wife, and was mistakenly poisoned by his second wife Deianira.

**Herat** capital of Herat province, and the largest city in western Afghanistan, on the north banks of the Hari Rud River; population (1988) 177,000. A principal road junction, it was a great city in ancient and medieval times.

**herb** any plant (usually a flowering plant) tasting sweet, bitter, aromatic, or pungent, used in cooking, medicine, or perfumery; technically, a herb is any plant in which the aerial parts do not remain above ground at the end of the growing season.

**herbalism** in alternative medicine, the prescription and use of plants and their derivatives for medication. Herbal products are favoured by alternative practitioners as 'natural medicine', as opposed to modern synthesized medicines and drugs, which are regarded with suspicion because of the dangers of side effects and dependence.

**Herbert, George** (1593–1633) English poet. His volume of religious poems, *The Temple,* appeared in 1633, shortly before his death. His intense though quiet poems embody his religious struggles ('The Temper', 'The Collar') or poignantly contrast mortality and eternal truth ('Vertue', 'Life') in a deceptively simple language.

**herbicide** any chemical used to destroy plants or check their growth.

**herbivore** animal that feeds on green plants (or photosynthetic single-celled organisms) or their products, including seeds, fruit, and nectar. The most numerous type of herbivore is thought to be the zooplankton, tiny invertebrates in the surface waters of the oceans that feed on small photosynthetic algae. Herbivores are more numerous than other animals because their food is the most abundant. They form a vital link in the food chain between plants and carnivores.

**Herculaneum** ancient city of Italy between Naples and Pompeii. Along with Pompeii, it was buried when Vesuvius erupted AD 79. It was excavated from the 18th century onwards.

**Hercules** in Roman mythology, Roman form of the deified Greek hero ◊Heracles. Possibly the first foreign cult accepted in Rome, he was popular with merchants due to his legendary travel and ability to ward off evil, and was seen as the personification of strength.

**heredity** in biology, the transmission of traits from parent to offspring. See also ◊genetics.

**Herefordshire** unitary authority in west England, created in 1998 from part of the former county of Hereford and Worcester
*area* 2,288 sq km/884 sq mi
*towns and cities* Hereford (administrative headquarters), Leominster, Ross-on-Wye, Ledbury
*features* River Wye; Herefordshire Beacon (340 m/1,115 ft) Iron Age fort; Hereford Cathedral (11th century) houses the late 13th/early 14th-century Mappa Mundi, and the Chained Library, with over 1,400 chained books and 200 manuscripts dating from the 8th to 12th centuries; Waterworks Museum (Hereford) in restored Victorian pump house; Croft Castle (Leominster); St Mary's Church (Kempley) with medieval wall paintings; The Prospect, a walled clifftop garden in Ross-on-Wye designed by John Kyrle in the 17th century; Norman Church (Kilpeck) with notable carvings
*industries* agriculture, orchards and cider industry, agricultural services and machinery, precision engineering, light engineering, plastics manufacture
*population* (1996) 166,100
*famous people* Thomas Knight, John Kyrle, Walter Map, John Masefield.

**heresy** (Greek *hairesis* 'parties' of believers) any doctrine opposed to orthodox belief, especially in religion. Those holding ideas considered heretical by the Christian church have included Gnostics, Arians, Pelagians, Montanists, Albigenses, Waldenses, Lollards, and Anabaptists.

**Hereward the Wake** (lived 11th century) legendary Saxon hero of the English resistance to the Normans, who defended Ely in 1070–71.

Outlawed by Edward the Confessor in 1062, Hereward returned home after 1066 to find his father dead, his brother murdered, and the Norman lord Peter de Bourne in possession. Hereward killed him in revenge and led 40 men to the last English strongpoint at the abbey of Ely. When William the Conqueror took the island in 1071, Hereward retreated into the forest.

**hermaphrodite** organism that has both male and female sex organs. Hermaphroditism is the norm in such species as earthworms and snails, and is common in flowering plants. Cross-fertilization is the rule among hermaphrodites, with the parents functioning as male and female simultaneously, or as one or the other sex at different stages in their development. Human hermaphrodites are extremely rare.

**Hermes** in Greek mythology, the messenger of the gods; son of Zeus and Maia, one of the Pleiades. Homer's *Odyssey* presented the god as the conductor of the dead (shades) to ◊Hades, in which capacity he became associated with the underworld and dreams. Identified with the Roman ◊Mercury and ancient Egyptian ◊Thoth, he protected thieves, travellers, and merchants. As a god of good fortune, he presided over some forms of popular divination, public competitions, and games of dice.

**hernia** or *rupture*, protrusion of part of an internal organ through a weakness in the surrounding muscular wall, usually in the groin. The appearance is that of a rounded soft lump or swelling.

**Herod Antipas** (21 BC–AD 39) Tetrarch (governor) of the Roman province of Galilee, northern Palestine, 4 BC–AD 39, son of Herod the Great. He divorced his wife to marry his niece Herodias, and was responsible for the death of John the Baptist. Jesus was brought before him on Pontius Pilate's discovery that he was a Galilean and hence of Herod's jurisdiction, but Herod returned him without giving any verdict. In AD 38 Herod Antipas went to Rome to try to persuade Emperor Caligula to give him the title of king, but was instead banished.

**Herodotus** (lived 5th century BC) Greek historian, described as the 'Father of History'. He wrote a nine-book account of the Greek-Persian struggle that culminated in the defeat of the Persian invasion attempts in 490 and 480 BC. The work contains lengthy digressions on peoples, places, and earlier history. Herodotus was the first historian to apply critical evaluation to his material while also recording divergent opinions.

**Herod the Great** (74–4 BC) King of the Roman province of Judaea, southern Palestine, from 40 BC. With the aid of Mark Antony, he established his government in Jerusalem 37 BC. He rebuilt the Temple in Jerusalem, but his Hellenizing tendencies made him suspect to orthodox Jewry. His last years were a reign of terror, and in the New Testament Matthew alleges that he ordered the slaughter of all the infants in Bethlehem to ensure the death of Jesus, whom he foresaw as a rival. He was the father of Herod Antipas.

**heroin** or *diamorphine*, powerful opiate analgesic, an acetyl derivative of ◊morphine. It is more addictive than morphine but causes less nausea.

**heron** large to medium-sized wading bird belonging to the same family as bitterns, egrets, night herons, and boatbills. Herons have sharp bills, broad wings, long legs, slender bodies, and soft plumage. They are found mostly in tropical and subtropical regions, but also in temperate zones, on lakes, fens, and mudflats, where they wade searching for prey. (Genera include *Ardea, Butorides,* and *Nycticorax;* family Ardeidae, order Ciconiiformes.)

**herpes** any of several infectious diseases caused by viruses of the herpes group. *Herpes simplex I* is the causative agent of a common inflammation, the cold sore. *Herpes simplex II* is responsible for genital herpes, a highly contagious, sexually transmitted disease characterized by painful blisters in the genital area. It can be transmitted in the birth canal from mother to newborn. *Herpes zoster* causes ◊shingles; another herpes virus causes chickenpox.

**Herrick, Robert** (1591–1674) English poet and cleric. He published *Hesperides: or the Works both Humane and Divine of Robert Herrick* (1648), a collection of verse admired for its lyric quality, including the well-known poems 'Gather ye rosebuds' and 'Cherry ripe'.

**herring** any of various marine fishes belonging to the herring family, but especially the important food fish *Clupea harengus*. A silvered greenish blue, it swims close to the surface, and may be 25–40 cm/10–16 in long. Herring travel in schools several kilometres long and wide. They are found in large quantities off the east coast of North America, and the shores of northeastern Europe. Overfishing and pollution have reduced their numbers. (Family Clupeidae.)

**Herschel, (Frederick) William** (1738–1822) German-born English astronomer. He was a skilled telescope maker, and pioneered the study of binary stars and nebulae. He discovered the planet Uranus in 1781 and infrared solar rays in 1801. He catalogued over 800 double stars, and found over 2,500 nebulae, catalogued by his sister Caroline Herschel; this work was continued by his son John Herschel. By studying the distribution of stars, William established the basic form of our Galaxy, the Milky Way. Knighted 1816.

**Hertfordshire** county of southeast England
**area** 1,630 sq km/629 sq mi
**towns and cities** Hertford (administrative headquarters), Bishop's Stortford, Hatfield, Hemel Hempstead, Letchworth (the first garden city; followed by Welwyn in 1919), Stevenage (the first new town, designated in 1946), St Albans, Watford, Hitchin
**physical** rivers Lea, Stort, Colne; part of the Chiltern Hills
**features** Hatfield House; Knebworth House (home of Lord Lytton); Brocket Hall (home of Palmerston and Melbourne); home of George Bernard ◊Shaw at Ayot St Lawrence;

Berkhamsted Castle (Norman); Rothamsted agricultural experimental station
**agriculture** barley for brewing industry, dairy farming, market gardening, horticulture
**industries** aircraft, computer electronics, electrical goods, engineering, paper and printing, plastics, pharmaceuticals, tanning, sand and gravel are worked in the south
**population** (1996) 1,015,800
**famous people** Henry Bessemer, Graham Greene, Cecil Rhodes.

**hertz** SI unit (symbol Hz) of frequency (the number of repetitions of a regular occurrence in one second). Radio waves are often measured in megahertz (MHz), millions of hertz, and the clock rate of a computer is usually measured in megahertz. The unit is named after German physicist Heinrich Hertz.

**Hertzsprung–Russell diagram** in astronomy, a graph on which the surface temperatures of stars are plotted against their luminosities. Most stars, including the Sun, fall into a narrow band called the *main sequence*. When a star grows old it moves from the main sequence to the upper right part of the graph, into the area of the giants and supergiants. At the end of its life, as the star shrinks to become a white dwarf, it moves again, to the bottom left area. It is named after the Danish astronomer Ejnar Hertzsprung and the US astronomer Henry Norris Russell, who independently devised it in the years 1911–13.

**Herzegovina** or *Hercegovina*, part of Bosnia-Herzegovina (which was formerly, until 1991, a republic of Yugoslavia).

**Herzl, Theodor** (1860–1904) Austrian founder of the Zionist movement. The ◊Dreyfus case convinced him that the only solution to the problem of anti-Semitism was the resettlement of the Jews in a state of their own. His book *Jewish State* (1896) launched political ◊Zionism, and he became the first president of the World Zionist Organization in 1897.

**Heseltine, Michael (Ray Dibdin)** (1933– ) British Conservative politician, deputy prime minister 1995–97. A member of Parliament from 1966 (for Tavistock 1966–74 and for Henley from 1974), he was secretary of state for the environment 1990–92 and for trade and industry 1992–95.

**Hess, (Walter Richard) Rudolf** (1894–1987) German Nazi leader. Imprisoned with Adolf Hitler 1924–25, he became his private secretary, taking down *Mein Kampf* from his dictation. In 1933 he was appointed deputy *Führer* to Hitler, a post he held until replaced by Goering in September 1939. On 10 May 1941 he landed by air in the UK with his own compromise peace proposals and was held a prisoner of war until 1945, when he was tried at Nürnberg as a war criminal and sentenced to life imprisonment. He died in Spandau prison, Berlin.

**Hesse** German *Hessen*, administrative region (German *Land*) in central Germany, bordered on the west by the state of Rhineland-Palatinate,

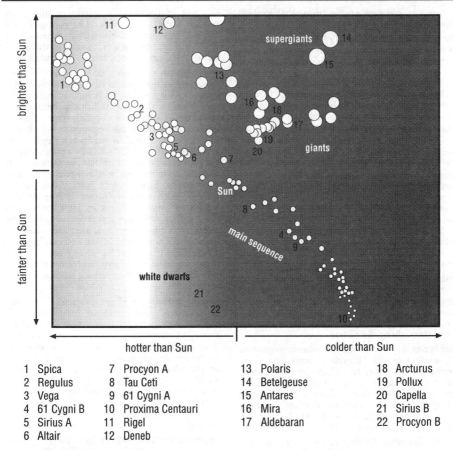

| 1 | Spica | 7 | Procyon A | 13 | Polaris | 18 | Arcturus |
|---|-------|---|-----------|----|---------|----|----------|
| 2 | Regulus | 8 | Tau Ceti | 14 | Betelgeuse | 19 | Pollux |
| 3 | Vega | 9 | 61 Cygni A | 15 | Antares | 20 | Capella |
| 4 | 61 Cygni B | 10 | Proxima Centauri | 16 | Mira | 21 | Sirius B |
| 5 | Sirius A | 11 | Rigel | 17 | Aldebaran | 22 | Procyon B |
| 6 | Altair | 12 | Deneb | | | | |

**Hertzsprung–Russell diagram** *The Hertzsprung–Russell diagram relates the brightness (or luminosity) of a star to its temperature. Most stars fall within a narrow diagonal band called the main sequence. A star moves off the main sequence when it grows old. The Hertzsprung–Russell diagram is one of the most important diagrams in astrophysics.*

on the south by Bavaria and Baden-Württemberg, on the east by Thuringia, and on the north by North Rhine-Westphalia and Lower Saxony

**area** 21,100 sq km/8,145 sq mi

**capital** Wiesbaden

**towns and cities** Frankfurt-am-Main, Kassel, Darmstadt, Fulda, Giessen, Offenbach-am-Main

**physical** valleys of the rivers Rhine, Main, and Fulda; Taunus Mountains; Vogelsberg Mountains; Odenwald Forest; see also ⬦Swabia

**industries** timber, chemicals (including the Hoechst plant on the outskirts of Frankfurt-am-Main), textiles, automobiles, electrical engineering, optical instruments, computers, telecommunications, printing, publishing

**agriculture** oats, wheat, potatoes, barley, flax, and sugar beet; wine is produced in the west of the state, in the Rheingau area bordering the Rhine

**population** (1995) 6,120,000

**religion** Protestant 61%, Roman Catholic 33%

**history** Hesse was formed after World War II

from the northwest part of the US occupation zone; the new *Land* comprised all or most of three historical provinces, with their respective centres at the towns of Kassel, Darmstadt, and Nassau.

**Hesse, Hermann** (1877–1962) German writer, a Swiss citizen from 1923. A conscientious objector in World War I and a pacifist opponent of Hitler, he published short stories, poetry, and novels, including *Peter Camenzind* (1904), *Siddhartha* (1922), and *Steppenwolf* (1927). Later works, such as *Das Glasperlenspiel/The Glass Bead Game* (1943), show the influence of Indian mysticism and Jungian psychoanalysis. Above all, Hesse was the prophet of individualism. Nobel Prize for Literature 1946.

**heterosexuality** sexual preference for, or attraction mainly to, persons of the opposite sex.

**heterotroph** any living organism that obtains its energy from organic substances produced by other organisms. All animals and fungi are heterotrophs, and they include herbivores, carnivores, and saprotrophs (those that feed on dead animal and plant material).

**hexadecimal number system** or *hex,* number system to the base 16, used in computing. In hex the decimal numbers 0–15 are represented by the characters 0, 1, 2, 3, 4, 5, 6, 7, 8, 9, A, B, C, D, E, F.

Hexadecimal numbers are easy to convert to the computer's internal ◊binary code and are more compact than binary numbers.

**Hezbollah** or *Hizbollah* (Party of God), extremist Muslim organization founded by the Iranian Revolutionary Guards who were sent to Lebanon after the 1979 Iranian revolution. Its aim is to spread the Islamic revolution of Iran among the Shiite population of Lebanon. Hezbollah is believed to be the umbrella movement of the groups that held many of the Western hostages taken from 1984.

In 1996 Hezbollah guerrillas, opposed to the Middle East peace process, engaged in renewed hostilities with Israeli forces stationed in southern Lebanon.

**hibernation** state of dormancy in which certain animals spend the winter. It is associated with a dramatic reduction in all metabolic processes, including body temperature, breathing, and heart rate. It is a fallacy that animals sleep throughout the winter.

**hibiscus** any of a group of plants belonging to the mallow family. Hibiscuses range from large herbaceous plants to trees. Popular as ornamental plants because of their brilliantly coloured, red to white, bell-shaped flowers, they include *H. syriacus* and *H. rosa-sinensis* of Asia and the rose mallow (*H. palustris*) of North America. (Genus *Hibiscus,* family Malvaceae.)

**Hick, Graeme Ashley** (1966– ) Rhodesian-born cricketer who became Zimbabwe's youngest professional cricketer at the age of 17. A prolific right-handed batsman, he joined Worcestershire, England, in 1984. He achieved the highest score in England in the 20th century in 1988 against Somerset with 405 not out. He made his Test debut for England in 1991 after a seven-year qualification period. He has not been able to reproduce his county form at Test level, and in particular has struggled against the top fast bowlers. Many of his best performances for England have come in one-day cricket. In 1999 he was appointed Worcestershire captain from 2000.
*career highlights*
*all first-class cricket* matches: 363; innings: 595; not out: 59; runs: 29,777; average: 55.55; hundreds: 103; best: 405 not out (Worcestershire v. Somerset 1988); catches: 441
*Test cricket* (1991– matches: 54; innings: 94; not out: 6; runs: 3,005; average: 34.14; hundreds: 5; catches: 76; bowling: 22–1,256 (average: 57.09)
*One-day internationals* (1991– ) matches: 96; innings: 95; not out: 11; runs: 3,271; average: 38.94; best: 126 not out; catches: 51; bowling: 21–804 (average 38.28)

**hickory** tree belonging to the walnut family, native to North America and Asia. It provides a valuable timber, and all species produce nuts, though some are inedible. The pecan (*C. illinoensis*) is widely cultivated in the southern USA, and the shagbark (*C. ovata*) in the northern USA. (Genus *Carya,* family Juglandaceae.)

**hieroglyphic** (Greek 'sacred carved writing') Egyptian writing system of the mid-4th millennium BC–3rd century AD, which combines picture signs with those indicating letters. The direction of writing is normally from right to left, the signs facing the beginning of the line. It was deciphered 1822 by the French Egyptologist J F Champollion (1790–1832) with the aid of the ◊*Rosetta Stone,* which has the same inscription carved in hieroglyphic, demotic, and Greek. The earliest hieroglyphics were discovered by German archaeologist Gunter Dreyer on clay tablets in southern Egypt in 1998 and record linen and oil deliveries and taxes paid. From the tomb of King Scorpion I, they are dated to between 3300 BC and 3200 BC and challenge the widely-held belief that Sumerians were the first people to write. Hieroglyphics were replaced for everyday use by cursive writing from about 700 BC onwards.

**Higgs boson** or *Higgs particle,* postulated ◊elementary particle whose existence would explain why particles have mass. The current theory of elementary particles, called the standard model, cannot explain how mass arises. To overcome this difficulty, Peter Higgs (1929– ) of the University of Edinburgh and Thomas Kibble (1932– ) of Imperial College, London proposed in 1964 a new particle that binds to other particles and gives them their mass. The Higgs boson has not yet been detected experimentally.

**high-definition television** (HDTV), ◊television system offering a significantly greater number of scanning lines, and therefore a clearer picture, than that provided by conventional systems. Typically, HDTV has about twice the horizontal and vertical resolution of current 525-line (such as the American standard, NTSC) or 625-line standards (such as the British standard, PAL); a frame rate of at least 24 Hz; and a picture aspect ratio of 9:16 instead of the current 3:4. HDTV systems have been in development since the mid-1970s.

**Higher** in Scottish education, a public examination taken at the age of 17, one year after the Scottish O grade. Highers are usually taken in four or five subjects and qualify students for entry to ◊higher education. About 90% of Scottish undergraduates choose to study in Scotland.

**higher education** in most countries, education beyond the age of 18 leading to a university or college degree or similar qualification.

**high jump** field event in athletics in which competitors leap over a horizontal crossbar held between rigid uprights at least 3.66 m/12 ft apart. The bar is placed at increasingly higher levels. Elimination occurs after three consecutive failures to clear the bar.

**Highland** unitary authority in northern Scotland, created from the region bearing the same name in 1996
*area* 26,157 sq km/10,100 sq mi (one-third of Scotland)
*towns* ◊Inverness (administrative headquarters), Thurso, Wick, Fort William, Aviemore
*physical* mainland Highland consists of a series of glaciated ancient plateau masses dissected by narrow glens and straths (valleys); in the northeast (Caithness), old red sandstone rocks give a softer, lower topography; Ben Nevis (1,343 m/4,406 ft), Cairngorm Mountains; Loch Ness; Cuillin Hills, Skye; includes many of the Inner Hebridean islands
*features* Caledonian Canal; John O'Groats; Skye Road Bridge
*industries* winter sports, timber, aluminium smelting, pulp and paper production, whisky distilling, cottage and croft industries
*agriculture* salmon fishing, sheep farming, grouse and deer hunting
*population* (1996) 207,500
*history* location of many key historical moments in Scottish history, including the 'massacre' of Glencoe, the Battle of Culloden and the Highland Clearances.

**Highland Clearances** forced removal of tenants from large estates in Scotland during the early 19th century, as landowners 'improved' their estates by switching from arable to sheep farming. It led ultimately to widespread emigration to North America.

**Highlands** one of the three geographical divisions of Scotland, lying to the north of a geological fault line that stretches from Stonehaven in the North Sea to Dumbarton on the Clyde. It is a mountainous region of hard rocks, shallow infertile soils, and high rainfall.

**High Tech** abbreviation for *high technology*, in architecture, an approach to design, originating in the UK in the 1970s, which concentrates on technical innovation, often using exposed structure and services as a means of creating exciting forms and spaces. The Hong Kong and Shanghai Bank, Hong Kong (1986), designed by Norman ◊Foster, is a masterpiece of High Tech architecture.

**highwayman** in English history, a thief on horseback who robbed travellers on the highway (those who did so on foot were known as *footpads*). Highwaymen continued to flourish well into the 19th century.

**hijacking** illegal seizure or taking control of a vehicle and/or its passengers or goods. The term dates from 1923 and originally referred to the robbing of freight lorries. Subsequently it (and its derivative 'skyjacking') has been applied to the seizure of aircraft, usually in flight, by an individual or group, often with some political aim. International treaties (Tokyo 1963, The Hague 1970, and Montréal 1971) encourage cooperation against hijackers and make severe penalties compulsory.

**Hijrah** or *Hegira,* (Arabic 'flight') the flight from Mecca to Medina of the prophet Muhammad, which took place AD 622 as a result of the persecution of the prophet and his followers. The Muslim calendar dates from this event, and the day of the Hijrah is celebrated as the Muslim New Year.

**Hill, Rowland** (1795–1879) English Post Office official who invented adhesive stamps. His pamphlet *Post Office Reform* (1837) prompted the introduction of the penny prepaid post in 1840 (previously the addressee paid, according to distance, on receipt).

**Hill and Adamson** David Octavius Hill (1802–1870) and Robert R Adamson (1821–1848) Scottish photographers who worked together 1843–48. They made extensive use of the ◊calotype process in their portraits of leading members of the Free Church of Scotland and their views of Edinburgh and the Scottish fishing village of Newhaven. They produced some 2,500 calotypes. Their work was rediscovered around 1900.

**Hillary, Edmund (Percival)** (1919– ) New Zealand mountaineer. In 1953, with Nepalese Sherpa mountaineer Tenzing Norgay, he reached the summit of Mount Everest, the first to climb the world's highest peak. As a member of the Commonwealth Transantarctic Expedition 1957–58, he was the first person since R F Scott to reach the South Pole overland, on 3 January 1958.

**hill fort** European Iron Age site with massive banks and ditches for defence, used as both a military camp and a permanent settlement. Examples found across Europe, in particular France, central Germany, and the British Isles, include Heuneberg near Sigmaringen, Germany, Spinans Hill in County Wicklow, Ireland, and Maiden Castle, Dorset, England.

**Hilliard, Nicholas** (*c.* 1547–1619) English miniaturist and goldsmith. Court artist to Elizabeth I and James I, he painted many leading figures of Tudor and Stuart society, including Francis Drake, Walter Raleigh, and Mary Queen of Scots, as well as several portraits of Elizabeth I herself. Some of his minatures, in particular *An Unknown Young Man Amid Roses* (*c.* 1590, Victoria and Albert Museum, London), place the sitter in a closely observed natural setting.

**Himachal Pradesh** state of northwest India, to the south of Kashmir and west of Tibet
*area* 55,700 sq km/21,500 sq mi
*capital* Shimla, lying at 2,213 m/7,200 ft
*physical* mountainous, stretching from the Shiwaliks in the south to Himalayan peaks of more than 6,700 m/22,000 ft; Chenab, Ravi and Beas rivers in the west, Sutlej and Yamuna rivers in the east
*features* mainly agricultural state, one-third forested, with softwood timber industry; Bhakra dam across the Sutlej, for irrigation and power generation; the mountain scenery attracts increasing numbers of tourists
*agriculture* fruit, grain, rice, seed potatoes
*industry* timber, small-scale mining of slate, gypsum, limestone; iron foundry; resin, fertilizer and turpentine production; electronics

**population** (1994 est) 5,530,000; mainly Hindu; some Buddhists
**language** Pahari, Hindi
**history** British forces entered the area in the early 19th century to protect 30 small hill states from Nepalese expansion. British annexation of the area in 1846 was followed by the choice of Shimla as the summer capital. Himachal Pradesh was centrally administered after independence before becoming a Union Territory in 1948, incorporating some hill areas from the former Punjab state. It became a state in 1971, formed from Hindi-speaking parts of the former Central Provinces, various princely states, and the Bastar region.

**Himalaya** vast mountain system of central Asia, extending from the Indian states of Kashmir in the west to Assam in the east, covering the southern part of Tibet, Nepal, Sikkim, and Bhutan. It is the highest mountain range in the world. The two highest peaks are Mount ◊Everest and ◊K2. Other peaks include ◊Kanchenjunga, Makalu, Annapurna, and Nanga Parbat, all over 8,000 m/26,000 ft.

**Himmler, Heinrich** (1900–1945) German Nazi leader, head of the ◊SS elite corps from 1929, the police and the ◊Gestapo secret police from 1936, and supervisor of the extermination of the Jews in Eastern Europe. During World War II he replaced Hermann Goering as Hitler's second-in-command. He was captured in May 1945 and committed suicide.

**Hindenburg, Paul Ludwig Hans Anton von Beneckendorf und Hindenburg** (1847–1934) German field marshal and right-wing politician. During World War I he was supreme commander and, with Erich von Ludendorff, practically directed Germany's policy until the end of the war. He was president of Germany 1925–33.

**Hindi language** member of the Indo-Iranian branch of the Indo-European language family, the official language of the Republic of India, although resisted as such by the Dravidian-speaking states of the south. Hindi proper is used by some 30% of Indians, in such northern states as Uttar Pradesh and Madhya Pradesh.

**Hinduism** (Hindu *sanatana dharma* 'eternal tradition') religion originating in northern India about 4,000 years ago, which is superficially and in some of its forms polytheistic, but has a concept of the supreme spirit, ◊Brahman, above the many divine manifestations. These include the triad of chief gods (the Trimurti): ◊Brahma, ◊Vishnu, and ◊Siva (creator, preserver, and destroyer). Central to Hinduism are the beliefs in reincarnation and ◊karma; the oldest scriptures are the ◊*Vedas*. Temple worship is almost universally observed and there are many festivals. There are over 805 million Hindus worldwide. Women are not regarded as the equals of men but should be treated with kindness and respect. Muslim influence in northern India led to the veiling of women and the restriction of their movements from about the end of the 12th century.

**Hindu Kush** mountain range in central Asia, length 800 km/500 mi, greatest height Tirich Mir, 7,690 m/25,239 ft, in Pakistan. The narrow *Khyber Pass* (53 km/33 mi long) connects Pakistan with Afghanistan and was used by ◊Babur and other invaders of India. The present road was built by the British in the Afghan Wars.

**Hindustan** ('land of the Hindus') the whole of India, but more specifically the plain of the ◊Ganges and Yamuna rivers, or that part of India north of the Deccan.

**Hindustani** member of the Indo-Iranian branch of the Indo-European language family, closely related to Hindi and Urdu and originating in the bazaars of Delhi. It is a ◊lingua franca in many parts of the Republic of India.

**Hingis, Martina** (1980–  ) Czech-born Swiss tennis player. In 1996 she became the youngest ever winner of a Grand Slam title when she won the Wimbledon women's doubles title at the age of 15 years 282 days. In January 1997, at 16 years 92 days, she won the women's singles at the Australian Open. Three months later she became the youngest player to be ranked as number one in the world since the women's official rankings began. In 1997, at 16 years 279 days she became the youngest winner of a singles title at Wimbledon since Lottie Dod won the women's singles in 1887 at the age of 15 years 285 days. In the same year she won the US Open singles champion. In early 1998 she retained her Australian Open singles titles defeating the 1994 Wimbledon champion Conchita Martinez of Spain in the final.

She has won the women's singles at the Australian Open for the third year in a row in January 1999. She also achieved her third successive doubles title at the championships.
**career highlights**
**Grand Slam singles titles**
**Wimbledon** 1997
**US Open** 1997
**Australian Open** 1997, 1998, 1999.

**hippie** member of a youth movement of the late 1960s, also known as *flower power,* which originated in San Francisco, California, and was characterized by nonviolent anarchy, concern for the environment, and rejection of Western materialism. The hippies formed a politically outspoken, antiwar, artistically prolific counter-culture in North America and Europe. Their colourful psychedelic style, inspired by drugs such as ◊LSD, emerged in fashion, graphic art, and music by bands such as Love (1965–71), the ◊Grateful Dead, Jefferson Airplane (1965–74), and ◊Pink Floyd.

**Hippocrates** (*c.* 460–*c.* 377 BC) Greek physician, often called the founder of medicine. Important Hippocratic ideas include cleanliness (for patients and physicians), moderation in eating and drinking, letting nature take its course, and living where the air is good. He believed that health was the result of the 'humours' of the body being in balance; imbalance caused disease. These ideas were later adopted by ◊Galen.

**hippopotamus** (Greek 'river horse') large herbivorous, short-legged, even-toed hoofed mammal. The *common hippopotamus*

(*Hippopotamus amphibius*) is found in Africa. It weighs up to 3,200 kg/7,040 lb, stands about 1.6 m/5.25 ft tall, and has a brown or slate-grey skin. It is an endangered species. (Family Hippopotamidae.)

**hire purchase** (HP), form of credit under which the buyer pays a deposit and makes instalment payments at fixed intervals over a certain period for a particular item. The buyer has immediate possession, but does not own the item until the final instalment has been paid.

**Hirohito** regnal era name *Shōwa* (1901–1989) Emperor of Japan from 1926, when he succeeded his father Taishō (Yoshihito). After the defeat of Japan in World War II in 1945, he was made a figurehead monarch by the US-backed constitution of 1946. He is believed to have played a reluctant role in General Tōjō's prewar expansion plans. He was succeeded by his son ◊Akihito.

**Hiroshige, Andō** (1797–1858) Japanese artist. He was one of the leading exponents of ◊ukiyo-e prints, an art form whose flat, decorative style and choice of everyday subjects influenced such artists as James Whistler and Vincent van Gogh. His landscape prints, often employing snow or rain to create atmosphere, include *Tōkaidō gojūsan tsugi/53 Stations on the Tōkaidō Highway* (1833).

**Hiroshima** industrial city and port on the south coast of Honshu island, Japan; population (1994) 1,077,000. On 6 August 1945 it was destroyed by the first wartime use of an atomic bomb. The city has largely been rebuilt since then. The main industries include food processing and the manufacture of cars and machinery.

**Hispaniola** Spanish 'little Spain', West Indian island, first landing place of Columbus in the New World, 6 December 1492; it is now divided into Haiti and the Dominican Republic.

**histamine** inflammatory substance normally released in damaged tissues, which also accounts for many of the symptoms of ◊allergy. It is an amine, $C_5H_9N_3$. Substances that neutralize its activity are known as ◊antihistamines. Histamine was first described in 1911 by British physiologist Henry Dale (1875–1968).

**histology** in medicine, the laboratory study of cells and tissues.

**history** record of the events of human societies. The earliest surviving historical records are inscriptions concerning the achievements of Egyptian and Babylonian kings. As a literary form in the Western world, historical writing, or *historiography,* began in the 5th century BC with the Greek Herodotus, who first to pass beyond the limits of a purely national outlook. Contemporary historians make extensive use of statistics, population figures, and primary records to justify historical arguments.

**Hitchcock, Alfred (Joseph)** (1899–1980) English film director, a US citizen from 1955. A master of the suspense thriller, he was noted for his meticulously drawn storyboards that determined his camera angles and for his cameo

walk-ons in his own films. His *Blackmail* (1929) was the first successful British talking film. *The Thirty-Nine Steps* (1935) and *The Lady Vanishes* (1938) are British suspense classics. He went to Hollywood in 1940, and his work there included *Rebecca* (1940), *Notorious* (1946), *Strangers on a Train* (1951), *Rear Window* (1954), *Vertigo* (1958), *North by Northwest* (1959), *Psycho* (1960), and *The Birds* (1963).

**Hitler, Adolf** (1889–1945) German Nazi dictator, born in Austria. He was *Führer* (leader) of the Nazi Party from 1921 and wrote *Mein Kampf/My Struggle* (1925–27). As chancellor of Germany from 1933 and head of state from 1934, he created a dictatorship by playing party and state institutions against each other and continually creating new offices and appointments. His position was not seriously challenged until the July Plot of 1944, which failed to assassinate him. In foreign affairs, he reoccupied the Rhineland and formed an alliance with the Italian Fascist Benito ◊Mussolini in 1936, annexed Austria in 1938, and occupied Sudeten under the ◊Munich Agreement. The rest of Czechoslovakia was annexed in March 1939. The ◊Ribbentrop–Molotov pact was followed in September by the invasion of Poland and the declaration of war by Britain and France (see ◊World War II). He committed suicide as Berlin fell.

**Hitler–Stalin pact** another name for the ◊Ribbentrop–Molotov pact.

**Hittite** member of any of a succession of peoples who inhabited Anatolia and northern Syria from the 3rd millennium to the 1st millennium BC. The city of Hattusas (now Boğazköy in central Turkey) became the capital of a strong kingdom which overthrew the Babylonian Empire. After a period of eclipse the Hittite New Empire became a great power (about 1400–1200 BC), which successfully waged war with Egypt. The Hittite language is an Indo-European language.

**HIV** abbreviation for *human immunodeficiency virus,* the infectious agent that is believed to cause ◊AIDS. It was first discovered in 1983 by Luc Montagnier of the Pasteur Institute in Paris, who called it lymphocyte-associated virus (LAV). Independently, US scientist Robert Gallo of the National Cancer Institute in Bethesda, Maryland, claimed its discovery in 1984 and named it human T-lymphocytotrophic virus 3 (HTLV-III).

**Hobbes, Thomas** (1588–1679) English political philosopher and the first thinker since Aristotle to attempt to develop a comprehensive theory of nature, including human behaviour. In *Leviathan* (1651), he advocates absolutist government as the only means of ensuring order and security; he saw this as deriving from the social contract.

**Ho Chi Minh** adopted name of Nguyen Tat Thanh (1890–1969) North Vietnamese communist politician, prime minister 1954–55, and president 1954–69. Having trained in Moscow shortly after the Russian Revolution, he headed the communist Vietminh from 1941 and fought against the French during the ◊Indochina War

1946–54, becoming president and prime minister of the republic at the armistice. Aided by the communist bloc, he did much to develop industrial potential. He relinquished the premiership in 1955, but continued as president. In the years before his death, Ho successfully led his country's fight against US-aided South Vietnam in the ◊Vietnam War 1954–75.

**Ho Chi Minh City** until 1976 *Saigon,* chief port and industrial city of South Vietnam; population (1989) 3,169,100. Industries include shipbuilding, textiles, rubber, and food products. Saigon was the capital of the Republic of Vietnam (South Vietnam) from 1954 to 1976, when it was renamed.

**Hockney, David** (1937– ) English painter, printmaker, and designer, resident in California. One of the best-known figures in British Pop art, he developed a distinctive figurative style, as in his portrait *Mr and Mrs Clark and Percy* (1971; Tate Gallery, London). He has experimented prolifically with technique, and produced drawings; etchings, including *Six Fairy Tales from the Brothers Grimm* (1970); photo collages; and opera sets for Glyndebourne, East Sussex, La Scala, Milan, and the Metropolitan, New York.

**Hodgkin's disease** or *lymphadenoma,* rare form of cancer mainly affecting the lymph nodes and spleen. It undermines the immune system, leaving the sufferer susceptible to infection.

However, it responds well to radiotherapy and cytotoxic drugs, and long-term survival is usual.

**hog** any member of the ◊pig family. The *river hog* (*Potamochoerus porcus*) lives in Africa, south of the Sahara. Reddish or black, up to 1.3 m/4.2 ft long plus tail, and 90 cm/3 ft at the shoulder, this gregarious animal roots for food in many types of habitat. The *giant forest hog* (*Hylochoerus meinerzthageni*) lives in thick forests of central Africa and grows up to 1.9 m/6 ft long. The ◊*wart hog* is another African wild pig. The *pygmy hog Sus salvanus,* the smallest of the pig family, is about 65 cm/26 in long (25 cm /10 in at the shoulder) and weighs 8–9 kg/18–20 lb.

**Hogarth, William** (1697–1764) English painter and engraver. He produced portraits and moralizing genre scenes, such as the story series of prints *A Rake's Progress* (1735; Soane Museum, London). His portraits are remarkably direct and full of character, for example *Heads of Six of Hogarth's Servants* (about 1750–55; Tate Gallery) and his oil sketch masterpiece *The Shrimp Girl* (National Gallery).

**Hohenstaufen** German family of princes, several members of which were Holy Roman Emperors 1138–1208 and 1214–54. They were the first German emperors to make use of associations with Roman law and tradition to aggrandize their office, and included Conrad III; Frederick I (Barbarossa), the first to use the title Holy Roman Emperor (previously the title Roman emperor was used); Henry VI; and Frederick II.

**Hohenzollern** German family, originating in Württemberg, the main branch of which held the titles of elector of Brandenburg from 1415, king of Prussia from 1701, and German emperor from 1871. The last emperor, Wilhelm II, was dethroned 1918 after the disastrous course of World War I. Another branch of the family were kings of Romania 1881–1947.

**Hohhot** or *Huhehot;* formerly *Kweisui,* city and capital of ◊Inner Mongolia Autonomous Region, China; population (1993) 730,000. It is an important industrial centre and trading hub between north and west China and Mongolia. Cotton textiles, wool, fur, steel, building materials, machinery, electronics, chemicals, flour, dairy goods, and diesel engines are produced. Hohhot contains Lamaist monasteries and temples.

**Hokkaido** formerly (until 1868) *Yezo* or *Ezo,* (Japanese *hoku* 'north'; *kai* 'sea'; *do* 'road') northernmost and second-largest of the four main islands of Japan, separated from Honshu to the south by Tsugaru Strait (20 km/12 mi wide), and from Sakhalin (Russia) to the north by Soya Strait

*area* 83,500 sq km/32,239 sq mi

*capital* ◊Sapporo

*cities* Hakodate, Asahikawa, Otaru, Muroran

*features* artificial harbour at Tomakomai; the undersea rail tunnel, the Seikan Tunnel, linking the old port of Hakodate with Aomori on Honshu opened in 1988

*physical* unspoiled dramatic scenery of active volcanoes, forests and a large lake; snow-covered for half the year; five national parks

*industries* coal, mercury, manganese, oil, natural gas and tourism

*agriculture* rice, dairying, forestry and fishing

*population* (1995) 5,692,000, including 16,000 Ainus

*history* little developed until the Meiji Restoration in 1868 when disbanded samurai were settled here; intensive exploitation followed World War II, including heavy and chemical industrial plants, development of electric power, and dairy farming.

**Hokusai, Katsushika** (1760–1849) Japanese artist. He was the leading printmaker of his time and a major exponent of ◊ukiyo-e. He published *Fugaku sanjū-rokkei/36 Views of Mount Fuji* (about 1823–29), and produced outstanding pictures of almost every kind of subject – birds, flowers, courtesans, and scenes from legend and everyday life. *Under the Wave at Kanagawa* (British Museum, London) is typical.

**Holbein, Hans,** *the Younger* (1497–1543) German painter and woodcut artist who spent much of his career as a portrait artist at the court of Henry VIII of England. One of the finest graphic artists of his age, he executed a woodcut series *Dance of Death* (about 1525), and designed title pages for Luther's New Testament and Thomas More's *Utopia.*

**Holiday, Billie** stage name of Eleanora Gough McKay (1915–1959) US jazz singer, also known as 'Lady Day'. She made her debut in clubs in Harlem, New York, and became known for her emotionally charged delivery and idiosyncratic phrasing. Holiday brought a blues feel to her performances with swing bands. Songs she made her own include 'Stormy Weather', 'Strange Fruit', 'I Cover the Waterfront', 'That Ole Devil Called Love', and 'Lover Man (Oh, Where can You Be?)'.

**holism** in philosophy, the concept that the whole is greater than the sum of its parts.

**holistic medicine** umbrella term for an approach that virtually all alternative therapies profess, which considers the overall health and lifestyle profile of a patient, and treats specific ailments not primarily as conditions to be alleviated but rather as symptoms of more fundamental disease.

**Holland** popular name for the Netherlands; also two provinces of the Netherlands, see ◊North Holland and ◊South Holland.

**holly** any of a group of trees or shrubs that includes the English Christmas holly (*I. aquifolium*), an evergreen with spiny, glossy leaves, small white flowers, and poisonous scarlet berries on the female tree. Leaves of the Brazilian holly (*I. paraguayensis*) are used to make the tea *yerba maté*. (Genus *Ilex,* family Aquifoliaceae.)

**Holly, Buddy** stage name of Charles Hardin Holley (1936–1959) US rock-and-roll singer, guitarist, and songwriter. He had a distinctive, hiccuping vocal style and was an early experimenter with recording techniques. Many of his hits with his band, the Crickets, such as 'That'll Be the Day' (1957), 'Peggy Sue' (1957), and 'Maybe Baby' (1958), have become classics. His albums include *The Chirping Crickets* (1958) and *Buddy Holly* (1958). He died in a plane crash.

**hollyhock** tall flowering plant belonging to the mallow family. *A. rosea*, originally a native of Asia, produces spikes of large white, yellow, pink, or red flowers, 3 m/10 ft high when cultivated as a biennial; it is a popular cottage garden plant. (Genus *Althaea,* family Malvaceae.)

**Hollywood** district in the city of Los Angeles, California; the centre of the US film industry from 1911. It is the home of film studios such as Twentieth Century Fox, MGM, Paramount, Columbia Pictures, United Artists, Disney, and Warner Bros. Many film stars' homes are situated nearby in Beverly Hills and other communities adjacent to Hollywood.

**Holmes, Sherlock** fictitious private detective, created by the English writer Arthur Conan ◊Doyle in *A Study in Scarlet* (1887) and recurring in novels and stories until 1927. Holmes' ability to make inferences from slight clues always astonishes the narrator, Dr Watson.

**holmium** (Latin *Holmia* 'Stockholm') silvery, metallic element of the ◊lanthanide series, symbol Ho, atomic number 67, relative atomic mass 164.93. It occurs in combination with other rareearth metals and in various minerals such as gadolinite. Its compounds are highly magnetic.

**Holocaust, the** the annihilation of an estimated 16 million people by the Hitler regime between 1933 and 1945, principally in the numerous extermination and ◊concentration camps, most notably ◊Auschwitz (Oświęcim), Sobibor, Treblinka, and Maidanek in Poland, and Belsen, ◊Buchenwald, and ◊Dachau in Germany. Of the victims around 6 million were Jews (over 67% of European Jews); around 10 million Ukrainian, Polish, and Russian civilians and prisoners of war, Romanies, socialists, homosexuals, and others (labelled 'defectives') were also imprisoned and/or exterminated. Victims were variously starved, tortured, experimented on, and worked to death. Millions were executed in gas chambers, shot, or hanged. It was euphemistically termed the final solution (of the Jewish question). The precise death toll will never be known. Holocaust museums and memorial sites have been established in Israel and in other countries.

**Holocene** epoch of geological time that began 10,000 years ago, the second and current epoch of the Quaternary period. During this epoch the glaciers retreated, the climate became warmer, and humans developed significantly.

**holography** method of producing three-dimensional (3-D) images, called holograms, by means of ◊laser light. Holography uses a photographic technique (involving the splitting of a laser beam into two beams) to produce a picture, or hologram, that contains 3-D information about the object photographed. Some holograms show meaningless patterns in ordinary light and produce a 3-D image only when laser light is projected through them, but reflection holograms produce images when ordinary light is reflected from them (as found on credit cards). *See illustration on page 418.*

**Holy Communion** another name for the ◊Eucharist, a Christian sacrament.

**Holy Grail** in medieval Christian legend, the dish or cup used by Jesus at the Last Supper; credited with supernatural powers and a symbol of Christian grace. In certain stories incorporated in Arthurian legend, it was an object of quest by King Arthur's knights, together with the spear with which Jesus was wounded at the Crucifixion. ◊Galahad was the only knight to achieve the mission.

**Holy Roman Empire** empire of Charlemagne and his successors, and the German Empire 962–1806, both being regarded as the Christian (hence 'holy') revival of the Roman Empire. At its height it comprised much of western and central Europe. See ◊Habsburg. *See table on page 419.*

**Holy Spirit** third person of the Christian ◊Trinity, also known as the Holy Ghost or the Paraclete, usually depicted as a white dove.

**Home Counties** those counties in close proximity to London, England: Hertfordshire, Essex, Kent, Surrey, Buckinghamshire, and formerly Berkshire and Middlesex.

**homeland** or *Bantustan,* before 1980, name for the ◊Black National States in the Republic of South Africa.

**homeopathy** or *homoeopathy,* system of alternative medicine based on the principle that symptoms of disease are part of the body's self-healing processes, and on the practice of

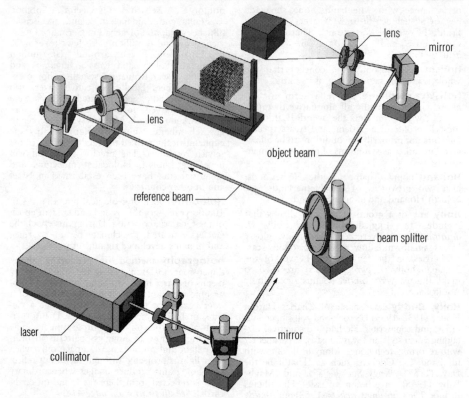

**holography** *Recording a transmission hologram. Light from a laser is divided into two beams. One beam goes directly to the photographic plate. The other beam reflects off the object before hitting the photographic plate. The two beams combine to produce a pattern on the plate which contains information about the 3-D shape of the object. If the exposed and developed plate is illuminated by laser light, the pattern can be seen as a 3-D picture of the object.*

administering extremely diluted doses of natural substances found to produce in a healthy person the symptoms manifest in the illness being treated. Developed by the German physician Samuel Hahnemann (1755–1843), the system is widely practised today as an alternative to allopathic (orthodox) medicine, and many controlled tests and achieved cures testify its efficacy.

**homeostasis** maintenance of a constant environment around living cells, particularly with regard to pH, salt concentration, temperature, and blood sugar levels. Stable conditions are important for the efficient functioning of the ◊enzyme reactions within the cells. In humans, homeostasis in the blood (which provides fluid for all tissues) is ensured by several organs. The ◊kidneys regulate pH, urea, and water concentration. The lungs regulate oxygen and carbon dioxide (see ◊breathing). Temperature is regulated by the liver and the skin. Glucose levels in the blood are regulated by the ◊liver and the pancreas.

**Homer** according to ancient tradition, the author of the Greek narrative epics, the ◊*Iliad* and the ◊*Odyssey* (both derived from oral tradition). Little is known about the man, but modern research suggests that both poems should be assigned to the 8th century BC, with the *Odyssey* the later of the two.

**Home Rule, Irish** movement to repeal the Act of ◊Union of 1801 that joined Ireland to Britain, and to establish an Irish Parliament responsible for internal affairs. In 1870 Isaac Butt (1813–1879) formed the Home Rule Association and the movement was led in Parliament from 1880 by Charles ◊Parnell. After 1918 the demand for an independent Irish republic replaced that for home rule.

**homicide** in law, the killing of a human being. This may be unlawful, lawful, or excusable, depending on the circumstances. Unlawful homicides include ◊murder, ◊manslaughter, infanticide, and causing death by dangerous driving. Lawful homicide occurs where, for example, a police officer is justified in killing a criminal in the course of apprehension or when a person is killed in self-defence or defence of others.

**homoeopathy** variant spelling of ◊*homeopathy.*

## HOLY ROMAN EMPERORS

| Reign | Name |
|---|---|
| *Carolingian Kings and Emperors* | |
| 800–14 | Charlemagne (Charles the Great) |
| 814–40 | Louis the Pious |
| 840–55 | Lothair I |
| 855–75 | Louis II |
| 875–77 | Charles (II) the Bald |
| 881–87 | Charles (III) the Fat |
| 891–94 | Guido of Spoleto |
| 892–98 | Lambert of Spoleto (co-emperor) |
| 896–901 | Arnulf (rival) |
| 901–05 | Louis III of Provence |
| 905–24 | Berengar |
| 911–18 | Conrad (I) of Franconia (rival) |
| *Saxon Kings and Emperors* | |
| 918–36 | Henry I the Fowler |
| 936–73 | Otto (I) the Great |
| 973–83 | Otto II |
| 983–1002 | Otto III |
| 1002–24 | Henry (II) the Saint |
| *Franconian (Salian) Emperors* | |
| 1024–39 | Conrad II |
| 1039–56 | Henry (III) the Black |
| 1056–1106 | Henry IV |
| 1077–80 | Rudolf of Swabia (rival) |
| 1081–93 | Hermann of Luxembourg (rival) |
| 1093–1101 | Conrad of Franconia (rival) |
| 1106–25 | Henry V |
| 1126–37 | Lothair II |
| *Hohenstaufen Kings and Emperors* | |
| 1138–52 | Conrad III |
| 1152–90 | Frederick Barbarossa |
| 1190–97 | Henry VI |
| 1198–1215 | Otto IV |
| 1198–1208 | Philip of Swabia (rival) |
| 1215–50 | Frederick II |
| 1246–47 | Henry Raspe of Thuringia (rival) |
| 1247–56 | William of Holland (rival) |

| Reign | Name |
|---|---|
| 1250–54 | Conrad IV |
| 1254–73 | no ruler (the Great Interregnum) |
| *Rulers from Various Noble Families* | |
| 1257–72 | Richard of Cornwall (rival) |
| 1257–73 | Alfonso X of Castile (rival) |
| 1273–91 | Rudolf I, Habsburg |
| 1292–98 | Adolf I of Nassau |
| 1298–1308 | Albert I, Habsburg |
| 1308–13 | Henry VII, Luxembourg |
| 1314–47 | Louis IV of Bavaria |
| 1314–25 | Frederick of Habsburg (co-regent) |
| 1347–78 | Charles IV, Luxembourg |
| 1378–1400 | Wenceslas of Bohemia |
| 1400 | Frederick III of Brunswick |
| 1400–10 | Rupert of the Palatinate |
| 1411–37 | Sigismund, Luxembourg |
| *Habsburg Emperors* | |
| 1438–39 | Albert II |
| 1440–93 | Frederick III |
| 1493–1519 | Maximilian I |
| 1519–56 | Charles V |
| 1556–64 | Ferdinand I |
| 1564–76 | Maximilian II |
| 1576–1612 | Rudolf II |
| 1612–19 | Matthias |
| 1619–37 | Ferdinand II |
| 1637–57 | Ferdinand III |
| 1658–1705 | Leopold I |
| 1705–11 | Joseph I |
| 1711–40 | Charles VI |
| 1742–45 | Charles VII of Bavaria |
| *Habsburg-Lorraine Emperors* | |
| 1745–65 | Francis I of Lorraine |
| 1765–90 | Joseph II |
| 1790–92 | Leopold II |
| 1792–1806 | Francis II |

**homologous** in biology, a term describing an organ or structure possessed by members of different taxonomic groups (for example, species, genera, families, orders) that originally derived from the same structure in a common ancestor. The wing of a bat, the arm of a monkey, and the flipper of a seal are homologous because they all derive from the forelimb of an ancestral mammal.

**homologous series** any of a number of series of organic chemicals with similar chemical properties in which members differ by a constant relative molecular mass.

**homosexuality** sexual preference for, or attraction to, persons of one's own sex; in women it is referred to as ◊lesbianism.

Both sexes use the term 'gay'. Men and women who are attracted to both sexes are referred to as bisexual. The extent to which homosexual behaviour is caused by biological or psychological factors is an area of disagreement among experts.

**Honan** alternative name of ◊Henan, a province of China.

**Honda** Japanese vehicle manufacturer, founded 1948. By the late 1980s the company was producing more than 1.5 million cars and 3 million motorcycles annually.

**Honduras** Republic of
**national name** *República de Honduras*

**area** 112,100 sq km/43,281 sq mi
**capital** Tegucigalpa
**major towns/cities** San Pedro Sula, La Ceiba, El Progreso, Choluteca, Juticalpa, Danlí
**major ports** La Ceiba, Puerto Cortés

**physical features** narrow tropical coastal plain with mountainous interior, Bay Islands, Caribbean reefs
**head of state and government** Carlos Flores from 1997
**political system** democracy
**political parties** Liberal Party of Honduras (PLH), centre left; National Party of Honduras (PNH), right wing
**currency** lempira
**GNP per capita (PPP)** (US$) 2,140 (1998)
**exports** bananas, lobsters and prawns, zinc, meat. Principal market: USA 73.2% (1998)
**population** 6,315,000 (1999 est)
**language** Spanish (official); English, American Indian languages
**religion** Roman Catholic
**life expectancy** 68 (men); 72 (women) (1995–2000)
**Chronology**
**c. AD 250–900** Part of culturally advanced Maya civilization.
**1502** Visited by Christopher Columbus, who named the country Honduras ('depths') after the deep waters off the north coast.
**1525** Colonized by Spain, who founded the town of Trujillo, but met with fierce resistance from the American Indian population.
**17th century onwards** The northern 'Mosquito Coast' fell under the control of British buccaneers, as the Spanish concentrated on the inland area, with a British protectorate being established over the coast until 1860.
**1821** Achieved independence from Spain and became part of Mexico.
**1823** Became part of United Provinces (Federation) of Central America, also embracing Costa Rica, El Salvador, Guatemala, and Nicaragua, with the Honduran liberal Gen Francisco Morazan, president of the Federation from 1830.
**1838** Achieved full independence when federation dissolved.
**1880** Capital transferred from Comayagua to Tegucigalpa.
**later 19th–early 20th centuries** The USA's economic involvement significant, with banana production, which provided two-thirds of exports in 1913, being controlled by the United Fruit Company; political instability, with frequent changes of constitution and military coups.
**1925** Brief civil war.
**1932–49** Under a right-wing National Party (PNH) dictatorship, led by Gen Tiburcio Carias Andino.
**1963–74** Following a series of military coups, Gen Oswaldo López Arelano held power, before resigning after allegedly accepting bribes from a US company.
**1969** Brief 'Football War' with El Salvador, which attacked Honduras at the time of a football competition between the two states, following evictions of thousands of Salvadoran illegal immigrants from Honduras.
**1980** The first civilian government in more than a century was elected, with Dr Roberto Suazo of the centrist Liberal Party (PLH) as president, but the commander in chief of the army, Gen

Gustavo Alvárez, retained considerable power.
**1983** There was close involvement with the USA in providing naval and air bases and allowing Nicaraguan counter-revolutionaries ('Contras') to operate from Honduras.
**1984** Alvarez was ousted in a coup led by junior officers and Gen Walter López Reyes, resulting in a policy review towards USA and Nicaragua.
**1986** José Azcona del Hoyo (PLH) was elected president after the electoral law was changed, making Suazo ineligible for presidency, despite receiving fewer votes than his opponent.
**1989** The government and opposition declared support for a Central American peace plan to demobilize Nicaraguan Contras (thought to number 55,000 with their dependents) based in Honduras. PNH won assembly elections; its leader, Rafael Leonardo Callejas Romero, was elected president.
**1992** A border dispute with El Salvador dating from 1861 was finally resolved.
**1993** PLH, under Carlos Roberto Reina Idiaquez, won assembly and presidential elections.
**1997** Carlos Flores (PLH) was elected president.

**Honecker, Erich** (1912–1994) German communist politician, in power in East Germany 1973–89, elected chair of the council of state (head of state) in 1976. He governed in an outwardly austere and efficient manner and, while favouring East–West détente, was a loyal ally of the USSR. In 1989, following a wave of prodemocracy demonstrations, he was replaced as leader of the Socialist Unity Party (SED) and head of state by Egon Krenz, and expelled from the Communist Party. He died in exile in Chile.

**honey** sweet syrup produced by honey ◊bees from the nectar of flowers. It is stored in honeycombs and made in excess of their needs as food for the winter. Honey comprises various sugars, mainly laevulose and dextrose, with enzymes, colouring matter, acids, and pollen grains. It has antibacterial properties and was widely used in ancient Egypt, Greece, and Rome as a wound salve. It is still popular for sore throats, in hot drinks or in lozenges.

**honeyeater** or *honey-sucker,* any of a group of small, brightly coloured birds with long, curved beaks and long tails, native to Australia. They have a long tongue divided into four at the end to form a brush for collecting nectar from flowers. (Family Meliphagidae.)

**honeysuckle** vine or shrub found in temperate regions of the world. The common honeysuckle or woodbine (*L. periclymenum*) of Europe is a climbing plant with sweet-scented flowers, reddish and yellow-tinted outside and creamy white inside; it now grows in the northeastern USA. (Genus *Lonicera,* family Caprifoliaceae.)

**Hong Kong** special administrative region in the southeast of China, comprising Hong Kong Island; the Kowloon Peninsula; many other islands, of which the largest is Lantau; and the mainland New Territories. A former British crown colony, it reverted to Chinese control in July 1997

**area** 1,070 sq km/413 sq mi
**capital** Victoria (Hong Kong City)
**towns and cities** Kowloon, Tsuen Wan (in the New Territories)
**features** an enclave of Guangdong province, China, it has one of the world's finest natural harbours; Hong Kong Island is connected with Kowloon by undersea railway and ferries; a world financial centre, its stock market has four exchanges
**environment** world's most densely populated city; surrounding waters heavily polluted
**exports** textiles, clothing, electronic goods, clocks, watches, cameras, plastic products; a large proportion of the exports and imports of southern China are transshipped here; tourism is important
**currency** Hong Kong dollar
**population** (1995 est) 6,189,800; 57% Hong Kong Chinese, most of the remainder refugees from the mainland
**language** English, Chinese
**religion** Confucianist, Buddhist, Taoist, with Muslim and Christian minorities
**government** Hong Kong is a Special Administrative Region within China, with a chief executive, Tung Chee-hwa, from 1997. There is an executive council, which comprises a mixture of business and political figures, and, from May 1998, an elected legislative council. Until reversion to Chinese control in July 1997 Hong Kong was a British dependency administered by a crown-appointed governor who presided over an unelected executive council, composed of 4 ex-officio and 11 nominated members, and a legislative council composed of 3 ex-officio members, 18 appointees, and 39 elected members
**history** formerly part of China, Hong Kong Island was occupied by Britain in 1841, during the first of the ◊Opium Wars, and ceded by China under the 1842 Treaty of Nanking. The Kowloon Peninsula was acquired under the 1860 Beijing (Peking) Convention and the New Territories secured under a 99-year lease from 1898. The colony, which developed into a major centre for Sino-British trade during the late 19th and early 20th centuries, was occupied by Japan from 1941 to 1945. The restored British administration promised, after 1946, to increase self-government. These plans were shelved, however, after the 1949 communist revolution in China.

During the 1950s almost 1 million Chinese (predominantly Cantonese) refugees fled to Hong Kong. Immigration continued during the 1960s and 1970s, raising the colony's population from 1 million in 1946 to 5 million in 1980, leading to the imposition of strict border controls during the 1980s. From 1975, 160,000 Vietnamese ◊boat people fled to Hong Kong; in 1991 some 61,000 remained. The UK government began forced repatriation in 1989. Hong Kong's economy expanded rapidly during the corresponding period and the colony became one of Asia's major commercial, financial, and industrial centres, boasting the world's busiest container port from 1987.

As the date (1997) for the termination of the New Territories' lease approached, negotiations on Hong Kong's future were opened between Britain and China in 1982. These culminated in 1984 in an agreement that Britain would transfer full sovereignty of the islands and New Territories to China in 1997 in return for Chinese assurance that Hong Kong's social and economic freedom and capitalist lifestyle would be preserved for at least 50 years.

As plans for the transfer became more detailed, fears that China would exert more control than agreed led to tensions between the UK and China. Tung Chee-hwa, a Shanghai-born shipping magnate who had studied in Britain and the USA before running, with Chinese financial help, a large ocean fleet out of Taiwan and Hong Kong, was elected by a 400-member Chinese-established selection committee, to become the first chief executive (replacing the British-appointed governor) of the Hong Kong Special Administrative Region (HKSAR) when Hong Kong reverted to Chinese sovereignty in July 1997.

In January 1997 Tung announced that the new executive council would comprise a mixture of business and political figures with strong links with mainland China. In February 1997 the Chinese parliament voted to dilute substantially Hong Kong's bill of rights and freedoms of association and assembly after the July 1997 handover.

The Hong Kong economy contracted by 4% during the first half of 1998, the stock market crashed to a 5-year-low, and the unemployment level reached a 15-year high, as the region suffered from the financial crisis that had engulfed southeast Asia since 1997. The approval rating of Tung fell as a consequence. GDP fell by 5% during 1998, as the region endured its worst ever economic recession and unemployment rose to above 5%.

**Honiara** port and capital of the Solomon Islands, on the northwest coast of Guadalcanal Island, on the River Mataniko; population (1989) 33,750.

**honi soit qui mal y pense** (French 'shame on him or her who thinks evil of it') motto of England's Order of the Garter.

**Honolulu** or *Honolulu on Oaha,* (Hawaiian 'sheltered bay') statecapital and port of ◊Hawaii, USA, on the south coast of Oahu; seat of Honolulu County; population (1994 est) 386,000. The city is the economic centre of Hawaii. It has a natural harbour (formed by a lagoon within the coral reef) with extensive shipping facilities. Honolulu is a trading centre for European and Indian goods, and is the principal point of entry to the islands. It is often called the 'Crossroads of the Pacific'. With its warm climate and tropical vegetation, Honolulu has become a holiday resort. In addition to tourism, other industries include food processing, machinery, clothing, and building materials. It was incorporated as a city in 1907.

**Honshu** principal island of Japan, lying between Hokkaido to the northeast and Kyushu to the southwest. Its landmass is approximately four-fifths of the country.

*area* 231,100 sq km/89,228 sq mi, including 382 smaller islands
*capital* ◊Tokyo
*cities* Yokohama, Osaka, Kobe, Nagoya, Hiroshima
*features* linked by bridges and tunnels with the islands of Hokkaido, Kyushu, and Shikoku
*physical* a chain of volcanic mountains runs along the island; frequent earthquakes
*population* (1995) 100,995,000.

**hoof** horny covering that protects the sensitive parts of the foot of an animal. The possession of hooves is characteristic of the orders Artiodactyla (even-toed ungulates such as deer and cattle), and Perissodactyla (horses, tapirs, and rhinoceroses).

**Hooke, Robert** (1635–1703) English scientist and inventor, originator of ◊*Hooke's law,* and considered the foremost mechanic of his time. His inventions included a telegraph system, the spirit level, marine barometer, and sea gauge. He coined the term 'cell' in biology.

**Hooker, John Lee** (1917– ) US blues guitarist, singer, and songwriter. He was one of the foremost blues musicians. His first record, 'Boogie Chillen' 1948, was a blues hit and his percussive guitar style made him popular with a rock audience from the 1950s. His albums include *Urban Blues* (1968) and *Boom Boom* (1992) (also the title of his 1962 song).

**Hooke's law** law stating that the deformation of a body is proportional to the magnitude of the deforming force, provided that the body's elastic limit (see ◊elasticity) is not exceeded. If the elastic limit is not reached, the body will return to its original size once the force is removed. The law was discovered by English physicist Robert Hooke in 1676.

**hookworm** parasitic roundworm (see ◊worm) with hooks around its mouth. It lives mainly in tropical and subtropical regions, but also in humid areas in temperate climates. The eggs are hatched in damp soil, and the larvae bore into the host's skin, usually through the soles of the feet. They make their way to the small intestine, where they live by sucking blood. The eggs are expelled with faeces, and the cycle starts again. The human hookworm causes anaemia, weakness, and abdominal pain. It is common in areas where defecation occurs outdoors. (Genus *Necator.*)

**hoopoe** bird slightly larger than a thrush, with a long, thin, slightly downward-curving bill and a bright pinkish-buff crest tipped with black that expands into a fan shape on top of the head. The wings and tail are banded with black and white, and the rest of the plumage is buff-coloured. The hoopoe is found throughout southern Europe and Asia down to southern Africa, India, Malaya. (Species *Upupa epops,* family Upupidae, order Coraciiformes.)

**Hoover, Herbert (Clark)** (1874–1964) 31st president of the USA 1929–33, a Republican. He was secretary of commerce 1921–28. Hoover lost public confidence after the stock-market crash of 1929, when he opposed direct government aid for the unemployed in the Depression that followed.

**Hoover, J(ohn) Edgar** (1895–1972) US lawyer and director of the Federal Bureau of Investigation (FBI) from 1924 until his death. He built up a powerful network for the detection of organized crime, including a national fingerprint collection. His drive against alleged communist activities after World War II and his opposition to the Kennedy administration brought much criticism for abuse of power.

**Hopei** alternative transcription of ◊Hebei, a province of China.

**Hopkins, Anthony (Philip)** (1937– ) Welsh actor. A successful stage actor both in London and on Broadway, Hopkins won acclaim for his performance as Richard the Lion-Heart in his second film, *The Lion in Winter* (1968). His performance as a cannibalistic serial killer in *The Silence of the Lambs* (1991) gained him an Academy Award.

**Hopkins, Gerard Manley** (1844–1889) English poet and Jesuit priest. His works are marked by originality of diction and rhythm and include 'The Wreck of the Deutschland' (1876), and 'The Windhover' and 'Pied Beauty' (both 1877). His collected works were published posthumously in 1918 by his friend the poet Robert Bridges. His employment of 'sprung rhythm' (the combination of traditional regularity of stresses with varying numbers of syllables in each line) greatly influenced later 20th-century poetry.

**Hopper, Edward** (1882–1967) US painter and etcher, one of the foremost American Realists. His views of life in New England and New York in the 1930s and 1940s, painted in rich, dark colours, convey a brooding sense of emptiness and solitude, as in *Nighthawks* (1942; Art Institute, Chicago).

**hops** female fruit heads of the hop plant *Humulus lupulus,* family Cannabiaceae; these are dried and used as a tonic and in flavouring beer. In designated areas in Europe, no male hops may be grown, since seedless hops produced by the unpollinated female plant contain a greater proportion of the alpha acid that gives beer its bitter taste.

**Horace** (65–8 BC) full name Quintus Horatius Flaccus, Roman lyric poet and satirist. He became a leading poet under the patronage of Emperor Augustus. His works include *Satires* 35–30 BC); the four books of *Odes,* (about 25–24 BC); *Epistles,* a series of verse letters; and an influential critical work, *Ars poetica.* They are distinguished by their style, wit, discretion, and patriotism.

**horehound** any of a group of plants belonging to the mint family. The white horehound (*M. vulgare*), found in Europe, North Africa, and western Asia and naturalized in North America, has a thick hairy stem and clusters of dull white flowers; it has medicinal uses. (Genus *Marrubium,* family Labiatae.)

**horizon** the limit to which one can see across the surface of the sea or a level plain, that is, about 5 km/3 mi at 1.5 m/5 ft above sea level, and about 65 km/40 mi at 300 m/1,000 ft.

**hormone** in biology, chemical secretion of the ductless ◊endocrine glands and specialized nerve cells concerned with control of body functions. The major glands are the thyroid, parathyroid, pituitary, adrenal, pancreas, ovary, and testis. There are also hormone-secreting cells in the kidney, liver, gastrointestinal tract, thymus (in the neck), pineal (in the brain), and placenta. Hormones bring about changes in the functions of various organs according to the body's requirements. The ◊hypothalamus, which adjoins the pituitary gland at the base of the brain, is a control centre for overall coordination of hormone secretion; the thyroid hormones determine the rate of general body chemistry; the adrenal hormones prepare the organism during stress for 'fight or flight'; and the sexual hormones such as oestrogen and testosterone govern reproductive functions.

**hormone-replacement therapy** (HRT), use of ◊oestrogen and progesterone to help limit the unpleasant effects of the menopause in women. The treatment was first used in the 1970s.

**Hormuz** or *Ormuz,* small island in the Strait of Hormuz belonging to Iran; area 41 sq km/16 sq mi. It is strategically important because oil tankers leaving the Gulf for Japan and the West have to pass through the strait to reach the Arabian Sea.

**horn** broad term for a hardened processes on the heads of some members of order Artiodactyla: deer, antelopes, cattle, goats, and sheep; and the rhinoceroses in order Perissodactyla. They are used usually for sparring rather than serious fighting, often between members of the same species rather than against predators.

**hornbeam** any of a group of trees belonging to the birch family. They have oval leaves with toothed edges and hanging clusters of flowers, each with a nutlike seed attached to the base. The trunk is usually twisted, with smooth grey bark. (Genus *Carpinus,* family Betulaceae.)

**hornbill** any of a group of omnivorous birds found in Africa, India, and Malaysia. They are about 1 m/3 ft long, and have powerful down-curved beaks, usually surmounted by a bony growth or casque. During the breeding season, the female walls herself into a hole in a tree and does not emerge until the young are hatched. There are about 45 species. (Family Bucerotidae, order Coraciiformes.)

**hornblende** green or black rock-forming mineral, one of the amphiboles. It is a hydrous ◊silicate composed mainly of calcium, iron, magnesium, and aluminium in addition to the silicon and oxygen that are common to all silicates. Hornblende is found in both igneous and metamorphic rocks and can be recognized by its colour and prismatic shape.

**Horn, Cape** (Spanish *Cabo de Hornos*) southernmost point of South America, in Magallanes region, Chile; situated on Horn Island to the south of ◊Tierra del Fuego archipelago. The cape is notorious for gales and heavy seas, and was the sea route between the Atlantic and the Pacific Oceans until the opening of the Panama Canal in 1914. Cape Horn was discovered in 1616 by Dutch explorer Willem Schouten (1580–1625), and named after his birthplace (Hoorn).

**hornet** type of ◊wasp.

**hornwort** nonvascular plant (with no 'veins' to carry water and food), related to the ◊liverworts and ◊mosses. Hornworts are found in warm climates, growing on moist shaded soil. (Class Anthocerotae, order Bryophyta.)

The name is also given to a group of aquatic flowering plants which are found in slow-moving water. They have whorls of finely divided leaves and may grow up to 2 m/7 ft long. (Genus *Ceratophyllum,* family Ceratophyllaceae.)

**horse** hoofed, odd-toed, grazing mammal belonging to the same family as zebras and asses. The many breeds of domestic horse of Euro-Asian origin range in colour from white to grey, brown, and black. The yellow-brown *Mongolian wild horse,* or *Przewalski's horse* (*Equus przewalskii*), named after its Polish 'discoverer' about 1880, is the only surviving species of wild horse. (Species *Equus caballus,* family Equidae.)

**horse chestnut** any of a group of trees, especially *A. hippocastanum,* originally from southeastern Europe but widely planted elsewhere. Horse chestnuts have large palmate (five-lobed) leaves, showy upright spikes of white, pink, or red flowers, and large, shiny, inedible seeds (*conkers*) in prickly green capsules. The horse chestnut is not related to the true chestnut. In North America it is called buckeye. (Genus *Aesculus,* family Hippocastanaceae.)

**horsefly** any of over 2,500 species of fly. The females suck blood from horses, cattle, and humans; the males live on plants and suck nectar. The larvae are carnivorous. (Family Tabanidae.)

**horse racing** sport of racing mounted or driven horses. Two forms in Britain are *flat racing,* for thoroughbred horses over a flat course, and *National Hunt racing,* in which the horses have to clear obstacles.

**horseradish** hardy perennial plant, native to southeastern Europe but naturalized elsewhere. The thick cream-coloured root is strong-tasting and is often made into a savoury sauce to accompany food. (*Armoracia rusticana,* family Cruciferae.)

**horsetail** plant related to ferns and club mosses; some species are also called *scouring rush.* There are about 35 living species, bearing their spores on cones at the stem tip. The upright stems are ribbed and often have spaced whorls of branches. Today they are of modest size, but hundreds of millions of years ago giant treelike forms existed. (Genus *Equisetum,* order Equisetales.)

**Horthy, Miklós Horthy de Nagybánya** (1868–1957) Hungarian politician and admiral.

Leader of the counter-revolutionary White government, he became regent in 1920 on the overthrow of the communist Bela ◊Kun regime by Romanian and Czechoslovak intervention. He represented the conservative and military class, and retained power until World War II, trying (although allied to Hitler) to retain independence of action. In 1944 he tried to negotiate a surrender to the USSR but Hungary was taken over by the Nazis and he was deported to Germany. He was released from German captivity the same year by the Western Allies. He was not tried at Nuremberg, however, but instead allowed to go to Portugal, where he died.

**horticulture** art and science of growing flowers, fruit, and vegetables. Horticulture is practised in gardens and orchards, along with millions of acres of land devoted to vegetable farming. Some areas, like California, have specialized in horticulture because they have the mild climate and light fertile soil most suited to these crops.

**Horus** the Elder *Haroeris,* in ancient Egyptian mythology, the falcon-headed sky god whose eyes were the Sun and the Moon; adult son of the principal goddess ◊Isis or Hathor (otherwise his wife), whom she magically conceived by the dead ◊Osiris, ruler of the underworld. He injured his eye while avenging his father's murder by ◊Set, the good eye being the Sun and the bad representing the Moon. The pharaohs declared themselves his incarnation, becoming Osiris on death.

**Hoskins, Bob (Robert William)** (1942–  ) English character actor. He progressed to fame from a series of supporting roles, and has played a range of both comic and dramatic roles, effortlessly shifting from humorous sidekick or love interest to menacing sociopath. Films include *The Long Good Friday* (1980), *The Cotton Club* (1984), *Mona Lisa* (1986), *A Prayer for the Dying* (1987), *Who Framed Roger Rabbit?* (1988), *Mermaids* (1990), *Shattered* (1991), *Nixon* (1995), in which he played the FBI chief J Edgar Hoover.

**hostage** person taken prisoner as a means of exerting pressure on a third party, usually with threats of death or injury.

**hot spot** in geology, isolated rising plume of molten mantle material that may rise to the surface of the Earth's crust creating features such as volcanoes, chains of ocean islands, seamounts, and rifts in continents. Hot spots occur beneath the interiors of tectonic plates and so differ from areas of volcanic activity at plate margins (see ◊plate tectonics). Examples of features made by hot spots are Iceland in the Atlantic Ocean, and in the Pacific Ocean the Hawaiian Islands and Emperor Seamount chain, and the Galápagos Islands.

**Houphouët-Boigny, Félix** (1905–1993) Côte d'Ivoire right-wing politician, president 1960–93. He held posts in French ministries, and became president of the Republic of Côte d'Ivoire on independence in 1960, maintaining close links with France, which helped to boost an already thriving economy and encourage political stability. Pro-Western and opposed to communist intervention in Africa, Houphouët-Boigny was strongly criticized for maintaining diplomatic relations with South Africa. He was re-elected for a seventh term in 1990 in multiparty elections, amid allegations of ballot rigging and political pressure.

**hour** period of time comprising 60 minutes; 24 hours make one calendar day.

**housefly** fly found in and around human dwellings, especially *M. domestica,* a common worldwide species. Houseflies are grey and have mouthparts adapted for drinking liquids and sucking moisture from food and manure. (Genus *Musca.*)

**house music** dance music of the 1980s originating in the inner-city clubs of Chicago, USA, combining funk with European high-tech pop, and using dub, digital sampling, and cross-fading. *Acid house* has minimal vocals and melody, instead surrounding the mechanically emphasized 4/4 beat with stripped-down synthesizer riffs and a wandering bass line. Other variants include *hip house,* with rap elements, and *handbag* (mainstream).

**House of Commons** see ◊Commons, House of.

**House of Lords** see ◊Lords, House of.

**House of Representatives** lower chamber of the US ◊Congress, with 435 members elected at regular two-year intervals, every even year, in November. States are represented in proportion to their population. The Speaker of the House is the majority party's leader.

**housing** provision of residential accommodation. All countries have found some degree of state housing provision or subsidy essential, even in free-enterprise economies such as the USA. In the UK, flats and houses to rent (intended for people with low incomes) are built by local authorities under the direction of the secretary of state for environment, but houses in England and Wales would have to last 2,500 years at the rate of replacement being achieved by local authorities 1991.

**Houston** city and port in southeastern Texas, USA; linked by the *Houston Ship Canal* to the Gulf of Mexico, in the Gulf Coastal Plain; population (1994 est) 1,702,000; population of metropolitan area (1994 est) 4,099,000. A major centre of finance and commerce, Houston is also one of the busiest US ports. Industrial products include refined petroleum, oilfield equipment, and petrochemicals, chief of which are synthetic rubber, plastics, insecticides, and fertilizers. Other products include iron and steel, electrical and electronic machinery, paper products, and milled rice. The Lyndon B Johnson Space Centre (1961), the command post for flights by US astronauts, is located here.

**hovercraft** vehicle that rides on a cushion of high-pressure air, free from all contact with the surface beneath, invented by English engineer Christopher Cockerell in 1959. Hovercraft need a smooth terrain when operating overland and are best adapted to use on waterways. They are useful in places where harbours have not been established.

**hoverfly** brightly coloured winged insect. Hoverflies usually have spots, stripes, or bands of yellow or brown against a dark-coloured background, sometimes with dense hair covering the body surface. Many resemble bees, bumble bees, and wasps (displaying Batesian mimicry) and most adults feed on nectar and pollen.

*classification* Hoverflies are members of the large family Syrphidae (numbering over 2,500 species), suborder Cyclorrhapha, order Diptera, class Insecta, phylum Arthropoda.

**Howard, Catherine** (c. 1520–1542) Queen consort of ◊Henry VIII of England from 1540. In 1541 the archbishop of Canterbury, Thomas Cranmer, accused her of being unchaste before marriage to Henry and she was beheaded 1542 after Cranmer made further charges of adultery.

**Howard, John** (1726–1790) English philanthropist whose work to improve prison conditions is continued today by the *Howard League for Penal Reform* (a charity formed in 1921 by the amalgamation of the Prison Reform League and the Howard Association).

**Howe, (Richard Edward) Geoffrey** Baron Howe of Aberavon (1926– ) British Conservative politician, member of Parliament for Surrey East. As chancellor of the Exchequer 1979–83 under Margaret Thatcher, he put into practice the monetarist policy that reduced inflation at the cost of a rise in unemployment. In 1983 he became foreign secretary, and in 1989 deputy prime minister and leader of the House of Commons. On 1 November 1990 he resigned in protest at Thatcher's continued opposition to the UK's greater integration in Europe.

**Hoxha, Enver** (1908–1985) Albanian communist politician, the country's leader from 1954. He founded the Albanian Communist Party in 1941, and headed the liberation movement 1939–44. He was prime minister 1944–54, also handling foreign affairs 1946–53, and from 1954 was first secretary of the Albanian Party of Labour. In policy he was a Stalinist and independent of both Chinese and Soviet communism.

**Hsuan Tung** name adopted by Henry ◊P'u-i on becoming emperor of China 1908.

**Hua Guofeng** or *Hua Kuofeng* (1920– ) Chinese politician, leader of the Chinese Communist Party (CCP) 1976–81, premier 1976–80. He dominated Chinese politics 1976–77, seeking economic modernization without major structural reform. From 1978 he was gradually eclipsed by Deng Xiaoping. Hua was ousted from the Politburo in September 1982 but remained a member of the CCP Central Committee.

**Huang He** or *Hwang Ho;* English *Yellow River,* river in China, named after its muddy waters; length 5,464 km/3,395 mi. Rising in Qinghai province in the west of the country, it winds eastwards to the Bohai Gulf. Sometimes known as 'China's sorrow' because of disastrous floods, it is now largely controlled through hydroelectric works, dykes, and embankments. The barriers, however, are ceasing to work because silt is continually raising the river bed.

**Hubble, Edwin (Powell)** (1889–1953) US astronomer. He discovered the existence of ◊galaxies outside our own, and classified them according to their shape. His theory that the universe is expanding is now generally accepted.

**Hubble's law** law that relates a galaxy's distance from us to its speed of recession as the universe expands, announced in 1929 by US astronomer Edwin Hubble. He found that galaxies are moving apart at speeds that increase in direct proportion to their distance apart. The rate of expansion is known as Hubble's constant.

**Hubble Space Telescope** (HST), space-based astronomical observing facility, orbiting the Earth at an altitude of 610 km/380 mi. It consists of a 2.4 m/94 in telescope and four complimentary scientific instruments, is roughly cylindrical, 13 m/43 ft long, and 4 m/13 ft in diameter, with two large solar panels. HST produces a wealth of scientific data, and allows astronomers to observe the birth of stars, find planets around neighbouring stars, follow the expanding remnants of exploding stars, and search for black holes in the centre of galaxies. HST is a cooperative programme between the European Space Agency (ESA) and the US agency NASA, and is the first spacecraft specifically designed to be serviced in orbit as a permanent space-based observatory. It was launched in 1990.

**Hubei** *Hupei* or *Hupeh,* province of central China, bounded to the north by Henan, to the east by Anhui, to the south by Jiangxi and Hunan, and to the west by Sichuan and Shaanxi provinces

*area* 187,500 sq km/72,375 sq mi

*capital* Wuhan

*cities and towns* Huangshi, Shashi, Yichang, Xiangfan

*physical* high land in the west; Chang Jiang River and gorges; fertile land; many lakes

*industries* copper, gypsum, iron ore, phosphorus, salt mining; steel, machinery, domestic appliances, textiles, food processing, fibre optic cables

*agriculture* rice, cotton, rapeseed, wheat, beans, vegetables

*population* (1996) 58,250,000.

**hubris** in Greek thought, an act of transgression or overweening pride. In ancient Greek tragedy, hubris was believed to offend the gods, and to lead to retribution.

**Hudson** river in northeastern USA; length 485 km/300 mi. It rises in the Adirondack Mountains and flows south, emptying into a bay of the Atlantic Ocean at New York City. The Hudson forms the boundary between New Jersey and New York, and the states are linked by bridges and tunnels. The New York Barge

Canal system links the Hudson to Lake Champlain, Lake Erie, and the St Lawrence River. It is navigable by small ocean-going vessels as far upstream as Albany and Troy, about 240 km/150 mi from its mouth, and for eight months of the year barge traffic can reach the Great Lakes.

**Hudson, Henry** (c. 1565–1611) English explorer. Under the auspices of the Muscovy Company (1607–08), he made two unsuccessful attempts to find the Northeast Passage to China. In September 1609, commissioned by the Dutch East India Company, he reached New York Bay and sailed 240 km/150 mi up the river that now bears his name, establishing Dutch claims to the area. In 1610 he sailed from London in the *Discovery* and entered what is now the Hudson Strait. After an icebound winter, he was turned adrift by a mutinous crew in what is now Hudson Bay.

**Hudson Bay** inland sea of northeastern Canada, linked with the Atlantic Ocean by *Hudson Strait* and with the Arctic Ocean by Foxe Channel and the Gulf of Boothia; area 1,233,000 sq km/476,000 sq mi. It is bordered by (clockwise) the provinces of Québec, Ontario, Manitoba, and the Northwest Territories. It is named after Henry Hudson, who reached it in 1610.

**Hudson's Bay Company** chartered company founded by Prince ◊Rupert 1670 to trade in furs with North American Indians. In 1783 the rival North West Company was formed, but in 1851 this became amalgamated with the Hudson's Bay Company. It is still Canada's biggest fur company, but today also sells general merchandise through department stores and has oil and natural gas interests.

**Hughes, Ted (Edward James)** (1930–1998) English poet. He was the poet laureate from 1984 until his death. His work is characterized by its harsh portrayal of the crueller aspects of nature, by its reflection of the agonies of personal experience, and by the employment of myths of creation and being, as in *Crow* (1970) and *Gaudete* (1977). His free-verse renderings, *Tales from Ovid* won the 1997 Whitbread Book of the Year prize, and his collection *Birthday Letters* was awarded the 1998 Forward Prize and the 1998 Whitbread Book of the Year Award.

**Hugo, Victor (Marie)** (1802–1885) French novelist, poet, and dramatist. The verse play *Hernani* (1830) firmly established Hugo as the leader of French Romanticism. This was the first of a series of dramas produced in the 1830s and early 1840s, including *Le Roi s'amuse* (1832) and *Ruy Blas* (1838). His melodramatic novels include *Notre-Dame de Paris* (1831), and *Les Misérables* (1862).

**Huguenot** French Protestant in the 16th century; the term referred mainly to Calvinists. Persecuted under Francis I and Henry II, the Huguenots survived both an attempt to exterminate them (the Massacre of ◊St Bartholomew on 24 August 1572) and the religious wars of the

next 30 years. In 1598 ◊Henry IV (himself formerly a Huguenot) granted them toleration under the Edict of Nantes. Louis XIV revoked the edict in 1685, attempting their forcible conversion, and 400,000 emigrated.

**Hui** one of the largest minority ethnic groups in China, numbering about eight and a half million. Members of the Hui live all over China, but are concentrated in the northern central region. They have been Muslims since the 10th century, for which they have suffered persecution both before and since the communist revolution.

**Hull** shortened name of ◊*Kingston upon Hull,* a city and unitary authority on the north bank of the Humber estuary, northeast England.

**Hull, Cordell** (1871–1955) US Democratic politician. As F D Roosevelt's secretary of state 1933–44, he was a vigorous champion of free trade, and opposed German and Japanese aggression. He was identified with the Good Neighbor policy of nonintervention in Latin America. An advocate of collective security after World War II, he was called by Roosevelt 'the father of the United Nations'. Nobel Peace Prize 1945.

**human body** the physical structure of the human being. It develops from the single cell of the fertilized ovum, is born at 40 weeks, and usually reaches sexual maturity between 11 and 18 years of age. The bony framework (skeleton) consists of more than 200 bones, over half of which are in the hands and feet. Bones are held together by joints, some of which allow movement. The circulatory system supplies muscles and organs with blood, which provides oxygen and food and removes carbon dioxide and other waste products. Body functions are controlled by the nervous system and hormones. In the upper part of the trunk is the thorax, which contains the lungs and heart. Below this is the abdomen, containing the digestive system (stomach and intestines); the liver, spleen, and pancreas; the urinary system (kidneys, ureters, and bladder); and, in women, the reproductive organs (ovaries, uterus, and vagina). In men, the prostate gland and seminal vesicles only of the reproductive system are situated in the abdomen, the testes being in the scrotum, which, with the penis, is suspended in front of and below the abdomen. The bladder empties through a small channel (urethra); in the female this opens in the upper end of the vulval cleft, which also contains the opening of the vagina, or birth canal; in the male, the urethra is continued into the penis. In both sexes, the lower bowel terminates in the anus, a ring of strong muscle situated between the buttocks. *See illustration on page 427.*

**Human Genome Project** research scheme, begun in 1988, to map the complete nucleotide (see ◊nucleic acid) sequence of human ◊DNA. There are approximately 100,000 (though a 1999 estimate by a participating US company was as high as 140,000) different ◊genes in the human genome, and one gene may contain more than 2 million nucleotides. The programme aims to collect 10–15,000 genetic specimens from 722 ethnic groups whose genetic make-up is to

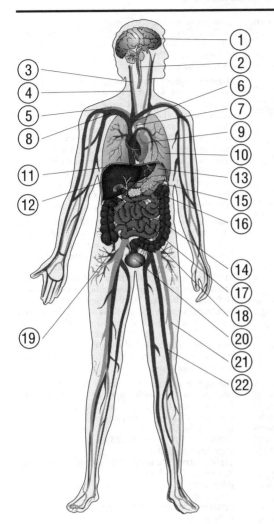

**Key**
1. brain
2. spinal cord
3. carotid artery
4. jugular vein
5. subclavian artery
6. superior vena cava
7. aorta
8. subclavian vein
9. heart
10. lungs
11. diaphragm
12. liver
13. stomach
14. gall bladder
15. kidney
16. pancreas
17. small intestine or ileum
18. large intestine or colon
19. appendix
20. bladder
21. popliteal artery
22. popliteal vein

**human body** *The adult human body has approximately 650 muscles, 100,000 km/60,000 mi of blood vessels and 13,000 nerve cells. There are 206 bones in the adult body, nearly half of them in the hands and feet.*

be preserved for future use and study. The knowledge gained is expected to help prevent or treat many crippling and lethal diseases, but there are potential ethical problems associated with knowledge of an individual's genetic make-up, and fears that it will lead to genetic discrimination.

In March 1999 the Human Genome Project announced that they aim to have a 'working draft' (about 90%) of the human genome by spring 2000. This would be 18 months ahead of the schedule announced at the end of 1998.

**humanism** belief in the high potential of human nature rather than in religious or tran-scendental values. Humanism culminated as a cultural and literary force in 16th-century Renaissance Europe in line with the period's enthusiasm for classical literature and art, grow-ing individualism, and the ideal of the all-round

male who should be statesman and poet, scholar and warrior. ◊Erasmus is a great exemplar of Renaissance humanism.

**human reproduction** an example of ◊sexual reproduction, where the male produces sperm and the female eggs. These gametes contain only half the normal number of chromosomes, 23 instead of 46, so that on fertilization the resulting cell has the correct genetic complement. Fertilization is internal, which increases the chances of concep-tion; unusually for mammals, copulation and pregnancy can occur at any time of the year. Human beings are also remarkable for the length of childhood and for the highly complex systems of parental care found in society. The use of con-traception and the development of laboratory methods of insemination and fertilization are issues that make human reproduction more than a merely biological phenomenon.

**Human Rights, Universal Declaration of**
charter of civil and political rights drawn up by
the United Nations 1948. They include the right
to life, liberty, education, and equality before the
law; to freedom of movement, religion, association, and information; and to a nationality.

Under the *European Convention of Human
Rights* 1950, the Council of Europe established
the *European Commission of Human Rights*,
which investigates complaints by states or individuals. Its findings are examined by the
*European Court of Human Rights* (established
1959), whose compulsory jurisdiction has been
recognized by a number of states, including the
UK.

**human species, origins of** evolution of
humans from ancestral ◊primates. The African
apes (gorilla and chimpanzee) are shown by
anatomical and molecular comparisons to be the
closest living relatives of humans. The oldest
known *hominids* (of the human group), the australopithecines, found in Africa, date from
3.5–4.4 million years ago. The first to use tools
came 2 million years later, and the first
humanoids to use fire and move out of Africa
appeared 1.7 million years ago. ◊Neanderthals
were not direct ancestors of the human species.
Modern humans are all believed to descend
from one African female of 200,000 years ago,
although there is a rival theory that humans
evolved in different parts of the world simultaneously.

**Humber** estuary in northeast England formed
by the Ouse and Trent rivers, which meet east of
Goole and flow east for 60 km/38 mi to enter
the North Sea below Spurn Head. It is an important commercial waterway, and the main ports
are ◊Kingston upon Hull on the north side, and
Grimsby on the south side. The Humber Bridge
(1981) joins the two banks.

**Humberside** former county of northeast England, created in 1974 out of north Lincolnshire
and parts of the East and West Ridings of
Yorkshire. It was abolished in 1996 when the
unitary authorities of East Riding of Yorkshire,
Kingston upon Hull, North East Lincolnshire,
and North Lincolnshire were created.

**Humbert** anglicized form of Umberto, two
kings of Italy.

**Hume, David** (1711–1776) Scottish philosopher whose *Treatise of Human Nature* (1739–
40) is a central text of British ◊empiricism (the
theory that experience is the only source of
knowledge). Examining meticulously our modes
of thinking, he concluded that they are more
habitual than rational. Consequently, he not
only rejected the possibility of knowlege that
goes beyond the bounds of experience (specula-
tive metaphysics), but also arrived at generally
sceptical positions about reason, causation,
necessity, identity, and the self.

**humidity** the quantity of water vapour in a
given volume of the atmosphere (absolute
humidity), or the ratio of the amount of water
vapour in the atmosphere to the saturation value
at the same temperature (relative humidity). At
dew point the relative humidity is 100% and the
air is said to be saturated. Condensation (the
conversion of vapour to liquid) may then occur.
Relative humidity is measured by various types
of hygrometer.

**hummingbird** any of various small, brilliantly
coloured birds found in the Americas. The name
comes from the sound produced by the rapid
vibration of their wings when hovering near
flowers to feed. Hummingbirds have long,
needlelike bills and tongues to obtain nectar
from flowers and capture insects. They are the
only birds able to fly backwards. The Cuban *bee
hummingbird* (*Mellisuga helenae*), the world's
smallest bird, is 5.5 cm/2 in long and weighs less
than 2.5 g/0.1 oz. There are over 300 species.
(Family Trochilidae, order Apodiformes.)

**Hun** member of any of a number of nomad
Mongol peoples who were first recorded histor-
ically in the 2nd century BC, raiding across the
Great Wall into China. They entered Europe
about AD 372, settled in the area that is now
Hungary, and imposed their supremacy on the
Ostrogoths and other Germanic peoples. Under
the leadership of Attila they attacked the
Byzantine Empire, invaded Gaul, and threatened
Rome. After Attila's death in 453 their power
was broken by a revolt of their subject peoples.
The *White Huns*, or Ephthalites, a kindred people, raided Persia and northern India in the 5th
and 6th centuries.

**Hunan** province of south central China,
bounded to the north by Hubei, to the east by
Jiangxi, to the south by Guangdong and
Guangxi Zhuang Autonomous Region, and to
the west by Guizhou and Sichuan
*area* 210,500 sq km/81,253 sq mi
*capital* Changsha
*cities and towns* Hengyang, Shaoyang,
Xiangtan, Zhuzhou
*physical* hills and plains; many rivers;
Dongting Lake
*features* farmhouse birthplace of Mao Zedong
in Shaoshan
*industries* nonferrous minerals, engineering,
chemicals, electrical goods
*agriculture* rice, tea, tobacco, rapeseed
*population* (1996) 64,280,000.

**Hundred Years' War** series of conflicts between England and France from 1337 to 1453
that finally ended any significant involvement of
the kings of England in Continental Europe. Its
origins lay with the English kings' possession of
Gascony (southwest France), which the French
kings claimed as their fief, and with trade rivalries over ◊Flanders. The two kingdoms had a
long history of strife before 1337, and the
Hundred Years' War has sometimes been interpreted as merely an intensification of these
struggles. It was caused by fears of French intervention in Scotland, which the English were trying to subdue, and by the claim of England's
Edward III (through his mother Isabella, daughter of Philip IV of France) to the crown of
France.

**Hungary** Republic of
*national name* Magyar Köztársaság

**area** 93,032 sq km/35,919 sq mi
**capital** Budapest
**major towns/cities** Miskolc, Debrecen, Szeged, Pécs, Gyor, Nyiregyháza, Székesfehérvár, Kecskemét
**physical features** Great Hungarian Plain covers eastern half of country; Bakony Forest, Lake Balaton, and Transdanubian Highlands in the west; rivers Danube, Tisza, and Raba; more than 500 thermal springs
**head of state** Arpád Göncz from 1990
**head of government** Viktor Orban from 1998
**political system** emergent democracy
**political parties** over 50, including Hungarian Socialist Party (HSP), reform-socialist; Alliance of Free Democrats (AFD), centrist, radical free market; Hungarian Democratic Forum (MDF), nationalist, centre right; Independent Smallholders Party (ISP), right of centre, agrarian; Christian Democratic People's Party (KDNP), right of centre; Federation of Young Democrats, liberal, anticommunist; Fidesz, right of centre
**currency** forint
**GNP per capita (PPP)** (US$) 7,320 (1998 est)
**exports** raw materials, semi-finished products, industrial consumer goods, food and agricultural products, transport equipment. Principal market: Germany 36.6% (1998)
**population** 10,075,000 (1999 est)
**language** Hungarian (or Magyar), one of the few languages of Europe with non-Indo-European origins; it is grouped with Finnish, Estonian, and others in the Finno-Ugric family
**religion** Roman Catholic 67%, Calvinist 20%, other Christian denominations, Jewish
**life expectancy** 67 (men); 75 (women) (1995–2000)
**Chronology**
**1st century** AD Region formed part of Roman Empire.
**4th century** Germanic tribes overran central Europe.

**c. 445** Attila the Hun established a short-lived empire, including Hungarian nomads living far to the east.
**c. 680** Hungarians settled between the Don and Dniepr rivers under Khazar rule.
**9th century** Hungarians invaded central Europe; ten tribes united under Árpád, chief of the Magyar tribe, who conquered the area corresponding to modern Hungary 896.
**10th century** Hungarians colonized Transylvania and raided their neighbours for plunder and slaves.
**955** Battle of Lech: Germans led by Otto the Great defeated Hungarians.
**1001** St Stephen founded Hungarian kingdom to replace tribal organization and converted Hungarians to Christianity.
**12th century** Hungary became a major power when King Béla III won temporary supremacy over the Balkans.
**1308–86** Angevin dynasty ruled after Arpádian line died out.
**1456** Battle of Belgrade: János Hunyadi defeated Ottoman Turks and saved Hungary from invasion.
**1458–90** Under Mátyás I Corvinus, Hungary enjoyed military success and cultural renaissance.
**1526** Battle of Mohács: Turks under Suleiman the Magnificent decisively defeated Hungarians.
**16th century** Partition of Hungary between Turkey, Austria, and semi-autonomous Transylvania.
**1699** Treaty of Karlowitz: Austrians expelled the Turks from Hungary, which was reunified under Habsburg rule.
**1707** Prince Ferenc Rákóczi II led uprising against Austrians, who promised to respect Hungarian constitution in 1711.
**1780–90** Joseph II's attempts to impose uniform administration throughout Austrian Empire provoked nationalist reaction among Hungarian nobility.
**early 19th century** 'National Revival' movement led by Count Stephen Széchenyi and Lajos Kossuth.
**1848** Hungarian Revolution: nationalists proclaimed self-government; Croat minority resisted Hungarian rule.
**1849** Kossuth repudiated Habsburg monarchy; Austrians crushed revolution with Russian support.
**1867** Austria conceded equality to Hungary within the dual monarchy of Austria-Hungary.
**1918** Austria-Hungary collapsed in military defeat; Count Mihály Károlyi proclaimed Hungarian Republic.
**1919** Communists took power under Béla Kun; Romanians invaded; Admiral Miklós Horthy overthrew Béla Kun.
**1920** Treaty of Trianon: Hungary lost 72% of its territory to Czechoslovakia, Romania, and Yugoslavia; Horthy restored Kingdom of Hungary with himself as regent.
**1921** Count István Bethlen became prime minister of authoritarian aristocratic regime.
**1938–41** Diplomatic collaboration with Germany allowed Hungary to regain territories lost in 1920; Hungary declared war on USSR in alliance with Germany in 1941.

**1944** Germany occupied Hungary and installed Nazi regime.
**1945** USSR 'liberated' Hungary; Smallholders' Party won free elections, but communists led by Mátyás Rákosi took over by stages 1946–49.
**1947** Peace treaty restored 1920 frontiers.
**1949** Hungary became a Soviet-style dictatorship; Rákosi pursued Stalinist policies of collectivization and police terror.
**1956** Hungarian uprising: anti-Soviet demonstrations led prime minister Imre Nagy to propose democratic reforms and neutrality; USSR invaded, crushed dissent, and installed János Kádár as communist leader.
**1961** Kádár began to introduce pragmatic liberal reforms of a limited kind.
**1988** Károly Grosz replaced Kádár and accelerated reform; Hungarian Democratic Forum was formed by opposition groups.
**1989** The communist dictatorship was dismantled, and a transitional constitution restored multiparty democracy. The opening of the border with Austria destroyed the 'Iron Curtain'.
**1990** Elections were won by a centre–right coalition led by József Antall, who pursued radical free-market reforms.
**1991** The withdrawal of Soviet forces was completed.
**1994** Gyula Horn, the leader of the ex-communist Hungarian Socialist Party, became prime minister, pledging to continue reform policies.
**1996** A friendship treaty with the Slovak Republic was signed, as was a cooperation treaty with Romania.
**1997** Hungary was invited to join NATO and to begin negotiations for membership of the European Union. A referendum showed clear support in favour of joining NATO.
**1998** Viktor Orban, leader of right-of-centre Fidesz, became prime minister after the general election. Negotiations for full EU membership commenced.
**1999** Hungary became a full member of NATO.

**Hun Sen** (1950–  ) Cambodian political leader, prime minister 1985–93, deputy prime minister from 1993, and single effective leader from July 1997. His leadership was characterized by the promotion of economic liberalization and a thawing in relations with exiled non-Khmer opposition forces as a prelude to a compromise political settlement. After the defeat of his Cambodian People's Party (CCP) in the 1993 elections, Hun Sen agreed to participate in a power-sharing arrangement as second premier. In July 1997 he launched a successful coup to oust first deputy prime minister, Prince Norodom Ranariddh, and secure full effective control over Cambodia. In February 1998 he accepted a Japanese-brokered peace plan to allow for Ranariddh's return, after he was found guilty in a March 1998 show trial and then pardoned by his father, king Norodom Sihanouk.

Following the November 1998 elections in which Hun Sen's CCP won 41% of the vote, Hun Sen formed a coalition between the two main rival political parties, FUNCINPEC and the CCP.

**Hunt, (William) Holman** (1827–1910) English painter, one of the founders of the ◊Pre-Raphaelite Brotherhood in 1848. His paintings, characterized both by a meticulous attention to detail and a clear moral and religious symbolism, include *The Awakening Conscience* (1853; Tate Gallery, London) and *The Light of the World* (1854; Keble College, Oxford).

**hunting dog** or *painted dog,* wild dog (weight 23–35 kg/51–77 lb) that once roamed over virtually the whole of sub-Saharan Africa. A pack might have a range of almost 4,000 km/ 2,500 mi, hunting zebra, antelope, and other game. Individuals can run at 50 kph/30 mph for up to 5 km/3 mi, with short bursts of even higher speeds. The number of hunting dogs that survive has been reduced to a fraction of the original population. According to a 1997 International Union for the Conservation of Nature (IUCN) report, there were fewer than 3,000 hunting dogs remaining in the wild, with many existing populations too small to be viable. (Species *Lycaon pictus,* family Canidae.)

**Huntington's chorea** rare hereditary disease of the nervous system that mostly begins in middle age. It is characterized by involuntary movements (chorea), emotional disturbances, and rapid mental degeneration progressing to ◊dementia. There is no known cure but the genetic mutation giving rise to the disease was located 1993, making it easier to test individuals for the disease and increasing the chances of developing a cure.

**Hupei** alternative transcription of ◊Hebei, a province of China.

**Hurd, Douglas (Richard)** (1930–  ) British Conservative politician, home secretary 1985–89 and foreign secretary 1989–95. In November 1990 he was an unsuccessful candidate in the Tory leadership contest following Margaret Thatcher's unexpected resignation.

**Huron, Lake** second largest of the ◊Great Lakes of North America, on the US–Canadian border; area 60,000 sq km/23,160 sq mi. Lake Huron is 331 km/205 mi long, lies at 177 m/581 ft above sea level, and reaches a depth of 230 m/ 755 ft. It is bounded on the north and east by Ontario, and on the west and southwest by Michigan. There are several small ports on its shores, and lumbering and fishing are important economic activities in the region.

**hurricane** *tropical cyclone* or *typhoon,* a severe ◊depression (region of very low atmospheric pressure) in tropical regions, called *typhoon* in the North Pacific. It is a revolving storm originating at latitudes between 5° and 20° N or S of the Equator, when the surface temperature of the ocean is above 27°C/80°F. A central calm area, called the eye, is surrounded by inwardly spiralling winds (anticlockwise in the northern hemisphere) of up to 320 kph/200 mph. A hurricane is accompanied by lightning and torrential rain, and can cause extensive damage. In meteorology, a hurricane is a wind of force 12 or more on the ◊Beaufort scale.

**Husák, Gustáv** (1913–1991) Czechoslovak politician, leader of the Communist Party of Czechoslovakia (CCP) 1969–87 and president

1975–89. After the 1968 Prague Spring of liberalization, his task was to restore control, purge the CCP, and oversee the implementation of a new, federalist constitution. He was deposed in the popular uprising of November–December 1989 and expelled from the CCP in February 1990.

**Hussein, Saddam** (1937– ) Iraqi politician, in power from 1968, president from 1979. He presided over the Iran-Iraq war 1980–88, and harshly repressed Kurdish rebels in northern Iraq. He annexed Kuwait 1990 but was driven out by a US-dominated coalition army February 1991. Defeat in the ◊Gulf War led to unrest, and both the Kurds in the north and Shiites in the south rebelled. His savage repression of both revolts led to charges of genocide. In 1995, to counter evidence of rifts among his closest supporters, he called a presidential election, in which he was elected (unopposed) with 99.6% of the vote. In September 1996 his involvement in Kurdish faction fighting in northern Iraq provoked air retaliation by US forces. In March 1998 a major confrontation with the UN over the inspection of weapons of mass destruction held by Iraq, was narrowly averted.

**Hussein ibn Talal** (1935–1999) King of Jordan 1952–99. By 1967 he had lost all his kingdom west of the river Jordan in the Arab-Israeli Wars, and in 1970 suppressed the Palestine Liberation Organization acting as a guerrilla force against his rule on the remaining East Bank territories. Subsequently, he became a moderating force in Middle Eastern politics, and in 1994 signed a peace agreement with Israel, ending a 46-year-old state of war between the two countries.

**Husserl, Edmund Gustav Albrecht** (1859–1938) German philosopher, regarded as the founder of phenomenology, the study of mental states as consciously experienced. His early phenomenology resembles linguistic philosophy because he examined the meaning and our understanding of words.

**Huston, John (Marcellus)** (1906–1987) US film director, screenwriter, and actor. An impulsive and individualistic filmmaker, he often dealt with the themes of greed, treachery in human relationships, and the loner. His works as a director include *The Maltese Falcon* (1941), *The Treasure of the Sierra Madre* (1948), *The Asphalt Jungle* (1950), *The African Queen* (1951), and *The Dead* (1987).

**Hutton, James** (1726–1797) Scottish geologist, known as the 'founder of geology', who formulated the concept of uniformitarianism. In 1785 he developed a theory of the igneous origin of many rocks.

**Hutu** member of the majority ethnic group of Burundi and Rwanda, numbering around 9.5 million. The Hutu tend to live as peasant farmers. They have been dominated by the ◊Tutsi minority since the 14th century and there is a long history of violent conflict between the two groups. The Hutu language belongs to the Bantu branch of the Niger-Congo family.

**Huxley, Aldous (Leonard)** (1894–1963) English writer of novels, essays, and verse. From the disillusionment and satirical eloquence of *Crome Yellow* (1921), *Antic Hay* (1923), and *Point Counter Point* (1928), Huxley developed towards the Utopianism exemplified by *Island* (1962). His most popular work, the science fiction novel *Brave New World* (1932) shows human beings mass-produced in laboratories and rendered incapable of freedom by indoctrination and drugs.

**Huxley, Thomas Henry** (1825–1895) English scientist and humanist. Following the publication of Charles Darwin's *On the Origin of Species* (1859), he became known as 'Darwin's bulldog', and for many years was a prominent champion of evolution. In 1869 he coined the word 'agnostic' to express his own religious attitude, and is considered the founder of scientific humanism.

**Hu Yaobang** (1915–1989) Chinese politician, Communist Party (CCP) chair 1981–87. A protégé of the communist leader Deng Xiaoping, Hu presided over a radical overhaul of the party structure and personnel 1982–86. His death ignited the prodemocracy movement, which was eventually crushed in ◊Tiananmen Square in June 1989.

**Huygens, Christiaan** or *Huyghens* (1629–1695) Dutch mathematical physicist and astronomer. He proposed the wave theory of light, developed the pendulum clock in 1657, discovered polarization, and observed Saturn's rings. He made important advances in pure mathematics, applied mathematics, and mechanics, which he virtually founded. His work in astronomy was an impressive defence of the Copernican view of the Solar System.

**hyacinth** any of a group of bulb-producing plants belonging to the lily family, native to the eastern Mediterranean and Africa. The cultivated hyacinth (*H. orientalis*) has large, scented, cylindrical heads of pink, white, or blue flowers. (Genus *Hyacinthus*, family Liliaceae.) The ◊water hyacinth is unrelated, a floating plant from South America.

**hybrid** offspring from a cross between individuals of two different species, or two inbred lines within a species. In most cases, hybrids between species are infertile and unable to reproduce sexually. In plants, however, doubling of the chromosomes can restore the fertility of such hybrids.

**Hyderabad** capital city of the southern central Indian state of ◊Andhra Pradesh, on the River Musi; population (1991) 4,280,000. Products include carpets, silks, and metal inlay work. More recently industries such as textiles, pharmaceuticals, electrical machinery, and chemicals have become important. It was formerly the capital of the state of Hyderabad. Buildings include the Jama Masjid mosque and Golconda fort. It is an important educational and research centre, with Osmania University founded by the Nizam in 1939.

**Hyderabad** city in Sind province, southeast Pakistan, lying 10 km/6 mi east of the ◊Indus River, 150 km/95 mi northeast of Karachi; population (1991) 1,000,000. It produces gold, pottery, glass, embroidered leather saddles for camels, and furniture. Industries include textiles, cement, glass and soap, and there is a thermal power station nearby.

**Hydra** in Greek mythology, a huge monster with nine heads. If one were cut off, two would grow in its place. One of the 12 labours of ◊Heracles was to kill it.

**hydra** in zoology, any of a group of freshwater polyps, belonging among the ◊coelenterates. The body is a double-layered tube (with six to ten hollow tentacles around the mouth), 1.25 cm/0.5 in long when extended, but capable of contracting to a small knob. Usually fixed to waterweed, hydras feed on minute animals that are caught and paralysed by stinging cells on the tentacles. (Genus *Hydra*, family Hydridae, phylum Coelenterata, subphylum Cnidaria.)

**hydrangea** any of a group of flowering shrubs belonging to the saxifrage family, native to Japan. Cultivated varieties of *H. macrophylla* normally produce round heads of pink flowers, but these may be blue if there are certain chemicals in the soil, such as alum or iron. The name comes from the Greek for 'water vessel', after the cuplike seed capsules. (Genus *Hydrangea*, family Hydrangeaceae.)

**hydraulics** field of study concerned with utilizing the properties of water and other liquids, in particular the way they flow and transmit pressure, and with the application of these properties in engineering. It applies the principles of ◊hydrostatics and hydrodynamics. The oldest type of hydraulic machine is the *hydraulic press*, invented by Joseph Bramah in England in 1795. The hydraulic principle of pressurized liquid

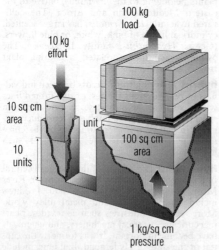

*hydraulics* The hydraulic jack transmits the pressure on a small piston to a larger one. A larger total force is developed by the larger piston but it moves a smaller distance than the small piston.

increasing a force is commonly used on vehicle braking systems, the forging press, and the hydraulic systems of aircraft and excavators.

**hydrocarbon** any of a class of chemical compounds containing only hydrogen and carbon (for example, the alkanes and alkenes). Hydrocarbons are obtained industrially principally from petroleum and coal tar.

**hydrochloric acid** HCl highly corrosive solution of hydrogen chloride (a colourless, acidic gas) in water. The concentrated acid is about 35% hydrogen chloride and is corrosive. The acid is a typical strong, monobasic acid forming only one series of salts, the chlorides. It has many industrial uses, including recovery of zinc from galvanized scrap iron and the production of chlorine. It is also produced in the stomachs of animals for the purposes of digestion.

**hydrodynamics** branch of physics dealing with fluids (liquids and gases) in motion.

**hydroelectric power** electricity generated by moving water. In a typical scheme, water stored in a reservoir, often created by damming a river, is piped into water ◊turbines, coupled to electricity generators. In pumped storage plants, water flowing through the turbines is recycled. A tidal power station exploits the rise and fall of the tides. About one-fifth of the world's electricity comes from hydroelectric power.

**hydrofoil** wing that develops lift in the water in much the same way that an aeroplane wing develops lift in the air. A hydrofoil boat is one whose hull rises out of the water owing to the lift, and the boat skims along on the hydrofoils. The first hydrofoil was fitted to a boat in 1906. The first commercial hydrofoil went into operation in 1956. One of the most advanced hydrofoil boats is the Boeing ◊jetfoil. Hydrofoils are now widely used for fast island ferries in calm seas.

**hydrogen** (Greek *hydro* + *gen* 'water generator') colourless, odourless, gaseous, nonmetallic element, symbol H, atomic number 1, relative atomic mass 1.00797. It is the lightest of all the elements and occurs on Earth chiefly in combination with oxygen as water. Hydrogen is the most abundant element in the universe, where it accounts for 93% of the total number of atoms and 76% of the total mass. It is a component of most stars, including the Sun, whose heat and light are produced through the nuclear-fusion process that converts hydrogen into helium. When subjected to a pressure 500,000 times greater than that of the Earth's atmosphere, hydrogen becomes a solid with metallic properties, as in one of the inner zones of Jupiter. Hydrogen's common and industrial uses include the hardening of oils and fats by hydrogenation, the creation of high-temperature flames for welding, and as rocket fuel. It has been proposed as a fuel for road vehicles.

**hydrogen bomb** bomb that works on the principle of nuclear ◊fusion. Large-scale explosion results from the thermonuclear release of energy when hydrogen nuclei are fused to form helium nuclei. The first hydrogen bomb was exploded at Enewetak Atoll in the Pacific Ocean by the USA in 1952.

**hydrogen carbonate** or *bicarbonate,* compound containing the ion $HCO_3^-$, an acid salt of carbonic acid (solution of carbon dioxide in water). When heated or treated with dilute acids, it gives off carbon dioxide. The most important compounds are sodium hydrogen carbonate (bicarbonate of soda), and calcium hydrogen carbonate.

**hydrography** study and charting of Earth's surface waters in seas, lakes, and rivers.

**hydrological cycle** alternative name for the ◊water cycle, by which water is circulated between the Earth's surface and its atmosphere.

**hydrophyte** plant adapted to live in water, or in waterlogged soil.

**hydroplane** on a submarine, a movable horizontal fin angled downwards or upwards when the vessel is descending or ascending. It is also a highly manoeuvrable motorboat with its bottom rising in steps to the stern, or a ◊hydrofoil boat that skims over the surface of the water when driven at high speed.

**hydroponics** cultivation of plants without soil, using specially prepared solutions of mineral salts. Beginning in the 1930s, large crops were grown by hydroponic methods, at first in California but since then in many other parts of the world.

**hydrostatics** in physics, the branch of ◊statics dealing with fluids in equilibrium – that is, in a static condition. Practical applications include shipbuilding and dam design.

**hyena** any of three species of carnivorous doglike mammals living in Africa and Asia. Hyenas have extremely powerful jaws. They are scavengers, feeding on the remains of animals killed by predators such as lions, although they will also attack and kill live prey. (Genera *Hyaena* and *Crocuta,* family Hyaenidae, order Carnivora.)

**Hymen** in Greek mythology, the god of the marriage ceremony; personification of the refrain of a wedding song. In art, he is represented as a boy crowned with flowers, carrying a burning bridal torch.

**hyperactivity** condition of excessive activity in young children, combined with restlessness, inability to concentrate, and difficulty in learning. There are various causes, ranging from temperamental predisposition to brain disease. In some cases food ◊additives have come under suspicion; in such instances modification of the diet may help. Mostly there is improvement at puberty, but symptoms may persist in the small proportion diagnosed as having ◊attention-deficit hyperactivity disorder.

**hyperbola** in geometry, a curve formed by cutting a right circular cone with a plane so that the angle between the plane and the base is greater than the angle between the base and the side of the cone. All hyperbolae are bounded by two asymptotes (straight lines which the hyperbola moves closer and closer to but never reaches).

A hyperbola is a member of the family of curves known as ◊conic sections.

**hypermetropia** or *long-sightedness,* defect of vision in which a person is able to focus on objects in the distance, but not on close objects. It is caused by the failure of the lens to return to its normal rounded shape, or by the eyeball being too short, with the result that the image is focused on a point behind the retina. Hypermetropia is corrected by wearing glasses fitted with converging lenses, each of which acts like a magnifying glass.

**hypertension** abnormally high ◊blood pressure due to a variety of causes, leading to excessive contraction of the smooth muscle cells of the walls of the arteries. It increases the risk of kidney disease, stroke, and heart attack.

**hypertext** system for viewing information (both text and pictures) on a computer screen in such a way that related items of information can easily be reached. For example, the program might display a map of a country; if the user clicks (with a ◊mouse) on a particular city, the program will display information about that city. *See illustration on page 434.*

**hypnosis** artificially induced state of relaxation or altered attention characterized by heightened suggestibility. There is evidence that, with susceptible persons, the sense of pain may be diminished, memory of past events enhanced, and illusions or hallucinations experienced. Posthypnotic amnesia (forgetting what happened during hypnosis) and posthypnotic suggestion (performing an action after hypnosis that had been suggested during it) have also been demonstrated.

**hypocaust** floor raised on tile piers, heated by hot air circulating beneath it. It was first used by the Romans for baths about 100 BC, and was later introduced to private houses.

**hypotenuse** the longest side of a right-angled triangle, opposite the right angle. It is of particular application in Pythagoras' theorem (the square of the hypotenuse equals the sum of the squares of the other two sides), and in trigonometry where the ratios ◊sine and ◊cosine are defined as the ratios opposite/hypotenuse and adjacent/hypotenuse respectively.

**hypothalamus** region of the brain below the cerebrum which regulates rhythmic activity and physiological stability within the body, including water balance and temperature. It regulates the production of the pituitary gland's hormones and controls that part of the ◊nervous system governing the involuntary muscles.

**hypothermia** condition in which the deep (core) temperature of the body falls below 35°C. If it is not discovered, coma and death ensue. Most at risk are the aged and babies (particularly if premature).

**hyrax** any of a group of small, rodentlike, herbivorous mammals that live among rocks in desert areas, and in forests in Africa, Arabia, and Syria. They are about the size of a rabbit, with a plump body, short legs, short ears,

WWW address (URL)

icons link to required audio
and video plug-ins

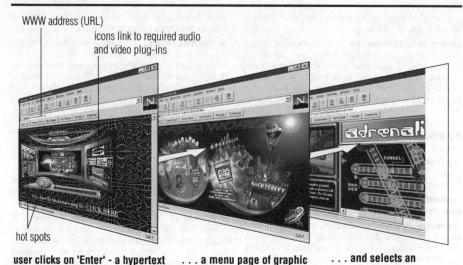

hot spots

**user clicks on 'Enter' - a hypertext
link to . . .**     **. . . a menu page of graphic
hotspots . . .**     **. . . and selects an
interactive game**

**hypertext** *An example of how pages on the World Wide Web may be linked to take the user to
additional pages of information.*

brownish fur, and long, curved front teeth.
(Family Procaviidae, order Hyracoidea.)

**hyssop** aromatic herb belonging to the mint
family, found in Asia, southern Europe, and
around the Mediterranean. It has blue flowers,
oblong leaves, and stems that are woody near
the ground but herbaceous (fleshy) above.
(*Hyssopus officinalis,* family Labiatae.)

**hysterectomy** surgical removal of all or part
of the uterus (womb). The operation is performed to treat fibroids (benign tumours growing in the uterus) or cancer; also to relieve heavy
menstrual bleeding. A woman who has had a
hysterectomy will no longer menstruate and
cannot bear children.

**Ibadan** city in southwest Nigeria, capital of Oyo State, 145 km/90 mi northeast of Lagos; population (1992 est) 1,295,000. Ibadan is the second-largest city in the country, and is a major commercial, industrial, and administrative centre. It is a marketplace for cocoa and other local agricultural produce. Industries include chemicals, electronics, plastics, and motor vehicle assembly.

**ibex** any of various wild goats found in mountainous areas of Europe, northeastern Africa, and Central Asia. They grow to 100 cm/3.5 ft, and have brown or grey coats and heavy horns. They are herbivorous and live in small groups.

**ibis** any of various wading birds, about 60 cm/2 ft tall, belonging to the same family as spoonbills. Ibises have long legs and necks, and long, downward-curved beaks, rather blunt at the end; the upper part is grooved. Their plumage is generally black and white. Various species occur in the warmer regions of the world. (Family Threskiornidae, order Ciconiiformes.)

**Ibiza** one of the ◊Balearic Islands, a popular tourist resort; area 596 sq km/230 sq mi; population (1990 est) 71,000. The capital and port, also called Ibiza, has a cathedral, built sometime between the 14th and 16th centuries.

**Ibn Saud, Abdul Aziz al-Saud** (1880–1953) First king of Saudi Arabia from 1932. His personal hostility to Hussein ibn Ali, the British-supported political and religious leader of the Al Hijaz (Hejaz) region of western Arabia, meant that he stood back from the Arab Revolt of World War I, organized by T E ◊Lawrence and in which ◊Abdullah ibn Hussein and Faisal I, of Iraq, participated. However, after the war, supported by the Wahhabi-inspired Ikhwan (Brethren), Ibn Saud extended his dominions to the Red Sea coast, capturing Jedda and the Muslim holy cities of Mecca and Medina (with their lucrative pilgrimage revenue). By 1921, all central Arabia had been brought under his rule, and in 1924 he successfully invaded the Hejaz, defeating Hussein ibn Ali, who, in 1919, had proclaimed himself king of all the Arab countries. In January 1926, at Mecca, he was proclaimed King of Hejaz and Nejd and in 1932 the territories were unified, under the title 'Kingdom of Saudi Arabia'. In 1934 Saudi forces attacked Yemen and captured further territories in the south, including the towns of Najran and Jizan.

Oil was discovered in 1938, with oil concessions being leased to US and British companies, and exports began in 1946. Between 1947–52, during the 'first oil boom', the country was transformed from a poor pastoral kingdom into an affluent modernizing state, as annual oil revenues increased from $10 million to $212 million. During World War II, Ibn Saud remained neutral, but sympathetic towards the UK and the USA. In 1945 he founded the Arab League to encourage Arab unity.

**Ibo** or *Igbo,* member of a West African people occupying southeastern Nigeria and numbering about 18 million. Primarily subsistence farmers, they also trade and export palm oil and kernels, and make pottery, woodcarvings, and music. They are divided into five main groups, and their languages belong to the Kwa branch of the Niger-Congo family.

**Ibsen, Henrik (Johan)** (1828–1906) Norwegian dramatist and poet. His realistic and often controversial plays revolutionized Euro-pean theatre. Driven into voluntary exile 1864–91 by opposition to the satirical *Kjærlighedens komedie/Love's Comedy* (1862), he wrote the symbolic verse dramas *Brand* (1866) and *Peer Gynt* (1867), followed by realistic plays dealing with social issues, including *Samfundets støtter/Pillars of Society* (1877), *Et dukkehjem/ A Doll's House* (1879), *Gengangere/Ghosts* (1881), *En folkefiende/An Enemy of the People* (1882), and *Hedda Gabler* (1890). By the time he returned to Norway, he was recognized as the country's greatest living writer.

**IC** abbreviation for ◊*integrated circuit.*

**Icarus** in Greek mythology, the son of ◊Daedalus, who with his father escaped from the labyrinth in Crete by making wings of feathers fastened with wax. Icarus plunged to his death when he flew too near the Sun and the wax melted.

**ice age** any period of glaciation occurring in the Earth's history, but particularly that in the Pleistocene epoch, immediately preceding historic times. On the North American continent, ◊glaciers reached as far south as the Great Lakes, and an ice sheet spread over northern Europe, leaving its remains as far south as Switzerland.

There were several glacial advances separated by interglacial stages during which the ice melted and temperatures were higher than today.

**ice hockey** game played on ice between two teams of six, developed in Canada from field hockey or bandy. Players, who wear skates and protective clothing, use a curved stick to advance the puck (a rubber disc) and shoot it at the opponents' goal, a netted cage, guarded by the goalminder, or goalie. The other positions are the left and right defencemen and the left wing, centre, and right wing. The latter three are offensive players. The team with the most goals scored at the end of the three 20-minute periods wins; an overtime period may be played if a game ends in a tie.

**Iceland** Republic of
**national name** Lýdveldid Ísland

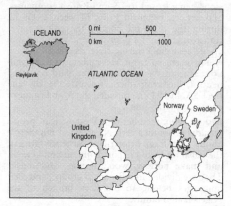

**area** 103,000 sq km/39,768 sq mi
**capital** Reykjavík
**major towns/cities** Akureyri, Akranes, Kópavogur, Hafnerfjördur, Vestmannaeyjar
**physical features** warmed by the Gulf Stream; glaciers and lava fields cover 75% of the country; active volcanoes (Hekla was once thought the gateway to Hell), geysers, hot springs, and new islands created offshore (Surtsey in 1963); subterranean hot water heats 85% of Iceland's homes; Sidujokull glacier moving at 100 metres a day
**head of state** Ìlafur Ragnar Grímsson from 1996
**head of government** Davíd Oddsson from 1991
**political system** democracy
**political parties** Independence Party (IP), right of centre; Progressive Party (PP), radical socialist; People's Alliance (PA), socialist; Social Democratic Party (SDP), moderate, left of centre; Citizens' Party, centrist; Women's Alliance, women- and family-oriented
**currency** krona
**GNP per capita (PPP)** (US$) 22,830 (1998)
**exports** fish products, aluminium, ferrosilicon, diatomite, fertilizer, animal products. Principal market: UK 19% (1998)
**population** 279,000 (1999 est)
**language** Icelandic, the most archaic Scandinavian language
**religion** Evangelical Lutheran
**life expectancy** 77 (men); 81 (women) (1995–2000)
**Chronology**
**7th century** Iceland discovered by Irish seafarers.
**874** First Norse settler, Ingólfr Arnarson, founded a small colony at Reykjavík.
**c. 900** Norse settlers came in larger numbers, mainly from Norway.
**930** Settlers established an annual parliament, the Althing, to make laws and resolve disputes.
**985** Eric the Red left Iceland to found a settlement in Greenland.
**1000** Icelanders adopted Christianity.
**1263** Icelanders recognized authority of the king of Norway after brief civil war.

**1397** Norway and Iceland united with Denmark and Sweden under a single monarch.
**15th century** Norway and Iceland were increasingly treated as appendages of Denmark, especially after Sweden seceded in 1449.
**1602** Denmark introduced a monopoly on Icelandic trade.
**1783** Poisonous volcanic eruption caused great loss of life.
**1814** Norway passed to the Swedish crown; Iceland remained under Danish rule.
**1845** Althing re-established in modernized form.
**1854** Danish monopoly on trade abolished.
**1874** New constitution gave Iceland limited autonomy.
**1918** Iceland achieved full self-government under the Danish crown.
**1940** British forces occupied Iceland after Germany invaded Denmark; US troops took over in 1941.
**1944** Iceland became an independent republic under President Sveinn Björnsson.
**1949** Iceland became a member of NATO.
**1953** Iceland joined the Nordic Council.
**1958** The introduction of exclusive 19-km/12-mi fishing limit led to the first 'Cod War', when Icelandic patrol boats clashed with British fishing boats.
**1972–73** Iceland extended its fishing limit to 80 km/50 mi, renewing confrontations with Britain.
**1975–76** The further extension of the fishing limit to 341 km/200 mi caused the third 'Cod War' with the UK.
**1980** Vigdis Finnbogadóttir became the first woman president of Iceland.
**1985** Iceland declared itself a nuclear-free zone.
**1992** Iceland defied a world ban to resume its whaling industry.
**1996** Ìlafur Ragnar Grímsson was elected president.

**Iceni** ancient people of eastern England, who revolted against Roman occupation under the chieftainship of ◊Boudicca.

**ice-skating** see ◊skating.

**ichneumon fly** any of a large group of parasitic wasps. There are several thousand species in Europe, North America, and other regions. They have slender bodies, and the females have unusually long, curved ovipositors (egg-laying instruments) that can pierce several inches of wood. The eggs are laid in the eggs, larvae, or pupae of other insects, usually butterflies or moths. (Family Ichneumonidae.)

**icon** in computing, a small picture on the computer screen, or ◊VDU, representing an object or function that the user may manipulate or otherwise use. It is a feature of ◊graphical user interface (GUI) systems. Icons make computers easier to use by allowing the user to point to and click with a ◊mouse on pictures, rather than type commands.

**icon** in the Greek or Eastern Orthodox Church, a representation of Jesus, Mary, an angel, or a saint, in painting, low relief, or mosaic. The painted icons were traditionally done on wood. After the 17th century and mainly in Russia, a *riza*, or gold and silver covering that leaves only the face and hands visible (and may be adorned with jewels presented by the faithful in thanksgiving), was often added as protection.

**iconography** in art history, significance attached to symbols that can help to identify subject matter (for example, a saint holding keys usually represents St Peter) and place a work of art in its historical context. The pioneer of this approach was the German art historian Erwin Panofsky.

**id** in Freudian psychology, the mass of motivational and instinctual elements of the human mind, whose activity is largely governed by the arousal of specific needs. It is regarded as the ◊unconscious element of the human psyche, and is said to be in conflict with the ◊ego and the ◊superego.

**Idaho** state of northwestern USA. It is nicknamed Gem State. Idaho, one of the Mountain States, was admitted to the Union in 1890 as the 43rd US state. It is bordered to the east by Montana and Wyoming, to the south by Utah and Nevada, to the west by Oregon and Washington, and to the north by British Columbia, Canada
*population* (1995) 1,163,300
*area* 216,500 sq km/83,569 sq mi
*capital* Boise
*towns and cities* Pocatello, Idaho Falls, Nampa, Lewiston
*industries and products* potatoes, wheat, livestock, timber, silver, lead, zinc, antimony, tourism, leisure industry.

**idealism** in philosophy, the theory that states that the external world is fundamentally immaterial and a dimension of the mind. Objects in the world exist but, according to this theory, they lack substance.

**Ides** in the Roman calendar, the 15th day of March, May, July, and October, and the 13th day of all other months (the word originally indicated the full moon); Julius Caesar was assassinated on the Ides of March 44 BC.

**igneous rock** rock formed from cooling magma or lava, and solidifying from a molten state. Igneous rocks are largely composed of silica ($SiO_2$) and they are classified according to their crystal size, texture, method of formation, or chemical composition, for example by the proportions of light and dark minerals.

**Iguaçu Falls** or *Iguassú Falls,* waterfall in South America, on the border between Brazil and Argentina. The falls lie 19 km/12 mi above the junction of the River Iguaçu with the Paraná. The falls are divided by forested rocky islands and form a spectacular tourist attraction. The water plunges in 275 falls, many of which have separate names. They have a height of 82 m/269 ft and a width of about 4 km/2.5 mi.

**iguana** any of about 700 species of lizard, chiefly found in the Americas. The *common iguana* (*I. iguana*) of Central and South America

is a vegetarian and may reach 2 m/6 ft in length. (Especially genus *Iguana,* family Iguanidae.)

**iguanodon** plant-eating ◊dinosaur whose remains are found in deposits of the Lower ◊Cretaceous age, together with the remains of other dinosaurs of the same order (ornithiscians) such as stegosaurus and ◊triceratops. It was 5–10 m/16–32 ft long and, when standing upright, 4 m/13 ft tall. It walked on its hind legs, using its long tail to balance its body. (Order *Ornithiscia.*)

**IJsselmeer** lake in the Netherlands, area 1,217 sq km/470 sq mi. It was formed in 1932 after the ◊Zuider Zee was cut off from the North Sea by a dyke 32 km/20 mi long (the *Afsluitdijk*); it has been freshwater since 1944. The rivers Vecht, IJssel, and Zwatewater flow into the lake.

**Ikhnaton** another name for ◊Akhenaton, pharaoh of Egypt.

**Ile-de-France** region of northern France; area 12,000 sq km/4,632 sq mi; population (1990) 10,660,600. It includes the French capital, ◊Paris, and the towns of Versailles, Sèvres, and St-Cloud, and comprises the *départements* of Essonne, Val-de-Marne, Val-d'Oise, Ville de Paris, Seine-et-Marne, Hauts-de-Seine, Seine-St-Denis, and Yvelines. From here the early French kings extended their authority over the whole country.

**ileum** part of the small intestine of the ◊digestive system, between the duodenum and the colon, that absorbs digested food.

*Iliad* Greek epic poem, product of an oral tradition; it was possibly written down by 700 BC and is attributed to ◊Homer. The title is derived from Ilion, the Greek name for Troy. Its subject is the wrath of the Greek hero Achilles at the loss of his concubine Briseis, and at the death of his friend Patroclus, during the Greek siege of Troy. The poems ends with the death of the Trojan hero Hector at the hands of Achilles.

**Iliescu, Ion** (1930– ) Romanian president 1990–96. A former member of the Romanian Communist Party (PCR) and of Nicolae Ceauşescu's government, Iliescu swept into power on Ceauşescu's fall as head of the National Salvation Front.

**Ilium** in classical mythology, an alternative name for the city of ◊Troy, taken from its founder Ilus.

**Illinois** midwestern state of the USA. It is nicknamed Prairie State. Illinois was admitted to the Union in 1818 as the 21st US state. A major agricultural state, Illinois is bordered to the east by Indiana, to the southeast by Kentucky, with the Ohio River serving as a boundary, to the west by Missouri and Iowa, with the Mississippi River as a boundary, and to the north by Wisconsin. In the northeast, it has a shore of about 100 km/60 mi on Lake Michigan, occupied by Chicago and its northern suburbs
*population* (1995) 11,829,900
*area* 146,100 sq km/56,395 sq mi
*capital* Springfield

***towns and cities*** Chicago, Rockford, Peoria, Decatur, Aurora

***industries and products*** soybeans, cereals, meat and dairy products, livestock, machinery, electrical and electronic equipment.

**Illyria** ancient name for the eastern coastal region of the Adriatic, north of the Gulf of Corinth. Its three constituent districts were Dalmatia, Iapydia, and Liburnia. It later formed the Roman province of Illyricum. The Albanians are the survivors of its ancient peoples.

**imaginary number** term often used to describe the non-real element of a ◊complex number. For the complex number (*a* + *ib*), *ib* is the imaginary number where i = √–1, and *b* any real number.

**Imagism** movement in Anglo-American poetry that flourished from 1912 to 1914 and affected much US and British poetry and critical thinking thereafter. A central figure was Ezra ◊Pound, who asserted the principles of free verse, complex imagery, and poetic impersonality.

**imago** sexually mature stage of an ◊insect.

**IMF** abbreviation for ◊*International Monetary Fund.*

**Imhotep** (born c. 2630 BC) Egyptian physician and architect, adviser to King Zoser (3rd dynasty). He is thought to have designed the step pyramid at Sakkara, and his tomb (believed to be in the north Sakkara cemetery) became a centre of healing. He was deified as the son of ◊Ptah and was identified with Aesculapius, the Greek god of medicine.

**Immaculate Conception** in the Roman Catholic Church, the belief that the Virgin Mary was, by a special act of grace, preserved free from original sin from the moment she was conceived. This article of the Catholic faith was for centuries the subject of heated controversy, opposed by St Thomas Aquinas and other theologians, but generally accepted from about the 16th century. It became a dogma in 1854 under Pope Pius IX.

**immunity** the protection that organisms have against foreign micro-organisms, such as bacteria and viruses, and against cancerous cells (see ◊cancer). The cells that provide this protection are called white blood cells, or leucocytes, and make up the immune system. They include neutrophils and ◊macrophages, which can engulf invading organisms and other unwanted material, and natural killer cells that destroy cells infected by viruses and cancerous cells. Some of the most important immune cells are the B cells and T cells. Immune cells coordinate their activities by means of chemical messengers or ◊lymphokines, including the antiviral messenger ◊interferon. The lymph nodes play a major role in organizing the immune response.

**immunization** conferring immunity to infectious disease by artificial methods. The most widely used technique is ◊vaccination.

Immunization is an important public health measure. If most of the population has been immunized against a particular disease, it is impossible for an epidemic to take hold.

**immunocompromised** lacking a fully effective immune system. The term is most often used in connection with infections such as ◊AIDS where the virus interferes with the immune response (see ◊immunity).

**immunoglobulin** human globulin ◊protein that can be separated from blood and administered to confer immediate immunity on the recipient. It participates in the immune reaction as the antibody for a specific ◊antigen (disease-causing agent).

**impala** African ◊antelope found from Kenya to South Africa in savannas and open woodland. The body is sandy brown. Males have lyre-shaped horns up to 75 cm/2.5 ft long. Impalas grow up to 1.5 m/5 ft long and 90 cm/3 ft tall. They live in herds and spring high in the air when alarmed. (Species *Aepyceros melampus*, family Bovidae.)

**impeachment** judicial procedure by which government officials are accused of wrongdoing and brought to trial before a legislative body. In the USA the House of Representatives may impeach offenders to be tried before the Senate, as in the case of President Andrew Johnson in 1868. Richard ◊Nixon resigned the US presidency in 1974 when threatened by impeachment. President Bill ◊Clinton's impeachment trial took place in 1999.

**imperialism** policy of extending the power and rule of a government beyond its own boundaries. A country may attempt to dominate others by direct rule and settlement – the establishment of a colony – or by less obvious means such as control of markets for goods or raw materials. These less obvious means are often called neocolonialism.

**imperial system** traditional system of units developed in the UK, based largely on the foot, pound, and second (f.p.s.) system.

**import** product or service that one country purchases from another for domestic consumption, or for processing and re-exporting (Hong Kong, for example, is heavily dependent on imports for its export business). Imports may be visible (goods) or invisible (services). If an importing country does not have a counterbalancing value of exports, it may experience balance-of-payments difficulties and accordingly consider restricting imports by some form of protectionism (such as an import tariff or import quotas).

**Impressionism** movement in painting that originated in France in the 1860s and had enormous influence in European and North American painting in the late 19th century. The Impressionists wanted to depict real life, to paint straight from nature, and to capture the changing effects of light. The term was first used abusively to describe Claude Monet's painting *Impression: Sunrise* (1872). The other leading Impressionists included Paul Cézanne, Edgar Degas, Edouard Manet, Camille Pissarro, Pierre-Auguste Renoir, and Alfred Sisley, but only Monet remained devoted to Impressionist ideas throughout his career.

**improvisation** creating a play, a poem, or any other imaginative work, without preparation.

The term is used in GCSE English for the unprepared piece of drama most students undertake as part of their assessment in the Speaking and Listening section of their examination.

The word has already been twisted from its original meaning in this context, and the term 'prepared improvisation' is being used to show that some preparation time has been allowed.

**in** abbreviation for ◊*inch*, a measure of distance.

**Inca** member of an ancient Peruvian civilization of Quechua-speaking American Indians that began in the Andean highlands about AD 1200. By the time the Spanish conquered the region in the 1530s, the Inca people ruled an area that stretched from Ecuador in the north to Chile in the south. Inca means 'king', and was the title of the ruler as well as the name of the people.

**incarnation** assumption of living form (plant, animal, human) by a deity; for example, the gods of Greece and Rome, Hinduism, and Christianity (Jesus as the second person of the Trinity).

**incendiary bomb** bomb containing inflammable matter. Usually dropped by aircraft, incendiary bombs were used in World War I and incendiary shells were used against Zeppelin aircraft. Incendiary bombs were a major weapon in attacks on cities in World War II, causing widespread destruction. To hinder firefighters, delayed-action high-explosive bombs were usually dropped with them. In the Vietnam War, US forces used ◊napalm in incendiary bombs.

**incest** sexual intercourse between persons thought to be too closely related to marry; the exact relationships that fall under the incest taboo vary widely from society to society. A biological explanation for the incest taboo is based on the necessity to avoid inbreeding.

**inch** imperial unit of linear measure, a twelfth of a foot, equal to 2.54 centimetres.

**Inchon** formerly *Chemulpo,* chief port of Seoul, South Korea; population (1990) 1,818,300. It produces steel and textiles.

**income support** in the UK, ◊social security benefit payable to people who are unemployed or who work for less than 24 hours per week and whose financial resources fall below a certain level. It replaced supplementary benefit in 1988. Originally payable to anyone over 18 not in full-time employment and without adequate resources, as of October 1996 it was restricted to groups such as pensioners or long-term disabled who were not required to be available for work. Payments were reduced if savings exceeded a set amount.

**indemnity** in law, an undertaking to compensate another for damage, loss, trouble, or expenses, or the money paid by way of such compensation – for example, under fire-insurance agreements.

**Independence Day** public holiday in the USA, commemorating the adoption of the ◊Declaration of Independence 4 July 1776.

**independent school** in the UK, a school run privately without direct assistance from the state. Just over 7% of children (1998) attend private fee-paying schools. There are some 2,420 independent schools in Britain, with about 600,000 pupils. A group of old-established and prestigious independent schools are known as public schools.

**Independent Television** (ITV), Independent television in the UK, paid for by advertising, dating from 1955. There are currently fifteen ITV licensees, including two for London, with one national breakfast channel. The current ten-year licences were granted from January 1993. Independent television companies are regulated by the Independent Television Commission (ITC), and are required to provide quality, independent productions, with provision for viewers with disabilities.

**indeterminacy principle** alternative name for ◊uncertainty principle.

**index** in economics, an indicator of a general movement in wages and prices over a specified period.

**index** plural *indices,* (Latin 'sign, indicator') in mathematics, another term for ◊exponent, the number that indicates the power to which a term should be raised.

**India** Republic of
*national name* Hindi *Bharat*

*area* 3,166,829 sq km/1,222,713 sq mi
*capital* Delhi
*major towns/cities* Bombay, Calcutta, Chennai (Madras), Bangalore, Hyderabad, Ahmadabad, Kanpur, Pune, Nagpur, Bhopal, Jaipur, Lucknow, Surat
*major ports* Calcutta, Bombay, Chennai (Madras)
*physical features* Himalaya mountains on northern border; plains around rivers Ganges, Indus, Brahmaputra; Deccan peninsula south of the Narmada River forms plateau between Western and Eastern Ghats mountain ranges; desert in west; Andaman and Nicobar Islands,

Lakshadweep (Laccadive Islands)
**head of state** Kocheril Raman Narayanan from 1997
**head of government** Atal Behari Vajpayee from 1998
**political system** liberal democratic federal republic
**political parties** All India Congress Committee, or Congress, cross-caste and cross-religion coalition, left of centre; Janata Dal (People's Party), secular, left of centre; Bharatiya Janata Party (BJP), radical right wing, Hindu-chauvinist; Communist Party of India (CPI), Marxist-Leninist; Communist Party of India–Marxist (CPI–M), West Bengal–based moderate socialist
**currency** rupee
**GNP per capita (PPP)** (US$) 1,700 (1998)
**exports** tea (world's largest producer), coffee, fish, iron and steel, leather, textiles, clothing, polished diamonds, handmade carpets, engineering goods, chemicals. Principal market: USA 22.8% (1998)
**population** 998,056,000 (1999 est)
**language** Hindi, English, and 17 other official languages: Assamese, Bengali, Gujarati, Kannada, Kashmiri, Konkani, Malayalam, Manipur, Marathi, Nepali, Oriya, Punjabi, Sanskrit, Sindhi, Tamil, Telugu, Urdu; more than 1,650 dialects
**religion** Hindu 83%, Sunni Muslim 11%, Christian 2.5%, Sikh 2%
**life expectancy** 62 (men); 63 (women) (1995–2000)
**Chronology**
**c. 2500–1500 BC** The earliest Indian civilization evolved in the Indus Valley with the city states of Harappa and Mohenjo Daro.
**c. 1500–1200 BC** Aryan peoples from the northwest overran northern India and the Deccan; Brahmanism (a form of Hinduism) developed.
**321 BC** Chandragupta, founder of the Mauryan dynasty, began to unite northern India in a Hindu Empire.
**268–232 BC** Mauryan Empire reached its height under Asoka, who ruled two-thirds of India from his capital Pataliputra.
**c. 180 BC** Shunga dynasty replaced the Mauryans; Hindu Empire began to break up into smaller kingdoms.
**AD 320–480** Gupta dynasty reunified northern India.
**c. 500** Raiding Huns from central Asia destroyed the Gupta dynasty; India reverted to many warring kingdoms.
**11th–12th centuries** Rajput princes of northern India faced repeated Muslim invasions by Arabs, Turks, and Afghans, and in 1206 the first Muslim dynasty was established at Delhi.
**14th–16th centuries** Muslim rule extended over northern India and the Deccan; south remained independent under the Hindu Vijayanagar dynasty.
**1498** Explorer Vasco da Gama reached India, followed by Portuguese, Dutch, French, and English traders.
**1526** Last Muslim invasion: Zahir ud-din Muhammad (Babur) defeated the Sultan of Delhi at Battle of Panipat and established the

Mogul Empire, which was consolidated by Akbar the Great (1556–1605).
**1600** East India Company founded by English merchants, who settled in Madras, Bombay, and Calcutta.
**17th century** Mogul Empire reached its zenith under Jahangir (1605–27), Shah Jehan (1628–58), and Aurangzeb (1658–1707).
**1739** Persian king Nadir Shah invaded India and destroyed Mogul prestige; British and French supported rival Indian princes in subsequent internal wars.
**1757** Battle of Plassey: Robert Clive defeated Siraj al-Daulah, nawab of Bengal; Bengal came under control of British East India Company.
**1772–85** Warren Hastings, British governor general of Bengal, raised Indian army and pursued expansionist policies.
**early 19th century** British took control (directly or indirectly) throughout India by defeating powerful Indian states in a series of regional wars.
**1858** 'Indian Mutiny': mutiny in Bengal army erupted into widespread anti-British revolt; rebels sought to restore powers of Mogul emperor.
**1858** British defeated the rebels; East India Company dissolved; India came under the British crown.
**1885** Indian National Congress founded in Bombay as focus for nationalism.
**1909** Morley–Minto Reforms: Indians received right to elect members of Legislative Councils; Hindus and Muslims formed separate electorates.
**1919** British forces killed 379 Indian demonstrators at Amritsar; India Act (Montagu–Chelmsford Reforms) conceded a measure of provincial self-government.
**1920–22** Mohandas Gandhi won control of the Indian National Congress, which launched campaign of civil disobedience in support of demand for complete self-rule.
**1935** India Act provided for Indian control of federal legislature, with defence and external affairs remaining the viceroy's responsibility.
**1940** Muslim League called for India to be partitioned along religious lines.
**1947** British India partitioned into two independent dominions of India (mainly Hindu) and Pakistan (mainly Muslim) amid bloody riots; Jawaharlal Nehru of Congress Party became prime minister.
**1950** India became a republic within the Commonwealth.
**1962** India lost brief border war with China; retained Kashmir in war with Pakistan in 1965.
**1966** Indira Gandhi, daughter of Nehru, became prime minister.
**1971** India defeated Pakistan in a war and helped East Pakistan become independent as Bangladesh.
**1975** Found guilty of electoral corruption, Mrs Gandhi declared a state of emergency and arrested opponents.
**1977–79** The Janata Party formed a government under Morarji Desai.
**1980** Mrs Gandhi, heading a Congress Party splinter group, Congress (I) ('I' for Indira), was returned to power.

**1984** Troops cleared Sikh separatists from the Golden Temple, Amritsar; Mrs Gandhi was assassinated by Sikh bodyguards; her son Rajiv Gandhi became prime minister.

**1989** After financial scandals, Congress ('I' was removed after Mrs Gandhi's assassination) lost elections; V P Singh formed a Janata Dal minority government.

**1990** Direct rule was imposed on Jammu and Kashmir after an upsurge in Muslim separatist violence; rising interethnic and religious conflict was seen in the Punjab and elsewhere.

**1991** Rajiv Gandhi was assassinated during an election campaign; P V Narasimha Rao formed a minority Congress government.

**1992** The destruction of a mosque at Ayodhya, northern India, by Hindu extremists resulted in widespread violence.

**1996** H D Deve Gowda became prime minister of a coalition government. Madras was renamed Chennai. Rao resigned as the Congress Party president and was replaced by Sitaram Kesri. Direct central rule was imposed on Uttar Pradesh after inconclusive assembly elections.

**1997** Deve Gowda's government was defeated in a confidence vote. The United Front government was reformed and led by Inder Kumar Gujral. Kocheril Raman Narayanan became the first 'untouchable' to be elected president.

**1998** Atal Behari Vajpayee, leader of the Bharatiya Janata party, was elected prime minister. Sonia Gandhi became leader of the Congress Party. The creation of three new states was proposed. India carried out five underground nuclear explosions, meeting with international condemnation. There were floods in Uttar Pradesh. Congress polled strongly in state elections in northern and central India, reflecting disenchantment with the BJP federal government.

**1999** The Indian government renounced further nuclear weapons testing and promised to sign the Comprehensive Test Ban Treaty. April: BJP-led coalition government defeated on confidence vote. Parliament was dissolved and general election planned for late September or October. May: Sonia Gandhi resigned Congress Party presidency and then withdrew the resignation. India used air power to attack 'infiltrators' in Kashmir. June: Kashmir peace talks offered to Pakistan.

**Indiana** state of the midwest USA. It is nicknamed the Hoosier State. Indiana was admitted to the Union in 1816 as the 19th US state. It is bordered to the northeast by Michigan, to the east by Ohio, to the south and southeast by Kentucky, and to the west by Illinois. In the northwest, Indiana has a shoreline of about 72 km/ 45 mi on Lake Michigan

**population** (1995) 5,803,500

**area** 93,700 sq km/36,168 sq mi

**capital** ◊Indianapolis

**towns and cities** Fort Wayne, Gary, Evansville, South Bend

**industries and products** maize, pigs, cattle, soybeans, limestone, machinery, electrical goods, coal, steel, iron, chemicals, glass, oil.

**Indianapolis** state capital and largest city of ◊Indiana, on the White River, 300 km/186 mi southeast of Chicago; seat of Marion County; population (1994 est) 752,000; population of metropolitan area (1992) 1,424,000. Situated in the rich Corn Belt agricultural region, the city is an industrial centre; products include electronic components, pharmaceuticals, processed foods, machinery, plastics, and rubber. It is the venue for the Indianapolis 500 car race.

**Indian languages** traditionally, the languages of the subcontinent of India; since 1947, the languages of the Republic of India. These number some 200, depending on whether a variety is classified as a language or a dialect. They fall into five main groups, the two most widespread of which are the Indo-European languages (mainly in the north) and the Dravidian languages (mainly in the south).

**Indian Mutiny** also Sepoy Rebellion or Mutiny, revolt of Indian soldiers (sepoys) against the British in India from 1857 to 1858. The uprising was confined to the north, from Bengal to the Punjab, and central India. It led to the end of rule by the ◊British East India Company and its replacement by direct British crown administration.

**Indian Ocean** ocean between Africa and Australia, with India to the north, and the southern boundary being an arbitrary line from Cape Agulhas to south Tasmania; area 73,500,000 sq km/28,371,000 sq mi; average depth 3,872 m/12,708 ft. The greatest depth is the Java Trench 7,725 m/25,353 ft. It includes two great bays on either side of the Indian peninsula, the Bay of Bengal to the east, and the Arabian Sea with the gulfs of Aden and Oman to the west.

**indicator** in chemistry, a compound that changes its structure and colour in response to its environment. The commonest chemical indicators detect changes in ◊pH (for example, ◊litmus and universal indicator), or in the oxidation state of a system (redox indicators).

**indigo** violet-blue vegetable dye obtained from various tropical plants such as the anil, but now replaced by a synthetic product. It was once a major export crop of India. (Plant genus *Indigofera*, family Leguminosae.)

**indium** (Latin *indicum* 'indigo') soft, ductile, silver-white, metallic element, symbol In, atomic number 49, relative atomic mass 114.82. It occurs in nature in some zinc ores, is resistant to abrasion, and is used as a coating on metal parts. It was discovered in 1863 by German metallurgists Ferdinand Reich (1799–1882) and Hieronymus Richter (1824–1898), who named it after the two indigo lines of its spectrum.

**individualism** in politics, a view in which the individual takes precedence over the collective: the opposite of ◊collectivism. The term *possessive individualism* has been applied to the writings of John ◊Locke and Jeremy ◊Bentham, describing society as comprising individuals interacting through market relations.

**Indo-Aryan languages** another name for the ◊Indo-European languages.

**Indochina** French, name given by the French to their colonies in Southeast Asia: Cambodia, Laos, and Vietnam, which became independent after World War II.

**Indochina War** war of independence 1946–54 between the nationalist forces of what was to become Vietnam and France, the occupying colonial power.

**Indo-European languages** family of languages that includes some of the world's major classical languages (Sanskrit and Pali in India, Zend Avestan in Iran, Greek and Latin in Europe), as well as several of the most widely spoken languages (English worldwide; Spanish in Iberia, Latin America, and elsewhere; and the Hindi group of languages in northern India). Indo-European languages were once located only along a geographical band from India through Iran into northwestern Asia, Eastern Europe, the northern Mediterranean lands, northern and western Europe and the British Isles.

**Indo-Germanic languages** former name for the ◊Indo-European languages.

**Indonesia** Republic of
*national name* *Republik Indonesia*

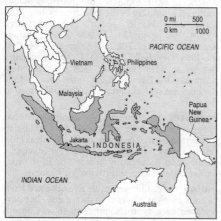

*area* 1,904,569 sq km/735,354 sq mi
*capital* Jakarta
*major towns/cities* Surabaya, Bandung, Yogyakarta (Java), Medan, Semarang (Java), Banda Aceh, Palembang (Sumatra), Ujung Pandang (Sulawesi), Denpasar (Bali), Kupang (Timor), Padang, Malang
*major ports* Tanjung Priok, Surabaya, Semarang (Java), Ujung Pandang (Sulawesi)
*physical features* comprises 13,677 tropical islands (over 6,000 of them are inhabited): the Greater Sundas (including Java, Madura, Sumatra, Sulawesi, and Kalimantan (part of Borneo)), the Lesser Sunda Islands/Nusa Tenggara (including Bali, Lombok, Sumbawa, Flores, Sumba, Alor, Lomblen, Timor, Roti, and Savu), Maluku/Moluccas (over 1,000 islands including Ambon, Ternate, Tidore, Tanimbar, and Halmahera), and Irian Jaya (part of New Guinea); over half the country is tropical rain-forest; it has the largest expanse of peatlands in the tropics
*head of state and government* B J Habibie from 1998
*political system* authoritarian nationalist republic
*political parties* Sekber Golkar, ruling military-bureaucrat-farmers' party; United Development Party (PPP), moderate Islamic; Indonesian Democratic Party (PDI), nationalist Christian
*currency* rupiah
*GNP per capita (PPP)* (US$) 2,790 (1998)
*exports* petroleum and petroleum products, natural and manufactured gas, textiles, rubber, palm oil, wood and wood products, electrical and electronic products, coffee, fishery products, coal, copper, tin, pepper, tea. Principal market: Japan 18.6% (1998)
*population* 210,126,000 (1999 est)
*language* Bahasa Indonesia (official), closely related to Malay; there are 583 regional languages and dialects; Javanese is the most widely spoken local language. Dutch is also spoken
*religion* Muslim 88%, Christian 10%, Buddhist and Hindu 2% (the continued spread of Christianity, together with an Islamic revival, have led to greater religious tensions)
*life expectancy* 63 (men); 67 (women) (1995–2000)
*Chronology*
*3000–500 BC* Immigrants from southern China displaced original Melanesian population.
*6th century AD* Start of Indian cultural influence; small Hindu and Buddhist kingdoms developed.
*8th century* Buddhist maritime empire of Srivijaya expanded to include all Sumatra and Malay peninsula.
*13th century* Islam introduced to Sumatra by Arab merchants; spread throughout the islands over next 300 years.
*14th century* Eastern Javanese kingdom of Majapahit destroyed Srivijaya and dominated the region.
*c. 1520* Empire of Majapahit disintegrated; Javanese nobles fled to Bali.
*16th century* Portuguese merchants broke Muslim monopoly of spice trade.
*1602* Dutch East India Company founded; it displaced the Portuguese and monopolized trade with the Spice Islands.
*1619* Dutch East India Company captured port of Jakarta in Java and renamed it Batavia.
*17th century* Dutch introduced coffee plants and established informal control over central Java through divide-and-rule policy among local rulers.
*1749* After frequent military intervention, the Dutch East India Company obtained formal sovereignty over Mataram.
*1799* The Netherlands took over interests of bankrupt Dutch East India Company.
*1808* French forces occupied Java; British expelled them in 1811 and returned Java to the Netherlands in 1816.
*1824* Anglo-Dutch Treaty: Britain recognized entire Indonesian archipelago as Dutch sphere of influence.

**1825–30** Java War: Prince Dipo Negoro led unsuccessful revolt against Dutch rule; further revolt 1894–96.

**19th century** Dutch formalized control over Java and conquered other islands; cultivation of coffee and sugar under tight official control made the Netherlands Indies one of the richest colonies in the world.

**1901** Dutch introduced 'Ethical Policy' supposed to advance local interests.

**1908** Dutch completed conquest of Bali.

**1927** Communist revolts suppressed; Achmed Sukarno founded Indonesian Nationalist Party (PNI) to unite diverse anti-Dutch elements.

**1929** Dutch imprisoned Sukarno and tried to suppress PNI.

**1942–45** Japanese occupation; PNI installed as anti-Western puppet government.

**1945** When Japan surrendered, President Sukarno declared an independent republic, but Dutch set about restoring colonial rule by force.

**1947** Dutch 'police action': all-out attack on Java and Sumatra conquered two-thirds of the republic.

**1949** Under US pressure, Dutch agreed to transfer sovereignty of the Netherlands Indies (except Dutch New Guinea or Irian Jaya) to the Republic of the United States of Indonesia.

**1950** President Sukarno abolished federalism and proclaimed unitary Republic of Indonesia dominated by Java; revolts in Sumatra and South Moluccas.

**1959** To combat severe political instability, Sukarno imposed authoritarian 'guided democracy'.

**1963** The Netherlands ceded Irian Jaya to Indonesia.

**1963–66** Indonesia tried to break up Malaysia by means of blockade and guerrilla attacks.

**1965–66** Clashes between communists and army; Gen Raden Suharto imposed emergency administration and massacred up to 700,000 alleged communists.

**1968** Suharto formally replaced Sukarno as president and proclaimed 'New Order' under strict military rule.

**1970s** Rising oil exports brought significant agricultural and industrial growth.

**1975** Indonesia invaded East Timor when Portuguese rule collapsed; 200,000 died in ensuing war.

**1986** After suppressing a revolt on Irian Jaya, Suharto introduced a programme to settle 65,000 Javanese there and on outer islands.

**1991** The Democracy Forum was launched to promote political dialogue.

**1993** President Suharto was re-elected for the sixth consecutive term.

**1996** The government initiated a crackdown on its opponents.

**1997** Hundreds were killed in ethnic riots in west Kalimantan province. There was a drought and a famine in Irian Jaya. Forest fires in Borneo and Sumatra blighted large areas of SE Asia with heavy smog, and caused catastrophic environmental damage.

**1998** Following mass riots, Suharto stepped down as president and was replaced by Vicepresident B J Habibie. There was partial withdrawal of troops from East Timor and partial autonomy was offered. Riots continued as GDP contracted by 15%. Irian Jaya's status as a military occupation zone ended, following a ceasefire agreement with separatist rebels. Troops killed 16 student demonstrators in Jakarta. The repressive legislation of the Suharto era was repealed in a special legislature session and political parties were legalized. Suharto was questioned over allegations of corruption.

**1999** Ethnic violence continued in Borneo, with over 500 people killed in March and April. The government promised a referendum in East Timor on a plan for autonomy, but violent clashes continued; over 25 East Timorese refugees were massacred by militia without the Indonesian army attempting to stop the attack.

**inductance** in physics, the phenomenon where a changing current in a circuit builds up a magnetic field which induces an ◊electromotive force either in the same circuit and opposing the current (self-inductance) or in another circuit (mutual inductance). The SI unit of inductance is the henry (symbol H).

**induction coil** type of electrical transformer, similar to an ignition coil, that produces an intermittent high-voltage alternating current from a low-voltage direct current supply.

**inductor** device included in an electrical circuit because of its inductance.

**indulgence** in the Roman Catholic Church, the total or partial remission of temporal punishment for sins that remain to be expiated after penitence and confession have secured exemption from eternal punishment. The doctrine of indulgence began as the commutation of church penances in exchange for suitable works of charity or money gifts to the church, and became a great source of church revenue. This trade in indulgences roused Martin Luther to initiate the Reformation in 1517. The Council of Trent in 1563 recommended moderate retention of indulgences, and they continue, notably in 'Holy Years'.

**Indus** river in Asia, rising in Tibet and flowing 3,180 km/1,975 mi to the Arabian Sea. In 1960 the use of its waters, including those of its five tributaries, was divided between India (rivers Ravi, Beas, Sutlej) and Pakistan (rivers Indus, Jhelum, Chenab). In the 3rd and 2nd millennia BC ◊Indus Valley civilization flourished at centres like Harappa and Mojenjo Daro.

**industrial design** branch of artistic activity that came into being as a result of the need to design machine-made products, introduced by the Industrial Revolution in the 18th century. The purpose of industrial design is to ensure that goods satisfy the demands of fashion, style, function, materials, and cost.

**industrial law** or *labour law,* the body of law relating to relationships between employers (and their representatives), employees (and their representatives), and government.

**industrial relations** relationship between employers and employees, and their dealings with each other. In most industries, wages and conditions are determined by *free collective bargaining* between employers and ◊trade unions. Some European and American countries have *worker participation* through profit-sharing and industrial democracy. Another solution is *co-ownership,* in which a company is entirely owned by its employees. The aim of good industrial relations is to achieve a motivated, capable workforce that sees its work as creative and fulfilling. A breakdown in industrial relations can lead to an industrial dispute where one party takes industrial action.

**Industrial Revolution** sudden acceleration of technical and economic development that began in Britain in the second half of the 18th century. The traditional agricultural economy was replaced by one dominated by machinery and manufacturing, made possible through technical advances such as the steam engine. This transferred the balance of political power from the landowner to the industrial capitalist and created an urban working class. From 1830 to the early 20th century, the Industrial Revolution spread throughout Europe and the USA and to Japan and the various colonial empires.

**industrial sector** any of the different groups into which industries may be divided: primary, secondary, tertiary, and quaternary. *Primary* industries extract or use raw materials; for example, mining and agriculture. *Secondary* industries are manufacturing industries, where raw materials are processed or components are assembled. *Tertiary* industries supply services such as retailing. The *quaternary* sector of industry is concerned with the professions and those services that require a high level of skill, expertise, and specialization. It includes education, research and development, administration, and financial services such as accountancy.

**industrial tribunal** independent panel that rules on disputes between employers and employees or trade unions relating to statutory terms and conditions of employment. Employment issues brought before it include unfair dismissal, redundancy, equal opportunities, and discrimination at work.

**industry** the extraction and conversion of raw materials, the manufacture of goods, and the provision of services. Industry can be either low technology, unspecialized, and labour-intensive, as in countries with a large unskilled labour force, or highly automated, mechanized, and specialized, using advanced technology, as in the industrialized countries. Major recent trends in industrial activity have been the growth of electronic, robotic, and microelectronic technologies, the expansion of the offshore oil industry, and the prominence of Japan and other Pacific-region countries in manufacturing and distributing electronics, computers, and motor vehicles.

**Indus Valley civilization** one of the four earliest ancient civilizations of the Old World (the other three being the ◊Sumerian civilization 3500 BC; Egypt 3000 BC; and China 2200 BC), developing in the northwest of the Indian sub-continent about 2500 BC.

**inert gas** or *noble gas,* any of a group of six elements (helium, neon, argon, krypton, xenon, and radon), so named because they were originally thought not to enter into any chemical reactions. This is now known to be incorrect: in 1962, xenon was made to combine with fluorine, and since then, compounds of argon, krypton, and radon with fluorine and/or oxygen have been described.

**inertia** in physics, the tendency of an object to remain in a state of rest or uniform motion until an external force is applied, as described by Isaac Newton's first law of motion (see ◊Newton's laws of motion).

**infection** invasio\n of the body by disease-causing organisms (pathogens, or germs) that become established, multiply, and produce symptoms. Bacteria and viruses cause most diseases, but diseases are also caused by other micro-organisms, protozoans, and other parasites.

**inferiority complex** in psychology, a ◊complex or cluster of repressed fears, described by Alfred Adler, based on physical inferiority. The term is popularly used to describe general feelings of inferiority and the overcompensation that often ensues.

**infertility** in medicine, inability to reproduce. In women, this may be due to blockage in the Fallopian tubes, failure of ovulation, a deficiency in sex hormones, or general ill health. In men, impotence, an insufficient number of sperm or abnormal sperm may be the cause of infertility. Clinical investigation will reveal the cause of the infertility in about 75% of couples and assisted conception may then be appropriate.

**infinity** mathematical quantity that is larger than any fixed assignable quantity; symbol ∞. By convention, the result of dividing any number by zero is regarded as infinity.

**inflation** in economics, a rise in the general level of prices. The many causes include cost-push inflation, which results from rising production costs. *Demand-pull inflation* occurs when overall demand exceeds supply. *Suppressed inflation* occurs in controlled economies and is reflected in rationing, shortages, and black-market prices. *Hyperinflation* is inflation of more than 50% in one month. *Deflation,* a fall in the general level of prices, is the reverse of inflation.

**influenza** any of various viral infections primarily affecting the air passages, accompanied by systemic effects such as fever, chills, headache, joint and muscle pains, and lassitude. Treatment is with bed rest and analgesic drugs such as aspirin or paracetamol.

**information technology** (IT), collective term for the various technologies involved in processing and transmitting information. They include computing, telecommunications, and microelectronics.

**infrared astronomy** study of infrared radiation produced by relatively cool gas and dust in space, as in the areas around forming stars. In 1983, the Infra-Red Astronomy Satellite (IRAS) surveyed the entire sky at infrared wavelengths. It found five new comets, thousands of galaxies undergoing bursts of star formation, and the possibility of planetary systems forming around several dozen stars.

**infrared radiation** invisible electromagnetic ◊radiation of wavelength between about 0.75 micrometres and 1 millimetre – that is, between the limit of the red end of the visible spectrum and the shortest microwaves. All bodies above the ◊absolute zero of temperature absorb and radiate infrared radiation. Infrared radiation is used in medical photography and treatment, and in industry, astronomy, and criminology.

**infrastructure** relatively permanent facilities that serve an industrial economy. Infrastructure usually includes roads, railways, other communication networks, energy and water supply, and education and training facilities. Some definitions also include sociocultural installations such as health-care and leisure facilities.

**Ingres, Jean-Auguste-Dominique** (1780–1867) French painter. A leading Neo-Classicist, he was a student of Jacques Louis ◊David. He studied and worked in Rome about 1807–20, where he began the *Odalisque* series of sensuous female nudes, then went to Florence, and returned to France 1824. His portraits painted in the 1840s–50s are meticulously detailed and highly polished.

**injunction** court order that forbids a person from doing something, or orders him or her to take certain action. Breach of an injunction is ◊contempt of court.

**Inkatha Freedom Party** IFP, (from the grass coil worn by Zulu women for carrying head loads; its many strands give it strength) South African political party, representing the nationalist aspirations of the country's largest ethnic group, the Zulus. It was founded as a paramilitary organization in 1975 by its present leader, Chief Gatsha ◊Buthelezi, with the avowed aim of creating a nonracial democratic political situation. The party entered South Africa's first multiracial elections in April 1994, after an initial violent boycott, and emerged with 10% of the popular vote.

**INLA** abbreviation for ◊Irish National Liberation Army.

**Innocent** thirteen popes, including:

**Innocent III** (*c*. 1161–1216) Pope from 1198. He asserted papal power over secular princes, in particular over the succession of Holy Roman emperors. He also made King ◊John of England his vassal, compelling him to accept Stephen Langton as archbishop of Canterbury. He promoted the fourth Crusade and crusades against the non-Christian Livonians and Letts, and the Albigensian heretics of southern France.

**Innsbruck** capital of Tirol state, west Austria; population (1995) 119,600. It is a tourist and winter sports centre, and a route junction for the Brenner Pass. Local industries include mechanical engineering, bellmaking, and bookbinding. The 1964 and 1976 Winter Olympics were held here.

**Inns of Court** four private legal societies in London, England: Lincoln's Inn, Gray's Inn, Inner Temple, and Middle Temple. All barristers (advocates in the English legal system) must belong to one of the Inns of Court. The main function of each Inn is the education, government, and protection of its members. Each is under the administration of a body of Benchers (judges and senior barristers).

**innuendo** indirect, unpleasant comment; a sly hint. 'I am sure you have brought up your child well – to the best of your ability.' 'I wouldn't take any books when you go to stay with Alan, if I were you. They have a habit of disappearing there.' The second example is more blatant than the first, but the essence of an innuendo is that it must be capable of an innocent explanation. The speaker must be able to charge the listener with misinterpretation or oversensitivity, if the innuendo is challenged.

**inoculation** injection into the body of dead or weakened disease-carrying organisms or their toxins (◊vaccine) to produce immunity by inducing a mild form of a disease.

**inorganic chemistry** branch of chemistry dealing with the chemical properties of the elements and their compounds, excluding the more complex covalent compounds of carbon, which are considered in ◊organic chemistry.

**input device** device for entering information into a computer. Input devices include keyboards, joysticks, mice, light pens, touch-sensitive screens, scanners, graphics tablets, speech-recognition devices, and vision systems. Compare ◊output device.

**inquest** inquiry held by a ◊coroner into an unexplained death. At an inquest, a coroner is assisted by a jury of between 7 and 11 people. Evidence is on oath, and medical and other witnesses may be summoned.

**insanity** in medicine and law, any mental disorder in which the patient cannot be held responsible for their actions. The term is no longer used to refer to psychosis.

**insect** any of a vast group of small invertebrate animals with hard, segmented bodies, three pairs of jointed legs, and, usually, two pairs of wings; they belong among the ◊arthropods and are distributed throughout the world. An insect's body is divided into three segments: head, thorax, and abdomen. On the head is a pair of feelers, or antennae. The legs and wings are attached to the thorax, or middle segment of the body. The abdomen, or end segment of the body, is where food is digested and excreted and where the reproductive organs are located.

Insects vary in size from 0.02 cm/0.008 in to 35 cm/13.5 in in length. The world's smallest insect is believed to be a 'fairy fly' wasp in the family Mymaridae, with a wingspan of 0.02 cm/0.008 in. (Class Insecta.) *See illustration on page 446.*

**insecticide** any chemical pesticide used to kill insects. Among the most effective insecticides are synthetic organic chemicals such as ◊DDT and dieldrin, which are chlorinated hydro-

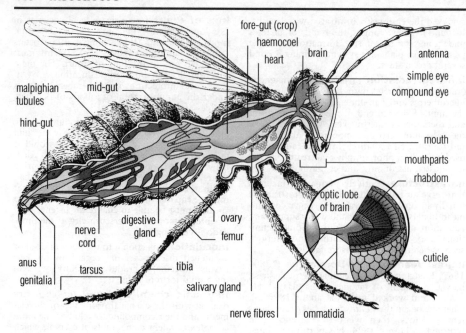

**insect** Body plan of an insect. The general features of the insect body include a segmented body divided into head, thorax, and abdomen, jointed legs, feelers or antennae, and usually two pairs of wings. Insects often have compound eyes (insert) with a large field of vision.

carbons. These chemicals, however, have proved persistent in the environment and are also poisonous to all animal life, including humans, and are consequently banned in many countries. Other synthetic insecticides include organic phosphorus compounds such as malathion. Insecticides prepared from plants, such as derris and pyrethrum, are safer to use but need to be applied frequently and carefully.

**insectivore** any animal whose diet is made up largely or exclusively of ◊insects. In particular, the name is applied to mammals of the order Insectivora, which includes the shrews, hedgehogs, moles, and tenrecs.

**insectivorous plant** plant that can capture and digest live prey (normally insects), to obtain nitrogen compounds that are lacking in its usual marshy habitat. Some are passive traps, for example, the pitcher plants *Nepenthes* and *Sarracenia*. One pitcher-plant species has container-traps holding 1.6 l/3.5 pt of the liquid that 'digests' its food, mostly insects but occasionally even rodents. Others, for example, sundews *Drosera*, butterworts *Pinguicula*, and Venus flytraps *Dionaea muscipula*, have an active trapping mechanism. Insectivorous plants have adapted to grow in poor soil conditions where the number of micro-organisms recycling nitrogen compounds is very much reduced. In these circumstances other plants cannot gain enough nitrates to grow. See also ◊leaf.

**insemination, artificial** see ◊artificial insemination.

**insider trading** or *insider dealing*, illegal use of privileged information in dealing on a stock exchange, for example, when a company takeover bid is imminent. Insider trading is in theory detected by the Securities and Exchange Commission (SEC) in the USA, and by the Securities and Investment Board (SIB) in the UK. Neither agency, however, has any legal powers other than public disclosure and they do not bring prosecutions themselves.

**instinct** in ◊ethology, behaviour found in all equivalent members of a given species (for example, all the males, or all the females with young) that is presumed to be genetically determined.

**insulin** protein ◊hormone, produced by specialized cells in the islets of Langerhans in the pancreas, that regulates the metabolism (rate of activity) of glucose, fats, and proteins. Insulin was discovered by Canadian physician Frederick ◊Banting and Canadian physiologist Charles ◊Best, who pioneered its use in treating ◊diabetes.

**insurance** contract guaranteeing compensation to the payer of a premium against loss by fire, death, accident, and so on, which is known as *assurance* in the case of a fixed sum and *insurance* where the payment is proportionate to the loss.

**intaglio** design cut into the surface of gems or seals by etching or engraving; an ◊engraving technique.

**integer** any whole number. Integers may be positive or negative; 0 is an integer, and is often considered positive. Formally, integers are members of the set

$$Z = \{... -3, -2, -1, 0, 1, 2, 3,... \}$$

Fractions, such as $\frac{1}{2}$ and 0.35, are known as non-integral numbers ('not integers').

**integral calculus** branch of mathematics using the process of integration. It is concerned with finding volumes and areas and summing infinitesimally small quantities.

**integrated circuit** (IC), popularly called silicon chip, miniaturized electronic circuit produced on a single crystal, or chip, of a semiconducting material – usually silicon. It may contain many millions of components and yet measure only 5 mm/0.2 in square and 1 mm/0.04 in thick. The IC is encapsulated within a plastic or ceramic case, and linked via gold wires to metal pins with which it is connected to a ◊printed circuit board and the other components that make up such electronic devices as computers and calculators.

**Integrated Services Digital Network** (ISDN), internationally developed telecommunications system for sending signals in digital format. It involves converting the 'local loop' – the link between the user's telephone (or private automatic branch exchange) and the digital telephone exchange – from an ◊analogue system into a digital system, thereby greatly increasing the amount of information that can be carried. The first large-scale use of ISDN began in Japan in 1988.

**intelligence** in military and political affairs, information, often secretly or illegally obtained, about other countries. *Counter-intelligence* is information on the activities of hostile agents. Much intelligence is gained by technical means, such as satellites and the electronic interception of data.

**interactive video** (IV), computer-mediated system that enables the user to interact with and control information (including text, recorded speech, or moving images) stored on video disk. IV is most commonly used for training purposes, using analogue video disks, but has wider applications with digital video systems such as CD-I (Compact Disc Interactive, from Philips and Sony) which are based on the CD-ROM format derived from audio compact discs.

**interest** in finance, a sum of money paid by a borrower to a lender in return for the loan, usually expressed as a percentage per annum. *Simple interest* is interest calculated as a straight percentage of the amount loaned or invested. In *compound interest,* the interest earned over a period of time (for example, per annum) is added to the investment, so that at the end of the next period interest is paid on that total.

**interference** in physics, the phenomenon of two or more wave motions interacting and combining to produce a resultant wave of larger or smaller amplitude (depending on whether the combining waves are in or out of phase with each other).

**interferon** naturally occurring cellular protein that makes up part of the body's defences against

viral disease. Three types (alpha, beta, and gamma) are produced by infected cells and enter the bloodstream and uninfected cells, making them immune to virus attack.

**Intermediate Nuclear Forces Treaty** agreement signed 8 December 1987 between the USA and the USSR to eliminate all ground-based nuclear missiles in Europe that were capable of hitting only European targets (including European Russia). It reduced the countries' nuclear arsenals by some 2,000 (4% of the total). The treaty included provisions for each country to inspect the other's bases.

**intermediate technology** application of mechanics, electrical engineering, and other technologies, based on inventions and designs developed in scientifically sophisticated cultures, but utilizing materials, assembly, and maintenance methods found in technologically less advanced regions (known as the Third World).

**internal-combustion engine** heat engine in which fuel is burned inside the engine, contrasting with an external-combustion engine (such as the steam engine) in which fuel is burned in a separate unit. The ◊diesel engine and ◊petrol engine are both internal-combustion engines. Gas ◊turbines and jet and ◊rocket engines are also considered to be internal-combustion engines because they burn their fuel inside their combustion chambers.

**International, the** coordinating body established by labour and socialist organizations, including:
*First International* or *International Working Men's Association* 1864–72, formed in London under Karl ◊Marx.
*Second International* 1889–1940, founded in Paris.
*Third (Socialist) International* or *Comintern* 1919–43, formed in Moscow by the Soviet leader Lenin, advocating from 1933 a popular front (communist, socialist, liberal) against the German dictator Hitler.
*Fourth International* or *Trotskyist International* 1938, somewhat indeterminate, anti-Stalinist.
*Revived Socialist International* 1951, formed in Frankfurt, Germany, a largely anticommunist association of social democrats.

**International Bank for Reconstruction and Development** specialized agency of the United Nations. Its popular name is the ◊World Bank.

**International Court of Justice** main judicial organ of the ◊United Nations, in The Hague, the Netherlands. It hears international law disputes as well as playing an advisory role to UN organs. It was set up by the UN charter in 1945 and superseded the World Court. There are 15 judges, each from a different member state.

**International Date Line** (IDL), imaginary line that approximately follows the 180° line of longitude. The date is put forward a day when crossing the line going west, and back a day when going east. The IDL was chosen at the International Meridian Conference in 1884.

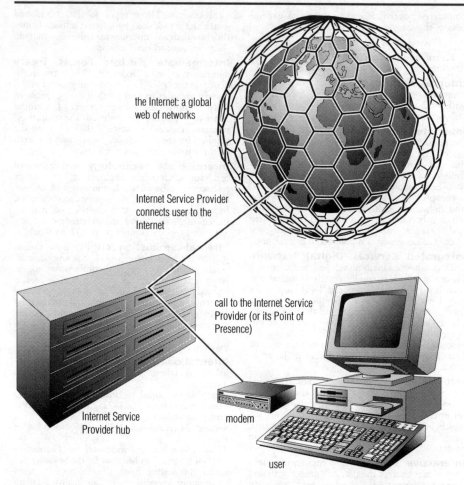

the Internet: a global
web of networks

Internet Service Provider
connects user to the
Internet

call to the Internet Service
Provider (or its Point of
Presence)

Internet Service
Provider hub

modem

user

**Internet** *The Internet is accessed by users via a modem to the service provider's hub, which handles all connection requests. Once connected, the user can access a whole range of information from many different sources, including the World Wide Web.*

**International Gothic** late Gothic style of painting and sculpture flourishing in Europe in the late 14th and 15th centuries. It is characterized by bright colours, a courtly elegance, and a naturalistic rendering of detail. Originally evolving in the court art of France and Burgundy, it spread to many parts of Europe, its leading exponents including the Italian Simone Martini and the Franco-Flemish Limbourg brothers.

**International Labour Organization** (ILO), specialized agency of the United Nations, originally established in 1919, which formulates standards for labour and social conditions. Its headquarters are in Geneva, Switzerland. It was awarded the Nobel Peace Prize in 1969. By 1997, the agency was responsible for over 70 international labour conventions.

**international law** body of rules generally accepted as governing the relations between countries, pioneered by Hugo ◊Grotius, especially in matters of human rights, territory, and war.

**International Monetary Fund** (IMF), specialized agency of the United Nations, headquarters Washington, DC, established under the 1944 ◊Bretton Woods agreement and operational since 1947. It seeks to promote international monetary cooperation and the growth of world trade, and to smooth multilateral payment arrangements among member states. IMF standby loans are available to members in balance-of-payments difficulties (the amount being governed by the member's quota), usually on the basis that the country must agree to take certain corrective measures.

**International Society for Krishna Consciousness** (ISKCON) or *Gaudiya Vaisnavism,* Hindu sect based on the demonstration of intense love for Krishna (an incarnation of the god Vishnu), especially by chanting the mantra 'Hare Krishna'. Members wear distinctive yellow robes, and men often have their heads partly shaven. Their holy books are the Hindu scriptures and particularly the *Bhagavad-Gītā*, which they study daily.

**International Style** or *International Modern*, architectural style, an early and influential phase of the ◊Modern Movement, originating in Western Europe in the 1920s but finding its fullest expression in the 1930s, notably in the USA. It is characterized by a dominance of geometric, especially rectilinear, forms; emphasis on asymmetrical composition; large expanses of glazing; and white rendered walls. Examples are Walter ◊Gropius's Bauhaus building, Dessau, Germany, (1925–26); ◊Le Corbusier's Villa Savoye, Poissy, France, (1927–31); Alvar ◊Aalto's Viipuri Library, Finland (now in Russia), (1927–35); and Mies van der Rohe's Barcelona Pavilion (1929).

**Internet** global computer network connecting governments, companies, universities, and many other networks and users. ◊Electronic mail, electronic conferencing, educational and chat services are all supported across the network, as is the ability to access remote computers and send and retrieve files. In 1997 around 60 million adults had access to the Internet in the USA alone. In 1998 the Internet generated $301 billion in revenue, according to a report released in June 1999 by researchers at the University of Texas, USA. The Internet also created 1.2 million jobs in 1998.

**Interpol** acronym for *International Criminal Police Organization*, agency founded following the Second International Judicial Police Conference in 1923 with its headquarters in Vienna, and reconstituted after World War II with its headquarters in Paris. It has an international criminal register, fingerprint file, and methods index.

**intestine** in vertebrates, the digestive tract from the stomach outlet to the anus. The human *small intestine* is 6 m/20 ft long, 4 cm/1.5 in in diameter, and consists of the duodenum, jejunum, and ileum; the *large intestine* is 1.5 m/5 ft long, 6 cm/2.5 in in diameter, and includes the caecum, colon, and rectum. Both are muscular tubes comprising an inner lining that secretes alkaline digestive juice, a submucous coat containing fine blood vessels and nerves, a muscular coat, and a serous coat covering all, supported by a strong peritoneum, which carries the blood and lymph vessels, and the nerves. The contents are passed along slowly by ◊peristalsis (waves of involuntary muscular action). The term intestine is also applied to the lower digestive tract of invertebrates.

**Intifada** (Arabic 'resurgence' or 'throwing off') Palestinian uprising; also the title of the involved *Liberation Army of Palestine*, a loosely organized group of adult and teenage Palestinians active 1987–93 in attacks on armed Israeli troops in the occupied territories of Palestine. Their campaign for self-determination included stone-throwing and petrol bombing. The 1993 peace accord between Israel and the Palestine Liberation Organization effectively liberated the occupied territories of Gaza and Jericho. However, extremist groups that had participated in the Intifada, notably the militant wing of the Hamas fundamentalist group, opposed the accord and continued a campaign of violence within Israel. Tensions around Jerusalem and the West Bank town of Hebron in October 1996 threatened to provoke a renewal of the Intifada.

**intrauterine device** (IUD) or *coil*, a contraceptive device that is inserted into the womb (uterus). It is a tiny plastic object, sometimes containing copper. By causing a mild inflammation of the lining of the uterus it prevents fertilized eggs from becoming implanted.

**introversion** in psychology, preoccupation with the self, generally coupled with a lack of sociability. The opposite of introversion is ◊extroversion.

**intrusion** mass of ◊igneous rock that has formed by 'injection' of molten rock, or magma, into existing cracks beneath the surface of the Earth, as distinct from a volcanic rock mass which has erupted from the surface. Intrusion features include vertical cylindrical structures such as stocks, pipes, and necks; sheet structures such as dykes that cut across the strata and sills that push between them; laccoliths, which are blisters that push up the overlying rock; and batholiths, which represent chambers of solidified magma and contain vast volumes of rock.

**intrusive rock** ◊igneous rock formed beneath the Earth's surface. Magma, or molten rock, cools slowly at these depths to form coarse-grained rocks, such as granite, with large crystals. (◊Extrusive rocks, which are formed on the surface, are usually fine-grained.) A mass of intrusive rock is called an intrusion.

**Inuit** (*inuk* 'a man') member of a people inhabiting the Arctic coasts of Alaska, the eastern islands of the Canadian Arctic, Labrador, and the ice-free coasts of Greenland. Until recent times there was a remarkable homogeneity in culture throughout this area, which traditionally relied on fish, sea mammals, and land animals for food, heat, light, clothing, tools, and shelter. The total number of Inuit (1993 est) is 125,000.

**Inverclyde** unitary authority in western Scotland, created in 1996 from Inverclyde district in Strathclyde region
*area* 161 sq km/62 sq mi
*towns* Greenock (administrative headquarters), Port Glasgow, Gourock
*physical* coastal lowland on the Firth of Clyde estuary, rising sharply to an inland plateau of 305 m/1,000 ft
*features* Inverkip Marina
*industries* electronics
*population* (1996) 90,000
*history* key part in the industrial history of Scotland as a port and a heavy engineering centre.

**Inverness** main town in, and the administrative centre of, ◊Highland unitary authority, Scotland, at the head of the Moray Firth, lying in a sheltered site at the mouth of the River Ness; population (1991) 41,200. It is a tourist centre with tanning, oil-related engineering, distilling, and electronics industries. Culloden Moor, scene of the massacre of clansmen loyal to Charles Edward Stuart by the English Army in April 1746, is situated to the east of Inverness.

**invertebrate** animal without a backbone. The invertebrates form all of the major divisions of the animal kingdom called phyla, with the exception of vertebrates. Invertebrates include the sponges, coelenterates, flatworms, nematodes, annelids, arthropods, molluscs, and echinoderms. Primitive aquatic chordates such as sea squirts and lancelets, which only have notochords and do not possess a vertebral column of cartilage or bone, are sometimes called invertebrate chordates, but this is misleading, since the notochord is the precursor of the backbone in advanced chordates.

**investment** in economics, the purchase of any asset with the potential to yield future financial benefit to the purchaser (such as a house, a work of art, stocks and shares, or even a private education).

**investment trust** public company that makes investments in other companies on behalf of its shareholders. It may issue shares to raise capital and issue fixed interest securities.

**in vitro fertilization** IVF; 'fertilization in glass', allowing eggs and sperm to unite in a laboratory to form embryos. The embryos (properly called pre-embryos) in their two- to eight-celled state) are stored by cooling to the temperature of liquid air (cryopreservation) until they are implanted into the womb of the otherwise infertile mother (an extension of ◊artificial insemination). The first baby to be produced by this method was born in 1978 in the UK. In cases where the Fallopian tubes are blocked, fertilization may be carried out by *intra-vaginal culture,* in which egg and sperm are incubated (in a plastic tube) in the mother's vagina, then transferred surgically into the uterus.

**iodide** compound formed between iodine and another element in which the iodine is the more electronegative element.

**iodine** (Greek *iodes* 'violet') greyish-black nonmetallic element, symbol I, atomic number 53, relative atomic mass 126.9044. It is a member of the ◊halogen group. Its crystals give off, when heated, a violet vapour with an irritating odour resembling that of chlorine. It only occurs in combination with other elements. Its salts are known as iodides, which are found in sea water. As a mineral nutrient it is vital to the proper functioning of the thyroid gland, where it occurs in trace amounts as part of the hormone thyroxine. Absence of iodine from the diet leads to ◊goitre. Iodine is used in photography, in medicine as an antiseptic, and in making dyes.

**IOM** abbreviation for *Isle of* ◊*Man,* an island in the Irish Sea.

**ion** atom, or group of atoms, that is either positively charged (◊cation) or negatively charged (◊anion), as a result of the loss or gain of electrons during chemical reactions or exposure to

certain forms of radiation. In solution or in the molten state, ionic compounds such as salts, acids, alkalis, and metal oxides conduct electricity. These compounds are known as electrolytes.

**Iona** island in the Inner Hebrides; area 850 hectares/2,100 acres. A centre of early Christianity, it is the site of a monastery founded 563 by St ◊Columba. It later became a burial ground for Irish, Scottish, and Norwegian kings. It has a 13th-century abbey.

**Ionesco, Eugène** (1912–1994) Romanian-born French dramatist. He was a leading exponent of the Theatre of the ◊Absurd. Most of his plays are in one act and concern the futility of language as a means of communication. These include *La Cantatrice chauve/The Bald Prima Donna* (1950) and *La Leçon/The Lesson* (1951). Later full-length plays include *Le Rhinocéros* (1958) and *Le Roi se meurt/Exit the King* (1961).

**Ionian** member of a Hellenic people from beyond the Black Sea who crossed the Balkans around 1980 BC and invaded Asia Minor. Driven back by the ◊Hittites, they settled all over mainland Greece, later being supplanted by the Achaeans.

**Ionian Sea** part of the Mediterranean Sea that lies between Italy and Greece, to the south of the Adriatic Sea, and containing the Ionian Islands.

**ionic bond** or *electrovalent bond,* bond produced when atoms of one element donate electrons to atoms of another element, forming positively and negatively charged ◊ions respectively. The attraction between the oppositely charged ions constitutes the bond. Sodium chloride ($Na^+Cl^-$) is a typical ionic compound.

**ionic compound** substance composed of oppositely charged ions. All salts, most bases, and some acids are examples of ionic compounds. They possess the following general properties: they are crystalline solids with a high melting point; are soluble in water and insoluble in organic solvents; and always conduct electricity when molten or in aqueous solution. A typical ionic compound is sodium chloride ($Na^+Cl^-$).

**ionosphere** ionized layer of Earth's outer ◊atmosphere (60–1,000 km/38–620 mi) that contains sufficient free electrons to modify the way in which radio waves are propagated, for instance by reflecting them back to Earth. The ionosphere is thought to be produced by absorption of the Sun's ultraviolet radiation.

The British Antarctic Survey estimates that the ionosphere is decreasing at a rate of 1 km/0.6 mi every five years, based on an analysis of data from 1960 to 1998. Global warming is the probable cause.

**IOW** abbreviation for *Isle of* ◊*Wight,* an island and unitary authority off the coast of southern England.

**Iowa** state of the midwest USA. It is nicknamed Hawkeye State. Iowa was admitted to the Union in 1846 as the 29th US state. It is a major constituent of the US Corn Belt, with grain and cereal crops and livestock-rearing historically comprising a significant proportion of

the state's income. Iowa is bordered to the south by Missouri, to the west by Nebraska and South Dakota, to the north by Minnesota, and to the east by Wisconsin and Illinois, with the Mississippi River forming the state boundary
**population** (1995) 2,841,800
**area** 145,800 sq km/56,279 sq mi
**capital** Des Moines
**towns and cities** Cedar Rapids, Davenport, Sioux City, Waterloo
**industries and products** cereals, soybeans, grasses and grains, pigs and cattle, poultry, dairy farming, chemicals, farm machinery, electrical goods, hardwood lumber, minerals, finance and insurance sectors.

**IQ** abbreviation for intelligence quotient, the ratio between a subject's 'mental' and chronological ages, multiplied by 100. A score of 100 ± 10 in an intelligence test is considered average.

**IRA** abbreviation for ◊*Irish Republican Army.*

**Iran** Islamic Republic of (formerly *Persia)*
**national name** *Jomhori-e-Islami-e-Irân*

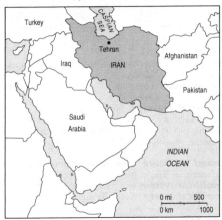

**area** 1,648,000 sq km/636,292 sq mi
**capital** Tehran
**major towns/cities** Esfahan, Mashhad, Tabriz, Shiraz, Ahvaz, Bakhtaran, Qom, Kara
**major ports** Abadan
**physical features** plateau surrounded by mountains, including Elburz and Zagros; Lake Rezayeh; Dasht-e-Kavir desert; occupies islands of Abu Musa, Greater Tunb and Lesser Tunb in the Gulf
**head of state and government** Seyyed Mohammad Khatami from 1997
**leader of the Islamic Revolution** Seyed Ali Khamenei from 1989
**political system** authoritarian Islamic republic
**political parties** none officially recognized
**currency** rial
**GNP per capita (PPP)** (US$) 3,920 (1998 est)
**exports** crude petroleum and petroleum products, agricultural goods, carpets, metal ores. Principal market: Japan 15.1% (1997)
**population** 66,796,000 (1999 est)
**language** Farsi (official), Kurdish, Turkish, Arabic, English, French

**religion** Shiite Muslim (official) 94%, Sunni Muslim, Zoroastrian, Christian, Jewish, Baha'i
**life expectancy** 69 (men); 70 (women) (1995–2000)
**Chronology**
**c. 2000 BC** Migration from southern Russia of Aryans, from whom Persians claim descent.
**612 BC** The Medes, from northwest Iran, destroyed Iraq-based Assyrian Empire to the west and established their own empire which extended into central Anatolia (Turkey-in-Asia).
**550 BC** Cyrus the Great overthrew Medes' empire and founded First Persian Empire, the Achaemenid, conquering much of Asia Minor, including Babylonia (Palestine and Syria) in 539 BC. Expansion continued into Afghanistan under Darius I, who ruled 521–486 BC.
**499–449 BC** The Persian Wars with Greece ended Persian domination of the ancient world.
**330 BC** Collapse of Achaemenid Empire following defeat by Alexander the Great of Macedon.
**AD 224** Sassanian Persian Empire founded by Ardashir, with its capital at Ctesiphon, in the northeast.
**637** Sassanian Empire destroyed by Muslim Arabs at battle of Qadisiya; Islam replaced Zoroastrianism.
**750–1258** Dominated by the Persianized Abbasid dynasty, who reigned as caliphs (Islamic civil and religious leaders), with a capital in Baghdad (Iraq).
**1380s** Conquered by the Mongol leader, Tamerlane.
**1501** Emergence of Safavids; the arts and architecture flourished, particularly under Abbas I, 'the Great', who ruled 1588–1629.
**1736** The Safavids were deposed by the warrior Nadir Shah Afshar, who ruled until 1747.
**1790** Rise of the Qajars, who transferred the capital from Esfahan in central Iran to Tehran, further north.
**19th century** Increasing influence in the north of tsarist Russia, which took Georgia and much of Armenia 1801–28. Britain exercised influence in the south and east, and fought Iran 1856–57 over claims to Herat (western Afghanistan).
**1906** Parliamentary constitution adopted after a brief revolution.
**1925** Weak and corrupt Qajar dynasty overthrown, with some British official help, in a coup by Col Reza Khan, a nationalist Iranian Cossack military officer, who was crowned shah ('king of kings'), with the title Reza Shah Pahlavi.
**1920s onwards** Economic modernization, Westernization, and secularization programme launched, which proved unpoular with traditionalist elements.
**1935** Name changed from Persia to Iran.
**1941** Owing to his pro-German sentiments, Pahlavi Shah was forced to abdicate during World War II by Allied occupation forces and was succeeded by his son Mohammad Reza Pahlavi, who continued the modernization programme.
**1946** British, US, and Soviet occupation forces left Iran.
**1951** Oilfields nationalized by radical prime minister Muhammad Mossadeq as anti-British and US sentiment increased.

**1953** Mossadeq deposed, the nationalization plan changed, and the US-backed shah, Muhammad Reza Shah Pahlavi, took full control of the government.

**1963** Hundreds of protesters, who demanded the release of the arrested fundamentalist Shiite Muslim leader Ayatollah Ruhollah Khomeini, were killed by troops.

**1970s** Spiralling world oil prices brought rapid economic expansion.

**1975** The shah introduced a single-party system.

**1977** The mysterious death in An Najaf of Mustafa, eldest son of the exiled Ayatollah Ruhollah Khomeini, sparked demonstrations by theology students, which were suppressed with the loss of six lives.

**1978** Opposition to the Shah was organized from France by Ayatollah Ruhollah Khomeini, who demanded a return to the principles of Islam. Hundreds of demonstrators were killed by troops in Jaleh Square, Tehran.

**1979** Amid mounting demonstrations by students and clerics, the shah left the country; Khomeini returned to create a nonparty theocratic Islamic state. Revolutionaries seized 66 US hostages at embassy in Tehran; US economic boycott.

**1980** Iraq invaded Iran, provoking a bitter war. The exiled shah died.

**1981** US hostages were released.

**1985–87** Fighting intensified in the Iran–Iraq War, with heavy loss of life.

**1988** There was a ceasefire in the war and talks with Iraq began.

**1989** Khomeini issued a fatwa (public order) for the death of British writer Salman Rushdie for blasphemy against Islam. On Khomeini's death, Ayatollah Ali Khamenei was elected interim Leader of the Revolution; and the speaker of Iranian parliament Hashemi Rafsanjani was elected president.

**1990** Generous peace terms with Iraq were accepted to close the Iran–Iraq war.

**1991** Nearly 1 million Kurds arrived from northwest Iraq, fleeing persecution by Saddam Hussein after the Gulf War between Iraq and UN forces.

**1993** President Rafsanjani re-elected, but with a smaller margin; free-market economic reforms were introduced.

**1996** Rafsanjani supporters won assembly elections.

**1997** Moderate politician Seyyed Mohammad Khatami was elected president.

**1998** There were signs of rapprochement with the West. There was increased tension with Afghanistan, after the murder of Iranian civilians by the Talibaan.

**1999** Diplomatic relations with the UK were to be restored.

**Irangate** US political scandal 1987 involving senior members of the Reagan administration (the name echoes the Nixon administration's ◊Watergate). Congressional hearings in 1986–87 revealed that the US government had secretly sold weapons to Iran in 1985 and traded them for hostages held in Lebanon by pro-Iranian militias, and used the profits to supply right-wing Contra guerrillas in Nicaragua with arms. The attempt to get around the law (Boland amendment) specifically prohibiting military assistance to the Contras also broke other laws in the process.

**Iraq** Republic of
**national name** al Jumhouriya al `Iraqia

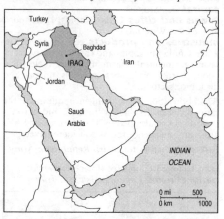

**area** 434,924 sq km/167,924 sq mi
**capital** Baghdad
**major towns/cities** Mosul, Basra, Kirkuk, Hilla, Najaf, Nasiriya
**major ports** Basra and Um Qass closed from 1980
**physical features** mountains in north, desert in west; wide valley of rivers Tigris and Euphrates running northwest–southeast; canal linking Baghdad and Persian Gulf opened in 1992
**head of state and government** Saddam Hussein al-Tikriti from 1979
**political system** one-party socialist republic
**political party** Arab Ba'ath Socialist Party, nationalist socialist
**currency** Iraqi dinar
**GNP per capita (PPP)** (US$) N/A
**exports** crude petroleum (accounting for more than 98% of total export earnings (1980–89), dates and other dried fruits. Principal market: Jordan 95% (1995)
**population** 22,450,000 (1999 est)
**language** Arabic (official); Kurdish, Assyrian, Armenian
**religion** Shiite Muslim 60%, Sunni Muslim 37%, Christian 3%
**life expectancy** 61 (men); 64 (women) (1995–2000)
**Chronology**
**c. 3400 BC** The world's oldest civilization, the Sumerian, arose in the land between the rivers Euphrates and Tigris, known as lower Mesopotamia, which lies in the heart of modern Iraq. Its cities included Lagash, Eridu, Uruk, Kish, and Ur.
**c. 2350 BC** The confederation of Sumerian city-states was forged into an empire by the Akkadian leader Sargon.
**7th century BC** In northern Mesopotamia, the Assyrian Empire, based around the River Tigris and formerly dominated by Sumeria and Euphrates-centred Babylonia, created a vast empire covering much of the Middle East.

**612 BC** The Assyrian capital of Nineveh was destroyed by Babylon and Mede (in northwest Iran).

**c. 550 BC** Mesopotamia came under Persian control.

**AD 114** Conquered by the Romans.

**266** Came under the rule of the Persian-based Sassanians.

**637** Sassanian Empire destroyed by Muslim Arabs at battle of Qadisiya, in southern Iraq; Islam spread.

**750–1258** Dominated by Abbasid dynasty, who reigned as caliphs (Islamic civil and religious leaders) in Baghdad.

**1258** Baghdad invaded and burned by Tatars.

**1401** Baghdad destroyed by Mongol ruler Tamerlane.

**1533** Annexed by Suleiman the Magnificent, becoming part of the Ottoman Empire until the 20th century, despite recurrent anti-Ottoman insurrections.

**1916** Occupied by Britain during World War I.

**1920** Iraq became a British League of Nations protectorate.

**1921** Hashemite dynasty established, with Faisal I installed by Britain as king.

**1932** Independence achieved from British protectorate status, with Gen Nuri-el Said as prime minister.

**1941–45** Occupied by Britain during World War II.

**1955** Signed the Baghdad Pact collective security treaty with the UK, Iran, Pakistan, and Turkey.

**1958** Monarchy overthrown in military-led revolution, in which King Faisal was assassinated; Iraq became a republic; joined Jordan in an Arab Federation; withdrew from Baghdad Pact as left-wing military regime assumed power.

**1963** Joint socialist-nationalist Ba'athist-military coup headed by Col Salem Aref and backed by US Central Intelligence Agency; reign of terror launched against the left.

**1968** Ba'athist military coup put Maj-Gen Ahmed Hassan al-Bakr in power.

**1979** Al-Bakr was replaced by Saddam Hussein of the Arab Ba'ath Socialist Party.

**1980** The war between Iraq and Iran broke out.

**1985–87** Fighting in the Iran–Iraq war intensified, with heavy loss of life.

**1988** There was a ceasefire and talks began with Iran. Iraq used chemical weapons against Kurdish rebels seeking greater autonomy in the northwest.

**1989** There was an unsuccessful coup against President Hussein; Iraq successfully launched a ballistic test missile.

**1990** A peace treaty favouring Iran was agreed. Iraq invaded and annexed Kuwait in August. US forces massed in Saudi Arabia at the request of King Fahd. The United Nations (UN) ordered Iraqi withdrawal and imposed total trade ban; further UN resolution sanctioned the use of force. All foreign hostages were released.

**1991** US-led Allied forces launched an aerial assault on Iraq and destroyed the country's infrastructure; a land–sea–air offensive to free Kuwait was successful. Uprisings of Kurds and Shiites were brutally suppressed by surviving Iraqi troops. Allied troops established 'safe havens' for Kurds in the north prior to the withdrawal, and left a rapid-reaction force near the Turkish border.

**1992** The UN imposed a 'no-fly zone' over southern Iraq to protect Shiites.

**1993** Iraqi incursions into the 'no-fly zone' prompted US-led alliance aircraft to bomb strategic targets in Iraq. There was continued persecution of Shiites in the south.

**1994** Iraq renounced its claim to Kuwait, but failed to fulfil the other conditions required for the lifting of UN sanctions.

**1995** The uncontested Hussein was elected in a closely monitored presidential election.

**1996** Iraqi-backed attacks on Kurds prompted US retaliation; these air strikes destroyed Iraqi military bases in the south.

**1997** Iraq continued to resist the US and Allied pressure to allow UN weapons inspections.

**1998** Iraq expelled UN weapons inspectors, provoking a build-up of US military strength in the Gulf. Military conflict was averted by an agreement secured by the UN secretary-general Kofi Annan. In April the UN inspectors' report showed that Iraq had failed to meet UN requirements on the destruction of chemical and biological weapons. In December US and UK forces launched Operation Desert Fox which lasted four days; there were further clashes between US–UK forces and Baghdad over the no-fly zone.

**1999** January: There were further clashes between US–UK forces and Baghdad over the no-fly zone. February: US–UK air strikes resumed. June: UK suggested the lifting of sanctions if Iraq resumed cooperation with the UN.

**Irbil** or **Arbil**, Kurdish capital city, in a governorate of the same name in northern Iraq; population (1987) 486,000. Occupied since Assyrian times, it was the site of a battle in 331 BC at which Alexander the Great defeated the Persians under Darius III. In 1974 Irbil became the capital of a Kurdish autonomous region set up by the Iraqi government. It was captured by the Kurdish Democratic Party in 1996 with the help of Saddam Hussein.

**Ireland** one of the British Isles, lying to the west of Great Britain, from which it is separated by the Irish Sea. It comprises the provinces of Ulster, Leinster, Munster, and Connacht, and is divided into the Republic of Ireland (which occupies the south, centre, and northwest of the island) and Northern Ireland (which occupies the northeastern corner and forms part of the United Kingdom).

## Ireland, Republic of

**national name** *Eire*

**area** 70,282 sq km/27,135 sq mi

**capital** Dublin

**major towns/cities** Cork, Limerick, Galway, Waterford, Wexford

**major ports** Cork, Dun Laoghaire, Limerick, Waterford, Galway

**physical features** central plateau surrounded by hills; rivers Shannon, Liffey, Boyne; Bog of Allen; Macgillicuddy's Reeks, Wicklow

Mountains; Lough Corrib, lakes of Killarney; Galway Bay and Aran Islands
**head of state** Mary McAleese from 1997
**head of government** Bertie Ahern from 1997
**political system** democracy
**political parties** Fianna Fáil (Soldiers of Destiny), moderate centre right; Fine Gael (Irish Tribe or United Ireland Party), moderate centre left; Labour Party, moderate left of centre; Progressive Democrats, radical free-enterprise
**currency** Irish pound (punt Eireannach)
**GNP per capita (PPP)** (US$) 18,340 (1998)
**exports** beef and dairy products, live animals, machinery and transport equipment, electronic goods, chemicals. Principal market: UK 22.2% (1998)
**population** 3,705,000 (1999 est)
**language** Irish Gaelic and English (both official)
**religion** Roman Catholic 95%, Church of Ireland, other Protestant denominations
**life expectancy** 74 (men); 79 (women) (1995–2000)
**Chronology**
**3rd century BC** The Gaels, a Celtic people, invaded Ireland and formed about 150 small kingdoms.
**AD c. 432** St Patrick introduced Christianity.
**5th–9th centuries** Irish Church remained a centre of culture and scholarship.
**9th–11th centuries** The Vikings raided Ireland until defeated by High King Brian Boru at Clontarf in 1014.
**12th–13th centuries** Anglo-Norman adventurers conquered much of Ireland, but no central government was formed and many became assimilated.
**14th–15th centuries** Irish chieftains recovered their lands, restricting English rule to the Pale around Dublin.
**1536** Henry VIII of England made ineffectual efforts to impose the Protestant Reformation on Ireland.
**1541** Irish Parliament recognized Henry VIII as king of Ireland; Henry gave peerages to Irish chieftains.
**1579** English suppressed Desmond rebellion,

confiscated rebel lands, and tried to 'plant' them with English settlers.
**1610** James I established plantation of Ulster with Protestant settlers from England and Scotland.
**1641** Catholic Irish rebelled against English rule; Oliver Cromwell brutally reasserted English control 1649–50; Irish landowners evicted and replaced with English landowners.
**1689–91** Williamite War: following the 'Glorious Revolution', the Catholic Irish unsuccessfully supported James II against Protestant William III in civil war. Penal laws barred Catholics from obtaining wealth and power.
**1720** Act passed declaring British Parliament's right to legislate for Ireland.
**1739–41** Famine killed one-third of population of 1.5 million.
**1782** Protestant landlords led by Henry Grattan secured end of restrictions on Irish trade and parliament.
**1798** British suppressed revolt by Society of United Irishmen (with French support) led by Wolfe Tone.
**1800** Act of Union abolished Irish parliament and created United Kingdom of Great Britain and Ireland, effective 1801.
**1829** Daniel O'Connell secured Catholic Emancipation Act, which permitted Catholics to enter parliament.
**1846–51** Potato famine reduced population by 20% through starvation and emigration.
**1870** Land Act increased security for tenants but failed to halt agrarian disorder; Isaac Butt formed political party to campaign for Irish Home Rule (devolution).
**1885** Home Rulers, led by Charles Stewart Parnell, held balance of power in parliament; first Home Rule Bill rejected 1886; second Home Rule Bill defeated in 1893.
**1905** Arthur Griffith founded the nationalist movement Sinn Féin ('Ourselves Alone').
**1914** Ireland came close to civil war as Ulster prepared to resist implementation of Home Rule Act (postponed because of World War I).
**1916** Easter Rising: nationalists proclaimed a republic in Dublin; British crushed revolt and executed 15 leaders.
**1919** Sinn Fein MPs formed Irish parliament in Dublin in defiance of British government.
**1919–21** Irish Republican Army (IRA) waged guerrilla war against British forces.
**1921** Anglo-Irish Treaty partitioned Ireland; northern Ireland (Ulster) remained part of the United Kingdom; southern Ireland won full internal self-government with dominion status.
**1922** Irish Free State proclaimed; IRA split over Anglo-Irish Treaty led to civil war 1922–23.
**1932** Anti-Treaty party, Fianna Fáil, came to power under Éamonn de Valéra.
**1937** New constitution established Eire (Gaelic name for Ireland) as a sovereign state and refused to acknowledge partition.
**1949** After remaining neutral in World War II, Eire left the Commonwealth and became the Republic of Ireland.
**1973** Ireland joined European Economic Community.

**1985** The Anglo-Irish Agreement gave the Republic of Ireland a consultative role, but no powers, in the government of Northern Ireland.
**1990** Mary Robinson became the first woman president of Ireland.
**1993** The Downing Street Declaration, a joint Anglo-Irish peace proposal for Northern Ireland, was issued.
**1998** A historic multiparty agreement (the Good Friday Agreement) was reached on the future of Northern Ireland. The subsequent referendum showed a large majority in favour of dropping Ireland's claim to the North. Strict legislation was passed against terrorism.

**Irian Jaya** western portion of the island of New Guinea, province of Indonesia
*area* 420,000 sq km/162,000 sq mi
*capital* Jayapura
*industries* copper, palm oil
*population* (1990) 1,648,700
*history* part of the Dutch East Indies 1828 as Western New Guinea; retained by the Netherlands after Indonesian independence 1949 but ceded to Indonesia 1963 by the United Nations and remained part of Indonesia by an 'Act of Free Choice' 1969. In the 1980s, 283,500 hectares/700,000 acres were given over to Indonesia's controversial transmigration programme for the resettlement of farming families from overcrowded Java, causing destruction of rainforests and displacing indigenous people. In 1989 Indonesia began construction of a space launching pad on the island of Biak, near the Equator, where the Earth's atmosphere is least thick. In May 1998 Indonesian officials found two new tribes in Irian Jaya. The tribes, known as Vahudate and Aukedate, communicate using sign language, and consist of 33 and 20 families respectively.

**iridium** (Latin *iridis* 'rainbow') hard, brittle, silver-white, metallic element, symbol Ir, atomic number 77, relative atomic mass 192.2. It is resistant to tarnish and corrosion. Iridium is one of the so-called platinum group of metals; it occurs in platinum ores and as a free metal (native metal) with osmium in osmiridium, a natural alloy that includes platinum, ruthenium, and rhodium.

**iris** in anatomy, the coloured muscular diaphragm that controls the size of the pupil in the vertebrate eye. It contains radial muscle that increases the pupil diameter and circular muscle that constricts the pupil diameter. Both types of muscle respond involuntarily to light intensity.

**iris** in botany, any of a group of perennial northern temperate flowering plants belonging to the iris family. The leaves are usually sword-shaped; the purple, white, or yellow flowers have three upright inner petals and three outward- and downward-curving ◊sepals. The wild yellow iris is called a flag. (Genus *Iris*, family Iridaceae.)

**Irish Gaelic** first official language of the Irish Republic, but much less widely used than the second official language, English. See ◊Gaelic language.

**Irish National Liberation Army** (INLA), guerrilla organization committed to the end of British rule in Northern Ireland and the incorporation of Ulster into the Irish Republic. The INLA was a 1974 offshoot of the Irish Republican Army (IRA). Among the INLA's activities was the killing of British politician Airey Neave in 1979. The INLA refused to participate in the August 1994 ceasefire declared by Sinn Fein, the political wing of the Irish Republican Army, but in April 1995 announced that it was renouncing the use of violence.
The group's leader, Gino Gallagher, was shot and killed in Belfast in January 1996, allegedly by feuding INLA members. The INLA carried out bomb attacks in London in 1998.

**Irish Republican Army** (IRA), militant Irish nationalist organization formed in 1919, the paramilitary wing of ◊Sinn Féin. Its aim is to create a united Irish socialist republic including Ulster. To this end, the IRA habitually carries out bombings and shootings. Despite its close association with Sinn Féin, it is not certain that the politicians have direct control of the military, the IRA usually speaking as a separate, independent organization. The chief common factor shared by Sinn Féin and the IRA is the aim of a united Ireland.

**Irkutsk** city in southern Siberian Russia, capital of Irkutsk oblast; population (1990) 635,000. Irkutsk is situated near Lake Baikal on the River Angara; there is a large hydroelectric station near the city. Coal is mined here, while manufactured goods include iron, steel, motor vehicles, and machine tools. Its industrial development dates from the arrival of the Trans-Siberian railway in 1898.

**iron** (Germanic *eis* 'strong') hard, malleable and ductile, silver-grey, metallic element, symbol Fe (from Latin *ferrum*), atomic number 26, relative atomic mass 55.847. It is the fourth most abundant element (the second most abundant metal, after aluminium) in the Earth's crust. Iron occurs in concentrated deposits as the ores hematite ($Fe_2O_3$), spathic ore ($FeCO_3$), and magnetite ($Fe_3O_4$). It sometimes occurs as a free metal, occasionally as fragments of iron or iron–nickel meteorites.

**Iron Age** developmental stage of human technology when weapons and tools were made from iron. Preceded by the Stone and Bronze ages, it is the last technological stage in the Three Age System framework for prehistory. Iron was produced in Thailand about 1600 BC, but was considered inferior in strength to bronze until about 1000 BC, when metallurgical techniques improved, and the alloy steel was produced by adding carbon during the smelting process.

**Iron Curtain** in Europe after World War II, the symbolic boundary between capitalist West and communist East during the ◊Cold War. The term was popularized by the UK prime minister Winston Churchill from 1945.

**iron pyrites** or *pyrite* ($FeS_2$), common iron ore. Brassy yellow, and occurring in cubic crystals, it is often called 'fool's gold', since only those who have never seen gold would mistake it.

**Irrawaddy** Myanmar *Ayeryarwady*, chief river of Myanmar (Burma), flowing roughly north–south for 2,090 km/1,300 mi across the centre of the country into the Bay of Bengal. Its sources are the Mali and N'mai rivers; its chief tributaries are the Chindwin and Shweli.

**irrigation** artificial water supply for dry agricultural areas by means of dams and channels. Drawbacks are that it tends to concentrate salts at the surface, ultimately causing soil infertility, and that rich river silt is retained at dams, to the impoverishment of the land and fisheries below them.

**Irving, Henry** stage name of John Henry Brodribb (1838–1905) English actor. He established his reputation from 1871, chiefly at the Lyceum Theatre in London, where he became manager in 1878. He staged a series of successful Shakespearean productions, including *Romeo and Juliet* (1882), with himself and Ellen Terry playing the leading roles. He was the first actor to be knighted, in 1895.

**Isaiah** (lived 8th century BC) in the Old Testament, the first major Hebrew prophet. The Book of Isaiah in the Old Testament was traditionally believed to be written by him, but it is now thought that large parts of it are the work of at least two other writers.

**ISBN** abbreviation for International Standard Book Number, code number used for ordering or classifying book titles. Every book printed now has a number on its back cover or jacket, preceded by the letters ISBN. It is a code to the country of origin and the publisher. The number is unique to the book, and will identify it anywhere in the world.

**ISDN** abbreviation for ◊Integrated Services Digital Network, a telecommunications system.

**Isherwood, Christopher (William Bradshaw)** (1904–1986) English novelist. He lived in Germany from 1929–33 just before Hitler's rise to power, a period that inspired *Mr Norris Changes Trains* (1935) and *Goodbye to Berlin* (1939), creating the character of Sally Bowles, the basis of the musical *Cabaret* (1968). Returning to England, he collaborated with W H ◊Auden in three verse plays.

**Ishiguro, Kazuo** (1954– ) Japanese-born British novelist. His novel *An Artist of the Floating World* won the 1986 Whitbread Prize, and *The Remains of the Day*, about an English butler coming to realize the extent of his self-sacrifice and self-deception, won the 1989 Booker Prize and was made into a successful film in 1993. His work is characterized by a sensitive style and subtle structure.

**Ishmael** in the Old Testament, the son of ◊Abraham and his wife Sarah's Egyptian maid Hagar; traditional ancestor of Muhammad and the Arab people. He and his mother were driven away by Sarah's jealousy. Muslims believe that it was Ishmael, not Isaac, whom God commanded Abraham to sacrifice, and that Ishmael helped Abraham build the Kaaba in Mecca.

**Ishtar** or *Istar,* Mesopotamian goddess of fertility, sexual love, wedlock, maternity, and war, worshipped by the Babylonians and Assyrians, and personified as the legendary queen Semiramis. She was the equivalent of the Canaanite and Syrian Astarte.

**Isis** (Ancient Egyptian 'seat') principal goddess of ancient Egypt; the daughter of Geb and Nut (Earth and Sky); and the personification of the throne of her brother-husband ◊Osiris. She searched for the body of Osiris after he was murdered by his brother, Set. Her son, the sky god ◊Horus, defeated and captured Set, but beheaded his mother because she would not allow Set to be killed. She was later identified with Hathor, and by the Greeks with ◊Demeter, goddess of agriculture, and Zeus' lover Io.

**Islam** (Arabic 'submission', that is, to the will of Allah) religion founded in the Arabian peninsula in the early AD 600s. It emphasizes the oneness of God, his omnipotence, beneficence, and inscrutability. Its sacred book is the *Koran,* which Muslims believe was divinely revealed to ◊Muhammad, the prophet or messenger of Allah. There are two main Muslim sects: ◊*Sunni* and ◊*Shiite.* Others include *Sufism,* a mystical movement which originated in the AD 700s. The word Muslim means 'one who makes his peace with God and Man'.

**Islamabad** capital of Pakistan from 1967 (replacing Karachi), in the Potwar district, at the foot of the Margala Hills and immediately northwest of Rawalpindi; population (1981) 201,000. The city was designed by Constantinos Doxiadis in the 1960s. Landmarks include the Shahrazad Hotel and national Assembly Building. The Federal Capital Territory of Islamabad has an area of 907 sq km/350 sq mi and a population (1985) of 379,000.

**island** area of land surrounded entirely by water. Australia is classed as a continent rather than an island, because of its size.

**Isle of Man** see ◊Man, Isle of.

**Isle of Wight** see ◊Wight, Isle of.

**Ismail** (1830–1895) Khedive (governor) of Egypt 1866–79. A grandson of Mehmet Ali, he became viceroy of Egypt 1863 and in 1866 received the title of khedive from the Ottoman sultan. He amassed huge foreign debts and in 1875 Britain, at Prime Minister Disraeli's suggestion, bought the khedive's Suez Canal shares for nearly £4 million, establishing Anglo-French control of Egypt's finances. In 1879 the UK and France persuaded the sultan to appoint Tewfik, his son, khedive in his place.

**Ismail I** (1486–1524) Shah of Persia from 1501. He was the founder of the *Safavi dynasty,* and established the first national government since the Arab conquest and Shiite Islam as the national religion.

**isobar** line drawn on maps and weather charts linking all places with the same atmospheric pressure (usually measured in millibars).

When used in weather forecasting, the distance between the isobars is an indication of the barometric gradient (the rate of change in pressure).

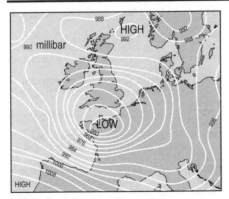

**isobar** *The isobars around a low-pressure area or depression. In the northern hemisphere, winds blow anticlockwise around lows, approximately parallel to the isobars, and clockwise around highs. In the southern hemisphere, the winds blow in the opposite directions.*

**isolationism** in politics, concentration on internal rather than foreign affairs; a foreign policy having no interest in international affairs that do not affect the country's own interests.

**Isolde** or *Iseult*, in Celtic and medieval legend, the wife of King Mark of Cornwall who was brought from Ireland by his nephew ◊Tristan. She and Tristan accidentally drank the aphrodisiac given to her by her mother for her marriage, were separated as lovers, and finally died together.

**isomer** chemical compound having the same molecular composition and mass as another, but with different physical or chemical properties owing to the different structural arrangement of its constituent atoms. For example, the organic compounds butane ($CH_3$ ($CH_2$)$_2CH_3$) and methyl propane ($CH_3CH(CH_3)CH_3$) are isomers, each possessing four carbon atoms and ten hydrogen atoms but differing in the way that these are arranged with respect to each other.

**isostasy** the theoretical balance in buoyancy of all parts of the Earth's crust, as though they were floating on a denser layer beneath. There are two theories of the mechanism of isostasy, the Airy hypothesis and the Pratt hypothesis, both of which have validity. In the *Airy hypothesis* crustal blocks have the same density but different depths: like ice cubes floating in water, higher mountains have deeper roots. In the *Pratt hypothesis,* crustal blocks have different densities allowing the depth of crustal material to be the same.

**isotope** one of two or more atoms that have the same atomic number (same number of protons), but which contain a different number of neutrons, thus differing in their atomic mass (see ◊relative atomic mass). They may be stable or radioactive (see ◊radioisotope), naturally occurring, or synthesized. For example, hydrogen has the isotopes $^2H$ (◊deuterium) and $^3H$ (◊tritium). The term was coined by English chemist Frederick Soddy, pioneer researcher in atomic disintegration.

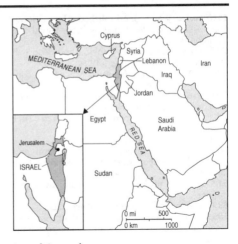

**Israel** State of
**national name** *Medinat Israel*
**area** 20,800 sq km/8,030 sq mi (as at 1949 armistice)
**capital** Jerusalem (not recognized by United Nations)
**major towns/cities** Tel Aviv-Yafo, Haifa, Bat-Yam, Holon, Ramat Gan, Petach Tikva, Rishon Leziyyon, Beersheba
**major ports** Tel Aviv-Yafo, Haifa, 'Akko (formerly Acre), Eilat
**physical features** coastal plain of Sharon between Haifa and Tel Aviv noted since ancient times for its fertility; central mountains of Galilee, Samaria, and Judea; Dead Sea, Lake Tiberias, and River Jordan Rift Valley along the east are below sea level; Negev Desert in the south; Israel occupies Golan Heights, West Bank, East Jerusalem, and Gaza Strip (the last was awarded limited autonomy, with West Bank town of Jericho, in 1993)
**head of state** Ezer Weizman from 1993
**head of government** Ehud Barak from 1999
**political system** democracy
**political parties** Israel Labour Party, moderate, left of centre; Consolidation Party (Likud), right of centre; Meretz (Vitality), left-of-centre alliance
**currency** shekel
**GNP per capita (PPP)** (US$) 17,310 (1997)
**exports** citrus fruits, worked diamonds, machinery and parts, military hardware, food products, chemical products, textiles and clothing. Principal market: USA 35.4% (1998)
**population** 6,101,000 (1999 est)
**language** Hebrew and Arabic (official); English, Yiddish, European and western Asian languages
**religion** Israel is a secular state, but the predominant faith is Judaism 85%; also Sunni Muslim, Christian, and Druze
**life expectancy** 76 (men); 80 (women) (1995–2000)
*Chronology*
*c. 2000 BC* Abraham, father of the Jewish people, is believed to have come to Palestine from Mesopotamia.
*c. 1225 BC* Moses led the Jews out of slavery in Egypt towards the promised land of Palestine.

**11th century BC** Saul established a Jewish kingdom in Palestine; developed by kings David and Solomon.

**586 BC** Jews defeated by Babylon and deported; many returned to Palestine 539 BC.

**333 BC** Alexander the Great of Macedonia conquered the entire region.

**3rd century BC** Control of Palestine contested by Ptolemies of Egypt and Seleucids of Syria.

**142 BC** Jewish independence restored after Maccabean revolt.

**63 BC** Palestine fell to Roman Empire.

**70 AD** Romans crushed Zealot rebellion and destroyed Jerusalem; start of dispersion of Jews (diaspora).

**614** Persians took Jerusalem from Byzantine Empire.

**637** Muslim Arabs conquered Palestine.

**1099** First Crusade captured Jerusalem; Christian kingdom lasted a century before falling to sultans of Egypt.

**1517** Palestine conquered by the Ottoman Turks.

**1897** Theodor Herzl organized the First Zionist Congress at Basel to publicize Jewish claims to Palestine.

**1917** The Balfour Declaration: Britain expressed support for the creation of a Jewish National Home in Palestine.

**1918** British forces expelled the Turks from Palestine, which became a British League of Nations mandate 1920.

**1929** Severe communal violence around Jerusalem caused by Arab alarm at doubling of Jewish population in ten years.

**1933** Jewish riots in protest at British attempts to restrict Jewish immigration.

**1937** The Peel Report, recommending partition, accepted by most Jews but rejected by Arabs; open warfare ensued 1937–38.

**1939** Britain postponed independence plans on account of World War II, and increased military presence.

**1946** Resumption of terrorist violence; Jewish extremists blew up British headquarters in Jerusalem.

**1947** United Nations (UN) voted for partition of Palestine.

**1948** Britain withdrew; Independent State of Israel proclaimed with David Ben-Gurion as prime minister; Israel repulsed invasion by Arab nations; many Palestinian Arabs settled in refugee camps in the Gaza Strip and West Bank.

**1952** Col Gamal Nasser of Egypt stepped up blockade of Israeli ports and support of Arab guerrillas in Gaza.

**1956** War between Israel and Egypt; Israeli invasion of Gaza and Sinai followed by withdrawal in 1957.

**1963** Levi Eshkol succeeded Ben-Gurion as prime minister.

**1964** Palestine Liberation Organization (PLO) founded to unite Palestinian Arabs with the aim of overthrowing the state of Israel.

**1967** Israel defeated Egypt, Syria, and Jordan in the Six-Day War; Gaza, West Bank, east Jerusalem, Sinai, and Golan Heights captured.

**1969** Golda Meir (Labour) elected prime minister; Yassir Arafat became chair of the PLO; escalation of terrorism and border raids.

**1973** Yom Kippur War: Israel repulsed surprise attack by Egypt and Syria.

**1974** Golda Meir succeeded by Yitzhak Rabin.

**1977** Right-wing Likud bloc took office under Menachem Begin; President Anwar Sadat of Egypt began peace initiative.

**1979** Camp David talks ended with signing of peace treaty between Israel and Egypt; Israel withdrew from Sinai.

**1980** United Jerusalem was declared the capital of Israel.

**1982** Israeli forces invaded southern Lebanon to drive out PLO guerrillas; occupation continued until 1985.

**1985** Labour and Likud formed a coalition government led by Shimon Peres 1985–86 and Yitzhak Shamir 1986–90.

**1988** The Israeli handling of Palestinian uprising (Intifada) in the occupied territories provoked international criticism.

**1990** Shamir headed the Likud government following the break-up of the coalition; PLO formally recognized the state of Israel.

**1991** Iraq launched missile attacks on Israel during the Gulf War; Middle East peace talks began in Madrid.

**1992** A Labour government was elected under Yitzhak Rabin.

**1993** Rabin and Arafat signed a peace accord; Israel granted limited autonomy to Gaza Strip and Jericho.

**1994** Arafat became the head of an autonomous Palestinian authority in Gaza and Jericho; a peace agreement was reached between Israel and Jordan.

**1995** Rabin was assassinated by a Jewish opponent of the peace accord; Peres became prime minister.

**1996** A Likud government was elected under Binjamin Netanyahu, a critic of the peace accord. A revival of communal violence was seen and the peace process was threatened. The opening of a 2,000-year-old tunnel near the Al-Aqsa mosque in Jerusalem provoked renewed Palestinian–Israeli conflict.

**1997** A Jewish settlement in east Jerusalem was widely condemned. There were suicide bombs by Hamas in Jerusalem. There was partial and limited withdrawal from the West Bank.

**1998** Violence flared on the West Bank between Palestinians and Israeli troops. Netanyahu demanded security guarantees from Palestinian Authorities and again the peace process stalled. A bomb exploded in Tel Aviv. The Wye Peace Agreement was signed with the PLO. A land-for-security deal was approved by the Knesset, and the promised Israeli withdrawal from the Lebanon was subsequently placed in doubt. President Clinton attempted to restart the peace process.

**1999** The South Lebanon 'security zone' was expanded. PLO leader Yasser Arafat delayed the declaration of an independent state until after the Israeli elections. In May, Labour Party candidate Ehud Barak was elected prime minister and restarted peace negotiations.

**Istanbul** city and chief seaport of Turkey; population (1990) urban area 6,407,200; city

6,293,400. It produces textiles, tobacco, cement, glass, and leather. Founded as *Byzantium* about 660 BC, it was renamed *Constantinople* AD 330 and was the capital of the ◊Byzantine Empire until captured by the Turks 1453. As *Istamboul* it was capital of the Ottoman Empire until 1922.

**IT** abbreviation for ◊*information technology.*

**Italy** Republic of
**national name** *Repubblica Italiana*

**area** 301,300 sq km/116,331 sq mi
**capital** Rome
**major towns/cities** Milan, Naples, Turin, Palermo, Genoa, Bologna
**major ports** Naples, Genoa, Palermo, Bari, Catania, Trieste
**physical features** mountainous (Maritime Alps, Dolomites, Apennines) with narrow coastal lowlands; continental Europe's only active volcanoes: Vesuvius, Etna, Stromboli; rivers Po, Adige, Arno, Tiber, Rubicon; islands of Sicily, Sardinia, Elba, Capri, Ischia, Lipari, Pantelleria; lakes Como, Maggiore, Garda
**head of state** Carlo Azeglio Ciampi from 1999
**head of government** Massimo d'Alema from 1998
**political system** democracy
**political parties** Forza Italia (Go Italy!), free market, right of centre; Northern League (LN), Milan-based, federalist, right of centre; National Alliance (AN), neofascist; Italian Popular Party (PPI), Catholic, centrist; Italian Renewal Party, centrist; Democratic Party of the Left (PDS), pro-European, moderate left wing (ex-communist); Italian Socialist Party (PSI), moderate socialist; Italian Republican Party (PRI), social democratic, left of centre; Democratic Alliance (AD), moderate left of centre; Christian Democratic Centre (CCD), Christian, centrist; Olive Tree alliance, centre left; Panella List, radical liberal; Union of the Democratic Centre (UDC), right of centre; Pact for Italy, reformist; Communist Refoundation (RC), Marxist; Verdi, environmentalist; La Rete (the Network), anti-Mafia

**currency** lira
**GNP per capita (PPP)** (US$) 20,200 (1998)
**exports** machinery and transport equipment, textiles, clothing, footwear, wine (leading producer and exporter), metals and metal products, chemicals, wood, paper and rubber goods. Principal market: Germany 16.5% (1998)
**population** 57,343,000 (1999 est)
**language** Italian; German, French, Slovene, and Albanian minorities
**religion** Roman Catholic 100% (state religion)
**life expectancy** 75 (men); 81 (women) (1995–2000)
**Chronology**
**4th and 3rd centuries BC** Italian peninsula united under Roman rule.
**AD 476** End of Western Roman Empire.
**568** Invaded by Lombards.
**756** Papal States created in central Italy.
**800** Charlemagne united Italy and Germany in Holy Roman Empire.
**12th and 13th centuries** Papacy and Holy Roman Empire contended for political supremacy; papal power reached its peak under Innocent III (1198–1216).
**1183** Cities of Lombard League (founded in 1164) became independent.
**14th century** Beginnings of Renaissance in northern Italy.
**15th century** Most of Italy ruled by five rival states: the city-states of Milan, Florence, and Venice; the Papal States; and the Kingdom of Naples.
**1494** Charles VIII of France invaded Italy.
**1529–59** Spanish Habsburgs secured dominance in Italy.
**17th century** Italy effectively part of Spanish Empire; economic and cultural decline.
**1713** Treaty of Utrecht gave political control of most of Italy to Austrian Habsburgs.
**1796–1814** France conquered Italy, setting up satellite states and introducing principles of French Revolution.
**1815** Old regimes largely restored; Italy divided between Austria, Papal States, Naples, Sardinia, and four duchies.
**1831** Giuseppe Mazzini founded 'Young Italy' movement with aim of creating unified republic.
**1848–49** Liberal revolutions occurred throughout Italy; reversed everywhere except Sardinia, which became centre of nationalism under leadership of Count Camillo di Cavour.
**1859** France and Sardinia forcibly expelled Austrians from Lombardy.
**1860** Sardinia annexed duchies and Papal States (except Rome); Giuseppe Garibaldi overthrew Neapolitan monarchy.
**1861** Victor Emmanuel II of Sardinia proclaimed King of Italy in Turin.
**1866** Italy gained Venetia after defeat of Austria by Prussia.
**1870** Italian forces occupied Rome in defiance of Pope, completing unification of Italy.
**1882** Italy joined Germany and Austria-Hungary in Triple Alliance.
**1896** Attempt to conquer Ethiopia defeated at Battle of Adowa.

**1900** King Umberto I assassinated by an anarchist.

**1912** Annexation of Libya and Dodecanese after Italo-Turkish War.

**1915** Italy entered World War I on side of Allies.

**1919** Peace treaties awarded Trentino, South Tyrol, and Trieste to Italy.

**1922** Mussolini established fascist dictatorship following period of strikes and agrarian revolts.

**1935–36** Conquest of Ethiopia.

**1939** Invasion of Albania.

**1940** Italy entered World War II as ally of Germany.

**1943** Allies invaded southern Italy; Mussolini removed from power; Germans occupied northern and central Italy.

**1945** Allies completed liberation.

**1946** Monarchy replaced by republic.

**1947** Peace treaty stripped Italy of its colonies.

**1948** New constitution adopted; Christian Democrats emerged as main party of government in political system marked by ministerial instability.

**1957** Italy became a founder member of European Economic Community (EEC).

**1963** Creation of first of long series of fragile centre-left coalition governments.

**1976** Communists attempt to join the coalition, the 'historic compromise', rejected by the Christian Democrats.

**1978** Christian Democrat Aldo Moro, the architect of historic compromise, was murdered by Red Brigade guerrillas infiltrated by Western intelligence agents.

**1983–87** Bettino Craxi, Italy's first Socialist prime minister, led the coalition. The economy improved.

**1993** A major political crisis was triggered by the exposure of government corruption and Mafia links, and governing parties were discredited. A new electoral system replaced proportional representation, with 75% majority voting.

**1994** Media tycoon Silvio Berlusconi created a new party, Forza Italia, and formed a right-wing coalition.

**1995** Lamberto Dini headed a nonparty government of 'experts'.

**1996** Olive Tree Alliance won the general election; Romano Prodi became the prime minister.

**1997** Prodi resigned, and 'grand coalition' was sought; communist support persuaded Prodi to continue. Berlusconi was sentenced for fraud but the sentence was quashed; Prodi was cleared of corruption charges.

**1998** Berlusconi was cleared of fraud charges. Prodi's Olive Tree Alliance coalition collapsed as Reformed Communists left. Massimo d'Alema formed a new communist-led coalition.

**1999** Carlo Azeglio Ciampi was elected president. Former prime minister Prodi became president of the new European Commission.

**Itagaki, Taisuke** (1837–1919) Japanese military and political leader. Involved in the overthrow of the ◊Tokugawa shogunate and the Meiji restoration of 1868, Itagaki became leader of the people's rights movement. He was the founder of Japan's first political party, the Jiyūtō (Liberal Party), in 1881.

**Itaipu Reservoir** world's largest hydroelectric plant, situated on the Paraná River, southwestern Brazil. A joint Brazilian-Paraguayan venture, it came into operation 1984; it supplies hydroelectricity to a wide area.

**Italian Somaliland** former Italian trust territory on the Somali coast of Africa extending to 502,300 sq km/194,999 sq mi. Established in 1892, it was extended in 1925 with the acquisition of Jubaland from Kenya; administered from Mogadishu; under British rule 1941–50. Thereafter it reverted to Italian authority before uniting with British Somaliland in 1960 to form the independent state of Somalia.

**Itō, Hirobumi** (1841–1909) Japanese politician, prime minister 1885–88, 1892–96, 1898, and 1900–01. He was a key figure in the modernization of Japan and was involved in the Meiji restoration of 1868 and in official missions to study forms of government in the USA and Europe in the 1870s and 1880s. He played a major role in drafting the Meiji constitution of 1889.

**Ivan** six rulers of Russia, including:

**Ivan (III) the Great** (1440–1505) Grand Duke of Muscovy from 1462. He revolted against Tatar overlordship by refusing tribute to Grand Khan Ahmed in 1480. He claimed the title of tsar (Caesar), and used the double-headed eagle as the Russian state emblem.

**Ivan (IV) the Terrible** (1530–1584) Grand Duke of Muscovy from 1533. He assumed power in 1544 and was crowned as first tsar of Russia in 1547. He conquered Kazan in 1552, Astrakhan in 1556, and Siberia in 1581. He reformed the legal code and local administration in 1555 and established trade relations with England. In his last years he alternated between debauchery and religious austerities, executing thousands and, in rage, his own son.

**IVF** abbreviation for ◊*in vitro fertilization*.

**ivory** hard white substance of which the teeth and tusks of certain mammals are made. Among the most valuable are elephants' tusks, which are of unusual hardness and density. Ivory is used in carving and other decorative work, and is so valuable that poachers continue to illegally destroy the remaining wild elephant herds in Africa to obtain it.

**ivy** any of an Old World group of woody climbing, trailing, or creeping evergreen plants. English or European ivy (*H. helix*) has shiny five-lobed leaves and clusters of small, yellowish-green flowers followed by black berries. It climbs by means of rootlike suckers put out from its stem, and causes damage to trees. (Genus *Hedera*, family Araliaceae.)

**Iwo Jima** or *Iojima*, largest of the three Japanese Volcano Islands in the western Pacific Ocean, 1,222 km/760 mi south of Tokyo; area 22 sq km/9 sq mi. Annexed by Japan in 1891, Iwo Jima, also known as Naka Iojima, was captured by the USA in 1945 after fierce fighting. It was returned to Japan in 1968.

**Iwo Jima, Battle of** intense fighting between Japanese and US forces 19 February–17 March 1945 during World War II. In February 1945, US marines landed on the island of Iwo Jima, a Japanese air base, intending to use it to prepare for a planned final assault on mainland Japan. The 22,000 Japanese troops put up a fanatical resistance but the island was finally secured 16 March. US casualties came to 6,891 killed and 18,700 wounded, while only 212 of the Japanese garrison survived.

**Izetbegović,     Alija** (1925–   ) Bosnia-Herzegovinan politician, president 1990–98.

**Izmir** formerly *Smyrna,* port and naval base in Turkey; population (1990) 1,757,400. Products include steel, electronics, and plastics. The largest annual trade fair in the Middle East is held here. It is the headquarters of ◊North Atlantic Treaty Organization SE Command.

**Iznik** modern name of ancient Nicaea, a town in Turkey noted for the richly decorated pottery and tiles produced there in the 15th and 16th centuries.

**J** in physics, the symbol for *joule,* the SI unit of energy.

**jacamar** insect-eating bird related to the woodpeckers, found in dense tropical forest in Central and South America. It has a long, straight, sharply-pointed bill, a long tail, and paired toes. The plumage is golden bronze with a steely lustre. Jacamars are usually seen sitting motionless on trees from which they fly out to catch insects on the wing, then return to crack them on a branch before eating them. The largest species is *Jacamerops aurea,* which is nearly 30 cm/12 in long. (Family Galbulidae, order Piciformes.)

**jacana** or *lily-trotter,* wading bird with very long toes and claws enabling it to walk on the floating leaves of water plants. There are seven species. Jacanas are found in Mexico, Central America, South America, Africa, South Asia, and Australia, usually in marshy areas. (Family Jacanidae, order Charadriiformes.)

**jacaranda** any of a group of tropical American trees belonging to the bignonia family, with fragrant wood and showy blue or violet flowers, commonly cultivated in the southern USA. (Genus *Jacaranda,* family Bignoniaceae.)

**jackal** any of several wild dogs found in South Asia, southern Europe, and North Africa. Jackals can grow to 80 cm/2.7 ft long, and have greyish-brown fur and a bushy tail. (Genus *Canis.*)

**jackdaw** bird belonging to the crow family, native to Europe and Asia. It is mainly black, but greyish on the sides and back of the head, and about 33 cm/1.1 ft long. It nests in tree holes or on buildings. Usually it lays five bluish-white eggs, mottled with tiny dark brown spots. Jackdaws feed on a wide range of insects, molluscs, spiders, worms, birds' eggs, fruit, and berries. (Species *Corvus monedula,* family Corvidae, order Passeriformes.)

**Jackson, Andrew** (1767–1845) 7th president of the USA 1829–37, a Democrat. A major general in the War of 1812, he defeated a British force at New Orleans 1815 (after the official end of the war 1814) and was involved in the war that led to the purchase of Florida 1819. The political organization he built as president, with Martin Van Buren (1782–1862), was the basis for the modern ◊Democratic Party.

**Jackson, Colin Ray** (1967– ) Welsh athlete who won the 110 metres hurdles gold medal at the 1993 World Championships at Stuttgart in a world record time of 12.91 sec. He gained a silver medal at the 1988 Olympic Games, and won three consecutive European titles 1990–98 and two consecutive Commonwealth titles, 1990–94. He also excelled indoors, and in 1994 set an indoor world 60 metres hurdles record of 7.30 sec. He won his fifth British indoor title at the AAA National Championships in Birmingham, England, in January 1999, and in March he won the 60 metre hurdles title at the World Indoor Championships in Maebashi, Japan. In July 1999 he became the first athlete to win nine AAA titles. At the world championships in Seville, Spain, he regained his 110 metres hurdles title, which he had previously won in 1993.

*career highlights*
**World Championships** bronze 1987; gold 1993; silver 1997; gold 1999
**Olympic Games** silver 1988
**European Championships** gold 1990; gold 1994; gold 1998
**Commonwealth Games** silver 1986; gold 1990; gold 1994
**World Indoor Games** gold 60 metre hurdles 1999; silver 60 metres hurdles 1989; silver 60 metres hurdles 1993; silver 60 metres hurdles 1997

**Jackson, Glenda** (1936– ) English actress and politician, Labour member of Parliament from 1992, and parliamentary undersecretary for transport from 1997. Her many stage appearances for the Royal Shakespeare Company include *Marat/Sade* (1966), Hedda in *Hedda Gabler* (1975), and Cleopatra in *Antony and Cleopatra* (1978). Among her films are the Oscar-winning *Women in Love* (1969), *Sunday Bloody Sunday* (1971), and *A Touch of Class* (1973). On television she played Queen Elizabeth I in *Elizabeth R* (1971).

**Jackson, Jesse Louis** (1941– ) US Democratic politician, a cleric and campaigner for minority rights. He contested his party's 1984 and 1988 presidential nominations in an effort to increase voter registration and to put black issues on the national agenda. He is an eloquent public speaker, and in 1998 emerged as a spiritual adviser to President Bill Clinton.

**Jackson, Michael Joseph** (1958– ) US rock singer and songwriter. His videos and live performances are meticulously choreographed. His first solo hit was 'Got to Be There' (1971); his worldwide popularity peaked with the albums *Thriller* (1982), *Bad* (1987), and *Dangerous* (1991). Jackson's career faltered after allegations of child abuse, but he returned with the album *History* (1995).

**Jacksonville** city and port in northeastern Florida, USA; population (1994 est) 665,000. It is one of the chief southern commercial centres on the Atlantic coast, with extensive rail, air, and highway connections; it is also a port of entry and a tourist resort. Manufactured goods include wood and paper products, ships, chemicals, cigars, and processed food. The port, situated on St John's River, has naval installations and ship-repair yards. To the north the Cross-Florida Barge Canal links the Atlantic with the Gulf of Mexico. Jacksonville dates from 1816, and was incorporated as a city in 1832.

**Jack the Ripper** popular name for the unidentified mutilator and murderer of at least five women prostitutes in the Whitechapel area of London in 1888.

**Jacob** in the Old Testament, Hebrew patriarch, son of Isaac and Rebecca, who obtained the rights of seniority from his twin brother Esau by trickery. He married his cousins Leah and Rachel, serving their father Laban seven years for each, and at the time of famine in Canaan joined his son Joseph in Egypt. His 12 sons were the traditional ancestors of the 12 tribes of Israel.

**Jacobean** style in the arts, particularly in architecture and furniture, during the reign of James I (1603–25) in England. Following the general lines of Elizabethan design, but using Classical features with greater complexity and with more profuse ornamentation, it adopted many motifs from contemporary Italian design.

**Jacobin** member of an extremist republican club of the French Revolution founded in Versailles 1789. Helped by ◊Danton's speeches, they proclaimed the French republic, had the king executed, and overthrew the moderate ◊Girondins 1792–93. Through the Committee of Public Safety, they began the Reign of Terror, led by ◊Robespierre. After his execution 1794, the club was abandoned and the name 'Jacobin' passed into general use for any left-wing extremist.

**Jacobite** in Britain, a supporter of the royal house of Stuart after the deposition of James II in 1688. They include the Scottish Highlanders, who rose unsuccessfully under Claverhouse in 1689; and those who rose in Scotland and northern England in 1715 under the leadership of ◊James Edward Stuart, the Old Pretender, and followed his son ◊Charles Edward Stuart in an invasion of England from 1745 to 1746 that reached Derby. After the defeat at ◊Culloden, Jacobitism disappeared as a political force.

**Jacquard, Joseph Marie** (1752–1834) French textile manufacturer. He invented a punched-card system for programming designs on a carpetmaking loom (the *Jacquard loom*). In 1801 he constructed looms that used a series of punched cards to control the pattern of longitudinal warp threads depressed before each sideways passage of the shuttle. On later machines the punched cards were joined to form an endless loop that represented the 'program' for the repeating pattern of a carpet.

**jade** semiprecious stone consisting of either jadeite, $NaAlSi_2O_6$ (a pyroxene), or nephrite, $Ca_2 (Mg,Fe)_5Si_8O_{22} (OH,F)_2$ (an amphibole), ranging from colourless through shades of green to black according to the iron content. Jade ranks 5.5–6.5 on the Mohs scale of hardness.

**Jade Emperor** or *Yu Huang*, in Chinese religion, the supreme god of pantheistic Taoism, also known as the *August Personage of Jade* and *Father Heaven,* who watches over human actions and is the ruler of life and death. His court inspects the earth annually, making a detailed account from which he apportions praise or blame; the gods could be promoted or lose their rank accordingly.

**Jaffa** Arabic *Yafa;* Hebrew *Yafo;* biblical *Joppa,* city and former port in west Israel, part of ◊Tel Aviv-Yafo from 1950. It is also a tourist centre.

**Jaffna** capital of Jaffna district, Northern Province, Sri Lanka; population (1990) 129,000. It was the focal point of Hindu Tamil nationalism and the scene of recurring riots during the 1980s.

**jaguar** largest species of cat in the Americas, formerly ranging from the southwestern USA to southern South America, but now extinct in most of North America. It can grow up to 2.5 m/8 ft long including the tail. Male jaguars weigh up to 150 kg/330 lb; females up to 90 kg/198 lb. The background colour of the fur varies from creamy white to brown or black, and is covered with black spots. The jaguar is usually solitary and lives approximately 11 years in the wild. (Species *Panthera onca,* family Felidae.)

**jaguarundi** wild cat found in forests in Central and South America. Up to 1.1 m/3.5 ft long, it is very slim with rather short legs and short rounded ears. It is uniformly coloured dark brown or chestnut. A good climber, it feeds on birds and small mammals and, unusually for a cat, has been reported to eat fruit. (Species *Felis yaguoaroundi,* family Felidae.)

**Jahangir** adopted name of Salim, ('Holder of the World') (1569–1627) third Mogul emperor of India (1605–27), succeeding his father ◊Akbar the Great. The first part of his reign was marked by peace, prosperity, and a flowering of the arts, but the latter half by rebellion and succession conflicts.

**Jainism** (Hindi *jaina* 'person who overcomes') ancient Indian religion, sometimes regarded as an offshoot of Hinduism. Jains emphasize the importance of not injuring living beings, and their code of ethics is based on sympathy and compassion for all forms of life. They also believe in ◊karma but not in any deity. It is a monastic, ascetic religion. There are two main sects: the Digambaras and the Swetambaras. Jainism practises the most extreme form of non-violence (*ahimsā*) of all Indian sects, and influenced the philosophy of Mahatma Gandhi. Jains number approximately 6 million; there are Jain communities throughout the world but the majority live in India.

**Jaipur** capital of Rajasthan, India, 240 km/150 mi southeast of Delhi; population (1991) 1,458,000. Products include textiles and metal products. Founded by Jai Singh II in 1728, it was formerly the capital of the state of Jaipur, which was merged with Rajasthan in 1949.

**Jakarta** or *Djakarta,* (formerly until 1949

*Batavia)* capital of Indonesia on the northwest coast of Java; population (1993) 9,000,000. Industries include textiles, chemicals, and plastics; a canal links it with its port of Tanjung Priok where rubber, oil, tin, coffee, tea, and palm oil are among its exports; also a tourist centre. Respiratory-tract infections caused by air pollution account for 12.6% of deaths annually. Jakarta was founded by Dutch traders in 1619.

**Jakeš, Miloš** (1922– ) Czech communist politician, a member of the Politburo from 1981 and party leader 1987–89. A conservative, he supported the Soviet invasion of Czechoslovakia 1968. He was forced to resign November 1989 following a series of prodemocracy mass rallies.

**Jalalabad** capital of Nangarhar province, east Afghanistan, on the road from Kabul to Peshawar in Pakistan; population (1988 est) 55,000. The city was besieged by ◊Mujahedin rebels after the withdrawal of Soviet troops from Afghanistan in 1989.

**Jamaica**

**area** 10,957 sq km/4,230 sq mi
**capital** Kingston
**major towns/cities** Montego Bay, Spanish Town, St Andrew, Portmore, May Pen
**physical features** mountainous tropical island; Blue Mountains (so called because of the haze over them)
**head of state** Elizabeth II from 1962, represented by governor general Howard Felix Hanlan Cooke from 1991
**head of government** Percival Patterson from 1992
**political system** constitutional monarchy
**political parties** Jamaica Labour Party (JLP), moderate, centrist; People's National Party (PNP), left of centre; National Democratic Union (NDM), centrist
**currency** Jamaican dollar
**GNP per capita (PPP)** (US$) 3,210 (1998)
**exports** bauxite, alumina, gypsum, sugar, bananas, garments, rum. Principal market: USA 33.3% (1997)
**population** 2,561,000 (1999 est)
**language** English, Jamaican creole
**religion** Protestant 70%, Rastafarian

**life expectancy** 73 (men); 77 (women) (1995–2000)
**Chronology**
**c. AD 900** Settled by Arawak Indians, who gave the island the name Jamaica ('well watered').
**1494** The explorer Christopher Columbus reached Jamaica.
**1509** Occupied by Spanish; much of Arawak community died from exposure to European diseases; black African slaves brought in to work sugar plantations.
**1655** Captured by Britain and became its most valuable Caribbean colony.
**1838** Slavery abolished.
**1870** Banana plantations established as sugar cane industry declined in face of competition from European beet sugar.
**1938** Serious riots during the economic depression and, as a sign of growing political awareness, the People's National Party (PNP) was formed by Norman Manley.
**1944** First constitution adopted.
**1958–62** Part of West Indies Federation.
**1959** Internal self-government granted.
**1962** Independence achieved within the Commonwealth, with Alexander Bustamante of the centre-right Jamaica Labour Party (JLP) as prime minister.
**1967** JLP re-elected under Hugh Shearer.
**1972** Michael Manley of the PNP became prime minister and pursued a policy of economic self-reliance.
**1980** The JLP was elected, with Edward Seaga as prime minister, following a violent election campaign.
**1981** Diplomatic links with Cuba were severed, and a free-market economic programme was pursued.
**1983** The JLP won all 60 seats in the general election.
**1988** The island was badly damaged by Hurricane Gilbert.
**1989** The PNP won a landslide victory with a newly moderate Manley returning as prime minister.
**1992** Manley retired and was succeeded by Percival Patterson.
**1993** The PNP increased its majority in the general election.
**1998** Violent crime increased as the economy declined.

**James, Henry** (1843–1916) US novelist, who lived in Europe from 1875 and became a naturalized British subject in 1915. His novels deal with the social, moral, and aesthetic issues arising from the complex relationship of European to American culture. His major novels include *The Portrait of a Lady* (1881), *The Bostonians* (1886), *What Maisie Knew* (1887), *The Ambassadors* (1903), and *The Golden Bowl* (1904). He also wrote more than a hundred shorter works of fiction, notably the novella *The Aspern Papers* (1888) and the supernatural/psychological riddle *The Turn of the Screw* (1898).

**James, Jesse Woodson** (1847–1882) US bank and train robber. He was a leader, with his brother Frank (1843–1915), of the Quantrill raiders, a Confederate guerrilla band in the Civil War.

Jesse was killed by Bob Ford, an accomplice; Frank remained unconvicted and became a farmer.

**James, P(hyllis) D(orothy)** Baroness James of Holland Park (1920– ) English detective novelist. She created the characters Superintendent Adam Dalgliesh and private investigator Cordelia Gray. She was a tax official, hospital administrator, and civil servant in the Home Office, involved with police matters, before turning to writing. Her books include *Death of an Expert Witness* (1977), *The Skull Beneath the Skin* (1982), *A Taste for Death* (1986), *Original Sin* (1994), and *Certain Justice* (1997). Baronesss 1991.

**James** two kings of Britain:

**James I** (1566–1625) King of England from 1603 and Scotland (as *James VI*) from 1567. The son of Mary Queen of Scots and her second husband, Lord Darnley, he succeeded to the Scottish throne on the enforced abdication of his mother and assumed power in 1583. He established a strong centralized authority, and in 1589 married Anne of Denmark (1574–1619).

As successor to Elizabeth I in England, he alienated the Puritans by his High Church views and Parliament by his assertion of ◊divine right, and was generally unpopular because of his favourites, such as ◊Buckingham, and his schemes for an alliance with Spain. He was succeeded by his son Charles I.

**James II** (1633–1701) King of England and Scotland (as *James VII*) from 1685. The second son of Charles I, he succeeded his brother, Charles II. In 1660 James married Anne Hyde (1637–1671, mother of Mary II and Anne) and in 1673 Mary of Modena (mother of James Edward Stuart). He became a Catholic in 1671, which led first to attempts to exclude him from the succession, then to the rebellions of Monmouth and Argyll, and finally to the Whig and Tory leaders' invitation to William of Orange to take the throne in 1688. James fled to France, then led an uprising in Ireland in 1689, but after defeat at the Battle of the ◊Boyne (1690) remained in exile in France.

**James** seven kings of Scotland:

**James I** (1394–1437) King of Scotland (1406–37), who assumed power in 1424. He was a cultured and strong monarch whose improvements in the administration of justice brought him popularity among the common people. He was assassinated by a group of conspirators led by the Earl of Atholl.

**James II** (1430–1460) King of Scotland from 1437, who assumed power in 1449. The only surviving son of James I, he was supported by most of the nobles and parliament. He sympathized with the Lancastrians during the Wars of the ◊Roses, and attacked English possessions in S Scotland. He was killed while besieging Roxburgh Castle.

**James III** (1451–1488) King of Scotland from 1460, who assumed power in 1469. His reign was marked by rebellions by the nobles, including his brother Alexander, Duke of Albany. He was

murdered during a rebellion supported by his son, who then ascended the throne as James IV.

**James IV** (1473–1513) King of Scotland from 1488. He came to the throne after his followers murdered his father, James III, at Sauchieburn. His reign was internally peaceful, but he allied himself with France against England, invaded in 1513, and was defeated and killed at the Battle of ◊Flodden. James IV was a patron of poets and architects as well as a military leader.

**James V** (1512–1542) King of Scotland from 1513, who assumed power in 1528. During the long period of his minority, he was caught in a struggle between pro-French and pro-English factions. When he assumed power, he allied himself with France and upheld Catholicism against the Protestants. Following an attack on Scottish territory by Henry VIII's forces, he was defeated near the border at Solway Moss in 1542.

**James VI** of Scotland. See ◊James I of England.

**James VII** of Scotland. See ◊James II of England.

**James Francis Edward Stuart** (1688–1766) British prince, known as the *Old Pretender* (for the ◊Jacobites, he was James III). Son of James II, he was born at St James's Palace and after the revolution of 1688 was taken to France. He landed in Scotland in 1715 to head a Jacobite rebellion but withdrew through lack of support. In his later years he settled in Rome.

**Jameson, Leander Starr** (1853–1917) Scottish colonial administrator, born in Edinburgh, Scotland. In South Africa, early in 1896, he led the *Jameson Raid* from Mafeking into the Transvaal to support the non-Boer colonists there, in an attempt to overthrow the government (for which he served some months in prison). Returning to South Africa, he succeeded Cecil ◊Rhodes as leader of the Progressive Party of Cape Colony, where he was prime minister 1904–08. 1st baronet 1911.

**Jammu and Kashmir** state of north India
**area** 222,200 sq km/85,791 sq mi
**capital** Jammu (winter); Srinagar (summer), the seat of state government
**towns and cities** Leh
**physical** semi-arid alluvial plains in the south; mountainous towards the north, to heights of 4,000 m/13,000 ft (◊Karakoram range), divided by river valleys (the Jhelum), and the Vale of Kashmir (1,600 m/5,250 ft), the most densely populated area
**agriculture** grain, rice, fruit round Dal Lake near Srinagar, in the Vale of Kashmir; sheep and goats in the far north
**industries** timber, silk, carpets, handicrafts; tourism is temporarily discouraged owing to the unsettled political situation
**population** (1994) 8,435,000 (Indian-occupied territory)
**history** Part of the Mogul Empire from 1586, Jammu came under the control of Gulab Singh in 1820. In 1947, although three-quarters of the population were Muslim, the Hindu Maharaja chose to become part of India after incursions by Pathan tribespeople from Pakistan. War between

India and Pakistan followed. It was ended by a ceasefire agreement in January 1949 and the ceasefire line became the *de facto* border. Dispute over the area (see ◊Kashmir) caused further hostilities in 1971 between India and Pakistan (ended by the Shimla agreement in 1972). Since then, separatist agitation has developed, complicating the territorial dispute between India and Pakistan. There are currently 150,000 Indian troops stationed in Kashmir, where Muslim separatists have been in revolt against the Indian authorities since 1990, with thousands of lives lost. In October 1996 the National Congress Party, which aims to retain the state within India, won the first local elections to be held since the separatist violence broke out in 1990.

**Janáček, Leoš** (1854–1928) Czech composer. He became director of the Conservatory at Brno 1919 and professor at the Prague Conservatory 1920. His music, highly original and influenced by Moravian folk music, includes arrangements of folk songs, operas (*Jenufa* (1904), *The Cunning Little Vixen* (1924), and the choral *Glagolitic Mass* (1926).

**Janus** in Roman mythology, the god of all openings, including doorways and passageways, and the beginning of the day, month, and year. January was dedicated to him. He is represented as having two faces, one looking forwards and one back, (in sculpture, a *herm*), and was associated with wisdom because he knew the past and could foresee the future. In Roman ritual he was invoked first in a list of gods, and at the beginning of any enterprise.

**Japan**
*national name Nippon*

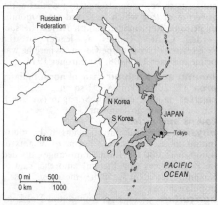

**area** 377,535 sq km/145,766 sq mi
**capital** Tokyo
**major towns/cities** Yokohama, Osaka, Nagoya, Fukuoka, Kitakyushu, Kyoto, Sapporo, Kobe, Kawasaki, Hiroshima
**major ports** Osaka, Nagoya, Yokohama, Kobe
**physical features** mountainous, volcanic (Mount Fuji, volcanic Mount Aso, Japan Alps); comprises over 1,000 islands, the largest of which are Hokkaido, Honshu, Kyushu, and Shikoku
**head of state** (figurehead) Emperor Akihito (Heisei) from 1989

**head of government** Keizo Obuchi from 1998
**political system** liberal democracy
**political parties** Liberal Democratic Party (LDP), right of centre; Shinshinto (New Frontier Party) opposition coalition, centrist reformist; Social Democratic Party of Japan (SDPJ, former Socialist Party), left of centre but moving towards centre; Shinto Sakigake (New Party Harbinger), right of centre; Japanese Communist Party (JCP), socialist; Democratic Party of Japan (DPJ), Sakigake and SDPJ dissidents
**currency** yen
**GNP per capita (PPP)** (US$) 23,180 (1998)
**exports** motor vehicles, electronic goods and components, chemicals, iron and steel products, scientific and optical equipment. Principal market: USA 30.5% (1998)
**population** 126,505,000 (1999 est)
**language** Japanese; also Ainu
**religion** Shinto, Buddhist (often combined), Christian
**life expectancy** 77 (men); 83 (women) (1995–2000)
*Chronology*
**660 BC** According to legend, Jimmu Tenno, descendent of the Sun goddess, became the first emperor of Japan.
**c. AD 400** The Yamato, one of many warring clans, unified central Japan; Yamato chiefs are the likely ancestors of the imperial family.
**5th–6th centuries** Writing, Confucianism, and Buddhism spread to Japan from China and Korea.
**646** Start of Taika Reform: Emperor Kotoku organized central government on Chinese model.
**794** Heian became imperial capital; later called Kyoto.
**858** Imperial court fell under control of Fujiwara clan, who reduced emperor to figurehead.
**11th century** Central government grew ineffectual; real power exercised by great landowners (daimyo) with private armies of samurai.
**1185** Minamoto clan seized power under Yoritomo, who established military rule.
**1192** Emperor gave Yoritomo the title of shogun (general); the shogun ruled in the name of the emperor.
**1274** Mongol conqueror Kublai Khan attempted to invade Japan, making a second attempt in 1281; on both occasions Japan was saved by a typhoon.
**1336** Warlord Takauji Ashikaga overthrew Minamoto shogunate; emperor recognized Ashikaga shogunate in 1338.
**16th century** Power of Ashikagas declined; constant civil war.
**1543** Portuguese sailors were first Europeans to reach Japan; followed by Spanish, Dutch, and English traders.
**1549** Spanish missionary St Francis Xavier began to preach Roman Catholic faith in Japan.
**1585–98** Warlord Hideyoshi took power and attempted to conquer Korea in 1592 and 1597.
**1603** Ieyasu Tokugawa founded new shogunate at Edo, reformed administration, and suppressed Christianity.

**1630s** Japan adopted policy of isolation: all travel forbidden and all foreigners expelled except small colony of Dutch traders in Nagasaki harbour.

**1853** USA sent warships to Edo with demand that Japan open diplomatic and trade relations; Japan conceded in 1854.

**1867** Revolt by isolationist nobles overthrew the Tokugawa shogunate.

**1868** Emperor Mutsuhito assumed full powers, adopted the title *Meiji* ('enlightened rule'), moved imperial capital from Kyoto to Edo (renamed Tokyo), and launched policy of swift Westernization.

**1894–95** Sino-Japanese War: Japan expelled Chinese from Korea.

**1902** Japan entered defensive alliance with Britain; ended in 1921.

**1904–05** Russo-Japanese War: Japan drove Russians from Manchuria and Korea; Korea annexed in 1910.

**1914** Japan entered World War I and occupied German possessions in Far East.

**1923** Earthquake destroyed much of Tokyo and Yokohama.

**1931** Japan invaded Chinese province of Manchuria and created puppet state of Manchukuo; Japanese government came under control of military and extreme nationalists.

**1937** Japan resumed invasion of China.

**1940** After Germany defeated France, Japan occupied French Indo-China.

**1941** Japan attacked US fleet at Pearl Harbor; USA and Britain declared war on Japan.

**1942** Japanese conquered Thailand, Burma, Malaya, Dutch East Indies, Philippines, and northern New Guinea.

**1945** USA dropped atomic bombs on Hiroshima and Nagasaki, Japan surrendered; US general Douglas MacArthur headed Allied occupation administration.

**1947** MacArthur supervised introduction of democratic 'Peace Constitution', accompanied by demilitarization and land reform.

**1952** Occupation ended.

**1955** Liberal Democratic Party (LDP) founded with support of leading business people.

**1956** Japan admitted to United Nations.

**1950s–70s** Rapid economic development; growth of manufacturing exports led to great prosperity.

**1993** An economic recession and financial scandals brought about the downfall of the LDP government in a general election. A coalition government was formed.

**1995** An earthquake devastated Kobe.

**1996** A general election produced an inconclusive result and a minority LDP government was formed, with Ryutaro Hashimoto as prime minister.

**1997** A financial crash occurred after bank failures.

**1998** Hashimoto resigned after the LDP polled poorly in upper house elections. Keizo Obuchi, leader of the LDP, became prime minister, with Kiichi Miyazawa as finance minister. The government introduced a new $200 billion economic stimulus package, after GDP contracted

2% in 1998 in the worst recession since World War II.

**1999** The ruling LDP formed a new coalition government with the Liberal Party.

**Jaruzelski, Wojciech Witold** (1923– ) Polish army general, appointed first secretary of the Polish United Workers Party (PUWP) in 1981. He was responsible for the imposition of martial law in Poland in December 1981. He was prime minister 1981–85 and president 1985–90. During martial law he attempted to suppress the ◊Solidarity trade union, interning its leaders and political dissidents. In 1989 he approved the 'Round Table' talks with the opposition that led to partially free parliamentary elections and to the appointment of a coalition government under a non-communist prime minister, Tadeusz Mazowiecki .

**jasmine** any of a group of subtropical plants with white or yellow flowers. The common jasmine (*J. officinale*) has fragrant pure white flowers that yield jasmine oil, used in perfumes; the Chinese winter jasmine (*J. nudiflorum*) has bright yellow flowers that appear before the leaves. (Genus *Jasminum,* family Oleaceae.)

**Jason** in Greek mythology, the leader of the Argonauts who sailed in the *Argo* to Colchis in search of the ◊Golden Fleece. He eloped with ◊Medea, daughter of the king of Colchis, who had helped him achieve his goal, but later deserted her.

**Jat** an ethnic group living in Pakistan and northern India, and numbering about 11 million; they are the largest group in northern India. The Jat are predominantly farmers. They speak Punjabi, a language belonging to the Iranian branch of the Indo-European family.

They are thought to be related to the Romany people.

**jaundice** yellow discoloration of the skin and whites of the eyes caused by an excess of bile pigment in the bloodstream. Approximately 60% of newborn babies exhibit some degree of jaundice, which is treated by bathing in white, blue, or green light that converts the bile pigment bilirubin into a water-soluble compound that can be excreted in urine. A serious form of jaundice occurs in rhesus disease (see ◊rhesus factor).

**Jaurès, (Auguste Marie Joseph) Jean (Léon)** (1859–1914) French socialist politician. He was considered a commanding intellectual presence within the socialist movement in France, through his writings (which included a magisterial social history of the French revolution), his oratory, and his journalism. In the decade leading up to the outbreak of World War I, Jaurès' impassioned opposition to the rising tide of militarism in Europe brought him centre stage within the Second International.

**Java** or *Jawa,* most populated island of Indonesia, situated between Sumatra and Bali

**area** (with the island of Madura) 132,000 sq km/51,000 sq mi

**capital** Jakarta (also capital of Indonesia)

**towns** ports include Surabaya and Semarang; Bandung

*physical* about half the island is under cultivation, the rest being thickly forested. Mountains and sea breezes keep temperatures down, but humidity is high, with heavy rainfall from December to March

*features* a chain of mountains, some of which are volcanic, runs along the centre, rising to 2,750 m/9,000 ft. The highest mountain, Semeru (3,676 m/12,060 ft), is in the east

*industries* rice, coffee, cocoa, tea, sugar, rubber, quinine, teak, petroleum, textiles

*population*    (with    Madura;    1990) 107,581,300, including people of Javanese, Sundanese, and Madurese origin, with differing languages

*religion* predominantly Muslim

*history* fossilized early human remains (*Homo erectus*) were discovered 1891–92. In central Java there are ruins of magnificent Buddhist monuments and of the Sivaite temple in Prambanan. The island's last Hindu kingdom, Majapahit, was destroyed about 1520 and followed by a number of short-lived Javanese kingdoms. The Dutch East India company founded a factory 1610. Britain took over during the Napoleonic period, 1811–16, and Java then reverted to Dutch control. Occupied by Japan 1942–45, Java then became part of the republic of Indonesia.

**javelin** spear used in athletics events. The men's javelin is about 260 cm/8.5 ft long, weighing 800 g/28 oz; the women's 230 cm/7.5 ft long, weighing 600 g/21 oz. It is thrown from a scratch line at the end of a run-up. The centre of gravity on the men's javelin was altered 1986 to reduce the vast distances (90 m/100 yd) that were being thrown.

**jay** any of several birds belonging to the crow family, generally brightly coloured and native to Europe, Asia, and the Americas. In the Eurasian *common jay* (*Garrulus glandarius*), the body is fawn with patches of white, blue, and black on the wings and tail. (Family Corvidae, order Passeriformes.)

**Jayawardene, Junius Richard** (1906– 1996) Sri Lankan politician. Leader of the United Nationalist Party from 1973, he became prime minister in 1977 and the country's first president 1978–88. Jayawardene embarked on a free-market economic strategy, but was confronted with increasing Tamil–Sinhalese ethnic unrest, forcing the imposition of a state of emergency in 1983.

**jazz** polyphonic syncopated music, characterized by solo virtuosic improvisation, which developed in the USA at the turn of the 20th century. Initially music for dancing, often with a vocalist, it had its roots in black American and other popular music. Developing from ◊blues and spirituals (religious folk songs) in the southern states, it first came to prominence in the early 20th century in New Orleans, St Louis, and Chicago, with a distinctive flavour in each city.

Traits common to all types of jazz are the modified rhythms of West Africa; the emphasis on improvisation; western European harmony emphasizing the dominant seventh and the clash of major and minor thirds; characteristic textures and ◊timbres, first exemplified by a singer and rhythm section (consisting of a piano, bass, drums, and guitar or a combination of these instruments), and later by the addition of other instruments such as the saxophone and various brass instruments, and later still by the adoption of electrically amplified instruments.

**Jedda** alternative spelling for the Saudi Arabian port ◊Jiddah.

**Jefferson, Thomas** (1743–1826) 3rd president of the USA 1801–09, founder of the Democratic Republican Party. He published *A Summary View of the Rights of America* 1774 and as a member of the Continental Congresses of 1775–76 was largely responsible for the drafting of the ◊Declaration of Independence. He was governor of Virginia 1779–81, ambassador to Paris 1785–89, secretary of state 1789–93, and vice-president 1797–1801.

**Jeffreys of Wem, George,** 1st Baron Jeffreys of Wem (1644–1689) Welsh judge, popularly known as 'the hanging judge'. He became Chief Justice of the King's Bench in 1683, and presided over many political trials, notably those of Philip Sidney, Titus Oates, and Richard Baxter, becoming notorious for his brutality.

**Jehovah** also *Jahweh*, in the Old Testament, the name of God, revealed to Moses; in Hebrew texts of the Old Testament the name was represented by the letters YHVH (without the vowels 'a o a') because it was regarded as too sacred to be pronounced.

**Jehovah's Witness** member of a religious organization originating in the USA 1872 under Charles Taze Russell (1852–1916). Jehovah's Witnesses attach great importance to Christ's second coming, which Russell predicted would occur 1914, and which Witnesses still believe is imminent. All Witnesses are expected to take part in house-to-house preaching; there are no clergy.

**Jekyll, Gertrude** (1843–1932) English landscape gardener and writer. She created over 300 gardens, many in collaboration with the architect Edwin ◊Lutyens. In her books, she advocated colour design in garden planning and natural gardens of the cottage type, with plentiful herbaceous borders.

**jellyfish** marine invertebrate, belonging among the ◊coelenterates, with an umbrella-shaped body made of a semitransparent jellylike substance, often tinted with blue, red, or orange colours, and stinging tentacles that trail in the water. Most adult jellyfish move freely, but during parts of their life cycle many are polyplike and attached to rocks, the seabed, or another underwater surface. They feed on small animals that are paralysed by stinging cells in the jellyfish tentacles. (Phylum Coelenterata, subphylum Cnidaria.)

**Jenkins, Roy Harris** Baron Jenkins of Hillhead (1920– ) British politician, born in Monmouthshire, Wales. He became a Labour

**jellyfish** *After fertilization, the gametes of a jellyfish may be released into the water as larvae (middle right) or retained in a brood pouch. After settling, the larvae change into a sedentary polyp stage (bottom right) similar to that of a coral. More polyps (bottom left) are produced by simple budding. These polyps may divide again to form the so-called ephyra larvae (middle left). These larvae eventually grow into the free-swimming medusa more familiarly known as a jellyfish (top).*

minister in 1964, was home secretary 1965–67 and 1974–76, and chancellor of the Exchequer 1967–70. He was president of the European Commission 1977–81. In 1981 he became one of the founders of the Social Democratic Party and was elected as an SDP MP in 1982, but lost his seat in 1987. In the same year, he was elected chancellor of Oxford University and made a life peer. In 1997 he was appointed head of a commission, set up by the Labour government, to recommend, in 1998, a new voting system for elections to Parliament.

**Jenner, Edward** (1749–1823) English physician who pioneered vaccination. In Jenner's day, smallpox was a major killer. His discovery in 1796 that inoculation with cowpox gives immunity to smallpox was a great medical breakthrough.

**jerboa** any of a group of small nocturnal rodents with long and powerful hind legs developed for leaping. There are about 25 species of jerboa, native to desert areas of North Africa and Southwest Asia. (Family Dipodidae.)

**Jeremiah** (lived 7th–6th century BC) Old Testament Hebrew prophet, whose ministry continued 626–586 BC. He was imprisoned during ◊Nebuchadnezzar's siege of Jerusalem on suspicion of intending to desert to the enemy. On the city's fall, he retired to Egypt.

**Jericho** town in the Jordan valley, west of the River Jordan and north of the Dead Sea, 24 km/15 mi northeast of Jerusalem; population (1987 est) 12,500. The site of the old city is the centre of a fertile district where palms, rose trees, grapes, and balsams are grown. It was occupied by Israel from 1967–94 when responsibility for its administration was transferred to the Palestine National Authority. Jericho was settled by 8000 BC, and by 6000 BC had become a walled city with 2,000 inhabitants. In the Old Testament it was the first Canaanite stronghold captured by the Israelites, and its walls, according to the Book of Joshua, fell to the blast of Joshua's trumpets. Successive archaeological excavations since 1907 show that the walls of the city were destroyed many times.

**Jerome, St** (*c.* 340–420) One of the early Christian leaders and scholars known as the Fathers of the Church. His Latin versions of the Old and New Testaments form the basis of the Roman Catholic Vulgate. He is usually depicted with a lion. Feast day 30 September.

**Jersey** largest of the ◊Channel Islands; capital St Helier; area 117 sq km/45 sq mi; population (1991) 85,200. It is governed by a lieutenant governor representing the English crown and an assembly. Jersey cattle were originally bred here. Jersey gave its name to a woollen garment

**Jerusalem** Arabic *al-Quds;* Hebrew *Yerushalayim,* ancient city of Palestine, 762 m/ 2,500 ft above sea level, situated in hills 55 km/ 34 mi from the Mediterranean, divided in 1948 between Jordan and the new republic of Israel; area (pre-1967) 37.5 sq km/14.5 sq mi, (post-1967) 108 sq km/42 sq mi, including areas of the West Bank; population (1995) 591,400. In 1950 the western New City was proclaimed as the Israeli capital, and, having captured from Jordan the eastern Old City in 1967, Israel affirmed in 1980 that the united city was the country's capital; the United Nations does not recognize East Jerusalem as part of Israel, and regards Tel Aviv as the capital.

**Jerusalem artichoke** a variety of ◊artichoke.

**Jesuit** member of the largest and most influential Roman Catholic religious order (also known as the *Society of Jesus)* founded by Ignatius Loyola 1534, with the aims of protecting Catholicism against the Reformation and carrying out missionary work. During the 16th and 17th centuries Jesuits were missionaries in

Japan, China, Paraguay, and among the North American Indians. The order had (1991) about 29,000 members (15,000 priests plus students and lay members). There are Jesuit schools and universities.

**Jesus** (*c.* 4 BC–AD 29 or 30) Hebrew preacher on whose teachings ◊Christianity was founded. According to the accounts of his life in the four Gospels, he was born in Bethlehem, Palestine, son of God and the Virgin Mary, and brought up by Mary and her husband Joseph as a carpenter in Nazareth. After adult baptism, he gathered 12 disciples, but his preaching antagonized the Roman authorities and he was executed by crucifixion. Three days later there came reports of his ◊resurrection and, later, his ascension to heaven.

**jetfoil** advanced type of ◊hydrofoil boat built by Boeing, propelled by water jets. It features horizontal, fully submerged hydrofoils fore and aft and has a sophisticated computerized control system to maintain its stability in all waters.

**Jew** follower of ◊Judaism, the Jewish religion. The term is also used to refer to those who claim descent from the ancient Hebrews, a Semitic people of the Middle East. Today, some may recognize their ethnic heritage but not practise the religious or cultural traditions. The term came into use in medieval Europe, based on the Latin name for Judeans, the people of Judah. Prejudice against Jews is termed ◊anti-Semitism.

**Jiang Jie Shi** or *Chiang Kai-shek* (1887– 1975) Chinese nationalist Kuomintang (◊Guomindang) general and politician, president of China 1928–31 and 1943–49, and of Taiwan from 1949, where he set up a US-supported rightwing government on his expulsion from the mainland by the communist forces.

**Jiang Qing** or *Chiang Ching* (1914–1991) Chinese communist politician, third wife of the party leader Mao Zedong. In 1960 she became minister for culture, and played a key role in the 1966–69 Cultural Revolution as the leading member of the Shanghai-based ◊Gang of Four, who attempted to seize power in 1976. She was imprisoned in 1981.

**Jiangsu** or *Kiangsu,* province on the coast of east China, bounded to the north by Shandong, to the east by the Yellow Sea, to the southeast by Shanghai, to the south by Zhejiang, and to the west by Anhui
*area* 102,200 sq km/39,449 sq mi
*capital* ◊Nanjing
**towns and cities** Suzhou, Wuxi, Lianyungang (port), Zhenjiang
*physical* Chang Jiang River delta
*features* independent municipality of Shanghai; Grand Canal
*industries* ceramics, machinery, textiles, chemicals, pharmaceuticals, electronics, computer components, coal, iron ore, copper, cement, salt
*agriculture* rice, winter wheat, tea, cotton, soybeans, rapeseed, fish, silk
*population* (1996) 71,100,000; the most densely populated province in China
*famous people* Zhou Enlai, premier of China

*history* Jiangsu was successively part of the ancient kingdoms of Wu, Yue, and Chu before being taken by the Qin dynasty (221–206 BC). *Wu* is still a traditional local name for the province. Later it became the heartland of the Southern Song dynasty (1127–1279). In 1667 it became a separate province. Nanjing was the capital of China under the Ming dynasty (1368–1644), and the Nationalist republic (1928–37 and 1945–49). Jiangsu's capture by Japan in 1937 was an important step in Japanese attempts to conquer China.

**Jiangxi** or *Kiangsi,* province of southeast China, bounded to the north by Hubei and Anhui, to the east by Zhejiang and Fujian, to the south by Guangdong, and to the west by Hunan
*area* 164,800 sq km/63,613 sq mi
*capital* ◊Nanchang
*cities and towns* Ganzhou, Ji'an, Jingdezhen, Jiujiang, Pingxiang
*physical* hills; Lake Poyang in central lowlands; Chang Jiang River
*industries* porcelain, coal, tungsten, copper, uranium
*agriculture* rice, tea, cotton, tobacco, timber
*population* (1996) 41,050,000.

**Jiang Zemin** (1926– ) Chinese communist politician, leader of the Chinese Communist Party from 1989 and state president from 1993. He succeeded ◊Zhao Ziyang as Communist Party leader after the Tiananmen Square massacre of 1989. He was re-elected state president in March 1998 by China's parliament, the National People's Congress and has continued to press on with a combination of market-centred economic reform, coupled with unswerving adherence to the CCP's 'political line'. He has also launched a campaign against official corruption.

**Jiddah** or *Jedda,* port in Hejaz, Saudi Arabia, on the eastern shore of the Red Sea, about 80 km/50 mi west of Mecca; population (1991 est) 1,500,000. The country's leading industrial centre, its industries include cement, steel, and oil refining. It exports hides, mother-of-pearl, coffee, and carpets. Pilgrims pass through here on their way to Mecca.

**jihad** (Arabic 'conflict') holy war undertaken by Muslims against nonbelievers. In the *Mecca Declaration* 1981, the Islamic powers pledged a jihad against Israel, though not necessarily military attack.

**Jilin** or *Kirin,* province of northeast China, bounded to the northeast by Heilongjiang, to the southeast by Russia, to the south by North Korea, to the southwest by Liaoning, and to the northwest by Inner Mongolia
*area* 187,000 sq km/72,182 sq mi
*capital* ◊Changchun
*cities and towns* Jilin, Tonghua, Baicheng, Liaoyuan
*physical* mountains; lowland
*industries* coal, iron ore, engineering, food-processing, chemicals
*agriculture* maize, sorghum, soybeans, millet
*population* (1996) 26,100,000.

**Ji'nan** *Tsinan* or *Chinan,* city and capital of ◊Shandong province, China; population (1993) 2,050,000. Industries include engineering, food processing, flour-milling, and the manufacture of textiles, iron, steel, heavy goods vehicles, machine tools, and chemicals.

**jingoism** blinkered, war-mongering patriotism. The term originated in 1878, when the British prime minister Disraeli developed a pro-Turkish policy, which nearly involved the UK in war with Russia. His supporters' war song included the line 'We don't want to fight, but by jingo if we do ...'.

**Jinnah, Muhammad Ali** (1876–1948) Indian politician, Pakistan's first governor general from 1947. He was president of the Muslim League 1916 and 1934–48, and by 1940 was advocating the need for a separate state of Pakistan. At the 1946 conferences in London he insisted on the partition of British India into Hindu and Muslim states.

**Jinsha Jiang** river rising in southwest China and forming the ◊Chang Jiang (Yangtze Kiang) at Yibin.

**Joan of Arc, St** also known as Jeanne d'Arc (*c.* 1412–1431) French military leader who inspired the French at Orléans in 1428–29 (see Orléans, Siege of) and at Patay, north of Orléans, in 1429. As a young peasant girl, she was the wrong age, class, and gender to engage in warfare, yet her 'heavenly voices' instructed her to expel the occupying English from northern France (see Hundred Years' War) and secure the coronation of Charles VII of France. Because of her strength of character, she achieved both aims. Her subsequent attempt to take Paris was overambitious, however, and she was captured May 1430 at Compiègne by the Burgundians, who sold her to the English. She was found guilty of witchcraft and heresy by a tribunal of French ecclesiastics who supported the English, and burned to death at the stake in Rouen 30 May 1431.

**jobseekers allowance** social security benefit included by the UK Conservative government in the Jobseekers Act, 1995. The allowance became effective from October 1996. It replaced unemployment benefit and ◊income support, combining them into one payment for the unemployed. The Labour government inherited the jobseekers allowance after winning the May 1997 general election, but some time before that it had established a commission to review and advise on the whole field of social security, the allowance forming part of that review.

**Jodhpur** city in Rajasthan, India, 490 km/310 mi southwest of Delhi; population (1991) 668,000. Handicraft industries such as ivory carving and lacquerware are important, and railway parts, textiles, and bicycles are manufactured here. It is a market centre. It was formerly capital of Jodhpur princely state, founded by Rao Jodha on the edge of the Thar Desert. A style of riding breeches is named after the town.

**Jodrell Bank** site in Cheshire, England, of the Nuffield Radio Astronomy Laboratories of the University of Manchester. Its largest instrument is the 76 m/250 ft radio dish (the Lovell Telescope), completed in 1957 and modified in 1970. A 38 × 25 m/125 × 82 ft elliptical radio dish was introduced in 1964, capable of working at shorter wave lengths.

**Joffre, Joseph Jacques Césaire** (1852–1931) Marshal of France during World War I. He was chief of general staff 1911. The German invasion of Belgium 1914 took him by surprise, but his stand at the Battle of the ◊Marne resulted in his appointment as supreme commander of all the French armies 1915. His failure to make adequate preparations at Verdun 1916 and the military disasters on the ◊Somme led to his replacement by Nivelle December 1916.

**Johannesburg** largest city of South Africa, situated on the Witwatersrand River in Gauteng Province; population (urban area, 1991) 1,916,100. It is the centre of a large gold-mining industry; other industries include engineering works, meat-chilling plants, and clothing factories.

**John, Augustus Edwin** (1878–1961) Welsh painter. He is known for his vivacious portraits, including *The Smiling Woman* (1910; Tate Gallery, London), portraying his second wife, Dorelia McNeill. His sitters included such literary figures as Thomas Hardy, Dylan Thomas, W B Yeats, T E Lawrence, and James Joyce.

**John, Elton** stage name of Reginald Kenneth Dwight (1947– ) English pop singer, pianist, and composer whose long and flamboyant career reached unparalleled heights in 1997 when he rewrote his 'Candle in the Wind' hit for the funeral of Diana, Princess of Wales, a personal friend. In the 1970s he had seven consecutive hit albums. *Goodbye Yellow Brick Road* (1973) includes the hit 'Bennie and the Jets'; among his many other highly successful songs are 'Rocket Man', 'Crocodile Rock', and 'Daniel' (all 1972), 'Candle in the Wind' (1973), 'Pinball Wizard' (1975), 'Blue Eyes' (1982), 'Nikita' (1985), and 'Sacrifice' (1989), the last from his album *Sleeping with the Past*. He wrote the Academy Award-winning music (with lyrics by Tim Rice) for the animated film and stage production *The Lion King* (1995).

**John (I) Lackland** (1167–1216) King of England from 1199 and acting king from 1189 during his brother Richard the Lion-Heart's absence on the Third Crusade.

He lost Normandy and almost all the other English possessions in France to Philip II of France by 1205. His repressive policies and excessive taxation brought him into conflict with his barons, and he was forced to seal the ◊Magna Carta in 1215. Later repudiation of it led to the first Barons' War (1215–17), during which he died. He was succeeded by his son Henry III.

**John I** (1357–1433) King of Portugal from 1385. An illegitimate son of Pedro I, he was elected by the Cortes (parliament). His claim was supported by an English army against the rival king of Castile, thus establishing the Anglo-Portuguese Alliance in 1386.

He married Philippa of Lancaster, daughter of ◊John of Gaunt.

**John Bull** imaginary figure who is a personification of England, similar to the American Uncle Sam. He is represented in cartoons and caricatures as a prosperous farmer of the 18th century.

**John Dory** marine bony fish also called a ◊dory.

**John of Gaunt** (1340–1399) English noble and politician, fourth (and third surviving) son of Edward III, Duke of Lancaster from 1362. He distinguished himself during the Hundred Years' War. During Edward's last years, and the years before Richard II attained the age of majority, he acted as head of government, and Parliament protested against his corrupt rule.

**John Paul II** Karol Jozef Wojtyla (1920– ) Pope from 1978, the first non-Italian to be elected pope since 1522. He was born near Kraków, Poland. He has upheld the tradition of papal infallibility and has condemned artificial contraception, women priests, married priests, and modern dress for monks and nuns – views that have aroused criticism from liberalizing elements in the church.

**Johns, Jasper** (1930– ) US painter, sculptor, and printmaker. He was one of the foremost exponents of ◊Pop art. He rejected abstract art, favouring such mundane subjects as flags, maps, and numbers as a means of exploring the relationship between image and reality. His work employs pigments mixed with wax (encaustic) to create a rich surface with unexpected delicacies of colour.

**John, St** (lived 1st century AD) New Testament apostle. Traditionally, he wrote the fourth Gospel and the Johannine Epistles (when he was bishop of Ephesus), and the Book of Revelation (while exiled to the Greek island of Patmos). His emblem is an eagle; his feast day 27 December.

**Johnson, Amy** (1903–1941) English aviator. She made a solo flight from England to Australia in 1930, in 9.5 days, and in 1932 made the fastest ever solo flight from England to Cape Town, South Africa. Her plane disappeared over the English Channel in World War II while she was serving with the Air Transport Auxiliary.

**Johnson, Andrew** (1808–1875) 17th president of the USA 1865–69, a Democrat. He was a congressman from Tennessee 1843–53, governor of Tennessee 1853–57, senator 1857–62, and vice-president 1865. He succeeded to the presidency on Abraham Lincoln's assassination (15 April 1865). His conciliatory policy to the defeated South after the Civil War involved him in a feud with the Radical Republicans, culminating in his impeachment 1868 before the Senate, which failed to convict him by one vote.

**Johnson, Jack (John Arthur)** (1878–1946) US heavyweight boxer. He overcame severe racial prejudice to become the first black heavyweight champion of the world in 1908 when he travelled to Australia to challenge Tommy Burns. The US authorities wanted Johnson 'dethroned' because of his colour but could not find suitable challengers until 1915, when he lost the title in a dubious fight decision to the giant Jess Willard.

*career highlights*
*professional fights* total: 107; wins: 86; draws: 11; defeats: 10.

**Johnson, Lyndon Baines** (1908–1973) 36th president of the USA 1963–69, a Democrat. He was a member of Congress 1937–49 and the Senate 1949–60. Born in Texas, he brought critical Southern support as J F Kennedy's vice-presidential running mate in 1960, and became president on Kennedy's assassination.

**Johnson, Philip Cortelyou** (1906– ) US architect and architectural historian. Originally designing in the style of Mies van der Rohe, he later became an exponent of ◊postmodernism. He designed the giant AT&T building in New York (1978), a pink skyscraper with a Chippendale-style cabinet top.

**Johnson, Samuel** Dr Johnson (1709–1784) English lexicographer, author, and critic. He was also a brilliant conversationalist and the dominant figure in 18th-century London literary society. His *Dictionary* (1755), provided in its method the pedigree for subsequent lexicography and remained authoritative for over a century. In 1764 he founded, at the suggestion of the painter Joshua Reynolds, a club, known from 1779 as the Literary Club, whose members at various times included also the political philosopher Edmund Burke, the dramatist Oliver Goldsmith, the actor David Garrick, and James ◊Boswell, Johnson's biographer.

**John the Baptist, St** (c. 12 BC–c. AD 27) In the New Testament, an itinerant preacher. After preparation in the wilderness, he proclaimed the coming of the Messiah and baptized Jesus in the River Jordan. He was later executed by ◊Herod Antipas at the request of Salome, who demanded that his head be brought to her on a platter.

**joint** in any animal with a skeleton, a point of movement or articulation. In vertebrates, it is the point where two bones meet. Some joints allow no motion (the sutures of the skull), others allow a very small motion (the sacroiliac joints in the lower back), but most allow a relatively free motion. Of these, some allow a gliding motion (one vertebra of the spine on another), some have a hinge action (elbow and knee), and others allow motion in all directions (hip and shoulder joints) by means of a ball-and-socket arrangement. The ends of the bones at a moving joint are covered with cartilage for greater elasticity and smoothness, and enclosed in an envelope (capsule) of tough white fibrous tissue lined with a membrane which secretes a lubricating and cushioning synovial fluid. The joint is further strengthened by ligaments. In invertebrates with an ◊exoskeleton, the joints are places where the exoskeleton is replaced by a more flexible outer covering, the arthrodial membrane, which allows the limb (or other body part) to bend at that point.

**Joliot-Curie** Frédéric (Jean) Joliot (1900–1958) and Irène (born Curie) (1897–1956), French physicists. They made the discovery of artificial ◊radioactivity, for which they were jointly awarded the 1935 Nobel Prize for Chemistry.

**Jonah** (lived 7th century BC) Hebrew prophet whose name is given to a book in the Old Testament. According to this, he fled by ship to evade his mission to prophesy the destruction of Nineveh. The crew threw him overboard in a storm, as a bringer of ill fortune, and he spent three days and nights in the belly of a whale before coming to land.

**Jonathan, Chief (Joseph) Leabua** (1914–1987) Lesotho politician. A leader in the drive for independence, Jonathan became prime minister of Lesotho in 1965. His rule was ended by a coup in 1986.

**Jones, Inigo** (1573–1652) English Classical architect. He introduced the Palladian style to England. He was employed by James I to design scenery for Ben Jonson's masques and was appointed Surveyor of the King's Works 1615–42. He designed the Queen's House, Greenwich, (1616–35), and the Banqueting House in Whitehall, London, (1619–22).

**jonquil** species of small ◊daffodil, with yellow flowers. It is native to Spain and Portugal, and is cultivated in other countries. (*Narcissus jonquilla*, family Amaryllidaceae.)

**Jonson, Ben(jamin)** (1572–1637) English dramatist, poet, and critic. *Every Man in his Humour* (1598) established the English 'comedy of humours', in which each character embodies a 'humour', or vice, such as greed, lust, or avarice. This was followed by *Cynthia's Revels* (1600) and *The Poetaster* (1601). His first extant tragedy is *Sejanus* (1603), with Burbage and Shakespeare as members of the original cast. His great comedies are *Volpone, or The Fox* (1606), *The Alchemist* (1610), and *Bartholomew Fair* (1614). He wrote extensively for court entertainment in the form of masques produced with scenic designer Inigo ◊Jones.

**Joplin, Scott** (1868–1917) US ◊ragtime pianist and composer. He first came to attention as a pianist at brothels in St Louis and Chicago, and was considered the leading exponent of 'classic rag', in which the standard syncopated rhythm was treated with some sophistication. His 'Maple Leaf Rag' (1899) was the first instrumental sheet music to sell a million copies, and 'The Entertainer', as the theme tune of the film *The Sting* (1973), revived his popularity. He was an influence on Jelly Roll Morton and other early jazz musicians.

**Jordan** Hashemite Kingdom of
*national name* Al Mamlaka al Urduniya al Hashemiyah
*area* 89,206 sq km/34,442 sq mi (West Bank 5,879 sq km/2,269 sq mi)
*capital* Amman
*major towns/cities* Zarqa, Irbid, Saet, Ma'an
*major ports* Aqaba
*physical features* desert plateau in east; Rift

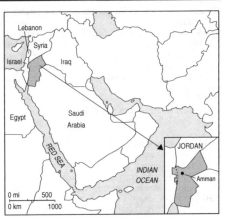

Valley separates east and west banks of River Jordan
*head of state* King Abdullah ibn Hussein from 1999
*head of government* Abdul-Raouf al-Rawabdeh from 1999
*political system* constitutional monarchy
*political parties* independent groups loyal to the king predominate; of the 21 parties registered since 1992, the most significant is the Islamic Action Front (IAF), Islamic fundamentalist
*currency* Jordanian dinar
*GNP per capita (PPP)* (US$) 3,230 (1998)
*exports* phosphate, potash, fertilizers, foodstuffs, pharmaceuticals, fruit and vegetables, cement. Principal market: India 9.2% (1998)
*population* 6,483,000 (1999 est)
*language* Arabic (official), English
*religion* Sunni Muslim 80%, Christian 8%
*life expectancy* 69 (men); 72 (women) (1995–2000)
*Chronology*
*13th century BC* Oldest known 'states' of Jordan, including Gideon, Ammon, Moab, and Edom, established.
*c. 1000 BC* East Jordan was part of kingdom of Israel, under David and Solomon.
*4th century BC* Southeast Jordan occupied by the independent Arabic-speaking Nabataeans.
*64 BC* Conquered by Romans and became part of province of Arabia.
*AD 636* Became largely Muslim after the Byzantine forces of Emperor Heraclius were defeated by Arab armies at battle of Yarmuk, in northern Jordan.
*1099–1187* Part of Latin Kingdom established by Crusaders in Jerusalem.
*from early 16th century* Part of Turkish Ottoman Empire, administered from Damascus.
*1920* Trans-Jordan (the area east of the River Jordan) and Palestine (which includes the West Bank) placed under British administration by League of Nations mandate.
*1923* Trans-Jordan separated from Palestine and recognized by Britain as a substantially independent state under the rule of Emir Abdullah ibn Hussein, a member of the Hashemite dynasty of Arabia.
*1946* Trans-Jordan achieved independence from

Britain, with Abd Allah as king; name changed to Jordan.
**1948** British mandate for Palestine expired, leading to fighting between Arabs and Jews, who each claimed the area.
**1950** Jordan annexed West Bank; 400,000 Palestinian refugees flooded into Jordan, putting pressure on economy.
**1951** King Abdullah assassinated in Jerusalem; succeeded by his son King Talal.
**1952** Partially democratic constitution introduced.
**1953** Hussein ibn Tal Abdulla el Hashim officially became king of Jordan, after his father, King Talal, stepped down.
**1958** Jordan and Iraq formed Arab Federation that ended when Iraqi monarchy was deposed.
**1967** Israel defeated Egypt, Syria, and Jordan in Arab–Israeli Six-Day War, and captured and occupied West Bank, including Arab Jerusalem. Martial law imposed.
**1970–71** Jordanians moved against increasingly radicalized Palestine Liberation Organization (PLO), which had launched guerrilla raids on Israel from Jordanian territory, resulting in bloody civil war, before PLO leadership fled abroad.
**1976** Lower house dissolved, political parties banned, elections postponed until further notice.
**1980** Jordan emerged as an important ally of Iraq in its war against Iran, an ally of Syria, with whom Jordan's relations were tense.
**1982** Hussein tried to mediate in the Arab–Israeli conflict, following the Israeli invasion of Lebanon.
**1984** Women voted for the first time; the parliament was recalled.
**1985** Hussein and PLO leader Yasser Arafat put forward a framework for a Middle East peace settlement. There was a secret meeting between Hussein and the Israeli prime minister.
**1988** Hussein announced his willingness to cease administering the West Bank as part of Jordan, passing responsibility to the PLO; parliament was suspended.
**1989** Prime Minister Zaid al-Rifai resigned; Hussein promised new parliamentary elections. There were riots over price increases of up to 50% following a fall in oil revenues. In the first parliamentary elections for 22 years the Muslim Brotherhood won 25 of 80 seats but were exiled from government. Martial law was lifted.
**1990** Hussein unsuccessfully tried to mediate after Iraq's invasion of Kuwait. There were huge refugee problems as thousands fled to Jordan from Kuwait and Iraq.
**1991** 24 years of martial law ended, the ban on political parties was lifted, and Jordan remained neutral during the Gulf War involving Iraq.
**1993** Candidates loyal to Hussein won a majority in the parliamentary elections; several leading Islamic fundamentalists lost their seats.
**1994** An economic cooperation pact was signed with the PLO. A peace treaty was signed with Israel, ending the 46-year-old state of war.
**1996** Abdul-Karim Kabariti was appointed prime minister.
**1997** There was success for government supporters in the assembly elections.

**1998** Fayez Tarawneh was appointed prime minister.
**1999** King Hussein died and his eldest son, Abdullah, succeeded him. Abdul-Raouf al-Rawabdeh was appointed prime minister. In May, Abdullah held talks with Yassir Arafat prior to Israeli peace negotiations.

**Joseph** in the New Testament, the husband of the Virgin Mary, a descendant of King David of the tribe of Judah, and a carpenter by trade.
Although Jesus was not the son of Joseph, Joseph was his legal father. According to Roman Catholic tradition, he had a family by a previous wife, and was an elderly man when he married Mary.

**Joseph II** (1741–1790) Holy Roman Emperor from 1765, son of Francis I (1708–1765).
The reforms he carried out after the death of his mother, ◊Maria Theresa, 1780, provoked revolts from those who lost privileges.

**Josephine, Marie Josèphe Rose Tascher de la Pagerie** (1763–1814) As wife of ◊Napoleon Bonaparte, she was empress of France 1804–1809. Born on the island of Martinique, she married in 1779 Alexandre de Beauharnais, who played a part in the French Revolution, and in 1796 Napoleon, who divorced her 1809 because she had not produced children.

**Joseph of Arimathaea, St** (lived 1st century AD) In the New Testament, a wealthy Hebrew, member of the Sanhedrin (supreme court), and secret supporter of Jesus. On the evening of the Crucifixion he asked the Roman procurator Pilate for Jesus' body and buried it in his own tomb. Feast day 17 March.

**Jospin, Lionel** (1937–  ) French socialist politician, first secretary of the Socialist Party (PS)1981–88 and 1995–97, then prime minister, under President Jacques ◊Chirac, from June 1997 heading a 'pluralist left' coalition with communist, green, and left radical parties.

**joule** SI unit (symbol J) of work and energy, replacing the ◊calorie (one joule equals 4.2 calories)

**Joule, James Prescott** (1818–1889) English physicist. His work on the relations between electrical, mechanical, and chemical effects led to the discovery of the first law of ◊thermodynamics.

**Joyce, James Augustine Aloysius** (1882–1941) Irish writer. His originality lies in evolving a literary form to express the complexity of the human mind, and he revolutionized the form of the English novel with his 'stream of consciousness' technique. His works include *Dubliners* (1914; short stories), *A Portrait of the Artist as a Young Man* (1916), *Ulysses* (1922), and *Finnegans Wake* (1939).

**joystick** in computing, an input device that signals to a computer the direction and extent of displacement of a hand-held lever. It is similar to the joystick used to control the flight of an aircraft.

**Juan Carlos** (1938–  ) King of Spain. The son of Don Juan, pretender to the Spanish throne, he married Princess Sofia, eldest daughter of King Paul of Greece, in 1962. In 1969 he was nominated by ◊Franco to succeed on the restoration of the monarchy intended to follow Franco's death; his father was excluded because of his known liberal views. Juan Carlos became king in 1975, and played a vital role in the smooth transition to democratic stability. He was instrumental in the defeat of an attempted military coup in 1981.

**Judah** or *Judaea,* district of southern Palestine. After the death of King Solomon in 922 BC, Judah adhered to his son Rehoboam and the Davidic line, whereas the rest of Israel elected Jeroboam as ruler of the northern kingdom. In New Testament times, Judah was the Roman province of Judaea, and in current Israeli usage it refers to the southern area of the West Bank.

**Judaism** the religion of the ancient Hebrews and their descendants the Jews, based, according to the Old Testament, on a covenant between God and Abraham about 2000 BC, and the renewal of the covenant with Moses about 1200 BC. Judaism is the oldest monotheistic faith, the forebear of Christianity and Islam. It rests on the concept of one eternal invisible God, whose will is revealed in the Torah and who has a special relationship with the Jewish people. The Torah comprises the first five books of the Bible (the Pentateuch), which contains the history, laws, and guide to life for correct behaviour. Besides those living in Israel, there are large Jewish populations in the USA, the former USSR (mostly Russia, Ukraine, Belarus, and Moldova), the UK and Commonwealth nations, and in Jewish communities throughout the world. There are approximately 18 million Jews, with about 9 million in the Americas, 5 million in Europe, and 4 million in Asia, Africa, and the Pacific.

**Judas Iscariot** (lived 1st century AD) In the New Testament, the disciple who betrayed Jesus Christ. Judas was the treasurer of the group. At the last Passover supper, he arranged, for 30 pieces of silver, to point out Jesus to the chief priests so that they could arrest him. Afterward Judas was overcome with remorse and committed suicide.

**judiciary** in constitutional terms, the system of courts and body of judges in a country. The independence of the judiciary from other branches of the central authority is generally considered to be an essential feature of a democratic political system. This independence is often written into a nation's constitution and protected from abuse by politicians.

**Judith** in the Old Testament, a Jewish widow who saved her community from a Babylonian siege by pretending to seduce and then beheading the enemy general Holofernes. Her story is much represented in Western art.

**judo** (Japanese *jū do,* 'gentle way') form of wrestling of Japanese origin. The two combatants wear loose-fitting, belted jackets and trousers to facilitate holds, and falls are broken by a square mat; when one has established a painful hold that the other cannot break, the latter signifies surrender by slapping the ground with a free hand. Degrees of proficiency are indicated by the colour of the belt: for novices, white, then yellow, orange (2 degrees), green (2 degrees), blue (2 degrees), brown (2 degrees), then black (Dan grades; 10 degrees, of which 1st to 5th Dan wear black belts, 6th to 9th wear red and white, and 10th wears solid red).

**Juggernaut** or *Jagannath,* a name for Vishnu, the Hindu god, meaning 'Lord of the World'. His temple is in Puri, Orissa, India. A statue of the god, dating from about 318, is annually carried in procession on a large vehicle (hence the word 'juggernaut'). Devotees formerly threw themselves beneath its wheels.

**jugular vein** one of two veins in the necks of vertebrates; they return blood from the head to the superior (or anterior) ◊vena cava and thence to the heart.

**jujube** any of a group of trees belonging to the buckthorn family, with berrylike fruits. The common jujube (*Z. jujuba*) of Asia, Africa, and Australia, cultivated in southern Europe and California, has fruit the size of small plums, known as Chinese dates when preserved in syrup. See also ◊lotus. (Genus *Zizyphus,* family Thamnaceae.)

**Julian the Apostate** (332–363) Roman emperor. Born in Constantinople, the nephew of Constantine the Great, he was brought up as a Christian but early in life became a convert to paganism. Sent by Constantius to govern Gaul 355, he was proclaimed emperor by his troops 360, and in 361 was marching on Constantinople when Constantius' death allowed a peaceful succession. He revived pagan worship and refused to persecute heretics. He was killed in battle against the Persians of the ◊Sassanian Empire.

**Julius II** born Giuliano della Rovere (1443–1513) Pope (1503–13). A politician who wanted to make the Papal States the leading power in Italy, he formed international alliances first against Venice and then against France. He began the building of St Peter's Church in Rome in 1506 and was a patron of the artists Michelangelo and Raphael.

**July Revolution** revolution 27–29 July 1830 in France that overthrew the restored Bourbon monarchy of Charles X and substituted the constitutional monarchy of Louis Philippe, whose rule (1830–48) is sometimes referred to as the July Monarchy.

**jumbo jet** popular name for a generation of huge wide-bodied airliners including the *Boeing 747,* which is 71 m/232 ft long, has a wingspan of 60 m/196 ft, a maximum takeoff weight of nearly 400 tonnes, and can carry more than 400 passengers.

**Juneau** ice-free port and state capital of ◊Alaska, USA, opposite Douglas Island on Gastineau Channel, in the south Alaskan panhandle (narrow strip of land that projects from one state into another); population (1992) 28,400. The city is the commercial and distribution centre for the fur-trading and mining industries of the panhandle region; also important are salmon fishing, fish processing, lumbering and tourism. Gold mining remained important here until the closure of the mine in 1944, but in the 1990s there has been some resumption of gold mining.

**Jung, Carl Gustav** (1875–1961) Swiss psychiatrist. He collaborated with Sigmund ◊Freud from 1907 until their disagreement 1914 over the importance of sexuality in causing psychological problems. Jung studied myth, religion, and dream symbolism, saw the unconscious as a source of spiritual insight, and distinguished between introversion and extroversion.

**juniper** any of a group of aromatic evergreen trees or shrubs of the cypress family, found throughout temperate regions. Its berries are used to flavour gin. Some junipers are mistakenly called ◊cedars. (Genus *Juniperus,* family Cupressaceae.)

**junk bond** derogatory term for a security officially rated as 'below investment grade'. It is issued in order to raise capital quickly, typically to finance a takeover to be paid for by the sale of assets once the company is acquired. Junk bonds have a high yield, but are a high-risk investment.

**Juno** in Roman mythology, the principal goddess, identified with the Greek ◊Hera. The wife of Jupiter and queen of heaven, she was concerned with all aspects of women's lives and also regarded as a patroness of commerce.

**Jupiter** fifth planet from the Sun, and the largest in the Solar System, with a mass equal to 70% of all the other planets combined, 318 times that of Earth's. It is largely composed of hydrogen and helium, liquefied by pressure in its interior, and probably with a rocky core larger than Earth. Its main feature is the Great Red Spot, a cloud of rising gases, 14,000 km/8,500 mi wide and 30,000 km/20,000 mi long, revolving anticlockwise.

*mean distance from the Sun* 778 million km/484 million mi
*equatorial diameter* 142,800 km/88,700 mi
*rotation period* 9 hr 51 min
*year* (complete orbit) 11.86 Earth years
*atmosphere* consists of clouds of white ammonia crystals, drawn out into belts by the planet's high speed of rotation (the fastest of any planet). Darker orange and brown clouds at lower levels may contain sulphur, as well as simple organic compounds. Further down still, temperatures are warm, a result of heat left over from Jupiter's formation, and it is this heat that drives the turbulent weather patterns of the planet.
*surface* although largely composed of hydrogen and helium, Jupiter probably has a rocky core larger than Earth.
In 1995, the *Galileo* probe revealed Jupiter's atmosphere to consist of 0.2% water, less than previously estimated.
*satellites* Jupiter has 16 moons. The four largest moons, Io, Europa (which is the size of our Moon), Ganymede, and Callisto, are the

*Galilean satellites,* discovered 1610 by *Galileo* (Ganymede, which is about the size of Mercury, is the largest moon in the Solar System). Three small moons were discovered 1979 by the Voyager space probes, as was a faint ring of dust around Jupiter's equator 55,000 km/34,000 mi above the cloud tops.

**Jupiter** or Jove, (Latin *Diovis pater* 'father of heaven') in Roman mythology, the supreme god reigning on Mount Olympus, identified with the Greek ◊Zeus; son of Saturn and Ops; and husband of Juno, his sister. His titles included Fulgur (thrower of lightning), Tonans (maker of thunder), Invictus (protector in battle), and Triumphator (bestower of victory). His main temple was on the Capitoline Hill in Rome; destination of the solemn triumphal processions of victorious generals. As the particular protector of Rome, he was honoured by consuls taking office.

**Jura Mountains** series of parallel mountain ranges running along the French–Swiss frontier between the Rivers Rhône and Rhine, a distance of 250 km/156 mi. The highest peak is Crête de la Neige (1,723 m/5,650 ft). The mountains give their name to the Jura *département* of France, and in 1979 a Jura canton was established in Switzerland, formed from the French-speaking areas of Berne.

**Jurassic** period of geological time 208–146 million years ago; the middle period of the Mesozoic era. Climates worldwide were equable, creating forests of conifers and ferns; dinosaurs were abundant, birds evolved, and limestones and iron ores were deposited.

**jurisprudence** the science of law in the abstract – that is, not the study of any particular laws or legal system, but of the principles upon which legal systems are founded.

**jury** body of lay people (usually 12) sworn to decide the facts of a case and reach a verdict in a court of law. Juries, used mainly in English-speaking countries, are implemented primarily in criminal cases, but also sometimes in civil cases; for example, inquests and libel trials.

**justice of the peace** (JP), in England, an unpaid ◊magistrate.
In the USA, where JPs receive fees and are usually elected, their courts are the lowest in the states, and deal only with minor offences, such as traffic violations; they may also conduct marriages.

**Justinian** Flavius Anicianus Justinianus (*c.* 483–565) East Roman emperor 527–65, renowned for overseeing the reconquest of Africa, Italy, and parts of Spain. He ordered the codification of Roman law, which has influenced European jurisprudence; he built the church of Hagia Sophia in Constantinople, and closed the university in Athens in 529. His achievements, however, were short-lived. His reconquests and ambitious building projects overstretched the empire's resources and within a few years of his death much of his newly conquered territory had been lost.

**jute** fibre obtained from two plants of the linden family: *C. capsularis* and *C. olitorius.* Jute is used for sacks and sacking, upholstery, webbing (woven strips used to support upholstery), string, and stage canvas. (Genus *Corchorus*, family Tiliaceae.)

**Jute** member of a Germanic people who originated in Jutland but later settled in Frankish territory. They occupied Kent, southeast England, in about 450, according to tradition under Hengist and Horsa, and conquered the Isle of Wight and the opposite coast of Hampshire in the early 6th century.

**Jutland** Danish *Jylland,* peninsula of northern Europe; area 29,500 sq km/11,400 sq mi. It is separated from Norway by the Skagerrak and from Sweden by the Kattegat, with the North Sea to the west. The larger northern part belongs to Denmark, the southern part to Germany.

**Juvenal** Decimus Junius Juvenalis (*c.* AD 60–140) Roman satirical poet. His 16 surviving *Satires* give an explicit and sometimes brutal picture of the corrupt Roman society of his time. Very little is known of his life, but his native place, if not his birthplace, was Aquinum (now Aquino, southern Italy). Juvenal is twice mentioned by ♢Martial, and he may be the author of a well-known dedication (probably to an altar to Ceres) by one Juvenal who held military rank and some civil offices at Aquinum. This reference to military service agrees with the story of Sidonius Apollinaris (5th century) that Juvenal quarrelled with Paris, a famous ballet dancer in the reign of Domitian, and was sent to the Egyptian frontier as an officer of a local garrison.

**K** symbol for *kelvin,* a scale of temperature.

**K2** or *Chogori,* second highest mountain above sea level, 8,611 m/28,261 ft, in the Karakoram range, in a disputed region of Pakistan. It was first climbed 1954 by an Italian expedition.

**kabbala** or *cabbala,* (Hebrew 'tradition') ancient esoteric Jewish mystical tradition of philosophy containing strong elements of pantheism, yet akin to neo-Platonism. Kabbalistic writing reached its peak between the 13th and 16th centuries. It is largely rejected by current Judaic thought as medieval superstition, but is basic to the Hasid sect.

**Kabul** capital of Afghanistan, 1,800 m/5,900 ft above sea level, on the *River Kabul;* population (1997 est) 500,000. Products include textiles, plastics, leather, and glass. It commands the strategic routes to Pakistan via the ◊Khyber Pass. The city was captured by the Taliban on 27 September 1996.

**Kádár, János** (1912–1989) Hungarian communist leader, in power 1956–88, after suppressing the national uprising. As leader of the Hungarian Socialist Workers' Party (HSWP) and prime minister 1956–58 and 1961–65, Kádár introduced a series of market-socialist economic reforms, while retaining cordial political relations with the USSR.

**Kafka, Franz** (1883–1924) Austrian novelist. He wrote in German. His three unfinished allegorical novels *Der Prozess/The Trial* (1925), *Das Schloss/The Castle* (1926), and *Amerika/America* (1927) were posthumously published despite his instructions that they should be destroyed. His short stories include 'Die Verwandlung/The Metamorphosis' 1915, in which a man turns into a huge insect. His vision of lonely individuals trapped in bureaucratic or legal labyrinths can be seen as a powerful metaphor for modern experience.

**Kaifeng** or *Pien-ching,* city in Henan province; population (1994) 788,500. Formerly the provincial capital and once a capital of China (907–1127), it lost its importance because of the silting-up of the nearby Huang He River. Industries include zinc smelting, and the manufacture of fertilizers, textiles, beverages, and agricultural machinery.

**Kairouan** or *Kairwan,* Arabic *al-Qayrawan,* Muslim holy city in Tunisia, south of Tunis; population (1994) 102,600. Chief products are carpets, leather goods, and copperware. The city, said to have been founded in AD 617, ranks after Mecca and Medina as a place of pilgrimage.

**Kaiser** title formerly used by the Holy Roman emperors, Austrian emperors 1806–1918, and German emperors 1871–1918. The word, like the Russian 'tsar', is derived from the Latin *Caesar.*

**kakapo** nocturnal flightless parrot that lives in burrows in New Zealand. It is green, yellow, and brown with a disc of brown feathers round its eyes, like an owl. It weighs up to 3.5 kg/7.5 lb. When in danger, its main defence is to remain perfectly still. Because of the introduction of predators such as dogs, cats, rats, and ferrets, it is in danger of extinction. In 1998 there were only 56 birds left in the wild. (Species *Strigops habroptilus,* order Psittaciformes.)

**Kalaallit Nunaat** Greenlandic name for ◊Greenland.

**Kalahari Desert** arid to semi-arid desert area forming most of Botswana and extending into Namibia, Zimbabwe, and South Africa; area about 900,000 sq km/347,400 sq mi. The only permanent river, the Okavango, flows into a delta in the northwest forming marshes rich in wildlife.

**kale** type of ◊cabbage.

**Kali** in Hindu mythology, the goddess of destruction and death. She is the wife of ◊Siva.

**Kalimantan** province of the republic of Indonesia occupying part of the island of Borneo; area 543,900 sq km/210,000 sq mi; population (urban area, 1990 est) 9,100,000. The land is mostly low-lying, with mountains in the north. Towns and cities include Banjarmasin and Balikpapan. Industries include petroleum, rubber, coffee, copra, pepper, and timber.

**Kaliningrad** formerly *Königsberg,* city and port in western Russia; population (1989) 871,000. Industries include shipbuilding, fisheries, engineering and paper manufacture. The port of Kaliningrad remains ice-free throughout the year; as well as being an important commercial centre, it is also the principal base of the Russian Baltic fleet. The city was the capital of East Prussia until this territory was divided between the USSR and Poland in 1945 under the Potsdam Agreement, when it was renamed in honour of Soviet President Mikhail Kalinin (1875–1946). As Königsberg, the city was the birthplace and residence of the German philosopher Immanuel Kant (1724–1804).

**Kamchatka Peninsula** mountainous region in the Russian Far East, separating the Sea of ◊Okhotsk from the Pacific Ocean and the Bering Sea. The Kamchatka Peninsula is over 1,200 km/746 mi long, covers an area of 370,000 sq km/142,857 sq mi, and contains a total of over 160 volcanoes (22 of them active), together with many hot springs and geysers. The region has an extremely severe climate and predominantly tundra vegetation, with forests in sheltered valleys. The Kamchatka Peninsula is home to a huge number of animal and bird species, including the brown bear, sea eagle, and sable. There are coal, sulphur, gold, mica, and other mineral deposits.

**Kampala** capital of Uganda, on Lake Victoria; population (1991) 773,500. It is linked by rail with Mombasa. Products include tea, coffee, fruit, and vegetables. Industries include engineering, chemicals, paint manufacture, textiles, footwear, brewing, distilling, and food processing.

**Kampuchea** former name (1975–89) of Cambodia.

**Kanchenjunga** Himalayan mountain on the Nepal–Sikkim border, 8,586 m/28,170 ft high, 120 km/75 mi southeast of Mount Everest. The name means 'five treasure houses of the great snows'. Kanchenjunga was first climbed by a British expedition 1955.

**Kandinsky, Vasily** (1866–1944) Russian-born painter. He was a pioneer of abstract art. Between 1910 and 1914 he produced the series *Improvisations* and *Compositions,* the first known examples of purely abstract work in 20th-century art. He was an originator of the Expressionist ◊*Blaue Reiter* movement 1911–12, and taught at the ◊Bauhaus school of design in Germany 1921–33.

**Kandy** city in central Sri Lanka, on the Mahaweli River; capital of a district of the same name; population (1990) 104,000. Products include tea. One of the most sacred Buddhist shrines, the Dalada Maligawa, is situated in Kandy; it contains an alleged tooth of the Buddha.

**kangaroo** any of a group of marsupials (mammals that carry their young in pouches) found in Australia, Tasmania, and New Guinea. Kangaroos are plant-eaters and most live in groups. They are adapted to hopping, the vast majority of species having very large, powerful back legs and feet compared with the small forelimbs. The larger types can jump 9 m/30 ft in a single bound. Most are nocturnal. Species vary from small rat kangaroos, only 30 cm/1 ft long, through the medium-sized wallabies, to the large red and great grey kangaroos, which are the largest living marsupials. These may be 1.8 m/5.9 ft long with 1.1 m/3.5 ft tails. (Family Macropodidae.)

**Ka Ngwane** former black homeland in Mpumalanga Province, South Africa; population (1991) 779,200.

**Kannada** or *Kanarese,* language spoken in southern India, the official state language of Karnataka; also spoken in Tamil Nadu and Maharashtra. There are over 20 million speakers of Kannada, which belongs to the Dravidian family. Written records in Kannada date from the 5th century AD.

**Kano** capital of Kano state in northern Nigeria, trade centre of an irrigated area; population (1992 est) 699,900. Kano is a major centre for the groundnut and cattle trade. Products include bicycles, glass, furniture, textiles, chemicals, flour, vegetable oil, and cereals. Kano is a tourist centre with trade in leather, brass, cloth,

silverware, and beads. Founded about 1000 BC, Kano is a walled city, with New Kano extending beyond the walls.

**Kanpur** formerly *Cawnpore,* commercial and industrial city and capital of Kanpur district, Uttar Pradesh, India, 65 km/40 mi southwest of Lucknow, on the River Ganges; population (1991) 2,111,300. Industries include cotton, wool, jute, chemicals, plastics, iron and steel. It has benefited from its rail links with Calcutta, particularly during the growth of its cotton industry in the last century.

**Kansas** state in central USA; it is nicknamed the Sunflower State. Kansas was admitted to the Union in 1861 as the 34th US state; it is considered both a part of the US Midwest and as one of the Great Plains states; it is bordered to the south by Oklahoma, to the west by Colorado, to the north by Nebraska, and to the east by Missouri
*population* (1995) 2,565,300
*area* 213,200 sq km/82,296 sq mi
*capital* Topeka
*towns and cities* Kansas City, Wichita, Overland Park
*industries and products* wheat, corn, sorghum, sunflowers, beef and dairy cattle, coal, petroleum, natural gas, lead, zinc, aircraft, minerals.

**Kansu** alternative spelling for the Chinese province ◊Gansu.

**Kant, Immanuel** (1724–1804) German philosopher. He believed that knowledge is not merely an aggregate of sense impressions but is dependent on the conceptual apparatus of the human understanding, which is itself not derived from experience. In ethics, Kant argued that right action cannot be based on feelings or inclinations but conforms to a law given by reason, the *categorical imperative.*

**Kaohsiung** city and port on the west coast of Taiwan; population (1992) 1,396,400. Industries include aluminium ware, fertilizers, cement, oil refineries, iron and steel works, shipyards, and food processing. Kaohsiung began to develop as a commercial port after 1858; its industrial development came about while it was occupied by Japan 1895–1945.

**kaolin** group of clay minerals, such as ◊kaolinite, $Al_2Si_2O_5(OH)_4$, derived from the alteration of aluminium silicate minerals, such as ◊feldspars and ◊mica. It is used in medicine to treat digestive upsets, and in poultices.

**kaolinite** white or greyish ◊clay mineral, hydrated aluminium silicate, $Al_2Si_2O_5(OH)_4$, formed mainly by the decomposition of feldspar in granite. It is made up of platelike crystals, the atoms of which are bonded together in two-dimensional sheets, between which the bonds are weak, so that they are able to slip over one another, a process made easier by a layer of water. China clay (kaolin) is derived from it. It is mined in France, the UK, Germany, China, and the USA.

**kapok** silky hairs that surround the seeds of certain trees, particularly the *kapok tree*

(*Bombax ceiba*) of India and Malaysia and the *silk-cotton tree* (*Ceiba pentandra*) of tropical America. Kapok is used for stuffing cushions and mattresses and for sound insulation; oil obtained from the seeds is used in food and soap.

**Karachi** largest city and chief port of Pakistan, northwest of the Indus delta; population (1996 est) 10 million; 4 million live in makeshift settlements. It is the capital of ◊Sind province. Industries include shipbuilding, engineering, chemicals, plastics, and textiles. A nuclear power plant has been developed at Paradise Point, 25 km/15 mi to the west of the city. It was the capital of Pakistan 1947–59, when it was replaced by ◊Islamabad.

**Karadžić, Radovan** (1945– ) Montenegrin-born leader of the Bosnian Serbs, leader of the community's unofficial government 1992–96. He cofounded the Serbian Democratic Party of Bosnia-Herzegovina (SDS-BH) in 1990 and launched the siege of Sarajevo in 1992, plunging the country into a prolonged and bloody civil war. A succession of peace initiatives for the region failed due to his ambitious demands for Serbian territory, and he was subsequently implicated in war crimes allegedly committed in Bosnia-Herzegovina. In the autumn of 1995, in the wake of a sustained NATO bombardment of Bosnian Serb positions around Sarajevo, Karadžić agreed to enter peace negotiations; in November he signed the US-sponsored Dayton peace accord, under the terms of which he was forced to step down as the Bosnian Serb prime minister. The accord divided Bosnia into separate Moslem, Croat, and Serb areas, and although this seemingly excluded him from further power, he remained a dominant backstage force. He was charged with genocide and crimes against humanity at the Yugoslav War Crimes Tribunal in The Hague, Netherlands, in November 1995 but subsequently defied NATO orders to arrest him on sight by continuing to travel openly about the region. He stepped down as party leader in July 1996. His position was further weakened when, in January 1998, the moderate Milorad Dodik became prime minister of the Bosnian Serb Republic.

**Karajan, Herbert von** (1908–1989) Austrian conductor. He dominated European classical music performance after 1947. He was principal conductor of the Berlin Philharmonic Orchestra 1955–89, artistic director of the Vienna State Opera 1957–64, and of the Salzburg Festival 1956–60. A perfectionist, he cultivated an orchestral sound of notable smoothness and transparency; he also staged operas and directed his own video recordings. He recorded the complete Beethoven symphonies three times, and had a special affinity with Mozart and Bruckner, although his repertoire extended from Bach to Schoenberg.

**Kara-Kalpak** or *Karakalpakstan*, large autonomous region in northwest Uzbekistan
**area** 158,000 sq km/61,000 sq mi
**physical** the north of the region consists mainly of lowland around the delta of the ◊Amu Darya, which formerly flowed into the Aral Sea, the southern half of which is within the region; plentiful salt deposits
**cities** Nukus (capital); Munyak
**industries** heavily irrigated cultivation of cotton, rice, and wheat; some viticulture and manufacture of leather goods
**history** named after the Kara-Kalpak ('black hood') people, who live south of the Aral Sea and were conquered by Russia in 1867. An autonomous Kara-Kalpak region was formed in 1926 within Kazakhstan, transferred to the Soviet republic in 1930, became an autonomous republic (incorporating part of the Uzbek SSR) in 1932, and was annexed to Uzbekistan in 1936. Soviet agricultural planning foresaw major grain production here, but large-scale irrigation schemes and excessive use of chemical fertilizers have deprived the Amu Darya and Aral Sea of water, and reduced the region to a dust bowl.

**Karakoram** mountain range in central Asia, divided among China, Pakistan, and India. Peaks include K2, Masharbrum, Gasharbrum, and Mustagh Tower. *Ladakh* subsidiary range is in northeastern Kashmir on the Tibetan border.

**Karamanlis, Konstantinos** (1907–1998) Greek politician of the New Democracy Party. A lawyer and an anticommunist, he was prime minister 1955–58, 1958–61, and 1961–63 (when he went into self-imposed exile because of a military coup). He was recalled as prime minister on the fall of the regime of the 'colonels' in July 1974, and was president 1980–85.

**karaoke** (Japanese 'empty orchestra') amateur singing in public to prerecorded backing tapes. Karaoke originated in Japan and spread to other parts of the world in the 1980s. Karaoke machines are jukeboxes of backing tracks to well-known popular songs, usually with a microphone attached and accompanying lyrics and video graphics displayed on a screen.

**karat** or *carat*, the unit of purity in gold in the US. Pure gold is 24-karat; 22-karat (the purest used in jewellery) is 22 parts gold and two parts alloy (to give greater strength); 18-karat is 75% gold.

**karate** (Japanese 'empty hand') one of the ◊martial arts. Karate is a type of unarmed combat derived from *kempo*, a form of the Chinese Shaolin boxing. It became popular in the West in the 1930s.

**Karen** member of any of a group of Southeast Asian peoples. Numbering 1.9 million, they live in eastern Myanmar (Burma), Thailand, and the Irrawaddy delta. Traditionally they practised ◊shifting cultivation. Buddhism and Christianity are their main religions, and their language belongs to the Thai division of the Sino-Tibetan family. In 1984 the Burmese government began a military campaign against the Karen National Liberation Army, the armed wing of the Karen National Union. The Myanmar State Law and Order Council (SLORC) increased the use of Karen civilians as forced labourers 1995–96, especially to build the Ye-Tavoy railway and road. Karen villages were also relocated, crops destroyed and property confiscated, forcing thousands to flee to Thailand.

**Karloff, Boris** Stage name of William Henry Pratt (1887–1969) English-born US actor. He achieved Hollywood stardom with his role as the monster in the film *Frankenstein* (1931). Several sequels followed, as well as appearances in such films as *The Mummy* (1932), *Scarface* (1932), *The Lost Patrol* (1934), *The Body Snatcher* (1945), and *The Raven* (1963).

**karma** Sanskrit 'action', in Hinduism, the sum of a human being's actions, carried forward from one life to the next, resulting in an improved or worsened fate. Buddhism has a similar belief, except that no permanent personality is envisaged, the karma relating only to volitional tendencies carried on from birth to birth, unless the power holding them together is dispersed in the attainment of nirvana.

**Karnataka** formerly (until 1973) *Mysore,* state in southwest India
***area*** 191,800 sq km/74,035 sq mi
***capital*** ◊Bangalore
***towns*** Mangalore (port)
***physical*** western coastal plain; inland the forested Western Ghats rise to heights of 1,250 m/4,000 ft; inland the drier, poor soils of the plateau; drained westwards by rivers Krishna, Tungabhadra, and Cauvery
***agriculture*** rice on the coastal western plain; inland millet, groundnuts, rice with irrigation; cotton in the north; coffee and tea on the slopes of the Western Ghats
***industry*** manganese, chromite, iron ore, bauxite, mica, copper, and India's only sources of gold (from the Kolar fields) and silver; teak and sandalwood processing; the Tungabhadra dam provides hydroelectricity, and irrigates up to 500,000 ha/1.23 million acres in Karnataka and Andhra Pradesh.
***population*** (1994) 48,150,000; mainly Hindu
***language*** Kannada
***famous people*** Haidar Ali, Tipu Sultan.

**Karoo** (Khoikhoi *karusa* 'hard') two areas of semi-desert in Eastern Cape Province, South Africa, divided into the **Great Karoo** and **Little Karoo** by the Swartberg Mountains. The two Karoos together have an area of about 260,000 sq km/100,000 sq mi.

**Karpov, Anatoly Yevgenyevich** (1951– ) Russian chess player. He succeeded Bobby Fischer of the USA as world champion 1975, and held the title until losing to Gary Kasparov 1985. He lost to Kasparov again 1990. In January 1998 Karpov won the FIDE World Chess Championship defeating Viswanathan Anand of India in the final.

**karst** landscape characterized by remarkable surface and underground forms, created as a result of the action of water on permeable limestone. The feature takes its name from the Karst region on the Adriatic coast in Slovenia and Croatia, but the name is applied to landscapes throughout the world, the most dramatic of which is found near the city of Guilin in the Guangxi province of China.

**karyotype** in biology, the set of ◊chromosomes characteristic of a given species. It is described as the number, shape, and size of the chromosomes in a single cell of an organism. In humans for example, the karyotype consists of 46 chromosomes, in mice 40, crayfish 200, and in fruit flies 8.

**Kashmir** former part of Jammu state in the north of British India with a largely Muslim population, ruled by a Hindu maharajah, who joined it to the republic of India 1947. There was fighting between the pro-India Hindu ruling class and the pro-Pakistan Muslim majority which involved Indian and Pakistani troops, until a UN ceasefire was agreed 30 October 1948. There was open war between the two countries 1965–66 and 1971. It is today divided under the terms of the 1972 Simla Agreement between the Pakistani area of Kashmir and the Indian state of ◊Jammu and Kashmir. Since 1990 it has been riven by Muslim separatist violence, with more than 150,000 Indian troops deployed in Kashmir 1993. These were criticized by human-rights groups for torture, rape, and killing. Estimates of casualties 1990–93 range from 8,000 to 20,000. Separatist violence escalated during 1995 and several Westerners were taken hostage, with one being killed by the militant separatist group Al-Faran. The main political party in Jammu and Kashmir, the separatist Jammu and Kashmir Liberation Front (JKLF), is divided into Indian- and Pakistan-based factions. In October 1996 the National Congress Party, which aims to retain the area within India, won the first local elections to be held since the separatist violence broke out in 1990. In September 1997 cross-border shelling by Pakistani and Indian forces led to 50 deaths. More than 100 were killed in August 1998 in intensified shelling duels between India and Pakistan.

**Kashmir** area occupied by Pakistan, 78,900 sq km/30,445 sq mi, in the northwest of the former state of Kashmir, now ◊Jammu and Kashmir; Azad ('free') Kashmir in the west has its own legislative assembly based in Muzaffarabad while Gilgit and Baltistan regions to the north and east are governed directly by Pakistan; the Northern Areas are claimed by India and Pakistan
***population*** 1,500,000
***towns and cities*** Gilgit, Skardu
***features*** west Himalayan peak Nanga Parbat (8,126 m/26,660 ft), Karakoram Pass, Indus River, Baltoro Glacier.

**Kasparov, Gary Kimovich** born Garri Weinstein (1963– ) Soviet chess player. When he beat his compatriot Anatoly Karpov to win the world title 1985, he was the youngest-ever champion at 22 years 210 days.

**Kathmandu** or *Katmandu,* capital of Nepal, situated at 1,370 m/4,500 ft in the southern Himalayas, in the Valley of Nepal, at the junction of the Baghmati and Vishnumati rivers; population (1991) 419,100. Tourism is an important economic activity.

**katydid** or *bush cricket* or *longhorn grasshopper,* one of over 4,000 insect species, most of which are tropical, related to grasshoppers.

**Kaunda, Kenneth David** (1924–  ) Zambian politician, president 1964–91. Imprisoned 1958–60 as founder of the Zambia African National Congress, in 1964 he became the first prime minister of Northern Rhodesia, then the first president of independent Zambia. In 1973 he introduced one-party rule. He supported the nationalist movement in Southern Rhodesia, now Zimbabwe, and survived a coup attempt in 1980 thought to have been promoted by South Africa. He was elected chair of the Organization of African Unity in 1970 and 1987. In November 1991 he lost the first multiparty elections to Frederick Chiluba.

In July 1995 he was elected president of the United National Independence Party (UNIP) and announced his return to active politics, though his decision was not widely applauded. In May 1996 the Zambian constitution was controversially amended, making it impossible for non-second-generation Zambians to stand for the presidency, thereby effectively debarring Kaunda from future contests. The move was criticized by Commonwealth observers. In 1998, while under house arrest, he was charged with concealing knowledge of an abortive coup in October 1997. In June 1998 he was freed, after a five-months' detention.

**Kawasaki** industrial city of Kanagawa prefecture, Honshu island, Japan; population (1994) 1,171,000. It is situated between Tokyo and Yokohama in the important Keihin industrial zone, the largest industrial zone in Japan, and is a major port for the import of raw materials. The main industries are iron, steel, shipbuilding, chemicals, and textiles. It is noted for its cherry blossoms at Inadazutsumi on the banks of the Tamagawa.

**Kazakh** or *Kazak,* a pastoral Kyrgyz people of Kazakhstan. Kazakhs also live in China (Xinjiang, Gansu, and Qinghai), Mongolia, and Afghanistan. There are 5–7 million speakers of Kazakh, a Turkic language belonging to the Altaic family. They are predominantly Sunni Muslim, although pre-Islamic customs have survived.

**Kazakhstan** Republic of
*national name Kazak Respublikasy*
*area* 2,717,300 sq km/1,049,150 sq mi
*capital* Astana (formerly called Akmola)
*major towns/cities* Karaganda, Pavlodar, Semipalatinsk, Petropavlovsk, Chimkent
*physical features* Caspian and Aral seas, Lake Balkhash; Steppe region; natural gas and oil deposits in the Caspian Sea
*head of state* Nursultan Nazarbayev from 1990
*head of government* Nurlan Balgimbayev from 1997
*political system* authoritarian nationalist
*political parties* Congress of People's Unity of Kazakhstan, moderate, centrist; People's Congress of Kazakhstan, moderate, ethnic; Socialist Party of Kazakhstan (SPK), left wing; Republican Party, right-of-centre coalition

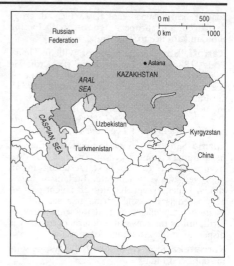

*currency* tenge
*GNP per capita (PPP)* (US$) 3,400 (1998)
*exports* ferrous and non-ferrous metals, mineral products (including petroleum and petroleum products), chemicals. Principal market: China 29.1% (1998)
*population* 16,269,000 (1999 est)
*language* Kazakh (official), related to Turkish; Russian
*religion* Sunni Muslim
*life expectancy* 63 (men); 73 (women) (1995–2000)
*Chronology*
*early Christian era* Settled by Mongol and Turkic tribes.
*8th century* Spread of Islam.
*10th century* Southward migration into east Kazakhstan of Kazakh tribes, displaced from Mongolia by the Mongols.
*13th–14th centuries* Part of Mongol Empire.
*late 15th century* Kazakhs emerged as distinct ethnic group from Kazakh Orda tribal confederation.
*early 17th century* The nomadic, cattle-breeding Kazakhs split into smaller groups, united in the three Large, Middle, and Lesser Hordes (federations), led by khans (chiefs).
*1731–42* Faced by attacks from the east by Oirot Mongols, protection was sought from the Russian tsars, and Russian control was gradually established.
*1822–48* Conquest by tsarist Russia completed; khans deposed. Large-scale Russian and Ukrainian peasant settlement of the steppes after the abolition of serfdom in Russia in 1861.
*1887* Alma-Alta (now Almaty), established in 1854 as a fortified trading centre and captured by the Russians in 1865, destroyed by earthquake.
*1916* 150,000 killed as anti-Russian rebellion brutally repressed.
*1917* Bolshevik coup in Russia followed by outbreak of civil war in Kazakhstan.
*1920* Autonomous republic in USSR.
*early 1930s* More than 1 million died of starvation during campaign to collectivize agriculture.

**1936** Joined USSR and became a full union republic.

**early 1940s** Volga Germans deported to the republic by Soviet dictator Joseph Stalin.

**1954–56** Part of Soviet leader Nikita Khrushchev's ambitious 'Virgin Lands' agricultural extension programme; large influx of Russian settlers made Kazakhs a minority in their own republic.

**1986** There were nationalist riots in Alma-Alta (now Almaty) after the reformist Soviet leader Mikhail Gorbachev ousted the local communist leader and installed an ethnic Russian.

**1989** Nursultan Nazarbayev, a reformist and mild nationalist, became leader of the Kazakh Communist Party (KCP) and instituted economic and cultural reform programmes, encouraging foreign inward investment.

**1990** Nazarbayev became head of state; economic sovereignty was declared.

**1991** Nazarbayev condemned the attempted anti-Gorbachev coup in Moscow; the KCP was abolished. The country joined the new Commonwealth of Independent States; and independence was recognized by the USA.

**1992** Kazakhstan was admitted into the United Nations and the Conference on Security and Cooperation in Europe (CSCE; now the Organization on Security and Cooperation in Europe, OSCE).

**1993** Presidential power was increased by a new constitution. A privatization programme was launched. START-1 (disarmament treaty) and Nuclear Non-Proliferation Treaty were both ratified by Kazakhstan.

**1994** There was economic, social, and military union with Kyrgyzstan and Uzbekistan.

**1995** An economic and military cooperation pact was signed with Russia. Kazakhstan achieved nuclear-free status. Nazarbayev's popular mandate was re-ratified in a national referendum.

**1997** Nurlan Balgimbayev was appointed prime minister. Major oil agreements were made with China. Astana (formerly known as Akmola) was designated as the new capital.

**1998** The opposition united to form the People's Front. The constitution was amended to end the restrictions of presidential terms. A treaty of 'eternal friendship' and a treaty of deepening economic cooperation was signed with Uzbekistan.

**1999** Nursultan Nazarbayev was re-elected president by a landslide margin, after his main rival was barred from standing.

**Kazan** city and port on the ◊Volga, capital and economic centre of Tatarstan, in the western Russian Federation; population (1996) 1,085,000. Kazan is the centre of Tatarstan culture. It has large engineering plants (manufacturing ships, machine tools, compressors, and dental equipment), chemical works (producing explosives, synthetic rubber, soap, and photographic materials), and a large leather and fur industry. It is also a major transportation centre, with its river port, airport, and location at a major railway junction.

**Kazan, Elia** born Elia Kazanjoglous (1909–　) Turkish-born US stage and film director. In the theatre he directed, among others, *The Skin of Our Teeth* (1942), *A Streetcar Named Desire* (1947), *Death of a Salesman* (1949), and *Cat on a Hot Tin Roof* (1955). He became a film director in (1944), and won Academy Awards for *Gentleman's Agreement* (1947) and *On the Waterfront* (1954).

**Keating, Paul John** (1944–　) Australian politician, Labor Party (ALP) leader and prime minister 1991–96. He was treasurer and deputy leader of the ALP 1983–91. In 1993 he announced plans for Australia to become a federal republic by the year 2001, which incited a mixed reaction among Australians. He and his party lost the February 1996 general election to John Howard, leader of the Liberal Party.

**Keaton, Buster (Joseph Francis)** (1896–1966) US comedian, actor, and film director. After being a star in vaudeville, he became one of the great comedians of the silent film era, with an inimitable deadpan expression masking a sophisticated acting ability. His films include *One Week* (1920), *The Navigator* (1924), *Sherlock, Jr* (1924), *The General* (1927), *The Cameraman* (1928), and *Steamboat Bill, Jr* (1928).

**Keats, John** (1795–1821) English Romantic poet. He produced work of the highest quality and promise before dying at the age of 25. *Poems* (1817), *Endymion* (1818), the great odes (particularly 'Ode to a Nightingale' and 'Ode on a Grecian Urn' written in 1819, published in 1820), and the narratives 'Isabella; or the Pot of Basil' (1818), 'Lamia' (1819), and 'The Eve of St Agnes' (1820), show his lyrical richness and talent for drawing on both classical mythology and medieval lore.

**kelim** oriental carpet or rug that is flat, pileless, and reversible.

Kelims are made by a tapestry-weave technique. Weft thread of one colour is worked to and fro in one area of the pattern; the next colour continues the pattern from the adjacent warp thread, so that no weft thread runs across the full width of the carpet.

**Kelly, Petra** (1947–1992) German politician and activist. She was a vigorous campaigner against nuclear power and other environmental issues and founded the German Green Party in 1972. She was a member of the Bundestag (parliament) 1983–90, but then fell out with her party.

**kelp** collective name for a group of large brown seaweeds. Kelp is also a term for the powdery ash of burned seaweeds, a source of iodine. (Typical families Fucaceae and Laminariaceae.)

**Kelvin, William Thomson** 1st Baron Kelvin (1824–1907) Irish physicist who introduced the *kelvin scale*, the absolute scale of temperature. His work on the conservation of energy in 1851 led to the second law of ◊thermodynamics. Knighted 1866, Baron 1892.

**kelvin scale** temperature scale used by scientists. It begins at ◊absolute zero (–273.15°C) and increases by the same degree intervals as the

Celsius scale; that is, 0°C is the same as 273.15 K and 100°C is 373.15 K.

**Kemal Atatürk, Mustafa** Turkish politician; see ◊Atatürk.

**Kempis, Thomas à** Medieval German monk and religious writer; see ◊Thomas à Kempis.

**Kennedy, Edward Moore ('Ted')** (1932– ) US Democratic politician. He aided his brothers John and Robert Kennedy in their presidential campaigns of 1960 and 1968, respectively, and entered politics as a senator for Massachusetts in 1962. He failed to gain the presidential nomination in 1980, largely because of questions about his delay in reporting a car crash at Chappaquiddick Island, near Cape Cod, Massachusetts, in 1969, in which his passenger, Mary Jo Kopechne, was drowned.

**Kennedy, John F(itzgerald) ('Jack')** (1917–1963) 35th president of the USA 1961–63, a Democrat; the first Roman Catholic and the youngest person to be elected president. In foreign policy he carried through the unsuccessful ◊Bay of Pigs invasion of Cuba, and secured the withdrawal of Soviet missiles from the island in 1962. His programme for reforms at home, called the *New Frontier*, was posthumously executed by Lyndon Johnson. Kennedy was assassinated while on a visit to Dallas, Texas, on 22 November 1963. Lee Harvey Oswald (1939–1963), who was within a few days shot dead by Jack Ruby (1911–1967), was named as the assassin.

**Kennedy, Nigel Paul** (1956– ) English violinist. He is credited with expanding the audience for classical music. His 1986 recording of Vivaldi's *Four Seasons* sold more than 1 million copies.

He retired from the classical concert platform in 1992.

**Kennedy, Robert Francis** (1925–1968) US Democratic politician and lawyer. He was presidential campaign manager for his brother John F ◊Kennedy in 1960, and as attorney general 1961–64 pursued a racket-busting policy and worked to enforce federal law in support of civil rights. He was assassinated during his campaign for the 1968 Democratic presidential nomination.

**Kennedy Space Center** ◊NASA launch site on Merritt Island, near Cape Canaveral, Florida, used for *Apollo* and space-shuttle launches. The first flight to land on the Moon (1969) and *Skylab*, the first orbiting laboratory (1973), were launched here.

**Kennelly–Heaviside layer** former term for the E layer of the ionosphere.

**Kenneth** two kings of Scotland:

**Kenneth I** called *MacAlpin* (died 860) King of Scotland from about 844. Traditionally, he is regarded as the founder of the Scottish kingdom (Alba) by virtue of his final defeat of the Picts about 844. He invaded Northumbria six times, and drove the Angles and the Britons over the River Tweed.

**Kent** county of southeast England, known as the 'garden of England' (since April 1998 Medway Towns has been a separate unitary authority)

*area* 3,730 sq km/1,440 sq mi

*towns and cities* Maidstone (administrative headquarters), Ashford, Canterbury, Deal, Dover (ferry terminus), Gravesend, Hythe, New Ash Green (a new town), Sevenoaks, Royal Tunbridge Wells; resorts: Folkestone, Margate, Ramsgate

*physical* the North Downs; White Cliffs of Dover; rivers: Thames, Darent, Medway (traditionally, a 'man of Kent' comes from east of the Medway and a 'Kentish man' from west Kent), Stour; marshes (especially Romney Marsh); the Isles of Grain, Thanet and Sheppey (on which is the resort of Sheerness, formerly a royal dockyard); the Weald (an agricultural area); Dungeness (peninsula and headland)

*features* Leeds Castle (converted to a palace by Henry VIII); Ightham Mote; Hever Castle (where Henry VIII courted Anne Boleyn); Chartwell (Churchill's country home), Knole, Sissinghurst Castle and gardens; the Brogdale Experimental Horticulture Station at Faversham has the world's finest collection of apple and other fruit trees; the former RAF Manston became Kent International Airport in 1989; Dungeness nuclear power station

*agriculture* cereals, hops, apples, soft fruit, vegetables; in Kent are found about half the orchards, half the hops, and one fifth of the soft fruit grown in England and Wales; livestock production

*industries* cement (Gravesend), paper, oil refining, shipbuilding, tourism; the East Kent coalfield ceased production in 1989

*population* (1996) 1,557,300

*famous people* Edward Heath, Christopher Marlowe.

**Kent, William** (1685–1748) English architect, landscape gardener, and interior designer. Working closely with Richard ◊Burlington, he was foremost in introducing the Palladian style to Britain from Italy, excelling in richly carved, sumptuous interiors and furnishings, as at Holkham Hall, Norfolk, begun in 1734.

Immensely versatile, he also worked in a Neo-Gothic style, and was a pioneer of Romantic landscape gardening, for example, the grounds of Stowe House, Buckinghamshire, and Rousham Park, Oxfordshire (1738–40). Horace Walpole called him 'the father of modern gardening'.

**Kentucky** state in south-central USA. It is nicknamed the Bluegrass State. Kentucky was admitted to the Union in 1792 as the 15th US state. Extending over 640 km/400 mi from east–west, Kentucky has the Ohio River along its entire northern boundary; across which are the states of Ohio, Indiana, and Illinois. To the east, the Tug Fork and Big Sandy rivers separate it from West Virginia. To the southeast, it is bordered by Virginia, with the Cumberland Gap at the extreme south; from this point along its southern boundary, as far as the Mississippi

River, it is bordered by Tennessee. Across a small stretch of the Mississippi, on the west, it faces the New Madrid region of Missouri
**population** (1995) 3,860,200
**area** 104,700 sq km/40,414 sq mi
**capital** Frankfort
**towns and cities** Louisville, Lexington, Owensboro, Covington, Bowling Green
**industries and products** tobacco, cereals, textiles, coal, whisky, horses, transport vehicles.

**Kenya** Republic of
**national name** *Jamhuri ya Kenya*

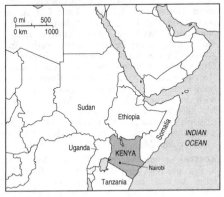

**area** 582,600 sq km/224,941 sq mi
**capital** Nairobi
**major towns/cities** Mombasa, Kisumu, Nakuru, Eldoret, Nyeri
**major ports** Mombasa
**physical features** mountains and highlands in west and centre; coastal plain in south; arid interior and tropical coast; semi-desert in north; Great Rift Valley, Mount Kenya, Lake Nakuru (salt lake with world's largest colony of flamingos), Lake Turkana (Rudolf)
**head of state and government** Daniel arap Moi from 1978
**political system** authoritarian nationalist
**political parties** Kenya African National Union (KANU), nationalist, centrist; Forum for the Restoration of Democracy–Kenya (FORD–Kenya), left of centre; Forum for the Restoration of Democracy–Asili (FORD–Asili), left of centre; Democratic Party (DP), centrist; Safina, centrist
**currency** Kenya shilling
**GNP per capita (PPP)** (US$) 1,130 (1998)
**exports** coffee, tea, petroleum products, soda ash, horticultural products. Principal market: Uganda 16.1% (1998)
**population** 29,549,000 (1999 est)
**language** Kiswahili (official), English; there are many local dialects
**religion** Roman Catholic, Protestant, Muslim, traditional tribal religions
**life expectancy** 51 (men); 53 (women) (1995–2000)
**Chronology**
**8th century** Arab traders began to settle along coast of East Africa.
**16th century** Portuguese defeated coastal states and exerted spasmodic control over them.

**18th century** Sultan of Oman reasserted Arab overlordship of East African coast, making it subordinate to Zanzibar.
**19th century** Europeans, closely followed by Christian missionaries, began to explore inland.
**1887** British East African Company leased area of coastal territory from sultan of Zanzibar.
**1895** Britain claimed large inland region as East African Protectorate.
**1903** Railway from Mombasa to Uganda built using Indian labourers, many of whom settled in the area; British and South African settlers began to farm highlands.
**1920** East African Protectorate became crown colony of Kenya, with legislative council elected by white settlers (and by Indians and Arabs soon afterwards).
**1923** Britain rejected demand for internal self-government by white settlers.
**1944** First African appointment to legislative council; Kenyan African Union (KAU) founded to campaign for African rights.
**1947** Jomo Kenyatta became leader of KAU, which was dominated by Kikuyu tribe.
**1952** Mau Mau (Kikuyu secret society) began terrorist campaign to drive white settlers from tribal lands; Mau Mau largely suppressed by 1954 but state of emergency lasted for eight years.
**1953** Kenyatta charged with management of Mau Mau activities and imprisoned by the British.
**1956** Africans allowed to elect members of legislative council on restricted franchise.
**1959** Kenyatta released from prison, but exiled to northern Kenya.
**1960** Britain announced plans to prepare Kenya for majority African rule.
**1961** Kenyatta allowed to return to help negotiate Kenya's independence.
**1963** Kenya achieved independence with Kenyatta as prime minister.
**1964** Kenya became a republic with Kenyatta as president.
**1967** East African Community (EAC) formed by Kenya, Tanzania, and Uganda to retain customs union inherited from colonial period.
**1969** Kenya became one-party state under Kenyan African National Union (KANU).
**1977** Political and economic disputes led to the collapse of the EAC.
**1978** The death of President Kenyatta who was succeeded by Daniel arap Moi.
**1984** There were violent clashes between government troops and the ethnic Somali population at Wajir.
**1989** Moi announced the release of political prisoners.
**1991** A multiparty system was conceded after an opposition group was launched.
**1997** There were demonstrations calling for democratic reform. Constitutional refoms were adopted.
**1998** A bomb exploded at the US embassy in Nairobi, killing over 230 people and injuring 5,000; an anti-American Islamic group claimed responsibility.

**Kenyatta, Jomo** assumed name of Kamau Ngengi (*c.* 1894–1978) Kenyan nationalist politician, prime minister from 1963, as well as the first president of Kenya from 1964 until his death. He led the Kenya African Union from 1947 (KANU from 1963) and was active in liberating Kenya from British rule.

**Kepler, Johannes** (1571–1630) German mathematician and astronomer. He formulated what are now called *Kepler's laws* of planetary motion: (1) the orbit of each planet is an ellipse with the Sun at one of the foci; (2) the radius vector of each planet sweeps out equal areas in equal times; (3) the squares of the periods of the planets are proportional to the cubes of their mean distances from the Sun. Kepler's laws are the basis of our understanding of the Solar System, and such scientists as Isaac ◊Newton built on his ideas.

**Kerala** state of southwest India
*area* 38,900 sq km/15,015 sq mi
*capital* Thiruvananthapuram
*towns* Kozhikode, Cochin
*physical* extends along the southwest coast from Karnataka almost to the southern tip of India; bounded on the east by the highlands of the Western Ghats; short dry season
*features* most densely populated (over 500 people per sq km/1,300 per sq mi in places), and most literate (60%), state of India, particularly amongst women who enjoy greater freedoms than is traditional in the country; strong religious and caste divisions make it politically unstable; wildlife sanctuary at Thekkady
*agriculture* tea, coffee, rice, coconuts, fruit, oilseed
*industries* textiles, chemicals, electrical goods, fish
*population* (1994 est) 30,555,000
*language* Malayalam, Kannada, Tamil
*religion* predominantly Hindu; 25% Christian and significant Jain, Muslim, Buddhist and Jewish minorities
*history* formed in 1956 from the former princely states of Travancore and Cochin, and part of Madras.

**keratin** fibrous protein found in the ◊skin of vertebrates and also in hair, nails, claws, hooves, feathers, and the outer coating of horns.

**Kerekou, Mathieu Ahmed** (1933–  ) Benin socialist politician and soldier, president 1980–91 and from 1996. In 1972, while deputy head of the Dahomey army, he led a coup to oust the ruling president and establish his own military government. He embarked on a programme of 'scientific socialism', changing his country's name to Benin to mark this change of direction. In 1987 he resigned from the army and confirmed a civilian administration. He was re-elected president in 1989, but lost to Nicéphore Soglo in the 1991 presidential elections. He surprisingly won the March 1996 presidential elections despite claims of fraud.

**kernel** the inner, softer part of a ◊nut, or of a seed within a hard shell.

**kerosene** thin oil obtained from the distillation of petroleum; a highly refined form is used in jet aircraft fuel. Kerosene is a mixture of hydrocarbons of the ◊paraffin series.

**Kerouac, Jack (Jean Louis)** (1922–1969) US novelist. He named and epitomized the ◊Beat Generation of the 1950s. The first of his autobiographical, myth-making books, *The Town and the City* (1950), was followed by the rhapsodic *On the Road* (1957). Other works written with similar free-wheeling energy and inspired by his interests in jazz and Buddhism include *The Dharma Bums* (1958), *Doctor Sax* (1959), and *Desolation Angels* (1965). His major contribution to poetry was *Mexico City Blues* (1959).

**Kerry** county of the Republic of Ireland, west of Cork, in the province of Munster; county town Tralee; area 4,700 sq km/1,814 sq mi; population (1991) 121,700. Industries include engineering, woollens, shoes, cutlery, fishing, and farming (dairy farming in the north, cattle grazing in the south). Tourism is important. Other towns include Caherciveen, Castleisland, Dingle, Killarney, and Listowel. Kerry is low-lying in the north and mountainous in the south, with the Slieve Mish and Caha Mountains, and Macgillycuddy's Reeks, where Carrauntoohill (Ireland's highest peak at 1,041m/3,417 ft) is situated; other peaks include Brandon (953 m/3,127 ft) and Mangerton (840 m/2,756 ft).

**kestrel** or *windhover,* small hawk that breeds in Europe, Asia, and Africa. About 30 cm/1 ft long, the male has a bluish-grey head and tail and is light chestnut brown back with black spots on the back and pale with black spots underneath. The female is slightly larger and reddish brown above, with bars; she does not have the bluish-grey head. The kestrel hunts mainly by hovering in midair while searching for prey. It feeds on small mammals, insects, frogs, and worms. (Species *Falco tinnunculus,* family Falconidae, order Falconiformes.)

**ketone** member of the group of organic compounds containing the carbonyl group ($C{=}O$) bonded to two atoms of carbon (instead of one carbon and one hydrogen as in ◊aldehydes). Ketones are liquids or low-melting-point solids, slightly soluble in water.

**key** in music, the ◊diatonic scale around which a piece of music is written. For example, a passage in the key of C major uses mainly the notes of the C major scale, and harmonies made up of the notes of that scale. The first note of the scale is known as the tonic; it gives the name of the key and is the note on which the music usually starts and finishes.

**Keynes, John Maynard** 1st Baron Keynes (1883–1946) English economist. His *General Theory of Employment, Interest, and Money* (1936) proposed the prevention of financial crises and unemployment by adjusting demand through government control of credit and currency. He is responsible for that part of economics that studies whole economies, now known as macroeconomics.

**kg** symbol for ◊*kilogram.*

**KGB** secret police of the USSR, the *Komitet Gosudarstvennoy Bezopasnosti* (Committee of State Security), which was in control of frontier and general security and the forced-labour system. KGB officers held key appointments in all fields of daily life, reporting to administration offices in every major town. On the demise of the USSR in 1991, the KGB was superseded by the Federal Counterintelligence Service, which was renamed the Federal Security Service (FSB) in April 1995, when its powers were expanded to enable it to combat corruption and organized crime, and to undertake foreign-intelligence gathering.

**Khabarovsk** large krai (territory) in the Russian Far East
**area** 824,600 sq km/318,378 sq mi
**cities** Khabarovsk (capital), Birobidzhan, Okhotsk, Komsomolsk-na-Amure, Sovetskaya Gavan
**physical** extends for over 2,000 km/1,243 mi along the eastern Siberian coast north of the Manchuria and the Amur River, almost entirely enclosing the Sea of Okhotsk; encompasses the Jewish Autonomous Region (Oblast); mountainous and extensively forested, with a cold monsoonal climate; mineral resources include gold, coal, tin, iron ore, manganese, and molybdenum
**industries** engineering, mining, metallurgy, pulp and paper production; lumbering and fishing
**population** (1996) 1,571,000; 81% urban
**history** the region was first reached and settled by Cossacks in the latter half of the 17th century. Civil disorder was rife (1917–20) until the establishment of the Far-Eastern Republic. The territory dates from 1938.

**Khaddhafi, Moamer al** or *Gaddafi* or *Qaddafi* (1942–  ) Libyan revolutionary leader. Overthrowing King Idris in 1969, he became virtual president of a republic, although he nominally gave up all except an ideological role in 1974. He favours territorial expansion in North Africa reaching as far as the Democratic Republic of Congo (formerly Zaire), has supported rebels in Chad, and has proposed mergers with a number of countries. During the ◊Gulf War, however, he advocated diplomacy rather than war. Imbued with Nasserism, he was to develop afterwards his own theories (*Green Book*), based on what he called 'natural socialism' of an egalitarian nature.

**Khalsa** the brotherhood of the Sikhs, created by Guru Gobind Singh at the festival of Baisakhi 1699. The Khalsa was originally founded as a militant group to defend the Sikh community from persecution.

**Khama, Seretse** (1921–1980) Botswanan politician, prime minister of Bechuanaland in 1965, and first president of Botswana 1966–80. He founded the Bechuanaland Democratic Party in 1962 and led his country to independence in 1966. Botswana prospered under his leadership, both economically and politically, and he won every post-independence election until his death in July 1980. He was knighted in 1966.

**Khan, Imran Niazi** (1952–  ) Pakistani cricketer. An all-rounder, he played cricket in England for Worcestershire and Sussex and made his test debut In 1971. He played 88 test matches for Pakistan, of which 48 were as captain. In 1992 he captained his country to victory in the World Cup. He scored 17,771 first-class runs at an average of 36.87, and took 1,287 wickets at an average of 22.32. He retired in 1992.
*career highlights*
**Test cricket** appearances: 88; runs: 3,807; average: 37.69; best: 136 (Pakistan v. Australia 1989–90); wickets: 362; average: 22.81; best: 8–58 (Pakistan v. Sri Lanka 1981–82)

**Khan, Jahangir** (1963–  ) Pakistani squash player. He won the world open championship a record six times 1981–85 and 1988, and was World Amateur champion in 1979, 1983, and 1985. He announced his retirement in 1993.
*career highlights*
**World Open champion** 1981–85, 1988
**World Amateur champion** 1979, 1983, 1985
*British Open champion* 1982–91

**Kharkov** Ukrainian *Kharkiv,* major city in eastern Ukraine, capital of the Kharkov oblast, 400 km/250 mi east of Kiev and 40km/25 mi south of the border with the Russian Federation; population (1990) 1,618,000. An important railway junction and industrial city, Kharkov is situated at the confluence of the Kharkov, Lopan, and Udy rivers, and lies close to the Donets Basin coalfield and Krivoy Rog iron mines. Its industrial enterprises include engineering and railway rolling-stock works, agricultural and mining machinery factories, and chemical plants.

**Khartoum** capital and trading centre of Sudan, in Khartoum State, at the junction of the Blue and White Nile rivers; population (1983) 561,000, and of Khartoum North, across the Blue Nile, 341,000. Omdurman is also a suburb of Khartoum, giving the urban area a population of over 1.3 million. The city is a transportation and trade centre with tanning, textiles, light engineering, and printing industries.

**Khmer** or *Kmer,* the largest ethnic group in Cambodia, numbering about 7 million. Khmer minorities also live in eastern Thailand and South Vietnam. The Khmer language belongs to the Mon-Khmer family of Austro-Asiatic languages.

**Khmer Republic** former name (1970–76) of Cambodia.

**Khmer Rouge** communist movement in Cambodia (Kampuchea) formed in the 1960s. Controlling the country 1974–78, it was responsible for mass deportations and executions under the leadership of ◊Pol Pot. Since then it has conducted guerrilla warfare, and in 1991 gained representation in the governing body.

**Khomeini, Ayatollah Ruhollah** (1900–1989) Iranian Shi'ite Muslim leader. Exiled from 1964 for his opposition to Shah Pahlavi, he returned when the shah left the country in 1979, and established a fundamentalist Islamic republic. His rule was marked by a protracted war with Iraq, and suppression of opposition within Iran, executing thousands of opponents.

**Khrushchev, Nikita Sergeyevich** (1894–1971) Soviet politician, secretary general of the Communist Party 1953–64, premier 1958–64. He emerged as leader from the power struggle following Stalin's death and was the first official to denounce Stalin, in 1956. His de-Stalinization programme gave rise to revolts in Poland and Hungary in 1956. Because of problems with the economy and foreign affairs (a breach with China in 1960; conflict with the USA in the ◊Cuban missile crisis of 1962), he was ousted by Leonid Brezhnev and Alexei Kosygin.

**Khuzestan** province of southwest Iran, on the northern shores of the Gulf; area 66,560 sq km/25,700 sq mi; population (1991) 3,175,900. It has Iran's chief oil resources. Cities include the administrative centre of ◊Ahvaz and the ports of ◊Abadan and Khorramshahr. A large proportion of the population is Arab. The province is often referred to by Arabs as Arabistan.

**Khwārizmī, al-, Muhammad ibn-Mūsā** (c. 780–c. 850) Persian mathematician. He wrote a book on algebra, from part of whose title (al-jabr) comes the word 'algebra', and a book in which he introduced to the West the Hindu–Arabic decimal number system.

The word 'algorithm' is a corruption of his name.

**Khyber Pass** pass through the mountain range that separates Pakistan from Afghanistan; length 53 km/33 mi; width varies from 140 m/460 ft at its widest to about 15 m/50 ft at its narrowest. On either side are rock faces rising to a height of 915 m/3,000 ft in some places, the highest point at Landi Kotal, 520 m/1,700 ft higher than Jamrud at the entrance to the pass. The Khyber Pass was used by invaders of India. The present road was constructed by the British during the Afghan Wars (1839–42 and 1878–80).

**kibbutz** Israeli communal collective settlement with collective ownership of all property and earnings, collective organization of work and decision-making, and communal housing for children. A modified version, the *Moshav Shitufi*, is similar to the collective farms that were typical of the USSR. Other Israeli cooperative rural settlements include the *Moshav Ovdim*, which has equal opportunity, and the similar but less strict *Moshav* settlement.

**kidnapping** the abduction of a person against his or her will. It often involves holding persons for ransom. It may also take place in child-custody disputes or involve psychosexual motives.

**kidney** in vertebrates, one of a pair of organs responsible for fluid regulation, excretion of waste products, and maintaining the ionic composition of the blood. The kidneys are situated on the rear wall of the abdomen. Each one consists of a number of long tubules (see ◊nephron); the outer parts filter the aqueous components of blood, and the inner parts selectively reabsorb vital salts, leaving waste products in the remaining fluid (urine), which is passed through the ureter to the bladder.

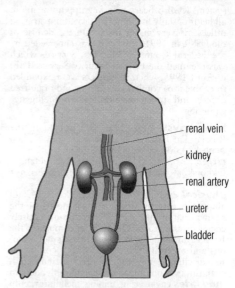

**kidney** Blood enters the kidney through the renal artery. The blood is filtered through the glomeruli to extract the nitrogenous waste products and excess water that make up urine. The urine flows through the ureter to the bladder; the cleaned blood then leaves the kidney via the renal vein.

**kidney machine** medical equipment used in ◊dialysis.

**Kierkegaard, Søren Aabye** (1813–1855) Danish philosopher and theologian, often considered to be the founder of ◊existentialism. He argued that no system of thought could explain the unique experience of the individual. He defended Christianity, suggesting that God cannot be known through reason, but only through a 'leap of faith'. His chief works are *Enten-Eller/Either-Or* (1843) and *Begrebet Angest/Concept of Dread* (1844).

**Kieślowski, Krzysztof** (1941–1996) Polish film director and screenwriter. One of the great European auteurs of the 1980s and 1990s, his films are often personal narratives with broader moral and political implications. His 'Three Colours' trilogy – *Trois couleurs: Bleu/Blue* (1993), *Trois couleurs: Blanc/White* (1993), and *Trois couleurs: Rouge/Red* (1994) – is based on the French flag and the concepts of liberty, equality, and fraternity.

**Kiev** Ukrainian *Kyiv*, capital and largest city of Ukraine, situated at the confluence of the Desna and Dnieper rivers; population (1990) 2,616,000. Kiev was the capital of Russia in the Middle Ages. It is a major industrial centre, producing chemicals, clothing, leather goods, machine tools, and electrical goods, and is also a market city for the abundant agricultural produce of the western Ukraine. Kiev University was founded in 1834.

*features* St Sophia cathedral, the oldest cathedral in Ukraine (11th century) and Kiev-Pechersky Monastery (both now museums) survive, together with the remains of the Golden Gate, an arched entrance to the old walled city, built in 1037. The gate is surmounted by the small Church of the Annunciation. The Kiev ballet and opera companies are renowned worldwide.

*history* Kiev was founded in the 5th century by ◊Vikings. The Slav domination of Russia began with the rise of Kiev, the 'mother of Russian cities'; Kiev replaced ◊Novgorod as the capital of the state of Kievan Rus in 882 and was the original centre of the Orthodox Christian faith from 988. It was for a long time an important trading centre on the route from the Baltic to the Black Sea, but declined in importance in the 12th century. The Russian capital was moved to Vladimir in 1169, and Kiev was sacked by Mongols under Batu Khan in 1240. From the 14th–late 17th centuries, the city was successively under Tatar, Lithuanian and Polish control. It was annexed by Russia in 1686. In World War II, Kiev, then the third-largest city of the USSR, was occupied and largely destrroyed by German forces 1941–43. During this period, around 200,000 of the city's inhabitants, including its entire Jewish population, were murdered.

**Kigali** capital of Rwanda, central Africa, 80 km/50 mi east of Lake Kivu; population (1993) 234,500. Products include coffee, tea, hides, textiles, cigarettes, shoes, paints, and varnishes.

**Kikuyu** member of the dominant ethnic group in Kenya, numbering about 3 million. The Kikuyu are primarily cultivators of millet, although many have entered the professions. Their language belongs to the Bantu branch of the Niger-Congo family.

**Kildare** county of the Republic of Ireland, in the province of Leinster; county town Naas; area 1,690 sq km/ 652 sq mi; population (1991) 122,500. The principal rivers are the Barrow, the Boyne, the Lesser Barrow, and the Liffey. Kildare is wet and boggy in the north with extensive grassy plains and rolling hills, and includes part of the Bog of Allen. The village of Maynooth has a training college for Roman Catholic priests. The Curragh, at Tully, is a plain that is the site of the national stud and headquarters of Irish horse racing; steeplechase racing also takes place at Punchestown. Cattle are grazed in the north, and in the south products include oats, barley, potatoes, and cattle. Other main towns include Athy, Droichead Nua, and *Kildare.*

**Kilimanjaro** volcano in Tanzania, the highest mountain in Africa, 5,895 m/19,340 ft. It is situated between Lake Victoria and the coast. It culminates in two peaks, Kibo (5,895 m/19,340 ft) and Mawenzi (5,149 m/16,893 ft), both craters of extinct volcanoes. The first recorded ascent was by the German geographer Hans Meyer and the Austrian mountaineer Ludwig Purtscheller in 1889.

**Kilkenny** county of the Republic of Ireland, in the province of Leinster; county town Kilkenny; area 2,060 sq km/795 sq mi; population (1991) 73,600. It has the rivers Nore, Suir, and Barrow. Industries include coal mining, clothing,

footwear, brewing, and agricultural activities cattle rearing and dairy farming. Principal towns include Castlecomer, Callan, Graiguenamanagh, and Thomastown.

**killer whale** or *orca,* toothed whale belonging to the dolphin family, found in all seas of the world. It is black on top, white below, and grows up to 9 m/30 ft long. It is the only whale that has been observed to prey on other whales, as well as on seals and seabirds. (Species *Orcinus orca,* family Delphinidae.)

**Killiecrankie, Battle of** in British history, during the first ◊Jacobite uprising, defeat on 7 May 1689 of General Mackay (for William of Orange) by John Graham of Claverhouse, a supporter of James II, at Killiecrankie, Scotland. Despite the victory, Claverhouse was killed and the revolt soon petered out; the remaining forces were routed on 21 August.

**kilobyte** (K or KB) in computing, a unit of memory equal to 1,024 ◊bytes. It is sometimes used, less precisely, to mean 1,000 bytes.

**kilogram** SI unit (symbol kg) of mass equal to 1,000 grams (2.24 lb). It is defined as a mass equal to that of the international prototype, a platinum-iridium cylinder held at the International Bureau of Weights and Measures in Sèvres, France.

**kilometre** unit of length (symbol km) equal to 1,000 metres, equivalent to 3,280.89 ft or 0.6214 (about 5/8) of a mile.

**kilowatt** unit (symbol kW) of power equal to 1,000 watts or about 1.34 horsepower.

**kilowatt-hour** commercial unit of electrical energy (symbol kWh), defined as the work done by a power of 1,000 watts in one hour and equal to 3.6 megajoules. It is used to calculate the cost of electrical energy taken from the domestic supply.

**kimberlite** an igneous rock that is ultramafic (containing very little silica); a type of alkaline peridotite with a porphyritic texture (larger crystals in a fine-grained matrix), containing mica in addition to olivine and other minerals. Kimberlite represents the world's principal source of diamonds.

**Kim Il Sung** (1912–1994) North Korean communist politician and marshal. He became prime minister in 1948 and led North Korea in the ◊Korean War 1950–53. He became president in 1972, retaining the presidency of the Communist Workers' party. He liked to be known as the 'Great Leader' and campaigned constantly for the reunification of Korea. His son *Kim Jong Il,* known as the 'Dear Leader', succeeded him.

**kimono** traditional Japanese costume. Worn in the Heian period (more than 1,000 years ago), it is still used by women for formal wear and informally by men.

**Kim Young Sam** (1927–  ) South Korean democratic politician, president 1993–98. In 1990 he merged the National Democratic Party (NNP) with the ruling party to form the Democratic Liberal Party (DLP), now known as the New

Korean Party. In the December 1992 presidential election he captured 42% of the national vote, assuming office in February 1993. As president, he encouraged greater political openness, some deregulation of the economy, and a globalization (segyehwa) initiative.

**kinesis** (plural *kineses*) in biology, a nondirectional movement in response to a stimulus; for example, woodlice move faster in drier surroundings. *Taxis* is a similar pattern of behaviour, but there the response is directional.

**kinetic energy** the energy of a body resulting from motion. It is contrasted with ◊potential energy.

**kinetics** the branch of chemistry that investigates the rates of chemical reactions.

**kinetics** branch of ◊dynamics dealing with the action of forces producing or changing the motion of a body; *kinematics* deals with motion without reference to force or mass.

**kinetic theory** theory describing the physical properties of matter in terms of the behaviour – principally movement – of its component atoms or molecules. The temperature of a substance is dependent on the velocity of movement of its constituent particles, increased temperature being accompanied by increased movement. A gas consists of rapidly moving atoms or molecules and, according to kinetic theory, it is their continual impact on the walls of the containing vessel that accounts for the pressure of the gas. The slowing of molecular motion as temperature falls, according to kinetic theory, accounts for the physical properties of liquids and solids, culminating in the concept of no molecular motion at ◊absolute zero (0K/–273°C).

**King, Billie Jean** born Moffitt (1943–   ) US tennis player. She won a record 20 Wimbledon titles 1961–79 and 39 Grand Slam titles, and fought for equal treatment and equal pay for women tennis players. In 1973 she formed the Women's Tennis Association and the Players' Union. In 1974, with Olympic swimmer Donna de Varona and others, she created the Women's Sports Foundation to support and promote women in sport. That same year, in front of a worldwide audience, she beat Bobby Riggs, a self-confessed chauvinist and critic of women in sport.

*career highlights*
*Wimbledon* singles: 1966–68, 1972–73, 1975; doubles: 1961–62, 1965, 1967–68, 1970–73, 1979; mixed: 1967, 1971, 1973–74
*US Open* singles: 1967, 1971–72, 1974; doubles: 1964, 1967, 1974, 1978, 1980; mixed: 1967, 1971, 1973, 1976
*French Open* singles: 1972; doubles: 1972; mixed: 1967, 1970
*Australian Open* singles: 1968; mixed: 1968

**King, Martin Luther, Jr** (1929–1968) US civil-rights campaigner, black leader, and Baptist minister. He first came to national attention as leader of the Montgomery, Alabama, bus boycott in 1955, and was one of the organizers of the march of 200,000 people on Washington, DC, in 1963 to demand racial equality. An advocate of nonviolence, he was awarded the Nobel Peace Prize 1964. On 4 April 1968 he was assassinated in Memphis, Tennessee, by James Earl Ray (1928–   ).

**king crab** or *horseshoe crab*, marine ◊arthropod found on the Atlantic coast of North America, and the coasts of Asia. The upper side of the body is entirely covered with a dark, rounded shell, and it has a long spinelike tail. It is up to 60 cm/2 ft long. It is unable to swim, and lays its eggs in the sand at the high-water mark. (Class Arachnida, subclass Xiphosura.)

**kingdom** the primary division in biological ◊classification. At one time, only two kingdoms were recognized: animals and plants. Today most biologists prefer a five-kingdom system, even though it still involves grouping together organisms that are probably unrelated. One widely accepted scheme is as follows: *Kingdom Animalia* (all multicellular animals); *Kingdom Plantae* (all plants, including seaweeds and other algae, except blue-green); *Kingdom Fungi* (all fungi, including the unicellular yeasts, but not slime moulds); *Kingdom Protista* or *Protoctista* (protozoa, diatoms, dinoflagellates, slime moulds, and various other lower organisms with eukaryotic cells); and *Kingdom Monera* (all prokaryotes – the bacteria and cyanobacteria, or ◊blue-green algae). The first four of these kingdoms make up the eukaryotes.

**kingfisher** any of a group of heavy-billed birds found near streams, ponds, and coastal areas around the world. The head is exceptionally large, and the long, angular bill is keeled; the tail and wings are relatively short, and the legs very short, with short toes. Kingfishers plunge-dive for fish and aquatic insects. The nest is usually a burrow in a riverbank. (Family Alcedinidae, order Coraciiformes.)

**Kingsley, Charles** (1819–1875) English author. A rector, he was known as the 'Chartist clergyman' because of such social novels as *Yeast* (1848) and *Alton Locke* (1850). His historical novels include *Westward Ho!* (1855) and *Hereward the Wake* (1866). He also wrote, for children, *The Water Babies* (1863).

**Kingston** capital and principal port of Jamaica, West Indies, the cultural and commercial centre of the island; population (1991) 587,800 (metropolitan area). Founded 1693, Kingston became the capital of Jamaica 1872.

**Kingston upon Hull** or *Hull*, city, port, and unitary authority, created in 1996 from part of the former county of Humberside, situated where the River Hull flows into the north side of the Humber estuary, northeast England
*area* 71 sq km/27 sq mi
*features* 13th-century Holy Trinity Church; restored docklands area; Town Docks Museum; Ferens Art Gallery (1927); University of Hull (1954) and University of Humberside (1992), formerly Humberside Polytechnic; linked with the south bank of the estuary by the Humber Bridge, the world's longest single-span suspension bridge
*industries* fish processing, flour milling, sawmilling, marine engineering, food processing,

and the manufacture of electrical goods, vegetable oils, paint, pharmaceuticals, chemicals, caravans, aircraft, and paper. There are 11 km/7 mi of modern docks located on the Humber estuary. The largest timber port in the UK, it also handles grain, oilseeds, wool, and the export/import of manufactured goods. There are ferries to Rotterdam and Zeebrugge. Following the building of the Queen Elizabeth Dock in 1971, the port's roll-on/roll-off freight traffic expanded rapidly.

***population*** (1996) 265,000

***famous people*** Amy Johnson, Stevie Smith, William Wilberforce; Philip Larkin was librarian at the University of Hull.

**Kingstown** capital and principal port of St Vincent and the Grenadines, West Indies, in the southwest of the island of St Vincent; population (1991) 26,200.

**kinkajou** Central and South American carnivorous mammal belonging to the raccoon family. Yellowish-brown, with a rounded face and slim body, the kinkajou grows to 55 cm/1.8 ft with a 50 cm/1.6 ft tail, and has short legs with sharp claws. It spends its time in trees and has a prehensile tail, which it uses as an extra limb when moving from branch to branch. It feeds largely on fruit. (Species *Potos flavus*, family Procyonidae.)

**Kinnock, Neil Gordon** (1942– ) British Labour politician, party leader 1983–92. Born and educated in Wales, he was elected to represent a Welsh constituency in Parliament in 1970 (Islwyn from 1983). He was further left than prime ministers Wilson and Callaghan, but as party leader (in succession to Michael Foot) adopted a moderate position, initiating a major policy review 1988–89. He resigned as party leader after Labour's defeat in the 1992 general election. In 1994 he left parliament to become a European commissioner and was given the transport portfolio. In July 1999 it was announced that Kinnock would become vice-president of the European Commission with responsibility for internal reform.

**Kinshasa** formerly (until 1966) *Léopoldville*, capital of the Democratic Republic of Congo on the Congo-Zaire River, 400 km/250 mi inland from the port of Matadi; population (1994 est) 4,655,300. Industries include shipbuilding and repairing, chemicals, textiles, engineering, food processing, and furniture. It was founded by the explorer Henry Morton Stanley in 1881. The National University of Kinshasa is here.

**kinship** in anthropology, human relationship based on blood or marriage, and sanctified by law and custom. Kinship forms the basis for most human societies and for such social groupings as the family, clan, or tribe.

**Kipling, (Joseph) Rudyard** (1865–1936) English writer, born in India. *Plain Tales from the Hills* (1888), about Anglo-Indian society, contains the earliest of his masterly short stories. His books for children, including *The Jungle Book* (1894–95), *Just So Stories* (1902), *Puck of Pook's Hill* (1906), and the picaresque novel *Kim* (1901), reveal his imaginative identification

with the exotic. Poems such as 'If–', 'Danny Deever', and 'Gunga Din', express an empathy with common experience, which contributed to his great popularity, together with a vivid sense of 'Englishness' (sometimes denigrated as a kind of jingoist imperialism).

**Kirchner, Ernst Ludwig** (1880–1938) German artist. He was a leading member of the Expressionist *die ◊Brücke* group in Dresden from 1905 and in Berlin from 1911. In Berlin he painted city scenes and portraits, using lurid colours and bold diagonal paint strokes recalling woodcut technique.

**Kirghizia** alternative form of Kyrgyzstan, a country in central Asia.

**Kiribati** Republic of (formerly part of the Gilbert and Ellice Islands)

***national name*** *Ribaberikin Kiribati*

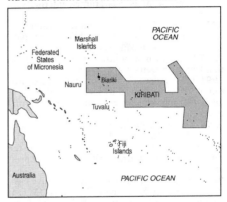

***area*** 717 sq km/277 sq mi

***capital*** Bairiki (on Tarawa Atoll) (and port)

***towns*** pricipal atolls: North Tarawa, Gilbert group, Abaiang, Tabiteuea

***major ports*** Betio (on Tarawa)

***physical features*** comprises 33 Pacific coral islands: the Kiribati (Gilbert), Rawaki (Phoenix), Banaba (Ocean Island), and three of the Line Islands including Kiritimati (Christmas Island); island groups crossed by Equator and International Date Line

***head of state and government*** Teburoro Tito from 1994

***political system*** liberal democracy

***political parties*** Maneaban Te Mauri (MTM), dominant faction; National Progressive Party (NPP), former governing faction 1979–94

***currency*** Australian dollar

***GNP per capita (PPP)*** (US$) 3,480 (1998)

***exports*** copra, fish, seaweed, bananas, breadfruit, taro. Principal market: USA (1996)

***population*** 77,000 (1999 est)

***Language*** English (official), Gilbertese

***religion*** Roman Catholic, Protestant (Congregationalist)

***life expectancy*** 61 (men); 65 (women) (1998 est)

***Chronology***

**1st millennium *BC*** Settled by Austronesian-speaking peoples.

**1606** Visited by Spanish explorers.
**late 18th century** Visited by British naval officers.
**1857** Christian mission established.
**1892** Gilbert (Kiribati) and Ellice (Tuvalu) Islands proclaimed a British protectorate.
**1916–39** Uninhabited Phoenix Islands, Christmas Island, Ocean Island, and Line Island (Banaba) added to colony.
**1942–43** Occupied by Japanese, it was the scene of fierce fighting with US troops.
**late 1950s** UK tested nuclear weapons on Christmas Island (Kiritimati).
**1963** Legislative council established.
**1974** Legislative council replaced by an elected House of Assembly.
**1975** The mainly Melanesian-populated Ellice Islands separated to become Tuvalu.
**1977** The predominantly Micronesian-populated Gilbert Islands was granted internal self-government.
**1979** Independence was achieved within the Commonwealth, as the Republic of Kiribati, with Ieremia Tabai as president.
**1985** Kiribati's first political party, the opposition Christian Democrats, was formed.
**1991** Tabai was re-elected but under the constitution was not allowed to serve a further term; Teatao Teannaki won the run-off presidential election.
**1994** The government resigned after losing a vote of confidence. The ruling National Progressive Party (NPP) were defeated in the general election. Teburoro Tito was elected president.
**1998** In the House of Assembly legislative elections the ruling Maneaban Te Mauru (MTM) and the opposition National Progressive Party (NPP) lost seats to independents. President Teburoro Tito, of the MTM, was re-elected for a second term by the House of Assembly.

**Kirkland, Gelsey** (1953–  ) US ballerina. She danced with effortless technique and innate musicality. She joined the New York City Ballet in 1968, where George ◊Balanchine staged a new *Firebird* for her (1970) and Jerome ◊Robbins chose her for his *Goldberg Variations* (1971) and other ballets. In 1974 Mikhail ◊Baryshnikov sought her out and she joined the American Ballet Theater in 1975, where they danced in partnership, for example in *Giselle*.

**Kissinger, Henry (Alfred)** (1923–  ) German-born US diplomat. After a brilliant academic career at Harvard University, he was appointed national security adviser in 1969 by President Nixon, and was secretary of state 1973–77. His missions to the USSR and China improved US relations with both countries, and he took part in negotiating US withdrawal from Vietnam in 1973 and in Arab-Israeli peace negotiations 1973–75. Nobel Peace Prize 1973.

**kiss of life** artificial ventilation, in first aid, another name for ◊artificial respiration.

**Kiswahili** another name for the ◊Swahili language.

**Kitchener, Horatio (Herbert)** 1st Earl Kitchener of Khartoum (1850–1916) Irish sol-
dier and administrator. He defeated the Sudanese at the Battle of Omdurman in 1898 and reoccupied Khartoum. In South Africa, he was commander in chief 1900–02 during the Boer War, and he commanded the forces in India 1902–09. Appointed war minister on the outbreak of World War I, he was successful in his campaign calling for voluntary recruitment.

**kitchen-sink painters** loose-knit group of British painters, active in the late 1940s and early 1950s. They depicted drab, everyday scenes with an aggressive technique and often brilliant, 'crude' colour. The best known were John Bratby, Derrick Greaves (1927–  ), Edward Middleditch (1923–1987), and Jack Smith (1928–  ).

**kite** quadrilateral with two pairs of adjacent equal sides. The geometry of this figure follows from the fact that it has one axis of symmetry.

**kite** any of a group of birds of prey found in all parts of the world. Kites have long, pointed wings and, usually, a forked tail. There are about 20 species. (Family Accipitridae, order Falconiformes.)

**kiwi** flightless bird found only in New Zealand. It has long hairlike brown plumage, minute wings and tail, and a very long beak with nostrils at the tip. It is nocturnal and insectivorous. It lays one or two white eggs per year, each weighing up to 450 g/15.75 oz. (Species *Apteryx australis*, family Apterygidae, order Apterygi-formes.)

**kiwi fruit** or *Chinese gooseberry*, fruit of a vinelike plant grown commercially on a large scale in New Zealand. Kiwi fruits are egg-sized, oval, and similar in flavour to gooseberries, though much sweeter, with a fuzzy brown skin. (*Actinidithia chinensis*, family Actinidiaceae.)

**Klammer, Franz** (1953–  ) Austrian skier. He won a record 35 World Cup downhill races between 1974 and 1985. Olympic gold medallist 1976. He was the combined world champion 1974, and the World Cup downhill champion 1975–78 and 1983.

**Klaus, Václav** (1941–  ) Czech politician and economist, prime minister of the Czech Republic 1993–97. Before the break-up of Czechoslovakia, he served in the government of Václav Havel and was chair of Civic Forum from 1990, breaking away to form the right-of-centre Civic Democratic Party (CDP) in 1991. The architect of Eastern Europe's initially most successful economic reform programme, he was a keen promoter of membership of the European Union.

**Klee, Paul** (1879–1940) Swiss painter and graphic artist. He was one of the most original and prolific artists of the 20th century. Endlessly inventive and playful, and suggesting a childlike innocence, his works are an exploration of the potential of line, plane, and colour. *Twittering Machine* (1922; Museum of Modern Art, New York) is typical.

**kleptomania** (Greek *kleptēs* 'thief') behavioural disorder characterized by an overpowering desire to possess articles for which one has no need. In kleptomania, as opposed to ordinary theft, there is no obvious need or use for what is stolen and sometimes the sufferer has no memory of the theft.

**Klimt, Gustav** (1862–1918) Austrian painter. He was influenced by *Jugendstil* (Art Nouveau) and was a founding member of the Vienna Sezession group 1897. His paintings, often sensual and erotic, have a jewelled effect similar to mosaics, for example *The Kiss* (1909; Musée des Beaux-Arts, Strasbourg). His many portraits include *Judith I* (1901; Österreichische Galerie, Vienna).

**Klondike** former gold-mining area in northwest ◊Yukon Territory , Canada, near Dawson, where the Klondike and Yukon rivers meet. It is named after the river valley (length 193 km/120 mi) near where gold was found in August 1896. By 1898, at the height of the 'Klondike Gold Rush', over 30,000 people had moved into the area.

**km** symbol for ◊*kilometre.*

**knapweed** any of several weedy plants belonging to the daisy family. In the common knapweed (*C. nigra*), also known as a *hardhead*, the hard, dark buds break open at the top into pale purple composite flowers. It is native to Europe and has been introduced to North America. (Genus *Centaurea*, family Compositae.)

**Kneller, Godfrey** born Gottfried Kniller (1646–1723) German-born portrait painter who lived in England from 1674. A successful and prolific painter of nearly 6,000 portraits, he dominated English portraiture of the late 17th and early 18th centuries. He was court painter to Charles II, James II, William III, and George I. Kneller was knighted in 1692 and made a baronet in 1715.

**knifefish** any of a group of fishes in which the body is deep at the front and drawn to a narrow or pointed tail at the rear, the main fin being the well-developed long ventral (stomach) fin that completes the knifelike shape. The ventral fin is rippled for forward or backward movement. Knifefishes produce electrical fields, which they use for navigation. (Genus *Gymnotus* and other allied genera, family Gymnotidae.)

**knighthood, orders of** fraternity carrying with it the rank of knight, admission to which is granted as a mark of royal favour or as a reward for public services. During the Middle Ages in Europe such fraternities fell into two classes: religious and secular. The first class, including the ◊*Templars* and the Knights of *St John*, consisted of knights who had taken religious vows and devoted themselves to military service against the Saracens (Arabs) or other non-Christians. The secular orders probably arose from bands of knights engaged in the service of a prince or great noble.

**Knock** village and parish in County Mayo, western Ireland, 11 km/7 mi northeast of Claremorris. A national place of pilgrimage, Knock is known as the site of alleged apparitions of the Virgin Mary (the first on 21 August 1879), and for its church shrine, the Basilica of Our Lady, 'Queen of Ireland', which seats

12,000 and was opened in 1976. Horan International Airport, opened in 1986, receives transatlantic flights; it was named after Monsignor James Horan, a parish priest who launched the project to attract pilgrims.

**Knossos** Middle and Late Bronze Age settlement, 8 km/5 mi south of present-day Iraklion, Crete. Knossos is one of the main cities of what is known as the Minoan civilization (a modern name derived from the legend of King Minos). The archaeological site, excavated by Arthur Evans in 1899–1935, includes the palace throne room, the remains of frescoes, and construction on more than one level. The Greek myth of Theseus' encounter with the Minotaur in a labyrinth was possibly derived from the ritual 'bull-leaping' by young people depicted in the palace frescoes and from the mazelike layout of the palace.

**knot** in navigation, unit by which a ship's speed is measured, equivalent to one ◊nautical mile per hour (one knot equals about 1.15 miles per hour). It is also sometimes used in aviation.

**knowledge-based system** (KBS), computer program that uses an encoding of human knowledge to help solve problems. It was discovered during research into ◊artificial intelligence that adding heuristics (rules of thumb) enabled programs to tackle problems that were otherwise difficult to solve by the usual techniques of computer science.

**Knox, John** (*c.* 1505–1572) Scottish Protestant reformer, founder of the Church of Scotland. He spent several years in exile for his beliefs, including a period in Geneva where he met John ◊Calvin. He returned to Scotland in 1559 to promote Presbyterianism. His books include *First Blast of the Trumpet Against the Monstrous Regiment of Women* (1558).

**koala** marsupial (mammal that carries its young in a pouch) found only in eastern Australia. It feeds almost entirely on eucalyptus shoots. It is about 60 cm/2 ft long, and resembles a bear (it is often incorrectly described as a 'koala bear'). The popularity of its greyish fur led to its almost complete extermination by hunters. Under protection since 1936, it rapidly increased in numbers, but recently numbers have fallen from 400,000 in 1985 to 40,000–80,000 in 1995. (Species *Phascolarctos cinereus*, family Phalangeridae.)

**Kobe** deep-water port on Osaka Bay in Hyogo prefecture, southern Honshu island, Japan; population (1994) 1,479,000. It was a ◊treaty port between 1868 and 1899, for foreigners exempt from Japanese law. *Port Island,* an artificial island of 5 sq km/3 sq mi in Kobe harbour, was created in 1960–68 from the rock of nearby mountains. It was one of the world's largest construction projects, and is now a residential and recreation area with a luxury hotel, amusement park, and conference centres. It is linked to the city by a driverless, computerized monorail.

**København** Danish name for ◊Copenhagen, the capital of Denmark.

**Koch, (Heinrich Hermann) Robert** (1843–1910) German bacteriologist. Koch and his assistants devised the techniques for culturing bacteria outside the body, and formulated the rules for showing whether or not a bacterium is the cause of a disease. Nobel Prize for Physiology or Medicine 1905.

**Koestler, Arthur** (1905–1983) Hungarian-born British writer. Imprisoned by the Nazis in France 1940, he escaped to England. His novel *Darkness at Noon* (1940), regarded as his masterpiece, is a fictional account of the Stalinist purges, and draws on his experiences as a prisoner under sentence of death during the Spanish Civil War. He also wrote extensively about creativity, science, parapsychology, politics, and culture.

**Kohl, Helmut** (1930–   ) German conservative politician, leader of the Christian Democratic Union (CDU) from 1976, West German chancellor (prime minister) 1982–90, and German chancellor from 1990 to 1998. He oversaw the reunification of East and West Germany 1989–90 and in 1990 won a resounding victory to become the first chancellor of a reunited Germany. His miscalculation of the true costs of reunification and their subsequent effects on the German economy led to a dramatic fall in his popularity, but as the economy recovered, so did his public esteem, enabling him to achieve a historic fourth electoral victory in 1994. In November 1996 Kohl entered his 15th year as chancellor, overtaking the record previously held by Konrad Adenauer, Kohl's political mentor. His close working relationship with President Mitterrand of France was the foundation for accelerating progress towards closer European integration, and Kohl was a strong backer of the project of a single European currency. His popularity slipped as a result of record levels of unemployment, which reached 12.6% in January 1998, and he lost office following his defeat by Gerhard Schroeder in the elections of September 1998.

**kohlrabi** variety of kale, which is itself a variety of ◊cabbage; it is used for food and resembles a turnip. The leaves of kohlrabi shoot from a round swelling on the main stem. (*Brassica oleracea caulorapa* or *B. oleracea gongylodes*, family Cruciferae.)

**Kokoschka, Oskar** (1886–1980) Austrian Expressionist painter. Initially influenced by the Vienna Sezession painters, he painted vivid landscapes, and highly charged allegories and portraits, for example *The Bride of the Wind* (*The Tempest*) (1914; Kunstmuseum, Basel). His writings include Expressionist plays and poetry.

**kola** alternative spelling of ◊cola, any of a group of tropical trees.

**Kola Peninsula** Russian *Kol'skiy Poluostrov*, peninsula in the far northwestern Russian Federation, between the Barents Sea and the White Sea. Administratively, it forms part of Murmansk oblast (region). Its total area is 129,500 sq km/50,000 sq mi, and it has a population of 1.3 million (of whom 2,000 are Saami). To the northwest the low-lying granite plateau adjoins Norway's thinly populated county of Finnmark.

**Kollontai, Alexandra Mikhailovna** born Domontovich (1872–1952) Russian revolutionary, politician, and writer. In 1905 she published *On the Question of the Class Struggle*, and, as commissar for public welfare, was the only female member of the first Bolshevik government. She campaigned for domestic reforms such as acceptance of free love, simplification of divorce laws, and collective child care.

**Kollwitz, Käthe** born Schmidt (1867–1945) German graphic artist and sculptor. One of the leading Expressionists, she is noted for the harrowing drawings, woodcuts, etchings, and lithographs on the themes of social injustice and human suffering, as in the woodcut cycle *Never Again War!* (1924).

**Köln** German form of ◊Cologne, a city in Germany.

**Kommunizma, Pik** or *Communism Peak;* formerly (to 1933) *Garmo Peak,* (1933–61) *Stalin Peak,* highest mountain in the ◊Pamirs, a mountain range in Tajikistan in Central Asia; height 7,495 m/24,590 ft. It was first climbed by a Soviet expedition in 1933.

**Kong Zi** Pinyin form of ◊Confucius, Chinese philosopher.

**Königsberg** former name of ◊Kaliningrad, a Baltic port in Russia.

**kookaburra** or *laughing jackass,* largest of the world's ◊kingfishers, found in Australia, with an extraordinary laughing call. It feeds on insects and other small creatures. The body and tail measure 45 cm/18 in, the head is greyish with a dark eye stripe, and the back and wings are flecked brown with grey underparts. It nests in shady forest regions, but will also frequent the vicinity of houses, and its cry is one of the most familiar sounds of the bush in eastern Australia. (Species *Dacelo novaeguineae,* family Alcedinidae, order Coraciiformes.)

**Koran** (alternatively transliterated as *Quran*) the sacred book of ◊Islam, written in Arabic.

It is said to have been divinely revealed through the angel Gabriel, or Jibra'el, to the prophet Muhammad between about AD 610 and 632. The Koran is the prime source of all Islamic ethical and legal doctrines.

**Korbut, Olga Valentinovna** (1955–   ) Soviet gymnast. She attracted world attention at the 1972 Olympic Games with her lively floor routine, winning three gold medals for the team, beam, and floor exercises.

*career highlights*
***Olympic Games*** gold: team, beam, floor exercise 1972; team: 1976

**Korda, Alexander (Laszlo)** (1893–1956) Hungarian-born British film producer and director. He was a dominant figure in the British film industry during the 1930s and 1940s. His films as director include *Marius* (1931), in France, and *The Private Life of Henry VIII* (1933), in England. He was the producer of *The Scarlet Pimpernel* (1935), *The Thief of Bagdad* (1940),

*The Third Man* (1949), and *Richard III* (1956), among many others.

**Korea** peninsula in East Asia, divided into north and south.

**Korean** person who is native to or an inhabitant of Korea; also the language and culture. There are approximately 33 million Koreans in South Korea, 15 million in North Korea, and 3 million elsewhere, principally in Japan, China (Manchuria), Russia, Kazakhstan, Uzbekistan, and the USA.

**Korean language** language of Korea, written from the 5th century AD in Chinese characters until the invention of an alphabet by King Sejong 1443. The linguistic affiliations of Korean are unclear, but it may be distantly related to Japanese.

**Korean War** war from 1950 to 1953 between North Korea (supported by China) and South Korea, aided by the United Nations (the troops were mainly US). North Korean forces invaded South Korea on 25 June 1950, and the Security Council of the United Nations, owing to a walkout by the USSR, voted to oppose them. The North Koreans held most of the South when US reinforcements arrived in September 1950 and forced their way through to the North Korean border with China. The Chinese retaliated, pushing them back to the original boundary by October 1950; truce negotiations began in 1951, although the war did not end until 1953.

**Kościusko, Mount** highest mountain in Australia (2,228 m/7,310 ft), in the Snowy Mountains of the Australian Alps in southeast New South Wales, close to the border with Victoria.

**Kościuszko, Tadeusz Andrzej** (1746–1817) Polish general and nationalist. He served with George Washington in the American Revolution (1776–83). He returned to Poland in 1784, fought against the Russian invasion that ended in the partition of Poland, and withdrew to Saxony. He returned in 1794 to lead the revolt against the occupation, but was defeated by combined Russian and Prussian forces and imprisoned until 1796.

**kosher** (Hebrew 'appropriate') conforming to religious law with regard to the preparation and consumption of food; in Judaism, conforming to the Mosaic law of the Book of Deuteronomy. For example, only animals that chew the cud and have cloven hooves (cows and sheep, but not pigs) may be eaten. There are rules governing their humane slaughter and their preparation (such as complete draining of blood) which also apply to fowl. Only fish with scales and fins may be eaten; not shellfish. Milk products may not be cooked or eaten with meat or poultry, or until four hours after eating them. Utensils for meat must be kept separate from those for milk.

**Kosovo** or *Kossovo*, autonomous region 1945–1990 of southern Serbia; capital Priština; area 10,900 sq km/4,207 sq mi; population (1991) 2,012,500, consisting of about 210,000 Serbs and about 1.8 million Albanians. Products include wine, nickel, lead, and zinc. Since it is

largely inhabited by Albanians and bordering on Albania, there have been demands for unification with that country, while in the late 1980s Serbians agitated for Kosovo to be merged with the rest of Serbia. A state of emergency was declared in February 1990 after fighting broke out between ethnic Albanians, police, and Kosovo Serbs. The parliament and government were dissolved in July 1990 and the Serbian parliament formally annexed Kosovo in September 1990. The Serbian invasion brought Kosovo to the brink of civil war; fighting and opposition efforts continued throughout the 1990s and escalated towards the end of the decade.

**Kosovo Liberation Army** KLA, also known as Ushtria Çlirimtare e Kosovës (UCK) in Albanian, paramilitary force operating in the predominantly ethnic Albanian province of Kosovo, Yugoslavia, and fighting for the independence of Kosovo. The KLA emerged as an organized movement in 1996, and by 1998 found itself in command of an uprising, which quickly spread across parts of the province. Labelled a terrorist organization by the Serb authorities (and Russia), the KLA took large tracts of land 1997–98, but the Serbs began to fight back in the summer of 1998 and by April 1999 – a month into a NATO offensive against Yugoslavia – the organization had been decimated. Thousands of new Kosovar recruits from European countries began to arrive. The KLA participated in the February 1999 Rambouillet peace talks and signed the agreement. It cooperated and coordinated its operations with NATO's air forces in its bombing campaign against Yugoslav military targets.

**Kossuth, Lajos** (1802–1894) Hungarian nationalist and leader of the revolution of 1848. He proclaimed Hungary's independence of Habsburg rule, became governor of a Hungarian republic in 1849, and, when it was defeated by Austria and Russia, fled first to Turkey and then to exile in Britain and Italy.

**Kosygin, Alexei Nikolaievich** (1904–1980) Soviet politician, prime minister 1964–80. He was elected to the Supreme Soviet in 1938, became a member of the Politburo in 1946, deputy prime minister in 1960, and succeeded Khrushchev as premier (while Brezhnev succeeded him as party secretary). In the late 1960s Kosygin's influence declined.

**Kowloon** peninsula on the Chinese coast, until July 1997 part of the British crown colony of Hong Kong; the city of Kowloon is a residential area.

**Krajina** region on the frontier between Croatia and Bosnia-Herzegovina; the chief town is Knin. Dominated by Serbs, the region proclaimed itself an autonomous Serbian province after Croatia declared its independence from Yugoslavia 1991. Krajina was the scene of intense inter-ethnic fighting during the civil war in Croatia 1991–92 and, following the ceasefire January 1992, 10,000 UN troops were deployed here and in eastern and western Slavonia.

**Krakatoa** Indonesian *Krakatau,* volcanic island in Sunda Strait, Indonesia, that erupted

1883, causing 36,000 deaths on Java and Sumatra by the tidal waves that followed. The island is now uninhabited.

**Kraków** or *Cracow,* city in Poland, on the River Vistula; population (1993) 751,300. It is an industrial centre producing railway wagons, paper, chemicals, and tobacco. It was capital of Poland about 1300–1595.

**Krasnodar** krai (territory) in the southwestern Russian Federation
*area* 83,600 sq km/32,278 sq mi
*cities* Krasnodar (capital), Armavir, Novorossiysk, Maikop, Sochi
*physical* in northwestern Caucasia, adjacent to the Black Sea and the Sea of Azov, and crossed by the River Kuban; lowland with black earth soil (*chernozem*) in the north; heavily forested northwestern part of the main Caucasian range in the south; oil, natural gas, and cement-marl deposits
*industries* food processing, engineering, oil extraction and refining, cement production, and manufacture of farm machinery; one of the main agricultural regions of the Russian Federation, growing wheat, sunflowers, rice, tobacco, fruit, and grapes; extensive livestock rearing
*population* (1996) 5,044,000; 54% urban
*history* the area north of the River Kuban formerly belonged to the Crimean Khanate (territory ruled by a *kahn*), which was annexed by Russia in 1783; the Black Sea littoral (coastal region) was captured from Turkey in 1829, and the Circassians south of the river were conquered by 1864. The first Russian and Ukrainian colonists were Don and Zaporozhye Cossacks. The Kuban region was one of the strongholds of anti-Bolshevik resistance in the Russian Civil War 1918–20, and in the campaign against the collectivization of agriculture 1929–33.

**Krasnoyarsk** krai (territory) in the Russian Federation, in central Siberia
*area* 2,401,600 sq km/927,258 sq mi (including Arctic Ocean Islands)
*cities* Krasnoyarsk (capital), Kansk, Norilsk
*physical* stretching some 3,000 km/1,870 mi north–south along the River Yenisey valley from the Arctic Ocean to the Sayan Mountains; lowland to the west of the Yenisey, plateau to the east; severe climate (permafrost in the north, within the Arctic Circle); largely covered with coniferous forests, but with tundra in the north and fertile steppe in the south; huge coal, graphite, iron-ore, gold, non-ferrous metals, and uranium deposits
*industries* coal and mineral mining, engineering, lumbering, textile manufacture, and food processing; hydroelectric power generation; agricultural activities are grain growing (spring wheat), cattle raising, and reindeer breeding; some fur trapping
*population* (1996) 3,106,000; 74% urban
*history* Krasnoyarsk krai was formerly an area of banishment and forced labour camps for criminal and political dissidents, but is now one of the most rapidly developing regions of Siberia.

**Kravchuk, Leonid** (1934–   ) Ukrainian politician, president 1990–94. Formerly a member of the Ukrainian Communist Party (UCP), he became its ideology chief in the 1980s. After the suspension of the UCP in August 1991, Kravchuk became an advocate of independence and market-centred economic reform. Faced with a rapidly deteriorating economic situation in 1993, he assumed direct control of government, eliminating the post of prime minister. He was, however, defeated by former prime minister Leonid Kuchma in the July 1994 presidential elections.

**Krebs, Hans Adolf** (1900–1981) German-born British biochemist. He discovered the citric acid cycle, also known as the ◊*Krebs cycle,* the final pathway by which food molecules are converted into energy in living tissues. For this work he shared the 1953 Nobel Prize for Physiology or Medicine. Knighted 1958.

**Krebs cycle** or *citric acid cycle* or *tricarboxylic acid cycle,* final part of the chain of biochemical reactions by which organisms break down food using oxygen to release energy (respiration). It takes place within structures called ◊mitochondria in the body's cells, and breaks down food molecules in a series of small steps, producing energy-rich molecules of ◊ATP.

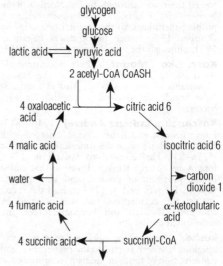

*Krebs cycle* The purpose of the Krebs (or citric acid) cycle is to complete the biochemical breakdown of food to produce energy-rich molecules, which the organism can use to fuel work. Acetyl coenzyme A (acetyl CoA) – produced by the breakdown of sugars, fatty acids, and some amino acids – reacts with oxaloacetic acid to produce citric acid, which is then converted in a series of enzyme-catalysed steps back to oxaloacetic acid. In the process, molecules of carbon dioxide and water are given off, and the precursors of the energy-rich molecules ATP are formed. (The numbers in the diagram indicate the number of carbon atoms in the principal compounds.)

**krill** any of several Antarctic ◊crustaceans, the most common species being *Euphausia superba*. Similar to a shrimp, it is up to 5 cm/2 in long, with two antennae, five pairs of legs, seven pairs of light organs along the body, and is coloured orange above and green beneath. It is the most abundant animal, numbering perhaps 600 trillion (million million). (Order Euphausiacea.)

**Krishna** incarnation of the Hindu god ◊Vishnu. The devotion of the bhakti movement is usually directed towards Krishna; an example of this is the ◊International Society for Krishna Consciousness. Many stories are told of Krishna's mischievous youth, and he is the charioteer of Arjuna in the *Bhagavad-Gītā*.

**Kristallnacht** 'night of (broken) glass' 9–10 November 1938 when the Nazi Sturmabteilung (SA) militia in Germany and Austria mounted a concerted attack on Jews, their synagogues, homes, and shops. It followed the assassination of a German embassy official in Paris by a Polish-Jewish youth. Subsequent measures included German legislation against Jews owning businesses or property, and restrictions on their going to school or leaving Germany. It was part of the ◊Holocaust.

**Kristiansen, Ingrid** (1956– ) Norwegian athlete, an outstanding long-distance runner of 5,000 metres, 10,000 metres, marathon, and cross-country races. She has won all the world's leading marathons. In 1986 she knocked 45.68 seconds off the world 10,000 metres record. She was the world cross-country champion in 1988 and won the London marathon 1984–85 and 1987–88.

*career highlights*
***World Cross-Country Champion*** 1988
***London Marathon*** 1984, 1985, 1987, 1988.

**Kruger, (Stephanus Johannes) Paul(us)** (1825–1904) President of the Transvaal 1883–1900. He refused to remedy the grievances of the uitlanders (English and other non-Boer white residents) and so precipitated the Second ◊South African War.

**krypton** (Greek *kryptos* 'hidden') colourless, odourless, gaseous, nonmetallic element, symbol Kr, atomic number 36, relative atomic mass 83.80. It is grouped with the inert gases and was long believed not to enter into reactions, but it is now known to combine with fluorine under certain conditions; it remains inert to all other reagents. It is present in very small quantities in the air (about 114 parts per million). It is used chiefly in fluorescent lamps, lasers, and gas-filled electronic valves.

**K-T boundary** geologists' shorthand for the boundary between the rocks of the ◊Cretaceous and the ◊Tertiary periods 65 million years ago. It coincides with the end of the extinction of the dinosaurs and in many places is marked by a layer of clay or rock enriched in the element iridium. Extinction of the dinosaurs at the K-T boundary and deposition of the iridium layer are thought to be the result of either impact of a meteorite (or comet) that crashed into the Yucatán Peninsula (forming the **Chicxulub**

*crater*) or the result of intense volcanism on the continent of India.

**Kuala Lumpur** capital of the Federation of Malaysia; area 240 sq km/93 sq mi; population (1991) 1,145,000. The city developed after 1873 with the expansion of tin and rubber trading; these are now its main industries. Formerly within the state of Selangor, of which it was also the capital, it was created a federal territory 1974.

**Kublai Khan** also *Khubilai* or *Kubla Khan* (*c.* 1216–1294) Mongol emperor of China from 1259. He completed his grandfather ◊Genghis Khan's conquest of northern China from 1240, and on his brother Mangu's death in 1259 established himself as emperor of China. He moved the capital to Khanbalik or Cambuluc (now the site of Beijing) and founded the Yuan dynasty, successfully expanding his empire into southern China, Tartary, and Tibet. He also conquered Indochina and Burma, and conducted campaigns in other neighbouring countries to secure tribute claims, but was defeated in an attempt to take Japan in 1281.

**Kubrick, Stanley** (1928–1999) US film director, producer, and screenwriter. His work was eclectic in subject matter and ambitious in scale and technique. It includes *Paths of Glory* (1957), *Dr Strangelove* (1964), *2001: A Space Odyssey* (1968), *A Clockwork Orange* (1971), and *Full Metal Jacket* (1987). His last film, *Eyes Wide Shut*, was completed just before his death and was released in 1999.

**kudu** either of two species of African antelope. The *greater kudu* (*T. strepsiceros*) is fawn-coloured with thin white vertical stripes, and stands 1.3 m/4.2 ft at the shoulder, with head and body 2.4 m/8 ft long. Males have long spiral horns. The greater kudu is found in bush country from Angola to Ethiopia. The similar *lesser kudu* (*T. imberbis*) lives in East Africa and is 1 m/3 ft at the shoulder. (Genus *Tragelaphus*, family Bovidae.)

**Ku Klux Klan** US secret society dedicated to white supremacy. It was founded in 1865 to oppose ◊Reconstruction in the Southern states after the American ◊Civil War and to deny political rights to the black population. Members wore hooded white robes to hide their identity, and burned crosses at their night-time meetings. In the late 20th century the Klan evolved into a paramilitary extremist group and forged loose ties with other white supremacist groups.

**kumquat** small orange-yellow fruit of any of several evergreen trees native to East Asia and cultivated throughout the tropics. The trees grow 2.4–3.6 m/8–12 ft high and have dark green shiny leaves and white scented flowers. The fruit is eaten fresh (the skin is edible), preserved, or candied. The oval or Nagami kumquat is the most common variety. (Genus *Fortunella*, family Rutaceae.)

**Kun, Béla** (1886–1937) Hungarian politician. He created a Soviet republic in Hungary in March 1919, which was overthrown in August 1919 by a Western blockade and Romanian military actions. The succeeding regime under Admiral ◊Horthy effectively liquidated both socialism and liberalism in Hungary.

**Kundera, Milan** (1929–   ) Czech writer. His first novel, *The Joke* (1967), brought him into official disfavour in Prague, and, unable to publish further works, he moved to France. Other novels include *The Book of Laughter and Forgetting* (1979) and *The Unbearable Lightness of Being* (1984; filmed 1988).

**kung fu** Chinese art of unarmed combat (Mandarin *ch'üan fa*), one of the ◊martial arts. It is practised in many forms, the most popular being *wing chun,* 'beautiful springtime'. The basic principle is to use attack as a form of defence.

**Kunming** formerly *Yünnan,* capital of ◊Yunnan province, China, on Lake Dianchi, about 2,000 m/6,500 ft above sea level; population (1990) 1,625,000. It is an important trading centre between the far west and central and south China. Industries include engineering and the manufacture of chemicals, textiles, iron, steel, machinery, cigarettes, heavy goods vehicles, plastics, and cement. Copper is smelted with nearby hydroelectric power.

**Kuomintang** original spelling of the Chinese nationalist party, now known (outside Taiwan) as ◊Guomindang.

**Kurd** member of a people living mostly in the Taurus and Sagros mountains of eastern Turkey, western Iran, and northern Iraq in the region called ◊Kurdistan. The Kurds have suffered repression in several countries, most brutally in Iraq, where in 1991 more than 1 million were forced to flee their homes. They speak an Indo-Iranian language and are predominantly Sunni Muslims, although there are some Shi'ites in Iran.

**Kurdish language** language belonging to the Indo-Iranian branch of the Indo-European family, closely related to Farsi (Persian). It is spoken by the Kurds, a geographically divided ethnic group. Its numerous dialects fall into two main groups: northern Kurmanji and southern Kurmanji (also known as Sorani). Around 60% of Kurds speak one of the northern Kurmanji dialects. Related languages include Zaza and Gurani. Three different alphabets are used – Arabic, Latin, and Cyrillic.

**Kurdistan** or *Kordestan,* mountain and plateau region in southwest Asia near Mount Ararat, where the borders of Iran, Iraq, Syria, Turkey, Armenia, and Azerbaijan meet; area 193,000 sq km/74,600 sq mi; total population 25–30 million. It is the home of the ◊Kurds and is the area over which Kurdish nationalists have traditionally fought to win sovereignty. It is also the name of a northwest Iranian province in the Zagros Mountains, covering 25,000 sq km/9,650 sq mi, population (1991) 1,233,500. The chief towns of the region are Kermanshah (Iran); Irbil, Sulaymaniyah, and Kirkuk (Iraq); Divarbakir, Erzurum, and Van (Turkey); and Qamishle (Syria).

**Kuril Islands** or *Kuriles,* chain of about 50 small islands stretching from the northeast of Hokkaido, Japan, to the south of Kamchatka, Russia, area 14,765 sq km/5,700 sq mi; population (1990) 25,000. Some of the islands are of volcanic origin with active volcanoes and hot springs. Two of the Kurils (Etorofu and Kunashiri) are claimed by Japan and Russia; they are of strategic importance and also have mineral deposits. The surrounding waters are rich in salmon and cod.

**Kurosawa, Akira** (1910–1998) Japanese director. His film *Rashōmon* (1950) introduced Western audiences to Japanese cinema. Epics such as *Shichinin no samurai/Seven Samurai* (1954) combine spectacle with intimate human drama. Kurosawa's films with a contemporary setting include *Yoidore tenshi/Drunken Angel* (1948) and *Ikiru/Living* (1952), both using illness as metaphor.

**Kuwait** State of
*national name Dowlat al Kuwait*

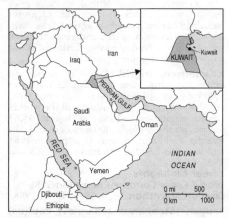

*area* 17,819 sq km/6,879 sq mi
*capital* Kuwait (also chief port)
*major towns/cities* as-Salimiya, Hawalli, Faranawiya, Abraq Kheetan, Jahra, Ahmadi, Fahaheel
*physical features* hot desert; islands of Failaka, Bubiyan, and Warba at northeast corner of Arabian Peninsula
*head of state* Sheikh Jabir al-Ahmad al-Jabir as-Sabah from 1977
*head of government* Crown Prince Sheikh Saad al-Abdullah as-Salinas as-Sabah from 1978
*political system* absolute monarchy
*political parties* none
*currency* Kuwaiti dinar
*GNP per capita (PPP)* (US$) 24,270 (1997)
*exports* petroleum and petroleum products (accounted for more than 93% of export revenue in 1994), chemical fertilizer, gas (natural and manufactured), basic manufactures. Principal market: Japan 24.1% (1997)
*population* 1,897,000 (1999 est)
*language* Arabic (official) 78%, Kurdish 10%, Farsi 4%, English
*religion* Sunni Muslim, Shiite Muslim, Christian
*life expectancy* 74 (men); 78 (women) (1995–2000)

**Chronology**

**c. 3000 BC** Archaeological evidence suggests that coastal parts of Kuwait may have been part of a commercial civilization contemporary with the Sumerian, based in Mesopotamia (the Tigris and Euphrates valley area of Iraq).

**c. 323 BC** Visited by Greek colonists at time of Alexander the Great.

**7th century AD** Islam introduced.

**late 16th century** Fell under nominal control of Turkish Ottoman Empire.

**1710** Control was assumed by the Utab, a member of the Anaza tribal confederation in northern Arabia, and Kuwait city was founded, soon developing from a fishing village into an important port.

**1756** Autonomous Sheikhdom of Kuwait founded by Abd Rahman of the al-Sabah family, a branch of the Utab.

**1776** British East India Company set up a base in the Gulf.

**1899** Concerned at the potential threat of growing Ottoman and German influence, Britain signed a treaty with Kuwait, establishing a self-governing protectorate in which the Emir received an annual subsidy from Britain in return for agreeing not to alienate any territory to a foreign power.

**1914** Britain recognized Kuwait as an 'independent government under British protection'.

**1922–33** Agreement on frontiers with Iraq, to the north, and Nejd (later Saudi Arabia) to the southwest.

**1938** Oil discovered; large-scale exploitation after World War II transformed the economy.

**1961** Full independence achieved from Britain, with Sheikh Abdullah al-Salem al-Sabah as emir. Attempted Iraqi invasion discouraged by dispatch of British troops to the Gulf.

**1962** Constitution introduced, with franchise restricted to 10% of the population.

**1965** Sheikh Abdullah died; succeeded by his brother, Sheikh Sabah al-Salem al-Sabah.

**1977** Sheikh Sabah died; he was succeeded by Crown Prince Jabir. The National Assembly was dissolved.

**1981** The National Assembly was reconstituted.

**1983** Shiite guerrillas bombed targets in Kuwait; 17 were arrested.

**1986** The National assembly was dissolved.

**1987** Kuwaiti oil tankers were reflagged and received US Navy protection; there were missile attacks by Iran.

**1988** Aircraft hijacked by pro-Iranian Shiites demanding the release of convicted guerrillas; Kuwait refused.

**1989** Two of the convicted guerrillas were released.

**1990** Prodemocracy demonstrations were suppressed. Kuwait was annexed by Iraq in August, causing extensive damage to property and environment. Emir set up a government in exile in Saudi Arabia.

**1991** US-led coalition forces defeated Iraqi forces in Kuwait in the Gulf War. The new government omitted any opposition representatives.

**1992** The reconstituted national assembly was elected, with opposition nominees, including Islamic candidates, winning the majority of seats.

**1993** Incursions by Iraq into Kuwait were repelled by US-led air strikes on Iraqi military sites.

**1994** The massing of Iraqi troops on the Kuwaiti border prompted a US-led response. Iraqi president Saddam Hussein publicly renounced any claim to Kuwait.

**Kuwait** Arabic *Al Kuwayt*) formerly *Qurein,* chief port and capital of the state of Kuwait, on the southern shore of Kuwait Bay; population (1993) 31,200. Kuwait is a banking and investment centre. It was heavily damaged during the Gulf War.

**Kwa Ndebele** former black homeland in former Transvaal Province, South Africa; now partly in Mpumalanga and partly in Gauteng.

**Kwangju** or *Kwangchu,* capital of South Cholla province, southwestern South Korea; population (1990) 1,144,700. It is at the centre of a rice-growing region. A museum in the city houses a large collection of Chinese porcelain dredged up in 1976 after lying for over 600 years on the ocean floor.

**kwashiorkor** severe protein deficiency in children under five years, resulting in retarded growth, lethargy, ◊oedema, diarrhoea, and a swollen abdomen. It is common in Third World countries with a high incidence of malnutrition.

**KwaZulu** former black homeland in former Natal Province, South Africa. In 1994 it became part of ◊KwaZulu-Natal Province. It achieved self-governing status in 1971. In 1994 it was placed under a state of emergency in the run-up to the first multiracial elections, after mounting violence by the Zulu-based ◊Inkatha party threatened to destabilize the election process. Homelands were to progressively disappear under the 1993 nonracial constitution, but Inkatha's leader (and the homeland's chief minister), Mangosuthu Buthelezi, won substantial concessions for KwaZulu prior to agreeing to participate in the elections.

**KwaZulu-Natal** province of the Republic of South Africa, formed from the former province of Natal and the former independent homeland of KwaZulu

**area** 91,481 sq km/35,321 sq mi

**capital** Pietermaritzburg

**towns and cities** Durban, Richards Bay

**physical** a narrow plain bounded by the Drakensberg Mountains to the west and the Indian Ocean to the east

**features** Ndumu Game Reserve; Kosi Bay Nature Reserve; Sodwana Bay National Park; Maple Lane Nature Reserve; St Lucia National Park, which extends from coral reefs of the Indian Ocean north of Umfolozi River (whales, dolphins, turtles, crayfish), over forested sandhills to inland grasslands and swamps of Lake St Lucia, 324 sq km/125 sq mi (reedbuck, buffalo, crocodiles, hippopotami, black rhinos, cheetahs, pelicans, flamingos, storks); it is under threat from titanium mining

**industries** oil refining, coal, iron and steel, engineering, food processing

*agriculture* sugar, maize, fruit, black wattle, maize, tobacco, vegetables
*population* (1995 est) 8,713,100; 75% Zulu
*history* British colony of Natal annexed Zululand 1897; became part of the Union of South Africa 1910; KwaZulu-Natal created May 1994
*languages* Zulu 80%, English 15%, Afrikaans 2%

**Kyd, Thomas** (*c.* 1557–1595) English dramatist. He was the author of a bloody revenge tragedy, *The Spanish Tragedy* (printed about 1590), which anticipated elements present in Shakespeare's *Hamlet.*

**Kyoto** or *Kioto,* former capital of Japan 794–1868 (when the capital was changed to Tokyo) on Honshu island, linked by canal with Lake Biwa, 510 km/317 mi west of Tokyo and 40 km/25 mi northeast of Osaka; population (1994) 1,391,000. Industries include electrical, chemical, and machinery plants; silk weaving; and the manufacture of porcelain, bronze, lacquerware, dolls, and fans.

**Kyprianou, Spyros** (1932–   ) Cypriot politician, president 1977–88. Foreign minister 1961–72, he founded the federalist, centre-left Democratic Front in 1976.

**Kyrgyzstan** Republic of
*national name Kyrgyz Respublikasy*

*area* 198,500 sq km/76,640 sq mi
*capital* Bishkek (formerly Frunze)
*major towns/cities* Osh, Przhevalsk, Kyzyl-Kiya, Tokmak, Djalal-Abad
*physical features* mountainous, an extension of the Tian Shan range
*head of state* Askar Akayev from 1990
*head of government* Amangeldy Mursadykovich Muraliyev from 1999
*political system* emergent democracy
*political parties* Party of Communists of Kyrgyzstan (banned 1991–92); Ata Meken, Kyrgyz-nationalist; Erkin Kyrgyzstan, Kyrgyz-nationalist; Social Democratic Party, nationalist,

pro-Akayev; Democratic Movement of Kyrgyzstan, nationalist reformist
*currency* som
*GNP per capita (PPP)* (US$) 2,200 (1998)
*exports* wool, cotton yarn, tobacco, electric power, electronic and engineering products, non-ferrous metallurgy, food and beverages. Principal market: Germany 37.4% (1998)
*population* 4,669,000 (1999 est)
*language* Kyrgyz, a Turkic language
*religion* Sunni Muslim
*life expectancy* 63 (men); 72 (women) (1995–2000)
*Chronology*
*8th century* Spread of Islam.
*10th century onwards* Southward migration of Kyrgyz people from upper Yenisey River region to Tian-Shan region; accelerated following rise of Mongol Empire in 13th century.
*13th–14th centuries* Part of Mongol Empire.
*1685* Came under control of Mongol Oirots following centuries of Turkic rule.
*1758* Kyrgyz people became nominal subjects of Chinese Empire, following Oirots' defeat by Chinese rulers, the Manchus.
*early 19th century* Came under suzerainty of Khanate (chieftaincy) of Kokand, to the west.
*1864–76* Incorporated into tsarist Russian Empire.
*1916–17* Many Kyrgyz migrated to China after Russian suppression of rebellion in Central Asia and outbreak of civil war following 1917 October Revolution in Russia, with local armed guerrillas (*basmachi*) resisting Bolshevik Red Army.
*1917–1924* Part of independent Turkestan republic.
*1920s* Land reforms resulted in settlement of many formerly nomadic Kyrgyz; literacy and education improved.
*1924* Became autonomous republic within USSR.
*1930s* Agricultural collectivization programme provoked *basmachi* resistance and local 'nationalist communists' were purged from Kyrgyz Communist Party (KCP).
*1936* Became full union republic within USSR.
*1990* A state of emergency was imposed in Bishkek after ethnic clashes. Askar Akayev, a reform communist, was chosen as president.
*1991* Akayev condemned the attempted coup in Moscow against the reformist Mikhail Gorbachev; Kyrgyzstan joined the new Commonwealth of Independent States (CIS) and its independence was recognized by the USA.
*1992* Kyrgyzstan joined the United Nations and Conference on Security and Cooperation in Europe (CSCE; now the Organization on Security and Cooperation in Europe, OSCE). A market-centred economic reform programme was instituted.
*1994* A national referendum overwhelmingly supported Akayev's presidency. The country joined the Central Asian Union, with Kazakhstan and Uzbekistan.
*1995* Pro-Akayev independents were successful in elections to a new bicameral legislature.
*1996* A constitutional amendment increased the powers of the president. An agreement was

made with Kazakhstan and Uzbekistan to create a single economic market.

**1997** Private ownership of land was legalized but the privatization programme was suspended. An agreement was made on border controls with Russia.

**1998** Kubanychbek Djumaliev became prime minister; he was soon replaced by Jumabek Ibraimov, following a sharp depreciation in the currency. A referendum approved the private ownership of land.

**Kyushu** or *Kiushu,* southernmost of the main islands of Japan, separated from Shikoku island by the Bungo Strait, from Honshu island by the Kammon Strait, and from Korea by the Korea Strait; connected to Honshu by bridge and rail tunnel

**area** 42,150 sq km/16,270 sq mi, including about 370 small islands

**capital** Nagasaki

**cities** Fukuoka, Kumamoto, Kagoshima, Kitakyushu

**physical** mountainous, with subtropical climate; volcanic: the active volcano Aso-take (1,592 m/5,225 ft), has the world's largest crater

**industries** semiconductors, coal, gold, silver, iron, tin, timber, tourism, cattle, hogs

**agriculture** rice, tea, oranges, tobacco, sweet potatoes

**population** (1995) 13,424,000.

**l** symbol for ◊*litre*, a measure of liquid volume.

**labellum** lower petal of an orchid flower; it is a different shape from the two lateral petals and gives the orchid its characteristic appearance. The labellum is more elaborate and usually larger than the other petals. It often has distinctive patterning to encourage ◊pollination by insects; sometimes it is extended backwards to form a hollow spur containing nectar.

**Labour Party** UK political party based on socialist principles, originally formed to represent workers. It was founded in 1900 and first held office in 1924. The first majority Labour government (1945–51) introduced ◊nationalization and the National Health Service, and expanded ◊social security. Labour was again in power 1964–70, 1974–79 and from 1997. The party leader (Tony ◊Blair from 1994) is elected by an electoral college, with a weighted representation of the Parliamentary Labour Party (30%), constituency parties (30%), and trade unions (40%).

**Labrador** area in northeastern Canada, part of the province of ◊Newfoundland, lying between Ungava Bay on the northwest, the Atlantic Ocean on the east, and the Strait of Belle Isle on the southeast; area 266,060 sq km/102,699 sq mi; population (1991) 30,000. The most easterly part of the North American mainland, Labrador consists primarily of a gently sloping plateau with an irregular coastline of numerous bays, fjords, inlets, and cliffs (60–120 m/200–400 ft high). Its industries include fisheries, timber and pulp, and the mining of various minerals, especially iron ore. Hydroelectric resources include Churchill Falls, where one of the world's largest underground power houses is situated (opened in 1971). There is a Canadian Air Force base at Goose Bay on Lake Melville.

**laburnum** any of a group of flowering trees or shrubs belonging to the pea family; the seeds develop in pealike pods but are poisonous. *L. anagyroides*, native to the mountainous parts of central Europe, is often grown as an ornamental tree. The flowers, in long drooping clusters, are bright yellow and appear in early spring; some varieties have purple or reddish flowers. (Genus *Laburnum*, family Leguminosae.)

**Labyrinth** in Greek legend, the maze designed by the Athenian artisan Daedalus at Knossos in Crete for King Minos, as a home for the Minotaur – a monster, half man and half bull. After killing the Minotaur, Theseus, the prince of Athens, was guided out of the Labyrinth by a thread given to him by the king's daughter Ariadne.

**Laccadive, Minicoy, and Amindivi Islands** former name of the Indian island group ◊Lakshadweep.

**lace** delicate, decorative, openwork textile fabric. Lace is a European craft with centres in Belgium, Italy, France, Germany, and England.

**lacewing** any of a group of insects found throughout the world. Lacewings take their name from the intricate veining of their two pairs of semitransparent wings. They have narrow bodies and long thin antennae. The larvae (called aphid lions) are predators, especially on aphids. (Families Hemerobiidae (brown lacewings) and Chrysopidae (green lacewings), order Neuroptera.)

**Laclos, Pierre-Ambroise-François Choderlos de** (1741–1803) French author. An army officer, he wrote a single novel in letter form, *Les Liaisons dangereuses/Dangerous Liaisons* in 1782, an analysis of moral corruption. A cynical and unscrupulous libertine, the Vicomte de Valmont, encouraged by the Marquise de Merteuil, seduces and destroys two innocent women. A moral twist is given at the end of the book when Valmont is killed in a duel and the Marquise de Merteuil is hideously disfigured by smallpox.

**lacquer** waterproof resinous varnish obtained from Oriental trees *Toxicodendron verniciflua*, and used for decorating furniture and art objects. It can be applied to wood, fabric, leather, or other materials, with or without added colours. The technique of making and carving small lacquerwork objects was developed in China, probably as early as the 4th century BC, and was later adopted in Japan.

**lacrosse** Canadian ball game, adopted from the North American Indians, and named after a fancied resemblance of the lacrosse stick (crosse) to a bishop's crosier. Thongs across the curved end of the crosse form a pocket to carry the small rubber ball.

The field is approximately 100 m/110 yd long and a minimum of 55 m/60 yd wide in the men's game, which is played with 10 players per side; the women's field is larger, and there are 12 players per side. The goals are just under 2 m/6 ft square, with loose nets. The world championship was first held in 1967 for men, and in 1969 for women.

**lactation** secretion of milk in mammals, from the mammary glands. In late pregnancy, the cells lining the lobules inside the mammary glands begin extracting substances from the blood to produce milk. The supply of milk starts shortly after birth with the production of colostrum, a clear fluid consisting largely of water, protein, antibodies, and vitamins. The production of milk continues practically as long as the baby continues to suckle.

**lactic acid** or *2-hydroxypropanoic acid,* $CH_3CHOHCOOH$ organic acid, a colourless, almost odourless liquid, produced by certain bacteria during fermentation and by active muscle cells when they are exercised hard and are experiencing oxygen debt. An accumulation of lactic acid in the muscles may cause cramp. It occurs in yogurt, buttermilk, sour cream, poor wine, and certain plant extracts, and is used in food preservation and in the preparation of pharmaceuticals.

**lactose** white sugar, found in solution in milk; it forms 5% of cow's milk. It is commercially prepared from the whey obtained in cheese-making. Like table sugar (sucrose), it is a disaccharide, consisting of two basic sugar units (monosaccharides), in this case, glucose and galactose. Unlike sucrose, it is tasteless.

**Ladoga, Lake** Russian *Ladozhskoye Ozero,* largest lake in Europe, and the second largest in the Russian Federation after the Caspian Sea, situated in the far northwest of the Russian Federation, in the Republic of Karelia and Leningrad oblast (region), northeast of the city of St Petersburg. Lake Ladoga covers an area of 17,700 sq km/6,384 sq mi (with its islands, 18,135 sq km/7,002 sq mi). The main feeder rivers are the Volkhov, Svir, and Vuoksa, and the lake's outlet is by way of the Neva River into the Gulf of Finland. Its average depth is 51 m/167 ft, and its maximum depth 230 m/755 ft. A valuable commercial fishing industry is based here.

**Lady** in the UK, the formal title of the daughter of an earl, marquess, or duke, and of any woman whose husband's rank is above that of baronet or knight; the title 'Lady' is prefixed to her first name. The wife of a baronet or a knight is also called 'Lady', but uses the title by courtesy only, and has it prefixed to her surname.

**ladybird** or *ladybug,* any of various small beetles, generally red or yellow in colour, with black spots. There are more than 5,200 species worldwide. As larvae and adults, they feed on aphids and scale-insect pests. (Family Coccinellidae, order Coleoptera.)

**Lady Day** British name for the Christian festival (25 March) of the Annunciation of the Virgin Mary; until 1752 it was the beginning of the legal year in England, and it is still a quarter day (date for the payment of quarterly rates or dues).

**Lafayette, Marie Joseph Paul Yves Roch Gilbert de Motier** Marquis de Lafayette (1757–1834) French soldier and politician. He fought against Britain in the American Revolution 1777–79 and 1780–82. During the French Revolution he sat in the National Assembly as a constitutional royalist and in 1789 presented the Declaration of the Rights of Man. After the storming of the ◊Bastille, he was given command of the National Guard. In 1792 he fled the country after attempting to restore the monarchy and was imprisoned by the Austrians until 1797. He supported Napoleon Bonaparte in 1815, sat in the chamber of deputies as a Liberal from 1818, and played a leading part in the revolution of 1830.

**La Fontaine, Jean de** (1621–1695) French poet. He was born at Château-Thierry, Champagne, and from 1656 lived largely in Paris, the friend of the playwrights Molière and Racine, and the poet Boileau. His works include *Contes et nouvelles en vers* (1665–74), a series of witty and bawdy tales in verse, and *Fables choisies mises en vers* (1668–94), his universally known verse fables.

**lagoon** coastal body of shallow salt water, usually with limited access to the sea. The term is normally used to describe the shallow sea area cut off by a ◊coral reef or barrier islands.

**Lagos** chief port and former capital of Nigeria, located at the western end of an island in a lagoon and linked by bridges with the mainland via Iddo Island; population (1992 est) 1,347,000. Industries include chemicals, metal products, fish, food processing, light engineering, chemicals, and brewing. Its surrounding waters are heavily polluted.

**Lahnda** language spoken by 15–20 million people in Pakistan and northern India. It is closely related to Punjabi and Romany, and belongs to the Indo-Iranian branch of the Indo-European language family.

**Lahore** capital of the province of ◊Punjab, Pakistan, situated on a tributary of the River Ravi, 50 km/30 mi west of Amritsar in India; population (1991) 3,200,000. Lahore is a commercial and banking centre, and industries include engineering, textiles, carpets, and chemicals. It is associated with the Mogul rulers ◊Akbar, ◊Jahangir, and ◊Aurangzeb, whose capital it was in the 16th and 17th centuries.

**Laibach** German name of ◊Ljubljana, a city in Slovenia.

**Laing, R(onald) D(avid)** (1927–1989) Scottish psychoanalyst. He was the originator of the social theory of mental illness; for example, that schizophrenia is promoted by family pressure for its members to conform to standards alien to themselves. His books include *The Divided Self* (1960) and *The Politics of the Family* (1971).

*laissez faire* (French 'let alone') theory that the state should not intervene in economic affairs, except to break up a monopoly. The phrase originated with the Physiocrats, 18th-century French economists whose maxim was *laissez faire et laissez passer* (literally, 'let go and let pass' – that is, leave the individual alone and let commodities circulate freely). The degree to which intervention should take place is still one of the chief problems of economics. The Scottish economist Adam ◊Smith justified the theory in *The Wealth of Nations* (1776).

**lake** body of still water lying in depressed ground without direct communication with the sea. Lakes are common in formerly glaciated regions, along the courses of slow rivers, and in low land near the sea. The main classifications are by origin: *glacial lakes,* formed by glacial scouring; *barrier lakes,* formed by landslides and glacial moraines; *crater lakes,* found in volcanoes; and *tectonic lakes,* occurring in natural fissures.

**Lake District** region in Cumbria, northwest England. It contains the principal English lakes, separated by wild uplands rising to many peaks, including Scafell Pike (978 m/3,210 ft), the highest peak in England. The area was made a national park in 1951, covering 2,292 sq km/882 sq mi, and is a popular tourist destination.

**Lakshadweep** group of 36 coral islands, 10 inhabited, in the Indian Ocean, 320 km/200 mi off the Malabar coast, forming a Union Territory of India; area 32 sq km/12 sq mi; population (1994 est) 56,000. The administrative headquarters are on Kavaratti Island. Products include coir, copra, and fish. There is a tourist resort on Bangarem, an uninhabited island with a large lagoon. The religion is Islam.

**Lakshmi** Hindu goddess of wealth and beauty, consort of Vishnu; her festival is ◊Diwali.

**Lalique, René** (1860–1945) French designer and manufacturer of ◊Art Nouveau glass, jewellery, and house interiors. The Lalique factory continues in production at Wingen-sur-Moder, Alsace, under his son Marc and granddaughter Marie-Claude.

**Lamaism** Buddhism of Tibet and Mongolia, a form of Mahāyāna Buddhism. Buddhism was introduced into Tibet AD 640, but the real founder of Tibetan Buddhism was the Indian missionary Padma Sambhava, who was active about 750. Tibetan Buddhism developed several orders, based on lineages of teachings transmitted by reincarnated lamas (teachers). In the 14th–15th centuries Tsong-kha-pa founded the sect of Geluk-Pa ('virtuous'), which became the most powerful order in the country. Its head is the ◊Dalai Lama, who is considered an incarnation of the Bodhisattva Avalokiteśvara.

**Lamarck, Jean Baptiste de** (1744–1829) French naturalist. His theory of evolution, known as *Lamarckism,* was based on the idea that acquired characteristics (changes acquired in an individual's lifetime) are inherited by the offspring, and that organisms have an intrinsic urge to evolve into better-adapted forms. *Philosophie zoologique/Zoological Philosophy* 1809 outlined his 'transformist' (evolutionary) ideas.

**Lamartine, Alphonse Marie Louis de** (1790–1869) French poet. He wrote romantic poems, including *Méditations poétiques/Poetical Meditations* 1820, followed by *Nouvelles méditations/New Meditations* 1823, and *Harmonies poétiques et religieuses/Poetical and Religious Harmonies* 1830. His *Histoire des Girondins/History of the Girondins* 1847 helped to inspire the revolution of 1848. Lamartine was the first to sound a more personal note in his poetry and to establish a direct bond between himself and his public.

**Lamb, Charles** (1775–1834) English essayist and critic. He collaborated with his sister *Mary Lamb* (1764–1847) on *Tales from Shakespeare* (1807), and his *Specimens of English Dramatic Poets Contemporary with Shakespeare, with Notes* (1808) revealed him as a penetrating critic and helped to revive interest in Elizabethan plays. As 'Elia' he contributed essays to the *London Magazine* from 1820 (collected 1823 and 1833).

**Lammas** ('loaf-mass') medieval festival of harvest, celebrated 1 August. At one time it was an English quarter day (date for payment of quarterly rates or dues), and is still a quarter day in Scotland.

**lammergeier** or *bearded vulture,* Old World vulture with a wingspan of 2.7 m/9 ft. It ranges over southern Europe, North Africa, and Asia, in wild mountainous areas. It feeds on offal and carrion and drops bones onto rocks to break them and so get at the marrow. (Species *Gypaetus barbatus,* family Accipitridae.)

**Lamont, Norman Stewart Hughson** (1942– ) British Conservative politician, chief secretary of the Treasury 1989–90, chancellor of the Exchequer 1990–93, born in the Shetland Islands. In September 1992, despite earlier assurances to the contrary, he was forced to suspend the UK's membership of the European Community (now the European Union) ◊Exchange Rate Mechanism (ERM). He was replaced as chancellor by Kenneth Clarke in May 1993, after which he became a fierce rightwing critic of the Major administration. He lost his House of Commons seat in the May 1997 general election.

**lamprey** any of various eel-shaped jawless fishes. A lamprey feeds on other fish by fixing itself by its round mouth to its host and boring into the flesh with its toothed tongue. Lampreys breed in fresh water, and the young live as larvae for about five years before migrating to the sea. (Family Petromyzontidae.)

**Lancashire** county of northwest England (since April 1998 Blackpool and Blackburn have been separate unitary authorities)
*area* 3,040 sq km/1,173 sq mi
*towns and cities* Preston (administrative headquarters), which forms part of Central Lancashire New Town from 1970 (together with Fulwood, Bamber Bridge, Leyland, and Chorley); Lancaster, Accrington, Burnley; ports Fleetwood and Heysham; seaside resorts Morecambe and Southport
*features* the River Ribble; the Pennines; the Forest of Bowland (moors and farming valleys); Pendle Hill
*industries* formerly a world centre of cotton manufacture, now replaced with high-technology aerospace, nuclear fuels, and electronics industries. There is dairy farming and market gardening
*population* (1996) 1,424,700
*famous people* Kathleen Ferrier, Gracie Fields, George Formby, Rex Harrison.

**Lancaster, House of** English royal house, a branch of the Plantagenets.

**lancelet** any of a variety of marine animals about 2.5 cm/1 in long. They have no skull, brain, eyes, heart, vertebral column, centralized brain, or paired limbs, but there is a notochord (a supportive rod) which runs from end to end of the body, a tail, and a number of gill slits.

Found in all seas, lancelets burrow in the sand but when disturbed swim freely. (Genus *Amphioxus,* phylum Chordata, subphylum Cephalocordata.)

**Land** (plural *Länder*) federal state of Germany or Austria.

**Land, Edwin Herbert** (1909–1991) US inventor of the ◊Polaroid Land camera 1947. The camera developed the film in one minute inside the camera and produced an 'instant' photograph.

**Land League** Irish peasant-rights organization, formed in 1879 by Michael Davitt and Charles ◊Parnell to fight against tenant evictions. Through its skilful use of the boycott against anyone who took a farm from which another had been evicted, it forced Gladstone's government to introduce a law in 1881 restricting rents and granting tenants security of tenure.

**Land Registry, HM** official body set up 1925 to register legal rights to land in England and Wales. There has been a gradual introduction, since 1925, of compulsory registration of land in different areas of the country. This requires the purchaser of land to register details of his or her title and all other rights (such as mortgages and easements) relating to the land. Once registered, the title to the land is guaranteed by the Land Registry, subject to those interests that cannot be registered; this makes the buying and selling of land easier and cheaper. The records are open to public inspection (since December 1990).

**Landsbergis, Vytautas** (1932– ) Lithuanian politician, president 1990–93. He became active in nationalist politics in the 1980s, founding and eventually chairing the anticommunist Sajudis independence movement in 1988. When Sajudis swept to victory in the republic's elections in March 1990, Landsbergis chaired the Supreme Council of Lithuania, becoming, in effect, president. He immediately drafted the republic's declaration of independence from the USSR, which, after initial Soviet resistance, was recognized in September 1991. In October 1996, after a general election, he took the chair of the new parliament.

**Landseer, Edwin Henry** (1802–1873) English painter, sculptor, and engraver of animal studies. Much of his work reflects the Victorian taste for sentimental and moralistic pictures, for example *Dignity and Impudence* (1839; Tate Gallery, London). His sculptures include the lions at the base of Nelson's Column in Trafalgar Square, London (1857–67). He was knighted in 1850.

**Land's End** promontory of southwest Cornwall, 15 km/9 mi southwest of Penzance, the westernmost point of England.

**landslide** sudden downward movement of a mass of soil or rocks from a cliff or steep slope. Landslides happen when a slope becomes unstable, usually because the base has been undercut or because materials within the mass have become wet and slippery.

**Landsteiner, Karl** (1868–1943) Austrian-born US immunologist. He discovered the ABO

◊blood group system 1900–02, and aided in the discovery of the Rhesus blood factors 1940. He also discovered the polio virus. Nobel prize 1930.

**Lang, Fritz** (1890–1976) Austrian film director. His films are characterized by a strong sense of fatalism and alienation. His German films include *Metropolis* (1927) and *M* (1931), in which Peter Lorre starred as a child-killer. His US films include *Rancho Notorious* (1952) and *The Big Heat* (1953).

**lang, k(athryn) d(awn)** (1961– ) Canadian singer. Her mellifluous voice and androgynous image have gained her a wide following beyond the country-music field where she first established herself. Her albums include *Angel With a Lariat* 1987, *Shadowland* 1988, *Absolute Torch and Twang* 1989, the mainstream *Ingénue* 1992, *Even Cowgirls get the Blues* 1993, and *All You Can Eat* 1995.

**Langland, William** (*c.* 1332–*c.* 1400) English poet. His alliterative *The Vision of William Concerning Piers the Plowman* (see *Piers Plowman*) was written in three (or possibly four) versions between about 1367 and 1386. The poem forms a series of allegorical visions, in which Piers develops from the typical poor peasant to a symbol of Jesus, and condemns the social and moral evils of 14th-century England. It is a masterpiece in combining the depiction of a spiritual pilgrimage with scenes of contemporary social life for a satirical purpose.

**Langobard** another name for ◊Lombard, member of a Germanic people.

**language** human communication through speech, writing, or both. Different nationalities or ethnic groups typically have different languages or variations on particular languages; for example, Armenians speaking the Armenian language, and British and Americans speaking distinctive varieties of the English language. One language may have various dialects, which may be seen by those who use them as languages in their own right. There are about 6,000 languages spoken worldwide, but 90% of these are in some danger of falling into disuse. More than half the world's population speaks one of just five languages – Chinese, English, Hindi, Russian, and Spanish.

The term language is also used for systems of communication with languagelike qualities, such as *animal language* (the way animals communicate), *body language* (gestures and expressions used to communicate ideas), *sign language* (gestures for the deaf or for use as a ◊lingua franca, as among American Indians), and *computer languages* (such as BASIC and COBOL).

**Languedoc** former province of southern France, bounded by the River Rhône, the Mediterranean Sea, and the regions of Guienne and Gascony. In 1791 Languedoc was replaced by the eight *départements* of Haute-Loire, Lozère, Ardèche, Aude, Tarn, Hérault, Gard, and Haute-Garonne. Lower Languedoc was united with the former province of Roussillon to form the modern region of ◊Languedoc-Roussillon.

**Languedoc-Roussillon** region of southern France, comprising the *départements* of Aude, Gard, Hérault, Lozère, and Pyrénées-Orientales; area 27,400 sq km/10,576 sq mi; population (1990) 2,115,000. The administrative centre is Montpellier. Products include fruit, vegetables, and wine.

**langur** any of various leaf-eating Old World monkeys that live in trees in South Asia. There are about 20 species. Langurs are related to the colobus monkey of Africa. (Genus *Presbytis* and other related genera.)

**lanolin** sticky, purified fat obtained from sheep's wool and used in cosmetics, soap, and leather preparation.

**lanthanide** any of a series of 15 metallic elements (also known as rare earths) with atomic numbers 57 (lanthanum) to 71 (lutetium).

One of its members, promethium, is radioactive. All occur in nature. Lanthanides are grouped because of their chemical similarities (most are trivalent, but some can be divalent or tetravalent), their properties differing only slightly with atomic number.

**lanthanum** (Greek *lanthanein* 'to be hidden') soft, silvery, ductile and malleable, metallic element, symbol La, atomic number 57, relative atomic mass 138.91, the first of the lanthanide series. It is used in making alloys. It was named 1839 by Swedish chemist Carl Mosander (1797–1858).

**Lanzarote** most easterly of the Spanish Canary Islands; area 795 sq km/307 sq mi; capital Arrecife. The desertlike volcanic landscape is dominated by the Montañas de Fuego ('Mountains of Fire') with more than 300 volcanic cones.

**Lanzhou** or *Lanchow,* capital of ◊Gansu province, China, on the Huang He River, 190 km/120 mi south of the Great Wall; population (1994) 1,612,600. Industries include oil-refining and the manufacture of chemicals, fertilizers, machinery, and synthetic rubber.

**Lao** people who live along the Mekong river system in Laos (2 million) and northern Thailand (9 million). The Lao language is a member of the Sino-Tibetan family. The majority of Lao live in rural villages. During the wet season, May–October, they grow rice in irrigated fields, though some shifting or swidden cultivation is practised on hillsides. Vegetables and other crops are grown during drier weather. The Lao are predominantly Buddhist, though a belief in spirits, *phi,* is included in Lao devotions. There are some Christians among the minority groups.

**Laocoön** in classical mythology, a Trojan priest of Apollo and a visionary, brother of Anchises. He and his sons were killed by serpents when he foresaw disaster for Troy in the ◊Trojan horse left by the Greeks. The scene of their death is the subject of a classical marble group, rediscovered in the Renaissance, and forms an episode in Virgil's *Aeneid.*

**Laois** or *Laoighis,* previously spelt *Leix;* also formerly known as *Queen's County,* county of

the Republic of Ireland, in the province of Leinster; county town Portlaoise; area 1,720 sq km/664 sq mi; population (1991) 52,300. Other towns are Abbeyleix, Mountmellick, Mountrath, and Portarlington. Laois is flat, except for the Slieve Bloom Mountains in the northwest, the highest point of which is Mount Arderin (529 m/1,734 ft), and there are many bogs. The Barrow and the Nore are the chief rivers. Agriculture includes dairying, and mixed cattle and arable farming (sugar beet), and industries include peat, woollens, and agricultural machinery. Part of the Leinster coalfield lies within the county. There is a large peat-fired power station near Portarlington, and at the Clonsast Bog (1,619 ha/4,000 acres) is an important peat industry.

**Laos** Lao People's Democratic Republic
*national name Saathiaranagroat Prachhathippatay Prachhachhon Lao*

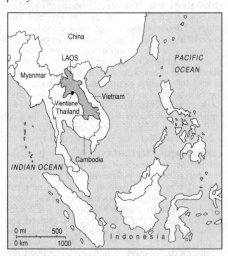

*area* 236,790 sq km/91,424 sq mi
*capital* Vientiane
*major towns/cities* Louangphrabang (the former royal capital), Pakse, Savannakhet
*physical features* landlocked state with high mountains in east; Mekong River in west; rainforest covers nearly 60% of land
*head of state* Gen Khamtay Siphandon from 1998
*head of government* Gen Sisavath Keobounphanh from 1998
*political system* communist, one-party state
*political party* Lao People's Revolutionary Party (LPRP, the only legal party)
*currency* new kip
*GNP per capita (PPP)* (US$) 1,300 (1998 est)
*exports* timber, textiles and garments, motorcycles, electricity, coffee, tin, gypsum. Principal market: Vietnam 42.7% (1997)
*population* 5,297,000 (1999 est)
*language* Lao (official), French, English
*religion* Theravāda Buddhist 85%, animist beliefs among mountain dwellers
*life expectancy* 52 (men); 55 (women) (1995–2000)

## Chronology

**c. 2000–500 BC** Early Bronze Age civilizations in central Mekong River and Plain of Jars regions.

**5th–8th centuries** Occupied by immigrants from southern China.

**8th century onwards** Theravāda Buddhism spread by Mon monks.

**9th–13th centuries** Part of the sophisticated Khmer Empire, centred on Angkor in Cambodia.

**12th century** Small independent principalities, notably Louangphrabang, established by Lao invaders from Thailand and Yunnan, southern China; they adopted Buddhism.

**14th century** United by King Fa Ngum; the first independent Laotian state, Lan Xang, formed. It was to dominate for four centuries, broken only by a period of Burmese rule 1574–1637.

**17th century** First visited by Europeans.

**1713** The Lan Xang kingdom split into three separate kingdoms, Louangphrabang, Vientiane, and Champassac, which became tributaries of Siam (Thailand) from the late 18th century.

**1893–1945** Laos was a French protectorate, comprising the three principalities of Louangphrabang, Vientiane, and Champassac.

**1945** Temporarily occupied by Japan.

**1946** Retaken by France, despite opposition by the Chinese-backed Lao Issara (Free Laos) nationalist movement.

**1950** Granted semi-autonomy in French Union, as an associated state under the constitutional monarchy of the king of Louangphrabang.

**1954** Independence achieved from France under the Geneva Agreements, but civil war broke out between a moderate royalist faction of the Lao Issara, led by Prince Souvanna Phouma, and the communist Chinese-backed Pathet Lao (Land of the Lao) led by Prince Souphanouvong (Souvanna's half-brother).

**1957** Coalition government, headed by Souvanna Phouma, established by Vientiane Agreement.

**1959** Savang Vatthana became king.

**1960** Right-wing pro-Western government seized power, headed by Prince Boun Gum.

**1962** Geneva Agreement established new coalition government, led by Souvanna Phouma, but civil war continued, the Pathet Lao receiving backing from the North Vietnamese, and Souvanna Phouma from the USA.

**1973** Vientiane ceasefire agreement divided the country between the communists and the Souvanna Phouma regime and brought the withdrawal of US, Thai, and North Vietnamese forces.

**1975** Communists seized power; republic proclaimed, with Prince Souphanouvong as head of state and the Communist Party leader Kaysone Phomvihane as the controlling prime minister.

**1979** Food shortages and the flight of 250,000 refugees to Thailand led to an easing of the drive towards nationalization and agricultural collectivization.

**1985** Greater economic liberalization received encouragement from the Soviet Union's reformist leader Mikhail Gorbachev.

**1989** The first assembly elections since communist takeover were held; Vietnamese troops were withdrawn from the country.

**1991** Kaysone Phomvihane was elected president and the army commander General Khamtay Siphandon became the prime minister. A security and cooperation pact was signed with Thailand, and an agreement reached on the phased repatriation of Laotian refugees.

**1992** Phomvihane died; he was replaced as president by Nouhak Phoumsavan.

**1995** The US lifted its 20-year aid embargo.

**1996** The military tightened its grip on political affairs, but inward investment and private enterprise continued to be encouraged, fuelling economic expansion.

**1997** Membership of theAssociation of South East Asian Nations (ASEAN) was announced.

**1998** Khamtay Siphandon became president and was replaced as prime minister by Sisavath Keobounphanh.

**Lao Zi** (*c.* 604–531 BC) or *Lao Tzu,* Chinese philosopher. He is commonly regarded as the founder of ◊Taoism, with its emphasis on the Tao, the inevitable and harmonious way of the universe. Nothing certain is known of his life. The *Tao Te Ching,* the Taoist scripture, is attributed to him but apparently dates from the 3rd century BC.

**La Paz** capital city of Bolivia, in Murillo province, 3,800 m/12,400 ft above sea level; population (1992) 711,000 (metropolitan area 1,126,000). It is in a canyon formed by the La Paz River, and is the world's highest capital city. Products include textiles and copper. It has been the seat of government since 1898, but Sucre is the legal capital and seat of the judiciary.

**lapis lazuli** rock containing the blue mineral lazurite in a matrix of white calcite with small amounts of other minerals. It occurs in silica-poor igneous rocks and metamorphic limestones found in Afghanistan, Siberia, Iran, and Chile. Lapis lazuli was a valuable pigment of the Middle Ages, also used as a gemstone and in inlaying and ornamental work.

**Laplace, Pierre Simon** Marquis de Laplace (1749–1827) French astronomer and mathematician. In 1796 he theorized that the Solar System originated from a cloud of gas (the nebular hypothesis). He studied the motion of the Moon and planets, and published a five-volume survey of ◊celestial mechanics, *Traité de méchanique céleste* 1799–1825. Among his mathematical achievements was the development of probability theory.

**Lapland** region of Europe within the Arctic Circle in Norway, Sweden, Finland and the Kola Peninsula of northwest Russia, without political definition. Its chief resources are chromium, copper, iron, timber, hydroelectric power, and tourism. The indigenous population are the Saami (formerly known as Lapps), 10% of whom are nomadic, the remainder living mostly in coastal settlements. Lapland has low temperatures, with two months of continuous daylight in summer and two months of continuous darkness in winter. There is summer agriculture.

**La Plata** capital of Buenos Aires province, Argentina, on the Río de la Plata 48 km/30 mi southeast of the city of Buenos Aires; population (1991) 542,600; metropolitan area (1992 est) 676,100. It is 9 km/6 mi from its port, Ensenada, the main outlet for produce from the Pampas. Industries include meat packing and petroleum refining. It has one of the country's best universities. The city was founded in 1882 by Governor Daroo Rocha.

**laptop computer** portable microcomputer, small enough to be used on the operator's lap. It consists of a single unit, incorporating a keyboard, ◊floppy disk and ◊hard disk drives, and a screen. The screen often forms a lid that folds back in use. It uses a liquid-crystal or gas-plasma display, rather than the bulkier and heavier cathode-ray tubes found in most display terminals. A typical laptop computer measures about 210 x 297 mm/8.3 x 11.7 in (A4), is 5 cm/2 in in depth, and weighs less than 3 kg/6 lb 9 oz. In the 1980s there were several types of laptop computer, but in the 1990s designs converged on systems known as notebook computers.

**lapwing** bird belonging to the plover family, also known as the **green plover** and, from its call, as the **peewit**. Bottle-green above and white below, with a long thin crest and rounded wings, it is about 30 cm/1 ft long. It inhabits moorland in Europe and Asia, making a nest scratched out of the ground, and is also often seen on farmland. (Species *Vanellus vanellus,* family Charadriidae.)

**Lara, Brian** (1969– ) Trinidadian cricket player. A left-handed batsman, he plays first-class cricket for Trinidad and Tobago and for Warwickshire. In April 1994 he broke the world individual test batting record with an innings of 375 against England, and 50 days later he broke the world record for an individual innings in first-class cricket with an unbeaten 501 for Warwickshire against Durham.

*career highlights*
***Test cricket (1990– )*** matches: 59; innings: 101 (3 not outs); runs: 4,860; average: 49.59; hundreds: 10; highest score: 375; catches: 80
***One-day internationals (1990– )*** matches: 137; innings: 135 (13 not outs); runs: 5,580; average: 46.59; highest score: 169; catches: 63

**larch** any of a group of trees belonging to the pine family. The common larch (*L. decidua*) grows to 40 m/130 ft. It is one of the few ◊conifers to shed its leaves annually. The small needlelike leaves are replaced every year by new bright-green foliage, which later darkens. (Genus *Larix,* family Pinaceae.)

**La Rioja** autonomous community of northern Spain; area 5,000 sq km/1,930 sq mi; population (1991) 261,600. The River Ebro passes through the region, but it is a tributary of the Río Oja, which gives its name to the region. La Rioja produces red and white wines with a characteristic flavour that derives from their storage in oak barrels. The capital is Logroño.

**lark** any of a group of songbirds found mainly in the Old World, but also in North America.

Larks are brownish-tan in colour and usually about 18 cm/7 in long; they nest on the ground in the open. The *skylark* (*Alauda arvensis*) sings as it rises almost vertically in the air. It is light brown and 18 cm/7 in long. (Family Alaudidae, order Passeriformes.)

**Larkin, Philip Arthur** (1922–1985) English poet. His perfectionist, pessimistic verse appeared in *The Less Deceived* (1955), and in the later volumes *The Whitsun Weddings* (1964), and *High Windows* (1974) which confirmed him as one of the most powerful and influential of 20th-century English poets. After his death, his letters and other writings, which he had instructed should be destroyed, revealed an intolerance and misanthropy not found in his published material. From 1955 until his death he was librarian at the University of Hull.

**larkspur** any of several plants included with the ◊delphiniums. (Genus *Delphinium,* family Ranunculaceae.)

**La Rochefoucauld, François** duc de (1613–1680) French writer. His 'Réflexions, ou sentences et maximes morales/Reflections, or Moral Maxims', published anonymously 1665, is a collection of brief, epigrammatic, and cynical observations on life and society, with the epigraph 'Our virtues are mostly our vices in disguise'. The work is remarkable for its literary excellence and its bitter realism in the dissection of basic human motives, making La Rochefoucauld a forerunner of modern 'psychological' writers.

**larva** stage between hatching and adulthood in those species in which the young have a different appearance and way of life from the adults. Examples include tadpoles (frogs) and caterpillars (butterflies and moths). Larvae are typical of the invertebrates, some of which (for example, shrimps) have two or more distinct larval stages. Among vertebrates, it is only the amphibians and some fishes that have a larval stage.

**laryngitis** inflammation of the larynx, causing soreness of the throat, a dry cough, and hoarseness. The acute form is due to a virus or other infection, excessive use of the voice, or inhalation of irritating smoke, and may cause the voice to be completely lost. With rest, the inflammation usually subsides in a few days.

**larynx** in mammals, a cavity at the upper end of the trachea (windpipe) containing the vocal cords. It is stiffened with cartilage and lined with mucous membrane. Amphibians and reptiles have much simpler larynxes, with no vocal cords. Birds have a similar cavity, called the *syrinx,* found lower down the trachea, where it branches to form the bronchi. It is very complex, with well-developed vocal cords.

**Lascaux** cave system near Montignac-sur-Vezère in the Dordogne, southwestern France, with prehistoric wall art, discovered 1940. It is richly decorated with realistic and symbolic paintings of aurochs (wild cattle), horses, and red deer of the Upper Palaeolithic period (Old Stone Age, about 15,000 BC), preserved under a glaze of calcite formation.

**laser** acronym for light amplification by stimulated emission of radiation, device for producing a narrow beam of light, capable of travelling over vast distances without dispersion, and of being focused to give enormous power densities ($10^8$ watts per $cm^2$ for high-energy lasers). The laser operates on a principle similar to that of the ◊maser (a high-frequency microwave amplifier or oscillator). The uses of lasers include communications (a laser beam can carry much more information than can radio waves), cutting, drilling, welding, satellite tracking, medical and biological research, and surgery. Sound wave vibrations from the window glass of a room can be picked up by a reflected laser beam. Lasers are also used as entertainment in theatres, concerts, and light shows.

**laser surgery** use of intense light sources to cut, coagulate, or vaporize tissue. Less invasive than normal surgery, it destroys diseased tissue gently and allows quicker, more natural healing. It can be used by way of a flexible endoscope to enable the surgeon to view the diseased area at which the laser needs to be aimed.

**Las Palmas** or *Las Palmas de Gran Canaria,* tourist resort on Gran Canaria, Canary Islands; population (1995) 373,800. Products include sugar and bananas. It lies in the northeast of the island on a narrow coastal strip, with the Atlantic Ocean on one side and cliffs containing rock houses on the other. There is a cathedral here, partly 15th century.

**Lassa fever** acute disease caused by an arenavirus, first detected 1969, and spread by a species of rat found only in West Africa. It is classified as a haemorrhagic fever and characterized by high fever, headache, muscle pain, and internal bleeding. There is no known cure, the survival rate being less than 50%.

**Las Vegas** city in southeastern Nevada, USA; seat of Clark County; population (1994 est) 328,000. With its many nightclubs and gambling casinos, Las Vegas attracts millions of visitors each year. It is also a major convention centre. Founded in 1855 in a ranching area, the modern community developed with the coming of the railroad in 1905 and was incorporated as a city in 1911. The first casino hotel opened here in 1947. Las Vegas is the easiest place to get married in the USA, with numerous chapels along the Strip (main street) and hotel chapels.

**latent heat** in physics, the heat absorbed or released by a substance as it changes state (for example, from solid to liquid) at constant temperature and pressure.

**latex** (Latin 'liquid') fluid of some plants (such as the rubber tree and poppy), an emulsion of resins, proteins, and other organic substances. It is used as the basis for making rubber. The name is also applied to a suspension in water of natural or synthetic rubber (or plastic) particles used in rubber goods, paints, and adhesives.

**Latin** Indo-European language of ancient Italy. Latin has passed through four influential phases: as the language of (1) republican Rome, (2) the Roman Empire, (3) the Roman Catholic Church, and (4) Western European culture, science, philosophy, and law during the Middle Ages and the Renaissance. During the third and fourth phases, much Latin vocabulary entered the English language. It is the parent form of the ◊Romance languages, noted for its highly inflected grammar and conciseness of expression.

**Latin America** large territory in the Western hemisphere south of the USA, consisting of Mexico, Central America, South America, and the West Indies. The main languages spoken are Spanish, Portuguese, and French.

**latitude and longitude** imaginary lines used to locate position on the globe. Lines of latitude are drawn parallel to the Equator, with 0° at the Equator and 90° at the north and south poles. Lines of longitude are drawn at right angles to these, with 0° (the Prime Meridian) passing through Greenwich, England.

*Point X lies on longitude 60°W*

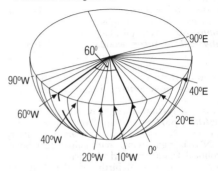

*Point X lies on latitude 20 °S*

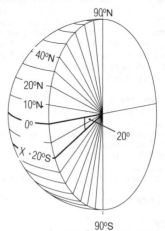

**latitude and longitude** *Locating a point on a globe using latitude and longitude. Longitude is the angle between the terrestrial meridian through a place and the standard meridian 0° passing through Greenwich, England. Latitude is the angular distance of a place from the equator.*

**Latvia** Republic of
*national name* *Latvijas Republika*
*area* 63,700 sq km/24,594 sq mi
*capital* Riga
*major towns/cities* Daugavpils, Leipāja, Jurmala, Jelgava, Ventspils
*major ports* Ventspils, Leipāja
*physical features* wooded lowland (highest point 312 m/1,024 ft), marshes, lakes; 472 km/293 mi of coastline; mild climate
*head of state* Vaira Vike-Freiberga from 1999
*head of government* Prime Minister Vilis Kristopans from 1998
*political system* emergent democracy
*political parties* Latvian Way, right of centre; Latvian National and Conservative Party (LNNK), right wing, nationalist; Economic-Political Union (formerly known as Harmony for Latvia and Rebirth of the National Economy), centrist; Ravnopravie (Equal Rights), centrist; For the Fatherland and Freedom (FFF), extreme nationalist; Latvian Peasants' Union (LZS), rural based, centre left; Union of Christian Democrats, centre right; Democratic Centre Party, centrist; Movement for Latvia, pro-Russian, populist; Master in Your Own Home (Saimnieks), ex-communist, populist; Latvian National Party of Reforms, right of centre nationalist coalition
*currency* lat
*GNP per capita (PPP)* (US$) 4,820 (1998 est)
*exports* timber and timber products, textiles, food and agricultural products, machinery and electrical equipment, metal industry products. Principal market: Germany 5.6% (1998)
*population* 2,389,000 (1999 est)
*language* Latvian
*religion* Lutheran, Roman Catholic, Russian Orthodox
*life expectancy* 63 (men); 74 (women) (1995–2000)
*Chronology*
**9th–10th centuries** Invaded by Vikings and Russians.
**13th century** Conquered by crusading German Teutonic Knights, who named the area Livonia and converted population to Christianity; Riga joined Hanseatic League, a northern European union of commercial towns.

**1520s** Lutheranism established as a result of Reformation.
**16th–17th centuries** Successively under Polish, Lithuanian, and Swedish rule.
**1721** Tsarist Russia took control.
**1819** Serfdom abolished.
**1900s** Emergence of independence movement.
**1914–18** Under partial German occupation during World War I.
**1918–19** Independence proclaimed and achieved after Russian Red Army troops expelled by German, Polish, and Latvian forces.
**1920s** Land reforms introduced by Farmers' Union government of Karlis Ulmanis.
**1934** Democracy overthrown and, at time of economic depression, Ulmanis established autocratic regime; Baltic Entente mutual defence pact with Estonia and Lithuania.
**1940** Incorporated into Soviet Union (USSR) as constituent republic, following secret German–Soviet agreement.
**1941–44** Occupied by Germany.
**1944** USSR regained control; mass deportations of Latvians to Central Asia, followed by immigration of ethnic Russians; agricultural collectivization.
**1960s and 1970s** Extreme repression of Latvian cultural and literary life.
**1980s** Nationalist dissent began to grow, influenced by the Polish Solidarity movement and Mikhail Gorbachev's *glasnost* ('openness') initiative in the USSR.
**1988** The Latvian Popular Front was established to campaign for independence. The prewar flag readopted and official status was given to the Latvian language.
**1989** The Latvian parliament passed a sovereignty declaration.
**1990** The Popular Front secured a majority in local elections and its leader, Ivan Godmanir, became the prime minister. The Latvian Communist Party split into pro-independence and pro-Moscow wings. The country entered a 'transitional period of independence' and the Baltic Council was reformed.
**1991** Soviet troops briefly seized key installations in Riga. There was an overwhelming vote for independence in a referendum. Full independence was achieved following the failure of the anti-Gorbachev coup attempt in Moscow; the Communist Party was outlawed. Joined United Nations (UN); a market-centred economic reform programme was instituted.
**1992** The curbing of rights of noncitizens prompted Russia to request minority protection by the UN.
**1993** The right-of-centre Latvian Way won the general election, and Valdis Birkavs became premier; a free-trade agreement was reached with Estonia and Lithuania.
**1994** The last Russian troops departed. Birkavs was replaced by Maris Gailis and economic growth resumed.
**1995** A trade and cooperation agreement was signed with European Union (EU). A general election produced a 'hung parliament' in which extremist parties received most support. Applied

for EU membership. The Independent Andris Skele became prime minister.

**1996** Guntis Ulmanis was re-elected president. The finance minister and deputy prime minister resigned from the eight-party coalition.

**1997** A new political party was formed, the Latvian National Party of Reforms. Prime Minister Skele was replaced by Guntar Krasts. Former Communist leader Alfreds Rubiks was released from prison.

**1998** The DPS withdrew from the government, leaving the coalition as a minority. Citizenship laws were relaxed to make it easier for ethnic Russians to acquire citizenship. A general election produced a hung parliament. Vilis Kristopans (Latvia's Way) became prime minister, heading a three-party minority coalition government, which pledged to continue privatization and improve relations with Russia.

**Latynina, Larissa Semyonovna** (1935– ) Soviet gymnast. She has won more Olympic medals than any person in any sport. She won 18 between 1956 and 1964, including nine gold medals. She won a total of 12 individual Olympic and world championship gold medals.

*career highlights*
***Olympic Games*** team champion: 1956, 1960, 1964; overall individual champion: 1956, 1960; floor exercise: 1956, 1960, 1964; vault: 1956
***World championship*** team: 1958, 1962; overall individual: 1958, 1962; vault: 1958; beam: 1958; floor exercise: 1962; asymmetric bars: 1958

**Laud, William** (1573–1645) English priest; archbishop of Canterbury from 1633. Laud's High Church policy, support for Charles I's unparliamentary rule, censorship of the press, and persecution of the Puritans all aroused bitter opposition, while his strict enforcement of the statutes against enclosures and of laws regulating wages and prices alienated the propertied classes. His attempt to impose the use of the Prayer Book on the Scots precipitated the English ◊Civil War. Impeached by Parliament in 1640, he was imprisoned in the Tower of London, summarily condemned to death, and beheaded.

**laudanum** alcoholic solution (tincture) of the drug ◊opium. Used formerly as a narcotic and painkiller, it was available in the 19th century from pharmacists on demand in most of Europe and the USA.

**laurel** any of a group of European evergreen trees with glossy aromatic leaves, yellowish flowers, and black berries. The leaves of sweet bay or poet's laurel (*L. nobilis*) are used in cooking. Several species are cultivated worldwide. (Genus *Laurus*, family Lauraceae.)

**Laurel and Hardy** Stan Laurel (stage name of Arthur Stanley Jefferson) (1890–1965) and Oliver Hardy (1892–1957) US film comedians. They were one of the most successful comedy teams in film history (Laurel was slim, Hardy rotund). Their partnership began in 1927, survived the transition from silent films to sound, and resulted in more than 200 short and feature-length films. Among these are *Pack Up Your*

*Troubles* (1932), *Our Relations* (1936), and *A Chump at Oxford* (1940). *The Music Box* (1932) won an Academy Award as Best Short Film. Laurel received a special Academy Award in 1960.

**lava** molten rock (usually 800–1,100°C/ 1,500–2,000°F) that erupts from a ◊volcano and cools to form extrusive ◊igneous rock. It differs from magma in that it is molten rock on the surface; *magma* is molten rock below the surface. Lava that is viscous and sticky does not flow far; it forms a steep-sided conical composite volcano. Less viscous lava can flow for long distances and forms a broad flat shield volcano.

**Laval, Pierre** (1883–1945) French extremerightwing politician, he gravitated between the wars from socialism through the centre ground (serving as prime minister and foreign secretary 1931–32 and again 1935–36) to the extreme right. As head of the Vichy government and foreign minister from 1942–44, he was responsible for the deportation of Jews and for requisitioning French labour to Germany.

**lavender** sweet-smelling   purple-flowering herb belonging to the mint family, native to western Mediterranean countries. The bushy low-growing species *L. angustifolia* has long, narrow, upright leaves of a silver-green colour. The small flowers, borne on spikes, vary in colour from lilac to deep purple and are covered with small fragrant oil glands. Lavender oil is widely used in pharmacy and perfumes. (Genus *Lavandula*, family Labiatae.)

**Lavoisier, Antoine Laurent** (1743–1794) French chemist. He proved that combustion needs only a part of the air, which he called oxygen, thereby destroying the theory of phlogiston (an imaginary 'fire element' released during combustion). With astronomer and mathematician Pierre de ◊Laplace, he showed in 1783 that water is a compound of oxygen and hydrogen. In this way he established the basic rules of chemical combination.

**law** body of rules and principles under which justice is administered or order enforced in a state or nation. In western Europe there are two main systems: Roman law and English law. US law is a modified form of English law.

**Law, Andrew Bonar** (1858–1923) British Conservative politician, born in New Brunswick, Canada, of Scottish descent. He succeeded Balfour as leader of the opposition in 1911, became colonial secretary in Asquith's coalition government (1915–16), chancellor of the Exchequer (1916–19), and Lord Privy Seal (1919–21) in Lloyd George's coalition. He formed a Conservative cabinet in 1922, but resigned on health grounds.

**Law Commission** in the UK, either of two statutory bodies established in 1965 (one for England and Wales and one for Scotland) which consider proposals for law reform and publish their findings. They also keep British law under constant review, systematically developing and reforming it by, for example, the repeal of obsolete and unnecessary enactments.

**law courts** bodies that adjudicate in legal disputes. Civil and criminal cases are usually dealt with by separate courts. In many countries there is a hierarchy of courts that provide an appeal system.

**law lords** in England, the ten Lords of Appeal in Ordinary who, together with the Lord Chancellor and other peers, make up the House of Lords in its judicial capacity. The House of Lords is the final court of appeal in both criminal and civil cases. Law lords rank as life peers.

**Lawrence, D(avid) H(erbert)** (1885–1930) English writer. His work expresses his belief in emotion and the sexual impulse as creative and true to human nature, but his ideal of the complete, passionate life is seen to be threatened by the encroachment of the modern and technological world. His writing first received attention after the publication of the semi-autobiographical *The White Peacock* (1911) and *Sons and Lovers* (1913). Other novels include *The Rainbow* (1915), *Women in Love* (1921), and *Lady Chatterley's Lover*, printed privately in Italy in 1928.

**Lawrence, T(homas) E(dward)** known as *Lawrence of Arabia* (1888–1935) British soldier, scholar, and translator. Appointed to the military intelligence department in Cairo, Egypt, during World War I, he took part in negotiations for an Arab revolt against the Ottoman Turks, and in 1916 attached himself to the emir Faisal. He became a guerrilla leader of genius, combining raids on Turkish communications with the organization of a joint Arab revolt, described in his book *The Seven Pillars of Wisdom* (1926).

**lawrencium** synthesized, radioactive, metallic element, the last of the actinide series, symbol Lr, atomic number 103, relative atomic mass 262. Its only known isotope, Lr-257, has a half-life of 4.3 seconds and was originally synthesized at the University of California at Berkeley in 1961 by bombarding californium with boron nuclei. The original symbol, Lw, was officially changed in 1963.

**Lawson, Nigel,** Baron Lawson of Blaby (1932– ) British Conservative politician. A former financial journalist, he was financial secretary to the Treasury 1979–81, secretary of state for energy 1981–83, and chancellor of the Exchequer 1983–89. He resigned as chancellor after criticism by government adviser Alan Walters, supported by prime minister Margaret Thatcher, over his policy of British membership of the ◊European Monetary System.

**laxative** substance used to relieve constipation (infrequent bowel movement). Current medical opinion discourages regular or prolonged use. Regular exercise and a diet high in vegetable fibre are believed to be the best means of preventing and treating constipation.

**Lazarus** in the New Testament, the brother of Martha, a friend of Jesus, raised by him from the dead. Lazarus is also the name of a beggar in a parable told by Jesus (Luke 16).

**Lazio** Roman *Latium,* region of west central Italy, comprising the provinces of Viterbo, Rieti, Rome, Frosinone, and Latina; area 17,200 sq km/6,639 sq mi; capital Rome; population (1992 est) 5,162,100. It is the third-largest region of Italy, over half its population living in the city of ◊Rome. Products include olives, wine, chemicals, pharmaceuticals, and textiles. Home of the Latins from the 10th century BC, it was dominated by the Romans from the 4th century BC.

**lb** (Latin 'libra') symbol for ◊*pound* (weight).

**lbw** abbreviation for *leg before wicket* (cricket).

**LCD** abbreviation for ◊liquid-crystal display.

**LEA** in the UK, abbreviation for *local education authority,* the body of local government responsible for the state schools and further education establishments in a district.

**lead** heavy, soft, malleable, grey, metallic element, symbol Pb (from Latin *plumbum*), atomic number 82, relative atomic mass 207.19. Usually found as an ore (most often in galena), it occasionally occurs as a free metal (native metal), and is the final stable product of the decay of uranium. Lead is the softest and weakest of the commonly used metals, with a low melting point; it is a poor conductor of electricity and resists acid corrosion. As a cumulative poison, lead enters the body from lead water pipes, lead-based paints, and leaded petrol. (In humans, exposure to lead shortly after birth is associated with impaired mental health between the ages of two and four.) The metal is an effective shield against radiation and is used in batteries, glass, ceramics, and alloys such as pewter and solder.

**leaded petrol** petrol that contains antiknock, a mixture of the chemicals tetraethyl lead and dibromoethane. The lead from the exhaust fumes enters the atmosphere, mostly as simple lead compounds, which are poisonous to the developing nervous systems of children.

**lead ore** any of several minerals from which lead is extracted. The primary ore is galena or lead sulphite PbS. This is unstable, and on prolonged exposure to the atmosphere it oxidizes into the minerals cerussite $PbCO_3$ and anglesite $PbSO_4$. Lead ores are usually associated with other metals, particularly silver – which can be mined at the same time – and zinc, which can cause problems during smelting.

**leaf** lateral outgrowth on the stem of a plant, and in most species the primary organ of ◊photosynthesis. The chief leaf types are cotyledons (seed leaves), scale leaves (on underground stems), foliage leaves, and bracts (in the axil of which a flower is produced).

**leaf insect** any of various insects about 10 cm/4 in long, with a green, flattened body, remarkable for closely resembling the foliage on which they live. They are most common in Southeast Asia. (Genus *Phyllium,* order Phasmida.)

**League of Nations** international organization formed after World War I to solve international disputes by arbitration. Established in Geneva, Switzerland, 1920, the League included representatives from states throughout the world, but was severely weakened by the US decision not to become a member, and had no power to enforce its decisions. It was dissolved in 1946. Its subsidiaries included the *International Labour Organization* and the *Permanent Court of International Justice* in The Hague, the Netherlands, both now under the auspices of the ◊United Nations (UN).

**Leakey, Louis Seymour Bazett** (1903–1972) Kenyan archaeologist, anthropologist, and palaeontologist. With his wife Mary ◊Leakey, he discovered fossils of extinct animals in the ◊Olduvai Gorge in Tanzania, as well as many remains of an early human type. Leakey's conviction that human origins lie in Africa was opposed to contemporary opinion.

**Leakey, Mary Douglas** born Nicol (1913– ) English archaeologist and anthropologist. In 1948 she discovered, on Rusinga Island, Lake Victoria, East Africa, the prehistoric ape skull known as *Proconsul*, about 20 million years old; and human footprints at Laetoli, to the south, about 3.75 million years old.

**Leakey, Richard Erskine Frere** (1944– ) Kenyan palaeoanthropologist. In 1972 he discovered at Lake Turkana, Kenya, an apelike skull estimated to be about 2.9 million years old; it had some human characteristics and a brain capacity of 800 cu cm/49 cu in. In 1984 his team found an almost complete skeleton of *Homo erectus* some 1.6 million years old. He is the son of Louis and Mary Leakey.

**Lean, David** (1908–1991) English film director. His films, painstakingly crafted, include early work codirected with the playwright Noël Coward, such as *Brief Encounter* (1946). Among his later films are such accomplished epics as *The Bridge on the River Kwai* (1957; Academy Award), *Lawrence of Arabia* (1962; Academy Award), and *Dr Zhivago* (1965).

**Lear, Edward** (1812–1888) English artist and humorist. His *Book of Nonsense* (1846) popularized the ◊limerick (a five-line humorous verse). His *Nonsense Songs, Botany and Alphabets* (1871), includes two of his best-known poems, 'The Owl and the Pussycat' and 'The Jumblies'.

**leasehold** in law, land or property held by a tenant (lessee) for a specified period (unlike ◊freehold, outright ownership), usually at a rent from the landlord (lessor).

**leather** material prepared from the hides and skins of animals, by tanning with vegetable tannins and chromium salts. Leather is a durable and water-resistant material, and is used for bags, shoes, clothing, and upholstery. There are three main stages in the process of converting animal skin into leather: cleaning, tanning, and dressing. Tanning is often a highly polluting process.

**Lebanon** Republic of
*national name* Jumhouria al-Lubnaniya
*area* 10,452 sq km/4,035 sq mi
*capital* Beirut (and port)
*major towns/cities* Tripoli, Zahlé, Baabda, Baalbek, Jezzine

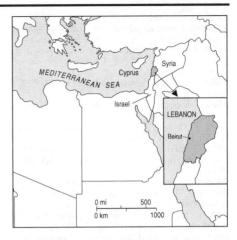

*major ports* Tripoli, Tyre, Sidon, Jounie
*physical features* narrow coastal plain; fertile Bekka valley running north–south between Lebanon and Anti-Lebanon mountain ranges
*head of state* Emile Lahoud from 1998
*head of government* Salim al-Hoss from 1998
*political system* emergent democracy
*political parties* Phalangist Party, Christian, radical, nationalist; Progressive Socialist Party (PSP), Druze, moderate, socialist; National Liberal Party (NLP), Maronite, centre left; National Bloc, Maronite, moderate; Lebanese Communist Party (PCL), nationalist, communist; Parliamentary Democratic Front, Sunni Muslim, centrist
*currency* Lebanese pound
*GNP per capita (PPP)* (US$) 6,150 (1998)
*exports* paper products, textiles, fruit and vegetables, jewellery. Principal market: Saudi Arabia 12.2% (1998)
*population* 3,236,000 (1999 est)
*language* Arabic (official), French, Armenian, English
*religion* Muslim 58% (Shiite 35%, Sunni 23%), Christian 27% (mainly Maronite), Druze 3%; other Christian denominations including Orthodox, Armenian, and Roman Catholic
*life expectancy* 68 (men); 72 (women) (1995–2000)
*Chronology*
**5th century BC–1st century AD** Part of the eastern Mediterranean Phoenician Empire.
**1st century** Came under Roman rule; Christianity introduced.
**635** Islam introduced by Arab tribes, who settled in southern Lebanon.
**11th century** Druze faith developed by local Muslims.
**1516** Became part of the Turkish Ottoman Empire.
**1860** Massacre of thousands of Christian Maronites by the Muslim Druze led to French intervention.
**1920–41** Administered by French under League of Nations mandate.
**1943** Independence achieved as a republic, with constitution that enshrined Christian and Muslim power-sharing.

**1945** Joined Arab League.

**1948–49** Lebanon joined first Arab war against Israel; Palestinian refugees settled in south.

**1958** Revolt by radical Muslims opposed to pro-Western policies of Christian president, Camille Chamoun.

**1964** Palestine Liberation Organization (PLO) founded in Beirut.

**1967** More Palestinian refugees settled in Lebanon following Arab–Israeli war.

**1971** PLO expelled from Jordan; established headquarters in Lebanon.

**1975** Outbreak of civil war between conservative Christians and leftist Muslims backed by PLO.

**1976** Ceasefire agreed; Syrian-dominated Arab deterrent force formed to keep the peace, but considered by Christians as an occupying force.

**1978** Israel launched limited invasion of southern Lebanon in search of PLO guerrillas. International United Nations peacekeeping force unable to prevent further fighting.

**1979** Part of southern Lebanon declared an 'independent free Lebanon' by right-wing army officer.

**1982** Bachir Gemayel, a Maronite Christian, was elected president but assassinated; he was succeeded by his brother Amin Gemayel. Israel again invaded Lebanon. Palestinians withdrew from Beirut under the supervision of an international peacekeeping force; the PLO moved its headquarters to Tunis.

**1983** An agreement was reached for withdrawal of Syrian and Israeli troops but abrogated under Syrian pressure; intense fighting was seen between Christian Phalangists and Muslim Druze militias.

**1984** Most of the international peacekeeping force were withdrawn. Radical Muslim militia took control of west Beirut.

**1985** Lebanon was in chaos; many foreigners were taken hostage and Israeli troops withdrawn.

**1987** Syrian troops were sent into Beirut.

**1988** An agreement on a Christian successor to Gemayel failed and Gen Michel Aoun was appointed to head the caretaker military government; Premier Selim el-Hoss set up a rival government; the threat of partition hung over the country.

**1989** Gen Aoun declared a 'war of liberation' against Syrian occupation; Arab League-sponsored talks resulted in a ceasefire and a revised constitution recognizing Muslim majority; René Mouhawad was assassinated after 17 days as president; Maronite Christian Elias Hrawi was named as his successor; Aoun occupied the presidential palace, rejecting the constitution.

**1990** The release of Western hostages began. Gen Aoun, crushed by Syrians, surrendered and legitimate government was restored.

**1991** The government extended its control to the whole country. A treaty of cooperation with Syria was signed.

**1992** The remaining Western hostages were released. A pro-Syrian administration was re-elected with Rafik al-Hariri as prime minister after many Christians boycotted general election.

**1993** Israel launched attacks against Shia fundamentalist Hezbollah strongholds in southern Lebanon before the USA and Syria brokered an agreement to avoid the use of force.

**1996** Israel launched a rocket attack on southern Lebanon in response to Hezbollah activity. USA, Israel, Syria, and Lebanon attempted to broker a new ceasefire.

**1998** Army chief General Emile Lahoud was elected president. Prime minister Rafik Hariri resigned and was replaced by Salim al-Hoss.

**1999** Israeli withdrawal from southern Lebanon.

**Lebowa** former black homeland assigned to the North Sotho people in former northern Transvaal Province, South Africa, now in Northern Transvaal. It consisted of five separate areas of territory. It achieved self-governing status in 1972.

**lecithin** lipid (fat), containing nitrogen and phosphorus, that forms a vital part of the cell membranes of plant and animal cells. The name is from the Greek *lekithos* 'egg yolk', eggs being a major source of lecithin.

**Leconte de Lisle, Charles Marie René** (1818–1894) French poet. He was born on the Indian Ocean Island of Réunion and settled in Paris 1846. He played an important part in formulating the aims of the anti-Romantic group *Les Parnassiens* and became their acknowledged leader. His work, characterized by classic regularity and faultlessness of form, drew inspiration from the ancient world; it includes *Poèmes antiques/Antique Poems* (1852), *Poèmes barbares/Barbaric Poems* (1862), and *Poèmes tragiques/Tragic Poems* (1884). Although he advocated impassivity, his poems express a pessimistic awareness of the transitoriness of things.

**Le Corbusier** assumed name of Charles-Edouard Jeanneret (1887–1965) Swiss-born French architect. He was an early and influential exponent of the ◊Modern Movement and one of the most innovative of 20th-century architects. His distinct brand of Functionalism first appears in his town-planning proposals of the early 1920s, which advocate 'vertical garden cities' with zoning of living and working areas and traffic separation as solutions to urban growth and chaos. From the 1940s several of his designs for multistorey villas were realized, notably his Unité d'habitation, Marseille, 1947–52 (now demolished), using his Modulor system of standard-sized units mathematically calculated according to the proportions of the human figure (see ◊Fibonacci, ◊golden section).

**LED** abbreviation for ◊light-emitting diode.

**Leda** in Greek mythology, wife of Tyndareus of Sparta and mother of ◊Clytemnestra. Zeus, transformed as a swan, was the father of her daughter ◊Helen of Troy and, in some traditions, the brothers Castor and Pollux (Greek Polydeuces). In other variants, Castor was fathered by Tyndareus or, according to Homer, both brothers were his sons.

**Led Zeppelin** UK rock group 1969–80, founders of the ◊heavy metal genre. Their overblown style, with long instrumental solos, was based on rhythm and blues. Many of their songs, such as 'Stairway to Heaven', 'Rock and Roll', 'Black Dog' and 'Kashmir', have become classics, most of them collected on the 1992 *Remasters* compilation. Among their most celebrated records were the group's untitled fourth album, popularly known as *Led Zeppelin IV* (1971) and their 1975 *Physical Graffiti.*

**Lee, Robert E(dward)** (1807–1870) US military strategist and Confederate general in the ◊American Civil War. As military adviser to Jefferson ◊Davis, president of the Confederacy, and as commander of the Army of Northern Virginia, he made several raids into Northern territory, but was defeated at ◊Gettysburg and surrendered in 1865 at ◊Appomattox.

**leech** any of a group of ◊annelid worms. Leeches live in fresh water, and in tropical countries infest damp forests. As bloodsucking animals they are injurious to people and animals, to whom they attach themselves by means of a strong mouth adapted to sucking. (Class Hirudinea.)

**Leeds** industrial city and metropolitan borough in West Yorkshire, England, 40 km/25 mi southwest of York, on the River Aire; population (1991) 424,200 (city), 680,700 (district). Industries include engineering, printing, chemicals, glass, woollens, clothing, plastics, paper, metal goods, and leather goods. Notable buildings include the Town Hall (1858) designed by Cuthbert Brodrick, the University of Leeds (1904), the Leeds City Art Gallery (1888), Temple Newsam House (early 16th century, altered in about 1630), and the Cistercian Abbey of Kirkstall (1147). It is a centre of communications where road, rail, and canals (to Liverpool and Goole) meet.

**leek** onionlike plant belonging to the lily family. The cultivated leek is a variety of the wild species *A. ampeloprasum* of the Mediterranean area and Atlantic islands. The lower leaf parts and white bulb are eaten as a vegetable. (Genus *Allium*, family Liliaceae.)

**Lee Kuan Yew** (1923–  ) Singaporean politician, prime minister from 1959–90. Lee founded the anticommunist Socialist People's Action Party in 1954 and entered the Singapore legislative assembly in 1955. He was elected the country's first prime minister in 1959, and took Singapore out of the Malaysian federation in 1965. He remained in power until his resignation in 1990, and was succeeded by Goh Chok Tong. Until 1992 he held on to the party leadership.

**Lee Teng-hui** (1923–  ) Taiwanese right-wing politician, vice-president 1984–88, president and Kuomintang (see ◊Guomindang) party leader from 1988. The country's first island-born leader, he was viewed as a reforming technocrat. He was directly elected president in March 1996, defying Chinese opposition to the democratic contest.

**Leeuwenhoek, Anton van** (1632–1723) Dutch pioneer of microscopic research. He ground his own lenses, some of which magnified up to 300 times. With these he was able to see individual red blood cells, sperm, and bacteria, achievements not repeated for more than a century.

**Leeward Islands** (1) group of islands, part of the ◊Society Islands, in ◊French Polynesia, South Pacific; (2) general term for the northern half of the Lesser ◊Antilles in the West Indies; (3) former British colony in the West Indies (1871–1956) comprising Antigua, Montserrat, St Kitts and Nevis, Anguilla, and the Virgin Islands.

**left wing** in politics, the socialist parties. The term originated in the French national assembly of 1789, where the nobles sat in the place of honour to the right of the president, and the commons sat to the left. This arrangement has become customary in European parliaments, where the progressives sit on the left and the conservatives on the right. It is also usual to speak of the right, left, and centre, when referring to the different elements composing a single party.

**legacy** in law, a gift of personal property made by a testator in a will and transferred on the testator's death to the legatee.
*Specific legacies* are definite named objects; a *general legacy* is a sum of money or item not specially identified; a *residuary legacy* is all the remainder of the deceased's personal estate after debts have been paid and the other legacies have been distributed.

**legal aid** public assistance with legal costs. In Britain it is given only to those below certain thresholds of income and unable to meet the costs. There are separate provisions for civil and criminal cases. Since 1989 legal aid is administered by the Legal Aid Board.

**Léger, Fernand** (1881–1955) French painter and designer. He was associated with ◊Cubism. From around 1909 he evolved a characteristic style of simplified forms, clear block outlines, and bold colours. Mechanical forms are constant themes in his work, which includes designs for the Swedish Ballet (1921–22), murals, and the abstract film *Ballet mécanique/Mechanical Ballet* 1924.

**legionnaires' disease** pneumonia-like disease, so called because it was first identified when it broke out at a convention of the American Legion in Philadelphia in 1976. Legionnaires' disease is caused by the bacterium *Legionella pneumophila,* which breeds in warm water (for example, in the cooling towers of air-conditioning systems). It is spread in minute water droplets, which may be inhaled. The disease can be treated successfully with antibiotics, though mortality can be high in elderly patients.

**legislature** lawmaking body or bodies in a political system. Some legislatures are unicameral (having one chamber), and some bicameral (with two).

**legume** plant of the family Leguminosae, which has a pod containing dry seeds. The family includes peas, beans, lentils, clover, and alfalfa (lucerne). Legumes are important in agriculture because of their specialized roots, which have nodules containing bacteria capable of fixing nitrogen from the air and increasing the fertility of the soil. The edible seeds of legumes are called *pulses*.

**Le Havre** industrial port in the *département* of Seine-Maritime in Normandy, northwest France, on the north side of the estuary of the River Seine, 90 km/56 mi from Rouen; population (1990) 197,200, conurbation 250,000. It is the second-largest port in France, and has cross-channel passenger links. The major industries include engineering, chemicals, car manufacturing, and oil refining.

**Leibniz, Gottfried Wilhelm** (1646–1716) German mathematician, philosopher, and diplomat. Independently of, but concurrently with, English scientist Isaac ◊Newton, he developed the branch of mathematics known as ◊calculus and was one of the founders of symbolic logic. Free from all concepts of space and number, his logic was the prototype of future abstract mathematics.

**Leicester, Robert** Dudley, Earl of Leicester (c. 1532–1588) English courtier. Son of the Duke of Northumberland, he was created Earl of Leicester in 1564. He led the disastrous military expedition (1585–87) sent to help the Netherlands against Spain. Despite this failure, he retained the favour of Queen Elizabeth I, who gave him command of the army prepared to resist the threat of Spanish invasion in 1588.

**Leicester City** industrial city and unitary authority in central England, on the River Soar. It was part of the county of Leicestershire to 1997
*area* 73 sq km/28 sq mi
*features* 14th-century Guildhall, St Martin's Cathedral, and two universities (University of Leicester, established in 1957, and De Montfort University, formerly Leicester Polytechnic, established in 1992); Bradgate House, the home of Lady Jane Grey, located in Bradgate Park, 10 km/6 mi northwest of Leicester; there is an Eco House in the city, an environment-friendly show home, demonstrating ways in which people can reduce the ecological impact of their homes
*industries* engineering, food processing, electronics, chemicals, and the manufacture of hosiery, footwear, knitwear, plastics, scientific and medical instruments, electrical products, and construction and woodworking machinery
*population* (1996) 270,500
*famous people* Joe Orton, C P Snow.

**Leicestershire** county of central England (since April 1997 Leicester City and Rutland have been separate unitary authorities)
*area* 2,084 sq km/804 sq mi
*towns and cities* Loughborough, Melton Mowbray, Market Harborough (administrative headquarters at Glenfield, Leicester)
*physical* rivers Soar and Wreake; Charnwood Forest (in the northwest); Vale of Belvoir (under which are large coal deposits)
*features* Belvoir Castle, seat of the dukes of Rutland since the time of Henry VIII, rebuilt by

James Wyatt in 1816; Donington Park motor-racing circuit, Castle Donington; Leicestershire has traditionally had several fox-hunts, including the Quorn hunt
*agriculture* good pasture with horses, cattle, and sheep (especially the New Leicester breed, first bred by Robert Bakewell in the 18th century at Dishley); dairy products (including Stilton cheese at Melton Mowbray); cereals
*industries* engineering (Loughborough); hosiery (at Earl Shilton, Hinckley, and Loughborough); footwear; bell founding; coal (Asfordby); quarrying of limestone (Barrow-on-Soar, Breedon-on-the-Hill), ironstone (in the northwest), and granite (Enderby, Stoney, and Mountsorrel, known for its paving stones)
*population* (1996) 927,500
*famous people* Thomas Babington Macaulay, Titus Oates, C P Snow.

**Leif Ericsson** (lived c. 970) Norse explorer, son of Eric the Red, who sailed west from Greenland to find a country first sighted by Norsemen in 986. He visited Baffin Island then sailed along the Labrador coast to Newfoundland, which was named 'Vinland' (Wine Land), because he discovered grape vines growing there.

**Leinster** southeastern historic province of the Republic of Ireland, comprising the counties of Carlow, Dublin, Kildare, Kilkenny, Laois, Longford, Louth, Meath, Offaly, Westmeath, Wexford, and Wicklow; area 19,630 sq km/7,577 sq mi; population (1991) 1,860,000.

**Leipzig** major commercial and industrial city in west Saxony, Germany, on the Weisse Elster (a tributary of the River Elbe), 145 km/90 mi southwest of Berlin; population (1995) 478,200. Industries include printing, publishing, and the production of furs, leather goods, paper, and musical instruments. It hosts numerous trade shows, including important industrial and book fairs. The city is also a centre for the arts, culture, and education, and has a university founded in 1409.

**leishmaniasis** any of several parasitic diseases caused by microscopic protozoans of the genus *Leishmania*, identified by William Leishman (1865–1926), and transmitted by sandflies.

It occurs in two main forms: *visceral* (also called kala-azar), in which various internal organs are affected, and *cutaneous,* where the disease is apparent mainly in the skin. Leishmaniasis occurs in the Mediterranean region, Africa, Asia, and Central and South America. There are 12 million cases of leishmaniasis annually. The disease kills 8,000 people a year in South America and results in hundreds of thousands more suffering permanent disfigurement and disability through skin lesions, joint pain, and swelling of the liver and spleen.

**leitmotif** German *Leitmotiv,* (German 'leading motive') in music, a recurring theme or motive used to illustrate a character or idea. Wagner frequently used this technique in his operas, and it was later adopted in music for film.

**Leitrim** county of the Republic of Ireland, in the province of Connacht, bounded on the northwest by Donegal Bay; county town Carrick-on-Shannon; area 1,530 sq km/591 sq mi; population (1991) 25,300. Carrick-on-Shannon, Mohill and Manorhamilton are the only important towns. The Rivers Shannon, Bonet, Drowes, and Duff run through Leitrim. There is some coal, and iron and lead in the mountainous areas, but the county is generally not very productive – even the soil is heavy – and is the poorest county in the Republic of Ireland. Potatoes and oats are grown, and some cattle and sheep are reared. Industries include linen, woollens, and potteries.

**lek** in biology, a closely spaced set of very small ◊territories each occupied by a single male during the mating season. Leks are found in the mating systems of several ground-dwelling birds (such as grouse) and a few antelopes, and in some insects.

**Lely, Peter** adopted name of Pieter van der Faes (1618–1680) Dutch painter. He was active in England from 1641, painting fashionable portraits in the style of van Dyck. His subjects included Charles I, Cromwell, and Charles II. He painted a series of admirals, *Flagmen* (National Maritime Museum, London), and one of *The Windsor Beauties* (Hampton Court, Richmond), fashionable women of Charles II's court.

**Lemaître, Georges Edouard** (1894–1966) Belgian cosmologist. He proposed the ◊Big Bang theory of the origin of the universe 1933. US astronomer Edwin ◊Hubble had shown that the universe was expanding, but it was Lemaître who suggested that the expansion had been started by an initial explosion, the Big Bang, a theory that is now generally accepted.

**Le Mans** industrial city and administrative centre of the Sarthe *département* in western France; population (1990) 148,500, conurbation 191,000. It has a motor-racing circuit where the annual endurance 24-hour race (established 1923) for sports cars and their prototypes is held at the Sarthe circuit. It is linked to Paris by a high-speed rail system.

**lemming** any of a group of small rodents distributed worldwide in northern latitudes. They are about 12 cm/5 in long, with thick brownish fur, a small head, and a short tail. Periodically, when their population exceeds the available food supply, lemmings undertake mass migrations. (Genus *Lemmus* and other related genera, family Cricetidae.)

**lemon** sharp-tasting yellow citrus fruit of the small, evergreen, semitropical lemon tree. It may have originated in northwestern India, and was introduced into Europe by the Spanish Moors in the 12th or 13th century. It is now grown in Italy, Spain, California, Florida, South Africa, and Australia, and is widely used for flavouring and as a garnish. (*Citrus limon,* family Rutaceae.)

**lemon balm** perennial herb belonging to the mint family, with lemon-scented leaves. It is widely used in teas, liqueurs, and medicines. (*Melissa officinalis,* family Labiatae.)

**lemur** any of various prosimian ◊primates found in Madagascar and the Comoros Islands. There are about 16 species, ranging from mouse-sized to dog-sized animals; the pygmy mouse lemur (*Microcebus myoxinus*), weighing 30 g/1 oz, is the smallest primate. The diademed sifaka, weighing 7 kg/15 lb, is the largest species of lemur. Lemurs are arboreal, and some species are nocturnal. They have long, bushy tails, and feed on fruit, insects, and small animals. Many are threatened with extinction owing to loss of their forest habitat and, in some cases, from hunting. (Family Lemuridae.)

**Lena** one of the largest rivers of the Russian Federation, in eastern Siberia; length 4,400 km/2,734 mi; total drainage area 490,000 sq km/189,189 sq mi. The Lena rises in the Baikal Mountains, west of Lake Baikal, and flows northeast to Yakutsk, then north into the Laptev Sea (an inlet of the Arctic Ocean), where it forms a large delta 400 km/240 mi wide and covering some 30,000 sq km/11,583 sq mi. The river is navigable almost throughout its course, but is frozen for eight months of the year. Its main tributaries are the Vitim, Olekma, and Aldan on the right, and the Vilyui on the left. The main ports on the Lena's course are Osetrovo (since 1954 part of Ust-Kut) and Yakutsk.

**Lendl, Ivan** (1960– ) Czech-born American lawn-tennis player. He won eight Grand Slam singles titles, including the US and French titles three times each, taking more than $15 million in prize money. He retired from the game in December 1994, citing a degenerative spinal condition.
*career highlights*
*US Open* 1985–87
*French Open* 1984, 1986–87
*Australian Open* 1989–90
*Grand Prix Masters* 1982–83, 1986–87
*Davis Cup* 1980 (member of Czechoslovakian team)

**Lenin, Vladimir Ilyich** adopted name of Vladimir Ilyich Ulyanov (1870–1924) Russian revolutionary, first leader of the USSR, and communist theoretician. Active in the 1905 Revolution, Lenin had to leave Russia when it failed, settling in Switzerland in 1914. He returned to Russia after the February revolution of 1917 (see ◊Russian Revolution). He led the Bolshevik revolution of November 1917 and became leader of a Soviet government, concluded peace with Germany, and organized a successful resistance to White Russian (pro-tsarist) uprisings and foreign intervention 1918–20. His modification of traditional Marxist doctrine to fit conditions prevailing in Russia became known as *Marxism-Leninism,* the basis of communist ideology.

**Leningrad** former name (1924–91) of the Russian city ◊St Petersburg.

**Leninism** modification of ◊Marxism by ◊Lenin which argues that in a revolutionary situation the industrial proletariat is unable to develop a truly revolutionary consciousness without strong leadership.

**Lennon, John Winston** (1940–1980) UK rock singer, songwriter, and guitarist; a founder member of the ◊Beatles. He lived in the USA from 1971. Both before the band's break-up in 1970 and in his solo career, he collaborated intermittently with his wife *Yoko Ono* (1933– ). 'Give Peace a Chance', a hit in 1969, became an anthem of the peace movement. His solo work alternated between the confessional and the political, as on the album *Imagine* (1971). He was shot dead by a fan.

**lens** in optics, a piece of a transparent material, such as glass, with two polished surfaces – one concave or convex, and the other plane, concave, or convex – that modifies rays of light. A convex lens brings rays of light together; a concave lens makes the rays diverge. Lenses are essential to spectacles, microscopes, telescopes, cameras, and almost all optical instruments.

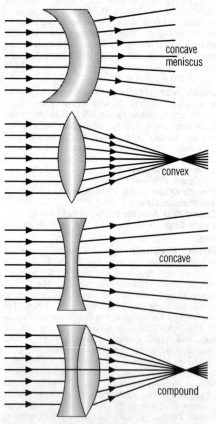

concave meniscus

convex

concave

compound

*lens* The passage of light through lenses. The concave lens diverges a beam of light from a distant source. The convex and compound lenses focus light from a distant source to a point. The distance between the focus and the lens is called the focal length. The shorter the focus, the more powerful the lens.

**Lent** in the Christian church, the 40-day period of fasting that precedes Easter, beginning on Ash Wednesday, but omitting Sundays.

**lentil** annual Old World plant belonging to the pea family. The plant, which resembles vetch, grows 15–45 cm/6–18 in high and has white, blue, or purplish flowers. The seeds, contained in pods about 1.6 cm/0.6 in long, are widely used as food. (*Lens culinaris,* family Leguminosae.)

**Leo** zodiacal constellation in the northern hemisphere, represented as a lion. The Sun passes through Leo from mid-August to mid-September. Its brightest star is first-magnitude Regulus at the base of a pattern of stars called the Sickle. In astrology, the dates for Leo are between about 23 July and 22 August (see ◊precession).

**Leo** thirteen popes, including:

**Leo (I) the Great, (St Leo)** (*c.* 390–461) Pope from 440. He helped to establish the Christian liturgy.

Leo summoned the Chalcedon Council where his Dogmatical Letter was accepted as the voice of St Peter. Acting as ambassador for the emperor Valentinian III (425–455), Leo saved Rome from devastation by the Huns by buying off their king, Attila.

**Leo III** (*c.* 750–816) Pope from 795. After the withdrawal of the Byzantine emperors, the popes had become the real rulers of Rome. Leo III was forced to flee because of a conspiracy in Rome and took refuge at the court of the Frankish king Charlemagne. He returned to Rome 799 and crowned Charlemagne emperor on Christmas Day 800, establishing the secular sovereignty of the pope over Rome under the suzerainty of the emperor (who became the Holy Roman Emperor).

**Leo X, Giovanni de' Medici** (1475–1521) Pope from 1513. The son of Lorenzo the Magnificent of Florence, he was created a cardinal at 13. He bestowed on Henry VIII of England the title of Defender of the Faith. A patron of the arts, he sponsored the rebuilding of St Peter's Church, Rome. He raised funds for this by selling indulgences (remissions of punishment for sin), a practice that led the religious reformer Martin Luther to rebel against papal authority. Leo X condemned Luther in the bull *Exsurge domine* (1520) and excommunicated him in 1521.

**León** capital of León province in Castilla–León, northwest Spain, situated on a plateau 821 m/2,694 ft high at the confluence of the Torio and Bernesga rivers; population (1991) 144,100. Linen, chemicals, pottery, and leather are manufactured. León was built on the site of a Roman camp. In the 10th century, after its recapture from the Moors, it became the capital of the kingdom of León until 1230, when it was merged with Castile. It has an 11th-century church, a Gothic cathedral, and parts of the old walls remain.

**Leonardo da Vinci** (1452–1519) Italian painter, sculptor, architect, engineer, and scientist. One of the greatest figures of the Italian Renaissance, he was active in Florence, Milan, and, from 1516, France. As state engineer and court painter to the Duke of Milan, he painted the *Last Supper* mural about 1495 (Sta Maria delle Grazie, Milan), and on his return to Florence painted the *Mona Lisa* about 1503–06 (Louvre, Paris). His notebooks and drawings show an immensely inventive and enquiring mind, studying aspects of the natural and scientific world from anatomy and botany to aerodynamics and hydraulics.

**leopard** or *panther,* large wild cat found in Africa and Asia. The background colour of the coat is golden, and the black spots form rosettes that differ according to the variety; *black panthers* are simply a colour variation and retain the patterning as a 'watered-silk' effect. The leopard is 1.5–2.5 m/5–8 ft long, including the tail, which may measure 1 m/3 ft. (Species *Panthera pardus,* family Felidae.)

**Leopold** three kings of the Belgians:

**Leopold I** (1790–1865) King of the Belgians from 1831. He was elected to the throne on the creation of an independent Belgium. Through his marriage, when prince of Saxe-Coburg, to Princess Charlotte Augusta, he was the uncle of Queen Victoria of Great Britain and had considerable influence over her.

**Leopold III** (1901–1983) King of the Belgians 1934–51. Against the prime minister's advice he surrendered to the German army in World War II in 1940. Post-war charges against his conduct led to a regency by his brother Charles and his eventual abdication in 1951 in favour of his son Baudouin.

**Lepanto, Battle of** sea battle on 7 October 1571 between the Ottoman Empire and 'Holy League' forces from Spain, Venice, Genoa, and the Papal States jointly commanded by the Spanish soldier Don John of Austria. The battle took place in the Mediterranean Gulf of Corinth off Lepanto (the Greek port of *Naupaktos),* then in Turkish possession. It was not decisive, but the combined western fleets halted Turkish expansion and broke Muslim sea power.

**Le Pen, Jean-Marie** (1928– ) French extreme-rightwing politician. He was the founder of the National Front (FN) in 1972. His talents as a public speaker, his demagogic mixing of nationalism with law-and-order populism – calling for immigrant repatriation, stricter nationality laws, and the restoration of capital punishment – and his hostility to the European Union attracted a wide swathe of electoral support in the 1980s and 1990s.

**leprosy** or *Hansen's disease,* chronic, progressive disease caused by a bacterium *Mycobacterium leprae* closely related to that of tuberculosis. The infection attacks the skin and nerves. Once common in many countries, leprosy is still endemic in 28 countries and confined almost entirely to the tropics. It is controlled with drugs. In 1998 there were an estimated 1.5 million cases of leprosy, with 60% of these being in India.

**lepton** any of a class of light $\lozenge$elementary particles that are not affected by the strong nuclear force; they do not interact strongly with other particles or nuclei. The leptons are comprised of the $\lozenge$electron, $\lozenge$muon, and $\lozenge$tau, and their $\lozenge$neutrinos (the electron neutrino, muon neutrino, and tau neutrino), plus their six $\lozenge$antiparticles.

**lesbianism** homosexuality (sexual attraction to one's own sex) between women, so called from the Greek island of Lesbos (now Lesvos), the home of $\lozenge$Sappho the poet and her followers to whom the behaviour was attributed.

**Lesbos** alternative spelling of $\lozenge$Lesvos, an island in the Aegean Sea.

**Lesotho** Kingdom of

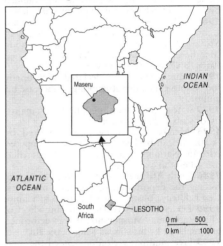

*area* 30,355 sq km/11,720 sq mi
*capital* Maseru
*major towns/cities* Qacha's Nek, Teyateyaneng, Mafeteng, Hlotse, Roma, Quthing
*physical features* mountainous with plateaux, forming part of South Africa's chief watershed
*head of state* King Letsie III from 1996
*head of government* Bethuel Pakulitha Mosisili from 1998
*political system* constitutional monarchy
*political parties* Basotho National Party (BNP), traditionalist, nationalist, right of centre; Basutoland Congress Party (BCP), left of centre
*currency* loti
*GNP per capita (PPP)* (US$) 2,320 (1998 est)
*exports* clothing, footwear, furniture, food and live animals (cattle), hides, wool and mohair, baskets. Principal market: SACU 65.1% (1998)
*population* 2,108,000 (1999 est)
*language* Sesotho, English (official), Zulu, Xhosa
*religion* Protestant 42%, Roman Catholic 38%, indigenous beliefs
*life expectancy* 55 (men); 57 (women) (1995–2000)
*Chronology*
*18th century* Formerly inhabited by nomadic hunter-gatherer San, Zulu-speaking Ngunis, and

Sotho-speaking peoples settled in the region.

**1820s** Under the name of Basutoland, Sotho nation founded by Moshoeshoe I, who united the people to repulse Zulu attacks from south.

**1843** Moshoeshoe I negotiated British protection as tension with South African Boers increased.

**1868** Became British territory, administered by Cape Colony (in South Africa) from 1871.

**1884** Became British crown colony, after revolt against Cape Colony control; Basuto chiefs allowed to govern according to custom and tradition, but rich agricultural land west of the Caledon River was lost to South Africa.

**1900s** Served as a migrant labour reserve for South Africa's mines and farms.

**1952** Left-of-centre Basutoland African Congress, later Congress Party (BCP), founded by Ntsu Mokhehle to campaign for self rule.

**1966** Independence achieved within Commonwealth, as Kingdom of Lesotho, with Moshoeshoe II as king and Chief Leabua Jonathan of conservative Basotho National Party (BNP) as prime minister.

**1970** State of emergency declared; king briefly forced into exile after attempting to increase his authority.

**1973** State of emergency lifted; BNP won majority of seats in general election.

**1975** Members of ruling party attacked by South African-backed guerrillas, who opposed African National Congress (ANC) guerrillas using Lesotho as a base.

**1986** South Africa imposed a border blockade, forcing the deportation of 60 ANC members. Gen Lekhanya ousted Chief Jonathan in a coup.

**1990** Lekhanya was replaced in coup by Col Elias Ramaema; Moshoeshoe II was dethroned and replaced by his son, as King Letsie III.

**1993** Free multiparty elections ended the military rule; Ntsu Mokhehle (BCP) became prime minister.

**1994** Fighting between rival army factions was ended by a peace deal, brokered by the Organization of African Unity.

**1995** King Letsie III abdicated to restore King Moshoeshoe II to the throne.

**1996** King Moshoeshoe II was killed in car accident; King Letsie III was restored to the throne.

**1998** The LCD attained general election victory amidst claims of rigged polls; public demonstrations followed. South Africa sent troops to support the government. Government talks with the opposition were not progressing, and there were violent demonstrations in the capital. An interim political authority was appointed prior to the new elections.

**Lesseps, Ferdinand Marie,** Vicomte de Lesseps (1805–1894) French engineer. He designed and built the ◊Suez Canal 1859–69. He began work on the Panama Canal 1881, but withdrew after failing to construct it without locks.

**Lessing, Doris May** born Tayler (1919–  ) English novelist and short-story writer, brought up in Rhodesia. Concerned with social and political themes, particularly the place of women in society, her work includes *The Grass*

*is Singing* (1950), the five-novel series *Children of Violence* (1952–69), *The Golden Notebook* (1962), *The Good Terrorist* (1985), *The Fifth Child* (1988), *London Observed* (1992), and *Love Again. Under My Skin* (1994) and *Walking in the Shade* (1997) are volumes of autobiography.

**Lesvos** Greek island in the Aegean Sea, near the coast of Turkey

**area** 2,154 sq km/831 sq mi

**capital** Mytilene

**industries** olives, wine, grain

**population** (1991) 103,700

**history** ancient name Lesbos; an Aeolian settlement, the home of the poets Alcaeus and Sappho; conquered by the Turks from Genoa 1462; annexed to Greece 1913.

**lettuce** annual plant whose large edible leaves are commonly used in salads. There are many varieties, including the cabbage lettuce, with round or loose heads, the Cos lettuce, with long, upright heads, and the Iceberg lettuce, with tight heads of crisp leaves. They are all believed to have been derived from the wild species *L. serriola*. (Genus *Lactuca*, especially *L. sativa*, family Compositae.)

**leucocyte** another name for a ◊white blood cell.

**leukaemia** any one of a group of cancers of the blood cells, with widespread involvement of the bone marrow and other blood-forming tissue. The central feature of leukaemia is runaway production of white blood cells that are immature or in some way abnormal. These rogue cells, which lack the defensive capacity of healthy white cells, overwhelm the normal ones, leaving the victim vulnerable to infection. Treatment is with radiotherapy and cytotoxic drugs to suppress replication of abnormal cells, or by bone-marrow transplantation.

**Levellers** democratic party in the English Civil War. The Levellers found wide support among Cromwell's New Model Army and the yeoman farmers, artisans, and small traders, and proved a powerful political force from 1647 to 1649. Their programme included the establishment of a republic, government by a parliament of one house elected by male suffrage, religious toleration, and sweeping social reforms.

**lever** simple machine consisting of a rigid rod pivoted at a fixed point called the fulcrum, used for shifting or raising a heavy load or applying force. Levers are classified into orders according to where the effort is applied, and the load-moving force developed, in relation to the position of the fulcrum.

**leveraged buyout** in business, the purchase of a controlling proportion of the shares of a company by its own management, financed almost exclusively by borrowing. It is so called because the ratio of a company's long-term debt to its equity (capital assets) is known as its 'leverage'.

**Lewinsky, Monica** (1973–  ) US former White House intern who became the centre of scandal in 1998 after President Bill Clinton eventually admitted having had an 'inappropriate relationship' with her, and the House of Representatives moved to impeach him. Lewinsky was a recent college graduate when she worked in 1995 as an unpaid White House intern. Her internship led to a paid position in the office of legislative affairs in December 1995, and in April 1996 she moved to the Pentagon as the confidential assistant to Kenneth Bacon, the assistant secretary of defense for public affairs. After news broke of her alleged involvement with the president in January 1988, she became the focus of worldwide media attention.

**Lewis** or *Lewis-with-Harris,* largest and most northerly island in the Outer ◊Hebrides, Western Isles; area 2,220 sq km/857 sq mi; population (1991) 21,700. Its main town is Stornoway. It is separated from northwest Scotland by the Minch. The island is 80 km/50 mi long from north to south, and its greatest breadth is 45 km/28 mi. There are many lochs and peat moors. The Callanish standing stones on the west coast are thought to be up to 5,000 years old, second only to Stonehenge in archaeological significance in the UK.

**Lewis, Lennox Claudius** (1966– ) English boxer who won the WBC world heavyweight title in 1992, becoming the first British boxer to do so this century. He was awarded the title when the reigning champion, Riddick Bowe, refused to fight him. After defending the title successfully for nearly two years, he lost to Oliver McCall in September 1994. However, he regained the title in February 1997.
*career highlights*
*professional record (1989– )* fights: 36; wins: 34 (27 within the distance); draws: 1; defeats: 1
*Olympic super-heavyweight champion* 1988
*WBC heavyweight champion* 1992–94, 1997–

**Lewis, Carl (Frederick Carlton)** (1961– ) US track and field athlete. He won nine gold medals and one silver in four successive Olympic Games. At the 1984 Olympic Games he equalled the performance of Jesse ◊Owens, winning gold medals in the 100 and 200 metres, 400-metre relay, and long jump. He officially ended his career in 1997 at the age of 36.
*career highlights*
*Olympic Games* gold 100 metres 1984, 1988; gold 200 metres 1984; gold 4 x 100 metres relay 1984, 1992; gold long jump 1984, 1988, 1992, 1996; silver 200 metres 1988
*World championships* gold 100 metres 1983, 1991; gold 4 x 100 metres relay 1983, 1987, 1991; gold long jump 1983, 1987; silver 100 metres 1987; silver long jump 1991

**Lewis, (Percy) Wyndham** (1882–1957) English writer and artist. He pioneered Vorticism, which, with its feeling of movement, sought to reflect the age of industry. He had a hard and aggressive style in both his writing and his painting. His literary works include the novel *The Apes of God* (1930); the essay collection *Time and Western Man* (1927); and an autobiography, *Blasting and Bombardiering* (1937). In addition to paintings of a semi-abstract kind, he made a number of portraits; among his sitters were the poets Edith Sitwell, Ezra Pound, and T S Eliot.

**Lhasa** 'the Forbidden City', capital of the autonomous region of ◊Tibet, China, at 5,000 m/16,400 ft; population (1992) 124,000. Products include handicrafts and light industry. The holy city of ◊Lamaism, Lhasa was closed to Westerners until 1904, when members of a British expedition led by Col Francis E Younghusband visited the city. It was annexed with the rest of Tibet in 1950–51 by China, and the spiritual and temporal head of state, the Dalai Lama, fled in 1959 after a popular uprising against Chinese rule. Monasteries have been destroyed and monks killed, and an influx of Chinese settlers has generated resentment. In 1988 and 1989 nationalist demonstrators were shot by Chinese soldiers.

**liability** in accounting, a financial obligation. Liabilities are placed alongside assets on a balance sheet to show the wealth of the individual or company concerned at a given date. Business organizations often distinguish between *current liabilities* such as overdrafts, trade credit, and provisions, and *long-term liabilities* such as debentures, mortgages, and unsecured loans.

**liana** woody, perennial climbing plant with very long stems, which grows around trees right up to the top, where there is more sunlight. Lianas are common in tropical rainforests, where individual stems may grow up to 78 m/255 ft long. They have an unusual stem structure that makes them flexible, despite being woody.

**Liaoning** province of northeast China, bounded to the east by Jilin, to the southeast by North Korea, to the south by Korea Bay and the Gulf of Liaodong, to the southwest by Hebei, and to the northwest by Inner Mongolia
*area* 151,000 sq km/58,300 sq mi
*capital* ◊Shenyang
*cities and towns* Anshan, Fushun, Liaoyang, Dalian (port)
*physical* Dongbei (Manchurian) Plain; grasslands of Mongolian Plateau
*features* one of China's most heavily industrialized areas
*industries* coal, iron, salt, oil
*agriculture* cereals
*population* (1996) 41,160,000
*history* developed by Japan between 1905 and 1945, including the *Liaodong Peninsula,* whose ports had been conquered from the Russians.

**Liaquat Ali Khan, Nawabzada** (1895–1951) Indian politician, deputy leader of the Muslim League 1940–47, first prime minister of Pakistan from 1947. He was assassinated by objectors to his peace policy with India.

**libel** in law, defamation published in a permanent form, such as in a newspaper, book, or broadcast.

**Liberal Democrats** in UK politics, common name for the ◊Social and Liberal Democrats.

**liberalism** political and social theory that favours representative government, freedom of the press, speech, and worship, the abolition of class privileges, the use of state resources to protect the welfare of the individual, and international ◊free trade. It is historically associated with the Liberal Party in the UK and the Democratic Party in the USA.

**Liberal Party** British political party, the successor to the ◊Whig Party, with an ideology of liberalism. In the 19th century it represented the interests of commerce and industry. Its outstanding leaders were Palmerston, Gladstone, and Lloyd George. From 1914 it declined, and the rise of the Labour Party pushed the Liberals into the middle ground. The Liberals joined forces with the Social Democratic Party (SDP) as the Alliance for the 1983 and 1987 elections. In 1988 a majority of the SDP voted to merge with the Liberals to form the ◊Social and Liberal Democrats.

**Liberia** Republic of

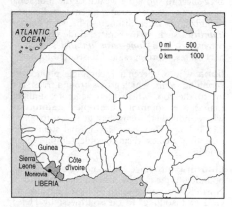

**area** 111,370 sq km/42,999 sq mi
**capital** Monrovia (and port)
**major towns/cities** Bensonville, Saniquillie, Gbarnga, Voinjama, Buchanan
**major ports** Buchanan, Greenville
**physical features** forested highlands; swampy tropical coast where six rivers enter the sea
**head of state and government** Ruth Perry from 1996
**political system** emergent democracy
**political parties** National Democratic Party of Liberia (NDPL), nationalist, left of centre; National Patriotic Front of Liberia (NPFL), left of centre; United Democratic Movement of Liberia for Democracy (Ulimo), left of centre; National Patriotic Party (NPP)
**currency** Liberian dollar
**GNP per capita (PPP)** (US$) N/A
**exports** iron ore, rubber, timber, coffee, cocoa, palm-kernel oil, diamonds, gold. Principal market: Belgium/Luxembourg 36.2% (1997)
**population** 2,930,000 (1999 est)
**language** English (official), over 20 Niger-Congo languages

**religion** animist, Sunni Muslim, Christian
**life expectancy** 46 (men); 49 (women) (1995–2000)
**Chronology**
**1821** Purchased by philanthropic American Colonization Society and turned into settlement for liberated black slaves from southern USA.
**1847** Recognized as an independent republic.
**1869** The True Whig Party founded, which was to dominate politics for more than a century, providing all presidents.
**1926** Large concession sold to Firestone Rubber Company as foreign indebtedness increased.
**1944** William Tubman, descendant of US slaves, elected president.
**1971** Tubman died and was succeeded by William Tolbert.
**1980** Tolbert was assassinated in military coup led by Sgt Samuel Doe, who banned political parties and launched an anticorruption drive.
**1984** A new constitution was approved in a referendum. The National Democratic Party (NDPL) was founded by Doe as political parties were relegalized.
**1985** Doe and the NDPL won decisive victories in the allegedly rigged elections.
**1990** Doe was killed as bloody civil war broke out, involving Charles Taylor and Gen Hezekiah Bowen, who led rival rebel armies, the National Patriotic Front (NPFL) and the Armed Forces of Liberia (AFL). The war left 150,000 dead and 2 million homeless. A West African peacekeeping force was drafted in. Amos Sawyer, with NPFL backing, became the interim head of government.
**1992** Monrovia was under siege by Taylor's rebel forces.
**1993** A peace agreement was signed, but soon collapsed.
**1995** Ghanaian-backed peace proposals were accepted by rebel factions; an interim Council of State was established, comprising leaders of three main rebel factions and chaired by Wilton Sankawulo.
**1996** There was renewed fighting in the capital. A peace plan was reached in talks convened by the Economic Community of West African States (ECOWAS); Ruth Perry became Liberia's first female head of state.
**1997** The National Patriotic Party (NPP), led by Charles Taylor, won a majority in assembly elections.
**1998** There was fighting in Monrovia between President Taylor's forces and opposition militias.

**libido** in Freudian psychology, the energy of the sex instinct, which is to be found even in a newborn child. The libido develops through a number of phases, described by Sigmund Freud in his theory of infantile sexuality. The source of the libido is the ◊id.

**Libra** faint zodiacal constellation on the celestial equator (see ◊celestial sphere) adjoining Scorpius, and represented as the scales of justice. The Sun passes through Libra during November. The constellation was once considered to be a part of Scorpius, seen as the scorpion's claws. In astrology, the dates for Libra are between about 23 September and 23 October (see ◊precession).

**Libreville** (French 'free town') capital of Gabon, on the northern shore of the Gabon River estuary; population (1993) 419,600. Products include timber, oil, cement, and minerals (including uranium and manganese). It is the main port and transport centre of the country, together with Owendo on the southern edge of the town. Libreville was founded in 1849 as a refuge for slaves freed by the French. Since the 1970s the city has developed rapidly due to the oil trade.

**Libya** Great Socialist People's Libyan Arab Republic
*national name Jamahiriya al-Arabiya al-Libya al-Shabiya al-Ishtirakiya al-Uzma*

*area* 1,759,540 sq km/679,358 sq mi
*capital* Tripoli
*towns and cities* Benghazi, Misurata, Az-Zaiwa, Tobruk, Ajdabiya, Derna
*major ports* Benghazi, Misurata, Az-Zaiwa, Tobruk, Ajdabiya, Derna
*physical features* flat to undulating plains with plateaux and depressions stretch southwards from the Mediterranean coast to an extremely dry desert interior
*head of state and government* Moamer al-Khaddhafi (Gadafi) from 1969
*political system* one-party socialist state
*political party* Arab Socialist Union (ASU), radical, left wing
*currency* Libyan dinar
*GNP per capita (PPP)* (US$) 5,470 (1994 est)
*exports* crude petroleum (accounted for 94% of 1991 export earnings), chemicals and related products. Principal market: Italy 41.3% (1997)
*population* 5,470,000 (1999 est)
*language* Arabic
*religion* Sunni Muslim
*life expectancy* 68 (men); 72 (women) (1995–2000)
*Chronology*
**7th century BC** Tripolitania, in western Libya, was settled by Phoenicians, who founded Tripoli; it became an eastern province of Carthaginian kingdom, which was centred on Tunis to the west.
**4th century BC** Cyrenaica, in eastern Libya, colonized by Greeks, who called it Libya.

**74 BC** Became a Roman province, with Tripolitania part of Africa Nova province and Cyrenaica combined with Crete as a province.
**19 BC** The desert region of Fezzan (Phazzania), inhabited by Garmante people, was conquered by Rome.
**6th century AD** Came under control of Byzantine Empire.
**7th century** Conquered by Arabs, who spread Islam: Egypt ruled Cyrenaica and Morrocan Berber Almohads controlled Tripolitania.
**mid-16th century** Became part of Turkish Ottoman Empire, who combined the three ancient regions into one regency in Tripoli.
**1711** Karamanli (Qaramanli) dynasty established virtual independence from Ottomans.
**1835** Ottoman control reasserted.
**1911–12** Conquered by Italy.
**1920s** Resistance to Italian rule by Sanusi order and Umar al-Mukhtar.
**1934** Colony named Libya.
**1942** Italians ousted, and area divided into three provinces: Fezzan (under French control), Cyrenaica, and Tripolitania (under British control).
**1951** Achieved independence as United Kingdom of Libya, under King Idris, former Amir of Cyrenaica and leader of Sanusi order.
**1959** Discovery of oil transformed economy, but also led to unsettling social changes.
**1969** King deposed in military coup led by Col Moamer al-Khaddhafi. Revolution Command Council set up and Arab Socialist Union (ASU) proclaimed the only legal party in a new puritanical Islamic-socialist republic which sought Pan-Arab unity.
**1970s** Economic activity collectivized, oil industry nationalized, opposition suppressed by Khaddhafi's revolutionary regime.
**1972** Proposed federation of Libya, Syria, and Egypt abandoned.
**1980** A proposed merger with Syria was abandoned. Libyan troops began fighting in northern Chad.
**1986** The US bombed Khaddhafi's headquarters, following allegations of his complicity in terrorist activities.
**1988** Diplomatic relations with Chad were restored; political prisoners were freed; and the economy was liberalized.
**1989** The US navy shot down two Libyan planes. There was a reconciliation with Egypt.
**1992** Khaddhafi came under international pressure to extradite the suspected Lockerbie and UTA (Union de Transports Aérians) bombers for trial outside Libya. United Nations sanctions were imposed; several countries severed diplomatic and air links with Libya.
**1995** There was an antigovernment campaign of violence by Islamicists. Hundreds of Palestinians and thousands of foreign workers were expelled.
**1999** Lockerbie suspects were handed over for trial in the Netherlands, to be tried by Scottish judges. Diplomatic relations with UK restored.

**lichen** any organism of a unique group that consists of associations of a specific ◊fungus and a specific ◊alga living together in a mutually beneficial relationship. Found as coloured patches or spongelike masses on trees, rocks, and other surfaces, lichens flourish in harsh conditions. (Group Lichenes.)

**Lichtenstein, Roy** (1923–1997) US Pop artist. He is best known for using advertising imagery and comic-strip techniques, often focusing on popular ideals of romance and heroism, as in *Whaam!* 1963 (Tate Gallery, London). He has also produced sculptures in brass, plastic, and enamelled metal.

**Liechtenstein** Principality of
**national name** *Fürstentum Liechtenstein*

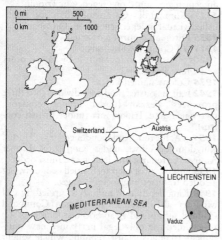

**area** 160 sq km/62 sq mi
**capital** Vaduz
**major towns/cities** Balzers, Schaan, Ruggell, Triesen, Eschen
**physical features** landlocked Alpine; includes part of Rhine Valley in west
**head of state** Prince Hans Adam II from 1989
**head of government** Mario Frick from 1993
**political system** constitutional monarchy
**political parties** Patriotic Union (VU), conservative; Progressive Citizens' Party (FBP), conservative
**currency** Swiss franc
**GNP per capita (PPP)** (US$) 25,100 (1995 est)
**exports** small machinery, artificial teeth and other material for dentistry, stamps, precision instruments, ceramics. Principal market: Switzerland 14.5% (1996)
**population** 32,000 (1999 est)
**language** German (official); an Alemannic dialect is also spoken
**religion** Roman Catholic (87%), Protestant
**life expectancy** 78 (men); 83 (women) (1995–2000)
**Chronology**
**c. AD 500** Settled by Germanic-speaking Alemanni tribe.
**1342** Became sovereign state.
**1434** Present boundaries established.
**1719** Former independent lordships of Schellenberg and Vaduz were united by Princes of Liechtenstein to form present state.
**1815–66** A member of German Confederation.
**1868** Abolished standing armed forces.

**1871** Liechtenstein was only German principality to stay outside newly formed German Empire.
**1918** Patriotic Union (VU) party founded, drawing most support from the mountainous south.
**1919** Switzerland replaced Austria as foreign representative of Liechtenstein.
**1921** Adopted Swiss currency; constitution created a parliament.
**1923** United with Switzerland in customs and monetary union.
**1938** Prince Franz Josef II came to power.
**1970** After 42 years as main governing party, northern-based Progressive Citizens' Party (FBP) defeated by VU which, except for 1974–78, became dominant force in politics.
**1978** Joined Council of Europe.
**1984** Prince Franz Josef II handed over power to the Crown Prince Hans Adam. The franchise was extended to women in the national elections.
**1989** Prince Franz Josef II died; he was succeeded by Hans Adam II.
**1990** Joined the United Nations.
**1991** Became the seventh member of the European Free Trade Association.
**1993** Mario Frick of VU became Europe's youngest head of government, aged 28, after two general elections.
**1997** Mario Frick and ruling VU–FBP government retained power after a general election. The FBP withdrew from the coalition.

**lied** (German 'song', plural *lieder*) musical dramatization of a poem, usually for solo voice and piano; referring to Romantic songs of Schubert, Schumann, Brahms, and Hugo Wolf.

**lie detector** instrument that records graphically certain body activities, such as thoracic and abdominal respiration, blood pressure, pulse rate, and galvanic skin response (changes in electrical resistance of the skin). Marked changes in these activities when a person answers a question may indicate that the person is lying.

**liege** in the feudal system, the allegiance owed by a vassal to his or her lord (the liege lord).

**Liège** Flemish *Luik*, industrial city, capital of Liège province in eastern Belgium, southeast of Brussels, almost bisected by the River Meuse, and bounded on the east side by Germany; population (1997) 189,500. It is one of the largest river ports in Europe. Weapons, textiles, paper, and chemicals are manufactured here. The city has a university, founded in 1817, and several ancient churches; the oldest, St Martin's, dates from 692.

**life** the ability to grow, reproduce, and respond to such stimuli as light, heat, and sound. Life on Earth may have began about 4 billion years ago when a chemical reaction produced the first organic substance. Over time, life has evolved from primitive single-celled organisms to complex multicellular ones. There are now some 10 million different species of plants and animals living on the Earth. The earliest fossil evidence of life is threadlike chains of cells discovered in 1980 in deposits in northwestern Australia;

these have been dated as being 3.5 billion years old.

◊Biology is the study of living organisms – their evolution, structure, functioning, classification, and distribution – while ◊biochemistry is the study of the chemistry of living organisms. Biochemistry is especially concerned with the function of the chemical components of organisms such as proteins, carbohydrates, lipids, and nucleic acids.

**life cycle** in biology, the sequence of developmental stages through which members of a given species pass. Most vertebrates have a simple life cycle consisting of ◊fertilization of sex cells or ◊gametes, a period of development as an ◊embryo, a period of juvenile growth after hatching or birth, an adulthood including ◊sexual reproduction, and finally death. Invertebrate life cycles are generally more complex and may involve major reconstitution of the individual's appearance (◊metamorphosis) and completely different styles of life. Plants have a special type of life cycle with two distinct phases, known as ◊alternation of generations. Many insects such as cicadas, dragonflies, and mayflies have a long larvae or pupae phase and a short adult phase. Dragonflies live an aquatic life as larvae and an aerial life during the adult phase. In many invertebrates and protozoa there is a sequence of stages in the life cycle, and in parasites different stages often occur in different host organisms.

**ligament** strong, flexible connective tissue, made of the protein ◊collagen, which joins bone to bone at moveable joints and sometimes encloses the joints. Ligaments prevent bone dislocation (under normal circumstances) but allow joint flexion. The ligaments around the joints are composed of white fibrous tissue. Other ligaments are composed of yellow elastic tissue, which is adapted to support a continuous but varying stress, as in the ligament connecting the various cartilages of the ◊larynx (voice box).

**light** ◊electromagnetic waves in the visible range, having a wavelength from about 400 nanometres in the extreme violet to about 770 nanometres in the extreme red. Light is considered to exhibit particle and wave properties, and the fundamental particle, or quantum, of light is called the photon. The speed of light (and of all electromagnetic radiation) in a vacuum is approximately 300,000 km/186,000 mi per second, and is a universal constant denoted by $c$.

**light-emitting diode** (LED), electronic component that converts electrical energy into light or infrared radiation in the range of 550 nm (green light) to 1300 nm (infrared). They are used for displaying symbols in electronic instruments and devices. An LED is a ◊diode made of ◊semiconductor material, such as gallium arsenide phosphide, that glows when electricity is passed through it. The first digital watches and calculators had LED displays, but many later models use ◊liquid-crystal displays.

**lighthouse** structure carrying a powerful light to warn ships or aeroplanes that they are approaching a place (usually land) dangerous or important to navigation. The light is magnified and directed out to the horizon or up to the zenith by a series of mirrors or prisms. Increasingly lighthouses are powered by electricity and automated rather than staffed; the more recent models also emit radio signals.

**lightning** high-voltage electrical discharge between two charged rainclouds or between a cloud and the Earth, caused by the build-up of electrical charges. Air in the path of lightning ionizes (becomes conducting), and expands; the accompanying noise is heard as thunder. Currents of 20,000 amperes and temperatures of 30,000°C/54,000°F are common. Lightning causes nitrogen oxides to form in the atmosphere and approximately 25% of the atmospheric nitrogen oxides are formed in this way.

**light year** in astronomy, the distance travelled by a beam of light in a vacuum in one year, approximately 9.46 trillion (million million) km/5.88 trillion miles.

**lignin** naturally occurring substance produced by plants to strengthen their tissues. It is difficult for ◊enzymes to attack lignin, so living organisms cannot digest wood, with the exception of a few specialized fungi and bacteria. Lignin is the essential ingredient of all wood and is, therefore, of great commercial importance.

**Liguria** coastal region of northwest Italy, which lies between the western Alps and the Gulf of Genoa in the Mediterranean, comprising the provinces of Genova, La Spezia, Imperia, and Savona; area 5,418 sq km/2,093 sq mi; population (1992 est) 1,668,900. ◊Genoa is the chief city and port. The region includes the resorts of the Italian Riviera and tourism is very important. Industries include shipbuilding, heavy engineering, horticulture, and the production of chemicals, metals, and textiles.

**lilac** any of a group of flowering Old World shrubs, with clusters (panicles) of small, sweetly scented, white or purple flowers on the main stems. The common lilac (*S. vulgaris*) is a popular garden ornamental. (Genus *Syringa,* family Oleaceae.)

**Lilienthal, Otto** (1848–1896) German aviation pioneer who inspired US aviators Orville and Wilbur ◊Wright. From 1891 he made and successfully flew many gliders, including two biplanes, before he was killed in a glider crash.

**Lille** Flemish *Ryssel* or *Russel;* Latin *Insula,* (*l'île* 'island') industrial city and administrative centre of the Nord *département* in the Nord-Pas-de-Calais region of France, on the River Deûle; population (1990) 178,300, metropolitan area 936,000. The world's first entirely automatic underground train system was opened here in 1982. The Eurostar train stops here, at the new Eurolille station. Industries include textiles, chemicals, engineering, and distilling.

**Lillee, Dennis Keith** (1949– ) Australian cricketer. He is regarded as the best fast bowler of his generation. He made his Test debut in the 1970–71 season and subsequently played for his country 70 times. Lillee took 355 wickets in Test cricket. He played Sheffield Shield cricket for

Western Australia and at the end of his career made a comeback with Tasmania.

*career highlights*
*Test cricket* appearances: 70; wickets: 355; average: 23.92

**Lilongwe** capital of Malawi since 1975, on the Lilongwe River; population (1993) 268,000. Products include tobacco, groundnuts, and textiles. Capital Hill, 5 km/3 mi from the old city, is the site of government buildings and offices. The city was founded in 1947.

**lily** any of a group of plants belonging to the lily family, of which there are about 80 species, most with showy, trumpet-shaped flowers growing from bulbs. The lily family includes hyacinths, tulips, asparagus, and plants of the onion genus. The name 'lily' is also applied to many lilylike plants of related genera and families. (Genus *Lilium,* family Liliaceae.)

**lily of the valley** plant belonging to the lily family, growing in woods in Europe, northern Asia, and North America. The small bell-shaped white flowers hang downwards from short stalks attached to a central stem; they are strongly scented. The plant is often cultivated. (*Convallaria majalis,* family Liliaceae.)

**Lima** capital and largest city of Peru, on the River Rímac, 13 km/8 mi from its Pacific port of Callao; population (1993) 5,706,100. It comprises about one-third of the country's total population. Industries include textiles, chemicals, glass, and cement.

**limbo** in Christian theology, a region for the souls of those who were not admitted to the divine vision. *Limbus infantum* was a place where unbaptized infants enjoyed inferior blessedness, and *limbus patrum* was where the prophets of the Old Testament dwelt. The word was first used in this sense in the 13th century by Thomas Aquinas.

**Limbourg** Flemish *Limburg,* province of northeast Belgium, bounded north and east by the Netherlands; the River Meuse marks the frontier
*area* 2,422 sq km/935 sq mi
*capital* Hasselt
*towns* Genk, Tongeren
*physical* River Demer; Kempen heathland in the north; rich coalfields; agriculture in the south
*industries* coal, sugar refining, food processing, chemicals, electronics, engineering, glass, metallurgy
*agriculture* dairy farming, market gardening
*population* (1997) 780,000
*history* the province was formerly part of the feudal duchy of Limburg (which was divided 1839 into today's Belgian and Dutch provinces).

**Limburg** southernmost province of the Netherlands, bounded by Germany to the east, Belgium to the west and south, and North Brabant to the north
*area* 2,170 sq km/838 sq mi
*capital* Maastricht
*towns* Kerkrade, Heerlen, Roermond
*physical* Maas (Meuse) and Roer rivers; sandy

soils in river plain, marl soils in the south; hilly towards the south
*features* a monument at the *Drielandenpunt,* where the Dutch, German, and Belgian borders meet; Kerkrade is alleged site of the first European coal mine
*industries* chemicals, cement, fertilizers
*agriculture* mixed arable farming, horticulture
*population* (1997) 1,136,200
*history* formerly part of the duchy of Limburg, which was divided in 1839 into today's Dutch and Belgian provinces; contains a small area of German territory transferred to Dutch sovereignty in 1949.

**lime** or *quicklime,* CaO (technical name *calcium oxide*) white powdery substance used in making mortar and cement. It is made commercially by heating calcium carbonate ($CaCO_3$), obtained from limestone or chalk, in a lime kiln. Quicklime readily absorbs water to become calcium hydroxide $Ca(OH)_2$, known as slaked lime, which is used to reduce soil acidity.

**lime** sharp-tasting green or greenish-yellow citrus fruit of the small thorny lime bush, native to India. The white flowers are followed by the fruits, which resemble lemons but are more round in shape; they are rich in vitamin C. (*Citrus aurantifolia,* family Rutaceae.)

**lime** or *linden,* any of a group of ◊deciduous trees native to the northern hemisphere. The leaves are heart-shaped and coarsely toothed, and the flowers are cream-coloured and fragrant. (Genus *Tilia,* family Tiliaceae.)

**limerick** five-line humorous verse, often nonsensical, which first appeared in England about 1820 and was popularized by Edward ◊Lear. An example is: 'There was a young lady of Riga, Who rode with a smile on a tiger; They returned from the ride With the lady inside, And the smile on the face of the tiger.'

**Limerick** county of the Republic of Ireland, in the province of Munster; county town Limerick; area 2,690 sq km/1,038 sq mi; population (1991) 161,900. The principal river is the ◊Shannon, and towns include Abbeyfeale, Kilmallock, Newcastle West, and Rathkeale. Limerick is hilly in the southwest (Mullaghreirk Mountains), and in the northeast (Galtee Mountains). The low-lying region in the west is very fertile, and is known as the 'Golden Vale'. Dairy cattle, sheep, pigs, and poultry are reared extensively, and corn, sugar-beet, and potatoes are grown. Lace is also produced.

**limestone** sedimentary rock composed chiefly of calcium carbonate $CaCO_3$, derived either from the shells of marine organisms or precipitated from solution, mostly in the ocean. Various types of limestone are used as building stone.

**limited company** company for whose debts the members are liable only to a limited extent. The capital of a limited company is divided into small units, and profits are distributed according to shareholding.

**Limousin** modern planning region and former province of central France; area 16,900 sq km/

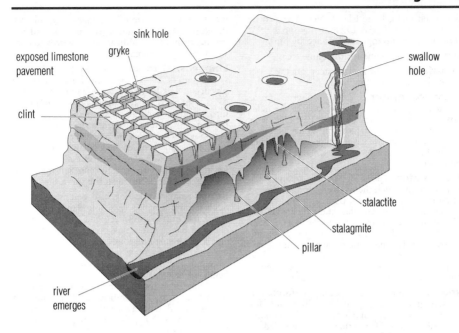

***limestone*** *The physical weathering and erosion of a limestone landscape. The freezing and thawing of rain and its mild acidic properties cause cracks and joints to enlarge, forming limestone pavements, potholes, caves and caverns.*

6,544 sq mi; population (1990) 722,900. The modern region consists of the *départements* of Corrèze, Creuse, and Haute-Vienne. The administrative centre is Limoges; Brive-la-Gaillarde, Tulle, and Gueret are the other towns of note. A thinly populated and largely infertile region, it is crossed by the mountains of the Massif Central. Fruit and vegetables are produced in the more fertile lowlands. Kaolin is mined here.

**limpet** any of various marine ◊snails belonging to several families and genera, found in the Atlantic and Pacific oceans. A limpet has a conical shell and adheres firmly to rocks by its disclike foot. Limpets leave their fixed positions only to graze on seaweeds, always returning to the same spot. The *common limpet* (*P. vulgata*) can be seen on rocks at low tide. (Especially genera *Acmaea* and *Patella*.)

**Limpopo** river in southeast Africa, rising in the Magaliesberg to the west of Pretoria in Gauteng Province, South Africa, and flowing through Mozambique to the Indian Ocean at Delagoa Bay; length 1,600 km/1,000 mi. It is also known as Crocodile River.

**Lin Biao** or *Lin Piao* (1908–1971) Chinese communist soldier and politician, deputy leader of the Chinese Communist Party 1969–71. He joined the communists in 1927, became a commander of ◊Mao Zedong's Red Army, and led the Northeast People's Liberation Army in the civil war after 1945. He became defence minister in 1959, and as vice chair of the party from 1969 he was expected to be Mao's successor. In 1972 the government announced that Lin had

been killed in an aeroplane crash in Mongolia on 17 September 1971 while fleeing to the USSR following an abortive coup attempt.

**Lincoln, Abraham** (1809–1865) 16th president of the USA 1861–65, a Republican. In the American ◊Civil War, his chief concern was the preservation of the Union from which the Confederate (Southern) slave states had seceded on his election. In 1863 he announced the freedom of the slaves with the Emancipation Proclamation. He was re-elected 1864 with victory for the North in sight, but was assassinated at the end of the war.

**Lincolnshire** county of eastern England
***area*** 5,890 sq km/2,274 sq mi
***towns and cities*** Lincoln (administrative headquarters), Skegness, Boston, Stamford
***physical*** hills of Lincoln Edge and the Wolds; marshy coastline; the Fens in the southeast; rivers Trent, Welland, Witham
***features*** Belton House, a Restoration mansion; Gibraltar Point National Nature Reserve
***agriculture*** cattle, sheep, horses; cereals (mainly barley); flower bulbs (largest bulb-growing industry in the UK, around Spalding); vegetables
***population*** (1996) 615,900
***famous people*** Isaac Newton, Alfred Tennyson, Margaret Thatcher, John Wesley.

**Lincs** abbreviation for ◊Lincolnshire, an English county.

**Lindbergh, Charles A(ugustus)** (1902–1974) US aviator. He made the first solo nonstop flight in 33.5 hours across the Atlantic

(Roosevelt Field, Long Island, New York, to Le Bourget airport, Paris) 1927 in the *Spirit of St Louis,* a Ryan monoplane designed by him.

**linden** another name for the ◊lime tree.

**Lindisfarne** site of a monastery off the coast of Northumberland, England.

**linear accelerator** or *linac,* in physics, a type of particle ◊accelerator in which the particles move along a straight tube. Particles pass through a linear accelerator only once – unlike those in a cyclotron (a ring-shaped accelerator), which make many revolutions, gaining energy each time.

**linear motor** type of electric motor, an induction motor in which the fixed stator and moving armature are straight and parallel to each other (rather than being circular and one inside the other as in an ordinary induction motor). Linear motors are used, for example, to power sliding doors. There is a magnetic force between the stator and armature; this force has been used to support a vehicle, as in the experimental ◊maglev linear motor train.

**Lineker, Gary** (1960– ) English footballer. He scored over 250 goals in 550 games for Leicester, Everton, Barcelona, and Tottenham. With 48 goals in 80 internationals he failed by one goal to equal Bobby Charlton's record of 49 goals for England. Lineker was elected Footballer of the Year in 1986 and 1992, and was leading scorer at the 1986 World Cup finals. In 1993 he moved to Japan to play for Nagoya Grampus Eight but retired a year later.
*career highlights*
*FA Cup* 1991 (with Tottenham)
*European Cup Winners Cup* 1989 (with Barcelona)
*Footballer of the Year* 1986, 1992

**linen** yarn spun and the textile woven from the fibres of the stem of the ◊flax plant. Used by the ancient Egyptians, linen was introduced by the Romans to northern Europe, where production became widespread. Religious refugees from the Low Countries in the 16th century helped to establish the linen industry in England, but here and elsewhere it began to decline in competition with cotton in the 18th century.

**ling** any of several deepwater long-bodied fishes of the cod family found in the North Atlantic. (Genus *Molva,* family Gadidae.)

**ling** another name for common ◊heather.

**lingua franca** (Italian 'Frankish tongue') any language that is used as a means of communication by groups who do not themselves normally speak that language; for example, English is a lingua franca used by Japanese doing business in Finland, or by Swedes in Saudi Arabia. The term comes from the mixture of French, Italian, Spanish, Greek, Turkish, and Arabic that was spoken around the Mediterranean from the time of the Crusades until the 18th century.

**linguistics** scientific study of language. Linguistics has many branches, such as origins (historical linguistics), the changing way language is pronounced (phonetics), derivation of words through various languages (etymology), development of meanings (semantics), and the arrangement and modifications of words to convey a message (grammar).

**Linnaeus, Carolus** (Latinized form of Carl von Linné) (1707–1778) Swedish naturalist and physician. His botanical work *Systema naturae* 1735 contained his system for classifying plants into groups depending on shared characteristics (such as the number of stamens in flowers), providing a much-needed framework for identification. He also devised the concise and precise system for naming plants and animals, using one Latin (or Latinized) word to represent the genus and a second to distinguish the species.

**linnet** small seed-eating bird belonging to the finch family, which is very abundant in Europe, Asia, and northwestern Africa. The male has a chestnut back with a pink breast and grey head, and a red breast and forehead during the breeding season; the female is mainly a dull brown. The linnet barely measures 13 cm/5 in in length, begins to breed in April, and generally chooses a low-lying bush for its home. The eggs, ranging from four to six in number, are a delicate pale blue streaked with a purplish brown. (Species *Acanthis cannabina,* family Fringillidae, order Passeriformes.)

**Lin Piao** alternative transliteration of ◊Lin Biao.

**linseed** seeds of the ◊flax plant, from which linseed oil is produced, the residue being used as cattle feed. The oil is used in paint, wood treatments and varnishes, and in the manufacture of linoleum floor coverings.

**lion** large wild cat with a tawny coat. The young have darker spot markings to camouflage them; these usually disappear in the adult. The male has a heavy mane and a tuft at the end of the tail. Head and body measure about 2 m/6 ft, plus 1 m/3 ft of tail; lionesses are slightly smaller. Lions produce litters of two to six cubs, and often live in groups (prides) of several adult males and females with young. They are carnivores (meat-eaters) and are found only in Africa, south of the Sahara desert, and in the Gir Forest of northwest India.

**lipase** enzyme responsible for breaking down fats into fatty acids and glycerol. It is produced by the ◊pancreas and requires a slightly alkaline environment. The products of fat digestion are absorbed by the intestinal wall.

**Li Peng** (1928– ) Chinese communist politician, a member of the Politburo from 1985, and prime minister 1987–98. During the prodemocracy demonstrations of 1989 he supported the massacre of students by Chinese troops and the subsequent execution of others. He sought improved relations with the USSR before its demise, and has favoured maintaining firm central and party control over the economy. In March 1998 Li stepped down as prime minister, being replaced by the more reformist Zhu Rongji. He was elected chairman of the National People's Congress (China's parliament), although an unprecedented 200 of the 2,950 delegates voted against his nomination.

**lipid** any of a large number of esters of fatty acids, commonly formed by the reaction of a fatty acid with glycerol. They are soluble in alcohol but not in water. Lipids are the chief constituents of plant and animal waxes, fats, and oils.

**Li Po** (*c*. 705–762) Taoist Chinese poet of the Tang dynasty (618–907). He used traditional literary forms, but his exuberance, the boldness of his imagination, and the intensity of his feeling have won him recognition as perhaps the greatest of all Chinese poets. Although he was mostly concerned with higher themes, he is also remembered for his celebratory verses on drinking.

**Lippi, Filippino** (*c*. 1457–1504) Florentine painter. He was trained by his father Filippo ◊Lippi and ◊Botticelli. His most important works are frescoes in the Strozzi Chapel of Sta Maria Novella in Florence, painted in a graceful but also dramatic and at times bizarre style.

**Lippi, Fra Filippo** (*c*. 1406–1469) Florentine painter. His most important works include frescoes depicting the lives of St Stephen and St John the Baptist (1452–66) (Prato Cathedral), which in their use of perspective and grouping of figures show the influence of ◊Masaccio. He also painted many altarpieces featuring the Madonna.

**liquefaction** the process of converting a gas to a liquid, normally associated with low temperatures and high pressures (see ◊condensation).

**liquid** state of matter between a ◊solid and a ◊gas. A liquid forms a level surface and assumes the shape of its container. Its atoms do not occupy fixed positions as in a crystalline solid, nor do they have freedom of movement as in a gas. Unlike a gas, a liquid is difficult to compress since pressure applied at one point is equally transmitted throughout (Pascal's principle). ◊Hydraulics makes use of this property.

**liquidation** in economics, the winding up of a company by converting all its assets into money to pay off its liabilities.

**liquid-crystal display** (LCD), display of numbers (for example, in a calculator) or pictures (such as on a pocket television screen) produced by molecules of a substance in a semiliquid state with some crystalline properties, so that clusters of molecules align in parallel formations. The display is a blank until the application of an electric field, which 'twists' the molecules so that they reflect or transmit light falling on them. There two main types of LCD are *passive matrix* and *active matrix*.

**liquorice** perennial European herb belonging to the ◊legume family. The long sweet root yields an extract which is made into a hard black paste and used in confectionery and medicines. (*Glycyrrhiza glabra*, family Leguminosae.)

**Lisbon** Portuguese *Lisboa*, capital of Portugal, and of the Lisboa district, in the southwest of the country, situated on a tidal lake and estuary formed by the River Tagus; population (1991) 677,800. It is a major commercial and industrial centre, and industries include steel, textiles, chemicals, pottery, shipbuilding, and fishing. Lisbon has been the Portugal's capital since 1260 and reached its peak of prosperity in the period of Portugal's empire during the 16th century. In 1755 an earthquake accompanied by a tidal wave killed 30,000–60,000 people (the estimates vary) and destroyed much of the city.

**Lister, Joseph** 1st Baron Lister (1827–1912) English surgeon. He was the founder of antiseptic surgery, influenced by Louis ◊Pasteur's work on bacteria. He introduced dressings soaked in carbolic acid and strict rules of hygiene to combat wound sepsis in hospitals. Baronet 1883, Baron 1897.

**Liszt, Franz** (1811–1886) Hungarian pianist and composer. An outstanding virtuoso of the piano, he was an established concert artist by the age of 12. His expressive, romantic, and frequently chromatic works include piano music (*Transcendental Studies, 1851*), Masses and oratorios, songs, organ music, and a symphony. Much of his music is programmatic; he also originated the symphonic poem. Liszt was taught by his father, then by Carl Czerny. He travelled widely in Europe, producing an operetta *Don Sanche* in Paris at the age of 14. As musical director and conductor at Weimar (1848–59), he championed the music of Berlioz and Wagner.

**litany** in the Christian church, a form of prayer or supplication led by a priest with set responses by the congregation. It was introduced in the 4th century.

**litchi** or *lychee*, evergreen tree belonging to the soapberry family. The delicately flavoured egg-shaped fruit has a rough brownish outer skin and a hard seed. The litchi is native to southern China, where it has been cultivated for 2,000 years. (*Litchi chinensis*, family Sapindaceae.)

**literacy** ability to read and write. The level at which functional literacy is set rises as society becomes more complex, and it becomes increasingly difficult for an illiterate person to find work and cope with the other demands of everyday life.

**literary criticism** the assessment and interpretation of literary works. The term 'criticism' is often taken to mean exclusively adverse comment, but in fact it refers to all literary assessment, whether positive or negative. Contemporary criticism offers analyses of literary works from structuralist, semiological, feminist, Marxist, and psychoanalytical perspectives, whereas earlier criticism tended to deal with moral or political ideas, or with a literary work as a formal object independent of its creator.

**literature** words set apart in some way from ordinary everyday communication. In the ancient oral traditions, before stories and poems were written down, literature had a mainly public function – mythic and religious. As literary works came to be preserved in writing, and, eventually, printed, their role became more private, serving as a vehicle for the exploration and expression of emotion and the human situation.

**lithium** (Greek *lithos* 'stone') soft, ductile, silver-white, metallic element, symbol Li, atomic number 3, relative atomic mass 6.941. It is one of the ɸalkali metals, has a very low density (far less than most woods), and floats on water (specific gravity 0.57); it is the lightest of all metals. Lithium is used to harden alloys, and in batteries; its compounds are used in medicine to treat manic depression.

**lithography** printmaking technique invented in 1798 by Aloys Senefelder, based on the mutual repulsion of grease and water. A drawing is made with greasy crayon on an absorbent stone, which is then wetted. The wet stone repels ink (which is greasy) applied to the surface and the crayon absorbs it, so that the drawing can be printed. Lithographic printing is used in book production, posters, and prints, and this basic principle has developed into complex processes.

**Lithuania** Republic of
*national name* *Lietuvos Respublika*

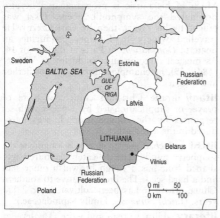

*area* 65,200 sq km/25,173 sq mi
*capital* Vilnius
*major towns/cities* Kaunas, Klaipeda, Siauliai, Panevezys
*physical features* central lowlands with gentle hills in west and higher terrain in southeast; 25% forested; some 3,000 small lakes, marshes, and complex sandy coastline; River Nemen
*head of state* Valdas Adamkus from 1998
*head of government* Rolandas Paksas from 1999
*political system* emergent democracy
*political parties* Lithuanian Democratic Labour Party (LDLP), reform-socialist (ex-communist); Homeland Union–Lithuanian Conservatives (Tevynes Santara), right of centre, nationalist; Christian Democratic Party of Lithuania, centre right; Lithuanian Social Democratic Party, left of centre
*currency* litas
*GNP per capita (PPP)* (US$) 4,310 (1998)
*exports* textiles, machinery and equipment, non-precious metals, animal products, timber. Principal market: Russia 16.5 (1998)

*population* 3,682,000 (1999 est)
*language* Lithuanian (official)
*religion* predominantly Roman Catholic; Lithuanian Lutheran Church
*life expectancy* 64 (men); 76 (women) (1995–2000)
*Chronology*
*late 12th century* Became a separate nation.
*1230* Mindaugas united Lithuanian tribes to resist attempted invasions by German and Livonian Teutonic Knights, and adopted Christianity.
*14th century* Strong Grand Duchy formed by Gediminas, founder of Vilnius and Jogaila dynasty, and his son, Algirdas; absorbing Ruthenian territories to east and south, it stretched from the Baltic to the Black Sea and east, nearly reaching Moscow.
*1410* Led by Duke Vytautas, and in alliance with Poland, the Teutonic Knights were defeated decisively at Battle of Tannenberg.
*1569* Joined Poland in a confederation, under the Union of Lublin, in which Poland had the upper hand and Lithuanian upper classes were Polonized.
*1795* Came under control of Tsarist Russia, following partition of Poland; 'Lithuania Minor' (Kaliningrad) fell to Germany.
*1831 and 1863* Failed revolts for independence.
*1880s* Development of organized nationalist movement.
*1914–18* Occupied by German troops during World War I.
*1918–19* Independence declared and, after uprising against attempted imposition of Soviet Union (USSR) control, was achieved as a democracy.
*1920–39* Province and city of Vilnius occupied by Poles.
*1926* Democracy overthrown in authoritarian coup by Antanas Smetona, who became president.
*1934* Baltic Entente mutual-defence pact signed with Estonia and Latvia.
*1939–40* Secret German–Soviet agreement brought most of Lithuania under Soviet influence as a constituent republic.
*1941* Lithuania revolted and established own government, but during World War II Germany again occupied the country and 210,000, mainly Jews, were killed.
*1944* USSR resumed rule.
*1944–52* Lithuanian guerrillas fought USSR, which persecuted the Catholic Church, collectivized agriculture, and deported half a million Balts to Siberia.
*1972* Demonstrations against Soviet government.
*1980s* There was a growth in nationalist dissent, influenced by the Polish Solidarity movement and the glasnost ('openness') initiative of reformist Soviet leader Mikhail Gorbachev.
*1988* Popular Front, the Sajudis, was formed to campaign for increased autonomy; the parliament declared Lithuanian the state language and readopted the flag of the interwar republic.
*1989* The Communist Party split into pro-Moscow and nationalist wings, and lost the

local monopoly of power; over 1 million took part in nationalist demonstrations.

**1990** Nationalist Sajudis won elections; their leader, Vytautas Landsbergis, became the president; a unilateral declaration of independence was rejected by the USSR, who imposed an economic blockade.

**1991** Soviet paratroopers briefly occupied key buildings in Vilnius, killing 13; the Communist Party was outlawed; Lithuanian independence was recognized by the USSR and Western nations; the country was admitted into the United Nations.

**1992** The ex-communist Democratic Labour Party (LDLP) won a majority in parliamentary elections as economic restructuring caused a contraction in GDP.

**1993** LDLP leader Algirdas Brazauskas was elected president, and Adolfas Slezevicius became prime minister. A free-trade agreement was reached with other Baltic states. The last Russian troops departed.

**1994** A friendship and cooperation treaty was signed with Poland.

**1994** A trade and cooperation agreement was reached with the European Union.

**1996** Slezevicius resigned over a banking scandal and was replaced by Laurynas Stankevicius. A new conservative coalition was formed, led by Gediminas Vagnorius.

**1997** A border treaty was signed with Russia.

**1998** Valdas Adamkus became president.

**litmus** dye obtained from various ◊lichens and used in chemistry as an indicator to test the acidic or alkaline nature of aqueous solutions; it turns red in the presence of acid, and blue in the presence of alkali.

**litre** metric unit of volume (symbol l), equal to one cubic decimetre (1.76 imperial pints/2.11 US pints). It was formerly defined as the volume occupied by one kilogram of pure water at 4°C at standard pressure, but this is slightly larger than one cubic decimetre.

**Little Bighorn** river in Montana, USA, a tributary of the Bighorn. On 25 June 1876 it was the scene of the Battle of the Little Bighorn.

**liturgy** in the Christian church, any written, authorized version of a service for public worship, especially the Roman Catholic ◊Mass.

**Liu Shaoqi** or *Liu Shao-chi* (1898–1969) Chinese communist politician, president 1960–65 and the most prominent victim of the 1966–69 leftist Cultural Revolution. A Moscow-trained labour organizer, he was a firm proponent of the Soviet style of government based around disciplined one-party control, the use of incentive gradings, and priority for industry over agriculture. This was opposed by ◊Mao Zedong (Tsetung), but began to be implemented by Liu while he was state president 1960–65. Liu was brought down during the ◊Cultural Revolution.

**liver** large organ of vertebrates, which has many regulatory and storage functions. The human liver is situated in the upper abdomen, and weighs about 2 kg/4.5 lb. It is divided into four lobes. The liver receives the products of digestion, converts glucose to glycogen (a long-chain carbohydrate used for storage), and then back to glucose when needed. In this way the liver regulates the level of glucose in the blood (see ◊homeostasis). It removes excess amino acids from the blood, converting them to urea, which is excreted by the kidneys. The liver also synthesizes vitamins, produces bile and blood-clotting factors, and removes damaged red cells and toxins such as alcohol from the blood.

**Liverpool** city, seaport, and metropolitan borough in Merseyside, northwest England; population (1991) 481,800. Liverpool is the UK's chief Atlantic port with miles of specialized, mechanized quays on the River Mersey, and 2,100 ha/5,187 acres of dockland. The port handles 27.8 million tonnes/28.25 million tons of cargo annually. Imports include crude oil, grain, ores, edible oils, timber, and containers. There are ferries to Ireland and the Isle of Man. Traditional industries, such as ship-repairing, have declined. Present-day industries include flour-milling, sugar refining, electrical engineering, food processing, and tanning; products include chemicals, soap, margarine, and motor vehicles. There are industrial estates at Aintree, Kirkby, and Speke. A rail tunnel, and Queensway Tunnel (1934) link Liverpool and Birkenhead; Kingsway Tunnel (1971), also known as the Mersey Tunnel, links Liverpool and Wallasey.

*features* Landmarks include the Bluecoat Chambers (1717); the Town Hall (1754); St George's Hall (1838–54), a good example of classical architecture; the Brown Library and Museum (1860); the Picton Library (1879); the Anglican Cathedral, designed by George Gilbert Scott (begun 1904, completed 1980); the Roman Catholic Metropolitan Cathedral of Christ the King, designed by Frederick Gibberd, consecrated in 1967; and the Tate Gallery in the North in the former Albert Dock (now restored as a shopping and leisure area), opened in 1987. The Walker Art Gallery (1877) and the Liverpool Philharmonic Orchestra, (founded in 1840, the Royal LPO since 1957), are here. The Grand National steeplechase takes place at Aintree. Outstanding buildings include the 16th-century Speke Hall, the Victoria Building of the University of Liverpool, the Dock Offices, the Port of Liverpool building (1907), Royal Liver Building (1911), and the Cunard Building (1916) on Pier Head. In the Canning Conservation Area, 600 Georgian and Victorian houses are being restored.

The Central Libraries (a conglomerate of several libraries) constitute one of the best public libraries in the country; the Picton Library (1879) for the humanities is a 19th-century building. There are two universities: the University of Liverpool (opened in 1903) and John Moores University. Britain's first International Garden Festival was held here in 1984. The ◊Beatles were born here. The Liverpool Institute for the Performing Arts, set up by former Beatle Paul McCartney and opened in 1995, occupies the old Liverpool Institute for Boys, where Paul McCartney and George Harrison went to school. It offers a bachelor's degree in the performing arts.

*history* Liverpool grew in importance during the 18th century as a centre of the slave trade, and until the early 20th century through the export of textiles from Lancashire and Yorkshire.

**Liverpool, Robert Banks Jenkinson,** 2nd Earl Liverpool (1770–1828) British Tory politician. He entered Parliament in 1790 and was foreign secretary 1801–03, home secretary 1804–06 and 1807–09, war minister 1809–12, and prime minister 1812–27. His government conducted the Napoleonic Wars to a successful conclusion, but its ruthless suppression of freedom of speech and of the press aroused such opposition that during 1815–20 revolution frequently seemed imminent. Earl 1808.

**liverwort** nonvascular plant (with no 'veins' to carry water and food), related to ◊hornworts and mosses; it is found growing in damp places. (Class Hepaticae, order Bryophyta.)

**Livingstone, David** (1813–1873) Scottish missionary explorer. In 1841 he went to Africa, reaching Lake Ngami in 1849. He followed the Zambezi to its mouth, saw the Victoria Falls in 1855, and went to East and Central Africa 1858–64, reaching Lakes Shirwa and Nyasa. From 1866, he tried to find the source of the River Nile, and reached Ujiji in Tanganyika in November 1871. British explorer Henry Stanley joined Livingstone in Ujiji.

**Livingstone, Ken(neth)** (1945– ) British left-wing Labour politician, leader of the Greater London Council (GLC) 1981–86 and member of Parliament for Brent East from 1987. He stood as a candidate for the Labour Party leadership elections in 1992 and declared himself a candidate for the mayorship of London in 1999, although he lacked backing from the Labour Party's leadership.

**Livonia** German *Livland*, one of the former ◊Baltic States, divided in 1918 between the modern states of Estonia and Latvia. Livonia belonged to the Teutonic Knights from the 13th to 16th centuries, to Poland from 1561, Sweden from 1629, and Russia from 1721.

**Livy** adopted name of Titus Livius (59 BC–AD 17) Roman historian. He was the author of a *History of Rome* from the city's foundation to 9 BC, based partly on legend. It was composed of 142 books, of which 35 survive, covering the periods from the arrival of Aeneas in Italy to 293 BC and from 218 to 167 BC.

**Li Xiannian** (1909–1992) Chinese communist politician, member of the Chinese Communist Party (CCP) Politburo from 1956, and state president 1983–88. He fell from favour during the 1966–69 Cultural Revolution, but was rehabilitated as finance minister in 1973, by ◊Zhou Enlai, and proceeded to implement cautious economic reform.

**lizard** reptile generally distinguishable from snakes, which belong to the same order, by having four legs, moveable eyelids, eardrums, and a fleshy tongue, although some lizards are legless and snakelike in appearance. There are over 3,000 species of lizard worldwide. (Suborder Lacertilia, order Squamata.)

**Lizard Point** southernmost point of mainland England in Cornwall. The coast is broken into small bays, overlooked by two cliff lighthouses.

**Ljubljana** German *Laibach,* capital and industrial city of Slovenia, near the confluence of the rivers Ljubljanica and Sava; population (1991) 276,100. Products include textiles, chemicals, paper, and leather goods. It has a nuclear research centre and is linked with southern Austria by the Karawanken road tunnel under the Alps (1979–83).

**llama** South American even-toed hoofed mammal belonging to the camel family, about 1.2 m/4 ft high at the shoulder. Llamas can be white, brown, or dark, sometimes with spots or patches. They are very hardy, and require little food or water. They spit when annoyed. (Species *Lama glama*, family Camelidae.)

**Llewelyn** two princes of Wales:

**Llewelyn I** (1173–1240) Prince of Wales from 1194. He extended his rule to all Wales not in Norman hands, driving the English from northern Wales in 1212, and taking Shrewsbury in 1215. During the early part of Henry III's reign, he was several times attacked by English armies. He was married to Joanna, the illegitimate daughter of King John.

**Llewelyn II ap Gruffydd** (*c.* 1225–1282) Prince of Wales from 1246, grandson of Llewelyn I. In 1277 Edward I of England compelled Llewelyn to acknowledge him as overlord and to surrender southern Wales. His death while leading a national uprising ended Welsh independence.

**Lloyd George, David,** 1st Earl Lloyd-George of Dwyfor (1863–1945) British Liberal politician, born in Manchester of Welsh parentage, prime minister 1916–22. A pioneer of social reform and the ◊welfare state, as chancellor of the Exchequer 1908–15 he introduced old-age pensions in 1908 and health and unemployment insurance in 1911. High unemployment, intervention in the Russian Civil War, and use of the military police force, the ◊Black and Tans, in Ireland eroded his support as prime minister, and the creation of the Irish Free State in 1921 and his pro-Greek policy against the Turks caused the collapse of his coalition government.

**Lloyd Webber, Andrew** (1948– ) English composer. His early musicals, with lyrics by Tim Rice, include *Joseph and the Amazing Technicolor Dreamcoat* (1968), *Jesus Christ Superstar* (1971), and *Evita* (1978), based on the life of the Argentine leader Eva Perón. He also wrote *Cats* (1981), based on T S Eliot's *Old Possum's Book of Practical Cats, Starlight Express* (1984), *The Phantom of the Opera* (1986), and *Aspects of Love* (1989).

**loach** carplike freshwater fish with a long narrow body and no teeth in the small downward-pointing mouth, which is surrounded by barbels (sensitive bristles). Loaches are native to Asian and European waters. (Family Cobitidae.)

**loam** type of fertile soil, a mixture of sand, silt, clay, and organic material. It is porous, which allows for good air circulation and retention of moisture.

**lobby** individual or pressure group that sets out to influence government action. The lobby is prevalent in the USA, where the term originated in the 1830s from the practice of those wishing to influence state policy waiting for elected representatives in the lobby of the Capitol.

**lobelia** any of a group of temperate and tropical plants with white to mauve flowers. Lobelias may grow to shrub size but are mostly small annual plants. (Genus *Lobelia*, family Lobeliaceae.)

**lobotomy** another name for the former brain operation, leucotomy.

**lobster** any of various large marine ◊crustaceans. Lobsters are grouped with freshwater ◊crayfish in the suborder Reptantia ('walking'), although both lobsters and crayfish can also swim, using their fanlike tails. Lobsters have eyes on stalks and long antennae, and are mainly nocturnal. They scavenge and eat dead or dying fish. (Family Homaridae, order Decapoda.)

**local government** that part of government dealing mainly with matters concerning the inhabitants of a particular area or town, usually financed at least in part by local taxes. In the USA and UK, local government has comparatively large powers and responsibilities.

**Locarno, Pact of** series of diplomatic documents initialled in Locarno, Switzerland, 16 October 1925 and formally signed in London 1 December 1925. The pact settled the question of French security, and the signatories – Britain, France, Belgium, Italy, and Germany – guaranteed Germany's existing frontiers with France and Belgium. Following the signing of the pact, Germany was admitted to the League of Nations.

**Lochner, Stephan** (*c.* 1400–1451) German painter. Active in Cologne from 1442, where most of his work still remains, notably the *Virgin in the Rose Garden* (*c.* 1440, Wallraf-Richartz Museum) and *Adoration of the Magi,* (1448, Cologne Cathedral). His work combines the indigenous German style with the naturalism of Flemish painting.

**Loch Ness** Scottish lake; see ◊Ness, Loch.

**lock** construction installed in waterways to allow boats or ships to travel from one level to another. The earliest form, the *flash lock,* was first seen in the East in 1st-century-AD China and in the West in 11th-century Holland. By this method barriers temporarily dammed a river and when removed allowed the flash flood to propel the waiting boat through or over any obstacle. This was followed in 12th-century China and 14th-century Holland by the *pound lock.* In this system the lock has gates at each end. Boats enter through one gate when the levels are the same both outside and inside. Water is then allowed in (or out of) the lock until the level rises (or falls) to the new level outside the other gate.

Locks are important to shipping where canals link oceans of differing levels, such as the Panama Canal, or where falls or rapids are replaced by these adjustable water 'steps'.

**Locke, John** (1632–1704) English philosopher. His *Essay Concerning Human Understanding* (1690) maintained that experience is the only source of knowledge (empiricism), and that 'we can have knowledge no farther than we have ideas' prompted by such experience. *Two Treatises on Government* (1690) helped to form contemporary ideas of liberal democracy.

**locomotive** engine for hauling railway trains. In 1804 Cornish engineer Richard Trevithick built the first steam engine to run on rails. Locomotive design did not radically improve until British engineer George Stephenson built the *Rocket* in 1829, which featured a multitube boiler and blastpipe, standard in all following *steam locomotives.* Today most locomotives are diesel or electric: *diesel locomotives* have a powerful diesel engine, and *electric locomotives* draw their power from either an overhead cable or a third rail alongside the ordinary track.

**locus** (Latin 'place') in mathematics, traditionally the path traced out by a moving point, but now defined as the set of all points on a curve satisfying given conditions. For example, the locus of a point that moves so that it is always at the same distance from another fixed point is a circle; the locus of a point that is always at the same distance from two fixed points is a straight line that perpendicularly bisects the line joining them. The locus of points a fixed distance from a line is two parallel lines running either side.

**locust** swarming grasshopper with short feelers, or antennae, and hearing organs on the abdomen (rear segment of the body). As winged adults, flying in swarms, locusts may be carried by the wind hundreds of miles from their breeding grounds; on landing they devour all vegetation. Locusts occur in nearly every continent. (Family Acrididae, order Orthoptera.)

**locust tree** another name for the ◊carob, a small tree of the Mediterranean region. It is also the name of several North American trees of the ◊legume family (Leguminosae).

**lode** geological deposit rich in certain minerals, generally consisting of a large vein or set of veins containing ore minerals. A system of veins that can be mined directly forms a lode, for example the mother lode of the California gold rush.

**Lódź** industrial city (textiles, machinery, dyes) in central Poland, 120 km/75 mi southwest of Warsaw; population (1993) 844,900.

**loganberry** hybrid between a ◊blackberry and a ◊raspberry with large, tart, dull-red fruit. It was developed in 1881 by US judge James H Logan.

**logarithm** or *log,* the ◊exponent or index of a number to a specified base – usually 10. For example, the logarithm to the base 10 of 1,000 is 3 because $10^3 = 1,000$; the logarithm of 2 is 0.3010 because $2 = 10^{0.3010}$. The whole-number part of a logarithm is called the *characteristic;* the fractional part is called the *mantissa.*

Before the advent of cheap electronic calculators, multiplication and division could be simplified by being replaced with the addition and subtraction of logarithms.

**logic** branch of philosophy that studies valid reasoning and argument. It is also the way in which one thing may be said to follow from, or be a consequence of, another (deductive logic). Logic is generally divided into the traditional formal logic of Aristotle and the symbolic logic derived from Friedrich Frege and Bertrand Russell.

**logical positivism** doctrine that the only meaningful propositions are those that can be verified empirically. Metaphysics, religion, and aesthetics are therefore meaningless. However, the doctrine itself cannot be verified empirically and so is self-refuting.

**Loire** longest river in France, rising in the Cévennes Mountains in the *département* of Ardèche at 1,350 m/4,430 ft near Mont Gerbier de Jonc, and flowing for over 1,000 km/620 mi north through Nevers to Orléans, then west through Tours and Nantes until it reaches the Bay of Biscay at St Nazaire. The Loire drains 116,550 sq km/45,000 sq mi of land, more than a fifth of France, and there are many châteaux and vineyards along its banks. The Loire gives its name to the *départements* of Loire, Haute-Loire, Loire-Atlantique, Indre-et-Loire, Maine-et-Loire, and Saône-et-Loire.

**Loki** in Norse mythology, the giant-born god and blood-brother of Odin, companion of the Aesir (principal warrior gods), but a source of trickery and evil, and the cause of dissension among the gods. Instrumental in the slaying of Balder, he hastened the coming of Ragnarök, the final battle of the gods. His children by the giantess Angrboda were the Midgard serpent Jörmungander, which girdles the Earth; the wolf Fenris; and Hel, goddess of death.

**Lollard** follower of the English religious reformer John ◊Wycliffe in the 14th century. The Lollards condemned the doctrine of the transubstantiation of the bread and wine of the Eucharist, advocated the diversion of ecclesiastical property to charitable uses, and denounced war and capital punishment. They were active from about 1377; after the passing of the statute *De heretico comburendo* ('The Necessity of Burning Heretics') in 1401 many Lollards were burned, and in 1414 they raised an unsuccessful revolt in London, known as Oldcastle's Rebellion.

**Lombard** or *Langobard,* member of a Germanic people who invaded Italy 568 and occupied Lombardy (named after them) and central Italy. Their capital was Monza. They were conquered by the Frankish ruler Charlemagne 774.

**Lombardy** Italian *Lombardia,* region of northern Italy, between the Alps and the River Po, comprising the provinces of Bergamo, Brescia, Como, Cremona, Mantua, Milan, Pavia, Sondrio, and Varese; area 23,900 sq km/ 9,225 sq mi; population (1992 est) 8,882,400.

Its capital is Milan. It is the country's chief industrial area with chemical, pharmaceutical, textile, and engineering operations, and its most productive agricultural region yielding wheat, maize, wine, meat, and dairy products.

**Lombardy League, The** Italian regional political party, committed to federalism. It models itself on the 12th–13th century Lombard League. In 1993 it became the core of a new conservative-populist political grouping, the Northern League, led by Umberto Bossi, and fought the 1994 general election as part of the right-wing Freedom Alliance.

**Lomé** capital, port, and administrative centre of Togo, on the Bight of Benin; population (1990) 450,000. It is a centre for gold, silver, and marble crafts. Industries include steel production, oil refining, brewing, plastics, cement, paper manufacturing, and food processing. Main exports include cacao, palm nuts, cotton, and coffee. It became capital of the independent Togo in 1960. The University of Benin was founded here in 1965.

**Lomond, Loch** largest freshwater Scottish lake, 37 km/21 mi long, area 70 sq km/27 sq mi. It is overlooked by the mountain **Ben Lomond** (973 m/3,192 ft) and is linked to the Clyde estuary.

**London** capital of England and the United Kingdom, located on the River Thames.

Since 1965 its metropolitan area has been known as ◊Greater London, consisting of the City of London and 32 boroughs; total area 1,580 sq km/610 sq mi; combined population (1995) for 31 boroughs, excluding the cities of London and Westminster, 7,001,900. The *City of London,* known as the 'square mile', is the financial and commercial centre of the UK; area 2.7 sq km/1 sq mi. London is the only major European capital without a strategic authority covering the whole area. Popular tourist attractions include the *Tower of London,* St Paul's Cathedral, Buckingham Palace, and Westminster Abbey. The Millennium Dome at Greenwich was the centrepiece of Britain's millennium celebrations.

**Londonderry** also known as *Derry;* until the 10th century known as *Derry-Calgaich,* (Irish 'oak wood'; *Derry-Calgaich* 'the oak wood of Calgaich' (a fierce warrior) historic city and port on the River Foyle, 35 km/22 mi from Lough Foyle, county town of County ◊Londonderry, Northern Ireland; population (1991) 95,400. Industries include textiles, chemicals, food processing, shirt manufacturing, and acetylene from naphtha.

*features* the Protestant Cathedral of St Columba dating from 1633; the Gothic revival Roman Catholic Cathedral of St Eugene (completed in 1833); the Guildhall (rebuilt in 1912), containing stained glass windows presented by livery companies of the City of London; the city walls, on which are modern iron statues by Anthony Gormley; four gates into the city still survive.

*history* Londonderry dates from the foundation of a monastery there by St Columba in AD 546. The city was subject to a number of sieges by the Danes between the 9th and 11th centuries, and by the Anglo-Normans in the 12th century; however, these were unsuccessful until James I of England captured the city in 1608. The king granted the borough and surrounding land to the citizens of London. The Irish Society was formed to build and administer the city and a large colony of English Protestants was established. The city, then governed by Major Henry Baker and the Reverend George Walker, was unsuccessfully besieged in 1689 by the armies of James II, who had fled England when William of Orange was declared joint sovereign with James' daughter Mary. James' army was led by Richard Talbot, Earl of Tyrconnell, in a conflict known as the *Siege of Derry,* when 13 Derry apprentices and citizens loyal to William of Orange locked the city gates against the Jacobite army. The siege lasted 15 weeks, during which many of the inhabitants died of starvation and disease because of the blockade.

**Londonderry** also known as *Derry,* county of Northern Ireland
*area* 2,070 sq km/799 sq mi
*towns and cities* ◊Londonderry (county town), Coleraine, Portstewart, Limavady
*physical* hilly moorland, coniferous forest; Sperrin Mountains; rivers Foyle, Bann, Roe, and Faughan; borders Lough Neagh
*industries* stone and lime quarrying, food processing, textiles and synthetic fibres, shirt manufacturing, light engineering, chemicals
*agriculture* farming is hindered by the very heavy rainfall; flax, cattle, sheep grazing on moorland, salmon and eel fisheries on the Bann
*population* (1981) 187,000
*famous people* Joyce Cary, Seamus ◊Heaney, William Massey, former prime minister of New Zealand.

**London, Greater** metropolitan area of ◊London, England, comprising the City of London, which forms a self-governing enclave, and 32 surrounding boroughs. Certain powers were exercised over this whole area by the Greater London Council (GLC) 1974–86
*area* 1,580 sq km/610 sq mi
*population* (1996) 7,074,200.

**lone pair** in chemistry, a pair of electrons in the outermost shell of an atom that are not used in bonding. In certain circumstances, they will allow the atom to bond with atoms, ions, or molecules (such as boron trifluoride, $BF_3$) that are deficient in electrons, forming coordinate covalent (dative) bonds in which they provide both of the bonding electrons.

**Longfellow, Henry Wadsworth** (1807–1882) US poet. He is remembered for his ballads ('Excelsior', 'The Village Blacksmith', 'The Wreck of the Hesperus') and the mythic narrative epics *Evangeline* 1847, *The Song of Hiawatha* 1855, and *The Courtship of Miles Standish* 1858.

**Longford** county of the Republic of Ireland, in the province of Leinster; county town Longford; area 1,040 sq km/401 sq mi; population (1991) 30,300. The county is low-lying (the highest point is Carn Clonhugh 279 m/916 ft), and the western border is formed of the River Shannon and part of Lough Ree, one of several lakes. Other rivers are the Camlin, a tributary of the Shannon, and the Inny, which flows into Lough Ree. Agricultural activities include cattle and sheep rearing, and the production of oats and potatoes.

**longhorn beetle** beetle with extremely long antennae, usually equalling the length of the entire body, and often twice its length. Their bodies are 2–150 mm/0.1–6 in long, usually cylindrical, and often mimic wasps, moss, or lichens. The larvae, white or yellow grubs, are wood-borers, mostly attacking decaying or dead wood, but they may bore into healthy trees causing much damage.
*classification* Longhorn beetles are in order Coleoptera, class Insecta, phylum Arthropoda.

**Long Island** island east of Manhattan and southeast of Connecticut, USA, separated from the mainland by Long Island Sound and the East River; 193 km/120 mi long by about 48 km/30 mi wide; area 3,627 sq km/1,400 sq mi; population (1990) 6,861,500. It is mainly a residential district with farming in the east. Henry Hudson discovered the island in 1609, and it was settled by the Dutch from New Amsterdam (in the west) and the English from New England (in the east) from the 1640s.

**longitude** see ◊latitude and longitude.

**long jump** field event in athletics in which competitors sprint up to and leap from a takeoff board into a sandpit measuring 9 metres in length. The takeoff board is 1 metre from the landing area. Each competitor usually has six attempts, and the winner is the one with the longest jump.

**Long March** in Chinese history, the 10,000-km/6,000-mi trek undertaken from 1934 to 1935 by ◊Mao Zedong and his communist forces from southeast to northwest China, under harassment from the Guomindang (nationalist) army.

**Long Parliament** English Parliament 1640–53 and 1659–60, which continued through the Civil War. After the Royalists withdrew in 1642 and the Presbyterian right was excluded in 1648, the remaining ◊Rump ruled England until expelled by Oliver Cromwell in 1653. Reassembled in 1659–60, the Long Parliament initiated the negotiations for the restoration of the monarchy.

**longship** Viking warship, probably developed in the 8th century. Longships were manoeuvrable and fast, well designed for raiding coastal settlements. They could carry 60 or more warriors and travelled under sail or by rowing. There were up to 30 rowing benches in standard longships (the 'great ships' of the late Viking Age had even more). The length-to-breadth ratio of the longship is greater than 6:1 (11.4:1 in one case) enabling them to cut swiftly through the water. Speed was further enhanced by lightness; the timbers of the shell were planed to a width of only 2 cm/0.8 in.

**long-sightedness** nontechnical term for ◊hypermetropia, a vision defect.

**loom** any machine for weaving yarn or thread into cloth. The first looms were used to weave sheep's wool about 5000 BC. A loom is a frame on which a set of lengthwise threads (warp) is strung.

A second set of threads (weft), carried in a shuttle, is inserted at right angles over and under the warp.

**Loos, Adolf** (1870–1933) Austrian architect. His buildings include private houses on Lake Geneva 1904 and the Steiner House in Vienna 1910. In his article 'Ornament and Crime' 1908 he rejected the ornamentation and curved lines of the Viennese *Jugendstil* movement (see ◊Art Nouveau).

**loosestrife** any of several plants belonging to the primrose family, including the yellow loosestrife (*L. vulgaris*), with spikes of yellow flowers, and the low-growing creeping jenny (*L. nummularia*). The striking purple loosestrife (*Lythrum saclicaria*) belongs to a different family. (Genus *Lysimachia*, family Primulaceae; purple loosestrife family Lythraceae.)

**Lope de Vega, (Carpio) Felix** Spanish poet and dramatist; see ◊Vega, Lope de.

**Lorca, Federico García** (1898–1936) Spanish poet and playwright. His plays include *Bodas de sangre/Blood Wedding* 1933, *Yerma* 1934, and *La casa de Bernarda Alba/The House of Bernarda Alba* 1936. His poems include the collection *Romancero gitano/Gypsy Balladbook* 1928 and the 'Lament' written for the bullfighter Ignacio Sánchez Mejías. Lorca was shot by the Falangists during the Spanish Civil War.

**Lord** (Old English *hlaford* 'bread keeper') in the UK, prefix used informally as a less formal alternative to the full title of a marquess, earl, or viscount, for example 'Lord Salisbury' instead of 'the Marquess of Salisbury'. Barons are normally referred to as lords, the term baron being used for foreign holders of that rank. 'Lord' is also used as a courtesy title before the forename and surname of younger sons of dukes and marquesses.

**Lord Advocate** chief law officer of the crown in Scotland who has ultimate responsibility for criminal prosecutions in Scotland. The Lord Advocate does not usually act in inferior courts, where prosecution is carried out by procurators-fiscal acting under the Lord Advocate's instructions.

**Lord Chancellor** UK state official.

**Lords, House of** upper chamber of the UK ◊Parliament. In 1998 there were 1,134 members; 631 hereditary peers and 477 life peers, including the two archbishops and 24 bishops. The Lords Temporal consist of 762 hereditary peers, and 435 life peers, of whom 26 are 'law lords'. In total there are 86 women peers. 304 of the hereditary peers are Conservatives and only 17 Labour. In contrast, 169 of the life peers are Conservatives, 139 are Labour, 42 are Liberal Democrats and 127 are independent 'crossbenchers'. The Labour government elected in May 1997 has introduced legislation to end the right of hereditary peers to sit and vote in the chamber. This will be the first stage in its democratization. The legislative powers of the Lords will not be changed. However, Prime Minister Blair made clear in 1998 that the government's long-term aim was to create a democratically elected second chamber.

**Lorelei** in Germanic folklore, a river ◊nymph of the Rhine who lures sailors onto the rock where she sits combing her hair. She features in several poems, including 'Die Lorelei' by the German Romantic writer Heinrich Heine. The *Lurlei* rock south of Koblenz is 130 m/430 ft high.

**Lorenz, Konrad Zacharias** (1903–1989) Austrian ethologist. He studied the relationship between instinct and behaviour, particularly in birds, and described the phenomenon of imprinting 1935. His books include *King Solomon's Ring* 1952 (on animal behaviour) and *On Aggression* 1966 (on human behaviour). In 1973 he shared the Nobel Prize for Physiology or Medicine with Nikolaas ◊Tinbergen and Karl von Frisch.

**loris** any of a group of small prosimian ◊primates native to Southeast Asia. Lorises are slow-moving, tree-dwelling, and nocturnal. They have very large eyes; true lorises have no tails. They climb without leaping, gripping branches tightly and moving on or hanging below them. (Family Lorisidae.)

**Lorrain, Claude** French painter; see ◊Claude Lorrain.

**Lorraine** German *Lothringen*, region and former province of northeast France in the upper reaches of the Meuse and Moselle rivers; bounded in the north by Belgium, Luxembourg, and Germany, and in the east by Alsace; area 23,600 sq km/9,095 sq mi; population (1990) 2,305,700. It comprises the *départements* of Meurthe-et-Moselle, Meuse, Moselle, and Vosges, and its chief cities are Metz, Nancy (the capital), Luneville, and Epinal. There are deposits of coal, iron ore, and salt; grain, fruit, and livestock are farmed. In 1871, after the Franco-Prussian War, the northern part of the region was ceded to Germany as part of ◊Alsace-Lorraine. The whole area saw heavy fighting in World War I.

**Los Angeles** city and port in southwestern California, USA; population (1994) 3,449,000; Los Angeles–Riverside–Orange County consolidated metropolitan area (also known as Greater Los Angeles) (1994) 15,302,000. In size of population it is the second-largest city and the second-largest metropolitan area in the USA. The city occupies 1,204 sq km/465 sq mi. Industries include aerospace, electronics, motor vehicles, chemicals, clothing, building materials, printing, food processing, and films. Los Angeles was established as a Spanish settlement in 1781.

**lost-wax technique** method of making sculptures.

**Lothair** two Holy Roman emperors:

**Lothair I** (795–855) Holy Roman Emperor from 817 in association with his father Louis I. On Louis's death 840, the empire was divided between Lothair and his brothers; Lothair took northern Italy and the valleys of the rivers Rhône and Rhine.

**Lothair II** (*c.* 1070–1137) Holy Roman Emperor from 1133 and German king from 1125. His election as emperor, opposed by the ◊Hohenstaufen family of princes, was the start of the feud between the Guelph and Ghibelline factions, who supported the papal party and the Hohenstaufens' claim to the imperial throne respectively.

**Lothian** former region of Scotland (1975–96), which was replaced by East Lothian, Midlothian, West Lothian, and City of Edinburgh unitary authorities.

**Lotto, Lorenzo** (*c.* 1480–1556) Venetian painter active in Bergamo, Treviso, Venice, Ancona, and Rome. His early works were influenced by Giovanni Bellini. He painted religious works but is best known for his portraits, which often convey a sense of unease or an air of melancholy.

**lotus** any of several different plants, especially the *water lily* (*Nymphaea lotus*), frequent in Egyptian art, and the pink *Asiatic lotus* (*Nelumbo nucifera*), a sacred symbol in Hinduism and Buddhism, whose flower head floats erect above the water.

**Lotus Sūtra** scripture of Mahāyāna Buddhism. The original is in Sanskrit (*Saddharmapundarīka Sūtra*) and is thought to date from some time after 100 BC.

**loudspeaker** electromechanical device that converts electrical signals into sound waves, which are radiated into the air. The most common type of loudspeaker is the *moving-coil speaker.* Electrical signals from, for example, a radio are fed to a coil of fine wire wound around the top of a cone. The coil is surrounded by a magnet. When signals pass through it, the coil becomes an electromagnet, which by moving causes the cone to vibrate, setting up sound waves.

**Louis, Joe** assumed name of Joseph Louis Barrow (1914–1981) US boxer, nicknamed 'the Brown Bomber'. He was world heavyweight champion 1937–49 and made a record 25 successful defences (a record for any weight).
*career highlights*
*professional fights* total: 66; wins: 63; knockouts: 49; defeats: 3
*first professional fight* 4 July 1934 v. Jack Kracken, USA
*last professional fight* 26 October 1951 v. Rocky Marciano, USA

**Louis** eighteen kings of France, including:

**Louis (I) the Pious** (788–840) Holy Roman Emperor from 814, when he succeeded his father Charlemagne.

**Louis III** (*c.* 863–882) King of northern France from 879, while his brother Carloman

(866–884) ruled southern France. He was the son of Louis II. Louis countered a revolt of the nobility at the beginning of his reign, and his resistance to the Normans made him a hero of epic poems.

**Louis XI** (1423–1483) King of France from 1461. He broke the power of the nobility (headed by ◊Charles the Bold) by intrigue and military power.

**Louis XIV** called *the Sun King* (1638–1715) King of France from 1643, when he succeeded his father Louis XIII; his mother was Anne of Austria. Until 1661 France was ruled by the chief minister, Jules Mazarin, but later Louis took absolute power, summed up in his saying *L'Etat c'est moi* ('I am the state'). Throughout his reign he was engaged in unsuccessful expansionist wars – 1667–68, 1672–78, 1688–97, and 1701–13 (the War of the ◊Spanish Succession) – against various European alliances, always including Britain and the Netherlands. He was a patron of the arts.

**Louis XV** (1710–1774) King of France from 1715, with the Duke of Orléans as regent until 1723. He was the great-grandson of Louis XIV. Indolent and frivolous, Louis left government in the hands of his ministers, the Duke of Bourbon and Cardinal Fleury (1653–1743). On the latter's death he attempted to rule alone but became entirely dominated by his mistresses, Madame de Pompadour and Madame Du Barry. His foreign policy led to French possessions in Canada and India being lost to England.

**Louis XVI** (1754–1793) King of France from 1774, grandson of Louis XV, and son of Louis the Dauphin. He was dominated by his queen, ◊Marie Antoinette, and French finances fell into such confusion that in 1789 the ◊States General (parliament) had to be summoned, and the ◊French Revolution began. Louis lost his personal popularity in June 1791 when he attempted to flee the country, and in August 1792 the Parisians stormed the Tuileries palace and took the royal family prisoner. Deposed in September 1792, Louis was tried in December, sentenced for treason in January 1793, and guillotined.

**Louis XVII** (1785–1795) Nominal king of France, the son of Louis XVI. During the French Revolution he was imprisoned with his parents in 1792 and probably died in prison.

**Louis XVIII** (1755–1824) King of France 1814–24, the younger brother of Louis XVI. He assumed the title of king in 1795, having fled into exile in 1791 during the French Revolution, but became king only on the fall of Napoleon I in April 1814. Expelled during Napoleon's brief return (the 'hundred days') in 1815, he resumed power after Napoleon's final defeat at Waterloo, pursuing a policy of calculated liberalism until ultra-royalist pressure became dominant after 1820.

**Louisiana** state in southern USA. It is nicknamed the Pelican State. Louisiana was admitted to the Union in 1818 as the 18th US state. It has been in the hands of the Spanish, French, and

Americans since the 16th century, and its culture also has been influenced by African slaves and their descendants, and Caribbean and French-Canadian immigrants; the Creoles of southern parishes were originally a mix of French and Spanish descendants; the Cajuns of the southwest were originally French immigrants who had been expelled from Acadia in modern-day Nova Scotia, Canada. Musically, the state is associated with the development of jazz and the blues, particularly in the city of New Orleans. Louisiana is bordered to the north by Arkansas, to the west by Texas, with the Sabine River and Toledo Bend Reservoir forming much of the boundary, and to the east by Mississippi, with the Mississippi and Pearl rivers forming much of the boundary. To the south, the state extends into the Gulf of Mexico, its area expanding continuously through the accretional growth of the delta of the Mississippi River; much of Louisiana consists literally of fragments of other states in the Mississippi-Missouri system

**population** (1995) 4,342,300; including Cajuns, descendants of 18th-century religious exiles from Canada, who speak a French dialect
**area** 135,900 sq km/52,457 sq mi
**capital** Baton Rouge
**towns and cities** New Orleans, Shreveport, Lafayette, Metairie
**industries and products** rice, cotton, sugar, soybeans, oil, natural gas, chemicals, sulphur, fish and shellfish, salt, processed foods, petroleum products, timber, paper, tourism, music industry.

**Louisiana Purchase** purchase by the USA from France in 1803 of an area covering about 2,144,000 sq km/828,000 sq mi, including the present-day states of Louisiana, Missouri, Arkansas, Iowa, Nebraska, North Dakota, South Dakota, and Oklahoma.

**Louis Philippe** (1773–1850) King of France 1830–48. Son of Louis Philippe Joseph, Duke of Orléans 1747–93; both were known as *Philippe Egalité* from their support of the 1792 Revolution. Louis Philippe fled into exile 1793–1814, but became king after the 1830 revolution with the backing of the rich bourgeoisie. Corruption discredited his regime, and after his overthrow, he escaped to the UK and died there.

**Lourdes** town in the *département* of Hautes-Pyrénées in the Midi-Pyrénées region of southwest France, on the Gave de Pau River; population (1990) 18,000. Its Christian shrine to St Bernadette has a reputation for miraculous cures, and Lourdes is an important Roman Catholic pilgrimage centre. In 1858 a young peasant girl, Bernadette Soubirous, claimed to have been shown the healing springs of the Grotte de Massabielle by a vision of the Virgin Mary.

**louse** parasitic insect that lives on mammals. It has a flat, segmented body without wings, and a tube attached to the head, used for sucking blood from its host. (Order Anoplura.)

**Louth** smallest county of the Republic of Ireland, in the province of Leinster; county town

Dundalk; area 820 sq km/317 sq mi; population (1991) 90,700. It is mainly fertile and low-lying. The chief towns are Dundalk at the north end of Dundalk bay, Drogheda, and Ardee, and the chief rivers are the Fane, Lagan, Glyde, and Dee. There is cattle-rearing and fishing; oats and potatoes are grown. Greenore on Carlingford Lough is a container-shipping port. Louth is rich in ancient buildings and remains, and was of strategic importance during the 12th–18th centuries. Important monastic sites with extensive remains include Monasterboice (founded in the 5th century), and Mellifont Abbey (founded in the 12th century).

**Low Countries** region of Europe that consists of Belgium and the Netherlands, and usually includes Luxembourg.

**Lower Austria** German *Niederösterreich*, largest federal state of Austria, bordered on the north by the Czech Republic, drained by the River Danube; area 19,200 sq km/7,411 sq mi; population (1994) 1,511,600. Its capital is St Pölten. The main towns are Wiener Neustadt and Krems. ◊Vienna is a provincial enclave within the province. In addition to wine, sugar beet, and grain, there are reserves of oil and natural gas. Manufactured products include textiles, chemicals, and metal goods. Agriculture and forestry are important.

**Lower Saxony** German *Niedersachsen*, administrative region (German *Land*) in northern Germany, bordered to the north by Schleswig-Holstein and the city-state of Hamburg, to the northeast by Mecklenburg-West Pomerania, to the south by North Rhine-Westphalia and Hesse, on the east and southeast by Saxony-Anhalt and Thuringia respectively, and on the west by the Netherlands
**area** 47,400 sq km/18,296 sq mi
**capital** Hannover
**towns and cities** Braunschweig (Brunswick), Osnabrück, Oldenburg, Göttingen, Wolfsburg, Salzgitter, Hildesheim
**physical** Lüneburg Heath; Harz Mountains; Elbe, Weser, Jade, and Ems rivers
**industries** cars (Volkswagen plant at Wolfsburg in the east of the state), machinery, electrical engineering, iron and steel production
**agriculture** cereals, oats and potatoes; livestock farming
**population** (1995) 7,823,000
**religion** 75% Protestant, 20% Roman Catholic
**history** formed in 1946 from Hannover and the former Prussian provinces of Oldenburg, Braunschweig, and Schaumburg-Lippe.

**Lowry, L(aurence) S(tephen)** (1887–1976) English painter. His works depict life in the industrial towns of the north of England. In the 1920s he developed a naive style characterized by matchstick figures, often in animated groups, and gaunt simplified factories and terraced houses, painted in an almost monochrome palette. *The Pond* (1950; Tate Gallery, London) is an example.

**LSD** abbreviation for *lysergic acid diethylamide*, psychedelic drug, a ◊hallucinogen.

Colourless, odourless, and easily synthesized, it is nonaddictive and nontoxic, but its effects are unpredictable. Its use is illegal in most countries.

**LSI** abbreviation for large-scale integration, technology that enables whole electrical circuits to be etched into a piece of semiconducting material just a few millimetres square.

**Luanda** formerly *Loanda,* capital and industrial port of Angola; population (1995) 2,250,000. Products include cotton, sugar, tobacco, timber, textiles, paper, fuel oil, and lubricants. Founded in 1575 by Portuguese settlers, it became a Portuguese colonial administrative centre as well as an outlet for slaves transported to Brazil.

**Lubbers, Rudolph Franz Marie (Ruud)** (1939– ) Dutch politician, prime minister of the Netherlands 1982–94. Leader of the right-of-centre Christian Democratic Appeal (CDA), he became minister for economic affairs in 1973.

**lubricant** substance used between moving surfaces to reduce friction. Carbon-based (organic) lubricants, commonly called grease and oil, are recovered from petroleum distillation.

**Lucerne** German *Luzern,* capital and tourist centre of Lucerne canton, Switzerland, 45 km/28 mi southwest of Zürich, on the River Reuss where it flows out of Lake Lucerne; population (1994) city 61,700; canton 337,700. Manufactured goods include chemicals, metal products, and textiles. The city developed around a Benedictine monastery established about 750, and owes its prosperity to its position on the St Gotthard road and railway.

**lucerne** another name for the plant ◊alfalfa.

**Lucerne, Lake** German *Vierwaldstättersee* 'lake of the four forest cantons', scenic lake surrounded by mountains in north-central Switzerland; area 114 sq km/44 sq mi. It lies at an altitude of 437 m/1,434 ft and its greatest depth is 215 m/705 ft. It has four main basins, connected by narrow channels. The lake is subject to sudden storms whipped up by the föhn wind.

**Lucifer** (Latin 'bearer of light') in Christian theology, another name for the ◊devil, the leader of the angels who rebelled against God. In Greek mythology, Lucifer is another name for the morning star (the planet ◊Venus).

**Lucknow** capital of the state of ◊Uttar Pradesh, India, on the Gumti River, 70 km/46 mi northeast of Kanpur on a railway junction; population (1991) 1,669,200. Industries include engineering, chemicals, textiles, and many handicrafts. The city has many beautiful mosques including the Great Mosque and the Pearl Mosque. It was the capital of the Nawabs of ◊Oudh in the 18th century. During the ◊Indian Mutiny against British rule, the British residency was besieged 2 July–16 November 1857.

**Lucretius** (*c.* 99–55 BC) Titus Lucretius Carus, Roman poet and ◊Epicurean philosopher. His *De Rerum natura/On the Nature of The Universe,* a didactic poem in six books, envisaged the whole universe as a combination of atoms, and had some concept of evolutionary theory.

**Luddite** one of a group of people involved in machine-wrecking riots in northern England 1811–16. The organizer of the Luddites was referred to as *General Ludd,* but may not have existed. Many Luddites were hanged or transported to penal colonies, such as Australia.

**Ludwig** three kings of Bavaria, including:

**Ludwig I** (1786–1868) King of Bavaria 1825–48, succeeding his father Maximilian Joseph I. He made Munich an international cultural centre, but his association with the dancer Lola Montez, who dictated his policies for a year, led to his abdication in 1848.

**Ludwig II** (1845–1886) King of Bavaria from 1864, when he succeeded his father Maximilian II. He supported Austria during the Austro-Prussian War 1866, but brought Bavaria into the Franco-Prussian War as Prussia's ally and in 1871 offered the German crown to the king of Prussia. He was the composer Richard Wagner's patron and built the Bayreuth theatre for him. Declared insane in 1886, he drowned himself soon after.

**Luftwaffe** German air force used both in World War I and (as reorganized by the Nazi leader Hermann Goering in 1933) in World War II. The Luftwaffe also covered anti-aircraft defence and the launching of the flying bombs V1 and V2.

**Lugosi, Bela** stage name of Bela Ferenc Denzso Blasko (1884–1956), Hungarian-born US film actor. Acclaimed for his performance in *Dracula* on Broadway 1927, Lugosi began acting in feature films 1930. His appearance in the film version of *Dracula* 1931 marked the start of Lugosi's long career in horror films – among them, *Murders in the Rue Morgue* 1932, *The Raven* 1935, and *The Wolf Man* 1941.

**lugworm** any of a group of marine ◊annelid worms that grow up to 10 in/25 cm long. They are common burrowers between tidemarks and are useful for their cleansing and powdering of the beach sand, of which they may annually bring to the surface about 5,000 tonnes per hectare/2,000 tons per acre. (Genus *Arenicola.*)

**Lukács, Georg** (1885–1971) Hungarian philosopher and literary critic, one of the founders of 'Western' or 'Hegelian' Marxism, a philosophy opposed to the Marxism of the official communist movement. He also wrote on aesthetics and the sociology of literature.

**Luke, St** (lived 1st century AD) Traditionally the compiler of the third Gospel and of the Acts of the Apostles in the New Testament. He is the patron saint of painters; his emblem is a winged ox, and his feast day is 18 October.

**lumbago** pain in the lower region of the back, usually due to strain or faulty posture. If it occurs with ◊sciatica, it may be due to pressure on spinal nerves by a slipped disc. Treatment includes rest, application of heat, and skilled manipulation. Surgery may be needed in rare cases.

**lumbar puncture** or *spinal tap,* insertion of a hollow needle between two lumbar (lower back) vertebrae to withdraw a sample of cerebrospinal fluid (CSF) for testing. Normally clear and colourless, the CSF acts as a fluid buffer around the brain and spinal cord. Changes in its quantity, colour, or composition may indicate neurological damage or disease.

**lumen** SI unit (symbol lm) of luminous flux (the amount of light passing through an area per second).

**Lumière** Auguste Marie Louis Nicolas (1862–1954) and Louis Jean (1864–1948, French brothers who pioneered cinematography. In February 1895 they patented their cinematograph, a combined camera and projector operating at 16 frames per second, screening short films for the first time on 22 March, and in December opening the world's first cinema in Paris. Among their first films were the simple documentaries *La Sortie des usines Lumière/ Workers Leaving the Lumière Factory* (1895) and *L'Arrivée d'un train en gare de La Ciotat/The Arrival of a Train at Ciotat Station* (1895), and the comedy *L'Arroseur arrosé/The Hoser Hosed* (1895).

**luminescence** emission of light from a body when its atoms are excited by means other than raising its temperature. Short-lived luminescence is called fluorescence; longer-lived luminescence is called phosphorescence.

**Lumumba, Patrice Emergy** (1925–1961) Congolese politician, prime minister of the Republic of the Congo (now the Democratic Republic of Congo) in 1960. Founder of the National Congolese Movement in 1958, he led his party to victory in the elections following independence in 1960. However, the country collapsed into civil war, and Lumumba was ousted in a coup led by Mobutu in September 1960, and murdered a few months later.

**lung** large cavity of the body, used for gas exchange. It is essentially a sheet of thin, moist membrane that is folded so as to occupy less space. Most tetrapod (four-limbed) vertebrates have a pair of lungs occupying the thorax. The lung tissue, consisting of multitudes of air sacs and blood vessels, is very light and spongy, and functions by bringing inhaled air into close contact with the blood so that oxygen can pass into the organism and waste carbon dioxide can be passed out. The efficiency of lungs is enhanced by ◊breathing movements, by the thinness and moistness of their surfaces, and by a constant supply of circulating blood.

**lung cancer** in medicine, cancer of the lung. The main risk factor is smoking, with almost nine out of ten cases attributed to it. Other risk factors include workspace exposure to carcinogenic substances such as asbestos, and radiation. Warning symptoms include a persistent and otherwise unexplained cough, breathing difficulties, and pain in the chest or shoulder. Treatment is with chemotherapy, radiotherapy, and surgery.

**lungfish** any of a group of fleshy-finned bony fishes found in South America, Australia, and Africa. They have elongated bodies, and grow to about 2 m/6 ft, and in addition to gills have 'lungs' with which they can breathe air during periods of drought conditions. (Genera *Lepidosiren, Neoceratodus,* and *Protopterus,* subclass Dipnoi.)

**Luo** or *Lwoo* or *Kavirondo,* member of the second-largest ethnic group of Kenya, living in the Lake Victoria region and numbering around 2,650,000 (1987). The Luo are a Nilotic people who traditionally lived by farming livestock. Many, however, now work as wage labourers throughout East Africa. Traditionally they had a strong clan system without centralized political authority. Their religion includes beliefs in a supreme creator, Nyasi, and ancestor worship. The Luo language is of the Nilo-Saharan family.

**Luoyang** or *Loyang,* city in Henan province, China, south of the Huang He River; population (1994) 1,340,000. Industries include oil-refining and the production of glass, machinery, and tractors. Luoyang was the capital of China for nearly eight centuries under the Eastern Zhou (8th–3rd century BC) and other dynasties, and an important Buddhist centre in the 5th and 6th centuries.

**Lupercalia** annual Roman festival of purification celebrated on 15 Feb. It has been associated with the Greek Lycaean ◊Pan, god of flocks and herds (identified with the Roman ◊Faunus), and the wolf (*lupus*) who supposedly suckled Romulus and Remus, the twin founders of Rome. Goats and dogs were sacrificed at the *Lupercal* at the foot of the Palatine Hill, near the cave of Lupercus, the wolf's lair.

**lupin** any of a group of leguminous plants (see ◊legume) that comprises about 300 species. Lupins are native to Mediterranean regions and parts of North and South America, and some species are naturalized in Britain. Their spikes of pealike flowers may be white, yellow, blue, or pink. *L. albus* is cultivated in some places for cattle fodder and for green manuring; other varieties are cultivated in Europe as cottage garden plants. (Genus *Lupinus,* family Leguminosae.)

**lupus** in medicine, any of various diseases characterized by lesions of the skin. One form (lupus vulgaris) is caused by the tubercle bacillus (see ◊tuberculosis). The organism produces ulcers that spread and eat away the underlying tissues. Treatment is primarily with standard antituberculous drugs, but ultraviolet light may also be used.

**Lusaka** capital of Zambia from 1964 (of Northern Rhodesia 1935–64), 370 km/230 mi northeast of Livingstone; population (1990) 982,000. It is a commercial, manufacturing, and agricultural centre. Industries include flour mills, tobacco factories, vehicle assembly, plastics, printing, cement, iron and steel, food processing, paints, plastics, fertilizers, funiture, and clothing.

**Lusitania** ancient area of the Iberian peninsula, roughly equivalent to Portugal. Conquered by Rome in 139 BC, the province of Lusitania rebelled periodically until it was finally conquered by Pompey (73–72 BC).

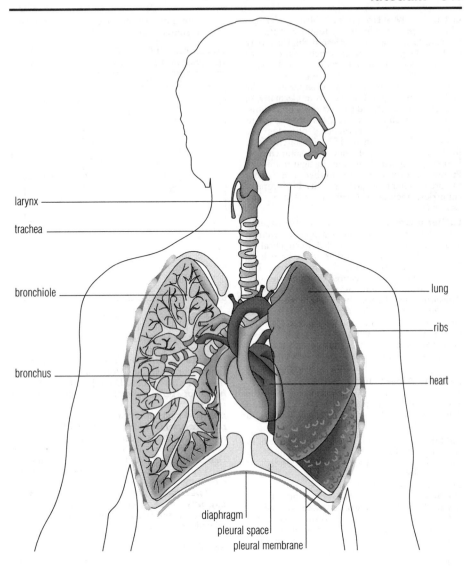

larynx

trachea

bronchiole

bronchus

lung

ribs

heart

diaphragm
pleural space
pleural membrane

*lung* The human lungs contain 300,000 million tiny blood vessels which would stretch for 2,400 km/1,500 mi if laid end to end. A healthy adult at rest breathes 12 times a minute; a baby breathes at twice this rate. Each breath brings 350 millilitres of fresh air into the lungs, and expels 150 millilitres of stale air from the nose and throat.

**lute** member of a family of plucked stringed musical instruments of the 14th–18th centuries, including the mandore, theorbo, and chitarrone. Lutes are pear-shaped with up to seven courses of strings (single or double), plucked with the fingers. Music for lutes is written in special notation called tablature and chords are played simultaneously, not arpeggiated as for guitar. Modern lutenists include Julian Bream and Anthony Rooley (1944–   ).

**luteinizing hormone** ◊hormone produced by the pituitary gland. In males, it stimulates the testes to produce androgens (male sex hormones). In females, it works together with follicle-stimulating hormone to initiate production of egg cells by the ovary. If fertilization occurs, it plays a part in maintaining the pregnancy by controlling the levels of the hormones oestrogen and progesterone in the body.

**lutetium** (Latin *Lutetia* 'Paris') silver-white, metallic element, the last of the ◊lanthanide series, symbol Lu, atomic number 71, relative atomic mass 174.97. It is used in the 'cracking', or breakdown, of petroleum and in other chemical processes. It was named by its discoverer, French chemist Georges Urbain, (1872–1938) after his native city.

**Luther,    Martin** (1483–1546)    German Christian church reformer, a founder of Protestantism. While he was a priest at the University of Wittenberg, he wrote an attack on the sale of indulgences (remissions of punishment for sin). The Holy Roman emperor Charles V summoned him to the Diet (meeting of dignitaries of the Holy Roman Empire) of Worms in Germany, in 1521, where he refused to retract his objections. Originally intending reform, his protest led to schism, with the emergence, following the Augsburg Confession in 1530 (a statement of the Protestant faith), of a new Protestant church. Luther is regarded as the instigator of the Protestant revolution, and ◊Lutheranism is now the predominant religion of many N European countries, including Germany, Sweden, and Denmark.

**Lutheranism** form of Protestant Christianity derived from the life and teaching of Martin ◊Luther; it is sometimes called Evangelical to distinguish it from the other main branch of European Protestantism, the Reformed. The most generally accepted statement of Lutheranism is that of the *Confession of Augsburg* in 1530, but Luther's Shorter Catechism also carries great weight. It is the largest Protestant body, including some 80 million persons, of whom 40 million are in Germany, 19 million in Scandinavia, 8.5 million in the USA and Canada, with most of the remainder in central Europe.

**Luthuli, Albert John** or *Lutuli* (*c.* 1898–1967) South African politician, president of the African National Congress 1952–67. Luthuli, a Zulu tribal chief, preached nonviolence and multiracialism.

**Luton** industrial town and unitary authority in south-central England, 48 km/30 mi north of London. It was part of the county of Bedfordshire to 1997
*area* 43 sq km/17 sq mi
*features* the Luton Hoo mansion (1767), designed and built by Robert Adam and with a park laid out by Capability Brown, is located south of the town; large church of St Mary (13th–15th centuries) is a cruciform building largely in the Decorated and Perpendicular styles
*industries* cars and trucks, chemicals, engineering components, and electrical goods. Luton airport is a secondary airport for London.
*population* (1996) 181,400.

**Lutyens, Edwin Landseer** (1869–1944) English architect. His designs ranged from the picturesque, such as Castle Drogo (1910–30), Devon, to Renaissance-style country houses, and ultimately evolved into a Classical style as seen in the Cenotaph, London (1919), and the Viceroy's House, New Delhi, India (1912–31). His complex use of space, interest in tradition, and distorted Classical language have proved of great interest to a number of postmodern architects, especially Robert Venturi.

**lux** SI unit (symbol lx) of illuminance or illumination (the light falling on an object). It is equivalent to one ◊lumen per square metre or to the

illuminance of a surface one metre distant from a point source of one ◊candela.

**Luxembourg** Grand Duchy of
*national name* *Grand-Duché de Luxembourg*

*area* 2,586 sq km/998 sq mi
*capital* Luxembourg
*major towns/cities* Esch-Alzette, Differdange, Dudelange, Petange
*physical features* on the River Moselle; part of the Ardennes (Oesling) forest in north
*head of state* Grand Duke Jean from 1964
*head of government* Jean-Claude Juncker from 1995
*political system* liberal democracy
*political parties* Christian Social Party (PCS), moderate, left of centre; Luxembourg Socialist Workers' Party (POSL), moderate, socialist; Democratic Party (PD), centre left; Communist Party of Luxembourg, pro-European left wing
*currency* Luxembourg franc
*GNP per capita (PPP)* (US$) 37,420 (1998)
*exports* base metals and manufactures, mechanical and electrical equipment, rubber and related products, plastics, textiles and clothing. Principal market: Germany 19% (1998)
*population* 426,000 (1999 est)
*language* French, German, local Letzeburgesch (all official)
*religion* Roman Catholic
*life expectancy* 73 (men); 80 (women) (1995–2000)
*Chronology*
*963* Luxembourg became autonomous within Holy Roman Empire under Siegfried, Count of Ardennes.
*1060* Conrad, descendent of Siegfried, took the title Count of Luxembourg.
*1354* Emperor Charles IV promoted Luxembourg to status of duchy.
*1441* Luxembourg ceded to dukes of Burgundy.
*1482* Luxembourg came under Habsburg control.
*1555* Luxembourg became part of Spanish Netherlands on division of Habsburg domains.
*1684–97* Much of Luxembourg occupied by France.

**1713** Treaty of Utrecht transferred Spanish Netherlands to Austria.
**1797** Conquered by revolutionary France.
**1815** Congress of Vienna made Luxembourg a grand duchy, under King William of the Netherlands.
**1830** Most of Luxembourg supported Belgian revolt against the Netherlands.
**1839** Western part of Luxembourg assigned to Belgium.
**1842** Luxembourg entered the Zollverein (German customs union).
**1867** Treaty of London confirmed independence and neutrality of Luxembourg to allay French fears about possible inclusion in a unified Germany.
**1870s** Development of iron and steel industry.
**1890** Link with Dutch crown ended on accession of Queen Wilhelmina, since Luxembourg's law of succession did not permit a woman to rule; Adolphe of Nassau-Weilburg became grand duke.
**1912** Revised law of succession allowed Marie-Adelaide to become grand duchess.
**1914–18** Occupied by Germany.
**1919** Plebiscite overwhelmingly favoured continued independence; Marie-Adelaide abdicated after allegations of collaboration with Germany; succeeded by Grand Duchess Charlotte.
**1921** Entered into close economic links with Belgium.
**1940** Invaded by Germany.
**1942–44** Annexed by Germany.
**1948** Luxembourg formed Benelux customs union with Belgium and the Netherlands.
**1949** Luxembourg became founding member of North Atlantic Treaty Organization (NATO).
**1958** Luxembourg became founding member of European Economic Community (EEC).
**1964** Grand Duchess Charlotte abdicated in favour of her son Jean.
**1974–79** The Christian Social Party was outside of the governing coalition for the first time since 1919.
**1994** Former premier Jacques Santer became the president of the European Commission (EC).
**1995** Jean-Claude Juncker became prime minister.

**Luxembourg** capital of the country of Luxembourg, on the Alzette and Pétrusse rivers, south of the Ardennes uplands; population (1997) 78,300. The 16th-century Grand Ducal Palace, European Court of Justice, and European Parliament secretariat are situated here, but plenary sessions of the parliament are now held only in Strasbourg, France. Industries include steel, chemicals, textiles, and processed food.

**Luxembourg** province of southeastern Belgium
**area** 4,400 sq km/1,698 sq mi
**capital** Arlon
**towns and cities** Bastogne, St Hubert, Bouillon
**industries** dairy products, iron and steel, tobacco
**physical** situated in the southeastern Ardennes and widely forested; rivers Ourthe, Semois, and Lesse
**population** (1995) 240,300

**history** formerly part of the Grand Duchy of Luxembourg, it became a Belgian province 1831.

**Luxemburg, Rosa** (1870–1919) Polish-born German communist. She helped found the Polish Social Democratic Party in the 1890s, the forerunner of the Polish Communist Party. She was a leader of the left wing of the German Social Democratic Party from 1898 where she collaborated with Karl Liebknecht in founding the Spartacus League in 1918 (see ◊Spartacist). Imprisoned during World War I for opposing the continuation of the war, she was also critical of the decision to launch an uprising in November 1918. She disagreed with leading Polish left-wing ideologists on the issue of Polish nationalism. Luxemburg was also the author of a Marxist critique of capitalist imperialism, *The Accumulation of Capital*. She was murdered, together with Liebknecht, in January 1919 by the Frei Corps who put down the Spartacist uprising.

**Luxor** Arabic *al-Uqsur,* city in Egypt on the east bank of the River Nile; population (1992) 146,000. The ancient city of Thebes is on the west bank, with the temple of Luxor built by Amenhotep III (*c.* 1411–1375 BC) and the tombs of the pharaohs in the Valley of the Kings.

**Luzon** largest island of the Philippines; area 108,130 sq km/41,750 sq mi; capital Quezon City; population (1970) 18,001,270. The chief city is Manila, capital of the Philippines. Industries include rice, timber, and minerals. It has US military bases.

**Lviv** Russian *Lvov;* Polish *Lwów;* German *Lemberg,* capital and industrial city of Lviv region (oblast), western Ukraine, 450 km/280 mi southwest of Kiev; population (1990) 798,000. Lviv is an important manufacturing centre and transport junction. There are chemical, metallurgical, and engineering industries in the city; manufactured goods include motor vehicles, agricultural equipment, textiles, and electronics. Lviv was the principal city of the historical region known as Galicia. The Ivan Franko University was founded in 1661. The city was the centre of the revival of Ukrainian nationalism and the resurgence of the Ukrainian Catholic Church in the 1980s.

**LW** abbreviation for *long wave,* a radio wave with a wavelength of over 1,000 m/3,300 ft; one of the main wavebands into which radio frequency transmissions are divided.

**lycanthropy** (Greek *lukos* 'wolf' + *anthropos* 'human') in folk belief, the transformation of a human being into a wolf (◊werewolf); or, in psychology, a delusion involving this belief.

**Lyceum** ancient Athenian gymnasium and garden, with covered walks, where the philosopher Aristotle taught. It was southeast of the city and named after the nearby temple of Apollo Lyceus.

**lychee** alternative spelling of ◊litchi, a fruit-bearing tree.

**Lycurgus** Spartan lawgiver. He was believed to have been a member of the royal house of the ancient Greek city-state of Sparta, who, while acting as regent, gave the Spartans their constitution and system of education. Many modern scholars believe him to be at least partly legendary.

**Lydia** ancient kingdom in Anatolia (7th–6th centuries BC), with its capital at Sardis. The Lydians were the first Western people to use standard coinage. Their last king, Croesus, was defeated by the Persians in 546 BC.

**Lyell, Charles** (1797–1875) Scottish geologist. In his *Principles of Geology* (1830–33), he opposed the French anatomist Georges Cuvier's theory that the features of the Earth were formed by a series of catastrophes, and expounded the Scottish geologist James ◊Hutton's view, known as uniformitarianism, that past events were brought about by the same processes that occur today – a view that influenced Charles ◊Darwin's theory of ◊evolution. Knighted 1848.

**lymph** fluid found in the lymphatic system of vertebrates.

**lymph nodes** small masses of lymphatic tissue in the body that occur at various points along the major lymphatic vessels. Tonsils and adenoids are large lymph nodes. As the lymph passes through them it is filtered, and bacteria and other micro-organisms are engulfed by cells known as macrophages.

**lymphocyte** type of white blood cell with a large nucleus, produced in the bone marrow. Most occur in the ◊lymph and blood, and around sites of infection. *B lymphocytes* or

B cells are responsible for producing ◊antibodies. *T lymphocytes* or T cells have several roles in the mechanism of ◊immunity.

**lymphokines** chemical messengers produced by lymphocytes that carry messages between the cells of the immune system (see ◊immunity). Examples include interferon, which initiates defensive reactions to viruses, and the interleukins, which activate specific immune cells.

**Lynch, Jack (John Mary)** (1917– ) Irish politician, Taoiseach (prime minister) 1966–73 and 1977–79, and leader of Fianna Fáil 1966–79.

**lynx** wild cat found in rocky and forested regions of North America and Europe. About 1 m/3 ft in length, it has a short tail and tufted ears, and the long, silky fur is reddish brown or grey with dark spots. The North American *bobcat* or *bay lynx* (*Felix rufus*) looks similar but is smaller. Some zoologists place the lynx, the bobcat, and the caracal in a separate genus, *Lynx*. (Species *Felis lynx*, family Felidae.)

**Lyon** English *Lyons*, industrial city and administrative centre of Rhône *département* in the Rhône-Alpes region, part of which lies on the long tongue of land between the Rivers Rhône and Saône, 275 km/170 mi north of Marseille; population (1990) 422,400, conurbation 1,221,000. Lyon is France's third-largest city and most important educational centre after Paris; its main industries are textiles, chemicals, machinery, and printing. Formerly a chief

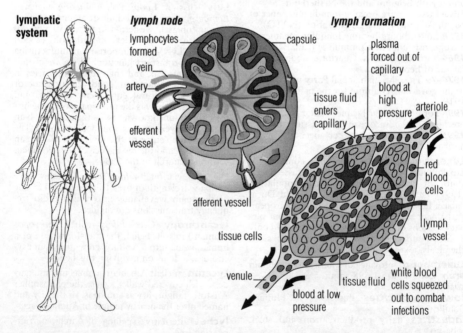

**lymphatic system**

**lymph node**
lymphocytes formed
vein
artery
efferent vessel
capsule
afferent vessel
tissue cells
venule

**lymph formation**
plasma forced out of capillary
blood at high pressure
arteriole
tissue fluid enters capillary
red blood cells
lymph vessel
blood at low pressure
tissue fluid
white blood cells squeezed out to combat infections

*lymph* Lymph is the fluid that carries nutrients and white blood cells to the tissues. Lymph enters the tissue from the capillaries (right) and is drained from the tissues by lymph vessels. The lymph vessels form a network (left) called the lymphatic system. At various points in the lymphatic system, lymph nodes (centre) filter and clean the lymph.

fortress of Franc, it was the ancient *Lugdunum,* taken by the Romans in 43 BC.

**lyre** stringed musical instrument of great antiquity. It consists of a hollow soundbox with two curved arms extended upwards to a crosspiece to which four to ten strings are attached. It is played with a plectrum or the fingers. It originated in Asia, and was widespread in ancient Greece and Egypt.

**lyrebird** either of two species of large birds found in southeastern Australia. They have very stout beaks and short, rounded wings; the tail has 16 feathers, and in the males the exterior pair of feathers are curved in the shape of a lyre; the tail of the female is long, broad, and normal in shape. Lyrebirds nest on the ground, and feed on insects, worms, and snails. (Genus *Menura,* family Menuridae, order Passeriformes.)

**Lysander** (died 395 BC) Spartan politician and admiral. He brought the ◊Peloponnesian War between Athens and Sparta to a successful conclusion by capturing the Athenian fleet at Aegospotami in 405 BC, and by starving Athens into surrender in the following year. He set up puppet governments in Athens and its former allies, and tried to secure for himself the Spartan kingship, but was killed in battle with the Thebans 395 BC.

**lysis** in biology, any process that destroys a cell by rupturing its membrane or cell wall (see ◊lysosome).

**lysosome** membrane-enclosed structure, or organelle, inside a ◊cell, principally found in animal cells. Lysosomes contain enzymes that can break down proteins and other biological substances. They play a part in digestion, and in the white blood cells known as phagocytes the lysosome enzymes attack ingested bacteria.

**m** symbol for ◊*metre*.

**M** Roman numeral for *1,000*.

**MA** abbreviation for the degree of *Master of Arts;* the state of ◊*Massachusetts.*

**Maastricht Treaty** treaty on European union which took effect on 1 November 1993, from which date the European Community (EC) became known as the ◊European Union (EU). Issues covered by the treaty included the EU's decision-making process and the establishment of closer links on foreign and military policy. A European Charter of Social Rights was approved by all member states except the UK, until a Labour government came to power in 1997.

**Mabuse, Jan** adopted name of *Jan Gossaert* (*c.* 1478–*c.* 1533) Flemish painter. His visit to Italy in 1508 started a new vogue in Flanders for Italianate ornament and Classical detail in painting, including sculptural nude figures, as in his *Neptune and Amphitrite* (*c.* 1516, Staatliche Museen, Berlin).

**macadamia** edible nut of a group of trees native to Australia, especially *M. ternifolia*), and cultivated in Hawaii, South Africa, Zimbabwe, and Malawi. The nuts are slow-growing; they are harvested when they drop. (Genus *Macadamia,* family Proteaceae.)

**McAleese, Mary Patricia** (1951– ) Irish lawyer and academic, president from 1997. When President Mary Robinson announced her resignation, McAleese was nominated by the ruling Fianna Fáil and Progressive Democrats as their candidate in preference to former prime minister Albert Reynolds. She asserted her opposition to violence and secured a clear victory over the Fine Gael nominated candidate, Mary Bannotti.

**macaque** any of a group of medium-sized Old World monkeys. Various species live in forests from the Far East to North Africa. The ◊rhesus monkey and the ◊Barbary ape belong to this group. (Genus *Macaca.*)

**MacArthur, Douglas** (1880–1964) US general in World War II, commander of US forces in the Far East and, from March 1942, of the Allied forces in the southwestern Pacific. After the surrender of Japan he commanded the Allied occupation forces there. During 1950 he commanded the UN forces in Korea, but in April 1951, after expressing views contrary to US and UN policy, he was relieved of all his commands by President Truman.

**Macau** Portuguese possession on the south coast of China, about 65 km/40 mi west of Hong Kong, from which it is separated by the estuary of the Pearl River; it consists of a peninsula and the islands of Taipa and Colôane
*area* 17 sq km/7 sq mi
*capital* Macau, on the peninsula
*features* the peninsula is linked to Taipa by a bridge and to Colôane by a causeway, both 2 km/1 mi long
*currency* pataca
*population* (1994 est) 395,300
*language* Cantonese; Portuguese (official)
*religion* Buddhist, with 6% Catholic minority.

**Macaulay, Thomas Babington** 1st Baron Macaulay (1800–1859) British historian, essayist, poet, and politician, secretary of war 1839–41. His *History of England* in five volumes (1849–61) celebrates the Glorious Revolution of 1688 as the crowning achievement of the Whig party. Baron 1857.

**macaw** any of a group of large, brilliantly coloured, long-tailed tropical American ◊parrots, such as the blue and yellow macaw *Ara ararauna.* They can be recognized by the massive beak, about half the size of the head, and by the extremely long tail. (Genera *Ara, Aratinga,* and *Anodorhynchus.*)

**Macbeth** (*c.* 1005–1057) King of Scotland from 1040. The son of Findlaech, hereditary ruler of Moray and Ross, he was commander of the forces of Duncan I, King of Scotland, whom he killed in battle in 1040. His reign was prosperous until Duncan's son Malcolm III led an invasion and killed him at Lumphanan in Aberdeenshire.

**Macedonia** Former Yugoslav Republic of (official international name); Republic of Macedon (official internal name)
*national name Republika Makedonija*

*area* 25,700 sq km/9,922 sq mi
*capital* Skopje
*major towns/cities* Bitolj, Prilep, Kumanovo, Tetovo
*physical features* mountainous; rivers: Struma, Vardar; lakes: Ohrid, Prespa, Scutari; partly Mediterranean climate with hot summers
*head of state* (acting) Stojan Andov from 1995
*head of government* Ljubco Georgievski from 1998
*political system* emergent democracy
*political parties* Socialist Party (SP); Social Democratic Alliance of Macedonia (SM) bloc, left of centre; Party for Democratic Prosperity (PDP), ethnic Albanian, left of centre; Internal Macedonian Revolutionary Organization–Democratic Party for Macedonian National Unity (VMRO–DPMNE), radical nationalist; Democratic Party of Macedonia (DPM), nationalist, free market
*currency* Macedonian denar
*GNP per capita (PPP)* (US$) 3,660 (1998)
*exports* manufactured goods, machinery and transport equipment, miscellaneous manufactured articles, sugar beet, vegetables, cheese, lamb, tobacco. Principal market: Germany 21.4% (1998)
*population* 2,011,000 (1999 est)
*language* Macedonian, closely allied to Bulgarian and written in Cyrillic
*religion* Christian, mainly Orthodox; Muslim 2.5%
*life expectancy* 71 (men); 75 (women) (1995–2000)
*Chronology*
*4th century BC* Part of ancient great kingdom of Macedonia, which included northern Greece and southwest Bulgaria and, under Alexander the Great, conquered a vast empire; Thessaloniki founded.
*146 BC* Macedonia became a province of the Roman Empire.
*395 AD* On the division of the Roman Empire, came under the control of Byzantine Empire, with its capital at Constantinople.
*6th century* Settled by Slavs, who later converted to Christianity.
*9th–14th centuries* Under successive rule by Bulgars, Byzantium, and Serbia.
*1371* Became part of Islamic Ottoman Empire.
*late 19th century* The 'Internal Macedonian Revolutionary Organization', through terrorism, sought to provoke Great Power intervention against Turks.
*1912–13* After First Balkan War, partitioned between Bulgaria, Greece, and the area that constitutes the current republic of Serbia.
*1918* Serbian part included in what was to become Yugoslavia; Serbian imposed as official language.
*1941–44* Occupied by Bulgaria.
*1945* Created a republic within Yugoslav Socialist Federation.
*1967* The Orthodox Macedonian archbishopric of Skopje, forcibly abolished 200 years earlier by the Turks, was restored.
*1980* The rise of nationalism was seen after the death of Yugoslav leader Tito.

*1990* Multiparty elections produced an inconclusive result.
*1991* Kiro Gligorov, a pragmatic former communist, became president. A referendum supported independence.
*1992* Independence was declared, and accepted by Serbia/Yugoslavia, but international recognition was withheld because of Greece's objections to the name.
*1993* Sovereignty was recognized by the UK and Albania; United Nations membership was won under the provisional name of the Former Yugoslav Republic of Macedonia; Greece blocked full European Union (EU) recognition.
*1994* Independence was recognized by the USA; a trade embargo was imposed by Greece, causing severe economic damage.
*1995* Independence was recognized by Greece and the trade embargo lifted. President Gligorov survived an assassination attempt.
*1997* Plans to reduce the strength of the UN Preventive Deployment Force (UNPREDEP) were abandoned. The government announced compensation for the public's losses in failed investment schemes.
*1998* The UN extended the mandate of UNPREDEP. A general election resulted in a right-wing coalition, with Ljubco Georgievski, the VRMO-DPMNE leader, as prime minister. The ethnic Albanian National Democratic Party (NDP) also joined the governing coalition. A 1,700-strong NATO force was deployed in Macedonia to safeguard the 2,000 ceasefire verification monitors in neighbouring Kosovo, Yugoslavia.

**Madagascar** Democratic Republic of
*national name* Repoblika Demokratika n`i Madagaskar

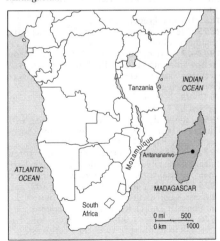

*area* 587,041 sq km/226,656 sq mi
*capital* Antananarivo
*major towns/cities* Antsirabe, Mahajanga, Fianarantsoa, Toamasina, Ambatondrazaka
*major ports* Toamasina, Antsiranana, Toliary, Mahajanga
*physical features* temperate central highlands;

humid valleys and tropical coastal plains; arid in south
**head of state** Didier Ratsiraka from 1996
**head of government** René Tantely Gabrio Andrianarivo from 1998
**political system** emergent democracy
**political parties** Vanguard for Economic and Social Recovery (ARES, also known as ARENA), left of centre; One Should Not Be Judged By One's Works (AVI), left of centre; Rally for Socialism and Democracy (RPSD), left of centre
**currency** Malagasy franc
**GNP per capita (PPP)** (US$) 900 (1998)
**exports** coffee, shrimps, cloves, vanilla, petroleum products, chromium, cotton fabrics. Principal market: France 39.5% (1998)
**population** 15,496,000 (1999 est)
**language** Malagasy (official); French, English
**religion** traditional beliefs, Roman Catholic, Protestant
**life expectancy** 56 (men); 59 (women) (1995–2000)
**Chronology**
**c. 6th–10th centuries AD** Settled by migrant Indonesians.
**1500** First visited by European navigators.
**17th century** Development of Merina and Sakalava kingdoms in the central highlands and west coast.
**1642–74** France established a coastal settlement at Fort-Dauphin, which they abandoned after a massacre by local inhabitants.
**late 18th–early 19th century** Merinas, united by their ruler Andrianampoinimerina, became dominant kingdom; court converted to Christianity.
**1861** Ban on Christianity (imposed in 1828) and entry of Europeans lifted by Merina king, Radama II.
**1885** Became French protectorate.
**1895** Merina army defeated by French and became a colony; slavery abolished.
**1942–43** British troops invaded to overthrow French administration allied to the pro-Nazi Germany Vichy regime and install anti-Nazi Free French government.
**1947–48** Nationalist uprising brutally suppressed by French.
**1960** Independence achieved from France, with Philibert Tsiranana, the leader of the Social Democratic Party (PSD), as president.
**1972** Merina-dominated army overthrew Tsiranana's government, dominated by the cotier (coastal tribes), as economy deteriorated.
**1975** Martial law imposed; new one-party state Marxist constitution adopted, with Lt-Commander Didier Ratsiraka as president.
**1978** More than 1,000 people were killed in race riots in Majunga city in the northwest.
**1980** Ratsiraka abandoned the Marxist experiment, which had involved nationalization and the severing of ties with France.
**1983** Ratsiraka was re-elected, despite strong opposition from the radical socialist movement under Monja Jaona.
**1990** Political opposition was legalized and 36 new parties were created.
**1991** Antigovernment demonstrations were

held. Ratsiraka formed a new unity government, which included opposition members.
**1992** Constitutional reform was approved by a referendum.
**1993** Albert Zafy was elected president and a pro-Zafy left-of-centre coalition won the majority in multiparty assembly elections.
**1995** A referendum backed the appointment of a prime minister by the president, rather than the assembly.
**1996** Norbert Ratsirahonana became prime minister and then interim president upon the parliament's removal of Zafy. Didier Ratsiraka was elected president.
**1997** Pascal Rakotomavo was appointed prime minister.
**1998** ARES largest party following election. Tantely Andrianarivo appointed prime minister.

**MacCarthy, Joe (Joseph Raymond)** (1908–1957) US right-wing Republican politician. His unsubstantiated claim in 1950 that the State Department had been infiltrated by communists started a wave of anticommunist hysteria, wild accusations, and blacklists, which continued until he was discredited in 1954. He was censured by the Senate for misconduct.

**McCartney, (James) Paul** (1942– ) British rock singer, songwriter, and bass guitarist. He was a member of the ◊Beatles, and leader of the pop group Wings 1971–81, in which his wife, Linda, also performed. His subsequent albums include *Off the Ground* (1993) and *Flaming Pie* (1997). Solo hits have included collaborations with Michael Jackson and Elvis Costello. Together with composer Carl Davis, McCartney wrote the *Liverpool Oratorio* (1991), his first work of classical music. Another classical composition, *Standing Stones*, achieved considerable success in the USA in the same year. He was knighted in 1997 and inducted into the US Rock and Roll Hall of Fame in March 1999.

**Macdonald, Flora** (1722–1790) Scottish heroine. She rescued Prince Charles Edward Stuart, the Young Pretender, after his defeat at Culloden in 1746. Disguising him as her maid, she escorted him from her home on South Uist in the Hebrides, to France. She was arrested and imprisoned in the Tower of London, but released in 1747.

**MacDonald, (James) Ramsay** (1866–1937) British politician, first Labour prime minister January–October 1924 and 1929–31, born in Morayshire, Scotland. He left the party to form a coalition government in 1931, which was increasingly dominated by Conservatives, until he was replaced by Stanley Baldwin in 1935.

**Macedonia** ancient region of Greece, forming parts of modern Greece, Bulgaria, and the Former Yugoslav Republic of Macedonia. Macedonia gained control of Greece after Philip II's victory at Chaeronea 338 BC. His son, Alexander the Great, conquered a vast empire. Macedonia became a Roman province 146 BC.

**Macedonia** Greek *Makedhonia*, mountainous region of northern Greece, part of the ancient country of Macedonia which was divided between Serbia, Bulgaria, and Greece after the

Balkan Wars of 1912–13. Greek Macedonia is bounded west and north by Albania and the Former Yugoslav Republic of Macedonia; area 34,177 sq km/13,200 sq mi; population (1991) 2,263,000. There are two regions, Macedonia Central, and Macedonia East and Thrace. The chief city is Thessaloniki. The Former Yugoslav Republic of Macedonia has refused to give up claims to the present Greek province of Macedonia, and has placed the star of Macedonia, symbol of the ancient Greek Kings of Macedonia, on its flag. Fertile valleys produce grain, olives, grapes, tobacco, and livestock. Mount Olympus rises to 2,918 m/9,570 ft on the border with Thessaly.

**Macedonian** people of Macedonian culture from the Former Yugoslav Republic of Macedonia and the surrounding area, especially Greece, Albania, and Bulgaria. Macedonian, a Slavic language belonging to the Indo-European family, has 1–1.5 million speakers. The Macedonians are predominantly members of the Greek Orthodox Church and write with a Cyrillic script. They are known for their folk arts.

**McGwire, Mark** (1963– ) US baseball player, a first baseman for the St Louis Cardinals who in 1998 set a new major league record of 70 home runs in a season, breaking the previous record of 61 set by Roger Maris of the New York Yankees in 1961. Also in 1998 he became the first player in major league history to hit 50 home runs or more in three consecutive seasons. In August 1999 he hit the 500th home run of his major league career. Only 15 players in major league history have hit more home runs. In September 1999 he became the first player in major league history to hit 50 home runs or more in four consecutive seasons.

**Machiavelli, Niccolò** (1469–1527) Italian politician and author. His name is synonymous with cunning and cynical statecraft. In his chief political writings, *Il principe/The Prince* (1513) and *Discorsi/Discourses* (1513–21), he discussed ways in which rulers can advance the interests of their states (and themselves) through an often amoral and opportunistic manipulation of other people.

**machine** device that allows a small force (the effort) to overcome a larger one (the load). There are three basic machines: the inclined plane (ramp), the lever, and the wheel and axle. All other machines are combinations of these three basic types. Simple machines derived from the inclined plane include the wedge, the gear, and the screw; the spanner is derived from the lever; the pulley from the wheel.

**Mach number** ratio of the speed of a body to the speed of sound in the undisturbed medium through which the body travels. Mach 1 is reached when a body (such as an aircraft) has a velocity greater than that of sound ('passes the sound barrier'), namely 331 m/1,087 ft per second at sea level. It is named after Austrian physicist Ernst Mach (1838–1916).

**Machu Picchu** ruined Inca city in the Peruvian Andes, northwest of Cuzco. This settlement and stronghold stands at the top of 300-m/1,000-ft-high cliffs above the Urabamba River and covers an area of 13 sq km/5 sq mi. Built in about AD 1500, the city's remote location saved it from being found and destroyed by the Spanish conquistadors, and the remains of its houses and temples are well preserved. Machu Picchu was discovered in 1911 by the US archaeologist Hiram L Bingham.

**McKellen, Ian Murray** (1939– ) English actor. Acclaimed as the leading Shakespearean player of his generation, his stage roles include Richard II (1968), Macbeth (1977), Max in Martin Sherman's *Bent* (1979), Platonov in Chekhov's *Wild Honey* (1986), Iago in *Othello* (1989), and Richard III (1990); he has also appeared in *Uncle Vanya* (1992) and *Enemy of the People* (1998). His films include *Priest of Love* (1982), *Plenty* (1985), *Scandal* (1990), *The Ballad of Little Jo* (1991), and *Last Action Hero* (1993). He was knighted in 1991.

**Mackenzie River** river in the Northwest Territories, northwestern Canada; about 1,705 km/1,060 mi long (from the Great Slave Lake to the Beaufort Sea). It originates as the Athabasca River in British Columbia and flows over 966 km/600 mi to Lake Athabasca; it then flows northwest from the Great Slave Lake until it enters the Beaufort Sea (part of the Arctic Ocean). The Mackenzie River is navigable from June to October, when it eventually freezes over. It is the main channel of the Finlay-Peace-Mackenzie system (4,241 km/2,635 mi long), the second longest system in North America.

**mackerel** any of various fishes of the mackerel family, especially the *common mackerel* (*Scomber scombrus*) found in the North Atlantic and Mediterranean. It weighs about 0.7 kg/1.5 lb, and is blue with irregular black bands down its sides, the sides and under surface having a metallic sheen. Like all mackerels, it has a deeply forked tail, and a sleek, streamlined body form. (Family Scombroidia.)

**McKinley, William** (1843–1901) 25th president of the USA 1897–1901, a Republican. His term as president was marked by the USA's adoption of an imperialist foreign policy, as exemplified by the Spanish-American War 1898 and the annexation of the Philippines. He sat in Congress 1876–91, apart from one term.

**McKinley, Mount** or *Denali*, highest peak in North America, situated in the ◊Rocky Mountains, Alaska; height 6,194 m/20,320 ft. It was named after US president William McKinley.

**Mackintosh, Charles Rennie** (1868–1928) Scottish architect, designer, and painter, whose highly original work represents a dramatic break with the late Victorian style. He worked initially in the ◊Art Nouveau idiom but later developed a unique style, both rational and expressive, that is more angular and stylized than the flowing, full-blown Art Nouveau style.

**Macmillan, (Maurice) Harold** 1st Earl of Stockton (1894–1986) British Conservative politician, prime minister 1957–63; foreign secretary 1955 and chancellor of the Exchequer 1955–57. In 1963 he attempted to negotiate British entry into the European Economic Community (EEC), but was blocked by the French president Charles de Gaulle. Much of his career as prime minister was spent defending the UK's retention of a nuclear weapon, and he was responsible for the purchase of US Polaris missiles in 1962.

**macrophage** type of ◊white blood cell, or leucocyte, found in all vertebrate animals. Macrophages specialize in the removal of bacteria and other micro-organisms, or of cell debris after injury. Like phagocytes, they engulf foreign matter, but they are larger than phagocytes and have a longer life span. They are found throughout the body, but mainly in the lymph and connective tissues, and especially the lungs, where they ingest dust, fibres, and other inhaled particles.

**mad cow disease** common name for ◊bovine spongiform encephalopathy, an incurable brain condition in cattle.

**madder** any of a group of plants bearing small funnel-shaped flowers, especially the perennial vine *R. tinctorum* which grows in Europe and Asia, the red root of which yields a red dye called alizarin (now made synthetically from coal tar). (Genus *Rubia,* family Rubiaceae.)

**Madeira Islands** group of islands forming an autonomous region of Portugal, off the northwest coast of Africa, about 420 km/260 mi north of the Canary Islands. Madeira, the largest, and Porto Santo are the only inhabited islands. The Desertas and Selvagens are uninhabited islets. Their mild climate makes them a popular, year-round tourist destination.
*area* 796 sq km/308 sq mi
*capital* Funchal, on Madeira
*physical* Pico Ruivo, on Madeira, is the highest mountain at 1,861 m/6,106 ft
*industries* Madeira (a fortified wine), sugar cane, fruit, fish, handicrafts, tourism
*population* (1994 est) 256,000
*history* Portuguese from the 15th century; occupied by Britain in 1801 and 1807–14. In 1980 Madeira gained partial autonomy but remains a Portuguese overseas territory.

**Madhya Pradesh** state of central India; the largest of the Indian states
*area* 443,400 sq km/171,196 sq mi
*capital* ◊Bhopal
*towns and cities* Indore, Jabalpur, Gwalior, Durg-Bhilainagar, Raipur, Ujjain
*physical* land-locked, mainly upland state; includes northern part of the Deccan plateau, drained by the rivers Narmada and Mahanadi, as well as the Betwa, Chambal, Tapti and Son; Vindhya and Satpura mountain ranges (rising to 600 m/2,000 ft), heavily forested particularly in the east
*industries* textiles, engineering, iron ore, steel (at Bhilai complex), coal, bauxite, manganese, paper, aluminium, limestone, diamonds, cement; hydroelectric power from the Chambal, ◊Narmada and Mahanadi rivers
*agriculture* rice in the wetter regions of the east, cotton, millet, wheat, oilseed, sugar, groundnuts, soya
*population* (1994 est) 71,950,000; about 20% are from tribes (Gonds, Bhils, Baigas, Korkus, Kols, Kamars and Marias)
*language* predominantly Hindi; Marathi
*history* formed in 1950 from the former British province of Central Provinces and Berar and the princely states of Makrai and Chattisgarh; lost some southwestern districts in 1956, including ◊Nagpur, and absorbed Bhopal, Madhya Bharat, and Vindhya Pradesh. In 1984 some 2,600 people died in ◊Bhopal from an escape of poisonous gas.

**Madonna** stage name of Madonna Louise Veronica Ciccone (1958–  ) US pop singer and actress who is arguably the most successful female artist in popular music. Her first hit was 'Like a Virgin' 1984; others include 'Material Girl' 1985 and 'Like a Prayer' 1989. Her films include *Desperately Seeking Susan* 1985, *Dick Tracy* 1990, the documentary *In Bed with Madonna* 1991, and *A League of Their Own* 1992.

**Madonna** Italian name for the Virgin ◊Mary, meaning 'my lady'.

**Madras** former name, to 1996, of ◊Chennai, an industrial port and capital of the state of Tamil Nadu, India.

**Madras** former name of ◊Tamil Nadu, a state of India.

**Madrid** autonomous community of central Spain; area 8,000 sq km/3,088 sq mi; population (1991) 4,845,900. Bounded by the Sierra de Guadarrama mountains in the northwest, and by the River Tagus in the southeast, it is arid plateau country. It is crossed by several rivers, including the Jarama, a tributary of the Tagus. Products include fruit and vegetables, grown in the south; timber from the forests in the northeast, and granite and gypsum from quarries in the mountains. The Escorial palace lies in the northwest; Aranjuez in the south a 15th-century royal palace and luxurious gardens. The capital is ◊Madrid.

**Madrid** city and capital of Spain and of ◊Madrid autonomous community, on the Manzanares River; population (1991) 2,909,800. Built on an elevated plateau in the centre of the country, at 655 m/2,183 ft it is the highest capital in Europe and has excesses of heat and cold. Industries include the production of food, electronics, pharmaceuticals, leather, chemicals, furniture, tobacco, and paper, and there is engineering and publishing.
*features* The Real Academia de Bellas Artes (1752); the Prado museum (1785); the royal palace (1764), built for Philip V; the 15th-century Retiro Park; the Plaza Mayor (1617–20); the Puerta de Alcalá arch; and the basilica of San Francisco el Grande (1761–84)
*history* Madrid began as the Moorish city of Magerit. It was captured in 1083 by King Alfonso VI of Castile. It remained a small provincial town until Philip II made it his capital in 1561 because of its position at the centre

of the Iberian peninsula; it became the national capital in 1607. In 1808 there was an uprising here against Napoleon's army of occupation. Madrid was the centre of opposition to Franco during the Spanish Civil War, and was besieged by the Nationalists 1936–39.

**maenad** in Greek mythology, one of the women participants in the orgiastic rites of ◊Dionysus; maenads were also known as *Bacchae.*

**Mafia** (Italian 'swank') secret society reputed to control organized crime such as gambling, loansharking, drug traffic, prostitution, and protection; connected with the Camorra of Naples. It originated in Sicily in the late Middle Ages and now operates chiefly there and in countries to which Italians have emigrated, such as the USA and Australia. During the early 1990s many centre and right-wing Italian politicians, such as the former Christian Democrat prime minister Giulio Andreotti, became discredited when it emerged that they had had dealings with the Mafia.

**mafic rock** plutonic rock composed chiefly of dark-coloured minerals containing abundant magnesium and iron, such as olivine and pyroxene. It is derived from *magnesium* and *ferric* (iron). The term *mafic* also applies to dark-coloured minerals rich in iron and magnesium as a group.

**magazine** publication brought out periodically, typically containing articles, essays, short stories, reviews, and illustrations. It is thought that the first magazine was *Le Journal des savants,* published in France in 1665. The first magazine in the UK was a penny weekly, the *Athenian Gazette,* better known later as the *Athenian Mercury* (1690–97). This was produced by a London publisher, John Dunton, to resolve 'all the most Nice and Curious Questions'. The US *Reader's Digest,* first published in 1922, with editions in many different countries and languages, was the world's best-selling magazine until overtaken by a Soviet journal in the mid-1980s.

**Magdeburg** industrial city and capital of ◊Saxony-Anhalt, Germany, on the River Elbe; population (1995) 263,000. Products include chemicals, precision instruments, paper, textiles, and machinery). A former capital of Saxony, Magdeburg became capital of Saxony-Anhalt on German reunification in 1990. In 1938 the city was linked by canal with the Rhine and Ruhr rivers.

**Magellan, Ferdinand** (*c.* 1480–1521) Portuguese navigator. In 1519 he set sail in the *Victoria* from Seville with the intention of reaching the East Indies by a westerly route. He sailed through the *Strait of Magellan* at the tip of South America, crossed an ocean he named the Pacific, and in 1521 reached the Philippines, where he was killed in a battle with the islanders. His companions returned to Seville in 1522, completing the voyage under del Cano.

**Magellanic Clouds** in astronomy, the two galaxies nearest to our own galaxy. They are irregularly shaped, and appear as detached parts of the ◊Milky Way, in the southern constellations Dorado, Tucana, and Mensa.

**maggot** soft, plump, limbless ◊larva of flies, a typical example being the larva of the blowfly which is deposited as an egg on flesh.

**magi** (singular *magus*) priests of the Zoroastrian religion of ancient Persia, noted for their knowledge of astrology. The term is used in the New Testament of the Latin Vulgate Bible where the Authorized Version gives 'wise men'. The magi who came to visit the infant Jesus with gifts of gold, frankincense, and myrrh (the *Adoration of the Magi)* were in later tradition described as 'the three kings' – Caspar, Melchior, and Balthazar.

**magic** art of controlling the forces of nature by supernatural means such as charms and ritual. The central ideas are that like produces like (*sympathetic magic)* and that influence carries by contagion or association; for example, by the former principle an enemy could be destroyed through an effigy, and by the latter principle through personal items such as hair or nail clippings.

**magic realism** in 20th-century literature, a fantastic situation realistically treated, as in the works of many Latin American writers such as Isabel Allende, Jorge Luis ◊Borges, and Gabriel ◊García Márquez.

**Maginot Line** French fortification system along the German frontier from Switzerland to Luxembourg built 1929–36 under the direction of the war minister, André Maginot. It consisted of semi-underground forts joined by underground passages, and was protected by antitank defences; lighter fortifications continued the line to the sea. In 1940 German forces pierced the Belgian frontier line and outflanked the Maginot Line.

**magistrate** in English law, a person who presides in a magistrates' court: either a justice of the peace (with no legal qualifications, and unpaid) or a stipendiary magistrate. Stipendiary magistrates are paid, qualified lawyers working mainly in London and major cities.

**maglev** acronym for *magnetic levitation,* high-speed surface transport using the repellent force of superconductive magnets (see ◊superconductivity) to propel and support, for example, a train above a track.

**magma** molten rock material beneath the Earth's (or any of the terrestrial planets) surface from which ◊igneous rocks are formed. ◊Lava is magma that has extruded on to the surface.

**Magna Carta** (Latin 'great charter') in English history, the charter granted by King John in 1215, traditionally seen as guaranteeing human rights against the excessive use of royal power. As a reply to the king's demands for excessive feudal dues and attacks on the privileges of the church, Archbishop Langton proposed to the barons the drawing-up of a binding document in 1213. John was forced to accept this at Runnymede (now in Surrey) on 15 June 1215.

**magnesia** common name for ◊magnesium oxide.

**magnesium** lightweight, very ductile and malleable, silver-white, metallic element, symbol Mg, atomic number 12, relative atomic mass 24.305. It is one of the ◊alkaline-earth metals, and the lightest of the commonly used metals. Magnesium silicate, carbonate, and chloride are widely distributed in nature. The metal is used in alloys and flash photography. It is a necessary trace element in the human diet, and green plants cannot grow without it since it is an essential constituent of the photosynthetic pigment ◊chlorophyll ($C_{55}H_{72}MgN_4O_5$).

**magnesium oxide** or *magnesia,* MgO white powder or colourless crystals, formed when magnesium is burned in air or oxygen; a typical basic oxide. It is used to treat acidity of the stomach, and in some industrial processes; for example, as a lining brick in furnaces, because it is very stable when heated (refractory oxide).

**magnet** any object that forms a magnetic field (displays ◊magnetism), either permanently or temporarily through induction, causing it to attract materials such as iron, cobalt, nickel, and alloys of these. It always has two magnetic poles, called north and south.

**magnetic field** region around a permanent magnet, or around a conductor carrying an electric current, in which a force acts on a moving charge or on a magnet placed in the field. The field can be represented by lines of force, which by convention link north and south poles and are parallel to the directions of a small compass needle placed on them. A magnetic field's magnitude and direction are given by the magnetic flux density, expressed in ◊teslas. See also ◊polar reversal.

**magnetic resonance imaging** (MRI), diagnostic scanning system based on the principles of nuclear magnetic resonance. MRI yields finely detailed three-dimensional images of structures within the body without exposing the patient to harmful radiation. The technique is invaluable for imaging the soft tissues of the body, in particular the brain and the spinal cord.

**magnetic storm** in meteorology, a sudden disturbance affecting the Earth's magnetic field, causing anomalies in radio transmissions and magnetic compasses. It is probably caused by ◊sunspot activity.

**magnetic tape** narrow plastic ribbon coated with an easily magnetizable material on which data can be recorded. It is used in sound recording, audiovisual systems (videotape), and computing. For mass storage on commercial mainframe computers, large reel-to-reel tapes are still used, but cartridges are becoming popular. Various types of cartridge are now standard on minis and PCs, while audio cassettes are sometimes used with home computers.

**magnetism** phenomena associated with ◊magnetic fields. Magnetic fields are produced by moving charged particles: in electromagnets, electrons flow through a coil of wire connected to a battery; in permanent magnets, spinning electrons within the atoms generate the field.

**magnification** measure of the enlargement or reduction of an object in an imaging optical system. *Linear magnification* is the ratio of the size (height) of the image to that of the object. *Angular magnification* is the ratio of the angle subtended at the observer's eye by the image to the angle subtended by the object when viewed directly.

**magnitude** in astronomy, measure of the brightness of a star or other celestial object. The larger the number denoting the magnitude, the fainter the object. Zero or first magnitude indicates some of the brightest stars. Still brighter are those of negative magnitude, such as Sirius, whose magnitude is –1.46. *Apparent magnitude* is the brightness of an object as seen from Earth; *absolute magnitude* is the brightness at a standard distance of 10 parsecs (32.6 light years).

**magnolia** any of a group of trees or shrubs belonging to the magnolia family, native to North America and East Asia, and cultivated as ornamentals. Magnolias vary in height from 60 cm/2 ft to 30 m/150 ft. The large, fragrant single flowers are white, pink, or purple. The southern magnolia (*M. grandiflora*) of the USA grows up to 24 m/80 ft tall and has white flowers 23 cm/9 in across. (Genus *Magnolia,* family Magnoliaceae.)

**magpie** any of various birds belonging to the crow family. They feed on insects, snails, young birds, and carrion, and are found in Europe, Asia, North Africa, and western North America. (Genus *Pica,* family Corvidae, order Passeriformes.)

**Magritte, René François Ghislain** (1898–1967) Belgian painter, one of the major figures in Surrealism. His work focuses on visual paradoxes and everyday objects taken out of context. Recurring motifs include bowler hats, apples, and windows, for example *Golconda* (1953; private collection), in which men in bowler hats are falling from the sky to a street below.

**Magyar** or *Hungarian,* member of the largest ethnic group in Hungary, comprising 92% of the population. Most are Roman Catholic. The Hungarian language belongs to the Uralic group.

**Maharashtra** state in west central India
*area* 307,700 sq km/118,802 sq mi
*capital* Mumbai
*towns and cities* Pune, Nagpur, Ulhasnagar, Sholapur, Nasik, Thana, Kolhapur, Aurangabad, Sangli, Amravati
*physical* divided by the heavily forested Western Ghats into the Konkan coastal plain and the Deccan plateau; the plain is subject to the southwest monsoon from June to September; the inland area receives only half the coastal rainfall; the Godavari and Krishna rivers rise in the Western Ghats and flow eastwards across the Deccan
*features* cave temples of Ajanta, containing 200 BC–7th century AD Buddhist murals and sculptures; Ellora cave temples 6th–9th century with Buddhist, Hindu, and Jain sculptures

*industries* cotton processing at Mumbai, Nagpur, Sholapur; oil refining at Bassein North; electrical goods, agricultural machinery, chemicals and plastics; manganese ore, coal, iron ore, bauxite, and copper ore; India's first nuclear power plant at Tarapur, 112 km/70 mi north of Mumbai

*agriculture* rice (on the coastal plain), cotton, millet and wheat on the Deccan, dairy farming, groundnuts, sugar, fruit

*population* (1991) 79,000,000

*language* Marathi 50%

*religion* Hindu 80%, Parsee, Jain, and Sikh minorities

*history* formed 1960 from the southern part of the former Mumbai state.

**maharishi** (Sanskrit *mahā* 'great', *rishi* 'sage') Hindu guru (teacher), or spiritual leader. The Maharishi Mahesh Yogi influenced the Beatles and other Westerners in the 1960s.

**Mahathir bin Mohamed** (1925– ) Malaysian politician, prime minister from 1981. Leader of the New United Malays' National Organization (UMNO Baru), his 'look east' economic policy, which emulated Japanese industrialization, met with considerable success, but faced its first serious challenge in 1997 when the Malaysian currency came under attack from international speculators. This forced austerity measures in 1998, including the repatriation of many foreign workers.

**Mahāyāna** (Sanskrit 'greater vehicle') one of the two major forms of ◊Buddhism, found in China, Korea, Japan, and Tibet. Veneration of bodhisattvas (those who achieve enlightenment but remain on the human plane in order to help other living beings) is a fundamental belief in Mahāyāna, as is the idea that everyone has within them the seeds of Buddhahood.

**Mahfouz, Naguib** (1911– ) Egyptian novelist and playwright. His novels, which deal with the urban working class, include the semi-autobiographical *Khan al-Kasrain/The Cairo Trilogy* 1956–57. His *Children of Gebelawi* 1959 was banned in Egypt because of its treatment of religious themes. He won the Nobel Prize for Literature 1988.

**mah-jong** or *mah-jongg* (Chinese 'sparrows'), originally an ancient Chinese card game, dating from the Song dynasty 960–1279. It is now usually played by four people with 144 small ivory tiles, divided into six suits.

**Mahler, Gustav** (1860–1911) Austrian composer and conductor. His epic symphonies express a world-weary Romanticism in visionary tableaux incorporating folk music and pastoral imagery. He composed nine large-scale symphonies, many with voices, including *Symphony No 2 'Resurrection'* (1884–86, revised 1893–96), and left a tenth unfinished. He also composed orchestral lieder (songs) including *Das Lied von der Erde/The Song of the Earth* (1909) and *Kindertotenlieder/Dead Children's Songs* (1901–04).

**Mahmud** two sultans of the Ottoman Empire:

**Mahmud I** (1696–1754) Ottoman sultan from 1730. After restoring order to the empire in Istanbul 1730, he suppressed the janissary rebellion 1731 and waged war against Persia 1731–46. He led successful wars against Austria and Russia, and concluded by the Treaty of Belgrade 1739. He was a patron of the arts and also carried out reform of the army.

**Mahmud II** (1785–1839) Ottoman sultan from 1808 who attempted to westernize the declining empire, carrying out a series of far-reaching reforms in the civil service and army. The pressure for Greek independence after 1821 led to conflict with Britain, France, and Russia, and he was forced to recognize Greek independence 1830.

**mahogany** timber from any of several trees found in the Americas and Africa. Mahogany is a tropical hardwood obtained chiefly by rainforest logging. It is a warm red colour and can be highly polished. True mahogany comes mainly from *S. mahagoni* and *S. macrophylla,* but other types come from the Spanish and Australian cedars, the Indian redwood, and other trees of the mahogany family, native to Africa and the East Indies. (True mahogany genus *Swietenia,* family Meliaceae.)

**maidenhair** any of a group of ferns, especially *A. capillus-veneris,* with delicately hanging hairlike fronds ending in small kidney-shaped spore-bearing lobes. It is widely distributed in the Americas, and is sometimes found in the British Isles. (Genus *Adiantum,* family Polypodiaceae.)

**Mailer, Norman Kingsley** (1923– ) US writer and journalist. One of the most prominent figures of post-war American literature, he gained wide attention with his first, bestselling book *The Naked and the Dead* (1948), a naturalistic war novel. His later works, which use sexual and scatological material, show his personal engagement with history, politics, and psychology. Always a pugnacious and controversial writer, his polemics on the theory and practice of violence-as-sex brought him into direct conflict with feminist Kate Millet in a series of celebrated debates during the 1970s.

**Maimonides, Moses (Moses Ben Maimon)** (1135–1204) Spanish-born Jewish rabbi and philosopher, one of the greatest Hebrew scholars. He attempted to reconcile faith and reason. His codification of Jewish law is known as the *Mishneh Torah/Torah Reviewed* 1180; he also formulated the **Thirteen Principles,** which summarize the basic beliefs of Judaism.

**Maine** northeasternmost state of the USA and the largest of the New England states. It is nicknamed the Pine Tree State. Maine was admitted to the Union in 1820 as the 23rd US state. It is bordered to the northwest by Québec, Canada, to the north and east by New Brunswick, Canada, to the east and south by the Atlantic Ocean, and to the west by New Hampshire; it is the sole US state to be contiguous with only one other US state. Maine's West Quoddy Head is the easternmost US point, the state (and region) is popularly known as 'Down East'

**population** (1995) 1,241,400
**area** 86,200 sq km/33,273 sq mi
**capital** Augusta
**towns and cities** Portland, Lewiston, Bangor
**industries and products** blueberries, dairy and market garden produce, paper, pulp, timber, footwear, leather, textiles, fish, lobster; tourism, shipbuilding.

**mainframe** large computer used for commercial data processing and other large-scale operations. Because of the general increase in computing power, the differences between the mainframe, ◊supercomputer, ◊minicomputer, and ◊microcomputer (personal computer) are becoming less marked.

**maintenance** in law, payments to support children or a spouse, under the terms of an agreement, or by a court order. In Britain, financial provision orders are made on divorce, but a court action can also be brought for maintenance without divorce proceedings. Applications for maintenance of illegitimate children are now treated in the same way as for legitimate children. Under the Child Support Act 1991 the Department of Social Security can assess suitable levels of maintenance and enforce payment.

**Maintenon, Françoise d'Aubigné**, Marquise de (1635–1719) second wife of Louis XIV of France from 1684, and widow of the writer Paul Scarron (1610–1660). She was governess to the children of Mme de Montespan by Louis, and his mistress from 1667. She secretly married the king after the death of Queen Marie Thérèse in 1683. Her political influence was considerable and, as a Catholic convert from Protestantism, her religious opinions were zealous.

**maize** North American *corn,* tall annual ◊cereal plant that produces spikes of yellow grains which are widely used as an animal feed. Grown extensively in all subtropical and warm temperate regions, its range has been extended to colder zones by hardy varieties developed in the 1960s. (*Zea mays.*)

**Major, John** (1943–  ) British Conservative politician, prime minister 1990–97. He was foreign secretary in 1989 and chancellor of the Exchequer 1989–90. As prime minister, his initially positive approach to European Community matters was hindered from 1991 by divisions within the Conservative Party. Despite continuing public dissatisfaction with the poll tax, the National Health Service, and the recession, Major was returned to power in the April 1992 general election. His subsequent handling of a series of domestic crises called into question his ability to govern the country effectively, but he won backing for his launch of a joint UK–Irish peace initiative on Northern Ireland in 1993, which led to a general ceasefire in 1994. On the domestic front, local and European election defeats and continuing divisions within the Conservative Party led to his dramatic and unexpected resignation of the party leadership in June 1995 in a desperate bid for party unity. He was narrowly re-elected to the post the following month. Criticized for weak leadership

of his divided party, he resigned as leader of the Conservative Party after a crushing defeat in the 1997 general election.

**Majorca** alternative spelling of ◊Mallorca.

**Makua** a people living to the north of the Zambezi River in Mozambique. With the Lomwe people, they make up the country's largest ethnic group. The Makua are mainly farmers, living in villages ruled by chiefs. The Makua language belongs to the Niger-Congo family, and has about 5 million speakers.

**Malabo** port and capital of Equatorial Guinea, on the north coast of the volcanic island of Bioko; population (1992) 35,000. It trades in cocoa, coffee, copra, and other agricultural products. It was founded in the 1820s by the British as *Port Clarence* (also *Clarencetown*). Under Spanish rule it was known as *Santa Isabel* (until 1973). It became the capital in 1968.

**Malacca** or *Melaka,* state of west Peninsular Malaysia; capital Malacca; area 1,700 sq km/656 sq mi; population (1993) 583,400 (about 70% Chinese). Products include rubber, tin, and wire. The town originated in the 13th century as a fishing village frequented by pirates, and later developed into a trading port. Portuguese from 1511, then Dutch from 1641, it was ceded to Britain 1824, becoming part of the Straits Settlements.

**malachite** common copper ore, basic copper carbonate, $Cu_2CO_3(OH)_2$. It is a source of green pigment and is used as an antifungal agent in fish farming, as well as being polished for use in jewellery, ornaments, and art objects.

**Málaga** industrial seaport and capital of Málaga province in Andalusia, southern Spain, situated at the mouth of the River Guadalmedina on the Mediterranean coast; population (1991) 512,100. Industries include sugar refining, distilling, brewing, and olive-oil pressing; it is also a holiday resort. Crude oil is unloaded from tankers offshore into a pipeline that transports it to Puertollano in the province of Ciudad Real.

**Malagasy** inhabitant of the island of Madagascar. The Malagasy language is divided into many dialects and has about 13 million speakers; it belongs to the Austronesian family.

**malapropism** amusing slip of the tongue, arising from the confusion of similar-sounding words; for example, 'the pineapple [pinnacle] of politeness'. The term derives from the French *mal à propos* (inappropriate); historically, it is associated with Mrs Malaprop, a character in Richard Sheridan's play *The Rivals* (1775).

**malaria** infectious parasitic disease of the tropics transmitted by mosquitoes, marked by periodic fever and an enlarged spleen. When a female mosquito of the *Anopheles* genus bites a human who has malaria, it takes in with the human blood one of four malaria protozoa of the genus *Plasmodium*. This matures within the insect and is then transferred when the mosquito bites a new victim. Malaria affects about 267

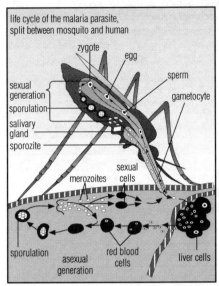

**malaria** *The life cycle of the malaria parasite is split between mosquito and human hosts. The parasites are injected into the human bloodstream by an infected Anopheles mosquito and carried to the liver. Here they attack red blood cells, and multiply asexually. The infected blood cells burst, producing spores, or merozoites, which reinfect the bloodstream. After several generations, the parasite develops into a sexual form. If the human host is bitten at this stage, the sexual form of the parasite is sucked into the mosquito's stomach. Here fertilization takes place, the zygotes formed reproduce asexually and migrate to the salivary glands ready to be injected into another human host, completing the cycle.*

million people in 103 countries, and in 1995 around 2.1 million people died of the disease. In sub-Saharan Africa alone between 1.5 and 2 million children die from malaria and its consequences each year. In November 1998, an agreement was reached to establish a multiagency programme for research and control of the disease. The agencies involved include the World Health Organization (WHO), the World Bank, the United Nations Children's Fund, and the United Nations Development Programme. The Roll Back Malaria campaign aims to halve deaths from malaria by 2010.

**Malawi** Republic of (formerly *Nyasaland*)
**national name** *Malawi*
**area** 118,484 sq km/45,735 sq mi
**capital** Lilongwe
**major towns/cities** Blantyre, Lilongwe, Mzuzu, Zomba
**physical features** landlocked narrow plateau with rolling plains; mountainous west of Lake Nyasa
**head of state and government** Bakili Muluzi from 1994
**political system** emergent democracy

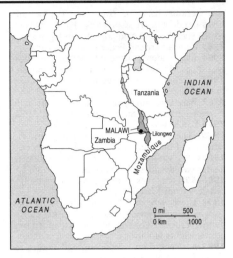

**political parties** Malawi Congress Party (MCP), multiracial, right wing; United Democratic Front (UDF), left of centre; Alliance for Democracy (AFORD), left of centre
**currency** Malawi kwacha
**GNP per capita (PPP)** (US$) 730 (1998)
**exports** tobacco, tea, sugar, cotton, groundnuts. Principal market: South Africa 12.8% (1997)
**population** 10,640,000 (1999 est)
**language** English, Chichewa (both official)
**religion** Christian 75%, Muslim 20%
**life expectancy** 39 (men); 40 (women) (1995–2000)
**Chronology**
**1st–4th centuries AD** Immigration by Bantu-speaking peoples.
**1480** Foundation of Maravi (Malawi) Confederacy, which covered much of central and southern Malawi and lasted into the 17th century.
**1530** First visited by the Portuguese.
**1600** Ngonde kingdom founded in northern Malawi by immigrants from Tanzania.
**18th century** Chikulamayembe state founded by immigrants from east of Lake Nyasa; slave trade flourished and Islam introduced in some areas.
**mid-19th century** Swahili-speaking Ngoni peoples, from South Africa, and Yao entered the region, dominating settled agriculturalists; Christianity introduced by missionaries, such as David Livingstone.
**1891** Became British protectorate of Nyasaland; cash crops, particularly coffee, introduced.
**1915** Violent uprising, led by Rev John Chilembwe, against white settlers who had moved into the fertile south, taking land from local population.
**1953** Became part of white-dominated Central African Federation, which included South Rhodesia (Zimbabwe) and North Rhodesia (Zambia).
**1958** Dr Hastings Kamuzu Banda returned to the country after working abroad for 40 years

and became head of conservative-nationalist Nyasaland/Malawi Congress Party (MCP), which spearheaded campaign for independence.
**1963** Central African Federation dissolved.
**1964** Independence achieved, within Commonwealth, as Malawi, with Banda as prime minister.
**1966** Became one-party republic, with Banda as president.
**1967** Banda became pariah of Black Africa by recognizing the apartheid regime of South Africa.
**1971** Banda was made president for life.
**1970s** There were reports of human-rights violations and the murder of Banda's opponents.
**1980s** The economy began to deteriorate after nearly two decades of expansion.
**1986–89** There was an influx of nearly a million refugees from Mozambique.
**1992** There were calls for a multiparty political system. Countrywide industrial riots caused many fatalities. Western aid was suspended over human-rights violations.
**1993** A referendum overwhelmingly supported the ending of one-party rule.
**1994** A new multiparty constitution was adopted. Bakili Muluzi, of the United Democratic Front (UDF), was elected president in the first free elections for 30 years. Assembly elections had inconclusive results.
**1995** Banda and the former minister of state John Tembo were charged with conspiring to murder four political opponents in 1983, but were cleared.

**Malawi, Lake** or *Lake Nyasa*, lake, bordered by Malawi, Tanzania, and Mozambique, formed in a section of the Great ◊Rift Valley. It is about 500 m/1,650 ft above sea level and 560 km/350 mi long, with an area of 28,749 sq km/11,100 sq mi and a depth of 700 m/2,296 ft, making it the ninth biggest lake in the world. It is intermittently drained to the south by the River Shire into the Zambezi.

**Malay** member of any of a large group of peoples comprising the majority population of the Malay Peninsula and archipelago, and also found in southern Thailand and coastal Sumatra and Borneo. Their language belongs to the western branch of the Austronesian family.

**Malayalam** southern Indian language, the official language of the state of Kerala. Malayalam is closely related to Tamil, also a member of the Dravidian language family; it is spoken by about 20 million people. Written records in Malayalam date from the 9th century AD.

**Malay language** member of the Western or Indonesian branch of the Malayo-Polynesian language family, used in the Malay peninsula and many of the islands of Malaysia and Indonesia. The Malay language can be written in either Arabic or Roman scripts. The dialect of the southern Malay peninsula is the basis of both Bahasa Malaysia and Bahasa Indonesia, the official languages of Malaysia and Indonesia. Bazaar Malay is a widespread pidgin variety used for trading and shopping.

**Malayo-Polynesian** family of languages spoken in Malaysia, better known as ◊*Austronesian*.

**Malaysia** Federation of (FOM)
**national name** *Persekutuan Tanah Malaysia*

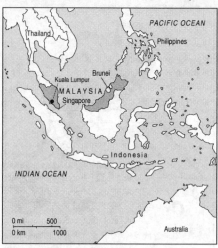

**area** 329,759 sq km/127,319 sq mi
**capital** Kuala Lumpur
**major towns/cities** Johor Baharu, Ipoh, George Town (Penang), Kuala Trengganu, Kuala Baharu, Petalong Jaya, Kelang, Kuching in Sarawak, Kota Kinabalu in Sabah
**major ports** Kelang
**physical features** comprises peninsular Malaysia (the nine Malay states – Johore, Kedah, Kelantan, Negri Sembilan, Pahang, Perak, Perlis, Selangor, Trengganu – plus Malacca and Penang); states of Sabah and Sarawak and federal territory of Kuala Lumpur; 75% tropical rainforest; central mountain range (Mount Kinabalu, the highest peak in southeast Asia); swamps in east; Niah caves (Sarawak)
**head of state** Tuanku Salehuddin Abdul Aziz Shah bin al-Marhum Hisamuddin Alam Shah from 1999
**head of government** Mahathir bin Mohamed from 1981
**political system** liberal democracy
**political parties** New United Malays' National Organization (UMNO Baru), Malay-oriented nationalist; Malaysian Chinese Association (MCA), Chinese-oriented, conservative; Gerakan Party, Chinese-oriented, socialist; Malaysian Indian Congress (MIC), Indian-oriented; Democratic Action Party (DAP), multiracial but Chinese-dominated, left of centre; Pan-Malayan Islamic Party (PAS), Islamic; Semangat '46 (Spirit of 1946), moderate, multiracial
**currency** ringgit
**GNP per capita (PPP)** (US$) 6,990 (1998 est)
**exports** palm oil, rubber, crude petroleum, machinery and transport equipment, timber, tin, textiles, electronic goods. Principal market: USA 21.6% (1998)
**population** 21,830,000 (1999 est)
**language** Malay (official), English, Chinese, Tamil, Iban
**religion** Muslim (official), Buddhist, Hindu, local beliefs

*life expectancy* 70 (men); 74 (women) (1995–2000)

**Chronology**

**1st century** AD Peoples of Malay peninsula influenced by Indian culture and Buddhism.

**8th–13th centuries** Malay peninsula formed part of Buddhist Srivijaya Empire based in Sumatra.

**14th century** Siam (Thailand) expanded to included most of Malay peninsula.

**1403** Muslim traders founded port of Malacca, which became a great commercial centre, encouraging spread of Islam.

**1511** Portuguese attacked and captured Malacca.

**1641** Portuguese ousted from Malacca by Dutch after seven-year blockade.

**1786** British East India Company established a trading post on island of Penang.

**1795–1815** Britain occupied Dutch colonies after France conquered the Netherlands.

**1819** Stamford Raffles of East India Company obtained Singapore from Sultan of Johore.

**1824** Anglo-Dutch Treaty ceded Malacca to Britain in return for territory in Sumatra.

**1826** British possessions of Singapore, Penang, and Malacca formed Straits Settlements, ruled by governor of Bengal; ports prospered and expanded.

**1840** Sultan of Brunei gave Sarawak to James Brooke, whose family ruled it as an independent state until 1946.

**1851** Responsibility for Straits Settlements assumed by governor general of India.

**1858** British government, through India Office, took over administration of Straits Settlements.

**1867** Straits Settlements became crown colony of British Empire.

**1874** British protectorates established over four Malay states of Perak, Salangor, Pahang, and Negri Sembilan, which federated in 1896.

**1888** Britain declared protectorate over northern Borneo (Sabah).

**late 19th century** Millions of Chinese and thousands of Indians migrated to Malaya to work in tin mines and on rubber plantations.

**1909–14** Britain assumed indirect rule over five northern Malay states after agreement with Siam (Thailand).

**1941–45** Japanese occupation.

**1946** United Malay National Organization (UMNO) founded to oppose British plans for centralized Union of Malaya.

**1948** Britain federated nine Malay states with Penang and Malacca to form single colony of Federation of Malaya.

**1948–60** Malayan emergency: British forces suppressed insurrection by communist guerrillas.

**1957** Federation of Malaya became independent with Prince Abdul Rahman (leader of UMNO) as prime minister.

**1963** Federation of Malaya combined with Singapore, Sarawak, and Sabah to form Federation of Malaysia.

**1963–66** 'The Confrontation' – guerrillas supported by Indonesia opposed federation with intermittent warfare.

**1965** Singapore withdrew from Federation of Malaysia.

**1968** Philippines claimed sovereignty over Sabah.

**1969** Malay resentment of Chinese economic dominance resulted in race riots in Kuala Lumpur.

**1971** *Bumiputra* policies which favoured ethnic Malays in education and employment introduced by Tun Abul Razak of UMNO.

**1981** Mahathir bin Muhammad (UMNO) became the prime minister; the government became increasingly dominated by Muslim Malays.

**1987** Malay–Chinese relations deteriorated; over 100 opposition activists were arrested.

**1988** UMNO split over Mahathir's leadership style; his supporters formed UMNO Baru (New UMNO), and his critics formed Semangat '46, a new multiracial party, in 1989.

**1991** An economic development policy was launched which aimed at 7% annual growth.

**1996** Semangat '46 rejoined UMNO Baru, which remained under Mahathir's leadership.

**1997** The currency was allowed to float. Parts of Borneo and Sumatra were covered by thick smog for several weeks following forest-clearing fires.

**1998** The repatriation of foreign workers commenced. Deputy prime minister Anwar Ibrahim was sacked and arrested on personal conduct and corruption charges. Anwar's wife, Wan Azizah Wan Ismail, set up a new opposition group, the Movement for Social Justice. Currency controls were introduced as the GDP contracted sharply.

**1999** Anwar Ibrahim was sentenced to six years in prison on corruption charges.

**Malcolm** four Celtic kings of Scotland, including:

**Malcolm III** called *Canmore* (c. 1031–1093) King of Scotland from 1058, the son of Duncan I. He fled to England in 1040 when the throne was usurped by ♢Macbeth, but recovered southern Scotland and killed Macbeth in battle in 1057. In 1070 he married Margaret (c. 1045–1093), sister of Edgar Atheling of England; their daughter Matilda (d. 1118) married Henry I of England. Malcolm was killed at Alnwick while invading Northumberland, England.

**Malcolm X** adopted name of Malcolm Little (1926–1965) US black nationalist leader. While serving a prison sentence for burglary 1946–53, he joined the Black Muslims sect. On his release he campaigned for black separatism, condoning violence in self-defence, but in 1964 modified his views to found the Islamic, socialist Organization of Afro-American Unity, preaching racial solidarity. He was assassinated.

**Maldini, Paolo** (1968– ) Italian footballer. A tall, left-sided defender, he made his international debut in 1988 at the age of 18, and by October 1999 had won 103 Italian caps, a total which only Dino Zoff with 112 has exceeded, scoring 7 goals. One of the game's greatest defenders, he was a member of the Italy side which reached the 1994 World Cup final, and also played in the 1990 and 1998 finals. An AC Milan first team player since the age of 16, he

has won the Italian league championship six times and the European Cup three times.
**career highlights**
**international appearances (1988–  )** 103 (7 goals)
**Italian league championship** 1988, 1992, 1993, 1994, 1996, 1999
**European Cup** 1989, 1990, 1994
**World Soccer** World Player of the Year, 1994

**Maldives** Republic of the
**national name** *Divehi Raajjeyge Jumhooriyaa*

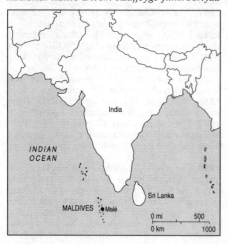

**area** 298 sq km/115 sq mi
**capital** Malé
**major towns/cities** Seenu, Kurehdhu, Kunfunadhoo, Dhiggiri, Anthimatha
**physical features** comprises 1,196 coral islands, grouped into 12 clusters of atolls, largely flat, none bigger than 13 sq km/5 sq mi, average elevation 1.8 m/6 ft; 203 are inhabited
**head of state and government** Maumoon Abd Gayoom from 1978
**political system** authoritarian nationalist
**political parties** none; candidates elected on basis of personal influence and clan loyalties
**currency** rufiya
**GNP per capita (PPP)** (US$) 3,100 (1998)
**exports** marine products (tuna bonito ('Maldive Fish'), clothing. Principal market: Germany 33% (1996)
**population** 278,000 (1999 est)
**language** Divehi (Sinhalese dialect), English
**religion** Sunni Muslim
**life expectancy** 66 (men); 63 (women) (1995–2000)
**Chronology**
**12th century AD** Islam introduced by seafaring Arabs, who displaced the indigenous Dravidian population.
**14th century** Ad-Din sultanate established.
**1558–73** Under Portuguese rule.
**1645** Became a dependency of Ceylon (Sri Lanka), which was ruled by the Dutch until 1796 and then by the British, with Sinhalese and Indian colonies being established.
**1887** Became internally self-governing British

protectorate, which remained a dependency of Sri Lanka until 1948.
**1932** Formerly hereditary, the sultanate became an elected position when Maldives' first constitution was introduced.
**1953** Maldive Islands became a republic within the Commonwealth, as the ad-Din sultanate was abolished.
**1954** Sultan restored.
**1959–60** Secessionist rebellion in Suvadiva (Huvadu) and Addu southern atolls.
**1965** Achieved full independence outside Commonwealth.
**1968** Sultan deposed after referendum; republic reinstated with Ibrahim Nasir as president.
**1975** The closure of a British air-force staging post on the southern island of Gan led to a substantial loss in income.
**1978** The autocratic Nasir retired and left the country; he was replaced by the progressive Maumoon Abd Gayoom.
**1980s** Economic growth was boosted by the rapid development of the tourist industry.
**1982** Rejoined the Commonwealth.
**1985** Became a founder member of the South Asian Association for Regional Cooperation.
**1986** The High Court sentenced the exiled Nasir in absentia to 25 years' banishment on charges of embezzlement of public funds, but a pardon was granted two years later.
**1988** A coup attempt by Sri Lankan mercenaries, thought to have the backing of former president Nasir, was foiled by Indian paratroops. President Gayoom was re-elected.
**1993** Gayoom was re-elected.
**1998** Gayoom was re-elected for a further presidential term.

**Malé** capital and chief atoll of the Maldives in the Indian Ocean; population (1990) 55,100. It trades in copra, breadfruit, fish, and palm products; it is also a growing tourist centre.

**Mali** Republic of
**national name** *République du Mali*

**area** 1,240,142 sq km/478,818 sq mi
**capital** Bamako
**major towns/cities** Mopti, Kayes, Ségou, Timbuktu, Sikasso
**physical features** landlocked state with River Niger and savanna in south; part of the Sahara

in north; hills in northeast; Senegal River and its branches irrigate the southwest

*head of state* Alpha Oumar Konare from 1992

*head of government* Ibrahim Boubaker Keita from 1994

*political system* emergent democracy

*political parties* Alliance for Democracy in Mali (ADEMA), left of centre; National Committee for Democratic Initiative (CNID), centre left; Assembly for Democracy and Progress (RDP), left of centre; Civic Society and the Democracy and Progress Party (PDP), left of centre; Malian People's Democratic Union (UDPM), nationalist socialist

*currency* franc CFA

*GNP per capita (PPP)* (US$) 720 (1998)

*exports* cotton, livestock, gold, miscellaneous manufactured articles. Principal market: Thailand 20.3% (1997)

*population* 10,960,000 (1999 est)

*language* French (official), Bambara

*religion* Sunni Muslim 90%, animist, Christian

*life expectancy* 52 (men); 55 (women) (1995–2000)

**Chronology**

*5th–13th centuries* Ghana Empire founded by agriculturist Soninke people, based on the Saharan gold trade for which Timbuktu became an important centre. At its height in the 11th century it covered much of the western Sahel, comprising parts of present-day Mali, Senegal, and Mauritania. Wars with Muslim Berber tribes from the north led to its downfall. Its capital was at Kumbi, 125 mi/200 km north of Bamako, in southeast Mauritania.

*13th–15th centuries* Ghana Empire superseded by Muslim Mali Empire of Malinke (Mandingo) people of southwest, from which Mali derives its name. At its peak, under Mansa Musa in the 14th century, it covered parts of Mali, Senegal, Gambia, and southern Mauritania.

*15th–16th centuries* Muslim Songhai Empire, centred around Timbuktu and Gao, superseded Mali Empire. Under Sonni Ali Ber, who ruled 1464–92, it covered Mali, Senegal, Gambia, and parts of Mauritania, Niger, and Nigeria, and included a professional army and civil service.

*1591* Songhai Empire destroyed by Moroccan Berbers, under Ahmad al-Mansur, who launched an invasion to take over the western Sudanese gold trade and took control over Timbuktu.

*18th–19th centuries* Niger valley region was divided between the nomadic Tuareg, in the area around Gao in the northeast, and the Fulani and Bambara kingdoms, around Macina and Bambara in the centre and southwest.

*late 18th century* Western Mali visited by Scottish explorer Mungo Park.

*mid-19th century* The Islamic Tukolor, as part of a jihad (holy war) conquered much of western Mali, including Fulani and Bambara kingdoms, while in the south, Samori Ture, a Muslim Malinke (Mandingo) warrior, created a small empire.

*1880–95* Region conquered by French, who overcame Tukolor and Samori resistance to establish colony of French Sudan.

*1904* Became part of federation of French West Africa.

*1946* French Sudan became an overseas territory within the French Union, with its own territorial assembly and representation in the French parliament; the pro-autonomy Sudanese Union and Sudanese Progressive Parties founded in Bamako.

*1959* With Senegal, formed the Federation of Mali.

*1960* Separated from Senegal and became independent Republic of Mali, with Modibo Keita, an authoritarian socialist of the Sudanese Union party, as president.

*1968* Keita replaced in army coup by Lt Moussa Traoré, as economy deteriorated: constitution suspended and political activity banned.

*1974* A new constitution made Mali a one-party state, dominated by Traoré's nationalistic socialist Malian People's Democratic Union (UDPM), formed in 1976.

*1979* More than a dozen were killed after a student strike was crushed.

*1985* There was a five-day conflict with Burkina Faso over a long-standing border dispute which was mediated by the International Court of Justice.

*late 1980s* Closer ties developed with the West and free-market economic policies were pursued, including privatization, as the Soviet influence waned.

*1991* Violent demonstrations and strikes against one-party rule led to 150 deaths; Traoré was ousted in a coup led by Lt-Col Amadou Toumani Toure.

*1992* A referendum endorsed a new democratic constitution. The opposition Alliance for Democracy in Mali (ADEMA) won multiparty elections; Alpha Oumar Konare was elected president. A coalition government was formed. A peace pact was signed with Tuareg rebels fighting in northern Mali for greater autonomy.

*1993–94* Student unrest forced two changes of prime minister. Ex-president Traoré was sentenced to death for his role in suppressing the 1991 riots.

*1997* President Konare was re-elected.

**Mali Empire** Muslim state in northwestern Africa during the 7th–15th centuries. Thriving on its trade in gold, it reached its peak in the 14th century under Mansa Musa (reigned 1312–37), when it occupied an area covering present-day Senegal, Gambia, Mali, and southern Mauritania. Mali's territory was similar to (though larger than) that of the Ghana Empire, and gave way in turn to the ◊Songhai Empire.

**mallard** common wild duck from which domestic ducks were bred, found almost worldwide. The male can grow to a length of 60 cm/ 2 ft and usually has a glossy green head, white collar, and chestnut brown breast with a pale grey body, while the female is mottled brown. Mallards are omnivorous dabbling ducks. (Species *Anas platyrhynchos,* subfamily Anatinae, order Anseriformes.)

**Mallarmé, Stéphane** (1842–1898) French poet. A leader of the Symbolist school, he became known as a poet's poet for his condensed, hermetic verse and unorthodox syntax, reaching for the ideal world of the intellect. His belief that poetry should be evocative and suggestive was reflected in *L'Après-midi d'un faune/Afternoon of a Faun* (1876) (illustrated by Manet), which inspired the composer Debussy. Later works are *Poésies complètes/Complete Poems* (1887), *Vers et prose/Verse and Prose* (1893), and the prose *Divagations/Digressions* (1897).

**Malle, Louis** (1932–1995) French film director. His early work anticipated the New Wave. Working in both France and the USA, he made such films as *Le Feu follet/A Time to Live and a Time to Die* (1963), *Atlantic City* (1980), and *Damage* (1993).

**mallee** any of a group of small eucalyptus trees and shrubs with many small stems and thick underground roots that retain water. Before irrigation farming began, dense thickets of mallee characterized most of northwestern Victoria, Australia, known as the mallee region. (Genus *Eucalyptus,* family Myrtaceae.)

**Mallorca** or *Majorca,* largest of the ◊Balearic Islands, belonging to Spain, in the western Mediterranean
*area* 3,640 sq km/1,405 sq mi
*capital* Palma
*features* the highest mountain is Puig Mayor (1,445 m/4,741 ft)
*industries* olives, figs, oranges, wine, brandy, timber, sheep; tourism is the mainstay of the economy
*population* (1990 est) 582,000
*history* captured in 797 by the Moors, it was taken by James I of Aragón in 1229 and became the kingdom of Mallorca in 1230. It was united with Aragón in 1349 and later incorporated into Spain when Aragón united with Castile in 1479. The composer Frédéric Chopin spent the winter of 1838–39 in the Carthusian monastery at Valldemosa.

**mallow** any flowering plant of the mallow family, including the European common mallow (*M. sylvestris*), the tree mallow (*L. arborea*), marsh mallow (*A. officinalis*), and hollyhock (*A. rosea*). Most mallows have pink or purple flowers. (Genera *Malva, Lavatera,* and *Althaea,* family Malvaceae.)

**Malmö** industrial port (shipbuilding, engineering, textiles) in southwestern Sweden, situated across the Øresund from Copenhagen, Denmark; population (1994 est) 242,700. Founded in the 12th century, Malmö is Sweden's third-largest city.

**malnutrition** condition resulting from a defective diet where certain important food nutrients (such as proteins, vitamins, or carbohydrates) are absent. It can lead to deficiency diseases. A related problem is undernourishment.

A high global death rate linked to malnutrition has arisen from famine situations caused by global warming, droughts, and the greenhouse effect as well as by sociopolitical factors, such as alcohol and drug abuse, poverty, and war.

**Malory, Thomas** (*c.* 1410–1471) English author. He is known for the prose romance *Le Morte D'Arthur* (*c.* 1470), printed in 1485, which relates the exploits of King Arthur's knights of the Round Table and the quest for the ◊Holy Grail. Knight of the shire from 1445.

**Malraux, André (Georges)** (1901–1976) French writer, art critic, and politician. An active antifascist, he gained international renown for his novel *La Condition humaine/Man's Estate* (1933), set during the Nationalist/Communist Revolution in China in the 1920s. *L'Espoir/Days of Hope* (1937) is set in Civil War Spain, where he was a bomber pilot in the International Brigade. In his revolutionary novels he frequently depicts individuals in situations where they are forced to examine the meaning of their own life. He also made an outstanding contribution to aesthetics with *La Psychologie de l'art* (1947–49), revised as *Les Voix du silence/The Voices of Silence* (1951).

**malt** in brewing, grain (barley, oats, or wheat) artificially germinated and then dried in a kiln. Malts are fermented to make beers or lagers, or fermented and then distilled to produce spirits such as whisky.

**Malta** Republic of
*national name* Repubblika Ta'Malta

*area* 320 sq km/124 sq mi
*capital* Valletta (and port)
*major towns/cities* Rabat, Birkirkara, Qormi, Sliema, Zetjun, Zabor
*major ports* Marsaxlokk, Valletta
*physical features* includes islands of Gozo 67 sq km/26 sq mi and Comino 3 sq km/1 sq mi
*head of state* Guido de Marco from 1999
*head of government* Edward Fenech Adami from 1998
*political system* liberal democracy
*political parties* Malta Labour Party (MLP), moderate, left of centre; Nationalist Party (PN), Christian, centrist, pro-European
*currency* Maltese lira

**GNP per capita (PPP)** (US$) 13,610 (1998)
**exports** machinery and transport equipment, manufactured articles (including clothing), beverages, chemicals, tobacco. Principal market: France 20.7% (1998)
**population** 386,000 (1999 est)
**language** Maltese, English (both official)
**religion** Roman Catholic 98%
**life expectancy** 75 (men); 79 (women) (1995–2000)
**Chronology**
**7th century BC** Invaded and subjugated by Carthaginians from North Africa.
**218 BC** Came under Roman control.
**AD 60** Converted to Christianity by the apostle Paul, who was shipwrecked here.
**395** On division of Roman Empire, became part of Eastern (Byzantine) portion, dominated by Constantinople.
**870** Came under Arab rule.
**1091** Arabs defeated by Norman Count Roger I of Sicily; Roman Catholic Church re-established.
**1530** Handed over by Holy Roman Emperor Charles V to religious military order, the Hospitallers (Knights of St John of Jerusalem).
**1798–1802** Briefly occupied by French.
**1814** Annexed to Britain by Treaty of Paris on condition that Roman Catholic Church was maintained and Maltese Declaration of Rights honoured.
**later 19th century–early 20th century** Became vital British naval base, with famous dockyard that developed as island's economic mainstay.
**1942** Awarded George Cross for valour in resisting severe Italian aerial attacks during World War II.
**1947** Achieved self-government.
**1955** Dom Mintoff of left-of-centre Malta Labour Party (MLP) became prime minister.
**1956** Referendum approved MLP's proposal for integration with UK. Plebiscite opposed and boycotted by right-of-centre Nationalist Party (PN).
**1958** MLP rejected final British integration proposal.
**1962** PN elected, with Giorgio Borg Olivier as prime minister.
**1964** Independence achieved from Britain, within Commonwealth. Ten-year defence and economic-aid treaty with UK signed.
**1971** Mintoff adopted policy of nonalignment and declared 1964 treaty invalid; negotiations began for leasing NATO base in Malta.
**1972** Seven-year NATO agreement signed.
**1974** Became a republic.
**1979** British military base closed; closer links were established with communist and Arab states, including Libya.
**1984** Mintoff retired and was replaced by Karmenu Mifsud Bonnici as prime minister and MLP leader.
**1987** Edward Fenech Adami (PN) was narrowly elected prime minister; he adopted a more pro-European and pro-American policy stance than the preceding administration.
**1990** A formal application was made for European Community membership.
**1994** Mifsud Bonnici was elected president.
**1998** The PN was returned to power after a snap election.

**Malthus, Thomas Robert** (1766–1834) English economist. His *Essay on the Principle of Population* (1798) (revised 1803) argued for population control, since populations increase in geometric ratio and food supply only in arithmetic ratio, and influenced Charles ◊Darwin's thinking on natural selection as the driving force of evolution.

**Maluku** or *Moluccas,* group of Indonesian islands; area 74,500 sq km/28,764 sq mi; population (urban area, 1990 est) 1,856,000. The capital is Ambon, on Ambon. As the Spice Islands, they were formerly part of the Netherlands East Indies; the southern Moluccas attempted secession from the newly created Indonesian republic from 1949; exiles continued agitation in the Netherlands.

**mamba** either of two venomous snakes belonging to the cobra family, found in Africa south of the Sahara. Unlike cobras, they are not hooded. (Genus *Dendroaspis,* family Elapidae.)

**Mameluke** member of a powerful political class that dominated Egypt from the 13th century until their massacre in 1811 by Mehmet Ali.

**Mamet, David (Alan)** (1947– ) US dramatist, screenwriter, and director. His plays use vivid, freewheeling language and urban settings. *American Buffalo* (1975), about a gang of hopeless robbers, was his first major success. *Glengarry Glen Ross* (1983) is a dark depiction of US business ethics. He made his directorial debut with *House of Games* (1987), which used gambling as a metaphor for relationships.

**mammal** any of a large group of warm-blooded vertebrate animals characterized by having ◊mammary glands in the female; these are used for suckling the young. Other features of mammals are ◊hair (very reduced in some species, such as whales); a middle ear formed of three small bones (ossicles); a lower jaw consisting of two bones only; seven vertebrae in the neck; and no nucleus in the red blood cells. (Class Mammalia.)

Mammals are divided into three groups: *placental mammals,* where the young develop inside the mother's body, in the ◊uterus, receiving nourishment from the blood of the mother via the ◊placenta; *marsupials,* where the young are born at an early stage of development and develop further in a pouch on the mother's body where they are attached to and fed from a nipple; and *monotremes,* where the young hatch from an egg outside the mother's body and are then nourished with milk.

The monotremes are the least evolved and have been largely displaced by more sophisticated marsupials and placentals, so that there are only a few types surviving (platypus and echidna). Placentals have spread to all parts of the globe, and where placentals have competed with marsupials, the placentals have in general displaced marsupial types. However, marsupials occupy many specialized niches in South America and, especially, Australasia.

According to the Red List of endangered species published by the World Conservation Union (IUCN) for 1996, 25% of mammal species are threatened with extinction.

**mammary gland** in female mammals, a milk-producing gland derived from epithelial cells underlying the skin, active only after the production of young. In all but monotremes (egg-laying mammals), the mammary glands terminate in teats which aid infant suckling. The number of glands and their position vary between species. In humans there are 2, in cows 4, and in pigs between 10 and 14.

**mammography** X-ray procedure used to screen for breast cancer. It can detect abnormal growths at an early stage, before they can be seen or felt.

**Mammon** evil personification of wealth and greed; originally a Syrian god of riches, cited in the New Testament as opposed to the Christian god.

**mammoth** extinct elephant, remains of which have been found worldwide. Some were 50% taller than modern elephants; others were much smaller. (Genus *Mammuthus* (or *Elephas*).)

**Managua** capital and chief industrial city of Nicaragua, and capital of a department of the same name; it is situated on the southern shore of Lake Managua 45km/28 mi from the Pacific coast and 138 km/86 mi from the main port of Corinto; population (1991 est) 615,000. One-fifth of the nation's population is resident here. It is Nicaragua's largest city and main industrial and commercial centre. Managua produces 60% of the nation's goods by value including cotton, drinks, and processed foods. Surrounding lowlands are very fertile, supporting maize, beans, sugar cane, and banana plantations.

**manatee** any of a group of plant-eating aquatic mammals found in marine bays and sluggish rivers, usually in thick, muddy water. They have flippers as forelimbs, no hindlimbs, and a short rounded and flattened tail used for swimming. The marine manatees can grow up to about 4.5 m/15 ft long and weigh up to 600 kg/1,323 lb. (Genus *Trichechus*, family Trichechidae, order Sirenia.)

**Manaus** capital of Amazonas federal unit (state), northwest Brazil, on the Río Negro, 16 km/10 mi from its confluence with the River Solimó which forms the River Amazon; population (1991) 996,700. It is the industrial trading and commercial centre of the state, and its chief port, although 1,600 km/1,000 mi from the Atlantic. Timber and rubber are the main exports, and there are sawmills and an oil refinery. Manaus is an important free-trade zone (established in 1966) that distributes products nationwide. It specializes in electrical goods.

**Manchester** metropolitan district of Greater Manchester, and city in northwest England, on the River Irwell, 50 km/31 mi east of Liverpool; population (1991) 402,900. A financial and manufacturing centre, its industries include banking and insurance; the production of cotton and synthetic textiles, petrochemicals, rubber, paper, machine tools, and processed foods; and heavy, light, and electrical engineering, also printing. It is linked to the River Mersey and the Irish Sea by the *Manchester Ship Canal*, opened in 1894. Only one dock is now open.

**Manchester, Greater** metropolitan county of northwest England, created in 1974; in 1986 most of the functions of the former county council were transferred to metropolitan district councils

*area* 1,290 sq km/498 sq mi

*towns and cities* Manchester, Bolton, Bury, Oldham, Rochdale, Salford, Stockport, Tameside, Trafford, Wigan

*features* Manchester Ship Canal links it with the River Mersey and the sea; Old Trafford cricket ground at Stretford, and the football ground of Manchester United

*industries* engineering, textiles, textile machinery, chemicals, plastics, electrical goods, electronic equipment, paper, printing, rubber, and asbestos

*population* (1996) 2,575,600

*famous people* Anthony Burgess, John Dalton, Gracie Fields, James Joule, Emmeline Pankhurst.

**Manchu** or *Qing*, last ruling dynasty in China, from 1644 until its overthrow 1912; its last emperor was the infant ◊P'u-i. Originally a nomadic people from Manchuria, they established power through a series of successful invasions from the north, then granted trading rights to the USA and Europeans, which eventually brought strife and the ◊Boxer Rebellion.

**Manchuria** European name for the northeastern region of China, comprising the provinces of Heilongjiang, Jilin, and Liaoning. It was united with China by the Manchu dynasty 1644, but as the Chinese Empire declined, Japan and Russia were rivals for its control.

The Russians were expelled after the ◊Russo-Japanese War 1904–05, and in 1932 Japan consolidated its position by creating a puppet state, *Manchukuo*, nominally led by the Chinese pretender to the throne Henry P'u-i. At the end of World War II the Soviets occupied Manchuria in a two-week operation August 1945. Japanese settlers were expelled when the region was returned to Chinese control.

**Mandalay** chief city of the Mandalay division of Myanmar (formerly Burma), on the River Irrawaddy, about 495 km/370 mi north of Yangon (Rangoon); population (1983) 533,000.

**mandarin** type of small ◊orange.

**Mandarin** (Sanskrit *mantrin* 'counsellor') standard form of the ◊Chinese language. Historically it derives from the language spoken by *mandarins*, Chinese imperial officials, from the 7th century onwards. It is used by 70% of the population and taught in schools of the People's Republic of China.

**mandate** in history, a territory whose administration was entrusted to Allied states by the League of Nations under the Treaty of Versailles after World War I. Mandated territories were former German and Turkish possessions (including Iraq, Syria, Lebanon, and Palestine). When the United Nations replaced the League of Nations in 1945, mandates that had not achieved independence became known as trust territories.

**Mandela, Nelson (Rolihlahla)** (1918– ) South African politician and lawyer, president 1994–99. He was president of the ◊African National Congress (ANC) 1991–97. Imprisoned from 1964, as organizer of the then banned ANC, he became a symbol of unity for the worldwide anti-◊apartheid movement. In February 1990 he was released, the ban on the ANC having been lifted, and entered into negotiations with the government about a multiracial future for South Africa. In May 1994 he was sworn in as South Africa's first post-apartheid president after the ANC won 62.65% of the vote in universal-suffrage elections. He shared the Nobel Prize for Peace in 1993 with South African president F W de Klerk.

**mandolin** plucked string instrument with four to six pairs of strings (courses), tuned like a violin, which flourished 1600–1800. The fingerboard is fretted to regulate intonation. It takes its name from its almond-shaped body (Italian *mandorla* 'almond'). Vivaldi composed two concertos for the mandolin about 1736.

**mandragora** or *mandrake,* any of a group of almost stemless Old World plants with narcotic (pain-killing and sleep-inducing) properties, belonging to the nightshade family. They have large leaves, pale blue or violet flowers, and round berries known as devil's apples. (Genus *Mandragora,* family Solanaceae.)

**mandrake** another name for the plant ◊mandragora.

**mandrill** large West African forest-living baboon, active mainly on the ground. It has large canine teeth like the drill (*M. leucophaeus*), to which it is closely related. The nose is bright red and the cheeks are striped with blue; the thick skin of the buttocks is also red, and the fur is brown, apart from a yellow beard. (Species *Mandrillus sphinx.*)

**Manet, Edouard** (1832–1883) French painter. One of the foremost French artists of the 19th century, he is often regarded as the father of modern painting. Rebelling against the academic tradition, he developed a clear and unaffected realist style that was one of the founding forces of ◊Impressionism. His subjects were mainly contemporary, such as *A Bar at the Folies-Bergère* (1882) (Courtauld Art Gallery, London).

**manganese** hard, brittle, grey-white metallic element, symbol Mn, atomic number 25, relative atomic mass 54.9380. It resembles iron (and rusts), but it is not magnetic and is softer. It is used chiefly in making steel alloys, also alloys with aluminium and copper.

It is used in fertilizers, paints, and industrial chemicals. It is a necessary trace element in human nutrition. The name is old, deriving from the French and Italian forms of Latin for

*magnesia* (MgO), the white tasteless powder used as an antacid from ancient times.

**mangelwurzel** or *mangold,* variety of the common beet *Beta vulgaris* used chiefly as feed for cattle and sheep.

**mango** evergreen tree belonging to the cashew family, native to India but now widely cultivated for its large oval fruits in other tropical and subtropical areas, such as the West Indies. (*Mangifera indica,* family Anacardiaceae.)

**mangold** another name for ◊mangelwurzel.

**mangrove** any of several shrubs and trees, especially of the mangrove family, found in the muddy swamps of tropical and subtropical coastlines and estuaries. By sending down aerial roots from their branches, they rapidly form close-growing mangrove thickets. Their timber is resistant to water penetration and damage by marine worms. Mangrove swamps are rich breeding grounds for fish and shellfish, but these habitats are being destroyed in many countries. (Genera *Rhizophora* and *Avicennia,* families Rhizophoraceae (mangrove) and Avicenniaceae (related).)

**Manhattan** island of the city of ◊New York, USA, forming most of a borough; population (1990) 1,488,000. It is 20 km/12.5 mi long and 4 km/2.5 mi wide, and lies between the Hudson and East rivers. The rocks from which it is formed rise to a height of more than 73 m/240 ft in the north of the island. Manhattan Island is bounded on the north and northeast by the Harlem River and Spuyten Duyvil Creek (which separate it from the Bronx); on the south by Upper New York Bay; on the west by the Hudson River (which separates it from New Jersey); and on the east by the East River (which separates it from Queens and Brooklyn). The borough of Manhattan also includes a small port at the Bronx mainland and several islands in the East River. Manhattan is the economic hub of New York City, although there are large residential and industrial areas here also. It includes the Wall Street business centre, Broadway and its theatres, Carnegie Hall (1891), the World Trade Centre (1973), the Empire State Building (1931), the United Nations headquarters (1952), Madison Square Garden, and Central Park.

**Manhattan Project** code name for the development of the ◊atom bomb in the USA in World War II, to which the physicists Enrico Fermi and J Robert Oppenheimer contributed.

**manic depression** or *bipolar disorder,* mental disorder characterized by recurring periods of either ◊depression or mania (inappropriate elation, agitation, and rapid thought and speech) or both.

Sufferers may be genetically predisposed to the condition. Some cases have been improved by taking prescribed doses of ◊lithium.

**Manila** industrial port (textiles, tobacco, distilling, chemicals, shipbuilding) and capital of the Philippines, on the island of Luzon; population of the metropolitan area (including

◊Quezon City) 9,000,000 (1994); city (1990) 1,601,000.

**manioc** another name for the plant ◊cassava.

**Manipur** state of northeast India; bordered south and east by Myanmar
**area** 22,300 sq km/8,610 sq mi
**capital** Imphal
**physical** mostly wooded and mountainous (mainly over 2,000 m/6,500 ft), with central valley containing Imphal
**features** Loktak Lake; original Indian home of polo
**industries** textiles, cement, handloom weaving
**agriculture** rice, grain, fruit, vegetables, sugar
**population** (1994 est) 2,010,000 (30% are hill tribes such as Nagas and Kukis)
**language** Manipuri, English
**religion** Hindu 70%
**history** former princely state administered from the state of Assam until 1947 when it became a Union Territory. It became a state in 1972. Women traders have a significant economic and political role in the state, with a powerful union.

**Man, Isle of** Gaelic *Ellan Vannin,* island in the Irish Sea, a dependency of the British crown, but not part of the UK
**area** 570 sq km/220 sq mi
**capital** Douglas
**towns and cities** Ramsey, Peel, Castletown
**features** Snaefell 620 m/2,035 ft; annual TT (Tourist Trophy) motorcycle races; gambling casinos, tax haven; tailless Manx cat
**industries** light engineering products; agriculture, fishing, tourism, banking, and insurance are important
**currency** the island produces its own coins and notes in UK currency denominations
**population** (1991) 69,800
**language** English (Manx, nearer to Scottish than Irish Gaelic, has been almost extinct since the 1970s)
**government** crown-appointed lieutenant-governor, a legislative council, and the representative House of Keys, which together make up the Court of Tynwald, passing laws subject to the royal assent. Laws passed at Westminster only affect the island if specifically so provided
**history** Norwegian until 1266, when the island was ceded to Scotland; it came under UK administration in 1765.

**Manitoba** (Algonquian *Manitou* 'great spirit') province in central Canada, the easternmost of the Prairie provinces. Bounded to the south, on the 49th Parallel, by the US states of Minnesota (in the east) and North Dakota (in the west); to the west by Saskatchewan; to the north, on the 60th Parallel, by the Northwest Territories and Hudson Bay; and to the east by Ontario
**area** 650,000 sq km/250,900 sq mi
**capital** ◊Winnipeg
**towns and cities** Brandon, Thompson, St Boniface, Churchill, Flin Flon, Portage La Prairie, The Pas
**population** (1996) 1,113,900
**physical** lakes Winnipeg, Winnipegosis, and Manitoba (area 4,700 sq km/1,814 sq mi); 50% forested

**industries** production of grain and food-processing; manufacture of machinery; fur-trapping; fishing; mining of nickel, zinc, copper, and the world's largest deposits of caesium (a metallic element used in the manufacture of photocells).

**Manley, Michael (Norman)** (1924–1997) Jamaican trade unionist, centre-left politician, leader of the socialist People's National Party from 1969, and prime minister (1972–80 and 1989–92). A charismatic orator, he was the son of Norman Manley, founder of the socialist People's National Party (PNP), and became leader of the PNP on his father's death in 1969. After a landslide victory in 1972, his 'democratic socialist' programme was beset by economic depression, losing him the election in 1980. He was re-elected on a more moderate manifesto in 1989, but ill health forced his resignation as prime minister in March 1992 and retirement from politics. He was succeeded as premier by Percival Patterson.

**Mann, Thomas** (1875–1955) German novelist and critic. A largely subjective artist, he drew his themes from his own experiences and inner thoughts. He was constantly preoccupied with the idea of death in the midst of life and with the position of the artist in relation to society. His first novel was *Buddenbrooks* (1901), a saga of a merchant family which traces through four generations the gradual growth of decay as culture slowly saps virility. *Der Zauberberg/The Magic Mountain* (1924), a vast symbolic work on the subject of disease in sick minds and bodies, and also the sickness of Europe, probes the question of culture in relation to life. Notable among his works of short fiction is 'Der Tod in Venedig/ Death in Venice' (1913). Nobel Prize for Literature 1929.

**Mannerism** in a general sense some idiosyncrasy, extravagance, or affectation of style or manner in art, though it has more specific reference to Italian painting in the 16th century and represents a distinct phase between the art of the High Renaissance and the rise of Baroque. It was largely based on an admiration for Michelangelo and a consequent exaggeration of the emphasis of his composition and the expressive distortion of his figures.

**manor** basic economic unit in ◊feudalism in Europe, established in England under the Norman conquest. It consisted of the lord's house and cultivated land, land rented by free tenants, land held by villagers, common land, woodland, and waste land.

**Man Ray** US photographer, painter, and sculptor; see Man ◊Ray.

**Mansfield, Katherine** pen-name of Kathleen Beauchamp (1888–1923) New Zealand writer. She lived most of her life in England. Her delicate artistry emerges not only in her volumes of short stories – such as *In a German Pension* (1911), *Bliss* (1920), and *The Garden Party* (1923) – but also in her 'Letters' and *Journal*.

**manslaughter** in English law, the unlawful killing of a human being in circumstances less culpable than ◊murder – for example, when the killer suffers extreme provocation, is in some way mentally ill (diminished responsibility), did not intend to kill but did so accidentally in the course of another crime or by behaving with criminal recklessness, or is the survivor of a genuine suicide pact that involved killing the other person.

**manta** another name for the ◊devil ray, a large fish.

**Mantegna, Andrea** (c. 1431–1506) Italian painter and engraver. He painted religious and mythological subjects, his works noted for their *all'antica* style taking elements from Roman antique architecture and sculpture, and for their innovative use of perspective.

**mantis** any of a group of carnivorous insects related to cockroaches. There are about 2,000 species of mantis, mainly tropical; some can reach a length of 20 cm/8 in. (Family Mantidae, order Dictyoptera.)

**mantra** in Hindu or Buddhist belief, a word repeatedly intoned to assist concentration and develop spiritual power; for example, *om,* which represents the names of Brahma, Vishnu, and Siva. Followers of a guru may receive their own individual mantra.

**Maoism** form of communism based on the ideas and teachings of the Chinese communist leader ◊Mao Zedong. It involves an adaptation of ◊Marxism to suit conditions in China and apportions a much greater role to agriculture and the peasantry in the building of socialism, thus effectively bypassing the capitalist (industrial) stage envisaged by Marx.

In addition, Maoism stresses ideological, as well as economic, transformation, based on regular contact between party members and the general population.

**Maori** (New Zealand *Maui* 'native' or 'indigenous') member of the Polynesian people of New Zealand. They number 435,000, about 15% of the total population, and around 89% live in the North Island. Maori civilization had particular strengths in warfare, cultivation, navigation, and wood- and stonework. Speechmaking and oral history, as well as woodcarving, were the main cultural repositories before the European introduction of writing, and Maori mythology and cosmology were highly developed. Their language, Maori, belongs to the eastern branch of the Austronesian family. The Maori Language Act 1987 recognized Maori as an official language of New Zealand.

**Mao Tse-tung** alternative transcription of ◊Mao Zedong.

**Mao Zedong** or *Mao Tse-tung* (1893–1976) Chinese communist politician and theoretician, leader of the Chinese Communist Party (CCP) 1935–76. Mao was a founder of the CCP in 1921, and became its leader in 1935. He organized the Long March 1934–35 and the war of liberation 1937–49, following which he established a People's Republic and communist rule in China. He was state president until 1959, and headed the CCP until his death. His influence diminished with the failure of his 1958–60

Great Leap Forward, but he emerged dominant again during the 1966–69 Cultural Revolution, which he launched in order to promote his own anti-bureaucratic line and to purge the party of 'revisionism'.

**map** diagrammatic representation of an area – for example, part of the Earth's surface or the distribution of the stars. Modern maps of the Earth are made using satellites in low orbit to take a series of overlapping stereoscopic photographs from which a three-dimensional image can be prepared. The earliest accurate large-scale maps appeared about 1580.

**maple** any of a group of deciduous trees with lobed leaves and green flowers, followed by two-winged fruits, or samaras. There are over 200 species, chiefly in northern temperate regions. (Genus *Acer,* family Aceraceae.)

**map projection** ways of depicting the spherical surface of the Earth on a flat piece of paper. Traditional projections include the *conic, azimuthal,* and *cylindrical.* The most famous cylindrical projection is the ◊Mercator projection, which dates from 1569. The weakness of these systems is that countries in high latitudes are shown disproportionately large, and lines of longitude and latitude appear distorted.

In 1973 German historian Arno Peters devised the *Peters projection* in which the countries of the world retain their relative areas. In 1992 the US physicist Mitchell Feigenbaum devised the *optimal conformal* projection, using a computer program designed to take data about the boundary of a given area and calculate the projection that produces the minimum of inaccuracies.

**Maputo** formerly (until 1975) *Lourenço Marques,* capital of Mozambique, and Africa's second-largest port, on Delagoa Bay; population (1993 est) 2,000,000. Linked by road and rail with Zimbabwe, Swaziland, and South Africa, it is a major outlet for minerals, steel, textiles, processed foods, and furniture.

**Marat, Jean Paul** (1743–1793) Swiss-born French Revolutionary leader, physician, and journalist. He was elected to the National Convention in 1792, where, as leader of the radical Montagnard faction, he carried on a long struggle with the right-wing ◊Girondins, which resulted in their overthrow in May 1793. In July he was murdered in his bath by Charlotte Corday, a Girondin supporter.

**Maratha** or *Mahratta,* member of a people living mainly in Maharashtra, western India. There are about 40 million speakers of Marathi, a language belonging to the Indo-European family. The Marathas are mostly farmers, and practise Hinduism. In the 17th and 18th centuries the Marathas formed a powerful military confederacy in rivalry with the Mogul emperors. The latter's Afghan allies defeated the Marathas at Panipat 1761, and, after a series of wars with the British 1779–1871, most of their territory was annexed. During the ◊Indian Mutiny and the rise of the movement of independence, the Marathas became a symbol of Hindu revival.

**marathon** athletics endurance race over 42.195 km/26 mi 385 yd. It was first included in the Olympic Games in Athens in 1896. The distance varied until it was standardized in 1924. More recently, races have been opened to wider participation, including social runners as well as those competing at senior level.

**Marathon, Battle of** battle fought in September 490 BC at the start of the Persian Wars, in which the Athenians and their allies from Plataea resoundingly defeated the Persian king Darius' invasion force. Fought on the Plain of Marathon about 40 km/25 mi northeast of Athens, it is one of the most famous battles of antiquity.

**Marbella** port and tourist resort in the province of Málaga in Andalusia, southern Spain, on the Costa del Sol between Málaga and Algeciras; population (1991) 76,800. There are three bullrings, a Moorish castle, and the remains of a medieval defensive wall.

**marble** rock formed by metamorphosis of sedimentary ◊limestone. It takes and retains a good polish, and is used in building and sculpture. In its pure form it is white and consists almost entirely of calcite $CaCO_3$. Mineral impurities give it various colours and patterns. Carrara, Italy, is known for white marble.

**Marc, Franz** (1880–1916) German Expressionist painter. He was associated with Wassily Kandinsky in founding the ◊*Blaue Reiter* movement. Animals played an essential part in his view of the world, and bold semi-abstracts of red and blue animals, particularly horses, are characteristic of his work.

**Marceau, Marcel** (1923– ) French mime artist. He is the creator of the clown-harlequin Bip and mime sequences such as 'Youth, Maturity, Old Age, and Death'.

**Marches** boundary areas of England with Wales, and England with Scotland. For several centuries from the time of William the Conqueror, these troubled frontier regions were held by lords of the Marches, those on the Welsh frontier called Marcher Lords, sometimes called *marchiones,* and those on the Scottish border known as earls of March. The first Marcher Lord was Roger de Mortimer (about 1286–1330); the first earl of March, Patrick Dunbar (died in 1285).

**Marconi, Guglielmo** (1874–1937) Italian electrical engineer and pioneer in the invention and development of radio. In 1895 he achieved radio communication over more than a mile, and in England 1896 he conducted successful experiments that led to the formation of the company that became Marconi's Wireless Telegraph Company Ltd. He shared the Nobel Prize for Physics 1909.

**Marco Polo** Venetian traveller and writer; see Marco ◊Polo.

**Marcos, Ferdinand Edralin** (1917–1989) Filipino right-wing politician, dictator-president 1965–86, when he was forced into exile in Hawaii by a popular front led by Corazon ◊Aquino.

**Marcos, Imelda Romualdez** (1930– ) Filipino politician and socialite, wife of the dictator-president Ferdinand ◊Marcos, and known as the 'Iron Butterfly'.

**Marcus Aurelius** adopted name of Marcus Annius Verus (AD 121–180) Roman emperor from 161 and Stoic philosopher who wrote the philosophical *Meditations.* He fought a series of campaigns against the Germanic tribes on the Rhine–Danube frontier, known collectively as the Marcomannic Wars, and died in Pannonia where he had gone to drive back the invading Marcomanni.

**Mardi Gras** (French 'fat Tuesday' from the custom of using up all the fat in the household before the beginning of ◊Lent) Shrove Tuesday. A festival was traditionally held on this day in Paris, and there are carnivals in many parts of the world, including New Orleans, Louisiana; Italy; and Brazil.

**Margaret, Rose** (1930– ) Princess of the UK, younger daughter of George VI and sister of Elizabeth II. In 1960 she married Anthony Armstrong-Jones, later created Lord Snowdon, but they were divorced in 1978. Their children are *David, Viscount Linley* (1961– ) and *Lady Sarah Chatto* (1964– ).

**Margaret of Anjou** (1430–1482) Queen of England from 1445, wife of ◊Henry VI of England. After the outbreak of the Wars of the ◊Roses in 1455, she acted as the leader of the Lancastrians, but was defeated and captured at the battle of Tewkesbury in 1471 by Edward IV.

**Margaret, St** (*c.* 1045–1093) Queen of Scotland, the granddaughter of King Edmund Ironside of England. She went to Scotland after the Norman Conquest, and soon after married Malcolm III. The marriage of her daughter Matilda to Henry I united the Norman and English royal houses.

**margarine** butter substitute made from animal fats and/or vegetable oils.
The French chemist Hippolyte Mège-Mouriès invented margarine in 1889. Today, margarines are usually made with vegetable oils, such as soya, corn, or sunflower oil, giving a product low in saturated fats (see ◊polyunsaturate) and fortified with vitamins A and D.

**margrave** German title (equivalent of marquess) for the 'counts of the march', who guarded the frontier regions of the Holy Roman Empire from Charlemagne's time. Later the title was used by other territorial princes. Chief among these were the margraves of Austria and of Brandenburg.

**Margrethe II** (1940– ) Queen of Denmark from 1972, when she succeeded her father Frederick IX. In 1967, she married the French diplomat Count Henri de Laborde de Monpezat, who took the title Prince Hendrik. Her heir is Crown Prince Frederick (1968– ).

**marguerite** European plant belonging to the daisy family. It is a shrubby perennial with white daisylike flowers. Marguerite is also the name of a cultivated variety of ◊chrysanthemum. (*Leucanthemum vulgare,* family Compositae.)

**Mariana Islands** or *Marianas,* archipelago in the northwest Pacific, east of the Philippines, divided politically into ◊*Guam* (an unincorporated territory of the USA) and the ◊*Northern Mariana Islands* (a commonwealth of the USA with its own internal government).

**Mariana Trench** lowest region on the Earth's surface; the deepest part of the sea floor. The trench is 2,400 km/1,500 mi long and is situated 300 km/200 mi east of the Mariana Islands, in the northwestern Pacific Ocean. Its deepest part is the gorge known as the Challenger Deep, which extends 11,034 m/36,210 ft below sea level.

**Maria Theresa** (1717–1780) Empress of Austria from 1740, when she succeeded her father, the Holy Roman Emperor Charles VI; her claim to the throne was challenged and she became embroiled, first in the War of the ◊Austrian Succession 1740–48, then in the ◊Seven Years' War 1756–63; she remained in possession of Austria but lost Silesia. The rest of her reign was peaceful and, with her son Joseph II, she introduced social reforms.

**Marie Antoinette** (1755–1793) Queen of France from 1774. She was the fourth daughter of Empress Maria Theresa of Austria and the Holy Roman Emperor Francis I, and married ◊Louis XVI of France in 1770. Her devotion to the interests of Austria, reputation for extravagance, and supposed connection with the scandal of the Diamond Necklace made her unpopular, and helped to provoke the ◊French Revolution of 1789. She was tried for treason in October 1793 and guillotined.

**Marie de' Medici** (1573–1642) Queen of France, wife of Henry IV from 1600, and regent (after his murder) for their son Louis XIII. She left the government to her favourites, the Concinis, until Louis XIII seized power and executed them in 1617. She was banished but, after she led a revolt in 1619, ◊Richelieu effected her reconciliation with her son. When she attempted to oust him again in 1630, she was exiled.

**marigold** any of several plants belonging to the daisy family, including pot marigold (*C. officinalis*) and the tropical American *T. patula,* commonly known as French marigold. (Genera *Calendula* and *Tagetes,* family Compositae.)

**marijuana** dried leaves and flowers of the hemp plant ◊cannabis, used as a drug; it is illegal in most countries. It is eaten or inhaled and causes euphoria, distortion of time, and heightened sensations of sight and sound. Mexico is the world's largest producer.

**marimba** musical instrument, a bass ◊xylophone, a Mexican variant of an instrument originating in Africa, with wooden rather than metal tubular resonators.

**marines** fighting force that operates both on land and at sea.

The *US Marine Corps* (1775) is constituted as an arm of the US Navy. It is made up of infantry and air support units trained and equipped for amphibious landings under fire.

**maritime law** that part of the law dealing with the sea: in particular, fishing areas, ships, and navigation. Seas are divided into *internal waters* governed by a state's internal laws (such as harbours, inlets); *territorial waters* (the area of sea adjoining the coast over which a state claims rights); the *continental shelf* (the seabed and subsoil that the coastal state is entitled to exploit beyond the territorial waters); and the *high seas,* where international law applies.

**marjoram** aromatic herb belonging to the mint family. Wild marjoram (*O. vulgare*) is found both in Europe and Asia and has become naturalized in the Americas; the sweet marjoram (*O. majorana*) used in cooking is widely cultivated. (Genus *Origanum* or *Marjorana,* family Labiatae.)

**Mark Antony** (*c.* 83–30 BC) also known as Marcus Antonius, Roman politician and soldier who was the last serious rival to Octavian's (later Augustus) domination of the Roman world. He served under Julius ◊Caesar in Gaul and during the civil war when he commanded the left wing at the final battle of Pharsalus. He was consul with Caesar in 44 when he tried to secure for him the title of king. After Caesar's assassination, he formed the Second Triumvirate with Octavian and Lepidus. In 42 he defeated Brutus and Cassius at Philippi. He took Egypt as his share of the empire and formed a liaison with the Egyptian queen Cleopatra, but returned to Rome in 40 to marry Octavia, the sister of Octavian. In 32 the Senate declared war on Cleopatra, and Antony, who had combined forces with Cleopatra, was defeated by Octavian at Actium, in 31. He returned to Egypt and committed suicide.

**marketing** promoting goods and services to consumers. In the 20th century, marketing has played an increasingly larger role in determining company policy, influencing product development, pricing, methods of distribution, advertising, and promotion techniques.

**Mark, St** (lived 1st century AD) In the New Testament, Christian apostle and evangelist whose name is given to the second Gospel. It was probably written AD 65–70, and used by the authors of the first and third Gospels. He is the patron saint of Venice, and his emblem is a winged lion; feast day 25 April.

**Marks & Spencer** UK chain store. The company was founded in 1884 by *Michael Marks* (1863–1907). In 1894 he was joined by *Thomas Spencer* (1852–1905), cashier at one of his suppliers. Simon Marks, the founder's son, became chairman in 1916 and with his brother-in-law, Israel Sieff, developed the company from a 'Penny Bazaar' to a national and international chain store.

**marlin** or *spearfish,* any of several open-sea fishes known as billfishes. Some 2.5 m/7 ft long, they are found in warmer waters and have elongated snouts and high-standing dorsal (back) fins. Members of the family include the *sailfish* (*Istiophorus platypterus*), the fastest of all fishes over short distances – reaching speeds of 100 kph/62 mph – and the *blue marlin* (*Makaira nigricans*), highly prized as a 'game' fish. (Family Istiophoridae, order Perciformes.)

**Marlowe, Christopher** (1564–1593) English poet and dramatist. His work includes the blank-verse plays *Tamburlaine the Great* in two parts (1587–88), *The Jew of Malta* (about 1591), *Edward II* (about 1592) and *Dr Faustus* (about 1594); the poem *Hero and Leander* (1598); and a translation of parts of ◊Ovid's *Amores*. Marlowe transformed the new medium of English blank verse into a powerful, melodic form of expression.

**marmoset** any of a group of small tree-dwelling monkeys found in South and Central America; some only reach a body length of 15 cm/6 in. Most species have characteristic tufted ears, clawlike nails, and a handsome tail, which is not prehensile (it cannot be used to grip branches in the same way as the arms and legs). Some marmosets are known as tamarins. (Genus *Callithrix* and related genera, family Callithricidae.)

**marmot** any of several large burrowing rodents belonging to the squirrel family. There are about 15 species, distributed throughout Canada and the USA, and from the Alps to the Himalayas. They eat plants and some insects, and live in colonies, make burrows (one to each family), and hibernate in winter (alpine marmots hibernate for six months of the year). In North America they are called *woodchucks* or *groundhogs*. (Genus *Marmota*, family Sciuridae.)

**Marne, Battles of the** in World War I, two unsuccessful German offensives in northern France. In the *First Battle* 6–9 September 1914 German advance was halted by French and British troops under the overall command of the French general Jospeh Joffre; in the *Second Battle* 15 July–4 August 1918, the German advance was defeated by British, French, and US troops under the French general Henri Pétain, and German morale crumbled.

**Maronite** member of a Christian sect deriving from refugee Monothelites (Christian heretics) of the 7th century. They were subsequently united with the Roman Catholic Church and number about 400,000 in Lebanon and Syria, with an equal number scattered in southern Europe and the Americas.

**Marquesas Islands** French *Iles Marquises*, island group in ◊French Polynesia, lying north of the Tuamotu Archipelago; area 1,270 sq km/490 sq mi; population (1988) 7,500. The administrative headquarters is Atuona on Hiva Oa. The islands were annexed by France 1842.

**marquess** or *marquis*, title and rank of a nobleman who in the British peerage ranks below a duke and above an earl. The wife of a marquess is a marchioness.

**marquetry** inlaying of various woods, bone, or ivory, usually on furniture, to create ornate patterns and pictures. *Parquetry* is the term used for geometrical inlaid patterns. The method is thought to have originated in Germany or Holland.

**Márquez, Gabriel García** Colombian novelist; see Gabriel ◊García Márquez.

**Marrakesh** or *Marrakech*, historic imperial city in Morocco in the foothills of the Atlas Mountains, about 210 km/130 mi south of Casablanca; population (1982) 439,700; urban area (1993) 602,000. It is a tourist centre, and has textile, leather, and food processing industries. Founded in 1062, it has a medieval palace and mosques, and was formerly the capital of Morocco.

**marram grass** coarse perennial grass that flourishes in sandy areas. Because of its tough, creeping roots, it is widely used to hold coastal dunes in place. (*Ammophila arenaria*, family Gramineae.)

**marriage** legally or culturally sanctioned union of one man and one woman (monogamy); one man and two or more women (polygamy); one woman and two or more men (polyandry). The basis of marriage varies considerably in different societies (romantic love in the West; arranged marriages in some other societies), but most marriage ceremonies, contracts, or customs involve a set of rights and duties, such as care and protection, and there is generally an expectation that children will be born of the union to continue the family line and maintain the family property.

In the 1990s the concept of marriage was extended in some countries to include the blessing or registration of homosexual relationships.

**marrow** or *vegetable marrow*, trailing vine that produces large pulpy fruits, used as vegetables and in preserves; the young fruits of one variety are known as courgettes (US zucchini). (*Cucurbita pepo*, family Cucurbitaceae.)

**Mars** fourth planet from the Sun. It is much smaller than Venus or Earth, with a mass 0.11 that of Earth. Mars is slightly pear-shaped, with a low, level northern hemisphere, which is comparatively uncratered and geologically 'young', and a heavily cratered 'ancient' southern hemisphere.

*mean distance from the Sun* 227.9 million km/141.6 million mi
*equatorial diameter* 6,780 km/4,210 mi
*rotation period* 24 hr 37 min
*year* 687 Earth days
*atmosphere* 95% carbon dioxide, 3% nitrogen, 1.5% argon, and 0.15% oxygen. Red atmospheric dust from the surface whipped up by winds of up to 450 kph/280 mph accounts for the light pink sky. The surface pressure is less than 1% of the Earth's atmospheric pressure at sea level
*surface* the landscape is a dusty, red, eroded lava plain. Mars has white polar caps (water ice and frozen carbon dioxide) that advance and retreat with the seasons
*satellites* two small satellites: Phobos and Deimos.

**Mars** *Mavors* or *Mamers*, in Roman mythology, the god of war (*Mars Gradivus*), depicted as a fearless warrior. The month of March is named after him. He was identified with the Greek ◊Ares, but achieved greater status.

**Marseille** English *Marseilles*, chief seaport and second city of France, and administrative centre of the *département* of Bouches-du-Rhône and of the ◊Provence-Alpes-Côte d'Azur region, situated on the Golfe du Lion on the Mediterranean Sea; population (1990) 807,700. Industries include chemicals, metallurgy, shipbuilding, and food processing, as well as oil-refining at the massive industrial complex of Fos-sur-Mer to the west.

**marsh** low-lying wetland. Freshwater marshes are common wherever groundwater, surface springs, streams, or run-off cause frequent flooding or more or less permanent shallow water. A marsh is alkaline whereas a ◊bog is acid. Marshes develop on inorganic silt or clay soils. Rushes are typical marsh plants. Large marshes dominated by papyrus, cattail, and reeds, with standing water throughout the year, are commonly called swamps. Near the sea, salt marshes may form.

**Marshall Islands** Republic of the (RMI)
**area** 181 sq km/70 sq mi

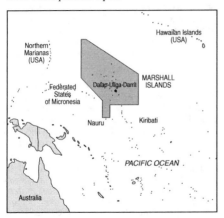

**capital** Dalap-Uliga-Darrit (on Majuro atoll)
**major towns/cities** Ebeye (the only other town)
**physical features** comprises the Ratak and Ralik island chains in the West Pacific, which together form an archipelago of 31 coral atolls, 5 islands, and 1,152 islets
**head of state and government** Imata Kabua from 1997
**political system** liberal democracy
**political parties** no organized party system, but in 1991 an opposition grouping, the Ralik Ratak Democratic Party, was founded to oppose the ruling group
**currency** US dollar
**GNP per capita (PPP)** (US$) 1,780 (1998 est)
**exports** coconut products, trochus shells, copra, handicrafts, fish, live animals. Principal market: USA
**population** 62,000 (1999 est)
**language** Marshallese, English (both official)
**religion** Christian (mainly Protestant) and Baha'i

*life expectancy* 63 (men); 66 (women) (1998 est)
*Chronology*
**after c. 1000 BC** Micronesians first settled the islands.
**1529** Visited by Spanish navigator Miguel de Saavedra and thereafter came under Spanish influence.
**1875** Spanish rule formally declared in face of increasing encroachment by German traders.
**1885** German protectorate established.
**1914** Seized by Japan on the outbreak of World War I.
**1920–44** Administered under League of Nations mandate by Japan and vigorously colonized.
**1944** Japanese removed after heavy fighting with US troops during World War II.
**1946–63** Eniwetok and Bikini atolls used for US atom-bomb tests; islanders later demanded rehabilitation and compensation for the damage.
**1947** Became part of United Nations (UN) Pacific Islands Trust Territory, administered by USA.
**1979** Amata Kabua was elected president as internal self-government was established.
**1986** The Compact of Free Association with the USA granted the islands self-government, with the USA retaining the responsibility for defence and security until 2001.
**1990** UN trust status was terminated.
**1991** Independence was agreed with Kabua as president; UN membership was granted.
**1996** Death of President Amata Kabua.
**1997** Imata Kabua was elected president.
**1998** President Imata Kabua's government survived two no-confidence votes.

**Marshall Plan** programme of US economic aid to Europe, set up at the end of World War II, totalling $13,000 billion between 1948 and 1952. Officially known as the European Recovery Programme, it was announced by Secretary of State George C Marshall in a speech at Harvard in June 1947, but it was in fact the work of a State Department group led by Dean Acheson. The perceived danger of a communist takeover in post-war Europe was the main reason for the aid effort.

**marsh marigold** plant belonging to the buttercup family, known as the kingcup in the UK and as the cowslip in the USA. It grows in moist, sheltered places and has brilliant yellow five-sepalled flowers. (*Caltha palustris*, family Ranunculaceae.)

**marsh rose** shrub native to South Africa, which grows to 1–4 m/3–13 ft high. It is under threat, partly because its beautiful flowers are frequently picked, but also because of fungi, probably introduced by footwear or equipment, and by changes in management practice that have prevented periodic fires which are necessary for seed germination. Ironically, numbers of the shrub are now so low that uncontrolled fires could wipe out the remaining adult specimens. Although protected, they remain highly threatened. (*Orothamnus zeyheri*.)

**Marston Moor, Battle of** battle fought in the English Civil War on 2 July 1644 on

Marston Moor, 11 km/7 mi west of York. The Royalists were conclusively defeated by the Parliamentarians and Scots.

**marsupial** (Greek *marsupion* 'little purse') mammal in which the female has a pouch where she carries her young (born tiny and immature) for a considerable time after birth. Marsupials include omnivorous, herbivorous, and carnivorous species, among them the kangaroo, wombat, opossum, phalanger, bandicoot, dasyure, and wallaby.

**marten** small bushy-tailed carnivorous mammal belonging to the weasel family. Martens live in North America, Europe, and temperate regions of Asia, and are agile tree climbers. (Genus *Martes,* family Mustelidae.)

**Martens, Wilfried** (1936– ) Belgian politician; prime minister 1979–92. He was president of the Dutch-speaking Social Christian Party (CVP) 1972–79 and, as prime minister, headed several coalition governments in the period 1979–92, when he was replaced by Jean-Luc Dehaene heading a new coalition.

**Martial, (Marcus Valerius Martialis)** (*c.* AD 41–*c.* 104) Latin poet and epigrammatist. Born in Bilbilis, Spain, Martial settled in Rome AD 64, where he lived a life of poverty and dependence. His poetry, often obscene, is keenly observant of all classes in contemporary Rome. Of his works the following survive: about 33 poems from *Liber Spectaculorum,* published AD 80 to commemorate the opening of the Colosseum; two collections of short mottoes entitled *Xenia* and *Apophoreta,* AD 84–85; and 12 books of *Epigrams,* published AD 86–102.

**martial arts** any of several styles of armed and unarmed combat developed in the East from ancient techniques and arts. Common martial arts include aikido, ◊judo, jujitsu, ◊karate, kendo, and ◊kung fu.

**martial law** replacement of civilian by military authorities in the maintenance of order.

**martin** any of several species of birds belonging to the swallow family. (Family Hirundinidae, order Passeriformes.)

**Martinique** French island in the West Indies (Lesser Antilles)
*area* 1,079 sq km/417 sq mi
*capital* Fort-de-France
*features* several active volcanoes; Napoleon's empress Josephine was born in Martinique, and her childhood home is now a museum
*industries* sugar, cocoa, rum, bananas, pineapples
*population* (1990) 359,600
*language* French (official), Creole
*history* Martinique was reached by Spanish navigators in 1493, became a French colony in 1635, an overseas department in 1946, and from 1974 also an administrative region of France.

**Martinmas** in the Christian calendar, the feast of St Martin, 11 November.

**martyr** (Greek 'witness') one who voluntarily suffers death for refusing to renounce a religious faith. The first recorded Christian martyr was St

Stephen, who was killed in Jerusalem shortly after the apostles began to preach.

**Marvell, Andrew** (1621–1678) English metaphysical poet and satirist. In 'To His Coy Mistress' (1650–52) and 'An Horatian Ode upon Cromwell's Return from Ireland' (1650) he produced, respectively, the most searching seduction and political poems in the language. He was committed to the Parliamentary cause, and was Member of Parliament for Hull from 1659. He devoted his last years mainly to verse satire and prose works attacking repressive aspects of the state and government.

**Marx, Karl Heinrich** (1818–1883) German philosopher, economist, and social theorist whose account of change through conflict is known as historical, or dialectical, materialism (see ◊Marxism). His *Das Kapital/Capital* (1867–95) is the fundamental text of Marxist economics, and his systematic theses on class struggle, history, and the importance of economic factors in politics have exercised an enormous influence on later thinkers and political activists.

**Marx Brothers** team of US film comedians: the silent *Harpo* (from the harp he played) 1888–1964; Julius *Groucho* (from his temper) 1890–1977; Leonard *Chico* (from the 'chicks' – women – he chased) 1891–1961; Adolph, Milton *Gummo* (from his gumshoes, or galoshes) *c.* 1892–1977, who left the team before they began making films; and Herbert *Zeppo* (born at the time of the first zeppelins) 1901–1979, part of the team until 1935. They made a total of 13 zany films 1929–49 including *Animal Crackers* (1930), *Monkey Business* (1931), *Duck Soup* (1933), *A Day at the Races* (1937), *A Night at the Opera* (1935), and *Go West* (1940).

**Marxism** philosophical system, developed by the 19th-century German social theorists ◊Marx and ◊Engels, also known as *dialectical materialism,* under which matter gives rise to mind (materialism) and all is subject to change (from dialectic; see ◊Hegel). As applied to history, it supposes that the succession of feudalism, capitalism, socialism, and finally the classless society is inevitable. The stubborn resistance of any existing system to change necessitates its complete overthrow in the *class struggle* – in the case of capitalism, by the proletariat – rather than gradual modification.

**Marxism–Leninism** term used by the Soviet dictator Stalin and his supporters to define their own views as the orthodox position of ◊Marxism as a means of refuting criticism. It has subsequently been employed by other communist parties as a yardstick for ideological purity.

**Mary Queen of Scots** (1542–1587) Queen of Scotland (1542–67). Also known as *Mary Stuart,* she was the daughter of James V. Mary's connection with the English royal line from Henry VII made her a threat to Elizabeth I's hold on the English throne, especially as she represented a champion of the Catholic cause. She was married three times. After her forced abdication she was imprisoned but escaped in 1568 to England. Elizabeth I held her prisoner, while the Roman Catholics, who regarded Mary as rightful queen of England, formed many conspiracies to place her on the throne, and for complicity in one of these she was executed.

**Mary** in the New Testament, the mother of Jesus through divine intervention (see ◊Annunciation), wife of ◊Joseph. The Roman Catholic Church maintains belief in her ◊Immaculate Conception and bodily assumption into heaven, and venerates her as a mediator. Feast day of the Assumption is 15 August.

**Mary** two queens of England:

**Mary I** called *Bloody Mary* (1516–1558) Queen of England from 1553. She was the eldest daughter of Henry VIII by Catherine of Aragón. When Edward VI died, Mary secured the crown without difficulty in spite of the conspiracy to substitute Lady Jane ◊Grey. In 1554 Mary married Philip II of Spain, and as a devout Roman Catholic obtained the restoration of papal supremacy and sanctioned the persecution of Protestants. She was succeeded by her half-sister Elizabeth I.

**Mary II** (1662–1694) Queen of England, Scotland, and Ireland from 1688. She was the Protestant elder daughter of the Catholic ◊James II, and in 1677 was married to her cousin ◊William of Orange. After the 1688 revolution she accepted the crown jointly with William.

**Maryland** state of eastern USA. It was nicknamed Old Line State or Free State. Maryland ratified the US Constitution in 1788, becoming the 7th state to join the Union. It is bordered to the north by Pennsylvania, along the old ◊Mason-Dixon Line, to the east by Delaware, with which it shares most of the Delmarva Peninsula, to the south by Virginia and West Virginia, with the latter of which it also shares a western boundary. At the Fall Line, where the Anacostia River joins the Potomac River, is the District of Columbia, which was carved out of Maryland and Virginia in 1790
*population* (1995) 5,042,400
*area* 31,600 sq km/12,198 sq mi
*capital* Annapolis
*towns and cities* Baltimore, Silver Spring, Dundalk, Bethesda
*industries and products* poultry, dairy products, machinery, steel, cars and parts, boatbuilding, electric and electronic equipment, chemicals, fish and shellfish, tourism.

**Mary Magdalene, St** (lived 1st century AD) in the New Testament, a woman whom Jesus cured of possession by evil spirits. She was present at the Crucifixion and burial, and was the first to meet the risen Jesus. She is often identified with the woman of St Luke's gospel who anointed Jesus' feet, and her symbol is a jar of ointment; feast day 22 July.

**Mary of Guise** or *Mary of Lorraine* (1515–1560) French-born second wife of James V of Scotland from 1538, and 1554–59 regent of Scotland for her daughter ◊Mary Queen of Scots. A Catholic, she moved from reconciliation with Scottish Protestants to repression, and died during a Protestant rebellion in Edinburgh.

**Masaccio, (Tommaso di Giovanni di Simone Guidi)** (1401–*c.* 1428) Florentine painter, one of the major figures of the early Italian Renaissance. His frescoes in the Brancacci Chapel of Santa Maria del Carmine, Florence (1425–28) show a decisive break with traditional styles. He was the first painter to apply the scientific laws of perspective, newly discovered by the architect Brunelleschi, and achieved a sense of space and volume that gives his pictures a sculptural quality.

**Masai** member of an East African people whose territory is divided between Tanzania and Kenya. They number about 250,000, and speak a Nilotic language belonging to the Nilo-Saharan family. Traditionally they are warriors and pastoral nomads, but much of their land was taken over by European colonists and today there is considerable pressure on them from the Kenyan government to settle as farmers.

**Masaryk, Tomáš Garrigue** (1850–1937) Czechoslovak nationalist politician. He directed the revolutionary movement against the Austrian Empire, founding with Edvard ◊Beneš and Milan Stefanik the Czechoslovak National Council. In 1918 he was elected first president of the newly formed Czechoslovak Republic. Three times re-elected, he resigned in 1935 in favour of Beneš.

**maser** acronym for microwave amplification by stimulated emission of radiation, in physics, a high-frequency microwave amplifier or oscillator in which the signal to be amplified is used to stimulate excited atoms into emitting energy at the same frequency. Atoms or molecules are raised to a higher energy level and then allowed to lose this energy by radiation emitted at a precise frequency. The principle has been extended to other parts of the electromagnetic spectrum as, for example, in the ◊laser.

**Maseru** capital of Lesotho, on the Caledon River at the border with Free State in South Africa; population (1992 est) 367,000. Founded in 1869 by the Basotho chief Mshweshwe I, it is a centre for trade, light manufacturing, and food processing. The National University of Lesotho (1975) is at nearby Roma.

**Masire, Quett Ketumile Joni** (1925– ) Botswanan politician; president 1980–98. In 1962, with Seretse ◊Khama, he founded the Botswana Democratic Party (BDP) and in 1965 was made deputy prime minister. After independence in 1966, he became vice-president and, on Khama's death in 1980, president, continuing a policy of nonalignment. He retired in March 1998 and was succeeded by Festus Mogae of the BDP.

**Mason–Dixon Line** in the USA, the boundary line between Maryland and Pennsylvania (latitude 39° 43' 26.3' N), named after Charles Mason (1730–1787) and Jeremiah Dixon (died 1777), English astronomers and surveyors who surveyed it 1763–67. It is popularly seen as dividing the North from the South.

**Mass** in music, the setting of the invariable parts of the Christian Mass, that is the *Kyrie,*

*Gloria, Credo, Sanctus* with *Benedictus,* and *Agnus Dei.* A notable example is J S Bach's *Mass in B Minor.*

**mass** in physics, the quantity of matter in a body as measured by its inertia. Mass determines the acceleration produced in a body by a given force acting on it, the acceleration being inversely proportional to the mass of the body. The mass also determines the force exerted on a body by ◊gravity on Earth, although this attraction varies slightly from place to place. In the SI system, the base unit of mass is the kilogram.

**Mass** in Christianity, the celebration of the ◊Eucharist.

**Massachusetts** state of northeast USA. It is nicknamed the Bay State or the Old Colony State. Massachusetts ratified the US Constitution in 1788, becoming the 6th state to join the Union. It is a region of great significance to US history, being the point of disembarkation for the *Mayflower* Pilgrims, as well as the site of key conflicts in the American Revolution. Massachusetts is bordered to the north by Vermont and New Hampshire, to the west by New York, to the south by Connecticut and Rhode Island, and to the southeast and east by the Atlantic Ocean
*population* (1995) 6,073,600
*area* 21,500 sq km/8,299 sq mi
*capital* ◊Boston
*towns and cities* Worcester, Springfield, Lowell, New Bedford, Brockton, Cambridge
*industries and products* electronic, communications, and optical equipment, precision instruments, non-electrical machinery, fish, cranberries, dairy products, tourism, academia and research, finance sector.

**massage** manipulation of the soft tissues of the body, the muscles, ligaments, and tendons, either to encourage the healing of specific injuries or to produce the general beneficial effects of relaxing muscular tension, stimulating blood circulation, and improving the tone and strength of the skin and muscles.

**mass–energy equation** Albert ◊Einstein's equation $E = mc^2$, denoting the equivalence of mass and energy, where $E$ is the energy in joules, $m$ is the mass in kilograms, and $c$ is the speed of light, in a vacuum, in metres per second.

**mass extinction** an event that produces the extinction of many species at about the same time. One notable example is the boundary between the Cretaceous and Tertiary periods (known as the ◊K-T boundary) that saw the extinction of the dinosaurs and other big reptiles, and many of the marine invertebrates as well. Mass extinctions have taken place frequently during Earth's history.

**Massif Central** upland region of south-central France with mountains and plateaux; area 93,000 sq km/36,000 sq mi, highest peak Puy de Sancy, 1,886 m/6,188 ft. It is a source of hydroelectricity.

**mass number** or *nucleon number,* sum (symbol *A*) of the numbers of protons and neutrons in the nucleus of an atom. It is used along with the ◊atomic number (the number of protons) in nuclear notation: in symbols that represent nuclear isotopes, such as $^{14}_6$C, the lower number is the atomic number, and the upper number is the mass number.

**Massorah** collection of philological notes on the Hebrew text of the Old Testament. It was at first an oral tradition, but was committed to writing in the Aramaic language at Tiberias, Palestine, between the 6th and 9th centuries.

**mass production** manufacture of goods on a large scale, a technique that aims for low unit cost and high output. In factories mass production is achieved by a variety of means, such as division and specialization of labour and mechanization. These speed up production and allow the manufacture of near-identical, interchangeable parts. Such parts can then be assembled quickly into a finished product on an assembly line.

**mastiff** breed of powerful dog, usually fawn in colour, that was originally bred in Britain for hunting purposes. It has a large head, wide-set eyes, and broad muzzle. It can grow up to 90 cm/36 in at the shoulder, and weigh 100 kg/220 lb.

**mastodon** any of an extinct family of mammals belonging to the elephant order. They differed from elephants and mammoths in the structure of their grinding teeth. There were numerous species, among which the *American mastodon* (*Mastodon americanum*), about 3 m/ 10 ft high, of the Pleistocene era, is well known. They were hunted by humans for food. (Family Mastodontidae, order Proboscidae.)

**Matabeleland** western portion of Zimbabwe between the Zambezi and Limpopo rivers, inhabited by the Ndebele people. It is divided into two administrative regions (Matabeleland North and Matabeleland South)
*area* 181,605 sq km/70,118 sq mi
*towns and cities* Bulawayo, Hwange
*physical* rich plains watered by tributaries of the Zambezi and Limpopo rivers
*industries* gold and other mineral mines, engineering
*agriculture* cotton, sugar, maize, cattle
*language* Ndebele
*famous people* Joshua Nkomo
*history* granted to the British South Africa Company 1889; occupied 1893 after attacks on white settlements in Mashonaland; included in Southern Rhodesia 1923; became part of independent Zimbabwe 1980.

**Mata Hari** stage name of Margaretha Geertruida Zelle (1876–1917) Dutch courtesan, dancer, and probable spy. In World War I she had affairs with highly placed military and government officials on both sides and told Allied secrets to the Germans. She may have been a double agent, in the pay of both France and Germany. She was shot by the French on espionage charges.

**materialism** philosophical theory that there is nothing in existence over and above matter and

## MATHEMATICAL SIGNS

| Symbol | Meaning | Symbol | Meaning |
|---|---|---|---|
| $a \rightarrow b$ | a implies b | $a-b=c$ | a–b, read as 'a minus b', denotes subtraction of b from a. a–b, or c, is the difference. Subtraction is the opposite of addition. |
| $\infty$ | infinity | | |
| lim | limiting value | | |
| $a \approx b$ | a approximately equal to b | | |
| $a=b$ | a equal to b | $a \times b=c$ | a×b, read as 'a multiplied by b', denotes multpilication of a by b. a×b, or c, is the product; a and b are factors of c. |
| $a>b$ | a greater than b | | |
| $a<b$ | a smaller than b | | |
| $a \neq b$ | a not equal to b | | |
| $b<a<c$ | a greater than b and smaller than c, that is a lies between b and c, but cannot equal either | $ab=c$ | a.b=c |
| | | $a:b=c$ | a:b, read as 'a divided by b', denotes division. a is the dividend, b is the divisor. a:b, or c, is the quotient. One aspect of division – repeated subtraction, is the opposite of multiplication – repeated addition. |
| ab | a equal to or greater than b, that is a at least as great as b | | |
| $a \leq b$ | a equal to or less than b, that is, a at most as great as b | | |
| $b \leq a \leq c$ | a lies between the values of b and c and could take the values of b and c | $a \div b=c$ | a/b=c |
| lal | absolute value of a; this is always positive, for example l–5l=5 | $a^b$ | $a^b$, read as 'a to the power b'. a is the base, b the exponent |
| + | addition sign, positive | $^b\sqrt{a}=c$ | $^b\sqrt{a}$ is the bth root of a, b being known as the root exponent. In the special case of 2 |
| – | subtraction sign, negative | | |
| × | multiplication sign, times | $\sqrt{a}=c$, 2 | $\sqrt{a}$ or c is known as the square root of a, ans the root exponent is usually omitted, that is 2 |
| : or ÷ or / | division sign, divided by | | |
| $a+b=c$ | a+b, read as 'a+b', denotes the addition of a nd b. The result of the addition, c, is also known as the sum. | $\sqrt{a}=\sqrt{a}.e$ | exponential constant and is the base of natural (napierian) logarithms = 2.7182818284... |
| $\int$ | indefinite integral | | |
| $_a\int^b(x)dx$ | definite integral, or integral between x=a and x=b | $\pi$ | pi, ratio of the circumference of a circle to its diameter = 3.1415925535 |

matter in motion. Such a theory excludes the possibility of deities. It also sees mind as an attribute of the physical, denying idealist theories that see mind as something independent of body; for example, Descartes' theory of 'thinking substance'.

**mathematics** science of relationships between numbers, between spatial configurations, and abstract structures. The main divisions of *pure mathematics* include geometry, arithmetic, algebra, calculus, and trigonometry. Mechanics, statistics, numerical analysis, computing, the mathematical theories of astronomy, electricity, optics, thermodynamics, and atomic studies come under the heading of *applied mathematics.*

**Matilda,** *the Empress Maud* (1102–1167) claimant to the throne of England. On the death of her father, Henry I, in 1135, the barons elected her cousin Stephen to be king. Matilda invaded England in 1139, and was crowned by her supporters in 1141. Civil war ensued until Stephen was finally recognized as king in 1153, with Henry II (Matilda's son) as his successor.

**Matisse, Henri Emile Benoît** (1869–1954) French painter, sculptor and illustrator. Matisse was one of the most original creative forces in early 20th-century art. He was a leading figure in ◊Fauvism and later developed a style characterized by strong, sinuous lines, surface pattern, and brilliant colour. *The Dance* (1910) (The Hermitage, St Petersburg) is characteristic. Later works include pure abstracts, as in his collages of coloured paper shapes (*gouaches découpées*).

**matriarchy** form of society where domestic and political life is dominated by women, where kinship is traced exclusively through the female line, and where religion is centred around the cult of a mother goddess. Its opposite concept is that of ◊patriarchy.

**matrix** in biology, usually refers to the extra-cellular matrix.

**matrix** in mathematics, a square ($n \times n$) or rectangular ($m \times n$) array of elements (numbers or algebraic variables) used to facilitate the study of problems in which the relation between the elements is important. They are a means of condensing information about mathematical systems and can be used for, among other things, solving simultaneous linear equations (see ◊simultaneous equations and ◊transformation).

**matter** in physics, anything that has mass. All matter is made up of ◊atoms, which in turn are made up of ◊elementary particles; it ordinarily exists in one of three physical states: solid, liquid, or gas.

**Matterhorn** French *le Cervin*, Italian *il Cervino*, mountain peak in the Alps on the Swiss-Italian border; 4,478 m/14,690 ft. It was first climbed 1865 by English mountaineer Edward Whymper (1840–1911); four members of his party of seven were killed when a rope broke during their descent.

**Matthews, Stanley** (1915–  ) English footballer who played for Stoke City, Blackpool, and England. He played nearly 700 Football League games, and won 54 international caps. He was

the first Footballer of the Year in 1948 (and again in 1963), the first European Footballer of the Year in 1956, and the first footballer to be knighted for services to the game in 1965.
**career highlights**
**Football League** appearances: 698; goals: 71
**international appearances** 54; goals: 11
**FA Cup** 1953
**Footballer of the Year** 1948, 1963
**European Footballer of the Year** 1956

**Matthew, St** (lived 1st century AD) Christian apostle and evangelist, the traditional author of the first Gospel. He is usually identified with Levi, who was a tax collector in the service of Herod Antipas, and was called by Jesus to be a disciple as he sat by the Lake of Galilee receiving customs dues. His emblem is a man with wings; feast day 21 September.

**Maugham, (William) Somerset** (1874–1965) English writer. His work includes the novels *Of Human Bondage* (1915), *The Moon and Sixpence* (1919), and *Cakes and Ale* (1930); the short-story collections *Ashenden* (1928) and *Rain and Other Stories* (1933); and the plays *Lady Frederick* (1907) and *Our Betters* (1917). There were new editions of *Collected Stories* in 1900 and *Selected Plays* in 1991. A penetrating observer of human behaviour, his writing is essentially anti-romantic and there is a vein of cynicism running through his work.

**Mau Mau** Kenyan secret guerrilla movement 1952–60, an offshoot of the Kikuyu Central Association banned in World War II. Its aim was to end British colonial rule. This was achieved 1960 with the granting of Kenyan independence and the election of Jomo Kenyatta as Kenya's first prime minister.

**Mauna Kea** astronomical observatory in Hawaii, USA, built on a dormant volcano at 4,200 m/13,784 ft above sea level. Because of its elevation high above clouds, atmospheric moisture, and artificial lighting, Mauna Kea is ideal for infrared astronomy. The first telescope on the site was installed in 1970.

**Mauna Loa** active volcano on the Pacific island of Hawaii, rising to a height of 4,169 m/13,678 ft. It has numerous craters, including the second-largest active crater in the world. Since the early 19th century there have been lava flows from the crater covering about half the island of Hawaii; averaging one eruption every 31/2 years, it is considered an effusive, rather than an explosive, volcano, with eruptions along fissures in its flank as well as in its central crater.

**Maundy Thursday** in the Christian church, the Thursday before Easter. The ceremony of washing the feet of pilgrims on that day was instituted in commemoration of Jesus' washing of the apostles' feet and observed from the 4th century to 1754.

**Maupassant, (Henry René Albert) Guy de** (1850–1893) French author. He established a reputation with the short story 'Boule de suif/Ball of Fat' (1880) and wrote some 300 short stories in all. His novels include *Une Vie/A Woman's Life*

(1883) and *Bel-Ami* (1885). He was encouraged as a writer by Gustave ◊Flaubert.

**Mauritania** Islamic Republic of
**national name** *République Islamique Arabe et Africaine de Mauritanie*

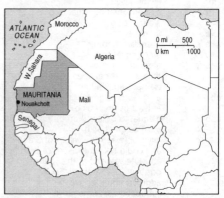

**area** 1,030,700 sq km/397,953 sq mi
**capital** Nouakchott (port)
**major towns/cities** Nouâdhibou, Kaédi, Zouerate, Kiffa, Rosso, Atar
**major ports** Nouâdhibou
**physical features** valley of River Senegal in south; remainder arid and flat
**head of state** Maaoya Sid'Ahmed Ould Taya from 1984
**head of government** Cheik el Avia Ould Muhammad Khouna from 1998
**political system** emergent democracy
**political parties** Democratic and Social Republican Party (PRDS), centre left, militarist; Rally for Democracy and National Unity (RDNU), centrist; Mauritian Renewal Party (MPR), centrist; Umma, Islamic fundamentalist
**currency** ouguiya
**GNP per capita (PPP)** (US$) 1,660 (1998 est)
**exports** fish and fish products, iron ore. Principal market: Japan 23.9% (1997)
**population** 2,598,000 (1999 est)
**language** French and Hasaniya Arabic (both official), African languages including Pulaar, Soninke, and Wolof
**religion** Sunni Muslim
**life expectancy** 52 (men); 55 (women) (1995–2000)
**Chronology**
**early Christian era** A Roman province with the name Mauritania, after the Mauri, its Berber inhabitants who became active in the long-distance salt trade.
**7th–11th centuries** Eastern Mauritania was incorporated in the larger Ghana Empire, centred on Mali to the east, but with its capital at Kumbi in southeast Mauritania. The Berbers were reduced to vassals and converted to Islam in the 8th century.
**11th–12th centuries** The area's Sanhadja Berber inhabitants, linked to the Morocco-based Almoravid Empire, destroyed the Ghana Empire and spread Islam among neighbouring peoples.

**13th–15th centuries** Southeast Mauritania formed part of Muslim Mali Empire, which extended to east and south.

**1441** Coast visited by Portuguese, who founded port of Arguin and captured Africans to sell as slaves.

**15th–16th centuries** Eastern Mauritania formed part of Muslim Songhai Empire, which spread across western Sahel, and Arab tribes migrated into the area.

**1817** Senegal Treaty recognized coastal region (formerly disputed by European nations) as French sphere of influence.

**1903** Formally became French protectorate.

**1920** Became French colony, within French West Africa.

**1960** Independence achieved, with Moktar Ould Daddah, leader of Mauritanian People's Party (PPM), as president. New capital built at Nouakchott.

**1968** Underlying tensions between agriculturalist black population of south and economically dominant semi-nomadic Arabo-Berber peoples, or Moors, of desert north became more acute after Arabic was made an official language (with French).

**1976** Western Sahara, to the northwest, ceded by Spain to Mauritania and Morocco. Mauritania occupied the southern area and Morocco the mineral-rich north. Polisario Front formed in Sahara to resist this occupation and guerrilla war broke out, with the Polisario receiving backing from Algeria and Libya.

**1978** Daddah deposed in bloodless coup; replaced by Col Mohamed Khouna Ould Haidalla in military government.

**1979** A peace accord was signed with the Polisario Front in Algiers, in which Mauritania, crippled by the cost of the military struggle over a largely uninhabited area, renounced its claims to southern Western Sahara (Tiris el Gharbia region) and recognized the Polisario regime; diplomatic relations were restored with Algeria.

**1981** Diplomatic relations with Morocco were broken after it annexed southern Western Sahara.

**1984** Haidalla was overthrown by Col Maaoya Sid'Ahmed Ould Taya.

**1985** Relations with Morocco were restored.

**1989** There were violent clashes in Mauritania and Senegal between Moors and black Africans, chiefly of Senegalese origins; over 50,000 Senegalese were expelled.

**1991** An amnesty was called for political prisoners, and there were calls for the resignation of President Taya. Political parties were legalized and a new multiparty constitution was approved in a referendum.

**1992** The first multiparty elections were largely boycotted by the opposition; Taya and his Social Democratic Republican Party (DSRP) were re-elected. Diplomatic relations with Senegal resumed.

**1998** Cheikh el Avia Ould Muhammad Khouna was appointed prime minister.

**Mauritius** Republic of

**area** 1,865 sq km/720 sq mi; the island of Rodrigues is part of Mauritius; there are several small island dependencies

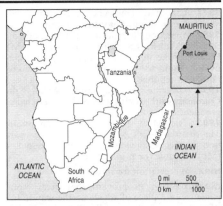

**capital** Port Louis (port)

**major towns/cities** Beau Bassin-Rose Hill, Curepipe, Quatre Bornes, Vacoas-Phoenix

**physical features** mountainous, volcanic island surrounded by coral reefs

**head of state** Cassam Uteem from 1992

**head of government** Navim Ramgoolam from 1995

**political system** liberal democracy

**political parties** Mauritius Socialist Movement (MSM), moderate socialist-republican; Mauritius Labour Party (MLP), democratic socialist, Hindu-oriented; Mauritius Social Democratic Party (PMSD), conservative, Francophile; Mauritius Militant Movement (MMM), Marxist-republican; Organization of Rodriguan People (OPR), left of centre

**currency** Mauritian rupee

**GNP per capita (PPP)** (US$) 9,400 (1998)

**exports** raw sugar, clothing, tea, molasses, jewellery. Principal market: UK 32.1% (1997)

**population** 1,149,000 (1999 est)

**language** English (official), French, Creole, Indian languages

**religion** Hindu, Christian (mainly Roman Catholic), Muslim

**life expectancy** 68 (men); 75 (women) (1995–2000)

**Chronology**

**1598** Previously uninhabited, the island was discovered by the Dutch and named after Prince Morris of Nassau.

**1710** Dutch colonists withdrew.

**1721** Island reoccupied by French East India Company, who renamed it Île de France, and established sugar cane and tobacco plantations worked by imported African slaves.

**1814** Ceded to Britain by Treaty of Paris.

**1835** Slavery abolished; indentured Indian and Chinese labourers imported to work the sugarcane plantations, which were later hit by competition from beet sugar.

**1903** Formerly administered with Seychelles, it became a single colony.

**1936** Mauritius Labour Party (MLP) founded, drawing strong support from sugar workers.

**1957** Internal self-government granted.

**1968** Independence achieved from Britain within Commonwealth, with Seewoosagur Ramgoolam of centrist Indian-dominated MLP as prime minister.

**1971** A state of emergency was temporarily imposed as a result of industrial unrest.

**1982** Aneerood Jugnauth, of the moderate socialist Mauritius Socialist Movement (MSM), became prime minister, pledging a programme of nonalignment, nationalization, and the creation of a republic.

**1992** Became a republic within the Commonwealth, with Cassam Uteem elected as president.

**1995** The MLP and the cross-community Mauritian Militant Movement (MMM) coalition won election victory; Navim Ramgoolam (MLP) became the prime minister.

**max.** abbreviation for *maximum*.

**maxim** saying or proverb that gives moral guidance or a piece of advice on the way to live ('First come, first served'; 'Better late than never').

**Maximilian I** (1459–1519) German king from 1486, Holy Roman Emperor from 1493. He was the son of the emperor Frederick III (1415–93). Through a combination of dynastic marriages and diplomacy backed up by military threats, Maximilian was able to build up the Habsburg inheritance. He married Mary of Burgundy in 1477, and after her death in 1582 held onto Burgundian lands. He married his son, Philip the Handsome, to Joanna, the daughter of ◊Ferdinand and Isabella, and undertook long wars with Italy and Hungary in attempts to extend Habsburg power. The eventual legatee of these arrangements was Maximilian's grandson, Charles V.

**Maxwell, (Ian) Robert** born Jan Ludvik Hoch (1923–1991) Czech-born British publishing and newspaper proprietor. He owned several UK national newspapers, including the *Daily Mirror*, the Macmillan Publishing Company; and the New York *Daily News*. At the time of his death, the Maxwell domain carried debts of about $3.9 billion.

**Maxwell, James Clerk** (1831–1879) Scottish physicist. His main achievement was in the understanding of ◊electromagnetic waves: *Maxwell's equations* bring together electricity, magnetism, and light in one set of relations. He studied gases, optics, and the sensation of colour, and his theoretical work in magnetism prepared the way for wireless telegraphy and telephony.

**maya** (Sanskrit 'illusion') in Hindu philosophy, mainly in the *Vedānta*, the cosmos which Isvara, the personal expression of Brahman, or the atman, has called into being. This is real, yet also an illusion, since its reality is not everlasting.

**Maya** American Indian civilization originating in the Yucatán Peninsula in Central America about 2600 BC, with later sites in Mexico, Guatemala, and Belize. It enjoyed a classical period AD 325–925, after which it declined as Toltecs from the Valley of Mexico moved south into the area, building new ceremonial centres and dominating the local people. Nevertheless, Maya sovereignty was maintained, for the most part, until late in the Spanish conquest (1560s)

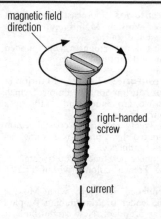

magnetic field direction

right-handed screw

current

***Maxwell, James Clerk*** *Maxwell's screw rule, named after the physicist James Maxwell, predicts the direction of the magnetic field produced around a wire carrying electric current. If a right-handed screw is turned so that it moves forward in the same direction as the current, its direction of rotation will give the direction of the magnetic field.*

in some areas. Today the Maya are Roman Catholic, and number 8–9 million (1994 est). They live in Yucatán, Guatemala, Belize, and western Honduras. Many still speak Maya, a member of the Totonac-Mayan (Penutian) language family, as well as Spanish. In the 1980s more than 100,000 Maya fled from Guatemala to Mexico.

**May Day** first day of May. In many countries it is a national holiday in honour of labour.

***Mayflower*** ship in which the ◊Pilgrims sailed in 1620 from Plymouth, England, to found Plymouth plantation and Plymouth colony in present-day Massachusetts.

**mayfly** any of a group of insects whose adult form lives only very briefly in the spring. The larval stage, which can last a year or more, is passed in water, the adult form developing gradually from the nymph through successive moults. The adult has transparent, net-veined wings. (Order Ephemerida.)

**Mayo** county of the Republic of Ireland, in the province of Connacht; county town Castlebar; area 5,400 sq km/2,084 sq mi; population (1991) 110,700. Its wild Atlantic coastline is about 400 km/249 mi long. The principal towns are Ballina, Ballinrobe, and Westport, and the principal rivers are the Moy, the Robe, and the Owenmore. Loughs Conn and Mask lie within the county. Agriculture includes pig, sheep, and cattle farming, and salmon fishing (particularly in the River Moy). The soil of the central plain is fertile, and crops include potatoes and oats. An excellent marble is found in the northwest district.

**mayor** title of the head of urban administration. In England, Wales, and Northern Ireland, the mayor is the principal officer of a district council that has been granted district-borough status under royal charter. In the USA a mayor is the elected head of a city or town. In 1996 the Labour Party floated proposals for directly elected mayors in Britain, which it confirmed when it came into power in 1997. A referendum in May 1998 approved establishing an elected mayor of London. A July 1998 government White Paper proposed allowing local authorites to introduce directly elected mayors, working in tandem with assemblies or executive commit-tees, as a way of reviving local democracy.

**mayweed** any of several species of the daisy family native to Europe and Asia and natural-ized elsewhere, including the European dog fen-nel or stinking daisy (*Anthemis cotula*), naturalized in North America, and the pineapple mayweed (*Matricaria matricarioides*), found in Europe and Asia. All have finely divided leaves. (Family Compositae.)

**Mazarin, Jules** born Giulio Raimondo Mazzarini (1602–1661) French politician who succeeded Richelieu as chief minister of France 1642. His attack on the power of the nobility led to the ◊Fronde and his temporary exile, but his diplomacy achieved a successful conclusion to the Thirty Years' War, and, in alliance with Oliver Cromwell during the British protectorate, he gained victory over Spain.

**mazurka** any of a family of traditional Polish dances from the 16th century, characterized by foot-stamping and heel-clicking, together with a turning movement. The music for the mazurka is in triple time (3/4), with dotted rhythms and the accentuation of weak beats, on which phrases also begin and end. It is found at a vari-ety of speeds, but is usually not as fast as the waltz, which is also formally a more rigid dance than the mazurka. During the 18th and 19th centuries, it spread throughout Europe and was made famous by Chopin's approximately 60 works in the genre. Other composers of the mazurka include Karol Szymanowski, Glinka, and Mussorgsky.

**Mazzini, Giuseppe** (1805–1872) Italian nationalist. He was a member of the revolution-ary society, the Carbonari, and founded in exile the nationalist movement Giovane Italia (Young Italy) 1831. Returning to Italy on the outbreak of the 1848 revolution, he headed a republican government established in Rome, but was forced into exile again on its overthrow 1849. He acted as a focus for the movement for Italian unity (see ◊Risorgimento).

**MBE** abbreviation for *Member (of the Order) of the British Empire,* an honour first awarded in 1917.

**MCC** abbreviation for *Marylebone Cricket Club.*

**ME** abbreviation for *myalgic encephalo-myelitis,* a popular name for ◊chronic fatigue syndrome.

**mead** alcoholic drink made from honey and water fermented with yeast, often with added spices. It was known in ancient times and was drunk by the Greeks, Britons, and Norse.

**mean** in mathematics, a measure of the aver-age of a number of terms or quantities. The sim-ple *arithmetic mean* is the average value of the quantities, that is, the sum of the quantities divided by their number. The *weighted mean* takes into account the frequency of the terms that are summed; it is calculated by multiplying each term by the number of times it occurs, sum-ming the results and dividing this total by the total number of occurrences. The *geometric mean* of *n* quantities is the *n*th root of their product. In statistics, it is a measure of central tendency of a set of data.

**meander** loop-shaped curve in a mature ◊river flowing sinuously across flat country. As a river flows, any curve in its course is accentuated by the current. On the outside of the curve the velocity, and therefore the erosion, of the current is greatest. Here the river cuts into the outside bank, producing a *cutbank* or *river cliff* and the river's deepest point, or *thalweg*. On the curve's inside the current is slow and deposits any trans-ported material, building up a gentle slip-off slope. As each meander migrates in the direction of its cutbank, the river gradually changes its course across the flood plain.

**mean deviation** in statistics, a measure of the spread of a population from the ◊mean.

**measles** acute virus disease (rubeola), spread by airborne infection.

Symptoms are fever, severe catarrh, small spots inside the mouth, and a raised, blotchy red rash appearing for about a week after two weeks' incubation. Prevention is by vaccination.

**Meath** county of the Republic of Ireland, in the province of Leinster; county town Navan; area 2,340 sq km/ 903 sq mi; population (1991) 105,600. The chief river is the Boyne, of which the Blackwater is a tributary. The principal towns are Kells, Trim, Athboy, Bettystown, and Laytown. Cattle and sheep are reared, and oats and potatoes are grown. The largest working lead-mine in Europe is located near Navan. Tara Hill, 155 m/509 ft high, was the site of a palace and was the coronation place of many kings of Ireland; St Patrick also preached here. The *Book of Kells* (now held in the Trinity College Library) was produced at Kells in the early 9th century.

**Mecca** Arabic *Makkah,* city in Saudi Arabia and, as birthplace of Muhammad, the holiest city of the Islamic world; population (1991 est) 633,000. In the centre of Mecca is the Great Mosque, in the courtyard of which is the Kaaba, the sacred shrine containing the black stone believed to have been given to Abraham by the angel Gabriel.

**mechanics** branch of physics dealing with the motions of bodies and the forces causing these motions, and also with the forces acting on bod-ies in equilibrium. It is usually divided into ◊dynamics and ◊statics.

**Meciar, Vladimír** (1942– ) Slovak politi-cian, prime minister of the Slovak Republic January 1993–March 1994 and again from October 1994–September 1998. He held a number of posts under the Czechoslovak communist regime until, as a dissident, he was expelled from the party in 1970. He joined the Public Against Violence (PAV) movement in 1989, campaigning for a free Czechoslovakia, then, as leader of the Movement for a Democratic Slovakia (HZDS) from 1990, sought an independent Slovak state. Under the federal system, Meciar became prime minister of the Slovak Republic in 1990 and the new state's first prime minister in January 1993. He resigned in March 1994 after a no-confidence vote in parliament, but was returned as premier in October 1994 following a general election victory. In 1999 he was defeated by Rudolf Schuster in the country's first direct presidential elections.

**Medea** in Greek mythology, the sorceress daughter of the king of Colchis. When ◊Jason reached Colchis, she fell in love with him, helped him acquire the ◊Golden Fleece, and they fled together. When Jason later married Creusa, daughter of the king of Corinth, Medea killed his bride with the gift of a poisoned garment, and then killed her own two children by Jason.

**Medellín** industrial city and capital of Antioquia department, northwest Colombia; situated at 1,538 m/5,048 ft above sea level in the Aburrá Valley, Central Cordillera of the Andes; population (1994) 1,608,000. It is the second city and main textile centre of Colombia, producing over 80% of the country's total output. Other main industries include gold and silver mining, chemicals, coffee-growing, and engineering. Medellín has also had a reputation for cocaine production.

**median** in mathematics and statistics, the middle number of an ordered group of numbers. If there is no middle number (because there is an even number of terms), the median is the ◊mean (average) of the two middle numbers. For example, the median of the group 2, 3, 7, 11, 12 is 7; that of 3, 4, 7, 9, 11, 13 is 8 (the average of 7 and 9).

In geometry, the term refers to a line from the vertex of a triangle to the midpoint of the opposite side.

**Medici, Cosimo de'** (1389–1464) Italian politician and banker. Regarded as the model for Machiavelli's *The Prince,* he dominated the government of Florence from 1434 and was a patron of the arts.

He was succeeded by his inept son *Piero de' Medici* (1416–1469).

**Medici, Cosimo de'** (1519–1574) Italian politician, ruler of Florence; duke of Florence from 1537 and 1st grand duke of Tuscany from 1569.

**Medici, Lorenzo de'**, *the Magnificent* (1449–1492) Italian politician, ruler of Florence from 1469. He was also a poet and a generous patron of the arts.

**Medici family** noble family that ruled the Italian city-state of Florence from the 15th to the 18th centuries. The Medici arrived in Florence in the 13th century and made their fortune in banking. The first family member to control the city, from 1434 to 1464, was Cosimo de' Medici ('the Elder'); he and his grandson Lorenzo ('the Magnificent'), who ruled from 1469 to 1492, made Florence the foremost city-state in ◊Renaissance Italy, and were famed as patrons of the arts and ◊humanist thought. Four Medici were elected pope, and others married into the royal families of Europe.

**medicine** the practice of preventing, diagnosing, and treating disease, both physical and mental; also any substance used in the treatment of disease. The basis of medicine is anatomy (the structure and form of the body) and physiology (the study of the body's functions).

**medicine, alternative** forms of medical treatment that do not use synthetic drugs or surgery in response to the symptoms of a disease, but aim to treat the patient as a whole (◊holism). The emphasis is on maintaining health (with diet and exercise) and on dealing with the underlying causes rather than just the symptoms of illness. It may involve the use of herbal remedies and techniques like ◊acupuncture, ◊homeopathy, and ◊chiropractic. Some alternative treatments are increasingly accepted by orthodox medicine, but the absence of enforceable standards in some fields has led to the proliferation of eccentric or untrained practitioners.

**Medina** Saudi Arabian city, about 355 km/220 mi north of Mecca; population (1991 est) 400,000. It is the second holiest city in the Islamic world, and contains the tomb of ◊Muhammad. It produces grain and fruit.

**meditation** act of spiritual contemplation, practised by members of many religions or as a secular exercise. It is a central practice in Buddhism (the Sanskrit term is *samādhi*) and the movement for ◊transcendental meditation.

**Mediterranean Sea** inland sea separating Europe from north Africa, with Asia to the east; extreme length 3,700 km/2,300 mi; area 2,966,000 sq km/1,145,000 sq mi. It is linked to the Atlantic Ocean (at the Strait of Gibraltar), Red Sea and Indian Ocean (by the Suez Canal), and the Black Sea (at the Dardanelles and Sea of Marmara). The main subdivisions are the Adriatic, Aegean, Ionian, and Tyrrhenian seas. It is highly polluted.

**medlar** small shrub or tree native to southeastern Europe. It is widely cultivated for its fruits, resembling small brown-green pears or quinces. These are palatable when they have begun to decay. (*Mespilus germanica,* family Rosaceae.)

**medulla** central part of an organ. In the mammalian kidney, the medulla lies beneath the outer cortex and is responsible for the reabsorption of water from the filtrate. In plants, it is a region of packing tissue in the centre of the stem. In the vertebrate brain, the medulla is the posterior region responsible for the coordination of basic activities, such as breathing and temperature control.

**medusa** the free-swimming phase in the life cycle of a coelenterate, such as a ◊jellyfish or ◊coral. The other phase is the sedentary *polyp.*

**Medusa** in Greek mythology, a mortal woman who was transformed into a snake-haired ◊Gorgon by Athena for defiling the goddess's temple with the god Poseidon. She was slain by the hero Perseus who watched her reflection in his shield, as her head was so hideous – even in death – that a direct beholder was turned to stone.

The winged horse ◊Pegasus and warrior Chrysaor were said to have sprung from her blood, her offspring with Poseidon.

**Medway Towns** unitary authority in southeast England, created in 1998 by combining the former city council of Rochester upon Medway with Gillingham borough council, both formerly in Kent
*area* 194 sq km/75 sq mi
*towns and cities* Rochester, Chatham, Gillingham, Strood (administrative headquarters)
*features* River Medway flows through Rochester; River Thames forms northern border of authority; reclaimed estuarine mudflats form the Isle of Grain; Charles Dickens Centre (Rochester) is housed in a 16th-century mansion; Royal Naval Dockyard (Chatham); Royal Engineers Museum (Gillingham); Upnor Castle (16th century) at Upper Upnor
*industries* oil refineries on Isle of Grain, heavy industry, engineering, maritime industries, Thamesport (privately-owned deep-water container port), avionics, financial services, information technology
*population* (1996) 240,000.
*famous people* William Jenner.

**meerkat** or *suricate,* small mammal with long soft grey fur, which is found in southern Africa, and belongs to the mongoose family. A third of its length of 35 cm/14 in is occupied by the tail. It feeds on succulent bulbs, insects, and small vertebrates, and is sociable, living in large extended family groups. Meerkat groups have a dominant breeding pair and up to 23 helpers to assist in the rearing of the babies. The dominant female produces 75% of the young.

**mega-** prefix denoting multiplication by a million. For example, a megawatt (MW) is equivalent to a million watts.

**megalith** (Greek *megas* 'great', *lithos* 'stone') prehistoric stone monument of the late Neolithic (New Stone Age) or early Bronze Age. Most common in Europe, megaliths include single large uprights or ◊menhirs (for example, the Five Kings, Northumberland, England); rows or *alignments* (for example, Carnac, Brittany, France); stone circles; and the hutlike remains of burial chambers after the covering earth has disappeared, known as dolmen (for example, Kits Coty, Kent, England, where only the entrance survives).

**megamouth** deep-sea shark that feeds on plankton. It has a bulbous head with protruding jaws and blubbery lips, is 4.5 m/15 ft long, and weighs 750 kg/1,650 lb. Although first discovered 1976, the first live specimen was found in 1992 off the coast of Los Angeles. The first female was found in 1994 in Hakata Bay, Kyushu, Japan; she was 4.8 m/16 ft long and weighed 790 kg/1,740 lb. (Species *Megachasma pelagios.*)

**megapode** or *mound-builder,* any of a group of chickenlike birds found in the Malay Archipelago and Australia. They pile up large mounds of vegetable matter, earth, and sand 4 m/13 ft across, in which to deposit their eggs, then cover the eggs and leave them to be incubated by the heat produced by the rotting vegetation. There are 19 species, all large birds, 50–70 cm/20–27.5 in in length, with very large feet. They include brush turkeys. (Family Megapodiidae, order Galliformes.)

**Meghalaya** state of northeast India, bordered to the north by Assam, to the south by Bangladesh
*area* 22,400 sq km/8,648 sq mi
*capital* Shillong
*physical* upland state with hills reaching 2,000 m/6,500 ft, rising steeply in the south away from its border with Bangladesh; heavy monsoon rainfall
*industries* mineral extraction includes 95% of India's sillimanite
*minerals* coal, limestone, white clay, corundum, mainly unexploited
*agriculture* cotton, potatoes, fruit, rice, maize, timber, jute
*population* (1994 est) 1,960,000, mainly Khasi, Jaintia, and Garo
*religion* Hindu 70%
*language* various
*history* the state was created in 1972 from the Khasi, Jaintia, Garo districts of ◊Assam, which were formerly small kingdoms inhabited by separate tribal groups.

**Mehmet Ali** or *Muhammad Ali* (1769–1849) Pasha (governor) of Egypt from 1805, and founder of the dynasty that ruled until 1953. An Albanian in the Ottoman service, he had originally been sent to Egypt to fight the French. As pasha, he established a European-style army and navy, fought his Turkish overlord 1831 and 1839, and conquered Sudan.

**meiosis** in biology, a process of cell division in which the number of ◊chromosomes in the cell is halved. It only occurs in ◊eukaryotic cells, and is part of a life cycle that involves sexual reproduction because it allows the genes of two parents to be combined without the total number of chromosomes increasing. *See illustration on page 580.*

**Meir, Golda** born Mabovitch, later Myerson (1898–1978) Israeli Labour politician; foreign minister 1956–66 and prime minister 1969–74. Criticism of the Israelis' lack of preparation for the 1973 Arab-Israeli War led to election losses for Labour and, unable to form a government, she resigned.

**meitnerium** synthesized radioactive element of the ◊transactinide series, symbol Mt, atomic number 109, relative atomic mass 266. It was first produced in 1982 at the Laboratory for Heavy Ion Research in Darmstadt, Germany, by fusing bismuth and iron nuclei; it took a week to obtain a single new, fused nucleus. It was named

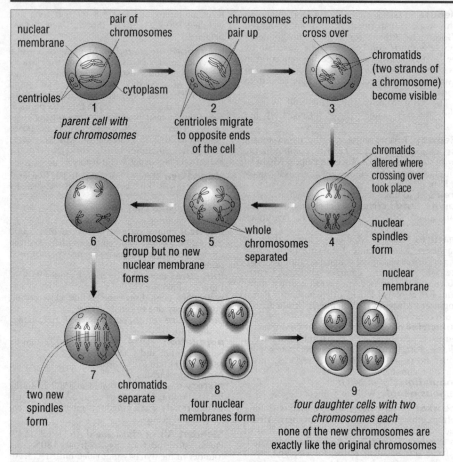

**meiosis** *Meiosis is a type of cell division that produces gametes (sex cells, sperm and egg). This sequence shows an animal cell but only four chromosomes are present in the parent cell (1). There are two stages in the division process. In the first stage (2–6), the chromosomes come together in pairs and exchange genetic material. This is called crossing over. In the second stage (7–9), the cell divides to produce four gamete cells, each with only one copy of each chromosome from the parent cell.*

in 1997 after the Austrian-born Swedish physicist Lise Meitner. Its temporary name was unnilennium.

**Mekong** river of China, rising as the Za Qu in Qinghai province, flowing through Tibet autonomous region and Yunnan province as the Lancang Jiang, and then through Laos, where part of its course forms the border with Thailand, Cambodia, and Vietnam; length 4,425 km/2,750 mi. The Mekong empties into the South China Sea through a vast delta, covering about 200,000 sq km/77,000 sq mi. It is being developed for irrigation and hydroelectricity by Cambodia, Laos, Thailand, and Vietnam.

**Melanesia** islands in the southwestern Pacific between Micronesia to the north and Polynesia to the east, embracing all the islands from the New Britain archipelago to the Fiji Islands.

**Melanesian** the indigenous inhabitants of Melanesia; any of the Pacific peoples of Melanesia. The Melanesian languages belong to the Austronesian family.

**Melanesian languages** see ◊Austronesian languages.

**melanin** brown pigment that gives colour to the eyes, skin, hair, feathers, and scales of many vertebrates. In humans, melanin helps protect the skin against ultraviolet radiation from sunlight. Both genetic and environmental factors determine the amount of melanin in the skin.

**melanoma** highly malignant tumour of the melanin-forming cells (melanocytes) of the skin. It develops from an existing mole in up to two thirds of cases, but can also arise in the eye or mucous membranes.

Malignant melanoma is the most dangerous of the skin cancers; it is associated with brief but excessive exposure to sunlight. It is easily treated if caught early but deadly once it has spread. There is a genetic factor in some cases.

**Melbourne** capital of the state of ◊Victoria, Australia; population (1996) 2,865,329. Australia's second-largest city, Melbourne is situated on the south-east coast of Australia, on Port Philip Bay, at the mouth of the River Yarra. It is separated from Tasmania by the Bass Strait. Industries include engineering, shipbuilding, electronics, printing, oil refining, food processing, brewing, flour-milling, and the manufacture of chemicals, cars, furniture, plastics, textiles, and clothing. It is an important port and the largest receiver of container vessels in Australia. Melbourne has seven universities, including the University of Melbourne (1853), Monash University (1961, the largest university in Australia), and La Trobe University (1964).

**melodrama** play or film with romantic and sensational plot elements, often concerned with crime, vice, or catastrophe. Originally a melodrama was a play with an accompaniment of music contributing to the dramatic effect. It became popular in the late 18th century, due to works like *Pygmalion* (1770), with pieces written by the French philosopher Jean-Jacques Rousseau. The early melodramas used extravagant theatrical effects to heighten violent emotions and actions artificially. By the end of the 19th century, melodrama had become a popular genre of stage play.

**melon** any of several large, juicy (95% water), thick-skinned fruits of trailing plants of the gourd family. The muskmelon (*Cucumis melo*), of which the honeydew melon is a variety, and the large red ◊watermelon (*Citrullus vulgaris*) are familiar edible varieties. (Family Cucurbitaceae.)

**meltdown** the melting of the core of a nuclear reactor, due to overheating.

To prevent such accidents all reactors have equipment intended to flood the core with water in an emergency. The reactor is housed in a strong containment vessel, designed to prevent radiation escaping into the atmosphere. The result of a meltdown would be an area radioactively contaminated for 25,000 years or more.

**melting point** temperature at which a substance melts, or changes from solid to liquid form. A pure substance under standard conditions of pressure (usually one atmosphere) has a definite melting point. If heat is supplied to a solid at its melting point, the temperature does not change until the melting process is complete. The melting point of ice is 0°C or 32°F.

**Melville, Herman** (1819–1891) US writer. His novel *Moby Dick* (1851) was inspired by his whaling experiences in the South Seas and is considered to be one of the masterpieces of American literature. *Billy Budd, Sailor,* completed just before his death and published 1924, was the basis of an opera by Benjamin ◊Britten (1951). Although most of his works were unappreciated during his lifetime, today he is one of the most highly regarded of US authors.

**membrane** in living things, a continuous layer, made up principally of fat molecules, that encloses a ◊cell or ◊organelles within a cell.

Small molecules, such as water and sugars, can pass through the cell membrane by ◊diffusion. Large molecules, such as proteins, are transported across the membrane via special channels, a process often involving energy input. The Golgi apparatus within the cell is thought to produce certain membranes.

**Memling, Hans** or *Memlinc* (*c.* 1430–1494) Flemish painter. He was probably a pupil of van der Weyden, but his style is calmer and softer. He painted religious subjects and also portraits, including *Tommaso Portinari and His Wife* (about 1480; Metropolitan Museum of Art, New York).

**memory** ability to store and recall observations and sensations. Memory does not seem to be based in any particular part of the brain; it may depend on changes to the pathways followed by nerve impulses as they move through the brain. Memory can be improved by regular use as the connections between ◊nerve cells (neurons) become 'well-worn paths' in the brain. Events stored in *short-term memory* are forgotten quickly, whereas those in *long-term memory* can last for many years, enabling recall of information and recognition of people and places over long periods of time.

**memory** in computing, the part of a system used to store data and programs either permanently or temporarily. There are two main types: immediate access memory and backing storage. Memory capacity is measured in ◊bytes or, more conveniently, in kilobytes (units of 1,024 bytes), megabytes (units of 1,024 kilobytes), or gigabytes (units of 1,024 megabytes).

**Memphis** industrial city and port on the Mississippi River, in southwestern Tennessee, USA, linked by a bridge with West Memphis, Arkansas, across the river; seat of Shelby County; population (1992) 610,300. It is a major cotton market, and one of the leading centres in the USA for the production of hardwood lumber; other industries include food processing and the manufacture of pharmaceuticals, chemicals, medical supplies, furniture, and tobacco products. A 1980s industry of handmade ultramodern furniture is called Memphis style and is copied by Italian and French firms.

**Memphis** ruined city beside the Nile, 19 km/ 12 mi southwest of Cairo, Egypt. Once the centre of the worship of Ptah, it was the earliest capital of a united Egypt under King Menes about 3050 BC, and acted intermittently as capital until *c.* 1300 BC.

**Mende** a West African people living in the rainforests of central east Sierra Leone and western Liberia. They number approximately 1 million. The Mende are farmers as well as hunter-gatherers, and each of their villages is led by a chief and a group of elders. The Mende language belongs to the Niger-Congo family.

**Mendeleyev, Dmitri Ivanovich** (1834–1907) Russian chemist who framed the periodic law in chemistry in 1869, which states that the chemical properties of the elements depend on their relative atomic masses. This law is the basis of the ◊periodic table of the elements, in which the elements are arranged by atomic number and organized by their related groups.

**Mendelism** in genetics, the theory of inheritance originally outlined by Austrian biologist Gregor Mendel. He suggested that, in sexually reproducing species, all characteristics are inherited through indivisible 'factors' (now identified with ◊genes) contributed by each parent to its offspring.

**Mendelssohn (-Bartholdy), (Jakob Ludwig) Felix** (1809–1847) German composer, also a pianist and conductor. His music has the lightness and charm of Classical music, applied to Romantic and descriptive subjects. Among his best-known works are *A Midsummer Night's Dream* (1827); the *Fingal's Cave* overture (1832); and five symphonies, which include the 'Reformation' (1830), the 'Italian' (1833), and the 'Scottish' (1842). He was instrumental in promoting the revival of interest in J S Bach's music.

**Mendoza** capital of Mendoza federal district, western Argentina, in the foothills of the Andes, 760 m/2,500 ft above sea level; population (1991) 121,700; metropolitan area (1992 est) 801,900. It is the commercial centre of an irrigated wine-producing and fruit-growing region. The city has an important university, and because of nearby oilfield, a growing industrial base. The city was founded in 1561 on the site of an Inca fort by the Spaniard Garcí Hurtado de Mendoza, after whom it is named. It developed because of its position on the Trans-Andean railway where the Argentine and Chilean rail lines link.

**Menem, Carlos (Saul)** (1930– ) Argentine politician, president from 1989; leader of the Peronist Justicialist Party. As president, he introduced sweeping privatization and cuts in public spending to address Argentina's economic crisis and stimulate the free market; released hundreds of political prisoners jailed under the Alfonsín regime; and sent two warships to the Gulf to assist the USA against Iraq in the 1992 Gulf War (the only Latin American country to offer support to the USA). He also improved relations with the UK.

**menhir** (Breton 'long stone') prehistoric tall, upright stone monument or ◊megalith. Menhirs may be found singly as ◊monoliths or in groups. They have a wide geographical distribution in the Americas (mainly as monoliths), and in Europe, Asia, and Africa, and belong to many different periods. Most European examples were erected in the late Neolithic (New Stone Age) or early Bronze Age.

**meningitis** inflammation of the meninges (membranes) surrounding the brain, caused by bacterial or viral infection. Bacterial meningitis, though treatable by antibiotics, is the more serious threat. Diagnosis is by ◊lumbar puncture.

**meniscus** in physics, the curved shape of the surface of a liquid in a thin tube, caused by the cohesive effects of ◊surface tension (capillary action). When the walls of the container are made wet by the liquid, the meniscus is concave, but with highly viscous liquids (such as mercury) the meniscus is convex. Meniscus is also the name of a concavo-convex or convexo-concave ◊lens.

**menopause** in women, the cessation of reproductive ability, characterized by menstruation (see ◊menstrual cycle) becoming irregular and eventually ceasing. The onset is at about the age of 50, but varies greatly. Menopause is usually uneventful, but some women suffer from symptoms such as hot flushes, excessive bleeding, and nervous disorders. Since the 1950s, ◊hormone-replacement therapy (HRT), using ◊oestrogen alone or with progestogen, a synthetic form of ◊progesterone, has been developed to counteract such effects.

**menorah** nine-branched candlestick used on the Jewish festival of ◊Hanukkah.

**Menorca** second largest of the ◊Balearic Islands in the Mediterranean.
*area* 689 sq km/266 sq mi
*towns and cities* Mahon (the capital), Ciudadela, Mercadal, Ferrerias, Fornells
*products* leather goods, costume jewellery, cheese and dairy products; tourism is important
*population* (1990 est) 62,000
*history* Menorca was occupied by British forces in 1708, during the War of Spanish Succession, and annexed to the British crown in 1713 by the Treaty of Utrecht. The French occupied the island during the Seven Years' War (1756–63); the British regained control until 1808, when the island reverted to the Spanish crown
*ecology* because its coastal ecosystem is unusually well preserved, the whole island was designated a Biosphere Reserve by UNESCO in 1993, and in 1995 a large area in the northeast of the island was declared a National Park of Spain, ensuring the protection of a wide variety of fauna and flora, especially bird species.

**Menshevik** (Russian *menshinstvo* 'minority') member of the minority of the Russian Social Democratic Party, who split from the ◊Bolsheviks in 1903. The Mensheviks believed in a large, loosely organized party and that, before socialist revolution could occur in Russia, capitalist society had to develop further. During the Russian Revolution they had limited power and set up a government in Georgia, but were suppressed in 1922.

**mens sana in corpore sano** (Latin) a healthy mind in a healthy body.

**menstrual cycle** cycle that occurs in female mammals of reproductive age, in which the body is prepared for pregnancy. At the beginning of the cycle, a Graafian (egg) follicle develops in the ovary, and the inner wall of the uterus forms a soft spongy lining. The egg is released from the ovary, and the uterus lining (endometrium) becomes vascularized (filled with blood vessels). If fertilization does not occur, the corpus luteum (remains of the Graafian follicle) degenerates, and the uterine lining breaks down, and is shed. This is what causes the loss of blood that marks menstruation. The cycle then begins again. Human menstruation takes place from puberty to menopause, except during pregnancy, occurring about every 28 days.

**mental disability** arrested or incomplete development of mental capacities. It can be very mild, but in more severe cases is associated with social problems and difficulties in living independently. A person may be born with a mental disability (for example, ◊Down's syndrome) or may acquire it through brain damage. Between 90 and 130 million people in the world suffer from such disabilities.

**mental illness** disordered functioning of the mind. Since normal working cannot easily be defined, the borderline between mild mental illness and normality is a matter of opinion (not to be confused with normative behaviour). It is broadly divided into two categories: ◊neurosis, in which the patient remains in touch with reality; and ◊psychosis, in which perception, thought, and belief are disordered.

**Menuhin, Yehudi, Baron Menuhin** (1916–1999) US-born violinist and conductor. His solo repertoire extended from Vivaldi to George Enescu. He recorded the Elgar *Violin Concerto* in 1932 with the composer conducting, and commissioned the *Sonata* for violin solo in 1944 from an ailing Bartók. He appeared in concert with sitar virtuoso Ravi Shankar, and with jazz violinist Stéphane Grappelli. In March 1997 he was awarded Germany's highest honour, the Great Order of Merit. He first played in Berlin in 1928, and was the first Jewish artist to play with the Berlin Philharmonic after World War II. He was also noted for his humanitarian activities.

**Meo** or *Miao*, another name (sometimes considered derogatory) for the Hmong, a Southeast Asian people.

**MEP** abbreviation for *member of the* ◊*European Parliament.*

**Mercalli scale** scale used to measure the intensity of an ◊earthquake. It differs from the ◊Richter scale, which measures *magnitude.* It is named after the Italian seismologist Giuseppe Mercalli (1850–1914).

**mercantilism** economic theory, held in the 16th–18th centuries, that a nation's wealth (in the form of bullion or treasure) was the key to its prosperity. To this end, foreign trade should be regulated to create a surplus of exports over imports, and the state should intervene where necessary (for example, subsidizing exports and taxing imports). The bullion theory of wealth was demolished by Adam ◊Smith in Book IV of *The Wealth of Nations* (1776).

**Mercator, Gerardus** Latinized form of *Gerhard Kremer* (1512–1594) Flemish mapmaker who devised *Mercator's projection* in which the parallels and meridians on maps are drawn uniformly at 90°. The projection continues to be used, in particular for navigational charts, because compass courses can be drawn as straight lines, but the true area of countries is increasingly distorted the further north or south they are from the Equator. For other types, see ◊map projection.

**mercenary** soldier hired by the army of another country or by a private army. Mercenary military service originated in the 14th century, when cash payment on a regular basis was the only means of guaranteeing soldiers' loyalty. In the 20th century mercenaries have been common in wars and guerrilla activity in Asia, Africa, and Latin America.

**merchant bank** financial institution that specializes in corporate finance and financial and advisory services for business. Originally developed in the UK in the 19th century, merchant banks now offer many of the services provided by the commercial banks.

**merchant navy** the passenger and cargo ships of a country. Most are owned by private companies. To avoid strict regulations on safety, union rules on crew wages, and so on, many ships are today registered under 'flags of convenience', that is, flags of countries that do not have such rules.

**Mercosur** South American Common Market; Portuguese: Mercosul, (Spanish *Mercado del Sur* 'Market of the South') free-trade organization, founded in March 1991 on signature of the Asunción Treaty by Argentina, Brazil, Paraguay, and Uruguay, and formally inaugurated on 1 January 1995. With a GNP of $800,000 million and a population of more than 190 million, Mercosur constitutes the world's fourth-largest free-trade bloc after the ◊European Economic Area, the North American Free Trade Agreement, and the Asia-Pacific Economic Cooperation Conference.

**Mercury** in astronomy, the closest planet to the Sun. Its mass is 0.056 that of Earth. On its sunward side the surface temperature reaches over 400°C/752°F, but on the 'night' side it falls to −170°C/−274°F.
*mean distance from the Sun* 58 million km/36 million mi
*equatorial diameter* 4,880 km/3,030 mi
*rotation period* 59 Earth days
*year* 88 Earth days
*atmosphere* Mercury has an atmosphere with minute traces of argon and helium
*surface* composed of silicate rock often in the form of lava flows. In 1974 the US space probe *Mariner 10* showed that Mercury's surface is cratered by meteorite impacts
*satellites* none.

**mercury** or *quicksilver*, (Latin *mercurius*) heavy, silver-grey, metallic element, symbol Hg (from Latin *hydrargyrum*), atomic number 80, relative atomic mass 200.59. It is a dense, mobile liquid with a low melting point (−38.87°C/−37.96°F). Its chief source is the mineral cinnabar, HgS, but it sometimes occurs in nature as a free metal.

**Mercury** or Mercurius, (Latin *merx* 'merchandizs') in Roman mythology, a god of commerce and gain, and messenger of the gods. He was identified with the Greek ◊Hermes, and similarly represented with winged sandals and a winged staff entwined with snakes.

**merganser** any of several diving ducks with long, slender, serrated bills for catching fish, widely distributed in the northern hemisphere. Most have crested heads. (Genus *Mergus,* family Anatidae.)

**meridian** half a great circle drawn on the Earth's surface passing through both poles and thus through all places with the same longitude. Terrestrial longitudes are usually measured from the Greenwich Meridian.

**merino** breed of sheep. Its close-set, silky wool is highly valued. Originally from Spain, the merino is now found all over the world, and is the breed on which the Australian wool industry is built.

**meristem** region of plant tissue containing cells that are actively dividing to produce new tissues (or have the potential to do so). Meristems found in the tip of roots and stems, the apical meristems, are responsible for the growth in length of these organs.

**Merit, Order of** British order (see ◊knighthood, order of), instituted in 1902 and limited in number to 24 men and women of eminence. It confers no precedence or knighthood.

**merlin** small ◊falcon of Europe, Asia, and North America, where it is also called a *pigeon hawk.* The male, 26 cm/10 in long, has a grey-blue back and reddish-brown barred front; the female, 32 cm/13 in long, has a dark brown back and lighter front with streaks. Merlins fly relatively low over the ground when hunting and 'stoop' quickly onto their prey, which consists mainly of small birds. (Species *Falco columbarius,* order Falconiformes.)

**Merlin** Welsh *Myrddin,* legendary magician, seer, and counsellor to King Arthur. Welsh bardic literature has a cycle of poems attributed to him, and he may have been a real person. His legend is related in *Vita Merlini* by the 12th-century chronicler Geoffrey of Monmouth.

**mermaid** (Old English *mere* 'lake', *maegth* 'maid') mythical sea creature (the male is a *merman),* having a human head and torso, often of great beauty, and a fish's tail. Suggested animals behind the myth include the dugong, manatee, and seal.

**Merovingian dynasty** (lived 5th–8th centuries) Frankish dynasty, named after its founder, *Merovech* (5th century AD). His descendants ruled France from the time of Clovis (481–511) to 751.

**Mersey** river in northwest England; length 112 km/70 mi. Formed by the confluence of the Goyt and Tame rivers at Stockport, it flows west through the south of Manchester, is joined by the Irwell at Flixton and by the Weaver at Runcorn, and enters the Irish Sea at Liverpool Bay. It drains large areas of the Lancashire and Cheshire plains. The Mersey is linked to the Manchester Ship Canal. Although plans were announced in 1990 to build a 1,800-m/5,907-ft barrage across the Mersey estuary to generate electricity from tides, these were abandoned in 1992 for financial reasons.

**Merseyside** metropolitan county of northwest England, created in 1974; in 1986, most of the functions of the former county council were transferred to metropolitan borough councils (The Wirral, Sefton, Liverpool, Knowsley, St Helens)
*area* 650 sq km/251 sq mi
*towns and cities* Liverpool, Bootle, Birkenhead, St Helens, Wallasey, Southport
*physical* River Mersey
*features* Merseyside Innovation Centre (MIC), linked with Liverpool and John Moores Universities; Prescot Museum of clock- and watch-making; Speke Hall (Tudor), and Croxteth Hall and Country Park (a working country estate open to the public)
*industries* brewing, chemicals, electrical goods, glassmaking, metal-working, pharmaceutical products, tanning, vehicles
*population* (1996) 1,420,400
*famous people* the Beatles, William Ewart Gladstone, George Stubbs.

**Merthyr Tydfil** unitary authority in south Wales, created in 1996 from part of the former county of Mid Glamorgan
*area* 111 sq km/43 sq mi
*towns* Merthyr Tydfil (administrative headquarters)
*features* area includes part of Brecon Beacons National Park
*industries* light engineering, electrical goods.
*population* (1996) 60,000.

**Meskhetian** a community of Turkish descent that formerly inhabited Meskhetia, on the then Turkish-Soviet border. They were deported by Stalin in 1944 to Kazakhstan and Uzbekistan, and have campaigned since then for a return to their homeland. In June 1989 at least 70 were killed in pogroms directed against their community in the Ferghana Valley of Uzbekistan by ethnic Uzbeks.

**Mesolithic** the Middle Stone Age developmental stage of human technology and of ◊prehistory.

**meson** in physics, a group of unstable subatomic particles made up of two indivisible elementary particles, a ◊quark and an antiquark. It has a mass intermediate between that of the electron and that of the proton, is found in cosmic radiation, and is emitted by nuclei under bombardment by very high-energy particles. There are believed to be 15 ordinary types. The last of these to be found was identified by physicists at Fermilab, USA in 1998.

**mesophyll** the tissue between the upper and lower epidermis of a leaf blade (lamina), consisting of parenchyma-like cells containing numerous ◊chloroplasts.

**Mesopotamia** the land between the Tigris and Euphrates rivers, now part of Iraq. The civilizations of Sumer and Babylon flourished here. The ◊Sumerian civilization (3500 BC) may have been the earliest urban civilization.

**mesosphere** layer in the Earth's ◊atmosphere above the stratosphere and below the thermosphere. It lies between about 50 km/31 mi and 80 km/50 mi above the ground.

**Mesozoic** era of geological time 245–65 million years ago, consisting of the Triassic, Jurassic, and Cretaceous periods. At the beginning of the era, the continents were joined together as Pangaea; dinosaurs and other giant reptiles dominated the sea and air; and ferns, horsetails, and cycads thrived in a warm climate worldwide. By the end of the Mesozoic era, the continents had begun to assume their present positions, flowering plants were dominant, and many of the large reptiles and marine fauna were becoming extinct.

**Messiaen, Olivier Eugène Prosper Charles** (1908–1992) French composer, organist, and teacher. His music is mystical in character, vividly coloured, and incorporates transcriptions of birdsong. Among his works are the *Quartet for the End of Time* (1941), the large-scale *Turangalîla Symphony* (1949), and solo organ and piano pieces. As a teacher at the Paris Conservatoire from 1942, he influenced three generations of composers.

**Messiah** (from Hebrew *māshīach* 'anointed') in Judaism and Christianity, the saviour or deliverer. Jews from the time of the Old Testament exile in Babylon have looked forward to the coming of the Messiah. Christians believe that the Messiah came in the person of ◊Jesus, and hence called him the Christ.

**Messina, Strait of** ancient *Siculum Fretum,* channel in the central Mediterranean separating Sicily from mainland Italy, joining the Tyrrhenian and Ionian seas; it is 35 km/22 mi long, and its width varies from 17 km/11 mi in the south to 3 km/2 mi in the north. In Greek legend the monster Scylla devoured sailors from a rock on the Italian shore, while another, Charybdis, created a whirlpool on the Sicilian side which sank ships. The classical hero Odysseus passed safely between them.

**metabolism** the chemical processes of living organisms enabling them to grow and to function. It involves a constant alternation of building up complex molecules (*anabolism)* and breaking them down (*catabolism).* For example, green plants build up complex organic substances from water, carbon dioxide, and mineral salts (◊photosynthesis); by digestion, animals partially break down complex organic substances, ingested as food, and subsequently resynthesize them for use in their own bodies (see ◊digestive system). Within cells, complex molecules are broken down by the process of ◊respiration. The waste products of metabolism are removed by ◊excretion.

**metal** any of a class of chemical elements with specific physical and chemical characteristics. Metallic elements compose about 75% of the 112 elements in the ◊periodic table of the elements.

Physical properties include a sonorous tone when struck, good conduction of heat and electricity, opacity but good reflection of light, malleability, which enables them to be cold-worked and rolled into sheets, ductility, which permits them to be drawn into thin wires, and the possible emission of electrons when heated (thermionic effect) or when the surface is struck by light (◊photoelectric effect).

**metal detector** electronic device for detecting metal, usually below ground, developed from the wartime mine detector. In the head of the metal detector is a coil, which is part of an electronic circuit. The presence of metal causes the frequency of the signal in the circuit to change, setting up an audible note in the headphones worn by the user.

**metallic bond** the force of attraction operating in a metal that holds the atoms together. In the metal the ◊valency electrons are able to move within the crystal and these electrons are said to be delocalized. Their movement creates short-lived, positively charged ions. The electrostatic attraction between the delocalized electrons and the ceaselessly forming ions constitutes the metallic bond.

**metallurgy** the science and technology of producing metals, which includes extraction, alloying, and hardening. *Extractive,* or *process, metallurgy* is concerned with the extraction of metals from their ◊ores and refining and adapting them for use. *Physical metallurgy* is concerned with their properties and application. *Metallography* establishes the microscopic structures that contribute to hardness, ductility, and strength.

**metamorphic rock** rock altered in structure and composition by pressure, heat, or chemically active fluids after original formation. (If heat is sufficient to melt the original rock, technically it becomes an igneous rock upon cooling.) The term was coined in 1833 by Scottish geologist Charles Lyell (1797–1875).

**metamorphism** geological term referring to the changes in rocks of the Earth's crust caused by increasing pressure and temperature. The resulting rocks are metamorphic rocks. All metamorphic changes take place in solid rocks. If the rocks melt and then harden, they become ◊igneous rocks.

**metamorphosis** period during the life cycle of many invertebrates, most amphibians, and some fish, during which the individual's body changes from one form to another through a major reconstitution of its tissues. For example, adult frogs are produced by metamorphosis from tadpoles, and butterflies are produced from caterpillars following metamorphosis within a pupa.

In classical thought and literature, metamorphosis is the transformation of a living being into another shape, either living or inanimate (for example Niobe). The Roman poet ◊Ovid wrote about this theme.

**metaphor** (Greek 'transfer') figure of speech using an analogy or close comparison between two things that are not normally treated as if they had anything in common. Metaphor is a common means of extending the uses and references of words. See also ◊simile.

**metaphysical poets** group of early 17th-century English poets whose work is characterized by ingenious, highly intricate wordplay and unlikely or paradoxical imagery. They used rhetorical and literary devices, such as paradox, hyperbole, and elaborately developed conceits, in such a way as to engage the reader by their humour, strangeness, or sheer outrageousness. Among the exponents of this genre are John ◊Donne, George ◊Herbert, Andrew ◊Marvell, Richard Crashaw, and Henry Vaughan.

**metaphysics** branch of philosophy that deals with first principles, in particular 'being' (ontology) and 'knowing' (◊epistemology), and that is concerned with the ultimate nature of reality. It has been maintained that no certain knowledge of metaphysical questions is possible.

**meteor** flash of light in the sky, popularly known as a *shooting* or *falling star,* caused by a particle of dust, a *meteoroid,* entering the atmosphere at speeds up to 70 kps/45 mps and burning up by friction at a height of around 100 km/60 mi. On any clear night, several *sporadic meteors* can be seen each hour.

**meteorite** piece of rock or metal from space that reaches the surface of the Earth, Moon, or other body. Most meteorites are thought to be fragments from asteroids, although some may be pieces from the heads of comets. Most are stony, although some are made of iron and a few have a mixed rock-iron composition.

**meteorology** scientific observation and study of the ◊atmosphere, so that weather can be accurately forecast.

Data from meteorological stations and weather satellites are collated by computer at central agencies, and forecast and weather maps based on current readings are issued at regular intervals.

**meter** any instrument used for measurement. The term is often compounded with a prefix to denote a specific type of meter: for example, ammeter, voltmeter, flowmeter, or pedometer.

**methanal** common name *formaldehyde,* HCHO gas at ordinary temperatures, condensing to a liquid at –21°C/–5.8°F. It has a powerful, penetrating smell. Dissolved in water, it is used as a biological preservative. It is used in the manufacture of plastics, dyes, foam, and in medicine.

**methane** $CH_4$ the simplest hydrocarbon of the paraffin series. Colourless, odourless, and lighter than air, it burns with a bluish flame and explodes when mixed with air or oxygen. It is the chief constituent of natural gas and also occurs in the explosive firedamp of coal mines. Methane emitted by rotting vegetation forms marsh gas, which may ignite by spontaneous combustion to produce the pale flame seen over marshland and known as will-o'-the-wisp.

**methanoic acid** common name *formic acid,* HCOOH, a colourless, slightly fuming liquid that freezes at 8°C/46.4°F and boils at 101°C/213.8°F. It occurs in stinging ants, nettles, sweat, and pine needles, and is used in dyeing, tanning, and electroplating.

**Methodism** evangelical Protestant Christian movement that was founded by John ◊Wesley in 1739 within the Church of England, but became a separate body in 1795. The Methodist Episcopal Church was founded in the USA in 1784. There are over 50 million Methodists worldwide.

**methylated spirit** alcohol that has been rendered undrinkable, and is used for industrial purposes, as a fuel for spirit burners or a solvent.

**metre** in music, the timescale represented by the beat. Metre is regular, whereas rhythm is irregular.

**metre** SI unit (symbol m) of length, equivalent to 1.093 yards or 39.37 inches. It is defined by scientists as the length of the path travelled by light in a vacuum during a time interval of 1/299,792,458 of a second.

**metric system** system of weights and measures developed in France in the 18th century and recognized by other countries in the 19th century. In 1960 an international conference on weights and measures recommended the universal adoption of a revised International System (Système International d'Unités, or SI), with seven prescribed 'base units': the metre (m) for length, kilogram (kg) for mass, second (s) for time, ampere (A) for electric current, kelvin (K) for thermodynamic temperature, candela (cd) for luminous intensity, and mole (mol) for quantity of matter.

**Metternich, Klemens Wenzel Nepomuk Lothar, Prince von Metternich** (1773–1859) Austrian politician, the leading figure in European diplomacy after the fall of Napoleon. As foreign minister 1809–48 (as well as chancellor from 1821), he tried to maintain the balance of power in Europe, supporting monarchy and repressing liberalism.

**Mexican War** war between the USA and Mexico 1846–48, begun in territory disputed between Texas (annexed by the USA 1845 but claimed by Mexico) and Mexico. It began when General Zachary Taylor invaded New Mexico after efforts to purchase what are now California and New Mexico failed. Mexico City was taken 1847, and under the Treaty of Guadaloupe Hidalgo that ended the war, the USA acquired New Mexico and California, as well as clear title to Texas for $15 million.

**Mexico** United States of
*national name* Estados Unidos Mexicanos
*area* 1,958,201 sq km/756,061 sq mi
*capital* Mexico City
*major towns/cities* Guadalajara, Monterrey, Puebla, Netzahualcóyotl, Ciudad Juárez, Tijuana
*major ports* 49 ocean ports
*physical features* partly arid central highlands; Sierra Madre mountain ranges east and west; tropical coastal plains; volcanoes, including Popocatepetl; Rio Grande
*head of state and government* Ernesto Zedillo Ponce de Leon from 1994
*political system* federal democracy
*political parties* Institutional Revolutionary Party (PRI), moderate, left wing; National Action Party (PAN), moderate, Christian, centre right; Party of the Democratic Revolution (PRD), centre left

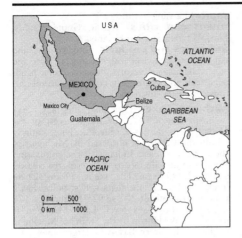

**currency** Mexican peso
**GNP per capita (PPP)** (US$) 8,190 (1998 est)
**exports** petroleum and petroleum products, engines and spare parts for motor vehicles, motor vehicles, electrical and electronic goods, fresh and preserved vegetables, coffee, cotton. Principal market: USA 81.9% (1998)
**population** 97,366,000 (1999 est)
**language** Spanish (official); Nahuatl, Maya, Zapoteco, Mixteco, Otomi
**religion** Roman Catholic
**life expectancy** 70 (men); 76 (women) (1995–2000)
**Chronology**
**c. 2600 BC** Mayan civilization originated in Yucatán peninsula.
**1000–500 BC** Zapotec civilization developed around Monte Albán in southern Mexico.
**4th–10th centuries AD** Mayan Empire at its height.
**10th–12th centuries** Toltecs ruled much of Mexico from their capital at Tula.
**12th century** Aztecs migrated south into valley of Mexico.
**c. 1325** Aztecs began building their capital Tenochtitlán on site of present-day Mexico City.
**15th century** Montezuma I built up Aztec Empire in central Mexico.
**1519–21** Hernán Cortes conquered Aztec Empire and secured Mexico for Spain.
**1520** Montezuma II, last king of the Aztecs, killed.
**1535** Mexico became Spanish viceroyalty of New Spain; plantations and mining developed with Indian labour.
**1519–1607** Indigenous population reduced from 21 million to 1 million, due mainly to lack of resistance to diseases transported from Old World.
**1810** Father Miguel Hidalgo led unsuccessful revolt against Spanish.
**1821** Independence proclaimed by Augustín de Iturbide with support of Church and landowners.
**1822** Iturbide overthrew provisional government and proclaimed himself Emperor Augustín I.
**1824** Federal republic established amid continuing public disorder.
**1824–55** Military rule of Antonio López de

Santa Anna, who imposed stability (he became president in 1833).
**1846–48** Mexican War: Mexico lost California and New Mexico to USA.
**1848** Revolt of Mayan Indians suppressed.
**1855** Benito Juárez aided overthrow of Santa Anna's dictatorship.
**1857–60** Sweeping liberal reforms and anticlerical legislation introduced by Juárez led to civil war with conservatives.
**1861** Mexico suspended payment on foreign debt leading to French military intervention; Juárez resisted with US support.
**1864** Supported by conservatives, France installed Archduke Maximilian of Austria as emperor of Mexico.
**1867** Maximilian shot by republicans as French troops withdrew; Juárez resumed presidency.
**1876** Gen Porfirio Diaz established dictatorship; Mexican economy modernized through foreign investment.
**1911** Revolution overthrew Diaz; liberal president Francisco Madero introduced radical land reform and labour legislation but political disorder increased.
**1914 and 1916–17** US military intervened to quell disorder.
**1917** New constitution, designed to ensure permanent democracy, adopted.
**1924–35** Government dominated by anti-clerical Gen Plutarco Calles, who introduced further social reforms.
**1929** Foundation of National Revolutionary Party (PRFN) (renamed PRI in 1946).
**1938** President Lázaro Cárdenas nationalized all foreign-owned oil wells in face of US opposition.
**1942** Mexico declared war on Germany and Japan (and so regained US favour).
**1946–52** Miguel Alemán first of succession of authoritarian PRI presidents to seek moderation and stability rather than further radical reform.
**1960s** Rapid industrial growth partly financed by borrowing.
**1976** Huge oil reserves were discovered in the southeastern state of Chiapas; oil production tripled in six years.
**1982** Falling oil prices caused a grave financial crisis; Mexico defaulted on debt.
**1985** An earthquake in Mexico City killed thousands.
**1994** There was an uprising in Chiapas by Zapatista National Liberation Army (EZLN), seeking rights for the Mayan Indian population; Mexico formed the North American Free Trade Agreement (NAFTA) with the USA and Canada.
**1995** The government agreed to offer greater autonomy to Mayan Indians in Chiapas.
**1996** There were short-lived peace talks with the EZLN; violent attacks against the government by the new leftist Popular Revolutionary Army (EPR) increased.
**1998** A lapsed peace accord with Zapatist rebels was reactivated, but talks between the government and the rebels broke down.

**Mexico City** Spanish *Ciudad de México*, capital, industrial (iron, steel, chemicals, textiles), and cultural centre of Mexico, 2,255 m/7,400 ft above sea level on the southern edge of the central plateau; population (1994) 15,500,000. It is thought to be one of the world's most polluted cities because of its position in a volcanic basin 2,000 m/7,400 ft above sea level.

**mg** symbol for *milligram*.

**mi** symbol for ◊*mile*.

**Miami** industrial city and port in southeastern Florida, USA, on the Atlantic coast of the Florida peninsula about 70 km/43 mi from its southern tip; seat of Dade County; population (1994 est) 373,000. It is the hub of finance, trade, and transport in the region, with air connections to Latin America and the Caribbean; industries include food processing, transportation and electronic equipment, clothing, furniture, and machinery. With its subtropical climate Miami is also a major tourist resort and a centre for oceanographic research. The first permanent European settlement dates from the 1870s; Miami was incorporated in 1896.

**mica** group of silicate minerals that split easily into thin flakes along lines of weakness in their crystal structure (perfect basal cleavage). They are glossy, have a pearly lustre, and are found in many igneous and metamorphic rocks. Their good thermal and electrical insulation qualities make them valuable in industry.

**Michael** (1921–   ) King of Romania 1927–30 and 1940–47. The son of Carol II, he succeeded his grandfather as king in 1927 but was displaced when his father returned from exile 1930. In 1940 he was proclaimed king again on his father's abdication, overthrew in 1944 the fascist dictatorship of Ion Antonescu (1882–1946), and enabled Romania to share in the victory of the Allies at the end of World War II. He abdicated and left Romania in 1947.

**Michelangelo** properly Michelangelo di Lodovico Buonarroti (1475–1564) Italian sculptor, painter, architect, and poet. He was active in his native Florence and in Rome. His giant talent dominated the High Renaissance. The marble *David*, (1501–04; Accademia, Florence) set a new standard in nude sculpture. His massive figure style was translated into fresco in the Sistine Chapel (1508–12 and 1536–41; Vatican). Other works in Rome include the dome of St Peter's basilica. His influence, particularly on the development of ◊Mannerism, was profound.

**Michigan** state in north-central USA. It is nicknamed the Wolverine State or the Great Lakes State. Michigan was admitted to the Union in 1837 as the 26th US state. It is situated in the Midwest and Great Lakes regions, and is comprised of two major peninsulas. The mitten-shaped, north–south oriented *Lower Peninsula* is bordered to the south by Ohio and Indiana, and faces Ontario, Canada, to the north and east across the Great Lakes. The east–west oriented *Upper Peninsula* is bordered to the south by Wisconsin, and also faces Ontario to the north and east across the lakes
*population* (1995) 9,549,400
*area* 151,600 sq km/58,518 sq mi

*capital* Lansing
*towns and cities* Detroit, Grand Rapids, Flint, Warren, Sterling Heights, Ann Arbor
*industries and products* motor vehicles and equipment, non-electrical machinery, iron and steel, chemicals, pharmaceuticals, dairy products, fruit and beans, salt, coal, oil, natural gas, music industry, tourism.

**Michigan, Lake** (Algonquian 'big lake') lake in north-central USA, the third largest of the ◊Great Lakes and the only one lying entirely within the USA; it is bordered by Michigan to the north and east, Indiana to the south, and Wisconsin and Illinois to the west; area 58,000 sq km/22,390 sq mi. The lake is 517 km/321 mi long, 190 km/118 mi at its widest point, has a maximum depth of 282 m/925 ft, and lies 176 m/577 ft above sea level. Lake Michigan is joined to Lake Huron by the Straits of Mackinac in the north. Green Bay is its largest inlet, and Chicago and Milwaukee are its main ports. The first European to see the Lake Michigan was the French explorer Jean Nicolet, in 1634.

**microbe** another name for ◊micro-organism.

**microbiology** the study of micro-organisms, mostly viruses and single-celled organisms such as bacteria, protozoa, and yeasts. The practical applications of microbiology are in medicine (since many micro-organisms cause disease); in brewing, baking, and other food and beverage processes, where the micro-organisms carry out fermentation; and in genetic engineering.

**microchip** popular name for the silicon chip, or ◊integrated circuit.

**microclimate** the climate of a small area, such as a woodland, lake, or even a hedgerow. Significant differences can exist between the climates of two neighbouring areas – for example, a town is usually warmer than the surrounding countryside (forming a heat island), and a woodland cooler, darker, and less windy than an area of open land.

**microcomputer** or *micro* or *personal computer*, small desktop or portable ◊computer, typically designed to be used by one person at a time, although individual computers can be linked in a network so that users can share data and programs.

Its central processing unit is a ◊microprocessor, contained on a single integrated circuit.

**micrometre** one-millionth of a ◊metre (symbol μm).

**Micronesia** Federated States of (FSM)
*area* 700 sq km/270 sq mi
*capital* Kolonia, in Pohnpei state
*major towns/cities* Weno, in Chuuk state; Lelu, in Kosrae state
*major ports* Teketik, Lepukos, Okak
*physical features* an archipelago of 607 equatorial, volcanic islands in the West Pacific
*head of state and government* Jacob Nena from 1997
*political system* democratic federal state

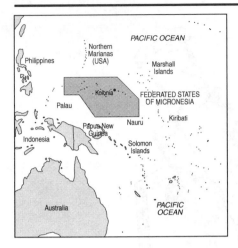

1991 Independence achieved, with Bailey Olter as president. Entered into UN membership.

**political parties** no formally organized political parties
**currency** US dollar
**GNP per capita (PPP)** (US$) 3,920 (1998 est)
**exports** copra, pepper, fish. Principal market: Japan 84.8% (1996)
**population** 116,000 (1999 est)
**language** English (official) and eight local languages
**religion** Christianity (mainly Roman Catholic in Yap state, Protestant elsewhere)
**life expectancy** 67 (men); 71 (women) (1995–2000)
**Chronology**
**c. 1000 BC** Micronesians first settled the islands.
**1525** Portuguese navigators first visited Yap and Ulithi islands in the Carolines (Micronesia).
**later 16th century** Fell under Spanish influence.
**1874** Spanish rule formally declared in face of increasing encroachment by German traders.
**1885** Yap seized by German naval forces, but restored to Spain after arbitration by Pope Leo XIII on condition that Germany was allowed freedom of trade.
**1899** Purchased for $4.5 million by Germany from Spain, after the latter's defeat in the Spanish–American War.
**1914** Occupied by Japan on outbreak of World War I.
**1919** Administered under League of Nations mandate by Japan, and vigorously colonized.
**1944** Occupied by USA after Japanese forces defeated in World War II.
**1947** Administered by USA as part of the United Nations (UN) Trust Territory of the Pacific Islands, under the name of the Federated States of Micronesia (FSM).
**1979** A constitution was adopted that established a federal system for its four constituent states (Yap, Chuuk, Pohnpei, and Kosrae) and internal self-government.
**1986** The Compact of Free Association was entered into with the USA, granting the islands self-government with the USA retaining responsibility for defence and security until 2001.
**1990** UN trust status was terminated.

**Micronesia** group of islands in the Pacific Ocean lying north of ◊Melanesia.

**Micronesian** any of the indigenous Australoid and Polynesian peoples of Micronesia, including Pacific islands north of the Equator, such as the Caroline, Marshall, Mariana, and Gilbert islands. Their languages belong to the Austronesian family.

**micro-organism** or *microbe,* living organism invisible to the naked eye but visible under a microscope. Micro-organisms include viruses and single-celled organisms such as bacteria, protozoa, yeasts, and some algae. The term has no taxonomic significance in biology. The study of micro-organisms is known as microbiology.

**microphone** primary component in a sound-reproducing system, whereby the mechanical energy of sound waves is converted into electrical signals by means of a ◊transducer. One of the simplest is the telephone receiver mouthpiece, invented by Scottish–US inventor Alexander Graham Bell in 1876; other types of microphone are used with broadcasting and sound-film apparatus.

**microprocessor** complete computer ◊central processing unit contained on a single ◊integrated circuit, or chip. The appearance of the first microprocessor in 1971 designed by Intel for a pocket calculator manufacturer heralded the introduction of the microcomputer. The microprocessor has led to a dramatic fall in the size and cost of computers, and dedicated computers can now be found in washing machines, cars, and so on. Examples of microprocessors are the Intel Pentium family and the IBM/Motorola PowerPC, used by Apple Computer.

**microscope** instrument for forming magnified images with high resolution for detail. Optical and electron microscopes are the ones chiefly in use; other types include acoustic, scanning tunnelling, and atomic force microscopes. *See illustration on page 590.*

**microsurgery** part or all of an intricate surgical operation – rejoining a severed limb, for example – performed with the aid of a binocular microscope, using miniaturized instruments. Sewing of the nerves and blood vessels is done with a nylon thread so fine that it is only just visible to the naked eye.

**microwave** ◊electromagnetic wave with a wavelength in the range 0.3 to 30 cm/0.1 in to 12 in, or 300–300,000 megahertz (between radio waves and ◊infrared radiation). Microwaves are used in radar, in radio broadcasting, and in microwave heating and cooking.

**microwave heating** heating by means of microwaves. Microwave ovens use this form of heating for the rapid cooking or reheating of foods, where heat is generated throughout the interior of the food. If food is not heated completely, there is a danger of bacterial growth that may lead to food poisoning. Industrially, microwave heating is used for destroying insects

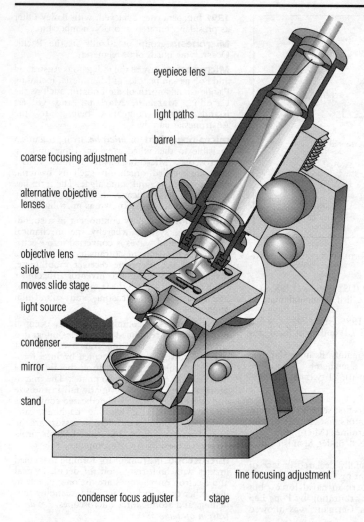

eyepiece lens

light paths

barrel

coarse focusing adjustment

alternative objective
lenses

objective lens

slide

moves slide stage

light source

condenser

mirror

stand

fine focusing adjustment

condenser focus adjuster          stage

***microscope*** *An optical microscope. In essence, the optical microscope consists of an eyepiece lens and an objective lens, which are used to produce an enlarged image of a small object by focusing light from a light source. Optical microscopes can achieve magnifications of up to 1,500–2,000. Higher magnifications and resolutions are obtained by electron microscopes.*

in grain and enzymes in processed food, pasteurizing and sterilizing liquids, and drying timber and paper.

**Midas** in Greek mythology, a king of Phrygia who was granted the ability to convert all he touched to gold by ◊Dionysus, god of wine and excess; the gift became a curse when his food and drink also turned to metal. In another story he was given ass's ears by Apollo for preferring the music of Pan in a contest between the two gods.

**Middle Ages, the** or *the Medieval period,* term used by Europeans to describe the period between ancient history and modern history. It is not a precise term, but is often taken to cover

the time from the fall of the Western Roman Empire in AD 476 to the fall of Constantinople (Istanbul) and the end of the Eastern Roman Empire in 1453. The term Dark Ages is sometimes used to cover the period from AD 476 to AD 1000, because it was a time when learning and the rule of law were at a low ebb in Europe. During the Middle Ages Germanic tribes overran Europe, bringing with them changes in language and culture.

**Middle East** indeterminate area now usually taken to include Egypt and the Arab states of the eastern Mediterranean and Arabian Peninsula, sometimes extended to the states of northwest Africa, Turkey, Iran, and Afghanistan.

**Middlesbrough** industrial town, port, and unitary authority, on the estuary of the River Tees, northeast England, created in 1996 from part of the former county of Cleveland. The town was the administrative headquarters of the county of Cleveland to 1996. It is the commercial centre of the Teesside industrial area, which also includes Stockton-on-Tees, Redcar, Billingham, Thornaby, and Eston

*area* 54 sq km/21 sq mi

*features* Transporter Bridge (1911) transports cars and passengers across the Tees to Hartlepool in a cable car; Newport Bridge (1934) was the first vertical lift bridge in England; the University of Teesside, formerly Teesside Polytechnic, was established in 1992; the Captain Cook Birthplace Museum commemorates the life of the naval explorer James Cook; the 18th-century National Trust-owned Ormesby Hall is located nearby

*industries* formerly a centre of heavy industry, it diversified its products in the 1960s; there are construction, electronics, engineering, and shipbuilding industries, and iron, steel, and chemicals are produced

*famous people* James Cook

*population* (1996) 146,000.

**midge** common name for many insects resembling ◊gnats, generally divided into biting midges (family Ceratopogonidae) that suck blood and non-biting midges (family Chironomidae).

**Mid Glamorgan** Welsh *Morgannwg Ganol,* former county of south Wales, 1974–1996, now divided between ◊Rhondda Cynon Taff, ◊Merthyr Tydfil, ◊Bridgend, and Vale of Glamorgan unitary authorities.

**Midi-Pyrénées** region of southwest France, comprising the *départements* of Ariège, Aveyron, Haute-Garonne, Gers, Lot, Hautes-Pyrénées, Tarn, and Tarn-et-Garonne; the capital is ◊Toulouse; area 45,300 sq km/17,486 sq mi; population (1990) 2,430,700. The region includes several spa towns (including ◊Lourdes), winter resorts, and prehistoric caves. It produces fruit, wine, and livestock, and industries include aerospace. There are two large universities. Other notable towns include Montauban, Cahors, and Rodez.

**Midlands** area of central England corresponding roughly to the Anglo-Saxon kingdom of Mercia. The *East Midlands* comprises Derbyshire, Leicestershire, Northamptonshire, and Nottinghamshire. The *West Midlands* covers the metropolitan district of ◊West Midlands created from parts of Staffordshire, Warwickshire, and Worcestershire, and split into the metropolitan boroughs of Dudley, Sandwell, Coventry, Birmingham, Walsall, Solihull, and Wolverhampton; and (often included) the *South Midlands* comprising Bedfordshire, Buckinghamshire, and Oxfordshire.

**midnight sun** the constant appearance of the Sun (within the Arctic and Antarctic circles) above the ◊horizon during the summer.

**Midway Islands** two coral islands in the Pacific, near the northwestern end of the Hawaiian Islands chain, USA, 1,800 km/1,120 mi northwest of Honolulu; area 5 sq km/2 sq mi. They form a naval base with no indigenous population. The islands are individually known as Eastern and Sand; they were annexed by the USA in 1867, and are now administered by the US Navy. The naval Battle of Midway (3–6 June 1942), between the USA and Japan, was a turning point in the Pacific in World War II; the US victory marked the end of Japanese expansion in the region.

**Midwest** or *Middle West,* large area of the north-central USA. It is loosely defined geographically, but is generally taken to comprise the states of Illinois, Iowa, Wisconsin, Minnesota, Nebraska, Kansas, Missouri, North Dakota, and South Dakota, and the portions of Montana, Wyoming, and Colorado that lie east of the Rocky Mountains. Ohio, Michigan, and Indiana are often variously included as well. In its broadest sense, the Midwest has an area of 986,800 sq mi/2,556,000 sq km and a population of about 61.5 million – roughly a quarter of the national total. The region is generally flat and well-watered, with good transportation links. Traditionally its economy is divided between agriculture and heavy industry. The main urban Midwest centre is Chicago. In the summer of 1993 the Midwest was devastated by floods, which left tens of thousands of people homeless.

**midwifery** assistance of women in childbirth. Traditionally, it was undertaken by experienced specialists; in modern medical training it is a nursing speciality for practitioners called midwives.

**migraine** acute, sometimes incapacitating headache (generally only on one side), accompanied by nausea, that recurs, often with advance symptoms such as flashing lights. No cure has been discovered, but ergotamine normally relieves the symptoms. Some sufferers learn to avoid certain foods, such as chocolate, which suggests an allergic factor.

**migrant labour** people who move from place to place to work or harvest seasonal crops. Economic or political pressures often cause people to leave their homelands to earn wages in this way, but some families live this way for several generations.

**migration** the movement, either seasonal or as part of a single life cycle, of certain animals, chiefly birds and fish, to distant breeding or feeding grounds.

**mildew** any ◊fungus that appears as a destructive growth on plants, paper, leather, or wood when they become damp for a certain length of time; such fungi usually form a thin white coating on the surface.

**mile** imperial unit of linear measure. A statute mile is equal to 1,760 yards (1.60934 km), and an international nautical mile is equal to 2,026 yards (1,852 m).

**Militant Tendency** in British politics, left-wing faction originally within the Labour Party, aligned with the publication *Militant*. It became active in the 1970s, with radical socialist policies based on Trotskyism (see ◊Trotsky), and gained some success in local government, for example in the inner-city area of Liverpool. In the mid-1980s the Labour Party considered it to be a separate organization within the party and banned it.

**militia** body of civilian soldiers, usually with some military training, who are on call in emergencies, distinct from professional soldiers. In Switzerland, the militia is the national defence force, and every able-bodied man is liable for service in it. In the UK the *Territorial Army* and in the USA the *National Guard* have supplanted earlier voluntary militias.

**milk** secretion of the ◊mammary glands of female mammals, with which they suckle their young (during ◊lactation). Over 85% is water, the remainder comprising protein, fat, lactose (a sugar), calcium, phosphorus, iron, and vitamins. The milk of cows, goats, and sheep is often consumed by humans, but regular drinking of milk after infancy is principally a Western practice.

**Milky Way** faint band of light crossing the night sky, consisting of stars in the plane of our Galaxy. The name Milky Way is often used for the Galaxy itself. It is a spiral ◊galaxy, 100,000 light years in diameter and 2,000 light years thick, containing at least 100 billion ◊stars. The Sun is in one of its spiral arms, about 25,000 light years from the centre, not far from its central plane.

**Mill, John Stuart** (1806–1873) English philosopher and economist who wrote *On Liberty* (1859), the classic philosophical defence of liberalism, and *Utilitarianism* (1863), a version of the 'greatest happiness for the greatest number' principle in ethics. His progressive views inspired *On the Subjection of Women* (1869).

**Millais, John Everett** (1829–1896) English painter, a founder member of the ◊Pre-Raphaelite Brotherhood in 1848. Among his best known works are *Ophelia* (1852; National Gallery, London) and *Autumn Leaves* (1856; City Art Galleries, Manchester). By the late 1860s he had left the Brotherhood, developing a more fluid and conventional style which appealed strongly to Victorian tastes.

**Millennium Bug** crisis that faced computer professionals and users at the end of the year 1999. The crisis arose because it was feared that computers would be unable to operate normally when faced with the unfamiliar date format of 2000. Information about the year was typically stored in a two-digit instead of a four-digit field in order to save memory space, which without remedial work would have meant that after the year 1999 ended the year could have appeared as '00', interpreted as 1900 or not recognized at all. The turn of the century itself passed without significant breakdowns of normal services. However, it was stressed that problems could continue to surface throughout 2000.

**Miller, Arthur** (1915– ) US dramatist. His plays deal with family relationships and contemporary American values, and include *Death of a Salesman* (1949, Pulitzer Prize), and *The Crucible*

(1953), based on the Salem witch trials and reflecting the communist witch-hunts of Senator Joe ◊McCarthy. He was married 1956–61 to the film star Marilyn Monroe, for whom he wrote the film *The Misfits* (1960).

**millet** any of several grasses of which the grains are used as a cereal food and the stems as animal fodder. Species include *Panicum miliaceum,* extensively cultivated in the warmer parts of Europe, and *Sorghum bicolor,* also known as durra. (Family Gramineae.)

**millimetre of mercury** unit of pressure (symbol mmHg), used in medicine for measuring blood pressure defined as the pressure exerted by a column of mercury one millimetre high, under the action of gravity.

**millipede** any of a group of ◊arthropods that have segmented bodies, each segment usually bearing two pairs of legs, and a pair of short clubbed antennae on the distinct head. Most millipedes are no more than 2.5 cm/1 in long; a few in the tropics are 30 cm/12 in. (Class Diplopoda.)

**Milošević, Slobodan** (1941– ) Serbian communist politician; party chief and president of Serbia 1986–97, and president of Yugoslavia from 1997. Milošević wielded considerable influence over the Serb-dominated Yugoslav federal army during the 1991–92 civil war and continued to back Serbian militia in Bosnia-Herzegovina 1992–94, although publicly disclaiming any intention to 'carve up' the newly independent republic. Widely believed to be the instigator of the conflict, Milošević changed tactics from 1993, adopting the public persona of peacemaker and putting pressure on his allies, the Bosnian Serbs, to accept negotiated peace terms; this contributed to the Dayton peace accord for Bosnia-Herzegovina in November 1995.

One of his first acts as president of Serbia in 1989 was to repeal the autonomy enjoyed by the province of Kosovo since 1974. In 1998 he faced international condemnation again for the brutal treatment of ethnic Albanians by Serbian forces in the province. In February 1999 there was fierce fighting between Serbian forces and Albanian separatist guerrillas in Kosovo, then representatives of the separatists agreed to attend Western-sponsored talks in Paris. A peace plan was accepted by the separatists but rejected by Serbia.

Following Milošević's rejection of the Rambouillet peace plan, NATO aircraft began a bombing campaign in March 1999 in an attempt to force the Yugoslav government to end its persecution of ethnic Albanians in Kosovo. In April, President Milošević dismissed his deputy, Vuk Draskovic, following his criticisms of the programme of 'ethnic cleansing' in Kosovo.

In June 1999 the International War Crimes Tribunal in The Hague indicted Milošević. In the same month Milošević accepted NATO's peace agreement.

**Milton, John** (1608–1674) English poet and prose writer. His epic *Paradise Lost* (1667) is one of the landmarks of English literature. Early poems, including *Comus* (a masque performed 1634) and *Lycidas* (an elegy, 1638), showed

Milton's superlative lyric gift. He also wrote many pamphlets and prose works, including *Areopagitica* (1644), which opposed press censorship, and he was Latin secretary to Oliver ◊Cromwell and the Council of State from 1649 until the restoration of Charles II.

**Milton Keynes** unitary authority in central England, formerly part of Buckinghamshire
**area** 311 sq km/120 sq mi
**towns and cities** Milton Keynes (administrative headquarters), Newport Pagnell, Olney, Bletchley, Stony Stratford, Woburn Sands, Wolverton
**features** Grand Union Canal; River Great Ouse; River Tove; Open University (established in Milton Keynes in 1971); Milton Keynes National Bowl (venue for outdoor events); National Badminton Centre (Milton Keynes); Bletchley Park, government centre of code-breaking during World War II; Ouse Valley Park with wetland habitats; Peace Pagoda (Milton Keynes), first to be built in northern hemisphere and surrounded by a thousand cherry and cedar trees planted in memory of all war victims; Milton Keynes' concrete cows, constructed in 1978 by a community artist and local schoolchildren; Open University and De Montfort University campuses
**industries** financial services, telecommunications, soft drinks, high technology industries, motor vehicle parts and manufacture (Aston Martin-Lagonda, Mercedes-Benz, Volkswagen-Audi), vellum and parchment
**population** (1996) 198,600.

**mimosa** any of a group of leguminous trees, shrubs, or herbs belonging to the mimosa family, found in tropical and subtropical regions. They all have small, fluffy, golden, ball-like flowers. A similar but unrelated plant, *Acacia dealbata*, is sold as mimosa by European florists. (True mimosa genus *Mimosa*, family Mimosaceae.)

**Mimosa** or *Becrux* or *Beta Crucis*, second-brightest star in the southern-hemisphere constellation of Crux, marking one of the four corners of the Southern Cross, and the 19th-brightest star in the night sky. It is a blue-white giant star of magnitude 0.8 around 460 light years from the Sun.

**min.** abbreviation for *minute* (time); *minimum*.

**Minangkabau** an Indonesian people of western Sumatra. In addition to approximately 3 million Minangkabau in western Sumatra, there are sizeable communities in the major Indonesian cities. The Minangkabau language belongs to the Austronesian family.

**mind** in philosophy, the presumed mental or physical being or faculty that enables a person to think, will, and feel; the seat of the intelligence and of memory; sometimes only the cognitive or intellectual powers, as distinguished from the will and the emotions.

**mineral** naturally formed inorganic substance with a particular chemical composition and a regularly repeating internal structure. Either in their perfect crystalline form or otherwise, minerals are the constituents of ◊rocks. In more general usage, a mineral is any substance economically valuable for mining (including coal and oil, despite their organic origins).

**mineral extraction** recovery of valuable ores from the Earth's crust. The processes used include open-cast mining, shaft mining, and quarrying, as well as more specialized processes such as those used for oil and sulphur.

**mineralogy** study of minerals. The classification of minerals is based chiefly on their chemical composition and the kind of chemical bonding that holds these atoms together. The mineralogist also studies their crystallographic and physical characters, occurrence, and mode of formation.

**Minerva** in Roman mythology, the goddess of wisdom and war, and of handicrafts and the arts, equivalent to the Greek ◊Athena. From the earliest days of ancient Rome, there was a temple to her on the Capitoline Hill, near the Temple of Jupiter.

**miniature painting** painting on a very small scale, notably early manuscript illumination, and later miniature portraits, sometimes set in jewelled cases, and Islamic paintings. Hans Holbein the Younger introduced miniature portrait painting into England, the form reaching its height in the works of Nicholas ◊Hilliard in the 16th century, though continuing well into the 19th century. There was also a very strong tradition of miniature portrait painting in France. Miniatures by Islamic artists flourished in India and Persia, their subjects often bird and flowers, or scenes from history and legend, rather than portraits.

**minicomputer** multiuser computer with a size and processing power between those of a ◊mainframe and a ◊microcomputer. Nowadays almost all minicomputers are based on ◊microprocessors.

**Minimalism** movement in abstract art (mostly sculpture) and music towards severely simplified composition. Minimal art developed in the USA in the 1950s in reaction to ◊Abstract Expressionism, shunning its emotive approach in favour of impersonality and elemental, usually geometric, shapes. It has found its fullest expression in sculpture, notably in the work of Carl Andre, who employs industrial materials in modular compositions. In music, from the 1960s, it manifested itself in large-scale statements, usually tonal or even diatonic, and highly repetitive, based on a few 'minimal' musical ideas. Major Minimalist composers are Steve ◊Reich and Philip ◊Glass.

**minimum lending rate** (MLR), in the UK, the rate of interest at which the Bank of England lends to the money market.

**mining** extraction of minerals from under the land or sea for industrial or domestic uses. Exhaustion of traditionally accessible resources has led to development of new mining techniques; for example, extraction of oil from offshore deposits and from land shale reserves.

Technology is also under development for the exploitation of minerals from entirely new sources such as mud deposits and mineral nodules from the sea bed.

**mink** either of two species of carnivorous mammals belonging to the weasel family, usually found in or near water. They have rich brown fur, and are up to 50 cm/1.6 ft long with bushy tails 20 cm/8 in long. They live in Europe and Asia (*M. lutreola*) and North America (*M. vison*). (Genus *Mustela*.)

**Minnesota** state in north Midwest USA. It is nicknamed the Gopher State or the North Star State. Minnesota was admitted to the Union in 1858 as the 32nd US state. One of the Great Lakes states, it is bordered to the south by Iowa, to the west by North and South Dakota, to the north by the Canadian states of Ontario and Manitoba, and to the east by Wisconsin
*population* (1995) 4,609,500
*area* 218,700 sq km/84,418 sq mi
*capital* St Paul
*towns and cities* Minneapolis, Duluth, Bloomington, Rochester
*industries and products* cereals, soybeans, livestock, meat and dairy products, iron ore (about two-thirds of US output), non-electrical machinery, electronic equipment, pulp, finance sector.

**minnow** any of various small freshwater fishes of the carp family, found in streams and ponds worldwide. Most species are small and dull in colour, but some are brightly coloured. They feed on larvae and insects. (Family Cyprinidae.)

**minor** legal term for those under the age of majority, which varies from country to country but is usually between 18 and 21. In the USA (from 1971 for voting, and in some states for nearly all other purposes) and certain European countries (in Britain since 1970) the age of majority is 18.

**Minotaur** in Greek mythology, a monster with a man's body and bull's head, offspring of Pasiphaë, wife of King Minos of Crete, and a bull sent by Poseidon. It was housed in a Labyrinth designed by ◊Daedalus at Knossos, and its victims were seven girls and seven youths sent in annual tribute by Athens. The beast was killed by ◊Theseus with the aid of Ariadne, daughter of Minos.

**mint** in botany, any aromatic plant of the mint family, widely distributed in temperate regions. The plants have square stems, creeping roots, and spikes of usually pink or purplish flowers. The family includes garden mint (*M. spicata*) and peppermint (*M. piperita*). (Genus *Mentha*, family Labiatae.)

**minuet** French country dance in three time adapted as a European courtly dance of the 17th century. The music was later used as the third movement of a classical four-movement symphony where its gentle rhythm provides a foil to the slow second movement and fast final movement.

**minute** unit of time consisting of 60 seconds; also a unit of angle equal to one sixtieth of a degree.

**Miocene** ('middle recent') fourth epoch of the Tertiary period of geological time, 23.5–5.2 million years ago. At this time grasslands spread over the interior of continents, and hoofed mammals rapidly evolved.

**Mira** or **Omicron Ceti**, brightest long-period pulsating ◊variable star, located in the constellation Cetus. Mira was the first star discovered to vary periodically in brightness.

**Mirabeau, Honoré Gabriel Riqueti, comte de** (1749–1791) French politician, leader of the National Assembly in the French Revolution. He wanted to establish a parliamentary monarchy on the English model. From May 1790 he secretly acted as political adviser to the king.

**miracle play** another name for ◊mystery play.

**Miró, Joan** (1893–1983) Spanish painter and sculptor, a major figure in ◊Surrealism. In the mid-1920s he developed an abstract style, lyrical and often witty, with amoeba shapes, some linear, some highly coloured, generally floating on a plain background. *Birth of the World* (1925; Museum of Modern Art New York) is typical of his more abstract works.

**mirror** any polished surface that reflects light; often made from 'silvered' glass (in practice, a mercury-alloy coating of glass). A plane (flat) mirror produces a same-size, erect 'virtual' image located behind the mirror at the same distance from it as the object is in front of it. A spherical concave mirror produces a reduced, inverted real image in front or an enlarged, erect virtual image behind it (as in a shaving mirror), depending on how close the object is to the mirror. A spherical convex mirror produces a reduced, erect virtual image behind it (as in a car's rear-view mirror).

**miscarriage** spontaneous expulsion of a fetus from the womb before it is capable of independent survival. Often, miscarriages are due to an abnormality in the developing fetus.

**missel thrush** bird belonging to the ◊thrush family.

**missile** rocket-propelled weapon, which may be nuclear-armed (see ◊nuclear warfare). Modern missiles are often classified as surface-to-surface missiles (SSM), air-to-air missiles (AAM), surface-to-air missiles (SAM), or air-to-surface missiles (ASM). A *cruise missile* is in effect a pilotless, computer-guided aircraft; it can be sea-launched from submarines or surface ships, or launched from the air or the ground.

**Mississippi** (American Indian *missi* 'big', *sipi* 'river') river in the USA, the main arm of the great river system draining the USA between the Appalachian and the Rocky mountain ranges. The length of the Mississippi is 3,778 km/2,348 mi; with its tributary the Missouri it totals 6,020 km/3,740 mi. The Mississippi rises in the lake region of northern Minnesota in the basin of Lake Itasca, and drops 20 m/65 ft over the St Anthony Falls at Minneapolis. Below the tributaries of the Minnesota, Wisconsin, Des Moines, and Illinois rivers, the confluence of the Missouri and Mississippi occurs at St Louis. Turning at the Ohio junction, it passes Memphis, and takes in the St Francis, Arkansas, Yazoo, and Red tributaries before reaching its delta on the Gulf of Mexico, beyond New Orleans. Altogether the Mississippi has 42 tributary streams and the whole Mississippi river system has a navigable length in excess of 25,900 km/16,100 mi.

**Mississippi** state in southeast USA. It is nicknamed the Magnolia State or the Bayou State. Mississippi was admitted to the Union in 1817 as the 20th US state. Part of the Deep South, it was historically associated with the cotton plantations, slavery, and the blues. Mississippi is bordered to the east by Alabama, to the north by Tennessee, and to the west by Arkansas and Louisiana. To the south the state has a coast c. 115 km/70 mi long on the Gulf of Mexico, with a number of islands in the Mississippi Sound
*population* (1995) 2,697,200
*area* 123,600 sq km/47,710 sq mi
*capital* Jackson
*towns and cities* Biloxi, Greenville, Meridian, Hattiesburg
*industries and products* cotton, rice, soybeans, chickens, fish and shellfish, lumber and wood products, petroleum and natural gas, transportation equipment, chemicals.

**Mississippian** US term for the Lower or Early ◊Carboniferous period of geological time, 363–323 million years ago. It is named after the state of Mississippi.

**Missouri** major river in central USA, largest tributary of the ◊Mississippi, which it joins north of St Louis; length 3,969 km/2,466 mi; drainage area 1,370,000 sq km/529,000 sq mi. It rises among the Rocky Mountains in Montana, and passes northwards through a 366-m/1200-ft gorge known as the 'Gate of the Mountains'. The river is formed by the confluence of the Jefferson, Gallatin, and Madison rivers near Gallatin City, southwestern Montana, and flows southeast through the states of Montana, North Dakota, and South Dakota to Sioux City, Iowa. It then turns south to form the borders between Iowa and Nebraska and between Kansas and Missouri, and enters the Mississippi channel 32 km/20 mi north of St Louis. Kansas City, Missouri, is the largest city on its banks.

**Missouri** state in central USA. It is nicknamed Show Me State or the Bullion State. Missouri was admitted ot the Union in 1821 as the 24th US state. Part of the Midwest, it is bordered to the south by Arkansas, to the west by Oklahoma, Kansas, and Nebraska, to the north by Iowa, and to the east by Illinois and, in the extreme southeast, by parts of Kentucky and Tennessee
*population* (1995) 5,323,500
*area* 180,600 sq km/69,712 sq mi
*capital* Jefferson City
*towns and cities* St Louis, Kansas City, Springfield, Independence

*industries and products* meat and other processed food, aerospace and transport equipment, lead, zinc, tourism.

**mistletoe** parasitic evergreen plant, native to Europe. It grows on trees as a small bush with translucent white berries. Used in many Western countries as a Christmas decoration, it also featured in the pagan religion ◊Druidism. (*Viscum album*, family Loranthaceae.)

**mite** minute ◊arachnid related to the ◊ticks. Some mites are free-living scavengers or predators. Some are parasitic, such as the *itch mite* (*Sarcoptes scabiei*), which burrows in skin causing scabies in humans and mange in dogs, and the *red mite* (*Dermanyssus gallinae*), which sucks blood from poultry and other birds. Others parasitize plants. (Order Acarina.)

**Mithras** or *Mithra*, in Persian mythology, the god of light, son of the sublime god, Ahura Mazda. Mithras represented the power of morality and goodness against Ahriman, the personification of evil, and promised his followers compensation for present evil after death. Mithraism was introduced into the Roman Empire in 68 BC and spread rapidly, gaining converts especially among soldiers; by about AD 250, it rivalled Christianity in strength.

**Mithridates VI Eupator the Great** (c. 120–60 BC) king of Pontus (on the Black Sea coast of modern Turkey), who became the greatest obstacle to Roman expansion in the east. He massacred 80,000 Romans while overrunning Asia Minor and went on to invade Greece. He was defeated by ◊Sulla during the first Mithridatic War in 88–84 BC, by Lucullus in the second 83–81, and by Pompey the Great in the third 74–64.

**mitochondria** singular *mitochondrion*, membrane-enclosed organelles within ◊eukaryotic cells, containing enzymes responsible for energy production during ◊aerobic respiration. Mitochondria absorb $O_2$ and glucose and produce energy in the form of ◊ATP by breaking down the glucose to $CO_2$ and $H_2O$. These rod-like or spherical bodies are thought to be derived from free-living bacteria that, at a very early stage in the history of life, invaded larger cells and took up a symbiotic way of life inside. Each still contains its own small loop of DNA called mitochondrial DNA, and new mitochondria arise by division of existing ones.

**mitosis** in biology, the process of cell division by which identical daughter cells are produced. During mitosis the DNA is duplicated and the chromosome number doubled, so new cells contain the same amount of DNA as the original cell.

The genetic material of ◊eukaryotic cells is carried on a number of ◊chromosomes. To control movements of chromosomes during cell division so that both new cells get the correct number, a system of protein tubules, known as the spindle, organizes the chromosomes into position in the middle of the cell before they replicate. The spindle then controls the movement of chromosomes as the cell goes through the stages of division:

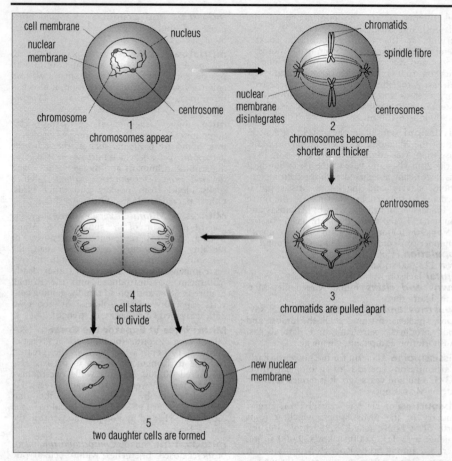

*mitosis* The stages of mitosis, the process of cell division that takes place when a plant or animal cell divides for growth or repair. The two daughter cells each receive the same number of chromosomes as were in the original cell.

*interphase, prophase, metaphase, anaphase,* and *telophase.* See also ◊meiosis.

**Mitsotakis, Constantine** (1918–  ) Greek politician, leader of the conservative New Democracy Party (ND) 1984–93, prime minister 1990–93. Minister for economic coordination in 1965 (a post he held again 1978–80), he was arrested by the military junta in 1967, but escaped from house arrest and lived in exile until 1974. In 1980–81 he was foreign minister. He resigned the leadership of the ND after its 1993 election defeat; in January 1996 proposed corruption charges against him were dropped.

**Mitterrand, François** (1916–1996) French socialist politician. After a successful ministerial career under the Fourth Republic, holding posts in 11 governments 1947–58, Mitterrand joined the new Socialist Party (PS) in 1971, establishing it as the most popular party in France before winning two successive terms as president, 1981–88 and 1988–95. From 1982 his adminis-

trations reverted from redistributive and reflationary policies to economic orthodoxy and maintenance of the 'strong franc' (linked to the Deutschmark), despite the high levels of unemployment this entailed, and vigorously pursued further European integration.

**Mizora** state of northeast India, lying between Bangladesh and Myanmar
*area* 21,100 sq km/8,145 sq mi
*capital* Aizawl
*physical* north–south ranges in the east rise to over 2,000 m/6,500 ft, densely forested
*products* rice, maize, hand-loom weaving
*population* (1994 est) 775,000
*religion* 84% Christian
*history* made a Union Territory in 1972 from the Mizo Hills District of Assam. Rebels carried on a guerrilla war 1966–76, but in 1976 acknowledged Mizoram as an integral part of India. It became a state in 1986.

**ml** symbol for *millilitre.*

**mm** symbol for *millimetre.*

**mmHg** symbol for ◊*millimetre of mercury.*

**Möbius strip** structure made by giving a half twist to a flat strip of paper and joining the ends together. It has certain remarkable properties, arising from the fact that it has only one edge and one side. If cut down the centre of the strip, instead of two new strips of paper, only one long strip is produced. It was invented by the German mathematician August Möbius.

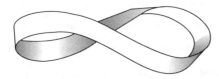

***Möbius strip** The Möbius strip has only one side and one edge. It consists of a strip of paper connected at its ends with a half-twist in the middle.*

**Mobutu, Sese Seko Kuku Ngbeandu Wa Za Banga** formerly Joseph Desire Mobutu (1930–1997) president of Zaire (now the Democratic Republic of Congo) 1965–97. The harshness of some of his policies and charges of corruption attracted widespread international criticism.

**mockingbird** North American songbird of the mimic thrush family, found in the USA and Mexico. About 25 cm/10 in long, it is brownish grey, with white markings on the black wings and tail. It is remarkable for its ability to mimic the songs of other species. (Species *Mimus polyglottos,* family Mimidae, order Passeriformes.)

**mock orange** or *syringa,* any of a group of deciduous shrubs, including *P. coronarius,* which has white, strongly scented flowers similar to those of the orange tree. (Genus *Philadelphus,* family Philadelphaceae.)

**mode** in mathematics, the element that appears most frequently in a given set of data. For example, the mode for the data 0, 0, 9, 9, 9, 12, 87, 87 is 9.

**Model Parliament** English parliament set up in 1295 by Edward I; it was the first to include representatives from outside the clergy and aristocracy, and was established because Edward needed the support of the whole country against his opponents: Wales, France, and Scotland. His sole aim was to raise money for military purposes, and the parliament did not pass any legislation.

**modern dance** 20th-century dance idiom that evolved in opposition to traditional ballet by those seeking a freer and more immediate means of dance expression. Leading exponents include Martha ◊Graham and Merce ◊Cunningham in the USA, Isadora ◊Duncan and Mary Wigman in Europe.

**Modernism** in the arts, a general term used to describe the 20th century's conscious attempt to

break with the artistic traditions of the 19th century; it is based on a concern with form and the exploration of technique as opposed to content and narrative. In the visual arts, direct representationalism gave way to abstraction (see ◊abstract art); in literature, writers experimented with alternatives to orthodox sequential storytelling, such as stream of consciousness; in music, the traditional concept of key was challenged by ◊atonality; and in architecture, Functionalism ousted decorativeness as a central objective (see ◊Modern Movement).

**Modern Movement** the dominant movement in 20th-century architecture, which grew out of the technological innovations of 19th-century industrial architecture, crystallized in the ◊International Style of the 1920s and 1930s, and has since developed various regional trends, such as ◊Brutalism. 'Truth to materials' and 'form follows function' are its two most representative dicta, although neither allows for the modernity of large areas of contemporary architecture, concerned with proportion, human scale, and attention to detail. Currently, architectural ◊postmodernism, a reaction to the movement, is developing alongside such Modernist styles as ◊High Tech.

**Modigliani, Amedeo** (1884–1920) Italian painter and sculptor, active in France from 1906. He is best known for graceful nudes and portraits. His paintings – for example, the portrait of his mistress Jeanne Hébuterne, painted 1919 (Guggenheim Museum, New York) – have a distinctive style, the forms elongated and sensual.

**modulation** in radio transmission, the variation of frequency, or amplitude, of a radio carrier wave, in accordance with the audio characteristics of the speaking voice, music, or other signal being transmitted.

**modulus** in mathematics, a number that divides exactly into the difference between two given numbers. Also, the multiplication factor used to convert a logarithm of one base to a logarithm of another base. Also, another name for ◊absolute value.

**Mogadishu** or *Muqdisho,* capital and chief port of Somalia; population (1987 est) 1,000,000. It is a centre for oil refining, food processing, and chemical production; there are uranium reserves nearby. During the civil war 1991–92, much of the city was devastated and many thousands killed. UN troops were stationed in the city after the war but were later forced to withdraw. The city has mosques dating from the 13th century; the cathedral, built 1925–28, was destroyed during the civil war.

**Mogul dynasty** northern Indian dynasty 1526–1858, established by ◊Babur, Muslim descendant of Tamerlane, the 14th-century Mongol leader. The Mogul emperors ruled until the last one, Bahadur Shah II, was dethroned and exiled by the British; they included ◊Akbar, ◊Aurangzeb, and ◊Shah Jahan. The Moguls established a more extensive and centralized empire than their Delhi sultanate forebears, and the Mogul era was one of great artistic achievement as well as urban and commercial development.

**Mohács, Battle of** comprehensive victory of a combined Austrian and Hungarian army under Charles of Lorraine over a Turkish army under Muhammad IV on 12 August 1687; the battle effectively meant the end of Turkish expansion into Europe. Named after the river port of that name on the Danube in Hungary, which is also the site of a Turkish victory 1526.

**Mohammed** alternative form of ◊Muhammad, founder of Islam.

**Mohawk** member of an ◊American Indian people, part of the Iroquois confederation, who lived in the Mohawk Valley, New York, and now live on reservations in Ontario, Québec, and New York State, as well as among the general population, and number about 10,000 (1990). Their language belongs to the Macro-Siouan group. In 1990 Mohawks south of Montréal mounted a blockade in a dispute over land with the government of Québec province.

**Mohegan** member of an Algonquian-speaking ◊American Indian people. Traditionally their economy was based on the cultivation of corn, and hunting, and fishing. They are closely related to the ◊Mohican.

**Mohican** or *Mahican*, member of an Algonquian-speaking ◊American Indian people. Traditionally their economy was based on the cultivation of corn, and hunting, and fishing. They are closely related to the Mohegan.

**Moholy-Nagy, Laszlo** (1895–1946) Hungarian-born painter, sculptor and photographer. Inspired by ◊Constructivism, he made abstract sculptures from the early 1920s and from 1923–29 taught at the Bauhaus school in Weimar and later in the USA. He experimented with a wide range of media, materials, and techniques, including the use of photographic techniques to achieve non-naturalistic effects.

**Mohs scale** scale of hardness for minerals (in ascending order): 1 talc; 2 gypsum; 3 calcite;

**MOHS SCALE**

| Number | Defining mineral | Other substances compared |
|--------|------------------|---------------------------|
| 1 | talc | |
| 2 | gypsum | $2\frac{1}{2}$ fingernail |
| 3 | calcite | $3\frac{1}{2}$ copper coin |
| 4 | fluorite | |
| 5 | apatite | $5\frac{1}{3}$ steel blade |
| 6 | orthoclase | $5\frac{3}{4}$ glass |
| 7 | quartz | 7 steel file |
| 8 | topaz | |
| 9 | corundum | |
| 10 | diamond | |

*Note that the scale is not regular; diamond, at number 10 the hardest natural substance, is 90 times harder in absolute terms than corundum, number 9*

4 fluorite; 5 apatite; 6 orthoclase; 7 quartz; 8 topaz; 9 corundum; 10 diamond.

**Moi, Daniel arap** (1924–   ) Kenyan politician, president from 1978. Leader of the Kenya African National Union (KANU), he became minister of home affairs in 1964, vice-president in 1967, and succeeded Jomo Kenyatta as president. He enjoyed the support of Western governments but was widely criticized for Kenya's poor human-rights record. His administration, first challenged by a coup attempt in 1982, became increasingly authoritarian. In 1991, in the face of widespread criticism, he promised the eventual introduction of multiparty politics. In 1992 he was elected president in the first free elections amid widespread accusations of vote rigging.

**molar** one of the large teeth found towards the back of the mammalian mouth. The structure of the jaw, and the relation of the muscles, allows a massive force to be applied to molars. In herbivores the molars are flat with sharp ridges of enamel and are used for grinding, an adaptation to a diet of tough plant material. Carnivores have sharp powerful molars called carnassials, which are adapted for cutting meat.

**Moldavian** member of the majority ethnic group living in Moldova, comprising almost two-thirds of the population; also, inhabitant of the Romanian province of Moldavia. The Moldavian language is a dialect of Romanian, and belongs to the Romance group of the Indo-European family. They are mostly Orthodox Christians.

**Moldova** Republic of
*national name Republica Moldoveneasca*

*area* 33,700 sq km/13,011 sq mi
*capital* Chişinău (Kishinev)
*major towns/cities* Tiraspol, Beltsy, Bendery
*physical features* hilly land lying largely between the rivers Prut and Dniester; northern Moldova comprises the level plain of the Beltsy Steppe and uplands; the climate is warm and moderately continental
*head of state* Petru Lucinschi from 1997
*head of government* Ion Sturza from 1999

*political system* emergent democracy
*political parties* Agrarian Democratic Party (ADP), nationalist, centrist; Socialist Party and Yedinstvo/Unity Movement, reform-socialist; Peasants and Intellectuals, Romanian nationalist; Christian Democratic Popular Front (CDPF), Romanian nationalist; Gagauz-Khalky (GKPM; Gagauz People's Movement), Gagauz separatist
*currency* leu
*GNP per capita (PPP)* (US$) 1,510 (1998 est)
*exports* food and agricultural products, machinery and equipment, textiles, clothing. Principal market: Russia 53% (1998)
*population* 4,379,000 (1999 est)
*language* Moldovan
*Religion* Russian Orthodox
*life expectancy* 64 (men); 72 (women) (1995–2000)
*Chronology*
**AD 106** The current area covered by Moldova, which lies chiefly between the Prut River, bordering Romania in the west, and the Dniestr River, with Ukraine in the east, was conquered by the Roman Emperor Trajan and became part of the Roman province of Dacia. It was known in earlier times as Bessarabia.
*mid-14th century* Formed part of an independent Moldovan principality, which included areas, such as Bukovina to the west, that are now part of Romania.
*late 15th century* Under Stephen IV 'the Great' the principality reached the height of its power.
*16th century* Became a tributary of the Ottoman Turks.
*1774–75* Moldovan principality, though continuing to recognize Turkish overlordship, was placed under Russian protectorship; Bukovina was lost to Austria.
*1812* Bessarabia ceded to tsarist Russia.
*1856* Remainder of Moldovan principality became largely independent of Turkish control.
*1859* Moldovan Assembly voted to unite with Wallachia, to the southwest, to form state of Romania, ruled by Prince Alexandru Ion Cuza. State became fully independent in 1878.
*1918* Following Russian Revolution, Bessarabia was seized and incorporated within Romania.
*1924* Moldovan autonomous Soviet Socialist Republic (SSR) created, as part of Soviet Union, comprising territory east of Dniestr River.
*1940* Romania returned Bessarabia, east of Prut River, to Soviet Union, which divided it between Moldovan SSR and Ukraine, with Trans-Dniestr region transferred from Ukraine to Moldova.
*1941* Moldovan SSR occupied by Romania and its wartime ally Germany.
*1944* Red Army reconquered Bessarabia.
*1946–47* Widespread famine as agriculture was collectivized; rich farmers and intellectuals liquidated.
*1950* Immigration by settlers from Russia and Ukraine as industries were developed.
*late 1980s* There was an upsurge in Moldovan nationalism, encouraged by the *glasnost* initiative of reformist Soviet leader Mikhail Gorbachev.

*1988* The Moldovan Movement in Support of Perestroika (economic restructuring) campaigned for accelerated political reform.
*1989* There were nationalist demonstrations in Kishinev (now Chişinău). The Moldovan Popular Front (MPF) founded; Moldovan was made the state language. There were campaigns for autonomy among ethnic Russians, strongest in industrialized Trans-Dniestr region, and the Turkish-speaking but Orthodox Christian Gagauz minority in southwest.
*1990* The MPF polled strongly in parliamentary elections and Mircea Snegur, a reform-nationalist communist, became president. Economic and political sovereignty was declared.
*1991* Independence was declared and the Communist Party outlawed after a conservative coup in Moscow against Gorbachev; joined Commonwealth of Independent States (CIS). There was insurrection in the Trans-Dniestr region.
*1992* Admitted into United Nations and the Conference on Security and Cooperation in Europe; a peace agreement was signed with Russia to end the civil war in Trans-Dniestr, giving special status to the region. The MPF-dominated government fell; A 'government of national accord' was formed, headed by Andrei Sangheli and dominated by the ADP.
*1993* A new currency, the leu, was introduced. A privatization programme was launched and closer ties were established with Russia.
*1994* Parliamentary elections were won by the ADP. Plebiscite rejected nationalist demands for a merger with Romania. Russia agreed to withdraw Trans-Dniestr troops by 1997.
*1995* Joined Council of Europe; economic growth resumed.
*1996* Petru Lucinschi was elected president. The president of the Dniestr region, Igor Smirnov, was re-elected.
*1997* Ion Cebuc was appointed prime minister. A new centrist party was formed, supporting President Lusinschi. There were major party realignments. A cooperation agreement was signed with the Dniestr region. A law was passed that provided for elections using proportional representation.
*1998* The Communist Party won the largest number of seats in the parliamentary election, but lacked a majority.
*1999* A new coalition government was formed, headed by Ion Sturza.

**mole** SI unit (symbol mol) of the amount of a substance. It is defined as the amount of a substance that contains as many elementary entities (atoms, molecules, and so on) as there are atoms in 12 g of the ◊isotope carbon-12.

**mole** small burrowing mammal with typically dark, velvety fur. Moles grow up to 18 cm/7 in long, and have acute senses of hearing, smell, and touch, but poor eyesight. They have short, muscular forelimbs and shovel-like, clawed front feet for burrowing in search of insects, grubs, and worms. Their fur lies without direction so that they can move forwards or backwards in their tunnels without discomfort. Moles are greedy eaters; they cannot live more than a few hours without food. (Family Talpidae, order Insectivora.)

**molecular biology** study of the molecular basis of life, including the biochemistry of molecules such as DNA, RNA, and proteins, and the molecular structure and function of the various parts of living cells.

**molecular solid** in chemistry, solid composed of molecules that are held together by relatively weak intermolecular forces. Such solids are low-melting and tend to dissolve in organic solvents. Examples of molecular solids are sulphur, ice, sucrose, and solid carbon dioxide.

**molecule** molecules are the smallest particles of an element or compound that can exist independently. Hydrogen ◊atoms, at room temperature, do not exist independently. They are bonded in pairs to form hydrogen molecules. A molecule of a compound consists of two or more different atoms bonded together. Molecules vary in size and complexity from the hydrogen molecule ($H_2$) to the large macromolecules of proteins. They may be held together by ionic bonds, in which the atoms gain or lose electrons to form ◊ions, or by covalent bonds, where electrons from each atom are shared in a new molecular orbital.

Each compound is represented by a chemical symbol, indicating the elements into which it can be broken down and the number of each type of atom present. The symbolic representation of a molecule is known as its formula. For example, one molecule of the compound water, having two atoms of hydrogen and one atom of oxygen, is shown as $H_2O$.

**mole rat, naked** small underground mammal, almost hairless, with a disproportionately large head. The mole rat is of importance to zoologists as one of the very few mammals that are eusocial, that is, living in colonies with sterile workers and one fertile female. (Species *Heterocephalus glaber.*)

**Molière** pen-name of Jean-Baptiste Poquelin (1622–1673) French satirical dramatist and actor. Modern French comedy developed from his work. After the collapse of the Paris-based Illustre Théâtre (of which he was one of the founders), Molière performed in the provinces 1645–58. In 1655 he wrote his first play, *L'Etourdi/The Blunderer,* and on his return to Paris produced *Les Précieuses ridicules/The Affected Ladies* (1659). His satires include *L'Ecole des femmes/The School for Wives* (1662), *Le Misanthrope* (1666), *Le Bourgeois Gentilhomme/The Would-Be Gentleman* (1670), and *Le Malade imaginaire/The Imaginary Invalid* (1673). Other satiric plays include *Tartuffe* (1664; banned for attacking the hypocrisy of the clergy; revised 1667; banned again until 1699), *Le Médecin malgré lui/Doctor in Spite of Himself* (1666), and *Les Femmes savantes/The Learned Ladies* (1672).

**mollusc** any of a group of invertebrate animals, most of which have a body divided into three parts: a head, a central mass containing the main organs, and a foot for movement; the more sophisticated octopuses and related molluscs have arms to capture their prey. The majority of molluscs are marine animals, but some live in fresh water, and a few live on dry land. They include clams, mussels, and oysters (bivalves), snails and slugs (gastropods), and cuttlefish, squids, and octopuses (cephalopods). The body is soft, without limbs (except for the cephalopods), and cold-blooded. There is no internal skeleton, but many species have a hard shell covering the body. (Phylum Mollusca.)

**Moloch** or *Molech,* in the Old Testament, a Phoenician deity worshipped in Jerusalem in the 7th century BC, to whom live children were sacrificed by fire.

**Molotov, Vyacheslav Mikhailovich** assumed name of Vyacheslav Mikhailovich Skriabin (1890–1986) Soviet communist politi-

amino acids, where R is one of many possible side chains

peptide bond

**molecule** A protein molecule is a long chain of amino acids linked by peptide bonds. The properties of a protein are determined by the order, or sequence, of amino acids in its molecule, and by the three-dimensional structure of the molecular chain. The chain folds and twists, often forming a spiral shape.

cian. He was chair of the Council of People's Commissars (prime minister) 1930–41 and foreign minister 1939–49 and 1953–56. He negotiated the 1939 nonaggression treaty with Germany (the ◊Ribbentrop–Molotov pact), and, after the German invasion in 1941, the Soviet partnership with the Allies. His post-war stance prolonged the Cold War and in 1957 he was expelled from the government for Stalinist activities.

**molybdenite** molybdenum sulphide, $MoS_2$, the chief ore mineral of molybdenum. It possesses a hexagonal crystal structure similar to graphite, has a blue metallic lustre, and is very soft (1–1.5 on Mohs scale).

**molybdenum** (Greek *molybdos* 'lead') heavy, hard, lustrous, silver-white, metallic element, symbol Mo, atomic number 42, relative atomic mass 95.94. The chief ore is the mineral molybdenite. The element is highly resistant to heat and conducts electricity easily. It is used in alloys, often to harden steels. It is a necessary trace element in human nutrition. It was named in 1781 by Swedish chemist Karl Scheele, after its isolation by P J Hjelm (1746–1813), for its resemblance to lead ore.

**Mombasa** industrial port and tourist resort in Kenya (the port also serves Uganda and Tanzania); population (1989) 461,800. It stands on Mombasa Island and the adjacent mainland. Industries include oil refining and cement. Mombasa was founded by Arab traders in the 11th century and was an important centre for ivory and slave trading until the 16th century.

**moment of a force** in physics, measure of the turning effect, or torque, produced by a force acting on a body. It is equal to the product of the force and the perpendicular distance from its line of action to the point, or pivot, about which the body will turn. Its unit is the newton metre.

**moment of inertia** in physics, the sum of all the point masses of a rotating object multiplied by the squares of their respective distances from the axis of rotation. It is analogous to the ◊mass of a stationary object or one moving in a straight line.

**Mon** or *Talaing*, a minority ethnic group living in the Irrawaddy delta region of lower Myanmar (Burma) and Thailand. The Mon founded the city of Bago in 573 and established kingdoms in the area in the 7th century, but much of their culture was absorbed by invaders such as the Toungoo in 1539, and Alaungpaya, founder of the Konbaung dynasty, in 1757.

**Monaco** Principality of
*national name* Principauté de Monaco
*area* 1.95 sq km/0.75 sq mi
*capital* Monaco-Ville
*major towns/cities* Monte Carlo, La Condamine; heliport Fontvieille
*physical features* steep and rugged; surrounded landwards by French territory
*head of state* Prince Rainier III from 1949
*head of government* Michel Leveque from 1998

*political system* constitutional monarchy under French protectorate
*political parties* no formal parties, but lists of candidates: Liste Campora, moderate, centrist; Liste Medecin, moderate, centrist
*currency* French franc
*GNP per capita (PPP)* (US$) 26,170 (1996 est)
*population* 32,200 (1999 est)
*language* French (official); English, Italian
*religion* Roman Catholic
*life expectancy* 75 (men); 82 (women) (1998 est)
*Chronology*
*1191* The Genoese took control of Monaco, which had formerly been part of the Holy Roman Empire.
*1297* Came under the rule of the Grimaldi dynasty, the current ruling family, who initially allied themselves to the French.
*1524–1641* Came under Spanish protection.
*1793* Annexed by France during French Revolutionary Wars. One member of ruling family was guillotined; the rest imprisoned.
*1815* Placed under protection of Sardinia.
*1848* The towns of Menton and Roquebrune, which had formed the greater part of the principality, seceded and later became part of France.
*1861* Franco-Monegasque treaty restored Monaco's independence under French protection; first casino built.
*1865* Customs union established with France.
*1918* France given veto over succession to throne and established that if reigning prince dies without a male heir, Monaco is to be incorporated into France.
*1941–45* Occupied successively by Italians and Germans during World War II.
*1949* Prince Rainier III ascended the throne.
*1956* Prince Rainier married US actress Grace Kelly.
*1958* Birth of male heir, Prince Albert.
*1959* Constitution of 1911 suspended and National Council dissolved.
*1962* A new, more liberal constitution was adopted and the National Council restored.
*1982* Princess Grace died in a car accident.
*1993* Joined United Nations.
*1998* Michel Leveque was reappointed head of government.

**Monaghan** Irish *Mhuineachain,* county of the Republic of Ireland, in the province of Ulster; county town Monaghan; area 1,290 sq km/498 sq mi; population (1991) 51,300. The county is low and rolling, with hills in the northwest, the highest point being Slieve Beagh (381 m/1,217 ft). The principal towns are Clones, Carrickmacross, and Castleblayney. Rivers include the Finn and the Glyde in the south, and the Blackwater in the north. Much of the county is fertile. The main form of agriculture is dairy farming, but cattle and pigs are also raised, and cereals and potatoes grown. Industries include leather, linen, knitwear, footwear, furniture, and lacemaking.

**monasticism** devotion to religious life under vows of poverty, chastity, and obedience, known to Judaism (for example the Essenes), Buddhism, and other religions, before Christianity. In Islam, the Sufis formed monastic orders from the 12th century.

**Monday** second day of the week, following Sunday. The name derives from its having been considered sacred to the Moon (Old English *Mōnandaeg* and Latin *Lunae dies*).

**Mondrian, Piet (Pieter Cornelis Mondriaan)** (1872–1944) Dutch painter. A founder member of the De ◊Stijl movement, he was the chief exponent of Neo-Plasticism, a rigorous abstract style based on the use of simple geometric forms and pure colours. Typically his works are frameworks of horizontal and vertical lines forming rectangles of white, red, yellow, and blue, as in *Composition in Red, Yellow and Blue* (1920; Stedelijk, Amsterdam).

**Monet, Claude** (1840–1926) French painter. He was a pioneer of Impressionism and a lifelong exponent of its ideals; his painting *Impression, Sunrise* (1872) gave the movement its name. In the 1870s he began painting the same subjects at different times of day to explore the ever-changing effects of light on colour and form; the *Haystacks* and *Rouen Cathedral* series followed in the 1890s, and from 1899 he painted a series of *Water Lilies* in the garden of his house at Giverny, Normandy (now a museum).

**monetarism** economic policy that proposes control of a country's money supply to keep it in step with the country's ability to produce goods, with the aim of curbing inflation. Cutting government spending is advocated, and the long-term aim is to return as much of the economy as possible to the private sector, allegedly in the interests of efficiency. Monetarism was first advocated by the economist Milton Friedman and the Chicago school of economists.

**money** any common medium of exchange acceptable in payment for goods or services or for the settlement of debts; legal tender. Money is usually coinage (invented by the Chinese in the second millennium BC) and paper notes (used by the Chinese from about AD 800). Developments such as the cheque and credit card fulfill many of the traditional functions of money. In 1994 Mondex electronic money was introduced experimentally in Swindon, Wiltshire, England.

**Mongol** member of any of the various Mongol (or Mongolian) ethnic groups of central Asia. Mongols live in Mongolia, Russia, Inner Mongolia (China), Tibet, and Nepal. The Mongol language belongs to the Altaic family, although some groups of Mongol descent speak languages in the Sino-Tibetan family.

**Mongol Empire** empire established by ◊Genghis Khan, a loosely constructed federation of tribal groups extending from Russia to northern China. Genghis became khan of the Mongol tribes in 1206. The empire was divided by his sons at his death in 1227 – Ogotai overcame the Jin and Sun dynasties of China in 1234, and another son, Batu, occupied Russia, parts of Hungary, and Georgia and Armenia, establishing the Kipchak Empire and other khanates. The Western Kipchaks, known as the ◊Golden Horde terrorized Europe from 1237. Genghis's grandson ◊Kublai Khan conquered China and used foreigners (such as the Venetian traveller Marco Polo) as well as subjects to administer his empire. Another grandson, Hulagu, conquered Baghdad and Syria. The Mongols lost China in 1367 and suffered defeats in the west in 1380; the empire broke up soon afterwards, fragmenting into separate chiefdoms.

**Mongolia** State of (*Outer Mongolia* until 1924; *People's Republic of Mongolia* until 1991)
*national name* *Mongol Uls*
*area* 1,565,000 sq km/604,246 sq mi

*capital* Ulaanbaatar (Ulan Bator)
*major towns/cities* Darhan, Choybalsan, Erdenet
*physical features* high plateau with desert and steppe (grasslands); Altai Mountains in southwest; salt lakes; part of Gobi desert in southeast; contains both the world's southernmost permafrost and northernmost desert
*head of state* Natsagiyn Bagabandi from 1997
*head of government* Janlaviyn Narantsatsralt from 1998
*political system* emergent democracy
*political parties* Mongolian People's Revolutionary Party (MPRP), reform-socialist (ex-communist); Mongolian National Demo-

cratic Party (MNDP), traditionalist, promarket economy; Union Coalition (UC, comprising the MNPD and the Social Democratic Party (SDP)), democratic, promarket economy
**currency** tugrik
**GNP per capita (PPP)** (US$) 1,520 (1998)
**exports** minerals and metals (primarily copper concentrate), consumer goods, foodstuffs, agricultural products. Principal market: China 30.1% (1998)
**population** 2,621,000 (1999 est)
**language** Khalkha Mongolian (official); Chinese, Russian, and Turkic languages
**religion** officially none (Tibetan Buddhist Lamaism suppressed in 1930s)
**life expectancy** 64 (men); 67 (women) (1995–2000)
**Chronology**
**AD 1206** Nomadic Mongol tribes united by Genghis Khan to form nucleus of vast Mongol Empire which, stretching across central Asia, reached its zenith under Genghis Khan's grandson, Kublai Khan.
**late 17th century** Conquered by China to become province of Outer Mongolia.
**1911** Independence proclaimed by Mongolian nationalists after Chinese 'republican revolution'; Tsarist Russia helped Mongolia to secure autonomy, under a traditionalist Buddhist monarchy in the form of a reincarnated lama.
**1915** Chinese sovereignty reasserted.
**1921** Chinese rule overthrown with Soviet help.
**1924** People's Republic proclaimed on death of king, when the monarchy was abolished; defeudalization programme launched, entailing collectivization of agriculture and suppression of Lama Buddhism.
**1932** Armed antigovernment uprising suppressed with Soviet assistance; 100,000 killed in political purges.
**1946** China recognized Mongolia's independence.
**1952** Death of Marshal Horloogiyn Choybalsan, the dominant force in the ruling communist Mongolian People's Revolutionary Party (MPRP) since 1939.
**1958** Yumjaagiyn Tsedenbal became dominant figure in MPRP and country.
**1962** Joined Comecon.
**1966** 20-year friendship, cooperation, and mutual-assistance pact signed with Soviet Union (USSR). Relations with China deteriorated.
**1984** Tsedenbal, the effective leader, retired; replaced by Jambyn Batmunkh.
**1987** There was a reduction in the number of Soviet troops; Mongolia's external contacts broadened. The tolerance of traditional social customs encouraged a nationalist revival.
**1989** Further Soviet troop reductions.
**1990** A demonstrations and democratization campaign was launched, influenced by events in Eastern Europe; Batmunkh resigned and was charged with corruption. Ex-communist MPRP elected in the first free multiparty elections; Punsalmaagiyn Ochirbat was indirectly elected president. Mongolian script was readopted.
**1991** A privatization programme was launched. GDP declined by 10%. Ochirbat resigned from

MPRP in the wake of the anti-Gorbachev attempted coup in the USSR.
**1992** The MPRP returned to power in assembly elections held under a new, noncommunist constitution. The economic situation worsened; GDP again declined by 10%.
**1993** Ochirbat won the first direct presidential elections.
**1996** The economy showed signs of revival. The Union Coalition won assembly elections, defeating the MPRP and ending 75 years of communist rule. A defence cooperation agreement was signed with the USA. Mendsayhany Enhsayhan became prime minister.
**1997** The ex-communist Natsagiyn Bagabandi was elected MPRP chairman. An economic shock therapy programme, supervised by IMF and World Bank, created unemployment and made the government unpopular. Bagabandi was elected president. All taxes and tariffs on trade were abolished.
**1998** National Democratic Party (DU) leader Tsakhiagiin Elbegdorj became prime minister. His government was toppled after losing a no-confidence vote. Attempts to form a new DU-led government, led by Rinchinnyamiin Amarjargal, failed. Janlaviyn Narantsatsralt, member of the MNDP, became prime minister.

**Mongolia, Inner** Chinese *Nei Mongol*, autonomous region of north China from 1947; bounded to the north by Mongolia and Russia; to the east by Heilongjiang and Jilin; to the southeast by Liaoning; to the south by Hebei, Shanxi, Shaanxi, and Ningxia Hui Autonomous Region; and to the west by Gansu
**area** 1,200,00 sq km/463,300 sq mi
**capital** ◊Hohhot
**towns** Baotou
**physical** grassland and desert
**industries** coal; reserves of iron ore, rare earth oxides europium, and yttrium at Bayan Obo; woollen textiles; dairy-processing; leather
**agriculture** cereals under irrigation, animal husbandry, forestry
**population** (1996) 23,070,000; less than one-sixth are Mongols.

**mongoose** any of a group of carnivorous tropical mammals. The *Indian mongoose* (*H. mungo*) is greyish in colour and about 50 cm/1.5 ft long, with a long tail. It can be tamed and is often kept for its ability to kill snakes. Like the snakes themselves, the acetylcholine receptors connecting the mongooses' nerves and muscle cells are unaffected by the venom. (Genera *Herpestes, Ichneumia*, and other related genera, family Viverridae.)

**monitor** any of various lizards found in Africa, South Asia, and Australasia. Monitors are generally large and carnivorous, with well-developed legs and claws and a long powerful tail that can be swung in defence. (Family Varanidae.)

**monkey** any of the various smaller, mainly tree-dwelling anthropoid ◊primates, excluding humans and the ◊apes. There are 125 species, living in Africa, Asia, and tropical Central and South America. Monkeys eat mainly leaves and fruit, and also small animals. Several species are endangered due to loss of forest habitat, for example the woolly spider monkey and black saki of the Amazonian forest.

**monkey puzzle** or *Chilean pine,* coniferous evergreen tree, native to Chile; its branches, growing in circular arrangements (whorls) around the trunk and larger branches, are covered in prickly, leathery leaves. (*Araucaria araucana,* family Araucariaceae.)

**Monmouthshire** Welsh *Trefynwy,* unitary authority in southeast Wales. A former county, between 1974 and 1996 it became (except for a small area on the border with Mid Glamorgan) the county of Gwent
*area* 851 sq km/328 sq mi
*towns* Cwmbran (administrative headquarters), Chepstow
*physical* rivers Wye and Usk; mountainous in north
*features* Chepstow and Raglan castles, Tintern Abbey, salmon and trout fishing; peak of Pen-y-Fal or Sugar Loaf (596 m/1,955 ft)
*agriculture* lowlands have rich mixed farming, with arable crops, including wheat, being important
*population* (1996) 80,400.

**monoclonal antibody** (MAB), antibody produced by fusing an antibody-producing lymphocyte with a cancerous myeloma (bone-marrow) cell. The resulting fused cell, called a hybridoma, is immortal and can be used to produce large quantities of a single, specific antibody. By choosing antibodies that are directed against antigens found on cancer cells, and combining them with cytotoxic drugs, it is hoped to make so-called magic bullets that will be able to pick out and kill cancers.

**monocotyledon** angiosperm (flowering plant) having an embryo with a single cotyledon, or seed leaf (as opposed to ◊dicotyledons, which have two). Monocotyledons usually have narrow leaves with parallel veins and smooth edges, and hollow or soft stems. Their flower parts are arranged in threes. Most are small plants such as orchids, grasses, and lilies, but some are trees such as palms.

**monolith** (Greek *monos* 'sole', *lithos* 'stone') single isolated stone or column, usually standing and of great size, used as a form of monument. Some are natural features, such as the Buck Stone in the Forest of Dean, England. Other monoliths may be quarried, resited, finished, or carved; those in Egypt of about 3000 BC take the form of obelisks. They have a wide distribution including Europe, South America, North Africa, and the Middle East.

**monologue** one person speaking, though the term is generally understood to mean a virtuoso solo performance. Literary monologues are often set pieces in which a character reveals his or her personality, sometimes unintentionally (as in the dramatic monologue); in drama the soliloquy performs a similar function.

A monologue can occur in a dialogue; for example, in a conversation where one person suddenly launches into a lengthy anecdote.

**monomer** chemical compound composed of simple molecules from which ◊polymers can be made. Under certain conditions the simple molecules (of the monomer) join together (polymerize) to form a very long chain molecule (macromolecule) called a polymer. For example, the polymerization of ethene (ethylene) monomers produces the polymer polyethene (polyethylene).

$$2n\mathrm{CH}_2 = \mathrm{CH}_2 \rightarrow (\mathrm{CH}_2\text{-}\mathrm{CH}_2\text{-}\mathrm{CH}_2\text{-}\ \mathrm{CH}_2)_n$$

**monopoly** in economics, the domination of a market for a particular product or service by a single company, which can therefore restrict competition and keep prices high. In practice, a company can be said to have a monopoly when it controls a significant proportion of the market (technically an oligopoly). In a communist country the state itself has the overall monopoly; in capitalist countries some services, such as transport or electricity supply, may be state monopolies.

**Monopoly** the world's biggest-selling copyrighted game, a board game of buying properties, building houses on them, and charging rent.

It was devised in the USA in 1934 by Charles B Darrow (1889–1967), with street names from Atlantic City, New Jersey, where he spent his holidays; he sold the game in 1935 to Parker Brothers, US game manufacturers, for a royalty.

**monorail** railway that runs on a single rail; the cars can be balanced on it or suspended from it. It was invented in 1882 to carry light loads, and when run by electricity was called a *telpher.*

**monosaccharide** or *simple sugar,* ◊carbohydrate that cannot be hydrolysed (split) into smaller carbohydrate units. Examples are glucose and fructose, both of which have the molecular formula $C_6H_{12}O_6$.

**monotreme** any of a small group of primitive egg-laying mammals, found in Australasia. They include the ◊echidnas (spiny anteaters) and the ◊platypus. (Order Monotremata.)

**Monroe, James** (1758–1831) 5th president of the USA 1817–25, a Democratic Republican. He served in the American Revolution, was minister to France 1794–96, and in 1803 negotiated the ◊Louisiana Purchase. He was secretary of state 1811–14 and 1815–17, and secretary of war 1814–15. His name is associated with the ◊Monroe Doctrine.

**Monroe, Marilyn** stage name of Norma Jean Mortenson or Baker (1926–1962) US film actress. The voluptuous blonde sex symbol of the 1950s, she made adroit comedies such as *Gentlemen Prefer Blondes* (1953), *How to Marry a Millionaire* (1953), *The Seven Year Itch* (1955), *Bus Stop* (1956), and *Some Like It Hot* (1959).

**Monroe Doctrine** declaration by US president James ◊Monroe 1823 that any further European colonial ambitions in the western hemisphere would be regarded as threats to US peace and security, made in response to proposed European intervention against newly independent former Spanish colonies in South America. In return for the quietening of such

European ambitions, the USA would not interfere in European affairs. The doctrine, subsequently broadened, has been a recurrent theme in US foreign policy, although it has no basis in US or international law.

**Monrovia** capital and port of Liberia; population (1992) 490,000. Industries include iron ore, rubber, cement, and petrol processing. Civil war damaged much of the infrastructure in and around Monrovia in the 1990s. The National Museum and the University of Liberia are here.

**monsoon** wind pattern that brings seasonally heavy rain to South Asia; it blows towards the sea in winter and towards the land in summer. The monsoon may cause destructive flooding all over India and Southeast Asia from April to September, leaving thousands of people homeless each year.

**monstera** or *Swiss cheese plant,* evergreen climbing plant belonging to the arum family, native to tropical America. *M. deliciosa* is grown as a house plant. Areas between the veins of the leaves dry up, forming deep notches and eventually holes. (Genus *Monstera,* family Araceae.)

**Montaigne, Michel Eyquem de** (1533–1592) French writer. He is regarded as the creator of the essay form. In 1580 he published the first two volumes of his *Essais;* the third volume appeared in 1588, and the definitive edition was issued posthumously in 1595. In his writings Montaigne considers all aspects of life from an urbanely sceptical viewpoint. He is critical of human pride and suspicious of philosophy and religion, seeking his own independent path to self-knowledge. Francis ◊Bacon was among the thinkers who have been challenged and stimulated by his work, and through the translation by John Florio in 1603, he influenced Shakespeare and other English writers.

**Montana** state in western USA, on the Canadian border. It is nicknamed the Treasure State. Montana was admitted to the Union in 1889 as the 41st US state. One of the Mountain States, it is bordered to the east by North Dakota and South Dakota, to the north by the Canadian states of Saskatchewan, Alberta, and British Columbia, to the west by Idaho, and to the south by Idaho and Wyoming
*population* (1995) 870,300
*area* 318,100 sq km/147,143 sq mi
*capital* Helena
*towns and cities* Billings, Great Falls, Butte
*industries and products* wheat, cattle, coal, copper, oil, natural gas, lumber, wood products, oil, natural gas, and strip-mined coal, tourism.

**Montanism** movement within the early Christian church that strove to return to the purity of primitive Christianity. It originated in Phrygia in about 156 with the teaching of a prophet named Montanus, and spread to Anatolia, Rome, Carthage, and Gaul. The theologian Tertullian was a Montanist.

**Mont Blanc** Italian *Monte Bianco,* the highest mountain in the ◊Alps, on the border between France and Italy, and one of the highest points in Europe at 4,807 m/15,772 ft. Lying 10 km/6 mi

south of Chamonix, it forms part of the Mont Blanc range. The peak was first climbed in 1786 by Jacques Balmat and Michel Paccard of Chamonix. In 1965 the longest road tunnel in the world (12 km/7.5 mi) was opened under the mountain, linking Chamonix to Courmayeur in Italy.

**Montcalm-Gozon, Louis-Joseph de** Marquis de Montcalm (1712–1759) French general, appointed military commander in Canada 1756. He won a succession of victories over the British during the French and Indian War, but was defeated in 1759 by James ◊Wolfe at Québec on the Plains of Abraham, where both he and Wolfe were killed; this battle marked the end of French rule in Canada.

**Monte Carlo** town and luxury resort in the principality of Monaco, situated on a rocky promontory northeast of Monaco town; population (1988 est) 28,000. It is a popular summer resort known for its casino (1878) designed by architect Charles Garnier; the Monte Carlo car rally and Monaco Grand Prix motor races; and its international television festival.

**Montego Bay** port and resort on the northwest coast of Jamaica; population (1991) 83,400. The fine beaches and climate attract tourists.

**Montenegrin** Slavic inhabitants of Montenegro (Yugoslavia) whose culture has much in common with the Serbs.

**Montenegro** Serbo-Croatian *Crna Gora,* constituent republic of Yugoslavia
*area* 13,800 sq km/5,327 sq mi
*capital* Podgorica
*towns and cities* Cetinje
*features* smallest of the republics; Skadarsko Jezero (Lake Scutari) shared with Albania; Mount Lovćen (1,749 m/5,738 ft)
*physical* mountainous and ◊karst region in southwest; forests and grasslands in the east
*population* (1991) 615,300, including *c.* 397,000 Montenegrins, 79,500 Muslims, and 39,500 Albanians
*language* Serbian variant of Serbo-Croat
*religion* Serbian Orthodox
*famous people* Milovan Djilas.

**Monteverdi, Claudio Giovanni Antonio** (1567–1643) Italian composer. He contributed to the development of the opera with *La favola d'Orfeo/The Legend of Orpheus* (1607) and *L'incoronazione di Poppea/The Coronation of Poppea* (1642). He also wrote madrigals, motets, and sacred music, notably the *Vespers* (1610).

**Montevideo** capital and chief port of Uruguay, situated on the northen shore of the Río de la Plata estuary; 210 km/130 mi east of Buenos Aires; population (1992) 1,383,700. It is Uruguay's chief industrial and commercial centre, and handles almost 90% of the country's imports and exports. Industries include meat packing, tanning, footwear, flour milling, and textiles. The main exports are grain, meat products, and hides. All Uruguay's railways converge on the city, and a large fishing fleet is based here.

Montevideo is also a tourist resort with extensive beaches.

**Montezuma II** (1466–1520) Aztec emperor of Mexico. He succeeded his uncle in 1502. Although he was a great warrior and legislator, heavy centralized taxation provoked resentment in outlying areas. When the Spanish conquistador Hernán ◊Cortés landed at Veracruz in 1519 and attempted to march on Tenochtitlán, he was well received by the inhabitants and made Montezuma his prisoner. The emperor was restored to his throne as a vassal of Spain, but dissident groups among his subjects rebelled and killed him.

**Montfort, Simon de** the Younger (*c.* 1208–1265) English politician and soldier. From 1258 he led the baronial opposition to Henry III's misrule during the second ◊Barons' War, and in 1264 defeated and captured the king at Lewes, Sussex. In 1265, as head of government, he summoned the first parliament in which the towns were represented; he was killed at the Battle of Evesham during the last of the Barons' Wars.

**Montgolfier** Joseph Michel (1740–1810) and Jacques Etienne (1745–1799, French brothers whose hot-air balloon was used for the first successful human flight 21 November 1783.

**Montgomery, Bernard Law** 1st Viscount Montgomery of Alamein (1887–1976) English field marshal. In World War II he commanded the 8th Army in North Africa in the Second Battle of El ◊Alamein in 1942. As commander of British troops in northern Europe from 1944, he received the German surrender in 1945.

**Montréal** inland port and commercial centre of Québec, Canada, on Montréal Island at the junction of the Ottawa and St Lawrence rivers; population of metropolitan area (1996 est) 3,326,500. It is the second-largest port on the North American east coast, the chief port of the St Lawrence–Great Lakes waterway system, and the world's farthest inland port, situated 1,600 km/1,000 mi from the Atlantic. Industries include oil-refining, engineering, food-processing, distilling, brewing, and the manufacture of steel, aircraft, ships, petrochemicals, tobacco products, clothing, pulp, and paper.

Founded by the French in 1642, Montréal became a British possession in 1763.

The city was badly affected by the great ice storm of January 1998 which coated electricity pylons with ice and brought many of them down, blacking out parts of Montréal and Québec.

**Montserrat** volcanic island in the West Indies, one of the Leeward group, a British crown colony; capital Plymouth; area 110 sq km/42 sq mi; population (1991) 11,957. Practically all buildings were destroyed by Hurricane Hugo in September 1989. The eruption of the Soufriere volcano in July 1997 buried the capital, Plymouth, under rock and ashes. Around 7,000 islanders were evacuated.

**Montserrat** (Spanish *monte serrado* 'serrated mountain') isolated mountain in Cataluña, northeast Spain, on the right bank of the River Llobregat, 37 km/23 mi north of Barcelona; so called because its uneven outline of eroded pinnacles resembles the edge of a saw. Its highest point is 1,240 m/4,070 ft.

**Moon** natural satellite of Earth, 3,476 km/2,160 mi in diameter, with a mass 0.012 (approximately one-eightieth) that of Earth.

Its surface gravity is only 0.16 (one-sixth) that of Earth. Its average distance from Earth is 384,400 km/238,855 mi, and it orbits in a west-to-east direction every 27.32 days (the *sidereal month*). It spins on its axis with one side permanently turned towards Earth. The Moon has no atmosphere and was thought to have no water till ice was discovered on its surface in 1998.

**moon** in astronomy, any natural ◊satellite that orbits a planet. Mercury and Venus are the only planets in the Solar System that do not have moons.

**Moor** any of the northwestern African Muslims, of mixed Arab and Berber origin, who conquered Spain and ruled its southern part from 711 to 1492, when they were forced to renounce their faith and became Christian (they were then known as *Moriscos*). The name (English form of Latin *Maurus*) was originally applied to an inhabitant of the Roman province of Mauritania, in northwestern Africa.

**moor** in earth science, a stretch of land, usually at a height, which is characterized by a vegetation of heather, coarse grass, and bracken. A moor may be poorly drained and contain boggy hollows.

**Moore, Bobby (Robert Frederick)** (1941–1993) English footballer who led the England team to victory against West Germany in the 1966 World Cup final. A superb defender, he played 108 games for England 1962–70 (until 1978, a world-record number of international appearances) and was captain 90 times. His Football League career, spent at West Ham 1968–74 and Fulham 1974–77, spanned 19 years and 668 matches.

*career highlights*
*Football League* appearances: 668; goals: 25
*international appearances* 108; goals: 2
*World Cup* 1966
*European Cup Winners Cup* 1965
*FA Cup* 1964
*Footballer of the Year* 1964
*World Cup Player of Players* 1966

**Moore, Henry (Spencer)** (1898–1986) English sculptor. His subjects include the reclining nude, mother-and-child groups, the warrior, and interlocking abstract forms. Many of his post-1945 works are in bronze or marble, including monumental semi-abstracts such as *Reclining Figure* (1957–58), outside the UNESCO building in Paris, and are often designed to be placed in landscape settings. He is considered one of the leading artists of the 20th century.

**moorhen** marsh bird belonging to the rail family, common in swamps, lakes, and ponds throughout Europe, Asia, Africa, and North and South America. It is about 33 cm/13 in long, brown above and dark grey below, with a red bill and forehead, a white stripe along the edge of the folded wings, a vivid white underside to the tail, and green legs. Its big feet are not webbed or lobed, but the moorhen can swim well. The nest is built by the waterside, and the eggs are buff-coloured with orange-brown spots. (Species *Gallinula chloropus,* family Rallidae, order Gruiformes.)

**moose** North American name for the ◊elk.

**moraine** rocky debris or till carried along and deposited by a ◊glacier. Material eroded from the side of a glaciated valley and carried along the glacier's edge is called a *lateral moraine;* that worn from the valley floor and carried along the base of the glacier is called a *ground moraine.* Rubble dropped at the snout of a melting glacier is called a *terminal moraine.*

**morality play** didactic medieval European verse drama, in part a development of the ◊mystery play (or miracle play), in which human characters are replaced by personified virtues and vices, the limited humorous elements being provided by the Devil. In England, morality plays, such as *Everyman,* flourished in the 15th century. They exerted an influence on the development of Elizabethan drama and comedy.

**Moravia** Czech *Morava,* area of central Europe, forming two regions of the Czech Republic: *South Moravia* (Czech Jihomoravský) and *North Moravia* (Czech Severomoravský). South Moravia has an area of 15,030 sq km/5,802 sq mi and a population (1991) of 2,048,900. Its capital is Brno. North Moravia has an area of 11,070 sq km/4,273 sq mi and a population (1991) of 1,961,500. Its capital is Ostrava.

**Mordred** in Arthurian legend, nephew and final opponent of King Arthur. What may be an early version of his name (Medraut) appears with Arthur in annals from the 10th century, listed under the year AD 537.

**Mordvin** or *Mordovian,* member of a Finnish people inhabiting the middle Volga Valley in western Asia. They are agriculturalists, known to have lived in the region since the 1st century AD. Although nominally Christian, their faith also includes non-Christian divinities. There are some 1 million speakers of Mordvin scattered throughout western Russia, about one-third of whom live in the Mordvinian republic. Mordvin is a Finno-Ugric language belonging to the Uralic family.

**More, (St) Thomas** (1478–1535) English politician and author. From 1509 he was favoured by ◊Henry VIII and employed on foreign embassies. He was a member of the privy council from 1518 and Lord Chancellor from 1529 but resigned over Henry's break with the pope. For refusing to accept the king as head of the church, he was executed. The title of his political book *Utopia* (1516) has come to mean any supposedly perfect society.

**morel** any of a group of edible ◊mushrooms. The common morel (*M. esculenta*) grows in Europe and North America. The yellowish-brown cap is pitted with holes like a sponge and is about 2.5 cm/1 in long. It is used for seasoning gravies, soups, and sauces and is second only to the ◊truffle as the world's most sought-after mushroom. (Genus *Morchella,* order Pezizales.)

**Morgan le Fay** in the romance and legend of the English king Arthur, an enchantress and healer, ruler of Avalon and sister of the king, whom she tended after his final battle. In *Morte d'Arthur* she revealed the intrigue between ◊Guinevere and Lancelot to her brother.

**Mormon** or *Latter-day Saint,* member of a Christian sect, the *Church of Jesus Christ of Latter-day Saints,* founded at Fayette, New York, in 1830 by Joseph Smith. According to Smith, Mormon was an ancient prophet in North America whose *Book of Mormon,* which Smith claimed was divinely revealed to him, is accepted by Mormons as part of the Christian scriptures. Originally persecuted, the Mormons migrated west to Salt Lake City, Utah, under Brigham Young's leadership and prospered; their headquarters are here. The Mormon Church is a missionary church with a worldwide membership of about 6 million.

**Moroccan Crises** two periods of international tension 1905 and 1911 following German objections to French expansion in Morocco. Their wider purpose was to break up the Anglo-French entente of 1904, but both crises served to reinforce the entente and isolate Germany. The first was resolved at the Algeciras Conference. The second brought Europe to the brink of war and is known as the Agadir Incident.

**Morocco** Kingdom of
*national name* al-Mamlaka al-Maghrebia

**area** 458,730 sq km/177,115 sq mi (excluding Western Sahara)
**capital** Rabat
**major towns/cities** Casablanca, Marrakesh, Fez, Oujda, Kenitra, Tetouan, Meknès
**major ports** Casablanca, Tangier, Agadir
**physical features** mountain ranges, including the Atlas Mountains northeast–southwest; fertile coastal plains in west
**head of state** Hassan II from 1961

**head of government** Abderrahmane Yous-soufi from 1998

**political system** constitutional monarchy

**political parties** Constitutional Union (UC), right wing; National Rally of Independents (RNI), royalist; Popular Movement (MP), moderate, centrist; Istiqlal, nationalist, centrist; Socialist Union of Popular Forces (USFP), progressive socialist; National Democratic Party (PND), moderate, nationalist

**currency** dirham (DH)

**GNP per capita (PPP)** (US$) 3,120 (1998)

**exports** phosphates and phosphoric acid, mineral products, seafoods and seafood products, citrus fruit, tobacco, clothing, hosiery. Principal market: France 31.7% (1997)

**population** 27,866,000 (1999 est)

**language** Arabic (official) 75%; Berber 25%, French, Spanish

**religion** Sunni Muslim

**life expectancy** 65 (men); 69 (women) (1995–2000)

**Chronology**

**10th–3rd centuries BC** Phoenicians from Tyre settled along north coast.

**1st century AD** Northwest Africa became Roman province of Mauritania.

**5th–6th centuries** Invaded by Vandals and Visigoths.

**682** Start of Arab conquest, followed by spread of Islam.

**8th century** King Idris I established small Arab kingdom.

**1056–1146** The Almoravids, a Berber dynasty based at Marrakesh, built an empire embracing Morocco and parts of Algeria and Spain.

**1122–1268** After a civil war, the Almohads, a rival Berber dynasty, overthrew the Almoravids; Almohads extended empire but later lost most of Spain.

**1258–1358** Beni Merin dynasty supplanted Almohads.

**14th century** Moroccan Empire fragmented into separate kingdoms, based in Fez and Marrakesh.

**15th century** Spain and Portugal occupied Moroccan ports; expulsion of Muslims from Spain in 1492.

**16th century** Saadian dynasty restored unity of Morocco and resisted Turkish invasion.

**1649** Foundation of current Alaouite dynasty of sultans; Morocco remained independent and isolated kingdom.

**1856** Under British pressure, sultan opened Morocco to European commerce.

**1860** Spain invaded Morocco, which was forced to cede the southwestern region of Ifni.

**1905** Major international crisis caused by German objections to increasing French influence in Morocco.

**1911** Agadir Crisis: further German objections to French imperialism in Morocco overcome by territorial compensation in central Africa.

**1912** Morocco divided into French and Spanish protectorates; sultan reduced to puppet ruler.

**1921** Moroccan rebels, the Riffs, led by Abd el-Krim, defeated large Spanish force at Anual.

**1923** City of Tangier separated from Spanish Morocco and made a neutral international zone.

**1926** French forces crushed Riff revolt.

**1944** Nationalist party, Istiqlal, founded to campaign for full independence.

**1948** Consultative assemblies introduced.

**1953–55** Serious anti-French riots.

**1956** French and Spanish forces withdrew; Morocco regained effective independence under Sultan Muhammad V, who took title of king in 1957.

**1961** Muhammad V succeeded by Hassan II.

**1962** First constitution adopted; replaced in 1970 and 1972.

**1965–77** King Hassan suspended constitution and ruled by decree.

**1969** Spanish overseas province of Ifni returned to Morocco.

**1975** Spain withdrew from Western Sahara, leaving Morocco and Mauritania to divide it between themselves.

**1976** Polisario Front, supported by Algeria, began guerrilla war in Western Sahara with aim of securing its independence as Sahrahwi Arab Democratic Republic.

**1979** Mauritania withdrew from its portion of Western Sahara, which Morocco annexed after major battles with Polisario.

**1984** Morocco signed mutual defence agreement with Libya, which had previously supported Polisario.

**1991** A UN-sponsored ceasefire came into effect in the Western Sahara.

**1992** The constitution was amended in an attempt to increase the influence of parliament.

**1994** Abd-al Latif Filali became prime minister.

**1996** A new two-chamber assembly was approved.

**1997** Assembly elections proved inconclusive.

**1998** Prime Minister Abderrahmane Youssoufi formed a centre–left coalition.

**Moroni** capital of the Comoros Republic, on Njazidja (Grand Comore); population (1992) 22,000. It has a small natural harbour from which coffee, cacao, and vanilla are exported. Local agricultural markets trade in coconuts, cassava, bananas, and rice.

**morphine** narcotic alkaloid $C_{17}H_{19}NO_3$ derived from ◊opium and prescribed only to alleviate severe pain. Its use produces serious side effects, including nausea, constipation, tolerance, and addiction, but it is highly valued for the relief of the terminally ill.

**morphology** in biology, the study of the physical structure and form of organisms, in particular their soft tissues.

**morphology** in the study of language, the analysis of the formation of words, the breaking-down of a language into morphemes.

**Morrigan** in Celtic mythology, a goddess of war and death who could take the shape of a crow.

**Morris, William** (1834–1896) English designer, socialist, and writer. A founder of the ◊Arts and Crafts movement, he condemned 19th-century mechanization and sought a revival of traditional crafts, such as furniture-making, book illustration, fabric design, and so on. He linked this to a renewal of society based on Socialist principles.

**morris dance** English folk dance. In early times it was usually performed by six men, one of whom wore girl's clothing while another portrayed a horse. The others wore costumes decorated with bells. Morris dancing probably originated in pre-Christian ritual dances and is still popular in the UK and USA.

**Morse code** international code for transmitting messages by wire or radio using signals of short (dots) and long (dashes) duration, originated by US inventor Samuel Morse for use on his invention, the telegraph (see ◊telegraphy).

**mortgage** transfer of property, usually a house, as a security for repayment of a loan. The loan is normally repaid to a bank or building society over a period of years.

**Mortimer, Roger de** 8th Baron of Wigmore and 1st Earl of March (*c.* 1287–1330) English politician and adventurer. He opposed Edward II and with Edward's queen, Isabella, led a rebellion against him in 1326, bringing about his abdication. From 1327 Mortimer ruled England as the queen's lover, until Edward III had him executed. Knighted 1306, Earl 1328.

**mosaic** design or picture, usually for a floor or wall, produced by setting small pieces (*tesserae*) of marble, glass, or other materials in a cement ground. The ancient Greeks were the first to use large-scale mosaic (in the Macedonian royal palace at Pella, for example). Mosaic was commonly used by the Romans for their baths and villas (a well-known example is Hadrian's Villa in Tivoli) and reached its highest development in the early Byzantine period (for example, in the church of San Vitale, Ravenna).

**Moscow** Russian *Moskva,* industrial and commercial city, capital of the Russian Federation and of the Moscow region, and formerly (1922–91) of the USSR; population (1990) 8,801,000. Moscow lies on the Moskva River 640 km/400 mi southeast of St Petersburg, and covers an area of some 880 sq km/340 sq mi. It is the main political, economic, and cultural centre of Russia. A major manufacturing city, its industries include aerospace technology and vehicle assembly, machine and precision tool manufacture, and the production of such diverse goods as electrical equipment, textiles, chemicals, and many food products. Moscow's State University was founded in 1755; other cultural institutions include the extensive Russian State Library and the Academy of Sciences. The city is home to the renowned Bolshoi Theatre of Opera and Ballet, the Pushkin Fine Arts Museum, the Tretyakov Gallery, and the Exhibition of Economic Achievements.

**Moses** (lived *c.* 13th century BC) Hebrew lawgiver and judge who led the Israelites out of Egypt to the promised land of Canaan. On Mount Sinai he claimed to have received from Jehovah the oral and written Law, including the *Ten Commandments* engraved on tablets of stone. The first five books of the Old Testament – in Judaism, the *Torah* – are ascribed to him.

**Moslem** alternative spelling of *Muslim,* a follower of ◊Islam.

**mosque** (Arabic *mesjid*) in Islam, a place of worship. Chief features are: the dome; the minaret, a balconied turret from which the faithful are called to prayer; the *mihrab*, or prayer niche, in one of the interior walls, showing the direction of the holy city of Mecca; and an open court surrounded by porticoes.

**mosquito** any of a group of flies in which the female has needlelike mouthparts and sucks blood before laying eggs. The males feed on plant juices. Some mosquitoes carry diseases such as ◊malaria. (Family Culicidae, order Diptera.)

**Mosquito Coast** Caribbean coast of Honduras and Nicaragua, characterized by swamp, lagoons, and tropical rainforest. The territory is inhabited by Miskito Indians, Garifunas, and Zambos, many of whom speak English. Between 1823 and 1860 Britain maintained a protectorate over the Mosquito Coast which was ruled by a succession of 'Mosquito Kings'.

**moss** small nonflowering plant of the class Musci (10,000 species), forming with the ◊liverworts and the ◊hornworts the order Bryophyta. The stem of each plant bears rhizoids that anchor it; there are no true roots. Leaves spirally arranged on its lower portion have sexual organs at their tips. Most mosses flourish best in damp conditions where other vegetation is thin. There are 1,000 British species of moss and more than 1,200 North American species.

**Mossi** member of the majority ethnic group living in Burkina Faso. Their social structure, based on a monarchy, aristocracy, commoners, and slaves, was established in the 13th–14th centures. There are about 4 million speakers of Mossi, a language belonging to the Gur branch of the Niger-Congo family.

**moth** any of a large number of mainly nightflying insects closely related to butterflies. Their wings are covered with microscopic scales. Most moths have a long sucking mouthpart (proboscis) for feeding on the nectar of flowers, but some have no functional mouthparts and rely instead upon stores of fat and other reserves built up during the caterpillar stage. At least 100,000 different species of moth are known. (Order Lepidoptera.)

**mother-of-pearl** or *nacre,* the smooth lustrous lining in the shells of certain molluscs – for example pearl oysters, abalones, and mussels. When this layer is especially thick it is used commercially for jewellery and decorations. Mother-of-pearl consists of calcium carbonate. See ◊pearl.

**Mother's Day** day set apart in the USA, UK, and many European countries for honouring mothers. It is thought to have originated in Grafton, West Virginia, USA, in 1908 when Anna Jarvis observed the anniversary of her mother's death.

**mot juste** (French) the right word, just the word to suit the occasion.

**motor** anything that produces or imparts

motion; a machine that provides mechanical power – for example, an electric motor. Machines that burn fuel (petrol, diesel) are usually called engines, but the internal-combustion engine that propels vehicles has long been called a motor, hence 'motoring' and 'motorcar'. Actually the motor is a part of the car engine.

**motorcycle** or *motorbike,* two-wheeled vehicle propelled by a ◊petrol engine. The first successful motorized bicycle was built in France in 1901, and British and US manufacturers first produced motorbikes in 1903.

**motorcycle racing** speed contests on motorcycles. It has many different forms: *road racing* over open roads; *circuit racing* over purpose-built tracks; *speedway* over oval-shaped dirt tracks; *motocross* over natural terrain, incorporating hill climbs; and *trials,* also over natural terrain, but with the addition of artificial hazards.

**motoring law** legislation affecting the use of vehicles on public roads. It covers the licensing of vehicles and drivers, and the criminal offences that can be committed by the owners and drivers of vehicles.

**motor neuron disease** (MND) or *amyotrophic lateral sclerosis,* chronic disease in which there is progressive degeneration of the nerve cells which instigate movement. It leads to weakness, wasting, and loss of muscle function and usually proves fatal within two to three years of onset. Motor neuron disease occurs in both familial and sporadic forms but its causes remain unclear. A gene believed to be implicated in familial cases was discovered in 1993.

**motor racing** competitive racing of motor vehicles. It has forms as diverse as hill-climbing, stock-car racing, rallying, sports-car racing, and Formula 1 Grand Prix racing. The first organized race was from Paris to Rouen, France, in 1894.

**Motown** first black-owned US record company, founded in Detroit (Mo[tor] Town) in 1959 by Berry Gordy, Jr (1929–   ). Its distinctive, upbeat sound (exemplified by the Four Tops and the Supremes) was a major element in 1960s pop music.

**mould** furlike growth caused by any of a group of fungi (see ◊fungus) living on foodstuffs and other organic matter; a few are parasitic on plants, animals, or each other. Many moulds are of medical or industrial importance; for example, the antibiotic penicillin comes from a type of mould.

**moulting** periodic shedding of the hair or fur of mammals, feathers of birds, or skin of reptiles. In mammals and birds, moulting is usually seasonal and is triggered by changes of day length.

**mountain** natural upward projection of the Earth's surface, higher and steeper than a hill. Mountains are at least 330 m/1000 ft above the surrounding topography. The process of mountain building (◊orogeny) consists of volcanism, folding, faulting, and thrusting, resulting from

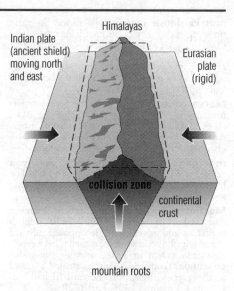

**mountain** *Mountains are created when two continental plates collide and no subduction takes place, resulting in the land at the collision zone being squeezed together and thrust upwards.*

the collision of two tectonic plates (see ◊plate tectonics) at a *convergent margin.* The existing rock is also subjected to high temperatures and pressures causing metamorphism. ◊Plutonic activity also can accompany mountain building.

**mountain ash** or *rowan,* European flowering tree. It grows to 15 m/50 ft and has pinnate leaves (leaflets growing either side of the stem) and large clusters of whitish flowers, followed by scarlet berries in autumn. (*Sorbus aucuparia,* family Rosaceae.)

**mountain biking** recreational sport that enjoyed increasing popularity in the 1990s. Mountain bikes were developed from the rugged 'clunkers' ridden by a small group of off-road riders on the steep, rocky hillsides of Marin County, California in the mid-70s. The fashion spread and the first mass-produced model appeared in the USA in 1981, and in the UK in 1984.

**mountaineering** art and practice of mountain climbing. For major peaks of the Himalayas it was formerly thought necessary to have elaborate support from Sherpas (local people), fixed ropes, and oxygen at high altitudes (*siege-style* climbing). In the 1980s the *Alpine style* was introduced. This dispenses with these aids, and relies on human ability to adapt, Sherpa-style, to high altitude.

**mountain gorilla** highly endangered ape found in bamboo and rainforest on the Rwanda, Democratic Republic of Congo (formerly Zaire), and Uganda borders in central Africa, with a total population of around 600 (1995). It is threatened by deforestation and illegal hunting for skins and the zoo trade. (Subspecies *Gorilla gorilla beringei.*)

**mountain lion** another name for the ◊puma.

**Mountbatten, Louis Francis Albert Victor Nicholas** 1st Earl Mountbatten of Burma (1900–1979) English admiral and administrator, a great-grandson of Queen Victoria. In World War II he became chief of combined operations in 1942 and commander in chief in southeast Asia in 1943. As last viceroy and governor general of India 1947–48, he oversaw that country's transition to independence. He was killed by an Irish Republican Army (IRA) bomb aboard his yacht at Mullaghmore, County Sligo, in the Republic of Ireland. KCVO 1922, Viscount 1945, Earl 1947.

**Mounties** popular name for the **Royal Canadian Mounted Police,** known for their uniform of red jacket and broad-brimmed hat. Their Security Service, established in 1950, was disbanded in 1981 and replaced by the independent Canadian Security Intelligence Service.

**mouse** in computing, an input device used to control a pointer on a computer screen. It is a feature of ◊graphical user interface (GUI) systems. The mouse is about the size of a pack of playing cards, is connected to the computer by a wire, and incorporates one or more buttons that can be pressed. Moving the mouse across a flat surface causes a corresponding movement of the pointer. In this way, the operator can manipulate objects on the screen and make menu selections.

**mouse** in zoology, one of a number of small rodents with small ears and a long, thin tail. The **house mouse** (*Mus musculus*) is distributed worldwide. It is 75 mm/3 in long, with a naked tail of the same length, and has a grey-brown body. (Family Muridae.)

**mouth** cavity forming the entrance to the digestive tract. In land vertebrates, air from the nostrils enters the mouth cavity to pass down the trachea. The mouth in mammals is enclosed by the jaws, cheeks, and palate.

**mouth organ** any of a family of small portable free-reed wind instruments originating in Eastern and South Asia. The compact **harmonica,** or European mouth organ, developed by Charles Wheatstone in 1829, has tuned metal free reeds of variable length contained in a narrow rectangular box and is played by blowing and sucking air while moving the instrument from side to side through the lips.

**Mozambique** People's Republic of
**national name** *República Popular de Moçambique*
**area** 799,380 sq km/308,640 sq mi
**capital** Maputo (and chief port)
**major towns/cities** Beira, Nampula, Nacala, Chimoio
**major ports** Beira, Nacala, Quelimane
**physical features** mostly flat tropical lowland; mountains in west; rivers Zambezi and Limpopo
**head of state** Joaquim Alberto Chissano from 1986
**head of government** Pascoal Mocumbi from 1994

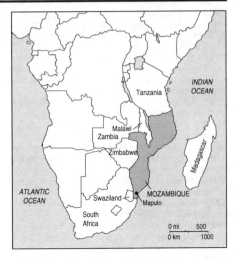

**political system** emergent democracy
**political parties** National Front for the Liberation of Mozambique (Frelimo), free market; Renamo, or Mozambique National Resistance (MNR), former rebel movement, right of centre
**currency** metical
**GNP per capita (PPP)** (US$) 850 (1998 est)
**exports** shrimps and other crustaceans, cashew nuts, raw cotton, sugar, copra, lobsters. Principal market: Spain 17.1% (1996)
**population** 19,286,000 (1999 est)
**language** Portuguese (official); 16 African languages
**religion** animist, Roman Catholic, Muslim
**life expectancy** 44 (men); 47 (women) (1995–2000)
*Chronology*
**1st–4th centuries AD** Bantu-speaking peoples settled in Mozambique.
**8th–15th century** Arab gold traders established independent city-states on coast.
**1498** Portuguese navigator Vasco da Gama was the first European visitor; at this time the most important local power was the Maravi kingdom of the Mwene Matapa peoples, who controlled much of the Zambezi basin.
**1626** The Mwene Matapa formally recognized Portuguese sovereignty. Portuguese soldiers set up private agricultural estates and used slave labour to exploit gold and ivory resources.
**late 17th century** Portuguese temporarily pushed south of Zambezi by the ascendant Rozwi kingdom.
**1752** First Portuguese colonial governor appointed; slave trade outlawed.
**late 19th century** Concessions given by Portugal to private companies to develop and administer parts of Mozambique.
**1930** Colonial Act established more centralized Portuguese rule, ending concessions to monopolistic companies and forging closer integration with Lisbon.
**1951** Became an overseas province of Portugal and, economically, a cheap labour reserve for South Africa's mines.

**1962** Frelimo (National Front for the Liberation of Mozambique) established in exile in Tanzania by Marxist guerrillas, including Samora Machel, to fight for independence.

**1964** Fighting broke out between Frelimo forces and Portuguese troops, starting a ten-year liberation war; Portugal despatched 70,000 troops to Mozambique.

**1969** Eduardo Mondlane, leader of Frelimo, was assassinated.

**1975** Following revolution in Portugal, independence achieved as a socialist republic, with Machel as president, Joaquim Chissano as prime minister, and Frelimo as sole legal party; Portuguese settlers left the country. Lourenço Marques renamed Maputo. Key enterprises nationalized.

**1977** Renamo resistance group formed, with covert backing of South Africa.

**1979** Machel encouraged Patriotic Front guerrillas in Rhodesia to accept Lancaster House Agreement, creating Zimbabwe.

**1983** Good relations were restored with Western powers.

**1984** The Nkomati Accord of nonaggression was signed with South Africa.

**1986** Machel was killed in air crash near the South African border and was succeeded by Chissano.

**1988** Tanzanian troops withdrawn from Mozambique.

**1989** Renamo continued attacks on government facilities and civilians.

**1990** One-party rule officially ended, and Frelimo abandoned Marxism–Leninism and embraced market economy.

**1992** A peace accord was signed with Renamo.

**1993** There were price riots in Maputo as a result of the implementation of IMF-promoted reforms to restructure the economy, which was devastated by war and drought.

**1994** The demobilization of contending armies was completed. Chissano and Frelimo were re-elected in the first multiparty elections; Renamo (now a political party) agreed to cooperate with the government.

**1995** Admitted to Commonwealth.

**Mozart, (Johann Chrysostom) Wolfgang Amadeus** (1756–1791) Austrian composer and performer who showed astonishing precocity as a child and was an adult virtuoso. He was trained by his father, *Leopold Mozart* (1719–1787). From an early age he composed prolifically, and his works include 27 piano concertos, 23 string quartets, 35 violin sonatas, and 41 symphonies including the E-flat K543, G minor K550, and C major K551 ('Jupiter') symphonies, all composed in 1788. His operas include *Idomeneo* (1780), *Entführung aus dem Serail/The Abduction from the Seraglio* (1782), *Le Nozze di Figaro/ The Marriage of Figaro* (1786), *Don Giovanni* (1787), *Così fan tutte/Thus Do All Women* (1790), and *Die Zauberflöte/The Magic Flute* (1791). Together with the work of Haydn, Mozart's music marks the height of the Classical age in its purity of melody and form.

**MP** abbreviation for *member of Parliament.*

**Mpumalanga** formerly *Eastern Transvaal,* province of the Republic of South Africa from 1994, formerly part of Transvaal province

*area* 81,816 sq km/31,589 sq mi

*capital* Nelspruit

*features* Limpopo River, Vaal River, Kruger National Park, Blyde River Canyon Nature Reserve, Mpumalanga Drakensberg Mountains

*industries* farming, coal

*population* (1995 est) 3,007,100

*languages* Siswati, Zulu, Afrikaans.

**MSc** in education, abbreviation for the degree of *Master of Science.* The US abbreviation is *MS.*

**Mubarak, Hosni** (1928– ) Egyptian politician, president from 1981. Vice-president to Anwar Sadat from 1975, Mubarak succeeded him on his assassination. He continued to pursue Sadat's moderate policies, and significantly increased the freedom of the press and of political association, while trying to repress the growing Islamic fundamentalist movement. He was re-elected (uncontested) in 1987 and 1993. He survived an assassination attempt in 1995.

**mucous membrane** thin skin lining all animal body cavities and canals that come into contact with the air (for example, eyelids, breathing and digestive passages, genital tract). It secretes mucus, a moistening, lubricating, and protective fluid.

**mucus** lubricating and protective fluid, secreted by mucous membranes in many different parts of the body. In the gut, mucus smooths the passage of food and keeps potentially damaging digestive enzymes away from the gut lining. In the lungs, it traps airborne particles so that they can be expelled.

**mudskipper** any of a group of fishes belonging to the goby family, found in brackish water and shores in the tropics, except for the Americas. It can walk or climb over mudflats, using its strong pectoral (chest) fins as legs, and has eyes set close together on top of the head. It grows up to 30 cm/12 in long. (Genus *Periophthalmus,* family Gobiidae.)

**Mugabe, Robert (Gabriel)** (1925– ) Zimbabwean politician, prime minister from 1980 and president from 1987. He was in detention in Rhodesia for nationalist activities 1964–74, then carried on guerrilla warfare from Mozambique. As leader of ZANU (Zimbabwe African National Union) he was in an uneasy alliance with Joshua ◊Nkomo of ZAPU (Zimbabwe African People's Union) from 1976.

**Muhammad** also known as Mohammed or Mahomet, (Arabic 'praised') (c. 570–632) Founder of Islam, born in Mecca on the Arabian peninsula. In about 616 he began to preach the worship of one God, who allegedly revealed to him the words of the Koran (it was later written down by his followers) through the angel Jibra'el (Gabriel). Muhammad fled from persecution to the town now known as Medina in 622: the flight, *Hijrah* or *Hegira,* marks the beginning of the Islamic era.

**Mujahedin** (Arabic *mujahid* 'fighters', from *jihad* 'holy war') Islamic fundamentalist guerrillas of contemporary Afghanistan and Iran.

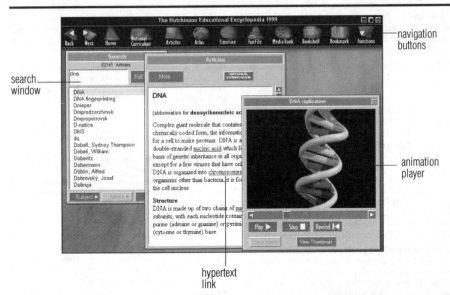

search window — navigation buttons — animation player — hypertext link

*multimedia* An example of how various elements can be combined to create a multimedia presentation. Text is combined with still images, and icons signify related video, audio, and hypertext links.

**mulberry** any of a group of trees consisting of a dozen species, including the black mulberry (*M. nigra*). It is native to western Asia and has heart-shaped, toothed leaves and spikes of whitish flowers. It is widely cultivated for its compound fruits, which resemble raspberries. The leaves of the Asiatic white mulberry (*M. alba*) are those used in feeding silkworms. (Genus *Morus*, family Moraceae.)

**mule** hybrid animal, usually the offspring of a male ass and a female horse.

**mullet** either of two species of fish. The *red mullet* (*Mullus surmuletus*) is found in the Mediterranean and warm Atlantic as far north as the English Channel. It is about 40 cm/16 in long, red with yellow stripes, and has long barbels (sensitive bristles) round the mouth. (Family Mullidae.)

The *grey mullet* (*Crenimugil labrosus*) lives in ponds and estuaries. It is greyish above, with horizontal dark stripes, and grows to 60 cm/24 in. (Family Mugilidae.)

**multimedia** computerized method of presenting information by combining audio and video components using text, sound, and graphics (still, animated, and video sequences). For example, a multimedia database of musical instruments may allow a user not only to search and retrieve text about a particular instrument but also to see pictures of it and hear it play a piece of music. Multimedia applications emphasize interactivity between the computer and the user.

**multinational corporation** company or enterprise operating in several countries, usually defined as one that has 25% or more of its output capacity located outside its country of origin.

**multiple birth** in humans, the production of more than two babies from one pregnancy.

Multiple births can be caused by more than two eggs being produced and fertilized (often as the result of hormone therapy to assist pregnancy), or by a single fertilized egg dividing more than once before implantation. See also ◊twin.

**multiple sclerosis** (MS) or *disseminated sclerosis,* incurable chronic disease of the central nervous system, occurring in young or middle adulthood. Most prevalent in temperate zones, it affects more women than men. It is characterized by degeneration of the myelin sheath that surrounds nerves in the brain and spinal cord.

**multitasking** or *multiprogramming,* in computing, a system in which one processor appears to run several different programs (or different parts of the same program) at the same time. All the programs are held in memory together and each is allowed to run for a certain period.

**Mumbai** industrial port, commercial centre, and capital of ◊Maharashtra, India; population (1994) 14,500,000. Industries include textiles, engineering, pharmaceuticals, and diamonds. It is the centre of the Hindi film industry.

**mummers' play** or *St George play,* British folk drama enacted in dumb show by a masked cast, performed on Christmas Day to celebrate the death of the old year and its rebirth as the new year. The plot usually consists of a duel between St George and an infidel knight, in which one of them is killed but later revived by a doctor. Mummers' plays are still performed in some parts of Britain, often by Morris dance teams.

**mummy** any dead body, human or animal, that has been naturally or artificially preserved. Natural mummification can occur through freezing (for example, mammoths in glacial ice from 25,000 years ago), drying, or preservation in bogs or oil seeps. Artificial mummification may be achieved by embalming (for example, the mummies of ancient Egypt) or by freeze-drying (cryonics).

**mumps** or *infectious parotitis,* virus infection marked by fever, pain, and swelling of one or both parotid salivary glands (situated in front of the ears). It is usually shortlived in children, although meningitis is a possible complication. In adults the symptoms are more serious and it may cause sterility in men.

**Munch, Edvard** (1863–1944) Norwegian painter and graphic artist, a major influence on ◊Expressionism. His highly charged paintings, characterized by strong colours and distorted forms, often focus on intense emotional states, as in one of his best-known works *The Scream* (1893). His works brought a new urgency and power to the two themes that dominated late 19th-century decadence, death and sexuality.

**Münchhausen's syndrome** emotional disorder in which a patient feigns or invents symptoms to secure medical treatment. It is the chronic form of factitious disorder, which is more common, and probably underdiagnosed. In some cases the patient will secretly ingest substances to produce real symptoms. It was named after the exaggerated tales of German storyteller Baron Münchhausen. Some patients invent symptoms for their children, a phenomenon known as Münchhausen's by proxy.

**Munda** any one of several groups living in northeastern and central India, numbering about 5 million (1983). Their most widely spoken languages are Santali and Mundari, languages of the Munda group, an isolated branch of the Austro-Asiatic family. The Mundas were formerly nomadic hunter-gatherers, but now practise shifting cultivation. They are Hindus, but retain animist beliefs.

**Munich** German *München,* capital of Bavaria, Germany, on the River Isar, about 520 m/1,706 ft above sea level, some 45 km/28 mi from the edge of the Alps; population (1995) 1,240,600. The main industries are brewing, printing, precision instruments, machinery, electrical goods, computers, telecommunications, fashion, and food processing.

**Munich Agreement** pact signed on 29 September 1938 by the leaders of the UK (Neville ◊Chamberlain), France (Edouard Daladier), Germany (Hitler), and Italy (Mussolini), under which Czechoslovakia was compelled to surrender its Sudeten-German districts (the *Sudeten)* to Germany. Chamberlain claimed it would guarantee 'peace in our time', but it did not prevent Hitler from seizing the rest of Czechoslovakia in March 1939.

**Munster** historic southern province of the Republic of Ireland, comprising the counties of Clare, Cork, Kerry, Limerick, North and South Tipperary, and Waterford; area 24,140 sq km/9,318 sq mi; population (1991) 1,008,400.

**muntjac** any of about nine species of small deer found in Southeast Asia. They live mostly in dense vegetation and do not form herds. The males have short spiked antlers and two sharp canine teeth forming tusks. They are sometimes called 'barking deer' because of their voices. (Genus *Muntiacus.*)

**muon** an ◊elementary particle similar to the electron except for its mass which is 207 times greater than that of the electron. It has a half-life of 2 millionths of a second, decaying into electrons and ◊neutrinos. The muon was originally thought to be a ◊meson and is thus sometimes called a mu meson, although current opinion is that it is a ◊lepton.

**mural painting** (Latin *murus* 'wall') decoration of the wall either by painting on the surface, or on a canvas which is subsequently affixed in position, the latter being a method frequently used in modern times. In painting directly on the wall, various media have been used, principal among them being fresco, though tempera, encaustic and oil also have their examples. Mural painting is found in all periods of art, but mainly, as distinct from the domestic easel picture, in palaces, churches, or the interiors of buildings of public use or significance.

**Murcia** autonomous community of southeast Spain, with a coastline on the Mediterranean Sea; area 11,300 sq km/4,362 sq mi; population (1991) 1,032,300. The River Segura and its tributaries (the Sangonera and the Quipar) flow through the region, which is very mountainous in the south and east. The irrigated area, the huerta of Murcia, is one of the most intensively farmed areas in Spain and is especially important for citrus fruits. Products include esparto grass (for weaving into simple products such as sandals), iron, olives, and fruit. There are large deposits of salt and minerals, especially lead and zinc. The main port is ◊Cartagena and the capital is Murcia.

**murder** unlawful killing of one person by another. In the USA, first-degree murder requires proof of premeditation; second-degree murder falls between first-degree murder and ◊manslaughter.

**Murdoch, (Keith) Rupert** (1931– ) Australian-born US media magnate with worldwide interests. His UK newspapers, generally rightwing, include the *Sun,* the *News of the World,* and *The Times;* in the USA, he has a 50% share of 20th Century Fox, six Metromedia TV stations, and newspaper and magazine publishing companies. He purchased a 50% stake in a Hungarian tabloid, *Reform,* in 1989.

**Murmansk** seaport and capital of the Murmansk oblast located 1000 km/624 mi north of St Petersburg on the Kola Peninsula in the northwest of the Russian Federation; population (1990) 472,000. Situated on an estuary 50 km/31 mi inland from the Barents Sea, it is the largest city in the Arctic, Russia's principal fishing port, and a base for icebreakers that keep the ◊Northeast Passage open. Shipbuilding is a major industry, and polar research institutes are located here.

**Murray** principal river of Australia, which rises in the Snowy Mountains of the Australian

Alps near Mount Kosciusko, in New South Wales; length 2,540 km/1,578 mi. The Murray flows west and northwest, for most of its length forming the boundary between New South Wales and Victoria, then turns south to reach the Southern Ocean at Encounter Bay, southeast of Adelaide in South Australia. The River Murray is an important source of hydroelectric power and irrigation. With its main tributary, the Darling, it is 3,750 km/2,330 mi long.

**Muscat** or *Masqat,* capital of Oman, east Arabia, adjoining the port of Matrah to the northwest, which has a deep-water harbour; combined population (1993) 40,900. It produces natural gas and chemicals.

**muscle** contractile animal tissue that produces locomotion and power, and maintains the movement of body substances. Muscle is made of long cells that can contract to between one-half and one-third of their relaxed length.

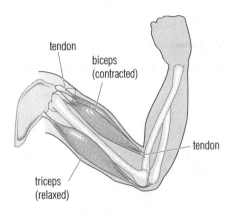

tendon
biceps
(contracted)
tendon
triceps
(relaxed)

*antagonistic muscle* Even simple movements such as bending and straightening the arm require muscle pairs to contract and relax synchronously.

**muscular dystrophy** any of a group of inherited chronic muscle disorders marked by weakening and wasting of muscle. Muscle fibres degenerate, to be replaced by fatty tissue, although the nerve supply remains unimpaired. Death occurs in early adult life.

**Muse** in Greek mythology, one of the nine inspiring deities of the creative arts: Clio, Euterpe, Thalia, Melpomene, Terpsichore, Erato, Polyhymnia, Urania, and Calliope; daughters of Zeus and Mnemosyne, goddess of memory. Reputedly born in Pieria, at the foot of Mount Olympus, they were originally only three in number, but became nine from the time of Hesiod.

**Museveni, Yoweri Kaguta** (1945–  ) Ugandan general and politician, president from 1986. He led the opposition to Idi Amin's regime 1971–78, and became minister of defence 1979–80. Unhappy with Milton Obote's autocratic leadership, he formed the National Resistance Army (NRA). When Obote was ousted in a coup in 1985, Museveni entered into

a brief power-sharing agreement with his successor, Tito Okello, before taking over as president. Museveni led a broad-based coalition government, and in 1993 reinstated the country's four tribal monarchies.

**mushroom** fruiting body of certain fungi (see ◊fungus), consisting of an upright stem and a spore-producing cap with radiating gills on the undersurface. There are many edible species belonging to the genus *Agaricus,* including the field mushroom (*A. campestris*). See also ◊toadstool.

**music** art of combining sounds into a coherent perceptual experience, typically in accordance with conventional patterns and for an aesthetic purpose. Music is generally categorized as classical, ◊jazz, ◊pop music, ◊country and western, and so on.

**musical** 20th-century form of dramatic musical performance, combining elements of song, dance, and the spoken word, often characterized by lavish staging and large casts. It developed from the operettas and musical comedies of the 19th century.

**music hall** British light theatrical entertainment, in which singers, dancers, comedians, and acrobats perform in 'turns'. The music hall's heyday was at the beginning of the 20th century, with such artistes as Marie Lloyd, Harry Lauder, and George Formby. The US equivalent is vaudeville.

**musk** in botany, perennial plant whose small oblong leaves give off the musky scent from which it takes its name; it is also called *monkey flower.* The name 'musk' is also given to several other plants with a similar scent, including the musk mallow (*Malva moschata*) and the musk rose (*Rosa moschata*). (*Mimulus moschatus,* family Scrophulariaceae.)

**musk deer** any of three species of small deer native to the mountains of central and northeastern Asia. A solitary animal, the musk deer is about 80–100 cm/30–40 in, sure-footed, and has large ears and no antlers. Males have long tusklike upper canine teeth. They are hunted and farmed for their musk (a waxy substance secreted by the male from a gland in the stomach area), which is used as medicine or perfume. (Genus *Moschus.*)

**musk ox** ruminant (cud-chewing) mammal native to the Arctic regions of North America. It has characteristics of both sheep and oxen, is about the size of a small domestic cow, and has long brown hair. At certain seasons it has a musky smell. (Species *Ovibos moschatus,* family Bovidae.)

**muskrat** North American rodent, about 30 cm/12 in long, that lives beside streams, rivers, and lakes. It has webbed hind feet, a side-to-side flattened tail, and shiny, light-brown fur. It builds up a store of food, plastering it over with mud, for winter consumption. It is hunted for its fur. (Species *Ondatra zibethicus,* family Cricetidae.)

**Muslim** or *Moslem,* a follower of ◊Islam.

**mussel** any of a group of shellfish, some of which are edible, such as the *common mussel* (*Mytilus edulis*) which has a blue-black hinged shell and is found in clusters attached to rocks around the North Atlantic and American coasts. Mussels are bivalve ◊molluscs. (Class Bivalvia, phylum Mollusca.)

**Mussolini, Benito Amilcare Andrea** (1883–1945) Italian dictator 1925–43. As founder of the Fascist Movement (see ◊fascism) in 1919 and prime minister from 1922, he became known as *Il Duce* ('the leader'). He invaded Ethiopia 1935–36, intervened in the Spanish Civil War 1936–39 in support of Franco, and conquered Albania in 1939. In June 1940 Italy entered World War II supporting Hitler. Forced by military and domestic setbacks to resign in 1943, Mussolini established a breakaway government in northern Italy 1944–45, but was killed trying to flee the country.

**Mussorgsky, Modest Petrovich** (1839–1881) Russian composer. He was a member of the group of five composers ('The Five'). His opera masterpiece *Boris Godunov* (1869, revised 1871–72), touched a political nerve and employed realistic transcriptions of speech patterns. Many of his works, including *Pictures at an Exhibition* (1874) for piano, were 'revised' and orchestrated by others, including Rimsky-Korsakov, Ravel, and Shostakovich, and some have only recently been restored to their original harsh beauty.

**mustard** any of several annual plants belonging to the cress family, with seed-bearing pods and sweet-smelling yellow flowers. Brown and white mustard are cultivated as an accompaniment to food in Europe and North America. The seeds of brown mustard (*B. juncea*) and white mustard (*Sinapis alba*) are used in the preparation of table mustard. (Genus mainly *Brassica*, family Cruciferae.)

**mutagen** any substance that increases the rate of gene ◊mutation. A mutagen may also act as a ◊carcinogen.

**mutation** in biology, a change in the genes produced by a change in the ◊DNA that makes up the hereditary material of all living organisms. Mutations, the raw material of evolution, result from mistakes during replication (copying) of DNA molecules. Only a few improve the organism's performance and are therefore favoured by ◊natural selection. Mutation rates are increased by certain chemicals and by radiation.

**mute** in music, any device used to dampen the vibration of an instrument and so affect the tone. Orchestral strings apply a form of clamp to the bridge – the change is used to dramatic effect by Bartók in the opening bars of *Music for Strings, Percussion, and Celesta* (1936). Brass instruments use the hand or a plug of metal or cardboard inserted in the bell.

**mutiny** organized act of disobedience or defiance by two or more members of the armed services. In naval and military law, mutiny has always been regarded as one of the most serious of crimes, punishable in wartime by death.

**mutualism** an association between two organisms of different species whereby both profit from the relationship; see ◊symbiosis.

**Muzorewa, Abel (Tendekayi)** (1925– ) Zimbabwean politician and Methodist bishop. He was president of the African National Council 1971–85 and prime minister of Rhodesia/Zimbabwe 1979–80. He was detained for a year in 1983–84. Muzorewa was leader of the minority United Africa National Council, which merged with the Zimbabwe Unity Movement (ZUM) in 1994. He pulled out of the 1996 presidential election contest at the last minute, claiming the electoral process was unfairly tilted in President Mugabe's favour.

**Mwinyi, Ali Hassan** (1925– ) Tanzanian socialist politician, succeeding Julius Nyerere as president 1985–95. He began a revival of private enterprise and control of state involvement and spending, and also instituted a multiparty political system in 1995. However in October he lost the first free presidential elections, and was succeeded by Benjamin Mkapa.

**Myanmar** Union of (formerly *Burma*, until 1989)
*national name* *Thammada Myanmar Naingngandaw*

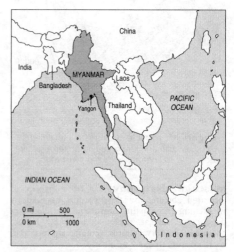

*area* 676,577 sq km/261,226 sq mi
*capital* Yangon (formerly Rangoon) (and chief port)
*major towns/cities* Mandalay, Mawlamyine, Bago, Bassein, Taunggyi, Sittwe, Manywa
*physical features* over half is rainforest; rivers Irrawaddy and Chindwin in central lowlands ringed by mountains in north, west, and east
*head of state and government* Than Shwe from 1992
*political system* military republic
*political parties* National Unity Party (NUP), military-socialist ruling party; National League for Democracy (NLD), pluralist opposition grouping
*currency* kyat
*GNP per capita (PPP)* (US$) 1,280 (1996 est)

**exports** teak, rice, pulses and beans, rubber, hardwood, base metals, gems, cement. Principal market: India 13.1% (1998)
**population** 45,039,000 (1999 est)
**language** Burmese (official), English
**religion** Hinayāna Buddhist 85%, animist, Christian, Muslim
**life expectancy** 59 (men); 62 (women) (1995–2000)
**Chronology**
**3rd century BC** Sittoung valley settled by Mons; Buddhism introduced by missionaries from India.
**3rd century AD** Arrival of Burmans from Tibet.
**1057** First Burmese Empire established by King Anawrahta, who conquered Thaton, established capital inland at Pagan, and adopted Theravāda Buddhism.
**1287** Pagan sacked by Mongols.
**1531** Founding of Toungoo dynasty, which survived until mid-18th century.
**1755** Nation reunited by Alaungpaya, with port of Rangoon as capital.
**1824–26** First Anglo-Burmese war resulted in Arakan coastal strip, between Chittagong and Cape Negrais, being ceded to British India.
**1852** Following defeat in second Anglo-Burmese war, Lower Burma, including Rangoon, was annexed by British.
**1886** Upper Burma ceded to British after defeat of Thibaw in third Anglo-Burmese war; British united Burma, which was administered as a province of British India.
**1886–96** Guerrilla warfare waged against British in northern Burma.
**early 20th century** Burma developed as major rice, teak and, later, oil exporter, drawing in immigrant labourers and traders from India and China.
**1937** Became British crown colony in Commonwealth, with a degree of internal self-government.
**1942** Invaded and occupied by Japan, who installed anti-British nationalist puppet government headed by Ba Maw.
**1945** Liberated from Japanese control by British, assisted by nationalists Aung San and U Nu, formerly ministers in puppet government, who had formed the socialist Anti Fascist People's Freedom League (AFPFL).
**1947** Assassination of Aung San and six members of interim government by political opponents.
**1948** Independence achieved from Britain as Burma, with U Nu as prime minister. Left Commonwealth. Quasi-federal state established.
**1958–60** Administered by emergency government, formed by army chief of staff Gen Ne Win.
**1962** Gen Ne Win reassumed power in left-wing army coup; he proceeded to abolish federal system and follow 'Burmese Way to Socialism', involving sweeping nationalization and international isolation, which crippled the economy.
**1973–74** Adopted presidential-style 'civilian' constitution.
**1975** The opposition National Democratic Front was formed by regionally-based minority groups, who mounted guerrilla insurgencies.

**1987** There were student demonstrations in Rangoon as food shortages worsened.
**1988** The government resigned after violent student demonstrations and workers' riots. Gen Saw Maung seized power in a military coup believed to have been organized by the ousted Ne Win; over 2,000 were killed.
**1989** Martial law was declared; thousands were arrested including advocates of democracy and human rights. The country was renamed Myanmar, and its capital Yangon.
**1990** The landslide general election victory for opposition National League for Democracy (NLD) was ignored by the military junta; NLD leaders U Nu and Suu Kyi, the daughter of Aung San, were placed under house arrest. A breakaway opposition group formed a parallel government.
**1991** Martial law and human-rights abuses continued. There was a government crackdown on Karen ethnic rebels in southeast. Suu Kyi, still imprisoned, was awarded the Nobel Peace Prize. There was a pogrom against the Muslim community in the Arakan province in southwest Myanmar. Western countries imposed sanctions.
**1992** Saw Maung was replaced by Than Shwe. Several political prisoners were released. Martial law was lifted, but restrictions on political freedom remained.
**1993** A ceasefire was agreed with Kachin rebels in the northeast.
**1995** Karen rebels were forced to flee to Thailand after a further military crackdown. Suu Kyi was released from house arrest, but her appointment as NLD leader was declared illegal. NLD boycotted the constitutional convention.
**1996** Karen rebels agreed to peace talks. Suu Kyi held the first party congress since her release; 200 supporters were detained by the government. There were major demonstrations in support of Suu Kyi.
**1997** Admission to Association of South East Asian Nations (ASEAN) granted, despite US sanctions for human-rights abuses. The currency came under threat from speculators.
**1998** Japan resumed a flow of aid, which had been stopped in 1988. The military junta ignored pro-democracy roadside protests by Aung San Suu Kyi and broke up student demonstrations. Junta leader Lt-Gen Khin Nyunt became chairman of a new political affairs committee. 300 members of the opposition NLD were released from detention.

**Mycenaean civilization** Bronze Age civilization that flourished in Crete, Cyprus, Greece, the Aegean Islands, and western Anatolia about 3000–1000 BC. During this period, magnificent architecture and sophisticated artefacts were produced.

**mycorrhiza** mutually beneficial (mutualistic) association occurring between plant roots and a soil fungus. Mycorrhizal roots take up nutrients more efficiently than non-mycorrhizal roots, and the fungus benefits by obtaining carbohydrates from the plant or tree.

**myelin sheath** insulating layer that surrounds nerve cells in vertebrate animals. It serves to speed up the passage of nerve impulses.

Myelin is made up of fats and proteins and is formed from up to a hundred layers, laid down by special cells, the *Schwann cells.*

**My Lai massacre** killing of 109 civilians in My Lai, a village in South Vietnam, by US troops in March 1968. An investigation in 1969 produced enough evidence to charge 30 soldiers with war crimes, but the only soldier convicted was Lt William Calley, commander of the platoon.

**mynah** any of various tropical starlings found in Southeast Asia. The glossy black *hill mynah* (*Gracula religiosa*) of India can realistically mimic sounds and human speech. It is up to 40 cm/16 in long with yellow wattles (loose folds of skin) on the head, and a yellow bill and legs. (Family Sturnidae, order Passeriformes.)

**myoglobin** globular protein, closely related to ◊haemoglobin and located in vertebrate muscle. Oxygen binds to myoglobin and is released only when the haemoglobin can no longer supply adequate oxygen to muscle cells.

**myopia** or *short-sightedness,* defect of the eye in which a person can see clearly only those objects that are close up. It is caused either by the eyeball being too long or by the cornea and lens system of the eye being too powerful, both of which cause the images of distant objects to be formed in front of the retina instead of on it. Nearby objects are sharply perceived. Myopia can be corrected by suitable glasses or contact lenses.

**myopia, low-luminance** poor night vision. About 20% of people have poor vision in twilight and nearly 50% in the dark. Low-luminance myopia does not show up in normal optical tests, but in 1989 a method was developed of measuring the degree of blurring by projecting images on a screen using a weak laser beam.

**myrrh** gum ◊resin produced by several small trees belonging to the bursera family, especially *C. myrrha,* found in Ethiopia and Arabia. In ancient times it was used for incense and perfume and in embalming dead bodies. (Genus *Commiphora,* family Burseraceae.)

**myrtle** any of a group of Old World evergreen shrubs belonging to the myrtle family. The commonly cultivated Mediterranean myrtle (*M. communis*) has oval opposite leaves and white flowers followed by purple berries, all of which are fragrant. (Genus *Myrtus,* family Myrtaceae.)

**mystery play** or *miracle play,* medieval religious drama based on stories from the Bible. Mystery plays were performed around the time of church festivals, reaching their height in Europe during the 15th and 16th centuries. A whole cycle running from the Creation to the Last Judgement was performed in separate scenes on mobile wagons by various town guilds, usually on the festival of Corpus Christi in midsummer.

**mystery religion** any of various cults of the ancient world that were open only to the initiated; for example, the cults of Demeter (Eleusinian Mysteries), Dionysus, Cybele, Isis, and Mithras. Underlying some of them is a fertility ritual, in which a deity undergoes death and resurrection and the initiates feed on the flesh and blood to attain communion with the divine and ensure their own life beyond the grave. The influence of mystery religions on early Christianity was considerable.

**mysticism** religious belief or spiritual experience based on direct, intuitive communion with the divine or apprehension of truths beyond the understanding. It does not always involve an orthodox deity, though it is found in all the main religions – for example, kabbalism in Judaism, Sufism in Islam, and the bhakti movement in Hinduism.

**mythology** (Greek *mythos, logos* 'storytelling' or a 'rationale of stories') body of traditional stories symbolically underlying a given culture. These stories describe gods and other supernatural beings with whom humans may have relationships, and are often intended to explain the workings of the universe, nature, or human history. Mythology is sometimes distinguished from legend as being entirely fictitious and imaginary, legend being woven around an historical figure or nucleus such as the tale of Troy, but such division is difficult as myth and legend are often closely interwoven.

**myxomatosis** contagious, usually fatal, virus infection of rabbits which causes much suffering. It has been deliberately introduced in the UK and Australia since the 1950s to reduce the rabbit population.

**Nabokov, Vladimir Vladimirovich** (1899–1977) US writer. He left his native Russia 1917 and began writing in English in the 1940s. His most widely known book is *Lolita* (1955), the story of the middle-aged Humbert Humbert's infatuation with a precocious girl of 12. His other books, remarkable for their word play and ingenious plots, include *Laughter in the Dark* (1938), *The Real Life of Sebastian Knight* (1945), *Pnin* (1957), and his memoirs *Speak, Memory* (1947).

**nadir** point on the celestial sphere vertically below the observer and hence diametrically opposite the *zenith*. The term is used metaphorically to mean the low point of a person's fortunes.

**Nagaland** state of northeast India, bordering Myanmar on the east, and the Indian states of Manipur to the south, and Assam to the north and west
*area* 16,600 sq km/6,409 sq mi
*capital* Kohima
*physical* mainly upland averaging over 1,500 m/4,900 ft, densely forested; wildlife includes tigers and elephants
*industries* timber, paper; petroleum at Dikhu
*agriculture* tea, sugar, coffee, rice, millet, maize, vegetables
*population* (1994 est) 1,410,000; the Naga population is made up of many different tribal groups
*religion* mainly Christian
*history* formerly part of Assam, the area was seized by Britain from Burma (now Myanmar) in 1826. The British sent 18 expeditions against the Naga peoples in the north 1832–87. After India attained independence in 1947, there was Naga guerrilla activity against the Indian government; the state of Nagaland was established in 1963 in response to demands for self-government, but fighting continued sporadically. A peace accord was struck with the guerrillas in 1975 but fighting resumed in 1980. Charges of serious human-rights violations have been filed against Indian forces operating in the area. The Naga guerrillas have links with other rebel groups in northeast India, but there is conflict between groups over protection money from the heroin trade, transport, and banking; by August 1993 they had forced the closure of 57 of the 63 bank branches in Nagaland and held hundreds of lorries to ransom on the Nagaland–Assam border.

**Nagasaki** industrial port (coal, iron, shipbuilding) on Kyushu island, Japan; population (1994) 438,000. Nagasaki was the only Japanese port open to European trade from the 16th century until 1859. The first modern Japanese shipyard opened here 1855–61. On 9 August 1945, an atom bomb was dropped on Nagasaki by the USA.

**Nagorno-Karabakh** (Russian 'mountainous Qarabagh') autonomous region of Azerbaijan
*area* 4,400 sq km/1,700 sq mi
*capital* Xankändi
*physical* lies on the eastern slopes of the Lesser ◊Caucasus Mountains, partly covered with oak and beech forests
*industries* cotton, grapes, wheat, silk; livestock raising (sheep, cattle, pigs, and horses)
*population* (1996) 200,000 (77% Armenian, 23% Azeri), the Christian Armenians forming an enclave within the predominantly Shiite Muslim Azerbaijan
*history* The region formed part of Armenia until the 7th century, but was subsequently taken by the Arabs, and ruled by them for 300 years. In the 11th century, the region came under the rule of the Bagratid kings of Georgia, who held the area until the Mongol invasion. After a century of Mongol rule, Karabakh fell into Turkish hands. In the early 1600s, Persia gained control of the region, and Abbās I allowed the local khan to rule in Karabakh. This line of khans was overthrown in 1805 by the Russians, who created a province of the region in 1822.

An autonomous protectorate following the Russian Revolution of 1917, Nagorno-Karabakh subsequently saw heavy fighting in the Civil War (1918–20), and was annexed to Azerbaijan in 1923 against the wishes of the largely Christian-Armenian population. From 1989, when the local council declared its intention to transfer control of the region to Armenia, the enclave was racked by fighting between local Armenian troops (reputedly backed by Armenia) and Azeri forces, both attempting to assert control.

After a declaration of independence on 6 January 1992 by the region's parliament (following a referendum on 10th December 1991), the conflict intensified and by June 1993 Armenian forces had overrun much of Nagorno-Karabakh. By February 1994, 18,000 Armenians and 5,000 Azeri were reported to have been killed in the conflict and one million people made refugees. In May of that year a ceasefire was agreed between Azerbaijan and Armenia, bringing hopes of an end to the conflict over Nagorno-Karabakh. By 1996, Nagorno-Kara-bakh was effectively an independent state. Arkady Gukasyan was elected president of Nagorno-Karabakh in 1997.

Border fighting between Azerbaijan and Armenia continued through 1997 and, in November 1998, the Azerbaijan government announced the rejection of the OSCE peace plan for the Nagoro-Karabakh dispute.

**Nagoya** industrial seaport, seat of Aichi prefecture, and capital of the ◊Chubu region, Honshu island, Japan; population (1994) 2,091,000. Situated at the head of Ise Bay, 260 km/162 mi west of Tokyo and 140 km/87 mi east of Osaka, Nagoya is the fourth-largest city of Japan and is a major port. Manufactured products include cars, textiles, and clocks. It has a shogun fortress, built 1610–14 and rebuilt in 1959, and a notable Shinto shrine, Atsuta Jingu.

**Nagpur** industrial city in Maharashtra, India, 710 km/440 mi east of Mumbai; population (1991) 1,661,000. Industries include textiles, metal goods, pharmaceuticals, cotton goods, and hosiery; oranges are traded. Nagpur was the centre of the Chanda Gond dynasty in the 10th–11th centuries, and was the former capital of Central Provinces and Berar, and Madhya Pradesh states. In 1956 it alternated with Mumbai as capital of Maharashtra state.

**Nagy, Imre** (1895–1958) Hungarian politician, prime minister 1953–55 and 1956. He led the Hungarian revolt against Soviet domination in 1956, for which he was executed.

**Nahayan, Sheikh Sultan bin Zayed al-** (1918– ) Emir of Abu Dhabi from 1969, when he deposed his brother, Sheikh Shakhbut. He was elected president of the supreme council of the United Arab Emirates in 1971. In 1991 he was implicated, through his majority ownership, in the international financial scandals associated with the Bank of Commerce and Credit International (BCCI), and in 1994 approved a payment by Abu Dhabi of $1.8 billion to BCCI creditors.

**Nairobi** capital of Kenya, in the central highlands at 1,660 m/5,450 ft; population (1993 est) 1,758,900. Industries include engineering, paints, brewing, and food processing. It is the headquarters of the United Nations Environment Programme (UNEP), and has the UN Centre for Human Settlements. It is one of Africa's largest and fastest-growing cities.

**naive art** fresh, childlike style of painting, employing bright colours and strong, rhythmic designs, usually the work of artists with no formal training. Outstanding naive artists include Henri Rousseau and Camille Bombois (1883–1970) in France, and Alfred Wallis (1855–1942) in England. The term is also used to describe the work of trained artists who employ naive techniques and effects, for example, L S Lowry.

**Najibullah, Ahmadzai** (1947–1996) Afghan communist politician, leader of the People's Democratic Party of Afghanistan (PDPA) from 1986, and state president 1986–92. Although his government initially survived the withdrawal of Soviet troops in February 1989, continuing pressure from the Mujaheddin forces resulted in his eventual overthrow. He was executed in September 1996 by the Talibaan (Islamic student army), who had seized control of most of Afghanistan.

**Nakasone, Yasuhiro** (1917– ) Japanese conservative politician, leader of the Liberal Democratic Party (LDP) and prime minister 1982–87. He increased military spending and Japanese participation in international affairs, with closer ties to the USA. He was forced to resign his party post in May 1989 as a result of having profited from insider trading in the Recruit scandal. After serving a two-year period of atonement, he rejoined the LDP in April 1991.

**Nakhichevan** autonomous region of Azerbaijan
*area* 5,500 sq km/2,124 sq mi
*cities* Nakhichevan (capital), Paragachay
*physical* an Azerbaijani enclave within the neighbouring state of Armenia, located on the Iranian frontier and separated from the rest of Azerbaijan by a narrow strip of Armenian territory; extremely arid, mountainous country with large salt deposits
*industries* irrigated agriculture (cotton, tobacco, grain), horticulture, and sheep raising; mining of salt, molybdenum, and lead; cotton ginning, silk spinning, fruit canning, meat packing and tobacco manufacture
*history* The area now covered by the republic was in Persian hands from the 13th to 19th centuries. It was annexed by Russia in 1828, and the republic was formed as an autonomous administrative unit of the Soviet Union in 1924. In 1990, it unilaterally declared its independence from the moribund USSR, and was thereafter the scene of inter-ethnic violence between Azeris and Armenians. Many Azeris have fled to Azerbaijan, and in January 1990 frontier posts and border fences with Iran were destroyed. In May 1992, Armenian forces made advances in the region, but Azeri forces soon regained control. The republic has sought independence from Azerbaijan.

**Namib Desert** coastal desert region between the Kalahari Desert and the Atlantic Ocean, extending some 2,800 km/1,740 mi from Luanda in Angola to St Helena Bay in South Africa. Its aridity is caused by the descent of dry air cooled by the cold Benguela current along the coast. The sand dunes of the Namib Desert are among the tallest in the world, reaching heights of 370 m/1,200 ft. In the most arid parts rainfall can be as little as 23 mm/0.9 in per year.

**Namibia** Republic of (formerly *South West Africa*)
*area* 824,300 sq km/318,262 sq mi
*capital* Windhoek
*major towns/cities* Swakopmund, Rehoboth, Rundu
*major ports* Walvis Bay
*physical features* mainly desert (Namib and Kalahari); Orange River; Caprivi Strip links Namibia to Zambezi River; includes the enclave of Walvis Bay (area 1,120 sq km/432 sq mi)
*head of state* Sam Nujoma from 1990
*head of government* Hage Geingob from 1990
*political system* democracy
*political parties* South West Africa People's Organization (SWAPO), socialist Ovambo-oriented; Democratic Turnhalle Alliance (DTA),

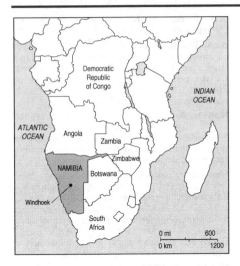

moderate, multiracial coalition; United Democratic Front (UDF), disaffected ex-SWAPO members; National Christian Action (ACN), white conservative
**currency** Namibia dollar
**GNP per capita (PPP)** (US$) 4,950 (1998 est)
**exports** diamonds, fish and fish products, live animals and meat, uranium, karakul pelts. Principal market: UK 33% (1998)
**population** 1,695,000 (1999 est)
**panguage** English (official), Afrikaans, German, indigenous languages
**religion** mainly Christian (Lutheran, Roman Catholic, Dutch Reformed Church, Anglican)
**life expectancy** 52 (men); 53 (women) (1995–2000)
**Chronology**
**1480s** Coast visited by European explorers.
**16th century** Bantu-speaking Herero migrated into northwest and Ovambo settled in northern-most areas.
**1840s** Rhenish Missionary Society began to spread German influence; Jonkar Afrikaner conquest state dominant in southern Namibia.
**1884** Germany annexed most of the area, calling it South West Africa, with Britain incorporating a small enclave around Walvis Bay in the Cape Colony of South Africa.
**1892** German farmers arrived to settle in the region.
**1903–04** Uprisings by the long-settled Nama (Khoikhoi) and Herero peoples brutally repressed by Germans, with over half the local communities slaughtered.
**1908** Discovery of diamonds led to a larger influx of Europeans.
**1915** German colony invaded and seized by South Africa during World War I, and the Ovambo, in the north, were conquered.
**1920** Administered by South Africa, under League of Nations mandate.
**1946** Full incorporation in South Africa refused by United Nations (UN).
**1949** White voters in South West Africa given representation in the South African parliament.
**1958** South West Africa People's Organization

(SWAPO) formed to campaign for racial equality and full independence.
**1960** Radical wing of SWAPO, led by Sam Nujoma, forced into exile.
**1964** UN voted to end South Africa's mandate, but South Africa refused to relinquish control or soften its policies towards the economically disenfranchised black majority.
**1966** South Africa's apartheid laws extended to the country; 60% of land was allocated to whites, who formed 10% of the population.
**1968** South West Africa redesignated Namibia by UN; SWAPO, drawing strong support from the Ovambo people of the north, began armed guerrilla struggle against South African rule, establishing People's Liberation Army of Namibia (PLAN).
**1971** Prolonged general strike by black Namibian contract workers.
**1973** The UN recognized SWAPO as the 'authentic representative of the Namibian people'.
**1975–76** The establishment of a new Marxist regime in independent Angola strengthened the position of SWAPO guerrilla movement, but also led to the increased military involvement of South Africa in the region.
**1978** UN Security Council Resolution 435 for the granting of full independence was accepted by South Africa, and then rescinded.
**1983** Direct rule was reimposed by Pretoria after the resignation of the Democratic Turnhalle Alliance (DTA), a conservative administration dominated by whites.
**1985** South Africa installed a new puppet administration, the Transitional Government of National Unity (TGNU), which tried to reform apartheid system, but was not recognized by the UN.
**1988** Peace talks between South Africa, Angola, and Cuba led to an agreement on troop withdrawals and full independence for Namibia.
**1989** UN peacekeeping force were stationed to oversee free elections to the assembly to draft a new constitution; SWAPO won the elections.
**1990** A liberal multiparty constitution was adopted and independence was achieved. Sam Nujoma, SWAPO's former guerrilla leader, was elected president. Joined the Commonwealth.
**1993** South Africa, with its new multiracial government, relinquished its claim to Walvis Bay sovereignty. Namibian dollar was launched with South African rand parity.
**1994** SWAPO won assembly elections; Nujoma was re-elected president.

**Nanak** (1469–c. 1539) Indian guru and founder of Sikhism, a religion based on the unity of God and the equality of all human beings. He was strongly opposed to caste divisions.

**Nanchang** capital of ◊Jiangxi province, China, on the River Gan, about 260 km/160 mi southeast of Wuhan; population (1994) 1,465,400. Motor vehicles, aircraft, tractors, textiles, glass, porcelain, soap, and lumber are produced. There is a considerable trade in rice, beans, linen, timber, paper, and tobacco.

**Nanjing** or *Nanking*, ('southern capital') inland port and capital of ◊Jiangsu province,

China, 270 km/165 mi northwest of Shanghai; population (1993) 2,430,000. It is a commercial centre and communications hub, with engineering, electronics, shipbuilding, chemical, and oil-refining industries. Textiles are a traditional manufacture. The bridge over the Chang Jiang River, built in 1968, is the longest in China at 6,705 m/22,000 ft.

**Nanning** river port and capital of ◊Guangxi Zhuang Autonomous Region, China, on the Yong Jiang River; population (1994) 1,181,200. It is an important trading centre, particularly in spices. Industries include sugar-refining, food-processing, and the manufacture of chemicals, machines, and cotton. It was a supply town during the Vietnam War and the Sino-Vietnamese confrontation of 1979. Almost a third of the population is of Zhuang cultural background.

**nanotechnology** experimental technology using individual atoms or molecules as the components of minute machines, measured by the nanometre, or millionth of a millimetre. Nanotechnology research in the 1990s focused on testing molecular structures and refining ways to manipulate atoms using a scanning tunnelling microscope. The ultimate aim is to create very small computers and molecular machines which could perform vital engineering or medical tasks.

**Nansen, Fridtjof** (1861–1930) Norwegian explorer and scientist. In 1893, he sailed to the Arctic in the *Fram,* which was deliberately allowed to drift north with an iceflow. Nansen, accompanied by F Hjalmar Johansen (1867–1923), continued north on foot and reached 86° 14' N, the highest latitude then attained. After World War I, Nansen became League of Nations high commissioner for refugees. Nobel Peace Prize 1922.

**Nantes** industrial port and administrative centre of the *département* of Loire-Atlantique and the ◊Pays de la Loire region in western France, situated on the right bank of the River Loire, 50 km/31 mi from its mouth; population (1990) 252,000. Industries include oil, sugar refining, metal goods, textiles, soap, biscuits, and tobacco. The city has many splendid buildings, including a cathedral constructed between 1434 and 1884 and a castle founded in 938.

**Nantucket** nickname 'the Little Grey Lady', island and resort in southeast Massachusetts, USA, 40 km/25 mi south of Cape Cod across Nantucket Sound; population of town (1990) 6,000. Extending over 120 sq km/46 sq mi, its beaches have made it a popular summer vacation area. The island was explored by the English in 1602, settled in 1659 by Quaker and Presbyterian families, and became part of Massachusetts in 1692. In the 18th–19th centuries, Nantucket Town was a whaling port.

**napalm** fuel used in flamethrowers and incendiary bombs. Produced from jellied petrol, it is a mixture of *na*phthenic and *palm*itic acids. Napalm causes extensive burns because it sticks to the skin even when aflame. It was widely used by the US Army during the Vietnam War, and by

Serb forces in the civil war in Bosnia-Herzegovina.

**naphtha** the mixtures of hydrocarbons obtained by destructive distillation of petroleum, coal tar, and shale oil. It is a raw material for the petrochemical and plastics industries. The term was originally applied to naturally occurring liquid hydrocarbons.

**Napier, John** 8th Laird of Merchiston (1550–1617) Scottish mathematician who invented ◊logarithms in 1614 and 'Napier's bones', an early mechanical calculating device for multiplication and division.

**Naples** Italian *Napoli,* (Greek *Neapolis* 'new city') industrial port and capital of Campania, Italy, on the Tyrrhenian Sea; population (1992) 1,071,700. Industries include shipbuilding, food-processing, and the manufacture of cars, textiles, and paper. To the south is the Isle of Capri, and behind the city is Mount Vesuvius, with the ruins of Pompeii at its foot.

**Naples, Kingdom of** state covering the southern part of Italy from the Middle Ages to 1860, when it was unified with the rest of Italy.

**Napoleon I** Napoleon Bonaparte (1769–1821), emperor of the French 1804–14 and 1814–15. A general from 1796 in the ◊Revolutionary Wars, in 1799 he overthrew the ruling Directory (see ◊French Revolution) and made himself dictator. From 1803 he conquered most of Europe (the ◊*Napoleonic Wars*) and installed his brothers as puppet kings (see ◊Bonaparte). After the Peninsular War and retreat from Moscow 1812, he was forced to abdicate 1814 and was banished to the island of Elba. In March 1815 he reassumed power but was defeated by British and Prussian forces at the Battle of ◊Waterloo and exiled to the island of St Helena. His internal administrative reforms and laws are still evident in France.

**Napoleon II** born François Charles Joseph Bonaparte (1811–1832), title given by the Bonapartists to the son of Napoleon I and Marie Louise; until 1814 he was known as the king of Rome and after 1818 as the duke of Reichstadt. After his father's abdication 1814 he was taken to the Austrian court, where he spent the rest of his life.

**Napoleon III** born Charles Louis Napoleon Bonaparte (1808–1873), emperor of the French 1852–70, known as *Louis-Napoleon.* After two attempted coups (in 1836 and 1840) he was jailed, then went into exile, returning for the revolution of 1848, when he became president of the Second Republic but proclaimed himself emperor in 1852. In 1870 he was manoeuvred by the German chancellor Bismarck into war with Prussia (see ◊Franco-Prussian war); he was forced to surrender at Sedan, northeastern France, and the empire collapsed.

**Napoleonic Wars** series of European wars (1803–15) conducted by ◊Napoleon I of France against an alliance of Britain, the German states, Spain, Portugal, and Russia, following the ◊Revolutionary Wars, and aiming for French conquest of Europe. At one time nearly all of

Europe was under Napoleon's domination. He was finally defeated at the ◊Battle of Waterloo in 1815.

**narcissism** in psychology, an exaggeration of normal self-respect and self-involvement which may amount to mental disorder when it precludes relationships with other people.

**narcissus** any of a group of bulbous plants belonging to the amaryllis family. Species include the daffodil, jonquil, and narcissus. All have flowers with a cup or trumpet projecting from the centre. (Genus *Narcissus,* family Amaryllidaceae.)

**Narcissus** in late Greek mythology, a beautiful youth who rejected the love of the nymph Echo and was condemned by Nemesis, goddess of retribution, to fall in love with his reflection in a pool. He pined away, and a flower which appeared at the spot was named after him.

**narcotic** pain-relieving and sleep-inducing drug. The term is usually applied to heroin, morphine, and other opium derivatives, but may also be used for other drugs which depress brain activity, including anaesthetic agents and hypnotics.

**Narmada** river that rises in the Maikala range in Madhya Pradesh state, central India, and flows 1,245 km/778 mi west and southwest to the Gulf of Khambat, an inlet of the Arabian Sea. Forming the traditional boundary between Hindustan and Deccan, the Narmada is a holy river of the Hindus.

**narwhal** toothed whale found only in the Arctic Ocean. It grows to 5 m/16 ft long, has a grey and black body, a small head, and short flippers. The male has a single spiral tusk growing straight out in front of its upper lip that can measure up to 2.7 m/9 ft long. (Species *Monodon monoceros,* family Monodontidae.)

**NASA** acronym for *National Aeronautics and Space Administration,* US government agency for spaceflight and aeronautical research, founded in 1958 by the National Aeronautics and Space Act. Its headquarters are in Washington, DC, and its main installation is at the ◊Kennedy Space Center in Florida. NASA's early planetary and lunar programmes included Pioneer spacecraft from 1958, which gathered data for the later crewed missions, the most famous of which took the first people to the Moon in *Apollo 11* on 16–24 July 1969.

**Naseby, Battle of** decisive battle of the English Civil War on 14 June 1645, when the Royalists, led by Prince Rupert, were defeated by the Parliamentarians ('Roundheads') under Oliver Cromwell and General Fairfax. It is named after the nearby village of Naseby, 32 km/20 mi south of Leicester.

**Nash, John** (1752–1835) English architect. His large country-house practice, established about 1796 with the landscape gardener Humphry Repton, used a wide variety of styles, and by 1798 he was enjoying the patronage of the Prince of Wales (afterwards George IV). Later he laid out Regent's Park, London, and its approaches, as well as Trafalgar Square and St

James's Park. Between 1811 and 1821 he planned Regent Street (later rebuilt), repaired and enlarged Buckingham Palace (for which he designed Marble Arch), and rebuilt the Royal Pavilion, Brighton, in flamboyant oriental style.

**Nash, Paul** (1889–1946) English painter. He was an official war artist in World Wars I and II. In the 1930s he was one of a group of artists promoting avant-garde style, and was deeply influenced by Surrealism. Two works which illustrate the visionary quality of his paintings are *Totes Meer/Dead Sea* (1940–41; Tate Gallery), London; and *Solstice of the Sunflower* (1945; National Gallery of Canada, Ottawa). 'Structural purpose' was an aim which led him into many forms of design, for textiles, ceramics, the stage and the book, but the Surrealist trend of the 1930s and the exhibition of 1936 brought out an imaginative and poetic feeling already apparent in his oils and watercolours.

**Nashville** capital and river port of ◊Tennessee, USA, on the Cumberland River; population (1996 est) 511,300. It is a banking and commercial centre, a major processing point for timber and agricultural produce, and has large car-manufacturing, printing, music-publishing, and recording industries. Nashville was settled in 1779 as Fort Nashborough.

**Nassau** capital and port of the Bahamas, on New Providence Island; population (1980) 135,000.

**Nasser, Gamal Abdel** (1918–1970) Egyptian politician, prime minister 1954–56 and from 1956 president of Egypt (the United Arab Republic 1958–71). In 1952 he was the driving power behind the Neguib coup, which ended the monarchy. His nationalization of the Suez Canal in 1956 led to an Anglo-French invasion and the ◊Suez Crisis, and his ambitions for an Egyptian-led union of Arab states led to disquiet in the Middle East (and in the West). Nasser was also an early and influential leader of the nonaligned movement.

**nastic movement** plant movement that is caused by an external stimulus, such as light or temperature, but is directionally independent of its source, unlike ◊tropisms. Nastic movements occur as a result of changes in water pressure within specialized cells or differing rates of growth in parts of the plant.

Examples include the opening and closing of crocus flowers following an increase or decrease in temperature (**thermonasty**), and the opening and closing of evening-primrose *Oenothera* flowers on exposure to dark and light (**photonasty**).

**nasturtium** any of a group of plants that includes watercress (*N. officinale*), a perennial aquatic plant of Europe and Asia, grown as a salad crop. Belonging to a different family altogether, the South American trailing nasturtiums include the cultivated species *T. majus,* with orange, scarlet, or yellow flowers, and *T. minus,* which has smaller flowers. (Genus *Nasturtium,* family Cruciferae; South American genus *Tropaeolum,* family Tropaeolaceae.)

**Natal** former province of South Africa to 1994, bounded on the east by the Indian Ocean. In 1994 it became part of ◊KwaZulu-Natal Province. It is called Natal ('of [Christ's] birth') because the Portuguese navigator Vasco da Gama reached it on Christmas Day in 1497.

**National Assembly for Wales** devolved parliamentary body for Wales, comprising 60 members and based in Cardiff. The Assembly was created by the July 1998 Government of Wales Act, which was passed following the Welsh electorate's narrow approval of government proposals in an 18 September 1997 referendum on devolution. Its temporary base is the Cardiff University Council Chamber and Crickhowell House on Cardiff Bay. A new building, designed by the architect Richard ◊Rogers, is to be built at Cardiff Bay to house the assembly from 2001.

**National Curriculum** in England and Wales from 1988, a course of study in ten subjects common to all primary and secondary state schools. The national curriculum is divided into three core subjects – English, maths, and science – and seven foundation subjects: geography, history, technology, a foreign language (for secondary school pupils), art, music, and physical education (plus Welsh in Wales). There are four key stages, on completion of which the pupil's work is assessed. The stages are for ages 5–7, 7–11, 11–14, and 14–16.

**national debt** debt incurred by the central government of a country to its own people and institutions and also to overseas creditors. A government can borrow from the public by means of selling interest-bearing bonds, for example, or from abroad. Traditionally, a major cause of national debt was the cost of war but in recent decades governments have borrowed heavily in order to finance development or nationalization, to support an ailing currency, or to avoid raising taxes.

**National Front** in the UK, extreme right-wing political party founded in 1967. In 1991 the party claimed 3,000 members. Some of its members had links with the National Socialist Movement of the 1960s (see ◊Nazism). It attracted attention during the 1970s through the violence associated with its demonstrations in areas with large black and Asian populations and, in response, the left-wing Anti Nazi League was formed to mount counter protests.

**National Health Service** (NHS), UK government medical scheme.

**national insurance** in the UK, state social-security scheme that provides child allowances, maternity benefits, and payments to the unemployed, sick, and retired, and also covers medical treatment. It is paid for by weekly or monthly contributions from employees and employers.

**nationalism** in politics, a movement that consciously aims to unify a nation, create a state, or liberate it from foreign or imperialistic rule. Nationalist movements became a potent factor in European politics during the 19th century; since 1900 nationalism has become a strong force in Asia and Africa and in the late 1980s revived strongly in Eastern Europe.

**nationalization** policy of bringing a country's essential services and industries under public ownership. It was pursued, for example, by the UK Labour government 1945–51. Subsequently the trend towards nationalization has slowed and in many countries (the UK, France, and Japan) reversed (◊privatization). Assets in the hands of foreign governments or companies may also be nationalized; for example, Iran's oil industry (see ◊Abadan), the ◊Suez Canal, and US-owned fruit plantations in Guatemala, all in the 1950s.

**National Security Agency** (NSA), largest and most secret of US intelligence agencies. Established 1952 to intercept foreign communications as well as to safeguard US transmissions, the NSA collects and analyses computer communications, telephone signals, and other electronic data, and gathers intelligence. Known as the Puzzle Palace, its headquarters are at Fort Meade, Maryland (with a major facility at Menwith Hill, England).

**national service** ◊conscription into the armed services in peacetime.

**National Socialism** official name for the ◊Nazi movement in Germany; see also ◊fascism.

**National Trust** British trust founded in 1895 for the preservation of land and buildings of historic interest or beauty, incorporated by an act of Parliament in 1907. It is the largest private landowner in Britain. The National Trust for Scotland was established in 1931.

**NATO** abbreviation for ◊*North Atlantic Treaty Organization.*

**natural gas** mixture of flammable gases found in the Earth's crust (often in association with petroleum). It is one of the world's three main fossil fuels (with coal and oil). Natural gas is a mixture of ◊hydrocarbons, chiefly methane (80%), with ethane, butane, and propane. Natural gas is usually transported from its source by pipeline, although it may be liquefied for transport and storage and is, therefore, often used in remote areas where other fuels are scarce and expensive. Prior to transportation, butane and propane are removed and liquefied to form 'bottled gas'.

**naturalism** in the arts generally, an approach that advocates the factual and realistic representation of the subject of a painting or novel with no stylization.

Specifically, *naturalism* refers to a movement in literature and drama that originated in France in the late 19th century with the writings of Emile ◊Zola and the brothers ◊Goncourt. Similar to ◊realism in that it was concerned with everyday life, naturalism also held that people's fates were determined by heredity, environment, and social forces beyond their control.

**natural selection** the process whereby gene frequencies in a population change through certain individuals producing more descendants than others because they are better able to survive and reproduce in their environment.

The accumulated effect of natural selection is to produce ◊adaptations such as the insulating coat of a polar bear or the spadelike forelimbs of a mole. The process is slow, relying firstly on random variation in the genes of an organism being produced by ◊mutation and secondly on the genetic ◊recombination of sexual reproduction. It was recognized by Charles ◊Darwin and English naturalist Alfred Russel Wallace as the main process driving ◊evolution.

**nature–nurture controversy** or *environment–heredity controversy,* long-standing dispute among philosophers and psychologists over the relative importance of environment, that is, upbringing, experience, and learning ('nurture'), and heredity, that is, genetic inheritance ('nature'), in determining the make-up of an organism, as related to human personality and intelligence.

**Nauru** Republic of
*national name Naoero*

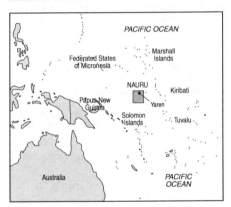

**area** 21 sq km/8.1 sq mi
**capital** (seat of government) Yaren District
**physical features** tropical coral island in southwest Pacific; plateau encircled by coral cliffs and sandy beaches
**head of state and government** Rene Harris from 1999
**political system** liberal democracy
**political parties** candidates are traditionally elected as independents, grouped into pro- and antigovernment factions; Democratic Party of Nauru (DPN), only formal political party, antigovernment
**currency** Australian dollar
**GNP per capita (PPP)** (US$) 11,800 (1994 est)
**exports** phosphates. Principal market: Australia
**population** 11,200 (1999 est)
**language** Nauruan (official), English
**religion** Protestant, Roman Catholic
**life expectancy** 64 (men); 69 (women) (1998 est)
**Chronology**
*1798* British whaler Capt John Fearn first visited Nauru and named it 'Pleasant Island'.
*1830s–80s* The island was a haven for white runaway convicts and deserters.

*1888* Annexed by Germany at the request of German settlers who sought protection from local clan unrest.
*1899* Phosphate deposits discovered; mining began eight years later, with indentured Chinese labourers brought in to work British Australian-owned mines.
*1914* Occupied by Australia on outbreak of World War I.
*1920* Administered by Australia on behalf of itself, New Zealand, and the UK until independence, except 1942–43, when occupied by Japan, and two-thirds of the population were deported briefly to Micronesia.
*1951* Local Government Council set up to replace Council of Chiefs.
*1956* Hammer DeRoburt became head chief of Nauru.
*1968* Independence achieved, with 'special member' British Commonwealth status. Hammer DeRoburt elected president.
*1976* Bernard Dowiyogo was elected president as criticism of DeRoburt's personal style of government mounted.
*1978* DeRoburt was re-elected.
*1986* DeRoburt was briefly replaced as president by opposition leader Kennan Adeang.
*1987* Adeang established the Democratic Party of Nauru.
*1989* DeRoburt was replaced by Kenas Aroi, who was later succeeded by Dowiyogo.
*1992* DeRoburt died.
*1994* Australia agreed to an out-of-court settlement of A$107 million, payable over 20 years, for environmental damage caused by phosphate mining which had left 80% of land agriculturally barren.
*1995* Lagumot Harris replaced Dowiyogo as president.
*1996* President Harris replaced by Bernard Dowiyogo, following a general election.
*1997* President Dowiyogo was defeated in a no-confidence motion. Kinza Clodumar became president after a new general election; the new cabinet included former presidents Dowiyogo and Kennan Adeang.
*1998* Clodumar was defeated in a no-confidence motion; replaced as president by Bernard Dowiyogo.

**nautical mile** unit of distance used in navigation, an internationally agreed-on standard (since 1959) equalling the average length of one minute of arc on a great circle of the Earth, or 1,852 m/6,076.12 ft. The term formerly applied to various units of distance used in navigation.

**nautilus** sea animal related to octopuses and squids, with many short, grasping tentacles surrounding a sharp beak, but different in that it has an outer shell. It is a ◊cephalopod, a type of ◊mollusc, and is found in the Indian and Pacific oceans. The well-known *pearly nautilus* (*N. pompilius*) has a chambered spiral shell about 20 cm/8 in in diameter. Its body occupies the outer chamber. (Genus *Nautilus,* class Cephalopoda.)

**Navajo** or Navaho, (Tena *Navahu* 'large planted field') member of the second-largest group of ◊American Indian people, numbering about 220,000 (1990) and living in Arizona, New Mexico, and Utah. They are related to the ◊Apache, and speak an Athabaskan language, belonging to the Na-Dené family. The Navajo were traditionally cultivators, although many now herd sheep, which they acquired from the Spanish. They are renowned for their artistry and earn an income from tourism, selling their painted pottery, woven rugs and blankets, and silver and turquoise jewellery.

**Navarino, Battle of** during the Greek war of liberation, the destruction on 20 October 1827 of a joint Turkish–Egyptian fleet by by the combined fleets of the British, French, and Russians under Vice-Admiral Edward Codrington (1770–1851). The destruction of their fleet left the Turks highly vulnerable in Greece as they had no protection to their rear and no supply line, and this proved to be the decisive battle of the war. Navarino is the Italian and historic name of Pylos Bay, Greece, on the southwest coast of the Peloponnese.

**Navarre** Spanish *Navarra*, autonomous community of northern Spain, bordered by France on the north; area 10,400 sq km/4,014 sq mi; population (1991) 516,300. The region is mountainous, containing spurs of the Pyrenees, and includes Monte Adi (1,503 m/4,933 ft high); the rivers Arga, Aragón, and Ebro flow through the area. Cereals and wine are produced in the lowlands. The capital is Pamplona.

**Navarre, Kingdom of** former kingdom comprising the Spanish province of Navarre and part of what is now the French *département* of Basses-Pyrénées. It resisted the conquest of the ◊Moors and was independent until it became French 1284 on the marriage of Philip IV to the heiress of Navarre. In 1479 Ferdinand of Aragón annexed Spanish Navarre, with French Navarre going to Catherine of Foix (1483–1512), who kept the royal title. Her grandson became Henry IV of France, and Navarre was absorbed in the French crown lands in 1620.

**navigation** the science and technology of finding the position, course, and distance travelled by a ship, plane, or other craft. Traditional methods include the magnetic ◊compass and ◊sextant. Today the gyrocompass is usually used, together with highly sophisticated electronic methods, employing beacons of radio signals, such as Decca, Loran, and Omega. Satellite navigation uses satellites that broadcast time and position signals.

**Navratilova, Martina** (1956– ) Czech tennis player who became a naturalized US citizen in 1981. The most outstanding woman player of the 1980s, she had 55 Grand Slam victories by 1991, including 18 singles titles. She won the Wimbledon singles title a record nine times, including six in succession 1982–87. She was defeated by Conchita Martinez in the final of her last Wimbledon as a singles player in 1994. She became a tennis coach in February 1997, and made her debut as captain of the defending champion US Fed Cup team, replacing Billie Jean King.

*career highlights*
**Wimbledon** singles: 1978–79, 1982–87, 1990; doubles: 1976, 1979, 1981–84, 1986; mixed: 1985, 1993, 1995
**US Open** singles: 1983–84, 1986–87; doubles: 1977–78, 1980, 1983–84, 1986–90; mixed: 1985, 1987
**French Open** singles: 1982, 1984; doubles: 1975, 1982, 1984–88; mixed: 1974, 1985
**Australian Open** singles: 1981, 1983, 1985; doubles: 1980, 1982–85, 1987–89

**navy** fleet of ships, usually a nation's warships and the organization to maintain them.

**Nazarbayev, Nursultan** (1940– ) Kazakh politician, president of Kazakhstan from 1990. In the Soviet period he was prime minister of the republic 1984–89 and leader of the Kazakh Communist Party 1989–91, which established itself as the independent Socialist Party of Kazakhstan in September 1991. He was an advocate of free-market policies, and yet also enjoyed the support of the environmentalist lobby.

**Nazareth** city in Galilee, northern Israel, 30 km/19 mi southeast of Haifa; population about 64,000. According to the New Testament it was the boyhood home of Jesus.

**Nazi** member of the *Nationalsozialistische Deutsche Arbeiterpartei*, usually abbreviated to the *Nazi Party*. The party was based on the ideology of ◊Nazism.

**Nazism** ideology based on racism, nationalism, and the supremacy of the state over the individual. The German Nazi party, the *Nationalsozialistische Deutsche Arbeiterpartei* (National Socialist German Workers' Party), was formed from the German Workers' Party (founded in 1919) and led by Adolf ◊Hitler from 1921 to 1945.

**Nazi–Soviet pact** another name for the ◊Ribbentrop–Molotov pact.

**Ndjamena** formerly (until 1973) Fort Lamy, capital of Chad, in the southwest of the country, at the confluence of the Chari and Logone rivers, on the Cameroon border; population (1993) 531,000. Industries include cotton, textiles, and meat packing. The city's agricultural markets trade in livestock, salt, dates, and grain. The Great Mosque built 1974–78 is an important landmark. It is a staging point for many pilgrims from West Africa to Mecca.

**Neagh, Lough** lake in Northern Ireland, 25 km/15 mi west of Belfast; area 396 sq km/153 sq mi. It is the largest lake in the British Isles and Ireland, being 27 km/17 mi long, 16 km/10 mi wide, with an average depth of 12 m/39 ft. The shores are mostly flat and marshy; there are a few islands of which Ram's Island is the largest, on which is an early round tower. The lake is famous for trout and eel fishing, and breeding waterbirds.

**Neanderthal** hominid of the Mid-Late Palaeolithic, named after the Neander Tal (valley) near Düsseldorf, Germany, where a skeleton was found in 1856. *Homo sapiens neanderthalensis* lived from about 150,000 to 35,000 years ago and was similar in build to present-day people, but slightly smaller, stockier, and heavier-featured with a strong jaw and prominent brow ridges on a sloping forehead. The condition of the Neanderthal teeth that have been found suggests that they were used as clamps for holding objects with the hands.

**Neath Port Talbot** unitary authority in south Wales, created in 1996 from part of the former county of West Glamorgan
*area* 442 sq km/171 sq mi
*towns* Port Talbot (administrative headquarters)
*physical* the terrain is dominated by the alternation of river valleys and high moorland interfluves
*features* Roman fort of Nidum is near Neath
*industries* coal mining, chemicals, various metalworks, variety of light industry
*population* (1996) 139,400.

**Nebraska** state in central USA. It is nicknamed the Cornhusker State or the Blackwater State. Nebraska was admitted to the Union in 1867 as the 37th US state. Pasrt of the Midwest, and on of the Great Plains states, it is bordered to the west by Wyoming, to the north by South Dakota, to the east by Iowa and Missouri, to the south by Kansas, and to the southwest by Colorado
*population* (1995) 1,637,100
*area* 200,400 sq km/77,354 sq mi
*capital* Lincoln
*towns and cities* Omaha, Grand Island, North Platte
*industries and products* cereals, livestock, processed foods, fertilizers, oil, natural gas, finance sector.

**Nebuchadnezzar** (*c.* 630–*c.* 562 BC) or *Nebuchadrezzar II,* king of Babylonia from 604 BC. Shortly before his accession he defeated the Egyptians at Carchemish and brought Palestine and Syria into his empire. Judah revolted, with Egyptian assistance, 596 and 587–586 BC; on both occasions he captured Jerusalem and took many Hebrews into captivity. He largely rebuilt Babylon and constructed the hanging gardens.

**nebula** cloud of gas and dust in space. Nebulae are the birthplaces of stars, but some nebulae are produced by gas thrown off from dying stars (see ◊planetary nebula; ◊supernova). Nebulae are classified depending on whether they emit, reflect, or absorb light.

**nectarine** smooth, shiny-skinned variety of ◊peach, usually smaller than other peaches and with firmer flesh. It arose from a natural variation of the original form.

**Nefertiti** or *Nofretete,* queen of Egypt in the 14th century BC, wife of the pharaoh ◊Akhenaton.

**negative/positive** in photography, a reverse image, which when printed is again reversed, restoring the original scene. It was invented by William Henry Fox Talbot about 1834.

**Negev** triangular desert region in southern Israel that tapers to the port of Elat, 120 km/75 mi wide at Beersheba, 13 km/8 mi at Elat; area 12,215 sq km/4,716 sq mi. It is fertile under irrigation, and minerals include oil and copper.

**Nehru, Jawaharlal** (1889–1964) Indian nationalist politician, prime minister from 1947. Before the partition (the division of British India into India and Pakistan), he led the socialist wing of the nationalist Congress Party, and was second in influence only to Mahatma Gandhi. He was imprisoned nine times by the British 1921–45 for political activities. As prime minister from the creation of the dominion (later republic) of India in August 1947, he originated the idea of nonalignment (neutrality towards major powers). His daughter was Prime Minister Indira Gandhi. His sister, Vijaya Lakshmi Pandit, was the UN General Assembly's first female president 1953–54.

**Nelson, Horatio** 1st Viscount Nelson (1758–1805) English admiral. He joined the navy in 1770. During the Revolutionary Wars against France he lost the sight in his right eye in 1794 and lost his right arm in 1797. He became a rear admiral and a national hero after the victory off Cape St Vincent, Portugal. In 1798 he tracked the French fleet to Aboukir Bay where he almost entirely destroyed it. In 1801 he won a decisive victory over Denmark at the Battle of ◊Copenhagen, and in 1805, after two years of blockading Toulon, he defeated the Franco-Spanish fleet at the Battle of ◊Trafalgar, near Gibraltar. KB 1797, Baron 1798, Viscount 1801.

**nematode** any of a group of unsegmented ◊worms that are pointed at both ends, with a tough, smooth outer skin. They include many free-living species found in soil and water, including the sea, but a large number are parasites, such as the roundworms and pinworms that live in humans, or the eelworms that attack plant roots. They differ from ◊flatworms in that they have two openings to the gut (a mouth and an anus). (Phylum Nematoda.)

**Nemesis** in late Greek mythology, the goddess of retribution, who especially punished hubris (Greek *hybris*), violent acts carried through in defiance of the gods and human custom.

**neoclassicism** movement in art, architecture, and design in Europe and North America about 1750–1850, characterized by a revival of Classical Greek and Roman styles. Leading figures of the movement were the architects Claude-Nicolas Ledoux and Robert Adam; the painters Jacques-Louis David, Jean Ingres, and Anton Mengs; the sculptors Antonio Canova, John Flaxman, Bertel Thorvaldsen, and Johann Sergel; and the designers Josiah Wedgwood, George Hepplewhite, and Thomas Sheraton.

**neo-Darwinism** the modern theory of ◊evolution, built up since the 1930s by integrating the 19th-century English scientist Charles ◊Darwin's theory of evolution through natural selection with the theory of genetic inheritance founded on the work of the Austrian biologist Gregor Mendel.

**neodymium** yellowish metallic element of the ◊lanthanide series, symbol Nd, atomic number 60, relative atomic mass 144.24. Its rose-coloured salts are used in colouring glass, and neodymium is used in lasers.

**neo-expressionism** style of modern painting in which the artist handles the materials in a rough and raw way, typically expressing violent emotion. It developed in the late 1970s and became a dominant force in avant-garde art during the 1980s, especially in the USA, Germany, and Italy. Pablo Picasso's late paintings, which are often aggressively sexual in subject and almost frenzied in brushwork, were a major source for the style. Neo-expressionist paintings often feature the human figure, but they are sometimes virtually abstract. In Italy neo-expressionism is sometimes known as the *Transavantgarde* ('beyond the avant-garde'), and in Germany its exponents are sometimes called *Neue Wilden* ('new wild ones'). Various alternative names have been used in the USA, including New Fauvism, Punk Art, and Bad Painting (the latter because, in spite of the commercial success enjoyed by several exponents, many critics find the work crude and ugly, flaunting a lack of conventional skills).

**neo-Impressionism** movement in French painting that developed from ◊Impressionism in the 1880s and flourished until the early years of the 20th century. The name was coined in 1886 in a review of the eighth and last Impressionist exhibition, held in Paris that year. Among the artists who exhibited there was Georges Seurat, who was the chief creator and outstanding exponent of neo-Impressionism.

**Neolithic** literally 'New Stone', the last period of the ◊Stone Age. It was characterized by settled agricultural communities who kept domesticated animals, and made pottery and sophisticated, finely finished stone tools.

The Neolithic period began and ended at different times in different parts of the world. For example, the earliest Neolithic communities appeared about 9000 BC in the Middle East, and were followed by those in Egypt, India, and China. In Europe farming began in about 6500 BC in the Balkans and Aegean Sea areas, spreading north and east by 1000 BC. The Neolithic period ended with the start of the ◊Bronze Age, when people began using metals. Some Stone Age cultures persisted into the 20th century, notably in remote parts of New Guinea.

**neon** (Greek *neos* 'new') colourless, odourless, nonmetallic, gaseous element, symbol Ne, atomic number 10, relative atomic mass 20.183. It is grouped with the ◊inert gases, is nonreactive, and forms no compounds. It occurs in small quantities in the Earth's atmosphere.

**neo-Nazism** the upsurge in racial and political intolerance in Eastern and Western Europe of the early 1990s. In Austria, Belgium, France, Germany, Russia, and Italy, the growth of extreme right-wing political groupings, coupled with racial violence, particularly in Germany, has revived memories of the Nazi period in Hitler's Germany. Ironically, the liberalization of politics in the post-Cold War world has unleashed anti-liberal forces hitherto checked by authoritarian regimes. The most significant parties in Western Europe described by the media as 'neo-Nazi' were the National Front in France,

led by Jean-Marie ◊Le Pen, and the National Alliance in Italy (although, by 1998, the National Alliance claimed to be a mainstream conservative party).

**neoplasm** (Greek 'new growth') any lump or tumour, which may be benign or malignant (cancerous).

**Neoplatonism** school of philosophy that flourished during the declining centuries of the Roman Empire (3rd–6th centuries AD). Neoplatonists argued that the highest stage of philosophy is attained not through reason and experience, but through a mystical ecstasy. Many later philosophers, including Nicholas of Cusa, were influenced by Neoplatonism.

**neorationalism** in architecture, a movement originating in Italy in the 1960s which rejected the functionalist and technological preoccupations of mainstream modernism, advocating a rationalist approach to design based on an awareness of formal properties. It developed in the light of a re-evaluation of the work of Giuseppe Terragni led by Aldo Rossi, and gained momentum through the work of Giorgio Grassi (1935– ). Characterized by elemental forms and an absence of detail, the style has adherents throughout Europe and the USA.

**neorealism** movement in Italian cinema that emerged in the 1940s. It is characterized by its naturalism, social themes, frequent use of nonprofessional actors, and the visual authenticity achieved through location filming. Exponents include the directors Vittorio de Sica, Luchino Visconti, and Roberto Rossellini.

**Nepal** Kingdom of
***national name*** *Nepal Adhirajya*

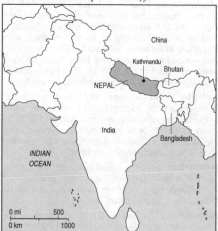

***area*** 147,181 sq km/56,826 sq mi
***capital*** Kathmandu
***major towns/cities*** Pátan, Moráng, Bhádgáon, Biratnagar, Lalitpur, Bhaktapur, Pokhara
***physical features*** descends from the Himalayan mountain range in the north through foothills to the River Ganges plain in the south; Mount Everest, Mount Kanchenjunga

**head of state** King Birendra Bir Bikram Shah Dev from 1972
**head of government** Krishna Prasad Bhattarai from 1999
**political system** constitutional monarchy
**political parties** Nepali Congress Party (NCP), left of centre; United Nepal Communist Party (UNCP; Unified Marxist–Leninist), left wing; Rashtriya Prajatantra Party (RPP), monarchist
**currency** Nepalese rupee
**GNP per capita (PPP)** (US$) 1,090 (1998)
**exports** woollen carpets, clothing, hides and skins, food grains, jute, timber, oil seeds, ghee, potatoes, medicinal herbs, cattle. Principal market: India 32.8% (1998)
**population** 23,386,000 (1999 est)
**language** Nepali (official); 20 dialects spoken
**religion** Hindu 90%; Buddhist, Muslim, Christian
**life expectancy** 58 (men); 57 (women) (1995–2000)
**Chronology**
**8th century BC** Kathmandu Valley occupied by Ahirs (shepherd kings), Tibeto-Burman migrants from northern India.
**c. 563 BC** In Lumbini in far south, Prince Siddhartha Gautama, the historic Buddha, was born.
**AD 300** Licchavis dynasty immigrated from India and introduced caste system.
**13th–16th centuries** Dominated by Malla dynasty, great patrons of the arts.
**1768** Nepal emerged as unified kingdom after ruler of the principality of the Gurkhas in the west, King Prithwi Narayan Shah, conquered Kathmandu Valley.
**1792** Nepal's expansion halted by defeat at the hands of Chinese in Tibet; commercial treaty signed with Britain.
**1815–16** Anglo-Nepali 'Gurkha War'; Nepal became British-dependent buffer state with British resident stationed in Kathmandu.
**1846** Fell under sway of Rana family, who became hereditary chief ministers, dominating powerless monarchy and isolating Nepal from outside world.
**1923** Full independence formally recognized by Britain.
**1951** Monarchy restored to power and Ranas overthrown in 'palace revolution' supported by Nepali Congress Party (NCP).
**1959** Constitution created elected legislature.
**1960–61** Parliament dissolved by King Mahendra; political parties banned after NCP's pro-India socialist leader B P Koirala became prime minister.
**1962** New constitution provided for tiered, traditional system of indirectly elected local councils (*panchayats*) and an appointed prime minister.
**1972** King Mahendra died; succeeded by his son, King Birendra Bikram Shah Dev.
**1980** A constitutional referendum was held, following popular agitation led by B P Koirala, resulted in the introduction of direct, but nonparty, elections to the National Assembly.
**1983** The monarch-supported prime minister was overthrown by directly elected deputies to the National Assembly.

**1986** New assembly elections returned a majority opposed to the *panchayat* system of partyless government.
**1988** Strict curbs were placed on opposition activity; over 100 supporters of the banned NCP were arrested, and censorship was imposed.
**1989** A border blockade was imposed by India during a treaty dispute.
**1990** The *panchayat* system collapsed after mass NCP-led violent prodemocracy demonstrations; a new democratic constitution was introduced, and the ban on political parties lifted.
**1991** The Nepali Congress Party, led by Girija Prasad Koirala, won the general election.
**1992** Communists led antigovernment demonstrations in Kathmandu and Pátan.
**1994** Koirala's government was defeated on a no-confidence motion; parliament was dissolved. A minority communist government was formed under Man Mohan Adhikari.
**1995** Parliament was dissolved by King Birendra at Prime Minister Adhikari's request; fresh elections were called but the Supreme Court ruled the move unconstitutional. Sher Bahadur Deuba (NCP) became prime minister.
**1997** Deuba was defeated in a vote of no-confidence. A new coalition was formed, led by the right-wing Rastriya Prajatantra Party under Prime Minister Lokendra Bahadur Chand. UCPN was successful in local elections. The coalition was divided; the government was defeated on a no-confidence vote. Former prime minister Surya Bahadur Thapa returned, pending a new election.
**1998** The government narrowly survived a no-confidence vote. Thapa stood down as prime minister and was replaced by G P Koirala of the NCP, who formed new coalition government.

**nephron** microscopic unit in vertebrate kidneys that forms **urine**. A human kidney is composed of over a million nephrons. Each nephron consists of a knot of blood capillaries called a glomerulus, contained in the Bowman's capsule, and a long narrow tubule enmeshed with yet more capillaries. Waste materials and water pass from the bloodstream into the tubule, and essential minerals and some water are reabsorbed from the tubule back into the bloodstream. The remaining filtrate (urine) is passed out from the body.

**Neptune** in astronomy, the eighth planet in average distance from the Sun. It is a giant gas (hydrogen, helium, methane) planet, with a mass 17.2 times that of Earth. It has the highest winds in the Solar System.
**mean distance from the Sun** 4.4 billion km/ 2.794 billion mi
**equatorial diameter** 48,600 km/30,200 mi
**rotation period** 16 hr 7 min
**year** 164.8 Earth years
**atmosphere** methane in its atmosphere absorbs red light and gives the planet a blue colouring. Consists primarily of hydrogen (85% with helium (13%) and methane (1–2%).
**surface** hydrogen, helium and methane. Its interior is believed to have a central rocky core covered by a layer of ice.
**satellites** of Neptune's eight moons, two

(Triton and Nereid) are visible from Earth. Six were discovered by the *Voyager 2* probe in 1989, of which Proteus (diameter 415 km/260 mi) is larger than Nereid (300 km/200 mi).

**rings** there are four faint rings: Galle, Le Verrier, Arago, and Adams (in order from Neptune). Galle is the widest at 1,700 km/1,060 mi. Leverrier and Arago are divided by a wide diffuse particle band called the plateau.

**Neptune** in Roman mythology, god of water, who became god of the sea only after his identification with the Greek ◊Poseidon.

**neptunium** silvery, radioactive metallic element of the ◊actinide series, symbol Np, atomic number 93, relative atomic mass 237.048. It occurs in nature in minute amounts in ◊pitchblende and other uranium ores, where it is produced from the decay of neutron-bombarded uranium in these ores. The longest-lived isotope, Np-237, has a half-life of 2.2 million years. The element can be produced by bombardment of U-238 with neutrons and is chemically highly reactive.

**Nereid** in Greek mythology, any of 50 sea goddesses, or ◊nymphs, who sometimes mated with mortals. Their father was Nereus, a sea god, and their mother was Doris.

**Nero** adopted name of Lucius Domitius Ahenobarbus (AD 37–68) Roman emperor from 54. In 59 he had his mother Agrippina and his wife Octavia put to death. The great fire at Rome in 64 was blamed on the Christians, whom he subsequently persecuted. In 65 a plot against Nero was discovered. Further revolts followed in 68, and he committed suicide.

**Neruda, Pablo** pen name of Neftalí Ricardo Reyes y Basoalto (1904–1973) Chilean poet and diplomat. His work includes lyrics and the epic poem of the American continent *Canto General* (1950). He was awarded the 1971 Nobel Prize for Literature. He served as consul and ambassador to many countries during the period 1927–44.

**nerve** bundle of nerve cells enclosed in a sheath of connective tissue and transmitting nerve impulses to and from the brain and spinal cord. A single nerve may contain both motor and sensory nerve cells, but they function independently.

**nerve cell** or *neuron*, elongated cell, the basic functional unit of the ◊nervous system that transmits information rapidly between different parts of the body. Each nerve cell has a cell body, containing the nucleus, from which trail processes called dendrites, responsible for receiving incoming signals. The unit of information is the *nerve impulse*, a travelling wave of chemical and electrical changes involving the membrane of the nerve cell. The cell's longest process, the ◊axon, carries impulses away from the cell body.

**nervous system** the system of interconnected ◊nerve cells of most invertebrates and all vertebrates. It is composed of the ◊central and ◊autonomic nervous systems. It may be as simple as the nerve net of coelenterates (for exam-

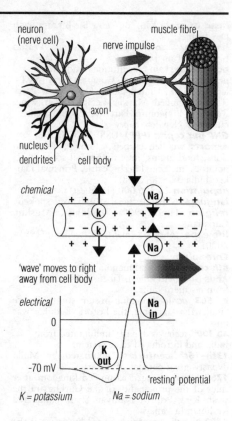

**nerve cell** *The anatomy and action of a nerve cell. The nerve cell or neuron consists of a cell body with the nucleus and projections called dendrites which pick up messages. An extension of the cell, the axon, connects one cell to the dendrites of the next. When a nerve cell is stimulated, waves of sodium ($Na^+$) and potassium ($K^+$) ions carry an electrical impulse down the axon.*

ple, jellyfishes) or as complex as the mammalian nervous system, with a central nervous system comprising ◊brain and ◊spinal cord and a peripheral nervous system connecting up with sensory organs, muscles, and glands.

**Ness, Loch** lake in the Highland unitary authority, Scotland, extending northeast to southwest. Forming part of the Caledonian Canal, it is 36 km/22.5 mi long, 2 km/1 mi wide (on average), 229 m/754 ft deep, and is the greatest expanse of fresh water in Europe. There have been unconfirmed reports of a Loch Ness monster since the 6th century.

**nest** place chosen or constructed by a bird or other animal for incubation of eggs, hibernation, and shelter. Nests vary enormously, from saucerlike hollows in the ground, such as the scrapes of hares, to large and elaborate structures, such as the 4-m/13-ft diameter mounds of the ◊megapode birds.

**Nestorianism** Christian doctrine held by the Syrian ecclesiastic Nestorius (died *c.* 451), patriarch of Constantinople 428–431. He asserted that Jesus had two natures, human and divine. He was banished for maintaining that Mary was the mother of the man Jesus only, and therefore should not be called the mother of God. Today the Nestorian Church is found in small communities in Syria, Iraq, Iran, and India.

**net** of a particular figure or price, calculated after the deduction of specific items such as commission, discounts, interest, and taxes. The opposite is ◊gross.

**net assets** either the total ◊assets of a company less its current liabilities (that is, the capital employed) or the total assets less current liabilities, debt capital, long-term loans and provisions, which would form the amount available to ordinary shareholders if the company were to be wound up.

**Netherlands, the** Kingdom of (popularly referred to as *Holland*)
*national name Koninkrijk der Nederlanden*

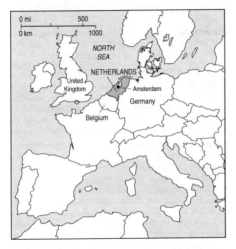

**area** 41,863 sq km/16,163 sq mi
*capital* Amsterdam
*major towns/cities* Rotterdam, The Hague (seat of government), Utrecht, Eindhoven, Groningen, Tilburg, Maastricht, Haarlem, Apeldoorn, Nijmegen, Enschede
*major ports* Rotterdam
*physical features* flat coastal lowland; rivers Rhine, Schelde, Maas; Frisian Islands
*territories* Aruba, Netherlands Antilles (Caribbean)
*head of state* Queen Beatrix Wilhelmina Armgard from 1980
*head of government* Wim Kok from 1994
*political system* constitutional monarchy
*political parties* Christian Democratic Appeal (CDA), Christian, right of centre; Labour Party (PvdA), democratic socialist, left of centre; People's Party for Freedom and Democracy (VVD), liberal, free enterprise; Democrats 66 (D66), ecologist, centrist; Political Reformed Party (SGP), moderate Calvinist; Evangelical Political Federation (RPF), radical Calvinist;

Reformed Political Association (GPV), fundamentalist Calvinist; Green Left, ecologist; General League of the Elderly (AOV), pensioner-oriented
*currency* guilder
*GNP per capita (PPP)* (US$) 21,620 (1998)
*exports* machinery and transport equipment, foodstuffs, live animals, petroleum and petroleum products, natural gas, chemicals, plants and cut flowers, plant-derived products. Principal market: Germany 26.5% (1997)
*population* 15,735,000 (1999 est)
*language* Dutch
*religion* Roman Catholic, Dutch Reformed Church
*life expectancy* 75 (men); 81 (women) (1995–2000)
*Chronology*
*55 BC* Julius Caesar brought lands south of River Rhine under Roman rule.
*4th century AD* Region overrun by Franks and Saxons.
*7th–8th centuries* Franks subdued Saxons north of Rhine and imposed Christianity.
*843–12th centuries* Division of Holy Roman Empire: the Netherlands repeatedly partitioned, not falling clearly into either French or German kingdoms.
*12th–14th centuries* Local feudal lords, led by count of Holland and bishop of Utrecht, became practically independent; Dutch towns became prosperous trading centres, usually ruled by small groups of merchants.
*15th century* Low Countries (Holland, Belgium, and Flanders) came under rule of dukes of Burgundy.
*1477* Low Countries passed by marriage to Habsburgs.
*1555* The Netherlands passed to Spain upon division of Habsburg domains.
*1568* Dutch rebelled under leadership of William the Silent, Prince of Orange, and fought a long war of independence.
*1579* Union of Utrecht: seven northern rebel provinces formed United Provinces.
*17th century* 'Golden Age': Dutch led world in trade, art, and science, and founded colonies in East and West Indies, primarily through Dutch East India Company, founded in 1602.
*1648* Treaty of Westphalia: United Provinces finally recognized as independent Dutch Republic.
*1652–54* Commercial and colonial rivalries led to naval war with England.
*1652–72* Johann de Witt ruled Dutch Republic as premier after conflict between republicans and House of Orange.
*1665–67* Second Anglo-Dutch war.
*1672–74* Third Anglo-Dutch war.
*1672* William of Orange became stadholder (ruling as chief magistrate) of the Dutch Republic, an office which became hereditary in the Orange family.
*1672–78* The Netherlands fought to prevent domination by King Louis XIV of France.
*1688–97 and 1701–13* War with France resumed.
*18th century* Exhausted by war, the Netherlands ceased to be a Great Power.

**1795** Revolutionary France conquered the Netherlands and established Batavian Republic.
**1806** Napoleon made his brother Louis king of Holland.
**1810** France annexed the Netherlands.
**1815** Northern and southern Netherlands (Holland and Belgium) unified as Kingdom of the Netherlands under King William I of Orange, who also became grand duke of Luxembourg.
**1830** Southern Netherlands rebelled and declared independence as Belgium.
**1848** Liberal constitution adopted.
**1890** Queen Wilhelmina succeeded to throne; dynastic link with Luxembourg broken.
**1894–96** Dutch suppressed colonial revolt in Java.
**1914–18** The Netherlands neutral during World War I.
**1940–45** Occupied by Germany during World War II.
**1948** The Netherlands formed Benelux customs union with Belgium and Luxembourg; Queen Wilhelmina abdicated in favour of her daughter Juliana.
**1949** Became founding member of North Atlantic Treaty Organization (NATO); most of Dutch East Indies became independent as Indonesia after four years of war.
**1953** Dykes breached by storm; nearly two thousand people and tens of thousands of cattle died in flood.
**1954** Remaining Dutch colonies achieved internal self-government.
**1958** The Netherlands became founding member of European Economic Community (EEC).
**1963** The Dutch colony of Western New Guinea was ceded to Indonesia.
**1975** Dutch Guiana became independent as Suriname.
**1980** Queen Juliana abdicated in favour of her daughter Beatrix.
**1994** Following an inconclusive general election, a three-party coalition was formed under PvdA leader Wim Kok.
**1998** There were Labour gains in the general election.
**1999** The coalition government resigned in May after the smallest party, Democrats 66 (D-66), withdrew.

**Netherlands Antilles** two groups of Caribbean islands, overseas territories of the Netherlands with full internal autonomy, comprising ◊Curaçao and Bonaire off the coast of Venezuela (◊Aruba is considered separately), and St Eustatius, Saba, and the southern part of St Maarten in the Leeward Islands, 800 km/500 mi to the northeast.
**area** 797 sq km/308 sq mi
**capital** Willemstad on Curaçao
**industries** oil from Venezuela refined here; tourism is important; rum; small manufacturing industries
**language** Dutch (official), Papiamento, English
**population** (1993 est) 197,100.

**nettle** any of a group of weedy plants with stinging hairs on oval, tooth-edged leaves; the hairs contain nerve poisons that penetrate the skin and cause a rash. The flowers are small and greenish, carried on spikes emerging at the same point where the leaves join the stem. The common nettle (*U. dioica*) grows on waste ground in Europe and North America, where it was introduced. (Genus *Urtica*, family Urticaceae.)

**network** in computing, a method of connecting computers so that they can share data and peripheral devices, such as printers. The main types are classified by the pattern of the connections – star or ring network, for example – or by the degree of geographical spread allowed; for example, local area networks (LANs) for communication within a room or building, and wide area networks (WANs) for more remote systems. Internet is the computer network that connects major English-speaking institutions throughout the world, with around 12 million users. JANET (joint academic network), a variant of Internet, is used in Britain. SuperJANET, launched in 1992, is an extension of this that can carry 1,000 million bits of information per second.

**neurology** medical speciality concerned with the study and treatment of disorders of the brain, spinal cord, and peripheral nerves.

**neuron** another name for a ◊nerve cell.

**neurosis** in psychology, a general term referring to emotional disorders, such as anxiety, depression, and phobias. The main disturbance tends to be one of mood; contact with reality is relatively unaffected, in contrast to ◊psychosis.

**neurotransmitter** chemical that diffuses across a ◊synapse, and thus transmits impulses between ◊nerve cells, or between nerve cells and effector organs (for example, muscles). Common neurotransmitters are noradrenaline (which also acts as a hormone) and acetylcholine, the latter being most frequent at junctions between nerve and muscle. Nearly 50 different neurotransmitters have been identified.

**neutrality** the legal status of a country that decides not to choose sides in a war. Certain states, notably Switzerland and Austria, have opted for permanent neutrality. Neutrality always has a legal connotation. In peacetime, neutrality towards the big power alliances is called *nonalignment* (see ◊nonaligned movement).

**neutralization** in chemistry, a process occurring when the excess acid (or excess base) in a substance is reacted with added base (or added acid) so that the resulting substance is neither acidic nor basic.

**neutrino** in physics, any of three uncharged ◊elementary particles (and their antiparticles) of the ◊lepton class, having a mass too close to zero to be measured. The most familiar type, the antiparticle of the electron neutrino, is emitted in the beta decay of a nucleus. The other two are the muon and tau neutrinos.

**neutron** one of the three main subatomic particles, the others being the ◊proton and the ◊electron. The neutron is a composite particle, being made up of three ◊quarks, and therefore belongs to the ◊baryon group of the ◊hadrons. Neutrons have about the same mass as protons but no electric charge, and occur in the nuclei of all atoms except hydrogen. They contribute to the mass of atoms but do not affect their chemistry.

**neutron bomb** or *enhanced radiation weapon,* small hydrogen bomb for battlefield use that kills by radiation, with minimal damage to buildings and other structures. See ◊nuclear warfare.

**neutron star** very small, 'superdense' star composed mostly of ◊neutrons. They are thought to form when massive stars explode as ◊supernovae, during which the protons and electrons of the star's atoms merge, owing to intense gravitational collapse, to make neutrons. A neutron star may have the mass of up to three Suns, compressed into a globe only 20 km/12 mi in diameter.

**Nevada** state in western USA. It is nicknamed the Silver State or the Sagebrush State. Nevada was admitted to the Union in 1864 as the 36th US state. It is famous as a gambling centre and, historically, especially in Reno, as a state in which marriages and divorces could be expedited. Nevada is bordered to the east by Utah and Arizona, to the west and southwest by California, and to the north by Oregon and Idaho.
*population* (1995) 1,530,100
*area* 286,400 sq km/110,550 sq mi
*capital* Carson City
*towns and cities* Las Vegas, Reno
*industries and products* mercury, barite, gold; tourism and gambling now generate more than half of the state's income.

**new age** movement of the late 1980s characterized by an emphasis on the holistic view of body and mind, alternative (or complementary) medicines, personal growth therapies, and a loose mix of theosophy, ecology, oriental mysticism, and a belief in the dawning of an astrological age of peace and harmony.

**New Brunswick** largest maritime province of eastern Canada. It is bounded on the north by Québec, with the Matapédia and Restigouche rivers forming part of the border; in the northeast Chaleur Bay separates New Brunswick's north shore from Québec's Gaspé Peninsula. Off its eastern coast is the Gulf of St Lawrence and in the southeast the Northumberland Strait, on the far side of which lies Prince Edward Island. Nova Scotia province is situated to its south and southeast, across the Bay of Fundy and the narrow land bridge known as the Chignecto Isthmus. To the southwest lies the US state of Maine, with the Saint John and Saint Croix rivers forming parts of the boundary
*area* 73,400 sq km/28,332 sq mi
*capital* Fredericton
*towns and cities* Saint John, Moncton
*population* (1991) 762,500; 33% French-speaking; 52% rural inhabitants
*physical* Grand Lake, Saint John River, Bay of Fundy, Hopewell Cape
*industries* production of wood, pulp, and paper; mining (lead, zinc, copper, nickel, silver, tungsten, gypsum, bismuth, antimony, coal, and potash); oil and natural-gas extraction; manufacturing includes heavy engineering, light industries (electronics, footwear), and production of building materials (bricks and tiles); arable farming (cereals, potatoes, apples), plus livestock-rearing and dairy industry; fishing (herring, lobster).

**New Caledonia** island group in the South Pacific, a French overseas territory between Australia and the Fiji Islands
*area* 18,576 sq km/7,170 sq mi
*capital* Nouméa
*physical* fertile, surrounded by a barrier reef
*industries* nickel (the world's third-largest producer), chrome, iron
*currency* CFP franc
*population* (1989) 164,200 (45% Kanak (Melanesian), 33% European, 7% Wallisian, 5% Vietnamese and Indonesian, 3% Polynesian)
*language* French (official)
*religion* Roman Catholic 60%, Protestant 30%
*government* The French high commissioner is Didier Cultiaux. In 1998 voters approved a referendum on the Noumea Accord, which provided for greater autonomy and a referendum on independence in 15–20 years' time. Turnout was 74% and 72% supported the government's proposals.
*history* New Caledonia was visited by Captain Cook in 1774 and became French in 1853. It has been a French Overseas Territory since 1958. In 1981 the French socialist government promised moves towards independence. The 1985 elections resulted in control of most regions by Kanaks, but not the majority of seats. In 1986 the French conservative government reversed the reforms. The Kanaks boycotted a referendum in September 1987 and a majority were in favour of remaining a French dependency. In 1988 New Caledonia was divided into three autonomous provinces. In 1989 the leader of the Socialist National Liberation front (the most prominent separatist group), Jean-Marie Tjibaou, was murdered.

**Newcastle upon Tyne** city and metropolitan borough in Tyne and Wear in northeast England on the River Tyne opposite Gateshead, 17 km/ 10 mi from the North Sea; population city (1991) 189,150, metropolitan district (1994) 274,000. It is the administrative centre of Tyne and Wear and regional centre of northeast England, as well as a centre for retail, commerce, communications, and the arts. Industries include engineering (including offshore technology), food processing, brewing, and the manufacture of electronics. Only 1% of the workforce is now in heavy industry, 80% are in the public or service sectors. The University of Newcastle was founded in 1963, and the University of Northumbria in 1992.
*features* Parts are preserved of a castle built by Henry II 1172–77 on the site of an older castle (1080). Other landmarks include the cathedral, formerly the parish church, which is chiefly 14th-century; a 12th-century church, and the

Guildhall (1658); the Metro underground; the Laing Art Gallery; the Newcastle Discovery Museum; the Hancock Museum; fine 19th-century classical buildings. The quayside area with its historic buildings has been restored, and is now a fashionable waterside area known for its nightlife, with clubs and pubs here, as well as in Bigg Market. Newcastle is connected with the neighbouring town of Gateshead by eight bridges and a tunnel.

*history* Newcastle stands on the site of a Roman settlement, *Pons Aelius.* Newcastle first began to trade in coal in the 13th century, and was an important centre for coal and ship-building until the 1980s. In 1826 ironworks were established by George ◊Stephenson, and the first engine used on the Stockton and Darlington railway was made in Newcastle.

**New Deal** in US history, the programme introduced by President Franklin D Roosevelt in 1933 to tackle the Great Depression, including employment on public works, farm loans at low rates, and social reforms such as old-age and unemployment insurance, prevention of child labour, protection of employees against unfair practices by employers, and loans to local authorities for slum clearance.

**New Delhi** capital of India, situated in the north of the country on the Yamuna River in the Union Territory of ◊Delhi; population (1991) 301,000. It lies near the old city of ◊Delhi, some 5 km/3 mi south of the Red Fort. Predominantly an administrative centre, it also produces chemicals, textiles, machine tools, electrical goods, and footwear.

**New England** region of northeast USA, comprising the states of Maine, New Hampshire, Vermont, Massachusetts, Rhode Island, and Connecticut. It is a geographic region rather than a political entity, with an area of 172,681 sq km/66,672 sq mi. Boston is the principal urban centre of the region, and Harvard and Yale are its major universities. First inhabited by the American Indian Algonquin peoples, New England was named by the explorer John Smith in 1614, and settled by Pilgrims and Puritans from England in the 17th century.

**Newfoundland** breed of large, gentle dog said to have originated in Newfoundland, Canada. Males can grow to 70 cm/27.5 in tall, and weigh 65 kg/145 lb; the females are slightly smaller. They have a dense, flat coat, usually dull black, and an oily, water-repellent undercoat, and they are excellent swimmers.

**Newfoundland** Canadian province on the Atlantic Ocean, the country's most easterly administrative region, comprising the island of Newfoundland and mainland ◊Labrador, separated by the Strait of Belle Isle. It is bounded on the west by Québec, while to the southwest lie the Gulf of St Lawrence and the provinces of Nova Scotia and Prince Edward Island
*area* 405,700 sq km/156,600 sq mi
*capital* St John's
*towns and cities* Corner Brook, Gander, Goose Bay (Labrador)
*population* (1996 est) 570,700

*physical* Newfoundland: Long Range Mountains, Burin and Avalon peninsulas; Labrador: Canadian Shield, Ungava Bay, Torngat Mountains, Churchill Falls
*industries* offshore oil extraction; fishing and fish-processing; mining (iron, copper, zinc, uranium); wood-processing and paper manufacture; hydroelectric power generation.

**New Guinea** island in the southwest Pacific, north of Australia, comprising Papua New Guinea and the Indonesian province of ◊Irian Jaya; total area about 885,780 sq km/342,000 sq mi. Part of the Dutch East Indies from 1828, West Irian was ceded by the United Nations to Indonesia in 1963 and renamed Irian Jaya ('victorious Irian') in 1973.

**New Hampshire** state in northeastern USA. It is nicknamed the Granite State. New Hampshire ratified the US Constitution in 1788, becoming the 9th state to join the Union. Part of New England, it is bordered to the east by Maine, to the north by Québec, Canada, to the west by ◊Vermont, and to the south by Massachusetts
*population* (1995) 1,148,300
*area* 24,000 sq km/9,264 sq mi
*capital* Concord
*towns and cities* Manchester, Nashua
*industries and products* dairy, poultry, fruits and vegetables, electrical and other machinery, pulp and paper, tourism, leisure industry.

**New Hebrides** former name (to 1980) of Vanuatu, a country in the South Pacific.

**New Jersey** state in northeastern USA. It is nicknamed the Garden State. New Jersey ratified the US Constitution in 1787, becoming the 3rd state to join the Union. The most densely populated US state, it lies within the suburban orbits of the cities of New York and Philadelphia. The New Jersey Turnpike, traversing a zone of heavy development, is the busiest highway in the country. New Jersey is bordered to the north by New York state. It lies largely between two rivers, the Hudson to the east and the Delaware to the west, with the Atlantic Ocean along its southeastern and southern boundaries. New York faces it across the Hudson River, Pennsylvania lies to the west, across the Delaware River, and to the southwest, across the river's mouth and Delaware Bay, is the state of Delaware
*population* (1995) 7,945,300
*area* 20,200 sq km/7,797 sq mi
*capital* Trenton
*towns and cities* Newark, Jersey City, Paterson, Elizabeth
*industries and products* fruits and vegetables, fish and shellfish, chemicals, pharmaceuticals, soaps and cleansers, transport equipment, petroleum refining, research centres, finance sector, tourism.

**Newman, John Henry** (1801–1890) English Roman Catholic theologian. While still an Anglican, he wrote a series of *Tracts for the Times,* which gave their name to the Tractarian Movement (subsequently called the ◊Oxford Movement) for the revival of Catholicism. He became a Catholic in 1845 and was made a cardinal in 1879. In 1864 his autobiography, *Apologia pro vita sua*, was published.

**New Mexico** state in southwestern USA. It is nicknamed the Land of Enchantment. New Mexico was admitted to the Union in 1912 as the 47th US state. One of the Mountain States, it is bordered to the east by Texas and the Oklahoma panhandle, and to the north by Colorado. In the northwest, at the 'Four Corners', it meets Colorado, Utah, and Arizona. Arizona also lies along its western border. To the south, it is bordered by the Mexican states of Sonora and Chihuahua, and by the Trans-Pecos section of Texas

*population* (1995) 1,685,400
*area* 315,000 sq km/121,590 sq mi
*capital* Santa Fe
*towns and cities* Albuquerque, Las Cruces, Roswell
*industries and products* uranium, potash, copper, oil, natural gas, petroleum and coal products, sheep farming, cotton, pecans, vegetables, chilli peppers, tourism.

**New Model Army** army created in 1645 by Oliver ◊Cromwell to support the cause of Parliament during the English ◊Civil War. It was characterized by organization and discipline. Thomas Fairfax was its first commander.

**New Orleans** nickname 'the Big Easy', city and river port in southeast Louisiana, USA, on the Mississippi River, and the Gulf of Mexico; population (1996 est) 476,600; metropolitan area (1992) 1,303,000. It is a commercial and manufacturing centre with shipbuilding, oil-refining, and petrochemical industries. Tourism is a major activity. New Orleans is regarded as the traditional birthplace of jazz, believed to have developed from the singing and voodoo rhythms of the weekly slave gatherings in Congo Square, during the 18th and 19th centuries. The city was founded by the French in 1718.

**Newport** unitary authority in south Wales, created in 1996 from part of the former county of Gwent
*area* 190 sq km/73 sq mi
*towns* Newport (administrative headquarters)
*physical* rivers Usk Ebbw, Afon Llwyd
*features* Legionary Museum and Roman amphitheatre at Caerleon
*industries* steel and aluminium production, engineering, chemicals, fertilizers, electronics
*population* (1996) 133,300.

**New South Wales** state of southeast Australia, including the dependency of Lord Howe Island; bounded by Queensland on the north, the Tasman Sea on the east, Victoria on the south, and South Australia on the west
*area* 801,600 sq km/309,418 sq mi
*capital* ◊Sydney
*towns and cities* Newcastle, Wollongong, Wagga Wagga, Broken Hill, Goulburn, Bathurst, Armidale, Coffs Harbour, Albury, Tamworth
*physical* ◊Great Dividing Range (including Blue Mountains) and part of the Australian Alps (including Snowy Mountains and Mount Kosciusko); rivers Murray, Darling, and Murrumbidgee; Riverina district, irrigated by the Murray-Darling-Murrumbidgee river system; Hunter Valley wine-producing area; Snowy River Scheme
*features* radio telescope at Parkes; Siding Spring Mountain 859 m/2,817 ft, northwest of Sydney, with telescopes that can observe the central sector of the Galaxy; Hume Reservoir; ◊Canberra forms an enclave within the state
*products* cereals, fruit, wine, sugar, tobacco, dairy products, meat, wool, gold, silver, copper, zinc, lead, coal, iron and steel, machinery, electrical appliances, cars, furniture, textiles and textile goods, hides and leather, tobacco, chemicals, paint, oil, paper, hydroelectric power from the Snowy River, mineral sands, glassware, timber, poultry, opals, fish and other seafood
*population* (1996) 6,038,700 (about 54% in Sydney)
*history* visited by Captain James ◊Cook in 1770; convict settlement 1788–1850; opened to free settlement by 1819; achieved self-government in 1855; became a state of the Commonwealth of Australia in 1901.

**newspaper** daily or weekly publication in the form of folded sheets containing news and comment. News-sheets became commercial undertakings after the invention of printing and were introduced in 1609 in Germany and 1616 in the Netherlands. In 1622 the first newspaper appeared in English, the *Weekly News*, edited by Nicholas Bourne and Thomas Archer. Improved ◊printing (steam printing in 1814, the rotary press in 1846 in the USA and in 1857 in the UK), newsprint (paper made from woodpulp), and a higher literacy rate led to the growth of newspapers. In the 20th century production costs fell with the introduction of new technology.

**newt** small ◊salamander found in Europe, Asia, northwestern Africa, and North America. (Family Salamandridae, order Urodela.)

**New Testament** the second part of the ◊Bible, recognized by the Christian church from the 4th century as sacred doctrine. The New Testament includes the Gospels, which tell of the life and teachings of Jesus, the history of the early church, the teachings of St Paul, and mystical writings. It was written in Greek during the 1st and 2nd centuries AD, and the individual sections have been ascribed to various authors by biblical scholars.

**newton** SI unit (symbol N) of ◊force. One newton is the force needed to accelerate an object with mass of one kilogram by one metre per second per second. The weight of a medium size (100 g/3 oz) apple is one newton.

**Newton, Isaac** (1642–1727) English physicist and mathematician who laid the foundations of physics as a modern discipline. During 1665–66, he discovered the binomial theorem, differential and integral calculus, and that white light is composed of many colours. He developed the three standard laws of motion (see ◊Newton's laws of motion) and the universal law of gravitation, set out in *Philosophiae naturalis principia mathematica* (1687), usually referred to as the *Principia*. Knighted 1705.

**Newton's laws of motion** in physics, three laws that form the basis of Newtonian mechanics. (1) Unless acted upon by an unbalanced force, a body at rest stays at rest, and a moving body continues moving at the same speed in the same straight line. (2) An unbalanced force applied to a body gives it an acceleration proportional to the force (and in the direction of the force) and inversely proportional to the mass of the body. (3) When a body A exerts a force on a body B, B exerts an equal and opposite force on A; that is, to every action there is an equal and opposite reaction.

**New World** the Americas, so called by the first Europeans who reached them. The term also describes animals and plants of the western hemisphere.

**New York** the most populous city in the USA, located on an inlet of the Atlantic Ocean in the far southeastern corner of ◊New York State; population (1996 est, excluding suburban metropolitan areas under separate administration) 7,380,900. New York is composed of five city boroughs that are also counties of New York State: ◊Manhattan (New York County); the Bronx (Bronx County); ◊Queens (Queens County); Brooklyn (Kings County); and Staten Island (Richmond County). As well as being the main port in North America, New York is one of the world's principal commercial and cultural centres. The many industries and services operating here include banking and other financial activities, publishing and printing, the electronic media, advertising, clothing manufacture and the fashion industry, and the production of food, chemicals, machinery, and textiles. With its great diversity of cultural institutions, places of entertainment, and sightseeing opportunities, the city also attracts a large number of tourists each year. New York is also known as the 'Big Apple'.

**New York** state in northeast USA. It is nicknamed the Empire State. New York ratified the US Constitution in 1788, becoming the 11th state to join the Union. It is bordered to the north by the Canadian states of Québec and Ontario, to the east by Vermont, Massachusetts, and Connecticut, and to the south by Pennsylvania and New Jersey. In the west is a strip of Pennsylvania that reaches north to Lake Erie. New York has shores on both lakes Eries Ontario, between which it faces part of the state of Ontario across the Niagara River. In the southeast it faces New Jersey across the lower Hudson River. Long Island extends east from New York Bay into the Atlantic Ocean, with Connecticut and Rhode Island lying to the north across Long Island Sound
**population** (1995) 18,136,100
**area** 127,200 sq km/49,099 sq mi
**capital** Albany
**towns and cities** New York City, Buffalo, Rochester, Yonkers, Syracuse
**industries and products** dairy products, apples, clothing, periodical and book printing and publishing, electronic components and accessories, office machines and computers, communications equipment, motor vehicles and

equipment, pharmaceuticals, aircraft and parts, finance sector, tourism.

**New Zealand** Dominion of
**area** 268,680 sq km/103,737 sq mi

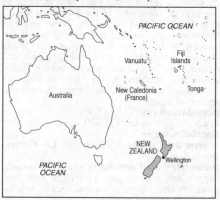

**capital** Wellington (and port)
**major towns/cities** Auckland, Hamilton, Palmerston North, Christchurch, Dunedin, Napier-Hastings
**major ports** Auckland
**physical features** comprises North Island, South Island, Stewart Island, Chatham Islands, and minor islands; mainly mountainous; Ruapehu in North Island, 2,797 m/9,180 ft, highest of three active volcanoes; geysers and hot springs of Rotorua district; Lake Taupo (616 sq km/238 sq mi), source of Waikato River; Kaingaroa state forest. In South Island are Southern Alps and Canterbury Plains
**territories** Tokelau (three atolls transferred in 1926 from former Gilbert and Ellice Islands colony); Niue Island (one of the Cook Islands, separately administered from 1903: chief town Alafi); Cook Islands are internally self-governing but share common citizenship with New Zealand; Ross Dependency in Antarctica
**head of state** Queen Elizabeth II from 1952, represented by governor general Catherine Tizard from 1990
**head of government** Jenny Shipley from 1997
**political system** constitutional monarchy
**political parties** Labour Party, moderate, left of centre; New Zealand National Party, free enterprise, centre right; Alliance Party bloc, left of centre, ecologists; New Zealand First Party (NZFP), centrist; United New Zealand Party (UNZ), centrist
**currency** New Zealand dollar
**GNP per capita (PPP)** (US$) 15,840 (1998)
**exports** meat, dairy products, wool, fish, timber and wood products, fruit and vegetables, aluminium, machinery. Principal market: Australia 21.2% (1998)
**population** 3,828,000 (1999 est)
**language** English (official), Maori
**religion** Christian
**life expectancy** 74 (men); 80 (women) (1995–2000)
**Chronology**
**1642** Dutch explorer Abel Tasman reached New

Zealand but indigenous Maoris prevented him from going ashore.

**1769** English explorer James Cook surveyed coastline of islands.

**1773 and 1777** Cook again explored coast.

**1815** First British missionaries arrived in New Zealand.

**1826** New Zealand Company founded in London to establish settlement.

**1839** New Zealand Company relaunched, after initial failure, by Edward Gibbon Wakefield.

**1840** Treaty of Waitangi: Maoris accepted British sovereignty; colonization began and large-scale sheep farming developed.

**1845–47** Maori revolt against loss of land.

**1851** Became separate colony (was originally part of Australian colony of New South Wales).

**1852** Colony procured constitution after dissolution of New Zealand Company; self-government fully implemented in 1856.

**1860–72** Second Maori revolt led to concessions, including representation in parliament.

**1891** New Zealand took part in Australasian Federal Convention in Sydney but rejected idea of joining Australian Commonwealth.

**1893** Became first country to give women the right to vote in parliamentary elections.

**1898** Liberal government under Richard Seddon introduced pioneering old-age pension scheme.

**1899–1902** Volunteers from New Zealand fought alongside imperial forces in Boer War.

**1907** New Zealand achieved dominion status within British Empire.

**1912–25** Government of Reform Party, led by William Massey, reflected interests of North Island farmers and strongly supported imperial unity.

**1914–18** 130,000 New Zealanders fought for British Empire in World War I.

**1916** Labour Party of New Zealand established.

**1931** Statute of Westminster affirmed equality of status between Britain and dominions, effectively granting independence to New Zealand.

**1935–49** Labour governments of Michael Savage and Peter Fraser introduced social reforms and encouraged state intervention in industry.

**1936** Liberal Party merged with Reform Party to create National Party.

**1939–45** New Zealand troops fought in World War II, notably in Crete, North Africa, and Italy.

**1947** Parliament confirmed independence of New Zealand within British Commonwealth.

**1951** New Zealand joined Australia and USA in ANZUS Pacific security treaty.

**1965–72** New Zealand contingent took part in Vietnam War.

**1973** British entry into European Economic Community (EEC) forced New Zealand to seek closer trading relations with Australia.

**1985** Non-nuclear military policy led to disagreements with France and USA.

**1986** The USA suspended defence obligations to New Zealand after it banned the entry of US warships.

**1988** A free-trade agreement was signed with Australia.

**1991** The Alliance Party was formed to challenge the two-party system.

**1997** Bolger was replaced as National Party leader and prime minister by Jenny Shipley.

**1998** The government was ordered to return more than £2 million worth of land confiscated from its Maori owners more than 30 years earlier.

**Ney, Michel** Duke of Elchingen, Prince of Ney (1769–1815) Marshal of France under ◊Napoleon I, who commanded the rearguard of the French army during the retreat from Moscow, and for his personal courage was called 'the bravest of the brave'. When Napoleon returned from Elba, Ney was sent to arrest him, but instead deserted to him and fought at Waterloo. He was subsequently shot for treason.

**NHS** abbreviation for *National Health Service,* the UK state-financed health service.

**Niagara Falls** two waterfalls on the Niagara River, on the Canada–USA border, between lakes Erie and Ontario and separated by Goat Island. The *American Falls* are 51 m/167 ft high, 330 m/1,080 ft wide; *Horseshoe Falls,* in Canada, are 49 m/160 ft high, 790 m/2,600 ft across.

**Niamey** port, capital, and administrative centre of Niger, in the southwest of the country, on the northeast bank of the Niger River; population (1988) 392,200. It produces textiles, chemicals, pharmaceuticals, and foodstuffs. It replaced Zinder as the capital in 1926. The National Museum is here.

**Nicaragua** Republic of
*national name Reṕublica de Nicaragua*

*area* 127,849 sq km/49,362 sq mi
*capital* Managua
*major towns/cities* León, Chinandega, Masaya, Granada
*major ports* Corinto, Puerto Cabezas, El Bluff
*physical features* narrow Pacific coastal plain separated from broad Atlantic coastal plain by volcanic mountains and lakes Managua and Nicaragua; one of world's most active earthquake regions
*head of state and government* Arnoldo Aleman from 1996

**political system** emergent democracy
**political parties** Sandinista National Liberation Front (FSLN), Marxist–Leninist; Opposition Political Alliance (APO, formerly National Opposition Union: UNO), loose US-backed coalition
**currency** cordoba
**GNP per capita (PPP)** (US$) 1,790 (1998 est)
**exports** coffee, meat, cotton, sugar, seafood, bananas, chemical products. Principal market: USA 34.8% (1998)
**population** 4,938,000 (1999 est)
**language** Spanish (official), Indian, English
**religion** Roman Catholic 95%
**life expectancy** 66 (men); 71 (women) (1995–2000)
**Chronology**
**10th century** AD Indians from Mexico and Mesoamerica migrated to Nicaragua's Pacific lowlands.
**1522** Visited by Spanish explorer Gil Gonzalez de Avila, who named the area Nicaragua after local Indian chief, Nicarao.
**1523–24** Colonized by the Spanish, under Francisco Hernandez de Cordoba, who was attracted by local gold deposits and founded cities of Granada and León.
**17th–18th centuries** British were dominant force on Caribbean side of Nicaragua, while Spain controlled Pacific lowlands.
**1821** Independence achieved from Spain; Nicaragua was initially part of Mexican Empire.
**1823** Became part of United Provinces (Fed-eration) of Central America, also embracing Costa Rica, El Salvador, Guatemala, and Honduras.
**1838** Became fully independent when it seceded from the Federation.
**1857–93** Ruled by succession of Conservative Party governments.
**1860** The British ceded control over Caribbean ('Mosquito') Coast to Nicaragua.
**1893** Liberal Party leader, José Santos Zelaya, deposed Conservative president and established dictatorship which lasted until overthrown by US marines in 1909.
**1912–25** At Nicaraguan government's request, with political situation deteriorating, USA estab-lished military bases and stationed marines.
**1927–33** Re-stationed US marines faced opposi-tion from anti-American guerrilla group led by Augusto César Sandino, who was assassinated in 1934 on the orders of the commander of the US-trained National Guard, Gen Anastasio Somoza Garcia.
**1937** Gen Somoza elected president; start of near-dictatorial rule by Somoza family, which amassed huge personal fortune.
**1956** Gen Somoza assassinated and succeeded as president by his elder son, Luis Somoza Debayle.
**1961** Left-wing Sandinista National Liberation Front (FSLN) formed to fight Somoza regime.
**1967** Luis Somoza died and was succeeded as president by his brother Anastasio Somoza Debayle, who headed an even more oppressive regime.
**1978** The Nicaraguan Revolution: Pedro Joaquin Chamorro, a popular publisher and leader of the anti-Somoza Democratic Liberation Union (UDEL), was assassinated, sparking a general strike and mass movement in which moderates joined with the FSLN to over-throw the Somoza regime.
**1979** The Somoza government was ousted by FSLN after a military offensive.
**1980** Anastasio Somoza was assassinated in Paraguay; a FSLN junta took power in Managua, headed by Daniel Ortega Saavedra; lands held by Somozas were nationalized and farming cooperatives established.
**1982** There was subversive activity against the government by right-wing Contra guerrillas, promoted by the USA, attacking from bases in Honduras. A state of emergency was declared.
**1984** US troops mined Nicaraguan harbours. The action was condemned by the World Court in 1986 and $17 billion in reparations ordered. FSLN won the assembly elections.
**1985** US president Ronald Reagan denounced the Sandinista government, vowing to 'remove it', and imposed a US trade embargo.
**1987** A Central American peace agreement was cosigned by Nicaraguan leaders.
**1988** The peace agreement failed. Nicaragua held talks with the Contra rebel leaders. A hur-ricane left 180,000 people homeless.
**1989** Demobilization of rebels and release of former Somozan supporters; the ceasefire ended but the economy was in ruins after the Contra war; there was 60% unemployment.
**1990** The FSLN was defeated by right-of-centre National Opposition Union (UNO), a US-backed coalition; Violeta Barrios de Chamorro, widow of the murdered Pedro Joaquin Cha-morro, was elected president. There were antigovernment riots.
**1992** Around 16,000 people were made home-less by an earthquake.
**1994** A peace accord was made with the remain-ing Contra rebels.
**1996** Right-wing candidate Arnoldo Aleman won the presidential elections.
**1998** Daniel Ortega was re-elected FSLN leader.

**Nice** city on the French ◊Riviera and adminis-trative centre of the *département* of Alpes-Maritimes, situated at the mouth of the River Paillon on the Baie des Anges, near the Italian frontier; population (1990) 345,700.

Founded in the 3rd century BC, it repeatedly changed hands between France and the Duchy of Savoy from the 14th to the 19th century. In 1860 it was finally transferred to France after a plebiscite. Nice is the fifth-largest city in France.

**Nicene Creed** one of the fundamental ◊creeds of Christianity, promulgated by the Council of Nicaea 325.

**niche** in ecology, the 'place' occupied by a species in its habitat, including all chemical, physical, and biological components, such as what it eats, the time of day at which the species feeds, temperature, moisture, the parts of the habitat that it uses (for example, trees or open grassland), the way it reproduces, and how it behaves.

**Nicholas** two tsars of Russia:

**Nicholas I** (1796–1855) Tsar of Russia from 1825. His Balkan ambitions led to war with Turkey 1827–29 and the Crimean War 1853–56.

**Nicholas II** (1868–1918) Tsar of Russia 1894–1917. He was dominated by his wife, Tsarina Alexandra, who was under the influence of the religious charlatan ◊Rasputin. His mismanagement of the Russo-Japanese War and of internal affairs led to the revolution of 1905, which he suppressed, although he was forced to grant limited constitutional reforms. He took Russia into World War I in 1914, was forced to abdicate in 1917 after the ◊Russian Revolution, and was executed with his family.

**Nicholas, St** (lived 4th century AD) also known as *Santa Claus,* In the Christian church, patron saint of Russia, children, merchants, sailors, and pawnbrokers; bishop of Myra (now in Turkey). His legendary gifts of dowries to poor girls led to the custom of giving gifts to children on the eve of his feast day, 6 December, still retained in some countries, such as the Netherlands; elsewhere the custom has been transferred to Christmas Day. His emblem is three balls.

**Nicholson, Ben(jamin Lauder)** (1894–1982) English abstract artist. After early experiments influenced by ◊Cubism and the Dutch ◊De Stijl group, Nicholson developed an elegant style of geometrical reliefs, notably a series of white reliefs (1933–38).

**Nicholson, Jack** (1937– ) US film actor and director. Films in which he has appeared include *One Flew Over the Cuckoo's Nest* (Academy Award) (1975), *The Shining* (1979), *Terms of Endearment* (Academy Award) (1983), and *Batman* 1989. In 1994 Nicholson received the American Film Institute's life achievement award. He was presented with an Academy Award for *As Good As It Gets* in 1998, and in the 1999 Golden Globe awards he received the Cecil B DeMille Lifetime Achievement Award.

**nickel** hard, malleable and ductile, silver-white metallic element, symbol Ni, atomic number 28, relative atomic mass 58.71. It occurs in igneous rocks and as a free metal (native metal), occasionally occurring in fragments of iron-nickel meteorites. It is a component of the Earth's core, which is held to consist principally of iron with some nickel. It has a high melting point, low electrical and thermal conductivity, and can be magnetized. It does not tarnish and therefore is much used for alloys, electroplating, and for coinage.

**Nicobar Islands** group of Indian islands, part of the Union Territory of ◊Andaman and Nicobar Islands.

**Nicosia** Greek *Lefkosia,* Turkish *Lefkosha,* capital of Cyprus, with leather, textile, and pottery industries; population (1993) 177,000. Nicosia was the residence of Lusignan kings of Cyprus 1192–1475. The Venetians, who took Cyprus 1489, surrounded Nicosia with a high wall, which still exists; the city fell to the Turks

1571. It was again partly taken by the Turks in the invasion 1974.

**nicotine** $C_{10}H_{14}N_2$ ◊alkaloid (nitrogenous compound) obtained from the dried leaves of the tobacco plant *Nicotiana tabacum* and used as an insecticide. A colourless oil, soluble in water, it turns brown on exposure to the air.

**Nietzsche, Friedrich Wilhelm** (1844–1900) German philosopher who rejected the accepted absolute moral values and the 'slave morality' of Christianity. He argued that 'God is dead' and therefore people were free to create their own values. His ideal was the *Übermensch,* or 'Superman', who would impose his will on the weak and worthless. Nietzsche claimed that knowledge is never objective but always serves some interest or unconscious purpose.

**Niger** Republic of
*national name République du Niger*

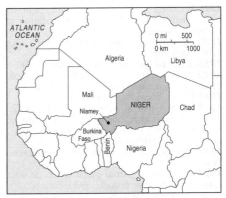

**area** 1,186,408 sq km/458,072 sq mi
**capital** Niamey
**major towns/cities** Zinder, Maradi, Tahoua, Agadez, Birui N'Konui
**physical features** desert plains between hills in north and savanna in south; River Niger in southwest, Lake Chad in southeast
**head of state** Daouda Mallam Wanke from 1999
**head of government** Ibrahim Hassane Mayaki from 1997
**political system** transitional
**political parties** National Movement for a Development Society (MNSD–Nassara), left of centre; Alliance of the Forces for Change (AFC), left-of-centre coalition; Party for Democracy and Socialism–Tarayya (PNDS–Tarayya), left of centre
**currency** franc CFA
**GNP per capita (PPP) (US$)** 830 (1998)
**exports** uranium ore, live animals, hides and skins, cow-peas, cotton. Principal market: USA 29.7% (1997)
**population** 10,401,000 (1999 est)
**language** French (official), Hausa, Djerma, and other minority languages
**religion** Sunni Muslim; also Christian, and traditional animist beliefs
**life expectancy** 47 (men); 50 (women) (1995–2000)

## Chronology

**10th–13th centuries** Kanem-Bornu Empire flourished in southeast, near Lake Chad, spreading Islam from the 11th century.

**15th century** Tuareg sultanate of Agades dominant in north.

**17th century** Songhai-speaking Djerma established an empire on Niger River.

**18th century** Powerful Gobir kingdom founded by Hausa people, who had migrated from south in 14th century.

**late 18th–early 19th centuries** Visited by European explorers, including the Scottish explorer, Mungo Park; Sultanate of Sokoto formed by Islamic revivalist Fulani, who had defeated the Hausa in a jihad (holy war).

**1890s** French conquered region and ended local slave trade.

**1904** Became part of French West Africa, although Tuareg resistance continued until 1922.

**1946** Became French overseas territory, with its own territorial assembly and representation in French Parliament.

**1958** Became autonomous republic within French community.

**1960** Achieved full independence; Hamani Diori of Niger Progressive Party (NPP) elected president, but maintained close ties with France.

**1971** Uranium production commenced.

**1974** Diori ousted in army coup led by Lt-Col Seyni Kountché after long Sahel drought had led to civil disorder; military government launched drive against corruption.

**1977** A cooperation agreement was signed with France.

**1984** There was a partial privatization of state firms due to further drought and increased government indebtedness as world uranium prices slumped.

**1987** Kountché died and was replaced by Gen Ali Saibu.

**1989** Ali Saibu was elected president without opposition.

**1991** Saibu was stripped of executive powers, and a transitional government was formed amid student and industrial unrest.

**1992** The transitional government collapsed amid economic problems and ethnic unrest among secessionist Tuareg in the north. A referendum approved of a new multiparty constitution.

**1993** The Alliance of the Forces for Change (AFC), a left-of-centre coalition, won an absolute majority in assembly elections. Mahamane Ousmane, a Muslim Hausa, was elected president in the first free presidential election.

**1994** A peace agreement was signed with northern Tuareg.

**1995** The AFC coalition won a general election with a reduced majority.

**1996** President Ousmane was ousted in a military coup led by Ibrahim Barre Mainassara. Civilian government was restored with Boukary Adji as premier; Mainassara was formally elected president.

**1999** President Mainassara was assassinated in coup; Major Daouda Mallam Wanke, the commander of Niger's presidential guard, assumed power.

**Niger** Semitic *Nihal,* third-longest river in Africa, 4,185 km/2,600 mi. It rises in the highlands bordering Sierra Leone and Guinea, flows northeast through Mali, then southeast through Niger and Nigeria to an inland delta on the Gulf of Guinea. Its total catchment area is 1.5 million sq km/579,150 sq mi. The flow is sluggish and the river frequently floods its banks. It was explored by the Scot Mungo Park 1795–1806, who was drowned in the river near Bussa.

**Nigeria** Federal Republic of

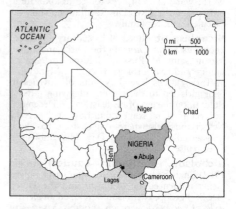

**area** 923,773 sq km/356,668 sq mi

**capital** Abuja

**major towns/cities** Ibadan, Lagos, Ogbomosho, Kano, Oshogbo, Ilorin, Abeokuta, Zaria, Ouitsha, Iwo, Kaduna

**major ports** Lagos, Port Harcourt, Warri, Calabar

**physical features** arid savanna in north; tropical rainforest in south, with mangrove swamps along coast; River Niger forms wide delta; mountains in southeast

**head of state and government** Olusegun Obasanjo from 1999

**political system** military republic

**political parties** Social Democratic Party (SDP), left of centre; National Republican Convention (NRC), right of centre

**currency** naira

**GNP per capita (PPP)** (US$) 820 (1998)

**exports** petroleum, cocoa beans, rubber, palm products, urea and ammonia, fish. Principal market: USA 36.9% (1997)

**population** 108,945,000 (1999 est)

**language** English (official), Hausa, Ibo, Yoruba

**religion** Sunni Muslim 50% (in north), Christian 40% (in south), local religions 10%

**life expectancy** 49 (men); 52 (women) (1995–2000)

## Chronology

**4th century BC–2nd century AD** Highly organized Nok culture flourished in northern Nigeria.

**9th century** Northeast Nigeria became part of empire of Kanem-Bornu, based around Lake Chad.

**11th century** Creation of Hausa states, including Kano and Katsina.

**13th century** Arab merchants introduced Islam in north.

**15th century** Empire of Benin at its height in south; first contact with European traders.

**17th century** Oyo Empire dominant in southwest; development of slave trade in Niger delta.

**1804–17** Islamic Fulani (or Sokoto) Empire established in north.

**1861** British traders procured Lagos; spread of Christian missionary activity in south.

**1884–1904** Britain occupied most of Nigeria by stages.

**1914** North and south protectorates united; growth of railway network and trade.

**1946** Nigerians allowed a limited role in decision-making in three regional councils.

**1951** Introduction of elected representation led to formation of three regional political parties.

**1954** New constitution increased powers of regions.

**1958** Oil discovered in southeast.

**1960** Achieved independence from Britain, within Commonwealth.

**1963** Became a republic, with Nnamdi Azikiwe as president.

**1966** Gen Aguiyi-Ironsi of Ibo tribe seized power and imposed unitary government; massacre of Ibo by Hausa in north; Gen Gowon seized power and restored federalism.

**1967** Conflict over oil revenues led to secession of eastern region as independent Ibo state of Biafra; ensuing civil war claimed up to a million lives.

**1970** Surrender of Biafra and end of civil war; development of oil industry financed more effective central government.

**1975** Gowon ousted in military coup; second coup put Gen Olusegun Obasanjo in power.

**1979** Civilian rule restored under President Shehu Shagari.

**1983** A bloodless coup was staged by Maj-Gen Muhammadu Buhari.

**1985** Buhari was replaced by Maj-Gen Ibrahim Babangida; Islamic northerners were dominant in the regime.

**1992** Multiparty elections were won by Babangida's SDP.

**1993** Moshood Abiola (SDP) won the first free presidential election; the results were suspended. Gen Sani Abacha restored military rule and dissolved political parties.

**1995** Commonwealth membership was suspended in protest at human-rights abuses by the military regime.

**1998** General Abdulsalam Abubakar took over as president following the death of Abacha. Nigeria's most prominent political prisoner, Moshood Abiola, died suddenly on the eve of his expected release. There were moves towards political liberalization, with the formation of new political parties and the release of some dissidents.

**1999** The People's Democratic Party won a Senate majority. Olusegun Obasanjo was elected president. Nigeria rejoined the Commonwealth.

**Niger-Congo languages** the largest group of languages in Africa. It includes about 1,000 languages and covers a vast area south of the Sahara desert, from the west coast to the east, and down the east coast as far as South Africa. It is divided into groups and subgroups; the most widely spoken Niger-Congo languages are Swahili (spoken on the east coast), the members of the Bantu group (southern Africa), and Yoruba (Nigeria).

**nightingale** songbird belonging to the thrush family; it sings with remarkable beauty by night as well as during the day. About 16.5 cm/6.5 in long, it is dull brown with a reddish-brown rounded tail; the breast is dull greyish-white, tinting to brown. It migrates in summer to Europe and winters in Africa. It feeds on insects, small animals, and occasionally fruit. It has a huge musical repertoire, built from about 900 melodic elements. (Species *Luscinia megarhyncos*, family Muscicapidae.)

**Nightingale, Florence** (1820–1910) English nurse, the founder of nursing as a profession. She took a team of nurses to Scutari (now Üsküdar, Turkey) in 1854 and reduced the ◊Crimean War hospital death rate from 42% to 2%. In 1856 she founded the Nightingale School and Home for Nurses in London.

**nightjar** any of about 65 species of night-hunting birds. They have wide, bristly mouths for catching flying insects. Their distinctive calls have earned them such names as 'whippoorwill' and 'church-will's-widow'. Some US species are called nighthawks. (Family Caprimulgidae, order Caprimulgiformes.)

**nightshade** any of several plants in the nightshade family. They include the annual herbaceous black nightshade (*S. nigrum*), with white flowers similar to those of the potato plant and black berries; the perennial shrubby bittersweet or woody nightshade (*S. dulcamara*), with purple, potatolike flowers and scarlet berries; and, belonging to a different genus, deadly nightshade or ◊belladonna (*A. belladonna*). (Genera *Solanum* and *Atropa,* family Solanaceae.)

**nihilism** the rejection of all traditional values, authority, and institutions. The term was coined in 1862 by Ivan Turgenev in his novel *Fathers and Sons,* and was adopted by the ◊Nihilists, the Russian radicals of the period. Despairing of reform, they saw change as possible only through the destruction of morality, justice, marriage, property, and the idea of God. Since then nihilism has come to mean a generally negative and destructive outlook.

**Nihilist** member of a group of Russian revolutionaries in the reign of Alexander II 1855–81. Despairing of reform, they saw change as possible only through the destruction of morality, justice, marriage, property, and the idea of God. In 1878 the Nihilists launched a guerrilla campaign leading to the murder of the tsar 1881.

**Nijinsky, Vaslav Fomich** (1890–1950) Russian dancer and choreographer. Noted for his powerful but graceful technique, he was a legendary member of ◊Diaghilev's Ballets Russes, for whom he choreographed Debussy's *Prélude à l'après-midi d'un faune* (1912) and *Jeux* (1913), and Stravinsky's *Le Sacre du printemps/ The Rite of Spring* (1913).

**Nile** (Semitic *nihal* 'river') river in Africa, the world's longest, 6,695 km/4,160 mi. The *Blue Nile* rises in Lake Tana, Ethiopia, the *White Nile* at Lake Victoria, and they join at Khartoum, Sudan. The river enters the Mediterranean Sea at a vast delta in northern Egypt.

**Nineveh** capital of the Assyrian Empire from the 8th century BC until its destruction by the Medes under King Cyaxares in 612 BC. It was situated on the River Tigris (opposite the present city of Mosul, Iraq) and was adorned with palaces.

**Ningxia Hui Autonomous Region** or *Ningxia;* formerly *Ninghsia*, administrative area of northwest China, bounded to the north by Inner Mongolia, to the east by Shaanxi, and to the south by Gansu
**area** 66,400 sq km/25,940 sq mi
**capital** Yinchuan
**physical** desert plateau; Huang He River
**industries** coal, chemicals
**agriculture** cereals and rice under irrigation, animal herding
**population** (1996) 5,210,000; one-third are Hui (Chinese Muslims); large Mongolian element in the north.

**niobium** soft, grey-white, somewhat ductile and malleable, metallic element, symbol Nb, atomic number 41, relative atomic mass 92.906. It occurs in nature with tantalum, which it resembles in chemical properties. It is used in making stainless steel and other alloys for jet engines and rockets and for making superconductor magnets.

**Nippon** or *Nihon*, English transliteration of the Japanese name for Japan.

**nirvana** (Sanskrit 'a blowing out') in Buddhism, and other Indian religions, the ultimate religious goal characterized by the attainment of perfect serenity, compassion, and wisdom by the eradication of all desires. When nirvana is attained, the cycle of life and death, known as transmigration, is broken and a state of liberty, free from pain and desire, is reached.

**nitrate** salt or ester of nitric acid, containing the $NO_3^-$ ion. Nitrates are used in explosives, in the chemical and pharmaceutical industries, in curing meat (see ◊nitre), and as fertilizers. They are the most water-soluble salts known and play a major part in the nitrogen cycle. Nitrates in the soil, whether naturally occurring or from inorganic or organic fertilizers, can be used by plants to make proteins and nucleic acids. However, runoff from fields can result in nitrate pollution.

**nitre** or *saltpetre*, potassium nitrate, $KNO_3$, a mineral found on and just under the ground in desert regions; used in explosives. Nitre occurs in Bihar, India, Iran, and Cape Province, South Africa. The salt was formerly used for the manufacture of gunpowder, but the supply of nitre for explosives is today largely met by making the salt from nitratine (also called Chile saltpetre, $NaNO_3$). Saltpetre is a preservative and is widely used for curing meats.

**nitric acid** or *aqua fortis*, $HNO_3$ fuming acid obtained by the oxidation of ammonia or the action of sulphuric acid on potassium nitrate. It is a highly corrosive acid, dissolving most metals, and a strong oxidizing agent. It is used in the nitration and esterification of organic substances, and in the making of sulphuric acid, nitrates, explosives, plastics, and dyes.

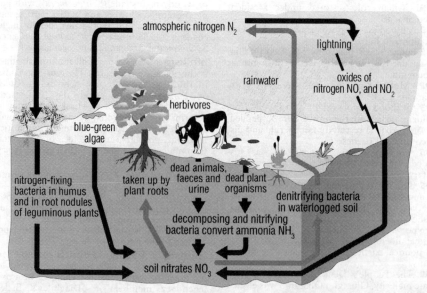

**nitrogen cycle** *The nitrogen cycle is one of a number of cycles during which the chemicals necessary for life are recycled. The carbon, sulphur, and phosphorus cycles are others. Since there is only a limited amount of these chemicals in the Earth and its atmosphere, the chemicals must be continuously recycled if life is to go on.*

**nitrification** process that takes place in soil when bacteria oxidize ammonia, turning it into nitrates. Nitrates can be absorbed by the roots of plants, so this is a vital stage in the ◊nitrogen cycle.

**nitrite** salt or ester of nitrous acid, containing the nitrite ion ($NO_2^-$). Nitrites are used as preservatives (for example, to prevent the growth of botulism spores) and as colouring agents in cured meats such as bacon and sausages.

**nitrogen** (Greek *nitron* 'native soda', sodium or potassium nitrate) colourless, odourless, tasteless, gaseous, nonmetallic element, symbol N, atomic number 7, relative atomic mass 14.0067. It forms almost 80% of the Earth's atmosphere by volume and is a constituent of all plant and animal tissues (in proteins and nucleic acids). Nitrogen is obtained for industrial use by the liquefaction and fractional distillation of air. Its compounds are used in the manufacture of foods, drugs, fertilizers, dyes, and explosives.

**nitrogen cycle** the process of nitrogen passing through the ecosystem. Nitrogen, in the form of inorganic compounds (such as nitrates) in the soil, is absorbed by plants and turned into organic compounds (such as proteins) in plant tissue. A proportion of this nitrogen is eaten by ◊herbivores, with some of this in turn being passed on to the carnivores, which feed on the herbivores. The nitrogen is ultimately returned to the soil as excrement and when organisms die and are converted back to inorganic form by decomposers.

**nitrogen fixation** the process by which nitrogen in the atmosphere is converted into nitrogenous compounds by the action of microorganisms, such as cyanobacteria (see ◊blue-green algae) and bacteria, in conjunction with certain legumes. Several chemical processes duplicate nitrogen fixation to produce fertilizers; see ◊nitrogen cycle.

**nitrogen oxide** any chemical compound that contains only nitrogen and oxygen. All nitrogen oxides are gases. Nitrogen monoxide and nitrogen dioxide contribute to air pollution. See also ◊nitrous oxide.

**nitroglycerine** $C_3H_5(ONO_2)_3$, flammable, explosive oil produced by the action of nitric and sulphuric acids on glycerol. Although poisonous, it is used in cardiac medicine. It explodes with great violence if heated in a confined space and is used in the preparation of dynamite, cordite, and other high explosives.

**nitrous oxide** or *dinitrogen oxide,* $N_2O$ colourless, nonflammable gas that, used in conjunction with oxygen, reduces sensitivity to pain. In higher doses it is an anaesthetic. Well tolerated, it is often combined with other anaesthetic gases to enable them to be used in lower doses. It may be self-administered; for example, in childbirth. It is a greenhouse gas; about 10% of nitrous oxide released into the atmosphere comes from the manufacture of nylon. It used to be known as 'laughing gas'.

**Niven, (James) David (Graham)** (1910–1983) Scottish-born US film actor. A suave and sophisticated leading man, he made films in Hollywood and Britain from the 1930s, often featuring in witty comedies and war films. His films include *Wuthering Heights* (1939), *Around the World in 80 Days* (1956), *Separate Tables* (1958) (Academy Award), *The Guns of Navarone* (1961), and *The Pink Panther* (1964).

**Nixon, Richard M(ilhous)** (1913–1994) 37th president of the USA 1969–74, a Republican. He attracted attention as a member of the House Un-American Activities Committee 1948, and was vice-president to Eisenhower 1953–61. As president he was responsible for US withdrawal from Vietnam, and the normalization of relations with communist China, but at home his culpability in the cover-up of the ◊Watergate scandal and the existence of a 'slush fund' for political machinations during his re-election campaign of 1972 led him to resign in 1974 when threatened with ◊impeachment.

**Nkomo, Joshua** (1917–1999) Zimbabwean trade unionist and politician, vice president 1990–99. As president of ZAPU (Zimbabwe African People's Union) from 1961, he was a leader of the black nationalist movement against the white Rhodesian regime. He was a member of Robert ◊Mugabe's cabinet 1980–82 and from 1987.

**Nkrumah, Kwame** (1909–1972) Ghanaian nationalist politician, prime minister of the Gold Coast (Ghana's former name) 1952–57 and of newly independent Ghana 1957–60. He became Ghana's first president in 1960 but was overthrown in a coup in 1966. His policy of 'African socialism' led to links with the communist bloc.

**Nō** or *Noh,* classical, aristocratic Japanese drama which developed from the 14th to the 16th centuries and is still performed. There is a repertory of some 250 pieces, of which five, one from each of the several classes devoted to different subjects, may be put on in a performance lasting a whole day. Dance, mime, music, and chanting develop the mythical or historical themes. All the actors are men, some of whom wear masks and elaborate costumes; scenery is limited. Nō influenced kabuki drama.

**Noah** in the Old Testament, the son of Lamech and father of Shem, Ham, and Japheth, who, according to God's instructions, built a ship, the ark, so that he and his family and specimens of all existing animals might survive the Flood. There is also a Babylonian version of the tale, the *Epic of* ◊*Gilgamesh.*

**nobelium** synthesized, radioactive, metallic element of the ◊actinide series, symbol No, atomic number 102, relative atomic mass 259. It is synthesized by bombarding curium with carbon nuclei.

**Nobel prize** annual international prize, first awarded in 1901 under the will of Alfred Nobel, Swedish chemist, who invented dynamite. The interest on the Nobel endowment fund is divided annually among the persons who have made the greatest contributions in the fields of physics, chemistry, medicine, literature, and world peace. The first four are awarded by academic committees based in Sweden, while the peace prize is awarded by a committee of the Norwegian parliament. A sixth prize, for economics, financed by the Swedish National Bank, was first awarded in 1969. The prizes have a large cash award and are given to organizations – such as the United Nations peacekeeping forces, which received the Nobel Peace Prize in 1988 – as well as individuals.

**noble gas** alternative name for ◊inert gas.

**nocturne** in music, a reflective character piece, often for piano, introduced by John Field (1782–1837) and adopted by Chopin.

**Nofretete** alternative name for ◊Nefertiti, queen of Egypt.

**nonaligned movement** countries adopting a strategic and political position of neutrality ('nonalignment') towards major powers, specifically the USA and former USSR. Although originally used by poorer states, the nonaligned position was later adopted by oil-producing nations. Its 113 members hold more than half the world's population and 85% of oil resources, but only 7% of global GDP (1995).

**Nonconformist** in religion, originally a member of the Puritan section of the Church of England clergy who, in the Elizabethan age, refused to conform to certain practices, for example the wearing of the surplice and kneeling to receive Holy Communion.

**nonmetal** one of a set of elements (around 20 in total) with certain physical and chemical properties opposite to those of metals. Nonmetals accept electrons and are sometimes called electronegative elements.

**noradrenaline** in the body, a catecholamine that acts directly on specific receptors to stimulate the sympathetic nervous system. Released by nerve stimulation or by drugs, it slows the heart mainly by constricting arterioles (small arteries) and so raising blood pressure. It is used therapeutically to treat ◊shock.

**Nord-Pas-de-Calais** region of northern France; area 12,400 sq km/4,786 sq mi; population (1990) 3,965,100. Its administrative centre is ◊Lille, and it consists of the *départements* of Nord and Pas-de-Calais.

**Norfolk** county of eastern England
**area** 5,360 sq km/2,069 sq mi
**towns and cities** ◊Norwich (administrative headquarters), King's Lynn, Great Yarmouth (ports); Cromer, Hunstanton (resorts)
**physical** low-lying with the Fens in the west and the ◊Norfolk Broads in the east; rivers Bure, Ouse, Waveney, Yare
**features** the Broads (a series of lakes famous for fishing and water fowl, and for boating); Halvergate Marshes wildlife area; traditional reed thatching; Grime's Graves (Neolithic flint mines); shrine of Our Lady of Walsingham, a medieval and present-day centre of pilgrimage; Blickling Hall (Jacobean, built 1619–24,

situated 14 km/7 mi south of Cromer); residence of Elizabeth II at Sandringham (built 1869–71)
**agriculture** cereals (wheat and barley); fruit and vegetables (beans, sugar beets, swedes, turnips); turkeys, geese, cattle; fishing centred on Great Yarmouth
**industries** agricultural implements; boots and shoes; brewing and malting; offshore natural gas; tanning; there are flour mills and mustard works
**population** (1996) 777,000
**famous people** Fanny Burney, John Sell Cotman, John Crome ('Old Crome'), Diana, Princess of Wales, Rider Haggard, Horatio Nelson, Thomas Paine.

**Norfolk Broads** area of interlinked shallow freshwater lakes in East Anglia, eastern England, between Norwich, Sea Palling, and Lowestoft. The area has about 200 km/125 mi of navigable waterways, and the region is a popular tourist destination for boating and fishing.

**Noriega Morena, Manuel (Antonio)** (1940– ) Panamanian soldier and politician, effective ruler of Panama from 1983, as head of the National Guard, until deposed by the USA in 1989. An informer for the US Central Intelligence Agency (CIA) from the late 1960s, he was known to be involved in drug trafficking as early as 1972.

He enjoyed US support until 1987. In the December 1989 US invasion of Panama, he was forcibly taken to the USA. He was tried and convicted of cocaine trafficking and money laundering in 1992.

**Norman** any of the descendants of the Norsemen (to whose chief, Rollo, Normandy was granted by Charles III of France in 911) who adopted French language and culture. During the 11th and 12th centuries they conquered England in 1066 (under William the Conqueror), Scotland in 1072, parts of Wales and Ireland, southern Italy, Sicily, and Malta, and took a prominent part in the Crusades.

**Norman Conquest** invasion and settlement of England by the ◊Normans, following the victory of ◊William the Conqueror at the Battle of ◊Hastings in 1066.

**Normandy** French *Normandie*, former duchy of northwest France now divided into two regions: ◊Haute-Normandie and ◊Basse-Normandie; area 29,900 sq km/11,544 sq mi; population (both parts, 1990) 3,146,500. Normandy was named after the Viking Norsemen (Normans) who conquered and settled in the area in the 9th century. As a French duchy it reached its peak under William the Conqueror and was renowned for its centres of learning established by Lanfranc and St Anselm. Normandy was united with England from 1100 to 1135. England and France fought over it during the Hundred Years' War, England finally losing it in 1449 to Charles VII. In World War II the Normandy beaches were the site of the Allied invasion on D-day, 6 June 1944.

**Normandy landings** alternative name for ◊D-day.

**Norse** early inhabitant of Norway or Scandinavia; also referring to their language and culture.

**Norsemen** early inhabitants of Norway. The term Norsemen is also applied to Scandinavian ◊Vikings who traded, explored, and raided far afield from their homelands during the 8th–11th centuries, settling in Iceland, Greenland, Russia, the British Isles, and northern France. The term is sometimes used to refer specifically to western Scandinavians or just to Norwegians.

**North, Frederick** 2nd Earl of Guilford, known as Lord North (1732–1792) English Tory politician. He entered Parliament in 1754, became chancellor of the Exchequer in 1767, and was prime minister in a government of Tories and 'king's friends' from 1770. His hard line against the American colonies was supported by George III, but in 1782 he was forced to resign by the failure of his policy. In 1783 he returned to office in a coalition with Charles ◊Fox. After its defeat, he retired from politics. Earl 1790.

**North, Oliver** (1943– ) US Marine lieutenant colonel. In 1981 he joined the staff of the National Security Council (NSC), where he supervised the mining of Nicaraguan harbours 1983, an air-force bombing raid on Libya 1986, and an arms-for-hostages deal with Iran 1985, which, when uncovered 1986 (◊Irangate), forced his dismissal and trial.

**North America** third largest of the continents (including Greenland and Central America), and over twice the size of Europe
*area* 24,000,000 sq km/9,400,000 sq mi
*largest cities* (population over 1 million) Mexico City, New York, Chicago, Toronto, Los Angeles, Montréal, Guadalajara, Monterrey, Philadelphia, Houston, Guatemala City, Vancouver, Detroit, San Diego, Dallas
*physical* occupying the northern part of the landmass of the western hemisphere between the Arctic Ocean and the tropical southeast tip of the isthmus that joins Central America to South America; the northernmost point on the mainland is the tip of Boothia Peninsula in the Canadian Arctic; the northernmost point on adjacent islands is Cape Morris Jesup on Greenland; the most westerly point on the mainland is Cape Prince of Wales, Alaska; the most westerly point on adjacent islands is Attu Island in the Aleutians; the most easterly point on the mainland lies on the southeast coast of Labrador; the highest point is Mount McKinley, Alaska, 6,194 m/20,320 ft; the lowest point is Badwater in Death Valley –86 m/–282 ft.
Perhaps the most dominating characteristic is the western cordillera running parallel to the coast from Alaska to Panama; it is called the ◊Rocky Mountains in the USA and Canada and its continuation into Mexico is called the ◊Sierra Madre. The cordillera is a series of ranges divided by intermontane plateaus and takes up about one-third of the continental area.
To the east of the cordillera lie the Great Plains, the agricultural heartland of North America, which descend in a series of steps to the depressions occupied by the ◊Great Lakes in the east and the Gulf of Mexico coastal lowlands in the southeast. The Plains are characterized by treeless expanses crossed by broad, shallow river valleys. To the north and east of the region lie the Laurentian Highlands of Canada, an ancient plateau or shield area. Glaciation has deeply affected its landscape. In the east are the Appalachian Mountains, flanked by the narrow coastal plain which widens further south. Erosion here has created a line of planed crests, or terraces, at altitudes between 300–1,200 m/985–3,935 ft. This has also formed a ridge-and-valley topography which was an early barrier to continental penetration. The Fall Line is the abrupt junction of plateau and coastal plain in the east.
*features* Lake Superior (the largest body of fresh water in the world); Grand Canyon on the Colorado River; Redwood National Park, California, has some of the world's tallest trees; San Andreas Fault, California; deserts: Death Valley, Mojave, Sonoran; rivers (over 1,600 km/1,000 mi) include Mississippi, Missouri, Mackenzie, Rio Grande, Yukon, Arkansas, Colorado, Saskatchewan-Bow, Columbia, Red, Peace, Snake.

**Northamptonshire** county of central England
*area* 2,370 sq km/915 sq mi
*towns and cities* Northampton (administrative headquarters), Kettering, Corby, Daventry, Wellingborough
*physical* rivers Avon, Cherwell, Leam, Nene, Ouse, and Welland
*features* Althorp Park, Spencer family home and burial place of Diana, Princess of Wales; Canons Ashby, Tudor house, home of the Drydens for 400 years; churches with broached spires (an octagonal spire on a square tower)
*agriculture* cereals (wheat and barley), sugar beet, sheep rearing; cattle rearing, especially in the Nene and Welland valleys, where there is rich pasture
*industries* engineering, food processing, printing, shoemaking; Northampton is the centre of the leather trade in England
*population* (1996) 604,300
*famous people* Robert Browne, John Dryden, Charles Kingsley, Richard III; the family of George Washington, first president of the USA, originated at Sulgrave Manor.

**Northants** abbreviation for ◊Northamptonshire, an English county.

**North Atlantic Treaty** agreement signed on 4 April 1949 by Belgium, Canada, Denmark, France, Iceland, Italy, Luxembourg, the Netherlands, Norway, Portugal, the UK, the USA; Greece, Turkey 1952; West Germany 1955; and Spain 1982. They agreed that 'an armed attack against one or more of them in Europe or North America shall be considered an attack against them all'. The ◊North Atlantic Treaty Organization (NATO) is based on this agreement.

**North Atlantic Treaty Organization** (NATO), association set up in April 1949 in response to the Soviet blockade of Berlin, to provide for the collective defence of the major Western European and North American states against the perceived threat from the USSR. The collapse of communism in eastern Europe from 1989 prompted the most radical review of its policy and defence strategy since its inception. After the Eastern European Warsaw Pact was disbanded in 1991, an adjunct to NATO, the *North Atlantic Cooperation Council* (NACC), was established, including all the former Soviet republics, with the aim of building greater security in Europe. In 1992 it was agreed that the Organization for Security and Cooperation in Europe would in future authorize all NATO's military responses within Europe.

At the 1994 Brussels summit a 'partnership for peace' (PFP) programme was formally launched, inviting former members of the Warsaw Pact and ex-Soviet republics to take part in a wide range of military cooperation arrangements, including training alongside NATO members and opening up defence plans. Romania was the first to join, followed by Estonia, Lithuania, and Poland; Russia agreed to participate in 1995. By 1996 the partnership included 27 countries, comprising the 15 former Soviet republics, Austria, Hungary, the Slovak Republic, Bulgaria, Malta, Albania, the Czech Republic, the Former Yugoslav Republic of Macedonia, Finland, and Sweden.

In May 1997, a NATO–Russia security pact, called the Founding Act on Mutual Relations, Cooperation and Security, was signed in Paris by all 16 NATO heads of government and Russian President Yeltsin. The charter gave Russia an assurance that NATO had no intention of siting nuclear weapons or allowing major troop deployments on the territories of new eastern European member-states. It also created a Russian–NATO advisory council, which, however, would have no veto over NATO actions.

NATO's secretary general, Javier Solana, announced in July 1997 the historic decision to invite Poland, Hungary, and the Czech Republic to join the alliance, signalling the biggest single expansion in NATO's history. In December 1997 the 1949 Washington Treaty was amended to allow these countries join NATO. The three states were invited during the Madrid summit to join NATO in 1999. The Madrid summit decision meant that countries with a population totalling 60 million, and armed forces of 382,000, would join NATO in 1999, increasing the military alliance's territory by 14%. The three countries officially became members of NATO in March 1999.

The US Senate voted in early May 1998 by a large majority to approve the inclusion of the Czech Republic, Hungary, and Poland in NATO. The vote was a foreign policy victory for President Clinton who had carefully steered the policy of NATO expansion through an initially sceptical political establishment. The vote made the USA the fifth country to ratify NATO expansion.

**North Ayrshire** unitary authority in western Scotland, created in 1996 from Cunninghame district in Strathclyde region

*area* 889 sq km/343 sq mi
*towns* Irvine (administrative headquarters), Kilwinning, Saltcoats, Largs, Kilbirnie
*physical* low-lying coastal plain on the mainland, rising inland to a plateau of over 305 m/ 1,000 ft; the islands of the Firth of Clyde are Arran, Holy Isle, Cumbraes; the rivers Irvine and Garnock reach the sea at Irvine; Goat Fell (874 m/2,867 ft)
*features* Pencil Monument, Largs; Scottish Maritime Museum, Irvine; Hunterston nuclear power station
*industries* chemicals, electronics, computer manufacturing
*agriculture* dairying, potatoes
*population* (1996) 139,200
*history* Eglinton Tournament (19th century); Battle of Largs (1263), when the Scots captured the Hebrides from the Norwegians.

**North Brabant** Dutch *Noord Brabant,* largest province of the Netherlands, located in the south of the country, lying between the Maas River (Meuse) and Belgium
*area* 4,940 sq km/1,907 sq mi
*capital* 's-Hertogenbosch
*towns and cities* Breda, Eindhoven, Tilburg
*physical* flat and marshy; former heathland is now under mixed farming
*industries* brewing, tobacco, engineering, microelectronics, textiles
*agriculture* cattle, wheat; sugar-beet in the northeast
*population* (1997) 2,304,100
*history* in the Middle Ages the duchy of Brabant included South Brabant, which is now a province of Belgium.

**North Cape** Norwegian *Nordkapp,* cape in the Norwegian county of Finnmark; the most northerly point of Europe.

**North Carolina** state in eastern USA. It is nicknamed the Tar Heel State or Old North State. North Carolina ratified the US Constitution in 1789, becoming the 12th state to join the Union. It is bordered to the north by Virginia, to the west and northwest by Tennessee, to the south by Georgia and South Carolina, and to the east by the Atlantic Ocean
*population* (1995) 7,195,100
*area* 136,400 sq km/52,650 sq mi
*capital* Raleigh
*towns and cities* Charlotte, Greensboro, Winston-Salem, Durham
*industries and products* tobacco, corn, soy bean, livestock, poultry, textiles, clothing, cigarettes, furniture, chemicals, machinery, tourism, finance sector, research.

**Northcliffe, Alfred Charles William Harmsworth** 1st Viscount Northcliffe (1865–1922) British newspaper proprietor, born in Dublin. Founding the *Daily Mail* in 1896, he revolutionized popular journalism, and with the *Daily Mirror* in 1903 introduced the illustrated paper. In 1908 he also obtained control of *The Times.*

**Northd** abbreviation for ◊*Northumberland,* an English county.

**North Dakota** state in the northern USA. It is nicknamed the Peace Garden State. North Dakota was admitted to the Union in 1889 as the 39th US state. Part of the Midwest, and one of the Great Plains states, it is bordered to the south by South Dakota, to the west by Montana, to the north by the Canadian states of Saskatchewan and Manitoba, and to the east by Minnesota. North Dakota remains the most rural of all the US states
*population* (1995) 641,400
*area* 183,100 sq km/70,677 sq mi
*capital* Bismarck
*towns and cities* Fargo, Grand Forks, Minot
*industries and products* cereals, meat products, farm equipment, oil, coal, tourism.

**North-East India** or *North-East Hill States,* area of India (Meghalaya, Assam, Mizoram, Tripura, Manipur,Nagaland, and Arunachal Pradesh) linked with the rest of India only by a narrow corridor, and bounded by Myanmar (Burma), China, Bhutan and Bangaladesh. There is opposition to immigration from Bangladesh and the rest of India, and demand for secession.

**North East Lincolnshire** unitary authority in eastern England created in 1996 from part of the former county of Humberside
*area* 192 sq km/74 sq mi
*towns and cities* Grimsby (administrative headquarters), Immingham, Cleethorpes, Humberston, New Waltham, Waltham, Healing, Laceby
*features* Humber Estuary forms east border of authority; River Freshney; Immingham Museum; National Fishing Heritage Centre (Grimsby)
*industries* fishing and associated industries, docks and shipping services at Immingham and Grimsby, chemical manufacture, heavy engineering, marine engineering, oil refining, tourism (Cleethorpes)
*population* (1996) 164,000.

**Northeast Passage** sea route from the North Atlantic, around Asia, to the North Pacific, pioneered by the Swedish explorer Nils Nordenskjöld 1878–79 and developed by the USSR in settling Northern Siberia from 1935.

**Northern Cape** province of the Republic of South Africa from 1994, formerly part of Cape Province
*area* 363,389 sq km/140,305 sq mi
*capital* Kimberley
*features* largest and most sparsely populated province; Orange River; Kalahari Desert; Kalahari-Gemsbok, Richtersveld, Augrabies Falls, and Vaalbos national parks
*industries* diamonds, iron, manganese, asbestos, cotton
*population* (1995 est) 742,000
*languages* Afrikaans 65%, Setswana (Tswana) 22%, Xhosa 4%.

**Northern Ireland Assembly** in the UK, power-sharing assembly based in Belfast, Northern Ireland. The assembly came into being as a result of the 10 April 1998 Good Friday Peace Agreement between the contending Unionist and Irish Nationalist communities in Northern Ireland. The agreement negotiated the devolution of a range of executive and legislative powers – in areas such as agriculture, economic development, education, the environment, finance, health, and social security – from the secretary of state for Northern Ireland to an elected assembly. The assembly effectively took over much of the work of the Northern Ireland Office, although the post of secretary of state for Northern Ireland remains. Elections were first held on 25 June 1998. The Assembly met for the first time on 1 July 1998, but did not become fully operational until later in 1999.

**northern lights** common name for the ◊aurora borealis.

**Northern Mariana Islands** archipelago in the northwestern Pacific, with ◊Guam known collectively as the Mariana Islands. The Northern Marianas are a commonwealth in union with the USA.
*area* 471 sq km/182 sq mi
*capital* Garapan on Saipan
*physical* 16 islands and atolls extending 560 km/350 mi north of Guam
*political system* liberal democracy
*political parties* Democratic Party, centre-left; Republican Party, right of centre; Territorial Party, nationalist
*currency* US dollar
*population* (1995 est) 47,200
*language* English
*religion* mainly Roman Catholicism
*history* came under Spanish control in 1565; sold to Germany in 1899; came under Japanese control in 1914 and Japanese rule under a League of Nations mandate in 1921. Taken by US marines in World War II, the islands became a UN Trust Territory administered by the USA in 1947 and a US commonwealth territory in 1978. Granted internal self-government and full US citizenship in 1986. UN Trusteeship status ended on 22 December 1990.

**Northern Province** formerly *Northern Transvaal,* province of the Republic of South Africa from 1994, formerly part of Transvaal
*area* 119,606 sq km/46,180 sq mi
*capital* Pietersburg
*features* Limpopo River, Soutpansberg Mountains
*industries* diamonds, copper, asbestos, iron, tourism. Many people in rural areas are migrant workers in Gauteng province.
*agriculture* wheat, maize, tobacco, groundnuts
*population* (1995 est) 5,397,200
*languages* Sepedi (North Sotho) 56%, Shangaan 22%, Venda 12%.

**Northern Rhodesia** former name (to 1964) of ◊Zambia, a country in Africa.

**Northern Territory** territory of north-central Australia, bounded on the north by the Timor and Arafura seas, on the east by Queensland, on the south by South Australia, and on the west by Western Australia
*area* 1,346,200 sq km/519,770 sq mi
*capital* ◊Darwin

***towns and cities*** Alice Springs, Katherine, Tennant Creek, Humpty Doo

***features*** Macdonnell Ranges (Mount Zeil 1,525 m/5,003 ft); ◊Arnhem Land; Kakadu National Park, with 50,000–60,000-year-old rock paintings of animals, birds, and fish; ◊Ayers Rock, the largest monolith in the world; Northern Territory University

***products*** beef, bauxite, gold, copper, uranium, manganese, tropical fruits, fish

***population*** (1996) 195,100

***government*** an administrator and a Legislative Assembly (25 elected members); represented in the federal parliament

***history*** part of New South Wales from 1827; annexed to South Australia in 1863; under the control of the Commonwealth of Australia government, 1911–1978; self-government introduced in 1978; mineral discoveries on land occupied by Aborigines led to a royalty agreement in 1979.

**Northern Transvaal** former name of ◊Northern Province, a province of the Republic of South Africa.

**North Holland** Dutch *Noord Holland,* lowlying coastal province of the Netherlands occupying the peninsula jutting northward between the North Sea and the IJsselmeer, bounded on the south by the provinces of South Holland and Utrecht, and including the island of *Texel* on the north side

***area*** 2,670 sq km/1,031 sq mi

***capital*** ◊Haarlem

***towns and cities*** Amsterdam, Hilversum, Den Helder; and the cheese centres, Alkmaar and Edam

***physical*** mostly below sea level, protected from the sea by a series of sand dunes and artificial dykes

***features*** mainly urban concentrations and dormitory towns; canals including the North Holland Canal and the North Sea Canal

***industries*** iron and steel works

***agriculture*** dairy products, flower bulbs, grain, and vegetables

***population*** (1997) 2,474,800

***history*** once part of the former county of Holland that was divided into two provinces (North and South) in 1840.

**North Korea** People's Democratic Republic of

***national name*** *Chosun Minchu-chui Inmin Konghwa-guk*

***area*** 120,538 sq km/46,539 sq mi

***capital*** Pyongyang

***major towns/cities*** Hamhung, Chongjin, Nampo, Wonsan, Sinuiji

***physical features*** wide coastal plain in west rising to mountains cut by deep valleys in interior

***head of state*** Kim Jong Il from 1994

***head of government*** Hong Song Nam from 1997

***political system*** communism

***political parties*** Korean Workers' Party (KWP), Marxist-Leninist (leads Democratic Front for the Reunification of the Fatherland, including Korean Social Democratic Party and Chondoist Chongu Party)

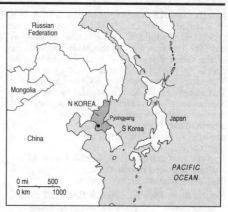

***currency*** won

***GNP per capita (PPP)*** (US$) 845 (1997 est)

***exports*** base metals, textiles, vegetable products, machinery and equipment. Principal market: Japan 27.9% (1995 est)

***population*** 23,702,000 (1999 est)

***language*** Korean

***religion*** Chondoist, Buddhist, Christian, traditional beliefs

***life expectancy*** 69 (men); 75 (women) (1995–2000)

***Chronology***

***2333 BC*** Legendary founding of Korean state by Tangun dynasty.

***1122 BC–4th century AD*** Period of Chinese Kija dynasty.

***668–1000*** Peninsula unified by Buddhist Shilla kingdom, with capital at Kyongju.

***1392–1910*** Period of Chosun, or Yi, dynasty, during which Korea became a vassal of China and Confucianism became dominant intellectual force.

***1910*** Korea formally annexed by Japan.

***1920s and 1930s*** Heavy industries developed in the coal-rich north, with Koreans forcibly conscripted as low-paid labourers; suppression of Korean culture led to development of resistance movement.

***1945*** Russian and US troops entered Korea at the end of World War II, forced surrender of Japanese, and divided the country in two at the 38th parallel. Soviet troops occupied North Korea.

***1946*** Soviet-backed provisional government installed, dominated by Moscow-trained Korean communists, including Kim Il Sung; radical programme of land reform and nationalization launched.

***1948*** Democratic People's Republic of Korea declared after pro-USA Republic of Korea founded in the south; Soviet troops withdrew.

***1950*** North Korea invaded South Korea to unite the nation, beginning the Korean War.

***1953*** Armistice agreed to end Korean War, which had involved US participation on the side of South Korea, and Chinese on that of North Korea. The war ended in stalemate, at a cost of 2 million lives.

***1961*** Friendship and mutual assistance treaty signed with China.

**1972** A new constitution, with an executive president, was adopted. Talks were held with South Korea about possible reunification.
**1983** Four South Korean cabinet ministers were assassinated in Rangoon, Burma (Myanmar), by North Korean army officers.
**1985** Relations improved with the USSR.
**1990** Diplomatic contacts with South Korea and Japan suggested a thaw in North Korea's relations with the rest of the world.
**1991** North Korea became a member of the United Nations. A nonaggression agreement with South Korea was signed.
**1992** The Nuclear Safeguards Agreement was signed, allowing international inspection of nuclear facilities. A pact was also signed with South Korea for mutual inspection of nuclear facilities.
**1994** Kim Il Sung died and was succeeded by his son, Kim Jong Il. An agreement was made to halt the nuclear-development programme in return for US aid, resulting in the easing of a 44-year-old US trade embargo.
**1996** US aid was sought in the face of a severe famine caused by floods; rice was imported from South Korea and food aid provided by the UN.
**1997** Kang Song San was replaced as prime minister by Hong Song Nam. Grave food shortages were revealed.
**1998** A UN food-aid operation was instituted in an effort to avert widespread famine. The first direct talks with South Korea since 1994 ended in a stalemate. Legislature elections were held for the first time since 1990. A ballistic missile test was fired over Japan. Deceased former leader Kim Il Sung was declared 'president for perpetuity'. Relations with the USA deteriorated when the USA demanded access to an underground site in Kumchangri suspected of being part of a renewed nuclear-weapons program.
**1999** Talks on possible reunification with South Korea were suspended.

**North Lanarkshire** unitary authority in central Scotland, created in 1996 from three districts of Strathclyde region
**area** 475 sq km/183 sq mi
**towns** Airdrie, Coatbridge, Cumbernauld, Motherwell (administrative headquarters)
**physical** low-lying, heavily urbanized area; River Clyde
**industries** paper, pharmaceuticals, engineering, electronics, light manufacturing, food and drink processing
**agriculture** dairying (around urban environment)
**population** (1995) 326,700
**history** former industrial region of central Scotland.

**North Lincolnshire** unitary authority in eastern England created in 1996 from part of the former county of Humberside
**area** 850 sq km/328 sq mi
**towns and cities** Scunthorpe (administrative headquarters), Brigg, Barton-upon-Humber, Barrow upon Humber, Epworth
**features** Humber Estuary forms north border; River Trent; Isle of Axholme; Stainforth and Keadby Canal; River Torne; Humber Bridge

southern landfall at Barton upon Humber; Julian's Bower (near Alkborough) – medieval maze cut in turf; wetland nature reserves at Barton Waterside and Blackroft Sands; Sandtoft Transport Centre with 60 trolley buses running on own circuit; Old Rectory (Epworth) where John Wesley, founder of Methodism, was born
**industries** steelworks and manufacture of steel products, computer equipment and electronics, food processing (Golden Wonder)
**population** (1996) 153,000
**famous people** Thomas Dunhill, David Hogarth, John Wesley.

**North Pole** the northern point where an imaginary line penetrates the Earth's surface by the axis around which it revolves; see also ◊pole, and ◊Arctic.

**North Rhine-Westphalia** German *Nordrhein-Westfalen,* administrative region (German *Land*) in northwestern Germany, bounded to the north and northeast by Lower Saxony, on the east by Hesse, on the south by the Rhineland-Palatinate, and on the west by Belgium and the Netherlands
**area** 34,100 sq km/13,163 sq mi
**capital** Düsseldorf
**towns and cities** Cologne, Essen, Dortmund, Duisburg, Bochum, Wuppertal, Bielefeld, Bonn, Gelsenkirchen, Münster, Mönchengladbach
**physical** valley of the Rhine; Teutoburger Wald (forest)
**features** Ruhr industrial district (*Ruhrgebiet*)
**industries** iron, steel, coal, lignite, electrical goods, fertilizers, synthetic textiles
**agriculture** dairy farming, cereals, wine-growing in the Rhine valley
**population** (1995) 17,920,000
**famous people** Josef Goebbels, Konrad Adenauer, Helmut Kohl
**religion** 53% Roman Catholic, 42% Protestant
**history** for history before 1945, see ◊Westphalia.

**North Sea** sea to the east of Britain and bounded by the coasts of Belgium, The Netherlands, Germany, Denmark, and Norway; part of the Atlantic Ocean; area 523,000 sq km/202,000 sq mi; average depth 55 m/180 ft, greatest depth 660 m/2,165 ft. The Dogger Bank extends east to west with shallows of as little as 11 m/36 ft, forming a traditionally well-stocked fishing ground. A deep channel follows the coast of Scandinavia reaching as far as the Skagerrak. In the northeast the North Sea joins the Norwegian Sea, and in the south it meets the Strait of Dover. It has 300 oil platforms, 10,000 km/6,200 mi of gas pipeline (gas was discovered in 1965), and fisheries (especially mackerel and herring).

**North Somerset** unitary authority in southwest England created in 1996 from part of the former county of Avon
**area** 372 sq km/144 sq mi
**towns and cities** Weston-Super-Mare (administrative headquarters), Clevedon, Portishead, Yatton, Congresbury
**features** Severn Estuary forms northwest border of authority; River Yea; River Avon forms northeast border; west end of the Mendips

including Bleadon Hill (134 m/440 ft); Clevedon Court – 14th/15th century manor house owned by Elton family; Weston Woods and Worlebury Hill Iron Age sites (Weston-Super-Mare); International Helicopter Museum (Weston-Super-Mare)

**industries** automotive components, rubber and plastics manufacture
**population** (1996) 177,000
**famous people** Hartley Coleridge, Portishead.

**Northumberland** county of northern England
**area** 5,030 sq km/1,942 sq mi
**towns and cities** Morpeth (administrative headquarters), Berwick-upon-Tweed, Hexham
**physical** Cheviot Hills; rivers Aln, Coquet, Rede, Till, Tweed, upper Tyne; Northumberland National Park in the west
**features** Holy Island (Lindisfarne); the Farne island group 8 km/5 mi east of Bamburgh, home to seal and bird colonies; part of Hadrian's Wall (a World Heritage site), including Housesteads Fort; Alnwick and Bamburgh castles; Thomas Bewick museum; Hexham Abbey; the walls of Berwick-upon-Tweed; large moorland areas used for military manoeuvres; Longstone Lighthouse from which Grace Darling rowed to rescue the crew of the *Forfarshire;* wild white cattle of Chillingham; Kielder Water (1982), the largest artificial lake in northern Europe
**agriculture** sheep, cattle; fishing
**industries** manufacturing of computer monitors (Cramlington); coal was formerly mined at several locations
**population** (1996) 307,400
**famous people** Thomas Bewick, Jack and Bobby Charlton, Grace Darling.

**Northumbria** Anglo-Saxon kingdom that covered northeast England and southeast Scotland. Comprising the 6th-century kingdoms of Bernicia (Forth–Tees) and Deira (Tees–Humber), united in the 7th century, it accepted the supremacy of Wessex in 827 and was conquered by the Danes in the late 9th century. It was not until the reign of William the Conqueror that Northumbria became an integral part of England.

**North West** province of the Republic of South Africa from 1994
**area** 118,710 sq km/45,834 sq mi
**capital** Mmabatho
**features** includes part of the former independent homeland of Bophuthatswana, Magaliesberg Mountains, Pilanesberg Game Reserve
**industries** platinum, chrome, iron
**agriculture** groundnuts
**population** (1995 est) 3,351,800
**languages** Setswana (Tswana) 63%, Xhosa 14%, Sesotho (Sotho) 8%.

**Northwest Passage** Atlantic–Pacific sea route around the north of Canada. Canada, which owns offshore islands, claims it as an internal waterway; the USA insists that it is an international waterway and sent an icebreaker through without permission 1985.

**Northwest Territories** northernmost and largest administrative area of Canada, extending into the ◊Arctic Circle. Covering one-third of the total area of the country, it comprises the mainland lying north of the 60th parallel (latitude 60° north) and the islands between the Canadian mainland and the North Pole, including all those in Hudson Bay, James Bay, and the Hudson Strait. Bounded by Yukon Territory in the west and Hudson Bay in the east, the Territories are also surrounded by the Beaufort Sea and the Arctic Ocean to the northwest and by Baffin Bay to the northeast
**area** 3,426,300 sq km/1,322,552 sq mi
**capital** Yellowknife
**towns and cities** Fort Smith, Hay River, Norman Wells, Inuvik, Echo Bay (Port Radium), Fort Laird, Fort McPherson
**population** (1996) 64,600 (39,670 in western Northwest Territories, 24,730 in Nunavut); over 50% indigenous peoples: Inuvialuit, Slavey, Dene, Métis, Inuit
**physical** Arctic Circle; Ellesmere Island; Victoria Island; Baffin Island; Hudson's Bay; Canadian Shield; Mackenzie and Big rivers; Great Slave and Great Bear lakes; Miles Canyon
**industries** oil and natural gas extraction; mining of zinc, lead and gold; fur-trapping; fishing.

**North Yorkshire** county of northeast England, created in 1974 from most of the North Riding and parts of the East and West Ridings of Yorkshire (since April 1996 York has been a separate unitary authority)
**area** 8,037 sq km/3,102 sq mi
**towns and cities** Northallerton (administrative headquarters); resorts: Harrogate, Scarborough, Whitby
**physical** England's largest county; rivers Derwent, Esk, Ouse; includes part of the Pennines; the Vale of York (a vast plain); the Cleveland Hills; North Yorkshire Moors, which form a national park (within which is Fylingdales radar station to give early warning – 4 minutes – of nuclear attack)
**features** Rievaulx Abbey; Yorkshire Dales National Park (including Swaledale, Wensleydale, and Bolton Abbey in Wharfedale); Fountains Abbey near Ripon, with Studley Royal Gardens (a World Heritage site); Castle Howard, designed by John Vanbrugh, has Britain's largest collection of 18th–20th-century costume; largest accessible cavern in Britain, the Battlefield Chamber, Ingleton
**agriculture** cereals, dairy products (Vale of York, Pickering); wool and meat from sheep (North York Moors)
**industries** coal, footwear, clothing, vehicles, plastics, foodstuffs, high technology industries, light industry
**population** (1996) 734,700
**famous people** Alcuin, W H Auden, Guy Fawkes.

**Norway** Kingdom of
**national name** *Kongeriket Norge*
**area** 387,000 sq km/149,420 sq mi (includes Svalbard and Jan Mayen)
**capital** Oslo
**major towns/cities** Bergen, Trondheim, Stavanger, Kristiansand, Drammen
**physical features** mountainous with fertile

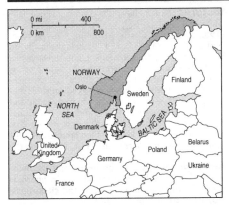

valleys and deeply indented coast; forests cover 25%; extends north of Arctic Circle
***territories*** dependencies in the Arctic (Svalbard and Jan Mayen) and in Antarctica (Bouvet and Peter I Island, and Queen Maud Land)
***head of state*** Harald V from 1991
***head of government*** Kjell Magne Bondevik from 1997
***political system*** constitutional monarchy
***political parties*** Norwegian Labour Party (DNA), moderate left of centre; Conservative Party, progressive, right of centre; Christian People's Party (KrF), Christian, centre left; Centre Party (Sp), left of centre, rural-oriented; Progress Party (FrP), right wing, populist
***currency*** Norwegian krone
***GNP per capita (PPP)*** (US$) 24,290 (1998)
***exports*** petroleum, natural gas, fish products, non-ferrous metals, wood pulp and paper. Principal market: UK 16.9% (1998)
***population*** 4,442,000 (1999 est)
***language*** Norwegian (official); there are Saami- (Lapp) and Finnish-speaking minorities
***religion*** Evangelical Lutheran (endowed by state)
***life expectancy*** 75 (men); 81 (women) (1995–2000)
***Chronology***
***5th century*** First small kingdoms established by Goths.
***c. 900*** Harald Fairhair created united Norwegian kingdom; it dissolved after his death.
***8th–11th centuries*** Vikings from Norway raided and settled in many parts of Europe.
***c. 1016–28*** Olav II (St Olav) reunited the kingdom and introduced Christianity.
***1217–63*** Haakon VI established royal authority over nobles and church and made monarchy hereditary.
***1263*** Iceland submitted to authority of king of Norway.
***1397*** Union of Kalmar: Norway, Denmark, and Sweden united under a single monarch.
***15th century*** Norway, the weakest of the three kingdoms, was increasingly treated as an appendage of Denmark.
***1523*** Secession of Sweden further undermined Norway's status.
***16th century*** Introduction of sawmill precipitated development of timber industry and growth of export trade.

***1661*** Denmark restored formal equality of status to Norway as a twin kingdom.
***18th century*** Norwegian merchants profited from foreign wars which increased demand for naval supplies.
***1814*** Treaty of Kiel: Denmark ceded Norway (minus Iceland) to Sweden; Norway retained its own parliament but cabinet appointed by king of Sweden.
***19th century*** Economic decline followed slump in timber trade due to Canadian competition; expansion of merchant navy and whaling industry.
***1837*** Democratic local government introduced.
***1884*** Achieved internal self-government when king of Sweden made Norwegian cabinet accountable to Norwegian parliament.
***1895*** Start of constitutional dispute over control of foreign policy: Norway's demand for a separate consular service refused by Sweden.
***1905*** Union with Sweden dissolved; Norway achieved independence under King Haakon VII.
***1907*** Norway became first European country to grant women the right to vote in parliamentary elections.
***early 20th century*** Development of industry based on hydroelectric power; long period of Liberal government committed to neutrality and moderate social reform.
***1935*** First Labour government took office.
***1940–45*** German occupation with Vidkun Quisling as puppet leader.
***1945–65*** Labour governments introduced economic planning and permanent price controls.
***1949*** Became a founding member of North Atlantic Treaty Organization (NATO).
***1952*** Joined Nordic Council.
***1957*** Olaf V succeeded his father King Haakon VII.
***1960*** Joined European Free Trade Association (EFTA).
***1972*** A national referendum rejected membership of European Economic Community (EEC).
***1975*** The export of North Sea oil began.
***1981*** Gro Harlem Brundtland (Labour) became Norway's first woman prime minister.
***1982*** Kare Willoch formed the first Conservative government since 1928.
***1986*** Falling oil prices caused a recession; Labour was re-elected under Brundtland.
***1991*** Olaf V was succeeded by his son Harald V.
***1994*** A national referendum rejected membership of European Union (EU).
***1996*** Brundtland resigned and was succeeded by Thorbjoern Jagland.
***1997*** Jagland failed to win a decisive majority in the general election. Kjell Magne Bondevik (KrF) became prime minister.
***1998*** There was a decline in the state of the economy.

**Norwich** cathedral city and administrative headquarters of ◊Norfolk, eastern England, on the River Wensum, 160 km/100 mi northeast of London; population (1991) 172,600. Industries include financial services and insurance, tourism, television and radio broadcasting, engineering, printing, high-technology industries, and the manufacture of shoes, mustard, clothing, chemicals, and confectionery. It is the largest medieval walled city in England.

**nose** in humans, the upper entrance of the respiratory tract; the organ of the sense of smell. The external part is divided down the middle by a septum of ◊cartilage. The nostrils contain plates of cartilage that can be moved by muscles and have a growth of stiff hairs at the margin to prevent foreign objects from entering. The whole nasal cavity is lined with a ◊mucous membrane that warms and moistens the air as it enters and ejects dirt. In the upper parts of the cavity the membrane contains 50 million olfactory receptor cells (cells sensitive to smell).

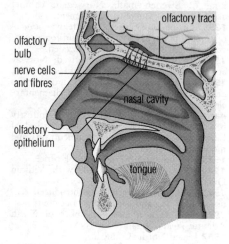

*detail of olfactory epithelium*

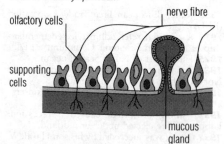

**nose** *The structure of the nose. The organs of smell are confined to a small area in the roof of the nasal cavity. The olfactory cells are stimulated when certain molecules reach them. Smell is one of our most subtle senses: tens of thousands of smells can be distinguished. By comparison, taste, although closely related to smell, is a crude sensation. All the subtleties of taste depend upon smell.*

**Nottingham City** industrial city and unitary authority in central England, on the River Trent, 200 km/124 mi northwest of London. It was the administrative headquarters of the county of Nottinghamshire to April 1998
**area** 74 sq km/29 sq mi

**features** Nottingham Playhouse (1963), the Theatre Royal (1866), the Royal Concert Hall (1982), and the Castle Museum; University of Nottingham (1881) and Nottingham Trent University (1992), formerly Trent Polytechnic; the Goose Fair, dating from the Middle Ages, is held every October; Nottingham has a race-course, and test matches are played on the Trent Bridge cricket ground; the Harvey Haddon sports stadium opened in 1964; the National Water Sports Centre is to the east of the city, near the village of Holme Pierrepont; a Tudor mansion, Holme Pierrepont Hall, is also in the village
**industries** tourism, engineering, and the manufacture of bicycles, textiles, knitwear, pharmaceuticals, tobacco, lace, hosiery, and electronics
**population** (1996) 285,000
**famous people** William Booth, Alan Sillitoe.

**Nottinghamshire** county of central England, which has contained the unitary authority Nottingham City since April 1998
**area** 2,160 sq km/834 sq mi
**towns and cities** West Bridgford (administrative headquarters), Mansfield, Newark, Worksop
**physical** rivers: Erewash Idle, Soar, Trent
**features** the remaining areas of Sherwood Forest (home of ◊Robin Hood) are included in the Dukeries, an area of estates; originally 32 km/20 mi long and 12 km/7 mi wide, the forest was formerly a royal hunting ground; Cresswell Crags (remains of prehistoric humans); D H Lawrence commemorative walk from Eastwood (where he lived) to Old Brinsley Colliery
**agriculture** cereals (barley, wheat), market gardening (potatoes), sugar beet; cattle, sheep; there are many orchards
**industries** cigarettes, coal mining, engineering, footwear, furniture, gravel, gypsum, ironstone, light engineering, limestone, oil, pharmaceuticals, sandstone, textiles
**population** (1996) 1,031,800
**famous people** Robin Hood, D H Lawrence.

**Notts** abbreviation for ◊*Nottinghamshire*, an English county.

**Nouakchott** capital of Mauritania, 270 mi/435 km northeast of Dakar, Senegal; population (1992) 600,000. It is the largest city in the Sahara. Products include salt, cement, insecticides, rugs, carpets, embroidery, and crafts. Exports include copper, petroleum, and phosphates. There is some light engineering.

**nouvelle cuisine** (French 'new cooking') contemporary French cooking style that avoids traditional rich sauces, emphasizing fresh ingredients and attractive presentation. The phrase was coined in the British magazine *Harpers & Queen* in June 1975.

**nova** plural *novae*, faint star that suddenly erupts in brightness by 10,000 times or more, remains bright for a few days, and then fades away and is not seen again for very many years, if at all. Novae are believed to occur in close ◊binary star systems, where gas from one star flows to a companion ◊white dwarf. The gas ignites and is thrown off in an explosion at speeds of 1,500 kps/930 mps or more. Unlike a ◊supernova, the star is not completely disrupted by the outburst. After a few weeks or months it subsides to its previous state; it may erupt many more times.

**Nova Scotia** maritime province of eastern Canada, comprising the peninsula of Nova Scotia, extending southeast from New Brunswick into the Atlantic Ocean, and Cape Breton Island, which is separated from the northeastern end of the mainland by the Canso Strait
**area** 55,500 sq km/21,423 sq mi
**capital** ◊Halifax (chief port)
**towns and cities** Dartmouth, Sydney, Annapolis Royal, Truro
**population** (1996 est) 942,800
**physical** Chignecto Isthmus; Cobequid Mountains; Cape Breton Highlands; Annapolis Valley; Bay of Fundy; Northumberland Strait; numerous lakes: Bras d'Or, St Andrew's Channel; fjord coastline
**industries** mineral extraction (coal, barite, gypsum); lumbering and paper-milling; fishing; agriculture (dairy produce, poultry, eggs, vegetables, and fruit); tourism.

**novel** extended fictional prose narrative, usually between 30,000 and 100,000 words, that deals imaginatively with human experience through the psychological development of the central characters and of their relationship with a broader world. The modern novel took its name and inspiration from the Italian *novella*, the short tale of varied character which became popular in the late 13th century. As the main form of narrative fiction in the 20th century, the novel is frequently classified according to genres and subgenres such as the historical novel, detective fiction, fantasy, and science fiction.

**Novgorod** city on the Volkhov River in the northwest Russian Federation and capital of Novgorod oblast, 500 km/311 mi northwest of Moscow; population (1990) 232,000. Novgorod is one of the oldest cities in Russia, and was the capital of the Russian state before the ascendancy of Moscow. Chemicals, clothing, electrical goods, furniture, and beer are manufactured.

**Novi Sad** industrial and commercial city (pottery and cotton), capital of the autonomous province of Vojvodina in northern Serbia, Yugoslavia, on the River Danube; population (1991) 179,600. Products include leather, textiles, and tobacco.

**Novosibirsk** formerly (1893–1925) *Novonikolayevsk*, capital city, economic and cultural centre of Novosibirsk oblast (region) in southwestern Siberia, Russian Federation; population (1996 est) 1,368,000. Sited on the River Ob and the Trans-Siberian Railway, it is the largest city in Siberia and one of the main industrial centres of the Russian Federation. It is at the hub of an extensive transport network; the Turksib (Turkestan–Siberian) Railway runs from here to Almaty, former capital of Kazakhstan. Novosibirsk has large engineering industries and varied light and food industries. Since the collapse of communism in 1991, there has been considerable development of financial, business, and other services.

**NT** abbreviation for ◊*Northern Territory,* Australia.

**Nu, U (Thakin)** (1907–1995) Myanmar politician, prime minister of Burma (now Myanmar) for most of the period from 1947 to the military coup of 1962. He was the country's first democratically elected prime minister. Exiled from 1966, U Nu returned to the country in 1980 and, in 1988, helped found the National League for Democracy opposition movement.

**nuclear energy** or *atomic energy,* energy released from the inner core, or ◊nucleus, of the atom. Energy produced by *nuclear* ◊*fission* (the splitting of uranium or plutonium nuclei) has been harnessed since the 1950s to generate electricity, and research continues into the possible controlled use of ◊*nuclear fusion* (the fusing, or combining, of atomic nuclei).

**nuclear fusion** process whereby two atomic nuclei are fused, with the release of a large amount of energy. Very high temperatures and pressures are thought to be required in order for the process to happen. Under these conditions the atoms involved are stripped of all their electrons so that the remaining particles, which together make up a *plasma,* can come close together at very high speeds and overcome the mutual repulsion of the positive charges on the atomic nuclei. At very close range the strong nuclear force will come into play, fusing the particles together to form a larger nucleus. As fusion is accompanied by the release of large amounts of energy, the process might one day be harnessed to form the basis of commercial energy production. Methods of achieving controlled fusion are therefore the subject of research around the world.

**nuclear physics** study of the properties of the nucleus of the ◊atom, including the structure of nuclei; nuclear forces; the interactions between particles and nuclei; and the study of radioactive decay. The study of elementary particles is ◊particle physics.

**nuclear reactor** device for producing ◊nuclear energy in a controlled manner. There are various types of reactor in use, all using nuclear ◊fission. In a *gas-cooled reactor,* a circulating gas under pressure (such as carbon dioxide) removes heat from the core of the reactor, which usually contains natural uranium. The efficiency of the fission process is increased by slowing neutrons in the core by using a moderator such as carbon. The reaction is controlled with neutron-absorbing rods made of boron. An *advanced gas-cooled reactor* (AGR) generally has enriched uranium as its fuel. A *water-cooled reactor,* such as the steam-generating heavy water (deuterium oxide) reactor, has water circulating through the hot core. The water is converted to steam, which drives turbo-alternators for generating electricity. The most widely used reactor is the *pressurized-water reactor* (PWR), which contains a sealed system of pressurized water that is heated to form steam in heat exchangers in an external circuit. The *fast reactor* has no moderator and uses fast neutrons to bring about fission. It uses a mixture of plutonium and uranium oxide as fuel. When operating, uranium is converted to plutonium, which can be extracted and used later as fuel. It is also called the fast breeder or breeder reactor because it produces more plutonium than it consumes. Heat is removed from the reactor by a coolant of liquid sodium.

**nuclear warfare** war involving the use of nuclear weapons. Nuclear-weapons research began in Britain in 1940, but was transferred to the USA after it entered World War II. The research programme, known as the Manhattan Project, was directed by J Robert Oppenheimer. The worldwide total of nuclear weapons in 1990 was about 50,000, and the number of countries possessing nuclear weapons stood officially at five – USA, USSR, UK, France, and China.

**nuclear waste** the radioactive and toxic by-products of the nuclear-energy and nuclear-weapons industries. Nuclear waste may have an active life of several thousand years. Reactor waste is of three types: *high-level* spent fuel, or the residue when nuclear fuel has been removed from a reactor and reprocessed; *intermediate,* which may be long-or short-lived; and *low-level,* but bulky, waste from reactors, which has only short-lived radioactivity. Disposal, by burial on land or at sea, has raised problems of safety, environmental pollution, and security.

**nuclear winter** possible long-term effect of a widespread nuclear war. In the wake of the destruction caused by nuclear blasts and the subsequent radiation, it has been suggested that atmospheric pollution by dust, smoke, soot, and ash could prevent the Sun's rays from penetrating for a period of time sufficient to eradicate most plant life on which other life depends, and create a new Ice Age.

**nucleic acid** complex organic acid made up of a long chain of nucleotides, present in the nucleus and sometimes the cytoplasm of the living cell. The two types, known as ◊DNA (deoxyribonucleic acid) and ◊RNA (ribonucleic acid), form the basis of heredity. The nucleotides are made up of a sugar (deoxyribose or ribose), a phosphate group, and one of four purine or pyrimidine bases. The order of the bases along the nucleic acid strand contains the genetic code.

**nucleon** in particle physics, either a ◊proton or a ◊neutron, when present in the atomic nucleus. *Nucleon number* is an alternative name for the ◊mass number of an atom.

**nucleus** in biology, the central, membrane-enclosed part of a eukaryotic cell, containing threads of DNA. During cell division these coil up to form chromosomes. The nucleus controls the function of the cell by determining which proteins are produced within it (see ◊DNA for details of this process). Because proteins are the chief structural molecules of living matter and, as enzymes, regulate all aspects of metabolism, it may be seen that the genetic code within the nucleus is effectively responsible for building and controlling the whole organism.

**nucleus** in physics, the positively charged central part of an ◊atom, which constitutes almost all its mass. Except for hydrogen nuclei, which have only protons, nuclei are composed of both protons and neutrons. Surrounding the nuclei are electrons, of equal and opposite charge to that of the protons, thus giving the atom a neutral charge.

**Nujoma, Sam** (1929– ) Namibian left-wing politician, founder and leader of SWAPO (the South West Africa People's Organization) from 1959, president from 1990. He was exiled in 1960, and controlled SWAPO's armed struggle against South Africa from Angolan bases in 1966. When the first free elections were held in 1989 under the United Nations peace plan, he returned to lead his party to victory, taking office in March 1990.

**Nuku'alofa** capital and port of Tonga on Tongatapu Island; population (1989) 29,000.

**number** symbol used in counting or measuring. In mathematics, there are various kinds of numbers. The everyday number system is the decimal ('proceeding by tens') system, using the base ten. ◊*Real numbers* include all rational numbers (integers, or whole numbers, and fractions) and irrational numbers (those not expressible as fractions). ◊*Complex numbers* include the real and imaginary numbers (real-number multiples of the square root of –1). The ◊binary number system, used in computers, has two as its base. The natural numbers, 0, 1, 2, 3, 4, 5, 6, 7, 8, and 9, give a counting system that, in the decimal system, continues 10, 11, 12, 13, and so on. These are whole numbers (integers), with fractions represented as, for example, 1/4, 1/2, 3/4, or as decimal fractions (0.25, 0.5, 0.75). They are also *rational numbers. Irrational numbers* cannot be represented in this way and require symbols, such as $\sqrt{2}$, $\pi$, and e. They can be expressed numerically only as the (inexact) approximations 1.414, 3.142, and 2.718 (to three places of decimals) respectively. The symbols $\pi$ and e are also examples of *transcendental numbers,* because they (unlike $\sqrt{2}$) cannot be derived by solving a polynomial equation (an equation with one ◊variable quantity) with rational ◊coefficients (multiplying factors). Complex numbers, which include the real numbers as well as imaginary numbers, take the general form $a + bi$, where $i = \sqrt{-1}$ (that is, $i^2 = -1$), and $a$ is the real part and $bi$ the imaginary part.

**Nuremberg** German *Nürnberg,* city in Bavaria, Germany, on the River Pegnitz, 149 km/ 92 mi northwest of Munich; population (1995) 494,100. Industries include electrical and other machinery, precision instruments, toys, and food processing. From 1933 the Nuremberg rallies were held here, and in 1945 the Nuremberg trials of war criminals.

**Nuremberg rallies** annual meetings 1933–38 of the German ◊Nazi Party. They were characterized by extensive torchlight parades, marches in party formations, and mass rallies addressed by Nazi leaders such as Hitler and Goebbels.

**Nuremberg trials** after World War II, the trials of the 24 chief ◊Nazi war criminals in November 1945–October 1946 by an international military tribunal consisting of four judges and four prosecutors: one of each from the USA, UK, USSR, and France. The German cabinet, general staff, high command, Nazi leadership corps, ◊SS, Sturmabteilung, and ◊Gestapo were also accused of criminal behaviour.

**Nureyev, Rudolf Hametovich** (1938–1993) Russian dancer and choreographer. A soloist with the Kirov Ballet, he defected to the West during a visit to Paris 1961. Mainly associated with the Royal Ballet (London) and as Margot ◊Fonteyn's principal partner, he was one of the most brilliant dancers of the 1960s and 1970s. Nureyev danced in such roles as Prince Siegfried in *Swan Lake* and Armand in *Marguerite and Armand,* which was created especially for Fonteyn and Nureyev. He also danced and acted in films and on television and choreographed several ballets. It was due to his enormous impact on the ballet world that the male dancer's role was elevated to the equivalent of the ballerina's.

**nursing** care of the sick, the very young, the very old, and the disabled. Organized training originated in 1836 in Germany, and was developed in Britain by the work of Florence ◊Nightingale, who, during the Crimean War, established standards of scientific, humanitarian care in military hospitals. Nurses give day-to-day care and carry out routine medical and surgical duties under the supervision of doctors.

**nut** any dry, single-seeded fruit that does not split open to release the seed, such as the chestnut. A nut is formed from more than one carpel, but only one seed becomes fully formed, the remainder aborting. The wall of the fruit, the pericarp, becomes hard and woody, forming the outer shell.

**nuthatch** any of a group of small birds with short tails and pointed beaks. Nuthatches climb head first up, down, and around tree trunks and branches, foraging for insects and their larvae. (Family Sittidae, order Passeriformes.)

**nutrition** the strategy adopted by an organism to obtain the chemicals it needs to live, grow, and reproduce. Also, the science of food, and its effect on human and animal life, health, and disease. Nutrition involves the study of the basic nutrients required to sustain life, their bioavailability in foods and overall diet, and the effects upon them of cooking and storage. It is also concerned with dietary deficiency diseases.

**Nyasa, Lake** alternative name for Lake Malawi (see ◊Malawi, Lake).

**Nyasaland** former name (to 1964) for Malawi.

**Nyerere, Julius Kambarage** (1922– ) Tanzanian socialist politician, president 1964–85. He devoted himself from 1954 to the formation of the Tanganyika African National Union and subsequent campaigning for independence. He became chief minister in 1960, was prime minister of Tanganyika 1961–62, president of the newly formed Tanganyika Republic 1962–64, and first president of Tanzania 1964–85.

**nylon** synthetic long-chain polymer similar in chemical structure to protein. Nylon was the first all-synthesized fibre, made from petroleum, natural gas, air, and water by the Du Pont firm in 1938. It is used in the manufacture of moulded articles, textiles, and medical sutures. Nylon fibres are stronger and more elastic than silk and are relatively insensitive to moisture and mildew. Nylon is used for hosiery and woven goods, simulating other materials such as silks and furs; it is also used for carpets.

**nymph** in entomology, the immature form of insects that do not have a pupal stage; for example, grasshoppers and dragonflies. Nymphs generally resemble the adult (unlike larvae), but do not have fully formed reproductive organs or wings.

**nymph** in Greek mythology, a guardian spirit of nature. ◊Dryads or *hamadryads* guarded trees; *naiads,* springs and pools; *oreads,* hills and rocks; *oceanids,* the open sea; and ◊Nereids, the Aegean.

**oak** any of a group of trees or shrubs belonging to the beech family, with over 300 known species widely distributed in temperate zones. Oaks are valuable for timber, the wood being durable and straight-grained. Their fruits are called ◊acorns. (Genus *Quercus,* family Fagaceae.)

**oarfish** any of a group of deep-sea bony fishes, found in warm parts of the Atlantic, Pacific, and Indian oceans. Oarfish are large, up to 9 m/30 ft long, elongated, and compressed, with a fin along the back and a manelike crest behind the head. They have a small mouth, no teeth or scales, and large eyes. They are often described as sea serpents. (Genus *Regalecidae.*)

**OAS** abbreviation for ◊*Organization of American States.*

**oasis** area of land made fertile by the presence of water near the surface in an otherwise arid region. The occurrence of oases affects the distribution of plants, animals, and people in the desert regions of the world.

**oat** type of annual grass, a ◊cereal crop. The plant has long narrow leaves and a stiff straw stem; the panicles of flowers (clusters around the main stem), and later of grain, hang downwards. The cultivated oat (*A. sativa*) is produced for human and animal food. (Genus *Avena.*)

**Oates, Titus** (1648–1705) English conspirator. A priest, he entered the Jesuit colleges at Valladolid, Spain, and St Omer, France, as a spy in 1677–78, and on his return to England announced he had discovered a 'Popish Plot' to murder Charles II and re-establish Catholicism. Although this story was almost entirely false, many innocent Roman Catholics were executed during 1678–80 on Oates's evidence.

**OAU** abbreviation for ◊*Organization of African Unity.*

**Ob** major river in Asian Russia, flowing 3,380 km/2,100 mi from the Altai Mountains through the western Siberian Plain to the Gulf of Ob in the Kara Sea (an inlet of the Arctic Ocean). With its main tributary, the *Irtysh,* the Ob is 5,600 km/3,480 mi long, and drains a total area of 2,990,000 sq km/1,154,439 sq mi.

**Oberammergau** village in Bavaria, Germany, 72 km/45 mi southwest of Munich; population (1980) 5,000. A Christian ◊passion play has been performed here every ten years since 1634 (except during the World Wars) to commemorate the ending of the Black Death plague.

**obesity** condition of being overweight (generally, 20% or more above the desirable weight for one's sex, build, and height). Obesity increases susceptibility to disease, strains the vital organs, and reduces life expectancy; it is usually remedied by controlled weight loss, healthy diet, and exercise.

**oboe** musical instrument of the woodwind family, a refined treble shawm of narrow tapering bore and exposed double reed. The oboe was developed by the Hotteterre family of instrument-makers about 1700 and was incorporated in the court ensemble of Louis XIV. In C, with a normal compass of about 21/2 octaves, it has a rich tone of elegant finish. Oboe concertos have been composed by Vivaldi, Albinoni, Richard Strauss, Martinu, and others. Heinz Holliger is a modern virtuoso oboist.

**Obote, (Apollo) Milton** (1924– ) Ugandan politician, prime minister 1962–66, and president 1966–71 and 1980–85. After forming the Uganda People's Congress (UPC) in 1959, he led the independence movement from 1961. As prime minister his rule became increasingly authoritarian, and in 1966 he suspended the constitution and declared himself president. He was ousted by Idi ◊Amin in 1971, fleeing to exile in Tanzania. Returning in 1979 after the collapse of the Amin regime, he was re-elected president in 1980 but failed to restore order and was deposed by Lieutenant General Tito Okello in 1985.

**obscenity law** UK law established by the Obscene Publications Act 1959 prohibiting the publishing of any material that tends to deprave or corrupt. In Britain, obscene material can be, for example, pornographic, violent, or can encourage drug taking. Publishing includes distribution, sale, and hiring of the material. There is a defence in support of the public good if the defendant can produce expert evidence to show that publication was in the interest of, for example, art, science, or literature.

**observatory** site or facility for observing astronomical or meteorological phenomena. The earliest recorded observatory was in Alexandria, North Africa, built by Ptolemy Soter in about 300 BC. The modern observatory dates from the invention of the telescope. Observatories may be ground-based, carried on aircraft, or sent into orbit as satellites, in space stations, and on the space shuttle.

**obsession** persistently intruding thought, emotion, or impulse, often recognized by the sufferer as irrational, but nevertheless causing distress. It may be a brooding on destiny or death, or chronic doubts interfering with everyday life (such as fearing the gas is not turned off and repeatedly checking), or an impulse leading to repetitive action, such as continually washing one's hands.

**obsessive-compulsive disorder** (OCD), in psychiatry, anxiety disorder that manifests itself in the need to check constantly that certain acts have been performed 'correctly'. Sufferers may, for example, feel compelled to repeatedly wash themselves or return home again and again to check that doors have been unlocked and appliances switched off. They may also hoard certain objects and insist in these being arranged in a precise way or be troubled by intrusive and unpleasant thoughts. In extreme cases normal life is disrupted through the hours devoted to compulsive actions. Treatment involves cognitive therapy and drug therapy with serotonin-blocking drugs such as Prozac.

**obsidian** black or dark-coloured glassy volcanic rock, chemically similar to ◊granite, but formed by cooling rapidly on the Earth's surface at low pressure.

**obstetrics** medical speciality concerned with the management of pregnancy, childbirth, and the immediate postnatal period.

**occult** (Latin 'hidden from general view') vague term describing a wide range of activities connected with the supernatural, from seances to black magic. The term has come to have largely sinister overtones and an association with Satanism and witchcraft.

**ocean** great mass of salt water. Strictly speaking three oceans exist – the Atlantic, Indian, and Pacific – to which the Arctic is often added. They cover approximately 70% or 363,000,000 sq km/140,000,000 sq mi of the total surface area of the Earth. Water levels recorded in the world's oceans have shown an increase of 10–15 cm/4–6 in over the past 100 years.

**Oceania** the groups of islands in the southern and central Pacific Ocean, comprising all those situated between the southeastern shores of Asia and the western shores of America.

**oceanography** study of the oceans. Its subdivisions deal with each ocean's extent and depth, the water's evolution and composition, its physics and chemistry, the bottom topography, currents and wind effects, tidal ranges, the biology, and the various aspects of human use.

**ocean ridge** mountain range on the seabed indicating the presence of a constructive plate margin (where tectonic plates are moving apart and magma rises to the surface; see ◊plate tectonics). Ocean ridges, such as the Mid-Atlantic Ridge, consist of many segments offset along transform ◊faults, and can rise thousands of metres above the surrounding seabed.

**ocean trench** deep trench in the seabed indicating the presence of a destructive margin (produced by the movements of ◊plate tectonics). The subduction or dragging downwards of one plate of the lithosphere beneath another means that the ocean floor is pulled down. Ocean trenches are found around the edge of the Pacific Ocean and the northeastern Indian Ocean; minor ones occur in the Caribbean and near the Falkland Islands.

**ocelot** wild cat of the southwestern USA, Mexico, and Central and South America. It is up to 1 m/3 ft long with a 45 cm/1.5 ft tail, weighs about 18 kg/40 lb, and has a pale yellowish coat

marked with horizontal stripes and blotches. As a result of being hunted for its fur, it is close to extinction. (Species *Felis pardalis,* family Felidae.)

**O'Connell, Daniel** (1775–1847) Irish lawyer and politician, known as 'the Liberator'. In 1823 he formed the Catholic Association, to campaign for Catholic emancipation and the repeal of the 1801 Act of Union between Britain and Ireland. He achieved the first objective in 1829, but failed in the second.

**octane rating** numerical classification of petroleum fuels indicating their combustion characteristics.

**octave** in music, a span of eight notes as measured on the white notes of a piano keyboard. It corresponds to the consonance of first and second harmonics.

**Octavian** original name of ◊Augustus, the first Roman emperor.

**October Revolution** second stage of the ◊Russian Revolution 1917, when, on the night of 24 October (6 November in the Western calendar), the Bolshevik forces under Trotsky, and on orders from Lenin, seized the Winter Palace and arrested members of the Provisional Government. The following day the Second All-Russian Congress of Soviets handed over power to the Bolsheviks.

**octopus** soft-bodied sea animal with a round or oval body and eight slender arms (tentacles) in a ring surrounding its mouth. They are solitary creatures, living alone in rocky dens. They feed on crabs and other small animals. There are about 50 different species of octopus living in all the oceans of the world. Some are small, having bodies only 8 cm/3 in long, but the largest deep-sea species can grow to lengths of 20 m/64 ft.

**ode** lyric poem of complex form. Odes originated in ancient Greece, where they were chanted to a musical accompaniment. Classical writers of odes include Sappho, Pindar, Horace, and Catullus. English poets who adopted the form include Spenser, Milton, Dryden, and Keats.

**Odessa** principal seaport of Ukraine, on the Black Sea, and capital of the Odessa region (oblast); population (1990) 1,106,400. Odessa is a commercial port, naval base, and tourist resort. The principal industries here are ship-building, fishing, steelmaking, and food processing. Products manufactured in the city include chemicals, pharmaceuticals, and machinery. Among the main goods handled in the port are grain, sugar, timber, and oil.

**Odin** Germanic Woden or Wotan, ('the raging one') chief god of Norse mythology, god of war, and the source of wisdom. A sky god, he lived in Asgard at the top of the world-tree Yggdrasil. From the ◊Valkyries, his divine maidens, he received the souls of half those heroes slain in battle, feasting with them in his great hall Valhalla; the remainder were feasted by ◊Freya. His son was ◊Thor, god of thunder. Wednesday or Woden's day is named after him.

**Odysseus** Latin Ulysses, ('son of wrath') chief character of Homer's *Odyssey*, king of the island of Ithaca (modern Thiaki or Levkas); he is also mentioned in the *Iliad* as one of the leaders of the Greek forces at the siege of Troy. Odysseus was distinguished among Greek leaders for his cleverness and cunning. He appears in other later tragedies, but his ten years' odyssey by sea after the fall of Troy is the most commonly known tradition.

**Odyssey** Greek epic poem; the product of an oral tradition, it was probably written before 700 BC and is attributed to ◊Homer. It describes the voyage home of Odysseus after the fall of Troy, and the vengeance he takes with his son Telemachus on the suitors of his wife Penelope on his return. During his ten-year wanderings, he encounters the Cyclops, the enchantress Circe, Scylla and Charybdis, and the Sirens.

**OECD** abbreviation for ◊*Organization for Economic Cooperation and Development.*

**oedema** any abnormal accumulation of fluid in tissues or cavities of the body; waterlogging of the tissues due to excessive loss of ◊plasma through the capillary walls. It may be generalized (the condition once known as dropsy) or confined to one area, such as the ankles.

**Oedipus** in Greek mythology, king of Thebes who unwittingly killed his father, Laius, and married his mother, Jocasta, in fulfilment of a prophecy. When he learned what he had done, he put out his eyes. His story was dramatized by the Greek tragedian ◊Sophocles.

**Oedipus complex** in psychology, the unconscious antagonism of a son to his father, whom he sees as a rival for his mother's affection. For a girl antagonistic to her mother, as a rival for her father's affection, the term is *Electra complex*. The terms were coined by Sigmund ◊Freud.

**oesophagus** muscular tube by which food travels from the mouth to the stomach. The human oesophagus is about 23 cm/9 in long. Its extends downwards from the pharynx, immediately behind the windpipe. It is lined with a mucous membrane which secretes lubricant fluid to assist the downward movement of food (◊peristalsis).

**oestrogen** any of a group of hormones produced by the ◊ovaries of vertebrates; the term is also used for various synthetic hormones that mimic their effects. The principal oestrogen in mammals is oestradiol. Oestrogens control female sexual development, promote the growth of female secondary sexual characteristics, stimulate egg production, and, in mammals, prepare the lining of the uterus for pregnancy.

**oestrus** in mammals, the period during a female's reproductive cycle (also known as the oestrus cycle or ◊menstrual cycle) when mating is most likely to occur. It usually coincides with ovulation.

**Offa** (died *c.* 796) king of the Anglo-Saxon kingdom of Mercia (west-central England) 757–97. He conquered Essex, Kent, Sussex, and Surrey; defeated the Welsh and the West Saxons; and established Mercian supremacy over all England south of the River Humber. He built the earthwork known as Offa's Dyke along the Welsh border to defend his frontier in the west.

**Offaly** county of the Republic of Ireland, in the province of Leinster, between Galway and Roscommon in the west and Kildare in the east; county town Tullamore; area 2,000 sq km/772 sq mi; population (1991) 58,500. It is low-lying, with part of the Bog of Allen to the north.

**Offa's Dyke** defensive earthwork dyke along the English–Welsh border, of which there are remains from the mouth of the River Dee to that of the River ◊Severn. It was built about AD 785 by King ◊Offa of Mercia, England, and represents the boundary secured by his wars with Wales.

**Official Secrets Act** UK act of Parliament 1989, prohibiting the disclosure of confidential material from government sources by employees; it remains an absolute offence for a member or former member of the security and intelligence services (or those working closely with them) to disclose information about their work. There is no public-interest defence, and disclosure of information already in the public domain is still a crime. Journalists who repeat disclosures may also be prosecuted.

**offset printing** the most common method of ◊printing, which uses smooth (often rubber) printing plates. It works on the principle of ◊lithography: that grease and water repel one another.

**O grade** in Scottish education, Ordinary Grade, formerly the equivalent of an English ◊GCSE now replaced by Standard Grade.

**Ogun** state of southwestern Nigeria; area 16,762 sq km/6,474 sq mi; capital Abeokuta; population (1991) 2,338,600.

**Ohio** state in northern central USA. It is nicknamed the Buckeye State. It was admitted to the Union in 1803 as the 17th US state. Part of the Midwest, it is bordered to the east by Pennsylvania, to the east and southeast by West Virginia, to the southwest by Kentucky, to the west by Indiana, to the northwest by Michigan's Lower Peninsula, and to the north by Lake Erie. Ohio comprises the eastern section of the US Corn Belt; heavily industrialized, it is also a quintessential Rust Belt state, today struggling with pollution and the need to diversify industrially
*population* (1995) 11,150,500
*area* 107,100 sq km/41,341 sq mi
*capital* Columbus
*towns and cities* Cleveland, Cincinnati, Dayton, Akron, Toledo, Youngstown, Canton
*industries and products* coal, cereals, livestock, dairy foods, machinery, chemicals, steel, motor vehicles, automotive and aircraft parts, rubber products, office equipment, refined petroleum, tourism.

**ohm** SI unit (symbol Ω) of electrical ◊resistance (the property of a conductor that restricts the flow of electrons through it).

**Ohm's law** law that states that the current flowing in a metallic conductor maintained at constant temperature is directly proportional to the potential difference (voltage) between its ends. The law was discovered by German physicist Georg Ohm in 1827.

**oil** flammable substance, usually insoluble in water, and composed chiefly of carbon and hydrogen. Oils may be solids (fats and waxes) or liquids. The three main types are: *essential oils,* obtained from plants; *fixed oils,* obtained from animals and plants; and *mineral oils,* obtained chiefly from the refining of ◊petroleum.

**oil crop** plant from whose seeds vegetable oils are pressed. Cool temperate areas grow rapeseed and linseed; warm temperate regions produce sunflowers, olives, and soybeans; tropical regions produce groundnuts (peanuts), palm oil, and coconuts.

**oil paint** painting medium in which ground pigment is bound with oil, usually linseed.

**oil palm** African ◊palm tree, the fruit of which yields valuable oils, used as food or processed into margarine, soaps, and livestock feeds. (*Elaeis guineensis.*)

**okapi** ruminant (cud-chewing) mammal related to the giraffe, although with a much shorter neck and legs, found in the tropical rainforests of central Africa. Its purplish brown body, creamy face, and black and white stripes on the legs and hindquarters provide excellent camouflage. Okapis have remained virtually unchanged for millions of years. (Species *Okapia johnstoni,* family Giraffidae.)

**Okavango Delta** marshy area in northwest Botswana covering about 20,000 km/7,722 sq mi, fed by the Okavango River, which rises in Angola and flows southeast about 1,600 km/1,000 mi. It is an important area for wildlife as it provides the main area of permanently available water in the Kalahari Desert.

**O'Keeffe, Georgia** (1887–1986) US painter. She is known chiefly for her large, semi-abstract studies of flowers and bones, such as *Black Iris* (1926; Metropolitan Museum of Art, New York) and the *Pelvis Series* of the 1940s. She was married 1924–46 to photographer and art exhibitor Alfred Stieglitz, in whose gallery her work was first shown.

**Okhotsk, Sea of** arm of the North Pacific Ocean between the Kamchatka Peninsula and Sakhalin and bordered to the south by the Kuril Islands, and the northern Japanese island of Hokkaido; area 937,000 sq km/361,700 sq mi, average depth 777 m/2,550 ft, maximum depth 3,372 m/11,062 ft. It is free of ice only in summer, and is often fog-bound. Magadan is the chief port, and the River Amur flows into it.

**Okinawa** group of islands, 520 km/323 mi from the Japanese mainland, forming part of the Japanese ◊Ryukyu Islands in the west Pacific; Okinawa is also the name of the largest island, and the name of a city on Okinawa
*area* 2,250 sq km/869 sq mi
*cities* Naha (capital), and Okinawa

*physical* the island of Okinawa is 106 km/66 mi long from north to south and 20 km/12 mi wide, with an irregular coastline
*features* Okinawa, the largest island of the group (area 1,176 sq km/454 sq mi; population (1990) 105,852), has a large US military base. As a region, Okinawa has a distinctive dialect and folk culture
*industry* manufacture of traditional textiles in a range of distinctive local dyes and weaves
*agriculture* sugar cane, pineapples
*population* (1995) 1,274,000
*history* virtually all buildings were destroyed in World War II. The principal island, Okinawa, was captured by the USA in the *Battle of Okinawa* 1 April–21 June 1945, with 47,000 US casualties (12,000 dead) and 60,000 Japanese (only a few hundred survived as prisoners). During the invasion over 150,000 Okinawans, mainly civilians, died; many were massacred by Japanese forces. The island was returned to Japan in 1972.

**Oklahoma** state in southern central USA. It is nicknamed the Sooner State. Oklahoma was admitted to the Union in 1907 as the 46th US state. It is bordered to the south by Texas, to the west, at the extreme of the Oklahoma panhandle, by New Mexico, to the north by Colorado and Kansas, and to the east by Missouri and Arkansas. Oklahoma is the US state most associated with American Indians; its name is a Choctaw coinage meaning 'red people'
*population* (1995) 3,277,700
*area* 181,100 sq km/69,905 sq mi
*capital* Oklahoma City
*towns and cities* Tulsa, Lawton, Norman, Enid
*industries and products* cereals, peanuts, cotton, livestock, oil, natural gas, helium, machinery and other metal products.

**Oklahoma City** capital of ◊Oklahoma, USA, on the North Canadian River; population (1996 est) 469,900. It is a major commercial, service, and distribution centre for a rich oil-producing and agricultural area; its cattle markets are among the largest and busiest in the world. Industries include oil-refining, food processing (meat and cereals), and the manufacture of iron, steel, machinery, cars, aircraft, electronic equipment, and cotton. A right-wing terrorist bomb attack occurred here in 1995, killing 168 people.

**okra** plant belonging to the Old World hibiscus family. Its red-and-yellow flowers are followed by long, sticky, green fruits known as *ladies' fingers* or *bhindi.* The fruits are cooked in soups and stews. (*Hibiscus esculentus,* family Malvaceae.)

**Old English** general name for the range of dialects spoken by Germanic settlers in England between the 5th and 12th centuries AD, also known as Anglo-Saxon. The literature of the period includes *Beowulf,* an epic in West Saxon dialect. See also ◊English language.

**Old Pretender** nickname of ◊James Edward Stuart, the son of James II of England.

**Old Testament** Christian term for the Hebrew ◊Bible, which is the first part of the

Christian Bible. It contains 39 (according to Christianity) or 24 (according to Judaism) books, which include the origins of the world, the history of the ancient Hebrews and their covenant with God, prophetical writings, and religious poetry. The first five books (*The five books of Moses*) are traditionally ascribed to Moses and known as the Pentateuch (by Christians) or the ♦Torah (by Jews).

**Olduvai Gorge** deep cleft in the Serengeti steppe, Tanzania, where Louis and Mary ♦Leakey found prehistoric stone tools in the 1930s. They discovered Pleistocene remains of prehumans and gigantic animals 1958–59. The gorge has given its name to the *Olduvai culture,* a simple stone-tool culture of prehistoric hominids, dating from 2–0.5 million years ago.

**Old World** the continents of the eastern hemisphere, so called because they were familiar to Europeans before the Americas. The term is used as an adjective to describe animals and plants that live in the eastern hemisphere.

**oleander** or *rose bay,* evergreen Mediterranean shrub belonging to the dogbane family, with pink or white flowers and aromatic leaves that produce and release the poison oleandrin. (*Nerium oleander,* family Apocynaceae.)

**oligarchy** (Greek *oligarchia* 'government of the few') rule of the few, in their own interests. It was first identified as a form of government by the Greek philosopher Aristotle. In modern times there have been a number of oligarchies, sometimes posing as democracies; the paramilitary rule of the ♦Duvalier family in Haiti, 1957–86, is an example.

**Oligocene** third epoch of the Tertiary period of geological time, 35.5–3.25 million years ago. The name, from Greek, means 'a little recent', referring to the presence of the remains of some modern types of animals existing at that time.

**olive** evergreen tree belonging to the olive family. Native to Asia but widely cultivated in Mediterranean and subtropical areas, it grows up to 15 m/50 ft high and has twisted branches and lance-shaped silvery leaves that grow opposite each other. The white flowers are followed by small green oval fruits that turn bluish-black when ripe. They are preserved in brine or oil; dried; or pressed to make olive oil. (*Olea europaea,* family Oleaceae.)

**olive branch** ancient symbol of peace; in the Bible (Genesis 9), an olive branch is brought back by the dove to Noah to show that the flood has abated.

**Olives, Mount of** range of hills east of Jerusalem, associated with the Christian religion: a former chapel (now a mosque) marks the traditional site of Jesus' ascension to heaven, with the Garden of Gethsemane at its foot.

**Olivier, Laurence (Kerr)** Baron Olivier (1907–1989) English actor and director. For many years associated with the Old Vic Theatre, he was director of the National Theatre company 1962–73. His stage roles include Henry V, Hamlet, Richard III, and Archie Rice in John Osborne's *The Entertainer* (1957; filmed 1960).

He directed and starred in filmed versions of Shakespeare's plays; for example, *Henry V* (1944) and *Hamlet* (1948) (Academy Award). He was knighted in 1947 and created a baron in 1970.

**Olympia** ancient sanctuary in the western Peloponnese, Greece, with a temple of Zeus, and the stadium (for foot races, boxing, wrestling) and hippodrome (for chariot and horse races), where the original Olympic Games, founded 776 BC, were held every four years. The gold and ivory statue of Zeus that was here, made by ♦Phidias, was one of the ♦Seven Wonders of the World. It was removed to Constantinople, where it was destroyed in a fire. The face of Zeus may have served as a model for the face of Christ Pantocrator in the dome of St Sophia.

**Olympic Games** sporting contests originally held in Olympia, ancient Greece, every four years during a sacred truce; records were kept from 776 BC. Women were forbidden to be present, and the male contestants were naked. The ancient Games were abolished in AD 394. The present-day games have been held every four years since 1896. Since 1924 there has been a separate winter Games programme; from 1994 the winter and summer Games are held two years apart.

**Olympus** Greek *Olimbos,* any of several mountains in Greece and elsewhere, one of which is *Mount Olympus* in northern Thessaly, Greece, 2,918 m/9,577 ft high. In ancient Greece it was considered the home of the gods.

**Om** sacred word in Hinduism, used to begin prayers and placed at the beginning and end of books. It is composed of three syllables, symbolic of the Hindu Trimurti, or trinity of gods.

**Oman** Sultanate of
*national name Saltanat `Uman*

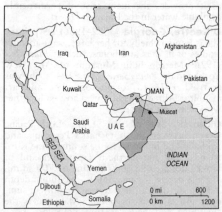

**area** 272,000 sq km/105,019 sq mi
**capital** Muscat
**major towns/cities** Salalah, Ibri, Sohar, Al-Buraimi, Nizwa
**major ports** Mina Qaboos, Mina Raysut
**physical features** mountains to north and south of a high arid plateau; fertile coastal strip;

Jebel Akhdar highlands; Kuria Muria Islands
*head of state and government* Qaboos bin
Said from 1970
*political system* absolute monarchy
*political parties* none
*currency* Omani rial
*GNP per capita (PPP)* (US$) 8,690 (1997)
*exports* petroleum, metals and metal goods,
textiles, animals and products. Principal market:
Japan 23.3% (1997)
*population* 2,460,000 (1999 est)
*language* Arabic (official); English, Urdu, other
Indian languages
*religion* Ibadhi Muslim 75%, Sunni Muslim,
Shiite Muslim, Hindu
*life expectancy* 69 (men); 73 (women) (1995–
2000)
**Chronology**
*c. 3000 BC* Archaeological evidence suggests
Oman may have been the semilegendary Magan,
a thriving seafaring state at the time of the
Sumerian Civilization of Mesopotamia (the
Tigris and Euphrates region of Iraq).
*9th century BC* Migration of Arab clans to
Oman, notably the Qahtan family from southwest Arabia and the Nizar from northwest
Arabia, between whom rivalry has continued.
*4th century BC–AD 800* North Oman under
Persian control.
*AD 630* Converted to Islam.
*751* Julanda ibn Masud was elected imam (spiritual leader); Oman remained under imam rule
until 1154.
*1151* Dynasty established by Banu Nabhan.
*1428* Dynastic rule came under challenge from
the imams.
*1507* Coastal area, including port city of
Muscat, fell under Portuguese control.
*1650* Portuguese ousted by Sultan ibn Sayf, a
powerful Ya'ariba leader.
*early 18th century* Civil war between the
Hinawis (descendents of the Qahtan) and the
Ghafiris (descendents of the Nizar).
*1749* Independent Sultanate of Muscat and
Oman established by Ahmad ibn Said, founder
of the Al Bu Said dynasty that still rules Oman.
*early-mid 19th century* Muscat and Oman
was most powerful state in Arabia, ruling
Zanzibar until 1861, and coastal parts of
Persia, Kenya, and Pakistan; came under
British protection.
*1951* The Sultanate of Muscat and Oman
achieved full independence from Britain. Treaty
of Friendship with Britain signed.
*1964* Discovery of oil led to transformation of
undeveloped kingdom into modern state.
*1970* After 38 years' rule, Sultan Said bin
Taimur replaced in bloodless coup by his son
Qaboos bin Said. Name changed to Sultanate of
Oman and modernization programme launched.
*1975* Left-wing rebels in Dhofar in the south,
who had been supported by South Yemen,
defeated with UK military assistance, ending a
ten-year insurrection.
*1981* The Consultative Council was set up;
Oman played a key role in the establishment of
a six-member Gulf Cooperation Council.
*1982* The Memorandum of Understanding with

the UK was signed, providing for regular consultation on international issues.
*1991* Joined the US-led coalition opposing Iraq's
occupation of Kuwait.

**Omar** alternative spelling of ◊Umar, 2nd caliph
of Islam.

**Omar Khayyám** (*c.* 1050–*c.* 1123) Persian
astronomer, mathematician, and poet. In the
West, he is chiefly known as a poet through
Edward Fitzgerald's version of 'The Rubaiyat of
Omar Khayyám' 1859.

**Omayyad dynasty** alternative spelling of
◊Umayyad dynasty.

**ombudsman** (Swedish 'commissioner') official who acts on behalf of the private citizen in
investigating complaints against the government. The post is of Scandinavian origin; it was
introduced in Sweden 1809, Denmark 1954,
and Norway 1962, and spread to other countries from the 1960s.

**omnivore** animal that feeds on both plant and
animal material. Omnivores have digestive
adaptations intermediate between those of
◊herbivores and ◊carnivores, with relatively
unspecialized digestive systems and gut micro-
organisms that can digest a variety of foodstuffs.
Omnivores include humans, the chimpanzee, the
cockroach, and the ant.

**Omsk** capital city, economic and cultural centre of Omsk oblast (region), Russian Federation;
population (1996 est) 1,160,000. Omsk is
located at the junction of the Om and Irtysh
rivers and lies on the Trans-Siberian Railway,
900 km/559 mi east of Yekaterinburg. The city
is a major industrial and commercial centre of
west Siberia. It contains engineering works, oil
refineries (linked with Tuimazy in Bashkortostan
by a 1,600-km/1,000-mi pipeline), wood-processing plants, and various food and other light
industrial factories.

**onager** wild ass found in western Asia.
Onagers are sandy brown, lighter underneath,
and about the size of a small horse. (Species
*Equus hemionus*.)

**oncogene** gene carried by a virus that induces
a cell to divide abnormally, giving rise to a cancer. Oncogenes arise from mutations in genes
(proto-oncogenes) found in all normal cells.
They are usually also found in viruses that are
capable of transforming normal cells to tumour
cells. Such viruses are able to insert their oncogenes into the host cell's DNA, causing it to
divide uncontrollably. More than one oncogene
may be necessary to transform a cell in this way.

**oncology** medical speciality concerned with
the diagnosis and treatment of ◊neoplasms,
especially cancer.

**Onega, Lake** Russian *Onezhskoye Ozero*,
lake in the far northwestern Russian Federation,
near the Finnish border. With an area of some
9,600 sq km/3,705 sq mi (excluding islands), it
is the second-largest lake in Europe. Lake Onega
is connected by the River Svir with Lake Ladoga
(the largest lake in Europe) and the Baltic Sea,

and by artificial waterways with the White Sea and the Volga (the 'Mariinsk' system).

**O'Neill, Eugene Gladstone** (1888–1953) US playwright. He is widely regarded as the greatest US dramatist. His plays, although tragic, are characterized by a down-to-earth quality and are often experimental in form, influenced by German expressionism, Strindberg, and Freud. They were a radical departure from the romantic and melodramatic American theatre entertainments. They include the Pulitzer prize-winning plays *Beyond the Horizon* (1920) and *Anna Christie* (1921), as well as *The Emperor Jones* (1920), *The Hairy Ape* (1922), *Desire Under the Elms* (1924), *The Iceman Cometh* (1946), and the posthumously produced autobiographical drama *A Long Day's Journey into Night* (1956; written 1941), also a Pulitzer prize winner. He was awarded the Nobel Prize for Literature 1936.

**onion** plant belonging to the lily family, whose bulb has a strong, distinctive smell and taste. Cultivated from ancient times, it may have originated in Asia. The bulb is edible; its pale concentric layers of leaf bases contain an oil that is released into the air when the onion is cut open, causing the eyes to water. Onions are used extensively in cooking. (*Allium cepa*, family Liliaceae.)

**online system** in computing, originally a system that allows the computer to work interactively with its users, responding to each instruction as it is given and prompting users for information when necessary. Since almost all the computers used now work this way, 'online system' is now used to refer to large databases, electronic mail, and conferencing systems accessed via a dial-up modem. These often have tens or hundreds of users from different places – sometimes from different countries – 'on line' at the same time.

**onomatopoeia** (Greek 'name-making') figure of speech that copies natural sounds. For example, the word 'cuckoo' imitates the sound that the cuckoo makes.

**Ontario** province of southeastern–central Canada, in area the country's second largest province, and its most populous. It is bounded to the north and northeast by Hudson Bay and James Bay, to the east by Québec (with the Ottawa River forming most of the boundary), and by Manitoba to the west. On the south it borders on, and extends into, all of the Great Lakes except Lake Michigan. From west to east along Ontario's southern boundary lie the US states of Minnesota, Wisconsin, Michigan, Ohio, Pennsylvania, and New York
*area* 1,068,600 sq km/412,480 sq mi
*capital* ◊Toronto (Canada's largest city)
*towns and cities* Hamilton, Ottawa (federal capital), London, Windsor, Kitchener, St Catharines, Oshawa, Thunder Bay, Sudbury
*population* (1996) 11,252,400
*physical* Canadian Shield; lakes Erie, Huron, Ontario, Superior; rivers Ottawa, Albany, St Lawrence; Georgian Bay; Niagara Falls
*industries* mining (nickel, iron, gold, copper,

uranium); manufacture of cars, aircraft, iron, steel, and high-tech goods; production of pulp, paper, oil, and chemicals; agriculture includes livestock rearing, cultivation of fruit, vegetables, and cereals.

**Ontario, Lake** smallest and easternmost of the ◊Great Lakes, on the US–Canadian border; area 19,200 sq km/7,400 sq mi. Extending for 310 km/194 mi, it has an average width of about 80 km/50 mi, and maximum depth of 244m/800 ft. It is connected to Lake Erie in the southeast by the Welland Ship Canal and the Niagara River, and drains into the ◊St Lawrence River to the northeast. The opening of the St Lawrence Seaway in 1959 made the lake accessible to large ocean-going vessels. Its main port is Toronto, Canada.

**ontogeny** process of development of a living organism, including the part of development that takes place after hatching or birth. The idea that 'ontogeny recapitulates phylogeny' (the development of an organism goes through the same stages as its evolutionary history), proposed by the German scientist Ernst Heinrich Haeckel, is now discredited.

**onyx** semiprecious variety of chalcedonic ◊silica ($SiO_2$) in which the crystals are too fine to be detected under a microscope, a state known as cryptocrystalline. It has straight parallel bands of different colours: milk-white, black, and red.

**oolite** limestone made up of tiny spherical carbonate particles, called *ooliths,* cemented together. Ooliths have a concentric structure with a diameter up to 2 mm/0.08 in. They were formed by chemical precipitation and accumulation on ancient sea floors.

**Oort, Jan Hendrik** (1900–1992) Dutch astronomer. In 1927, he calculated the mass and size of our Galaxy, the ◊Milky Way, and the Sun's distance from its centre, from the observed movements of stars around the Galaxy's centre. In 1950 Oort proposed that comets exist in a vast swarm, now called the ◊*Oort cloud,* at the edge of the Solar System.

**Oort cloud** spherical cloud of comets beyond Pluto, extending out to about 100,000 astronomical units (1.5 light years) from the Sun. The gravitational effect of passing stars and the rest of our Galaxy disturbs comets from the cloud so that they fall in towards the Sun on highly elongated orbits, becoming visible from Earth. As many as 10 trillion comets may reside in the Oort cloud, named after Dutch astronomer Jan Oort who postulated it in 1950.

**opal** form of hydrous ◊silica ($SiO_2.nH_2O$), often occurring as stalactites and found in many types of rock. The common opal is translucent, milk-white, yellow, red, blue, or green, and lustrous. Precious opal is opalescent, the characteristic play of colours being caused by close-packed silica spheres diffracting light rays within the stone.

**Op art** abbreviation for *Optical art,* type of abstract art, mainly painting, in which patterns are used to create the impression that the image is flickering or vibrating. This type of art began to emerge in about 1960 and the name was coined in 1964; it is a pun on ◊Pop art, a dominant style in the art world at the time in the late 1950s and '60s.

**OPEC** acronym for ◊*Organization of Petroleum-Exporting Countries.*

**Open College** in the UK, a network launched in 1987 by the Manpower Services Commission (now the Training Agency) to enable people to gain and update technical and vocational skills by means of distance teaching, such as correspondence, radio, and television.

**Open University** institution established in the UK in 1969 to enable adult students without qualifications to study to degree level without regular attendance. Open University teaching is based on a mixture of correspondence courses, TV and radio lectures and demonstrations, personal tuition organized on a regional basis, and summer schools.

**opera** dramatic musical work in which singing takes the place of speech. In opera the music accompanying the action has paramount importance, although dancing and spectacular staging may also play their parts. Opera originated in late 16th-century Florence when the musical declamation, lyrical monologues, and choruses of classical Greek drama were reproduced in current forms.

**operating system** (OS), in computing, a program that controls the basic operation of a computer. A typical OS controls the peripheral devices such as printers, organizes the filing system, provides a means of communicating with the operator, and runs other programs.

**operetta** light form of opera, with music, dance, and spoken dialogue. The story line is romantic and sentimental, often employing farce and parody. Its origins lie in the 19th-century *opéra comique*, and it is intended to amuse. Examples of operetta are Jacques Offenbach's *Orphée aux enfers/Orpheus in the Underworld* (1858), Johann Strauss' *Die Fledermaus/The Flittermouse* (1874), and Gilbert and Sullivan's *The Pirates of Penzance* (1879) and *The Mikado* (1885).

**ophthalmology** medical speciality concerned with diseases of the eye and its surrounding tissues.

**opium** drug extracted from the unripe seeds of the opium poppy (*Papaver somniferum*) of southwestern Asia. An addictive ◊narcotic, it contains several alkaloids, including *morphine,* one of the most powerful natural painkillers and addictive narcotics known, and *codeine,* a milder painkiller.

**Opium Wars** two wars, the First Opium War 1839–42 and the Second Opium War 1856–60, waged by Britain against China to enforce the opening of Chinese ports to trade in opium. Opium from British India paid for Britain's imports from China, such as porcelain, silk, and, above all, tea.

**opossum** any of a family of marsupials (mammals that carry their young in a pouch) native to North and South America. Most opossums are tree-living, nocturnal animals, with prehensile tails that can be used as an additional limb, and hands and feet well adapted for grasping. They range from 10 cm/4 in to 50 cm/20 in in length and are insectivorous, carnivorous, or, more commonly, omnivorous. (Family Didelphidae.)

**opposition** in astronomy, the moment at which a body in the Solar System lies opposite the Sun in the sky as seen from the Earth and crosses the ◊meridian at about midnight.

**optical character recognition** (OCR), in computing, a technique for inputting text to a computer by means of a document reader. First, a ◊scanner produces a digital image of the text; then character-recognition software makes use of stored knowledge about the shapes of individual characters to convert the digital image to a set of internal codes that can be stored and processed by computer.

**optical fibre** very fine, optically pure glass fibre through which light can be reflected to transmit images or data from one end to the other. Although expensive to produce and install, optical fibres can carry more data than traditional cables, and are less susceptible to interference. Standard optical fibre transmitters can send up to 10 billion bits of information per second by switching a laser beam on and off.

**optical illusion** scene or picture that fools the eye. An example of a natural optical illusion is that the Moon appears bigger when it is on the horizon than when it is high in the sky, owing to the ◊refraction of light rays by the Earth's atmosphere.

**optical mark recognition** (OMR), in computing, a technique that enables marks made in predetermined positions on computer-input forms to be detected optically and input to a computer. An *optical mark reader* shines a light beam onto the input document and is able to detect the marks because less light is reflected back from them than from the paler, unmarked paper.

**optic nerve** large nerve passing from the eye to the brain, carrying visual information. In mammals, it may contain up to a million nerve fibres, connecting the sensory cells of the retina to the optical centres in the brain. Embryologically, the optic nerve develops as an outgrowth of the brain.

**optics** branch of physics that deals with the study of ◊light and vision – for example, shadows and mirror images, lenses, microscopes, telescopes, and cameras. For all practical purposes light rays travel in straight lines, although Albert ◊Einstein demonstrated that they may be 'bent' by a gravitational field. On striking a surface they are reflected or refracted with some absorption of energy, and the study of this is known as geometrical optics.

**option** in business, a contract giving the owner the right (as opposed to the obligation, as with futures contracts; see ◊futures trading) to buy or sell a specific quantity of a particular commodity or currency at a future date and at an agreed price, in return for a premium. The buyer only can decide not to exercise the option if it would prove disadvantageous, but in this case would lose the premium paid.

**optoelectronics** branch of electronics concerned with the development of devices (based on the ◊semiconductor gallium arsenide) that respond not only to the ◊electrons of electronic data transmission, but also to ◊photons.

**oracle** (Latin *orare* 'to speak') sacred site where a deity gives answers or oracles, through the mouth of its priest, to a supplicant's questions about personal affairs or state policy. These were often ambivalent. There were more than 250 oracular seats in the Greek world. The earliest example was probably at Dodona (in ◊Epirus), where priests interpreted the sounds made by the sacred oaks of ◊Zeus, but the most celebrated was that of ◊Apollo, god of prophecy, at ◊Delphi.

**oral literature** stories that are or have been transmitted in spoken form, such as public recitation, rather than through writing or printing.

Most pre-literate societies have had a tradition of oral literature, including short folk tales, legends, myths, proverbs, and riddles as well as longer narrative works; and most of the ancient epics – such as the Greek *Odyssey* and the Mesopotamian *Gilgamesh* – seem to have been composed and added to over many centuries before they were committed to writing.

**Oran** Arabic *Wahran,* fortified seaport and commercial and manufacturing centre in Algeria, 5 km/3 mi from the port of Mers-el-Kebir; population (1989) 664,000. Products include iron, plastics, textiles, footwear, and processed food; the port trades in grain, wool, vegetables, and native esparto grass. Natural gas is brought to the city via a pipeline from the Sahara, and hydrocarbons are exported. There is an international airport.

**orange** round orange-coloured juicy citrus fruit of several species of evergreen trees, which bear white blossom and fruits at the same time. Thought to have originated in Southeast Asia, orange trees are commercially cultivated in Spain, Israel, the USA, Brazil, South Africa, and elsewhere. The sweet orange (*C. sinensis*) is the one commonly eaten fresh; the Jaffa, blood, and navel orange are varieties of this species. (Genus *Citrus*, family Rutaceae.)

**orang-utan** large ape found only in Borneo and Sumatra. Up to 1.65 m/5.5 ft in height, it is covered with long, red-brown hair and lives a largely solitary life in the trees, feeding mainly on fruit. Now an endangered species, it is officially protected because its habitat is being systematically destroyed by ◊deforestation. In 1998 there were less than 27,000 orang-utans in the wild, with an estimated 5,000–7,000 in Sumatra, 3,000–5,000 in Sabah (northeast Borneo), and 12,000–15,000 in Kalimantan (Indonesia). (Species *Pongo pygmaeus*.)

**oratorio** dramatic, nonscenic musical setting of religious texts, scored for orchestra, chorus, and solo voices. Its origins lie in the *Laude*

*spirituali* performed by St Philip Neri's Oratory in Rome in the 16th century, followed by the first definitive oratorio in the 17th century by Cavalieri. The form reached perfection in such works as J S Bach's *Christmas Oratorio,* and Handel's *Messiah*.

**orbit** path of one body in space around another, such as the orbit of Earth around the Sun, or the Moon around Earth. When the two bodies are similar in mass, as in a ◊binary star, both bodies move around their common centre of mass. The movement of objects in orbit follows Johann ◊Kepler's laws, which apply to artificial satellites as well as to natural bodies.

**orchestra** group of musicians playing together on different instruments. In Western music, an orchestra is typically based on the bowed, stringed instruments of the violin family, but often contains wind, brass, and percussion sections. The size and format may vary according to the requirements of composers.

**orchid** any plant of a large family that contains at least 15,000 species and 700 genera, distributed throughout the world except in the coldest areas, and most numerous in damp equatorial regions. The flowers are the most highly evolved of the plant kingdom; they have three ◊sepals and three petals and sometimes grow singly, but more usually appear with other flowers on spikes, growing up one side of the main stem, or all around the main stem, which may be upright or drooping. (Family Orchidaceae.)

**order** in classical architecture, the ◊column (including capital, shaft, and base) and the entablature, considered as an architectural whole. The five orders are Doric, Ionic, Corinthian, Tuscan, and Composite.

**order** in biological classification, a group of related ◊families. For example, the horse, rhinoceros, and tapir families are grouped in the order Perissodactyla, the odd-toed ungulates, because they all have either one or three toes on each foot. The names of orders are not shown in italic (unlike genus and species names) and by convention they have the ending '-formes' in birds and fish; '-a' in mammals, amphibians, reptiles, and other animals; and '-ales' in fungi and plants. Related orders are grouped together in a ◊class.

**ordinal number** in mathematics, one of the series first, second, third, fourth, ... . Ordinal numbers relate to order, whereas ◊cardinal numbers (1, 2, 3, 4, ... ) relate to quantity, or count.

**ordination** religious ceremony by which a person is accepted into the priesthood or monastic life in various religions. Within the Christian church, ordination authorizes a person to administer the sacraments.

**Ordovician** period of geological time 510–439 million years ago; the second period of the ◊Palaeozoic era. Animal life was confined to the sea: reef-building algae and the first jawless fish are characteristic.

**ore** body of rock, a vein within it, or a deposit of sediment, worth mining for the economically valuable mineral it contains. The term is usually applied to sources of metals. Occasionally metals are found uncombined (native metals), but more often they occur as compounds such as carbonates, sulphides, or oxides. The ores often contain unwanted impurities that must be removed when the metal is extracted.

**oregano** any of several perennial herbs belonging to the mint family, especially the aromatic O. *vulgare,* also known as wild marjoram. It is native to the Mediterranean countries and western Asia and naturalized in the Americas. Oregano is extensively used to season Mediterranean cooking. (Genus *Origanum,* family Labiatae.)

**Oregon** state in northwestern USA, on the Pacific coast. It is nicknamed Beaver State. Oregon was admitted to the Union in 1859 as the 33rd US state. It is bordered to the east by Idaho, to the north by Washington, to the south by California and Nevada, and to the west by the Pacific Ocean

*population* (1995) 3,140,600
*area* 251,500 sq km/97,079 sq mi
*capital* Salem
*towns and cities* Portland, Eugene, Gresham, Beaverton
*industries and products* wheat, fruit, dairy farming, livestock, salmon and tuna, timber, electronics, tourism, leisure industry.

**Orestes** in Greek mythology, the son of ◊Agamemnon and ◊Clytemnestra, who killed his mother on the instructions of Apollo because she and her lover Aegisthus had murdered his father. He was subsequently hounded by the ◊Furies until he was purified, and acquitted of the crime of matricide.

**organ** in biology, part of a living body that has a distinctive function or set of functions. Examples include the liver or brain in animals, or the leaf in plants. An organ is composed of a group of coordinated ◊tissues. A group of organs working together to perform a function is called an *organ system,* for example, the ◊digestive system comprises a number of organs including the stomach, the small intestine, the colon, the pancreas, and the liver.

**organ** musical wind instrument of ancient origin, in which sound is produced when a depressed key opens a valve, allowing compressed air to pass through a single pipe or a series of pipes; the number of pipes in total may vary, according to the size of the instrument. Apart from its continued use in serious compositions and for church music, the organ has been adapted for light entertainment.

**organelle** discrete and specialized structure in a living cell; organelles include mitochondria, chloroplasts, lysosomes, ribosomes, and the nucleus.

**organic chemistry** branch of chemistry that deals with carbon compounds. Organic compounds form the chemical basis of life and are more abundant than inorganic compounds. In a typical organic compound, each carbon atom forms bonds covalently with each of its neigh-

bouring carbon atoms in a chain or ring, and additionally with other atoms, commonly hydrogen, oxygen, nitrogen, or sulphur.

**organic farming** farming without the use of synthetic fertilizers (such as ◊nitrates and phosphates) or ◊pesticides (herbicides, insecticides, and fungicides) or other agrochemicals (such as hormones, growth stimulants, or fruit regulators). Food produced by genetic engineering cannot be described as organic.

**Organization for Economic Cooperation and Development** (OECD), international organization of 30 industrialized countries that provides a forum for discussion and coordination of member states' economic and social policies. Founded in 1961, with its headquarters in Paris, the OECD superseded the Organization for European Economic Cooperation (OEEC), which had been established in 1948 to implement the ◊Marshall Plan. The Commission of the European Union also participates in the OECD's work.

**Organization of African Unity** (OAU), association established in 1963 to eradicate colonialism and improve economic, cultural, and political cooperation in Africa. The secretary general is Salim Ahmed Salim of Tanzania. Its headquarters are in Addis Ababa, Ethiopia. There are now 53 members representing virtually the whole of central, southern, and northern Africa.

**Organization of American States** (OAS), association founded in 1948 at Bogotá, Colombia by a charter signed by representatives of North, Central, and South American states. It aims to maintain peace and solidarity within the hemisphere, and is also concerned with the social and economic development of Latin America.

**Organization of Petroleum-Exporting Countries** (OPEC), body established in 1960 to coordinate price and supply policies of oil-producing states. Its concerted action in raising prices in the 1970s triggered worldwide recession but also lessened demand so that its influence was reduced by the mid-1980s. OPEC members are: Algeria, Gabon, Indonesia, Iran, Iraq, Kuwait, Libya, Nigeria, Qatar, Saudi Arabia, the United Arab Emirates, and Venezuela. Ecuador, formerly a member, withdrew in 1993. OPEC's secretary-general is Rilwanu Lukman of Nigeria.

**orienteering** sport of cross-country running and route-finding. Competitors set off at one-minute intervals and have to find their way, using map and compass, to various checkpoints (approximately 0.8 km/0.5 mi apart), where their control cards are marked. World championships have been held since 1966.

**Orinoco** river in northern South America; it rises in the Sierra Parima range in southern Venezuela near the Brazilian border and flows north for about 2,400 km/1,500 mi through Venezuela, forming the boundary with Colombia for about 320 km/200 mi; tributaries include the Guaviare, Meta, Apure, Ventuari,

Caura, Arauca, and Caroni rivers. It is navigable by large steamers for 1,125 km/700 mi from its Atlantic delta; rapids obstruct the upper river. The Orinoco is South America's third-largest river; its drainage basin area is 962,000 sq km/371,428 sq mi.

**oriole** any of several brightly coloured songbirds belonging to two families: New World orioles belong to the family Icteridae, and Old World orioles are members of the family Oriolidae. They eat insects, seeds, and fruit.

**Orion** in astronomy, a very prominent constellation in the equatorial region of the sky (see ◊celestial sphere), identified with the hunter of Greek mythology.

**Orion nebula** luminous cloud of gas and dust 1,500 light years away, in the constellation Orion, from which stars are forming. It is about 15 light years in diameter, and contains enough gas to make a cluster of thousands of stars.

**Orissa** state of northeast India
*area* 155,700 sq km/60,115 sq mi
*capital* Bhubaneshwar
*towns and cities* Cuttack, Raurkela
*physical* coastal plain of Bay of Bengal, extending inland to the Eastern Ghats; the Mahanadi River valley and delta, containing the greatest population concentration; the shallow Chilka Lake with fisheries and game, set in the coastal swamps; the upland areas of the Ghats and Chota Nagpur plateau contain minerals
*features* temple of Jagannath or Juggernaut at Puri; Hirakud dam on the Mahanadi River provides irrigation and power; Utkal University; the Agricultural University at Bhubaneswar
*industries* chemicals, paper, steel; aluminium smelting at Hirakud using power from the dam; minerals include chromite (95% of India's output), dolomite, graphite, iron (for steel works at Raurkela), manganese, chromite, coal, bauxite, limestone
*agriculture* rice, wheat, oilseed, sugar
*population* (1994 est) 33,795,000
*language* Oriya (official)
*religion* 90% Hindu
*history* administered by the British 1803–1912 as a subdivision of Bengal, it joined with Bihar to become a province. In 1936 Orissa became a separate province, and in 1948–49 its area was almost doubled when 48 princely states merged with it before its designation as a state in 1950. In the 1960s, a drought resulted in the death of 1 million people from famine; the Hirakud dam complex has helped to reduce the risk of another catastrophe.

**Orkney Islands** island group and unitary authority off the northeast coast of Scotland
*area* 1,014 sq km/391 sq mi
*towns* Kirkwall (administrative headquarters), Stromness, both on Mainland (Pomona)
*physical* there are 90 islands and inlets in the group. The surface of the islands is irregular and indented by many arms of the sea. Next to Mainland, the most important of the islands are North and South Ronaldsay, Hoy, Rousay, Stronsay, Flotta, Shapinsay, Eday, Sanday, and Westray. The highest peak is Ward Hill in Hoy,

which has an elevation of 479 m/1,572 ft. The Old Man of Hoy is an isolated stack of red sandstone 137 m/450 ft high, off Hoy's northwest coast
*features* Skara Brae Neolithic village, and Maes Howe burial chamber; Scapa Flow; oil terminal on Flotta
*industries* offshore oil, woollen weaving, wind-powered electricity generation, distilling, boatbuilding, fish curing
*agriculture* fishing, beef cattle, dairy products
*population* (1996) 19,600
*famous people* Edwin Muir, John Rae
*history* population of Scandinavian descent; Harald I (Fairhair) of Norway conquered the islands in 876; pledged to James III of Scotland in 1468 for the dowry of Margaret of Denmark; Scapa Flow, between Mainland and Hoy, was a naval base in both World Wars, the German fleet scuttled itself here on 21 June 1919.

**Orléans** administrative centre of Loiret *département* in central France, situated on the right bank of the River Loire, 115 km/70 mi southwest of Paris; population (1990) 108,000, conurbation 243,000. Industries include engineering, textiles and food processing; there is also an extensive trade in agricultural produce and wine. Orléans is of pre-Roman origin. Joan of Arc, known as the Maid of Orléans, liberated the town from the English in 1429.

**Ormuzd** another name for *Ahura Mazda*, the good god of ◊Zoroastrianism.

**ornithology** study of birds. It covers scientific aspects relating to their structure and classification, and their habits, song, flight, and value to agriculture as destroyers of insect pests. Worldwide scientific banding (or the fitting of coded rings to captured specimens) has resulted in accurate information on bird movements and distribution. There is an International Council for Bird Preservation with its headquarters at the Natural History Museum, London.

**ornithophily** ◊pollination of flowers by birds. Ornithophilous flowers are typically brightly coloured, often red or orange. They produce large quantities of thin, watery nectar, and are scentless because most birds do not respond well to smell. They are found mostly in tropical areas, with hummingbirds being important pollinators in North and South America, and the sunbirds in Africa and Asia.

**orogeny** or *orogenesis*, the formation of mountains. It is brought about by the movements of the rigid plates making up the Earth's crust and upper-most mantle (described by ◊plate tectonics). Where two plates collide at a destructive margin rocks become folded and lifted to form chains of mountains (such as the Himalayas).

**Orpheus** mythical Greek poet and musician of Thrace; the son of ◊Apollo and the Muse Calliope. Orpheus ventured into Hades, the underworld, to bring back his wife Eurydice, who had died from a snakebite. His lyre playing was so charming that Pluto granted her return to life, but on condition that Orpheus walked ahead without looking back. He turned at the entrance and Eurydice was irretrievably lost. In his grief, he offended the ◊maenad women of Thrace, and they tore him to pieces.

**Ortega Saavedra, Daniel** (1945–  ) Nicaraguan socialist politician, head of state 1979–90. He was a member of the Marxist Sandinista Liberation Front (FSLN), which overthrew the regime of Anastasio Somoza Debayle in 1979, later becoming its secretary general. US-sponsored ◊Contra guerrillas opposed his government from 1982.

**orthodontics** branch of ◊dentistry concerned with ◊dentition, and with treatment of any irregularities, such as correction of malocclusion (faulty position of teeth).

**Orthodox Church** or *Eastern Orthodox Church* or *Greek Orthodox Church,* federation of self-governing Christian churches mainly found in Eastern Europe and parts of Asia. The centre of worship is the Eucharist. There is a married clergy, except for bishops; the Immaculate Conception is not accepted. The highest rank in the church is that of ecumenical patriarch, or bishop of Istanbul.

There are about 130 million adherents (1990).

**orthopaedics** (Greek *orthos* 'straight'; *pais* 'child') medical speciality concerned with the correction of disease or damage in bones and joints.

**Orwell, George** pen name of Eric Arthur Blair (1903–1950) English writer. His books include the satirical fable *Animal Farm* (1945), an attack on the Soviet Union and its leader, Stalin, which includes such slogans as 'All animals are equal, but some are more equal than others'; and the prophetic *Nineteen Eighty-Four* (1949), targeting Cold War politics, which portrays the catastrophic excesses of state control over the individual. He also wrote numerous essays. Orwell was distrustful of all political parties and ideologies, and a deep sense of social conscience and antipathy towards political dictatorship characterize his work.

**oryx** any of a group of large antelopes native to Africa and Asia. The *Arabian oryx* (*O. leucoryx*), at one time extinct in the wild, was successfully reintroduced into its natural habitat using stocks bred in captivity in 1982. By 1998 the oryx reintroduction project was seriously reduced through poaching. The population fell to 138, and 40 animals were returned to captivity as the population was believed to be no longer viable. By January 1999 there were less than 100 oryx remaining in wild and only 11 of these were female. (Genus *Oryx,* family Bovidae.)

**Osaka** industrial port on the Pacific coast of Honshu island, Japan, 24 km/15 mi from Kobe; population (1994) 2,481,000. It is Japan's third-largest city. Industries include iron, steel, shipbuilding, chemicals, and textiles. Emperor Kotoku established it as a capital in 645. *Osaka castle,* built in 1583, was the scene of a siege in 1614–15. The city is the home of the *bunraku* puppet theatre.

**Osborne, John James** (1929–1994) English dramatist. He became one of the first Angry Young Men (anti-establishment writers of the 1950s) of British theatre with his debut play, *Look Back in Anger* (1956). Other plays include *The Entertainer* (1957), *Luther* (1960), *Inadmissible Evidence* (1964), and *A Patriot for Me* (1965).

**oscillating universe** in astronomy, a theory that states that the gravitational attraction of the mass within the universe will eventually slow down and stop the expansion of the universe. The outward motions of the galaxies will then be reversed, eventually resulting in a 'Big Crunch' where all the matter in the universe would be contracted into a small volume of high density. This could undergo a further ◊Big Bang, thereby creating another expansion phase. The theory suggests that the universe would alternately expand and collapse through alternate Big Bangs and Big Crunches.

**oscilloscope** another name for ◊cathode-ray oscilloscope.

**Osiris** ancient Egyptian god, the embodiment of goodness, who ruled the underworld after being killed by ◊Set. The pharaohs were believed to be his incarnation. The sister-wife of Osiris was ◊Isis or Hathor; she miraculously conceived their son ◊Horus after the death of Osiris, and he eventually captured his father's murderer.

**Oslo** industrial port and capital of Norway; population (1996) 731,600. The main industries are shipbuilding, textiles, electrical equipment, engineering, machine tools, timber, and food processing. The first recorded settlement was made in the 11th century by Harald III Hardrada, but after a fire in 1624, it was entirely replanned by the Danish king Christian IV and renamed *Christiania* from 1624 to 1924. Following Norway's separation from Denmark (1814) and then Sweden (1905), the city reverted in 1925 to its original Norwegian name of Oslo.

**Osman I** or *Uthman I* (1259–1326) Turkish ruler from 1299. He began his career in the service of the Seljuk Turks, but in 1299 he set up a kingdom of his own in Bithynia, northwestern Asia, and assumed the title of sultan. He conquered a great part of Anatolia, so founding a Turkish empire. His successors were known as 'sons of Osman', from which the term ◊Ottoman Empire is derived.

**osmium** (Greek *osme* 'odour') hard, heavy, bluish-white, metallic element, symbol Os, atomic number 76, relative atomic mass 190.2. It is the densest of the elements, and is resistant to tarnish and corrosion. It occurs in platinum ores and as a free metal with iridium in a natural alloy called osmiridium, containing traces of platinum, ruthenium, and rhodium. Its uses include pen points and light-bulb filaments; like platinum, it is a useful catalyst.

**osmosis** movement of water through a selectively permeable membrane separating solutions of different concentrations. Water passes by ◊diffusion from a *weak solution* (high water

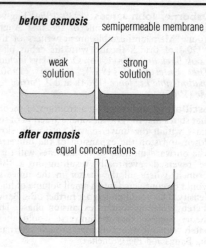

*before osmosis* semipermeable membrane

weak
solution

strong
solution

*after osmosis*
equal concentrations

**osmosis** *Apparatus for measuring osmotic pressure. In 1877 German physicist Wilhelm Pfeffer used this apparatus to make the first ever measurement of osmotic pressure and show that osmotic pressure varies according to temperature and the strength of the solute (dissolved substance).*

concentration) to a *strong solution* (low water concentration) until the two concentrations are equal. The selectively permeable membrane allows the diffusion of water but not of the solute (for example, sugar molecules). Many cell membranes behave in this way, and osmosis is a vital mechanism in the transport of fluids in living organisms – for example, in the transport of water from soil (weak solution) into the roots of plants (stronger solution of cell sap).

**osprey** bird of prey, sometimes called 'fish hawk' because it plunges feet first into the water to catch fish. It is dark brown above and a striking white below, and measures 60 cm/2 ft with a 2 m/6 ft wingspan. The nest is often built in trees near the seashore or lakeside, and two or three white eggs, blotched with crimson, are laid. Ospreys occur on all continents except Antarctica and have faced extinction in several areas. (Species *Pandion haliaetus*, family Pandionidae, order Falconiformes.)

**Ossetia** region in the Caucasus, on the border between Russia and Georgia. It is inhabited by the Ossets, who speak the Iranian language Ossetic, and who were conquered by the Russians in 1802.

Some live in Alania (formerly North Ossetia), an autonomous republic in the southwestern Russian Federation.

The rest live in ◊South Ossetia, an autonomous region of the Georgian republic. The region has been the scene of Osset–Georgian interethnic conflict since 1989. More than 100,000 Ossets from South Ossetia moved to Alania 1989–92, in turn causing the Ingush there to flee to Ingushetia.

**osteomyelitis** infection of bone, with spread of pus along the marrow cavity.

Now quite rare, it may follow from a compound fracture (where broken bone protrudes through the skin), or from infectious disease elsewhere in the body. It is more common in children whose bones are not yet fully grown.

**osteopathy** system of alternative medical practice that relies on physical manipulation to treat mechanical stress. It was developed over a century ago by US physician Andrew Taylor Still, who maintained that most ailments can be prevented or cured by techniques of spinal manipulation.

**osteoporosis** disease in which the bone substance becomes porous and brittle. It is common in older people, affecting more women than men. It may be treated with calcium supplements and etidronate. Approximately 1.7 million people worldwide, mostly women, suffer hip fractures, mainly due to osteoporosis. A single gene was discovered in 1993 to have a major influence on bone thinning.

**Ostia** ancient Roman town near the mouth of the Tiber. Founded about 330 BC, it was the port of Rome and had become a major commercial centre by the 2nd century AD. It was abandoned in the 9th century. The present-day seaside resort *Ostia Mare* is situated nearby.

**ostrich** large flightless bird. There is only one species, found in Africa. The male may be about 2.5 m/8 ft tall and weigh 135 kg/300 lb, and is the largest living bird. It has exceptionally strong legs and feet (two-toed) that enable it to run at high speed, and are also used in defence. It lives in family groups of one cock with several hens, each of which lays about 14 eggs. (Species *Struthio camelus*, order Struthioniformes.)

**Ostrogoth** member of a branch of the eastern Germanic people, the ◊Goths.

**Othman** alternative spelling of ◊Uthman, third caliph of Islam.

**otitis** inflammation of the ear. *Otitis externa*, occurring in the outer ear canal, is easily treated with antibiotics. Inflamed conditions of the middle ear (*otitis media*) or inner ear (*otitis interna*) are more serious, carrying the risk of deafness and infection of the brain. Treatment is with antibiotics or, more rarely, surgery.

**Ottawa** capital of Canada, in eastern Ontario, on the hills overlooking the Ottawa River, and divided by the Rideau Canal into the Upper (western) and Lower (eastern) towns; population (1996 est) of metropolitan area (with adjoining Hull, Québec) 1,030,500. Industries include engineering, food-processing, publishing, lumber, and the manufacture of pulp, paper, textiles, and leather products. Government, and community and health services employ a large section of the workforce. Ottawa was founded 1826–32 as Bytown, in honour of John By (1781–1836), whose army engineers were building the Rideau Canal. In 1854 it was renamed after the Ottawa River; the name deriving from the Outaouac, Native Canadian Algonquin people of the area.

**otter** any of various aquatic carnivores belonging to the weasel family, found on all continents except Australia. Otters have thick brown fur, short limbs, webbed toes, and long, compressed tails. They are social, playful, and agile.

**Otto** four Holy Roman emperors, including:

**Otto I** (912–973) Holy Roman Emperor from 962. He restored the power of the empire and asserted his authority over the pope and the nobles. His son, Liudolf, led a German rebellion allied with the Magyars, but Otto drew them from the siege of Augsburg (Bavaria) and ended the Magyar menace by his victory at Lechfeld in 955. He refounded the East Mark, or Austria, as a barrier against them.

**Otto IV** (c. 1174–1218) Holy Roman Emperor, elected in 1198. He was the son of Henry the Lion (1129–95), and was made Count of Poitou by his uncle, Richard (I) the Lionheart (1157–99). He clashed with Philip, Duke of Swabia, in rivalry for the empire. He engaged in controversy with Pope Innocent III (c. 1160–1216), and was defeated by the pope's ally Philip (II) Augustus of France at Bouvines in 1214. Otto lost the throne to Holy Roman Emperor ◊Frederick II, and retired to Brunswick (Germany).

**Otto cycle** alternative name for the ◊four-stroke cycle, introduced by the German engineer Nikolaus Otto (1832–1891) in 1876.

**Ottoman Empire** Muslim empire of the Turks from 1300 to 1920, the successor of the ◊Seljuk Empire. It was founded by ◊Osman I and reached its height with ◊Suleiman in the 16th century. Its capital was Istanbul (formerly Constantinople).

**OU** abbreviation for ◊*Open University*.

**Ouagadougou** also *Wagadugu*, capital and industrial centre of Burkina Faso, and of Kadiogo Province; population (1991 est) 634,000. Products include textiles, vegetable oil, beverages, and soap. Its pre-eminence as a commercial centre is challenged by Bobo-Dioulasso. The city has the palace of Moro Naba, emperor of the Mossi people, a neo-Romanesque cathedral, and a central avenue called the Champs Elysées. It was the capital of the Mossi empire from the 15th century.

**Oudh** region of north India, now part of Uttar Pradesh. An independent kingdom before it fell under Mogul rule, Oudh regained independence 1732–1856, when it was annexed by Britain. Its capital was Lucknow, centre of the ◊Indian Mutiny 1857–58. In 1877 it was joined with Agra, from 1902 as the United Provinces of Agra and Oudh, renamed Uttar Pradesh in 1950.

**Oughtred, William** (1575–1660) English mathematician, credited as the inventor of the slide rule in 1622. His major work *Clavis mathematicae/The Key to Mathematics* (1631) was a survey of the entire body of mathematical knowledge of his day. It introduced the '×' symbol for multiplication, as well as the abbreviations 'sin' for *sine* and 'cos' for *cosine*.

**output device** in computing, any device for displaying, in a form intelligible to the user, the results of processing carried out by a computer.

**ouzel** or *ousel*, ancient name for the blackbird. The *ring ouzel* (*Turdus torquatus*) is similar to a blackbird, but has a white band across the breast. It is found in Europe in mountainous and rocky country. *Water ouzel* is another name for the ◊dipper.

**ovary** in female animals, the organ that generates the ◊ovum. In humans, the ovaries are two whitish rounded bodies about 25 mm/1 in by 35 mm/1.5 in, located in the lower abdomen on either side of the uterus. Every month, from puberty to the onset of the menopause, an ovum is released from the ovary. This is called ovulation, and forms part of the ◊menstrual cycle. In botany, an ovary is the expanded basal portion of the ◊carpel of flowering plants, containing one or more ovules. It is hollow with a thick wall to protect the ovules. Following fertilization of the ovum, it develops into the fruit wall or pericarp.

**Overijssel** province of the east central Netherlands, extending from the IJsselmeer to the German border
*area* 3,340 sq km/1,290 sq mi
*capital* Zwolle
*towns and cities* Enschede, Hengelo, Deventer
*physical* the rivers rivers IJssel and Vecht; sandy flats, covered with waste stretches of heath and fen; some fertile pasture land along the IJsselmeer; land has been reclaimed in the east
*industries* textiles (cotton-spinning in the district of Twente)
*agriculture* livestock, dairy products, fishing
*population* (1997) 1,057,900
*history* ruled by the bishops of Utrecht during the Middle Ages; sold to Charles V of Spain in 1527; joined the revolt against Spanish authority to become one of the United Provinces of the Netherlands in 1579.

**overpopulation** too many people for the resources available in an area (such as food, land, and water). The consequences were first set out by English economist Thomas ◊Malthus at the start of the population explosion.

**overture** in music, the opening piece of a concert or opera, having the dual function of settling the audience and allowing the conductor and musicians to become acquainted with the ◊acoustic of a concert auditorium. See also ◊prelude.

**Ovid** Publius Ovidius Naso (43 BC–AD 17) Latin poet. His poetry deals mainly with the themes of love (*Amores* 20 BC, *Ars amatoria/The Art of Love* 1 BC), mythology (*Metamorphoses* AD 2), and exile (*Tristia* AD 9–12). Born at Sulmo, Ovid studied rhetoric in Rome in preparation for a legal career, but soon turned to literature. In AD 9 he was banished by Augustus to Tomis, on the Black Sea, where he died. Sophisticated, ironical, and self-pitying, his work was highly influential during the Middle Ages and Renaissance.

**ovoviviparous** method of animal reproduction in which fertilized eggs develop within the female (unlike oviparous), and the embryo gains no nutritional substances from the female (unlike viviparous). It occurs in some invertebrates, fishes, and reptiles.

**ovulation** in female animals, the process of releasing egg cells (ova) from the ◊ovary. In mammals it occurs as part of the ◊menstrual cycle.

**ovum** plural *ova,* female gamete (sex cell) before fertilization. In animals it is called an egg, and is produced in the ovaries. In plants, where it is also known as an egg cell or oosphere, the ovum is produced in an ovule. The ovum is nonmotile. It must be fertilized by a male gamete before it can develop further, except in cases of ◊parthenogenesis.

**Owen, David Anthony Llewellyn** (1938– ) British politician, Labour foreign secretary 1977–79. In 1981 he was one of the founders of the ◊Social Democratic Party (SDP), and became its leader in 1983. Opposed to the decision of the majority of the party to merge with the Liberals in 1987, Owen stood down but emerged in 1988 as leader of a rump SDP, which was eventually disbanded in 1990.

**Owen, Michael** (1979– ) English footballer. A striker of exceptional pace, he made his full England debut in February 1998 at the age of 18 years 59 days, then three months later became England's youngest ever goalscorer. He scored two goals at the 1998 World Cup finals, including what was widely regarded as the goal of the tournament against Argentina. In December 1998 he was voted the 1998 BBC Sports Personality of the Year. By October 1999 he had scored 6 goals in 16 England appearances.

**Owen, Wilfred Edward Salter** (1893–1918) English poet. His verse, owing much to the encouragement of Siegfried Sassoon, is among the most moving of World War I poetry; it shatters the illusion of the glory of war, revealing its hollowness and cruel destruction of beauty. Only four poems were published during his lifetime; he was killed in action a week before the Armistice. After Owen's death Sassoon collected and edited his *Poems* (1920). Among the best known are 'Dulce et Decorum Est' and 'Anthem for Doomed Youth', published in 1921. Benjamin ◊Britten used several of the poems in his *War Requiem* (1962).

**Owens, Jesse (James Cleveland)** (1913–1980) US track and field athlete who excelled in the sprints, hurdles, and the long jump. At the 1936 Berlin Olympics he won four gold medals.
*career highlights*
*Olympic Games* gold 100 metres, 200 metres, 4 x 100 metres relay, long jump (all in 1936)
*World Records* 100 metres 1936; 100 yards: 1935, 1936; 200 metres: 1935; 220 yards: 1935; 200 metres hurdles: 1935; 220 yards hurdles: 1935; 4 x 100 metres relay: 1936 (US National team); long jump: 1935

**owl** any of a group of mainly nocturnal birds of prey found worldwide. They have hooked beaks, heads that can turn quickly and far round on their very short necks, and forward-facing immobile eyes, surrounded by 'facial discs' of rayed feathers; they fly silently and have an acute sense of hearing. Owls comprise two families: typical owls (family Strigidae), of which there are about 120 species, and barn owls (family Tytonidae), of which there are 10 species. (Order Strigiformes.)

**ox** castrated male of domestic cattle, used in developing countries for ploughing and other

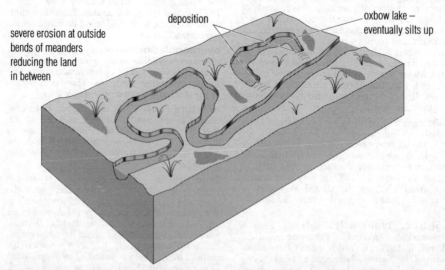

severe erosion at outside bends of meanders reducing the land in between

deposition

oxbow lake – eventually silts up

**oxbow lake** *The formation of an oxbow lake. As a river meanders across a flood plain, the outer bends are gradually eroded and the water channel deepens; as the loops widen, the neck of the loop narrows and finally gives way, allowing the water to flow in a more direct route, isolating the old water channel and forming an oxbow lake.*

agricultural work. Also the extinct wild ox or ◊aurochs of Europe, and surviving wild species such as buffaloes and yaks.

**oxalic acid** (COOH)$_2$.2H$_2$O white, poisonous solid, soluble in water, alcohol, and ether. Oxalic acid is found in rhubarb, and its salts (oxalates) occur in wood sorrel (genus *Oxalis,* family Oxalidaceae) and other plants. It also occurs naturally in human body cells. It is used in the leather and textile industries, in dyeing and bleaching, ink manufacture, metal polishes, and for removing rust and ink stains.

**oxbow lake** curved lake found on the flood plain of a river. Oxbows are caused by the loops of ◊meanders being cut off at times of flood and the river subsequently adopting a shorter course. In the USA, the term bayou is often used.

**Oxford** university city and administrative centre of ◊Oxfordshire in south central England, at the confluence of the rivers Thames (called the Isis around Oxford) and Cherwell, 84 km/52 mi northwest of London; population (1994 est) 121,000. Oxford University has 36 colleges, the oldest being University College (1249). Industries include motor vehicles at Cowley, steel products, electrical goods, publishing (Oxford University Press, Blackwells), and English language schools. Tourism is important.
*features* these include Christ Church cathedral (12th century); the Divinity School and Duke Humphrey's Library (1488); the Sheldonian Theatre, designed by Christopher ◊Wren 1663–69; the Ashmolean museum (1845); and the 17th-century Bodleian Library. Other museums include the University Museum (1855–60), designed by Benjamin Woodward, the Pitt-Rivers Museum, and the Museum of Modern Art. Features of the colleges include the 14th-century Mob Quad and library at Merton College; the Canterbury Quad (1636) and gardens laid out by Capability Brown at St John's College; and Holman Hunt's *The Light of the World* in Keble College. The Bate Collection of Historical Instruments is housed at the Faculty of Music. The Botanic Gardens (laid out in 1621) are the oldest in Britain. On 1 May (May morning) madrigals are sung at the top of Magdalen College tower. St Giles fair takes place every September.
*history* the town was first occupied in Saxon times as a fording point, and is first mentioned in written records in the Anglo-Saxon Chronicle of 912. The University of Oxford, the oldest in England, is first mentioned in the 12th century, when its growth was encouraged by the influx of English students expelled from Paris in 1167. The fame of the university grew steadily, until by the 14th century it was the equal of any in Europe. As the university grew, there was increasing antagonism between it and the town. Most of the university's buildings were built during the 15th, 16th, and 17th centuries. The earliest colleges were University College (1249), Balliol (1263), and Merton (1264).
During the Civil War, the university supported the Royalist cause while the city declared for Parliament. Oxford became the headquarters of the king and court in 1642, but yielded to the Parliamentary commander in chief, Gen Fairfax, in 1646.

By the beginning of the 20th century, the city had experienced rapid expansion and industrialization, and printing and publishing industries had become firmly established. In the 1920s the English industrial magnate William Morris (1877–1963), later Lord Nuffield, began a motor-car industry at Cowley, just outside the city, which became the headquarters of the Austin-Rover group.

**Oxford Movement** also known as *Tractarian Movement* or *Catholic Revival,* movement that attempted to revive Catholic religion in the Church of England. Cardinal Newman dated the movement from Keble's sermon in Oxford in 1833. The Oxford Movement by the turn of the century had transformed the Anglican communion, and survives today as Anglo-Catholicism.

**Oxfordshire** county of south central England
*area* 2,610 sq km/1,007 sq mi
*towns and cities* ◊Oxford (administrative headquarters), Abingdon, Banbury, Goring, Henley-on-Thames, Wallingford, Witney, Woodstock, Wantage, Chipping Norton, Thame
*physical* River Thames and tributaries (the Cherwell, Evenlode, Ock, Thame, and Windrush); Cotswold Hills (in the north) and Chiltern Hills (in the southeast)
*features* Vale of the White Horse (with a chalk hill figure 114 m/374 ft, below the hill camp known as Uffington Castle); Oxford University; Blenheim Palace (a World Heritage site), Woodstock (started in 1705 by Vanbrugh with help from Nicholas Hawksmoor, completed in 1722), with landscaped grounds by Capability ◊Brown; early 14th-century Broughton Castle; Rousham Park (1635), remodelled by William ◊Kent (1738–40), with landscaped garden; Ditchley Park, designed by James Gibbs in 1720; Europe's major fusion project JET (Joint European Torus) at the UK Atomic Energy Authority's fusion laboratories at Culham; the Manor House, Kelmscott (country house of William Morris, leader of the Arts and Crafts movement); Henley Regatta
*agriculture* cereals, sheep, dairy farming
*industries* agricultural implements (at Banbury); aluminium (at Banbury); bricks; cars (Cowley); cement; iron ore (in the north); high technology industries; medical electronic equipment; paper; publishing; nuclear research (Harwell); biotechnology
*population* (1996) 603,100
*famous people* Winston Churchill, William Davenant, Stephen Hawking, William Morris, Flora Thompson.

**oxidation** in chemistry, the loss of ◊electrons, gain of oxygen, or loss of hydrogen by an atom, ion, or molecule during a chemical reaction.

**oxide** compound of oxygen and another element, frequently produced by burning the element or a compound of it in air or oxygen.

**oxpecker** or *tick-bird,* either of two species of African birds belonging to the starling family.

They climb around on the bodies of large mammals, feeding on ticks and other parasites and on cattle earwax. They are usually seen in groups of seven or eight, attending a herd of buffaloes or antelopes, and may help to warn the host of approaching dangers. (Species *Buphagus africana*, family Sturnidae, order Passeriformes.)

**oxyacetylene torch** gas torch that burns ethyne (acetylene) in pure oxygen, producing a high-temperature flame (3,000°C/5,400°F). It is widely used in welding to fuse metals. In the cutting torch, a jet of oxygen burns through metal already melted by the flame.

**oxygen** (Greek *oxys* 'acid'; *genes* 'forming') colourless, odourless, tasteless, nonmetallic, gaseous element, symbol O, atomic number 8, relative atomic mass 15.9994. It is the most abundant element in the Earth's crust (almost 50% by mass), forms about 21% by volume of the atmosphere, and is present in combined form in water and many other substances. Oxygen is a by-product of ◊photosynthesis and the basis for ◊respiration in plants and animals.

**oxymoron** (Greek 'sharply dull' or 'pointedly foolish') figure of speech involving the combination of two or more words that are normally opposites, in order to startle. *Bittersweet* is an oxymoron, as are *cruel to be kind* and *beloved enemy*.

**oyster** edible shellfish with a rough, irregular hinged shell, found on the sea bottom in coastal areas. Oysters are bivalve ◊molluscs; the upper valve (shell) is flat, the lower hollow, like a bowl, and the two are hinged by an elastic ligament. The mantle, a protective layer of skin, lies against the shell, shielding the inner body, which includes the organs for breathing, digesting food, and reproduction. Oysters commonly change their sex once a year, sometimes more often; females can release up to a million eggs during a spawning period. (Family Ostreidae.)

**oyster catcher** any of several quite large, chunky shorebirds, with a long, heavy bill which is flattened at the sides and used to prise open the shells of oysters, mussels, and other shellfish. (Family Haematopodidae, order Charadriiformes.)

**Özal, Turgut** (1927–1993) Turkish Islamic right-wing politician, prime minister 1983–89, and president 1989–93. He was responsible for improving his country's relations with Greece, but his prime objective was to strengthen Turkey's alliance with the USA.

**Ozark Mountains** highland plateau region in south-central USA (shared by Arkansas, Illinois, Kansas, Missouri, Oklahoma) with ridges, valleys, and streams; area 130,000 sq km/50,000 sq mi. Extending between the Missouri and Arkansas rivers, it contains the *Ozark* and Springfield plateaux, the Boston Mountains, and the Salem uplands. Generally low in elevation, 300–400 m/984–1,312 ft, the highlands crest in the Boston Mountains at 800 m/2,625 ft. The area is heavily forested, with lead and zinc mining, agricultural, and recreational activities.

**ozone** $O_3$ highly reactive pale-blue gas with a penetrating odour. Ozone is an allotrope of oxygen (see ◊allotropy), made up of three atoms of oxygen. It is formed when the molecule of the stable form of oxygen ($O_2$) is split by ultraviolet radiation or electrical discharge. It forms the ◊ozone layer in the upper atmosphere, which protects life on Earth from ultraviolet rays, a cause of skin cancer.

**ozone depleter** any chemical that destroys the ozone in the stratosphere. Most ozone depleters are chemically stable compounds containing chlorine or bromine, which remain unchanged for long enough to drift up to the upper atmosphere. The best known are ◊chlorofluorocarbons (CFCs), but many other ozone depleters are known, including halons, used in some fire extinguishers; methyl chloroform and carbon tetrachloride, both solvents; some CFC substitutes; and the pesticide methyl bromide.

**ozone layer** thin layer of the gas ◊ozone in the upper atmosphere that shields the Earth from harmful ultraviolet rays. A continent-sized hole has formed over Antarctica as a result of damage to the ozone layer. This has been caused in part by ◊chlorofluorocarbons (CFCs), but many reactions destroy ozone in the stratosphere: nitric oxide, chlorine, and bromine atoms are implicated.

# P

**pacemaker** or *sinoatrial node* (SA node, in vertebrates, a group of muscle cells in the wall of the heart that contracts spontaneously and rhythmically, setting the pace for the contractions of the rest of the heart. The pacemaker's intrinsic rate of contraction is increased or decreased, according to the needs of the body, by stimulation from the ◊autonomic nervous system. The term also refers to a medical device implanted under the skin of a patient whose heart beats inefficiently. It delivers minute electric shocks to stimulate the heart muscles at regular intervals and restores normal heartbeat.

**Pacific Islands** former United Nations trust territory (1947–1990) in the western Pacific captured from Japan during World War II. The territory comprised over 2,000 islands and atolls and was assigned to the USA in 1947. The islands were divided into four governmental units: the *Northern Mariana Islands* (except Guam) which became a self-governing commonwealth in union with the USA in 1975 (inhabitants granted US citizenship in 1986); the Marshall Islands, the Federated States of Micronesia, and the Republic of Palau (formerly also known as Belau) became self-governing in 1979–80, signing agreements of free association with the USA in 1986. In December 1990 the United Nations Security Council voted to dissolve its trusteeship over the islands with the exception of Palau. The Marshall Islands and the Federated States of Micronesia were granted UN membership in 1991.

**Pacific Ocean** world's largest ocean, extending from Antarctica to the Bering Strait; area 166,242,500 sq km/64,170,000 sq mi; greatest breadth 16,000 km/9,942 mi, length 11,000 km/6,835 mi; average depth 4,188 m/13,749 ft; greatest depth of any ocean 11,524 m/37,808 ft in the Mindanao Trench, east of the Philippines.

**Pacific War** war 1879–83 fought by an alliance of Bolivia and Peru against Chile. Chile seized Antofagasta and the coast between the mouths of the rivers Loa and Paposo, rendering Bolivia landlocked, and also annexed the south Peruvian coastline from Arica to the mouth of the Loa, including the nitrate fields of the Atacama Desert.

**pacifism** belief that violence, even in self-defence, is unjustifiable under any conditions and that arbitration is preferable to war as a means of solving disputes. In the East, pacifism has roots in Buddhism, and nonviolent action was used by Mahatma ◊Gandhi in the struggle for Indian independence.

**Padua** Italian *Padova;* ancient *Patavium,* town in Veneto, northern Italy, on the canalized section of the River Bacchiglione, 38 km/24 mi west of Venice; population (1992) 213,700. Industries include engineering, and the manufacture of clothing and synthetic fibres. The astronomer Galileo taught at the university, founded in 1222.

**paediatrics** medical speciality concerned with the care of children. Paediatricians treat childhood diseases such as measles, chicken pox, and mumps, and immunize children against more serious infections such as diptheria. Their role also includes treating and identifying disorders caused by lack of proper nutrition or child abuse.

**Pagan** archaeological site in Myanmar, on the Irrawaddy River, with the ruins of the former capital (founded 847, taken by the Mongol leader Kublai Khan 1287). These include Buddhist pagodas, shrines, and temples with wall paintings of the great period of Burmese art (11th–13th centuries), during which the Pagan state controlled much of Burma (now Myanmar).

**pagan** (Latin *paganus* 'a person from the countryside') usually, a member of one of the pre-Christian cultures of northern Europe, primarily Celtic or Norse, linked to the stone circles and to an agricultural calendar of which the main festivals are the summer and winter solstices and Beltane, the spring festival.

**Pahlavi dynasty** Iranian dynasty founded by Reza Khan (1877–1944), an army officer who seized control of the government in 1921 and was proclaimed shah in 1925. During World War II, Britain and the USSR were nervous about his German sympathies and occupied Iran in 1941–46. They compelled him to abdicate in 1941 in favour of his son Muhammad Reza Shah Pahlavi who was deposed in the Islamic revolution of 1979.

**pain** sense that gives an awareness of harmful effects on or in the body. It may be triggered by stimuli such as trauma, inflammation, and heat. Pain is transmitted by specialized nerves and also has psychological components controlled by higher centres in the brain. Drugs that control pain are known as painkillers or ◊analgesics.

**Paine, Thomas** (1737–1809) English left-wing political writer. He was active in the American and French revolutions. His pamphlet *Common Sense* (1776) ignited passions in the American Revolution; others include *The Rights of Man* (1791) and *The Age of Reason* (1793). He advocated republicanism, deism, the abolition of slavery, and the emancipation of women.

**paint** any of various materials used to give a protective and decorative finish to surfaces or for making pictures. A paint consists of a pigment suspended in a vehicle, or binder, usually with added solvents. It is the vehicle that dries and hardens to form an adhesive film of paint. Among the most common kinds are cellulose paints (or lacquers), oil-based paints, emulsion (water-based) paints, and special types such as enamels and primers.

**painting** the application of coloured pigment to a surface. The chief methods of painting are: *tempera* emulsion painting, with a gelatinous (for example, egg yolk) rather than oil base – known in ancient Egypt; *fresco* watercolour painting on plaster walls – the palace of Knossos, Crete, contains examples from about 2,000 BC; *ink* developed in China for calligraphy in the Sung period and highly popular in Japan from the 15th century; *oil* ground pigments in linseed, walnut, or other oil, it spread from northern to southern Europe in the 15th century; *watercolour* pigments combined with gum arabic and glycerol, which are diluted with water – the method was developed in the 15th–17th centuries for wash drawings; *acrylic* synthetic pigments developed after World War II, the colours are very hard and brilliant.

**Paisley, Ian (Richard Kyle)** (1926– ) Northern Ireland politician, cleric, and leader of the Democratic Unionist Party (DUP) from 1971. An imposing and deeply influential member of the Protestant community, he remains staunchly committed to the union with Britain. His political career was one of high drama, marked by protests, resignations, fierce oratory, and a pugnacious and forthright manner.

**Pakistan** Islamic Republic of
*national name* Islami Jamhuriya e Pakistan

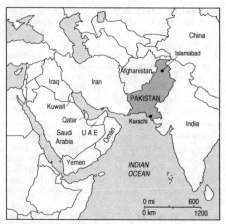

**area** 803,940 sq km/310,321 sq mi; one-third of Kashmir under Pakistani control
**capital** Islamabad
**major towns/cities** Lahore, Rawalpindi, Faisalabad, Karachi, Hyderabad, Multan, Peshawar, Gujranwala, Sialkot, Sargodha, Quetta, Islamabad
**major ports** Karachi, Port Qasim
**physical features** fertile Indus plain in east, Baluchistan plateau in west, mountains in north

and northwest; the 'five rivers' (Indus, Jhelum, Chenab, Ravi, and Sutlej) feed the world's largest irrigation system; K2 mountain; Khyber Pass
**head of state** Rafiq Tarar from 1997
**head of government** Nawaz Sharif from 1997
**political system** emergent democracy
**political parties** Islamic Democratic Alliance (IDA), conservative; Pakistan People's Party (PPP), moderate, Islamic, socialist; Pakistan Muslim League (PML), Islamic conservative (contains pro- and anti-government factions); Pakistan Islamic Front (PIF), Islamic fundamentalist, right wing; Awami National Party (ANP), left wing; National Democratic Alliance (NDA) bloc, left of centre; Mohajir National Movement (MQM), Sind-based *mohajir* settlers (Muslims previously living in India); Movement for Justice, reformative, anti-corruption
**currency** Pakistan rupee
**GNP per capita (PPP)** (US$) 1,560 (1998)
**exports** cotton, textiles, petroleum and petroleum products, clothing and accessories, leather, rice, food and live animals. Principal market: USA 21.5% (1998–99)
**population** 152,330,000 (1999 est)
**language** Urdu (official); English, Punjabi, Sindhi, Pashto, Baluchi, other local dialects
**religion** Sunni Muslim 75%, Shiite Muslim 20%; also Hindu, Christian, Parsee, Buddhist
**life expectancy** 63 (men); 65 (women) (1995–2000)
*Chronology*
*2500–1600 BC* The area was the site of the Indus Valley civilization, a sophisticated, city-based ancient culture.
*327 BC* Invaded by Alexander the Great of Macedonia.
*1st–2nd centuries* North Pakistan was the heartland of the Kusana Empire, formed by invaders from Central Asia.
*8th century* First Muslim conquests, in Baluchistan and Sind, followed by increasing immigration by Muslims from the west, from the 10th century.
*1206* Establishment of Delhi Sultanate, stretching from northwest Pakistan and across northern India.
*16th century* Sikh religion developed in Punjab.
*16th–17th centuries* Lahore served intermittently as a capital city for the Mogul Empire, which stretched across the northern half of the Indian subcontinent.
*1843–49* Sind and Punjab annexed by British and incorporated within empire of 'British India'.
*late 19th century* Major canal irrigation projects in West Punjab and the northern Indus Valley drew in settlers from the east, as wheat and cotton production expanded.
*1933* The name 'Pakistan' (Urdu for 'Pure Nation') invented by Choudhary Rahmat Ali, as Muslims within British India began to campaign for the establishment of an independent Muslim territory that would embrace the four provinces of Sind, Baluchistan, Punjab, and the Northwest Frontier.

**1940** The All-India Muslim League (established in 1906), led by Karachi-born Muhammad Ali Jinnah, endorsed the concept of a separate nation for Muslims in the Lahore Resolution.

**1947** Independence achieved from Britain, as dominion within the Commonwealth. Pakistan, which included East Bengal, a Muslim-dominated province more than 1,600 km/1,000 mi from Punjab, was formed following the partition of British India. Large-scale and violent cross-border migrations of Muslims, Hindus, and Sikhs followed, and a brief border war with India over disputed Kashmir.

**1948** Jinnah, the country's first governor general, died.

**1956** Proclaimed a republic.

**1958** Military rule imposed by Gen Ayub Khan.

**1965** Border war with India over disputed territory of Kashmir.

**1969** Power transferred to Gen Yahya Khan following strikes and riots.

**1970** General election produced clear majority in East Pakistan for pro-autonomy Awami League, led by Sheikh Mujibur Rahman, and in West Pakistan for Islamic socialist Pakistan People's Party (PPP), led by Zulfiqar Ali Bhutto.

**1971** East Pakistan secured independence, as Bangladesh, following a civil war in which it received decisive military support from India. Power was transferred from the military to the populist Bhutto in Pakistan.

**1977** Bhutto overthrown in military coup by Gen Zia ul-Haq following months of civil unrest; martial law imposed.

**1979** Bhutto executed for alleged murder; tight political restrictions imposed by Zia regime.

**1980** Three million refugees fled to the Northwest Frontier Province and Baluchistan as a result of the Soviet invasion of Afghanistan.

**1981** The broad-based Opposition Movement for the Restoration of Democracy was formed. The Islamization process was pushed forward by the government.

**1985** Martial law and the ban on political parties was lifted.

**1986** Agitation for free elections was launched by Benazir Bhutto, the daughter of Zulfiqar Ali Bhutto.

**1988** An Islamic legal code, the Shari'a, was introduced; Zia was killed in a military plane crash. Benazir Bhutto became prime minister after the (now centrist) PPP won the general election.

**1989** Tension with India was increased by outbreaks of civil war in Kashmir. Pakistan rejoined the Commonwealth, which it had left in 1972.

**1990** Bhutto was dismissed as prime minister by President Ghulam Ishaq Khan on charges of incompetence and corruption. The conservative Islamic Democratic Alliance (IDA), led by Nawaz Sharif, won the general election and launched a privatization and economic deregulation programme.

**1993** Khan and Sharif resigned. Benazir Bhutto and PPP were re-elected. Farooq Leghari (PPP) was elected president.

**1994** There was regional sectarian violence between Shia and Sunni Muslims, centred in Karachi.

**1996** Benazir Bhutto was dismissed by Leghari amid allegations of corruption.

**1997** The right-of-centre Pakistan Muslim League won in the general election, returning Nawaz Sharif to power as prime minister. President Leghari resigned. Rafiq Tarar was elected president.

**1998** There were antigovernment protests as the economy deteriorated. Sharif proposed introducing full Islamic law but this met with opposition within the parliament. Pakistan conducted its first ever nuclear tests, provoking international condemnation and sanctions by the USA. Benazir Bhutto and her husband were charged with corruption. Federal rule was imposed on Sindh as a result of escalating violence. A $5.5 billion economic bailout package was agreed with the IMF and World Bank.

**1999** Benazir Bhutto and her husband were found guilty of corruption, sentenced to five years in prison, and fined £5.3 million. In June India agreed to enter peace talks on Kashmir.

**Palaeocene** (Greek 'old' + 'recent') first epoch of the Tertiary period of geological time, 65–56.5 million years ago. Many types of mammals spread rapidly after the disappearance of the great reptiles of the Mesozoic. Flying mammals replaced the flying reptiles, swimming mammals replaced the swimming reptiles, and all the ecological niches vacated by the reptiles were adopted by mammals.

**Palaeolithic** the Old Stone Age period, the earliest stage of human technology; see ◊prehistory.

**palaeontology** in geology, the study of ancient life, encompassing the structure of ancient organisms and their environment, evolution, and ecology, as revealed by their ◊fossils. The practical aspects of palaeontology are based on using the presence of different fossils to date particular rock strata and to identify rocks that were laid down under particular conditions; for instance, giving rise to the formation of oil.

**Palaeozoic** era of geological time 570–245 million years ago. It comprises the Cambrian, Ordovician, Silurian, Devonian, Carboniferous, and Permian periods. The Cambrian, Ordovician, and Silurian constitute the Lower or Early Palaeozoic; the Devonian, Carboniferous, and Permian make up the Upper or Late Palaeozoic. The era includes the evolution of hard-shelled multicellular life forms in the sea; the invasion of land by plants and animals; and the evolution of fish, amphibians, and early reptiles. The earliest identifiable fossils date from this era.

**Palatinate** called the *Pfalz* in Germany, historic division of Germany, dating from before the 8th century. It was ruled by a *count palatine* (a count with royal prerogatives) and varied in size.

**Palau** Republic of (also known as *Belau)*
*area* 508 sq km/196 sq mi
*capital* Koror (on Koror Island)
*major towns/cities* Melekeiok, Garusuun, Malakal

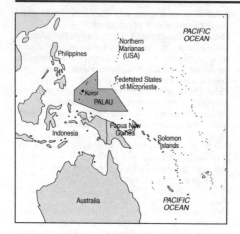

**physical features** more than 350 (mostly unin-habited) islands, islets, and atolls in the west Pacific; warm, humid climate, susceptible to typhoons
**head of state and government** Kuniwo Nakamura from 1992
**political system** liberal democracy
**political parties** there are no formally organized political parties
**currency** US dollar
**GNP per capita (PPP)** (US$) N/A
**exports** copra, coconut oil, handicrafts, trochus, tuna
**population** 19,000 (1999 est)
**language** Palauan and English
**Religion** Christian, principally Roman Catholic
**life expectancy** 65 (men); 71 (women) (1998 est)
**Chronology**
**c. 1000 BC** Micronesians first settled the islands.
**1543** First visited by Spanish navigator Ruy Lopez de Villalobos.
**16th century** Colonized by Spain.
**later 16th century** Fell under Spanish influence.
**1899** Purchased from Spain by Germany.
**1914** Occupied by Japan at the outbreak of World War I.
**1920** Administered by Japan under League of Nations mandate.
**1944** Occupied by USA after Japanese removed during World War II.
**1947** Became part of United Nations (UN) Pacific Islands Trust Territory, administered by USA.
**1981** Acquired autonomy as the Republic of Belau (Palau) under a constitution which prohibited the entry, storage, or disposal of nuclear or biological weapons.
**1982** The Compact of Free Association signed with the USA, providing for the right to maintain US military facilities in return for economic aid. However, the compact could not come into force since it contradicted the constitution, which could only be amended by a 75% vote in favour.
**1985** President Haruo Remeliik was assassinated; succeeded by Lazarus Salii.

**1988** President Salii committed suicide and was succeeded by Ngiratkel Etpison.
**1992** Kuniwo Nakamura was elected president.
**1993** A referendum approved a constitutional amendment allowing the implementation of the Compact of Free Association with the USA.
**1994** Independence was achieved and UN membership granted.

**Palermo** capital and seaport of Sicily; population (1992) 696,700. It is also capital of Palermo province. Palermo is situated on the northern coastal plain of the Conca d'Oro, on a bay of the Tyrrhenian Sea. Industries include shipbuilding, steel, glass, textiles, and chemicals. Palermo is the most important industrial centre and port with shipbuilding facilities in southern Italy after Naples. It was founded by the Phoenicians in the 8th century BC.

**Palestine** (Arabic *Falastin,* 'Philistine') historic geographical area at the eastern end of the Mediterranean sea, also known as the Holy Land because of its historic and symbolic importance for Jews, Christians, and Muslims. Early settlers included the Canaanites, Hebrews, and Philistines. Over the centuries it became part of the Egyptian, Assyrian, Babylonian, Macedonian, Ptolemaic, Seleucid, Roman, Byzantine, Arab, Ottoman, and British empires. Today it comprises parts of Israel and Jordan.

**Palestine Liberation Organization** (PLO), Arab organization founded in 1964 to bring about an independent state in Palestine. It consists of several distinct groupings, the chief of which is al-◊Fatah, led by Yassir ◊Arafat, the president of the PLO from 1969.

**Palestine Wars** another name for the ◊Arab-Israeli Wars.

**Pali** ancient Indo-European language of northern India, related to Sanskrit, and a classical language of Buddhism.

**palindrome** word, sentence, or verse that reads the same backwards as forwards (ignoring word breaks and punctuation). 'Madam, in Eden, I'm Adam.' 'Ten animals I slam in a net.'

**palisade cell** cylindrical cell lying immediately beneath the upper epidermis of a leaf. Palisade cells normally exist as one closely packed row and contain many chloroplasts. During the hours of daylight palisade cells are photosynthetic, using the energy of the sun to create carbohydrates from water and carbon dioxide.

**Palladio, Andrea** (1508–1580) Italian architect who created harmonious and balanced classical structures. He designed numerous palaces and country houses in and around Vicenza, making use of Roman Classical forms, symmetry, and proportion. The Villa Malcontenta and the Villa Rotonda are examples of houses designed from 1540 for patrician families of the Venetian Republic. He also designed churches in Venice and published his studies of classical form in several illustrated books.

**palladium** lightweight, ductile and malleable, silver-white, metallic element, symbol Pd, atomic number 46, relative atomic mass 106.4.

It is one of the so-called platinum group of metals, and is resistant to tarnish and corrosion. It often occurs in nature as a free metal in a natural alloy with platinum. Palladium is used as a catalyst, in alloys of gold (to make white gold) and silver, in electroplating, and in dentistry.

**Pallas** in Greek mythology, a title of the goddess ◊Athena, possibly meaning virgin.

**palm** any of a group of large treelike plants with a single tall stem that has a thick cluster of large palmate (five-lobed) leaves or pinnate leaves (leaflets either side of the stem) at the top. Most of the numerous species are tropical or subtropical. Some, such as the coconut, date, sago, and oil palms, are important economically. (Family Palmae.)

**Palma de Mallorca** port and capital of the ◊Balearic Islands autonomous community, Spain, situated on a wide bay on the southwest coast of the island of ◊Mallorca; population (1994) 322,000. Industries include textiles, cement, paper, pottery, and tourism. Palma was founded as a Roman colony in 276 BC. It has a Gothic cathedral, begun in 1229; the 14th-century Almudaina palace, a former royal residence; and the 13th-century church of St Francis of Assisi, which contains the tomb of the Mallorcan scholar Ramon Llull.

**Palmas, Las** port in the Canary Islands; see ◊Las Palmas.

**Palmer, Samuel** (1805–1881) English landscape painter and etcher. His early works, small pastoral scenes mostly painted in watercolour and sepia, have an intense, visionary quality, greatly influenced by a meeting with the aged William Blake, and the latter's engravings for Thornton's *Virgil*. From 1826 to 1835 he lived in Shoreham, Kent, with a group of artists who followed Blake, styling themselves 'the Ancients'.

**Palmerston, Henry John Temple, 3rd Viscount Palmerston** (1784–1865) British politician. He was prime minister 1855–58 (when he rectified Aberdeen's mismanagement of the Crimean War, suppressed the ◊Indian Mutiny, and carried through the Second Opium War), and 1859–65 (when he almost involved Britain in the American Civil War on the side of the South). Initially a Tory, in Parliament from 1807, he was secretary-at-war 1809–28. He broke with the Tories in 1830 and sat in the Whig cabinets of 1830–34, 1835–41, and 1846–51 as foreign secretary. Viscount 1802.

**Palm Sunday** in the Christian calendar, the Sunday before Easter and first day of Holy Week, commemorating Jesus' entry into Jerusalem, when the crowd strewed palm leaves in his path.

**Pamir** central Asian plateau mainly in Tajikistan, but extending into China and Afghanistan, traversed by mountain ranges. Its highest peak is Kommunizma Pik (Communism Peak 7,495 m/24,600 ft) in the Akademiya Nauk range.

**Pampas** flat treeless plains in central Argentina, lying between the foothills of the Andes and the Atlantic coast, and stretching north from the Río Colorado to the Gran Chaco; area 650,000 sq km/25,097 sq mi. it incorporates the provinces of Buenos Aires, La Pampa, Santa Fé, and Cordobá. The eastern Pampas consist of grasslands which support large cattle ranches and produce flax and over half the nation's output of grain; the western Pampas are arid and unproductive. The characteristic vegetation is the *pampas grass* which grows to a height of 2–3m/6–10 ft.

**pampas grass** any of a group of large grasses native to South America, especially C. *argentea*, which is grown in gardens and has tall leaves and large clusters of feathery white flowers growing around the tips of the flower-bearing stems. (Genus *Cortaderia*.)

**Pan** (Greek 'all') in Greek mythology, the god of flocks and herds. He is depicted as a man with the horns, ears, and hoofed legs of a goat, and plays a shepherd's syrinx or *panpipes,* an instrument he reputedly invented. Later he was regarded as the personification of nature, existing order of things. The Romans identified him with ◊Faunus and Silvanus.

**Pan-Africanist Congress** (PAC), South African political party, formed as a militant black nationalist group in 1959, when it broke away from the African National Congress (ANC), promoting a black-only policy for Africa. PAC was outlawed 1960–90; its military wing was called Poqo ('we alone'). It suspended its armed struggle in 1994, and transformed itself into a political party to contest the first multiracial elections. It is more radical than the ANC, advocating a radical redistribution of land and a state-run economy.

**Panamá** capital of the Republic of Panama, on the east bank of the Pacific entrance to the Panama Canal, with its port at Balboa in the Canal Zone; population (1990) 584,800. Products include oil, plastics, leather, food, and drink. The original old city was founded by the Spaniard Pedro Arias de Avila in 1519, on the site of an Indian fishing village; it was destroyed in 1671 by the Welsh buccaneer Henry Morgan, and rebuilt on its present site, 8 km/5 mi to the southwest, in 1673. It became capital in 1903 following independence from Colombia. The city developed rapidly following the completion of the Canal.

**Panama** Republic of
*national name* República de Panamá
*area* 77,100 sq km/29,768 sq mi
*capital* Panamá (or Panama City)
*major towns/cities* San Miguelito, Colón, David, La Chorrera, Santiago, Chitré
*major ports* Colón, Cristóbal, Balboa
*physical features* coastal plains and mountainous interior; tropical rainforest in east and northwest; Archipelago de las Perlas in Gulf of Panama; Panama Canal
*head of state and government* Mireya Moscoso from 1999
*political system* emergent democracy
*political parties* Democratic Revolutionary Party (PRD), right wing; Arnulfista Party (PA),

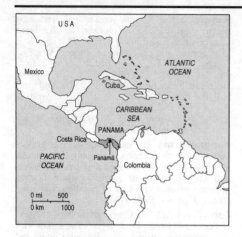

left of centre; Authentic Liberal Party (PLA), left
of centre; Nationalist Liberal Republican
Movement (MOLIRENA), right of centre; Papa
Ego Movement (MPE), moderate, centre left
**currency** balboa
**GNP per capita (PPP)** (US$) 6,940 (1998)
**exports** bananas, shrimps and lobsters, sugar,
clothing, coffee. Principal market: USA 39.9%
(1998)
**population** 2,812,000 (1999 est)
**language** Spanish (official), English
**religion** Roman Catholic
**life expectancy** 72 (men); 76 (women) (1995–
2000)
**Chronology**
**1502** Visited by Spanish explorer Rodrigo de
Bastidas, at which time it was inhabited by
Cuna, Choco, Guaymi, and other Indian groups.
**1513** Spanish conquistador Vasco Núñez de
Balboa explored Pacific Ocean from Darien isthmus; he was made governor of Panama (meaning 'abundance of fish'), but was later executed
as a result of Spanish court intrigue.
**1519** Spanish city established at Panama, which
became part of the Spanish viceroyalty of New
Andalucia (later New Granada).
**1572–95 and 1668–71** Spanish settlements
sacked by British buccaneers Francis Drake and
Henry Morgan.
**1821** Achieved independence from Spain; joined
confederacy of Gran Colombia, which included
Colombia, Venezuela, Ecuador, Peru, and
Bolivia.
**1830** Gran Colombia split up and Panama
became part of Colombia.
**1846** Treaty signed with USA, allowing it to
construct a railway across the isthmus.
**1880s** French attempt to build a Panama canal
connecting the Atlantic and Pacific Oceans
failed as a result of financial difficulties and the
death of 22,000 workers from yellow fever and
malaria.
**1903** Full independence achieved with US help
on separation from Colombia; USA bought
rights to build Panama Canal, and were given
control of a 10-mile strip, the Canal Zone, in
perpetuity.
**1914** Panama Canal opened.

**1939** Panama's status as a US protectorate was
terminated by mutual agreement.
**1968–81** Military rule of Gen Omar Torrijos
Herrera, leader of the National Guard, who
deposed the elected president and launched a
costly programme of economic modernization.
**1977** USA–Panama treaties transferred the canal
to Panama (effective from 2000), with the USA
guaranteeing protection and annual payment.
**1984** Nicolás Ardito Barletta of the right-wing
Democratic Revolutionary Party (PRD) elected
president by narrow margin.
**1985** Barletta resigned; replaced by Eric Arturo
del Valle, to the dissatisfaction of the USA.
**1987** Gen Manuel Noriega (head of the
National Guard and effective ruler since 1983)
resisted calls for his removal, despite suspension
of US military and economic aid.
**1988** Del Valle replaced by Manuel Solis Palma
after trying to oust Noriega. Noriega, charged
with drug smuggling by the USA, declared a
state of emergency after the coup against him
failed.
**1989** Assembly elections declared invalid when
won by opposition. 'State of war' with USA
announced, and US invasion (codenamed
'Operation Just Cause') deposed Noriega; 4,000
Panamanians died in the fighting. Guillermo
Endara, who had won earlier elections, was
installed as president in December.
**1991** An attempted antigovernment coup was
foiled. Constitutional reforms were approved by
the assembly, including the abolition of the
standing army; a privatization programme was
introduced.
**1992** Noriega was found guilty of drug offences
and given a 40-year prison sentence in USA. A
referendum rejected the proposed constitutional
reforms.
**1994** Ernesto Pérez Balladares (PRD) was
elected president. The constitution was amended
by assembly; the army was formally abolished.
**1998** Voters rejected a proposed constitutional
change to allow the president to run for a second term.
**1999** Mireya Moscoso, widow of former president Arnulfo Arias, became Panama's first
female head of state.

**Panama Canal** canal across the Panama isthmus in Central America, connecting the Pacific
and Atlantic oceans; length 80 km/50 mi, with
12 locks; average width 150 m/492 ft. It was
built by the USA 1904–14, after an unsuccessful
attempt by the French. The *Panama Canal
Zone* was acquired 'in perpetuity' by the USA in
1903, comprising land extending about 5 km/3
mi on either side of the canal. The zone passed
to Panama in 1979, and control of the canal
itself was ceded to Panama by the USA in
January 1990 under the terms of the Panama
Canal Treaty of 1977. The Canal Zone has several US military bases.

**panchromatic** in photography, a term
describing highly sensitive black-and-white film
made to render all visible spectral colours in correct grey tones. Panchromatic film is always
developed in total darkness.

**pancreas** in vertebrates, an accessory gland of the digestive system located close to the duodenum. When stimulated by the hormone secretin, it releases enzymes into the duodenum that digest starches, proteins, and fats. In humans, it is about 18 cm/7 in long, and lies behind and below the stomach. It contains groups of cells called the *islets of Langerhans,* which secrete the hormones insulin and glucagon that regulate the blood sugar level.

**panda** one of two carnivores of different families, native to northwestern China and Tibet. The *giant panda Ailuropoda melanoleuca* has black-and-white fur with black eye patches and feeds mainly on bamboo shoots, consuming about 8 kg/17.5 lb of bamboo per day. It can grow up to 1.5 m/4.5 ft long, and weigh up to 140 kg/300 lb. It is an endangered species. In 1999 there were only 1,000 remaining in the wild.

The *lesser,* or *red, panda Ailurus fulgens,* of the raccoon family, is about 50 cm/1.5 ft long, and is black and chestnut, with a long tail.

**Pandora** (Greek 'all gifts') in Greek mythology, the first mortal woman. Zeus sent her to Earth with a box containing every human woe to counteract the blessings brought to mortals by ◊Prometheus, whose gift of fire was stolen from the gods. In the most common tradition, she opened the box, and the evils flew out; only hope was left inside as a consolation.

**pangolin** or *scaly anteater,* toothless mammal of tropical Africa and Southeast Asia. They are long-tailed and covered with large, overlapping scales, except on the muzzle, sides of the head, throat, chest, and belly. They have an elongated skull and a long, extensible tongue. Pangolins measure 30–100 cm/12–39 in long, exclusive of the prehensile tail, which is about twice as long as the body.

Some are arboreal and others are terrestrial. All live on ants and termites. Pangolins comprise the order Pholidota. There is only one genus (*Manis*) and family Manidae, with seven species.

**Pankhurst, Emmeline** born Goulden (1858–1928) English ◊suffragette. Founder of the Women's Social and Political Union (WSPU) in 1903, she launched the militant suffragette campaign in 1905. In 1926 she joined the Conservative Party and was a prospective Parliamentary candidate for Whitechapel.

**pansy** cultivated plant derived from the European wild pansy (*Viola tricolor*) and including many different varieties and strains. The flowers are usually purple, yellow, or cream, or a mixture of these colours, and there are many highly developed varieties bred for size, colour, or special markings. Several of the 400 different species are scented. (Family Violaceae.)

**pantheism** (Greek *pan* 'all'; *theos* 'God') doctrine that regards all of reality as divine, and God as present in all of nature and the universe. It is expressed in Egyptian religion and Brahmanism; Stoicism, Neoplatonism, Judaism, Christianity, and Islam can be interpreted in pantheistic terms. Pantheistic philosophers include Giordano Bruno, Baruch Spinoza, J G Fichte, F W J Schelling, and G W F Hegel.

**panther** another name for the ◊leopard.

**pantomime** in the British theatre, a traditional Christmas entertainment. It has its origins in the harlequin spectacle of the 18th century and burlesque of the 19th century, which gave rise to the tradition of the principal boy being played by an actress and the dame by an actor. The harlequin's role diminished altogether as themes developed on folk tales such as 'The Sleeping Beauty' and 'Cinderella', and with the introduction of additional material such as popular songs, topical comedy, and audience participation. Popular television stars regularly feature in modern pantomime

**Papal States** area of central Italy in which the pope was temporal ruler from 756 until the unification of Italy 1870.

**Papandreou, Andreas** (1919–1996) Greek socialist politician, founder of the Pan-Hellenic Socialist Movement (PASOK); prime minister 1981–89, and again 1993–96. He lost the 1989 election after being implicated in an alleged embezzlement scandal, involving the diversion of funds to the Greek government from the Bank of Crete, headed by George Koskotas. In January 1992 a trial cleared Papandreou of all corruption charges.

**papaya** tropical evergreen tree, native from Florida to South America. Varieties are grown throughout the tropics. The edible fruits are like melons, with orange-coloured flesh and large numbers of blackish seeds in the centre; they can weigh up to 9 kg/20 lb. (*Carica papaya*, family Caricaceae.)

**Papeete** capital and port of French Polynesia on the northwest coast of Tahiti; population (1992) 24,200. Products include vanilla, copra, and mother-of-pearl.

**paper** thin, flexible material made in sheets from vegetable fibres (such as wood pulp) or rags and used for writing, drawing, printing, packaging, and various household needs. The name comes from papyrus, a form of writing material made from water reed, used in ancient Egypt. The invention of true paper, originally made of pulped fishing nets and rags, is credited to Tsai Lun, Chinese minister of agriculture, in AD 105.

**Pap test** or *Pap smear,* common name for ◊cervical smear.

**Papuan** native to or inhabitant of Papua New Guinea; speaker of any of various Papuan languages, used mainly on the island of New Guinea, although some 500 are used in New Britain, the Solomon Islands, and the islands of the southwest Pacific. The Papuan languages belong to the Indo-Pacific family.

**Papua New Guinea**
*area* 462,840 sq km/ 178,702 sq mi
*capital* Port Moresby (on East New Guinea) (also port)
*major towns/cities* Lae, Madang, Arawa, Wewak, Goroka, Rabaul, Mount Hagen
*major ports* Rabaul
*physical features* mountainous; swamps and

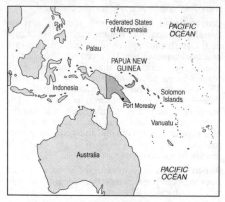

plains; monsoon climate; tropical islands of New Ireland, New Britain, and Bougainville; Admiralty Islands, D'Entrecasteaux Islands, and Louisiade Archipelago; active volcanoes Vulcan and Tavurvur

**head of state** Queen Elizabeth II, represented by governor general Silas Atopare from 1997

**head of government** Bill Skate from 1997

**political system** liberal democracy

**political parties** Papua New Guinea Party (Pangu Pati: PP), urban- and coastal-oriented nationalist; People's Democratic Movement (PDM), 1985 breakaway from the PP; National Party (NP), highlands-based, conservative; Melanesian Alliance (MA), Bougainville-based, pro-autonomy, left of centre; People's Progress Party (PPP), conservative; People's Action Party (PAP), right of centre

**currency** kina

**GNP per capita (PPP)** (US$) 2,700 (1998 est)

**exports** gold, copper ore and concentrates, crude petroleum, timber, coffee beans, coconut and copra products. Principal market: Australia 19.8% (1998)

**population** 4,702,000 (1999 est)

**language** English (official); pidgin English, 715 local languages

**religion** Protestant, Roman Catholic, local faiths

**life expectancy** 57 (men); 59 (women) (1995–2000)

**Chronology**

**c. 3000 BC** New settlement of Austronesian (Melanesian) immigrants.

**1526** Visited by Portuguese navigator Jorge de Menezes, who named the main island the Ilhos dos Papua after the 'frizzled' hair of the inhabitants.

**1545** Spanish navigator Ynigo Ortis de Retez gave the island the name of New Guinea, as a result of a supposed resemblance of the peoples with those of the Guinea coast of Africa.

**17th century** Regularly visited by Dutch merchants.

**1828** Dutch East India Company incorporated western part of New Guinea into Netherlands East Indies (becoming Irian Jaya, in Indonesia).

**1884** Northeast New Guinea annexed by Germany; the southeast was claimed by Britain.

**1870s** Visits by Western missionaries and traders increased.

**1890s** Copra plantations developed in German New Guinea.

**1906** Britain transferred its rights to Australia, which renamed the lands Papua.

**1914** German New Guinea occupied by Australia at outbreak of World War I; from the merged territories Papua New Guinea was formed.

**1920–42** Held as League of Nations mandate by Australia.

**1942–45** Occupied by Japan, who lost 150,000 troops resisting Allied counterattack.

**1947** Held as United Nations Trust Territory by Australia.

**1951** Legislative Council established.

**1964** Elected House of Assembly formed.

**1967** Pangu Party (Pangu Pati; PP) formed to campaign for home rule.

**1975** Independence achieved from Australia, within Commonwealth, with Michael Somare (PP) as prime minister.

**1980** Sir Julius Chan of People's Progress Party (PPP) became prime minister.

**1982** Somare returned to power.

**1985** Somare challenged by deputy prime minister Paias Wingti, who later left the PP and formed the People's Democratic Movement (PDM); he became head of a five-party coalition government.

**1988** Wingti defeated on no-confidence vote; replaced by Rabbie Namaliu (PP), heading coalition government. Joined Solomon Islands and Vanuatu to form Spearhead Group, aiming to preserve Melanesian cultural traditions.

**1989** State of emergency imposed on copper-rich Bougainville in response to separatist violence.

**1990** The Bougainville Revolutionary Army (BRA) issued a unilateral declaration of independence.

**1991** There was an economic boom as gold production doubled.

**1992** Wingti was appointed premier, heading a three-party coalition.

**1994** Wingti was replaced as premier by Sir Julius Chan. There was a short-lived peace agreement with BRA.

**1996** The prime minister of Bougainville was murdered, jeopardizing the peace process. Gerard Sinato was elected president of the transitional Bougainville government.

**1997** The army and police mutinied following the government's use of mercenaries against secessionist rebels. Bill Skate (PDM) was appointed prime minister. Silas Atopare was appointed governor general.

**1998** There was a truce with Bougainville secessionists. At least 1,500 people died and thousands were left homeless when tidal waves destroyed villages on the north coast. The PPP left the government, criticizing Skate for mismanaging the economy.

**1999** Bougainville Transitional Government (BTG) was replaced by the new interim Bougainville Reconciliation Government (BRG), headed by former rebel leader Joseph Kabui and BTG leader Gerard Sinato.

**papyrus** type of paper made by the ancient Egyptians. Typically papyrus was made by gluing together some 20 sheets of the pith of the papyrus or paper reed plant *Cyperus papyrus,* family Cyperaceae. These sheets were arranged in alternating layers aligned vertically, followed by horizontally. The strips were then covered with linen and beaten with a mallet. Finally, the papyrus was polished with a stone. Papyrus was in use before the First Dynasty.

**parabola** in mathematics, a curve formed by cutting a right circular cone with a plane parallel to the sloping side of the cone. A parabola is one of the family of curves known as ◊conic sections. The graph of $y = x^2$ is a parabola.

**paracetamol** analgesic, particularly effective for musculoskeletal pain. It is as effective as aspirin in reducing fever, and less irritating to the stomach, but has little anti-inflammatory action. An overdose can cause severe, often irreversible or even fatal, liver and kidney damage.

**parachute** any canopied fabric device strapped to a person or a package, used to slow down descent from a high altitude, or returning spent missiles or parts to a safe speed for landing, or sometimes to aid (through braking) the landing of a plane or missile. Modern designs enable the parachutist to exercise considerable control of direction, as in skydiving.

**paradise** (Persian 'pleasure garden') in various religions, a place or state of happiness. Examples are the Garden of Eden and the Messianic kingdom; the Islamic paradise of the Koran is a place of sensual pleasure.

**paradox** statement that seems contradictory but contains an element of truth. The truth is emphasized by the unexpected form of expression. The Bible is a rich source of paradox: 'Love your enemies'; 'The first shall be last and the last shall be first.'

**paraffin** common name for ◊alkane, any member of the series of hydrocarbons with the general formula $C_nH_{2n+2}$. The lower members are gases, such as methane (marsh or natural gas). The middle ones (mainly liquid) form the basis of petrol, kerosene, and lubricating oils, while the higher ones (paraffin waxes) are used in ointment and cosmetic bases.

**Paraguay** Republic of
*national name* Repúblíca del Paraguay
*area* 406,752 sq km/157,046 sq mi
*capital* Asunción (and port)
*major towns/cities* Ciudad del Este, Pedro Juan Caballero, San Lorenzo, Fernando de la Mora, Lambare, Concepción, Villartica, Encaración
*major ports* Concepción
*physical features* low marshy plain and marshlands; divided by Paraguay River; Paraná River forms southeast boundary
*head of state and government* Luis Gonzalez Macchi from 1999
*political system* emergent democracy
*political parties* National Republican Association (Colorado Party), right of centre; Authentic Radical Liberal Party (PLRA), centrist; National Encounter, right of centre; Radical Liberal Party (PLR), centrist; Liberal Party (PL), centrist

*currency* guaraní
*GNP per capita (PPP)* (US$) 3,650 (1998)
*exports* soybeans (and other oil seeds), cotton, timber and wood manufactures, hides and skins, meat. Principal market: Brazil 37.1% (1998)
*population* 5,359,000 (1999 est)
*language* Spanish 6% (official), Guaraní 90%
*religion* Roman Catholic (official religion); Mennonite, Anglican
*life expectancy* 68 (men); 72 (women) (1995–2000)
*Chronology*
**1526** Visited by Italian navigator Sebastian Cabot, who travelled up Paraná River; at this time the east of the country had long been inhabited by Guaraní-speaking Amerindians, who gave the country its name, which means 'land with an important river'.
**1537** Spanish made an alliance with Guaraní Indians against hostile Chaco Indians, enabling them to colonize interior plains; Asunción founded by Spanish.
**1609** Jesuits arrived from Spain to convert local population to Roman Catholicism and administer the country.
**1767** Jesuit missionaries expelled.
**1776** Formerly part of Spanish Viceroyalty of Peru, which covered much of South America, became part of Viceroyalty of La Plata, with capital at Buenos Aires (Argentina).
**1808** With Spanish monarchy overthrown by Napoleon Bonaparte, La Plata Viceroyalty became autonomous, but Paraguayans revolted against rule from Buenos Aires.
**1811** Independence achieved from Spain.
**1814** Under dictator Gen José Gaspar Rodriguez Francia ('El Supremo'), Paraguay became an isolated state.
**1840** Francia was succeeded by his nephew, Carlos Antonio Lopez, who opened country to foreign trade and whose son, Francisco Solano Lopez, as president from 1862, built up powerful army.
**1865–70** War with Argentina, Brazil, and Uruguay over access to sea; more than half the

population died and 150,000 sq km/58,000 sq mi of territory lost; President Lopez killed.

*later 1880s* Conservative Colorado Party and Liberal Party founded.

*1912* Liberal leader Edvard Schaerer came to power, ending decades of political instability.

*1932–35* Territory in west won from Bolivia during Chaco War (settled by arbitration in 1938).

*1940–48* Presidency of autocratic Gen Higinio Morínigo.

*1948–54* Political instability; six different presidents.

*1954* Gen Alfredo Stroessner seized power in a coup. He ruled as a ruthless autocrat, suppressing civil liberties; the country received initial US backing as economy expanded.

*1989* Stroessner was ousted in a coup led by Gen Andrés Rodríguez. Rodríguez was elected president; the right-of-centre military-backed Colorado Party won assembly elections.

*1992* A new democratic constitution was adopted.

*1993* The Colorado Party won the most seats in the first free multiparty elections, but no overall majority; its candidate, Juan Carlos Wasmosy, won the first free presidential elections.

*1998* The Colorado Party candidate Raul Cubas was elected president.

*1999* President Cubas resigned after threats of impeachment following the assassination of the vice-president, Luis Argana; he was replaced by senate leader Luis Gonzalez Macchi.

**parakeet** any of various small long-tailed ◊parrots, order Psittaciformes, with a moderate beak. They include the *ring-necked parakeets,* genus *Psittacula,* which are very common in India and Africa, and ◊cockatiels, and ◊budgerigars, natives of Australia. The *king parakeet* is about the size of a magpie and has a red head and breast and green wings.

**parallax** change in the apparent position of an object against its background when viewed from two different positions. In astronomy, nearby stars show a shift owing to parallax when viewed from different positions on the Earth's orbit around the Sun. A star's parallax is used to deduce its distance from the Earth.

**parallel lines and parallel planes** in mathematics, straight lines or planes that always remain a constant distance from one another no matter how far they are extended. This is a principle of Euclidean geometry. Some non-Euclidean geometries, such as elliptical and hyperbolic geometry, however, reject Euclid's parallel axiom.

**parallelogram** in mathematics, a quadrilateral (four-sided plane figure) with opposite pairs of sides equal in length and parallel, and opposite angles equal. The diagonals of a parallelogram bisect each other. Its area is the product of the length of one side and the perpendicular distance between this and the opposite side. In the special case when all four sides are equal in length, the parallelogram is known as a rhombus, and when the internal angles are right angles, it is a rectangle or square.

**parallel processing** emerging computer technology that allows more than one computation at the same time. Although in the 1980s this technology enabled only a small number of computer processor units to work in parallel, in theory thousands or millions of processors could be used at the same time.

**paralysis** loss of voluntary movement due to failure of nerve impulses to reach the muscles involved. It may result from almost any disorder of the nervous system, including brain or spinal cord injury, poliomyelitis, stroke, and progressive conditions such as a tumour or multiple sclerosis. Paralysis may also involve loss of sensation due to sensory nerve disturbance.

**Paramaribo** chief port and capital of Suriname, on the west bank of the Suriname River near its mouth on the Atlantic coast; population (1996) 150,000. Products include coffee, fruit, timber, and bauxite.

**paranoia** mental disorder marked by delusions of grandeur or persecution. In popular usage, paranoia means baseless or exaggerated fear and suspicion.

**paraplegia** paralysis of the lower limbs, involving loss of both movement and sensation; it is usually due to spinal injury.

**parapsychology** (Greek *para* 'beyond') study of paranormal phenomena, which are generally subdivided into two types: ◊extrasensory perception (ESP), or the paracognitive; and psychokinesis (PK), telekinesis, or the paraphysical – movement of an object without the use of physical force or energy.

**parasite** organism that lives on or in another organism (called the host) and depends on it for nutrition, often at the expense of the host's welfare. Parasites that live inside the host, such as liver flukes and tapeworms, are called *endoparasites;* those that live on the exterior, such as fleas and lice, are called *ectoparasites.*

**Pareto, Vilfredo** (1848–1923) Italian economist and political philosopher. A vigorous opponent of socialism and liberalism, he justified inequality of income and rule by elites on the grounds of his empirical observation (*Pareto's law*) that income distribution remained constant whatever efforts were made to change it. In some ways a classical liberal, his ideas nevertheless influenced Mussolini, who appointed him senator in 1922.

**Paris** port and capital of France, on the River Seine; *département* (*Ville de Paris*) in the Île-de-France region; area of the *agglomération parisienne* (comprising the *Ville de Paris* and 379 *communes* surrounding it) 105 sq km/40.5 sq mi; population *Ville de Paris* (1990) 2,152,000; *agglomération parisienne* (1990) 9,300,000. The city is the core of a highly centralized national administration, a focus of European transport networks, and France's leading centre for education, research, finance, and industry. Manufactured products include metal, electrical and luxury goods, chemicals, glass, and tobacco. As one of the world's principal historic and cultural centres, Paris attracts enormous numbers of tourists throughout the year.

**Paris** in Greek mythology, a Trojan prince whose abduction of ◊Helen, wife of Menelaus, caused the Trojan wars. Helen had been promised to him by the goddess Aphrodite as a bribe, during his judgement between her beauty and that of the goddesses, Hera and Athena. During the wars, he killed the Greek hero ◊Achilles by shooting an arrow into his heel, but was later mortally wounded by the archer Philoctetes.

**Paris Commune** name given to two separate periods in the history of Paris:
*The Paris municipal government 1789–94* was established after the storming of the ◊Bastille and remained powerful in the French Revolution until the fall of Robespierre 1794.
*The provisional national government 18 March–May 1871* was formed while Paris was besieged by the German troops during the Franco-Prussian War. It consisted of socialists and left-wing republicans, and is often considered the first socialist government in history. Elected after the right-wing National Assembly at Versailles tried to disarm the National Guard, it fell when the Versailles troops captured Paris and massacred 20,000–30,000 people 21–28 May.

**parity** of a number, the state of being either even or odd. In computing, the term refers to the number of 1s in the binary codes used to represent data. A binary representation has *even parity* if it contains an even number of 1s and *odd parity* if it contains an odd number of 1s.

**parity** in economics, equality of price, rate of exchange, wages, and buying power. Parity ratios may be used in the setting of wages to establish similar status to different work groups. Parity in international exchange rates means that those on a par with each other share similar buying power. In the USA, agricultural output prices are regulated by a parity system.

**Park, Mungo** (1771–1806) Scottish explorer who traced the course of the Niger River 1795–97. He disappeared and probably drowned during a second African expedition 1805–06. He published *Travels in the Interior of Africa* (1799).

**Park Chung Hee** (1917–1979) South Korean politician, president 1963–79. Under his rule South Korea had one of the world's fastest-growing economies, but recession and his increasing authoritarianism led to his assassination in 1979.

**Parker, Charlie** Charles Christopher 'Bird', 'Yardbird' (1920–1955) US alto saxophonist and jazz composer. He was associated with the trumpeter Dizzy Gillespie in developing the ◊bebop style. His skilful improvisations inspired performers on all jazz instruments.

**Parkinson's disease** or *parkinsonism* or *paralysis agitans,* degenerative disease of the brain characterized by a progressive loss of mobility, muscular rigidity, tremor, and speech difficulties. The condition is mainly seen in people over the age of 50.

**parliament** (French 'speaking') legislative body of a country. The world's oldest parliament is the Icelandic Althing, which dates from about 930. The UK Parliament is usually dated from 1265. The legislature of the USA is called ◊Congress and comprises the ◊House of Representatives and the ◊Senate.

**Parliament, European** governing body of the European Union (formerly the European Community); see ◊European Parliament.

**Parnassus** mountain in central Greece, height 2,457 m/8,200 ft, revered by the ancient Greeks as the abode of Apollo and the Muses. The sacred site of Delphi lies on its southern flank.

**Parnell, Charles Stewart** (1846–1891) Irish nationalist politician. He supported a policy of obstruction and violence to attain ◊Home Rule, and became the president of the Nationalist Party in 1877. In 1879 he approved the ◊Land League, and his attitude led to his imprisonment in 1881. His career was ruined in 1890 when he was cited as co-respondent in a divorce case. Because of his great influence over his followers, he was called 'the 'uncrowned king of Ireland'.

**parody** in literature and the other arts, a work that imitates the style of another work, usually with mocking or comic intent; it is related to satire.

**parrot** tropical bird found mainly in Australia and South America. These colourful birds have been valued as pets in the Western world for many centuries. Parrots have the ability to imitate human speech. They are mainly vegetarian, and range in size from the 8.5 cm/3.5 in pygmy parrot to the 100 cm/40 in Amazon parrot. The smaller species are commonly referred to as ◊parakeets. The plumage is often very colourful, and the call is usually a harsh screech. In most species the sexes are indistinguishable. Several species are endangered. Parrots are members of the family Psittacidae, of the order Psittaciformes.

**parsec** in astronomy, a unit (symbol pc) used for distances to stars and galaxies. One parsec is equal to 3.2616 ◊light years, 2.063 x $10^5$ ◊astronomical units, and 3.086 x $10^{13}$ km.

**parsley** herb belonging to the carrot family, cultivated for flavouring and garnishing in cookery and for its nutrient value, being rich in vitamin C and minerals. It can grow up to 45 cm/1.5 ft high and has aromatic, curled or flat pinnate leaves (leaflets either side of the stem) and delicate open clusters of yellow flowers. It is a biennial plant. (*Petroselinum crispum,* family Umbelliferae.)

**parsnip** temperate biennial plant belonging to the carrot family, found in Europe and Asia, and cultivated for its tapering, creamy-white, aromatic root, which is much used as a winter vegetable. (*Pastinaca sativa,* family Umbelliferae.)

**parthenogenesis** development of an ovum (egg) without any genetic contribution from a male. Parthenogenesis is the normal means of reproduction in a few plants (for example, dandelions) and animals (for example, certain fish).

Some sexually reproducing species, such as aphids, show parthenogenesis at some stage in their life cycle to accelerate reproduction to take advantage of good conditions.

**Parthia** ancient country in western Asia in what is now northeastern Iran, capital Ctesiphon. Parthian ascendancy began with the Arsacid dynasty in 248 BC, and reached the peak of its power under Mithridates I in the 2nd century BC; the region was annexed to Persia under the Sassanians in AD 226.

**particle detector** one of a number of instruments designed to detect subatomic particles and track their paths; they include the ◊cloud chamber, bubble chamber, spark chamber, and multiwire chamber.

**particle physics** study of the particles that make up all atoms, and of their interactions. More than 300 subatomic particles have now been identified by physicists, categorized into several classes according to their mass, electric charge, spin, magnetic moment, and interaction. Subatomic particles include the ◊elementary particles (◊quarks, ◊leptons, and ◊gauge bosons), which are believed to be indivisible and so may be considered the fundamental units of matter; and the ◊hadrons (baryons, such as the proton and neutron, and mesons), which are composite particles, made up of two or three quarks. The proton, electron, and neutrino are the only stable particles (the neutron being stable only when in the atomic nucleus). The unstable particles decay rapidly into other particles, and are known from experiments with particle accelerators and cosmic radiation. See ◊atomic structure.

**particle, subatomic** in physics, a particle that is smaller than an atom; see ◊particle physics.

**partisan** member of an armed group that operates behind enemy lines or in occupied territories during wars. The name 'partisans' was first given to armed bands of Russians who operated against Napoleon's army in Russia during 1812, but has since been used to describe Russian, Yugoslav, Italian, Greek, and Polish Resistance groups against the Germans during World War II. In Yugoslavia the communist partisans under their leader, Tito, played a major role in defeating the Germans.

**part of speech** grammatical function of a word, described in the grammatical tradition of the Western world, based on Greek and Latin. The four major parts of speech are the noun, verb, adjective, and adverb; the minor parts of speech vary according to schools of grammatical theory, but include the article, conjunction, preposition, and pronoun.

**partridge** any of various medium-sized ground-dwelling fowl of the family Phasianidae, order Galliformes, that also includes pheasants, quail, and chickens. Partridges are Old World birds, some of which have become naturalized in North America.

**pascal** SI unit (symbol Pa) of pressure, equal to one newton per square metre. It replaces bars and millibars ($10^5$ Pa equals one bar). It is named after the French mathematician Blaise Pascal.

**Pascal, Blaise** (1623–1662) French philosopher and mathematician. He contributed to the development of hydraulics, ◊calculus, and the mathematical theory of ◊probability.

**Pashto language** or *Pushto* or *Pushtu*, Indo-European language, the official language of Afghanistan, also spoken in northern Pakistan.

**Passchendaele, Battle of** in World War I, successful but costly British operation to capture the Passchendaele ridge in western Flanders, part of the third Battle of ◊Ypres October–November 1917; British casualties numbered nearly 400,000. The name is often erroneously applied to the whole of the battle of Ypres, but Passchendaele was in fact just part of that battle.

**passé** (French) out of date.

**passion flower** any of a group of tropical American climbing plants. They have distinctive flowers consisting of a saucer-shaped petal base, a fringelike corona or circle of leafy outgrowths inside the ring of petals, and a central stalk bearing five pollen-producing ◊stamens and three pollen-receiving ◊stigmas. The flowers can be yellow, greenish, purple, or red. Some species produce edible fruit. (Genus *Passiflora,* family Passifloraceae.)

**passion play** play representing the death and resurrection of Jesus, performed on Good Friday throughout medieval Europe. It has its origins in medieval ◊mystery plays. Traditionally, a passion play takes place every ten years at ◊Oberammergau, Germany.

**passive smoking** inhalation of tobacco smoke from other people's cigarettes; see ◊smoking.

**pass laws** South African laws that required the black population to carry passbooks (identity documents) at all times and severely restricted freedom of movement. The laws, a major cause of discontent, formed a central part of the policies of ◊apartheid. They were repealed 1986.

**Passover** also called *Pesach,* in Judaism, an eight-day spring festival which commemorates the exodus of the Israelites from Egypt and the passing over by the Angel of Death of the Jewish houses, so that only the Egyptian firstborn sons were killed, in retribution for Pharaoh's murdering of all Jewish male infants.

**pastel** sticklike drawing or painting material consisting of ground pigment bound with gum; also works produced in this medium. Pastel is a form of painting in dry colours and produces a powdery surface, which is delicate and difficult to conserve. Exponents include Rosalba Carriere (1675–1785), La Tour, Chardin, Degas, and Mary Cassatt.

**Pasternak, Boris Leonidovich** (1890–1960) Russian poet and novelist. His novel *Dr Zhivago* (1957) was banned in the USSR as a 'hostile act', and was awarded a Nobel prize (which Pasternak was later declined). The ban on *Dr Zhivago* was later lifted and Pasternak was posthumously rehabilitated.

**Pasteur, Louis** (1822–1895) French chemist and microbiologist who discovered that fermentation is caused by micro-organisms and developed the germ theory of disease. He also created a vaccine for ◊rabies, which led to the foundation of the Pasteur Institute in Paris in 1888.

**pasteurization** treatment of food to reduce the number of micro-organisms it contains and so protect consumers from disease. Harmful bacteria are killed and the development of others is delayed. For milk, the method involves heating it to 72°C/161°F for 15 seconds followed by rapid cooling to 10°C/50°F or lower. The process also kills beneficial bacteria and reduces the nutritive property of milk.

**Patagonia** geographic region of South America, in southern Argentina and Chile; area 780,000 sq km/301,158 sq mi. A thinly populated vast plateau area, it stretches from the Río Colorado in central Argentina to the Magellan Straits in the south, and slopes eastwards from the Andes to the Atlantic coast. It consists of the provinces of Neuquén, Rio Negro, Chubut, and Santa Cruz. The main towns are the port of Comodoro Rivadavia (Argentina) and Punta Arenas (Chile).

**patchouli** soft-wooded eastern Indian shrub belonging to the mint family; the leaves are the source of the perfume patchouli. (*Pogostemon heyneanus*, family Labiateae.)

**patella** or *kneecap*, flat bone embedded in the knee tendon of birds and mammals, which protects the joint from injury.

**patent** or *letters patent*, documents conferring the exclusive right to make, use, and sell an invention for a limited period. Ideas are not eligible; neither is anything not new.

**Pathan** or *Pathkun*, member of a people of northwestern Pakistan and Afghanistan, numbering about 14 million (1984). The majority are Sunni Muslims. The Pathans speak Pashto, a member of the Indo-Iranian branch of the Indo-European family.

**pathogen** (Greek 'disease producing') in medicine, any micro-organism that causes disease. Most pathogens are ◊parasites, and the diseases they cause are incidental to their search for food or shelter inside the host. Nonparasitic organisms, such as soil bacteria or those living in the human gut and feeding on waste foodstuffs, can also become pathogenic to a person whose immune system or liver is damaged. The larger parasites that can cause disease, such as nematode worms, are not usually described as pathogens.

**pathology** medical speciality concerned with the study of disease processes and how these provoke structural and functional changes in the body.

**patriarch** (Greek 'ruler of a family') in the Old Testament, one of the ancestors of the human race, and especially those of the ancient Hebrews, from Adam to Abraham, Isaac, Jacob, and his sons (who became patriarchs of the Hebrew tribes). In the Eastern Orthodox Church, the term refers to the leader of a national church.

**patriarchy** (Greek 'rule of the father') form of social organization in which a man heads and controls the family unit. By extension, in a patriarchal society men also control larger social and working groups as well as government. The definition has been broadened by feminists to describe the dominance of male values throughout society. The opposite concept is ◊matriarchy.

**patrician** member of a privileged class in ancient Rome, which originally dominated the ◊Senate. During the 5th and 4th centuries BC many of the rights formerly exercised by the patricians alone were extended to the plebeians, and patrician descent became a matter of prestige.

**Patrick, St** (*c.* 389–*c.* 461) patron saint of Ireland. Born in Britain, probably in South Wales, he was carried off by pirates to six years' slavery in Antrim, Ireland, before escaping either to Britain or Gaul – his poor Latin suggests the former – to train as a missionary. He is variously said to have landed again in Ireland in 432 or 456, and his work was a vital factor in the spread of Christian influence there. His symbols are snakes and shamrocks; feast day 17 March.

**patronage** power to give a favoured appointment to an office or position in politics, business, or the church; or sponsorship of the arts. Patronage was for centuries bestowed mainly by individuals (in Europe often royal or noble) or by the church. In the 20th century, patrons have tended to be political parties, the state, and – in the arts – private industry and foundations.

**Patten, Chris(topher Francis)** (1944–  ) British Conservative politician, governor of Hong Kong 1992–97. He was MP for Bath 1979–1992 and Conservative Party chair 1990–92, orchestrating the party's campaign for the 1992 general election, in which he lost his parliamentary seat. He accepted the governorship of Hong Kong for the crucial five years prior to its transfer to China in 1997. He went on to take part in the reform of the Royal Ulster Constabulary.

**Patton, George Smith** (1885–1945) US general in World War II, known as 'Old Blood and Guts'. During World War I, he formed the first US tank force and led it in action 1918. He was appointed to command the 2nd Armored Division 1940 and became commanding general of the First Armored Corps 1941. In 1942 he led the Western Task Force that landed at Casablanca, Morocco. After commanding the 7th Army in the invasion of Sicily, he led the 3rd Army across France and into Germany, and in 1945 took over the 15th Army.

**Pauling, Linus Carl** (1901–1994) US theoretical chemist and biologist. His ideas on chemical bonding are fundamental to modern theories of molecular structure. He also investigated the properties and uses of vitamin C as related to human health. He won the Nobel Prize for Chemistry in 1954 and the Nobel Peace Prize in 1962, having campaigned for a nuclear-test ban.

**Paul, St** (*c.* AD 3–*c.* AD 68) Christian missionary and martyr; in the New Testament, one of the apostles and author of 13 epistles. Originally opposed to Christianity, he took part in the stoning of St Stephen. He is said to have been converted by a vision on the road to Damascus. After his conversion he made great missionary journeys, for example to Philippi and Ephesus, becoming known as the Apostle of the Gentiles (non-Jews). His emblems are a sword and a book; feast day 29 June.

**Pavlov, Ivan Petrovich** (1849–1936) Russian physiologist who studied conditioned reflexes in animals (see ◊conditioning). His work had a great impact on behavioural theory (see ◊behaviourism) and learning theory. He was awarded the Nobel Prize for Physiology or Medicine in 1904.

**Pavlova, Anna** (1881–1931) Russian dancer. Prima ballerina of the Imperial Ballet from 1906, she left Russia 1913, and went on to become one of the world's most celebrated exponents of classical ballet. With London as her home, she toured extensively with her own company, influencing dancers worldwide with roles such as Mikhail Fokine's *The Dying Swan* solo in 1907. She was opposed to the modern reforms of Diaghilev's Ballets Russes, adhering strictly to conservative aesthetics.

**pawpaw** or *papaw,* small tree belonging to the custard-apple family, native to the eastern USA. It produces oblong fruits 13 cm/5 in long with yellowish edible flesh. The name 'pawpaw' is also used for the ◊papaya. (*Asimina triloba,* family Annonaceae.)

**Paxton, Joseph** (1801–1865) English architect. He was also garden superintendent to the Duke of Devonshire from 1826. He designed the Great Exhibition building 1851 (the Crystal Palace), which was revolutionary in its structural use of glass and iron. Knighted 1851.

**Pays de la Loire** agricultural region of western France, comprising the *départements* of Loire-Atlantique, Maine-et-Loire, Mayenne, Sarthe, and Vendée; area 32,100 sq km/12,391 sq mi; population (1990) 3,059,100. The administrative centre is ◊Nantes. Industries include shipbuilding and wine production.

**Paz, (Estenssoro) Victor** (1907– ) Bolivian president 1952–56, 1960–64, and 1985–89. He founded and led the Movimiento Nacionalista Revolucionario (MNR), which seized power in 1952. His regime extended the vote to Indians, nationalized the country's largest tin mines, embarked on a programme of agrarian reform, and brought inflation under control.

**Paz, Octavio** (1914–1998) Mexican poet, essayist, and political thinker. His works reflect many influences, including Marxism, Surrealism, and Aztec mythology. *El laberinto de la soledad/The Labyrinth of Solitude* (1980), the book which brought him to world attention, explores Mexico's heritage. His long poem *Piedra del sol/Sun Stone* (1957) uses contrasting images, centring on the Aztec Calendar Stone (representing the Aztec universe), to symbolize the loneliness of individuals and their search for

union with others. He was awarded the Nobel Prize for Literature in 1990.

**PC** abbreviation for *personal computer; politically correct; police constable; Privy Councillor.*

**pea** climbing leguminous plant (see ◊legume) with pods of round green edible seeds, grown since prehistoric times for food. The pea is a popular vegetable and is eaten fresh, canned, frozen, or dried. The *sweet pea* (*Lathyrus odoratus*) of the same family is grown for its scented red, purple, pink, and white butterfly-shaped flowers; it is a popular cottage garden plant. (Edible pea *Pisum sativum,* family Leguminosae.)

**peace movement** collective opposition to war. The Western peace movements of the late 20th century can trace their origins to the pacifists of the 19th century and conscientious objectors during World War I (see ◊pacifism). The campaigns after World War II have tended to concentrate on nuclear weapons, but there are numerous organizations devoted to peace, some wholly pacifist, some merely opposed to escalation.

**peach** yellow-reddish round edible fruit of the peach tree, which is cultivated for its fruit in temperate regions and has oval leaves and small, usually pink, flowers. The fruits have thick velvety skins; nectarines are a smooth-skinned variety. (*Prunus persica,* family Rosaceae.)

**peacock** technically, the male of any of various large ◊pheasants, order Galliformes. The name is most often used for the common peacock *Pavo cristatus,* a bird of the pheasant family, native to South Asia. It is rather larger than a pheasant. The male has a large fan-shaped tail, brightly coloured with blue, green, and purple 'eyes' on a chestnut background, that is raised during courtship displays. The female (peahen) is brown with a small tail.

**peanut** or *groundnut* or *monkey nut,* South American vinelike annual plant. After flowering, the flower stalks bend and force the pods into the earth to ripen underground. The nuts are a staple food in many tropical countries and are widely grown in the southern USA. They provide a valuable edible oil and are the basis for a large number of processed foods. (*Arachis hypogaea,* family Leguminosae.)

**pear** succulent, gritty-textured edible fruit of the pear tree, native to temperate regions of Europe and Asia. White flowers precede the fruits, which have a greenish-yellow and brown skin and taper towards the stalk. Pear trees are cultivated for their fruit which are eaten fresh or canned; a wine known as perry is made from pear juice. (*Pyrus communis,* family Rosaceae.)

**pearl** shiny, hard, rounded abnormal growth composed of nacre (or mother-of-pearl), a chalky substance. Nacre is secreted by many molluscs, and deposited in thin layers on the inside of the shell around a parasite, a grain of sand, or some other irritant body. After several years of the mantle (the layer of tissue between the shell and the body mass) secreting this nacre, a pearl is formed.

**Pearl Harbor** US Pacific naval base on Oahu island, Hawaii, USA, the scene of a Japanese aerial attack on 7 December 1941, which brought the USA into World War II. The attack took place while Japanese envoys were holding so-called peace talks in Washington. More than 2,000 members of the US armed forces were killed, and a large part of the US Pacific fleet was destroyed or damaged.

**Pearse, Patrick (Henry)** (1879–1916) Irish writer, educationalist and revolutionary. He was prominent in the Gaelic revival, and a leader of the ◊Easter Rising in 1916. Proclaimed president of the provisional government, he was court-martialled and shot after its suppression.

**Pearson, Lester Bowles** (1897–1972) Canadian politician, leader of the Liberal Party from 1958, prime minister 1963–68. As foreign minister 1948–57, he represented Canada at the United Nations, playing a key role in settling the ◊Suez Crisis of 1956. He was awarded the Nobel Peace Prize in 1957.

**Peary, Robert Edwin** (1856–1920) US polar explorer who, after several unsuccessful attempts, became the first person to reach the North Pole on 6 April 1909. In 1988 an astronomer claimed Peary's measurements were incorrect.

**Peasants' Revolt** the rising of the English peasantry in June 1381, the result of economic, social, and political disillusionment. It was sparked off by the imposition of a new poll tax, three times the rates of those imposed in 1377 and 1379. Led by Wat ◊Tyler and John ◊Ball, rebels from southeast England marched on London and demanded reforms. The authorities put down the revolt by deceit and force.

**peat** fibrous organic substance found in bogs and formed by the incomplete decomposition of plants such as sphagnum moss. Northern Asia, Canada, Finland, Ireland, and other places have large deposits, which have been dried and used as fuel from ancient times. Peat can also be used as a soil additive.

**pecan** nut-producing ◊hickory tree (*C. illinoensis* or *C. pecan*), native to the central USA and northern Mexico and now widely cultivated. The trees grow to over 45 m/150 ft, and the edible nuts are smooth-shelled, the kernel resembling a smooth, oval walnut. (Genus *Carya*, family Juglandaceae.)

**peccary** one of two species of the New World genus *Tayassu* of piglike hoofed mammals. A peccary has a gland in the middle of its back which secretes a strong-smelling substance. Peccaries are blackish in colour, covered with bristles, and have tusks that point downwards. Adults reach a height of 40 cm/16 in, and a weight of 25 kg/60 lb.

**Peel, Robert** (1788–1850) British Conservative politician. As home secretary 1822–27 and 1828–30, he founded the modern police force and in 1829 introduced Roman Catholic emancipation. He was prime minister 1834–35 and 1841–46, when his repeal of the ◊Corn Laws caused him and his followers to break with the party. 2nd baronet 1830.

**peerage** the high nobility; in the UK, holders, in descending order, of the titles of duke, marquess, earl, viscount, and baron. In the late 19th century the peerage was augmented by the Lords of Appeal in Ordinary (the nonhereditary life peers) and, from 1958, by a number of specially created life peers of either sex (usually long-standing members of the House of Commons). Since 1963 peers have been able to disclaim their titles, usually to enable them to take a seat in the Commons (where peers are disqualified from membership).

**peer group** in the social sciences, people who have a common identity based on such characteristics as similar social status, interests, age, or ethnic group. The concept has proved useful in analysing the power and influence of co-workers, school friends, and ethnic and religious groups in socialization and social behaviour.

**Pegasus** in Greek mythology, the winged horse that sprang from the blood of the ◊Gorgon Medusa when she was decapitated by the hero Perseus. He carried Bellerophon in his fight with the ◊chimera, and was later transformed into a constellation.

**Pei, I(eoh) M(ing)** (1917– ) Chinese-born US modernist architect. He is noted for his innovative high-tech structures, particularly the use of glass walls. His projects include the 70-storey Bank of China, Hong Kong (1987, Asia's tallest building at 368 m/1,209 ft), the glass pyramid in front of the Louvre, Paris, France (1989), and the Miho Museum (1997), in a nature reserve near Kyoto, Japan.

**Peking** alternative transcription of ◊Beijing, the capital of China.

**pekingese** breed of small long-haired dog first bred at the Chinese court as the 'imperial lion dog'. It has a flat skull and flat face, is typically less than 25 cm/10 in tall, and weighs less than 5 kg/11 lb.

**pelargonium** commonly called *geranium,* any of a group of shrubby, tender flowering plants belonging to the geranium family, grown extensively for their colourful white, pink, scarlet, and black-purple flowers. They are the familiar summer bedding and pot 'geraniums'. Ancestors of the garden hybrids came from southern Africa. (Genus *Pelargonium*, family Geraniaceae.)

**Pelé** Adopted name of Edson Arantes do Nascimento (1940– ) Brazilian soccer player. A prolific goal scorer, he appeared in four World Cup competitions 1958–70 and led Brazil to three championships (1958, 1962, 1970).
***career highlights***
***first-class appearances*** 1,363
***total first-class goals*** 1,281
***World Cup winner*** 1958, 1962, 1970
***Brazilian Cup*** 1962–64, 1968
***World Club Championship*** 1962–63

**pelican** large water bird of family Pelecanidae, order Pelecaniformes, remarkable for the pouch beneath the bill, which is used as a fishing net and temporary store for catches of fish. Some species grow up to 1.8 m/6 ft and have wingspans of 3 m/10 ft.

**Peloponnese** Greek *Peloponnesos,* peninsula forming the southern part of Greece; area 21,549 sq km/8,318 sq mi; population (1991) 1,077,000. It is joined to the mainland by the narrow isthmus of Corinth and is divided into the nomes (administrative areas) of Argolis, Arcadia, Achaea, Elis, Corinth, Lakonia, and Messenia, representing its seven ancient states. It is divided into two regions; Greece West (including Achaea and Elis), and Peloponnese (including Argolis, Arcadia, Corinth, Lakonia, and Messenia).

**Peloponnesian War** war fought 431–404 BC between Athens and Sparta and their respective allies, involving most of the Greek world from Asia Minor to Sicily and from Byzantium (present-day Istanbul, Turkey) to Crete. Sparked by Spartan fears about the growth of Athenian power, it continued until the Spartan general Lysander captured the Athenian fleet in 405 at Aegospotami and starved the Athenians into surrender in 404. As a result of this victory, Athens' political power collapsed.

**Peltier effect** in physics, a change in temperature at the junction of two different metals produced when an electric current flows through them. The extent of the change depends on what the conducting metals are, and the nature of change (rise or fall in temperature) depends on the direction of current flow. It is the reverse of the ♦Seebeck effect. It is named after the French physicist Jean Charles Peltier (1785–1845) who discovered it in 1834.

**pelvis** in vertebrates, the lower area of the abdomen featuring the bones and muscles used to move the legs or hindlimbs. The *pelvic girdle* is a set of bones that allows movement of the legs in relation to the rest of the body and provides sites for the attachment of relevant muscles.

**Pembrokeshire** Welsh *Sir Benfro,* unitary authority in southwest Wales; a former county, from 1974 to 1996 it was part of the county of Dyfed
*area* 1,588 sq km/613 sq mi
*towns* Haverfordwest (administrative headquarters), Milford Haven
*physical* bounded on the south by the Bristol Channel; valleys and hills inland; rivers East and West Cleddau
*features* Pembrokeshire Coast National Park
*industries* oil refinery at Milford Haven, agriculture, fishing, woollen milling.
*population* (1996) 117,700.

**Penang** Malay *Pulau Pinang,* state in west Peninsular Malaysia, formed of *Penang Island,* Province Wellesley, and the Dindings on the mainland; area 1,030 sq km/398 sq mi; capital Penang (George Town); population (1993) 1,141,500. Penang Island was bought by Britain from the ruler of Kedah in 1785; Province Wellesley was acquired in 1800.

**Penda** (*c.* 577–654) King of Mercia, an Anglo-Saxon kingdom in England, from about 632. He raised Mercia to a powerful kingdom, and defeated and killed two Northumbrian kings, Edwin in 632 and Oswald in 642. He was killed in battle by Oswy, king of Northumbria.

**Penelope** in Greek mythology, the wife of ♦Odysseus, king of Ithaca; their son was ♦Telemachus. She represented wifely faithfulness. While Odysseus was absent at the siege of Troy, she kept her many suitors at bay by asking them to wait while she completed a shroud for Laertes, her father-in-law; every night she unravelled her weaving. When Odysseus returned after 20 years, he and Telemachus killed her suitors.

**penguin** marine flightless bird, family Spheniscidae, order Sphenisciformes, mostly black and white, found in the southern hemisphere. They comprise 18 species in six genera. Males are usually larger than the females. Penguins range in size from 40 cm/1.6 ft to 1.2 m/4 ft tall, and have thick feathers to protect them from the intense cold. They are awkward on land (except on snow slopes down which they propel themselves at a rapid pace), but their wings have evolved into flippers, making them excellent swimmers. Penguins congregate to breed in 'rookeries', and often spend many months incubating their eggs while their mates are out at sea feeding. They feed on a mixture of fish, squid, and krill.

**penicillin** any of a group of ♦antibiotic (bacteria killing) compounds obtained from filtrates of moulds of the genus *Penicillium* (especially *P. notatum*) or produced synthetically. Penicillin was the first antibiotic to be discovered (by Alexander ♦Fleming); it kills a broad spectrum of bacteria, many of which cause disease in humans.

**Peninsular War** war of 1808–14 caused by the French emperor Napoleon's invasion of Portugal and Spain. British expeditionary forces under Sir Arthur Wellesley (Duke of ♦Wellington), combined with Spanish and Portuguese resistance, succeeded in defeating the French at Vimeiro in 1808, Talavera in 1809, Salamanca in 1812, and Vittoria in 1813. The results were inconclusive, and the war was ended by Napoleon's forced abdication in 1814.

**penis** male reproductive organ containing the ♦urethra, the channel through which urine and semen are voided. It transfers sperm to the female reproductive tract to fertilize the ovum. In mammals, the penis is made erect by vessels that fill with blood, and in most mammals (but not humans) is stiffened by a bone.

**Pennines, the** range of hills in northern England, known as the 'the backbone of England'; length (from the Scottish border to the Peaks in Derbyshire) 400 km/250 mi. The highest peak in the Pennines (which are sometimes referred to as mountains rather than hills) is Cross Fell (893 m/2,930 ft). It is the watershed for the main rivers of northeast England. The rocks are carboniferous limestone and millstone grit, the land high moorland and fell.

**Pennsylvania** state in northeastern USA. It is nicknamed the Keystone State. Pennsylvania ratified the US Constitution in 1787, becoming the 2nd state to join the Union. It is bordered to the north by New York, with a small coastal strip on Lake Erie, to the west by Ohio and the West

Virginia panhandle, to the south, on what was the ◊Mason-Dixon Line, by West Virginia, Maryland, and Delaware, and to the east by New Jersey, across the Delaware River. Pennsylvania was the hub of US industry in the late 19th and early 20th century

**population** (1995) 12,071,800
**area** 117,400 sq km/45,316 sq mi
**capital** Harrisburg
**towns and cities** Philadelphia, Pittsburgh, Erie, Allentown, Scranton
**industries and products** hay, cereals, mushrooms, cattle, poultry, dairy products, cement, limestone, coal, steel, petroleum products, pharmaceuticals, chemicals, motor vehicles and equipment, electronic components, textiles, tourism.

**pension** organized form of saving for retirement. Pension schemes, which may be government-run or privately administered, involve regular payment for a qualifying period; when the person retires, a payment is made each week or month from the invested pension fund. Pension funds have today become influential investors in major industries; 44% of UK shares are owned by pension funds (1995).

**Pentagon** the headquarters of the US Department of Defense, Arlington, Virginia from 1947, situated on the Potomac River opposite Washington DC. One of the world's largest office buildings (five storeys high and five-sided, with a pentagonal central court), it houses the administrative and command headquarters for the US armed forces and has become synonymous with the military establishment bureaucracy.

**pentagon** five-sided plane figure. The regular pentagon has ◊golden section proportions between its sides and diagonals. The five-pointed star formed by drawing all the diagonals of a regular pentagon is called a *pentagram.* This star has further golden sections.

**Pentecost** in Judaism, the festival of *Shavuot,* celebrated on the 50th day after ◊Passover in commemoration of the giving of the Ten Commandments to Moses on Mount Sinai, and the end of the grain harvest; in the Christian church, Pentecost is the day on which the apostles experienced inspiration of the Holy Spirit, commemorated on Whit Sunday.

**Pentecostal movement** Christian revivalist movement inspired by the baptism in the Holy Spirit with 'speaking in tongues' experienced by the apostles at the time of Pentecost. It represents a reaction against the rigid theology and formal worship of the traditional churches. It originated in the USA in 1906.

Pentecostalists believe in the literal word of the Bible and faith healing; glossalia, or speaking in tongues, often occurs. It is an intensely missionary faith, and recruitment has been rapid since the 1960s: worldwide membership is more than 10 million.

**peony** any of a group of perennial plants native to Europe, Asia, and North America, remarkable for their large, round, brilliant white, pink, or red flowers. Most popular in

gardens are the common peony (*P. officinalis*), the white peony (*P. lactiflora*), and the taller tree peony (*P. suffruticosa*). (Genus *Paeonia,* family Paeoniaceae.)

**Pepin the Short** (*c.* 714–*c.* 768) king of the Franks from 751. The son of Charles Martel, he acted as Mayor of the Palace to the last Merovingian king, Childeric III, deposed him and assumed the royal title himself, founding the Carolingian dynasty. He was ◊Charlemagne's father.

**pepper** climbing plant native to the East Indies. When gathered green, the berries are crushed to release the seeds for the spice called black pepper. When the berries are ripe, the seeds are removed and their outer skin is discarded, to produce white pepper. Chilli pepper, cayenne or red pepper, and the sweet peppers used as a vegetable come from ◊capsicums native to the New World. (*Piper nigrum,* family Piperaceae.)

**peppermint** perennial herb of the mint family, native to Europe, with oval aromatic leaves and purple flowers. Oil of peppermint is used in medicine and confectionery. (*Mentha piperita,* family Labiatae.)

**pepsin** enzyme that breaks down proteins during digestion. It requires a strongly acidic environment and is present in the stomach.

**peptide** molecule comprising two or more ◊amino acid molecules (not necessarily different) joined by *peptide bonds,* whereby the acid group of one acid is linked to the amino group of the other (–CO.NH). The number of amino acid molecules in the peptide is indicated by referring to it as a di-, tri-, or polypeptide (two, three, or many amino acids).

**Pepys, Samuel** (1633–1703) English naval administrator and diarist. His *Diary* (1660–69) is a unique record of the daily life of the period, the historical events of the Restoration, the manners and scandals of the court, naval administration, and Pepys's own interests, weaknesses, and intimate feelings. Written in shorthand, it was not deciphered until 1825.

**percentage** way of representing a number as a ◊fraction of 100. Thus 45 percent (45%) equals $\frac{45}{100}$, and 45% of 20 is $\frac{45}{100} \times 20 = 9$.

**perch** any of the largest order of spiny-finned bony fishes, the Perciformes, with some 8,000 species. This order includes the sea basses, cichlids, damselfishes, mullets, barracudas, wrasses, and gobies. Perches of the freshwater genus *Perca* are found in Europe, Asia, and North America. They have varied shapes and are usually a greenish colour. They are very prolific, spawning when about three years old, and have voracious appetites.

**percussion instrument** musical instrument played by being struck with the hand or a beater. Percussion instruments can be divided into those that can be tuned to produce a sound of definite pitch, such as the timpani, tubular bells, glockenspiel, xylophone, and piano, and those of indefinite pitch, including the bass drum, tambourine, triangle, cymbals, and castanets.

**perennating organ** in plants, that part of a ◊biennial plant or herbaceous perennial that allows it to survive the winter; usually a root, tuber, rhizome, bulb, or corm.

**perennial plant** plant that lives for more than two years. Herbaceous perennials have aerial stems and leaves that die each autumn. They survive the winter by means of an underground storage (perennating) organ, such as a bulb or rhizome. Trees and shrubs or woody perennials have stems that persist above ground throughout the year, and may be either ◊deciduous or ◊evergreen. See also ◊annual plant, ◊biennial plant.

**Peres, Shimon** (1923– ) Israeli Labour politician, prime minister 1984–86 and 1995–96. He was prime minister, then foreign minister, under a power-sharing agreement with the leader of the Likud Party, Yitzhak ◊Shamir. From 1989 to 1990 he was finance minister in a Labour–Likud coalition. As foreign minister in Yitzhak Rabin's Labour government from 1992, he negotiated the 1993 peace agreement with the Palestine Liberation Organization (PLO). He was awarded the 1994 Nobel Prize for Peace jointly with Rabin and PLO leader Yassir Arafat.

Following the assassination of Rabin in November 1995, Peres succeeded him as prime minister, and pledged to continue the peace process in which they had both been so closely involved, but in May 1996 he was defeated in Israel's first direct elections for prime minister.

*perestroika* (Russian 'restructuring') in Soviet politics, the wide-ranging economic and political reforms initiated from 1985 by Mikhail Gorbachev, finally leading to the demise of the Soviet Union. Originally, in the economic sphere, *perestroika* was conceived as involving 'intensive development' concentrating on automation and improved labour efficiency. It evolved to attend increasingly to market indicators and incentives ('market socialism') and the gradual dismantling of the Stalinist central-planning system, with decision-taking being devolved to self-financing enterprises.

**Pérez de Cuéllar, Javier** (1920– ) Peruvian diplomat, fifth secretary general of the United Nations 1982–91. He raised the standing of the UN by his successful diplomacy in ending the Iran–Iraq War in 1988 and in securing the independence of Namibia in 1989. He was a candidate in the Peruvian presidential elections of 1995, but was defeated by his opponent Alberto Fujimori.

**Pergamum** ancient Greek city in Mysia in western Asia Minor, which became the capital of an independent kingdom in 283 BC under the Attalid dynasty. As the ally of Rome it achieved great political importance in the 2nd century BC, and became a centre of art and culture. It had a famous library, the contents of which were transported to Alexandria when they were given by ◊Mark Antony to Cleopatra, queen of Egypt. Pergamum was the birthplace of the physician ◊Galen. Most of its territory became the Roman province of Asia in 133 BC. Close to its site is the modern Turkish town of Bergama.

**pericarp** wall of a ◊fruit. It encloses the seeds and is derived from the ◊ovary wall. In fruits such as the acorn, the pericarp becomes dry and hard, forming a shell around the seed. In fleshy fruits the pericarp is typically made up of three distinct layers. The *epicarp*, or *exocarp*, forms the tough outer skin of the fruit, while the *mesocarp* is often fleshy and forms the middle layers. The innermost layer or *endocarp*, which surrounds the seeds, may be membranous or thick and hard, as in the ◊drupe (stone) of cherries, plums, and apricots.

**Pericles** (c. 495–429 BC) Athenian politician under whom Athens reached the height of power. He persuaded the Athenians to reject Sparta's ultimata in 432 BC, and was responsible for Athenian strategy in the opening years of the Peloponnesian War. His policies helped to transform the Delian League into an empire, but the disasters of the ◊Peloponnesian War led to his removal from office in 430 BC. Although quickly reinstated, he died soon after.

**perihelion** point at which an object, travelling in an elliptical orbit around the Sun, is at its closest to the Sun. The point at which it is furthest from the Sun is the aphelion.

**periodic table of the elements** in chemistry, a table in which the elements are arranged in order of their atomic number. The table summarizes the major properties of the elements and enables predictions to be made about their behaviour. *See illustration on pages 692–693.*

**peripheral device** in computing, any item connected to a computer's ◊central processing unit (CPU). Typical peripherals include keyboard, mouse, monitor, and printer. Users who enjoy playing games might add a ◊joystick or a trackball; others might connect a modem, ◊scanner, or ◊integrated services digital network (ISDN) terminal to their machines.

**peristalsis** wavelike contractions, produced by the contraction of smooth muscle, that pass along tubular organs, such as the intestines. The same term describes the wavelike motion of earthworms and other invertebrates, in which part of the body contracts as another part elongates.

**periwinkle** in botany, any of several trailing blue-flowered evergreen plants of the dogbane family, native to Europe and Asia. They range in length from 20 cm/8 in to 1 m/3 ft. (Genus *Vinca*, family Apocynaceae.)

**periwinkle** in zoology, any marine snail of the family Littorinidae, found on the shores of Europe and eastern North America. Periwinkles have a conical spiral shell, and feed on algae.

**perjury** the offence of deliberately making a false statement on oath (or affirmation) when appearing as a witness in legal proceedings, on a point material to the question at issue. In Britain and the USA it is punishable by a fine, imprisonment, or both.

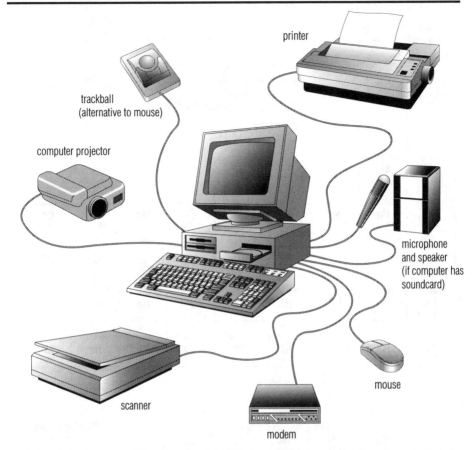

printer

trackball
(alternative to mouse)

computer projector

microphone
and speaker
(if computer has
soundcard)

mouse

scanner

modem

**peripheral device** *Some of the types of peripheral device that may be connected to a computer include printers, scanners, and modems.*

**Perm** formerly (1940–57) *Molotov,* capital city, economic and cultural centre of Perm oblast (region), in the west-central Russian Federation, in the southern foothills of the Urals; population (1996 est) 1,028,000. Perm, which lies on the River Kama 475 km/295 mi northeast of Kazan, is a major centre of commerce and transportation. It is also an important industrial centre, producing machinery, chemicals, oil by-products, and timber.

**permafrost** condition in which a deep layer of soil does not thaw out during the summer. Permafrost occurs under periglacial conditions. It is claimed that 26% of the world's land surface is permafrost.

**Permian** period of geological time 290–245 million years ago, the last period of the Palaeozoic era. Its end was marked by a significant change in marine life, including the extinction of many corals and trilobites. Deserts were widespread, terrestrial amphibians and mammal-like reptiles flourished, and cone-bearing plants (gymnosperms) came to prominence. In the oceans, 49% of families and 72% of genera vanished in

the late Permian. On land, 78% of reptile families and 67% of amphibian families disappeared.

**Perón, (María Estela) Isabel** born Martínez (1931– ) Argentine president 1974–76, and third wife of Juan Perón. She succeeded him after he died in office in 1974 (she had been elected vice-president in 1973), but labour unrest, inflation, and political violence pushed the country to the brink of chaos. Accused of corruption in 1976, she was held under house arrest for five years. She went into exile in Spain in 1981.

**Perón, Eva ('Evita') Duarte de** born María Eva Duarte (1919–1952) Argentine populist leader. A successful radio actress, she became the second wife of Juan ◊Perón in 1945. When he became president the following year, she became his chief adviser and virtually ran the health and labour ministries, devoting herself to helping the poor, improving education, and achieving women's suffrage. She founded a social welfare organization called the Eva Perón Foundation. She was politically astute and sought the vice-presidency in 1951, but was opposed by the

**Periodic table of the elements**

Legend:
- 1 — atomic number
- Hydrogen — name
- H — symbol
- 1.00794 — relative atomic mass

**element**

- nonmetals
- metals

| Group I | Group II | | | | | | | | |
|---|---|---|---|---|---|---|---|---|---|
| 1 Hydrogen **H** 1.00794 | | | | | | | | | |
| 3 Lithium **Li** 6.941 | 4 Beryllium **Be** 9.012 | | | | | | | | |
| 11 Sodium **Na** 22.98977 | 12 Magnesium **Mg** 24.305 | | | | | | | | |
| 19 Potassium **K** 30.098 | 20 Calcium **Ca** 40.06 | 21 Scandium **Sc** 44.9559 | 22 Titanium **Ti** 47.90 | 23 Vanadium **V** 50.9414 | 24 Chromium **Cr** 51.996 | 25 Manganese **Mn** 54.9380 | 26 Iron **Fe** 55.847 | 27 Cobalt **Co** 58.9332 | |
| 37 Rubidium **Rb** 85.4678 | 38 Strontium **Sr** 87.62 | 39 Yttrium **Y** 88.9059 | 40 Zirconium **Zr** 91.22 | 41 Niobium **Nb** 92.9064 | 42 Molybdenum **Mo** 95.94 | 43 Technetium **Tc** 97.9072 | 44 Ruthenium **Ru** 101.07 | 45 Rhodium **Rh** 102.9055 | |
| 55 Caesium **Cs** 132.9054 | 56 Barium **Ba** 137.34 | **La** | 72 Hafnium **Hf** 178.49 | 73 Tantalum **Ta** 180.9479 | 74 Tungsten **W** 183.85 | 75 Rhenium **Re** 186.207 | 76 Osmium **Os** 190.2 | 77 Iridium **Ir** 192.22 | |
| 87 Francium **Fr** 223.0197 | 88 Radium **Ra** 226.0254 | **Ac** | 104 Rutherfordium **Rf** 261.109 | 105 Dubnium **Db** 262.114 | 106 Seaborgium **Sg** 263.120 | 107 Bohrium **Bh** 262 | 108 Hassium **Hs** 265 | 109 Meitnerium **Mt** 266 | |

**Lanthanide series**

| 57 Lanthanum **La** 138.9055 | 58 Cerium **Ce** 140.12 | 59 Praeseodymium **Pr** 140.9077 | 60 Neodymium **Nd** 144.24 | 61 Promethium **Pm** 144.9128 | 62 Samarium **Sm** 150.36 |
|---|---|---|---|---|---|

**Actinide series**

| 89 Actinium **Ac** 227.0278 | 90 Thorium **Th** 232.0381 | 91 Protactinium **Pa** 231.0359 | 92 Uranium **U** 238.029 | 93 Neptunium **Np** 237.0482 | 94 Plutonium **Pu** 244.0642 |
|---|---|---|---|---|---|

army and withdrew. After her death from cancer in 1952, Juan Perón's political strength began to decline.

**Perón, Juan Domingo** (1895–1974) Argentine politician, dictator 1946–55 and from 1973 until his death. His populist appeal to the poor was enhanced by the charisma and political work of his second wife Eva ('Evita') Perón. After her death in 1952 his popularity waned and, with increasing economic difficulties and labour unrest, he was deposed in a military coup in 1955. He fled to Paraguay and, in 1960, to Spain. He returned from exile to the presidency in 1973, but died in office in 1974, and was succeeded by his third wife, Isabel Perón.

**perpendicular** in mathematics, at a right angle; also, a line at right angles to another or to a plane. For a pair of skew lines (lines in three dimensions that do not meet), there is just one common perpendicular, which is at right angles to both lines; the nearest points on the two lines are the feet of this perpendicular.

**perpetual motion** the idea that a machine can be designed and constructed in such a way that, once started, it will continue in motion indefinitely without requiring any further input of energy (motive power). Such a device would contradict at least one of the two laws of thermodynamics that state that (1) energy can neither be created nor destroyed (the law of conservation of energy) and (2) heat cannot by itself flow from a cooler to a hotter object. As a result, all practical (real) machines require a continuous supply of energy, and no heat

| | | | | III | IV | V | VI | VII | 0 |
|---|---|---|---|---|---|---|---|---|---|
| | | | | | | | | | 2 Helium **He** 4002.60 |
| | | | | 5 Boron **B** 10.81 | 6 Carbon **C** 12.011 | 7 Nitrogen **N** 14.0067 | 8 Oxygen **O** 15.9994 | 9 Fluorine **F** 18.99840 | 10 Neon **Ne** 20.179 |
| | | | | 13 Aluminium **Al** 26.98154 | 14 Silicon **Si** 28.066 | 15 Phosphorus **P** 30.9738 | 16 Sulphur **S** 32.06 | 17 Chlorine **Cl** 35.453 | 18 Argon **Ar** 39.948 |
| 28 Nickel **Ni** 58.70 | 29 Copper **Cu** 63.546 | 30 Zinc **Zn** 65.38 | | 31 Gallium **Ga** 69.72 | 32 Germanium **Ge** 72.59 | 33 Arsenic **As** 74.9216 | 34 Selenium **Se** 78.96 | 35 Bromine **Br** 79.904 | 36 Krypton **Kr** 83.80 |
| 46 Palladium **Pd** 106.4 | 47 Silver **Ag** 107.868 | 48 Cadmium **Cd** 112.40 | | 49 Indium **In** 114.82 | 50 Tin **Sn** 118.69 | 51 Antimony **Sb** 121.75 | 52 Tellurium **Te** 127.75 | 53 Iodine **I** 126.9045 | 54 Xenon **Xe** 131.30 |
| 78 Platinum **Pt** 195.09 | 79 Gold **Au** 196.9665 | 80 Mercury **Hg** 200.59 | | 81 Thallium **Tl** 204.37 | 82 Lead **Pb** 207.37 | 83 Bismuth **Bi** 207.2 | 84 Polonium **Po** 210 | 85 Astatine **At** 211 | 86 Radon **Rn** 222.0176 |
| 110 Ununnilium **Uun** 269 | 111 Unununium **Uuu** 272 | 112 Ununbium **Uub** 277 | | | | | | | |

| 63 Europium **Eu** 151.96 | 64 Gadolinium **Gd** 157.25 | 65 Terbium **Tb** 158.9254 | 66 Dysprosium **Dy** 162.50 | 67 Holmium **Ho** 164.9304 | 68 Erbium **Er** 167.26 | 69 Thulium **Tm** 168.9342 | 70 Ytterbium **Yb** 173.04 | 71 Lutetium **Lu** 174.97 |
|---|---|---|---|---|---|---|---|---|

| 95 Americium **Am** 243.0614 | 96 Curium **Cm** 247.0703 | 97 Berkelium **Bk** 247 | 98 Californium **Cf** 251.0786 | 99 Einsteinium **Es** 252.0828 | 100 Fermium **Fm** 257.0951 | 101 Mendelevium **Md** 258.0986 | 102 Nobelium **No** 259.1009 | 103 Lawrencium **Lr** 260.1054 |
|---|---|---|---|---|---|---|---|---|

engine is able to convert all the heat into useful work.

**Perry, Fred (Frederick John)** (1909–1995) English lawn-tennis player, the last Briton to win the men's singles at Wimbledon, in 1936. He also won the world table-tennis title in 1929. Perry later became a television commentator and a sports-goods manufacturer.

*career highlights*
*lawn tennis*
*Wimbledon* singles: 1934–36; mixed: 1935–36
*French Open* singles: 1935; doubles: 1933; mixed: 1932
*Australian Open* singles: 1934; doubles: 1934
*US Open* singles: 1933–34, 1936; mixed: 1932
*table tennis*
*world championships* singles: 1929
*English Championships* doubles: 1928–30; mixed: 1929

**Persephone** Roman *Proserpina*, in Greek mythology, the goddess and queen of the underworld; and the daughter of Zeus and ◊Demeter, goddess of agriculture. She was carried off to the underworld by ◊Pluto, also known as Hades, although Zeus later ordered that she should spend six months of the year above ground with her mother. The myth symbolizes the growth and decay of vegetation and the changing seasons.

**Persia, ancient** kingdom in southwestern Asia. The early Persians were a nomadic Aryan people who migrated through the Caucasus to the Iranian plateau. Cyrus organized the empire into provinces which were each ruled by Satraps. The royal house is known as the Achaemenids after the founder of the line. The administrative centre was Susa, with the royal palace at Persepolis.

Expansion led the Persians into conflicts with Greek cities, notably in the Ionian Revolt, Darius I's campaign that ended at the Athenian victory of Marathon (490 BC), and Xerxes I's full-blown invasion of the Greek mainland 480.

**Persian Gulf** or *Arabian Gulf,* large shallow inlet of the Arabian Sea; area 233,000 sq km/ 90,000 sq mi. It divides the Arabian peninsula from Iran and is linked by the Strait of Hormuz and the Gulf of Oman to the Arabian Sea. Oilfields producing about one-third of the world's oil surround it in the Gulf States of Bahrain, Iran, Iraq, Kuwait, Oman, Qatar, Saudi Arabia, and the United Arab Emirates.

**Persian language** language belonging to the Indo-Iranian branch of the Indo-European family; see ◊Farsi.

**Persian Wars** series of conflicts between Greece and Persia in 499–479 BC. Greek involvement with Persia began when ◊Cyrus (II) the Great (reigned 559–530 BC) conquered the Greek cities of western Asia Minor and ended with ◊Alexander (III) the Great's conquest of Persia, but the term 'Persian Wars' usually refers to the two Persian invasions of mainland Greece in 490 and 480/79. The Greek victory marked the end of Persian domination of the ancient world and the beginning of Greek supremacy.

**persimmon** any of a group of tropical trees belonging to the ebony family, especially the common persimmon (*D. virginiana*) of the southeastern USA. Growing up to 19 m/60 ft high, the persimmon has alternate oval leaves and yellow-green flowers. The small, sweet, orange fruits are edible. (Genus *Diospyros,* family Ebenaceae.)

**personification** figure of speech (poetic or imaginative expression) in which animals, plants, objects, and ideas are treated as if they were human or alive ('Clouds chased each other across the face of the Moon'; 'Nature smiled on their work and gave it her blessing'; 'The future beckoned eagerly to them').

**perspective** the realistic representation of a three-dimensional object in two dimensions. In a perspective drawing, vertical lines are drawn parallel from the top of the page to the bottom. Horizontal lines, however, are represented by straight lines which meet at one of two perspective points. These perspective points lie to the right and left of the drawing at a distance which depends on the view being taken of the object.

**Perspex** trade name for a clear, lightweight, tough plastic first produced in 1930. It is widely used for watch glasses, advertising signs, domestic baths, motorboat windscreens, aircraft canopies, and protective shields. Its chemical name is polymethylmethacrylate (PMMA). It is manufactured under other names: Plexiglas, Lucite, Acrylite, and Rhoplex (in the USA), and Oroglas (in Europe).

**Perth** capital of the state of ◊Western Australia; population (1996) 1,096,829. Perth is situated on the southwest coast of Australia, on the River Swan, 19 km/12 mi inland. Its port is at Fremantle, to the southwest at the mouth of the Swan. Industries include oil refining, electronics, food processing, shipbuilding, banking and finance, and tourism; products include textiles, nickel, alumina, fertilizers, cement, furniture, and motor vehicles. Perth is an important centre for the export of primary products: refined oil, minerals, wool, wheat, meat, fruit, timber, and dairy produce. Perth has four universities: the University of Western Australia (founded 1911); Murdoch University (1975); Curtin University of Technology (1987); Edith Cowan University (1990).

**Perth and Kinross** unitary authority in central Scotland, created in 1996 from the district bearing the same name in Tayside region
*area* 5,388 sq km/2,080 sq mi
*towns* Blairgowrie, Crieff, Kinross, Perth (administrative headquarters), Pitlochry, Aberfeldy
*physical* the geological fault that gives the distinctive character to lowland and highland Scotland passes southwest–northeast through the area. The population is largely centred in the lowlands, along wide fertile valleys such as Strathearn, and the Carse of Gowrie. To the north and west are the Grampians intersected by narrow glens with lochs in their valley floors. Among the highest elevations in the Grampians are Ben Lawers (1,214 m/3,984 ft) and Schiehallion (1,083 m/3,554 ft); in the south are the lower Ochil and Sidlaw Hills
*features* Highland Games at Pitlochry; Dunkeld Cathedral; Scone Palace; Glenshee Ski Development
*industries* woollen manufacture, whisky distilling and blending
*agriculture* highly productive and varied agricultural area with soft fruit (Carse of Gowrie), arable crops (to the south), livestock, salmon fisheries (to the north)
*population* (1996) 131,800.

**Peru** Republic of
*national name* República del Perú

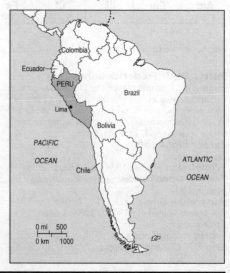

*area* 1,285,200 sq km/496,216 sq mi
*capital* Lima
*major towns/cities* Arequipa, Iquitos, Chiclayo, Trujillo, Cuzco, Piura, Chimbote
*major ports* Callao, Chimbote, Salaverry
*physical features* Andes mountains running northwest–southeast cover 27% of Peru, separating Amazon river-basin jungle in northeast from coastal plain in west; desert along coast north–south (Atacama Desert); Lake Titicaca
*head of state* Alberto Fujimori from 1990
*head of government* Alberto Pandolfi from 1998
*political system* democracy
*political parties* American Popular Revolutionary Alliance (APRA), moderate, left wing; United Left (IU), left wing; Change 90 (Cambio 90), centrist; New Majority (Nueva Mayoria), centrist; Popular Christian Party (PPC), right of centre; Liberal Party (PL), right wing
*currency* nuevo sol
*GNP per capita (PPP)* (US$) 4,910 (1998 est)
*exports* copper, fishmeal, zinc, gold, refined petroleum products. Principal market: USA 24.9% (1997)
*population* 25,230,000 (1999 est)
*language* Spanish, Quechua (both official), Aymara
*religion* Roman Catholic (state religion)
*life expectancy* 66 (men); 71 (women) (1995–2000)
**Chronology**
*4000 BC* Evidence of early settled agriculture in Chicama Valley.
*AD 700–1100* Period of Wari Empire, first expansionist militarized empire in Andes.
*1200* Manco Capac became first emperor of South American Indian Quechua-speaking Incas, who established a growing and sophisticated empire centred on the Andean city of Cuzco, and believed their ruler was descended from the Sun.
*late 15th century* At its zenith, Inca Empire stretched from Quito in Ecuador to beyond Santiago in southern Chile. It superseded Chimu civilization, which had flourished in Peru 1250–1470.
*1532–33* Incas defeated by Spanish conquistadores, led by Francisco Pizarro. King Atahualpa killed. Empire came under Spanish rule, as part of Viceroyalty of Peru, with capital in Lima, founded in 1535.
*1541* Pizarro assassinated as rivalries broke out among conquistadores.
*1780* Tupac Amaru, who claimed to be descended from last Inca chieftain, led failed native revolt against Spanish.
*1810* Peru became headquarters for Spanish government as European settlers rebelled elsewhere in Spanish America.
*1820–22* Fight for liberation from Spanish rule led by Gen José de San Martín and Army of Andes which, after freeing Argentina and Chile, invaded southern Peru.
*1824* Became last colony in Central and South America to achieve independence from Spain after attacks from north by Field Marshal Sucre, acting for freedom fighter Simón Bolívar.

*1836–39* Failed attempts at union with Bolivia.
*1845–62* Economic progress under rule of Gen Ramón Castilla.
*1849–74* Around 80,000–100,000 Chinese labourers arrived in Peru to fill menial jobs such as collecting guano.
*1866* Victorious naval war fought with Spain.
*1879–83* Pacific War fought in alliance with Bolivia and Chile over nitrate fields of the Atacama Desert in the south; three provinces along coastal south lost to Chile.
*1902* Boundary dispute with Bolivia settled.
*mid–1920s* After several decades of civilian government, series of right-wing dictatorships held power.
*1927* Boundary dispute with Colombia settled.
*1929* Tacna province, lost to Chile in 1880, was returned.
*1941* Brief war with Ecuador secured Amazonian territory.
*1945* Civilian government, dominated by left-of-centre American Popular Revolutionary Alliance (APRA, formed 1924), came to power after free elections.
*1948* Army coup installed military government led by Gen Manuel Odría, who remained in power until 1956.
*1963* Return to civilian rule, with centrist Fernando Belaúnde Terry as president.
*1968* Return of military government in bloodless coup by Gen Juan Velasco Alvarado, following industrial unrest. Populist land reform programme introduced.
*1975* Velasco replaced, in a bloodless coup, by Gen Morales Bermúdez.
*1980* Return to civilian rule, with Fernando Belaúnde as president; agrarian and industrial reforms pursued. Sendero Luminoso ('Shining Path') Maoist guerrilla group active.
*1981* Boundary dispute with Ecuador renewed.
*1985* Belaúnde succeeded by Social Democrat Alan García Pérez, who launched campaign to remove military and police 'old guard'.
*1987* President García delayed the nationalization of Peru's banks after a vigorous campaign against the proposal.
*1988* García was pressured to seek help from International Monetary Fund (IMF) as economy deteriorated. Sendero Luminoso increased its campaign of violence.
*1990* Right-of-centre Alberto Fujimori, the son of Japanese immigrants, defeated ex-communist writer Vargas Llosa in presidential elections. An assassination attempt on the president failed. Inflation rose to 400%; a privatization programme was launched.
*1992* Fujimori allied himself with the army and suspended the constitution, provoking international criticism. The Sendero Luminoso leader was arrested and sentenced to life imprisonment. A new single-chamber legislature was elected.
*1993* A new constitution was adopted, enabling Fujimori to seek re-election.
*1994* 6,000 Sendero Luminoso guerrillas surrendered to the authorities.
*1995* A border dispute with Ecuador was resolved after armed clashes. Fujimori was

re-elected. A controversial amnesty was granted to those previously convicted of human-rights abuses.

**1996** Prime Minister Dante Cordova resigned in protest against the rapid pace of market reform. Hostages were held in the Japanese embassy by Marxist Tupac Amaru Revolutionary Movement (MRTA) guerrillas.

**1997** The hostage siege ended.

**1998** Javier Valle Riestra was appointed prime minister, but resigned two months later. Alberto Pandolfi was appointed to succeed him. A border dispute that had lasted for 157 years was settled with Ecuador.

**Peru Current** formerly known as *Humboldt Current,* cold ocean ◊current flowing north from the Antarctic along the west coast of South America to southern Ecuador, then west. It reduces the coastal temperature, making the western slopes of the Andes arid because winds are already chilled and dry when they meet the coast.

**Peshawar** capital of North-West Frontier Province, Pakistan, 18 km/11 mi east of the Khyber Pass, on the Bara River; population (1981) 555,000. Historically a trading centre for India, Afghanistan and central Asia, products include fruit, textiles, leather, and copper.

**pest** in biology, any insect, fungus, rodent, or other living organism that has a harmful effect on human beings, other than those that directly cause human diseases. Most pests damage crops or livestock, but the term also covers those that damage buildings, destroy food stores, and spread disease.

**pesticide** any chemical used in farming, gardening, or indoors to combat pests. Pesticides are of three main types: *insecticides* (to kill insects), *fungicides* (to kill fungal diseases), and *herbicides* (to kill plants, mainly those considered weeds). Pesticides cause a number of pollution problems through spray drift on to surrounding areas, direct contamination of users or the public, and as residues on food. The World Health Organization (WHO) estimated in 1999 that 20,000 people die annually worldwide from pesticide poisoning incidents.

The safest pesticides include those made from plants, such as the insecticides pyrethrum and derris.

**Pétain, (Henri) Philippe Benoni Omer Joseph** (1856–1951) French general and head of state. Voted in as prime minister in June 1940, Pétain signed an armistice with Germany on 22 June before assuming full powers on 16 July. His authoritarian regime, established at Vichy, collaborated with the Germans and proposed a reactionary 'National Revolution' for France under the slogan 'Work, Family, Fatherland'. Convinced in 1940 of Britain's imminent defeat, Pétain accepted Germany's terms for peace, including the occupation of northern France. In December 1940 he dismissed his deputy Pierre ◊Laval, who wanted to side with the Axis powers, but bowed to German pressures to reinstate him in April 1942. With Germany occupying the whole of France from that November, Pétain found himself head, in name only, of a puppet state. Removed from France by the German army in 1944, he returned voluntarily and was tried and condemned to death for treason in August 1945. He died in prison on the Ile d'Yeu, his sentence having been commuted to life imprisonment.

**petal** part of a flower whose function is to attract pollinators such as insects or birds. Petals are frequently large and brightly coloured and may also be scented. Some have a nectary at the base and markings on the petal surface, known as honey guides, to direct pollinators to the source of the nectar. In wind-pollinated plants, however, the petals are usually small and insignificant, and sometimes absent altogether. Petals are derived from modified leaves, and are known collectively as a corolla.

**Peter** three tsars of Russia, including:

**Peter (I) the Great** (1672–1725) Tsar of Russia from 1682 on the death of his half-brother Tsar Feodor III; he assumed control of the government in 1689. He attempted to reorganize the country on Western lines. He modernized the army, had a fleet built, remodelled the administrative and legal systems, encouraged education, and brought the Russian Orthodox Church under state control. On the Baltic coast, where he had conquered territory from Sweden, Peter built a new city, St Petersburg, and moved the capital there from Moscow.

**Peterborough** unitary authority in eastern England, created in 1998 from part of Cambridgeshire

*area* 334 sq km/129 sq mi

*towns and cities* Peterborough (administrative headquarters), Wittering, Old Fletton, Thorney, Glinton, Northborough, Peakirk

*features* River Nene; western margins of the Fens; St Peter's Cathedral (Peterborough), 12th century, containing Catherine of Aragon's tomb; Wildfowl and Wetlands Centre at Peakirk

*industries* aluminium founding and manufacture, electronics, domestic appliances, plastics and rubber manufacture, precision engineering, telecommunications equipment, food manufacture and processing

*population* (1996) 156,900

*famous people* John Clare, L P Hartley.

**Peterloo massacre** the events in St Peter's Fields in Manchester, England, on 16 August 1819, when an open-air meeting in support of parliamentary reform was charged by yeomanry (voluntary cavalry soldiers) and hussars (regular cavalry soldiers). Eleven people were killed and 500 wounded. The name was given in analogy with the Battle of Waterloo.

**Peter, St** (lived 1st century) Christian martyr, the author of two epistles in the New Testament and leader of the apostles. He is regarded as the first bishop of Rome, whose mantle the pope inherits. His real name was Simon, but he was nicknamed Kephas ('Peter', from the Greek for 'rock') by Jesus, as being the rock upon which he would build his church. His emblem is two keys; feast day 29 June.

**Petipa, Marius** (1822–1910) French choreographer. He created some of the most important ballets in the classical repertory. For the Imperial Ballet in Russia he created masterpieces such as *Don Quixote* (1869), *La Bayadère* (1877), *The Sleeping Beauty* (1890), *Swan Lake* (1895; with Ivanov), and *Raymonda* (1898).

**Petra** Arabic Wadi Musa, ancient city carved out of the red rock at a site in Jordan, on the eastern slopes of the Wadi el Araba, 90 km/56 mi south of the Dead Sea. An Edomite stronghold and capital of the Nabataeans in the 2nd century, it was captured by the Roman emperor Trajan in 106 and destroyed by the Arabs in the 7th century. It was forgotten in Europe until 1812 when the Swiss traveller Johann Ludwig Burckhardt (1784–1817) came across it.

**Petrarch, Francesco** Italian *Petrarca* (1304–1374) Italian poet, humanist, and leader of the revival of classical learning. His *Il canzoniere/Songbook* (also known as *Rime Sparse/Scattered Lyrics*) contains madrigals, songs, and ◊sonnets in praise of his idealized love, 'Laura', whom he first saw 1327 (she was a married woman and refused to become his mistress). These were Petrarch's greatest contributions to Italian literature; they shaped the lyric poetry of the Renaissance and greatly influenced French and English love poetry. Although he did not invent the sonnet form, he was its finest early practitioner and the 'Petrarchan sonnet' was admired as an ideal model by later poets.

**petrel** any of various families of seabirds in the order Procellariiforme, including the worldwide *storm petrels* (family Hydrobatidae), which include the smallest seabirds (some only 13 cm/5 in long), and the *diving petrels* (family Pelecanoididae) of the southern hemisphere. All have a hooked bill, rudimentary hind toes, tubular nostrils, and feed by diving underwater. They include ◊fulmars and ◊shearwaters.

**Petrograd** former name (1914–24) of ◊St Petersburg, a city in Russia. It adopted this Russian-style name as a patriotic gesture at the outbreak of World War I, but was renamed Leningrad on the death of the USSR's first leader.

**petrol** mixture of hydrocarbons derived from petroleum, mainly used as a fuel for internal-combustion engines. It is colourless and highly volatile. *Leaded petrol* contains antiknock (a mixture of tetraethyl lead and dibromoethane), which improves the combustion of petrol and the performance of a car engine. The lead from the exhaust fumes enters the atmosphere, mostly as simple lead compounds. There is strong evidence that it can act as a nerve poison on young children and cause mental impairment. This has prompted a gradual switch to the use of *unleaded petrol* in the UK.

**petrol engine** the most commonly used source of power for motor vehicles, introduced by the German engineers Gottlieb Daimler and Karl Benz in 1885. The petrol engine is a complex piece of machinery made up of about 150 moving parts. It is a reciprocating piston engine, in which a number of pistons move up and down in cylinders. A mixture of petrol and air is introduced to the space above the pistons and ignited. The gases produced force the pistons down, generating power. The engine-operating cycle is repeated every four strokes (upward or downward movement) of the piston, this being known as the ◊four-stroke cycle. The motion of the pistons rotate a crankshaft, at the end of which is a heavy flywheel. From the flywheel the power is transferred to the car's driving wheels via the transmission system of clutch, gearbox, and final drive.

**petroleum** or *crude oil,* natural mineral oil, a thick greenish-brown flammable liquid found underground in permeable rocks. Petroleum consists of hydrocarbons mixed with oxygen, sulphur, nitrogen, and other elements in varying proportions. It is thought to be derived from ancient organic material that has been converted by, first, bacterial action, then heat, and pressure (but its origin may be chemical also).

From crude petroleum, various products are made by distillation and other processes; for example, fuel oil, petrol, kerosene, diesel, and lubricating oil. Petroleum products and chemicals are used in large quantities in the manufacture of detergents, artificial fibres, plastics, insecticides, fertilizers, pharmaceuticals, toiletries, and synthetic rubber.

**petrology** branch of geology that deals with the study of rocks, their mineral compositions, and their origins.

**Peugeot** France's second-largest car manufacturer, founded in 1885 when Armand Peugeot (1849–1915) began making bicycles; the company bought the rival firm Citroën in 1974 and the European operations of the American Chrysler Company in 1978.

**pewter** any of various alloys of mostly tin with varying amounts of lead, copper, or antimony. Pewter has been known for centuries and was once widely used for domestic utensils but is now used mainly for ornamental ware.

**peyote** spineless cactus of northern Mexico and the southwestern USA. It has white or pink flowers. Its buttonlike tops contain *mescaline,* which causes hallucinations and is used by American Indians in religious ceremonies. (*Lophopora williamsii,* family Cactaceae.)

**pH** scale from 0 to 14 for measuring acidity or alkalinity. A pH of 7.0 indicates neutrality, below 7 is acid, while above 7 is alkaline. Strong acids, such as those used in car batteries, have a pH of about 2; strong alkalis such as sodium hydroxide are pH 13.

**phage** another name for a ◊bacteriophage, a virus that attacks bacteria.

**phagocyte** type of ◊white blood cell, or leucocyte, that can engulf a bacterium or other invading micro-organism. Phagocytes are found in blood, lymph, and other body tissues, where they also ingest foreign matter and dead tissue. A ◊macrophage differs in size and life span.

**Phalangist** member of a Lebanese military organization (*Phalanges Libanaises*), since 1958 the political and military force of the ◊Maronite Church in Lebanon. The Phalangists' unbending right-wing policies and resistance to the introduction of democratic institutions were among the contributing factors to the civil war in Lebanon.

**phalanx** in ancient Greece and Macedonia, a battle formation using up to 16 lines of infantry with pikes about 4 m/13 ft long, protected to the sides and rear by cavalry. It was used by Philip II and Alexander the Great of Macedon, and though more successful than the conventional hoplite formation, it proved inferior to the Roman legion.

**phalarope** any of a genus *Phalaropus* of small, elegant shorebirds in the sandpiper family (Scolopacidae). They have the habit of spinning in the water to stir up insect larvae. They are native to North America, the UK, and the polar regions of Europe.

**Phanerozoic** (Greek *phanero* 'visible') eon in Earth history, consisting of the most recent 570 million years. It comprises the Palaeozoic, Mesozoic, and Cenozoic eras. The vast majority of fossils come from this eon, owing to the evolution of hard shells and internal skeletons. The name means 'interval of well-displayed life'.

**Pharaoh** Hebrew form of the Egyptian royal title Per-'o. This term, meaning 'great house', was originally applied to the royal household, and after about 950 BC to the king.

**Pharisee** (Hebrew 'separatist') member of a conservative Jewish sect that arose in Roman-occupied Palestine in the 2nd century BC in protest against all movements favouring compromise with Hellenistic culture. The Pharisees were devout adherents of the law, both as found in the Torah and in the oral tradition known as the Mishnah.

**pharmacology** study of the properties of drugs and their effects on the human body.

**phase** in astronomy, the apparent shape of the Moon or a planet when all or part of its illuminated hemisphere is facing the Earth.

The Moon undergoes a full cycle of phases from new (when between the Earth and the Sun) through first quarter (when at 90° eastern elongation from the Sun), full (when opposite the Sun), and last quarter (when at 90° western elongation from the Sun).

**pheasant** any of various large, colourful Asiatic fowls of the family Phasianidae, order Galliformes, which also includes grouse, quail, and turkey. The typical pheasants are in the genus *Phasianus,* which has two species: the Japanese pheasant, *P. versicolor,* found in Japan, and the Eurasian ring-necked or common pheasant, *P. colchicus,* also introduced to North America. The genus is distinguished by the very long wedge-shaped tail and the absence of a crest. The plumage of the male common pheasant is richly tinted with brownish-green, yellow, and red markings, but the female is a camouflaged brownish colour. The nest is made on the ground. The male is polygamous.

**phenol** member of a group of aromatic chemical compounds with weakly acidic properties, which are characterized by a hydroxyl (OH) group attached directly to an aromatic ring. The simplest of the phenols, derived from benzene, is also known as phenol and has the formula $C_6H_5OH$. It is sometimes called *carbolic acid* and can be extracted from coal tar.

**phenotype** in genetics, visible traits, those actually displayed by an organism. The phenotype is not a direct reflection of the ◊genotype because some alleles are masked by the presence of other, dominant alleles (see ◊dominance). The phenotype is further modified by the effects of the environment (for example, poor nutrition stunts growth).

**pheromone** chemical signal (such as an odour) that is emitted by one animal and affects the behaviour of others. Pheromones are used by many animal species to attract mates.

**Phidias** (lived mid-5th century BC) or *Pheidias,* Greek sculptor. Active in Athens, he supervised the sculptural programme for the Parthenon (most of it is preserved in the British Museum, London, and known as the ◊Elgin marbles). He also executed the colossal statue of Zeus at Olympia, one of the ◊Seven Wonders of the World. No surviving sculptures can be credited to him with certainty.

**Philadelphia** (Greek 'the city of brotherly love') river port and chief city in Pennsylvania, USA, on the Delaware River at the junction with the Schuykill River; population (1996 est) 1,478,000; metropolitan area (1992) 5,939,000. It is the world's largest freshwater port, the fifth largest city in the USA, and a financial, business, and research centre. Industries include oil-refining, food processing, electronics, printing, publishing, and the production of iron, steel, chemicals, textiles, carpets, and transportation equipment. It was originally settled by Swedish settlers in 1682, and was the capital of the USA 1790–1800.

**philanthropy** love felt by an individual towards humankind. It is expressed through acts of generosity and charity and seeks to promote the greater happiness and prosperity of humanity.

**philately** the collection and study of postage stamps. It originated as a hobby in France in about 1860.

**Philip, Duke of Edinburgh** (1921– ) prince of the UK, husband of Elizabeth II, a grandson of George I of Greece and a great-great-grandson of Queen Victoria. He was born in Corfu, Greece, but brought up in England.

**Philip** six kings of France, including:

**Philip II** also known as Philip Augustus (1165–1223) king of France from 1180. As part of his efforts to establish a strong monarchy and evict the English from their French possessions, he waged war in turn against the English kings ◊Henry II, Richard (I) the Lionheart (with whom he also went on the Third Crusade), and John (1167–1216).

**Philip VI** (1293–1350) king of France from 1328, first of the house of Valois, elected by the barons on the death of his cousin, Charles IV. His claim was challenged by Edward III of England, who defeated him at Crécy in 1346.

**Philip II of Macedon** (382–336 BC) king of ◊Macedonia from 359 BC. He seized the throne from his nephew, for whom he was regent, defeated the Greek city states at the battle of Chaeronea (in central Greece) in 338 and formed them into a league whose forces could be united against Persia. He was assassinated while he was planning this expedition, and was succeeded by his son Alexander the Great.

**Philip** five kings of Spain, including:

**Philip II** (1527–1598) king of Spain from 1556. He was born at Valladolid, the son of the Habsburg emperor Charles V, and in 1554 married Queen Mary of England. On his father's abdication in 1556 he inherited Spain, the Netherlands, and the Spanish possessions in Italy and the Americas, and in 1580 he annexed Portugal. His intolerance and lack of understanding of the Netherlanders drove them into revolt. Political and religious differences combined to involve him in war with England (sending the unsuccessful ◊Spanish Armada against them) and, after 1589, with France.

**Philippines** Republic of the
*national name Republika ng Pilipinas*

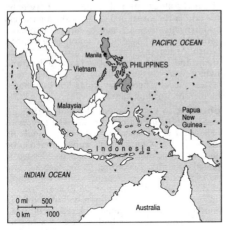

*area* 300,000 sq km/115,830 sq mi
*capital* Manila (on Luzon) (and chief port)
*major towns/cities* Quezon City (on Luzon), Davao, Caloocan, Cebu, Zamboanga
*major ports* Cebu, Davao (on Mindanao), Iloilo, Zamboanga (on Mindanao)
*physical features* comprises over 7,000 islands; volcanic mountain ranges traverse main chain north–south; 50% still forested. The largest islands are Luzon 108,172 sq km/41,754 sq mi and Mindanao 94,227 sq km/36,372 sq mi; others include Samar, Negros, Palawan, Panay, Mindoro, Leyte, Cebu, and the Sulu group; Pinatubo volcano (1,759 m/5,770 ft); Mindanao has active volcano Apo (2,954 m/ 9,690 ft) and mountainous rainforest
*head of state and government* Joseph Ejercito Estrada from 1998

*political system* emergent democracy
*political parties* Laban ng Demokratikong Pilipino (Democratic Filipino Struggle Party; LDP–DFSP), centrist, liberal-democrat coalition; Lakas ng Edsa (National Union of Christian Democrats; LNE–NUCD), centrist; Liberal Party, centrist; Nationalist Party (Nacionalista), right wing; New Society Movement (NSM; Kilusan Bagong Lipunan), conservative, pro-Marcos; National Democratic Front, left-wing umbrella grouping, including the Communist Party of the Philippines (CPP); Mindanao Alliance, island-based decentralist body
*currency* peso
*GNP per capita (PPP)* (US$) 3,540 (1998)
*exports* electronic products (notably semiconductors and microcircuits), garments, agricultural products (particularly fruit and seafood), woodcraft and furniture, lumber, chemicals, coconut oil. Principal market: USA 34.2% (1998)
*population* 74,454,000 (1999 est)
*language* Tagalog (Filipino, official); English and Spanish; Cebuano, Ilocano, and more than 70 other indigenous languages
*religion* mainly Roman Catholic; Protestant, Muslim, local religions
*life expectancy* 67 (men); 70 (women) (1995–2000)
*Chronology*
*14th century* Traders from Malay peninsula introduced Islam and created Muslim principalities of Manila and Jolo.
*1521* Portuguese navigator Ferdinand Magellan reached the islands, but was killed in battle with islanders.
*1536* Philippines named after Charles V's son (later Philip II of Spain) by Spanish navigator Ruy López de Villalobos.
*1565* Philippines conquered by Spanish army led by Miguel López de Lagazpi.
*1571* Manila was made capital of the colony, which was part of the viceroyalty of Mexico.
*17th century* Spanish missionaries converted much of lowland population to Roman Catholicism.
*1762–63* British occupied Manila.
*1834* End of Spanish monopoly on trade; British and American merchants bought sugar and tobacco.
*1896–97* Emilio Aguinaldo led revolt against Spanish rule.
*1898* Spanish-American War: US navy destroyed Spanish fleet in Manila Bay; Aguinaldo declared independence, but Spain ceded Philippines to USA.
*1898–1901* Nationalist uprising suppressed by US troops; 200,000 Filipinos killed.
*1907* Americans set up elected legislative assembly.
*1916* Bicameral legislature introduced on US model.
*1935* Philippines gained internal self-government with Manuel Quezon as president.
*1942–45* Occupied by Japan.
*1946* Philippines achieved independence from USA under President Manuel Roxas; USA retained military bases and supplied economic aid.

**1957–61** 'Filipino First' policy introduced by President Carlos García to reduce economic power of Americans and Chinese; official corruption increased.

**1965** Ferdinand Marcos elected president.

**1972** Marcos declared martial law and ended freedom of press; economic development financed by foreign loans, of which large sums were diverted by Marcos for personal use.

**1981** Martial law officially ended but Marcos retained sweeping emergency powers, ostensibly needed to combat long-running Muslim and communist insurgencies.

**1983** Opposition leader Benigno Aquino was murdered at Manila airport while surrounded by government troops.

**1986** Marcos falsified election results. Corazon Aquino (widow of Benigno Aquino) used 'people's power' to force Marcos to flee the country.

**1987** A 'Freedom constitution' was adopted; Aquino's People's Power won congressional elections.

**1989** A state of emergency was declared after the sixth coup attempt was suppressed with US aid.

**1991** The Philippine senate called for the withdrawal of US forces; US renewal of Subic Bay naval base lease was rejected.

**1992** Fidel Ramos was elected to succeed Aquino; a 'Rainbow Coalition' government was formed.

**1995** Imelda Marcos (the widow of Ferdinand Marcos) was elected to House of Representatives while on bail from prison on a sentence for corruption.

**1996** The LDP withdrew from LDP–DFSP coalition. A peace agreement was made between the government and Moro National Liberation Front (MNLF) after 25 years of civil unrest on Mindanao.

**1997** Preliminary peace talks took place between the government and the Muslim secessionist Moro Islamic Liberation Front (MILF). Major changes were made in political parties. The Supreme Court rejected a proposal to allow a second presidential term.

**1998** Joseph Estrada, the vice-president, was inaugurated as president and Gloria Macapagal Arroyo as vice-president. Imelda Marcos was acquitted of corruption charges. A dispute with China over the mineral-rich Spratly Islands was resolved with an agreement on the joint use of the resources.

**Philistine** member of a seafaring people of non-Semitic origin who founded city-states on the Palestinian coastal plain in the 12th century BC, adopting a Semitic language and religion.

**philology** (Greek 'love of language') in historical ◊linguistics, the study of the development of languages. It is also an obsolete term for the study of literature.

**philosophy** (Greek 'love of wisdom') systematic analysis and critical examination of fundamental problems such as the nature of reality, mind, perception, self, free will, causation, time and space, and moral judgements. Traditionally, philosophy has three branches: metaphysics (the nature of being), epistemology (theory of knowl-edge), and logic (study of valid inference). Modern philosophy also includes ethics, aesthetics, political theory, the philosophy of science, and the philosophy of religion.

**phloem** tissue found in vascular plants whose main function is to conduct sugars and other food materials from the leaves, where they are produced, to all other parts of the plant.

**phlox** any of a group of plants native to North America and Siberia. Phloxes are small with alternate leaves and clusters of showy white, pink, red, or purple flowers. (Genus *Phlox*, family Polemoniaceae.)

**Phnom Penh** capital of Cambodia, on the Mekong River, 210 km/130 mi northwest of Saigon; population (1994) 920,000. Industries include textiles and food processing. It has been Cambodia's capital since the 15th century, and has royal palaces, museums, and pagodas.

**phobia** excessive irrational fear of an object or situation – for example, agoraphobia (fear of open spaces and crowded places), acrophobia (fear of heights), and claustrophobia (fear of enclosed places). ◊Behaviour therapy is one form of treatment.

**Phoenicia** ancient Greek name for northern ◊Canaan on the east coast of the Mediterranean. The Phoenician civilization flourished from about 1200 BC until the capture of Tyre by Alexander the Great in 332 BC. Seafaring traders and artisans, they are said to have circumnavigated Africa and established colonies in Cyprus, North Africa (for example, Carthage), Malta, Sicily, and Spain. Their cities (Tyre, Sidon, and Byblos were the main ones) were independent states ruled by hereditary kings but dominated by merchant ruling classes.

**phoenix** in Egyptian and Oriental mythology, a sacred bird born from the sun. The Egyptians believed it was also connected with the soul and the obelisk. In China the phoenix signified good and its appearance prosperity; its departure boded calamity. According to the Greek historian Herodotus, the creature visited the temple of the sun at Heliopolis every 500 years to bury its dead father, embalmed in a ball of myrrh. In another version, the phoenix placed itself on the city's burning altar or built a nest as a funeral pyre, and rose rejuvenated from the ashes. Only one phoenix existed at a time.

**Phoenix** capital and largest city of ◊Arizona, USA, located on the Salt River; population (1996 est) 1,159,200. It is a commercial and industrial centre, an agricultural distribution point for the irrigated Salt River valley, and a popular winter resort. Products include steel, aluminium, aviation equipment, computers, electrical goods, cosmetics, clothing, and processed foods.

**phonetics** the identification, description, and classification of sounds used in articulate speech. These sounds are codified in the International Phonetic Alphabet (IPA), a highly modified version of the Roman alphabet.

**phosphate** salt or ester of phosphoric acid. Incomplete neutralization of phosphoric acid gives rise to acid phosphates. Phosphates are used as fertilizers, and are required for the development of healthy root systems. They are involved in many biochemical processes, often as part of complex molecules, such as ◊ATP.

**phosphor** any substance that is phosphorescent, that is, gives out visible light when it is illuminated by a beam of electrons or ultraviolet light. The television screen is coated on the inside with phosphors that glow when beams of electrons strike them. Fluorescent lamp tubes are also phosphor-coated. Phosphors are also used in Day-Glo paints, and as optical brighteners in detergents.

**phosphorescence** in physics, the emission of light by certain substances after they have absorbed energy, whether from visible light, other electromagnetic radiation such as ultraviolet rays or X-rays, or cathode rays (a beam of electrons). When the stimulating energy is removed phosphorescence ceases, although it may persist for a short time after (unlike ◊fluorescence, which stops immediately).

**phosphorus** (Greek *phosphoros* 'bearer of light') highly reactive, nonmetallic element, symbol P, atomic number 15, relative atomic mass 30.9738. It occurs in nature as phosphates (commonly in the form of the mineral apatite), and is essential to plant and animal life. Compounds of phosphorus are used in fertilizers, various organic chemicals, for matches and fireworks, and in glass and steel.

**photochemical reaction** any chemical reaction in which light is produced or light initiates the reaction. Light can initiate reactions by exciting atoms or molecules and making them more reactive: the light energy becomes converted to chemical energy. Many photochemical reactions set up a ◊chain reaction and produce ◊free radicals.

**photocopier** machine that uses some form of photographic process to reproduce copies of documents or illustrations. Most modern photocopiers, as pioneered by the Xerox Corporation, use electrostatic photocopying, or xerography ('dry writing').

**photoelectric effect** in physics, the emission of ◊electrons from a substance (usually a metallic surface) when it is struck by ◊photons (quanta of electromagnetic radiation), usually those of visible light or ultraviolet radiation.

**photography** process for reproducing images on sensitized materials by various forms of radiant energy, including visible light, ultraviolet, infrared, X-rays, atomic radiations, and electron beams.

Photography was developed in the 19th century; among the pioneers were Louis ◊Daguerre in France and Fox Talbot in the UK. Colour photography dates from the early 20th century.

**photogravure** ◊printing process that uses a plate prepared photographically, covered with a pattern of recessed cells in which the ink is held. See ◊gravure.

**photon** in physics, the ◊elementary particle or 'package' (quantum) of energy in which light and other forms of electromagnetic radiation are emitted. The photon has both particle and wave properties; it has no charge, is considered massless but possesses momentum and energy. It is one of the ◊gauge bosons, and is the carrier of the ◊electromagnetic force, one of the fundamental forces of nature.

**photosynthesis** process by which green plants trap light energy from the Sun. This energy is used to drive a series of chemical reactions which lead to the formation of carbohydrates. The carbohydrates occur in the form of simple sugar, or glucose, which provides the basic food for both plants and animals. For photosynthesis to occur, the plant must possess ◊chlorophyll and must have a supply of carbon dioxide and water. Photosynthesis takes place inside ◊chloroplasts which are found mainly in the leaf cells of plants.

The by-product of photosynthesis, oxygen, is of great importance to all living organisms, and virtually all atmospheric oxygen has originated by photosynthesis. *See illustration on page 702.*

**Phrygia** former kingdom of western Asia covering the Anatolian plateau. It was inhabited in ancient times by an Indo-European people and achieved great prosperity in the 8th century BC under a line of kings bearing in turn the names Gordius and Midas, but then fell under Lydian rule. From Phrygia the cult of the Earth goddess Cybele was introduced into Greece and Rome.

**phylloxera** plant-eating insect of the family Phylloxeridae, closely related to the aphids.

**phylogeny** historical sequence of changes that occurs in a given species during the course of its evolution. It was once erroneously associated with ontogeny (the process of development of a living organism).

**phylum** plural *phyla,* major grouping in biological classification. Mammals, birds, reptiles, amphibians, fishes, and tunicates belong to the phylum Chordata; the phylum Mollusca

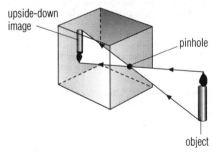

upside-down image

pinhole

object

*photography* A pinhole camera has no lens but can nevertheless produce a sharp inverted image because only one ray from a particular point can enter the tiny pinhole aperture, and so no blurring takes place. However, the very low amount of light entering the camera also means that the film at the back must be exposed for a long time before a photographic image is produced; the camera is therefore only suitable for photographing stationary objects.

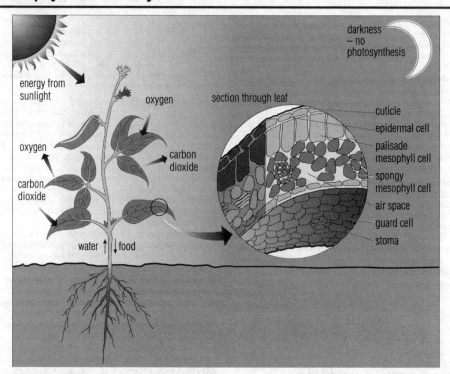

**energy from sunlight**

**darkness – no photosynthesis**

**oxygen**

**oxygen**

**carbon dioxide**

**carbon dioxide**

**section through leaf**

**cuticle**

**epidermal cell**

**palisade mesophyll cell**

**spongy mesophyll cell**

**air space**

**guard cell**

**stoma**

**water ↑ ↓ food**

**photosynthesis** *Process by which green plants and some bacteria manufacture carbohydrates from water and atmospheric carbon dioxide, using the energy of sunlight. Photosynthesis depends on the ability of chlorophyll molecules within plant cells to trap the energy of light to split water molecules, giving off oxygen as a by-product. The hydrogen of the water molecules is then used to reduce carbon dioxide to simple carbohydrates.*

consists of snails, slugs, mussels, clams, squid, and octopuses; the phylum Porifera contains sponges; and the phylum Echinodermata includes starfish, sea urchins, and sea cucumbers. In classifying plants (where the term 'division' often takes the place of 'phylum'), there are between four and nine phyla depending on the criteria used; all flowering plants belong to a single phylum, Angiospermata, and all conifers to another, Gymnospermata. Related phyla are grouped together in a ❑kingdom; phyla are subdivided into ❑classes.

**physical chemistry** branch of chemistry concerned with examining the relationships between the chemical compositions of substances and the physical properties that they display. Most chemical reactions exhibit some physical phenomenon (change of state, temperature, pressure, or volume, or the use or production of electricity), and the measurement and study of such phenomena has led to many chemical theories and laws.

**physics** branch of science concerned with the laws that govern the structure of the universe, and the investigation of the properties of matter and energy and their interactions. For convenience, physics is often divided into branches such as atomic physics, nuclear physics, particle physics, solid-state physics, molecular physics,

electricity and magnetism, optics, acoustics, heat, thermodynamics, quantum theory, and relativity. Before the 20th century, physics was known as *natural philosophy*.

**physiology** branch of biology that deals with the functioning of living organisms, as opposed to anatomy, which studies their structures.

**physiotherapy** treatment of injury and disease by physical means such as exercise, heat, manipulation, massage, and electrical stimulation.

**phytomenadione** one form of vitamin K, a fat-soluble chemical found in green vegetables. It is involved in the production of prothrombin, which is essential in blood clotting. It is given to newborns to prevent potentially fatal brain haemorrhages.

**pi** symbol π, the ratio of the circumference of a circle to its diameter. Pi is an irrational number; it cannot be expressed as the ratio of two integers, and its expression as a decimal never terminates and never starts recurring. The value of pi is 3.1415926, correct to seven decimal places. Common approximations to pi are 22/7 and 3.14, although the value 3 can be used as a rough estimation.

**piano** or *pianoforte,* (originally *fortepiano*) stringed musical instrument played by felt-covered hammers activated from a keyboard. It is therefore a form of mechanized dulcimer, a percussion instrument, unlike the earlier harpsichord, a mechanized harp in which the strings are plucked. It is capable of dynamic gradation between soft (Italian *piano*) and loud (Italian *forte*) tones, hence its name. The first piano was constructed in 1704 and introduced in 1709 by Bartolommeo Cristofori, a harpsichord maker from Padua. It uses a clever mechanism to make the keyboard touch sensitive. Extensively developed during the 18th century, the piano attracted admiration among many composers, although it was not until 1768 that Johann Christian Bach gave one of the first public recitals on the instrument.

**Picardy** French *Picardie,* region of northern France, including Aisne, Oise, and Somme *départements;* area 19,400 sq km/7,488 sq mi; population (1990) 1,810,700. Its industries include chemicals and metals. The main towns include Abbeville and Amiens; the latter is the administrative centre and was capital of the old province.

**picaresque** (Spanish *pícaro* 'rogue') genre of novel that takes a rogue or villain for its central character, telling his or her story in episodic form. The genre originated in Spain and was popular in the 18th century in Britain. Daniel Defoe's *Moll Flanders,* Tobias Smollett's *Roderick Random,* Henry Fielding's *Tom Jones,* and Mark Twain's *Huckleberry Finn* are typical picaresque novels. The device of using an outsider gave the author the opportunity to give fresh moral insights into society.

**Picasso, Pablo Ruiz y** (1881–1973) Spanish artist, chiefly active in France. He was one of the most inventive and prolific talents in 20th-century art. His Blue Period 1901–04 and Rose Period 1905–06 preceded the revolutionary *Les Demoiselles d'Avignon* (1907; Museum of Modern Art, New York), which paved the way for ◊Cubism. In the early 1920s he was considered a leader of the Surrealist movement. From the 1930s his work included sculpture, ceramics, and graphic works in a wide variety of media. Among his best-known paintings is *Guernica* (1937; Prado, Madrid), a comment on the bombing of civilians in the Spanish Civil War.

**piccolo** woodwind instrument, the smallest member of the ◊flute family, for which Vivaldi composed three concertos. Used adjectivally, 'piccolo' is also an alternative term for sopranino.

**Pickford, Mary** stage name of Gladys Mary Smith (1893–1979) Canadian-born US actress. The first star of the silent screen, she was known as 'America's Sweetheart,' and played innocent ingenue roles into her thirties. She and her second husband (from 1920), Douglas ◊Fairbanks, Sr, were known as 'the world's sweethearts'. With her husband, Charlie ◊Chaplin, and D W ◊Griffith she founded United Artists studio in 1919. For many years she was the wealthiest and most influential woman in Hollywood.

**Pict** Roman term for a member of the peoples of northern Scotland, possibly meaning 'painted' (tattooed). Of pre-Celtic origin, and speaking a Celtic language which died out in about the 10th century, the Picts are thought to have inhabited much of England before the arrival of the Celtic Britons. They were united with the Celtic Scots under the rule of Kenneth MacAlpin in 844. Their greatest monument is a series of carved stones, whose symbols remain undeciphered.

**pidgin language** any of various trade jargons, contact languages, or ◊lingua francas arising in ports and markets where people of different linguistic backgrounds meet for commercial and other purposes. Usually a pidgin language is a rough blend of the vocabulary of one (often dominant) language with the syntax or grammar of one or more other (often dependent) groups. Pidgin English in various parts of the world, *français petit negre,* and Bazaar Hindi or Hindustani are examples of pidgins that have served long-term purposes to the extent of being acquired by children as one of their everyday languages. At this point they become ◊creole languages.

**Piedmont** Italian *Piemonte,* region of northern Italy, comprising the provinces of Alessandria, Asti, Cuneo, Novara, Turin, and Vercelli; area 25,400 sq km/9,804 sq mi; population (1992 est) 4,303,800. It borders Switzerland to the north and France to the west, and is surrounded, except to the east, by the Alps and the Apennines. The regional capital is ◊Turin. Piedmont also includes the fertile Po Valley. Products include rice, fruit, grain, cattle, cars, and textiles. The movement for the unification of Italy started in the 19th century in Piedmont, under the House of Savoy.

**Piero della Francesca** (c. 1420–1492) painter from Borgo San Sepulcro in Umbria. Active in Arezzo and Urbino, he was one of the major artists of the 15th century. His work has a solemn stillness and unusually solid figures, luminous colour, and carefully calculated compositional harmonies. It includes several important fresco series, and panel paintings such as the *Flagellation of Christ* (c. 1455; Ducal Palace, Urbino), which is remarkable for its use of perspective.

**Pietism** religious movement within Lutheranism in the 17th century that emphasized spiritual and devotional faith rather than theology and dogma. It was founded by Philipp Jakob Spener (1635–1705), a minister in Frankfurt, Germany, who emphasized devotional meetings for 'groups of the Elect' rather than biblical learning; he wrote the *Pia Desideria* (1675).

**Pietro da Cortona, (Pietro Berrettini)** (1596–1669) Italian painter and architect. He was a major influence in the development of the High Baroque. His enormous fresco *Allegory of Divine Providence* (1633–39; Barberini Palace, Rome) glorifies his patron the pope, and the Barberini family, and gives a convincing illusion of reality.

**piezoelectric effect** property of some crystals (for example, quartz) to develop an electromotive force or voltage across opposite faces when subjected to tension or compression, and, conversely, to expand or contract in size when subjected to an electromotive force. Piezoelectric crystal oscillators are used as frequency standards (for example, replacing balance wheels in watches), and for producing ultrasound.

**pig** any even-toed hoofed mammal of the family Suidae. They are omnivorous, and have simple, non-ruminating stomachs and thick hides. The Middle Eastern *wild boar Sus scrofa* is the ancestor of domesticated breeds; it is 1.5 m/4.5 ft long and 1 m/3 ft high, with formidable tusks, but not naturally aggressive. The smallest member of the pig family is the *pygmy hog Sus salvanus*. Males are 65 cm long (25 cm at the shoulder) and weigh 8–9 kg.

**pigeon** or *dove,* bird of the family Columbidae, order Columbiformes, distinguished by its large crop, which becomes glandular in the breeding season and secretes a milky fluid ('pigeon's milk') that aids digestion of food for the young. There are many species, and they are found worldwide.

**Piggott, Lester Keith** (1935– ) English jockey. He adopted a unique high riding style and is renowned as a brilliant tactician. A champion jockey 11 times between 1960 and 1982, he rode a record nine ◊Derby winners. Piggott retired from riding in 1985 and took up training. In 1987 he was imprisoned for tax evasion. He returned to racing in 1990 and has ridden 4,460 winners, including a record 30 classics to the start of the 1994 season. He retired as a jockey for the second time in September 1995.
*career highlights*
*champion jockey* 1960, 1964–71, 1981–82
*Derby* 1954, 1957, 1960, 1968, 1970, 1972, 1976–77, 1983
*Oaks* 1957, 1959, 1966, 1975, 1981, 1984
*St Leger* 1960–61, 1967–68, 1970–72, 1984
*1,000 Guineas* 1970, 1981
*2,000 Guineas* 1957, 1968, 1970, 1985, 1992
*Irish 2,000 Guineas* 1992

**pig iron** or *cast iron,* the quality of iron produced in a ◊blast furnace. It contains around 4% carbon plus some other impurities.

**Pigs, Bay of** inlet on the south coast of Cuba about 145 km/90 mi southwest of Havana. It was the site of an unsuccessful invasion attempt by 1,500 US-sponsored Cuban exiles 17–20 April 1961; 1,173 were taken prisoner.

**pika** or *mouse-hare,* any small mammal of the family Ochotonidae, belonging to the order Lagomorpha (rabbits and hares). The single genus *Ochotona* contains about 15 species, most of which live in mountainous regions of Asia, although two species are native to North America.

**pike** any of a family Esocidae in the order Salmoniformes, of slender, freshwater bony fishes with narrow pointed heads and sharp, pointed teeth. The northern pike *Esox lucius,* of North America and Eurasia, may reach a length of 2.2 m/7 ft and a weight of 9 kg/20 lb.

**Pilate, Pontius** (died *c.* AD 36) Roman procurator of Judea AD 26–36. The New Testament

Gospels describe his reluctant ordering of Jesus' crucifixion, but there has been considerable debate about his actual role in it.

**pilchard** any of various small, oily members of the herring family, Clupeidae, especially the commercial sardine of Europe *Sardina pilchardus,* and the California sardine *Sardinops sagax.*

**pilgrimage** journey to sacred places inspired by religious devotion. For Hindus, the holy places include Varanasi and the purifying River Ganges; for Buddhists, the places connected with the crises of Buddha's career; for the ancient Greeks, the shrines at Delphi and Ephesus, among others; for Jews, the Western Wall in Jerusalem; and for Muslims, Mecca and Medina.

**Pilgrimage of Grace** rebellion against Henry VIII of England 1536–37, originating in Yorkshire and Lincolnshire. The uprising was directed against the policies of the monarch (such as the dissolution of the monasteries and the effects of the enclosure of common land).

**Pilgrims** or *Pilgrim Fathers,* the emigrants who sailed from Plymouth, Devon, England, in the *Mayflower* on 16 September 1620 to found the first colony in New England, North America, at New Plymouth, Massachusetts. Of the 102 passengers about a third were Puritan refugees.

**Pill, the** commonly used term for the contraceptive pill, based on female hormones. The combined pill, which contains synthetic hormones similar to oestrogen and progesterone, stops the production of eggs, and makes the mucus produced by the cervix hostile to sperm. It is the most effective form of contraception apart from sterilization, being more than 99% effective.

**pimento** or *allspice,* any of several evergreen trees belonging to the myrtle family, found in tropical parts of the New World. The dried berries of the species *P. dioica* are used as a spice (allspice). Also, a sweet variety of ◊capsicum pepper (more correctly spelled *pimiento*). (Pimento genus *Pimenta,* family Myrtaceae.)

**pimpernel** any of a group of plants belonging to the primrose family, comprising about 30 species mostly native to Western Europe. The European scarlet pimpernel (*A. arvensis*) grows in cornfields, the small star-shaped flowers opening only in full sunshine. It is naturalized in North America. (Genus *Anagallis,* family Primulaceae.)

**Pinatubo, Mount** active volcano on Luzon Island, the Philippines, 88 km/55 mi north of Manila. Dormant for 600 years, it erupted June 1991, killing 343 people and leaving as many as 200,000 homeless. Surrounding rice fields were covered with 3 m/10 ft of volcanic ash.

**Pindling, Lynden (Oscar)** (1930– ) Bahamian politician, prime minister 1967–92. In the 1960s he became leader of the centrist Progressive Liberal Party (PLP), formed in 1953. Attracting support from the islands' demographically dominant black community, the PLP won the 1967 House of Assembly elections, the first to be held on a full adult voting register, and Pindling became the Bahamas' first black prime minister. He led the country to independence, within the British Commonwealth, in 1973 and successfully expanded the tourist industry, but accusations of government corruption grew in the 1980s and the PLP lost power in 1992. After further electoral defeat in 1997, Pindling retired as PLP leader.

**pine** any of a group of coniferous, ◊resin-producing trees with evergreen needle-shaped leaves; there are about 70–100 species of pines, making them the largest family of ◊conifers. (Genus *Pinus,* family Pinaceae.)

**pineal body** or *pineal gland,* a cone-shaped outgrowth of the vertebrate brain. In some lower vertebrates, it develops a rudimentary lens and retina, which show it to be derived from an eye, or pair of eyes, situated on the top of the head in ancestral vertebrates. In fishes that can change colour to match their background, the pineal perceives the light level and controls the colour change. In birds, the pineal detects changes in daylight and stimulates breeding behaviour as spring approaches. Mammals also have a pineal gland, but it is located deeper within the brain. It secretes a hormone, melatonin, thought to influence rhythms of activity. In humans, it is a small piece of tissue attached by a stalk to the rear wall of the third ventricle of the brain.

**pineapple** large, juicy fruit of the pineapple plant, which belongs to the bromeliad family and is native to South and Central America but now cultivated in many other tropical areas, such as Hawaii and Queensland, Australia. The plant's mauvish flowers are produced in the second year, and afterwards join with their bracts (specialized leaves protecting the buds) to form the fleshy fruit, which looks like a giant cone. (*Ananas comosus,* family Bromeliaceae.)

**Pinero, Arthur Wing** (1855–1934) English dramatist. A leading exponent of the 'well-made' play, he enjoyed great contemporary success with his farces, beginning with *The Magistrate* (1885). More substantial social drama followed with *The Second Mrs Tanqueray* (1893), and comedies including *Trelawny of the 'Wells'* (1898). He was knighted in 1909.

**pink** any of a group of annual or perennial plants that have stems with characteristic swellings (nodes) and scented flowers ranging in colour from white through pink to purple. Members of the pink family include carnations, sweet williams, and baby's breath (*Gypsophila paniculata*). (Genus *Dianthus,* family Carophyllaceae.)

**Pink Floyd** British psychedelic rock group, formed in 1965. The original members were Syd Barrett (1946– ), Roger Waters (1944– ), Richard Wright (1945– ), and Nick Mason (1945– ). Dave Gilmour (1946– ) joined the band in 1968. Their albums include *The Dark*

*Side of the Moon* (1973) and *The Wall* (1979), with its spin-off film starring Bob Geldof.

**pinnate leaf** leaf that is divided up into many small leaflets, arranged in rows along either side of a midrib, as in ash trees (*Fraxinus*). It is a type of compound leaf. Each leaflet is known as a *pinna,* and where the pinnae are themselves divided, the secondary divisions are known as pinnules.

**Pinochet (Ugarte), Augusto** (1915– ) Chilean military dictator from 1973, when a coup backed by the US Central Intelligence Agency ousted and killed President Salvador Allende, until 1989. Pinochet took over the presidency as the result of the coup and governed ruthlessly, crushing all political opposition (including more than 3,000 people who 'vanished' or were killed) but also presiding over the country's economic expansion in the 1980s, stimulated further by free-market reforms. In 1988 he called and lost a plebiscite to ratify him as sole nominee for the presidency. He was voted out of power when general elections were held in December 1989 but remained head of the armed forces until March 1998 when he became senator for life, which gave him instant legal immunity.

**pint** imperial dry or liquid measure of capacity equal to 20 fluid ounces, half a quart, one-eighth of a gallon, or 0.568 litre. In the USA, a liquid pint is equal to 0.473 litre, while a dry pint is equal to 0.550 litre.

**Pinter, Harold** (1930– ) English dramatist, originally an actor. He specializes in the tragicomedy of the breakdown of communication, broadly in the tradition of the Theatre of the ◊Absurd – for example, *The Birthday Party* (1958) and *The Caretaker* (1960). Later plays include *The Homecoming* (1965), *Old Times* (1971), *Betrayal* (1978), and *Moonlight* (1993). His *Various Voices: Prose, Poetry, Politics, 1948–1998* was published in 1998.

**pinworm** ◊nematode worm *Enterobius vermicularis,* an intestinal parasite of humans.

**Pinyin** Chinese phonetic alphabet approved 1956 by the People's Republic of China, and used since 1979 in transcribing all names of people and places from Chinese ideograms into other languages using the English/Roman alphabet. For example, the former transcription Chou En-lai became Zhou Enlai, Hua Kuo-feng became Hua Guofeng, Teng Hsiao-ping became Deng Xiaoping, Peking became Beijing.

**pipit** any of various sparrow-sized ground-dwelling songbirds of the genus *Anthus* of the family Motacillidae, order Passeriformes.

**piracy** the taking of a ship, aircraft, or any of its contents, from lawful ownership, punishable under international law by the court of any country where the pirate may be found or taken. When the craft is taken over to alter its destination, or its passengers held to ransom, the term is ◊hijacking. Piracy is also used to describe infringement of ◊copyright.

**Pirandello, Luigi** (1867–1936) Italian dramatist, novelist, and short-story writer. His plays, which often deal with the themes of illusion and reality, and the tragicomic absurdity of life, include *Sei personaggi in cerca d'autore/Six Characters in Search of an Author* (1921), and *Enrico IV/Henry IV* (1922). Among his novels are *L'esclusa/The Outcast* (1901), *Il fu Mattia Pascal/The Late Mattia Pascal* (1904), and *I vecchi e i giovani/The Old and the Young* (1909). He was awarded the Nobel Prize for Literature in 1934.

**piranha** any South American freshwater fish of the genus *Serrusalmus,* in the same order as cichlids. They can grow to 60 cm/2 ft long, and have razor-sharp teeth; some species may rapidly devour animals, especially if attracted by blood.

**Pisa** ancient *Pisae,* town in Tuscany, Italy, on the River Arno, 70 km/43 mi southwest of Florence; population (1991) 101,000. Industries include tourism, engineering, and the production of glass and textiles. Its famous campanile (bell-tower), the *Leaning Tower of Pisa,* is 55 m/ 180 ft high and about 5 m/16.5 ft out of perpendicular, its shallow foundations being on unstable ground.

**Pisces** inconspicuous zodiac constellation, mainly in the northern hemisphere between ◊Aries and ◊Aquarius, near Pegasus. It is represented as two fish tied together by their tails. The Circlet, a delicate ring of stars, marks the head of the western fish in Pisces. The constellation contains the *vernal equinox,* the point at which the Sun's path around the sky (the *ecliptic)* crosses the celestial equator (see ◊celestial sphere). The Sun reaches this point around 21 March each year as it passes through Pisces from mid-March to late April. In astrology, the dates for Pisces are between about 19 February and 20 March (see ◊precession).

**pistachio** deciduous tree of the cashew family, native to Europe and Asia, whose green nuts are eaten salted or used to enhance and flavour food, especially ice cream. (*Pistacia vera,* family Anacardiaceae.)

**pistil** general term for the female part of a flower, either referring to one single ◊carpel or a group of several fused carpels.

**piston** barrel-shaped device used in reciprocating engines (steam, petrol, diesel oil) to harness power. Pistons are driven up and down in cylinders by expanding steam or hot gases. They pass on their motion via a connecting rod and crank to a crankshaft, which turns the driving wheels. In a pump or compressor, the role of the piston is reversed, being used to move gases and liquids. See also ◊internal-combustion engine.

**pit bull terrier** or *American pit bull terrier,* variety of dog that was developed in the USA solely as a fighting dog. It usually measures about 50 cm/20 in at the shoulder and weighs roughly 23 kg/50 lb, but there are no established criteria since it is not recognized as a breed by either the American or British Kennel Clubs. Selective breeding for physical strength and aggression has created a dog unsuitable for life in the modern community.

**Pitcairn Islands** British colony in Polynesia, 5,300 km/3,300 mi northeast of New Zealand
**area** 35.5 sq km/22 sq mi
**capital** Adamstown
**physical** Pitcairn Island (area 4.6 sq km/2.9 sq mi); the uninhabited Henderson Islands, an unspoiled coral atoll with a rare ecology, which has been a World Heritage Site since 1989; tiny Ducie and Oeno islands
**products** coconuts, bananas, breadfruit, yams, pineapples, tomatoes, oranges, and pineapples; souvenirs are sold to passing ships
**population** (1996) 58 (only Pitcairn Island is inhabited)
**language** English
**government** the governor is the British high commissioner in New Zealand
**history** visited by British sailor Philip Carteret in 1767; settled in 1790 by nine mutineers from the British ship the *Bounty* together with some Tahitians; their occupation remained unknown until 1808. Pitcairn Island annexed by Britain in 1887, and Henderson, Ducie, and Oeno islands in 1902.

**pitch** in chemistry, a black, sticky substance, hard when cold, but liquid when hot, used for waterproofing, roofing, and paving. It is made by the destructive distillation of wood or coal tar, and has been used since antiquity for caulking wooden ships.

**pitch** in mechanics, the distance between the adjacent threads of a screw or bolt. When a screw is turned through one full turn it moves a distance equal to the pitch of its thread. A screw thread is a simple type of machine, acting like a rolled-up inclined plane, or ramp (as may be illustrated by rolling a long paper triangle around a pencil). A screw has a mechanical advantage greater than one.

**pitch** in music, how high or low a note is. This depends on the frequency of vibration of the sound and is measured in Hertz (Hz), or cycles per second. It also means the standard to which instruments are tuned, nowadays using the A above middle C (A4 or a') with a frequency of 440Hz as a reference tone. This is often known as *concert pitch.*

Pitch can now be measured accurately by electronic tuning devices, which are beginning to replace the traditional tuning fork, but it is still normal practice for orchestras to tune to an oboe playing a', despite the inherent inaccuracy of this practice.

**pitchblende** or *uraninite,* brownish-black mineral, the major constituent of uranium ore, consisting mainly of uranium oxide ($UO_2$). It also contains some lead (the final, stable product of uranium decay) and variable amounts of most of the naturally occurring radioactive elements, which are products of either the decay or the fissioning of uranium isotopes. The uranium yield is 50–80%; it is also a source of radium, polonium, and actinium. Pitchblende was first studied by Pierre and Marie ◊Curie, who found radium and polonium in its residues in 1898.

**pitcher plant** any of various ◊insectivorous plants, the leaves of which are shaped like a pitcher and filled with a fluid that traps and digests insects. (Genera especially *Nepenthes* and *Sarracenia,* family Sarraceniaceae.)

**Pitot tube** instrument that measures fluid (gas and liquid) flow. It is used to measure the speed of aircraft, and works by sensing pressure differences in different directions in the airstream.

It was invented in the 1730s by the French scientist Henri Pitot (1695–1771).

**Pitt, William,** *the Elder* 1st Earl of Chatham (1708–1778) British Whig politician, 'the Great Commoner'. As paymaster of the forces 1746–55, he broke with tradition by refusing to enrich himself; he was dismissed for attacking the Duke of Newcastle, the prime minister. He served effectively as prime minister in coalition governments 1756–61 (successfully conducting the Seven Years' War) and 1766–68. He was created an earl in 1766.

**Pitt, William,** *the Younger* (1759–1806) British Tory prime minister 1783–1801 and 1804–06. He raised the importance of the House of Commons, clamped down on corruption, carried out fiscal reforms, and effected the union with Ireland. He attempted to keep Britain at peace but underestimated the importance of the French Revolution and became embroiled in wars with France from 1793; he died on hearing of Napoleon's victory at Austerlitz.

**Pittsburgh** nickname 'City of Bridges', second-largest city in Pennsylvania, USA, at the confluence of the Allegheny and Monongahela rivers, forming the Ohio River; population (1996 est) 350,400; metropolitan area (1992) 2,406,000. It is a business and financial centre with one of the largest river ports in the world. High technology and healthcare services dominate an economy formerly based on iron, steel, heavy engineering, and glass industries.

**pituitary gland** major ◊endocrine gland of vertebrates, situated in the centre of the brain. It is attached to the ◊hypothalamus by a stalk. The pituitary consists of two lobes. The posterior lobe is an extension of the hypothalamus, and is in effect nervous tissue. It stores two hormones synthesized in the hypothalamus: ADH and oxytocin. The anterior lobe secretes six hormones, some of which control the activities of other glands (thyroid, gonads, and adrenal cortex); others are direct-acting hormones affecting milk secretion and controlling growth.

**Pius** 12 popes, including:

**Pius V, Antonio Etrislieri** (1504–1572) pope from 1566. His early career was in the Inquisition, a role which brought him the support of Paul IV who made him a cardinal in 1558. From the beginning of his own pontificate, he stressed his determination to carry out the reforms of the Council of Trent. He also excommunicated Elizabeth I of England, and organized the expedition against the Turks that won the victory of ◊Lepanto.

**Pius IX** (1792–1878) pope from 1846. He never accepted the incorporation of the papal states and of Rome in the kingdom of Italy. He proclaimed the dogmas of the Immaculate Conception of the Virgin in 1854 and papal infallibility in 1870; his pontificate was the longest in history.

**Pius XII** Eugenio Pacelli (1876–1958) pope from 1939. He was conservative in doctrine and politics, and condemned modernism. In 1950 he proclaimed the dogma of the bodily assumption of the Virgin Mary, and in 1951 restated the doctrine (strongly criticized by many) that the life of an infant must not be sacrificed to save a mother in labour. He was criticized for failing to speak out against atrocities committed by the Germans during World War II and has been accused of collusion with the Nazis.

**pixel** derived from picture element, single dot on a computer screen. All screen images are made up of a collection of pixels, with each

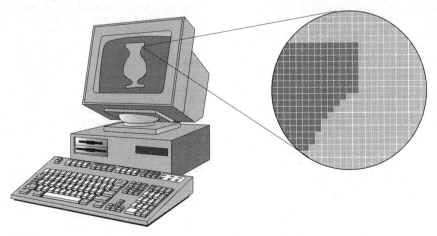

**pixel** *Computer screen images are made of a number of pixels('dots'). The greater the number of pixels the greater the resolution of the image; most computer screens are set at 640 × 480 pixels, although higher resolutions are available.*

pixel being either off (dark) or on (illuminated, possibly in colour). The number of pixels available determines the screen's resolution. Typical resolutions of microcomputer screens vary from 320 x 200 pixels to 800 x 600 pixels, but screens with 1,024 x 768 pixels or more are now common for high-quality graphic (pictorial) displays.

**Pizarro, Francisco** (1475–1541) Spanish conquistador. He took part in the expeditions of Vasco Núñez de ◊Balboa and others. He began exploring the northwest coast of South America in 1524, and, with the permission of the king of Spain, conquered Peru in 1531 with 180 followers. The Inca king Atahualpa was seized and murdered. In 1535 Pizarro founded the Peruvian city of Lima. Internal feuding led to his assassination.

**placebo** (Latin 'I will please') any harmless substance, often called a 'sugar pill', that has no active ingredient, but may nevertheless bring about improvement in the patient's condition.

**placenta** organ that attaches the developing ◊embryo or ◊fetus to the ◊uterus in placental mammals (mammals other than marsupials, platypuses, and echidnas). Composed of maternal and embryonic tissue, it links the blood supply of the embryo to the blood supply of the mother, allowing the exchange of oxygen, nutrients, and waste products. The two blood systems are not in direct contact, but are separated by thin membranes, with materials diffusing across from one system to the other. The placenta also produces hormones that maintain and regulate pregnancy. It is shed as part of the afterbirth.

**plague** term applied to any epidemic disease with a high mortality rate, but it usually refers to the bubonic plague. This is a disease transmitted by fleas (carried by the black rat) which infect the sufferer with the bacillus *Yersinia pestis*. An early symptom is swelling of lymph nodes, usually in the armpit and groin; such swellings are called 'buboes'. It causes virulent blood poisoning and the death rate is high.

**plaice** fish *Pleuronectes platessa* belonging to the flatfish group, abundant in the North Atlantic. It is white beneath and brownish with orange spots on the 'eyed' side. It can grow to 75 cm/2.5 ft long, and weigh about 2 kg/4.5 lb.

**Plaid Cymru** (Welsh 'Party of Wales') Welsh nationalist political party established in 1925, dedicated to an independent Wales. In 1966 the first Plaid Cymru member of Parliament was elected. Four Plaid Cymru MPs were returned in the 1997 general election. The Labour Party's 1997 devolution proposals for Wales were criticized by Plaid Cymru as being too cautious. Nevertheless, the party supported the 'Yes' vote in the subsequent referendum.

**plain** or *grassland,* land, usually flat, upon which grass predominates. The plains cover large areas of the Earth's surface, especially between the deserts of the tropics and the rainforests of the Equator, and have rain in one season only. In such regions the climate belts move

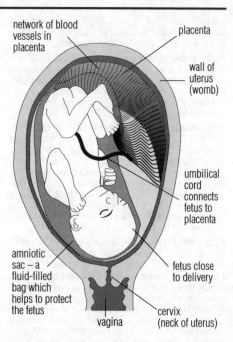

**placenta** *The placenta is a disc-shaped organ about 25 cm/10 in in diameter and 3 cm/1 in thick. It is connected to the fetus by the umbilical cord.*

north and south during the year, bringing rainforest conditions at one time and desert conditions at another. Temperate plains include the North European Plain, the High Plains of the USA and Canada, and the Russian Plain, also known as the steppe.

**Planck, Max Karl Ernst** (1858–1947) German physicist who framed the ◊quantum theory in 1900. His research into the manner in which heated bodies radiate energy led him to report that energy is emitted only in indivisible amounts, called 'quanta', the magnitudes of which are proportional to the frequency of the radiation. His discovery ran counter to classical physics and is held to have marked the commencement of the modern science. He was awarded the Nobel Prize for Physics in 1918.

**Planck's constant** in physics, a fundamental constant (symbol $h$) that relates the energy ($E$) of one quantum of electromagnetic radiation (the smallest possible 'packet' of energy; see ◊quantum theory) to the frequency ($f$) of its radiation by $E = hf$.

Its value is $6.6261 \times 10^{-34}$ joule seconds.

**plane** in botany, any of several trees belonging to the plane family. Species include the oriental plane (*P. orientalis*), a favourite plantation tree of the Greeks and Romans, and the American plane or buttonwood (*P. occidentalis*). A hybrid of these two is the London plane (*P. x acerifolia*), with palmate, usually five-lobed leaves, which is widely planted in cities for its resistance to air pollution. (Genus *Platanus*, family Platanaceae.)

**THE PLANETS**

(– = not applicable.)

| Planet | Main constituents | Atmosphere | Average distance from the Sun km (millions) | mi (millions) | Orbital period (Earth yrs) | Diameter km (thousands) | mi (thousands) | Average density (water = 1 unit) |
|---|---|---|---|---|---|---|---|---|
| Mercury | rock, ferrous | – | 58 | 36 | 0.241 | 4.88 | 3.03 | 5.4 |
| Venus | rock, ferrous | carbon dioxide | 108 | 67 | 0.615 | 12.10 | 7.51 | 5.2 |
| Earth | rock, ferrous | nitrogen, oxygen | 150 | 93 | 1.00 | 12.76 | 7.92 | 5.5 |
| Mars | rock | carbon dioxide | 228 | 141 | 1.88 | 6.78 | 4.21 | 3.9 |
| Jupiter | liquid hydrogen, helium | – | 778 | 483 | 11.86 | 142.80 | 88.73 | 1.3 |
| Saturn | hydrogen, helium | – | 1,427 | 886 | 29.46 | 120.00 | 74.56 | 0.7 |
| Uranus | ice, hydrogen, helium | hydrogen, helium | 2,870 | 1,783 | 84.00 | 50.80 | 31.56 | 1.3 |
| Neptune | ice, hydrogen, helium | hydrogen, helium | 4,497 | 2,794 | 164.80 | 48.60 | 30.20 | 1.6 |
| Pluto | ice, rock | methane | 5,900 | 3,666 | 248.50 | 2.27 | 1.41 | ~2 |

**planet** (Greek 'wanderer') large celestial body in orbit around a star, composed of rock, metal, or gas. There are nine planets in the ◊Solar System: Mercury, Venus, Earth, Mars, Jupiter, Saturn, Neptune, Uranus, and Pluto. The inner four, called the *terrestrial planets,* are small and rocky, and include the planet Earth. The outer planets, with the exception of Pluto, are called the *major planets,* and consist of large balls of rock, liquid, and gas; the largest is Jupiter, which contains a mass equivalent to 70% of all the other planets combined. Planets do not produce light, but reflect the light of their parent star.

**planetary nebula** shell of gas thrown off by a star at the end of its life. Planetary nebulae have nothing to do with planets. They were named by William Herschel, who thought their rounded shape resembled the disc of a planet. After a star such as the Sun has expanded to become a ◊red giant, its outer layers are ejected into space to form a planetary nebula, leaving the core as a ◊white dwarf at the centre.

**plankton** small, often microscopic, forms of plant and animal life that live in the upper layers of fresh and salt water, and are an important source of food for larger animals. Marine plankton is concentrated in areas where rising currents bring mineral salts to the surface.

**plant** organism that carries out ◊photosynthesis, has cellulose cell walls and complex cells, and is immobile. A few parasitic plants have lost the ability to photosynthesize but are still considered to be plants.

Plants are ◊autotrophs, that is, they make carbohydrates from water and carbon dioxide, and are the primary producers in all food chains, so that all animal life is dependent on them. They play a vital part in the carbon cycle, removing carbon dioxide from the atmosphere and generating oxygen. The study of plants is known as ◊botany.

**Plantagenet** English royal house, which reigned from 1154 to1399, and whose name comes from the nickname of Geoffrey, Count of Anjou (1113–1151), father of Henry II, who often wore in his hat a sprig of broom, *planta genista*. In the 1450s, Richard, Duke of York, took 'Plantagenet' as a surname to emphasize his superior claim to the throne over that of Henry VI.

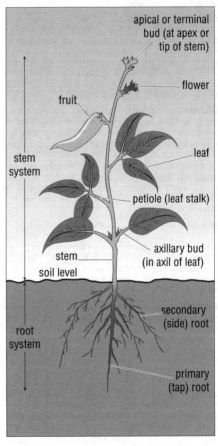

apical or terminal bud (at apex or tip of stem)

flower

fruit

stem system

leaf

petiole (leaf stalk)

stem

soil level

axillary bud (in axil of leaf)

root system

secondary (side) root

primary (tap) root

*plant* The external anatomy of a typical flowering plant.

**plantain** any of a group of northern temperate plants. The great plantain (*P. major*) is low-growing with large oval leaves close to the ground, grooved stalks, and spikes of green flowers with purple anthers (in which the pollen matures) followed by seeds, which are used in bird food. (Genus *Plantago*, family Plantaginaceae.)

**plant classification** taxonomy or classification of plants. Originally the plant kingdom included bacteria, diatoms, dinoflagellates, fungi, and slime moulds, but these are not now thought of as plants. The groups that are always classified as plants are the bryophytes (mosses and liverworts), pteridophytes (ferns, horsetails, and club mosses), gymnosperms (conifers, yews, cycads, and ginkgos), and angiosperms (flowering plants). The angiosperms are split into monocotyledons (for example, orchids, grasses, lilies) and dicotyledons (for example, oak, buttercup, geranium, and daisy).

**plant hormone** substance produced by a plant that has a marked effect on its growth, flowering, leaf fall, fruit ripening, or some other process. Examples include ◊auxin, ◊gibberellin, ◊ethene, and cytokinin.

**plaque** any abnormal deposit on a body surface, especially the thin, transparent film of sticky protein (called mucin) and bacteria on tooth surfaces. If not removed, this film forms tartar (calculus), promotes tooth decay, and leads to gum disease. Another form of plaque is a deposit of fatty or fibrous material in the walls of blood vessels causing atheroma.

**plasma** in biology, the liquid component of the ◊blood. It is a straw-coloured fluid, largely composed of water (around 90%), in which a number of substances are dissolved. These include a variety of proteins (around 7%) such as fibrinogen (important in ◊blood clotting), inorganic mineral salts such as sodium and calcium, waste products such as ◊urea, traces of ◊hormones, and ◊antibodies to defend against infection.

**plasma** in physics, an ionized gas produced at extremely high temperatures, as in the Sun and other stars, which contains positive and negative charges in equal numbers. It is a good electrical conductor. In thermonuclear reactions the plasma produced is confined through the use of magnetic fields.

**plasmid** small, mobile piece of ◊DNA found in bacteria and used in ◊genetic engineering. Plasmids are separate from the bacterial chromosome but still multiply during cell growth. Their size ranges from 3% to 20% of the size of the chromosome. There is usually only one copy of a single plasmid per cell, but occasionally several are found. Some plasmids carry 'fertility genes' that enable them to move from one bacterium to another and transfer genetic information between strains. Plasmid genes determine a wide variety of bacterial properties including resistance to antibiotics and the ability to produce toxins.

**plastic** any of the stable synthetic materials that are fluid at some stage in their manufacture, when they can be shaped, and that later set to rigid or semi-rigid solids. Plastics today are chiefly derived from petroleum. Most are polymers, made up of long chains of identical molecules.

**plate** or tectonic plate, one of several sections of lithosphere approximately 100 km/60 mi thick and at least 200 km/120 mi across, which together comprise the outermost layer of the Earth like the pieces of the cracked surface of a hard-boiled egg.

**plateau** elevated area of fairly flat land, or a mountainous region in which the peaks are at the same height. An *intermontane plateau* is one surrounded by mountains. A *piedmont plateau* is one that lies between the mountains and low-lying land. A *continental plateau* rises abruptly from low-lying lands or the sea, such as the Massif Central in France.

**platelet** tiny disc-shaped structure found in the blood, which helps it to clot. Platelets are not true cells, but membrane-bound cell fragments without nuclei that bud off from large cells in the bone marrow.

**plate tectonics** theory formulated in the 1960s to explain the phenomena of ◊continental drift and seafloor spreading, and the formation of the major physical features of the Earth's surface. The Earth's outermost layer, the lithosphere, is regarded as a jigsaw puzzle of rigid major and minor plates that move relative to each other, probably under the influence of convection currents in the mantle beneath. At the margins of the plates, where they collide or move apart, major landforms such as ◊mountains, ◊volcanoes, ◊ocean trenches, and *ocean ridges* are created. The rate of plate movement is at most 15 cm/6 in per year.

**Plath, Sylvia** (1932–1963) US poet and novelist. Her powerful, highly personal poems, often expressing a sense of desolation, are distinguished by their intensity and sharp imagery. Her *Collected Poems* (1981) was awarded a Pulitzer prize. Her autobiographical novel *The Bell Jar* (1961) deals with the events surrounding a young woman's emotional breakdown.

**platinum** (Spanish *platina* 'little silver' (*plata* 'silver') heavy, soft, silver-white, malleable and ductile, metallic element, symbol Pt, atomic number 78, relative atomic mass 195.09. It is the first of a group of six metallic elements (platinum, osmium, iridium, rhodium, ruthenium, and palladium) that possess similar traits, such as resistance to tarnish, corrosion, and attack by acid, and that often occur as free metals (native metals). They often occur in natural alloys with each other, the commonest of which is osmiridium. Both pure and as an alloy, platinum is used in dentistry, jewellery, and as a catalyst.

**Plato** (c. 427–347 BC) Greek philosopher. He was a pupil of Socrates, teacher of Aristotle, and founder of the Academy school of philosophy. He was the author of philosophical dialogues on such topics as metaphysics, ethics, and politics. Central to his teachings is the notion of Forms, which are located outside the everyday world – timeless, motionless, and absolutely real.

**platypus** monotreme, or egg-laying, mammal *Ornithorhynchus anatinus,* found in Tasmania and eastern Australia. Semiaquatic, it has small eyes and no external ears, and jaws resembling a duck's beak. It lives in long burrows along river banks, where it lays two eggs in a rough nest. It

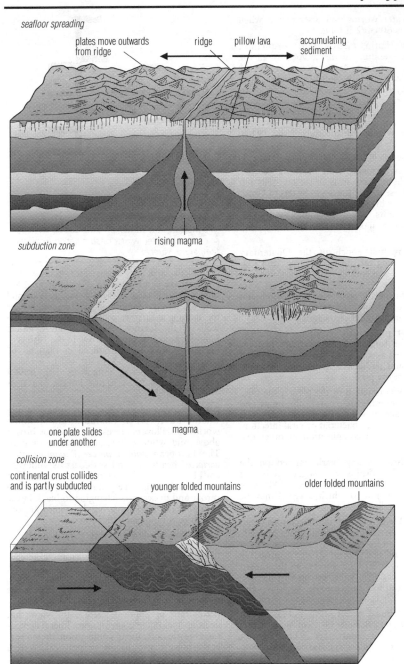

*seafloor spreading*

plates move outwards
from ridge

ridge   pillow lava   accumulating
sediment

rising magma

*subduction zone*

one plate slides
under another

magma

*collision zone*

continental crust collides
and is partly subducted

younger folded mountains

older folded mountains

**plate tectonics** *The three main types of action in plate tectonics. (top) Seafloor spreading. The upwelling of magma forces apart the crust plates, producing new crust at the joint. Rapid extrusion of magma produces a domed ridge; more gentle spreading produces a central valley. (middle) The drawing downwards of an oceanic plate beneath a continent produces a range of volcanic fold mountains parallel to the plate edge. (bottom) Collision of continental plates produces immense fold mountains, such as the Himalayas. Younger mountains are found near the coast with older ranges inland. The plates of the Earth's lithosphere are always changing in size and shape of each plate as material is added at constructive margins and removed at destructive margins. The process is extremely slow, but it means that the tectonic history of the Earth cannot be traced back further than about 200 million years.*

feeds on water worms and insects, and when full-grown is 60 cm/2 ft long.

**plebiscite** (Latin *plebiscitium* 'ordinance, decree') ◊referendum or direct vote by all the electors of a country or district on a specific question. Since the 18th century plebiscites have been employed on many occasions to decide to what country a particular area should belong; for example, in Upper Silesia and elsewhere after World War I, and in the Saar in 1935.

The term fell into disuse during the 1930s, after the widespread abuse by the Nazis in Germany to legitimize their regime.

**Pleiades** in astronomy, an open star cluster about 400 light years away in the constellation Taurus, represented as the Seven Sisters of Greek mythology. Its brightest stars (highly luminous, blue-white giants only a few million years old) are visible to the naked eye, but there are many fainter ones.

**Pleistocene** first epoch of the Quaternary period of geological time, beginning 1.64 million years ago and ending 10,000 years ago. The polar ice caps were extensive and glaciers were abundant during the ice age of this period, and humans evolved into modern *Homo sapiens sapiens* about 100,000 years ago.

**plesiosaur** prehistoric carnivorous marine reptile of the Jurassic and Cretaceous periods, which reached a length of 12 m/36 ft, and had a long neck and paddlelike limbs. The pliosaurs evolved from the plesiosaurs.

**pleurisy** inflammation of the pleura, the thin, secretory membrane that covers the lungs and lines the space in which they rest. Pleurisy is nearly always due to bacterial or viral infection, but may also be a complication of other diseases.

**Plimsoll line** loading mark painted on the hull of merchant ships, first suggested by the 19th-century English politician Samuel Plimsoll. It shows the depth to which a vessel may be safely (and legally) loaded.

**Pliny the Elder** Gaius Plinius Secundus (*c*. AD 23–79) Roman scientific encyclopedist and historian. Many of his works have been lost, but in *Historia naturalis/Natural History*, probably completed in AD 77, Pliny surveys all the known sciences of his day, notably astronomy, meteorology, geography, mineralogy, zoology, and botany.

**Pliocene** ('almost recent') fifth and last epoch of the Tertiary period of geological time, 5.2–1.64 million years ago. The earliest hominid, the humanlike ape *Australopithecines*, evolved in Africa.

**PLO** abbreviation for ◊*Palestine Liberation Organization*, founded in 1964 to bring about an independent state of Palestine.

**Plough, the** in astronomy, a popular name for the most prominent part of the constellation ◊Ursa Major.

**plough** agricultural implement used for tilling the soil. The plough dates from about 3500 BC, when oxen were used to pull a simple wooden

| TF | Tropical fresh water |
| F | Fresh water |
| T | Tropical salt water |
| S | Salt water in summer |
| W | Salt water in winter |
| WNA | Winter in North Atlantic |
| LR | Lloyd's Register |

***Plimsoll line*** *The Plimsoll line on the hull of a ship indicates the maximum safe loading levels for sea or fresh water, winter or summer, in tropical or temperate waters.*

blade, or ard. In about 500 BC the iron ploughshare came into use. By about AD 1000 horses as well as oxen were being used to pull wheeled ploughs, equipped with a ploughshare for cutting a furrow, a blade for forming the walls of the furrow (called a coulter), and a mouldboard to turn the furrow. In the 18th century an innovation introduced in England by Robert Ransome (1753–1830), led to a reduction in the number of animals used to draw a plough: from 8–12 oxen, or 6 horses, to a 2- or 4-horse plough.

**plover** any shore bird of the family Charadriidae, order Charadriiformes, found worldwide. Plovers are usually black or brown above and white below, and have short bills. The European *golden plover Pluviatilis apricaria*, of heathland and sea coast, is about 28 cm/11 in long. In winter the upper parts are a sooty black with large yellow spots, and white throat and underparts, changing to black in the spring. It nests on the ground, laying four yellowish eggs blotched with brown.

**plum** smooth-skinned, oval, reddish-purple or green edible fruit of the plum tree. There are many varieties, including the Victoria, czar, eggplum, greengage, and damson; the wild sloe (*P. spinosa*), which is the fruit of the ◊blackthorn, is closely related. Dried plums are known as prunes. (*Prunus domestica*, family Rosaceae.)

**pluralism** in political science, the view that decision-making in contemporary liberal democracies is the outcome of competition among several interest groups in a political system characterized by free elections, representative institutions, and open access to the organs of power. This concept is opposed by corporatism and other approaches that perceive power to be centralized in the state and its principal elites (the Establishment).

**Plutarch** (*c*. AD 46–*c*. 120) Greek biographer and essayist. He is best remembered for his *Lives*, a collection of short biographies of famous figures from Greek and Roman history arranged in contrasting pairs (for example,

Alexander the Great and Julius Caesar are paired). He also wrote *Moralia,* a collection of essays on moral and social themes.

**Pluto** in astronomy, the smallest and, usually, outermost planet of the Solar System. The existence of Pluto was predicted by calculation by Percival Lowell and the planet was located by Clyde Tombaugh in 1930. Its highly elliptical orbit occasionally takes it within the orbit of Neptune, as in 1979–99. Pluto has a mass about 0.002 of that of Earth.

**mean distance from the Sun** 5.8 billion km/ 3.6 billion mi

**equatorial diameter** 2,300 km/1,438 mi
**rotation period** 6.39 Earth days
**year** 248.5 Earth years
**atmosphere** thin atmosphere with small amounts of methane gas
**surface** low density, composed of rock and ice, primarily frozen methane; there is an ice cap at Pluto's north pole
**satellites** one moon, Charon.

**Pluto** or *Hades,* in Greek mythology, lord of ◊Hades, the underworld and also his original name. His Roman counterpart was *Dis* (also Orcus). He was the son of the Titans ◊Kronos and Rhea; and brother of Zeus, Poseidon, Hera, Hestia, and Demeter. He abducted and married ◊Persephone, daughter of the goddess of agriculture ◊Demeter, causing winter on Earth; Persephone was eventually allotted six months of each year in Hades, and six with her mother.

**plutonic rock** igneous rock derived from magma that has cooled and solidified deep in the crust of the Earth; granites and gabbros are examples of plutonic rocks.

**plutonium** silvery-white, radioactive, metallic element of the ◊actinide series, symbol Pu, atomic number 94, relative atomic mass 239.13. It occurs in nature in minute quantities in ◊pitchblende and other ores, but is produced in quantity only synthetically. It has six allotropic forms (see ◊allotropy) and is one of three fissile elements (elements capable of splitting into other elements – the others are thorium and uranium).

**Plymouth** city, seaport, and unitary authority in southwest England, at the mouth of the River Plym; until April 1998 it was part of the county of Devon

**area** 79 sq km/31 sq mi
**features** dockyard and naval base at Devonport; three harbours, Sutton Pool, Catwater (Cattewater), and the Hamoaze, which unite in Plymouth Sound, a bay with a breakwater over 1 km/0.6 mi in length across the entrance; ferry links with France and Spain; Plymouth University, formerly South West Polytechnic, established in 1992; ramparts of a 17th-century citadel, built to guard the harbour soon after the Civil War; Eddystone Rocks lighthouse 22 km/14 mi to the south; the Hoe, an esplanade overlooking Plymouth Sound, with many monuments including a statue of Sir Francis Drake, and Smeaton's Tower, originally erected in 1759 on the Eddystone Rocks and replaced in 1882; Plymouth Dome illustrates the history of the city; aquarium of the Marine Biological Association, which has its headquarters in Plymouth
**industries** marine and machine tools industries, and clothing, radio equipment, and processed foods are produced
**population** (1996) 257,000
**famous people** John Hawkins, John Northcote, Robert Falcon Scott (Scott of the Antarctic)
**history** the city rises north of the Hoe headland, where tradition has it that the explorer Francis Drake played bowls as the Spanish Armada approached in 1588. The *Mayflower* ◊Pilgrims sailed from here to North America in 1620. The naval explorer James Cook led his first (1768–71) and third (1776–79) Pacific voyages from Plymouth. The first meeting in England of the fundamentalist Christian Protestant sect, the Plymouth Brethren, was held here in 1831. The three separate towns of Devonport, East Stonehouse, and Plymouth were amalgamated in 1914 under the inclusive name of Plymouth. The city centre was reconstructed after heavy bombing in World War II.

**pneumatic drill** drill operated by compressed air, used in mining and tunnelling, for drilling shot holes (for explosives), and in road repairs for breaking up pavements. It contains an air-operated piston that delivers hammer blows to the drill bit many times a second. The French engineer Germain Sommeiller (1815–1871) developed the pneumatic drill in 1861 for tunnelling in the Alps.

**pneumonia** inflammation of the lungs, generally due to bacterial or viral infection but also to particulate matter or gases. It is characterized by a build-up of fluid in the alveoli, the clustered air sacs (at the ends of the air passages) where oxygen exchange takes place.

**Po** Greek *Eridanos;* Latin *Padus,* longest river in Italy, flowing from the Cottian Alps to the Adriatic Sea; length 668 km/415 mi. Its valley is fertile and contains natural gas. The river is heavily polluted.

**pochard** any of various diving ducks found in Europe and North America, especially the genus *Aythya.* They feed largely on water plants. The nest is made in long grass on the borders of lakes and pools.

**pod** in botany, a type of fruit that is characteristic of legumes (plants belonging to the Leguminosae family), such as peas and beans. It develops from a single ◊carpel and splits down both sides when ripe to release the seeds.

**Poe, Edgar Allan** (1809–1849) US writer and poet. His short stories are renowned for their horrific atmosphere, as in 'The Fall of the House of Usher' (1839) and 'The Masque of the Red Death' (1842), and for their acute reasoning (ratiocination), as in 'The Gold Bug' (1843) and 'The Murders in the Rue Morgue' (1841; in which the investigators Legrand and Dupin anticipate Conan Doyle's Sherlock Holmes). His poems include 'The Raven' (1845). His novel *The Narrative of Arthur Gordon Pym of Nantucket* (1838) has attracted critical attention.

**poet laureate** poet of the British royal household or of the USA, so called because of the laurel wreath awarded to eminent poets in the Graeco-Roman world. Early UK poets with unofficial status were John Skelton, Samuel Daniel, Ben ◊Jonson, and William Davenant. John ◊Dryden was the first to receive the title by letters-patent in 1668 and from then on the post became a regular institution. Ted ◊Hughes was poet laureate 1984–1998; he was succeeded in 1999 by Andrew Motion.

**poetry** the imaginative expression of emotion, thought, or narrative, frequently in metrical form and often using figurative language. Poetry has traditionally been distinguished from prose (ordinary written language) by rhyme or the rhythmical arrangement of words (metre), the employment of the line as a formal unit, heightened vocabulary, and freedom of syntax. Poetic images are presented using a variety of techniques, of which the most universal is the use of metaphor and simile to evoke a range of associations through implicit or explicit comparison. Although not frequently encountered in modern verse, alliteration has been used, chiefly for rhetoric or emphasis, in works dating back to Old English.

**pogrom** (Russian 'destruction') unprovoked violent attack on an ethnic group, particularly Jews, carried out with official sanction. The Russian pogroms against Jews began in 1881, after the assassination of Tsar Alexander II, and again in 1903–06; persecution of the Jews remained constant until the Russian Revolution. Later there were pogroms in Eastern Europe, especially in Poland after 1918, and in Germany under Hitler (see ◊Holocaust).

**poikilothermy** the condition in which an animal's body temperature is largely dependent on the temperature of the air or water in which it lives. It is characteristic of all animals except birds and mammals, which maintain their body temperatures by homeothermy (they are 'warm-blooded').

**poinsettia** or *Christmas flower,* winter-flowering shrub with large red leaves encircling small greenish-yellow flowers. It is native to Mexico and tropical America and is a popular houseplant in North America and Europe. (*Euphorbia pulcherrima,* family Euphorbiaceae.)

**pointer** any of several breeds of gun dog, bred especially to scent the position of game and indicate it by standing, nose pointed towards it, often with one forefoot raised, in silence. English pointers have smooth coats, mainly white mixed with black, tan, or dark brown. They stand about 60 cm/24 in tall, and weigh 28 kg/62 lb.

**Pointillism** or *Divisionism,* technique in oil painting developed in the 1880s by the neo-Impressionist Georges Seurat. He used small dabs of pure colour laid side by side to create form and an impression of shimmering light when viewed from a distance.

**poison** or *toxin,* any chemical substance that, when introduced into or applied to the body, is capable of injuring health or destroying life.

The liver removes some poisons from the blood. The majority of poisons may be divided into *corrosives,* such as sulphuric, nitric, and hydrochloric acids; *irritants,* including arsenic and copper sulphate; *narcotics* such as opium, and carbon monoxide; and *narcotico-irritants* from any substances of plant origin including carbolic acid and tobacco.

**Poitiers** administrative centre of the *département* of Vienne and of the ◊Poitou-Charentes region in western France, at the confluence of the Rivers Clain and Boivre; population (1990) 82,500. Products include chemicals, electrical and metal goods, and clothing. The theme park of Mirapolis is nearby. The Merovingian king Clovis I defeated the Visigoths, for whom it was an important town, under Alaric II here in 507; ◊Charles Martel stemmed the Saracen advance in 732; and ◊Edward the Black Prince of England, with English and Gascon forces, defeated the French troops of Jean le Bon (John II) here in 1356, and took him prisoner.

**Poitou-Charentes** region of west-central France, comprising the *départements* of Charente, Charente-Maritime, Deux-Sèvres, and Vienne; area 25,800 sq km/9,959 sq mi; population (1990) 1,595,100. Its administrative centre is ◊Poitiers. Industries include dairy products, wheat, chemicals, and metal goods; brandy is made at Cognac.

**Poland** Republic of
***national name*** *Rzeczpospolita Polska*

***area*** 312,683 sq km/120,726 sq mi
***capital*** Warsaw
***major towns/cities*** Lódź, Kraków (Cracow), Wroclaw (Breslau), Poznań (Posen), Gdańsk (Danzig), Szczecin (Stettin), Katowice (Kattowitz), Bydgoszcz (Bromberg), Lublin
***major ports*** Gdańsk (Danzig), Szczecin (Stettin), Gdynia (Gdingen)
***physical features*** part of the great plain of Europe; Vistula, Oder, and Neisse rivers; Sudeten, Tatra, and Carpathian mountains on southern frontier

**head of state** Aleksander Kwaśniewski from 1995
**head of government** Jerzy Buzek from 1997
**political system** emergent democracy
**political parties** Democratic Left Alliance (SLD), reform socialist (ex-communist); Polish Peasant Party (PSL), moderate, agrarian; Freedom Union (UW), moderate, centrist; Labour Union (UP), left wing; Non-Party Bloc in Support of Reforms (BBWR), Christian Democrat, right of centre, pro-Wałęsa; Confederation for an Independent Poland (KPN), right wing; Solidarity Electoral Action (AWS), Christian, right wing
**currency** złoty
**GNP per capita (PPP)** (US$) 6,740 (1998)
**exports** machinery and transport equipment, textiles, chemicals, coal, coke, copper, sulphur, steel, food and agricultural products, clothing and leather products, wood and paper products. Principal market: Germany 36% (1998)
**population** 38,741,000 (1999 est)
**language** Polish
**religion** Roman Catholic 95%
**life expectancy** 68 (men); 77 (women) (1995–2000)
**Chronology**
**966** Polish Slavic tribes under Mieszko I, leader of Piast dynasty, adopted Christianity and united region around Poznań to form first Polish state.
**1241** Devastated by Mongols.
**13th–14th centuries** German and Jewish refugees settled among Slav population.
**1386** Jagellonian dynasty came to power: golden age for Polish culture.
**1569** Poland united with Lithuania to become largest state in Europe.
**1572** Jagellonian dynasty became extinct; future kings were elected by nobility and gentry, who formed 10% of the population.
**mid-17th century** Defeat in war against Russia, Sweden, and Brandenburg (in Germany) set in a process of irreversible decline.
**1772–95** Partitioned between Russia, which ruled the northeast; Prussia, the west, including Pomerania; and Austria in the south-centre, including Galicia, where there was greatest autonomy.
**1815** After Congress of Vienna, Russian eastern portion of Poland re-established as kingdom within Russian Empire.
**1830 and 1863** Uprisings against repressive Russian rule.
**1892** Nationalist Polish Socialist Party (PPS) founded.
**1918** Independent Polish republic established after World War I, with Marshal Józef Piłsudski, founder of the PPS, elected president.
**1919–21** Abortive advance into Lithuania and Ukraine.
**1926** Piłsudski seized full power in coup and established autocratic regime.
**1935** On Piłsudski's death, military regime held power under Marshal Śmigly-Rydz.
**1939** Invaded by Germany; western Poland incorporated into Nazi Reich (state) and the rest became a German colony; 6 million Poles – half of them Jews – were slaughtered in the next five years.

**1944–45** Liberated from Nazi rule by Soviet Union's Red Army; boundaries redrawn westwards at Potsdam Conference. One half of 'old Poland', 180,000 sq km/70,000 sq mi in the east, was lost to the USSR; 100,000 sq km/40,000 sq mi of ex-German territory in Silesia, along the Oder and Neisse rivers, was added, shifting the state 240 km/150 mi westwards; millions of Germans were expelled.
**1947** Communist people's republic proclaimed after manipulated election.
**1949** Joined Comecon.
**early 1950s** Harsh Stalinist rule under communist leader Boleslaw Bierut: nationalization; rural collectivization; persecution of Catholic Church members.
**1955** Joined Warsaw Pact defence organization.
**1956** Poznań strikes and riots. The moderate Wladyslaw Gomulka installed as Polish United Workers' Party (PUWP) leader.
**1960s** Private farming reintroduced and Catholicism tolerated.
**1970** Gomulka replaced by Edward Gierek after Gdańsk riots against food price rises.
**1970s** Poland heavily indebted to foreign creditors after failed attempt to boost economic growth.
**1980** Solidarity, led by Lech Wałęsa, emerged as free trade union following Gdańsk disturbances.
**1981** Martial law imposed by General Wojciech Jaruzelski, trade-union activity banned, and Solidarity leaders and supporters arrested.
**1983** Martial law ended.
**1984** Amnesty for 35,000 political prisoners.
**1988** Solidarity-led strikes and demonstrations for pay increases. Reform-communist Mieczyslaw Rakowski became prime minister.
**1989** Agreement to relegalize Solidarity, allow opposition parties, and adopt a more democratic constitution, after round-table talks involving Solidarity, the Communist Party, and the Catholic Church. Widespread success for Solidarity in first open elections for 40 years; noncommunist 'grand coalition' government was formed, headed by Tadeusz Mazowiecki of Solidarity; an economic austerity and free-market restructuring programme began.
**1990** The PUWP was dissolved and re-formed as the Democratic Left Alliance (SLD). Wałęsa was elected president and Jan Bielecki became prime minister.
**1991** A shock-therapy economic restructuring programme, including large-scale privatization, produced a sharp fall in living standards and a rise in the unemployment rate to 11%. The unpopular Bielecki resigned and, after inconclusive elections, Jan Olszewski formed a fragile centre–right coalition government.
**1992** The political instability continued, with Waldemar Pawlak of the centre-left Polish Peasant Party (PSL) and Hanna Suchocka of the centrist Democratic Union successively replacing Olszewski as prime minister.
**1993** The economy became the first in Central Europe to grow since the collapse of communism. After new elections, Pawlak formed a coalition government with the ex-communist SLD, which pledged to continue to build a market-based economy and seek early entry into the European Union (EU).

**1994** Poland joined the NATO 'partnership for peace' programme; the last Russian troops left the country.
**1995** Ex-communist Józef Oleksy replaced Pawlak as prime minister. Wałęsa was narrowly defeated by Aleksander Kwaśniewski, leader of the SLD, in a presidential election.
**1996** Oleksy resigned as prime minister amid allegations of spying for Russia's secret service; he was replaced by Wlodzimierz Cimoszewicz.
**1997** Further structural reform and privatization took place and a new constitution was approved. Poland was invited to join NATO and begin negotiations to join the EU. A general election was won by Solidarity Electoral Action (AWS). A coalition government was formed, led by Jerzy Buzek.
**1998** Full EU membership negotiations commenced. The government was weakened by defections to the opposition. The number of provinces was reduced from 49 to 16.
**1999** Poland became a full member of NATO.

**Polanski, Roman** (1933– ) Polish film director. His films include *Repulsion* (1965), *Cul de Sac* (1966), *Rosemary's Baby* (1968), *Tess* (1979), *Frantic* (1988), *Bitter Moon* (1992), and *Death and the Maiden* (1995).

**polar bear** large white-coated bear that lives in the Arctic. Polar bears are normally solitary, except for females when rearing cubs. They feed mainly on seals but will eat berries and scavenge when food is scarce. Males weigh 400–800 kg/880–1,760 lb and are up to 2.5 m/8.25 ft in length (twice as large as females, 200–400 kg). The estimated world population in 1997 was 20,000–30,000 bears.

**Polaris** or *Pole Star* or *North Star,* bright star closest to the north celestial pole, and the brightest star in the constellation ◊Ursa Minor. Its position is indicated by the 'pointers' in ◊Ursa Major. Polaris is a yellow ◊supergiant about 500 light years away. It is also known as *Alpha Ursae Minoris.*

**Polaroid camera** instant-picture camera, invented by Edwin Land in the USA in 1947. The original camera produced black-and-white prints in about one minute. Modern cameras can produce black-and-white prints in a few seconds, and colour prints in less than a minute. An advanced model has automatic focusing and exposure.
It ejects a piece of film on paper immediately after the picture has been taken.

**Polar Regions** see ◊Antarctica, ◊Antarctic Ocean, ◊Arctic, the, ◊Arctic Ocean.

**polar reversal** change in polarity of Earth's magnetic field. Like all magnets, Earth's magnetic field has two opposing regions, or poles, one of attraction and one of repulsion, positioned approximately near geographical North and South Poles. During a period of normal polarity the region of attraction corresponds with the North Pole. Today, a compass needle, like other magnetic materials, aligns itself parallel to the magnetizing force and points to the North Pole. During a period of reversed polarity, the region of attraction would change to the South Pole and the needle of a compass would point south.
Studies of the magnetism retained in rocks at the time of their formation (like little compasses frozen in time) have shown that the polarity of the magnetic field has reversed repeatedly throughout geological time.

**polder** area of flat reclaimed land that used to be covered by a river, lake, or the sea. Polders have been artificially drained and protected from flooding by building dykes. They are common in the Netherlands, where the total land area has been increased by nearly one-fifth since AD 1200. Such schemes as the Zuider Zee project have provided some of the best agricultural land in the country.

**pole** either of the geographic north and south points of the axis about which the Earth rotates. The geographic poles differ from the magnetic poles, which are the points towards which a freely suspended magnetic needle will point.

**Pole** people of Polish culture from Poland and the surrounding area.
There are 37–40 million speakers of Polish (including some in the USA), a Slavic language belonging to the Indo-European family. The Poles are predominantly Roman Catholic, though there is an Orthodox Church minority. They are known for their distinctive cooking, folk festivals, and folk arts.

**polecat** Old World weasel *Mustela putorius* with a brown back and dark belly and two yellow face patches. The body is about 50 cm/20 in long and it has a strong smell from anal gland secretions. It is native to Asia, Europe, and North Africa. In North America, ◊skunks are sometimes called polecats. A ferret is a domesticated polecat.

**Pole Star** another name for ◊Polaris, the northern pole star. There is no bright star near the southern celestial pole.

**police** civil law-and-order force. In the UK, it is responsible to the Home Office, with 56 autonomous police forces, generally organized on a county basis; mutual aid is given in circumstances such as mass picketing in the 1984–85 miners' strike, but there is no national police force or police riot unit (such as the French CRS riot squad). The predecessors of these forces were the ineffective medieval watch and London's Bow Street runners, introduced in 1749 by Henry ◊Fielding, which formed a model for the London police force established by Robert ◊Peel's government in 1829 (hence 'peelers' or 'bobbies'); the system was introduced throughout the country from 1856.

**polio** short for poliomyelitis, viral infection of the central nervous system affecting nerves that activate muscles. The disease used to be known as infantile paralysis since children were most often affected. Two kinds of vaccine are available, one injected (see ◊Salk) and one given by mouth. The Americas were declared to be polio-free by the Pan American Health Organization in 1994. In 1997 the World Health Organization (WHO) reported that causes of polio had dropped by nearly 90% since 1988 when the organization began its programme to eradicate the disease by the year 2000. Most remaining cases are in Africa and southeast Asia (in 1998 India accounted for over 30% of the world's polio cases).

**Polish language** member of the Slavonic branch of the Indo-European language family, spoken mainly in Poland. Polish is written in the Roman and not the Cyrillic alphabet and its standard form is based on the dialect of Poznań in western Poland.

**Politburo** contraction of 'political bureau', the executive committee (known as the Presidium 1952–66) of the Supreme Soviet in the USSR, which laid down party policy. It consisted of about 12 voting and 6 candidate (nonvoting) members.

**Polk, James Knox** (1795–1849) 11th president of the USA 1845–49, a Democrat. Presiding over a period of westward expansion, he allowed Texas admission to the Union, and forced the war on Mexico that resulted in the annexation of California and New Mexico.

**pollack** marine fish *Pollachius virens* of the cod family, growing to 75 cm/2.5 ft, and found close to the shore on both sides of the North Atlantic.

**Pollack, Sydney** (1934–   ) US director, actor, and producer. He directed *Out of Africa,* which won the Academy Awards for best picture and best director in 1985. He also directed *The Way We Were* (1973), *The Electric Horseman* (1979), *Absence of Malice* (1981), *Tootsie* (1982), *The Firm* (1993), *Sabrina* (1995), and *Random Hearts* (1999). He appeared in such films as *Husbands and Wives* (1992), *The Player* (1992), and *Eyes Wide Shut* (1999).

**pollen** the grains of ◊seed plants that contain the male gametes. In ◊angiosperms (flowering plants) pollen is produced within ◊anthers; in most ◊gymnosperms (cone-bearing plants) it is produced in male cones. A pollen grain is typically yellow and, when mature, has a hard outer wall. Pollen of insect-pollinated plants (see ◊pollination) is often sticky and spiny and larger than the smooth, light grains produced by wind-pollinated species.

**pollen tube** outgrowth from a pollen grain that grows towards the ovule, following germination of the grain on the ◊stigma. In ◊angiosperms (flowering plants) the pollen tube reaches the ovule by growing down through the ◊style, carrying the male gametes inside. The gametes are discharged into the ovule and one fertilizes the egg cell.

**pollination** the process by which pollen is transferred from one plant to another. The male ◊gametes are contained in pollen grains, which must be transferred from the anther to the stigma in ◊angiosperms (flowering plants), and from the male cone to the female cone in ◊gymnosperms (cone-bearing plants). Fertilization (not the same as pollination) occurs after the growth of the pollen tube to the ovary. Self-

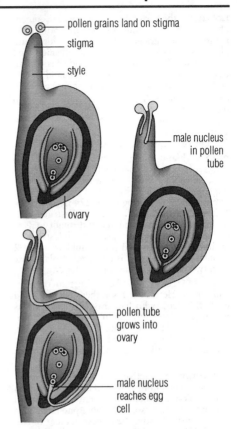

**pollen** *Pollination, the process by which pollen grains transfer their male nuclei (gametes) to the ovary of a flower. The pollen grains land on the stigma and form a pollen tube that grows down into the ovary. The male nuclei travel along the pollen tube.*

pollination occurs when pollen is transferred to a stigma of the same flower, or to another flower on the same plant; cross-pollination occurs when pollen is transferred to another plant. This involves external pollen-carrying agents, such as wind (see anemophily), water (hydrophily), insects, birds (see ◊ornithophily), bats, and other small mammals.

**Pollock, (Paul) Jackson** (1912–1956) US painter. He was a pioneer of abstract expressionism and one of the foremost exponents of ◊action painting. His style is characterized by complex networks of swirling, interwoven lines of great delicacy and rhythmic subtlety.

**poll tax** tax levied on every individual, without reference to income or property. Being simple to administer, it was among the earliest sorts of tax (introduced in England in 1379), but because of its indiscriminate nature (it is a regressive tax, in that it falls proportionately more heavily on poorer people) it has often proved unpopular.

**pollution** the harmful effect on the environment of by-products of human activity, principally industrial and agricultural processes – for example, noise, smoke, car emissions, chemical and radioactive effluents in air, seas, and rivers, pesticides, radiation, sewage, and household waste. Pollution contributes to the ◊greenhouse effect.

**Pollux** or *Beta Geminorum,* brightest star in the constellation ◊Gemini and the 17th-brightest star in the night sky. Pollux is a yellow star with a true luminosity 45 times that of the Sun. It is 35 light years away from the Sun.

**polo** stick-and-ball game played between two teams of four on horseback. It originated in Iran, spread to India and was first played in England 1869. Polo is played on the largest field of any game, measuring up to 274 m/300 yd by 182 m/200 yd. A small solid ball is struck with the side of a longhandled mallet through goals at each end of the field. A typical match lasts about an hour, and is divided into 'chukkas' of 71/2 minutes each. No pony is expected to play more than two chukkas in the course of a day.

**Polo, Marco** (1254–1324) Venetian traveller and writer. He joined his father (Niccolo) and uncle (Maffeo), who had travelled to China as merchants (1260–69), when they began a journey overland back to China (1271). Once there, he learned Mongolian and served the emperor Kubla Khan until he returned to Europe by sea 1292–95.

**polonium** radioactive, metallic element, symbol Po, atomic number 84, relative atomic mass 210. Polonium occurs in nature in small amounts and was isolated from ◊pitchblende. It is the element having the largest number of isotopes (27) and is 5,000 times as radioactive as radium, liberating considerable amounts of heat. It was the first element to have its radioactive properties recognized and investigated.

**Pol Pot** also known as *Saloth Sar, Tol Saut,* and *Pol Porth* (c. 1925–1998) Cambodian politician and leader of the Khmer Rouge communist movement that overthrew the government in 1975. After widespread atrocities against the civilian population, his regime was deposed by a Vietnamese invasion in 1979. Pol Pot continued to help lead the Khmer Rouge despite officially resigning from all positions in 1989. He was captured in 1997 but escaped from Cambodia, reportedly to Thailand, in January 1998 to avoid facing an international court for his crimes against humanity. The Cambodian government announced mid-April 1998 that he had been captured inside Thailand. However, a few days later reports of Pol Pot's death were confirmed. He died following a heart attack, in a Cambodian village two miles from the Thai border.

**polyandry** system whereby a woman has more than one husband at the same time. It is found in various parts of the world, for example, in Madagascar, Malaysia, and certain Pacific isles, and among certain Inuit and American Indian groups. In Tibet and parts of India, polyandry takes the form of the marriage of one woman to several brothers, as a means of keeping intact a family's heritage and property.

**polyester** synthetic resin formed by the condensation of polyhydric alcohols (alcohols containing more than one hydroxyl group) with dibasic acids (acids containing two replaceable hydrogen atoms). Polyesters are thermosetting ◊plastics, used in making synthetic fibres, such as Dacron and Terylene, and constructional plastics. With glass fibre added as reinforcement, polyesters are used in car bodies and boat hulls.

**polyethylene** or *polyethene,* polymer of the gas ethylene (technically called ethene, $C_2H_4$). It is a tough, white, translucent, waxy thermoplastic (which means it can be repeatedly softened by heating). It is used for packaging, bottles, toys, wood preservation, electric cable, pipes and tubing.

**polygamy** the practice of having more than one spouse at the same time. It is found among many peoples. Normally it has been confined to the wealthy and to chiefs and nobles who can support several women and their offspring, as among ancient Egyptians, Teutons, Irish, and Slavs. Islam limits the number of legal wives a man may have to four. Certain Christian sects – for example, the Anabaptists of Münster, Germany, and the Mormons – have practised polygamy because it was the norm in the Old Testament.

**polygon** in geometry, a plane (two-dimensional) figure with three or more straight-line sides. Common polygons have names which define the number of sides (for example, triangle (3), quadrilateral (4), pentagon(5), hexagon (6), heptagon (7), octagon (8), and so on. *Regular polygons* have sides of the same length and all the exterior angles are equal.

**polymer** compound made up of a large long-chain or branching matrix composed of many repeated simple units (*monomers*) linked together by polymerization. There are many polymers, both natural (cellulose, chitin, lignin) and synthetic (polyethylene and nylon, types of plastic). Synthetic polymers belong to two groups: thermosoftening and thermosetting (see ◊plastic).

**polymorphism** in genetics, the coexistence of several distinctly different types in a population (groups of animals of one species). Examples include the different blood groups in humans, different colour forms in some butterflies, and snail shell size, length, shape, colour, and stripiness.

**Polynesia** islands of Oceania east of 170° E latitude, including Hawaii, Kiribati, Tuvalu, Fiji Islands, Tonga, Tokelau, Samoa, Cook Islands, and French Polynesia.

**Polynesian languages** family of languages spoken throughout Polynesia.

**polysaccharide** long-chain ◊carbohydrate made up of hundreds or thousands of linked simple sugars (monosaccharides) such as glucose and closely related molecules.

**Polythene** trade name for a variety of
◊polyethylene.

**polyunsaturate** type of ◊fat or oil containing
a high proportion of triglyceride molecules
whose ◊fatty acid chains contain several double
bonds. By contrast, the fatty-acid chains of the
triglycerides in saturated fats (such as lard) contain only single bonds. Medical evidence suggests that polyunsaturated fats, used widely in
margarines and cooking fats, are less likely to
contribute to cardiovascular disease than saturated fats, but there is also some evidence that
they may have adverse effects on health.

**polyvinyl chloride** (PVC), type of ◊plastic
used for drainpipes, floor tiles, audio discs,
shoes, and handbags. It is derived from vinyl
chloride ($CH_2=CHCl$).

**pomegranate** round, leathery, reddish-yellow fruit of the pomegranate tree, a deciduous
shrub or small tree native to southwestern Asia
but cultivated widely in tropical and subtropical
areas. The fruit contains a large number of seeds
that can be eaten fresh or made into wine.
(*Punica granatum*, family Punicaceae.)

**Pompeii** ancient city in Italy, near the volcano
◊Vesuvius, 21 km/13 mi southeast of Naples.
    In AD 63 an earthquake destroyed much of the
city, which had been a Roman port and pleasure
resort; it was completely buried beneath volcanic ash when Vesuvius, a composite – and
therefore explosive – ◊volcano erupted in AD 79.
Over 2,000 people were killed. Pompeii was
rediscovered in 1748 and the systematic excavation begun in 1763 still continues.

**Pompey the Great** (106–48 BC) Gnaeus
Pompeius Magnus, Roman soldier and politician. From 60 BC to 53 BC, he was a member of
the First Triumvirate with Julius Caesar and
Marcus Livius Crassus. Originally a supporter
of Sulla, Pompey became consul with Crassus in
70 BC. He defeated ◊Mithridates VI Eupator of
Pontus, and annexed Syria and Palestine. He
married Caesar's daughter Julia (died 54 BC) in
59 BC. When the Triumvirate broke down after
53 BC, Pompey was drawn into leadership of the
senatorial faction. On the outbreak of civil war
49 BC he withdrew to Greece, was defeated by
Caesar at Pharsalus 48 BC, and was murdered in
Egypt.
    Considered one of Rome's greatest generals,
Pompey had already commanded several armies
before being admitted to the Senate as consul in
70 BC. After the death of his father Pompeius
Strabo, he raised an army from his father's veterans and clients which fought for ◊Sulla in the
Social War. For this, Sulla gave Pompey the perhaps mocking title Magnus ('The Great'). He
suppressed a rebellion in Italy in 77, then fought
Sertorius in Spain the following year. He enjoyed
some success with Sertorius' subordinates before
being checked by Sertorius himself near the river
Sucro (probably the modern Ebro). The conflict
ended when Sertorius was murdered, and
Pompey returned to Rome where he helped
defeat the Spartacus Revolt before entering the
Senate. In 67 BC Pompey received the extraordinary command to clear the Mediterranean of
pirates, which he completed in three months.
Sent to conclude the war with Mithridates (VI)
Eupator of Pontus, Pompey defeated him at
Lycus (see Lycus, Battle of) in 66 BC then
received the surrender of Tigranes (I) the Great
of Armenia. In 63, he intervened in a civil war in
Judaea, storming Jerusalem where he entered
the Holy of Holies of the Jewish temple but left
its treasures undisturbed. He later consolidated
and organized Rome's eastern provinces, shaping their administrative structure for centuries to
come. Political failures led to his alliance with
◊Caesar and Marcus Licinius ◊Crassus (the
Elder), the so-called First Triumvirate. After
Crassus' death, Pompey refused to treat Caesar
as an equal and supported his opponents in the
Senate, culminating in the civil war of 49 BC. He
abandoned Italy and built up a large army in
Macedon which he planned to lead back to
Rome. However, he was greatly hindered by the
many prominent senators who fled to his camp
and questioned his orders, perhaps causing his
rather lacklustre generalship in the final campaign. Though far less experienced and confident than Caesar's legions, Pompey's army
nearly defeated them at Dyrrachium (see
Dyrrachium, Battle of 49–8 BC) but was soundly
beaten at Pharsalus. Pompey fled to Egypt where
he was murdered.

**Pompidou, Georges Jean Raymond**
(1911–1974) French Gaullist politician and
head of state, President ◊de Gaulle's second
prime minister 1962–68 and his successor as
president 1969–74. As prime minister he played
a key role in managing the Gaullist party but his
moderate and pragmatic conservativism brought
a rift with de Gaulle in May–June 1968, when
he negotiated the Grenelle Agreement with
employers and unions to end the strike movement. Their political divergences were confirmed
when, during his own presidency, he authorized
a devaluation of the franc (which de Gaulle had
vetoed in 1968), agreed to British entry into the
European Community (which de Gaulle had
twice vetoed in the 1960s), and approved initial
steps towards a European Monetary System.
Pompidou died in office before completing his
full seven-year presidential term.

**Ponce de León, Juan** (*c.* 1460–1521)
Spanish soldier and explorer. He is believed to
have sailed to the Americas with Christopher
Columbus in 1493, and served in Hispaniola
1502–04. He conquered Puerto Rico in 1508,
and was made governor in 1509. In 1513 he was
the first European to reach Florida.

**Pondicherry** Union Territory of southeast
India; area 480 sq km/185 sq mi; population
(1994 est) 894,000. Its capital is Pondicherry
which lies on the Coromandel Coast, 196 km/
122 mi south of Chennai. Its products include
rice, millet, groundnuts, cotton, and sugar;
industry is based on textiles and coastal trade.

**pond-skater** water ◊bug (insect of the
Hemiptera order with piercing mouth parts)
that rows itself across the surface by using its
middle legs. It feeds on smaller insects.

**pondweed** any of a group of aquatic plants
that either float on the surface of the water or are

submerged. The leaves of floating pondweeds are broad and leathery, whereas leaves of the submerged forms are narrower and translucent; the flowers grow in green spikes. (Genus *Potamogeton,* family Potamogetonaceae.)

**Pontefract** or *Pomfret,* industrial town in West Yorkshire, northern England, 34 km/21 mi southwest of York, near the junction of the rivers Aire and Calder; population (1991) 28,400. Industries include coalmining, iron founding, engineering, tanning, brewing, corn milling, market gardening, and the manufacture of furniture and confectionery. The town gives its name to liquorice Pontefract or Pomfret cakes. Features include the remains of the Norman castle (built in 1069) where Richard II was murdered in 1399.

**pony** small ◊horse under 1.47 m/4.5 ft (14.2 hands) shoulder height. Although of Celtic origin, all the pony breeds have been crossed with thoroughbred and Arab stock, except for the smallest – the hardy Shetland, which is less than 105 cm/42 in shoulder height.

**poodle** breed of gun dog, including standard (above 38 cm/15 in at shoulder), miniature (below 38 cm/15 in), and toy (below 28 cm/11 in) varieties. The dense curly coat, usually cut into an elaborate style, is often either black or white, although greys and browns are also bred.

**Poole** unitary authority in southwest England, created in 1997 from part of Dorset
*area* 64 sq km/25 sq mi
*towns and cities* Poole (administrative headquarters), Broadstone, Hillbournes, Sandbanks
*features* River Stour formers northern border of authority; Poole Harbour; Holes Bay; Pergins Island; Maritime Museum (Poole); Compton Acres themed gardens (including water, rock, heather, Japanese, Roman, Italian); Canford Heath, tumuli field; Sandbanks spit guarding entrance to harbour; ferry from Poole to Brownsea Island and the Channel Islands
*industries* boatbuilding and repair, tourism, electromechanical engineering, marine engineering and marine electronics, electrical systems, aeronautical instruments
*population* (1996) 138,100.

**Poona** former spelling of ◊Pune, a city in India; after independence in 1947 the form Poona was gradually superseded by Pune.

**poor law** English system for poor relief, established by the Poor Relief Act of 1601. Each parish was responsible for its own poor, paid for by a parish tax. The care of the poor was transferred to the Ministry of Health in 1918, but the poor law remained in force until 1930.

**Pop art** movement in modern art that took its imagery from the glossy world of advertising and from popular culture such as comic strips, films, and television; it developed in the 1950s and flourished in the 1960s, notably in Britain and the USA. The term was coined by the British critic Lawrence Alloway (1926–1990) in about 1955, to refer to works of art that drew upon popular culture. Richard Hamilton, one of the leading British pioneers and exponents of Pop

art, defined it in 1957 as 'popular, transient, expendable, low-cost, mass-produced, young, witty, sexy, gimmicky, glamorous, and Big Business'. In its eclecticism and sense of irony and playfulness, Pop art helped to prepare the way for the ◊postmodernism that has been a feature of Western culture since the 1970s.

**pope** the bishop of Rome, head of the Roman Catholic Church, which claims he is the spiritual descendant of St Peter. Elected by the Sacred College of Cardinals, a pope dates his pontificate from his coronation with the tiara, or triple crown, at St Peter's Basilica, Rome. The pope had great political power in Europe from the early Middle Ages until the Reformation.

**Pope, Alexander** (1688–1744) English poet and satirist. He established his poetic reputation with the precocious *Pastorals* (1709) and *An Essay on Criticism* (1711), which were followed by a parody of the heroic epic, *The Rape of the Lock* (1712–14), *The Temple of Fame* (1715), and 'Eloisa to Abelard' (1717). The highly Neo-Classical translations of Homer's *Iliad* and *Odyssey* (1715–26) were very successful but his edition of Shakespeare (1725) attracted scholarly ridicule, which led Pope to write a satire on scholarly dullness, *The Dunciad* (1728). His finest mature works are his *Imitations of the Satires of Horace* (1733–38) and his personal letters.

**poplar** any of a group of deciduous trees with characteristically broad leaves. The white poplar (*P. alba*) has a smooth grey trunk and leaves with white undersides. (Genus *Populus,* family Salicaceae.)

**pop music** or *popular music,* any contemporary music not categorizable as jazz or classical. Characterized by strong rhythms of African origin, simple harmonic structures often repeated to strophic melodies, and the use of electrically amplified instruments, pop music generically includes the areas of rock, country and western, rhythm and blues, soul, and others. Pop became distinct from folk music with the advent of sound-recording techniques; electronic amplification and other technological innovations have played a large part in the creation of new styles. The traditional format is a song of roughly three minutes with verse, chorus, and middle eight bars.

**Popper, Karl Raimund** (1902–1994) British philosopher of science, who was born in Austria and became a naturalized British subject in 1945. His theory of falsificationism states that although scientific generalizations cannot be conclusively verified, they can be conclusively falsified by a counterinstance; therefore, science is not certain knowledge but a series of 'conjectures and refutations', approaching, though never reaching, a definitive truth. For Popper, psychoanalysis and Marxism are falsifiable and therefore unscientific.

**poppy** any of a group of plants belonging to the poppy family. They have brightly coloured mainly red and orange flowers, often with dark centres, and yield a milky sap. Species include the crimson European field poppy (*P. rhoeas*) and the Asian opium poppy (*P. somniferum*), source of the drug ◊opium. Closely related are the California poppy (*Eschscholtzia californica*) and the yellow horned or sea poppy (*Glaucium flavum*). (Poppy genus *Papaver,* family Papaveraceae.)

**population** the number of people living in a specific area or region, such as a town or country, at any one time. The study of populations, their distribution and structure, resources, and patterns of ◊migration, is called ◊demography. Information on population is obtained in a number of ways, such as through the registration of births and deaths. These figures are known as 'vital statistics'. However, more detailed information on population distribution, density, and change is necessary to enable governments to plan for education, health, housing, and transport on local and national levels. This information is usually obtained from ◊censuses (population counts), which provide data on sex, age, occupation, and nationality.

**population cycle** in biology, regular fluctuations in the size of a population, as seen in lemmings, for example. Such cycles are often caused by density-dependent mortality: high mortality due to overcrowding causes a sudden decline in the population, which then gradually builds up again. Population cycles may also result from an interaction between a predator and its prey.

**population explosion** the rapid and dramatic rise in world population that has occurred over the last few hundred years. Between 1959 and 1995, the world's population increased from 2.5 billion to 5.6 billion people. It had reached 6 billion by the end of the 20th century.

**porcelain** hardpaste, translucent ceramic material with a shining finish, see ◊pottery and porcelain.

**porcupine** any ◊rodent with quills on its body, belonging to either of two families: Old World porcupines (family Hystricidae), terrestrial in habit and having long black-and-white quills; or New World porcupines (family Erethizontidae), tree-dwelling, with prehensile tails and much shorter quills.

**porpoise** any small whale of the family Delphinidae that, unlike dolphins, have blunt snouts without beaks. Common porpoises of the genus *Phocaena* can grow to 1.8 m/6 ft long; they feed on fish and crustaceans.

**Port-au-Prince** capital and industrial port (sugar, rum, textiles, plastics) of Haiti; population (1992) 1,255,100.

**Porter, Cole (Albert)** (1892–1964) US composer and lyricist. He wrote mainly musical comedies. His witty, sophisticated songs like 'Let's Do It' (1928), 'I Get a Kick Out of You' (1934), and 'Don't Fence Me In' (1944) have been widely recorded and admired. His shows, many of which were made into films, include *The Gay Divorce* (1932, filmed 1934 as *The Gay Divorcee*) and *Kiss Me Kate* (1948). He also wrote movie musicals, such as *Born to Dance* (1936) and *High Society* (1956).

**Portland, William Henry Cavendish Bentinck** 3rd Duke of Portland (1738–1809) English Whig politician. He was prime minister in 1783 and 1807–09, each time as titular leader of a government dominated by stronger characters. He served as home secretary in William Pitt's Tory administration 1794–1801.

**Port Moresby** capital and port of Papua New Guinea, on the south coast of New Guinea; population (1990) 193,200. The port trades in coffee, copper, gold, copra, palm oil, and timber.

**Pôrto** English *Oporto,* industrial city and capital of Pôrto district, northwest Portugal, 280 km/174 mi north of Lisbon, on the River Douro, 5 km/3 mi from its mouth on the Atlantic coast; population (1987) 350,000. Port wine is exported, and industries include textiles, leather, and pottery. Pôrto is built on terraces cut into the steep northern slopes of the Douro gorge. It is connected to the southern suburb of Vila Nova de Gaia by the two-storey bridge of Dom Luis I, built by ◊Eiffel, and which crosses the river in a single span of 160 m/525 ft at a height of 36 m/118 ft.

**Pôrto Alegre** industrial port and capital of Río Grande do Sul federal unit (state), southeast Brazil; population (1991) 1,254,600; (metrolitan area 3,757,500). The port is situated on the eastern bank Río Guaíba (formed by the confluence of five rivers), at the northwestern end of Lagôa dos Patos, a freshwater lagoon which flows into the Atlantic; the lagoon is accessible to ocean-going vessels via the port of Rio Grande. It is southern Brazil's chief industrial and commercial centre; there are shipyards, iron foundries, textile, chemical, and food processing industries. Chief exports include pinewood, meat, rice, wheat, hides, and wool. The city has a cathedral, whose foundations are built over a church that dates back to 1772, and two universities. It was founded in 1755.

**Port-of-Spain** port and capital of Trinidad and Tobago, on the island of Trinidad; population (1990) 58,400. It has a cathedral (1813–28) and the San Andres Fort (1785).

**Porto-Novo** port and capital of Benin, on Porto-Novo lagoon; population (1994) 179,000. It trades in palm oil, palm kernels, and cotton. A former Portuguese centre for the slave and tobacco trade with Brazil, it became a French protectorate in 1863. The National Museum of Ethnography is here.

**Port Said** port in Egypt, on reclaimed land at the north end of the ◊Suez Canal; population (1992) 460,000. During the 1967 Arab–Israeli War the city was damaged and the canal blocked; Port Said was evacuated by 1969 but by 1975 had been largely reconstructed.

**Portsmouth** city, naval port, and unitary authority in southern England, 118 km/73 mi southwest of London, on the peninsula of Portsea Island, opposite the Isle of Wight; it was part of the county of Hampshire until 1997
*area* 42 sq km/16 sq mi
*features* 12th-century cathedral; UK headquar-

ters of IBM (UK) Ltd, Pall Europe Ltd, and Zurich Insurance Group; Portsmouth University, formerly Portsmouth Polytechnic, was established in 1992; the city has won a Millennium Award for a harbour development that will create a maritime leisure complex; Tudor warship *Mary Rose* and Admiral Horatio Nelson's flagship HMS *Victory* are exhibited here **industries** high-technology and manufacturing industries, including aircraft engineering, electronics, shipbuilding, and ship maintenance; naval dockyard was closed in 1981, although some naval facilities remain; it is a continental ferry port
**population** (1996) 189,300
**famous people** Walter Besant, Isambard Kingdom Brunel, Charles Dickens, Jonas Hanway, Captain Frederick Marryat, George Meredith.

**Portugal** Republic of
**national name** *República Portuguesa*

**area** 92,000 sq km/35,521 sq mi (including the Azores and Madeira)
**capital** Lisbon
**major towns/cities** Porto, Coimbra, Amadora, Setúbal, Guarde, Portalegre
**major ports** Porto, Setúbal
**physical features** mountainous in the north (Serra da Estrêla mountains); plains in the south; rivers Minho, Douro, Tagus (Tejo), Guadiana
**head of state** Jorge Sampaio from 1996
**head of government** Antonio Guterres from 1995
**political system** democracy
**political parties** Social Democratic Party (PSD), moderate left of centre; Socialist Party (PS), centre left; People's Party (PP), right wing, anti-European integration
**currency** escudo
**GNP per capita (PPP)** (US$) 14,380 (1998)
**exports** textiles, clothing, footwear, pulp and waste paper, wood and cork manufactures, tinned fish, electrical equipment, wine, refined petroleum. Principal market: Germany 19.8% (1998)
**population** 9,873,000 (1999 est)

**language** Portuguese
**religion** Roman Catholic 97%
**life expectancy** 72 (men); 79 (women) (1995–2000)
**Chronology**
**2nd century BC** Romans conquered Iberian peninsula.
**5th century AD** Iberia overrun by Vandals and Visigoths after fall of Roman Empire.
**711** Visigoth kingdom overthrown by Muslims invading from North Africa.
**997–1064** Christians resettled northern area, which came under rule of Léon and Castile.
**1139** Afonso I, son of Henry of Burgundy, defeated Muslims; the area became an independent kingdom.
**1340** Final Muslim invasion defeated.
**1373** Anglo-Portuguese alliance signed.
**15th century** Age of exploration: Portuguese mariners surveyed coast of Africa, opened sea route to India (Vasco da Gama), and reached Brazil (Pedro Cabral).
**16th century** 'Golden Age': Portugal flourished as commercial and colonial power.
**1580** Philip II of Spain took throne of Portugal.
**1640** Spanish rule overthrown in bloodless coup; Duke of Braganza proclaimed as King John IV.
**1668** Spain recognized Portuguese independence.
**1755** Lisbon devastated by earthquake.
**1755–77** Politics dominated by chief minister Sebastiao de Carlvalho, Marquis of Pombal, who introduced secular education and promoted trade.
**1807** Napoleonic France invaded Portugal; Portuguese court fled to Brazil.
**1807–11** In the Peninsular War British forces played leading part in liberating Portugal from French.
**1820** Liberal revolution forced King John VI to return from Brazil and accept constitutional government.
**1822** Brazil declared independence; first Portuguese constitution adopted.
**1826** First constitution replaced by more conservative one.
**1828** Dom Miguel blocked succession of his niece, Queen Maria, and declared himself absolute monarch; civil war ensued between liberals and conservatives.
**1834** Queen Maria regained throne with British, French, and Brazilian help; constitutional government restored.
**1840s** Severe disputes between supporters of radical 1822 constitution and more conservative 1826 constitution.
**1851** 'Regeneration' to promote order and economic growth launched by Duke of Saldanha after coup.
**late 19th century** Government faced severe financial difficulties; rise of socialist, anarchist, and republican parties.
**1908** Assassination of King Carlos I.
**1910** Portugal became republic after three-day insurrection forced King Manuel II to flee.
**1911** New regime adopted liberal constitution, but republic proved unstable, violent, and corrupt.

*1916–18* Portugal fought in World War I on Allied side.

*1926–51* Popular military coup installed Gen António de Fragoso Carmona as president.

*1928* António de Oliveira Salazar became finance minister and introduced successful reforms.

*1932* Salazar became prime minister with dictatorial powers.

*1933* Authoritarian 'Estado Novo' ('New State') constitution adopted; living conditions improved, but Salazar resisted political change at home and in colonies.

*1949* Portugal became founding member of North Atlantic Treaty Organization (NATO).

*1968* Salazar retired; succeeded by Marcello Caetano.

*1974* Army seized power to end stalemate situation in African colonial wars; Gen Antó Ribeiro de Spínola became president; succeeded by Gen Francisco da Costa Gomes.

*1975* Portuguese colonies achieved independence; Gomes narrowly averted communist coup.

*1976* First free elections in 50 years resulted in minority government under socialist leader Mario Soares; Gen António Ramahlo Eanes won presidency.

*1980* Francisco Balsemão (PSD) formed a centre-party coalition.

*1986* Soares became the first civilian president in 60 years; Portugal joined the European Community (EC).

*1989* The Social Democrat government started to dismantle the socialist economy and privatize major industries.

*1996* Jorge Sampaio (PS) was elected president.

**Portuguese** inhabitants of Portugal. The Portuguese have a mixed cultural heritage that can be traced back to the Lusitanian Celts who were defeated by the Romans about 140 BC. In the 5th century AD the Suebi, a Germanic group, overran the Iberian peninsula, and were later subdued by the Visigoths. In the 8th century AD southern Portugal was invaded by the Moors. The Portuguese are predominantly Roman Catholic.

**Portuguese language** member of the Romance branch of the Indo-European language family; spoken by 120–135 million people worldwide, it is the national language of Portugal, closely related to Spanish and strongly influenced by Arabic. Portuguese is also spoken in Brazil, Angola, Mozambique, and other former Portuguese colonies.

**Portuguese man-of-war** any of a genus *Physalia* of phylum *Coelenterata* (see ◊coelenterate). They live in the sea, in colonies, and have a large air-filled bladder (or 'float') on top and numerous hanging tentacles made up of feeding, stinging, and reproductive individuals. The float can be 30 cm/1 ft long.

**Port-Vila** port and capital of Vanuatu, on the southwest of Efate Island; population (1989) 19,400.

**Poseidon** Roman *Neptune,* in Greek mythology, the chief god of the sea, brother of Zeus and Pluto. The brothers dethroned their father, ◊Kronos, and divided his realm, Poseidon taking the sea. Husband of Amphitrite, his sons were the merman sea god ◊Triton and the Cyclops Polyphemus.

**positivism** theory that confines genuine knowledge within the bounds of science and observation. The theory is associated with the French philosopher Auguste Comte and ◊empiricism. *Logical positivism* developed in the 1920s. It rejected any metaphysical world beyond everyday science and common sense, and confined statements to those of formal logic or mathematics.

**positron** in physics, the antiparticle of the electron; an ◊elementary particle having the same mass as an electron but exhibiting a positive charge. The positron was discovered in 1932 by US physicist Carl Anderson at Caltech, USA, its existence having been predicted by the British physicist Paul Dirac in 1928.

**positron emission tomography** (PET) an imaging technique which enables doctors to observe the metabolic activity of the human body by following the progress of a radioactive chemical that has been inhaled or injected, detecting ◊gamma radiation given out when ◊positrons emitted by the chemical are annihilated. The technique has been used to study a wide range of conditions, including schizophrenia, Alzheimer's disease, and Parkinson's disease.

**possum** another name for the ◊opossum, a marsupial animal with a prehensile tail found in North, Central and South America. The name is also used for many of the smaller marsupials found in Australia.

**poster** public notice used for advertising or propaganda, often illustrated. Ancestors of the modern poster were *handbills* with woodcut illustrations, which were posted up in public places. The French artist Jules Chéret pioneered the medium of colour lithography in his posters of the early 1860s, but the 1890s were the classic age of the poster, notable exponents being Toulouse-Lautrec, Aubrey Beardsley, and the 'Beggarstaff Brothers' (William Nicholson and James Pryde). Poster design flourished again in the 1960s with the advent of Psychedelic art, and artists such as Rick Griffin (1944–1991) and Stanley Mouse (1921–  ) in the USA, and Michael English (1942–  ) in the UK.

**post-Impressionism** broad term covering various developments in French painting that developed out of ◊Impressionism in the period from about 1880 to about 1905. Some of these developments built on the achievements of Impressionism, but others were reactions against its concentration on surface appearances, seeking to reintroduce a concern with emotional and symbolic values.

**postmodernism** late 20th-century movement in architecture and the arts that rejects the preoccupation of ◊modernism with purity of form and technique. Postmodernists use an amalgam of style elements from the past, such as the classical and the baroque, and apply them to spare modern forms, often with ironic effect. Their slightly off-key familiarity creates a more immediate appeal than the austerities of modernism.

Exponents include the architects Robert Venturi and Michael Graves and the novelists David Lodge and Thomas Pynchon. In literary criticism and critical theory, postmodernism denotes a differently conceived resumption rather than a repudiation of modernist radicalism.

**postmortem** or autopsy, (Latin 'after death') dissection of a dead body to determine the cause of death.

**postnatal depression** mood change occurring in many mothers a few days after the birth of a baby, also known as 'baby blues'. It is usually a shortlived condition but can sometimes persist; one in five women suffer a lasting depression after giving birth. The most severe form of post-natal depressive illness, *puerperal psychosis,* requires hospital treatment.

**potash** general name for any potassium-containing mineral, most often applied to potassium carbonate ($K_2CO_3$) or potassium hydroxide (KOH). Potassium carbonate, originally made by roasting plants to ashes in earthenware pots, is commercially produced from the mineral sylvite (potassium chloride, KCl) and is used mainly in making artificial fertilizers, glass, and soap.

**potassium** (Dutch *potassa* 'potash') soft, waxlike, silver-white, metallic element, symbol K (Latin *kalium*), atomic number 19, relative atomic mass 39.0983. It is one of the ◊alkali metals and has a very low density – it floats on water, and is the second lightest metal (after lithium). It oxidizes rapidly when exposed to air and reacts violently with water. Of great abundance in the Earth's crust, it is widely distributed with other elements and found in salt and mineral deposits in the form of potassium aluminium silicates.

**potato** perennial plant with edible tuberous roots that are rich in starch and are extensively eaten as a vegetable. Used by the Andean Indians for at least 2,000 years before the Spanish Conquest, the potato was introduced to Europe by the mid-16th century, and reputedly to England by the explorer Walter Raleigh. (*Solanum tuberosum,* family Solanaceae.)

**potential difference** pd, difference in the electrical potential (see ◊potential, electric) of two points, being equal to the electrical energy converted by a unit electric charge moving from one point to the other. The SI unit of potential difference is the volt (V). The potential difference between two points in a circuit is commonly referred to as voltage. See also ◊Ohm's law.

**potential, electric** in physics, the relative electrical state of an object. The potential at a point is equal to the energy required to bring a unit electric charge from infinity to the point. The SI unit of potential is the volt (V). Positive electric charges will flow 'downhill' from a region of high potential to a region of low potential.

**potential energy** (PE), in physics, ◊energy possessed by an object by virtue of its relative position or state (for example, in a compressed spring or a muscle). It is contrasted with kinetic energy, the form of energy possessed by moving bodies. An object that has been raised up is described as having gravitational potential energy.

**potentiometer** in physics, an electrical resistor that can be divided so as to compare, measure, or control voltages. In radio circuits, any rotary variable resistance (such as volume control) is referred to as a potentiometer.

**Potsdam Conference** conference held in Potsdam, Germany, 17 July–2 August 1945, between representatives of the USA, the UK, and the USSR. They established the political and economic principles governing the treatment of Germany in the initial period of Allied control at the end of World War II, and sent an ultimatum to Japan demanding unconditional surrender on pain of utter destruction.

**Potter, (Helen) Beatrix** (1866–1943) English writer and illustrator of children's books. Her first book was *The Tale of Peter Rabbit* (1900), followed by *The Tailor of Gloucester* (1902), based on her observation of family pets and wildlife. Other books in the series include *The Tale of Mrs Tiggy-Winkle* (1904), *The Tale of Jeremy Fisher* (1906), and a sequel to Peter Rabbit, *The Tale of the Flopsy Bunnies* (1909). Her tales are told with a childlike wonder, devoid of sentimentality, and accompanied by delicate illustrations.

**pottery and porcelain** ceramics in domestic and ornamental use, including earthenware, stoneware, and *bone china* (or softpaste porcelain). Made of 5% bone ash and china clay, bone china was first made in the West in imitation of Chinese porcelain. The standard British bone china was developed about 1800, with a body of clay mixed with ox bones; a harder version, called *parian,* was developed in the 19th century and was used for figurine ornaments.

Hardpaste *porcelain* is characterized by its hardness, ringing sound when struck, translucence, and shining finish, like that of a cowrie shell (Italian *porcellana*). It is made of kaolin and petuntse (fusible feldspar consisting chiefly of silicates reduced to a fine white powder); it is high-fired at 1,400°C/2,552°F. Porcelain first evolved from stoneware in China in about the 6th century AD. A formula for making porcelain was developed in the 18th century in Germany, also in France, Italy, and Britain. It was first produced in the USA in the early 19th century.

**potto** arboreal, nocturnal, African prosimian primate *Perodicticus potto* belonging to the ◊loris family. It has a thick body, strong limbs, and grasping feet and hands, and grows to 40 cm/16 in long, with horny spines along its backbone, which it uses in self-defence. It climbs slowly, and eats insects, snails, fruit, and leaves.

**poultry** domestic birds such as chickens, turkeys, ducks, and geese. They were domesticated for meat and eggs by early farmers in China, Europe, Egypt, and the Americas. Chickens were domesticated from the Southeast Asian jungle fowl *Gallus gallus* and then raised in the East as well as the West. Turkeys are New World birds, domesticated in ancient Mexico. Geese and ducks were domesticated in Egypt, China, and Europe.

**pound** imperial unit (abbreviation lb) of mass. The commonly used avoirdupois pound, also called the *imperial standard pound* (7,000 grains/0.45 kg), differs from the *pound troy* (5,760 grains/0.37 kg), which is used for weighing precious metals. It derives from the Roman *libra*, which weighed 0.327 kg.

**pound** British standard monetary unit, issued as a gold sovereign before 1914, as a note 1914–83, and as a circular yellow metal-alloy coin from 1983. The pound is also the name given to the unit of currency in Egypt, Lebanon, Malta, Sudan, and Syria.

**Pound, Ezra Loomis** (1885–1972) US poet and cultural critic. He is regarded as one of the most important figures of 20th-century literature, and his work revolutionized modern poetry. His *Personae* and *Exultations* (1909) established and promoted the principles of ◊imagism, and influenced numerous poets, including T S ◊Eliot. His largest work was his series of *Cantos* (1925–69), a highly complex, eclectic collage that sought to create a unifying, modern cultural tradition.

**Poussin, Nicolas** (1594–1665) French painter. Active chiefly in Rome, he was the foremost exponent of 17th-century Baroque Classicism. He painted several major religious works, but is best known for his mythological and literary scenes executed in an austere classical style, for example, *Et in Arcadia Ego* (1638–39; Louvre, Paris). His style had a profound effect on the development of French art.

**poverty trap** situation where a person reduces his or her net income by taking a job, or gaining a higher wage, which disqualifies him/her from claiming social security benefits or raises his/her tax liability.

**Powell, Colin (Luther)** (1937–  ) US general, chair of the Joint Chiefs of Staff from 1989–93 and, as such, responsible for the overall administration of the Allied forces in Saudi Arabia during the ◊Gulf War of 1991. A Vietnam War veteran, he first worked in government in 1972 and was national security adviser 1987–89. Following intense media speculation, in November 1995 Powell announced that he would not seek the Republican party's presidential nomination in 1996, citing family reasons.

**Powell, Michael (Latham)** (1905–1990) English film director and producer. In collaboration with the Hungarian-born screenwriter Emeric ◊Pressburger, he produced a succession of ambitious and richly imaginative films, including *I Know Where I'm Going!* (1945), *A Matter of Life and Death* (1946), and *The Red Shoes* (1948).

**power** in mathematics, that which is represented by an ◊exponent or index, denoted by a superior small numeral. A number or symbol raised to the power of 2 – that is, multiplied by itself – is said to be squared (for example, $3^2$,

$x^2$), and when raised to the power of 3, it is said to be cubed (for example, $2^3$, $y^3$). Any number to the power zero always equals 1.

**power** in physics, the rate of doing work or consuming energy. It is measured in watts (joules per second) or other units of work per unit time.

**Powys** unitary authority in central Wales, created in 1996 from the former county of Powys
*area* 5,179 sq km/1,999 sq mi
*towns* Llandrindod Wells (administrative headquarters), Brecon, Builth Wells, Newtown, Welshpool
*physical* mountainous to the north, Black Mountains, rivers Wye and ◊Severn, which both rise on the eastern slopes of Plynlimon
*features* the Brecon Beacons National Park, Lake Vyrnwy (an artificial reservoir supplying Liverpool and Birmingham), alternative-technology centre near Machynlleth
*industries* agriculture, tourism
*agriculture* arable and dairy farming, sheep-rearing
*population* (1996) 123,600.

**Poznań** German *Posen*, industrial city (machinery, aircraft, beer) in western Poland; population (1993) 590,000. Founded in 970, it was settled by German immigrants in 1253 and passed to Prussia in 1793; it was restored to Poland in 1919.

**Prado** (Real Museo de Pintura del Prado) Spanish art museum containing the national collection of pictures. The building was designed as a natural history museum and begun in 1785; it became an art gallery in 1818 under Ferdinand VII.

**pragmatism** philosophical tradition that interprets truth in terms of the practical effects of what is believed and, in particular, the usefulness of these effects. The US philosopher Charles Peirce is often accounted the founder of pragmatism; it was further advanced by William James.

**Prague** Czech *Praha*, city and capital of the Czech Republic on the River Vltava; population (1993) 1,217,300. Industries include cars, aircraft, chemicals, paper and printing, clothing, brewing, and food processing. It was the capital of Czechoslovakia 1918–93.

**Prague Spring** the 1968 programme of liberalization, begun under a new Communist Party leader in Czechoslovakia. In August 1968 Soviet tanks invaded Czechoslovakia and entered the capital Prague to put down the liberalization movement initiated by the prime minister Alexander Dubček, who had earlier sought to assure the Soviets that his planned reforms would not threaten socialism. Dubček was arrested but released soon afterwards. Most of the Prague Spring reforms were reversed.

**Praia** port and capital of the Republic of Cape Verde, on the island of São Tiago (Santiago); population (1990) 61,600. Industries include fishing, shipping, and tourism.

**prairie** the central North American plain, formerly grass-covered, extending over most of the region between the Rocky Mountains, to the west, and the Great Lakes and Ohio River, to the east.

**prairie dog** any of the North American genus *Cynomys* of burrowing rodents in the squirrel family (Sciuridae). They grow to 30 cm/12 in, plus a short 8 cm/3 in tail. Their 'towns' can contain up to several thousand individuals. Their barking cry has given them their name. Persecution by ranchers has brought most of the five species close to extinction.

**Prakrit** general name for the ancient Indo-European dialects of northern India, contrasted with the sacred classical language Sanskrit.

The word is itself Sanskrit, meaning 'natural', as opposed to *Sanskrit,* which means 'perfected'. The Prakrits are considered to be the ancestors of such modern northern Indian languages as Hindi, Punjabi, and Bengali.

**Prasad, Rajendra** (1884–1963) Indian politician. He was president of the Indian National Congress several times between 1934 and 1948 and India's first president after independence 1950–62.

**praseodymium** (Greek *prasios* 'leek-green' + *didymos* 'twin') silver-white, malleable, metallic element of the ◊lanthanide series, symbol Pr, atomic number 59, relative atomic mass 140.907. It occurs in nature in the minerals monzanite and bastnaesite, and its green salts are used to colour glass and ceramics. It was named in 1885 by Austrian chemist Carl von Welsbach (1858–1929).

**prawn** any of various ◊shrimps of the suborder Natantia ('swimming'), of the crustacean order Decapoda, as contrasted with lobsters and crayfishes, which are able to 'walk'. Species called prawns are generally larger than species called shrimps.

**Praxiteles** (lived mid-4th century BC) Greek sculptor. His *Aphrodite of Cnidus* (about 350 BC) is thought to have initiated the tradition of life-size free-standing female nudes in Greek sculpture. It was destroyed by fire in AD 475, but a Roman copy exists in the Vatican.

**praying mantis** another name for ◊mantis.

**Precambrian** in geology, the time from the formation of Earth (4.6 billion years ago) up to 570 million years ago. Its boundary with the succeeding Cambrian period marks the time when animals first developed hard outer parts (exoskeletons) and so left abundant fossil remains. It comprises about 85% of geological time and is divided into two periods: the Archaean, in which no life existed, and the Proterozoic, in which there was life in some form.

**precession** slow wobble of the Earth on its axis, like that of a spinning top. The gravitational pulls of the Sun and Moon on the Earth's equatorial bulge cause the Earth's axis to trace out a circle on the sky every 25,800 years. The position of the celestial poles (see ◊celestial sphere) is constantly changing owing to precession, as are the positions of the equinoxes (the

points at which the celestial equator intersects the Sun's path around the sky). The *precession of the equinoxes* means that there is a gradual westward drift in the ecliptic – the path that the Sun appears to follow – and in the coordinates of objects on the celestial sphere.

**precipitation** in chemistry, the formation of an insoluble solid in a liquid as a result of a reaction within the liquid between two or more soluble substances. If the solid settles, it forms a *precipitate;* if the particles of solid are very small, they will remain in suspension, forming a *colloidal precipitate* (see ◊colloid).

**precipitation** in meteorology, water that falls to the Earth from the atmosphere. It is part of the ◊hydrological cycle. Forms of precipitation include rain, snow, sleet, ◊hail, ◊dew, and ◊frost.

**predestination** in Christian theology, the doctrine asserting that God has determined all events beforehand, including the ultimate salvation or damnation of the individual human soul. Today Christianity in general accepts that humanity has free will, though some forms, such as Calvinism, believe that salvation can only be attained by the gift of God. The concept of predestination is also found in Islam.

**pregnancy** in humans, the process during which a developing embryo grows within the woman's womb. It begins at conception and ends at birth, and the normal length is 40 weeks, or around nine months.

**prehistory** period of human culture before the use of writing. The study of prehistory is mainly dependent on archaeology. General chronological dividing lines between prehistoric eras, or history and prehistory, are difficult to determine because communities had developed at differing rates. The Three Age System of classification (published in 1836 by the Danish archaeologist Christian Thomsen) is based on the predominant materials used by early humans for tools and weapons: ◊Stone Age, ◊Bronze Age, and ◊Iron Age.

**prelude** in music, a composition intended as the preface to further music, especially preceding a ◊fugue, forming the opening piece of a suite, or setting the mood for a stage work, as in Wagner's *Lohengrin.* As used by Chopin, a prelude is a short self-contained piano work.

**Premadasa, Ranasinghe** (1924–1993) Sri Lankan right-wing politician, prime minister 1978–88, president from 1988. He gained popularity through overseeing a major house-building and poverty-alleviation programme. He sought peace talks with the Tamil Tiger guerrillas. He was assassinated in office by a suicide bomber in the centre of Colombo; the Tamil Tigers denied responsibility.

**premenstrual tension** (PMT) or *premenstrual syndrome,* medical condition caused by hormone changes and comprising a number of physical and emotional symptoms that occur cyclically before menstruation and disappear with its onset. These include mood changes, breast tenderness, a feeling of bloatedness, and headache.

**Pre-Raphaelite Brotherhood** (PRB), group of British painters (1848–53); Dante Gabriel ◊Rossetti, John Everett ◊Millais, and Holman Hunt – at this time young students at the Royal Academy – were the leading figures among the seven founders. They aimed to paint serious subjects, to study nature closely, and to return to the sincerity of spirit of painters before the time of ◊Raphael Sanzio (1483–1520). Their subjects were mainly biblical and literary, painted with obsessive naturalism and attention to detail. The group was short-lived but added a new realism to the art of the 1850s, and influenced many painters.

In his later work only Hunt remained true to Pre-Raphaelite ideals, but the name stuck to Rossetti, the least committed of the original group, and was applied to his later dreamily romantic pictures although these had moved away from the movement's founding ideas. A 'second wave' of Pre-Raphaelitism in the late 19th century, stimulated by Ruskin and Rossetti, was associated with the revival of handicrafts and the art of design. William Morris and Edward Burne-Jones were among the many artists influenced at this time.

**Presbyterianism** system of Christian Protestant church government, expounded during the Reformation by John Calvin in Geneva, Switzerland, which gives its name to the established Church of Scotland, and is also practised in England, Wales, Ireland, Switzerland, North America, and elsewhere. There is no compulsory form of worship and each congregation is governed by presbyters or elders (clerical or lay), who are of equal rank.

Congregations are grouped in presbyteries, synods, and general assemblies.

**Presley, Elvis Aron** (1935–1977) US singer and guitarist, the most influential performer of the rock-and-roll era. With his recordings for Sun Records in Memphis, Tennessee, 1954–55 and early hits such as 'Heartbreak Hotel', 'Hound Dog' and 'Love Me Tender' (all 1956), he created an individual vocal style, influenced by Southern blues, gospel music, country music, and rhythm and blues. His records continued to sell in their millions into the 1990s.

**Pressburger, Emeric** Adopted name of Imre József Pressburger (1902–1988) Hungarian-born film producer, screenwriter, and novelist. He worked on films in Germany, France, and the UK. Together with Michael ◊Powell, he made 14 films between 1942 and 1956, including such classics of the British cinema as *The Life and Death of Colonel Blimp* (1943), *A Canterbury Tale* (1944), and *The Red Shoes* (1948).

**pressure** in a fluid, the force that would act normally (at right angles) per unit surface area of a body immersed in the fluid. The SI unit of pressure is the pascal (Pa), equal to a pressure of one newton per square metre. In the atmosphere, the pressure declines with height from about 100 kPa at sea level to zero where the atmosphere fades into space. Pressure is commonly measured with a ◊barometer, manometer, or ◊Bourdon gauge. Other common units of pressure are the bar and the torr.

**pressure group** or *interest group* or *lobby,* association that puts pressure on governments, businesses, or parties to ensure laws and treatment favourable to its own interest. Pressure groups have played an increasingly prominent role in contemporary Western democracies. In general they fall into two types: groups concerned with a single issue, such as nuclear disarmament, and groups attempting to promote their own interest, such as oil producers.

**Pretoria** city in Gauteng Province, South Africa, and the country's administrative capital; population (1991) 1,080,200. Industries include engineering, chemicals, iron, steel, cement, diamonds, granite quarrying, chemicals, and food processing. Founded in 1855, it was named after Boer leader Andries Pretorius (1799–1853). It was the administrative capital of the Union of South Africa from 1910 and capital of Transvaal Province 1860–1994.

**Previn, André George** (1929– ) German-born US conductor and composer. He was principal conductor of the London Symphony Orchestra 1968–79 and was appointed music director of Britain's Royal Philharmonic Orchestra in 1985 (a post he relinquished the following year, staying on as principal conductor until 1991). He was also principal conductor of the Los Angeles Philharmonic 1986–89 and is now a guest conductor of many orchestras in Europe and the USA. He was one of the recipients of the 1998 Kennedy Center Honors.

After early success as a composer and arranger for film, he studied conducting with Pierre Monteux in 1951. His compositions include concertos for piano (1971) and guitar (1984); he has conducted Gershwin and Mozart concertos from the keyboard and recorded many US and British composers.

**Priapus** in Greek mythology, the god of fertility, son of Dionysus and Aphrodite, represented as grotesquely ugly, with an exaggerated phallus. He was later a Roman god of gardens, where his image was frequently used as a scarecrow.

**prickly pear** any of several cacti (see ◊cactus) native to Central and South America, mainly Mexico and Chile, but naturalized in southern Europe, North Africa, and Australia, where it is a pest. The common prickly pear (*O. vulgaris*) is low-growing, with flat, oval stem joints, bright yellow flowers, and prickly, oval fruit; the flesh and seeds of the peeled fruit have a pleasant taste. (Genus *Opuntia,* family Cactaceae.)

**Priestley, J(ohn) B(oynton)** (1894–1984) English novelist and dramatist. His first success was a novel about travelling theatre, *The Good Companions* (1929). He followed it with a realist novel about London life, *Angel Pavement* (1930). His career as a dramatist began with *Dangerous Corner* (1932), one of several plays in which time is a preoccupation. His best-known plays are the enigmatic *An Inspector Calls* (1945) and *The Linden Tree* (1948), a study of post-war social issues.

**Primakov, Yevgeny Maksimovich** (1928– ) Russian politician, prime minister 1998–99. He was appointed to succeed Andrei Kozyrev as foreign minister in 1995 in order to give President Boris ◊Yeltsin some credibility with those who supported the communists and nationalists. He was no more successful than Kozyrev in stopping decline, but his championing of Russia's interests and his willingness to use anti-Western rhetoric restored some of the damage done to injured pride. Still, it was a surprise when Yeltsin, reeling under the shock of economic collapse in the summer of 1998, appointed him prime minister with what seemed almost an anti-reform mandate. Primakov, though far from an old-fashioned communist and relatively subtle in his private diplomacy, still saw the achievement of consensus as more important than reform, and refused to adopt an economic programme that could attract the support of the IMF. The result was that political peace was preserved, at the cost of a disastrously declining economy – though it was clear to no-one what plan could assist Russia's revival. Primakov was sacked by Yeltsin in a surprise move in May 1999.

**primary** in presidential election campaigns in the USA, a statewide ballot in which voters indicate their candidate preferences for the two main parties. Held in 41 states, primaries begin with New Hampshire in February and continue until June; they operate under varying complex rules. Primaries are also held to choose candidates for other posts, such as Congressional seats.

**primate** in zoology, any member of the order of mammals that includes monkeys, apes, and humans (together called *anthropoids*), as well as lemurs, bushbabies, lorises, and tarsiers (together called *prosimians*).

Generally, they have forward-directed eyes, gripping hands and feet, opposable thumbs, and big toes. They tend to have nails rather than claws, with gripping pads on the ends of the digits, all adaptations to the arboreal, climbing mode of life.

**prime number** number that can be divided only by 1 and itself, that is, having no other factors. There is an infinite number of primes, the first ten of which are 2, 3, 5, 7, 11, 13, 17, 19, 23, and 29 (by definition, the number 1 is excluded from the set of prime numbers). The number 2 is the only even prime because all other even numbers have 2 as a factor.

**primitivism** the influence on modern art (Ernst Kirchner, Amedeo Modigliani, Pablo Picasso, Paul Gauguin, and others) of the indigenous arts of Africa, Oceania, the Americas, and also of Western folk art.

**primrose** any of a group of plants belonging to the primrose family, with showy five-lobed flowers. The common primrose (*P. vulgaris*) is a woodland plant, native to Europe, with abundant pale yellow flowers in spring. Related to it is the ◊cowslip. (Genus *Primula*, family Primulaceae.)

**Prince** former stage name of Prince Rogers Nelson (1958– ) US pop musician. He composes, arranges, and produces his own records and often plays all the instruments. His albums, including *1999* (1982) and *Purple Rain* (1984), contain elements of rock, funk, and jazz. His stage shows are energetic and extravagant. Prince has now changed his name to a symbol.

**Prince Edward Island** smallest province of Canada, situated in the Gulf of St Lawrence, separated from Nova Scotia (to the south and east) and New Brunswick (to the west) by the Northumberland Strait
*area* 5,700 sq km/2,200 sq mi
*capital* Charlottetown
*towns and cities* Montague, Summerside, Georgetown, Kensington
*population* (1996) 137,300; 94% English-speaking; 1,100 American Indians; most densely populated province

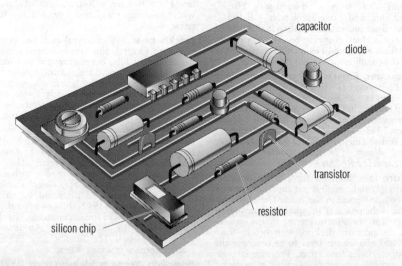

**printed circuit board** *A typical microcomputer printed circuit board (PCB). The PCB contains sockets for the integrated circuits, or chips, and the connecting tracks.*

**physical** Hillsborough River, Prince Edward Island National Park

**industries** fishing (lobsters, oysters, mussels); agriculture includes the cultivation of potatoes, and dairy produce; food processing; manufacture of farm vehicles.

**printed circuit board** (PCB), electrical circuit created by laying (printing) 'tracks' of a conductor such as copper on one or both sides of an insulating board. The PCB was invented in 1936 by Austrian scientist Paul Eisler, and was first used on a large scale in 1948.

**printer** in computing, an output device for producing printed copies of text or graphics. Types include the daisywheel printer, which produces good-quality text but no graphics; the dot matrix printer, which produces text and graphics by printing a pattern of small dots; the ink-jet printer, which creates text and graphics by spraying a fine jet of quick-drying ink onto the paper; and the laser printer, which uses electrostatic technology very similar to that used by a photocopier to produce high-quality text and graphics.

**printing** reproduction of multiple copies of text or illustrative material on paper, as in books or newspapers, or on an increasing variety of materials; for example, on plastic containers. The first printing used woodblocks, followed by carved wood type or moulded metal type and hand-operated presses. Modern printing is effected by electronically controlled machinery. Current printing processes include electronic phototypesetting with ◊offset printing, and ◊gravure print.

**printmaking** creating a picture or design by printing from a plate (woodblock, stone, or metal sheet) that holds ink or colour. The oldest form of print is the woodcut, common in medieval Europe, followed by line ◊engraving (from the 15th century), and ◊etching (from the 17th century); coloured woodblock prints flourished in Japan from the 18th century. ◊Lithography was invented in 1796.

**prion** acronym for proteinaceous infectious particle, infectious agent, a hundred times smaller than a virus. Composed of protein, and without any detectable nucleic acid (genetic material), it is strongly linked to a number of fatal degenerative brain diseases in mammals, such as bovine spongiform encephalopathy (BSE) in cattle, scrapie in sheep, and Creutzfeldt–Jakob disease (CJD) and kuru in humans.

**prism** in mathematics, a solid figure whose cross section is constant in planes drawn perpendicular to its axis. A cube, for example, is a rectangular prism with all faces (bases and sides) the same shape and size.

**prism** in optics, a triangular block of transparent material (plastic, glass, silica) commonly used to 'bend' a ray of light or split a beam into its spectral colours. Prisms are used as mirrors to define the optical path in binoculars, camera viewfinders, and periscopes. The dispersive property of prisms is used in the ◊spectroscope.

**prison** place of confinement for those accused or convicted of contravening the laws of the state; after conviction, most countries claim to aim also at rehabilitation and deterrence as well as punishment. For major crimes, life imprisonment (or death in some countries or US states) may be the sentence.

The average number of people in prison in the UK in 1995 was 58,375; 12,669 on ◊remand (awaiting trial or sentence), 45,052 sentenced, and 654 other. Of these, 56,189 were male and 2,186 female.

**private finance initiative** (PFI), an idea floated by the UK Labour Party when in opposition before 1997, and particularly by the deputy leader, John Prescott, who argued that the country's infrastructure could be improved by combining public expenditure with private finance. Since assuming office in May 1997 the Labour government has kept the initiative alive by gaining the support of major companies for its investment plans and inviting prominent industrialists to work in or with the administration.

**private sector** the part of the economy that is owned and controlled by private individuals and business organizations such as private and public limited companies. In a ◊free enterprise economy, the private sector is responsible for allocating most of the resources within the economy. This contrasts with the ◊public sector, where economic resources are owned and controlled by the state.

**privatization** policy or process of selling or transferring state-owned or public assets and services (notably nationalized industries) to private investors. Privatization of services involves the government contracting private firms to supply services previously supplied by public authorities.

**privet** any of a group of evergreen shrubs with dark green leaves, belonging to the olive family. They include the European common privet (*L. vulgare*) with white flowers and black berries, naturalized in North America, and the native North American California privet (*L. ovalifolium*), also known as hedge privet. (Genus *Ligustrum*, family Oleaceae.)

**Privy Council** council composed originally of the chief royal officials of the Norman kings in Britain; under the Tudors and early Stuarts it became the chief governing body. It was replaced from 1688 by the ◊cabinet, originally a committee of the council, and the council itself now retains only formal powers in issuing royal proclamations and orders in council. In 1998 there were over 200 Privy Counsellors. Cabinet ministers are automatically members, and it is presided over by the Lord President of the Council.

**privy purse** personal expenditure of the British sovereign, which derives from his/her own resources (as distinct from the civil list, which now finances only expenses incurred in pursuance of official functions and duties). The office that deals with this expenditure is also known as the Privy Purse.

**probability** likelihood, or chance, that an event will occur, often expressed as odds, or, in mathematics, numerically as a fraction or decimal.

In general, the probability that *n* particular events will happen out of a total of *m* possible events is *n/m*. A certainty has a probability of 1; an impossibility has a probability of 0. Empirical probability is defined as the number of successful events divided by the total possible number of events.

**probate** formal proof of a will. In the UK, if a will's validity is unquestioned, it is proven in 'common form'; the executor, in the absence of other interested parties, obtains at a probate registry a grant upon his or her own oath. Otherwise, it must be proved in 'solemn form': its validity established at a probate court (in the Chancery Division of the High Court), those concerned being made parties to the action.

**probation** in law, the placing of offenders under supervision of probation officers in the community, as an alternative to prison.

**processor** in computing, another name for the ◊central processing unit or ◊microprocessor of a computer.

**procurator fiscal** officer of a Scottish sheriff's court who (combining the role of public prosecutor and coroner) inquires into suspicious deaths and carries out the preliminary questioning of witnesses to crime.

**Procyon** or *Alpha Canis Minoris,* brightest star in the constellation ◊Canis Minor and the eighth-brightest star in the night sky. Procyon is a white star 11.4 light years from the Sun, with a mass of 1.7 Suns. It has a ◊white dwarf companion that orbits it every 40 years.

**productivity** in economics, the output produced by a given quantity of labour, usually measured as output per person employed in the firm, industry, sector, or economy concerned. Productivity is determined by the quality and quantity of the fixed ◊capital used by labour, and the effort of the workers concerned.

**progesterone** ◊steroid hormone that occurs in vertebrates. In mammals, it regulates the menstrual cycle and pregnancy. Progesterone is secreted by the corpus luteum (the ruptured Graafian follicle of a discharged ovum).

**program** in computing, a set of instructions that controls the operation of a computer. There are two main kinds: ◊applications programs, which carry out tasks for the benefit of the user – for example, word processing; and systems programs, which control the internal workings of the computer. A utility program is a systems program that carries out specific tasks for the user. Programs can be written in any of a number of ◊programming languages but are always translated into machine code before they can be executed by the computer.

**programming** writing instructions in a programming language for the control of a computer. *Applications programming* is for end-user programs, such as accounts programs or word-processing packages. *Systems programming* is for operating systems and the like, which are concerned more with the internal workings of the computer.

**programming language** in computing, a special notation in which instructions for controlling a computer are written. Programming languages are designed to be easy for people to write and read, but must be capable of being mechanically translated (by a ◊compiler or an interpreter) into the machine code that the computer can execute. Programming languages may be classified as high-level languages or low-level languages.

**progression** sequence of numbers each occurring in a specific relationship to its predecessor. An *arithmetic progression* has numbers that increase or decrease by a common sum or difference (for example, 2, 4, 6, 8); a *geometric progression* has numbers each bearing a fixed ratio to its predecessor (for example, 3, 6, 12, 24); and a *harmonic progression* has numbers whose ◊reciprocals are in arithmetical progression, for example $1, \frac{1}{2}, \frac{1}{3}, \frac{1}{4}$.

**Prohibition** in US history, the period 1920–33 when the 18th Amendment to the US Constitution was in force, and the manufacture, transportation, and sale of alcohol was illegal. This led to ◊bootlegging (the illegal distribution of liquor, often illicitly distilled), to the financial advantage of organized crime.

**prokaryote** in biology, an organism whose cells lack organelles (specialized segregated structures such as nuclei, mitochondria, and chloroplasts). Prokaryote DNA is not arranged in chromosomes but forms a coiled structure called a *nucleoid.* The prokaryotes comprise only the *bacteria* and *cyanobacteria* (see ◊blue-green algae); all other organisms are eukaryotes.

**Prokofiev, Sergey Sergeyevich** (1891–1953) Russian composer. His music includes operas such as *The Love for Three Oranges* (1921); ballets for Sergei Diaghilev, including *Romeo and Juliet* (1935); seven symphonies including the *Classical Symphony* (1916–17); music for film, including Eisenstein's *Alexander Nevsky* (1938); piano and violin concertos; songs and cantatas (for example, that composed for the 30th anniversary of the October Revolution); and *Peter and the Wolf* (1936) for children, to his own libretto after a Russian folk tale.

**PROM** acronym for programmable read-only memory, in computing, a memory device in the form of an integrated circuit (chip) that can be programmed after manufacture to hold information permanently. PROM chips are empty of information when manufactured, unlike ROM (read-only memory) chips, which have information built into them. Other memory devices are ◊EPROM (erasable programmable read-only memory) and ◊RAM (random-access memory).

**Prometheus** (Greek 'forethought') in Greek mythology, a ◊Titan who stole fire from heaven for the human race. In revenge, Zeus chained him to a rock and sent an eagle to gnaw at his liver by day; the organ grew back each night. ◊Heracles rescued him from the torture.

**promethium** radioactive, metallic element of the ◊lanthanide series, symbol Pm, atomic number 61, relative atomic mass 145. It occurs in nature only in minute amounts, produced as a fission product/by-product of uranium in ◊pitchblende and other uranium ores; for a long time it was considered not to occur in nature. The longest-lived isotope has a half-life of slightly more than 20 years.

**prominence** bright cloud of gas projecting from the Sun into space 100,000 km/60,000 mi or more. *Quiescent prominences* last for months, and are held in place by magnetic fields in the Sun's corona. *Surge prominences* shoot gas into space at speeds of 1,000 kps/600 mps. *Loop prominences* are gases falling back to the Sun's surface after a solar ◊flare.

**pronghorn** ruminant mammal *Antilocapra americana* constituting the family Antilocapridae, native to the western USA. It is not a true antelope. It is light brown and about 1 m/3 ft high. It sheds its horns annually and can reach speeds of 100 kph/60 mph. The loss of prairie land to agriculture, as well as excessive hunting, has brought this unique animal close to extinction.

**propaganda** systematic spreading (propagation) of information or disinformation, usually to promote a religious or political doctrine with the intention of instilling particular attitudes or responses. As a system of disseminating information it was considered a legitimate instrument of government, but became notorious through the deliberate distortion of facts or the publication of falsehoods by totalitarian regimes, notably Nazi Germany.

**propane** $C_3H_8$ gaseous hydrocarbon of the ◊alkane series, found in petroleum and used as fuel.

**propanone** $CH_3COCH_3$ (common name *acetone*) colourless flammable liquid used extensively as a solvent, in nail-varnish remover. It boils at 56.5°C/133.7°F, mixes with water in all proportions, and has a characteristic odour.

**propellant** substance burned in a rocket for propulsion. Two propellants are used: oxidizer and fuel are stored in separate tanks and pumped independently into the combustion chamber. Liquid oxygen (oxidizer) and liquid hydrogen (fuel) are common propellants, used, for example, in the space-shuttle main engines. The explosive charge that propels a projectile from a gun is also called a propellant.

**propeller** screwlike device used to propel some ships and aeroplanes. A propeller has a number of curved blades that describe a helical path as they rotate with the hub, and accelerate fluid (liquid or gas) backwards during rotation. Reaction to this backward movement of fluid sets up a propulsive thrust forwards. The marine screw propeller was developed by Francis Pettit Smith in the UK and Swedish-born John Ericson in the USA and was first used in 1839.

**propene** $CH_3CH{=}CH_2$ (common name *propy- lene)* second member of the alkene series of hydrocarbons. A colourless, flammable gas, it is widely used by industry to make organic chemicals, including polypropylene plastics.

**property** the right to control the use of a thing (such as land, a building, a work of art, or a computer program). In English law, a distinction is made between *real property,* which involves a degree of geographical fixity, and *personal property,* which does not. Property is never absolute, since any society places limits on an individual's property (such as the right to transfer that property to another). Different societies have held widely varying interpretations of the nature of property and the extent of the rights of the owner of that property.

**prophet** person thought to speak from divine inspiration or one who foretells the future. Prophets whose words and actions are recorded in the Bible include Moses, Samuel, Elijah, Isaiah, and Jeremiah. In Islam, ◊Muhammad is believed to be the last and greatest of a long line of prophets beginning with Adam and including Moses and Jesus.

**prophylaxis** any measure taken to prevent disease, including exercise and ◊vaccination. Prophylactic (preventive) medicine is an aspect of public-health provision that is receiving increasing attention.

**proportional representation** (PR), electoral system in which distribution of party seats corresponds to their proportion of the total votes cast, and minority votes are not wasted (as opposed to a simple majority, or 'first past the post', system). Forms include:
*party list* (PLS) or additional member system (AMS). As recommended by the Hansard Society in 1976 for introduction in the UK, three-quarters of the members would be elected in single-member constituencies on the traditional majority-vote system, and the remaining seats be allocated according to the overall number of votes cast for each party (a variant of this, the additional member system, is used in Germany, where half the members are elected from lists by proportional representation, and half fight for single-member 'first past the post' constituencies). Proportional representation is used for the new Scottish Parliament and National Assembly for Wales, elected in 1999, and for the European Parliament elections in Britain.
*single transferable vote* (STV), in which candidates are numbered in order of preference by the voter, and any votes surplus to the minimum required for a candidate to win are transferred to second preferences, as are second-preference votes from the successive candidates at the bottom of the poll until the required number of elected candidates is achieved. This is in use in the Republic of Ireland and for European Parliament elections in Northern Ireland.

**prop root** or *stilt root,* modified root that grows from the lower part of a stem or trunk down to the ground, providing a plant with extra support. Prop roots are common on some woody plants, such as mangroves, and also occur on a few herbaceous plants, such as maize. *Buttress roots* are a type of prop root found at the base of tree trunks, extended and flattened along the upper edge to form massive triangular buttresses; they are common on tropical trees.

**prose** spoken or written language without metrical regularity; in literature, prose corresponds more closely to the patterns of everyday speech than ◊poetry.

**prosecution** in law, the party instituting legal proceedings. In the UK, the prosecution of a criminal case is begun by bringing the accused (defendant) before a magistrate, either by warrant or summons, or by arrest without warrant. Most criminal prosecutions are conducted by the ◊Crown Prosecution Service, although other government departments may also prosecute some cases; for example, the Department of Inland Revenue. An individual may bring a private prosecution, usually for assault.

**Prosecution Service, Crown** body established by the Prosecution of Offences Act 1985, responsible for prosecuting all criminal offences in England and Wales. It is headed by the Director of Public Prosecutions (DPP), and brings England and Wales in line with Scotland (see ◊procurator fiscal) in having a prosecution service independent of the police.

**Proserpina** in Roman mythology, the goddess of the underworld. Her Greek equivalent is ◊Persephone.

**Prost, Alain Marie Pascal** (1955–   ) French motor-racing driver who was world champion in 1985, 1986, 1989, and 1993, and the first French world drivers' champion. To the end of the 1993 season he had won 51 Grand Prix from 199 starts. He retired in 1993.
*career highlights*
***World champion*** 1985 (Marlboro McLaren–TAG), 1986 (Marlboro McLaren–TAG), 1989 (Marlboro McLaren–Honda), 1993 (Williams–Renault)
***Formula 1 Grand Prix*** 199; wins: 51 (record).

**prostaglandin** any of a group of complex fatty acids present in the body that act as messenger substances between cells. Effects include stimulating the contraction of smooth muscle (for example, of the womb during birth), regulating the production of stomach acid, and modifying hormonal activity. In excess, prostaglandins may produce inflammatory disorders such as arthritis. Synthetic prostaglandins are used to induce labour in humans and domestic animals.

**prostate gland** gland surrounding and opening into the ◊urethra at the base of the ◊bladder in male mammals.

**prosthesis** artificial device used to substitute for a body part which is defective or missing. Prostheses include artificial limbs, hearing aids, false teeth and eyes, heart ◊pacemakers and plastic heart valves and blood vessels.

**protactinium** (Latin *protos* 'before' + *aktis* 'first ray') silver–grey, radioactive, metallic element of the ◊actinide series, symbol Pa, atomic number 91, relative atomic mass 231.036. It occurs in nature in very small quantities, in ◊pitchblende and other uranium ores. It has 14 known isotopes; the longest-lived, Pa-231, has a half-life of 32,480 years.

**protectionism** in economics, the imposition of heavy duties or import quotas by a government as a means of discouraging the import of foreign goods likely to compete with domestic products. Price controls, quota systems, and the reduction of surpluses are among the measures taken for agricultural products in the European Union. The opposite practice is ◊free trade.

**protectorate** formerly in international law, a small state under the direct or indirect control of a larger one. The 20th-century equivalent was a trust territory. In English history the rule of Oliver and Richard Cromwell 1653–59 is referred to as *the Protectorate*.

**protein** complex, biologically important substance composed of amino acids joined by ◊peptide bonds. Proteins are essential to all living organisms. As ◊enzymes they regulate all aspects of metabolism. Structural proteins such as *keratin* and *collagen* make up the skin, claws, bones, tendons, and ligaments; *muscle* proteins produce movement; *haemoglobin* transports oxygen; and *membrane* proteins regulate the movement of substances into and out of cells. For humans, protein is an essential part of the diet, and is found in greatest quantity in soy beans and other grain legumes, meat, eggs, and cheese.

**protein engineering** the creation of synthetic proteins designed to carry out specific tasks. For example, an enzyme may be designed to remove grease from soiled clothes and remain stable at the high temperatures in a washing machine.

**Proterozoic** eon of geological time, 3.5 billion to 570 million years ago, the second division of the Precambrian. It is defined as the time of simple life, since many rocks dating from this eon show traces of biological activity, and some contain the fossils of bacteria and algae.

**Protestantism** one of the main divisions of Christianity, which emerged from Roman Catholicism at the time of the ◊Reformation. The chief denominations are the Anglican Communion (Church of England in the UK and Episcopal Church in the USA), Baptists, Christian Scientists, Congregationalists (United Church of Christ), Lutherans, Methodists, Pentecostals, and Presbyterians, with a total membership of about 300 million.

**protist** in biology, a single-celled organism which has a eukaryotic cell, but which is not a member of the plant, fungal, or animal kingdoms. The main protists are ◊protozoa.

**proton** (Greek 'first') in physics, a positively charged subatomic particle, a constituent of the nucleus of all atoms. It belongs to the ◊baryon subclass of the ◊hadrons. A proton is extremely long-lived, with a lifespan of at least $10^{32}$ years. It carries a unit positive charge equal to the negative charge of an ◊electron. Its mass is almost 1,836 times that of an electron, or $1.67 \times 10^{-27}$ kg. Protons are composed of two up ◊quarks and one down quark held together by ◊gluons. The number of protons in the atom of an element is equal to the atomic number of that element.

**proton number** alternative name for ◊atomic number.

**protoplasm** contents of a living cell. Strictly speaking it includes all the discrete structures (organelles) in a cell, but it is often used simply to mean the jellylike material in which these float. The contents of a cell outside the nucleus are called ◊cytoplasm.

**protozoa** group of single-celled organisms without rigid cell walls. Some, such as amoeba, ingest other cells, but most are ◊saprotrophs or parasites. The group is polyphyletic (containing organisms which have different evolutionary origins).

**Proust, Marcel** (1871–1922) French novelist and critic. His immense autobiographical work *A la Recherche du temps perdu/Remembrance of Things Past* (1913–27), consisting of a series of novels, is the expression of his childhood memories coaxed from his subconscious; it is also a precise reflection of life in France at the end of the 19th century.

**Provence-Alpes-Côte d'Azur** region of southeast France, comprising the *départements* of Alpes-de-Haute-Provence, Hautes-Alpes, Alpes-Maritimes, Bouches-du-Rhône, Var, and Vaucluse; area 31,400 sq km/12,120 sq mi; the administrative centre is ◊Marseille; population (1990) 4,257,900. The Côte d'Azur, on the Mediterranean, is a tourist centre. Provence was an independent kingdom in the 10th century, and the area still has its own traditional language, Provençal.

**Proxima Centauri** closest star to the Sun, 4.2 light years away. It is a faint ◊red dwarf, visible only with a telescope, and is a member of the Alpha Centauri triple-star system.

**proxy** in law, a person authorized to stand in another's place; also the document conferring this right. The term usually refers to voting at meetings, but marriages by proxy are possible.

**Prussia** northern German state 1618–1945 on the Baltic coast. It was an independent kingdom until 1867, when it became, under Otto von ◊Bismarck, the military power of the North German Confederation and part of the German Empire 1871 under the Prussian king Wilhelm I. West Prussia became part of Poland under the Treaty of ◊Versailles, and East Prussia was largely incorporated into the USSR after 1945.

**prussic acid** former name for hydrocyanic acid.

**Prut** or *Pruc, Prutul,* river in eastern Europe; length 900 km/565 mi. The Prut rises in the Carpathian Mountains in southwestern Ukraine, and flows south to meet the Danube at Reni. For most of its course it forms the frontier between Romania and Moldova.

**psalm** sacred poem or song of praise. The Book of Psalms in the Old Testament is divided into five books containing 150 psalms, traditionally ascribed to David, the second king of Israel. In the Christian church they may be sung antiphonally in plainsong or set by individual composers to music in a great variety of styles,

from Josquin Desprez's *De profundis* to Igor Stravinsky's *Symphony of Psalms* (1930).

**pseudocarp** in botany, a fruitlike structure that incorporates tissue that is not derived from the ovary wall. The additional tissues may be derived from floral parts such as the ◊receptacle and ◊calyx. For example, the coloured, fleshy part of a strawberry develops from the receptacle and the true fruits are small achenes – the 'pips' embedded in its outer surface. Rose hips are a type of pseudocarp that consists of a hollow, fleshy receptacle containing a number of achenes within. Different types of pseudocarp include pineapples, figs, apples, and pears.

**pseudocopulation** attempted copulation by a male insect with a flower. It results in ◊pollination of the flower and is common in the orchid family, where the flowers of many species resemble a particular species of female bee. When a male bee attempts to mate with a flower, the pollinia (groups of pollen grains) stick to its body. They are transferred to the stigma of another flower when the insect attempts copulation again.

**psoriasis** chronic, recurring skin disease characterized by raised, red, scaly patches, on the scalp, elbows, knees, and elsewhere. Tar preparations, steroid creams, and ultraviolet light are used to treat it, and sometimes it disappears spontaneously. Psoriasis may be accompanied by a form of arthritis (inflammation of the joints). Psoriasis affects 100 million people worldwide.

**Psyche** late Greek personification of the soul as a winged girl or young woman. In Greek mythology, she was the youngest and most beautiful of three princesses. Incensed by her beauty, Aphrodite ordered her son Eros, the god of love, to inspire Psyche with desire for the vilest creatures. Instead, he fell in love with her, in some traditions by accidently grazing himself with his arrow.

**psychedelic drug** any drug that produces hallucinations or altered states of consciousness. Such sensory experiences may be in the auditory, visual, tactile, olfactory, or gustatory fields or in any combination. Among drugs known to have psychedelic effects are LSD (lysergic acid diethylamide), mescaline, and, to a mild degree, marijuana, along with a number of other plant-derived or synthetically prepared substances.

**psychiatry** branch of medicine dealing with the diagnosis and treatment of mental disorder, normally divided into the areas of *neurotic conditions,* including anxiety, depression, and hysteria, and *psychotic disorders,* such as schizophrenia. Psychiatric treatment consists of drugs, analysis, or electroconvulsive therapy.

**psychoanalysis** theory and method of treatment for neuroses, developed by Sigmund ◊Freud in the 1890s. Psychoanalysis asserts that the impact of early childhood sexuality and experiences, stored in the ◊unconscious, can lead to the development of adult emotional problems. The main treatment method involves the free association of ideas, and their interpretation by patient and analyst, in order to discover these long-buried events and to grasp their significance to the patient, linking aspects of the patient's historical past with the present relationship to the analyst. Psychoanalytic treatment aims to free the patient from specific symptoms and from irrational inhibitions and anxieties.

**psychology** systematic study of human and animal behaviour. The first psychology laboratory was founded in 1879 by Wilhelm Wundt at Leipzig, Germany. The subject includes diverse areas of study and application, among them the roles of instinct, heredity, environment, and culture; the processes of sensation, perception, learning, and memory; the bases of motivation and emotion; and the functioning of thought, intelligence, and language. Significant psychologists have included Gustav Fechner, founder of psychophysics; Wolfgang Köhler, one of the Gestalt or 'whole' psychologists; Sigmund Freud and his associates Carl Jung and Alfred Adler; William James, Jean Piaget; Carl Rogers; Hans Eysenck; J B Watson; and B F Skinner.

**psychopathy** personality disorder characterized by chronic antisocial behaviour (violating the rights of others, often violently) and an absence of feelings of guilt about the behaviour.

**psychosis** or *psychotic disorder,* general term for a serious mental disorder where the individual commonly loses contact with reality and may experience hallucinations (seeing or hearing things that do not exist) or delusions (fixed false beliefs). For example, in a paranoid psychosis, an individual may believe that others are plotting against him or her. A major type of psychosis is ◊schizophrenia.

**psychosomatic** of a physical symptom or disease thought to arise from emotional or mental factors.

**psychotherapy** any treatment for psychological problems that involves talking rather than surgery or drugs. Examples include cognitive therapy and ◊psychoanalysis.

**pt** symbol for ◊*pint.*

**Ptah** Egyptian god, the divine potter, a personification of the creative force. Worshipped at ◊Memphis, he was portrayed as a primitive human statue or mummy holding an ankh, symbol of life. He was said to be the father of ◊Imhotep, the physician and architect.

**ptarmigan** hardy, northern ground-dwelling bird of genus *Lagopus,* family Phasianidae (which also includes ◊grouse), with feathered legs and feet.

**pteridophyte** simple type of ◊vascular plant. The pteridophytes comprise four classes: the Psilosida, including the most primitive vascular plants, found mainly in the tropics; the Lycopsida, including the club mosses; the Sphenopsida, including the horsetails; and the Pteropsida, including the ferns. They do not produce seeds.

**pterodactyl** genus of ◊pterosaur.

**pterosaur** extinct flying reptile of the order Pterosauria, existing in the Mesozoic age. They ranged from the size of a starling to the 12 m/39 ft wingspan of *Arambourgiania philadelphiae;* the largest of the pterosaurs discovered so far. Some had horns on their heads that, when in flight, made a whistling to roaring sound.

**Ptolemy** Claudius Ptolemaeus (*c.* AD 100–*c.* AD 170) Egyptian astronomer and geographer. His *Almagest* developed the theory that Earth is the centre of the universe, with the Sun, Moon, and stars revolving around it. In 1543 the Polish astronomer ◊Copernicus proposed an alternative to the *Ptolemaic system.* Ptolemy's *Geography* was a standard source of information until the 16th century.

**puberty** stage in human development when the individual becomes sexually mature. It may occur from the age of ten upwards. The sexual organs take on their adult form and pubic hair grows. In girls, menstruation begins, and the breasts develop; in boys, the voice breaks and becomes deeper, and facial hair develops.

**public corporation** company structure that is similar in organization to a public limited company but with no shareholder rights. Such corporations are established to carry out state-owned activities, but are financially independent of the state and are run by a board. The first public corporation to be formed in the UK was the Central Electricity Board in the 1920s.

**public inquiry** in English law, a legal investigation where witnesses are called and evidence is produced in a similar fashion to a court of law. Inquiries may be held as part of legal procedure, or into a matter of public concern.

**public limited company** (plc) in the UK, registered company in which shares and debentures may be offered to the public. It must have a minimum of two shareholders and there is no upper limit. The company's financial records must be available for any member of the public to scrutinize, and the company's name must carry the words 'public limited company' or initials 'plc'. A public company can raise large sums of money to fuel its development and expansion by inviting the public to buy shares.

**Public Order Act** UK act of Parliament 1986 that abolished the common-law offences of riot, rout, unlawful assembly, and affray and created a new expanded range of statutory offences: riot, violent disorder, affray, threatening behaviour, and disorderly conduct. These are all arrestable offences that may be committed in both private and public places. Prosecution for riot requires the consent of the Director of Public Prosecutions.

**public sector** the part of the economy that is owned and controlled by the state, namely central government, local government, and government enterprises. In a command economy, the public sector allocates most of the resources in the economy. The opposite of the public sector is the ◊private sector, where resources are allocated by private individuals and business organizations.

**public spending** expenditure by government, covering the military, health, education, infrastructure, development projects, and the cost of servicing overseas borrowing.

**Puccini, Giacomo (Antonio Domenico Michele Secondo Maria)** (1858–1924) Italian opera composer. His music shows a strong gift for melody and dramatic effect and his operas combine exotic plots with elements of *verismo* (realism). They include *Manon Lescaut* (1893), *La Bohème* (1896), *Tosca* (1900), *Madama Butterfly* (1904), and the unfinished *Turandot* (1926).

**pueblo** (Spanish 'village') settlement of flat-roofed stone or adobe houses that are the communal dwelling houses of the Hopi, Zuni, and other American Indians of Arizona and New Mexico. The word has also come to refer to the pueblo-dwelling American Indians of the southwest themselves.

**Puerto Rico** the Commonwealth of; easternmost island of the Greater Antilles, situated between the US Virgin Islands and the Dominican Republic
*area* 9,000 sq km/3,475 sq mi
*capital* San Juan
*towns and cities* ports Mayagüez, Ponce
*features* volcanic mountains run east–west; the islands of Vieques and Culebra belong to Puerto Rico
*exports* sugar, tobacco, rum, pineapples, textiles, plastics, chemicals, processed foods, vegetables, coffee
*currency* US dollar
*population* (1992 est) 3,336,000
*language* Spanish and English (official)
*religion* Roman Catholic
*government* under the constitution of 1952, similar to that of the USA, with a governor elected for four years, and a legislative assembly with a senate and house of representatives. Residents are US citizens, represented in US Congress by an elected Resident Commissioner with a seat in the House of Representatives.
*history* visited in 1493 by Columbus; annexed by Spain in 1509; ceded to the USA after the ◊Spanish-American War in 1898; known as *Porto Rico* ('Rich Port') 1898–1932; achieved commonwealth status with local self-government in 1952.

**puffball** ball-shaped fruiting body of certain fungi (see ◊fungus) that cracks open when it ripens, releasing the enclosed spores in the form of a brown powder; for example, the common puffball (*L. perlatum*). (Genera *Lycoperdon* and *Calvatia*.)

**puffer fish** fish of the family Tetraodontidae. As a means of defence it inflates its body with water until it becomes spherical and the skin spines become erect. Puffer fish are mainly found in warm waters, where they feed on molluscs, crustaceans, and coral.

**puffin** any of various sea birds of the genus *Fratercula* of the ◊auk family, found in the northern Atlantic and Pacific. The puffin is about 35 cm/14 in long, with a white face and front, red legs, and a large deep bill, very brightly coloured in summer. Having short wings and webbed feet, puffins are poor fliers but excellent swimmers. They nest in rock crevices, or make burrows, and lay a single egg.

**pug** breed of small dog with short wrinkled face, hanging ears, chunky body, and tail curled over the hip. It weighs 6–8 kg/13–18 lb. Its short coat may be black, beige or grey; the beige or grey dogs have black on the face and ears.

**Puget Sound** inlet of the Pacific Ocean on the west coast of Washington State, USA, extending southwards for about 160 km/100 mi, from the eastern end of the Strait of Juan de Fuca to Olympia, the state capital. It covers an area of about 5,180 sq km/1,990 sq mi, and contains a number of islands; Whidbey, Vashon, and Bainbridge are the largest. The major port of ◊Seattle lies on its eastern shore, and a government naval yard is situated at Bremerton. The sound contains two main branches, Admiralty Inlet and Hood Canal, and receives rivers from the Cascade Range. Its waterways serve a rich industrial and agricultural area, and timber is rafted from its well-wooded shores to lumber and paper mills along the coast.

**Pugin, Augustus Welby Northmore** (1812–1852) English architect and designer. He collaborated with Charles ◊Barry in the detailed design of the New Palace of Westminster (Houses of Parliament). He did much to instigate the Gothic Revival in England, largely through his books *Contrasts: or a Parallel between the Architecture of the 15th and 19th Centuries* (1836) and *Gothic Ornaments from Ancient Buildings in England and France* (1828–31).

**Puglia** Italian form of ◊Apulia, a region of Italy.

**P'u-i, Henry** or *Pu-Yi* (1906–1967) last Manchu Qing emperor of China (as Hsuan Tung) from 1908 until he was deposed in the republican revolution of 1912; he was restored for a week in 1917. After his deposition he chose to be called Henry. He was president 1932–34 and emperor 1934–45 of the Japanese puppet state of Manchukuo (see ◊Manchuria).

**pulley** simple machine consisting of a fixed, grooved wheel, sometimes in a block, around which a rope or chain can be run. A simple pulley serves only to change the direction of the applied effort (as in a simple hoist for raising loads). The use of more than one pulley results in a mechanical advantage, so that a given effort can raise a heavier load.

**pulmonary** pertaining to the ◊lungs.

**pulsar** celestial source that emits pulses of energy at regular intervals, ranging from a few seconds to a few thousandths of a second. Pulsars are thought to be rapidly rotating ◊neutron stars, which flash at radio and other wavelengths as they spin. They were discovered in 1967 by Jocelyn Bell-Burnell and Antony Hewish at the Mullard Radio Astronomy Observatory, Cambridge, England. By 1998 1,000 pulsars had been discovered since the initial identification in 1967.

**pulse** impulse transmitted by the heartbeat throughout the arterial systems of vertebrates. When the heart muscle contracts, it forces blood into the aorta (the chief artery). Because the arteries are elastic, the sudden rise of pressure causes a throb or sudden swelling through them. The actual flow of the blood is about 60 cm/2 ft a second in humans. The average adult pulse rate is generally about 70 per minute. The pulse can be felt where an artery is near the surface, for example in the wrist or the neck.

**pulse** crop such as peas and beans. Pulses are grown primarily for their seeds, which provide a concentrated source of vegetable protein, and make a vital contribution to human diets in poor countries where meat is scarce, and among vegetarians. Soybeans are the major temperate protein crop in the West; most are used for oil production or for animal feed. In Asia, most are processed into soymilk and beancurd. Peanuts dominate pulse production in the tropical world and are generally consumed as human food.

**puma** also called *cougar* or *mountain lion,* large wild cat *Felis concolor* found in North and South America. Tawny-coated, it is 1.5 m/4.5 ft long with a 1-m/3-ft tail. Pumas live alone, with each male occupying a distinct territory; they eat deer, rodents, and cattle. Pumas need large territories, with females maintaining up to 100 sq km and males even more. Two to four cubs are born and will remain with the mother till they are 18–24 months old (they are completely weaned at 6 months).

**pumice** light volcanic rock produced by the frothing action of expanding gases during the solidification of lava. It has the texture of a hard sponge and is used as an abrasive.

**pump** any device for moving liquids and gases, or compressing gases.

Some pumps, such as the traditional *lift pump* used to raise water from wells, work by a reciprocating (up-and-down) action. Movement of a piston in a cylinder with a one-way valve creates a partial vacuum in the cylinder, thereby sucking water into it.

**pumpkin** creeping plant whose large round fruit has a thick orange rind, pulpy flesh, and many seeds. Pumpkins are used in cookery (especially pies and soups) and are hollowed out to form candle lanterns at Halloween. (*Cucurbita pepo,* family Cucurbitaceae.)

**pun** figure of speech, a play on words, or double meaning that is technically known as *paronomasia* (Greek 'adapted meaning'). Double meaning can be accidental, often resulting from homonymy, or the multiple meaning of words; puns, however, are deliberate, intended as jokes or as clever and compact remarks.

**punctuation** system of conventional signs (punctuation marks) and spaces employed to organize written and printed language in order to make it as readable, clear, and logical as possible.

**Pune** formerly *Poona,* city in Maharashtra, India, 100 km/60 mi southeast of Mumbai on the Mutha River; population (1991) 2,494,000.

Products include chemicals, rubber, rice, sugar, cotton, paper, and jewellery. Industries include cars, trucks, scooters, and motorbikes; pumps, cables, machinery, arms and ammunitions, cutting tools, televisions, boilers, and generators.

**Punic** (Latin *Punicus* 'a Phoenician') relating to ◊Carthage, ancient city in North Africa founded by the Phoenicians.

**Punic Wars** three wars between ◊Rome and ◊Carthage: *First Punic War* 264–241 BC, resulted in the defeat of the Carthaginians under ◊Hamilcar Barca and the cession of Sicily to Rome; *Second Punic War* 218–201 BC, Hannibal invaded Italy, defeated the Romans at Trebia, Trasimene, and at Cannae (under Fabius Maximus), but was finally defeated himself by Scipio Africanus Major at Zama (now in Algeria); *Third Punic War* 149–146 BC, ended in the destruction of Carthage, and its possessions becoming the Roman province of Africa.

**Punjab** (Sanskrit 'five rivers': the Indus tributaries Jhelum, Chenab, Ravi, Beas, and Sutlej) former state of British India, now divided between India and Pakistan. Punjab was annexed by Britain in 1849 after the Sikh Wars (1845–46 and 1848–49), and formed into a province with its capital at Lahore. Under the British, West Punjab was extensively irrigated, and land was granted to Indians who had served in the British army.

**Punjab** state of northwest India, bordering Pakistan
*area* 50,400 sq km/19,454 sq mi
*capital* ◊Chandigarh
*towns and cities* Amritsar, Jalandhar, Faridkot, Ludhiana
*physical* rivers Sutlej and Beas, tributaries of the ◊Indus flow through the gently sloping alluvial plain which makes up most of the state
*features* mainly agricultural, crops chiefly under irrigation through schemes such as the Bhakra Nangal dam on the Sutlej; ruins from the ◊Indus Valley civilization 2500 to 1600 BC
*industry* textiles, sewing machines
*agriculture* wheat, rice, sugar, maize, millet, barley, cotton
*population* (1994 est) 21,695,000 (highest life expectancy rates in India – 59 for women, 64 for men)
*language* Punjabi
*religion* 60% Sikh, 30% Hindu; there is friction between the two groups
*history* in 1919 unrest led to the Punjab riots. The present state was formed at the partition of India in 1947 (see ◊Punjab massacres). The Indian Punjab was further divided into three areas: Himachal Pradesh, the Patiala and East Punjab States Union, and the state of East Punjab. In 1956 the latter two were merged to form Punjab (India), which was again divided in 1966 along linguistic lines to create three states: the predominantly Hindu states of Himachal Pradesh and Haryana (which shares the capital Chandigarh with Punjab); the remaining Punjab state, with mostly Punjabi-speaking Sikhs.

**Punjab** state of northeast Pakistan
*area* 205,344 sq km/79,263 sq mi

*capital* ◊Lahore
*physical* semi-arid alluvial plain, drained by the ◊Indus River and its tributaries, the Jhelum, Chenab, Ravi and Sutlej rivers; to the north, the Himalayan foothills, and Salt Range mountains (containing oil) between the Indus and Jhelum valleys
*features* ruins from the ◊Indus Valley civilization 2500 to 1600 BC
*agriculture* wheat cultivation (by irrigation)
*population* (1993 est) 72,300,000
*language* Punjabi, Urdu
*religion* Islam
*history* formed as West Punjab state in 1947 upon partition of India and the formation of Pakistan.

**Punjabi** the majority ethnic group living in the Punjab. Approximately 37 million live in the Pakistan half of Punjab, while another 14 million live on the Indian side of the border. In addition to Sikhs, there are Rajputs in Punjab, some of whom have adopted Islam. The Punjabi language belongs to the Indo-Iranian branch of the Indo-European family. It is considered by some to be a variety of Hindi, by others to be a distinct language.

**Punjab massacres** violent episode occurring after the partition of India in 1947, in which more than a million people died while relocating in the Punjab. The eastern section became an Indian state, while the western area, dominated by the Muslims, went to Pakistan. Violence occurred as Muslims fled from eastern Punjab, and Hindus and Sikhs moved from Pakistan to India.

**punk** movement of disaffected youth of the late 1970s, manifesting itself in fashions and music designed to shock or intimidate. *Punk rock* began in the UK and stressed aggressive performance within a three-chord, three-minute format, as exemplified by the Sex Pistols. The punk aesthetic continued to be revived periodically with the nostalgia boom of the 1990s, supported by the growth of a neo-punk movement in the USA and by groups such as the Clash being accorded the status of rock 'n' roll 'classics'.

**pupa** nonfeeding, largely immobile stage of some insect life cycles, in which larval tissues are broken down, and adult tissues and structures are formed.

**Purcell, Henry** (*c.* 1659–1695) English Baroque composer. His music balances high formality with melodic expression of controlled intensity, for example, the opera *Dido and Aeneas* (1689) and music for Dryden's *King Arthur* (1691) and for *The Fairy Queen* (1692). He wrote more than 500 works, ranging from secular operas and incidental music for plays to cantatas and church music.

**purdah** (Persian and Hindu 'curtain') seclusion of women practised by some Islamic and Hindu peoples. It had begun to disappear with the adoption of Western culture, but the fundamentalism of the 1980s revived it; for example, the wearing of the chador (an all-enveloping black mantle) in Iran.

**purgatory** in Roman Catholic belief, a purificatory state or place where the souls of those who have died in a state of grace can expiate their venial sins, with a limited amount of suffering.

**Purim** Jewish festival celebrated in February or March (the 14th of Adar in the Jewish calendar), commemorating Esther, who saved the Jews from destruction in 473 BC during the Persian occupation.

**Puritan** from 1564, a member of the Church of England who wished to eliminate Roman Catholic survivals in church ritual, or substitute a presbyterian for an episcopal form of church government. The term also covers the separatists who withdrew from the church altogether.

**pus** yellowish fluid that forms in the body as a result of bacterial infection; it includes white blood cells (leucocytes), living and dead bacteria, dead tissue, and serum. An enclosed collection of pus is called an abscess.

**Pusan** or *Busan,* chief industrial port (textiles, rubber, salt, fishing) of South Korea; population (1990) 3,797,600. It was invaded by the Japanese in 1592 and opened to foreign trade in 1883.

**Pushkin, Aleksandr Sergeyevich** (1799–1837) Russian poet and writer. His works include the novel in verse *Eugene Onegin* 1823–31 and the tragic drama *Boris Godunov* 1825. Pushkin's range was wide, and his willingness to experiment freed later Russian writers from many of the archaic conventions of the literature of his time.

**Pushtu** another name for the ◊Pashto language of Afghanistan and northern Pakistan.

**Puttnam, David (Terence)** (1941– ) English film producer. He played a major role in reviving the British film industry internationally in the 1980s, and has been involved in an eclectic range of films with a variety of filmmakers. They include *Midnight Express* (1978), *Chariots of Fire* (1981) (Academy Award for best film), *The Killing Fields* (1984), and *Memphis Belle* (1990). He was head of Columbia Pictures 1986–87.

**Pu-Yi** alternative transliteration of the name of the last Chinese emperor, Henry ◊P'u-i.

**Pygmalion** in Greek mythology, a king of Cyprus who fell in love with an ivory statue he had carved. When Aphrodite breathed life into it, he married the woman and named her Galatea. Their children were Paphos and Metharme.

**Pygmy** sometimes *Negrillo,* member of any of several groups of small-statured, dark-skinned peoples living in the equatorial jungles of Africa. The most important groups are the Twa, Aka, Mbuti, Binga, Baka, Gelli Efé; their combined population is less than 200,000. They were probably the aboriginal inhabitants of the region, before the arrival of farming peoples from elsewhere. They live nomadically in small groups, as hunter-gatherers; they also trade with settled people in the area.

**pyramid** four-sided building with triangular sides. Pyramids were used in ancient Egypt to enclose a royal tomb; for example, the Great Pyramid of Khufu/Cheops at El Gîza, near Cairo, 230 m/755 ft square and 147 m/481 ft high. The three pyramids at Gîza were considered one of the ◊Seven Wonders of the World. In Babylon and Assyria, broadly stepped pyramids (◊ziggurats) were used as the base for a shrine to a god: the Tower of ◊Babel was probably one of these.

**Pyrenees** French *Pyrénées;* Spanish *Pirineos,* mountain range in southwest Europe between France and Spain; length about 435 km/270 mi; highest peak Aneto (French Néthon) 3,404 m/ 11,172 ft. Andorra lies entirely within the range. Hydroelectric power has encouraged industrial development in the foothills.

**pyrethrum** popular name for several cultivated chrysanthemums. The ornamental species *C. coccineum,* and hybrids derived from it, are commonly grown in gardens. Pyrethrum powder, made from the dried flower heads of some species, is a powerful pesticide for aphids and mosquitoes. (Genus *Chrysanthemum,* family Compositae.)

**pyridine** $C_5H_5N$ a heterocyclic compound. It is a liquid with a sickly smell and occurs in coal tar. It is soluble in water, acts as a strong ◊base, and is used as a solvent, mainly in the manufacture of plastics.

**Pyrrhus** (319–272 BC) king of Epirus (an area of northwestern Greece and southern Albania) from 307 BC. In the early years of his reign he struggled to maintain his throne and retain independence from Macedonian control. In 280 BC he invaded Italy as an ally of the Tarentines against Rome. He twice defeated the Romans, but with such heavy losses that a 'Pyrrhic victory' has come to mean a victory not worth winning. He returned to Epirus in 275 after his defeat at Beneventum, and was killed in street fighting at Argos.

**Pythagoras** (*c.* 580–500 BC) Greek mathematician and philosopher who formulated ◊Pythagoras' theorem.

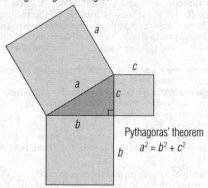

*for right-angled triangles*

Pythagoras' theorem
$$a^2 = b^2 + c^2$$

**Pythagoras' theorem** *Pythagoras' theorem for right-angled triangles is likely to have been known long before the time of Pythagoras. It was probably used by the ancient Egyptians to lay out the pyramids.*

**Pythagoras' theorem** in geometry, a theorem stating that in a right-angled triangle, the area of the square on the hypotenuse (the longest side) is equal to the sum of the areas of the squares drawn on the other two sides. If the hypotenuse is $h$ units long and the lengths of the other sides are $a$ and $b$, then $h^2 = a^2 + b^2$.

**python** any constricting snake of the Old World subfamily Pythoninae of the family Boidae, which also includes ◊boas and the ◊anaconda. Pythons are found in the tropics of Africa, Asia, and Australia. Unlike boas, they lay eggs rather than produce living young. Some species are small, but the reticulated python *Python reticulatus* of Southeast Asia can grow to 10 m/33 ft.

**Qaboos bin Said** (1940– ) Sultan of Oman, the 14th descendant of the Albusaid family. Opposed to the conservative views of his father, he overthrew him in 1970 in a bloodless coup and assumed the sultanship. Subsequently, he followed more liberal and expansionist policies, while maintaining his country's position of international nonalignment.

**Qaddafi** alternative form of ◊Khaddhafi, Libyan leader.

**qat** or *kat* or *khat,* evergreen shrub with white flowers belonging to the staff-tree family, native to Africa and Asia. The leaves are chewed as a mild narcotic drug in some Arab countries. Its use was banned in Somalia 1983. (*Catha edulis,* family Celastraceae.)

**Qatar** State of
*national name Dawlat Qatar*

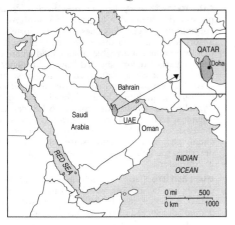

**area** 11,400 sq km/4,401 sq mi
**capital** Doha (and chief port)
**major towns/cities** Dukhan, centre of oil production; Halul, terminal for offshore oilfields; Umm Said, Ruwais, Wakra, Al-Khour
**physical features** mostly flat desert with salt flats in south
**head of state and government** Sheikh Hamad bin Khalifa al-Thani from 1995
**political system** absolute monarchy
**political parties** none

**currency** Qatari riyal
**GNP per capita (PPP)** (US$) 20,100 (1997 est)
**exports** petroleum. Principal market: Japan 49.7% (1997)
**population** 589,000 (1999 est)
**language** Arabic (official); English
**Religion** Sunni Muslim
**life expectancy** 70 (men); 75 (women) (1995–2000)
**Chronology**
**7th century AD** Islam introduced.
**8th century** Developed into important trading centre during time of Abbasid Empire.
**1783** The al-Khalifa family, who had migrated to northeast Qatar from west and north of the Arabian Peninsula, foiled Persian invasion and moved their headquarters to Bahrain Island, while continuing to rule the area of Qatar.
**1867–68** After the Bahrain-based al-Khalifa had suppressed a revolt by their Qatari subjects, destroying the town of Doha, Britain intervened and installed Muhammad ibn Thani al-Thani, from the leading family of Qatar, as the ruling sheikh (or emir). A British Resident was given power to arbitrate disputes with Qatar's neighbours.
**1871–1914** Nominally part of Turkish Ottoman Empire, although in 1893 sheik's forces inflicted a defeat on Ottomans.
**1916** Qatar became British protectorate after treaty signed with Sheikh Abdullah al-Thani.
**1949** Oil production began at onshore Dukhan field in west.
**1960** Sheikh Ahmad al-Thani became new emir.
**1968** Britain's announcement that it would remove its forces from the Persian Gulf by 1971 led Qatar to make an abortive attempt to arrange a federation of Gulf states.
**1970** Constitution adopted, confirming emirate as absolute monarchy.
**1971** Independence achieved from Britain.
**1972** Emir Sheikh Ahmad replaced in bloodless coup by his cousin, the Crown prince and prime minister Sheikh Khalifa ibn Hamad al-Thani.
**1991** Qatar forces joined the United Nations (UN) coalition in the Gulf War against Iraq.
**1995** Sheikh Khalifa was ousted by his son, Crown Prince Sheikh Hamad bin Khalifa al-Thani.
**1996** The announcement of plans to introduce democracy were followed by an assassination attempt on Sheikh Hamad.

**QC** abbreviation for ◊*Queen's Counsel.*

**Qinghai** or *Tsinghai;* Mongolian *Koko Nor;* Tibetan *Amdo,* province of northwest China, bounded to the north by Gansu, to the south by Sichuan, to the west by Tibet, and to the northwest by Xinjiang Uygur Autonomous Region
**area** 721,000 sq km/278,306 sq mi
**capital** Xining
**towns** Golmud
**physical** mountains and plateaus in the west and south; Huang He River valley in the east; Qinghai Lake
**industries** minerals, chemicals, livestock, oil, medical products
**agriculture** animal rearing, bee-keeping

*population* (1996) 4,448,000; minorities include 900,000 Tibetans (mostly nomadic herders).

**Qom** or *Qum, Kom, Kum,* holy city of Shiite Muslims, in central Iran, 145 km/90 mi south of Tehran on the Qom River; population (1991) 681,300. Pottery, textiles, shoes, and glass are the main industries. The Islamic academy of Madresseh Faizieh in 1920 became the headquarters of Ayatollah ◊Khomeini.

**quadratic equation** in mathematics, a polynomial equation of second degree (that is, an equation containing as its highest power the square of a variable, such as $x^2$). The general formula of such equations is

$$ax^2 + bx + c = 0$$

in which *a, b,* and *c* are real numbers, and only the coefficient *a* cannot equal 0.

In ◊coordinate geometry, a quadratic function represents a ◊parabola.

**Quadruple Alliance** in European history, three military alliances of four nations:
*the Quadruple Alliance* 1718 Austria, Britain, France, and the United Provinces (Netherlands) joined forces to prevent Spain from annexing Sardinia and Sicily;
*the Quadruple Alliance* 1813 Austria, Britain, Prussia, and Russia allied to defeat the French emperor Napoleon; renewed 1815 and 1818.
*the Quadruple Alliance* 1834 Britain, France, Portugal, and Spain guaranteed the constitutional monarchies of Spain and Portugal against rebels in the Carlist War.

**quaestor** junior Roman magistrate whose primary role was to oversee the finances of individual provinces under the Republic. Quaestors originated as assistants to the consuls. They often commanded units in the army when the governor of the province fought a campaign.

**quail** any of several genera of small ground-dwelling birds of the family Phasianidae, which also includes grouse, pheasants, bobwhites, and prairie chickens. Species are found in Africa, India, Australia, North America, and Europe.

**Quaker** popular name, originally derogatory, for a member of the Society of ◊Friends.

**qualitative analysis** in chemistry, a procedure for determining the identity of the component(s) of a single substance or mixture. A series of simple reactions and tests can be carried out on a compound to determine the elements present.

**quango** acronym for *quasi-autonomous non-governmental organization,* any administrative body that is nominally independent but relies on government funding; for example, the British Council (1935) and the Equal Opportunities Commission (1975) in the UK, and the Environmental Protection Agency (1970) in the USA.

**Quant, Mary** (1934– ) English fashion designer. She popularized the miniskirt in the UK and was one of the first designers to make clothes specifically for the teenage and early twenties market, producing bold, simple outfits which were in tune with the 'swinging London' of the 1960s. Her designs were sharp, angular, and streetwise, and she combined spots, stripes, and checks in an original way. Her boutique in Chelsea's King's Road, opened in 1955, was named Bazaar. In the 1970s she extended into cosmetics and textile design.

**quantitative analysis** in chemistry, a procedure for determining the precise amount of a known component present in a single substance or mixture. A known amount of the substance is subjected to particular procedures.

*Gravimetric analysis* determines the mass of each constituent present; *volumetric analysis* determines the concentration of a solution by ◊titration against a solution of known concentration.

**quantum mechanics** branch of physics dealing with the interaction of ◊matter and ◊radiation, the structure of the ◊atom, the motion of atomic particles, and with related phenomena (see ◊elementary particle and ◊quantum theory).

**quantum number** in physics, one of a set of four numbers that uniquely characterize an ◊electron and its state in an ◊atom. The *principal quantum number n* defines the electron's main energy level. The *orbital quantum number l* relates to its angular momentum. The *magnetic quantum number m* describes the energies of electrons in a magnetic field. The *spin quantum number $m_s$* gives the spin direction of the electron.

**quantum theory** or *quantum mechanics,* in physics, the theory that ◊energy does not have a continuous range of values, but is, instead, absorbed or radiated discontinuously, in multiples of definite, indivisible units called quanta. Just as earlier theory showed how light, generally seen as a wave motion, could also in some ways be seen as composed of discrete particles (◊photons), quantum theory shows how atomic particles such as electrons may also be seen as having wavelike properties. Quantum theory is the basis of particle physics, modern theoretical chemistry, and the solid-state physics that describes the behaviour of the silicon chips used in computers.

**quarantine** (from French *quarantaine* '40 days') any period for which people, animals, plants, or vessels may be detained in isolation to prevent the spread of contagious disease.

**quark** in physics, the ◊elementary particle that is the fundamental constituent of all ◊hadrons (subatomic particles that experience the strong nuclear force and divide into baryons, such as neutrons and protons, and mesons). Quarks have electric charges that are fractions of the electronic charge (+2/3 or –1/3 of the electronic charge). There are six types, or 'flavours': up, down, top, bottom, strange, and charmed, each of which has three varieties, or 'colours': red, green, and blue (visual colour is not meant, although the analogy is useful in many ways). To each quark there is an antiparticle, called an antiquark.

**quartz** crystalline form of ⟡silica $SiO_2$, one of the most abundant minerals of the Earth's crust (12% by volume). Quartz occurs in many different kinds of rock, including sandstone and granite. It ranks 7 on the Mohs scale of hardness and is resistant to chemical or mechanical breakdown. Quartzes vary according to the size and purity of their crystals. Crystals of pure quartz are coarse, colourless, transparent, show no cleavage, and fracture unevenly; this form is usually called rock crystal. Impure coloured varieties, often used as gemstones, include ⟡agate, citrine quartz, and ⟡amethyst. Quartz is also used as a general name for the cryptocrystalline and noncrystalline varieties of silica, such as chalcedony, chert, and opal.

Quartz is used in ornamental work and industry, where its reaction to electricity makes it valuable in electronic instruments (see ⟡piezoelectric effect). Quartz can also be made synthetically.

**quasar** from *quasi*-stell*ar* object or QSO, one of the most distant extragalactic objects known, discovered in 1963. Quasars appear starlike, but each emits more energy than 100 giant galaxies. They are thought to be at the centre of galaxies, their brilliance emanating from the stars and gas falling towards an immense ⟡black hole at their nucleus. Most quasars are found in elliptical galaxies.

**quassia** any of a group of tropical American trees with bitter bark and wood. The heartwood of *Q. amara* is a source of quassiin, an infusion of which was formerly used as a tonic; it is now used in insecticides. (Genus *Quassia*, family Simaroubaceae.)

**Quaternary** period of geological time that began 1.64 million years ago and is still in process. It is divided into the ⟡Pleistocene and ⟡Holocene epochs.

**Quatre Bras, Battle of** battle fought on 16 June 1815 during the ⟡Napoleonic Wars, in which the British commander Wellington defeated French forces under Marshal Ney. It is named after a hamlet in Brabant, Belgium, 32 km/20 mi southeast of Brussels.

**Quayle, (James) Dan(forth)** (1947– ) US Republican politician, vice president 1989–93. A congressman for Indiana 1977–81, he became a senator in 1981.

**Québec** (Iroquois *Kebec*, 'a place where waters narrow') capital and port of ⟡Québec province, Canada, at the junction of the Saint-Charles and St Lawrence rivers, Canada; population (1991) 167,500, metropolitan area (1996) 697,600. It is a major inland seaport, and a commercial, financial, and administrative centre. Industries include printing and publishing; and the production of paper, pulp, wood products, electronic goods, textiles, and leather. Lumber and wheat are exported. It is a centre of French culture, and most of its inhabitants are French-speaking.

**Québec** province of eastern Canada; the largest province, second only in area among the nation's administrative subdivisions to the Northwest Territories. Québec is bordered on the northeast by Labrador, on the east by Newfoundland, on the southeast by New Brunswick and Nova Scotia, and on the west and southwest by Ontario. On its southern border lie (west–east) the US states of New York, Vermont, New Hampshire, and Maine

*area* 1,540,700 sq km/594,710 sq mi

*capital* Québec

*towns and cities* Montréal, Laval, Sherbrooke, Verdun, Hull, Trois Rivières

*population* (1991) 6,811,800

*physical* Canadian Shield, including the Laurentian and Torngat mountain ranges; extensive lakes and rivers provide resources for major hydroelectric schemes; St Lawrence, Ottawa, and Grande Rivière rivers; Appalachian mountains

*industries* mining (iron, copper, gold, and zinc); arable farming (cereals, potatoes, and maple syrup 70% of world's output; fishing; paper and textile manufacture).

**Québec Conference** two conferences of Allied leaders in the city of Québec during World War II. The *first conference* in 1943 approved British admiral Mountbatten as supreme Allied commander in Southeast Asia and made plans for the invasion of France, for which US general Eisenhower was to be supreme commander. The *second conference* in September 1944 adopted plans for intensified air attacks on Germany, created a unified strategy against Japan, and established a post-war policy for a defeated Germany.

**quebracho** any of several South American trees belonging to the cashew family, with very hard, tannin-rich wood; chiefly the red quebracho (*S. lorentzii*), used in the tanning of leather. (Genus *Schinopsis*, family Anacardiaceae.)

**Quechua** or *Quichua* or *Kechua*, the largest group of American Indians living in South America. The Quechua live in the Andean region. Their ancestors included the Inca, who established the Quechua language in the region, now the second official language of Peru and widely spoken as a lingua franca in Ecuador, Bolivia, Columbia, Argentina, and Chile; it belongs to the Andean-Equatorial family.

**Queen** British glam-rock group 1971–91 credited with making the first successful pop video, for their hit 'Bohemian Rhapsody' (1975). The operatic flamboyance of lead singer Freddie Mercury (1946–1991) was the cornerstone of their popularity. Among their other hits are 'We Will Rock You' (1977) and the rockabilly pastiche 'Crazy Little Thing Called Love' (1980).

**Queens** largest borough and county of New York City, USA; population (1996 est) 1,980,600. Situated at the western end of ⟡Long Island, it covers an area of 280 sq km/108 sq mi. Mainly residential, its districts include Jackson Heights, Forest Hills, and Flushing. Industries are concentrated in Long Island City, a railroad and shipping terminus, and Maspeth. Products include processed foods, metalware, paint, furniture, stonemasonry, clothes, and electronic and office equipment.

**Queen's Counsel** (QC), in England, a barrister appointed to senior rank by the Lord Chancellor. When the monarch is a king the term is *King's Counsel* (*KC*). A QC wears a silk gown, and takes precedence over a junior member of the Bar.

**Queensland** state in northeast Australia, including the adjacent islands in the Pacific Ocean and in the Gulf of Carpentaria; bordered on the west by Northern Territory, on the southwest by South Australia, on the south by New South Wales, on the east by the Pacific Ocean, and on the extreme northwest by the Gulf of Carpentaria
*area* 1,727,200 sq km/666,699 sq mi
*capital* ◊Brisbane
*towns and cities* Toowoomba, Townsville, Cairns, Rockhampton, Bundaberg, Mackay, Ipswich, Maryborough
*features* second-largest of the Australian states; Great Dividing Range, including Mount Bartle Frere 1,622 m/5,321 ft; Great Barrier Reef (collection of coral reefs and islands about 2,000 km/1,250 mi long, off the east coast); Mount Isa mining area; Gold Coast, south of Brisbane; Sunshine Coast, north of Brisbane
*products* sugar, wheat, pineapples, beef, cotton, wool, tobacco, copper, gold, silver, lead, zinc, coal, nickel, bauxite, uranium, natural gas, oil, fish
*population* (1996) 3,368,850, concentrated in the southeast
*history* visited by Captain Cook in 1770; first settlement a penal colony at Moreton Bay in 1824; opened to free settlers in 1842; part of New South Wales from 1788 to 1859, when it became self-governing.

**quetzal** long-tailed Central American bird *Pharomachus mocinno* of the ◊trogon family, order Trogoniformes. The male is brightly coloured, with green, red, blue, and white feathers. It has a train of blue-green plumes (tail coverts) that hang far beyond the true tail feathers. There is a crest on the head and decorative drooping feathers on the wings. It is about 1.3 m/4.3 ft long including tail. The female is smaller and lacks the tail and plumage.

**Quetzalcoatl** in pre-Columbian cultures of Central America, a feathered serpent god of air and water. In his human form, he was said to have been fair-skinned and bearded and to have reigned on Earth during a golden age. He disappeared across the eastern sea, with a promise to return; the Spanish conquistador Hernán ◊Cortés exploited the myth in his own favour when he invaded. Ruins of Quetzalcoatl's temples survive in various ancient Mesoamerican ceremonial centres, including the one at Teotihuacán in Mexico. (See also ◊Aztec, ◊Mayan, and ◊Toltec civilizations.)

**Quezon City** former capital of the Philippines 1948–76, northeastern part of metropolitan ◊Manila (the present capital), on Luzon Island; population (1990) 1,166,800. It was named after the Philippines' first president, Manuel Luis Quezon (1878–1944).

**quicksilver** another name for the element ◊mercury.

**quince** small tree native to western Asia but widely cultivated elsewhere. The bitter, yellow, pear-shaped fruit is used in preserves. Flowering quinces are cultivated mainly for their attractive flowers. (*Cydonia oblonga;* flowering quince genus *Chaenomeles;* family Rosaceae.)

**quinine** antimalarial drug extracted from the bark of the cinchona tree. Peruvian Indians taught French missionaries how to use the bark in 1630, but quinine was not isolated until 1820. It is a bitter alkaloid, with the formula $C_{20}H_{24}N_2O_2$.

**Quinn, Anthony (Rudolph Oaxaca)** (1916– ) Mexican-born US actor. His roles frequently displayed volatile machismo and he often played larger-than-life characters, such as the title role in *Zorba the Greek* (1964). Other films include *Viva Zapata!* (1952) (Academy Award for best supporting actor) and Federico Fellini's *La strada* (1954).

**Quisling, Vidkun Abraham Lauritz Jonsson** (1887–1945) Norwegian politician. Leader from 1933 of the Norwegian Fascist Party, he aided the Nazi invasion of Norway 1940 by delaying mobilization and urging nonresistance. He was made premier by Hitler in 1942, and was arrested and shot as a traitor by the Norwegians in 1945. His name became a generic term for a traitor who aids an occupying force.

**Quito** industrial city, capital of Ecuador and of Pichincha province; situated on a plateau in the Andes, 22 km/14 mi south of the equator, at an altitude of 2,850 m/9,350 ft; population (1990) 1,101,000. Industries include textiles, chemicals, leather, gold, and silver. Quito lies at the foot of the volcano Pichincha (4,794 m/15,728 ft), which last erupted in 1666, in an area prone to earthquakes. It has a temperate climate all year round. The city has been declared a World Cultural Heritage Site by UNESCO.

**QwaQwa** former black homeland for South Sotho people in Orange Free State (now Free State), South Africa.

# R

**Rabat** capital and industrial port of Morocco, on the Atlantic coast, 177 km/110 mi west of Fès; population (urban area, 1991) 519,000; Rabat-Salé 1,494,000. It is situated on the Bou Regreg River, opposite Salé. Industries include textiles, asbestos, carpets, pottery, leather goods, fishing; other exports include skins, wax, cork, slippers, and beans. Founded in 1190, it is named after its original *ribat* or fortified monastery.

**rabbit** any of several genera of hopping mammals of the order Lagomorpha, which together with ◊hares constitute the family Leporidae. Rabbits differ from hares in bearing naked, helpless young and in occupying burrows.

**Rabelais, François** (*c.* 1495–1553) French satirist, monk, and physician. His name has become synonymous with bawdy humour. He was educated in the humanist tradition and was the author of satirical allegories, including a cycle known as Gargantua and Pantagruel which included *La Vie estimable du grand Gargantua, père de Pantagruel/The Inestimable Life of the Great Gargantua, Father of Pantagruel*, the first to be written, but published in 1534, two years after *Les Horribles et Épouvantables Faits et prouesses du très renommé Pantagruel/The Horrible and Dreadful Deeds and Prowess of the Very Renowned Pantagruel* (1532).

**rabies** or *hydrophobia,* (Greek 'fear of water') viral disease of the central nervous system that can afflict all warm-blooded creatures. It is caused by a lyssavirus. It is almost invariably fatal once symptoms have developed. Its transmission to humans is generally by a bite from an infected animal. Rabies continues to kill hundreds of thousands of people every year; almost all of these deaths occur in Asia, Africa, and South America.

**Rabin, Yitzhak** (1922–1995) Israeli Labour politician, prime minister from 1974–77 and 1992–95. As a former soldier, he was a national hero in the Arab-Israeli Wars. His policy of favouring Palestinian self-government in the occupied territories contributed to the success of the centre-left party in the 1992 elections. In September 1993 he signed a historic peace agreement with the Palestinian Liberation Organization (PLO), providing for a phased withdrawal of Israeli forces. He was awarded the 1994 Nobel Prize for Peace jointly with Israeli foreign minister Shimon Peres and PLO leader Yassir Arafat. He was shot and killed by a young Israeli extremist while attending a peace rally in Tel Aviv in November 1995.

**Rabuka, Sitiveni** (1948– ) Fijian soldier and politician, prime minister from 1992. When the April 1987 elections produced a new left-of-centre government, headed by Timoci Bavadra, which was determined to end discrimination against the country's ethnic Indian community, Rabuka staged two successive coups, in May and September 1987. Within months of the second coup, he stepped down, allowing a civilian government headed by Kamisese Mara to take over. In 1992 Rabuka was nominated as the new Fijian premier. He was re-elected to the post in 1994 and, after revising the constitution so as not to discriminate against the ethnic Indian community, secured Fiji's re-admission to the Commonwealth in October 1997.

**raccoon** any of several New World species of carnivorous mammals of the genus *Procyon,* in the family Procyonidae. The common raccoon *P. lotor* is about 60 cm/2 ft long, with a grey-brown body, a black-and-white ringed tail, and a black 'mask' around its eyes. The crab-eating raccoon *P. cancrivorus* of South America is slightly smaller and has shorter fur.

**race** term sometimes applied to a physically distinctive group of people, on the basis of their difference from other groups in skin colour, head shape, hair type, and physique. Formerly, anthropologists divided the human race into three hypothetical racial groups: Caucasoid, Mongoloid, and Negroid. Others postulated from 6 to 30 races. Scientific studies, however, have produced no proof of definite genetic racial divisions. Race is a cultural, political, and economic concept, not a biological one. Genetic differences do exist between populations but they do not define historical lineages, and are minimal compared to the genetic variation between individuals. Most anthropologists today, therefore, completely reject the concept of race, and social scientists tend to prefer the term 'ethnic group'.

**Rachmaninov, Sergei Vasilevich** (1873–1943) Russian composer, conductor, and pianist. After the 1917 Revolution he emigrated to the USA. His music is melodious and emotional and includes operas, such as *Francesca da Rimini* 1906, three symphonies, four piano concertos, piano pieces, and songs. Among his other works are the *Prelude in C-Sharp Minor* 1892 and *Rhapsody on a Theme of Paganini* 1934 for piano and orchestra.

**Racine, Jean Baptiste** (1639–1699) French dramatist. He was an exponent of the classical tragedy in French drama, taking his subjects from Greek mythology and observing the rules of classical Greek drama. Most of his tragedies have women in the title role, for example *Andromaque* 1667, *Iphigénie* 1674, and *Phèdre* 1677.

**racism** belief in, or set of implicit assumptions about, the superiority of one's own ◊race or ethnic group, often accompanied by prejudice against members of an ethnic group different from one's own. Racism may be used to justify ◊discrimination, verbal or physical abuse, or even genocide, as in Nazi Germany, or as practised by European settlers against American Indians in both North and South America.

**rad** unit of absorbed radiation dose, now replaced in the SI system by the ◊gray (one rad equals 0.01 gray), but still commonly used. It is defined as the dose when one kilogram of matter absorbs 0.01 joule of radiation energy (formerly, as the dose when one gram absorbs 100 ergs).

**radar** acronym for *radio direction and ranging*, device for locating objects in space, direction finding, and navigation by means of transmitted and reflected high-frequency radio waves.

**radar astronomy** bouncing of radio waves off objects in the Solar System, with reception and analysis of the 'echoes'. Radar contact with the Moon was first made in 1945 and with Venus in 1961. The travel time for radio reflections allows the distances of objects to be determined accurately. Analysis of the reflected beam reveals the rotation period and allows the object's surface to be mapped. The rotation periods of Venus and Mercury were first determined by radar. Radar maps of Venus were obtained first by Earth-based radar and subsequently by orbiting space probes.

**radian** SI unit (symbol rad) of plane angles, an alternative unit to the ◊degree. It is the angle at the centre of a circle when the centre is joined to the two ends of an arc (part of the circumference) equal in length to the radius of the circle. There are $2\pi$ (approximately 6.284) radians in a full circle (360°).

**radiation** in physics, emission of radiant ◊energy as particles or waves – for example, heat, light, alpha particles, and beta particles (see ◊electromagnetic waves and ◊radioactivity). See also ◊atomic radiation.

**radiation sickness** sickness resulting from exposure to radiation, including X-rays, gamma rays, neutrons, and other nuclear radiation, as from weapons and fallout. Such radiation ionizes atoms in the body and causes nausea, vomiting, diarrhoea, and other symptoms. The body cells themselves may be damaged even by very small doses, causing leukaemia and other cancers.

**radiation units** units of measurement for radioactivity and radiation doses. In SI units, the activity of a radioactive source is measured in becquerels (symbol Bq), where one becquerel is equal to one nuclear disintegration per second (an older unit is the curie). The exposure is measured in coulombs per kilogram ($C$ $kg^{-1}$); the amount of ionizing radiation (X-rays or gamma rays) which produces one coulomb of charge in one kilogram of dry air (replacing the roentgen). The absorbed dose of ionizing radiation is measured in grays (symbol Gy) where one gray is equal to one joule of energy being imparted to one kilogram of matter (the rad is the previously used unit). The dose equivalent, which is a measure of the effects of radiation on living organisms, is the absorbed dose multiplied by a suitable factor which depends upon the type of radiation. It is measured in sieverts (symbol Sv), where one sievert is a dose equivalent of one joule per kilogram (an older unit is the rem).

**Radical** in Britain, supporter of parliamentary reform before the Reform Bill of 1832. As a group the Radicals later became the progressive wing of the Liberal Party. During the 1860s (led by Cobden, Bright, and J S Mill) they campaigned for extension of the franchise, free trade, and ◊laissez-faire, but after 1870, under the leadership of Joseph Chamberlain and Charles Dilke, they adopted a republican and semi-socialist programme. With the growth of ◊socialism in the later 19th century, Radicalism ceased to exist as an organized movement.

**radical** in chemistry, a group of atoms forming part of a molecule, which acts as a unit and takes part in chemical reactions without disintegration, yet often cannot exist alone for any length of time; for example, the methyl radical $-CH_3$, or the carboxyl radical $-COOH$.

**radical** in politics, anyone with opinions more extreme than the main current of a country's major political party or parties. It is more often applied to those with left-wing opinions, although the radical right also exists.

**radio** transmission and reception of radio waves. In radio transmission a microphone converts sound waves (pressure variations in the air) into ◊electromagnetic waves that are then picked up by a receiving aerial and fed to a loudspeaker, which converts them back into sound waves.

**radioactive decay** process of disintegration undergone by the nuclei of radioactive elements, such as radium and various isotopes of uranium and the transuranic elements. This changes the element's atomic number, thus transmuting one element into another, and is accompanied by the emission of radiation. Alpha and beta decay are the most common forms.

**radioactivity** spontaneous alteration of the nuclei of radioactive atoms, accompanied by the emission of radiation. It is the property exhibited by the radioactive ◊isotopes of stable elements and all isotopes of radioactive elements, and can be either natural or induced. See ◊radioactive decay.

**radio astronomy** study of radio waves emitted naturally by objects in space, by means of a ◊radio telescope. Radio emission comes from hot gases (*thermal radiation*); electrons spiralling in magnetic fields (*synchrotron radiation*); and specific wavelengths (*lines*) emitted by atoms and molecules in space, such as the 21-cm/8-in line emitted by hydrogen gas.

**radiocarbon dating** or *carbon dating*, method of dating organic materials (for example, bone or wood), used in archaeology. Plants take up carbon dioxide gas from the atmosphere and incorporate it into their tissues, and some of that carbon dioxide contains the radioactive isotope of carbon, $^{14}C$ or carbon-14. As this decays

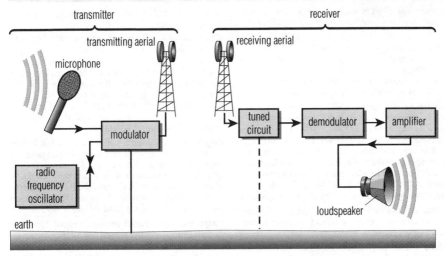

*radio* Radio transmission and reception. The radio frequency oscillator generates rapidly varying electrical signals, which are sent to the transmitting aerial. In the aerial, the signals produce radio waves (the carrier wave), which spread out at the speed of light. The sound signal is added to the carrier wave by the modulator. When the radio waves fall on the receiving aerial, they induce an electrical current in the aerial. The electrical current is sent to the tuning circuit, which picks out the signal from the particular transmitting station desired. The demodulator separates the sound signal from the carrier wave and sends it, after amplification, to the loudspeaker.

at a known rate (half of it decays every 5,730 years), the time elapsed since the plant died can be measured in a laboratory. Animals take carbon-14 into their bodies from eating plant tissues and their remains can be similarly dated. After 120,000 years, so little carbon-14 is left that no measure is possible (see ◊half-life).

**radiochemistry** chemical study of radioactive isotopes and their compounds (whether produced from naturally radioactive or irradiated materials) and their use in the study of other chemical processes.

**radio frequencies and wavelengths** see ◊electromagnetic waves.

**radio galaxy** galaxy that is a strong source of electromagnetic waves of radio wavelengths. All galaxies, including our own, emit some radio waves, but radio galaxies are up to a million times more powerful.

**radiography** branch of science concerned with the use of radiation (particularly ◊X-rays) to produce images on photographic film or fluorescent screens. X-rays penetrate matter according to its nature, density, and thickness. In doing so they can cast shadows on photographic film, producing a radiograph. Radiography is widely used in medicine for examining bones and tissues and in industry for examining solid materials; for example, to check welded seams in pipelines.

**radioisotope** contraction of *radioactive isotope*, in physics, a naturally occurring or synthetic radioactive form of an element. Most radioisotopes are made by bombarding a stable element with neutrons in the core of a nuclear

reactor (see ◊fission). The radiations given off by radioisotopes are easy to detect (hence their use as tracers), can in some instances penetrate substantial thicknesses of materials, and have profound effects (such as genetic ◊mutation) on living matter.

**radio telescope** instrument for detecting radio waves from the universe in ◊radio astronomy. Radio telescopes usually consist of a metal bowl that collects and focuses radio waves the way a concave mirror collects and focuses light waves. Radio telescopes are much larger than optical telescopes, because the wavelengths they are detecting are much longer than the wavelength of light. The largest single dish is 305 m/ 1,000 ft across, at Arecibo, Puerto Rico.

**radiotherapy** treatment of disease by ◊radiation from X-ray machines or radioactive sources. Radiation, which reduces the activity of dividing cells, is of special value for its effect on malignant tissues, certain nonmalignant tumours, and some diseases of the skin.

**radio wave** electromagnetic wave possessing a long wavelength (ranging from about $10^{-3}$ to $10^4$ m) and a low frequency (from about $10^5$ to $10^{11}$ Hz). Included in the radio-wave part of the spectrum are ◊microwaves, used for both communications and for cooking; ultra high- and very high-frequency waves, used for television and FM (◊frequency modulation) radio communications; and short, medium, and long waves, used for AM (◊amplitude modulation) radio communications. Radio waves that are used for communications have all been modulated (see ◊modulation) to carry information. Certain astronomical objects emit radio waves, which may be detected and studied using ◊radio telescopes.

**radish** annual herb native to Europe and Asia, and cultivated for its fleshy, pungent, edible root, which is usually reddish but sometimes white or black; it is eaten raw in salads. (*Raphanus sativus,* family Cruciferae.)

**radium** (Latin *radius* 'ray') white, radioactive, metallic element; symbol Ra, atomic number 88, relative atomic mass 226.02. It is one of the ◊alkaline-earth metals, found in nature in ◊pitchblende and other uranium ores. Of the 16 isotopes, the commonest, Ra-226, has a half-life of 1,620 years. The element was discovered and named in 1898 by Pierre and Marie ◊Curie, who were investigating the residues of pitchblende.

**radius** a straight line from the centre of a circle to its circumference, or from the centre to the surface of a sphere.

**radon** colourless, odourless, gaseous, radioactive, nonmetallic element; symbol Rn, atomic number 86, relative atomic mass 222. It is grouped with the ◊inert gases and was formerly considered nonreactive, but is now known to form some compounds with fluorine. Of the 20 known isotopes, only three occur in nature; the longest half-life is 3.82 days (Rn-222).

**Raffles, (Thomas) Stamford** (1781–1826) British colonial administrator, born in Jamaica. He served in the British ◊East India Company, took part in the capture of Java from the Dutch in 1811, and while governor of Sumatra (1818–23) was responsible for the acquisition and founding of Singapore in 1819. He was knighted in 1817.

**rafflesia** or *stinking corpse lily,* any of a group of parasitic plants without stems, native to Malaysia, Indonesia, and Thailand. There are 14 species, several of which are endangered by the destruction of the forests where they grow. The fruit is used locally for medicine. The largest flowers in the world are produced by *R. arnoldiana.* About 1 m/3 ft across, they exude a smell of rotting flesh, which attracts flies to pol-

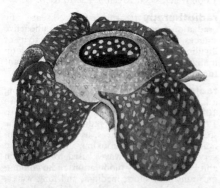

**rafflesia** *The rafflesia, or stinking corpse lily, is the largest flower of all, about 1 m/3 ft across and weighing 7 kg/15 lb. It gives off a smell of rotting meat to attract flies to pollinate it.*

linate them. (Genus *Rafflesia,* family Rafflesiaceae.)

**Rafsanjani, Hojatoleslam Ali Akbar Hashemi** (1934–   ) Iranian politician and cleric, president 1989–97. When his former teacher Ayatollah ◊Khomeini returned after the revolution of 1979–80, Rafsanjani became the speaker of the Iranian parliament and, after Khomeini's death, state president and effective political leader. He was succeeded in 1997 by Seyyed Muhammad Khatami.

**raga** (Sanskrit *rāga* 'tone' or 'colour') in Indian music, a scale of notes and style of ornament for music associated with a particular mood or time of day; the equivalent term in rhythm is *tala.* A choice of raga and tala forms the basis of improvised music; however, a written composition may also be based on (and called) a raga.

**ragtime** syncopated music ('ragged time') in 2/4 rhythm, usually played on piano. It developed in the USA among black musicians in the late 19th century; it was influenced by folk tradition, minstrel shows, and marching bands, and was later incorporated into jazz. Scott ◊Joplin was a leading writer of ragtime pieces, called 'rags'.

**ragwort** any of several European perennial plants, usually with yellow flower heads; some are poisonous. (Genus *Senecio,* family Compositae.)

**Rahman, Tunku (Prince) Abdul** (1903–1990) Malaysian politician, first prime minister of independent Malaya 1957–63 and of Malaysia 1963–70.

**rail** any wading bird of the family Rallidae, including the rails proper (genus *Rallus*), coots, moorhens, and gallinules. Rails have dark plumage, a short neck and wings, and long legs. They are 10–45 cm/4–18 in long.

**Railtrack** British company responsible for the commercial operation of the railway network in Britain. In May 1996 it was privatized, and the 20 British Rail service companies that had previously provided Railtrack's infrastructure support functions were sold into the private sector.

**railway** method of transport in which trains convey passengers and goods along a twin rail track. Following the work of British steam pioneers such as the Scottish engineer James ◊Watt, the English engineer George ◊Stephenson built the first public steam railway, from Stockton to Darlington, England, in 1825. This heralded extensive railway building in Britain, continental Europe, and North America, providing a fast and economical means of transport and communication. After World War II, steam engines were replaced by electric and diesel engines. At the same time, the growth of road building, air services, and car ownership brought to an end the supremacy of the railways.

**rainforest** dense forest usually found on or near the ◊Equator where the climate is hot and wet. Moist air brought by the converging tradewinds rises because of the heat, producing heavy rainfall. Over half of the tropical rainforests are in Central and South America, primarily the lower Amazon and the coasts of Ecuador and Columbia. The rest are in Southeast Asia (Malaysia, Indonesia, and New Guinea) and in West Africa and the Congo.

Tropical rainforest once covered 14% of the Earth's land surface, but are now being destroyed at an increasing rate as their valuable timber is harvested and the land cleared for agriculture, causing problems of ◊deforestation. Although by 1991 over 50% of the world's rainforest had been removed, they still comprise about 50% of all growing wood on the planet, and harbour at least 40% of the Earth's species (plants and animals).

**Raj, the** the period of British rule in India before independence in 1947.

**Rajasthan** state of northwest India
*area* 342,200 sq km/132,089 sq mi
*capital* ◊Jaipur
*towns* Jaisalmer, Bikaner, Ajmer, Udaipur
*physical* the larger part of the Thar Desert, where India's first nuclear test was carried out; Ranthambhor wildlife reserve, in the Southwest, formerly the private hunting ground of the maharajahs of Jaipur, with tigers, deer, antelope, wild boar, crocodiles, and sloth bears; the Aravalli hills
*industries* textiles, cement, glass, asbestos, chemicals; minerals include coal (Bikaner), salt (Sambhar salt lake), limestone, mica, zinc (smelted at Udaipur), copper, gypsum, phosphate, silver, marble
*agriculture* millet, wheat, barley; oilseed, cotton, sugar; cattle, sheep, camels in drier areas; dependant on irrigation schemes such as the Indira Gandhi and Chambal canals
*population* (1994 est) 48,040,000
*language* Rajasthani, Hindi
*religion* 90% Hindu, 3% Muslim; 12% belong to tribal groups (mainly Bhils) and have a guaranteed representation in the legislative assembly
*history* was formed in 1948 from former Rajput princely states (Rajputana); enlarged in 1956.

**Raleigh, Walter** or *Ralegh* (c. 1552–1618) English adventurer, writer, and courtier to Queen Elizabeth I. He organized expeditions to colonize North America 1584–87, all unsuccessful, and made exploratory voyages to South America 1595 and 1616. His aggressive actions against Spanish interests, including attacks on Spanish ports, brought him into conflict with the pacific James I. He was imprisoned for treason 1603–16 and executed on his return from an unsuccessful final expedition to South America. He is traditionally credited with introducing the potato to Europe and popularizing the use of tobacco.

**RAM** acronym for random-access memory, in computing, a memory device in the form of a collection of integrated circuits (chips), frequently used in microcomputers. Unlike ◊ROM (read-only memory) chips, RAM chips can be both read from and written to by the computer, but their contents are lost when the power is switched off.

**Rama** incarnation of ◊Vishnu, the supreme spirit of Hinduism. He is the hero of the epic poem the *Rāmāyana,* and regarded as an example of morality and virtue.

**Ramadan** in the Muslim ◊calendar, the ninth month of the year. Throughout Ramadan a strict fast is observed during the hours of daylight; Muslims are encouraged to read the whole Koran in commemoration of the Night of Power (which falls during the month) when, it is believed, Muhammad first received his revelations from the angel Gabriel.

**Rambert, Marie** adopted name of Cyvia Myriam Rambam (1888–1982) Polish-born British ballet dancer and teacher. One of the major innovative and influential figures in modern ballet, she worked with Vaslav Nijinsky on *The Rite of Spring* for the Diaghilev ballet in Paris 1912–13, opened the Rambert School in London in 1920, and in 1926 founded the Ballet Rambert which she directed. It became a modern dance company from 1966 and was renamed the Rambert Dance Company in 1987. Rambert became a British citizen in 1918. She was created a DBE in 1962.

**Rambert Dance Company** British modern-dance company, founded as the Ballet Rambert by Marie ◊Rambert in 1926. In 1966 she handed the direction over to her protégé Norman Morrice, who began the process of transforming the company into one more focused on new creations and modern work. Richard Alston was appointed artistic director in 1986 and changed the company name to Rambert Dance Company in 1987. The company was relaunched on an expanded scale in 1994 under the direction of Christopher Bruce, working from a more 'classical' contemporary base.

**Rameses** alternative spelling of ◊Ramses, name of kings of ancient Egypt.

**Ramos, Fidel (Eddie)** (1928– ) Filipino centre-right politician, president 1992–98. He launched a commission to consult with Muslim secessionist rebel groups on Mindanao, which produced a peace deal with one of the rebel groups in September 1996. In addition, as part of a government move to end corruption and human-rights abuses, he purged the police force. These and other initiatives won him popular support, and in the May 1995 congressional elections, with the economy booming, his supporters won a sweeping victory. However, from 1997 the economic situation deteriorated, with the peso being devalued in July 1997. Ramos was prevented by the constitution from seeking a second term in 1998, and was succeeded by the former vice president Joseph Estrada.

**Ramsay, William** (1852–1916) Scottish chemist who, with Lord Rayleigh, discovered argon in 1894. In 1895 Ramsay produced helium and in 1898, in cooperation with Morris Travers, identified neon, krypton, and xenon. In 1903, with Frederick Soddy, he noted the transmutation of radium into helium, which led to the discovery of the density and relative atomic mass of radium. He was awarded a Nobel prize in 1904 and made a KCB in 1902.

**Ramses** or *Rameses,* 11 kings (pharaohs) of ancient Egypt, including:

**Ramses II** or *Rameses II;* known as *Ramses the Great,* King (pharaoh) of ancient Egypt about 1279–1213 BC, the son of Seti I. He campaigned successfully against the Hittites, and built two rock temples at Abu Simbel in southern Egypt.

**Ramses III** or *Rameses III,* King (pharaoh) of ancient Egypt about 1187–1156 BC. He won victories over the Libyans and the ◊Sea Peoples and asserted his control over Palestine.

**Ramsey, Alf(red) Ernest** (1920–1999) English football player and manager. England's most successful manager ever, he won the 1966 World Cup. Of the 113 matches in which he was in charge of the national side between 1963 and 1974, England had 69 victories, 27 draws, and only 17 defeats. Shrewd, pragmatic, and single-minded, he was not afraid to go against traditional football wisdom, most notably in 1966 when he decided to play without wingers; a step which was greeted with widespread scepticism, but subsequently was hailed as a masterstroke when England won the World Cup. He led England to the quarter-finals of the 1970 World Cup, but was sacked four years later after the team failed to qualify for the 1974 finals.

**Rangoon** former name (to 1989) of ◊Yangon, the capital of Myanmar (Burma).

**Rao, P(amulaparti) V(enkata) Nara-simha** (1921–  ) Indian politician, prime minister 1991–96 and Congress leader 1991–96. He governed the state of Andhra Pradesh as chief minister 1971–73, and served in the cabinets of Indira and Rajiv Gandhi as minister of external affairs 1980–85 and 1988–90 and of human resources 1985–88. He took over the Congress party leadership after the assassination of Rajiv Gandhi. Elected prime minister the following month, he instituted a market-centred and outward looking reform of the economy. He survived a vote of no confidence in 1993. After Congress was defeated in national elections in May 1996, Rao resigned as prime minister and dissolved parliament. He resigned as Congress leader in September 1996 as allegations mounted over his alleged involvement in political bribery.

**rape** in law, sexual intercourse without the consent of the subject. Most cases of rape are of women by men. In Islamic law a rape accusation requires the support of four independent male witnesses.

**rape** in botany, either of two plant species of the mustard family grown for their seeds, which yield a pungent edible oil. The common turnip is a variety of *B. rapa* and the swede turnip is a variety of of *B. napus.* (*Brassica rapa* and *B. napus,* family Cruciferae.)

**Raphael Sanzio** *Raffaello Sanzio* (1483–1520) Painter and architect born in Urbino and eventually settled in Rome. He painted portraits and mythological and religious works, noted for their harmony of colour and composition. He

was active in Perugia, Florence, and (from 1508) Rome, where he painted frescoes in the Vatican. Among his best-known works are *The Marriage of the Virgin* (1504) (Brera, Milan) and the fresco *The School of Athens* (1509–11, Vatican, Rome).

**rap music** rapid, rhythmic chant over a prerecorded repetitive backing track. Rap emerged in New York in 1979 as part of the hip-hop culture, although the macho, swaggering lyrics that initially predominated have roots in ritual boasts and insults. Different styles were flourishing by the 1990s, such as jazz rap, gangsta rap, and reggae rap.

**rare-earth element** alternative name for ◊lanthanide.

**Ras el Khaimah** or *Ra's al Khaymah,* emirate on the Gulf; area 1,690 sq km/652 sq mi; population (1995) 144,400. Products include oil, pharmaceuticals, and cement. It is one of the seven members of the United Arab Emirates.

**raspberry** any of a group of prickly cane plants native to Europe, Asia, and North America, and widely cultivated. They have white flowers followed by hollow red composite fruits, which are eaten fresh as a delicacy and used for making jam and wine. (Genus *Rubus,* family Rosaceae.)

**Rasputin** Russian 'dissolute'; born Grigory Efimovich Novykh (1871–1916) Siberian Eastern Orthodox mystic. He acquired influence over the Tsarina Alexandra, wife of ◊Nicholas II, and was able to make political and ecclesiastical appointments. His abuse of power and notorious debauchery (reputedly including the tsarina) led to his murder by a group of nobles.

**Rastafarianism** religion originating in the West Indies, based on the ideas of Marcus ◊Garvey, who called on black people to return to Africa and set up a black-governed country there. When Haile Selassie (*Ras Tafari,* 'Lion of Judah') was crowned emperor of Ethiopia 1930, this was seen as a fulfilment of prophecy and some Rastafarians acknowledged him as an incarnation of God (*Jah*), others as a prophet. The use of ganja (marijuana) is a sacrament. There are no churches. There were about 1 million Rastafarians by 1990.

**rat** any of numerous long-tailed ◊rodents (especially of the families Muridae and Cricetidae) larger than mice and usually with scaly, naked tails. The genus *Rattus* in the family Muridae includes the rats found in human housing.

**rate of reaction** the speed at which a chemical reaction proceeds. It is usually expressed in terms of the concentration (usually in ◊moles per litre) of a reactant consumed, or product formed, in unit time; so the units would be moles per litre per second (mol $l^{-1}$ $s^{-1}$). The rate of a reaction may be affected by the concentration of the reactants, the temperature of the reactants (or the amount of light in the case of a photochemical reaction), and the presence of a ◊catalyst. If the reaction is entirely in the gas

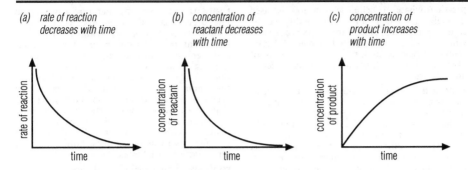

(a) *rate of reaction decreases with time*

(b) *concentration of reactant decreases with time*

(c) *concentration of product increases with time*

**rate of reaction** *The rate of reaction decreases with time whilst the concentration of product increases.*

state, the rate is affected by pressure, and, where one of the reactants is a solid, it is affected by the particle size.

**rates** in the UK, a local government tax levied on industrial and commercial property (business rates) and, until the introduction of the community charge (see ◊poll tax) 1989–90, also on residential property to pay for local amenities such as roads, footpaths, refuse collection and disposal, and community and welfare activities. The water companies also use a rating system to charge most householders for water supply.

**ratio** measure of the relative size of two quantities or of two measurements (in similar units), expressed as a proportion. For example, the ratio of vowels to consonants in the alphabet is 5:21; the ratio of 500 m to 2 km is 500:2,000, or 1:4. Ratios are normally expressed as whole numbers, so 2:3.5 would become 4:7 (the ratio remains the same provided both numbers are multiplied or divided by the same number).

**rationalism** in theology, the belief that human reason rather than divine revelation is the correct means of ascertaining truth and regulating behaviour. In philosophy, rationalism takes the view that self-evident a priori propositions (deduced by reason alone) are the sole basis of all knowledge. It is usually contrasted with ◊empiricism, which argues that all knowledge must ultimately be derived from the senses.

**rattlesnake** any of various New World pit ◊vipers of the genera *Crotalus* and *Sistrurus* (the massasaugas and pygmy rattlers), distinguished by horny flat segments of the tail, which rattle when vibrated as a warning to attackers. They can grow to 2.5 m/8 ft long. The venom injected by some rattlesnakes can be fatal.

**Rauschenberg, Robert** born Milton Rauschenberg (1925– ), US Pop artist. He has created happenings and multimedia works, called 'combined painting', such as *Monogram* 1959 (Moderna Museet, Stockholm), a stuffed goat daubed with paint and wearing a car tyre around its body. In the 1960s he returned to painting and used the silk-screen printing process to transfer images to canvas.

**Ravel, (Joseph) Maurice** (1875–1937) French composer and pianist. His work is characterized by its sensuousness, exotic harmonics, and dazzling orchestral effects. His opera *L'enfant et les sortilèges* 1924 illustrates most of the various styles which influenced him at different times. Other works include the piano pieces *Pavane pour une infante défunte/Pavane for a Dead Infanta* 1899 and *Jeux d'eau/ Waterfall* 1901, and the ballets *Daphnis et Chloë* 1912 and *Boléro* 1928.

**raven** any of several large ◊crows, genus *Corvus*, of the Corvidae family, order Passeriformes. The common raven *C. corax* is about 60 cm/2 ft long with a wingspan of nearly 1 m/3 ft, and has black, lustrous plumage; the beak and mouth, tongue, legs, and feet are also black. It is a scavenger, and is found only in the northern hemisphere.

**Rawalpindi** city in Punjab province, Pakistan, on the north bank of the River Leh, 175 km/110 mi southeast of Peshawar in the foothills of the Himalayas; population (1981) 928,400. Industries include oil refining, iron, chemicals, locomotives and furniture. A former military station, it is strategically positioned on the route into Kashmir; it was capital of Pakistan 1959–67 during the construction of ◊Islamabad.

**ray** any of several orders (especially Ragiformes) of cartilaginous fishes with a flattened body, winglike pectoral fins, and a whiplike tail.

**Ray, Man** adopted name of Emmanuel Rabinovich Rudnitsky (1890–1976) US photographer, painter, and sculptor. He was active mainly in France and was associated with the ◊Dada movement and then ◊Surrealism. One of his best-known sculptures is *Gift* 1921, a Surrealist ready-made consisting of an iron on to which a row of nails has been glued.

**Ray, Satyajit** (1921–1992) Indian film director. He became internationally known with his trilogy of life in his native Bengal: *Pather Panchali, Unvanquished,* and *The World of Apu* 1955–59. Later films include *The Music Room* 1963, *Charulata* 1964, *The Chess Players* 1977, and *The Home and the World* 1984.

**rayon** any of various shiny textile fibres and fabrics made from ◊cellulose. It is produced by pressing whatever cellulose solution is used through very small holes and solidifying the resulting filaments. A common type is ◊viscose, which consists of regenerated filaments of pure cellulose. Acetate and triacetate are kinds of rayon consisting of filaments of cellulose acetate and triacetate.

**reaction** in chemistry, the coming together of two or more atoms, ions, or molecules with the result that a chemical change takes place; that is, a change that occurs when two or more substances interact with each other, resulting in the production of different substances with different chemical compositions. The nature of the reaction is portrayed by a ◊chemical equation.

**Reading** industrial town and unitary authority in southern England, on the River Thames where it meets the Kennet, 61 km/38 mi west of London; it was the administrative headquarters of the county of Berkshire until April 1998
*area* 37 sq km/14 sq mi
*features* remains of a 12th-century Benedictine abbey where Henry I is buried; the Museum of Reading includes Roman and Saxon relics, and a full-size Victorian reproduction of the Bayeaux Tapestry; the Museum of English Rural Life is also here; Reading hosts an annual pop festival
*industries* biscuits, brewing, boats, engineering, printing, and electronics; it is an agricultural and horticultural centre with seed-testing grounds, and is a major bulb producer
*population* (1996) 131,000
*famous people* William Laud, archbishop of Canterbury from 1633; the writer Oscar Wilde spent two years in Reading jail (1895–97)
*history* Reading was a Danish encampment in 871. By the time of the Domesday survey of 1086, 'Radynges', as it was then known, had 30 religious houses. The Benedictine abbey was founded in 1121 and consecrated in 1164. In the 16th century the town was important in the cloth industry. The university was established in 1892 as a college affiliated to the University of Oxford and gained independent university status in 1926. The city was extensively rebuilt after World War II.

**Reagan, Ronald (Wilson)** (1911–   ) 40th president of the USA 1981–89, a Republican. He was governor of California 1966–74, and a former Hollywood actor. Reagan was a hawkish and popular president. He adopted an aggressive policy in Central America, attempting to overthrow the government of Nicaragua, and invading Grenada in 1983. In 1987, ◊Irangate was investigated by the Tower Commission; Reagan admitted that USA–Iran negotiations had become an 'arms for hostages deal', but denied knowledge of resultant funds being illegally sent to the Contra guerrillas in Nicaragua. He increased military spending (sending the national budget deficit to record levels), cut social programmes, introduced the deregulation of domestic markets, and cut taxes. His ◊Strategic Defense Initiative, announced 1983, proved controversial owing to the cost and unfeasibility. He was succeeded by Vice President George Bush.

**realism** in the arts and literature generally, an unadorned, naturalistic approach to subject matter. More specifically, *Realism* refers to a movement in mid-19th-century European art and literature, a reaction against Romantic and Classical idealization and a rejection of conventional academic themes (such as mythology, history, and sublime landscapes) in favour of everyday life and carefully observed social settings. The movement was particularly important in France, where it had political overtones; the painters Gustave ◊Courbet and Honoré Daumier, two leading Realists, both used their art to expose social injustice.

**realism** in philosophy, the theory that universals (properties such as 'redness') have an existence independent of the human mind. Realists hold that the essence of things is objectively given in nature, and that our classifications are not arbitrary. As such, realism is contrasted with nominalism, the theory that universals are merely names or general terms.

**real number** in mathematics, any of the rational numbers (which include the integers) or irrational numbers. Real numbers exclude ◊imaginary numbers, found in ◊complex numbers of the general form $a + bi$ where $i = \sqrt{-1}$, although these do include a real component $a$.

**real-time system** in computing, a program that responds to events in the world as they happen. For example, an automatic-pilot program in an aircraft must respond instantly in order to correct deviations from its course. Process control, robotics, games, and many military applications are other examples of real-time systems.

**receiver** in law, a person appointed by a court to collect and manage the assets of an individual, company, or partnership in serious financial difficulties. In the case of bankruptcy, the assets may be sold and distributed by a receiver to creditors.

**receptacle** the enlarged end of a flower stalk to which the floral parts are attached. Normally the receptacle is rounded, but in some plants it is flattened or cup-shaped. The term is also used for the region on that part of some seaweeds which becomes swollen at certain times of the year and bears the reproductive organs.

**recession** in economics, a fall in business activity lasting more than a few months, causing stagnation in a country's output.

**recessive gene** in genetics, an ◊allele (alternative form of a gene) that will show in the ◊phenotype (observed characteristics of an organism) only if its partner allele on the paired chromosome is similarly recessive. Such an allele will not show if its partner is dominant, that is if the organism is heterozygous for a particular characteristic. Alleles for blue eyes in humans, and for shortness in pea plants are recessive. Most mutant alleles are recessive and therefore are only rarely expressed (see ◊haemophilia and ◊sickle-cell disease).

**reciprocal** in mathematics, the result of dividing a given quantity into 1. Thus the reciprocal of 2 is 1/2; of 2/3 is 3/2; of $x^2$ is $1/x^2$ or $x^{-2}$.

Reciprocals are used to replace division by multiplication, since multiplying by the reciprocal of a number is the same as dividing by that number.

**recombination** in genetics, any process that recombines, or 'shuffles', the genetic material, thus increasing genetic variation in the offspring. The two main processes of recombination both occur during meiosis (reduction division of cells). One is *crossing over,* in which chromosome pairs exchange segments; the other is the random reassortment of chromosomes that occurs when each gamete (sperm or egg) receives only one of each chromosome pair.

**Reconstruction** in US history, the period 1865–77 after the Civil War during which the nation was reunited under the federal government after the defeat of the Southern Confederacy.

**recorder** any of a widespread range of woodwind instruments of the whistle type which flourished in consort ensembles in the Renaissance and Baroque eras, along with viol consorts, as an instrumental medium for polyphonic music. Unlike the flute, the recorder is held vertically and blown into through a mouthpiece in which the air is diverted by an obstructive block called the 'fipple' and produces a milder tone than that of the flute. A modern consort may include a sopranino in F5, soprano (descant) in C4, alto (treble) in F3, tenor in C3, bass in F2, and great bass in C2.

**record player** device for reproducing recorded sound stored as a spiral groove on a vinyl disc. A motor-driven turntable rotates the record at a constant speed, and a stylus or needle on the head of a pick-up is made to vibrate by the undulations in the record groove. These vibrations are then converted to electrical signals by a ◊transducer in the head (often a ◊piezoelectric crystal). After amplification, the signals pass to one or more loudspeakers, which convert them into sound. Alternative formats are ◊compact disc and magnetic ◊tape recording.

**rectangle** quadrilateral (four-sided plane figure) with opposite sides equal and parallel and with each interior angle a right angle (90°). Its area $A$ is the product of the length $l$ and height $h$; that is, $A = l \times h$. A rectangle with all four sides equal is a square.

**rectifier** in electrical engineering, a device used for obtaining one-directional current (DC) from an alternating source of supply (AC). (The process is necessary because almost all electrical power is generated, transmitted, and supplied as alternating current, but many devices, from television sets to electric motors, require direct current.) Types include plate rectifiers, thermionic ◊diodes, and ◊semiconductor diodes.

**recycling** processing of industrial and household waste (such as paper, glass, and some metals and plastics) so that the materials can be reused. This saves expenditure on scarce raw materials, slows down the depletion of nonrenewable resources, and helps to reduce pollution. Aluminium is frequently recycled because

of its value and special properties that allow it to be melted down and re-pressed without loss of quality, unlike paper and glass, which deteriorate when recycled.

**red blood cell** or *erythrocyte,* the most common type of blood cell, responsible for transporting oxygen around the body. It contains haemoglobin, which combines with oxygen from the lungs to form oxyhaemoglobin. When transported to the tissues, these cells are able to release the oxygen because the oxyhaemoglobin splits into its original constituents.

**Redcar and Cleveland** unitary authority in northeast England created in 1996 from part of the former county of Cleveland
*area* 240 sq km/93 sq mi
*towns and cities* Redcar (administrative headquarters), Skelton, Guisborough, Marske-by-the-Sea, Saltburn-by-the-Sea, Brotton, Loftus
*features* North Sea coast; River Tees forms northwest border; Boulby Cliffs are highest cliffs on England's east coast (203 m/666 ft); 12th-century Priory at Guisborough; Cleveland Way long-distance path reaches coast at Saltburn; RNLI Zetland Lifeboat Museum (Redcar); Ironstone Mining Museum (Saltburn-by-the-Sea)
*industries* manufacture of steel products (British Steel), engineering, fertilizers and potash products, textiles
*population* (1996) 144,000.

**Red Cross** International Federation of the Red Cross, international relief agency founded by the Geneva Convention in 1863 at the instigation of the Swiss doctor Henri Dunant to assist the wounded and prisoners in war. Its symbol is a symmetrical red cross on a white ground. In addition to dealing with associated problems of war, such as refugees and the care of the disabled, the Red Cross is concerned with victims of natural disasters – floods, earthquakes, epidemics, and accidents. It was awarded the Nobel Peace Prize in 1917 and 1944.

**red deer** large deer widely distributed throughout Europe, Asia and North Africa. A full-grown male (stag or hart) stands 1.2 m/4 ft at the withers, and typical antlers measure about 80 cm/31 in in length with a spread of about the same. During the breeding season the colour is a rich brown, turning grey at the approach of winter. The young are spotted with white.

**red dwarf** any star that is cool, faint, and small (about one-tenth the mass and diameter of the Sun). Red dwarfs burn slowly, and have estimated lifetimes of 100 billion years. They may be the most abundant type of star, but are difficult to see because they are so faint. Two of the closest stars to the Sun, ◊Proxima Centauri and Barnard's Star, are red dwarfs.

**Redford, (Charles) Robert** (1937– ) US actor and film director. His blond good looks and versatility earned him his first starring role in *Barefoot in the Park* (1967), followed by *Butch Cassidy and the Sundance Kid* (1969) and *The Sting* (1973), both with Paul Newman.

**red giant** any large bright star with a cool surface. It is thought to represent a late stage in the evolution of a star like the Sun, as it runs out of hydrogen fuel at its centre and begins to burn heavier elements, such as helium, carbon, and silicon. Because of more complex nuclear reactions that then occur in the red giant's interior, it eventually becomes gravitationally unstable and begins to collapse and heat up. The result is either explosion of the star as a ◊supernova, leaving behind a ◊neutron star, or loss of mass by more gradual means to produce a ◊white dwarf.

**Redgrave, Michael (Scudamore)** (1908–1985) English actor. His stage roles included Hamlet and Lear (Shakespeare), Uncle Vanya (Chekhov), and the schoolmaster in Terence Rattigan's *The Browning Version* (filmed 1951). On screen he appeared in *The Lady Vanishes* (1938), *The Importance of Being Earnest* (1952), and *Goodbye Mr Chips* (1969). He was knighted in 1959.

**Redgrave, Steven Geoffrey** (1962– ) English oarsman, gold medallist at four successive Olympics, winning the coxed fours in 1984, the coxless pairs in 1988 and 1992, and the coxless fours in 1996. He also won nine gold medals at the World Championships 1986–99, a gold at the World Indoor Championships in 1991, and was a member of the winning four-man bobsleigh team at the national bobsleigh championships in 1989.
*career highlights*
**Olympic Games** gold coxed fours 1984, 1988, 1992, 1996 (coxless pairs)
**World Championships** gold 1986 (coxed pairs), 1987, 1991, 1993, 1994, 1995 (coxless pairs), 1997, 1998, 1999 (coxless fours)

**Redgrave, Vanessa** (1937– ) English actress. She has played Shakespeare's Lady Macbeth and Cleopatra on the stage, Ellida in Ibsen's *Lady From the Sea* (1976 and 1979), and Olga in Chekhov's *Three Sisters* (1990). She won an Academy Award for best supporting actress for the title role in the film *Julia* (1976); other films include *Wetherby* (1985), *Howards End* (1992), *Mother's Boys* (1994), *The House of the Spirits* (1993), and *A Month by the Lake* (1995). She is active in left-wing politics.

**red-hot poker** any of a group of perennial plants native to Africa, in particular *K. uvaria*, with a flame-coloured spike of flowers. (Genus *Kniphofia*, family Liliaceae.)

**Red Sea** branch of the Indian Ocean, formed from a submerged section of the Great ◊Rift Valley, extending northwest from the Gulf of Aden. It is 2,000 km/1,200 mi long and up to 320 km/200 mi wide, reaching depths of over 2,300 m/7,545 ft. Egypt, Sudan, Ethiopia, and Eritrea (in Africa) and Saudi Arabia (Asia) are on its shores. At its northern end, it divides into the gulfs of Suez and Aqaba, separated by the Sinai peninsula.

**red shift** in astronomy, the lengthening of the wavelengths of light from an object as a result of the object's motion away from us. It is an example of the ◊Doppler effect. The red shift in light from galaxies is evidence that the universe is expanding.

**redstart** any bird of the genus *Phoenicurus*, a member of the thrush family Muscicapidae, order Passeriformes. It winters in Africa and spends the summer in Eurasia. The *American redstart Setophaga ruticulla* belongs to the family Parulidae.

**reduction** in chemistry, the gain of electrons, loss of oxygen, or gain of hydrogen by an atom, ion, or molecule during a chemical reaction.

**redwood** giant coniferous tree, one of the two types of ◊sequoia.

**reed** any of various perennial tall, slender grasses found growing in wet or marshy environments; also the hollow, jointed stalks of any

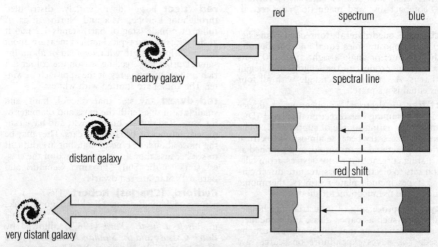

**red shift** *The red shift causes lines in the spectra of galaxies to be shifted towards the red end of the spectrum. More distant galaxies have greater red shifts than closer galaxies. The red shift indicates that distant galaxies are moving apart rapidly, as the universe expands.*

of these plants. The common reed (*P. australis*) reaches a height of 3 m/10 ft, having stiff, upright leaves and straight stems with a plume of purplish flowers at the top. (Especially species of the genera *Phragmites* and *Arundo*, family Gramineae.)

**Reed, Lou (Louis Firbank)** (1942– ) US rock singer, songwriter, and guitarist. He was a member (1965–70 and 1993) of the New York avant-garde group the Velvet Underground, perhaps the most influential band of the period. His solo work deals largely with urban alienation and angst, and includes the albums *Berlin* (1973), *Street Hassle* (1978), and *New York* (1989). His best-known recording is 'Walk on the Wild Side' from the album *Transformer* (1972).

**referendum** procedure whereby a decision on proposed legislation is referred to the electorate for settlement by direct vote of all the people. It is most frequently employed in Switzerland, the first country to use it, but has become increasingly widespread.

**refining** any process that purifies or converts something into a more useful form. Metals usually need refining after they have been extracted from their ores by such processes as ◊smelting. Petroleum, or crude oil, needs refining before it can be used; the process involves fractional distillation, the separation of the substance into separate components or 'fractions'.

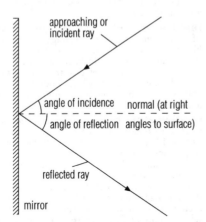

**reflection** *The law of reflection: the angle of incidence of a light beam equals the angle of reflection of the beam.*

**reflection** the throwing back or deflection of waves, such as ◊light or sound waves, when they hit a surface. The *law of reflection* states that the angle of incidence (the angle between the ray and a perpendicular line drawn to the surface) is equal to the angle of reflection (the angle between the reflected ray and a perpendicular to the surface).

**reflex** in animals, a very rapid involuntary response to a particular stimulus. It is controlled by the ◊nervous system. A reflex involves only a few nerve cells, unlike the slower but more complex responses produced by the many processing nerve cells of the brain.

**reflex camera** camera that uses a mirror and prisms to reflect light passing through the lens into the viewfinder, showing the photographer the exact scene that is being shot. When the shutter button is released the mirror springs out of the way, allowing light to reach the film. The most common type is the single-lens reflex (◊SLR) camera. The twin-lens reflex (TLR) camera has two lenses: one has a mirror for viewing, the other is used for exposing the film.

**reflexology** in alternative medicine, manipulation and massage of the feet to ascertain and treat disease or dysfunction elsewhere in the body.

**Reform Acts** in the UK, acts of Parliament in 1832, 1867, and 1884 that extended voting rights and redistributed parliamentary seats; also known as ◊Representation of the People Acts.

**Reformation** religious and political movement in 16th-century Europe to reform the Roman Catholic Church, which led to the establishment of Protestant churches. Anticipated from the 12th century by the Waldenses, Lollards, and Hussites, it was set off by German priest Martin ◊Luther in 1517, and became effective when the absolute monarchies gave it support by challenging the political power of the papacy and confiscating church wealth.

**refraction** the bending of a wave when it passes from one medium into another. It is the effect of the different speeds of wave propagation in two substances that have different densities. The amount of refraction depends on the densities of the media, the angle at which the wave strikes the surface of the second medium, and the amount of bending and change of velocity corresponding to the wave's frequency (dispersion). Refraction occurs with all types of progressive waves – ◊electromagnetic waves,

**refraction** *Refraction is the bending of a light beam when it passes from one transparent medium to another. This is why a spoon appears bent when standing in a glass of water and pools of water appear shallower than they really are. The quantity sini/sin r has a constant value, for each material, called the refractive index.*

sound waves, and water waves – and differs from ◊reflection, which involves no change in velocity.

**refractory** (of a material) able to resist high temperature, for example ◊ceramics made from clay, minerals, or other earthy materials. Furnaces are lined with refractory materials such as silica and dolomite.

**refrigeration** use of technology to transfer heat from cold to warm, against the normal temperature gradient, so that a body can remain substantially colder than its surroundings. Refrigeration equipment is used for the chilling and deep-freezing of food in food technology, and in air conditioners and industrial processes.

**refugee** according to international law, a person fleeing from oppressive or dangerous conditions (such as political, religious, or military persecution) and seeking refuge in a foreign country. In 1995 there were an estimated 27 million refugees worldwide; their resettlement and welfare is the responsibility of the United Nations High Commission for Refugees (UNHCR). An estimated average of 10,000 people a day become refugees. Women and children make up 75% of all refugees and displaced persons. Many more millions are 'economic' or 'environmental' refugees, forced to emigrate because of economic circumstances, lack of access to land, or environmental disasters.

**Regency** in Britain, the years 1811–20 during which ◊George IV (then Prince of Wales) acted as regent for his father ◊George III, who was finally declared insane and unfit to govern in December 1810. The Regency was marked by the Prince Regent's turbulent private life, his dissolute public image, and the fashionable society he patronized.

**Regency style** style of architecture and interior furnishings popular in England during the late 18th and early 19th centuries. It is characterized by restrained simplicity and the imitation of ancient classical elements, often Greek.

**regeneration** in biology, regrowth of a new organ or tissue after the loss or removal of the original. It is common in plants, where a new individual can often be produced from a 'cutting' of the original. In animals, regeneration of major structures is limited to lower organisms; certain lizards can regrow their tails if these are lost, and new flatworms can grow from a tiny fragment of an old one. In mammals, regeneration is limited to the repair of tissue in wound healing and the regrowth of peripheral nerves following damage.

**reggae** predominant form of West Indian popular music of the 1970s and 1980s, characterized by a heavily accented offbeat and a thick bass line. The lyrics often refer to ◊Rastafarianism.

Musicians include Bob Marley, Lee 'Scratch' Perry (1940–  , performer and producer), and the group Black Uhuru (1974–  ). Reggae is also played in the UK, South Africa, and elsewhere.

**Reich, Steve** (1936–  ) US composer. His Minimalist music employs simple patterns carefully superimposed and modified to highlight constantly changing melodies and rhythms; examples are *Phase Patterns* for four electronic organs 1970, *Music for Mallet Instruments, Voices, and Organ* 1973, and *Music for Percussion and Keyboards* 1984.

**Reims** English *Rheims*, city in the *département* of Marne, and largest commercial centre of the ◊Champagne-Ardenne region, France, situated 130 km/80 mi northeast of Paris on the right bank of the River Vesle, a tributary of the Aisne; population (1990) 185,200, conurbation 206,000. From 987 all but six French kings were crowned here. The western facade of its cathedral, Notre Dame, is one of the masterpieces of the Middle Ages. In World War II the German High Command formally surrendered here to US general Eisenhower on 7 May 1945. Reims is the centre of the ◊champagne trade, and has textile, chemical, mechanical, metallurgical, and foodstuff manufactures.

**reincarnation** or *transmigration* or *metempsychosis,* belief that after death the human soul or the spirit of a plant or animal may live again in another human or animal. It is part of the teachings of many religions and philosophies; for example, ancient Egyptian and Greek (the philosophies of Pythagoras and Plato), Buddhism, Hinduism, Jainism, Sikhism, certain Christian heresies (such as the Cathars), and theosophy.

**reindeer** or *caribou,* deer *Rangifer tarandus* of Arctic and subarctic regions, common to North America and Eurasia. About 1.2 m/4 ft at the shoulder, it has a thick, brownish coat and broad hooves well adapted to travel over snow. It is the only deer in which both sexes have antlers; these can grow to 1.5 m/5 ft long, and are shed in winter.

**relative atomic mass** the mass of an atom relative to one-twelfth the mass of an atom of carbon-12. It depends primarily on the number of protons and neutrons in the atom, the electrons having negligible mass. If more than one ◊isotope of the element is present, the relative atomic mass is calculated by taking an average that takes account of the relative proportions of each isotope, resulting in values that are not whole numbers. The term *atomic weight,* although commonly used, is strictly speaking incorrect.

**relativism** philosophical position that denies the possibility of objective truth independent of some specific social or historical context or conceptual framework.

**relativity** in physics, the theory of the relative rather than absolute character of motion and mass, and the interdependence of matter, time, and space, as developed by German-born US physicist Albert ◊Einstein in two phases:
*special theory of relativity* (1905) Starting with the premises that (1) the laws of nature are the same for all observers in unaccelerated motion, and (2) the speed of light is independent

of the motion of its source, Einstein arrived at some rather unexpected consequences. Intuitively familiar concepts, like mass, length, and time, had to be modified. For example, an object moving rapidly past the observer will appear to be both shorter and heavier than when it is at rest (that is, at rest relative to the observer), and a clock moving rapidly past the observer will appear to be running slower than when it is at rest. These predictions of relativity theory seem to be foreign to everyday experience merely because the changes are quite negligible at speeds less than about 1,500 km s$^{-1}$, and they only become appreciable at speeds approaching the speed of light.

**general theory of relativity** (1915) The geometrical properties of space-time were to be conceived as modified locally by the presence of a body with mass. A planet's orbit around the Sun (as observed in three-dimensional space) arises from its natural trajectory in modified space-time; there is no need to invoke, as Isaac ◊Newton did, a force of ◊gravity coming from the Sun and acting on the planet. Einstein's general theory accounts for a peculiarity in the behaviour of the motion of the perihelion of the orbit of the planet Mercury that cannot be explained in Newton's theory. The new theory also said that light rays should bend when they pass by a massive object. The predicted bending of starlight was observed during the eclipse of the Sun 1919. A third corroboration is found in the shift towards the red in the spectra of the Sun and, in particular, of stars of great density – white dwarfs such as the companion of Sirius.

**relay** in electrical engineering, an electromagnetic switch. A small current passing through a coil of wire wound around an iron core attracts an ◊armature whose movement closes a pair of sprung contacts to complete a secondary circuit, which may carry a large current or activate other devices. The solid-state equivalent is a thyristor switching device.

**relief** in sculpture, particularly architectural sculpture, carved figures and other forms that project from the background. The Italian terms *basso-rilievo* (low relief), *mezzo-rilievo* (middle relief), and *alto-rilievo* (high relief) are used according to the extent to which the sculpture projects. The French term *bas-relief* is commonly used to mean low relief.

**religion** (Latin *religare* 'to bind'; bond of humans to God) code of belief or philosophy that often involves the worship of a ◊God or gods. Belief in a supernatural power is not essential (absent in, for example, Buddhism and Confucianism), but faithful adherence is usually considered to be rewarded; for example, by escape from human existence (Buddhism), by a future existence (Christianity, Islam), or by worldly benefit (Sōka Gakkai Buddhism). Religions include:

*ancient and pantheist* religions of Babylonia, Assyria, Egypt, Greece, and Rome;

*animist or polytheistic* traditional central African religions, voodoo and related beliefs in Latin America and the Caribbean, traditional faiths of American Indians, Maoris, Australian Aborigines, and Javanese;

*oriental* Hinduism, Buddhism, Jainism, Zoroastrianism, Confucianism, Taoism, and Shinto;

*'religions of a book'* Judaism, Christianity (the principal divisions are Roman Catholic, Eastern Orthodox, and Protestant), and Islam (the principal divisions are Sunni and Shiite);

*combined derivation* these include Baha'ism, the Unification church, and Mormonism.

**rem** acronym of *roentgen equivalent man,* unit of radiation dose equivalent.

**remand** in law, the committing of an accused but not convicted person into custody or to release on bail pending a court hearing.

**Rembrandt, Harmensz van Rijn** (1606–1669) Dutch painter and etcher. He was one of the most prolific and significant artists in Europe of the 17th century. Between 1629 and 1669 he painted about 60 penetrating self-portraits. He also painted religious subjects, and produced about 300 etchings and over 1,000 drawings. His major group portraits include *The Anatomy Lesson of Dr Tulp* 1632 (Mauritshuis, The Hague) and *The Night Watch* 1642 (Rijksmuseum, Amsterdam).

**Remington, Philo** (1816–1889) US inventor and businessman. He designed the breech-loading rifle that bears his name. He began manufacturing typewriters in 1873, using the patent of Christopher Sholes, and made improvements that resulted five years later in the first machine with a shift key, thus providing lower-case letters as well as capital letters.

**remora** any of a family of warm-water fishes that have an adhesive disc on the head, by which they attach themselves to whales, sharks, and turtles. These provide the remora with shelter and transport, as well as food in the form of parasites on the host's skin.

**remote sensing** gathering and recording information from a distance. Space probes have sent back photographs and data about planets as distant as Neptune. In archaeology, surface survey techniques provide information without disturbing subsurface deposits.

**REM sleep** acronym for *rapid-eye-movement* sleep, phase of sleep that recurs several times nightly in humans and is associated with dreaming. The eyes flicker quickly beneath closed lids.

**Renaissance** or *Revival of Learning,* period in European cultural history that began in Italy around 1400 and lasted there until the end of the 1500s. Elsewhere in Europe it began later, and lasted until the 1600s. One characteristic of the Renaissance was the rediscovery of classical literature, led by the writers Giovanni ◊Boccaccio and Francesco ◊Petrarch. A central theme of the Renaissance was ◊humanism, the belief in the active rather than the contemplative life, and a faith in the republican ideal. The greatest expression of the Renaissance was in the arts and learning. The term 'Renaissance' (French for 'rebirth') to describe this period of cultural history was invented by historians in the 1800s.

**René, France-Albert** (1935– ) the Seychelles left-wing politician. He became the country's first prime minister after independence, and president from 1977 after a coup. He followed a non-nuclear policy of nonalignment. In 1993 René and his party, the People's Progressive Front, won the country's first free elections in 16 years.

**renewable energy** power from any source that replenishes itself. Most renewable systems rely on ◊solar energy directly or through the weather cycle as ◊wave power, ◊hydroelectric power, or wind power via ◊wind turbines, or solar energy collected by plants (alcohol fuels, for example). In addition, the gravitational force of the Moon can be harnessed through tidal power stations, and the heat trapped in the centre of the Earth is used via ◊geothermal energy systems.

**renewable resource** natural resource that is replaced by natural processes in a reasonable amount of time. Soil, water, forests, plants, and animals are all renewable resources as long as they are properly conserved. Solar, wind, wave, and geothermal energies are based on renewable resources.

**rennet** extract, traditionally obtained from a calf's stomach, that contains the enzyme rennin, used to coagulate milk in the cheesemaking process. The enzyme can now be chemically produced.

**Renoir, Jean** (1894–1979) French film director. His films, characterized by their humanism and naturalistic technique, include *Boudu sauvé des eaux/Boudu Saved from Drowning* 1932, *La Grande Illusion* 1937, and *La Règle du jeu/The Rules of the Game* 1939.

**Renoir, Pierre-Auguste** (1841–1919) French Impressionist painter. He met Claude ◊Monet and Alfred Sisley in the early 1860s, and together they formed the nucleus of ◊Impressionism. He developed a lively, colourful painting style with feathery brushwork (known as his 'rainbow style') and painted many scenes of everyday life, such as *The Luncheon of the Boating Party* 1881 (Phillips Collection, Washington, DC), and also female nudes, such as *The Bathers* about 1884–87 (Philadelphia Museum of Art).

**repetitive strain injury** (RSI), inflammation of tendon sheaths, mainly in the hands and wrists, which may be disabling. It is found predominantly in factory workers involved in constant repetitive movements, and in those who work with computer keyboards. The symptoms include aching muscles, weak wrists, tingling fingers and in severe cases, pain and paralysis. Some victims have successfully sued their employers for damages. In 1999 RSI affected more than a million people annually in Britain and the USA.

**replication** in biology, production of copies of the genetic material DNA; it occurs during cell division (◊mitosis and ◊meiosis). Most mutations are caused by mistakes during replication.

**Representation of the People Acts** series of UK acts of Parliament from 1867 that extended voting rights, creating universal suffrage in 1928. The 1867 and 1884 acts are known as the second and third ◊Reform Acts.

**repression** in psychology, a mental process that ejects and excludes from consciousness ideas, impulses, or memories that would otherwise threaten emotional stability.

**reproduction** in biology, the process by which a living organism produces other organisms more or less similar to itself. The ways in which species reproduce differ, but the two main methods are by ◊asexual reproduction and ◊sexual reproduction. Asexual reproduction involves only one parent without the formation of ◊gametes: the parent's cells divide by ◊mitosis to produce new cells with the same number and kind of ◊chromosomes as its own. Thus offspring produced asexually are clones of the parent and there is no variation. Sexual reproduction involves two parents, one male and one female. The parents' sex cells divide by ◊meiosis, producing gametes, which contain only half the number of chromosomes of the parent cell. In this way, when two sets of chromosomes combine during ◊fertilization, a new combination of genes is produced. Hence the new organism will differ from both parents, and variation is introduced. The ability to reproduce is considered one of the fundamental attributes of living things.

**reptile** any member of a class (Reptilia) of vertebrates. Unlike amphibians, reptiles have hard-shelled, yolk-filled eggs that are laid on land and from which fully formed young are born. Some snakes and lizards retain their eggs and give birth to live young. Reptiles are cold-blooded, and their skin is usually covered with scales. The metabolism is slow, and in some cases (certain large snakes) intervals between meals may be months. Reptiles date back over 300 million years.

**republic** (Latin *res publica* 'the state'; from *res* 'affair', and *publica* 'public') country where the head of state is not a monarch, either hereditary or elected, but usually a president, whose role may or may not include political functions.

**Republican Party** one of the two main political parties of the USA, formed 1854. It is more right-wing than the Democratic Party, favouring capital and big business and opposing state subvention and federal controls. In the late 20th century most presidents have come from the Republican Party, but in Congress Republicans have generally been outnumbered. In 1992 Republican George Bush lost the presidency to Democrat Bill Clinton, who in 1996 was re-elected for a second term (the first Democrat to be elected to a second term since Franklin D Roosevelt) although the Republicans retained control of Congress and had governors in 32 of the country's 50 states.

**requiem** in the Roman Catholic Church, a Mass for the dead. Musical settings include those by Palestrina, Mozart, Berlioz, Verdi, Fauré, and Britten.

**reserve currency** in economics, a country's holding of internationally acceptable means of payment (major foreign currencies or gold); central banks also hold the ultimate reserve of money for their domestic banking sector. On the asset side of company balance sheets, undistributed profits are listed as reserves.

**resin** substance exuded from pines, firs, and other trees in gummy drops that harden in air. Varnishes are common products of the hard resins, and ointments come from the soft resins.

**resistance** in physics, that property of a conductor that restricts the flow of electricity through it, associated with the conversion of electrical energy to heat; also the magnitude of this property. Resistance depends on many factors, such as the nature of the material, its temperature, dimensions, and thermal properties; degree of impurity; the nature and state of illumination of the surface; and the frequency and magnitude of the current. The SI unit of resistance is the ◊ohm.

resistance = voltage/current

This is known as ◊Ohm's law.

**resistance movement** opposition movement in a country occupied by an enemy or colonial power, especially in the 20th century; for example, the French resistance to Nazism in World War II.

**resonance** rapid amplification of a vibration when the vibrating object is subject to a force varying at its natural frequency. In a trombone, for example, the length of the air column in the instrument is adjusted until it resonates with the note being sounded. Resonance effects are also produced by many electrical circuits. Tuning a radio, for example, is done by adjusting the natural frequency of the receiver circuit until it coincides with the frequency of the radio waves falling on the aerial.

**respiration** metabolic process in organisms in which food molecules are broken down to release energy. The cells of all living organisms need a continuous supply of energy, and in most plants and animals this is obtained by *aerobic* respiration. In this process, oxygen is used to

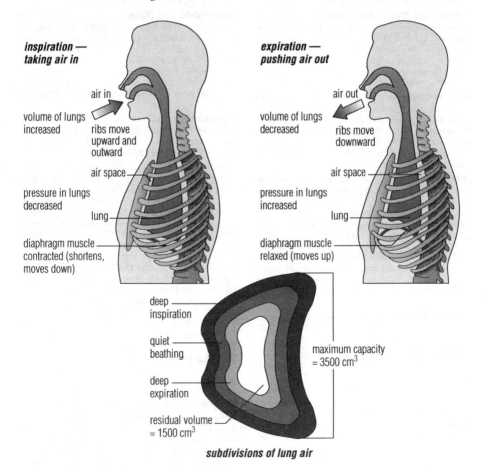

*respiration* The two phases of the process of respiration. Gas exchange occurs in the alveoli, tiny air tubes in the lungs.

break down the glucose molecules in food. This releases energy in the form of energy-carrying molecules (◊ATP), and produces carbon dioxide and water as by-products. Respiration sometimes occurs without oxygen, and this is called *anaerobic* respiration. In this case, the end products are energy and either lactose acid or ethanol (alcohol) and carbon dioxide; this process is termed ◊fermentation.

**Restoration** in English history, the period when the monarchy, in the person of Charles II, was re-established after the English Civil War and the fall of the ◊Protectorate in 1660.

**Restoration comedy** style of English theatre, dating from the ◊Restoration (1660). It witnessed the first appearance of women on the English stage, most notably in the 'breeches part', specially created in order to costume the actress in male attire, thus revealing her figure to its best advantage. The genre placed much emphasis on wit and sexual intrigues. Examples include Wycherley's *The Country Wife* (1675), Congreve's *The Way of the World* (1700), and Farquhar's *The Beaux' Stratagem* (1707).

**restrictive trade practice** any agreement between people in a particular trade or business that restricts free trade in a market. For example, several producers may join together to form a ◊cartel and fix prices; or a manufacturer may refuse to supply goods to a retailer if the retailer stocks the products of a rival company.

**resurrection** in Christian, Jewish, and Muslim belief, the rising from the dead that all souls will experience at the Last Judgement. The Resurrection also refers to Jesus rising from the dead on the third day after his crucifixion, a belief central to Christianity and celebrated at Easter.

**resuscitation** steps taken to revive anyone on the brink of death. The most successful technique for life-threatening emergencies, such as electrocution, near-drowning, or heart attack, is mouth-to-mouth resuscitation. Medical and paramedical staff are trained in cardiopulmonary resuscitation (CPR): the use of specialized equipment and techniques to attempt to restart the breathing and/or heartbeat and stabilize the patient long enough for more definitive treatment. CPR has a success rate of less than 30%.

**retail-price index** (RPI), indicator of variations in the cost of living, superseded in the USA by the consumer price index.

**retina** light-sensitive area at the back of the ◊eye connected to the brain by the optic nerve. It has several layers and in humans contains over a million rods and cones, sensory cells capable of converting light into nervous messages that pass down the optic nerve to the brain.

**retinol** or *vitamin A*, fat-soluble chemical derived from ß-carotene and found in milk, butter, cheese, egg yolk, and liver. Lack of retinol in the diet leads to the eye disease *xerophthalmia.*

**retriever** any of several breeds of hunting dogs, often used as guide dogs for the blind. The commonest breeds are the *Labrador retriever,* large, smooth-coated, and usually black or yellow; and the *golden retriever,* with either flat or wavy coat. They can grow to 60 cm/2 ft high and weigh 40 kg/90 lb.

**retrovirus** any of a family of ◊viruses (Retroviridae) containing the genetic material ◊RNA rather than the more usual ◊DNA.

**Réunion** French island of the Mascarenes group, in the Indian Ocean, 650 km/400 mi east of Madagascar and 180 km/110 mi southwest of Mauritius
*area* 2,512 sq km/970 sq mi
*capital* St Denis
*physical* forested, rising in Piton de Neiges to 3,069 m/10,072 ft
*features* administers five uninhabited islands, also claimed by Madagascar
*industries* sugar, maize, vanilla, tobacco, rum
*population* (1995 est) 653,400
*history* explored by Portuguese (the first European visitors) 1513; annexed by Louis XIII of France 1642; overseas *département* of France 1946; overseas region 1972.

**reversible reaction** chemical reaction that proceeds in both directions at the same time, as the product decomposes back into reactants as it is being produced. Such reactions do not run to completion, provided that no substance leaves the system. Examples include the manufacture of ammonia from hydrogen and nitrogen, and the oxidation of sulphur dioxide to sulphur trioxide.

**revisionism** political theory derived from Marxism that moderates one or more of the basic tenets of Karl Marx, and is hence condemned by orthodox Marxists.

**revolution** any rapid, far-reaching, or violent change in the political, social, or economic structure of society. It is usually applied to political change: examples include the American Revolution, where the colonists broke free from their colonial ties and established a sovereign, independent nation; the ◊French Revolution, where an absolute monarchy was overthrown by opposition from inside the country and a popular uprising; and the ◊Russian Revolution, where a repressive monarchy was overthrown by those seeking to institute widespread social and economic changes based on a socialist model. In 1989–90 the Eastern Bloc nations demonstrated against and voted out the Communist Party, in many cases creating a prodemocracy revolution.

**Revolutionary Wars** series of wars from 1791 to 1802 between France and the combined armies of England, Austria, Prussia, and others, during the period of the ◊French Revolution and ◊Napoleon's campaign to conquer Europe.

**revolutions of 1848** series of revolts in various parts of Europe against monarchical rule. Although some of the revolutionaries had republican ideas, many more were motivated by economic grievances. The revolution began in France with the overthrow of Louis Philippe and then spread to Italy, the Austrian Empire, and

Germany, where the short-lived Frankfurt Parliament put forward ideas about political unity in Germany. None of the revolutions enjoyed any lasting success, and most were violently suppressed within a few months.

**revolutions of 1989** popular uprisings in many countries of Eastern Europe against communist rule, prompted by internal reforms in the USSR that permitted dissent within its sphere of influence. By 1990 nearly all of the Warsaw Pact countries had moved from one-party to pluralist political systems, in most cases peacefully but with growing hostility between various nationalist and ethnic groups.

**revue** stage presentation involving short satirical and topical items in the form of songs, sketches, and monologues; it originated in the late 19th century.

**Reykjavik** chief port and capital (from 1918) of Iceland, on the southwest coast on Faxa Bay; population (1994) 103,000. Fish processing is the main industry. Most of the city is heated by an underground water mains system, built in 1945, the source of the hot water being volcanic springs and geysers. It was a seat of Danish administration from 1801 to 1918, and has been the seat of the Parliament since 1843. Reykjavik is the world's most northerly capital.

**Reynolds, Albert** (1932– ) Irish Fianna Fáil politician, Taoiseach (prime minister) from 1992–94. He was minister for industry and commerce (1987–88) and minister of finance (1988–92). In December 1993 Reynolds and UK prime minister John Major issued a joint peace initiative for Northern Ireland, the Downing Street Declaration, which led to a ceasefire by both the Irish Republican Army (IRA) and the loyalist paramilitaries the following year.

**Reynolds, Joshua** (1723–1792) English painter. One of the greatest portraitists of the 18th century, he displayed a facility for striking and characterful compositions in the 'Grand Manner', a style based on Classical and Renaissance art. He often borrowed classical poses, for example *Mrs Siddons as the Tragic Muse* (1784; San Marino, California). His elegant portraits are mostly of wealthy patrons, though he also painted such figures as the writers Laurence Sterne and Dr Johnson, and the actor David Garrick. Active in London from 1752, he became the first president of the Royal Academy in 1768 and founded the Royal Academy schools. He was knighted in 1769.

**rhea** one of two flightless birds of the family Rheidae, order Rheiformes. The common rhea *Rhea americana* is 1.5 m/5 ft high and is distributed widely in South America. The smaller Darwin's rhea *Pterocnemia pennata* occurs only in the south of South America and has shorter, feathered legs, and mottled plumage. Rheas differ from the ostrich in their smaller size and in having a feathered neck and head, three-toed feet, and no plumelike tail feathers.

**rhenium** (Latin *Rhenus* 'Rhine') heavy, silver-white, metallic element, symbol Re, atomic number 75, relative atomic mass 186.2. It has

chemical properties similar to those of manganese and a very high melting point (3,180°C/5,756°F), which makes it valuable as an ingredient in alloys.

**rhesus factor** group of ♦antigens on the surface of red blood cells of humans which characterize the rhesus blood group system. Most individuals possess the main rhesus factor (Rh+), but those without this factor (Rh−) produce ♦antibodies if they come into contact with it. The name comes from rhesus monkeys, in whose blood rhesus factors were first found.

**rhesus monkey** macaque monkey *Macaca mulatta* found in northern India and Southeast Asia. It has a pinkish face, red buttocks, and long, straight, brown-grey hair. It can grow up to 60 cm/2 ft long, with a 20 cm/8 in tail.

**rhetoric** (Greek *rhetor* 'orator') traditionally, the art of public speaking and debate. Rhetorical skills are valued in such occupations as politics, teaching, law, religion, and broadcasting.

**rheumatic fever** or *acute rheumatism,* acute or chronic illness characterized by fever and painful swelling of joints. Some victims also experience involuntary movements of the limbs and head, a form of chorea. It is now rare in the developed world.

**rheumatism** nontechnical term for a variety of ailments associated with inflammation and stiffness of the joints and muscles.

**Rhine** German *Rhein,* French *Rhin,* Dutch *Rijn,* European river rising in Switzerland and reaching the North Sea via Germany and the Netherlands; length 1,320 km/820 mi. It drains an area of some 220,000 sq km/85,000 sq mi and is navigable for 805 km/500 mi. Tributaries include the Moselle and the Ruhr. The Rhine is linked with the Mediterranean by the Rhine–Rhône Waterway, and with the Black Sea by the Rhine–Main–Danube Waterway.

**Rhineland-Palatinate** German *Rheinland-Pfalz,* administrative region (German *Land*) of Germany, bordered on the north by North Rhine-Westphalia, on the east by Hesse and Baden-Württemberg, on the south by France, on the southwest by the Saarland, and on the west by Luxembourg and Belgium
*area* 19,800 sq km/7,643 sq mi
*capital* Mainz
*towns and cities* Ludwigshafen, Koblenz, Trier, Worms, Kaiserslautern
*physical* wooded mountain country, river valleys of Rhine and Moselle, the Eifel plateau
*industries* motor vehicles, mechanical and electrical engineering, chemicals, machinery, leather goods, pottery, glass, beverages
*agriculture* wine (75% of German output), potatoes, cereals, sugar beet, fruit, tobacco, stock rearing
*population* (1995) 4,015,000
*history* formed in 1946 of the Rhenish ♦Palatinate and parts of Hesse, Rhine province, and Hesse-Nassau.

**rhinoceros** large grazing mammal with one or more horns on its snout. Rhinoceroses have thick, loose skin with little hair, stumpy, powerful legs with three toes on each foot. The largest species (the one-horned Indian rhinoceros) can grow up to 2 m/6 ft high at the shoulder and weigh 2,300–4,000 kg/5,060–8,800 lb. Rhinoceroses eat grass, leafy twigs, and shrubs, and are solitary. They have poor eyesight but excellent hearing and smell. Although they look clumsy, rhinos can reach speeds of 56 kph/35 mph. In the wild they are thought to live for about 25 years, and up to 47 in captivity. There are five species: three Asian and two African, all in danger of extinction.

**rhizome** or **rootstock**, horizontal underground plant stem. It is a ◊perennating organ in some species, where it is generally thick and fleshy, while in other species it is mainly a means of ◊vegetative reproduction, and is therefore long and slender, with buds all along it that send up new plants. The potato is a rhizome that has two distinct parts, the tuber being the swollen end of a long, cordlike rhizome.

**Rhode Island** smallest state of the USA, located in New England. It is nicknamed Little Rhody or the Ocean State, and is officially known as *Rhode Island and Providence Plantations*. Rhode Island ratified the US Constitution in 1790, becoming the 13th state to join the Union. It is bordered to the north and east by Massachusetts, to the west by Connecticut, and to the south by the Atlantic Ocean
**population** (1995) 989,800
**area** 3,100 sq km/1,197 sq mi
**capital** Providence
**towns and cities** Warwick, Cranston, Newport, Woonsocket
**industries and products** electronics, machine tools, jewellery, textiles, silverware, rubber, and plastics. Agriculture is limited by the rocky terrain but is important in rural areas, the main crops being apples and potatoes. Rhode Island Red hens were developed here from the 19th century.

**Rhodes** Greek *Ródhos*, Greek island, largest of the Dodecanese, in the eastern Aegean Sea
**area** 1,412 sq km/545 sq mi
**capital** Rhodes
**industries** grapes, olives
**population** (1981) 88,000
**history** settled by Greeks about 1000 BC; the Colossus of Rhodes (fell 224 BC) was one of the ◊Seven Wonders of the World; held by the Knights Hospitallers of St John 1306–1522; taken from Turkish rule by the Italian occupation 1912; ceded to Greece 1947.

**Rhodes, Cecil John** (1853–1902) South African politician, born in the UK, prime minister of Cape Colony 1890–96. Aiming at the formation of a South African federation and the creation of a block of British territory from the Cape to Cairo, he was responsible for the annexation of Bechuanaland (now Botswana) in 1885. He formed the British South Africa Company in 1889, which occupied Mashonaland and Matabeleland, thus forming ◊*Rhodesia* (now Zambia and Zimbabwe).

**Rhodesia** former name of Zambia (Northern Rhodesia) and Zimbabwe (Southern Rhodesia), in southern Africa.

**rhodium** (Greek *rhodon* 'rose') hard, silver-white, metallic element, symbol Rh, atomic number 45, relative atomic mass 102.905. It is one of the so-called platinum group of metals and is resistant to tarnish, corrosion, and acid. It occurs as a free metal in the natural alloy osmiridium and is used in jewellery, electroplating, and thermocouples.

**rhododendron** any of numerous, mostly evergreen shrubs belonging to the heath family. The leaves are usually dark and leathery, and the large funnel-shaped flowers, which grow in tight clusters, occur in all colours except blue. They thrive on acid soils. ◊Azaleas belong to the same genus. (Genus *Rhododendron*, family Ericaceae.)

**rhombus** in geometry, an equilateral (all sides equal) ◊parallelogram. Its diagonals bisect each other at right angles, and its area is half the product of the lengths of the two diagonals. A rhombus whose internal angles are 90° is called a square.

**Rhondda Cynon Taff** unitary authority in south Wales, created in 1996 from part of the former county of Mid Glamorgan
**area** 440 sq km/170 sq mi
**towns** Clydach Vale (administrative headquarters)
**physical** rivers Rhondda Fawr and Rhondda Fach
**industries** light industries
**population** (1996) 232,600.

**Rhône** river of southern Europe; length 810 km/500 mi. It rises at the Rhône Glacier (altitude 1,825 m/5,987 ft) in the canton of Valais in Switzerland and flows through Lake Geneva to Lyon in France, where, at its confluence with the Saône, the upper limit of navigation is reached. The river then turns due south and passes Vienne and Avignon. Near Arles it divides into the *Grand* and *Petit Rhône*, flowing respectively southeast and southwest into the Mediterranean west of Marseille. Here it forms a two-armed delta; the area between the tributaries is the marshy region known as the Camargue.

**Rhône-Alpes** region of eastern France in the upper reaches of the ◊Rhône; area 43,700 sq km/16,868 sq mi; population (1992) 5,344,000. It consists of the *départements* of Ain, Ardèche, Drôme, Isère, Loire, Rhône, Savoie, and Haute-Savoie. The capital is ◊Lyon. There are several wine-producing areas, including Chenas, Fleurie, and Beaujolais. Industrial products include chemicals, textiles, and motor vehicles.

**rhubarb** perennial plant grown for its pink edible leaf stalks. The large leaves contain ◊oxalic acid, and are poisonous. There are also wild rhubarbs native to Europe and Asia. (*Rheum rhaponticum*, family Polygonaceae.)

**rhythm and blues** R & B, US popular music of the 1940s–60s, which drew on swing and jump-jazz rhythms and blues vocals, and was an important influence on rock and roll. It diversified into soul, funk, and other styles. R & B artists include Bo Diddley, Jackie Wilson (1934–84), and Etta James (c. 1938– ).

**Ribbentrop–Molotov pact** nonaggression treaty signed by Germany and the USSR 23 August 1939. Under the terms of the treaty both countries agreed to remain neutral and to refrain from acts of aggression against each other if either went to war. Secret clauses allowed for the partition of Poland – German Nazi dictator Adolf Hitler was to acquire western Poland, Soviet dictator Joseph Stalin the eastern part. On 1 September 1939 Hitler invaded Poland. The pact ended when Hitler invaded Russia 22 June 1941. See also ◊World War II.

**riboflavin** or *vitamin B₂* ◊vitamin of the B complex important in cell respiration. It is obtained from eggs, liver, and milk. A deficiency in the diet causes stunted growth.

**ribonucleic acid** full name of ◊RNA.

**ribosome** in biology, the protein-making machinery of the cell. Ribosomes are located on the endoplasmic reticulum (ER) of eukaryotic cells, and are made of proteins and a special type of ◊RNA, ribosomal RNA. They receive messenger RNA (copied from the ◊DNA) and ◊amino acids, and 'translate' the messenger RNA by using its chemically coded instructions to link amino acids in a specific order, to make a strand of a particular protein.

**Ricardo, David** (1772–1823) English economist. Among his discoveries were the principle of *comparative advantage* (that countries can benefit by specializing in goods they produce efficiently and trading internationally to buy others), and the *law of diminishing returns* (that continued increments of capital and labour applied to a given quantity of land will eventually show a declining rate of increase in output). He wrote *Principles of Political Economy* 1817.

**rice** principal ◊cereal of the wet regions of the tropics, derived from wild grasses probably native to India and Southeast Asia. Rice is unique among cereal crops in that it is grown standing in water. The yield is very large, and rice is said to be the staple food of one-third of the world's population. (*Oryza sativa.*)

**Richard (I) the Lion-Heart** French *Coeur-de-Lion* (1157–1199) king of England 1189–99. He spent all but six months of his reign abroad. He was the third son of Henry II, against whom he twice rebelled. In the third ◊Crusade 1191–92 he won victories at Cyprus, Acre, and Arsuf (against ◊Saladin), but failed to recover Jerusalem. While returning overland he was captured by the Duke of Austria, who handed him over to the emperor Henry VI, and he was held prisoner until a large ransom was raised. He then returned briefly to England, where his brother John had been ruling in his stead. His later years were spent in warfare in France, where he was killed by a crossbow bolt while besieging Châlus-Chabrol in 1199. He left no heir.

**Richard II** or *Richard of Bordeaux* (1367–1400) King of England from 1377, effectively from 1389, son of Edward the Black Prince. He reigned in conflict with Parliament; they executed some of his associates in 1388, and he executed some of the opposing barons in 1397, whereupon he made himself absolute. Two years later, forced to abdicate in favour of ◊Henry IV, he was jailed and probably assassinated.

**Richard III** (1452–1485) King of England from 1483. The son of Richard, Duke of York, he was created Duke of Gloucester by his brother Edward IV, and distinguished himself in the Wars of the ◊Roses. On Edward's death 1483 he became protector to his nephew Edward V, and soon secured the crown for himself on the plea that Edward IV's sons were illegitimate. He proved a capable ruler, but the suspicion that he had murdered Edward V and his brother undermined his popularity. In 1485 Henry, Earl of Richmond (later ◊Henry VII), raised a rebellion, and Richard III was defeated and killed at ◊Bosworth.

**Richards, Viv (Isaac Vivian Alexander)** (1952– ) West Indian cricketer. He was captain of the West Indies team 1986–91. He has played for the Leeward Islands and, in the UK, for Somerset and Glamorgan. A prolific run-scorer, he holds the record for the greatest number of runs made in Test cricket in one calendar year (1,710 runs in 1976). He retired from international cricket after the West Indies tour of England in 1991 and from first-class cricket at the end of the 1993 season.
*career highlights*
*all first-class cricket* runs: 36,212; average: 49.33; best: 322 (Somerset v. Warwickshire 1985); wickets: 223; average: 45.15; best: 5 for 88 (West Indies v. Queensland 1981–82)
*Test cricket* appearances: 121; runs: 8,540; average: 50.23; best: 291 (v. England 1976); wickets: 32; average: 61.37; best: 2 for 17 (v. Pakistan 1988)

**Richardson, Ralph (David)** (1902–1983) English actor. He played many stage parts, including Falstaff (Shakespeare), Peer Gynt (Ibsen), and Cyrano de Bergerac (Rostand). He shared the management of the Old Vic Theatre with Laurence ◊Olivier 1944–50. In later years he revealed himself as an accomplished deadpan comic.

**Richardson, Samuel** (1689–1761) English novelist. He was one of the founders of the modern novel. *Pamela* (1740–41), written in the form of a series of letters and containing much dramatic conversation, was sensationally popular all across Europe, and was followed by *Clarissa* (1747–48) and *Sir Charles Grandison* (1753–54).

**Richelieu, Armand Jean du Plessis de** (1585–1642) French cardinal and politician, chief minister from 1624. He aimed to make the monarchy absolute; he ruthlessly crushed opposition by the nobility and destroyed the political power of the ◊Huguenots, while leaving them religious freedom. Abroad, he sought to establish French supremacy by breaking the power of the

## RICHTER SCALE

The Richter scale is based on measurement of seismic waves, used to determine the magnitude of an earthquake at its epicenter. The magnitude of an earthquake differs from its intensity, measured by the Mercalli scale, which is subjective and varies from place to place for the same earthquake. The Richter scale was named after US seismologist Charles Richter (1900–1985). The relative amount of energy released indicates the ratio of energy between earthquakes of different magnitude.

| Magnitude | Relative amount of energy released | Examples | Year |
|---|---|---|---|
| 1 | 1 | | |
| 2 | 31 | | |
| 3 | 960 | | |
| 4 | 30,000 | Carlisle, England (4.7) | 1979 |
| 5 | 920,000 | Wrexham, Wales (5.1) | 1990 |
| 6 | 29,000,000 | San Fernando (CA) (6.5) | 1971 |
| | | northern Armenia (6.8) | 1988 |
| 7 | 890,000,000 | Loma Prieta (CA) (7.1) | 1989 |
| | | Kobe, Japan (7.2) | 1995 |
| | | Rasht, Iran (7.7) | 1990 |
| | | San Francisco (CA) (7.7–7.9)[1] | 1906 |
| 8 | 28,000,000,000 | Tangshan, China (8.0) | 1976 |
| | | Gansu, China (8.6) | 1920 |
| | | Lisbon, Portugal (8.7) | 1755 |
| 9 | 850,000,000,000 | Prince William Sound (AK) (9.2) | 1964 |

[1] Richter's original estimate of a magnitude of 8.3 has been revised by two recent studies carried out by the California Institute of Technology and the US Geological Survey.

---

Habsburgs; he therefore supported the Swedish king Gustavus Adolphus and the German Protestant princes against Austria and in 1635 brought France into the Thirty Years' War.

**Richter scale** scale based on measurement of seismic waves, used to determine the magnitude of an ◊earthquake at its epicentre. The magnitude of an earthquake differs from its intensity, measured by the ◊Mercalli scale, which is subjective and varies from place to place for the same earthquake. The scale is named after US seismologist Charles Richter.

**rickets** defective growth of bone in children due to an insufficiency of calcium deposits. The bones, which do not harden adequately, are bent out of shape. It is usually caused by a lack of vitamin D and insufficient exposure to sunlight. Renal rickets, also a condition of malformed bone, is associated with kidney disease.

**rifle** ◊firearm that has spiral grooves (rifling) in its barrel. When a bullet is fired, the rifling makes it spin, thereby improving accuracy. Rifles were first introduced in the late 18th century.

**Rift Valley, Great** longest 'split' in the Earth's surface; see ◊Great Rift Valley.

**Riga** capital and port of Latvia; population (1995) 840,000. Industries include engineering, brewing, food processing, and the manufacture of textiles and chipboard.

**Rigel** or *Beta Orionis*, brightest star in the constellation Orion. It is a blue-white supergiant, with an estimated diameter 50 times that of the Sun. It is 900 light years from the Sun, and is intrinsically the brightest of the first-magnitude stars, its true luminosity being about 100,000 times that of the Sun. It is the seventh-brightest star in the night sky.

**Rights of Man and the Citizen, Declaration of the** historic French document. According to the statement of the French National Assembly 1789, these rights include representation in the legislature; equality before the law; equality of opportunity; freedom from arbitrary imprisonment; freedom of speech and religion; taxation in proportion to ability to pay; and security of property. In 1946 were added equal rights for women; right to work, join a union, and strike; leisure, social security, and support in old age; and free education.

**right wing** the more conservative or reactionary section of a political party or spectrum. It originated in the French national assembly of 1789, where the nobles sat in the place of honour on the president's right, whereas the commons were on his left (hence ◊left wing).

**Rig-Veda** oldest of the ◊Vedas, the chief sacred writings of Hinduism. It consists of hymns to the Aryan gods, such as Indra, and to nature gods.

**Riley, Bridget Louise** (1931– ) English painter. A pioneer of ◊Op art, she developed her characteristic style in the early 1960s, arranging hard-edged black lines in regular patterns to create disturbing effects of scintillating light and movement. *Fission* (1963; Museum of Modern Art, New York) is an example.

**Rilke, Rainer Maria** (1875–1926) Austrian writer. His prose works include the semi-autobiographical *Die Aufzeichnungen des Malte Laurids Brigge/The Notebook of Malte Laurids Brigge* 1910. His verse is characterized by a form of mystic pantheism that seeks to achieve a state of ecstasy in which existence can be apprehended as a whole.

**Rimbaud, (Jean Nicolas) Arthur** (1854–1891) French Symbolist poet. His verse was chiefly written before the age of 20, notably *Les Illuminations* published 1886. From 1871 he lived with the poet Paul Verlaine.

**Rimsky-Korsakov, Nikolai Andreievich** (1844–1908) Russian composer. His operas include *The Maid of Pskov* (1873), *The Snow Maiden* (1882), *Mozart and Salieri* (1898), and *The Golden Cockerel* (1907), a satirical attack on despotism that was banned until 1909. He also wrote an influential text on orchestration.

**ringworm** any of various contagious skin infections due to related kinds of fungus, usually resulting in circular, itchy, discoloured patches covered with scales or blisters. The scalp and feet (athlete's foot) are generally involved. Treatment is with antifungal preparations.

**Rio de Janeiro** (Portuguese 'river of January') port and resort in southeast Brazil; capital of Rio de Janeiro federal unit (state), and former national capital (1763–1960); population (1991) 5,480,800 (metropolitan area 10,389,400). It is situated on the southwest shore of Guanabara Bay, an inlet of the Atlantic Ocean; Sugar Loaf Mountain (a huge cone-shaped rock outcrop, composed of granite, quartz and felspar) stands at the entrance to the harbour, and the city is dominated by the 30 m/100 ft-high figure of Christ on the top of Corcovado, a jagged peak 690 m/2,264 ft high. Industries include ship-repair, sugar refining, textiles, and the manufacture of foodstuffs; coffee, sugar, and iron ore are exported.

**Rio Grande** Mexican *Río Bravo del Norte,* river of the USA and Mexico, rising in the Rocky Mountains in southern Colorado, it flows southeast, through New Mexico and Texas, to the Gulf of Mexico near Brownsville; length 3,050 km/1,900 mi. From El Paso, the river forms the US-Mexican border for the last 2,400 km/1,500 mi of its course. Insufficient water is carried for the demands of irrigation on both sides of the border, and the Rio Grande is eventually reduced to a trickle in its lower reaches. Its rate of flow is subject to international agreements.

**Rio Grande do Norte** federal unit (state) of northeast Brazil, bounded on the north and east by the Atlantic Ocean; area 53,100 sq km/20,500 sq mi; population (1991) 2,414,100; capital Natal. Apart from a narrow coastal zone with abundant rainfall, most of the state lies on a semi-arid plateau, crossed by several rivers, where there is stock-raising, and cotton, sugar, and cassava are grown. There are oil, textile, and agricultural industries. It produces 90% of the nation's salt. Carnauba wax is extensively produced from the carnauba palm.

**Rio Grande do Sul** southernmost federal unit (state) of Brazil, to the east of the Uruguay River, bounded on the east by the Atlantic Ocean, on the west by Argentina, and on the south by Uruguay; area 282,184 sq km/108,993 sq mi; population (1991) 9,138,700; capital ◊Pôrto Alegre. The region consists mainly of vast grasslands where there is extensive stock-raising (cattle, sheep, pigs); wine, rice, and soybeans are produced, and industries are centred around agricultural production and processing. The state produces 90% of the national wine production.

**Rioja, La** see ◊La Rioja, a region of Spain.

**riot** disturbance caused by a potentially violent mob. In the UK, riots formerly suppressed under the Riot Act are now governed by the Public Order Act 1986. Methods of riot control include plastic bullets, stun bags (soft canvas pouches filled with buckshot which spread out in flight), water cannon, and CS gas (tear gas).

**ripple tank** in physics, shallow water-filled tray used to demonstrate various properties of waves, such as reflection, refraction, diffraction, and interference.

**RISC** acronym for reduced instruction-set computer, in computing, a microprocessor (processor on a single chip) that carries out fewer instructions than other (CISC) microprocessors in common use in the 1990s. Because of the low number and the regularity of machine code instructions, the processor carries out those instructions very quickly.

**Risorgimento** 19th-century movement for Italian national unity and independence, begun 1815. Leading figures in the movement included ◊Cavour, ◊Mazzini, and ◊Garibaldi. Uprisings of 1848–49 failed, but with help from France in a war against Austria – to oust it from Italian provinces in the north – an Italian kingdom was founded in 1861. Unification was finally completed with the addition of Venetia in 1866 and the Papal States in 1870.

**rite of passage** ritual that accompanies any of the most significant moments or transitions (birth, puberty, marriage, and so on) in an individual's life. In Hinduism there are 14, called samskaras.

**river** large body of water that flows down a slope along a channel restricted by adjacent banks and levées. A river originates at a point called its *source,* and enters a sea or lake at its *mouth.* Along its length it may be joined by smaller rivers called *tributaries;* a river and its tributaries are contained within a drainage basin. The point at which two rivers join is called the *confluence.* See illustration on page 764.

**Rivera, Diego** (1886–1957) Mexican painter. He was one of the most important muralists of the 20th century. An exponent of Social Realism, he received many public commissions for murals depicting the Mexican revolution, his vivid style influenced by Mexican folk art. A vast cycle on historical themes (National Palace, Mexico City) was begun 1929.

**Riviera** the Mediterranean coast of France and Italy from Hyères to La Spezia. The most exclusive stretch of the Riviera, with the finest climate, is the Côte d'Azur, from Menton to St-Tropez, which includes Monaco.

**Riyadh** Arabic *Ar Riyad,* capital of Saudi Arabia and of the Nejd region, situated in an

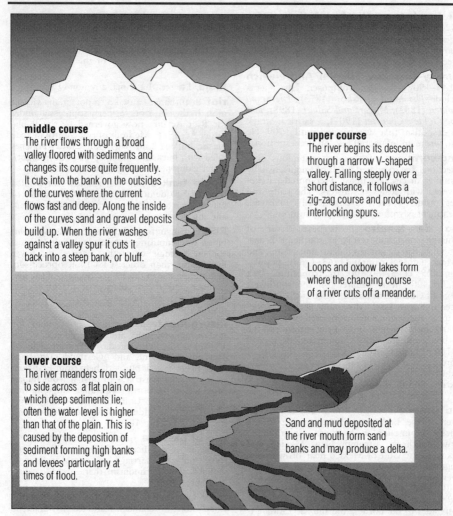

**middle course**
The river flows through a broad valley floored with sediments and changes its course quite frequently. It cuts into the bank on the outsides of the curves where the current flows fast and deep. Along the inside of the curves sand and gravel deposits build up. When the river washes against a valley spur it cuts it back into a steep bank, or bluff.

**upper course**
The river begins its descent through a narrow V-shaped valley. Falling steeply over a short distance, it follows a zig-zag course and produces interlocking spurs.

Loops and oxbow lakes form where the changing course of a river cuts off a meander.

**lower course**
The river meanders from side to side across a flat plain on which deep sediments lie; often the water level is higher than that of the plain. This is caused by the deposition of sediment forming high banks and levees' particularly at times of flood.

Sand and mud deposited at the river mouth form sand banks and may produce a delta.

*river* The course of a river from its source of a spring or melting glacier, through to maturity where it flows into the sea.

oasis and connected by rail with Dammam 450 km/280 mi away on the Arabian Gulf; population (1994) 1,500,000.

**RNA** abbreviation for ribonucleic acid, nucleic acid involved in the process of translating the genetic material ◊DNA into proteins. It is usually single-stranded, unlike the double-stranded DNA, and consists of a large number of nucleotides strung together, each of which comprises the sugar ribose, a phosphate group, and one of four bases (uracil, cytosine, adenine, or guanine). RNA is copied from DNA by the formation of ◊base pairs, with uracil taking the place of thymine.

**roach** any freshwater fish of the Eurasian genus *Rutilus*, of the carp family, especially *R. rutilus* of northern Europe. It is dark green above, whitish below, with reddish lower fins; it grows to 35 cm/1.2 ft.

**robbery** in law, a variety of theft: stealing from a person, using force, or the threat of force, to intimidate the victim.

**Robbia, della** Italian family of sculptors and architects. They were active in Florence. *Luca della Robbia* (1400–1482) created a number of major works in Florence, notably the marble *cantoria* (singing gallery) in the cathedral (1431– 38) (Museo del Duomo), with lively groups of choristers. Luca also developed a characteristic style of glazed terracotta work.

**Robbins, Jerome** (1918–1998) US dancer and choreographer. He was co-director of the New York City Ballet 1969–83 (with George ◊Balanchine). His ballets were internationally renowned and he was considered the greatest US-born ballet choreographer. He also choreographed the musicals *The King and I* (1951),

*West Side Story* (1957), and *Fiddler on the Roof* (1964).

**Robert (I) the Devil** Duke of Normandy from 1027. Also known as *the Magnificent,* he was the father of William the Conqueror, and was legendary for his cruelty. He became duke after the death of his brother Richard III, in which he may have been implicated.

**Robert (II) Curthose** (*c.* 1054–1134) Duke of Normandy 1087–1106. He was the son of William the Conqueror, and a noted crusader (1096–1100). When the English throne passed to his younger brother William II in 1087, Robert was unable to recover it by war. In 1106 Robert again attempted to recover England from Henry I, but was defeated at Tinchebrai and imprisoned until his death.

**Robert** three kings of Scotland:

**Robert (I) the Bruce** (1274–1329) king of Scots from 1306, successful guerrilla fighter, and grandson of Robert de Bruce. In 1307 he displayed his tactical skill in the Battle of Loudon Hill against the English under Edward I, and defeated the English again under Edward II at Bannockburn in 1314. In 1328 the Treaty of Northampton recognized Scotland's independence and Robert the Bruce as king.

Large English expeditions of 1322 and 1327 were beaten by Robert's 'scorched earth' policy, apparently his deathbed advice on how best to conduct warfare.

**Robert II** (1316–1390) King of Scotland from 1371. He was the son of Walter (1293–1326), steward of Scotland, and Marjory, daughter of Robert the Bruce. He acted as regent during the exile and captivity of his uncle David II, whom he eventually succeeded. He was the first king of the house of Stuart.

**Robert III** (*c.* 1340–1406) King of Scotland from 1390, son of Robert II. He was unable to control the nobles, and the government fell largely into the hands of his brother, Robert, Duke of Albany (*c.* 1340–1420).

**Robespierre, Maximilien François Marie Isidore de** (1758–1794) French politician in the ◊French Revolution. As leader of the ◊Jacobins in the National Convention (1792), he supported the execution of Louis XVI and the overthrow of the right-wing republican Girondins, and in July 1793 was elected to the Committee of Public Safety. A year later he was guillotined; many believe that he was a scapegoat for the Reign of ◊Terror since he ordered only 72 executions personally.

**robin** migratory songbird *Erithacus rubecula* of the thrush family Muscicapidae, order Passeriformes, found in Europe, West Asia, Africa, and the Azores. About 13 cm/5 in long, both sexes are olive brown with a red breast. Two or three nests are constructed during the year in sheltered places, and from five to seven white freckled eggs are laid.

**Robin Hood** in English legend, an outlaw and champion of the poor against the rich, said to have lived in Sherwood Forest, Nottinghamshire, during the reign of Richard I (1189–99). He feuded with the sheriff of Nottingham, accompanied by Maid Marian and a band of followers known as his 'merry men'. He appears in many popular ballads from the 13th century, but his first datable appearance is in William Langland's *Piers Plowman* in the late 14th century. He became popular in the 15th century.

**Robinson, Mary** (1944– ) Irish Labour politician, president 1990–97. She became a professor of law at the age of 25. A strong supporter of women's rights, she campaigned for the liberalization of Ireland's laws prohibiting divorce and abortion.

**Robinson, Sugar Ray** Adopted name of Walker Smith (1920–1989) US boxer. He was world welterweight champion 1945–51; he defended his title five times. Defeating Jake LaMotta in 1951, he took the middleweight title. He lost the title six times and won it seven times. He retired at the age of 45.
*career highlights*
*professional fights* total: 202; wins: 175; draws: 6; defeats: 19; no contests: 2

**Robinson, W(illiam) Heath** (1872–1944) English cartoonist and illustrator. He made humorous drawings of bizarre machinery for performing simple tasks, such as raising one's hat. A clumsily designed apparatus is often described as a 'Heath Robinson' contraption.

**robot** any computer-controlled machine that can be programmed to move or carry out work. Robots are often used in industry to transport materials or to perform repetitive tasks. For instance, robotic arms, fixed to a floor or workbench, may be used to paint machine parts or assemble electronic circuits. Other robots are designed to work in situations that would be dangerous to humans – for example, in defusing bombs or in space and deep-sea exploration.

**rock** constituent of the Earth's crust composed of ◊minerals or materials of organic origin that have consolidated into hard masses as ◊igneous, ◊sedimentary, or ◊metamorphic rocks. Rocks are formed from a combination (or aggregate) of minerals, and the property of a rock will depend on its components. Where deposits of economically valuable minerals occur they are termed ◊ores. As a result of ◊weathering, rock breaks down into very small particles that combine with organic materials from plants and animals to form ◊soil. In ◊geology the term 'rock' can also include unconsolidated materials such as ◊sand, mud, ◊clay, and ◊peat.

**rock and roll** pop music born of a fusion of rhythm and blues with country and western, and based on electric guitar and drums. In the mid-1950s, with the advent of Elvis Presley, it became the heartbeat of teenage rebellion in the West and also had considerable impact on other parts of the world. It found perhaps its purest form in late-1950s rockabilly, the style of white Southerners in the USA; the blanket term 'rock' later came to comprise a multitude of styles.

**Rockefeller, John D(avison)** (1839–1937) US millionaire. He was the founder of Standard Oil in 1870 (which achieved control of 90% of US refineries by 1882). He also founded the philanthropic *Rockefeller Foundation* (1913), to which his son *John D(avison) Rockefeller Jr* (1874– 1960) devoted his life.

**rocket** projectile driven by the reaction of gases produced by a fast-burning fuel. Unlike jet engines, which are also reaction engines, modern rockets carry their own oxygen supply to burn their fuel and do not require any surrounding atmosphere. For warfare, rocket heads carry an explosive device.

**Rocky Mountains** or *Rockies,* largest North American mountain system, extending for 4,800 km/3,000 mi from the Mexican plateau near Sante Fe, north through the west-central states of the USA, and through Canada to the Alaskan border. They form part of the Continental Divide, which separates rivers draining into the Atlantic or Arctic oceans from those flowing toward the Pacific Ocean. To the east lie the Great Plains, and to the west, the plateaux separating the Rocky Mountains from parallel Pacific coast ranges. Mount Elbert is the highest peak, 4,400 m/14,433 ft. Some geographers consider the Yukon and Alaskan ranges as part of the system, making the highest point Mount McKinley (Denali), 6,194 m/20,320 ft, and its total length 5,150 km/3,219 mi.

**Rococo** movement in the arts and architecture in 18th-century Europe, tending towards lightness, elegance, delicacy, and decorative charm. The term 'Rococo' is derived from the French *rocaille* (rock- or shell-work), a style of interior decoration based on S-curves and scroll-like forms. Jean-Antoine Watteau's paintings and Sèvres porcelain belong to the French Rococo vogue. In the 1730s the movement became widespread in Europe, notably in the churches and palaces of southern Germany and Austria. Chippendale furniture is an English example of the French Rococo style.

**rodent** any mammal of the worldwide order Rodentia, making up nearly half of all mammal species. Besides ordinary 'cheek teeth', they have a single front pair of incisor teeth in both upper and lower jaw, which continue to grow as they are worn down.

**Rodgers, Richard Charles** (1902–1979) US composer. He collaborated with librettist Lorenz Hart (1895–1943) on songs like 'Blue Moon' 1934 and musicals like *On Your Toes* 1936. With Oscar Hammerstein II, he wrote many musicals, including *Oklahoma!* 1943, *South Pacific* 1949, *The King and I* 1951, and *The Sound of Music* 1959.

**Rodin, (René François) Auguste** (1840– 1917) French sculptor. He is considered the greatest of his day. He freed sculpture from the idealizing conventions of the time by his realistic treatment of the human figure, introducing a new boldness of style and expression. Examples are *Le Penseur/The Thinker* 1904 (Musée Rodin, Paris), *Le Baiser/The Kiss* 1886 (marble version in the Louvre, Paris), and *The Burghers*

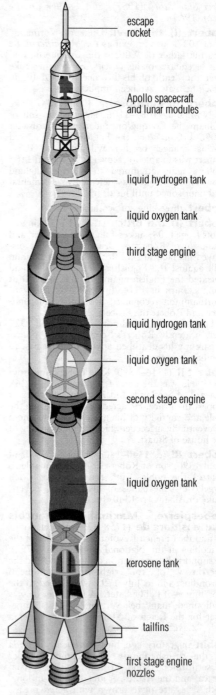

escape rocket

Apollo spacecraft and lunar modules

liquid hydrogen tank

liquid oxygen tank

third stage engine

liquid hydrogen tank

liquid oxygen tank

second stage engine

liquid oxygen tank

kerosene tank

tailfins

first stage engine nozzles

**rocket** *The three-stage Saturn V rocket used in the Apollo moonshots of the 1960s and 1970s. It stood 111 m/365 ft high, as tall as a 30-storey skyscraper, weighed 2,700 tonnes/3,000 tons when loaded with fuel, and developed a power equivalent to 50 Boeing 747 jumbo jets.*

*of Calais* 1884–86 (copy in Embankment Gardens, Westminster, London).

**roentgen** or *röntgen,* unit (symbol R) of radiation exposure, used for X-rays and gamma rays. It is defined in terms of the number of ions produced in one cubic centimetre of air by the radiation. Exposure to 1,000 roentgens gives rise to an absorbed dose of about 870 rads (8.7 grays), which is a dose equivalent of 870 rems (8.7 sieverts).

**Rogers, Richard George** (1933–   ) English High Tech architect. His works include the Pompidou Centre in Paris (1977), with Renzo Piano; the Lloyd's of London building in London (1986); and the Reuters building at Blackwall Yard, London (1992), which won him a RIBA award. He was knighted in 1991.

**Roh Tae-woo** (1932–   ) South Korean right-wing politician and general, president 1988–93. He held ministerial office from 1981 under President Chun, and became chair of the ruling Democratic Justice Party in 1985. He was elected president in 1988, amid allegations of fraud and despite being connected with the massacre of 2,000 anti-government demonstrators in 1980. In October 1995 Roh admitted publicly to having secretly amassed £400 million during his term in office, of which he retained £140 million for personal use. He was arrested in November on corruption charges, along with former president Chun, and placed on trial in 1996, on charges of sedition and military rebellion in 1980. He was found guilty in August 1996, heavily fined, and sentenced to 22 years' imprisonment. In December 1996 an appeal court reduced his prison sentence to 17 years.

**Roland** (died *c.* 778) French hero. His real and legendary deeds of valour and chivalry inspired many medieval and later romances, including the 11th-century *Chanson de Roland* and Ariosto's *Orlando furioso.* A knight of ◊Charlemagne, Roland was killed in 778 with his friend Oliver and the 12 peers of France at Roncesvalles (in the Pyrenees) by Basques. He headed the rearguard during Charlemagne's retreat from his invasion of Spain.

**roller** any brightly coloured bird of the Old World family Coraciidae, resembling crows but in the same order as kingfishers and hornbills. Rollers grow up to 32 cm/13 in long. The name is derived from the habit of some species of rolling over in flight.

**rolling** common method of shaping metal. Rolling is carried out by giant mangles, consisting of several sets, or stands, of heavy rollers positioned one above the other. Red-hot metal slabs are rolled into sheet and also (using shaped rollers) girders and rails. Metal sheets are often cold-rolled finally to impart a harder surface.

**Rolling Stones, the** British band formed in 1962, once notorious as the 'bad boys' of rock. Original members were Mick Jagger (1943–   ), Keith Richards (1943–   ), Brian Jones (1942–1969), Bill Wyman (1936–   ), Charlie Watts (1941–   ), and the pianist Ian Stewart (1938–1985). A rock-and-roll institution, the Rolling

Stones were still performing and recording in the 1990s.

**Rollo** 1st duke of Normandy, or Hrolfr (*c.* 860–*c.* 932) first Viking ruler and Duke of Normandy (although he never used the title). He founded the duchy of Normandy and established the dynasty of ◊William (I) the Conqueror. The city of Rouen is named after him.

**Rolls, Master of the** British judge.

**ROM** acronym for read-only memory, in computing, a memory device in the form of a collection of integrated circuits (chips), frequently used in microcomputers. ROM chips are loaded with data and programs during manufacture and, unlike ◊RAM (random-access memory) chips, can subsequently only be read, not written to, by computer. However, the contents of the chips are not lost when the power is switched off, as happens in RAM.

**Romagna** area of Italy on the Adriatic coast, under papal rule 1278–1860 and now part of the region of ◊Emilia-Romagna.

**Roman Britain** period in British history from the two expeditions by Julius Caesar in 55 and 54 BC to the early 5th century AD. Roman relations with Britain began with Caesar's expeditions, but the actual conquest was not begun until AD 43. During the reign of the emperor Domitian, the governer of the province, Agricola, campaigned in Scotland. After several unsuccessful attempts to conquer Scotland, the northern frontier was fixed between the Solway and the Tyne at ◊Hadrian's Wall.

**Roman Catholicism** one of the main divisions of the Christian religion, separate from the Eastern Orthodox Church from 1054, and headed by the pope. For history and beliefs, see ◊Christianity. Membership in 1995 was about 970 million worldwide, concentrated in southern Europe, Latin America, and the Philippines.

**romance** in literature, tales of love and chivalric adventure, in verse or prose, that became popular in France about 1200 and spread throughout Europe.

**Romance languages** branch of Indo-European languages descended from the Latin of the Roman Empire ('popular' or 'vulgar' as opposed to 'classical' Latin). The present-day Romance languages with national status are French, Italian, Portuguese, Romanian, and Spanish.

**Roman Empire** from 27 BC to the 5th century AD; see ◊Rome, ancient.

**Romanesque architecture** style of Western European ◊architecture of the 10th to 12th centuries, marked by rounded arches, solid volumes, and emphasis on perpendicular elements. In England the style is also known as Norman architecture.

## Romania
*national name* România
**area** 237,500 sq km/91,698 sq mi
*capital* Bucharest

0 mi      200
0 km         400

**major towns/cities** Braşov, Timişoara, Cluj-Napoca, Iaşl, Constanţa, Galaţi, Craiova, Ploieşti
**major ports** Galaţi, Constanţa, Brăila
**physical features** mountains surrounding a plateau, with river plains in south and east. Carpathian Mountains, Transylvanian Alps; River Danube; Black Sea coast; mineral springs
**head of state** Emil Constantinescu from 1996
**head of government** Radu Vasile from 1998
**political system** emergent democracy
**political parties** Democratic Convention of Romania (DCR), centre-right coalition; Social Democratic Union (SDU), reformist; Social Democracy Party of Romania (PSDR), social democrat; Romanian National Unity Party (RNUP), Romanian nationalist, right wing, anti-Hungarian; Greater Romania Party (Romania Mare), far right, ultranationalist, anti-Semitic; Democratic Party–National Salvation Front (DP–NSF), promarket; National Salvation Front (NSF), centre left; Hungarian Democratic Union of Romania (HDUR), ethnic Hungarian; Christian Democratic–National Peasants' Party (CD–PNC), centre right, promarket; Socialist Labour Party (SLP), ex-communist
**currency** leu
**GNP per capita (PPP)** (US$) 3,970 (1998)
**exports** base metals and metallic articles, textiles and clothing, machinery and equipment, mineral products, foodstuffs. Principal market: Italy 19.5% (1997)
**population** 22,402,000 (1999 est)
**language** Romanian (official), Hungarian, German
**religion** mainly Romanian Orthodox
**life expectancy** 66 (men); 74 (women) (1995–2000)
**Chronology**
**106** Formed heartland of ancient region of Dacia, which was conquered by Roman Emperor Trajan and became a province of Roman Empire; Christianity introduced.
**275** Taken from Rome by invading Goths, a Germanic people.
**4th–10th centuries** Invaded by successive waves of Huns, Avars, Bulgars, Magyars, and Mongols.

**c. 1000** Transylvania, in north, became an autonomous province under Hungarian crown.
**mid-14th century** Two Romanian principalities emerged, Wallachia in south, around Bucharest, and Moldova in northeast.
**15th–16th centuries** The formerly autonomous principalities of Wallachia, Moldova, and Transylvania became tributaries to Ottoman Turks, despite peasant uprisings and resistance from Vlad Tepes ('the Impaler'), ruling prince of Wallachia.
**late 17th century** Transylvania conquered by Austrian Habsburgs.
**1829** Wallachia and Moldova brought under tsarist Russian suzerainty.
**1859** Under Prince Alexandru Ion Cuza, Moldova and Wallachia united to form Romanian state.
**1878** Romania's independence recognized by Great Powers in Congress of Berlin.
**1881** Became kingdom under Carol I.
**1916–18** Fought on Triple Entente side (Britain, France, and Russia) during World War I; acquired Transylvania and Bukovina, in north, from dismembered Austro-Hungarian Empire, and Bessarabia, in east, from Russia. This made it largest state in Balkans.
**1930** To counter growing popularity of fascist and antisemitic 'Iron Guard' mass movement, King Carol II abolished democratic institutions and established dictatorship.
**1940** Forced to surrender Bessarabia and northern Bukovina, adjoining Black Sea, to Soviet Union, and northern Transylvania to Hungary; King Carol II abdicated, handing over effective power to Gen Ion Antonescu, who signed Axis Pact with Germany.
**1941–44** Fought on Germany's side against Soviet Union; thousands of Jews massacred.
**1944** Antonescu ousted; Romania joined war against Germany.
**1945** Occupied by Soviet Union; communist-dominated government installed.
**1947** Paris Peace Treaty reclaimed Transylvania for Romania, but lost southern Dobruja to Bulgaria and northern Bukovina and Bessarabia to Soviet Union; King Michael, son of Carol II, abdicated and People's Republic proclaimed.
**1948–49** New Soviet-style constitution; joined Comecon; nationalization and agricultural collectivization.
**1955** Romania joined Warsaw Pact.
**1958** Soviet occupation forces removed.
**1965** Nicolae Ceauşescu replaced Gheorghe Gheorghiu-Dej as Romanian Communist Party leader, and pursued foreign policy autonomous of Moscow, refusing to participate in Warsaw Pact manoeuvres.
**1975** Ceauşescu made president.
**1985–86** Winters of austerity and power cuts as Ceauşescu refused to liberalize the economy.
**1987** Workers' demonstrations against austerity programme brutally crushed at Braşov.
**1988–89** Relations with Hungary deteriorated over 'systematization programme', designed to forcibly resettle ethnic Hungarians in Transylvania.
**1989** Bloody overthrow of Ceauşescu regime in 'Christmas Revolution'; Ceauşescu and wife

tried and executed; estimated 10,000 dead in civil war. Power assumed by NSF, headed by Ion Iliescu.

**1990** Securitate secret police was replaced by new Romanian Intelligence Service; Eastern Orthodox Church and private farming were re-legalized; the systematization programme was abandoned.

**1991** A privatization law was passed. Prime Minister Petre Roman resigned following riots by striking miners; he was succeeded by Theodor Stolojan heading a new cross-party coalition government.

**1992** NSF split; Iliescu was re-elected president; Nicolai Vacaroiu was appointed prime minister of a minority coalition government.

**1994** A military cooperation pact was made with Bulgaria. Far-right parties were brought into the governing coalition.

**1996** There were signs of economic growth; parliamentary elections were won by the DCR, who formed a coalition government with the SDU; Emil Constantinescu of the Democratic Convention was elected president; Victor Ciorbea was appointed prime minister.

**1997** An economic reform programme and drive against corruption were announced; there was a sharp increase in inflation. Former King Michael returned from exile. The finance minister was dismissed in a shake-up of economic ministries.

**1998** The Social Democrats withdrew support from ruling coalition, criticizing the slow pace of reform. Ciorbea resigned as prime minister, and was replaced by Radu Vasile (CD–PNC). Full EU membership negotiations commenced. GDP contracted by 6% in 1998, following a 6.6% fall in 1997; the level of foreign debt increased sharply and unemployment rose to more than 10%.

**1999** Roadblocks were imposed by tanks north of Bucharest to prevent 10,000 striking miners entering Bucharest.

**Romanian** people of Romanian culture from Romania, Yugoslavia, Moldova, and the surrounding area. There are 20–25 million speakers of the Romanian language.

**Romanian language** member of the Romance branch of the Indo-European language family, spoken in Romania, Macedonia, Albania, and parts of northern Greece. It has been strongly influenced by the Slavonic languages and by Greek. The Cyrillic alphabet was used until the 19th century, when a variant of the Roman alphabet was adopted.

**Roman law** legal system of ancient Rome that is now the basis of ◊civil law, one of the main European legal systems.

**Roman numerals** ancient European number system using symbols different from Arabic numerals (the ordinary numbers 1, 2, 3, 4, 5, and so on). The seven key symbols in Roman numerals, as represented today, are I (1), V (5), X (10), L (50), C (100), D (500), and M (1,000). There is no zero, and therefore no place-value as is fundamental to the Arabic system. The first ten Roman numerals are I, II, III, IV (or IIII), V, VI, VII, VIII, IX, and X. When a Roman symbol is preceded by

a symbol of equal or greater value, the values of the symbols are added (XVI = 16).

When a symbol is preceded by a symbol of less value, the values are subtracted (XL = 40). A horizontal bar over a symbol indicates a multiple of 1,000 ($\bar{X}$ = 10,000). Although addition and subtraction are fairly straightforward using Roman numerals, the absence of a zero makes other arithmetic calculations (such as multiplication) clumsy and difficult.

**Romanov dynasty** rulers of Russia from 1613 to the ◊Russian Revolution 1917. Under the Romanovs, Russia developed into an absolutist empire.

**Roman religion** religious system that retained early elements of animism (with reverence for stones and trees) and totemism (see ◊Romulus and Remus), and had a strong domestic base in the lares and penates, the cult of Janus and Vesta. It also had a main pantheon of gods derivative from the Greek system, which included Jupiter and Juno, Mars and Venus, Minerva, Diana, Ceres, and many lesser deities.

**Romanticism** in literature and the visual arts, a style that emphasizes the imagination, emotions, and creativity of the individual artist. Romanticism also refers specifically to late-18th- and early-19th-century European culture, as contrasted with 18th-century ◊Classicism.

**Romanticism** in music, a preoccupation with subjective emotion expressed primarily through melody, a use of folk idioms, and a cult of the musician as visionary artist and hero (virtuoso). Often linked with nationalistic feelings, the Romantic movement reached its height in the late 19th century, as in the works of Robert Schumann and Richard Wagner.

**Romany** or *Gypsy,* member of a nomadic people believed to have originated in northwestern India and now living throughout the world. They used to be thought of as originating in Egypt, hence the name Gypsy (a corruption of 'Egyptian'). The Romany language, spoken in several different dialects, belongs to the Indic branch of the Indo-European family.

**Rome** Italian *Roma,* capital of Italy and of Lazio region, on the River Tiber, 27 km/17 mi from the Tyrrhenian Sea; population (1992) 2,723,300.

Rome is an important road, rail, and cultural centre. A large section of the population finds employment in government and other offices: the headquarters of the Roman Catholic church (the Vatican City State, a separate sovereign area within Rome) and other international bodies, such as the Food and Agriculture Organization (FAO), are here; it is also a destination for many tourists and pilgrims. Industries have developed, mainly to the south and east of the city; these include engineering, printing, food-processing, electronics, and the manufacture of chemicals, pharmaceuticals, plastics, and clothes. The city is a centre for the film and fashion industries. Among the remains of the ancient city (see ◊Rome, ancient) are the Forum, ◊Colosseum, and Pantheon.

**Rome, ancient history** Ancient Rome was a civilization based on the city of Rome. It lasted for about 800 years. Traditionally founded as a kingdom in 753 BC, Rome became a republic in 510 BC following the expulsion of its last king, Tarquinius Superbus. From then, its history is one of almost continual expansion until the murder of Julius Caesar and the foundation of the empire in 27 BC under ◊Augustus and his successors. At its peak under ◊Trajan, the Roman Empire stretched from Britain to Mesopotamia and the Caspian Sea. A long line of emperors ruling by virtue of military, rather than civil, power marked the beginning of Rome's long decline; under Diocletian the empire was divided into two parts – East and West – although it was temporarily reunited under ◊Constantine, the first emperor to formally adopt Christianity. The end of the Roman Empire is generally dated by the deposition of the last emperor in the west in AD 476. The Eastern Empire continued until 1453 with its capital at Constantinople (modern Istanbul).

**Rome, Treaties of** two international agreements signed 25 March 1957 by Belgium, France, West Germany, Italy, Luxembourg, and the Netherlands, which established the European Economic Community (now the ◊European Union) and the European Atomic Energy Commission (EURATOM).

**Rommel, Erwin Johannes Eugen** (1891–1944) German field marshal. He served in World War I, and in World War II he played an important part in the invasions of central Europe and France. He was commander of the North African offensive from 1941 (when he was nicknamed 'Desert Fox') until defeated in the Battles of El ◊Alamein and he was expelled from Africa in March 1943.

**Romney, George** (1734–1802) English painter. Active in London from 1762, he became, with Thomas Gainsborough and Joshua Reynolds, one of the most successful portrait painters of the late 18th century. His best work is to be found in the straightforward realism of *The Beaumont Family* (National Gallery, London) or the simple charm of *The Parson's Daughter* (Tate Gallery, London).

**Romulus** in Roman legend, the founder and first king of Rome; the son of Mars and Rhea Silvia, daughter of Numitor, king of Alba Longa.

Romulus and his twin brother Remus were thrown into the Tiber by their great-uncle Amulius, who had deposed Numitor, but the infants were saved and suckled by a she-wolf, and later protected by the shepherd Faustulus. On reaching adulthood they killed Amulius, restored Numitor, and founded the city of Rome on the River Tiber.

**Ronaldo** born Luiz de Nazario de Lima Ronaldo (1976– ) Brazilian footballer who was voted FIFA World Player of the Year in 1996 and 1997. A prolific goalscorer, he has twice been transferred for world-record fees, moving from PSV Eindhoven to Barcelona for £13.25 million in 1996, then a year later to Inter Milan for an estimated £21 million. He made his full international debut in 1994 and by October 1999 he had scored 36 goals in 53 internationals.

**Rondônia** federal unit (state) of northwest Brazil, within the drainage basin of the Amazon River, and bordered on the southwest by Bolivia; the centre of Amazonian tin and gold mining and a frontier region of agricultural colonization; area 238,400 sq km/92,000 sq mi; population (1991) 1,130,900; capital Pôrto Velho. Its principal products are rubber and brazil nuts. Known as the Federal Territory of *Guaporé* until 1956, Rondônia became a state in 1981.

**röntgen** alternative spelling for ◊roentgen, unit of X- and gamma-ray exposure.

**Röntgen, Wilhelm Konrad** or *Roentgen* (1845–1923) German physicist. He discovered ◊X-rays 1895. While investigating the passage of electricity through gases, he noticed the ◊fluorescence of a barium platinocyanide screen. This radiation passed through some substances opaque to light, and affected photographic plates. Developments from this discovery revolutionized medical diagnosis. He won the Nobel Prize for Physics in 1901.

**rook** gregarious European ◊crow *Corvus frugilegus*. The plumage is black and lustrous and the face bare; the legs, toes, and claws are also black. A rook can grow to 45 cm/18 in long. Rooks nest in colonies (rookeries) at the tops of trees. They feed mainly on invertebrates found just below the soil surface. The last 5 mm/0.2 in of beak tip is mostly cartilage containing lots of nerve endings to enable the rook to feel for hidden food.

**Roosevelt, Franklin D(elano)** (1882–1945) 32nd president of the USA (1933–45), a Democrat. He served as governor of New York from 1929–33. Becoming president during the Great ◊Depression, he launched the ◊*New Deal* economic and social reform programme, which made him popular with the people. After the outbreak of World War II he introduced lend-lease for the supply of war materials and services to the Allies and drew up the Atlantic Charter of solidarity. Once the USA had entered the war in 1941, he spent much time in meetings with Allied leaders.

**Roosevelt, Theodore** (1858–1919) 26th president of the USA (1901–09), a Republican. After serving as governor of New York from 1898–1900 he became vice president to ◊McKinley, whom he succeeded as president on McKinley's assassination in 1901. He campaigned against the great trusts (associations of enterprises that reduce competition), while carrying on a jingoist foreign policy designed to enforce US supremacy over Latin America.

**root** the part of a plant that is usually underground, and whose primary functions are anchorage and the absorption of water and dissolved mineral salts. Roots usually grow downwards and towards water (that is, they are positively geotropic and hydrotropic; see ◊tropism). Plants such as epiphytic orchids, which grow above ground, produce aerial roots that absorb moisture from the atmosphere.

Others, such as ivy, have climbing roots arising from the stems, which serve to attach the plant to trees and walls.

**root** of an equation, a value that satisfies the equality. For example, $x = 0$ and $x = 5$ are roots of the equation $x^2 - 5x = 0$.

**root** in language, the basic element from which a word is derived. The root is a morpheme, a unit that cannot be subdivided. The Latin word *dominus* ('master'), for example, is a root from which many English words are derived, such as 'dominate', 'dominion', and 'domino'.

**root crop** plant cultivated for its swollen edible root (which may or may not be a true root). Potatoes are the major temperate root crop; the major tropical root crops are cassava, yams, and sweet potatoes. Root crops are second in importance only to cereals as human food. Roots have a high carbohydrate content, but their protein content rarely exceeds 2%. Consequently, communities relying almost exclusively upon roots may suffer from protein deficiency. Food production for a given area from roots is greater than from cereals.

**roots music** term originally denoting ◊reggae, later encompassing any music indigenous to a particular culture; see ◊world music.

**rootstock** another name for ◊rhizome, an underground plant organ.

**Rorschach test** in psychology, a method of diagnosis involving the use of inkblot patterns that subjects are asked to interpret, to help indicate personality type, degree of intelligence, and emotional stability. It was invented by the Swiss psychiatrist Hermann Rorschach (1884–1922).

**Roscommon** (originally *Ros-Comain*, 'wood around a monastery') county of the Republic of Ireland, in the province of Connacht; county town *Roscommon;* area 2,460 sq km/950 sq mi; population (1991) 51,900. It has rich pastures and is bounded on the east by the River Shannon, with bogs and lakes, including Lough Key and Lough Gara. The three largest lakes (loughs Allen, Boderg, and Ree) lie only partly within the county. There is agriculture, especially cattle rearing. Roscommon was established as a county in about 1580. Other important towns are Castlerea, Elphin, and Boyle.

**rose** any shrub or climbing plant belonging to the rose family, with prickly stems and fragrant flowers in many different colours. Numerous cultivated forms have been derived from the sweetbrier or eglantine (*R. rubiginosa*) and dogrose (*R. canina*) native to Europe and Asia. There are many climbing varieties, but the forms most commonly grown in gardens are bush roses and standards (cultivated roses grafted on to a brier stem). (Genus *Rosa*, family Rosaceae.)

**Roseau** formerly *Charlotte Town*, capital of Dominica, West Indies, on the southwest coast of the island; population (1981) 20,000.

**Rosebery, Archibald Philip Primrose, 5th Earl of Rosebery** (1847–1929) British Liberal politician. He was foreign secretary in 1886 and 1892–94, when he succeeded Gladstone as prime minister, but his government survived less than a year. After 1896 his imperialist views gradually placed him further from the mainstream of the Liberal Party. Earl 1868.

**rosemary** evergreen shrub belonging to the mint family, native to the Mediterranean and western Asia, with small, narrow, scented leaves and clusters of pale blue or purple flowers. It is widely cultivated as a herb for use in cooking and for its aromatic oil, used in perfumery and pharmaceuticals. Rosemary is a traditional symbol of remembrance. (*Rosmarinus officinalis,* family Labiatae.)

**Roses, Wars of the** civil wars in England 1455–85 between the houses of ◊Lancaster (badge, red rose) and York (badge, white rose), both of whom claimed the throne through descent from the sons of Edward III. As a result of ◊Henry VI's lapse into insanity in 1453, Richard, Duke of York, was installed as protector of the realm. Upon his recovery, Henry forced York to take up arms in self-defence.

**Rosetta Stone** slab of basalt with inscriptions from 197 BC, found near the town of Rosetta, Egypt, 1799. Giving the same text in three versions – Greek, hieroglyphic, and demotic script – it became the key to deciphering other Egyptian inscriptions.

**Rosh Hashanah** two-day holiday that marks the start of the Jewish New Year (first new Moon after the autumn equinox), traditionally announced by blowing a ram's horn (a shofar).

**Rosicrucians** group of early 17th-century philosophers who claimed occult powers and employed the terminology of ◊alchemy to expound their mystical doctrines (said to derive from Paracelsus). The name comes from books published 1614 and 1615, attributed to Christian Rosenkreutz ('rosy cross'), most probably a pen-name but allegedly a writer living around 1460. Several societies have been founded in Britain and the USA that claim to be their successors, such as the Rosicrucian Fraternity (1614 in Germany, 1861 in the USA).

**Ross, James Clark** (1800–1862) English explorer. He discovered the north magnetic pole 1831. He also went to the Antarctic 1839; Ross Island, Ross Sea, and Ross Dependency are named after him. Knighted 1843.

**Ross Dependency** all the Antarctic islands and territories between 160° east and 150° west longitude, and situated south of 60° south latitude; it includes Edward VII Land, Ross Sea and its islands (including the Balleny Isles), and parts of Victoria Land. It is claimed by New Zealand
*area* 450,000 sq km/173,745 sq mi
*features* the *Ross Ice Shelf* (or Ross Barrier), a permanent layer of ice across the Ross Sea about 425 m/1,394 ft thick
*population* scientific personnel only
*history* claimed by the UK in 1923, with the claim subsequently transferred to New Zealand. It is probable that marine organisms beneath the ice shelf had been undisturbed from the Pleistocene period until drillings were made in 1976.

**Rossellini, Roberto** (1906–1977) Italian film director. His World War II trilogy, *Roma città aperta/Rome, Open City* (1945), *Paisà/ Paisan* (1946), and *Germania anno zero/ Germany Year Zero* (1947), reflects his humanism and is considered a landmark of European cinema.

**Rossetti, Christina Georgina** (1830– 1894) English poet and a devout High Anglican (see ◊Oxford movement). Her best-known work is *Goblin Market and Other Poems* (1862); among others are *The Prince's Progress* (1866), *Annus Domini* (1874), and *A Pageant* (1881). She was the sister of Dante Gabriel ◊Rossetti.

**Rossetti, Dante Gabriel** (1828–1882) English painter and poet. He was a founding member of the ◊*Pre-Raphaelite Brotherhood* (PRB) in 1848. As well as romantic medieval scenes, he produced many idealized portraits of women, including the *Beata Beatrix* (1864). His verse includes 'The Blessed Damozel' (1850). His sister was the poet Christina ◊Rossetti.

**Rossini, Gioacchino Antonio** (1792– 1868) Italian composer. His first success was the opera *Tancredi* 1813. In 1816 his opera buffa *Il barbiere di Siviglia/The Barber of Seville* was produced in Rome. He was the most successful opera composer of his time, producing 20 operas in the period 1815–23. He also created (with Donizetti and Bellini) the 19th-century Italian operatic style.

**Rostov-na-Donu** capital of Rostov oblast (region), southwestern Russian Federation; population (1996 est) 1,025,000. A major industrial and commercial city and the centre of a fertile agricultural region, it lies on the River Don, 46 km/29 mi from its mouth. Rostov is home to many large engineering concerns manufacturing chemicals, agricultural machinery, aircraft, and ships; there are also tobacco and food-processing plants, shoe factories, and textile mills. The city is an important transportation centre; railway lines from Moscow and Kiev converge here, and river cruises run up the Don and Volga. Rostov has been called the 'Gateway to the Caucasus'.

**Roth, Philip Milton** (1933– ) US novelist. His witty, sharply satirical, and increasingly fantastic novels depict the moral and sexual anxieties of 20th-century Jewish-American life, most notably in *Goodbye Columbus* (1959) and *Portnoy's Complaint* (1969). In 1998 he was awarded the National Medal of Arts.

**Rothermere, Vere Harold Esmond Harmsworth, 3rd Viscount Rothermere** (1925–1998) British newspaper proprietor. He became chair of Associated Newspapers in 1971, controlling the right-wing *Daily Mail* (founded by his great-uncle Lord ◊Northcliffe) and *Mail on Sunday* (launched in 1982), the London *Evening Standard,* and a string of regional newspapers.

**Rothko, Mark** Adopted name of Marcus Rothkovich (1903–1970) Russian-born US painter. He was a leading exponent of ◊Abstract Expressionism and a pioneer, towards the end of his life, of Colour Field painting. Typically, his works are canvases covered in large hazy rectangles of thin paint, the colours subtly modulated, as in *Light Red over Black* (Tate Gallery, London).

**rotifer** any of the tiny invertebrates, also called 'wheel animalcules', of the phylum Rotifera. Mainly freshwater, some marine, rotifers have a ring of ◊cilia that carries food to the mouth and also provides propulsion. They are the smallest of multicellular animals – few reach 0.05 cm/0.02 in.

**Rotterdam** industrial city and port in South Holland province, the Netherlands, in the Rhine-Maas delta, 90 km/56 mi southwest of Amsterdam; population (1997) 590,000. The Rotterdam-Europoort complex is the biggest oil refining centre in the world, and one of its foremost ocean cargo ports. Other industries include brewing, distilling, shipbuilding, sugar and petroleum refining, margarine, and tobacco. A canal, the New Waterway (*Nieuwe Waterweg*), links Rotterdam with the North Sea.

**Rottweiler** breed of dog originally developed in Rottweil, Germany, as a herding and guard dog, and subsequently used as a police dog. Powerfully built, the dog is about 63–66 cm/ 25–27 in high at the shoulder, black with tan markings. It has a short coat and docked tail.

**Rouault, Georges Henri** (1871–1958) French painter, etcher, illustrator, and designer. He was one of the major religious artists of the 20th century. Early in his career he was associated with the ◊Fauves, but created his own highly distinctive style using rich, dark colours and heavy outlines. His subjects include clowns, prostitutes, lawyers, and religious figures, as in *Christ Mocked* (1932) (Museum of Modern Art, New York).

**Roubiliac, Louis François** or *Roubillac* (*c.* 1705–1762) French sculptor. A Huguenot, he fled religious persecution to settle in England in 1732. He became a leading sculptor of the day, creating a statue of German composer Georg Handel for Vauxhall Gardens, London, 1737.

**Roundhead** member of the Parliamentary party during the English Civil War 1640–60, opposing the Royalist Cavaliers. The term referred to the short hair then worn only by men of the lower classes.

**Rousseau, Henri Julien Félix** 'Le Douanier' (1844–1910) French painter. A self-taught naive artist, he painted scenes of the Parisian suburbs, portraits, and exotic scenes with painstaking detail, as in *Tropical Storm with a Tiger* 1891 (National Gallery, London). He was much admired by artists such as Gauguin and Picasso, and writers such as the poet Apollinaire.

**Rousseau, Jean-Jacques** (1712–1778) French social philosopher and writer. His book *Du Contrat social/Social Contract* (1762), emphasizing the rights of the people over those of the government, was a significant influence on the French Revolution. In the novel *Emile* (1762), he outlined a new theory of education.

**rowan** another name for the European ◊mountain ash tree.

**rowing** propulsion of a boat by oars, either by one rower with two oars (sculling) or by crews (two, four, or eight persons) with one oar each, often with a coxswain. Major events include the world championship, first held in 1962 for men and 1974 for women, and the Boat Race (between England's Oxford and Cambridge universities), first held in 1829.

**Rowlandson, Thomas** (1757–1827) English painter and illustrator. One of the greatest caricaturists of 18th-century England, his fame rests on his humorous, often bawdy, depictions of the vanities and vices of Georgian social life. He illustrated many books, including *Tour of Dr Syntax in Search of the Picturesque* (1809), which was followed by two sequels between 1812 and 1821.

**royal assent** in the UK, formal consent given by a British sovereign to the passage of a bill through Parliament, after which it becomes an ◊act of Parliament. The last instance of a royal refusal was the rejection of the Scottish Militia Bill of 1702 by Queen Anne.

**royal commission** in the UK and Canada, a group of people appointed by the government (nominally by the sovereign) to investigate a matter of public concern and make recommendations on any actions to be taken in connection with it, including changes in the law. In cases where agreement on recommendations cannot be reached, a minority report can be submitted by dissenters.

**Royal Doulton** British pottery firm. See Henry ◊Doulton.

**Royal Greenwich Observatory** originally one of the two UK national astronomical observatories run by the Particle Physics and Astronomy Research Council (PPARC). It was founded in 1675 at Greenwich, East London, to provide navigational information to sailors. After World War II it moved to Herstmonceux Castle in Sussex, where the 2.5-m/8.2-ft Isaac Newton Telescope (INT) was constructed in 1967. Following the relocation of the INT to the island of La Palma, in the Canary Islands, RGO was relocated to Cambridge in 1988–90. In 1998 the Cambridge site was closed and the RGO merged with the Royal Observatory Edinburgh to form a new Astronomy Technology Centre on the Edinburgh site.

**Royalist** term often used to describe monarchist factions. In England, it is used especially for those who supported Charles I during the English ◊Civil War. They are also known as 'Cavaliers', and their opponents as 'Parliamentarians' or ◊ Roundheads.

**royal prerogative** powers, immunities, and privileges recognized in common law as belonging to the crown. Most prerogative acts in the UK are now performed by the government on behalf of the crown. The royal prerogative belongs to the Queen as a person as well as to the institution called the crown, and the award of some honours and dignities remain her personal choice. As by prerogative 'the king can do no wrong', the monarch is immune from prosecution.

**royalty** in law, payment to the owner for rights to use or exploit literary or artistic copyrights and patent rights in new inventions of all kinds.

**Rozwi empire** or *Changamire,* highly advanced empire in southeastern Africa, located south of the Zambezi River and centred on the stone city of Great Zimbabwe. It replaced the gold-trading empire of Mwene Mutapa from the 15th century. The Rozwi empire survived until the Mfecane of the 1830s, when overpopulation to the south drove the Nguni and Ndebele people northwards into Rozwi territory in search of more land.

**RSI** abbreviation for ◊repetitive strain injury, a condition affecting workers, such as typists, who repeatedly perform certain movements with their hands and wrists.

**Ruanda** part of the former Belgian territory of Ruanda-Urundi until it achieved independence as ◊Rwanda, a country in central Africa.

**rubato** (from Italian *tempo rubato,* 'rubbed time') in music, a pushing or dragging against the beat for expressive effect.

**rubber** coagulated ◊latex of a variety of plants, mainly from the New World. Most important is Para rubber, which comes from the tree *Hevea brasiliensis,* belonging to the spurge family. It was introduced from Brazil to Southeast Asia, where most of the world supply is now produced, the chief exporters being Peninsular Malaysia, Indonesia, Sri Lanka, Cambodia, Thailand, Sarawak, and Brunei. At about seven years the tree, which may grow to 20 m/60 ft, is ready for tapping. Small cuts are made in the trunk and the latex drips into collecting cups. In its pure form, rubber is white and has the chemical formula $(C_5H_8)_n$.

**rubber plant** Asiatic tree belonging to the mulberry family, native to Asia and North Africa, which produces ◊latex in its stem. It has shiny, leathery, oval leaves, and young specimens are grown as house plants. (*Ficus elastica,* family Moraceae.)

**rubella** technical term for ◊German measles.

**Rubens, Peter Paul** (1577–1640) Flemish painter. He was one of the greatest figures of the ◊Baroque. Bringing the exuberance of Italian Baroque to N Europe, he created innumerable religious and allegorical paintings for churches and palaces. These show mastery of drama and movement in large compositions, and a love of rich colour and texture. He also painted portraits and, in his last years, landscapes. *The Rape of the Daughters of Leucippus* of 1617 (Alte Pinakothek, Munich) is typical.

**Rubicon** ancient name of the small river flowing into the Adriatic that, under the Roman Republic, marked the boundary between Italy proper and Cisalpine Gaul. When Caesar led his army across it in 49 BC, he therefore declared war on the Republic; hence to 'cross the Rubicon' means to take an irrevocable step.

**rubidium** (Latin *rubidus* 'red') soft, silver-white, metallic element, symbol Rb, atomic number 37, relative atomic mass 85.47. It is one of the ◊alkali metals, ignites spontaneously in air, and reacts violently with water. It is used in photocells and vacuum-tube filaments.

**ruby** the red transparent gem variety of the mineral ◊corundum $Al_2O_3$ aluminium oxide. Small amounts of chromium oxide, $Cr_2O_3$, substituting for aluminium oxide, give ruby its colour. Natural rubies are found mainly in Myanmar (Burma), but rubies can also be produced artificially and such synthetic stones are used in ◊lasers.

**rudd** or *red eye,* freshwater bony fish allied to the ◊roach. It is tinged with bronze, and has reddish fins, the dorsal being farther back than that of the roach. It is found in British and European lakes and sluggish streams. The largest weigh over 1 kg/2.2 lb and may be as much as 45 cm/18 in long.

The rudd *Scardinius erythropthalmus* belongs to the order Cypriniformes, class Osteichthyes.

**Rudolph** two Holy Roman Emperors:

**Rudolph I** (1218–1291) Holy Roman Emperor from 1273. Originally count of Habsburg, he was the first Habsburg emperor and expanded his dynasty by investing his sons with the duchies of Austria and Styria.

**Rudolph II** (1552–1612) Holy Roman Emperor from 1576, when he succeeded his father Maximilian II. His policies led to unrest in Hungary and Bohemia, which led to the surrender of Hungary to his brother Matthias in 1608 and religious freedom for Bohemia.

**rue** shrubby perennial herb native to southern Europe and temperate Asia. It bears clusters of yellow flowers. An oil extracted from the strongly scented blue-green leaves is used in perfumery. (*Ruta graveolens,* family Rutaceae.)

**ruff** bird *Philomachus pugnax* of the sandpiper family Scolopacidae. The name is taken from the frill of erectile purple-black feathers developed in the breeding season around the neck of the male. The females (reeves) have no ruff; they lay four spotted green eggs in a nest of coarse grass made amongst reeds or rushes. The ruff is found across northern Europe and Asia, and migrates south in winter. It is a casual migrant throughout North America.

**Rugby League** professional form of rugby football founded in England in 1895 as the Northern Union when a dispute about pay caused northern clubs to break away from the Rugby Football Union. The game is similar to ◊Rugby Union, but the number of players was reduced from 15 to 13 in 1906, and other rule changes have made the game more open and fast-moving.

**Rugby Union** form of rugby in which there are 15 players on each side. Points are scored by 'tries', scored by 'touching down' the ball beyond the goal line or by kicking goals from penalties. The Rugby Football Union was formed in 1871

and has its headquarters in England (Twickenham, Middlesex). Formerly an amateur game, the game's status was revoked in August 1995 by the International Rugby Football Board, which lifted restrictions on players moving between Rugby Union and Rugby League.

**Ruhr** river in Germany, length 235 km/146 mi. It rises in the Rothaargebirge Mountains at the eastern boundary of North Rhine-Westphalia, and flows west to join the Rhine at Duisburg. The *Ruhr Valley,* a metropolitan industrial area, produces petrochemicals, cars, iron, and steel at Duisburg and Dortmund; it is also a coal-mining area.

**Ruisdael, Jacob Isaakszoon van** or *Ruysdael* (*c.* 1628–1682) Dutch artist. He is widely considered the greatest of the Dutch landscape painters. He painted scenes near his native town of Haarlem and in Germany, his works often concentrating on the dramatic aspects of nature. A notable example of his atmospheric style is *The Jewish Cemetery,* about 1660 (Gemäldegalerie, Dresden).

**rule of law** doctrine that no individual, however powerful, is above the law. The principle had a significant influence on attempts to restrain the arbitrary use of power by rulers and on the growth of legally enforceable human rights in many Western countries.

It is often used as a justification for separating legislative from judicial power.

**ruminant** any even-toed hoofed mammal with a rumen, the 'first stomach' of its complex digestive system. Plant food is stored and fermented before being brought back to the mouth for chewing (chewing the cud) and then is swallowed to the next stomach. Ruminants include cattle, antelopes, goats, deer, and giraffes, all with a four-chambered stomach. Camels are also ruminants, but they have a three-chambered stomach.

**Rump, the** English parliament formed between December 1648 and November 1653 after Pride's purge of the ◊Long Parliament to ensure a majority in favour of trying Charles I. It was dismissed in 1653 by Cromwell, who replaced it with the ◊Barebones Parliament.

**Rundstedt, (Karl Rudolf) Gerd von** (1875–1953) German field marshal in World War II. Largely responsible for the German breakthrough in France in 1940, he was defeated on the Ukrainian front in 1941. As commander in chief in France from 1942, he resisted the Allied invasion in 1944 and in December launched the temporarily successful Ardennes offensive.

**rune** character in the oldest Germanic script, chiefly adapted from the Latin alphabet, the earliest examples being from the 3rd century and found in Denmark. Runes were scratched on wood, metal, stone, or bone.

**runner** or *stolon,* in botany, aerial stem that produces new plants.

**Rupert, Prince** or *Rupert of the Rhine* (1619–1682) English Royalist general and admiral, born in Prague, son of the Elector Palatine Frederick V and James I's daughter Elizabeth. Defeated by Cromwell at ◊Marston Moor and ◊Naseby in the Civil War, he commanded a privateering fleet (1649–52), until routed by Admiral Robert Blake, and, returning after the Restoration, was a distinguished admiral in the Dutch Wars. He founded the ◊Hudson's Bay Company. He was created Duke of Cumberland and Earl of Holderness in 1644.

**rush** any of a group of grasslike plants found in wet places in cold and temperate regions. The round stems and flexible leaves of some species have been used for making mats and baskets since ancient times. (Genus *Juncus*, family Juncaceae.)

**Rushdie, (Ahmed) Salman** (1947– ) British writer. He was born in India of a Muslim family. His book *Midnight's Children* (1981) deals with India from the date of independence and won the Booker Prize. His novel *The Satanic Verses* (1988) (the title refers to verses deleted from the Koran) offended many Muslims with alleged blasphemy. In 1989 the Ayatollah Khomeini of Iran placed a religious *fatwa* on Rushdie, calling for him and his publishers to be killed.

**Ruskin, John** (1819–1900) English art and social critic. Much of his finest art criticism appeared in two widely influential works, *Modern Painters* (1843–60) and *The Seven Lamps of Architecture* (1849). He was a keen advocate of painters considered unorthodox at the time, such as J M W ◊Turner and members of the ◊Pre-Raphaelite Brotherhood. His later writings were concerned with social and economic problems.

**Russell, Bertrand Arthur William** 3rd Earl Russell (1872–1970) English philosopher, mathematician, and peace campaigner. He contributed to the development of modern mathematical logic and wrote about social issues. His works include *Principia Mathematica* (1910–13; with A N Whitehead), in which he attempted to show that mathematics could be reduced to a branch of logic; *The Problems of Philosophy* (1912); and *A History of Western Philosophy* (1946). He was an outspoken liberal pacifist. He was awarded the Nobel Prize for Literature in 1950. He became the earl in 1931.

**Russell, John** 1st Earl Russell, known until 1861 as Lord John Russell (1792–1878) British Liberal politician, son of the 6th Duke of Bedford. He entered the House of Commons in 1813 and supported Catholic emancipation and the Reform Bill. He held cabinet posts (1830–41), became prime minister (1846–52), and was again a cabinet minister until becoming prime minister again (1865–66). He retired after the defeat of his Reform Bill in 1866.

**Russia** country name originally designating the prerevolutionary Russian Empire (until 1917), now used to refer informally to the Russian Federation.

**Russian** or *Great Russian*, member of the majority ethnic group living in Russia. Russians

are also often the largest minority in neighbouring republics. The Russian language is a member of the East Slavonic branch of the Indo-European language family and was the official language of the USSR. It has 130–150 million speakers and is written in the Cyrillic alphabet. The ancestors of the Russians migrated from central Europe in the 6th–8th centuries AD.

**Russian Federation** (formerly to 1991 *Russian Soviet Federal Socialist Republic (RSFSR)*)

**national name** *Rossiskaya Federatsiya*
**area** 17,075,400 sq km/6,592,811 sq mi
**capital** Moscow
**major towns/cities** St Petersburg (Leningrad), Nizhniy Novgorod (Gorky), Rostov-na-Donu, Samara (Kuibyshev), Tver (Kalinin), Volgograd, Vyatka (Kirov), Yekaterinburg (Sverdlovsk), Novosibirsk, Chelyabinsk, Kazan, Omsk, Perm, Ufa
**physical features** fertile Black Earth district; extensive forests; the Ural Mountains with large mineral resources; Lake Baikal, world's deepest lake
**head of state** Boris Yeltsin from 1991
**head of government** Sergei Stepashin from 1999
**political system** emergent democracy
**political parties** Russia is Our Home, centrist; Party of Unity and Accord (PRUA), moderate reformist; Communist Party of the Russian Federation (CPRF), left wing, conservative (ex-communist); Agrarian Party, rural-based, centrist; Liberal Democratic Party, far right, ultranationalist; Congress of Russian Communities, populist, nationalist; Russia's Choice, reformist, centre right; Yabloko, gradualist free market; Russian Social Democratic People's Party (Derzhava), communist-nationalist; Patriotic Popular Union of Russia (PPUR), communist-led; Russian People's Republican Party (RPRP)
**currency** rouble
**GNP per capita (PPP)** (US$) 3,950 (1998)
**exports** mineral fuels, ferrous and non-ferrous metals and derivatives, precious stones, chemical products, machinery and transport equip-

ment, weapons, timber and paper products. Principal market: Ukraine 9.1% (1998)
**population** 147,195,000 (1999 est)
**language** Russian
**religion** traditionally Russian Orthodox
**life expectancy** 61 (men); 73 (women) (1995–2000)
**Chronology**
**9th–10th centuries** Viking chieftains established own rule in Novgorod, Kiev, and other cities.
**10th–12th centuries** Kiev temporarily united Russian peoples into its empire. Christianity introduced from Constantinople 988.
**13th century** Mongols (Golden Horde) overran the southern steppes in 1223, compelling Russian princes to pay tribute.
**14th century** Byelorussia and Ukraine came under Polish rule.
**1462–1505** Ivan the Great, grand duke of Muscovy, threw off Mongol yoke and united lands in northwest.
**1547–84** Ivan the Terrible assumed title of tsar and conquered Kazan and Astrakhan; colonization of Siberia began.
**1613** First Romanov tsar, Michael, elected after period of chaos.
**1667** Following Cossack revolt, eastern Ukraine reunited with Russia.
**1682–1725** Peter the Great modernized the bureaucracy and army; he founded a navy and a new capital, St Petersburg, introduced Western education, and wrested the Baltic seaboard from Sweden. By 1700 colonization of Siberia had reached the Pacific.
**1762–96** Catherine the Great annexed the Crimea and part of Poland and recovered western Ukraine and Byelorussia.
**1798–1814** Russia intervened in Revolutionary and Napoleonic Wars (1798–1801, 1805–07); repelled Napoleon, and took part in his overthrow (1812–14).
**1827–29** Russian attempts to dominate Balkans led to war with Turkey.
**1853–56** Crimean War.
**1856–64** Caucasian War of conquest completed annexation of northern Caucasus, causing more than a million people to emigrate.
**1858–60** Treaties of Aigun 1858 and Peking 1860 imposed on China, annexing territories north of the Amur and east of the Ussuri rivers; Vladivostok founded on Pacific coast.
**1861** Serfdom abolished (on terms unfavourable to peasants). Rapid growth of industry followed, a working-class movement developed, and revolutionary ideas spread, culminating in assassination of Alexander II in 1881.
**1877–78** Russo-Turkish War.
**1898** Social Democratic Party founded by Russian Marxists; split into Bolshevik and Menshevik factions in 1903.
**1904–05** Russo-Japanese War caused by Russian expansion in Manchuria.
**1905** A revolution, though suppressed, forced tsar to accept parliament (Duma) with limited powers.

**1914** Russo-Austrian rivalry in Balkans was a major cause of outbreak of World War I; Russia fought in alliance with France and Britain.
**1917** Russian Revolution: tsar abdicated, provisional government established; Bolsheviks seized power under Vladimir Lenin.
**1918** Treaty of Brest-Litovsk ended war with Germany; murder of former tsar; Russian Empire collapsed; Finland, Poland, and Baltic States seceded.
**1918–22** Civil War between Red Army, led by Leon Trotsky, and White Russian forces with foreign support; Red Army ultimately victorious; control regained over Ukraine, Caucasus, and Central Asia.
**1922** Former Russian Empire renamed Union of Soviet Socialist Republics.
**1924** Death of Lenin.
**1928** Joseph Stalin emerged as absolute ruler after ousting Trotsky.
**1928–33** First Five-Year Plan collectivized agriculture by force; millions died in famine.
**1936–38** The Great Terror: Stalin executed his critics and imprisoned millions of people on false charges of treason and sabotage.
**1939** Nazi-Soviet nonaggression pact; USSR invaded eastern Poland and attacked Finland.
**1940** USSR annexed Baltic States.
**1941–45** 'Great Patriotic War' against Germany ended with Soviet domination of eastern Europe and led to 'Cold War' with USA and its allies.
**1949** Council for Mutual Economic Assistance (Comecon) created to supervise trade in Soviet bloc.
**1953** Stalin died; 'collective leadership' in power.
**1955** Warsaw Pact created.
**1956** Nikita Khrushchev made 'secret speech' criticizing Stalin; USSR invaded Hungary.
**1957–58** Khrushchev ousted his rivals and became effective leader, introducing limited reforms.
**1960** Rift between USSR and Communist China.
**1962** Cuban missile crisis: Soviet nuclear missiles installed in Cuba but removed after ultimatum from USA.
**1964** Khrushchev ousted by new 'collective leadership' headed by Leonid Brezhnev and Alexei Kosygin.
**1968** USSR and allies invaded Czechoslovakia.
**1970s** 'Détente' with USA and western Europe.
**1979** USSR invaded Afghanistan; fighting continued until Soviet withdrawal ten years later.
**1982** Brezhnev died; Uri Andropov became leader.
**1984** Andropov died; Konstantin Chernenko became leader.
**1985** Chernenko died; Mikhail Gorbachev became leader and announced wide-ranging reform programme (*perestroika*).
**1986** Chernobyl nuclear disaster.
**1988** Special All-Union Party Congress approved radical constitutional changes and market reforms; start of open nationalist unrest in Caucasus and Baltic republics.
**1989** Multi-candidate elections held in move towards 'socialist democracy'; collapse of Soviet

satellite regimes in eastern Europe; end of Cold War.

**1990** Anticommunists and nationalists polled strongly in multiparty local elections; Baltic and Caucasian republics defied central government; Boris Yeltsin became president of Russian Federation and left the Communist Party.

**1991** There was an unsuccessful coup by hard-line communists; republics declared independence; communist rule dissolved in the Russian Federation; the USSR was replaced by a loose Commonwealth of Independent States (CIS).

**1992** Russia assumed former USSR seat on the United Nations (UN) Security Council; a new constitution was devised; end of price controls.

**1993** There was a power struggle between Yeltsin and the Congress of People's Deputies; congress was dissolved; an attempted coup was foiled; a new parliament was elected.

**1994** Russia joined NATO 'Partnership for Peace'; Russian forces invaded the breakaway republic of Chechnya.

**1995** The bloody civil war in Chechnya continued.

**1996** President Yeltsin was re-elected. A peace plan was forged and Russian troops withdrew from Chechnya.

**1997** A peace treaty was signed with Chechnya. Yeltsin signed an agreement on cooperation with NATO. Russia gained effective admission to the G-7 group.

**1998** President Yeltsin sacked the government and appointed Sergei Kiriyenko as prime minister. The rouble was heavily devalued. Kiriyenko was sacked as prime minister, and former communist spy chief, Yevgeny Primakov, became the new prime minister, heading a government including prominent figures associated with Soviet state planning, as market-centred reform was abandoned. Yury Luzhkov, the popular mayor of Moscow, formed a new centrist movement, Otechestvo (Fatherland). The USA pledged aid of over 3 million tonnes of grain and meat, after a 5% contraction in GDP in 1998.

**1999** Primakov's government dismissed by President Yeltsin; Sergei Stepashin was appointed prime minister; Yeltsin resigned.

**Russian Orthodox Church** another name for the ◊Orthodox Church.

**Russian Revolution** two revolutions of February and October 1917 (Julian ◊calendar) that began with the overthrow of the Romanov dynasty and ended with the establishment of a communist soviet (council) state, the Union of Soviet Socialist Republics (USSR). In October Bolshevik workers and sailors, led by Vladimir Ilyich ◊Lenin, seized government buildings and took over power.

**Russian revolution, 1905** political upheaval centred in and around St Petersburg, Russia (1905–1906), leading up to the February and October revolutions of 1917. On 22 January 1905 thousands of striking unarmed workers marched to Tsar Nicholas II's Winter Palace in St Petersburg, to ask for reforms. Government troops fired on the crowd, killing many people. After this 'Bloody Sunday' slaughter the

revolution gained strength, culminating in a general strike which paralysed the whole country in October 1905. Revolutionaries in St Petersburg formed a 'soviet' (council) called the Soviet of Workers' Deputies. Nicholas II then granted the Duma (parliament) the power to pass or reject proposed laws. Although these measures satisfied the liberal element, the revolution continued to gain ground and came to a head when the army crushed a serious uprising in December 1905.

**Soviet Federal Socialist Republic** (RSFSR), the largest republic of the former Soviet Union; it became independent as the Russian Federation in 1991.

**Russo-Japanese War** war between Russia and Japan (1904–05), which arose from conflicting ambitions in Korea and ◊Manchuria, specifically, the Russian occupation of Port Arthur (modern Lüshun) in 1897 and of the Amur province in 1900. Japan successfully besieged Port Arthur from May in 1904–January 1905, took Mukden (modern Shenyang) on 29 February–10 March, and on 27 May defeated the Russian Baltic fleet, which had sailed halfway around the world to Tsushima Strait. A peace was signed 23 August 1905. Russia surrendered its lease on Port Arthur, ceded southern Sakhalin to Japan, evacuated Manchuria, and recognized Japan's interests in Korea.

**russula** any of a large group of fungi (see ◊fungus), containing many species. They are medium-to-large mushrooms with flattened caps, and many are brightly coloured. (Genus *Russula*.)

**rust** in botany, the common name for a group of minute parasitic fungi (see ◊fungus) that appear on the leaves of their hosts as orange-red spots, later becoming darker. The commonest is the wheat rust (*Puccinia graminis*). (Order Uredinales.)

**rust** reddish-brown oxide of iron formed by the action of moisture and oxygen on the metal. It consists mainly of hydrated iron(III) oxide ($Fe_2O_3.H_2O$) and iron(III) hydroxide ($Fe(OH)_3$). Rusting is the commonest form of ◊corrosion.

**Ruthenia** or *Carpathian Ukraine,* a region of central Europe, on the southern slopes of the Carpathian Mountains, home of the Ruthenes or Russniaks. Dominated by Hungary from the 10th century, it was part of Austria-Hungary until World War I. In 1918 it was divided between Czechoslovakia, Poland, and Romania; independent for a single day in 1938, it was immediately occupied by Hungary, captured by the USSR in 1944 and incorporated from 1945–47 (as the Transcarpathian Region) into Ukraine Republic, which became independent as Ukraine in 1991.

**ruthenium** hard, brittle, silver-white, metallic element, symbol Ru, atomic number 44, relative atomic mass 101.07. It is one of the so-called platinum group of metals; it occurs in platinum ores as a free metal and in the natural alloy osmiridium. It is used as a hardener in alloys and as a catalyst; its compounds are used as colouring agents in glass and ceramics.

**Rutherford, Ernest**, 1st Baron Rutherford of Nelson (1871–1937) New Zealand-born British physicist. He was a pioneer of modern atomic science. His main research was in the field of ◊radioactivity, and he discovered alpha, beta, and gamma rays. He was the first to recognize the nuclear nature of the atom in 1911. He was awarded a Nobel prize in 1908.

**rutherfordium** synthesized, radioactive, metallic element, symbol Rf. It is the first of the ◊transactinide series, atomic number 104, relative atomic mass 262. It is produced by bombarding californium with carbon nuclei and has ten isotopes, the longest-lived of which, Rf-262, has a half-life of 70 seconds.

**Ruysdael, Jacob van** Dutch painter; see Jacob van ◊Ruisdael.

**Rwanda** Republic of
*national name* *Republika y'u Rwanda*

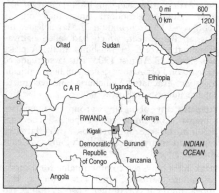

**area** 26,338 sq km/10,169 sq mi
**capital** Kigali
**major towns/cities** Butare, Ruhengeri, Gisenyi
**physical features** high savanna and hills, with volcanic mountains in northwest; part of lake Kivu; highest peak Mount Karisimbi 4,507 m/ 14,792 ft; Kagera River (whose headwaters are the source of the Nile)
**head of state** Pasteur Bizimungu from 1994
**head of government** Pierre Celestin Rwigema from 1995
**political system** transitional
**political parties** National Revolutionary Development Movement (MRND), nationalist-socialist, Hutu-oriented; Social Democratic Party (PSD), left of centre; Christian Democratic Party (PDC), Christian, centrist; Republican Democratic Movement (MDR), Hutu nationalist; Liberal Party (PL), moderate centrist; Rwanda Patriotic Front (FPR), Tutsi-led but claims to be multiethnic
**currency** Rwanda franc
**GNP per capita (PPP)** (US$) 690 (1998)
**exports** coffee, tea, tin ores and concentrates, pyrethrum, quinquina. Principal market: Belgium–Luxembourg 36.1% (1997)
**population** 7,235,000 (1999 est)
**language** Kinyarwanda, French (official); Kiswahili

**religion** Roman Catholic 54%, animist 23%, Protestant 12%, Muslim 9%
**life expectancy** 39 (men); 42 (women) (1995– 2000)
***Chronology***
***10th century onwards*** Hutu peoples settled in region formerly inhabited by hunter-gatherer Twa Pygmies, becoming peasant farmers.
***14th century onwards*** Majority Hutu community came under dominance of cattle-owning Tutsi peoples, immigrants from the east, who became a semi-aristocracy and established control through land and cattle contracts.
***15th century*** Ruganzu Bwimba, a Tutsi leader, founded kingdom near Kigali.
***17th century*** Central Rwanda and outlying Hutu communities subdued by Tutsi mwami (king) Ruganzu Ndori.
***late 19th century*** Under the great Tutsi king, Kigeri Rwabugiri, a unified state with a centralized military structure was established.
***1890*** Known as Ruandi, the Tutsi kingdom, along with neighbouring Burundi, came under nominal German control, as Ruanda-Urundi.
***1916*** Occupied by Belgium, during World War I.
***1923*** Belgium granted League of Nations mandate to administer Ruanda-Urundi; they were to rule 'indirectly' through Tutsi chiefs.
***1959*** Interethnic warfare between Hutu and Tutsi, forcing mwami (king) Kigeri V into exile.
***1961*** Republic proclaimed after mwami deposed.
***1962*** Independence from Belgium achieved as Rwanda, with Hutu Grégoire Kayibanda as president; many Tutsis left the country.
***1963*** 20,000 killed in interethnic clashes, after Tutsis exiled in Burundi had launched a raid.
***1973*** Kayibanda ousted in military coup led by Hutu Maj-Gen Juvenal Habyarimana; this was caused by resentment of Tutsis, who held some key government posts.
***1981*** Elections created civilian legislation, but dominated by Hutu socialist National Revolutionary Development Movement (MRND), in a one-party state.
***1988*** Hutu refugees from Burundi massacres streamed into Rwanda.
***1990*** The government was attacked by the Rwanda Patriotic Front (FPR), a Tutsi refugee military-political organization based in Uganda, which controlled parts of northern Rwanda.
***1992*** There was a peace accord with FPR.
***1993*** A United Nations (UN) mission was sent to monitor the peace agreement.
***1994*** President Habyarimana and Burundian Hutu president Ntaryamira were killed in an air crash; involvement of FPR was suspected. Half a million people were killed in the ensuing civil war, with many Tutsi massacred by Hutu death squads and the exodus of 2 million refugees to neighbouring countries. The government fled as FPR forces closed in. French peacekeeping troops established 'safe zone' in the southwest. An interim coalition government was installed, with moderate Hutu and FPR leader, Pasteur Bizimungu, as president.

**1995** A war-crimes tribunal opened and government human-rights abuses were reported.
**1996** Rwanda and Zaire (Democratic Republic of Congo) were on the brink of war after Tutsi killings of Hutu in Zaire. A massive Hutu refugee crisis was narrowly averted as thousands were allowed to return to Rwanda.
**1997** There were further Tutsi killings by Hutus.
**1998** 378 rebels were killed by the Rwandan army.

**rye** tall annual ◊cereal grass grown extensively in northern Europe and other temperate regions. The flour is used to make dark-coloured ('black') breads. Rye is grown mainly as a food crop for animals, but the grain is also used to make whisky and breakfast cereals. (*Secale cereale.*)

**Ryle, Martin** (1918–1984) English radio astronomer. At the Mullard Radio Astronomy Observatory, Cambridge, he developed the technique of sky-mapping using 'aperture synthesis', combining smaller dish aerials to give the characteristics of one large one. His work on the distribution of radio sources in the universe brought confirmation of the ◊Big Bang theory. He was knighted in 1966, and won, with his co-worker the English radio astronomer Antony Hewish, the Nobel Prize for Physics in 1974.

**Ryukyu Islands** or *Riukiu* or *Nansei,* southernmost island group of Japan, stretching towards Taiwan and including Okinawa, Miyako, and Ishigaki
**area** 2,254 sq km/870 sq mi
**capital** Naha (on Okinawa)
**features** 73 islands, some uninhabited; subject to typhoons
**industries** sugar, pineapples, fish
**population** (1985) 1,179,000
**history** originally an independent kingdom; ruled by China from the late 14th century until seized by Japan in 1609 and controlled by the Satsuma feudal lords from 1611 until 1868, when the Japanese government took over. Chinese claims to the islands were relinquished in 1895. In 1945, during World War II, the islands were taken by the USA (see ◊Okinawa); northernmost group, Oshima, restored to Japan in 1953, the rest in 1972.

**S** abbreviation for *south*.

**Saarinen, (Gottlieb) Eliel** (1873–1950) Finnish-born US architect and town planner. He founded the Finnish Romantic school. His best-known European project is the Helsinki railway station (1905–14). In 1923 he emigrated to the USA, where he is remembered for his designs for the Cranbrook Academy of Art in Bloomfield Hills, Michigan (1926–43), and Christ Church, Minneapolis (1949).

**Saarinen, Eero** (1910–1961) Finnish-born US architect. He was renowned for his wide range of innovative modernist designs, experimenting with different structures and shapes. His works include the US embassy, London (1955–61); the TWA terminal at John F Kennedy Airport, New York City (1956–62); and Dulles Airport, Washington, DC (1958–63). He collaborated on a number of projects with his father, Eliel ◊Saarinen.

**Saarland** French *Sarre,* administrative region (German *Land*) in southwest Germany, bordered by Rhineland-Palatinate and the French *departement* of Moselle
**area** 2,570 sq km/992 sq mi
**capital** Saarbrücken
**towns and cities** Neunkirchen, Völklingen, Saarlouis
**physical**   one-third   forest;   crossed northwest–south by the River Saar
**industries** motor vehicles, mechanical and electrical engineering; former flourishing coal and steel industries survive only by government subsidy
**agriculture** cereals and other crops; cattle, pigs, poultry
**population** (1995) 1,103,000
**history** Saar district administered in 1919 by France under the auspices of the League of Nations; returned by plebiscite to Germany in 1935; given the name Saarbrücken by Hitler; part of French zone of occupation in 1945; included in the economic union with France in 1947; returned to Germany in 1957.

**Sabah** self-governing state of the federation of Malaysia, occupying northeast Borneo, forming (with Sarawak) East Malaysia
**area** 73,613 sq km/28,415 sq mi
**capital** Kota Kinabalu (formerly Jesselton)
**physical** chiefly mountainous (highest peak Mount Kinabalu 4,098 m/13,450 ft) and forested
**industries** hardwoods (25% of the world's supplies), rubber, fish, cocoa, palm oil, copper, copra, and hemp
**population** (1990) 1,736,900, of which the Kadazans form the largest ethnic group at 30%; also included are 250,000 immigrants from Indonesia and the Philippines
**language** Malay (official) and English
**religion** Sunni Muslim and Christian (the Kadazans, among whom there is unrest about increasing Muslim dominance)
**government** consists of a constitutional head of state with a chief minister, cabinet, and legislative assembly
**history** In 1877–78 the sultan of Sulu made concessions to the North Borneo Company, which was eventually consolidated with Labuan as a British colony in 1946, and became the state of Sabah within Malaysia in 1963. The Philippines advanced territorial claims on Sabah in 1962 and 1968 on the grounds that the original cession by the sultan was illegal, Spain having then been sovereign in the area.

**Sabah, Sheikh Jabir al-Ahmad al-Jabir al-** (1928–   ) Emir of Kuwait from 1977. He suspended the national assembly in 1986 after mounting parliamentary criticism, ruling in a feudal, paternalistic manner. On the invasion of Kuwait by Iraq in 1990 he fled to Saudi Arabia, returning to Kuwait in March in 1991. In 1992 a reconstituted national assembly was elected.

**Sabatini, Gabriela** (1970–   ) Argentine tennis player. In 1986 she became the youngest Wimbledon semifinalist for 99 years. She was ranked number three in the world behind Monica Seles and Steffi Graf in 1991. She retired from professional tennis in October 1996.

**Sabbath** (Hebrew *shābath,* 'to rest') the seventh day of the week, commanded by God in the Old Testament as a sacred day of rest; in Judaism, from sunset Friday to sunset Saturday; in Christianity, Sunday (or, in some sects, Saturday).

**Sabine** member of an ancient people of central Italy, conquered by the Romans and amalgamated with them in the 3rd century BC. The so-called *rape of the Sabine women* – a mythical attempt by ◊Romulus in the early days of Rome to carry off the Sabine women to colonize the new city – is frequently depicted in art.

**sable** marten *Martes zibellina,* about 50 cm/20 in long and usually brown. It is native to northern Eurasian forests, but now found mainly in eastern Siberia. The sable has diminished in numbers because of its valuable fur, which has long attracted hunters.
   Conservation measures and sable farming have been introduced to save it from extinction.

**saccharide** another name for a ◊sugar molecule.

**saccharin** or *ortho-sulpho benzimide,* $C_7H_5NO_3S$ sweet, white, crystalline solid derived from coal tar and substituted for sugar.

Since 1977 it has been regarded as potentially carcinogenic. Its use is not universally permitted and it has been largely replaced by other sweetening agents.

**sacrament** in Christian usage, observances forming the visible sign of inward grace. In the Roman Catholic Church there are seven sacraments: baptism, Holy Communion (Eucharist or Mass), confirmation, rite of reconciliation (confession and penance), holy orders, matrimony, and the anointing of the sick.

**Sacramento** capital and deep-water port of ◊California, USA, 130 km/80 mi northeast of San Francisco; population (1996 est) 376,200; metropolitan area (1992) 1,563,000. Situated in Central Valley, the city lies on the Sacramento River as it curves towards San Francisco Bay. It is the commercial, manufacturing, and distribution centre for a rich irrigated farming area, and provides government, military, and tourist services. Industries include the manufacture of detergents, jet aircraft, arms, and processed foods; almonds, peaches, and pears are local agricultural specialities.

**Sadat, (Muhammad) Anwar** (1918– 1981) Egyptian politician, president 1970–81. Succeeding ◊Nasser as president in 1970, he restored morale by his handling of the Egyptian campaign in the 1973 war against Israel. In 1974 his plan for economic, social, and political reform to transform Egypt was unanimously adopted in a referendum. In 1977 he visited Israel to reconcile the two countries, and shared the Nobel Peace Prize with Israeli prime minister Menachem Begin in 1978. Although feted by the West for pursuing peace with Israel, Sadat was denounced by the Arab world. He was assassinated by Islamic fundamentalists and succeeded by Hosni Mubarak.

**Sadducee** Hebrew 'righteous', member of the ancient Hebrew political party and sect of ◊Judaism that formed in pre-Roman Palestine in the first century BC. They were the group of priestly aristocrats in Jerusalem until the final destruction of the Temple in AD 70.

**Sade, Donatien Alphonse François, comte de** known as *the Marquis de Sade* (1740–1814) French writer. He was imprisoned for sexual offences and finally committed to an asylum. He wrote plays and novels dealing explicitly with a variety of sexual practices, including ◊sadism, deriving pleasure or sexual excitement from inflicting pain on others.

**sadism** tendency to derive pleasure (usually sexual) from inflicting physical or mental pain on others. The term is derived from the Marquis de ◊Sade.

**safflower** thistlelike Asian plant with large orange-yellow flowers. It is widely grown for the oil from its seeds, which is used in cooking, margarine, and paints and varnishes; the leftovers are used as cattle feed. (*Carthamus tinctorius,* family Compositae.)

**saffron** crocus plant belonging to the iris family, probably native to southwestern Asia, and formerly widely cultivated in Europe; also the dried orange-yellow ◊stigmas of its purple flowers, used for colouring and flavouring in cookery. (*Crocus sativus,* family Iridaceae.)

**saga** prose narrative written down in the 11th–13th centuries in Norway and Iceland. The sagas range from family chronicles, such as the *Landnamabok* of Ari (1067–1148), to legendary and anonymous works such as *Njal's Saga.*

**sage** perennial herb belonging to the mint family, with grey-green aromatic leaves used for flavouring in cookery. It grows up to 50 cm/20 in high and has bluish-lilac or pink flowers. (*Salvia officinalis,* family Labiatae.)

**Sagittarius** bright zodiac constellation in the southern hemisphere, represented as a centaur aiming a bow and arrow at neighbouring Scorpius. The Sun passes through Sagittarius from mid-December to mid-January, including the winter solstice, when it is farthest south of the Equator. The constellation contains many nebulae and globular clusters, and open star clusters. Kaus Australis and Nunki are its brightest stars. The centre of our Galaxy, the ◊Milky Way, is marked by the radio source Sagittarius A. In astrology, the dates for Sagittarius are about 22 November–21 December (see ◊precession).

**sago** starchy material obtained from the pith of the sago palm *Metroxylon sagu.* It forms a nutritious food and is used for manufacturing glucose and sizing textiles.

**Sahara** Arabic *Sahra* 'wilderness', largest desert in the world, occupying around 9,000,000 sq km/3,500,000 sq mi of north Africa from the Atlantic to the Nile, covering: west Egypt; part of west Sudan; large parts of Mauritania, Mali, Niger, and Chad; and southern parts of Morocco, Algeria, Tunisia, and Libya. Small areas in Algeria and Tunisia are below sea level, but it is mainly a plateau with a central mountain system, including the Ahaggar Mountains in Algeria, the Aïr Massif in Niger, and the Tibesti Massif in Chad, of which the highest peak is Emi Koussi, 3,415 m/11,208 ft.

**Sahel** (Arabic *sahil* 'coast') marginal area to the south of the Sahara, from Senegal to Somalia, which experiences desert-like conditions during periods of low rainfall. The ◊desertification is partly due to climatic fluctuations but has also been caused by the pressures of a rapidly expanding population, which has led to overgrazing and the destruction of trees and scrub for fuelwood. In recent years many famines have taken place in the area.

**Saigon** former name (to 1976) of ◊Ho Chi Minh City, Vietnam.

**Saigon, Battle of** during the Vietnam War, battle from 29 January to 23 February 1968, when 5,000 Vietcong were expelled by South Vietnamese and US forces. The city was finally taken by North Vietnamese forces 30 April 1975, after South Vietnamese withdrawal from the central highlands.

**sailing** sport involving cruising or racing a small vessel; see ◊yachting.

**saint** holy man or woman respected for his or her wisdom, spirituality, and dedication to their faith. Within the Roman Catholic Church a saint is officially recognized through canonization by the pope. Many saints are associated with miracles and canonization usually occurs after a thorough investigation of the lives and miracles attributed to them. For individual saints, see under forename; for example, ◊Paul, St.

**St Andrews** town in Fife, Scotland, 19 km/12 mi southeast of Dundee; population (1991) 11,100. Its university (1411) is the oldest in Scotland. It is considered to be the 'home of golf', with a famous Old Course. The Royal and Ancient Club (1754) is the ruling body of golf. There is a ruined cathedral, founded in 1160 and consecrated in 1318.

**St Bartholomew, Massacre of** slaughter of ◊Huguenots (Protestants) in Paris, (24 August–17 September 1572, and until 3 October in the provinces). About 25,000 people are believed to have been killed. When ◊Catherine de' Medici's plot to have Admiral Coligny assassinated failed, she resolved to have all the Huguenot leaders killed, persuading her son Charles IX that it was in the interest of public safety.

**St Christopher–Nevis** alternate form of St Kitts and Nevis.

**Saint-Exupéry, Antoine Marie Roger de** (1900–1944) French author and pilot. He wrote the autobiographical *Vol de nuit/Night Flight* 1931 and *Terre des hommes/Wind, Sand, and Stars* 1939. His children's book *Le Petit Prince/The Little Prince* 1943 is also an adult allegory.

**St George's** port and capital of Grenada, on the southwest coast; population (1989) 35,700. It was founded in 1650 by the French.

**St Helena** British island in the south Atlantic, 1,900 km/1,200 mi west of Africa, area 122 sq km/47 sq mi; population (1997) 5,644. Its capital is Jamestown, and it exports fish and timber. Ascension and Tristan da Cunha islands are dependencies.

**St Helens, Mount** volcanic mountain in Skamania County, Washington. It is located on the western flank of the Cascade Range, 56 km/35 mi east of Kelso, in the Gifford Pinchot National Forest. Dormant since 1857, it erupted on 18 May 1980, devastating an area of 600 sq km/230 sq mi, and killing 60 people; its height was reduced from 2,950 m/9,682 ft to 2,560 m/8,402 ft. The Mount St Helens National Volcanic Monument now surrounds the peak.

**St John's** port and capital of Antigua and Barbuda, on the northwest coast of Antigua; population (1992) 38,000. It exports rum, cotton, and sugar.

**Saint-Just, Louis Antoine Léon Florelle de** (1767–1794) French revolutionary. A close associate of ◊Robespierre, he became a member of the Committee of Public Safety in 1793, and was guillotined with Robespierre.

**St Kitts and Nevis** (or St Christopher and Nevis) Federation of

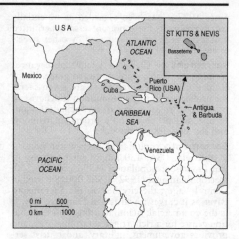

**area** 262 sq km/101 sq mi (St Kitts 168 sq km/65 sq mi, Nevis 93 sq km/36 sq mi)
**capital** Basseterre (on St Kitts) (and chief port)
**major towns/cities** Charlestown (largest on Nevis), Newcastle, Sandy Point Town, Dieppe Bay Town
**physical features** both islands are volcanic; fertile plains on coast; black beaches
**head of state** Queen Elizabeth II from 1983, represented by governor general Clement Arrindell from 1983
**head of government** Denzil Douglas from 1995
**political system** federal constitutional monarchy
**political parties** People's Action Movement (PAM), centre right; Nevis Reformation Party (NRP), Nevis-separatist, centrist; Labour Party (SKLP), moderate left of centre
**currency** East Caribbean dollar
**GNP per capita (PPP)** (US$) 7,940 (1998)
**exports** sugar, manufactures, postage stamps; sugar and sugar products accounted for approximately 40% of export earnings in 1992. Principal market: USA 46.6% (1996)
**population** 42,000 (1999 est)
**language** English (official)
**religion** Anglican 36%, Methodist 32%, other Protestant 8%, Roman Catholic 10%
**life expectancy** 65 (men); 71 (women) (1998 est)
*Chronology*
**1493** Visited by the explorer Christopher Columbus, after whom the main island is named, but for next two centuries the islands were left in the possession of the indigenous Caribs.
**1623 and 1628** St Kitts and Nevis islands successively settled by British as their first Caribbean colony, with 2,000 Caribs brutally massacred in 1626.
**1783** In the Treaty of Versailles, France, which had long disputed British possession, rescinded its claims to the islands, on which sugar cane plantations developed, worked by imported African slaves.
**1816** Anguilla was joined politically to the two islands.

**1834** Abolition of slavery.
**1871–1956** Part of the Leeward Islands Federation.
**1932** Centre-left Labour Party founded to campaign for independence.
**1937** Internal self-government granted.
**1952** Universal adult suffrage granted.
**1958–62** Part of the Federation of the West Indies.
**1967** St Kitts, Nevis, and Anguilla achieved internal self-government, within the British Commonwealth, with Robert Bradshaw, Labour Party leader, as prime minister.
**1970** NRP formed, calling for separation for Nevis.
**1971** Anguilla returned to being a British dependency after rebelling against domination by St Kitts.
**1978** Bradshaw died; succeeded by Paul Southwell.
**1979** Southwell died; succeeded by Lee L Moore.
**1980** People's Action Movement (PAM) and NRP centrist coalition government, led by Kennedy Simmonds, formed after inconclusive general election.
**1983** Full independence was achieved within the Commonwealth.
**1993** Simmonds continued in office despite criticism of his leadership. Antigovernment demonstrations followed an inconclusive general election.
**1994** A three-week state of emergency was imposed after violent antigovernment riots by Labour Party supporters in Basseterre.
**1995** Labour Party won a general election; Denzil Douglas became prime minister.
**1997** Nevis withdrew from the federation.
**1998** Nevis referendum on secession failed to secure support.

**Saint-Laurent, Yves Henri Donat Mathieu** (1936– ) French fashion designer. He has had an exceptional influence on fashion in the second half of the 20th century. He began working for Christian ◊Dior 1955 and succeeded him as designer on Dior's death 1957. He established his own label 1962 and went on to create the first 'power-dressing' looks for men and women: classic, stylish city clothes.

**St Lawrence** river in eastern North America. With the ◊Great Lakes and linking canals such as the Welland Ship Canal, it forms the St Lawrence Seaway, an inland route for small ocean-going ships from the Gulf of St Lawrence, an arm of the Atlantic Ocean, to Thunder Bay at the head of Lake Superior; larger vessels stop at ◊Montréal. The river is 1,200 km/745 mi long and icebound for four months each year. Enormous quantities of hydroelectric power are generated along its course.

**St Louis** city and riverport in Missouri, USA, on the Mississippi River; population (1996 est) 351,6000; metropolitan area (1996 est) 2,600,000. Occupying a central US location, it is a warehousing and distribution hub, and a major market for livestock, grain, wool, and lumber. The port handles oil, coal, sulphur, cement, and agricultural and manufactured goods. Products include aerospace and transport equipment, pharmaceuticals, refined oil, rubber, printed materials, processed metals, tobacco, and food.

**St Lucia**

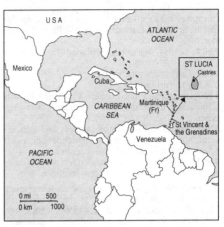

**area** 617 sq km/238 sq mi
**capital** Castries
**major towns/cities** Soufrière, Vieux-Fort, Laborie
**major ports** Vieux-Fort
**physical features** mountainous island with fertile valleys; mainly tropical forest; volcanic peaks; Gros and Petit Pitons
**head of state** Queen Elizabeth II from 1979, represented by governor general Stanislaus A James from 1992
**head of government** Kenny Anthony from 1997
**political system** constitutional monarchy
**political parties** United Workers' Party (UWP), moderate left of centre; St Lucia Labour Party (SLP), moderate left of centre; Progressive Labour Party (PLP), moderate left of centre
**currency** East Caribbean dollar
**GNP per capita (PPP)** (US$) 4,610 (1998)
**exports** bananas, coconut oil, cocoa beans, copra, beverages, tobacco, miscellaneous articles. Principal market: UK 50% (1995)
**population** 154,000 (1999 est)
**language** English; French patois
**religion** Roman Catholic 90%
**life expectancy** 68 (men); 75 (women) (1998 est)
**Chronology**
**1502** Sighted by the explorer Christopher Columbus on St Lucia's day but not settled for more than a century due to hostility of the island's Carib Indian inhabitants.
**1635** Settled by French, who brought in slaves to work sugar cane plantations as Carib community was annihilated.
**1814** Ceded to Britain as a crown colony, following Treaty of Paris; black African slaves brought in to work sugar cane plantations.
**1834** Slavery abolished.
**1860s** A major coal warehousing centre until the switch to oil and diesel fuels in 1930s.

**1871–1956** Part of Leeward Islands Federation.
**1951** Universal adult suffrage granted.
**1967** Acquired internal self-government as a West Indies associated state.
**1979** Independence achieved within Commonwealth with John Compton, leader of United Workers' Party (UWP), as prime minister; Compton was replaced by Allan Louisy, leader of the St Lucia Labour Party (SLP), following elections.
**1981** Louisy resigned; replaced by Winston Cenac.
**1982** Compton returned to power at head of UWP government.
**1991** Integration with other Windward Islands (Dominica, Grenada, and St Vincent) was proposed.
**1993** Unrest and strikes by farmers and agricultural workers arose as a result of depressed prices for the chief cash crop, bananas.
**1997** SLP won a general election; Kenny Anthony was appointed prime minister.

**St Petersburg** capital of the St Petersburg region, Russian Federation, at the head of the Gulf of Finland; population (1994) 4,883,000. Industries include shipbuilding, machinery, chemicals, and textiles. It was renamed *Petrograd* 1914 and was called *Leningrad* 1924–91, when its original name was restored.

Built on a low and swampy site, St Petersburg is split up by the mouths of the River Neva, which connects it with Lake Ladoga. The climate is severe. The city became a seaport when it was linked with the Baltic by a ship canal built 1875–93. It is also linked by canal and river with the Caspian and Black seas, and in 1975 a seaway connection was completed via lakes Onega and Ladoga with the White Sea near Belomorsk, allowing naval forces to reach the Barents Sea free of NATO surveillance.

**St-Pierre and Miquelon** territorial collectivity of France, comprising eight small islands off the south coast of Newfoundland, Canada
**area** St-Pierre group 26 sq km/10 sq mi; Miquelon-Langlade group 216 sq km/83 sq mi
**capital** St-Pierre
**physical** Dune of Langdale, barren, rocky, peat bogs, marshes
**features** the last surviving remnant of France's North American empire
**industries** fishing; tourism
**agriculture** cattle, subsistence farming
**currency** French franc
**population** (1990) 6,400
**language** French
**religion** Roman Catholic
**history** settled in the 17th century by Breton and Basque fishing people; ceded to Britain under Treaty of Utrecht (1713); returned to France (1763); taken by Britain (1794); returned to France by Treaty of Paris (1814); French territory (1816–1976); overseas *département* until 1985 when it became a Territorial Collectivity; violent protests in 1989 when France tried to impose its claim to a 320-km/200-mi fishing zone around the islands; Canada maintains that there is only a 19-km/12-mi zone. Used as an alcohol-smugglers' base during American

Prohibition (1920–33). Was occupied by the Free French troops of General Charles de Gaulle during World War II.

**Saint-Saëns, (Charles) Camille** (1835–1921) French composer, pianist, and organist. Saint-Saëns was a master of technique and a prolific composer; among his many lyrical Romantic pieces are concertos, the symphonic poem *Danse macabre* 1875, the opera *Samson et Dalila* 1877, and the uncharacteristic orchestral piece *Le carnaval des animaux/The Carnival of the Animals* 1886, his most popular work.

## St Vincent and the Grenadines

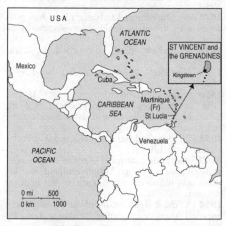

**area** 388 sq km/150 sq mi, including islets of the Northern Grenadines (43 sq km/17 sq mi)
**capital** Kingstown
**major towns/cities** Georgetown, Châteaubelair, Layon, Baronallie
**physical features** volcanic mountains, thickly forested; La Soufrière volcano
**head of state** Queen Elizabeth II from 1979, represented by governor-general David Jack from 1989
**head of government** James Mitchell from 1984
**political system** constitutional monarchy
**political parties** New Democratic Party (NDP), right of centre; St Vincent Labour Party (SVLP), moderate left of centre
**currency** East Caribbean dollar
**GNP per capita (PPP)** (US$) 4,090 (1998)
**exports** bananas, eddoes, dasheen, sweet potatoes, flour, ginger, tannias, plantains. Principal market: UK 38.5% (1996)
**population** 120,000 (1999 est)
**language** English; French patois
**religion** Anglican, Methodist, Roman Catholic
**life expectancy** 72 (men); 76 (women) (1998 est)
**Chronology**
**1498** Main island visited by the explorer Christopher Columbus on St Vincent's day.
**17th–18th centuries** Possession disputed by France and Britain, with fierce resistance from the indigenous Carib community.

*1783* Recognized as British crown colony by Treaty of Versailles.

*1795–97* Carib uprising, with French support, resulted in deportation of 5,000 to Belize and Honduras.

*1834* Slavery abolished.

*1902* Over 2,000 killed by the eruption of La Soufrière volcano.

*1951* Universal adult suffrage granted.

*1958–62* Part of West Indies Federation.

*1969* Achieved internal self-government.

*1979* Achieved full independence within Commonwealth, with Milton Cato of centre-left St Vincent Labour Party (SVLP) as prime minister.

*1981* General strike against new industrial-relations legislation at a time of economic recession.

*1984* James Mitchell, of the centre-right New Democratic Party (NDP), replaced Cato as prime minister.

*1989* James Mitchell and the NDP were re-elected.

*1991* Integration with other Windward Islands (Dominica, Grenada, and St Lucia) was proposed.

*1994* The NDP was re-elected. A new opposition left-of-centre party, the United Labour Party (ULP), was formed.

**Sakharov, Andrei Dmitrievich** (1921–1989) Soviet physicist. He was an outspoken human-rights campaigner, who with Igor Tamm (1895–1971) developed the hydrogen bomb. He later protested against Soviet nuclear tests and was a founder of the Soviet Human Rights Committee in 1970, winning the Nobel Peace Prize in 1975. For criticizing Soviet action in Afghanistan, he was sent into internal exile (1980–86).

**Saladin** or *Salah al-Din Yusuf ibn Ayyub* (c. 1138–1193) Kurdish conqueror of the Kingdom of Jerusalem. He was tutored in the military arts by his uncle, a general in Aleppo, before becoming the ruler of Egypt in 1169 and Aleppo in 1183. He recovered Jerusalem from the Christians in 1187, precipitating the Third ◊Crusade, but was later defeated by Richard (I) the Lionheart. Renowned for knightly courtesy, Saladin made peace with Richard in 1192.

**salamander** tailed amphibian of the order Urodela. They are sometimes confused with ◊lizards, but unlike lizards they have no scales or claws. Salamanders have smooth or warty moist skin. The order includes some 300 species, arranged in nine families, found mainly in the northern hemisphere. Salamanders include hellbenders, mudpuppies, olms, waterdogs, sirens, mole salamanders, ◊newts, and lungless salamanders (dusky, woodland, and spring salamanders).

**Salamis** ancient city on the east coast of Cyprus, the capital under the early Ptolemies until its harbour silted up in about 200 BC, when it was succeeded by Paphos in the southwest.

**Salamis, Battle of** in the Persian Wars, a sea battle fought in the Strait of Salamis west of Athens, Greece, in 480 BC between the Greeks and the invading Persians. Despite being heavily outnumbered, the Greeks inflicted a crushing defeat on the invading Persians which effectively destroyed their fleet.

**Salazar, António de Oliveira** (1889–1970) Portuguese prime minister 1932–68 who exercised a virtual dictatorship. During World War II he maintained Portuguese neutrality but fought long colonial wars in Africa (Angola and Mozambique) that impeded his country's economic development as well as that of the colonies.

**salicylic acid** $HOC_6H_4COOH$ the active chemical constituent of aspirin, an analgesic drug. The acid and its salts (salicylates) occur naturally in many plants; concentrated sources include willow bark and oil of wintergreen.

**Salinas de Gortari, Carlos** (1948– ) Mexican politician, president (1988–94), a member of the dominant Institutional Revolutionary Party (PRI). During his presidency he promoted economic reform, including privatization, and signed a North American Free Trade Agreement (NAFTA) with the USA and Canada in December 1992. However, he was also confronted with problems of drug trafficking and violent crime, including the murder of his nominated successor, Luis Donaldo Colosio, in 1994. He went into exile in 1995 after his brother Raúl was implicated in the assassination of another high-ranking PRI official and held in jail. It was later revealed that his brother had amassed more than $84 million in a Swiss bank account.

**Salinger, J(erome) D(avid)** (1919– ) US writer. He wrote the classic novel of mid-20th-century adolescence, *The Catcher in the Rye* (1951). He developed his lyrical Zen themes in *Franny and Zooey* (1961) and *Raise High the Roof Beam, Carpenters* and *Seymour: An Introduction* (1963), short stories about a Jewish family named Glass, after which he stopped publishing. He also wrote *For Esmé – With Love and Squalor* (1953).

**Salisbury, Robert Arthur Talbot Gascoyne-Cecil,** 3rd Marquess of Salisbury (1830–1903) British Conservative politician. He entered the Commons in 1853 and succeeded to his title in 1868. As foreign secretary (1878–80), he took part in the Congress of Berlin, and as prime minister (1885–86, 1886–92), and (1895–1902) gave his main attention to foreign policy, remaining also as foreign secretary for most of this time.

**Salk, Jonas Edward** (1914–1995) US physician and microbiologist. In 1954 he developed the original vaccine that led to virtual eradication of paralytic ◊polio in industrialized countries. He was director of the Salk Institute for Biological Studies, University of California, San Diego, from 1963 to 1975.

**Sallust, Gaius Sallustius Crispus** (86– c. 34 BC) Roman historian. He served under Julius ◊Caesar in Gaul (France) and during the civil war, but retired from public life after a scandal involving his governorship of Africa. He wrote histories of the Catiline conspiracy and the Jugurthine War, as well as a Roman history of which only fragments survive.

**salmon** any of the various bony fishes of the family Salmonidae. More specifically the name is applied to several species of game fishes of the genera Salmo and Oncorhynchus of North America and Eurasia that mature in the ocean but, to spawn, return to the freshwater streams where they were born. Their normal colour is silvery with a few dark spots, but the colour changes at the spawning season.

**salmonella** any of a very varied group of bacteria, genus *Salmonella*, that colonize the intestines of humans and some animals. Some strains cause typhoid and paratyphoid fevers, while others cause salmonella ◊food poisoning, which is characterized by stomach pains, vomiting, diarrhoea, and headache. It can be fatal in elderly people, but others usually recover in a few days without antibiotics. Most cases are caused by contaminated animal products, especially poultry meat.

**Salop** abbreviation and former official name (1972–80) of ◊Shropshire, a county in England.

**salt** in chemistry, any compound formed from an acid and a base through the replacement of all or part of the hydrogen in the acid by a metal or electropositive radical. *Common salt* is sodium chloride (see ◊salt, common).

**SALT** abbreviation for ◊*Strategic Arms Limitation Talks,* a series of US–Soviet negotiations (1969–79).

**salt, common** or *sodium chloride,* NaCl, white crystalline solid, found dissolved in sea water and as rock salt (the mineral halite) in large deposits and salt domes. Common salt is used extensively in the food industry as a preservative and for flavouring, and in the chemical industry in the making of chlorine and sodium.

**Salt Lake City** capital of ◊Utah, USA, on the River Jordan, 605 km/378 mi northwest of Denver, Colorado; population (1992) 165,900. It is the commercial centre and world capital of the Church of Jesus Christ of the Latter-day Saints (the ◊Mormon Church). Industries include mineral-refining, food-processing, and the manufacture of textiles, footwear, and electronic and mining equipment. Copper, silver, lead, zinc, coal, and iron mines are worked nearby. In 1995 Salt Lake City was chosen as the site for the 2002 Winter Olympic Games.

**saltpetre** former name for potassium nitrate ($KNO_3$), the compound used in making gunpowder (from about 1500). It occurs naturally, being deposited during dry periods in places with warm climates, such as India.

**saluki** ancient breed of hunting dog resembling the greyhound. It is about 65 cm/26 in high at the shoulder and has a silky coat, which is usually fawn, cream, or white.

**Salvador** port, resort, and naval base, capital of Bahía federal unit (state), northeast Brazil, on the inner side of a peninsula separating Todos los Santos Bay from the Atlantic Ocean; population (1991) 2,075,400 (metropolitan area 3,134,900). Chief industries include oil refining, petrochemicals, and tourism; fruit, cocoa, sisal, soybeans, and petrochemical products are exported. The city is built on two distinct levels; the Cidade Alta (upper city), the site of the original settlement where there are many examples of colonial architecture, and Cidade Baixa (lower city), comprising the commercial, financial and port district. It was the first capital of Brazil (1549–1763).

**Salvador, El** republic in Central America.

**Salvation Army** Christian evangelical, socialservice, and social-reform organization, originating in 1865 in London, England, with the work of William ◊Booth. Originally called the Christian Revival Association, it was renamed the East London Christian Mission in 1870 and from 1878 has been known as the Salvation Army, now a worldwide organization. It has military titles for its officials, is renowned for its brass bands, and its weekly journal is the *War Cry.*

**Salyut** (Russian 'salute') series of seven space stations launched by the USSR (1971–82). The Salyut was cylindrical in shape, 15 m/50 ft long, and weighed 19 tonnes/21 tons. It housed two or three cosmonauts at a time, for missions lasting up to eight months.

**Salzburg** capital of the federal state of ◊Salzburg, west Austria, on the River Salzach; population (1995) 142,000. There are textile industries, and stock rearing, dairy farming, forestry, tourism, and the manufacture of musical instruments all contribute to the local economy. The city is dominated by the Hohensalzburg fortress (founded 1077, present buildings 1465–1519). It is the seat of an archbishopric founded by St Boniface in about 700 and has a 17th-century cathedral. It is also a conference centre. There are numerous fine Romanesque, Gothic, and Baroque churches. It is the birthplace of the composer Wolfgang Amadeus Mozart and an annual music festival in August has been held here since 1920. The Mozart Museum of Sound and Film opened in 1991.

**Salzburg** federal state of Austria, bounded on the northwest by Bavaria; area 7,200 sq km/2,779 sq mi; population (1994) 504,300. It lies mainly in the Salzburg Alps. Its capital is Salzburg. The chief industries are cattle rearing, dairy-farming, forestry, and tourism. It was annexed by Germany in 1938 but reunited with Austria in 1945.

**Samara** formerly (1935–91) *Kuibyshev,* capital city and river port of Samara oblast (region), west-central Russian Federation; population (1996 est) 1,175,000. Samara is located on the River Volga and the main Trans-Siberian Railway, 820 km/510 mi southeast of Moscow. It is a major industrial centre, with large heavy-engineering industries (producing road vehicles and railway rolling stock), as well as chemical, oil-processing, wood-processing, and light industries.

**Samaria** region of ancient Israel. The town of Samaria (now *Sebastiyeh*) on the west bank of the River Jordan was the capital of Israel in the 10th–8th centuries BC. It was renamed *Sebarte* in the 1st century BC by the Roman administrator Herod the Great. Extensive remains have been excavated.

**Samaritan** members or descendants of the colonists forced to settle in Samaria (now northern Israel) by the Assyrians after their occupation of the ancient kingdom of Israel in 722 BC. Samaritans adopted a form of Judaism, but adopted only the Pentateuch, the five books of Moses of the Old Testament, and regarded their temple on Mount Gerizim as the true sanctuary.

**samarium** hard, brittle, grey-white, metallic element of the ◊lanthanide series, symbol Sm, atomic number 62, relative atomic mass 150.4. It is widely distributed in nature and is obtained commercially from the minerals monzanite and bastnaesite. It is used only occasionally in industry, mainly as a catalyst in organic reactions. Samarium was discovered by spectroscopic analysis of the mineral samarskite and named in 1879 by French chemist Paul Lecoq de Boisbaudran (1838–1912) after its source.

**Samarkand** Uzbek *Samarqand,* city in eastern Uzbekistan, capital of Samarkand wiloyat (oblast), near the River Zerafshan, 217 km/135 mi east of Bukhara; population (1996) 370,000. Industries include cotton-ginning, silk manufacture, production of foodstuffs, and engineering. Samarkand is one of the oldest cities in Central Asia, dating from the 3rd or 4th millennium BC. The Registan – a collection of mosques, courtyards and former Muslim theological seminaries ('madrasahs') – forms the centrepiece of the historic town. A university is situated here.

**samba** Latin American ballroom dance; the music for this. Samba originated in Brazil and became popular in the West in the 1940s. There are several different samba rhythms; the bossa nova is a samba-jazz fusion.

**Samoa** Independent State of
**national name** *Malotutu'atasi o Samoa i Sisifo*

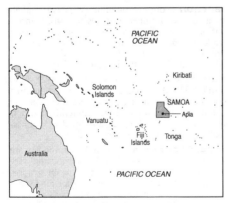

**area** 2,830 sq km/1,092 sq mi
**capital** Apia (on Upolu island) (and chief port)
**major towns/cities** Lalomanu, Falevai, Tuasivi, Falealupo
**physical features** comprises South Pacific islands of Savai'i and Upolu, with two smaller tropical islands and uninhabited islets; moun-

tain ranges on main islands; coral reefs; over half forested
**head of state** King Malietoa Tanumafili II from 1962
**head of government** Tuila'epa Sa'ilele Malielegaoi from 1998
**political system** liberal democracy
**political parties** Human Rights Protection Party (HRPP), led by Tofilau Eti Alesana; Samoa Democratic Party (SDP), led by Le Tagaloa Pita; Samoa National Development Party (SNDP), led by Tupuola Taisi Efi and Va'ai Kolone. All 'parties' are personality-based groupings
**currency** tala, or Samoa dollar
**GNP per capita (PPP)** (US$) 3,440 (1998)
**exports** coconut cream, beer, cigarettes, taro, copra, cocoa, bananas, timber. Principal market: Australia 69.8% (1997)
**population** 177,000 (1999 est)
**language** English, Samoan (official)
**religion** Congregationalist; also Roman Catholic, Methodist
**life expectancy** 69 (men); 74 (women) (1995–2000)
**Chronology**
**c. 1000 BC** Settled by Polynesians from Tonga.
**AD 950–1250** Ruled by Tongan invaders; the Matai (chiefly) system was developed.
**15th century** United under the Samoan Queen Salamasina.
**1722** Visited by Dutch traders.
**1768** Visted by the French navigator Louis Antoine de Bougainville.
**1830** Christian mission established and islanders were soon converted to Christianity.
**1887–89** Samoan rebellion against German attempt to depose paramount ruler and install its own puppet regime.
**1889** Under the terms of the Act of Berlin, Germany took control of the nine islands of Western Samoa, while the USA was granted American Samoa, and Britain Tonga and the Solomon Islands.
**1900s** More than 2,000 Chinese brought in to work coconut plantations.
**1914** Occupied by New Zealand on the outbreak of World War I.
**1918** Nearly a quarter of the population died in an influenza epidemic.
**1920s** Development of nationalist movement, the Mau, which resorted to civil disobedience.
**1920–61** Administered by New Zealand under League of Nations and, later, United Nations mandate.
**1959** Local government established, headed by chief minister Fiame Mata'afa Mulinu'u.
**1961** Referendum favoured independence.
**1962** Independence achieved within Commonwealth, with Mata'afa as prime minister, a position he retained (apart from a short break 1970–73) until his death in 1975.
**1976** Tupuola Taisi Efi became first nonroyal prime minister.
**1982** Va'ai Kolone, the head of the opposition Human Rights Protection Party (HRPP), became prime minister, but was forced to resign over charges of electoral malpractice. The new HRPP leader, Tofilau Eti Alesana, became prime minister.
**1985** Tofilau Eti Alesana resigned after

opposition to budget; head of state invited Va'ai Kolone to lead the government.

**1988** Elections produced hung parliament, with first Tupuola Efi as prime minister and then Tofilau Eti Alesana.

**1990** Universal adult suffrage was introduced and the power of Matai (elected clan leaders) reduced.

**1991** Fiame Naome became the first woman in cabinet; major damage was caused by 'Cyclone Val'.

**1998** Name was changed officially to 'Samoa'. Tofilau Eti Alesana stepped down, for health reasons, to become senior minister without portfolio and his deputy, Tuila'epa Sa'ilele Malielegaoi, of the HRPP, became the new prime minister.

**Samoa** volcanic island chain in the southwestern Pacific. It is divided into Samoa and American Samoa.

**Samoa, American** group of islands 4,200 km/2,610 mi south of Hawaii, administered by the USA

*area* 200 sq km/77 sq mi

*capital* Pago Pago

*physical* five volcanic islands, including Tutuila, Tau, and Swains Island, and two coral atolls; virgin rainforest; flying foxes

*features* the national park (1988) includes the prehistoric village of Saua

*exports* canned tuna, handicrafts, copra

*currency* US dollar

*population* (1993) 52,900

*language* Samoan and English

*religion* Christian

*government* as a non-self-governing territory of the USA, it is constitutionally an unincorporated territory of the USA, administered by the Department of the Interior

*history* the islands were acquired by the USA December 1899 by agreement with Britain and Germany under the Treaty of Berlin. A constitution was adopted in 1960 and revised in 1967. Around 85,000 American Samoans were living in the USA in 1990.

**Sampras, Pete** (1971–  ) US tennis player. At the age of 19 years and 28 days, he became the youngest winner of the US Open in 1990. A fine server and volleyer, Sampras also won the inaugural Grand Slam Cup in Munich in 1990. In 1997 he won the men's singles at Wimbledon for the fourth time in five years. He finished 1997 at the top of the ATP men's world rankings for an unprecedented fifth consecutive year. In 1998 he won the Wimbledon tournament again, thus joining Sweden's Björn Borg as the only player to win five Wimbledon men's singles titles since the abolition of the Challenge Round in 1922. In August 1999 he beat Ivan Lendl's all-time record of 270 weeks at the top of the ATP Tour world rankings.

*career highlights*

*Wimbledon* singles: 1993–95, 1997, 1998

*Australian Open* singles: 1994, 1997

*US Open* singles: 1990, 1993, 1995–96

*Grand Slam Cup* 1990

*ATP Tour World Championship* 1991, 1994, 1996, 1997

**samurai** or bushi, (Japanese 'one who serves'): Japanese term for the warrior class which became the ruling military elite for almost 700 years. A samurai was an armed retainer of a *daimyō* (large landowner) with specific duties and privileges and a strict code of honour. The system was abolished in 1869 and all samurai were pensioned off by the government.

**San'a** or *Sana'a*, capital of Yemen, southwest Arabia, 320 km/200 mi north of Aden on the central plateau, 2,210 m/7,250 ft above sea level; population (1995) 972,000. A walled city, with fine mosques and traditional architecture, it is rapidly being modernized. Weaving and jewellery are local handicrafts.

**San Andreas fault** geological fault stretching for 1,125 km/700 mi northwest–southeast through the state of California, USA. It marks a conservative plate margin, where two plates slide past each other (see ◊plate tectonics).

**San Antonio** or *San Antonio de Bejar,* city in southern Texas, USA, on the *San Antonio River;* population (1996 est) 1,067,800. It is a commercial, financial, and military centre. Industries include tourism, aircraft maintenance, oil-refining, and meat-packing. Fort Sam Houston, four Air Force bases, the South Texas Medical Center, and the Southwest Research Center lie within the city limits and play an important part in the economy.

**San Cristóbal** capital of Tachirá state, western Venezuela, situated 800 m/26,250 ft above sea level in the northern Andes overlooking the River Torbes, 56 km/35 mi from the Colombian border; population (1990) 220,700. It is the centre of a coffee-growing region, and other products include textiles, cement, leather goods, and tobacco. San Cristóbal was founded by Spanish settlers in 1561 and stands on the Pan-American Highway.

**sanction** economic or military measure taken by a state or number of states to enforce international law. The first use of sanctions, as a trade embargo, was the attempted economic boycott of Italy (1935–36) during the Abyssinian War by the League of Nations.

**sand** loose grains of rock, sized 0.0625–2.00 mm/0.0025–0.08 in in diameter, consisting most commonly of ◊quartz, but owing their varying colour to mixtures of other minerals. Sand is used in cement-making, as an abrasive, in glass-making, and for other purposes.

**Sand, George** pen-name of Amandine Aurore Lucie Dupin (1804–1876) French author. Her prolific literary output was often autobiographical. In 1831 she left her husband after nine years of marriage and, while living in Paris as a writer, had love affairs with Alfred de Musset, Chopin, and others. Her first novel *Indiana* (1832) was a plea for women's right to independence.

**sandalwood** fragrant heartwood of any of several Asiatic and Australian trees, used for ornamental carving, in perfume, and burned as incense. (Genus *Santalum,* family Santalaceae.)

**sandgrouse** any bird of the family Pteroclidae, order Columbiformes. They look like long-tailed grouse, but are actually closely related to pigeons. They live in warm, dry areas of Europe, Asia, and Africa and have long wings, short legs and bills, a wedge-shaped tail, and thick skin. They are sandy coloured and feed on vegetable matter and insects.

**sand hopper** or *beachflea,* any of various small crustaceans belonging to the order Amphipeda, with laterally compressed bodies, that live in beach sand and jump like fleas. The eastern sand hopper *Orchestia agilis* of North America is about 1.3 cm/0.5 in long.

**San Diego** city and US naval air station, on the Pacific Ocean, and on the border of Mexico, in California, USA; population (1996 est) 1,171,100; metropolitan area (1992) 2,601,000. San Diego is linked to Tijuana, Mexico, by a 26-km/16-mi transit line (1981), popular with tourists. It is an important fishing port. Manufacturing includes aerospace and electronic equipment, metal fabrication, printing and publishing, seafood-canning, and shipbuilding. San Diego is the oldest Spanish settlement in California; a Spanish mission and fort were established here in 1769.

**Sandinista** member of a Nicaraguan left-wing organization (Sandinist National Liberation Front, FSLN) named after Augusto César Sandino, a guerrilla leader killed 1934. It was formed 1962 and obtained widespread support from the trade unions, the church, and the middle classes, which enabled it to overthrow the regime of General Anastasio Somoza in July 1979.

The FSLN dominated the Nicaraguan government and fought a civil war against US-backed Contra guerrillas until 1988. The FSLN was defeated in elections of 1990 by a US-backed coalition, but remained the party with the largest number of seats.

**sandpiper** shorebird with a long, slender bill, which is compressed and grooved at the tip. They belong to the family Scolopacidae, which includes godwits, ◊curlews, and ◊snipes, order Charadriiformes.

**sandstone** ◊sedimentary rocks formed from the consolidation of sand, with sand-sized grains (0.0625–2 mm/0.0025–0.08 in) in a matrix or cement. Their principal component is quartz. Sandstones are commonly permeable and porous, and may form freshwater ◊aquifers. They are mainly used as building materials.

**San Francisco** chief Pacific port in California, USA, on the tip of a peninsula in San Francisco Bay; population (1996 est) 735,300; metropolitan area of San Francisco and Oakland 3,686,600. The entrance channel from the Pacific to San Francisco Bay was named the Golden Gate in 1846; its strait was crossed in 1937 by the world's second-longest single-span bridge, 1,280 m/4,200 ft in length. Manufactured goods include textiles, machinery and metalware, electrical equipment, petroleum products, and pharmaceuticals. San Francisco is also a financial, trade, corporate, and diversified service centre. Tourism is a major industry. A Spanish fort (the Presidio) and the San Francisco de Asis Mission were established here in 1776. San Francisco has the largest Chinese community outside Asia.

**Sanger, Frederick** (1918– ) English biochemist. He was the first person to win a Nobel Prize for Chemistry twice: the first in 1958 for determining the structure of ◊insulin, and the second in 1980 for work on the chemical structure of ◊genes.

**San José** capital of Costa Rica, and of San José province; population (1991 est) 299,400. It is situated in the broad fertile valley of the central plateau. Products include coffee, cocoa, sugar cane, textiles, and pharmaceuticals. There is a cathedral, and the University of Costa Rica, which was founded in 1843. It was founded in 1737 and became capital in 1823, replacing the former capital Cartago because it had a better all-year-round climate.

**San José** city in California, USA, in Santa Clara Valley, at the head of the southern arm of San Francisco Bay; population (1996) 838,700. It is situated at one end of 'Silicon Valley', the site of many high-technology electronic firms turning out semiconductors and other computer components. There are also electrical, aerospace, missile, rubber, metal, and machine industries, and it is a commercial and transportation centre for orchard crops and wines produced in the area.

**San Juan** industrial city and capital of Puerto Rico; population (1990) 437,750. It is a major port, exporting sugar, tobacco, coffee, and tropical fruits, mostly to the US mainland, and providing the world's busiest cruise ship base. Products include chemicals, pharmaceuticals, machine tools, electronic equipment, textiles, plastics, and rum. Banking, metalworking, publishing, and tourism are also important to the local economy. The main campus of the University of Puerto Rico (1903) is here.

**San Marino** Most Serene Republic of
*national name* Serenissima Repubblica di San Marino
*area* 61 sq km/24 sq mi

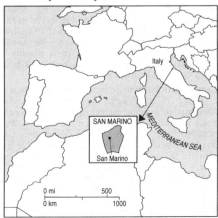

**capital** San Marino
**major towns/cities** Serravalle (industrial centre), Faetano, Fiorentino, Monte Giardino
**physical features** the slope of Mount Titano
**head of state and government** two captains regent, elected for a six-month period
**political system** direct democracy
**political parties** San Marino Christian Democrat Party (PDCS), Christian centrist; Progressive Democratic Party (PDP) (formerly the Communist Party: PCS), moderate left wing; Socialist Party (PS), left of centre
**currency** Italian lira
**GNP per capita (PPP)** (US$) 20,000 (1997 est)
**exports** wood machinery, chemicals, wine, olive oil, textiles, tiles, ceramics, varnishes, building stone, lime, chestnuts, hides. Principal market: Italy
**population** 25,000 (1999 est)
**language** Italian
**religion** Roman Catholic 95%
**life expectancy** 78 (men); 85 (women) (1998 est)

**Chronology**
**c. AD 301** Founded as a republic (the world's oldest surviving) by St Marinus and a group of Christians who settled there to escape persecution.
**12th century** Self-governing commune.
**1600** Statutes (constitution) provided for a parliamentary form of government, based around the Great and General Council.
**1815** Independent status of the republic recognized by the Congress of Vienna.
**1862** Treaty with Italy signed; independence recognized under Italy's protection.
**1945–57** Communist–Socialist administration in power, eventually ousted in a bloodless 'revolution'.
**1957–86** Governed by a series of left-wing and centre-left coalitions.
**1971** Treaty with Italy renewed.
**1986** A communist and centre-right Christian Democrat (PDCS) 'grand coalition' was formed.
**1992** San Marino joined the United Nations (UN). PDCS withdrew from the 'grand coalition' to form an alliance with the Socialist Party.
**1998** The ruling PDCS–PSS coalition remained in power after a general election.

**San Martín, José de** (1778–1850) South American revolutionary leader. He served in the Spanish army during the Peninsular War, but after 1812 he devoted himself to the South American struggle for independence, playing a large part in the liberation of Argentina, Chile, and Peru from Spanish rule.

**San Pedro Sula** main industrial and commercial city in northwest Honduras, near the Guatemalan border, capital of ◊Cortés department and the second-largest city in the country; population (1991 est) 325,900. Situated in the fertile valley of the Ulúa River, and 45 km/28 mi south of the port of Puerto Cortés, it is a trading centre and key distribution point for the north and northwest regions, which produce bananas, coffee, sugar, and timber; industries include steel, textiles, plastics, furniture, and cement. One of Central America's fastest growing cities,

it was founded in 1536 by the Spaniard Pedro de Alvarado.

**San Salvador** capital of El Salvador and of San Salvador department; situated at the foot of San Salvador volcano (2,548 m/8,360 ft) on the River Acelhuate, 48 km/30 mi from the Pacific Ocean; population (1992) 422,600. Industries include coffee, food-processing, pharmaceuticals, and textiles. One-third of the country's industrial output comes from the city. Founded in 1525, it was destroyed by an earthquake in 1854 and rebuilt on the present site. It is now a modern city with architecture conditioned to seismic activity, to which the region is prone, although many buildings collapsed during a further earthquake in 1986.

**Sanskrit** the dominant classical language of the Indian subcontinent, a member of the Indo-Iranian group of the Indo-European language family, and the sacred language of Hinduism. The oldest form of Sanskrit is *Vedic*, the variety used in the *Vedas* and *Upanishads* (about 1500–700 BC).

**Santa Anna, Antonio López de** (c. 1795–1876) Mexican revolutionary. He became general and dictator of Mexico for most of the years between 1824 and 1855. He led the attack on the Alamo fort in Texas 1836.

**Santa Fe** capital of ◊New Mexico, USA, on the *Santa Fe River*, 65 km/40 mi west of Las Vegas; population (1996 est) 66,500, many Spanish-speaking. It is situated in the Rio Grande Valley, over 2,000 m/6,500 ft above sea level, on the western slopes of the Sangre de Cristo Mountains. Santa Fe is the cultural and tourist capital of the southwest, home to many artists, theatre, and opera. Precision instruments, pottery, and American Indian jewellery and textiles are produced.

**Santiago** capital of Chile, on the Mapocho River; population (1992) 4,385,500 (metropolitan area 5,180,800). It is the fifth largest city in South America and the country's cultural, commercial, and manufacturing centre. Industries include textiles, chemicals, and food processing. It has three universities, and several theatres, libraries, and museums.

**Santo Domingo** capital and chief sea port of the Dominican Republic; population (1991 est) 2,055,000. Founded 1496 by Bartolomeo, brother of Christopher Columbus, it is the oldest colonial city in the Americas. Its cathedral was built 1515–40.

**São Paulo** industrial city and capital of São Paulo federal unit (state), southeast Brazil, 72 km/45 mi northwest of its port Santos, and 400 km/249 mi southwest of Rio de Janeiro; population (1992) 9,646,200 (metropolitan area 16,567,300). It is Latin America's second-largest city after Mexico City. It is 900 m/3,000 ft above sea level, and 2° south of the Tropic of Capricorn. It is also South America's leading industrial city, producing electronics, steel, and chemicals; it has meat-packing plants and is the centre of Brazil's coffee trade. The city has a cathedral and four universities (the University of

Sáo Paulo is the largest in Brazil). The Butantã Snake Farm is a biomedical research institute for the production of antidotes for snakebite.

**São Tomé and Príncipe** Democratic Republic of
**national name** *República Democrática de São Tomé e Príncipe*

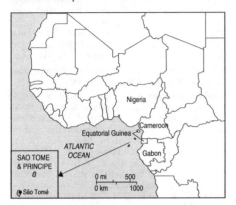

**area** 1,000 sq km/386 sq mi
**capital** São Tomé
**major towns/cities** São António, Santana, Porto-Alegre
**physical features** comprises two main islands and several smaller ones, all volcanic; thickly forested and fertile
**head of state** Miguel Trovoada from 1991
**head of government** Carlos da Graca from 1994
**political system** emergent democracy
**political parties** Movement for the Liberation of São Tomé e Príncipe–Social Democratic Party (MLSTP–PSD), nationalist socialist; Democratic Convergence Party–Reflection Group (PCD–GR), moderate left of centre; Independent Democratic Action (ADI), centrist
**currency** dobra
**GNP per capita (PPP)** (US$) 1,350 (1998)
**exports** cocoa, copra, coffee, bananas, palm oil. Principal market: the Netherlands 50.9% (1997)
**population** 154,000 (1999 est)
**language** Portuguese (official); Fang (a Bantu language)
**religion** Roman Catholic 80%, animist
**life expectancy** 63 (men); 66 (women) (1998 est)
**Chronology**
**1471** First visited by the Portuguese, who imported convicts and slaves to work on sugar plantations in the formerly uninhabited islands.
**1522** Became a province of Portugal.
**1530** Slaves successfully revolted, forcing plantation owners to flee to Brazil; thereafter became a key staging post for Congo-Americas slave trade.
**19th century** Forced contract labour used to work coffee and cocoa plantations.
**1953** More than 1,000 striking plantation workers gunned down by Portuguese troops.
**1960** First political party formed, the forerunner

of the socialist-nationalist Movement for the Liberation of São Tomé e Príncipe (MLSTP).
**1974** Military coup in Portugal led to strikes, demonstrations, and army mutiny in São Tomé; thousands of Portuguese settlers fled the country.
**1975** Independence achieved, with Manuel Pinto da Costa (MLSTP) as president; close links developed with communist bloc, and plantations nationalized.
**1984** Formally declared a nonaligned state as economy deteriorated.
**1988** Coup attempt against da Costa foiled by Angolan and East European troops.
**1990** Influenced by collapse of communism in Eastern Europe, MLSTP abandoned Marxism; a new pluralist constitution was approved in a referendum.
**1991** In the first multiparty elections, the ruling MLSTP lost its majority and the independent Miguel Trovoada, MLSTP prime minister before 1978, was elected president.
**1994** MLSTP returned to power with Carlos da Graca as prime minister.
**1995** There was an abortive coup by junior army officers.
**1998** MLSTP–PSD won an absolute majority in the assembly.

**São Tomé** port and capital of São Tomé e Príncipe, on the northeast coast of São Tomé island, Gulf of Guinea; population (1991) 43,400. It exports sugar, cocoa, and coffee.

**saponification** in chemistry, the hydrolysis (splitting) of an ◊ester by treatment with a strong alkali, resulting in the liberation of the alcohol from which the ester had been derived and a salt of the constituent fatty acid. The process is used in the manufacture of soap.

**sapphire** deep-blue, transparent gem variety of the mineral ◊corundum $Al_2O_3$, aluminium oxide. Small amounts of iron and titanium give it its colour. A corundum gem of any colour except red (which is a ruby) can be called a sapphire; for example, yellow sapphire.

**Sappho** (*c.* 610–*c.* 580 BC) Greek lyric poet. A native of Lesbos and contemporary of the poet Alcaeus, she was famed for her female eroticism (hence lesbianism). The surviving fragments of her poems express a keen sense of loss, and delight in the worship of the goddess ◊Aphrodite.

**Sapporo** capital of ◊Hokkaido prefecture, Japan, on the Ishikari River; population (1994) 1,719,000. Industries include rubber, food processing, printing, brewing beer, and lead and zinc mining. It is a winter sports centre and was the site of the 1972 Winter Olympics. Giant figures are sculpted in ice at the annual snow festival. The city has an underground railway.

**saprotroph** formerly *saprophyte,* organism that feeds on the excrement or the dead bodies or tissues of others. They include most fungi (the rest being parasites); many bacteria and protozoa; animals such as dung beetles and vultures; and a few unusual plants, including several orchids. Saprotrophs cannot make food for themselves, so they are a type of ◊heterotroph.

They are useful scavengers, and in sewage farms and refuse dumps break down organic matter into nutrients easily assimilable by green plants.

**Saracen** ancient Greek and Roman term for an Arab, used in the Middle Ages by Europeans for all Muslims. The equivalent term used in Spain was ◊Moor.

**Sarajevo** capital of Bosnia-Herzegovina; population (1991) 526,000. Industries include engineering, brewing, chemicals, carpets, and ceramics. A Bosnian, Gavrilo Princip, assassinated Archduke ◊Franz Ferdinand here in 1914, thereby precipitating World War I. From April 1992 the city was the target of a siege by Bosnian Serb forces in their fight to carve up the newly independent republic. A United Nations ultimatum and the threat of NATO bombing led to a ceasefire in February 1994 and the effective end of the siege as Serbian heavy weaponry was withdrawn from the high points surrounding the city.

**Sarawak** state of Malaysia, on the northwest corner of the island of Borneo
*area* 124,400 sq km/48,018 sq mi
*capital* Kuching
*physical* mountainous; the rainforest, which may be 10 million years old, contains several thousand tree species. A third of all its plant species are endemic to Borneo. 30% of the forest was cut down between 1963 and 89; timber is expected to run out by 1995 to 2001
*industries* timber, oil, rice, pepper, rubber, coconuts, and natural gas
*population* (1991) 1,669,000; 24 ethnic groups make up almost half this number
*history* Sarawak was granted by the Sultan of Brunei to English soldier James Brooke in 1841, who became 'Rajah of Sarawak'. It was a British protectorate from 1888 until captured by the Japanese in World War II. It was a crown colony from 1946 to 1963, when it became part of Malaysia.

**sarcoma** malignant ◊tumour arising from the fat, muscles, bones, cartilage, or blood and lymph vessels and connective tissues. Sarcomas are much less common than ◊carcinomas.

**sardine** common name for various small fishes (◊pilchards) in the herring family.

**Sardinia** Italian *Sardegna,* mountainous island and special autonomous region of Italy, about 240 km/150 mi southwest of the Orbetello promontory in Tuscany; area 24,100 sq km/9,303 sq mi; population (1992 est) 1,651,900. It is the second-largest Mediterranean island and comprises the provinces of Cagliari, Nuoro, Oristano, and Sassari; its capital is Cagliari. Cork, fruit, grain, tobacco, minerals (lead, zinc, manganese), and petrochemicals are exported. Features include the Costa Smeralda (Emerald Coast) tourist area in the northeast and *nuraghi* (fortified Bronze Age dwellings). After centuries of foreign rule, Sardinia became linked with Piedmont in 1720, and this dual kingdom became the basis of a united Italy in 1861.

**Sartre, Jean-Paul** (1905–1980) French author and philosopher. He was a leading proponent of ◊existentialism. He published his first novel, *La Nausée/Nausea*, in 1937, followed by the trilogy *Les Chemins de la liberté/Roads to Freedom* (1944–45) and many plays, including *Les Mouches/The Flies* (1943), *Huis clos/In Camera* (1944), and *Les Séquestrés d'Altona/The Condemned of Altona* (1960). *L'Etre et le néant/Being and Nothingness* (1943), his first major philosophical work, sets out a radical doctrine of human freedom. In the later work *Critique de la raison dialectique/Critique of Dialectical Reason* (1960) he tried to produce a fusion of existentialism and Marxism.

**SAS** abbreviation for ◊*Special Air Service;* also for *Scandinavian Airlines System.*

**Saskatchewan** nickname 'Canada's breadbasket', (Cree *Kis-is-ska-tche-wan* 'swift flowing') province of west-central Canada, the middle Prairie province, bordered to the west by Alberta and to the east by Manitoba. To the north of Saskatchewan (above the 60th Parallel) are the Northwest Territories, while to the south (below the 49th Parallel) lie the US states of North Dakota and Montana
*area* 652,300 sq km/251,788 sq mi
*capital* Regina
*towns and cities* Saskatoon, Moose Jaw, Prince Albert, Yorkton, Swift Current
*population* (1997) 1,023,500; Native Canadian 75,400; British, French, German, Scandinavian, and Slav cultures
*physical* Canadian Shield; northern forests, lakes, and subarctic tundra; southern prairies; Cypress Hills; Saskatchewan River; Athabasca Lake
*industries* extraction of oil, natural gas, uranium, zinc, potash (world's largest reserves), copper, and helium (the only western reserves outside the USA); manufacture of cement, chemicals, fertilizers, wood products; agriculture centres on cultivation of wheat (over 60% of Canada's production), oats, barley, rye, and flax; cattle-rearing; manufacture of dairy produce.

**Sassanian Empire** Persian empire founded AD 224 by Ardashir, a chieftain in the area of what is now Fars, in Iran, who had taken over ◊Parthia; it was named after his grandfather, Sasan. The capital was Ctesiphon, near modern ◊Baghdad, Iraq. After a rapid period of expansion, when it contested supremacy with Rome, it was destroyed in 637 by Muslim Arabs at the Battle of Qadisiya.

**Sassau-Nguesso, Denis** (1943– ) Congolese socialist politician, president 1979–92 and from 1997. He progressively consolidated his position within the ruling left-wing Congolese Labour Party (PCT), at the same time as improving relations with France and the USA. In 1990, in response to public pressure, he agreed that the PCT should abandon Marxism-Leninism and that a multiparty system should be introduced. He returned to power in November 1997.

**Satan** a name for the ◊devil.

**satellite** any small body that orbits a larger one, either natural or artificial. Natural satellites that orbit planets are called moons. The first *artificial satellite, Sputnik 1,* was launched into orbit around the Earth by the USSR in 1957. Artificial satellites are used for scientific purposes, communications, weather forecasting, and military applications. The brightest artificial satellites can be seen by the naked eye.

**satellite television** transmission of broadcast signals through artificial communications satellites. Mainly positioned in ◊geostationary orbit, satellites have been used since the 1960s to relay television pictures around the world.

Higher-power satellites have more recently been developed to broadcast signals to cable systems or directly to people's homes.

**Satie, Erik (Alfred Leslie)** (1866–1925) French composer. His piano pieces, such as the three *Gymnopédies* (1888), are precise and tinged with melancholy, and parody romantic expression with surreal commentary. His aesthetic of ironic simplicity, as in the *Messe des pauvres/Poor People's Mass* (1895), acted as a nationalist antidote to the perceived excesses of German Romanticism.

**saturated fatty acid** ◊fatty acid in which there are no double bonds in the hydrocarbon chain.

**Saturn** in astronomy, the second-largest planet in the Solar System, sixth from the Sun, and encircled by bright and easily visible equatorial rings. Viewed through a telescope it is ochre. Its polar diameter is 12,000 km/7,450 mi smaller than its equatorial diameter, a result of its fast rotation and low density, the lowest of any planet. Its mass is 95 times that of Earth, and its magnetic field 1,000 times stronger.
*mean distance from the Sun* 1.427 billion km/0.886 billion mi
*equatorial diameter* 120,000 km/75,000 mi
*rotational period* 10 hr 14 min at equator, 10 hr 40 min at higher latitudes
*year* 29.46 Earth years
*atmosphere* visible surface consists of swirling clouds, probably made of frozen ammonia at a temperature of –170°C/–274°F, although the markings in the clouds are not as prominent as Jupiter's. The space probes *Voyager 1* and *2* found winds reaching 1,800 kph/1,100 mph
*surface* Saturn is believed to have a small core of rock and iron, encased in ice and surrounded by a deep layer of liquid hydrogen
*satellites* 18 known moons, more than for any other planet. The largest moon, ◊Titan, has a dense atmosphere. Other satellites include Epimetheus, Janus, Pandor, and Prometheus. The rings visible from Earth begin about 14,000 km/9,000 mi from the planet's cloudtops and extend out to about 76,000 km/47,000 mi. Made of small chunks of ice and rock (averaging 1 m/3 ft across), they are 275,000 km/170,000 mi rim to rim, but only 100 m/300 ft thick. The Voyager probes showed that the rings actually consist of thousands of closely spaced ringlets, looking like the grooves in a gramophone record.

**Saturn** or *Saturnus,* in Roman mythology, the god of agriculture, identified by the Romans with the Greek god ◊Kronos. His period of rule

was the ancient Golden Age, when he introduced social order and the arts of civilization. Saturn was dethroned by his sons Jupiter, Neptune, and Dis. At the *Saturnalia,* his festival in December, gifts were exchanged, and slaves were briefly treated as their masters' equals.

**Saudi Arabia** Kingdom of
*national name Mamlaka al-'Arabiya as-Sa'udiya*

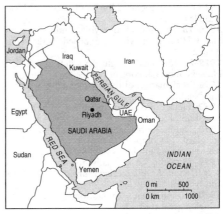

*area* 2,200,518 sq km/849,620 sq mi
*capital* Riyadh
*major towns/cities* Jiddah, Mecca, Medina, Taif, Dammam, Hufuf
*major ports* Jiddah, Dammam, Jubail, Jizan, Yanbu
*physical features* desert, sloping to the Persian Gulf from a height of 2,750 m/9,000 ft in the west
*head of state and government* King Fahd Ibn Abdul Aziz from 1996
*political system* absolute monarchy
*political parties* none
*currency* rial
*GNP per capita (PPP)* (US$) 9,200 (1998 est)
*exports* crude and refined petroleum, petrochemicals, wheat. Principal market: Japan 17% (1997)
*population* 20,899,000 (1999 est)
*language* Arabic
*religion* Sunni Muslim; there is a Shiite minority
*life expectancy* 70 (men); 73 (women) (1995–2000)
*Chronology*
**622** Muhammad began to unite Arabs in Muslim faith.
**7th–8th centuries** Muslim Empire expanded, ultimately stretching from India to Spain, with Arabia itself being relegated to a subordinate part.
**12th century** Decline of Muslim Empire; Arabia grew isolated and internal divisions multiplied.
**13th century** Mameluke sultans of Egypt became nominal overlords of Hejaz in western Arabia.
**1517** Hejaz became a nominal part of Ottoman Empire after Turks conquered Egypt.
**18th century** Al Saud family united tribes of Nejd in central Arabia in support of the Wahhabi religious movement.

*c. 1830* The Al Saud established Riyadh as the Wahhabi capital.

*c. 1870* Turks took effective control of Hejaz and also Hasa on Persian Gulf.

*late 19th century* Rival Wahhabi dynasty of Ibn Rashid became leaders of Nejd.

*1902* Ibn Saud organized Bedouin revolt and regained Riyadh.

*1913* Ibn Saud completed the reconquest of Hasa from Turks.

*1915* Britain recognized Ibn Saud as emir of Nejd and Hasa.

*1916–18* British-backed revolt, under aegis of Sharif Hussein of Mecca, expelled Turks from Arabia.

*1919–25* Ibn Saud fought and defeated Sharif Hussein and took control of Hejaz.

*1926* Proclamation of Ibn Saud as king of Hejaz and Nejd.

*1932* Hejaz and Nejd renamed the United Kingdom of Saudi Arabia.

*1933* Saudi Arabia allowed American-owned Standard Oil Company to prospect for oil, which was discovered in Hasa 1938.

*1939–45* Although officially neutral in World War II, Saudi Arabia received subsidies from USA and Britain.

*1940s* Commercial exploitation of oil began, bringing great prosperity.

*1953* Ibn Saud died; succeeded by his eldest son, Saud.

*1964* King Saud forced to abdicate; succeeded by his brother, Faisal.

*1975* King Faisal assassinated; succeeded by his half-brother, Khalid.

*1982* King Khalid died; succeeded by his brother, Fahd.

*1987* Rioting by Iranian pilgrims caused 400 deaths in Mecca and a breach in diplomatic relations with Iran.

*1990* Iraqi troops invaded Kuwait and massed on the Saudi Arabian border, prompting King Fahd to call for assistance from US and UK forces.

*1991* Saudi Arabia fought on the Allied side against Iraq in the Gulf War.

*1992* Under international pressure to move towards democracy, King Fahd formed a 'consultative council' to assist in the government of the kingdom.

*1995* King Fahd suffered a stroke and transferred power to Crown Prince Abdullah.

*1996* King Fahd resumed power.

**Saul** (lived 11th century BC) in the Old Testament, the first king of Israel. He was anointed by Samuel and warred successfully against the neighbouring Ammonites and Philistines, but fell from God's favour in his battle against the Amalekites. He became jealous and suspicious of ◊David and turned against him and Samuel. After being wounded in battle with the Philistines, in which his three sons died, he committed suicide.

**savanna** or *savannah,* extensive open tropical grasslands, with scattered trees and shrubs. Savannas cover large areas of Africa, North and South America, and northern Australia. The soil is acidic and sandy and generally considered suitable only as pasture for low-density grazing.

**Savimbi, Jonas Malheiro** (1934– ) Angolan soldier and right-wing revolutionary, founder and leader of the National Union for the Total Independence of Angola (UNITA). From 1975 UNITA, under Savimbi's leadership, tried to overthrow the government. A peace agreement was signed in 1994. Savimbi rejected the offer of vice presidency in a coalition government in 1996; however, in 1998, UNITA was demilitarized and accepted as a national political party.

**savings** unspent income, after deduction of tax, put aside through bank deposits or other financial schemes offering ◊interest to savers on their deposits. In economics a distinction is made between ◊investment, involving the purchase of capital goods, such as buying a house, and saving (where capital goods are not directly purchased; for example, buying shares as a way of earning an income).

**Savonarola, Girolamo** (1452–1498) Italian reformer, a Dominican friar and an eloquent preacher. His crusade against political and religious corruption won him popular support, and in 1494 he led a revolt in Florence that expelled the ruling Medici family and established a democratic republic. His denunciations of Pope ◊Alexander VI led to his excommunication (1497), and in 1498 he was arrested, tortured, hanged, and burned for heresy.

**Savoy** area of France between the Alps, Lake Geneva, and the River Rhône. A medieval duchy, it was made into the *départements* of Savoie and Haute-Savoie, in the Rhône-Alpes region.

**sawfish** any fish of the order Pristiformes of large, sharklike ◊rays, characterized by a flat, sawlike snout edged with teeth. The common sawfish *Pristis pectinatus,* also called the smalltooth, is more than 6 m/19 ft long. It has some 24 teeth along an elongated snout (2 m/6 ft) that can be used as a weapon.

**sawfly** any of several families of insects of the order Hymenoptera, related to bees, wasps, and ants, but lacking a 'waist' on the body. The egg-laying tube (ovipositor) of the female is surrounded by a pair of sawlike organs, which it uses to make a slit in a plant stem to lay its eggs. Horntails are closely related.

**Saxe-Coburg-Gotha** Saxon duchy. Albert, the Prince Consort of Britain's Queen Victoria, was a son of the 1st Duke, Ernest I (1784–1844), who was succeeded by Albert's elder brother, Ernest II (1818–1893). It remained the name of the British royal house until 1917, when it was changed to Windsor.

**saxifrage** any of a group of plants belonging to the saxifrage family, found growing in rocky, mountainous, and alpine areas in the northern hemisphere. They are low plants with groups of small white, pink, or yellow flowers. (Genus *Saxifraga,* family Saxifragaceae.)

**Saxon** member of a Germanic tribe once inhabiting the Danish peninsula and northern Germany. The Saxons migrated from their homelands in the early Middle Ages, under pressure from the Franks, and spread into various parts of Europe, including Britain (see ◊Anglo-Saxon). They also undertook piracy in the North Sea and the English Channel.

**Saxony** German *Sachsen,* administrative *Land* (state) of Germany
**area** 17,036 sq km/6,580 sq mi
**capital** Dresden
**towns** Leipzig, Chemnitz, Zwickau
**physical** on the plain of the River Elbe north of the Erzgebirge mountain range
**products** electronics, textiles, vehicles, machinery, chemicals, coal
**population** (1995) 4,602,000
**history** conquered by Charlemagne 792, Saxony became a powerful medieval German duchy. The electors of Saxony were also kings of Poland 1697–1763. Saxony was part of East Germany 1946–90, forming a region with Anhalt.

**Saxony-Anhalt** administrative *Land* (state) of Germany
**area** 20,450 sq km/10,000 sq mi
**capital** Magdeburg
**towns** Halle, Dessau
**industries** chemicals, electronics, rolling stock, footwear, cereals, vegetables
**population** (1995) 2,735,000
**history** Anhalt became a duchy 1863 and a member of the North German Confederation 1866. Between 1946 and 1990 it was joined to the former Prussian province of Saxony as a region of East Germany.

**saxophone** member of a hybrid brass instrument family of conical bore, with a single-reed woodwind mouthpiece and keyworks, invented about in 1840 by Belgian instrument-maker Adolphe Sax (1814–1894). Soprano, alto, tenor, and baritone forms remain current. The soprano saxophone is usually straight; the others are characteristically curved back at the mouthpiece and have an upturned bell. Initially a concert instrument of suave tone, the saxophone was incorporated into dance bands of the 1930s and 1940s, and assumed its modern guise as an abrasive solo jazz instrument after 1945. It has a voicelike ability to bend a note.

**Say's law** in economics, the 'law of markets' formulated by Jean-Baptiste Say (1767–1832) to the effect that supply creates its own demand and that resources can never be underused.

**scabies** contagious infection of the skin caused by the parasitic itch mite *Sarcoptes scabiei,* which burrows under the skin to deposit eggs. Treatment is by antiparasitic creams and lotions.

**scabious** any of a group of plants belonging to the teasel family, native to Europe and Asia, with many small, usually purplish-blue flowers borne in a single head on a tall stalk. The small scabious (*S. columbaria*) and the Mediterranean sweet scabious (*S. atropurpurea*) are often cultivated. (Genus *Scabiosa,* family Dipsacaceae.)

**scale** in chemistry, ◊calcium carbonate deposits that form on the inside of a kettle or boiler as a result of boiling ◊hard water.

**scale** in music, a sequence of pitches that establishes a key, and in some respects the character of a composition. A scale is defined by its starting note and may be *major* or *minor* depending on the order of intervals. A *chromatic scale* is the full range of 12 notes: it has no key because there is no fixed starting point.

**scale insect** any small plant-sucking insect, order Homoptera, of the superfamily Coccoidea. Some species are major pests – for example, the citrus mealy bug (genus *Pseudococcus*), which attacks citrus fruits in North America. The female is often wingless and legless, attached to a plant by the head and with the body covered with a waxy scale. The rare males are winged.

**scallop** any marine bivalve ◊mollusc of the family Pectinidae, with a fan-shaped shell. There are two 'ears' extending from the socketlike hinge. Scallops use water-jet propulsion to move through the water to escape predators such as starfish. The giant Pacific scallop found from Alaska to California can reach 20 cm/8 in width.

**scaly anteater** another name for the ◊pangolin.

**Scandinavia** peninsula in northwestern Europe, comprising Norway and Sweden; politically and culturally it also includes Denmark, Iceland, the Faroe Islands, and Finland. (See separate entries for all of these.)

**scandium** silver-white, metallic element of the ◊lanthanide series, symbol Sc, atomic number 21, relative atomic mass 44.956.

Its compounds are found widely distributed in nature, but only in minute amounts. The metal has little industrial importance.

**scanner** in computing, a device that can produce a digital image of a document for input and storage in a computer. It uses technology similar to that of a photocopier. Small scanners can be passed over the document surface by hand; larger versions have a flat bed, like that of a photocopier, on which the input document is placed and scanned.

**scanning** in medicine, the noninvasive examination of body organs to detect abnormalities of structure or function. Detectable waves – for example, ◊ultrasound, gamma, or ◊X-rays – are passed through the part to be scanned. Their absorption pattern is recorded, analysed by computer, and displayed pictorially on a screen.

**scarab** any of a family Scarabaeidae of beetles, often brilliantly coloured, and including ◊cockchafers, June beetles, and dung beetles. The *Scarabeus sacer* was revered by the ancient Egyptians as the symbol of resurrection.

**Scargill, Arthur** (1938– ) British trade-union leader. Elected president of the National Union of Miners (NUM) in 1981, he embarked on a collision course with the Conservative government of Margaret Thatcher. The damaging strike of 1984–85 split the miners' movement. In 1995, criticizing what he saw as the Labour Party's lurch to the right, he announced that he would establish a rival party, the independent

Socialist Labour Party. This proved to be largely ineffectual, and made little impact in consequent elections. By 1997 membership of the NUM had fallen to 10,000.

**Scarlatti, (Giuseppe) Domenico** (1685–1757) Italian composer. The eldest son of Alessandro ◊Scarlatti, he lived most of his life in Portugal and Spain in the service of the Queen of Spain. He wrote over 500 sonatas for harpsichord, short pieces in binary form demonstrating the new freedoms of keyboard composition and inspired by Spanish musical idioms.

**Scarlatti, (Pietro) Alessandro (Gaspare)** (1660–1725) Italian Baroque composer. He was maestro di capella at the court of Naples and developed the opera form. He composed more than 100 operas, including *Tigrane* (1715), as well as church music and oratorios.

**scarlet fever** or *scarlatina,* acute infectious disease, especially of children, caused by the bacteria in the *Streptococcus pyogenes* group. It is marked by fever, vomiting, sore throat, and a bright red rash spreading from the upper to the lower part of the body. The rash is followed by the skin peeling in flakes. It is treated with antibiotics.

**scarp and dip** in geology, the two slopes formed when a sedimentary bed outcrops as a landscape feature. The scarp is the slope that cuts across the bedding plane; the dip is the opposite slope which follows the bedding plane. The scarp is usually steep, while the dip is a gentle slope.

**scepticism** ancient philosophical view that absolute knowledge of things is ultimately unobtainable, hence the only proper attitude is to suspend judgement. Its origins lay in the teachings of the Greek philosopher Pyrrho, who maintained that peace of mind lay in renouncing all claims to knowledge.

**Scheherazade** the storyteller in the *Arabian Nights.*

**Schiele, Egon** (1890–1918) Austrian artist. Strongly influenced by ◊Art Nouveau, and in particular Gustav ◊Klimt, he developed an angular, contorted style, employing garish colours, that made him an important pioneer of ◊Expressionism. His subject matter includes portraits and openly erotic nudes.

**Schiller, Johann Christoph Friedrich von** (1759–1805) German dramatist, poet, and historian. He wrote *Sturm und Drang* ('storm and stress') verse and plays, including the dramatic trilogy *Wallenstein* (1798–99). He was an idealist, and much of his work concerns the aspiration for political freedom and the avoidance of mediocrity.

**schist** ◊metamorphic rock containing ◊mica or another platy or elongate mineral, whose crystals are aligned to give a foliation (planar texture) known as schistosity. Schist may contain additional minerals such as ◊garnet.

**schizophrenia** mental disorder, a psychosis of unknown origin, which can lead to profound changes in personality, behaviour, and perception, including delusions and hallucinations. It is more common in males and the early-onset form is more severe than when the illness develops in later life. Modern treatment approaches include drugs, family therapy, stress reduction, and rehabilitation.

**Schleswig-Holstein** adminstrative region (German *Land*) in north Germany, bounded on the north by Denmark, on the east by the Baltic Sea and Mecklenberg-West Pomerania, on the south by Lower Saxony and Hamburg, and on the west by the north Sea and the Heligoland Bight

*area* 15,700 sq km/6,060 sq mi

*capital* Kiel

*towns* Lübeck, Flensburg, Schleswig, Neumünster, Rendsburg

*physical* Elbe River, Kiel Canal, Heligoland; Schleswig in the north is divided from Holstein in the south by the River Eider

*industries* shipbuilding, mechanical and electrical engineering, food processing, textiles

*agricuIuture* fisheries, cattle, sheep, pigs, poultry

*population* (1995) 2,708,000

*religion* 87% Protestant; 6% Catholic

*history* Schleswig (Danish *Slesvig*) and Holstein were two duchies held by the kings of Denmark from 1460, but were not part of the kingdom; a number of the inhabitants were German, and Holstein was a member of the Confederation of the Rhine formed in 1815. Possession of the duchies had long been disputed by Prussia, and when Frederick VII of Denmark died without an heir in 1863, Prussia, supported by Austria, fought and defeated the Danes in 1864, and in 1866 annexed the two duchies. A plebiscite held in 1920 gave the northern part of Schleswig to Denmark, which made it the province of Haderslev and Aabenraa; the rest, with Holstein, remained part of Germany.

**Schliemann, Heinrich** (1822–1890) German archaeologist. In 1870 he began excavating at Hissarlik, Turkey, the traditional site of ◊Troy, and uncovered its ruins and those of other cities on the site. His later excavations were at Mycenae, Greece, (1874–76), where he discovered the ruins of the ◊Mycenaean civilization.

**Schlüter, Poul Holmskov** (1929–  ) Danish right-wing politician, leader of the Conservative People's Party (KF) from 1974 and prime minister (1982–93). His centre-right coalition survived the 1990 election and was reconstituted, with Liberal support. In January 1993 Schlüter resigned, accused of dishonesty over his role in an incident involving Tamil refugees. He was succeeded by Poul Nyrup Rasmussen.

**Schmidt, Helmut Heinrich Waldemar** (1918–  ) German socialist politician, member of the Social Democratic Party (SPD), chancellor of West Germany (1974–83). As chancellor, Schmidt introduced social reforms and continued Brandt's policy of Ostpolitik. With the French president Giscard d'Estaing, he instigated annual world and European economic summits. He was a firm supporter of ◊NATO and of the deployment of US nuclear missiles in West Germany during the early 1980s.

**Schoenberg, Arnold Franz Walter** (1874–1951) Austro-Hungarian composer, a US citizen from 1941. After Romantic early works such as *Verklärte Nacht/Transfigured Night* (1899) and the *Gurrelieder/Songs of Gurra* (1900–11), he experimented with ◊atonality (absence of key), producing works such as *Pierrot lunaire/ Moonstruck Pierrot* (1912) for chamber ensemble and voice, before developing the ◊twelve-tone system of musical composition.

**scholasticism** the theological and philosophical systems and methods taught in the schools of medieval Europe, especially in the 12th–14th centuries. Scholasticism tried to integrate orthodox Christian teaching with Aristotelian and some Platonic philosophy. The scholastic method involved surveying different opinions and the reasons given for them, and then attempting solutions of the problems raised, using logic and dialectic.

**Schopenhauer, Arthur** (1788–1860) German philosopher. His *The World as Will and Idea* (1818), inspired by Immanuel Kant and ancient Hindu philosophy, expounded an atheistic and pessimistic world view: an irrational will is considered as the inner principle of the world, producing an ever-frustrated cycle of desire, of which the only escape is aesthetic contemplation or absorption into nothingness.

**Schrödinger, Erwin** (1887–1961) Austrian physicist. He advanced the study of wave mechanics to describe the behaviour of electrons in atoms. He produced in 1926 a solid mathematical explanation of the ◊quantum theory and the structure of the atom. Nobel prize in 1933.

**Schubert, Franz Peter** (1797–1828) Austrian composer. His ten symphonies include the incomplete eighth in B minor (the 'Unfinished') and the 'Great' in C major. He wrote chamber and piano music, including the 'Trout Quintet', and over 600 lieder (songs) combining the Romantic expression of emotion with pure melody. They include the cycles *Die schöne Müllerin/The Beautiful Maid of the Mill* (1823) and *Die Winterreise/The Winter Journey* (1827).

**Schumacher, (Fritz) E(rnst) F(riedrich)** (1911–1977) German economist who made his career in the UK. He believed that the increasing size of institutions, coupled with unchecked economic growth, creates a range of social and environmental problems. He argued his case in books such as *Small is Beautiful* (1973), and established the Intermediate Technology Development Group.

**Schumacher, Michael** (1969– ) German motor-racing driver. He began his career in the Mercedes-Benz junior team; he joined the Jordan Formula 1 team in 1991, but was poached by Benetton almost immediately. He won his first Grand Prix in Belgium in 1992. Hailed by many as a gifted 'natural' driver, he won the world drivers' championship title for the first time in 1994, and again in 1995. He joined Ferrari at the end of the 1995 season. In July 1998 Schumacher won the British Grand Prix for the first time and signed a new £100 million contract with Ferrari that would keep him with the Italian team until 2002. At the beginning of the 1999 Grand Prix season he had a career total of 33 wins from 118 Grands Prix. Only Alain ◊Prost with 51 and Ayrton ◊Senna with 41 have won more Grand Prix. With his subsequent win in the 1999 Monaco Grand Prix in May 1999 he broke the record for the most number of Grand Prix wins by a Ferrari driver. It was his 16th victory for the Italian team – one more than that achieved by Austrian driver Niki Lauda.

**Schumann, Robert Alexander** (1810–1856) German composer and writer. His songs and short piano pieces portray states of emotion with great economy. Among his compositions are four symphonies, a violin concerto, a piano concerto, sonatas, and song cycles, such as *Dichterliebe/Poet's Love* (1840). Mendelssohn championed many of his works.

**Schwarzkopf, Norman** nicknamed 'Stormin' Norman' (1934– ) US general. He was supreme commander of the Allied forces in the ◊Gulf War (1991). He planned and executed a blitzkrieg campaign, 'Desert Storm', sustaining remarkably few Allied casualties in the liberation of Kuwait. He was a battalion commander in the Vietnam War and deputy commander of the US invasion of Grenada in 1983.

**sciatica** persistent pain in the back and down the outside of one leg, along the sciatic nerve and its branches. Causes of sciatica include inflammation of the nerve or pressure of a displaced disc on a nerve root leading out of the lower spine.

**science** (Latin *scientia* 'knowledge') any systematic field of study or body of knowledge that aims, through experiment, observation, and deduction, to produce reliable explanations of phenomena, with reference to the material and physical world.

**Scientology** (Latin *scire* 'to know' and Greek *logos* 'branch of learning') 'applied religious philosophy' based on dianetics, founded in California in 1952 by L Ron Hubbard as the *Church of Scientology*, and claiming to 'increase man's spiritual awareness'. Its headquarters from 1984 have been in Los Angeles.

**scilla** any of a group of bulbous plants belonging to the lily family, with blue, pink, or white flowers; they include the spring ◊squill (*S. verna*). (Genus *Scilla*, family Liliaceae.)

**Scilly, Isles of** or *Scilly Isles/Islands,* or *Scillies,* group of 140 islands and islets lying 40 km/25 mi southwest of Land's End, England; administered by the Duchy of Cornwall; area 16 sq km/6.3 sq mi; population (1991) 2,050. The five inhabited islands are *St Mary's,* the largest, on which is Hugh Town, capital of the Scillies; *Tresco,* the second largest, with subtropical gardens; *St Martin's,* noted for its beautiful shells; *St Agnes;* and *Bryher.*

**Scipio, Publius Cornelius** (236– *c.* 183 BC) also known as Scipio Africanus Major, Roman general whose tactical and strategic abilities turned the tide of the Second Punic War in 208–201 BC and established his reputation as one of Rome's greatest commanders. He defeated the Carthaginians in Spain in 210–206 BC and invaded Africa in 204 BC. At Zama in 202 BC he defeated the Carthaginian general ◊Hannibal to win the war for Rome. He adopted the name 'Africanus' in recognition of the place of his greatest victory, but he felt that his achievements had not been sufficiently rewarded and retired to his villa embittered.

**Scipio Africanus Minor, Publius Cornelius** (*c.* 185–129 BC) Roman general, the adopted grandson of Scipio Africanus Major, also known as *Scipio Aemilianus.* He destroyed Carthage 146, and subdued Spain 133. He was opposed to his brothers-in-law, the Gracchi.

**sclerenchyma** plant tissue whose function is to strengthen and support, composed of thick-walled cells that are heavily lignified (toughened). On maturity the cell inside dies, and only the cell walls remain.

**sclerosis** any abnormal hardening of body tissues, especially the nervous system or walls of the arteries. See ◊multiple sclerosis and ◊atherosclerosis.

**scorpion** any arachnid of the order Scorpiones, common in the tropics and subtropics. Scorpions have four pairs of walking legs, large pincers, and long tails ending in upcurved poisonous stings, though the venom is not usually fatal to a healthy adult human. Some species reach 25 cm/10 in. There are about 600 different species.

**Scorpius** bright zodiacal constellation in the southern hemisphere between ◊Libra and ◊Sagittarius, represented as a scorpion. The Sun passes briefly through Scorpius in the last week of November. The heart of the scorpion is marked by the bright red supergiant star ◊Antares. Scorpius contains rich ◊Milky Way star fields, plus the strongest ◊X-ray source in the sky, Scorpius X-1. The whole area is rich in clusters and nebulae. In astrology, the dates for Scorpius are about 24 October–21 November (see ◊precession).

**Scorsese, Martin** (1942–  ) US director, screenwriter, and producer. One of the most influential figures in modern American cinema, he has made such contemporary classics as *Mean Streets* (1973), *Taxi Driver* (1976), *Raging Bull* (1980), *GoodFellas* (1990), and *The Age of Innocence* (1993).

**Scot** inhabitant of Scotland, part of Britain; or a person of Scottish descent. Originally the Scots were a Celtic (Gaelic) people of Northern Ireland who migrated to Scotland in the 5th century.

**Scotland** Roman *Caledonia,* the northernmost part of Britain, formerly an independent country, now part of the UK
*area* 78,470 sq km/30,297 sq mi
*capital* Edinburgh
*cities* Glasgow, Dundee, Aberdeen
*features* the Highlands in the north (with the Grampian Mountains); central Lowlands, including valleys of the Clyde and Forth, with most of the country's population and industries; Southern Uplands (including the Lammermuir Hills); and islands of the Orkneys, Shetlands, and Western Isles; the world's greatest concentration of nuclear weapons are at the UK and US bases on the Clyde, near Glasgow; 8,000-year-old pinewood forests once covered 1,500,000 ha/3,706,500 acres, now reduced to 12,500 ha/30,900 acres; there were at least 104,876 ha/ 259,150 acres of native woodlands remaining in the Highlands in 1994, covering only 2% of the total area. The 1995 Millennium Commission award will fund the creation of the Millennium Forest, and double Scotland's forests
*industry* electronics, marine and aircraft engines, oil, natural gas, chemicals, textiles, clothing, printing, paper, food processing, tourism, whisky, coal, computer industries (Scotland's 'Silicon Glen' produces over 35% of Europe's personal computers)
*currency* pound sterling
*population* (1993 est) 5,120,000
*languages* English; ◊Scots, a lowland dialect (derived from Northumbrian Anglo-Saxon); Gaelic spoken by 1.3%, mainly in the Highlands
*religions* Presbyterian (Church of Scotland), Roman Catholic
*famous people* Robert Bruce, Walter Scott, Robert Burns, Robert Louis Stevenson, Adam Smith
*government* Scotland sends 72 members to the UK Parliament at Westminster. The Local Government (Scotland) Bill of 1994 abolished the two-tier system of local government. Since 1996 there have been 32 unitary authorities. There is a differing legal system to England (see ◊Scottish law).

Scots voted overwhelmingly in favour of a Scottish parliament and the beginning of devolution in a referendum held in September 1997. Scotland's last legislature vanished with the Union of 1707. The Scottish Parliament was backed by 75% of the 2.4 million people who voted in the two-question referendum and 63% agreed that it should have tax-varying powers. There was a 61.4% turnout.

Elections to the 129-member assembly were planned for spring 1999, with the Parliament coming into being on a site in Edinburgh to be decided by the turn of the millennium. It will have charge over most of Scotland's domestic affairs, including education, the health service, local government, and agriculture, and will be headed by a First Minister.

**Scots language** the form of the English language as traditionally spoken and written in Scotland, regarded by some scholars as a distinct language. Scots derives from the Northumbrian dialect of Anglo-Saxon or Old English, and has been a literary language since the 14th century.

**Scott, (George) Gilbert** (1811–1878) English architect. As the leading practical architect of the mid-19th-century Gothic Revival in England, Scott was responsible for the building or restoration of many public buildings and monuments, including the Albert Memorial (1863–72), the Foreign Office in Whitehall (1862–73), and the St Pancras Station Hotel (1868–74), all in London.

**Scott, Giles Gilbert** (1880–1960) English architect. He was the grandson of Gilbert ◊Scott. He designed Liverpool Anglican Cathedral (begun 1903; completed 1978), Cambridge University Library (1931–34), Battersea Power Station (1932–34), and Waterloo Bridge, London (1939–45). He also designed and supervised the rebuilding of the House of Commons chamber at the Palace of Westminster in a modern Gothic style after World War II.

**Scott, Robert Falcon** known as *Scott of the Antarctic* (1868–1912) English explorer who commanded two Antarctic expeditions, in 1901–04 and 1910–12. On 18 January 1912 he reached the South Pole, shortly after the Norwegian Roald ◊Amundsen, but on the return journey he and his companions died in a blizzard only a few miles from their base camp. His journal was recovered and published in 1913.

**Scott, Walter** (1771–1832) Scottish novelist and poet. His first works were translations of German ballads and collections of Scottish ballads, which he followed with narrative poems of his own, such as *The Lay of the Last Minstrel* (1805), *Marmion* (1808), and *The Lady of the Lake* (1810). He gained a European reputation for his historical novels such as *Waverley* (1814), *Rob Roy* (1817), *The Heart of Midlothian* (1818), and *Ivanhoe* (1819), all published anonymously.

**Scottish Borders** unitary authority in southeast Scotland, created in 1996 to replace the former Borders region
*area* 4,733 sq km/1,827 sq mi
*towns* Galashiels, Hawick, Jedburgh, Kelso, Newtown St Boswells (administrative headquarters), Peebles, Selkirk
*physical* much of the west part of the area is upland (Lammermuir, Moorfoot and Pentland Hills); Broad Law (840 m/2,756 ft), near Tweedsmuir, is the highest point. The principal river, the Tweed, traverses the region west–east; its tributaries include the River Teviot. The largest loch is St Mary's, and the only substantial area of low-lying agricultural land is the Merse in the southeast, near the English border. The coast is generally precipitous
*features* Walter Scott's home at Abbotsford; Field Marshal Haig and Walter Scott buried at Dryburgh Abbey; Melrose Abbey (12th century)
*famous people* Mungo Park, James Hogg (Scottish poet 'the Ettrick Shepherd'), Walter Scott
*industries* electronics, timber, knitwear, tweed
*agriculture* sheep and cattle; cereals and root crops; fishing
*population* (1996) 105,300.

**Scottish Gaelic language** see ◊Gaelic language.

**Scottish law** the legal system of Scotland. Owing to its separate development, Scotland has a system differing from the rest of the UK, being based on ◊civil law. Its continued separate existence was guaranteed by the Act of Union with England in 1707.

**Scottish Parliament** devolved legislative body of Scotland. It comprises 129 members and was created by the November 1998 Scotland Act, which was passed following the Scottish electorate's overwhelming approval of government proposals in an 11 September 1997 referendum on devolution. The first elections to the parliament were held on 6 May 1999 and the parliament opened on 1 July 1999. Its temporary base is the Church of Scotland General Assembly Hall and City of Edinburgh Council buildings, in the Lawnmarket and on George IV Bridge, in Edinburgh. A permanent home is being built on the Royal Mile, next to Holyrood House, by a design team led by the architect Enric Miralles (1955– ) of Barcelona, with completion planned for the autumn of 2001.

**Scouts** worldwide youth organization that emphasizes character, citizenship, and outdoor life. It was founded (as the Boy Scouts) in England in 1908 by Robert ◊Baden-Powell. His book *Scouting for Boys* (1908) led to the incorporation in the UK of the Boy Scout Association by royal charter in 1912. There are some 25 million members of the World Organization of the Scout Movement (1998).

**scrapie** fatal disease of sheep and goats that attacks the central nervous system, causing deterioration of the brain cells, and leading to characteristic staggering gait and other behavioural abnormalities, before death. It is caused by the presence of an abnormal version of the brain protein PrP and is related to ◊bovine spongiform encephalopathy, the disease of cattle known as 'mad cow disease', and Creutzfeldt–Jakob disease in humans. It is a transmissible spongiform encephalopathy.

**screen** in computing, another name for monitor.

**scuba** acronym for *self-contained underwater breathing apparatus,* another name for ◊aqualung.

**Scudamore, Peter Michael** (1958– ) British National Hunt jockey. He was champion jockey in 1982 (shared with John Francome) and from 1986 to 1992. In 1988–89 he rode a record 221 winners, a total surpassed in 1997–98 by Tony McCoy. In April 1993 he announced his retirement from the sport, with a world record 1,677 winners.

**sculpture** artistic shaping of materials such as wood, stone, clay, metal, and, more recently, plastic and other synthetics. The earliest prehistoric human artefacts include sculpted stone figurines, and all ancient civilizations have left behind examples of sculpture. Many indigenous cultures have maintained rich traditions of sculpture. Those of Africa, South America, and the Caribbean in particular have been influential in the development of contemporary Western sculpture.

Historically, most sculpture has been religious in intent. Chinese, Japanese, and Indian sculptures are usually Buddhist or Hindu images. African, American Indian, and Oceanic sculptures reflect spirit cults and animist beliefs.

There are two main techniques traditionally employed in sculpture: *carving,* involving the cutting away of hard materials such as wood or stone to reveal an image; and *modelling,* involving the building up of an image from malleable materials, such as clay or wax, which may then be cast in bronze. In the 20th century various techniques for 'constructing' sculptures have been developed, for example metal welding and assemblage.

*ancient    sculpture*  Egyptian and Mesopotamian sculpture took the form of monumental ◊reliefs in palace and temple decoration. Standing sculptures of the period were intended to be seen only from the front and sides. The first sculptures in the round (to be seen from all sides) were Greek. The development of vigorous poses (contrapposto) and emotional expressiveness elevated Greek sculpture to the pinnacle of artistic achievement (see ◊Phidias, ◊Praxiteles), and much of subsequent Western sculpture has been imitative of Greek ideals. Lifelike portrait sculpture was introduced by the Romans.

*medieval    sculpture*  Sculpture of the medieval period is epitomized by niche figures carved in stone for churches (for example, Chartres Cathedral, France) and by delicate ivory carvings. The work of Nicola Pisano began a great tradition of Italian sculpture.

*Renaissance  sculpture*  Greek supremacy was challenged by the reintroduction of free-standing sculptures, notably Michelangelo's *David* (1501–04), and by superlative bronze casting, for example, Donatello's equestrian monument of *Gattamelata* (1447–50, Piazza del Santo, Padua). In the work of Lorenzo Ghiberti, Luca della Robbia, and Andrea del Verrocchio, figure sculpture attained a new dignity and power. The work of Benvenuto Cellini and Giovanni Bologna (1524–1608) exemplified the Mannerist style.

Pedro Berruguete, a pupil of Michelangelo, introduced the Renaissance to Spain. In France, Jean Goujon developed Mannerism. However, it was the High Renaissance style of Michelangelo that was later encouraged by Louis XIV, who commissioned numerous busts and figure groups, notably by François Girardon.

*Baroque and Rococo sculpture*  Relief rather than free-standing sculptures came to the fore. The limpid virtuosity of such sculptors as Giovanni Bernini seemed to defy the nature of the materials they used. The style was represented in France by Etienne Falconet, and in Spain by Alonso Cano.

*neoclassical  sculpture*  Sculpture of the 18th century concentrated on smooth perfection of form and surface, notably the work of Antonio Canova. The last great exponent of sculpture in the Classical tradition was Auguste Rodin. The work of Aristide Maillol and Antoine Bourdelle (1861–1929) emphasized formal qualities, rejecting both realism and Impressionism.

*20th century*  Sculptors such as Henry Moore, Barbara Hepworth, and Jacob Epstein used traditional materials and techniques to create forms inspired by 'primitive' art and nature. The work of Amedeo Modigliani and Henri Gaudier-Brzeska also reflects such influences. Abstract sculpture was pioneered by Alexander Archipenko and Ossip Zadkine, both exponents of Cubism, and Constantin Brancusi and Alberto Giacometti, who developed three-dimensional abstract forms from natural materials. Followers of the nonrepresentational school include Jacques Lipchitz, Jean Arp, Naum Gabo and Antoine Pevsner (pioneers of Russian Constructivism), Reg Butler, and Anthony Caro. Among more traditional sculptors whose work powerfully expresses the modern idiom are Marino Marini in Italy and Frank Dobson (1888–1963) in England.

Other sculptors have broken with the past entirely, rejecting both carving and modelling. Today the term sculpture applies to the mobiles of Alexander Calder, assemblages of various materials, 'environment sculpture' and earthworks (pioneered by Carl André), and 'installations'.

Another development has been the sculpture garden; for example, Hakore open-air museum in Japan and the Grizedale Forest sculpture project in the Lake District, England.

**scurvy**  disease caused by deficiency of vitamin C (ascorbic acid), which is contained in fresh vegetables and fruit. The signs are weakness and aching joints and muscles, progressing to bleeding of the gums and other spontaneous haemorrhage, and drying-up of the skin and hair. It is reversed by giving the vitamin.

**Scylla and Charybdis**  in Greek mythology, a sea monster and a whirlpool, between which ◊Odysseus had to sail. Later writers located them at the northern end of the Straits of Messina, between Sicily and Italy.

**Scythia**  region north of the Black Sea between the Carpathian Mountains and the River Don, inhabited by the Scythians in the 7th–1st centuries BC. From the middle of the 4th century, they were slowly superseded by the Sarmatians. The Scythians produced ornaments and vases in gold and electrum with animal decoration. Although there is no surviving written work, there are spectacular archaeological remains, including vast royal burial mounds which often contain horse skeletons.

**SDLP**  abbreviation for ◊*Social Democratic Labour Party,* a Northern Ireland political party.

**SDP**  abbreviation for ◊*Social Democratic Party,* former British political party.

**sea anemone**  invertebrate marine animal of the phylum Cnidaria with a tubelike body attached by the base to a rock or shell. The other end has an open 'mouth' surrounded by stinging tentacles, which capture crustaceans and other small organisms. Many sea anemones are beautifully coloured, especially those in tropical waters.

**seaborgium** synthesized radioactive element of the ◊transactinide series, symbol Sg, atomic number 106, relative atomic mass 263. It was first synthesized in 1974 in the USA and given the temporary name unnilhexium. The discovery was not confirmed until 1993. It was officially named in 1997 after US nuclear chemist Glenn Seaborg.

**sea cucumber** any echinoderm of the class Holothuroidea with a cylindrical body that is tough-skinned, knobbed, or spiny. The body may be several feet in length. Sea cucumbers are sometimes called 'cotton-spinners' from the sticky filaments they eject from the anus in self-defence.

**seafloor spreading** growth of the ocean crust outwards (sideways) from ocean ridges. The concept of seafloor spreading has been combined with that of continental drift and incorporated into ◊plate tectonics.

**seagull** see ◊gull.

**sea horse** any marine fish of several related genera, especially *Hippocampus*, of the family Syngnathidae, which includes the pipefishes. The body is small and compressed and covered with bony plates raised into tubercles or spines. The tail is prehensile, and the tubular mouth sucks in small shellfish and larvae as food. The head and foreparts, usually carried upright, resemble those of a horse. They swim vertically and beat their fins up to 70 times a second.

**seakale** perennial European coastal plant with broad, fleshy leaves and white flowers; it is cultivated in Europe and the young shoots are eaten as a vegetable. (*Crambe maritima*, family Cruciferae.)

**seal** aquatic carnivorous mammal of the families Otariidae and Phocidae (sometimes placed in a separate order, the Pinnipedia). The eared seals or sea lions (Otariidae) have small external ears, unlike the true seals (Phocidae). Seals have a streamlined body with thick blubber for insulation, and front and hind flippers. They are able to close their nostrils as they dive, and obtain oxygen from their blood supply while under water. They feed on fish, squid, or crustaceans, and are commonly found in Arctic and Antarctic seas, but also in Mediterranean, Caribbean, and Hawaiian waters.

**sea lily** any ◊echinoderm of the class Crinoidea. In most, the rayed, cuplike body is borne on a sessile stalk (permanently attached to a rock) and has feathery arms in multiples of five encircling the mouth. However, some sea lilies are free-swimming and unattached.

**sea lion** any of several genera of ◊seals of the family Otariidae (eared seals), which also includes the fur seals. These streamlined animals have large fore flippers which they use to row themselves through the water. The hind flippers can be turned beneath the body to walk on land.

**Sea Peoples** unidentified seafaring warriors who may have been Achaeans, Etruscans, or ◊Philistines, who ravaged and settled the Mediterranean coasts in the 12th–13th centuries BC. They were defeated by Ramses III of Egypt in 1191 BC.

**search engine** in computing, remotely accessible program to help users find information on the Internet. Commercial search engines such as AltaVista and Lycos comprise databases of documents, URLs, USENET articles, and more, which can be searched by keying in a key word or phrase. The databases are compiled by a mixture of automated agents (spiders) and webmasters registering their sites.

**sea slug** any of an order (Nudibranchia) of marine gastropod molluscs in which the shell is reduced or absent. The order includes some very colourful forms, especially in the tropics. They are largely carnivorous, feeding on hydroids and ◊sponges.

**season** period of the year having a characteristic climate. The change in seasons is mainly due to the change in attitude of the Earth's axis in relation to the Sun, and hence the position of the Sun in the sky at a particular place. In temperate latitudes four seasons are recognized: spring, summer, autumn (fall), and winter. Tropical regions have two seasons – the wet and the dry. Monsoon areas around the Indian Ocean have three seasons: the cold, the hot, and the rainy.

**seasonal affective disorder** (SAD), form of depression that occurs in winter and is relieved by the coming of spring. Its incidence decreases closer to the Equator. One type of SAD is associated with increased sleeping and appetite.

**sea squirt** or *tunicate,* any solitary or colonial-dwelling saclike ◊chordate of the class Ascidiacea. A pouch-shaped animal attached to a rock or other base, it draws in food-carrying water through one siphon and expels it through another after straining it through numerous gill slits. The young are free-swimming tadpole-shaped organisms, which, unlike the adults, have a notochord.

**Seattle** nickname 'Emerald City', port on Lake Washington, USA; the largest city in the Pacific Northwest; population (1996 est) 524,700, metropolitan area with Everett (1995 est) 3,020,000. It is the main transit point for supplies to Alaska. Industries include aerospace (it is the headquarters of the Boeing Corporation), timber, tourism, banking and insurance, paper industries, electronics (Microsoft is based in adjoining Redmond), ocean science, shipbuilding and repair, and fishing. Coffee has been an important product since the development of the Starbucks Company in the 1970s. Trade with Japan is important.

**sea urchin** any of various orders of the class Echinoidea among the ◊echinoderms. They all have a globular body enclosed with plates of lime and covered with spines. Sometimes the spines are anchoring organs, and they also assist in locomotion. Sea urchins feed on seaweed and the animals frequenting them, and some are edible, as is their roe.

**seaweed** any of a vast group of simple multi-cellular plant forms belonging to the ◊algae and found growing in the sea, brackish estuaries, and salt marshes, from about the high-tide mark to depths of 100–200 m/300–600 ft. Many sea-weeds have holdfasts (attaching them to rocks or other surfaces), stalks, and fronds, sometimes with air bladders to keep them afloat, and are green, blue-green, red, or brown.

**Sebastiano del Piombo** Sebastiano Luciani (*c.* 1485–1547) Venetian painter; he was a pupil of ◊Giorgione and developed a similar style. In 1511 he moved to Rome, where his friendship with Michelangelo (and rivalry with Raphael) inspired his finest works, such as *The Raising of Lazarus* (1517–19; National Gallery, London).

**Sebastian, St** (died *c.* 258) Roman soldier. He was traditionally a member of Emperor Diocletian's bodyguard until his Christian faith was discovered. He was condemned to be killed by arrows. Feast day 20 January.

**secession** Latin *secessio,* in politics, the with-drawal from a federation of states by one or more of its members, as in the secession of the Confederate states from the Union in the USA (1860), Singapore from the Federation of Malaysia (1965), and Croatia and Slovenia from the Yugoslav Federation (1991).

**second** basic ◊SI unit (symbol sec or s) of time, one-sixtieth of a minute. It is defined as the duration of 9,192,631,770 cycles of regulation (periods of the radiation corresponding to the transition between two hyperfine levels of the ground state) of the caesium-133 isotope. In mathematics, the second is a unit (symbol ΄) of angular measurement, equalling one-sixtieth of a minute, which in turn is one-sixtieth of a degree.

**Second World War** alternative name for ◊World War II, 1939–45.

**secretary bird** ground-hunting, long-legged, mainly grey-plumaged bird of prey *Sagittarius serpentarius.* It is about 1.2 m/4 ft tall, with an erectile head crest tipped with black. It is pro-tected in southern Africa because it eats poiso-nous snakes.

**secretary of state** in the UK, a title held by a number of ministers; for example, the secre-tary of state for foreign and commonwealth affairs.

**secretin** ◊hormone produced by the small intestine of vertebrates that stimulates the pro-duction of digestive secretions by the pancreas and liver.

**sect** small ideological group, usually religious in nature, that may have moved away from a main group, often claiming a monopoly of access to truth or salvation. Sects are usually highly exclusive. They demand strict conformity, total commitment to their code of behaviour, and complete personal involvement, sometimes to the point of rejecting mainstream society alto-gether in terms of attachments, names, posses-sions, and family.

**sector** in geometry, part of a circle enclosed by two radii and the arc that joins them. A *minor sector* has an angle at the centre of the circle of less than 180°. A *major sector* has an angle at the centre of the circle of more than 180°.

**secularization** the process through which religious thinking, practice, and institutions lose their religious and/or social significance. The concept is based on the theory, held by some sociologists, that as societies become industrial-ized their religious morals, values, and institu-tions give way to secular ones and some religious traits become common secular prac-tices.

**Security Council** the most important body of the United Nations; see ◊United Nations.

**sedative** any drug that has a calming effect, reducing anxiety and tension.
Sedatives will induce sleep in larger doses. Examples are ◊barbiturates, ◊narcotics, and ◊benzodiazepines.

**sedge** any of a group of perennial grasslike plants, usually with three-cornered solid stems, common in low water or on wet and marshy ground. (Genus *Carex,* family Cyperaceae.)

**Sedgemoor, Battle of** in English history, a battle on 6 July 1685 in which Monmouth's rebellion was crushed by the forces of James II, on a tract of marshy land 5 km/3 mi southeast of Bridgwater, Somerset.

**sediment** any loose material that has 'settled' – deposited from suspension in water, ice, or air, generally as the water current or wind speed decreases. Typical sediments are, in order of increasing coarseness, clay, mud, silt, sand, gravel, pebbles, cobbles, and boulders.

**sedimentary rock** rock formed by the accu-mulation and cementation of deposits that have been laid down by water, wind, ice, or gravity. Sedimentary rocks cover more than two-thirds of the Earth's surface and comprise three major categories: clastic, chemically precipitated, and organic (or biogenic). Clastic sediments are the largest group and are composed of fragments of pre-existing rocks; they include clays, sands, and gravels.
Chemical precipitates include some lime-stones and evaporated deposits such as gypsum and halite (rock salt). Coal, oil shale, and lime-stone made of fossil material are examples of organic sedimentary rocks.

**sedition** in the UK, the offence of inciting unlawful opposition to the crown and govern-ment. Unlike treason, sedition does not carry the death penalty.

**Seebeck effect** in physics, the generation of a voltage in a circuit containing two different met-als, or semiconductors, by keeping the junctions between them at different temperatures. Discovered by the German physicist Thomas Seebeck (1770–1831), it is also called the ther-moelectric effect, and is the basis of the ◊thermocouple. It is the opposite of the ◊Peltier effect (in which current flow causes a tempera-ture difference between the junctions of different metals).

**seed** the reproductive structure of higher plants (◊angiosperms and ◊gymnosperms). It develops from a fertilized ovule and consists of an embryo and a food store, surrounded and protected by an outer seed coat, called the testa. The food store is contained either in a specialized nutritive tissue, the endosperm, or in the ◊cotyledons of the embryo itself. In angiosperms the seed is enclosed within a ◊fruit, whereas in gymnosperms it is usually naked and unprotected, once shed from the female cone.

Following ◊germination the seed develops into a new plant.

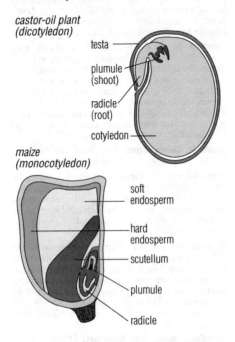

*castor-oil plant (dicotyledon)*

testa
plumule (shoot)
radicle (root)
cotyledon

*maize (monocotyledon)*

soft endosperm
hard endosperm
scutellum
plumule
radicle

**seed** *The structure of seeds. The castor-oil plant is a dicotyledon, a plant in which the developing plant has two leaves, developed from the cotyledon. In maize, a monocotyledon, there is a single leaf developed from the scutellum.*

**seed plant** any seed-bearing plant; also known as a *spermatophyte.*

The seed plants are subdivided into two classes: the ◊angiosperms, or flowering plants, and the ◊gymnosperms, principally the cycads and conifers.

Together, they comprise the major types of vegetation found on land.

**Seine** French river rising on the Langres plateau in the *département* of Côte d'Or, 30 km/19 mi northwest of Dijon, and flowing 774 km/472 mi northwest through ◊Paris and Rouen to join the English Channel at Le Havre. It is the third longest, but economically the most important, river in the country.

**seismic wave** energy wave generated by an ◊earthquake or an artificial explosion. There are two types of seismic waves: *body waves* that travel through the Earth's interior, and *surface waves* that travel through the surface layers of the crust and can be felt as the shaking of the ground, as in an earthquake.

**seismology** study of earthquakes and how their shock waves travel through the Earth. By examining the global pattern of waves produced by an earthquake, seismologists can deduce the nature of the materials through which they have passed. This leads to an understanding of the Earth's internal structure.

**Selangor** state of the Federation of Malaysia; area 7,956 sq km/3,071 sq mi; population (1993 est) 1,981,200. It was under British protection from 1874 and was a federated state from 1895–1946. The capital was transferred to Shah Alam from Kuala Lumpur in 1973. Klang is the seat of the sultan and a centre for rubber-growing and tin-mining; Port Kelang (or Klang), formerly Port Swettenham, exports tin and rubber.

**select committee** any of several long-standing committees of the UK House of Commons, such as the Environment Committee and the Treasury and Civil Service Committee. These were intended to restore parliamentary control of the executive, improve the quality of legislation, and scrutinize public spending and the work of government departments. Select committees represent the major parliamentary reform of the 20th century, and a possible means – through their all-party membership – of avoiding the automatic repeal of one government's measures by its successor.

**Selene** in Greek mythology, the goddess of the Moon; daughter of the Titan Hyperion; and sister of the Sun god ◊Helios and Eos, goddess of the dawn. In later times she was identified with ◊Artemis.

**selenium** (Greek *Selene* 'Moon') grey, non-metallic element, symbol Se, atomic number 34, relative atomic mass 78.96. It belongs to the sulphur group and occurs in several allotropic forms that differ in their physical and chemical properties. It is an essential trace element in human nutrition.

Obtained from many sulphide ores and selenides, it is used as a red colouring for glass and enamel.

**Seleucus (I) Nicator** (c. 358–281 BC) Macedonian general under ◊Alexander (III) the Great and founder of the Seleucid dynasty of Syria. After Alexander's death in 323 BC, Seleucus became governor and then, in 312 BC, ruler of Babylonia, founding the city of Seleucia on the River Tigris. He conquered Syria and had himself crowned king in 306 BC, but his expansionist policies brought him into conflict with the Ptolemies of Egypt and he was assassinated. He was succeeded by his son Antiochus I.

**Seljuk Empire** empire of the Turkish people (converted to Islam during the 7th century) under the leadership of the invading Tatars or Seljuk Turks. The Seljuk Empire (1055–1243) included Iran, Iraq, and most of Anatolia and Syria. It was a loose confederation whose centre was in Iran, jointly ruled by members of the family and led by a great sultan exercising varying degrees of effective power. It was succeeded by the ◊Ottoman Empire.

**Sellafield** site of a nuclear power station on the coast of Cumbria, northwest England. It was known as *Windscale* until 1971, when the management of the site was transferred from the UK Atomic Energy Authority to British Nuclear Fuels Ltd. It reprocesses more than 1,000 tonnes of spent fuel from nuclear reactors annually. The plant is the world's greatest discharger of radioactive waste: between 1968 and 1979, 180 kg/400 lb of plutonium was discharged into the Irish Sea. According to a report published in January 1999, by Britain's nuclear safety watchdog, the Nuclear Installations Inspectorate (NII), the storage facilities are in poor structural condition, presenting a significant risk of leakage.

**Sellers, Peter** stage name of Richard Henry Sellers (1925–1980) English comedian and film actor. He was particularly skilled at mimicry. He made his name in the madcap British radio programme *The Goon Show* (1949–60). His films include *The Ladykillers* (1955), *I'm All Right Jack* (1960), *Dr Strangelove* (1964), five *Pink Panther* films (1964–78) (as the bumbling Inspector Clouseau), and *Being There* (1979).

**Selznick, David O(liver)** (1902–1965) US film producer. His early work includes *King Kong, Dinner at Eight,* and *Little Women,* all 1933. His independent company, Selznick International (1935–40), made such lavish films as *Gone With the Wind* (1939), *Rebecca* (1940), and *Duel in the Sun* (1946). His last film was *A Farewell to Arms* (1957).

**semantics** branch of linguistics dealing with the meaning of words and sentences. Semantics asks how we can use language to express things about the real world and how the meanings of linguistic expressions can reflect people's thoughts. Semantic knowledge is *compositional;* the meaning of a sentence is based on the meanings of the words it contains and the order they appear in. For example, the sentences 'Teachers love children' and 'Children love teachers' both involve people loving other people but because of the different order of words they mean different things.

**semaphore** visual signalling code in which the relative positions of two moveable pointers or hand-held flags stand for different letters or numbers. The system is used by ships at sea and for railway signals.

**Semarang** port in north Java, Indonesia; population (1990) 1,005,300. There is a shipbuilding industry, and exports include coffee, teak, sugar, tobacco, kapok, and petroleum from nearby oilfields.

**semiconductor** material with electrical conductivity intermediate between metals and insulators and used in a wide range of electronic devices. Certain crystalline materials, most notably silicon and germanium, have a small number of free electrons that have escaped from the bonds between the atoms. The atoms from

which they have escaped possess vacancies, called holes, which are similarly able to move from atom to atom and can be regarded as positive charges. Current can be carried by both electrons (negative carriers) and holes (positive carriers). Such materials are known as *intrinsic semiconductors.*

**semiology** or *semiotics,* the study of the function of signs and symbols in human communication, both in language and by various nonlinguistic means. Beginning with the notion of the Swiss linguist Ferdinand de Saussure that no word or other sign (*signifier*) is intrinsically linked with its meaning (*signified*), it was developed as a scientific discipline, especially by Claude Lévi-Strauss and Roland ◊Barthes.

**Semite** any of the peoples of the Middle East originally speaking a Semitic language, and traditionally said to be descended from Shem, a son of Noah in the Bible. Ancient Semitic peoples include the Hebrews, Ammonites, Moabites, Edomites, Babylonians, Assyrians, Chaldaeans, Phoenicians, and Canaanites. The Semitic peoples founded the monotheistic religions of Judaism, Christianity, and Islam.

**Semitic languages** branch of the Hamito-Semitic language; see ◊Afro-Asiatic language.

**Semtex** plastic explosive, manufactured in the Czech Republic. It is safe to handle (it can only be ignited by a detonator) and difficult to trace, since it has no smell. It has been used by extremist groups in the Middle East and by the IRA in Northern Ireland.

**Senate** in ancient Rome, the 'council of elders'. Originally consisting of the heads of patrician families, it was recruited from ex-magistrates and persons who had rendered notable public service, but was periodically purged by the censors. Although nominally advisory, it controlled finance and foreign policy. Sulla doubled its size to 600.

**Sendak, Maurice Bernard** (1928– ) US writer and book illustrator. His children's books with their deliberately arch illustrations include *Where the Wild Things Are* (1963), *In the Night Kitchen* (1970), and *Outside Over There* (1981).

**Sendero Luminoso** Shining Path, Maoist guerrilla group active in Peru, formed 1980 to overthrow the government; until 1988 its activity was confined to rural areas. From 1992 its attacks intensified in response to a government crackdown. By 1997 the 17-year war had caused 30,000 deaths.

**Seneca, Lucius Annaeus** (*c.* 4 BC–AD *c.* 65) Roman stoic playwright, author of essays and nine tragedies. He was tutor to the future emperor Nero but lost favour after Nero's accession to the throne and was ordered to commit suicide. His tragedies were accepted as classical models by 16th-century dramatists.

**Senegal** Republic of
*national name Republique du Senegal*
*area* 196,200 sq km/75,752 sq mi
*capital* Dakar (and chief port)

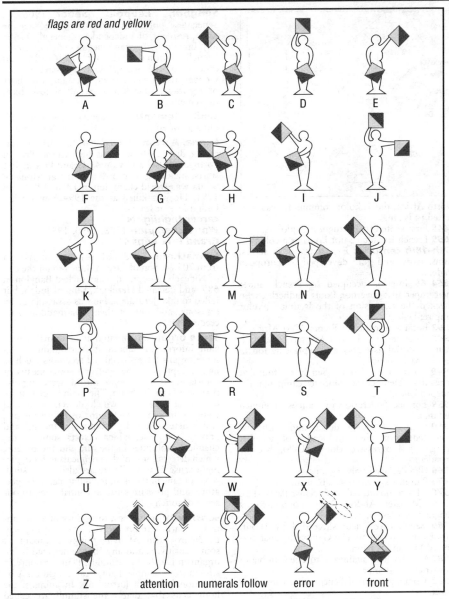

flags are red and yellow

A B C D E
F G H I J
K L M N O
P Q R S T
U V W X Y
Z attention numerals follow error front

**semaphore** *The semaphore signals for the letters of the alphabet and some special signals.*

**major towns/cities** Thiès, Kaolack, Saint-Louis, Ziguinchor, Diourbel
**physical features** plains rising to hills in southeast; swamp and tropical forest in southwest; River Senegal; The Gambia forms an enclave within Senegal
**head of state** Abdou Diouf from 1981
**head of government** Mamadou Lamine Loum from 1998
**political system** emergent socialist democracy
**political parties** Senegalese Socialist Party (PS), democratic socialist; Senegalese Democratic Party (PDS), centrist

**currency** franc CFA
**GNP per capita (PPP)** (US$) 1,710 (1998)
**exports** fresh and processed fish, refined petroleum products, chemicals, groundnuts and related products, calcium phosphates and related products. Principal market: India 25.6% (1997)
**population** 9,240,000 (1999 est)
**language** French (official); Wolof
**religion** mainly Sunni Muslim
**life expectancy** 51 (men); 54 (women) (1995–2000)
**Chronology**
**10th–11th centuries** Links established with

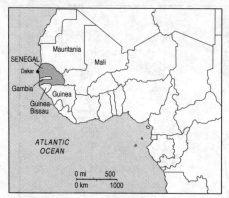

North Africa; the Tukolor community was converted to Islam.
**1445** First visited by Portuguese explorers.
**1659** French founded Saint-Louis as a colony.
**17th–18th centuries** Export trades in slaves, gums, ivory, and gold developed by European traders.
**1854–65** Interior occupied by French under their imperialist governor, Louis Faidherbe, who checked the expansion of the Islamic Tukulor Empire; Dakar founded.
**1902** Became territory of French West Africa.
**1946** Became French overseas territory, with own territorial assembly and representation in French parliament.
**1948** Leopold Sedar Senghor founded Senegalese Democratic Bloc to campaign for independence.
**1959** Formed Federation of Mali with French Sudan.
**1960** Achieved independence and withdrew from federation. Senghor, leader of socialist Senegalese Progressive Union (UPS), became president.
**1966** UPS declared only legal party.
**1974** Pluralist system re-established.
**1976** UPS reconstituted as Socialist Party (PS). Prime Minister Abdou Diouf nominated as Senghor's successor.
**1980** Senghor resigned; succeeded by Diouf. Troops sent to defend The Gambia against suspected Libyan invasion.
**1981** Military help again sent to The Gambia to thwart coup attempt.
**1982** Confederation of Senegambia came into effect.
**1983** Diouf re-elected. Post of prime minister abolished.
**1989** Diplomatic links with Mauritania severed after 450 died in violent clashes; over 50,000 people repatriated from both countries. Senegambia federation abandoned.
**1992** The post of prime minister was reinstated. Diplomatic links with Mauritania were re-established.
**1993** Assembly and presidential elections were won by the ruling PS.
**1998** PS won the general election despite claims of fraud. Abdou Diouf became 'president for life'.
**1999** A new 60-member Senate was created as Senegal's second legislative chamber.

**Senghor, Léopold Sédar** (1906– ) Senegalese politician and writer. He was the first president of independent Senegal (1960–80). Previously he was Senegalese deputy to the French national assembly (1946–58), and founder of the Senegalese Progressive Union. He was also a well-known poet and a founder of *négritude,* a black literary and philosophical movement.

**senile dementia** ▷dementia associated with old age, often caused by ▷Alzheimer's disease.

**Senna, Ayrton** (1960–1994) Brazilian motor-racing driver. He won his first Grand Prix in Portugal (1985) and won 41 Grand Prix in 161 starts, including a record six wins at Monaco. Senna was world champion in 1988, 1990, and 1991. He was killed at the 1994 San Marino Grand Prix at Imola.
*career highlights*
***World champion*** 1988, 1990, 1991
***Grand Prix wins*** 41

**Sennacherib** (died 681 BC) king of Assyria from 705 BC. Son of Sargon II, he rebuilt the city of Nineveh on a grand scale, sacked Babylon in 689, and defeated Hezekiah, King of Judah, but failed to take Jerusalem. He was assassinated by his sons, and one of them, Esarhaddon, succeeded him.

**sense organ** any organ that an animal uses to gain information about its surroundings. All sense organs have specialized receptors (such as light receptors in the eye) and some means of translating their response into a nerve impulse that travels to the brain. The main human sense organs are the eye, which detects light and colour (different wavelengths of light); the ear, which detects sound (vibrations of the air) and gravity; the nose, which detects some of the chemical molecules in the air; and the tongue, which detects some of the chemicals in food, giving a sense of taste. There are also many small sense organs in the skin, including pain, temperature, and pressure sensors, contributing to our sense of touch.

**sensitivity** in biology, the ability of an organism, or part of an organism, to detect changes in the environment. All living things are capable of some sensitivity, and any change detected by an organism is called a stimulus. Plant response to stimuli (for example, light, heat, moisture) is by directional growth (▷tropism). In animals, the body cells that detect the stimuli are called receptors, and these are often contained within a ▷sense organ. For example, the eye is a sense organ, within which the retina contains rod and cone cells which are receptors. The part of the body that responds to a stimulus, such as a muscle, is called an effector, and the communication of stimuli from *receptors* to effectors is termed 'coordination'; messages are passed from receptors to *effectors* either via the ▷nerves or by means of chemicals called ▷hormones. Rapid communication and response to stimuli, such as light, sound, and scent, can be essential to an animal's well-being and survival, and evolution has led to the development of highly complex mechanisms for this purpose.

**sentence** in law, the judgement of a court stating the punishment to be imposed following a plea of guilty or a finding of guilt by a jury. Before a sentence is imposed, the *antecedents* (criminal record) and any relevant reports on the defendant are made known to the judge and the defence may make a plea in mitigation of the sentence.

**Seoul** or *Sŏul,* capital of South Korea (Republic of Korea), near the Han River, and with its chief port at Inchon; population (1994) 11,500,000. Industries include engineering, textiles, food processing, electrical and electronic equipment, chemicals, and machinery.

**sepal** part of a flower, usually green, that surrounds and protects the flower in bud. The sepals are derived from modified leaves, and are collectively known as the ◊calyx.

**separation of powers** limiting the powers of government by separating government functions into the executive, legislative, and judiciary. The concept has its fullest prectical expression in the US constitution.

**Sephardi** plural *Sephardim,* Jews descended from those expelled from Spain and Portugal in the 15th century, or from those forcibly converted during the Inquisition to Christianity (Marranos). Many settled in North Africa and in the Mediterranean countries, as well as in the Netherlands, England, and Dutch colonies in the New World. Sephardim speak Ladino, a 15th-century Romance dialect, as well as the language of their nation.

**sepia** brown pigment produced from the black fluid of cuttlefish. After 1870 it replaced the use of bistre (made from charred wood) in wash drawings due to its warmer range of colours. Sepia fades rapidly in bright light.

**Sepoy Rebellion** alternative name for the ◊Indian Mutiny, a revolt of Indian soldiers against the British in India 1857–58.

**sepsis** general term for infectious change in the body caused by bacteria or their toxins.

**septicaemia** general term for any form of ◊blood poisoning.

**septic shock** life-threatening fall in blood pressure caused by blood poisoning (septicaemia). Toxins produced by bacteria infecting the blood induce a widespread dilation of the blood vessels throughout the body, and it is this that causes the patient's collapse. Septic shock can occur following bowel surgery, after a penetrating wound to the abdomen, or as a consequence of infection of the urinary tract. It is usually treated in an intensive care unit and has a high mortality rate.

**sequencing** in biochemistry, determining the sequence of chemical subunits within a large molecule. Techniques for sequencing amino acids in proteins were established in the 1950s, insulin being the first for which the sequence was completed. The ◊Human Genome Project is attempting to determine the sequence of the 3 billion base pairs within human ◊DNA.

**sequoia** either of two species of ◊conifer tree belonging to the redwood family, native to the western USA. The *redwood* (*Sequoia sempervirens*) is a long-living timber tree, and one specimen, the Howard Libbey Redwood, is the world's tallest tree at 110 m/361 ft, with a trunk circumference of 13.4 m/44 ft. The *giant sequoia* (*Sequoiadendron giganteum*) reaches up to 30 m/100 ft in circumference at the base of the trunk, and grows almost as tall as the redwood. It is also (except for the bristlecone pine) the oldest living tree, some specimens being estimated at over 3,500 years of age. (Family Taxodiaceae.)

**Serapis** or *Sarapis,* ancient Graeco-Egyptian god, a combination of Apis, the bull of Memphis who carried the dead, and Osiris, ruler of the underworld. Invented by Ptolemy I to unify his Greek and Egyptian subjects, he became the official deity of the kingdom replacing Osiris. He was worshipped in Greek at the *Serapeum,* a Greek-style temple and statue in Alexandria, and was mainly regarded as a healer of the sick.

**Serb** Yugoslavia's largest ethnic group, found mainly in Serbia, but also in the neighbouring independent republics of Bosnia-Herzegovina and Croatia. Their language is generally recognized to be the same as Croat and is hence known as ◊Serbo-Croatian.

**Serbia** Serbo-Croatian *Srbija,* constituent republic of Yugoslavia, which includes Kosovo and Vojvodina
*area* 88,400 sq km/34,122 sq mi
*capital* Belgrade
*physical* fertile Danube plains in the north, mountainous in the south (Dinaric Alps, Sar Mountains, northern Albanian Alps, Balkan Mountains); rivers Sava, Tisza, Morava
*features* includes the former autonomous provinces of ◊*Kosovo,* capital Priština, of which the predominantly Albanian population demands unification with Albania, and ◊*Vojvodina,* capital Novi Sad, largest town Subotica, with a predominantly Serbian population and a large Hungarian minority
*population* (1991) 9,791,400
*language* the Serbian variant of Serbo-Croatian
*religion* Serbian Orthodox
*history* The Serbs settled in the Balkans in the 7th century and became Christians in the 9th century. They were united as one kingdom in about 1169; the Serbian hero Stephan Dushan (1331–1355) founded an empire covering most of the Balkans. After their defeat at Kosovo in 1389 they came under the domination of the Turks, who annexed Serbia in 1459. Uprisings of 1804–16, led by Kara George and Miloš Obrenović, forced the Turks to recognize Serbia as an autonomous principality under Miloš. The assassination of Kara George on Obrenović's orders gave rise to a long feud between the two houses. After a war with Turkey in 1876–78, Serbia became an independent kingdom. On the assassination of the last Obrenović in 1903 the Karageorgević dynasty came to the throne.
The two Balkan Wars in 1912–13 greatly

enlarged Serbia's territory at the expense of Turkey and Bulgaria. Serbia's designs on Bosnia-Herzegovina, backed by Russia, led to friction with Austria, culminating in the outbreak of war in 1914. Serbia was overrun in 1915–16 and was occupied until 1918, when it became the nucleus of the new kingdom of the Serbs, Croats, and Slovenes, and subsequently Yugoslavia. Rivalry between Croats and Serbs continued within the republic. During World War II Serbia was under a puppet government set up by the Germans (94% of Serbian Jews were killed in 1941–44); after the war it became a constituent republic of Yugoslavia.

From 1986 Slobodan ◊Milošević as Serbian communist party chief and president waged a populist campaign to end the autonomous status of the provinces of Kosovo and Vojvodina. Despite a violent Albanian backlash in Kosovo in 1989–90 and growing pressure in Croatia and Slovenia to break away from the federation, Serbia formally annexed Kosovo and Vojvodina in September 1990.

The 1991 civil war in Yugoslavia arose from the Milošević nationalist government attempting the forcible annexation of Serb-dominated regions in Croatia, making use of the largely Serbian federal army. In October 1991 Milošević renounced territorial claims on Croatia, pressured by threats of European Community (EC, now European Union) and United Nations (UN) sanctions, but the fighting continued until a cease-fire was agreed in January 1992. EC recognition of Slovenia's and Croatia's independence in January 1992 and Bosnia-Herzegovina's in April left Serbia dominating a greatly reduced 'rump' Yugoslavia. In March 1992, and again in June, thousands of Serbs marched through Belgrade, demanding the ousting of Milošević and an end to the war in Bosnia-Herzegovina. However, Milošević was re-elected in December 1992.

The Socialist authorities refused to recognize opposition victories in November 1996 municipal elections, and rejected opposition demands for fresh elections. Western governments said that the verdict of the electorate must be acknowledged before Serbia can return to international respectability. Pro-democracy demonstrations took place in Belgrade in December 1996.

Despite the 1996–97 winter civil unrest, Milošević was elected in July 1997 to the Yugoslav presidency.

Early 1998 saw growing civil unrest in the province of Kosovo where fighting erupted between Serb paramilitary forces and ethnic Albanians. In April Western countries imposed a freeze on Serb-held assets overseas as the government refused to enter into negotiations with Albanian separatists, and in May NATO announced a ban on investment in Serbia. Despite these sanctions, both President Milošević and Albanian leader in Kosovo, Ibrahim Rugova, rejected the possibility of settlement talks. After a period of escalating violence and atrocities, NATO issued an ultimatum to both warring sides on 28 January 1999,

demanding the withdrawal of Serbian forces from Kosovo and an end to fighting and unprovoked attacks, and indicating that NATO was ready to react if these measures, together with peace negotiations, were not put into place.

In March 1999 NATO began a bombing campaign in an attempt to force the government to end its persecution of ethnic Albanians, and in September 1999 anti-government parties stepped up their campaign to oust Milošević.

**Serbo-Croatian** or *Serbo-Croat*, the most widely spoken language in Yugoslavia and its former constituent republics, it is a member of South Slavonic branch of the Indo-European family, and has over 17 million speakers.

The different dialects of Serbo-Croatian tend to be written by the Greek Orthodox Serbs in the Cyrillic script, and by the Roman Catholic Croats in the Latin script.

**serenade** musical piece for chamber orchestra or wind instruments in several movements, originally intended for informal evening entertainment, such as Mozart's *Eine kleine Nachtmusik/ A Little Night Music.*

**serfdom** the legal and economic status of peasants under ◊feudalism. Serfs could not be sold like slaves, but they were not free to leave their master's estate without his permission. They had to work the lord's land without pay for a number of days every week and pay a percentage of their produce to the lord every year. They also served as soldiers in the event of conflict. Serfs also had to perform extra labour at harvest time and other busy seasons; in return they were allowed to cultivate a portion of the estate for their own benefit.

**Sergius, St** of Radonezh, originally Barfolomay Kirillovich, (1314–1392) Patron saint of Russia, who founded the Eastern Orthodox monastery of the Blessed Trinity near Moscow, over the Tatar khan Mamai at Kulikowo, on the upper Don, 1380.

**serialism** in music, a later form of the ◊twelve-tone system of composition.

**series circuit** electrical circuit in which the components are connected end to end, so that the current flows through them all one after the other.

**Serpens** constellation on the celestial equator, represented as a serpent coiled around the body of Ophiuchus. It is the only constellation divided into two halves: *Serpens Caput*, the head (on one side of Ophiuchus), and *Serpens Cauda*, the tail (on the other side). Its main feature is the Eagle nebula.

**serpentine** group of minerals, hydrous magnesium silicate, $Mg_3Si_2O_5(OH)_4$, occurring in soft metamorphic rocks and usually dark green. The fibrous form *chrysotil* is a source of asbestos; other forms are *antigorite* and *lizardite*. Serpentine minerals are formed by hydration of ultramafic rocks during metamorphism. Rare snake-patterned forms are used in ornamental carving.

**serum** clear fluid that separates out from clotted blood. It is blood plasma with the anticoagulant proteins removed, and contains ◊antibodies and other proteins, as well as the fats and sugars of the blood. It can be produced synthetically, and is used to protect against disease.

**serval** African wild cat *Felis serval*. It is a slender, long-limbed cat, about 1 m/3 ft long, with a yellowish-brown, black-spotted coat. It has large, sensitive ears, with which it locates its prey, mainly birds and rodents.

**servomechanism** automatic control system used in aircraft, motor cars, and other complex machines. A specific input, such as moving a lever or joystick, causes a specific output, such as feeding current to an electric motor that moves, for example, the rudder of the aircraft. At the same time, the position of the rudder is detected and fed back to the central control, so that small adjustments can continually be made to maintain the desired course.

**sesame** annual herbaceous plant, probably native to Southeast Asia, and widely cultivated in India. It produces oily seeds used in cooking and soap making. (*Sesamum indicum*, family Pedaliaceae.)

**set** or *class,* in mathematics, any collection of defined things (elements), provided the elements are distinct and that there is a rule to decide whether an element is a member of a set. It is usually denoted by a capital letter and indicated by curly brackets {}.

**Set** also Seth or Setekh, in Egyptian mythology, the god of night, the desert, and of all evils. Portrayed as a grotesque animal with long ears and a tail, Set was the murderer of his brother ◊Osiris, later ruler of the underworld.

**Settlement, Act of** in Britain, a law passed in 1701 during the reign of King William III, designed to ensure a Protestant succession to the throne by excluding the Roman Catholic descendants of James II in favour of the Protestant House of Hanover. Elizabeth II still reigns under this act.

**Seurat, Georges Pierre** (1859–1891) French artist. One of the major Post-Impressionists, he originated, with Paul Signac, the technique of ◊Pointillism (painting with small dabs rather than long brushstrokes). One of his best-known works is *A Sunday Afternoon on the Island of La Grande Jatte* (1886) (Art Institute of Chicago).

**seven deadly sins** in Christian theology, anger, avarice, envy, gluttony, lust, pride, and sloth (or dejection). These vices are considered fundamental to all other sins.

**Seven Weeks' War** war in 1866 between Austria and Prussia, engineered by the German chancellor ◊Bismarck. It was nominally over the possession of ◊Schleswig-Holstein, but was actually to confirm Prussia's superseding Austria as the leading German state. The Prussian victory at the Battle of Sadowa was the culmination of General von Moltke's victories.

**Seven Wonders of the World** in antiquity, the pyramids of Egypt, the Hanging Gardens of Babylon, the temple of Artemis at ◊Ephesus, the Greek sculptor Phidias' chryselephantine statue of Zeus at ◊Olympia, the Mausoleum at Halicarnassus, the Colossus of Rhodes, and the lighthouse on the island of Pharos in the Bay of Alexandria.

**Seven Years' War** fighting in North America known as the *French and Indian War,* war in 1756–63 arising from the conflict between Austria and Prussia, and between France and Britain over colonial supremacy. Britain and Prussia defeated France, Austria, Spain, and Russia; Britain gained control of India and many of France's colonies, including Canada.

Spain ceded Florida to Britain in exchange for Cuba. Fighting against great odds, Prussia was eventually successful in becoming established as one of the great European powers. The war ended with the Treaty of Paris (1763), signed by Britain, France, and Spain.

**Severn** Welsh *Hafren,* river in Britain, which rises on the slopes of Plynlimon, in Ceredigion, west Wales, and flows east and then south, finally forming a long estuary leading into the Bristol Channel; length 336 km/208 mi. The Severn is navigable for 290 km/180 mi, up to Welshpool (Trallwng) on the Welsh border. The principal towns on its course are Shrewsbury, Worcester, and Gloucester. England and South Wales are linked by two road bridges and a railway tunnel crossing the Severn (Severn Bridge). A remarkable feature of the river is a tidal wave known as the 'Severn Bore' that flows for some miles upstream and can reach a height of 2 m/6 ft.

**Severus, Lucius Septimius** (AD 146–211) Roman emperor 193–211. After holding various commands under the emperors ◊Marcus Aurelius and Commodus, Severus was appointed commander-in-chief of the army on the Danube, in the Roman provinces, Pannonia and Illyria. After the murder of Pertinax (Roman emperor 193), he was proclaimed emperor by his troops. Severus was an able administrator. He was born in North Africa at Leptis Magna, and was the only native of Africa to become emperor. He died at York.

**Seville** Spanish *Sevilla,* capital of Seville province and of the autonomous community of ◊Andalusia, southern Spain, on the River Guadalquivir, 96 km/60 mi north of Cádiz; population (1991) 659,100. Products include machinery, spirits, porcelain, pharmaceuticals, silk, and tobacco. Although 80 km/50 mi from the sea, Seville has a historically important port (now little used), and during the 16th century it had a monopoly of trade with the West Indies.

**sewing machine** apparatus for the mechanical sewing of cloth, leather, and other materials by a needle, powered by hand, treadle, or belted electric motor. The popular lockstitch machine, using a double thread, was invented independently in the USA by both Walter Hunt in 1834 and Elias Howe in 1846. Howe's machine was the basis of the machine patented in 1851 by US inventor Isaac Singer.

**sex determination** process by which the sex of an organism is determined. In many species, the sex of an individual is dictated by the two sex chromosomes (X and Y) it receives from its parents. In mammals, some plants, and a few insects, males are XY, and females XX; in birds, reptiles, some amphibians, and butterflies the reverse is the case. In bees and wasps, males are produced from unfertilized eggs, females from fertilized eggs.

Environmental factors can affect some fish and reptiles, such as turtles, where sex is influenced by the temperature at which the eggs develop. In 1991 it was shown that maleness is caused by a single gene, 14 base pairs long, on the Y chromosome.

**sex hormone** steroid hormone produced and secreted by the gonads (testes and ovaries). Sex hormones control development and reproductive functions and influence sexual and other behaviour.

**sexism** belief in (or set of implicit assumptions about) the superiority of one's own sex, often accompanied by a ⟩stereotype or preconceived idea about the opposite sex. Sexism may also be accompanied by ⟩discrimination on the basis of sex, generally as practised by men against women.

**sex linkage** in genetics, the tendency for certain characteristics to occur exclusively, or predominantly, in one sex only. Human examples include red-green colour blindness and haemophilia, both found predominantly in males. In both cases, these characteristics are ⟩recessive and are determined by genes on the ⟩X chromosome.

**sextant** navigational instrument for determining latitude by measuring the angle between some heavenly body and the horizon. It was invented in 1730 by John Hadley (1682–1744) and can be used only in clear weather.

**sexually transmitted disease** (STD), any disease transmitted by sexual contact, involving transfer of body fluids. STDs include not only traditional ⟩venereal disease, but also a growing list of conditions, such as ⟩AIDS and scabies, which are known to be spread primarily by sexual contact. Other diseases that are transmitted sexually include viral ⟩hepatitis. The WHO estimate that there are 356,000 new cases of STDs daily worldwide (1995).

**sexual reproduction** reproductive process in organisms that requires the union, or ⟩fertilization, of gametes (such as eggs and sperm). These are usually produced by two different individuals, although self-fertilization occurs in a few ⟩hermaphrodites such as tapeworms. Most organisms other than bacteria and cyanobacteria (⟩blue-green algae) show some sort of sexual process. Except in some lower organisms, the gametes are of two distinct types called eggs and sperm. The organisms producing the eggs are called females, and those producing the sperm, males. The fusion of a male and female gamete produces a *zygote*, from which a new individual develops. See ⟩reproduction.

**sexual selection** process similar to ⟩natural selection but relating exclusively to success in finding a mate for the purpose of sexual reproduction and producing offspring. Sexual selection

occurs when one sex (usually but not always the female) invests more effort in producing young than the other. Members of the other sex compete for access to this limited resource (usually males competing for the chance to mate with females).

**Seychelles** Republic of

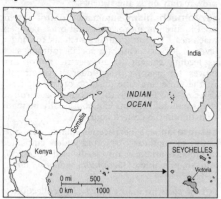

**area** 453 sq km/174 sq mi
**capital** Victoria (on Mahé island) (and chief port)
**major towns/cities** Cascade, Port Glaud, Misere
**physical features** comprises two distinct island groups: one, the Granitic group, concentrated, the other, the Outer or Coralline group, widely scattered; totals over 100 islands and islets
**head of state and government** France-Albert René from 1977
**political system** emergent democracy
**political parties** Seychelles People's Progressive Front (SPPF), nationalist socialist; Democratic Party (DP), left of centre
**currency** Seychelles rupee
**GNP per capita (PPP)** (US$) 10,530 (1998)
**exports** fresh and frozen fish, canned tuna, shark fins, cinnamon bark, refined petroleum products. Principal market: France 18.7% (1997)
**population** 79,000 (1999 est)
**language** creole (Asian, African, European mixture) 95%, English, French (all official)
**religion** Roman Catholic
**life expectancy** 66 (men); 76 (women) (1998 est)
**Chronology**
**early 16th century** First sighted by European navigators.
**1744** Became French colony.
**1756** Claimed as French possession and named after an influential French family.
**1770s** French colonists brought African slaves to settle the previously uninhabited islands; plantations established.
**1794** Captured by British during French Revolutionary Wars.
**1814** Ceded by France to Britain; incorporated as dependency of Mauritius.
**1835** Slavery abolished by British, leading to influx of liberated slaves from Mauritius and Chinese and Indian immigrants.

**1903** Became British crown colony, separate from Mauritius.
**1963–64** First political parties formed.
**1976** Independence achieved from Britain as republic within Commonwealth, with a moderate, James Mancham, of the centre-right Seychelles Democratic Party (SDP) as president.
**1977** More radical France-Albert René ousted Mancham in armed bloodless coup and took over presidency; white settlers emigrated.
**1979** Nationalistic socialist Seychelles People's Progressive Front (SPPF) became sole legal party under new constitution; became nonaligned state.
**1981** An attempted coup by South African mercenaries was thwarted.
**1991** Multiparty politics were promised.
**1993** A new multiparty constitution was adopted. René defeated Mancham, who had returned from exile, in competitive presidential elections; SPPF won parliamentary elections.
**1998** President René was re-elected. SPUP won assembly elections.

**Seyfert galaxy** galaxy whose small, bright centre is caused by hot gas moving at high speed around a massive central object, possibly a ◊black hole. Almost all Seyferts are spiral galaxies. They seem to be closely related to ◊quasars, but are about 100 times fainter. They are named after their discoverer Carl Seyfert (1911–1960).

**Seymour, Jane** (c. 1509–1537) English noble, third wife of Henry VIII, whom she married in 1536. She died soon after the birth of her son Edward VI.

**Shaanxi** or *Shensi*, province of northwest China, bounded to the north by Inner Mongolia, to the east by Shanxi and Henan, to the south by Hubei and Sichuan, and to the west by Gansu and Ningxia Hui Autonomous Region
**area** 195,800 sq km/75,579 sq mi
**capital** ◊Xi'an
**towns** Baoji, Yan'an, Tongchuan
**physical** mountains; loess (loamy) soil; Huang He River valley
**industries** coalmining, iron, steel, textiles, aerospace
**agriculture** wheat, maize, rice, fruit, tea
**population** (1996) 35,430,000.

**Shackleton, Ernest Henry** (1874–1922) Irish Antarctic explorer. In 1908–09, he commanded the British Antarctic expedition that reached 88° 23' S latitude, located the magnetic South Pole, and climbed Mount ◊Erebus. He was knighted in 1909.

**shad** any of several marine fishes, especially the genus *Alosa*, the largest (60 cm/2 ft long and 2.7 kg/6 lb in weight) of the herring family (Clupeidae). They migrate in shoals to breed in rivers.

**shadow** area of darkness behind an opaque object that cannot be reached by some or all of the light coming from a light source in front. Its presence may be explained in terms of light rays travelling in straight lines and being unable to bend around obstacles. A point source of light produces an *umbra*, a completely black shadow

with sharp edges. An extended source of light produces both a central umbra and a *penumbra*, a region of semidarkness with blurred edges where darkness gives way to light.

**shadow cabinet** the chief members of the British parliamentary opposition, each of whom is responsible for commenting on the policies and performance of a government ministry.

**Shaftesbury, Anthony Ashley Cooper**, 1st Earl of Shaftesbury (1621–1683) English politician, a supporter of the Restoration of the monarchy. He became Lord Chancellor in 1672, but went into opposition in 1673 and began to organize the ◊Whig Party. He headed the Whigs' demand for the exclusion of the future James II from the succession, secured the passing of the Habeas Corpus Act of 1679, then, when accused of treason in 1681, fled to Holland. He became baronet in 1631, baron in 1661, and was created Earl in 1672.

**shag** waterbird *Phalacrocorax aristoclis,* order Pelecaniformes, related to the ◊cormorant. It is smaller than the cormorant, with a green tinge to its plumage and a crest in the breeding season. Its food consists mainly of sand eels for which it dives, staying underwater for up to 54 seconds. It breeds on deeply fissured cliffs, and on rocky parts of isolated islands.

**shah** (more formally, *shahanshah* 'king of kings') traditional title of ancient Persian rulers, and also of those of the recent ◊Pahlavi dynasty in Iran.

**Shah Jahan** (1592–1666) Mogul emperor of India from 1628, under whom the dynasty reached its zenith. Succeeding his father ◊Jahangir, he extended Mogul authority into the Deccan plateau (eastern India), subjugating Ahmadnagar, Bijapur, and Golconda in 1636, but lost Kandahar in the northwest to the Persians 1653. His reign marked the high point of Indo-Muslim architecture, with Delhi being rebuilt as Shahjahanabad, while the Taj Mahal and Pearl Mosque were constructed at Agra. On falling seriously ill in 1658, he was dethroned and imprisoned by his son ◊Aurangzeb.

**Shaka** or *Chaka* (c. 1787–1828) Zulu chief who formed a Zulu empire in southeastern Africa. He seized power from his half-brother in 1816 and then embarked on a bloody military campaign to unite the Zulu clans. He was assassinated by his two half-brothers.

**Shaker** member of the Christian sect of the *United Society of Believers in Christ's Second Appearing,* called Shakers because of their ecstatic trembling and shaking during worship. The movement was founded by James and Jane Wardley in England about 1747, and taken to North America in 1774 by Ann Lee (1736–1784).

**Shakespeare, William** (1564–1616) English dramatist and poet. He is considered the greatest English dramatist. His plays, written in blank verse with some prose, can be broadly divided into lyric plays, including *Romeo and Juliet* and *A Midsummer Night's Dream;* comedies,

## SHAKESPEARE'S PLAYS

| Title | First performed/ written (approximate) |
|---|---|
| **Early Plays** | |
| Henry VI Part I | 1589–92 |
| Henry VI Part II | 1590–91 |
| Henry VI Part III | 1590–92 |
| The Comedy of Errors | 1591–93 |
| The Taming of the Shrew | 1593–94 |
| Titus Andronicus | 1593–94 |
| The Two Gentlemen of Verona | 1590–95 |
| Love's Labour's Lost | 1593–95 |
| Romeo and Juliet | 1594–95 |
| **Histories** | |
| Richard III | 1592–93 |
| Richard II | 1595–97 |
| King John | 1595–97 |
| Henry IV Part I | 1596–97 |
| Henry IV Part II | 1596–97 |
| Henry V | 1599 |
| **Roman Plays** | |
| Julius Caesar | 1599 |
| Antony and Cleopatra | 1606–07 |
| Coriolanus | 1608 |
| **The 'Great' or 'Middle' Comedies** | |
| A Midsummer Night's Dream | 1594–95 |
| The Merchant of Venice | 1596–98 |
| Much Ado About Nothing | 1598 |
| As You Like It | 1599–1600 |
| The Merry Wives of Windsor | 1597 |
| Twelfth Night | 1600–02 |
| **The Great Tragedies** | |
| Hamlet | 1601–02 |
| Othello | 1604 |
| King Lear | 1605–06 |
| Macbeth | 1606 |
| Timon of Athens | 1607–08 |
| **The 'Dark' Comedies** | |
| Troilus and Cressida | 1601–02 |
| All's Well That Ends Well | 1602–03 |
| Measure for Measure | 1604 |
| **Late Plays** | |
| Pericles | 1606–08 |
| Cymbeline | 1609–10 |
| The Winter's Tale | 1611 |
| The Tempest | 1611 |
| Henry VIII | 1613 |

including *The Comedy of Errors, As You Like It, Much Ado About Nothing,* and *Measure For Measure;* historical plays, such as *Henry VI* (in three parts), *Richard III,* and *Henry IV* (in two parts), which often showed cynical political wisdom; and tragedies, including *Hamlet, Othello, King Lear,* and *Macbeth.* He also wrote numerous sonnets.

**shale** fine-grained and finely layered ◊sedimentary rock composed of silt and clay. It is a weak rock, splitting easily along bedding planes to form thin, even slabs (by contrast, mudstone splits into irregular flakes). Oil shale contains kerogen, a solid bituminous material that yields ◊petroleum when heated.

**shaman** (Tungu *samân*) ritual leader who acts as intermediary between society and the supernatural world in many indigenous cultures of Asia, Africa, and the Americas. Also known as a *medicine man, seer,* or *sorcerer,* the shaman is expected to use special powers to cure illness and control good and evil spirits.

**Shamir, Yitzhak Yernitsky** (1915– ) Polish-born Israeli right-wing politician; prime minister (1983–84 and 1986–92); leader of the Likud (Consolidation Party) until 1993. He was foreign minister under Menachem Begin (1980–83), and again foreign minister in Shimon ◊Peres's unity government (1984–86).

**shamrock** any of several leguminous plants (see ◊legume) whose leaves are divided into three leaflets, including ◊clovers. St Patrick is said to have used one to illustrate the doctrine of the Holy Trinity, and it was made the national badge of Ireland. (Family Leguminosae.)

**Shandong** or *Shantung,* province of east China, bounded to the north by the Bohai Gulf, to the east by the Yellow Sea, to the south by Jiangsu and Anhui, and to the west by Henan and Hebei provinces
**area** 153,300 sq km/59,174 sq mi
**capital** ◊Jinan
**towns and ports** Zibo, Yantai, Weihai, Qingdao
**physical** Huang He River; Shandong Peninsula
**features** ◊Grand Canal
**industries** coal, oil, petrochemicals, engineering, textiles
**agriculture** cereals, cotton, peanuts, wild silk, wine
**population** (1996) 83,430,000; one of the most densely populated provinces in China

**Shanghai** largest urban settlement and mainland port in China, in Jiangsu province, on the Huangpu and Wusong rivers, 24 km/15 mi from the Chang Jiang estuary; population (1993) 8,760,000. The municipality of Shanghai has an area of 5,800 sq km/2,239 sq mi; population (1996) 14,190,000. Shanghai is China's principal commercial and financial centre. Textiles, paper, chemicals, steel, vehicles, agricultural machinery, precision instruments, shipbuilding, and flour are produced; other industries include vegetable-oil milling and oil-refining. Administratively independent of Jiangsu, Shanghai answers directly to the central government.

**Shankar, Ravi** (1920– ) Indian composer and musician. A virtuoso of the sitar, he has been influential in popularizing Indian music in the West. He has composed two concertos for sitar and orchestra (1971 and 1981), and film music, including scores for Satyajit Ray's *Pather Panchali* (1955) and Richard Attenborough's *Gandhi* (1982), and founded music schools in Bombay and Los Angeles.

**Shannon** longest river in Ireland, rising 105 m/344 ft above sea level in the Cuilcagh Mountains in County Cavan, and flowing 386 km/240 mi to the Atlantic Ocean past Athlone, and through Loughs Allen, Boderg, Forbes, Ree, and Derg. The estuary, which is 110 km/68 mi long and 3–16 km/3–10 wide, forms the northern boundary of

County Limerick. The river is navigable as far as Limerick city, above which are the rapids of Doonas and Castletroy. The river is known for its salmon farms, Castleconnell being an important centre. It also has the first and largest hydroelectric scheme in the Republic of Ireland (constructed 1925–29), with hydroelectric installations at and above Ardnacrusha, 5 km/3 mi north of Limerick.

**Shantung** alternative transliteration of the Chinese province of ◊Shandong.

**Shanxi** or *Shansi*, province of north China, bounded to the north by Inner Mongolia, to the east by Hebei, to the south by Henan, and to the west by Shaanxi
*area* 157,100 sq km/60,641 sq mi
*capital* Taiyuan
*towns* Datong
*physical* loess-covered plateau; Huang He and Fen He rivers; Taihang Mountains
*features* partly surrounded by the ◊Great Wall of China
*industries* coal, iron, machinery, mining equipment, chemicals
*agriculture* fruit, cereals, meat
*population* (1996 ) 31,090,000.

**share** in finance, that part of the ◊capital of a company held by a member (shareholder). Shares may be numbered and are issued as units of definite face value; shareholders are not always called on to pay the full face value of their shares, though they bind themselves to do so.

**Shari'a** the law of ◊Islam believed by Muslims to be based on divine revelation, and drawn from a number of sources, including the Koran, the Hadith, and the consensus of the Muslim community. Under this law, *qisās*, or retribution, allows a family to exact equal punishment on an accused; *diyat*, or blood money, is payable to a dead person's family as compensation.

**shark** any member of various orders of cartilaginous fishes (class Chondrichthyes), found throughout the oceans of the world. There are about 400 known species of shark. They have tough, usually grey skin covered in denticles (small toothlike scales). A shark's streamlined body has side pectoral fins, a high dorsal fin, and a forked tail with a large upper lobe. Five open gill slits are visible on each side of the generally pointed head. They shed and replace their teeth continually, even before birth. Teeth may be replaced as frequently as every week. Most sharks are fish-eaters, and a few will attack humans. They range from several feet in length to the *great white shark Carcharodon carcharias*, 9 m/30 ft long, and the harmless plankton-feeding *whale shark Rhincodon typus*, over 15 m/50 ft in length.

**Sharpeville** black township in South Africa, 65 km/40 mi south of Johannesburg and north of Vereeniging; 69 people were killed here when police fired on a crowd of anti-apartheid demonstrators 21 March 1960.

**Shatt-al-Arab** ('river of Arabia') waterway formed by the confluence of the rivers

◊Euphrates and ◊Tigris; length 190 km/120 mi to the Gulf. Basra, Khorramshahr, and Abadan stand on it. Its main tributary is the Karun River.

**Shaw, George Bernard** (1856–1950) Irish dramatist. He was also a critic and novelist, and an early member of the socialist ◊Fabian Society, although he resigned in 1911. His plays combine comedy with political, philosophical, and polemic aspects, aiming to make an impact on his audience's social conscience as well as their emotions. They include *Arms and the Man* (1894), *Devil's Disciple* (1897), *Man and Superman* (1903), *Pygmalion* (1913), and *St Joan* (1923). He was awarded the Nobel Prize for Literature in 1925.

**Shearer, Alan** (1970– ) English footballer. In 1996 he was transferred to Newcastle United from Blackburn Rovers for what was then a world record fee of £15 million. A strongly-built centre-forward, he made his England debut in 1992 and by October 1999 had scored 28 goals in 55 internationals.

**shearwater** any sea bird of the genus *Puffinus*. All the species are oceanic, and either dark above and white below or all dark. Shearwaters are members of the same family (Procellariidae), as the diving ◊petrels, order Procellariiformes. They get their name from their habit of skimming low over the sea on still wings.

**Sheba** ancient name for southern Yemen (Sha'abijah). It was once renowned for gold and spices. According to the Old Testament, its queen visited Solomon; until 1975 the Ethiopian royal house traced its descent from their union.

**sheep** any of several ruminant, even-toed, hoofed mammals of the family Bovidae. Wild species survive in the uplands of central and eastern Asia, North Africa, southern Europe and North America. The domesticated breeds are all classified as *Ovis aries*.
  Various breeds of sheep are reared worldwide for meat, wool, milk, and cheese, and for rotation on arable land to maintain its fertility.

**sheepdog** any of several breeds of dog, bred originally for herding sheep. The dog now most commonly used by shepherds and farmers in Britain to tend sheep is the border collie. Non-pedigree dogs of the border collie type, though more variable in size and colour, are referred to as working sheepdogs. Other recognized British breeds are the ◊Old English and Shetland sheepdogs. Many countries have their own breeds of sheepdog, such as the Belgian sheepdog, Australian kelpie, and Hungarian puli.

**Sheffield** industrial city and metropolitan borough on the River Don, South Yorkshire, England; population of metropolitan district (1991) 501,200. From the 12th century, iron smelting was the chief industry, and by the 14th century, Sheffield cutlery, silverware, and plate were being made. During the Industrial Revolution the iron and steel industries developed rapidly. It now produces alloys and special steels, cutlery of all kinds, permanent magnets, drills, and precision tools. Other industries include electroplating, type-founding, and the manufacture of optical glass. It is an important conference centre.

**sheikh** leader or chief of an Arab family or village; also Muslim title meaning 'religious scholar'.

**shelduck** duck *Tadorna tadorna* of family Anatidae, order Anseriformes. It has a dark-green head and red bill, with the rest of the plumage strikingly marked in black, white, and chestnut. The drake is about 60 cm/24 in long. Widely distributed in Europe and Asia, it lays 10–12 white eggs in rabbit burrows on sandy coasts, and is usually seen on estuary mudflats.

**shell** the hard outer covering of a wide variety of invertebrates. The covering is usually mineralized, normally with large amounts of calcium. The shell of birds' eggs is also largely made of calcium.

**shellac** resin derived from secretions of the lac insect.

**Shelley, Mary Wollstonecraft** born Godwin (1797–1851) English writer. She is best known as the author of the Gothic horror story *Frankenstein* (1818), which is considered to be the origin of modern science fiction, and her other novels include *The Last Man* (1826) and *Valperga* (1823). In 1814 she eloped to Switzerland with the poet Percy Bysshe Shelley, whom she married in 1816 on the death of his first wife Harriet. She was the daughter of Mary Wollstonecraft and William Godwin.

**Shelley, Percy Bysshe** (1792–1822) English lyric poet and critic. With his skill in poetic form and metre, his intellectual capacity and searching mind, his rebellious but constructive nature, and his notorious moral nonconformity, he is a commanding figure of the Romantic movement. He fought all his life against religion and for political freedom. This is reflected in his early poems such as *Queen Mab* (1813). He later wrote tragedies including *The Cenci* (1818), lyric dramas such as *Prometheus Unbound* (1820), and lyrical poems such as 'Ode to the West Wind'. He drowned while sailing in Italy.

**shellfish** popular name for molluscs and crustaceans, including the whelk and periwinkle, mussel, oyster, lobster, crab, and shrimp.

**shell shock** or *combat neurosis* or *battle fatigue,* any of the various forms of mental disorder that affect soldiers exposed to heavy explosions or extreme ◊stress. Shell shock was first diagnosed during World War I.

**Shenyang** or *Mukden,* capital of ◊Liaoning province, China; population (1994) 4,699,000. It is the region's main trading city, and one of China's principal metal-fabricating and machine-building centres. It was the capital of the Manchu emperors from 1625 to 1644; their tombs are nearby.

**Shenzhen** special economic zone on the coast of Guangdong province, south China, established in 1980 opposite Hong Kong; population (1993) 2,400,000. A poor rural area in 1979, with a population of 20,000, it grew spectacu-

larly with the relocation of toy, textiles, and electronics factories from Hong Kong. Diverse light industries have subsequently been introduced, particularly the manufacture of chemicals and electrical goods. It is also an international financial centre, housing one of China's two stock exchanges. The zone is fenced off, and immigration strictly controlled.

**Sheraton, Thomas** (1751–1806) English designer of elegant inlaid Neo-Classical furniture. He was influenced by his predecessors Hepplewhite and ◊Chippendale.

**Sheridan, Philip Henry** (1831–1888) Union general in the American ◊Civil War. Recognizing Sheridan's aggressive spirit, General Ulysses S ◊Grant gave him command of his cavalry in 1864, and soon after of the Army of the Shenandoah Valley, Virginia. Sheridan laid waste to the valley, cutting off grain supplies to the Confederate armies. In the final stage of the war, Sheridan forced General Robert E ◊Lee to retreat to Appomattox Court House and surrender.

**Sheridan, Richard Brinsley** (1751–1816) Irish dramatist and politician. His social comedies include *The Rivals* (1775), celebrated for the character of Mrs Malaprop, and *The School for Scandal* (1777). He also wrote a burlesque, *The Critic* (1779). In 1776 he became lessee of the Drury Lane Theatre. He became a member of Parliament in 1780.

**sheriff** (Old English *scīr* 'shire', *gerēfa* 'reeve') in England and Wales, the crown's chief executive officer in a county for ceremonial purposes; in Scotland, the equivalent of the English county-court judge, but also dealing with criminal cases; and in the USA the popularly elected head law-enforcement officer of a county, combining judicial authority with administrative duties.

**Sherman, William Tecumseh** (1820–1891) Union general in the American ◊Civil War. In 1864 he captured and burned Atlanta; continued his march eastward, to the sea, laying Georgia waste; and then drove the Confederates northward. He was US Army Chief of Staff from 1869 to 1883.

**Sherpa** member of a Mongolian people who originally migrated from Tibet and now live in northeastern Nepal. They are related to the Tibetans. Skilled mountaineers, they frequently work as support staff and guides for climbing expeditions.

**Shetland Islands** (Old Norse *Hjaltland* 'high land' or 'Hjalte's land') islands and unitary authority off the north coast of Scotland, 80 km/50 mi northeast of the Orkney Islands, an important centre of the North Sea oil industry, and the most northerly part of the UK
*area* 1,452 sq km/560 sq mi
*towns* Lerwick (administrative headquarters), on Mainland, largest of 12 inhabited islands
*physical* the 100 islands are mostly bleak, hilly, and clad in moorland. The climate is moist, cool, and windy; in summer there is almost perpetual daylight, whilst winter days are very

short. On clear winter nights, the aurora borealis ('northern lights') can frequently be seen in the sky

*industries* processed fish, handknits from Fair Isle and Unst, herring fishing, salmon farming, cattle and sheep farming; large oil and gas fields west of Shetland; Europe's largest oil port is Sullom Voe, Mainland; production at Foinaven oilfield, the first to be developed in Atlantic waters; tourism

*population* (1996) 22,500

*history* dialect derived from Norse, the islands having been a Norse dependency from the 9th century until 1472 when they were annexed by Scotland.

**Shevardnadze, Edvard Amvrosievich** (1928– ) Georgian politician, Soviet foreign minister 1985–91, head of the state of Georgia from 1992. A supporter of Mikhail ◊Gorbachev, he was first secretary of the Georgian Communist Party from 1972 and an advocate of economic reform. In 1985 he became a member of the Politburo, working for détente and disarmament. In July 1991 he resigned from the Soviet Communist Party (CPSU) and, along with other reformers and leading democrats, established the Democratic Reform Movement. In March 1992 he was chosen as chair of Georgia's ruling military council, and in October was elected speaker of parliament (equivalent to president). He survived assassination attempts in 1995 and in February 1998.

**Shiah** see ◊Shiite.

**shifting cultivation** farming system where farmers move on from one place to another when the land becomes exhausted. The most common form is *slash-and-burn* agriculture: land is cleared by burning, so that crops can be grown. After a few years, soil fertility is reduced and the land is abandoned. A new area is cleared while the old land recovers its fertility.

**Shi Huangdi** (*c.* 259– *c.* 210 BC) or *Shih Huang Ti,* Emperor of China. He succeeded to the throne of the state of Qin in 246 BC and had reunited China as an empire by 228 BC. He burned almost all existing books in 213 to destroy ties with the past; rebuilt the ◊Great Wall of China; and was buried in Xi'an, Shaanxi province, in a tomb complex guarded by 10,000 life-size terracotta warriors (excavated in the 1980s).

**Shiite** or *Shiah,* member of a sect of ◊Islam that believes that ◊Ali was ◊Muhammad's first true successor. The Shiites are doctrinally opposed to the Sunni Muslims. They developed their own law differing only in minor directions, such as inheritance and the status of women. In Shi'ism, the clergy are empowered to intervene between God and humans, whereas among the Sunni, the relationship with God is direct and the clergy serve as advisers.

The Shiites are prominent in Iran, the Lebanon, and Indo-Pakistan, and are also found in Iraq and Bahrain.

**Shijiazhuang** or *Shihchiachuang,* capital of ◊Hebei province, China, at the foot of the Taihang Mountains; population (1993) 1,210,000. It is a major railway junction and agricultural distribution point. Industries include printing, light engineering, and the manufacture of chemicals, petrochemicals, and electronics.

**Shikoku** smallest of the four main islands of Japan, south of Honshu, east of Kyushu; area 18,800 sq km/7,257 sq mi; population (1995) 4,183,000. The island consists of four prefectures, Kagawa, Tokushima, Ehime, and Kochi. The chief towns are Matsuyama and Takamatsu. The population is largely concentrated in the small coastal plains which front the Inland Sea. Products include rice, wheat, soybeans, sugar cane, orchard fruits, salt, and copper.

**shingles** common name for ◊herpes zoster, a disease characterized by infection of sensory nerves, with pain and eruption of blisters along the course of the affected nerves.

**Shinto** (Chinese *shin tao* 'way of the gods') the indigenous religion of Japan. It combines an empathetic oneness with natural forces and loyalty to the reigning dynasty as descendants of the Sun goddess, Amaterasu-Omikami. An aggressive nationalistic form of Shinto, known as State Shinto, was developed under the Emperor Meiji (1868–1912) and remained official until 1945, when it was discarded.

**ship** large seagoing vessel. The Greeks, Phoenicians, Romans, and Vikings used ships extensively for trade, exploration, and warfare. The 14th century was the era of European exploration by sailing ship, largely aided by the invention of the compass. In the 15th century Britain's Royal Navy was first formed, but in the 16th–19th centuries Spanish and Dutch fleets dominated the shipping lanes of both the Atlantic and Pacific.

The ultimate sailing ships, the fast US and British tea clippers, were built in the 19th century. Also in the 19th century, iron was first used for some shipbuilding instead of wood. Steampropelled ships of the late 19th century were followed by compound engine and turbinepropelled vessels from the early 20th century.

**Shipley, Jenny** (1952– ) New Zealand right-of-centre politician, prime minister from 1997. She joined the conservative National Party at the age of 23 and, after a spell as a local councillor, was elected to the House of Representatives in 1987. When the National Party came to power in 1990, Shipley entered Jim ◊Bolger's government as minister of social welfare and women's affairs (1990–93), health and women's affairs (1993–94), and minister of transport and state services (1996–97). She provoked controversy through benefit-cutting and introducing an internal market into the health service.

On the right wing of the National Party, Shipley became increasingly disillusioned with Bolger's cautious policy approach and began to challenge his leadership in 1997. During Bolger's absence at the Commonwealth heads of government conference in the UK, in November 1997, she consolidated her position and on his return warned him that she had enough support within the parliamentary party to force his resignation. This persuaded Bolger to resign as party leader and she was elected as his replacement and became, in December 1997, New Zealand's first female prime minister. She headed a coalition with the New Zealand First Party, led by Winston Peters.

**shire** administrative area formed in Britain for the purpose of raising taxes in Anglo-Saxon times. By AD 1000 most of southern England had been divided into shires with fortified strongholds at their centres. The Midland counties of England are still known as *the Shires;* for example Derbyshire, Nottinghamshire, and Staffordshire.

**Shiva** alternative spelling of ◊Siva, Hindu god.

**shock** in medicine, circulatory failure marked by a sudden fall of blood pressure and resulting in pallor, sweating, fast (but weak) pulse, and sometimes complete collapse. Causes include disease, injury, and psychological trauma.

**shogun** Japanese term for military dictator and abbreviation for '*seii tai shogun*' – 'great barbarian-conquering general'. Technically an imperial appointment, the office was treated as hereditary and was held by a series of clans, the Minamoto (1192–1219), the Ashikaga (1336–1573), and the ◊Tokugawa (1603–1868). The shogun held legislative, judicial, and executive power.

**Shona** a Bantu-speaking people of South Africa, comprising approximately 80% of the population of Zimbabwe. They also occupy the land between the Save and Pungure rivers in Mozambique, and smaller groups are found in South Africa, Botswana, and Zambia. The Shona are mainly farmers, living in scattered villages. The Shona language belongs to the Niger-Congo family.

**short circuit** unintended direct connection between two points in an electrical circuit.

◊Resistance is proportional to the length of wire through which current flows. By bypassing the rest of the circuit, the short circuit has low resistance and a large current flows through it. This may cause the circuit to overheat dangerously.

**shorthand** any system of rapid writing, such as the abbreviations practised by the Greeks and Romans. The first perfecter of an entirely phonetic system was Isaac Pitman, by which system speeds of about 300 words a minute are said to be attainable.

**Short Parliament** the English Parliament that was summoned by Charles I on 13 April 1640 to raise funds for his war against the Scots. It was succeeded later in the year by the ◊Long Parliament.

**short-sightedness** nontechnical term for ◊myopia.

**short story** short work of prose fiction, usually consisting of between 500 and 10,000 words, which typically either sets up and resolves a single narrative point or depicts a mood or an atmosphere.

**Shostakovich, Dmitri Dmitrievich** (1906–1975) Russian composer. His music is tonal, expressive, and sometimes highly dramatic; it was not always to official Soviet taste. He wrote 15 symphonies, chamber and film music, ballets, and operas, the latter including *Lady Macbeth of the Mtsensk District* (1934), which was suppressed as 'too divorced from the proletariat', but revived as *Katerina Izmaylova* (1963). His symphonies are among the greatest of the 20th century.

**shot put** or *putting the shot,* in athletics, the sport of throwing (or putting) overhand from the shoulder a metal ball (or shot). Standard shot weights are 7.26 kg/16 lb for men and 4 kg/8.8 lb for women.

**shrew** insectivorous mammal of the family Soricidae, order Insectivora, found in the Americas and Eurasia. It is mouselike, but with a long nose and pointed teeth. Its high metabolic rate means that it must eat almost constantly.

**shrike** or *butcher-bird,* bird of the family Laniidae, of which there are over 70 species, living mostly in Africa, but also in Eurasia and North America. They often impale insects and small vertebrates on thorns. They can grow to 35 cm/14 in long, have grey, black, or brown plumage, sharply clawed feet, and hooked beaks.

**shrimp** crustacean related to the ◊prawn. It has a cylindrical, semi-transparent body, with ten jointed legs. Some shrimps grow as large as 25 cm/10 in long.

**Shropshire** county of western England, which has contained the unitary authority of Telford and Wrekin since April 1998. Sometimes abbreviated to *Salop,* Shropshire was officially known by this name from 1974 until local protest reversed the decision in 1980

*area* 3,490 sq km/1,347 sq mi

*towns* Shrewsbury (administrative headquarters), Ludlow, Oswestry

*physical* Shropshire is bisected, on the Welsh border, northwest–southeast by the River Severn; River Teme; Ellesmere (47 ha/116 acres), the largest of several lakes; the Clee Hills rise to about 610 m/1,800 ft (Brown Clee) in the southwest

*features* Ironbridge Gorge open-air museum of industrial archaeology, with the Iron Bridge (1779), the world's first cast-iron bridge; Market Drayton is famous for its gingerbread, and Wem for its sweet peas

*agriculture* cereals (barley, oats, wheat), sugar beet, mangolds (a root vegetable used for cattle feed), vegetables (turnips, swedes), sheep and cattle; dairy farming; forestry

*industries* brick-making; engineering; limestone; manufacturing: machine tools, agricultural implements (Shrewsbury, Market Drayton, Prees, Whitchurch, Ellesmere), carpets and radio receivers (Bridgnorth), clocks (Whitchurch); Shropshire is the principal iron-producing county of England.

**population** (1996) 421,200
**famous people** Charles Darwin, A E Housman, Wilfred Owen, Gordon Richards

**Shushkevich, Stanislav** (1934– ) Belorussian politician, president from 1991–94. He was elected to parliament as a nationalist 'reform communist' in 1990 and played a key role in the creation of the Commonwealth of Independent States (CIS) as the successor to the USSR. A supporter of free-market reforms, he opposed the alignment of Belarus's economic and foreign policy with that of neighbouring Russia.

**SI** abbreviation for *Système International d'Unités* (French 'International System of Metric Units'); see ◊SI units.

**siamang** the largest ◊gibbon *Symphalangus syndactylus,* native to Malaysia and Sumatra. Siamangs have a large throat pouch to amplify the voice, making the territorial 'song' extremely loud.

**Sibelius, Jean Julius Christian** (1865–1957) Finnish composer. His works include nationalistic symphonic poems such as *En saga* (1893) and *Finlandia* (1900), a violin concerto (1904), and seven symphonies. In 1940 he abruptly ceased composing and spent the rest of his life as a recluse. Restoration of many works to their original state has helped to dispel his conservative image and reveal unexpectedly radical features.

**Siberia** Asian region of Russia, extending from the Ural Mountains to the Pacific Ocean
**area** 12,050,000 sq km/4,650,000 sq mi
**towns** Novosibirsk, Omsk, Krasnoyarsk, Irkutsk, Tomsk
**features** continental climate, bringing long and extremely cold winters; the world's largest remaining native forests (*taiga*), covering about 5,000,000 sq km/1,930,000 sq mi; Lake Baikal; volcanoes (on the Kamchatka Peninsula); Ussuriland, domain of the world's largest cat, the Siberian tiger
**industries** hydroelectric power from rivers Lena, Ob, and Yenisey; forestry and agriculture; vast mineral resources, including coal (in the Kuznetsk Basin), gold, diamonds, oil, natural gas, iron, copper, nickel, cobalt.

**Sibyl** in Roman mythology, one of many priestesses who prophesied under a deity's direct inspiration; most notably the Sibyl of Cumae, near Naples. A priestess of ◊Apollo, she guided ◊Aeneas to Hades, and offered to sell nine collections of prophecies, the *Sibylline Books,* to the legendary king of Rome, ◊Tarquinius Superbus. The price was too high, but after she had destroyed all but three, he bought those surviving for the initial sum. They were kept in the Capitol for consultation in emergency by order of the Senate.

**Sichuan** or *Szechwan,* ('four rivers') province of central China, bounded to the north by Qinghai, Gansu, and Shaanxi; to the east by Hubei and Hunan; to the south by Guizhou and Yunnan; and to the west by Tibet
**area** 539,000 sq km/208,000 sq mi

**capital** ◊Chengdu
**towns and cities** Nanchong, Neijiang, Zigong, Panzhihua
**physical** mountains in west, plain in east
**features** nuclear research centres
**industries** coal, natural gas, iron ore, salt brine, textiles, engineering, electronics
**agriculture** rice, wheat, maize
**population** (1996) 84,300,000
**famous people** Deng Xiaoping (1904–1997), Chinese Communist Party leader.

**Sicily** Italian *Sicilia,* the largest Mediterranean island and an autonomous region of Italy, divided from the Italian mainland by the Strait of Messina; area 25,700 sq km/9,920 sq mi; population (1992) 4,997,700. It consists of nine provinces: Agrigento, Caltanissetta, Catania, Enna, Messina, Palermo, Ragusa, Syracuse, and Trapani; its capital is Palermo. Exports include Marsala wine, olives, citrus, refined oil and petrochemicals, pharmaceuticals, potash, asphalt, and marble. The region also incorporates the islands of Lipari, Egadi, Ustica, and Pantelleria. Etna, 3,323 m/10,906 ft high, is the highest volcano in Europe; its last major eruption was in 1993.

**sick building syndrome** malaise diagnosed in the early 1980s among office workers and thought to be caused by such pollutants as formaldehyde (from furniture and insulating materials), benzene (from paint), and the solvent trichloroethene, concentrated in air-conditioned buildings. Symptoms include headache, sore throat, tiredness, colds, and flu. Studies have found that it can cause a 40% drop in productivity and a 30% rise in absenteeism.

**Sickert, Walter Richard** (1860–1942) English artist. His works, broadly Impressionist in style, capture subtleties of tone and light, often with a melancholic atmosphere, their most familiar subjects being the rather shabby cityscapes and domestic and music-hall interiors of late Victorian and Edwardian London. *Ennui* (about 1913; Tate Gallery, London) is a typical interior painting. His work inspired the ◊Camden Town Group.

**sickle-cell disease** also called sickle-cell anaemia, hereditary chronic blood disorder common among people of black African descent; also found in the eastern Mediterranean, parts of the Persian Gulf, and in northeastern India. It is characterized by distortion and fragility of the red blood cells, which are lost too rapidly from the circulation. This often results in ◊anaemia.

**sidewinder** rattlesnake *Crotalus cerastes* that lives in the deserts of the southwestern USA and Mexico, and moves by throwing its coils into a sideways 'jump' across the sand. It can grow up to 75 cm/30 in long.

**Sidney, Philip** (1554–1586) English poet and incompetent soldier. He wrote the sonnet sequence *Astrophel and Stella* (1591), *Arcadia* (1590), a prose romance, and *Apologie for Poetrie* (1595). Politically, Sidney became a charismatic, but hardly powerful, figure supporting a 'forward' foreign policy that would help the Protestant Netherlands against the Spanish.

**Siegfried** legendary Germanic and Norse hero. His story, which may contain some historical elements, occurs in the German *Nibelungenlied/Song of the Nibelung* and in the Norse *Elder* or *Poetic Edda* and the prose *Völsunga Saga* (in the last two works, the hero is known as Sigurd).

Siegfried wins Brunhild for his liege lord and marries his sister, but is eventually killed in the intrigues that follow.

He is the hero of the last two operas in Wagner's *The Ring of the Nibelung* cycle.

**siemens** SI unit (symbol S) of electrical conductance, the reciprocal of the ⏻resistance of an electrical circuit. One siemens equals one ampere per volt. It was formerly called the mho or reciprocal ohm.

**Sierra Leone** Republic of

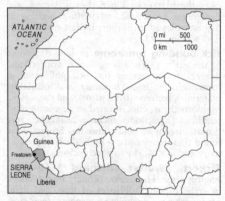

**area** 71,740 sq km/27,698 sq mi
**capital** Freetown
**major towns/cities** Koidu, Bo, Kenema, Makeni
**major ports** Bonthe-Sherbro
**physical features** mountains in east; hills and forest; coastal mangrove swamps
**head of state and government** Ahmad Tejan Kabbah from 1998
**political system** transitional
**political parties** All People's Congress (APC), moderate socialist; United Front of Political Movements (UNIFORM), centre left. Party political activity suspended from 1992
**currency** leone
**GNP per capita (PPP)** (US$) 390 (1998)
**exports** rutile, diamonds, bauxite, gold, coffee, cocoa beans. Principal market: Belgium – Luxembourg 48.9% (1997)
**population** 4,717,000 (1999 est)
**language** English (official), Krio (a creole language)
**religion** animist 52%, Muslim 39%, Protestant 6%, Roman Catholic 2% (1980 est)
**life expectancy** 36 (men); 39 (women) (1995–2000)

*Chronology*
**15th century** Mende, Temne, and Fulani peoples moved from Senegal into region formerly populated by Bulom, Krim, and Gola peoples. The Portuguese, who named the area Serra Lyoa, established a coastal fort, trading manufactured goods for slaves and ivory.
**17th century** English trading posts established on Bund and York islands.
**1787–92** English abolitionists and philanthropists bought land to establish settlement for liberated and runaway African slaves (including 1,000 rescued from Canada), known as Freetown.
**1808** Became a British colony and Freetown a base for British naval operations against slave trade, after parliament declared it illegal.
**1896** Hinterland conquered and declared British protectorate.
**1951** First political party, Sierra Leone People's Party (SLPP), formed by Dr Milton Margai, who became 'leader of government business', in 1953.
**1961** Independence achieved within Commonwealth, with Margai as prime minister.
**1964** Margai died; succeeded by his half-brother, Albert Margai.
**1965** Free-trade area pact signed with Guinea, Liberia, and the Côte d'Ivoire.
**1967** Election won by All People's Congress (APC), led by Siaka Stevens, but disputed by army, who set up National Reformation Council and forced governor general to leave the country.
**1968** Army revolt brought back Stevens as prime minister.
**1971** New constitution made Sierra Leone a republic, with Stevens as president.
**1978** New constitution made APC the only legal party.
**1985** Stevens retired and was succeeded as president and APC leader by Maj-Gen Joseph Momoh.
**1989** An attempted coup against President Momoh was foiled.
**1991** A referendum endorsed multiparty politics and new constitution. A Liberian-based rebel group began guerrilla activities.
**1992** President Momoh was overthrown by the military, and party politics were suspended as the National Provisional Ruling Council was established under Capt Valentine Strasser; 500,000 Liberians fled to Sierra Leone as a result of the civil war.
**1995** The ban on political parties was lifted. A coup attempt was foiled.
**1996** Strasser was overthrown by his deputy, Julius Maada Bio, who was replaced as president by Ahmad Tejan Kabbah after multiparty elections.
**1997** President Kabbah's civilian government was ousted in a bloody coup. Maj Johnny Paul Koroma seized the presidency and the Revolutionary Council was formed.
**1998** A Nigerian-led peacekeeping force drove out Maj Koroma's junta; President Kabbah returned from exile. Former members of military government were executed for treason.
**1999** Fighting between government and rebel

forces continued. Diplomatic efforts were spear-headed by the Organization of African Unity; a ceasefire and peace agreement were reached with rebels.

**Sierra Madre** chief mountain system of Mexico, consisting of three ranges, the Sierra Madre Oriental, the Sierra Madre del Sur, and the Sierra Madre Occidental, enclosing the central plateau of the country; the highest is Citlaltepetl (5,700 m/18,700 ft). The Sierra Madre del Sur ('of the south') runs along the southwest Pacific coast.

**Sierra Nevada** mountain range of southern Spain, mainly in the province of Granada, but also extending east into Almería. The highest point is Mulhacén (3,481 m/11,425 ft high). It has several winter sports resorts; the main centre is Sol y Nieve.

**Sierra Nevada** mountain range in eastern California, extending for about 640 km/400 mi, with a general ridge line at over 2,500 m/8,202 ft. Its highest point is Mount Whitney, which rises to 4,418 m/14,500 ft. The Sierra Nevada includes the King's Canyon, ◊Yosemite, and Sequoia national parks.

**sievert** SI unit (symbol Sv) of radiation dose equivalent. It replaces the rem (1 Sv equals 100 rem). Some types of radiation do more damage than others for the same absorbed dose – for example, an absorbed dose of alpha radiation causes 20 times as much biological damage as the same dose of beta radiation. The equivalent dose in sieverts is equal to the absorbed dose of radiation in grays multiplied by the relative biological effectiveness. Humans can absorb up to 0.25 Sv without immediate ill effects; 1 Sv may produce radiation sickness; and more than 8 Sv causes death.

**Sigismund** (1368–1437) Holy Roman Emperor from 1411, king of Hungary (1387–1437), and king of Bohemia (1419–37). Sigismund's reign was overshadowed by two religious issues: the Great Schism and the agitation of the reformer John Huss. Sigismund demonstrated his ability as a European leader in working to end the schism by arranging the Council of Constance in 1414–18; his weakness was manifest in his continual failure to suppress the Hussites.

**Sihanouk, Norodom** (1922– ) Cambodian politician, king in 1941–55 and from 1993. He was prime minister in 1955–70, when his government was overthrown in a military coup led by Lon Nol. With ◊Pol Pot's resistance front, he overthrew Lon Nol in 1975 and again became prime minister in 1975–76, when he was forced to resign by the ◊Khmer Rouge. He returned from exile in November 1991 under the auspices of a United Nations-brokered peace settlement to head a coalition intended to comprise all Cambodia's warring factions (the Khmer Rouge, however, continued fighting). He was re-elected king after the 1993 elections, in which the royalist party won a majority; in 1996, however, it was announced that he was suffering from a brain tumour and might abdicate. In October 1997, three months after a successful coup by communists, he left for China and his return was uncertain. In March 1998 he pardoned his son, prince Norodom Ranariddh, who had been sentenced to 30 years' imprisonment for smuggling arms and colluding with the Khmer Rouge.

**Sikhism** religion professed by 14 million Indians, living mainly in the Punjab. Sikhism was founded by Nanak (1469–c. 1539). Sikhs believe in a single God who is the immortal creator of the universe and who has never been incarnate in any form, and in the equality of all human beings; Sikhism is strongly opposed to caste divisions.

Their holy book is the *Guru Granth Sahib*. Guru Gobind Singh (1666–1708) instituted the *Khanda-di-Pahul*, the baptism of the sword, and established the Khalsa ('pure'), the company of the faithful. The Khalsa wear the five Ks: *kes*, long hair; *kangha*, a comb; *kirpan*, a sword; *kachh*, short trousers; and *kara*, a steel bracelet. Sikh men take the last name 'Singh' ('lion') and women 'Kaur' ('princess').

**Sikh Wars** two wars in India between the Sikhs and the British:

The *First Sikh War (1845–46)* followed an invasion of British India by Punjabi Sikhs. The Sikhs were defeated and part of their territory annexed.

The *Second Sikh War (1848–49)* arose from a Sikh revolt in Multan. They were defeated, and the British annexed the Punjab.

**Sikkim** or *Denjong*, upland state of northeast India, bounded by Nepal to the west, Bhutan to the east, Tibet (China) to the north and West Bengal state to the south. Formerly a protected state, it was absorbed by India in 1975, the monarchy being abolished. China does not recognize India's sovereignty.

*area* 7,100 sq km/2,741 sq mi

*capital* Gangtok

*features* Mount Kanchenjunga (8,586 m/28,210 ft), the third highest in the world; wildlife including birds, butterflies, and orchids; River Tista, a tributary of the Brahmaputra, joined by the rivers Rangit, Rangpo

*industries* carpets, textiles, cigarettes, food processing

*minerals* copper, lead, zinc, coal, iron ore, garnet, graphite, pyrites, marble, gold, silver

*agriculture* cardamom, tea, grain, fruit, soybeans, livestock

*population* (1994 est) 444,000

*language* Bhutia, Lepcha, Khaskura (Nepalese) – all official

*religion* Mahāyāna Buddhism, Hinduism

*history* the Lepchas are regarded as the indigenous inhabitants of the region. Sikkim was ruled by the Namgyol dynasty from the 14th century to 1975, when the last chogyal, or king, was deposed. Allied to Britain in 1886, Sikkim became a protectorate of India in 1950 and a state of India in 1975. The border with Tibet was closed at the outbreak of hostilities between India and China in 1961.

**Sikorski, Wladyslaw Eugeniusz** (1881–1943) Polish general and politician; prime minister 1922–23, and 1939–43 in the Polish government in exile in London during World War II. He was killed in an aeroplane crash near Gibraltar in controversial circumstances.

**Sikorsky, Igor Ivan** (1889–1972) Ukrainian-born US engineer. He built the first successful helicopter in 1939 (commercially produced from 1943). His first biplane flew in 1910, and in 1929 he began to construct multi-engined flying boats.

**silage** fodder preserved through controlled fermentation in a silo, an airtight structure that presses green crops. It is used as a winter feed for livestock. The term also refers to stacked crops that may be preserved indefinitely.

**Silesia** region of Europe that has long been disputed because of its geographical position, mineral resources, and industrial potential; now in Poland and the Czech Republic with metallurgical industries and a coalfield in Polish Silesia. Dispute began in the 17th century with claims on the area by both Austria and Prussia. It was seized by Prussia's Frederick the Great, which started the War of the ◊Austrian Succession; this was finally recognized by Austria in 1763, after the Seven Years' War. After World War I, it was divided (1919) among newly formed Czechoslovakia, revived Poland, and Germany, which retained the largest part. In 1945, after World War II, all German Silesia east of the Oder-Neisse line was transferred to Polish administration; about 10 million inhabitants of German origin, both there and in Czechoslovak Silesia, were expelled.

**silica** silicon dioxide, $SiO_2$, the composition of the most common mineral group, of which the most familiar form is quartz. Other silica forms are ◊chalcedony, chert, opal, tridymite, and cristobalite.

Common sand consists largely of silica in the form of quartz.

**silicate** one of a group of minerals containing silicon and oxygen in tetrahedral units of $SiO_4$, bound together in various ways to form specific structural types. Silicates are the chief rock-forming minerals. Most rocks are composed, wholly or in part, of silicates (the main exception being limestones). Glass is a manufactured complex polysilicate material in which other elements (boron in borosilicate glass) have been incorporated.

**silicon** (Latin *silex* 'flint') brittle, nonmetallic element, symbol Si, atomic number 14, relative atomic mass 28.086. It is the second-most abundant element (after oxygen) in the Earth's crust and occurs in amorphous and crystalline forms. In nature it is found only in combination with other elements, chiefly with oxygen in silica (silicon dioxide, $SiO_2$) and the silicates. These form the mineral ◊quartz, which makes up most sands, gravels, and beaches.

**silicon chip** ◊integrated circuit with microscopically small electrical components on a piece of silicon crystal only a few millimetres square.

**Silicon Valley** nickname given to a region of southern California, approximately 32 km/20 mi long, between Palo Alto and San Jose. It is the site of many high-technology electronic firms, whose prosperity is based on the silicon chip.

**silk** fine soft thread produced by the larva of the ◊silkworm moth when making its cocoon. It is soaked, carefully unwrapped, and used in the manufacture of textiles. The introduction of synthetics originally harmed the silk industry, but rising standards of living have produced an increased demand for real silk. It is manufactured in China, India, Japan, and Thailand.

**Silk Road** ancient and medieval overland route of about 6,400 km/4,000 mi by which silk was brought from China to Europe in return for trade goods; it ran west via the Gobi Desert, Samarkand, and Antioch to Mediterranean ports in Greece, Italy, the Middle East, and Egypt.

Buddhism came to China via this route, which was superseded from the 16th century by sea trade.

**silk-screen printing** or *serigraphy,* method of ◊printing based on stencilling. It can be used to print on most surfaces, including paper, plastic, cloth, and wood. An impermeable stencil (either paper or photosensitized gelatin plate) is attached to a finely meshed silk screen that has been stretched on a wooden frame, so that the ink passes through to the area beneath only where an image is required. The design can also be painted directly on the screen with varnish. A series of screens can be used to add successive layers of colour to the design.

**silkworm** usually the larva of the *common silkworm moth Bombyx mori.* After hatching from the egg and maturing on the leaves of white mulberry trees (or a synthetic substitute), it spins a protective cocoon of fine silk thread 275 m/900 ft long. To keep the thread intact, the moth is killed before emerging from the cocoon, and several threads are combined to form the commercial silk thread woven into textiles.

**Silurian** period of geological time 439–409 million years ago, the third period of the Palaeozoic era. Silurian sediments are mostly marine and consist of shales and limestone. Luxuriant reefs were built by coral-like organisms. The first land plants began to evolve during this period, and there were many ostracoderms (armoured jawless fishes). The first jawed fishes (called acanthodians) also appeared.

**silver** white, lustrous, extremely malleable and ductile, metallic element, symbol Ag (from Latin *argentum*), atomic number 47, relative atomic mass 107.868. It occurs in nature in ores and as a free metal; the chief ores are sulphides, from which the metal is extracted by smelting with lead. It is one of the best metallic conductors of both heat and electricity; its most useful compounds are the chloride and bromide, which darken on exposure to light and are the basis of photographic emulsions.

**silverfish** wingless insect, a type of ◊bristletail.

**Simenon, Georges Joseph Christian** (1903–1989) Belgian crime writer. Initially a pulp fiction writer, in 1931 he created Inspector

Maigret of the Paris Sûreté who appeared in a series of detective novels.

**simile** (Latin 'likeness') figure of speech that in English uses the conjunctions *like* and *as* to express comparisons between two things of different kinds ('run like the devil'; 'as deaf as a post'). It is sometimes confused with ◊metaphor. The simile makes an explicit comparison, while the metaphor's comparison is implicit.

**Simon, Paul** (1942– ) US pop singer and songwriter. In a folk-rock duo with Art Garfunkel, he had such hits as 'Mrs Robinson' (1968) and 'Bridge Over Troubled Water' (1970). Simon's solo work includes the critically acclaimed album *Graceland* (1986), for which he drew on Cajun and African music.

**Simpson, Wallis Warfield, Duchess of Windsor** (1896–1986) US socialite, twice divorced. She married ◊Edward VIII 1937, who abdicated in order to marry her. He was given the title Duke of Windsor by his brother, George VI, who succeeded him.

**simultaneous equations** in mathematics, one of two or more algebraic equations that contain two or more unknown quantities that may have a unique solution. For example, in the case of two linear equations with two unknown variables, such as: (i) $x + 3y = 6$ and (ii) $3y - 2x = 4$ the solution will be those unique values of $x$ and $y$ that are valid for both equations. Linear simultaneous equations can be solved by using algebraic manipulation to eliminate one of the variables, ◊coordinate geometry, or matrices (see ◊matrix).

**sin** transgression of the will of God or the gods, as revealed in the moral code laid down by a particular religion. In Roman Catholic theology, a distinction is made between *mortal sins,* which, if unforgiven, result in damnation, and *venial sins,* which are less serious. In Islam, the one unforgivable sin is *shirk,* denial that Allah is the only god.

**Sinai** Egyptian peninsula, largely desert, at the head of the Red Sea; area 65,000 sq km/25,000 sq mi. Resources include oil, natural gas, manganese, and coal; irrigation water from the River Nile is carried under the Suez Canal. The main towns are Al-Arish (the capital of South Sinai governorate) and Al-Tur (capital of North Sinai governorate). It is the ancient source of turquoise. Tourism is of increasing importance.

**Sinai, Mount** or *Horeb,* mountain near the tip of the Sinai Peninsula; height 2,285 m/7,500 ft. According to the Old Testament this is where ◊Moses received the Ten Commandments from God. Its identity is not absolutely certain, but it is traditionally thought to be Jebel Musa ('Mountain of Moses').

**Sinan** (1489–1588) Ottoman architect. He was chief architect to Suleiman the Magnificent from 1538. Among the hundreds of buildings he designed are the Suleimaniye mosque complex in Istanbul (1551–58) and the Selimiye mosque in Adrinople (now Edirne) (1569–74).

**Sinatra, Frank (Francis Albert)** (1915–1998) US singer and film actor. Celebrated for his phrasing and emotion, especially on love ballads, he was particularly associated with the song 'My Way'. His films included *From Here to Eternity* (1953), for which he won an Academy Award, *Some Came Running* (1959), and the political thriller *The Manchurian Candidate* (1963).

**Sind** province of southeast Pakistan, mainly in the Indus delta
*area* 140,914 sq km/54,393 sq mi
*capital* and chief port ◊Karachi
*physical* the last 480 km/300 mi of the Indus Valley; to the east is the Thar Desert; low rainfall averages make the region dependant on irrigation
*features* Sukkur Barrage, which enables water from the Indus River to be used for irrigation of over 2 million ha/4.9 million acres; down river at Kotri, a second barrage irrigates over 1 million ha/2.46 million acres; rail link with India via Hyderabad
*industry* shipbuilding at Karachi, cement, textiles, foundries; assisted by hydroelectric and natural gas power sources; salt is mined
*agriculture* wheat, rice, cotton, barley, oilseeds, vegetables; red Sindhi cattle, buffaloes, camels
*population* (1993 est) 28,930,000
*language* 60% Sindi; others include Urdu, Punjabi, Baluchi, Pashto
*history* annexed 1843, it became a province of British India, and part of Pakistan on independence. There is agitation for its creation as a separate state, Sindhudesh.

**Sindhi** the majority ethnic group living in the Pakistani province of Sind. The Sindhi language is spoken by about 15 million people. Since the partition of India and Pakistan 1947, large numbers of Urdu-speaking refugees have moved into the region from India, especially into the capital, Karachi.

**sine** in trigonometry, a function of an angle in a right-angled triangle which is defined as the ratio of the length of the side opposite the angle to the length of the hypotenuse (the longest side).

**sine rule** in trigonometry, a rule that relates the sides and angles of a triangle, stating that the ratio of the length of each side and the sine of the angle opposite is constant (twice the radius of the circumscribing circle). If the sides of a triangle are $a$, $b$, and $c$, and the angles opposite are $A$, $B$, and $C$, respectively, then the sine rule may be expressed as

$$a/\sin A = b/\sin B = c/\sin C$$

**sinfonietta** orchestral work that is of a shorter, lighter nature than a ◊symphony, for example Janáček's *Sinfonietta* 1926. It is also the name for a small-scale orchestra specializing in such works, for example the London Sinfonietta.

**Singapore** Republic of
*area* 622 sq km/240 sq mi
*capital* Singapore City
*major towns/cities* Jurong, Changi
*physical features* comprises Singapore Island, low and flat, and 57 small islands; Singapore

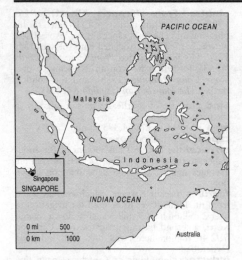

Island is joined to the mainland by a causeway across the Strait of Johore

**head of state** Ong Teng Cheong from 1993

**head of government** Goh Chok Tong from 1990

**political system** liberal democracy with strict limits on dissent

**political parties** People's Action Party (PAP), conservative, free market, multi-ethnic; Workers' Party (WP), socialist; Singapore Democratic Party (SDP), liberal pluralist

**currency** Singapore dollar

**GNP per capita (PPP)** (US$) 28,260 (1998)

**exports** electrical and nonelectrical machinery, transport equipment, petroleum products, chemicals, rubber, foodstuffs, clothing, metal products, iron and steel, orchids and other plants, aquarium fish. Principal market: USA 19.9% (1998)

**population** 3,522,000 (1999 est)

**language** Malay (national tongue), Chinese, Tamil, English (all official)

**religion** Buddhist, Taoist, Muslim, Hindu, Christian

**life expectancy** 75 (men); 80 (women) (1995–2000)

**Chronology**

**12th century** First trading settlement established on Singapore Island.

**14th century** Settlement destroyed, probably by Javanese Empire of Mahapahit.

**1819** Stamford Raffles of British East India Company obtained Singapore from sultan of Johore.

**1826** Straits Settlements formed from British possessions of Singapore, Penang, and Malacca ruled by governor of Bengal.

**1832** Singapore became capital of Straits Settlements; the port prospered, attracting Chinese and Indian immigrants.

**1851** Responsibility for Straits Settlements fell to governor general of India.

**1858** British government, through the India Office, took over administration of Straits Settlements.

**1867** Straits Settlements became crown colony of British Empire.

**1922** Singapore chosen as principal British military base in Far East.

**1942** Japan captured Singapore, taking 70,000 British and Australian prisoners.

**1945** British rule restored after defeat of Japan.

**1946** Singapore became separate crown colony.

**1959** Internal self-government achieved as State of Singapore with Lee Kuan Yew (PAP) as prime minister.

**1960s** Rapid development as leading commercial and financial centre.

**1963** Singapore combined with Federation of Malaya, Sabah, and Sarawak to form Federation of Malaysia.

**1965** Became independent republic after withdrawing from Federation of Malaysia in protest at alleged discrimination against ethnic Chinese.

**1971** Last remaining British military bases closed.

**1984** Two opposition members elected to national assembly for first time.

**1986** Opposition leader convicted of perjury and prohibited from standing for election.

**1988** Ruling PAP won all but one of available assembly seats; increasingly authoritarian rule.

**1990** Lee Kuan Yew retired from the premiership after 31 years and was succeeded by Goh Chok Tong.

**1992** Lee Kuan Yew surrendered the PAP leadership to Goh Chok Tong.

**1993** Ong Teng Cheong was elected president with increased powers.

**1996** Constitutional change was introduced, allowing better representation of minority races.

**1997** The PAP, led by Prime Minister Goh Chok Tong, won a general election.

**1998** Pay cuts were introduced as Singapore slipped into recession for the first time in 13 years.

**Singapore** capital of Singapore, on the southeast coast of the island of Singapore; population (1993) 2,874,000. Major industries include trade, shipping, banking, electronics, shipbuilding, and oil refining. Formerly a British colonial town, it was occupied by Japanese forces during World War II.

**Singer, Isaac Bashevis** (1904–1991) Polish-born US novelist and short-story writer. He lived in the USA from 1935. His works, written in Yiddish, often portray traditional Jewish life in Poland and the USA, and the loneliness of old age. They include *The Family Moskat* (1950) and *Gimpel the Fool and Other Stories* (1957). Nobel prize (1978).

**singularity** in astrophysics, the point in ◊space-time at which the known laws of physics break down. Singularity is predicted to exist at the centre of a black hole, where infinite gravitational forces compress the infalling mass of a collapsing star to infinite density. It is also thought, according to the Big Bang model of the origin of the universe, to be the point from which the expansion of the universe began.

**Sinhalese** the majority ethnic group of Sri Lanka (70% of the population). Sinhalese is the official language of Sri Lanka; it belongs to the Indo-Iranian branch of the Indo-European family, and is written in a script derived from the Indian Pali form. The Sinhalese are Buddhists. Since 1971 they have been involved in a violent struggle with the Tamil minority, who are seeking independence.

The Veddas of the central highlands are thought to be the descendants of the original inhabitants of Sri Lanka. Around 550 BC the island was invaded by Aryans from the mainland, though it seems likely that these people had already become mixed with the Dravidian inhabitants of southern India. The name Sinhalese is derived from the lion, *sinha*, symbol which occurs in the legends of origin.

Buddhism was flourishing by the 3rd century BC and during the 5th century AD the Sinhalese began to keep a Buddhist chronicle. Their script is based on the Indian Pali form. The Hīnayāna (Lesser Vehicle) Buddhists of Sri Lanka have had an impact on Southeast Asian religion, especially in Myanmar. During the 11th century there were Tamil incursions and by the time of the arrival of the Portuguese the Tamils were firmly established in the north. Today there is a large Tamil minority especially around Jaffna. There are also mixed populations, the descendants of islanders who married European seafarers, and small Arab communities along the coast. Trading and fishing remain important activities in coastal regions, while further inland rice is cultivated in irrigated fields.

**Sinn Féin** (Gaelic 'we ourselves') Irish political party founded in 1905, whose aim is the creation of a united republican Ireland. The driving political force behind Irish nationalism between 1916 and 1921, Sinn Féin returned to prominence with the outbreak of violence ('the Troubles') in Northern Ireland in the late 1960s, when it split into 'Provisional' and 'Official' wings at the same time as the ◊Irish Republican Army (IRA), with which it is closely associated. From the late 1970s 'Provisional' Sinn Féin assumed a more active political role, putting up candidates to stand in local and national elections. Sinn Féin won two seats in the 1997 UK general election and one seat in the 1997 Irish general election. Gerry ◊Adams became party president in 1978. Sinn Féin participated in the multiparty negotiations (known as the Stormont Talks) and became a signatory of the agreement reached on Good Friday, 10 April 1998. The party gained 17.6% of votes in the June 1998 elections to the 108-seat Belfast assembly. In September a historic meeting between Gerry Adams and the Ulster Unionist leader, David Trimble, took place at Stormont; Sinn Féin also agreed to appoint a contact with the international body overseeing the decommissioning of arms – the party's chief negotiator, Martin McGuinness.

**Sino-Japanese Wars** two wars waged by Japan against China 1894–95 and 1931–45 to expand to the mainland. Territory gained in the First Sino-Japanese War (Korea) and in the 1930s (Manchuria, Shanghai) was returned at the end of World War II.

**Sino-Tibetan languages** group of languages spoken in Southeast Asia. This group covers a large area, and includes Chinese and Burmese, both of which have numerous dialects. Some classifications include the Tai group of languages (including Thai and Lao) in the Sino-Tibetan family.

**sinusitis** painful inflammation of one of the sinuses, or air spaces, that surround the nasal passages. Most cases clear with antibiotics and nasal decongestants, but some require surgical drainage.

**Sioux** or *Dakota,* (Chippewa 'enemies') member of the largest group of American Indian Plains Indians, numbering about 103,000 (1990) in the USA and 60,000 in Canada (1991), and now living on reservations in North and South Dakota and Nebraska, and scattered throughout the country. Their language belongs to the Macro-Siouan family.

**siren** in Greek mythology, a sea ◊nymph, half woman and half bird, who lured sailors to shipwreck along rocky coasts with her irresistible singing, before devouring them. ◊Odysseus, on the advice of the enchantress Circe, tied himself to the mast of his ship in order to hear the sirens safely, and plugged his crew's ears with wax.

**Sirius** or *the Dog Star* or *Alpha Canis Majoris,* brightest star in the night sky, 8.6 light years from the Sun in the constellation ◊Canis Major. Sirius is a white star with a mass 2.3 times that of the Sun, a diameter 1.8 times that of the Sun, and a true luminosity of 23 Suns. It is orbited every 50 years by a ◊white dwarf, Sirius B, also known as the Pup.

**sirocco** hot, normally dry and dust-laden wind that blows from the deserts of North Africa across the Mediterranean into southern Europe. It occurs mainly in the spring. The name 'sirocco' is also applied to any hot oppressive wind.

**sisal** strong fibre made from various species of ◊agave, such as *Agave sisalina.*

**Sisulu, Walter Max Ulyate** (1912– ) South African civil-rights activist, deputy president of the African National Congress (ANC). In 1964 he became, with Nelson Mandela, one of the first full-time secretaries general of the ANC. He was imprisoned following the 1964 Rivonia Trial for opposition to the apartheid system and released in 1989, at the age of 77, as a gesture of reform by President F W ◊de Klerk. In 1991, when Mandela became ANC president, Sisulu became his deputy.

**Sisyphus** in Greek mythology, a king of Corinth who was condemned to Tartarus, a region of the underworld for the wicked. As punishment for his evil life, he was forced to roll a huge stone uphill for eternity; it always fell back before he could reach the top.

**Sita** in Hinduism, the wife of Rama, an avatar (manifestation) of the god Vishnu; a character in the *Rāmāyana* epic, characterized by chastity and kindness.

**Sitting Bull** Indian name *Tatanka Iyotake* (c. 1834–1890) American Indian chief who agreed to ◊Sioux resettlement 1868. When the treaty was broken by the USA, he led the Sioux against Lieutenant Colonel ◊Custer at the Battle of the ◊Little Bighorn 1876.

**situationism** in ethics, the doctrine that any action may be good or bad depending on its context or situation. Situationists argue that no moral rule can apply in all situations and that what may be wrong in most cases may be right if the end is sufficiently good. In general, situationists believe moral attitudes are more important than moral rules.

**SI units** French *Système International d'Unités,* standard system of scientific units used by scientists worldwide.

Originally proposed in 1960, it replaces the m.k.s., ◊c.g.s., and f.p.s. systems. It is based on seven basic units: the metre (m) for length, kilogram (kg) for mass, second (s) for time, ampere (A) for electrical current, kelvin (K) for temperature, mole (mol) for amount of substance, and candela (cd) for luminosity.

**Siva** or *Shiva,* (Sanskrit 'propitious') in Hinduism, the third chief god (with Brahma and Vishnu). As Mahadeva (great lord), he is the creator, symbolized by the phallic *lingam,* who restores what as Mahakala he destroys. He is often sculpted as Nataraja, performing his fruitful cosmic dance.

His consort or female principle (*sakti*) is Parvati, otherwise known as Durga or Kali.

**Six Counties** the six counties that form Northern Ireland: Antrim, Armagh, Down, Fermanagh, Londonderry, and Tyrone.

**Six-Day War** another name for the third ◊Arab-Israeli War.

**skate** any of several species of flatfish of the ray group. The common skate *Raja batis* is up to 1.8 m/6 ft long and greyish, with black specks. Its egg cases ('mermaids' purses') are often washed ashore by the tide.

**skateboard** single flexible board mounted on wheels and steerable by weight positioning. As a land alternative to surfing, skateboards developed in California in the 1960s and became a worldwide craze in the 1970s. Skateboarding is practised in urban environments and has enjoyed a revival since the late 1980s.

**skating** self-propulsion on ice by means of bladed skates, or on other surfaces by skates with small rollers (wheels of wood, metal, or plastic).

The chief competitive ice-skating events are figure skating, for singles or pairs, ice-dancing, and simple speed skating. The first world ice-skating championships were held in 1896.

**skeleton** the rigid or semirigid framework that supports and gives form to an animal's body, protects its internal organs, and provides anchorage points for its muscles. The skeleton may be composed of bone and cartilage (vertebrates), chitin (arthropods), calcium carbonate (molluscs and other invertebrates), or silica (many protists). The human skeleton is composed of 206 bones, with the ◊vertebral column (spine) forming the central supporting structure.

**skiing** self-propulsion on snow by means of elongated runners (skis) for the feet, slightly bent upward at the tip. It is a popular recreational sport, as cross-country ski touring or as downhill runs on mountain trails; events include downhill; slalom, in which a series of turns between flags have to be negotiated; cross-country racing; and ski jumping, when jumps of over 150 m/490 ft are achieved from ramps up to 90 m/295 ft high. Speed-skiing uses skis approximately one-third longer and wider than normal with which speeds of up to 200 kph/125 mph have been recorded. Recently, *snowboarding* (or monoboarding), the use of a single, very broad ski, similar to a surf board, used with the feet facing the front and placed together, has become increasingly popular.

**skin** the covering of the body of a vertebrate. In mammals, the outer layer (epidermis) is dead and its cells are constantly being rubbed away and replaced from below; it helps to protect the body from infection and to prevent dehydration. The lower layer (dermis) contains blood vessels, nerves, hair roots, and sweat and sebaceous glands, and is supported by a network of fibrous and elastic cells. The medical speciality concerned with skin diseases is called dermatology.

**skink** lizard of the family Scincidae, a large family of about 700 species found throughout the tropics and subtropics. The body is usually long and the legs are reduced. Some skinks are legless and rather snakelike. Many are good burrowers, or can 'swim' through sand, like the *sandfish* genus *Scincus* of North Africa. Some skinks lay eggs, others bear live young.

**Skinner, B(urrhus) F(rederic)** (1904–1990) US psychologist. He was a radical behaviourist who rejected mental concepts, seeing the organism as a 'black box' where internal processes are not significant in predicting behaviour. He studied operant conditioning (influencing behaviour patterns by reward or punishment) and held that behaviour is shaped and maintained by its consequences.

**Skopje** capital and industrial city of the Former Yugoslav Republic of Macedonia; population (1991) 563,300. Industries include iron, steel, chromium mining, and food processing.

**skua** dark-coloured gull-like seabird, living in Arctic and Antarctic waters. Skuas can grow up to 60 cm/2 ft long, with long, well-developed wings and short, stout legs; in colour they are greyish above and white below. They are aggressive scavengers, and seldom fish for themselves but force gulls to disgorge their catch, and also eat chicks of other birds. Skuas are in the family Stercorariidae, order Charadriiformes.

**skull** in vertebrates, the collection of flat and irregularly shaped bones (or cartilage) that enclose the brain and the organs of sight, hearing, and smell, and provide support for the jaws. In most mammals, the skull consists of 22 bones joined by fibrous immobile joints called sutures. The floor of the skull is pierced by a large hole (*foramen magnum*) for the spinal cord and a number of smaller apertures through which other nerves and blood vessels pass.

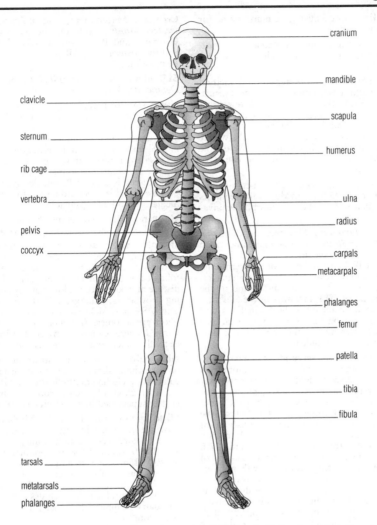

- cranium
- mandible
- scapula
- humerus
- ulna
- radius
- carpals
- metacarpals
- phalanges
- femur
- patella
- tibia
- fibula

- clavicle
- sternum
- rib cage
- vertebra
- pelvis
- coccyx
- tarsals
- metatarsals
- phalanges

**skeleton** *There are 206 bones in the adult body, nearly half of them in the hands and feet. The adult human body also has approximately 100 joints.*

**skunk** North American mammal of the weasel family. The common skunk *Mephitis mephitis* has a long, arched body, short legs, a bushy tail, and black fur with white streaks on the back. In self-defence, it discharges a foul-smelling fluid.

**Skye** largest island of the Inner ◊Hebrides, Highland region, off the west coast of Scotland; area 1,740 sq km/672 sq mi; population (1991) 8,900. It is separated from the mainland to the southeast by the Sound of Sleat and by the islands of Raasay and Scalpay to the northeast. The chief port and town is Portree. The economy is based on crofting, craft industries, tourism, and livestock. The *Skye Bridge,* a privately financed toll bridge to Kyleakin on the island from the Kyle of Lochalsh, was completed in 1995.

**skylab** US space station, launched 14 May 1973, made from the adapted upper stage of a Saturn V rocket. At 75 tonnes/82.5 tons, it was the heaviest object ever put into space, and was 25.6 m/84 ft long. *Skylab* contained a workshop for carrying out experiments in weightlessness, an observatory for monitoring the Sun, and cameras for photographing the Earth's surface.

**skylark** a type of ◊lark.

**skyscraper** building so tall that it appears to 'scrape the sky', developed 1868 in New York, USA, where land prices were high and the geology allowed such methods of construction. Skyscrapers are now found in cities throughout the world. The world's tallest free-standing structure is the CN (Canadian National) Tower, Toronto, at 555 m/1,821 ft.

**slag** in chemistry, the molten mass of impurities that is produced in the smelting or refining of metals.

**slaked lime** in chemistry, common name for ◊calcium hydroxide.

**slander** spoken defamatory statement; if written, or broadcast on radio or television, it constitutes ◊libel.

**slash and burn** simple agricultural method whereby natural vegetation is cut and burned, and the clearing then farmed for a few years until the soil loses its fertility, whereupon farmers move on and leave the area to regrow. Although this is possible with a small, widely dispersed population, it becomes unsustainable with more people and is now a cause of ◊deforestation.

**slate** fine-grained, usually grey metamorphic rock that splits readily into thin slabs along its cleavage planes. It is the metamorphic equivalent of ◊shale.

**Slav** or *Slavonian, Slowene,* or *Slowane,* (from *Slawa* or *Slowo* 'articulate') member of an Indo-European people in central and Eastern Europe, the Balkans, and parts of northern Asia, speaking closely related ◊Slavonic languages, some written in the Cyrillic and some in the Roman alphabet. The ancestors of the Slavs are believed to have included the Sarmatians and ◊Scythians. Moving west from central Asia, they settled in eastern and southeastern Europe during the 2nd and 3rd millennia BC.

**slavery** the enforced servitude of one person (a slave) to another or one group to another. A slave has no personal rights and is the property of another person through birth, purchase, or capture. Slavery goes back to prehistoric times but declined in Europe after the fall of the Roman Empire. During the imperialism of Spain, Portugal, and Britain in the 16th to 18th centuries and in the American South in the 17th to 19th centuries, slavery became a mainstay of an agricultural factory economy, with millions of Africans sold to work on plantations in North and South America. Millions more died in the process, but the profits from this trade were enormous. Slavery was abolished in the British Empire in 1833 and in the USA at the end of the Civil War (1863–65), but continues illegally in some countries.

**Slavonia** region of eastern Croatia bounded by the Sava, Drava, and Danube rivers; Osijek is the largest town. Eastern and western Slavonia declared themselves autonomous provinces of Serbia following Croatia's declaration of independence from Yugoslavia (1991), and the region was the scene of fierce fighting between Croatian forces and Serb-dominated Yugoslav federal troops (1991–92). After the ceasefire in 1992, 10,000 UN troops were deployed in eastern and western Slavonia and contested Krajina. Rebel Serbs in Croatia agreed in November 1995 to return the region of eastern Slavonia to Croatian control.

**Slavonic languages** or *Slavic languages,* branch of the Indo-European language family spoken in central and Eastern Europe, the Balkans, and parts of northern Asia. The family comprises the *southern group* (Slovene, Serbo-Croatian, Macedonian, and Bulgarian); the *western group* (Czech and Slovak, Sorbian in Germany, and Polish and its related dialects); and the *eastern group* (Russian, Ukrainian, and Belorussian).

**SLD** abbreviation for ◊*Social and Liberal Democrats,* British political party.

**sleep** state of natural unconsciousness and inactivity that occurs at regular intervals in most mammals and birds, though there is considerable variation in the amount of time spent sleeping. Sleep differs from hibernation in that it occurs daily rather than seasonally, and involves less drastic reductions in metabolism. The function of sleep is unclear. People deprived of sleep become irritable, uncoordinated, forgetful, hallucinatory, and even psychotic.

**sleeping pill** any ◊sedative that induces sleep; in small doses, such drugs may relieve anxiety.

**sleeping sickness** infectious disease of tropical Africa, a form of ◊trypanosomiasis. Early symptoms include fever, headache, and chills, followed by ◊anaemia and joint pains. Later, the disease attacks the central nervous system, causing drowsiness, lethargy, and, if left untreated, death. Sleeping sickness is caused by either of two trypanosomes, *Trypanosoma gambiense* or *T. rhodesiense.* Control is by eradication of the tsetse fly, which transmits the disease to humans.

**slide rule** mathematical instrument with pairs of logarithmic sliding scales, used for rapid calculations, including multiplication, division, and the extraction of square roots. It has been largely superseded by the electronic calculator.

**Sligo** county of the Republic of Ireland, in the province of Connacht, situated on the Atlantic coast of northwest Ireland; county town Sligo; area 1,800 sq km/695 sq mi; population (1991) 54,700. Limestone mountains rise behind a boggy coastal plain. There is some mineral wealth, including barytes, coal, lead, and copper. Agricultural activity includes cattle farming and dairy farming. The other principal town is Ballymote.

**slime mould** or *myxomycete,* extraordinary organism that shows some features of ◊fungus and some of ◊protozoa. Slime moulds are not closely related to any other group, although they are often classed, for convenience, with the fungi. There are two kinds, cellular slime moulds and plasmodial slime moulds, differing in their complex life cycles.

**sloe** fruit of the ◊blackthorn bush.

**sloth** slow-moving South American mammal, about 70 cm/2.5 ft long, family Bradypodidae, order Edentata. Sloths are greyish brown and have small rounded heads, rudimentary tails, and prolonged forelimbs. Each foot has long curved claws adapted to clinging upside down from trees. On the ground the animals cannot walk, but drag themselves along. They are vegetarian.

**Slough** industrial town and unitary authority in southern England, near Windsor, 32 km/20 west of London; it was part of the county of

Berkshire to April 1998
**area** 28 sq km/11 sq mi
**features** the home of astronomer William Herschel is now a museum; the history of the town is recorded in Slough Museum
**industries** pharmaceuticals, electronics, engineering, aviation support services, and the manufacture of chocolate, paint, and power tools; a trading estate was developed here in the 1920s, the first of its kind to be established in England
**population** (1996) 105,000.

## Slovak Republic
**national name** *Slovenská Republika*

**area** 49,035 sq km/18,932 sq mi
**capital** Bratislava
**major towns/cities** Košice, Nitra, Prešov, Banská Bystrica, Žilina, Trnava
**physical features** Western range of Carpathian Mountains, including Tatra and Beskids in north; Danube plain in south; numerous lakes and mineral springs
**head of state** Rudolf Schuster from 1999
**head of government** Mikulas Dzurinda from 1998
**political system** emergent democracy
**political parties** Movement for a Democratic Slovakia (MDS), centre left, nationalist-populist; Democratic Union of Slovakia (DUS), centrist; Christian Democratic Movement (KSDH), right of centre; Slovak National Party (SNP), nationalist; Party of the Democratic Left (PDL), reform socialist, (ex-communist); Association of Workers of Slovakia, left wing; Hungarian Coalition, ethnic Hungarian
**currency** Slovak koruna (based on Czechoslovak koruna)
**GNP per capita (PPP)** (US$) 6,600 (1998 est)
**exports** basic manufactures, machinery and transport equipment, miscellaneous manufactured articles. Principal market: Germany 28.9% (1998)
**population** 5,381,000 (1999 est)
**language** Slovak (official)
**religion** Roman Catholic (over 50%), Lutheran, Reformist, Orthodox

**life expectancy** 69 (men); 77 (women) (1995–2000)
**Chronology**
**9th century** Part of kingdom of Greater Moravia, in Czech lands to west, founded by Slavic Prince Sviatopluk; Christianity adopted.
**906** Came under Magyar (Hungarian) domination and adopted Roman Catholicism.
**1526** Came under Austrian Habsburg rule.
**1867** With creation of dual Austro-Hungarian monarchy, came under separate Hungarian rule; policy of forced Magyarization stimulated a revival of Slovak national consciousness.
**1918** Austro-Hungarian Empire dismembered; Slovaks joined Czechs to form independent state of Czechoslovakia. Slovak-born Tomas Masaryk remained president until 1935, but political and economic power became concentrated in Czech lands.
**1939** Germany annexed Czechoslovakia, which became Axis puppet state under the Slovak autonomist leader Monsignor Jozef Tiso; Jews persecuted.
**1944** Popular revolt against German rule ('Slovak Uprising').
**1945** Liberated from German rule by Soviet troops; Czechoslovakia re-established.
**1948** Communists assumed power in Czechoslovakia.
**1950s** Heavy industry introduced into previously rural Slovakia; Slovak nationalism and Catholic Church forcibly suppressed.
**1968–69** 'Prague Spring' political reforms introduced by Slovak-born Communist Party leader Alexander Dubček; Warsaw Pact forces invaded Czechoslovakia to stamp out reforms; Slovak Socialist Republic, with autonomy over local affairs, created under new federal constitution; Slovak-born Gustáv Husák became Communist Party leader in Czechoslovakia.
**1989** Prodemocracy demonstrations in Bratislava; new political parties, including centre-left People Against Violence (PAV), formed and legalized; Communist Party stripped of powers; new government formed, with ex-dissident playwright Václav Havel as president.
**1990** Slovak nationalists polled strongly in multiparty elections, with Vladimir Meciar (PAV) becoming prime minister.
**1991** There was increasing Slovak separatism as the economy deteriorated. Meciar formed a PAV splinter group, Movement for a Democratic Slovakia (HZDS), pledging greater autonomy for Slovakia. Pro-Meciar rallies in Bratislava followed his dismissal.
**1992** Meciar returned to power following an electoral victory for the HZDS. Slovak parliament's declaration of sovereignty led to Havel's resignation; 'velvet divorce' agreement on separate Czech and Slovak states established a free-trade customs union.
**1993** The Slovak Republic joined the United Nations (UN) and Council of Europe as a sovereign state, with Meciar as prime minister and Michal Kovac, formerly of HZDS, as president.
**1994** The Slovak Republic joined NATO's 'Partnership for Peace' programme. Meciar was ousted on no-confidence vote, but later returned after new elections, heading a

coalition government that included ultrana-
tionalists and socialists.

**1995** A second wave of mass privatization was
postponed; Slovak was made the sole official
language; a Treaty of Friendship and
Cooperation was signed with Hungary, easing
tensions among the Hungarian minority community.

**1996** An anti-Meciar coalition, the Slovak
Democratic Coalition, was formed, comprising
five opposition parties.

**1997** A referendum on NATO membership and
presidential elections was declared invalid after
confusion over voting papers.

**1998** Presidential powers were assumed by
Meciar after failure to elect new president. The
national council chair, Ivan Gasparović, became
acting head of state. Meciar stepped down as
prime minister after the opposition Slovak
Democratic Coalition (SDC) polled strongly in a
general election. A new SDC-led coalition was
formed under Mikulas Dzurinda. The koruna
was devalued by 6%.

**Slovakia** one of the two republics that formed
the Federative Republic of Czechoslovakia.
Settled in the 5th–6th centuries by Slavs; it was
occupied by the Magyars in the 10th century,
and was part of the kingdom of Hungary until
1918, when it became a province of Czechoslovakia. Slovakia was a puppet state under
German domination in 1939–45, and was abolished as an administrative division in 1949. Its
capital and chief town was Bratislava. It was re-
established as a sovereign state, the Slovak
Republic, after the break-up of Czechoslovakia
in 1993.

**Slovene** member of the southern ◊Slav people
of ◊Slovenia and parts of the Alpine provinces of
Styria and Carinthia in Austria, and Gorizia and
Carniola in Italy. Formerly under ◊Hapsburg
rule, they united with the Serbs and Croats to
form the state of Yugoslavia after World War II.
There are 1.5–2 million speakers of Slovene, a
language belonging to the South Slavonic
branch of the Indo-European family. The
Slovenes use the Roman alphabet and the majority belong to the Roman Catholic Church.

**Slovenia** Republic of
**national name** *Republika Slovenija*
**area** 20,251 sq km/7,818 sq mi
**capital** Ljubljana
**major towns/cities** Maribor, Kranj, Celji,
Velenje, Koper (Capodistria)
**major ports** Koper
**physical features** mountainous; Sava and
Drava rivers
**head of state** Milan Kučan from 1990
**head of government** Janez Drnovšek from
1992
**political system** emergent democracy
**political parties** Slovenian Christian
Democrats (SKD), right of centre; Slovenian
People's Party (SPP), conservative; Liberal
Democratic Party of Slovenia (LDS), centrist;
Slovenian Nationalist Party (SNS), right-wing
nationalist; Democratic Party of Slovenia (LDP),
left of centre; United List of Social Democrats

(ZLSD) left of centre, ex-communist
**currency** tolar
**GNP per capita (PPP)** (US$) 12,730 (1998 est)
**exports** raw materials, semi-finished goods,
machinery, electric motors, transport equipment, foodstuffs, clothing, pharmaceuticals, cosmetics. Principal market: Germany 28.4%
(1998)
**population** 1,989,000 (1999 est)
**language** Slovene, resembling Serbo-Croat,
written in Roman characters
**religion** Roman Catholic
**life expectancy** 71 (men); 78 (women) (1995–
2000)
**Chronology**
**1st century BC** Came under Roman rule.
**AD 395** In division of Roman Empire, stayed in
west, along with Croatia and Bosnia.
**6th century** Settled by the Slovene South Slavs.
**7th century** Adopted Christianity as Roman
Catholics.
**8th–9th centuries** Under successive rule of
Franks and dukes of Bavaria.
**907–55** Came under Hungarian domination.
**1335** Was absorbed in Austro-Hungarian
Habsburg Empire, as part of Austrian crown-
lands of Carniola, Styria, and Carinthia.
**1848** Slovene struggle for independence began.
**1918** On collapse of Habsburg Empire, Slovenia
united with Serbia, Croatia, and Montenegro to
form the 'Kingdom of Serbs, Croats and
Slovenes', under Serbian Karageorgevic dynasty.
**1929** Kingdom became known as Yugoslavia.
**1941–45** Occupied by Nazi Germany and Italy
during World War II; anti-Nazi Slovene
Liberation Front formed and became allies of
Marshal Tito's communist-led Partisans.
**1945** Slovenia became a constituent republic of
the Yugoslav Socialist Federal Republic.
**mid-1980s** The Slovenian Communist Party liberalized itself and agreed to free elections.
Yugoslav counterintelligence (KOV) began
repression.
**1989** The constitution was changed to allow
secession from the federation.
**1990** A Nationalist Democratic Opposition of
Slovenia (DEMOS) coalition secured victory in

the first multiparty parliamentary elections; Milan Kučan, a reform communist, became president. Sovereignty was declared. Independence was overwhelmingly approved in a referendum.

**1991** Slovenia seceded from the Yugoslav federation, along with Croatia; 100 people were killed after the Yugoslav federal army intervened; a ceasefire brokered by the European Community (EC) brought the withdrawal of the Yugoslav army.

**1992** Janez Drnovšek, a centrist Liberal Democrat, was appointed prime minister; independence was recognized by the EC and the USA. Slovenia was admitted into the United Nations (UN). Liberal Democrats and Christian Democrats won assembly elections.

**1996** The governing coalition was weakened by the withdrawal of ZLSD. LDS failed to win an overall majority in assembly elections.

**1997** A new government was formed by the ruling LDS, led by Prime Minister Janez Drnovsek. President Kucan was re-elected. The European Union (EU) agreed to open membership talks with Slovenia.

**slow-worm** harmless species of lizard *Anguis fragilis*, once common in Europe, now a protected species in Britain. Superficially resembling a snake, it is distinguished by its small mouth and movable eyelids. It is about 30 cm/1 ft long, and eats worms and slugs.

**SLR** abbreviation for *single-lens reflex*, a type of ◊camera in which the image can be seen through the lens before a picture is taken.

**slug** soft-bodied land-living gastropod (type of ◊mollusc) related to the snails, but without a shell, or with a much reduced shell. All slugs have a protective coat of slime and a distinctive head with protruding tentacles. The eyes are at the end of the tentacles, which are also used to smell and locate food. Slugs eat dead animal matter and plants; some species are carnivorous and eat other slugs, snails, and earthworms. Slugs are hermaphrodite (having both male and female organs). They can fertilize themselves, but usually mate with another. Slugs can live for up to three years, and are invertebrates (animals without backbones).

**small arms** one of the two main divisions of firearms: guns that can be carried by hand. The first small arms were portable handguns in use in the late 14th century, supported on the ground and ignited by hand. Today's small arms range from breech-loading single-shot rifles and shotguns to sophisticated automatic and semi-automatic weapons.

**smallpox** acute, highly contagious viral disease, marked by aches, fever, vomiting, and skin eruptions leaving pitted scars. Widespread vaccination programmes have wiped out this often fatal disease.

**smart card** plastic card with an embedded microprocessor and memory. It can store, for example, personal data, identification, and bank-account details, to enable it to be used as a credit or debit card. The card can be loaded with credits, which are then spent electronically, and reloaded as needed. Possible other uses range from hotel door 'keys' to passports.

**smart drug** any drug or combination of nutrients (vitamins, amino acids, minerals, and sometimes herbs) said to enhance the functioning of the brain, increase mental energy, lengthen the span of attention, and improve the memory. As yet there is no scientific evidence to suggest that these drugs have any significant effect on healthy people.

**smart weapon** programmable bomb or missile that can be guided to its target by laser technology, TV homing technology, or terrain-contour matching (TERCOM). A smart weapon relies on its pinpoint accuracy to destroy a target rather than on the size of its warhead.

**smell** sense that responds to chemical molecules in the air. It works by having receptors for particular chemical groups, into which the airborne chemicals must fit to trigger a message to the brain.

**smelt** small fish, usually marine, although some species are freshwater.

They occur in Europe and North America. The most common European smelt is the sparling *Osmerus eperlanus*.

**smelting** processing a metallic ore in a furnace to produce the metal. Oxide ores such as iron ore are smelted with coke (carbon), which reduces the ore into metal and also provides fuel for the process.

**Smetana, Bedřich** (1824–1884) Bohemian composer. He established a Czech nationalist style in, for example, the operas *Prodaná Nevěsta/The Bartered Bride* (1866) and *Dalibor* (1868), and the symphonic suite *Má Vlast/My Country* (1875–80). He conducted at the National Theatre of Prague (1866–74).

**Smith, Adam** (1723–1790) Scottish economist. He is often regarded as the founder of political economy. His *The Wealth of Nations* (1776) defined national wealth in terms of consumable goods and the labour that produces them, rather than in terms of bullion, as prevailing economic theories assumed. The ultimate cause of economic growth is explained by the division of labour – dividing a production process into several repetitive operations, each carried out by different workers, is more efficient. Smith advocated the free working of individual enterprise, and the necessity of 'free trade'.

**Smith, Ian (Douglas)** (1919–  ) Rhodesian politician. He was a founder of the Rhodesian Front in 1962 and prime minister (1964–79). In 1965 he made a unilateral declaration of Rhodesia's independence and, despite United Nations sanctions, maintained his regime with tenacity.

In 1979 he was succeeded as prime minister by Bishop Abel Muzorewa, when the country was renamed Zimbabwe. He was suspended from the Zimbabwe parliament in April 1987 and resigned in May as head of the white opposition party. In 1992 he helped found a new opposition party, the United Front.

**Smith, John** (1580–1631) English colonist. After an adventurous early life he took part in the colonization of Virginia, acting as president of the North American colony (1608–09). He explored New England in 1614, which he named, and published pamphlets on America and an autobiography. His trade with the Indians may have kept the colonists alive in the early years.

**Smith, William** (1769–1839) English geologist. He produced the first geological maps of England and Wales, setting the pattern for geological cartography. Often called the founder of stratigraphical geology, he determined the succession of English strata across the whole country, from the Carboniferous up to the Cretaceous. He also established their fossil specimens.

**smokeless fuel** fuel that does not give off any smoke when burned, because all the carbon is fully oxidized to carbon dioxide ($CO_2$). Natural gas, oil, and coke are smokeless fuels.

**smoking** inhaling the fumes from burning substances, generally ◊tobacco in the form of cigarettes. The practice is habit-forming and is dangerous to health, since carbon monoxide and other toxic materials result from the combustion process. A direct link between lung cancer and tobacco smoking was established in 1950; the habit is also linked to respiratory and coronary heart diseases. In the West, smoking is now forbidden in many public places because even *passive smoking* – breathing in fumes from other people's cigarettes – can be harmful.

**Smollett, Tobias George** (1721–1771) Scottish novelist. He wrote the picaresque novels *Roderick Random* (1748), *Peregrine Pickle* (1751), *Ferdinand Count Fathom* (1753), *Sir Launcelot Greaves* (1760–62), and *Humphrey Clinker* (1771). His novels are full of gusto and vivid characterization.

**smuggling** illegal import or export of prohibited goods or the evasion of customs duties on dutiable goods. Smuggling has a long tradition in most border and coastal regions; goods smuggled include tobacco, spirits, diamonds, gold, and illegal drugs.

**Smuts, Jan Christian** (1870–1950) South African politician and soldier; prime minister (1919–24 and 1939–48). He supported the Allies in both world wars and was a member of the British imperial war cabinet (1917–18).

**snail** air-breathing gastropod mollusc with a spiral shell. There are thousands of species, on land and in water. The typical snails of the genus *Helix* have two species in Europe. The common garden snail *H. aspersa* is very destructive to plants.

**snake** reptile of the suborder Serpentes of the order Squamata, which also includes lizards. Snakes are characterized by an elongated limbless body, possibly evolved because of subterranean ancestors. However, a team of US and Israeli palaeontologists rediscovered a fossil collection in 1996 which suggested that snakes evolved from sea-dwelling predators.

One of the striking internal modifications is the absence or greatly reduced size of the left lung. The skin is covered in scales, which are markedly wider underneath where they form. There are 3,000 species found in the tropical and temperate zones, but none in New Zealand, Ireland, Iceland, and near the poles. Only three species are found in Britain: the adder, smooth snake, and grass snake.

**snapdragon** perennial herbaceous plant belonging to the figwort family, with spikes of brightly coloured two-lipped flowers. (*Antirrhinum majus*, family Scrophulariaceae.)

**Snell's law of refraction** in optics, the rule that when a ray of light passes from one medium to another, the sine of the angle of incidence divided by the sine of the angle of refraction is equal to the ratio of the indices of refraction in the two media. For a ray passing from medium 1 to medium 2:

$$n_2/n_1 = \sin i/\sin r$$

where $n_1$ and $n_2$ are the refractive indices of the two media. The law was devised by the Dutch physicist, Willebrord Snell.

**snipe** marsh bird of the family Scolopacidae, order Charadriiformes, closely related to the ◊woodcock. Snipes use their long, straight bills to probe marshy ground for worms, insects, and molluscs. Their nests are made on the grass, and they lay four eggs.

**snooker** indoor game derived from ◊billiards (via pool). It is played with 22 balls: 15 red, one each of yellow, green, brown, blue, pink, and black, and one white cueball. A tapered pole (cue) is used to move the balls across the table. Red balls are worth one point when sunk, while the coloured balls have ascending values from two points for the yellow to seven points for the black. The world professional championship was first held in 1927. The world amateur championship was first held in 1963. A snooker World Cup team event was inaugurated at Bangkok, Thailand, in 1996. The International Olympic Committee recognized snooker as an Olympic sport in 1998; snooker is likely to make its Olympic debut at the Athens games in 2004.

**Snowdon** Welsh *Eryri*, highest mountain in Wales, 1,085 m/3,560 ft above sea level. Situated 16 km/10 mi southeast of the Menai Strait, it consists of a cluster of five peaks. At the foot of Snowdon are the Llanberis, Aberglaslyn, and Rhyd-ddu passes. A rack railway ascends to the summit from Llanberis. Snowdonia, the surrounding mountain range, was made a national park in 1951. It covers 2,188 sq km/845 sq mi of mountain, lakes, and forest land.

**snowdrop** small bulbous European plant; its white bell-shaped hanging flowers, tinged with green, are among the first to appear in early spring. (*Galanthus nivalis*, family Amaryllidaceae.)

**snow leopard** a type of ◊leopard.

**Soane, John** (1753–1837) English architect. His refined Neo-Classical designs anticipated contemporary taste. Soane was a master of the established conventions of Classical architecture; he also developed a highly individual style based on an elegantly mannered interpretation of Neo-Classicism. He designed his own house in Lincoln's Inn Fields, London (1812–13), now *Sir John Soane's Museum,* which he bequeathed to the nation in 1835, together with his collection of antiques, architectural elements and casts, papers, and drawings. Little remains of his extensive work at the Bank of England, London (rebuilt 1930–40).

**soap** mixture of the sodium salts of various ◊fatty acids: palmitic, stearic, and oleic acid. It is made by the action of sodium hydroxide (caustic soda) or potassium hydroxide (caustic potash) on fats of animal or vegetable origin. Soap makes grease and dirt disperse in water in a similar manner to a ◊detergent.

**Soares, Mario Alberto Nobre Lopes** (1924– ) Portuguese socialist politician, president 1986–96. Exiled in 1970, he returned to Portugal in 1974, and, as leader of the Portuguese Socialist Party, was prime minister 1976–78. He resigned as party leader in 1980, but in 1986 he was elected Portugal's first socialist president.

**Sobchak, Anatoly** (1937– ) Soviet centrist politician, mayor of St Petersburg (1990–96), cofounder of the Democratic Reform Movement (with former foreign minister ◊Shevardnadze), and member of the Soviet parliament (1989–91). He prominently resisted the abortive anti-Gorbachev coup of August 1991.

**Sobers, Garry (Garfield St Auburn)** (1936– ) West Indian Test cricketer, arguably the world's finest ever all rounder. He held the world individual record for the highest Test innings with 365 not out, until beaten by Brian Lara in 1994. He played county cricket for Nottinghamshire and, in a match against Glamorgan at Swansea in 1968, he became the first to score six sixes in an over in first-class cricket. He played for the West Indies on 93 occasions, and was captain 39 times. He was knighted for services to cricket in 1975.

*career highlights*
*all first-class cricket* runs: 28,315; average: 54.87; best: 365 not out (West Indies v. Pakistan 1957–58); wickets: 1,043; average: 27.74; best: 9–49 (West Indies v. Kent 1966)
*Test cricket* runs: 8,032; average: 57.78; best: 365 not out (v. Pakistan 1957–58); wickets: 235; average: 34.03; best: 6–73 (v. Australia 1968–69)

**soca** Latin Caribbean dance music, a mixture of *so*ul and *ca*lypso but closer to the latter. A soca band is likely to include conga drums, synthesizer, and a small horn section, as well as electric guitar, bass, and drums. Soca originated on Trinidad in the 1970s.

**Social and Liberal Democrats** official name for the British political party formed in 1988 from the former Liberal Party and most of the Social Democratic Party. The common name for the party is the *Liberal Democrats.*

**social costs and benefits** in economics, the costs and benefits to society as a whole that result from economic decisions. These include private costs (the financial cost of production incurred by firms) and benefits (the profits made by firms and the value to people of consuming goods and services) and external costs and benefits (affecting those not directly involved in production or consumption); pollution is one of the external costs.

**social democracy** political ideology or belief in the gradual evolution of a democratic ◊socialism within existing political structures. The earliest was the German Sozialde-mokratische Partei (SPD) in 1891 (today one of the two main German parties), which had been created in 1875 by the amalgamation of other groups including August Bebel's earlier German Social Democratic Workers' Party, founded in 1869. Parties along the lines of the German model were founded in the last two decades of the 19th century in a number of countries, including Austria, Belgium, the Netherlands, Hungary, Poland, and Russia. The British Labour Party is in the social democratic tradition.

**Social Democratic and Labour Party** (SDLP), Northern Ireland left-of-centre political party, formed in 1970. It aims ultimately at Irish unification, but has distanced itself from violent tactics, adopting a constitutional, conciliatory role. Its leader, John Hume, played a key role in the negotiations which ended in the 1998 Good Friday Agreement on power-sharing. It secured 24 of the 108 seats in the new Northern Ireland Assembly, elected in June 1998; the party's deputy leader, Seamus Mallon, was voted deputy first minister (to Ulster Unionist David Trimble) by the first meeting of the Assembly.

**Social Democratic Party** (SDP), British centrist political party 1981–90, formed by members of Parliament who resigned from the Labour Party. The 1983 and 1987 general elections were fought in alliance with the Liberal Party as the *Liberal/SDP Alliance.* A merger of the two parties was voted for by the SDP in 1987, and the new party became the ◊Social and Liberal Democrats, leaving a rump SDP that folded in 1990.

**social history** branch of history that documents the living and working conditions of people rather than affairs of state. In recent years, television programmes, books, and museums have helped to give social history a wide appeal.

**socialism** movement aiming to establish a classless society by substituting public for private ownership of the means of production, distribution, and exchange. The term has been used to describe positions as widely apart as anarchism and social democracy. Socialist ideas appeared in classical times; in early Christianity; among later Christian sects such as the ◊Anabaptists and ◊Diggers; and, in the 18th and early 19th centuries, were put forward as systematic political aims by Jean-Jacques Rousseau, Claude Saint-Simon, François Fourier, and Robert Owen, among others. See also Karl ◊Marx and Friedrich ◊Engels.

**Socialist Realism** officially approved type of art in the former USSR and other communist countries; in line with communist doctrine, art was expected to educate and inspire the people with optimistic works extolling the virtues of work and patriotism, but in effect it was mainly devoted to glorifying the state. In Soviet Russia, as in other totalitarian countries, the government controlled all artistic organizations, and all forms of artistic experimentation were seen as a sign of decadent Western influence. Although the term is used mainly with reference to painting, it can apply to literature and music.

**Social Realism** in painting, art that realistically depicts subjects of social concern, such as poverty and deprivation. Those described as Social Realists include: in the USA, members of the Ashcan School and Ben Shahn; in the UK, the 'kitchen-sink group', for example John Bratby; and in Mexico, the muralists José Orozco and Diego Rivera.

**social science** the group of academic disciplines that investigate how and why people behave the way they do, as individuals and in groups. The term originated with the 19th-century French thinker Auguste ◊Comte. The academic social sciences are generally listed as sociology, economics, anthropology, political science, and psychology.

**social security** state provision of financial aid to alleviate poverty. The term 'social security' was first applied officially in the USA, in the Social Security Act of 1935. In Britain it was first used officially in 1944, and following the Beveridge Report of 1942 a series of acts was passed from 1945 to widen the scope of social security. Basic entitlements of those paying National Insurance contributions in Britain include an old-age pension, unemployment benefit (known as jobseeker's allowance from October 1996), widow's pension, incapacity benefit, and payment during a period of sickness in one's working life (Statutory Sick Pay). Other benefits, which are non-contributory, include family credit, ◊income support, child benefit, and attendance allowance for those looking after sick or disabled people. It was announced in the March 1998 budget that family credit and the disabled working allowance would be replaced from October 1999 by a working families tax credit and disabled persons tax credit, to be administered by the Inland Revenue.

**Society Islands** French *Archipel de la Société,* archipelago in ◊French Polynesia, divided into the Windward Islands and the Leeward Islands; area 1,685 sq km/650 sq mi; population (1988) 162,600. The administrative headquarters is Papeete on ◊Tahiti. The *Windward Islands* (French *Iles du Vent)* have an area of 1,200 sq km/460 sq mi and a population (1988) of 140,300. They comprise Tahiti, Moorea (area 132 sq km/51 sq mi; population 7,000), Maio (or Tubuai Manu; 9 sq km/3.5 sq mi; population 200), and the smaller Tetiaroa and Mehetia. The *Leeward Islands* (French *Iles sous le Vent)* have an area of 404 sq km/156 sq mi and a population of 22,200 (1988). They comprise the volcanic islands of Raiatea (including the main town of Uturoa), Huahine, Bora-Bora, Maupiti, Tahaa, and four small atolls. Claimed by France in 1768, the group became a French protectorate in 1843 and a colony 1880.

**sociobiology** study of the biological basis of all social behaviour, including the application of population genetics to the evolution of behaviour. It builds on the concept of inclusive fitness, contained in the notion of the 'selfish gene'. Contrary to some popular interpretations, it does not assume that all behaviour is genetically determined.

**sociology** systematic study of the origin and constitution of human society, in particular of social order and social change, social conflict and social problems. It studies institutions such as the family, law, and the church, as well as concepts such as norm, role, and culture. Sociology attempts to study people in their social environment according to certain underlying moral, philosophical, and political codes of behaviour.

**Socrates** (c. 469–399 BC) Athenian philosopher. He wrote nothing but was immortalized in the dialogues of his pupil Plato. In his desire to combat the scepticism of the ◊sophists, Socrates asserted the possibility of genuine knowledge. In ethics, he put forward the view that the good person never knowingly does wrong. True knowledge emerges through dialogue and systematic questioning and an abandoning of uncritical claims to knowledge.

**Socratic method** method of teaching used by Socrates, in which he aimed to guide pupils to clear thinking on ethics and politics by asking questions and then exposing their inconsistencies in cross-examination. This method was effective against the ◊sophists.

**sodium** soft, waxlike, silver-white, metallic element, symbol Na (from Latin *natrium*), atomic number 11, relative atomic mass 22.989. It is one of the ◊alkali metals and has a very low density, being light enough to float on water. It is the sixth-most abundant element (the fourth-most abundant metal) in the Earth's crust. Sodium is highly reactive, oxidizing rapidly when exposed to air and reacting violently with water. Its most familiar compound is sodium chloride (common salt), which occurs naturally in the oceans and in salt deposits left by dried-up ancient seas.

**sodium chloride** or *common salt* or *table salt,* NaCl white, crystalline compound found widely in nature. It is a typical ionic solid with a high melting point (801°C/1,474°F); it is soluble in water, insoluble in organic solvents, and is a strong electrolyte when molten or in aqueous solution. Found in concentrated deposits, it is widely used in the food industry as a flavouring and preservative, and in the chemical industry in the manufacture of sodium, chlorine, and sodium carbonate.

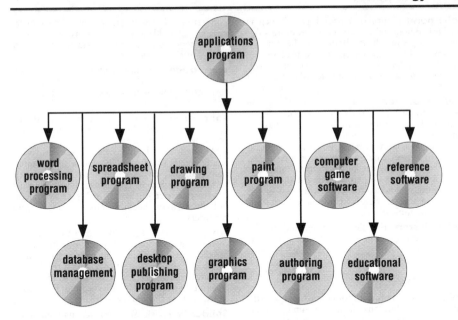

**software** *The various types of software application program that are available for computer systems.*

**sodium hydroxide** or *caustic soda,* NaOH the commonest alkali. The solid and the solution are corrosive. It is used to neutralize acids, in the manufacture of soap, and in oven cleaners. It is prepared industrially from sodium chloride by the ◊electrolysis of concentrated brine.

**Sofia** or *Sofiya,* capital of Bulgaria since 1878; population (1991) 1,221,000. Industries include textiles, rubber, machinery, and electrical equipment. It lies at the foot of the Vitosha Mountains.

**software** in computing, a collection of programs and procedures for making a computer perform a specific task, as opposed to ◊hardware, the physical components of a computer system. Software is created by programmers and is either distributed on a suitable medium, such as the ◊floppy disk, or built into the computer in the form of firmware. Examples of software include ◊operating systems, ◊compilers, and applications programs such as payrolls or word processors. No computer can function without some form of software.

**soft water** water that contains very few dissolved metal ions such as calcium ($Ca^{2+}$) or magnesium ($Mg^{2+}$). It lathers easily with soap, and no ◊scale is formed inside kettles or boilers. It has been found that the incidence of heart disease is higher in soft-water areas.

**soil** loose covering of broken rocky material and decaying organic matter overlying the bedrock of the Earth's surface. It is comprised of minerals, organic matter (called humus) derived from decomposed plants and organisms, living organisms, air, and water. Soils differ according to climate, parent material, rainfall, relief of the bedrock, and the proportion of organic material. The study of soils is *pedology.*

**soil erosion** the wearing away and redistribution of the Earth's soil layer.

It is caused by the action of water, wind, and ice, and also by improper methods of ◊agriculture. If unchecked, soil erosion results in the formation of deserts (◊desertification). It has been estimated that 20% of the world's cultivated topsoil was lost between 1950 and 1990.

**Sokoto** state in Nigeria, established 1976; capital Sokoto; area 102,500 sq km/39,565 sq mi; population (1991) 4,392,400. It was an Islamic Fula sultanate from the 16th century until occupied by the British in 1903.

**solar energy** energy derived from the Sun's radiation. The amount of energy falling on just 1 sq km/0.3861 sq mi is about 4,000 megawatts, enough to heat and light a small town. In one second the Sun gives off 13 million times more energy than all the electricity used in the USA in one year. *Solar heaters* have industrial or domestic uses. They usually consist of a black (heat-absorbing) panel containing pipes through which air or water, heated by the Sun, is circulated, either by thermal ◊convection or by a pump.

Solar energy may also be harnessed indirectly using *solar cells* (photovoltaic cells) made of panels of ◊semiconductor material (usually silicon), which generate electricity when illuminated by sunlight. Although it is difficult to generate a high output from solar energy compared to sources such as nuclear or fossil fuels, it is a major nonpolluting and renewable energy source used as far north as Scandinavia as well as in the southwestern USA and in Mediterranean countries.

**solar pond** natural or artificial 'pond', such as the Dead Sea, in which salt becomes more soluble in the Sun's heat. Water at the bottom becomes saltier and hotter, and is insulated by the less salty water layer at the top. Temperatures at the bottom reach about 100°C/212°F and can be used to generate electricity.

**solar radiation** radiation given off by the Sun, consisting mainly of visible light, ◊ultraviolet radiation, and ◊infrared radiation, although the whole spectrum of ◊electromagnetic waves is present, from radio waves to X-rays. High-energy charged particles, such as electrons, are also emitted, especially from solar ◊flares. When these reach the Earth, they cause magnetic storms (disruptions of the Earth's magnetic field), which interfere with radio communications.

**Solar System** the ◊Sun (a star) and all the bodies orbiting it: the nine ◊planets (Mercury, Venus, Earth, Mars, Jupiter, Saturn, Uranus, Neptune, and Pluto), their moons, the asteroids, and the comets. The Sun contains 99.86% of the mass of the Solar System.

**solar wind** stream of atomic particles, mostly protons and electrons, from the Sun's corona, flowing outwards at speeds of between 300 kps/200 mps and 1,000 kps/600 mps.

**solder** any of various alloys used when melted for joining metals such as copper, its common alloys (brass and bronze), and tin-plated steel, as used for making food cans.

**soldier beetle** reddish beetle with soft, black elytra (wing cases) and a black patch and black legs. It reaches a length of 15 mm/0.5 in and can be found in the daytime during the months of April to July on field, garden, and forest plants. It feeds particularly on aphids. Its larvae are black, and are to be found in the soil or among moss.

The soldier beetle is in family Cantharidae, order Coleoptera, class Insecta, phylum Arthropoda.

**sole** flatfish found in temperate and tropical waters. The *common sole Solea solea,* also called *Dover sole,* is found in the southern seas of northwestern Europe. Up to 50 cm/20 in long, it is a prized food fish, as is the *sand* or *French sole Pegusa lascaris* further south.

**solenodon** rare insectivorous shrewlike mammal, genus *Solenodon.* There are two species, one each on Cuba and Hispaniola. They are about 30 cm/12 in long with a 25 cm/10 in naked tail, shaggy hair, long, pointed snouts, and strong claws, and they produce venomous saliva. They are slow-moving, come out mostly at night, and eat insects, worms, and other invertebrate animals. They are threatened with extinction owing to introduced predators.

**solenoid** coil of wire, usually cylindrical, in which a magnetic field is created by passing an electric current through it (see ◊electromagnet). This field can be used to move an iron rod placed on its axis.

Mechanical valves attached to the rod can be operated by switching the current on or off, so converting electrical energy into mechanical energy. Solenoids are used to relay energy from the battery of a car to the starter motor by means of the ignition switch.

**sole trader** or *sole proprietor,* one person who runs a business, receiving all profits and responsible for all liabilities. Many small businesses are sole traders.

**solicitor** in the UK, a member of one of the two branches of the English legal profession, the other being a ◊barrister.

A solicitor is a lawyer who provides all-round legal services (making wills, winding up estates, conveyancing, divorce, and litigation). A solicitor cannot appear at High Court level, but must brief a barrister on behalf of his or her client. Solicitors may become circuit judges and recorders.

**solid** in physics, a state of matter that holds its own shape (as opposed to a liquid, which takes up the shape of its container, or a gas, which totally fills its container). According to ◊kinetic theory, the atoms or molecules in a solid are not free to move but merely vibrate about fixed positions, such as those in crystal lattices.

**Solidarity** Polish *Solidarność,* national confederation of independent trade unions in Poland, formed under the leadership of Lech ◊Wałęsa in September 1980. An illegal organization from 1981 to 1989, it was then elected to head the Polish government. Divisions soon emerged in the leadership and in 1990 its political wing began to fragment (Wałęsa resigned as chairman in December of that year). In the September 1993 elections Solidarity gained less than 5% of the popular vote but, in September 1997, under the leadership of Marian Krzaklewski, Solidarity Electoral Action (AWS) won 34% of the vote and led the subsequent coalition government with Jerzy Buzek as prime minister.

**solid-state circuit** electronic circuit where all the components (resistors, capacitors, transistors, and diodes) and interconnections are made at the same time, and by the same processes, in or on one piece of single-crystal silicon. The small size of this construction accounts for its use in electronics for space vehicles and aircraft.

**solipsism** in philosophy, a view that maintains that the self is the only thing that can be known to exist. It is an extreme form of ◊scepticism. The solipsist sees himself or herself as the only individual in existence, assuming other people to be a reflection of his or her own consciousness.

**Solomon** (c. 974– c. 922 BC) In the Old Testament, third king of Israel, son of David by Bathsheba. During a peaceful reign, he was famed for his wisdom and his alliances with Egypt and Phoenicia. The much later biblical Proverbs, Ecclesiastes, and Song of Songs are attributed to him. He built the temple in Jerusalem with the aid of heavy taxation and forced labour, resulting in the revolt of northern Israel.

### Solomon Islands
*area* 27,600 sq km/10,656 sq mi
*capital* Honiara (on Guadalcanal) (and chief port)

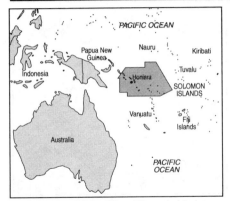

**major towns/cities** Gizo, Kieta, Auki
**major ports** Yandina
**physical features** comprises all but the northernmost islands (which belong to Papua New Guinea) of a Melanesian archipelago stretching nearly 1,500 km/900 mi. The largest is Guadalcanal (area 6,500 sq km/2,510 sq mi); others are Malaita, San Cristobal, New Georgia, Santa Isabel, Choiseul; mainly mountainous and forested
**head of state** Queen Elizabeth II, represented by governor general Moses Pitakaka from 1994
**head of government** Bartholomew Ulufa'alu from 1997
**political system** constitutional monarchy
**political parties** Group for National Unity and Reconciliation (GNUR), centrist coalition; National Coalition Partners (NCP), broad-based coalition; People's Progressive Party (PPP); People's Alliance Party (PAP)
**currency** Solomon Island dollar
**GNP per capita (PPP)** (US$) 2,080 (1998)
**exports** timber, fish products, oil palm products, copra, cocoa, coconut oil. Principal market: Japan 59.2% (1997)
**population** 430,000 (1999 est)
**language** English (official); there are some 120 Melanesian dialects spoken by 85% of the population, and Papuan and Polynesian languages
**religion** Anglican, Roman Catholic, South Sea Evangelical, other Protestant
**life expectancy** 70 (men); 74 (women) (1995–2000)
**Chronology**
**1568** The islands, rumoured in South America to be the legendary gold-rich 'Islands of Solomon', were first sighted by Spanish navigator Alvaro de Mendana, journeying from Peru.
**1595 and 1606** Unsuccessful Spanish efforts to settle the islands, which had long been peopled by Melanesians.
**later 18th century** Visited again by Europeans.
**1840s** Christian missions established.
**1870s** Development of copra export trade and shipment of islanders to work on sugar cane plantations in Australia and Fiji Islands.
**1886** Northern Solomon Islands became German protectorate.
**1893** Southern Solomon Islands placed under British protection.

**1899** Germany ceded Solomon Islands possessions to Britain in return for British recognition of its claims to Western Samoa.
**1900** Unified British Solomon Islands Protectorate formed and placed under jurisdiction of Western Pacific High Commission (WPHC), with its headquarters in Fiji Islands.
**1942–43** Occupied by Japan. Site of fierce fighting, especially on Guadalcanal, which was recaptured by US forces, with the loss of 21,000 Japanese and 5,000 US troops.
**1943–50** Development of Marching Rule (Ma'asina Ruru) cargo cult populist movement on Malaita island, campaigning for self-rule.
**1945** Headquarters of WPHC moved to Honiara.
**1960** Legislative and executive councils established by constitution.
**1974** Became substantially self-governing, with Solomon Mamaloni of centre-left People's Progressive Party (PPP) as chief minister.
**1976** Became fully self-governing, with Peter Kenilorea of right-of-centre Solomon Islands United Party (SIUPA) as chief minister.
**1978** Independence achieved from Britain within Commonwealth, with Kenilorea as prime minister.
**1981** Mamaloni (PPP) became prime minister, pledging to decentralize power.
**1984** Kenilorea returned to power, heading a coalition government.
**1986** Kenilorea resigned after allegations of corruption; he was replaced by his deputy, Ezekiel Alebua.
**1988** Kenilorea was elected deputy prime minister. The Solomon Islands joined Vanuatu and Papua New Guinea to form the Spearhead Group, aiming to preserve Melanesian cultural traditions.
**1989** Mamaloni, now leader of People's Alliance Party (PAP), was appointed prime minister.
**1990** Mamaloni resigned as PAP party leader, but continued as head of a government of national unity, which included Kenilorea as foreign minister.
**1993** A new Mamaloni-led coalition won the largest number of seats in a general election, but Francis Billy Hilly, an independent politician, was appointed prime minister.
**1994** Billy Hilly resigned; Mamaloni returned to power.
**1997** Bartholomew Ulufa'alu was elected prime minister.
**1998** Ulufa'alu's Alliance for Change government narrowly survived a no-confidence vote.

**Solomon's seal** any of a group of perennial plants belonging to the lily family, native to Europe and found growing in moist, shady woodland areas. They have drooping bell-like white or greenish-white flowers which appear just above the point where the leaves join the arching stems, followed by blue or black berries. (Genus *Polygonatum*, family Liliaceae.)

**Solon** (c. 638–c. 558 BC) Athenian statesman. As one of the chief magistrates about 594 BC, he carried out the cancellation of all debts from which land or liberty was the security and the revision of the constitution that laid the foundations of Athenian democracy. He was one of the Seven Sages of Greece.

**solstice** either of the days on which the Sun is farthest north or south of the celestial equator each year. The *summer solstice,* when the Sun is farthest north, occurs around 21 June; the *winter solstice* around 22 December.

**solubility** measure of the amount of solute (usually a solid or gas) that will dissolve in a given amount of solvent (usually a liquid) at a particular temperature. Solubility may be expressed as grams of solute per 100 grams of solvent or, for a gas, in parts per million (ppm) of solvent.

**solute** substance that is dissolved in another substance (see ◊solution).

**solution** two or more substances mixed to form a single, homogenous phase. One of the substances is the *solvent* and the others (*solutes*) are said to be dissolved in it.

**solution** in earth science, the process by which the minerals in a rock are dissolved in water. It is also referred to as *corrosion.* Solution is one of the processes of ◊erosion as well as ◊weathering (in which the dissolution of rock occurs without transport of the dissolved material). An example of this is when weakly acidic rainfall causes carbonation.

**solvent** substance, usually a liquid, that will dissolve another substance (see ◊solution). Although the commonest solvent is water, in popular use the term refers to low-boiling-point organic liquids, which are harmful if used in a confined space. They can give rise to respiratory problems, liver damage, and neurological complaints.

**Solyman I** alternative spelling of ◊Suleiman, Ottoman sultan.

**Solzhenitsyn, Alexander Isayevich** (1918– ) Soviet novelist. He became a US citizen (1974). He was in prison and exile from 1945–57 for anti-Stalinist comments. Much of his writing is semi-autobiographical and highly critical of the system, including *One Day in the Life of Ivan Denisovich* (1962), which deals with the labour camps under Stalin, and *The Gulag Archipelago* (1973), an exposé of the whole Soviet labour-camp network. This led to his expulsion from the USSR in 1974. He was awarded a Nobel prize in 1970.

**Somali** member of a group of East African peoples from the Horn of Africa. Although the majority of Somalis live in the Somali Republic, there are minorities in Ethiopia and Kenya. Primarily nomadic pastoralists and traders, they live in families, grouped in clans, under an elective or hereditary chieftain. They are mainly Sunni Muslims. Their Cushitic language belongs to the Hamitic branch of the Afro-Asiatic family.

**Somalia** Somali Democratic Republic
*national name Jamhuriyadda Dimugradiga ee Soomaliya*
*area* 637,700 sq km/246,215 sq mi

*capital* Mogadishu (and port)
*major towns/cities* Hargeysa, Berbera, Kismayo, Marka
*major ports* Berbera, Marka, Kismayo
*physical features* mainly flat, with hills in north
*head of state and government (interim)* Hussein Aidid from 1996
*political system* transitional
*political parties* parties are mainly clan-based and include the United Somali Congress (USC), Hawiye clan; Somali Patriotic Movement (SPM), Darod clan; Somali Southern Democratic Front (SSDF), Majertein clan; Somali Democratic Alliance (SDA), Gadabursi clan; United Somali Front (USF), Issa clan; Somali National Movement (SNM) based in self-proclaimed Somaliland Republic
*currency* Somali shilling
*GNP per capita (PPP)* (US$) 620 (1996 est)
*exports* livestock, skins and hides, bananas, fish and fish products, myrrh. Principal market: Saudi Arabia 57.9% (1997)
*population* 9,672,000 (1999 est)
*language* Somali, Arabic (both official), Italian, English
*religion* Sunni Muslim
*life expectancy* 45 (men); 49 (women) (1995–2000)
*Chronology*
**8th–10th centuries** Arab ancestors of Somali clan families migrated to the region and introduced Sunni Islam; coastal trading cities, including Mogadishu, were formed by Arabian immigrants and developed into sultanates.
**11th–14th century** Southward and westward movement of Somalis and Islamization of Christian Ethiopian interior.
**early 16th century** Portuguese contacts with coastal region.
**1820s** First British contacts with northern Somalia.
**1884–87** British protectorate of Somaliland established in north.
**1889** Italian protectorate of Somalia established in south.
**1927** Italian Somalia became a colony and part of Italian East Africa from 1936.
**1941** Italian Somalia occupied by Britain during World War II.
**1943** Somali Youth League (SYL) formed as nationalist party.

*1950* Italy resumed control over Italian Somalia under UN trusteeship.
*1960* Independence achieved from Italy and Britain as Somalia, with Aden Abdullah Osman as president.
*1963* Border dispute with Kenya; diplomatic relations broken with Britain for five years.
*1967* Dr Abdirashid Ali Shermarke (SYL) became president.
*1969* President Ibrahim Egal assassinated in army coup led by Maj-Gen Muhammad Siad Barre; constitution suspended, political parties banned, Supreme Revolutionary Council set up, and socialist-Islamic state formed.
*1972* 20,000 died in severe drought.
*1978* Defeated in eight-month war with Ethiopia fought on behalf of Somali guerrillas in Ogaden to the southwest. Armed insurrection began in north and hundreds of thousands became refugees.
*1979* New constitution for socialist one-party state dominated by Somali Revolutionary Socialist Party (SRSP).
*1982* The antigovernment Ethiopian-backed Somali National Movement (SNM) was formed in the north, followed by oppressive counter-measures by the government.
*late 1980s* Guerrilla activity increased in the north as the civil war intensified.
*1991* Mogadishu was captured by rebels; Barre fled; Ali Mahdi Muhammad was named president; free elections were promised. The secession of northeast Somalia, as the Somaliland Republic, was announced but not recognized internationally.
*1992* There was widespread famine. Western food-aid convoys were hijacked by 'warlords'. United Nations (UN) peacekeeping troops, led by US Marines, were sent in to protect relief operations.
*1993* Leaders of armed factions (except the Somaliland-based faction) agreed to a federal system of government. US-led UN forces destroyed the headquarters of warlord Gen Muhammad Farah Aidid after the killing of Pakistani peacekeepers.
*1994* Ali Mahdi Muhammad and Aidid signed a truce. Most Western peacekeeping troops were withdrawn, but clan-based fighting continued.
*1995* The last UN peacekeepers were withdrawn.
*1996* Aidid was killed in renewed faction fighting; his son Hussein Aidid succeeded him as interim president.
*1998* A peace plan was agreed.
*1999* In June the Ethiopian army, supporting opponents of Aidid, invaded Somalia.

**Somaliland** region of Somali-speaking peoples in eastern Africa including the former British Somaliland Protectorate (established in 1887) and Italian Somaliland (made a colony in 1927, conquered by Britain in 1941, and administered by Britain until 1950) – which both became independent in 1960 as the Somali Democratic Republic, the official name for Somalia – and former French Somaliland, which was established in 1888, became known as the Territory of the Afars and Issas in 1967, and became independent as Djibouti in 1977.

**Somerset** county of southwest England
*area* 3,460 sq km/1,336 sq mi
*towns* Taunton (administrative headquarters); Bridgwater, Frome, Glastonbury, Wells, Yeovil; Burnham-on-Sea, Minehead (coastal resorts)
*physical* rivers Avon, Axe, Brue, Exe, Parret (the principal river), and Yeo; marshy coastline on the Bristol Channel; Mendip Hills; Quantock Hills; Exmoor; Blackdown Hills
*features* Cheddar Gorge and Wookey Hole, a series of limestone caves where Stone Age flint implements and bones of extinct animals have been found; Glastonbury Tor
*agriculture* apples; dairy farming; cereals (wheat, barley, oats), vegetables (turnips, mangolds (a root vegetable used as animal feed)); cider; cattle and sheep rearing; willows (withies) for wickerwork
*industries* agricultural implements; Bath-bricks (manufactured at Bridgwater from the sand of the Parret); chemicals; dairy products (including Cheddar cheese); engineering; food processing; helicopters; leather; mineral working (iron, lead, zinc); stone quarrying (slate); textiles; tourism
*population* (1996) 482,600
*famous people* Roger Bacon, Ernest Bevin, Arthur C Clarke, Henry Fielding, John Locke, John Pym.

**Somerset, Edward Seymour**, 1st Duke of Somerset (*c.* 1506–1552) English politician. Created Earl of Hertford after Henry VIII's marriage to his sister Jane, he became Duke of Somerset and protector (regent) for Edward VI in 1547. His attempt to check ◊enclosure (the transfer of land from common to private ownership) offended landowners and his moderation in religion upset the Protestants, and he was eventually beheaded on a treason charge in 1552. Knighted in 1523, viscount in 1536, earl in 1537.

**Somme** river in northern France, on which Amiens and Abbeville stand; length 245 km/152 mi. It rises in Aisne *département* near St-Quentin and flows west through Somme *département* to the English Channel near St Valéry-sur-Somme. It is connected by canal with the Oise and the Schelde (French Escaut). Its tributaries include the rivers Ancre and Avre.
Some of the heaviest fighting of World War I took place on the banks of the Somme, especially in July–November 1916 (see ◊Somme, Battle of the).

**Somme, Battle of the** Allied offensive in World War I during July–November 1916 on the River Somme in northern France, during which severe losses were suffered by both sides. It was planned by the Marshal of France, Joseph Joffre, and UK commander-in-chief Douglas Haig; the Allies lost over 600,000 soldiers and advanced 13 km/8 mi. It was the first battle in which tanks were used. The German offensive around St Quentin during March–April 1918 is sometimes called the Second Battle of the Somme.

**Somoza (García), Anastasio** (1896–1956) Nicaraguan soldier and politician, president from 1937–47 and 1950–56. As head of the

Nicaraguan army, he deposed President Juan Bautista Sacasa, his uncle, in 1936 and assumed the presidency the following year, ruling as a virtual dictator from 1937 until his assassination in 1956. He exiled most of his political opponents and amassed a considerable fortune in land and businesses. Members of his family retained control of the country until 1979, when they were overthrown by popular forces.

**sonar** acronym for *sound navigation and ranging,* method of locating underwater objects by the reflection of ultrasonic waves. The time taken for an acoustic beam to travel to the object and back to the source enables the distance to be found since the velocity of sound in water is known. Sonar devices, or *echo sounders,* were developed in 1920, and are the commonest means of underwater navigation.

**sonata** (Italian 'sounded') in music, an essay in instrumental composition for a solo player or a small ensemble and consisting of a single movement or series of movements. The name signifies that the work is not beholden to a text or existing dance form, but is self-sufficient.

**song** a setting of words to music for one or more singers, with or without instrumental accompaniment. Song may be sacred, for example a psalm, motet, or cantata, or secular, for example a folk song or ballad. In verse song, the text changes in mood while the music remains the same; in ◊lied and other forms of art song, the music changes in response to the emotional development of the text.

**song cycle** sequence of songs related in mood and sung as a group, used by romantic composers such as Schubert, Schumann, and Wolf.

**Songhai Empire** former kingdom of northwestern Africa, founded in the 8th century, which developed into a powerful Muslim empire under the rule of Sonni Ali (reigned 1464–92). It superseded the ◊Mali Empire and extended its territory, occupying an area that included parts of present-day Guinea, Burkina Faso, Senegal, Gambia, Mali, Mauritania, Niger, and Nigeria. In 1591 it was invaded and overthrown by Morocco.

**sonic boom** noise like a thunderclap that occurs when an aircraft passes through the ◊sound barrier, or begins to travel faster than the speed of sound. It happens when the cone-shaped shock wave caused by the plane touches the ground.

**sonnet** fourteen-line poem of Italian origin introduced to England by Thomas Wyatt in the form used by Petrarch (rhyming *abba abba cdcdcd* or *cdecde*) and followed by Milton and Wordsworth; Shakespeare used the form *abab cdcd efef gg.*

**sophist** (Greek *sophistes* 'wise man') in ancient Greece, one of a group of 5th-century BC itinerant lecturers on culture, rhetoric, and politics. Sceptical about the possibility of achieving genuine knowledge, they applied bogus reasoning and were concerned with winning arguments rather than establishing the truth. ◊Plato regarded them as dishonest and *sophistry* came

to mean fallacious reasoning. In the 2nd century AD the term was linked to the art of public speaking.

**Sophocles** (*c.* 496–406 BC) Athenian dramatist. He is attributed with having developed tragedy by introducing a third actor and scene-painting, and ranked with ◊Aeschylus and ◊Euripides as one of the three great tragedians. He wrote some 120 plays, of which seven tragedies survive. These are *Antigone* (443 BC), *Oedipus the King* (429), *Electra* (410), *Ajax, Trachiniae, Philoctetes* (409 BC), and *Oedipus at Colonus* (401) (produced after his death).

**soprano** the highest range of the female voice, stretching from around D4 to A6. Some operatic roles require the extended upper range of a ◊coloratura soprano, reaching to around F6, for example Kiri ◊Te Kanawa. Some instruments use the prefix soprano for those models which sound in the compass of the soprano voice.

**sorghum** or *great millet* or *Guinea corn,* any of a group of ◊cereal grasses native to Africa but cultivated widely in India, China, the USA, and southern Europe. The seeds are used for making bread. Durra is a member of the genus. (Genus *Sorghum.*)

**sorrel** (Old French *sur* 'sour') any of several plants belonging to the buckwheat family. *R. acetosa* is grown for its bitter salad leaves. ◊Dock plants are of the same genus. (Genus *Rumex,* family Polygonaceae.)

**SOS** internationally recognized distress signal, using letters of the ◊Morse code (... – – – ...).

**Sotho** a large ethnic group in southern Africa, numbering about 7 million (1987) and living mainly in Botswana, Lesotho, and South Africa. The Sotho are predominantly farmers, living in small village groups. They speak a variety of closely related languages belonging to the Bantu branch of the Niger-Congo family. With English, Sotho is the official language of Lesotho.

**soul music** emotionally intense style of ◊rhythm and blues sung by, among others, Sam Cooke, Aretha Franklin, and Al Green. A synthesis of blues, gospel music, and jazz, it emerged in the 1950s. Sometimes all popular music made by African-Americans is labelled soul music.

**sound** physiological sensation received by the ear, originating in a vibration that communicates itself as a pressure variation in the air and travels in every direction, spreading out as an expanding sphere. All sound waves in air travel with a speed dependent on the temperature; under ordinary conditions, this is about 330 m/1,070 ft per second. The pitch of the sound depends on the number of vibrations imposed on the air per second (◊frequency), but the speed is unaffected. The loudness of a sound is dependent primarily on the amplitude of the vibration of the air.

**sound barrier** concept that the speed of sound, or sonic speed (about 1,220 kph/760 mph at sea level), constitutes a speed limit to flight through the atmosphere, since a badly designed aircraft suffers severe buffeting at near sonic speed owing to the formation of shock waves. US test pilot Chuck Yeager first flew through the 'barrier' in 1947 in a Bell X-1 rocket plane. Now, by careful design, such aircraft as Concorde can fly at supersonic speed with ease, though they create in their wake a ◊sonic boom.

**sound synthesis** the generation of sound (usually music) by electronic ◊synthesizer.

**soundtrack** band at one side of a cine film on which the accompanying sound is recorded. Usually it takes the form of an optical track (a pattern of light and shade). The pattern is produced on the film when signals from the recording microphone are made to vary the intensity of a light beam. During playback, a light is shone through the track on to a photocell, which converts the pattern of light falling on it into appropriate electrical signals. These signals are then fed to loudspeakers to recreate the original sounds.

**South Africa** Republic of
***national name*** *Republiek van Suid-Afrika*

**area** 1,222,081 sq km/471,845 sq mi
**capital** Cape Town (legislative) (and port), Pretoria (administrative), Bloemfontein (judicial)
***major towns/cities*** Johannesburg, Durban, Port Elizabeth, Vereeniging, East London, Pietermaritzburg, Kimberley
***major ports*** Durban, Port Elizabeth, East London
***physical features*** southern end of large plateau, fringed by mountains and lowland coastal margin; Drakensberg Mountains, Table Mountain; Limpopo and Orange rivers
**territories** Marion Island and Prince Edward Island in the Antarctic
***head of state and government*** Thabo Mbeki from 1999
***political system*** liberal democracy
***political parties*** African National Congress (ANC), left of centre; National Party (NP), right

of centre; Inkatha Freedom Party (IFP), centrist, multiracial (formerly Zulu nationalist); Freedom Front (FF), right wing; Democratic Party (DP), moderate, centre left, multiracial; Pan-Africanist Congress (PAC), black, left wing; African Christian Democratic Party (ACDP), Christian, right of centre
**currency** rand
***GNP per capita (PPP)*** (US$) 6,990 (1998 est)
**exports** metals and metal products, gold, precious and semiprecious stones, mineral products and chemicals, natural cultured pearls, machinery and mechanical appliances, wool, maize, fruit, sugar. Principal market: UK 10.1% (1997)
***population*** 39,900,000 (1999 est)
***language*** English and Afrikaans (both official); main African languages: Xhosa, Zulu, and Sesotho (all official)
***religion*** Dutch Reformed Church and other Christian denominations, Hindu, Muslim
***life expectancy*** 52 (men); 58 (women) (1995–2000)
***Chronology***
***1652*** Dutch East India Company established colony at Cape Town as a port of call.
***1795*** Britain occupied Cape after France conquered the Netherlands.
***1814*** Britain bought Cape Town and hinterland from the Netherlands for £6 million.
***1820s*** Zulu people established military kingdom under Shaka.
***1836–38*** The Great Trek: 10,000 Dutch settlers (known as Boers, meaning 'farmers') migrated north to escape British rule.
***1843*** Britain established colony of Natal on east coast.
***1852–54*** Britain recognized Boer republics of Transvaal and Orange Free State.
***1872*** The Cape became self-governing colony within British Empire.
***1877*** Britain annexed Transvaal.
***1879*** Zulu War: Britain destroyed power of Zulus.
***1881*** First Boer War: Transvaal Boers defeated British at Majuba Hill and regained independence.
***1886*** Discovery of gold on Witwatersrand attracted many migrant miners (uitlanders) to Transvaal, which denied them full citizenship.
***1895*** Jameson Raid: uitlanders, backed by Cecil Rhodes, tried to overthrow President Paul Kruger of Transvaal.
***1899–1902*** Second South African War (also known as Boer War): dispute over rights of uitlanders led to conflict which ended with British annexation of Boer republics.
***1907*** Britain granted internal self-government to Transvaal and Orange Free State on whites-only franchise.
***1910*** Cape Colony, Natal, Transvaal, and Orange Free State formed Union of South Africa, with Louis Botha as prime minister.
***1912*** Gen Barry Hertzog founded (Boer) Nationalist Party; ANC formed to campaign for rights of black majority.
***1914*** Boer revolt in Orange Free State suppressed; South African troops fought for British Empire in World War I.

**1919** Jan Smuts succeeded Botha as premier; South West Africa (Namibia) became South African mandate.

**1924** Hertzog became prime minister, aiming to sharpen racial segregation and loosen ties with British Empire.

**1939–45** Smuts led South Africa into World War II despite neutralism of Hertzog; South African troops fought with Allies in Middle East, East Africa, and Italy.

**1948** Policy of apartheid ('separateness') adopted when National Party (NP) took power under Daniel Malan; continued by his successors Johannes Strijdom 1954–58, Hendrik Verwoerd 1958–66, B J Vorster 1966–78, and P J Botha 1978–89.

**1950** Entire population classified by race; Group Areas Act segregated blacks and whites; ANC responded with campaign of civil disobedience.

**1960** 70 black demonstrators killed at Sharpville; ANC banned.

**1961** South Africa left Commonwealth and became republic.

**1964** ANC leader Nelson Mandela sentenced to life imprisonment.

**1967** Terrorism Act introduced indefinite detention without trial.

**1970s** Over 3 million people forcibly resettled in black 'homelands'.

**1976** Over 600 killed in clashes between black protesters and security forces in Soweto.

**1984** New constitution gave segregated representation to coloureds and Asians, but continued to exclude blacks.

**1985** Growth of violence in black townships led to proclamation of state of emergency.

**1986** USA and Commonwealth imposed limited economic sanctions against South Africa.

**1989** F W de Klerk succeeded P W Botha as president; public facilities were desegregated; many ANC activists were released.

**1990** The ban on the ANC was lifted; Mandela was released; talks began between the government and the ANC; there was a daily average of 35 murders.

**1991** De Klerk repealed the remaining apartheid laws; sanctions were lifted; however, there was severe fighting between the ANC and the Zulu Inkatha movement.

**1993** An interim majority rule constitution was adopted; de Klerk and Mandela agreed to form a government of national unity after free elections.

**1994** The ANC were victorious in the first nonracial elections; Mandela became president; Commonwealth membership was restored.

**1996** De Klerk withdrew the NP from the coalition after the new constitution failed to provide for power-sharing after 1999.

**1997** A new constitution was signed by President Mandela. De Klerk announced his retirement from politics.

**1999** Mandela retired as state president; he was succeeded by Thabo Mbeki; ANC won assembly majority in election.

**South African Wars** two wars between the Boers (settlers of Dutch origin) and the British; essentially fought for the gold and diamonds of the Transvaal.

The *War of 1881* was triggered by the attempt of the Boers of the ◊Transvaal to reassert the independence surrendered in 1877 in return for British aid against African peoples. The British were defeated at Majuba, and the Transvaal again became independent.

The *War of 1899–1902*, also known as the *Boer War,* was preceded by the armed Jameson Raid into the Boer Transvaal, a failed attempt, inspired by the Cape Colony prime minister Cecil Rhodes, to precipitate a revolt against Paul Kruger, the Transvaal president. The *uitlanders* (non-Boer immigrants) were still not given the vote by the Boers, negotiations failed, and the Boers invaded British territory, besieging Ladysmith, Mafeking (now Mafikeng), and Kimberley. The war ended with the Peace of Vereeniging following the Boer defeat.

**South America** fourth largest of the continents, nearly twice as large as Europe (13% of the world's land surface), extending south from ◊Central America

*area* 17,864,000 sq km/6,900,000 sq mi

*largest cities* (population over 3.5 million) Buenos Aires, São Paulo, Rio de Janeiro, Bogotá, Santiago, Lima, Caracas

*features* Lake Titicaca (the world's highest navigable lake); La Paz (highest capital city in the world); Atacama Desert; Inca ruins at Machu Picchu; rivers include the Amazon (world's largest and second longest), Paraná, Madeira, São Francisco, Purús, Paraguay, Orinoco, Araguaia, Negro, Uruguay

*physical* occupying the southern part of the landmass of the western hemisphere, the South American continent stretches from Point Gallinas on the Caribbean coast of Colombia to Cape Horn at the southern tip of Horn Island, which lies adjacent to Tierra del Fuego; the most southerly point on the mainland is Cape Froward on the Brunswick peninsula, southern Chile; at its maximum width (5,120 km/3,200 mi) the continent stretches from Point Pariñas, Peru, in the extreme west to Point Coqueiros, just north of Recife, Brazil, in the east; five-sixths of the continent lies in the southern hemisphere and two-thirds within the tropics.

**Southampton** industrial city, seaport, and unitary authority in southern England, at the head of Southampton Water, 20 km/12 mi southwest of Winchester; it was part of the county of Hampshire to 1997

*area* 52 sq km/20 sq mi

*features* Southampton University, established in 1952; ferry link to the Isle of Wight; the port is a base for many liners, including P&O's *Oriana;* Southampton City Art Gallery; parts of the medieval town wall survive, including four of the town-wall towers, and Bargate, the elaborate old north gateway to the city; the partly Norman St Michael's Church has an 18th-century spire 50 m/164 ft high; the 14th-century Wool House now houses a maritime museum; Tudor House Museum, situated in a half-timbered 15th-century building; the hospital of God's House was originally founded in 1185 for

pilgrims going either to the shrine of St Swithin at Winchester, or to Canterbury; 15th-century God's House Tower houses a museum of archaeology; Norman House and Canute's Palace are among the oldest examples of Norman domestic architecture in Britain; a memorial column marks the place of embarkation of the *Mayflower;* the headquarters of the Ordnance Survey are here
*industries* marine engineering, chemicals, plastics, flour-milling, tobacco, the manufacture of cables and electrical goods, and financial services. It is a major passenger and container port. There is an oil refinery nearby at Fawley
*population* (1996) 207,100
*famous people* Donald Griffin, Benny Hill, George Saintsbury, George Thomas.

**South Australia** state of south-central Australia, including Kangaroo Island and other islands in the Indian Ocean; bounded on the northeast by Queensland, on the east by New South Wales, on the southeast by Victoria, on the south by the Indian Ocean, and on the west by Western Australia
*area* 984,381 sq km/379,971 sq mi
*capital* ◊Adelaide (chief port)
*towns* Whyalla, Mount Gambier, Port Pirie, Port Augusta
*features* Murray Valley irrigated area, including wine-growing Barossa Valley; salt lakes ◊Eyre and Torrens; Mount Lofty, Musgrave, and Flinders ranges; parts of the Nullarbor Plain, and Great Victoria and Simpson deserts; experimental rocket range in the arid north at Woomera (Woomera Prohibited Area)
*products* meat, wool, wine, wheat, barley, almonds, oranges and other citrus fruits, dried and canned fruit, coal, copper, uranium, silver, zinc, gold, steel, jade, slate, opals, marble, granite, household and electrical goods, vehicles, oil, natural gas
*population* (1996) 1,428,000
*history* possibly known to the Dutch in the 16th century; surveyed by Dutch navigator Abel ◊Tasman in 1644; first European settlement in 1834; became a province in 1836 and a state in 1901.

**South Ayrshire** unitary authority in southwest Scotland, created in 1996 from Kyle and Carrick district (1975–96), Strathclyde region
*area* 1,245 sq km/480 sq mi
*towns* Ayr (administrative headquarters), Prestwick, Girvan, Troon, Maybole
*physical* coastal plain which rises to higher ground inland (500 m/1,640 ft); rivers Ayr, Stinchar, Water of Girvan; Brown Carrick Hill (287 m/942 ft); Ailsa Craig; many beaches interspersed with cliffs and caves
*features* Glasgow Prestwick Airport; Culzean Castle; Crossraguel Abbey; Royal Troon and Turnberry championship golf courses; Ayr racecourse
*industries* aerospace, high technology, tourism
*agriculture* fishing (Ayr), dairying, beef cattle, potatoes
*population* (1996) 114,000
*history* birthplace of Robert Burns.

**South Carolina** state in southeastern USA. It is nicknamed the Palmetto State. South Carolina ratified the US Constitution in 1788, becoming the 8th state to join the Union. Part of the Deep South, it is bordered to the north and east by North Carolina, to the west and south by Georgia, and to the southeast by the Atlantic Ocean. South Carolina was one of the original US plantation states, associated with slavery
*population* (1995) 3,673,300
*area* 80,600 sq km/31,112 sq mi
*capital* Columbia
*towns and cities* Charleston, North Charleston, Greenville, Spartanburg
*industries and products* tobacco, soybeans, lumber, textiles, clothing, paper, wood pulp, chemicals, nonelectrical machinery, primary and fabricated metals, tourism, leisure industry.

**South Dakota** state in western USA. It is nicknamed the Coyote or Sunshine State. South Dakota was admitted to the Union in 1889 as the 40th US state. It is bordered to the north by North Dakota, to the west by Montana and Wyoming, to the south by Nebraska, and to the east by Minnesota and Iowa
*population* (1995) 729,000
*area* 199,800 sq km/77,123 sq mi
*capital* Pierre
*towns and cities* Sioux Falls, Rapid City, Aberdeen
*industries and products* cereals, hay, livestock, gold (second-largest US producer), meat products, tourism.

**Southend** resort and unitary authority in eastern England, on the Thames estuary, 60 km/37 mi east of London, the nearest seaside resort to London; it was part of the county of Essex to April 1998
*area* 42 sq km/16 sq mi
*features* a pier, 2 km/1.25 mi long, said to be the longest in the world; 11 km/7 mi of seafront, an aquarium, amusement facilities, and many public parks and gardens, including the Cliff Gardens; well known for its flowers, including carpet bedding displays and a Floral Trail Tour; nearly a third of all land in the area is managed for nature conservation, including Belfairs Wood Nature Reserve and Leigh National Nature Reserve on Two Tree Island
*industries* tourism, financial services, light engineering, and boatbuilding
*population* (1996) 171,000.

**Southern Cross** popular name for the constellation Crux.

**Southern Uplands** one of the three geographical divisions of Scotland, being most of the hilly Scottish borderland to the south of a geological fault line that stretches from Dunbar, East Lothian, on the North Sea to Girvan, South Ayrshire, on the Firth of Clyde. The Southern Uplands, largely formed by rocks of the Silurian and Ordovician age, are intersected by the broad valleys of the Nith and Tweed rivers.

**South Georgia** island in the South Atlantic, a British crown colony administered, with the South Sandwich Islands, from the Falkland

Islands by a commissioner; area 3,757 sq km/1,450 sq mi. The average temperature on the island is -2°C/28.4°F.

There has been no permanent population since the whaling station was abandoned in 1966. South Georgia lies 1,300 km/800 mi southeast of the Falkland Islands, of which it was a dependency until 1985. The British Antarctic Survey has a station on nearby Bird Island.

**South Glamorgan** Welsh *De Morgannwg,* former county of south Wales, 1974–1996, now divided between ◊Cardiff and ◊Vale of Glamorgan unitary authorities.

**South Gloucestershire** unitary authority in southwest England created in 1996 from part of the former county of Avon
*area* 497 sq km/192 sq mi
*towns and cities* Thornbury (administrative headquarters), Patchway, Yate, Chipping Sodbury
*features* River Severn borders northwest; Vale of Berkeley; Severn Road Bridge; Marshfield has one of Britain's longest village streets with 17th-century almshouses; 13th-century church of St Peter (Dyrham); late 17th century Dyrham Park Mansion
*industries* agriculture and associated industries
*population* (1996) 220,000.

**South Holland** Dutch *Zuid Holland,* low-lying coastal province of the Netherlands, bounded to the north by North Holland, to the east by Utrecht and North Brabant, to the south by Zeeland, and to the west by the North Sea
*area* 2,910 sq km/1,124 sq mi
*capital* ◊The Hague
*towns* Rotterdam, Dordrecht, Leiden, Delft, Gouda
*physical* mostly below sea level
*features* major ports at Rotterdam and the Hook of Holland
*industries* chemicals, textiles, distilleries, petroleum refineries
*agriculture* bulbs, horticulture, livestock, dairy products
*population* (1997) 3,344,700
*history* It was once part of the former county of Holland, which was divided into two provinces in 1840.

**South Korea** Republic of Korea
*national name* Daehan Min-kuk
*area* 98,799 sq km/38,146 sq mi
*capital* Seoul
*major towns/cities* Pusan, Taegu, Inchon, Kwangju, Taejon
*major ports* Pusan, Inchon
*physical features* southern end of a mountainous peninsula separating the Sea of Japan from the Yellow Sea
*head of state* Kim Dae Jung from 1998
*head of government* Kim Jong Pil from 1998
*political system* emergent democracy
*political parties* New Korea Party (NKP, formerly Democratic Liberal Party (DLP)), right of centre; National Congress for New Politics (NCNP), centre left; Democratic Party (DP), left

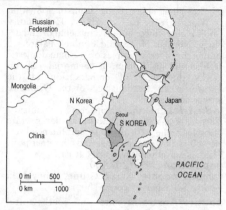

of centre; New Democratic Party (NDP), centrist, pro-private enterprise; United Liberal Democratic Party (ULD), ultra-conservative, pro-private enterprise
*currency* won
*GNP per capita (PPP)* (US$) 12,270 (1998)
*exports* electrical machinery, textiles, clothing, footwear, telecommunications and sound equipment, chemical products, ships ('invisible export' – overseas construction work). Principal market: USA 17.2% (1998)
*population* 46,479,000 (1999 est)
*language* Korean
*religion* Shamanist, Buddhist, Confucian, Protestant, Roman Catholic
*life expectancy* 69 (men); 76 (women) (1995–2000)
*Chronology*
*2333 BC* Traditional date of founding of Korean state by Tangun (mythical son from union of bear-woman and god).
*1122 BC* Ancient texts record founding of kingdom in Korea by Chinese nobleman Kija.
*194 BC* Northwest Korea united under warlord, Wiman.
*108 BC* Korea conquered by Chinese.
*1st–7th centuries AD* Three Korean kingdoms – Koguryo, Paekche, and Silla – competed for supremacy.
*668* Korean peninsula unified by Buddhist Silla kingdom; culture combining Chinese and Korean elements flourished.
*935* Silla dynasty overthrown by Wang Kon of Koguryo, who founded Koryo dynasty in its place.
*1258* Korea accepted overlordship of Mongol Yüan Empire.
*1392* Yi dynasty founded by Gen Yi Song-gye, vassal of Chinese Ming Empire; Confucianism replaced Buddhism as official creed; extreme conservatism characterized Korean society.
*1592 and 1597* Japanese invasions repulsed by Korea.
*1636* Manchu invasion forced Korea to sever ties with Ming dynasty.
*18th–19th centuries* Korea resisted change in political and economic life and rejected contact with Europeans.
*1864* Attempts to reform government and strengthen army by Taewongun (who ruled in

name of his son, King Kojong); converts to Christianity persecuted.

**1873** Taewongun forced to cede power to Queen Min; reforms reversed; government authority collapsed.

**1882** Chinese occupied Seoul and installed governor.

**1894–95** Sino-Japanese War: Japan forced China to recognize independence of Korea; Korea fell to Japanese influence.

**1896** Fearing for his life, King Kojong sought protection of Russian legation.

**1904–05** Russo-Japanese War: Japan ended Russian influence in Korea.

**1910** Korea formally annexed by Japan; Japanese settlers introduced modern industry and agriculture; Korean language banned.

**1919** 'Samil' nationalist movement suppressed by Japanese.

**1945** After defeat of Japan in World War II, Russia occupied regions of Korea north of 38th parallel (demarcation line agreed at Yalta Conference) and USA occupied regions south of it.

**1948** The USSR refused to permit United Nations (UN) supervision of elections in the northern zone; the southern zone became independent as the Republic of Korea, with Syngman Rhee as president.

**1950** North Korea invaded South Korea; UN forces (mainly from the USA) intervened to defend South Korea; China intervened in support of North Korea.

**1953** The Korean War ended with an armistice which restored the 38th parallel; no peace treaty was agreed and US troops remained in South Korea.

**1960** President Syngman Rhee was forced to resign by student-led protests against corruption and fraudulent elections.

**1961** Military coup placed Gen Park Chung Hee in power; a major programme of industrial development began.

**1972** Martial law was imposed and presidential powers increased.

**1979** President Park was assassinated. The interim government of President Choi Kyu-Hah introduced liberalizing reforms.

**1979** Gen Chun Doo Hwan assumed power after anti-government riots; Korea emerged as a leading shipbuilding nation and exporter of electronic goods.

**1987** The constitution was made more democratic as a result of Liberal pressure; ruling Democratic Justice Party (DJP) candidate Roh Tae Woo Was elected president amid allegations of fraud.

**1988** The Olympic Games were held in Seoul.

**1991** Large-scale antigovernment protests were forcibly suppressed; South Korea joined the UN.

**1992** South Korea established diplomatic relations with China; Kim Young Sam was elected president.

**1994** The US military presence was stepped up in response to the perceived threat from North Korea.

**1996** Roh Tae Woo and Chun Doo Hwan were charged with treason for their alleged role in the massacre of demonstrators in 1980.

**1997** South Korea was admitted to the OECD. Kim Dae Jung, former dissident and political prisoner, became the first opposition politician to lead South Korea.

**1998** Kim Dae Jung was sworn in as president, with Kim Jong Pil as prime minister. New labour laws ended lifetime employment and the financial system was opened up. More than 2,000 prisoners were released, including 74 political prisoners. There was continuing labour unrest as the GDP contracted by 5%.

**1999** Talks on possible reunification with North Korea were suspended.

**South Lanarkshire** unitary authority in south central Scotland, created in 1996 from three districts of Strathclyde region

***area*** 1,772 sq km/684 sq mi

***towns*** Hamilton (administrative headquarters), Lanark, Rutherglen, East Kilbride, Carluke, Cambuslang

***physical*** area of stark contrast: predominantly rural to the south and urban to the north. The River Clyde flows through the area. Tinto (707 m/2,320 ft) is a key landmark to the south

***features*** Craignethan Castle; Carstairs State Hospital, New Lanark

***industries*** textiles, electronics, engineering

***agriculture*** fruit cultivation in the valleys of the Clyde; less intensive grazing and stock rearing in the upland south; dairying around the urban core in the north

***population*** (1996) 307,100

***history*** New Lanark village is a World Heritage Site, significant for the attempt to improve living conditions for workers and their families.

**South Ossetia** autonomous region of the Georgian republic; population (1990) 99,800; capital Tshkinvali, population (1989) 34,000. See ◊Ossetia.

**South Pole** the southern point where an imaginary line penetrates the Earth's surface by the axis about which it revolves; see also ◊pole and ◊Antarctica.

**South Sea Bubble** financial crisis in Britain in 1720. The South Sea Company, founded in 1711, which had a monopoly of trade with South America, offered in 1719 to take over more than half the national debt in return for further concessions. Its 100 shares rapidly rose to 1,000, and an orgy of speculation followed. When the 'bubble' burst, thousands were ruined.

The discovery that cabinet ministers had been guilty of corruption led to a political crisis.

**South, the** historically, the states of the USA bounded on the north by the ◊Mason–Dixon Line, the Ohio River, and the eastern and northern borders of Missouri, with an agrarian economy based on plantations worked by slaves, and which seceded from the Union 1861, beginning the American Civil War, as the ◊Confederacy. The term is now loosely applied in a geographical and cultural sense, with Texas often regarded as part of the Southwest rather than the South.

**South Yorkshire** metropolitan county of northeast England, created in 1974; in 1986, most of the functions of the former county council were transferred to the metropolitan borough councils

**area** 1,560 sq km/602 sq mi

**towns** Barnsley, Doncaster, Rotherham, Sheffield (all administrative centres for the districts of the same name)

**physical** River Don; part of Peak District National Park; the county contains a rich diversity of rural landscapes between the barren Pennine moors in the southwest and the very low, flat carr-lands (a mixture of marsh and copses) in the east

**features** the Earth Centre for Environmental Research

**agriculture** sheep; dairy and arable farming

**industries** metal-work, coal, engineering, iron, and steel

**population** (1996) 1,304,800

**famous people** Ian Botham, Arthur Scargill.

**sovereignty** absolute authority within a given territory. The possession of sovereignty is taken to be the distinguishing feature of the state, as against other forms of community. The term has an internal aspect, in that it refers to the ultimate source of authority within a state, such as a parliament or monarch, and an external aspect, where it denotes the independence of the state from any outside authority.

**soviet** (Russian 'council') originally a strike committee elected by Russian workers in the 1905 revolution; in 1917 these were set up by peasants, soldiers, and factory workers. The soviets sent delegates to the All-Russian Congress of Soviets to represent their opinions to a future government. They were later taken over by the ◊Bolsheviks.

**Soviet Union** alternative name for the former Union of Soviet Socialist Republics (USSR).

**Soweto** acronym for *South West Township,* urban settlement in South Africa, southwest of Johannesburg; population (1991) 597,000. It experienced civil unrest during the ◊apartheid regime. Industries include wood pulp and paper manufacturing.

**soybean** leguminous plant (see ◊legume), native to East Asia, in particular Japan and China. Originally grown as a food crop for animals, it is increasingly used for human consumption in cooking oils and margarine, as a flour, soya milk, soy sauce, or processed into tofu, miso, or textured vegetable protein (TVP). (*Glycine max*)

**Soyinka, Wole** pen-name of Akinwande Oluwole Soyinka (1934–　) Nigerian author and dramatist. His plays explore Yoruba myth, ritual, and culture, with the early *Swamp Dwellers* (1958) and *The Lion and the Jewel* (1959), culminating with *A Dance of the Forests* (1960), written as a tragic vision of Nigerian independence. Tragic inevitability is the theme of *Madmen and Specialists* (1970) and of *Death and the King's Horseman* (1976), but he has also written sharp satires, from *The Jero Plays* (1960 and 1973) to the indictment of African dictatorship in *A Play of Giants* (1984). He was the first African to receive the Nobel Prize for Literature,

(1986). A recent volume of poetry, *From Zia with Love,* appeared (1992).

Soyinka was charged with treason by the Nigerian government in March 1997 over a spate of bomb blasts in the country. From December 1996 a series of blasts on army buses had killed three soldiers and wounded dozens more. Soyinka and 11 other dissidents were charged and if convicted they face the death penalty. Soyinka was among the four opposition figures who had fled Nigeria in 1995 to Europe and the USA. The charges would pave the way for Nigeria to try to have Soyinka extradited back home.

**Soyuz** (Russian 'union') Soviet series of spacecraft, capable of carrying up to three cosmonauts. Soyuz spacecraft consist of three parts: a rear section containing engines; the central crew compartment; and a forward compartment that gives additional room for working and living space. They are now used for ferrying crews up to space stations, though they were originally used for independent space flight.

**space** or *outer space,* void that exists beyond Earth's atmosphere. Above 120 km/75 mi, very little atmosphere remains, so objects can continue to move quickly without extra energy. The space between the planets is not entirely empty, but filled with the tenuous gas of the ◊solar wind as well as dust specks.

**Spacelab** small space station built by the European Space Agency, carried in the cargo bay of the US space shuttle, in which it remains throughout each flight, returning to Earth with the shuttle. Spacelab consists of a pressurized module in which astronauts can work, and a series of pallets, open to the vacuum of space, on which equipment is mounted.

**space probe** any instrumented object sent beyond Earth to collect data from other parts of the Solar System and from deep space. The first probe was the Soviet *Lunik 1,* which flew past the Moon in 1959. The first successful planetary probe was the US *Mariner 2,* which flew past Venus in 1962, using transfer orbit. The first space probe to leave the Solar System was *Pioneer 10* in 1983. Space probes include *Galileo, Giotto, Magellan, Mars Observer, Ulysses,* the Moon probes, and the Mariner, Pioneer, Viking, and Voyager series.

**space shuttle** reusable crewed spacecraft. The first was launched 12 April 1981 by the USA. It was developed by NASA to reduce the cost of using space for commercial, scientific, and military purposes. After leaving its payload in space, the space-shuttle orbiter can be flown back to Earth to land on a runway, and is then available for reuse.

**space station** any large structure designed for human occupation in space for extended periods of time. Space stations are used for carrying out astronomical observations and surveys of Earth, as well as for biological studies and the processing of materials in weightlessness. The first space station was ◊*Salyut 1,* and the USA has launched ◊*Skylab.*

**space-time** in physics, combination of space and time used in the theory of ⏀relativity. When developing relativity, Albert Einstein showed that time was in many respects like an extra dimension (or direction) to space. Space and time can thus be considered as entwined into a single entity, rather than two separate things.

**Spain** Kingdom of
**national name** *Reino de España*

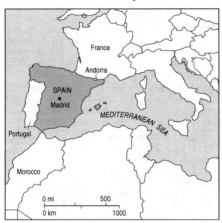

**area** 504,750 sq km/194,883 sq mi
**capital** Madrid
**major towns/cities** Barcelona, Valencia, Zaragoza, Seville, Málaga, Bilbao, Las Palmas de Gran Canarias, Murcia, Córdoba, Palma de Mallorca, Granada
**major ports** Barcelona, Valencia, Cartagena, Málaga, Cádiz, Vigo, Santander, Bilbao
**physical features** central plateau with mountain ranges, lowlands in south; rivers Ebro, Douro, Tagus, Guadiana, Guadalquivir; Iberian Plateau (Meseta); Pyrenees, Cantabrian Mountains, Andalusian Mountains, Sierra Nevada
**territories** Balearic and Canary Islands; in North Africa: Ceuta, Melilla, Alhucemas, Chafarinas Islands, Peñón de Vélez
**head of state** King Juan Carlos I from 1975
**head of government** José Maria Aznar from 1996
**political system** constitutional monarchy
**political parties** Socialist Workers' Party (PSOE), democratic socialist; Popular Party (PP), centre right
**currency** peseta
**GNP per capita (PPP)** (US$) 16,060 (1998)
**exports** motor vehicles, machinery and electrical equipment, vegetable products, metals and their manufactures, foodstuffs. Principal market: France 19.6% (1998)
**population** 39,633,000 (1999 est)
**language** Spanish (Castilian, official), Basque, Catalan, Galician
**religion** Roman Catholic
**life expectancy** 75 (men); 82 (women) (1995–2000)
**Chronology**
**2nd century BC** Romans conquered the Iberian

peninsula, which became the province of Hispania.
**5th century AD** After the fall of the Roman Empire, Iberia was overrun by Vandals and Visigoths.
**711** Muslims invaded from North Africa and overthrew Visigoth kingdom.
**9th century** Christians in northern Spain formed kingdoms of Asturias, Aragón, Navarre, and León, and county of Castile.
**10th century** Abd-al-Rahman III established caliphate of Córdoba; Muslim culture at its height in Spain.
**1230** León and Castile united under Ferdinand III, who drove the Muslims from most of southern Spain.
**14th century** Spain consisted of Christian kingdoms of Castile, Aragón, and Navarre, and the Muslim emirate of Granada.
**1469** Marriage of Ferdinand of Aragón and Isabella of Castile; kingdoms united on their accession in 1479.
**1492** Conquest of Granada ended Muslim rule in Spain.
**1494** Treaty of Tordesillas; Spain and Portugal divided newly discovered America; Spain became a world power.
**1519–56** Emperor Charles V was both King of Spain and Archduke of Austria; he also ruled Naples, Sicily, and the Low Countries; Habsburgs dominant in Europe.
**1555** Charles V divided his domains between Spain and Austria before retiring; Spain retained the Low Countries and southern Italy as well as South American colonies.
**1568** Dutch rebelled against Spanish rule; Spain recognized independence of Dutch Republic in 1648.
**1580** Philip II of Spain inherited the throne of Portugal, where Spanish rule lasted until 1640.
**1588** Spanish Armada: attempt to invade England defeated.
**17th century** Spanish power declined amid wars, corruption, inflation, and loss of civil and religious freedom.
**1701–14** War of the Spanish Succession: allied powers fought France to prevent Philip of Bourbon inheriting throne of Spain.
**1713–14** Treaties of Utrecht and Rastat: Bourbon dynasty recognized, but Spain lost Gibraltar, southern Italy, and Spanish Netherlands.
**1793** Spain declared war on revolutionary France; reduced to a French client state in 1795.
**1808** Napoleon installed his brother Joseph as King of Spain.
**1808–14** Peninsular War: British forces played a large part in liberating Spain and restoring Bourbon dynasty.
**1810–30** Spain lost control of its South American colonies.
**1833–39** Carlist civil war: Don Carlos (backed by conservatives) unsuccessfully contested the succession of his niece Isabella II (backed by liberals).
**1870** Offer of Spanish throne to Leopold of Hohenzollern-Sigmaringen sparked Franco-Prussian War.

**1873–74** First republic ended by military coup which restored Bourbon dynasty with Alfonso XII.

**1898** Spanish-American War: Spain lost Cuba and Philippines.

**1923–30** Dictatorship of Gen Primo de Rivera with support of Alfonso XIII.

**1931** Proclamation of Second Republic, initially dominated by anticlerical radicals and socialists.

**1933** Moderates and Catholics won elections; insurrection by socialists and Catalans in 1934.

**1936** Left-wing Popular Front narrowly won fresh elections; General Francisco Franco launched military rebellion.

**1936–39** Spanish Civil War: Nationalists (with significant Italian and German support) defeated Republicans (with limited Soviet support); Franco became dictator of nationalist-fascist regime.

**1941** Though officially neutral in World War II, Spain sent 40,000 troops to fight USSR.

**1955** Spain admitted to the United Nations (UN).

**1975** Death of Franco; he was succeeded by King Juan Carlos I.

**1978** A referendum endorsed democratic constitution.

**1982** Socialists took office under Felipe González; Spain joined the North Atlantic Treaty Organization (NATO); Basque separatist organization (ETA) stepped up its terrorist campaign.

**1986** Spain joined the European Economic Community (EEC).

**1996** José Maria Aznar formed a minority PP government.

**1997** 23 Basque nationalist leaders were jailed for terrorist activities.

**1998** ETA announced an indefinite ceasefire. The government announced that it would begin peace talks.

**spaniel** any of several breeds of small and medium-sized gundog, characterized by large, drooping ears and a wavy, long, silky coat. Spaniels are divided into two groups: those that are still working gundogs – Clumber, cocker, Irish water, springer, and Sussex – and the toy breeds that are kept as pets – including the Japanese, King Charles, papillon, and Tibetan.

**Spanish-American War** brief war 1898 between Spain and the USA over Spanish rule in Cuba and the Philippines; the complete defeat of Spain made the USA a colonial power. The Treaty of Paris ceded the Philippines, Guam, and Puerto Rico to the USA; Cuba became independent. The USA paid $20 million to Spain. This ended Spain's colonial presence in the Americas.

**Spanish Armada** fleet sent by Philip II of Spain against England in 1588. Consisting of 130 ships, it sailed from Lisbon and carried on a running fight up the Channel with the English fleet of 197 small ships under Howard of Effingham and Francis ♢Drake. The Armada anchored off Calais but fire ships forced it to put to sea, and a general action followed off Gravelines. What remained of the Armada escaped around the north of Scotland and west of Ireland, suffering many losses by storm and shipwreck on the way. Only about half the original fleet returned to Spain.

**Spanish Civil War** 1936–39. See ♢Civil War, Spanish.

**Spanish language** member of the Romance branch of the Indo-European language family, traditionally known as Castilian and originally spoken only in northeastern Spain. As the language of the court, it has been the standard and literary language of the Spanish state since the 13th century. It is now a world language, spoken in Mexico and all South and Central American countries (except Brazil, Guyana, Suriname, and French Guiana) as well as in the Philippines, Cuba, Puerto Rico, and much of the USA.

**Spanish Main** common term for the Caribbean Sea in the 16th–17th centuries, but more properly the South American mainland between the River Orinoco and Panama.

**Spanish Succession, War of the** war 1701–14 of Britain, Austria, the Netherlands, Portugal, and Denmark (the Allies) against France, Spain, and Bavaria. It was caused by Louis XIV's acceptance of the Spanish throne on behalf of his grandson, Philip, in defiance of the Partition Treaty of 1700, under which it would have passed to Archduke Charles of Austria (later Holy Roman Emperor Charles VI).

**spark plug** plug that produces an electric spark in the cylinder of a petrol engine to ignite the fuel mixture. It consists essentially of two electrodes insulated from one another. High-voltage (18,000 V) electricity is fed to a central electrode via the distributor. At the base of the electrode, inside the cylinder, the electricity jumps to another electrode earthed to the engine body, creating a spark.

**sparrow** any of a family (Passeridae) of small Old World birds of the order Passeriformes with short, thick bills, but applied particularly to the different members of the genus *Passer* in the family Ploceidae, order Passeriformes.

Many numbers of the New World family Emberizidae, which includes ♢warblers, orioles, and buntings, are also called sparrows; for example, the North American song sparrow *Melospize melodia.*

**sparrow hawk** small woodland ♢hawk *Accipiter nisus,* of the family Falconidae, order Falconiformes, found in Eurasia and North Africa. It is bluish-grey, with brown and white markings, and has a long tail and short wings. The male grows to 28 cm/11 in long, and the female to 38 cm/15 in. It hunts small birds and mice.

**Sparta** ancient Greek city-state in the southern Peloponnese (near Sparte), developed from Dorian settlements in the 10th century BC. The Spartans, known for their military discipline and austerity, took part in the ♢Persian and ♢Peloponnesian Wars.

**Spartacist** member of a group of left-wing radicals in Germany at the end of World War I, founders of the *Spartacus League,* which became the German Communist Party in 1919. The league participated in the Berlin workers' revolt of January 1919, which was suppressed by the Freikorps on the orders of the socialist government. The agitation ended with the murder of Spartacist leaders Karl Liebknecht and Rosa ◊Luxemburg.

**Spartacus** (died 71 BC) Thracian gladiator. In 73 BC he led a revolt of gladiators and slaves in Capua, near Naples, and swept through southern Italy and Cisalpine Gaul. He was eventually caught by Roman general Crassus in 71 BC. The fate of Spartacus is not known, although his followers were executed in mass crucifixions.

**spastic** term applied generally to limbs with impaired movement, stiffness, and resistance to passive movement, and to any body part (such as the colon) affected with spasm.

**spa town** town with a spring, the water of which, it is claimed, has the power to cure illness and restore health. Spa treatment involves drinking and bathing in the naturally mineralized spring water.

**speakeasy** bar that illegally sold alcoholic beverages during the ◊Prohibition period (1920–33) in the USA. The term is probably derived from the need to speak quickly or quietly to the doorkeeper in order to gain admission.

**Speaker** presiding officer charged with the preservation of order in the legislatures of various countries. In the UK the equivalent of the Speaker in the House of Lords is the Lord Chancellor; in the House of Commons the Speaker is elected for each parliament, usually on an agreed basis among the parties, but often holds the office for many years. The original appointment dates from 1377. In 1992 Betty Boothroyd became the first female Speaker of the House of Commons.

**spearmint** perennial herb belonging to the mint family, with aromatic leaves and spikes of purple flowers; the leaves are used for flavouring in cookery. (*Mentha spicata*, family Labiatae.)

**Special Air Service** (SAS), specialist British regiment recruited from regiments throughout the army. It has served in Malaysia, Oman, Yemen, the Falklands, Northern Ireland, and during the 1991 Gulf War, as well as against international urban guerrillas, as in the siege of the Iranian embassy in London 1980.

**Special Branch** section of the British police originally established in 1883 to deal with Irish Fenian activists. All 42 police forces in Britain now have their own Special Branches. They act as the executive arm of MI5 (British ◊intelligence) in its duty of preventing or investigating espionage, subversion, and sabotage; carry out duties at air and sea ports in respect of naturalization and immigration; and provide armed bodyguards for public figures.

**speciation** emergence of a new species during evolutionary history. One cause of speciation is the geographical separation of populations of the parent species, followed by reproductive

isolation and selection for different environments so that they no longer produce viable offspring when they interbreed. Other causes are ◊assortative mating and the establishment of a polyploid population.

**species** in biology, a distinguishable group of organisms that resemble each other or consist of a few distinctive types (as in ◊polymorphism), and that can all interbreed to produce fertile offspring. Species are the lowest level in the system of biological classification.

**specific gravity** alternative term for relative density.

**specific heat capacity** in physics, quantity of heat required to raise unit mass (1 kg) of a substance by one ◊kelvin (1 K). The unit of specific heat capacity in the SI system is the ◊joule per kilogram kelvin ($J\ kg^{-1}\ K^{-1}$).

**specific latent heat** in physics, the heat that changes the physical state of a unit mass (one kilogram) of a substance without causing any temperature change.

**Spector, Phil** (1940– ) US record producer. He is known for the 'wall of sound', created using a large orchestra, which distinguished his work in the early 1960s with vocal groups such as the Crystals and the Ronettes. He withdrew into semi-retirement in 1966 but his influence can still be heard.

**spectroscopy** study of spectra (see ◊spectrum) associated with atoms or molecules in solid, liquid, or gaseous phase. Spectroscopy can be used to identify unknown compounds and is an invaluable tool in science, medicine, and industry (for example, in checking the purity of drugs).

**spectrum** plural *spectra,* in physics, an arrangement of frequencies or wavelengths when electromagnetic radiations are separated into their constituent parts. Visible light is part of the electromagnetic spectrum and most sources emit waves over a range of wavelengths that can be broken up or 'dispersed'; white light can be separated into red, orange, yellow, green, blue, indigo, and violet. The visible spectrum was first studied by Isaac ◊Newton, who showed in 1672 how white light could be broken up into different colours.

**speech recognition** or *voice input,* in computing, any technique by which a computer can understand ordinary speech. Spoken words are divided into 'frames', each lasting about one-thirtieth of a second, which are converted to a wave form. These are then compared with a series of stored frames to determine the most likely word. Research into speech recognition started in 1938, but the technology did not become sufficiently developed for commercial applications until the late 1980s.

**speech synthesis** or *voice output,* computer-based technology for generating speech. A speech synthesizer is controlled by a computer, which supplies strings of codes representing basic speech sounds (phonemes); together these make up words. Speech-synthesis applications include children's toys, car and aircraft warning systems, and talking books for the blind.

**speed** the rate at which an object moves. The average speed $v$ of an object may be calculated by dividing the distance $s$ it has travelled by the time $t$ taken to do so, and may be expressed as:

$$v = \frac{s}{t}$$

The usual units of speed are metres per second or kilometres per hour.

**speed of light** speed at which light and other ◊electromagnetic waves travel through empty space. Its value is 299,792,458 m/186,281 mi per second. The speed of light is the highest speed possible, according to the theory of ◊relativity, and its value is independent of the motion of its source and of the observer. It is impossible to accelerate any material body to this speed because it would require an infinite amount of energy.

**speed of sound** speed at which sound travels through a medium, such as air or water. In air at a temperature of 0°C/32°F, the speed of sound is 331 m/1,087 ft per second. At higher temperatures, the speed of sound is greater; at 18°C/64°F it is 342 m/1,123 ft per second.

It is greater in liquids and solids; for example, in water it is around 1,440 m/4,724 ft per second, depending on the temperature.

**speedway** sport of motorcycle racing on a dirt track. Four riders compete in each heat over four laps. A series of heats make up a match or competition. In Britain there are two leagues, the British League and the National League. World championships exist for individuals, pairs (first held 1970), four-rider teams (first held 1960), long-track racing, and ice speedway.

**speedwell** any of a group of flowering plants belonging to the snapdragon family. Of the many wild species, most are low-growing with small bluish flowers. (Genus *Veronica*, family Scrophulariaceae.)

**Speer, Albert** (1905–1981) German architect and minister in the Nazi government during World War II. He was appointed Hitler's architect and, like his counterparts in Fascist Italy, chose an overblown Classicism to glorify the state, for example, his plan for the Berlin and Nürnberg Party Congress Grounds in 1934. He built the New Reich Chancellery, Berlin, in 1938–39 (now demolished), but his designs for an increasingly megalomaniac series of buildings in a stark Classical style were never realized.

**speleology** scientific study of caves, their origin, development, physical structure, flora, fauna, folklore, exploration, mapping, photography, cave-diving, and rescue work. *Potholing*, which involves following the course of underground rivers or streams, has become a popular sport.

**Spencer, Stanley** (1891–1959) English painter. He was born and lived in Cookham-on-Thames, and recreated the Christian story in a Cookham setting. Typically his dreamlike compositions combine a dry, meticulously detailed, and often humorous depiction of everyday life

with an elaborate religious symbolism, as in *The Resurrection, Cookham* (1924–26; Tate Gallery, London).

**Spender, Stephen (Harold)** (1909–1995) English poet and critic. His early poetry has a left-wing political content. With Cyril Connolly he founded the magazine *Horizon* (of which he was co-editor in 1939–41), and Spender was co-editor of *Encounter* (1953–66). His *Journals* (1939–83) and *Collected Poems* (1928–1985) were published in 1985. He was knighted in 1983.

**Spenser, Edmund** (*c.* 1552–1599) English poet. His major work is the allegorical epic *The Faerie Queene*, of which six books survive (three published in 1590 and three in 1596). Other books include *The Shepheard's Calendar* (1579), *Astrophel* (1586), the love sonnets *Amoretti*, and the marriage poem *Epithalamion* (1595).

**sperm** or *spermatozoon,* in biology, the male ◊gamete of animals. Each sperm cell has a head capsule containing a nucleus, a middle portion containing ◊mitochondria (which provide energy), and a long tail (flagellum). See ◊sexual reproduction.

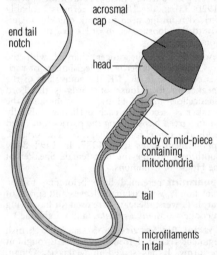

acrosmal cap

end tail notch

head

body or mid-piece containing mitochondria

tail

microfilaments in tail

**sperm** *Only a single sperm is needed to fertilize an egg, or ovum. Yet up to 500 million may start the journey towards the egg. Once a sperm has fertilized an egg, the egg's wall cannot be penetrated by other sperm. The unsuccessful sperm die after about three days.*

**spermatophore** small capsule containing ◊sperm and other nutrients produced in invertebrates, newts, and cephalopods.

**spermatophyte** in botany, another name for a ◊seed plant.

**spermicide** any cream, jelly, pessary, or other preparation that kills the ◊sperm cells in semen. Spermicides are used for contraceptive purposes, usually in combination with a ◊condom or

◊diaphragm. Sponges impregnated with spermicide have been developed but are not yet in widespread use. Spermicide used alone is only 75% effective in preventing pregnancy.

**sphere** in mathematics, a perfectly round object with all points on its surface the same distance from the centre. This distance is the radius of the sphere. For a sphere of radius $r$, the volume $V = 4/3\pi r^3$ and the surface area $A = 4\pi r^2$.

**Sphinx** mythological creature, depicted in Egyptian, Assyrian, and Greek art as a lion with a human head. The Greek *Sphinx of Thebes* was winged with a woman's breasts, and was adopted as an emblem of wisdom. She killed all those who failed to answer her riddle about which animal went on four, then two, and finally three legs: the answer being humanity (baby, adult, and old person with stick). When ◊Oedipus gave the right reply, she committed suicide.

**Spica** or *Alpha Virginis,* brightest star in the constellation Virgo and the 16th-brightest star in the night sky. Spica has a true luminosity of over 1,500 times that of the Sun. It is a spectroscopic binary star, the components of which orbit each other every four days. It is 140 light years from the Sun.

**spice** any aromatic vegetable substance used as a condiment and for flavouring food. Spices are mostly obtained from tropical plants, and include pepper, nutmeg, ginger, and cinnamon. They have little food value but increase the appetite and may help digestion.

**spider** any arachnid (eight-legged animal) of the order Araneae. There are about 30,000 known species, mostly a few centimetres in size, although a few tropical forms attain great size, for example, some bird-eating spiders attain a body length of 9 cm/3.5 in. Spiders produce silk, and many spin webs to trap their prey. They are found everywhere in the world except Antarctica. Many species are found in woods and dry commons; a few are aquatic. Spiders are predators; they bite their prey, releasing a powerful toxin from poison glands which causes paralysis, together with digestive juices. They then suck out the juices and soft parts.

**spider plant** African plant belonging to the lily family. Two species (*C. comosum* and *C. elatum*) are popular house plants. They have long, narrow, variegated leaves and produce flowering shoots from which the new plants grow, hanging below the main plant. The flowers are small and white. Spider plants absorb toxins from the air and therefore help to purify the atmosphere around them. (Genus *Chlorophytum*, family Liliaceae.)

**Spielberg, Steven** (1947– ) US film director, writer, and producer. Immensely popular, Spielberg's films often combine heartfelt sentimentality and a childlike sensibility. His credits include such phenomenal box-office successes as *Jaws* (1975), *Close Encounters of the Third Kind* (1977), *Raiders of the Lost Ark* (1981), *ET The Extra-Terrestrial* (1982), *Jurassic Park* (1992), the multi-award-winning *Schindler's List* (1993), and *Saving Private Ryan* (1998). He was the recipient of the American Film Institute's life achievement award in 1995. The US financial magazine *Forbes* listed him in 1997 as the biggest earner in showbusiness.

**spikelet** in botany, one of the units of a grass inflorescence. It comprises a slender axis on which one or more flowers are borne.

**spin** in physics, the intrinsic angular momentum of a subatomic particle, nucleus, atom, or molecule, which continues to exist even when the particle comes to rest. A particle in a specific energy state has a particular spin, just as it has a particular electric charge and mass. According to ◊quantum theory, this is restricted to discrete and indivisible values, specified by a spin ◊quantum number. Because of its spin, a charged particle acts as a small magnet and is affected by magnetic fields.

**spina bifida** congenital defect in which part of the spinal cord and its membranes are exposed, due to incomplete development of the spine (vertebral column). It is a neural tube defect.

**spinach** annual plant belonging to the goosefoot family. It is native to Asia and widely cultivated for its leaves, which are eaten as a vegetable. (*Spinacia oleracea*, family Chenopodiaceae.)

**spinal cord** major component of the ◊central nervous system in vertebrates. It consists of bundles of nerves enveloped in three layers of membrane (the meninges) and is bathed in cerebrospinal fluid. The spinal cord is encased and protected by the vertebral column, lying within the vertebral canal formed by the posterior arches of successive vertebrae.

**spinal tap** another term for ◊lumbar puncture, a medical test.

**spine** backbone of vertebrates. In most mammals, it contains 26 small bones called *vertebrae,* which enclose and protect the *spinal cord* (which links the peripheral nervous system to the brain). The spine articulates with the skull, ribs, and hip bones, and provides attachment for the back muscles. *See illustration on page 850.*

**spinning** art of drawing out and twisting fibres (originally wool or flax) into a long thread, or yarn, by hand or machine. Synthetic fibres are extruded as a liquid through the holes of a spinneret.

Spinning was originally done by hand, then with the spinning wheel, and in about 1764 in England James ◊Hargreaves built the *spinning jenny,* a machine that could spin 8, then 16, bobbins at once. Later, Samuel Crompton's *spinning mule* (1779) had a moving carriage carrying the spindles; this is still in use today.

**Spinoza, Benedict** or *Baruch* (1632–1677) Dutch philosopher. He believed in a rationalistic pantheism that owed much to René ◊Descartes's mathematical appreciation of the universe. Mind and matter are two modes of an infinite substance that he called God or Nature, good and evil being relative. He was a determinist,

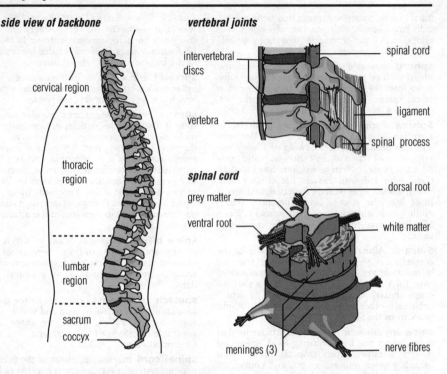

**side view of backbone**

cervical region

thoracic region

lumbar region

sacrum

coccyx

**vertebral joints**

intervertebral discs

vertebra

spinal cord

ligament

spinal process

**spinal cord**

grey matter

ventral root

meninges (3)

dorsal root

white matter

nerve fibres

**spine** *The human spine extends every night during sleep. During the day, the cartilage discs between the vertebra are squeezed when the body is in a vertical position, standing or sitting, but at night, with pressure released, the discs swell and the spine lengthens by about 8 mm/0.3 in.*

believing that human action was motivated by self-preservation.

**spiny anteater** alternative name for ◊echidna.

**spiracle** in insects, the opening of a ◊trachea, through which oxygen enters the body and carbon dioxide is expelled. In cartilaginous fishes (sharks and rays), the same name is given to a circular opening that marks the remains of the first gill slit.

**spiraea** any of a group of herbaceous plants or shrubs, which includes many cultivated species with ornamental sprays of white or pink flowers; their delicate appearance has given rise to the popular name bridal wreath. (Genus *Spiraea*, family Rosaceae.)

**spiritualism** belief in the survival of the human personality and in communication between the living and those who have died. The spiritualist movement originated in the USA in 1848. Adherents practise *mediumship*, which claims to allow clairvoyant knowledge of distant events and spirit healing. The writer Arthur Conan ◊Doyle and the Victorian prime minister William ◊Gladstone were converts.

**spit** ridge of sand or shingle projecting from the land into a body of water. It is formed by the interruption of longshore drift due wave interaction with tides, currents, or a bend in the coastline. The consequent decrease in wave energy causes more material to be deposited than is transported down the coast, building up a finger of sand that points in the direction of the longshore drift. Deposition in the brackish water behind a spit may result in the formation of a salt marsh.

**Spitsbergen** mountainous island with a deeply indented coastline, situated in the Arctic Ocean between Franz Josef Land and Greenland. It is the main island in the Norwegian archipelago of ◊Svalbard, 657 km/408 mi north of Norway, and now owned by that country; area 39,043 sq km/15,075 sq mi. Fishing, hunting, and coal mining are the chief economic activities. The Norwegian Polar Research Institute operates an all-year scientific station on the west coast. The highest point is Newtontoppen, which rises to 1,713 m/5,620 ft. The island was formerly called West Spitsbergen when part of the Svalbard archipeligo was named Spitsbergen.

**spleen** organ in vertebrates, part of the reticuloendothelial system, which helps to process ◊lymphocytes. It also regulates the number of red blood cells in circulation by destroying old cells, and stores iron. It is situated on the left side of the body, behind the stomach.

**Split** Italian *Spalato*, port in Croatia, on the Adriatic coast; population (1991) 189,400. Industries include engineering, cement, and textiles.

Split was bombed during 1991 as part of Yugoslavia's blockade of the Croatian coast.

**Spode, Josiah** (1754–1827) English potter. Around 1800, he developed bone porcelain (made from bone ash, china stone, and china clay), which was produced at all English factories in the 19th century. He became potter to King George III in 1806.

**sponge** any saclike simple invertebrate of the phylum Porifera, usually marine. A sponge has a hollow body, its cavity lined by cells bearing flagellae, whose whiplike movements keep water circulating, bringing in a stream of food particles. The body walls are strengthened with protein (as in the bath sponge) or small spikes of silica, or a framework of calcium carbonate.

**spontaneous combustion** burning that is not initiated by the direct application of an external source of heat. A number of materials and chemicals, such as hay and sodium chlorate, can react with their surroundings, usually by oxidation, to produce so much internal heat that combustion results.

**spoonbill** any of several large wading birds of the ibis family Threskiornithidae, order Ciconiiformes, characterized by a long, flat bill, dilated at the tip in the shape of a spoon. Spoonbills are white or pink, and up to 90 cm/3 ft tall. Their feet are adapted for wading, and the birds obtain their food, consisting chiefly of fish, frogs, molluscs, and crustaceans, from shallow water.

**spoonerism** exchange of elements in a flow of words. Usually a slip of the tongue, a spoonerism can also be contrived for comic effect (for example 'a troop of Boy Scouts' becoming 'a scoop of Boy Trouts'). William Spooner (1844–1930) gave his name to the phenomenon.

**spore** small reproductive or resting body, usually consisting of just one cell. Unlike a ◊gamete, it does not need to fuse with another cell in order to develop into a new organism. Spores are produced by the lower plants, most fungi, some bacteria, and certain protozoa. They are generally light and easily dispersed by wind movements.

Plant spores are haploid and are produced by the sporophyte, following ◊meiosis; see ◊alternation of generations.

**spreadsheet** in computing, a program that mimics a sheet of ruled paper, divided into columns down the page, and rows across. The user enters values into cells within the sheet, then instructs the program to perform some operation on them, such as totalling a column or finding the average of a series of numbers. Highly complex numerical analyses may be built up from these simple steps.

**spring** device, usually a metal coil, that returns to its original shape after being stretched or compressed. Springs are used in some machines (such as clocks) to store energy, which can be released at a controlled rate. In other machines (such as engines) they are used to close valves.

**spring** in geology, a natural flow of water from the ground, formed at the point of intersection of the water table and the ground's surface. The source of water is rain that has percolated through the overlying rocks. During its underground passage, the water may have dissolved mineral substances that may then be precipitated at the spring (hence, a mineral spring).

**springbok** South African antelope *Antidorcas marsupialis* about 80 cm/30 in at the shoulder, with head and body 1.3 m/4 ft long. It may leap 3 m/10 ft or more in the air when startled or playing, and has a fold of skin along the middle of the back which is raised to a crest in alarm. Springboks once migrated in herds of over a million, but are now found only in small numbers where protected.

**Springsteen, Bruce** (1949– ) US rock singer, songwriter, and guitarist. His music combines melodies in traditional rock idiom and reflective lyrics about working-class life and the pursuit of the American dream on such albums as *Born to Run* (1975), *Born in the USA* (1984), and *Human Touch* (1992). His retrospective collection of songs, *Tracks,* was released in November 1998. He was inducted into the Rock and Roll Hall of Fame in March 1999.

**spruce** coniferous tree belonging to the pine family, found over much of the northern hemisphere. Pyramidal in shape, spruces have rigid, prickly needles and drooping, leathery cones. Some are important forestry trees, such as the sitka spruce (*P. sitchensis*), native to western North America, and the Norway spruce (*P. abies*), now planted widely in North America. (Genus *Picea*, family Pinaceae.)

**Sputnik** (Russian 'fellow traveller') series of ten Soviet Earth-orbiting satellites. *Sputnik 1* was the first artificial satellite, launched 4 October 1957. It weighed 84 kg/185 lb, with a 58 cm/23 in diameter, and carried only a simple radio transmitter which allowed scientists to track it as it orbited Earth. It burned up in the atmosphere 92 days later. Sputniks were superseded in the early 1960s by the Cosmos series.

**sq** abbreviation for *square* (measure).

**square root** in mathematics, a number that when squared (multiplied by itself) equals a given number. For example, the square root of 25 (written $\sqrt{25}$) is $\pm 5$, because $5 \times 5 = 25$, and $(-5) \times (-5) = 25$. As an ◊exponent, a square root is represented by $\frac{1}{2}$, for example, $16^{\frac{1}{2}} = 4$.

**squash** or *squash rackets,* racket-and-ball game usually played by two people on an enclosed court, derived from rackets. Squash became a popular sport in the 1970s and later gained competitive status. There are two forms of squash: the American form, which is played in North and some South American countries, and the English, which is played mainly in Europe and Commonwealth countries such as Pakistan, Australia, and New Zealand.

**squatter** person illegally occupying someone else's property; for example, some of the urban homeless in contemporary Britain making use of vacant houses. Squatters commit a criminal offence if they take over property where there is a 'residential occupier'; for example, by moving in while the owner is on holiday.

**squill** bulb-forming perennial plant belonging to the lily family, found growing in dry places near the sea in Western Europe. Cultivated species usually bear blue flowers, either singly or in clusters, at the top of the stem. (Genus *Scilla*, family Liliaceae.)

**squint** or *strabismus*, common condition in which one eye deviates in any direction. A squint may be convergent (with the bad eye turned inwards), divergent (outwards), or, in rare cases, vertical. A convergent squint is also called *cross-eye*.

**squirrel** rodent of the family Sciuridae. Squirrels are found worldwide except for Australia, Madagascar, and polar regions. Some are tree dwellers; these generally have bushy tails, and some, with membranes between their legs, are called ɸflying squirrels. Others are terrestrial, generally burrowing forms called ground squirrels; these include chipmunks, gophers, marmots, and prairie dogs.

**Sri Lanka** Democratic Socialist Republic of (formerly to 1972 *Ceylon*)
**national name** *Sri Lanka Prajathanthrika Samajawadi Janarajaya*

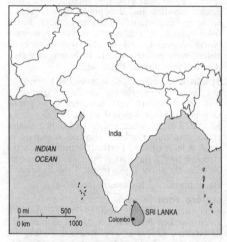

**area** 65,610 sq km/25,332 sq mi
**capital** Colombo (and chief port)
**major towns/cities** Kandy, Dehiwala-Mount Lavinia, Moratuwa, Jaffna, Kotte
**major ports** Jaffna, Galle, Negombo, Trincomalee
**physical features** flat in north and around coast; hills and mountains in south and central interior
**head of state** Chandrika Bandaranaike Kumaratunga from 1994
**head of government** Sirimavo Bandaranaike from 1994
**political system** liberal democracy
**political parties** United National Party (UNP), right of centre; Sri Lanka Freedom Party (SLFP), left of centre; Democratic United National Front (DUNF), centre left; Tamil United Liberation Front (TULF), Tamil autonomy (banned from 1983); Eelam People's Revolutionary Liberation

Front (EPRLF), Indian-backed Tamil-secessionist 'Tamil Tigers'; People's Liberation Front (JVP), Sinhalese-chauvinist, left wing (banned 1971–77 and 1983–88)
**currency** Sri Lankan rupee
**GNP per capita (PPP)** (US$) 2,300 (1998 est)
**exports** clothing and textiles, tea (world's largest exporter and third-largest producer), precious and semi-precious stones, coconuts and coconut products, rubber. Principal market: USA 39.9% (1998)
**population** 18,639,000 (1999 est)
**language** Sinhala, Tamil, English
**religion** Buddhist 69%, Hindu 15%, Muslim 8%, Christian 7%
**life expectancy** 71 (men); 75 (women) (1995–2000)
*Chronology*
*c. 550 BC* Arrival of the Sinhalese, led by Vijaya, from northern India, displacing long-settled Veddas.
*5th century BC* Sinhalese kingdom of Anuradhapura founded by King Pandukabaya.
*c. 250–210 BC* Buddhism, brought from India, became established in Sri Lanka.
*AD 992* Downfall of Anuradhapura kingdom, defeated by South Indian Colas.
*1070* Overthrow of Colas by Vijayabahu I and establishment of the Sinhalese kingdom of Polonnaruva, which survived for more than two centuries before a number of regional states arose.
*late 15th century* Kingdom of Kandy established in central highlands.
*1505* Arrival of Portuguese navigator Lorenço de Almeida, attracted by spice trade developed by Arab merchants who had called the island Serendip.
*1597–1618* Portuguese controlled most of Sri Lanka, with the exception of Kandy.
*1658* Dutch conquest of Portuguese territories.
*1795–98* British conquest of Dutch territories.
*1802* Treaty of Amiens recognized island as British colony of Ceylon.
*1815* British won control of Kandy, becoming first European power to rule whole island.
*1830s* Immigration of south Indian Hindu Tamil labourers to work central coffee plantations.
*1880s* Tea and rubber become chief cash crops after blight ended production of coffee.
*1919* Formation of the Ceylon National Congress to campaign for self rule; increasing conflicts between Sinhalese majority community and Tamil minority.
*1931* Universal adult suffrage introduced for elected legislature and executive council in which power was shared with British.
*1948* Ceylon achieved independence from Britain within Commonwealth, with Don Senanayake of conservative United National Party (UNP) as prime minister.
*1949* Indian Tamils disenfranchised.
*1952* Death of Don Senanayake, who was succeeded as prime minister by his son, Dudley.
*1956* Sinhala established as official language; Solomon Bandaranaike became prime minister.
*1959* Bandaranaike assassinated.

**1960** Sirimavo Bandaranaike, the widow of Solomon, won general election and formed an SLFP government, which nationalized oil industry.
**1965** General election won by UNP; Dudley Senanayake became prime minister.
**1970** Sirimavo Bandaranaike returned to power as prime minister, leading United Front government.
**1971** Sinhalese Marxist uprising, led by students and People's Liberation Army (JVP).
**1972** Socialist Republic of Sri Lanka proclaimed; Buddhism given 'foremost place' in new state, antagonizing Tamils.
**1976** Tamil United Liberation Front formed to fight for independent Tamil state ('Eelam') in north and east Sri Lanka.
**1978** Presidential constitution adopted by new free-market government headed by Junius Jayawardene of UNP.
**1983** Ethnic riots as Tamil guerrilla violence escalated; state of emergency imposed; more than 1,000 Tamils killed by Sinhalese mobs.
**1987** President Jayawardene and Indian prime minister Rajiv Gandhi signed Colombo Accord aimed at creating new provincial councils, disarming Tamil militants ('Tamil Tigers'), and stationing 7,000-strong Indian Peace Keeping Force. Violence continued despite ceasefire policed by Indian troops.
**1988** Left-wing JVP guerrillas campaigned against Indo-Sri Lankan peace pact. Prime Minister Ranasinghe Premadasa elected president.
**1989** Dingiri Banda Wijetunga became prime minister. Leaders of Tamil Tigers and banned Sinhala extremist JVP assassinated.
**1990** The Indian peacekeeping force was withdrawn. Violence continued, with a death toll of over a thousand a month.
**1991** Defence Minister Ranjan Wijeratne was assassinated; the Sri Lankan army killed 2,552 Tamil Tigers at Elephant Pass in the northern Jaffna region. An impeachment motion against President Premadasa failed. A new party, the Democratic National United Front (DUNF), was formed by former members of UNP.
**1992** Several hundred Tamil Tiger rebels were killed in an army offensive, code-named 'Strike Force Two'.
**1993** President Premadasa was assassinated by Tamil Tiger terrorists; he was succeeded by Dingiri Banda Wijetunga.
**1994** The UNP were narrowly defeated in a general election; Chandrika Kumaratunga became prime minister in an SLFP-led left-of-centre coalition. Peace talks opened with the Tamil Tigers. Kumaratunga was elected the first female president; her mother, Sirimavo Bandaranaike, became prime minister.
**1995** Renewed bombing campaign by Tamil Tigers. A major offensive drove out Tamil Tigers from Jaffna city.
**1996** A state of emergency was extended nationwide after Tamils bombed the capital. Government forces launched a major new offensive against the Tamil Tigers.
**1997** Clashes with Tamil separatists threatened to derail the government's peace initiative.

**1998** The Tamil Tigers were outlawed after the bombing of Sri Lanka's holiest Buddhist site. In September over 1,300 Sri Lankan soldiers and Tamil Tiger rebels died in renewed fighting in the north. In October the Tamil Tigers captured the strategic northern town of Kilinochchi, killing more than 600 government troops; the government launched a new military operation against the Tamil Tigers.

**SS** German Schutz-Staffel 'protective squadron', Nazi elite corps established in 1925. Under ◊Himmler its 500,000 membership included the full-time **Waffen-SS** (armed SS), which fought in World War II, and spare-time members. The SS performed state police duties and was brutal in its treatment of the Jews and others in the concentration camps and occupied territories. It was condemned as an illegal organization at the Nuremberg Trials of war criminals.

**stadholder** or **stadtholder,** leader of the United Provinces of the Netherlands from the 15th to the 18th century.

**Staffordshire** county of west central England (since April 1997 Stoke-on-Trent has been a separate unitary authority)
**area** 2,720 sq km/1,050 sq mi
**towns** Stafford (administrative headquarters), Newcastle-under-Lyme, Lichfield, Tamworth, Leek, Uttoxeter
**physical** largely flat, with hilly regions in the north (part of the Peak district) and southwest; River Trent and its tributaries (the Churnet, Dove, Penk, Sow, and Tame); Cannock Chase (a large open area in the middle of the county)
**features** castles at Chartley, Tamworth, and Tutbury; Lichfield Cathedral; Keele University (1962); Shugborough Hall (17th century), seat of the earls of Lichfield; Staffordshire bull terriers
**agriculture** dairy farming
**industries** breweries (Burton-upon-Trent); china and earthenware in the Potteries and the upper Trent basin (including Wedgwood); tractors and agricultural equipment (Uttoxeter); electrical engineering; electronics
**population** (1996) 555,700
**famous people** Arnold Bennett, Clarice Cliff, David Garrick, John Jervis, Samuel Johnson, Robert Peel, Isaak Walton, Josiah Wedgwood, Peter de Wint.

**Staffs** abbreviation for ◊*Staffordshire,* an English county.

**stagflation** (combination of *stagnation* and *inflation*) economic condition (experienced in the USA and Europe in the 1970s) in which rapid inflation is accompanied by stagnating, even declining, output and by increasing unemployment. Its cause is often sharp increases in costs of raw materials and/or labour. It is a recently coined term to explain a condition that violates many of the suppositions of classical economics.

**stainless steel** widely used ◊alloy of iron, chromium, and nickel that resists rusting. Its chromium content also gives it a high tensile strength. It is used for cutlery and kitchen fittings, and in surgical instruments. Stainless steel was first produced in the UK in 1913 and in Germany in 1914.

**stakeholder economy** an idea floated by Will Hutton, former economics editor of *The Guardian* newspaper, and subsequently editor of *The Observer*, which put forward the prospect of greater worker involvement in companies on something of the German model. In his best-selling book *The State We're In* (1996), Hutton ranged far wider than industrial democracy and called for a major review of Britain's constitution.

**stalactite and stalagmite** cave structures formed by the deposition of calcite dissolved in ground water. *Stalactites* grow downwards from the roofs or walls and can be icicle-shaped, straw-shaped, curtain-shaped, or formed as terraces. *Stalagmites* grow upwards from the cave floor and can be conical, fir-cone shaped, or resemble a stack of saucers. Growing stalactites and stalagmites may meet to form a continuous column from floor to ceiling.

**Stalin, Joseph** Russian 'steel', adopted name of Joseph Vissarionovich Djugashvili (1879–1953) Soviet politician. A member of the October Revolution committee of 1917, Stalin became general secretary of the Communist Party in 1922. After ◊Lenin's death in 1924, Stalin sought to create 'socialism in one country' and clashed with ◊Trotsky, who denied the possibility of socialism inside Russia until revolution had occurred in Western Europe. Stalin won this ideological struggle by 1927, and a series of five-year plans was launched to collectivize industry and agriculture from 1928. All opposition was eliminated in the Great Purge 1936–38. During World War II, Stalin intervened in the military direction of the campaigns against Nazi Germany. He managed not only to bring the USSR through the war but to help it emerge as a superpower, although only at an immense cost in human suffering to his own people. After the war, Stalin quickly turned Eastern Europe into a series of Soviet satellites and maintained an autocratic rule domestically. His role was denounced after his death by Khrushchev and other members of the Soviet regime.

**Stalingrad** former name (1925–61) of the Russian city of ◊Volgograd.

**stamen** male reproductive organ of a flower. The stamens are collectively referred to as the androecium. A typical stamen consists of a stalk, or filament, with an anther, the pollen-bearing organ, at its apex, but in some primitive plants, such as *Magnolia*, the stamen may not be markedly differentiated.

**Stamp Act** UK act of Parliament in 1765 that sought to raise enough money from the American colonies to cover the cost of their defence.

Refusal to use the required tax stamps and a blockade of British merchant shipping in the colonies forced a repeal of the act the following year. It helped to precipitate the ◊American Revolution.

**standard deviation** in statistics, a measure (symbol σ or s) of the spread of data. The deviation (difference) of each of the data items from the mean is found, and their values squared. The mean value of these squares is then calculated. The standard deviation is the square root of this mean.

**standard form** or *scientific notation*, method of writing numbers often used by scientists, particularly for very large or very small numbers. The numbers are written with one digit before the decimal point and multiplied by a power of 10. The number of digits given after the decimal point depends on the accuracy required. For example, the ◊speed of light is $2.9979 \times 10^8$ m/$1.8628 \times 10^5$ mi per second.

**standard of living** in economics, the measure of consumption and welfare of a country, community, class, or person. Individual standard-of-living expectations are heavily influenced by the income and consumption of other people in similar jobs.

**standard temperature and pressure** (STP), in chemistry, a standard set of conditions for experimental measurements, to enable comparisons to be made between sets of results. Standard temperature is 0°C/32°F (273K) and standard pressure 1 atmosphere (101,325 Pa).

**Stanislavsky, Konstantin Sergeivich Alekseyev** (1863–1938) Russian actor, director, and teacher of acting. He rejected the declamatory style of acting in favour of a more realistic approach, concentrating on the psychological basis for the development of character. The Actors Studio is based on his methods. As a director, he is acclaimed for his productions of the great plays of ◊Chekhov.

**Stanley, Henry Morton** Adopted name of John Rowlands (1841–1904) Welsh-born US explorer and journalist who made four expeditions to Africa. He and David ◊Livingstone met at Ujiji in 1871 and explored Lake Tanganyika. He traced the course of the Congo-Zaire River to the sea (1874–77), established the Congo Free State (Democratic Republic of Congo) (1879–84), and charted much of the interior (1887–89). GCB 1899.

**Stanton, Elizabeth** born Cady (1815–1902) US feminist. With Susan B Anthony, she founded the National Woman Suffrage Association 1869, the first women's movement in the USA, and was its first president. She and Anthony wrote and compiled the *History of Women's Suffrage* 1881–86. Stanton also worked for the abolition of slavery.

**stanza** (Italian 'resting or stopping place') group of lines in a poem. A stanza serves the same function in poetry as a paragraph in prose. Stanzas are often of uniform length and separated by a blank line.

**star** luminous globe of gas, mainly hydrogen and helium, which produces its own heat and light by nuclear reactions. Although stars shine for a very long time – many billions of years – they are not eternal, and have been found to change in appearance at different stages in their lives.

**starch** widely distributed, high-molecular-mass ◊carbohydrate, produced by plants as a food store; main dietary sources are cereals, legumes, and tubers, including potatoes. It consists of varying proportions of two ◊glucose polymers (◊polysaccharides): straight-chain (amylose) and branched (amylopectin) molecules.

**Star Chamber** in English history, a civil and criminal court, named after the star-shaped ceiling decoration of the room in the Palace of Westminster, London, where its first meetings were held. Created in 1487 by Henry VII, the Star Chamber comprised some 20 or 30 judges. It was abolished in 1641 by the ◊Long Parliament.

**starfish** or *sea star,* any ◊echinoderm of the subclass Asteroidea with arms radiating from a central body. Usually there are five arms, but some species have more. They are covered with spines and small pincerlike organs. There are also a number of small tubular processes on the skin surface that assist in locomotion and respiration. Starfish are predators, and vary in size from 1.2 cm/0.5 in to 90 cm/3 ft.

**star fruit** fruit of the carambola tree.

**starling** any member of a large widespread Old World family (Sturnidae) of chunky, dark, generally gregarious birds of the order Passeriformes. The European starling *Sturnus vulgaris,* common in northern Eurasia, has been naturalized in North America from the late 19th century. The black, speckled plumage is glossed with green and purple. The feathers on the upper parts are tipped with buff, and the wings are greyish-black, with a reddish-brown fringe. The female is less glossy and lustrous than the male. Its own call is a bright whistle, but it is a mimic of the songs of other birds. It is about 20 cm/8 in long.

**Star Wars** popular term for the ◊Strategic Defense Initiative announced by US president Reagan in 1983.

**States General** former French parliament that consisted of three estates: nobility, clergy, and commons. First summoned in 1302, it declined in importance as the power of the crown grew. It was not called at all from 1614–1789 when the crown needed to institute fiscal reforms to avoid financial collapse. Once called, the demands made by the States General formed the first phase in the ◊French Revolution. States General is also the name of the Dutch parliament.

**states of matter** forms (solid, liquid, or gas) in which material can exist. Whether a material is solid, liquid, or gaseous depends on its temperature and the pressure on it. The transition between states takes place at definite temperatures, called melting point and boiling point.

**static electricity** ◊electric charge that is stationary, usually acquired by a body by means of electrostatic induction or friction. Rubbing different materials can produce static electricity, as seen in the sparks produced on combing one's hair or removing a nylon shirt. In some processes static electricity is useful, as in paint spraying where the parts to be sprayed are charged with electricity of opposite polarity to that on the paint droplets, and in xerography.

**statics** branch of mechanics concerned with the behaviour of bodies at rest and forces in equilibrium, and distinguished from ◊dynamics.

**statistics** branch of mathematics concerned with the collection and interpretation of data. For example, to determine the ◊mean age of the children in a school, a statistically acceptable answer might be obtained by calculating an average based on the ages of a representative sample, consisting, for example, of a random tenth of the pupils from each class. ◊Probability is the branch of statistics dealing with predictions of events.

**status** in the social sciences, an individual's social position, or the esteem in which he or she is held by others in society. Both within and between most occupations or social positions there is a status hierarchy. *Status symbols,* such as insignia of office or an expensive car, often accompany high status.

**status quo** (Latin 'the state in which') the current situation, without change.

**Stavropol** krai (territory) in the southwestern Russian Federation
*area* 80,600 sq km/31,120 sq mi
*cities* Stavropol (capital), Pyatigorsk, Kislovodsk
*physical* situated in northern Caucasia, in the foothills of the main Caucasus Mountains; dry steppe in the northeast; rich deposits of natural gas, and mineral springs; main rivers are the Kuban and the Kuma; administratively, the Karachayevo-Cherkess Republic forms part of the territory
*industries* on the steppe, wheat and sunflowers are grown, and cattle and sheep are raised; natural gas is piped to Moscow and St Petersburg, and there is a variety of food-processing industries; spas and health resorts around Mineralnye Vody
*population* (1996) 2,667,000; 54% urban
*history* the region saw heavy fighting during the Russian Civil War (1918–20); the area now covered by Stavropol krai was first constituted as the Southeastern Oblast in 1924, changing to its present designation in 1943; Stavropol was occupied by German forces 1942–43.

**STD** abbreviation for ◊sexually transmitted disease.

**steady-state theory** in astronomy, a rival theory to that of the ◊Big Bang, which claims that the universe has no origin but is expanding because new matter is being created continuously throughout the universe. The theory was proposed in 1948 by Hermann Bondi, Thomas Gold (1920– ), and Fred Hoyle, but was dealt a severe blow in 1964 by the discovery of ◊cosmic background radiation (radiation left over from the formation of the universe) and is now largely rejected.

**stealth technology** methods used to make an aircraft as invisible as possible, primarily to radar detection but also to detection by visual means and heat sensors. This is achieved by a combination of aircraft-design elements: smoothing off all radar-reflecting sharp edges; covering the aircraft with radar-absorbent materials; fitting engine coverings that hide the exhaust and heat signatures of the aircraft; and other, secret technologies.

**steam** in chemistry, a dry, invisible gas formed by vaporizing water.

The visible cloud that normally forms in the air when water is vaporized is due to minute suspended water particles. Steam is widely used in chemical and other industrial processes and for the generation of power.

**steam engine** engine that uses the power of steam to produce useful work. It was the principal power source during the British Industrial Revolution in the 18th century. The first successful steam engine was built in 1712 by English inventor Thomas Newcomen at Dudley, West Midlands; it was developed further by Scottish mining engineer James Watt from 1769 and by English mining engineer Richard Trevithick, whose high-pressure steam engine of 1802 led to the development of the steam locomotive.

**stearic acid** $CH_3 (CH_2)_{16}COOH$ saturated long-chain ◊fatty acid, soluble in alcohol and ether but not in water. It is found in many fats and oils, and is used to make soap and candles and as a lubricant. The salts of stearic acid are called stearates.

**steel** alloy or mixture of iron and up to 1.7% carbon, sometimes with other elements, such as manganese, phosphorus, sulphur, and silicon. The USA, Russia, Ukraine, and Japan are the main steel producers. Steel has innumerable uses, including ship and car manufacture, skyscraper frames, and machinery of all kinds.

**steel band** musical ensemble common in the West Indies, consisting mostly of percussion instruments made from oil drums that give a sweet, metallic ringing tone.

**Steele, Richard** (1672–1729) Irish essayist, playwright, and politician. He founded the journal *The Tatler* (1709–11), in which Joseph ◊Addison collaborated. They continued their joint work in the *Spectator*, also founded by Steele (1711–12), and the *Guardian* (1713). He also wrote plays, such as *The Conscious Lovers* (1722).

**Stefan–Boltzmann law** in physics, a law that relates the energy, $E$, radiated away from a perfect emitter (a black body), to the temperature, $T$, of that body. It has the form $E = \sigma T^4$, where $E$ is the energy radiated per unit area per second, $T$ is the temperature, and $\sigma$ is the *Stefan–Boltzmann constant*. Its value is $5.6705 \times 10^{-8}$ W m$^{-2}$ K$^{-4}$. The law was derived by the Austrian physicists Josef Stefan and Ludwig Boltzmann.

**Stegosaurus** genus of late Jurassic North American dinosaurs of the order Ornithischia. They were ungainly herbivores, with very small heads, a double row of triangular plates along the back, and spikes on the tail.

**Stein, Gertrude** (1874–1946) US writer. She influenced authors Ernest ◊Hemingway, Sherwood Anderson, and F Scott ◊Fitzgerald with her radical prose style. Drawing on the stream-of-consciousness psychology of William James and on the geometry of Cézanne and the Cubist painters in Paris, she evolved a 'continuous present' style made up of constant repetition and variation of simple phrases. Her work includes the self-portrait *The Autobiography of Alice B Toklas* (1933).

**Steinbeck, John Ernst** (1902–1968) US novelist. His realist novels, such as *In Dubious Battle* (1936), *Of Mice and Men* (1937), and *The Grapes of Wrath* (1939; Pulitzer prize; filmed 1940), portray agricultural life in his native California, where migrant farm labourers from the Oklahoma dust bowl struggled to survive. He was awarded the Nobel Prize for Literature in 1962.

**Steinem, Gloria** (1934– ) US journalist and liberal feminist. She emerged as a leading figure in the US women's movement in the late 1960s. She was also involved in radical protest campaigns against racism and the Vietnam War. She cofounded the Women's Action Alliance in 1970 and *Ms* magazine. In 1983 a collection of her articles was published as *Outrageous Acts and Everyday Rebellions*.

**Steiner, Rudolf** (1861–1925) Austrian philosopher, occultist, and educationalist. He formulated his own mystic and spiritual teaching, which he called anthroposophy. This rejected materialism and aimed to develop the whole human being, intellectually, socially, and, above all, spiritually. A number of Steiner schools follow a curriculum laid down by him with a strong emphasis on the arts.

**Stella, Frank Philip** (1936– ) US painter. He was a pioneer of the severe, hard-edged geometric trend in abstract art that followed ◊Abstract Expressionism. From around 1960 he also experimented with shaped canvases.

**stem** main supporting axis of a plant that bears the leaves, buds, and reproductive structures; it may be simple or branched. The plant stem usually grows above ground, although some grow underground, including ◊rhizomes, ◊corms, ◊rootstocks, and ◊tubers. Stems contain a continuous vascular system that conducts water and food to and from all parts of the plant.

**Stendhal** pen-name of Marie Henri Beyle (1783–1842) French novelist. His novels *Le Rouge et le Noir/The Red and the Black* 1830 and *La Chartreuse de Parme/The Charterhouse of Parma* 1839 were pioneering works in their treatment of disguise and hypocrisy and outstanding for their psychological analysis; a review of the latter by fellow novelist ◊Balzac 1840 furthered Stendhal's reputation, but he was not fully understood during his lifetime.

**Stephen** (*c.* 1097–1154) King of England from 1135. A grandson of William the Conqueror, he was elected king in 1135, although he had previously recognized Henry I's daughter ◊Matilda as heiress to the throne. Matilda landed in England in 1139, and civil war disrupted the country until 1153, when Stephen acknowledged Matilda's son, Henry II, as his own heir.

**Stephen, St** (lived *c.* AD 35) The first Christian martyr; he was stoned to death. Feast day 26 December.

**Stephenson, George** (1781–1848) English engineer. He built the first successful steam locomotive. He also invented a safety lamp independently of Humphrey ◊Davy in 1815. He was appointed engineer of the Stockton and Darlington Railway, the world's first public railway, in 1821, and of the Liverpool and Manchester Railway in 1826. In 1829 he won a prize with his locomotive *Rocket*.

**Stephenson, Robert** (1803–1859) English civil engineer. He constructed railway bridges such as the high-level bridge at Newcastle-upon-Tyne, England, and the Menai and Conway tubular bridges in Wales. He was the son of George ◊Stephenson.

**steppe** the temperate grasslands of Europe and Asia. Sometimes the term refers to other temperate grasslands and semi-arid desert edges.

**steradian** SI unit (symbol sr) of measure of solid (three-dimensional) angles, the three-dimensional equivalent of the ◊radian. One steradian is the angle at the centre of a sphere when an area on the surface of the sphere equal to the square of the sphere's radius is joined to the centre.

**stereotype** (Greek 'fixed impression') in sociology, a fixed, exaggerated, and preconceived description about a certain type of person, group, or society.

It is based on prejudice rather than fact, but by repetition and with time, stereotypes become fixed in people's minds, resistant to change or factual evidence to the contrary.

**sterilization** the killing or removal of living organisms such as bacteria and fungi. A sterile environment is necessary in medicine, food processing, and some scientific experiments. Methods include heat treatment (such as boiling), the use of chemicals (such as disinfectants), irradiation with gamma rays, and filtration. See also ◊asepsis.

**sterilization** any surgical operation to terminate the possibility of reproduction. In women, this is normally achieved by sealing or tying off the ◊Fallopian tubes (tubal ligation) so that fertilization can no longer take place. In men, the transmission of sperm is blocked by ◊vasectomy.

**sterling silver** ◊alloy containing 925 parts of silver and 75 parts of copper. The copper hardens the silver, making it more useful.

**Sterne, Laurence** (1713–1768) Irish writer. He created the comic anti-hero Tristram Shandy in *The Life and Opinions of Tristram Shandy, Gent* (1759–67), an eccentrically whimsical and bawdy novel in which associations of ideas on the principles of John Locke, and other devices, foreshadow in part some of the techniques associated with the 20th-century novel such as stream-of-consciousness. His other works include *A Sentimental Journey through France and Italy* (1768).

**steroid** in biology, any of a group of cyclic, unsaturated alcohols (lipids without fatty acid components), which, like sterols, have a complex molecular structure consisting of four carbon rings. Steroids include the sex hormones, such as ◊testosterone, the corticosteroid hormones produced by the ◊adrenal gland, bile acids, and ◊cholesterol.

The term is commonly used to refer to ◊anabolic steroid. In medicine, synthetic steroids are used to treat a wide range of conditions.

**sterol** any of a group of solid, cyclic, unsaturated alcohols, with a complex structure that includes four carbon rings; cholesterol is an example. Steroids are derived from sterols.

**stethoscope** instrument used to ascertain the condition of the heart and lungs by listening to their action. It consists of two earpieces connected by flexible tubes to a small plate that is placed against the body. It was invented in 1819 in France by René Théophile Hyacinthe Laënnec.

**Stevenson, Robert Louis Balfour** (1850–1894) Scottish novelist and poet. He wrote the adventure stories *Treasure Island* (1883), *Kidnapped* (1886), and *The Master of Ballantrae* (1889), notable for their characterization as well as their action. He was a master also of shorter fiction such as *The Strange Case of Dr Jekyll and Mr Hyde* (1886), and of stories of the supernatural such as *Thrawn Janet* (1881).

**stick insect** insect of the order Phasmida, closely resembling a stick or twig. The eggs mimic plant seeds. Many species are wingless. The longest reach a length of 30 cm/1 ft.

**stickleback** any fish of the family Gasterosteidae, found in marine and fresh waters of the northern hemisphere. It has a long body that can grow to 18 cm/7 in. The spines along a stickleback's back take the place of the first dorsal fin, and can be raised to make the fish difficult to eat for predators. After the eggs have been laid the female takes no part in rearing the young: the male builds a nest for the eggs, which he then guards and rears for the first two weeks.

**stigma** in a flower, the surface at the tip of a ◊carpel that receives the ◊pollen. It often has short outgrowths, flaps, or hairs to trap pollen and may produce a sticky secretion to which the grains adhere.

**Stijl, De** (Dutch 'the style') influential movement in art, architecture, and design founded 1917 in the Netherlands. Attempting to bring art and design together in a single coherent system, the members of De Stijl developed an austere simplification of style, based on simple geometrical shapes and primary colour. Its best-known member was the abstract painter Piet ◊Mondrian. The group's main theorist and publicist was Theo van Doesburg (1883–1931), and his death in 1931 effectively marked its end.

**still life** in painting and other visual arts, a depiction of inanimate objects, such as flowers, fruit, or tableware. Pictures of dead animals are also embraced by the term. Still-life painting was popular among the ancient Greeks and Romans (who also made still-life mosaics), but thereafter it was sidelined in European art for centuries, as art was overwhelmingly devoted to religious subjects during the Middle Ages. It reappeared during the Renaissance and became established as a distinctive branch of painting in the 17th century, flourishing first in the Netherlands, where the Reformation had discouraged religious imagery and artists were seeking new subjects.

**Stilwell, Joseph Warren** 'Vinegar Joe' (1883–1946) US general in World War II. In 1942 he became US military representative in China, when he commanded the Chinese forces cooperating with the British (with whom he quarrelled) in Burma (now Myanmar). He later commanded all US forces in China, Burma, and India until recalled to the USA in 1944 after differences over nationalist policy with the ◊Guomindang (nationalist) leader Chiang Kaishek. Subsequently he commanded the US 10th Army on the Japanese island of Okinawa.

**stimulant** any substance that acts on the brain to increase alertness and activity; for example, ◊amphetamine. When given to children, stimulants may have a paradoxical, calming effect. Stimulants cause liver damage, are habit-forming, have limited therapeutic value, and are now prescribed only to treat narcolepsy and severe obesity.

**Stirling** unitary authority in central Scotland, created in 1996 from Stirling district, Central region
*area* 2,196 sq km/848 sq mi
*towns* Dunblane, Stirling (administrative headquarters), Aberfoyle
*physical* mountainous to the north, including the forested Trossachs, and the open moorland north and west of Breadalbane, within the flood plain of the River Forth to the south around Sterling. The area contains many famous Scottish lochs (Tay, Katrine, Lomond) and Scotland's only lake (Lake of Menteith). Peaks include Ben More (1,174 m/3,852 ft) and Ben Venue (727 m/2,385 ft)
*features* Bannockburn Heritage Centre; Stirling Castle (most visited paid attraction in Scotland outside Edinburgh)
*industries* tourism, light engineering
*agriculture* forestry and stock rearing in the uplands, while in the lowlands some of the richest agricultural lands in Scotland may be found, including the Carse of Gowrie
*population* (1996) 82,000
*history* William Wallace won battle of Stirling Bridge in 1297; English defeated at Bannockburn by Robert the Bruce in 1314; battle at Sheriffmuir in 1715 between Jacobites and Hanoverians.

**Stirling, James Frazer** (1926–1992) Scottish architect. He was possibly the most influential of his generation. While in partnership with James Gowan (1924– ), he designed an influential housing estate at Ham Common, Richmond (1958), and the Leicester University Engineering Building (1959–63) in a Constructivist vein. He later adopted a more eclectic approach, exemplified in his considered masterpiece, the Staatsgalerie, Stuttgart, Germany (1977–83), which blended Constructivism, Modernism, and several strands of Classicism. He also designed the Clore Gallery (1980–86) extension to the Tate Gallery, London. He was knighted in 1983.

**stoat** carnivorous mammal *Mustela erminea* of the northern hemisphere, in the weasel family, about 37 cm/15 in long including the black-tipped tail. It has a long body and a flattened head. The upper parts and tail are red-brown, and the underparts are white. In the colder regions, the coat turns white (ermine) in winter. Its young are called kits.

**stock** in botany, any of a group of herbaceous plants commonly grown as garden ornamentals. Many cultivated varieties, including simple-stemmed, queen's, and ten-week stocks, have been derived from the wild stock (*M. incana*); night-scented (or evening) stock (*M. bicornis*) becomes aromatic at night. (Genus *Matthiola*, family Cruciferae.)

**stock** in finance, the UK term for the fully paid-up capital of a company. It is bought and sold by subscribers not in units or shares, but in terms of its current cash value. In US usage the term stock generally means an ordinary share. See also ◊stocks and shares.

**stock exchange** institution for the buying and selling of stocks and shares (securities). The world's largest stock exchanges are London, New York (Wall Street), and Tokyo. The oldest stock exchanges are Antwerp (1460), Hamburg (1558), Amsterdam (1602), New York (1790), and London (1801). The former division on the London Stock Exchange between brokers (who bought shares from jobbers to sell to the public) and jobbers (who sold them only to brokers on commission, the 'jobbers' turn') was abolished in 1986.

**Stockhausen, Karlheinz** (1928– ) German composer of avant-garde music. He has continued to explore new musical sounds and compositional techniques since the 1950s. His major works include *Gesang der Jünglinge* (1956), *Kontakte* (1960) (electronic music), and *Sirius* (1977).

**Stockholm** capital and industrial port of Sweden; population (1994 est) 703,600. It is built on a number of islands. Industries include engineering, brewing, electrical goods, paper, textiles, and pottery.

**stocks and shares** investment holdings (securities) in private or public undertakings. Although distinctions have become blurred, in the UK stock usually means fixed-interest securities – for example, those issued by central and local government – while ◊shares represent a stake in the ownership of a trading company which, if they are ordinary shares, yield to the

*structure*

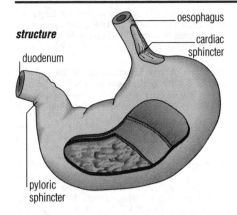

oesophagus

cardiac sphincter

duodenum

pyloric sphincter

*detail of stomach wall*

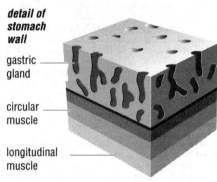

gastric gland

circular muscle

longitudinal muscle

**stomach** *The human stomach can hold about 1.5 l/2.6 pt of liquid. The digestive juices are acidic enough to dissolve metal. To avoid damage, the cells of the stomach lining are replaced quickly – 500,000 cells are replaced every minute, and the whole stomach lining every three days.*

owner dividends reflecting the success of the company. In the USA the term stock generally signifies what in the UK is an ordinary share.

**Stockton-on-Tees** unitary authority in north-east England created in 1996 from part of the former county of Cleveland
*area* 200 sq km/77 sq mi
*towns and cities* Stockton-on-Tees (administrative headquarters), Billingham, Yarm, Longnewton
*features* River Tees forms east border; Tees Barrage; Yarm viaduct; Preston Hall Museum and Park (Stockton); Castlegate Quay (Stockton) includes full-scale replica of *HMS Endeavour*
*industries* chemicals, polythene film, light and heavy engineering, insulation products, plastics, electronics
*population* (1996) 176,600.

**stoicism** (Greek *stoa* 'porch') Greek school of philosophy, founded about 300 BC by Zeno of Citium. The stoics were pantheistic materialists who believed that happiness lay in accepting the law of the universe. They emphasized human

brotherhood, denounced slavery, and were internationalist. The name is derived from the porch on which Zeno taught.

**Stoke-on-Trent** city and unitary authority in central England, on the River Trent, 23 km/14 mi north of Stafford; it was part of the county of Staffordshire to 1997
*area* 93 sq km/36 sq mi
*features* the Gladstone Pottery Museum is a working pottery museum
*industries* it is the heart of the Potteries, a major ceramic centre, and the largest clayware producer in the world; the ceramics factories of Minton, ◊Wedgwood, Spode, and Royal Doulton are all based here. Other industries include the manufacture of steel, chemicals, engineering machinery, paper, rubber, and tyres. Michelin has its headquarters in the town
*population* (1996) 254,200
*famous people* Arnold Bennett, John Wain, Robbie Williams
*history* Stoke was formed in 1910 from Burslem, Hanley, Longton, Stoke-upon-Trent, Fenton, and Tunstall.

**stomach** the first cavity in the digestive system of animals. In mammals it is a bag of muscle situated just below the diaphragm. Food enters it from the oesophagus, is digested by the acid and ◊enzymes secreted by the stomach lining, and then passes into the duodenum. Some plant-eating mammals have multichambered stomachs that harbour bacteria in one of the chambers to assist in the digestion of ◊cellulose.

The gizzard is part of the stomach in birds.

**stone** plural stone, imperial unit (abbreviation st) of mass. One stone is 14 pounds (6.35 kg).

**Stone Age** the developmental stage of humans in ◊prehistory before the use of metals, when tools and weapons were made chiefly of stone, especially flint. The Stone Age is subdivided into the Old or *Palaeolithic*, when flint implements were simply chipped into shape; the Middle or *Mesolithic*; and the New or *Neolithic*, when implements were ground and polished. Palaeolithic people were hunters and gatherers; by the Neolithic period people were taking the first steps in agriculture, the domestication of animals, weaving, and pottery.

**stonecrop** any of a group of plants belonging to the orpine family, succulent herbs with fleshy leaves and clusters of red, yellow, or white star-like flowers. Stonecrops are characteristic of dry, rocky places and some grow on walls. (Genus *Sedum*, family Crassulaceae.)

**stonefish** any of a family (Synanceiidae) of tropical marine bony fishes with venomous spines and bodies resembling encrusted rocks.

**Stonehenge** (Old English 'hanging stones') megalithic monument on Salisbury Plain, 3 km/ 1.9 mi west of Amesbury in Wiltshire, England. The site developed over various periods from a simple henge (earthwork circle and ditch), dating from about 3000 BC, to a complex stone structure, from about 2100 BC, which included a circle of 30 upright stones, their tops linked by lintel stones to form a continuous circle about 30 m/100 ft across.

**Stoppard, Tom** originally Thomas Straussler (1937–   ) Czechoslovak-born British dramatist. His works use wit and wordplay to explore logical and philosophical ideas. His play *Rosencrantz and Guildenstern are Dead* (1967) was followed by comedies including *The Real Inspector Hound* (1968), *Jumpers* (1972), *Travesties* (1974), *Dirty Linen* (1976), *The Real Thing* (1982), *Hapgood* (1988), *Arcadia* (1993), and *Indian Ink* (1995). He has also written for radio, television, and the cinema.

**stork** any of the 17 species of the Ciconiidae, a family of long-legged, long-necked wading birds with long, powerful wings, and long conical bills used for spearing prey. Some species grow up to 1.5 m/5 ft tall.

**Stormont** village 8 km/5 mi east of Belfast, Northern Ireland. It is the site of the new Northern Ireland Assembly, elected as a result of the Good Friday Agreement in 1998. It was the seat of the government of Northern Ireland 1921–72.

**Strachey, (Giles) Lytton** (1880–1932) English critic and biographer. He was a member of the ◊Bloomsbury Group of writers and artists. His *Landmarks in French Literature* was written in 1912. The mocking and witty treatment of Cardinal Manning, Florence Nightingale, Thomas Arnold, and General Gordon in *Eminent Victorians* (1918) won him recognition. His biography of *Queen Victoria* (1921) was more affectionate.

**Stradivari, Antonio** Latin form *Stradivarius* (*c.* 1644–1737) Italian stringed instrument maker, generally considered the greatest of all violin makers. He produced more than 1,100 instruments from his family workshops, over 600 of which survive; they have achieved the status (and sale-room prices) of works of art.

**Strafford, Thomas Wentworth, 1st Earl of Strafford** (1593–1641) English politician. He was originally an opponent of Charles I, but from 1628 he was on the Royalist side. He ruled despotically as Lord Deputy of Ireland (1632–39), when he returned to England as Charles's chief adviser and received an earldom. He was impeached in 1640 by Parliament, abandoned by Charles as a scapegoat, and beheaded. He was knighted in 1611, became Baron in 1628, and created Earl in 1640.

**Straits Settlements** former province of the ◊East India Company (1826–58), a British crown colony (1867–1946); it comprised Singapore, Malacca, Penang, Cocos Islands, Christmas Island, and Labuan.

**Strasbourg** German *Strassburg,* administrative centre of the Bas-Rhin *département* and of ◊Alsace region, northeast France, situated near the German border on the River Ill, 3 km/1.9 mi west of the Rhine near its confluence with the Rhine–Rhône and Rhine and Marne canals; population (1990) 255,900, conurbation 388,000. Industries include car manufacture, tobacco, printing and publishing, and preserves.

The town was selected as the headquarters for the ◊Council of Europe in 1949, and sessions of the European Parliament alternate between here and Luxembourg. It has an 11th–15th-century cathedral.

**Strategic Arms Limitation Talks** (SALT), series of US-Soviet discussions (1969–79) aimed at reducing the rate of nuclear-arms build-up (as opposed to ◊disarmament, which would reduce the number of weapons, as discussed in ◊Strategic Arms Reduction Talks [START]). The accords of the 1970s sought primarily to prevent the growth of nuclear arsenals.

**Strategic Arms Reduction Talks** (START), phase in peace discussions dealing with ◊disarmament, initially involving the USA and the Soviet Union, from 1992 the USA and Russia, and from 1993 Belarus and the Ukraine.

It began with talks in Geneva, Switzerland, in 1983, leading to the signing of the ◊Intermediate Nuclear Forces Treaty in 1987. In 1989 proposals for reductions in conventional weapons were added to the agenda. As the Cold War drew to a close from 1989, negotiations moved rapidly. Reductions of about 30% in strategic nuclear weapons systems were agreed in Moscow in July 1991 (START) and more significant cuts were agreed in January 1993 (START II); the latter treaty was ratified by the US Senate in January 1996.

**Strategic Defense Initiative** SDI) also called *Star Wars,* attempt by the USA to develop a defence system against incoming nuclear missiles, based in part outside the Earth's atmosphere. It was announced by President Reagan in March 1983, and the research had by 1990 cost over $16.5 billion. In 1988, the Joint Chiefs of Staff announced that they expected to be able to intercept no more than 30% of incoming missiles.

**Stratford-upon-Avon** market town on the River Avon, in Warwickshire, England, 35 km/22 mi southeast of Birmingham; population (1991) 22,200. It is the birthplace of William ◊Shakespeare and has the Royal Shakespeare Theatre (1932), the Swan Theatre, and The Other Place. Stratford receives over 2 million tourists a year. Industries include canning, aluminium ware, and boat building.

**stratosphere** that part of the atmosphere 10–40 km/6–25 mi from the Earth's surface, where the temperature slowly rises from a low of −55°C/−67°F to around 0°C/32°F. The air is rarefied and at around 25 km/15 mi much ◊ozone is concentrated.

**Strauss, Richard (Georg)** (1864–1949) German composer and conductor. He followed the German Romantic tradition but had a strongly personal style, characterized by his bold, colourful orchestration. He first wrote tone poems such as *Don Juan* (1889), *Till Eulenspiegel's Merry Pranks* (1895), and *Also sprach Zarathustra/Thus Spake Zarathustra* (1896). He then moved on to opera with *Salome* (1905) and *Elektra* (1909), both of which have elements of polytonality. He reverted to a more traditional style with *Der Rosenkavalier/The Knight of the Rose* (1909–10).

**Stravinsky, Igor Fyodorovich** (1882–1971) Russian composer, later of French (1934) and US (1945) nationality. He studied under ◊Rimsky-Korsakov and wrote the music for the Diaghilev ballets *The Firebird* (1910), *Petrushka* (1911), and *The Rite of Spring* (1913) (controversial at the time for their unorthodox rhythms and harmonies). His works also include symphonies, concertos (for violin and piano), chamber music, and operas; for example, *The Rake's Progress* (1951) and *The Flood* (1962).

**strawberry** low-growing perennial plant widely cultivated for its red, fleshy fruits, which are rich in vitamin C. Commercial cultivated forms bear one crop of fruit in summer, with the berries resting on a bed of straw to protect them from the damp soil, and multiply by runners. The flowers are normally white, although pink-flowering varieties are cultivated as ornamentals. (Genus *Fragaria*, family Rosaceae.)

**stress** in psychology, any event or situation that makes heightened demands on a person's mental or emotional resources. Stress can be caused by overwork, anxiety about exams, money, job security, unemployment, bereavement, poor relationships, marriage breakdown, sexual difficulties, poor living or working conditions, and constant exposure to loud noise.

**stress and strain** in the science of materials, measures of the deforming force applied to a body (stress) and of the resulting change in its shape (strain). For a perfectly elastic material, stress is proportional to strain (◊Hooke's law).

**stridulatory organs** in insects, organs that produce sound when rubbed together. Crickets rub their wings together, but grasshoppers rub a hind leg against a wing. Stridulation is thought to be used for attracting mates, but may also serve to mark territory.

**strike** stoppage of work by employees, often as members of a trade union, to obtain or resist change in wages, hours, or conditions. A *lock-out* is a weapon of an employer to thwart or enforce such change by preventing employees from working. Another measure is *work to rule*, when production is virtually brought to a halt by strict observance of union rules.

**Strindberg, (Johan) August** (1849–1912) Swedish dramatist and novelist. His plays are in a variety of styles including historical dramas, symbolic dramas (the two-part *Dödsdansen/The Dance of Death;* 1901), and 'chamber plays' such as *Spöksonaten/The Ghost [Spook] Sonata* (1907). *Fadren/The Father* (1887) and *Fröken Julie/ Miss Julie* (1888) are among his best-known works.

**string quartet** ◊chamber music ensemble consisting of first and second violins, viola, and cello. The 18th-century successor to the domestic viol consort, the string quartet with its stronger and more rustic tone formed the basis of the symphony orchestra. Important composers for the string quartet include Haydn (more than 80 string quartets), Mozart (27), Schubert (20), Beethoven (17), Dvořák (8), Bartók (6), and Shostakovich (15).

**stroke** or *cerebrovascular accident* or *apoplexy*, interruption of the blood supply to part of the brain due to a sudden bleed in the brain (cerebral haemorrhage) or embolism or ◊thrombosis. Strokes vary in severity from producing almost no symptoms to proving rapidly fatal. In between are those (often recurring) that leave a wide range of impaired function, depending on the size and location of the event.

**stromatolite** mound produced in shallow water by mats of algae that trap mud particles. Another mat grows on the trapped mud layer and this traps another layer of mud and so on. The stromatolite grows to heights of a metre or so. They are uncommon today but their fossils are among the earliest evidence for living things – over 2,000 million years old.

**strong nuclear force** one of the four fundamental ◊forces of nature, the other three being the gravitational force or gravity, the electromagnetic force, and the weak nuclear force. The strong nuclear force was first described by the Japanese physicist Hideki Yukawa in 1935. It is the strongest of all the forces, acts only over very small distances within the nucleus of the atom ($10^{-13}$ cm), and is responsible for binding together ◊quarks to form ◊hadrons, and for binding together protons and neutrons in the atomic nucleus. The particle that is the carrier of the strong nuclear force is the ◊gluon, of which there are eight kinds, each with zero mass and zero charge.

**strontium** soft, ductile, pale-yellow, metallic element, symbol Sr, atomic number 38, relative atomic mass 87.62. It is one of the ◊alkaline-earth metals, widely distributed in small quantities only as a sulphate or carbonate. Strontium salts burn with a red flame and are used in fireworks and signal flares.

**structuralism** 20th-century philosophical movement that has influenced such areas as linguistics, anthropology, and literary criticism. Inspired by the work of the Swiss linguist Ferdinand de Saussure, structuralists believe that objects should be analysed as systems of relations, rather than as positive entities.

**strychnine** $C_{21}H_{22}O_2N_2$ bitter-tasting, poisonous alkaloid. It is a poison that causes violent muscular spasms, and is usually obtained by powdering the seeds of plants of the genus *Strychnos* (for example *S. nux vomica*). Curare is a related drug.

**Stuart** or *Stewart*, royal family that inherited the Scottish throne in 1371 and the English throne in 1603, holding it until 1714, when Queen Anne died without heirs; the house of Stuart was succeeded by the house of Hanover. The claimants to the British throne James Francis Edward Stuart (the 'Old Pretender', son of the deposed James VII of Scotland and II of England) and his son Charles Edward Stuart (the 'Young Pretender') both attempted unsuccessful invasions of England in support of their claims, in 1715 and 1745 (see ◊Jacobites).

**Stubbs, George** (1724–1806) English artist. He is renowned for his paintings of horses, such as *Mares and Foals* (about 1763; Tate Gallery, London). After the publication of his book of engravings *The Anatomy of the Horse* (1766), he was widely commissioned as an animal painter. The dramatic *Lion Attacking a Horse* (1770; Yale University Art Gallery, New Haven, Connecticut) and the peaceful *Reapers* (1786; Tate Gallery, London) show the variety of mood in his painting.

**sturgeon** any of a family of large, primitive, bony fishes with five rows of bony plates, small sucking mouths, and chin barbels used for exploring the bottom of the water for prey.

**Stuttgart** capital of Baden-Württemberg, on the River Neckar, Germany; population (1995) 587,000. Industries include the manufacture of vehicles, electronics, mechanical and electrical engineering, precision instruments, foodstuffs, textiles, papermaking and publishing; it is a fruit-growing and wine-producing centre. There are two universities. Stuttgart was founded in the 10th century.

**style** in flowers, the part of the ◊carpel bearing the ◊stigma at its tip. In some flowers it is very short or completely lacking, while in others it may be long and slender, positioning the stigma in the most effective place to receive the pollen.

**Styx** (Greek 'hateful') in Greek mythology, the river surrounding ◊Hades, the underworld. When an oath was sworn by Styx, its waters were taken to seal the promise. Gods who broke such a vow suffered a year's unconsciousness and nine years' exile, while to mortal transgressors its waters were deadly poison. The tradition may have derived from some form of trial by ordeal.

**subatomic particle** in physics, a particle that is smaller than an atom. Such particles may be indivisible ◊elementary particles, such as the ◊electron and ◊quark, or they may be composites, such as the ◊proton, ◊neutron, and ◊alpha particle. See also ◊particle physics.

**subduction zone** region where two plates of the Earth's rigid lithosphere collide, and one plate descends below the other into the weaker asthenosphere. Subduction occurs along ocean trenches, most of which encircle the Pacific Ocean; portions of the ocean plate slide beneath other plates carrying continents.

**sublimation** in chemistry, the conversion of a solid to vapour without passing through the liquid phase.

**submarine** underwater warship. The first underwater boat was constructed in 1620 for James I of England by the Dutch scientist Cornelius van Drebbel (1572–1633). A naval submarine, or submersible torpedo boat, the *Gymnote*, was launched by France in 1888. The conventional submarine of World War I was driven by diesel engine on the surface and by battery-powered electric motors underwater. The diesel engine also drove a generator that produced electricity to charge the batteries.

**submersible** vessel designed to operate under water, especially a small submarine used by engineers and research scientists as a ferry craft to support diving operations. The most advanced submersibles are the so-called lock-out type, which have two compartments: one for the pilot, the other to carry divers. The diving compartment is pressurized and provides access to the sea.

**subpoena** (Latin 'under penalty') in law, an order requiring someone who might not otherwise come forward of his or her own volition to give evidence before a court or judicial official at a specific time and place. A witness who fails to comply with a subpoena is in ◊contempt of court.

**substitution reaction** in chemistry, the replacement of one atom or ◊functional group in an organic molecule by another.

**succession** in ecology, a series of changes that occur in the structure and composition of the vegetation in a given area from the time it is first colonized by plants (*primary succession*), or after it has been disturbed by fire, flood, or clearing (*secondary succession*).

**Sucre** legal capital and seat of the judiciary of Bolivia, also capital of Chuquisaca department; population (1992) 131,000. It stands on the central plateau in the Andes at an altitude of 2,840 m/9,320 ft. It is the commercial centre for the surrounding agricultural area and has an oil refinery.

**sucrose** or *cane sugar* or *beet sugar,* $C_{12}H_{22}O_{11}$ a sugar found in the pith of sugar cane and in sugar beets. It is popularly known as ◊sugar.

**Sudan** Democratic Republic of
*national name Jamhuryat es-Sudan*

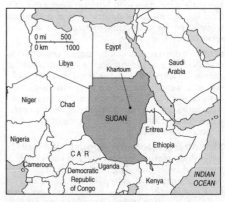

**area** 2,505,800 sq km/967,489 sq mi
**capital** Khartoum
**major towns/cities** Omdurman, Port Sudan, Juba, Wadi Medani, al-Obeid, Kassala, Atbara, al-Qadarif, Kosti
**major ports** Port Sudan
**physical features** fertile Nile valley separates Libyan Desert in west from high rocky Nubian Desert in east
**head of state and government** Gen Omar Hassan Ahmed al-Bashir from 1989

*political system* emergent democracy
*political parties* officially banned from 1989, but an influential grouping is the fundamentalist National Islamic Front
*currency* Sudanese dinar
*GNP per capita (PPP)* (US$) 1,360 (1998)
*exports* cotton, sesame seed, gum arabic, sorghum, livestock, hides and skins. Principal market: Saudi Arabia 21.3% (1997)
*population* 28,882,000 (1999 est)
*language* Arabic 51% (official), local languages
*religion* Sunni Muslim; also animist and Christian
*life expectancy* 54 (men); 56 (women) (1995–2000)
*Chronology*
**c. 600 BC–AD 350** Meroë, near Khartoum, was capital of the Nubian Empire, which covered southern Egypt and northern Sudan.
**6th century** Converted to Coptic Christianity.
**7th century** Islam first introduced by Arab invaders, but did not spread widely until the 15th century.
**16th–18th centuries** Arab-African Fur and Fung Empires established in central and northern Sudan.
**1820** Invaded by Muhammad Ali and brought under Egyptian control.
**1881–85** Revolt led to capture of Khartoum by Sheik Muhammad Ahmed, a self-proclaimed Mahdi ('messiah'), and the killing of British general Charles Gordon.
**1898** Anglo-Egyptian offensive led by Lord Kitchener subdued Mahdi revolt at Battle of Omdurman in which 20,000 Sudanese died.
**1899** Sudan administered as Anglo-Egyptian condominium.
**1923** White Flag League formed by Sudanese nationalists in north; British instituted policy of reducing contact between northern and southern Sudan, with the aim that the south would eventually become part of federation of eastern African states.
**1955** Civil war between the dominant Arab Muslim north and black African Christian and animist south broke out.
**1956** Sudan achieved independence from Britain and Egypt as a republic.
**1958** Military coup replaced civilian government with Supreme Council of the Armed Forces.
**1964** Civilian rule reinstated after October Revolution of student demonstrations.
**1969** Coup led by Col Gaafar Mohammed al-Nimeri abolished political institutions and concentrated power in a leftist Revolutionary Command Council.
**1971** Nimeri confirmed as president and the Sudanese Socialist Union (SSU) declared the only legal party by a new constitution.
**1972** Plans to form Federation of Arab Republics, comprising Sudan, Egypt, and Syria, abandoned due to internal opposition. To end 17-year-long civil war, Nimeri agreed to give south greater autonomy.
**1974** National assembly established.
**1980** Country reorganized into six regions, each with own assembly and effective autonomy.

**1983** Shari'a (Islamic law) imposed. Sudan People's Liberation Movement (SPLM) formed in south as civil war broke out again.
**1985** Nimeri deposed in a bloodless coup led by Gen Swar al-Dahab following industrial unrest in north.
**1986** Coalition government formed after general election, with Sadiq al-Mahdi, great-grandson of the Mahdi, as prime minister.
**1987** Civil war with Sudan People's Liberation Army (SPLA); drought and famine in south and refugee influx from Ethiopa and Chad.
**1988** A peace pact was signed with SPLA, but fighting continued.
**1989** Al-Mahdi was overthrown in a coup led by Islamic fundamentalist Gen Omar Hassan Ahmed el-Bashir. All political activity was suspended.
**1991** A federal system was introduced, with division of the country into nine states as the civil war continued.
**1996** The first presidential and parliamentary elections were held since the coup of 1989.
**1998** Civil war continued between the SPLA and the the Islamist government. There was famine in the south, where millions faced starvation. The USA launched a missile attack on a suspected chemical weapons-producing site in retaliation for bombings of US embassies in Nairobi and Dar es Salaam. There was a temporary ceasefire by the SPLA.
**1999** Multiparty politics were reintroduced.

**sudden infant death syndrome** (SIDS), in medicine, the technical term for ◊cot death.

**Sudeten** mountainous region in northeast Bohemia, Czech Republic, extending eastwards along the border with Poland. Sudeten was annexed by Germany under the ◊Munich Agreement 1938; it was returned to Czechoslovakia in 1945.

Germany and the Czech Republic sought to bury decades of mutual antagonism in January 1997 by signing a joint declaration aimed at drawing a line under the vexed issue of the Sudetenland. Germany apologised for the suffering caused during the Nazi occupation. For their part, the Czechs expressed regret over the 'injustices' that took place during the expulsion of more than 2.5 million Sudetenland Germans after World War II. It took over two years to reach agreement.

**Suetonius, (Gaius Suetonius Tranquillus)** (*c.* AD 69–*c.* 140) Roman historian. He was the author of *Lives of the Caesars* (Julius Caesar to Domitian).

**Suez Canal** artificial waterway from Port Said to the Suez, linking the Mediterranean and Red Seas; 160 km/100 mi long. It separates Africa from Asia and provides the shortest eastwards sea route from Europe. It was opened in 1869, nationalized in 1956, blocked by Egypt during the Arab-Israeli War in 1967, and not reopened until 1975.

**Suez Crisis** military confrontation from October to December 1956 following the nationalization of the Suez Canal by President Nasser of Egypt. In an attempt to reassert international control of the canal, Israel launched an attack, after which British and French troops landed. Widespread international censure forced the withdrawal of the British and French. The crisis resulted in the resignation of British prime minister Eden.

**Suffolk** county of eastern England
*area* 3,800 sq km/1,467 sq mi
*towns* Ipswich (administrative headquarters), Aldeburgh, Beccles, Bury St Edmunds, Felixstowe, Lowestoft, Sudbury, Southwold
*physical* undulating lowlands in the south and west; flat coastline; rivers Waveney (the boundary with Norfolk), Alde, Deben, Orwell, Stour (the boundary with Essex), Little Ouse; part of the Norfolk Broads
*features* Minsmere marshland bird reserve, near Aldeburgh; the Sandlings (heathlands and birds); bloodstock rearing and horse racing at Newmarket; ◊Sutton Hoo (7th-century ship burial); Sizewell B, Britain's first pressurized-water nuclear reactor plant; Aldeburgh Festival, held every June at Snape Maltings
*agriculture* cereals (barley, oats, wheat), sugar beet; cattle, sheep, and pig rearing; fishing (for which Lowestoft is the main centre)
*industries* agricultural machinery; chemicals; coconut matting; electronics; fertilizers; food processing; motor vehicle components; North Sea oil and gas exploration; printing; telecommunications research; silk; timber; brewing
*population* (1996) 661,600
*famous people* Benjamin Britten, John Constable, George Crabbe, Thomas Gainsborough, Elizabeth Garrett Anderson.

**suffragette** or *suffragist,* woman fighting for the right to vote. In the UK, women's suffrage bills were repeatedly introduced and defeated in Parliament between 1886 and 1911, and a militant campaign was launched in 1906 by Emmeline ◊Pankhurst and her daughters. In 1918 women were granted limited franchise; in 1928 it was extended to all women over 21. In the USA the 19th amendment to the constitution in 1920 gave women the vote in federal and state elections.

**Sufism** mystical movement of ◊Islam that originated in the 8th century. Sufis believe that deep intuition is the only real guide to knowledge. The movement has a strong strain of asceticism. The name derives from Arabic *suf,* a rough woollen robe worn as an indication of disregard for material things. There are a number of groups or brotherhoods within Sufism, each with its own method of meditative practice, one of which is the whirling dance of the dervishes.

**sugar** or *sucrose,* sweet, soluble, crystalline carbohydrate found in the pith of sugar cane and in sugar beet. It is a *disaccharide* sugar, each of its molecules being made up of two simple-sugar (*monosaccharide*) units: glucose and fructose. Sugar is easily digested and forms a major source of energy in humans, being used in cooking and in the food industry as a sweetener and, in high concentrations, as a preservative. A high consumption is associated with obesity and

tooth decay. In the UK, sucrose may not be used in baby foods.

**Suharto, Thojib I** (1921– ) Indonesian politician and general. He was president from 1967–98. His authoritarian rule met with domestic opposition from the left, but the Indonesian economy enjoyed significant growth until 1997. He was re-elected in 1973, 1978, 1983, 1988, 1993, and, unopposed, in March 1998. This was despite his deteriorating health and the country's economy being weakened by a sharp decline in value of the Indonesian currency, which had provoked student unrest and food riots. After mounting civil unrest reached a critical point, on 21 May 1998 he handed over the presidency to the vice president, Bacharuddin Jusuf Habibie.

**suicide** the act of intentionally killing oneself; also someone who does this. The frequency of attempted suicide is 20 times higher than actual suicide. Three times more women than men attempt suicide, and three times more men succeed. Men tend to use more violent methods like gunshot wounds to the head; women are more likely to take an overdose. Over 6,000 people in the USA use handguns to kill themselves each year. The highest suicide rate for both sexes is in the over-75 age group. Hungary has the highest suicide rate in this age category at 108 per 100,000 (1992). Suicide among people aged 18–24, although relatively infrequent, is the third leading cause of death, after accidents and homicides, in the UK.

**Sukarno, Achmed** (1901–1970) Indonesian nationalist, president 1945–67. During World War II he cooperated in the local administration set up by the Japanese, replacing Dutch rule. After the war he became the first president of the new Indonesian republic, becoming president-for-life in 1966; he was ousted by ◊Suharto.

**Sulawesi** formerly *Celebes,* island in eastern Indonesia, one of the Sunda Islands; area (with dependent islands) 190,000 sq km/73,000 sq mi; population (1990) 12,520,700. It is mountainous and forested and produces copra and nickel.

**Suleiman** or *Solyman* (c. 1494–1566) Ottoman sultan from 1520, known as *the Magnificent* and *the Lawgiver.* Under his rule, the Ottoman Empire flourished and reached its largest extent. He made conquests in the Balkans, the Mediterranean, Persia, and North Africa, but was defeated at Vienna in 1529 and Valletta (on Malta) in 1565. He was a patron of the arts, a poet, and an administrator.

**Sulla, Publius Cornelius** (138 BC–78 BC) Roman general and dictator. He was elected consul in 88 BC after defeating the Samnites several times during the Italian Social War. In the same year, Marius tried to deprive him of the command against the king of Pontus, Mithridates (VI) Eupator (120–60 BC). Sulla's unprecedented response was to march on Rome, executing or putting to flight his rivals. His campaign against Mithridates ended successfully in 85 BC, and Sulla returned to Italy in 83 where his opponents had raised armies against him. Sulla defeated them in 82 and massacred all his opponents. After holding supreme power as dictator and carrying out a series of political reforms, he retired to private life in 80 BC.

**Sullivan, Arthur Seymour** (1842–1900) English composer. He wrote operettas in collaboration with William Gilbert, including *HMS Pinafore* (1878), *The Pirates of Penzance* (1879), and *The Mikado* (1885). Their partnership broke down in 1896. Sullivan also composed serious instrumental, choral, and operatic works – for example, the opera *Ivanhoe* (1890) – which he valued more highly than the operettas.

**sulphate** $SO_4^{2-}$ salt or ester derived from sulphuric acid. Most sulphates are water soluble (the exceptions are lead, calcium, strontium, and barium sulphates), and require a very high temperature to decompose them.

**sulphide** compound of sulphur and another element in which sulphur is the more electronegative element. Sulphides occur in a number of minerals. Some of the more volatile sulphides have extremely unpleasant odours (hydrogen sulphide smells of bad eggs).

**sulphite** $SO_3^{2-}$ salt or ester derived from sulphurous acid.

**sulphonamide** any of a group of compounds containing the chemical group sulphonamide $(SO_2NH_2)$ or its derivatives, which were, and still are in some cases, used to treat bacterial diseases. Sulphadiazine $(C_{10}H_{10}N_4O_2S)$ is an example.

**sulphur** brittle, pale-yellow, nonmetallic element, symbol S, atomic number 16, relative atomic mass 32.064. It occurs in three allotropic forms: two crystalline (called rhombic and monoclinic, following the arrangements of the atoms within the crystals) and one amorphous. It burns in air with a blue flame and a stifling odour. Insoluble in water but soluble in carbon disulphide, it is a good electrical insulator. Sulphur is widely used in the manufacture of sulphuric acid (used to treat phosphate rock to make fertilizers) and in making paper, matches, gunpowder and fireworks, in vulcanizing rubber, and in medicines and insecticides.

**sulphur dioxide** $SO_2$ pungent gas produced by burning sulphur in air or oxygen. It is widely used for disinfecting food vessels and equipment, and as a preservative in some food products. It occurs in industrial flue gases and is a major cause of ◊acid rain.

**sulphuric acid** or *oil of vitriol*, $H_2SO_4$ a dense, viscous, colourless liquid that is extremely corrosive. It gives out heat when added to water and can cause severe burns. Sulphuric acid is used extensively in the chemical industry, in the refining of petrol, and in the manufacture of fertilizers, detergents, explosives, and dyes. It forms the acid component of car batteries.

**sulphurous acid** $H_2SO_3$ solution of sulphur dioxide $(SO_2)$ in water. It is a weak acid.

**Sumatra** or *Sumatera,* second-largest island of Indonesia, one of the Sunda Islands; area 473,600 sq km/182,800 sq mi; population (1990) 36,505,700. East of a longitudinal volcanic mountain range is a wide plain; both are heavily forested. Products include rubber, rice, tobacco, tea, timber, tin, and petroleum.

**Sumerian civilization** the world's earliest civilization, dating from about 3500 BC and located at the confluence of the Tigris and Euphrates rivers in lower Mesopotamia (present-day Iraq). It was a city-state with priests as secular rulers. After 2300 BC, Sumer declined.

**summons** in law, a court order officially delivered, requiring someone to appear in court on a certain date.

**sumo wrestling** national sport of Japan. Fighters of larger than average size (rarely less than 130 kg/21 st or 285 lb) try to push, pull, or throw each other out of a circular ring.

**Sun** the ◊star at the centre of the Solar System. Its diameter is 1,392,000 km/865,000 mi; its temperature at the surface is about 5,800K (5,500°C/9,900°F), and at the centre 15,000,000K (15,000,000°C/27,000,000°F). It is composed of about 70% hydrogen and 30% helium, with other elements making up less than 1%. The Sun's energy is generated by nuclear fusion reactions that turn hydrogen into helium at its centre. The gas core is far denser than mercury or lead on Earth. The Sun is about 4.7 billion years old, with a predicted lifetime of 10 billion years. *See illustration on page 866.*

**Sundanese** the second-largest ethnic group in the Republic of Indonesia. There are more than 20 million speakers of Sundanese, a member of the western branch of the Austronesian family. Like their neighbours, the Javanese, the Sundanese are predominantly Muslim.

They are known for their performing arts, especially *jaipongan* dance traditions, and distinctive batik fabrics.

**sundew** any of a group of insectivorous plants found growing in bogs; sticky hairs on the leaves catch and digest insects that land on them. (Genus *Drosera,* family Droseraceae.)

**sunfish** marine fish *Mola mola* with a disc-shaped body 3 m/10 ft long found in all temperate and tropical oceans. The term also applies to fish of the North American freshwater Centrarchidae family, which have compressed, almost circular bodies, up to 80 cm/30 in long, and are nestbuilders and avid predators.

**sunflower** tall, thick-stemmed plant with a large, single, yellow-petalled flower, belonging to the daisy family. The common or giant sunflower (*H. annuus*), probably native to Mexico, can grow up to 4.5 m/15 ft high. It is commercially cultivated in central Europe, the USA, Russia, Ukraine, and Australia for the oil-bearing seeds that ripen in the central disc of the flower head; sunflower oil is widely used as a cooking oil and in margarine. (Genus *Helianthus,* family Compositae.)

**Sunni** member of the larger of the two main sects of ◊Islam, with about 680 million adherents. Sunni Muslims believe that the first three

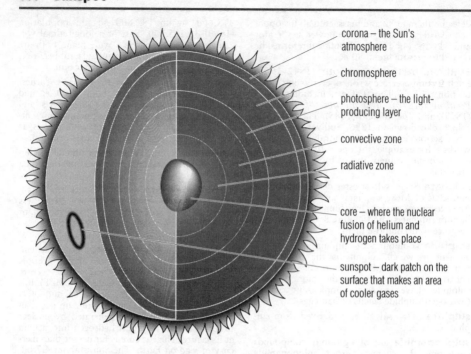

corona – the Sun's atmosphere

chromosphere

photosphere – the light-producing layer

convective zone

radiative zone

core – where the nuclear fusion of helium and hydrogen takes place

sunspot – dark patch on the surface that makes an area of cooler gases

**Sun** *The structure of the Sun. Nuclear reactions at the core releases vast amounts of energy in the form of light and heat that radiate out to the photosphere and corona. Surges of glowing gas rise as prominences from the surface of the Sun, and cooler areas known as sunspots appear as dark patches on the giant star's surface.*

caliphs were all legitimate successors of the prophet Muhammad, and that guidance on belief and life should come from the Koran and the Hadith, and from the Shari'a, not from a human authority or spiritual leader. Imams in Sunni Islam are educated lay teachers of the faith and prayer leaders.

**sunspot** dark patch on the surface of the Sun, actually an area of cooler gas, thought to be caused by strong magnetic fields that block the outward flow of heat to the Sun's surface. Sunspots consist of a dark central *umbra*, about 4,000K (3,700°C/6,700°F), and a lighter surrounding *penumbra*, about 5,500K (5,200°C/9,400°F). They last from several days to over a month, ranging in size from 2,000 km/1,250 mi to groups stretching for over 100,000 km/62,000 mi.

**Sun Zhong Shan** or *Sun Yat-sen* (1867–1925) Chinese revolutionary leader. He was the founder of the Kuomintang (◊Guomindang, nationalist party) in 1894, and provisional president of the Republic of China 1912 after playing a vital part in deposing the emperor. He was president of a breakaway government from 1921.

**superbug** popular name given to an infectious bacterium that has developed resistance to most or all known antibiotics.

**supercomputer** fastest, most powerful type of computer, capable of performing its basic operations in picoseconds (trillionths of a second), rather than nanoseconds (billionths of a second), like most other computers.

**superconductivity** in physics, increase in electrical conductivity at low temperatures. The resistance of some metals and metallic compounds decreases uniformly with decreasing temperature until at a critical temperature (the superconducting point), within a few degrees of absolute zero (0K/–273.15°C/–459.67°F), the resistance suddenly falls to zero. The phenomenon was discovered by Dutch scientist Heike Kamerlingh Onnes in 1911.

**supercooling** the cooling of a liquid below its freezing point without freezing taking place; or the cooling of a saturated solution without crystallization taking place, to form a supersaturated solution. In both cases supercooling is possible because of the lack of solid particles around which crystals can form. Crystallization rapidly follows the introduction of a small crystal (seed) or agitation of the supercooled solution.

**superego** in Freudian psychology, the element of the human mind concerned with the ideal, responsible for ethics and self-imposed standards of behaviour. It is characterized as a form of conscience, restraining the ◊ego, and responsible for feelings of guilt when the moral code is broken.

**superfluid** fluid that flows without viscosity or friction and has a very high thermal conductivity. Liquid helium at temperatures below 2K (–271°C/–456°F) is a superfluid: it shows unexpected behaviour; for instance, it flows uphill in apparent defiance of gravity and, if placed in a container, will flow up the sides and escape.

**supergiant** largest and most luminous type of star known, with a diameter of up to 1,000 times that of the Sun and absolute magnitudes of between –5 and –9. Supergiants are likely to become ◊supernovae.

**Superior, Lake** largest and deepest of the ◊Great Lakes and the largest freshwater lake in the world; area 82,100 sq km/31,700 sq mi. Extending east–west for 616 km/385 mi, it reaches a maximum width of 260 km/163 mi and depth of 407 m/1,335 ft. The lake is bordered by the Canadian province of Ontario and the US states of Minnesota, Wisconsin, and Michigan. As the westernmost of the Great Lakes, Superior is at the western end of the St Lawrence Seaway.

**supernova** explosive death of a star, which temporarily attains a brightness of 100 million Suns or more, so that it can shine as brilliantly as a small galaxy for a few days or weeks. Very approximately, it is thought that a supernova explodes in a large galaxy about once every 100 years. Many supernovae – astronomers estimate some 50% – remain undetected because of obscuring by interstellar dust.

**supersonic speed** speed greater than that at which sound travels, measured in ◊Mach numbers. In dry air at 0°C/32°F, sound travels at about 1,170 kph/727 mph, but decreases its speed with altitude until, at 12,000 m/39,000 ft, it is only 1,060 kph/658 mph.

**superstring theory** in physics, a mathematical theory developed in the 1980s to explain the properties of ◊elementary particles and the forces between them (in particular, gravity and the nuclear forces) in a way that combines ◊relativity and ◊quantum theory.

In string theory, the fundamental objects in the universe are not pointlike particles but extremely small stringlike objects. These objects exist in a universe of ten dimensions, although, for reasons not yet understood, only three space dimensions and one dimension of time are discernible.

**supersymmetry** in physics, a theory that relates the two classes of elementary particle, the ◊fermions and the ◊bosons. According to supersymmetry, each fermion particle has a boson partner particle, and vice versa. It has not been possible to marry up all the known fermions with the known bosons, and so the theory postulates the existence of other, as yet undiscovered fermions, such as the photinos (partners of the photons), gluinos (partners of the gluons), and gravitinos (partners of the gravitons). Using these ideas, it has become possible to develop a theory of gravity – called *supergravity* – that extends Einstein's work and considers the gravitational, nuclear, and electromagnetic forces to be manifestations of an underlying superforce. Supersymmetry has been incorporated into the ◊superstring theory, and appears to be a crucial

ingredient in the 'theory of everything' sought by scientists.

**supply-side economics** school of economic thought advocating government policies that allow market forces to operate freely, such as privatization, cuts in public spending and income tax, reductions in trade-union power, and cuts in the ratio of unemployment benefits to wages. Supply-side economics developed as part of the monetarist (see ◊monetarism) critique of Keynesian economics.

**Supreme Court** highest US judicial tribunal, composed since 1869 of a chief justice (William Rehnquist from 1986) and eight associate justices. Appointments are made for life by the president, with the advice and consent of the Senate, and justices can be removed only by impeachment.

**surface tension** in physics, the property that causes the surface of a liquid to behave as if it were covered with a weak elastic skin; this is why a needle can float on water. It is caused by the exposed surface's tendency to contract to the smallest possible area because of cohesive forces between ◊molecules at the surface. Allied phenomena include the formation of droplets, the concave profile of a meniscus, and the capillary action by which water soaks into a sponge.

**surfing** sport of riding on the crest of large waves while standing on a narrow, keeled surfboard, usually of light synthetic material such as fibreglass, about 1.8 m/6 ft long (or about 2.4–7 m/8–9 ft known as the Malibu), as first developed in Hawaii and Australia. ◊Windsurfing is a recent development.

**surgeon fish** any fish of the tropical marine family Acanthuridae. It has a flat body up to 50 cm/20 in long, is brightly coloured, and has a movable spine on each side of the tail that can be used as a weapon.

**surgery** branch of medicine concerned with the treatment of disease, abnormality, or injury by operation. Traditionally it has been performed by means of cutting instruments, but today a number of technologies are used to treat or remove lesions, including ultrasonic waves and laser surgery.

**Suriname** Republic of (formerly *Dutch Guiana*)
*national name* Republiek Suriname
*area* 163,820 sq km/63,250 sq mi
*capital* Paramaribo
*major towns/cities* Nieuw Nickerie, Moengo, Pontoetoe, Brokopondo, Nieuw Amsterdam
*physical features* hilly and forested, with flat and narrow coastal plain; Suriname River
*head of state* Jules Wijdenbosch from 1996
*head of government* Prataapnarain Shawh Radhecheran Radhakishun from 1996
*political system* emergent democracy
*political parties* New Front (NF), alliance of four left-of-centre parties: Party for National Unity and Solidarity (KTPI), Suriname National Party (NPS), Progressive Reform Party (VHP), Suriname Labour Party (SPA); National Democratic Party (NDP), left of centre;

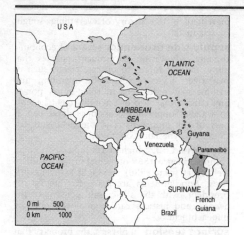

Democratic Alternative 1991 (DA '91), alliance of three left-of-centre parties
**currency** Suriname guilder
**GNP per capita (PPP)** (US$) 3,680 (1997 est)
**exports** alumina, aluminium, shrimps, bananas, plantains, rice, wood and wood products. Principal market: USA 16.4% (1997)
**population** 416,000 (1998 est)
**language** Dutch (official), Sranan (creole), English, Hindi, Javanese, Chinese. Spanish is the main working language
**religion** Christian, Hindu, Muslim
**life expectancy** 68 (men); 73 (women) (1995–2000)
**Chronology**
AD **1593** Visited and claimed by Spanish explorers; the name Suriname derived from the country's earliest inhabitants, the Surinen, who were driven out by other Amerindians in the 16th century.
**1602** Dutch settlements established.
**1651** British colony founded by settlers sent from Barbados.
**1667** Became a Dutch colony, received in exchange for New Amsterdam (New York) by Treaty of Breda.
**1682** Coffee and sugar cane plantations introduced, worked by imported African slaves.
**1795–1802 and 1804–16** Under British rule.
**1863** Slavery abolished and indentured labourers brought in from China, India, and Java.
**1915** Bauxite discovered and gradually became main export.
**1954** Achieved internal self-government as Dutch Guiana.
**1958–69** Politics dominated by Johan Pengel, charismatic leader of the mainly Creole Suriname National Party (NPS).
**1975** Independence achieved, with Dr Johan Ferrier as president and Henck Arron (NPS) as prime minister; 40% of population emigrated to the Netherlands.
**1980** Arron's government overthrown in army coup; Ferrier refused to recognize military regime; appointed Dr Henk Chin A Sen of the Nationalist Republican Party (PNR) to lead civilian administration. Army replaced Ferrier with Dr Chin A Sen.

**1982** Army, led by Lt Col Desi Bouterse, seized power, setting up a Revolutionary People's Front; economic aid from the Netherlands and US cut off after opposition leaders, charged with plotting a coup, were executed.
**1985** Ban on political activities lifted.
**1986** Antigovernment rebels brought economic chaos to Suriname.
**1988** Ramsewak Shankar of the combined opposition parties elected president under new constitution.
**1989** Bouterse rejected peace accord reached by President Shankar with guerrilla insurgents, the Bush Negro (descendents of escaped slaves) maroons, and vowed to continue fighting.
**1990** Shankar was deposed in an army coup engineered by Bouterse.
**1991** Johan Kraag (NPS) became interim president. A New Front opposition alliance won an assembly majority. Ronald Venetiaan was elected president.
**1992** A peace accord was reached with guerrilla groups.
**1996** Jules Wijdenbosch was elected president.
**1999** Former dictator and presidential adviser Desi Bouterse was awaiting trial for cocaine trafficking.

**Surrealism** movement in art, literature, and film that developed out of ◊Dada around 1922. Led by André ◊Breton, who produced the *Surrealist Manifesto* in 1924, the Surrealists were inspired by the thoughts and visions of the subconscious mind. They explored varied styles and techniques, and the movement became the dominant force in Western art between World Wars I and II.

**Surrey** county of southern England
**area** 1,660 sq km/641 sq mi
**towns** Kingston upon Thames (administrative headquarters), Farnham, Guildford, Leatherhead, Reigate, Woking, Epsom, Dorking
**physical** rivers Mole, Thames, and Wey; Box Hill (183 m/600 ft), Gibbet Hill (277 m/909 ft), and Leith Hill (299 m/981 ft, 5 km/3 mi south of Dorking, the highest hill in southeast England); North Downs
**features** Kew Palace and Royal Botanic Gardens, Kew; Yehudi Menuhin School (one of four specialist music schools in England)
**agriculture** vegetables; sheep rearing; dairy farming; horticulture
**industries** service industries; sand and gravel quarrying; fuller's earth extraction (near Reigate)
**population** (1996) 1,047,100
**famous people** Eric Clapton, John Galsworthy, Aldous Huxley, Laurence Olivier.

**surveying** the accurate measuring of the Earth's crust, or of land features or buildings. It is used to establish boundaries, and to evaluate the topography for engineering work. The measurements used are both linear and angular, and geometry and trigonometry are applied in the calculations.

**suspension** mixture consisting of small solid particles dispersed in a liquid or gas, which will settle on standing. An example is milk of magnesia, which is a suspension of magnesium hydroxide in water.

**Sussex** former county of England, on the south coast, now divided into ◊East Sussex and ◊West Sussex.

**Sutherland, Graham Vivian** (1903–1980) English painter, graphic artist, and designer. He was active mainly in France from the 1940s. A leading figure of the Neo-Romantic movement (1935–55), which revived the spirit of 19th-century Romanticism in a more modern idiom, he executed portraits, landscapes, and religious subjects, often using a semi-abstract style. In the late 1940s he turned increasingly to portraiture. His portrait of Winston Churchill (1954) was disliked by its subject and eventually burned on the instructions of Lady Churchill (studies survive). He was awarded the OM in 1960.

**Sutton Hoo** archaeological site in Suffolk, England, where in 1939 a Saxon ship burial was excavated. It may be the funeral monument of Raedwald, King of the East Angles, who died about 624 or 625. The jewellery, armour, and weapons discovered were placed in the British Museum, London.

**Suu Kyi, Aung San** (1945– ) Myanmar (Burmese) politician and human-rights campaigner, leader of the National League for Democracy (NLD), the main opposition to the military junta. Despite Suu Kyi being placed under house arrest in 1989, the NLD won the 1990 elections, although the junta refused to surrender power. She was awarded the Nobel Prize for Peace in 1991 in recognition of her 'nonviolent struggle for democracy and human rights' in Myanmar. Finally released from house arrest in 1995, she was banned from resuming any leadership post within the NLD by the junta. She is the daughter of former Burmese premier ◊Aung San.

**Suzhou** or *Soochow;* formerly (1912–49) *Wuhsien,* city in Jiangsu province, China, south of the Chang Jiang River delta and east of the ◊Grand Canal; population (1994) 1,050,000. Dating from about 1000 BC, it is popularly known as the 'Venice of the East' because of its network of ancient bridges and canals. Traditional silk, embroidery, and other handicrafts have been augmented by papermaking and the production of chemicals, electronics, and telecommunications equipment.

**Svalbard** Norwegian archipelago in the Arctic Ocean; population (1995) 2,900 (41% being Norwegian). The main island is ◊Spitsbergen, which includes the largest town, Longyearbyen; other islands include Edgeøya, Barentsøya, Svenskøya, Nordaustlandet, Prins Karls Foreland, Wilhelmøya, Lågøya, Storøya, Danskøya, and Sørkappøya. The other main centres of population are the Russian mining settlements of Barentsburg and Grumantbyen. The total land area is 62,000 sq km/23,938 sq mi.

**Swabia** German *Schwaben,* historic region of southwestern Germany, an independent duchy in the Middle Ages. It includes Augsburg and Ulm and forms part of the *Länder* (states) of Baden-Württemberg, Bavaria, and Hessen.

**Swahili** or Kiswahili, (Arabic *sawahil* 'language of the coast') language belonging to the Bantu branch of the Niger-Congo family, widely used in east and central Africa. Swahili originated on the East African coast as a *lingua franca* used among traders, and contains many Arabic loan words. It is an official language in Kenya and Tanzania.

**swallow** any bird of the family Hirundinidae of small, insect-eating birds in the order Passeriformes, with long, narrow wings, and deeply forked tails. Swallows feed while flying, capturing winged insects in the mouth, which is lined with bristles made viscid (sticky) by a salivary secretion.

**swan** large water bird, with a long slender neck and webbed feet, closely related to ducks and geese. The four species of swan found in the northern hemisphere are white; the three species found in the southern hemisphere are all or partly black. The male (cob) and female (pen) are similar in appearance, and they usually pair for life. They nest on or near water in every continent, except Africa and Antarctica. Swans produce a clutch of 4–6 greenish coloured eggs and their young are known as cygnets. Cygnets are covered with a grey down and only become fully feathered and able to fly after 14–16 weeks.

Swans feed mainly on aquatic plants. They are among the largest and heaviest birds that can fly and because of this require large areas of water to take off. They fly with a slow, graceful wing beat and when migrating, fly in a distinctive V-shaped flock.

The *mute swan* is the most common species. It is native to northern Europe and Asia, but has been introduced and is now widespread in North America. The mute swan has white feathers, black legs and a bright orange flattened bill with a black knob on the upper bill, near the eyes. It may be as long as 150 cm/5 ft in length and weigh as much as 14 kg/30 lb. It hisses loudly when angry.

*classification* Swans belong to animal phylum Chordata, class Aves (birds), order Anseriformes, family Anatidae. They belong to the genus *Cygnus.* There are seven species: the mute swan (*Cygnus olor*), the whooper swan (*C. cygnus*), Bewick's swan (*C. bewicki* ), the tundra (whistling) swan (*C. columbianus*), the North American trumpeter swan (*C. buccinator* ), the black swan of Australia (*C. atratus*), and the South American black-necked swan (*C. melanocoryphus*). The North American trumpeter swan is the largest, with a wingspan of 2.4 m/8 ft.

**Swansea** unitary authority in south Wales, created in 1996 from part of the former county of West Glamorgan

*area* 377 sq km/156 sq mi

*towns* Swansea (administrative headquarters)

*physical* River Tawe

*features* Gower Peninsula (an area of outstanding natural beauty)

*industries* tinplate manufacture, chemicals, oil refineries.

*population* (1996) 232,000.

**swastika** (Sanskrit *svasti* 'prosperity') cross in which the bars are extended at right angles in the same clockwise or anticlockwise direction. Its origin is uncertain, but it appears frequently as an ancient good-luck and religious symbol in both the Old World and the New. A swastika with clockwise bars was adopted as the emblem of the Nazi Party and incorporated into the German national flag 1935–45.

**Swazi kingdom** South African kingdom, established by Sobhuza I (died 1839), and named after his successor Mswati (ruled 1840–75).

**Swaziland** Kingdom of
*national name Umbuso we Swatini*

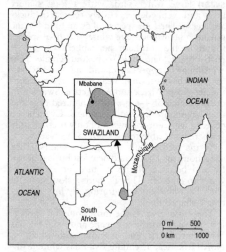

**area** 17,400 sq km/6,718 sq mi
**capital** Mbabane
**major towns/cities** Manzini, Big Bend, Mhlume, Havelock Mine, Nhlangano
**physical features** central valley; mountains in west (Highveld); plateau in east (Lowveld and Lubombo plateau)
**head of state** King Mswati III from 1986
**head of government** Barnabas Sibusiso Dlamini from 1996
**political system** transitional absolute monarchy
**political parties** Imbokodvo National Movement (INM), nationalist monarchist; Swaziland United Front (SUF), left of centre; Swaziland Progressive Party (SPP), left of centre; People's United Democratic Movement, left of centre
**currency** lilangeni
**GNP per capita (PPP)** (US$) 3,580 (1998)
**exports** sugar, wood pulp, cotton yarn, canned fruits, asbestos, coal, diamonds, gold. Principal market: South Africa 74% (1997)
**population** 980,000 (1999 est)
**language** Swazi, English (both official)
**religion** Christian, animist
**life expectancy** 58 (men); 63 (women) (1995–2000)
*Chronology*
**late 16th century** King Ngwane II crossed Lubombo mountains from the east and settled in

southeast Swaziland; his successors established a strong centralized Swazi kingdom, dominating the long-settled Nguni and Sothi peoples.
**mid-19th century** Swazi nation was ruled by the warrior King Mswati who, at the height of his power, controlled an area three times the size of the present-day state.
**1882** Gold was discovered in the northwest, attracting European fortune hunters who coerced Swazi rulers into granting land concessions.
**1894** Came under joint rule of Britain and the Boer republic of Transvaal.
**1903** Following the South African War, Swaziland became a special British protectorate, or High Commission territory, against South Africa's wishes.
**1922** King Sobhuza II succeeded to the Swazi throne.
**1968** Independence achieved within the Commonwealth, as the Kingdom of Swaziland, with King (or Ngwenyama) Sobhuza II as head of state.
**1973** The king suspended the constitution, banned political activity, and assumed absolute powers after the opposition deputies had been elected to parliament.
**1977** King announced substitution of traditional tribal communities (*tinkhundla*) for the parliamentary system, arguing it was more suited to Swazi values.
**1982** King Sobhuza died; his place was taken by one of his wives, Queen Dzeliwe, until his son, Prince Makhosetive, reached the age of 21.
**1983** Queen Dzeliwe ousted by a younger wife, Queen Ntombi, as real power passed to the prime minister, Prince Bhekimpi Dlamini.
**1984** After a royal power struggle it was announced that the crown prince would become king at 18.
**1986** The crown prince was formally invested as King Mswati III.
**1993** Direct elections of *tinkhundla* candidates were held for the first time; Prince Jameson Mbilini Dlamini was appointed premier.
**1998** Prince Dlamini was reappointed.

**Sweden** Kingdom of
*national name Konungariket Sverige*
**area** 450,000 sq km/173,745 sq mi
**capital** Stockholm (and chief port)
**major towns/cities** Göteborg, Malmö, Uppsala, Norrköping, Västerås, Linköping, Orebro, Jönköping, Helsingborg, Borås
**major ports** Helsingborg, Malmö, Göteborg
**physical features** mountains in west; plains in south; thickly forested; more than 20,000 islands off the Stockholm coast; lakes, including Vänern, Vättern, Mälaren, and Hjälmaren
**head of state** King Carl XVI Gustaf from 1973
**head of government** Goran Persson from 1996
**political system** constitutional monarchy
**political parties** Christian Democratic Community Party (KdS), Christian, centrist; Left Party (Vp), European, Marxist; Social Democratic Party (SAP), moderate, left of centre; Moderate Party (M), right of centre; Liberal Party (Fp), centre left; Centre Party (C), centrist;

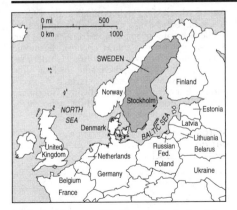

Ecology Party (MpG), ecological; New Democracy (NG), right wing, populist
**currency** Swedish krona
**GNP per capita (PPP)** (US$) 19,480 (1998)
**exports** forestry products (wood, pulp, and paper), machinery, motor vehicles, power-generating non-electrical machinery, chemicals, iron and steel. Principal market: Germany 11.2% (1998)
**population** 8,892,000 (1999 est)
**language** Swedish; there are Finnish- and Saami-speaking minorities
**religion** Evangelical Lutheran (established national church)
**life expectancy** 76 (men); 81 (women) (1995–2000)
**Chronology**
**8th century** Kingdom of the Svear, based near Uppsala, extended its rule across much of southern Sweden.
**9th–11th centuries** Swedish Vikings raided and settled along the rivers of Russia.
**c. 1000** Olaf Skötkonung, king of the Svear, adopted Christianity and united much of Sweden (except south and west coasts, which remained Danish until 17th century).
**11th–13th centuries** Sweden existed as isolated kingdom under the Stenkil, Sverker, and Folkung dynasties; series of crusades incorporated Finland.
**1397** Union of Kalmar: Sweden, Denmark, and Norway united under a single monarch; Sweden effectively ruled by succession of regents.
**1448** Breach with Denmark: Sweden alone elected Charles VIII as king.
**1523** Gustavus Vasa, leader of insurgents, became king of fully independent Sweden.
**1527** Swedish Reformation: Gustavus confiscated Church property and encouraged Lutherans.
**1544** Swedish crown became hereditary in House of Vasa.
**1592–1604** Sigismund Vasa, a Catholic, was king of both Sweden and Poland until ousted from Swedish throne by his Lutheran uncle Charles IX.
**17th century** Sweden, a great military power under Gustavus Adolphus (1611–32), Charles X (1654–60), and Charles XI (1660–97), fought

lengthy wars with Denmark, Russia, Poland, and Holy Roman Empire.
**1709** Battle of Poltava: Russians inflicted major defeat on Swedes under Charles XII.
**1720** Limited monarchy established; political power passed to *Riksdag* (parliament) dominated by nobles.
**1721** Great Northern War ended with Sweden losing nearly all its conquests of the previous century.
**1741–43** Sweden defeated in disastrous war with Russia; further conflict 1788–90.
**1771–92** Gustavus III increased royal power and introduced wide-ranging reforms; assassinated at a masked ball.
**1809** Russian invaders annexed Finland; Swedish nobles staged coup and restored powers of Riksdag.
**1810** Napoleonic marshal, Jean-Baptiste Bernadotte, elected crown prince of Sweden, as Charles XIII had no heir.
**1812** Bernadotte allied Sweden with Russia against France.
**1814** Treaty of Kiel: Sweden obtained Norway from Denmark.
**1818–44** Bernadotte reigned in Sweden as Charles XIV John.
**1846** Free enterprise established by abolition of trade guilds and monopolies.
**1866** Series of liberal reforms culminated in new two-chambered *Riksdag* dominated by bureaucrats and farmers.
**late 19th century** Development of large-scale forestry and iron-ore industry; neutrality adopted in foreign affairs.
**1905** Union with Norway dissolved.
**1907** Adoption of proportional representation and universal suffrage.
**1920s** Economic boom transformed Sweden from an agricultural to an industrial economy.
**1932** Social Democrat government of Per Halbin Hansson introduced radical public-works programme to combat trade slump.
**1940–43** Under duress, neutral Sweden permitted limited transit of German forces through its territory.
**1946–69** Social Democrat government of Tage Erlander developed comprehensive welfare state.
**1959** Sweden joined European Free Trade Association.
**1969–76** SAP in power, under Prime Minister Olaf Palme.
**1971** Constitution amended to create single-chamber Riksdag.
**1975** Remaining constitutional powers of monarch removed.
**1976–82** Centre–right coalition government under Prime Minister Thorbjörn Fälldin ended 44 years of Social Democrat dominance.
**1982** Olaf Palme (SAP) regained position of prime minister.
**1986** Palme was assassinated and succeeded by Ingvar Carlsson.
**1991** Ingvar Carlsson resigned, and the leader of the Moderate Party, Carl Bildt, headed up a coalition of the Moderate, Centre, Liberal, and Christian Democratic parties.

**1994** The SAP returned to power with Carlsson as prime minister.
**1995** Sweden became a member of the European Union.
**1996** Ingvar Carlsson resigned and Goran Persson (SAP) became prime minister.
**1998** The SAP were narrowly re-elected in a general election.

**swede** annual or biennial plant widely cultivated for its edible root, which is purple, white, or yellow. It is similar in taste to the turnip but is of greater food value, firmer fleshed, and can be stored for a longer time. (*Brassica napus,* family Cruciferae.)

**sweet pea** plant belonging to the ◊pea family.

**sweet potato** tropical American plant belonging to the morning-glory family; the white-orange tuberous root is used as a source of starch and alcohol and eaten as a vegetable. (*Ipomoea batatas,* family Convolvulaceae.)

**swift** fast-flying, short-legged bird of the family Apodidae, order Apodiformes, of which there are about 75 species, found largely in the tropics. They are 9–23 cm/4–11 in long, with brown or grey plumage, long, pointed wings, and usually a forked tail. They are capable of flying at 110 kph/70 mph.

**Swift, Jonathan** (1667–1745) Irish satirist and Anglican cleric. He wrote *Gulliver's Travels* (1726), an allegory describing travel to lands inhabited by giants, miniature people, and intelligent horses. His other works include *The Tale of a Tub* (1704), attacking corruption in religion and learning and the satirical pamphlet *A Modest Proposal* (1729), which suggested that children of the poor should be eaten. His lucid prose style is simple and controlled and he imparted his views with fierce indignation and wit.

**swim bladder** thin-walled, air-filled sac found between the gut and the spine in bony fishes. Air enters the bladder from the gut or from surrounding capillaries (see ◊capillary), and changes of air pressure within the bladder maintain buoyancy whatever the water depth.

**swimming** self-propulsion of the body through water. There are four strokes in competitive swimming: freestyle, breaststroke, backstroke, and butterfly. Distances of races vary between 50 and 1,500 metres. Olympic-size pools are 50 m/55 yd long and have eight lanes.

**Swindon** unitary authority in southwest England, created in 1997 from the former district council of Thamesdown
**area** 230 sq km/89 sq mi
**towns and cities** Swindon (administrative headquarters); villages of Stanton, Fitzwarren, Highworth
**features** River Thames forms northern border of authority; Barbury Castle, Iron Age hill fort on Marlborough Downs; Great Western Railway Museum and National Monuments Records Centre (Swindon)
**industries** insurance, motor vehicle manufacturing, publishing, energy services, high technology industries, information technology
**population** (1996) 170,000.

**swing music** jazz style popular in the 1930s–40s, a big-band dance music with a simple harmonic base of varying tempo from the rhythm section (percussion, guitar, piano), harmonic brass and woodwind sections (sometimes strings), and superimposed solo melodic line from, for example, trumpet, clarinet, or saxophone. Exponents included Benny Goodman, Duke Ellington, and Glenn Miller, who introduced jazz to a mass white audience.

**Switzerland** Swiss Confederation
**national name** German *Schweiz,* French *Suisse,* Romansch *Svizra*

**area** 41,300 sq km/15,945 sq mi
**capital** Bern (Berne)
**major towns/cities** Zürich, Geneva, Basel, Lausanne, Luzern, St Gallen, Winterthur
**major ports** river port Basel (on the Rhine)
**physical features** most mountainous country in Europe (Alps and Jura mountains); highest peak Dufourspitze 4,634 m/15,203 ft in Apennines
**head of state and government** Ruth Dreifuss from 1999
**government** federal democracy
**political parties** Radical Democratic Party (FDP/PRD), radical, centre left; Social Democratic Party (SP/PS), moderate, left of centre; Christian Democratic People's Party (CVP/PDC), Christian, moderate, centrist; Swiss People's Party (SVP/UDC), centre left; Liberal Party (LPS/PLS), federalist, right of centre; Green Party (GPS/PES), ecological
**currency** Swiss franc
**GNP per capita (PPP)** (US$) 26,620 (1998)
**exports** machinery and equipment, pharmaceutical and chemical products, foodstuffs, precision instruments, clocks and watches, metal products. Principal market: Germany 23.6% (1998)
**population** 7,345,000 (1999 est)
**language** German 64%, French 19%, Italian 8%, Romansch 0.6% (all official)
**religion** Roman Catholic 50%, Protestant 48%

**life expectancy** 75 (men); 82 (women) (1995–2000)

**Chronology**

**58 BC** Celtic Helvetii tribe submitted to Roman authority after defeat by Julius Caesar.

**4th century AD** Region overrun by Germanic tribes, Burgundians, and Alemannians.

**7th century** Formed part of Frankish kingdom and embraced Christianity.

**9th century** Included in Charlemagne's Holy Roman Empire.

**12th century** Many autonomous feudal holdings developed as power of Holy Roman Empire declined.

**13th century** Habsburgs became dominant as overlords of eastern Switzerland.

**1291** Cantons of Schwyz, Uri, and Lower Unterwalden formed Everlasting League, a loose confederation to resist Habsburg control.

**1315** Battle of Morgarten: Swiss Confederation defeated Habsburgs.

**14th century** Luzern, Zürich, Basel, and other cantons joined Swiss Confederation, which became independent of Habsburgs.

**1523–29** Zürich, Bern, and Basel accepted Reformation but rural cantons remained Roman Catholic.

**1648** Treaty of Westphalia recognized Swiss independence from Holy Roman Empire.

**1798** French invasion established Helvetic Republic, a puppet state with centralized government.

**1803** Napoleon's Act of Mediation restored considerable autonomy to cantons.

**1814** End of French domination; Switzerland reverted to loose confederation of sovereign cantons with a weak federal parliament.

**1815** Great Powers recognized 'Perpetual Neutrality' of Switzerland.

**1845** Seven Catholic cantons founded Sonderbund league to resist any strengthening of central government by Liberals.

**1847** Federal troops defeated Sonderbund in brief civil war.

**1848** New constitution introduced greater centralization; Bern chosen as capital.

**1874** Powers of federal government increased; principle of referendum introduced.

**late 19th century** Development of industry, railways, and tourism led to growing prosperity.

**1920** League of Nations selected Geneva as its headquarters.

**1923** Switzerland formed customs union with Liechtenstein.

**1960** Joined European Free Trade Association (EFTA).

**1971** Women gained right to vote in federal elections.

**1986** A proposal for membership of the United Nations (UN) was rejected in a referendum.

**1992** Closer ties with the European Community (EC) were rejected in a national referendum.

**1996** Jean-Paul Delamuraz was elected president.

**1997** Arnold Koller was elected president.

**1998** Ruth Dreifuss was elected president (to take office from 1999), the first woman to hold the post in Switzerland.

**swordfish** marine bony fish *Xiphias gladius,* the only member of its family (Xiphiidae), characterized by a long swordlike beak protruding from the upper jaw. It may reach 4.5 m/15 ft in length and weigh 450 kg/1,000 lb.

**sycamore** deciduous tree native to Europe. The leaves are five-lobed, and the hanging clusters of flowers are followed by winged fruits. The timber is used for furniture making. (*Acer pseudoplatanus.*)

**Sydney** principal port of Australia and capital of the state of ◊New South Wales; population (1996) 3,276,500. Founded in 1788, Sydney is situated on Port Jackson inlet on the southeast coast of Australia, and is built around a number of bays and inlets that form an impressive natural harbour. Industries include financial services, oil refining, engineering, electronics, and the manufacture of scientific equipment, chemicals, clothing, and furniture. Notable architectural landmarks are the Harbour Bridge, the nearby Sydney Opera House, and Centre Point Tower. There are many parks, as well as coastal beaches ideal for surfing, such as Bondi and Manly. In 1994 Sydney was chosen to host the Olympic Games in the year 2000.

**syllable** unit of pronunciation within a word, or as a monosyllabic word, made by a vowel or a combination of vowels and consonants. For example, the word 'competition' contains four syllables: 'com/pe/ti/tion'.

**syllogism** set of philosophical statements devised by Aristotle in his work on logic. It establishes the conditions under which a valid conclusion follows or does not follow by deduction from given premises. The following is an example of a valid syllogism: 'All men are mortal, Socrates is a man, therefore Socrates is mortal.'

**symbiosis** any close relationship between two organisms of different species, and one where both partners benefit from the association. A well-known example is the pollination relationship between insects and flowers, where the insects feed on nectar and carry pollen from one flower to another. This is sometimes known as ◊mutualism.

**Symbolism** in the arts, the use of symbols as a device for concentrating or intensifying meaning. The Symbolist movement in art flourished during the last two decades of the 19th century. Symbolist painters rejected realism and Impressionism, seeking to express moods and psychological states through colour, line, and form. Their subjects were often mythological, mystical, or fantastic. Gustave Moreau was a leading Symbolist painter. Others included Pierre Puvis de Chavannes and Odilon Redon in France, Arnold Böcklin in Switzerland, Edward Burne-Jones in Britain, and Jan Theodoor Toorop in the Netherlands.

**Symbolism** late 19th-century movement in French poetry, which inspired a similar trend in French painting. The Symbolist poets used words for their symbolic rather than concrete meaning. Leading exponents were Paul Verlaine, Stéphane Mallarmé, and Arthur Rimbaud.

**symmetry** exact likeness in shape about a given line (axis), point, or plane. A figure has symmetry if one half can be rotated and/or reflected onto the other. (Symmetry preserves length, angle, but not necessarily orientation.) In a wider sense, symmetry exists if a change in the system leaves the essential features of the system unchanged; for example, reversing the sign of electric charges does not change the electrical behaviour of an arrangement of charges.

**symphony** abstract musical composition for orchestra, traditionally in four separate but closely related movements. It developed from the smaller ◊sonata form, the Italian ◊overture, and the concerto grosso.

**synagogue** in Judaism, a place of worship; in the USA a synagogue is also called a temple by the non-Orthodox. As an institution it dates from the destruction of the Temple in Jerusalem in AD 70, though it had been developing from the time of the Babylonian exile as a substitute for the Temple. In antiquity it was a public meeting hall where the Torah was also read, but today it is used primarily for prayer and services. A service requires a quorum (*minyan*) of ten adult Jewish men.

**synapse** junction between two ◊nerve cells, or between a nerve cell and a muscle (a neuromuscular junction), across which a nerve impulse is transmitted. The two cells are separated by a narrow gap called the *synaptic cleft*. The gap is bridged by a chemical ◊neurotransmitter, released by the nerve impulse.

**syndicalism** (French *syndicat* 'trade union') political movement in 19th-century Europe that rejected parliamentary activity in favour of direct action, culminating in a revolutionary general strike to secure worker ownership and control of industry. After 1918 syndicalism was absorbed in communism, although it continued to have an independent existence in Spain until the late 1930s.

**Synge, J(ohn) M(illington)** (1871–1909) Irish dramatist. He was a leading figure in the Irish dramatic revival of the early 20th century. His six plays reflect the speech patterns of the Aran Islands and western Ireland. They include *In the Shadow of the Glen* (1903), *Riders to the Sea* (1904), and *The Playboy of the Western World* (1907), which caused riots at the Abbey Theatre, Dublin, when first performed.

**syntax** the structure of language; the ways in which words are ordered and combined to convey meaning. Syntax applies principally to grammar, and a grammatically correct sentence is also syntactically correct, but syntax has a wider significance.

**synthesis** in chemistry, the formation of a substance or compound from more elementary compounds. The synthesis of a drug can involve several stages from the initial material to the final product; the complexity of these stages is a major factor in the cost of production.

**synthesizer** musical device for the simulation of vocal or instrumental ◊timbre by mechanical or electro-acoustic means.

**synthetic** any material made from chemicals. Since the 1900s, more and more of the materials used in everyday life are synthetics, including plastics (polythene, polystyrene), synthetic fibres (nylon, acrylics, polyesters), synthetic resins, and synthetic rubber. Most naturally occurring organic substances are now made synthetically, especially pharmaceuticals.

**syphilis** sexually transmitted disease caused by the spiral-shaped bacterium (spirochete) *Treponema pallidum*. Untreated, it runs its course in three stages over many years, often starting with a painless hard sore, or chancre, developing within a month on the area of infection (usually the genitals). The second stage, months later, is a rash with arthritis, hepatitis, and/or meningitis. The third stage, years later, leads eventually to paralysis, blindness, insanity, and death. The Wassermann test is a diagnostic blood test for syphilis.

**Syracuse** Italian *Siracusa,* industrial port (chemicals, salt) in eastern Sicily; population (1992) 126,800. It has a cathedral and remains of temples, aqueducts, catacombs, and an amphitheatre. Founded in 734 BC by the Corinthians, it became a centre of Greek culture under the elder and younger ◊Dionysius. After a three-year siege it was taken by Rome 212 BC. In AD 878 it was destroyed by the Arabs, and the rebuilt town came under Norman rule in the 11th century.

**Syria** Syrian Arab Republic
*national name* al-Jamhuriya al-Arabya as-Suriya

*area* 185,200 sq km/71,505 sq mi
*capital* Damascus
*major towns/cities* Aleppo, Homs, Latakia, Hama
*major ports* Latakia
*physical features* mountains alternate with fertile plains and desert areas; Euphrates River
*head of state and government* Hafez al-Assad from 1971
*political system* socialist republic
*political parties* National Progressive Front (NPF), pro-Arab, socialist coalition, including

the Communist Party of Syria, the Arab Socialist Party, the Arab Socialist Unionist Party, the Syrian Arab Socialist Union Party, the Ba'ath Arab Socialist Party

**currency** Syrian pound

**GNP per capita (PPP)** (US$) 3,000 (1998)

**exports** crude petroleum, textiles, vegetables, fruit, raw cotton, natural phosphate. Principal market: Italy 17.5% (1997)

**population** 15,725,000 (1999 est)

**language** Arabic 89% (official); Kurdish 6%, Armenian 3%

**religion** Sunni Muslim 90%; other Islamic sects, Christian

**life expectancy** 67 (men); 71 (women) (1995–2000)

**Chronology**

**c.1750 BC** Syria became part of Babylonian Empire; during the next millennium it was successively conquered by Hittites, Assyrians, Chaldeans, and Persians.

**333 BC** Alexander the Great of Macedonia conquered Persia and Syria.

**301 BC** Seleucus I, one of the generals of Alexander the Great, founded kingdom of Syria, which the Seleucid dynasty ruled for over 200 years.

**64 BC** Syria became part of Roman Empire.

**4th century AD** After division of Roman Empire, Syria came under Byzantine rule.

**634** Arabs conquered most of Syria and introduced Islam.

**661–750** Damascus was capital of Muslim Empire.

**1055** Seljuk Turks overran Syria.

**1095–99** First Crusade established Latin states on Syrian coast.

**13th century** Mameluke sultans of Egypt took control.

**1516** Ottoman Turks conquered Syria.

**1831** Egyptians led by Mehemet Ali drove out Turks.

**1840** Turkish rule restored; Syria opened up to European trade.

**late 19th century** French firms built ports, roads, and railways in Syria.

**1916** Sykes-Picot Agreement: secret Anglo-French deal to partition Turkish Empire allotted Syria to France.

**1918** British expelled Turks with help of Arab revolt.

**1919** Syrian national congress called for independence under Emir Faisal and opposed transfer to French rule.

**1920** Syria became League of Nations protectorate, administered by France.

**1925** People's Party founded to campaign for independence and national unity; insurrection by Druze religious sect against French control.

**1936** France promised independence within three years, but martial law imposed in 1939.

**1941** British forces ousted Vichy French regime in Damascus and occupied Syria in conjunction with Free French.

**1944** Syrian independence proclaimed but French military resisted transfer of power.

**1946** Syria achieved effective independence when French forces withdrew.

**1948–49** Arab–Israeli War: Syria joined unsuccessful invasion of newly independent Israel.

**1958** Syria and Egypt merged to form United Arab Republic (UAR).

**1959** USSR agreed to give financial and technical aid to Syria.

**1961** Syria seceded from UAR.

**1964** Ba'ath Socialist Party established military dictatorship.

**1967** Six-Day War: Syria lost Golan Heights to Israel.

**1970–71** Syria invaded Jordan in support of Palestinian guerrillas.

**1970** Hafez al-Assad staged a coup.

**1971** Hafez al-Assad was elected president.

**1973** Yom Kippur War: Syrian attack on Israel repulsed.

**1976** Start of Syrian military intervention in Lebanese civil war.

**1978** Syria opposed peace deal between Egypt and Israel.

**1986** Britain broke off diplomatic relations, accusing Syria of involvement in international terrorism.

**1990** Diplomatic links with Britain were restored.

**1991** Syria contributed troops to a US-led coalition in Gulf War against Iraq. A US–Middle East peace plan was approved by Assad.

**1994** Israel offered a partial withdrawal from the Golan Heights in return for peace, but Syria remained sceptical.

**1995** A security framework agreement was made with Israel.

**systems analysis** in computing, the investigation of a business activity or clerical procedure, with a view to deciding if and how it can be computerized. The analyst discusses the existing procedures with the people involved, observes the flow of data through the business, and draws up an outline specification of the required computer system. The next step is ◊systems design.

**systems design** in computing, the detailed design of an applications package. The designer breaks the system down into component programs, and designs the required input forms, screen layouts, and printouts. Systems design forms a link between systems analysis and ◊programming.

**Szechwan** alternative spelling for the central Chinese province of ◊Sichuan.

**Table Bay** wide bay on the north coast of the Cape of Good Hope, South Africa, on which Cape Town stands. It is overlooked by Table Mountain.

**table tennis** or *ping pong,* indoor game played on a rectangular table by two or four players. It was developed in Britain in about 1880 and derived from lawn tennis. World championships were first held in 1926.

**Tachisme** (French 'blotting, staining') French style of abstract painting current in the 1940s and 1950s, the European equivalent to ◊Abstract Expressionism. Breaking free from the restraints of ◊Cubism, the Tachistes adopted a novel, spontaneous approach to brushwork, typified by all-over blotches of impastoed colour and dribbled paint, or swirling calligraphy applied straight from the tube, as in the work of Georges Mathieu (1921– ). The terms *L'Art Informel,* meaning gestural or ◊action painting, and **abstraction lyrique** ('lyrical abstraction') are also used to describe the style.

**tachograph** combined speedometer and clock that records a vehicle's speed and the length of time the vehicle is moving or stationary. It is used to monitor a lorry driver's working hours.

**Tacitus, Publius Cornelius** (c. AD 56–c. 120) Roman historian. A public orator in Rome, he was consul under Nerva 97–98 and proconsul of Asia 112–113. He wrote histories of the Roman empire, *Annales* and *Historiae,* covering the years AD 14–68 and 69–97 respectively. He also wrote a *Life of Agricola* (97) (he married Agricola's daughter in 77) and a description of the Germanic tribes, *Germania* (98).

**Taegu** third-largest city in South Korea, situated between Seoul and Pusan; population (1990) 2,228,800. Nearby is the Haeinsa Temple, one of the country's largest monasteries and repository of the *Triptaka Koreana,* a collection of 80,000 wood blocks on which the Buddhist scriptures are carved. Grain, fruit, textiles, and tobacco are produced.

**tae kwon do** Korean ◊martial art similar to ◊karate, which includes punching and kicking. It was included in the 1988 Olympic Games as a demonstration sport, and will become a full medal discipline at the Sydney 2000 Olympic Games.

**Taft, William Howard** (1857–1930) 27th president of the USA) 1909–13, a Republican. He was secretary of war 1904–08 in Theodore Roosevelt's administration, but as president his conservatism provoked Roosevelt to stand against him in the 1912 election. Taft served as chief justice of the Supreme Court in 1921–30.

**Tagalog** the majority ethnic group living around Manila on the island of Luzon, in the Philippines, who number about 10 million (1988). The Tagalog live by fishing and trading. In its standardized form, known as Pilipino, Tagalog is the official language of the Philippines, and belongs to the Western branch of the Austronesian family. The Tagalog religion is a mixture of animism, Christianity, and Islam.

**tagging, electronic** long-distance monitoring of the movements of people charged with or convicted of a crime, thus enabling them to be detained in their homes rather than in prison.

**Tagore, Rabindranath** (1861–1941) Bengali Indian writer. He translated into English his own verse *Gitanjali/Song Offerings* (1912) and his verse play *Chitra* (1896). He was awarded the Nobel Prize for Literature in 1913.

**Tagus** Spanish *Tajo,* Portuguese *Tejo,* river in Spain and Portugal; length 1,007 km/626 mi. It rises in the Sierra de Albarracín, Spain, on the border between the provinces of Cuenca and Teruel. It flows west past Toledo and Alcántara, then follows the Spanish-Portuguese frontier for 50 km/31 mi, and crosses Portugal to the Atlantic Ocean at Lisbon.

**Tahiti** largest of the Society Islands, in ◊French Polynesia; area 1,042 sq km/402 sq mi; population (1988) 115,800. Its capital is Papeete. Tahiti was visited by Capt James ◊Cook (1769) and by Admiral ◊Bligh of the *Bounty* (1788). It came under French control in 1843 and became a colony in 1880.

**Tai** member of any of the groups of Southeast Asian peoples who speak Tai languages, all of which belong to the Sino-Tibetan language family. There are over 60 million speakers, the majority of whom live in Thailand. Tai peoples are also found in southwestern China, northwestern Myanmar (Burma), Laos, and North Vietnam.

**T'ai Chi** series of 108 complex, slow-motion movements, each named (for example, the White Crane Spreads Its Wings) and designed to ensure effective circulation of the *chi,* or intrinsic energy of the universe, through the mind and body. It derives partly from the Shaolin ◊martial arts of China and partly from ◊Taoism.

**taiga** or *boreal forest,* Russian name for the forest zone south of the ◊tundra, found across the northern hemisphere. Here, dense forests of conifers (spruces and hemlocks), birches, and poplars occupy glaciated regions punctuated with cold lakes, streams, bogs, and marshes. Winters are prolonged and very cold, but the summer is warm enough to promote dense growth.

**taipan** species of small-headed cobra *Oxyuranus scutellatus,* found in northeastern Australia and New Guinea. It is about 3 m/10 ft long, and has a brown back and yellow belly. Its venom is fatal within minutes.

**Taiwan** Republic of China
*national name Chung Hua Min Kuo*

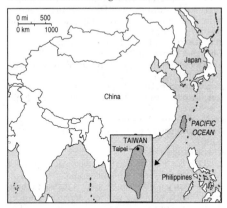

**area** 36,179 sq km/13,968 sq mi
**capital** Taipei
**major towns/cities** Kaohsiung, Taichung, Tainan, Panchiao, Yunlin
**major ports** Kaohsiung, Keelung
**physical features** island (formerly Formosa) off People's Republic of China; mountainous, with lowlands in west; Penghu (Pescadores), Jinmen (Quemoy), Mazu (Matsu) islands
**head of state** Lee Teng-hui from 1988
**head of government** Vincent Siew from 1997
**political system** emergent democracy
**political parties** Nationalist Party of China (Kuomintang: KMT; known as Guomindang outside Taiwan), anticommunist, Chinese nationalist; Democratic Progressive Party (DPP), centrist-pluralist, pro-self-determination grouping; Workers' Party (Kuntang), left of centre
**currency** New Taiwan dollar
**GNP per capita (PPP)** (US$) 18,950 (1998 est)
**exports** electronic products, base metals and metal articles, textiles and clothing, machinery, information and communication products, plastic and rubber products, vehicles and transport equipment, footwear, headwear, umbrellas, toys, games, sports equipment. Principal market: USA 26.6% (1998)
**population** 22,113,000 (1999 est)
**language** Mandarin Chinese (official); Taiwan, Hakka dialects
**religion** officially atheist; Taoist, Confucian, Buddhist, Christian
**life expectancy** 74 (men); 80 (women) (1998 est)
**Chronology**
**7th century AD** Island was occupied by aboriginal community of Malayan descent; immigration of Chinese from mainland began, but remained limited before 15th century.
**1517** Sighted by Portuguese vessels en route to Japan and named Ilha Formosa ('beautiful island').

**1624** Occupied and controlled by Dutch.
**1662** Dutch defeated by Chinese Ming general, Cheng Ch'eng-kung (Koxinga), whose family came to rule Formosa for a short period.
**1683** Annexed by China's rulers, the Manchu Qing.
**1786** Major rebellion against Chinese rule.
**1860** Ports opened to Western trade.
**1895** Ceded 'in perpetuity' to Japan under Treaty of Shominoseki at end of Sino-Japanese war.
**1945** Recovered by China's Nationalist Guomindang government at end of World War II.
**1947** Rebellion against Chinese rule brutally suppressed.
**1949** Flight of Nationalist government, led by Generalissimo Jiang Jie Shi (Chiang Kai-shek), to Taiwan after Chinese communist revolution. They retained the designation of Republic of China (ROC), claiming to be the legitimate government for all China, and were recognized by USA and United Nations (UN).
**1950s onwards** Rapid economic growth as Taiwan became successful export-orientated Newly Industrializing Country (NIC) and land was redistributed from the gentry 'to-the-tiller'.
**1954** US–Taiwanese mutual defence treaty.
**1971** Expulsion from UN as USA adopted new policy of détente towards communist China.
**1972** Commencement of legislature elections as programme of gradual democratization and Taiwanization launched by mainlander-dominated Guomindang.
**1975** President Jiang Jie Shi died; replaced as Guomindang leader by his son, Jiang Ching-kuo.
**1979** USA severed diplomatic relations and annulled 1954 security pact.
**1986** Centrist Democratic Progressive Party (DPP) formed as opposition to nationalist Guomindang.
**1987** Martial law lifted; opposition parties legalized; press restrictions lifted.
**1988** President Jiang Ching-kuo died; replaced by Taiwanese-born Lee Teng-hui.
**1990** Chinese-born Guomindang members became a minority in parliament.
**1991** President Lee Teng-hui declared an end to the civil war with China. The constitution was amended. Guomindang won a landslide victory in elections to the new National Assembly, the 'superparliament'.
**1993** A cooperation pact was signed with China.
**1995** The ruling Guomindang retained a majority in working assembly (Legislative Yuan) by a slim margin.
**1996** Lee Teng-hui was elected president in the first ever Chinese democratic elections.
**1997** The government narrowly survived a no-confidence motion. Vincent Siew became prime minister.
**1998** Lin Yi-shiung became leader of the opposition Democratic Progressive Party. President Lee Teng-hui announced that reunion with mainland China was impossible until Beijing adopted democracy. The ruling KMT increased its majority in parliamentary and local elections.

**Taipei** or *Taibei,* capital and commercial centre of Taiwan; population (1995) 2,639,300. Industries include electronics, plastics, textiles, and machinery. The National Palace Museum (1965) houses the world's greatest collection of Chinese art, brought here from the mainland in 1948.

**Taiping Rebellion** popular revolt in 1850–64 that undermined China's Qing dynasty (see ◊Manchu. By 1853 the rebels had secured control over much of the central and lower Chang Jiang valley region, instituting radical, populist land reforms. Civil war continued until 1864, when the Taipings, weakened by internal dissension, were overcome by the provincial Hunan army of Zeng Guofan and the Ever-Victorious Army, led by American F T Ward and British soldier Charles Gordon.

**Tajik** or *Tadzhik,* member of the majority ethnic group in Tajikistan. Tajiks also live in Afghanistan and parts of Pakistan and western China. The Tajiki language belongs to the West Iranian sub-branch of the Indo-European family, and is similar to Farsi; it is written in the Cyrillic script. The Tajiks have long been associated with neighbouring Turkic peoples and their language contains Altaic loan words. The majority of the Tajik people are Sunni Muslims; there is a Shiite minority in Afghanistan.

**Taj Mahal** white marble mausoleum built 1630–53 on the River Yamuna near Agra, India. Erected by Shah Jahan to the memory of his favourite wife, it is a celebrated example of Indo-Islamic architecture, the fusion of Muslim and Hindu styles.

**Tajikistan** Republic of
*national name Respublika i Tojikiston*

**area** 143,100 sq km/55,250 sq mi
**capital** Dushanbe
**major towns/cities** Khodzhent (formerly Leninabad), Kurgan-Tyube, Kulyab
**physical features** mountainous, more than half of its territory lying above 3,000 m/10,000 ft; huge mountain glaciers, which are the source of many rapid rivers
**head of state** Imamali Rakhmanov from 1994
**head of government** Yahya Azimov from 1996
**political system** authoritarian nationalist
**political parties** Communist Party of Tajikistan (CPT), pro-Rakhmanov; Democratic Party of Tajikistan (DP), anticommunist (banned from 1993); Party of Popular Unity and Justice, anticommunist
**currencies** Tajik and Russian rouble
**GNP per capita (PPP)** (US$) 1,310 (1998 est)
**exports** aluminium, cotton lint. Principal market: Uzbekistan 36.8% (1997)
**population** 6,104,000 (1999 est)
**language** Tajik (official), similar to Farsi (Persian)
**religion** Sunni Muslim
**life expectancy** 64 (men); 70 (women) (1995–2000)
**Chronology**
*c. 330* Formed an eastern part of empire of Alexander the Great of Macedonia.
*8th century* Tajiks established as distinct ethnic group, with semi-independent territories under the tutelage of the Uzbeks, to the west; spread of Islam.
*13th century* Conquered by Genghis Khan and became part of Mongol Empire.
*1860–1900* Northern Tajikistan came under tsarist Russian rule, while the south was annexed by Emirate of Bukhara, to the west.
*1917–18* Attempts to establish Soviet control after Bolshevik revolution in Russia resisted initially by armed guerrillas (basmachi).
*1921* Became part of Turkestan Soviet Socialist Autonomous Republic.
*1924* Tajik Autonomous Soviet Socialist Republic formed.
*1929* Became constituent republic of Soviet Union (USSR).
*1930s* Stalinist era of collectivization led to widespread repression of Tajiks.
*1978* 13,000 participated in anti-Russian riots.
*late 1980s* Resurgence in Tajik consciousness, stimulated by the *glasnost* initiative of Soviet leader Mikhail Gorbachev.
*1989* Rastokhez ('Revival') Popular Front established and Tajik declared state language. New mosques constructed.
*1990* Violent interethnic Tajik–Armenian clashes in Dushanbe; a state of emergency was imposed.
*1991* President Kakhar Makhkamov, local communist leader since 1985, was forced to resign after supporting a failed anti-Gorbachev coup in Moscow. Independence was declared. Rakhman Nabiyev, communist leader 1982–85, was elected president. Joined new Commonwealth of Independent States (CIS).
*1992* Joined Muslim Economic Cooperation Organization, the Conference on Security and Cooperation in Europe (CSCE; now the Organization on Security and Cooperation in Europe, OSCE), and the United Nations. Violent demonstrations by Islamic and prodemocracy groups forced Nabiyev to resign. Civil war between pro- and anti-Nabiyev forces claimed

20,000 lives, made 600,000 refugees, and wrecked the economy. Imamali Rakhmanov, a communist sympathetic to Nabiyev, took over as head of state.

**1993** Government forces regained control of most of the country. CIS peacekeeping forces were drafted in to patrol the border with Afghanistan, the base of the pro-Islamic rebels.

**1994** A ceasefire was agreed. Rakhmanov was popularly elected president under a new constitution.

**1995** Parliamentary elections were won by Rakhmanov's supporters. There was renewed fighting on the Afghan border.

**1996** Pro-Islamic rebels captured towns in the southwest. There was a UN-sponsored ceasefire between government and pro-Islamic rebels.

**1997** A four-stage peace plan was signed. President Rakhmanov was seriously injured by a grenade. There was a peace accord with the Islamic rebel group the United Tajik Opposition (UTO).

**1998** Members of UTO were appointed to the government as part of a peace plan. The UN military observer mission (UNMOT) suspended its operations, following the killing of four UN workers. More than 200 people were killed in clashes in Leninabad between the army and rebel forces loyal to the renegade Tajik army commander Col Makhmud Khudoberdiyev; the deputy leader of the Islamic-led UTO, Ali Akbar Turadzhonzada, was appointed first deputy prime minister. Tajikistan joined the CIS.

**takahe** flightless bird *Porphyrio mantelli* of the rail family, order Gruiformes, native to New Zealand. It is about 60 cm/2 ft tall and weighs just over 2 kg/4.4 lb, with blue and green plumage and a red bill. The takahe was thought to have become extinct at the end of the 19th century, but in 1948 small numbers were rediscovered in the tussock grass of a mountain valley on South Island.

**takeover** in business, the acquisition by one company of a sufficient number of shares in another company to have effective control of that company – usually 51%, although a controlling stake may be as little as 30%.

**talc** $Mg_3Si_4O_{10}(OH)_2$, mineral, hydrous magnesium silicate. It occurs in tabular crystals, but the massive impure form, known as *steatite* or *soapstone,* is more common. It is formed by the alteration of magnesium compounds and is usually found in metamorphic rocks. Talc is very soft, ranked 1 on the Mohs scale of hardness. It is used in powdered form in cosmetics, lubricants, and as an additive in paper manufacture.

**Taliesin** (lived *c.* 550) Legendary Welsh poet, a bard at the court of the king of Rheged in Scotland. Taliesin allegedly died at Taliesin (named after him) in Dyfed, Wales.

**Talleyrand-Périgord, Charles Maurice de** (1754–1838) French politician and diplomat. As bishop of Autun in 1789–91 he supported moderate reform during the ◊French Revolution, was excommunicated by the pope, and fled to the USA during the Reign of Terror (persecution

of anti-revolutionaries). He returned and became foreign minister under the Directory (1797–99) and under Napoleon (1799–1807). He represented France at the Congress of Vienna (1814–15).

**Tallinn** German *Reval;* Russian *Revel,* naval port and capital of Estonia, 300 km/186 mi west of St Petersburg on the Gulf of Finland; population (1990) 505,100. Industries include the manufacture of electrical and oil-drilling machinery, textiles, and paper production. It is a major cultural centre, containing the Estonian Academy of Sciences and a number of polytechnic, arts, and other institutes. Founded as a Danish fortress in 1219, Tallinn was a member of the ◊Hanseatic League throughout the Middle Ages; it came under the control of the ◊Teutonic Knights in 1346, Sweden in 1561, and Russia in 1750. It was occupied by German forces in both World Wars, and suffered widespread damage.

**Tallis, Thomas** (*c.* 1505–1585) English composer. He was a master of ◊counterpoint. His works include *Tallis's Canon* ('Glory to thee my God this night') (1567), the antiphonal *Spem in alium non habui* (*c.* 1573) for 40 voices in various groupings, and a collection of 34 motets, *Cantiones sacrae* (1575), of which 16 are by Tallis and 18 by Byrd.

**Talmud** the two most important works of post-Biblical Jewish literature. The Babylonian and the Palestinian (or Jerusalem) Talmud provide a compilation of ancient Jewish law and tradition. The Babylonian Talmud was edited at the end of the 5th century AD and is the more authoritative version for later Judaism; both Talmuds are written in a mix of Hebrew and Aramaic. They contain the commentary (*gemara*) on the *Mishnah* (early rabbinical commentaries compiled about AD 200), and the material can be generally divided into *halakhah,* consisting of legal and ritual matters, and *aggadah* (or *haggadah*), concerned with ethical, theological, and folklorist matters.

**tamandua** tree-living toothless anteater *Tamandua tetradactyla* found in tropical forests and tree savanna from southern Mexico to Brazil. About 56 cm/1.8 ft long with a prehensile tail of equal length, it has strong foreclaws with which it can break into nests of tree ants and termites, which it licks up with its narrow tongue.

**tamarind** evergreen tropical tree native to the Old World, with pinnate leaves (leaflets either side of the stem) and reddish-yellow flowers, followed by pods. The pulp surrounding the seeds is used in medicine and as a flavouring. (*Tamarindus indica,* family Leguminosae.)

**tamarisk** any of a group of small trees or shrubs that flourish in warm, salty, desert regions of Europe and Asia where no other vegetation is found. The common tamarisk *T. gallica,* which grows in European coastal areas, has small, scalelike leaves on feathery branches and produces spikes of small pink flowers. (Genus *Tamarix,* family Tamaricaceae.)

**tambourine** musical percussion instrument of ancient origin, almost unchanged since Roman times, consisting of a shallow frame drum with a single skin and loosely set jingles in the rim which add their noise when the drum skin is struck or rubbed, or sound separately when the instrument is shaken.

**Tamerlane** also known as Timur Leng or Timur the Lame (1335–1405) Turco-Mongol ruler of Samarkand, in Uzbekistan, from 1369 who conquered Persia, Azerbaijan, Armenia, and Georgia. He defeated the ◊Golden Horde in 1395, sacked Delhi in 1398, invaded Syria and Anatolia, and captured the Ottoman sultan Bayezid I (*c.* 1360–1403) in Ankara in 1402; he died invading China.

**Tamil** the majority ethnic group living in the Indian state of Tamil Nadu (formerly Madras). Tamils also live in southern India, northern Sri Lanka, Malaysia, Singapore, and South Africa, totalling 35–55 million worldwide. Tamil belongs to the Dravidian family of languages; written records in Tamil date from the 3rd century BC. The 3 million Tamils in Sri Lanka are predominantly Hindu, unlike the Sinhalese, the majority group there, who are mainly Buddhist. The *Tamil Tigers,* most prominent of the various Tamil groups, are attempting to create a separate homeland in northern Sri Lanka through both political and military means.

**Tamil Nadu** formerly (until 1968) Madras State, state of southeast India bounded on the north by Karnataka and Andhra Pradesh, Kerala on the west, and the Bay of Bengal and Indian Ocean on the east and south
*area* 130,100 sq km/50,219 sq mi
*capital* ◊Chennai (formerly Madras)
*physical* coastal plains, including the Cauvery delta; inland the Nilgiri Hills and extensions of the Western Ghats; rainfall is unreliable, derived mainly from the northeast monsoon
*features* hydroelectric power schemes at Mettur and Moyar; coal-powered power stations at Neyveli and Ennore
*industries* cotton, leather, sugar refining are the main industries; also electrical machinery, tractors, rubber, cars, chemicals, oil refining, fertilizers, cement, cycles; film industry; most industry concentrated in Chennai, as well as in Coimbatore, Salem, and Tiruchchirappalli
*agriculture* tea, coffee, spices, sugar cane, coconuts as cash crops; rice, millet, groundnuts; frequently dependent on tank and well irrigation; fishing
*population* (1994 est) 58,840,000
*language* Tamil; Telugu spoken in the north by 10%
*history* the present state was formed 1956. Tamil Nadu comprises part of the former British Madras presidency (later province) formed from areas taken from France and Tipu Sahib, the sultan of Mysore, in the 18th century, which became a state of the Republic of India in 1950. The northeast was detached to form Andhra Pradesh in 1953; in 1956 other areas went to Kerala and Mysore (now Karnataka), and the Laccadive Islands (now Lakshadweep) became a separate Union Territory.

**Tampere** Swedish *Tammerfors,* city in southwestern Finland; population (1994) 179,000, metropolitan area 258,000. Industries include textiles, paper, footwear, and turbines. It is the second-largest city in Finland.

**Tanabata** (Japanese 'star festival') festival celebrated annually on 7 July, introduced to Japan from China in the 8th century. It is dedicated to Altair and Vega, two stars in the constellations Aquila and Lyra respectively, separated by the Milky Way. According to legend they represent two star-crossed lovers allowed by the gods to meet on that night.

**tanager** New World bird of the family Emberizidae, order Passeriformes. There are about 230 species in forests of Central and South America, all brilliantly coloured. They are 10–20 cm/4–8 in long, with plump bodies and conical beaks. The tanagers of North America all belong to the genus *Piranga.*

**Tanganyika, Lake** lake 772 m/2,534 ft above sea level in the Great Rift Valley, East Africa, with the Democratic Republic of Congo to the west, Zambia to the south, and Tanzania and Burundi to the east. It is about 645 km/400 mi long, with an area of about 31,000 sq km/12,000 sq mi, and is the deepest lake (1,435 m/4,710 ft) in Africa, and the second-deepest freshwater lake in the world. The mountains around its shores rise to about 2,700 m/8,860 ft. The chief ports on the lake are Bujumbura (Burundi), Kigoma (Tanzania), and Kalémié (Democratic Republic of Congo).

**Tang dynasty** the greatest of China's imperial dynasties, which ruled from 618 to 907. Founded by the Sui official Li Yuan (566–635), it extended Chinese authority into central Asia, Tibet, Korea, and Annam, establishing what was then the world's largest empire. The dynasty's peak was reached during the reign of Emperor Minghuang or Hsuan-tsung (712–56) .

**tangent** in geometry, a straight line that touches a curve and gives the gradient of the curve at the point of contact. At a maximum, minimum, or point of inflection, the tangent to a curve has zero gradient. Also, in trigonometry, a function of an acute angle in a right-angled triangle, defined as the ratio of the length of the side opposite the angle to the length of the side adjacent to it; a way of expressing the gradient of a line.

**tangerine** small type of ◊orange.

**Tangier** or *Tangiers* or *Tanger,* Arabic *Tanjah,* port in north Morocco, on the Strait of Gibraltar, 58 km/36 mi southwest of Gibraltar; population (urban area, 1993) 307,000. Cigarette manufacturing is the most important industry, and there are fisheries, market gardens, and preserving industries. It is the northern terminus of the Tangier–Fès railway. It was a Phoenician trading centre in the 15th century BC. Captured by the Portuguese in 1471, it passed to England in 1662 as part of the dowry of Catherine of Braganza, but was abandoned in 1684, and later became a lair of Barbary Coast pirates. From 1923 Tangier and a small surrounding enclave became an international zone, administered by Spain (1940–45). In 1956 it was transferred to independent Morocco and became a free port in 1962.

**tango** dance for couples, developed in Argentina during the early 20th century, or the music for it. The dance consists of two long steps followed by two short steps then one long step, using stylized body positions. The music is in moderately slow duple time (2/4) and employs syncopated rhythms. Similar to the habanera, from which it evolved, the tango consists of two balanced sections, the second usually in the ♭dominant key or the relative minor of the first section. William Walton uses a tango in his suite *Facade* 1923.

**tangram** puzzle made by cutting up a square into seven pieces.

**tank** armoured fighting vehicle that runs on tracks and is fitted with weapons systems capable of defeating other tanks and destroying life and property. The term was originally a code name for the first effective tracked and armoured fighting vehicle, invented by the British soldier and scholar Ernest Swinton, and first used in the Battle of the Somme 1916.

**tansy** perennial herb belonging to the daisy family, native to Europe. The yellow flower heads grow in clusters on stalks up to 120 cm/4 ft tall, and the aromatic leaves are used in cookery. (*Tanacetum vulgare,* family Compositae.)

**tantalum** hard, ductile, lustrous, grey-white, metallic element, symbol Ta, atomic number 73, relative atomic mass 180.948. It occurs with niobium in tantalite and other minerals. It can be drawn into wire with a very high melting point and great tenacity, useful for lamp filaments subject to vibration. It is also used in alloys, for corrosion-resistant laboratory apparatus and chemical equipment, as a catalyst in manufacturing synthetic rubber, in tools and instruments, and in rectifiers and capacitors.

**Tantalus** in Greek mythology, a king of Lydia, son of Zeus, and father of Pelops and Niobe. He offended the gods by divulging their secrets and serving them human flesh at a banquet. His crimes were punished in Tartarus (a part of the underworld for the wicked) by the provision of food and drink he could not reach. The word 'tantalize' derives from his torment.

**Tantrism** forms of Hinduism and Buddhism that emphasize the division of the universe into male and female forces which maintain its unity by their interaction. Tantric Hinduism is associated with magical and sexual yoga practices that imitate the union of Siva and Sakti, as described in scriptures known as the *Tantras.* In Buddhism, the *Tantras* are texts attributed to the Buddha, describing magical ritual methods of attaining enlightenment.

**Tanzania** United Republic of
**national name** *Jamhuri ya Muungano wa Tanzania*
**area** 945,000 sq km/364,864 sq mi
**capital** Dodoma (since 1983)

**major towns/cities** Zanzibar Town, Mwanza, Tabora, Mbeya, Tanga
**major ports** (former capital) Dar es Salaam
**physical features** central plateau; lakes in north and west; coastal plains; lakes Victoria, Tanganyika, and Nyasa; half the country is forested; comprises islands of Zanzibar and Pemba; Mount Kilimanjaro, 5,895 m/19,340 ft, the highest peak in Africa; Olduvai Gorge; Ngorongoro Crater, 14.5 km/9 mi across, 762 m/2,500 ft deep
**head of state** Benjamin Mkapa from 1995
**head of government** Cleoopa Msuya from 1994
**political system** emergent democracy
**political parties** Revolutionary Party of Tanzania (CCM), African, socialist; Civic Party (Chama Cha Wananchi), left of centre; Tanzania People's Party (TPP), left of centre; Democratic Party (DP), left of centre; Justice and Development Party, left of centre; Zanzibar United Front (Kamahuru), Zanzibar-based, centrist
**currency** Tanzanian shilling
**GNP per capita (PPP)** (US$) 490 (1998)
**exports** coffee beans, raw cotton, tobacco, tea, cloves, cashew nuts, minerals, petroleum products. Principal market: India 11.6% (1997)
**population** 32,793,000 (1999 est)
**language** Kiswahili, English (both official)
**Religion** Muslim, Christian, traditional religions
**life expectancy** 50 (men); 53 (women) (1995–2000)
**Chronology**
**8th century** Growth of city states along coast after settlement by Arabs from Oman.
**1499** Portuguese navigator Vasco da Gama visited island of Zanzibar.
**16th century** Portuguese occupied Zanzibar, defeated coastal states, and exerted spasmodic control over them.
**1699** Portuguese ousted from Zanzibar by Arabs of Oman.
**18th century** Sultan of Oman reasserted Arab overlordship of East African coast, which became subordinate to Zanzibar.

**1744–1837** Revolt of ruler of Mombasa against Oman spanned 93 years until final victory of Oman.

**1822** Moresby Treaty: Britain recognized regional dominance of Zanzibar, but protested against slave trade.

**1840** Sultan Seyyid bin Sultan moved his capital from Oman to Zanzibar; trade in slaves and ivory flourished.

**1861** Sultanates of Zanzibar and Oman separated on death of Seyyid.

**19th century** Europeans started to explore inland, closely followed by Christian missionaries.

**1884** German Colonization Society began to acquire territory on mainland in defiance of Zanzibar.

**1890** Britain obtained protectorate over Zanzibar, abolished slave trade, and recognized German claims to mainland.

**1897** German East Africa formally established as colony.

**1905–06** Maji Maji revolt suppressed by German troops.

**1916** Conquest of German East Africa by British and South African forces, led by Gen Jan Smuts.

**1919** Most of German East Africa became British League of Nations mandate of Tanganyika.

**1946** Britain continued to govern Tanganyika as United Nations (UN) trusteeship.

**1954** Julius Nyerere organized the Tanganyikan African National Union (TANU) to campaign for independence.

**1961** Tanganyika achieved independence from Britain with Nyerere as prime minister.

**1962** Tanganyika became republic under President Nyerere.

**1963** Zanzibar achieved independence.

**1964** Arab-dominated sultanate of Zanzibar overthrown by Afro-Shirazi Party in violent revolution; Zanzibar merged with Tanganyika to form United Republic of Tanzania.

**1967** East African Community (EAC) formed by Tanzania, Kenya, and Uganda; Nyerere pledged to build socialist state.

**1977** Revolutionary Party of Tanzania (CCM) proclaimed as only legal party; EAC dissolved.

**1979** Tanzanian troops intervened in Uganda to help overthrow President Idi Amin.

**1985** Nyerere retired as president; he was succeeded by Ali Hassan Mwinyi.

**1992** Multiparty politics were permitted.

**1995** Benjamin Mkapa of CCM was elected president.

**1998** A bomb exploded at the US embassy in Dar es Salaam, killing 6 people and injuring 60; an anti-American Islamic group claimed responsibility.

**Taoiseach** Gaelic title for the prime minister of the Irish Republic.

**Taoism** Chinese philosophical system, traditionally founded by the Chinese philosopher Lao Zi in the 6th century BC. He is also attributed authorship of the scriptures, *Tao Te Ching*, although these were apparently compiled 3rd century BC. The 'tao' or 'way' denotes the hidden principle of the universe, and less stress is laid on good deeds than on harmonious interaction with the environment, which automatically ensures right behaviour. The magical side of Taoism is illustrated by the *I Ching* or *Book of Changes*, a book of divination.

**tap dancing** rapid step dance, derived from clog dancing. Its main characteristic is the tapping of toes and heels accentuated by steel taps affixed to the shoes. It was popularized in vaudeville and in 1930s films by such dancers as Fred Astaire and Bill 'Bojangles' Robinson (1878–1949).

**tape recording, magnetic** method of recording electric signals on a layer of iron oxide, or other magnetic material, coating a thin plastic tape. The electrical signals from the microphone are fed to the electromagnetic recording head, which magnetizes the tape in accordance with the frequency and amplitude of the original signal. The impulses may be audio (for sound recording), video (for television), or data (for computer). For playback, the tape is passed over the same, or another, head to convert magnetic into electrical signals, which are then amplified for reproduction. Tapes are easily demagnetized (erased) for reuse, and come in cassette, cartridge, or reel form.

**tapeworm** any of various parasitic flatworms of the class Cestoda. They lack digestive and sense organs, can reach 15 m/50 ft in length, and attach themselves to the host's intestines by means of hooks and suckers. Tapeworms are made up of hundreds of individual segments, each of which develops into a functional hermaphroditic reproductive unit capable of producing numerous eggs. The larvae of tapeworms usually reach humans in imperfectly cooked meat or fish, causing anaemia and intestinal disorders.

**tapioca** granular starch used in cooking, produced from the ◊cassava root.

**tapir** any of the odd-toed hoofed mammals (perissodactyls) of the single genus *Tapirus,* now constituting the family Tapiridae. There are four species living in the American and Malaysian tropics. They reach 1 m/3 ft at the shoulder and weigh up to 350 kg/770 lb. Their survival is in danger because of destruction of the forests.

Tapirs have thick, hairy, black skin, short tails, and short trunks. They are vegetarian, harmless, and shy. They are related to the ◊rhinoceros, and slightly more distantly to the horse.

**taproot** in botany, a single, robust, main ◊root that is derived from the embryonic root, or radicle, and grows vertically downwards, often to considerable depth. Taproots are often modified for food storage and are common in biennial plants such as the carrot *Daucus carota,* where they act as ◊perennating organs.

**tar** dark brown or black viscous liquid obtained by the destructive distillation of coal, shale, and wood. Tars consist of a mixture of hydrocarbons, acids, and bases. Creosote and ◊paraffin are produced from wood tar.

**tarantella** southern Italian dance in very fast compound time (6/8); also a piece of music composed for, or in the rhythm of, this dance. It is commonly believed to be named after the tarantula spider which was (incorrectly) thought to cause tarantism (hysterical ailment), at one time epidemic in the southern Italian town of Taranto, and whose cure was thought to involve wild dancing. The dance became popular during the 19th century, several composers writing tarantellas employing a perpetuum mobile in order to generate intense energy. Examples include those by Chopin, Liszt, and Weber.

**Taranto** Greek *Tarantum,* naval base and port in Apulia region, southeast Italy, on the Gulf of Taranto, 80 km/50 mi southeast of Bari; population (1992) 230,200. It is an important commercial centre, and its steelworks are part of the new industrial complex of southern Italy. There are chemical and oil-refining industries, and oyster and mussel fisheries. It was founded in the 8th century BC by ◊Sparta, and was captured by the Romans in 272 BC.

**tarantula** wolf spider *Lycosa tarantula* (family Lycosidae) with a 2.5 cm/1 in body. It spins no web, relying on its speed in hunting to catch its prey. The name 'tarantula' is also used for any of the numerous large, hairy spiders of the family Theraphosidae, with large poison fangs, native to the southwestern USA and tropical America.

**tariff** tax or duty placed on goods when they are imported into a country or trading bloc (such as the European Union) from outside. The aim of tariffs is to reduce imports by making them more expensive.

**Tarkovsky, Andrei Arsenyevich** (1932–1986) Soviet film director. His work is characterized by an epic style combined with intense personal spirituality. His films include *Solaris* (1972), *Zerkalo/Mirror* (1975), *Stalker* (1979), and *Offret/The Sacrifice* (1986).

**taro** or *eddo,* plant belonging to the arum family, native to tropical Asia; the tubers (underground stems) are edible and are the source of Polynesian poi (a fermented food). (*Colocasia esculenta,* family Araceae.)

**tarot cards** fortune-telling aid consisting of 78 cards: the 56 *minor arcana* in four suits (resembling playing cards) and the *major arcana,* 22 cards with densely symbolic illustrations that have links with astrology and the ◊kabbala.

**Tarquinius Superbus** (lived 6th century BC) Tarquin the Proud, last king of Rome 534–510 BC. He abolished certain rights of Romans, and made the city powerful. According to legend, he was deposed when his son Sextus raped Lucretia.

**tarragon** perennial bushy herb belonging to the daisy family, native to the Old World. It grows up to 1.5 m/5 ft tall and has narrow leaves and small green-white flower heads arranged in groups. Tarragon contains an aromatic oil; its leaves are used to flavour salads, pickles, and tartar sauce. It is closely related to wormwood. (*Artemisia dracunculus,* family Compositae.)

**Tarragona** port and capital of Tarragona province in Cataluña, northeast Spain, at the mouth of the Francoli River on the Mediterranean coast; population (1991) 110,000. Industries include petrochemicals, pharmaceuticals, and electrical goods. It has a cathedral and Roman remains, including an aqueduct and amphitheatre.

**Tarshish** city mentioned in the Old Testament, probably the Phoenician settlement of Tartessus in Spain.

**tarsier** any of three species of the prosimian primates, genus *Tarsius,* of the East Indies and the Philippines. These survivors of early primates are about the size of a rat with thick, light-brown fur, very large eyes, and long feet and hands. They are nocturnal, arboreal, and eat insects and lizards.

**tartan** woollen cloth woven in specific chequered patterns individual to Scottish clans, with stripes of different widths and colours crisscrossing on a coloured background; it is used in making skirts, kilts, trousers, and other articles of clothing.

**Tartar** variant spelling of ◊Tatar, member of a Turkic people now living mainly in the autonomous region of Tatarstan, Russia.

**tartrazine** (E102), yellow food colouring produced synthetically from petroleum. Many people are allergic to foods containing it. Typical effects are skin disorders and respiratory problems. It has been shown to have an adverse effect on hyperactive children.

**Tartu** German *Dorpat;* Russian *Yurev,* city in Estonia, 150 km/93 mi southeast of Tallinn and 50 km/31 mi west of Lake Peipus; population (1990) 115,400. Industries include light engineering, food processing, and lumber. Founded by Russians in 1030, it was a stronghold of the ◊Teutonic Knights from 1224 onwards. Tartu was captured by Russia in 1558 and subsequently held by Sweden and Poland, but returned to Russian control in 1704. It was occupied by German forces in both World Wars.

**Tarzan** fictitious hero inhabiting the African rainforest, created by US writer Edgar Rice ◊Burroughs in *Tarzan of the Apes* 1914, with numerous sequels. He and his partner Jane have featured in films, comic strips, and television series.

**Tashkent** Uzbek *Toshkent,* capital of Uzbekistan and of Tashkent wiloyat (oblast), located in the western foothills of the Tien Shan mountain range and in the valley of the River Chirchiq. With a population (1996) of some 2,300,000, it is the largest city in Central Asia. It is an important transit centre for the region; there is an international airport terminal here. Industrial activity includes the manufacture of mining machinery, chemicals, textiles, and leather goods. Tashkent suffered severe damage in an earthquake in 1966, but was rapidly rebuilt.

**Tasman, Abel Janszoon** (1603–1659) Dutch navigator. In 1642, he was the first

European to see ◊Tasmania. He also made the first European sightings of New Zealand, Tonga, and the Fiji Islands.

**Tasmania** formerly (1642–1856) *Van Diemen's Land,* island in the Indian Ocean, southeast of Australia, separated from the mainland by Bass Strait; state of Australia
*area* about 68,000 sq km/26,248 sq mi
*capital* Hobart
*towns and cities* Launceston (chief port), Devonport, Burnie, Queenstown
*features* the smallest of the Australian states; territory includes numerous smaller islands; World Heritage Area in the southwest; unique flora and fauna, including the Huon pine and the Tasmanian devil (a marsupial found only in Tasmania)
*products* wool, dairy products, apples and other fruit, processed foods, timber, paper, iron, tungsten, copper, silver, coal, cement
*population* (1996) 459,700
*history* the first European to visit was Abel ◊Tasman in 1642; British penal colony established at Risdon Cove in 1803; part of New South Wales until 1825; name changed to Tasmania in 1856; became a state of the Australian Commonwealth in 1901.

**Tasmanian devil** carnivorous marsupial *Sarcophilus harrisii,* in the same family (Dasyuridae) as native 'cats'. It is about 65 cm/2.1 ft long with a 25 cm/10 in bushy tail. It has a large head, strong teeth, and is blackish with white patches on the chest and hind parts. It is nocturnal, carnivorous, and can be ferocious when cornered. It has recently become extinct in the Australian mainland and survives only in remote parts of Tasmania.

**Tasmanian wolf** or *thylacine,* carnivorous marsupial *Thylacinus cynocephalus,* in the family Dasyuridae. It is doglike in appearance with a long tail, characteristic dark stripes on back and hindquarters, and measures nearly 2 m/6 ft from nose to tail tip. It was hunted to probable extinction in the 1930s, but there are still occasional unconfirmed reports of sightings, both on the Australian mainland and in the Tasmanian mountains, its last known habitat.

**taste** sense that detects some of the chemical constituents of food. The human ◊tongue can distinguish only four basic tastes (sweet, sour, bitter, and salty) but it is supplemented by the sense of smell. What we refer to as taste is really a composite sense made up of both taste and smell.

**Tatar** or *Tartar,* member of a Turkic people, the descendants of the mixed Mongol and Turkic followers of ◊Genghis Khan. The Tatars now live mainly in the Russian autonomous republic of Tatarstan, western Siberia, Turkmenistan, and Uzbekistan (where they were deported from the Crimea in 1944). There are over 5 million speakers of the Tatar language, which belongs to the Turkic branch of the Altaic family.

**tatting** lacework in cotton, made since medieval times by knotting and looping a single thread with a small shuttle.

**tau** ◊elementary particle with the same electric charge as the electron but a mass nearly double that of a proton. It has a lifetime of around 3 × $10^{-13}$ seconds and belongs to the ◊lepton family of particles – those that interact via the electromagnetic, weak nuclear, and gravitational forces, but not the strong nuclear force.

**Taurus** conspicuous zodiacal constellation in the northern hemisphere near ◊Orion, represented as a bull. The Sun passes through Taurus from mid-May to late June. In astrology, the dates for Taurus are between about 20 April and 20 May (see ◊precession).

**taxation** raising of money from individuals and organizations by the state in order to pay for the goods and services it provides. Taxation can be *direct* (a deduction from income) or *indirect* (added to the purchase price of goods or services, that is, a tax on consumption). The standard form of indirect taxation in Europe is *value-added tax* (*VAT*). *Income tax* is the most common form of direct taxation.

**tax avoidance** conducting of financial affairs in such a way as to keep tax liability to a minimum within the law.

**tax evasion** failure to meet tax liabilities by illegal action, such as not declaring income. Tax evasion is a criminal offence.

**taxonomy** another name for the ◊classification of living organisms.

**Tay** longest river in Scotland; length 193 km/120 mi, it flows northeast through *Loch Tay,* then east and southeast past Perth to the *Firth of Tay,* crossed at Dundee by the *Tay Bridge,* before joining the North Sea. The Tay has salmon fisheries; its main tributaries are the Tummel, Isla, and Earn, Braan, and Almond.

**TB** abbreviation for the infectious disease ◊tuberculosis.

**Tbilisi** formerly *Tiflis,* capital and cultural centre of Georgia, located on the Kura River in the ◊Caucasus Mountains; population (1996) 1,200,000. It is a major economic, transportation and industrial centre. Industries include the manufacture of textiles, machinery, ceramics and tobacco. In the lead-up to the collapse of the USSR in 1989 and Georgian independence, the city was the scene of bloody clashes between Russian security forces and nationalist demonstrators.

**Tchaikovsky, Pyotr Il'yich** (1840–1893) Russian composer. His strong sense of melody, personal expression, and brilliant orchestration are clear throughout his many Romantic works, which include six symphonies, three piano concertos, a violin concerto, operas (including *Eugene Onegin* 1879), ballets (including *The Nutcracker* 1891–92), orchestral fantasie (including *Romeo and Juliet* 1870), and chamber and vocal music.

**tea** evergreen shrub or small tree whose fermented, dried leaves are soaked in hot water to make a refreshing drink, also called tea. Known in China as early as 2737 BC, tea was first brought to Europe in AD 1610 and rapidly became a popular drink. In 1823 the shrub was found growing wild in northern India, and plantations were later established in Assam and Sri Lanka; producers today include Africa, South America, Georgia, Azerbaijan, Indonesia, and Iran. (*Camellia sinensis,* family Theaceae.)

**teak** tropical Asian timber tree with yellowish wood used in furniture and shipbuilding. (*Tectona grandis,* family Verbenaceae.)

**teal** any of various small, short-necked dabbling ducks of the genus *Anas,* order Anseriformes, but particularly *A. crecca.* The male is dusky grey; its tail feathers ashy grey; the crown of its head deep cinnamon or chestnut; its eye is surrounded by a black band, glossed with green or purple, which unites on the nape; its wing markings are black and white; and its bill is black and resembles that of the widgeon. The female is mottled brown. The total length is about 35cm/14 in.

**tear gas** any of various volatile gases that produce irritation and watering of the eyes, used by police against crowds and used in chemical warfare. The gas is delivered in pressurized, liquid-filled canisters or grenades, thrown by hand or launched from a specially adapted rifle. Gases (such as Mace) cause violent coughing and blinding tears, which pass when the victim breathes fresh air, but there are no lasting effects.

**teasel** upright prickly biennial herb, native to Europe and Asia. It grows up to 1.5 m/5 ft, has prickly stems and leaves, and a large prickly head of purple flowers. The dry, spiny seed heads were once used industrially to tease or fluff up the surface fibres of cloth. (*Dipsacus fullonum,* family Dipsacaceae.)

**tea tree** shrub or small tree native to Australia and New Zealand. It is thought that some species of tea tree were used by the explorer Captain Cook to brew tea; it was used in the first years of settlement for this purpose. (Genus *Leptospermum,* family Myrtaceae.)

**technetium** (Greek *technetos* 'artificial') silver-grey, radioactive, metallic element, symbol Tc, atomic number 43, relative atomic mass 98.906. It occurs in nature only in extremely minute amounts, produced as a fission product from uranium in ◊pitchblende and other uranium ores. Its longest-lived isotope, Tc-99, has a half-life of 216,000 years. It is a superconductor and is used as a hardener in steel alloys and as a medical tracer.

**technology** the use of tools, power, and materials, generally for the purposes of production. Almost every human process for getting food and shelter depends on complex technological systems, which have been developed over a 3-million-year period. Significant milestones include the advent of the ◊steam engine in 1712, the introduction of ◊electricity and the ◊internal combustion engine in the mid-1870s, and recent developments in communications, ◊electronics, and the nuclear and space industries. The *advanced technology* (highly automated and specialized) on which modern industrialized society depends is frequently contrasted with the *low technology* (labour-intensive and unspecialized) that characterizes some developing countries. ◊*Intermediate technology* is an attempt to adapt scientifically advanced inventions to less developed areas by using local materials and methods of manufacture. *Appropriate technology* refers to simple and small-scale tools and machinery of use to developing countries.

**Tecumseh** (1768–1813) American Indian chief of the Shawnee. He attempted to unite the Indian peoples from Canada to Florida against the encroachment of white settlers, but the defeat of his brother **Tenskwatawa**, 'the Prophet', at the battle of Tippecanoe in November 1811 by W H Harrison, governor of the Indiana Territory, largely destroyed the confederacy built up by Tecumseh.

**tefillin** or *phylacteries,* in Judaism, two small leather boxes containing scrolls from the Torah, that are strapped to the left arm and the forehead by Jewish men for daily prayer.

**Teflon** trade name for polytetrafluoroethene (PTFE), a tough, waxlike, heat-resistant plastic used for coating nonstick cookware and in gaskets and bearings.

**Tegucigalpa** capital of Honduras; situated at an altitude of 975 m/3,199 ft in the highlands of south-central Honduras, on the River Choluteca at the foot of the extinct El Pichacho volcano; population (1991 est) 670,100. Industries include textiles, chemicals, and food-processing, mostly for domestic consumption. It was founded by the Spanish in the 16th century as a gold- and silver-mining centre, and became capital in 1880 (the former capital was Comayagua). Tocontín international airport is 6 km/4 mi to the south. The city has some fine colonial architecture including an 18th-century cathedral, and the church of Saint Francis, completed in 1592.

**Tehran** or *Teheran,* capital of Iran; population (1991) 6,475,500. Industries include textiles, chemicals, engineering, and tobacco. It is built at an average altitude of 1,220 m/3,937 ft on a slope running south from the Elburz Mountains.

**Te Kanawa, Kiri Janette** (1944–  ) New Zealand soprano. Te Kanawa's first major role was the Countess in Mozart's *The Marriage of Figaro* at Covent Garden, London (1971). Her voice combines the purity and intensity of the upper range with an extended lower range of great richness and resonance. Apart from classical roles, she has also featured popular music in her repertoire, such as the 1984 recording of Leonard Bernstein's *West Side Story.* DBE 1982.

**tektite** (from Greek *tektos* 'molten') small, rounded glassy stone, found in certain regions of the Earth, such as Australasia. Tektites are probably the scattered drops of molten rock thrown out by the impact of a large ◊meteorite.

**Tel Aviv-Yafo** or *Tel Aviv-Jaffa,* city in Israel, situated on the coast of Sharon Plain, 77 km/48 mi northwest of Jerusalem; population (1995)

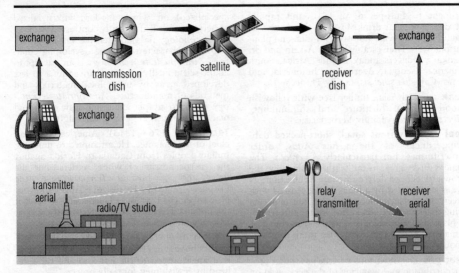

**telecommunications** *The international telecommunications system relies on microwave and satellite links for long-distance international calls. Cable links are increasingly made of optical fibres. The capacity of these links is enormous. The TDRS-C (tracking data and relay satellite communications) satellite, the world's largest and most complex satellite, can transmit in a single second the contents of a 20-volume encyclopedia, with each volume containing 1,200 pages of 2,000 words. A bundle of optical fibres, no thicker than a finger, can carry 10,000 phone calls – more than a copper wire as thick as an arm.*

355,900. Industries include textiles, chemicals, sugar, printing, publishing, and tourism. Tel Aviv was founded in 1909 as a Jewish residential area in the Arab town of ◊Jaffa, with which it was combined in 1949; their ports were superseded in 1965 by Ashdod to the south. During the ◊Gulf War of 1991, Tel Aviv became a target for Iraqi missiles as part of Saddam Hussein's strategy to break up the Arab alliance against him. It is regarded by the UN as the capital of Israel.

**telecommunications** communications over a distance, generally by electronic means. Long-distance voice communication was pioneered in 1876 by Scottish scientist Alexander Graham Bell when he invented the telephone. Today it is possible to communicate internationally by telephone cable or by satellite or microwave link, with over 100,000 simultaneous conversations and several television channels being carried by the latest satellites.

**telegraphy** transmission of messages along wires by means of electrical signals. The first modern form of telecommunication, it now uses printers for the transmission and receipt of messages. Telex is an international telegraphy network.

**Telemachus** in Greek mythology, son of ◊Odysseus and ◊Penelope. He was a child when his father set out for the Trojan wars. In Homer's *Odyssey*, he attempted to control his mother's suitors while his father was believed dead, but on Odysseus' return after 20 years, he helped him to kill them, with the support of the goddess ◊Athena.

**Telemann, Georg Philipp** (1681–1767) German Baroque composer, organist, and conductor. He was the best-known German composer of his time with a contemporary reputation much greater than Johann Sebastian Bach's. His prolific output of concertos for both new and old instruments, including violin, viola da gamba, recorder, flute, oboe, trumpet, horn, and bassoon, represents a methodical and fastidious investigation into the tonal resonances and structure of the new Baroque orchestra, research which was noted by Bach. Other works include 25 operas, numerous sacred cantatas, and instrumental fantasias.

**telepathy** 'the communication of impressions of any kind from one mind to another, independently of the recognized channels of sense', as defined by the English essayist F W H Myers (1843–1901), cofounder in 1882 of the Psychical Research Society, who coined the term. It is a form of ◊extrasensory perception.

**telephone** instrument for communicating by voice along wires, developed by Scottish inventor Alexander Graham ◊Bell in 1876. The transmitter (mouthpiece) consists of a carbon microphone, with a diaphragm that vibrates when a person speaks into it. The diaphragm vibrations compress grains of carbon to a greater or lesser extent, altering their resistance to an electric current passing through them. This sets up variable electrical signals, which travel along the telephone lines to the receiver of the person being called. There they cause the magnetism of an electromagnet to vary, making a diaphragm above the electromagnet vibrate and give out sound waves, which mirror those that entered the mouthpiece originally.

**telephone tapping** or *telephone bugging,* listening in on a telephone conversation, without the knowledge of the participants; in the UK and the USA this is a criminal offence if done without a warrant or the consent of the person concerned.

**teleprinter** or *teletypewriter,* transmitting and receiving device used in telecommunications to handle coded messages. Teleprinters are automatic typewriters keyed telegraphically to convert typed words into electrical signals (using a five-unit Baudot code, see ◊baud) at the transmitting end, and signals into typed words at the receiving end.

**telescope** optical instrument that magnifies images of faint and distant objects; any device for collecting and focusing light and other forms of electromagnetic radiation. It is a major research tool in astronomy and is used to sight over land and sea; small telescopes can be attached to cameras and rifles. A telescope with a large aperture, or opening, can distinguish finer detail and fainter objects than one with a small aperture. The *refracting telescope* uses lenses, and the *reflecting telescope* uses mirrors. A third type, the *catadioptric telescope,* is a combination of lenses and mirrors. See also ◊radio telescope.

**teletext** broadcast system of displaying information on a television screen. The information – typically about news items, entertainment, sport, and finance – is constantly updated. Teletext is a form of ◊videotext, pioneered in Britain by the British Broadcasting Corporation (BBC) with Ceefax and by Independent Television (ITN) with Teletext.

**television** (TV), reproduction of visual images at a distance using radio waves. For transmission, a television camera converts the pattern of light it takes in into a pattern of electrical charges. This is scanned line by line by a beam of electrons from an electron gun, resulting in variable electrical signals that represent the picture. These signals are combined with a radio carrier wave and broadcast as electromagnetic waves. The TV aerial picks up the wave and feeds it to the receiver (TV set). This separates out the vision signals, which pass to a cathode-ray tube where a beam of electrons is made to scan across the screen line by line, mirroring the action of the electron gun in the TV camera. The result is a recreation of the pattern of light that entered the camera.

**telex** acronym for *tel*eprinter *ex*change, international telecommunications network that handles telegraph messages in the form of coded signals. It uses ◊teleprinters for transmitting and receiving, and makes use of land lines (cables) and radio and satellite links to make connections between subscribers.

**Telford, Thomas** (1757–1834) Scottish civil engineer. He opened up northern Scotland by building roads and waterways. He constructed many aqueducts and canals, including the Caledonian Canal (1802–23), and erected the Menai road suspension bridge between Wales

*telescope* Three kinds of telescope. The refracting telescope uses a large objective lens to gather light and form an image which the smaller eyepiece lens magnifies. A reflecting telescope uses a mirror to gather light. The Cassegrain telescope uses a corrective lens to achieve a wide field of view. It is one of the most widely used tools of astronomy.

and Anglesey (1819–26), a type of structure scarcely tried previously in the UK. In Scotland he constructed over 1,600 km/1,000 mi of road and 1,200 bridges, churches, and harbours.

**Telford and Wrekin** unitary authority in west England, created in 1998 from part of Shropshire
*area* 291 sq km/112 sq mi
*towns and cities* Telford (administrative headquarters), Newport
*features* The *Wrekin,* isolated hill (407 m/ 1,334 ft); Ironbridge Gorge (World Heritage Site) includes world's first iron bridge, built across River Severn in 1779 by Abraham Darby, and Ironbridge Gorge Museum Trust (seven industrial history museums including Museum of the River, Museum of Iron, Blists Hill Open Air Museum, Coalport China Museum)
*industries* iron founding, agriculture, dairy farming, food processing, confectionery, audio and tape manufacture, electronic tools and equipment, vehicle parts, plastics, clothing manufacture, information technology
*population* (1996) 144,600.

**Tell, Wilhelm (William),** legendary 14th-century Swiss archer, said to have refused to salute the Habsburg badge at Altdorf on Lake Lucerne. Sentenced to shoot an apple from his son's head, he did so, then shot the tyrannical Austrian ruler Gessler, symbolizing his people's refusal to submit to external authority.

**tellurium** (Latin *Tellus* 'Earth') silver-white, semi-metallic (metalloid) element, symbol Te, atomic number 52, relative atomic mass 127.60. Chemically it is similar to sulphur and selenium, and it is considered one of the sulphur group. It occurs naturally in telluride minerals, and is used in colouring glass blue-brown, in the electrolytic refining of zinc, in electronics, and as a catalyst in refining petroleum.

**Telugu** language spoken in southeastern India. It is the official language of Andhra Pradesh, and is also spoken in Malaysia, giving a total number of speakers of around 50 million. Written records in Telugu date from the 7th century AD. Telugu belongs to the Dravidian family.

**tempera** painting medium in which powdered pigments are mixed with a water-soluble binding agent such as egg yolk. Tempera is noted for its strong, translucent colours. A form of tempera was used in ancient Egypt, and egg tempera was the foremost medium for panel painting in late Medieval and early Renaissance Europe. It was gradually superseded by oils from the late 15th century onwards.

**temperance movement** societies dedicated to curtailing the consumption of alcohol by total prohibition, local restriction, or encouragement of declarations of personal abstinence ('the pledge'). Temperance movements were first set up in the USA, Ireland, and Scotland, then in northern England in the 1830s.

**temperature** degree or intensity of heat of an object and the condition that determines whether it will transfer heat to another object or receive heat from it, according to the laws of ◊thermodynamics. The temperature of an object is a measure of the average kinetic energy possessed by the atoms or molecules of which it is composed. The SI unit of temperature is the kelvin (symbol K) used with the Kelvin scale. Other measures of temperature in common use are the Celsius scale and the Fahrenheit scale.

**tempering** heat treatment for improving the properties of metals, often used for steel alloys. The metal is heated to a certain temperature and then cooled suddenly in a water or oil bath.

**Templars** or *Knights Templar* or *Order of Poor Knights of Christ and of the Temple of Solomon,* military religious order founded in Jerusalem (1119–20) to protect pilgrims travelling to the Holy Land. They played an important part in the ◊Crusades of the 12th and 13th centuries. Innocent II placed them under direct papal authority in 1139, and their international links allowed them to adapt to the 13th-century decline of the Crusader states by becoming Europe's bankers. The Templars' independence, power, and wealth, rather than their alleged heresy, probably motivated Philip IV of France, helped by the Avignon pope Clement V, to suppress the order in 1307–14.

**Temple of Jerusalem** centre of Jewish national worship in Jerusalem, Israel, in both ancient and modern days. The **Wailing Wall** is the surviving part of the western wall of the enclosure of Herod's Temple. Since the destruction of the Temple in AD 70, Jews have gone there to pray and to mourn their dispersion and the loss of their homeland.

**tempo** (Italian 'time') in music, the speed at which a piece should be played. One way of indicating the tempo of a piece of music is to give a metronome marking, which states the number of beats per minute; for example, 'crotchet = 60' means that there should be 60 crotchet beats to the minute. Modern electronic metronomes measure tempo very accurately, but performers often change or even ignore metronome markings, playing at a tempo that suits their interpretation of the music.

**Temuco** capital of Araucanía region, south-central Chile, situated to the north of the Lake District on the River Cautín, 675 km/420 mi south of Santiago; population (1992) 240,900. Cereals, timber, and apples are produced in the surrounding region, and industries include coal mining, and the manufacture of steel and textiles. It is a market town for the Mapuche Indians, who trade their produce and crafts. The great majority of them live in the forest land around Temuco. Founded in 1881, the city is the gateway to the Lake District region.

**tench** European freshwater bony fish *Tinca tinca,* a member of the carp family, now established in North America. It is about 45 cm/18 in long, weighs 2 kg/4.5 lb, and is coloured olive-green above and grey beneath. The scales are small and there is a barbel at each side of the mouth.

**Ten Commandments** in the Old Testament, the laws given by God to the Hebrew leader Moses on Mount Sinai, engraved on two tablets of stone.

They are: to have no other gods besides Jehovah; to make no idols; not to misuse the name of God; to keep the sabbath holy; to honour one's parents; not to commit murder, adultery, or theft; not to give false evidence; and not to be covetous. They form the basis of Jewish and Christian moral codes; the 'tablets of the Law' given to Moses are also mentioned in the Koran. The giving of the Ten Commandments is celebrated in the Jewish festival of *Shavuot* (see ◊Pentecost).

**tendon** or *sinew,* in vertebrates, a cord of very strong, fibrous connective tissue that joins muscle to bone. Tendons are largely composed of bundles of fibres made of the protein collagen, and because of their inelasticity are very efficient at transforming muscle power into movement.

**tendril** in botany, a slender, threadlike structure that supports a climbing plant by coiling around suitable supports, such as the stems and branches of other plants. It may be a modified stem, leaf, leaflet, flower, leaf stalk, or stipule (a small appendage on either side of the leaf stalk), and may be simple or branched. The tendrils of Virginia creeper *Parthenocissus quinquefolia* are modified flower heads with suckerlike pads at the end that stick to walls, while those of the grapevine *Vitis* grow away from the light and thus enter dark crevices where they expand to anchor the plant firmly.

**Tenerife** largest of the ◊Canary Islands, in the province of Santa Cruz de Tenerife, Spain; area 2,060 sq km/795 sq mi; population (1991) 706,900. Fruit and vegetables are produced, especially bananas and tomatoes, and the island is a popular tourist resort. Santa Cruz is the main town here, and Pico de Teide, an active volcano, is the highest peak in Spain (3,713 m/ 12,186 ft high).

**Tennessee** state in eastern central USA. It is nicknamed the Volunteer State. Tennessee was admitted to the Union in 1796 as the 16th US state. It is bordered to the east by North Carolina, to the south by Georgia, Alabama, and Mississippi, to the west by Arkansas and Missouri, across the Mississippi River, and to the north by Kentucky and Virginia. Historically, Tennessee was a plantation state, associated with slavery. Culturally, it is one of the centres of country music
**population** (1995) 5,256,100
**area** 109,200 sq km/42,151 sq mi
**capital** Nashville
**towns and cities** Memphis, Knoxville, Chattanooga, Clarksville
**industries and products** cereals, cotton, tobacco, soybeans, livestock, timber, coal, zinc, copper, chemicals, power generation, automobiles, aluminium, music industry, tourism.

**tennis** racket-and-ball game invented towards the end of the 19th century. Although played on different surfaces (grass, wood, shale, clay, concrete), it is also called 'lawn tennis'. The aim of the two or four players (in singles or doubles matches) is to strike the ball into the prescribed area of the court, with oval-headed rackets (strung with gut or nylon), in such a way that it cannot be returned. The game is won by those first winning four points (called 15, 30, 40, game), unless both sides reach 40 (deuce), when two consecutive points are needed to win. A set is won by winning six games with a margin of two over opponents, though a tie-break system operates, that is at six games to each side (or in some cases eight) except in the final set. A match lasts a maximum of five sets for men, three for women.

**Tennyson, Alfred** 1st Baron Tennyson (1809– 1892) English poet. He was poet laureate from 1850–92. His verse has a majestic, musical quality, and few poets have surpassed his precision and delicacy of language. His works include 'The Lady of Shalott' (1833), 'The Lotus Eaters' (1833), 'Ulysses' (1842), 'Break, Break, Break' (1842), and 'The Charge of the Light Brigade' (1854); the longer narratives *Locksley Hall* (1832) and *Maud* (1855); the elegy *In Memoriam* (1850); and a long series of poems on the Arthurian legends, *The Idylls of the King* (1859–89).

**tenpin bowling** indoor sport popular in North America and Britain. As in skittles, the object is to bowl a ball down an alley at pins

(ten as opposed to nine). The game is usually between two players or teams. A game of tenpins is made up of ten 'frames'. The frame is the bowler's turn to play and in each frame he or she may bowl twice. One point is scored for each pin knocked down, with bonus points for knocking all ten pins down in either one ball or two. The player or team making the greater score wins.

**tequila** Mexican alcoholic drink distilled from the ◊agave plant. It is named after the place, near Guadalajara, where the conquistadors first developed it from Aztec *pulque,* which would keep for only a day.

**terbium** soft, silver-grey, metallic element of the ◊lanthanide series, symbol Tb, atomic number 65, relative atomic mass 158.925. It occurs in gadolinite and other ores, with yttrium and ytterbium, and is used in lasers, semiconductors, and television tubes. It was named in 1843 by Swedish chemist Carl Mosander (1797–1858) for the town of Ytterby, Sweden, where it was first found.

**Terence** (c. 190– c. 159 BC) Publius Terentius Afer, Roman dramatist. Born in Carthage, he was taken as a slave to Rome where he was freed and came under the patronage of the Roman general Scipio Africanus Minor. His surviving six comedies (including *The Eunuch,* 161 BC) are subtly characterized and based on Greek models. They were widely read and performed during the Middle Ages and the Renaissance.

**Teresa, Mother** born Agnes Gonxha Bojaxhiu (1910–1997) Roman Catholic nun who devoted her life to working among the sick and poor of Calcutta, India. She established the Misssionaries of Charity, now a multinational organization with 517 centres around the world: More than 4,000 nuns staff the missionaries of Charity orphanages, Aids hospices, mental homes and basic medical clinics, alongside numerous volunteers. Mother Teresa was awarded the Nobel Peace Prize in 1979.

**terminal** in computing, a device consisting of a keyboard and display screen (◊VDU) to enable the operator to communicate with the computer. The terminal may be physically attached to the computer or linked to it by a telephone line (remote terminal). A 'dumb' terminal has no processor of its own, whereas an 'intelligent' terminal has its own processor and takes some of the processing load away from the main computer.

**termite** any member of the insect order Isoptera. Termites are soft-bodied social insects living in large colonies which include one or more queens (of relatively enormous size and producing an egg every two seconds), much smaller kings, and still smaller soldiers, workers, and immature forms. Termites build galleried nests of soil particles that may be 6 m/20 ft high.

**tern** any of various lightly built seabirds in the gull family Laridae, order Charadriiformes, with pointed wings and bill, and usually a forked tail. Terns plunge-dive after aquatic prey. They are 20–50 cm/8–20 in long, and usually coloured in combinations of white and black. They are extensively distributed, especially in temperate climates.

**terracotta** (Italian 'baked earth') brownish-red baked clay, usually unglazed, used in building, sculpture, and pottery. The term is specifically applied to small figures or figurines, such as those found at Tanagra in central Greece. Excavations at Xi'an, China, have revealed life-size terracotta figures of the army of the Emperor Shi Huangdi dating from the 3rd century BC.

**terra firma** (Latin) dry land; solid ground.

**terrapin** member of some species of the order Chelonia (◊turtles and ◊tortoises). Terrapins are small to medium-sized, aquatic or semi-aquatic, and are found widely in temperate zones. They are omnivorous, but generally eat aquatic animals. Some species are in danger of extinction owing to collection for the pet trade; most of the animals collected die in transit.

**terrier** any of various breeds of highly intelligent, active dogs. They are usually small. Types include the bull, cairn, fox, Irish, Scottish, Sealyham, Skye, and Yorkshire terriers. They were originally bred for hunting rabbits and following quarry such as foxes down into burrows.

**territory** in animal behaviour, a fixed area from which an animal or group of animals excludes other members of the same species. Animals may hold territories for many different reasons; for example, to provide a constant food supply, to monopolize potential mates, or to ensure access to refuges or nest sites.

The size of a territory depends in part on its function: some nesting and mating territories may be only a few square metres, whereas feeding territories may be as large as hundreds of square kilometres.

**terrorism** systematic violence in the furtherance of political aims, often by small ◊guerrilla groups.

**Terror, Reign of** phase of the ◊French Revolution when the ◊Jacobins were in power (October 1793 to July 1794) under ◊Robespierre and began systematically to murder their political opponents. The Terror was at its height in the early months of 1794. Across France, it is thought that between 17,000 and 40,000 people were executed, mainly by guillotine, until public indignation rose and Robespierre was overthrown and guillotined in July 1794.

**Tertiary** period of geological time 65–1.64 million years ago, divided into five epochs: Palaeocene, Eocene, Oligocene, Miocene, and Pliocene. During the Tertiary period, mammals took over all the ecological niches left vacant by the extinction of the dinosaurs, and became the prevalent land animals. The continents took on their present positions, and climatic and vegetation zones as we know them became established. Within the geological time column the Tertiary follows the Cretaceous period and is succeeded by the Quaternary period.

**tesla** SI unit (symbol T) of magnetic flux density. One tesla represents a flux density of one ◊weber per square metre, or $10^4$ gauss. It is named after the Croatian–born US physicist Nikola Tesla.

**Test Ban Treaty** agreement signed by the USA, the USSR, and the UK on 5 August 1963 contracting to test nuclear weapons only underground. In the following two years 90 other nations signed the treaty, the only major nonsignatories being France and China, which continued underwater and ground-level tests. In January 1996 France announced the ending of its test programme, and supported the implementation of a universal test ban.

**testis** plural *testes,* the organ that produces ◊sperm in male (and hermaphrodite) animals. In vertebrates it is one of a pair of oval structures that are usually internal, but in mammals (other than elephants and marine mammals), the paired testes (or testicles) descend from the body cavity during development, to hang outside the abdomen in a scrotal sac. The testes also secrete the male sex hormone ◊androgen.

**testosterone** in vertebrates, hormone secreted chiefly by the testes, but also by the ovaries and the cortex of the adrenal glands. It promotes the development of secondary sexual characteristics in males. In animals with a breeding season, the onset of breeding behaviour is accompanied by a rise in the level of testosterone in the blood.

**tetanus** or *lockjaw,* acute disease caused by the toxin of the bacillus *Clostridium tetani,* which usually enters the body through a wound. The bacterium is chiefly found in richly manured soil. Untreated, in seven to ten days tetanus produces muscular spasm and rigidity of the jaw spreading to other parts of the body, convulsions, and death. There is a vaccine, and the disease may be treatable with tetanus antitoxin and antibiotics.

**tête-à-tête** (French 'head-to-head') private meeting between two people.

**Tethys Sea** sea that in the Mesozoic era separated Laurasia from Gondwanaland. The formation of the Alpine fold mountains caused the sea to separate into the Mediterranean, the Black, the Caspian, and the Aral seas.

**tetra** any of various brightly coloured tropical freshwater bony fishes of the family Characidae, formerly placed in the genus *Tetragonopterus.* Tetras are found mainly in tropical South America, and also in Africa.

**tetrachloromethane** $CCl_4$ or *carbon tetra-chloride* chlorinated organic compound that is a very efficient solvent for fats and greases, and was at one time the main constituent of household dry-cleaning fluids and of fire extinguishers used with electrical and petrol fires. Its use became restricted after it was discovered to be carcinogenic and it has now been largely removed from educational and industrial laboratories.

**tetracycline** one of a group of antibiotic compounds having in common the four-ring structure of chlortetracycline, the first member of the group to be isolated. They are prepared synthetically or obtained from certain bacteria of the genus *Streptomyces*. They are broad-spectrum antibiotics, effective against a wide range of disease-causing bacteria.

**tetrahedron** plural *tetrahedra*, in geometry, a solid figure (polyhedron) with four triangular faces; that is, a pyramid on a triangular base. A regular tetrahedron has equilateral triangles as its faces.

**Teutonic Knight** member of a German Christian military order, the *Knights of the Teutonic Order,* founded in 1190 by Hermann of Salza in Palestine. They crusaded against the pagan Prussians and Lithuanians from 1228 and controlled Prussia until the 16th century. Their capital was Marienburg (now Malbork, Poland).

**Texas** state in southwestern USA. It is nicknamed the Lone Star State. Texas was admitted to the Union in 1845 as the 28th US state. One of the Great Plains states, it is bordered to the east by Louisiana, to the northeast by Arkansas, to the north by Oklahoma, to the west by New Mexico, to the southwest by the Mexican states of Chihuahua, Coahuil, Nuevo Léon, and Tamaulipas, and to the southeast by the Gulf of Mexico. Texas is the largest state in the lower 48 US states.
*population* (1995) 18,724,000
*area* 691,200 sq km/266,803 sq mi
*capital* Austin
*towns and cities* Houston, Dallas, Fort Worth, San Antonio, El Paso, Corpus Christi, Lubbock
*industries and products* rice, cotton, sorghum, wheat, hay, livestock, shrimps, meat products, lumber, wood and paper products, petroleum (nearly one-third of US production), natural gas, sulphur, salt, uranium, chemicals, petrochemicals, nonelectrical machinery, fabricated metal products, transportation equipment, electric and electronic equipment, aerospace equipment, computer and high-tech machinery, finance sector, tourism.

**Thackeray, William Makepeace** (1811–1863) English novelist and essayist. He was a regular contributor to *Fraser's Magazine* and *Punch*. His first novel was *Vanity Fair* (1847–48), significant for the breadth of its canvas as well as for the depth of the characterization. This was followed by *Pendennis* (1848), *Henry Esmond* (1852) (and its sequel *The Virginians,* 1857–59), and *The Newcomes* (1853–55), in which Thackeray's tendency to sentimentality is most marked.

**Thai** the majority ethnic group living in Thailand and northern Myanmar (Burma). Thai peoples also live in southwestern China, Laos, and North Vietnam. They speak Tai languages, all of which belong to the Sino-Tibetan language family. There are over 60 million speakers, the majority of whom live in Thailand. Most Thais are Buddhists, but the traditional belief in spirits, *phi,* remains.

**Thailand** Kingdom of
*national name* Prathet Thai or Muang Thai

*area* 513,115 sq km/198,113 sq mi
*capital* Bangkok (and chief port)
*major towns/cities* Chiangmai, Hat Yai, Khon Kaen, Songkhla, Chon Buri, Nakhon Si Thammarat, Lampang, Phitsannlok, Ratchasima
*major ports* Nakhon Sawan
*physical features* mountainous, semi-arid plateau in northeast, fertile central region, tropical isthmus in south; rivers Chao Phraya, Mekong, and Salween
*head of state* King Bhumibol Adulyadej from 1946
*head of government* Chavalit Yongchaiyudh from 1996
*political system* military-controlled emergent democracy
*political parties* Democrat Party (DP), centre left; Thai Nation (Chart Thai), right wing, pro-private enterprise; New Aspiration Party (NAP), centrist; Palang Dharma Party (PDP), anti-corruption, Buddhist; Social Action Party (SAP), moderate, conservative; Chart Pattana (National Development), conservative
*currency* baht
*GNP per capita (PPP)* (US$) 5,840 (1998)
*exports* textiles and clothing, electronic goods, rice, rubber, gemstones, sugar, cassava (tapioca), fish (especially prawns), machinery and manufactures, chemicals. Principal market: USA 22.3% (1998)
*population* 60,858,000 (1999 est)
*language* Thai and Chinese (both official); Lao, Chinese, Malay, Khmer
*religion* Buddhist
*life expectancy* 66 (men); 72 (women) (1995–2000)
*Chronology*
*13th century* Siamese (Thai) people migrated south and settled in valley of Chao Phraya River in Khmer Empire.
*1238* Siamese ousted Khmer governors and formed new kingdom based at Sukhothai.

**14th and 15th centuries** Siamese expanded at expense of declining Khmer Empire.

**1350** Siamese capital moved to Ayatthaya (which also became name of kingdom).

**1511** Portuguese traders first reached Siam.

**1569** Conquest of Ayatthaya by Burmese ended years of rivalry and conflict.

**1589** Siamese regained independence under King Naresuan.

**17th century** Foreign trade under royal monopoly developed with Chinese, Japanese, and Europeans.

**1690s** Siam expelled European military advisers and missionaries and adopted policy of isolation.

**1767** Burmese invaders destroyed city of Ayatthaya, massacred ruling families, and withdrew, leaving Siam in a state of anarchy.

**1782** Reunification of Siam after civil war under Gen Phraya Chakri, who founded new capital at Bangkok and proclaimed himself King Rama I.

**1824–51** King Rama III reopened Siam to European diplomats and missionaries.

**1851–68** King Mongkut employed European advisers to help modernize government, legal system, and army.

**1856** Royal monopoly on foreign trade ended.

**1868–1910** King Chulalongkorn continued modernization and developed railway network using Chinese immigrant labour; Siam became major exporter of rice.

**1896** Anglo-French agreement recognized Siam as independent buffer state between British Burma and French Indo-China.

**1932** Bloodless coup forced King Rama VII to grant a constitution with mixed civilian-military government.

**1939** Siam changed its name to Thailand (briefly reverting to Siam 1945–49).

**1941** Japanese invaded; Thailand became puppet ally of Japan under Field Marshal Phibun Songkhram.

**1945** Japanese withdrawal; Thailand compelled to return territory taken from Laos, Cambodia, and Malaya.

**1946** King Ananda Mahidol assassinated.

**1947** Phibun regained power in military coup, reducing monarch to figurehead; Thailand adopted strongly pro-American foreign policy.

**1955** Political parties and free speech introduced.

**1957** State of emergency declared; Phibun deposed in bloodless coup; military dictatorship continued under Gen Sarit Thanarat (1957–63) and Gen Thanom Kittikachorn (1963–73).

**1967–72** Thai troops fought in alliance with USA in Vietnam War.

**1973** Military government overthrown by student riots.

**1974** Adoption of democratic constitution, followed by civilian coalition government.

**1976** Military reassumed control in response to mounting strikes and political violence.

**1978** Gen Kriangsak Chomanan introduced constitution with mixed civilian–military government.

**1980** Gen Prem Tinsulanonda assumed power.

**1983** Prem relinquished army office to head civilian government; martial law maintained.

**1988** Chatichai Choonhavan succeeded Prem as prime minister.

**1991** A military coup imposed a new military-oriented constitution despite mass protests.

**1992** A general election produced a five-party coalition; riots forced Prime Minister Suchinda Kraprayoon to flee; Chuan Leekpai formed a new coalition government.

**1995** The ruling coalition collapsed; Banharn Silpa-archa was appointed premier.

**1996** Banharn resigned; a general election resulted in a new six-party coalition led by Chavalit Yongchaiyudh.

**1997** A major financial crisis led to floating of currency. An austerity rescue plan was agreed with the International Monetary Fund (IMF).

**1998** Repatriation of foreign workers commenced, as the economy contracted sharply in response to IMF-inspired austerity measures. An economic restructuring plan was welcomed by the IMF. The opposition Chart Patthana party was brought into the coalition government of Chuan Leekpai, increasing its majority to push through reforms.

**thalassaemia** or *Cooley's anaemia,* any of a group of chronic hereditary blood disorders that are widespread in the Mediterranean countries, Africa, the Far East, and the Middle East. They are characterized by an abnormality of the red blood cells and bone marrow, with enlargement of the spleen. The genes responsible are carried by about 100 million people worldwide. The diseases can be diagnosed prenatally.

**Thalia** (Greek 'bloom') in Greek mythology, the ◊Muse of comedy and pastoral or idyllic poetry. In art she is shown with a comic mask, shepherd's staff, or ivy wreath. She is also one of the three ◊Graces of classical mythology.

**thallium** (Greek *thallos* 'young green shoot') soft, bluish-white, malleable, metallic element, symbol Tl, atomic number 81, relative atomic mass 204.38. It is a poor conductor of electricity. Its compounds are poisonous and are used as insecticides and rodent poisons; some are used in the optical-glass and infrared-glass industries and in photocells.

**Thames** river in south England, flowing through London; length 338 km/210 mi. The longest river in England, it rises in the Cotswold Hills above Cirencester and is tidal as far as Teddington. Below London there is protection from flooding by means of the *Thames Barrier* (1982). The headstreams unite at Lechlade.

**Thanksgiving** Day, national holiday in the USA (fourth Thursday in November) and Canada (second Monday in October), first celebrated by the Pilgrim settlers in Massachusetts after their first harvest in 1621.

**Thatcher, Margaret Hilda** born Roberts, Baroness Thatcher (1925– ) British Conservative politician, prime minister (1979–90). She was education minister (1970–74) and Conservative Party leader (1975–90). In 1982 she sent British troops to recapture the Falkland Islands from Argentina. She confronted trade-union power during the miners' strike (1984–85), sold off majority stakes in many public utilities to the private sector, and reduced the influence of local government through such measures as the abolition of metropolitan councils, the control of expenditure through 'rate-capping', and the introduction of the community charge, or ◊poll tax, in 1989. In 1990, splits in the cabinet over the issues of Europe and consensus government forced her resignation. An astute parliamentary tactician, she tolerated little disagreement, either from the opposition or from within her own party.

**Thatcherism** political outlook comprising a belief in the efficacy of market forces, the need for strong central government, and a conviction that self-help is preferable to reliance on the state, combined with a strong element of ◊nationalism. The ideology is associated with the former UK premier Margaret Thatcher, but stems from an individualist view found in Britain's 19th-century Liberal and 20th-century Conservative parties, and is no longer confined to Britain. Since leaving public office, Baroness Thatcher has established her own 'Foundation'.

**theatre** a place or building in which dramatic performances for an audience take place; these include ◊drama, dancing, music, mime, ◊opera, ◊ballet, and puppets. Theatre history can be traced to Egyptian religious ritualistic drama as long ago as 3200 BC. The first known European theatres were in Greece from about 600 BC.

The earliest theatres were natural amphitheatres. By the Hellenistic period came the development of the stage, a raised platform on which the action took place. In medieval times, temporary stages of wood and canvas, one for every scene, were set up in churches and market squares for the performance of mimes and ◊miracle plays. With the Renaissance came the creation of scenic illusion, with the actors appearing within a proscenium arch; in the 19th century the introduction of the curtain and interior lighting further heightened this illusion. In the 20th century, alternative types of theatre were developed, including open stage, thrust stage, theatre-in-the-round, and studio theatre.

Famous theatre companies include the ◊Comédie Française in Paris (founded by Louis XIV in 1690 and given a permanent home in 1792), the first national theatre. The Living Theater was founded in New York in 1947 by Julian Beck and Judith Malina. In Britain the National Theatre company was established in 1963; other national theatres exist in Stockholm, Moscow, Athens, Copenhagen, Vienna, Warsaw, and elsewhere.

For traditional Japanese theatre, see ◊Nō.

**Thebes** Greek name of an ancient city (*Niut-Amen*) in Upper Egypt, on the Nile. Probably founded under the first dynasty, it was the centre of the worship of Amen, and the Egyptian capital under the New Kingdom from about 1550 BC. Temple ruins survive near the villages of Karnak and Luxor, and in the nearby *Valley of the Kings* are buried the 18th–20th dynasty kings, including Tutankhamen and Amenhotep III.

**Thebes** capital of Boeotia in ancient Greece. In the Peloponnesian War it was allied with Sparta

against Athens. For a short time after 371 BC when Thebes defeated Sparta at Leuctra, it was the most powerful state in Greece. Alexander the Great destroyed it in 336 BC and although it was restored, it never regained its former power.

**theism** belief in the existence of gods, but more specifically in that of a single personal God, at once immanent (active) in the created world and transcendent (separate) from it.

**Themistocles** (*c.* 524– *c.* 460 BC) Athenian admiral and politician. His success in persuading the Athenians to build a navy is credited with saving Greece from Persian conquest. During the Persian War, he fought with distinction in the battles of Artemisium and ◊Salamis in 480 BC. After the war he pursued an anti-Spartan line which got him ostracized, possibly in 471. Some years later he fled to Asia Minor where he died.

**theodolite** instrument for the measurement of horizontal and vertical angles, used in surveying. It consists of a small telescope mounted so as to move on two graduated circles, one horizontal and the other vertical, while its axes pass through the centre of the circles.

**Theodora** (*c.* 508–548) Byzantine empress from 527. She was originally the mistress of Emperor Justinian before marrying him in 525. She earned a reputation for charity, courage, and championing the rights of women.

**Theodoric the Great** (*c.* 455–526) king of the Ostrogoths 471–526. He led the Ostrogoths from the Danube frontier regions of the Roman Empire to conquer Italy, where he established a peaceful and prosperous kingdom. Although remembered for his benevolent rule in later years, Theodoric was ruthless in his efforts to attain power. He had no strong successor and his kingdom eventually became part of the Byzantine Empire of Justinian.

**theology** study of God or gods, either by reasoned deduction from the natural world (natural theology) or through divine revelation (revealed theology), as in the scriptures of Christianity, Islam, or other religions.

**theorbo** musical instrument, a bass ◊lute or archlute developed around 1500 and incorporating dual sets of strings, a set of freely vibrating bass strings for plucking with the thumb in addition to five to seven courses over a fretted fingerboard. It survived to form part of the Italian Baroque orchestra in about 1700.

**theorem** mathematical proposition that can be deduced by logic from a set of axioms (basic facts that are taken to be true without proof). Advanced mathematics consists almost entirely of theorems and proofs, but even at a simple level theorems are important.

**theory** in science, a set of ideas, concepts, principles, or methods used to explain a wide set of observed facts. Among the major theories of science are ◊relativity, ◊quantum theory, ◊evolution, and ◊plate tectonics.

**Theravāda** one of the two major forms of ◊Buddhism, common in Southeast Asia (Sri

Lanka, Thailand, Cambodia, and Myanmar); the other is the later Mahāyāna.

**Thérèse of Lisieux, St** originally Thérèse Martin (1873–1897) French saint. She was born in Alençon, and entered a Carmelite convent in Lisieux at 15, where her holy life induced her superior to ask her to write her spiritual autobiography. She advocated the 'Little Way of Goodness' in small things in everyday life, and became known as the 'Little Flower of Jesus'. She died of tuberculosis and was canonized in 1925.

**thermal conductivity** in physics, the ability of a substance to conduct heat. Good thermal conductors, like good electrical conductors, are generally materials with many free electrons (such as metals).

**thermal reactor** nuclear reactor in which the neutrons released by fission of uranium-235 nuclei are slowed down in order to increase their chances of being captured by other uranium-235 nuclei, and so induce further fission. The material (commonly graphite or heavy water) responsible for doing so is called a *moderator*. When the fast newly-emitted neutrons collide with the nuclei of the moderator's atoms, some of their kinetic energy is lost and their speed is reduced. Those that have been slowed down to a speed that matches the thermal (heat) energy of the surrounding material are called *thermal neutrons*, and it is these that are most likely to induce fission and ensure the continuation of the chain reaction. See ◊nuclear reactor and ◊nuclear energy.

**Thermidor** 11th month of the French Revolutionary calendar, which gave its name to the period after the fall of the Jacobins and the proscription of Robespierre by the National Convention 9 Thermidor 1794.

**thermocouple** electric temperature measuring device consisting of a circuit having two wires made of different metals welded together at their ends. A current flows in the circuit when the two junctions are maintained at different temperatures (◊Seebeck effect). The electromotive force generated – measured by a millivoltmeter – is proportional to the temperature difference.

**thermodynamics** branch of physics dealing with the transformation of heat into and from other forms of energy. It is the basis of the study of the efficient working of engines, such as the steam and internal combustion engines. The three laws of thermodynamics are: (1) energy can be neither created nor destroyed, heat and mechanical work being mutually convertible; (2) it is impossible for an unaided self-acting machine to convey heat from one body to another at a higher temperature; and (3) it is impossible by any procedure, no matter how idealized, to reduce any system to the ◊absolute zero of temperature (0K/–273°C/–459°F) in a finite number of operations. Put into mathematical form, these laws have widespread applications in physics and chemistry.

**thermography** photographic recording of heat patterns. It is used medically as an imaging technique to identify 'hot spots' in the body – for example, tumours, where cells are more active than usual. Thermography was developed in the 1970s and 1980s by the military to assist night vision by detecting the body heat of an enemy or the hot engine of a tank. It uses a photographic method (using infrared radiation) employing infrared-sensitive films.

**thermometer** instrument for measuring temperature. There are many types, designed to measure different temperature ranges to varying degrees of accuracy. Each makes use of a different physical effect of temperature. Expansion of a liquid is employed in common *liquid-in-glass thermometers*, such as those containing mercury or alcohol. The more accurate *gas thermometer* uses the effect of temperature on the pressure of a gas held at constant volume. A *resistance thermometer* takes advantage of the change in resistance of a conductor (such as a platinum wire) with variation in temperature. Another electrical thermometer is the ◊thermocouple. Mechanically, temperature change can be indicated by the change in curvature of a *bimetallic strip* (as commonly used in a ◊thermostat).

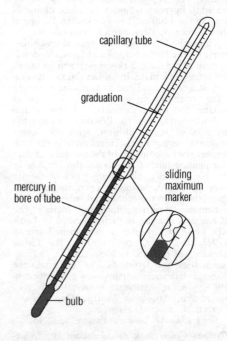

*thermometer* Maximum and minimum thermometers are universally used in weather-reporting stations. The maximum thermometer, shown here, includes a magnet that fits tightly inside a capillary tube and is moved up it by the rising mercury. When the temperature falls, the magnet remains in position, thus enabling the maximum temperature to be recorded.

**Thermopylae, Battle of** battle between the Greeks under the Spartan king Leonidas and the invading Persians under Xerxes I. They clashed at the narrow mountain pass of Thermopylae, leading from Thessaly to Locrish in central Greece. Although the Greeks were defeated, the heroism of those who fought to the last against the Persians boosted Greek morale.

**thermosphere** layer in the Earth's ◊atmosphere above the mesosphere and below the exosphere. Its lower level is about 80 km/50 mi above the ground, but its upper level is undefined. The ionosphere is located in the thermosphere. In the thermosphere the temperature rises with increasing height to several thousand degrees Celsius. However, because of the thinness of the air, very little heat is actually present.

**thermostat** temperature-controlling device that makes use of feedback. It employs a temperature sensor (often a bimetallic strip) to operate a switch or valve to control electricity or fuel supply. Thermostats are used in central heating, ovens, and car engines.

**Theseus** in Greek mythology, a hero of ◊Attica, who was believed to have united the states of the area under a constitutional government in Athens. He killed the monstrous ◊Minotaur with the aid of ◊Ariadne, fought the ◊Amazons, and took part in the expedition of the ◊Argonauts.

**Thessaloníki** English *Salonika*, port in Macedonia, northeastern Greece, at the head of the Gulf of Thessaloníki; the second-largest city in Greece; population (1991) 378,000. Industries include textiles, shipbuilding, chemicals, brewing, and tanning. It was founded from Corinth by the Romans in 315 BC as *Thessalonica* (to whose inhabitants St Paul addressed two epistles), captured by the Saracens in AD 904 and by the Turks in 1430, and restored to Greece in 1912.

**Thessaly** Greek *Thessalia*, region of eastern central Greece, on the Aegean; area 13,904 sq km/5,367 sq mi; population (1991) 731,200. It is a major area of cereal production. It was an independent state in ancient Greece and later formed part of the Roman province of ◊Macedonia. It was Turkish from the 14th century until incorporated into Greece in 1881.

**Thetis** in Greek mythology, the most beautiful ◊Nereid (a sea goddess), and mother of ◊Achilles. She dipped the baby in the ◊Styx, rendering him invulnerable except for the heel which she held. In Homer's *Iliad* she also gave Achilles armour forged by Hephaestus. Fated to have a son more powerful than his father, she was married by the gods against her will to a mortal, Peleus.

**thiamine** or *vitamin B₁* a water-soluble vitamin of the B complex. It is found in seeds and grain. Its absence from the diet causes the disease ◊beriberi.

**Thimphu** capital since 1962 of the Himalayan state of Bhutan; population (1993) 30,300. There is a 13th-century fortified monastery, Tashichoedzong, and the Memorial Charter to the Third King (1974).

**Third Reich** Third Empire, Germany during the years of Hitler's dictatorship after 1933. The idea of the Third Reich was based on the existence of two previous German empires: the medieval Holy Roman Empire, and the second empire of 1871 to 1918.

**Third World** or *developing world,* those countries that are less developed than the industrialized free-market countries of the West (First World) and the industrialized former Communist countries (Second World). Third World countries are the poorest, as measured by their income per head of population, and are concentrated in Asia, Africa, and Latin America.

The early 1970s saw the beginnings of attempts by Third World countries to act together in confronting the powerful industrialized countries over such matters as the level of prices of primary products, with the nations regarding themselves as a group that had been exploited in the past by the developed nations and that had a right to catch up with them (see ◊nonaligned movement).

**Thirteen Colonies** 13 American colonies that signed the ◊Declaration of Independence from Britain in 1776. Led by George ◊Washington, the Continental Army defeated the British army in the ◊American Revolution (1776–81) to become the original 13 United States of America: Connecticut, Delaware, Georgia, Maryland, Massachusetts, New Hampshire, New Jersey, New York, North Carolina, Pennsylvania, Rhode Island, South Carolina, and Virginia. They were united first under the Articles of ◊Confederation and from 1789, the US ◊constitution.

**38th parallel** demarcation line between North (People's Democratic Republic of) and South (Republic of) Korea, agreed at the Yalta Conference in 1945 and largely unaltered by the Korean War (1950–53).

**Thirty-Nine Articles** set of articles of faith defining the doctrine of the Anglican Church; see under ◊Anglican Communion.

**Thirty Years' War** major war (1618–48) in central Europe. Beginning as a German conflict between Protestants and Catholics, it was gradually transformed into a struggle to determine whether the ruling Austrian Habsburg family could gain control of all Germany. The war caused serious economic and demographic problems in central Europe. Under the *Peace of Westphalia* the German states were granted their sovereignty and the emperor retained only nominal control.

**thistle** any of a group of prickly plants with spiny stems, soft cottony purple flower heads, and deeply indented leaves with prickly edges. The thistle is the national emblem of Scotland. (Genera include *Carduus, Carlina, Onopordum,* and *Cirsium;* family Compositae.)

**Thomas, Dylan Marlais** (1914–1953) Welsh poet. His poems, characterized by complex imagery and a strong musicality, include the celebration of his 30th birthday 'Poem in October' and the evocation of his youth 'Fern Hill'

(1946). His 'play for voices' *Under Milk Wood* (1954) describes with humour and compassion a day in the life of the residents of a small Welsh fishing village, Llareggub. The short stories of *Portrait of the Artist as a Young Dog* (1940) are autobiographical.

**Thomas à Kempis** adopted name of *Thomas Hämmerken* (*c.* 1380–1471) German Augustinian monk, author of *De Imitatio Christi/Imitation of Christ* (1441), a devotional handbook of the *devotio moderna*. The work proved quickly popular, being translated into Dutch and French.

**Thomas Aquinas** medieval philosopher; see ◊Aquinas, St Thomas.

**Thompson, Emma** (1959– ) English actress. She has worked in cinema, theatre, and television, ranging from song-and-dance to Shakespeare, often playing variations on the independent woman. She won an Academy Award for her performance in *Howards End* (1992) and another for her film adaptation (1995) of Jane Austen's novel *Sense and Sensibility*, in which she also played the role of Elinor.

**Thomson, George Paget** (1892–1975) English physicist whose work on ◊interference phenomena in the scattering of electrons by crystals helped to confirm the wavelike nature of particles. He shared a Nobel prize in 1937. He was knighted in 1943.

**Thomson, J(oseph) J(ohn)** (1856–1940) English physicist. He discovered the ◊electron in 1897. His work inaugurated the electrical theory of the atom, and his elucidation of positive rays and their application to an analysis of neon led to the discovery of ◊isotopes. He was awarded a Nobel prize in 1906 and was knighted in 1908.

**Thor** in Norse and Teutonic mythology, the god of thunder (his hammer), represented as a man of enormous strength defending humanity against demons and the frost giants. He was the son of Odin and Freya, and one of the Aesir (warrior gods). Thursday is named after him.

**thorax** in four-limbed vertebrates, the part of the body containing the heart and lungs, and protected by the ribcage; in arthropods, the middle part of the body, between the head and abdomen.

**Thoreau, Henry David** (1817–1862) US author. One of the most influential figures of 19th-century US literature, he is best known for his vigorous defence of individualism and the simple life. His work *Walden, or Life in the Woods* (1854) stimulated the back-to-nature movement, and he completed some 30 volumes based on his daily nature walks. His essay 'Civil Disobedience' (1849), prompted by his refusal to pay taxes, advocated peaceful resistance to unjust laws and had a wide impact, even in the 20th century.

**thorium** dark-grey, radioactive, metallic element of the ◊actinide series, symbol Th, atomic number 90, relative atomic mass 232.038. It occurs throughout the world in small quantities in minerals such as thorite and is widely distributed in monazite beach sands. It is one of three fissile elements (the others are uranium and plutonium), and its longest-lived isotope has a half-life of $1.39 \times 10^{10}$ years. Thorium is used to strengthen alloys. It was discovered by Jöns Berzelius in 1828 and was named by him after the Norse god Thor.

**thoroughbred** horse bred for racing purposes. All racehorses are thoroughbreds, and all are direct descendants of one of three stallions imported into Britain during the 17th and 18th centuries: the Darley Arabian, Byerley Turk, and Godolphin Barb.

**Thoth** Greek *Hermes Trismegistos*, in Egyptian mythology, the god of wisdom, learning, and magic. Inventor of ◊hieroglyphic writing, he was the patron of scribes, and associated with the Moon, whose phases were used for reckoning. He was represented as a dog-faced baboon or as a scribe with the head of an ibis; the bird was sacred to him.

**Thrace** Greek *Thráki*, ancient region of the Balkans, southeastern Europe, formed by parts of modern Greece and Bulgaria. It was held successively by the Greeks, Persians, Macedonians, and Romans.

**Three Kingdoms** period in Chinese history from 220 to 581, an era of disruptive, intermittent warfare between three powers. Sometimes the term is used to cover only the period 220 to 280 following the end of the Han dynasty when the Wei, Shu, and Wu fought for supremacy.

**Three Mile Island** island in the Shenandoah River near Harrisburg, Pennsylvania. It is the site of a nuclear power station which was put out of action following a serious accident in March 1979. Opposition to nuclear power in the USA was reinforced after this accident and safety standards reassessed.

**thrift** or *sea pink,* any of several perennial low-growing coastal plants. The common sea pink *A. maritima* occurs in clumps on seashores and cliffs throughout Europe. The leaves are small and linear and the dense round heads of pink flowers rise on straight stems. (Genus *Armeria,* family Plumbaginaceae.)

**thrips** any of a number of tiny insects of the order Thysanoptera, usually with feathery wings. Many of the 3,000 species live in flowers and suck their juices, causing damage and spreading disease. Others eat fungi, decaying matter, or smaller insects.

**throat** in human anatomy, the passage that leads from the back of the nose and mouth to the ◊trachea and ◊oesophagus. It includes the pharynx and the ◊larynx, the latter being at the top of the trachea. The word 'throat' is also used to mean the front part of the neck, both in humans and other vertebrates; for example, in describing the plumage of birds. In engineering, it is any narrowing entry, such as the throat of a carburettor.

**thrombosis** condition in which a blood clot forms in a vein or artery, causing loss of circulation to the area served by the vessel. If it breaks away, it often travels to the lungs, causing pulmonary embolism.

**thrush** any bird of the large family Turdidae, order Passeriformes, found worldwide and known for their song. Thrushes are usually brown with speckles of other colours. They are 12–30 cm/5–12 in long.

**thrush** in medicine, infection usually of the mouth (particularly in infants), but also sometimes of the vagina, caused by a yeastlike fungus (*Candida*). It is seen as white patches on the mucous membranes.

**Thrust 2** jet-propelled car in which British driver Richard Noble set a world land speed record in the Black Rock desert of Nevada, USA, on 4 October 1983. The record speed was 1,019.4 kph/633.468 mph. In 1996 Noble attempted to break the sound barrier in *Thrust SCC. Thrust SCC* has two Rolls-Royce Spey engines (the same kind used in RAF Phantom jets) that provide 110,000 horsepower; it weighs 6,350 kg/13,970 lb, and is 16.5 m/54 ft in length. It was driven by RAF fighter pilot Andy Green to break the sound barrier in September 1997, setting a speed of 1,149.272 kph/714.144 mph.

**Thucydides** (c. 455 BC–c. 400 BC) Athenian historian. He was briefly a general during the ◊Peloponnesian War with Sparta, but as a result of his failure to save Amphipolis from the Spartan general Brasidas, he was banished from Athens in 424. His *History of the Peloponnesian War* gives a detailed account of the conflict to 411.

**thulium** soft, silver-white, malleable and ductile, metallic element of the ◊lanthanide series, symbol Tm, atomic number 69, relative atomic mass 168.94. It is the least abundant of the rare earth metals, and was first found in gadolinite and various other minerals. It is used in arc lighting.

**Thunderbird** legendary bird of the North American Indians, the creator of storms. It is said to produce thunder by flapping its wings and lightning by opening and closing its eyes.

**Thurrock** unitary authority in eastern England, created in 1998 from part of Essex
*area* 163 sq km/63 sq mi
*towns and cities* Grays (administrative headquarters), Purfleet, Tilbury, Chadwell, St Mary, Stanford-le-Hope, Corringham, South Ockendon
*features* located on north bank of River Thames; Holehaven Creek forms eastern border of authority; Tilbury Marshes; Mucking Marshes; Dartford Tunnel and Queen Elizabeth II bridge have northern approach through Thurrock; 17th-century Tilbury Fort, with three moats; Alexandra Lake; Lakeside shopping centre
*industries* oil refineries, power station at west Tilbury Marshes, sand and gravel extraction, cement works, soap, margarine, timber products
*population* (1996) 130,600.

**thylacine** another name for the ◊Tasmanian wolf.

**thyme** any of several herbs belonging to the mint family. Garden thyme *T. vulgaris*, native to

the Mediterranean, grows to 30 cm/1 ft high and has small leaves and pinkish flowers. Its aromatic leaves are used for seasoning in cookery. (Genus *Thymus*, family Labiatae.)

**thymus** organ in vertebrates, situated in the upper chest cavity in humans. The thymus processes ◊lymphocyte cells to produce T-lymphocytes (T denotes 'thymus-derived'), which are responsible for binding to specific invading organisms and killing them or rendering them harmless.

**thyroid** ◊endocrine gland of vertebrates, situated in the neck in front of the trachea. It secretes several hormones, principally thyroxine, an iodine-containing hormone that stimulates growth, metabolism, and other functions of the body. The thyroid gland may be thought of as the regulator gland of the body's metabolic rate. If it is overactive, as in hyperthyroidism, the sufferer feels hot and sweaty, has an increased heart rate, diarrhoea, and weight loss. Conversely, an underactive thyroid leads to *myxoedema*, a condition characterized by sensitivity to the cold, constipation, and weight gain. In infants, an underactive thyroid leads to *cretinism*, a form of mental retardation.

**Tiananmen Square** (Chinese 'Square of Heavenly Peace') paved open space in central Beijing (Peking), China, the largest public square in the world (area 0.4 sq km/0.14 sq mi). On 3–4 June 1989 more than 1,000 unarmed protesters were killed by government troops in a massacre that crushed China's emerging prodemocracy movement.

**Tiberius** Tiberius Claudius Nero (42 BC–AD 37) Roman emperor, the stepson, adopted son, and successor of Augustus from AD 14. He was a cautious ruler whose reign was marred by the heavy incidence of trials for treason or conspiracy. Tiberius fell under the influence of Sejanus who encouraged the emperor's fear of assassination and was instrumental in Tiberius' departure from Rome to Caprae (Capri). He never returned to Rome.

**Tibet** autonomous region of southwestern China (Pinyin form *Xizang*);
*area* 1,221,600 sq km/471,538 sq mi
*capital* Lhasa
*features* Tibet occupies a barren plateau bounded to the south and southwest by the Himalayas and north by the Kunlun Mountains, traversed west to east by the Bukamagna, Karakoram, and other mountain ranges, and having an average elevation of 4,000–4,500 m/13,000–15,000 ft. The Sutlej, Brahmaputra, and Indus rivers rise in Tibet, which has numerous lakes, many of which are salty. The ◊yak is the main domestic animal
*government* Tibet is an autonomous region of China, with its own People's Government and People's Congress. The controlling force in Tibet is the Communist Party of China, represented locally by First Secretary Wu Jinghua from 1985. Tibetan nationalists regard the province as being under colonial rule. There is a government-in-exile in Dharmsala, Himachel Pradesh, India, where the ◊Dalai Lama lives

*industries* wool, borax, salt, horn, musk, herbs, furs, gold, iron pyrites, lapis lazuli, mercury, textiles, chemicals, agricultural machinery. Tibet has the largest uranium reserves in the world: uranium processing and extraction is causing pollution, and human and animal birth deformities

*population* (1993) 2,290,000; many Chinese have settled in Tibet; 2 million Tibetans live in China outside Tibet

*religion* traditionally Lamaist (a form of Mahāyāna Buddhism)

*history* Tibet was an independent kingdom from the 5th century AD. It came under nominal Chinese rule about 1700.

From 1910–13 the capital, Lhasa, was occupied by Chinese troops, after which independence was re-established. China regained control in 1951 when the historic ruler and religious leader, the ◊Dalai Lama, was driven from the country and the monks (who formed 25% of the population) were forced out of the monasteries. The Chinese People's Liberation Army (PLA) controlled Tibet 1951–59, although the Dalai Lama returned as nominal spiritual and temporal head of state. In 1959 a Tibetan uprising spread from bordering regions to Lhasa and was supported by Tibet's local government. The rebellion was suppressed by the PLA, prompting the Dalai Lama and 9,000 Tibetans to flee to India. The Chinese proceeded to dissolve the Tibet local government, abolish serfdom, collectivize agriculture, and suppress ◊Lamaism. In 1965 Tibet became an autonomous region of China. Chinese rule continued to be resented, however, and the economy languished.

**Tibetan** a Mongolian people inhabiting Tibet who practise a form of Mahāyāna Buddhism, introduced in the 7th century. Since China's Cultural Revolution in 1966–68, refugee communities have formed in India and Nepal. The Tibetan language belongs to the Sino-Tibetan language family.

**Tibetan mastiff** large breed of dog regarded as the ancestor of many present breeds. It is a very powerful animal with a long black or black and tan coat. It is about 71 cm/28 in in height and 60 kg/132 lb in weight.

**tibia** the anterior of the pair of bones in the leg between the ankle and the knee. In humans, the tibia is the shinbone. It articulates with the femur above to form the knee joint, the ◊fibula externally at its upper and lower ends, and with the talus below, forming the ankle joint.

**tick** any of the arachnid family Ixodoidae, order Acarina, of large bloodsucking mites. They have flat bodies protected by horny shields. Many carry and transmit diseases to mammals (including humans) and birds.

**tidal wave** common name for a ◊tsunami.

**tide** the rhythmic rise and fall of the sea level in the Earth's oceans and their inlets and estuaries due to the gravitational attraction of the Moon and, to a lesser extent, the Sun, affecting regions of the Earth unequally as it rotates. Water on the side of the Earth nearest the Moon feels the

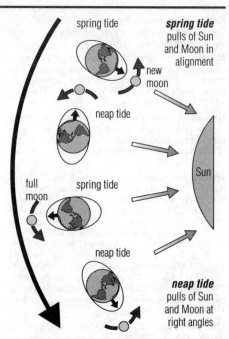

spring tide

**spring tide** pulls of Sun and Moon in alignment

new moon

neap tide

full moon    spring tide

Sun

neap tide

**neap tide** pulls of Sun and Moon at right angles

**tide** *The gravitational pull of the Moon is the main cause of the tides. Water on the side of the Earth nearest the Moon feels the Moon's pull and accumulates directly under the Moon. When the Sun and the Moon are in line, at new and full moon, the gravitational pull of Sun and Moon are in line and produce a high spring tide. When the Sun and Moon are at right angles, lower neap tides occur.*

Moon's pull and accumulates directly below it producing high tide.

**Tiepolo, Giovanni Battista (Giambattista)** (1696–1770) Italian painter. He was one of the first exponents of Italian Rococo and created monumental decorative schemes in palaces and churches in northeastern Italy, southwestern Germany, and Madrid. His style is light-hearted, his colours light and warm, and he made great play with illusion.

**Tierra del Fuego** island group separated from the southern extremity of South America by the Strait of Magellan; Cape Horn is at the southernmost point. There are oil, natural gas, and sheep farming industries. Tourism is also important. The largest island is Tierra del Fuego, or *Isla Grande*, with an area of 48,100 sq km/ 18,571 sq mi; half of this island, and the islands west of it, belong to Chile, and form part of the Magallanes region, the capital and chief town of which is Punta Arenas. The eastern part of the archipelago belongs to Argentina, forming the federal district of Tierra del Fuego; its capital, Ushuaia, is the world's most southerly town.

**tiger** largest of the great cats, *Panthera tigris* (family Felidae, order Carnivora), formerly found in much of central and South Asia, from

Siberia south to Sumatra, but nearing extinction (5,000 in 1997) because of hunting and the high prices paid for the pelt, as well as the destruction of its natural habitat.

The male tiger can grow to 3.6 m/12 ft long, while the female averages about 2.6 m/8.5 ft. It weighs up to 300 kg/660 lb, and has a yellow-orange coat with black stripes. Tigers are solitary, and largely nocturnal. They will eat carrion, but generally kill for themselves. Their food consists mainly of deer, antelopes, and smaller animals, but they sometimes kill wild boar. Human-eating tigers are rare and are the result of weakened powers or shortage of game.

**Tigré** a people of northern Ethiopia. The Tigré language is spoken by about 2.5 million people; it belongs to the southeastern Semitic branch of the Afro-Asiatic (Hamito-Semitic) family. *Tigrinya* is a closely related language spoken slightly to the south.

**Tigré** or *Tigray*, region in the northern highlands of Ethiopia; area 65,900 sq km/25,444 sq mi. The chief town is Mek'elē. The region had an estimated population of 2.4 million in 1984, at a time when drought and famine led to a movement of Tigrayans to fertile land in the south or into neighbouring Sudan. In 1978 a guerrilla group known as the Tigré People's Liberation Front (TPLF) began fighting for regional autonomy. In 1989 government troops were forced from the province, and the TPLF advanced towards Addis Ababa, playing the key role in the fall of the Ethiopian government in May 1991.

**Tigris** Arabic *Dijla*, river flowing through Turkey and Iraq (see also ◊Mesopotamia), joining the ◊Euphrates 80 km/50 mi northwest of Basra, where it forms the ◊Shatt-al-Arab; length 1,600 km/1,000 mi.

**Tijuana** city and resort in northwestern Mexico; population (1990) 742,700. It is known for horse races and casinos. ◊San Diego adjoins it across the US border.

**timber** wood used in construction, furniture, and paper pulp. *Hardwoods* include tropical mahogany, teak, ebony, rosewood, temperate oak, elm, beech, and eucalyptus. All except eucalyptus are slow-growing, and world supplies are almost exhausted. *Softwoods* comprise the ◊conifers (pine, fir, spruce, and larch), which are quick to grow and easy to work but inferior in quality of grain. *White woods* include ash, birch, and sycamore; all have light-coloured timber, are fast-growing, and can be used as veneers on cheaper timber.

**timbre** (French 'tone') in music, the tone colour, or quality of tone, of a particular ◊sound. Different instruments playing a note at the same ◊pitch have different sound qualities, and it is the timbre that enables the listener to distinguish the sound of, for example, a trumpet from that of a violin. The tone quality of a sound depends on several things, including its waveform, the strength of its harmonics, and its attack and decay – the 'shape' of the sound. The study of the elements of sound quality is part of the science of acoustics.

**Timisoara** capital of Timiş county, western Romania; population (1993) 325,000. Industries include electrical engineering, chemicals, pharmaceuticals, textiles, food processing, metal, and footwear. The revolt against the Ceauşescu regime began here in December 1989 when demonstrators prevented the arrest and deportation of a popular Protestant minister who was promoting the rights of ethnic Hungarians. This soon led to large prodemocracy rallies.

**Timor** largest and most easterly of the Lesser Sunda Islands, part of Indonesia; area 33,610 sq km/12,973 sq mi. Its indigenous people were the Atoni; successive migrants have included the Malay, Melanesian, Chinese, Arab, and Gujerati.

The Dutch were established in Kupang in 1613, with the Portuguese in the north and east. Portugal established a colonial administration in Timor in 1702, but the claim was disputed by the Dutch, as well as by the Timorese, who frequently rebelled. Timor was divided into *West Timor* and ◊*East Timor* by treaties of 1859 and 1913 and subjected to Dutch and Portuguese control respectively; during World War II both parts were occupied by Japan. West Timor (capital Kupang) became part of Indonesia in 1949. East Timor (capital Dili) comprises the enclave on the northwest coast, and the islands of Atauro and Jaco. It was seized by Indonesia in 1975, and became an Indonesian province in 1976 (East Timor is the English name for the Indonesian province of Timor Timur). The annexation is not recognized by the United Nations, and guerrilla warfare by local people seeking independence continues. Since 1975 over 500,000 Timorese have been killed by Indonesian troops or have resettled in West Timor. Civilians demonstrating in Dili 1991 were massacred by Indonesian troops.

Products include coffee, maize, rice, and coconuts.

**tin** soft, silver-white, malleable and somewhat ductile, metallic element, symbol Sn (from Latin *stannum*), atomic number 50, relative atomic mass 118.69. Tin exhibits ◊allotropy, having three forms: the familiar lustrous metallic form above 13.2°C/55.8°F; a brittle form above 161°C/321.8°F; and a grey powder form below 13.2°C/55.8°F (commonly called tin pest or tin disease). The metal is quite soft (slightly harder than lead) and can be rolled, pressed, or hammered into extremely thin sheets; it has a low melting point. In nature it occurs rarely as a free metal. It resists corrosion and is therefore used for coating and plating other metals.

**Tinbergen, Niko(laas)** (1907–1988) Dutch-born British zoologist. He specialized in the study of instinctive behaviour in animals. One of the founders of ◊ethology, the scientific study of animal behaviour in natural surroundings, he shared a Nobel prize in 1973 with Konrad ◊Lorenz (with whom he worked on several projects) and Karl von Frisch.

**tinnitus** in medicine, constant buzzing or ringing in the ears. The phenomenon may originate from prolonged exposure to noisy conditions (drilling, machinery, or loud music) or from damage to or disease of the middle or inner ear. The sufferer may become overwhelmed by the relentless noise in the head.

**tin ore** mineral from which tin is extracted, principally cassiterite, $SnO_2$. The world's chief producers are Malaysia, Thailand, and Bolivia.

**Tintoretto** adopted name of *Jacopo Robusti* (1518–1594) Venetian painter who produced portraits and religious works of great intensity. Outstanding among his many works is a series of religious works in the Scuola di S Rocco in Venice (1564–88), the dramatic figures lit by a flickering, unearthly light, the space around them distorted into long perspectives. Among his best-known works is *St George and the Dragon* (*c*.1570, National Gallery, London).

**Tipperary** county of the Republic of Ireland, in the province of Munster, divided into North and South Ridings; county town Clonmel; area 4,255 sq km/1,643 sq mi; population (1991) 132,600. It includes part of the Golden Vale, a fertile dairy-farming region. Agriculture is the chief industry; barley and oats are the main crops, but potatoes and turnips are also grown. Cattle are reared in large numbers, and there are flour mills and butter factories. There is also horse and greyhound breeding. Other main towns are Cahir, Carrick-on-Suir, Cashel, Templemore, Tipperary, Thurles, Nenagh, and Roscrea.

**TIR** abbreviation for *Transports Internationaux Routiers* (French 'International Road Transport').

**Tirana** or *Tiranë,* capital (since 1920) of Albania; population (1991) 251,000. Industries include metallurgy, cotton textiles, soap, and cigarettes. It was founded in the early 17th century by Turks when part of the Ottoman Empire. Although the city is now largely composed of recent buildings, some older districts and mosques have been preserved.

**tire** US spelling of tyre, an inflatable rubber hoop fitted round the rims of bicycle, car, and other road-vehicle wheels.

**Tiresias** or *Teiresias,* in Greek mythology, a man of Thebes blinded by the gods and given the ability to predict the future.

**Tirol** federal state of Austria; area 12,600 sq km/4,864 sq mi; population (1995) 655,200. Its capital is Innsbruck, and it produces diesel engines, optical instruments, and hydroelectric power. Tirol was formerly a province (from 1363) of the Austrian Empire, divided in 1919 between Austria and Italy.

**tissue** in biology, any kind of cellular fabric that occurs in an organism's body. Several kinds of tissue can usually be distinguished, each consisting of cells of a particular kind bound together by cell walls (in plants) or extracellular matrix (in animals). Thus, nerve and muscle are different kinds of tissue in animals, as are parenchyma and ◊sclerenchyma in plants.

**tissue culture** process by which cells from a plant or animal are removed from the organism and grown under controlled conditions in a sterile medium containing all the necessary nutrients. Tissue culture can provide information on cell growth and differentiation, and is also used in plant propagation and drug production.

**tit** or *titmouse,* any of 65 species of insectivorous, acrobatic bird of the family Paridae, order Passeriformes. Tits are 8–20 cm/3–8 in long and have grey or black plumage, often with blue or yellow markings. They are found in Eurasia and Africa, and also in North America, where they are called *chickadees.*

**Titan** in astronomy, the largest moon of the planet Saturn, with a diameter of 5,150 km/3,200 mi and a mean distance from Saturn of 1,222,000 km/759,000 mi. It was discovered in 1655 by Dutch mathematician and astronomer Christiaan ◊Huygens, and is the second-largest moon in the Solar System (Ganymede, of Jupiter, is larger).

**Titan** in Greek mythology, any of the giant children of ◊Uranus, the primeval sky god, and ◊Gaia, goddess of the Earth, whose six sons and six daughters included ◊Kronos, Rhea, Themis, and Oceanus. Kronos and Rhea were in turn the parents of Zeus, who ousted his father as ruler of the world.

**Titanic** British passenger liner, supposedly unsinkable, that struck an iceberg and sank off the Grand Banks of Newfoundland on its first voyage on the 14–15 April 1912; estimates of the number of lives lost, largely due to inadequate provision of lifeboats, vary between 1,503 and 1,517. In 1985 it was located by robot submarine 4 km/2.5 mi down in an ocean canyon, preserved by the cold environment. In 1987 salvage operations began.

**titanium** strong, lightweight, silver-grey, metallic element, symbol Ti, atomic number 22, relative atomic mass 47.90. The ninth-most abundant element in the Earth's crust, its compounds occur in practically all igneous rocks and their sedimentary deposits. It is very strong and resistant to corrosion, so it is used in building high-speed aircraft and spacecraft; it is also widely used in making alloys, as it unites with almost every metal except copper and aluminium. Titanium oxide is used in high-grade white pigments.

**titanium ore** any mineral from which titanium is extracted, principally ilmenite ($FeTiO_3$) and rutile ($TiO_2$). Brazil, India, and Canada are major producers. Both these ore minerals are found either in rock formations or concentrated in heavy mineral sands.

**tithe** formerly, payment exacted from the inhabitants of a parish for the maintenance of the church and its incumbent; some religious groups continue the practice by giving 10% of members' incomes to charity.

**Titian** anglicized form of Tiziano Vecellio (*c*. 1487–1576) Italian painter. He was one of the greatest artists of the High Renaissance. During his long career he was court painter to Charles V, Holy Roman Emperor, and to his son, Philip

II of Spain. He produced a vast number of portraits, religious paintings, and mythological scenes, including *Bacchus and Ariadne* (1520–23; National Gallery, London) and *Venus and Adonis* (1554; Prado, Madrid).

**Titicaca, Lake** lake in the Andes, 3,810 m/12,500 ft above sea level and 1,220 m/4,000 ft above the tree line; area 8,300 sq km/3,200 sq mi, the largest lake in South America, and the world's highest navigable body of water. It is divided between Bolivia (port at Guaqui) and Peru (ports at Puno (principal port) and Huancane). The lake is fed by several streams which originate in the snow-capped surrounding mountains. The lake contains enormous frogs, which are farmed, the legs being an edible delicacy, and there is some trout farming. The herding of alpacas and llamas is also common. It is one of the few places in the world where reed boats are still made by the Uru tribal peoples (Lake Tana in Ethiopia is another). The lake is also used for irrigation.

**titration** in analytical chemistry, a technique to find the concentration of one compound in a solution by determining how much of it will react with a known amount of another compound in solution.

**Tlingit** member of an ◊American Indian people living on the west coast of southern Alaska and northern British Columbia and numbering about 14,000 (1990). The Tlingit are known for their dugout canoes, their potlatch ceremonies, where food and gifts are distributed to guests in order to gain status, and their carved wooden 'totem' poles representing their family crests, and which show such animals as the raven, whale, octopus, beaver, bear, wolf, and the mythical ◊Thunderbird. Their language belongs to the Na-Dene branch of the the Athabaskan language family.

**TM** abbreviation for ◊*transcendental meditation.*

**TNT** (abbreviation for *trinitrotoluene*) $CH_3C_6H_2(NO_2)_3$, a powerful high explosive. It is a yellow solid, prepared in several isomeric forms from ◊toluene by using sulphuric and nitric acids.

**toad** any of the more terrestrial warty-skinned members of the tailless amphibians (order Anura). The name commonly refers to members of the genus *Bufo*, family Bufonidae, which are found worldwide, except for Australia (where the marine or ◊cane toad *B. marinus* has been introduced), Madagascar, and Antarctica. They differ from ◊frogs chiefly by the total absence of teeth, and in certain other anatomical features.

**toadflax** any of a group of small plants belonging to the snapdragon family, native to Western Europe and Asia. Toadflaxes have spurred, two-lipped flowers, commonly purple or yellow, and grow 20–80 cm/8–32 in tall. (Genus *Linaria*, family Scrophulariaceae.)

**toadstool** common name for many umbrella-shaped fruiting bodies of fungi (see ◊fungus). The term is normally applied to those that are inedible or poisonous.

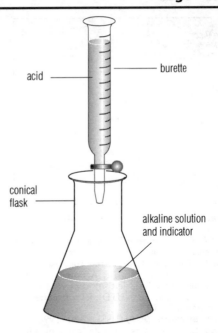

acid — burette
conical flask —
alkaline solution and indicator

*titration A method used to find the concentration of an acid or an alkali. Typically a burette is filled with an acid of unknown concentration which is slowly (drop by drop) added to an alkali of a known concentration, mixed with an indicator (such as phenolphthalein). The volume of acid needed to neutralize the alkali in the flask can be used to calculate the concentration of the acid.*

**tobacco** any of a group of large-leaved plants belonging to the nightshade family, native to tropical parts of the Americas. The species *N. tabacum* is widely cultivated in warm, dry climates for use in cigars and cigarettes, and in powdered form as snuff. (Genus *Nicotiana*, family Solanaceae.)

**Tobago** island in the West Indies; part of the republic of Trinidad and Tobago.

**Tocqueville, Alexis Charles Henri Clérel de** (1805–1859) French politician, sociologist, and historian. He was the author of the first analytical study of the strengths and weaknesses of US society, *De la Démocratie en Amérique/ Democracy in America* (1835). He also wrote a penetrating description of France before the Revolution, *L'Ancien Régime et la Révo-lution/ The Old Regime and the Revolution* (1856).

**Togo** Republic of (formerly *Togoland*)
*national name* République Togolaise
*area* 56,800 sq km/21,930 sq mi
*capital* Lomé
*major towns/cities* Sokodé, Kpalimé, Kara, Atakpamé, Bassar, Tsévié
*physical features* two savanna plains, divided by a range of hills northeast–southwest; coastal lagoons and marsh; Mono Tableland, Oti Plateau, Oti River

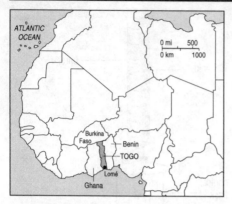

**head of state** Etienne Gnassingbé Eyadéma from 1967
**head of government** Kwasi Klutse from 1996
**political system** emergent democracy
**political parties** Rally of the Togolese People (RPT), nationalist, centrist; Action Committee for Renewal (CAR), left of centre; Togolese Union for Democracy (UTD), left of centre
**currency** franc CFA
**GNP per capita (PPP)** (US$) 1,390 (1998)
**exports** phosphates (mainly calcium phosphates), ginned cotton, green coffee, cocoa beans. Principal market: Canada 7.6% (1997)
**population** 4,512,000 (1999 est)
**language** French (official), Ewe, Kabre, Gurma
**religion** animist, Catholic, Muslim, Protestant
**life expectancy** 48 (men); 50 (women) (1995–2000)
*Chronology*
**15th–17th centuries** Formerly dominated by Kwa peoples in southwest and Gur-speaking Voltaic peoples in north, Ewe clans immigrated from Nigeria and the Ane (Mina) from Ghana and the Côte d'Ivoire.
**18th century** Coastal area held by Danes.
**1847** Arrival of German missionaries.
**1884–1914** Togoland was a German protectorate until captured by Anglo-French forces; cocoa and cotton plantations developed, using forced labour.
**1922** Divided between Britain and France under League of Nations mandate.
**1946** Continued under United Nations trusteeship.
**1957** British Togoland, comprising one-third of the area and situated in the west, integrated with Ghana, following a plebiscite.
**1960** French Togoland, situated in the east, achieved independence from France as Republic of Togo with Sylvanus Olympio, leader of United Togolese (UP) party, as head of state.
**1963** Olympio killed in a military coup. His brother-in-law, Nicolas Grunitzky, became president.
**1967** Grunitzky replaced by Lt-Gen Etienne Gnassingbé Eyadéma in bloodless coup; political parties banned.
**1969** Assembly of the Togolese People (RPT) formed by Eyadéma as sole legal political party.
**1975** EEC Lomé convention signed in Lomé,

establishing trade links with developing countries.
**1977** Assassination plot against Eyadéma, allegedly involving Olympio family, thwarted.
**1979** Eyadéma returned in election. Further EEC Lomé convention signed.
**1986** Attempted coup failed and situation stabilized with help of French troops.
**1990** There were casualties as violent antigovernment demonstrations in Lomé were suppressed; Eyadéma relegalized political parties.
**1991** Gilchrist Olympio returned from exile. Eyadéma was forced to call a national conference that limited the president's powers, and elected Joseph Kokou Koffigoh head of an interim government. Three attempts by Eyadéma's troops to unseat the government failed.
**1992** There were strikes in southern Togo; Olympio was attacked by soldiers and fled to France. A referendum showed overwhelming support for multiparty politics. A new constitution was adopted.
**1993** Eyadéma won the first multiparty presidential elections amid widespread opposition.
**1994** An antigovernment coup was foiled. The opposition CAR polled strongly in assembly elections. Eyadéma appointed Edem Kodjo of the minority UTD prime minister.
**1996** Kwasi Klutse was appointed prime minister.
**1998** President Eyadéma was re-elected.

**Tokay** sweet white wine made near the Hungarian town of Tokaj; also the grape from which it is made.

**Tokugawa** military family which controlled Japan as ◊shoguns from 1603 to 1868. *Tokugawa Ieyasu* (1542–1616) was the Japanese general and politician who established the Tokugawa shogunate. The Tokugawa were feudal lords who ruled about one-quarter of Japan. Undermined by increasing foreign incursions, they were overthrown by an attack of provincial forces from Chōshū, Satsuma, and Tosa, who restored the Meiji emperor to power.

**Tokyo** capital of Japan, on Honshu island; population (1994) 7,874,000. It is Japan's main cultural, financial, and industrial centre (engineering, chemicals, textiles, electrical goods).

Founded in the 16th century as *Yedo* (or *Edo*), it was renamed when the emperor moved his court here from Kyoto in 1868. By the end of the 18th century, Yedo, with 1 million people, was the largest city in the world. An earthquake in 1923 killed 58,000 people and destroyed much of the city, which was again severely damaged by Allied bombing in World War II when 60% of Tokyo's housing was destroyed; US firebomb raids of 1945 were particularly destructive with over 100,000 people killed in just one night of bombing on 9 March. The subsequent rebuilding has made it into one of the world's most modern cities.

**Tokyo trials** war-crimes trials (1946–48) of Japan's wartime leaders, held during the Allied occupation after World War II. Former prime minister Tōjō was among the seven sentenced to death by an international tribunal, while 16 were given life imprisonment.

Political considerations allowed Emperor ◊Hirohito (Shōwa) to escape trial.

**Toledo** capital of Toledo province in Castilla–La Mancha, central Spain, built on a rock above the River Tagus; population (1990) 60,700. It was the capital of the Visigoth kingdom from 534–711 (see ◊Goth), then became a Moorish city, and was the Castilian capital from 1085–1560. Knives, silks, and ceramics are manufactured here. There is a Gothic cathedral (13th–17th centuries) and several churches which preserve paintings by El Greco. The alcazar (fortified palace) was rebuilt after the successful Nationalist defence of Toledo in the Spanish Civil War (1936–39) and became a Nationalist shrine.

**Tolpuddle Martyrs** six farm labourers of Tolpuddle, a village in Dorset, southwest England, who were transported to Australia in 1834 after being sentenced for 'administering unlawful oaths' – as a 'union', they had threatened to withdraw their labour unless their pay was guaranteed, and had been prepared to put this in writing. They were pardoned two years later, after nationwide agitation. They returned to England and all but one migrated to Canada.

**Tolstoy, Leo Nikolaievich** (1828–1910) Russian novelist. He wrote *War and Peace* (1863–69) and *Anna Karenina* (1873–77). He was offended by the materialism of western Europe and in the 1860s and 1870s he became a pioneer of 'free education'. From 1880 he underwent a profound spiritual crisis and took up various moral positions, including passive resistance to evil, rejection of authority (religious or civil) and private ownership, and a return to basic mystical Christianity. He was excommunicated by the Orthodox Church, and his later works were banned.

**Toltec** ('builder') member of an ancient American Indian people who ruled much of Mexico and Central America in the 10th–12th centuries, with their capital and religious centre at Tula or Tollán, northeast of Mexico City. They also occupied and extended the ancient Maya city of Chichen Itzá in Yucatán. After the fall of the Toltecs the Aztecs took over much of their former territory, except for the regions regained by the Maya.

**toluene** or *methyl benzene,* $C_6H_5CH_3$ colourless, inflammable liquid, insoluble in water, derived from petroleum. It is used as a solvent, in aircraft fuels, in preparing phenol (carbolic acid, used in making resins for adhesives, pharmaceuticals, and as a disinfectant), and the powerful high explosive ◊TNT.

**tomato** annual plant belonging to the nightshade family, native to South America. It is widely cultivated for its shiny, round, red fruit containing many seeds (technically a berry), which is widely used in salads and cooking. (*Lycopersicon esculentum*, family Solanaceae.)

**Tombouctou** or *Timbuktu*, town in Mali, near the most northerly point on the Niger River; population (1996) 20,500 (town); (1987) 453,000 (region). It was a Tuareg camel caravan centre on the fringe of the Sahara from the 11th century. Since 1960 the area surrounding the town has become increasingly arid, and the former canal link with the River Niger is dry. Products include salt.

**tomography** the technique of using X-rays or ultrasound waves to procure images of structures deep within the body for diagnostic purposes. In modern medical imaging there are several techniques, such as the ◊CAT scan (computerized axial tomography).

**ton** imperial unit of mass. The *long ton,* used in the UK, is 1,016 kg/2,240 lb; the *short ton,* used in the USA, is 907 kg/2,000 lb. The *metric ton* or *tonne* is 1,000 kg/2,205 lb.

**ton** in shipping, unit of volume equal to 2.83 cubic metres/100 cubic feet. *Gross tonnage* is the total internal volume of a ship in tons; *net register tonnage* is the volume used for carrying cargo or passengers. *Displacement tonnage* is the weight of the vessel, in terms of the number of imperial tons of seawater displaced when the ship is loaded to its load line; it is used to describe warships.

**tonality** in music, a sense of key orientation in relation to form, for example the step pattern of a dance as expressed by corresponding changes of direction from a tonic or 'home' key to a related key. Most popular and folk music worldwide recognizes an underlying tonality or reference pitch against which the movement of a melody can be clearly heard. The opposite of tonality is atonality.

**tone poem** in music, an alternative name for symphonic poem.

**Tonga** Kingdom of (or *Friendly Islands) national name Pule'anga Fakatu'i 'o Tonga*

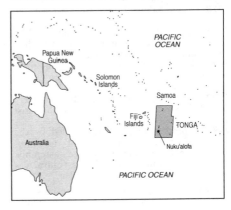

**area** 750 sq km/290 sq mi
**capital** Nuku'alofa (on Tongatapu Island)
**major towns/cities** Pangai, Neiafu
**physical features** three groups of islands in southwest Pacific, mostly coral formations, but actively volcanic in west; of the 170 islands in the Tonga group, 36 are inhabited

**head of state** King Taufa'ahau Tupou IV from 1965

**head of government** Baron Vaea from 1991

**political system** constitutional monarchy

**political parties** legally none, but one prodemocracy grouping, the People's Party

**currency** Tongan dollar or pa'anga

**GNP per capita (PPP)** (US$) 3,860 (1998)

**exports** vanilla beans, pumpkins, coconut oil and other coconut products, watermelons, knitted clothes, cassava, yams, sweet potatoes, footwear. Principal market: Japan 52.9% (1997)

**population** 98,000 (1999 est)

**language** Tongan (official); English

**religion** Free Wesleyan Church

**life expectancy** 68 (men); 72 (women) (1998 est)

**Chronology**

**c. 1000 BC** Settled by Polynesian immigrants from the Fiji Islands.

**c. AD 950** The legendary Aho'eitu became the first hereditary Tongan king (Tu'i Tonga).

**13th–14th centuries** Tu'i Tonga kingdom at the height of its power.

**1643** Visited by the Dutch navigator, Abel Tasman.

**1773** Islands visited by British navigator Capt James Cook, who named them the 'Friendly Islands'.

**1826** Methodist mission established.

**1831** Tongan dynasty founded by a Christian convert and chief of Ha'apai, Prince Taufa'ahau Tupou, who became king 14 years later.

**1845–93** Reign of King George Tupou I, during which the country was reunited after half a century of civil war; Christianity was spread and a modern constitution adopted in 1875.

**1900** Friendship ('Protectorate') treaty signed between King George Tupou II and Britain, establishing British control over defence and foreign affairs, but leaving internal political affairs under Tongan control.

**1918** Queen Salote Tupou III ascended the throne.

**1965** Queen Salote died; she was succeeded by her son, King Taufa'ahau Tupou IV, who had been prime minister since 1949.

**1970** Tonga achieved independence from Britain, but remained within the Commonwealth.

**1993** Six prodemocracy candidates were elected. There were calls for reform of absolutist power.

**1996** A prodemocracy movement led by the People's Party won a majority of the 'commoner' seats in the legislative assembly. Prodemocracy campaigner Akilisis Pohiva was released after a month's imprisonment.

**tongue** in tetrapod vertebrates, a muscular organ usually attached to the floor of the mouth. It has a thick root attached to a U-shaped bone (hyoid), and is covered with a ◊mucous membrane containing nerves and taste buds. It is the main organ of taste. The tongue directs food to the teeth and into the throat for chewing and swallowing. In humans, it is crucial for speech; in other animals, for lapping up water and for grooming, among other functions. In some ani-

mals, such as frogs, it can be flipped forwards to catch insects; in others, such as anteaters, it serves to reach for food found in deep holes.

**tonne** the metric ton of 1,000 kg/2,204.6 lb; equivalent to 0.9842 of an imperial ◊ton.

**tonsillitis** inflammation of the ◊tonsils.

**tonsils** in higher vertebrates, masses of lymphoid tissue situated at the back of the mouth and throat (palatine tonsils), and on the rear surface of the tongue (lingual tonsils). The tonsils contain many ◊lymphocytes and are part of the body's defence system against infection.

**Tonton Macoute** member of a private army of death squads on Haiti. The Tontons Macoutes were initially organized by François ◊Duvalier, president of Haiti 1957–71, and continued to terrorize the population under his successor J C Duvalier. It is alleged that the organization continued to operate after Duvalier's exile to France.

**tooth** in vertebrates, one of a set of hard, bonelike structures in the mouth, used for biting and chewing food, and in defence and aggression. In humans, the first set (20 milk teeth) appear from age six months to two and a half years. The permanent ◊dentition replaces these from the sixth year onwards, the wisdom teeth (third molars) sometimes not appearing until the age of 25 or 30. Adults have 32 teeth: two incisors, one canine (eye tooth), two premolars, and three molars on each side of each jaw. Each tooth consists of an enamel coat (hardened calcium deposits), dentine (a thick, bonelike layer), and an inner pulp cavity, housing nerves and blood vessels. Mammalian teeth have roots surrounded by cementum, which fuses them into their sockets in the jawbones.

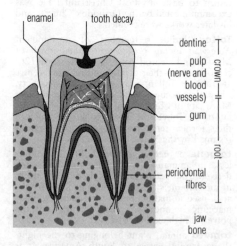

**tooth** *Adults have 32 teeth: two incisors, one canine, two premolars, and three molars on each side of each jaw. Each tooth has three parts: crown, neck, and root. The crown consists of a dense layer of mineral, the enamel, surrounding hard dentine with a soft centre, the pulp.*

The neck of the tooth is covered by the gum, while the enamel-covered crown protrudes above the gum line.

**topaz** mineral, aluminium fluorosilicate, $Al_2(F_2SiO_4)$. It is usually yellow, but pink if it has been heated, and is used as a gemstone when transparent. It ranks 8 on the Mohs scale of hardness.

**topography** the surface shape and composition of the landscape, comprising both natural and artificial features, and its study. Topographical features include the relief and contours of the land; the distribution of mountains, valleys, and human settlements; and the patterns of rivers, roads, and railways.

**topology** branch of geometry that deals with those properties of a figure that remain unchanged even when the figure is transformed (bent, stretched) – for example, when a square painted on a rubber sheet is deformed by distorting the sheet.

Topology has scientific applications, as in the study of turbulence in flowing fluids.

**Torah** in ◊Judaism, the first five books of the Hebrew Bible (Christian Old Testament). It contains a traditional history of the world from the Creation to the death of Moses; it also includes the Hebrew people's covenant with their one God, rules for religious observance, and guidelines for social conduct, including the Ten Commandments.

**Torfaen** unitary authority in south Wales, created in 1996 from part of the former county of Gwent
*area* 98 sq km/38 sq mi
*towns* Pontypool (administrative headquarters), Cwmbran (the first new town in Wales)
*physical* Coity Mountain in the north, River Afon Llwyd
*industries* advanced electronics, automotive, engineering
*population* (1996) 90,700.

**tornado** extremely violent revolving storm with swirling, funnel-shaped clouds, caused by a rising column of warm air propelled by strong wind. A tornado can rise to a great height, but with a diameter of only a few hundred metres or less. Tornadoes move with wind speeds of 160–480 kph/100–300 mph, destroying everything in their path. They are common in the central USA and Australia.

**Toronto** (Huron 'place of meeting') port and capital of ◊Ontario, Canada, at the mouths of the Humber and Don rivers on Lake Ontario; population (1991) 635,400, metropolitan area (1996) 4,444,700. It is a major shipping point on the St Lawrence Seaway, and Canada's main financial, business, commercial, and manufacturing centre. Industries include shipbuilding, food-processing, publishing, and the production of fabricated metals, aircraft, farm machinery, cars, chemicals, and clothing. It is also a tourist and cultural centre, with theatres and a film industry.

**torpedo** or *electric ray,* any species of the order Torpediniformes of mainly tropical rays (cartilaginous fishes), whose electric organs between the pectoral fin and the head can give a powerful shock. They can grow to 180 cm/6 ft in length.

**torpedo** self-propelled underwater missile, invented in 1866 by British engineer Robert Whitehead. Modern torpedoes are homing missiles; some resemble mines in that they lie on the seabed until activated by the acoustic signal of a passing ship. A television camera enables them to be remotely controlled, and in the final stage of attack they lock on to the radar or sonar signals of the target ship.

**torque** the turning effect of force on an object. A turbine produces a torque that turns an electricity generator in a power station. Torque is measured by multiplying the force by its perpendicular distance from the turning point.

**torr** unit of pressure equal to 1/760 of an ◊atmosphere, used mainly in high-vacuum technology.

**torsion** in physics, the state of strain set up in a twisted material; for example, when a thread, wire, or rod is twisted, the torsion set up in the material tends to return the material to its original state. The *torsion balance,* a sensitive device for measuring small gravitational or magnetic forces, or electric charges, balances these against the restoring force set up by them in a torsion suspension.

**tort** in law, a wrongful act for which someone can be sued for damages in a civil court. It includes such acts as libel, trespass, injury done to someone (whether intentionally or by negligence), and inducement to break a contract (although breach of contract itself is not a tort).

**tortoise** reptile of the order Chelonia, family Testudinidae, with the body enclosed in a hard shell. Tortoises are related to the ◊terrapins and ◊turtles, and range in length from 10 cm/4 in to 150 cm/5 ft. The shell consists of a curved upper carapace and flattened lower plastron joined at the sides; it is generally more domed than that of turtles. The head and limbs is withdrawn into it when the tortoise is in danger. Most land tortoises are herbivorous, feeding on plant material, and have no teeth. The mouth forms a sharp-edged beak. They occur in the warmer regions of all continents except Australia. Tortoises have been known to live for 150 years.

**totalitarianism** government control of all activities within a country, overtly political or otherwise, as in fascist or communist dictatorships. Examples of totalitarian regimes are Italy under Benito ◊Mussolini (1922–45); Germany under Adolf ◊Hitler (1933–45); the USSR under Joseph ◊Stalin from the 1930s until his death in 1953; and more recently Romania under Nicolae ◊Ceauşescu (1974–89).

**totalizator** or *Tote,* system of betting on racehorses or greyhounds. All money received is divided in equal shares among winning ticket owners, less expenses. It was first introduced 1928; see ◊betting.

**totemism** (Algonquin Indian 'mark of my family') the belief in individual or clan kinship with an animal, plant, or object. This totem is sacred to those concerned, and they are forbidden to eat or desecrate it; marriage within the clan is usually forbidden. Totemism occurs among Pacific Islanders and Australian Aborigines, and was formerly prevalent throughout Europe, Africa, and Asia. Most American Indian societies had totems as well.

**toucan** any South and Central American forest-dwelling bird of the genus *Ramphastos,* family Ramphastidae, order Piciformes. Toucans have very large, brilliantly coloured beaks and often handsome plumage. They live in small flocks and eat fruits, seeds, and insects. They nest in holes in trees, where the female lays 2–4 eggs; both parents care for the eggs and young. There are 37 species, ranging from 30 cm/1 ft to 60cm/2ft in size.

**touch** sensation produced by specialized nerve endings in the skin. Some respond to light pressure, others to heavy pressure. Temperature detection may also contribute to the overall sensation of touch. Many animals, such as nocturnal ones, rely on touch more than humans do. Some have specialized organs of touch that project from the body, such as whiskers or antennae.

**Toulouse** administrative centre of Haute-Garonne *département* in southwest France, 200 km/125 mi southeast of Bordeaux on the River Garonne; population (1990) 365,900, conurbation 650,000. It is the fourth city of France, a centre of communications, and the seat of an archbishopric and a university, founded in 1229. The town is a marketing, publishing, and banking centre, and its chief industries are textiles, chemicals, metallurgical goods, and aircraft construction; Concorde was built here. It has also become a major European centre of scientific research, especially in aerospace, electronics, data processing, and agriculture.

**Toulouse-Lautrec, Henri (Marie Raymond de)** (1864–1901) French artist. He was active in Paris, where he painted entertainers and prostitutes in a style characterized by strong colours, bold design, and brilliant technical skill. From 1891 his lithographic posters were a great success, skilfully executed and yet retaining the spontaneous character of sketches. His later work was to prove vital to the development of ◊poster art.

**touraco** or *turaco,* any fruit-eating African bird of the family Musophagidae, order Cuculiformes. The touraco has a small high bill, notched and serrated mandibles, a long tail, erectile crest, and short, rounded wings. The largest are 70 cm/28 in long.

**Tour de France** French road race for professional cyclists held annually over approximately 4,800 km/3,000 mi of primarily French roads. The race takes about three weeks to complete and the route varies each year, often taking in adjoining countries, but always ending in Paris. A separate stage is held every day, and the overall leader at the end of each stage wears the coveted 'yellow jersey' (French *maillot jaune*).

**Tower of London** fortress on the bank of the River Thames to the east of the City of London, England. William (I) the Conqueror established a camp here immediately after his coronation in 1066, and in 1078 Gundulf of Bec, Bishop of Rochester, began building the White Tower on the site of British and Roman fortifications. It is the centrepiece of the fortress and probably the finest and best-preserved Norman keep in existence. It is surrounded by two strong walls and a ditch, now dry, and was for centuries a royal residence and the principal state prison.

**toxaemia** another term for ◊blood poisoning; *toxaemia of pregnancy* is another term for pre-eclampsia.

**toxic shock syndrome** rare condition marked by rapid onset of fever, vomiting, and low blood pressure, sometimes leading to death. It is caused by a toxin of the bacterium *Staphylococcus aureus,* normally harmlessly present in the body. It is seen most often in young women using tampons during menstruation.

**toxic waste** dumped ◊hazardous waste.

**toxin** any poison produced by another living organism (usually a bacterium) that can damage the living body. In vertebrates, toxins are broken down by ◊enzyme action, mainly in the liver.

**toxoplasmosis** disease transmitted to humans by animals, often in pigeon or cat excrement, or in undercooked meat. It causes flulike symptoms and damages the central nervous system, eyes, and visceral organs. It is caused by a protozoan, *Toxoplasma gondii.* Congenital toxoplasmosis, transmitted from an infected mother to her unborn child, can lead to blindness and retardation.

**trace element** chemical element necessary in minute quantities for the health of a plant or animal. For example, magnesium, which occurs in chlorophyll, is essential to photosynthesis, and iodine is needed by the thyroid gland of mammals for making hormones that control growth and body chemistry.

**trachea** tube that forms an airway in air-breathing animals. In land-living ◊vertebrates, including humans, it is also known as the *windpipe* and runs from the larynx to the upper part of the chest. Its diameter is about 1.5 cm/0.6 in and its length 10 cm/4 in. It is strong and flexible, and reinforced by rings of ◊cartilage. In the upper chest, the trachea branches into two tubes: the left and right bronchi, which enter the lungs. Insects have a branching network of tubes called tracheae, which conduct air from holes (<◊spiracles) in the body surface to all the body tissues. The finest branches of the tracheae are called tracheoles.

**tracheotomy** or *tracheostomy,* surgical opening in the windpipe (trachea), usually created for the insertion of a tube to enable the patient to breathe. It is done either to bypass an airway impaired by disease or injury, or to safeguard it during surgery or a prolonged period of mechanical ventilation.

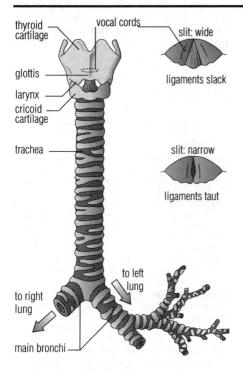

thyroid cartilage

vocal cords

slit: wide

ligaments slack

glottis

larynx

cricoid cartilage

trachea

slit: narrow

ligaments taut

to left lung

to right lung

main bronchi

*trachea* The human trachea, or windpipe. The larynx, or voice box, lies at the entrance to the trachea. The two vocal cords are membranes that normally remain open and still. When they are drawn together, the passage of air makes them vibrate and produce sounds.

**trachoma** chronic eye infection, resembling severe ◊conjunctivitis. The conjunctiva becomes inflamed, with scarring and formation of pus, and there may be damage to the cornea. It is caused by a viruslike organism (◊chlamydia), and is a disease of dry tropical regions. Although it responds well to antibiotics, numerically it remains the biggest single cause of blindness worldwide. In 1999 there were 146 million people suffering with trachoma worldwide, mostly in developing countries.

**tradescantia** any of a group of plants native to North and Central America, with variegated or striped leaves. The spiderwort *T. virginiana* is a cultivated garden plant; the wandering jew *T. albiflora* is a common house plant, with green oval leaves tinged with pink or purple or silver-striped. They are named after English botanist John Tradescant the Younger. (Genus *Tradescantia*, family Commelinaceae.)

**trade union** organization of workers that exists to promote and defend the interests of its members. Trade unions are particularly concerned with pay, working conditions, job security, and redundancy. Four types of trade union are often distinguished: general unions, craft unions, industrial unions, and white-collar unions.

**trade wind** prevailing wind that blows towards the Equator from the northeast and southeast. Trade winds are caused by hot air rising at the Equator and the consequent movement of air from north and south to take its place. The winds are deflected towards the west because of the Earth's west-to-east rotation.

The unpredictable calms known as the ◊doldrums lie at their convergence.

**Trafalgar, Battle of** during the ◊Napoleonic Wars, victory of the British fleet, commanded by Admiral Horatio Nelson, over a combined French and Spanish fleet on 21 October 1805; Nelson was mortally wounded during the action. The victory laid the foundation for British naval supremacy throughout the 19th century. It is named after Cape Trafalgar, a low headland in southwest Spain, near the western entrance to the Straits of Gibraltar.

**tragedy** in the ◊theatre, a play dealing with a serious theme, traditionally one in which a character meets disaster as a result either of personal failings or circumstances beyond his or her control. Historically the classical view of tragedy, as expressed by the Greek tragedians Aeschylus, Euripides, and Sophocles, and the Roman tragedian Seneca, has been predominant in the Western tradition. In the 20th century, tragedies dealing with exalted or heroic figures in an elevated manner have virtually died out. Tragedy has been replaced by dramas with 'tragic' implications or overtones, as in the work of Ibsen, O'Neill, Tennessee Williams, and Osborne, for example, or by the problem plays of Pirandello, Brecht, and Beckett.

**tragicomedy** drama that contains elements of tragedy and comedy; for example, Shakespeare's 'reconciliation' plays, such as *The Winter's Tale*, which reach a tragic climax but then lighten to a happy conclusion. A tragicomedy is the usual form for plays in the tradition of the Theatre of the ◊Absurd, such as Samuel ◊Beckett's *En attendant Godot/Waiting for Godot* (1952) and Tom ◊Stoppard's *Rosencrantz and Guildenstern are Dead* (1967).

**Training Agency** UK government-sponsored organization responsible for retraining of unemployed workers. Founded as the *Manpower Services Commission* in 1974, the organization has operated such schemes as the Training Opportunities Scheme (TOPS) (1974), the Youth Opportunities Programme (YOP) (1978), the Youth Training Scheme (YTS) (1983), and the Technical and Vocational Initiative (TVEI) (1983).

**Trajan** Marcus Ulpius Trajanus (AD 52–117) Roman emperor from AD 98. He conquered Dacia (Romania) in 101–07 and much of ◊Parthia in 113–17, bringing the empire to its greatest extent.

**trampolining** gymnastics performed on a sprung canvas sheet which allows the performer to reach great heights before landing again. Marks are gained for carrying out difficult manoeuvres. Synchronized trampolining and tumbling are also popular forms of the sport.

**tranquillizer** common name for any drug for reducing anxiety or tension (anxiolytic), such as ◊benzodiazepines, barbiturates, antidepressants, and beta-blockers. The use of drugs to control anxiety is becoming much less popular, because most of the drugs available are capable of inducing dependence.

**transactinide element** any of a series of eight radioactive, metallic elements with atomic numbers that extend beyond the ◊actinide series, those from 104 (rutherfordium) to 111 (unununium). They are grouped because of their expected chemical similarities (they are all bivalent), the properties differing only slightly with atomic number. All have ◊half-lives that measure less than two minutes.

**Trans-Alaskan Pipeline** one of the world's greatest civil engineering projects, the construction of a pipeline to carry petroleum (crude oil) 1,285 km/800 mi from northern Alaska to the ice-free port of Valdez. It was completed in 1977 after three years' work and much criticism by ecologists. In 1997 the Pipeline delivered more than 20% of US oil production.

**Trans-Amazonian Highway** or *Transamazonica,* road in Brazil, linking Recife in the east with the provinces of Rondonia, Amazonas, and Acre in the west.

**transcendentalism** philosophy inaugurated in the 18th century by the German philosopher Immanuel Kant. As opposed to metaphysics in the traditional sense, transcendental philosophy is concerned with the conditions of possibility of experience, rather than the nature of being. It seeks to show the necessary structure of our 'point of view' on the world.

**transcendental meditation** (TM), technique of focusing the mind, based in part on Hindu meditation. Meditators are given a mantra (a special word or phrase) to repeat over and over in the mind; such meditation is believed to benefit the practitioner by relieving stress and inducing a feeling of wellbeing and relaxation. It was introduced to the West by Maharishi Mahesh Yogi and popularized by the ◊Beatles in the late 1960s.

**transducer** device that converts one form of energy into another. For example, a thermistor is a transducer that converts heat into an electrical voltage, and an electric motor is a transducer that converts an electrical voltage into mechanical energy. Transducers are important components in many types of sensor, converting the physical quantity to be measured into a proportional voltage signal.

**transformation** in mathematics, a mapping or ◊function, especially one which causes a change of shape or position in a geometric figure. Reflection, rotation, enlargement, and translation are the main geometrical transformations.

**transformer** device in which, by electromagnetic induction, an alternating current (AC) of one voltage is transformed to another voltage, without change of ◊frequency. Transformers are widely used in electrical apparatus of all kinds, and in particular in power transmission where high voltages and low currents are utilized.

**transfusion** intravenous delivery of blood or blood products (plasma, red cells) into a patient's circulation to make up for deficiencies due to disease, injury, or surgical intervention.

Cross-matching is carried out to ensure the patient receives the right blood group. Because of worries about blood-borne disease, there is a growing interest in autologous transfusion with units of the patient's own blood 'donated' over the weeks before an operation.

**transistor** solid-state electronic component, made of ◊semiconductor material, with three or more ◊electrodes, that can regulate a current passing through it. A transistor can act as an amplifier, oscillator, photocell, or switch, and (unlike earlier thermionic valves) usually operates on a very small amount of power. Transistors commonly consist of a tiny sandwich of ◊germanium or ◊silicon, alternate layers having different electrical properties because they are impregnated with minute amounts of different impurities.

**transition metal** any of a group of metallic elements that have incomplete inner electron shells and exhibit variable valency – for example, cobalt, copper, iron, and molybdenum. They are excellent conductors of electricity, and generally form highly coloured compounds.

**transparency** in photography, a picture on slide film. This captures the original in a positive image (direct reversal) and can be used for projection or printing on positive-to-positive print material, for example by the Cibachrome or Kodak R-type process.

**transpiration** the loss of water from a plant by evaporation. Most water is lost from the leaves through pores known as stomata, whose primary function is to allow gas exchange between the plant's internal tissues and the atmosphere. Transpiration from the leaf surfaces causes a continuous upward flow of water from the roots via the ◊xylem, which is known as the transpiration stream.

**transplant** in medicine, the transfer of a tissue or organ from one human being to another or from one part of the body to another (skin grafting). In most organ transplants, the operation is for life-saving purposes, although the immune system tends to reject foreign tissue. Careful matching and immunosuppressive drugs must be used, but these are not always successful.

**transsexual** person who identifies himself or herself completely with the opposite sex, believing that the wrong sex was assigned at birth. Unlike *transvestites,* who desire to dress in clothes traditionally worn by the opposite sex; transsexuals think and feel emotionally in a way typically considered appropriate to members of the opposite sex, and may undergo surgery to modify external sexual characteristics.

**Trans-Siberian Railway** the world's longest single-service railway, connecting the cities of European Russia with Omsk, Novosibirsk, Irkutsk, and Khabarovsk, and terminating at

Nakhodka on the Pacific coast east of Vladivostok. The line was built between 1891 and 1915, and has a total length of 9,289 km/5,772 mi, from Moscow to Vladivostok.

**transubstantiation** in Christian theology, the doctrine that the whole substance of the bread and wine changes into the substance of the body and blood of Jesus when consecrated in the ◊Eucharist.

**transuranic element** or *transuranium element,* chemical element with an atomic number of 93 or more – that is, with a greater number of protons in the nucleus than has uranium. All transuranic elements are radioactive. Neptunium and plutonium are found in nature; the others are synthesized in nuclear reactions.

**Transvaal** former province of northeast South Africa to 1994, when it was divided into Mpumalanga, Northern, and Gauteng provinces. It bordered Zimbabwe to the north, Botswana to the northwest, and Swaziland and Mozambique to the east. It was settled by *Voortrekkers,* Boers who left Cape Colony in the Great Trek from 1831. Independence was recognized by Britain in 1852, until the settlers' difficulties with the conquered Zulus led to British annexation in 1877. It was made a British colony after the South African War (1899–1902), and in 1910 became a province of the Union of South Africa.

**Transylvania** mountainous area of central and northwestern Romania, bounded to the south by the Transylvanian Alps (an extension of the ◊Carpathian Mountains). Formerly a principality, with its capital at Cluj-Napoca, it was part of Hungary from about 1000 until its people voted to unite with Romania in 1918. It is the home of the vampire legends. In a 1996 treaty Hungary renounced its claims on Transylvania.

**trapezium** US trapezoid, in geometry, a four-sided plane figure (quadrilateral) with two of its sides parallel. If the parallel sides have lengths $a$ and $b$ and the perpendicular distance between them is $h$ (the height of the trapezium), its area $A=\frac{1}{2}h\,(\,a+b)$.

**Trappist** member of a Roman Catholic order of monks and nuns, renowned for the strictness of their rule, which includes the maintenance of silence, manual labour, and a vegetarian diet. The order was founded in 1664 at La Trappe, in Normandy, France, by Armand de Rancé (1626–1700) as a reformed version of the Cistercian order.

**travel sickness** nausea and vomiting caused by the motion of cars, boats, or other forms of transport. Constant vibration and movement may stimulate changes in the fluid of the semicircular canals (responsible for balance) of the inner ear, to which the individual fails to adapt, and to which are added visual and psychological factors. Some proprietary remedies contain ◊antihistamine drugs.

**treasure trove** in England, any gold or silver, plate or bullion, found concealed in a house or the ground, the owner being unknown.

Normally, treasure originally hidden, and not abandoned, belongs to the crown, but if the treasure was casually lost or intentionally abandoned, the first finder is entitled to it against all but the true owner. Objects buried with no intention of recovering them, for example in a burial mound, do not rank as treasure trove, and belong to the owner of the ground.

**treaty port** port in Asia where the Western powers had special commercial privileges in the 19th century. As a result of the enforced unequal treaties, treaty ports were established mainly in China, from 1842; and Japan, from 1854 to 1899. Foreigners living in 'concessions' in the ports were not subject to local taxes or laws.

**tree** perennial plant with a woody stem, usually a single stem (trunk), made up of ◊wood and protected by an outer layer of ◊bark. It absorbs water through a ◊root system. There is no clear dividing line between shrubs and trees, but sometimes a minimum achievable height of 6 m/20 ft is used to define a tree.

**trefoil** any of several ◊clover plants of a group belonging to the pea family, the leaves of which are divided into three leaflets. The name is also used for other plants with leaves divided into three lobes. (Genus *Trifolium,* family Leguminosae.)

**trematode** parasitic flatworm with an oval non-segmented body, of the class Trematoda, including the ◊fluke.

**tremor** minor ◊earthquake.

**Trent, Council of** conference held in 1545–63 by the Roman Catholic Church at Trento, northern Italy, initiating the so-called ◊Counter-Reformation; see also ◊Reformation.

**trespass** going on to the land of another without authority. In law, a landowner has the right to eject a trespasser by the use of reasonable force and can sue for any damage caused.

**trial** in law, the determination of an accused person's innocence or guilt by means of the judicial examination of the issues of the case in accordance with the law of the land. The two parties in a trial, the defendant and plaintiff, or their counsels, put forward their cases and question the witnesses; on the basis of this evidence the jury or other tribunal body decides on the innocence or guilt of the defendant.

**trial by ordeal** in the Middle Ages, a test of guilt or innocence.

**triangle** in geometry, a three-sided plane figure, the sum of whose interior angles is 180°. Triangles can be classified by the relative lengths of their sides. A *scalene triangle* has three sides of unequal length; an *isosceles triangle* has at least two equal sides; an *equilateral triangle* has three equal sides (and three equal angles of 60°).

**Triassic** period of geological time 245–208 million years ago, the first period of the Mesozoic era. The continents were fused together to form the world continent Pangaea. Triassic sediments contain remains of early dinosaurs and other reptiles now extinct. By late Triassic times, the first mammals had evolved.

There was a mass extinction of 95% of plants at the end of the Triassic caused by rising temperatures.

**triathlon** test of stamina involving three sports: swimming 3.8 km/2.4 mi, cycling 180 km/112 mi, and running a marathon 42.195 km/26 mi 385 yd, each one immediately following the last.

**tribunal** strictly, a court of justice, but used in English law for a body appointed by the government to arbitrate in disputes, or investigate certain matters. Tribunals usually consist of a lawyer as chair, sitting with two lay assessors.

**tribune** Roman magistrate of plebeian family, elected annually to defend the interests of the common people; only two were originally chosen in the early 5th century BC, but there were later ten. They could veto the decisions of any other magistrate.

**triceratops** any of a genus *Triceratops* of massive, horned dinosaurs of the order Ornithischia. They had three horns and a neck frill and were up to 8 m/25 ft long; they lived in the Cretaceous period.

**Trident** nuclear missile deployed on certain US nuclear-powered submarines and in the 1990s also being installed on four UK submarines. Each missile has eight warheads (MIRVs) and each of the four submarines will have 16 Trident D-5 missiles. The Trident replaced the earlier Polaris and Poseidon missiles.

**Trieste** Slovenian *Trst;* ancient *Tergeste,* port in Friuli-Venezia Giulia, Italy, on the Adriatic coast, opposite Venice; population (1992) 228,400, including a large Slovene minority. It is the largest seaport on the Adriatic, extending for 13 km/8 mi along the Gulf of Trieste. There are large shipyards, and an oil pipeline linked with refineries in Germany and Austria. It is the site of the International Centre for Theoretical Physics, established in 1964.

**triggerfish** any marine bony fish of the family Balistidae, with a laterally compressed body, up to 60 cm/2 ft long, and a deep belly. They have small mouths but strong jaws and teeth. The first spine on the dorsal fin locks into an erect position, allowing them to fasten themselves securely in crevices for protection; it can only be moved by depressing the smaller third ('trigger') spine.

**triglyceride** chemical name for a ◊fat comprising three fatty acids reacted with a glycerol.

**trigonometry** branch of mathematics that solves problems relating to plane and spherical triangles. Its principles are based on the fixed proportions of sides for a particular angle in a right-angled triangle, the simplest of which are known as the ◊sine, ◊cosine, and ◊tangent (so-called trigonometrical ratios). Trigonometry is of practical importance in navigation, surveying, and simple harmonic motion in physics.

**trilobite** any of a large class (Trilobita) of extinct, marine, invertebrate arthropods of the Palaeozoic era, with a flattened, oval body, 1–65 cm/0.4–26 in long. The hard-shelled body was

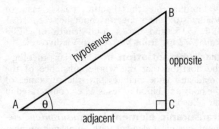

for any right-angled triangle with angle θ as shown the trigonometrical ratios are

$$\sin(\theta) = \frac{BC}{AB} = \frac{\text{opposite}}{\text{hypotenuse}}$$

$$\cos\theta = \frac{AC}{AB} = \frac{\text{adjacent}}{\text{hypotenuse}}$$

$$\tan\theta = \frac{BC}{AC} = \frac{\text{opposite}}{\text{adjacent}}$$

*trigonometry At its simplest level, trigonometry deals with the relationships between the sides and angles of triangles. Unknown angles or lengths are calculated by using trigonometrical ratios such as sine, cosine, and tangent. The earliest applications of trigonometry were in the fields of navigation, surveying, and astronomy, and usually involved working out an inaccessible distance such as the distance of the Earth from the Moon.*

divided by two deep furrows into three lobes. Some were burrowers, others were swimming and floating forms. Their worldwide distribution, many species, and the immense quantities of their remains make them useful in geological dating.

**Trinidad and Tobago** Republic of
***area*** 5,130 sq km/1,980 sq mi including smaller islands (Trinidad 4,828 sq km/1,864 sq mi and Tobago 300 sq km/115 sq mi)

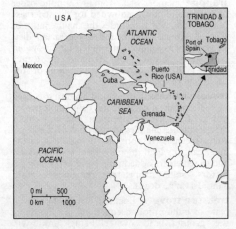

**capital** Port-of-Spain (and port)
**major towns/cities** San Fernando, Arima, Point Fortin
**major ports** Scarborough, Point Lisas
**physical features** comprises two main islands and some smaller ones in Caribbean Sea; coastal swamps and hills east–west
**head of state** Noor Hassanali from 1987
**head of government** Basdeo Panday from 1995
**political system** democracy
**political parties** National Alliance for Reconstruction (NAR), nationalist, left of centre; People's National Movement (PNM), nationalist, moderate, centrist; United National Congress (UNC), left of centre; Movement for Social Transformation (Motion), left of centre
**currency** Trinidad and Tobago dollar
**GNP per capita (PPP)** (US$) 6,720 (1998)
**exports** mineral fuels and lubricants, chemicals, basic manufactures, food. Principal market: USA 39.7% (1997)
**population** 1,288,000 (1999 est)
**language** English (official); Hindi, French, Spanish
**religion** Roman Catholic, Anglican, Hindu, Muslim
**life expectancy** 72 (men); 76 (women) (1995–2000)
**Chronology**
**1498** Visited by the explorer Christopher Columbus, who named Trinidad after the three peaks at its southeastern tip and Tobago after the local form of tobacco pipe. Carib and Arawak Indians comprised the indigenous community.
**1532** Trinidad colonized by Spain.
**1630s** Tobago settled by Dutch, who introduced sugar-cane growing.
**1797** Trinidad captured by Britain and ceded by Spain five years later under Treaty of Amiens.
**1814** Tobago ceded to Britain by France.
**1834** Abolition of slavery resulted in indentured labourers being brought in from India, rather than Africa, to work sugar plantations.
**1889** Trinidad and Tobago amalgamated as British colony.
**1956** The People's National Movement (PNM) founded by Eric Williams, a moderate nationalist.
**1958–62** Part of West Indies Federation.
**1959** Achieved internal self-government, with Williams as chief minister.
**1962** Independence achieved within Commonwealth, with Williams as prime minister.
**1970** Army mutiny and violent Black Power riots directed against minority East Indian population; state of emergency imposed for two years.
**1976** Became a republic, with former governor general Ellis Clarke as president and Williams as prime minister.
**1981** Williams died; succeeded by George Chambers.
**1986** Tobago-based National Alliance for Reconstruction (NAR), headed by Arthur Robinson, won general election.
**1987** Noor Hassanali became president.

**1990** An attempted antigovernment coup by Islamic fundamentalists was foiled.
**1991** A general election resulted in victory for PNM, with Patrick Manning as prime minister.
**1995** The UNC and PNM tied in general election; a UNC–NAR coalition was formed, led by Basdeo Panday.

**Trinity** in Christianity, the union of three persons – Father, Son, and Holy Ghost/Spirit – in one godhead. The precise meaning of the doctrine has been the cause of unending dispute, and was the chief cause of the split between the Eastern Orthodox and Roman Catholic churches. *Trinity Sunday* occurs on the Sunday after Pentecost (Whitsun).

**Triple Alliance** pact from 1882 between Germany, Austria-Hungary, and Italy to offset the power of Russia and France. It was last renewed in 1912, but during World War I Italy's initial neutrality gradually changed and it denounced the alliance in 1915. The term also refers to other alliances: 1668 – England, Holland, and Sweden; 1717 – Britain, Holland, and France (joined in 1718 by Austria); 1788 – Britain, Prussia, and Holland; 1795 – Britain, Russia, and Austria.

**Triple Entente** alliance of Britain, France, and Russia from 1907–17. In 1911 this became a military alliance and formed the basis of the Allied powers in World War I against the Central Powers, Germany and Austria-Hungary.

**triple nose-leaf bat** one of many threatened bats in Africa, *Triaenops persicus* is found scattered along much of the coastal regions of East Africa and faces threats from disturbance of the caves in which it breeds. Tourism development, resulting in disturbance to coral caves which the bats inhabit, is a particular problem.

**Tripura** hill state of northeast India since 1972, formerly a princely state, between Bangladesh and Assam
**area** 10,500 sq km/4,053 sq mi
**capital** Agartala
**physical** four main valleys, separating hills which rise to about 1,000 m/3,300 ft; the south is forested; the Deo, Khowai and Dhalai rivers drain northwards, while the River Gumti flows to the south
**industries** steel, jute, timber, rubber
**agriculture** rice, millet, maize, fruit, cotton, tea, sugar cane
**population** (1994 est) 3,055,000
**language** Bengali, Kokbarak, Manipuri
**religion** Hinduism

**trireme** (Anglicized Latin 'three-oared') ancient Greek warship with three banks of oars. They were used at the Battle of ◊Salamis and by the Romans until the 4th century AD.

**Tristan** or *Tristram*, legendary Celtic hero of a tragic romance. He fell in love with Isolde, the bride he was sent to win for his uncle King Mark of Cornwall. The story became part of the Arthurian cycle and is the subject of Richard Wagner's opera *Tristan und Isolde* (1865).

**tritium** radioactive isotope of hydrogen, three times as heavy as ordinary hydrogen, consisting of one proton and two neutrons. It has a half-life of 12.5 years.

**Triton** in Greek mythology, a merman sea god with the lower body of a dolphin; the son of ◊Poseidon and the sea goddess Amphitrite. Traditionally, he is shown blowing on a conch shell to raise or calm a storm.

**trogon** (Greek *trogein* 'to gnaw') any species of the family Trogonidae, order Trogoniformes, of tropical birds, up to 50 cm/1.7 ft long, with resplendent plumage, living in the Americas, Africa, and Asia. They are primarily birds of forest or woodland, living in trees. Their diet consists mainly of insects and other arthropods, and sometimes berries and other fruit. Most striking is the ◊quetzal.

**Trojan horse** seemingly innocuous but treacherous gift from an enemy. In Greek mythology, during the siege of Troy, an enormous wooden horse left by the Greek army outside the gates of the city. When the Greeks had retreated, the Trojans, believing it to be a religious offering, brought the horse in. Greek soldiers then emerged from within the hollow horse and opened the city gates to enable Troy to be captured.

**trombone** brass wind instrument of mainly cylindrical bore, incorporating a movable slide which allows a continuous glissando (slide) in pitch over a span of half an octave. The longer the tube length, the lower the note. All the notes of the chromatic scale are therefore available by placing the slide in any of seven basic positions, and blowing a harmonic series of notes built upon each basic note. A descendant of the Renaissance sackbut, the Baroque trombone has a shallow cup mouthpiece and modestly flared bell giving a firm, noble tone, to which the modern wide bell adds a brassy sheen. The tenor and bass trombones are staple instruments of the orchestra and brass band, also of Dixieland and jazz bands, either separately or as a tenor-bass hybrid. The hybrid has a switch which lowers the pitch a fourth from B-flat to F.

**trompe l'oeil** (French 'deceives the eye') painting that gives a convincing illusion of three-dimensional reality. As an artistic technique, it has been in common use in most stylistic periods in the West, originating in Classical Greek art.

**Trondheim** fishing port, and county town of Sor-Trondelag, Norway, at the mouth of the Nid on Trondheim Fjord, 135 km/84 mi northeast of Kristiansund; population (1996) 135,900. It has canning, textile, margarine and soap industries. Originally called Nidaros, it was the medieval capital of Norway. Norwegian kings are crowned in the cathedral (1066–93), which is one of the most celebrated in Scandinavia. Trondheim was occupied by the Germans 1940–45 and used as a U-boat base, and the town was frequently bombed by the Allies.

**tropics** the area between the tropics of Cancer and Capricorn, defined by the parallels of latitude approximately 23°30' north and south of the Equator. They are the limits of the area of Earth's surface in which the Sun can be directly overhead. The mean monthly temperature is over 20°C/68°F.

**tropism** or *tropic movement,* the directional growth of a plant, or part of a plant, in response to an external stimulus such as gravity or light. If the movement is directed towards the stimulus it is described as positive; if away from it, it is negative. *Geotropism* for example, the response of plants to gravity, causes the root (positively geotropic) to grow downwards, and the stem (negatively geotropic) to grow upwards.

**troposphere** lower part of the Earth's ◊atmosphere extending about 10.5 km/6.5 mi from the Earth's surface, in which temperature decreases with height to about –60°C/–76°F except in local layers of temperature inversion. The *tropopause* is the upper boundary of the troposphere, above which the temperature increases slowly with height within the atmosphere. All of the Earth's weather takes place within the troposphere.

**Trotsky, Leon** adopted name of Lev Davidovitch Bronstein (1879–1940) Russian revolutionary. He joined the Bolshevik party and took a leading part in the seizure of power in 1917 and in raising the Red Army that fought the Civil War 1918–20. In the struggle for power that followed ◊Lenin's death in 1924, ◊Stalin defeated Trotsky, and this and other differences with the Communist Party led to his exile in 1929. He settled in Mexico, where he was assassinated at Stalin's instigation. Trotsky believed in world revolution and in permanent revolution (see ◊Trotskyism), and was an uncompromising, if liberal, idealist.

**Trotskyism** form of Marxism advocated by Leon Trotsky. Its central concept is that of *permanent revolution.* In his view a proletarian revolution, leading to a socialist society, could not be achieved in isolation, so it would be necessary to spark off further revolutions throughout Europe and ultimately worldwide. This was in direct opposition to the Stalinist view that socialism should be built and consolidated within individual countries.

**trotting** another name for the sport of ◊harness racing.

**trout** any of various bony fishes in the salmon family, popular for sport and food, usually speckled and found mainly in fresh water. They are native to the northern hemisphere. Trout have thick bodies and blunt heads, and vary in colour. The common trout *Salmo trutta* is widely distributed in Europe, occurring in British fresh and coastal waters. Sea trout are generally silvery and river trout olive-brown, both with spotted fins and sides.

**Troy** also known as Ilium, ancient city in Asia Minor (modern Hissarlik in Turkey), just south of the Dardanelles. It has a long and complex history dating from about 3000 BC to AD 1200. In 1820 the city was identified as Troy, the site of the legendary ten-year Trojan War described in Homer's epic *Iliad,* but its actual name is unknown.

**Troyes** administrative centre of the *département* of Aube in the Champagne-Ardenne region of northeast France, situated on the River Seine 150 km/93 mi southeast of Paris; population (1990) 60,800, conurbation 120,000. The town has an agricultural market, but is also an industrial city manufacturing textiles, machinery and foodstuffs. The hosiery industry remains important. The *Treaty of Troyes* signed by Henry V of England and Charles VI in 1420 recognized Henry as heir to the French throne.

**troy system** system of units used for precious metals and gems. The pound troy (0.37 kg) consists of 12 ounces (each of 120 carats) or 5,760 grains (each equal to 65 mg).

**truffle** any of a group of underground fungi (see ◊fungus), certain of which are highly valued as edible delicacies; in particular, the species *Tuber melanosporum*, generally found growing under oak trees. It is native to the Périgord region of France but is cultivated in other areas as well. It is rounded, blackish-brown, externally covered with warts, and has blackish flesh. (Order Tuberales.)

**Truman, Harry S** (1884–1972) 33rd president of the USA (1945–53), a Democrat. In January 1945 he became vice-president to Franklin D Roosevelt, and president when Roosevelt died in April that year. He used the atomic bomb against Japan to end World War II, launched the ◊Marshall Plan to restore Western Europe's post-war economy, and nurtured the European Community (now the European Union) and NATO (including the rearmament of West Germany).

**trumpet** member of an ancient family of lip-reed instruments existing worldwide in a variety of forms and materials, and forming part of the brass section in a modern orchestra. Its distinguishing features are a generally cylindrical bore and straight or coiled shape, producing a penetrating tone of stable pitch for signalling and ceremonial use. Valve trumpets were introduced around 1820, giving access to the full range of chromatic pitches.

**trust** arrangement whereby a person or group of people (the trustee or trustees) hold property for others (the beneficiaries) entitled to the beneficial interest. A trust can be a legal arrangement under which A is empowered to administer property belonging to B for the benefit of C. A and B may be the same person; B and C may not.

**trypanosomiasis** any of several debilitating long-term diseases caused by a trypanosome (protozoan of the genus *Trypanosoma*). They include sleeping sickness in Africa, transmitted by the bites of ◊tsetse flies, and ◊Chagas's disease in Central and South America, spread by assassin bugs.

**tsetse fly** any of a number of blood-feeding African flies of the genus *Glossina*, some of which transmit the disease nagana to cattle and sleeping sickness to human beings. Tsetse flies may grow up to 1.5 cm/0.6 in long.

**tsunami** Japanese 'harbour wave', ocean wave generated by vertical movements of the sea floor resulting from ◊earthquakes or volcanic activity. Unlike waves generated by surface winds, the entire depth of water is involved in the wave motion. In the open ocean the tsunami takes the form of several successive waves, rarely in excess of 1 m/3 ft in height but travelling at speeds of 650–800 kph/400–500 mph. In the coastal shallows tsunamis slow down and build up, producing huge swells over 15 m/45 ft high in some cases and over 30 m/90 ft in rare instances. The waves sweep inland, often causing great loss of life and property. On 26 May 1983, an earthquake in the Pacific Ocean caused tsunamis up to 14 m/42 ft high, which killed 104 people along the west coast of Japan near Minehama, Honshu.

**Tswana** member of the majority ethnic group living in Botswana. The Tswana are divided into four subgroups: the Bakwena, Bamangwato, Bangwaketse, and Batawana. The Tswana language belongs to the Bantu branch of the Niger-Congo family.

**Tuareg** plural same, (Arabic *tawarek* 'God-forsaken') member of one of a group of eight nomadic peoples, mainly stock breeders, from west and central Sahara and Sahel (Algeria, Libya, Mali, Niger, and Burkina Faso). Their language, Tamashek, belongs to the Berber branch of the Hamito-Semitic family and is spoken by 500,000–850,000 people. Many are Muslims.

**tuatara** lizardlike reptile of the genus *Sphenodon*. It grows up to 70 cm/2.3 ft long, is greenish black, and has a spiny crest down its back. On the top of its head is the ◊pineal body, or so-called 'third eye', linked to the brain, which probably acts as a kind of light meter. It is the sole survivor of the reptilian order Rhynchocephalia. It lays eggs in burrows that it shares with seabirds, and has the longest incubation period of all reptiles (up to 15 months).

**tuba** member of a family of valved lip-reed brass instruments of conical bore and deep, mellow tone, introduced around 1830 as bass members of the orchestra brass section and the brass band. The tuba is surprisingly agile and delicate for its size and pitch, qualities exploited by Berlioz, Ravel, and Vaughan Williams.

**tuber** swollen region of an underground stem or root, usually modified for storing food. The potato is a *stem tuber*, as shown by the presence of terminal and lateral buds, the 'eyes' of the potato. *Root tubers*, for example dahlias, developed from adventitious roots (growing from the stem, not from other roots) lack these. Both types of tuber can give rise to new individuals and so provide a means of ◊vegetative reproduction. *See illustration on page 914.*

**tuberculosis** (TB) formerly known as *consumption* or *phthisis*, infectious disease caused by the bacillus *Mycobacterium tuberculosis*. It takes several forms, of which pulmonary tuberculosis is by far the most common. A vaccine, ◊BCG, was developed around 1920 and the first antituberculosis drug, streptomycin, in 1944. The bacterium is mostly kept in check by the body's immune system; about 5% of those infected develop the disease. Treatment of

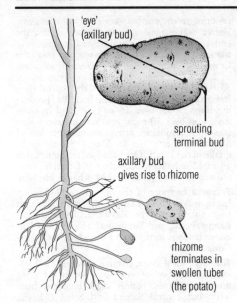

'eye'
(axillary bud)

sprouting
terminal bud

axillary bud
gives rise to rhizome

rhizome
terminates in
swollen tuber
(the potato)

**tuber** *Tubers are produced underground from stems, as in the potato, or from roots, as in the dahlia. Tubers can grow into new plants.*

patients with a combination of anti-TB medicines for 6–8 months produces a cure rate of 80%. There are 7 million new cases of TB annually worldwide (1998) and 3 million deaths.

**TUC** abbreviation for *Trades Union Congress.*

**Tucson** (Papago 'foot of the mountain') city in southeast Arizona, USA, on the Santa Cruz and Rillito rivers, 105 km/66 mi north of the Mexican border; population (1996 est) 449,000. It stands 760 m/2,500 ft above sea level in the Sonora Desert; the Santa Catalina Mountains rise to about 2,750 m/9,000 ft to the northeast. The area's winter sports and mild, dry, sunny winter climate have made the city a popular winter residence and resort. Industries include copper-smelting, and the manufacture of aircraft and electronics. Cotton and cattle are marketed and processed from the surrounding irrigated agricultural area.

**Tudjman, Franjo** (1922–  ) Croatian nationalist leader and historian, president from 1990. As leader of the centre-right Croatian Democratic Union (CDU), he led the fight for Croatian independence. During the 1991–92 civil war, his troops were hampered by lack of arms and the military superiority of the Serb-dominated federal army, but Croatia's independence was recognized following a successful United Nations-negotiated ceasefire in January 1992. Tudjman was re-elected in August 1992 and again in October 1995. Despite suffering from stomach cancer, he was re-elected president in June 1997.

**Tudor dynasty** English dynasty 1485–1603, founded by Henry VII, who became king by overthrowing Richard III (the last of the York dynasty) at the Battle of Bosworth. Henry VII reigned from 1485 to 1509, and was succeeded by Henry VIII (reigned 1509–47); Edward VI (reigned 1547–53); Mary (reigned 1553–58); and Elizabeth I (reigned 1558–1603). Elizabeth died childless and the throne of England passed to her cousin James VI of Scotland, who thus became James I of England and the first of the Stuart line.

**tufa** or *travertine,* soft, porous, ◊limestone rock, white in colour, deposited from solution from carbonate-saturated ground water around hot springs and in caves.

**tulip** any of a group of spring-flowering bulbous plants belonging to the lily family, usually with single goblet-shaped flowers on the end of an upright stem and narrow oval leaves with pointed ends. Tulips come in a large range of shapes, sizes, and colours and are widely cultivated as a garden flower. (Genus *Tulipa,* family Liliaceae.)

**tumour** overproduction of cells in a specific area of the body, often leading to a swelling or lump. Tumours are classified as *benign* or *malignant* (see ◊cancer). Benign tumours grow more slowly, do not invade surrounding tissues, do not spread to other parts of the body, and do not usually recur after removal. However, benign tumours can be dangerous in areas such as the brain. The most familiar types of benign tumour are warts on the skin. In some cases, there is no sharp dividing line between benign and malignant tumours.

**tuna** any of various large marine bony fishes of the mackerel family, especially the genus *Thunnus,* popular as food and game. *Albacore T. alalunga, bluefin tuna T. thynnus,* and *yellowfin tuna T. albacares* are commercially important.

**tundra** region of high latitude almost devoid of trees, resulting from the presence of ◊permafrost. The vegetation consists mostly of grasses, sedges, heather, mosses, and lichens. Tundra stretches in a continuous belt across northern North America and Eurasia. Tundra is also used to describe similar conditions at high altitudes.

**tungsten** (Swedish *tung sten* 'heavy stone') hard, heavy, grey-white, metallic element, symbol W (from German *Wolfram*), atomic number 74, relative atomic mass 183.85. It occurs in the minerals wolframite, scheelite, and hubertite. It has the highest melting point of any metal (3,410°C/6,170°F) and is added to steel to make it harder, stronger, and more elastic; its other uses include high-speed cutting tools, electrical elements, and thermionic couplings. Its salts are used in the paint and tanning industries.

**Tunguska Event** explosion at Tunguska, central Siberia, Russia, in June 1908, which devastated around 6,500 sq km/2,500 sq mi of forest. It is thought to have been caused by either a cometary nucleus or a fragment of Encke's comet about 200 m/220 yards across, or possibly an asteroid. The magnitude of the explosion was equivalent to an atom bomb (10–20 megatons) and produced a colossal shock wave; a bright falling object was seen 600 km/375 mi away and was heard up to 1,000 km/625 mi away.

**tunicate** any marine ◊chordate of the subphylum Tunicata (Urochordata), for example the ◊sea squirt. Tunicates have transparent or translucent tunics made of cellulose. They vary in size from a few millimetres to 30 cm/1 ft in length, and are cylindrical, circular, or irregular in shape. There are more than 1,000 species.

**Tunis** capital and chief port of Tunisia; population (1994) 674,100. Industries include chemicals, textiles, engineering, lead smelting, and distilling. Velvets, silks, linen, and fez caps are also manufactured. Exports include phosphates, iron ore, fruit, and vegetables. Founded by the Arabs, it was captured by the Turks in 1533, then occupied by the French in 1881 and by the Axis powers 1942–43. The ruins of ancient ◊Carthage are to the northeast.

**Tunisia** Tunisian Republic
*national name* al-Jumhuriya at-Tunisiya

*area* 164,150 sq km/63,378 sq mi
*capital* Tunis (and chief port)
*major towns/cities* Sfax, Ariana, Bizerte, Djerba, Gabès, Sousse, Kairouan, Bardo, La Goulette
*major ports* Sfax, Sousse, Bizerte
*physical features* arable and forested land in north graduates towards desert in south; fertile island of Jerba, linked to mainland by causeway (identified with island of lotus-eaters); Shott el Jerid salt lakes
*head of state* Zine el-Abidine Ben Ali from 1987
*head of government* Hamed Karoui from 1989
*political system* emergent democracy
*political parties* Constitutional Democratic Rally (RCD), nationalist, moderate, socialist; Popular Unity Movement (MUP), radical, left of centre; Democratic Socialists Movement (MDS), left of centre; Renovation Movement (MR), reformed communists
*currency* Tunisian dinar

*GNP per capita (PPP)* (US$) 5,160 (1998)
*exports* textiles and clothing, crude petroleum, phosphates and fertilizers, olive oil, fruit, leather and shoes, fishery products, machinery and electrical appliances. Principal market: France 27% (1998)
*population* 9,460,000 (1999 est)
*language* Arabic (official); French
*religion* Sunni Muslim; Jewish, Christian
*life expectancy* 68 (men); 71 (women) (1995–2000)
*Chronology*
*814 BC* Phoenician emigrants from Tyre, in Lebanon, founded Carthage, near modern Tunis, as a trading post. By 6th century BC Carthaginian kingdom dominated western Mediterranean.
*146 BC* Carthage destroyed by Punic Wars with Rome, which began 264 BC; Carthage became part of Rome's African province.
*AD 533* Came under control of Byzantine Empire.
*7th century* Invaded by Arabs, who introduced Islam. Succession of Islamic dynasties followed, including Aghlabids (9th century), Fatimids (10th century), and Almohads (12th century).
*1574* Became part of Islamic Turkish Ottoman Empire and a base for 'Barbary Pirates' who operated against European shipping until 19th century.
*1705* Husayn Bey founded local dynasty, which held power under rule of Ottomans.
*early 19th century* Ahmad Bey launched programme of economic modernization, which was to nearly bankrupt the country.
*1881* Became French protectorate, with Bey retaining local power.
*1920* Destour (Constitution) Party, named after original Tunisian constitution of 1861, founded to campaign for equal Tunisian participation in French-dominated government.
*1934* Habib Bourguiba founded radical splinter party, the Neo-Destour Party, to spearhead nationalist movement.
*1942–43* Brief German occupation during World War II.
*1956* Independence achieved as monarchy under Bey, with Bourguiba as prime minister.
*1957* Bey deposed; Tunisia became one-party republic with Bourguiba as president.
*1975* Bourguiba made president for life.
*1979* Headquarters for Arab League moved to Tunis after Egypt signed Camp David Accords with Israel.
*1981* Multiparty elections held, as a sign of political liberalization, but were won by Bourguiba's Destourian Socialist Party (DSP).
*1982* Allowed Palestine Liberation Organization (PLO) to use Tunis for its headquarters.
*1985* Diplomatic relations with Libya severed; Israel attacked PLO headquarters.
*1987* Zine el-Abidine Ben Ali, new prime minister, declared Bourguiba (now aged 84) incompetent for government and seized power as president.
*1988* 2,000 political prisoners freed; privatization initiative. Diplomatic relations with Libya restored. DSP renamed RCD.

**1990** The Arab League's headquarters returned to Cairo, Egypt.

**1991** There was opposition to US actions during the Gulf War, and a crackdown on religious fundamentalists.

**1992** Human-rights transgressions provoked Western criticism.

**1994** Ben Ali and the RCD were re-elected. The PLO transferred its headquarters to Gaza City in Palestine.

**tunnel** passageway through a mountain, under a body of water, or underground. Tunnelling is a significant branch of civil engineering in both mining and transport. The difficulties naturally increase with the size, length, and depth of tunnel, but with the mechanical appliances now available no serious limitations are imposed. Granite or other hard rock presents little difficulty to modern power drills. In recent years there have been notable developments in linings (for example, concrete segments and steel liner plates), and in the use of rotary diggers and cutters and explosives.

**tunny** another name for ◊tuna.

**turbine** engine in which steam, water, gas, or air is made to spin a rotating shaft by pushing on angled blades, like a fan. Turbines are among the most powerful machines. Steam turbines are used to drive generators in power stations and ships' propellers; water turbines spin the generators in hydroelectric power plants; and gas turbines (as jet engines) power most aircraft and drive machines in industry.

**turbocharger** turbine-driven device fitted to engines to force more air into the cylinders, producing extra power. The turbocharger consists of a 'blower', or compressor, driven by a turbine, which in most units is driven by the exhaust gases leaving the engine.

**turbofan** jet engine of the type used by most airliners, so called because of its huge front fan. The fan sends air not only into the engine for combustion but also around the engine for additional thrust. This results in a faster and more fuel-efficient propulsive jet.

**turbot** any of various flatfishes of the flounder group prized as food, especially *Scophthalmus maximus* found in European waters. It grows up to 1 m/3 ft long and weighs up to 14 kg/30 lb. It is brownish above and whitish underneath.

**Turin** Italian *Torino;* ancient *Augusta Taurinorum,* capital of Piedmont, northwest

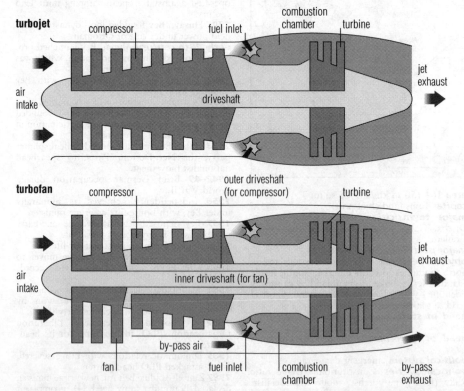

**turbofan** *Two forms of jet engine. In the turbojet, air passing into the air intake is compressed by the compressor and fed into the combustion chamber where fuel burns. The hot gases formed are expelled at high speed from the rear of the engine, driving the engine forwards and turning a turbine which drives the compressor. In the turbofan, some air flows around the combustion chamber and mixes with the exhaust gases. This arrangement is more efficient and quieter than the turbojet.*

Italy, at the confluence of the rivers Po and Dora Riparia; population (1992) 952,700. It stands at the foot of the Alps, commanding road and rail routes between France and Italy. Iron, steel, cars, silk and other textiles, fashion goods, chocolate, and wine are produced. There is a university (1404), and a 15th-century cathedral. Turin was the first capital of united Italy (1861–64).

**Turin shroud** ancient piece of linen bearing the image of a body, claimed to be that of Jesus. Independent tests carried out 1988 by scientists in Switzerland, the USA, and the UK showed that the cloth of the shroud dated from between 1260 and 1390. The shroud, property of the pope, is kept in Turin Cathedral, Italy. A more detailed 20-year study published 1997 revealed that the shroud was made, around 1325, by daubing a man in red ochre paint and then wrapping him tightly in the linen sheet. Vermillion paint was then splashed on the head and wrists to suggest blood stains. Why it was made, and by whom, remains a mystery.

**Turk** or *Turkic,* member of any of the Turkic-speaking peoples of Asia and Europe, especially the principal ethnic group of Turkey. Turkic languages belong to the Altaic family and include Uzbek, Ottoman, Turkish, Azeri, Turkoman, Tatar, Kirghiz, and Yakut. The ancestors of the Turks were pastoral nomads in central Asia. Islam was introduced during the 7th century.

**Turkestan** historical area of Central Asia extending from the Caspian Sea in the west to the Gobi desert in the east. It is now divided among Kazakhstan, Kyrgyzstan, Tajikistan, Turkmenistan, Uzbekistan, Afghanistan (Northeast province), and China (part of Xinjiang Uygur province). It formerly covered an area of some 2,600,000 sq km/1,003,680 sq mi; its principal cities were ◊Tashkent, ◊Samarkand, and ◊Bukhara.

**Turkey** Republic of
*national name Türkiye Cumhuriyeti*

**area** 779,500 sq km/300,964 sq mi
**capital** Ankara
**major towns/cities** Istanbul, Izmir, Adana, Bursa, Antakya, Gaziantep, Konya, Mersin, Kayseri, Edirne, Antalya
**major ports** Istanbul and Izmir
**physical features** central plateau surrounded by mountains, partly in Europe (Thrace) and partly in Asia (Anatolia); Bosporus and Dardanelles; Mount Ararat (highest peak Great Ararat, 5,137 m/16,854 ft); Taurus Mountains in southwest (highest peak Kaldi Dag, 3,734 m/12,255 ft); sources of rivers Euphrates and Tigris in east
**head of state** Suleiman Demirel from 1993
**head of government** Bülent Ecevit from 1999
**political system** democracy
**political parties** Motherland Party (ANAP), Islamic, nationalist, right of centre; Republican People's Party (CHP), centre left; True Path Party (DYP), centre right, pro-Western; Virtue Party (FP), Islamic fundamentalist
**currency** Turkish lira
**GNP per capita (PPP)** (US$) 5,830 (1998 est)
**exports** textiles and clothing, agricultural products and foodstuffs (including figs, nuts, and dried fruit), tobacco, leather, glass, refined petroleum and petroleum products. Principal market: Germany 20.3% (1998)
**population** 65,546,000 (1999 est)
**language** Turkish (official); Kurdish, Arabic
**religion** Sunni Muslim; Orthodox, Armenian churches
**life expectancy** 67 (men); 72 (women) (1995–2000)
*Chronology*
**1st century BC** Asia Minor became part of Roman Empire, later passing to Byzantine Empire.
**6th century AD** Turkic peoples spread from Mongolia into Turkestan, where they adopted Islam.
**1055** Seljuk Turks captured Baghdad; their leader Tughrul took title of sultan.
**1071** Battle of Manzikert: Seljuk Turks defeated Byzantines and conquered Asia Minor.
**13th century** Ottoman Turks, driven west by Mongols, became vassals of Seljuk Turks.
**c. 1299** Osman I founded small Ottoman kingdom, which quickly displaced Seljuks to include all Asia Minor.
**1354** Ottoman Turks captured Gallipoli and began their conquests in Europe.
**1389** Battle of Kossovo: Turks defeated Serbs to take control of most of Balkan peninsula.
**1453** Constantinople, capital of Byzantine Empire, fell to the Turks; became capital of Ottoman Empire as Istanbul.
**16th century** Ottoman Empire reached its zenith under Suleiman the Magnificent 1520–66; Turks conquered Egypt, Syria, Arabia, Mesopotamia, Tripoli, Cyprus, and most of Hungary.
**1683** Failure of Siege of Vienna marked start of decline of Ottoman Empire.
**1699** Treaty of Karlowitz: Turks forced out of Hungary by Austrians.
**1774** Treaty of Kuchuk Kainarji: Russia drove Turks from Crimea and won the right to intervene on behalf of Christian subjects of the sultan.
**19th century** 'The Eastern Question': Ottoman weakness caused intense rivalry between powers

to shape future of Near East.

**1821–29** Greek war of independence: Greeks defeated Turks with help of Russia, Britain, and France.

**1854–56** Crimean War: Britain and France fought to defend Ottoman Empire from further pressure by Russians.

**1877–78** Russo-Turkish War ended with Treaty of Berlin and withdrawal of Turks from Bulgaria.

**1908** Young Turk revolution forced sultan to grant constitution; start of political modernization.

**1911–12** Italo-Turkish War: Turkey lost Tripoli (Libya).

**1912–13** Balkan War: Greece, Serbia, and Bulgaria expelled Turks from Macedonia and Albania.

**1914** Ottoman Empire entered World War I on German side.

**1919** Following Turkish defeat, Mustapha Kemal launched nationalist revolt to resist foreign encroachments.

**1920** Treaty of Sèvres partitioned Ottoman Empire, leaving no part of Turkey fully independent.

**1922** Kemal, having defied Allies, expelled Greeks, French, and Italians from Asia Minor; sultanate abolished.

**1923** Treaty of Lausanne recognized Turkish independence; secular republic established by Kemal, who imposed rapid westernization.

**1935** Kemal adopted surname Atatürk ('Father of the Turks').

**1938** Death of Kemal Atatürk; succeeded as president by Ismet Inönü.

**1950** First free elections won by opposition Democratic Party; Adnan Menderes became prime minister.

**1952** Turkey became a member of NATO.

**1960** Military coup led by Gen Cemal Gürsel deposed Menderes, who was executed in 1961.

**1961** Inönü returned as prime minister; politics dominated by the issue of Cyprus.

**1965** Justice Party came to power under Suleyman Demirel.

**1971–73** Prompted by strikes and student unrest, army imposed military rule.

**1974** Turkey invaded northern Cyprus.

**1980–83** Political violence led to further military rule.

**1984** Kurds began guerrilla war in quest for greater autonomy.

**1989** Application to join European Community rejected.

**1990–91** Turkey joined the UN coalition against Iraq in the Gulf War.

**1995** Turkish offensives against Kurdish bases in northern Iraq; the Islamicist Welfare Party won the largest number of seats in general election.

**1997** Plans were agreed for the curbing of Muslim fundamentalism. Mesut Yilmaz appointed prime minister. Agreement was reached with Greece on the peaceful resolution of disputes.

**1998** The Islamic Welfare Party (RP) was banned by Constitutional Court, and regrouped as the Virtue Party (FP). Prime Minister Mesut Yilmaz lost a vote of confidence and was replaced by Yalim Erez.

**1999** Yalim Erez failed in early January 1999 to form a government and was replaced as prime minister by Bülent Ecevit. Ecevit's ruling centre-left party won the majority of seats in a general election.

**turkey** any of several large game birds of the pheasant family, Meleagrididae, order Galliformes, native to the Americas. The wild turkey *Meleagris galloparvo* reaches a length of 1.3 m/4.3 ft, and is native to North and Central American woodlands. The domesticated turkey derives from the wild species. Turkeys in the wild lay a single clutch of 12 eggs every spring, whereas domestic turkeys lay 120 over 27 weeks. Wild turkeys weigh up to 10 kg/22 lb; domestic turkeys up to 30 kg/66 lb. The ocellated turkey *Agriocharis ocellata* is found in Central America; it has eyespots on the tail.

**Turkish language** language of central and West Asia, the national language of Turkey. It belongs to the Altaic language family. Varieties of Turkish are spoken in northwestern Iran and several of the Central Asian Republics, and all have been influenced by Arabic and Persian. Originally written in Arabic script, it has been written within Turkey in a variant of the Roman alphabet since 1928.

**Turkmenistan** Republic of

**area** 488,100 sq km/188,455 sq mi
**capital** Ashgabat
**major towns/cities** Chardzhov, Mary (Merv), Nebit-Dag, Krasnovodsk
**major ports** Turkmenbashi
**physical** about 90% of land is desert including the Kara Kum 'Black Sands' desert (area 310,800 sq km/120,000 sq mi)
**head of state and government** Saparmurad piyazov from 1991
**political system** authoritarian nationalist

**political parties** Democratic Party of Turkmenistan, ex-communist, pro-Niyazov; Turkmen Popular Front (Agzybirlik), nationalist
**currency** manat
**GNP per capita (PPP)** (US$) 1,480 (1998 est)
**exports** natural gas, cotton yarn, electric energy, petroleum and petroleum products. Principal market: Ukraine 43.6% (1997)
**population** 4,384,000 (1999 est)
**language** West Turkic, closely related to Turkish
**religion** Sunni Muslim
**life expectancy** 62 (men); 69 (women) (1995–2000)
**Chronology**
**6th century BC** Part of Persian Empire of Cyrus the Great.
**4th century BC** Part of empire of Alexander the Great of Macedonia.
**7th century** Spread of Islam into Transcaspian region, followed by Arab rule from 8th century.
**10th–13th centuries** Immigration from northeast by nomadic Oghuz Seljuk and Mongol tribes, whose Turkic-speaking descendants now dominate the country; conquest by Genghis Khan.
**16th century** Came under dominance of Persia, to the south.
**1869–81** Fell under control of tsarist Russia after 150,000 Turkmen were killed in Battle of Gok Tepe in 1881; became part of Russia's Turkestan Governor-Generalship.
**1916** Turkmen revolted violently against Russian rule; autonomous Transcaspian government formed after Russian Revolution of 1917.
**1919** Brought back under Russian control following invasion by the Soviet Red Army.
**1921** Part of Turkestan Soviet Socialist Autonomous Republic.
**1925** Became constituent republic of USSR.
**1920s–30s** Soviet programme of agricultural collectivization and secularization provoked sporadic guerrilla resistance and popular uprisings.
**1960–67** Lenin Kara-Kum Canal built, leading to dramatic expansion in cotton production in previously semidesert region.
**1985** Saparmurad Niyazov replaced Muhammad Gapusov, local communist leader since 1971, whose regime had been viewed as corrupt.
**1989** Stimulated by *glasnost* initiative of reformist Soviet leader Mikhail Gorbachev, Agzybirlik 'popular front' formed by Turkmen intellectuals.
**1990** Economic and political sovereignty was declared. Niyazov was elected state president.
**1991** Niyazov initially supported an attempted anti-Gorbachev coup in Moscow. Independence was later declared; Turkmenistan joined the new Commonwealth of Independent States (CIS).
**1992** Joined the Muslim Economic Cooperation Organization and the United Nations; a new constitution was adopted.
**1993** A new currency, the manat, was introduced and a programme of cautious economic reform introduced, with foreign investment in the country's huge oil and gas reserves encouraged. The economy continued to contract.

**1994** A nationwide referendum overwhelmingly backed Niyazov's presidency. Ex-communists won most seats in parliamentary elections.
**1997** Private land ownership was legalized.

**Turkoman** or *Turkman* (plural Turkomen) member of the majority ethnic group in Turkmenistan. They live to the east of the Caspian Sea, around the Kara Kum Desert, and along the borders of Afghanistan, Iraq, Syria, Turkey, and Iran. Their language belongs to the Turkic branch of the Altaic family and is closely related to the language of Turkey.

**Turks and Caicos Islands** British crown colony in the West Indies, the southeastern archipelago of the Bahamas
**area** 430 sq km/166 sq mi
**capital** Cockburn Town on Grand Turk
**features** a group of 30 islands, of which six are inhabited. The largest is the uninhabited *Grand Caicos;* others include *Grand Turk* (1990 population 3,761), *South Caicos* (1,220), *Middle Caicos* (275), *North Caicos* (1,305), *Providenciales* (5,586), and *Salt Cay* (213); since 1982 the Turks and Caicos have developed as a tax haven
**government** governor, with executive and legislative councils (chief minister from 1993 Charles W Misick)
**exports** crayfish and conch (flesh and shell); tourism is important
**currency** US dollar
**population** (1990 est) 12,400, 90% of African descent
**language** English, French Creole
**religion** Christian
**history** uninhabited islands discovered by the Spanish in 1512; they remained unoccupied until British settlers from Bermuda established a salt panning industry in 1678. Secured by Britain in 1766 against French and Spanish claims, the islands were a Jamaican dependency (1873–1962), and became a separate colony in 1962.

**Turku** Swedish *Åbo,* port in southwestern Finland, near the mouth of the River Aura, on the Gulf of Bothnia; population (1992) 160,000. Industries include shipbuilding, engineering, textiles, and food processing. It was the capital of Finland until 1812.

**turmeric** perennial plant belonging to the ginger family, native to India and the East Indies; also the ground powder from its tuberous rhizomes (underground stems), used in curries to give a yellow colour and as a dyestuff. (*Curcuma longa,* family Zingiberaceae.)

**Turner, Joseph Mallord William** (1775–1851) English painter. He was one of the most original artists of his day. He travelled widely in Europe, and his landscapes became increasingly Romantic, with the subject often transformed in scale and flooded with brilliant, hazy light. Many later works anticipate Impressionism, for example *Rain, Steam and Speed* (1844; National Gallery, London).

**Turner Prize** annual prize established in 1984 to encourage discussion about new developments in contemporary British art. £20,000 is awarded to a British artist under the age of 50 for an outstanding exhibition or other presentation of his or her work in the preceding 12 months; the winner is usually announced in November or early December. The Turner Prize has often attracted criticism for not celebrating what is traditionally considered to be art.

**turnip** biennial plant widely cultivated in temperate regions for its edible white- or yellow-fleshed root and young leaves, which are used as a green vegetable. Closely allied to it is the ◊swede (*B. napus*). (*Brassica rapa,* family Cruciferae.)

**turnover** in finance, the value of sales of a business organization over a period of time. For example, if a shop sells 10,000 items in a week at an average price of £2 each, then its weekly turnover is £20,000. The profit of a company is not only affected by the total turnover but also by the rate of turnover.

**turnpike road** road with a gate or barrier preventing access until a toll had been paid, common from the mid-16th to 19th centuries. In 1991, a plan for the first turnpike road to be built in the UK since the 18th century was announced: the privately funded Birmingham northern relief road, 50 km/31 mi long.

**turpentine** solution of resins distilled from the sap of conifers, used in varnish and as a paint solvent but now largely replaced by white spirit.

**Turpin, Dick (Richard)** (1705–1739) English highwayman. The son of an innkeeper, he turned to highway robbery, cattle-thieving, and smuggling, and was hanged at York, England.

**turquoise** mineral, hydrous basic copper aluminium phosphate, $CuAl_6 (PO_4)_4 (OH)_8 5H_2O$. Blue-green, blue, or green, it is a gemstone. Turquoise is found in Australia, Egypt, Ethiopia, France, Germany, Iran, Turkestan, Mexico, and southwestern USA. It was originally introduced into Europe through Turkey, from which its name is derived.

**turtle** freshwater or marine reptile whose body is protected by a shell. Turtles are related to tortoises, and some species can grow to a length of up to 2.5 m/8 ft. Turtles often travel long distances to lay their eggs on the beaches where they were born. Many species have suffered through destruction of their breeding sites as well as being hunted for food and their shells. Unlike tortoises, turtles cannot retract their heads into their shells.

**Tuscany** Italian *Toscana;* Roman *Etruria,* region of north central Italy, on the west coast, comprising the provinces of Massa e Carrara, Arezzo, Florence, Grosseto, Livorno, Lucca, Pisa, Pistoia, and Siena; area 23,000 sq km/8,878 sq mi; population (1992 est) 3,528,700. Its capital is ◊Florence, and its cities include Pisa, Livorno, and Siena. The area is mainly agricultural, producing cereals, wine (Chianti hills), olives (Lucca) and tobacco (plain of Arno); it also has mining of lignite (upper

Arno) and iron (Elba) and marble quarries (Carrara, Apuan Alps). The Tuscan dialect has been adopted as the standard form of Italian.

**Tussaud, Madame** born Anne Marie Grosholtz (1761–1850) French wax-modeller. In 1802 she established an exhibition of wax models of celebrities in London. It was destroyed by fire in 1925, but reopened in 1928.

**Tutankhamen** King (pharaoh) of ancient Egypt of the 18th dynasty, about 1333–1323 BC. A son of Akhenaton (also called Amenhotep IV), he was about 11 at his accession. In 1922 his tomb was discovered by the British archaeologists Lord Carnarvon and Howard Carter in the Valley of the Kings at Luxor, almost untouched by tomb robbers. The contents included many works of art and his solid-gold coffin, which are now displayed in a Cairo museum.

**Tutsi** member of a minority ethnic group living in Rwanda and Burundi. They have politically dominated the ◊Hutu majority and the Twa (or ◊Pygmies) since their arrival in the area in the 14th century. In Burundi, positions of power were monopolized by the Tutsis, who carried out massacres in response to Hutu rebellions, notably in 1972 and 1988. In Rwanda, where the balance of power is more even, Tutsis were massacred in their thousands by Hutu militia during the 1994 civil war.

**Tutu, Desmond Mpilo** (1931– ) South African priest, Anglican archbishop of Cape Town (1986–96) and general secretary of the South African Council of Churches (1979–84). One of the leading figures in the struggle against ◊apartheid in the Republic of South Africa, he was awarded the 1984 Nobel Peace Prize.

**Tuvalu** South West Pacific State of (formerly *Ellice Islands*)

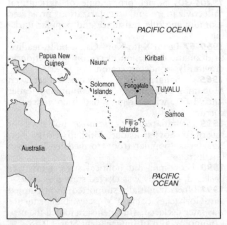

**area** 25 sq km/9.6 sq mi
**capital** Fongafale (on Funafuti atoll)
*major towns/cities* Vaitupu, Niutao, Nanumea
*physical features* nine low coral atolls forming a chain of 579 km/650 mi in the Southwest Pacific

**head of state** Queen Elizabeth II from 1978, represented by governor general Tulaga Manuella from 1994
**head of government** Ionatana Ionatana from 1999
**political system** liberal democracy
**political parties** none; members are elected to parliament as independents
**currency** Australian dollar
**GNP per capita (PPP)** (US$) 1,435 (1996)
**exports** copra. Principal market: Australia
**population** 11,000 (1999 est)
**language** Tuvaluan, English
**religion** Christian (mainly Protestant)
**life expectancy** 63 (men); 66 (women) (1998 est)
**Chronology**
**c. 300 BC** First settled by Polynesian peoples.
**16th century** Invaded and occupied by Samoans.
**1765** Islands first reached by Europeans.
**1850–75** Population decimated by European slave traders capturing Tuvaluans to work in South America and by exposure to European diseases.
**1856** The four southern islands, including Funafuti, claimed by USA.
**1865** Christian mission established.
**1877** Came under control of British Western Pacific High Commission (WPHC), with its headquarters in the Fiji Islands.
**1892** Known as the Ellice Islands, they were joined with Gilbert Islands (now Kiribati) to form British protectorate.
**1916** Gilbert and Ellice Islands colony formed.
**1942–43** Became base for US airforce operations when Japan occupied Gilbert Islands during World War II.
**1975** Following referendum, the predominantly Melanesian-peopled Ellice Islands, fearing domination by Micronesian-peopled Gilbert Islands in an independent state, were granted separate status.
**1978** Independence achieved within Commonwealth, with Toaripi Lauti as prime minister; reverted to former name Tuvalu ('eight standing together').
**1979** The USA signed friendship treaty, relinquishing its claim to the four southern atolls in return for continued access to military bases.
**1981** Dr Tomasi Puapua became premier after Louti implicated in alleged investment scandal.
**1986** Islanders rejected proposal for republican status.
**1989** Bikenibeu Paeniu became prime minister.
**1993** Kamuta Laatasi became prime minister.
**1995** The union flag was removed from the national flag, presaging a move towards republican status.
**1996** Bikenibeu Paeniu became prime minister.
**1999** Ionatana Ionatana became prime minister.

**Twa** ethnic group comprising 1% of the populations of Burundi and Rwanda. The Twa are the aboriginal inhabitants of the region. They are a pygmoid people, and live as nomadic hunter-gatherers in the forests.

**Twain, Mark** pen-name of Samuel Langhorne Clemens (1835–1910) US writer. He established his reputation with the comic masterpiece *The Innocents Abroad* (1869) and two classic American novels, in dialect, *The Adventures of Tom Sawyer* (1876) and *The Adventures of Huckleberry Finn* (1885). He also wrote satire, as in *A Connecticut Yankee at King Arthur's Court* (1889). He is recognized as one of America's finest and most characteristic writers.

**Twelve Tables** in ancient Rome, the earliest law code, drawn from religious and secular custom. It was published on tablets of bronze or wood at the Roman forum *c.* 450 BC, and although these were destroyed in the sack of Rome by Celts in 387 BC, the code survived to have influence into the later Republic.

**twelve-tone system** or *twelve-note system,* method of musical composition invented by Arnold ◊Schoenberg in about 1921 in which all 12 notes of the ◊chromatic scale are arranged in a particular order of the composer's choice, without repeating any of the notes. Such an arrangement is called a 'series' or 'tone row'. The initial series may be transposed, divided, and otherwise mutated to provide a complete resource for all melodic and harmonic material in a work.

**twin** one of two young produced from a single pregnancy. Human twins may be genetically identical (monozygotic), having been formed from a single fertilized egg that splits into two cells, both of which became implanted. Nonidentical (fraternal or dizygotic) twins are formed when two eggs are fertilized at the same time.

**two-stroke cycle** operating cycle for internal combustion piston engines. The engine cycle is completed after just two strokes (up or down) of the piston, which distinguishes it from the more common ◊four-stroke cycle. Power mowers and lightweight motorcycles use two-stroke petrol engines, which are cheaper and simpler than four-strokes.

**Tyler, Wat** (died 1381) English leader of the ◊Peasants' Revolt of 1381. He was probably born in Kent or Essex, and may have served in the French wars. After taking Canterbury, he led the peasant army to Blackheath, outside London, and went on to invade the city. King Richard II met the rebels at Mile End and promised to redress their grievances, which included the imposition of a poll tax. At a further conference at Smithfield, London, Tyler was murdered.

**Tyndale, William** (*c.* 1492–1536) English translator of the Bible. The printing of his New Testament was begun in Cologne in 1525 and, after he had been forced to flee, completed in Worms. Tyndale introduced some of the most familiar phrases to the English language, such as 'filthy lucre', and 'God forbid'. He was strangled and burned as a heretic at Vilvorde in Belgium.

**typesetting** means by which text, or copy, is prepared for ◊printing, now usually carried out by computer.
    Text is keyed on a typesetting machine in a

similar way to typing. Laser or light impulses are projected on to light-sensitive film that, when developed, can be used to make plates for printing.

**typewriter** keyboard machine that produces characters on paper. The earliest known typewriter design was patented by Henry Mills in England in 1714. However, the first practical typewriter was built in 1867 in Milwaukee, Wisconsin, USA, by Christopher Sholes, Carlos Glidden, and Samuel Soulé. By 1873 Remington and Sons, US gunmakers, had produced under contract the first typing machines for sale and in 1878 they patented the first with lower-case as well as upper-case (capital) letters.

**typhoid fever** acute infectious disease of the digestive tract, caused by the bacterium *Salmonella typhi,* and usually contracted through a contaminated water supply. It is characterized by bowel haemorrhage and damage to the spleen. Treatment is with antibiotics.

**typhoon** violent revolving storm, a ♢hurricane in the western Pacific Ocean.

**typhus** any one of a group of infectious diseases caused by bacteria transmitted by lice, fleas, mites, and ticks. Symptoms include fever, headache, and rash. The most serious form is epidemic typhus, which also affects the brain, heart, lungs, and kidneys and is associated with insanitary overcrowded conditions. Treatment is by antibiotics.

**typography** design and layout of the printed word. Typography began with the invention of writing and developed as printing spread throughout Europe after the invention of metal moveable type by Johann ♢Gutenberg in about 1440. Hundreds of variations have followed since, but the basic design of the Frenchman Nicholas Jensen in about 1420–1480), with a few modifications, is still the ordinary ('roman') type used in printing.

Typography, for centuries the domain of engravers and printers, is now a highly-computerized process, and can be carried out on a PC using specialist software.

**tyrannosaur** any of a genus *Tyrannosaurus* of gigantic flesh-eating ♢dinosaurs, order Saurischia, that lived in North America and Asia about 70 million years ago. They had two feet, were up to 15 m/50 ft long, 6.5 m/20 ft tall, weighed 10 tonnes, and had teeth 15 cm/6 in long.

**Tyrol** variant spelling of ♢Tirol, a state of Austria.

**Tyrone** county of Northern Ireland
*area* 3,160 sq km/1,220 sq mi
*towns and cities* Omagh (county town), Dungannon, Strabane, Cookstown
*features* rivers: Derg, Blackwater, Foyle; Lough Neagh; Sperrin Mountains
*industries* mainly agricultural: barley, flax, potatoes, turnips, cattle, sheep, brick making, linen, hosiery, shirts
*population* (1991) 158,500.

**Tyrrhenian Sea** arm of the Mediterranean Sea surrounded by mainland Italy, Sicily, Sardinia, Corsica, and the Ligurian Sea. It is connected to the Ionian Sea through the Straits of Messina. Islands include Elba, Ustica, Capri, Stromboli, and the Lipari Islands. It has a deep seabed plain reaching a maximum depth of 3,620 m/11,876 ft

U

**U2** Irish rock group formed in Dublin, Ireland, in 1977. U2 became one of the most popular and successful rock bands of the 1980s and 1990s, managing to sustain their fanbase throughout two decades by clever reinvention. The group are known for their political views, combining their music with political messages, for example in 'Sunday, Bloody Sunday' (1983) which was an expression of the band's feelings about the violence and conflict in Northern Ireland. The album *The Joshua Tree* (1987) propelled the band to super-stardom, and the band continued to release highly successful and critically acclaimed albums, including *Achtung Baby* in 1992, and *Zooropa* in 1993.

**uakari** any of several rare South American monkeys of the genus *Cacajao*. There are three species, all with bald faces and long fur. About 55 cm/1.8 ft long in head and body, and with a comparatively short 15 cm/6 in tail, they rarely leap, but are good climbers, remaining in the tops of the trees in swampy forests and feeding largely on fruit. The black uakari is in danger of extinction because it is found in such small numbers already, and the forests where it lives are fast being destroyed.

**UCAS** the Universities and Colleges Admissions Service, central applications service for full-time undergraduate higher-education courses in the UK. Candidates can apply through UCAS for up to six courses at various institutions, and the applications and the responses from the universities and colleges concerned are coordinated through the applications service.

**Uccello, Paolo** adopted name of *Paolo di Dono* (1397–1475) Florentine painter. He was one of the first to experiment with perspective, though his love of detail, decorative colour, and graceful line remained traditional. His works include *St George and the Dragon* (c. 1460, National Gallery, London) and *A Hunt* (c. 1460, Ashmolean Museum, Oxford).

**Ufa** capital of Bashkortostan, central Russian Federation, loacted on the River Belaya, in the western Urals; population (1990) 1,094,000. Ufa is situated near the Tuymazy and Ishimbay fields in the Volga–Ural oil region, and is a centre for oil refining and the production of petrochemicals. One of the main manufacturing cities of the Urals, its industries include aerospace technology, electronic engineering, distilling, and lumbering.

**UFO** abbreviation for ⬦*unidentified flying object.*

**Uganda** Republic of
*area* 236,600 sq km/91,351 sq mi

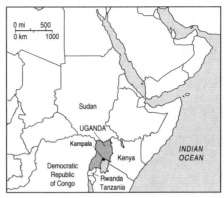

*capital* Kampala
*major towns/cities* Jinja, Mbale, Entebbe, Masaka, Bugembe
*physical features* plateau with mountains in the west (Ruwenzori Range, with Mount Margherita, 5,110 m/16,765 ft); forest and grassland; 18% is lakes, rivers, and wetlands (Owen Falls on White Nile where it leaves Lake Victoria; Lake Albert in west); arid in northwest
*head of state* Yoweri Museveni from 1986
*head of government* Apolo Nsibambi from 1999
*political system* emergent democracy
*political parties* National Resistance Movement (NRM), left of centre; Democratic Party (DP), centre left; Conservative Party (CP), centre right; Uganda People's Congress (UPC), left of centre; Uganda Freedom Movement (UFM), left of centre. From 1986, political parties were forced to suspend activities
*currency* Uganda new shilling
*GNP per capita (PPP)* (US$) 1,170 (1998 est)
*exports* coffee, cotton, tea, tobacco, oil seeds and oleaginous fruit; hides and skins, textiles. Principal market: Spain 14.4% (1997)
*population* 21,143,000 (1999 est)
*language* English (official), Kiswahili, Bantu and Nilotic languages
*religion* Christian 50%, animist 40%, Muslim 10%
*life expectancy* 39 (men); 40 (women) (1995–2000)
*Chronology*
**16th century** Bunyoro kingdom founded by immigrants from southeastern Sudan.
**17th century** Rise of kingdom of Buganda people, which became particularly powerful from 17th century.
**mid-19th century** Arabs, trading ivory and slaves, reached Uganda; first visits by European explorers and Christian missionaries.
**1885–87** Uganda Martyrs: Christians persecuted by Buganda ruler, Mwanga.
**1890** Royal Charter granted to British East African Company, a trading company whose

agent, Frederick Lugard, concluded treaties with local rulers, including the Buganda and the western states of Ankole and Toro.

**1894** British protectorate established, with Buganda retaining some autonomy under its traditional prince (Kabaka) and other resistance being crushed.

**1904** Cotton growing introduced by Buganda peasants.

**1958** Internal self-government granted.

**1962** Independence achieved from Britain, within Commonwealth, with Milton Obote of Uganda People's Congress (UPC) as prime minister.

**1963** Proclaimed federal republic with King Mutesa II (of Buganda) as president and Obote as prime minister.

**1966** King Mutesa, who opposed creation of one-party state, ousted in coup led by Obote, who ended federal status and became executive president.

**1969** All opposition parties banned after assassination attempt on Obote; key enterprises nationalized.

**1971** Obote overthrown in army coup led by Maj-Gen Idi Amin Dada; constitution suspended and ruthlessly dictatorial regime established; nearly 49,000 Ugandan Asians expelled; over 300,000 opponents of regime killed.

**1976** Relations with Kenya strained by Amin's claims to parts of Kenya.

**1979** After annexing part of Tanzania, Amin forced to leave country by opponents backed by Tanzanian troops. Provisional government set up with Yusuf Lule as initial president and then Godfrey Binaisa.

**1978–79** Fighting broke out against Tanzanian troops.

**1980** Binaisa overthrown by army. Elections held and Milton Obote returned to power.

**1985** After opposition by pro-Lule National Resistance Army (NRA), and indiscipline in army, Obote ousted by Gen Tito Okello; constitution suspended; power-sharing agreement entered into with NRA leader Yoweri Museveni.

**1986** Museveni became president, heading broad-based coalition government.

**1993** The King of Buganda was reinstated as formal monarch, in the person of Ronald Muwenda Mutebi II.

**1996** A landslide victory was won by Museveni in the first direct presidential elections.

**1997** Allied Democratic Forces (ADF) led uprisings by rebels.

**UHF** abbreviation for *ultra high frequency,* referring to radio waves of very short wavelength, used, for example, for television broadcasting.

**Uigur** or *Uygur,* member of a Turkic people living in northwestern China, Uzbekistan, Kazakhstan, and Kirgizia; they form about 80% of the population of the Chinese province of Xinjiang Uygur. There are about 5 million speakers of Uigur, a language belonging to the Turkic branch of the Altaic family; it is the official language of the province.

**ukiyo-e** (Japanese 'pictures of the floating world') Japanese colour print depicting scenes from everyday life, the dominant art form in 18th- and 19th-century Japan. Aiming to satisfy the tastes of the increasingly affluent merchant classes, ukiyo-e artists employed bright colours and strong designs, made possible by improvements in block printing, and featured actors, prostitutes, and landscapes among their favoured subjects; over a quarter of all the illustrated ukiyo-e works produced were erotic works. ◊Hiroshige, Utamaro, ◊Hokusai, and Suzuki were leading exponents. The flat decorative colour and lively designs of ukiyo-e prints were later to influence many prominent French avant-garde artists.

## Ukraine

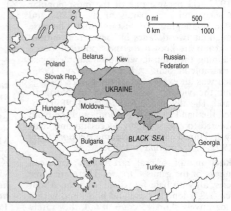

**area** 603,700 sq km/233,088 sq mi
**capital** Kiev
**major towns/cities** Kharkov, Donetsk, Dnepropetrovsk, Lugansk (Voroshilovgrad), Lviv (Lvov), Mariupol (Zhdanov), Krivoy Rog, Zaporozhye, Odessa
**physical features** Russian plain; Carpathian and Crimean Mountains; rivers: Dnieper (with the Dnieper dam 1932), Donetz, Bug
**head of state** Leonid Kuchma from 1994
**head of government** Valery Pustovoitenko from 1997
**political system** emergent democracy
**political parties** Ukrainian Communist Party (UCP), left wing, anti-nationalist (banned 1991–93); Peasants' Party of the Ukraine (PPU), conservative agrarian; Ukrainian Socialist Party (SPU), left wing, anti-nationalist; Ukrainian People's Movement (Rukh), Ukrainian Republican Party (URP), Congress of Ukrainian Nationalists (CUN), and Democratic Party of Ukraine (DPU) – all moderate nationalist; Social Democratic Party of Ukraine (SDPU), federalist
**currency** hryvna
**GNP per capita (PPP)** (US$) 2,420 (1998 est)
**exports** grain, coal, oil, various minerals. Principal market: Russia 23% (1998)
**population** 50,658,000 (1999 est)
**language** Ukrainian (a Slavonic language)
**religion** traditionally Ukrainian Orthodox; also Ukrainian Catholic

*life expectancy* 64 (men); 74 (women) (1995–2000)

**Chronology**

**9th century** Rus' people established state centred on Kiev and adopted Eastern Orthodox Christianity 988.

**1199** Reunification of southern Rus' lands, after period of fragmentation, under Prince Daniel of Galicia-Volhynia.

**13th century** Mongol-Tatar Golden Horde sacked Kiev and destroyed Rus' state.

**14th century** Poland annexed Galicia; Lithuania absorbed Volhynia and expelled Tatars; Ukraine peasants became serfs of Polish and Lithuanian nobles.

**1569** Poland and Lithuania formed single state; clergy of Ukraine formed Uniate Church, which recognized papal authority but retained Orthodox rites, to avoid Catholic persecution.

**16th and 17th centuries** Runaway serfs known as Cossacks ('outlaws') formed autonomous community in eastern borderlands.

**1648** Cossack revolt led by Gen Bogdan Khmelnitsky drove out Poles from central Ukraine; Khmelnitsky accepted Russian protectorate in 1654.

**1660–90** 'Epoch of Ruins': Ukraine devastated by civil war and invasions by Russians, Poles, and Turks; Poland regained western Ukraine.

**1687** Gen Ivan Mazepa entered into alliance with Sweden in effort to regain Cossack autonomy from Russia.

**1709** Battle of Poltava: Russian victory over Swedes ended hopes of Cossack independence.

**1772–95** Partition of Poland: Austria annexed Galicia, Russian annexations included Volhynia.

**1846–47** Attempt to promote Ukrainian national culture through formation of Cyril and Methodius Society.

**1899** Revolutionary Ukrainian Party founded.

**1917** Revolutionary parliament (Rada), proclaimed Ukrainian autonomy within a federal Russia.

**1918** Ukraine declared full independence; civil war ensued between Rada (backed by Germans) and Reds (backed by Russian Bolsheviks).

**1919** Galicia united with Ukraine; conflict escalated between Ukrainian nationalists, Bolsheviks, anarchists, White Russians, and Poles.

**1921** Treaty of Riga: Russia and Poland partitioned Ukraine.

**1921–22** Several million people perished in famine.

**1922** Ukrainian Soviet Socialist Republic (Ukrainian SSR) became part of Union of Soviet Socialist Republics (USSR).

**1932–33** Enforced collectivization of agriculture caused another catastrophic famine with more than 7.5 million deaths.

**1939** USSR annexed eastern Poland and added Galicia-Volhynia to Ukrainian SSR.

**1940** USSR seized northern Bukhovina from Romania and added it to Ukrainian SSR.

**1941–44** Germany occupied Ukraine; many Ukrainians collaborated; millions of Ukrainians and Ukrainian Jews enslaved and exterminated by Nazis.

**1945** USSR annexed Ruthenia from Czechoslovakia and added it to Ukrainian SSR, which became a nominal member of United Nations (UN).

**1946** Uniate Church forcibly merged with Russian Orthodox Church.

**1954** Crimea transferred from Russian Federation to Ukrainian SSR.

**1986** Major environmental disaster caused by explosion of nuclear reactor at Chernobyl, north of Kiev.

**1989** Rukh (nationalist movement) established as political party; ban on Uniate Church lifted.

**1990** Ukraine declared its sovereignty under President Leonid Kravchuk, leader of the CP.

**1991** Ukraine declared its independence from USSR; President Kravchuk left the CP; Ukraine joined the newly formed Commonwealth of Independent States (CIS).

**1992** Crimean sovereignty was declared but then rescinded.

**1994** Election gains were made by radical nationalists in western Ukraine and by Russian unionists in eastern Ukraine; Leonid Kuchma succeeded Kravchuk as president.

**1996** A new constitution replaced the Soviet system, making the presidency stronger; remaining nuclear warheads were returned to Russia for destruction; a new currency was introduced.

**1997** New government appointments were made to speed economic reform. A treaty of friendship was signed with Russia, solving the issue of the Russian Black Sea fleet. Prime Minister Lazarenko was replaced by Valery Pustovoitenko. A loan of $750 million from the International Monetary Fund (IMF) was approved.

**1998** The communists won the largest number of seats in parliamentary elections, but fell short of an absolute majority. The value of the hryvnya fell by over 50% against the US dollar after the neighbouring Russian currency crisis. The government survived a no-confidence vote tabled by left-wing factions that opposed the government's economic program.

**Ukrainian** the majority ethnic group living in Ukraine; there are minorities in Siberian Russia, Kazakhstan, Poland, Slovakia, and Romania. There are 40–45 million speakers of Ukrainian, a member of the East Slavonic branch of the Indo-European family, closely related to Russian. Ukrainian-speaking communities are also found in Canada and the USA.

**Ulaanbaatar** or *Ulan Bator* (formerly until 1924 *Urga,* capital of the Mongolian Republic; a trading centre producing carpets, textiles, and vodka; population (1993) 600,500.

**ulcer** any persistent breach in a body surface (skin or mucous membrane). It may be caused by infection, irritation, or tumour and is often inflamed. Common ulcers include aphthous (mouth), gastric (stomach), duodenal, decubitus ulcers (pressure sores), and those complicating varicose veins.

**Ulster** a former kingdom and province in the north of Ireland, annexed by England in 1461. From Jacobean times it was a centre of English, and later Scottish, settlement on land confiscated from its owners; divided in 1921 into Northern Ireland (counties Antrim, Armagh, Down, Fermanagh, Londonderry, and Tyrone) and the Republic of Ireland (counties Cavan, Donegal, and Monaghan).

**Ulster Defence Association** (UDA), Northern Ireland Protestant paramilitary organization responsible for a number of sectarian killings. Fanatically loyalist, it established a paramilitary wing (the Ulster Freedom Fighters) to combat the ◊Irish Republican Army (IRA) on its own terms and by its own methods. No political party has acknowledged any links with the UDA. In 1994, following a cessation of military activities by the IRA, the UDA, along with other Protestant paramilitary organizations, declared a ceasefire.

**Ulster Freedom Fighters** (UFF), paramilitary wing of the ◊Ulster Defence Association.

**Ulster Unionist Party** also known as the *Official Unionist Party* (*OUP*), the largest political party in Northern Ireland. Right-of-centre in orientation, it advocates equality for Northern Ireland within the UK and opposes union with the Republic of Ireland. The party has the broadest support of any Ulster party, and has consistently won a large proportion of parliamentary and local seats. Its central organization, dating from 1905, is formally called the Ulster Unionist Council. Its leader from 1995 is David Trimble. It secured 28 of the 108 seats in the new Northern Ireland Assembly, elected in June 1998, and Trimble was elected Northern Ireland's first minister at the Assembly's first meeting on 1 July.

**ultrasonics** branch of physics dealing with the theory and application of ultrasound: sound waves occurring at frequencies too high to be heard by the human ear (that is, above about 20 kHz).

**ultrasound scanning** or *ultrasonography,* in medicine, the use of ultrasonic pressure waves to create a diagnostic image. It is a safe, noninvasive technique that often eliminates the need for exploratory surgery.

**ultraviolet radiation** electromagnetic radiation invisible to the human eye, of wavelengths from 400 to 4 nm (where the ◊X-ray range begins). Physiologically, ultraviolet radiation is extremely powerful, producing sunburn and causing the formation of vitamin D in the skin.

**Ulysses** Roman name for ◊Odysseus, the Greek mythological hero.

**Umar** (*c.* 581–644) Muslim caliph (civic and religious leader of Islam) in 634–44, succeeding Abu Bakr. He laid the foundations of a regular, organized Muslim army, employing the brilliant Khalid ibn al-Walid to lead his armies in battle, and conquered Syria, Palestine, Egypt, and Persia. He was murdered by a Persian slave. The Mosque of Omar in Jerusalem is attributed to him.

**Umayyad dynasty** Arabian dynasty of the Islamic Empire who reigned as caliphs (civic and religious leaders of Islam) from 661 to 750, when they were overthrown by Abbasids. A member of the family, Abd al-Rahmam, escaped to Spain and in 756 assumed the title of Emir of Córdoba. His dynasty, which took the title of caliph in 929, ruled in Córdoba until the early 11th century.

**umbrella bird** any of three species of bird of tropical South and Central America, family Cotingidae, order Passeriformes, about 45 cm/18 in long. The Amazonian species *Cephalopterus ornatus,* the *ornate umbrella bird,* has an inflatable wattle at the neck to amplify its humming call, and in display elevates a long crest (12 cm/4 in) lying above the bill so that it rises umbrella-like above the head. These features are less noticeable in the female, which is brownish, while the male is blue-black.

**Umbria** mountainous region of Italy in the central Apennines, including the provinces of Perugia and Terni; area 8,500 sq km/3,281 sq mi; population (1992 est) 815,000. Its capital is Perugia, and the River Tiber rises in the region. Industries include textiles, chemicals, and metalworking. Wine is produced (Orvieto), and tobacco, grain, and olives (Lake Trasimene) are grown. This is the home of the Umbrian school of artists, including Raphael.

**UN** abbreviation for ◊*United Nations.*

**uncertainty principle** or *indeterminacy principle,* in quantum mechanics, the principle that it is impossible to know with unlimited accuracy the position and momentum of a particle. The principle arises because in order to locate a particle exactly, an observer must bounce light (in the form of a ◊photon) off the particle, which must alter its position in an unpredictable way.

**unconformity** surface of erosion or nondeposition eventually overlain by younger ◊sedimentary rock strata and preserved in the geologic record. A surface where the ◊beds above and below lie at different angles is called an *angular unconformity.* The boundary between older igneous or metamorphic rocks that are truncated by erosion and later covered by younger sedimentary rocks is called a *nonconformity.*

**unconscious** in psychoanalysis, a part of the personality of which the individual is unaware, and which contains impulses or urges that are held back, or repressed, from conscious awareness.

**underground** (US *subway*), rail service that runs underground. The first underground line in the world was in London, opened in 1863; it was essentially a roofed-in trench. The London Underground is still the longest underground system, with over 400 km/250 mi of routes. Many large cities throughout the world have similar systems, and Moscow's underground, the Metro, handles up to 6.5 million passengers a day.

**Underground Railroad** in US history, a network established in the North before the

◊American Civil War to provide sanctuary and assistance for escaped black slaves. Safe houses, transport facilities, and 'conductors' existed to lead the slaves to safety in the North and Canada, although the number of fugitives who secured their freedom by these means may have been exaggerated.

**unemployment** lack of paid employment. The unemployed are usually defined as those out of work who are available for and actively seeking work. Unemployment is measured either as a total or as a percentage of those who are available for work, known as the working population, or labour force. Periods of widespread unemployment in Europe and the USA in the 20th century include 1929–1930s, and the years since the mid-1970s. According to a report released by the UN's International Labour Organization November 1995, nearly 1 billion people, about 30% of the global workforce, were out of work or underemployed. The reduction in job opportunities was attributed to lower growth rates in industrialized countries since 1973, and the failure of most developing nations to recover fully from the economic crisis of the early 1980s. The ILO contended that despite increasing worldwide competition, the 1996 jobless figures were neither politically nor socially sustainable. Unemployment in industrialized countries (the members of the ◊Organization for Economic Cooperation and Development (OECD)) in 1995 averaged 7.5%, and in the European Union (EU) 11.1%. Within the OECD group the country with the lowest percentage of unemployed in 1995 was Japan (3%) and the highest was Spain (22.6%).

**UNESCO** (acronym for *United Nations Educational, Scientific, and Cultural Organization)* specialized agency of the United Nations, established in 1946, to promote international cooperation in education, science, and culture, with its headquarters in Paris.

**ungulate** general name for any hoofed mammal. Included are the odd-toed ungulates (perissodactyls) and the even-toed ungulates (artiodactyls), along with subungulates such as elephants.

**Uniate Church** any of the ◊Orthodox Churches that accept the Catholic faith and the supremacy of the pope and are in full communion with the Roman Catholic Church, but retain their own liturgy and separate organization.

**unicellular organism** animal or plant consisting of a single cell. Most are invisible without a microscope but a few, such as the giant ◊amoeba, may be visible to the naked eye. The main groups of unicellular organisms are bacteria, protozoa, unicellular algae, and unicellular fungi or yeasts. Some become disease-causing agents, ◊pathogens.

**unicorn** mythical animal referred to by classical writers, said to live in India and resembling a horse, but with one spiralled horn growing from the forehead.

**unidentified flying object** or *UFO,* any light or object seen in the sky whose immediate identity is not apparent. Despite unsubstantiated claims, there is no evidence that UFOs are alien spacecraft. On investigation, the vast majority of sightings turn out to have been of natural or identifiable objects, notably bright stars and planets, meteors, aircraft, and satellites, or to have been perpetrated by pranksters. The term *flying saucer* was coined in 1947.

**Unification Church** or *Moonies,* church founded in Korea in 1954 by the Reverend Sun Myung Moon. The number of members (often called 'Moonies') is about 200,000 worldwide. The theology unites Christian and Taoist ideas and is based on Moon's book *Divine Principle,* which teaches that the original purpose of creation was to set up a perfect family, in a perfect relationship with God.

**unified field theory** in physics, the theory that attempts to explain the four fundamental forces (strong nuclear, weak nuclear, electromagnetic, and gravity) in terms of a single unified force (see ◊particle physics).

**Union, Acts of** act of Parliament of 1707 that brought about the union of England and Scotland; that of 1801 united England and Ireland.

**Union Movement** British political group. Founded as the *New Party* by Oswald Mosley and a number of Labour members of Parliament in 1931, it developed into the *British Union of Fascists* in 1932. In 1940 the organization was declared illegal and its leaders interned, but it was revived as the Union Movement in 1948, characterized by racist doctrines including anti-Semitism.

**UNISON** Britain's largest trade union with 1,368,796 members (1998): 966,370 female, and 402,426 male. It was formed on 1 July 1993 by the merging of the National Union of Public Employees (NUPE), the Confederation of Health Service Employees, and the National Local Government Officers Association (NALGO).

**UNITA** acronym for *Uniao Nacional para a Independencia Total de Angola* (National Union for the Total Independence of Angola), Angolan nationalist movement founded by Jonas ◊Savimbi in 1966. Backed by South Africa, UNITA continued to wage guerrilla warfare against the ruling People's Movement for the Liberation of Angola (MPLA) after the latter gained control of the country in 1976. A peace agreement was signed in May 1991, but fighting recommenced in September 1992, after Savimbi disputed an election victory for the ruling party, and escalated into a bloody civil war in 1993. A peace agreement was signed in 1994. Savimbi later turned down the vice-presidency in a coalition government. In 1998 UNITA was demilitarized and formally legalized.

**unitary authority** administrative unit of Great Britain. Since 1996 the two-tier structure of local government has ceased to exist in Scotland and Wales, and in some parts of England, and has been replaced by unitary authorities, responsible for all local government services.

**United Arab Emirates** (UAE) federation of the emirates of Abu Dhabi, Ajman, Dubai, Fujairah, Ras al Khaimah, Sharjah, Umm al Qaiwain

*national name* Ittihad al-Imarat al-Arabiyah

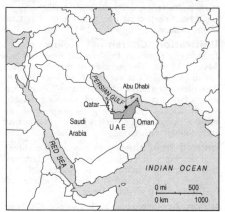

**area** 83,657 sq km/32,299 sq mi
**capital** Abu Dhabi
**major towns/cities** Dubai, Sharjah, Ras al-Khaimah, Ajman, Fujairah
**major ports** Dubai
**physical features** desert and flat coastal plain; mountains in east
**head of state** Sheikh Zayed bin Sultan al-Nahayan of Abu Dhabi from 1971
**head of government** Maktum bin Rashid al-Maktum of Dubai from 1990
**political system** absolutism
**political parties** none
**currency** UAE dirham
**GNP per capita (PPP)** (US$) 19,720 (1998)
**exports** crude petroleum, natural gas, re-exports (mainly machinery and transport equipment). Principal market: Japan 36.3% (1997)
**population** 2,397,000 (1999 est)
**language** Arabic (official), Farsi, Hindi, Urdu, English
**religion** Muslim 96%; Christian, Hindu
**life expectancy** 74 (men); 77 (women) (1995–2000)
*Chronology*
**7th century** AD Islam introduced.
**early 16th century** Portuguese established trading contacts with Persian Gulf states.
**18th century** Rise of trade and seafaring among Qawasim and Bani Yas, respectively in Ras al-Khaimah and Sharjah in north and Abu Dhabi and Dubai in desert of south. Emirates' current ruling families are descended from these peoples.
**early 19th century** Britain signed treaties ('truces') with local rulers, ensuring that British shipping through the Gulf was free from 'pirate' attacks and bringing Emirates under British protection.
**1892** Trucial Sheiks signed Exclusive Agreements with Britain, agreeing not to cede, sell, or mortgage territory to another power.

**1952** Trucial Council established by seven sheikdoms of Abu Dhabi, Ajman, Dubai, Fujairah, Ras al Khaimah, Sharjah, and Umm al Qawain, with a view to later forming a federation.
**1958** Large-scale exploitation of oil reserves led to rapid economic progress.
**1968** Britain's announcement that it would remove its forces from the Persian Gulf by 1971 led to abortive attempt to arrange federation between seven Trucial States and Bahrain and Qatar.
**1971** Bahrain and Qatar ceded from the Federation of Arab Emirates, which was dissolved. Six Trucial States formed the United Arab Emirates, with the ruler of Abu Dhabi, Sheikh Zayed, as president. A provisional constitution was adopted. The UAE joined the Arab League and the United Nations (UN).
**1972** Seventh state, Ras al Khaimah, joined federation.
**1976** Sheikh Zayed threatened to relinquish presidency unless progress towards centralization became more rapid.
**1985** Diplomatic and economic links with the Soviet Union and China were established.
**1987** Diplomatic relations with Egypt were restored.
**1990–91** UAE opposed the Iraqi invasion of Kuwait, and UAE troops fought as part of the UN coalition.
**1991** The Bank of Commerce and Credit International (BCCI), partly owned and controlled by Abu Dhabi's ruler Zayed bin Sultan al-Nahayan, collapsed at cost to the UAE of $10 billion.
**1992** There was a border dispute with Iran.
**1994** Abu Dhabi agreed to pay BCCI creditors $1.8 billion.

**United Arab Republic** union formed in 1958, broken in 1961, between Egypt and Syria. Egypt continued to use the name after the breach up until 1971.

**United Kingdom** of Great Britain and Northern Ireland (UK)

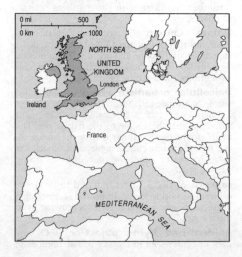

**area** 244,100 sq km/94,247 sq mi

**capital** London

**major towns/cities** Birmingham, Glasgow, Leeds, Sheffield, Liverpool, Manchester, Edinburgh, Bradford, Bristol, Coventry, Belfast, Newcastle upon Tyne, Cardiff

**major ports** London, Grimsby, Southampton, Liverpool

**physical features** became separated from European continent in about 6000 BC; rolling landscape, increasingly mountainous towards the north, with Grampian Mountains in Scotland, Pennines in northern England, Cambrian Mountains in Wales; rivers include Thames, Severn, and Spey

**territories** Anguilla, Bermuda, British Antarctic Territory, British Indian Ocean Territory, British Virgin Islands, Cayman Islands, Falkland Islands, Gibraltar, Montserrat, Pitcairn Islands, St Helena and Dependencies (Ascension, Tristan da Cunha), Turks and Caicos Islands; the Channel Islands and the Isle of Man are not part of the UK but are direct dependencies of the crown

**head of state** Queen Elizabeth II from 1952

**head of government** Tony Blair from 1997

**political system** liberal democracy

**political parties** Conservative and Unionist Party, right of centre; Labour Party, moderate left of centre; Social and Liberal Democrats, centre left; Scottish National Party (SNP), Scottish nationalist; Plaid Cymru (Welsh Nationalist Party), Welsh nationalist; Official Ulster Unionist Party (OUP), Democratic Unionist Party (DUP), Ulster People's Unionist Party (UPUP), all Northern Ireland right of centre, in favour of remaining part of UK; Social Democratic Labour Party (SDLP), Northern Ireland, moderate left of centre; Green Party, ecological

**currency** pound sterling (£)

**GNP per capita (PPP)** (US$) 20,640 (1998)

**exports** industrial and electrical machinery, automatic data-processing equipment, motor vehicles, petroleum, chemicals, finished and semi-finished manufactured products, agricultural products and foodstuffs. Principal market: USA 13.3% (1998)

**population** 58,744,000 (1999 est)

**language** English, Welsh, Gaelic

**religion** Church of England (established Church); other Protestant denominations, Roman Catholic, Muslim, Jewish, Hindu, Sikh

**life expectancy** 75 (men); 80 (women) (1995–2000)

**Chronology**

**c. 400–200 BC** British Isles conquered by Celts.

**55–54 BC** Romans led by Julius Caesar raided Britain.

**AD 43–60** Romans conquered England and Wales, which formed the province of Britannia; Picts stopped them penetrating further north.

**5th–7th centuries** After Romans withdrew, Anglo-Saxons overran most of England and formed kingdoms, including Wessex, Northumbria, and Mercia; Wales was stronghold of Celts.

**500** The Scots, a Gaelic-speaking tribe from Ireland, settled in the kingdom of Dalriada (Argyll).

**5th–6th centuries** British Isles converted to Christianity.

**829** King Egbert of Wessex accepted as overlord of all England.

**c. 843** Kenneth McAlpin unified Scots and Picts to become first king of Scotland.

**9th–11th centuries** Vikings raided British Isles, conquering north and east England and northern Scotland.

**1066** Normans led by William I defeated Anglo-Saxons at Battle of Hastings and conquered England.

**12th–13th centuries** Anglo-Norman adventurers conquered much of Ireland, but effective English rule remained limited to area around Dublin.

**1215** King John of England forced to sign Magna Carta, which placed limits on royal powers.

**1265** Simon de Montfort summoned the first English parliament in which the towns were represented.

**1284** Edward I of England invaded Scotland; Scots defeated English at Battle of Stirling Bridge in 1297.

**1314** Robert the Bruce led Scots to victory over English at Battle of Bannockburn; England recognized Scottish independence in 1328.

**1455–85** Wars of the Roses: House of York and House of Lancaster disputed English throne.

**1513** Battle of Flodden: Scots defeated by English; James IV of Scotland killed.

**1529** Henry VIII founded Church of England after break with Rome; Reformation effective in England and Wales, but not in Ireland.

**1536–43** Acts of Union united Wales with England, with one law, one parliament, and one official language.

**1541** Irish parliament recognized Henry VIII of England as king of Ireland.

**1557** First Covenant established Protestant faith in Scotland.

**1603** Union of crowns: James VI of Scotland became James I of England also.

**1607** First successful English colony in Virginia marked start of three centuries of overseas expansion.

**1610** James I established plantation of Ulster in Northern Ireland with Protestant settlers from England and Scotland.

**1642–52** English Civil War between king and Parliament, with Scottish intervention and Irish rebellion, resulted in victory for Parliament.

**1649** Execution of Charles I; Oliver Cromwell appointed Lord Protector in 1653; monarchy restored in 1660.

**1689** 'Glorious Revolution' confirmed power of Parliament; replacement of James II by William III resisted by Scottish Highlanders and Catholic Irish.

**1707** Act of Union between England and Scotland created United Kingdom of Great Britain, governed by a single parliament.

**1721–42** Cabinet government developed under Robert Walpole, in effect the first prime minister.

**1745** 'The Forty-Five': rebellion of Scottish Highlanders in support of Jacobite pretender to throne; defeated 1746.

*c. 1760–1850* Industrial Revolution: Britain became the first industrial nation in the world.

*1775–83* American Revolution: Britain lost 13 American colonies; empire continued to expand in Canada, India, and Australia.

*1793–1815* Britain at war with revolutionary France, except for 1802–03.

*1800* Act of Union created United Kingdom of Great Britain and Ireland, governed by a single parliament; effective 1801.

*1832* Great Reform Act extended franchise; further extensions in 1867, 1884, 1918, and 1928.

*1846* Repeal of Corn Laws reflected shift of power from landowners to industrialists.

*1870* Home Rule Party formed to campaign for restoration of separate Irish parliament.

*1880–90s* Rapid expansion of British Empire in Africa.

*1906–14* Liberal governments introduced social reforms and curbed the power of the House of Lords.

*1914–18* The UK played a leading part in World War I; the British Empire expanded in the Middle East.

*1919–21* The Anglo-Irish war ended with the secession of southern Ireland as the Irish Free State; Ulster remained within the United Kingdom of Great Britain and Northern Ireland with some powers devolved to a Northern Irish parliament.

*1924* The first Labour government was led by Ramsay MacDonald.

*1926* A general strike arose from a coal dispute. Equality of status was recognized between the UK and Dominions of the British Commonwealth.

*1931* A National Government coalition was formed to face a growing economic crisis; unemployment reached 3 million.

*1939–45* The UK played a leading part in World War II.

*1945* The first Scottish Nationalist MP was elected.

*1945–51* The Labour government of Clement Attlee created the welfare state and nationalized major industries.

*1947–71* Decolonization brought about the end of the British Empire.

*1966* The first Welsh Nationalist MP was elected.

*1969* Start of the Troubles in Northern Ireland; the Northern Irish Parliament was suspended in 1972.

*1973* The UK joined the European Economic Community.

*1979–90* The Conservative government of Margaret Thatcher pursued radical free-market economic policies.

*1982* Unemployment reached over 3 million. The Falklands War with Argentina over the disputed sovereignty of the Falkland Islands cost more than a thousand lives but ended with the UK retaining control of the islands.

*1983* Coal pits were closed by the Conservative government and the miners went on strike.

*1990* John Major took over from Margaret Thatcher as leader of the Conservative Party and prime minister.

*1991* British troops took part in a US-led war against Iraq under a United Nations (UN) umbrella. Following the economic successes of the 1980s there was a period of severe economic recession and unemployment.

*1992* The Conservative Party and John Major won a general election.

*1993* A peace proposal for Northern Ireland, the Downing Street Declaration, was issued jointly with the Irish government.

*1994* The IRA and Protestant paramilitary declared a ceasefire in Northern Ireland.

*1996* The IRA renewed its bombing campaign in London.

*1997* The Labour Party won a landslide victory in a general election; Tony Blair became prime minister. Blair launched a new Anglo-Irish peace initiative. Princess Diana was killed in a car crash. Blair met with Sinn Fein leader Gerry Adams; all-party peace talks began in Northern Ireland. Scotland and Wales voted in favour of devolution.

*1998* A historic multiparty agreement (the 'Good Friday Agreement') was reached on the future of Northern Ireland; a peace plan was approved by referenda in Northern Ireland and the Irish Republic. The UUP leader, David Trimble, was elected first minister.

*1999* The Scottish Parliament and the Welsh Assembly opened, with Labour the largest party in both. Talks on Northern Ireland foundered on the issues of decommissioning of arms and prisoner release. The Conservative Party polled strongly in local and European elections.

**United Nations** (UN), association of states for international peace, security, and cooperation, with its headquarters in New York. The UN was established in 1945 by 51 states as a successor to the ◊League of Nations, and has played a role in many areas, such as refugees, development assistance, disaster relief, cultural cooperation, and peacekeeping. Its membership in 1996 stood at 185 states, and the total proposed budget for 1995–96 (raised by the member states) was $2,600 million supporting more than 50,000 staff. Kofi Annan became secretary-general in 1997 and in January 1998 Louise Frechette was elected its first deputy secretary-general. There are six official working languages: English, French, Russian, Spanish, Chinese, and Arabic. The name 'United Nations' was coined by the US president Franklin D Roosevelt.

The principal institutions are the General Assembly, the Security Council, the Economic and Social Council, the Trusteeship Council, all based in New York; and the International Court of Justice in The Hague, Netherlands. At a July 1998 UN conference in Rome, attended by 160 countries, a treaty was agreed to set up a permanent international criminal court to try individuals accused of war crimes, genocide, and crimes against humanity.

The UN operates many specialized agencies, involved either in promoting communication between states (such as the International Telecommunication Union, ITU), or concerned with the welfare of states, such as the World

Health Organization (WHO), the UN Educational, Scientific and Cultural Organization (UNESCO), and the International Bank for Reconstruction and Development (World Bank). Much of the work of the specialized welfare agencies concerns the developing countries, and consists mainly of research and field work. However, they also provide international standards relevant to all countries in their respective fields.

Though autonomous, the specialized agencies are related to the UN by special arrangements and work with the UN and each other through the coordinating machinery of the Economic and Social Council.

## United States of America

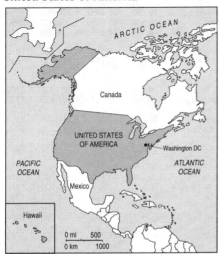

**area** 9,372,615 sq km/3,618,766 sq mi
**capital** Washington DC
**major towns/cities** New York, Los Angeles, Chicago, Philadelphia, Detroit, San Francisco, Washington, Dallas, San Antonio, San Diego, Houston, Boston, Baltimore, Phoenix, Indianapolis, Memphis, Honolulu, San José
**physical features** topography and vegetation from tropical (Hawaii) to arctic (Alaska); mountain ranges parallel with east and west coasts; the Rocky Mountains separate rivers emptying into the Pacific from those flowing into the Gulf of Mexico; Great Lakes in north; rivers include Hudson, Mississippi, Missouri, Colorado, Columbia, Snake, Rio Grande, Ohio
**territories** the commonwealths of Puerto Rico and Northern Marianas; Guam, the US Virgin Islands, American Samoa, Wake Island, Midway Islands, and Johnston and Sand Islands
**head of state and government** Bill Clinton from 1993
**political system** liberal democracy
**political parties** Democratic Party, liberal centre; Republican Party, centre right
**currency** US dollar
**GNP per capita (PPP)** (US$) 29,340 (1998)
**exports** machinery, motor vehicles, agricultural products and foodstuffs, aircraft, weapons,

chemicals, electronics. Principal market: Canada 23.3% (1998)
**population** 276,219,000 (1999 est)
**language** English, Spanish
**religion** Christian 86.5% (Roman Catholic 26%, Baptist 19%, Methodist 8%, Lutheran 5%); Jewish 1.8%; Muslim 0.5%; Buddhist and Hindu less than 0.5%
**life expectancy** 73 (men); 80 (women) (1995–2000)
**Chronology**
**c. 15,000 BC** First evidence of human occupation in North America.
**1513** Ponce de Léon of Spain explored Florida in search of the Fountain of Youth; Francisco Coronado explored southwest region of North America 1540–42.
**1565** Spanish founded St Augustine (Florida), the first permanent European settlement in North America.
**1585** Sir Walter Raleigh tried to establish English colony on Roanoke Island in what he called Virginia.
**1607** English colonists founded Jamestown, Virginia, and began growing tobacco.
**1620** The Pilgrim Fathers founded Plymouth Colony (near Cape Cod); other English Puritans followed them to New England.
**1624** Dutch formed colony of New Netherlands; Swedes formed New Sweden in 1638; both taken by England in 1664.
**17th–18th centuries** Millions of Africans were sold into slavery on American cotton and tobacco plantations.
**1733** Georgia became thirteenth British colony on east coast.
**1763** British victory over France in Seven Years' War secured territory as far west as Mississippi River.
**1765** British first attempted to levy tax in American colonies with Stamp Act; protest forced repeal in 1767.
**1773** 'Boston Tea Party': colonists boarded ships and threw cargoes of tea into sea in protest at import duty.
**1774** British closed Boston harbour and billeted troops in Massachusetts; colonists formed First Continental Congress.
**1775** American Revolution: colonies raised Continental Army led by George Washington to fight against British rule.
**1776** American colonies declared independence; France and Spain supported them in war with Britain.
**1781** Americans defeated British at Battle of Yorktown; rebel states formed loose confederation, codified in Articles of Confederation.
**1783** Treaty of Paris: Britain accepted loss of colonies.
**1787** 'Founding Fathers' devised new constitution for United States of America.
**1789** Washington elected first president of USA.
**1791** Bill of Rights guaranteed individual freedom.
**1803** Louisiana Purchase: France sold former Spanish lands between Mississippi River and Rocky Mountains to USA.

**UNITED STATES OF AMERICA: STATES**

| State | Nickname(s) | Abbre-viation | Capital | Area sq km | Area sq mi | Population (1995) | Joined the union |
|---|---|---|---|---|---|---|---|
| Alabama | Heart of Dixie/Camellia State | AL | Montgomery | 134,700 | 51,994 | 4,253,000 | 1819 |
| Alaska | Mainland State/The Last Frontier | AK | Juneau | 1,531,100 | 591,005 | 603,600 | 1959 |
| Arizona | Grand Canyon State/ Apache State | AZ | Phoenix | 294,100 | 113,523 | 4,217,900 | 1912 |
| Arkansas | Bear State/Land of Opportunity | AR | Little Rock | 137,800 | 53,191 | 2,483,800 | 1836 |
| California | Golden State | CA | Sacramento | 411,100 | 158,685 | 31,589,200 | 1850 |
| Colorado | Centennial State | CO | Denver | 269,700 | 104,104 | 3,746,600 | 1876 |
| Connecticut | Constitution State/ Nutmeg State | CT | Hartford | 13,000 | 5018 | 3,274,700 | 1788 |
| Delaware | First State/Diamond State | DE | Dover | 5,300 | 2,046 | 717,200 | 1787 |
| Florida | Sunshine State/Everglade State | FL | Tallahassee | 152,000 | 58,672 | 14,165,600 | 1845 |
| Georgia | Empire State of the South/ Peach State | GA | Atlanta | 152,600 | 58,904 | 7,200,900 | 1788 |
| Hawaii | Aloha State | HI | Honolulu | 16,800 | 6,485 | 1,186,800 | 1959 |
| Idaho | Gem State | ID | Boise | 216,500 | 83,569 | 1,163,300 | 1890 |
| Illinois | Inland Empire/Prairie State/ Land of Lincoln | IL | Springfield | 146,100 | 56,395 | 11,829,900 | 1818 |
| Indiana | Hoosier State | IN | Indianapolis | 93,700 | 36,168 | 5,803,500 | 1816 |
| Iowa | Hawkeye State/Corn State | IA | Des Moines | 145,800 | 56,279 | 2,841,800 | 1846 |
| Kansas | Sunflower State/Jayhawker State | KS | Topeka | 213,200 | 82,295 | 2,565,300 | 1861 |
| Kentucky | Bluegrass State | KY | Frankfort | 104,700 | 40,414 | 3,860,200 | 1792 |
| Louisiana | Pelican State/Sugar State/ Creole State | LA | Baton Rouge | 135,900 | 52,457 | 4,342,300 | 1792 |
| Maine | Pine Tree State | ME | Augusta | 86,200 | 33,273 | 1,241,400 | 1812 |
| Maryland | Old Line State/Free State | MD | Annapolis | 31,600 | 12,198 | 5,042,400 | 1788 |
| Massachusetts | Bay State/Old Colony | MA | Boston | 21,500 | 8,299 | 6,073,550 | 1788 |
| Michigan | Great Lakes State/Wolverine State | MI | Lansing | 151,600 | 58,518 | 9,549,400 | 1837 |
| Minnesota | North Star State/Gopher State | MN | St Paul | 218,700 | 84,418 | 4,609,500 | 1858 |
| Mississippi | Magnolia State | MS | Jackson | 123,600 | 47,710 | 2,697,200 | 1817 |
| Missouri | Show Me State/Bullion State | MO | Jefferson City | 180,600 | 69,712 | 5,323,500 | 1821 |
| Montana | Treasure State/Big Sky Country | MT | Helena | 381,200 | 147,143 | 870,300 | 1889 |
| Nebraska | Cornhusker State/Beef State | NE | Lincoln | 200,400 | 77,354 | 1,637,100 | 1867 |
| Nevada | Sagebrush State/Silver State/ Battleborn State | NV | Carson City | 286,400 | 110,550 | 1,530,100 | 1864 |
| New Hampshire | Granite State | NH | Concord | 24,000 | 9,264 | 1,148,300 | 1788 |
| New Jersey | Garden State | NJ | Trenton | 20,200 | 7,797 | 7,945,300 | 1787 |
| New Mexico | Land of Enchantment/ Sunshine State | NM | Santa Fé | 315,000 | 121,590 | 1,685,400 | 1912 |
| New York | Empire State | NY | Albany | 127,200 | 49,099 | 18,136,100 | 1788 |
| North Carolina | Tar Heel State/Old North State | NC | Raleigh | 136,400 | 52,650 | 7,195,100 | 1789 |
| North Dakota | Peace Garden State | ND | Bismarck | 183,100 | 70,677 | 641,400 | 1889 |
| Ohio | Buckeye State | OH | Columbus | 107,100 | 41,341 | 11,150,500 | 1803 |
| Oklahoma | Sooner State | OK | Oklahoma City | 181,100 | 69,905 | 3,277,700 | 1907 |
| Oregon | Beaver State/Sunset State | OR | Salem | 251,500 | 97,079 | 3,140,600 | 1859 |
| Pennsylvania | Keystone State | PA | Harrisburg | 117,400 | 45,316 | 12,071,800 | 1787 |
| Rhode Island | Little Rhody/Ocean State | RI | Providence | 3,100 | 1,197 | 989,800 | 1790 |
| South Carolina | Palmetto State | SC | Columbia | 80,600 | 31,112 | 3,673,300 | 1788 |
| South Dakota | Coyote State/Mount Rushmore State | SD | Pierre | 199,800 | 77,123 | 729,000 | 1889 |
| Tennessee | Volunteer State | TN | Nashville | 109,200 | 42,151 | 5,256,100 | 1796 |
| Texas | Lone Star State | TX | Austin | 691,200 | 266,803 | 18,724,000 | 1845 |
| Utah | Beehive State/Mormon State | UT | Salt Lake City | 219,900 | 84,881 | 1,951,400 | 1896 |
| Vermont | Green Mountain State | VT | Montpelier | 24,900 | 9,611 | 584,800 | 1791 |
| Virginia | Old Dominion State/ Mother of Presidents | VA | Richmond | 105,600 | 40,762 | 6,618,400 | 1788 |
| Washington | Evergreen State/Chinook State | WA | Olympia | 176,700 | 68,206 | 5,430,900 | 1889 |
| West Virginia | Mountain State/ Panhandle State | WV | Charleston | 62,900 | 24,279 | 1,828,100 | 1863 |
| Wisconsin | Badger State/America's Dairyland | WI | Madison | 145,500 | 56,163 | 5,122,900 | 1848 |
| Wyoming | Equality State | WY | Cheyenne | 253,400 | 97,812 | 480,200 | 1890 |
| District of Columbia (Federal District) | – | DC | Washington | 180 | 69 | 554,300 | (est. by Act of Congress 1790–91) |

**1812–14** War with Britain arose from dispute over blockade rights during Napoleonic Wars.

**1819** USA bought Florida from Spain.

**19th century** Mass immigration from Europe; settlers moved westwards, crushing Indian resistance and claiming 'manifest destiny' of USA to control North America. By end of century, number of states in the Union had increased from 17 to 45.

**1846–48** Mexican War: Mexico ceded vast territory to USA.

**1854** Kansas–Nebraska Act heightened controversy over slavery in southern states; abolitionists formed Republican Party.

**1860** Abraham Lincoln (Republican) elected president.

**1861** Civil war broke out after 11 southern states, wishing to retain slavery, seceded from USA and formed Confederate States of America under Jefferson Davis.

**1865** USA defeated Confederacy; slavery abolished; President Lincoln assassinated.

**1867** Alaska bought from Russia.

**1869** Railway linked east and west coasts; rapid growth of industry and agriculture 1870–1920 made USA very rich.

**1876** Sioux Indians defeated US troops at Little Big Horn; Indians finally defeated at Wounded Knee in 1890.

**1898** Spanish–American War: USA gained Puerto Rico and Guam; also Philippines (until 1946) and Cuba (until 1901); USA annexed Hawaii.

**1913** 16th amendment to constitution gave federal government power to levy income tax.

**1917–18** USA intervened in World War I; President Woodrow Wilson took leading part in peace negotiations in 1919, but USA rejected membership of League of Nations.

**1920** Women received right to vote; sale of alcohol prohibited, until 1933.

**1924** American Indians made citizens of USA by Congress.

**1929** 'Wall Street Crash': stock market collapse led to Great Depression with 13 million unemployed by 1933.

**1933** President Franklin Roosevelt launched 'New Deal' with public works to alleviate Depression.

**1941** Japanese attacked US fleet at Pearl Harbor, Hawaii; USA declared war on Japan; Germany declared war on USA, which henceforth played a leading part in World War II.

**1945** USA ended war in Pacific by dropping two atomic bombs on Hiroshima and Nagasaki, Japan.

**1947** 'Truman Doctrine' pledged US aid for nations threatened by communism; start of Cold War between USA and USSR.

**1950–53** US forces engaged in Korean War.

**1954** Racial segregation in schools deemed unconstitutional; start of campaign to secure civil rights for black Americans.

**1962** Cuban missile crisis: USA forced USSR to withdraw nuclear weapons from Cuba.

**1963** President Kennedy assassinated.

**1964–68** President Lyndon Johnson introduced 'Great Society' programme of civil-rights and welfare measures.

**1961–75** USA involved in Vietnam War.

**1969** US astronaut Neil Armstrong was first person on Moon.

**1974** 'Watergate' scandal: evidence of domestic political espionage compelled President Richard Nixon to resign.

**1979–80** Iran held US diplomats hostage, humiliating President Jimmy Carter.

**1981–89** Tax-cutting policies of President Ronald Reagan led to large federal budget deficit.

**1986** 'Irangate' scandal: secret US arms sales to Iran illegally funded Contra guerrillas in Nicaragua.

**1990** President George Bush declared an end to the Cold War.

**1991** USA played leading part in expelling Iraqi forces from Kuwait in the Gulf War.

**1992** Democrat Bill Clinton won presidential elections.

**1996** Clinton was re-elected. US launched missile attacks on Iraq in response to Hussein's incursions into Kurdish safe havens.

**1997** Reform in welfare law brought a substantial drop in the number of welfare recipients.

**1998** President Clinton testified before a grand jury that he had misled the public about his relationship with White House intern Monica Lewinsky. The House of Representatives voted to impeach him on the grounds of perjury and obstruction of justice. Clinton's national approval rating remained high, and Democrats made gains in congressional midterm elections. In response to bombings of US embassies in Tanzania and Kenya by an Islamic group, the USA bombed suspected sites in Afghanistan and Sudan. The USA also led air strikes against Iraq following the expulsion of UN weapons inspectors by Saddam Hussein.

**1999** The Senate voted against impeaching Clinton in trial arising from the Monica Lewinsky affair. Clinton projected a 1999 federal budget surplus of $76 billion. US forces led NATO air strikes against Yugoslavia in protest against Serb violence against ethnic Albanians in Kosovo.

**unit trust** company that invests its clients' funds in other companies. The units it issues represent holdings of shares, which means unit shareholders have a wider spread of capital than if they bought shares on the stock market.

**universe** all of space and its contents, the study of which is called ◊cosmology. The universe is thought to be between 10 billion and 20 billion years old, and is mostly empty space, dotted with ◊galaxies for as far as telescopes can see. The most distant detected galaxies and ◊quasars lie 10 billion light years or more from Earth, and are moving farther apart as the universe expands. Several theories attempt to explain how the universe came into being and evolved; for example, the ◊Big Bang theory of an expanding universe originating in a single explosive event, and the contradictory ◊steady-state theory.

**UNIX** multiuser ◊operating system designed for minicomputers but becoming increasingly popular on microcomputers, workstations, mainframes, and supercomputers.

**unleaded petrol** petrol manufactured without the addition of antiknock. It has a slightly lower octane rating than leaded petrol, but has the advantage of not polluting the atmosphere with lead compounds. Many cars can be converted to run on unleaded petrol by altering the timing of the engine, and most new cars are designed to do so. Cars fitted with a ◊catalytic converter must use unleaded fuel.

**unnilennium** temporary name assigned to the element ◊meitnerium, atomic number 109.

**unnilhexium** temporary name assigned to the element ◊seaborgium (1974–97).

**unniloctium** temporary name assigned to the element ◊hassium, atomic number 108.

**unnilpentium** temporary name assigned to the element ◊dubnium.

**unnilquadium** temporary name assigned to the element ◊rutherfordium (1964–97).

**unnilseptium** temporary name assigned to the element ◊bohrium (1964–97).

**unsaturated compound** chemical compound in which two adjacent atoms are linked by a double or triple covalent bond.

**Unzen** active volcano on the Shimbara peninsula, Kyushu island, Japan, opposite the city of Kumamoto. Its eruption in June 1991 led to the evacuation of 10,000 people. It is the main feature of Unzen-Amakusa National Park. The highest peak, Fugendake, is 1,359 m/4,459 ft high. There have been hot springs in the area since the 8th century and wild azaleas (*miyamakirishima*) grow locally.

**Upanishad** one of a collection of Hindu sacred treatises, written in Sanskrit, connected with the ◊Vedas but composed later, from about 800–200 BC. Metaphysical and ethical, their doctrine equated the atman (self) with the Brahman (supreme spirit) – 'Tat tvam asi' ('Thou art that') – and developed the theory of the transmigration of souls.

**Updike, John Hoyer** (1932–  ) US writer. Associated with the *New Yorker* magazine from 1955, he soon established a reputation for polished prose, poetry, and criticism. His novels include *The Poorhouse Fair* (1959), *The Centaur* (1963), *Couples* (1968), *The Witches of Eastwick* (1984), *Roger's Version* (1986), and *S.* (1988), and deal with the tensions and frustrations of contemporary US middle-class life and their effects on love and marriage. Updike was awarded the Medal for Distinguished Contribution to American Letters in the 1998 National Book Awards.

**Upper Austria** German *Oberösterreich*, mountainous federal state of Austria, drained by the Danube, and bordered on the north by the Czech Republic and on the west by Bavaria; area 12,000 sq km/4,632 sq mi; population (1995) 1,385,500. Its capital is Linz and the main towns are Steyr and Wels. Agricultural products include fruit, wine, sugar beet, and grain. There

are reserves of oil, and salt and lignite are mined. Textiles, chemicals, and metal and electronic goods are manufactured. The population density is the highest of all the provinces except Vienna.

**Upper Volta** former name (to 1984) of Burkina Faso.

**Uppsala** city in Sweden, northwest of Stockholm; population (1994) 181,200. Industries include engineering and pharmaceuticals. The university was founded in 1477; there are Viking relics and a Gothic cathedral. The botanist Carolus Linnaeus lived here.

**Ur** ancient city of the ◊Sumerian civilization, in modern Iraq. Excavations by the British archaeologist Leonard Woolley show that it was inhabited from about 3500 BC. He discovered evidence of a flood that may have inspired the *Epic of* ◊*Gilgamesh* as well as the biblical account, and remains of ziggurats, or step pyramids.

**Ural Mountains** Russian *Ural'skiy Khrebet*, mountain system extending for over 2,000 km/1,242 mi from the Arctic Ocean to the Caspian Sea, and traditionally regarded as separating Europe from Asia. The highest peak is Naradnaya, 1,894 m/6,214 ft. The mountains hold vast mineral wealth.

**uranium** hard, lustrous, silver-white, malleable and ductile, radioactive, metallic element of the ◊actinide series, symbol U, atomic number 92, relative atomic mass 238.029. It is the most abundant radioactive element in the Earth's crust, its decay giving rise to essentially all radioactive elements in nature; its final decay product is the stable element lead. Uranium combines readily with most elements to form compounds that are extremely poisonous. The chief ore is ◊pitchblende, in which the element was discovered by German chemist Martin Klaproth in 1789; he named it after the planet Uranus, which had been discovered in 1781.

**Uranus** seventh planet from the Sun, discovered by William ◊Herschel in 1781. It is twice as far out as the sixth planet, Saturn. Uranus has a mass 14.5 times that of Earth. The spin axis of Uranus is tilted at 98°, so that one pole points towards the Sun, giving extreme seasons.
*mean distance from the Sun* 2.9 billion km/1.8 billion mi
*equatorial diameter* 50,800 km/31,600 mi
*rotation period* 17.2 hr
*year* 84 Earth years
*atmosphere* deep atmosphere composed mainly of hydrogen and helium
*surface* composed primarily of hydrogen and helium but may also contain heavier elements, which might account for Uranus's mean density being higher than Saturn's
*satellites* 17 moons (two discovered in 1997); 11 thin rings around the planet's equator were discovered in 1977.

**Uranus** in Greek mythology, the primeval sky god, whose name means 'Heaven'. He was responsible for both the sunshine and the rain, and was the son and husband of ◊Gaia, the

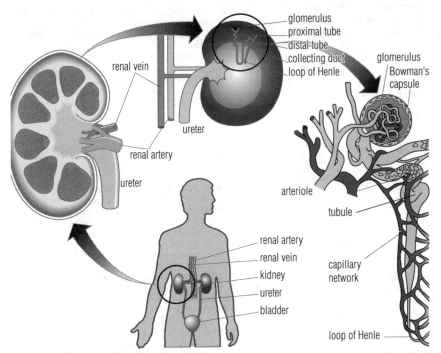

**urinary system** *The human urinary system. At the bottom centre the complete system in outline; on the left, the arrangement of blood vessels connected to the kidney; at the top right, a detail of the network of vessels within a kidney.*

goddess of the Earth. Uranus and Gaia were the parents of ◊Kronos and his fellow ◊Titans, the one-eyed giant Cyclops, and the 100-handed *Hecatoncheires*.

**Urdu language** member of the Indo-Iranian branch of the Indo-European language family, related to Hindi and written not in Devanagari but in Arabic script. Urdu is strongly influenced by Farsi (Persian) and Arabic. It is the official language of Pakistan and is used by Muslims in India.

**urea** $CO(NH_2)_2$ waste product formed in the mammalian liver when nitrogen compounds are broken down. It is filtered from the blood by the kidneys, and stored in the bladder as urine prior to release. When purified, it is a white, crystalline solid. In industry it is used to make urea-formaldehyde plastics (or resins), pharmaceuticals, and fertilizers.

**ureter** tube connecting the kidney to the bladder. Its wall contains fibres of smooth muscle whose contractions aid the movement of urine out of the kidney.

**urethra** in mammals, a tube connecting the bladder to the exterior. It carries urine and, in males, semen.

**uric acid** $C_5H_4N_4O_3$ nitrogen-containing waste substance, formed from the breakdown of food and body protein.

It is only slightly soluble in water. Uric acid is the normal means by which most land animals

that develop in a shell (birds, reptiles, insects, and land gastropods) deposit their waste products. The young are unable to get rid of their excretory products while in the shell and therefore store them in this insoluble form.

**urinary system** system of organs that removes nitrogenous waste products and excess water from the bodies of animals. In vertebrates, it consists of a pair of kidneys, which produce urine; ureters, which drain the kidneys; and (in bony fishes, amphibians, some reptiles, and mammals) a bladder that stores the urine before its discharge. In mammals, the urine is expelled through the urethra; in other vertebrates, the urine drains into a common excretory chamber called a cloaca, and the urine is not discharged separately.

**Ursa Major** (Latin 'Great Bear') third-largest constellation in the sky, in the north polar region. Its seven brightest stars make up the familiar shape or asterism of the *Big Dipper* or *Plough*. The second star of the handle of the dipper, called Mizar, has a companion star, Alcor.

Two stars forming the far side of the bowl act as pointers to the north pole star, ◊Polaris. Dubhe, one of them, is the constellation's brightest star.

**Ursa Minor** (Latin 'Little Bear') small constellation of the northern hemisphere. It is shaped like a dipper, with the bright north pole star ◊Polaris at the end of the handle.

**Uruguay** Oriental Republic of
**national name** *República Oriental del Uruguay*
**area** 176,200 sq km/68,030 sq mi
**capital** Montevideo
**major towns/cities** Salto, Paysandú, Las Piedras
**physical features** grassy plains (pampas) and low hills; rivers Negro, Uruguay, Río de la Plata
**head of state and government** Julio Maria Sanguinetti from 1994
**political system** democracy
**political parties** Colorado Party (PC), progressive, centre left; National (Blanco) Party (PN), traditionalist, right of centre; New Space (NE), moderate, left wing; Progressive Encounter (EP), left wing
**currency** Uruguayan peso
**GNP per capita (PPP)** (US$) 9,480 (1998)
**exports** textiles, meat (chiefly beef), live animals and by-products (mainly hides and leather products), cereals, footwear. Principal market: Brazil 34.7% (1998)
**population** 3,313,000 (1999 est)
**language** Spanish (official)
**religion** mainly Roman Catholic
**life expectancy** 71 (men); 78 (women) (1995–2000)
*Chronology*
**1516** Río de la Plata visited by Spanish navigator Juan Diaz de Solis, who was killed by native Charrua Amerindians. This discouraged European settlement for more than a century.
**1680** Portuguese from Brazil founded Nova Colonia do Sacramento on Río de la Plata estuary.
**1726** Spanish established fortress at Montevideo and wrested control over Uruguay from Portugal, with much of the Amerindian population being killed.
**1776** Became part of Viceroyalty of La Plata, with capital at Buenos Aires.
**1808** With Spanish monarchy overthrown by Napoleon Bonaparte, La Plata Viceroyalty became autonomous, but Montevideo remained

loyal to Spanish Crown and rebelled against Buenos Aires control.
**1815** Dictator José Gervasio Artigas overthrew Spanish and Buenos Aires control.
**1820** Artigas ousted by Brazil, which disputed control of Uruguay with Argentina.
**1825** Independence declared after fight led by Juan Antonio Lavalleja.
**1828** Independence recognized by country's neighbours.
**1836** Civil war between Reds and Whites, after which Colorado and Blanco parties were named.
**1840** Merino sheep introduced by British traders, who later established meat processing factories for export trade.
**1865–70** Fought successfully alongside Argentina and Brazil in war against Paraguay.
**1903** After period of military rule, José Battle y Ordonez, a progressive from centre-left Colorado Party, became president. As president 1903–07 and 1911–15, he gave women the franchise and created an advanced welfare state as a successful ranching economy developed.
**1930** First constitution adopted, but period of military dictatorship followed during Depression period.
**1958** After 93 years out of power, right-of-centre Blanco Party returned to power.
**1967** Colorado Party in power, with Jorge Pacheco Areco as president. Period of labour unrest and urban guerrilla activity by left-wing Tupamaros.
**1972** Juan María Bordaberry Arocena of Colorado Party became president.
**1973** Parliament dissolved and Bordaberry shared power with military dictatorship, which crushed Tupamaros and banned left-wing groups.
**1976** Bordaberry deposed by army; Dr Aparicio Méndez Manfredini became president.
**1981** Gen Grigorio Alvárez Armellino became new military ruler.
**1984** Violent antigovernment protests after ten years of repressive rule and deteriorating economy.
**1985** Agreement reached between army and political leaders for return to constitutional government and freeing of political prisoners. Colorado Party won general election; Dr Julio María Sanguinetti became president.
**1986** Government of national accord established under President Sanguinetti.
**1989** Luis Alberto Lacalle Herrera of the Blanco Party was elected president.
**1992** The public voted against privatization in a national referendum.
**1994** Colorado candidate Julio Maria Sanguinetti was elected president.

**Urumqi** *Urumchi* or *Wulumuqi;* until 1953 *Dihau,* industrial city and capital of Xinjiang Uygur Autonomous Region, northwest China, on the Urumqi River, at the northern foot of the Tian Shan Mountains; population (1994) 1,240,000. Industries include oil-refining, food-processing, brewing, and the manufacture of cotton textiles, cement, iron, steel, plastics, and agricultural equipment.

**user interface** in computing, the procedures and methods through which the user operates a program. These might include menus, input forms, error messages, and keyboard procedures. A ◊graphical user interface (GUI or WIMP) is one that makes use of icons (small pictures) and allows the user to make menu selections with a mouse.

**Ushuaia** southernmost town in the world, at the tip of Tierra del Fuego, Argentina, less than 1,000 km/620 mi from Antarctica; population (1991) 29,700. It is a free port and naval base. Industries include lumbering, sheeprearing, and fishing.

**Ustaše** Croatian nationalist terrorist organization founded in 1929 and led by Ante Pavelić against the Yugoslav state. During World War II, it collaborated with the Nazis and killed thousands of Serbs, Romanies, and Jews. It also carried out deportations and forced conversions to Roman Catholicism in its attempt to create a 'unified' Croatian state.

**Utah** state in western USA. It is nicknamed the Beehive State or the Mormon State. Utah was admitted to the Union in 1896 as the 45th US state. One of the Mountain States, it is bordered to the east by Colorado, to the north by Wyoming, to the west by Nevada, and to the south by Arizona. At the 'Four Corners', in the southeast, it also touches New Mexico
*population* (1995) 1,951,400
*area* 219,900 sq km/84,881 sq mi
*capital* Salt Lake City
*towns and cities* Provo, Ogden, West Valley City
*industries and products* wool, gold, silver, copper, coal, oil, potash, salt, steel, aerospace and military-dependent industries, tourism.

**uterus** hollow muscular organ of female mammals, located between the bladder and rectum, and connected to the Fallopian tubes above and the vagina below. The embryo develops within the uterus, and in placental mammals is attached to it after implantation via the ◊placenta and umbilical cord. The lining of the uterus changes during the ◊menstrual cycle. In humans and other higher primates, it is a single structure, but in other mammals it is paired.

**Uthman** (*c.* 574–656) Third caliph (leader of the Islamic Empire) from 644, a son-in-law of the prophet Muhammad. Under his rule the Arabs became a naval power and extended their rule to North Africa and Cyprus, but Uthman's personal weaknesses led to his assassination. He was responsible for the compilation of the authoritative version of the Koran, the sacred book of Islam.

**Uthman I** another name for the Turkish sultan ◊Osman I.

**utilitarianism** philosophical theory of ethics outlined by the philosopher Jeremy ◊Bentham and developed by John Stuart Mill. According to utilitarianism, an action is morally right if it has consequences that lead to happiness, and wrong if it brings about the reverse. Thus society should aim for the greatest happiness of the greatest number.

**Utopia** (Greek 'no place') in literature, any ideal state, named after philosopher Thomas More's ideal commonwealth in his book *Utopia* 1516. Other versions include Plato's *Republic*, Francis Bacon's *New Atlantis*, and *City of the Sun* by the Italian Tommaso Campanella (1568–1639). Utopias are a common subject in science fiction.

**Utrecht** province of the Netherlands, lying southeast of Amsterdam, and south of the IJsselmeer, on the Kromme Rijn (Crooked Rhine)
*area* 1,330 sq km/514 sq mi
*capital* Utrecht
*towns and cities* Amersfoort, Zeist, Nieuwegeun, Veenendaal
*physical* sandy, barren soil in the east; more fertile in the west
*industries* petrochemicals, textiles, electrical goods, engineering, steelworks, railway workshops, furniture
*agriculture* livestock, dairy products, fruit, vegetables, cereals
*population* (1997) 1,079,400
*history* ruled by the bishops of Utrecht in the Middle Ages; sold to the emperor Charles V of Spain in 1527; became a centre of Protestant resistance to Spanish rule; with the signing of the Treaty of Utrecht, became one of the seven United Provinces of the Netherlands in 1579.

**Utrecht, Union of** in 1579, the union of seven provinces of the northern Netherlands – Holland, Zeeland, Friesland, Groningen, Utrecht, Gelderland, and Overijssel – that, as the United Provinces, became the basis of opposition to the Spanish crown and the foundation of the present-day Dutch state.

**Uttar Pradesh** state of north India, bordered by Nepal and China to the northeast, and Indian states to the south and west
*area* 294,400 sq km/113,638 sq mi
*capital* ◊Lucknow
*towns and cities* Kanpur, Varanasi, Agra, Allahabad, Meerut, Haridwar
*physical* Gangetic plain covers three-quarters of the state, which rises to the Himalaya in the northwest (Nanda Devi, 7,818 m/25,655 ft); the Ganges rises in the northwest, and flows southeast; the Yamuna and Ghaghara rivers also drain southeastwards; to the south are the Shiwalik hills
*features* most populous state; Tehri Dam project
*industries* sugar, oil refining, textiles, leatherwork, cement, chemicals, coal, silica, handicrafts (Varanasi, Lucknow)
*agriculture* wheat, rice, millet, barley, sugar cane, groundnuts, peas, cotton, oilseed, potatoes, livestock, fruit; new strains of wheat have increased yields since the 1960s
*population* (1994 est) 150,695,000
*famous people* Indira Gandhi, Ravi Shankar
*language* Hindi
*religion* 80% Hinduism; religious sites in the state include Varanasi, Haridwar, Allahabad; 15% Muslim

*history* formerly the heart of the Mogul Empire and generating point of the ◊Indian Mutiny in 1857 and subsequent opposition to British rule; see also ◊Agra and ◊Oudh. There are secessionist demands for a new hill state carved out of Uttar Pradesh.

**Uzbek** or *Uzbeg,* member of the majority ethnic group (almost 70%) living in Uzbekistan. Minorities live in Turkmenistan, Tajikistan, Kazakhstan, and Afghanistan and include ◊Turkomen, ◊Tatars, ◊Armenians, Kazakhs, and Kirghiz. There are 10–14 million speakers of the Uzbek language, which belongs to the Turkic branch of the Altaic family. Uzbeks are predominantly Sunni Muslims but retain aspects of shamanism.

**Uzbekistan** Republic of
*national name* *Ozbekistan Respublikasy*

*area* 447,400 sq km/172,741 sq mi
*capital* Tashkent
*major towns/cities* Samarkand, Bukhara, Namangan, Andizhan
*physical features* oases in deserts; rivers: Amu Darya, Syr Darya; Ferghana Valley; rich in mineral deposits
*head of state* Islam Karimov from 1990
*head of government* Otkir Sultonov from 1995
*political system* authoritarian nationalist
*political parties* People's Democratic Party of Uzbekistan (PDP), reform socialist (ex-communist); Fatherland Progress Party (FP; Vatan Taraqioti), pro-private enterprise; Erk (Freedom Democratic Party), mixed economy; Social Democratic Party of Uzbekistan, pro-Islamic; National Revival Democratic Party, centrist, intelligentsia-led
*currency* som
*GNP per capita (PPP)* (US$) 2,900 (1998)
*exports* cotton fibre, textiles, machinery, food and energy products, gold. Principal market: Russia 14.9% (1998)
*population* 23,941,000 (1999 est)
*language* Uzbek, a Turkic language

*religion* Sunni Muslim
*life expectancy* 64 (men); 71 (women) (1995–2000)
*Chronology*
*6th century BC* Part of Persian Empire of Cyrus the Great.
*4th century BC* Part of empire of Alexander the Great of Macedonia.
*1st century BC* Samarkand (Maracanda) developed as transit point on strategic Silk Road trading route between China and Europe.
*7th century* City of Tashkent founded; spread of Islam.
*12th century* Tashkent taken by Turks; Khorezem (Khiva), in northwest, became centre of large Central Asian polity, stretching from Caspian Sea to Samarkand in the east.
*13th–14th centuries* Conquered by Genghis Khan and became part of Mongol Empire, with Samarkand serving as capital for Tamerlane.
*18th–19th centuries* Dominated by independent emirates and khanates (chiefdoms) of Bukhara in southwest, Kokand in east, and Samarkand in centre.
*1865–67* Tashkent was taken by Russia and made capital of Governor-Generalship of Turkestan.
*1868–76* Tsarist Russia annexed emirate of Bukhara (1868); and khanates of Samarkand (1868), Khiva (1873), and Kokand (1876).
*1917* Following Bolshevik revolution in Russia, Tashkent soviet ('people's council') established, which deposed the emir of Bukhara and other khans in 1920.
*1918–22* Mosques closed and Muslim clergy persecuted as part of secularization drive by new communist rulers, despite nationalist guerrilla (basmachi) resistance.
*1921* Part of Turkestan Soviet Socialist Autonomous Republic.
*1925* Became constituent republic of USSR.
*1930s* Skilled ethnic Russians immigrated into urban centres as industries developed.
*1944* About 160,000 Meskhetian Turks forcibly transported from their native Georgia to Uzbekistan by Soviet dictator Joseph Stalin.
*1950s–80s* Major irrigation projects stimulated cotton production, but led to desiccation of Aral Sea.
*late 1980s* Upsurge in Islamic consciousness stimulated by *glasnost* initiative of Soviet Union's reformist leader Mikhail Gorbachev.
*1989* Birlik ('Unity'), nationalist movement, formed. Violent attacks on Meskhetian and other minority communities in Ferghana Valley.
*1990* Economic and political sovereignty was declared by the increasingly nationalist UCP, led by Islam Karimov, who became president.
*1991* An attempted anti-Gorbachev coup by conservatives in Moscow was initially supported by President Karimov. Independence was declared. Uzbekistan joined the new Commonwealth of Independent States (CIS); Karimov was re-elected president.
*1992* There were violent food riots in Tashkent. Uzbekistan joined the Economic Cooperation Organization and the United Nations (UN). A new constitution was adopted.
*1993* There was a crackdown on Islamic funda-

mentalists as the economy deteriorated.

**1994** Economic, military, and social union was forged with Kazakhstan and Kyrgyzstan, and an economic integration treaty was signed with Russia. Links with Turkey were strengthened and foreign inward investment encouraged.

**1995** The ruling PDP (formerly UCP) won a general election, from which opposition was banned from participating. Karimov's tenure was extended for a further five-year term by national plebiscite.

**1996** An agreement was made with Kazakhstan and Kyrgyzstan to create a single economic market.

**1998** A treaty of eternal friendship and deepening economic cooperation was signed with Kazakhstan.

**1999** Uzbekistan threatened to end participation in a regional security treaty, accusing Russia of seeking to integrate the former Soviet republics into a superstate.

**V** in physics, symbol for ◊velocity.

**V** Roman numeral for *five;* in physics, symbol for ◊volt.

**vaccine** any preparation of modified pathogens (viruses or bacteria) that is introduced into the body, usually either orally or by a hypodermic syringe, to induce the specific ◊antibody reaction that produces ◊immunity against a particular disease.

**vacuole** in biology, a fluid-filled, membrane-bound cavity inside a cell. It may be a reservoir for fluids that the cell will secrete to the outside, or may be filled with excretory products or essential nutrients that the cell needs to store. Plant cells usually have a large central vacuole containing sap (sugar and salts in solution) which serves both as a store of food and as a key factor in maintaining turgor. In amoebae (single-celled animals), vacuoles are the sites of digestion of engulfed food particles.

**vacuum** in general, a region completely empty of matter; in physics, any enclosure in which the gas pressure is considerably less than atmospheric pressure (101,325 pascals).

**vacuum flask** or *Dewar flask* or *Thermos flask,* container for keeping things either hot or cold. It has two silvered glass walls with a vacuum between them, in a metal or plastic outer case. This design reduces the three forms of heat transfer: radiation (prevented by the silvering), conduction, and convection (both prevented by the vacuum). A vacuum flask is therefore equally efficient at keeping cold liquids cold or hot liquids hot. It was invented by the British scientist James Dewar in about 1872, to store liquefied gases.

**Vaduz** capital of the European principality of Liechtenstein; population (1995) 5,100. The economic base is now tourism and financial services. It trades in wine, fruit, and vegetables. Above the town stands the castle of the ruling prince.

**vagina** the lower part of the reproductive tract in female mammals, linking the uterus to the exterior. It admits the penis during sexual intercourse, and is the birth canal down which the baby passes during delivery.

**Valencia** city and capital of Valencia province in the ◊Valencian Community, eastern Spain, on the estuary of the Guadalaviar River; population (1991) 752,900. It is the centre of a very rich agricultural plain noted for the high quality of its citrus fruits, particularly oranges; industries include textiles, chemicals, ship repair, and wine.

**Valencian Community** Spanish *Comunidad Valenciana,* autonomous community of western Spain, comprising the provinces of Alicante, Castellón, and Valencia; area 23,307 sq km/8,999 sq mi; population (1995) 3,857,200. There is a rich agricultural area on the coastal plain, producing oranges, and rice, and industries include iron and steel production and car manufacture. The capital is ◊Valencia.

**valency** in chemistry, the measure of an element's ability to combine with other elements, expressed as the number of atoms of hydrogen (or any other standard univalent element) capable of uniting with (or replacing) its atoms. The number of electrons in the outermost shell of the atom dictates the combining ability of an element.

**Valentine, St** according to tradition, a bishop of Terni martyred in Rome, now omitted from the calendar of saints' days as probably nonexistent. His festival was 14 February, but the custom of sending 'valentines' to a loved one on that day seems to have arisen because the day accidentally coincided with the Roman mid-February festival of ◊Lupercalia.

**Valentino, Rudolph** adopted name of Rodolfo Alfonso Guglielmi di Valentina d'Antonguolla (1895–1926) Italian-born US film actor and dancer. He was the archetypal romantic lover of the Hollywood silent era. His screen debut was 1919, but his first starring role was in *The Four Horsemen of the Apocalypse* (1921). His subsequent films include *The Sheik* (1921) and *Blood and Sand* (1922).

**Vale of Glamorgan** unitary authority in south Wales, created in 1996 from parts of the former counties of Mid Glamorgan and South Glamorgan
*area* 337 sq km/130 sq mi
*towns* Barry (administrative headquarters), Penarth
*physical* lowland area
*agriculture* sheep farming, varied agriculture
*population* (1996) 119,500.

**Valhalla** in Norse mythology, the golden hall in ◊Odin's palace in Asgard, where he feasted with the souls of half those heroes killed in battle (*valr*) chosen by his female attendants, the ◊Valkyries; the remainder celebrated in Sessrumnir with ◊Freya, goddess of love and war.

**Valkyrie** (Old Norse *valr* 'slain', *kjosa* 'choose') in Norse mythology, any of the female attendants of ◊Odin. They directed the course of battles and selected the most valiant warriors to die; half being escorted to ◊Valhalla, and the remainder to Sessrumnir, the hall of ◊Freya.

**Valladolid** capital of Valladolid province, in Castilla–León, Spain; population (1994) 328,400. Industries include food processing, textiles, engineering, and vehicle manufacture. It has a university (founded in 1346) and a 16th-century cathedral.

**Valletta** capital and port of Malta; population (1995) 9,129 (inner harbour area 102,600).

**Valley of the Kings** burial place of ancient kings opposite ◊Thebes, Egypt, on the left bank of the Nile. It was established as a royal cemetery during the reign of Thotmes I (*c.* 1500 BC) and abandoned during the reign of Ramses XI (*c.* 1100 BC).

**Valparaíso** industrial port, naval base, and capital of Valparaiso region, central Chile, situated on a broad bay on the Pacific coast at the foot of a spur of hills, 120 km/75 mi northwest of Santiago; population (1992) 276,700. It is Chile's major port and second-largest city, an administrative centre, and the seat of the Chilean parliament. Both the law courts and the new National Congress are located here. Industries include textiles, chemicals, oil, sugar refining, and leather goods. Fruit and mining products are exported. It is the seat of the Chilean Naval Academy.

**value-added tax** (VAT), tax on goods and services. VAT is imposed by the European Union (EU) on member states. The tax varies from state to state. An agreed proportion of the tax money is used to fund the EU.

**valve** in animals, a structure for controlling the direction of the blood flow. In humans and other vertebrates, the contractions of the beating heart cause the correct blood flow into the arteries because a series of valves prevents back flow. Diseased valves, detected as 'heart murmurs', have decreased efficiency. The tendency for low-pressure venous blood to collect at the base of limbs under the influence of gravity is counteracted by a series of small valves within the veins. It was the existence of these valves that prompted the 17th-century physician William Harvey to suggest that the blood circulated around the body.

**valvular heart disease** damage to the heart valves, leading to either narrowing of the valve orifice when it is open (stenosis) or leaking through the valve when it is closed (regurgitation).

**vampire** (Hungarian *vampir* (and similar forms in other Slavonic languages) in Hungarian and Slavonic folklore, an 'undead' corpse that sleeps in its coffin by day and sucks the blood of the living by night, often in the form of a bat. ◊Dracula is a vampire in popular fiction, based on the creation of Bram Stoker.

**vampire bat** South and Central American bat of the family Desmodontidae, of which there are three species. The ***common vampire Desmodus rotundus*** is found from northern Mexico to central Argentina; its head and body grow to 9 cm/3.5 in. Vampire bats feed on the blood of birds and mammals; they slice a piece of skin from a sleeping animal with their sharp incisor teeth and lap up the flowing blood. They chiefly approach their prey by flying low then crawling and leaping.

**vanadium** silver-white, malleable and ductile, metallic element, symbol V, atomic number 23, relative atomic mass 50.942. It occurs in certain iron, lead, and uranium ores and is widely distributed in small quantities in igneous and sedimentary rocks. It is used to make steel alloys, to which it adds tensile strength.

**Van Allen radiation belts** two zones of charged particles around the Earth's magnetosphere, discovered in 1958 by US physicist James Van Allen. The atomic particles come from the Earth's upper atmosphere and the ◊solar wind, and are trapped by the Earth's magnetic field. The inner belt lies 1,000–5,000 km/620–3,100 mi above the Equator, and contains ◊protons and ◊electrons. The outer belt lies 15,000–25,000 km/9,300–15,500 mi above the Equator, but is lower around the magnetic poles. It contains mostly electrons from the solar wind.

**Vanbrugh, John** (1664–1726) English Baroque architect, dramatist, and soldier. Although entirely untrained as an architect, he designed the huge mansions of Castle Howard (1699–1726), Blenheim (1705–16; completed by Nicholas Hawksmoor 1722–25), Seaton Delaval (1720–29), and many others, as well as much of Greenwich Hospital (1718 onwards). He also wrote the comic dramas *The Relapse* (1696) and *The Provok'd Wife* (1697).

**Vancouver** chief Pacific seaport of Canada, on the mainland of British Columbia; population (1991) 471,800, metropolitan area (1996) 1,891,400. A major commercial, distribution, and tourist centre, it is the terminus of transcontinental rail and road routes, and a 1,144-km/715-mi pipeline from the Alberta oilfields. Industries include oil-refining, engineering, shipbuilding, fishing and fish-canning, brewing, timber-milling, and the manufacture of aircraft, pulp and paper, and textiles.

**Vandal** member of a Germanic people related to the ◊Goths. In the 5th century AD the Vandals invaded Roman ◊Gaul and Spain, many settling in Andalusia (formerly Vandalitia) and others reaching North Africa in 429. They sacked Rome in 455 but were defeated by Belisarius, general of the emperor Justinian, in the 6th century.

**van de Graaff generator** electrostatic generator capable of producing a voltage of over a million volts. It consists of a continuous vertical conveyor belt that carries electrostatic charges (resulting from friction) up to a large hollow sphere supported on an insulated stand. The lower end of the belt is earthed, so that charge accumulates on the sphere. The size of the voltage built up in air depends on the radius of the sphere, but can be increased by enclosing the generator in an inert atmosphere, such as nitrogen.

**van der Waals' law** modified form of the ◊gas laws that includes corrections for the non-ideal behaviour of real gases (the molecules of ideal gases occupy no space and exert no forces on each other). It is named after the Dutch physicist J D van der Waals (1837–1923).

**van Dyck, Anthony** Flemish painter; see ◊Dyck, Anthony van.

**van Eyck, Jan** Flemish painter; see ◊Eyck, Jan van.

**van Gogh, Vincent** Dutch painter; see ◊Gogh, Vincent van.

**vanilla** any of a group of climbing orchids native to tropical America but cultivated elsewhere, with large, fragrant white or yellow flowers. The dried and fermented fruit, or podlike capsules, of the species *V. planifolia* are the source of the vanilla flavouring used in cookery and baking. (Genus *Vanilla*.)

**Vanuatu** Republic of
*national name Ripablik blong Vanuatu*

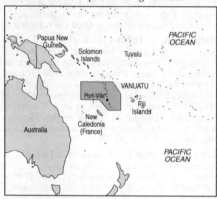

*area* 14,800 sq km/5,714 sq mi
*capital* (and chief port) Port-Vila (on Efate)
*major towns/cities* Luganville (on Espíritu Santo)
*major ports* Santo
*physical features* comprises around 70 inhabited islands, including Espíritu Santo, Malekula, and Efate; densely forested, mountainous; three active volcanoes; cyclones on average twice a year
*head of state* John Bernard Bani from 1999
*head of government* Donald Kalpokas from 1998
*political system* democracy
*political parties* Union of Moderate Parties (UMP), Francophone centrist; National United Party (NUP), formed by Walter Lini; Vanua'aku Pati (VP), Anglophone centrist; Melanesian Progressive Party (MPP), Melanesian centrist; Fren Melanesian Party
*currency* vatu
*GNP per capita (PPP)* (US$) 3,160 (1998 est)
*exports* copra, beef, timber, cocoa, shells. Principal market: Japan 32.1% (1997)
*population* 186,000 (1999 est)
*language* Bislama 82%, English, French (all official)
*religion* Christian 80%, animist
*life expectancy* 66 (men); 70 (women) (1995–2000)
*Chronology*
*1606* First visited by Portuguese navigator Pedro Fernandez de Queiras, who named the islands Espíritu Santo.

*1774* Visited by British navigator Capt James Cook, who named them the New Hebrides, after the Scottish islands.
*1830s* European merchants attracted to islands by sandalwood trade. Christian missionaries arrived, but many were attacked by the indigenous Melanesians who, in turn, were ravaged by exposure to European diseases.
*later 19th century* Britain and France disputed control; islanders were shipped to Australia, the Fiji Islands, Samoa, and New Caledonia to work as plantation labourers.
*1906* The islands were jointly administered by France and Britain as the Condominium of the New Hebrides.
*1963* Indigenous Na-Griamel (NG) political grouping formed on Espíritu Santo to campaign against European acquisition of more than a third of the land area.
*1975* A representative assembly was established following pressure from the VP, formed in 1972 by English-speaking Melanesian Protestants.
*1978* A government of national unity was formed, with Father Gerard Leymang as chief minister.
*1980* A revolt on the island of Espíritu Santo by French settlers and pro-NG plantation workers delayed independence but it was achieved within the Commonwealth, with George Kalkoa (adopted name Sokomanu) as president and left-of-centre Father Walter Lini (VP) as prime minister.
*1988* The dismissal of Lini by Sokomanu led to Sokomanu's arrest for treason. Lini was later reinstated.
*1989* Sokomanu was succeeded as president by Fred Timakata.
*1991* Lini was voted out by party members and replaced by Donald Kalpokas. A general election produced a coalition government of the Francophone Union of Moderate Parties (UMP) and Lini's new National United Party (NUP) under Maxime Carlot Korman.
*1993* A cyclone caused extensive damage.
*1994* Timakata was succeeded as president by Jean Marie Leye.
*1995* The governing UMP–NUP coalition won a general election, but Serge Vohor of the VP-dominated Unity Front became prime minister in place of Carlot Korman.
*1996* Vohor was briefly replaced by Maxime Carlot Korman, but Vohor returned to power leading a new coalition after the Carlot government was implicated in financial scandal. The VP, led by Donald Kalpokas, joined the governing coalition.
*1997* Prime Minister Vohor formed a new coalition. The legislature was dissolved and new elections called after a no-confidence motion against Vohor.
*1998* A two-week state of emergency followed rioting in the capital. Donald Kalpokas was elected prime minister after an early election, heading a VP–NUP coalition.
*1999* John Bernard Bani elected president.

**vapour density** density of a gas, expressed as the ◊mass of a given volume of the gas divided by the mass of an equal volume of a reference gas (such as hydrogen or air) at the same temperature and pressure. It is equal approximately to half the relative molecular weight (mass) of the gas.

**vapour pressure** pressure of a vapour given off by (evaporated from) a liquid or solid, caused by vibrating atoms or molecules continuously escaping from its surface. In an enclosed space, a maximum value is reached when the number of particles leaving the surface is in equilibrium with those returning to it; this is known as the *saturated vapour pressure* or *equilibrium vapour pressure*.

**Varanasi** or *Benares* or *Banaras*, city in Uttar Pradesh, India, one of the seven holy cities of Hinduism, on the River Ganges; population (1991) 932,000. There are 1,500 golden shrines, and a 5 km/3 mi frontage to the Ganges with sacred stairways (ghats) for purification by bathing. Varanasi is also a sacred centre of ◊Jainism, ◊Sikhism, and ◊Buddhism: Buddha came to Varanasi from Gaya and is believed to have preached in the Deer Park. One-third of its inhabitants are Muslim.

**variable** in mathematics, a changing quantity (one that can take various values), as opposed to a ◊constant. For example, in the algebraic expression $y = 4x^3 + 2$, the variables are $x$ and $y$, whereas 4 and 2 are constants.

**variable star** in astronomy, a star whose brightness changes, either regularly or irregularly, over a period ranging from a few hours to months or years. The ◊Cepheid variables regularly expand and contract in size every few days or weeks.

**varicose veins** or *varicosis,* condition where the veins become swollen and twisted. The veins of the legs are most often affected; other vulnerable sites include the rectum (◊haemorrhoids) and testes.

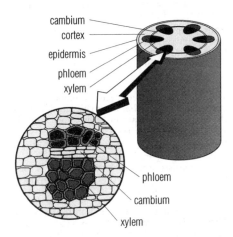

**vascular bundle** *The fluid-carrying tissue of most plants is normally arranged in units called vascular bundles. The vascular tissue is of two types: xylem and phloem. The xylem carries water up through the plant; the phloem distributes food made in the leaves to all parts of the plant.*

**vascular bundle** in botany, strand of primary conducting tissue (a 'vein') in vascular plants, consisting mainly of water-conducting tissues, metaxylem and protoxylem, which together make up the primary ◊xylem, and nutrient-conducting tissue, ◊phloem. It extends from the roots to the stems and leaves. Typically the phloem is situated nearest to the epidermis and the xylem towards the centre of the bundle. In plants exhibiting secondary growth, the xylem and phloem are separated by a thin layer of vascular ◊cambium, which gives rise to new conducting tissues.

**vascular plant** plant containing vascular bundles. ◊Pteridophytes (ferns, horsetails, and club mosses), ◊gymnosperms (conifers and cycads), and ◊angiosperms (flowering plants) are all vascular plants.

**vas deferens** in male vertebrates, a tube conducting sperm from the testis to the urethra. The sperm is carried in a fluid secreted by various glands, and can be transported very rapidly when the smooth muscle in the wall of the vas deferens undergoes rhythmic contraction, as in sexual intercourse.

**vasectomy** male sterilization; an operation to cut and tie the ducts (see ◊vas deferens) that carry sperm from the testes to the penis. Vasectomy does not affect sexual performance, but the semen produced at ejaculation no longer contains sperm.

**VAT** abbreviation for ◊*value-added tax.*

## Vatican City State
*national name* Stato della Città del Vaticano
*area* 0.4 sq km/0.2 sq mi
*physical features* forms an enclave in the heart of Rome, Italy
*head of state* John Paul II from 1978
*head of government* Cardinal Sebastiano Baggio
*political system* absolute Catholicism
*currency* Vatican City lira; Italian lira
*GNP per capita (PPP)* see Italy
*population* 1,000 (1999 est)
*language* Latin (official), Italian
*religion* Roman Catholic
*life expectancy* see Italy
*Chronology*
**AD 64** Death of St Peter, a Christian martyr who, by legend, was killed in Rome and became regarded as the first bishop of Rome. The Pope, as head of the Roman Catholic Church, is viewed as the spiritual descendent of St Peter.
**756** The Pope became temporal ruler of the Papal States, which stretched across central Italy, centred around Rome.
**11th–13th centuries** Under Gregory VII and Innocent III the papacy enjoyed its greatest temporal power.
**1377** After seven decades in which the papacy was based in Avignon (France), Rome once again became the headquarters for the Pope, with the Vatican Palace becoming the official residence.
**1860** Umbria, Marche, and much of Emilia Romagna which, along with Lazio formed the

from 1500 or 2000 BC. The four main collections are: the *Rig-veda* (hymns and praises); *Yajur-Veda* (prayers and sacrificial formulae); *Sâma-Veda* (tunes and chants); and *Atharva-Veda,* or Veda of the Atharvans, the officiating priests at the sacrifices.

**Vedda** (Sinhalese 'hunter') member of any of the aboriginal peoples of Sri Lanka, who occupied the island before the arrival of the Aryans about 550 BC. Formerly cave-dwelling hunter-gatherers, they have now almost died out or merged with the dominant Sinhalese and Tamil populations. They speak a Sinhalese language, belonging to the Indo-European family.

**Vega** or *Alpha Lyrae,* brightest star in the constellation Lyra and the fifth-brightest star in the night sky. It is a blue-white star, 25 light years from the Sun, with a true luminosity 50 times that of the Sun.

**Vega, Lope Felix de (Carpio)** (1562–1635) Spanish poet and dramatist. He was one of the founders of modern Spanish drama. He wrote epics, pastorals, odes, sonnets, novels, and over 500 plays (of which 426 are still in existence), mostly tragicomedies. He set out his views on drama in *Arte nuevo de hacer comedias/The New Art of Writing Plays* (1609), in which he defended his innovations while reaffirming the Classical forms. *Fuenteovejuna* (c. 1614) has been acclaimed as the first proletarian drama.

**vegetative reproduction** type of ◊asexual reproduction in plants that relies not on spores, but on multicellular structures formed by the parent plant. Some of the main types are stolons and runners, gemmae, bulbils, sucker shoots produced from roots (such as in the creeping thistle *Cirsium arvense*), ◊tubers, ◊bulbs, ◊corms, and ◊rhizomes. Vegetative reproduction has long been exploited in horticulture and agriculture, with various methods employed to multiply stocks of plants.

**vein** in animals with a circulatory system, any vessel that carries blood from the body to the heart. Veins contain valves that prevent the blood from running back when moving against gravity. They carry blood at low pressure, so their walls are thinner than those of arteries. They always carry deoxygenated blood, with the exception of the *pulmonary vein,* leading from the lungs to the heart in birds and mammals, which carries newly oxygenated blood.

**Velázquez, Diego Rodríguez de Silva y** (1599–1660) Spanish painter. One of the outstanding artists of the 17th century, he was court painter to Philip IV in Madrid, where he produced many portraits of the royal family as well as occasional religious paintings, genre scenes, and other works. Notable among his portraits is *Las Meninas/The Maids of Honour* (1656; Prado, Madrid), while *Women Frying Eggs* (1618; National Gallery of Scotland, Edinburgh) is a typical genre scene.

**veldt** subtropical grassland in South Africa, equivalent to the ◊Pampas of South America.

**velocity** speed of an object in a given direction. Velocity is a vector quantity, since its

Papal States, were annexed by the new unified Italian state.
**1870** First Vatican Council defined as a matter of faith the absolute primacy of the Pope and the infallibility of his pronouncements on 'matters of faith and morals'.
**1870–71** French forces, which had been protecting the Pope, were withdrawn, allowing Italian nationalist forces to capture Rome, which became the capital of Italy; Pope Pius IX retreated into the Vatican Palace, from which no Pope was to emerge until 1929.
**1929** The Lateran Agreement, signed by the Italian fascist leader Benito Mussolini and Pope Pius XI, restored full sovereign jurisdiction over the Vatican City State to the bishopric of Rome (Holy See) and declared the new state to be a neutral and inviolable territory.
**1947** A new Italian constitution confirmed the sovereignty of the Vatican City State.
**1962** The Second Vatican Council was called by Pope John XXIII.
**1978** John Paul II became the first non-Italian pope for more than 400 years.
**1985** A new concordat was signed under which Roman Catholicism ceased to be Italy's state religion.
**1992** Relations with East European states were restored.

**Vatican Council** either of two Roman Catholic ecumenical councils called by Pope Pius IX 1869 (which met 1870) and by Pope John XXIII 1959 (which met 1962). These councils deliberated over elements of church policy.

**Vaughan Williams, Ralph** (1872–1958) English composer. His style was tonal and often evocative of the English countryside through the use of folk themes. Among his works are the orchestral *Fantasia on a Theme by Thomas Tallis* (1910); the opera *Sir John in Love* (1929), featuring the Elizabethan song 'Greensleeves'; and nine symphonies (1909–57).

**VDU** abbreviation for ◊*visual display unit.*

**Veda** (Sanskrit 'divine knowledge') the most sacred of the Hindu scriptures, hymns written in an old form of Sanskrit; the oldest may date direction is important as well as its magnitude (or speed).

**velvet** fabric of silk, cotton, nylon, or other textile, with a short, thick pile. Utrecht in the Netherlands and Genoa, Italy, are traditional centres of manufacture. It is woven on a double loom, then cut between the centre pile to form velvet nap.

**vena cava** either of the two great veins of the trunk, returning deoxygenated blood to the right atrium of the ◊heart. The *superior vena cava,* beginning where the arches of the two innominate veins join high in the chest, receives blood from the head, neck, chest, and arms; the *inferior vena cava,* arising from the junction of the right and left common iliac veins, receives blood from all parts of the body below the diaphragm.

**venereal disease** (VD), any disease mainly transmitted by sexual contact, although commonly the term is used specifically for gonorrhoea and syphilis, both occurring worldwide, and chancroid ('soft sore') and lymphogranuloma venerum, seen mostly in the tropics. The term ◊*sexually transmitted disease* (STD) is more often used to encompass a growing list of conditions passed on primarily, but not exclusively, by sexual contact.

**Veneto** region of northeast Italy, comprising the provinces of Belluno, Padua, Treviso, Rovigo, Venice, and Vicenza; area 18,400 sq km/7,102 sq mi; population (1992 est) 4,395,300. Its capital is ◊Venice, and towns include Padua, Verona, and Vicenza. The Veneto forms part of the north Italian plain, with the delta of the River Po; it includes part of the Alps and Dolomites, and Lake Garda. Products include cereals, fruit, vegetables, wine, tobacco, chemicals, ships, and textiles.

**Venezuela** Republic of
*national name República de Venezuela*

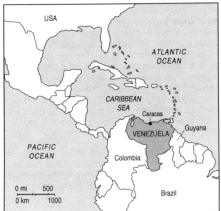

**area** 912,100 sq km/352,161 sq mi
**capital** Caracas
**major towns/cities** Maracaibo, Maracay, Barquisimeto, Valencia, Ciudad Guayana, San Cristóbal

**major ports** Maracaibo
**physical features** Andes Mountains and Lake Maracaibo in northwest; central plains (llanos); delta of River Orinoco in east; Guiana Highlands in southeast
**head of state and government** Hugo Chavez from 1998
**political system** federal democracy
**political parties** Democratic Action Party (AD), moderate left of centre; Christian Social Party (COPEI), Christian, centre right; National Convergence (CN), broad coalition grouping; Movement towards Socialism (MAS), left of centre; Radical Cause (LCR), left wing
**currency** bolívar
**GNP per capita (PPP)** (US$) 8,190 (1998)
**exports** petroleum and petroleum products, metals (mainly aluminium and iron ore), natural gas, chemicals, basic manufactures, motor vehicles and parts. Principal market: USA 56.7% (1997)
**population** 23,706,000 (1999 est)
**language** Spanish (official), Indian languages 2%
**religion** Roman Catholic
**life expectancy** 70 (men); 76 (women) (1995–2000)
***Chronology***
**1st millennium BC** Beginnings of settled agriculture.
**AD 1498–99** Visited by Christopher Columbus and Alonso de Ojeda, at which time the principal indigenous Indian communities were the Caribs, Arawaks, and Chibchas; it was named Venezuela ('little Venice') since the coastal Indians lived in stilted thatched houses.
**1521** Spanish settlement established on the northeast coast and was ruled by Spain from Santo Domingo (Dominican Republic).
**1567** Caracas founded by Diego de Losada.
**1739** Became part of newly created Spanish Viceroyalty of New Granada, with capital at Bogotá (Colombia), but, lacking gold mines, retained great autonomy.
**1749** First rebellion against Spanish colonial rule.
**1806** Rebellion against Spain, led by Francisco Miranda.
**1811–12** First Venezuelan Republic declared by patriots, taking advantage of Napoleon Bonaparte's invasion of Spain, but Spanish Royalist forces re-established their authority.
**1813–14** The Venezuelan, Simón Bolívar, 'El Libertador' (the Liberator), created another briefly independent republic, before being forced to withdraw to Colombia.
**1821** After battle of Carabobo, Venezuelan independence achieved within Republic of Gran Colombia (which also comprised Colombia, Ecuador, and Panama).
**1829** Became separate state of Venezuela after leaving Republic of Gran Colombia.
**1830–48** Gen José Antonio Páez, the first of a series of caudillos (military leaders), established political stability.
**1870–88** Antonio Guzmán Blanco ruled as benevolent liberal–conservative dictator, modernizing infrastructure and developing agriculture (notably coffee) and education.

**1899** International arbitration tribunal found in favour of British Guiana (Guyana) in long-running dispute over border with Venezuela.

**1902** Ports blockaded by British, Italian, and German navies as a result of Venezuela's failure to repay loans.

**1908–35** Harsh rule of dictator Juan Vicente Gómez, during which period Venezuela became world's largest exporter of oil, which had been discovered in 1910.

**1947** First truly democratic elections held, but the new president, Rómulo Gallegos, was removed within eight months by the military in the person of Col Marcos Pérez Jimenez.

**1958** Overthrow of Perez and establishment of an enduring civilian democracy, headed by leftwing Romulo Betancourt of Democratic Action Party (AD).

**1964** Dr Raúl Leoni (AD) became president in first-ever constitutional handover of civilian power.

**1969** Dr Rafael Caldera Rodríguez, of centreright Christian Social Party (COPEI), became president.

**1974** Carlos Andrés Pérez (AD) became president, with economy remaining buoyant through oil revenues. Oil and iron industries nationalized.

**1979** Dr Luis Herrera (COPEI) became president.

**1984** Dr Jaime Lusinchi (AD) became president; social pact established between government, trade unions, and business; national debt rescheduled as oil revenues plummetted.

**1987** Widespread social unrest triggered by inflation; student demonstrators shot by police.

**1989** Carlos Andrés Pérez (AD) was elected president. An economic austerity programme was instigated. Price increases triggered riots known as 'Caracazo'; 300 people were killed. Martial law was declared and a general strike followed. Elections were boycotted by opposition groups.

**1992** An attempted antigovernment coup failed, at a cost of 120 lives.

**1993** Pérez resigned, accused of corruption; Ramon José Velasquez succeeded him as interim head of state. Former president Dr Rafael Caldera (COMEI) was re-elected.

**1996** Pérez was found guilty on corruption charges and imprisoned.

**1998** Hugo Chavez was elected president.

**1999** Hugo Chavez was inaugurated as president.

**Venice** Italian *Venezia*, city, port, and naval base on the northeast coast of Italy; population (1992) 305,600. It is the capital of Veneto region.

The old city is built on piles on low-lying islands in a salt-water lagoon, sheltered from the Adriatic Sea by the Lido and other small strips of land. There are about 150 canals crossed by some 400 bridges. Apart from tourism (it draws 8 million tourists a year), industries include glass, jewellery, textiles, and lace. Venice was an independent trading republic from the 10th century, ruled by a doge, or chief magistrate, and was one of the centres of the Italian Renaissance. It was renowned as a centre of early publishing; 15% of all printed books before 1500 were printed in Venice.

**Venn diagram** in mathematics, a diagram representing a ◊set or sets and the logical relationships between them. The sets are drawn as circles. An area of overlap between two circles (sets) contains elements that are common to both sets, and thus represents a third set. Circles that do not overlap represent sets with no elements in common (disjoint sets). The method is named after the English logician John Venn.

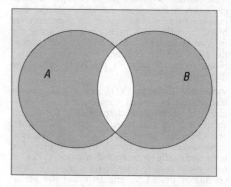

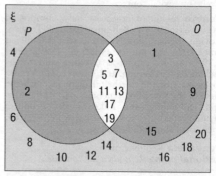

**Venn diagram** *Sets and their relationships are often represented by Venn diagrams. The sets are drawn as circles – the area of overlap between the circles shows elements that are common to each set, and thus represent a third set. Here (a) is a Venn diagram of two intersecting sets and (b) a Venn diagram showing the set of whole numbers from 1 to 20 and the subsets P and O of prime and odd numbers, respectively. The intersection of P and O contains all the prime numbers that are also odd.*

**ventral surface** the front of an animal. In vertebrates, the side furthest from the backbone; in invertebrates, the side closest to the ground. The positioning of the main nerve pathways on the ventral side is a characteristic of invertebrates.

**ventricle** in zoology, either of the two lower chambers of the heart that force blood to circulate by contraction of their muscular walls. The term also refers to any of four cavities within the brain in which cerebrospinal fluid is produced.

**Venus** in Roman mythology, the goddess of love and beauty, equivalent to the Greek ◊Aphrodite. The patricians of Rome claimed descendance from her son, the Trojan prince ◊Aeneas, and she was consequently venerated as the guardian of the Roman people. Venus was also worshipped as a goddess of military victory and patroness of spring.

**Venus** second planet from the Sun. It can approach Earth to within 38 million km/24 million mi, closer than any other planet. Its mass is 0.82 that of Earth. Venus rotates on its axis more slowly than any other planet, from east to west, the opposite direction to the other planets (except Uranus and possibly Pluto).
**mean distance from the Sun** 108.2 million km/67.2 million mi
**equatorial diameter** 12,100 km/7,500 mi
**rotation period** 243 Earth days
**year** 225 Earth days
**atmosphere** Venus is shrouded by clouds of sulphuric acid droplets that sweep across the planet from east to west every four days. The atmosphere is almost entirely carbon dioxide, which traps the Sun's heat by the ◊greenhouse effect and raises the planet's surface temperature to 480°C/900°F, with an atmospheric pressure of 90 times that at the surface of the Earth.
**surface** consists mainly of silicate rock and may have an interior structure similar to that of Earth: an iron–nickel core, a mantle composed of more mafic rocks (rocks made of one or more ferromagnesian, dark-coloured minerals), and a thin siliceous outer crust. The surface is dotted with deep impact craters. Some of Venus's volcanoes may still be active.
**satellites** no moons.

**Venus flytrap** insectivorous plant belonging to the sundew family, native to the southeastern USA. Its leaves have two hinged surfaces that rapidly close together to trap any insect which brushes against the sensitive leaf hairs; digestive juices then break down the insect body so that it can be absorbed by the plant. (*Dionaea muscipula*, family Droseraceae.)

**verbena** any of a group of plants containing about 100 species, mostly found in the American tropics. The leaves are fragrant and the tubular flowers are arranged in close spikes in colours ranging from white to rose, violet, and purple. The garden verbena is a hybrid annual. (Genus *Verbena*, family Verbenaceae.)

**Verdi, Giuseppe Fortunino Francesco** (1813–1901) Italian opera composer of the Romantic period. He took his native operatic style to new heights of dramatic expression. In 1842 he wrote the opera *Nabucco*, followed by *Ernani* (1844) and *Rigoletto* (1851). Other works include *Il trovatore* and *La traviata* (both 1853), *Aïda* (1871), and the masterpieces of his old age, *Otello* (1887) and *Falstaff* (1893). His *Requiem* (1874) commemorates the poet and novelist Alessandro Manzoni.

**verdigris** green-blue coating of copper ethanoate that forms naturally on copper, bronze, and brass. It is an irritating, poisonous compound made by treating copper with ethanoic acid, and was formerly used in wood preservatives, antifouling compositions, and green paints.

**Verdun** fortress town in northeast France in the *département* of the Meuse, 280 km/174 mi east of Paris. During World War I it became a symbol of French resistance and was the centre of a series of bitterly fought actions between French and German forces, finally being recaptured in September 1918.

**Vermeer, Jan** (1632–1675) Dutch painter, active in Delft. He painted quiet, everyday scenes that are characterized by an almost abstract simplicity, subtle colour harmonies, and a remarkable ability to suggest the fall of light on objects. Examples are *The Lacemaker* about (1655; Louvre, Paris) and *Maidservant Pouring Milk* (about 1658) (Rijksmuseum, Amsterdam).

**Vermont** state in northeastern USA. It is nicknamed the Green Mountain State. Vermont was admitted to the Union in 1791 as the 14th US state. It is bordered to the north by Québec, Canada, to the east by New Hampshire, to the south by Massachusetts, and to the west by New York
**population** (1995) 584,800
**area** 24,900 sq km/9,611 sq mi
**capital** Montpelier
**towns and cities** Burlington, Rutland, Barre
**industries and products** apples, maple syrup, dairy products, china clay, granite, marble, slate, business machines, paper and allied products, computers and high-tech manufacturing, tourism, leisure industry.

**Verne, Jules** (1828–1905) French author. He wrote tales of adventure that anticipated future scientific developments: *Five Weeks in a Balloon* (1862), *Journey to the Centre of the Earth* (1864), *Twenty Thousand Leagues under the Sea* (1870), and *Around the World in Eighty Days* (1873).

**Verona** town in Veneto, Italy, on the Adige River, 100 km/62 mi west of Venice; population (1992) 255,500. It lies at the junction of the Brenner Pass road with the Venice–Milan motorway. Industries include printing, engineering, and the manufacture of paper, plastics, furniture, and pasta. It is one of Italy's main marketing centres for fruit and vegetables.

**Veronese, Paolo (Paolo Caliari)** (*c.* 1528–1588) Italian painter, born in Verona. He was the pupil of Antonio Badile, but also learned from the study of Titian and ◊Tintoretto. Some part of his youth was spent in the shop of his brother Antonio, who dealt in the embroidery and rich stuffs that were to play an important decorative part in his painting. From 1555 he lived in Venice, producing those huge decorative compositions with the representation of splendid architecture and crowds of luxuriously dressed figures for which he is famous. He was active mainly in Venice. He specialized in grand decorative schemes, such as his ceilings in the Doge's Palace, noted for their rich colouring, broad composition, *trompe l'oeil* effects, and inventive detail. Religious, mythological, historical, or allegorical, his paintings – usually of banquets and scenes of pageantry – celebrated the power and splendour of Venice.

**Versailles, Treaty of** peace treaty after World War I between the Allies and Germany, signed on 28 June 1919. It established the ◊League of Nations. Germany surrendered Alsace-Lorraine to France, and large areas in the east to Poland, and made smaller cessions to Czechoslovakia, Lithuania, Belgium, and Denmark. The Rhineland was demilitarized, German rearmament was restricted, and Germany agreed to pay reparations for war damage. The treaty was never ratified by the USA, which made a separate peace with Germany and Austria in 1921.

**vertebral column** the backbone, giving support to an animal and protecting its spinal cord. It is made up of a series of bones or vertebrae running from the skull to the tail, with a central canal containing the nerve fibres of the spinal cord. In tetrapods the vertebrae show some specialization with the shape of the bones varying according to position. In the chest region the upper or thoracic vertebrae are shaped to form connections to the ribs. The backbone is only slightly flexible to give adequate rigidity to the animal structure.

**vertebrate** any animal with a backbone. The 41,000 species of vertebrates include mammals, birds, reptiles, amphibians, and fishes. They include most of the larger animals, but in terms of numbers of species are only a tiny proportion of the world's animals. The zoological taxonomic group Vertebrata is a subgroup of the ◊phylum Chordata.

**vertigo** dizziness; a whirling sensation accompanied by a loss of any feeling of contact with the ground. It may be due to temporary disturbance of the sense of balance (as in spinning for too long on one spot), psychological reasons, disease such as labyrinthitis, or intoxication.

**Verulamium** Romano-British town near St Albans, Hertfordshire, occupied until about AD 450. Verulamium superseded a nearby Belgic settlement and was first occupied by the Romans in 44–43 BC. The earliest English martyr, St Alban, was martyred here, perhaps during the reign of Septimus ◊Severus. A fragmentary inscription from the site of the forum records the name of the Roman governor ◊Agricola. The site became deserted in the late 5th or 6th century.

**Vesalius, Andreas** (1514–1564) Belgian physician who revolutionized anatomy by performing postmortem dissections and making use of illustrations to teach anatomy. Vesalius upset the authority of ◊Galen, and his book – the first real textbook of anatomy – marked the beginning of biology as a science.

**Vespasian** also known as Titus Flavius Vespasianus (9–79) Roman emperor from AD 69. Proclaimed emperor by his soldiers while he was campaigning in Palestine, he reorganized the eastern provinces, and was a capable administrator. He was responsible for the construction of the Colosseum in Rome, which was completed by his son Titus.

**Vesta** in Roman mythology, the goddess of the hearth, equivalent with the Greek Hestia. In Rome, the sacred flame in her shrine at the Forum represented the spirit of the community, and was kept constantly alight by the six *Vestal Virgins*.

**Vesuvius** Italian *Vesuvio,* active volcano in Campania, Italy, 15 km/9 mi southeast of Naples, Italy; height 1,277 m/4,190 ft. In AD 79 it destroyed the cities of Pompeii, Herculaneum, and Stabiae.

**Veterans Day** in the USA, the name adopted in 1954 for ◊Armistice Day and from 1971 observed by most states on 11 November. The equivalent in the UK and Canada is Remembrance Sunday.

**veto** (Latin 'I forbid') exercise by a sovereign, branch of legislature, or other political power, of the right to prevent the enactment or operation of a law, or the taking of some course of action.

**VHF** abbreviation for *very high frequency,* referring to radio waves that have very short wavelengths (10 m–1 m). They are used for interference-free FM transmissions (see ◊frequency modulation). VHF transmitters have a relatively short range because the waves cannot be reflected over the horizon like longer radio waves.

**vibraphone** electrophonic percussion instrument resembling a ◊xylophone but with metal keys. Electrically driven discs spin within resonating tubes under each key to add a tremulant effect that can be controlled in length with a foot pedal.

**viburnum** any of a group of small trees or shrubs belonging to the honeysuckle family, found in temperate and subtropical regions, including the wayfaring tree, the laurustinus, and the guelder rose of Europe and Asia, and the North American blackhaws and arrowwoods. (Genus *Viburnum,* family Caprifoliaceae.)

**vice versa** (Latin) the other way around.

**Vichy government** in World War II, the right-wing government of unoccupied France after the country's defeat by the Germans in June 1940, named after the spa town of Vichy, France, where the national assembly was based under Prime Minister Pétain until the liberation in 1944. *Vichy France* was that part of France not occupied by German troops until November 1942. Authoritarian and collaborationist, the Vichy regime cooperated with the Germans even after they had moved to the unoccupied zone November 1942. It imprisoned some 135,000 people, interned another 70,000, deported some 76,000 Jews, and sent 650,000 French workers to Germany.

**Victoria** state of southeast Australia; bounded on the north and northeast by New South Wales, from which it is separated by the River Murray; on the west by South Australia; and on the south and southeast by the Southern Ocean, Bass Strait, and the Pacific Ocean
*area* 227,600 sq km/87,876 sq mi
*capital* ◊Melbourne

**towns and cities** Geelong, Ballarat, Bendigo
**features** part of the Great Dividing Range,
running east–west and including the larger part
of the Australian Alps; Aboriginal rock paintings in the Grampians; Gippsland lake district;
the ◊mallee shrub region
**agriculture** wool, beef, dairy products,
tobacco, wheat, wine, dried fruit, orchard fruits,
vegetables
**industries** mining of gold, brown coal, gypsum, kaolin, and bauxite, extraction of oil and
natural gas, oil refining, electronics, food processing, chemicals, pharmaceuticals, machinery,
cars, textiles, wine, aquaculture, wool, building
materials
**population** (1996) 4,373,500
**history** annexed for Britain by Captain James
◊Cook in 1770; settled in the 1830s; after being
part of New South Wales, known as the Port
Philip district, became a separate colony in
1851, named after Queen Victoria; gold was discovered at Ballarat in 1851; ◊Eureka Stockade
miners' revolt in 1854; became a state in 1901.

**Victoria** (1819–1901) Queen of the UK from
1837, when she succeeded her uncle William IV,
and Empress of India from 1877. In 1840 she
married Prince ◊Albert of Saxe-Coburg and
Gotha. Her relations with her prime ministers
ranged from the affectionate (Melbourne and
Disraeli) to the stormy (Peel, Palmerston, and
Gladstone). Her golden jubilee in 1887 and diamond jubilee in 1897 marked a waning of
republican sentiment, which had developed with
her withdrawal from public life on Albert's
death in 1861.

**Victoria Cross** British decoration for conspicuous bravery in wartime, instituted by Queen
Victoria in 1856.

**Victoria, Lake** or *Victoria Nyanza,* largest
lake in Africa and third-largest freshwater lake
in the world; area over 68,800 sq km/26,560 sq
mi; length 410 km/255 mi; average depth .80
m/260 ft. It lies on the Equator at an altitude of
1,136 m/3,728 ft, bounded by Uganda, Kenya,
and Tanzania. It is a source of the River Nile.

**Victorian** style of architecture, furnituremak-
ing, and decorative art covering the reign of
Queen Victoria, from 1837 to 1901. The era
was influenced by significant industrial and
urban development, and the massive expansion
of the ◊British Empire.
Victorian style was often very ornate,
markedly so in architecture, where there was
more than one 'revival' of earlier styles, beginning with a lengthy competition between the
*Classic* and *Gothic* schools. Gothic Revival
drew on the original Gothic architecture of
medieval times. The Gothic boom had begun in
1818, when Parliament voted a million pounds
for building 214 new Anglican churches. No less
than 174 of them were constructed in a Gothic
or near-Gothic style, and for nearly a century,
most churches in England were Gothic in design.
Despite the popularity of extravagant decoration, Renaissance or Classic styles were also
favoured for public buildings, examples being St

George's Hall, Liverpool (1815), and
Birmingham Town Hall (1832–50).
Many people, such as John ◊Ruskin, believed
in designing objects and architecture primarily
for their function, and not for mere appearance.
Increasing mass production by machines threatened the existence of craft skills, and encouraged
the development of the ◊Arts and Crafts movement, with its nostalgia for the medieval way of
life. In the last quarter of the century there were
revivals of *Jacobean* and finally of *Queen Anne*
architecture.

**vicuna** ◊ruminant mammal *Lama vicugna* of
the camel family that lives in herds on the
Andean plateau. It can run at speeds of 50 kph/
30 mph. It has good eyesight, fair hearing, and a
poor sense of smell. Hunted close to extinction
for its meat and soft brown fur, which was used
in textile manufacture, the vicuna is now a protected species. Its populations are increasing
thanks to strict conservation measures; by 1996
they had reached 100,000–200,000. The vicuna
is listed on CITES Appendix 2 (vulnerable).
It is related to the ◊alpaca, the ◊guanaco, and
the ◊llama.

**video camera** or *camcorder,* portable television camera that records moving pictures electronically on magnetic tape. It produces an
electrical output signal corresponding to rapid
line-by-line scanning of the field of view. The
output is recorded on video cassette and is
played back on a television screen via a ◊video
cassette recorder. *See illustration on page 950.*

**video cassette recorder** (VCR), device for
recording on and playing back video cassettes; see
◊videotape recorder. *See illustration on page 950.*

**video disk** disk with pictures and sounds
recorded on it, played back by laser. The video
disk is a type of ◊compact disc.

**videotape recorder** (VTR), device for
recording pictures and sound on cassettes or
spools of magnetic tape. The first commercial
VTR was launched in 1956 for the television
broadcasting industry, but from the late 1970s
cheaper models developed for home use, to
record broadcast programmes for future viewing
and to view rented or owned video cassettes of
commercial films.

**videotext** system in which information (text
and simple pictures) is displayed on a television
(video) screen. There are two basic systems,
known as ◊teletext and viewdata. In the teletext
system information is broadcast with the ordinary
television signals, whereas in the viewdata system
information is relayed to the screen from a central
data bank via the telephone network. Both systems require the use of a television receiver (or a
connected VTR) with special decoder.

**Vienna** German *Wien,* capital of Austria, on
the River Danube at the foot of the Wiener Wald
(Vienna Woods); population (1995) 1,531,200.
Although within the territory of Lower Austria,
it is a separate province. Industries include engineering, electrical goods, electronics, clothing,
precision and musical instruments, and beer. It is
a major cultural and tourist centre.

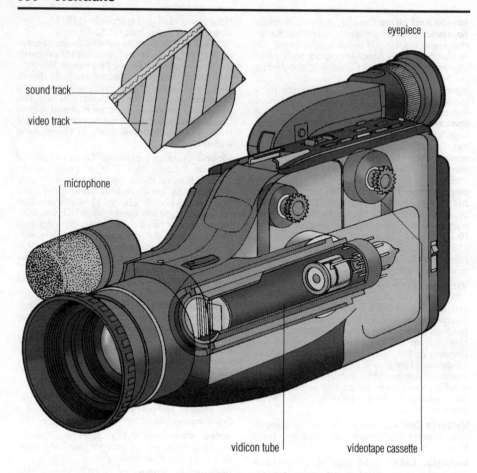

**video camera** *The heart of the video camera is the vidicon tube which converts light entering the front lens to an electrical signal. An image is formed on a light-sensitive surface at the front of the tube. The image is then scanned by an electron beam, to give an output signal corresponding to the image brightness. The signal is recorded as a magnetic track traversing the tape diagonally. The sound track, which records the sounds picked up by the microphone, runs along the edge of the tape.*

**Vientiane** Lao *Vieng Chan,* capital and chief port of Laos on the Mekong River; population (1992) 449,000. Noted for its pagodas, canals, and houses on stilts, it is a trading centre for forest products and textiles. The Temple of the Heavy Buddha, the Pratuxai triumphal arch, and the Black Stupa are here. The Great Sacred Stupa to the northeast of the city is the most important national monument in Laos.

**Vietnam** Socialist Republic of
**national name** *Công Hòa Xã Hôi Chu Nghia Viêt Nam*
**area** 329,600 sq km/127,258 sq mi
**capital** Hanoi
**major towns/cities** Ho Chi Minh City (formerly Saigon), Haiphong, Da Nang, Can Tho, Nha Trang, Nam Dinh
**major ports** Ho Chi Minh City (formerly Saigon), Da Nang, Haiphong
**physical features** Red River and Mekong

deltas, centre of cultivation and population; tropical rainforest; mountainous in north and northwest
**head of state** Tran Duc Luong from 1997
**head of government** Phan Van Khai from 1997
**political system** communism
**political party** Communist Party
**currency** dong
**GNP per capita (PPP)** (US$) 1,690 (1998)
**exports** rice (leading exporter), crude petroleum, coal, coffee, marine products, handicrafts, light industrial goods, rubber, nuts, tea, garments, tin. Principal market: Japan 18.2% (1997)
**population** 78,705,000 (1999 est)
**language** Vietnamese (official); French, English, Khmer, Chinese, local languages
**religion** Taoist, Buddhist, Roman Catholic
**life expectancy** 65 (men); 70 (women) (1995–2000)
**Chronology**
**300 BC** Rise of Dong Son culture.
**111 BC** Came under Chinese rule.
**1st–6th centuries AD** Southern Mekong delta region controlled by independent Indianized Funan kingdom.
**939** Chinese overthrown by Ngo Quyen at battle of Bach Dang River; first Vietnamese dynasty founded.
**11th century** Theravāda Buddhism promoted.
**15th century** North and South Vietnam united, as kingdom of Champa in the south was destroyed in 1471.
**16th century** Contacts with French missionaries and European traders as political power became decentralized.
**early 19th century** Under Emperor Nguyen Anh authority was briefly recentralized.
**1858–84** Conquered by France and divided into protectorates of Tonkin (North Vietnam) and Annam (South Vietnam).
**1887** Became part of French Indo-China Union, which included Cambodia and Laos.
**late 19th–early 20th century** Development of colonial economy based in south on rubber and rice, drawing migrant labourers from north.
**1930** Indochinese Communist Party (ICP) formed by Ho Chi Minh to fight for independence.
**1941** Occupied by Japanese during World War II; ICP formed Vietminh as guerrilla resistance force designed to overthrow Japanese-installed puppet regime headed by Bao Dai, Emperor of Annam.
**1945** Japanese removed from Vietnam at end of World War II; Vietminh, led by Ho Chi Minh, in control of much of the country, declared independence.
**1946** Vietminh war began against French, who tried to reassert colonial control and set up non-communist state in south 1949.
**1954** France decisively defeated at Dien Bien Phu. Vietnam divided along 17th parallel between communist-controlled North and US-backed South.
**1963** Ngo Dinh Diem, leader of South Vietnam, overthrown in military coup by Lt-Gen Nguyen Van Thieu.

**1964** US combat troops entered Vietnam War as North Vietnamese army began to attack South and allegedly attacked US destroyers in the Tonkin Gulf.
**1969** Death of Ho Chi Minh, who was succeeded as Communist Party leader by Le Duan. US forces, which numbered 545,000 at their peak, gradually began to be withdrawn from Vietnam as a result of domestic opposition to the rising casualty toll.
**1973** Paris ceasefire agreement provided for withdrawal of US troops and release of US prisoners of war.
**1975** Saigon captured by North Vietnam, violating Paris Agreements.
**1976** Socialist Republic of Vietnam proclaimed. Hundreds of thousands of southerners became political prisoners; many more fled abroad. Collectivization extended to south.
**1978** Diplomatic relations severed with China. Admission into Comecon. Vietnamese invasion of Cambodia.
**1979** Sino-Vietnamese 17-day border war; 700,000 Chinese and middle-class Vietnamese fled abroad as refugee 'boat people'.
**1986** Death of Le Duan and retirement of 'old guard' leaders; pragmatic Nguyen Van Linh became Communist Party leader and encouraged the private sector through *doi moi* ('renovation') initiative.
**1987–88** Over 10,000 political prisoners released.
**1989** Troops were fully withdrawn from Cambodia.
**1991** Economic reformer Vo Van Kiet replaced Do Muoi as prime minister. A Cambodia peace agreement was signed. Relations with China were normalized.
**1992** A new constitution was adopted, guaranteeing economic freedoms. The conservative Le Duc Anh was elected president. Relations with South Korea were normalized.
**1994** The US 30-year trade embargo was removed.
**1995** Full diplomatic relations were re-established with the USA. Vietnam became a full member of ASEAN.
**1996** The economic upturn gained pace.
**1997** Diplomatic relations with the USA were restored. Tran Duc Luong and Phan Van Khai were elected president and prime minister respectively. The size of the standing army was reduced.
**1998** The Vietnamese currency was devalued. Corruption charges were made against a senior communist, Pham The Duyet. A new emphasis was placed on agricultural development after export and GDP growth slumped to 3% in 1998.
**1999** Tran Do, a former high-ranking communist, was expelled from the Communist Party after urging democratization.

**Vietnam War** (1954–75), war between communist North Vietnam and US-backed South Vietnam, in which North Vietnam aimed to conquer South Vietnam and unite the country as a communist state; the USA, in supporting the South against the North, aimed to prevent the spread of communism in Southeast Asia. Some 200,000 South Vietnamese soldiers, 1 million North Vietnamese soldiers, and 500,000 civilians were killed; 56,555 US soldiers were killed 1961–75, a fifth of them by their own troops. The war destroyed 50% of the country's forest cover and 20% of agricultural land. Cambodia, a neutral neighbour, was bombed by the USA 1969–75, with 1 million killed or wounded. At the end of the war North and South Vietnam were reunited as a socialist republic.

**Viking** or *Norseman,* the inhabitants of Scandinavia in the period 800–1100. They traded with, and raided, much of Europe, and often settled there. In their narrow, shallow-draught, highly manoeuvrable longships, the Vikings penetrated far inland along rivers. They plundered for gold and land, and were equally energetic as colonists – with colonies stretching from North America to central Russia – and as traders, with main trading posts at Birka (near Stockholm) and Hedeby (near Schleswig). The Vikings had a sophisticated literary culture, with ◊sagas and runic inscriptions, and an organized system of government with an assembly ('thing'). Their kings and chieftains were buried with their ships, together with their possessions.

**Viking probes** two US space probes to Mars, each one consisting of an orbiter and a lander. They were launched on 20 August and 9 September 1975. They transmitted colour pictures and analysed the soil.

**villeinage** system of serfdom that prevailed in Europe in the Middle Ages.

A villein was a peasant who gave dues and services to his lord in exchange for land. In France until the 13th century, 'villeins' could refer to rural or urban non-nobles, but after this, it came to mean exclusively rural non-noble freemen. In Norman England, it referred to free peasants of relatively high status. At the time of the Domesday Book, the villeins were the most numerous element in the English population, providing the labour force for the manors.

**Villeneuve, Jacques** (1971–  ) Canadian racing driver. The son of the Formula 1 driver Gilles Villeneuve, he rose to prominence in 1995 when he won the Indy Car World Series and the Indianapolis 500. Two years later, driving for Williams, he became the first Canadian to win the Formula 1 World Drivers' Championship. In 1999 he left Williams for the new British American Racing (BAR) team.

*career highlights*
*Formula 1 World Driver's Champion* 1997
*Formula 1 Grand Prix wins (1995–97)* 11
*Indy Car world series champion* 1995
*Indianapolis 500* 1995

**villus** (plural *villi*) small fingerlike projection extending into the interior of the small intestine and increasing the absorptive area of the intestinal wall. Digested nutrients, including sugars and amino acids, pass into the villi and are carried away by the circulating blood.

**Vilnius** German *Wilna;* Russian *Vilna;* Polish *Wilno,* capital of Lithuania, situated on the River Neris; population (1991) 593,000. Vilnius is an important railway crossroads and commercial centre. Its industries include electrical engineering, woodworking, and the manufacture of textiles, chemicals, and foodstuffs.

**Vimy Ridge** hill in northern France, taken in World War I by Canadian troops during the battle of Arras, April 1917, at the cost of 11,285 lives. It is a spur of the ridge of Notre Dame de Lorette, 8 km/5 mi northeast of Arras.

**vincristine** ◊alkaloid extracted from the blue periwinkle plant *Vinca rosea.* Developed as an anticancer agent, it has revolutionized the treatment of childhood acute leukaemias; it is also included in ◊chemotherapy regimens for some lymphomas (cancers arising in the lymph tissues) and lung and breast cancers. Side effects, such as nerve damage and loss of hair, are severe but usually reversible.

**vine** or *grapevine,* any of a group of climbing woody plants, especially *V. vinifera,* native to Asia Minor and cultivated from antiquity. The fruits (grapes) are eaten or made into wine or other fermented drinks; dried fruits of certain varieties are known as raisins and currants. Many other species of climbing plant are also called vines. (Genus *Vitis,* family Vitaceae.)

**viol** member of a Renaissance family of bowed six-stringed musical instruments with flat backs, fretted fingerboards, and narrow shoulders that flourished particularly in England from about 1540–1700, before their role was taken by the violins. Normally performing as an ensemble or consort, their repertoire is a development of madrigal style with idiomatic decoration.

**viola** bowed, stringed musical instrument, the alto member of the violin family. Its four strings are tuned C3, G3, D4, and A5. With its dark, vibrant tone, it is often used for music of reflective character, as in Stravinsky's *Elegy* (1944) or Britten's *Lachrymae* (1950). Its principal function is harmonic in string quartets and orchestras. Concertos have been written for the viola by composers such as Telemann, Berlioz, Walton, Hindemith, and Bartók.

**violet** any of a group of perennial herbaceous plants found in temperate regions; they have heart-shaped leaves and mauve, blue, or white five-petalled flowers, for example the dog violet *V. canina,* found on sandy heaths, and the fragrant sweet violet *V. odorata.* A ◊pansy is a kind of violet. (Genus *Viola,* family Violaceae.)

**violin** bowed, four-stringed musical instrument, the smallest and highest pitched (treble) of the violin family. The strings are tuned in fifths (G3, D4, A5, and E5).

**viper** any front-fanged venomous snake of the family Viperidae. Vipers range in size from 30 cm/1 ft to 3 m/10 ft, and often have diamond or jagged markings. Most give birth to live young.

**Virgil** (70–19 BC) Publius Vergilius Maro, Roman poet. He wrote the *Eclogues* (37 BC), a series of pastoral poems; the *Georgics* (30 BC), four books on the art of farming; and his epic masterpiece, the *Aeneid* (30–19 BC). He was patronized by Maecenas on behalf of Octavian (later the emperor Augustus).

**virginal** plucked stringed keyboard instrument of the 16th and 17th centuries, often called 'virginals' or 'a pair of virginals' in England, where the term was applied to any quilled keyboard instrument well into the 17th century. The virginal is rectangular or polygonal in shape and is distinguished from the ◊harpsichord and spinet by its strings being set at right angles to the keys, rather than parallel with them.

**Virginia** state in eastern USA. It is nicknamed Old Dominion. Officially known as the *Commonwealth of Virginia,* it ratified the US Constitution in 1788, becoming the 10th US state. It is bordered to the north by Maryland and the District of Columbia, to the west by Kentucky and West Virginia, and to the south by North Carolina and Tennessee. In the east it occupies the southern tip of the Delamarva Peninsula and is bordered by the Atlantic Ocean. Virginia was the northeasternmost state of the Confederacy
*population* (1995) 6,618,400
*area* 105,600 sq km/40,762 sq mi
*capital* Richmond
*towns and cities* Norfolk, Virginia Beach, Newport News, Hampton, Chesapeake, Portsmouth
*industries and products* sweet potatoes, maize, tobacco, apples, peanuts, coal, ships, lorries, paper, chemicals, processed food, textiles, tourism, leisure industry.

**Virgin Islands** group of about 100 small islands, northernmost of the Leeward Islands in the Antilles, West Indies. Tourism is the main industry.

They comprise the *US Virgin Islands*: St Thomas (with the capital, Charlotte Amalie), St Croix, St John, and about 50 small islets; area 350 sq km/135 sq mi; population (1990) 101,800; and the *British Virgin Islands*: Tortola (with the capital, Road Town), Virgin Gorda, Anegada, and Jost van Dykes, and about 40 islets (11 islands are inhabited); area 150 sq km/58 sq mi; population (1991) 16,100.

**Virgo** zodiacal constellation of the northern hemisphere, the second-largest in the sky. It is represented as a maiden holding an ear of wheat, marked by first-magnitude ◊Spica, Virgo's brightest star. The Sun passes through Virgo from late September to the end of October. In astrology, the dates for Virgo are between about 23 August and 22 September (see ◊precession).

**virtual reality** advanced form of computer simulation, in which a participant has the illusion of being part of an artificial environment. The participant views the environment through two tiny television screens (one for each eye) built into a visor. Sensors detect movements of the participant's head or body, causing the apparent viewing position to change. Gloves (datagloves) fitted with sensors may be worn, which allow the participant seemingly to pick up and move objects in the environment.

**virus** infectious particle consisting of a core of nucleic acid (DNA or RNA) enclosed in a protein shell. Viruses are acellular and able to function and reproduce only if they can invade a living cell to use the cell's system to replicate themselves. In the process they may disrupt or alter the host cell's own DNA. The healthy human body reacts by producing an antiviral protein, ◊interferon, which prevents the infection spreading to adjacent cells.

There are around 5,000 species of virus known to science (1998), though there may be as many as 0.5 million actually in existence.

**viscose** yellowish, syrupy solution made by treating cellulose with sodium hydroxide and carbon disulphide. The solution is then regenerated as continuous filament for the making of ◊rayon and as cellophane.

**viscosity** in physics, the resistance of a fluid to flow, caused by its internal friction, which makes it resist flowing past a solid surface or other layers of the fluid. It applies to the motion of an object moving through a fluid as well as to the motion of a fluid passing by an object.

**Vishnu** in Hinduism, the second in the triad of gods (with Brahma and Siva) representing three aspects of the supreme spirit. He is the *Preserver,* and is believed to have assumed human appearance in nine *avatāra*s, or incarnations, in such forms as Rama and Krishna. His worshippers are the Vaishnavas.

**Visigoth** member of the western branch of the ◊Goths, an East Germanic people.

**vision defect** any abnormality of the eye that causes less-than-perfect sight. Common defects are short-sightedness or ◊myopia; long-sightedness or ◊hypermetropia; lack of ◊accommodation or presbyopia; and ◊astigmatism. Other eye defects include colour blindness.

**visual display unit** (VDU), computer terminal consisting of a keyboard for input data and a screen for displaying output. The oldest and most popular type of VDU screen is the ◊cathode-ray tube (CRT), which uses essentially the same technology as a television screen. Other types use plasma display technology and ◊liquid-crystal displays.

**vitamin** any of various chemically unrelated organic compounds that are necessary in small quantities for the normal functioning of the human body. Many act as coenzymes, small molecules that enable ◊enzymes to function effectively. Vitamins must be supplied by the diet because the body cannot make them. They are normally present in adequate amounts in a balanced diet. Deficiency of a vitamin may lead to a metabolic disorder ('deficiency disease'), which can be remedied by sufficient intake of the vitamin. They are generally classified as *water-soluble* (B and C) or *fat-soluble* (A, D, E, and K). See separate entries for individual vitamins, also nicotinic acid and ◊folic acid.

**vitamin A** another name for ◊retinol.

**vitamin B₁** another name for ◊thiamine.

**vitamin B**₁₂ another name for ◊cyanocobalamin.

**vitamin B**₂ another name for ◊riboflavin.

**vitamin B**₆ another name for pyridoxine.

**vitamin C** another name for ascorbic acid.

**vitamin D** another name for cholecalciferol.

**vitamin E** another name for tocopherol.

**vitamin H** another name for biotin.

**vitamin K** another name for ◊phytomenadione.

**vitriol** any of a number of sulphate salts. Blue, green, and white vitriols are copper, ferrous, and zinc sulphate, respectively. *Oil of vitriol* is sulphuric acid.

**Vivaldi, Antonio Lucio** (1678–1741) Italian Baroque composer, violinist, and conductor. One of the most prolific composers of his day, he was particularly influential through his concertos, several of which were transcribed by Johann Sebastian Bach. He wrote 23 symphonies; 75 sonatas; over 400 concertos, including *The Four Seasons* (1725) for violin and orchestra; over 40 operas; and much sacred music. His work was largely neglected until the 1930s.

**viviparous** in animals, a method of reproduction in which the embryo develops inside the body of the female from which it gains nourishment (in contrast to oviparous and ◊ovoviviparous). Vivipary is best developed in placental mammals, but also occurs in some arthropods, fishes, amphibians, and reptiles that have placentalike structures. In plants, it is the formation of young plantlets or bulbils instead of flowers. The term also describes seeds that germinate prematurely, before falling from the parent plant.

**vivisection** literally, cutting into a living animal. Used originally to mean experimental surgery or dissection practised on a live subject, the term is often used by antivivisection campaigners to include any experiment on animals, surgical or otherwise.

**Vladivostok** city on the western shore of the Sea of Japan, on a peninsula extending into Peter the Great Bay; population (1996 est) 627,000. It is the capital of the Primorski (Maritime) Krai of the Russian Federation, and one of the most important economic and cultural centres of the Russian Far East, where it is the largest city. Vladivostok is a terminus of the Trans-Siberian Railway (9,224 km/mi from Moscow) and the Northern Sea Route, centre of communications for the Pacific territories, the largest Russian port on the Pacific, and the chief base of the Pacific Fleet. The port is kept open by icebreakers during winter.

**vocal cords** the paired folds, ridges, or cords of tissue within a mammal's larynx, and a bird's syrinx. Air constricted between the folds or membranes makes them vibrate, producing sounds. Muscles in the larynx change the pitch of the sounds produced, by adjusting the tension of the vocal cords.

**vodka** strong colourless alcoholic beverage distilled from rye, potatoes, or barley.

**Vojvodina** autonomous province in northern Serbia, Yugoslavia, 1945–1990; area 21,500 sq km/8,299 sq mi; population (1991) 2,012,500, including 1,110,000 Serbs and 390,000 Hungarians, as well as Croat, Slovak, Romanian, and Ukrainian minorities. Its capital is Novi Sad. In September 1990 Serbia effectively stripped Vojvodina of its autonomous status, causing antigovernment and anticommunist riots in early 1991.

**volatile** in chemistry, term describing a substance that readily passes from the liquid to the vapour phase. Volatile substances have a high ◊vapour pressure.

**volcanic rock** another name for ◊extrusive rock, igneous rock formed on the Earth's surface.

**volcano** crack in the Earth's crust through which hot magma (molten rock) and gases well up. The magma is termed lava when it reaches the surface. A volcanic mountain, usually cone

composite
volcano

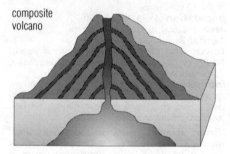

cinder
cone

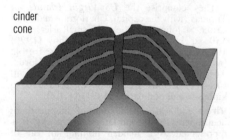

shield volcano

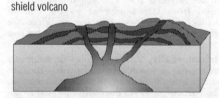

**volcano** *There are two main types of volcano, but three distinctive cone shapes. Composite volcanoes emit a stiff, rapidly solidifying lava which forms high, steep-sided cones. Volcanoes that regularly throw out ash build up flatter domes known as cinder cones. The lava from a shield volcano is not ejected violently, flowing over the crater rim and forming a broad low profile.*

shaped with a crater on top, is formed around the opening, or vent, by the build-up of solidified lava and ashes (rock fragments). Most volcanoes arise on plate margins (see ◊plate tectonics), where the movements of plates generate magma or allow it to rise from the mantle beneath. However, a number are found far from plate-margin activity, on 'hot spots' where the Earth's crust is thin.

**vole** any of various rodents of the family Cricetidae, subfamily Microtinae, distributed over Europe, Asia, and North America, and related to hamsters and lemmings. They are characterized by stout bodies and short tails. They have brown or grey fur, and blunt noses, and some species reach a length of 30 cm/12 in. They feed on grasses, seeds, aquatic plants, and insects. Many show remarkable fluctuations in numbers over 3–4 year cycles.

**Volga** ancient *Rha,* longest river in Europe, entirely within the territory of the Russian Federation. The Volga has a total length of 3,685 km/2,290 mi, 3,540 km/2,200 mi of which are navigable. It rises in the Valdai plateau northwest of Moscow, and flows into the Caspian Sea 88 km/55 mi below the city of Astrakhan. The Volga basin drains most of the central and eastern parts of European Russia, its total drainage area being 1,360,000 sq km/ 525,100 sq mi.

**Volgograd** formerly (until 1925) *Tsaritsyn* and (1925–61) *Stalingrad,* industrial city in southwest Russian Federation, on the River Volga; population (1994) 1,000,000. Industries include the manufacture of metal goods and machinery, sawmilling, and oil refining.

**volleyball** indoor and outdoor team game played on a court between two teams of six players each. A net is placed across the centre of the court, and players hit the ball with their hands over it, the aim being to ground it in the opponents' court.

**volt** SI unit of electromotive force or electric potential. A small battery has a potential of 1.5 volts, whilst a high-tension transmission line may carry up to 765,000 volts. The domestic electricity supply in the UK is 230 volts (lowered from 240 volts in 1995); it is 110 volts in the USA.

**Volta** main river in Ghana, about 1,600 km/1,000 mi long, with two main upper branches, the Black and White Volta. It has been dammed at Akosombo to provide power.

**voltage** commonly used term for ◊potential difference (pd) or ◊electromotive force (emf).

**Voltaire** pen-name of François-Marie Arouet (1694–1778) French writer. He is the embodiment of the 18th-century ◊Enlightenment. He wrote histories, books of political analysis and philosophy, essays on science and literature, plays, poetry, and the satirical fable *Candide* (1759), his best-known work. A trenchant satirist of social and political evils, he was often forced to flee from his enemies and was twice imprisoned. His works include *Lettres philosophiques sur les Anglais/Philosophical Letters on the English* (1733) (essays in favour of English ways, thought, and political practice), *Le Siècle de Louis XIV/The Age of Louis XIV* (1751), and *Dictionnaire philosophique/ Philosophical Dictionary* (1764).

**voodoo** set of magical beliefs and practices, followed in some parts of Africa, South America, and the West Indies, especially Haiti. It arose in the 17th century on slave plantations as a combination of Roman Catholicism and West African religious traditions; believers retain membership in the Roman Catholic church. It was once practiced in New Orleans and other areas of southern USA by African-Americans. Beliefs include the existence of *loa,* spirits who closely involve themselves in human affairs, and some of whose identities mesh with those of Christian saints. The loa are invoked by the priest (*houngan*) or priestess (*manbo*) at ceremonies, during which members of the congregation become possessed by the spirits and go into a trance.

**vote** expression of opinion by ◊ballot, show of hands, or other means. In systems that employ direct vote, the ◊plebiscite and ◊referendum are fundamental mechanisms. In parliamentary elections the results can be calculated in a number of ways. The main electoral systems are: *simple plurality* or *first past the post,* with single-member constituencies (USA, UK, India, Canada); *absolute majority,* achieved for example by the *alternative vote,* where the voter, in single-member constituencies, chooses a candidate by marking preferences (Australia), or by the *second ballot,* where, if a clear decision is not reached immediately, a second ballot is held (France, Egypt); ◊*proportional representation,* achieved for example by the *party list* system (Israel, most countries of Western Europe, and several in South America), the *additional member* system or AMS (Germany), the *single transferable vote* (Ireland and Malta), and the *limited vote* (Japan's upper house and Liechtenstein). Revised voting systems were adopted by Italy and New Zealand in 1993, in which both houses were elected by a combination of simple majority voting and proportional representation on the AMS model. In Japan AMS was adopted for the lower house in 1994.

**Vulcan** or *Vulcanus,* in Roman mythology, the god of fire and destruction, later identified with the Greek god ◊Hephaestus.

**vulture** any of various carrion-eating birds of prey in the order Falconiformes, with naked heads and necks, strong hooked bills, and keen senses of sight and smell. Vultures are up to 1 m/3.3 ft long, with wingspans of up to 3.7 m/12 ft. The plumage is usually dark, and the head brightly coloured.

**W** abbreviation for *west;* in physics, symbol for *watt.*

**wadi** in arid regions of the Middle East, a steep-sided valley containing an intermittent stream that flows in the wet season.

**Wagner, (Wilhelm) Richard** (1813–1883) German opera composer. He revolutionized the 19th-century conception of opera, envisaging it as a wholly new art form in which musical, poetic, and scenic elements should be unified through such devices as the ◊leitmotif. His operas include *Tannhäuser* (1845), *Lohengrin* (1848), and *Tristan und Isolde* (1865). In 1872 he founded the Festival Theatre in Bayreuth; his masterpiece *Der Ring des Nibelungen/The Ring of the Nibelung,* a sequence of four operas, was first performed there in 1876. His last work, *Parsifal,* was produced in 1882.

**Wagner, Otto** (1841–1918) Viennese architect. Initially working in the Art Nouveau style, for example the Vienna Stadtbahn 1894–97, he later rejected ornament for Rationalism, as in the Post Office Savings Bank, Vienna, 1904–06. He influenced such Viennese architects as Josef Hoffmann, Adolf Loos, and Joseph Olbrich.

**wagtail** slim, narrow-billed bird of the genus *Motacilla,* in the family Motacillidae, order Passeriformes, about 18 cm/7 in long, with a characteristic flicking movement of the tail. There are about 30 species, found mostly in Eurasia and Africa.

**Wahabi** puritanical Saudi Islamic sect founded by Muhammad ibn-Abd-al-Wahab (1703–1792), which regards all other sects as heretical. By the early 20th century it had spread throughout the Arabian peninsula; it still remains the official ideology of the Saudi Arabian kingdom.

**Wailing Wall** or (in Judaism) *Western Wall,* the remaining part of the ◊Temple in Jerusalem, a sacred site of pilgrimage and prayer for Jews. There they offer prayers either aloud ('wailing') or on pieces of paper placed between the stones of the wall.

**Waite, Terry (Terence Hardy)** (1939– ) English religious adviser to the archbishop of Canterbury (then Dr Robert Runcie) from 1980–87. As the archbishop's special envoy, Waite disappeared on 20 January 1987 while engaged in secret negotiations to free European hostages in Beirut, Lebanon. He was taken hostage by an Islamic group and released on 18 November 1991.

**Walachia** alternative spelling of ◊Wallachia, part of Romania.

**Wales** Welsh *Cymru,* Principality of; constituent part of the UK, in the west between the British Channel and the Irish Sea
*area* 20,780 sq km/8,021 sq mi
*capital* Cardiff
*towns and cities* Swansea, Wrexham, Newport, Carmarthen
*features* Snowdonia Mountains (Snowdon 1,085 m/3,560 ft, the highest point in England and Wales) in the northwest and in the southeast the Black Mountains, Brecon Beacons, and Black Forest ranges; rivers Severn, Wye, Usk, and Dee
*industries* traditional industries have declined, but varied modern and high-technology ventures are being developed. There are oil refineries and open-cast coal mining. The last deep coal mine in north Wales closed in 1996. Wales has the largest concentration of Japanese-owned plants in the UK. It also has the highest density of sheep in the world and a dairy industry; tourism is important
*currency* pound sterling
*population* (1993 est) 2,906,000
*language* English, 19% Welsh-speaking
*religion* Nonconformist Protestant denominations; Roman Catholic minority
*government* returns 40 members to the UK Parliament; in April 1996, the 8 counties were replaced by 22 county and county borough unitary authorities; devolved National Assembly for Wales (approved by referendum in 1997) is due to sit in Cardiff from 1999

**Wałęsa, Lech** (1943– ) Polish trade-union leader, president of Poland from 1990–95; one of the founding members of the ◊Solidarity free-trade-union movement, which emerged to challenge the communist government during strikes in the Gdańsk shipyards in August 1980. Wałęsa led the movement to become a national force. He was awarded the Nobel Prize for Peace in 1983. After his election as president, he gradually became estranged from Solidarity. In 1997 he formed a Christian Democratic party, which was, however, unlikely to make a significant impact on Polish political life.

**Wales, Prince of** title conferred on the eldest son of the UK's sovereign. Prince ◊Charles was invested as 21st prince of Wales at Caernarfon in 1969 by his mother, Elizabeth II.

**Walker, Alice Malsenior** (1944– ) US poet, novelist, critic, and essay writer. She has been active in the US civil-rights movement since the 1960s and, as a black woman, wrote about the double burden of racist and sexist oppression, about colonialism, and the quest for political and spiritual recovery. Her novel *The Color Purple* (1982, filmed 1985), told in the form of letters, won a Pulitzer prize. Her other works include *Possessing the Secret of Joy* (1992), which deals passionately with female circumcision, and *By the Light of My Father's Smile* (1998).

**Wallachia** independent medieval principality, founded in 1290, with allegiance to Hungary until 1330 and under Turkish rule 1387–1861, when it was united with the neighbouring principality of Moldavia to form Romania.

**wallflower** European perennial cottage garden plant with fragrant spikes of red, orange, yellow, brown, or purple flowers in spring. (*Cheiranthus cheiri,* family Cruciferae.)

**Walloon** a French-speaking people of southeastern Belgium and adjacent areas of France. The name 'Walloon' is etymologically linked to 'Welsh'.

**Wall Street** the financial centre of the USA, a street on lower Manhattan Island, New York City, on which the New York Stock Exchange is situated; also a synonym for stock dealing in the USA. Office skyscrapers house many of the major banks, trust companies, insurance corporations, and financial institutions of the city; coffee, cotton, metal, produce, and corn exchanges are sited here. Its narrow course follows the line of a stockade wall erected by the Dutch to protect New Amsterdam in 1653.

**Wall Street Crash, 1929** panic selling on the New York Stock Exchange following an artificial boom from 1927 to 1929 fed by speculation. On 24 October 1929, 13 million shares changed hands, with further heavy selling on 28 October and the disposal of 16 million shares on 29 October. Many shareholders were ruined, banks and businesses failed, and in the ◊Depression that followed, unemployment rose to approximately 17 million.

**walnut** deciduous tree, probably originating in southeastern Europe and now widely cultivated elsewhere. It can grow up to 30 m/100 ft high, and produces a full crop of edible nuts about 12 years after planting; the timber is used in furniture and the oil is used in cooking. (*Juglans regia,* family Juglandaceae.)

**Walpole, Robert** 1st Earl of Orford (1676–1745) British Whig politician, the first 'prime minister'. As First Lord of the Treasury and chancellor of the Exchequer (1715–17 and 1721–42) he encouraged trade and tried to avoid foreign disputes (until forced into the War of Jenkins' Ear with Spain in 1739).

**walrus** Arctic marine carnivorous mammal *Odobenus rosmarus* of the same family (Otaridae) as the eared ◊seals. It can reach 4 m/13 ft in length, and weigh up to 1,400 kg/3,000 lb. It has webbed flippers, a bristly moustache, and large tusks. It is gregarious except at breeding time and feeds mainly on molluscs. It has been hunted for its ivory tusks, hide, and blubber; the Alaskan walrus is close to extinction.

**waltz** ballroom dance in moderate triple time (3/4) that developed in Germany and Austria during the late 18th century from the Austrian *Ländler* (traditional peasants' country dance). Associated particularly with Vienna and the Strauss family, the waltz has remained popular up to the present day and has inspired composers including Chopin, Brahms, and Ravel.

**wapiti** or *elk,* species of deer *Cervus canadensis,* native to North America, Europe, and Asia, including New Zealand. It is reddish-brown in colour, about 1.5 m/5 ft at the shoulder, weighs up to 450 kg/1,000 lb, and has antlers up to 1.2 m/4 ft long. It is becoming increasingly rare, although the wapiti population in Yellowstone National Park, USA, was a thriving 25,000 in 1998. In North America, the wapiti is also called an elk.

**Warbeck, Perkin** (*c.* 1474–1499) Flemish pretender to the English throne. Claiming to be Richard, brother of Edward V, he led a rising against Henry VII in 1497, and was hanged after attempting to escape from the Tower of London.

**War between the States** another (usually Southern) name for the American ◊Civil War.

**warble fly** large, brownish, hairy flies, with mouthparts that are reduced or vestigial. The larva is a large maggot covered with spines. They cause myiasis (invasion of the tissues by fly larvae) in animals.

**warbler** any of two families of songbirds, order Passeriformes. The Old World warblers are in the family Sylviidae, while the New World warblers are members of the Parulidae.

**warfarin** poison that induces fatal internal bleeding in rats; neutralized with sodium hydroxide, it is used in medicine as an anticoagulant in the treatment of ◊thrombosis: it prevents blood clotting by inhibiting the action of vitamin K. It can be taken orally and begins to act several days after the initial dose.

**Warhol, Andy** adopted name of Andrew Warhola (1928–1987) US Pop artist and filmmaker. He made his name in 1962 with paintings of Campbell's soup cans, Coca-Cola bottles, and film stars. In his New York studio, the Factory, he and his assistants produced series of garish silk-screen prints. His films include *Chelsea Girls* (1966) and *Trash* (1970).

**warning coloration** in biology, an alternative term for aposematic coloration.

**War of 1812** war between the USA and Britain caused by British interference with US trade (shipping) as part of Britain's economic warfare against Napoleonic France. Tensions between the Americans and the British in Canada led to plans for a US invasion but these were never realized and success was limited to the capture of Detroit and a few notable naval victories. In 1814 British forces occupied Washington, DC, and burned the White House and the Capitol. A treaty signed in Ghent, Belgium, in December 1814 ended the conflict.

**Warrington** unitary authority in northwest England, created in 1998 from part of Cheshire
*area* 176 sq km/68 sq mi
*towns and cities* ◊Warrington (administrative headquarters), Lymm, Great Sankey
*features* River Mersey; Manchester Ship Canal; Warrington Museum and Art Gallery includes over 1,000 paintings; Risley Moss bog and woodland with nature trails and visitors' centre

*industries* chemicals, food and soft drinks processing, brewing, printing, manufacturing of clothing, leather, metal goods, timber products *population* (1996) 151,000.

**Warrington** industrial town and, from April 1998, administrative headquarters of ◊Warrington unitary authority in northwest England, on the River Mersey, 25 km/16 mi from both Liverpool and Manchester; population (1994 est) 151,000. It was part of the county of Cheshire to April 1998. Industries include the manufacture of metal goods and chemicals, brewing, iron founding, tanning, engineering, and high technology industries. A trading centre since Roman times, it was designated a new town in 1968.

**Warsaw** Polish *Warszawa,* capital of Poland, on the River Vistula; population (1993) 1,653,300. Industries include engineering, food processing, printing, clothing, and pharmaceuticals.

**wart** protuberance composed of a local overgrowth of skin. The common wart (*Verruca vulgaris*) is due to a virus infection. It usually disappears spontaneously within two years, but can be treated with peeling applications, burning away (cautery), freezing (cryosurgery), or laser treatment.

**wart hog** African wild ◊pig *Phacochoerus aethiopicus,* which has a large head with a bristly mane, fleshy pads beneath the eyes, and four large tusks. It has short legs and can grow to 80 cm/2.5 ft at the shoulder.

**Warwick, Richard Neville,** 1st or 16th Earl of Warwick (1428–1471) English politician, called *the Kingmaker.* During the Wars of the ◊Roses he fought at first on the Yorkist side against the Lancastrians, and was largely responsible for placing Edward IV on the throne. Having quarrelled with him, he restored Henry VI in 1470, but was defeated and killed by Edward at Barnet, Hertfordshire. Earl in 1449.

**Warwickshire** county of central England
*area* 1,980 sq km/764 sq mi
*towns and cities* Warwick (administrative headquarters), Nuneaton, Royal Leamington Spa, Rugby, Stratford-upon-Avon (the birthplace of Shakespeare)
*physical* rivers Avon, Stour, and Tame; remains of the 'Forest of Arden' (portrayed by Shakespeare in *As You Like It*)
*features* Kenilworth and Warwick castles; Edgehill, site of the Battle of Edgehill in 1642, during the English Civil War; annual Royal Agricultural Show held at Stoneleigh
*agriculture* cereals (oats and wheat); dairy farming; fruit; market gardening
*industries* cement; engineering; ironstone, and lime are worked in the east and south; motor industry; textiles; tourism
*population* (1996) 500,600
*famous people* Rupert Brooke, George Eliot, William Shakespeare.

**Wash, the** bay of the North Sea between Norfolk and Lincolnshire, eastern England; 24 km/15 mi long, 40 km/25 mi wide. The rivers Nene, Ouse, Welland, and Witham drain into the Wash. In 1992, 10,120 ha/25,000 acres of the mudflats, marshes, and sand banks on its shores were designated a national nature reserve.

**Washington** state in northwestern USA. It is nicknamed the Evergreen State. Washington was admitted to the Union in 1889 as the 42nd US state. It is bordered to the east by Idaho, to the south by Oregon, to the north by British Columbia, Canada, and to the west by the Pacific Ocean. Washington's Cape Alava is the westernmost point in the lower 48 US states
*population* (1995) 5,430,900 (including 1.4% American Indians, mainly of the Yakima people)
*area* 176,700 sq km/68,206 sq mi
*capital* Olympia
*towns and cities* Seattle, Spokane, Tacoma, Bellevue, Everett
*industries and products* apples and other fruits, potatoes, livestock, fish and shellfish, timber, processed food, wood products, paper and allied products, aircraft and aerospace equipment, aluminium, computer software.

**Washington, George** (1732–1799) Commander of the American forces during the American Revolutionary War and 1st president of the USA from 1789–97; known as 'the father of his country'. An experienced soldier, he had fought in campaigns against the French during the French and Indian War. He was elected to the Virginia House of Burgesses 1759 and was a leader of the Virginia militia, gaining valuable exposure to wilderness fighting. As a strong opponent of British government's policy, he sat in the Continental Congresses of 1774 and 1775, and on the outbreak of the ◊American Revolution was chosen commander in chief of the Continental army. After many setbacks, he accepted the surrender of British general Cornwallis at Yorktown in 1781.

After the war Washington retired to his Virginia estate, Mount Vernon, but in 1787 he re-entered politics as president of the Constitutional Convention in Philadelphia, and was elected US president in 1789. He attempted to draw his ministers from all factions, but his aristocratic outlook and acceptance of the fiscal policy championed by Alexander ◊Hamilton alienated his secretary of state, Thomas Jefferson, who resigned in 1793, thus creating the two-party system.

Washington was re-elected president in 1793 but refused to serve a third term, setting a precedent that stood until 1940. He died and was buried at Mount Vernon.

**Washington, DC** District of Columbia, capital of the US, on the Potomac River; the world's first planned national capital. It was named Washington, DC, to distinguish it from Washington state, and because it is coextensive with the ◊District of Columbia, hence DC; population (1996 est) 543,200; metropolitan area extending outside the District of Columbia (1990) 3,923,600. The District of Columbia, the federal district of the USA, is an area of 174 sq km/69 sq mi. Its site was chosen by President

George Washington, and the first structures date from 1793. Washington, DC, operates the national executive, legislative, and judicial government of the USA, and is a centre for international diplomacy and finance. Federal and district government are key employers, though numbers employed in both are decreasing. Public, trade, business, and social organizations maintain a presence, as well as law and other service agencies. Tourism is a major industry.

**Wasim Akram** (1966–  ) Pakistan cricketer. A left-arm fast bowler and hard-hitting batsman, he made his Test debut in 1985 at the age of 18 and soon established himself as one of the world's leading players. He has taken more wickets in one-day internationals than any other player, and is also the only player to have taken 300 wickets or more in both Test and one-day international cricket. He has played county cricket for Lancashire since 1988, and in September 1998 captained the team to victory in the Natwest Trophy and helped them clinch the AXA League title. He led Pakistan to the final of the 1999 World Cup where they were defeated by Australia.

*career highlights*
**Test cricket (1985–)** bowling: matches: 79; overs: 2,987; runs: 7,705; wickets: 341; average: 22.59; best: 7–119; batting: innings: 109 (15 not outs); runs: 2,018; average: 257; hundreds: 2; highest score: 257 not out
**One-day internationals** matches: 275; overs: 2,357; runs: 9,057; wickets: 386; average: 23.46; best: 5–15; batting: 2,824 runs (average 15.86); catches: 75.

**wasp** any of several families of winged stinging insects of the order Hymenoptera, characterized by a thin stalk between the thorax and the abdomen. Wasps can be social or solitary. Among social wasps, the queens devote themselves to egg laying, the fertilized eggs producing female workers; the males come from unfertilized eggs and have no sting. The larvae are fed on insects, but the mature wasps feed mainly on fruit and sugar. In winter, the fertilized queens hibernate, but the other wasps die.

**waste** materials that are no longer needed and are discarded. Examples are household waste, industrial waste (which often contains toxic chemicals), medical waste (which may contain organisms that cause disease), and ◊nuclear waste (which is radioactive). By ◊recycling, some materials in waste can be reclaimed for further use. In 1990 the industrialized nations generated 2 billion tonnes of waste. In the USA, 40 tonnes of solid waste are generated annually per person, roughly twice as much as in Europe or Japan.

**water** is a chemical compound of hydrogen and oxygen elements, $H_2O$. It can exist as a solid (ice), liquid (water), or gas (water vapour). Water is the most common element on Earth and vital to all living organisms. It covers 70% of the Earth's surface, and provides a habitat for large numbers of aquatic organisms. It is the largest constituent of all living organisms – the human body consists of about 65% water. Pure water is a colourless, odourless, tasteless liquid which freezes at 0°C/32°F, and boils at 100°C/212°F. Natural water in the environment is never pure and always contains a variety of dissolved substances. Some 97% of the Earth's water is in the oceans; a further 2% is in the form of snow or ice, leaving only 1% available as fresh water for plants and animals. The recycling and circulation of water through the ◊biosphere is termed the *water cycle,* or 'hydrological cycle'; regulation of the water balance in organisms is termed osmoregulation.

**water beetle** aquatic beetle with an oval, flattened, streamlined shape. The head is sunk into

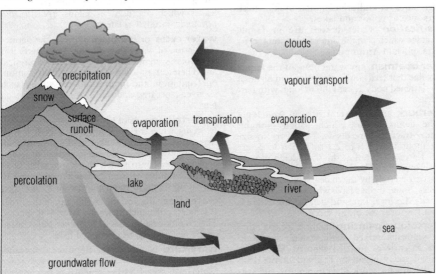

*water cycle* About one-third of the solar energy reaching the Earth is used in evaporating water. About 380,000 cubic km/95,000 cubic mi is evaporated each year. The entire contents of the oceans would take about one million years to pass through the water cycle.

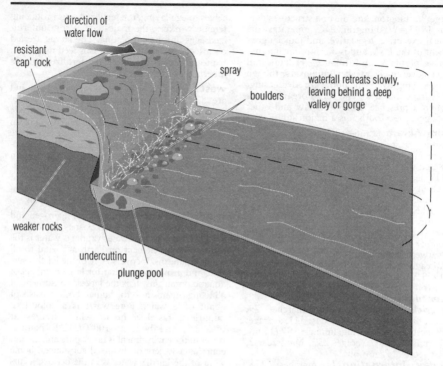

direction of
water flow

resistant
'cap' rock

spray

boulders

waterfall retreats slowly,
leaving behind a deep
valley or gorge

weaker rocks

undercutting

plunge pool

**waterfall** *When water flows over hard rock and soft rock, the soft rocks erode creating waterfalls. As the erosion processes continue, the falls move backwards, in the opposite direction of the water.*

the thorax and the hindlegs are flattened into flippers for swimming; there is a wide variation in size within the species; they are usually dark or black in colour and the entire body has a resplendent sheen. Both the adults and larvae are entirely aquatic, and are common in still, fresh waters such as ponds and lakes.
**classification** Water beetles are in family Dytiscidae which is in the order Coleoptera, class Insecta, phylum Arthropoda.

**water boatman** any water ◊bug of the family Corixidae that feeds on plant debris and algae. It has a flattened body 1.5 cm/0.6 in long, with oarlike legs.

**waterbuck** any of several African ◊antelopes of the genus *Kobus* which usually inhabit swampy tracts and reedbeds. They vary in size from about 1.8m/6 ft to 2.1 m/7.25 ft long, are up to 1.4 m/4.5 ft tall at the shoulder, and have long brown fur. The large curved horns, normally carried only by the males, have corrugated surfaces. Some species have white patches on the buttocks. Lechwe, kor, and defassa are alternative names for some of the species.

**watercolour painting** method of painting with pigments mixed with water, known in China as early as the 3rd century. The art as practised today began in England in the 18th century with the work of Paul Sandby and was developed by Thomas Girtin, John Sell Cotman, and J M W Turner. Other outstanding watercolourists were Raoul Dufy, Paul Cézanne, and

John Marin. The technique of watercolour painting requires great skill since its transparency rules out overpainting.

**watercress** perennial aquatic plant found in Europe and Asia and cultivated for its pungent leaves which are used in salads. (*Nasturtium officinale*, family Cruciferae.)

**water cycle** or *hydrological cycle,* the natural circulation of water through the ◊biosphere. It is a complex system involving a number of physical and chemical processes (such as ◊evaporation, ◊precipitation, and infiltration) and stores (such as rivers, oceans, and soil). *See illustration on page 959.*

**waterfall** cascade of water in a river or stream. It occurs when a river flows over a bed of rock that resists erosion; weaker rocks downstream are worn away, creating a steep, vertical drop and a plunge pool into which the water falls. Over time, continuing erosion causes the waterfall to retreat upstream forming a deep valley, or gorge.

**water flea** any aquatic crustacean in the order Cladocera, of which there are over 400 species. The commonest species is *Daphnia pulex,* used in the pet trade to feed tropical fish.

**Waterford** county of the Republic of Ireland, in the province of Munster; county town Waterford; area 1,840 sq km/710 sq mi; population (1991) 91,600. Other towns include Dungarvon, Lismore, and Tramore. The chief rivers are the Suir and the Blackwater; the

Comeragh and Monavallagh mountain ranges lie in the north and centre of the county. Agriculture and dairy farming are important; wheat, barley, and vegetables are also grown. Industries include glassware, pharmaceuticals, and electronics, and there are tanneries, bacon factories, and flour mills.

**waterfowl** any water bird, but especially any member of the family Anatidae, which consists of ducks, geese, and swans.

**Watergate** US political scandal, named after the building in Washington, DC, which housed the headquarters of the Democratic National Committee in the 1972 presidential election. Five men, hired by the Republican Committee for the Re-election of the President (popularly known as CREEP), were caught after breaking into the Watergate with complex electronic surveillance equipment. Investigations revealed that the White House was implicated in the break-in, and that there was a 'slush fund', used to finance unethical activities, including using the CIA and the Internal Revenue Service for political ends, setting up paramilitary operations against opponents, altering and destroying evidence, and bribing defendants to lie or remain silent. In August 1974, President ◊Nixon was forced by the Supreme Court to surrender to Congress tape recordings of conversations he had held with administration officials, which indicated his complicity in a cover-up. Nixon resigned rather than face impeachment for obstruction of justice and other crimes.

**water glass** common name for sodium metasilicate ($Na_2SiO_3$). It is a colourless, jelly-like substance that dissolves readily in water to give a solution used for preserving eggs and fireproofing porous materials such as cloth, paper, and wood. It is also used as an adhesive for paper and cardboard and in the manufacture of soap and silica gel, a substance that absorbs moisture.

**water hyacinth** tropical aquatic plant belonging to the pickerelweed family. In one growing season 25 plants can produce 2 million new plants. It is liable to choke waterways, removing nutrients from the water and blocking out the sunlight, but it can be used to purify sewage-polluted water as well as in making methane gas, compost, concentrated protein, paper, and baskets. Originating in South America, it now grows in more than 50 countries. (*Eichhornia crassipes,* family Pontederiaceae.)

**water lily** any of a group of aquatic plants belonging to the water lily family. The fleshy roots are embedded in mud and the large round leaves float on the surface of the water. The cup-shaped flowers may be white, pink, yellow, or blue. (Genera *Nymphaea* and *Nuphar,* family Nymphaeaceae.)

**Waterloo, Battle of** final battle of the Napoleonic Wars on 18 June 1815 in which a coalition force of British, Prussian, and Dutch troops under the Duke of Wellington defeated Napoleon near the village of Waterloo, 13 km/8 mi south of Brussels, Belgium. Napoleon found

Wellington's army isolated from his allies and began a direct offensive to smash them, but the British held on until joined by the Prussians under Marshal Gebhard von Blücher. Four days later Napoleon abdicated for the second and final time.

**watermelon** large ◊melon belonging to the gourd family, native to tropical Africa, with a dark green rind and reddish juicy flesh studded with a large number of black seeds. It is widely cultivated in subtropical regions. (*Citrullus vulgaris,* family Cucurbitaceae.)

**water pollution** any addition to fresh or sea water that disrupts biological processes or causes a health hazard. Common pollutants include nitrates, pesticides, and sewage, although a huge range of industrial contaminants, such as chemical byproducts and residues created in the manufacture of various goods, also enter water – legally, accidentally, and through illegal dumping.

**water polo** water sport developed in England 1869, originally called 'soccer-in-water'. The aim is to score goals, as in soccer, at each end of a swimming pool. It is played by teams of seven on each side (from squads of 13).

**water skiing** water sport in which a person is towed across water on a ski or skis, wider than those used for skiing on snow, by means of a rope (23 m/75 ft long) attached to a speedboat. Competitions are held for overall performances, slalom, tricks, and jumping.

**water supply** distribution of water for domestic, municipal, or industrial consumption. Water supply in sparsely populated regions usually comes from underground water rising to the surface in natural springs, supplemented by pumps and wells. Urban sources are deep artesian wells, rivers, and reservoirs, usually formed from enlarged lakes or dammed and flooded valleys, from which water is conveyed by pipes, conduits, and aqueducts to filter beds. As water seeps through layers of shingle, gravel, and sand, harmful organisms are removed and the water is then distributed by pumping or gravitation through mains and pipes.

**water treatment** Often other substances are added to the water, such as chlorine and fluoride; aluminium sulphate, a clarifying agent, is the most widely used chemical in water treatment. In towns, domestic and municipal (road washing, sewage) needs account for about 135 l/30 gal per head each day. In coastal desert areas, such as the Arabian peninsula, desalination plants remove salt from sea water. The Earth's waters, both fresh and saline, have been polluted by industrial and domestic chemicals, some of which are toxic and others radioactive (see ◊water pollution).

**water table** the upper level of ground water (water collected underground in porous rocks). Water that is above the water table will drain downwards; a spring forms where the water table cuts the surface of the ground. The water table rises and falls in response to rainfall and the rate at which water is extracted, for example, for irrigation and industry.

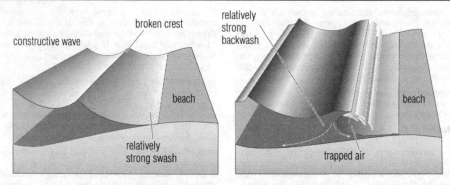

**wave** *The low gentle crests of a constructive wave, with the energy of the wave flowing up the beach in a strong swash and depositing material, contrasts with the high steep crested more forceful motions of destructive waves which crash in at an angle to the beach directing all their energy into plunging waves which tear up the sand and shingle and carry it out with the strong backwash.*

**Watson, James Dewey** (1928–  ) US biologist. His research on the molecular structure of ◊DNA and the genetic code, in collaboration with Francis ◊Crick, earned him a shared Nobel prize in 1962. Based on earlier works, they were able to show that DNA formed a double helix of two spiral strands held together by base pairs.

**watt** SI unit (symbol W) of power (the rate of expenditure or consumption of energy) defined as one joule per second. A light bulb, for example, may use 40, 60, 100, or 150 watts of power; an electric heater will use several kilowatts (thousands of watts). The watt is named after the Scottish engineer James Watt.

**Watt, James** (1736–1819) Scottish engineer who developed the steam engine in the 1760s, making Thomas Newcomen's engine vastly more efficient by cooling the used steam in a condenser separate from the main cylinder. He eventually made a double-acting machine that supplied power with both directions of the piston and developed rotary motion. He also invented devices associated with the steam engine, artistic instruments and a copying process, and devised the horsepower as a description of an engine's rate of working. The modern unit of power, the watt, is named after him.

**wattle** any of certain species of ◊acacia in Australia, where their fluffy golden flowers are the national emblem. The leathery leaves are adapted to drought conditions and avoid loss of water through ◊transpiration by turning their edges to the direct rays of the sun. Wattles are used for tanning leather and in fencing.

**wattle and daub** method of constructing walls consisting of upright stakes bound together with withes (strong flexible shoots or twigs, usually of willow), and covered in mud or plaster. This was the usual way of building houses in medieval Europe; it was also the traditional method used in Australia, Africa, the Middle East, and the Far East.

**Waugh, Evelyn (Arthur St John)** (1903–1966) English novelist. His humorous social satires include *Decline and Fall* (1928), *Vile Bodies* (1930), *Scoop* (1938), and *The Loved One* (1948). He developed a serious concern with religious issues in *Brideshead Revisited* (1945) (successfully dramatized for television in the 1980s). *The Ordeal of Gilbert Pinfold* (1957) is largely autobiographical.

**wave** in the oceans, a ridge or swell formed by wind or other causes. The power of a wave is determined by the strength of the wind and the distance of open water over which the wind blows (the fetch). Waves are the main agents of ◊coastal erosion and deposition: sweeping away or building up beaches, creating ◊spits and berms, and wearing down cliffs by their hydraulic action and by the corrosion of the sand and shingle that they carry. A ◊tsunami (misleadingly called a 'tidal wave') is formed after a submarine earthquake.

**wave** in physics, waves are oscillations that are propagated from a source. Mechanical waves require a medium through which to travel. Electromagnetic waves do not; they can travel through a vacuum. Waves carry energy but they do not transfer matter. There are two types: in a longitudinal wave, such as a sound wave, the disturbance is parallel to the wave's direction of travel; in a transverse wave, such as an electromagnetic wave, it is perpendicular. The medium (for example the Earth, for seismic waves) is not permanently displaced by the passage of a wave.

**wavelength** the distance between successive crests of a ◊wave. The wavelength of a light wave determines its colour; red light has a wavelength of about 700 nanometres, for example. The complete range of wavelengths of electromagnetic waves is called the electromagnetic ◊spectrum.

**wave power** power obtained by harnessing the energy of water waves. Various schemes have been advanced since 1973 when oil prices rose dramatically and an energy shortage threatened. In 1974 the British engineer Stephen Salter developed the duck – a floating boom, the segments of which nod up and down with the waves. The nodding motion can be used to drive pumps and spin generators. Another device, developed in Japan, uses an oscillating water column to harness wave power. A major breakthrough will be required if wave power is ever to contribute significantly to the world's energy needs, although several ideas have reached prototype stage.

**wax** solid fatty substance of animal, vegetable, or mineral origin.

Waxes are composed variously of ◊esters, ◊fatty acids, free ◊alcohols, and solid hydrocarbons.

**waxbill** any of a group of small, mainly African, seed-eating birds in the family Estrildidae, order Passeriformes, which also includes the grass finches of Australia. Waxbills grow to 15 cm/6 in long, are brown and grey with yellow, red, or brown markings, and have waxy-looking red or pink beaks.

**waxwing** any of several fruit-eating birds of the family Bombycillidae, order Passeriformes. They are found in the northern hemisphere. The Bohemian waxwing *Bombycilla garrulus* of North America and Eurasia is about 18 cm/7 in long, and is greyish-brown above with a redish-chestnut crest, black streak at the eye, and variegated wings. It undertakes mass migrations in some years.

**wayfaring tree** European shrub belonging to the honeysuckle family, with clusters of fragrant white flowers, found on limy soils; it is naturalized in the northeastern USA. (*Viburnum lantana*, family Caprifoliaceae.)

**Wayne, John** 'Duke', stage name of Marion Michael Morrison (1907–1979) US actor. He played the archetypal western hero: plain-speaking, brave, and solitary. His films include *Stagecoach* (1939), *Red River* (1948), *She Wore a Yellow Ribbon* (1949), *The Searchers* (1956), *Rio Bravo* (1959), *The Man Who Shot Liberty Valance* (1962), and *True Grit* (1969) (Academy Award).

**weak nuclear force** or *weak interaction,* one of the four fundamental ◊forces of nature, the other three being the gravitational force or gravity, the electromagnetic force, and the strong nuclear force. It causes radioactive beta decay and other subatomic reactions. The particles that carry the weak force are called ◊weakons (or intermediate vector bosons) and comprise the positively and negatively charged W particles and the neutral Z particle.

**weakon** or *intermediate vector boson,* in physics, a ◊gauge boson that carries the weak nuclear force, one of the fundamental forces of nature. There are three types of weakon, the positive and negative W particle and the neutral Z particle.

**weapon** any implement used for attack and defence, from simple clubs, spears, and bows and arrows in prehistoric times to machine guns and nuclear bombs in modern times. The first revolution in warfare came with the invention of ◊gunpowder and the development of cannons and shoulder-held guns. Many other weapons

now exist, such as grenades, shells, torpedoes, rockets, and guided missiles. The ultimate in explosive weapons are the atomic (fission) and hydrogen (fusion) bombs. They release the enormous energy produced when atoms split or fuse together (see ◊nuclear warfare). There are also chemical and bacteriological weapons, which release poisons or disease.

**Wear** river in northeast England; length 107 km/67 mi. From its source near Wearhead in the Pennines in County Durham, it flows eastwards along a narrow valley, Weardale, to Bishop Auckland and then northeast past Durham and Chester-le-Street, to meet the North Sea at Sunderland.

**weasel** any of various small, short-legged, lithe carnivorous mammals with bushy tails, especially the genus *Mustela,* found worldwide except Australia. They feed mainly on small rodents although some, like the mink *M. vison,* hunt aquatic prey. Most are 12–25 cm/5–10 in long, excluding the tail.

**weathering** process by which exposed rocks are broken down on the spot by the action of rain, frost, wind, and other elements of the weather. It differs from ◊erosion in that no movement or transportation of the broken-down material takes place. Two types of weathering are recognized: physical (or mechanical) and chemical. They usually occur together.

**weaver** any small bird of the family Ploceidae, order Passeriformes; they are mostly about 15 cm/6 in long. The majority of weavers are African, a few Asian. The males use grasses to weave elaborate globular nests in bushes and trees. The nests are entered from beneath, and the male hangs from it calling and flapping his wings to attract a female. Their bodies are somewhat elongated and the tails long, and the prominent conical bill is very powerful. They eat insects and may eat cultivated grain. Males are often more brightly coloured than females.

**weaving** the production of textile fabric by means of a loom. The basic process is the interlacing at right angles of longitudinal threads (the warp) and horizontal threads (the weft), the latter being carried across from one side of the loom to the other by a type of bobbin called a shuttle.

**weber** SI unit (symbol Wb) of magnetic flux (the magnetic field strength multiplied by the area through which the field passes). It is named after German chemist Wilhelm Weber. One weber equals $10^8$ maxwells.

**Weber, Carl Maria Friedrich Ernst von** (1786–1826) German composer. He established the Romantic school of opera with *Der Freischütz/The Marksman* (1821) and *Euryanthe* (1823). He was Kapellmeister (chief conductor) at Breslau (1804–06), Prague (1813–16), and Dresden in (1816). He died during a visit to London, where he produced his opera *Oberon* (1826), written for the Covent Garden Theatre.

**Webern, Anton (Friedrich Wilhelm von)** (1883–1945) Austrian composer. He wrote spare, enigmatic miniatures combining a pastoral poetic with severe structural rigour. A Renaissance musical scholar, he became a pupil of Arnold ◊Schoenberg, whose twelve-tone system he reinterpreted as abstract design in works such as the *Concerto for Nine Instruments* (1931–34) and the *Second Cantata* (1941–43). His constructivist aesthetic influenced the postwar generation of advanced composers.

**Webster, John** (*c.* 1580–*c.* 1625) English dramatist. His reputation rests on two tragedies, *The White Devil* (1612) and *The Duchess of Malfi* (*c.*1613). Though both show the preoccupation with melodramatic violence and horror typical of the Jacobean revenge tragedy, they are also remarkable for their poetry and psychological insight. He collaborated with a number of other dramatists, notably with Thomas Dekker on the comedy *Westward Ho* (*c.*1606).

**Webster, Noah** (1758–1843) US lexicographer whose books on grammar and spelling and *American Dictionary of the English Language* (1828) standardized US English.

**Weddell Sea** arm of the Southern Atlantic Ocean that cuts into the Antarctic continent southeast of Cape Horn; area 8,000,000 sq km/ 3,088,800 sq mi. Much of it is covered with thick pack ice for most of the year.

**Wedgwood, Josiah** (1730–1795) English pottery manufacturer. He set up business in Staffordshire in the early 1760s to produce his agateware as well as unglazed blue or green stoneware (jasper) decorated with white neo-Classical designs, using pigments of his own invention.

**weever fish** any of a family (Trachinidae) of marine bony fishes of the perch family, especially the genus *Trachinus,* with poison glands on the dorsal fin and gill cover that can give a painful sting. It grows up to 5 cm/2 in long, has eyes near the top of the head, and lives on sandy seabeds.

**weevil** any of a superfamily (Curculionoidea) of ◊beetles, usually less than 6 mm/0.25 in long, and with a head prolonged into a downward beak, which is used for boring into plant stems and trees for feeding.

**weight** the force exerted on an object by ◊gravity. The weight of an object depends on its mass – the amount of material in it – and the strength of the Earth's gravitational pull, which decreases with height. Consequently, an object weighs less at the top of a mountain than at sea level. On the surface of the Moon, an object has only one-sixth of its weight on Earth, because the Moon's surface gravity is one-sixth that of the Earth.

**weightlifting** sport of lifting the heaviest possible weight above one's head to the satisfaction of judges. In international competitions there are two standard lifts: *snatch* and *jerk.*

**weights and measures** see under ◊c.g.s. system, f.p.s. system, m.k.s. system, ◊SI units.

**Weights and Measures Act 1963** in Britain, act of Parliament which makes it illegal for businesses to give short weights or short measures to consumers. For example, it is illegal to sell a consumer half a pint of milk when it states on the carton that it contains one pint of milk. Trading standards departments are responsible for enforcing the Weights and Measures Act.

**Weill, Kurt Julian** (1900–1950) German composer; a US citizen from 1943. He wrote chamber and orchestral music and collaborated with Bertolt ◊Brecht on operas such as *Die Dreigroschenoper/The Threepenny Opera* (1928) and *Aufstieg und Fall der Stadt Mahagonny/The Rise and Fall of the City of Mahagonny* (1929), both of which attacked social corruption (*Mahagonny,* which satirized US frontier values, caused a riot at its premiere in Leipzig). He tried to evolve a new form of music theatre, using subjects with a contemporary relevance and the simplest musical means. In 1933 he left Germany, and from 1935 was in the USA, where he wrote a number of successful scores for Broadway, among them the antiwar musical *Johnny Johnson* (1936), *Knickerbocker Holiday* (1938) (including the often covered 'September Song'), and *Street Scene* (1947), based on an Elmer Rice play set in the Depression.

**Weil's disease** or *leptospirosis,* infectious disease of animals that is occasionally transmitted to human beings, usually by contact with water contaminated with rat urine. It is characterized by acute fever, and infection may spread to the brain, liver, kidneys, and heart. It has a 10% mortality rate.

**Weimar Republic** constitutional republic in Germany from 1919 to 1933, which was crippled by the election of antidemocratic parties to the Reichstag (parliament), and then subverted by the Nazi leader Hitler after his appointment as chancellor in 1933. It took its name from the city where in February 1919 a constituent assembly met to draw up a democratic constitution.

**Weizmann, Chaim Azriel** (1874–1952) Zionist leader, the first president of Israel 1948–52. He conducted the negotiations leading up to the Balfour Declaration, by which the UK declared its support for an independent Jewish state.

**Weizsäcker, Richard, Baron von** (1920–   ) German Christian Democrat politician, president 1984–94. He began his career as a lawyer and was also active in the German Protestant church and in Christian Democratic Union party politics. He was elected to the West German Bundestag (parliament) in 1969 and served as mayor of West Berlin from 1981, before being elected federal president in 1984.

**welding** joining pieces of metal (or nonmetal) at faces rendered plastic or liquid by heat or pressure (or both). The principal processes today are gas and arc welding, in which the heat from a gas flame or an electric arc melts the faces to be joined. Additional 'filler metal' is usually added to the joint.

**welfare state** political system under which the state (rather than the individual or the private sector) has responsibility for the welfare of its citizens. Services such as unemployment and sickness benefits, family allowances and income supplements, pensions, medical care, and education may be provided and financed through state insurance schemes and taxation.

**welfare to work** programme introduced by UK ◊Labour Party's to reduce unemployment, particularly among young people, by getting them off welfare into work. In January 1998, the chancellor of the Exchequer, Gordon Brown, announced a 'national crusade to end unemployment', targeting at first the under-25s, and then older people.

**Welles, (George) Orson** (1915–1985) US actor, screenwriter, and film and theatre director. His first and greatest film was *Citizen Kane* (1941), which he produced, directed, and starred in. Later work includes the *films noirs The Lady from Shanghai* (1948) and *Touch of Evil* (1958). As an actor, he created the character of Harry Lime in the film *The Third Man* (1949).

**Wellington** capital and industrial port of New Zealand, in the province of the same name on North Island, on the Cook Strait; population (1996) 335,500 (urban area). Industries in the city include woollen textiles, chemicals, engineering, and electrical goods. The harbour was sighted by Captain James Cook in 1773.

**Wellington, Arthur Wellesley, 1st Duke of Wellington** (1769–1852) Irish-born British soldier and Tory politician. As commander in the ◊Peninsular War, he expelled the French from Spain in 1814. He defeated Napoleon Bonaparte at Quatre-Bras and Waterloo in 1815, and was a member of the Congress of Vienna. As prime minister (1828–30), he was forced to concede Roman Catholic emancipation. KB 1804, Viscount 1809, Earl 1812, Marquess 1812, Duke 1814.

**Wells, H(erbert) G(eorge)** (1866–1946) English writer. He was a pioneer of science fiction with such novels as *The Time Machine* (1895) and *The War of the Worlds* (1898), which describes a Martian invasion of Earth and brought him nationwide recognition. His later novels had an anti-establishment, anti-conventional humour remarkable in its day, for example *Kipps* (1905) and *Tono-Bungay* (1909). He was originally a Fabian and later became a Labour party supporter. He was a Labour candidate for London University in 1921 and 1922.

**Welsh** people of ◊Wales; see also ◊Celt. The term is thought to be derived from an old Germanic term for 'foreigner', and so linked to Walloon (Belgium) and Wallachian (Romania). It may also derive from the Latin *Volcae*, the name of a Celtic people of France.

**Welsh Assembly** devolved governmental body based in Cardiff; see ◊National Assembly for Wales.

**Welsh corgi** breed of dog with a foxlike head and pricked ears, originally bred for cattle herding. The coat is dense, with several varieties of colouring. Corgis are about 30 cm/12 in at the shoulder, and weigh up to 12 kg/27 lb.

**Welsh language** in Welsh, *Cymraeg*, member of the Celtic branch of the Indo-European language family, spoken chiefly in the rural north and west of Wales. Spoken by 18.7% of the Welsh population, it is the strongest of the surviving ◊Celtic languages.

**welwitschia** woody plant found in the deserts of southwestern Africa. It has a long, water-absorbent taproot and can live for up to 100 years. (*Welwitschia mirabilis*, order Gnetales.)

**Wenceslas, St** (*c.* 907–929) Duke of Bohemia. He attempted to Christianize his people and was murdered by his brother. He is patron saint of the Czech Republic and the 'good King Wenceslas' of a popular carol. Feast day 28 September.

**werewolf** in folk belief, a human being either turned into a wolf by a spell or having the ability to assume a wolf form. The symptoms of porphyria may have fostered the legends.

**Wesley, John** (1703–1791) English founder of ◊Methodism. When the pulpits of the Church of England were closed to him and his followers, he took the gospel to the people. For 50 years he rode about the country on horseback, preaching daily, largely in the open air. His sermons became the doctrinal standard of the Wesleyan Methodist Church.

**Wessex** kingdom of the West Saxons in Britain, said to have been founded by Cerdic about AD 500, covering Hampshire, Dorset, Wiltshire, Somerset, Devon, and the former county of Berkshire. In 829 Egbert established West Saxon supremacy over all England.

**West, Rebecca** pen name of Cicily Isabel Fairfield (1892–1983) English journalist and novelist, an active feminist from 1911. Her novels, of which the semi-autobiographical *The Fountain Overflows* (1956) and *The Birds Fall Down* (1966) are regarded as the best, demonstrate a social and political awareness.

**West Bank** area (5,879 sq km/2,270 sq mi) on the west bank of the River Jordan; population (1994) 1,122,900. The area has been occupied by Israel since 1967; Israel refers to the area as Judaea and ◊Samaria.

**West Bengal** state of northeast India
*area* 88,700 sq km/34,247 sq mi
*capital* ◊Calcutta
*towns and cities* Asansol, Durgarpur, Burdwan, Burnpur
*physical* occupies the west part of the vast alluvial plain created by the rivers Ganges and Brahmaputra, with the Hooghly River; Damodar, Bhagirathi rivers flow into Hooghly delta; western part of Sunderbunds mangrove swamps in the estuary area; annual rainfall more than 250 cm/100 in; Himalayan uplands to the north
*industries* jute (particularly at Hooghly industrial complex), iron and steel (at Durgapur, Asansol, based on the Raniganj coalfield), cars, locomotives, aluminium, fertilizers, chemicals, cotton, printing
*agriculture* rice, jute, tea (in Darjiling and Jalpaiguri); oilseed, sugar, pulses, tobacco; fishing

**population** (1994 est) 73,600,000
**language** 85% Bengali; Hindi, Urdu, tribal languages
**famous people** Rabindranath Tagore.

**West Berkshire** unitary authority in southeast England, created in 1998 from part of the former county of Berkshire
**area** 705 sq km/272 sq mi
**towns and cities** Newbury (administrative headquarters), Hungerford, Lambourn
**features** River Kennet; River Cambourn; Kennet and Avon Canal; Snelsmore Common Country Park covers 59 ha/ 146 acres including wetland habitats; Inkpen Hill (291 m/854 ft) with a Stone Age tomb and Walbury Hill (297 m/974 ft) with its Iron Age fort are the highest chalk hills in England; Thatcham Moors reedbeds are designated Sites of Special Scientific Interest (SSSI); Greenham Common Women's Peace Camp has been the site of campaigning against nuclear weapons development at Greenham, Burghfield, and Aldermaston since 1981
**industries** race horse industry, agriculture, dairy cattle, pig farming (including local Berkshire pig)
**population** (1996) 142,600.
**famous people** Francis Baily, John Langley, George Sanger.

**West Dunbartonshire** unitary authority in west central Scotland, created in 1996 from parts of two districts of Strathclyde region
**area** 177 sq km/68 sq mi
**towns** Dumbarton (administrative headquarters), Clydebank, Alexandria
**physical** Leven valley and coastal land of Firth of Clyde rise toward the upland plateau of the Kilpatrick Hills
**features** Dumbarton Castle
**industries** whisky distilling, light manufacturing
**agriculture** sheep; not significant
**population** (1996) 97,800
**history** industrial area of west central Scotland, targeted by Germans and bombed in World War II; heart of ancient kingdom of Strathclyde.

**Western Australia** state of Australia, bounded on the north and west by the Indian Ocean, on the east by Northern Territory and South Australia, on the south by the Southern Ocean
**area** 2,525,500 sq km/974,843 sq mi
**capital** ◊Perth
**towns and cities** Fremantle (main port), Bunbury, Geraldton, Kalgoorlie-Boulder, Albany, Broome
**features** largest state in Australia, occupying nearly one-third of the continent; territory includes the Monte Bello Islands; Cocos Islands; Christmas Island; Nullarbor Plain; Gibson, Sandy, and Great Victoria deserts; Ningaloo Reef; Purnululu National Park; Shark Bay World Heritage Area; much unusual flora and fauna (karri, jarrah, and tingle trees; more than 8,000 species of wildflowers; black swan)
**products** wheat, fresh and dried fruit, beef,

dairy products, wool, wine, natural gas, oil, iron, gold, nickel, diamonds, bauxite, cultured and freshwater pearls, timber, fish
**population** (1996) 1,726,100
**history** first European to land was Dutch navigator Dirck Hartog in 1616; visited by Englishman William Dampier in 1688; a short-lived convict settlement at King George Sound in 1826; first non-convict settlement founded on Swan River (at Perth) in 1829; governed at first by New South Wales; became self-governing in 1890; became a state in 1901.

**Western Cape** province of the Republic of South Africa from 1994, formerly part of Cape Province
**area** 129,386 sq km/49,956 sq mi
**capital** Cape Town
**towns and cities** Simonstown, Stellenbosch, George, Knysna, Beaufort West, Paarl, Mossel Bay
**physical** Table Mountain (highest point McClear's Beacon 1,087 m/3,566 ft), Little Karoo, Great Karoo
**industries** copper, oil refining, chemicals, engineering, tourism
**agriculture** fruit, wine, wheat, tobacco
**population** (1995 est) 3,721,200
**languages** Afrikaans 63% English 20%, Xhosa 16%.

**Western Front** battle zone in World War I between Germany and its enemies France and Britain, extending as lines of trenches from Nieuport on the Belgian coast through Ypres, Arras, Albert, Soissons, and Rheims to Verdun, constructed by both Germany and the Allies.

**Western Isles** island administrative unitary authority area in Scotland, also known as the Outer Hebrides, including the major islands of Lewis, Harris, North and South Uist, Benbecula, and Barra
**area** 3,057 sq km/1,180 sq mi
**towns** Stornoway on Lewis (administrative headquarters), Castlebay, Lochboisdale, Lochmaddy, Tarbert
**physical** open to the Atlantic Ocean on the west and the stormy Minch to the east, the islands are almost treeless and have extensive peat bogs. There are areas of hills and mountains on all the islands. The only fertile land is the sandy Machair on the west coast. The islands are mainly composed of the oldest rock in Britain, the Lewisian gneiss. Lewis is divided from the mainland by the Minch channel. The islands south of Lewis are divided from the Inner Hebrides by the Little Minch and the Sea of the Hebrides; uninhabited islands include St Kilda and Rockall
**features** Callanish monolithic Stone Age circles on Lewis
**industries** Harris tweed, tourism
**agriculture** sheep, cattle, fishing
**population** (1996) 27,800.

**Western Sahara** formerly Spanish Sahara, disputed territory in northwest Africa bounded to the north by Morocco, to the east and south by Mauritania, and to the west by the Atlantic Ocean

**area** 266,800 sq km/103,011 sq mi
**capital** Laâyoune (Arabic *El Aaiún*)
**towns and cities** Dakhla
**features** electrically monitored fortified wall enclosing the phosphate areas
**exports** phosphates, iron ore
**currency** dirham
**population** (1993 est) 214,000; another estimated 196,000 live in refugee camps near Tindouf, southwest Algeria. Ethnic composition: Sawrawis (traditionally nomadic herders)
**language** Arabic
**religion** Sunni Muslim
**government** administered by Morocco.

**West Germany**   see ◊Germany, West.

**West Glamorgan** Welsh *Gorllewin Morgannwg*, former county of southwest Wales, 1974–1996, now divided into ◊Neath Port Talbot, and ◊Swansea unitary authorities.

**West Indian** inhabitant of or native to the West Indies, or person of West Indian descent. The West Indies are culturally heterogeneous; in addition to the indigenous Carib and Arawak Indians, there are peoples of African, European, and Asian descent, as well as peoples of mixed descent.

**West Indies** archipelago of about 1,200 islands, dividing the Atlantic Ocean from the Gulf of Mexico and the Caribbean Sea. The islands are divided into:
*Bahamas; Greater Antilles* Cuba, Hispaniola (Haiti, Dominican Republic), Jamaica, and Puerto Rico;
*Lesser Antilles* Aruba, Netherlands Antilles, Trinidad and Tobago, the Windward Islands (Grenada, Barbados, St Vincent, St Lucia, Martinique, Dominica, Guadeloupe), the Leeward Islands (Montserrat, Antigua, St Kitts and Nevis, Barbuda, Anguilla, St Martin, British and US Virgin Islands), and many smaller islands.

**Westmeath** county of the Republic of Ireland, in the province of Leinster; county town Mullingar; area 1,760 sq km/679 sq mi; population (1991) 61,900. The Rivers Brosna, Inny, and Shannon flow through the county, and its principal lakes are Loughs Ree (the largest, and an extension of the River Shannon), Ennell, Owel, and Sheelin. The Royal Canal cuts through the county but is now disused. The land is low-lying, about 76 m/249 ft above sea-level, with much pasture. The main agricultural activity is cattle fattening and dairy farming. Limestone is found, and textiles are also important. Angling for trout is popular. Other principal towns are Athlone and Moate.

**West Midlands** metropolitan county of central England, created in 1974; in 1986, most of the functions of the former county council were transferred to the metropolitan borough councils
**area** 900 sq km/347 sq mi
**towns and cities** Birmingham, Coventry, Dudley, Solihull, Walsall, Wolverhampton (all administrative centres for districts of the same name), Oldbury (administrative centre for Sandwell)

**industries** aircraft components; chemicals; coal mining; engineering; electrical equipment; glass; machine tools; motor vehicles, including Land Rover at Solihull; motor components
**population** (1996) 2,642,500
**famous people** Edward Burne-Jones, Neville Chamberlain, John Curry, Francis Galton, Jerome K Jerome, Philip Larkin, John Marston, Henry Morton, Frank Whittle.

**Westphalia** independent medieval duchy, incorporated in Prussia by the Congress of Vienna in 1815, and made a province in 1816 with Münster as its capital. Since 1946 it has been part of the German *Land* (region) of ◊North Rhine–Westphalia.

**Westphalia, Treaty of** agreement of 1648 ending the ◊Thirty Years' War. The peace marked the end of the supremacy of the Holy Roman Empire and the emergence of France as a dominant power. It recognized the sovereignty of the German states, Switzerland, and the Netherlands; Lutherans, Calvinists, and Roman Catholics were given equal rights.

**West Sussex** county of southern England, created in 1974, formerly part of Sussex
**area** 1,990 sq km/768 sq mi
**towns and cities** Chichester (administrative headquarters), Crawley, Horsham, Haywards Heath, Shoreham (port); Bognor Regis, Littlehampton, Worthing (resorts)
**physical** the Weald; South Downs; rivers Adur, Arun, and West Rother
**features** Arundel and Bramber castles; Chichester cathedral; Goodwood House and racecourse; Petworth House (17th century); Wakehurst Place, where the Royal Botanic Gardens, Kew, have additional grounds; Uppark House (1685–90); the Weald and Downland Open Air Museum at Singleton; Fishbourne villa (important Roman site near Chichester); Selsey (reputed landing place of the South Saxons in 447); Gatwick Airport
**agriculture** cereals (wheat and barley); fruit; market gardening (mainly on the coastal plain); dairy produce; forestry
**industries** electronics; light engineering
**population** (1996) 737,300
**famous people** Richard Cobden, William Collins, Percy Bysshe Shelley.

**West Virginia** state in eastern central USA. It is nicknamed the Mountain State. West Virginia was admitted to the Union in 1863 as the 35th US state. It is bordered to the south and east by Virginia, to the north by Ohio, Pennsylvania, and Maryland, and to the west by Ohio and Kentucky. West Virginia is composed essentially of those Virginia counties that, unsympathetic to the plantation South, refused to join Virginia in its 1861 secession from the Union
**population** (1995) 1,828,100
**area** 62,900 sq km/24,279 sq mi
**capital** Charleston
**towns and cities** Huntington, Wheeling, Parkersburg
**industries and products** apples, maize, poultry, dairy and meat products, coal, natural gas,

oil, chemicals, synthetic fibres, plastics, steel, glass, pottery, tourism.

**West Yorkshire** metropolitan county of northeast England, created in 1974; in 1986, most of the functions of the former county council were transferred to the metropolitan borough councils
**area** 2,040 sq km/787 sq mi
**towns and cities** Bradford, Leeds, Wakefield (administrative centres for districts of the same name), Halifax (administrative centre of Calderdale district), Huddersfield (administrative centre of Kirklees district)
**physical** Ilkley Moor, Haworth Moor; high Pennine moorlands in the west, Vale of York to the east; rivers Aire, Calder, Colne, Wharfe
**features** Haworth Parsonage; part of the Peak District National Park; British Library, Boston Spa (scientific, technical, and business documents)
**industries** woollen textiles, financial services; coal mining is in decline
**population** (1996) 2,109,300
**famous people** the Brontës, David Hockney, Henry Moore, J B Priestley.

**wetland** permanently wet land area or habitat. Wetlands include areas of ◊marsh, fen, ◊bog, flood plain, and shallow coastal areas. Wetlands are extremely fertile. They provide warm, sheltered waters for fisheries, lush vegetation for grazing livestock, and an abundance of wildlife. Estuaries and seaweed beds are more than 16 times as productive as the open ocean.

**Wexford** county of the Republic of Ireland, in the province of Leinster; county town Wexford; 2,350 sq km/907 sq mi; population (1991) 102,000. Wexford is one of the most intensively cultivated areas in Ireland. The main crops are wheat, barley, beet, and potatoes. Fishing is important, the main fishing port being Kilmore Quay in the south; sheep and cattle rearing are also significant, as is dairy farming. Industries include agricultural machinery and food processing. Wexford was the first part of Ireland to be colonized from England; Normans arrived in 1169.

**whale** any marine mammal of the order Cetacea. The only mammals to have adapted to living entirely in water, they have front limbs modified into flippers and no externally visible traces of hind limbs. They have horizontal tail flukes. When they surface to breathe, the hot air they breathe out condenses to form a 'spout' through the blowhole (single or double nostrils) in the top of the head. Whales are intelligent and have a complex communication system, known as 'songs'. They occur in all seas of the world.

The order is divided into two groups: the toothed whales (Odontoceti) and the baleen whales (Mysticeti). Toothed whales are predators, feeding on fish and squid. They include ◊dolphins and ◊porpoises, along with large forms such as sperm whales. The largest whales are the baleen whales, with plates of modified mucous membrane called baleen (whalebone) in the mouth; these strain the food, mainly microscopic plankton, from the water. Baleen whales include the finback and right whales, and the blue whale, the largest animal that has ever lived, of length up to 30 m/100 ft.

Whales have been hunted for hundreds of years (see ◊whaling); today they are close to extinction. Of the 11 great whale species, 7 were listed as either endangered or vulnerable in 1996. Whale-watching, as an economic alternative to whaling, generated $121 million worldwide in 1994.

**whaling** the hunting of whales. Whales have been killed by humans since at least the Middle Ages. There were hundreds of thousands of whales at the beginning of the 20th century, but the invention of the harpoon in 1870 and improvements in ships and mechanization have led to the near-extinction of several species of whale. Commercial whaling was largely discontinued in 1986, although Norway and Japan have continued commercial whaling.

Traditional whaling areas include the coasts of Greenland and Newfoundland, but the Antarctic, in the summer months, supplies the bulk of the catch.

Practically the whole of the animal can be utilized in one form or another: whales are killed for whale oil (made from the thick layer of fat under the skin called 'blubber'), which is used as a lubricant, or for making soap, candles, and margarine; for the large reserve of oil in the head of the sperm whale, used in the leather industry; and for **ambergris**, a waxlike substance from the intestines of the sperm whale, used in making perfumes. Whalebone was used by corset manufacturers and in the brush trade; there are now synthetic substitutes for all these products. Whales have also been killed for use in petfood manufacture in the USA and Europe, and as a food in Japan. The flesh and ground bones are used as soil fertilizers.

**wheat** cereal plant derived from the wild *Triticum*, a grass native to the Middle East. It is the chief cereal used in breadmaking and is widely cultivated in temperate climates suited to its growth. Wheat is killed by frost, and damp makes the grains soft, so warm, dry regions produce the most valuable grain.

**wheatear** small (15 cm/6 in long) migratory bird *Oenanthe oenanthe* of the family Muscicapidae, order Passeriformes (which includes thrushes). Wheatears are found throughout the Old World and also breed in far northern parts of North America. The plumage is light grey above and white below with a buff tinge on the breast, a black face-patch, and black and white wings and tail. In flight a white patch on the lower back and tail is conspicuous. The wheatear's food consists chiefly of insects.

**whelk** any of various families of large marine snails with a thick spiral shell, especially the family Buccinidae. Whelks are scavengers, and also eat other shellfish. The largest grow to 40 cm/16 in long. Tropical species, such as the conches, can be very colourful.

**Whig Party** in the UK, predecessor of the Liberal Party. The name was first used of rebel

◊Covenanters and then of those who wished to exclude James II from the English succession (as a Roman Catholic). They were in power continuously 1714–60 and pressed for industrial and commercial development, a vigorous foreign policy, and religious toleration. During the French Revolution, the Whigs demanded parliamentary reform in Britain, and from the passing of the Reform Bill of 1832 became known as Liberals.

**whimbrel** wading bird *Numenius phaeopus,* order Charadriiformes, with a medium-sized down-curved bill, streaked brown plumage, and striped head. About 40 cm/1.3 ft long, it breeds in the Arctic, and winters in Africa, southern North America, South America, and South Asia. It is related to the ◊curlew.

**whip** (the whipper-in of hounds at a foxhunt) in UK politics, the member of Parliament who ensures the presence of colleagues in the party when there is to be a vote in Parliament at the end of a debate. The written appeal sent by the whips to MPs is also called a whip; this letter is underlined once, twice, or three times to indicate its importance. A *three-line whip* is the most urgent, and every MP is expected to attend and vote with their party. An MP who fails to attend may be temporarily suspended from the party, a penalty known as 'having the whip withdrawn'.

**whippet** breed of dog resembling a small greyhound. It grows to 56 cm/22 in at the shoulder, and 9 kg/20 lb in weight.

**whip snake** or *coachwhip,* any of the various species of nonpoisonous slender-bodied tree-dwelling snakes of the New World genus *Masticophis,* family Colubridae. They are closely allied to members of the genus *Coluber* of southwestern North America, Eurasia, Australasia, and North Africa, some of which are called whip snakes in the Old World, but racers in North America.

**whirlwind** rapidly rotating column of air, often synonymous with a ◊tornado. On a smaller scale it produces the dust-devils seen in deserts.

**whisky** or whiskey, (Gaelic *uisge beatha,* water of life) distilled spirit made from cereals: Scotch whisky from malted barley, Irish whiskey usually from barley, and North American whiskey and bourbon from maize and rye. Scotch is usually blended; pure malt whisky is more expensive. Whisky is generally aged in wooden casks for 4 to 12 years.

**whist** card game for four, predecessor of ◊bridge, in which the partners try to win a majority of the 13 tricks (the highest card played being the winner of the trick).

**Whistler, James Abbott McNeill** (1834–1903) US painter and etcher. Active in London from 1859, he was a leading figure in the ◊Aesthetic Movement. Influenced by Japanese prints, he painted riverscapes and portraits that show subtle composition and colour harmonies, for example *Arrangement in Grey and Black: Portrait of the Painter's Mother* (1871; Musée d'Orsay, Paris).

**Whitby, Synod of** council summoned by King Oswy of Northumbria in 664, which decided to adopt the Roman rather than the Celtic form of Christianity for Britain.

**White, Patrick Victor Martindale** (1912–1990) Australian writer. He did more than any other to put Australian literature on the international map. His partly allegorical novels explore the lives of early settlers in Australia and often deal with misfits or inarticulate people. They include *The Aunt's Story* (1948), written during his voyage back to Australia, *The Tree of Man* (1955), *Voss* (1957), based on the ill-fated 19th-century explorer Ludwig Leichhardt, and *Riders in the Chariot* (1961), exploring suburban life (Nobel Prize for Literature 1973). White became a fervent republican after the dismissal of the Gough Whitlam government in 1975, returning his Order of Australia in 1976, and supported conservation causes in his later years.

**whitebait** any of the fry (young) of various silvery fishes, especially ◊herring. It is also the name for a Pacific smelt *Osmerus mordax.*

**whitebeam** tree native to southern Europe, usually found growing on chalk or limestone. It can reach 20 m/60 ft in height. It takes its name from the dense coat of short white hairs on the underside of the leaves. (*Sorbus aria,* family Rosaceae.)

**white blood cell** or *leucocyte,* one of a number of different cells that play a part in the body's defences and give immunity against disease. Some (neutrophils and ◊macrophages) engulf invading micro-organisms, others kill infected cells, while ◊lymphocytes produce more specific immune responses. White blood cells are colourless, with clear or granulated cytoplasm, and are capable of independent amoeboid movement. They occur in the blood, ◊lymph, and elsewhere in the body's tissues.

**white dwarf** small, hot ◊star, the last stage in the life of a star such as the Sun. White dwarfs make up 10% of the stars in the Galaxy; most have a mass 60% of that of the Sun, but only 1% of the Sun's diameter, similar in size to the Earth. Most have surface temperatures of 8,000°C/14,400°F or more, hotter than the Sun. Yet, being so small, their overall luminosities may be less than 1% of that of the Sun. The Milky Way contains an estimated 50 billion white dwarfs.

**whitefish** any of various freshwater fishes, genera *Coregonus* and *Prosopium,* of the salmon family, found in lakes and rivers of North America and Eurasia. They include the *whitefish C. clupeaformis* and *cisco C. artedi.*

**White Horse** any of 17 hill figures in England, found particularly in the southern chalk downlands. The Uffington White Horse below Uffington Castle, a hill fort on the Berkshire Downs, is 110 m/360 ft long and probably a tribal totem of the late Bronze Age.

**whitethroat** any of several Old World warblers of the genus *Sylvia* in the family Muscicapidae, order Passeriformes. They are found in scrub, hedges, and wood clearings of

Eurasia in summer, migrating to Africa in winter. They are about 14 cm/5.5 in long.

**whiting** predatory fish *Merlangius merlangus* common in shallow sandy northern European waters. It grows to 70 cm/2.3 ft.

**Whitman, Walt(er)** (1819–1892) US poet. He published *Leaves of Grass* in 1855, which contains the symbolic 'Song of Myself'. It used unconventional free verse (with no rhyme or regular rhythm) and scandalized the public by its frank celebration of sexuality.

**Whit Sunday** Christian church festival held seven weeks after Easter, commemorating the descent of the Holy Spirit on the Apostles. The name is probably derived from the white garments worn by candidates for baptism at the festival. Whit Sunday corresponds to the Jewish festival of Shavuot (Pentecost).

**Whittle, Frank** (1907–1996) British engineer. He patented the basic design for the turbojet engine in 1930. In the Royal Air Force he worked on jet propulsion from 1937–46. In May 1941 the Gloster E 28/39 aircraft first flew with the Whittle jet engine. Both the German (first operational jet planes) and the US jet aircraft were built using his principles. He was knighted in 1948.

**WHO** acronym for ◊*World Health Organization,* an agency of the United Nations established to prevent the spread of diseases.

**whooping cough** or *pertussis,* acute infectious disease, seen mainly in children, caused by colonization of the air passages by the bacterium *Bordetella pertussis.* There may be catarrh, mild fever, and loss of appetite, but the main symptom is violent coughing, associated with the sharp intake of breath that is the characteristic 'whoop', and often followed by vomiting and severe nose bleeds. The cough may persist for weeks.

**whydah** any of various African birds of the genus *Vidua,* order Passeriformes, of the weaver family. They lay their eggs in the nests of ◊waxbills, which rear the young. Young birds resemble young waxbills, but the adults do not resemble adult waxbills. Males have long tail feathers used in courtship displays.

**Wicklow** county of the Republic of Ireland, in the province of Leinster; county town Wicklow; area 2,030 sq km/784 sq mi; population (1991) 97,300. It includes the *Wicklow Mountains,* the Rivers Slaney, Avoca, Vartry, and Liffey, and the coastal resort Bray. Other towns include Arklow, Greystones, and Baltinglass. The village of Shillelagh gave its name to rough cudgels of oak or blackthorn made there. Agriculture is important; there is livestock rearing (in particular a special breed of mountain sheep), and dairy farming. Wheat and oats are grown, and seed potatoes and bulbs are produced. Granite is mined at Aughrim and Ballyknockan.

**wigeon** either of two species of dabbling duck of genus *Anas,* order Anseriformes. The *American wigeon A. americana,* about 48 cm/19 in long, is found along both coasts in winter and breeds inland. Males have a white-capped head and a green eye stripe.

**Wight, Isle of** island and unitary authority of southern England
*area* area 380 sq km/147 sq mi
*towns* Newport (the administrative headquarters); Ryde, Sandown, Shanklin, Ventnor (all resorts)
*physical* chalk cliffs and downs, and deep ravines, known locally as 'chines'; the highest point is St Boniface Down (240 m/787 ft); the Needles, a group of pointed chalk rocks up to 30 m/100 ft high in the sea to the west; the Solent, the sea channel between Hampshire and the island
*features* Benedictine monastery at Quarr Abbey; Parkhurst Prison, just outside Newport; Cowes, venue of Regatta Week and headquarters of the Royal Yacht Squadron; Osborne House, built for Queen Victoria in 1845
*agriculture* fruit and vegetables grown in south of island
*industries* aircraft components, electronics, marine engineering, plastics, boatbuilding, sawmills, tourism
*population* (1996) 130,000
*famous people* Thomas Arnold, Robert Hooke, Alfred Tennyson
*history* the Isle of Wight was called *Vectis* ('separate division') by the Romans, who conquered it in AD 43; there are Roman villas at Newport and Brading. Charles I was imprisoned (1647–48) in Carisbrooke Castle, now ruined.

**Wilberforce, William** (1759–1833) English reformer. He was instrumental in abolishing slavery in the British Empire. He entered Parliament in 1780; in 1807 his bill banning the trade in slaves from the West Indies was passed, and in 1833, largely through his efforts, slavery was eradicated throughout the empire. He died shortly before the Slavery Abolition Act was passed.

**Wilde, Oscar (Fingal O'Flahertie Wills)** (1854–1900) Irish writer. With his flamboyant style and quotable conversation, he dazzled London society and, on his lecture tour in 1882, the USA. He published his only novel, *The Picture of Dorian Gray,* in 1891, followed by a series of sharp comedies, including *A Woman of No Importance* (1893) and *The Importance of Being Earnest* (1895). In 1895 he was imprisoned for two years for homosexual offences; he died in exile.

**wildebeest** or *gnu,* either of two species of African ◊antelope, with a cowlike face, a beard and mane, and heavy curved horns in both sexes. The body is up to 1.3 m/4.2 ft high at the shoulder and slopes away to the hindquarters. (Genus *Connochaetes.*)

**wilderness** area of uninhabited land that has never been disturbed by humans, usually located some distance from towns and cities. According to estimates by US group Conservation International, 52% (90 million sq km/35 million sq mi) of the Earth's total land area was still undisturbed in 1994.

**wildlife trade** international trade in live plants and animals, and in wildlife products such as skins, horns, shells, and feathers. The trade has made some species virtually extinct, and whole ecosystems (for example, coral reefs) are threatened. Wildlife trade is to some extent regulated by CITES (Convention on International Trade in Endangered Species).

**wild type** in genetics, the naturally occurring gene for a particular character that is typical of most individuals of a given species, as distinct from new genes that arise by mutation.

**Wilkins, Maurice Hugh Frederick** (1916– ) New Zealand-born British molecular biologist. In 1962 he shared the Nobel Prize for Physiology or Medicine with Francis ◊Crick and James ◊Watson for his work on the molecular structure of nucleic acids, particularly ◊DNA, using X-ray diffraction.

**William** full name William Arthur Philip Louis (1982– ) Prince of the UK, first child of the Prince and Princess of Wales.

**William** four kings of England:

**William (I) the Conqueror** (c. 1027–1087) King of England from 1066. He was the illegitimate son of Duke Robert the Devil and succeeded his father as duke of Normandy in 1035. Claiming that his relative King Edward the Confessor had bequeathed him the English throne, William invaded the country in 1066, defeating ◊Harold II at Hastings, Sussex, and was crowned king of England.

**William (II) Rufus** 'William the Red' (c. 1056–1100) king of England from 1087, the third son of William (I) the Conqueror. He spent most of his reign attempting to capture Normandy from his brother ◊Robert (II) Curthose , Duke of Normandy. His extortion of money led his barons to revolt and caused confrontation with Bishop Anselm. He was killed while hunting in the New Forest, Hampshire, and was succeeded by his brother Henry I.

**William (III) of Orange** (1650–1702) King of Great Britain and Ireland from 1688, the son of William II of Orange and Mary, daughter of Charles I. He was offered the English crown by the parliamentary opposition to James II. He invaded England in 1688 and in 1689 became joint sovereign with his wife, ◊Mary II. He spent much of his reign campaigning, first in Ireland, where he defeated James II at the Battle of ◊Boyne in 1690, and later against the French in Flanders. He died childless and was succeeded by Mary's sister, Anne.

**William IV** (1765–1837) King of Great Britain and Ireland from 1830, when he succeeded his brother George IV. Third son of George III, he was created Duke of Clarence in 1789, and married Adelaide of Saxe-Meiningen (1792–1849) in 1818. During the Reform Bill crisis he secured its passage by agreeing to create new peers to overcome the hostile majority in the House of Lords. He was succeeded by his niece Victoria.

**William I** (1797–1888) King of Prussia from 1861 and emperor of Germany from 1871; the son of Friedrich Wilhelm III. He served in the Napoleonic Wars (1814–15) and helped to crush the 1848 revolution. After he succeeded his brother Friedrich Wilhelm IV to the throne of Prussia, his policy was largely dictated by his chancellor ◊Bismarck, who secured his proclamation as emperor.

**William II** German *Wilhelm II* (1859–1941) Emperor of Germany from 1888, the son of Frederick III and Victoria, daughter of Queen Victoria of Britain. In 1890 he forced Chancellor Bismarck to resign in an attempt to assert his own political authority. The result was an exacerbation of domestic and international political instability, although his personal influence declined in the 1900s. He was an enthusiastic supporter of Admiral Tirpitz's plans for naval expansion. In 1914 he first approved Austria's ultimatum to Serbia and then, when he realized war was inevitable, tried in vain to prevent it. In 1918 he fled to Doorn in the Netherlands after Germany's defeat and his abdication.

**William the Lion** (1143–1214) king of Scotland from 1165. He was captured by Henry II while invading England in 1174, and forced to do homage, but Richard I abandoned the English claim to suzerainty for a money payment in 1189. In 1209 William was forced by King John to renounce his claim to Northumberland.

**William the Silent** (1533–1584) Prince of Orange from 1544. Leading a revolt against Spanish rule in the Netherlands from 1573, he briefly succeeded in uniting the Catholic south and Protestant northern provinces, but the former provinces submitted to Spain while the latter formed a federation in 1579 (Union of Utrecht) which repudiated Spanish suzerainty in 1581.

**William (I) the Conqueror** (1028–1087) king of England from 25 December 1066. He was the illegitimate son of Duke Robert the Devil whom he succeeded as Duke of Normandy in 1035. Claiming that his relative King Edward the Confessor had bequeathed him the English throne, William invaded England in 1066, defeating ◊Harold (II) Godwinson at the Battle of Hastings on 14 October 1066, and was crowned king of England.

**Williams, Tennessee (Thomas Lanier)** (1911–1983) US dramatist. His work is characterized by fluent dialogue and searching analysis of the psychological deficiencies of his characters. His plays, usually set in the Deep South against a background of decadence and degradation, include *The Glass Menagerie* (1945), *A Streetcar Named Desire* (1947), and *Cat on a Hot Tin Roof* (1955), the last two of which earned Pulitzer prizes.

**Willis, Norman David** (1933– ) English trade-union leader. A trade-union official since leaving school, he was the general secretary of the Trades Union Congress (TUC) 1984–93 and president of the European TUC 1991–93.

**willow** any of a group of trees or shrubs containing over 350 species, found mostly in the northern hemisphere, flourishing in damp places. The leaves are often lance-shaped, and the male and female catkins are borne on separate trees. (Genus *Salix*, family Salicaceae.)

**willowherb** any of a group of perennial flowering plants belonging to the evening primrose family. The *rosebay willowherb* or *fireweed* (*C. angustifolium*) is common in woods and wasteland. It grows to 1.2 m/4 ft with tall upright spikes of red or purplish flowers. (Genera *Epilobium* and *Chamaenerion*, family Onagraceae.)

**Wilson, (James) Harold** Baron Wilson of Rievaulx (1916–1995) British Labour politician, party leader from 1963, prime minister 1964–70 and 1974–76. His premiership was dominated by the issue of UK admission to membership of the European Community (now the European Union), the social contract (unofficial agreement with the trade unions), and economic difficulties.

**Wilson, (Thomas) Woodrow** (1856–1924) 28th president of the USA 1913–21, a Democrat. He kept the USA out of World War I until 1917, and in January 1918 issued his 'Fourteen Points' as a basis for a just peace settlement.

At the peace conference in Paris he secured the inclusion of the ◊League of Nations in individual peace treaties, but these were not ratified by Congress, so the USA did not join the League. He was awarded the Nobel Peace Prize in 1919.

**Wilts** abbreviation for ◊Wiltshire, an English county.

**Wiltshire** county of southwest England (since April 1997 Swindon has been a separate unitary authority)
*area* 3,480 sq km/1,343 sq mi
*towns and cities* Trowbridge (administrative headquarters), Salisbury, Wilton, Devizes, Chippenham, Warminster
*physical* Marlborough Downs; Savernake Forest; rivers Kennet, Wylye, Avons (Salisbury and Bristol); Salisbury Plain (32 km/20 mi by 25 km/16 mi, lying at about 120 m/394 ft above sea-level), a military training area used since Napoleonic times
*features* Longleat House (Marquess of Bath); Wilton House (Earl of Pembroke); Stourhead, with 18th-century gardens; Neolithic Stonehenge, Avebury, Silbury Hill, West Kennet Long Barrow, finest example of a long barrow in Wiltshire, dating from the 3rd millennium BC; Stonehenge, Avebury, and associated sites are a World Heritage site; Salisbury Cathedral, which has the tallest spire in Britain (123 m/404 ft)
*agriculture* cereals (wheat); cattle; dairy-farming (condensed milk, cheese); pig and sheep farming
*industries* brewing (Devizes); computing; electronics; engineering (Chippenham); pharmaceuticals; plastics; quarrying (Portland stone); rubber (Bradford-on-Avon, Melksham); tobacco (Devizes)
*population* (1996) 593,300
*famous people* Isaac Pitman, William Talbot, Christopher Wren.

**Wimbledon** English lawn-tennis centre used for international championship matches, situated in south London. There are currently 18 courts.

**WIMP** acronym for windows, icons, menus, pointing device, in computing, another name for ◊graphical user interface (GUI).

**Winchester** cathedral city and administrative headquarters of ◊Hampshire, England, on the River Itchen, 19 km/12 mi northeast of Southampton; population (1991) 36,100. Tourism is important, and there is also light industry. Originally a Roman town, Winchester was capital of the Anglo-Saxon kingdom of Wessex, and later of England. Winchester Cathedral (1079–93) is the longest medieval church in Europe and was remodelled from Norman-Romanesque to Perpendicular Gothic under the patronage of William of Wykeham (founder of Winchester College in 1382), who is buried there, as are Saxon kings, St Swithun, and the writers Izaac Walton and Jane Austen.

**wind** the lateral movement of the Earth's atmosphere from high-pressure areas (anticyclones) to low-pressure areas (depression). Its speed is measured using an ◊anemometer or by studying its effects on, for example, trees by using the ◊Beaufort scale. Although modified by features such as land and water, there is a basic worldwide system of ◊trade winds, westerlies, and polar easterlies.

**wind-chill factor** or *wind-chill index*, estimate of how much colder it feels when a wind is blowing. It is the sum of the temperature (in °F below zero) and the wind speed (in miles per hour). So for a wind of 15 mph at an air temperature of –5°F, the wind-chill factor is 20.

**Windermere** largest lake in England, in the ◊Lake District, Cumbria, northwest England; length 17 km/10.5 mi; width 1.6 km/1 mi. Windermere is the principal centre of tourism in the Lake District. The town of the same name extends towards Bowness on the eastern shore of the lake.

**Windhoek** capital of Namibia, and administrative centre of Khomas region; population (1992) 126,000. It is just north of the Tropic of Capricorn, in the Khomas Highlands, 290 km/180 mi from the west coast. It is the world centre of the karakul (breed of sheep) industry; other industries include engineering and food processing.

**Windows** in computing, originally Microsoft's ◊graphical user interface (GUI) for IBM PCs and clones running MS-DOS. Windows has developed into a family of operating systems that run on a wide variety of computers from pen-operated palmtop organizers to large, multiprocessor computers in corporate data centres.

**wind power** the harnessing of wind energy to produce power. The wind has long been used as a source of energy: sailing ships and windmills are ancient inventions. After the energy crisis of the 1970s ◊wind turbines began to be used to produce electricity on a large scale.

**Windscale** former name of ◊Sellafield, a nuclear power station in Cumbria, England.

**Windsor and Maidenhead** unitary authority in southeast England, created in 1998 from part of the former county of Berkshire
*area* 198 sq km/76 sq mi
*towns and cities* Windsor, Maidenhead (administrative headquarters)
*features* River Thames; Windsor Castle, royal residence originally built by William the Conqueror; Windsor Great Park, remnant of royal hunting ground; Eton College, founded by Henry VI in 1440; Household Cavalry Museum (Windsor); Stanley Spencer (1891–1959) Gallery (Cookham on Thames); Ascot Racecourse
*industries* tourism and service industries, electrical systems and components, chemicals, motor vehicle components, telecommunications, publishing, scientific equipment
*population* (1996) 140,200

**windsurfing** or *boardsailing* or *sailboarding,* water sport combining elements of surfing and sailing, first developed in the USA in 1968. The windsurfer stands on a board that is propelled and steered by means of a sail attached to a mast that is articulated at the foot. Since 1984 the sport has been included in the Olympic Games as part of the yachting events. From 1992 men and women have had to compete in separate categories. There are also annual boardsailing world championships.

**wind turbine** windmill of advanced aerodynamic design connected to an electricity generator and used in wind-power installations. Wind turbines can be either large propeller-type rotors mounted on a tall tower, or flexible metal strips fixed to a vertical axle at top and bottom.

**wine** alcoholic beverage, usually made from fermented grape pulp, although wines have also traditionally been made from many other fruits such as damsons and elderberries. *Red wine* is the product of the grape with the skin; *white wine* of the inner pulp of the grape. The sugar content is converted to ethyl alcohol by the yeast *Saccharomyces ellipsoideus,* which lives on the skin of the grape. The largest wine-producing countries are Italy, France, Russia, Georgia, Moldova, Armenia, and Spain; others include almost all European countries, Australia, South Africa, the USA, and Chile.
*types of wine* For *dry wine* the fermentation is allowed to go on longer than for *sweet* or *medium;* ◊champagne (sparkling wine from the Champagne region of France) is bottled while still fermenting, but other sparkling wines are artificially carbonated. Some wines are fortified with additional alcohol obtained from various sources, and with preservatives. Some of the latter may cause dangerous side effects (see ◊additive). For this reason, organic wines, containing no preservatives, have recently become popular.

**wing** in biology, the modified forelimb of birds and bats, or the membranous outgrowths of the ◊exoskeleton of insects, which give the power of flight. Birds and bats have two wings. Bird wings

*wing* Birds can fly because of the specialized shape of their wings: a rounded leading edge, flattened underneath and round on top. This aerofoil shape produces lift in the same way that an aircraft wing does. The outline of the wing is related to the speed of flight. Fast birds of prey have a streamlined shape. Larger birds, such as the eagle, have large wings with separated tip feathers which reduce drag and allow slow flight. Insect wings are not aerofoils. They push downwards to produce lift, in the same way that oars are used to push through water.

have feathers attached to the fused digits ('fingers') and forearm bones, while bat wings consist of skin stretched between the digits. Most insects have four wings, which are strengthened by wing veins.

**Winnipeg** nickname 'Gateway to the West', (Cree *win-nipuy* 'muddy water') capital of Manitoba, Canada, at the confluence of the Red and Assiniboine rivers, 65 km/40 mi south of Lake Winnipeg, 30 km/20 mi north of the US border; population (1991) 616,800, metropolitan area (1996) 676,700. It is a focus for trans-Canada and Canada–US traffic, and a market and transhipment point for wheat and other produce from the prairie provinces: Manitoba, Alberta, and Saskatchewan. Processed-foods, textiles, farming machinery, and transport equipment are manufactured. Established as Winnipeg in 1870 on the site of earlier forts, the city expanded with the arrival of the Canadian Pacific Railroad in 1881.

**wintergreen** any of a group of plants belonging to the heath family, especially the species *G. procumbens* of northeastern North America, which creeps underground and sends up tiny shoots. Oil of wintergreen, used in treating rheumatism, is extracted from its leaves.

Wintergreen is also the name for various plants belonging to the wintergreen family Pyrolaceae, including the green pipsissewa *C. maculata* of northern North America, Europe, and Asia. (Genus *Gaultheria,* family Ericaceae; also genera *Pyrola, Chimaphila, Orthilia,* and *Moneses,* family Pyrolaceae.)

**Wisconsin** state in northern central USA. It is nicknamed the Badger State. Wisconsin was admitted to the Union in 1848 as the 30th US state. Part of the Midwest, it is bordered to the south by Illinois, to the west by Iowa and Minnesota, to the north by Lake Superior and the Upper Peninsula of Michigan, and to the east by Lake Michigan

*population* (1995) 5,122,900

*area* 145,500 sq km/56,163 sq mi

*capital* Madison

*towns and cities* Milwaukee, Green Bay, Racine

*industries and products* leading US dairy state; maize, hay, industrial and agricultural machinery, engines and turbines, precision instruments, paper products, cars and lorries, plumbing equipment, research, tourism.

**wisent** another name for the European ◊bison.

**wisteria** any of a group of climbing leguminous shrubs (see ◊legume), including *W. sinensis,* native to the eastern USA and East Asia. Wisterias have hanging clusters of bluish, white, or pale mauve flowers, and pinnate leaves (leaflets on either side of the stem). They are grown against walls as ornamental plants. (Genus *Wisteria,* family Leguminosae.)

**witch doctor** alternative name for a ◊shaman.

**witch hazel** any of a group of flowering shrubs or small trees belonging to the witch hazel family, native to North America and East Asia, especially *H. virginiana.* An astringent extract prepared from the bark or leaves is used in medicine as an eye lotion and a liniment to relieve pain or stiffness. (Genus *Hamamelis,* family Hamamelidaceae.)

**witch-hunt** persecution of minority political opponents or socially nonconformist groups without any regard for their guilt or innocence. Witch-hunts are often accompanied by a degree of public hysteria; for example, the ◊McCarthy anticommunist hearings during the 1950s in the USA.

**witness** in law, a person who was present at some event (such as an accident, a crime, or the signing of a document) or has relevant special knowledge (such as a medical expert) and can be called on to give evidence in a court of law.

**Wittgenstein, Ludwig Josef Johann** (1889–1951) Austrian philosopher. *Tractatus Logico-Philosophicus* (1922) postulated the 'picture theory' of language: that words represent things according to social agreement. He subsequently rejected this idea, and developed the idea that usage was more important than convention.

**Witwatersrand** or *the Rand,* (Afrikaans 'ridge of white water') economic heartland of Gauteng Province, South Africa. Its reef, which stretches nearly 100 km/60 mi, produces over half the world's gold. Gold was first found here in 1853. The chief city of the region is Johannesburg. Forming a watershed between the Vaal and the Olifant rivers, the Rand comprises a series of parallel ranges which extend 100 km/60 mi east–west and rise to 1,525–1,830 m/5,000–6,000 ft above sea level. Gold occurs in reefs that are mined at depths of up to 3,050 m/10,000 ft.

**woad** biennial plant native to Europe, with arrow-shaped leaves and clusters of small yellow flowers. It was formerly cultivated for a blue dye extracted from its leaves. Ancient Britons used the blue dye as a body paint in battle. (*Isatis tinctoria,* family Cruciferae.)

**Wodehouse, P(elham) G(renville)** (1881–1975) English novelist. He became a US citizen in 1955. His humorous novels and stories portray the accident-prone world of such characters as the socialite Bertie Wooster and his invaluable and impeccable manservant Jeeves, and Lord Emsworth of Blandings Castle with his prize pig, the Empress of Blandings.

**Woden** or *Wodan,* the foremost Anglo-Saxon god, whose Norse counterpart is ◊Odin.

**Wokingham** unitary authority in southeast England, created in 1998 from part of the former county of Berkshire

*area* 179 sq km/69 sq mi

*towns and cities* Wokingham (administrative headquarters), Twyford

*features* River Thames forms northern border of authority; Royal Electrical and Mechanical Engineering Corps Museum (Arborfield); Swallowfield Park, house built for 2nd Earl of Clarendon in 1690; National Dairy Museum; Henley Regatta course; large areas of mixed woodland including remnants of old Royal Chase of Windsor Forest and tree-lined avenues; Finchampstead Ridges

*industries* light engineering, electronics and information technology, telecommunications, computer components and software, plastics

*population* (1996) 142,000.

**wolf** any of two species of large wild dogs of the genus *Canis.* The *grey* or *timber wolf C. lupus,* of North America and Eurasia, is highly social, measures up to 90 cm/3 ft at the shoulder, and weighs up to 45 kg/100 lb. It has been greatly reduced in numbers except for isolated wilderness regions. The *red wolf C. rufus,* generally more slender and smaller (average weight about 15 kg/35 lb) and tawnier in colour, may not be a separate species, but a grey wolf–coyote hybrid. It used to be restricted to southern central USA, but is now thought to be extinct in the wild.

**Wolfe, James** (1727–1759) English soldier. He served in Canada and commanded a victorious expedition against the French general Montcalm in Quebec on the Plains of Abraham, during which both commanders were killed. The British victory established their supremacy over Canada.

**wolfram** alternative name for ◊tungsten.

**Wollstonecraft, Mary** (1759–1797) British feminist. She was a member of a group of radical intellectuals called the English Jacobins. Her book *A Vindication of the Rights of Women* (1792) demanded equal educational opportunities for women. She married William Godwin in 1797 and died giving birth to a daughter, Mary (later Mary ◊Shelley).

**Wolof** the majority ethnic group living in Senegal. There is also a Wolof minority in Gambia. There are about 2 million speakers of Wolof, a language belonging to the Niger-Congo family. The Wolof are Muslims.

**Wolsey, Thomas** (*c.* 1475–1530) English cleric and politician. In Henry VIII's service from 1509, he became archbishop of York in 1514, cardinal and lord chancellor in 1515, and began the dissolution of the monasteries.

His reluctance to further Henry's divorce from Catherine of Aragon led to his downfall in 1529. He was charged with high treason in 1530 but died before being tried.

**Wolverhampton** industrial town in West Midlands, central England, 20 km/12 mi northwest of Birmingham; population (1994) 256,100. Industries include metalworking, engineering, and the manufacture of chemicals, tyres, aircraft, bicycles, locks and keys, and commercial vehicles. Europe's first power station fuelled by waste tyres opened here in 1993.

**wolverine** *Gulo gulo,* largest land member of the weasel family (Mustelidae), found in Europe, Asia, and North America.

It is stocky in build, and about 1 m/3.3 ft long. Its long, thick fur is dark brown on the back and belly and lighter on the sides. It covers food that it cannot eat with an unpleasant secretion. Destruction of habitat and trapping for its fur have greatly reduced its numbers.

**womb** common name for the ◊uterus.

**wombat** any of a family (Vombatidae) of burrowing, herbivorous marsupials, native to Tasmania and southern Australia. They are about 1 m/3.3 ft long, heavy, with a big head, short legs and tail, and coarse fur.

**women's movement** campaign for the rights of women, including social, political, and economic equality with men. Early European campaigners of the 17th–19th centuries fought for women's right to own property, to have access to higher education, and to vote (see ◊suffragette). Once women's suffrage was achieved in the 20th century, the emphasis of the movement shifted to the goals of equal social and economic opportunities for women, including employment. A continuing area of concern in industrialized countries is the contradiction between the now generally accepted principle of equality and the inequalities that remain between the sexes in state policies and in everyday life.

**wood** the hard tissue beneath the bark of many perennial plants; it is composed of water-conducting cells, or secondary ◊xylem, and

gains its hardness and strength from deposits of ◊lignin. *Hardwoods,* such as oak, and *softwoods,* such as pine, have commercial value as structural material and for furniture.

**woodcock** either of two species of wading birds, genus *Scolopax,* of the family Scolopacidae, which have barred plumage and long bills, and live in wet woodland areas. They belong to the long-billed section of the snipes, order Charadriiformes.

**woodcut** print made by a woodblock in which a picture or design has been cut in relief along the grain of the wood. The woodcut is the oldest method of ◊printing, invented in China in the 5th century AD. In the Middle Ages woodcuts became popular in Europe, illustrating early printed books and broadsides.

**woodland** area in which trees grow more or less thickly; generally smaller than a forest. Temperate climates, with four distinct seasons a year, tend to support a mixed woodland habitat, with some conifers but mostly broad-leaved and deciduous trees, shedding their leaves in autumn and regrowing them in spring. In the Mediterranean region and parts of the southern hemisphere, the trees are mostly evergreen.

**woodlouse** crustacean of the order Isopoda. Woodlice have segmented bodies, flattened undersides, and 14 legs. The eggs are carried by the female in a pouch beneath the thorax. They often live in high densities: as many as 8,900 per square metre.

**woodmouse** or *long-tailed field mouse, Apodemus sylvaticus,* rodent that lives in woodlands, hedgerows, and sometimes open fields in Britain and Europe. About 9 cm/3.5 in long, with a similar length of tail, it is yellow-brown above, white below, and has long oval ears.

It is nocturnal and feeds largely on seeds, but eats a range of foods, including some insects.

**woodpecker** bird of the family Picidae, order Piciformes. They are adapted for climbing up the bark of trees, and picking out insects to eat from the crevices. The feet, though very short, are usually strong; the nails are broad and crooked and the toes placed in pairs, two forward and two backward. As an additional support their tail feathers terminate in points, and are uncommonly hard. Woodpeckers have a long extensile tongue, which has muscles enabling the bird to dart it forth and to retract it again quickly. There are about 200 species worldwide.

**Woods, Tiger** born Eldrick Woods (1976– ) US golfer. He has made a phenomenal impact on the game since 1994 when he became the youngest player, at the age of 18, to win the US Amateur Championship, the first of an unprecedented three successive titles. Previously he had won the US Junior Championship on three successive occasions from 1991–93. After his third Amateur Championship triumph, he turned professional in 1996, immediately becoming one of the wealthiest men in US sport as a result of endorsement deals worth £40 million. In his first six months as a professional he won four

tournaments on the US PGA circuit, then in 1997 he won Mercedes Championships, the Honda Asian Classic (Bangkok), and the US Masters. Woods was voted the 1997 Associated Press Male Athlete of the Year, only the 5th golfer to win this award and the first since Lee Trevino. He made a remarkable comeback in the Thai Open at Phuket, overcoming an 11-stroke deficit going into the final two rounds to win a sudden- death playoff for the championship against the South African US Open champion Ernie Els. In August 1999 he won the second major of his career, the 1999 US PGA championship at Medinah, Chicago. This victory earned him $630,000 and a return to the number 1 ranking in the world golf ranking. In 1999 he played in the US team which won the Ryder Cup.
*career highlights*
*US Amateur* 1994–96
*US Masters* 1997
*US PGA championship* 1999

**Woodstock** the first free rock festival, held near Bethel, New York State, USA, over three days in August 1969. It was attended by 400,000 people, and performers included the Band, Country Joe and the Fish, the Grateful Dead, Jimi Hendrix, Jefferson Airplane, and the Who. The festival was a landmark in the youth culture of the 1960s (see ◊hippie) and was recorded in the film *Woodstock* (1970).

**woodworm** common name for the larval stage of certain wood-boring beetles. Dead or injured trees are their natural target, but they also attack structural timber and furniture.

**wool** the natural hair covering of the sheep, and also of the llama, angora goat, and some other ◊mammals. The domestic sheep *Ovis aries* provides the great bulk of the fibres used in textile production. Lanolin is a by-product.

**Woolf, (Adeline) Virginia** born Stephen (1882–1941) English novelist and critic. In novels such as *Mrs Dalloway* (1925), *To the Lighthouse* (1927), and *The Waves* (1931), she used a 'stream of consciousness' technique to render inner experience. In *A Room of One's Own* (1929) (nonfiction), *Orlando* (1928), and *The Years* (1937), she examines the importance of economic independence for women and other feminist principles.

**Worcestershire** two-tier county of west central England. Herefordshire and Worcestershire existed as counties until 1974, when they were amalgamated to form the county of Hereford and Worcester; in 1998 this county was divided back into Worcestershire and Herefordshire, which regained their pre-1974 boundaries
*area* 1,640 sq km/1,020 sq mi
*towns and cities* Worcester (administrative headquarters), Bewdley, Bromsgrove, Evesham, Kidderminster, Pershore, Stourport, Tenbury Wells
*physical* Malvern Hills in the southwest (highest point Worcester Beacon 425 m/1,394 ft); rivers Severn with tributaries Stour, Teme, and Avon (running through the fertile Vale of Evesham)

*features* Droitwich, once a Victorian spa, reopened its baths in 1985 (the town lies over a subterranean brine reservoir); Three Choirs Festival at Great Malvern
*agriculture* cereals (oats, wheat), fruit (apples, pears), hops, vegetables; cider; much of the county is under cultivation, a large part being devoted to permanent pasture, notably for Hereford cattle
*industries* carpets (Kidderminster), chemicals, engineering, food processing, needles and fishing tackle (Redditch), porcelain (Worcester), salt
*population* (1996) 535,700
*famous people* Richard Baxter, Samuel Butler, Edward Elgar, A E Housman, William Langland, Francis Brett Young.

**Wordsworth, William** (1770–1850) English Romantic poet. In 1797 he moved with his sister Dorothy Wordsworth to Somerset, where he lived near Samuel Taylor ◊Coleridge and collaborated with him on *Lyrical Ballads* (1798) (which included 'Tintern Abbey', a meditation on his response to nature). From 1799 he lived in the Lake District. His most notable individual poems were published in *Poems* (1807) (including 'Intimations of Immortality'). At intervals between then and 1839 he revised *The Prelude* (posthumously published in 1850), the first part of his uncompleted philosophical, creative, and spiritual autobiography in verse. He was appointed poet laureate in 1843.

**work** in physics, a measure of the result of transferring energy from one system to another to cause an object to move. Work should not be confused with ◊energy (the capacity to do work, which is also measured in joules) or with ◊power (the rate of doing work, measured in joules per second).

**workhouse** in the UK, a former institution to house and maintain people unable to earn their own living. Groups of parishes in England combined to build workhouses for the poor, the aged, the disabled, and orphaned children from about 1815 until about 1930.

**World Bank** popular name for the *International Bank for Reconstruction and Development*, specialized agency of the United Nations that borrows in the commercial market and lends on commercial terms. It was established 1945 under the 1944 Bretton Woods agreement, which also created the International Monetary Fund. The *International Development Association* is an arm of the World Bank.

**World Cup** the most prestigious competition in international soccer; World Cup events are also held in rugby union, cricket, and other sports.

**World Health Organization** (WHO), specialized agency of the United Nations established in 1946 to prevent the spread of diseases and to eradicate them. In 1996–97 it had a budget of $842.654 million. Its headquarters are in Geneva, Switzerland. The WHO's greatest achievement to date has been the eradication of smallpox.

**world music** or *roots music,* popular music which has its roots in ◊folk music, especially non-European folk music. It is usually performed by artists from the country it comes from, and has a distinct regional character. Examples are West African mbalax, East African soukous, South African mbaqanga, French Antillean zouk, Latin American salsa and lambada, and Cajun music, as well as combinations of these with European folk music or rural ◊blues.

The term is sometimes used to include non-western classical music, such as the Javanese gamelan and Spanish flamenco, or simply to describe any music other than Western classical music.

**World Trade Organization** (WTO), specialized agency of the United Nations, world trade monitoring body established in January 1995, on approval of the Final Act of the Uruguay round of the ◊General Agreement on Tariffs and Trade (GATT). Under the Final Act, the WTO, a permanent trading body with a status commensurate with that of the International Monetary Fund or the World Bank, effectively replaced GATT. The WTO monitors agreements to reduce barriers to trade, such as tariffs, subsidies, quotas, and regulations which discriminate against imported products.

All members of GATT automatically became members of the WTO on their parliaments' ratification of the Uruguay round; new members, without exception, would have to meet the criteria established by the Uruguay round. WTO headquarters are in Geneva, Switzerland, and its director-general has Renato Ruggiero, of Italy. The organization has 129 members.

**World War I** (1914–18), war between the Central European Powers (Germany, Austria-Hungary, and allies) on one side and the Triple Entente (Britain and the British Empire, France, and Russia) and their allies, including the USA (which entered 1917), on the other side. An estimated 10 million lives were lost and twice that number were wounded. It was fought on the eastern and western fronts, in the Middle East, in Africa, and at sea.

**World War II** (1939–45), war between Germany, Italy, and Japan (the Axis powers) on one side, and Britain, the Commonwealth, France, the USA, the USSR, and China (the Allied powers) on the other. An estimated 55 million lives were lost (20 million of them citizens of the USSR), and 60 million people in Europe were displaced because of bombing raids. The war was fought in the Atlantic and Pacific theatres.

It is estimated that, during the course of the war, for every tonne of bombs dropped on the UK, 315 fell on Germany.

In 1945, Germany surrendered (May) but Japan fought on until the USA dropped atomic bombs on Hiroshima and Nagasaki (August).

**World Wide Fund for Nature** WWF, formerly the *World Wildlife Fund,* international organization established in 1961 to raise funds for conservation by public appeal. Projects include conservation of particular species, for example, the tiger and giant panda, and special areas, such as the Simen Mountains, Ethiopia.

**worm** any of various elongated limbless invertebrates belonging to several phyla. Worms include the ◊flatworms, such as ◊flukes and ◊tapeworms; the roundworms or ◊nematodes, such as the eelworm and the hookworm; the marine ribbon worms or nemerteans; and the segmented worms or ◊annelids.

**WORM** acronym for *write once read many times,* in computing, a storage device, similar to a ◊CD-ROM. The computer can write to the disk directly, but cannot later erase or overwrite the same area. WORMs are mainly used for archiving and backup copies.

**Worms** ancient city and river port in Rhineland-Palatinate, Germany, on the River Rhine, 25 km/15 mi north of Ludwigshafen; population (1995) 79,700. Industries include food processing and the manufacture of chemicals, paint, machinery, furniture, and worsted. The vineyards of the Liebfrauenkirche (14th to 15th century) produced the original Liebfraumilch wine; it is now produced by many growers around Worms. The Protestant reformer Martin Luther appeared before the *Diet* (Assembly) *of Worms* in 1521 and was declared an outlaw by the Roman Catholic church. It is one of the oldest cities in Germany.

**wormwood** any of a group of plants belonging to the daisy family and mainly found in northern temperate regions, especially the aromatic herb *A. absinthium,* the leaves of which are used in the alcoholic drink absinthe. Tarragon is closely related to wormwood. (Genus *Artemisia,* family Compositae.)

**Wounded Knee** site on the Oglala Sioux Reservation, South Dakota, USA, of a confrontation between the US Army and American Indians; the last 'battle' of America's Indian Wars. On 15 December 1890 Chief ◊Sitting Bull was killed, supposedly resisting arrest, and on 29 December a group of Indians involved in the Ghost Dance Movement (aimed at resumption of Indian control of North America with the aid of the spirits of dead braves) were surrounded by the 7th Cavalry; 153 Indians were gunned down.

**W particle** in physics, an ◊elementary particle, one of the weakons responsible for transmitting the ◊weak nuclear force.

**wrack** any of the large brown ◊seaweeds characteristic of rocky shores. The bladder wrack *F. vesiculosus* has narrow, branched fronds up to 1 m/3.3 ft long, with oval air bladders, usually in pairs on either side of the midrib or central vein. (Genus *Fucus.*)

**wrasse** any bony fish of the family Labridae, found in temperate and tropical seas. They are slender and often brightly coloured, with a single long dorsal fin. They have elaborate courtship rituals, and some species can change their colouring and sex. Species vary in size from 5 cm/2 in to 2 m/6.5 ft.

**wren** any of the family Troglodytidae of small birds of the order Passeriformes, with slender, slightly curved bills, and uptilted tails.

**Wren, Christopher** (1632–1723) English architect. His ingenious use of a refined and sober Baroque style can be seen in his best-known work, St Paul's Cathedral, London (1675–1711), and in the many churches he built in London including St Mary-le-Bow, Cheapside (1670–77), and St Bride's, Fleet Street (1671–78). His other works include the Sheldonian Theatre, Oxford (1664–69), Greenwich Hospital, London (begun 1694), and Marlborough House, London (1709–10; now much altered).

**wrestling** sport popular in ancient Egypt, Greece, and Rome, and included in the Olympics from 704 BC. The two main modern international styles are *Greco-Roman*, concentrating on above-waist holds, and *freestyle*, which allows the legs to be used to hold or trip; in both the aim is to throw the opponent to the ground.

**Wrexham** unitary authority in northeast Wales, created in 1996 from part of the former county of Clwyd
*area* 500 sq km/193 sq mi
*towns* Wrexham (administrative headquarters), Holt, Ruabon
*physical* western side is mountainous, including Ruabon Mountain; River Dee
*features* Clywedog Valley, with notable countryside and industrial archaeology
*industries* food manufacture, plastics, pharmaceuticals, high-technology industries
*population* (1996) 123,500.

**Wright, Frank Lloyd** (1869–1959) US architect. He is known for 'organic architecture', in which buildings reflect their natural surroundings. From the 1890s, he developed his celebrated *prairie house* style, a series of low, spreading houses with projecting roofs. He later diversified, employing reinforced concrete to explore a variety of geometric forms. Among his buildings are his Wisconsin home, Taliesin East (1925), in prairie-house style; Falling Water, near Pittsburgh, Pennsylvania (1936), a house of cantilevered terraces straddling a waterfall; and the Guggenheim Museum, New York (1959), a spiral ramp rising from a circular plan.

**Wright brothers** Orville (1871–1948) and Wilbur (1867–1912) US inventors; brothers who pioneered piloted, powered flight. Inspired by Otto ◊Lilienthal's gliding, they perfected their piloted glider in 1902. In 1903 they built a powered machine, a 12-hp 341-kg/750-lb plane, and became the first to make a successful powered flight, near Kitty Hawk, North Carolina. Orville flew 36.6 m/120 ft in 12 seconds; Wilbur, 260 m/852 ft in 59 seconds.

**writing** any written form of communication using a set of symbols: see ◊alphabet, ◊cuneiform, ◊hieroglyphic. The last two used ideographs (picture writing) and phonetic word symbols side by side, as does modern Chinese. Syllabic writing, as in Japanese, develops from the continued use of a symbol to represent the sound of a short word. Some 8,000-year-old inscriptions, thought to be pictographs, were found on animal bones and tortoise shells in Henan province, China, at a Neolithic site at Jiahu. They are thought to predate by 2,500 years the oldest known writing (Mesopotamian cuneiform of 3,500 BC and Egyptian hieroglyphics of c 3300–3200 BC).

**Wrocław** formerly *Breslau*, industrial river port in Poland, on the River Oder; population (1993) 643,600. Industries include shipbuilding, engineering, textiles, and electronics. It was the capital of the German province of Lower Silesia until 1945.

**wrought iron** fairly pure iron containing some beads of slag, widely used for construction work before the days of cheap steel. It is strong, tough, and easy to machine. It is made in a puddling furnace, invented by Henry Colt in England in 1784. Pig iron is remelted and heated strongly in air with iron ore, burning out the carbon in the metal, leaving relatively pure iron and a slag containing impurities. The resulting pasty metal is then hammered to remove as much of the remaining slag as possible. It is still used in fences and gratings.

**Wuhan** river port and capital of ◊Hubei province, central China, at the confluence of the Han and Chang Jiang rivers; population (1994) 4,436,100. It was formed in 1950 as one of China's greatest industrial areas by the amalgamation of Hankou, Hanyang, and Wuchang. Iron, steel, machine tools, textiles, food and drinks, fibre optic cables, and fertilizer are manufactured.

**Wyclif, John** or *Wycliffe* (c. 1320–1384) English religious reformer. Allying himself with the party of John of Gaunt, which was opposed to ecclesiastical influence at court, he attacked abuses in the church, maintaining that the Bible rather than the church was the supreme authority. He criticized such fundamental doctrines as priestly absolution, confession, and indulgences, and set disciples to work on translating the Bible into English.

**Wyoming** state in western USA. It is nicknamed the Equality State. Wyoming was admitted to the Union in 1890 as the 44th US state. One of the Mountain States, it is bordered to the east by Nebraska and South Dakota, to the north by Montana, to the west by Montana, Idaho, and Utah, and to the south by Utah and Colorado
*population* (1995) 480,200
*area* 253,400 sq km/97,812 sq mi
*capital* Cheyenne
*towns and cities* Casper, Laramie
*industries and products* oil, natural gas, sodium salts, coal, uranium, sheep, beef.

**WYSIWYG** acronym for what you see is what you get, in computing, a program that attempts to display on the screen a faithful representation of the final printed output. For example, a WYSIWYG word processor would show actual page layout – line widths, page breaks, and the sizes and styles of type.

**Xavier, St Francis** (1506–1552) Spanish Jesuit missionary. He went to the Portuguese colonies in the East Indies, arriving at Goa in 1542. He was in Japan 1549–51, establishing a Christian mission that lasted for 100 years. He returned to Goa in 1552, and sailed for China, but died of fever there. He was canonized in 1622.

**X chromosome** larger of the two sex chromosomes, the smaller being the ◊Y chromosome. These two chromosomes are involved in sex determination. Females have two X chromosomes, males have an X and a Y. Genes carried on the X chromosome produce the phenomenon of ◊sex linkage.

**xenon** (Greek *xenos* 'stranger') colourless, odourless, gaseous, non-metallic element, symbol Xe, atomic number 54, relative atomic mass 131.30. It is grouped with the ◊inert gases and was long believed not to enter into reactions, but is now known to form some compounds, mostly with fluorine. It is a heavy gas present in very small quantities in the air (about one part in 20 million).

**Xenophon** (c. 430– c. 350 BC) Greek soldier and writer who was a disciple of ◊Socrates (described in Xenophon's *Symposium*). He joined the Persian prince Cyrus the Younger against his brother Artaxerxes II in 401 BC, and after the Battle of Cunaxa the same year took command. His book *Anabasis* describes how he led 10,000 Greek mercenaries on a 1,600-km/1,000-mile march home across enemy territory.

**xerophyte** plant adapted to live in dry conditions. Common adaptations to reduce the rate of ◊transpiration include a reduction of leaf size, sometimes to spines or scales; a dense covering of hairs over the leaf to trap a layer of moist air (as in edelweiss); water storage cells; sunken stomata; and permanently rolled leaves or leaves that roll up in dry weather (as in marram grass). Many desert cacti are xerophytes.

**Xerxes I** (c. 519–465 BC) Achaemenid king of Persia from 486–465 BC, the son and successor of Darius (I) the Great. He suppressed Babylonian revolts in 484 and 482, then in 480, at the head of a great army supported by a fleet, he crossed the Hellespont (Dardanelles) on bridges of boats and marched through Thrace into Greece. He occupied Athens, but the Persian fleet was defeated at Salamis and Xerxes was forced to retreat. His general Mardonius remained behind, but was defeated by the Greeks at Plataea in 479 BC.

**Xhosa** plural Xhosa, member of a Bantu people of South Africa, living mainly in the Eastern Cape province. Traditionally, the Xhosa were farmers and cattle herders, cattle having great social and religious importance to them. Their social structure is based on a monarchy. Their Bantu language belongs to the Niger-Congo family.

**Xia dynasty** or *Hsia dynasty,* China's first legendary ruling family, *c.* 2200–*c.* 1500 BC, reputedly founded by the model emperor Yu the Great. He is believed to have controlled floods by constructing dykes. Archaeological evidence suggests that the Xia dynasty really did exist, as a Bronze Age civilization where writing was being developed, with its capital at Erlidou (Erhli-t'ou) in Henan (Honan).

**Xi'an** ('western peace') industrial city and capital of ◊Shaanxi province, China, on the Wei He River; population (1993) 2,360,000. It produces chemicals, machinery, electrical and electronic equipment, aircraft, and fertilizers.

**Xinjiang Uygur Autonomous Region** *Xinjiang* or *Sinkiang Uighur Autonomous Region,* autonomous region of northwest China, bounded to the north by Kyrgyzstan, Kazakhstan, and Russia; to the east by Mongolia and Gansu; to the south by Qinghai and Tibet; and to the west by Jammu and Kashmir, Afghanistan, and Tajikistan
**area** 1,646,800 sq km/635,665 sq mi
**capital** ◊Urumqi
**physical** Dzungarian Basin (Junggar Pendi), Tarim Basin, mountains, and desert
**industries** oil, chemicals, iron, textiles, coal, copper, tourism
**agriculture** cereals, cotton, fruit, animal husbandry
**population** (1996) 16,890,000; 13 recognized ethnic minorities, including over 7 million Uigurs (Turkic Muslim group)
**religion** 50% Muslim
**history** conquered by Turkic people of Muslim culture in the 8th century, Chinese control was not re-established until the Qing dynasty subdued the area in the mid-18th century. Large sections were ceded to Russia in 1864 and 1881.

**Xiongnu** also known as Hsiung-nu, nomadic confederacy, possibly of Turkish origin, that fought against the Chinese states in the 3rd century BC. Their power began in Mongolia in about 200 BC, but they were forced back to the Gobi Desert in 119 BC by China's Han-dynasty emperor Wudi (Wu-ti) (reigned 141–87 BC) and Qin Shi Huangdi built the Great Wall of China against them. They were eventually conquered and the survivors were employed as frontier troops.

**X-ray** band of electromagnetic radiation in the wavelength range $10^{-11}$ to $10^{-9}$ m (between gamma rays and ultraviolet radiation; see ◊electromagnetic waves). Applications of X-rays make use of their short wavelength (as in ◊X-ray diffraction) or their penetrating power (as in medical X-rays of internal body tissues). X-rays are dangerous and can cause cancer.

**X-ray astronomy** detection of X-rays from intensely hot gas in the universe. Such X-rays are prevented from reaching the Earth's surface by the atmosphere, so detectors must be placed in rockets and satellites. The first celestial X-ray source, Scorpius X-1, was discovered by a rocket flight in 1962.

**X-ray diffraction** method of studying the atomic and molecular structure of crystalline substances by using ◊X-rays. X-rays directed at such substances spread out as they pass through the crystals owing to ◊diffraction (the slight spreading of waves around the edge of an opaque object) of the rays around the atoms. By using measurements of the position and intensity of the diffracted waves, it is possible to cal-culate the shape and size of the atoms in the crystal. The method has been used to study substances such as ◊DNA that are found in living material.

**xylem** tissue found in ◊vascular plants, whose main function is to conduct water and dissolved mineral nutrients from the roots to other parts of the plant. Xylem is composed of a number of different types of cell, and may include long, thin, usually dead cells known as tracheids; fibres (schlerenchyma); thin-walled parenchyma cells; and conducting vessels.

**xylophone** musical ◊percussion instrument of African and Indonesian origin, consisting of a series of hardwood bars of varying lengths, each with its own distinct pitch, arranged in sequence over a resonator or resonators, and played with hard sticks. It first appeared as an orchestral instrument in Saint-Saëns's *Danse macabre* (1874), illustrating dancing skeletons.

**yachting** pleasure cruising or racing a small and light vessel, whether sailing or power-driven. At the 1996 Olympic Games there were eight sail-driven categories: Laser, 470, Tornado, Soling, Mistral, Star, Finn, and Europe. The Laser, Mistral, Finn, and Europe are solo events; the Soling class is for three-person crews; all other classes are for crews of two. The International Sailing Federation (ISF) World Sailing Championships were inaugurated in 1994 and are held every four years. Additionally, separate world championships are held annually in each of the Olympic classes and in others such as the Melges 24 or Mumm 30.

**yak** species of cattle *Bos grunniens,* family Bovidae, which lives in wild herds at high altitudes in Tibet. It stands about 2 m/6 ft at the shoulder and has long shaggy hair on the underparts. It has large, upward-curving horns and humped shoulders. It is in danger of becoming extinct.

*yakuza* (Japanese 'good for nothing') Japanese gangster. Organized crime in Japan is highly structured, and the various syndicates between them employed some 110,000 people 1989, with a turnover of an estimated 1.5 trillion yen. The *yakuza* have been unofficially tolerated and are very powerful.

**Yalta Conference** strategic conference held from 4–11 February 1945 in Yalta (a Soviet holiday resort in the Crimea) by the main Allied leaders in World War II. At this, the second of three key meetings between the 'Big Three' – Winston Churchill (UK), Franklin D Roosevelt (USA), and Joseph Stalin (USSR) – plans were drawn up for the final defeat and disarmament of Nazi Germany, the post-war partition of Europe (see ◊Cold War), and the foundation of the ◊United Nations.

**yam** any of a group of climbing plants cultivated in tropical regions; the starchy tubers (underground stems) are eaten as a vegetable. The Mexican yam (*D. composita*) contains a chemical that is used in the contraceptive pill. (Genus *Dioscorea,* family Dioscoreaceae.)

**Yamoussoukro** capital since 1983 of Côte d'Ivoire; population (1990 est) 120,000. The economy is based on tourism, agricultural trade and production, and petroleum distribution to the surrounding region. Other industries include forestry and perfume manufacture.

**Yanamamo** or *Yanomamo* (plural *Yanamami,* a semi-nomadic Native South American people, numbering approximately 22,000 (9,500 in northern Brazil and the rest in Venezuela), where most continue to follow their traditional way of life. The Yanamamo language belongs to the Macro-Chibcha family. In November 1991 Brazil granted the Yanamami possession of their original land, 58,395 km/36,293 sq mi on its northern border.

**Yangon** formerly (until 1989) *Rangoon,* capital and chief port of Myanmar (Burma) on the Yangon River, 32 km/20 mi from the Indian Ocean; population (1983) 2,459,000. Products include timber, oil, and rice. The city *Dagon* was founded on the site AD 746; it was given the name Rangoon (meaning 'end of conflict') by King Alaungpaya in 1755.

**Yang Shangkun** (1907–1998) Chinese communist politician. He held a senior position in the Central Committee of the Communist Party of China (CCP) 1956–66 but was demoted during the Cultural Revolution. He was rehabilitated in 1978, elected to the Politburo in 1982, and served as state president 1988–93.

**Yao** a people living in southern China, North Vietnam, northern Laos, Thailand, and Myanmar (Burma), and numbering about 4 million (1984). The Yao language may belong to either the Sino-Tibetan or the Thai language family. The Yao incorporate elements of ancestor worship in their animist religion.

**Yaoundé** capital of Cameroon, 210 km/130 mi east of the port of Douala; population (1991) 750,000. Industries include tourism, oil refining, food production, and textile manufacturing. It is linked by the Transcameroon railway to Douala and to Ngaoundere in the north.

**yapok** nocturnal ◊opossum *Chironectes minimus* found in tropical South and Central America. It is about 33 cm/1.1 ft long, with a 40 cm/1.3 ft tail. It has webbed hind feet and thick fur, and is the only aquatic marsupial. The female has a watertight pouch.

**yard** unit (symbol yd) of length, equivalent to 3 feet (0.9144 m).

**yarrow** or *milfoil,* perennial herb belonging to the daisy family, with feathery, scented leaves and flat-topped clusters of white or pink flowers. It is native to Europe and Asia. (*Achillea millefolium,* family Compositae.)

**yaws** contagious tropical disease common in the West Indies, West Africa, and some Pacific islands, characterized by red, raspberrylike eruptions on the face, toes, and other parts of the body, sometimes followed by lesions of the bones; these may progress to cause gross disfigurement. It is caused by a spirochete (*Treponema pertenue*), a bacterium related to the one that causes ◊syphilis. Treatment is by antibiotics.

**Y chromosome** smaller of the two sex chromosomes. In male mammals it occurs paired with the other type of sex chromosome (X), which carries far more genes. The Y chromosome is the smallest of all the mammalian chromosomes and is considered to be largely inert (that is, without direct effect on the physical body). There are only 20 genes discovered so far on the human Y chromosome, much fewer than on all other human chromosomes. See also ◊sex determination.

**yd** abbreviation for ◊yard.

**yeast** one of various single-celled fungi (see ◊fungus) that form masses of tiny round or oval cells by budding. When placed in a sugar solution the cells multiply and convert the sugar into alcohol and carbon dioxide. Yeasts are used as fermenting agents in baking, brewing, and the making of wine and spirits. Brewer's yeast (*S. cerevisiae*) is a rich source of vitamin B. (Especially genus *Saccharomyces;* also other related genera.)

**yeast artificial chromosome** (YAC), fragment of ◊DNA from the human genome inserted into a yeast cell. The yeast replicates the fragment along with its own DNA. In this way the fragments are copied to be preserved in a gene library. YACs are characteristically between 250,000 and 1 million base pairs in length. A cosmid works in the same way.

**Yeats, W(illiam) B(utler)** (1865–1939) Irish poet. He was a leader of the Celtic revival and a founder of the Abbey Theatre in Dublin. His early work was romantic and lyrical, as in the poem 'The Lake Isle of Innisfree' and the plays *The Countess Cathleen* (1892) and *The Land of Heart's Desire* (1894). His later poetry, which includes *The Wild Swans at Coole* (1917) and *The Winding Stair* (1929), was also much influenced by European and Eastern thought. He was a senator of the Irish Free State (1922–28), and won the Nobel Prize for Literature in 1923.

**Yedo** or *Edo,* former name of ◊Tokyo, Japan, until 1868.

**yeheb nut** small tree found in Ethiopia and Somalia, formerly much valued for its nuts as a food source. Although cultivated as a food crop in Kenya and Sudan, it is now critically endangered in the wild and is only known to survive at three sites. Overgrazing by cattle and goats has prevented regrowth, and the taking of nuts for consumption prevents reseeding. Although reintroduction would be possible from cultivated trees, the continuing grazing pressure would make establishment unlikely without proper management. (*Cordeauxia adulis.*)

**yellow archangel** flowering plant belonging to the mint family, found over much of Europe. It grows up to 60 cm/2 ft tall and has nettlelike leaves and rings, or whorls, of yellow flowers growing around the main stem; the lower lips of the flowers are streaked with red in early summer. (*Lamiastrum galeobdolon,* family Labiatae.)

**yellow fever** or *yellow jack,* acute tropical viral disease, prevalent in the Caribbean area, Brazil, and on the west coast of Africa. The yellow fever virus is an arbovirus transmitted by mosquitoes. Its symptoms include a high fever, headache, joint and muscle pains, vomiting, and yellowish skin (jaundice, possibly leading to liver failure); the heart and kidneys may also be affected. The mortality rate is 25%, with 91% of all cases occurring in Africa.

**yellowhammer** Eurasian bird *Emberiza citrinella* of the bunting family Emberizidae, order Passeriformes. About 16.5 cm/6.5 in long, the male has a yellow head and underside, a chestnut rump, and a brown-streaked back. The female is duller.

**Yellow River** English name for the ◊Huang He River, China.

**Yellow Sea** Chinese *Huang Hai,* gulf of the Pacific Ocean between China and Korea; length approximately 1,000 km/620 mi, greatest width 700 km/435 mi; area 466,200 sq km/180,000 sq mi. To the north are the gulfs of Korea, Chihli, and Liaotung. There are many small islands to the east near the Korean coast. It receives the Huang He (Yellow River) and Chang Jiang (Yangtze Kiang), which transport yellow mud down into the shallow waters (average depth 44 m/144 ft).

**Yellowstone National Park** oldest US nature reserve, and largest in the lower 48 states, situated on a broad plateau in the ◊Rocky Mountains, chiefly in northwest Wyoming, but also projecting about 3 km/2 mi into southwest Montana and eastern Idaho; area 8,983 sq km/3,469 sq mi. The park contains more than 3,000 geysers and hot springs, including periodically erupting Old Faithful. Established in 1872, it is now a World Heritage Site and one of the world's greatest wildlife refuges. In 1988 naturally-occurring forest fires burned 36% of the park.

**Yeltsin, Boris Nikolayevich** (1931–   ) Russian politician, president of the Russian Soviet Federative Socialist Republic (RSFSR) 1990–91, and president of the newly independent Russian Federation from 1991. He directed the Federation's secession from the USSR and the formation of a new, decentralized confederation, the ◊Commonwealth of Independent States (CIS), with himself as the most powerful leader. A referendum in 1993 supported his policies of price deregulation and accelerated privatization, despite severe economic problems and civil unrest. He survived a coup attempt later the same year, but was subsequently forced to compromise on the pace of his reforms after far-right electoral gains, and lost considerable public support. He suffered two heart attacks in 1995, yet still contested the June 1996 presidential elections, in which he secured re-election by defeating Communist Party leader Gennady Zyuganov. He resigned at the end of 1999.

**Yemen** Republic of
*national name* Jamhuriya al Yamaniya
*area* 531,900 sq km/205,366 sq mi
*capital* San'a
*major towns/cities* Aden, Ta'izz, Al Mukalla, Hodeida, Ibb, Dhamar

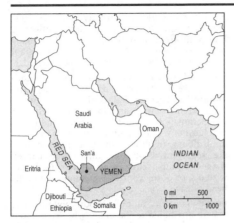

**major ports** Aden
**physical features** hot, moist coastal plain, rising to plateau and desert
**head of state** Ali Abdullah Saleh from 1990
**head of government** Abdul Ali al-Rahman al-Iryani from 1998
**political system** emergent democracy
**political parties** General People's Congress (GPC), left of centre; Yemen Socialist Party (YSP), left wing; Yemen Reform Group (al-Islah), Islamic, right of centre; National Opposition Front, left of centre
**currency** riyal (North); dinar (South), both legal currency throughout the country
**GNP per capita (PPP)** (US$) 740 (1998)
**exports** petroleum and petroleum products, cotton, basic manufactures, clothing, live animals, hides and skins, fish, rice, coffee. Principal market: China 30.9% (1997)
**population** 17,488,000 (1999 est)
**language** Arabic
**religion** Sunni Muslim 63%, Shiite Muslim 37%
**life expectancy** 57 (men); 58 (women) (1995–2000)
**Chronology**
**1st millennium BC** South Yemen (Aden) divided between economically advanced Qataban and Hadramawt kingdoms.
**c. 5th century BC** Qataban fell to the Sabaeans (Shebans) of North Yemen (Sana).
**c. 100 BC–AD 525** All of Yemen became part of Himyarite kingdom.
**AD 628** Islam introduced.
**1174–1229** Under control of Egyptian Ayyubids.
**1229–1451** 'Golden age' for arts and sciences under the Rasulids, who had served as governors of Yemen under the Ayyubids.
**1538** North Yemen came under control of Turkish Ottoman Empire.
**1636** Ottomans left North Yemen and power fell into hands of Yemeni Imams, based on local Zaydi tribes, who also held South Yemen until 1735.
**1839** Aden became a British territory. Port developed into important ship refuelling station after opening of Suez Canal 1869; protectorate was gradually established over 23 Sultanates inland.

**1870s** The Ottomans re-established control over North Yemen.
**1918** North Yemen became independent, with Imam Yahya from Hamid al-Din family as king.
**1937** Aden became British crown colony.
**1948** Imam Yahya assassinated by exiled Free Yemenis nationalist movement, but uprising was crushed by his son, Imam Ahmad.
**1959** Federation of South Arabia formed by Britain between city of Aden and feudal Sultanates (Aden Protectorate).
**1962** Military coup on death of Imam Ahmad; North Yemen declared Yemen Arab Republic (YAR), with Abdullah al-Sallal as president. Civil war broke out between royalists (supported by Saudi Arabia) and republicans (supported by Egypt).
**1963** Armed rebellion by National Liberation Front (NLF) began against British rule in Aden.
**1967** Civil war ended with republicans victorious. Sallal deposed and replaced by Republican Council. The Independent People's Republic of South Yemen formed after British withdrawal from Aden. Many fled to north as repressive communist NLF regime took over in south.
**1970** People's Republic of South Yemen renamed People's Democratic Republic of Yemen.
**1971–72** War between South Yemen and YAR; union agreement brokered by Arab League signed but not kept.
**1974** The pro-Saudi Col Ibrahim al-Hamadi seized power in North Yemen; Military Command Council set up.
**1977** Hamadi assassinated; replaced by Col Ahmed ibn Hussein al-Ghashmi.
**1978** Constituent people's assembly appointed in North Yemen and Military Command Council dissolved. Ghashmi killed by envoy from South Yemen; succeeded by Ali Abdullah Saleh. War broke out again between two Yemens. South Yemen president deposed and executed; Yemen Socialist Party (YSP) formed in south by communists.
**1979** A ceasefire was agreed with commitment to future union.
**1980** YSP leader Ali Nasser Muhammad became head of state in South Yemen.
**1986** There was civil war in South Yemen; the autocratic Ali Nasser was dismissed. A new administration was formed under the more moderate Haydar Abu Bakr al-Attas, who was committed to negotiating union with the north because of the deteriorating economy in the south.
**1989** A draft multiparty constitution for a single Yemen state was published.
**1990** The border between the two Yemens was opened; the countries were formally united on 22 May as the Republic of Yemen.
**1991** The new constitution was approved; Yemen opposed US-led operations against Iraq in the Gulf War.
**1992** There were antigovernment riots.
**1993** Saleh's General People's Congress (GPC) won most seats in a general election but no overall majority; a five-member presidential council was elected, including Saleh as president, YSP

leader Ali Salim al-Baidh as vice-president, and Bakr al-Attas as prime minister.

**1994** Fighting erupted between northern forces, led by President Saleh, and southern forces, led by Vice-president al-Baidh, as southern Yemen announced its secession. Saleh inflicted a crushing defeat on al-Baidh and a new GPC coalition was appointed.

**1997** GPC won the election. Farag Said Ben Ghanem was appointed prime minister.

**1998** A new government was headed by Abdul Ali al-Rahman al-Iryani.

**Yenisey** or *Yenisei,* one of the main rivers in Russia, rising in the Sayan Mountains in the Asian Tuva region and flowing generally north across the Siberian plain into the Arctic Ocean; length 4,100 km/2,550 mi. The Yenisey has a drainage basin of 2,580,000 sq km/996,138 sq mi. Navigable throughout almost its entire course, its chief ports are Dudinka, Igarka, and Krasnoyarsk.

**Yerevan** capital city, economic, and cultural centre of the independent Republic of Armenia, situated in the southern Caucasus 25 km/16 mi north of the Turkish border; population (1996) 1,200,000. Yerevan stands on the Razdan River, and is a major industrial city, manufacturing machine tools, agricultural equipment, chemicals, bricks, bicycles, and wine. Other industries include the production of aluminium, plastics, and textiles, fruit canning, and distilling.

**yeti** (Tibetan *yeh* 'rocky place', *teh* 'animal') name given by the Sherpas of east Nepal to an unidentified animal of the Himalayas, also known as the abominable snowman.

**Yevtushenko, Yevgeny Aleksandrovich** (1933–  ) Soviet poet. He aroused controversy with his anti-Stalinist 'Stalin's Heirs' in 1956, published with Khrushchev's support, and 'Babi Yar' in 1961, which attacked Russian as well as Nazi anti-Semitism. His other works include the long poem *Zima Junction* (1956), the novel *Berries* (1981), and *Precocious Autobiography* (1963).

**yew** any of a group of evergreen coniferous trees native to the northern hemisphere. The dark green flat needlelike leaves and bright red berrylike seeds are poisonous; the wood is hard and close-grained. (Genus *Taxus,* family Taxaceae.)

**Yi** plural Yi, member of a people living in the mountainous regions of southwestern China, northern Vietnam, Laos, Thailand, and Myanmar, totalling about 5.5 million (1987). The Yi are farmers, producing both crops and livestock, and opium as a cash crop. Traditionally they were stratified into princes, aristocrats, commoners, and debt slaves. Their language belongs to the Sino-Tibetan family; their religion is animist.

**Yiddish language** member of the west Germanic branch of the Indo-European language family, deriving from 13th–14th-century Rhineland German and spoken by northern, central, and eastern European Jews, who have carried it to Israel, the USA, and many other parts of the world. It is written in the Hebrew alphabet and has many dialects reflecting European areas of residence, as well as many borrowed words from Polish, Russian, Lithuanian, and other languages encountered.

**yin and yang** (Chinese 'dark' and 'bright') the passive (characterized as feminine, negative, intuitive) and active (characterized as masculine, positive, intellectual) principles of nature. Their interaction is believed to maintain equilibrium and harmony in the universe and to be present in all things. In Taoism and Confucianism they are represented by two interlocked curved shapes within a circle, one white, one black, with a spot of the contrasting colour within the head of each.

**yoga** (Sanskrit 'union') Hindu philosophical system attributed to Patanjali, who lived about 150 BC at Gonda, Uttar Pradesh, India. He preached mystical union with a personal deity through the practice of self-hypnosis and a rising above the senses by abstract meditation, adoption of special postures, and ascetic practices. As practised in the West, yoga is more a system of mental and physical exercise, and of induced relaxation as a means of relieving stress.

**yogurt** or *yoghurt* or *yoghourt,* semisolid curd-like dairy product made from milk fermented with bacteria. It was originally made by nomadic tribes of Central Asia, from mare's milk in leather pouches attached to their saddles. It is drunk plain throughout the Asian and Mediterranean region, to which it spread, but honey, sugar, and fruit were added in Europe and the USA, and the product was made solid and creamy, to be eaten by a spoon.

**Yogyakarta** city in Java, Indonesia, capital 1945–1949; population (1990) 412,400. The chief industries are batik textiles, handicrafts, and tourism. It is the cultural centre of the Javanese ethnic group.

**yolk** store of food, mostly in the form of fats and proteins, found in the ◊eggs of many animals. It provides nourishment for the growing embryo.

**Yom Kippur** the Jewish Day of ◊Atonement.

**Yom Kippur War** the surprise attack on Israel in October 1973 by Egypt and Syria; see ◊Arab-Israeli Wars; Israel, *the Fourth Arab–Israeli War.* It is named after the Jewish national holiday on which it began, the holiest day of the Jewish year.

**York** cathedral and industrial city and administrative headquarters of ◊York unitary authority in northern England, on the River Ouse; population (1991) 127,700. It was the administrative headquarters of the county of North Yorkshire until 1996. Industries include tourism and the manufacture of scientific instruments, sugar, chocolate, and glass. Founded in AD 71 as the Roman provincial capital *Eboracum,* York retains many of its medieval streets and buildings and much of its 14th-century city wall; the Gothic York Minster, England's largest medieval cathedral, includes fine 15th-century stained glass. The city is visited by some 3 million tourists a year.

**York** unitary authority in northeast England created in 1996 from part of the county of North Yorkshire
*area* 271 sq km/105 sq mi
*towns* ◊York (administrative headquarters)
*features* River Ouse; River Fosse; York Minster – largest medieval cathedral in England, with 15th-century stained glass; York Castle and Museum; National Railway Museum; city walls built by Henry III in the 13th century with 4 gates and 39 towers; Jorvik Viking Centre; the Shambles medieval streets
*industries* agriculture and agricultural services, mechanical engineering, circuit boards, tourism, scientific instruments, confectionery, glass
*population* (1996) 174,800
*famous people* W H Auden, Alcuin, Guy Fawkes, John Flaxman.

**Yorkshire** former county in northeast England on the North Sea divided administratively into North, East, and West Ridings (thirds), but reorganized to form a number of new counties in 1974: the major part of *Cleveland* and *Humberside, North Yorkshire, South Yorkshire,* and *West Yorkshire.* Small outlying areas also went to Durham, Cumbria, Lancashire, and Greater Manchester. In 1996 Cleveland and Humberside were abolished, and a number of unitary authorities were created to replace them.

**Yoruba** the majority ethnic group living in southwestern Nigeria; there is a Yoruba minority in eastern Benin. They number approximately 20 million in all, and their language belongs to the Kwa branch of the Niger-Congo family. The Yoruba established powerful city states in the 15th century, known for their advanced culture which includes sculpture, art, and music.

**Yosemite** region in the Sierra Nevada, eastern California, USA, a national park from 1890; area 3,079 sq km/1,189 sq mi. Embracing 12 km/8 mi of the Yosemite Valley, its main features are Yosemite Gorge, cut by the Merced River; Yosemite Falls, the highest waterfall in the USA, plunging 739 m/2,425 ft in three leaps; Half Dome Mountain, a 2 km/1mi-high sheer cliff on El Capitan, the largest body of exposed granite in the world; Mount Lyell, rising to 3,997 m/13,114 ft; and groves of giant sequoia trees. It is a World Heritage Site.

**Young, Neil** (1945– ) Canadian rock guitarist, singer, and songwriter. He lived in the USA from 1966. His high, plaintive voice and loud, abrasive guitar make his work instantly recognizable, despite abrupt changes of style throughout his career. *Rust Never Sleeps* (1979) and *Arc Weld* (1991) (both with the group Crazy Horse) are among his best work.

**Young Pretender** nickname of ◊Charles Edward Stuart, claimant to the Scottish and English thrones.

**Young Turk** member of a reformist movement of young army officers in the Ottoman Empire founded 1889. The movement was instrumental

in the constitutional changes of 1908 and the abdication of Sultan Abd al-Hamid II in 1909. It gained prestige during the Balkan Wars (1912–13) and encouraged Turkish links with the German empire. Its influence diminished after 1918. The term is now used for a member of any radical or rebellious faction within a party or organization.

**Youth Training Scheme** (YTS) in the UK, a one- or two-year course of training and work experience for unemployed school leavers aged 16 and 17, from 1989 provided by employer-led Training and Enterprise Councils at local levels and renamed Youth Training.

**Ypres, Battles of** (Flemish *Ieper*), in World War I, three major battles 1914–17 between German and Allied forces near Ypres, a Belgian town in western Flanders, 40 km/25 mi south of Ostend. Neither side made much progress in any of the battles, despite heavy casualties, but the third battle in particular (also known as Passchendaele) July–November 1917 stands out as an enormous waste of life for little return. The Menin Gate (1927) is a memorial to British soldiers lost in these battles.

**ytterbium** soft, lustrous, silvery, malleable and ductile element of the ◊lanthanide series, symbol Yb, atomic number 70, relative atomic mass 173.04. It occurs with (and resembles) yttrium in gadolinite and other minerals, and is used in making steel and other alloys.

**yttrium** silver-grey, metallic element, symbol Y, atomic number 39, relative atomic mass 88.905. It is associated with and resembles the rare earth elements ( ◊lanthanides), occurring in gadolinite, xenotime, and other minerals. It is used in colour-television tubes and to reduce steel corrosion.

**yucca** any of a group of plants belonging to the lily family, with over 40 species found in Latin America and the southwestern USA. The leaves are stiff and sword-shaped and the flowers, which grow on upright central spikes, are white and bell-shaped. (Genus *Yucca,* family Liliaceae.)

**Yukon** river in North America, 3,185 km/1,979 mi long, flowing from Lake Tagish in Yukon Territory into Alaska, where it empties into the Bering Sea.

**Yugoslavia** Federal Republic of
*national name* *Federativna Republika Jugoslavija*
*area* 58,300 sq km/22,509 sq mi
*capital* Belgrade
*major towns/cities* Priština, Novi Sad, Niš, Rijeka, Kragujevac, Podgorica (formerly Titograd), Subotica
*physical features* federation of republics of Serbia and Montenegro and two former autonomous provinces, Kosovo and Vojvodina
*head of state* Slobodan Milošević from 1997
*head of government* Momir Bulatović from 1998
*political system* socialist pluralist republic
*political parties* Socialist Party of Serbia (SPS),

Serb nationalist, reform socialist (ex-communist); Montenegrin Social Democratic Party (SDPCG), federalist, reform socialist (ex-communist); Serbian Radical Party (SRS), Serb nationalist, extreme right wing; People's Assembly Party, Christian democrat, centrist; Democratic Party (DS), moderate nationalist; Democratic Party of Serbia (DSS), moderate nationalist; Democratic Community of Vojvodina Hungarians (DZVM), ethnic Hungarian; Democratic Party of Albanians/Party of Democratic Action (DPA/PDA), ethnic Albanian; New Socialist Party of Montenegro (NSPM), left of centre
**currency** new Yugoslav dinar
**GNP per capita (PPP)** (US$) 5,880 (1997 est)
**exports** basic manufactures, machinery and transport equipment, clothing, miscellaneous manufactured articles, food and live animals. Principal market: Italy 11.5% (1997)
**population** 10,637,000 (1999 est)
**language** Serbo-Croatian; Albanian (in Kosovo)
**religion** Serbian and Montenegrin Orthodox; Muslim in southern Serbia
**life expectancy** 70 (men); 76 (women) (1995–2000)
**Chronology**
**3rd century BC** Serbia (then known as Moesia Superior) conquered by Romans; empire was extended to Belgrade centuries later by Emperor Augustus.
**6th century AD** Slavic tribes, including Serbs, Croats, and Slovenes, crossed River Danube and settled in Balkan Peninsula.
**879** Serbs converted to Orthodox Church by St Cyril and St Methodius.
**mid-10th–11th centuries** Serbia broke free briefly from Byzantine Empire to establish independent state.
**1217** Independent Serbian kingdom re-established, reaching its height in mid-14th century under Stefan Dushan, when it controlled much of Albania and northern Greece.
**1389** Serbian army defeated by Ottoman Turks

at Battle of Kosovo; area became Turkish *pashalik* (province). Montenegro in southwest survived as sovereign principality. Croatia and Slovenia in northwest became part of Habsburg Empire.
**18th century** Vojvodina enjoyed protection from the Austrian Habsburgs.
**1815** Uprisings against Turkish rule secured autonomy for Serbia.
**1878** Independence achieved as Kingdom of Serbia, after Turks defeated by Russians in war over Bulgaria.
**1912–13** During Balkan Wars, Serbia expanded its territory at expense of Turkey and Bulgaria.
**1918** Joined Croatia and Slovenia, formerly under Austrian Habsburg control, to form Kingdom of Serbs, Croats, and Slovenes under Serbian Peter Karageorgević (Peter I); Montenegro's citizens voted to depose their ruler, King Nicholas, and join the union.
**1929** New name of Yugoslavia ('Land of the Southern Slavs') adopted; Serbian-dominated military dictatorship established by King Alexander I as opposition mounted from Croatian federalists.
**1934** Alexander I assassinated by a Macedonian with Croatian terrorist links; his young son Peter II succeeded, with Paul, his uncle, as regent; Nazi Germany and fascist Italy increased their influence.
**1941** Following coup by pro-Allied air-force officers, Nazi Germany invaded. Peter II fled to England. Armed resistance to German rule began, spearheaded by pro-royalist, Serbian-based Chetniks ('Army of the Fatherland'), led by Gen Draza Mihailović, and communist Partisans ('National Liberation Army'), led by Marshal Tito. An estimated 900,000 Yugoslavs died in the war, including more than 400,000 Serbs and 200,000 Croats.
**1943** Provisional government formed by Tito at liberated Jajce in Bosnia.
**1945** Yugoslav Federal People's Republic formed under leadership of Tito; communist constitution introduced.
**1948** Split with Soviet Union after Tito objected to Soviet 'hegemonism'; expelled from Cominform.
**1953** Workers' self-management principle enshrined in constitution and private farming supported; Tito became president.
**1961** Nonaligned movement formed under Yugoslavia's leadership.
**1971** In response to mounting separatist demands in Croatia, new system of collective and rotating leadership introduced.
**1980** Tito died; collective leadership assumed power.
**1981–82** Armed forces suppressed demonstrations in Kosovo province, southern Serbia, by Albanians demanding full republic status.
**1986** Slobodan Milošević, a populist-nationalist hardliner who had the ambition of creating a 'Greater Serbia', became leader of communist party in the Serbian republic.
**1988** Economic difficulties: 1,800 strikes, 250% inflation, 20% unemployment. Ethnic unrest in Montenegro and Vojvodina, and separatist

demands in rich northwestern republics of Croatia and Slovenia; 'market socialist' reform package, encouraging private sector, inward investment, and liberalizing prices combined with austerity wage freeze.

**1989** Reformist Croatian Ante Marković became prime minister. Ethnic riots in Kosovo province against Serbian attempt to end autonomous status of Kosovo and Vojvodina; at least 30 were killed and a state of emergency imposed.

**1990** Multiparty systems were established in the republics; Kosovo and Vojvodina were stripped of autonomy. In Croatia, Slovenia, Bosnia, and Macedonia, elections brought to power new noncommunist governments seeking a looser confederation.

**1991** Demonstrations against Serbian president Slobodan Milošević in Belgrade were crushed by riot police and tanks. Slovenia and Croatia declared their independence, resulting in clashes between federal and republican armies; Slovenia accepted a peace pact sponsored by the European Community (EC), but fighting intensified in Croatia, where Serb militias controlled over a third of the republic; Federal President Stipe Mesic and Prime Minister Marković resigned.

**1992** There was an EC-brokered ceasefire in Croatia; the EC and the USA recognized Slovenia's and Croatia's independence. Bosnia-Herzegovina and Macedonia then declared their independence, and Bosnia-Herzegovina's independence was recognized by the EC and the USA. A New Federal Republic of Yugoslavia (FRY) was proclaimed by Serbia and Montenegro but not internationally recognized; international sanctions were imposed and UN membership was suspended. Ethnic Albanians proclaimed a new 'Republic of Kosovo', but it was not recognized.

**1993** Pro-Milošević Zoran Lilic became Yugoslav president. There was antigovernment rioting in Belgrade. Macedonia was recognized as independent under the name of the Former Yugoslav Republic of Macedonia. The economy was severely damaged by international sanctions.

**1994** A border blockade was imposed by Yugoslavia against Bosnian Serbs; sanctions were eased as a result.

**1995** Serbia played a key role in the US-brokered Dayton peace accord for Bosnia-Herzegovina and accepted the separate existence of Bosnia and Croatia.

**1996** Diplomatic relations were restored between Serbia and Croatia, and UN sanctions against Serbia were lifted. Allies of Milošević were successful in parliamentary elections. Diplomatic relations were established with Bosnia-Herzegovina. There was mounting opposition to Milošević's government following its refusal to accept opposition victories in municipal elections.

**1997** Milošević was elected president and the pro-democracy mayor of Belgrade was ousted. The validity of Serbian presidential elections continued to be questioned. The anti-Milošević candidate was elected president of Montenegro.

**1998** A Serb military offensive against ethnic Albanian separatists in Kosovo led to a refugee and humanitarian crisis, with hundreds of people killed and hundreds of thousands displaced. The offensive against the Kosovo Liberation Army (KLA) was condemned by the international community and NATO military intervention was threatened.

**1999** Fighting continued between Serbians and Albanian separatists in Kosovo. March: following the failure of efforts to reach a negotiated settlement, NATO began a bombing campaign against the Serbs; the ethnic cleansing of Kosovars by Serbs intensified and the refugee crisis in neighbouring countries worsened as hundreds of thousands of ethnic Albanians fled Kosovo. May: President Milošević was indicted for crimes against humanity by the International War Crimes Tribunal in The Hague. June: peace agreed on NATO terms. Refugees began returning to Kosovo.

**Yukon Territory** (Dené *you-kon* 'great water') most northwesterly administrative division of Canada, bordered by the Beaufort Sea to the north, the Northwest Territories to the east, British Columbia to the south (below the 60th Parallel), and Alaska, USA to the west
*area* 483,500 sq km/186,631 sq mi
*capital* Whitehorse
*towns and cities* Dawson, Mayo
*population* (1996) 31,500, including 6,200 American Indians
*physical* Yukon River; Mount Logan, the highest point in Canada; Mackenzie, Ogilvie, Selwyn, and St Elias mountain ranges
*industries* mining of gold, silver, lead, coal, and zinc; oil and natural-gas extraction; lumbering; fur-trapping; fishing

**Yunnan** province of southwest China, bounded to the north by Tibet and Sichuan, to the east by Guizhou and Guangxi Zhuang Autonomous Region, to the south by Vietnam and Laos, and to the west by Myanmar (formerly Burma)
*area* 436,200 sq km/168,373 sq mi
*capital* Kunming
*cities and towns* Dongchuan, Gejiu, Lijiang, Wuding
*physical* Chang Jiang, Salween, Mekong rivers; mountainous and well forested
*features* crossed by the Burma Road
*industries* tin, copper, lead, gold, zinc, coal, salt, cigarettes
*agriculture* rice, tea, timber, wheat, cotton, tobacco, rubber
*population* (1996) 40,420,000.

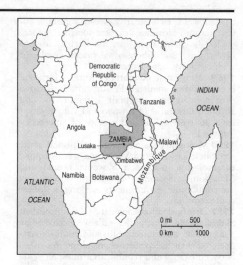

**Zagreb** industrial city (leather, linen, carpets, paper, and electrical goods) and capital of Croatia, on the Sava River; population (1991) 726,800. Zagreb was a Roman city (*Aemona*) and has a Gothic cathedral. Its university was founded in 1874. The city was damaged by bombing in October 1991 during the Croatian civil war.

**Zahir Shah, Muhammad** (1914–  ) King of Afghanistan 1933–73. Zahir, educated in Kabul and Paris, served in the government 1932–33 before being crowned king. He was overthrown in 1973 by a republican coup and went into exile. He became a symbol of national unity for the ♢Mujaheddin Islamic fundamentalist resistance groups.

**Zahir ud-Din Muhammad** first Mogul emperor of India; see ♢Babur.

**Zambezi** or *Zambesi,* river in central and southeast Africa; length 2,650 km/1,650 mi from northwest Zambia through Mozambique to the Indian Ocean, with a wide delta near Chinde. Major tributaries include the Kafue in Zambia. It is interrupted by rapids, and includes on the Zimbabwe–Zambia border the Victoria Falls (Mosi-oa-tunya) and Kariba Dam, which forms the reservoir of Lake Kariba with large fisheries. Its drainage area is about 1,347,000 sq km/520,077 sq mi.

**Zambia** Republic of (formerly *Northern Rhodesia)*
**area** 752,600 sq km/290,578 sq mi
**capital** Lusaka
**major towns/cities** Kitwe, Ndola, Kabwe, Mufulira, Chingola, Luanshya, Livingstone
**physical features** forested plateau cut through by rivers; Zambezi River, Victoria Falls, Kariba Dam
**head of state and government** Frederick Chiluba from 1991
**political system** emergent democracy
**political parties** United National Independence Party (UNIP), African socialist; Movement for Multiparty Democracy (MMD), moderate, left of centre; Multiracial Party (MRP), moderate, left of centre, multiracial; National Democratic Alliance (NADA), left of centre; Democratic Party (DP), left of centre
**currency** Zambian kwacha
**GNP per capita (PPP)** (US$) 860 (1998)
**exports** copper, zinc, lead, cobalt, tobacco. Principal market: Japan 11.6% (1997)

**population** 8,976,000 (1999 est)
**language** English (official); Bantu languages
**religion** Christian, animist, Hindu, Muslim
**life expectancy** 40 (men); 41 (women) (1995–2000)
**Chronology**
**16th century** Immigration of peoples from Luba and Lunda Empires of Zaire, to the northwest, who set up small kingdoms.
**late 18th century** Visited by Portuguese explorers.
**19th century** Instability with immigration of Ngoni from east, Kololo from west, establishment of Bemba kingdom in north, and slave-trading activities of Portuguese and Arabs from East Africa.
**1851** Visited by British missionary and explorer David Livingstone.
**1889** As Northern Rhodesia, came under administration of British South Africa Company of Cecil Rhodes, and became involved in copper mining, especially from 1920s.
**1924** Became a British protectorate.
**1948** Northern Rhodesia African Congress (NRAC) formed by black Africans to campaign for self-rule.
**1953** Became part of Central African Federation, which included South Rhodesia (Zimbabwe) and Nyasaland (Malawi).
**1960** UNIP was formed by Kenneth Kaunda as a breakaway from NRAC, as African socialist body to campaign for independence and dissolution of federation dominated by South Rhodesia's white minority.
**1963** The federation was dissolved and internal self-government achieved.
**1964** Independence was achieved within the Commonwealth as the Republic of Zambia, with Kaunda of the UNIP as president.
**later 1960s** Key enterprises were brought under state control.
**1972** UNIP was declared the only legal party.
**1975** The opening of the Tan-Zam railway from the Zambian copperbelt, 322 mi/200 km north of Lusaka, to port of Dar es Salaam in Tanzania, reduced Zambia's dependence on the rail route

via Rhodesia (Zimbabwe) for its exports.

**1976** Zambia declared its support for Patriotic Front (PF) guerrillas fighting to topple the white-dominated regime in Rhodesia (Zimbabwe).

**1980** There was an unsuccessful South African-promoted coup against President Kaunda; relations with Zimbabwe improved when the PF came to power.

**1985** Kaunda was elected chair of African Front Line States.

**1991** A new multiparty constitution was adopted. The MMD won a landslide election victory, and its leader Frederick Chiluba became president in what was the first democratic change of government in English-speaking black Africa.

**1993** A state of emergency was declared after rumours of a planned antigovernment coup. A privatization programme was launched.

**1996** Kaunda was effectively barred from future elections by an amendment to the constitution; President Chiluba was re-elected.

**1997** There was an abortive antigovernment coup.

**1998** Former president Kaunda was placed under house arrest after alleged involvement in the antigovernment coup. Kaunda was charged but the charges were subsequently dropped.

**Zanzibar** island region of Tanzania
**area** 1,658 sq km/640 sq mi (80 km/50 mi long)
**towns and cities** Zanzibar
**agriculture** cloves, copra
**population** (1988) 375,500
**history** settled by Arab traders in the 7th century; occupied by the Portuguese in the 16th century; became a sultanate in the 17th century; under British protection from 1890–1963. Together with the island of Pemba, some nearby islets, and a strip of mainland territory, it became a republic in 1963. It merged with Tanganyika as Tanzania in 1964.

**Zapata, Emiliano** (1879–1919) Mexican Indian revolutionary leader. He led a revolt against dictator Porfirio Díaz from 1910 under the slogan 'Land and Liberty', to repossess for the indigenous Mexicans the land taken by the Spanish. By 1915 he was driven into retreat, and was assassinated in his stronghold, Morelos, by an agent of Venustiano Carranza.

**Zapotec** an American Indian people of southern Mexico, now numbering approximately 250,000, living mainly in Oaxaca. The Zapotec language, which belongs to the Oto-Mangean family, has nine dialects. The ancient Zapotec built the ceremonial centre of Monte Albán 1000–500 BC. They developed one of the classic Mesoamerican civilizations by AD 300, but declined under pressure from the Mixtecs from 900 until the Spanish Conquest in the 1530s.

**Zaragoza** English *Saragossa*, capital of Zaragoza province and of ◊Aragón; autonomous community, northeast Spain, on the River Ebro; population (1994) 607,000. Industries include iron, steel, chemicals, plastics, and canned food. The medieval city walls and bridges over the River Ebro still remain, and there is a 15th-century university.

**zebra** black and white striped member of the horse genus *Equus* found in Africa; the stripes serve as camouflage or dazzle and confuse predators. It is about 1.5 m/5 ft high at the shoulder, with a stout body and a short, thick mane. Zebras live in family groups and herds on mountains and plains, and can run at up to 60 kph/40 mph. Males are usually solitary.

**zebu** any of a species of ◊cattle *Bos indicus* found domesticated in East Asia, India, and Africa. It is usually light-coloured, with large horns and a large fatty hump near the shoulders. It is used for pulling loads, and is held by some Hindus to be sacred. There are about 30 breeds.

**Zedekiah** (lived early 6th century) last king of Judah 597–586 BC. Placed on the throne by Nebuchadnezzar, he rebelled, was forced to witness his sons' execution, then was blinded and sent to Babylon. The witness to these events was the prophet Jeremiah, who describes them in the Old Testament.

**Zeebrugge** small Belgian ferry port on the North Sea, linked to Bruges by a canal (built 1896–1907), 14 km/9 mi long. It was occupied by the Germans in World War I and developed as a major naval base. In March 1987 it was the scene of a disaster in which over 180 passengers lost their lives when the car ferry *Herald of Free Enterprise* put to sea from Zeebrugge with its car-loading doors still open.

**Zeeland** province of southwest Netherlands, consisting of five islands lying in the Schelde river estuary, and the region north of the Belgian province of East Flanders
**area** 1,790 sq km/691 sq mi
**capital** Middelburg
**towns and cities** Vlissingen
**physical** mostly below sea level; protected by a system of dykes; fertile soil; islands of North and South *Beveland,* and *Walcheren* in Schelde estuary; the Delta Project, a series of barrages, links all the islands
**industries** shipbuilding, engineering, petrochemicals
**agriculture** livestock, dairy products, cereals, potatoes
**population** (1997) 368,400
**history** disputed by the counts of Flanders and Holland during the Middle Ages; annexed to Holland 1323 by Count William III.

**Zen** (abbreviation of Japanese *zenna* 'quiet mind concentration') form of ◊Buddhism introduced from India to Japan via China in the 12th century. *Kōan* (paradoxical questions), intense meditation, and sudden enlightenment are elements of Zen practice. Soto Zen was spread by the priest Dōgen (1200–1253), who emphasized work, practice, discipline, and philosophical questions to discover one's Buddha-nature in the 'realization of self'.

**zenith** uppermost point of the celestial horizon, immediately above the observer; the ◊nadir is below, diametrically opposite. See ◊celestial sphere.

**Zeno of Elea** (c. 490– c. 430 BC) Greek philosopher. He pointed out several paradoxes that raised 'modern' problems of space and time. For example, motion is an illusion, since an arrow in flight must occupy a determinate space at each instant, and therefore must be at rest.

**Zeppelin, Ferdinand Adolf August Heinrich**, Count von Zeppelin (1838– 1917) German ◊airship pioneer. His first airship was built and tested in 1900. During World War I a number of *zeppelins* bombed England. They were also used for luxury passenger transport but the construction of hydrogen-filled airships with rigid keels was abandoned after several disasters in the 1920s and 1930s. Zeppelin also helped to pioneer large multi-engine bomber planes.

**Zeus** in Greek mythology, the chief of the Olympian gods (Roman ◊Jupiter). He was the son of ◊Kronos, whom he overthrew; his brothers included Pluto and Poseidon, his sisters Demeter, Hestia, and Hera. As the supreme god he dispensed good and evil and was the father and ruler of all humankind, the fount of kingly power and law and order. His emblems were the thunderbolt and aegis (shield), representing the thundercloud. The colossal ivory and gold statue of the seated god, made by Phidias for the temple of Zeus in the Peloponnese, was one of the ◊Seven Wonders of the World.

**Zhangjiakou** or *Changchiakow;* Mongolian *Kalgan,* historic city and trading centre in Hebei province, China, on the Great Wall, 160 km/100 mi northwest of Beijing; population (1990) 670,000. Zhangjiakou used to be an important border post between China and Mongolia on the road and railway to Ulaanbaatar; its Mongolian name means 'gate'. It developed under the Qing dynasty, and was the centre of the tea trade from China to Russia. In 1998 an earthquake centred on Zhangbei, 40 km/25 mi north of the city, caused widespread destruction in the city and its surrounding region.

**Zhao Ziyang** (1919– ) Chinese politician, prime minister from 1980–87 and leader of the Chinese Communist Party from 1987–89. His reforms included self-management and incentives for workers and factories. He lost his secretaryship and other posts after the Tiananmen Square massacre in Beijing in June 1989.

**Zhejiang** or *Chekiang,* coastal province of southeast China, bounded to the north by Jiangsu, to the east by the East China Sea, to the south by Fujian, and to the west by Jiangxi and Anhui
*area* 101,800 sq km/39,295 sq mi
*capital* ◊Hangzhou
*towns* Ningbo, Wenzhou
*physical* Chang Jiang delta, hills in south
*features* West Lake gardens and pavilions, and early Zen (Chan) Buddhist Lingyin Temple at Hangzhou; Tianyige Library (1516), Ningbo, China's oldest surviving library; Putuoshan Island, a Buddhist holy mountain and mythical home of Guanyin, goddess of mercy and fertility
*industries* silk, chemical fibres, canning, tea-processing, handicrafts
*agriculture* rice, cotton, sugar, silkworms, jute, maize, timber, fish
*population* (1996) 43,430,000.

**Zhelev, Zhelyu** (1935– ) Bulgarian politician, president 1990–96. In 1989 he became head of the opposition Union Democratic Forces (UDF) coalition. He was a proponent of market-centred economic reform and social peace.

**Zhengzhou** or *Chengchow,* capital of ◊Henan province, China, on the Huang He River; population (1993) 2,009,000. Industries include light engineering, food-processing, and the manufacture of chemicals, building materials, and cotton textiles.

**Zhou dynasty** or *Chou dynasty,* Chinese succession of rulers *c.* 1066–256 BC, during which cities emerged and philosophy flourished. The dynasty was established by the Zhou, a semi-nomadic people from the Wei Valley region, west of the great bend in the Huang He (Yellow River). Zhou influence waned from 403 BC, as the Warring States era began.

**Zhou Enlai** or *Chou En-lai* (1898–1976) Chinese communist politician. Zhou, a member of the Chinese Communist Party (CCP) from the 1920s, was prime minister 1949–76 and foreign minister 1949–58. He was a moderate Maoist and weathered the Cultural Revolution. He played a key role in foreign affairs.

**zidovudine** formerly *AZT,* antiviral drug used in the treatment of ◊AIDS. It is not a cure for AIDS but is effective in prolonging life; it does not, however, delay the onset of AIDS in people carrying the virus.

**ziggurat** in ancient Babylonia and Assyria, a step pyramid of sun-baked brick faced with glazed bricks or tiles on which stood a shrine. The Tower of Babel as described in the Bible may have been a ziggurat.

**Zimbabwe** Republic of (formerly *Southern Rhodesia*)

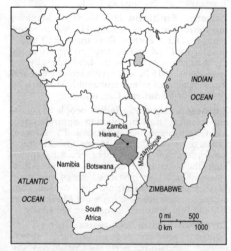

*area* 390,300 sq km/150,694 sq mi
*capital* Harare
*major towns/cities* Bulawayo, Gweru, Kwekwe, Mutare, Hwange, Chitungwiza
*physical features* high plateau with central

high veld and mountains in east; rivers Zambezi, Limpopo; Victoria Falls

**head of state and government** Robert Mugabe from 1987

**political system** effectively one-party socialist republic

**political parties** Zimbabwe African National Union–Patriotic Front (ZANU–PF), African socialist; opposition parties exist but none have mounted serious challenge to ruling party

**currency** Zimbabwe dollar

**GNP per capita (PPP)** (US$) 2,150 (1998)

**exports** tobacco, metals and metal alloys, textiles and clothing, cotton lint. Principal market: South Africa 12.1% (1997)

**population** 11,529,000 (1999 est)

**language** English (official), Shona, Sindebele

**religion** Christian, Muslim, Hindu, animist

**life expectancy** 44 (men); 45 (women) (1995–2000)

**Chronology**

**13th century** Shona people settled Mashonaland (eastern Zimbabwe), erecting stone buildings (hence name Zimbabwe, 'stone house').

**15th century** Shona Empire reached its greatest extent.

**16th–17th centuries** Portuguese settlers developed trade with Shona states and achieved influence over kingdom of Mwanamutapa in northern Zimbabwe in 1629.

**1837** Ndebele (or Matabele) people settled in southwest Zimbabwe after being driven north from Transvaal by Boers; Shona defeated by Ndebele led by King Mzilikazi who formed military empire based at Bulawayo.

**1870** King Lobengula succeeded King Mzilikazi.

**1889** Cecil Rhodes' British South Africa Company (BSA Co) obtained exclusive rights to exploit mineral resources in Lobengula's domains.

**1890** Creation of white colony in Mashonaland and founding of Salisbury (Harare) by Leander Starr Jameson, associate of Rhodes.

**1893** Matabele War: Jameson defeated Lobengula; white settlers took control of country.

**1895** Matabeleland, Mashonaland, and Zambia named Rhodesia after Cecil Rhodes.

**1896** Matabele revolt suppressed.

**1898** Southern Rhodesia (Zimbabwe) became British protectorate administered by BSA Co; farming, mining, and railways developed.

**1922** Union with South Africa rejected by referendum among white settlers.

**1923** Southern Rhodesia became self-governing colony; Africans progressively disenfranchised.

**1933–53** Prime Minister Godfrey Huggins (later Lord Malvern) pursued 'White Rhodesia' policy of racial segregation.

**1950s** Immigration doubled white population to around 250,000, while indigenous African population stood at around 6 million.

**1953** Southern Rhodesia formed part of Federation of Rhodesia and Nyasaland.

**1961** Zimbabwe African People's Union (ZAPU) formed with Joshua Nkomo as leader; declared illegal a year later.

**1962** Rhodesia Front party of Winston Field took power in Southern Rhodesia, pledging to preserve white rule.

**1963** Federation of Rhodesia and Nyasaland dissolved as Zambia and Malawi moved towards independence; Zimbabwe African National Union (ZANU) formed, with Robert Mugabe as secretary; declared illegal a year later.

**1964** Ian Smith became prime minister; he rejected British terms for independence which required moves towards black majority rule; Nkomo and Mugabe imprisoned.

**1965** Smith made unilateral declaration of independence (UDI); Britain broke off all relations.

**1966–68** United Nations (UN) imposed economic sanctions on Rhodesia, which still received help from South Africa and Portugal.

**1969** Rhodesia declared itself a republic.

**1972** Britain rejected draft independence agreement as unacceptable to African population.

**1974** Nkomo and Mugabe released and jointly formed Patriotic Front to fight Smith regime in mounting civil war.

**1975** Geneva Conference between British, Smith regime, and African nationalists failed to reach agreement.

**1978** At height of civil war, whites were leaving Rhodesia at rate of 1,000 per month.

**1979** Rhodesia became Zimbabwe-Rhodesia with new 'majority' constitution which nevertheless retained special rights for whites; Bishop Abel Muzorewa became premier; Mugabe and Nkomo rejected settlement; Lancaster House Agreement temporarily restored Rhodesia to British rule.

**1980** Zimbabwe achieved independence from Britain with full transition to African majority rule; Mugabe became prime minister with Rev. Canaan Banana as president.

**1981** There was a rift between Mugabe (ZANU–PF) and Nkomo (ZAPU).

**1982** Nkomo was dismissed from the cabinet.

**1984** A ZANU–PF party congress agreed to the principle of a one-party state.

**1987** Mugabe combined the posts of head of state and prime minister as executive president; Nkomo became vice-president.

**1989** ZANU–PF and ZAPU formally merged; the Zimbabwe Unity Movement was founded by Edgar Tekere to oppose the one-party state.

**1992** The United Party was formed to oppose ZANU–PF. Mugabe declared drought and famine a national disaster.

**1996** Mugabe was re-elected president.

**1998** Mugabe issued new rules banning strikes and restricting political and public gatherings. The government's radical land distribution plans were watered down after pressure from aid donors. There were violent antigovernment demonstrations.

**1999** Further violent antigovernment protests took place. In June the human rights group African Rights produced a scathing report on Mugabe's government.

**zinc** (Germanic *zint* 'point') hard, brittle, bluish-white, metallic element, symbol Zn, atomic number 30, relative atomic mass 65.37. The principal ore is sphalerite or zinc blende (zinc sulphide, ZnS). Zinc is hardly affected by air or moisture at ordinary temperatures; its chief uses are in alloys such as brass and in coating metals (for example, galvanized iron). Its compounds include ◊zinc oxide, used in ointments (as an astringent) and cosmetics, paints, glass, and printing ink.

Zinc is an essential trace element in most animals; adult humans have 2–3 g/0.07–0.1 oz zinc in their bodies. There are more than 300 known enzymes that contain zinc.

**zinc ore** mineral from which zinc is extracted, principally sphalerite $(Zn,Fe)S$, but also zincite, $ZnO_2$, and smithsonite, $ZnCO_3$, all of which occur in mineralized veins. Ores of lead and zinc often occur together, and are common worldwide; Canada, the USA, and Australia are major producers.

**zinc oxide** ZnO white powder, yellow when hot, that occurs in nature as the mineral zincite. It is used in paints and as an antiseptic in zinc ointment; it is the main ingredient of calamine lotion.

**zinnia** any of a group of annual plants belonging to the daisy family, native to Mexico and South America; notably the cultivated hybrids of *Z. elegans* with brightly coloured daisylike flowers. (Genus *Zinnia,* family Compositae.)

**Zinoviev, Grigory Yevseyevich** (1883–1936) Russian communist politician whose name was attached to a forgery, the *Zinoviev letter,* inciting Britain's communists to rise, which helped to topple the Labour government in 1924.

**Zion** Jebusite (Amorites of Canaan) stronghold in Jerusalem captured by King David, and the hill on which he built the Temple, symbol of Jerusalem and of Jewish national life.

**Zionism** national liberation movement advocating the re-establishment of a Jewish homeland (the *Eretz Israel*) in Palestine. Here, in the 'promised land' of the Bible, its adherents called for the Jewish people to be granted a sovereign state with its capital at Jerusalem, the 'city of Zion'. The movement was founded by the Hungarian writer Theodor ◊Herzl, who in 1897 convened the First Zionist Congress in the Swiss city of Basel. Zionism was the driving force behind the creation of the state of Israel in 1948.

**zip fastener** fastening device used in clothing, invented in the USA by Whitcomb Judson in 1891, originally for doing up shoes. It has two sets of interlocking teeth, meshed by means of a slide that moves up and down. It became widely used in the clothing industry in the 1930s.

**zircon** zirconium silicate, $ZrSiO_4$, a mineral that occurs in small quantities in a wide range of igneous, sedimentary, and metamorphic rocks. It is very durable and is resistant to erosion and weathering. It is usually coloured brown, but can be other colours, and when transparent may be used as a gemstone.

**zirconium** (Germanic *zircon,* from Persian *zargun* 'golden') lustrous, greyish-white, strong, ductile, metallic element, symbol Zr, atomic number 40, relative atomic mass 91.22. It occurs in nature as the mineral zircon (zirconium silicate), from which it is obtained commercially. It is used in some ceramics, alloys for wire and filaments, steel manufacture, and nuclear reactors, where its low neutron absorption is advantageous.

**zither** member of a family of musical instruments consisting of one or more strings stretched over a resonating frame or soundbox, played horizontally. The modern concert zither has up to 45 strings of which five, passing over frets, are plucked with a plectrum for melody, and the remainder are plucked with the fingers for harmonic accompaniment.

**Zi Xi** or *Tz'u-hsi* (c. 1834–1908) Empress dowager of China. She was presented as a concubine to the emperor Xianfeng. On his death in 1861 she became regent for her young son Tongzhi (1856–1875) until 1873 and, after his death, for her nephew Guangxu (1871–1908) until 1889. A ruthless conservative, she blocked the Hundred Days' Reform launched in 1898 and assumed power again, having Guangxu imprisoned. Her policies helped deny China a peaceful transition to political and economic reform.

**zodiac** zone of the heavens containing the paths of the Sun, Moon, and planets. When this was devised by the ancient Greeks, only five planets were known, making the zodiac about 16° wide. In astrology, the zodiac is divided into 12 signs, each 30° in extent: Aries, Taurus, Gemini, Cancer, Leo, Virgo, Libra, Scorpio, Sagittarius, Capricorn, Aquarius, and Pisces. These do not cover the same areas of sky as the astronomical constellations.

**Zoë** (c. 978–1050) Byzantine empress who ruled from 1028 until 1050. She gained the title by marriage to the heir apparent Romanus III Argyrus, but was reputed to have poisoned him (1034) in order to marry her lover Michael. He died in 1041 and Zoë and her sister Theodora were proclaimed joint empresses. Rivalry led to Zoë marrying Constantine IX Monomachus with whom she reigned until her death.

**Zola, Émile Edouard Charles Antoine** (1840–1902) French novelist and social reformer. He made his name with *Thérèse Raquin* (1867), a grim, powerful story of remorse. With *La Fortune des Rougon/The Fortune of the Rougons* (1867) he began a series of some 20 naturalistic novels collectively known as *Le Rougon-Macquart,* portraying the fortunes of a French family under the Second Empire. They include *Le Ventre de Paris/The Underbelly of Paris* (1873), *Nana* (1880), and *La Débâcle/The Debacle* (1892). In 1898 he published *J'accuse/I Accuse,* a pamphlet indicting the persecutors of Alfred ◊Dreyfus, for which he was prosecuted for libel but later pardoned.

**zombie** corpse believed to be reanimated by a spirit and enslaved. The idea, widespread in Haiti, possibly arose from voodoo priests using the nerve poison tetrodotoxin (from the puffer fish) to produce a semblance of death from which the victim afterwards physically recovers. Those eating incorrectly prepared puffer fish in Japan have been similarly affected.

**zoo** abbreviation for *zoological gardens,* place where animals are kept in captivity. Originally created purely for visitor entertainment and education, zoos have become major centres for the breeding of endangered species of animals; a 1984 report identified 2,000 vertebrate species in need of such maintenance.

**zoology** branch of biology concerned with the study of animals. It includes any aspect of the study of animal form and function – the study of present-day animals, the study of evolution of animal forms, ◊anatomy, ◊physiology, ◊embryology, behaviour, and geographical distribution.

**zoonosis** any infectious disease that can be transmitted to humans by other vertebrate animals. Probably the most feared example is ◊rabies. The transmitted micro-organism sometimes causes disease only in the human host, leaving the animal host unaffected.

**Zoroastrianism** pre-Islamic Persian religion founded by the Persian prophet Zoroaster in the 6th century BC, and still practised by the Parsees in India. The *Zend-Avesta* are the sacred scriptures of the faith. The theology is dualistic, *Ahura Mazda* or *Ormuzd* (the good God) being perpetually in conflict with *Ahriman* (the evil God), but the former is assured of eventual victory. There are approximately 100,000 (1991) Zoroastrians worldwide; membership is restricted to those with both parents belonging to the faith.

**Z particle** in physics, an ◊elementary particle, one of the weakons responsible for carrying the ◊weak nuclear force.

**zucchini** another name for the courgette, a type of ◊marrow.

**Zuider Zee** former sea inlet in the northwestern Netherlands, closed off from the North Sea by a 32-km/20-mi dyke in 1932; much of it has been reclaimed as land. The remaining lake is called the ◊IJsselmeer.

**Zulu** member of a group of southern African peoples mainly from Kwa Zulu-Natal, South Africa. They are traditionally agriculturalists. The Zulu language, closely related to Xhosa, belongs to the Bantu branch of the Niger-Congo family. Many Zulus are supporters of the political organization ◊Inkatha.

**Zürich** city and capital of **Switzerland,** situated at the exit of the Limmat River from Lake Zürich; population (1995) 422,700. Lying at the foot of the Alps, it is the capital of Zürich canton, the principal financial and business centre of Switzerland, and one of the world's leading international banking and insurance centres (the 'Gnomes of Zürich'). Manufactured goods include machinery, electrical goods, textiles, and printed works. It is the largest city in Switzerland.

**Zwingli, Ulrich** (1484–1531) Swiss Protestant reformer. He was ordained a Roman Catholic priest in 1506, but by 1519 was a Reformer and led the Reformation in Switzerland with his insistence on the sole authority of the Scriptures. He was killed in a skirmish at Kappel during a war against the cantons that had not accepted the Reformation.

**zwitterion** ion that has both a positive and a negative charge, such as an ◊amino acid in neutral solution. For example, glycine contains both a basic amino group ($NH_2$) and an acidic carboxyl group (COOH); when these are both ionized in aqueous solution, the acid group loses a proton to the amino group, and the molecule is positively charged at one end and negatively charged at the other.

**zygote** ◊ovum (egg) after ◊fertilization but before it undergoes cleavage to begin embryonic development.

## ARCHAEOLOGY: CHRONOLOGY

| | |
|---|---|
| 14th–16th centuries | Interest revived in Classical Greek and Roman art and architecture, including ruins and buried art and artefacts. |
| 1748 | The Roman city of Pompeii is discovered buried under volcanic ash from Vesuvius. |
| 1784 | Thomas Jefferson excavates an Indian burial mound on the Rivanna River in Virginia and writes a report on his finds. |
| 1790 | John Frere identifies Old Stone Age (Palaeolithic) tools together with large extinct animals. |
| 1822 | Jean François Champollion deciphers Egyptian hieroglyphics. |
| 1836 | Christian Thomsen devises the Stone, Bronze, and Iron Age classification (Three Age System). |
| 1840s | Austen Layard excavates the Assyrian capital of Nineveh. |
| 1868 | The Great Zimbabwe ruins in southern Africa are first seen by Europeans. |
| 1871 | Heinrich Schliemann begins excavations at Troy. |
| 1879 | Ice Age paintings are first discovered at Altamira, Spain. |
| 1880s | Augustus Pitt-Rivers develops the concept of stratigraphy (identification of successive layers of soil within a site with successive archaeological stages, the most recent being at the top). |
| 1891 | Flinders Petrie begins excavating Akhetaton in Egypt. |
| 1899–1935 | Arthur Evans excavates Minoan Knossos in Crete. |
| 1900–44 | Max Uhle begins the systematic study of the civilizations of Peru. |
| 1911 | The Inca city of Machu Picchu is discovered by Hiram Bingham in the Andes. |
| 1914–18 | Osbert Crawford develops the technique of aerial survey of sites. |
| 1917–27 | John Eric Thompson investigates the great Maya sites in Yucatán, Mexico. |
| 1922 | Tutankhamen's tomb in Egypt is opened by Howard Carter. |
| 1926 | A kill site in Folsom, New Mexico, is found with chipped stone spearpoints in association with ancient bison. |
| 1935 | Dendrochronology (dating events in the distant past by counting tree rings) is developed by A E Douglass. |
| 1939 | An Anglo-Saxon ship-burial treasure is found at Sutton Hoo, England. |
| 1947 | First of the Dead Sea Scrolls discovered. |
| 1948 | The 'Proconsul' prehistoric ape is discovered by Mary Leakey in Kenya. |
| 1950s–1970s | Several early hominid fossils are found by Louis and Mary Leakey in Olduvai Gorge. |
| 1953 | Michael Ventris deciphers Minoan Linear B. |
| 1960s | Radiocarbon and thermoluminescence measurement techniques are developed as aids for dating remains. |
| 1961 | The Swedish warship *Wasa* is raised at Stockholm. |
| 1963 | Walter Emery pioneers rescue archaeology at Abu Simbel before the site is flooded by the Aswan Dam. |
| 1969 | Human remains found at Lake Mungo, |

| | |
|---|---|
| | Australia, are dated at 26,000 years; earliest evidence of ritual cremation. |
| 1974 | The tomb of Shi Huangdi, with its terracotta army, is discovered in China; the partial skeleton of a 3.18-million year old hominid nicknamed 'Lucy' is found in Ethiopia, and hominid footprints, 3.8 million years old, at Laetoli in Tanzania. |
| 1978 | The tomb of Philip II of Macedon (Alexander the Great's father) is discovered in Greece. |
| 1979 | The Aztec capital Tenochtitlán is excavated beneath a zone of Mexico City. |
| 1982 | Henry VIII's warship *Mary Rose* of 1545 is raised and studied with new techniques in underwater archaeology. |
| 1985 | The tomb of Maya, Tutankhamen's treasurer, is discovered at Sakkara, Egypt. |
| 1988 | The Turin Shroud is established as being of medieval origin by radiocarbon dating. |
| 1989 | The remains of the Globe and Rose Theatres, where many of Shakespeare's plays were originally performed, are discovered in London. |
| 1991 | Clothed body of man from 5,300 years ago, with bow, arrows, copper axe, and other implements, is found preserved in ice in the Italian Alps. |
| 1992 | The world's oldest surviving wooden structure, a well 15 m/49 ft deep made of huge oak timbers at Kückhoven, Germany, is dated by tree-rings to 5090 BC. The world's oldest sea-going vessel, dating from about 1400 BC, is discovered at Dover, southern England. |
| 1993 | Drawings done in charcoal on the walls of the Cosquer Cave (near Marseille, France, discovered 1991) were dated by radiocarbon to be 27,110 and c. 19,000 years old; a fragment of cloth found on a tool handle unearthed in Çayönü, southeast Turkey in 1988 is carbon-dated at 9,000 years old, making it the oldest cloth ever found. |
| 1994 | Grotte Chauvet, (a network of hundreds of Palaeolithic cave drawings, dating from 30,000 years ago) is found in southeast France. |
| 1995 | A vast underground tomb believed to be the burial site of 50 of the sons of Ramses II is discovered. It is the largest yet found in the Valley of the Kings. |
| 1998 | Stone tools, belonging to *Homo erectus* and dated at about 8,000 years old, are discoverd by Australian palaeontologists on Flores, an island near Bali. The discovery provides strong evidence that *Homo erectus* are seafarers and had the language abilities and social structure to organize the colonization of new islands. |
| 1999 | The earliest playable wind instruments were excavated from Neolithic site in Henan Province, China, in 1999. The six bone flutes date from between 7000 and 5700 BC. |

## ASTRONOMY: CHRONOLOGY

**2300 BC** Chinese astronomers make their earliest observations.

**2000** Babylonian priests make their first observational records.

**1900** Stonehenge is constructed: first phase.

**434** Anaxagoras claims the Sun is made up of hot rock.

**365** The Chinese observe the satellites of Jupiter with the naked eye.

**3rd century** Aristarchus argues that the Sun is the centre of the Solar System.

**2nd century AD** Ptolemy's complicated Earth-centred system is promulgated, which dominates the astronomy of the Middle Ages.

**1543** Copernicus revives the ideas of Aristarchus in *De Revolutionibus*.

**1608** Hans Lippershey invents the telescope, which is first used by Galileo in 1609.

**1609** Johannes Kepler's first two laws of planetary motion are published (the third appears in 1619).

**1632** The world's first official observatory is established in Leiden in the Netherlands.

**1633** Galileo's theories are condemned by the Inquisition.

**1675** The Royal Greenwich Observatory is founded in England.

**1687** Newton's *Principia* is published, including his 'law of universal gravitation'.

**1705** Edmond Halley correctly predicts that the comet that had passed the Earth in 1682 will return in 1758; the comet is later known by his name.

**1781** William Herschel discovers Uranus and recognizes stellar systems beyond our Galaxy.

**1796** Pierre Laplace elaborates his theory of the origin of the Solar System.

**1801** Giuseppe Piazzi discovers the first asteroid, Ceres.

**1814** Joseph von Fraunhofer first studies absorption lines in the solar spectrum.

**1846** Neptune is identified by Johann Galle, following predictions by John Adams and Urbain Leverrier.

**1859** Gustav Kirchhoff explains dark lines in the Sun's spectrum.

**1887** The earliest photographic star charts are produced.

**1889** Edward Barnard takes the first photographs of the Milky Way.

**1908** Fragment of comet falls at Tunguska, Siberia.

**1920** Arthur Eddington begins the study of interstellar matter.

**1923** Edwin Hubble proves that the galaxies are systems independent of the Milky Way, and by 1930 has confirmed the concept of an expanding universe.

**1930** The planet Pluto is discovered by Clyde Tombaugh at the Lowell Observatory, Arizona, USA.

**1931** Karl Jansky founds radio astronomy.

**1945** Radar contact with the Moon is established by Z Bay of Hungary and the US Army Signal Corps Laboratory.

**1948** The 5-m/200-in Hale reflector telescope is installed at Mount Palomar, California, USA.

**1957** The Jodrell Bank telescope dish in England is completed.

**1957** The first Sputnik satellite (USSR) opens the age of space observation.

**1962** The first X-ray source is discovered in Scorpius.

**1963** The first quasar is discovered.

**1967** The first pulsar is discovered by Jocelyn Bell and Antony Hewish.

**1969** The first crewed Moon landing is made by US astronauts.

**1977** Uranus is discovered to have rings.

**1977** The spacecraft *Voyager* 1 and 2 are launched, passing Jupiter and Saturn 1979–1981.

**1978** The spacecraft *Pioneer Venus* 1 and 2 reach Venus.

**1978** A satellite of Pluto, Charon, is discovered by James Christy of the US Naval Observatory.

**1986** Halley's comet returned. *Voyager 2* flies past Uranus and discovers six new moons.

**1987** Supernova SN1987A flares up, becoming the first supernova to be visible to the naked eye since 1604. The 4.2-m/165-in William Herschel Telescope on La Palma, Canary Islands, and the James Clerk Maxwell Telescope on Mauna Kea, Hawaii, begins operation.

**1988** The most distant individual star is recorded – a supernova, 5 billion light years away, in the AC118 cluster of galaxies.

**1989** *Voyager 2* flies by Neptune and discovers eight moons and three rings.

**1990** Hubble Space Telescope is launched into orbit by the US space shuttle.

**1991** The space probe *Galileo* flies past the asteroid Gaspra, approaching it to within 26,000 km/16,200 mi.

**1992** COBE satellite detects ripples from the Big Bang that mark the first stage in the formation of galaxies.

**1994** Fragments of comet Shoemaker–Levy strike Jupiter.

**1997** Data from the satellite *Hipparcos* improves estimates of the age of the universe, and the distances to many nearby stars. Two new moons are discovered circling Uranus, bringing its total number of moons up to 17.

**1998** NASA announces the discovery of up to 300 million tonnes of ice on the surface of the Moon. The ice exists as a thin layer of crystals inside some craters that are permanently in shadow.

**1999** Cosmonauts aboard *Mir* return to Earth, permanently abandoning the space station, more than a decade after its first occupation.

## BIOLOGY: CHRONOLOGY

**c. 500 BC** First studies of the structure and behaviour of animals, by the Greek Alcmaeon of Croton.

**c. 450** Hippocrates of Kos undertakes the first detailed studies of human anatomy.

**c. 350** Aristotle lays down the basic philosophy of the biological sciences and outlines a theory of evolution.

**c. 300** Theophrastus carries out the first detailed studies of plants.

**C. AD 175** Galen establishes the basic principles of anatomy and physiology.

**c. 1500** Leonardo da Vinci studies human anatomy to improve his drawing ability and produces detailed anatomical drawings.

**1628** William Harvey describes the circulation of the blood.

**1665** Robert Hooke uses a microscope to describe the cellular structure of plants.

**1672** Marcelle Malphigi undertakes the first studies in embryology by describing the development of a chicken egg.

**1677** Anton van Leeuwenhoek greatly improves the microscope and uses it to describe spermatozoa as well as many micro-organisms.

**1736** Carolus (Carl) Linnaeus publishes his systematic classification of plants, so establishing taxonomy.

**1768–79** James Cook's voyages of discovery in the Pacific reveal a great diversity of living species, prompting the development of theories to explain their origin.

**1796** Edward Jenner establishes the practice of vaccination against smallpox, laying the foundations for theories of antibodies and immune reactions.

**1809** Jean-Baptiste Lamarck advocates a theory of evolution through inheritance of acquired characteristics.

**1839** Theodor Schwann proposes that all living matter is made up of cells.

**1857** Louis Pasteur establishes that micro-organisms are responsible for fermentation, beginning microbiology.

**1859** Charles Darwin publishes 'On the Origin of Species', expounding his theory of the evolution of species by natural selection.

**1865** Gregor Mendel pioneers the study of inheritance with his experiments on peas, but achieves little recognition.

**1883** August Weismann proposes his theory of the continuity of the germ plasm.

**1900** Mendel's work is rediscovered and the science of genetics founded.

**1935** Konrad Lorenz publishes the first of many major studies of animal behaviour, which founds the discipline of ethology.

**1953** James Watson and Francis Crick describe the molecular structure of the genetic material DNA.

**1964** William Hamilton recognizes the importance of inclusive fitness, so paving the way for the development of sociobiology.

**1975** Discovery of endogenous opiates (the brain's own painkillers) opens up a new phase in the study of brain chemistry.

**1976** Har Gobind Khorana and his colleagues construct the first artificial gene to function naturally when inserted into a bacterial cell, a major step in genetic engineering.

**1982** Gene databases are established at Heidelberg, Germany, for the European Molecular Biology Laboratory, and at Los Alamos, USA, for the US National Laboratories.

**1985** The first human cancer gene, retinoblastoma, is isolated by US researchers.

**1988** The Human Genome Organization (HUGO) is established in Washington DC with the aim of mapping the complete sequence of DNA.

**1991** *Biosphere 2*, an experiment that attempts to reproduce the world's biosphere in miniature within a sealed glass dome, is launched in Arizona, USA.

**1992** Researchers at the University of California, USA, stimulate the multiplication of isolated brain cells of mice, overturning the axiom that mammalian brains cannot produce replacement cells once birth has taken place.

**1994** Scientists from Pakistan and the USA unearth a 50-million-year-old fossil whale with hind legs that would have enabled it to walk on land.

**1995** A new phylum is identified and named Cycliophora. It contains a single known species, *Symbion pandora*, a parasite of the lobster.

**1996** The sequencing of the genome of brewer's yeast *Saccharomyces cerevisiae* is completed, the first time this has been achieved for an organism more complex than a bacterium. The 12 million base pairs took 300 scientists six years to map. A new muscle is discovered by two US dentists. It is 3 cm/1 in long, and runs from the jaw to behind the eye socket.

**1997** The first mammal to be cloned from a nonreproductive cell is born. The lamb (named Dolly) has been cloned from an udder cell from a six-year-old ewe.

**1999** Canadian researchers engineer an artificial chromosome that can be inserted into mammal cells and then transmitted from one generation to the next.

## CHEMISTRY: CHRONOLOGY

**c. 3000 BC** Egyptians are producing bronze – an alloy of copper and tin.

**c. 450 BC** Greek philosopher Empedocles proposes that all substances are made up of a combination of four elements – earth, air, fire, and water – an idea that is developed by Plato and Aristotle and persists for over 2,000 years.

**c. 400 BC** Greek philosopher Democritus theorizes that matter consists ultimately of tiny, indivisible particles, *atomos*.

**AD 1** Gold, silver, copper, lead, iron, tin, and mercury are known.

**200** The techniques of solution, filtration, and distillation are known.

**7th–17th centuries** Chemistry is dominated by alchemy, the attempt to transform nonprecious metals such as lead and copper into gold. Though misguided, it leads to the discovery of many new chemicals and techniques, such as sublimation and distillation.

**1661** Robert Boyle defines an element as any substance that cannot be broken down into still simpler substances and asserts that matter is composed of 'corpuscles' (atoms) of various sorts and sizes, capable of arranging themselves into groups, each of which constitutes a chemical substance.

**1662** Boyle describes the inverse relationship between the volume and pressure of a fixed mass of gas (Boyle's law).

**1697** Georg Stahl proposes the erroneous theory that substances burn because they are rich in a substance called phlogiston.

**1755** Joseph Black discovers carbon dioxide.

**1774** Joseph Priestley discovers oxygen, which he calls 'dephlogisticated air'. Antoine Lavoisier demonstrates his law of conservation of mass.

**1781** Henry Cavendish shows water to be a compound.

**1792** Alessandra Volta demonstrates the electrochemical series.

**1807** Humphry Davy passes an electric current through molten compounds (the process of electrolysis) in order to isolate elements, such as potassium, that have never been separated by chemical means.

**1808** John Dalton publishes his atomic theory, which states that every element consists of similar indivisible particles – called atoms – which differ from the atoms of other elements in their mass; he also draws up a list of relative atomic masses.

**1811** Amedeo Avogadro's hypothesis on the relation between the volume and number of molecules of a gas, and its temperature and pressure, is published.

**1813–14** Berzelius devises the chemical symbols and formulae still used to represent elements and compounds.

**1828** Franz Wöhler converts ammonium cyanate into urea – the first synthesis of an organic compound from an inorganic substance.

**1832–33** Michael Faraday expounds the laws of electrolysis, and adopts the term 'ion' for the particles believed to be responsible for carrying current.

**1846** Thomas Graham expounds his law of diffusion.

**1858** Stanislao Cannizzaro differentiates between atomic and molecular weights (masses).

**1861** Organic chemistry is defined by German chemist Friedrich Kekulé as the chemistry of carbon compounds.

**1864** John Newlands devises the first periodic table of the elements.

**1869** Dmitri Mendeleyev expounds his periodic table of the elements (based on atomic mass), leaving gaps for elements that have not yet been discovered.

**1884** Svante Arrhenius suggests that electrolytes (solutions or molten compounds that conduct electricity) dissociate into ions, atoms or groups of atoms that carry a positive or negative charge.

**1894** William Ramsey and Lord Rayleigh discover the first inert gases, argon.

**1897** The electron is discovered by J J Thomson.

**1901** Mikhail Tsvet invents paper chromatography as a means of separating pigments.

**1909** Sören Sörensen devises the pH scale of acidity.

**1912** Max von Laue shows crystals to be composed of regular, repeating arrays of atoms by studying the patterns in which they diffract X-rays.

**1913–14** Henry Moseley equates the atomic number of an element with the positive charge on its nuclei, and draws up the periodic table, based on atomic number, that is used today.

**1916** Gilbert Newton Lewis explains covalent bonding between atoms as a sharing of electrons.

**1927** Nevil Sidgwick publishes his theory of valency, based on the numbers of electrons in the outer shells of the reacting atoms.

**1930** Electrophoresis, which separates particles in suspension in an electric field, is invented by Arne Tiselius.

**1932** Deuterium (heavy hydrogen), an isotope of hydrogen, is discovered by Harold Urey.

**1940** Edwin McMillan and Philip Abelson show that new elements with a higher atomic number than uranium can be formed by bombarding uranium with neutrons, and synthesize the first transuranic element, neptunium.

**1950** Derek Barton deduces that some properties of organic compounds are affected by the orientation of their functional groups (the study of which becomes known as conformational analysis).

**1981** Quantum mechanics is applied to predict the course of chemical reactions by US chemist Roald Hoffmann and Kenichi Fukui of Japan.

**1985** Fullerenes, a new class of carbon solids made up of closed cages of carbon atoms, are discovered by Harold Kroto and David Walton

**1999** Russian scientists create element 114 by colliding isotopes calcium 48 and plutonium 44. Shortly afterwards, US physicists create element 118, which decays into another new element, 116, by bombarding lead with krypton.

## PHYSICS: CHRONOLOGY

**c. 400 BC** The first 'atomic' theory is put forward by Democritus.

**c. 250** Archimedes' principle of buoyancy is established.

**AD 1600** William Gilbert describes magnetism.

**1608** Hans Lippershey invents the refracting telescope.

**c. 1610** The principle of falling bodies descending to earth at the same speed is established by Galileo.

**1642** The principles of hydraulics are put forward by Blaise Pascal.

**1643** The mercury barometer is invented by Evangelista Torricelli.

**1656** The pendulum clock is invented by Christiaan Huygens.

**1662** Boyle's law concerning the behaviour of gases is established by Robert Boyle.

**c. 1665** Isaac Newton puts forward the law of gravity, stating that the Earth exerts a constant force on falling bodies.

**1690** The wave theory of light is propounded by Christiaan Huygens.

**1704** The corpuscular theory of light is put forward by Isaac Newton.

**1714** The mercury thermometer is invented by Daniel Fahrenheit.

**1764** Specific and latent heats are described by Joseph Black.

**c. 1787** Charles's law relating the pressure, volume, and temperature of a gas is established by Jacques Charles.

**1798** The link between heat and friction is discovered by Benjamin Rumford.

**1800** Alessandro Volta invents the Voltaic cell.

**1801** Interference of light is discovered by Thomas Young.

**1808** The 'modern' atomic theory is propounded by John Dalton.

**1811** Avogadro's hypothesis relating volumes and numbers of molecules of gases is proposed by Amedeo Avogadro.

**1815** Refraction of light is explained by Augustin Fresnel.

**1820** The discovery of electromagnetism is made by Hans Oersted.

**1821** The dynamo principle is described by Michael Faraday; the thermocouple is invented by Thomas Seebeck.

**1822** The laws of electrodynamics are established by André Ampère.

**1824** Thermodynamics as a branch of physics is proposed by Sadi Carnot.

**1827** Ohm's law of electrical resistance is established by Georg Ohm; Brownian movement resulting from molecular vibrations is observed by Robert Brown.

**1829** The law of gaseous diffusion is established by Thomas Graham.

**1831** Electromagnetic induction is discovered by Faraday.

**1834** Faraday discovers self-induction.

**1842** The principle of conservation of energy is observed by Julius von Mayer.

**c. 1847** The mechanical equivalent of heat is described by James Joule.

**1849** A measurement of speed of light is put forward by Armand Fizeau.

**1851** The rotation of the Earth is demonstrated by Jean Foucault.

**1859** Spectrographic analysis is made by Robert Bunsen and Gustav Kirchhoff.

**1880** Piezoelectricity discovered by Pierre Curie.

**1887** The existence of radio waves is predicted by Heinrich Hertz.

**1895** Wilhelm Röntgen discovers X-rays.

**1896** The discovery of radioactivity is made by Antoine Becquerel.

**1897** J J Thomson discovers the electron.

**1899** Ernest Rutherford discovers alpha and beta rays.

**1900** Quantum theory is propounded by Max Planck; the discovery of gamma rays is made by Paul-Ulrich Villard.

**1902** Oliver Heaviside discovers the ionosphere.

**1904** The theory of radioactivity is put forward by Rutherford and Frederick Soddy.

**1905** Albert Einstein propounds his special theory of relativity.

**1911** The discovery of the atomic nucleus is made by Rutherford.

**1913** The orbiting electron atomic theory is propounded by Danish physicist Niels Bohr.

**1915** X-ray crystallography is discovered by William and Lawrence Bragg.

**1916** Einstein puts forward his general theory of relativity; mass spectrography is discovered by William Aston.

**1924** Edward Appleton makes his study of the Heaviside layer.

**1926** Wave mechanics is introduced by Erwin Schrödinger.

**1927** The uncertainty principle is established by Werner Heisenberg.

**1931** The cyclotron is developed by Ernest Lawrence.

**1932** The discovery of the neutron is made by James Chadwick.

**1933** The positron, the antiparticle of the electron, is discovered by Carl Anderson.

**1934** Artificial radioactivity is developed by Frédéric and Irène Joliot-Curie.

**1939** The discovery of nuclear fission is made by Otto Hahn and Fritz Strassmann.

**1942** The first controlled nuclear chain reaction is achieved by Enrico Fermi.

**1956** The neutrino is discovered by Clyde Cowan and Fred Reines.

**1960** The Mössbauer effect of atom emissions is discovered by Rudolf Mössbauer; the first laser and the first maser are developed by Theodore Maiman.

**1964** Murray Gell-Mann and George Zweig discover the quark.

**1979** James W Cronin and Val L Fitch discover the asymmetry of elementary particles.

**1983** Evidence of the existence of weakons (W and Z particles) is confirmed at CERN, validating the link between the weak nuclear force and the electromagnetic force.

**1986** The first high-temperature superconductor is able to conduct electricity without resistance at $-238°C/-396°F$.

**1989** CERN's Large Electron Positron Collider (LEP) particle accelerator comes into operation.

**1999** Scientists succeed in slowing down the speed of light from its normal speed of 299,792 km/186,282 mi per second to 61 km/38 mi per hour.

## COMPUTING: CHRONOLOGY

| | |
|---|---|
| **1614** | John Napier invents logarithms. |
| **1615** | William Oughtred invents the slide rule. |
| **1623** | Wilhelm Schickard (1592–1635) invents the mechanical calculating machine. |
| **1645** | Blaise Pascal produces a calculator. |
| **1672–74** | Gottfried Leibniz builds his first calculator, the Stepped Reckoner. |
| **1801** | Joseph-Marie Jacquard develops an automatic loom controlled by punch cards. |
| **1820** | The first mass-produced calculator, the Arithometer, is developed by Charles Thomas de Colmar. |
| **1822** | Charles Babbage completes his first model for the difference engine. |
| **1830s** | Babbage creates the first design for the analytical engine. |
| **1890** | Herman Hollerith develops the punched-card ruler for the US census. |
| **1936** | Alan Turing publishes the mathematical theory of computing. |
| **1938** | Konrad Zuse constructs the first binary calculator, using Boolean algebra. |
| **1939** | US mathematician and physicist J V Atanasoff becomes the first to use electronic means for mechanizing arithmetical operations. |
| **1943** | The Colossus electronic code-breaker is developed at Bletchley Park, England. The Harvard University Mark I or Automatic Sequence Controlled Calculator (partly financed by IBM) becomes the first program-controlled calculator. |
| **1946** | ENIAC (acronym for electronic numerator, integrator, analyser, and computer), the first general purpose, fully electronic digital computer, is completed at the University of Pennsylvania, USA. |
| **1948** | Manchester University (England) Mark I, the first stored-program computer, is completed. William Shockley of Bell Laboratories invents the transistor. |
| **1951** | Launch of Ferranti Mark I, the first commercially produced computer. Whirlwind, the first real-time computer, is built for the US air-defence system. Grace Murray Hopper of Remington Rand invents the compiler computer program. |
| **1952** | EDVAC (acronym for electronic discrete variable computer) is completed at the Institute for Advanced Study, Princeton, USA (by John Von Neumann and others). |
| **1953** | Magnetic core memory is developed. |
| **1958** | The first integrated circuit is constructed. |
| **1963** | The first minicomputer is built by Digital Equipment (DEC). The first electronic calculator is built by Bell Punch Company. |
| **1964** | Launch of IBM System/360, the first compatible family of computers. John Kemeny and Thomas Kurtz of Dartmouth College invent BASIC (Beginner's All-purpose Symbolic Instruction Code). |
| **1965** | The first supercomputer, the Control Data |

| | |
|---|---|
| | CD6600, is developed. |
| **1971** | The first microprocessor, the Intel 4004, is announced. |
| **1974** | CLIP–4, the first computer with a parallel architecture, is developed by John Backus at IBM. |
| **1975** | Altair 8800, the first personal computer (PC), or microcomputer, is launched. |
| **1981** | The Xerox Star system, the first WIMP system (acronym for windows, icons, menus, and pointing devices), is developed. IBM launches the IBM PC. |
| **1984** | Apple launches the Macintosh computer. |
| **1985** | The Inmos T414 transputer, the first 'off-the-shelf' microprocessor for building parallel computers, is announced. |
| **1988** | The first optical microprocessor, which uses light instead of electricity, is developed. |
| **1989** | Wafer-scale silicon memory chips, able to store 200 million characters, are launched. |
| **1990** | Microsoft releases Windows 3, a popular windowing environment for PCs. |
| **1992** | Philips launches the CD-I (Compact-Disc Interactive) player, based on CD audio technology, to provide interactive multimedia programs for the home user. |
| **1993** | Intel launches the Pentium chip containing 3.1 million transistors and capable of 100 MIPs (millions of instructions per second). The Personal Digital Assistant (PDA), which recognizes users' handwriting, goes on sale. |
| **1995** | Intel launches the Pentium Pro microprocessor (formerly codenamed P6). |
| **1996** | IBM's computer Deep Blue beats grand master Garry Kasparov at chess, the first time a computer has beaten a human grand master. |
| **1997** | The US Justice Department rules that Microsoft's bundling of its web browser with its operating system is unfair trading and an attempt to dominate the market. Microsoft is ordered to sell the browser separately to prevent it from building a monopoly. |
| **1997** | A computer employee in Virginia ignores malfunction warnings and causes seven of the world's nine root servers to corrupt all the data sent to them, causing the Internet to break down. Millions of e-mail messages are returned all over the world, prompting speculation about the dangers of the over-centralization of information. |
| **1999** | A computer virus spreads via e-mail to more than 100,000 computers around the world. Named Melissa, it reportedly spreads more widely and quickly than any previous virus. Computer programmer David Smith is arrested in New Jersey and charged with its creation. |

## EARTH SCIENCE: CHRONOLOGY

**1735**   George Hadley describes the circulation of the atmosphere as large-scale convection currents centred on the equator.

**1743**   Christopher Packe produces the first geological map, of southern England.

**1744**   The first map using modern surveying principles is produced by César-François Cassini in France.

**1745**   In Russia, Mikhail Vasilievich Lomonosov publishes a catalogue of over 3,000 minerals.

**1746**   A French expedition to Lapland proves the Earth to be flattened at the poles.

**1760**   Lomonosov explains the formation of icebergs. John Mitchell proposes that earthquakes are produced when one layer of rock rubs against another.

**1766**   The fossilized bones of a huge animal (later called *Mosasaurus*) are found in a quarry near the River Meuse, the Netherlands.

**1776**   James Keir suggests that some rocks, such as those making up the Giant's Causeway in Ireland, may have formed as molten material that cooled and then crystallized.

**1779**   Comte George de Buffon speculates that the Earth may be much older than the 6,000 years suggested by the Bible.

**1785**   James Hutton proposes the theory of uniformitarianism: all geological features are the result of processes that are at work today, acting over long periods of time.

**1786**   Johann von Carpentier describes the European ice age.

**1793**   Jean Baptiste Lamarck argues that fossils are the remains of once-living animals and plants.

**1804**   Jean Biot and Joseph Gay-Lussac study the atmosphere from a hot-air balloon.

**1809**   The first geological survey of the eastern USA is produced by William Maclure.

**1815**   In England, William Smith shows how rock strata (layers) can be identified on the basis of the fossils found in them.

**1822**   In Germany, Friedrich Mohs introduces a scale for specifying mineral hardness.

**1825**   Georges Cuvier proposes his theory of catastrophes as the cause of the extinction of large groups of animals.

**1839**   In the USA, Louis Agassiz describes the motion and laying down of glaciers, confirming the reality of the ice ages.

**1842**   Richard Owen coins the name 'dinosaur' for the reptiles, now extinct, that lived about 175 million years ago.

**1850**   Matthew Fontaine Maury maps the Atlantic Ocean, noting that it is deeper near its edges than at the centre.

**1852**   Edward Sabine in Ireland shows a link between sunspot activity and changes in the Earth's magnetic field.

**1853**   James Coffin describes the three major wind bands that girdle each hemisphere.

**1854**   George Airy calculates the mass of the Earth by measuring gravity at the top and bottom of a coal mine.

**1872**   The beginning of the world's first major oceanographic expedition, the four-year voyage of the *Challenger*.

**1884**   Vladimir Köppen introduces a classification of the world's temperature zones.

**1890**   Arthur Holmes uses radioactivity to date rocks, establishing the Earth to be 4.6 billion years old.

**1895**   In the USA, Jeanette Picard launches the first balloon to be used for stratospheric research.

**1896**   Svante Arrhenius discovers a link between the amount of carbon dioxide in the atmosphere and the global temperature.

**1897**   Jacob Bjerknes and his father Vilhelm develop the mathematical theory of weather forecasting.

**1906**   Richard Dixon Oldham proves the Earth to have a molten core by studying seismic waves.

**1909**   Andrija Mohorovičić discovers a discontinuity in the Earth's crust, about 30 km/18 mi below the surface, that forms the boundary between the crust and the mantle.

**1912**   In Germany, Alfred Wegener proposes the theory of continental drift and the existence of a supercontinent, Pangaea, in the distant past.

**1913**   Charles Fabry discovers the ozone layer in the upper atmosphere.

**1914**   Beno Gutenberg discovers the discontinuity that marks the boundary between the Earth's mantle and the outer core.

**1925**   A German expedition discovers the Mid-Atlantic Ridge by means of sonar. Edward Appleton discovers a layer of the atmosphere that reflects radio waves; it is later named after him.

**1935**   Charles Richter establishes a scale for measuring the magnitude of earthquakes.

**1939**   In Germany, Walter Maurice Elsasser proposes that eddy currents in the molten iron core cause the Earth's magnetism.

**1956**   Bruce Charles Heezen and Maurice Ewing discover a global network of oceanic ridges and rifts that divide the Earth's surface into plates.

**1958**   Using rockets, James Van Allen discovers a belt of radiation (later named after him) around the Earth.

**1960**   The world's first weather satellite, *TIROS 1*, is launched. US geologist Harry Hammond Hess shows that the sea floor spreads out from ocean ridges and descends back into the mantle at deep-sea trenches.

**1963**   Fred Vine and Drummond Matthews analyse the magnetism of rocks in the Atlantic Ocean floor and find conclusive proof of seafloor spreading.

**1985**   A British expedition to the Antarctic discovers a hole in the ozone layer above the South Pole.

**1991**   A borehole in the Kola Peninsula in Arctic Russia, begun in the 1970s, reaches a depth of 12,261 m/40,240 ft (where the temperature is found to be 210°C/410°F).

**1996**   US geophysicists detect a difference between the spinning time of the core and that of the rest of the Earth.

## CINEMA: CHRONOLOGY

**1826–34** Various machines are invented to show moving images: the stroboscope, zoetrope, and thaumatrope.

**1872** Eadweard Muybridge demonstrates movement of horses' legs by using 24 cameras.

**1877** Invention of Praxinoscope; it is developed as a projector of successive images on screen 1879 in France.

**1878–95** Marey, a French physiologist, develops various types of camera for recording human and animal movements.

**1887** Augustin le Prince produces the first series of images on a perforated film; Thomas A Edison, having developed the phonograph, takes the first steps in developing a motion-picture recording and reproducing device to accompany recorded sound.

**1888** William Friese-Greene shows the first celluloid film and patents a movie camera.

**1889** Edison invents 35-mm film.

**1890–94** Edison, using perforated film, develops his Kinetograph camera and Kinetoscope individual viewer; developed commercially in New York, London, and Paris.

**1895** The Lumière brothers project, to a paying audience, a film of an oncoming train arriving at a station. Some of the audience flee in terror.

**1896** Charles Pathé introduces the Berliner gramophone, using discs in synchronization with film. Lack of amplification, however, makes the performances ineffective.

**1899** Edison tries to improve amplification by using banks of phonographs.

**1900** Attempts to synchronize film and disc are made by Leon Gaumont in France and Goldschmidt in Germany, leading later to the Vitaphone system of the USA.

**1902** Georges Méliès makes *Le Voyage dans la lune/A Trip to the Moon*.

**1903** The first Western is made in the USA – *The Great Train Robbery* by Edwin Porter.

**1906** The earliest colour film (Kinemacolor) is patented in Britain by George Albert Smith.

**1907–11** The first films are shot in the Los Angeles area called Hollywood. In France, Émile Cohl (1857–1938) experiments with film animation.

**1910** With the influence of US studios and fan magazines, film actors and actresses begin to become international stars.

**1911** The first Hollywood studio, Horsley's Centaur Film Company, is established, followed in 1915 by Carl Laemmle's Universal City and Thomas Ince's studio.

**1912** In Britain, Eugene Lauste designs experimental 'sound on film' systems.

**1914–18** There is full newsreel coverage of World War I.

**1915** *The Birth of a Nation*, D W Griffith's epic on the American Civil War, is released in the USA.

**1917** 35-mm is officially adopted as the standard format for motion picture film by the Society of Motion Picture Engineers of America.

**1918–19** A sound system called Tri-Ergon is developed in Germany, which leads to sound being recorded on film photographically. Photography with sound is also developed in the USA by Lee De Forest in his Phonofilm system.

**1923** First sound film (as Phonofilm) demonstrated.

**1926** *Don Juan*, a silent film with a synchronized music score, is released.

**1927** Release of the first major sound film, *The Jazz Singer*, consisting of some songs and a few moments of dialogue, by Warner Brothers, New York City. The first Academy Awards (Oscars) are presented.

**1928** Walt Disney releases his first Mickey Mouse cartoon, *Steamboat Willie*. The first all-talking film, *Lights of New York*, is released.

**1930** *The Big Trail*, a Western filmed and shown in 70-mm rather than the standard 35-mm format, is released. 70-mm is still used, mainly for big-budget epics such as *Lawrence of Arabia*.

**1932** The technicolor (three-colour) process is introduced and used for a Walt Disney cartoon film.

**1935** *Becky Sharp*, the first film in three-colour Technicolor, is released.

**1937** Walt Disney releases the first feature-length (82 minutes) cartoon, *Snow White and the Seven Dwarfs*.

**1939** *Gone With the Wind*, regarded as one of Hollywood's greatest achievements, is released.

**1952** Cinerama, a wide-screen presentation using three cameras and three projectors, is introduced in New York.

**1953** Commercial 3-D (three-dimensional) cinema and wide-screen CinemaScope are launched in the USA. CinemaScope uses a single camera and projector to produce a wide-screen effect with an anamorphic lens. The 3-D cameras are clumsy and the audiences dislike wearing the obligatory glasses. The new wide-screen cinema is accompanied by the introduction of Stereographic sound, which eventually becomes standard.

**1959** The first film in Smell-O-Vision, *The Scent of Mystery*, is released. The process does not catch on.

**1980** Most major films are released in Dolby stereo.

**1988** Robert Zemeckis' (1952– ) *Who Framed Roger Rabbit* sets new technical standards in combining live action with animation.

**1995** *Toy Story* becomes the first feature film in which every single frame is generated by computer.

**1997** *Titanic* opens, starring Leonardo DiCaprio and Kate Winslet. The film is reportedly the most expensive film of all time, costing over $250 million to make. It wins 11 Academy Awards.

**1999** *Star Wars Episode 1: The Phantom Menace* opens. A prequel to the original Star Wars trilogy (1977–1983), it contains cutting-edge special effects, including the pod race which became the basis for a PlayStation computer game of the same name.

## MUSIC, WESTERN: CHRONOLOGY

**AD 590** St Gregory the Great is elected pope. Under his rule, music attains new heights, initiating Gregorian chant.

**600s** The system of notation known as 'neumes' is devised, giving the approximate pitch and rhythm of plainchant.

**800s** Early medieval polyphony known as 'organum' consists of two voice parts singing parallel lines.

**1000s** Composers begin using polyphony involving two independent voice parts.

**1026** The Italian monk Guido d'Arezzo completes his treatise *Micrologus.* He founds modern notation and tonic sol-fa.

**1240** The earliest known canon, *Sumer is Icumen In,* is composed around this year.

**1280** *Carmina Burana,* a collection of students' songs, is compiled in Benediktbuern, Bavaria; Carl Orff is later inspired by their subject matter.

**1320** Ars nova, a tract by the French composer Philippe de Vitry, gives its name to a new, more graceful era in music.

**1364** Music's first large-scale masterpiece, the *Notre Dame Mass* of Guillaume de Machaut, is performed in Reims to celebrate the coronation of Charles V of France.

**1473** The earliest known printed music, the *Collectorium super Magnificat* by Johannes Gerson, is published in Esslingen, near Stuttgart, Germany.

**1597** The first opera, *La Dafne* by Jacopo Peri, is staged privately at the Corsi Palazzo in Florence.

**1637** The world's first opera house opens in Venice.

**1721** J S Bach completes his six *Brandenburg Concertos* for Baroque orchestra.

**1722** Jean-Philippe Rameau's book *Traité de l'harmonie* is published, founding modern harmonic theory.

**1725** Antonio Vivaldi's set of four violin concertos *The Four Seasons* is published in Amsterdam.

**1788** Wolfgang Amadeus Mozart completes his last three symphonies, numbers 39–41, in six weeks.

**1805** Ludwig van Beethoven's 'Eroica' Symphony is first performed; it vastly expands the horizons of orchestral music.

**1815** Franz Schubert's output for this year includes two symphonies, two masses, 20 waltzes, and 145 songs.

**1830** Hector Berlioz's dazzlingly avant-garde and programmatic *Symphonie fantastique* startles Paris concertgoers.

**1839** Verdi's first opera, *Oberto,* is produced at La Scala, Milan.

**1854** In Weimar, Germany, Franz Liszt conducts the premieres of his first symphonic poems.

**1865** Richard Wagner's opera *Tristan and Isolde* scales new heights of expressiveness using unprecedented chromaticism. Schubert's *Unfinished Symphony* (1822) is premiered in Vienna.

**1875** The first of a series of collaborations between Arthur Sullivan and the librettist W S Gilbert, *Trial by Jury,* is given its premiere.

**1876** Wagner's *The Ring of the Nibelung* is produced in Bayreuth. Johannes Brahms's *First Symphony* is performed in Karlsruhe.

**1894** Claude Debussy's *Prélude à l'après-midi d'un faune* anticipates 20th-century composition with its use of the whole-tone scale.

**1897** Mahler becomes director of the Vienna Court Opera.

**1911** Irving Berlin has his first big success as a songwriter with 'Alexander's Ragtime Band'.

**1913** Igor Stravinsky's ballet *The Rite of Spring* precipitates a riot at its premiere in Paris.

**1925** Louis Armstrong makes his first jazz records with the Hot Five. Duke Ellington's Washingtonians also starts recording.

**1927** Jerome Kern's *Show Boat,* with libretto by Oscar Hammerstein II, lays the foundations of the US musical.

**1930s** Big-band music becomes popular.

**1940** Walt Disney's *Fantasia* introduces classical music, conducted by Leopold Stokowski, to a worldwide audience of filmgoers.

**1940s** Bebop jazz is initiated. The jazz greats Charlie Parker and Dizzy Gillespie first record together. Big bands, such as those led by Duke Ellington and Glen Miller, reach their height of popularity.

**1942** In Chicago, John Cage conducts the premiere of his *Imaginary Landscape No 3,* scored for marimbula, gongs, tin cans, buzzers, plucked coil, electric oscillator, and generator.

**1954** Edgard Varèse's *Déserts,* the first work to combine instruments and prerecorded magnetic tape, is performed in Paris. Elvis Presley makes his first rock-and-roll recordings in Memphis, Tennesee.

**1955** The Miles Davis Quintet with John Coltrane unites two of the most important innovators in jazz.

**1957** Leonard Bernstein's *West Side Story* is premiered in New York.

**1965** Robert Moog invents a synthesizer that considerably widens the scope of electronic music. Bob Dylan turns to electric instrumentation on *Highway 61 Revisited.*

**1967** The Beatles' album *Sgt Pepper's Lonely Hearts Club Band,* which took over 500 hours to record, is released.

**1972** Bob Marley's LP *Catch a Fire* begins the popularization of reggae beyond Jamaica.

**1976** Punk rock arrives with the Sex Pistols' 'Anarchy in the UK'.

**1983** Olivier Messiaen's only opera, *Saint François d'Assise,* is given its first performance in Paris.

**1998** British composer Harrison Birtwistle's orchestral work *Exody,* completed earlier in the year, is performed at the Proms in London, England.

## PAINTING: CHRONOLOGY OF WESTERN PAINTING

**27000–13000 BC** Cave art in southwest Europe.

**3000–100** Egyptian wall paintings combine front and side views of the human body in a flat 'diagrammatic' style.

**2000–1450** The Minoan civilization, based at Knossos, evolve bright wall paintings.

**1000–400** Greek painting by the finest artists survives mainly as vase decorations.

**330–1453** Byzantine art expresses Orthodox Christian values in formalized mosaics and painted icons.

**680–800** Celtic Christian art illuminated religious texts, such as the *Book of Kells.*

**1290–1337** Italian painting emerges from the Byzantine style with the new depth and realism of Giotto, the first great painter of the Italian Renaissance period.

**1315–1425** Italian Gothic and then International Gothic evolves an elegant and decorative style.

**1420–92** Fra Angelico, Piero della Francesca, and Botticelli bring a new freshness of vision to Italian painting.

**1425–50** A new and vivid realism, owing much to the use of high-quality oil paints, appears in the early Renaissance painters of the North such as Jan van Eyck.

**1470–1569** The Northern Renaissance produces a series of disparate geniuses, including Dürer, Bosch, and Brueghel, who express the religious anxieties of the age.

**1472–1519** Leonardo da Vinci brings a new psychological depth to painting.

**1500–64** Michelangelo rediscovers classical grandeur and harnesses it to Christian subjects as in the Sistine Chapel frescoes.

**1506–94** The Venetian Renaissance is manifested in the warm sensuality of Titian, Giorgione, Tintoretto, and Veronese.

**1520–1600** Mannerists, such as Romano, Pontormo and Parmigianino, apply the discoveries of the High Renaissance in more stylized forms.

**1525–1792** The tradition of portrait painting in Britain begins with Holbein and continues to Reynolds and Gainsborough.

**1560–1609** Caravaggio, a master of dramatic light and shade, leads the way towards the Baroque style.

**1570–1682** The great age of Spanish painting lasts from the tortured religious idealism of El Greco through to Velázquez.

**1577–1640** Rubens is the supreme master of the Baroque grand style.

**1620–70** Dutch genre painting produces masters of portraiture, landscapes, and still life.

**1626–69** Rembrandt brings an unparalled psychological and emotional depth to biblical scenes and portraits.

**1706–1806** The elegance of French rococo is captured by Watteau, Boucher, and Fragonard.

**1780–1851** The Romantic spirit is expressed in the vision of painters such as Goya, Turner, Constable, and Delacroix.

**1780–1867** Ingres and David sustains the classicism of the French revolutionary and post-revolutionary periods.

**1863** Eschewing half-tones and contemporary pictorial conventions, Manet heralds a new era in art.

**1870–90** Symbolists and Pre-Raphaelites portrays visionary ideas through the use of symbols and rich colours.

**1874** Monet, Renoir, and Degas exhibits at the first Impressionist exhibiton with paintings composed of broken surfaces of light.

**1883–1903** Gauguin's spiritual and sensual odyssey to Tahiti looks forward to Expressionism and Fauvism.

**1885–90** Van Gogh's personal vision invests ordinary scenes with unparalleled emotion and spirituality through broad strokes of bright colour.

**1886–1906** Cézanne creates a new kind of painting with solid forms built with a mosaic of brush strokes.

**1892–1926** Munch, and later the Expressionists, uses colour and form to express emotions.

**1907** *Les Demoiselles d'Avignon* by Picasso heralds the Cubist movement by rejecting conventional naturalistic representation from only one viewpoint and conventional ideas of beauty.

**1910** Kandinsky develops a purely abstract art.

**1913–44** A geometrical abstract art is developed by Malevitch, Tatlin, and Mondrian.

**From 1914** Duchamp and the Dadaists bring an anarchist element to painting that questioned traditional notions of art.

**From 1924** Surrealist painters, notably Dali, Magritte and Miró, reach for unconscious sources of inspiration.

**1940s** Abstract Expressionism, developed in New York by Jackson Pollock and Arshile Gorky, adds an element of uninhibited expression to pure abstraction.

**Late 1940s–50s** European post-war anxiety finds expression in the *art brut* of Jean Dubuffet, and the Expressionism of the COBRA group, including Karel Appel.

**Late 1950s–60s** Pop Art returned to representation, drawing on popular images and commercial techniques. Artists includes Richard Hamilton, David Hockney, Jasper Johns, and Andy Warhol.

**From late 50s** The broadly based 'London School' continues the British figurative tradition: Francis Bacon, Frank Auerbach, and Lucien Freud.

**From 1960s** In the USA, super-Realist artists (Malcolm Morley and Richard Estes) strive for a photographic realism. Op art extends the range of abstraction.

**Mid-1970s–80s** In the USA, graffiti, seen as an urban folk art, is exploited by artists such as Keith Haring and Jean-Michel Basquiat.

**Late 1970s–80s** Neo-Expressionism flourishes in Germany (Anselm Keifer and Georg Baselitz), Italy (Francesco Clemente and Enzo Cucchi), and the USA (Julian Schnabel).

**1997** The controversial and provocative *Sensation* exhibition is held at the Royal Acadamy, London. It includes works such as Damien Hirst's 'pickled animal' sculptures, and a portrait of child murderer, Myra Hindley.

## THEATRE: CHRONOLOGY

**c. 3200 BC** Beginnings of Egyptian religious drama, essentially ritualistic.

**c. 600** Choral performances (dithyrambs) in honour of Dionysus formed the beginnings of Greek tragedy, according to Aristotle.

**500–300** Great age of Greek drama which included tragedy, comedy, and satyr plays (grotesque farce).

**468** Sophocles' first victory at the Athens festival. His use of a third actor altered the course of the tragic form.

**458** Aeschylus' *Oresteia* first performed.

**c. 425–388** Comedies of Aristophanes including *The Birds* 414, *Lysistrata* 411, and *The Frogs* 405. In tragedy the importance of the chorus diminished under Euripides, author of *The Bacchae* c. 405.

**c. 320** Menander's 'New Comedy' of social manners developed.

**c. 240 BC–AD 100** Emergence of Roman drama, adapted from Greek originals. Plautus, Terence, and Seneca were the main dramatists.

**c. AD 400** *Kālidāsa's Sakuntalā* marked the height of Sanskrit drama in India.

**c. 1250 –1500** European mystery (or miracle) plays flourished, first in the churches and later in marketplaces, and were performed in England by town guilds.

**c. 1375** *Nō* (Noh) drama developed in Japan.

**c. 1495** *Everyman*, the best known of all the morality plays, was first performed.

**1525– 1750** Italian commedia dell'arte troupes performed popular, improvised comedies; they were to have a large influence on Molière and on English harlequinade and pantomime.

**c. 1576** The first English playhouse, The Theatre, was built by James Burbage in London.

**c. 1587** Christopher Marlowe's play *Tamburlaine the Great* marked the beginning of the great age of Elizabethan and Jacobean drama in England.

**c. 1590– 1612** Shakespeare's greatest plays, including *Hamlet* and *King Lear,* were written.

**1642** An act of Parliament closed all English theatres.

**1660** With the restoration of Charles II to the English throne, dramatic performances recommenced. The first professional actress appeared as Desdemona in Shakespeare's *Othello.*

**1667** Jean Racine's first success, *Andromaque,* was staged.

**1680** The Comédie Française was formed by Louis XIV.

**1737** The Stage Licensing Act in England required all plays to be approved by the Lord Chamberlain before performance.

**1773** In England, Oliver Goldsmith's *She Stoops to Conquer* and Richard Sheridan's *The Rivals* 1775 established the 'comedy of manners'.

**1830** Victor Hugo's *Hernani* caused riots in Paris. His work marked the beginning of a new Romantic drama.

**1879** Henrik Ibsen's *A Doll's House,* an early example of realism in European theatre.

**1893** George Bernard Shaw wrote *Mrs Warren's Profession* (banned until 1902 because it deals with prostitution).

**1895** Oscar Wilde's comedy *The Importance of Being Earnest.*

**1896** The first performance of Anton Chekhov's *The Seagull* failed. Alfred Jarry's *Ubu Roi,* a forerunner of Surrealism, was produced in Paris.

**1920** *Beyond the Horizon,* Eugene O'Neill's first play, marked the beginning of serious theatre in the USA.

**1921** Luigi Pirandello's *Six Characters in Search of an Author.*

**1928** Bertolt Brecht's *Die Dreigroschenoper/The Threepenny Opera* with score by Kurt Weill; other political satires by Karel Čapek and Elmer Rice.

**1930s** US social-protest plays of Clifford Odets, Lillian Hellman, Thornton Wilder, and William Saroyan.

**1944** Jean-Paul Sartre's *Huis Clos/In Camera;* Jean Anouilh's *Antigone.*

**post-1945** Resurgence of German-language theatre, including Wolfgang Borchert, Max Frisch, Friedrich Dürrenmatt, and Peter Weiss.

**1947** Tennessee Williams' *A Streetcar Named Desire.* First Edinburgh Festival, Scotland, with fringe theatre events.

**1949** Bertolt Brecht and Helene Weigel founded the Berliner Ensemble in East Germany.

**1953** Arthur Miller's *The Crucible* opened in the USA; *En attendant Godot/Waiting for Godot* by Samuel Beckett exemplified the Theatre of the Absurd.

**1956** The English Stage Company was formed at the Royal Court Theatre to provide a platform for new dramatists. John Osborne's *Look Back in Anger* was included in its first season.

**1960s** Off-off-Broadway theatre, a more daring and experimental type of drama, began to develop in New York. Fringe theatre developed in Britain.

**1961** The Royal Shakespeare Company was formed in the UK under the directorship of Peter Hall.

**1963–64** The UK National Theatre Company was formed at the Old Vic under the directorship of Laurence Olivier.

**1967** Athol Fugard founded the Serpent Players as an integrated company in Port Elizabeth, South Africa; Tom Stoppard's *Rosencrantz and Guildenstern are Dead* was produced in London.

**1970** Peter Brook founded his international company, the International Centre for Theatre Research, in Paris; first festival of Chicano theatre in the USA.

**1980** Howard Brenton's *The Romans in Britain* led in the UK to a private prosecution of the director for obscenity.

**1993** Construction of the new Globe Theatre, a replica of the Elizabethan Globe Playhouse, began in London, near the site of the original Globe.

**1996** The Prologue Season at the new Globe Theatre in London opened with *The Two Gentlemen of Verona.*

## IMPERIAL AND METRIC CONVERSION FACTORS

| To convert from imperial to metric | Multiply by | Multiply by | To convert from metric to imperial |
|---|---|---|---|
| *Length* | | | |
| inches | 25.4 | 0.0393701 | millimetres |
| feet | 0.3048 | 3.28084 | metres |
| yards | 0.9144 | 1.09361 | metres |
| furlongs | 0.201168 | 4.97097 | kilometres |
| miles | 1.609344 | 0.621371 | kilometres |
| *Area* | | | |
| square inches | 6.4516 | 0.1550 | square centimetres |
| square feet | 0.092903 | 10.7639 | square metres |
| square yards | 0.836127 | 1.19599 | square metres |
| square miles | 2.589988 | 0.386102 | square kilometres |
| acres | 4046.856422 | 0.000247 | square metres |
| acres | 0.404685 | 2.471054 | hectares |
| *Volume/capacity* | | | |
| cubic inches | 16.387064 | 0.061024 | cubic centimetres |
| cubic feet | 0.028317 | 35.3147 | cubic metres |
| cubic yards | 0.764555 | 1.30795 | cubic metres |
| cubic miles | 4.1682 | 0.239912 | cubic kilometres |
| fluid ounces (imperial) | 28.413063 | 0.035195 | millilitres |
| fluid ounces (US) | 29.5735 | 0.033814 | millilitres |
| pints (imperial) | 0.568261 | 1.759754 | litres |
| pints (US) | 0.473176 | 2.113377 | litres |
| quarts (imperial) | 1.136523 | 0.879877 | litres |
| quarts (US) | 0.946353 | 1.056688 | litres |
| gallons (imperial) | 4.54609 | 0.219969 | litres |
| gallons (US) | 3.785412 | 0.364172 | litres |
| *Mass/weight* | | | |
| ounces | 28.349523 | 0.035274 | grams |
| pounds | 0.453592 | 2.20462 | kilograms |
| stone (14 lb) | 6.350293 | 0.157473 | kilograms |
| tons (imperial) | 1016.046909 | 0.000984 | kilograms |
| tons (US) | 907.18474 | 0.001102 | kilograms |
| tons (imperial) | 1.016047 | 0.984207 | metric tonnes |
| tons (US) | 0.907185 | 1.10231 | metric tonnes |
| *Speed* | | | |
| miles per hour | 1.609344 | 0.621371 | kilometres per hour |
| feet per second | 0.3048 | 3.28084 | metres per second |
| *Force* | | | |
| pound-force | 4.44822 | 0.224809 | newton |
| kilogram-force | 9.80665 | 0.101972 | newton |
| *Pressure* | | | |
| pound-force per square inch | 6.89476 | 0.145038 | kilopascals |
| tons-force per square inch (imperial) | 15.4443 | 0.064779 | megapascals |
| atmospheres | 10.1325 | 0.098692 | newtons per square centimetre |
| atmospheres | 14.695942 | 0.068948 | pound-force per square inch |
| *Energy* | | | |
| calorie | 4.1868 | 0.238846 | joule |
| watt hour | 3,600 | 0.000278 | joule |
| *Power* | | | |
| horsepower | 0.7457 | 1.34102 | kilowatts |
| *Fuel consumption* | | | |
| miles per gallon (imperial) | 0.3540 | 2.824859 | kilometres per litre |
| miles per gallon (US) | 0.4251 | 2.3521 | kilometres per litre |
| gallons per mile (imperial) | 2.824859 | 0.3540 | litres per kilometre |
| gallons per mile (US) | 2.3521 | 0.4251 | litres per kilometre |

## SI UNITS

(French *Système International d'Unités*) A standard system of scientific units used by scientists worldwide. Originally proposed in 1960, it replaces the mks (metre, kilogram, second), cgs (centimetre, gram, second), and fps (foot, pound, second) systems. It is based on seven basic units: the metre (m) for length, kilogram (kg) for mass, second (s) for time, ampere (A) for electrical current, kelvin (K) for temperature, mole (mol) for amount of substance, and candela (cd) for luminosity.

| Quantity | SI unit | Symbol |
|---|---|---|
| absorbed radiation dose | gray | Gy |
| amount of substance | mole[1] | mol |
| electric capacitance | farad | F |
| electric charge | coulomb | C |
| electric conductance | siemens | S |
| electric current | ampere[1] | A |
| energy or work | joule | J |
| force | newton | N |
| frequency | hertz | Hz |
| illuminance | lux | lx |
| inductance | henry | H |
| length | metre[1] | m |
| luminous flux | lumen | lm |

| Quantity | SI unit | Symbol |
|---|---|---|
| luminous intensity | candela[1] | cd |
| magnetic flux | weber | Wb |
| magnetic flux density | tesla | T |
| mass | kilogram[1] | kg |
| plane angle | radian | rad |
| potential difference | volt | V |
| power | watt | W |
| pressure | pascal | Pa |
| radiation dose equivalent | sievert | Sv |
| radiation exposure | roentgen | R |
| radioactivity | becquerel | Bq |
| resistance | ohm | Ω |
| solid angle | steradian | sr |

[1]SI base unit.

## PHYSICAL CONSTANTS

Physical constants, or fundamental constants, are standardized values whose parameters do not change.

| Constant | Symbol | Value in SI units |
|---|---|---|
| acceleration of free fall | $g$ | $9.80665$ m s$^{-2}$ |
| Avogadro's constant | $N_A$ | $6.0221367 \times 10^{23}$ mol$^{-1}$ |
| Boltzmann's constant | $k$ | $1.380658 \times 10^{-23}$ J K$^{-1}$ |
| elementary charge | $e$ | $1.60217733 \times 10^{-19}$ C |
| electronic rest mass | $m_e$ | $9.1093897 \times 10^{-31}$ kg |
| Faraday's constant | $F$ | $9.6485309 \times 10^{4}$ C mol$^{-1}$ |
| gas constant | $R$ | $8.314510$ J K$^{-1}$ mol$^{-1}$ |
| gravitational constant | $G$ | $6.672 \times 10^{-11}$ N m$^2$ kg$^{-2}$ |
| Loschmidt's number | $N_L$ | $2.686763 \times 10^{25}$ m$^{-3}$ |
| neutron rest mass | $m_n$ | $1.6749286 \times 10^{-27}$ kg |
| Planck's constant | $h$ | $6.6260755 \times 10^{-34}$ J s |
| proton rest mass | $m_p$ | $1.6726231 \times 10^{-27}$ kg |
| speed of light in a vacuum | $c$ | $2.99792458 \times 10^{8}$ m s$^{-1}$ |
| standard atmosphere | atm | $1.01325 \times 10^{5}$ Pa |
| Stefan–Boltzmann constant | $\sigma$ | $5.67051 \times 10^{-8}$ W m$^{-2}$ K$^{-4}$ |

## MISCELLANEOUS UNITS

| Unit | Definition |
|---|---|
| acoustic ohm | cgs unit of acoustic impedance (the ratio of sound pressure on a surface to sound flux through the surface) |
| acre | traditional English land measure; 1 acre = 4,480 sq yd (4,047 sq m or 0.4047 ha) |
| acre-foot | unit sometimes used to measure large volumes of water such as reservoirs; 1 acre-foot = 1,233.5 cu m/43,560 cu ft |
| astronomical unit | unit (symbol AU) equal to the mean distance of the Earth from the Sun: 149,597,870 km/92,955,808 mi |
| atmosphere | unit of pressure (abbreviation atm); 1 standard atmosphere = 101,325 Pa |
| barn | unit of area, especially the cross-sectional area of an atomic nucleus; 1 barn = $10^{-28}$ sq m |
| barrel | unit of liquid capacity; the volume of a barrel depends on the liquid being measured and the country and state laws. In the USA, 1 barrel of oil = 42 gal (159 l/34.97 imperial gal), but for federal taxing of fermented liquor (such as beer), 1 barrel = 31 gal (117.35 l/25.81 imperial gal). Many states fix a 36-gallon barrel for cistern measurement and federal law uses a 40-gallon barrel to measure 'proof spirits'. 1 barrel of beer in the UK = 163.66 l (43.23 US gal/36 imperial gal) |
| base box | imperial unit of area used in metal plating; 1 base box = 20.232 sq m/31,360 sq in |
| baud | unit of electrical signalling speed equal to 1 pulse per second |
| brewster | unit (symbol B) for measuring reaction of optical materials to stress |
| British thermal unit | imperial unit of heat (symbol Btu); 1 Btu = approximately 1,055 J |

| Unit | Definition |
|---|---|
| bushel | measure of dry and (in the UK) liquid volume. 1 bushel (struck measure) = 8 dry US gallons (64 dry US pt/35.239 l/2,150.42 cu in). 1 heaped US bushel = 1,278 bushels, struck measure (81.78 dry pt/45.027 l/2,747.715 cu in), often referred to a $1\frac{1}{4}$ bushels, struck measure. In the UK, 1 bushel = 8 imperial gallons (64 imperial pt); 1 UK bushel = 1.03 US bushels |
| cable | unit of length used on ships, taken as $\frac{1}{10}$ of a nautical mile (185.2 m/607.6 ft) |
| calorie | cgs unit of heat, now replaced by the joule; 1 calorie = 4.1868 J |
| carat | unit for measuring mass of precious stones; 1 carat = 0.2 g/0.00705 oz |
| carat | unit of purity in gold; pure gold is 24-carat |
| carcel | obsolete unit of luminous intensity |
| cental | name for the short hundredweight; 1 cental = 45.36 kg/100 lb |
| chaldron | obsolete unit measuring capacity; 1 chaldron = 1.309 cu m/46.237 cu ft |
| clausius | in engineering, a unit of entropy; defined as the ratio of energy to temperature above absolute zero |
| cleanliness unit | unit for measuring air pollution; equal to the number of particles greater than 0.5 μm in diameter per cu ft of air |
| clo | unit of thermal insulation of clothing; standard clothes have insulation of about 1 clo, the warmest have about 4 clo per 2.5 cm/1 in of thickness |
| clusec | unit for measuring the power of a vacuum pump |
| condensation number | in physics, the ratio of the number of molecules condensing on a surface to the number of molecules touching that surface |
| cord | unit for measuring the volume of wood cut for fuel; 1 cord = 3.62 cu m/128 cu ft, or a stack 2.4 m/8 ft long, 1.2 m/4 ft wide and 1.2 m/4 ft high |
| crith | unit of mass for weighing gases; 1 crith = the mass of 1 litre of hydrogen gas at standard temperature and pressure |
| cubit | earliest known unit of length; 1 cubit = approximately 45.7 cm/18 in, the length of the human forearm from the tip of the middle finger to the elbow |
| curie | former unit of radioactivity (symbol Ci); 1 curie = $3.7 \times 10^{10}$ becquerels |
| dalton | international atomic mass unit, equivalent to $\frac{1}{12}$ of the mass of a neutral carbon-12 atom |
| darcy | cgs unit (symbol D) of permeability, used mainly in geology to describe the permeability of rock |
| darwin | unit of measurement of evolutionary rate of change |
| decontamination factor | unit measuring the effectiveness of radiological decontamination; the ratio of original contamination to the radiation remaining |
| demal | unit measuring concentration; 1 demal = 1 gram-equivalent of solute in 1 cu dm of solvent |
| denier | unit used to measure the fineness of yarns; 9,000 m of 15 denier nylon weighs 15 g/0.5 oz |
| dioptre | optical unit measuring the power of a lens; the reciprocal of the focal length in metres |
| dram | unit of apothecaries' measure; 1 dram = 60 grains/3.888 g |
| dyne | cgs unit of force; $10^5$ dynes = 1 N |
| einstein unit | unit for measuring photoenergy in atomic physics |
| eotvos unit | unit (symbol E) for measuring small changes in the intensity of the Earth's gravity with horizontal distance |
| erg | cgs unit of work; equal to the work done by a force of 1 dyne moving through 1 cm |
| erlang | unit for measuring telephone traffic intensity; for example, 90 minutes of carried traffic measured over 60 minutes = 1.5 erlangs ('carried traffic' refers to the total duration of completed calls made within a specified period) |
| fathom | unit of depth measurement in mining and seafaring; 1 fathom = 1.83 m/6 ft |
| finsen unit | unit (symbol FU) for measuring intensity of ultraviolet light |
| fluid ounce | measure of capacity; equivalent in the USA to $\frac{1}{16}$ of a pint ($\frac{1}{20}$ of a pint in the UK and Canada) |
| foot | imperial unit of length (symbol ft), equivalent to 0.3048 m |
| foot-candle | unit of illuminance, replaced by the lux; 1 foot-candle = 10.76391 lux |
| foot-pound | imperial unit of energy (symbol ft-lb); 1 ft-lb = 1.356 joule |
| frigorie | unit (symbol fg) used in refrigeration engineering to measure heat energy, equal to a rate of heat extraction of 1 kilocalorie per hour |
| furlong | unit of measurement, originating in Anglo-Saxon England, equivalent to 201.168 m/220 yd |
| galileo | unit (symbol Gal) of acceleration; 1 galileo = $10^{-2}$ m s$^{-2}$ |
| gallon | imperial liquid or dry measure subdivided into 4 quarts or 8 pints; 1 US gal = 3.785 l; 1 imperial gal = 4.546 l |
| gauss | cgs unit (symbol) of magnetic flux density, replaced by the tesla; 1 gauss = $1 \times 10^{-4}$ tesla |
| gill | imperial unit of volume for liquid measure; equal to $\frac{1}{4}$ of a pint (in the USA, 4 fl oz/0.118 l; in the UK, 5 fl oz/0.142 l) |
| grain | smallest unit of mass in the three English systems of measurement (avoirdupois, troy, apothecaries' weights) used in the UK and USA; 1 grain = 0.0648 g |

| Unit | Definition |
| --- | --- |
| hand | unit used in measuring the height of a horse from front hoof to shoulder (withers); 1 hand = 10.2 cm/4 in |
| hardness number | unit measuring hardness of materials. There are many different hardness scales: Brinell, Rockwell, and Vickers scales measure the degree of indentation or impression of materials; Mohs' scale measures resistance to scratching against a standard set of minerals |
| hartree | atomic unit of energy, equivalent to atomic unit of charge divided by atomic unit of length; 1 hartree = $4.850 \times 10^{-18}$ J |
| haze factor | unit of visibility in mist or fog; the ratio of brightness of mist compared with that of the object |
| Hehner number | unit measuring concentration of fatty acids in oils; a Hehner number of 1 = 1 kg of fatty acid in 100 kg of oil or fat |
| hide | unit of measurement used in the 12th century to measure land; 1 hide = 60–120 acres/25–50 ha |
| horsepower | imperial unit (abbreviation hp) of power; 1 horsepower = 746 W |
| hundredweight | imperial unit (abbreviation cwt) of mass; 1 cwt = 45.36 kg/100 lb in the USA and 50.80 kg/112 lb in the UK |
| inch | imperial unit (abbreviation in) of linear measure, $\frac{1}{12}$ of a ft; 1 in = 2.54 cm |
| inferno | unit used in astrophysics for describing the temperature inside a star; 1 inferno = 1 billion K (degrees Kelvin) |
| iodine number | unit measuring the percentage of iodine absorbed in a substance, expressed as grams of iodine absorbed by 100 grams of material |
| jansky | unit used in radio astronomy to measure radio emissions or flux densities from space; 1 jansky = $10^{-26}$ W m$^{-2}$ Hz$^{-1}$. Flux density is the energy in a beam of radiation which passes through an area normal to the beam in a single unit of time. A jansky is a measurement of the energy received from a cosmic radio source per unit area of detector in a single time unit |
| kayser | unit used in spectroscopy to measure wave number (number of waves in a unit length); a wavelength of 1 cm has a wave number of 1 kayser |
| knot | unit used in navigation to measure a ship's speed; 1 knot = 1 nautical mile per hour, or about 1.15 miles per hour |
| league | obsolete imperial unit of length; 1 league = 3 nautical mi/5.56 km or 3 statute mi/4.83 km |
| light year | unit used in astronomy to measure distance; the distance travelled by light in one year, approximately $9.46 \times 10^{12}$ km/$5.88 \times 10^{12}$ mi |
| mache | obsolete unit of radioactive concentration; 1 mache = $3.7 \times 10^{-7}$ curies of radioactive material per cu m of a medium |
| maxwell | cgs unit (symbol Mx) of magnetic flux, the strength of a magnetic field in an area multiplied by the area; 1 maxwell = $10^{-8}$ weber |
| megaton | measurement of the explosive power of a nuclear weapon; 1 megaton = 1 million tons of trinitrotoluene (TNT) |
| mil | (a) one-thousandth of a litre; contraction of the word millilitre; (b) imperial measure of length, equal to one-thousandth of an inch; also known as the thou |
| mile | imperial unit of linear measure; 1 statute mile = 1.60934 km/5,280 ft; 1 international nautical mile = 1.852 km/6,076 ft |
| millimetre of mercury | unit of pressure (symbol mmHg) used in medicine for measuring blood pressure |
| morgan | arbitrary unit used in genetics; 1 morgan is the distance along the chromosome in a gene that gives a recombination frequency of 1% |
| nautical mile | unit of distance used in navigation, equal to the average length of 1 minute of arc on a great circle of the Earth; 1 international nautical mile = 1.852 km/6,076 ft |
| neper | unit used in telecommunications; gives the attenuation of amplitudes of currents or powers as the natural logarithm of the ratio of the voltage between two points or the current between two points |
| oersted | cgs unit (symbol Oe) of magnetic field strength, now replaced by amperes per metre (1 Oe = 79.58 amp per m) |
| ounce | unit of mass, $\frac{1}{16}$ of a pound avoirdupois, equal to 437.5 grains/28.35 g; or 14.6 pound troy, equal to 480 grains/31.10 g |
| parsec | unit (symbol pc) used in astronomy for distances to stars and galaxies; 1 pc = 3.262 light years, $2.063 \times 10^5$ astronomical units, or $3.086 \times 10^{13}$ km |
| peck | obsolete unit of dry measure, equal to 8 imperial quarts or 1 quarter bushel (8.1 l in the USA or 9.1 l in the UK) |
| pennyweight | imperial unit of mass; 1 pennyweight = 24 grains = $1.555 \times 10^{-3}$ kg |
| perch | obsolete imperial unit of length; 1 perch = $5\frac{1}{2}$ yards = 5.029 m, also called the rod or pole |
| pint | imperial unit of liquid or dry measure; in the USA, 1 liquid pint = 16 fl oz/0.473 l, while 1 dry pint = 0.551 l; in the UK, 1 pt = 20 fl oz, $\frac{1}{2}$ quart, $\frac{1}{8}$ gal, or 0.568 l |
| point | metric unit of mass used in relation to gemstones; 1 point = 0.01 metric carat = $2 \times 10^{-3}$ g |
| poise | cgs unit of dynamic viscosity; 1 poise = 1 dyne-second per sq cm |
| pound | imperial unit (abbreviation lb) of mass; the avoirdupois pound or imperial standard |

| Unit | Definition |
|---|---|
| | pound = 0.45 kg/7,000 grains, while the pound troy (used for weighing precious metals) = 0.37 kg/5,760 grains |
| poundal | imperial unit (abbreviation pdl) of force; 1 poundal = 0.1383 newton |
| quart | imperial liquid or dry measure; in the USA, 1 liquid quart = 0.946 l, while 1 dry quart = 1.101 l; in the UK, 1 quart = 2 pt/1.137 l |
| rad | unit of absorbed radiation dose, replaced in the SI system by the gray; 1 rad = 0.01 joule of radiation absorbed by 1 kg of matter |
| relative biological effectiveness | relative damage caused to living tissue by different types of radiation |
| roentgen | unit (symbol R) of radiation exposure, used for X- and gamma rays |
| rood | imperial unit of area; 1 rood = $\frac{1}{4}$ acre = 1,011.7 sq m |
| rydberg | atomic unit of energy; 1 rydberg = $2.425 \times 10^{-18}$ J |
| sabin | unit of sound absorption, used in acoustical engineering; 1 sabin = absorption of 1 sq ft (0.093 sq m) of a perfectly absorbing surface |
| scruple | imperial unit of apothecaries' measure; 1 scruple = 20 grains = $1.3 \times 10^{-3}$ kg |
| shackle | unit of length used at sea for measuring cable or chain; 1 shackle = 15 fathoms (90 ft/27 m) |
| slug | obsolete imperial unit of mass; 1 slug = 14.59 kg/32.17 lb |
| snellen | unit expressing the visual power of the eye |
| sone | unit of subjective loudness |
| standard volume | in physics, the volume occupied by 1 kilogram molecule (molecular mass in kilograms) of any gas at standard temperature and pressure; approximately 22.414 cu m |
| stokes | cgs unit (symbol St) of kinematic viscosity; 1 stokes = $10^{-4}$ m$^2$ s$^{-1}$ |
| stone | imperial unit (abbreviation st) of mass; 1 stone = 6.35 kg/14 lb |
| strontium unit | measures concentration of strontium-90 in an organic medium relative to the concentration of calcium |
| tex | metric unit of line density; 1 tex is the line density of a thread with a mass of 1 gram and a length of 1 kilometre |
| tog | measure of thermal insulation of a fabric, garment, or quilt; the tog value is equivalent to 10 times the temperature difference (in °C) between the two faces of the article, when the flow of heat across it is equal to 1 W per sq m |
| tonne | 1 unit of mass; the long ton (UK) = 1,016 kg/2,240 lb; 1 short ton (USA) = 907 kg/2,000 lb; 1 metric tonne = 1000 kg/2205 lb |
| yard | imperial unit (symbol yd) of length, equivalent to 0.9144 m/3 ft |

## TABLE OF EQUIVALENT TEMPERATURES

Celsius and Fahrenheit temperatures can be interconverted as follows: $C = (F - 32) \times 100/180$; $F = (C \times 180/100) + 32$.

| °C | °F | °C | °F | °C | °F | °C | °F |
|---|---|---|---|---|---|---|---|
| 100 | 212.0 | 70 | 158.0 | 40 | 104.0 | 10 | 50.0 |
| 99 | 210.2 | 69 | 156.2 | 39 | 102.2 | 9 | 48.2 |
| 98 | 208.4 | 68 | 154.4 | 38 | 100.4 | 8 | 46.4 |
| 97 | 206.6 | 67 | 152.6 | 37 | 98.6 | 7 | 44.6 |
| 96 | 204.8 | 66 | 150.8 | 36 | 96.8 | 6 | 42.8 |
| 95 | 203.0 | 65 | 149.0 | 35 | 95.0 | 5 | 41.0 |
| 94 | 201.2 | 64 | 147.2 | 34 | 93.2 | 4 | 39.2 |
| 93 | 199.4 | 63 | 145.4 | 33 | 91.4 | 3 | 37.4 |
| 92 | 197.6 | 62 | 143.6 | 32 | 89.6 | 2 | 35.6 |
| 91 | 195.8 | 61 | 141.8 | 31 | 87.8 | 1 | 33.8 |
| 90 | 194.0 | 60 | 140.0 | 30 | 86.0 | 0 | 32.0 |
| 89 | 192.2 | 59 | 138.2 | 29 | 84.2 | −1 | 30.2 |
| 88 | 190.4 | 58 | 136.4 | 28 | 82.4 | −2 | 28.4 |
| 87 | 188.6 | 57 | 134.6 | 27 | 80.6 | −3 | 26.6 |
| 86 | 186.8 | 56 | 132.8 | 26 | 78.8 | −4 | 24.8 |
| 85 | 185.0 | 55 | 131.0 | 25 | 77.0 | −5 | 23.0 |
| 84 | 183.2 | 54 | 129.2 | 24 | 75.2 | −6 | 21.2 |
| 83 | 181.4 | 53 | 127.4 | 23 | 73.4 | −7 | 19.4 |
| 82 | 179.6 | 52 | 125.6 | 22 | 71.6 | −8 | 17.6 |
| 81 | 177.8 | 51 | 123.8 | 21 | 69.8 | −9 | 15.8 |
| 80 | 176.0 | 50 | 122.0 | 20 | 68.0 | −10 | 14.0 |
| 79 | 174.2 | 49 | 120.2 | 19 | 66.2 | −11 | 12.2 |
| 78 | 172.4 | 48 | 118.4 | 18 | 64.4 | −12 | 10.4 |
| 77 | 170.6 | 47 | 116.6 | 17 | 62.6 | −13 | 8.6 |
| 76 | 168.8 | 46 | 114.8 | 16 | 60.8 | −14 | 6.8 |
| 75 | 167.0 | 45 | 113.0 | 15 | 59.0 | −15 | 5.0 |
| 74 | 165.2 | 44 | 111.2 | 14 | 57.2 | −16 | 3.2 |
| 73 | 163.4 | 43 | 109.4 | 13 | 55.4 | −17 | 1.4 |
| 72 | 161.6 | 42 | 107.6 | 12 | 53.6 | −18 | −0.4 |
| 71 | 159.8 | 41 | 105.8 | 11 | 51.8 | −19 | −2.2 |

## TIME ZONES AND RELATIVE TIMES IN CITIES THROUGHOUT THE WORLD

The surface of the Earth is divided into 24 time zones. Each zone represents 15° of longitude or 1 hour of time. Countries to the east of London and the Greenwich meridian are ahead of Greenwich Mean Time (GMT) and countries to the west are behind. The time indicated in the table below is fixed by law and is called standard time. Use of daylight saving time (such as British Summer Time) varies widely. At 12:00 noon, GMT, the standard time elsewhere around the world is as follows:

| City | Time | City | Time |
|---|---|---|---|
| Abu Dhabi, United Arab Emirates | 16:00 | Jakarta, Indonesia | 19:00 |
| Accra, Ghana | 12:00 | Jerusalem, Israel | 14:00 |
| Addis Ababa, Ethiopia | 15:00 | Johannesburg, South Africa | 14:00 |
| Adelaide, Australia | 21:30 | Karachi, Pakistan | 17:00 |
| Alexandria, Egypt | 14:00 | Kiev, Ukraine | 14:00 |
| Algiers, Algeria | 13:00 | Kuala Lumpur, Malaysia | 20:00 |
| Al Manamah (also called Bahrain), Bahrain | 15:00 | Kuwait City, Kuwait | 15:00 |
| Amman, Jordan | 14:00 | Kyoto, Japan | 21:00 |
| Amsterdam, Netherlands | 13:00 | Lagos, Nigeria | 13:00 |
| Anchorage (AK), USA | 03:00 | Le Havre, France | 13:00 |
| Ankara, Turkey | 14:00 | Lima, Peru | 07:00 |
| Athens, Greece | 14:00 | Lisbon, Portugal | 12:00 |
| Auckland, New Zealand | 24:00 | London, England | 12:00 |
| Baghdad, Iraq | 15:00 | Luanda, Angola | 13:00 |
| Bahrain (also called Al Manamah), Bahrain | 15:00 | Luxembourg, Luxembourg | 13:00 |
| Bangkok, Thailand | 19:00 | Lyon, France | 13:00 |
| Barcelona, Spain | 13:00 | Madrid, Spain | 13:00 |
| Beijing, China | 20:00 | Manila, Philippines | 20:00 |
| Beirut, Lebanon | 14:00 | Marseille, France | 13:00 |
| Belgrade, Yugoslavia | 13:00 | Mecca, Saudi Arabia | 15:00 |
| Berlin, Germany | 13:00 | Melbourne, Australia | 22:00 |
| Bern, Switzerland | 13:00 | Mexico City, Mexico | 06:00 |
| Bogotá, Colombia | 07:00 | Milan, Italy | 13:00 |
| Bombay, India | 17:30 | Minsk, Belarus | 14:00 |
| Bonn, Germany | 13:00 | Monrovia, Liberia | 12:00 |
| Brazzaville, Republic of the Congo | 13:00 | Montevideo, Uruguay | 09:00 |
| Brisbane, Australia | 22:00 | Montréal, Canada | 07:00 |
| Brussels, Belgium | 13:00 | Moscow, Russian Federation | 15:00 |
| Bucharest, Romania | 14:00 | Munich, Germany | 13:00 |
| Budapest, Hungary | 13:00 | Nairobi, Kenya | 15:00 |
| Buenos Aires, Argentina | 09:00 | New Orleans (LA), USA | 06:00 |
| Cairo, Egypt | 14:00 | New York (NY), USA | 07:00 |
| Calcutta, India | 17:30 | Nicosia, Cyprus | 14:00 |
| Canberra, Australia | 22:00 | Oslo, Norway | 13:00 |
| Cape Town, South Africa | 14:00 | Ottawa, Canada | 07:00 |
| Caracas, Venezuela | 08:00 | Panamá, Panama | 07:00 |
| Casablanca, Morocco | 12:00 | Paris, France | 13:00 |
| Chennai (formerly Madras), India | 17:30 | Perth, Australia | 20:00 |
| Chicago (IL), USA | 06:00 | Port Said, Egypt | 14:00 |
| Cologne, Germany | 13:00 | Prague, Czech Republic | 13:00 |
| Colombo, Sri Lanka | 18:00 | Rawalpindi, Pakistan | 17:00 |
| Copenhagen, Denmark | 13:00 | Reykjavík, Iceland | 12:00 |
| Damascus, Syria | 14:00 | Rio de Janeiro, Brazil | 09:00 |
| Dar es Salaam, Tanzania | 15:00 | Riyadh, Saudi Arabia | 15:00 |
| Darwin, Australia | 21:30 | Rome, Italy | 13:00 |
| Delhi, India | 17:30 | San Francisco (CA), USA | 04:00 |
| Denver (CO), USA | 05:00 | Santiago, Chile | 08:00 |
| Dhaka, Bangladesh | 18:00 | Seoul, South Korea | 21:00 |
| Dubai, United Arab Emirates | 16:00 | Shanghai, China | 20:00 |
| Dublin, Republic of Ireland | 12:00 | Singapore City, Singapore | 20:00 |
| Florence, Italy | 13:00 | Sofia, Bulgaria | 14:00 |
| Frankfurt am Main, Germany | 13:00 | St Petersburg, Russian Federation | 15:00 |
| Gdańsk, Poland | 13:00 | Stockholm, Sweden | 13:00 |
| Geneva, Switzerland | 13:00 | Sydney, Australia | 22:00 |
| Gibraltar | 13:00 | Taipei, Taiwan | 20:00 |
| Hague, The, Netherlands | 13:00 | Tashkent, Uzbekistan | 17:00 |
| Harare, Zimbabwe | 14:00 | Tehran, Iran | 15:30 |
| Havana, Cuba | 07:00 | Tel Aviv-Yafo, Israel | 14:00 |
| Helsinki, Finland | 14:00 | Tenerife, Canary Islands | 12:00 |
| Hobart, Australia | 22:00 | Tokyo, Japan | 21:00 |
| Ho Chi Minh City, Vietnam | 19:00 | Toronto, Canada | 07:00 |
| Hong Kong, China | 20:00 | Tripoli, Libya | 13:00 |
| Istanbul, Turkey | 14:00 | Tunis, Tunisia | 13:00 |

| City | Time | City | Time |
|------|------|------|------|
| Valparaiso, Chile | 08:00 | Warsaw, Poland | 13:00 |
| Vancouver, Canada | 04:00 | Wellington, New Zealand | 24:00 |
| Vatican City | 13:00 | Yangon (formerly Rangoon), Myanmar | 18:30 |
| Venice, Italy | 13:00 | Yokohama, Japan | 21:00 |
| Vienna, Austria | 13:00 | Zagreb, Croatia | 13:00 |
| Vladivostok, Russian Federation | 22:00 | Zürich, Switzerland | 13:00 |
| Volgograd, Russian Federation | 16:00 | | |

## LARGEST COUNTRIES BY POPULATION SIZE

Source: United Nations Population Division, Department of Economic and Social Affairs

Countries with a population of over 100 million, 1998 and 2050.

| Rank | Country | Population (millions) | % of world population | Rank | Country | Population (millions) | % of world population |
|------|---------|----------------------|----------------------|------|---------|----------------------|----------------------|
| **1998** | | | | 4 | Pakistan | 346 | 3.88 |
| 1 | China | 1,256 | 21.28 | 5 | Indonesia | 312 | 3.50 |
| 2 | India | 982 | 16.64 | 6 | Nigeria | 244 | 2.73 |
| 3 | United States | 274 | 4.64 | 7 | Brazil | 244 | 2.73 |
| 4 | Indonesia | 206 | 3.49 | 8 | Bangladesh | 213 | 2.39 |
| 5 | Brazil | 166 | 2.81 | 9 | Ethiopia | 170 | 1.90 |
| 6 | Pakistan | 148 | 2.50 | 10 | Congo, Democratic Republic of | 160 | 1.79 |
| 7 | Russian Federation | 147 | 2.49 | | | | |
| 8 | Japan | 126 | 2.13 | 11 | Mexico | 147 | 1.65 |
| 9 | Bangladesh | 125 | 2.11 | 12 | Philippines | 131 | 1.47 |
| 10 | Nigeria | 106 | 1.79 | 13 | Vietnam | 127 | 1.42 |
| **World total** | | 5,901 | | 14 | Russian Federation | 122 | 1.42 |
| | | | | 15 | Iran | 115 | 1.29 |
| **2050 (projected)** | | | | 16 | Egypt | 115 | 1.29 |
| 1 | India | 1,529 | 17.16 | 17 | Japan | 105 | 1.17 |
| 2 | China | 1,478 | 16.58 | 18 | Turkey | 101 | 1.13 |
| 3 | United States | 349 | 3.91 | **World total** | | 8,909 | |

## RELIGION: FESTIVALS

| Date | Festival | Religion | Event commemorated |
|------|----------|----------|--------------------|
| 6 Jan | Epiphany | Western Christian | coming of the Magi |
| 6–7 Jan | Christmas | Orthodox Christian | birth of Jesus |
| 18–19 Jan | Epiphany | Orthodox Christian | coming of the Magi |
| Jan–Feb | New Year | Chinese | Return of kitchen god to heaven |
| Feb–March | Shrove Tuesday | Christian | day before Lent |
| | Ash Wednesday | Christian | first day of Lent |
| | Purim | Jewish | story of Esther |
| | Mahashivaratri | Hindu | Siva |
| March–April | Palm Sunday | Western Christian | Jesus' entry into Jerusalem |
| | Good Friday | Western Christian | crucifixion of Jesus |
| | Easter Sunday | Western Christian | resurrection of Jesus |
| | Passover | Jewish | escape from slavery in Egypt |
| | Holi | Hindu | Krishna |
| Holi Mohalla | Sikh | (coincides with Holi) | |
| | Rama Naumi | Hindu | birth of Rama |
| | Ching Ming | Chinese | remembrance of the dead |
| 13 April | Baisakhi | Sikh | founding of the Khalsa |
| April–May | Easter | Orthodox Christian | death and resurrection of Jesus |
| May–June | Shavuot | Jewish | giving of Ten Commandments to Moses |
| | Pentecost (Whitsun) | Western Christian | Jesus' followers receiving the Holy Spirit |
| | Wesak | Buddhist | day of the Buddha's birth, enlightenment and death |
| | Martyrdom of Guru Arjan | Sikh | death of fifth guru of Sikhism |
| June | Dragon Boat Festival | Chinese | Chinese martyr |
| | Pentecost | Orthodox Christian | Jesus' followers receiving the Holy Spirit |
| July | Dhammacakka | Buddhist | preaching of Buddha's first sermon |
| Aug | Raksha Bandhan | Hindu | family |
| Aug–Sept | Janmashtami | Hindu | birthday of Krishna |
| Sept | Moon Festival | Chinese | Chinese hero |
| Sept–Oct | Rosh Hashana | Jewish | start of Jewish New Year |
| | Yom Kippur | Jewish | day of atonement |
| | Succot | Jewish | Israelites' time in the wilderness |
| Oct | Dusshera | Hindu | goddess Devi |

| Date | Festival | Religion | Event commemorated |
|------|----------|----------|--------------------|
| Oct–Nov | Diwali | Hindu | goddess Lakshmi |
| | Diwali | Sikh | release of Guru Hargobind from prison |
| Nov | Guru Nanak's birthday | Sikh | founder of Sikhism |
| Nov–Dec | Bodhi Day | Buddhist (Mahayana) | Buddha's enlightenment |
| Dec | Hanukkah | Jewish | recapture of Temple of Jerusalem |
| | Winter Festival | Chinese | time of feasting |
| 25 Dec | Christmas | Western Christian | birth of Christ |
| Dec–Jan | Birthday of Guru Gobind Sind | Sikh | last (tenth) human guru of Sikhism |
| | Martyrdom of Guru Tegh Bahadur | Sikh | ninth guru of Sikhism |

## LARGEST DESERTS IN THE WORLD

| Desert | Location | Area[1] | |
|--------|----------|---------|---|
| | | sq km | sq mi |
| Sahara | northern Africa | 9,065,000 | 3,500,000 |
| Gobi | Mongolia/northeastern China | 1,295,000 | 500,000 |
| Patagonian | Argentina | 673,000 | 260,000 |
| Rub al-Khali | southern Arabian peninsula | 647,500 | 250,000 |
| Kalahari | southwestern Africa | 582,800 | 225,000 |
| Chihuahuan | Mexico/southwestern USA | 362,600 | 140,000 |
| Taklimakan | northern China | 362,600 | 140,000 |
| Great Sandy | northwestern Australia | 338,500 | 130,000 |
| Great Victoria | southwestern Australia | 338,500 | 130,000 |
| Kyzyl Kum | Uzbekistan/Kazakhstan | 259,000 | 100,000 |
| Thar | India/Pakistan | 259,000 | 100,000 |
| Sonoran | Mexico/southwestern USA | 181,300 | 70,000 |
| Simpson | Australia | 103,600 | 40,000 |
| Mojave | southwestern USA | 65,000 | 25,000 |

[1] Desert areas are very approximate because clear physical boundaries may not occur.

## LARGEST LAKES IN THE WORLD

| Lake | Location | Area | |
|------|----------|------|---|
| | | sq km | sq mi |
| Caspian Sea | Azerbaijan/Russia/Kazakhstan/Turkmenistan/Iran | 370,990 | 143,239 |
| Superior | USA/Canada | 82,071 | 31,688 |
| Victoria | Tanzania/Kenya/Uganda | 69,463 | 26,820 |
| Aral Sea | Kazakhstan/Uzbekistan | 64,500 | 24,903 |
| Huron | USA/Canada | 59,547 | 22,991 |
| Michigan | USA | 57,735 | 22,291 |
| Tanganyika | Tanzania/Democratic Republic of Congo/Zambia/Burundi | 32,880 | 12,695 |
| Baikal | Russia | 31,499 | 12,162 |
| Great Bear | Canada | 31,316 | 12,091 |
| Malawi (or Nyasa) | Malawi/Tanzania/Mozambique | 28,867 | 11,146 |
| Great Slave | Canada | 28,560 | 11,027 |
| Erie | USA/Canada | 25,657 | 9,906 |
| Winnipeg | Canada | 25,380 | 9,799 |
| Ontario | USA/Canada | 19,010 | 7,340 |
| Balkhash | Kazakhstan | 18,421 | 7,112 |
| Ladoga | Russia | 17,695 | 6,832 |
| Chad | Chad/Cameroon/Nigeria | 16,310 | 6,297 |
| Maracaibo | Venezuela | 13,507 | 5,215 |

## HIGHEST MOUNTAINS IN THE WORLD AND FIRST ASCENTS

| Mountain | Location | Height m | ft | Year of first ascent | Expedition nationality (leader) |
|---|---|---|---|---|---|
| Everest | China/Nepal | 8,848 | 29,028 | 1953 | British/New Zealander (J Hunt) |
| K2 | Kashmir/Jammu | 8,611 | 28,251 | 1954 | Italian (A Desio) |
| Kangchenjunga | India/Nepal | 8,598 | 28,208 | 1955 | British (C Evans; by the southwest face) |
| Lhotse | China/Nepal | 8,511 | 27,923 | 1956 | Swiss (E Reiss) |
| Yalung Kang (formerly Kangchenjunga West Peak) | India/Nepal | 8,502 | 27,893 | 1973 | Japanese (Y Ageta) |
| Kangchenjunga South Peak | India/Nepal | 8,488 | 27,847 | 1978 | Polish (W Wróż) |
| Makalu I | China/Nepal | 8,481 | 27,824 | 1955 | French (J Couzy) |
| Kangchenjunga Middle Peak | India/Nepal | 8,475 | 27,805 | 1973 | Polish (W Wróż) |
| Lhotse Shar | China/Nepal | 8,383 | 27,503 | 1970 | Austrian (S Mayerl) |
| Dhaulagiri | Nepal | 8,172 | 26,811 | 1960 | Swiss/Austrian (K Diemberger) |
| Manaslu | Nepal | 8,156 | 26,759 | 1956 | Japanese (T Imanishi) |
| Cho Oyu | China/Nepal | 8,153 | 26,748 | 1954 | Austrian (H Tichy) |
| Nanga Parbat | Kashmir/Jammu | 8,126 | 26,660 | 1953 | German (K M Herrligkoffer) |
| Annapurna I | Nepal | 8,078 | 26,502 | 1950 | French (M Herzog) |
| Gasherbrum I | Kashmir/Jammu | 8,068 | 26,469 | 1958 | US (P K Schoening; by the southwest ridge) |
| Broad Peak | Kashmir/Jammu | 8,047 | 26,401 | 1957 | Austrian (M Schmuck) |
| Gasherbrum II | Kashmir/Jammu | 8,034 | 26,358 | 1956 | Austrian (S Larch; by the southwest spur) |
| Gosainthan | China | 8,012 | 26,286 | 1964 | Chinese (195-strong team; accounts are inconclusive) |
| Broad Peak (Middle) | Kashmir/Jammu | 8,000 | 26,246 | 1975 | Polish (K Glazek) |
| Gasherbrum III | Kashmir/Jammu | 7,952 | 26,089 | 1975 | Polish (J Onyszkiewicz) |
| Annapurna II | Nepal | 7,937 | 26,040 | 1960 | British (C Bonington) |
| Gasherbrum IV | Kashmir/Jammu | 7,923 | 25,994 | 1958 | Italian (W Bonatti, C Mouri) |
| Gyachung Kang | Nepal | 7,921 | 25,987 | 1964 | Japanese (Y Kato, K Sakaizqwa) |
| Disteghil Shar | Kashmir | 7,884 | 25,866 | 1960 | Austrian (G Stärker, D Marchart) |
| Himalchuli | Nepal | 7,864 | 25,800 | 1960 | Japanese (M Harada, H Tanabe) |
| Nuptse | Nepal | 7,841 | 25,725 | 1961 | British (D Davis, C Bonington, L Brown) |
| Manaslu II | Nepal | 7,835 | 25,705 | 1970 | Japanese (H Watanabe, Lhakpa Tsering) |
| Masherbrum East | Kashmir | 7,821 | 25,659 | 1960 | Pakistani/US (G Bell, W Unsoeld) |
| Nanda Devi | India | 7,817 | 25,646 | 1936 | British (H W Tilman) |
| Chomo Lonzo | Nepal | 7,815 | 25,639 | 1954 | French (J Couzy, L Terry) |

## MAJOR OCEANS AND SEAS IN THE WORLD

| Ocean/sea | Area[1] sq km | sq mi | Average depth m | ft |
|---|---|---|---|---|
| Pacific Ocean | 166,242,000 | 64,186,000 | 3,939 | 12,925 |
| Atlantic Ocean | 86,557,000 | 33,420,000 | 3,575 | 11,730 |
| Indian Ocean | 73,429,000 | 28,351,000 | 3,840 | 12,598 |
| Arctic Ocean | 13,224,000 | 5,106,000 | 1,038 | 3,407 |
| South China Sea | 2,975,000 | 1,149,000 | 1,464 | 4,802 |
| Caribbean Sea | 2,754,000 | 1,063,000 | 2,575 | 8,448 |
| Mediterranean Sea | 2,510,000 | 969,000 | 1,501 | 4,926 |
| Bering Sea | 2,261,000 | 873,000 | 1,491 | 4,893 |
| Sea of Okhotsk | 1,580,000 | 610,000 | 973 | 3,192 |
| Gulf of Mexico | 1,544,000 | 596,000 | 1,614 | 5,297 |
| Sea of Japan | 1,013,000 | 391,000 | 1,667 | 5,468 |
| Hudson Bay | 730,000 | 282,000 | 93 | 305 |
| East China Sea | 665,000 | 257,000 | 189 | 620 |
| Andaman Sea | 565,000 | 218,000 | 1,118 | 3,667 |

| Ocean/sea | Area[1] | | Average depth | |
| --- | --- | --- | --- | --- |
| | sq km | sq mi | m | ft |
| Black Sea | 461,000 | 178,000 | 1,190 | 3,906 |
| Red Sea | 453,000 | 175,000 | 538 | 1,764 |
| North Sea | 427,000 | 165,000 | 94 | 308 |
| Baltic Sea | 422,000 | 163,000 | 55 | 180 |
| Yellow Sea | 294,000 | 114,000 | 37 | 121 |
| Persian Gulf | 230,000 | 89,000 | 100 | 328 |
| Gulf of California | 153,000 | 59,000 | 724 | 2,375 |
| English Channel | 90,000 | 35,000 | 54 | 177 |
| Irish Sea | 89,000 | 34,000 | 60 | 197 |

[1] All figures are approximate, as boundaries of oceans and seas cannot be exactly determined

## LONGEST RIVERS IN THE WORLD

| River | Location | Approximate length | | River | Location | Approximate length | |
| --- | --- | --- | --- | --- | --- | --- | --- |
| | | km | mi | | | km | mi |
| Nile | Africa | 6,695 | 4,160 | Rio Grande | USA/Mexico | 3,058 | 1,900 |
| Amazon | South America | 6,570 | 4,083 | Indus | Tibet/Pakistan | 2,897 | 1,800 |
| | | | | Danube | central and eastern Europe | 2,858 | 1,776 |
| Chang Jiang (Yangtze) | China | 6,300 | 3,915 | | | | |
| | | | | Japura | Brazil | 2,816 | 1,750 |
| Mississippi–Missouri– Red Rock | USA | 6,020 | 3,741 | Salween | Myanmar/ China | 2,800 | 1,740 |
| Huang He (Yellow River) | China | 5,464 | 3,395 | Brahmaputra | Asia | 2,736 | 1,700 |
| | | | | Euphrates | Iraq | 2,736 | 1,700 |
| Ob–Irtysh | China/ Kazakhstan/ Russia | 5,410 | 3,362 | Tocantins | Brazil | 2,699 | 1,677 |
| | | | | Zambezi | Africa | 2,650 | 1,647 |
| | | | | Orinoco | Venezuela | 2,559 | 1,590 |
| Amur–Shilka | Asia | 4,416 | 2,744 | Paraguay | Paraguay | 2,549 | 1,584 |
| Lena | Russia | 4,400 | 2,734 | Amu Darya | Tajikistan/ Turkmenistan/ Uzbekistan | 2,540 | 1,578 |
| Congo–Zaire | Africa | 4,374 | 2,718 | | | | |
| Mackenzie–Peace– Finlay | Canada | 4,241 | 2,635 | Ural | Russia/ Kazakhstan | 2,535 | 1,575 |
| Mekong | Asia | 4,180 | 2,597 | | | | |
| Niger | Africa | 4,100 | 2,548 | Kolyma | Russia | 2,513 | 1,562 |
| Yenisei | Russia | 4,100 | 2,548 | Ganges | India/ Bangladesh | 2,510 | 1,560 |
| Paraná | Brazil | 3,943 | 2,450 | | | | |
| Mississippi | USA | 3,779 | 2,348 | Arkansas | USA | 2,344 | 1,459 |
| Murray–Darling | Australia | 3,751 | 2,331 | Colorado | USA | 2,333 | 1,450 |
| Missouri | USA | 3,726 | 2,315 | Dnieper | Russia/Belarus/ Ukraine | 2,285 | 1,420 |
| Volga | Russia | 3,685 | 2,290 | | | | |
| Madeira | Brazil | 3,241 | 2,014 | Syr Darya | Asia | 2,205 | 1,370 |
| Purus | Brazil | 3,211 | 1,995 | Irrawaddy | Myanmar | 2,152 | 1,337 |
| São Francisco | Brazil | 3,199 | 1,988 | Orange | South Africa | 2,092 | 1,300 |
| Yukon | USA/Canada | 3,185 | 1,979 | | | | |

## MAJOR VOLCANOES ACTIVE IN THE 20TH CENTURY

As of 15 January 1999.

| Volcano | Height | | Location | Date of last |
|---|---|---|---|---|
| | **m** | **ft** | | eruption or activity |
| *Africa* | | | | |
| Cameroon | 4,096 | 13,353 | isolated mountain, Cameroon | 1986 |
| Nyiragongo | 3,470 | 11,385 | Virungu, Democratic Republic of Congo | 1994 |
| Nyamuragira | 3,056 | 10,028 | Democratic Republic of Congo | 1998 |
| Ol Doinyo Lengai | 2,886 | 9,469 | Tanzania | 1993 |
| Lake Nyos | 918 | 3,011 | Cameroon | 1986 |
| Erta-Ale | 503 | 1,650 | Ethiopia | 1995 |
| *Antarctica* | | | | |
| Erebus | 4,023 | 13,200 | Ross Island, McMurdo Sound | 1995 |
| Deception Island | 576 | 1,890 | South Shetland Island | 1970 |
| *Asia* | | | | |
| Kerinci | 3,800 | 12,467 | Sumatra, Indonesia | 1987 |
| Rindjani | 3,726 | 12,224 | Lombok, Indonesia | 1966 |
| Semeru | 3,676 | 12,060 | Java, Indonesia | 1995 |
| Slamet | 3,428 | 11,247 | Java, Indonesia | 1989 |
| Raung | 3,322 | 10,932 | Java, Indonesia | 1993 |
| Agung | 3,142 | 10,308 | Bali, Indonesia | 1964 |
| On-Taka | 3,063 | 10,049 | Honshu, Japan | 1991 |
| Merapi | 2,911 | 9,551 | Java, Indonesia | 1998 |
| Marapi | 2,891 | 9,485 | Sumatra, Indonesia | 1993 |
| Asama | 2,530 | 8,300 | Honshu, Japan | 1990 |
| Nigata Yake-yama | 2,475 | 8,111 | Honshu, Japan | 1989 |
| Mayon | 2,462 | 8,084 | Luzon, Philippines | 1993 |
| Canlaon | 2,459 | 8,070 | Negros, Philippines | 1993 |
| Chokai | 2,225 | 7,300 | Honshu, Japan | 1974 |
| Galunggung | 2,168 | 7,113 | Java, Indonesia | 1984 |
| Azuma | 2,042 | 6,700 | Honshu, Japan | 1977 |
| Sangeang Api | 1,935 | 6,351 | Lesser Sunda Island, Indonesia | 1988 |
| Pinatubo | 1,759 | 5,770 | Luzon, Philippines | 1995 |
| Kelut | 1,730 | 5,679 | Java, Indonesia | 1990 |
| Unzen | 1,360 | 4,462 | Japan | 1996 |
| Krakatoa | 818 | 2,685 | Sumatra, Indonesia | 1996 |
| Taal | 300 | 984 | Philippines | 1977 |
| *Atlantic Ocean* | | | | |
| Pico de Teide | 3,716 | 12,192 | Tenerife, Canary Islands, Spain | 1909 |
| Fogo | 2,835 | 9,300 | Cape Verde Islands | 1995 |
| Beerenberg | 2,277 | 7,470 | Jan Mayen Island, Norway | 1985 |
| Hekla | 1,491 | 4,920 | Iceland | 1991 |
| Krafla | 654 | 2,145 | Iceland | 1984 |
| Helgafell | 215 | 706 | Iceland | 1973 |
| Surtsey | 174 | 570 | Iceland | 1967 |
| *Caribbean* | | | | |
| La Grande Soufrière | 1,467 | 4,813 | Basse-Terre, Guadeloupe | 1977 |
| Pelée | 1,397 | 4,584 | Martinique | 1932 |
| La Soufrière | | | | |
| St Vincent | 1,234 | 4,048 | St Vincent and the Grenadines | 1979 |
| Soufriere Hills/ | | | | |
| Chances | | | | |
| Peak | 968 | 3,176 | Montserrat | 1999 |
| *Central America* | | | | |
| Acatenango | 3,960 | 12,992 | Sierra Madre, Guatemala | 1972 |
| Fuego | 3,835 | 12,582 | Sierra Madre, Guatemala | 1991 |
| Tacana | 3,780 | 12,400 | Sierra Madre, Guatemala | 1988 |
| Santa Maria | 3,768 | 12,362 | Sierra Madre, Guatemala | 1993 |
| Irazú | 3,452 | 11,325 | Cordillera Central, Costa Rica | 1992 |
| Turrialba | 3,246 | 10,650 | Cordillera Central, Costa Rica | 1992 |
| Póas | 2,721 | 8,930 | Cordillera Central, Costa Rica | 1994 |
| Pacaya | 2,543 | 8,346 | Sierra Madre, Guatemala | 1998 |
| San Miguel | 2,131 | 6,994 | El Salvador | 1986 |
| Arenal | 1,552 | 5,092 | Costa Rica | 1998 |
| *Europe* | | | | |
| Kliuchevskoi | 4,750 | 15,584 | Kamchatka Peninsula, Russia | 1997 |
| Koryakskaya | 3,456 | 11,339 | Kamchatka Peninsula, Russia | 1957 |

| Volcano | Height | | Location | Date of last |
|---|---|---|---|---|
| | m | ft | | eruption or activity |
| Sheveluch | 3,283 | 10,771 | Kamchatka Peninsula, Russia | 1997 |
| Etna | 3,236 | 10,625 | Sicily, Italy | 1999 |
| Bezymianny | 2,882 | 9,455 | Kamchatka Peninsula, Russia | 1997 |
| Alaid | 2,335 | 7,662 | Kurile Islands, Russia | 1986 |
| Tiatia | 1,833 | 6,013 | Kurile Islands, Russia | 1981 |
| Sarychev Peak | 1,512 | 4,960 | Kurile Islands, Russia | 1989 |
| Vesuvius | 1,289 | 4,203 | Italy | 1944 |
| Stromboli | 931 | 3,055 | Lipari Islands, Italy | 1998 |
| Santorini (Thera) | 584 | 1,960 | Cyclades, Greece | 1950 |
| *Indian Ocean* | | | | |
| Karthala | 2,440 | 8,000 | Comoros | 1991 |
| Piton de la Fournaise | 1,823 | 5,981 | Réunion Island, France | 1998 |
| (Le Volcan) | | | | |
| *Mid-Pacific* | | | | |
| Mauna Loa | 4,170 | 13,681 | Hawaii, USA | 1984 |
| Kilauea | 1,247 | 4,100 | Hawaii, USA | 1998 |
| *North America* | | | | |
| Popocatépetl | 5,452 | 17,887 | Altiplano de México, Mexico | 1998 |
| Colima | 4,268 | 14,003 | Altiplano de México, Mexico | 1999 |
| Spurr | 3,374 | 11,070 | Alaska Range (AK) USA | 1953 |
| Lassen Peak | 3,186 | 10,453 | California, USA | 1921 |
| Redoubt | 3,108 | 10,197 | Alaska Range (AK) USA | 1991 |
| Iliamna | 3,052 | 10,016 | Alaska Range (AK) USA | 1978 |
| Shishaldin | 2,861 | 9,387 | Aleutian Islands (AK) USA | 1997 |
| St Helens | 2,549 | 8,364 | Washington, USA | 1998 |
| Pavlof | 2,517 | 8,261 | Alaska Range (AK) USA | 1997 |
| Veniaminof | 2,507 | 8,225 | Alaska Range (AK) USA | 1995 |
| Novarupta (Katmai) | 2,298 | 7,540 | Alaska Range (AK) USA | 1931 |
| El Chichon | 2,225 | 7,300 | Altiplano de México, Mexico | 1982 |
| Makushin | 2,036 | 6,680 | Aleutian Islands (AK) USA | 1987 |
| *Oceania* | | | | |
| Ruapehu | 2,796 | 9,175 | New Zealand | 1997 |
| Ulawun | 2,296 | 7,532 | Papua New Guinea | 1993 |
| Ngauruhoe | 2,290 | 7,515 | New Zealand | 1977 |
| Bagana | 1,998 | 6,558 | Papua New Guinea | 1993 |
| Manam | 1,829 | 6,000 | Papua New Guinea | 1998 |
| Lamington | 1,780 | 5,844 | Papua New Guinea | 1956 |
| Karkar | 1,499 | 4,920 | Papua New Guinea | 1979 |
| Lopevi | 1,450 | 4,755 | Vanuatu | 1982 |
| Ambrym | 1,340 | 4,376 | Vanuatu | 1991 |
| Tarawera | 1,149 | 3,770 | New Zealand | 1973 |
| Langila | 1,093 | 3,586 | Papua New Guinea | 1996 |
| Rabaul | 688 | 2,257 | Papua New Guinea | 1997 |
| Pagan | 570 | 1,870 | Mariana Islands | 1993 |
| White Island | 328 | 1,075 | New Zealand | 1999 |
| *South America* | | | | |
| San Pedro | 6,199 | 20,325 | Andes, Chile | 1960 |
| Guallatiri | 6,060 | 19,882 | Andes, Chile | 1993 |
| Lascar | 5,990 | 19,652 | Andes, Chile | 1995 |
| San José | 5,919 | 19,405 | Andes, Chile | 1931 |
| Cotopaxi | 5,897 | 19,347 | Andes, Ecuador | 1975 |
| Tutupaca | 5,844 | 19,160 | Andes, Ecuador | 1902 |
| Ubinas | 5,710 | 18,720 | Andes, Peru | 1969 |
| Tupungatito | 5,640 | 18,504 | Andes, Chile | 1986 |
| Islunga | 5,566 | 18,250 | Andes, Chile | 1960 |
| Nevado del Ruiz | 5,435 | 17,820 | Andes, Colombia | 1992 |
| Tolima | 5,249 | 17,210 | Andes, Colombia | 1943 |
| Sangay | 5,230 | 17,179 | Andes, Ecuador | 1996 |

## SOVEREIGNS OF ENGLAND AND THE UNITED KINGDOM FROM 899

| Reign | Name | Relationship |
|---|---|---|
| *West Saxon Kings* | | |
| 899–924 | Edward the Elder | son of Alfred the Great |
| 924–39 | Athelstan | son of Edward the Elder |
| 939–46 | Edmund | half-brother of Athelstan |
| 946–55 | Edred | brother of Edmund |
| 955–59 | Edwy | son of Edmund |
| 959–75 | Edgar | brother of Edwy |
| 975–78 | Edward the Martyr | son of Edgar |
| 978–1016 | Ethelred (II) the Unready | son of Edgar |
| 1016 | Edmund Ironside | son of Ethelred (II) the Unready |
| *Danish Kings* | | |
| 1016–35 | Canute | son of Sweyn I of Denmark who conquered England in 1013 |
| 1035–40 | Harold I | son of Canute |
| 1040–42 | Hardicanute | son of Canute |
| *West Saxon Kings (restored)* | | |
| 1042–66 | Edward the Confessor | son of Ethelred (II) the Unready |
| 1066 | Harold II | son of Godwin |
| *Norman Kings* | | |
| 1066–87 | William I | illegitimate son of Duke Robert the Devil |
| 1087–1100 | William II | son of William I |
| 1100–35 | Henry I | son of William I |
| 1135–54 | Stephen | grandson of William II |
| *House of Plantagenet* | | |
| 1154–89 | Henry II | son of Matilda (daughter of Henry I) |
| 1189–99 | Richard I | son of Henry II |
| 1199–1216 | John | son of Henry II |
| 1216–72 | Henry III | son of John |
| 1272–1307 | Edward I | son of Henry III |
| 1307–27 | Edward II | son of Edward I |
| 1327–77 | Edward III | son of Edward II |
| 1377–99 | Richard II | son of the Black Prince |
| *House of Lancaster* | | |
| 1399–1413 | Henry IV | son of John of Gaunt |

| Reign | Name | Relationship |
|---|---|---|
| 1413–22 | Henry V | son of Henry IV |
| 1422–61, 1470–71 | Henry VI | son of Henry V |
| *House of York* | | |
| 1461–70, 1471–83 | Edward IV | son of Richard, Duke of York |
| 1483 | Edward V | son of Edward IV |
| 1483–85 | Richard III | brother of Edward IV |
| *House of Tudor* | | |
| 1485–1509 | Henry VII | son of Edmund Tudor, Earl of Richmond |
| 1509–47 | Henry VIII | son of Henry VII |
| 1547–53 | Edward VI | son of Henry VIII |
| 1553–58 | Mary I | daughter of Henry VIII |
| 1558–1603 | Elizabeth I | daughter of Henry VIII |
| *House of Stuart* | | |
| 1603–25 | James I | great-grandson of Margaret (daughter of Henry VII) |
| 1625–49 | Charles I | son of James I |
| 1649–60 | the Commonwealth | |
| *House of Stuart (restored)* | | |
| 1660–85 | Charles II | son of Charles I |
| 1685–88 | James II | son of Charles I |
| 1689–1702 | William III and Mary | son of Mary (daughter of Charles I); daughter of James II |
| 1702–14 | Anne | daughter of James II |
| *House of Hanover* | | |
| 1714–27 | George I | son of Sophia (granddaughter of James I) |
| 1727–60 | George II | son of George I |
| 1760–1820 | George III | son of Frederick (son of George II) |
| 1820–30 | George IV (regent 1811–20) | son of George III |
| 1830–37 | William IV | son of George III |
| 1837–1901 | Victoria | daughter of Edward (son of George III) |
| *House of Saxe-Coburg* | | |
| 1901–10 | Edward VII | son of Victoria |
| *House of Windsor* | | |
| 1910–36 | George V | son of Edward VII |
| 1936 | Edward VIII | son of George V |
| 1936–52 | George VI | son of George V |
| 1952– | Elizabeth II | daughter of George VI |

## SCOTTISH MONARCHS 1005–1603

This table covers the period from the unification of Scotland to the union of the crowns of Scotland and England.

| Reign | Name | Reign | Name |
|---|---|---|---|
| *Celtic Kings* | | *English Domination* | |
| 1005–34 | Malcolm II | 1292–96 | John Baliol |
| 1034–40 | Duncan I | 1296–1306 | annexed to England |
| 1040–57 | Macbeth | *House of Bruce* | |
| 1057–93 | Malcolm III Canmore | | |
| 1093–94 | Donald III Donalbane | 1306–29 | Robert I the Bruce |
| 1094 | Duncan II | 1329–71 | David II |
| 1094–97 | Donald III (restored) | *House of Stuart* | |
| 1097–1107 | Edgar | | |
| 1107–24 | Alexander I | 1371–90 | Robert II |
| 1124–53 | David I | 1390–1406 | Robert III |
| 1153–65 | Malcolm IV | 1406–37 | James I |
| 1165–1214 | William the Lion | 1437–60 | James II |
| 1214–49 | Alexander II | 1460–88 | James III |
| 1249–86 | Alexander III | 1488–1513 | James IV |
| 1286–90 | Margaret of Norway | 1513–42 | James V |
| | | 1542–67 | Mary |
| | | 1567–1625 | James VI[1] |

[1] After the union of crowns in 1603, he became James I of England.

## PRIME MINISTERS OF GREAT BRITAIN AND THE UK

| Term | Name | Party |
|---|---|---|
| 1721–42 | Robert Walpole[1] | Whig |
| 1742–43 | Spencer Compton, Earl of Wilmington | Whig |
| 1743–54 | Henry Pelham | Whig |
| 1754–56 | Thomas Pelham-Holles, 1st Duke of Newcastle | Whig |
| 1756–57 | William Cavendish, 4th Duke of Devonshire | Whig |
| 1757–62 | Thomas Pelham-Holles, 1st Duke of Newcastle | Whig |
| 1762–63 | John Stuart, 3rd Earl of Bute | Tory |
| 1763–65 | George Grenville | Whig |
| 1765–66 | Charles Watson Wentworth, 2nd Marquess of Rockingham | Whig |
| 1766–68 | William Pitt, 1st Earl of Chatham | Tory |
| 1768–70 | Augustus Henry Fitzroy, 3rd Duke of Grafton | Whig |
| 1770–82 | Frederick North, Lord North[2] | Tory |
| 1782 | Charles Watson Wentworth, 2nd Marquess of Rockingham | Whig |
| 1782–83 | William Petty-Fitzmaurice, 2nd Earl of Shelburne[3] | Whig |
| 1783 | William Henry Cavendish-Bentinck, 3rd Duke of Portland | Whig |
| 1783–1801 | William Pitt, The Younger | Tory |
| 1801–04 | Henry Addington | Tory |
| 1804–06 | William Pitt, The Younger | Tory |
| 1806–07 | William Wyndham Grenville, 1st Baron Grenville | Whig |
| 1807–09 | William Henry Cavendish-Bentinck, 3rd Duke of Portland | Whig |
| 1809–12 | Spencer Perceval | Tory |
| 1812–27 | Robert Banks Jenkinson, 2nd Earl of Liverpool | Tory |
| 1827 | George Canning | Tory |
| 1827–28 | Frederick John Robinson, 1st Viscount Goderich | Tory |
| 1828–30 | Arthur Wellesley, 1st Duke of Wellington | Tory |
| 1830–34 | Charles Grey, 2nd Earl Grey | Whig |
| 1834 | William Lamb, 2nd Viscount Melbourne | Whig |
| 1834 | Arthur Wellesley, 1st Duke of Wellington | Tory |
| 1834–35 | Sir Robert Peel, 2nd Baronet | Tory |
| 1835–41 | William Lamb, 2nd Viscount Melbourne | Whig |
| 1841–46 | Sir Robert Peel, 2nd Baronet | Conservative |
| 1846–52 | John Russell, Lord Russell | Whig-Liberal |
| 1852 | Edward Geoffrey Stanley, 14th Earl of Derby | Conservative |
| 1852–55 | George Hamilton-Gordon, 4th Earl of Aberdeen | Peelite |
| 1855–58 | Henry John Temple, 3rd Viscount Palmerston | Liberal |
| 1858–59 | Edward Geoffrey Stanley, 14th Earl of Derby | Conservative |
| 1859–65 | Henry John Temple, 3rd Viscount Palmerston | Liberal |
| 1865–66 | John Russell, 1st Earl Russell | Liberal |
| 1866–68 | Edward Geoffrey Stanley, 14th Earl of Derby | Conservative |
| 1868 | Benjamin Disraeli | Conservative |
| 1868–74 | William Ewart Gladstone | Liberal |
| 1874–80 | Benjamin Disraeli[4] | Conservative |

| Term | Name | Party |
|------|------|-------|
| 1880–85 | William Ewart Gladstone | Liberal |
| 1885–86 | Robert Cecil, 3rd Marquess of Salisbury | Conservative |
| 1886 | William Ewart Gladstone | Liberal |
| 1886–92 | Robert Cecil, 3rd Marquess of Salisbury | Conservative |
| 1892–94 | William Ewart Gladstone | Liberal |
| 1894–95 | Archibald Philip Primrose, 5th Earl of Rosebery | Liberal |
| 1895–1902 | Robert Cecil, 3rd Marquess of Salisbury | Conservative |
| 1902–05 | Arthur James Balfour | Conservative |
| 1905–08 | Sir Henry Campbell-Bannerman | Liberal |
| 1908–16 | Herbert Henry Asquith | Liberal |
| 1916–22 | David Lloyd George | Liberal |
| 1922–23 | Bonar Law | Conservative |
| 1923–24 | Stanley Baldwin | Conservative |
| 1924 | Ramsay Macdonald | Labour |
| 1924–29 | Stanley Baldwin | Conservative |
| 1929–35 | Ramsay Macdonald | Labour |
| 1935–37 | Stanley Baldwin | Conservative |
| 1937–40 | Neville Chamberlain | Conservative |
| 1940–45 | Winston Churchill | Conservative |
| 1945–51 | Clement Attlee | Labour |
| 1951–55 | Winston Churchill[5] | Conservative |
| 1955–57 | Sir Anthony Eden | Conservative |
| 1957–63 | Harold Macmillan | Conservative |
| 1963–64 | Sir Alec Douglas-Home | Conservative |
| 1964–70 | Harold Wilson | Labour |
| 1970–74 | Edward Heath | Conservative |
| 1974–76 | Harold Wilson | Labour |
| 1976–79 | James Callaghan | Labour |
| 1979–90 | Margaret Thatcher | Conservative |
| 1990–97 | John Major | Conservative |
| 1997– | Tony Blair | Labour |

[1] From 1725, Sir Robert Walpole.
[2] From 1790, 2nd Earl of Guilford.
[3] From 1784, 1st Marquess of Lansdowne.
[4] From 1876, Earl of Beaconsfield.
[5] From 1953, Sir Winston Churchill.

## US PRESIDENTS

| Year elected/ took office | President | Party | Losing candidate(s) | Party |
|------|------|------|------|------|
| 1789 | 1 George Washington | Federalist | no opponent | |
| 1792 | re-elected | | no opponent | |
| 1796 | 2 John Adams | Federalist | Thomas Jefferson | Democrat–Republican |
| 1800 | 3 Thomas Jefferson | Democrat–Republican | Aaron Burr | Democrat–Republican |
| 1804 | re-elected | | Charles Pinckney | Federalist |
| 1808 | 4 James Madison | Democrat–Republican | Charles Pinckney | Federalist |
| 1812 | re-elected | | DeWitt Clinton | Federalist |
| 1816 | 5 James Monroe | Democrat–Republican | Rufus King | Federalist |
| 1820 | re-elected | | John Quincy Adams | Democrat–Republican |
| 1824 | 6 John Quincy Adams | Democrat–Republican | Andrew Jackson | Democrat–Republican |
| | | | Henry Clay | Democrat–Republican |
| | | | William H Crawford | Democrat–Republican |
| 1828 | 7 Andrew Jackson | Democrat | John Quincy Adams | National Republican |
| 1832 | re-elected | | Henry Clay | National Republican |
| 1836 | 8 Martin Van Buren | Democrat | William Henry Harrison | Whig |
| 1840 | 9 William Henry Harrison | Whig | Martin Van Buren | Democrat |
| 1841 | 10 John Tyler[1] | Whig | | |
| 1844 | 11 James K Polk | Democrat | Henry Clay | Whig |
| 1848 | 12 Zachary Taylor | Whig | Lewis Cass | Democrat |
| 1850 | 13 Millard Fillmore[2] | Whig | | |
| 1852 | 14 Franklin Pierce | Democrat | Winfield Scott | Whig |
| 1856 | 15 James Buchanan | Democrat | John C Fremont | Republican |
| 1860 | 16 Abraham Lincoln | Republican | Stephen Douglas | Democrat |
| | | | John Breckinridge | Democrat |
| | | | John Bell | Constitutional Union |
| 1864 | re-elected | | George McClellan | Democrat |
| 1865 | 17 Andrew Johnson[3] | Democrat | | |

| Year elected/ took office | President | Party | Losing candidate(s) | Party |
|---|---|---|---|---|
| 1868 | 18 Ulysses S Grant | Republican | Horatio Seymour | Democrat |
| 1872 | re-elected | | Horace Greeley | Democrat–Liberal Republican |
| 1876 | 19 Rutherford B Hayes | Republican | Samuel Tilden | Democrat |
| 1880 | 20 James A Garfield | Republican | Winfield Hancock | Democrat |
| 1881 | 21 Chester A Arthur[4] | Republican | | |
| 1884 | 22 Grover Cleveland | Democrat | James Blaine | Republican |
| 1888 | 23 Benjamin Harrison | Republican | Grover Cleveland | Democrat |
| 1892 | 24 Grover Cleveland | Democrat | Benjamin Harrison | Republican |
| | | | James Weaver | People's |
| 1896 | 25 William McKinley | Republican | William J Bryan | Democrat–People's |
| 1900 | re-elected | | William J Bryan | Democrat |
| 1901 | 26 Theodore Roosevelt[5] | Republican | | |
| 1904 | re-elected | | Alton B Parker | Democrat |
| 1908 | 27 William Howard Taft | Republican | William J Bryan | Democrat |
| 1912 | 28 Woodrow Wilson | Democrat | Theodore Roosevelt | Progressive |
| | | | William Howard Taft | Republican |
| 1916 | re-elected | | Charles E Hughes | Republican |
| 1920 | 29 Warren G Harding | Republican | James M Cox | Democrat |
| 1923 | 30 Calvin Coolidge[6] | Republican | | |
| 1924 | re-elected | | John W Davis | Democrat |
| | | | Robert M LaFollette | Progressive |
| 1928 | 31 Herbert Hoover | Republican | Alfred E Smith | Democrat |
| 1932 | 32 Franklin D Roosevelt | Democrat | Herbert C Hoover | Republican |
| | | | Norman Thomas | Socialist |
| 1936 | re-elected | | Alfred Landon | Republican |
| 1940 | re-elected | | Wendell Willkie | Republican |
| 1944 | re-elected | | Thomas E Dewey | Republican |
| 1945 | 33 Harry S Truman[7] | Democrat | | |
| 1948 | re-elected | | Thomas E Dewey | Republican |
| | | | J Strom Thurmond | States' Rights |
| | | | Henry A Wallace | Progressive |
| 1952 | 34 Dwight D Eisenhower | Republican | Adlai E Stevenson | Democrat |
| 1956 | re-elected | | Adlai E Stevenson | Democrat |
| 1960 | 35 John F Kennedy | Democrat | Richard M Nixon | Republican |
| 1963 | 36 Lyndon B Johnson[8] | Democrat | | |
| 1964 | re-elected | | Barry M Goldwater | Republican |
| 1968 | 37 Richard M Nixon | Republican | Hubert H Humphrey | Democrat |
| | | | George C Wallace | American Independent |
| 1972 | re-elected | | George S McGovern | Democrat |
| 1974 | 38 Gerald R Ford[9] | Republican | | |
| 1976 | 39 James Earl Carter | Democrat | Gerald R Ford | Republican |
| 1980 | 40 Ronald Reagan | Republican | James Earl Carter | Democrat |
| | | | John B Anderson | Independent |
| 1984 | re-elected | | Walter Mondale | Democrat |
| 1988 | 41 George Bush | Republican | Michael Dukakis | Democrat |
| | | | Ross Perot | Independent |
| 1992 | 42 Bill Clinton | Democrat | George Bush | Republican |
| 1996 | re-elected | | Bob Dole | Republican |
| | | | Ross Perot | Reform |

[1] Became president on death of Harrison.
[2] Became president on death of Taylor.
[3] Became president on assassination of Lincoln.
[4] Became president on assassination of Garfield.
[5] Became president on assassination of McKinley.
[6] Became president on death of Harding.
[7] Became president on death of F D Roosevelt.
[8] Became president on assassination of Kennedy.
[9] Became president on resignation of Nixon.